THE ARDEN
SHAKESPEARE
COMPLETE WORKS

The editors and publisher would like to thank Jane Armstrong, Project Manager; Tom Adair, who compiled the glossary; and Christine Ames and her colleagues at Multiplex Techniques.

Picture research by Image Select.

The general editors of the Arden Shakespeare have been
W.J. Craig and R.H. Case (first series 1899-1944)
Una Ellis-Fermor, Harold F. Brooks, Harold Jenkins and
Brian Morris (second series 1946-82)

Present general editors (third series)
Richard Proudfoot, Ann Thompson and David Scott Kastan

The Arden Shakespeare Complete Works
first published 1998 by Thomas Nelson and Sons Ltd

Thomas Nelson and Sons Ltd
Nelson House Mayfield Road
Walton-on-Thames Surrey
KT12 5PL UK

I(T)P® Thomas Nelson is an International Thomson Publishing Company
I(T)P® is used under licence

Editorial matter © 1998 Richard Proudfoot, Ann Thompson,
David Scott Kastan

Typeset by Multiplex Techniques
Printed in China

British Library Cataloguing in Publication Data
A catalogue record for this book is available from the British Library
Library of Congress Cataloguing in Publication Data
A catalogue record has been applied for

ISBN 0-17-443615-7

NPN 9 8 7 6 5 4 3 2 1

THE ARDEN
SHAKESPEARE
COMPLETE WORKS

Edited by Richard Proudfoot, Ann Thompson and David Scott Kastan

Consultant Editor Harold Jenkins

CONTENTS

LIST OF ILLUSTRATIONS

General Editors' Preface

The texts in this volume were edited for the second and third series of the Arden Shakespeare. The second series (Arden 2; General Editors: Una Ellis-Fermor, Harold F. Brooks, Harold Jenkins and Brian Morris) was published in thirty-eight volumes between 1951 and 1982. The third series (Arden 3; General Editors: Richard Proudfoot, Ann Thompson and David Scott Kastan) began publication in 1995. At the time of writing, Arden 3 has replaced five volumes published early in Arden 2: *Antony and Cleopatra*, *King Henry V*, *King Lear*, *Othello* and *Titus Andronicus*; and has added two, *The Two Noble Kinsmen* and *Shakespeare's Sonnets*, which Arden 2 did not include. Despite some changes in editorial convention and the minor inconsistencies resulting from them, we have decided to include texts from Arden 3 in this collected volume. The other possible courses, to reissue Arden 2 texts which have been replaced, or to wait many years for completion of Arden 3, had less to recommend them.

Some conventions of presentation and layout newly introduced for Arden 3 have been adopted throughout this volume. These include: the use of arabic numerals for act and scene numbers and the reduced prominence of those numbers on the page; the adoption of unabbreviated names for use as speech prefixes; removal of all editorial notes of location of action (most of which were the inventions of eighteenth-century editors and relate to the theatre of that period); substitution of 'List of Roles' for '*Dramatis Personae*' and translation of Latin stage directions with the exception of the familiar *Exit.* ([s]he goes out) and *Exeunt.* (they go out).

Minor inconsistency will be found in the seven Arden 3 texts in respect of (a) treatment of elided syllables; (b) spelling; (c) forms of stage directions.

(a) No elisions are marked in Arden 3 texts unless they indicate pronunciation differing from late twentieth-century English usage. For metrical reasons, the '-ed' ending of past participles was sometimes sounded in verse passages, contrary to normal pronunciation. After his earliest plays, Shakespeare made sparing use of this licence and Arden 3, accordingly, does not adopt the familiar practice of drawing attention to such usage in the text. The convention used by Arden 2 was to print non-syllabic '-ed' as '-'d', which usually indicates normal modern pronunciation by use of an obsolete spelling form. Where conventional scene divisions have been altered, the rejected scene and line numbers are recorded in square brackets for purposes of reference.

(b) Arden 2 editors were encouraged to retain obsolete spellings from the early editions if they believed that they might indicate the Elizabethan pronunciation of a word. Arden 3 adopts the practice of thorough modernization, on the grounds that the relation of spelling to pronunciation is imperfectly understood and was certainly variable and erratic. What has been clearly demonstrated is that, in the period before modern English spelling was stabilized, printers were already understood to be responsible for the spelling of books they printed – and also for punctuation (as they still are today). Consequently, few authorial spellings are likely to be present in the early editions, and those few are impossible to identify, in the absence of surviving manuscripts in Shakespeare's hand which might identify them. Variations in spelling are included in the glossary where they might otherwise cause confusion.

(c) Where stage directions have been added by editors (as very many have), Arden 3 prefers active verbs to present participles: e.g. [*Reads.*], not [*reading*]. The exact wording of stage directions throughout should be regarded as editorial, though in substance they most frequently derive from the source texts.

(d) More radical differences of convention relate to *King Lear*. Several recent editions of the play, accepting the theory that the first Quarto of 1608 and the first Folio of 1623 print incompatible and separate versions of the play, have printed the two as separate plays, either in sequence or in parallel. The Arden 3 editor, regarding this as unnecessary, has instead engaged in the deliberate experiment of presenting a single edited text in which readers are made aware of some main differences between Quarto and Folio. Arden 3, accordingly, presents a Folio-based edited text which incorporates all further words and passages present only in the Quarto. Words, phrases and longer passages unique to the Quarto are enclosed within superscript ^{QQ}, those unique to the Folio between ^{FF}. Words or phrases in stage directions which are of editorial origin and appear in neither Quarto nor Folio are enclosed in square brackets. The convention of superscript markers has also been used for three passages in *Titus Andronicus* which are taken from sources other than the first Quarto of 1594. The Arden 3 editors of *Henry V* and *Othello* have chosen the more conventional course of not indicating readings and passages unique to the earlier quartos incorporated into their Folio–based edited texts of those plays.

Mr. WILLIAM
SHAKESPEARES
COMEDIES,
HISTORIES, &
TRAGEDIES.

Published according to the True Originall Copies.

LONDON
Printed by Isaac Iaggard, and Ed. Blount. 1623.

1 Title-page, with a portrait of Shakespeare engraved by Droeshout, from the First Folio, printed by Isaac Jaggard and Edward Blount, 1623.

Introduction

WHY SHAKESPEARE?

What is 'Shakespeare'? A worldwide cultural phenomenon, a brand-name, a logo, an image that appears on T-shirts and credit cards, a mainstay of theatre, film and video production, a compulsory component of education, a label that sells thousands of books, a household name. Also an individual human being, born in a small English country town in 1564, a man who went to London and had a successful career as an actor, playwright and shareholder in the theatre. By all accounts an agreeable and modest man who did not seek to draw attention to himself, even by publishing his plays, though he does seem to have hoped that the fame of his *Sonnets* would outlive him. His surname has nevertheless become so familiar that his first name, William, does not need to be mentioned – is not indeed mentioned on the covers or title-pages of his works as published in 'The Arden Shakespeare': a person from another planet might work carefully through an entire volume in our series without discovering the first name of the author, but on our planet 'everyone' knows who he is. It has even become a kind of perverse tribute to him that periodically people attempt to prove that he didn't write anything after all, that the works ascribed to him were in fact written by somebody else entirely.

The names of some of this man's works have become so familiar themselves that we can even drop 'Shakespeare' without fear of being misunderstood when we talk of 'Orson Welles's *Othello*' or 'Kenneth Branagh's *Henry V*'. Certain images have become instantly recognizable: a man dressed in black holding a skull 'means' *Hamlet*, a man talking to a woman above him on a moon-lit balcony 'means' *Romeo and Juliet*. We quote Shakespeare all the time, sometimes unconsciously, using phrases that have dropped into common usage: 'to have one's pound of flesh' (*Merchant of Venice* 1.3.145-6 and subsequently); 'to the manner born' (*Hamlet* 1.4.15); 'more honoured in the breach than the observance' (*Hamlet* 1.4.16); 'at one fell swoop' (*Macbeth* 4.3.219). Compilers of crossword puzzles and quiz games routinely rely on Shakespearean quotations and references.

Words and phrases from the plays and poems have provided the titles of hundreds of novels, plays and films: one might cite Edith Wharton's *The Glimpses of the Moon* (*Hamlet* 1.4.53), William Faulkner's *The Sound and the Fury* (*Macbeth* 5.5.27), Aldous Huxley's *Brave New World* (*The Tempest* 5.1.183), Margaret Millar's *How Like an Angel* (*Hamlet* 2.2.306), Agatha Christie's *By the Pricking of My Thumbs* – Ray Bradbury completed the rhyme with his *Something Wicked This Way Comes* (*Macbeth* 4.1.44-5) – and H.E. Bates's *The Darling Buds of May* (Sonnet 18, 3). The plays are still being performed live all over the world, and film and video versions have made them accessible to millions of people who never go to the theatre. They continue to inspire adaptations and spin-offs such as Peter Greenaway's film *Prospero's Books* (1991), Gus Van Sant's film *My Own Private Idaho* (1992) and Alan Isler's novel *The Prince of West End Avenue* (1994), all of which assume a prior knowledge of a Shakespeare text on the part of their viewers or readers.

How and why has this happened? Four hundred years after the heyday of Shakespeare's own dramatic career we find ourselves arguing about whether his extraordinary fame and influence were somehow inevitable, a direct result of the intrinsic qualities of his works themselves, or a piece of sustained hype, the manipulation of a myth by those with a personal stake in its perpetuation – performers, teachers, publishers, Stratford-upon-Avon hoteliers – and by those with a more general interest in promoting British 'high' culture: Shakespeare has become 'the Bard of Avon', the ultimate canonical figure who is taken to represent the genius and values of an entire nation.

Shakespeare did do well during his lifetime out of what was the nearest thing Elizabethan and Jacobean London had to a mass entertainment industry. Unlike other dramatists of the time, he did most of his work for a single theatrical company, the Lord Chamberlain's Men, under Elizabeth I, who became the King's Men under James I. This stability in itself probably provided him with reasonably good working conditions and the opportunity to develop his work with known performers and business associates; it made it relatively easy for his complete works to be collected and published after he died. Other dramatists such as Thomas Middleton, who produced work for a number of different companies, had a less stable working environment and less chance of having their work collected or even identified.

The First Folio of Shakespeare's plays was published in 1623, seven years after his death, and reprinted in 1632, but in 1642 the theatres were closed, and were to remain closed for nearly twenty years during the Civil War and Commonwealth period, potentially jeopardizing the chances of Shakespeare or any other dramatist achieving lasting fame. With the Restoration of the monarchy in 1660, however, the theatres reopened and Shakespeare's plays came back into the repertory, albeit in truncated and altered versions. During the eighteenth century his reputation was consolidated by the publication of a number of scholarly editions and monographs, the erection of a monument in Westminster Abbey (1741) and the promotion of Stratford-upon-Avon as his birthplace and the site of David Garrick's festival or 'Jubilee' (1769). While the plays were often rewritten wholesale for the contemporary stage, their texts were simultaneously being 'restored' with great care (and even more ingenuity) by editors who contributed largely to the 'canonization' of the author. This has essentially been the story of Shakespeare's reception and cultural survival ever since: we still (in the total absence of manuscripts) pursue the chimaera of 'what Shakespeare really wrote', while on the other hand treating his texts as endlessly adaptable, available for rewriting, rereading and reinterpreting by each generation.

The plays have turned out to be equally suitable for export, and Shakespeare has been enthusiastically appropriated by many countries around the world. In Germany, for example, Ferdinand Freiligrath's 1844 poem beginning '*Deutschland ist Hamlet*' ('Germany is Hamlet') spelt out a long-lasting identification of the character of Hamlet with the German Romantic self-image of a people capable of profound reflection but incapable of action. In the United States, on the other hand, Shakespeare became a kind of symbol of racial and cul-

tural integration and democracy, perhaps especially during the period when silent films made his work accessible to people who did not know English. In Japan, which imported Shakespeare relatively late in the nineteenth century, he quickly came to represent the essence of westernization and modernization. All these countries now have thriving Shakespeare industries of their own.

The globalization of Shakespeare was of course assisted by the political and economic spread of the British Empire in the nineteenth century and by the continuing dominance of English as a worldwide language after the decline of that Empire. What remains remarkable is that Shakespeare is actually quite a difficult writer linguistically – much harder to read today than most of his contemporaries such as Ben Jonson, Thomas Middleton or John Fletcher. His syntax is often complex, his figures of speech elaborate and his ideas hard to grasp. Some of this may be offset by the larger patterns of satisfaction we find in his plots and characters, and indeed it could be said that the difficulty itself leaves room for our explanations and interpretations. Shakespeare still 'works' in the theatre, but at school we have to be taught to 'appreciate' Shakespeare: is this indoctrination or something more benign – an educational process involving the 'recognition' of intrinsic merit?

In his essay *Of the Standard of Taste*, written in 1742, the philosopher David Hume argued that there is such a thing as intrinsic excellence in literature and that it is the continuity of a work's reputation that proves it. What he calls 'catholic and universal beauty' in various art forms is demonstrated by 'the durable admiration which attends those works that have survived all the caprices of mode and fashion, all the mistakes of ignorance and envy'. To support this he claims that 'The same Homer who pleased at Athens two thousand years ago, is still admired at Paris and London'. Shakespeare can be said to have passed the survival test, but perhaps it is not 'the same Shakespeare' now as four hundred years ago, and not 'the same Shakespeare' in Berlin, New York or Tokyo

2 Shakespeare as twentieth-century cultural icon, selling lager

as in London or Stratford-upon-Avon. One of the secrets of Shakespeare's success may be his changeability, the openness of his works to take on new meanings in contexts he cannot have anticipated.

SHAKESPEARE: THE LIFE

William Shakespeare was a successful man of the emerging entertainment industry of Elizabethan England. He was an actor, a 'sharer' in the acting company (that is, no mere hireling but a partner entitled to share in its profits) and, of course, a leading playwright.

He began, however, more humbly. We know a remarkable amount, for this period, about Shakespeare and his family. He was born late in April 1564 in Stratford-upon-Avon. The parish church records his baptism on 26 April; his unrecorded birthdate is conventionally set three days earlier on the 23 April, St George's Day (and also, apparently, the date of Shakespeare's death). His father was John Shakespeare, a glover and later a wool merchant, and his mother was Mary Arden, daughter of a well-established farmer in the nearby village of Wilmcote. Though the records have not survived, we can safely assume that he attended the King's New School, the Stratford grammar school with its strenuous classically based curriculum, but we know for certain that at the age of eighteen he married Anne Hathaway, also of Stratford, and that a daughter, Susanna, was born to them, as the parish records note, on 26 May 1583. On 2 February 1585 the register records the birth of twins, Hamnet and Judith.

Shakespeare was well established in London by the early 1590s as an actor and as a playwright. In 1592 a book appeared in which Robert Greene criticized an unnamed actor, 'an upstart Crow', for his presumption in writing plays, supposing himself 'as well able to bombast out a blank verse' as any and imagining himself 'the only Shake-scene in a country'. Since Greene's attack contains a parody of a line from *3 Henry VI*, it seems certain that it is Shakespeare that he aims at. By 1592, then, Shakespeare had already established himself in the theatre and drawn the ire of a jealous rival. In 1594, Court records indicate payments to Shakespeare and two other sharers in the Lord Chamberlain's Men for 'two several comedies or interludes showed by them before her Majesty in Christmas time last'. References to Shakespeare's activity in the theatre abound, and in 1598 Francis Meres claimed that Shakespeare could be compared with Seneca for the writing of tragedy and with Plautus for comedy, indeed that among English writers he was 'the best of both kinds for the stage'. But he wrote nondramatic poetry as well. When a severe outbreak of plague beginning in the summer of 1592 forced the closing of the theatres until the spring of 1594, Shakespeare wrote two narrative poems, *Venus and Adonis* and *The Rape of Lucrece*, both dedicated to Henry Wriothesley, the third Earl of Southampton, and printed by a former fellow-resident of Stratford, Richard Field, in 1593 and 1594 respectively; and an edition of *Shakespeare's Sonnets* was published by Thomas Thorpe in 1609.

But Shakespeare's primary work was in the theatre, and it was the theatre that made him a wealthy man. His money, however, came neither from commissions nor from royalties for his plays but from his position as a sharer in the Lord Chamberlain's Men (who, with the accession of James to the throne in 1603, became the King's Men), by which he was entitled to one-tenth of the company's profits, a share handsome enough to permit him considerable investment in real estate. In 1597 he bought for £60 the substantial freehold house in Stratford known as New Place, the second largest dwelling in the town; in 1602, he purchased 107 acres of land in the manorial fields to the north of Stratford for £320, and later that year a cottage in Stratford on Chapel Lane; in 1605 he bought a half-interest in a Stratford tithe farm for an additional £440; and in 1613, with three other investors, he acquired a 'tenement' in Blackfriars for £140.

If Shakespeare's business dealings can be traced in the Court Rolls, his family's lives and deaths can be traced in the Stratford parish register. His son Hamnet died at the age of eleven and was buried on 11 August 1596. Shakespeare's father died in September 1601, his mother in 1608. Shakespeare's elder daughter, Susanna, married John Hall, a well-respected Stratford physician, in Holy Trinity church on 5 June 1607. His younger daughter, Judith, married Thomas Quiney on 10 February 1616. Shakespeare's wife died on 6 August 1623; she had lived to see a monument to her husband installed in Holy Trinity, but passed away just before the publication of the First Folio of his plays, the more lasting monument to his memory.

Shakespeare himself had died in late April of 1616, and was buried on the north side of the chancel of Holy Trinity, having left a will written that January. He left ten pounds for 'the poor of Stratford', remembered local friends and his extended family, and allotted 16s. 8d. each for memorial rings for his theatrical colleagues, Richard Burbage, John Heminges and Henry Condell. He left £150 to his daughter Judith, and another £150 to be paid if 'she or any issue of her body be living' three years from the execution of the will, but the bulk of the estate was left to Susanna. His wife is mentioned only once, in an apparent afterthought to the document: 'Item, I give unto my wife my second best bed with the furniture.' The bequest of the bed and bedding has led many to speculate that this was a deliberate slight, but English customary law provided the widow with a third of the estate, and the 'second best bed' was almost certainly their own, the best being saved for guests.

Yet in spite of the detailed records that remain, allowing us to trace major and minor events in the lives of Shakespeare and his family, as well as to see his vital presence in the life of the London stage, some critics have passionately held that the author of the plays was someone other than 'the man from Stratford'. It was not until the eighteenth century that anyone questioned Shakespeare's authorship, but since then many, including Mark Twain, Henry James and Sigmund Freud, have been attracted to the anti-Stratfordian heresy. Various candidates have been proposed. Christopher Marlowe, Francis Bacon, Edward de Vere, the seventeenth Earl of Oxford, Queen Elizabeth, even Daniel Defoe (who was not born until 1661) have all been suggested as the 'real' author of 'Shakespeare's' plays and poems. The controversy, however, has little to recommend it except its unintended humour; anti-Stratfordian champions have sometimes had unfortunate names, including Looney, Battey and Silliman. Although usually energetically asserted, the belief that someone other than Shakespeare wrote the plays seemingly derives from simple, if unattractive, social snobbery: a certainty that only someone educated at university or at court would be capable of such artistry. The desire to give the plays a more socially distinguished patrimony than they in fact had at least attests to the importance they have come to assume in our culture. All in all, however, there seems little doubt that William Shakespeare, the glover's son from Stratford, wrote the plays that bear his name, though their greatness can hardly be illuminated or intensified by the evidence of the life of their author.

SHAKESPEARE AND THE THEATRE

At an unknown date between 1585 and 1591, William Shakespeare left Stratford-upon-Avon and became an actor and playwright. Early tradition holds that he was for a few years before this a country schoolmaster (which might help to explain his close knowledge of some Latin texts, including plays by Plautus and Seneca). In 1587 the Queen's Men visited Stratford shortly after they lost a leading actor, William Knell, killed in a duel at Thame in Oxfordshire. Whether or not this may be imagined as Shakespeare's opportunity to join the players, plays from the Queen's Men's repertoire were, on the evidence of later allusions in his plays, well known to him. His name is, however, more often associated with two other companies, Lord Strange's (Derby's) Men and its offshoot the Earl of Pembroke's Men, which collapsed in the summer of 1593. A new play, called 'harey the vj' and usually identified as *King Henry VI, Part 1*, was performed by Strange's Men at the Rose playhouse on 3 March 1592 and thereafter. *Titus Andronicus*, played by the Earl of Sussex's Men, followed on 23 January 1594: in June two more performances of it were given by the Lord Admiral's Men and the Lord Chamberlain's Men. By June 1594 Shakespeare had become a leading member of a newly-formed company, the Lord Chamberlain's Men. He would remain with them for the rest of his career. Of his repertoire as an actor we know almost nothing. His name heads the list of 'principal actors in all these plays' prefaced to the First Folio in 1623. It had earlier appeared in the similar lists for Ben Jonson's *Every Man in his Humour* (1598) and *Sejanus, His Fall* (1603), printed in the Jonson Folio of 1616. Beyond this, we have only late seventeenth-century traditions that he played Adam in *As You Like It* and the Ghost in *Hamlet*.

1594 saw the stabilization in London of the leading playing companies. The Admiral's Men, led by Edward Alleyn, under the management of Philip Henslowe, were at Henslowe's theatre, the Rose, on Bankside in Southwark (whose foundations were partially revealed by archaeologists in the spring of 1989, before being covered once more for the construction above them of an office block). The Chamberlain's Men, led by Richard Burbage and managed by his father, James, acted at the Theatre, north of the Thames, in Finsbury (not far from the modern Barbican Centre). The Theatre, built in 1576 for James Burbage, was the first building to be erected in the

suburbs of London expressly for the presentation of plays. Henslowe's Rose followed in 1587; after it came the Swan (1595); the Globe (1599), replacing the Theatre and built with its structural timbers, bodily removed through London and across the River Thames from Finsbury to Southwark; the Fortune (1600), built in north London to replace the Rose; the Red Bull (1605); and the Hope (1614). The building of the Globe was an important event for Shakespeare, and we can see in the first plays he wrote for it, perhaps *As You Like It* and *King Henry V*, more surely *Julius Caesar* and *Hamlet*, a renewed awareness of the propositions that 'all the world's a stage' and that every man and woman is a performer in the wider theatre of the world. Not for nothing was it called the Globe.

Before 1576 plays had been performed, as they continued to be throughout the lifetime of Shakespeare, in a wide variety of locations, indoors and out. In London, the yards of coaching inns were used as theatres (and sometimes adapted for the purpose at considerable expense). Throughout the country the halls of schools, towns, colleges and noble houses were used for occasional performances by visiting players. Models for the public playhouses in London included inn yards as well as the baiting rings on the south bank used for bull- and bear-baiting. A large auditorium (with 20 sides and a diameter of 100 feet in the case of the Globe), had seats arranged in three galleries, and contained within it the separate structure of a stage and backstage building. The

3 Portrait of Richard Burbage, leading actor of the Chamberlain's Men

4 The Globe Theatre, as recreated in the 1990s on London's Bankside

stage was covered by a canopy, or 'heavens', which could house winding-gear for lowering large properties or descending gods, and it was accessible from below through a trapdoor. At the back of the stage, behind a wall with two or three large doors in it, lay the 'tiring-house' (dressing rooms and wings combined), above which was a gallery, reached by a stair and divided into a number of 'rooms' or boxes, where the most important members of the audience could sit to see and to be seen. When necessary, one or more of these boxes could be used to represent a window, or walls, if required by action 'above' or 'aloft', and they may also have housed the musicians.

Indoor acting continued throughout the period at smaller 'private' playhouses, of which the earliest were set up in the halls of former monastic buildings within the city of London. Holding an audience of some 600 or 700 (against the 2,500-3,000 capacity attributed to the public playhouses) these theatres were used for plays appealing to a more restricted and wealthier audience. While you could stand in the yard at the Globe for a penny, the cheapest seat at the Blackfriars or St Paul's theatre would cost sixpence. The indoor playhouses were associated with companies of boy players, composed of choristers of the Chapel Royal and of St Paul's Cathedral. The play-

5 Detail from Wenzel Hollar's engraving *A Long Bird's-Eye View of London*, 1647, showing the rebuilt Globe

The Workes of William Shakespeare,
containing all his Comedies, Histories, and Tragedies: Truely set forth, according to their first *ORIGINALL.*

The Names of the Principall Actors in all these Playes.

William Shakespeare.	Samuel Gilburne.
Richard Burbadge.	Robert Armin.
John Hemmings.	William Ostler.
Augustine Phillips.	Nathan Field.
William Kempt.	John Underwood.
Thomas Poope.	Nicholas Tooley.
George Bryan.	William Ecclestone.
Henry Condell.	Joseph Taylor.
William Slye.	Robert Benfield.
Richard Cowly.	Robert Goughe.
John Lowine.	Richard Robinson.
Samuell Crosse.	John Shancke.
Alexander Cooke.	John Rice.

6 The principal actors in the King's Men, as listed in the First Folio of 1623

houses Shakespeare wrote for were the Theatre (and its substitute the Curtain), the Globe and, after 1608 or 1609, the Blackfriars private theatre.

During the lifetime of Shakespeare adult playing companies grew to a size and achieved a stability which justified the expense of building permanent theatres around London. Such companies consisted of some dozen to fifteen men and three to five boys, who trained as the apprentices of leading members and played female and juvenile roles. Earlier in the century, companies were much smaller – sometimes as small as three men and a boy – and playwrights had developed writing techniques to allow a cast of five to double in up to seventeen roles. Survival of such techniques accounts for the very large number of roles for Shakespeare's histories and tragedies, where most actors would have played two or more parts, some of them appearing for no more than a scene or two.

In sixteenth- and early seventeenth-century Europe the prohibition of public acting by women and the convention of all-male casting were peculiar to England. Though easily accepted by audiences, the playing of female roles by boys led writers to emphasize the femininity of the women in their plays to an extent that the use of female performers would have rendered unnecessary. Shakespeare had much to do with the popularity of female roles in which a girl spends much of the action in male disguise. While this may have been an easier convention to accept when the role was played by a boy, it also meant that the performer's skill was required, not to impersonate a young man, but to keep the audience aware that 'he' was 'really' a girl under the male costume. In the early Jacobean years the King's Men evidently had a boy or young man of exceptional talent, if we assume that the roles of Lady Macbeth, Cleopatra and Volumnia in *Coriolanus* may have been written for the same actor; the same must be true of such roles as Queen Margaret in the *King Henry VI* plays and Katherine in *The Taming of the Shrew* in the early 1590s, and of the comic heroines of *Much Ado About Nothing*, *As You Like It* and *Twelfth Night* around the turn of the century.

As the plays indicate, the skills demanded of an actor included singing, dancing and sword-fighting as well as the rhetorician's arts of speech and significant gesture. We know little, however, about acting styles in the period; nevertheless, it is not fanciful to suppose that the changing style of the plays written between 1590 and 1620 reflects a change by actors from a broad style, dependent on resonant vocal delivery and confident use of expansive gesture, such as suited open-air playhouses, to a subtler and more intimate manner, less dependent on emphatic speech and allowing a wider range of gesture and even facial expression, which could register with most of the audience in the smaller space of a private playhouse. The contrast is clear if *The Tempest* is compared with the *King Henry VI* plays or *Titus Andronicus*.

It is likely that Shakespeare's own plays were instrumental in changing styles of acting between 1590 and 1614. He had the unparalleled good fortune to work in the same company for some twenty years, as actor and as principal dramatist. He wrote for actors who were also his business partners and co-owners of the playhouses they played in. We must presume that he had some say in how the plays he wrote for them were presented. The strength of the company is reflected in the demands his plays make on actors. The Jacobean plays, in particular, regularly require strong performances in ten or a dozen significant roles – a hard requirement for any company to fulfil. The identification of actor with role – the building of a 'character' – is a commonplace of twentieth-century theatre. In Shakespeare's time it seems to have been something of an innovation: indeed a 'character' would have been understood to mean a stock or stereotyped stage figure such as the old man, the melancholy lover or the country clown. Richard Burbage, Shakespeare's

leading actor, attracted comment for (exceptionally) remaining in character when he came off-stage during a performance. Not the least of Shakespeare's achievements was the writing of dramatic roles a few hundred lines in length which can reward close and subtle verbal, moral or psychological analysis, three-dimensional fictions which create the illusion of the authentically recognizable inconsistency of human individuals.

Career and chronology

We do not know the dates of composition of all of Shakespeare's plays. Such evidence as there is is circumstantial: dates when they (or works on which they are certainly based) were published, or dated references to, and comments on, early performances can narrow the limits for many of them, while a very few allude to datable events of the time. On such evidence, supported by internal features of style, metre and subject, the plays can be arranged, with varying degrees of certainty, in groups relating to five phases of his theatrical career.

First come the plays Shakespeare had probably already written before the forming of the Chamberlain's Men in the summer of 1594. These are *The Two Gentlemen of Verona*, *The Taming of the Shrew* and possibly *The Comedy of Errors*, the three parts of *King Henry VI*, *King Richard III* and *Titus Andronicus*. Plays written for the new company at the Theatre in the five years from 1594 until the opening of the Globe in the autumn of 1599, in possible sequence of composition, are *Romeo and Juliet*, *Love's Labour's Lost*, *A Midsummer Night's Dream*, *King Richard II*, *King John*, *The Merchant of Venice*, the two parts of *King Henry IV*, *Much Ado About Nothing*, *The Merry Wives of Windsor* and (at some date before summer 1598) the lost *Love's Labour's Won*. *As You Like It* and *King Henry V* may belong in this group, though both show signs of having been written with the Globe in mind.

Plays for the Globe from 1599 until the death of Queen Elizabeth I in the spring of 1603 are *Julius Caesar*, *Hamlet*, *Twelfth Night*, *Troilus and Cressida*, *Othello* and possibly *All's Well That Ends Well*. As a leading member of the King's Men, Shakespeare seems to have reduced his output from the previous average of two plays per year. His new plays from 1603 to 1608 were: *Measure for Measure*, *Timon of Athens*, *King Lear*, *Macbeth*, *Antony and Cleopatra*, *Pericles* and *Coriolanus*. The final period, from the company's recovery of the indoor Blackfriars Theatre for winter use in 1608–9 to 1613–14, saw composition of *The Winter's Tale*, *Cymbeline*, *The Tempest* and of three plays written in collaboration with John Fletcher, *King Henry VIII*, the lost *Cardenio* and *The Two Noble Kinsmen*.

SHAKESPEARE IN PRINT

Shakespeare's literary career in his own lifetime strikingly resists the very notions of artistic autonomy and authority that his name has come triumphantly to represent. He had no specific literary and little direct financial interest in his plays. He wrote scripts to be performed, scripts that once they were turned over to the acting company no longer belonged to him in any legal sense and immediately

7 The earliest illustration of a work by Shakespeare; a scene from *Titus Andronicus*, attributed to Henry Peacham, *c.*1595, 1605 or 1615

escaped his artistic control, as staging requirements and actors' temperaments inevitably enforced their changes upon them. He involved himself with the printing and publication of none of them, and held no copyright. In the absence of anything like modern copyright law, which dates in Britain only from 1709, the scripts belonged to the acting company (and as they remained in the repertory they would be subject to continued revision as the actors sought to keep their property current).

Except that, as an experienced actor and sharer in his company, he could no doubt exert influence over production as an independent playwright could not, Shakespeare's relation to the plays he wrote was in no way unusual. Like all playwrights, he wrote so that his plays could be acted; his words were intended to be heard, not read. In spite of Ben Jonson's efforts to establish his own plays as a form of high culture, plays remained sub-literary, the piece-work of an emerging entertainment industry. 'Riffe-raffe', Thomas Bodley called them in 1612, and ordered his librarian not to collect such 'idle books' in order to protect his Oxford library against the 'scandal' that would be caused by their presence.

A play was generally written on demand for an acting company, and the completed script then belonged to the company that had commissioned it. Under certain circumstances, and with no necessary regard for the author's wishes or interests, the companies would sell their rights in a play to a publisher, who would have it printed in an edition of about 800 copies, usually in a quarto format and selling for sixpence. The author would receive no money from the sale of the manuscript or from any subsequent sale of books. Neither were the literary ambitions of the playwrights usually a factor in publication. Ben Jonson's aggressive effort to create himself as a literary figure is, of course, the exception that proves the rule, his 1616 Folio's characteristic 'The Author, B.I.' on the individual title-pages revealingly anomalous; indeed Jonson is the *only* playwright in the period ever identified as an 'author' on a title-page.

Shakespeare displayed no similarly proprietary artistic impulses. At the time of his death, eighteen plays had reached print (many in more than one edition), but he had prepared none of the texts for publication and had overseen none through the press. The eighteen play-texts each appeared in a hastily-printed quarto volume; none has a dedication or an epistle from the author; none displays any sign of Shakespeare's interest or involvement in its printing. On the other hand, his two long poems, *Venus and Adonis* (1593) and *The Rape of Lucrece* (1594), printed by fellow-Stratfordian Richard Field, are obviously produced with care, and each is issued with a signed dedication to the Earl of Southampton. The texts of the plays show nothing comparable.

In the course of Shakespeare's lifetime twenty different publishers brought forth editions of individual plays, but not one took any unusual care to ensure that the text was authoritative or the printing exact. The texts are of varied quality and provenance, some seemingly printed from manuscripts that appear authorial, others apparently

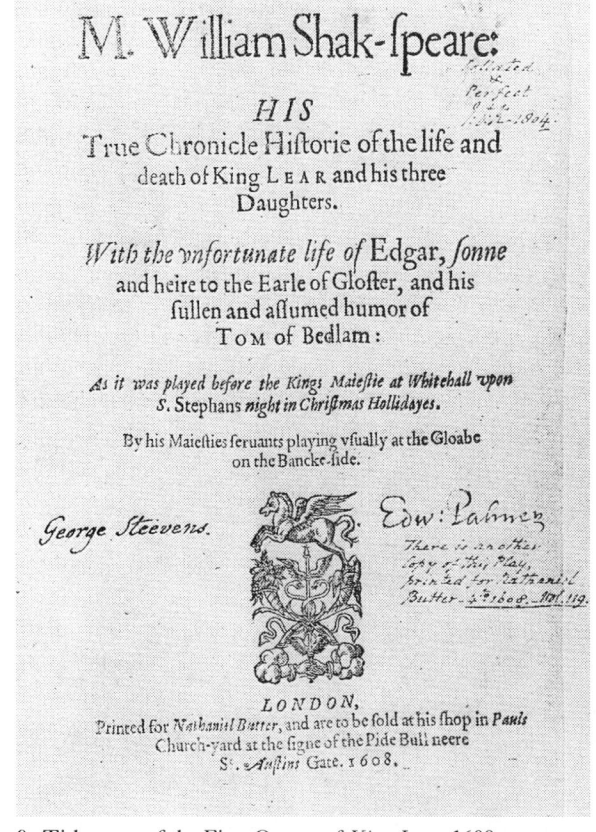

8 Title-page of the First Quarto of *Love's Labour's Lost*, 1598

9 Title-page of the First Quarto of *King Lear*, 1608

from copy showing the inevitable cuts and interpolations of the theatre, still others printed from transcripts, as fellow-playwright Thomas Heywood claims, 'Corrupt and mangled (coppied by the eare)', reported texts reconstructing performances witnessed or acted. In any case no manuscript of a Shakespeare play survives (unless it be the so-called 'Hand D' in the manuscript of *The Booke of Sir Thomas More* which, if indeed Shakespeare's own, bears witness to Shakespeare as collaborator, merely one of five playwrights who collaborated in writing the play).

Though today Shakespeare's literary pre-eminence has made the publication of his plays a thriving cultural industry, his earliest publishers did not seem much to care about his authorship. The 1594 edition of *Titus Andronicus* omits Shakespeare's name from the title-page, giving information rather about the printer and where the play could be bought. The play is advertised – and title-pages were explicitly forms of advertising, hung up as posters on bookstalls – not as by William Shakespeare but by the acting company that performed it: 'As it was Plaide by the Right Honourable the Earle of *Darbie*, Earle of *Pembrooke*, and Earle of *Sussex* their seruants.' And when it was reprinted, first in 1600 and then in 1611, neither bibliographic scruple nor thought of commercial advantage led the publisher to add Shakespeare's name to the title-page.

Indeed, until 1598 none of Shakespeare's plays that appeared in print identifies Shakespeare as its author. Not merely *Titus* or the early Quartos of *2* and *3 Henry VI*, which could be thought immature efforts of a young playwright whose achievement did not yet merit nor permit a publisher to capitalize on his name on the title-page, but even his later and more successful plays refuse to acknowledge or exploit Shakespeare's authorship. *Romeo and Juliet* appeared in 1597, identified only 'As it hath been often (with great applause) plaid publiquely, by the right Honourable L. of Hunsdon his seruants'; and its next two printings, in 1599 and 1609, while claiming that the text has now been 'Newly corrected, augmented, and amended', still make no mention of its author (or corrector), again only identifying the acting company that performed it as the source of its authority. *Richard II* and *King Henry IV, Part 1* similarly first appear with no mention of Shakespeare on the title-page, or anywhere else for that matter.

In fact seven plays appeared before one was issued with Shakespeare's name. In 1598 Cuthbert Burby published *Love's Labour's Lost* with the title-page identifying the play in small type as 'Newly corrected and augmented by *W. Shakespere*'. Whatever this assertion is, it is certainly no ardent proclamation of Shakespeare's authorship. The unequivocal evidence of the early Quartos is, then, that Shakespeare had no interest in their publication and what is perhaps more surprising, that his publishers had as little interest in him.

At least the latter would soon change. The 1608 'Pide Bull' Quarto (so called after the name of the shop where it was sold) of *King Lear* does indeed proudly assert Shakespeare's authorship, emblazoning his name across the title-page in a typeface substantially larger than any other. But the text, it must be said, shows no sign of Shakespeare's involvement in its publication. It is poorly printed. (It was the first play that its printer had attempted,

and noticeably so.) An author overseeing the printing would have insisted on changes, but nonetheless the publisher, Nathaniel Butter, spectacularly identifies the printed play as Shakespeare's.

What has happened is not that Shakespeare's rights as an author had suddenly been recognized and were here being celebrated but that Shakespeare's name was now of value to the publisher. For Butter, identifying his *King Lear* as 'M. William Shak-speare: / *HIS* / True Chronicle Historie of the life and / death of King LEAR' served to differentiate his property from another play about King Lear (*The True Chronicle Historie of King Leir*) that had been published in 1605 and was available in the bookstalls. Shakespeare's name functioned on the title-page at least as much to identify the play*book* as the play*wright*, though already it was becoming evident that Shakespeare's name could sell books. As the publisher of *Othello* in 1622 later asserted: 'the Authors name is sufficient to vent his worke'.

But in truth it is only in 1623 with the publication of the First Folio edition of his plays that Shakespeare truly enters English literature as an author, though this, of course, was neither his own idea nor of any direct benefit to him. He had died in 1616, seven years before the Folio appeared, and to the end showed no sign of any literary ambition for his plays. But the Folio assumes that Shakespeare is indeed an author to be read and not merely the provider of scripts to be acted. The play-texts in the Folio are stripped of their theatrical association. Unlike the early Quartos, there is no mention in the Folio that any text is 'as it was played', indeed, though 'The Names of the Principall Actors in all these Playes' are listed, Shakespeare's own at the head of them, no acting company is ever mentioned by name; rather the texts are described, no doubt too confidently, as perfect and purely authorial, presented here exactly 'as he conceiued them'.

It is not clear whose idea the collected volume was or even what was the precise motivation for it (beyond a general hope of making some money). The volume's two principal publishers, Edward Blount and Isaac Jaggard, apparently negotiated with two of Shakespeare's old friends and fellow-actors, John Heminges and Henry Condell, for the rights to the plays that had not yet been printed, and they then worked to secure the publishing rights to those that had. Eventually they acquired them all (except for *Pericles*, which had been published in a Quarto in 1609 as the work of Shakespeare, and *The Two Noble Kinsmen*, not published until 1634 but identified then as the work of Shakespeare and John Fletcher), and the Folio was published in 1623. It includes thirty-six plays, eighteen of which had never before appeared in print, a dedication and an epistle, prefatory verses, and an engraved title-page with a three-quarter-page portrait of Shakespeare and a facing poem.

Printing had begun early in 1622 and took about twenty-one months to complete. The volume sold for £1 with a plain calf binding, for somewhat less when more cheaply bound; and unbound, as many books were sold, it could be bought for 15*s*. Its very appearance in folio, a format usually reserved for theological or historical works or for collected editions of canonical authors, itself marks a major shift in the cultural positioning of

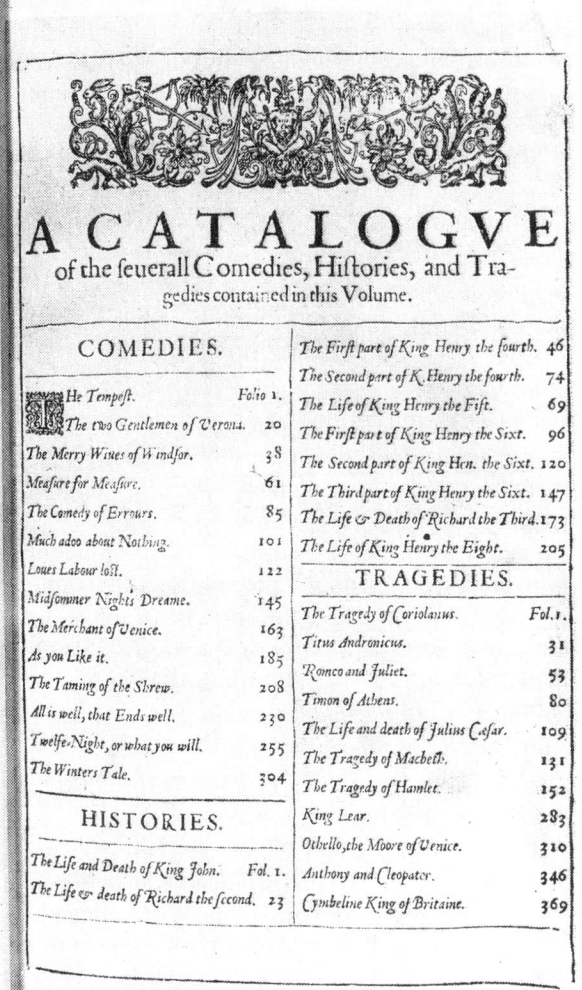

A CATALOGVE
of the feuerall Comedies, Hiftories, and Tragedies contained in this Volume.

COMEDIES.

He Tempeft.	Folio 1.
The two Gentlemen of Verona.	20
The Merry Wiues of Windfor.	38
Meafure for Meafure.	61
The Comedy of Errours.	85
Much adoo about Nothing.	101
Loues Labour loft.	122
Midfommer Nights Dreame.	145
The Merchant of Venice.	163
As you Like it.	185
The Taming of the Shrew.	208
All is well, that Ends well.	230
Twelfe-Night, or what you will.	255
The Winters Tale.	304

HISTORIES.

The Life and Death of King John.	Fol. 1.
The Life & death of Richard the fecond.	23

The Firft part of King Henry the fourth.	46
The Second part of K. Henry the fourth.	74
The Life of King Henry the Fift.	69
The Firft part of King Henry the Sixt.	96
The Second part of King Hen. the Sixt.	120
The Third part of King Henry the Sixt.	147
The Life & Death of Richard the Third.	173
The Life of King Henry the Eight.	205

TRAGEDIES.

The Tragedy of Coriolanus.	Fol. 1.
Titus Andronicus.	31
Romeo and Juliet.	53
Timon of Athens.	80
The Life and death of Julius Cæfar.	109
The Tragedy of Macbeth.	131
The Tragedy of Hamlet.	152
King Lear.	283
Othello, the Moore of Venice.	310
Anthony and Cleopater.	346
Cymbeline King of Britaine.	369

10 The catalogue of 35 of Shakespeare's plays as listed in the First Folio, 1623: *Troilus and Cressida* is not listed

To the great Variety of Readers.

From the moft able, to him that can but fpell: There you are number'd. We had rather you were weighd. Efpecially, when the fate of all Bookes depends vpon your capacities : and not of your heads alone, but of your purfes. Well ! It is now publique, & you wil ftand for your priuiledges weeknow: to read, and cenfure. Do fo, but buy it firft. That doth beft commend a Booke, the Stationer faies. Then, how odde foeuer your braines be, or your wifedomes, make your licence the fame, and fpare not. Iudge your fixe-pen'orth, your fhillings worth, your fiue fhillings worth at a time, or higher, fo you rife to the iuft rates, and welcome. But, what euer you do, Buy. Cenfure will not driue a Trade, or make the Iacke go. And though you be a Magiftrate of wit, and fit on the Stage at *Black-Friers*, or the *Cock-pit*, to arraigne Playes dailie, know, thefe Playes haue had their triall alreadie, and ftood out all Appeales; and do now come forth quitted rather by a Decree of Court, then any purchas'd Letters of commendation.

It had bene a thing, we confeffe, worthie to haue bene wifhed, that the Author himfelfe had liu'd to haue fet forth, and ouerfeen his owne writings; But fince it hath bin ordain'd otherwife, and he by death departed from that right, we pray you do not envie his Friends, the office of their care, and paine, to haue collected & publifh'd them; and fo to haue publifh'd them, as where (before) you were abus'd with diuerfe ftolne, and furreptitious copies, maimed, and deformed by the frauds and ftealthes of iniurious impoftors, that expos'd them: euen thofe, are now offer'd to your view cur'd, and perfect of their limbes; and all the reft, abfolute in their numbers, as he conceiued thē. Who, as he was a happie imitator of Nature, was a moft gentle expreffer of it. His mind and hand went together: And what he thought, he vttered with that eafineffe, that wee haue fcarfe receiued from him a blot in his papers. But it is not our prouince, who onely gather his works, and giue them you, to praife him. It is yours that reade him. And there we hope, to your diuers capacities, you will finde enough, both to draw, and hold you : for his wit can no more lie hid, then it could be loft. Reade him, therefore; and againe, and againe : And if then you doe not like him, furely you are in fome manifeft danger, not to vnderftand him. And fo we leaue you to other of his Friends, whom if you need, can bee your guides : if you neede them not, you can leade your felues, and others. And fuch Readers we wifh him.

A 3   *John Heminge.*
       Henrie Condell.

11 The second epistle 'To the great variety of readers', prefacing the First Folio, 1623, and signed by John Heminges and Henry Condell

Shakespeare, a shift confirmed within a few months of publication when Thomas Bodley, who, as we have seen, in 1612 forbade the collection of play-texts, accepted a copy for his library and had it bound in fine leather and stamped with the Oxford University seal.

Today it seems obvious that the Folio published by Blount and Jaggard was a necessary and appropriate memorial to England's greatest playwright, but at the time all that was clear to the publishers was that they had undertaken a complex and expensive project with no guarantee of recovering their considerable investment. In the event, of course, they did. The book sold well, and a second edition appeared only nine years later, remarkable evidence of its popularity. For later generations, with no financial stake, the book is of even greater value. Without the Folio the eighteen plays that first appeared in it might well have been lost; and without the Folio, Shakespeare might never have emerged as the singular figure of English literature he has become, for it is that book that first established Shakespeare as the author he never aspired to be.

The second *Epistle* to the First Folio
By the autumn of 1623 John Heminges and Henry Condell were the senior surviving members of the King's

Men. In April 1616 they and their colleague, Richard Burbage, who died in 1619, had been left small bequests in the will of William Shakespeare to buy memorial rings. The publication of the First Folio was a different kind of memorial to 'so worthy a friend and fellow . . . as . . . our Shakespeare', as the dead dramatist is described in the first of two epistles prefaced to the volume and signed with the names of Heminges and Condell. That epistle dedicates the book to William Herbert, Earl of Pembroke and Lord Chamberlain, and his brother Philip, Earl of Montgomery, and calls on them to act as guardians to Shakespeare's orphaned plays. The second epistle (reproduced here in facsimile) urges 'the great variety of readers' to buy 'these plays', which 'have had their trial already, and stood out all appeals' in the theatre.

The second paragraph makes several claims which have important implications for actors, readers and editors of Shakespeare. Heminges and Condell claim to have done the best they could, in the absence of their dead friend, to collect and verify the texts of his plays for publication. Three of their claims have been the source of dispute and controversy, and need some qualification. The mention of adding 'all the rest' to the plays already in print leads readers to expect the Folio to contain the complete plays of Shakespeare. It does not. Not only are two collaborative late plays, *Pericles* and *The Two Noble Kinsmen*, omitted, but the volume initially went on sale without *Troilus and Cressida* (as its absence from the 'catalogue', or table of contents, testifies). *Troilus* was soon added to the volume – though not to the catalogue: its late arrival is best explained as the result of difficulties experienced by Isaac Jaggard and Edward Blount, the principal publishers, in obtaining permission to reprint it from the copyright holder, Henry Walley. Exclusion from the Folio is accordingly not conclusive evidence that a play may not have had Shakespeare's hand in it.

More teasing is the warning to readers against previous editions of the plays (half of which were already in print in quarto). What Heminges and Condell meant by 'diverse stolen and surreptitious copies, maimed and deformed by the frauds and stealths of injurious imposters that exposed them' has been much debated. They were clearly aware that some earlier quarto editions of plays by Shakespeare differed radically from the texts they were printing. Among those, a handful are conspicuous by the extent to which they differ from the texts printed in the Folio in length, wording, names and natures of characters, and even scenic sequence or particulars of action. They are *The Taming of a Shrew* (1594), *The First Part of the Contention* (i.e. *King Henry VI Part 2*) (1594), *The True Tragedy of Richard, Duke of York* (i.e. *King Henry VI Part 3*) (1595), *Romeo and Juliet* (1597), *King Henry V* (1600), *Sir John Falstaff* (i.e. *The Merry Wives of Windsor*) (1602) and *Hamlet* (1603). Modern scholarship (unhappily) has dubbed these the 'bad' Quartos. They do seem, however, to merit the description 'maimed and deformed', at least in relation to their Folio counterparts (or to later 'good' Quartos in the cases of *Romeo* and *Hamlet*).

Variation in a further group of Quartos is less radical, though often pervasive. These are *King Richard III* (1597), *King Henry IV Part 2* (1600), *Hamlet* (1604/5), *King Lear* (1608), *Troilus and Cressida* (1609) and *Othello* (1622). Where the seven 'bad' Quartos seem to demand exceptional circumstances of textual transmission, such as someone's attempt to reconstruct them from memory, to account for their very approximate resemblance to the equivalent 'good' texts, the other six may be adequately accounted for as products of various usual processes of stage abridgement or adaptation, or of authorial revision, to which they may have been subjected.

What is clear is that Heminges and Condell cannot have intended a blanket condemnation of all earlier published versions, but that their focus must have been on the 'bad' texts and, to a lesser degree, on those plays which they could offer in texts reflecting a later stage in their evolution than that represented by the Quartos. They had no qualms about simply reprinting Quartos they found reliable, like *The Merchant of Venice* or *Much Ado About Nothing*, with the minimum of editorial intervention.

The myth of Shakespeare's fluency in composition originates in the Folio *Epistle*. Where Heminges and Condell saw that fluency as a virtue, others, and especially

Ben Jonson, demurred. Jonson was later to respond to the claim that Shakespeare rarely 'blotted' a line – that is, deleted and revised it – with the wish that he 'had blotted a thousand'. In his own contribution to the preliminary matter of the Folio, his verses 'To the memory of my beloved, the Author, Mr. William Shakespeare: and what he hath left us', Jonson took pains to offer an alternative view of Shakespeare as a conscious and painstaking poetic craftsman, ready to:

> strike the second heat
> Upon the Muses' anvil: turn the same,
>   (And himself with it) that he thinks to
>   frame;
> Or for the laurel, he may gain a scorn;
>   For a good Poet's made, as well as born:
> And such wert thou.

Although nearly half of his plays had been printed in his lifetime, Shakespeare only became an author to be read as well as a dramatist to be performed seven years after his death, with the publication of his histories, comedies and tragedies in the First Folio of 1623. During the eighteen-year period between the closure of the theatres in 1642 and the Restoration of Charles II in 1660, his plays could only be read. The first published criticism of him, in Margaret Cavendish's *Sociable Letters* (1664), reflects this shift, claiming that 'those that could Read his Playes, could not be so Foolish as to Condemn them'. The shift was radical and irreversible. By 1660, the theatrical company Shakespeare wrote for was long dispersed, though survivors would act again and some had distant or second-hand memories of him. The split between progressive revision and adaptation of the plays for theatres with new facilities and constantly changing audiences, and an increasingly conservative scholarly concern to preserve or restore the plays as reading texts had begun. Shakespeare the book and Shakespeare the dramatist were set on their divergent paths.

SHAKESPEARE'S READING AND READING SHAKESPEARE

Elizabethan playwrights worked in a repertory system which constantly demanded new plays. Their natural expedient, encouraged by a literary climate which set store by creative imitation of existing models, was to base many, even most, of their plays on familiar stories. Shakespeare was no exception, other than in the range of subjects he dramatized. Almost all his plays can be shown to follow, broadly or closely, what scholars have designated as his 'sources' – that is, earlier texts he had read or otherwise knew of. Often he combined material from two or more sources into a single play, particularly in his comedies. His reading was wide and multifarious: history – Greek, Roman and English; prose fiction (chiefly translated into English from continental originals); earlier plays, ancient and modern, in Latin, Italian and English; pamphlets and other ephemera – all were grist to his mill. He had favourite authors, such as Chaucer, Spenser and Sir Philip Sidney among English writers, or Montaigne, whose essays he seems to have known by the time he wrote *Hamlet* (about 1600). His Latin favourites were Ovid's *Metamorphoses* and the comedies of Plautus, but he also knew Virgil, Seneca and Horace, and Plutarch's *Lives of the Noble Grecians and Romans*, written originally in Greek, were well known to him in Thomas North's English translation. Playwrights of his own and the previous generation, notably John Lyly, Thomas Kyd, Robert Greene and Christopher Marlowe, had much to offer him by way of example, and he must also have learned from his interaction with such rivals as Ben Jonson and from his collaborators, John Fletcher and (less certainly) Thomas Middleton. In addition he was, as an actor, deeply immersed in the repertoires of his successive companies.

Reading Shakespeare four hundred years later, we encounter the English language of a period now described as Early Modern, before any notion of correctness of usage, whether of grammar, syntax, spelling or punctuation, had acquired wide currency, let alone authority. The primary language of education, both in schools and universities, was still Latin, a language which required the formal understanding of its rules and structures. Shakespeare had his own schooling in Latin, a schooling which included the standard subjects of grammar, logic and (most important of the three for an aspiring poet) rhetoric, the art of appropriate use of language for all practical and literary purposes. The fluidity of English in the late sixteenth century was a gift to a linguistically inventive generation of writers. Shakespeare did as much as any to exploit and extend the wide range of literary styles and linguistic registers available to him. His characters speak in all styles, from the artificial rhyming verse of *Love's Labour's Lost* or *Romeo and Juliet* to the uneducated prose of Dogberry or the regional dialect of Fluellen. It was to his plays that Samuel Johnson turned, while compiling his great *Dictionary* (1755), for illustrations of 'the diction of common life'.

Blank verse, already the norm of dramatic language in the 1580s, was adopted by Shakespeare and developed into the flexible and versatile medium of his Jacobean plays. The forging of a dramatic prose which could range from low comedy to Hamlet's philosophical musings or the inexhaustible improvisations of Falstaff was among his major stylistic achievements. The conciseness which is so marked a feature of his dramatic writing was learned, in part, from the experience of writing sonnets.

Readers of Shakespeare have long needed the assistance of a glossary to help with the unfamiliar vocabulary or idiom and the semantic changes which constitute one initial obstacle to full enjoyment and understanding. The glossary in this volume is based on the commentaries in the Arden editions whose texts are reprinted in it. It aims at giving answers to readers' most likely questions but makes no attempt at full explanation of the sources of difficulty. Readers should always remember that Shakespeare's plays were written to be heard, not read – least of all silently read. The attempt at full understanding of linguistic detail and subtlety (if such an aim were attainable) should always be seen as secondary to the experience of the play as a whole. Fuller comprehension of detail will follow with subsequent rereadings.

AFTERLIFE

While 'Shakespeare' has been a stable element in English culture for four hundred years, and has been successfully exported to numerous other cultures, there is considerable variation in the reputation and influence of individual works. Each generation seems able to find something (its own image?) in 'Shakespeare', but it has always been possible to choose a different text or a different interpretation. Some plays, such as *Julius Caesar*, *Romeo and Juliet* and *The Taming of the Shrew*, have an almost continuous history of performance and appear regularly on school and college syllabuses; others, such as *Timon of Athens*, *Troilus and Cressida* and *Pericles*, are rarely either performed or set for study; others again, such as *Cymbeline*, *King John* and *King Henry VIII*, were far more popular in the past than they are today. During his lifetime it would seem that Shakespeare's most highly esteemed tragedy was *Titus Andronicus*; for the next 350 years it was *Hamlet*; since about 1960 it has been *King Lear*. There is a similar degree of variation in the extent to which works have been adapted, translated and filmed. Broadly speaking, the 'afterlife' of the plays and poems has depended on and can be measured by four things: publication, performance, criticism, and adaptation and creative influence.

Publication

Publication is taken first as even performers need to read plays before they stage them. About half of Shakespeare's plays were published during his lifetime as single pocket-size paperback volumes known from their method of printing and small size as Quartos. All the plays in the present volume apart from *Pericles* and *The Two Noble Kinsmen* were printed (or reprinted) after his death in the large-format 1623 First Folio. Until 1709 two separate traditions of publication continued independently of each other: the First Folio was followed by the Second (1632), Third (1663) and Fourth (1685) Folios – 'literary' collections of the almost-complete works which found their way into the libraries of individuals and institutions – while many of the Quartos were reprinted as play-texts, used by actors and bought by playgoers.

In 1709 Nicholas Rowe published *The Works of Mr William Shakespear, Revised and Corrected* in eight volumes, the first of a line of eighteenth-century edited texts. He based his text on the Folio but also began the tradition of including passages which had previously appeared only in the Quartos. He and later eighteenth-century editors also provided commentaries in which they often disagreed with each other over variant readings, emendations and interpretations. These editions were usually published by subscription and were relatively expensive, but cheap acting editions continued to be available, for example the rival sets published in the 1730s by Robert Walker and Jacob Tonson or Bell's Shakespeare (1773-4). The nineteenth century saw the publication of cheaper mass-market texts and, after the Bowdlers' *Family Shakespeare* (1807), a proliferation of expurgated texts explicitly aimed at women and children. In the twentieth century, Shakespeare remains big business for

12 The three witches in the television cartoon version of
Macbeth (1993)

publishers and editors, with hot competition for school, college and university markets, and the consequent provision both of popular versions of Shakespeare and of increasingly specialist series such as *Shakespeare in Performance*, which provides detailed annotation of stage business, and *Shakespearean Originals*, which offers reprints of the earliest texts.

Shakespeare has also, of course, been translated into many languages. Some translations have become 'classics' in their own right – François-Victor Hugo's translations into French, August Wilhelm Schlegel's translations into German, and Boris Pasternak's translations into Russian – but it has also seemed necessary for each generation to produce new translations, just as each generation of English speakers produces new editions.

Performance

Our records of performances in Shakespeare's lifetime are poor, possibly because of the fire which destroyed the first Globe Theatre (and presumably its papers) in 1613. The title-pages of play-texts sometimes give misleading information about whether plays were (or were not) performed and where; sometimes we have to rely on chance diary entries or on what we can deduce from passing references by contemporaries – evidence for pre-1623 performances is provided in the introductions to individual plays in this volume. We do know that the plays were not performed at all after 1642 when the theatres were closed during the Civil War and the Commonwealth period, but that they returned as staple fare when the theatres reopened at the Restoration of the monarchy in 1660. At this time Shakespeare was popular but not as popular as the Jacobean dramatists Beaumont and Fletcher. Two significant innovations in 1660 were the use of stage scenery and the introduction of female performers; before 1640 women's roles had been played by boys.

The Restoration theatres were relatively small, indoor and expensive, attracting patrons from upper- and middle-class circles. In this they were like the Blackfriars Theatre, used by the King's Men before the Civil War, and unlike the large outdoor Globe which had cheap standing room for those who could not afford a seat. Attendance at a Shakespearean performance had thus become more of a minority pursuit, though touring companies continued to flourish in the British provinces and abroad in the eighteenth and nineteenth and indeed twentieth centuries.

Shakespeare reached a mass market again with the invention of film and video in the twentieth century. The versions performed in the Restoration and in the eighteenth century were regularly cut (partly in order to allow time for changing the scenery and trimming the candles) and often substantially rewritten. Despite a first attempt by the famous actor David Garrick in the mid-eighteenth century to restore more of Shakespeare's lines, the performance tradition continued to give audiences far less of the texts than was available in published versions.

A fashion for historical accuracy and heavily pictorial staging in the nineteenth century further weighted the plays with unnecessary baggage, and it was not until the 1880s that, under the influence of William Poel, a serious attempt was made to return to fluid 'Elizabethan' staging with minimal props and scenery. In Britain in the twentieth century the performance of Shakespeare became institutionalized with the foundation of the Shakespeare Memorial Theatre (originally built 1879, rebuilt after a fire in 1932) and later, in 1961, of the Royal Shakespeare Company, which currently performs in three theatres in Stratford-upon-Avon and two in London and undertakes national and international tours.

Shakespeare's plays were widely performed in Europe from the very beginning (English actors toured to Germany, Poland and other countries), and a strong acting tradition grew up in America in the nineteenth century, but the silent cinema brought a new and powerful means of internationalization. Dozens of silent versions were made, in America, England, Germany, France and Italy, usually abbreviating the plots but often finding inventive ways of replacing Shakespeare's language with visual images. This tradition continued into the sound period after 1929 when, perhaps ironically, it has been precisely those films which have not been 'hampered' by Shakespeare's text which have been seen as the most successful screen versions: Akira Kurosawa's Japanese *Macbeth* (*Throne of Blood*, 1957), for example, and Grigori Kozintsev's Russian *Hamlet* (1964) and *King Lear* (1970). A few English-language directors have nevertheless managed to make creditable films, notably Laurence Olivier (*Henry V*, 1944, *Hamlet*, 1948, *Richard III*, 1955), Orson Welles (*Macbeth*, 1948, *Othello*, 1952, *Chimes at Midnight* (the Falstaff plays), 1966) and Kenneth Branagh (*Henry V*, 1989, *Much Ado About Nothing*, 1993, *Hamlet*, 1996). Many Shakespeare films are commercially available on video; the British Broadcasting Company and the American Time-Life Corporation sponsored a series of the complete works for television from 1979 to 1985 which, while proving uneven aesthetically, has become an invaluable resource for those without access to live performances.

Criticism

The first person to publish a critical essay on Shakespeare was Margaret Cavendish, Duchess of Newcastle, in 1664. She was a poet, dramatist and essayist, and in effect inaugurated a tradition of critical writing on Shakespeare by people who were themselves creative writers: John Dryden, Samuel Johnson, William Hazlitt, Samuel Taylor Coleridge and T.S. Eliot are examples of such influential critics whose work is still read today. While from the

LEAR.

MACBETH.

RICHARD III.d

HAMLET.

Mr GARRICK in Four of his Principal Tragic Characters.

13 David Garrick in four of his most famous Shakespearean roles, from a contemporary engraving

14 Ellen Terry as Mistress Page in *The Merry Wives of Windsor*

15 A modern production of *A Midsummer Night's Dream* (Royal Shakespeare Company, 1994)

beginning Shakespeare was highly praised for his dramatic skills, particularly in the construction of lifelike characters, late seventeenth- and eighteenth-century writers were often critical of what they saw as his grammatical incorrectness, his undisciplined elaboration of metaphors and his carelessness with plotting and historical accuracy. During the nineteenth century the general tone became more adulatory and the focus on character increased: many studies treated Shakespeare's men and women as if they were real people or at least characters in realistic novels. The publication by famous performers of their reminiscences enhanced this tendency. At the same time, the introduction of English Literature as a subject for study at universities brought about a professionalization of criticism and resulted in the situation we have today where most Shakespeare criticism is written by people with full-time academic posts in university departments of English or Drama.

Modern criticism is diverse and alarmingly prolific: the American journal *Shakespeare Quarterly* publishes listings which show that around two hundred items (editions, translations, books and essays) are currently published every year on *King Lear*, and around four hundred on *Hamlet*. As in the past, critics today aim in various ways to elucidate Shakespeare for audiences and readers. They study his language and the literary and dramatic conventions of his time. They explore the circumstances in which the texts were originally produced – how and where they were performed, how they were copied and printed. They are also perhaps more attentive than their predecessors were to the circumstances in which the texts are continually reproduced – how and why we keep rereading and even rewriting Shakespeare for our own purposes. Dominant in recent criticism are issues of power and gender: 'power' in the sense of Shakespeare's relation to analysis of early modern political structures and also in the sense of the power of 'Shakespeare' as a cultural artefact; 'gender' in the sense of his representations of gender identity and sexual

relations when seen from the perspective of the continuing struggle of women, gay men and lesbians for acceptance and equality.

Adaptation and creative influence

While he was still alive, some of Shakespeare's works were already exerting an influence on other writers. John Fletcher's play *The Woman's Prize, or The Tamer Tamed* (1611) is a 'sequel' to *The Taming of the Shrew*, and Fletcher and Francis Beaumont's *Philaster* (1609) could not have been written without *Hamlet*; if we read the plays of the next generation of dramatists such as John Ford, Philip Massinger, Thomas Middleton and John Webster, we keep encountering echoes of Shakespeare in characters, situations, lines and phrases. In the Restoration period playwrights 'adapted' his plays for their own stage by cutting them and 'improving' the language, correcting Shakespeare's grammar and clarifying his difficult metaphors. They also began to rewrite the plays substantially, producing hybrids which are clearly dependent on their Shakespearean originals but sometimes very different in their handling of the plots. John Dryden and William Davenant's 1667 *The Enchanted Island*, for example, a version of *The Tempest*, introduces a sister for Miranda and Hippolito, a man who has never seen a woman; Dryden's 1678 *All for Love* is a version of *Antony and Cleopatra* in which Antony's wife Octavia confronts Cleopatra (who never wavers in her commitment to Antony); Nahum Tate's 1681 *King Lear* leaves Lear and Gloucester alive at the end and Cordelia about to marry Edgar.

In later centuries, the plays inspired works in other genres: operas, novels, films and musicals. Neither Henry Purcell's opera *The Fairy Queen* (1692) nor Benjamin Britten's opera (1960) would exist without *A Midsummer Night's Dream*; *Hamlet* inspired countless works in the nineteenth century from Johann Wolfgang von Goethe's novel *Wilhelm Meister's Apprenticeship* (1795) and Charles Dickens's *Great Expectations* (1860-1) to Anton Chekhov's play *The Seagull* (1896); such musicals as Cole Porter's *Kiss Me Kate* (1948) and Jerome Robbins's and Leonard Bernstein's *West Side Story* (1957) depend on *The Taming of the Shrew* and *Romeo and Juliet* respectively. In recent times *King Lear* has inspired Akira Kurosawa's film

16 (above) Sir Henry Beerbohm Tree in the surviving silent
film fragment of *King John*, 1899

17 (right) Laurence Olivier as the King in the 1944 film of
Henry V

18 (below) Akira Kurosawa's Japanese film version of
Macbeth, *Throne of Blood*, 1957

Ran (1984) and Jane Smiley's novel *A Thousand Acres* (1991); *The Tempest* has inspired Suniti Namjoshi's poem sequence *Snapshots of Caliban* (1984) and Marina Warner's novel *Indigo* (1992).

Shakespeare's fame and influence began early and show no sign of abating. In the volume of his notebooks covering the years 1661–3, John Ward, vicar of Stratford-upon-Avon from 1662 to 1681, wrote of his most famous deceased parishioner:

> I have heard that Mr. Shakespeare was a natural wit, without any art at all; he frequented the plays all his younger time, but in his elder days lived at Stratford, and supplied the stage with 2 plays every year, and for that had an allowance so large, that he spent at the rate of a thousand pounds a year, as I have heard.

He continued with a note to himself: 'Remember to peruse Shakespeare's plays, and be versed in them, that I may not be ignorant in that matter'. We can think of no better advice to give our readers, and to repeat with it the encouragement of his first editors inviting the public to 'read and censure' their volume of the collected works. 'Do so', they exhort frankly, 'but buy it first':

> Then, how odd soever your brains be, or your wisdoms, make your licence the same, and spare not. Judge your six penn'orth, your shilling's worth, your five shillings' worth at a time, or higher, so you rise to the just rates, and welcome. But whatever you do, buy. Censure will not drive a trade, or make the jack go. And though you be a magistrate of wit, and sit on the stage at Blackfriars or the Cockpit to arraign plays daily, know: these plays have had their trial already and stood out all appeals, and do now come forth quitted rather by a decree of court than any purchased letters of commendation.

Like Heminges and Condell and all our distinguished predecessor editors, we urge you to buy and read or reread Shakespeare, confident that 'if then you do not like him, surely you are in some manifest danger not to understand him'.

Shakespeare's Sonnets and A Lover's Complaint

On the evidence of Francis Meres in *Palladis Tamia*, by 1598 Shakespeare was known to have written 'sugared sonnets' and to have circulated them among his 'private friends'. In 1599 four sonnets by him were printed in *The Passionate Pilgrim* together with a further collection of lyrical poems, several of which, despite a general title-page attribution of the small book to 'W. Shakespeare', are known to be the work of other poets. Two of those sonnets had already been printed in 1598, in the Quarto of *Love's Labour's Lost*, the other two were to be numbered 138 and 144 in *Shakespeare's Sonnets*, printed together with *A Lover's Complaint* in 1609. Surviving manuscript copies of various sonnets probably all date from later than Shakespeare's death in 1616 and none is earlier than the 1609 edition. The celebrated dedication of the *Sonnets* by their publisher T[homas] T[horpe] to 'Mr. W.H.' as 'only begetter of these ensuing sonnets' will continue to provoke conjecture and controversy. The most plausible identifications of 'W.H.' are: William Herbert, Earl of Pembroke, which fits if the poems are of early seventeenth-century date; Henry Wriothesley, Earl of Southampton, which only makes sense if they were written in the early 1590s; and William Shakespeare – assuming that the 'H' is a misprint for 'S'.

Though other views have long prevailed, the *Sonnets* can be seen as an authorized publication in which the 154 sonnets appear in a significant order determined by Shakespeare, and the *Complaint* (whose characters and situation bear some resemblance to those in *Troilus*, *Othello*, *All's Well* and *Measure for Measure*) is also a planned feature of the volume. Few of the sonnets admit of certain dating, but 138 and 144 were written before 1599 and 107 may well relate to the death of Queen Elizabeth I in the spring of 1603 and to the coronation of King James I in the following spring. This likelihood is a caution against too ready an assumption that all the sonnets must have been written in the mid-1590s, at the height of the sonneteering vogue. The final line of 94 occurs also in a play called *The Reign of King Edward III*, printed in 1596, but it remains unclear which was the debtor, and the possibility of common authorship cannot be ruled out.

The relationships and narrative implicit in Shakespeare's sonnets contrast strongly with the conventional pattern in which courtship of a woman by a male lover leads to acceptance (as in Spenser's *Amoretti* (1594)), or to a final rejection (as in Sidney's *Astrophil and Stella* (1595)), or to the death of the lady and the continuance of celebration by her lover (as in the *Canzoniere* of Petrarch (1358–74)). Shakespeare's sonnets are poems of introspection in which no character but the poet has a name, which makes it easy for the reader to identify with him. Sonnets 1-126 are mainly addressed to a man younger and of higher social standing than the poet; sonnets 127-52 to an unfaithful mistress, whose other lovers include the young man. The last two sonnets, on the traditional theme of Cupid and Diana, stand apart from this pattern. In the *Complaint*, a young woman abandoned by a lying and faithless lover recounts her story to a stranger, re-enacting the seduction to which she concludes that she would still be vulnerable.

The earliest reprint of the sonnets, in the volume of Shakespeare's poems published by John Benson in 1640, rearranged them, changed many male pronouns to their female equivalents and added titles describing them in terms of address to a mistress. Interest in the sonnets waned until 1780, when Edmond Malone republished them in an influential edition. Nineteenth-century attempts to read them as Shakespeare's amatory autobiography have persisted throughout the twentieth century, but without reaching any stable conclusions. To Wordsworth's claim that 'With this key, Shakespeare unlocked his heart', Robert Browning's rejoinder was, 'Did Shakespeare? If so – the less Shakespeare he'. Oscar Wilde's notorious interest in the sonnets as homosexual love poems articulated a source of unease felt by many scholars and readers since 1780 and led to half a century of nervous evasion of any such unseemly possibility. The question that will always divide opinion is whether or not, and if so in what sense, these poems reflect the lived experience of their playwright-poet.

The Arden text is based on the 1609 First Quarto.

TO. THE. ONLY. BEGETTER. OF.
THESE. ENSUING. SONNETS.
Mr. W.H. ALL. HAPPINESS.
AND. THAT. ETERNITY.
PROMISED.
BY.
OUR. EVER-LIVING. POET.
WISHETH.
THE. WELL-WISHING.
ADVENTURER. IN.
SETTING.
FORTH.
T.T.

1

From fairest creatures we desire increase,
That thereby beauty's rose might never die,
But as the riper should by time decease
His tender heir might bear his memory:
But thou, contracted to thine own bright eyes,
Feed'st thy light's flame with self-substantial fuel,
Making a famine where abundance lies,
Thyself thy foe, to thy sweet self too cruel.
Thou that art now the world's fresh ornament,
And only herald to the gaudy spring,
Within thine own bud buriest thy content,
And, tender churl, mak'st waste in niggarding.
    Pity the world, or else this glutton be,
    To eat the world's due, by the grave and thee.

2

When forty winters shall besiege thy brow,
And dig deep trenches in thy beauty's field,
Thy youth's proud livery, so gazed on now,
Will be a tattered weed of small worth held:
Then being asked, where all thy beauty lies,
Where all the treasure of thy lusty days,
To say, within thine own deep-sunken eyes,
Were an all-eating shame and thriftless praise.
How much more praise deserved thy beauty's use
If thou couldst answer, 'This fair child of mine
Shall sum my count, and make my old excuse',
Proving his beauty by succession thine:
    This were to be new made when thou art old,
    And see thy blood warm when thou feel'st it cold.

3

Look in thy glass, and tell the face thou viewest
Now is the time that face should form another,
Whose fresh repair if now thou not renewest
Thou dost beguile the world, unbless some mother.
For where is she so fair whose uneared womb
Disdains the tillage of thy husbandry?
Or who is he so fond will be the tomb
Of his self-love, to stop posterity?
Thou art thy mother's glass, and she in thee
Calls back the lovely April of her prime:
So thou through windows of thine age shalt see,
Despite of wrinkles, this thy golden time.
    But if thou live remembered not to be,
    Die single, and thine image dies with thee.

4

Unthrifty loveliness, why dost thou spend
Upon thyself thy beauty's legacy?
Nature's bequest gives nothing, but doth lend,
And being frank, she lends to those are free:
Then, beauteous niggard, why dost thou abuse
The bounteous largesse given thee to give?
Profitless usurer, why dost thou use
So great a sum of sums, yet canst not live?
For having traffic with thyself alone,
Thou of thyself thy sweet self dost deceive;
Then how, when nature calls thee to be gone,
What acceptable audit canst thou leave?
    Thy unused beauty must be tombed with thee,
    Which used, lives th'executor to be.

5

Those hours that with gentle work did frame
The lovely gaze where every eye doth dwell
Will play the tyrants to the very same,
And that unfair which fairly doth excel.
For never-resting time leads summer on
To hideous winter, and confounds him there,
Sap checked with frost and lusty leaves quite gone,
Beauty o'er-snowed and bareness everywhere;
Then were not summer's distillation left,
A liquid prisoner pent in walls of glass,
Beauty's effect with beauty were bereft,
Nor it, nor no remembrance what it was.
    But flowers distilled, though they with winter
      meet,
    Leese but their show; their substance still lives
      sweet.

6

Then let not winter's ragged hand deface
In thee thy summer, ere thou be distilled:
Make sweet some vial, treasure thou some place
With beauty's treasure, ere it be self-killed.
That use is not forbidden usury
Which happies those that pay the willing loan;
That's for thyself to breed another thee,
Or ten times happier, be it ten for one:
Ten times thyself were happier than thou art,
If ten of thine ten times refigured thee;
Then what could death do if thou shouldst depart,
Leaving thee living in posterity?
   Be not self-willed, for thou art much too fair
   To be death's conquest and make worms thine
      heir.

7

Lo, in the Orient when the gracious light
Lifts up his burning head, each under eye
Doth homage to his new appearing sight,
Serving with looks his sacred majesty;
And having climbed the steep-up heavenly hill,
Resembling strong youth in his middle age,
Yet mortal looks adore his beauty still,
Attending on his golden pilgrimage:
But when from high-most pitch with weary car
Like feeble age he reeleth from the day,
The eyes, fore-duteous, now converted are
From his low tract, and look another way:
   So thou, thyself out-going in thy noon,
   Unlooked on diest, unless thou get a son.

8

Music to hear, why hear'st thou music sadly?
Sweets with sweets war not, joy delights in joy;
Why lov'st thou that which thou receiv'st not gladly,
Or else receiv'st with pleasure thine annoy?
If the true concord of well-tuned sounds
By unions married, do offend thine ear,
They do but sweetly chide thee, who confounds
In singleness the parts that thou shouldst bear:
Mark how one string, sweet husband to another,
Strikes each in each by mutual ordering,
Resembling sire, and child, and happy mother,
Who all in one, one pleasing note do sing:
   Whose speechless song being many, seeming one,
   Sings this to thee: 'Thou single wilt prove none.'

9

Is it for fear to wet a widow's eye
That thou consum'st thyself in single life?
Ah, if thou issueless shalt hap to die,
The world will wail thee like a makeless wife;
The world will be thy widow, and still weep
That thou no form of thee hast left behind,
When every private widow well may keep,
By children's eyes, her husband's shape in mind:
Look what an unthrift in the world doth spend,
Shifts but his place, for still the world enjoys it;
But beauty's waste hath in the world an end,
And kept unused the user so destroys it:
   No love toward others in that bosom sits
   That on himself such murd'rous shame commits.

10

For shame deny that thou bear'st love to any,
Who for thyself art so unprovident;
Grant, if thou wilt, thou art beloved of many,
But that thou none lov'st is most evident:
For thou art so possessed with murd'rous hate
That 'gainst thyself thou stick'st not to conspire,
Seeking that beauteous roof to ruinate
Which to repair should be thy chief desire:
O change thy thought, that I may change my mind;
Shall hate be fairer lodged than gentle love?
Be as thy presence is, gracious and kind;
Or to thyself at least kind-hearted prove,
   Make thee another self for love of me,
   That beauty still may live in thine or thee.

11

As fast as thou shalt wane, so fast thou grow'st
In one of thine, from that which thou departest;
And that fresh blood which youngly thou bestow'st
Thou mayst call thine, when thou from youth
    convertest;
Herein lives wisdom, beauty and increase;
Without this, folly, age and cold decay.
If all were minded so, the times should cease,
And threescore year would make the world away:
Let those whom nature hath not made for store,
Harsh, featureless and rude, barrenly perish;
Look whom she best endowed, she gave the more,
Which bounteous gift thou shouldst in bounty cherish:
   She carved thee for her seal, and meant thereby
   Thou shouldst print more, not let that copy die.

12

When I do count the clock that tells the time,
And see the brave day sunk in hideous night;
When I behold the violet past prime,
And sable curls all silvered o'er with white:
When lofty trees I see barren of leaves,
Which erst from heat did canopy the herd,
And summer's green all girded up in sheaves
Borne on the bier with white and bristly beard:
Then of thy beauty do I question make,
That thou among the wastes of time must go,
Since sweets and beauties do themselves forsake,
And die as fast as they see others grow,
    And nothing 'gainst time's scythe can make defence
    Save breed to brave him, when he takes thee hence.

13

O that you were yourself! But, love, you are
No longer yours, than you yourself here live;
Against this coming end you should prepare,
And your sweet semblance to some other give:
So should that beauty which you hold in lease
Find no determination; then you were
Yourself again after yourself's decease,
When your sweet issue your sweet form should bear.
Who lets so fair a house fall to decay,
Which husbandry in honour might uphold
Against the stormy gusts of winter's day
And barren rage of death's eternal cold?
    O none but unthrifts, dear my love you know:
    You had a father; let your son say so.

14

Not from the stars do I my judgement pluck;
And yet, methinks, I have astronomy,
But not to tell of good or evil luck,
Of plagues, of dearths, or seasons' quality;
Nor can I fortune to brief minutes tell,
Pointing to each his thunder, rain and wind;
Or say with princes if it shall go well
By aught predict that I in heaven find;
But from thine eyes my knowledge I derive,
And, constant stars, in them I read such art
As truth and beauty shall together thrive
If from thyself, to store thou wouldst convert:
    Or else of thee this I prognosticate,
    Thy end is truth's and beauty's doom and date.

15

When I consider everything that grows
Holds in perfection but a little moment;
That this huge stage presenteth naught but shows
Whereon the stars in secret influence comment;
When I perceive that men as plants increase,
Cheered and checked even by the self-same sky,
Vaunt in their youthful sap, at height decrease,
And wear their brave state out of memory:
Then the conceit of this inconstant stay
Sets you, most rich in youth, before my sight,
Where wasteful time debateth with decay
To change your day of youth to sullied night:
    And all in war with time for love of you
    As he takes from you, I engraft you new.

16

But wherefore do not you a mightier way
Make war upon this bloody tyrant, time,
And fortify yourself in your decay
With means more blessed than my barren rhyme?
Now stand you on the top of happy hours,
And many maiden gardens, yet unset,
With virtuous wish would bear your living flowers,
Much liker than your painted counterfeit:
So should the lines of life that life repair,
Which this, time's pencil or my pupil pen,
Neither in inward worth nor outward fair,
Can make you live yourself in eyes of men:
    To give away yourself keeps yourself still,
    And you must live drawn by your own sweet skill.

17

Who will believe my verse in time to come,
If it were filled with your most high deserts?
Though yet, heaven knows, it is but as a tomb,
Which hides your life, and shows not half your parts:
If I could write the beauty of your eyes,
And in fresh numbers number all your graces,
The age to come would say, 'This poet lies;
Such heavenly touches ne'er touched earthly faces.'
So should my papers (yellowed with their age)
Be scorned, like old men of less truth than tongue,
And your true rights be termed a poet's rage,
And stretched metre of an antique song;
    But were some child of yours alive that time,
    You should live twice: in it, and in my rhyme.

18

Shall I compare thee to a summer's day?
Thou art more lovely and more temperate:
Rough winds do shake the darling buds of May,
And summer's lease hath all too short a date:
Sometime too hot the eye of heaven shines,
And often is his gold complexion dimmed;
And every fair from fair sometime declines,
By chance, or nature's changing course, untrimmed:
But thy eternal summer shall not fade,
Nor lose possession of that fair thou ow'st,
Nor shall death brag thou wander'st in his shade
When in eternal lines to time thou grow'st:
    So long as men can breathe or eyes can see,
    So long lives this, and this gives life to thee.

19

Devouring time, blunt thou the lion's paws,
And make the earth devour her own sweet brood;
Pluck the keen teeth from the fierce tiger's jaws,
And burn the long-lived Phoenix in her blood;
Make glad and sorry seasons as thou fleet'st,
And do whate'er thou wilt, swift-footed time,
To the wide world and all her fading sweets:
But I forbid thee one most heinous crime,
O carve not with thy hours my love's fair brow,
Nor draw no lines there with thine antique pen;
Him in thy course untainted do allow
For beauty's pattern to succeeding men.
    Yet do thy worst, old Time, despite thy wrong,
    My love shall in my verse ever live young.

20

A woman's face with nature's own hand painted
Hast thou, the master mistress of my passion;
A woman's gentle heart, but not acquainted
With shifting change, as is false women's fashion;
An eye more bright than theirs, less false in rolling,
Gilding the object whereupon it gazeth;
A man in hue, all hues in his controlling,
Which steals men's eyes and women's souls amazeth;
And for a woman wert thou first created,
Till nature as she wrought thee fell a-doting,
And by addition me of thee defeated,
By adding one thing to my purpose nothing:
    But since she pricked thee out for women's pleasure,
    Mine be thy love, and thy love's use their treasure.

21

So is it not with me as with that Muse,
Stirred by a painted beauty to his verse,
Who heaven itself for ornament doth use,
And every fair with his fair doth rehearse,
Making a couplement of proud compare
With sun and moon, with earth and sea's rich gems;
With April's first-born flowers and all things rare
That heaven's air in this huge rondure hems;
O let me true in love but truly write,
And then believe me: my love is as fair
As any mother's child, though not so bright
As those gold candles fixed in heaven's air:
    Let them say more that like of hearsay well,
    I will not praise, that purpose not to sell.

22

My glass shall not persuade me I am old
So long as youth and thou are of one date;
But when in thee time's furrows I behold,
Then look I death my days should expiate:
For all that beauty that doth cover thee
Is but the seemly raiment of my heart,
Which in thy breast doth live, as thine in me;
How can I then be elder than thou art?
O therefore love be of thyself so wary
As I not for myself, but for thee will,
Bearing thy heart, which I will keep so chary
As tender nurse her babe from faring ill:
    Presume not on thy heart when mine is slain;
    Thou gav'st me thine not to give back again.

23

As an unperfect actor on the stage,
Who with his fear is put besides his part;
Or some fierce thing, replete with too much rage,
Whose strength's abundance weakens his own heart;
So I, for fear of trust, forget to say
The perfect ceremony of love's right,
And in mine own love's strength seem to decay,
O'ercharged with burden of mine own love's might:
O let my books be then the eloquence
And dumb presagers of my speaking breast,
Who plead for love, and look for recompense,
More than that tongue that more hath more
    expressed:
    O learn to read what silent love hath writ!
    To hear with eyes belongs to love's fine wit.

24

Mine eye hath played the painter, and hath steeled
Thy beauty's form in table of my heart;
My body is the frame wherein 'tis held,
And perspective it is best painter's art;
For through the painter must you see his skill,
To find where your true image pictured lies,
Which in my bosom's shop is hanging still,
That hath his windows glazed with thine eyes:
Now see what good turns eyes for eyes have done:
Mine eyes have drawn thy shape, and thine for me
Are windows to my breast, wherethrough the sun
Delights to peep, to gaze therein on thee;
    Yet eyes this cunning want to grace their art:
    They draw but what they see, know not the heart.

25

Let those who are in favour with their stars
Of public honour and proud titles boast,
Whilst I, whom fortune of such triumph bars,
Unlooked for joy in that I honour most;
Great princes' favourites their fair leaves spread
But as the marigold at the sun's eye,
And in themselves their pride lies buried,
For at a frown they in their glory die.
The painful warrior famoused for worth,
After a thousand victories once foiled,
Is from the book of honour razed quite,
And all the rest forgot for which he toiled:
    Then happy I, that love and am beloved
    Where I may not remove, nor be removed.

26

Lord of my love, to whom in vassalage
Thy merit hath my duty strongly knit:
To thee I send this written embassage,
To witness duty, not to show my wit;
Duty so great, which wit so poor as mine
May make seem bare, in wanting words to show it;
But that I hope some good conceit of thine
In thy soul's thought (all naked) will bestow it:
Till whatsoever star that guides my moving
Points on me graciously with fair aspect,
And puts apparel on my tattered loving,
To show me worthy of thy sweet respect;
    Then may I dare to boast how I do love thee;
    Till then, not show my head where thou mayst
        prove me.

27

Weary with toil, I haste me to my bed,
The dear repose for limbs with travail tired;
But then begins a journey in my head
To work my mind, when body's work's expired:
For then my thoughts, from far where I abide,
Intend a zealous pilgrimage to thee,
And keep my drooping eyelids open wide,
Looking on darkness which the blind do see;
Save that my soul's imaginary sight
Presents thy shadow to my sightless view,
Which like a jewel hung in ghastly night
Makes black night beauteous, and her old face new:
    Lo, thus by day my limbs, by night my mind,
    For thee, and for myself, no quiet find.

28

How can I then return in happy plight
That am debarred the benefit of rest?
When day's oppression is not eased by night,
But day by night and night by day oppressed,
And each, though enemies to either's reign,
Do in consent shake hands to torture me,
The one by toil, the other to complain
How far I toil, still farther off from thee.
I tell the day to please him, thou art bright,
And dost him grace, when clouds do blot the
        heaven;
So flatter I the swart-complexioned night,
When sparkling stars twire not thou gild'st the even;
    But day doth daily draw my sorrows longer,
    And night doth nightly make grief's length seem
        stronger.

29

When in disgrace with fortune and men's eyes
I all alone beweep my outcast state,
And trouble deaf heav'n with my bootless cries,
And look upon myself, and curse my fate,
Wishing me like to one more rich in hope,
Featured like him, like him with friends possessed,
Desiring this man's art and that man's scope,
With what I most enjoy contented least;
Yet in these thoughts myself almost despising,
Haply I think on thee, and then my state,
Like to the lark at break of day arising,
From sullen earth sings hymns at heaven's gate;
    For thy sweet love remembered such wealth brings
    That then I scorn to change my state with kings.

30

When to the sessions of sweet silent thought
I summon up remembrance of things past,
I sigh the lack of many a thing I sought,
And with old woes new wail my dear time's waste;
Then can I drown an eye (unused to flow)
For precious friends hid in death's dateless night,
And weep afresh love's long since cancelled woe,
And moan th'expense of many a vanished sight.
Then can I grieve at grievances foregone,
And heavily from woe to woe tell o'er
The sad account of fore-bemoaned moan,
Which I new pay, as if not paid before;
    But if the while I think on thee, dear friend,
    All losses are restored, and sorrows end.

31

Thy bosom is endeared with all hearts
Which I, by lacking, have supposed dead;
And there reigns love, and all love's loving parts,
And all those friends which I thought buried.
How many a holy and obsequious tear
Hath dear religious love stol'n from mine eye,
As interest of the dead, which now appear
But things removed that hidden in thee lie:
Thou art the grave where buried love doth live,
Hung with the trophies of my lovers gone,
Who all their parts of me to thee did give;
That due of many, now is thine alone.
    Their images I loved, I view in thee,
    And thou, all they, hast all the all of me.

32

If thou survive my well-contented day,
When that churl death my bones with dust shall
    cover,
And shalt by fortune once more re-survey
These poor rude lines of thy deceased lover:
Compare them with the bett'ring of the time,
And though they be outstripped by every pen,
Reserve them for my love, not for their rhyme,
Exceeded by the height of happier men.
O then vouchsafe me but this loving thought:
'Had my friend's Muse grown with this growing age,
A dearer birth than this his love had brought,
To march in ranks of better equipage:
    But since he died and poets better prove,
    Theirs for their style I'll read, his for his love.'

33

Full many a glorious morning have I seen
Flatter the mountain tops with sovereign eye,
Kissing with golden face the meadows green,
Gilding pale streams with heavenly alchemy;
Anon permit the basest clouds to ride
With ugly rack on his celestial face,
And from the forlorn world his visage hide,
Stealing unseen to west with this disgrace:
Even so my sun one early morn did shine
With all triumphant splendour on my brow;
But out alack, he was but one hour mine,
The region cloud hath masked him from me now.
    Yet him for this, my love no whit disdaineth:
    Suns of the world may stain, when heaven's sun
        staineth.

34

Why didst thou promise such a beauteous day
And make me travail forth without my cloak,
To let base clouds o'ertake me in my way,
Hiding thy brav'ry in their rotten smoke?
'Tis not enough that through the cloud thou break,
To dry the rain on my storm-beaten face,
For no man well of such a salve can speak
That heals the wound and cures not the disgrace;
Nor can thy shame give physic to my grief;
Though thou repent, yet I have still the loss;
Th'offender's sorrow lends but weak relief
To him that bears the strong offence's loss.
    Ah, but those tears are pearl which thy love sheds,
    And they are rich, and ransom all ill deeds.

35

No more be grieved at that which thou hast done;
Roses have thorns, and silver fountains mud;
Clouds and eclipses stain both moon and sun,
And loathsome canker lives in sweetest bud.
All men make faults, and even I, in this,
Authorizing thy trespass with compare,
Myself corrupting, salving thy amiss,
Excusing these sins more than these sins are:
For to thy sensual fault I bring in sense;
Thy adverse party is thy advocate,
And 'gainst myself a lawful plea commence:
Such civil war is in my love and hate
    That I an accessory needs must be
    To that sweet thief which sourly robs from me.

36

Let me confess that we two must be twain,
Although our undivided loves are one;
So shall those blots that do with me remain,
Without thy help, by me be borne alone.
In our two loves there is but one respect,
Though in our lives a separable spite;
Which, though it alter not love's sole effect,
Yet doth it steal sweet hours from love's delight.
I may not evermore acknowledge thee,
Lest my bewailed guilt should do thee shame,
Nor thou with public kindness honour me,
Unless thou take that honour from thy name:
　　But do not so; I love thee in such sort,
　　As thou being mine, mine is thy good report.

37

As a decrepit father takes delight
To see his active child do deeds of youth,
So I, made lame by fortune's dearest spite,
Take all my comfort of thy worth and truth:
For whether beauty, birth, or wealth, or wit,
Or any of these all, or all, or more,
Entitled in thy parts do crowned sit,
I make my love engrafted to this store:
So then I am not lame, poor, nor despised,
Whilst that this shadow doth such substance give
That I in thy abundance am sufficed,
And by a part of all thy glory live:
　　Look what is best, that best I wish in thee;
　　This wish I have, then ten times happy me.

38

How can my Muse want subject to invent
While thou dost breathe, that pour'st into my verse
Thine own sweet argument, too excellent
For every vulgar paper to rehearse?
O give thyself the thanks, if aught in me
Worthy perusal stand against thy sight:
For who's so dumb, that cannot write to thee,
When thou thyself dost give invention light?
Be thou the tenth Muse, ten times more in worth
Than those old nine which rhymers invocate;
And he that calls on thee, let him bring forth
Eternal numbers to outlive long date.
　　If my slight Muse do please these curious days,
　　The pain be mine, but thine shall be the praise.

39

O how thy worth with manners may I sing,
When thou art all the better part of me?
What can mine own praise to mine own self bring,
And what is't but mine own, when I praise thee?
Even for this, let us divided live,
And our dear love lose name of single one,
That by this separation I may give
That due to thee which thou deserv'st alone.
O absence, what a torment wouldst thou prove,
Were it not thy sour leisure gave sweet leave
To entertain the time with thoughts of love,
Which time and thoughts so sweetly dost deceive,
　　And that thou teachest how to make one twain
　　By praising him here who doth hence remain.

40

Take all my loves, my love; yea, take them all;
What hast thou then more than thou hadst before?
No love, my love, that thou mayst true love call;
All mine was thine, before thou hadst this more:
Then if for my love thou my love receivest,
I cannot blame thee, for my love thou usest;
But yet be blamed, if thou thyself deceivest
By wilful taste of what thyself refusest.
I do forgive thy robb'ry, gentle thief,
Although thou steal thee all my poverty;
And yet love knows it is a greater grief
To bear love's wrong, than hate's known injury.
　　Lascivious grace, in whom all ill well shows,
　　Kill me with spites; yet we must not be foes.

41

Those pretty wrongs that liberty commits
When I am sometime absent from thy heart,
Thy beauty and thy years full well befits;
For still temptation follows where thou art.
Gentle thou art, and therefore to be won;
Beauteous thou art, therefore to be assailed;
And when a woman woos, what woman's son
Will sourly leave her till he have prevailed?
Ay me, but yet thou mightst my seat forbear,
And chide thy beauty and thy straying youth
Who lead thee in their riot even there
Where thou art forced to break a twofold truth:
　　Hers by thy beauty tempting her to thee,
　　Thine by thy beauty being false to me.

42

That thou hast her it is not all my grief,
And yet it may be said I loved her dearly;
That she hath thee is of my wailing chief,
A loss in love that touches me more nearly.
Loving offenders, thus I will excuse ye:
Thou dost love her, because thou knowst I love her,
And for my sake even so doth she abuse me,
Suff'ring my friend for my sake to approve her;
If I lose thee, my loss is my love's gain,
And losing her, my friend hath found that loss;
Both find each other, and I lose both twain,
And both for my sake lay on me this cross:
    But here's the joy, my friend and I are one;
    Sweet flattery! Then she loves but me alone.

43

When most I wink, then do mine eyes best see;
For all the day they view things unrespected,
But when I sleep, in dreams they look on thee,
And darkly bright, are bright in dark directed.
Then thou whose shadow shadows doth make bright,
How would thy shadow's form form happy show
To the clear day with thy much clearer light,
When to unseeing eyes thy shade shines so?
How would (I say) mine eyes be blessed made
By looking on thee in the living day,
When in dead night thy fair imperfect shade
Through heavy sleep on sightless eyes doth stay?
    All days are nights to see till I see thee,
    And nights bright days when dreams do show
        thee me.

44

If the dull substance of my flesh were thought,
Injurious distance should not stop my way;
For then, despite of space, I would be brought
From limits far remote, where thou dost stay;
No matter then although my foot did stand
Upon the farthest earth removed from thee,
For nimble thought can jump both sea and land
As soon as think the place where he would be.
But ah, thought kills me, that I am not thought,
To leap large lengths of miles when thou art gone,
But that so much of earth and water wrought,
I must attend time's leisure with my moan;
    Receiving naughts by elements so slow
    But heavy tears, badges of either's woe.

45

The other two, slight air, and purging fire,
Are both with thee, wherever I abide:
The first my thought, the other my desire,
These, present absent, with swift motion slide;
For when these quicker elements are gone
In tender embassy of love to thee,
My life being made of four, with two alone
Sinks down to death, oppressed with melancholy,
Until life's composition be recured
By those swift messengers returned from thee
Who even but now come back again assured
Of thy fair health, recounting it to me.
    This told, I joy; but then no longer glad,
    I send them back again and straight grow sad.

46

Mine eye and heart are at a mortal war
How to divide the conquest of thy sight;
Mine eye, my heart thy picture's sight would bar;
My heart, mine eye the freedom of that right;
My heart doth plead that thou in him dost lie,
A closet never pierced with crystal eyes;
But the defendant doth that plea deny,
And says in him thy fair appearance lies.
To 'cide this title is empanelled
A quest of thoughts, all tenants to the heart,
And by their verdict is determined
The clear eyes' moiety, and the dear heart's part:
    As thus, mine eyes' due is thy outward part,
    And my heart's right, thy inward love of heart.

47

Betwixt mine eye and heart a league is took,
And each doth good turns now unto the other;
When that mine eye is famished for a look,
Or heart in love with sighs himself doth smother,
With my love's picture then my eye doth feast,
And to the painted banquet bids my heart;
Another time mine eye is my heart's guest,
And in his thoughts of love doth share a part.
So either by thy picture or my love,
Thyself away, art present still with me:
For thou no further than my thoughts canst move,
And I am still with them, and they with thee;
    Or if they sleep, thy picture in my sight
    Awakes my heart to heart's and eye's delight.

48

How careful was I, when I took my way,
Each trifle under truest bars to thrust,
That to my use it might unused stay
From hands of falsehood, in sure wards of trust;
But thou, to whom my jewels trifles are,
Most worthy comfort, now my greatest grief,
Thou best of dearest, and mine only care,
Art left the prey of every vulgar thief.
Thee have I not locked up in any chest,
Save where thou art not, though I feel thou art,
Within the gentle closure of my breast,
From whence at pleasure thou mayst come and part;
   And even thence thou wilt be stol'n, I fear;
   For truth proves thievish for a prize so dear.

49

Against that time, if ever that time come,
When I shall see thee frown on my defects;
Whenas thy love hath cast his utmost sum,
Called to that audit by advised respects;
Against that time when thou shalt strangely pass,
And scarcely greet me with that sun, thine eye;
When love, converted from the thing it was,
Shall reasons find of settled gravity;
Against that time do I ensconce me here,
Within the knowledge of mine own desert,
And this my hand against myself uprear,
To guard the lawful reasons on thy part:
   To leave poor me, thou hast the strength of laws,
   Since why to love, I can allege no cause.

50

How heavy do I journey on the way
When what I seek, my weary travel's end,
Doth teach that ease and that repose to say,
'Thus far the miles are measured from thy friend.'
The beast that bears me, tired with my woe,
Plods dully on to bear that weight in me,
As if by some instinct the wretch did know
His rider loved not speed being made from thee:
The bloody spur cannot provoke him on
That sometimes anger thrusts into his hide,
Which heavily he answers with a groan,
More sharp to me than spurring to his side,
   For that same groan doth put this in my mind:
   My grief lies onward and my joy behind.

51

Thus can my love excuse the slow offence
Of my dull bearer, when from thee I speed:
From where thou art, why should I haste me thence?
Till I return, of posting is no need.
O what excuse will my poor beast then find,
When swift extremity can seem but slow?
Then should I spur, though mounted on the wind;
In winged speed no motion shall I know;
Then can no horse with my desire keep pace;
Therefore desire, of perfect'st love being made,
Shall neigh no dull flesh in his fiery race,
But love, for love, thus shall excuse my jade:
   Since from thee going he went wilful slow,
   Towards thee I'll run, and give him leave to go.

52

So am I as the rich, whose blessed key
Can bring him to his sweet up-locked treasure,
The which he will not every hour survey,
For blunting the fine point of seldom pleasure;
Therefore are feasts so solemn and so rare,
Since, seldom coming, in the long year set,
Like stones of worth they thinly placed are,
Or captain jewels in the carcanet.
So is the time that keeps you as my chest,
Or as the wardrobe which the robe doth hide,
To make some special instant special blessed
By new unfolding his imprisoned pride.
   Blessed are you, whose worthiness gives scope,
   Being had, to triumph; being lacked, to hope.

53

What is your substance, whereof are you made,
That millions of strange shadows on you tend?
Since every one hath every one one shade,
And you, but one, can every shadow lend;
Describe Adonis, and the counterfeit
Is poorly imitated after you;
On Helen's cheek all art of beauty set
And you in Grecian tires are painted new;
Speak of the spring, and foison of the year:
The one doth shadow of your beauty show,
The other as your bounty doth appear,
And you in every blessed shape we know.
   In all external grace you have some part,
   But you like none, none you, for constant heart.

54

O how much more doth beauty beauteous seem
By that sweet ornament which truth doth give!
The rose looks fair, but fairer we it deem
For that sweet odour which doth in it live;
The canker blooms have full as deep a dye
As the perfumed tincture of the roses,
Hang on such thorns, and play as wantonly,
When summer's breath their masked buds discloses;
But for their virtue only is their show
They live unwooed, and unrespected fade,
Die to themselves. Sweet roses do not so;
Of their sweet deaths are sweetest odours made;
    And so of you, beauteous and lovely youth;
    When that shall vade, by verse distils your truth.

55

Not marble, nor the gilded monuments
Of princes, shall outlive this powerful rhyme;
But you shall shine more bright in these contents
Than unswept stone, besmeared with sluttish time.
When wasteful war shall statues overturn
And broils root out the work of masonry,
Nor Mars his sword, nor war's quick fire, shall burn
The living record of your memory:
'Gainst death, and all oblivious enmity,
Shall you pace forth; your praise shall still find room
Even in the eyes of all posterity
That wear this world out to the ending doom.
    So till the judgement that yourself arise,
    You live in this, and dwell in lovers' eyes.

56

Sweet love, renew thy force; be it not said
Thy edge should blunter be than appetite,
Which but today by feeding is allayed,
Tomorrow sharpened in his former might;
So, love, be thou; although today thou fill
Thy hungry eyes even till they wink with fullness,
Tomorrow see again, and do not kill
The spirit of love with a perpetual dullness;
Let this sad interim like the ocean be
Which parts the shore, where two contracted new
Come daily to the banks, that when they see
Return of love, more blessed may be the view;
    Or call it winter, which being full of care
    Makes summer's welcome thrice more wished,
        more rare.

57

Being your slave, what should I do but tend
Upon the hours and times of your desire?
I have no precious time at all to spend,
Nor services to do, till you require;
Nor dare I chide the world-without-end hour
Whilst I, my sovereign, watch the clock for you,
Nor think the bitterness of absence sour
When you have bid your servant once adieu;
Nor dare I question with my jealous thought
Where you may be, or your affairs suppose,
But like a sad slave stay and think of naught,
Save, where you are, how happy you make those.
    So true a fool is love, that in your will,
    Though you do anything, he thinks no ill.

58

That god forbid, that made me first your slave,
I should in thought control your times of pleasure,
Or at your hand th'account of hours to crave,
Being your vassal bound to stay your leisure.
O let me suffer, being at your beck,
Th'imprisoned absence of your liberty,
And patience tame, to sufferance bide each check,
Without accusing you of injury.
Be where you list, your charter is so strong
That you yourself may privilege your time
To what you will; to you it doth belong
Yourself to pardon of self-doing crime.
    I am to wait, though waiting so be hell,
    Not blame your pleasure be it ill or well.

59

If there be nothing new, but that which is
Hath been before, how are our brains beguiled,
Which, labouring for invention, bear amiss
The second burden of a former child?
O that record could with a backward look
Even of five hundred courses of the sun
Show me your image in some antique book,
Since mind at first in character was done,
That I might see what the old world could say
To this composed wonder of your frame;
Whether we are mended, or whe'er better they,
Or whether revolution be the same.
    O sure I am, the wits of former days
    To subjects worse have given admiring praise.

60

Like as the waves make towards the pebbled shore,
So do our minutes hasten to their end,
Each changing place with that which goes before,
In sequent toil all forwards do contend.
Nativity, once in the main of light,
Crawls to maturity; wherewith being crowned
Crooked eclipses 'gainst his glory fight,
And time, that gave, doth now his gift confound.
Time doth transfix the flourish set on youth,
And delves the parallels in beauty's brow;
Feeds on the rarities of nature's truth,
And nothing stands but for his scythe to mow.
    And yet to times in hope my verse shall stand,
    Praising thy worth, despite his cruel hand.

61

Is it thy will thy image should keep open
My heavy eyelids to the weary night?
Dost thou desire my slumbers should be broken
While shadows like to thee do mock my sight?
Is it thy spirit that thou send'st from thee
So far from home into my deeds to pry,
To find out shames and idle hours in me,
The scope and tenor of thy jealousy?
O no, thy love, though much, is not so great;
It is my love that keeps mine eye awake,
Mine own true love that doth my rest defeat,
To play the watchman ever for thy sake.
    For thee watch I, whilst thou dost wake elsewhere,
    From me far off, with others all too near.

62

Sin of self-love possesseth all mine eye,
And all my soul, and all my every part;
And for this sin there is no remedy,
It is so grounded inward in my heart.
Methinks no face so gracious is as mine,
No shape so true, no truth of such account,
And for myself mine own worth do define
As I all other in all worths surmount.
But when my glass shows me myself indeed,
Beated and chopped with tanned antiquity,
Mine own self-love quite contrary I read;
Self, so self-loving, were iniquity;
    'Tis thee (myself) that for myself I praise,
    Painting my age with beauty of thy days.

63

Against my love shall be as I am now,
With time's injurious hand crushed and o'erworn;
When hours have drained his blood, and filled his brow
With lines and wrinkles; when his youthful morn
Hath travailed on to age's steepy night,
And all those beauties whereof now he's king
Are vanishing, or vanished out of sight,
Stealing away the treasure of his spring;
For such a time do I now fortify
Against confounding age's cruel knife,
That he shall never cut from memory
My sweet love's beauty, though my lover's life.
    His beauty shall in these black lines be seen,
    And they shall live, and he in them still green.

64

When I have seen by time's fell hand defaced
The rich proud cost of outworn buried age;
When sometime lofty towers I see down razed,
And brass eternal slave to mortal rage;
When I have seen the hungry ocean gain
Advantage on the kingdom of the shore,
And the firm soil win of the wat'ry main,
Increasing store with loss, and loss with store;
When I have seen such interchange of state,
Or state itself confounded, to decay,
Ruin hath taught me thus to ruminate:
That time will come and take my love away.
    This thought is as a death, which cannot choose
    But weep to have that which it fears to lose.

65

Since brass, nor stone, nor earth, nor boundless sea,
But sad mortality o'er-sways their power,
How with this rage shall beauty hold a plea,
Whose action is no stronger than a flower?
O how shall summer's honey breath hold out
Against the wrackful siege of batt'ring days
When rocks impregnable are not so stout,
Nor gates of steel so strong, but time decays?
O fearful meditation! Where, alack,
Shall time's best jewel from time's chest lie hid?
Or what strong hand can hold his swift foot back,
Or who his spoil o'er beauty can forbid?
    O none, unless this miracle have might:
    That in black ink my love may still shine bright.

66

Tired with all these for restful death I cry:
As to behold desert a beggar born,
And needy nothing trimmed in jollity,
And purest faith unhappily forsworn,
And gilded honour shamefully misplaced,
And maiden virtue rudely strumpeted,
And right perfection wrongfully disgraced,
And strength by limping sway disabled,
And art made tongue-tied by authority,
And folly, doctor-like, controlling skill,
And simple truth miscalled simplicity,
And captive good attending captain ill:
    Tired with all these, from these would I be gone,
    Save that to die I leave my love alone.

67

Ah, wherefore with infection should he live,
And with his presence grace impiety,
That sin by him advantage should achieve,
And lace itself with his society?
Why should false painting imitate his cheek,
And steal dead seeing of his living hue?
Why should poor beauty indirectly seek
Roses of shadow, since his rose is true?
Why should he live, now nature bankrupt is,
Beggared of blood to blush through lively veins?
For she hath no exchequer now but his,
And proud of many, lives upon his gains.
    O, him she stores, to show what wealth she had
    In days long since, before these last so bad.

68

Thus is his cheek the map of days outworn,
When beauty lived and died as flowers do now,
Before these bastard signs of fair were borne,
Or durst inhabit on a living brow;
Before the golden tresses of the dead,
The right of sepulchres, were shorn away,
To live a second life on second head;
Ere beauty's dead fleece made another gay:
In him those holy antique hours are seen,
Without all ornament, itself and true,
Making no summer of another's green,
Robbing no old to dress his beauty new;
    And him as for a map doth nature store
    To show false art what beauty was of yore.

69

Those parts of thee that the world's eye doth view
Want nothing that the thought of hearts can mend;
All tongues, the voice of souls, give thee that due,
Utt'ring bare truth, even so as foes commend:
Thy outward thus with outward praise is crowned.
But those same tongues that give thee so thine own
In other accents do this praise confound,
By seeing further than the eye hath shown;
They look into the beauty of thy mind,
And that in guess they measure by thy deeds;
Then churls their thoughts (although their eyes were
    kind)
To thy fair flower add the rank smell of weeds.
    But why thy odour matcheth not thy show,
    The soil is this, that thou dost common grow.

70

That thou art blamed shall not be thy defect,
For slander's mark was ever yet the fair;
The ornament of beauty is suspect,
A crow that flies in heaven's sweetest air.
So thou be good, slander doth but approve
Thy worth the greater, being wooed of time;
For canker vice the sweetest buds doth love,
And thou present'st a pure unstained prime.
Thou hast passed by the ambush of young days,
Either not assailed, or victor, being charged;
Yet this thy praise cannot be so thy praise,
To tie up envy, evermore enlarged:
    If some suspect of ill masked not thy show
    Then thou alone kingdoms of hearts shouldst owe.

71

No longer mourn for me when I am dead
Than you shall hear the surly sullen bell
Give warning to the world that I am fled
From this vile world, with vilest worms to dwell:
Nay, if you read this line, remember not
The hand that writ it, for I love you so
That I in your sweet thoughts would be forgot,
If thinking on me then should make you woe.
O if (I say) you look upon this verse,
When I, perhaps, compounded am with clay,
Do not so much as my poor name rehearse,
But let your love even with my life decay;
    Lest the wise world should look into your moan,
    And mock you with me after I am gone.

72

O, lest the world should task you to recite
What merit lived in me that you should love,
After my death (dear love) forget me quite,
For you in me can nothing worthy prove;
Unless you would devise some virtuous lie
To do more for me than mine own desert,
And hang more praise upon deceased I
Than niggard truth would willingly impart;
O, lest your true love may seem false in this,
That you for love speak well of me untrue,
My name be buried where my body is,
And live no more to shame nor me, nor you:
 For I am shamed by that which I bring forth,
 And so should you, to love things nothing worth.

73

That time of year thou mayst in me behold,
When yellow leaves, or none, or few do hang
Upon those boughs which shake against the cold,
Bare ruined choirs where late the sweet birds sang;
In me thou seest the twilight of such day
As after sunset fadeth in the west,
Which by and by black night doth take away,
Death's second self that seals up all in rest;
In me thou seest the glowing of such fire
That on the ashes of his youth doth lie,
As the deathbed, whereon it must expire,
Consumed with that which it was nourished by;
 This thou perceiv'st, which makes thy love more
  strong,
 To love that well, which thou must leave ere long.

74

But be contented when that fell arrest
Without all bail shall carry me away;
My life hath in this line some interest,
Which for memorial still with thee shall stay.
When thou reviewest this, thou dost review
The very part was consecrate to thee;
The earth can have but earth, which is his due,
My spirit is thine, the better part of me;
So then thou hast but lost the dregs of life,
The prey of worms, my body being dead,
The coward conquest of a wretch's knife,
Too base of thee to be remembered:
 The worth of that, is that which it contains,
 And that is this, and this with thee remains.

75

So are you to my thoughts as food to life,
Or as sweet seasoned showers to the ground;
And for the peace of you I hold such strife
As 'twixt a miser and his wealth is found:
Now proud as an enjoyer, and anon
Doubting the filching age will steal his treasure;
Now counting best to be with you alone,
Then bettered that the world may see my pleasure;
Sometime all full with feasting on your sight,
And by and by clean starved for a look,
Possessing or pursuing no delight
Save what is had, or must from you be took.
 Thus do I pine and surfeit day by day,
 Or gluttoning on all, or all away.

76

Why is my verse so barren of new pride,
So far from variation or quick change?
Why with the time do I not glance aside
To new-found methods and to compounds strange?
Why write I still all one, ever the same,
And keep invention in a noted weed,
That every word almost doth tell my name,
Showing their birth, and where they did proceed?
O know, sweet love, I always write of you,
And you and love are still my argument:
So all my best is dressing old words new,
Spending again what is already spent:
 For as the sun is daily new and old,
 So is my love still telling what is told.

77

Thy glass will show thee how thy beauties wear,
Thy dial how thy precious minutes waste,
The vacant leaves thy mind's imprint will bear,
And of this book, this learning mayst thou taste:
The wrinkles which thy glass will truly show
Of mouthed graves will give thee memory;
Thou by thy dial's shady stealth mayst know
Time's thievish progress to eternity;
Look what thy memory cannot contain,
Commit to these waste blanks, and thou shalt find
Those children nursed, delivered from thy brain,
To take a new acquaintance of thy mind.
 These offices, so oft as thou wilt look,
 Shall profit thee, and much enrich thy book.

78

So oft have I invoked thee for my Muse,
And found such fair assistance in my verse,
As every alien pen hath got my use,
And under thee their poesy disperse.
Thine eyes, that taught the dumb on high to sing,
And heavy ignorance aloft to fly,
Have added feathers to the learned's wing,
And given grace a double majesty.
Yet be most proud of that which I compile,
Whose influence is thine, and born of thee:
In others' works thou dost but mend the style,
And arts with thy sweet graces graced be;
    But thou art all my art, and dost advance,
    As high as learning, my rude ignorance.

79

Whilst I alone did call upon thy aid
My verse alone had all thy gentle grace;
But now my gracious numbers are decayed,
And my sick Muse doth give another place.
I grant, sweet love, thy lovely argument
Deserves the travail of a worthier pen;
Yet what of thee thy poet doth invent
He robs thee of, and pays it thee again;
He lends thee virtue, and he stole that word
From thy behaviour; beauty doth he give,
And found it in thy cheek; he can afford
No praise to thee, but what in thee doth live:
    Then thank him not for that which he doth say,
    Since what he owes thee, thou thyself dost pay.

80

O how I faint when I of you do write,
Knowing a better spirit doth use your name,
And in the praise thereof spends all his might,
To make me tongue-tied speaking of your fame.
But since your worth, wide as the ocean is,
The humble as the proudest sail doth bear,
My saucy bark, inferior far to his,
On your broad main doth wilfully appear.
Your shallowest help will hold me up afloat,
Whilst he upon your soundless deep doth ride;
Or, being wracked, I am a worthless boat,
He of tall building, and of goodly pride.
    Then if he thrive, and I be cast away,
    The worst was this: my love was my decay.

81

Or I shall live, your epitaph to make;
Or you survive, when I in earth am rotten;
From hence your memory death cannot take,
Although in me each part will be forgotten.
Your name from hence immortal life shall have,
Though I, once gone, to all the world must die;
The earth can yield me but a common grave,
When you entombed in men's eyes shall lie.
Your monument shall be my gentle verse,
Which eyes not yet created shall o'er-read,
And tongues to be your being shall rehearse,
When all the breathers of this world are dead.
    You still shall live, such virtue hath my pen,
    Where breath most breathes, even in the mouths
      of men.

82

I grant thou wert not married to my Muse,
And therefore mayst without attaint o'erlook
The dedicated words which writers use
Of their fair subject, blessing every book.
Thou art as fair in knowledge as in hue,
Finding thy worth a limit past my praise,
And therefore art enforced to seek anew
Some fresher stamp of the time-bettering days,
And do so love; yet when they have devised
What strained touches rhetoric can lend,
Thou, truly fair, wert truly sympathized
In true plain words, by thy true-telling friend;
    And their gross painting might be better used
    Where cheeks need blood; in thee it is abused.

83

I never saw that you did painting need,
And therefore to your fair no painting set;
I found (or thought I found) you did exceed
The barren tender of a poet's debt;
And therefore have I slept in your report,
That you yourself, being extant, well might show
How far a modern quill doth come too short,
Speaking of worth, what worth in you doth grow.
This silence for my sin you did impute,
Which shall be most my glory, being dumb;
For I impair not beauty, being mute,
When others would give life, and bring a tomb.
    There lives more life in one of your fair eyes
    Than both your poets can in praise devise.

84

Who is it that says most? Which can say more,
Than this rich praise: that you alone are you,
In whose confine immured is the store
Which should example where your equal grew?
Lean penury within that pen doth dwell
That to his subject lends not some small glory;
But he that writes of you, if he can tell
That you are you, so dignifies his story.
Let him but copy what in you is writ,
Not making worse what nature made so clear,
And such a counterpart shall fame his wit,
Making his style admired everywhere.
    You to your beauteous blessings add a curse,
    Being fond on praise, which makes your praises
        worse.

85

My tongue-tied Muse in manners holds her still,
While comments of your praise richly compiled
Reserve your character with golden quill,
And precious phrase by all the Muses filed;
I think good thoughts, whilst other write good words,
And like unlettered clerk still cry 'Amen'
To every hymn that able spirit affords
In polished form of well-refined pen.
Hearing you praised, I say, ''Tis so, 'tis true',
And to the most of praise add something more;
But that is in my thought, whose love to you
(Though words come hindmost) holds his rank
        before;
    Then others for the breath of words respect,
    Me for my dumb thoughts, speaking in effect.

86

Was it the proud full sail of his great verse,
Bound for the prize of all-too-precious you,
That did my ripe thoughts in my brain in-hearse,
Making their tomb the womb wherein they grew?
Was it his spirit, by spirits taught to write
Above a mortal pitch, that struck me dead?
No, neither he, nor his compeers by night,
Giving him aid, my verse astonished.
He, nor that affable familiar ghost
Which nightly gulls him with intelligence,
As victors of my silence cannot boast;
I was not sick of any fear from thence.
    But when your countenance filled up his line,
    Then lacked I matter, that enfeebled mine.

87

Farewell, thou art too dear for my possessing,
And like enough thou knowst thy estimate;
The charter of thy worth gives thee releasing;
My bonds in thee are all determinate.
For how do I hold thee but by thy granting,
And for that riches where is my deserving?
The cause of this fair gift in me is wanting,
And so my patent back again is swerving.
Thyself thou gav'st, thy own worth then not
        knowing,
Or me, to whom thou gav'st it, else mistaking;
So thy great gift upon misprision growing
Comes home again, on better judgement making.
    Thus have I had thee as a dream doth flatter,
    In sleep a king, but waking no such matter.

88

When thou shalt be disposed to set me light
And place my merit in the eye of scorn,
Upon thy side, against myself, I'll fight,
And prove thee virtuous, though thou art forsworn:
With mine own weakness being best acquainted,
Upon thy part I can set down a story
Of faults concealed, wherein I am attainted,
That thou, in losing me, shall win much glory;
And I by this will be a gainer too,
For bending all my loving thoughts on thee,
The injuries that to myself I do,
Doing thee vantage, double vantage me:
    Such is my love, to thee I so belong,
    That for thy right myself will bear all wrong.

89

Say that thou didst forsake me for some fault,
And I will comment upon that offence;
Speak of my lameness, and I straight will halt,
Against thy reasons making no defence.
Thou canst not, love, disgrace me half so ill,
To set a form upon desired change,
As I'll myself disgrace, knowing thy will;
I will acquaintance strangle and look strange,
Be absent from thy walks, and in my tongue
Thy sweet beloved name no more shall dwell,
Lest I, too much profane, should do it wrong,
And haply of our old acquaintance tell.
    For thee, against myself I'll vow debate;
    For I must ne'er love him whom thou dost hate.

90

Then hate me when thou wilt, if ever, now,
Now, while the world is bent my deeds to cross,
Join with the spite of fortune, make me bow,
And do not drop in for an after-loss.
Ah, do not, when my heart hath 'scaped this sorrow,
Come in the rearward of a conquered woe;
Give not a windy night a rainy morrow,
To linger out a purposed overthrow.
If thou wilt leave me, do not leave me last,
When other petty griefs have done their spite;
But in the onset come, so shall I taste
At first the very worst of fortune's might;
    And other strains of woe, which now seem woe,
    Compared with loss of thee, will not seem so.

91

Some glory in their birth, some in their skill,
Some in their wealth, some in their bodies' force,
Some in their garments, though new-fangled ill,
Some in their hawks and hounds, some in their horse,
And every humour hath his adjunct pleasure,
Wherein it finds a joy above the rest;
But these particulars are not my measure;
All these I better in one general best.
Thy love is better than high birth to me,
Richer than wealth, prouder than garments' cost,
Of more delight than hawks or horses be;
And having thee, of all men's pride I boast –
    Wretched in this alone, that thou mayst take
    All this away, and me most wretched make.

92

But do thy worst to steal thyself away;
For term of life thou art assured mine,
And life no longer than thy love will stay,
For it depends upon that love of thine.
Then need I not to fear the worst of wrongs,
When in the least of them my life hath end;
I see a better state to me belongs
Than that which on thy humour doth depend.
Thou canst not vex me with inconstant mind,
Since that my life on thy revolt doth lie.
O what a happy title do I find,
Happy to have thy love, happy to die!
    But what's so blessed fair that fears no blot?
    Thou mayst be false, and yet I know it not.

93

So shall I live, supposing thou art true,
Like a deceived husband; so love's face
May still seem love to me, though altered new,
Thy looks with me, thy heart in other place;
For there can live no hatred in thine eye,
Therefore in that I cannot know thy change.
In many's looks, the false heart's history
Is writ in moods and frowns and wrinkles strange;
But heaven in thy creation did decree
That in thy face sweet love should ever dwell;
Whate'er thy thoughts or thy heart's workings be,
Thy looks should nothing thence but sweetness tell.
    How like Eve's apple doth thy beauty grow,
    If thy sweet virtue answer not thy show.

94

They that have power to hurt, and will do none,
That do not do the thing they most do show,
Who, moving others, are themselves as stone,
Unmoved, cold, and to temptation slow:
They rightly do inherit heaven's graces,
And husband nature's riches from expense;
They are the lords and owners of their faces,
Others, but stewards of their excellence.
The summer's flower is to the summer sweet,
Though to itself it only live and die,
But if that flower with base infection meet,
The basest weed outbraves his dignity:
    For sweetest things turn sourest by their deeds;
    Lilies that fester smell far worse than weeds.

95

How sweet and lovely dost thou make the shame
Which like a canker in the fragrant rose
Doth spot the beauty of thy budding name:
O in what sweets dost thou thy sins enclose!
That tongue that tells the story of thy days,
Making lascivious comments on thy sport,
Cannot dispraise; but in a kind of praise,
Naming thy name, blesses an ill report.
O what a mansion have those vices got,
Which for their habitation chose out thee,
Where beauty's veil doth cover every blot,
And all things turns to fair that eyes can see!
    Take heed, dear heart, of this large privilege;
    The hardest knife ill used doth lose his edge.

96

Some say thy fault is youth, some wantonness;
Some say thy grace is youth and gentle sport;
Both grace and faults are loved of more and less;
Thou mak'st faults graces, that to thee resort:
As on the finger of a throned queen
The basest jewel will be well esteemed,
So are those errors that in thee are seen
To truths translated, and for true things deemed.
How many lambs might the stern wolf betray
If like a lamb he could his looks translate?
How many gazers mightst thou lead away
If thou wouldst use the strength of all thy state?
　　But do not so; I love thee in such sort,
　　As thou being mine, mine is thy good report.

97

How like a winter hath my absence been
From thee, the pleasure of the fleeting year!
What freezings have I felt, what dark days seen,
What old December's bareness everywhere!
And yet this time removed was summer's time,
The teeming autumn big with rich increase
Bearing the wanton burden of the prime,
Like widowed wombs after their lords' decease:
Yet this abundant issue seemed to me
But hope of orphans, and unfathered fruit;
For summer and his pleasures wait on thee,
And thou away, the very birds are mute;
　　Or if they sing, 'tis with so dull a cheer
　　That leaves look pale, dreading the winter's near.

98

From you have I been absent in the spring,
When proud pied April, dressed in all his trim,
Hath put a spirit of youth in everything,
That heavy Saturn laughed, and leaped with him.
Yet nor the lays of birds, nor the sweet smell
Of different flowers in odour and in hue,
Could make me any summer's story tell,
Or from their proud lap pluck them where they grew;
Nor did I wonder at the lily's white,
Nor praise the deep vermilion in the rose;
They were but sweet, but figures of delight,
Drawn after you, you pattern of all those.
　　Yet seemed it winter still, and, you away,
　　As with your shadow I with these did play.

99

The forward violet thus did I chide:
'Sweet thief, whence didst thou steal thy sweet that
　　smells,
If not from my love's breath? The purple pride
Which on thy soft cheek for complexion dwells
In my love's veins thou hast too grossly dyed.'
The lily I condemned for thy hand,
And buds of marjoram had stol'n thy hair;
The roses fearfully on thorns did stand,
One blushing shame, another white despair;
A third, nor red, nor white, had stol'n of both,
And to his robb'ry had annexed thy breath;
But for his theft, in pride of all his growth,
A vengeful canker ate him up to death.
　　More flowers I noted, yet I none could see,
　　But sweet, or colour, it had stol'n from thee.

100

Where art thou, Muse, that thou forget'st so long
To speak of that which gives thee all thy might?
Spend'st thou thy fury on some worthless song,
Dark'ning thy power to lend base subjects light?
Return, forgetful Muse, and straight redeem,
In gentle numbers, time so idly spent;
Sing to the ear that doth thy lays esteem,
And gives thy pen both skill and argument.
Rise, resty Muse: my love's sweet face survey,
If time have any wrinkle graven there;
If any, be a satire to decay,
And make time's spoils despised everywhere:
　　Give my love fame faster than time wastes life,
　　So thou prevent'st his scythe and crooked knife.

101

O truant Muse, what shall be thy amends
For thy neglect of truth in beauty dyed?
Both truth and beauty on my love depends;
So dost thou, too, and therein dignified:
Make answer, Muse, wilt thou not haply say,
'Truth needs no colour with his colour fixed,
Beauty no pencil, beauty's truth to lay,
But best is best if never intermixed'?
Because he needs no praise, wilt thou be dumb?
Excuse not silence so, for't lies in thee
To make him much outlive a gilded tomb,
And to be praised of ages yet to be.
　　Then do thy office, Muse: I teach thee how
　　To make him seem long hence as he shows now.

102

My love is strengthened, though more weak in
    seeming;
I love not less, though less the show appear.
That love is merchandised, whose rich esteeming
The owner's tongue doth publish everywhere.
Our love was new, and then but in the spring,
When I was wont to greet it with my lays,
As Philomel in summer's front doth sing,
And stops her pipe in growth of riper days.
Not that the summer is less pleasant now
Than when her mournful hymns did hush the night;
But that wild music burdens every bough,
And sweets grown common lose their dear delight:
    Therefore, like her, I sometime hold my tongue,
    Because I would not dull you with my song.

103

Alack, what poverty my Muse brings forth,
That, having such a scope to show her pride,
The argument all bare is of more worth
Than when it hath my added praise beside.
O blame me not if I no more can write!
Look in your glass, and there appears a face
That overgoes my blunt invention quite,
Dulling my lines, and doing me disgrace.
Were it not sinful, then, striving to mend,
To mar the subject that before was well?
For to no other pass my verses tend
Than of your graces and your gifts to tell;
    And more, much more, than in my verse can sit
    Your own glass shows you, when you look in it.

104

To me, fair friend, you never can be old;
For as you were when first your eye I eyed,
Such seems your beauty still: three winters cold
Have from the forests shook three summers' pride;
Three beauteous springs to yellow autumn turned
In process of the seasons have I seen;
Three April perfumes in three hot Junes burned,
Since first I saw you fresh, which yet art green.
Ah, yet doth beauty, like a dial hand,
Steal from his figure, and no pace perceived;
So your sweet hue, which methinks still doth stand,
Hath motion, and mine eye may be deceived;
    For fear of which, hear this, thou age unbred,
    Ere you were born was beauty's summer dead.

105

Let not my love be called idolatry,
Nor my beloved as an idol show,
Since all alike my songs and praises be,
To one, of one, still such, and ever so.
Kind is my love today, tomorrow kind,
Still constant in a wondrous excellence;
Therefore my verse, to constancy confined,
One thing expressing, leaves out difference.
Fair, kind and true is all my argument;
Fair, kind and true, varying to other words,
And in this change is my invention spent,
Three themes in one, which wondrous scope affords.
    Fair, kind and true have often lived alone,
    Which three, till now, never kept seat in one.

106

When in the chronicle of wasted time
I see descriptions of the fairest wights,
And beauty making beautiful old rhyme,
In praise of ladies dead, and lovely knights;
Then in the blazon of sweet beauties best,
Of hand, of foot, of lip, of eye, of brow,
I see their antique pen would have expressed
Even such a beauty as you master now:
So all their praises are but prophecies
Of this our time, all you prefiguring;
And for they looked but with divining eyes
They had not skill enough your worth to sing;
    For we which now behold these present days
    Have eyes to wonder, but lack tongues to praise.

107

Not mine own fears, nor the prophetic soul
Of the wide world, dreaming on things to come,
Can yet the lease of my true love control,
Supposed as forfeit to a confined doom.
The mortal moon hath her eclipse endured,
And the sad augurs mock their own presage;
Uncertainties now crown themselves assured,
And peace proclaims olives of endless age.
Now with the drops of this most balmy time
My love looks fresh, and death to me subscribes,
Since 'spite of him I'll live in this poor rhyme,
While he insults o'er dull and speechless tribes;
    And thou in this shalt find thy monument,
    When tyrants' crests and tombs of brass are spent.

108

What's in the brain that ink may character
Which hath not figured to thee my true spirit?
What's new to speak, what new to register,
That may express my love, or thy dear merit?
Nothing, sweet boy; but yet, like prayers divine,
I must each day say o'er the very same,
Counting no old thing old; thou mine, I thine,
Even as when first I hallowed thy fair name:
So that eternal love, in love's fresh case,
Weighs not the dust and injury of age,
Nor gives to necessary wrinkles place
But makes antiquity for aye his page,
    Finding the first conceit of love there bred,
    Where time and outward form would show it dead.

109

O never say that I was false of heart,
Though absence seemed my flame to qualify;
As easy might I from myself depart
As from my soul which in thy breast doth lie:
That is my home of love; if I have ranged,
Like him that travels I return again,
Just to the time, not with the time exchanged,
So that myself bring water for my stain;
Never believe, though in my nature reigned
All frailties that besiege all kinds of blood,
That it could so preposterously be stained,
To leave for nothing all thy sum of good:
    For nothing this wide universe I call,
    Save thou, my rose; in it thou art my all.

110

Alas, 'tis true, I have gone here and there,
And made myself a motley to the view,
Gored mine own thoughts, sold cheap what is most
    dear,
Made old offences of affections new.
Most true it is that I have looked on truth
Askance and strangely; but by all above,
These blenches gave my heart another youth,
And worse essays proved thee my best of love.
Now all is done, save what shall have no end;
Mine appetite I never more will grind
On newer proof, to try an older friend,
A god in love, to whom I am confined:
    Then give me welcome, next my heaven the best,
    Even to thy pure and most most loving breast.

111

O, for my sake do you with Fortune chide,
The guilty goddess of my harmful deeds,
That did not better for my life provide
Than public means, which public manners breeds;
Thence comes it that my name receives a brand,
And almost thence my nature is subdued
To what it works in, like the dyer's hand;
Pity me, then, and wish I were renewed,
Whilst like a willing patient I will drink
Potions of eisell 'gainst my strong infection;
No bitterness that I will bitter think,
Nor double penance to correct correction.
    Pity me then, dear friend, and I assure ye,
    Even that your pity is enough to cure me.

112

Your love and pity doth th'impression fill
Which vulgar scandal stamped upon my brow;
For what care I who calls me well or ill
So you o'er-green my bad, my good allow?
You are my all-the-world, and I must strive
To know my shames and praises from your tongue;
None else to me, nor I to none, alive,
That my steeled sense o'er-changes right or wrong.
In so profound abysm I throw all care
Of others' voices, that my adder's sense
To critic and to flatterer stopped are.
Mark how with my neglect I do dispense:
    You are so strongly in my purpose bred
    That all the world besides me thinks you're dead.

113

Since I left you, mine eye is in my mind,
And that which governs me to go about
Doth part his function, and is partly blind;
Seems seeing, but effectually is out:
For it no form delivers to the heart
Of bird, of flower, or shape which it doth latch;
Of his quick objects hath the mind no part,
Nor his own vision holds what it doth catch:
For if it see the rud'st or gentlest sight,
The most sweet-favoured or deformed'st creature,
The mountain, or the sea, the day, or night,
The crow, or dove, it shapes them to your feature.
    Incapable of more, replete with you,
    My most true mind thus maketh mine untrue.

114

Or whether doth my mind, being crowned with you,
Drink up the monarch's plague, this flattery?
Or whether shall I say mine eye saith true,
And that your love taught it this alchemy,
To make of monsters and things indigest
Such cherubins as your sweet self resemble,
Creating every bad a perfect best
As fast as objects to his beams assemble?
O, 'tis the first, 'tis flatt'ry in my seeing,
And my great mind most kingly drinks it up:
Mine eye well knows what with his gust is greeing,
And to his palate doth prepare the cup.
   If it be poisoned, 'tis the lesser sin,
   That mine eye loves it and doth first begin.

115

Those lines that I before have writ do lie,
Even those that said I could not love you dearer;
Yet then my judgement knew no reason why
My most full flame should afterwards burn clearer.
But reckoning time, whose millioned accidents
Creep in 'twixt vows, and change decrees of kings,
Tan sacred beauty, blunt the sharp'st intents,
Divert strong minds to th' course of alt'ring things;
Alas, why, fearing of time's tyranny,
Might I not then say, 'Now I love you best',
When I was certain o'er uncertainty,
Crowning the present, doubting of the rest?
   Love is a babe; then might I not say so,
   To give full growth to that which still doth grow?

116

Let me not to the marriage of true minds
Admit impediments; love is not love
Which alters when it alteration finds,
Or bends with the remover to remove.
O no, it is an ever-fixed mark,
That looks on tempests and is never shaken;
It is the star to every wand'ring bark,
Whose worth's unknown, although his height be taken.
Love's not Time's fool, though rosy lips and cheeks
Within his bending sickle's compass come;
Love alters not with his brief hours and weeks,
But bears it out even to the edge of doom.
   If this be error and upon me proved,
   I never writ, nor no man ever loved.

117

Accuse me thus: that I have scanted all
Wherein I should your great deserts repay,
Forgot upon your dearest love to call,
Whereto all bonds do tie me day by day;
That I have frequent been with unknown minds,
And given to time your own dear-purchased right;
That I have hoisted sail to all the winds
Which should transport me farthest from your sight.
Book both my wilfulness and errors down,
And on just proof surmise accumulate;
Bring me within the level of your frown,
But shoot not at me in your wakened hate:
   Since my appeal says I did strive to prove
   The constancy and virtue of your love.

118

Like as, to make our appetites more keen,
With eager compounds we our palate urge;
As, to prevent our maladies unseen,
We sicken to shun sickness when we purge;
Even so, being full of your ne'er-cloying sweetness,
To bitter sauces did I frame my feeding,
And, sick of welfare, found a kind of meetness
To be diseased ere that there was true needing.
Thus policy in love, t'anticipate
The ills that were not, grew to faults assured,
And brought to medicine a healthful state
Which, rank of goodness, would by ill be cured;
   But thence I learn, and find the lesson true,
   Drugs poison him that so fell sick of you.

119

What potions have I drunk of siren tears
Distilled from limbecks foul as hell within,
Applying fears to hopes, and hopes to fears,
Still losing when I saw myself to win?
What wretched errors hath my heart committed,
Whilst it hath thought itself so blessed never?
How have mine eyes out of their spheres been fitted
In the distraction of this madding fever?
O benefit of ill: now I find true
That better is by evil still made better,
And ruined love when it is built anew
Grows fairer than at first, more strong, far greater:
   So I return rebuked to my content,
   And gain by ills thrice more than I have spent.

120

That you were once unkind befriends me now,
And for that sorrow, which I then did feel,
Needs must I under my transgression bow,
Unless my nerves were brass or hammered steel:
For if you were by my unkindness shaken,
As I by yours, you've passed a hell of time,
And I, a tyrant, have no leisure taken
To weigh how once I suffered in your crime.
O that our night of woe might have remembered
My deepest sense how hard true sorrow hits,
And soon to you, as you to me then, tendered
The humble salve which wounded bosoms fits!
 But that your trespass now becomes a fee;
 Mine ransoms yours, and yours must ransom me.

121

'Tis better to be vile than vile esteemed,
When not to be, receives reproach of being,
And the just pleasure lost, which is so deemed
Not by our feeling, but by others' seeing.
For why should others' false adulterate eyes
Give salutation to my sportive blood?
Or on my frailties why are frailer spies,
Which in their wills count bad what I think good?
No, I am that I am, and they that level
At my abuses, reckon up their own;
I may be straight, though they themselves be bevel.
By their rank thoughts my deeds must not be shown,
 Unless this general evil they maintain:
 All men are bad, and in their badness reign.

122

Thy gift, thy tables, are within my brain
Full charactered with lasting memory,
Which shall above that idle rank remain
Beyond all date, even to eternity;
Or at the least, so long as brain and heart
Have faculty by nature to subsist;
Till each to razed oblivion yield his part
Of thee, thy record never can be missed.
That poor retention could not so much hold,
Nor need I tallies thy dear love to score;
Therefore to give them from me was I bold,
To trust those tables that receive thee more;
 To keep an adjunct to remember thee
 Were to import forgetfulness in me.

123

No! Time, thou shalt not boast that I do change;
Thy pyramids, built up with newer might,
To me are nothing novel, nothing strange;
They are but dressings of a former sight:
Our dates are brief, and therefore we admire
What thou dost foist upon us that is old,
And rather make them born to our desire
Than think that we before have heard them told:
Thy registers and thee I both defy,
Not wond'ring at the present, nor the past,
For thy records, and what we see doth lie,
Made more or less by thy continual haste:
 This I do vow, and this shall ever be,
 I will be true despite thy scythe and thee.

124

If my dear love were but the child of state
It might, for fortune's bastard, be unfathered,
As subject to time's love or to time's hate,
Weeds among weeds, or flowers with flowers
 gathered.
No, it was builded far from accident;
It suffers not in smiling pomp, nor falls
Under the blow of thralled discontent,
Whereto th'inviting time our fashion calls:
It fears not policy, that heretic,
Which works on leases of short-numbered hours,
But all alone stands hugely politic,
That it nor grows with heat, nor drowns with showers.
 To this I witness call the fools of time,
 Which die for goodness, who have lived for crime.

125

Were't ought to me I bore the canopy,
With my extern the outward honouring,
Or laid great bases for eternity,
Which proves more short than waste or ruining?
Have I not seen dwellers on form and favour
Lose all, and more, by paying too much rent,
For compound sweet forgoing simple savour,
Pitiful thrivers, in their gazing spent?
No, let me be obsequious in thy heart,
And take thou my oblation, poor but free,
Which is not mixed with seconds, knows no art,
But mutual render, only me for thee.
 Hence, thou suborned informer, a true soul
 When most impeached, stands least in thy control.

126

O thou my lovely Boy, who in thy power
Dost hold time's fickle glass, his sickle hour,
Who hast by waning grown, and therein show'st
Thy lover's withering, as thy sweet self grow'st;
If nature, sovereign mistress over wrack,
As thou goest onwards still will pluck thee back,
She keeps thee to this purpose: that her skill
May time disgrace, and wretched minute kill.
Yet fear her, O thou minion of her pleasure:
She may detain, but not still keep, her treasure!
Her audit, though delayed, answered must be,
And her quietus is to render thee.
    (   )
    (   )

127

In the old age black was not counted fair,
Or if it were, it bore not beauty's name;
But now is black beauty's successive heir,
And beauty slandered with a bastard shame:
For since each hand hath put on nature's power,
Fairing the foul with art's false borrowed face,
Sweet beauty hath no name, no holy bower,
But is profaned, if not lives in disgrace.
Therefore my mistress' eyes are raven black,
Her eyes so suited, and they mourners seem
At such who, not born fair, no beauty lack,
Sland'ring creation with a false esteem;
    Yet so they mourn, becoming of their woe,
    That every tongue says beauty should look so.

128

How oft when thou, my music, music play'st
Upon that blessed wood whose motion sounds
With thy sweet fingers, when thou gently sway'st
The wiry concord that mine ear confounds,
Do I envy those jacks that nimble leap,
To kiss the tender inward of thy hand,
Whilst my poor lips, which should that harvest reap,
At the wood's boldness by thee blushing stand?
To be so tickled they would change their state
And situation with those dancing chips,
O'er whom thy fingers walk with gentle gait,
Making dead wood more blessed than living lips.
    Since saucy jacks so happy are in this,
    Give them thy fingers, me thy lips to kiss.

129

Th'expense of spirit in a waste of shame
Is lust in action; and till action, lust
Is perjured, murd'rous, bloody, full of blame,
Savage, extreme, rude, cruel, not to trust;
Enjoyed no sooner but despised straight;
Past reason hunted, and no sooner had,
Past reason hated as a swallowed bait,
On purpose laid to make the taker mad;
Mad in pursuit, and in possession so,
Had, having, and in quest to have, extreme;
A bliss in proof, and proved, a very woe;
Before, a joy proposed; behind, a dream.
    All this the world well knows, yet none knows well
    To shun the heaven that leads men to this hell.

130

My mistress' eyes are nothing like the sun;
Coral is far more red than her lips' red;
If snow be white, why then her breasts are dun;
If hairs be wires, black wires grow on her head;
I have seen roses damasked, red and white,
But no such roses see I in her cheeks;
And in some perfumes is there more delight
Than in the breath that from my mistress reeks.
I love to hear her speak, yet well I know
That music hath a far more pleasing sound;
I grant I never saw a goddess go;
My mistress when she walks treads on the ground.
    And yet, by heaven, I think my love as rare
    As any she belied with false compare.

131

Thou art as tyrannous, so as thou art,
As those whose beauties proudly make them cruel;
For well thou knowst, to my dear doting heart
Thou art the fairest and most precious jewel.
Yet in good faith some say, that thee behold,
Thy face hath not the power to make love groan;
To say they err, I dare not be so bold,
Although I swear it to myself alone;
And to be sure that is not false, I swear
A thousand groans but thinking on thy face;
One on another's neck do witness bear
Thy black is fairest in my judgement's place.
    In nothing art thou black save in thy deeds,
    And thence this slander, as I think, proceeds.

132

Thine eyes I love, and they, as pitying me,
Knowing thy heart torment me with disdain,
Have put on black, and loving mourners be,
Looking with pretty ruth upon my pain;
And truly, not the morning sun of heaven
Better becomes the grey cheeks of the East,
Nor that full star that ushers in the even
Doth half that glory to the sober West
As those two mourning eyes become thy face:
O let it then as well beseem thy heart
To mourn for me, since mourning doth thee grace,
And suit thy pity like in every part:
    Then will I swear beauty herself is black,
    And all they foul that thy complexion lack.

133

Beshrew that heart that makes my heart to groan
For that deep wound it gives my friend and me;
Is't not enough to torture me alone,
But slave to slavery my sweet'st friend must be?
Me from myself thy cruel eye hath taken,
And my next self thou harder hast engrossed:
Of him, myself and thee I am forsaken,
A torment thrice threefold thus to be crossed.
Prison my heart in thy steel bosom's ward;
But then my friend's heart let my poor heart bail.
Whoe'er keeps me, let my heart be his guard;
Thou canst not then use rigour in my jail.
    And yet thou wilt, for I being pent in thee,
    Perforce am thine, and all that is in me.

134

So now I have confessed that he is thine,
And I myself am mortgaged to thy will,
Myself I'll forfeit, so that other mine
Thou wilt restore to be my comfort still;
But thou wilt not, nor he will not be free,
For thou art covetous, and he is kind;
He learned but surety-like to write for me,
Under that bond that him as fast doth bind.
The statute of thy beauty thou wilt take,
Thou usurer, that put'st forth all to use,
And sue a friend, came debtor for my sake:
So him I lose through my unkind abuse.
    Him have I lost; thou hast both him and me;
    He pays the whole, and yet am I not free.

135

Whoever hath her wish, thou hast thy Will,
And Will to boot, and Will in overplus;
More than enough am I, that vex thee still,
To thy sweet will making addition thus.
Wilt thou, whose will is large and spacious,
Not once vouchsafe to hide my will in thine?
Shall will in others seem right gracious,
And in my will no fair acceptance shine?
The sea, all water, yet receives rain still,
And in abundance addeth to his store;
So thou, being rich in Will, add to thy Will
One will of mine, to make thy large Will more:
    Let no unkind, no fair beseechers kill;
    Think all but one, and me in that one Will.

136

If thy soul check thee that I come so near,
Swear to thy blind soul that I was thy Will,
And will, thy soul knows, is admitted there;
Thus far for love my love-suit sweet fulfil.
Will will fulfil the treasure of thy love,
Ay, fill it full with wills, and my will one;
In things of great receipt with ease we prove
Among a number one is reckoned none.
Then in the number let me pass untold,
Though in thy store's account I one must be.
For nothing hold me, so it please thee hold
That nothing, me, a something sweet to thee.
    Make but my name thy love, and love that still;
    And then thou lov'st me, for my name is Will.

137

Thou blind fool love, what dost thou to mine eyes,
That they behold, and see not what they see?
They know what beauty is, see where it lies,
Yet what the best is, take the worst to be.
If eyes, corrupt by over-partial looks,
Be anchored in the bay where all men ride,
Why of eyes' falsehood hast thou forged hooks,
Whereto the judgement of my heart is tied?
Why should my heart think that a several plot
Which my heart knows the wide world's common
    place?
Or mine eyes, seeing this, say this is not,
To put fair truth upon so foul a face?
    In things right true my heart and eyes have erred,
    And to this false plague are they now transferred.

138

When my love swears that she is made of truth,
I do believe her, though I know she lies,
That she might think me some untutored youth
Unlearned in the world's false subtleties.
Thus vainly thinking that she thinks me young,
Although she knows my days are past the best,
Simply I credit her false-speaking tongue;
On both sides thus is simple truth suppressed.
But wherefore says she not she is unjust?
And wherefore say not I that I am old?
O love's best habit is in seeming trust,
And age in love loves not t' have years told:
  Therefore I lie with her, and she with me,
  And in our faults by lies we flattered be.

139

O call not me to justify the wrong
That thy unkindness lays upon my heart;
Wound me not with thine eye, but with thy tongue;
Use power with power, and slay me not by art.
Tell me thou lov'st elsewhere; but in my sight,
Dear heart, forbear to glance thine eye aside.
What need'st thou wound with cunning, when thy
    might
Is more than my o'er-pressed defence can bide?
Let me excuse thee: ah, my love well knows
Her pretty looks have been mine enemies,
And therefore from my face she turns my foes
That they elsewhere might dart their injuries.
  Yet do not so, but since I am near slain,
  Kill me outright with looks, and rid my pain.

140

Be wise as thou art cruel, do not press
My tongue-tied patience with too much disdain,
Lest sorrow lend me words, and words express
The manner of my pity-wanting pain.
If I might teach thee wit, better it were,
Though not to love, yet love to tell me so,
As testy sick men, when their deaths be near,
No news but health from their physicians know:
For if I should despair, I should grow mad,
And in my madness might speak ill of thee;
Now this ill-wresting world is grown so bad,
Mad slanderers by mad ears believed be.
  That I may not be so, nor thou belied,
  Bear thine eyes straight, though thy proud heart go
    wide.

141

In faith, I do not love thee with mine eyes,
For they in thee a thousand errors note;
But 'tis my heart that loves what they despise,
Who in despite of view is pleased to dote.
Nor are mine ears with thy tongue's tune delighted,
Nor tender feeling to base touches prone,
Nor taste, nor smell, desire to be invited
To any sensual feast with thee alone:
But my five wits, nor my five senses, can
Dissuade one foolish heart from serving thee,
Who leaves unswayed the likeness of a man,
Thy proud heart's slave and vassal wretch to be:
  Only my plague thus far I count my gain,
  That she that makes me sin, awards me pain.

142

Love is my sin, and thy dear virtue hate,
Hate of my sin, grounded on sinful loving;
O but with mine compare thou thine own state,
And thou shalt find it merits not reproving;
Or if it do, not from those lips of thine,
That have profaned their scarlet ornaments,
And sealed false bonds of love as oft as mine,
Robbed others' beds' revenues of their rents.
Be it lawful I love thee as thou lov'st those
Whom thine eyes woo, as mine importune thee,
Root pity in thy heart, that when it grows,
Thy pity may deserve to pitied be.
  If thou dost seek to have what thou dost hide,
  By self-example mayst thou be denied.

143

Lo, as a careful housewife runs to catch
One of her feathered creatures broke away,
Sets down her babe, and makes all swift dispatch
In pursuit of the thing she would have stay;
Whilst her neglected child holds her in chase,
Cries to catch her whose busy care is bent
To follow that which flies before her face,
Not prizing her poor infant's discontent:
So run'st thou after that which flies from thee,
Whilst I, thy babe, chase thee afar behind.
But if thou catch thy hope, turn back to me,
And play the mother's part, kiss me, be kind:
  So will I pray that thou mayst have thy Will,
  If thou turn back and my loud crying still.

144

Two loves I have, of comfort and despair,
Which, like two spirits, do suggest me still:
The better angel is a man right fair,
The worser spirit a woman coloured ill.
To win me soon to hell my female evil
Tempteth my better angel from my side,
And would corrupt my saint to be a devil,
Wooing his purity with her foul pride;
And whether that my angel be turned fiend
Suspect I may, yet not directly tell;
But being both from me both to each friend,
I guess one angel in another's hell.
    Yet this shall I ne'er know, but live in doubt,
    Till my bad angel fire my good one out.

145

Those lips that love's own hand did make
Breathed forth the sound that said 'I hate',
To me, that languished for her sake;
But when she saw my woeful state,
Straight in her heart did mercy come,
Chiding that tongue that, ever sweet,
Was used in giving gentle doom,
And taught it thus anew to greet:
'I hate' she altered with an end
That followed it as gentle day
Doth follow night, who like a fiend
From heaven to hell is flown away.
    'I hate' from 'hate' away she threw,
    And saved my life, saying 'not you'.

146

Poor soul, the centre of my sinful earth,
Feeding these rebel powers that thee array,
Why dost thou pine within and suffer dearth,
Painting thy outward walls so costly gay?
Why so large cost, having so short a lease,
Dost thou upon thy fading mansion spend?
Shall worms, inheritors of this excess,
Eat up thy charge? Is this thy body's end?
Then soul, live thou upon thy servant's loss,
And let that pine to aggravate thy store;
Buy terms divine in selling hours of dross,
Within be fed, without be rich no more:
    So shalt thou feed on death, that feeds on men,
    And death once dead, there's no more dying then.

147

My love is as a fever, longing still
For that which longer nurseth the disease,
Feeding on that which doth preserve the ill,
Th'uncertain sickly appetite to please:
My reason, the physician to my love,
Angry that his prescriptions are not kept,
Hath left me, and I, desperate, now approve
Desire is death, which physic did except.
Past cure I am, now reason is past care,
And frantic mad with ever more unrest;
My thoughts and my discourse as madmen's are,
At random from the truth vainly expressed:
    For I have sworn thee fair, and thought thee bright,
    Who art as black as hell, as dark as night.

148

O me! What eyes hath love put in my head,
Which have no correspondence with true sight?
Or if they have, where is my judgement fled,
That censures falsely what they see aright?
If that be fair whereon my false eyes dote,
What means the world to say it is not so?
If it be not, then love doth well denote,
Love's eye is not so true as all men's: no,
How can it? O how can love's eye be true,
That is so vexed with watching and with tears?
No marvel then though I mistake my view:
The sun itself sees not, till heaven clears.
    O cunning love, with tears thou keep'st me blind,
    Lest eyes well seeing thy foul faults should find.

149

Canst thou, O cruel, say I love thee not,
When I against myself with thee partake?
Do I not think on thee, when I forgot
Am of myself, all, tyrant, for thy sake?
Who hateth thee, that I do call my friend?
On whom frown'st thou, that I do fawn upon?
Nay, if thou lour'st on me, do I not spend
Revenge upon myself with present moan?
What merit do I in myself respect
That is so proud thy service to despise,
When all my best doth worship thy defect,
Commanded by the motion of thine eyes?
    But, love, hate on; for now I know thy mind:
    Those that can see thou lov'st, and I am blind.

150

O from what power hast thou this powerful might,
With insufficiency my heart to sway,
To make me give the lie to my true sight,
And swear that brightness doth not grace the day?
Whence hast thou this becoming of things ill,
That in the very refuse of thy deeds
There is such strength and warrantise of skill
That in my mind thy worst all best exceeds?
Who taught thee how to make me love thee more,
The more I hear and see just cause of hate?
O, though I love what others do abhor,
With others thou shouldst not abhor my state:
    If thy unworthiness raised love in me,
    More worthy I to be beloved of thee.

151

Love is too young to know what conscience is:
Yet who knows not conscience is born of love?
Then, gentle cheater, urge not my amiss,
Lest guilty of my faults thy sweet self prove;
For, thou betraying me, I do betray
My nobler part to my gross body's treason;
My soul doth tell my body that he may
Triumph in love; flesh stays no further reason,
But rising at thy name doth point out thee
As his triumphant prize, proud of this pride:
He is contented thy poor drudge to be,
To stand in thy affairs, fall by thy side.
    No want of conscience hold it that I call
    Her 'love', for whose dear love I rise and fall.

152

In loving thee thou knowst I am forsworn;
But thou art twice forsworn to me love swearing,
In act thy bed-vow broke and new faith torn,
In vowing new hate after new love bearing.
But why of two oaths' breach do I accuse thee,
When I break twenty? I am perjured most,
For all my vows are oaths but to misuse thee,
And all my honest faith in thee is lost:
For I have sworn deep oaths of thy deep kindness,
Oaths of thy love, thy truth, thy constancy,
And to enlighten thee gave eyes to blindness,
Or made them swear against the thing they see:
    For I have sworn thee fair: more perjured eye,
    To swear against the truth so foul a lie.

153

Cupid laid by his brand, and fell asleep;
A maid of Dian's this advantage found,
And his love-kindling fire did quickly steep
In a cold valley-fountain of that ground,
Which borrowed from this holy fire of love
A dateless lively heat still to endure,
And grew a seething bath, which yet men prove
Against strange maladies a sovereign cure:
But at my mistress' eye love's brand new fired,
The boy for trial needs would touch my breast;
I, sick withal, the help of bath desired,
And thither hied, a sad distempered guest,
    But found no cure; the bath for my help lies
    Where Cupid got new fire: my mistress' eye.

154

The little love-god lying once asleep,
Laid by his side his heart-inflaming brand,
Whilst many nymphs, that vowed chaste life to keep,
Came tripping by; but in her maiden hand
The fairest votary took up that fire
Which many legions of true hearts had warmed;
And so the general of hot desire
Was, sleeping, by a virgin hand disarmed.
This brand she quenched in a cool well by,
Which from love's fire took heat perpetual,
Growing a bath and healthful remedy
For men diseased; but I, my mistress' thrall,
    Came there for cure, and this by that I prove:
    Love's fire heats water, water cools not love.

A Lover's Complaint

From off a hill whose concave womb reworded
A plaintful story from a sist'ring vale,
My spirits t'attend this double voice accorded,
And down I laid to list the sad-tuned tale;
Ere long espied a fickle maid full pale,   5
Tearing of papers, breaking rings a-twain,
Storming her world with sorrow's wind and rain.

Upon her head a plaited hive of straw,
Which fortified her visage from the sun,
Whereon the thought might think sometime it saw   10
The carcass of a beauty spent and done;
Time had not scythed all that youth begun,
Nor youth all quit, but spite of heaven's fell rage
Some beauty peeped through lattice of seared age.

Oft did she heave her napkin to her eyne,   15
Which on it had conceited characters,
Laund'ring the silken figures in the brine
That seasoned woe had pelleted in tears,
And often reading what contents it bears;
As often shrieking undistinguished woe,   20
In clamours of all size, both high and low.

Sometimes her levelled eyes their carriage ride,
As they did batt'ry to the spheres intend;
Sometime, diverted, their poor balls are tied
To th'orbed earth; sometimes they do extend   25
Their view right on; anon their gazes lend
To every place at once, and nowhere fixed,
The mind and sight distractedly commixed.

Her hair, nor loose, nor tied in formal plait,
Proclaimed in her a careless hand of pride;   30
For some untucked descended her sheaved hat,
Hanging her pale and pined cheek beside;
Some in her threaden fillet still did bide,
And, true to bondage, would not break from thence,
Though slackly braided in loose negligence.   35

A thousand favours from a maund she drew,
Of amber, crystal and of beaded jet,
Which, one by one, she in a river threw,
Upon whose weeping margent she was set,
Like usury, applying wet to wet,   40
Or monarch's hands, that lets not bounty fall
Where want cries 'Some!', but where excess begs, 'All!'

Of folded schedules had she many a one,
Which she perused, sighed, tore and gave the flood;
Cracked many a ring of posied gold and bone,   45
Bidding them find their sepulchres in mud;
Found yet moe letters, sadly penned in blood,
With sleided silk, feat and affectedly
Enswathed and sealed to curious secrecy.

These often bathed she in her fluxive eyes,   50
And often kissed, and often gave to tear;
Cried, 'O false blood, thou register of lies,
What unapproved witness dost thou bear!
Ink would have seemed more black and damned here.'
This said, in top of rage the lines she rents,   55
Big discontent so breaking their contents.

A reverend man, that grazed his cattle nigh,
Sometime a blusterer, that the ruffle knew
Of court, of city, and had let go by
The swiftest hours observed as they flew,   60
Towards this afflicted fancy fastly drew,
And, privileged by age, desires to know
In brief the grounds and motives of her woe.

So slides he down upon his grained bat,
And comely distant sits he by her side,   65
When he again desires her, being sat,
Her grievance with his hearing to divide:
If that from him there may be aught applied
Which may her suffering ecstasy assuage,
'Tis promised in the charity of age.   70

'Father,' she says, 'though in me ye behold
The injury of many a blasting hour,
Let it not tell your judgement I am old:
Not age, but sorrow, over me hath power.
I might as yet have been a spreading flower,   75
Fresh to myself, if I had self-applied
Love to myself, and to no love beside.

'But woe is me! Too early I attended
A youthful suit; it was to gain my grace;
O, one by nature's outwards so commended   80
That maidens' eyes stuck over all his face;
Love lacked a dwelling, and made him her place;
And when in his fair parts she did abide
She was new-lodged and newly deified.

'His browny locks did hang in crooked curls,   85
And every light occasion of the wind
Upon his lips their silken parcels hurls;
What's sweet to do, to do will aptly find;
Each eye that saw him did enchant the mind:
For on his visage was in little drawn   90
What largeness thinks in paradise was sawn.

'Small show of man was yet upon his chin;
His phoenix down began but to appear,
Like unshorn velvet, on that termless skin,
Whose bare out-bragged the web it seemed to wear;   95
Yet showed his visage by that cost more dear,
And nice affections wavering stood in doubt
If best were as it was, or best without.

'His qualities were beauteous as his form:
For maiden-tongued he was, and thereof free;
Yet if men moved him, was he such a storm
As oft 'twixt May and April is to see,
When winds breathe sweet, unruly though they be.
His rudeness so with his authorized youth
Did livery falseness in a pride of truth.

'Well could he ride, and often men would say,
"That horse his mettle from his rider takes,
Proud of subjection, noble by the sway,
What rounds, what bounds, what course, what stop
   he makes!"
And controversy hence a question takes,
Whether the horse by him became his deed,
Or he his manage, by th' well-doing steed.

'But quickly on this side the verdict went:
His real habitude gave life and grace
To appertainings and to ornament,
Accomplished in himself, not in his case;
All aids, themselves made fairer by their place,
Came for additions; yet their purposed trim
Pieced not his grace, but were all graced by him.

'So on the tip of his subduing tongue
All kind of arguments and question deep,
All replication prompt, and reason strong,
For his advantage still did wake and sleep,
To make the weeper laugh, the laugher weep:
He had the dialect and different skill,
Catching all passions in his craft of will.

'That he did in the general bosom reign
Of young, of old, and sexes both enchanted
To dwell with him in thoughts, or to remain
In personal duty, following where he haunted;
Consent's bewitched, ere he desire have granted,
And dialogued for him what he would say,
Asked their own wills, and made their wills obey.

'Many there were that did his picture get
To serve their eyes, and in it put their mind,
Like fools, that in th'imagination set
The goodly objects which abroad they find,
Of lands and mansions, theirs in thought assigned,
And labouring in moe pleasures to bestow them
Than the true gouty landlord which doth owe them.

'So many have, that never touched his hand,
Sweetly supposed them mistress of his heart:
My woeful self that did in freedom stand,
And was my own fee-simple, not in part,
What with his art in youth, and youth in art,
Threw my affections in his charmed power,
Reserved the stalk and gave him all my flower.

'Yet did I not, as some, my equals, did,
Demand of him; nor, being desired, yielded,
Finding myself in honour so forbid:
With safest distance I mine honour shielded.
Experience for me many bulwarks builded
Of proofs new-bleeding, which remained the foil
Of this false jewel and his amorous spoil.

'But ah! Who ever shunned by precedent
The destined ill she must herself assay,
Or forced examples 'gainst her own content,
To put the by-passed perils in her way?
Counsel may stop a while what will not stay:
For when we rage, advice is often seen
By blunting us to make our wits more keen.

'Nor gives it satisfaction to our blood
That we must curb it upon others' proof,
To be forebode the sweets that seems so good,
For fear of harms that preach in our behoof:
O appetite, from judgement stand aloof!
The one a palate hath that needs will taste,
Though reason weep and cry, "It is thy last!"

'For further, I could say, "This man's untrue",
And knew the patterns of his foul beguiling;
Heard where his plants in others' orchards grew;
Saw how deceits were gilded in his smiling;
Knew vows were ever brokers to defiling;
Thought characters and words merely but art,
And bastards of his foul adulterate heart.

'And long upon these terms I held my city,
Till thus he 'gan besiege me: "Gentle maid,
Have of my suffering youth some feeling pity
And be not of my holy vows afraid:
That's to ye sworn to none was ever said,
For feasts of love I have been called unto,
Till now, did ne'er invite, nor never woo.

' "All my offences that abroad you see
Are errors of the blood, none of the mind:
Love made them not; with acture they may be
Where neither party is nor true nor kind;
They sought their shame that so their shame did find,
And so much less of shame in me remains,
By how much of me their reproach contains.

' "Among the many that mine eyes have seen,
Not one whose flame my heart so much as warmed,
Or my affection put to th' smallest teen,
Or any of my leisures ever charmed:
Harm have I done to them, but ne'er was harmed;
Kept hearts in liveries, but my own was free,
And reigned commanding in his monarchy.

'"Look here what tributes wounded fancies sent me,
Of pallid pearls and rubies red as blood,
Figuring that they their passions likewise lent me
200 Of grief and blushes, aptly understood,
In bloodless white and the encrimsoned mood,
Effects of terror and dear modesty,
Encamped in hearts, but fighting outwardly.

'"And lo! Behold these talons of their hair,
205 With twisted metal amorously empleached,
I have received from many a several fair,
Their kind acceptance weepingly beseeched,
With th'annexions of fair gems enriched,
And deep-brained sonnets, that did amplify
210 Each stone's dear nature, worth and quality.

'"The diamond? Why, 'twas beautiful and hard,
Whereto his invised properties did tend:
The deep green emerald, in whose fresh regard
Weak sights their sickly radiance do amend;
215 The heaven-hued sapphire and the opal blend
With objects manifold; each several stone
With wit well-blazoned smiled, or made some moan.

'"Lo, all these trophies of affections hot,
Of pensived and subdued desires the tender,
220 Nature hath charged me that I hoard them not,
But yield them up where I myself must render,
That is, to you, my origin and ender:
For these of force must your oblations be;
Since I their altar, you empatron me.

225 '"O then advance of yours that phraseless hand,
Whose white weighs down the airy scale of praise;
Take all these similes to your own command,
Hallowed with sighs that burning lungs did raise:
What me, your minister for you, obeys,
230 Works under you; and to your audit comes
Their distract parcels in combined sums.

'"Lo, this device was sent me from a nun,
Or sister sanctified, of holiest note,
Which late her noble suit in court did shun,
235 Whose rarest havings made the blossoms dote;
For she was sought by spirits of richest coat,
But kept cold distance, and did thence remove
To spend her living in eternal love.

'"But O, my sweet, what labour is't to leave
240 The thing we have not, mast'ring what not strives,
Planing the place which did no form receive,
Playing patient sports in unconstrained gyves;
She that her fame so to herself contrives
The scars of battle 'scapeth by the flight,
245 And makes her absence valiant, not her might.

'"O pardon me, in that my boast is true;
The accident which brought me to her eye
Upon the moment did her force subdue,
And now she would the caged cloister fly,
Religious love put out religion's eye; 250
Not to be tempted would she be immured,
And now to tempt all liberty procured.

'"How mighty then you are, O hear me tell!
The broken bosoms that to me belong
Have emptied all their fountains in my well, 255
And mine I pour your ocean all among:
I strong o'er them, and you o'er me being strong,
Must for your victory us all congest,
As compound love, to physic your cold breast.

'"My parts had power to charm a sacred nun, 260
Who, disciplined, I dieted in grace,
Believed her eyes, when they t'assail begun,
All vows and consecrations giving place.
O most potential love! Vow, bond, nor space,
In thee hath neither sting, knot, nor confine, 265
For thou art all and all things else are thine.

'"When thou impressest, what are precepts worth
Of stale example? When thou wilt inflame,
How coldly those impediments stand forth,
Of wealth, of filial fear, law, kindred, fame? 270
Love's arms are peace, 'gainst rule, 'gainst sense,
'gainst shame,
And sweetens in the suff'ring pangs it bears
The aloes of all forces, shocks and fears.

'"Now all these hearts that do on mine depend,
Feeling it break, with bleeding groans they pine, 275
And supplicant their sighs to you extend,
To leave the batt'ry that you make 'gainst mine,
Lending soft audience to my sweet design
And credent soul to that strong-bonded oath
That shall prefer and undertake my troth." 280

'This said, his wat'ry eyes he did dismount,
Whose sights till then were levelled on my face;
Each cheek a river running from a fount
With brinish current downward flowed apace.
O how the channel to the stream gave grace, 285
Who glazed with crystal gate the glowing roses
That flame through water which their hue encloses!

'O father, what a hell of witchcraft lies
In the small orb of one particular tear!
But with the inundation of the eyes 290
What rocky heart to water will not wear?
What breast so cold that is not warmed here?
O cleft effect! Cold modesty, hot wrath,
Both fire from hence and chill extincture hath.

'For lo, his passion, but an art of craft,   295
Even there resolved my reason into tears;
There my white stole of chastity I daffed,
Shook off my sober guards and civil fears,
Appeared to him as he to me appears,
All melting, though our drops this diff'rence bore: 300
His poisoned me, and mine did him restore.

'In him a plenitude of subtle matter,
Applied to cautels, all strange forms receives,
Of burning blushes, or of weeping water,
Or swooning paleness; and he takes and leaves   305
In either's, aptness, as it best deceives,
To blush at speeches rank, to weep at woes,
Or to turn white and swoon at tragic shows.

'That not a heart which in his level came
Could 'scape the hail of his all-hurting aim,   310
Showing fair nature is both kind and tame;
And veiled in them, did win whom he would maim.
Against the thing he sought he would exclaim;
When he most burned in heart-wished luxury
He preached pure maid, and praised cold chastity.   315

'Thus, merely with the garment of a grace,
The naked and concealed fiend he covered,
That th'unexperient gave the tempter place
Which, like a cherubin, above them hovered.
Who, young and simple, would not be so lovered?   320
Ay me, I fell, and yet do question make
What I should do again for such a sake.

'O, that infected moisture of his eye!
O, that false fire which in his cheek so glowed!
O, that forced thunder from his heart did fly!   325
O, that sad breath his spongy lungs bestowed!
O, all that borrowed motion, seeming owed,
Would yet again betray the fore-betrayed,
And new pervert a reconciled maid.'

Venus and Adonis; Lucrece; The Passionate Pilgrim; 'The Phoenix and Turtle'

The first published works to name William Shakespeare as their author were two long narrative poems. *Venus and Adonis* was published in April 1593, a few days before its author's twenty-ninth birthday, *Lucrece* (or *The Rape of Lucrece*), a year later. Their printer, Richard Field, was, like Shakespeare, a native of Stratford-upon-Avon. Both poems were dedicated to Henry Wriothesley (probably pronounced 'Risely' or 'Rosely'), Earl of Southampton, a prominent member of the circle that surrounded Robert Devereux, second Earl of Essex, the rising star of the 1590s. The dedicatory epistle to *Venus and Adonis* describes it as 'the first heir of my invention' and vows to Southampton that if he likes it it will be followed by 'some graver labour' as a more fitting gift. That 'graver labour', *Lucrece*, had gone through nine editions by 1655: *Venus and Adonis* – on this evidence the most popular of all Shakespeare's works in his own time – went through sixteen editions by 1640. A marginal note by Gabriel Harvey, made no later than February 1601, records that while *Venus and Adonis* delights 'the younger sort', *Lucrece* and *Hamlet* 'have it in them, to please the wiser sort'.

The poems complement each other. *Venus and Adonis* rewrites the classical myth, best known from Ovid's version in Book 10 of his *Metamorphoses*, turning it into a contest between Venus' passion for a sulky, adolescent Adonis and his greater passion for hunting the boar (which leads to his death). The poem has been interpreted as an erotic celebration of love, a satire on the indignities of sex, or a platonic myth. What can safely be claimed is that it offers, in the predicament of Venus, a sharply defined embodiment of the urgency, perversity and contrariety of love – 'She's love, she loves, and yet she is not lov'd' – as well as justifying her prophecy that love will always be attended by disaster and that 'They that love best, their loves shall not enjoy'.

Lucrece handles a crucial episode from early Roman history, in which the rape of the chaste wife of the Roman general Collatinus by the king's son, Sextus Tarquinius,

and her subsequent suicide became the flint to fire the republican rebellion which expelled the Tarquin kings from Rome. This story, known to Shakespeare from Chaucer, Ovid and Livy, provided him with his first serious tragic theme, and his poem is replete with ideas and images that were to remain in his imagination for the rest of his career. Tarquin is his first self-destructive self-deceiver, whose lust destroys him as surely as it destroys his victim. The lengthy complaint of Lucrece is written in a familiar tradition of poems of female lamentation. After it, she likens her situation to the siege and fall of Troy, as represented in a picture, in Shakespeare's first extended treatment of that most familiar *topos* of tragic deceit, loss and suffering. The poem has provoked new interest and has found a new readership among modern feminists.

William Jaggard's unauthorized anthology *The Passionate Pilgrim*, 'By W. Shakespeare' (1599), contains only five poems which are certainly by him (three from *Love's Labour's Lost* (3, 5 and 16) and *Sonnets* 138 and 144 (1 and 2)). Shakespeare is known to have been displeased by the publication, as another author, Thomas Heywood (himself misappropriated by Jaggard in a later edition), has left on record.

'The Phoenix and Turtle' is Shakespeare's most enigmatic work. It was published in a book entitled *Love's Martyr* (1601), compiled and largely written by Robert Chester, who also commissioned contributions from other poets. Shakespeare's poem relates to the subject matter of Chester's book and may call to mind the 'metaphysical' manner of John Donne, but it also belongs in a long tradition of bird poems whose most famous English examples include Chaucer's *Parlement of Foules* and the closing songs of Shakespeare's own *Love's Labour's Lost*.

The Arden text is based on the first editions of *Venus and Adonis* (1593), *Lucrece* (1594), *The Passionate Pilgrim* (1599) and Robert Chester's *Love's Martyr* (1601).

Venus and Adonis

Vilia miretur vulgus: mihi flavus Apollo
Pocula Castalia plena ministret aqua.

To the Right Honourable
Henry Wriothesley, Earl of Southampton,
and Baron of Titchfield.

Right Honourable,

I know not how I shall offend in dedicating my
unpolished lines to your Lordship, nor how the world
will censure me for choosing so strong a prop to support
so weak a burden. Only, if your Honour seem but pleased,
I account myself highly praised; and vow to take
advantage of all idle hours, till I have honoured you with
some graver labour. But if the first heir of my invention
prove deformed, I shall be sorry it had so noble a
godfather, and never after ear so barren a land, for fear it
yield me still so bad a harvest. I leave it to your
Honourable survey, and your Honour to your heart's
content, which I wish may always answer your own wish,
and the world's hopeful expectation.

Your Honour's in all duty,
William Shakespeare.

Even as the sun with purple-colour'd face
Had ta'en his last leave of the weeping morn,
Rose-cheek'd Adonis hied him to the chase;
Hunting he lov'd, but love he laugh'd to scorn.
    Sick-thoughted Venus makes amain unto him,
    And like a bold-fac'd suitor 'gins to woo him.

'Thrice fairer than myself,' thus she began,
'The field's chief flower, sweet above compare;
Stain to all nymphs, more lovely than a man,
More white and red than doves or roses are:
    Nature that made thee with herself at strife,
    Saith that the world hath ending with thy life.

'Vouchsafe, thou wonder, to alight thy steed,
And rein his proud head to the saddle-bow;
If thou wilt deign this favour, for thy meed
A thousand honey secrets shalt thou know.
    Here come and sit, where never serpent hisses,
    And being set, I'll smother thee with kisses.

'And yet not cloy thy lips with loath'd satiety,
But rather famish them amid their plenty,
Making them red, and pale, with fresh variety:
Ten kisses short as one, one long as twenty.
    A summer's day will seem an hour but short,
    Being wasted in such time-beguiling sport.'

With this she seizeth on his sweating palm,   25
The precedent of pith and livelihood,
And trembling in her passion, calls it balm,
Earth's sovereign salve to do a goddess good:
    Being so enrag'd, desire doth lend her force
    Courageously to pluck him from his horse.   30

Over one arm the lusty courser's rein,
Under her other was the tender boy,
Who blush'd and pouted in a dull disdain,
With leaden appetite, unapt to toy:
    She red and hot as coals of glowing fire,   35
    He red for shame, but frosty in desire.

The studded bridle on a ragged bough
Nimbly she fastens – O how quick is love! –
The steed is stalled up, and even now
To tie the rider she begins to prove: 40
    Backward she push'd him, as she would be thrust,
    And govern'd him in strength, though not in lust.

So soon was she along as he was down,
Each leaning on their elbows and their hips;
Now doth she stroke his cheek, now doth he frown,   45
And 'gins to chide, but soon she stops his lips,
    And kissing speaks, with lustful language broken,
    'If thou wilt chide, thy lips shall never open.'

He burns with bashful shame, she with her tears
Doth quench the maiden burning of his cheeks;   50
Then with her windy sighs and golden hairs
To fan and blow them dry again she seeks.
    He saith she is immodest, blames her miss;
    What follows more, she murders with a kiss.

Even as an empty eagle, sharp by fast,   55
Tires with her beak on feathers, flesh and bone,
Shaking her wings, devouring all in haste,
Till either gorge be stuff'd or prey be gone:
    Even so she kiss'd his brow, his cheek, his chin,
    And where she ends she doth anew begin.   60

Forc'd to content, but never to obey,
Panting he lies and breatheth in her face.
She feedeth on the steam as on a prey,
And calls it heavenly moisture, air of grace,
    Wishing her cheeks were gardens full of flowers,   65
    So they were dew'd with such distilling showers.

Look how a bird lies tangled in a net,
So fasten'd in her arms Adonis lies;
Pure shame and aw'd resistance made him fret,
Which bred more beauty in his angry eyes: 70
    Rain added to a river that is rank
    Perforce will force it overflow the bank.

Still she entreats, and prettily entreats,
For to a pretty ear she tunes her tale.
75 Still is he sullen, still he lours and frets,
'Twixt crimson shame and anger ashy pale.
  Being red, she loves him best, and being white,
  Her best is better'd with a more delight.

Look how he can, she cannot choose but love;
80 And by her fair immortal hand she swears,
From his soft bosom never to remove
Till he take truce with her contending tears,
  Which long have rain'd, making her cheeks all
    wet:
  And one sweet kiss shall pay this comptless debt.

85 Upon this promise did he raise his chin,
Like a dive-dapper peering through a wave,
Who being look'd on, ducks as quickly in:
So offers he to give what she did crave,
  But when her lips were ready for his pay,
90 He winks, and turns his lips another way.

Never did passenger in summer's heat
More thirst for drink than she for this good turn.
Her help she sees, but help she cannot get;
She bathes in water, yet her fire must burn.
95 'Oh pity,' 'gan she cry, 'flint-hearted boy,
  'Tis but a kiss I beg, why art thou coy?

'I have been woo'd as I entreat thee now,
Even by the stern and direful god of war,
Whose sinewy neck in battle ne'er did bow,
100 Who conquers where he comes in every jar;
  Yet hath he been my captive and my slave,
  And begg'd for that which thou unask'd shalt
    have.

'Over my altars hath he hung his lance,
His batter'd shield, his uncontrolled crest;
105 And for my sake hath learn'd to sport and dance,
To toy, to wanton, dally, smile and jest,
  Scorning his churlish drum and ensign red,
  Making my arms his field, his tent my bed.

'Thus he that overrul'd I oversway'd,
110 Leading him prisoner in a red rose chain:
Strong-temper'd steel his stronger strength obey'd,
Yet was he servile to my coy disdain.
  Oh be not proud, nor brag not of thy might,
  For mast'ring her that foil'd the god of fight!

115 'Touch but my lips with those fair lips of thine –
Though mine be not so fair, yet are they red –
The kiss shall be thine own as well as mine.
What see'st thou in the ground? hold up thy head,
  Look in mine eye-balls, there thy beauty lies:
120 Then why not lips on lips, since eyes in eyes?

'Art thou asham'd to kiss? then wink again,
And I will wink; so shall the day seem night.
Love keeps his revels where there are but twain;
Be bold to play, our sport is not in sight.
  These blue-vein'd violets whereon we lean   125
  Never can blab, nor know not what we mean.

'The tender spring upon thy tempting lip
Shows thee unripe; yet mayst thou well be tasted.
Make use of time, let not advantage slip;
Beauty within itself should not be wasted.   130
  Fair flowers that are not gather'd in their prime
  Rot, and consume themselves in little time.

'Were I hard-favour'd, foul, or wrinkled old,
Ill-nurtur'd, crooked, churlish, harsh in voice,
O'erworn, despised, rheumatic and cold,   135
Thick-sighted, barren, lean, and lacking juice,
  Then mightst thou pause, for then I were not for
    thee;
  But having no defects, why dost abhor me?

'Thou canst not see one wrinkle in my brow,
Mine eyes are grey and bright and quick in turning.   140
My beauty as the spring doth yearly grow,
My flesh is soft and plump, my marrow burning.
  My smooth moist hand, were it with thy hand felt,
  Would in thy palm dissolve, or seem to melt.

'Bid me discourse, I will enchant thine ear,   145
Or like a fairy trip upon the green,
Or like a nymph, with long dishevell'd hair,
Dance on the sands, and yet no footing seen.
  Love is a spirit all compact of fire,
  Not gross to sink, but light, and will aspire.   150

'Witness this primrose bank whereon I lie:
These forceless flowers like sturdy trees support me.
Two strengthless doves will draw me through the sky
From morn till night, even where I list to sport me.
  Is love so light, sweet boy, and may it be   155
  That thou should think it heavy unto thee?

'Is thine own heart to thine own face affected?
Can thy right hand seize love upon thy left?
Then woo thyself, be of thyself rejected;
Steal thine own freedom, and complain on theft.   160
  Narcissus so himself himself forsook,
  And died to kiss his shadow in the brook.

'Torches are made to light, jewels to wear,
Dainties to taste, fresh beauty for the use,
Herbs for their smell, and sappy plants to bear: 165
Things growing to themselves are growth's abuse.
  Seeds spring from seeds, and beauty breedeth
    beauty;
  Thou wast begot, to get it is thy duty.

'Upon the earth's increase why shouldst thou feed,
170 Unless the earth with thy increase be fed?
By law of nature thou art bound to breed,
That thine may live when thou thyself art dead;
    And so in spite of death thou dost survive,
    In that thy likeness still is left alive.'

175 By this the love-sick queen began to sweat,
For where they lay, the shadow had forsook them;
And Titan, tired in the mid-day heat,
With burning eye did hotly overlook them,
    Wishing Adonis had his team to guide,
180   So he were like him and by Venus' side.

And now Adonis with a lazy sprite,
And with a heavy, dark, disliking eye,
His louring brows o'erwhelming his fair sight,
Like misty vapours when they blot the sky:
185   Souring his cheeks, cries, 'Fie, no more of love!
    The sun doth burn my face, I must remove.'

'Ay me,' quoth Venus, 'young, and so unkind!
What bare excuses mak'st thou to be gone!
I'll sigh celestial breath, whose gentle wind
190 Shall cool the heat of this descending sun
    I'll make a shadow for thee of my hairs;
    If they burn too, I'll quench them with my tears.

'The sun that shines from heaven shines but warm,
And lo I lie between that sun and thee:
195 The heat I have from thence doth little harm,
Thine eye darts forth the fire that burneth me;
    And were I not immortal, life were done,
    Between this heavenly and earthly sun.

'Art thou obdurate, flinty, hard as steel?
200 Nay more than flint, for stone at rain relenteth;
Art thou a woman's son and canst not feel
What 'tis to love, how want of love tormenteth?
    O had thy mother borne so hard a mind,
    She had not brought forth thee, but died unkind.

205 'What am I that thou shouldst contemn me this,
Or what great danger dwells upon my suit?
What were thy lips the worse for one poor kiss?
Speak, fair, but speak fair words, or else be mute.
    Give me one kiss, I'll give it thee again,
210   And one for int'rest, if thou wilt have twain.

'Fie, lifeless picture, cold and senseless stone,
Well-painted idol, image dull and dead,
Statue contenting but the eye alone,
Thing like a man, but of no woman bred!
215   Thou art no man, though of a man's complexion,
    For men will kiss even by their own direction.'

This said, impatience chokes her pleading tongue,
And swelling passion doth provoke a pause.
Red cheeks and fiery eyes blaze forth her wrong;
Being judge in love, she cannot right her cause. 220
    And now she weeps, and now she fain would
        speak,
    And now her sobs do her intendments break.

Sometime she shakes her head, and then his hand,
Now gazeth she on him, now on the ground.
Sometime her arms infold him like a band: 225
She would, he will not in her arms be bound.
    And when from thence he struggles to be gone,
    She locks her lily fingers one in one.

'Fondling,' she saith, 'since I have hemm'd thee
    here
Within the circuit of this ivory pale, 230
I'll be a park, and thou shalt be my deer:
Feed where thou wilt, on mountain or in dale;
    Graze on my lips, and if those hills be dry,
    Stray lower, where the pleasant fountains lie.

'Within this limit is relief enough, 235
Sweet bottom grass and high delightful plain,
Round rising hillocks, brakes obscure and rough,
To shelter thee from tempest and from rain:
    Then be my deer, since I am such a park,
    No dog shall rouse thee, though a thousand bark.' 240

At this Adonis smiles as in disdain,
That in each cheek appears a pretty dimple;
Love made those hollows, if himself were slain,
He might be buried in a tomb so simple,
    Foreknowing well, if there he came to lie, 245
    Why there love liv'd, and there he could not die.

These lovely caves, these round enchanting pits,
Open'd their mouths to swallow Venus' liking:
Being mad before, how doth she now for wits?
Struck dead before, what needs a second striking? 250
    Poor queen of love, in thine own law forlorn,
    To love a cheek that smiles at thee in scorn!

Now which way shall she turn? what shall she say?
Her words are done, her woes the more increasing;
The time is spent, her object will away, 255
And from her twining arms doth urge releasing.
    'Pity,' she cries, 'some favour, some remorse!'
    Away he springs, and hasteth to his horse.

But lo from forth a copse that neighbours by,
A breeding jennet, lusty, young and proud, 260
Adonis' trampling courser doth espy,
And forth she rushes, snorts and neighs aloud:
    The strong-neck'd steed being tied unto a tree,
    Breaketh his rein, and to her straight goes he.

265 Imperiously he leaps, he neighs, he bounds
And now his woven girths he breaks asunder;
The bearing earth with his hard hoof he wounds,
Whose hollow womb resounds like heaven's thunder;
    The iron bit he crusheth 'tween his teeth,
270   Controlling what he was controlled with.

His ears up-prick'd, his braided hanging mane
Upon his compass'd crest now stand on end;
His nostrils drink the air, and forth again
As from a furnace, vapours doth he send;
275   His eye which scornfully glisters like fire
    Shows his hot courage and his high desire.

Sometime he trots, as if he told the steps,
With gentle majesty and modest pride;
Anon he rears upright, curvets and leaps,
280 As who should say 'Lo thus my strength is tried:
    And this I do to captivate the eye
    Of the fair breeder that is standing by.'

What recketh he his rider's angry stir,
His flattering 'holla' or his 'Stand, I say'?
285 What cares he now for curb or pricking spur,
For rich caparisons or trappings gay?
    He sees his love, and nothing else he sees,
    For nothing else with his proud sight agrees.

Look when a painter would surpass the life
290 In limning out a well-proportion'd steed,
His art with nature's workmanship at strife,
As if the dead the living should exceed:
    So did this horse excel a common one,
    In shape, in courage, colour, pace and bone.

295 Round-hoof'd, short-jointed, fetlocks shag and long,
Broad breast, full eye, small head, and nostril wide,
High crest, short ears, straight legs and passing
        strong,
Thin mane, thick tail, broad buttock, tender hide:
    Look what a horse should have he did not lack,
300   Save a proud rider on so proud a back.

Sometime he scuds far off, and there he stares;
Anon he starts at stirring of a feather.
To bid the wind a base he now prepares,
And where he run or fly, they know not whether,
305   For through his mane and tail the high wind sings,
    Fanning the hairs, who wave like feather'd wings.

He looks upon his love, and neighs unto her:
She answers him, as if she knew his mind.
Being proud, as females are, to see him woo her,
310 She puts on outward strangeness, seems unkind,
    Spurns at his love, and scorns the heat he feels,
    Beating his kind embracements with her heels.

Then like a melancholy malcontent,
He vails his tail that like a falling plume
Cool shadow to his melting buttock lent; 315
He stamps, and bites the poor flies in his fume.
    His love perceiving how he was enrag'd,
    Grew kinder, and his fury was assuag'd.

His testy master goeth about to take him,
When lo the unback'd breeder, full of fear, 320
Jealous of catching, swiftly doth forsake him;
With her the horse, and left Adonis there:
    As they were mad unto the wood they hie them,
    Outstripping crows that strive to overfly them.

All swoln with chafing, down Adonis sits, 325
Banning his boist'rous and unruly beast.
And now the happy season once more fits
That love-sick love by pleading may be blest;
    For lovers say, the heart hath treble wrong,
    When it is barr'd the aidance of the tongue. 330

An oven that is stopp'd, or river stay'd,
Burneth more hotly, swelleth with more rage:
So of concealed sorrow may be said
Free vent of words love's fire doth assuage;
    But when the heart's attorney once is mute, 335
    The client breaks, as desperate in his suit.

He sees her coming, and begins to glow,
Even as a dying coal revives with wind;
And with his bonnet hides his angry brow,
Looks on the dull earth with disturbed mind, 340
    Taking no notice that she is so nigh,
    For all askance he holds her in his eye.

O what a sight it was, wistly to view
How she came stealing to the wayward boy!
To note the fighting conflict of her hue, 345
How white and red each other did destroy!
    But now her cheek was pale, and by and by
    It flash'd forth fire, as lightning from the sky.

Now was she just before him as he sat,
And like a lowly lover down she kneels; 350
With one fair hand she heaveth up his hat,
Her other tender hand his fair cheek feels:
    His tend'rer cheek receives her soft hand's print,
    As apt as new-fall'n snow takes any dint.

Oh what a war of looks was then between them! 355
Her eyes petitioners to his eyes suing,
His eyes saw her eyes, as they had not seen them,
Her eyes woo'd still, his eyes disdain'd the wooing;
    And all this dumb play had his acts made plain
    With tears, which chorus-like her eyes did rain. 360

Full gently now she takes him by the hand,
A lily prison'd in a gaol of snow,
Or ivory in an alablaster band:
So white a friend engirts so white a foe.
365   This beauteous combat, wilful and unwilling,
    Show'd like two silver doves that sit a-billing.

Once more the engine of her thoughts began:
'O fairest mover on this mortal round,
Would thou wert as I am, and I a man,
370 My heart all whole as thine, thy heart my wound!
    For one sweet look thy help I would assure thee,
    Though nothing but my body's bane would cure
    thee.'

'Give me my hand,' said he, 'why dost thou feel it?'
'Give me my heart,' saith she, 'and thou shalt have it.
375 O give it me lest thy hard heart do steel it,
And being steel'd, soft sighs can never grave it.
    Then love's deep groans I never shall regard,
    Because Adonis' heart hath made mine hard.'

'For shame,' he cries, 'let go, and let me go:
380 My day's delight is past, my horse is gone,
And 'tis your fault I am bereft him so.
I pray you hence, and leave me here alone,
    For all my mind, my thought, my busy care,
    Is how to get my palfrey from the mare.'

385 Thus she replies: 'Thy palfrey as he should,
Welcomes the warm approach of sweet desire.
Affection is a coal that must be cool'd;
Else, suffer'd, it will set the heart on fire.
    The sea hath bounds, but deep desire hath none;
390   Therefore no marvel though thy horse be gone.

'How like a jade he stood tied to the tree,
Servilely master'd with a leathern rein!
But when he saw his love, his youth's fair fee,
He held such petty bondage in disdain,
395   Throwing the base thong from his bending crest,
    Enfranchising his mouth, his back, his breast.

'Who sees his true-love in her naked bed,
Teaching the sheets a whiter hue than white,
But when his glutton eye so full hath fed,
400 His other agents aim at like delight?
    Who is so faint that dares not be so bold
    To touch the fire, the weather being cold?

'Let me excuse thy courser, gentle boy,
And learn of him, I heartily beseech thee,
405 To take advantage on presented joy;
Though I were dumb, yet his proceedings teach thee.
    O learn to love, the lesson is but plain,
    And once made perfect, never lost again.'

'I know not love,' quoth he, 'nor will not know it,
Unless it be a boar, and then I chase it.   410
'Tis much to borrow, and I will not owe it:
My love to love is love but to disgrace it,
    For I have heard, it is a life in death,
    That laughs and weeps, and all but with a breath.

'Who wears a garment shapeless and unfinish'd?   415
Who plucks the bud before one leaf put forth?
If springing things be any jot diminish'd,
They wither in their prime, prove nothing worth;
    The colt that's back'd and burden'd being young,
    Loseth his pride, and never waxeth strong.   420

'You hurt my hand with wringing, let us part,
And leave this idle theme, this bootless chat;
Remove your siege from my unyielding heart,
To love's alarms it will not ope the gate.
    Dismiss your vows, your feigned tears, your flatt'ry,   425
    For where a heart is hard they make no batt'ry.'

'What, canst thou talk?' quoth she, 'hast thou a
    tongue?
O would thou hadst not, or I had no hearing!
Thy mermaid's voice hath done me double wrong;
I had my load before, now press'd with bearing: 430
    Melodious discord, heavenly tune harsh-sounding,
    Ears' deep sweet music, and heart's deep sore
    wounding!

'Had I no eyes but ears, my ears would love
That inward beauty and invisible;
Or were I deaf, thy outward parts would move   435
Each part in me that were but sensible:
    Though neither eyes nor ears, to hear nor see,
    Yet should I be in love by touching thee.

'Say that the sense of feeling were bereft me,
And that I could not see, nor hear, nor touch,   440
And nothing but the very smell were left me,
Yet would my love to thee be still as much;
    For from the stillitory of thy face excelling
    Comes breath perfum'd, that breedeth love by
    smelling.

'But oh what banquet wert thou to the taste,   445
Being nurse and feeder of the other four!
Would they not wish the feast might ever last,
And bid suspicion double-lock the door,
    Lest jealousy, that sour unwelcome guest,
    Should by his stealing in disturb the feast?'   450

Once more the ruby-colour'd portal open'd,
Which to his speech did honey passage yield,
Like a red morn that ever yet betoken'd
Wrack to the seaman, tempest to the field,
 Sorrow to shepherds, woe unto the birds,
 Gusts and foul flaws to herdmen and to herds.

This ill presage advisedly she marketh:
Even as the wind is hush'd before it raineth,
Or as the wolf doth grin before he barketh,
Or as the berry breaks before it staineth,
 Or like the deadly bullet of a gun,
 His meaning struck her ere his words begun.

And at his look she flatly falleth down,
For looks kill love, and love by looks reviveth:
A smile recures the wounding of a frown.
But blessed bankrout, that by love so thriveth!
 Thy silly boy, believing she is dead,
 Claps her pale cheek, till clapping makes it red.

And all amaz'd brake off his late intent,
For sharply did he think to reprehend her,
Which cunning love did wittily prevent:
Fair fall the wit that can so well defend her!
 For on the grass she lies as she were slain,
 Till his breath breatheth life in her again.

He wrings her nose, he strikes her on the cheeks,
He bends her fingers, holds her pulses hard,
He chafes her lips; a thousand ways he seeks
To mend the hurt that his unkindness marr'd.
 He kisses her, and she by her good will
 Will never rise, so he will kiss her still.

The night of sorrow now is turn'd to day:
Her two blue windows faintly she up-heaveth,
Like the fair sun when in his fresh array
He cheers the morn, and all the earth relieveth;
 And as the bright sun glorifies the sky,
 So is her face illumin'd with her eye.

Whose beams upon his hairless face are fix'd,
As if from thence they borrow'd all their shine.
Were never four such lamps together mix'd,
Had not his clouded with his brow's repine;
 But hers, which through the crystal tears gave
  light,
 Shone like the moon in water seen by night.

'O where am I?' quoth she, 'in earth or heaven?
Or in the ocean drench'd, or in the fire?
What hour is this, or morn, or weary even?
Do I delight to die, or life desire?
 But now I liv'd, and life was death's annoy;
 But now I died, and death was lively joy.

'O thou didst kill me, kill me once again!   500
Thy eyes' shrewd tutor, that hard heart of thine,
Hath taught them scornful tricks, and such disdain,
That they have murder'd this poor heart of mine;
 And these mine eyes, true leaders to their queen,
 But for thy piteous lips no more had seen.

'Long may they kiss each other for this cure!   505
Oh never let their crimson liveries wear,
And as they last, their verdour still endure,
To drive infection from the dangerous year:
 That the star-gazers, having writ on death,
 May say, the plague is banish'd by thy breath.   510

'Pure lips, sweet seals in my soft lips imprinted,
What bargains may I make, still to be sealing?
To sell myself I can be well contented,
So thou wilt buy, and pay, and use good dealing:
 Which purchase if thou make, for fear of slips,   515
 Set thy seal manual on my wax-red lips.

'A thousand kisses buys my heart from me,
And pay them at thy leisure, one by one,
What is ten hundred touches unto thee?
Are they not quickly told and quickly gone?   520
 Say for non-payment that the debt should double,
 Is twenty hundred kisses such a trouble?'

'Fair queen,' quoth he, 'if any love owe me,
Measure my strangeness with my unripe years.
Before I know myself, seek not to know me: 525
No fisher but the ungrown fry forbears;
 The mellow plum doth fall, the green sticks fast,
 Or being early pluck'd, is sour to taste.

'Look the world's comforter with weary gait
His day's hot task hath ended in the west;   530
The owl, night's herald, shrieks, 'tis very late;
The sheep are gone to fold, birds to their nest,
 And coal-black clouds that shadow heaven's light
 Do summon us to part, and bid good night.

'Now let me say good night, and so say you;   535
If you will say so, you shall have a kiss.'
'Good night,' quoth she, and ere he says adieu,
The honey fee of parting tender'd is:
 Her arms do lend his neck a sweet embrace;
 Incorporate then they seem, face grows to face.   540

Till breathless he disjoin'd, and backward drew
The heavenly moisture, that sweet coral mouth,
Whose precious taste her thirsty lips well knew,
Whereon they surfeit, yet complain on drouth.
 He with her plenty press'd, she faint with dearth,   545
 Their lips together glued, fall to the earth.

Now quick desire hath caught the yielding prey,
And glutton-like she feeds, yet never filleth.
Her lips are conquerors, his lips obey,
550 Paying what ransom the insulter willeth;
    Whose vulture thought doth pitch the price so high
    That she will draw his lips' rich treasure dry.

And having felt the sweetness of the spoil,
With blindfold fury she begins to forage;
555 Her face doth reek and smoke, her blood doth boil,
And careless lust stirs up a desperate courage,
    Planting oblivion, beating reason back,
    Forgetting shame's pure blush and honour's wrack.

Hot, faint and weary with her hard embracing,
Like a wild bird being tam'd with too much
560   handling,
Or as the fleet-foot roe that's tir'd with chasing,
Or like the froward infant still'd with dandling:
    He now obeys, and now no more resisteth,
    While she takes all she can, not all she listeth.

565 What wax so frozen but dissolves with temp'ring,
And yields at last to very light impression?
Things out of hope are compass'd oft with vent'ring,
Chiefly in love, whose leave exceeds commission:
    Affection faints not like a pale-fac'd coward,
    But then woos best when most his choice is
570   froward.

When he did frown, O had she then gave over,
Such nectar from his lips she had not suck'd.
Foul words and frowns must not repel a lover;
What though the rose have prickles, yet 'tis pluck'd.
575   Were beauty under twenty locks kept fast,
    Yet love breaks through, and picks them all at last.

For pity now she can no more detain him;
The poor fool prays her that he may depart.
She is resolv'd no longer to restrain him,
580 Bids him farewell, and look well to her heart,
    The which by Cupid's bow she doth protest
    He carries thence encaged in his breast.

'Sweet boy,' she says, 'this night I'll waste in
        sorrow,
For my sick heart commands mine eyes to watch.
585 Tell me, love's master, shall we meet tomorrow?
Say, shall we, shall we? wilt thou make the match?'
    He tells her no, tomorrow he intends
    To hunt the boar with certain of his friends.

'The boar,' quoth she: whereat a sudden pale,
Like lawn being spread upon the blushing rose, 590
Usurps her cheek; she trembles at his tale,
And on his neck her yoking arms she throws.
    She sinketh down, still hanging by his neck;
    He on her belly falls, she on her back.

Now is she in the very lists of love, 595
Her champion mounted for the hot encounter.
All is imaginary she doth prove;
He will not manage her, although he mount her:
    That worse than Tantalus' is her annoy,
    To clip Elizium and to lack her joy. 600

Even so poor birds deceiv'd with painted grapes
Do surfeit by the eye and pine the maw:
Even so she languisheth in her mishaps,
As those poor birds that helpless berries saw.
    The warm effects which she in him finds missing 605
    She seeks to kindle with continual kissing.

But all in vain; good queen, it will not be.
She hath assay'd as much as may be prov'd:
Her pleading hath deserv'd a greater fee;
She's love, she loves, and yet she is not lov'd. 610
    'Fie, fie,' he says, 'you crush me; let me go,
    You have no reason to withhold me so.'

'Thou hadst been gone,' quoth she, 'sweet boy, ere
        this,
But that thou told'st me, thou wouldst hunt the boar.
Oh be advis'd, thou know'st not what it is, 615
With javelin's point a churlish swine to gore,
    Whose tushes never sheath'd he whetteth still,
    Like to a mortal butcher, bent to kill.

'On his bow-back he hath a battle set
Of bristly pikes that ever threat his foes; 620
His eyes like glow-worms shine when he doth fret,
His snout digs sepulchres where'er he goes;
    Being mov'd, he strikes whate'er is in his way,
    And whom he strikes his crooked tushes slay.

'His brawny sides with hairy bristles armed 625
Are better proof than thy spear's point can enter;
His short thick neck cannot be easily harmed;
Being ireful, on the lion he will venture.
    The thorny brambles and embracing bushes,
    As fearful of him, part; through whom he rushes. 630

'Alas, he naught esteems that face of thine,
To which love's eyes pays tributary gazes;
Nor thy soft hands, sweet lips and crystal eyne,
Whose full perfection all the world amazes:
    But having thee at vantage – wondrous dread! – 635
    Would root these beauties as he roots the mead.

'Oh let him keep his loathsome cabin still!
Beauty hath naught to do with such foul fiends.
Come not within his danger by thy will:
640 They that thrive well, take counsel of their friends.
　　When thou didst name the boar, not to dissemble,
　　I fear'd thy fortune, and my joints did tremble.

'Didst thou not mark my face, was it not white?
Saw'st thou not signs of fear lurk in mine eye?
645 Grew I not faint, and fell I not downright?
Within my bosom, whereon thou dost lie,
　　My boding heart pants, beats, and takes no rest,
　　But like an earthquake, shakes thee on my breast.

'For where love reigns, disturbing jealousy
650 Doth call himself affection's sentinel;
Gives false alarms, suggesteth mutiny,
And in a peaceful hour doth cry "Kill, kill!"
　　Distemp'ring gentle love in his desire,
　　As air and water do abate the fire.

655 'This sour informer, this bate-breeding spy,
This canker that eats up love's tender spring,
This carry-tale, dissentious jealousy,
That sometime true news, sometime false doth bring,
　　Knocks at my heart, and whispers in mine ear,
660 　　That if I love thee, I thy death should fear.

'And more than so, presenteth to mine eye
The picture of an angry chafing boar,
Under whose sharp fangs on his back doth lie
An image like thyself, all stain'd with gore;
665 　　Whose blood upon the fresh flowers being shed,
　　Doth make them droop with grief and hang the
　　　　head.

'What should I do, seeing thee so indeed,
That tremble at th'imagination?
The thought of it doth make my faint heart bleed,
670 And fear doth teach it divination:
　　I prophesy thy death, my living sorrow,
　　If thou encounter with the boar tomorrow.

'But if thou needs wilt hunt, be rul'd by me:
Uncouple at the timorous flying hare,
675 Or at the fox which lives by subtlety,
Or at the roe which no encounter dare;
　　Pursue these fearful creatures o'er the downs,
　　And on thy well-breath'd horse keep with thy
　　　　hounds.

'And when thou hast on foot the purblind hare,
680 Mark the poor wretch, to overshoot his troubles,
How he outruns the wind, and with what care
He cranks and crosses with a thousand doubles;
　　The many musits through the which he goes
　　Are like a labyrinth to amaze his foes.

'Sometime he runs among a flock of sheep,　　685
To make the cunning hounds mistake their smell;
And sometime where earth-delving conies keep,
To stop the loud pursuers in their yell;
　　And sometime sorteth with a heard of deer:
　　Danger deviseth shifts, wit waits on fear.　　690

'For there his smell with others being mingled,
The hot scent-snuffing hounds are driven to doubt,
Ceasing their clamorous cry, till they have singled
With much ado the cold fault cleanly out;
　　Then they do spend their mouths: echo replies,　　695
　　As if another chase were in the skies.

'By this, poor Wat, far off upon a hill,
Stands on his hinder-legs with list'ning ear,
To hearken if his foes pursue him still.
Anon their loud alarums he doth hear;　　700
　　And now his grief may be compared well
　　To one sore sick, that hears the passing bell.

'Then shalt thou see the dew-bedabbled wretch
Turn, and return, indenting with the way.
Each envious briar his weary legs do scratch,　　705
Each shadow makes him stop, each murmur stay:
　　For misery is trodden on by many,
　　And being low, never reliev'd by any.

'Lie quietly, and hear a little more;
Nay, do not struggle, for thou shalt not rise.　　710
To make thee hate the hunting of the boar,
Unlike myself thou hear'st me moralise,
　　Applying this to that, and so to so,
　　For love can comment upon every woe.

'Where did I leave?' 'No matter where,' quoth he;　　715
'Leave me, and then the story aptly ends:
The night is spent.' 'Why, what of that?' quoth she.
'I am,' quoth he, 'expected of my friends,
　　And now 'tis dark, and going I shall fall.'
　　'In night,' quoth she, 'desire sees best of all.　　720

'But if thou fall, oh then imagine this:
The earth in love with thee thy footing trips,
And all is but to rob thee of a kiss.
Rich preys make true men thieves; so do thy lips
　　Make modest Dian cloudy and forlorn,　　725
　　Lest she should steal a kiss and die forsworn.

'Now of this dark night I perceive the reason:
Cynthia for shame obscures her silver shine,
Till forging nature be condemn'd of treason,
For stealing moulds from heaven, that were divine;　　730
　　Wherein she fram'd thee, in high heaven's despite,
　　To shame the sun by day and her by night.

'And therefore hath she brib'd the destinies
To cross the curious workmanship of nature,
735 To mingle beauty with infirmities
And pure perfection with impure defeature,
    Making it subject to the tyranny
    Of mad mischances and much misery:

'As burning fevers, agues pale and faint,
740 Life-poisoning pestilence and frenzies wood,
The marrow-eating sickness whose attaint
Disorder breeds by heating of the blood;
    Surfeits, imposthumes, grief and damn'd despair,
    Swear nature's death, for framing thee so fair.

745 'And not the least of all these maladies
But in one minute's fight brings beauty under;
Both favour, savour, hue and qualities,
Whereat th'impartial gazer late did wonder,
    Are on the sudden wasted, thaw'd and done,
750   As mountain snow melts with the midday sun.

'Therefore despite of fruitless chastity,
Love-lacking vestals and self-loving nuns,
That on the earth would breed a scarcity
And barren dearth of daughters and of sons,
755   Be prodigal; the lamp that burns by night
    Dries up his oil to lend the world his light.

'What is thy body but a swallowing grave,
Seeming to bury that posterity,
Which by the rights of time thou needs must have,
760 If thou destroy them not in dark obscurity?
    If so, the world will hold thee in disdain,
    Sith in thy pride so fair a hope is slain.

'So in thyself thyself art made away;
A mischief worse than civil home-bred strife,
765 Or theirs whose desperate hands themselves do slay,
Or butcher sire that reaves his son of life.
    Foul cank'ring rust the hidden treasure frets,
    But gold that's put to use more gold begets.'

'Nay then,' quoth Adon, 'you will fall again
770 Into your idle over-handled theme.
The kiss I gave you is bestow'd in vain,
And all in vain you strive against the stream;
    For by this black-fac'd night, desire's foul nurse,
    Your treatise makes me like you worse and worse.

775 'If love have lent you twenty thousand tongues,
And every tongue more moving than your own,
Bewitching like the wanton mermaid's songs,
Yet from my heart the tempting tune is blown;
    For know, my heart stands armed in mine ear,
780   And will not let a false sound enter there;

'Lest the deceiving harmony should run
Into the quiet closure of my breast,
And then my little heart were quite undone,
In his bedchamber to be barr'd of rest.
    No, lady, no; my heart longs not to groan, 785
    But soundly sleeps, while now it sleeps alone.

'What have you urg'd that I cannot reprove?
The path is smooth that leadeth on to danger.
I hate not love, but your device in love
That lends embracements unto every stranger. 790
    You do it for increase: O strange excuse,
    When reason is the bawd to lust's abuse!

'Call it not love, for love to heaven is fled,
Since sweating lust on earth usurp'd his name;
Under whose simple semblance he hath fed 795
Upon fresh beauty, blotting it with blame;
    Which the hot tyrant stains and soon bereaves,
    As caterpillars do the tender leaves.

'Love comforteth like sunshine after rain,
But lust's effect is tempest after sun; 800
Love's gentle spring doth always fresh remain,
Lust's winter comes ere summer half be done;
    Love surfeits not, lust like a glutton dies;
    Love is all truth, lust full of forged lies.

'More I could tell, but more I dare not say: 805
The text is old, the orator too green.
Therefore in sadness, now I will away;
My face is full of shame, my heart of teen,
    Mine ears that to your wanton talk attended
    Do burn themselves, for having so offended.' 810

With this he breaketh from the sweet embrace
Of those fair arms which bound him to her breast,
And homeward through the dark laund runs apace;
Leaves love upon her back deeply distress'd.
    Look how a bright star shooteth from the sky, 815
    So glides he in the night from Venus' eye;

Which after him she darts, as one on shore
Gazing upon a late embarked friend,
Till the wild waves will have him seen no more,
Whose ridges with the meeting clouds contend: 820
    So did the merciless and pitchy night
    Fold in the object that did feed her sight.

Whereat amaz'd, as one that unaware
Hath dropp'd a precious jewel in the flood,
Or 'stonish'd as night-wand'rers often are, 825
Their light blown out in some mistrustful wood:
    Even so confounded in the dark she lay,
    Having lost the fair discovery of her way.

And now she beats her heart, whereat it groans,
830 That all the neighbour caves, as seeming troubled,
Make verbal repetition of her moans;
Passion on passion deeply is redoubled:
    'Ay me,' she cries, and twenty times, 'Woe, woe,'
    And twenty echoes twenty times cry so.

835 She marking them, begins a wailing note,
And sings extemporally a woeful ditty:
How love makes young men thrall, and old men dote,
How love is wise in folly, foolish witty.
    Her heavy anthem still concludes in woe,
840   And still the quire of echoes answer so.

Her song was tedious, and outwore the night,
For lovers' hours are long, though seeming short.
If pleas'd themselves, others they think delight
In such like circumstance, with such like sport.
845   Their copious stories oftentimes begun,
    End without audience, and are never done.

For who hath she to spend the night withal,
But idle sounds resembling parasites,
Like shrill-tongu'd tapsters answering every call,
850 Soothing the humour of fantastic wits?
    She says ''Tis so,' they answer all ''Tis so,'
    And would say after her, if she said 'No.'

Lo here the gentle lark, weary of rest,
From his moist cabinet mounts up on high,
855 And wakes the morning, from whose silver breast
The sun ariseth in his majesty;
    Who doth the world so gloriously behold
    That cedar tops and hills seem burnish'd gold.

Venus salutes him with this fair good-morrow,
860 'Oh thou clear god, and patron of all light,
From whom each lamp and shining star doth borrow
The beauteous influence that makes him bright:
    There lives a son that suck'd an earthly mother,
    May lend thee light, as thou dost lend to other.'

865 This said, she hasteth to a myrtle grove,
Musing the morning is so much o'erworn,
And yet she hears no tidings of her love;
She hearkens for his hounds and for his horn.
    Anon she hears them chant it lustily,
870   And all in haste she coasteth to the cry.

And as she runs, the bushes in the way,
Some catch her by the neck, some kiss her face,
Some twine about her thigh to make her stay;
She wildly breaketh from their strict embrace,
875   Like a milch doe, whose swelling dugs do ache,
    Hasting to feed her fawn, hid in some brake.

By this she hears the hounds are at a bay,
Whereat she starts like one that spies an adder
Wreath'd up in fatal folds just in his way,
The fear whereof doth make him shake and shudder: 880
    Even so the timorous yelping of the hounds
    Appals her senses and her spirit confounds.

For now she knows it is no gentle chase,
But the blunt boar, rough bear, or lion proud,
Because the cry remaineth in one place,   885
Where fearfully the dogs exclaim aloud;
    Finding their enemy to be so curst,
    They all strain court'sy who shall cope him first.

This dismal cry rings sadly in her ear,
Through which it enters to surprise her heart;   890
Who overcome by doubt and bloodless fear,
With cold pale weakness numbs each feeling part:
    Like soldiers when their captain once doth yield,
    They basely fly, and dare not stay the field.

Thus stands she in a trembling ecstasy,   895
Till cheering up her senses all dismay'd,
She tells them 'tis a causeless fantasy,
And childish error, that they are afraid;
    Bids them leave quaking, bids them fear no more,
    And with that word, she spied the hunted boar: 900

Whose frothy mouth bepainted all with red,
Like milk and blood being mingled both together,
A second fear through all her sinews spread,
Which madly hurries her she knows not whither.
    This way she runs, and now she will no further,   905
    And back retires, to rate the boar for murther.

A thousand spleens bear her a thousand ways,
She treads the path that she untreads again;
Her more than haste is mated with delays
Like the proceedings of a drunken brain,   910
    Full of respects, yet naught at all respecting,
    In hand with all things, naught at all effecting.

Here kennell'd in a brake she finds a hound,
And asks the weary caitiff for his master;
And there another licking of his wound,   915
'Gainst venom'd sores the only sovereign plaster.
    And here she meets another sadly scowling,
    To whom she speaks, and he replies with howling.

When he hath ceas'd his ill-resounding noise,
Another flap-mouth'd mourner, black and grim,   920
Against the welkin volleys out his voice;
Another and another answer him,
    Clapping their proud tails to the ground below,
    Shaking their scratch'd ears, bleeding as they go.

Look how the world's poor people are amazed
At apparitions, signs and prodigies,
Whereon with fearful eyes they long have gazed,
Infusing them with dreadful prophecies:
    So she at these sad signs draws up her breath,
930   And sighing it again, exclaims on death.

'Hard-favour'd tyrant, ugly, meagre, lean,
Hateful divorce of love,' thus chides she death:
'Grim-grinning ghost, earth's worm, what dost thou
    mean,
To stifle beauty and to steal his breath?
935   Who when he liv'd, his breath and beauty set
       Gloss on the rose, smell to the violet.

'If he be dead, – O no, it cannot be,
Seeing his beauty, thou shouldst strike at it, –
O yes, it may, thou hast no eyes to see,
940 But hatefully at randon dost thou hit:
       Thy mark is feeble age, but thy false dart
       Mistakes that aim, and cleaves an infant's heart.

'Hadst thou but bid beware, then he had spoke,
And hearing him, thy power had lost his power.
945 The destinies will curse thee for this stroke:
They bid thee crop a weed, thou pluck'st a flower.
       Love's golden arrow at him should have fled,
       And not death's ebon dart to strike him dead.

'Dost thou drink tears, that thou provok'st such
    weeping?
950 What may a heavy groan advantage thee?
Why hast thou cast into eternal sleeping
Those eyes that taught all other eyes to see?
       Now nature cares not for thy mortal vigour,
       Since her best work is ruin'd with thy rigour.'

955 Here overcome, as one full of despair,
She vail'd her eyelids, who like sluices stopp'd
The crystal tide that from her two cheeks fair
In the sweet channel of her bosom dropp'd;
       But through the flood-gates breaks the silver rain,
960   And with his strong course opens them again.

O how her eyes and tears did lend and borrow!
Her eye seen in the tears, tears in her eye:
Both crystals where they view'd each other's sorrow,
Sorrow that friendly sighs sought still to dry;
965   But like a stormy day, now wind, now rain,
       Sighs dry her cheeks, tears make them wet again.

Variable passions throng her constant woe,
As striving who should best become her grief;
All entertain'd, each passion labours so,
970 That every present sorrow seemeth chief,
       But none is best: then join they all together,
       Like many clouds consulting for foul weather.

By this, far off she hears some huntsman holla:
A nurse's song ne'er pleas'd her babe so well.
The dire imagination she did follow   975
This sound of hope doth labour to expel;
    For now reviving joy bids her rejoice,
       And flatters her it is Adonis' voice.

Whereat her tears began to turn their tide,
Being prison'd in her eye like pearls in glass;   980
Yet sometimes falls an orient drop beside,
Which her cheek melts, as scorning it should pass
    To wash the foul face of the sluttish ground,
    Who is but drunken when she seemeth drown'd.

O hard-believing love, how strange it seems   985
Not to believe, and yet too credulous!
Thy weal and woe are both of them extremes;
Despair and hope makes thee ridiculous:
    The one doth flatter thee in thoughts unlikely,
    In likely thoughts the other kills thee quickly.   990

Now she unweaves the web that she hath wrought:
Adonis lives, and death is not to blame;
It was not she that call'd him all to naught;
Now she adds honours to his hateful name:
    She clepes him king of graves, and grave for kings,   995
    Imperious supreme of all mortal things.

'No, no,' quoth she, 'sweet death, I did but jest;
Yet pardon me, I felt a kind of fear
Whenas I met the boar, that bloody beast,
Which knows no pity, but is still severe: 1000
    Then, gentle shadow, – truth I must confess, –
    I rail'd on thee, fearing my love's decease.

' 'Tis not my fault, the boar provok'd my tongue:
Be wreak'd on him, invisible commander.
'Tis he, foul creature, that hath done thee wrong: 1005
I did but act, he's author of thy slander.
    Grief hath two tongues, and never woman yet
    Could rule them both, without ten women's wit.'

Thus hoping that Adonis is alive,
Her rash suspects she doth extenuate;   1010
And that his beauty may the better thrive,
With death she humbly doth insinuate;
    Tells him of trophies, statues, tombs, and stories
    His victories, his triumphs and his glories.

'O love,' quoth she, 'how much a fool was I,   1015
To be of such a weak and silly mind,
To wail his death who lives, and must not die
'Till mutual overthrow of mortal kind!
    For he being dead, with him is beauty slain,
    And beauty dead, black Chaos comes again.   1020

'Fie, fie, fond love, thou art as full of fear
As one with treasure laden, hemm'd with thieves!
Trifles unwitnessed with eye or ear
Thy coward heart with false bethinking grieves.'
    Even at this word she hears a merry horn,
    Whereat she leaps that was but late forlorn. 1025

As falcons to the lure, away she flies;
The grass stoops not, she treads on it so light,
And in her haste unfortunately spies
The foul boar's conquest on her fair delight: 1030
    Which seen, her eyes as murder'd with the view,
    Like stars asham'd of day, themselves withdrew.

Or as the snail, whose tender horns being hit,
Shrinks backward in his shelly cave with pain,
And there all smother'd up in shade doth sit, 1035
Long after fearing to creep forth again:
    So at his bloody view her eyes are fled
    Into the deep dark cabins of her head.

Where they resign their office and their light
To the disposing of her troubled brain, 1040
Who bids them still consort with ugly night
And never wound the heart with looks again;
    Who like a king perplexed in his throne
    By their suggestion, gives a deadly groan.

Whereat each tributary subject quakes, 1045
As when the wind imprison'd in the ground,
Struggling for passage, earth's foundation shakes;
Which with cold terror doth men's minds confound.
    This mutiny each part doth so surprise
    That from their dark beds once more leap her 1050
        eyes:

And being open'd threw unwilling light
Upon the wide wound that the boar had trench'd
In his soft flank, whose wonted lily-white
With purple tears that his wound wept, was
    drench'd. 1055
    No flower was nigh, no grass, herb, leaf or weed,
    But stole his blood and seem'd with him to bleed.

This solemn sympathy poor Venus noteth;
Over one shoulder doth she hang her head.
Dumbly she passions, franticly she doteth:
She thinks he could not die, he is not dead. 1060
    Her voice is stopp'd, her joints forget to bow,
    Her eyes are mad, that they have wept till now.

Upon his hurt she looks so steadfastly
That her sight dazzling makes the wound seem three;
And then she reprehends her mangling eye, 1065
That makes more gashes, where no breach should be.
    His face seems twain, each several limb is doubled,
    For oft the eye mistakes, the brain being troubled.

'My tongue cannot express my grief for one,
And yet,' quoth she, 'behold two Adons dead! 1070
My sighs are blown away, my salt tears gone;
Mine eyes are turn'd to fire, my heart to lead.
    Heavy heart's lead melt at mine eyes' red fire!
    So I shall die by drops of hot desire.

'Alas, poor world, what treasure hast thou lost! 1075
What face remains alive that's worth the viewing?
What tongue is music now? what canst thou boast
Of things long since, or any thing ensuing?
    The flowers are sweet, their colours fresh and
       trim,
    But true sweet beauty liv'd and died with him. 1080

'Bonnet nor veil henceforth no creature wear:
Nor sun nor wind will ever strive to kiss you.
Having no fair to lose, you need not fear:
The sun doth scorn you and the wind doth hiss you.
    But when Adonis liv'd, sun and sharp air 1085
    Lurk'd like two thieves to rob him of his fair.

'And therefore would he put his bonnet on,
Under whose brim the gaudy sun would peep:
The wind would blow it off, and being gone,
Play with his locks; then would Adonis weep, 1090
    And straight, in pity of his tender years,
    They both would strive who first should dry his
       tears.

'To see his face the lion walk'd along,
Behind some hedge, because he would not fear him.
To recreate himself, when he hath sung, 1095
The tiger would be tame and gently hear him.
    If he had spoke, the wolf would leave his prey,
    And never fright the silly lamb that day.

'When he beheld his shadow in the brook,
The fishes spread on it their golden gills; 1100
When he was by, the birds such pleasure took
That some would sing, some other in their bills
    Would bring him mulberries and ripe red cherries:
    He fed them with his sight, they him with berries.

But this foul, grim, and urchin-snouted boar, 1105
Whose downward eye still looketh for a grave,
Ne'er saw the beauteous livery that he wore;
Witness the entertainment that he gave.
    If he did see his face, why then I know
    He thought to kiss him, and hath kill'd him so. 1110

'Tis true, 'tis true, thus was Adonis slain:
He ran upon the boar with his sharp spear,
Who did not whet his teeth at him again,
But by a kiss thought to persuade him there;
    And nuzzling in his flank, the loving swine 1115
    Sheath'd unaware the tusk in his soft groin.

'Had I been tooth'd like him, I must confess,
With kissing him I should have kill'd him first.
But he is dead, and never did he bless
1120 My youth with his; the more am I accurst.'
    With this she falleth in the place she stood,
    And stains her face with his congealed blood.

She looks upon his lips, and they are pale;
She takes him by the hand, and that is cold.
1125 She whispers in his ears a heavy tale,
As if they heard the woeful words she told.
    She lifts the coffer-lids that close his eyes,
    Where lo, two lamps burnt out in darkness lies.

Two glasses where herself herself beheld
1130 A thousand times, and now no more reflect;
Their virtue lost, wherein they late excell'd,
And every beauty robb'd of his effect.
    'Wonder of time,' quoth she, 'this is my spite,
    That thou being dead, the day should yet be light.

1135 'Since thou art dead, lo here I prophesy,
Sorrow on love hereafter shall attend:
It shall be waited on with jealousy,
Find sweet beginning, but unsavoury end;
    Ne'er settled equally, but high or low,
1140   That all love's pleasure shall not match his woe.

'It shall be fickle, false and full of fraud;
Bud, and be blasted, in a breathing while;
The bottom poison, and the top o'erstraw'd
With sweets that shall the truest sight beguile;
1145   The strongest body shall it make most weak,
    Strike the wise dumb, and teach the fool to speak.

'It shall be sparing, and too full of riot,
Teaching decrepit age to tread the measures;
The staring ruffian shall it keep in quiet,
1150 Pluck down the rich, enrich the poor with treasures;
    It shall be raging mad, and silly mild,
    Make the young old, the old become a child.

'It shall suspect where is no cause of fear,
It shall not fear where it should most mistrust;
1155 It shall be merciful, and too severe,
And most deceiving when it seems most just;
    Perverse it shall be, where it shows most toward;
    Put fear to valour, courage to the coward.

'It shall be cause of war and dire events,
And set dissension 'twixt the son and sire;   1160
Subject and servile to all discontents,
As dry combustious matter is to fire.
    Sith in his prime death doth my love destroy,
    They that love best, their loves shall not enjoy.'

By this the boy that by her side lay kill'd   1165
Was melted like a vapour from her sight,
And in his blood that on the ground lay spill'd,
A purple flower sprung up, checker'd with white,
    Resembling well his pale cheeks and the blood
    Which in round drops upon their whiteness stood.   1170

She bows her head, the new-sprung flower to smell,
Comparing it to her Adonis' breath,
And says within her bosom it shall dwell,
Since he himself is reft from her by death.
    She crops the stalk, and in the breach appears   1175
    Green-dropping sap, which she compares to tears.

'Poor flower,' quoth she, 'this was thy father's
    guise, –
Sweet issue of a more sweet-smelling sire, –
For every little grief to wet his eyes;
To grow unto himself was his desire,   1180
    And so 'tis thine; but know, it is as good
    To wither in my breast as in his blood.

'Here was thy father's bed, here in my breast;
Thou art the next of blood, and 'tis thy right.
Lo in this hollow cradle take thy rest;   1185
My throbbing heart shall rock thee day and night:
    There shall not be one minute in an hour
    Wherein I will not kiss my sweet love's flower.'

Thus weary of the world, away she hies,
And yokes her silver doves, by whose swift aid   1190
Their mistress mounted through the empty skies,
In her light chariot quickly is convey'd,
    Holding their course to Paphos, where their queen
    Means to immure herself and not be seen.

Lucrece

To the Right Honourable
Henry Wriothesley, Earl of Southampton,
and Baron of Titchfield.

The love I dedicate to your Lordship is without end;
whereof this pamphlet without beginning is but a
superfluous moiety. The warrant I have of your Honourable
disposition, not the worth of my untutored lines, makes it
assured of acceptance. What I have done is yours, what I
have to do is yours, being part in all I have devoted yours.
Were my worth greater, my duty would show greater;
meantime, as it is, it is bound to your Lordship, to whom I
wish long life still lengthened with all happiness.

Your Lordship's in all duty,
William Shakespeare.

THE ARGUMENT

Lucius Tarquinius (for his excessive pride surnamed
Superbus), after he had caused his own father-in-law
Servius Tullius to be cruelly murdered, and, contrary to
the Roman laws and customs, not requiring or staying for
the people's suffrages, had possessed himself of the
kingdom, went, accompanied with his sons and other
noblemen of Rome, to besiege Ardea. During which siege,
the principal men of the army meeting one evening at the
tent of Sextus Tarquinius, the King's son, in their
discourses after supper everyone commended the virtues of
his own wife; among whom Collatinus extolled the
incomparable chastity of his wife Lucretia. In that pleasant
humour they all posted to Rome, and, intending by their
secret and sudden arrival to make trial of that which
everyone had before avouched, only Collatinus finds his
wife, though it were late in the night, spinning amongst her
maids; the other ladies were all found dancing and
revelling, or in several disports. Whereupon the noblemen
yielded Collatinus the victory, and his wife the fame. At
that time Sextus Tarquinius, being inflamed with Lucrece'
beauty, yet smothering his passions for the present,
departed with the rest back to the camp; from whence he
shortly after privily withdrew himself, and was, according
to his estate, royally entertained and lodged by Lucrece at
Collatium. The same night he treacherously stealeth into
her chamber, violently ravished her, and early in the
morning speedeth away. Lucrece, in this lamentable plight,
hastily despatcheth messengers, one to Rome for her father,
another to the camp for Collatine. They came, the one
accompanied with Junius Brutus, the other with Publius
Valerius; and finding Lucrece attired in mourning habit,
demanded the cause of her sorrow. She, first taking an oath
of them for her revenge, revealed the actor, and whole
manner of his dealing, and withal suddenly stabbed herself.
Which done, with one consent they all vowed to root out
the whole hated family of the Tarquins and, bearing the
dead body to Rome, Brutus acquainted the people with the
doer and manner of the vile deed, with a bitter invective
against the tyranny of the King. Wherewith the people
were so moved, that with one consent and a general
acclamation the Tarquins were all exiled, and the state
government changed from kings to consuls.

From the besieged Ardea all in post,
Borne by the trustless wings of false desire,
Lust-breathed Tarquin leaves the Roman host
And to Collatium bears the lightless fire,
Which in pale embers hid, lurks to aspire,   5
    And girdle with embracing flames the waist
    Of Collatine's fair love, Lucrece the chaste.

Haply that name of 'chaste' unhapp'ly set
This bateless edge on his keen appetite,
When Collatine unwisely did not let   10
To praise the clear unmatched red and white
Which triumph'd in that sky of his delight;
    Where mortal stars as bright as heaven's beauties,
    With pure aspects did him peculiar duties.

For he the night before, in Tarquin's tent   15
Unlock'd the treasure of his happy state:
What priceless wealth the heavens had him lent,
In the possession of his beauteous mate;
Reck'ning his fortune at such high proud rate
    That kings might be espoused to more fame,   20
    But king nor peer to such a peerless dame.

O happiness enjoy'd but of a few,
And if possess'd, as soon decay'd and done
As is the morning's silver melting dew
Against the golden splendour of the sun!   25
An expir'd date cancell'd ere well begun!
    Honour and beauty in the owner's arms,
    Are weakly fortress'd from a world of harms.

Beauty itself doth of itself persuade
The eyes of men without an orator;   30
What needeth then apologies be made,
To set forth that which is so singular?
Or why is Collatine the publisher
    Of that rich jewel he should keep unknown
    From thievish ears, because it is his own?   35

Perchance his boast of Lucrece' sov'reignty
Suggested this proud issue of a king;
For by our ears our hearts oft tainted be.
Perchance that envy of so rich a thing,
Braving compare, disdainfully did sting   40
    His high-pitch'd thoughts, that meaner men
        should vaunt
    That golden hap which their superiors want.

But some untimely thought did instigate
His all-too-timeless speed, if none of those;
His honour, his affairs, his friends, his state,   45
Neglected all, with swift intent he goes
To quench the coal which in his liver glows.
    O rash false heat, wrapp'd in repentant cold,
    Thy hasty spring still blasts and ne'er grows old!

50 When at Collatium this false lord arrived,
Well was he welcom'd by the Roman dame,
Within whose face beauty and virtue strived
Which of them both should underprop her fame.
When virtue bragg'd, beauty would blush for shame;
55   When beauty boasted blushes, in despite
         Virtue would stain that o'er with silver white.

But beauty in that white entituled
From Venus' doves, doth challenge that fair field;
Then virtue claims from beauty beauty's red,
60 Which virtue gave the golden age to gild
Their silver cheeks, and call'd it then their shield;
     Teaching them thus to use it in the fight,
         When shame assail'd, the red should fence the
             white.

This heraldry in Lucrece' face was seen,
65 Argu'd by beauty's red and virtue's white;
Of either's colour was the other queen,
Proving from world's minority their right.
Yet their ambition makes them still to fight;
     The sov'reignty of either being so great,
70   That oft they interchange each other's seat.

This silent war of lilies and of roses,
Which Tarquin view'd in her fair face's field,
In their pure ranks his traitor eye encloses;
Where, lest between them both it should be kill'd,
75 The coward captive vanquished doth yield
     To those two armies, that would let him go
         Rather than triumph in so false a foe.

Now thinks he that her husband's shallow tongue, –
The niggard prodigal that prais'd her so, –
80 In that high task hath done her beauty wrong,
Which far exceeds his barren skill to show.
Therefore that praise which Collatine doth owe
     Enchanted Tarquin answers with surmise,
         In silent wonder of still-gazing eyes.

85 This earthly saint adored by this devil,
Little suspecteth the false worshipper;
For unstain'd thoughts do seldom dream on evil,
Birds never lim'd no secret bushes fear:
So guiltless she securely gives good cheer
90   And reverend welcome to her princely guest,
         Whose inward ill no outward harm express'd.

For that he colour'd with his high estate,
Hiding base sin in pleats of majesty,
That nothing in him seem'd inordinate,
95 Save sometime too much wonder of his eye,
Which having all, all could not satisfy;
     But poorly rich, so wanteth in his store
         That cloy'd with much, he pineth still for more.

But she that never cop'd with stranger eyes,
Could pick no meaning from their parling looks, 100
Nor read the subtle shining secrecies
Writ in the glassy margents of such books;
She touch'd no unknown baits, nor fear'd no hooks:
     Nor could she moralize his wanton sight,
         More than his eyes were open'd to the light. 105

He stories to her ears her husband's fame,
Won in the fields of fruitful Italy;
And decks with praises Collatine's high name,
Made glorious by his manly chivalry
With bruised arms and wreaths of victory. 110
     Her joy with heav'd-up hand she doth express,
         And wordless so greets heaven for his success.

Far from the purpose of his coming thither,
He makes excuses for his being there;
No cloudy show of stormy blust'ring weather 115
Doth yet in his fair welkin once appear,
Till sable night, mother of dread and fear,
     Upon the world dim darkness doth display,
         And in her vaulty prison stows the day.

For then is Tarquin brought unto his bed, 120
Intending weariness with heavy sprite;
For after supper long he questioned
With modest Lucrece, and wore out the night.
Now leaden slumber with life's strength doth fight,
     And every one to rest themselves betake, 125
         Save thieves and cares and troubled minds that wake.

As one of which doth Tarquin lie revolving
The sundry dangers of his will's obtaining,
Yet ever to obtain his will resolving,
Though weak-built hopes persuade him to
     abstaining. 130
Despair to gain doth traffic oft for gaining,
     And when great treasure is the meed proposed,
         Though death be adjunct, there's no death
             supposed.

Those that much covet are with gain so fond
That what they have not, that which they possess 135
They scatter and unloose it from their bond;
And so by hoping more they have but less,
Or gaining more, the profit of excess
     Is but to surfeit, and such griefs sustain,
         That they prove bankrout in this poor rich gain. 140

The aim of all is but to nurse the life
With honour, wealth and ease, in waning age;
And in this aim there is such thwarting strife
That one for all or all for one we gage:
As life for honour in fell battle's rage, 145
     Honour for wealth; and oft that wealth doth cost
         The death of all, and all together lost.

So that in vent'ring ill we leave to be
The things we are, for that which we expect;
150 And this ambitious foul infirmity,
In having much, torments us with defect
Of that we have: so then we do neglect
    The thing we have, and all for want of wit,
    Make something nothing by augmenting it.

155 Such hazard now must doting Tarquin make,
Pawning his honour to obtain his lust;
And for himself himself he must forsake.
Then where is truth if there be no self-trust?
When shall he think to find a stranger just,
160   When he himself himself confounds, betrays
    To sland'rous tongues and wretched hateful days?

Now stole upon the time the dead of night,
When heavy sleep had clos'd up mortal eyes.
No comfortable star did lend his light,
165 No noise but owls' and wolves' death-boding cries;
Now serves the season that they may surprise
    The silly lambs: pure thoughts are dead and still,
    While lust and murder wakes to stain and kill.

And now this lustful lord leap'd from his bed,
170 Throwing his mantle rudely o'er his arm;
Is madly toss'd between desire and dread:
Th'one sweetly flatters, th' other feareth harm.
But honest fear, bewitch'd with lust's foul charm,
    Doth too too oft betake him to retire,
175   Beaten away by brain-sick rude desire.

His falchion on a flint he softly smiteth,
That from the cold stone sparks of fire do fly;
Whereat a waxen torch forthwith he lighteth,
Which must be lodestar to his lustful eye:
180 And to the flame thus speaks advisedly:
    'As from this cold flint I enforc'd this fire,
    So Lucrece must I force to my desire.'

Here pale with fear he doth premeditate
The dangers of his loathsome enterprise;
185 And in his inward mind he doth debate
What following sorrow may on this arise.
When looking scornfully, he doth despise
    His naked armour of still slaughter'd lust,
    And justly thus controls his thoughts unjust:

190 'Fair torch, burn out thy light, and lend it not
To darken her whose light excelleth thine;
And die, unhallow'd thoughts, before you blot
With your uncleanness that which is divine;
Offer pure incense to so pure a shrine.
195   Let fair humanity abhor the deed
    That spots and stains love's modest snow-white
        weed.

'O shame to knighthood and to shining arms!
O foul dishonour to my household's grave!
O impious act including all foul harms!
A martial man to be soft fancy's slave! 200
True valour still a true respect should have.
    Then my digression is so vile, so base,
    That it will live engraven in my face.

'Yea, though I die the scandal will survive
And be an eye-sore in my golden coat; 205
Some loathsome dash the herald will contrive,
To cipher me how fondly I did dote:
That my posterity sham'd with the note,
    Shall curse my bones, and hold it for no sin
    To wish that I their father had not been. 210

'What win I if I gain the thing I seek?
A dream, a breath, a froth of fleeting joy.
Who buys a minute's mirth to wail a week,
Or sells eternity to get a toy?
For one sweet grape who will the vine destroy? 215
    Or what fond beggar, but to touch the crown,
    Would with the sceptre straight be strucken
        down?

'If Collatinus dream of my intent,
Will he not wake, and in a desp'rate rage
Post hither, this vile purpose to prevent? – 220
This siege that hath engirt his marriage,
This blur to youth, this sorrow to the sage,
    This dying virtue, this surviving shame,
    Whose crime will bear an ever-during blame.

'O what excuse can my invention make 225
When thou shalt charge me with so black a deed?
Will not my tongue be mute, my frail joints shake,
Mine eyes forgo their light, my false heart bleed?
The guilt being great, the fear doth still exceed;
    And extreme fear can neither fight nor fly, 230
    But coward-like with trembling terror die.

'Had Collatinus kill'd my son or sire,
Or lain in ambush to betray my life;
Or were he not my dear friend, this desire
Might have excuse to work upon his wife, 235
As in revenge or quittal of such strife:
    But as he is my kinsman, my dear friend,
    The shame and fault finds no excuse nor end.

'Shameful it is, – ay, if the fact be known.
Hateful it is, – there is no hate in loving. 240
I'll beg her love, – but she is not her own.
The worst is but denial and reproving.
My will is strong past reason's weak removing:
    Who fears a sentence or an old man's saw
    Shall by a painted cloth be kept in awe.' 245

Thus graceless holds he disputation
'Tween frozen conscience and hot burning will,
And with good thoughts makes dispensation,
Urging the worser sense for vantage still;
250   Which in a moment doth confound and kill
    All pure effects, and doth so far proceed
    That what is vile shows like a virtuous deed.

Quoth he, 'She took me kindly by the hand,
And gaz'd for tidings in my eager eyes,
255 Fearing some hard news from the warlike band
Where her beloved Collatinus lies.
O how her fear did make her colour rise!
    First red as roses that on lawn we lay,
    Then white as lawn, the roses took away.

260 'And how her hand in my hand being lock'd,
Forc'd it to tremble with her loyal fear!
Which strook her sad, and then it faster rock'd,
Until her husband's welfare she did hear;
  Whereat she smiled with so sweet a cheer
265   That had Narcissus seen her as she stood,
    Self-love had never drown'd him in the flood.

'Why hunt I then for colour or excuses?
All orators are dumb when beauty pleadeth.
Poor wretches have remorse in poor abuses;
270 Love thrives not in the heart that shadows dreadeth.
Affection is my captain, and he leadeth;
    And when his gaudy banner is display'd,
    The coward fights, and will not be dismay'd.

'Then childish fear avaunt, debating die!
275 Respect and reason wait on wrinkled age!
My heart shall never countermand mine eye:
Sad pause and deep regard beseems the sage;
My part is youth, and beats these from the stage.
    Desire my pilot is, beauty my prize;
280   Then who fears sinking where such treasure lies?'

As corn o'ergrown by weeds, so heedful fear
Is almost chok'd by unresisted lust.
Away he steals with open list'ning ear,
Full of foul hope and full of fond mistrust;
285 Both which, as servitors to the unjust,
    So cross him with their opposite persuasion
    That now he vows a league, and now invasion.

Within his thought her heavenly image sits,
And in the self-same seat sits Collatine.
290 That eye which looks on her confounds his wits;
That eye which him beholds, as more divine,
Unto a view so false will not incline,
    But with a pure appeal seeks to the heart,
    Which once corrupted takes the worser part:

And therein heartens up his servile powers, 295
Who flatter'd by their leader's jocund show,
Stuff up his lust, as minutes fill up hours;
And as their captain, so their pride doth grow,
Paying more slavish tribute than they owe.
    By reprobate desire thus madly led, 300
    The Roman lord marcheth to Lucrece' bed.

The locks between her chamber and his will,
Each one by him enforc'd, retires his ward;
But as they open, they all rate his ill,
Which drives the creeping thief to some regard. 305
The threshold grates the door to have him heard;
    Night-wand'ring weasels shriek to see him there:
    They fright him, yet he still pursues his fear.

As each unwilling portal yields him way,
Through little vents and crannies of the place 310
The wind wars with his torch to make him stay,
And blows the smoke of it into his face,
Extinguishing his conduct in this case;
    But his hot heart, which fond desire doth scorch,
    Puffs forth another wind that fires the torch. 315

And being lighted, by the light he spies
Lucretia's glove, wherein her needle sticks;
He takes it from the rushes where it lies,
And gripping it, the needle his finger pricks,
As who should say, 'This glove to wanton tricks 320
    Is not inur'd; return again in haste;
    Thou seest our mistress' ornaments are chaste.'

But all these poor forbiddings could not stay him;
He in the worst sense consters their denial.
The doors, the wind, the glove, that did delay him, 325
He takes for accidental things of trial;
Or as those bars which stop the hourly dial,
    Who with a ling'ring stay his course doth let,
    Till every minute pays the hour his debt.

'So, so,' quoth he, 'these lets attend the time, 330
Like little frosts that sometime threat the spring,
To add a more rejoicing to the prime,
And give the sneaped birds more cause to sing.
Pain pays the income of each precious thing:
    Huge rocks, high winds, strong pirates, shelves
      and sands 335
    The merchant fears, ere rich at home he lands.'

Now is he come unto the chamber door
That shuts him from the heaven of his thought,
Which with a yielding latch, and with no more,
Hath barr'd him from the blessed thing he sought. 340
So from himself impiety hath wrought,
    That for his prey to pray he doth begin,
    As if the heavens should countenance his sin.

But in the midst of his unfruitful prayer,
Having solicited th' eternal power
That his foul thoughts might compass his fair fair,
And they would stand auspicious to the hour,
Even there he starts; quoth he, 'I must deflower:
    The powers to whom I pray abhor this fact;
    How can they then assist me in the act?

345

350

'Then love and fortune be my gods, my guide!
My will is back'd with resolution;
Thoughts are but dreams till their effects be tried;
The blackest sin is clear'd with absolution.
Against love's fire fear's frost hath dissolution:
    The eye of heaven is out, and misty night
    Covers the shame that follows sweet delight.'

355

This said, his guilty hand pluck'd up the latch,
And with his knee the door he opens wide.
The dove sleeps fast that this night-owl will catch;
Thus treason works ere traitors be espied.
Who sees the lurking serpent steps aside;
    But she, sound sleeping, fearing no such thing,
    Lies at the mercy of his mortal sting.

360

Into the chamber wickedly he stalks,
And gazeth on her yet unstained bed.
The curtains being close, about he walks,
Rolling his greedy eyeballs in his head;
By their high treason is his heart misled,
    Which gives the watch-word to his hand full soon,
    To draw the cloud that hides the silver moon.

365

370

Look as the fair and fiery-pointed sun
Rushing from forth a cloud, bereaves our sight:
Even so, the curtain drawn, his eyes begun
To wink, being blinded with a greater light.
Whether it is that she reflects so bright,
    That dazzleth them, or else some shame supposed;
    But blind they are, and keep themselves enclosed.

375

O had they in that darksome prison died,
Then had they seen the period of their ill!
Then Collatine again by Lucrece' side
In his clear bed might have reposed still.
But they must ope, this blessed league to kill;
    And holy-thoughted Lucrece to their sight
    Must sell her joy, her life, her world's delight.

380

385

Her lily hand her rosy cheek lies under,
Coz'ning the pillow of a lawful kiss;
Who therefore angry, seems to part in sunder,
Swelling on either side to want his bliss:
Between whose hills her head entombed is,
    Where like a virtuous monument she lies,
    To be admir'd of lewd unhallowed eyes.

390

Without the bed her other fair hand was,
On the green coverlet; whose perfect white
Show'd like an April daisy on the grass,
With pearly sweat resembling dew of night.
Her eyes like marigolds had sheath'd their light,
    And canopied in darkness sweetly lay,
    Till they might open to adorn the day.

395

Her hair like golden threads play'd with her breath:
O modest wantons, wanton modesty!
Showing life's triumph in the map of death,
And death's dim look in life's mortality.
Each in her sleep themselves so beautify,
    As if between them twain there were no strife,
    But that life liv'd in death and death in life.

400

405

Her breasts like ivory globes circled with blue,
A pair of maiden worlds unconquered;
Save of their lord, no bearing yoke they knew,
And him by oath they truly honoured.
These worlds in Tarquin new ambition bred;
    Who like a foul usurper went about,
    From this fair throne to heave the owner out.

410

What could he see but mightily he noted?
What did he note but strongly he desired?
What he beheld, on that he firmly doted,
And in his will his wilful eye he tired.
With more than admiration he admired
    Her azure veins, her alablaster skin,
    Her coral lips, her snow-white dimpled chin.

415

420

As the grim lion fawneth o'er his prey,
Sharp hunger by the conquest satisfied;
So o'er this sleeping soul doth Tarquin stay,
His rage of lust by gazing qualified, –
Slak'd not suppress'd, for standing by her side,
    His eye which late this mutiny restrains,
    Unto a greater uproar tempts his veins.

425

And they like straggling slaves for pillage fighting,
Obdurate vassals fell exploits effecting,
In bloody death and ravishment delighting,
Nor children's tears nor mothers' groans respecting,
Swell in their pride, the onset still expecting.
    Anon his beating heart, alarum striking,
    Gives the hot charge, and bids them do their
        liking.

430

His drumming heart cheers up his burning eye,
His eye commends the leading to his hand;
His hand, as proud of such a dignity,
Smoking with pride, march'd on to make his stand
On her bare breast, the heart of all her land;
    Whose ranks of blue veins, as his hand did scale,
    Left their round turrets destitute and pale.

435

440

They must'ring to the quiet cabinet
Where their dear governess and lady lies,
Do tell her she is dreadfully beset,
445 And fright her with confusion of their cries.
She much amaz'd, breaks ope her lock'd-up eyes,
    Who peeping forth this tumult to behold,
    Are by his flaming torch dimm'd and controll'd.

Imagine her as one in dead of night
450 From forth dull sleep by dreadful fancy waking,
That thinks she hath beheld some ghastly sprite,
Whose grim aspect sets every joint a-shaking:
What terror 'tis! but she in worser taking,
    From sleep disturbed, heedfully doth view
455   The sight which makes supposed terror true.

Wrapp'd and confounded in a thousand fears,
Like to a new-kill'd bird she trembling lies.
She dares not look, yet winking there appears
Quick-shifting antics, ugly in her eyes.
460 Such shadows are the weak brain's forgeries;
    Who, angry that the eyes fly from their lights,
    In darkness daunts them with more dreadful
        sights.

His hand that yet remains upon her breast, –
Rude ram, to batter such an ivory wall! –
465 May feel her heart, poor citizen! distress'd,
Wounding itself to death, rise up and fall, –
Beating her bulk, that his hand shakes withal:
    This moves in him more rage and lesser pity,
    To make the breach and enter this sweet city.

470 First like a trumpet doth his tongue begin
To sound a parley to his heartless foe,
Who o'er the white sheet peers her whiter chin,
The reason of this rash alarm to know;
Which he by dumb demeanour seeks to show:
475   But she with vehement prayers urgeth still
    Under what colour he commits this ill.

Thus he replies: 'The colour in thy face,
That even for anger makes the lily pale
And the red rose blush at her own disgrace,
480 Shall plead for me and tell my loving tale.
Under that colour am I come to scale
    Thy never-conquer'd fort: the fault is thine,
    For those thine eyes betray thee unto mine.

'Thus I forestall thee, if thou mean to chide:
485 Thy beauty hath ensnar'd thee to this night,
Where thou with patience must my will abide,
My will that marks thee for my earth's delight;
Which I to conquer sought with all my might:
    But as reproof and reason beat it dead,
490   By thy bright beauty was it newly bred.

'I see what crosses my attempt will bring,
I know what thorns the growing rose defends;
I think the honey guarded with a sting:
All this beforehand counsel comprehends.
But will is deaf, and hears no heedful friends; 495
    Only he hath an eye to gaze on beauty,
    And dotes on what he looks, 'gainst law or duty.

'I have debated even in my soul,
What wrong, what shame, what sorrow I shall breed;
But nothing can affection's course control, 500
Or stop the headlong fury of his speed.
I know repentant tears ensue the deed,
    Reproach, disdain and deadly enmity;
    Yet strive I to embrace mine infamy.'

This said, he shakes aloft his Roman blade, 505
Which like a falcon tow'ring in the skies,
Coucheth the fowl below with his wings' shade,
Whose crooked beak threats, if he mount he dies:
So under his insulting falchion lies
    Harmless Lucretia, marking what he tells 510
    With trembling fear, as fowl hear falcons' bells.

'Lucrece,' quoth he, 'this night I must enjoy thee.
If thou deny, then force must work my way:
For in thy bed I purpose to destroy thee;
That done, some worthless slave of thine I'll slay, 515
To kill thine honour with thy life's decay;
    And in thy dead arms do I mean to place him,
    Swearing I slew him, seeing thee embrace him.

'So thy surviving husband shall remain
The scornful mark of every open eye; 520
Thy kinsmen hang their heads at this disdain,
Thy issue blurr'd with nameless bastardy.
And thou, the author of their obloquy,
    Shalt have thy trespass cited up in rhymes
    And sung by children in succeeding times. 525

'But if thou yield, I rest thy secret friend;
The fault unknown is as a thought unacted.
A little harm done to a great good end
For lawful policy remains enacted.
The poisonous simple sometime is compacted 530
    In a pure compound; being so applied,
    His venom in effect is purified.

'Then for thy husband and thy children's sake,
Tender my suit; bequeath not to their lot
The shame that from them no device can take, 535
The blemish that will never be forgot,
Worse than a slavish wipe or birth-hour's blot:
    For marks descried in men's nativity
    Are nature's faults, not their own infamy.'

Here with a cockatrice' dead-killing eye 540
He rouseth up himself, and makes a pause;
While she, the picture of pure piety,
Like a white hind under the gripe's sharp claws,
Pleads in a wilderness where are no laws,
    To the rough beast that knows no gentle right, 545
    Nor aught obeys but his foul appetite.

But when a black-fac'd cloud the world doth threat,
In his dim mist th' aspiring mountains hiding
From earth's dark womb some gentle gust doth get,
Which blow these pitchy vapours from their biding, 550
Hind'ring their present fall by this dividing:
    So his unhallowed haste her words delays,
    And moody Pluto winks while Orpheus plays.

Yet, foul night-waking cat, he doth but dally,
While in his hold-fast foot the weak mouse panteth. 555
Her sad behaviour feeds his vulture folly,
A swallowing gulf that even in plenty wanteth.
His ear her prayers admits, but his heart granteth
    No penetrable entrance to her plaining:
    Tears harden lust, though marble wear with 560
        raining.

Her pity-pleading eyes are sadly fixed
In the remorseless wrinkles of his face.
Her modest eloquence with sighs is mixed,
Which to her oratory adds more grace.
She puts the period often from his place, 565
    And 'midst the sentence so her accent breaks
    That twice she doth begin ere once she speaks.

She conjures him by high almighty Jove,
By knighthood, gentry, and sweet friendship's oath,
By her untimely tears, her husband's love, 570
By holy human law and common troth,
By heaven and earth, and all the power of both,
    That to his borrowed bed he make retire,
    And stoop to honour, not to foul desire.

Quoth she, 'Reward not hospitality 575
With such black payment as thou hast pretended.
Mud not the fountain that gave drink to thee,
Mar not the thing that cannot be amended.
End thy ill aim before thy shoot be ended;
    He is no woodman that doth bend his bow 580
    To strike a poor unseasonable doe.

'My husband is thy friend; for his sake spare me.
Thyself art mighty; for thine own sake leave me.
Myself a weakling; do not then ensnare me.
Thou look'st not like deceit; do not deceive me. 585
My sighs like whirlwinds labour hence to heave thee;
    If ever man were mov'd with woman's moans,
    Be moved with my tears, my sighs, my groans.

'All which together, like a troubled ocean,
Beat at thy rocky and wrack-threat'ning heart, 590
To soften it with their continual motion;
For stones dissolv'd to water do convert.
O if no harder than a stone thou art,
    Melt at my tears and be compassionate!
    Soft pity enters at an iron gate. 595

'In Tarquin's likeness I did entertain thee:
Hast thou put on his shape to do him shame?
To all the host of heaven I complain me,
Thou wrong'st his honour, wound'st his princely
        name;
Thou art not what thou seem'st, and if the same, 600
    Thou seem'st not what thou art, a god, a king:
    For kings like gods should govern everything.

'How will thy shame be seeded in thine age,
When thus thy vices bud before thy spring?
If in thy hope thou dar'st do such outrage, 605
What dar'st thou not when once thou art a king?
O be remember'd, no outrageous thing
    From vassal actors can be wip'd away:
    Then kings' misdeeds cannot be hid in clay.

'This deed will make thee only lov'd for fear; 610
But happy monarchs still are fear'd for love.
With foul offenders thou perforce must bear,
When they in thee the like offences prove.
If but for fear of this, thy will remove,
    For princes are the glass, the school, the book, 615
    Where subjects' eyes do learn, do read, do look.

'And wilt thou be the school where lust shall learn?
Must he in thee read lectures of such shame?
Wilt thou be glass wherein it shall discern
Authority for sin, warrant for blame? 620
To privilege dishonour in thy name,
    Thou back'st reproach against long-living laud,
    And mak'st fair reputation but a bawd.

'Hast thou command? by him that gave it thee,
From a pure heart command thy rebel will. 625
Draw not thy sword to guard iniquity,
For it was lent thee all that brood to kill.
Thy princely office how canst thou fulfil,
    When pattern'd by thy fault, foul sin may say
    He learn'd to sin, and thou didst teach the way? 630

'Think but how vile a spectacle it were,
To view thy present trespass in another.
Men's faults do seldom to themselves appear;
Their own transgressions partially they smother.
This guilt would seem death-worthy in thy brother. 635
    O how are they wrapp'd in with infamies,
    That from their own misdeeds askance their eyes!

'To thee, to thee, my heav'd-up hands appeal,
Not to seducing lust, thy rash relier.
640 I sue for exil'd majesty's repeal:
Let him return, and flatt'ring thoughts retire;
His true respect will prison false desire,
    And wipe the dim mist from thy doting eyne,
    That thou shalt see thy state, and pity mine.'

645 'Have done,' quoth he, 'my uncontrolled tide
Turns not, but swells the higher by this let.
Small lights are soon blown out, huge fires abide,
And with the wind in greater fury fret;
The petty streams that pay a daily debt
650   To their salt sovereign, with their fresh falls' haste
    Add to his flow, but alter not his taste.'

'Thou art,' quoth she, 'a sea, a sovereign king,
And lo there falls into thy boundless flood
Black lust, dishonour, shame, misgoverning,
655 Who seek to stain the ocean of thy blood.
If all these petty ills shall change thy good,
    Thy sea within a puddle's womb is hearsed,
    And not the puddle in thy sea dispersed.

'So shall these slaves be king, and thou their slave:
660 Thou nobly base, they basely dignified;
Thou their fair life, and they thy fouler grave;
Thou loathed in their shame, they in thy pride.
The lesser thing should not the greater hide:
    The cedar stoops not to the base shrub's foot,
665   But low shrubs wither at the cedar's root.

'So let thy thoughts, low vassals to thy state' –
'No more,' quoth he, 'by heaven I will not hear
        thee.
Yield to my love: if not, enforced hate
Instead of love's coy touch, shall rudely tear thee.
670 That done, despitefully I mean to bear thee
    Unto the base bed of some rascal groom,
    To be thy partner in this shameful doom.'

This said, he sets his foot upon the light,
For light and lust are deadly enemies:
675 Shame folded up in blind concealing night,
When most unseen, then most doth tyrannize.
The wolf hath seiz'd his prey, the poor lamb cries,
    Till with her own white fleece her voice controll'd
    Entombs her outcry in her lips' sweet fold.

680 For with the nightly linen that she wears
He pens her piteous clamours in her head,
Cooling his hot face in the chastest tears
That ever modest eyes with sorrow shed.
O that prone lust should stain so pure a bed!
685   The spots whereof could weeping purify,
    Her tears should drop on them perpetually.

But she hath lost a dearer thing than life,
And he hath won what he would lose again.
This forced league doth force a further strife;
This momentary joy breeds months of pain; 690
This hot desire converts to cold disdain.
    Pure chastity is rifled of her store,
    And lust the thief, far poorer than before.

Look as the full-fed hound or gorged hawk,
Unapt for tender smell or speedy flight, 695
Make slow pursuit, or altogether balk
The prey wherein by nature they delight:
So surfeit-taking Tarquin fares this night.
    His taste delicious, in digestion souring,
    Devours his will that liv'd by foul devouring. 700

O deeper sin than bottomless conceit
Can comprehend in still imagination!
Drunken desire must vomit his receipt,
Ere he can see his own abomination.
While lust is in his pride no exclamation 705
    Can curb his heat or rein his rash desire,
    Till, like a jade, self-will himself doth tire.

And then with lank and lean discolour'd cheek,
With heavy eye, knit brow, and strenghtless pace,
Feeble desire, all recreant, poor and meek, 710
Like to a bankrout beggar wails his case.
The flesh being proud, desire doth fight with grace;
    For there it revels, and when that decays,
    The guilty rebel for remission prays.

So fares it with this faultful lord of Rome, 715
Who this accomplishment so hotly chased;
For now against himself he sounds this doom,
That through the length of times he stands
        disgraced.
Besides, his soul's fair temple is defaced,
    To whose weak ruins muster troops of cares, 720
    To ask the spotted princess how she fares.

She says her subjects with foul insurrection
Have batter'd down her consecrated wall,
And by their mortal fault brought in subjection
Her immortality, and made her thrall 725
To living death and pain perpetual:
    Which in her prescience she controlled still,
    But her foresight could not forestall their will.

Ev'n in this thought through the dark night he
        stealeth,
A captive victor that hath lost in gain, 730
Bearing away the wound that nothing healeth,
The scar that will despite of cure remain;
Leaving his spoil perplex'd in greater pain:
    She bears the load of lust he left behind,
    And he the burden of a guilty mind. 735

He like a thievish dog creeps sadly thence,
She like a wearied lamb lies panting there;
He scowls, and hates himself for his offence,
She desperate, with her nails her flesh doth tear.
740   He faintly flies, sweating with guilty fear;
    She stays, exclaiming on the direful night,
    He runs, and chides his vanish'd loath'd delight.

He thence departs a heavy convertite,
She there remains a hopeless castaway;
745   He in his speed looks for the morning light,
She prays she never may behold the day:
'For day,' quoth she, 'night's 'scapes doth open lay,
    And my true eyes have never practis'd how
    To cloak offences with a cunning brow.

750   'They think not but that every eye can see
The same disgrace which they themselves behold;
And therefore would they still in darkness be,
To have their unseen sin remain untold.
For they their guilt with weeping will unfold,
755   And grave like water that doth eat in steel,
    Upon my cheeks, what helpless shame I feel.'

Here she exclaims against repose and rest,
And bids her eyes hereafter still be blind.
She wakes her heart by beating on her breast,
760   And bids it leap from thence, where it may find
Some purer chest, to close so pure a mind.
    Frantic with grief, thus breathes she forth her
      spite
    Against the unseen secrecy of night:

'O comfort-killing night, image of hell,
765   Dim register and notary of shame,
Black stage for tragedies and murders fell,
Vast sin-concealing Chaos, nurse of blame!
Blind muffled bawd, dark harbour for defame,
    Grim cave of death, whisp'ring conspirator
770   With close-tongued treason and the ravisher!

'O hateful, vaporous and foggy night,
Since thou art guilty of my cureless crime,
Muster thy mists to meet the eastern light,
Make war against proportion'd course of time:
775   Or if thou wilt permit the sun to climb
    His wonted height, yet ere he go to bed,
    Knit poisonous clouds about his golden head.

'With rotten damps ravish the morning air;
Let their exhal'd unwholesome breaths make sick
780   The life of purity, the supreme fair,
Ere he arrive his weary noontide prick.
And let thy musty vapours march so thick,
    That in their smoky ranks his smother'd light
    May set at noon and make perpetual night.

'Were Tarquin night, as he is but night's child,   785
The silver-shining queen he would distain;
Her twinkling handmaids too, by him defil'd,
Through night's black bosom should not peep again.
So should I have co-partners in my pain;
    And fellowship in woe doth woe assuage,   790
    As palmers' chat makes short their pilgrimage.

'Where now I have no one to blush with me,
To cross their arms and hang their heads with mine,
To mask their brows and hide their infamy;
But I alone, alone must sit and pine,   795
Seasoning the earth with showers of silver brine,
    Mingling my talk with tears, my grief with groans,
    Poor wasting monuments of lasting moans.

'O night, thou furnace of foul reeking smoke,
Let not the jealous day behold that face   800
Which underneath thy black all-hiding cloak
Immodestly lies martyr'd with disgrace!
Keep still possession of thy gloomy place,
    That all the faults which in thy reign are made
    May likewise be sepulchred in thy shade.   805

'Make me not object to the tell-tale day:
The light will show character'd in my brow
The story of sweet chastity's decay,
The impious breach of holy wedlock vow;
Yea, the illiterate that know not how   810
    To cipher what is writ in learned books,
    Will quote my loathsome trespass in my looks.

'The nurse to still her child will tell my story,
And fright her crying babe with Tarquin's name.
The orator to deck his oratory   815
Will couple my reproach to Tarquin's shame.
Feast-finding minstrels tuning my defame,
    Will tie the hearers to attend each line,
    How Tarquin wronged me, I Collatine.

'Let my good name, that senseless reputation,   820
For Collatine's dear love be kept unspotted.
If that be made a theme for disputation,
The branches of another root are rotted,
And undeserv'd reproach to him allotted
    That is as clear from this attaint of mine   825
    As I ere this was pure to Collatine.

'O unseen shame, invisible disgrace!
O unfelt sore, crest-wounding private scar!
Reproach is stamp'd in Collatinus' face,
And Tarquin's eye may read the mot afar,   830
How he in peace is wounded, not in war:
    Alas how many bear such shameful blows,
    Which not themselves, but he that gives them
      knows!

'If, Collatine, thine honour lay in me,
From me by strong assault it is bereft:
My honey lost, and I a drone-like bee,
Have no perfection of my summer left,
But robb'd and ransack'd by injurious theft;
 In thy weak hive a wand'ring wasp hath crept,
 And suck'd the honey which thy chaste bee kept.

'Yet am I guilty of thy honour's wrack;
Yet for thy honour did I entertain him:
Coming from thee I could not put him back,
For it had been dishonour to disdain him.
Besides, of weariness he did complain him,
 And talk'd of virtue: O unlook'd-for evil,
 When virtue is profan'd in such a devil!

'Why should the worm intrude the maiden bud,
Or hateful cuckoos hatch in sparrows' nests?
Or toads infect fair founts with venom mud,
Or tyrant folly lurk in gentle breasts?
Or kings be breakers of their own behests?
 But no perfection is so absolute
 That some impurity doth not pollute.

'The aged man that coffers up his gold
Is plagu'd with cramps and gouts and painful fits,
And scarce hath eyes his treasure to behold;
But like still-pining Tantalus he sits,
And useless barns the harvest of his wits,
 Having no other pleasure of his gain
 But torment that it cannot cure his pain.

'So then he hath it when he cannot use it,
And leaves it to be master'd by his young,
Who in their pride do presently abuse it;
Their father was too weak, and they too strong,
To hold their cursed-blessed fortune long:
 The sweets we wish for turn to loathed sours
 Even in the moment that we call them ours.

'Unruly blasts wait on the tender spring;
Unwholesome weeds take root with precious flowers;
The adder hisses where the sweet birds sing;
What virtue breeds iniquity devours.
We have no good that we can say is ours,
 But ill-annexed opportunity
 Or kills his life, or else his quality.

'O opportunity, thy guilt is great!
'Tis thou that execut'st the traitor's treason;
Thou sets the wolf where he the lamb may get;
Whoever plots the sin, thou poinst the season.
'Tis thou that spurn'st at right, at law, at reason;
 And in thy shady cell where none may spy him,
 Sits sin to seize the souls that wander by him.

'Thou mak'st the vestal violate her oath;
Thou blow'st the fire when temperance is thaw'd;
Thou smother'st honesty, thou murder'st troth,
Thou foul abettor, thou notorious bawd!
Thou plantest scandal, and displacest laud:
 Thou ravisher, thou traitor, thou false thief!
 Thy honey turns to gall, thy joy to grief.

'Thy secret pleasure turns to open shame,
Thy private feasting to a public fast,
Thy smoothing titles to a ragged name,
Thy sugar'd tongue to bitter wormwood taste;
Thy violent vanities can never last.
 How comes it then, vile opportunity,
 Being so bad, such numbers seek for thee?

'When wilt thou be the humble suppliant's friend,
And bring him where his suit may be obtained?
When wilt thou sort an hour great strifes to end,
Or free that soul which wretchedness hath chained?
Give physic to the sick, ease to the pained?
 The poor, lame, blind, halt, creep, cry out for thee;
 But they ne'er meet with opportunity.

'The patient dies while the physician sleeps;
The orphan pines while the oppressor feeds;
Justice is feasting while the widow weeps;
Advice is sporting while infection breeds.
Thou grant'st no time for charitable deeds;
 Wrath, envy, treason, rape, and murder's rages,
 Thy heinous hours wait on them as their pages.

'When truth and virtue have to do with thee,
A thousand crosses keep them from thy aid;
They buy thy help, but sin ne'er gives a fee:
He gratis comes, and thou art well appaid,
As well to hear as grant what he hath said.
 My Collatine would else have come to me
 When Tarquin did, but he was stay'd by thee.

'Guilty thou art of murder and of theft,
Guilty of perjury and subornation,
Guilty of treason, forgery and shift,
Guilty of incest, that abomination:
An accessory by thine inclination
 To all sins past and all that are to come
 From the creation to the general doom.

'Mis-shapen time, copesmate of ugly night,
Swift subtle post, carrier of grisly care,
Eater of youth, false slave to false delight,
Base watch of woes, sin's pack-horse, virtue's snare!
Thou nurses all, and murder'st all that are:
 O hear me then, injurious shifting time!
 Be guilty of my death, since of my crime.

'Why hath thy servant opportunity
Betray'd the hours thou gav'st me to repose,
Cancell'd my fortunes and enchained me
935 To endless date of never-ending woes?
Time's office is to fine the hate of foes,
    To eat up errors by opinion bred,
    Not spend the dowry of a lawful bed.

'Time's glory is to calm contending kings,
940 To unmask falsehood and bring truth to light,
To stamp the seal of time in aged things,
To wake the morn and sentinel the night,
To wrong the wronger till he render right,
    To ruinate proud buildings with thy hours,
945 And smear with dust their glitt'ring golden tow'rs;

'To fill with worm-holes stately monuments,
To feed oblivion with decay of things,
To blot old books and alter their contents,
To pluck the quills from ancient ravens' wings,
950 To dry the old oak's sap and cherish springs,
    To spoil antiquities of hammer'd steel,
    And turn the giddy round of fortune's wheel;

'To show the beldam daughters of her daughter,
To make the child a man, the man a child,
955 To slay the tiger that doth live by slaughter,
To tame the unicorn and lion wild,
To mock the subtle in themselves beguil'd,
    To cheer the ploughman with increaseful crops,
    And waste huge stones with little water-drops.

960 'Why work'st thou mischief in thy pilgrimage,
Unless thou could'st return to make amends?
One poor retiring minute in an age
Would purchase thee a thousand thousand friends,
Lending him wit that to bad debtors lends:
    O this dread night, would'st thou one hour come
965   back,
    I could prevent this storm and shun thy wrack!

'Thou ceaseless lackey to eternity,
With some mischance cross Tarquin in his flight;
Devise extremes beyond extremity,
970 To make him curse this cursed crimeful night.
Let ghastly shadows his lewd eyes affright,
    And the dire thought of his committed evil
    Shape every bush a hideous shapeless devil.

'Disturb his hours of rest with restless trances,
975 Afflict him in his bed with bedrid groans;
Let there bechance him pitiful mischances,
To make him moan, but pity not his moans.
Stone him with harden'd hearts harder than stones,
    And let mild women to him lose their mildness,
980 Wilder to him than tigers in their wildness.

'Let him have time to tear his curled hair,
Let him have time against himself to rave,
Let him have time of time's help to despair,
Let him have time to live a loathed slave,
Let him have time a beggar's orts to crave,   985
    And time to see one that by alms doth live
    Disdain to him disdained scraps to give.

'Let him have time to see his friends his foes,
And merry fools to mock at him resort;
Let him have time to mark how slow time goes   990
In time of sorrow, and how swift and short
His time of folly and his time of sport:
    And ever let his unrecalling crime
    Have time to wail th'abusing of his time.

'O time, thou tutor both to good and bad,   995
Teach me to curse him that thou taught'st this ill!
At his own shadow let the thief run mad,
Himself, himself seek every hour to kill:
Such wretched hands such wretched blood should
    spill,
    For who so base would such an office have   1000
    As sland'rous deathsman to so base a slave?

'The baser is he, coming from a king,
To shame his hope with deeds degenerate;
The mightier man the mightier is the thing
That makes him honour'd or begets him hate,   1005
For greatest scandal waits on greatest state.
    The moon being clouded presently is miss'd,
    But little stars may hide them when they list.

'The crow may bathe his coal-black wings in mire,
And unperceiv'd fly with the filth away;   1010
But if the like the snow-white swan desire,
The stain upon his silver down will stay.
Poor grooms are sightless night, kings glorious day;
    Gnats are unnoted wheresoe'er they fly,
    But eagles gaz'd upon with every eye.   1015

'Out idle words, servants to shallow fools,
Unprofitable sounds, weak arbitrators!
Busy yourselves in skill-contending schools,
Debate where leisure serves with dull debaters;
To trembling clients be you mediators: 1020
    For me, I force not argument a straw,
    Since that my case is past the help of law.

'In vain I rail at opportunity,
At time, at Tarquin, at uncheerful night;
In vain I cavil with mine infamy,   1025
In vain I spurn at my confirm'd despite;
This helpless smoke of words doth me no right:
    The remedy indeed to do me good
    Is to let forth my foul defiled blood.

'Poor hand, why quiver's thou at this decree?   1030
Honour thyself to rid me of this shame:
For if I die, my honour lives in thee,
But if I live, thou liv'st in my defame.
Since thou could'st not defend thy loyal dame,
    And wast afeard to scratch her wicked foe,   1035
    Kill both thyself and her for yielding so.'

This said, from her betumbled couch she starteth,
To find some desp'rate instrument of death;
But this no slaughterhouse no tool imparteth
To make more vent for passage of her breath,   1040
Which thronging through her lips so vanisheth
    As smoke from Aetna, that in air consumes,
    Or that which from discharged cannon fumes.

'In vain,' quoth she, 'I live, and seek in vain
Some happy mean to end a hapless life.   1045
I fear'd by Tarquin's falchion to be slain,
Yet for the self-same purpose seek a knife;
But when I fear'd I was a loyal wife:
    So am I now, – O no, that cannot be!
    Of that true type hath Tarquin rifled me.   1050

'O that is gone for which I sought to live,
And therefore now I need not fear to die!
To clear this spot by death, at least I give
A badge of fame to slander's livery,
A dying life to living infamy: 1055
    Poor helpless help, the treasure stol'n away,
    To burn the guiltless casket where it lay!

'Well well, dear Collatine, thou shalt not know
The stained taste of violated troth;
I will not wrong thy true affection so,   1060
To flatter thee with an infringed oath.
This bastard graff shall never come to growth:
    He shall not boast who did thy stock pollute,
    That thou art doting father of his fruit.

'Nor shall he smile at thee in secret thought,   1065
Nor laugh with his companions at thy state;
But thou shalt know thy int'rest was not bought
Basely with gold, but stol'n from forth thy gate.
For me, I am the mistress of my fate,
    And with my trespass never will dispense,   1070
    Till life to death acquit my forc'd offence.

'I will not poison thee with my attaint,
Nor fold my fault in cleanly-coin'd excuses;
My sable ground of sin I will not paint,
To hide the truth of this false night's abuses.   1075
My tongue shall utter all, mine eyes like sluices,
    As from a mountain-spring that feeds a dale,
    Shall gush pure streams to purge my impure tale.'

By this, lamenting Philomel had ended
The well-tun'd warble of her nightly sorrow,   1080
And solemn night with slow sad gait descended
To ugly hell; when lo, the blushing morrow
Lends light to all fair eyes that light will borrow;
    But cloudy Lucrece shames herself to see,
    And therefore still in night would cloister'd be.   1085

Revealing day through every cranny spies,
And seems to point her out where she sits weeping;
To whom she sobbing speaks, 'O eye of eyes,
Why pry'st thou through my window? leave thy
    peeping,
Mock with thy tickling beams eyes that are sleeping;   1090
    Brand not my forehead with thy piercing light,
    For day hath naught to do what's done by night.'

Thus cavils she with every thing she sees.
True grief is fond and testy as a child,
Who wayward once, his mood with naught agrees;   1095
Old woes, not infant sorrows, bear them mild.
Continuance tames the one; the other wild,
    Like an unpractis'd swimmer plunging still,
    With too much labour drowns for want of skill.

So she deep-drenched in a sea of care,   1100
Holds disputation with each thing she views,
And to herself all sorrow doth compare;
No object but her passion's strength renews,
And as one shifts another straight ensues.
    Sometime her grief is dumb and hath no words,   1105
    Sometime 'tis mad and too much talk affords.

The little birds that tune their morning's joy
Make her moans mad with their sweet melody,
For mirth doth search the bottom of annoy;
Sad souls are slain in merry company,   1110
Grief best is pleas'd with grief's society:
    True sorrow then is feelingly suffic'd
    When with like semblance it is sympathis'd.

'Tis double death to drown in ken of shore;
He ten times pines that pines beholding food;   1115
To see the salve doth make the wound ache more;
Great grief grieves most at that would do it good;
Deep woes roll forward like a gentle flood,
    Who being stopp'd, the bounding bank o'erflows;
    Grief dallied with, nor law nor limit knows.   1120

'You mocking birds,' quoth she, 'your tunes entomb
Within your hollow swelling feather'd breasts,
And in my hearing be you mute and dumb;
My restless discord loves no stops nor rests.
A woeful hostess brooks not merry guests.   1125
    Relish your nimble notes to pleasing ears;
    Distress likes dumps, when time is kept with
        tears.

'Come Philomel, that sing'st of ravishment,
Make thy sad grove in my dishevel'd hair;
1130 As the dank earth weeps at thy languishment,
So I at each sad strain will strain a tear
And with deep groans the diapason bear;
    For burden-wise I'll hum on Tarquin still,
    While thou on Tereus descants better skill.

1135 'And whiles against a thorn thou bear'st thy part
To keep thy sharp woes waking, wretched I
To imitate thee well, against my heart
Will fix a sharp knife to affright mine eye,
Who if it wink shall thereon fall and die:
1140   These means as frets upon an instrument
    Shall tune our heart-strings to true languishment.

'And for, poor bird, thou sing'st not in the day,
As shaming any eye should thee behold,
Some dark deep desert seated from the way,
1145 That knows not parching heat nor freezing cold,
Will we find out; and there we will unfold
    To creatures stern, sad tunes to change their kinds:
    Since men prove beasts, let beasts bear gentle
        minds.'

As the poor frighted deer that stands at gaze,
1150 Wildly determining which way to fly,
Or one encompass'd with a winding maze,
That cannot tread the way out readily;
So with herself is she in mutiny,
    To live or die which of the twain were better,
1155   When life is sham'd and death reproach's debtor.

'To kill myself,' quoth she, 'alack what were it,
But with my body my poor soul's pollution?
They that lose half with greater patience bear it
Than they whose whole is swallowed in confusion.
1160 That mother tries a merciless conclusion,
    Who having two sweet babes, when death takes
        one,
    Will slay the other and be nurse to none.

'My body or my soul, which was the dearer,
When the one pure, the other made divine?
1165 Whose love of either to myself was nearer,
When both were kept for heaven and Collatine?
Ay me, the bark pill'd from the lofty pine,
    His leaves will wither and his sap decay;
    So must my soul, her bark being pill'd away.

1170 'Her house is sack'd, her quiet interrupted,
Her mansion batter'd by the enemy,
Her sacred temple spotted, spoil'd, corrupted,
Grossly engirt with daring infamy.
Then let it not be call'd impiety,
1175   If in this blemish'd fort I make some hole,
    Through which I may convey this troubled soul.

'Yet die I will not, till my Collatine
Have heard the cause of my untimely death,
That he may vow in that sad hour of mine
Revenge on him that made me stop my breath.   1180
My stained blood to Tarquin I'll bequeath,
    Which by him tainted shall for him be spent,
    And as his due writ in my testament.

'My honour I'll bequeath unto the knife
That wounds my body so dishonoured.   1185
'Tis honour to deprive dishonour'd life;
The one will live, the other being dead.
So of shame's ashes shall my fame be bred,
    For in my death I murder shameful scorn:
    My shame so dead, mine honour is new born.   1190

'Dear lord of that dear jewel I have lost,
What legacy shall I bequeath to thee?
My resolution, love, shall be thy boast,
By whose example thou reveng'd mayst be.
How Tarquin must be us'd, read it in me: 1195
    Myself thy friend will kill myself thy foe,
    And for my sake serve thou false Tarquin so.

'This brief abridgement of my will I make:
My soul and body to the skies and ground;
My resolution, husband, do thou take;   1200
Mine honour be the knife's that makes my wound;
My shame be his that did my fame confound;
    And all my fame that lives disbursed be
    To those that live and think no shame of me.

'Thou Collatine, shalt oversee this will;   1205
How was I overseen that thou shalt see it!
My blood shall wash the slander of mine ill;
My life's foul deed my life's fair end shall free it.
Faint not, faint heart, but stoutly say "So be it";
    Yield to my hand, my hand shall conquer thee: 1210
    Thou dead, both die, and both shall victors be.'

This plot of death when sadly she had laid,
And wip'd the brinish pearl from her bright eyes,
With untun'd tongue she hoarsely calls her maid,
Whose swift obedience to her mistress hies;   1215
For fleet-wing'd duty with thought's feathers flies.
    Poor Lucrece' cheeks unto her maid seem so
    As winter meads when sun doth melt their snow.

Her mistress she doth give demure good-morrow,
With soft slow tongue, true mark of modesty,   1220
And sorts a sad look to her lady's sorrow,
For why her face wore sorrow's livery;
But durst not ask of her audaciously
    Why her two suns were cloud-eclipsed so,
    Nor why her fair cheeks over-wash'd with woe. 1225

But as the earth doth weep, the sun being set,
Each flower moisten'd like a melting eye,
Even so the maid with swelling drops 'gan wet
Her circled eyne, enforc'd by sympathy
1230 Of those fair suns set in her mistress' sky,
    Who in a salt-way'd ocean quench their light;
    Which makes the maid weep like the dewy night.

A pretty while these pretty creatures stand,
Like ivory conduits coral cisterns filling.
1235 One justly weeps, the other takes in hand
No cause, but company, of her drops' spilling;
Their gentle sex to weep are often willing,
    Grieving themselves to guess at others' smarts,
    And then they drown their eyes or break their
        hearts.

1240 For men have marble, women waxen, minds,
And therefore are they form'd as marble will;
The weak oppress'd, th' impression of strange kinds
Is form'd in them by force, by fraud, or skill.
Then call them not the authors of their ill,
1245   No more than wax shall be accounted evil,
    Wherein is stamp'd the semblance of a devil.

Their smoothness, like a goodly champaign plain,
Lays open all the little worms that creep;
In men as in a rough-grown grove remain
1250 Cave-keeping evils that obscurely sleep;
Through crystal walls each little mote will peep;
    Though men can cover them with bold stern looks,
    Poor women's faces are their own faults' books.

No man inveigh against the withered flower,
1255 But chide rough winter that the flower hath kill'd;
Not that devour'd, but that which doth devour
Is worthy blame; O let it not be hild
Poor women's faults, that they are so fulfill'd
    With men's abuses! those proud lords to blame
1260   Make weak-made women tenants to their shame.

The precedent whereof in Lucrece view,
Assail'd by night with circumstances strong
Of present death, and shame that might ensue
By that her death, to do her husband wrong;
1265 Such danger to resistance did belong,
    That dying fear through all her body spread;
    And who cannot abuse a body dead?

By this, mild patience bid fair Lucrece speak
To the poor counterfeit of her complaining.
1270 'My girl,' quoth she, 'on what occasion break
Those tears from thee, that down thy cheeks are
        raining?
If thou dost weep for grief of my sustaining,
    Know, gentle wench, it small avails my mood:
    If tears could help, mine own would do me good.

'But tell me, girl, when went' – and there she stay'd, 1275
Till after a deep groan – 'Tarquin from hence?'
'Madam, ere I was up,' replied the maid,
'The more to blame my sluggard negligence.
Yet with the fault I can thus far dispense:
    Myself was stirring ere the break of day, 1280
    And ere I rose was Tarquin gone away.

'But lady, if your maid may be so bold,
She would request to know your heaviness.'
'O peace,' quoth Lucrece, 'if it should be told,
The repetition cannot make it less; 1285
For more it is than I can well express,
    And that deep torture may be call'd a hell,
    When more is felt than one hath power to tell.

'Go get me hither paper, ink and pen;
Yet save that labour, for I have them here. 1290
– What should I say? – One of my husband's men
Bid thou be ready by and by to bear
A letter to my lord, my love, my dear:
    Bid him with speed prepare to carry it;
    The cause craves haste, and it will soon be writ.' 1295

Her maid is gone, and she prepares to write,
First hovering o'er the paper with her quill;
Conceit and grief an eager combat fight,
What wit sets down is blotted straight with will:
This is too curious-good, this blunt and ill. 1300
    Much like a press of people at a door,
    Throng her inventions, which shall go before.

At last she thus begins: 'Thou worthy lord
Of that unworthy wife that greeteth thee,
Health to thy person! next, vouchsafe t'afford – 1305
If ever, love, thy Lucrece thou wilt see –
Some present speed to come and visit me.
    So I commend me, from our house in grief;
    My woes are tedious, though my words are brief.'

Here folds she up the tenure of her woe, 1310
Her certain sorrow writ uncertainly.
By this short schedule Collatine may know
Her grief, but not her grief's true quality;
She dares not thereof make discovery,
    Lest he should hold it her own gross abuse, 1315
    Ere she with blood had stain'd her stain'd excuse.

Besides, the life and feeling of her passion
She hoards, to spend when he is by to hear her,
When sighs and groans and tears may grace the
        fashion
Of her disgrace, the better so to clear her 1320
From that suspicion which the world might bear her:
    To shun this blot, she would not blot the letter
    With words, till action might become them better.

To see sad sights moves more than hear them told,
For then the eye interprets to the ear
The heavy motion that it doth behold,
When every part a part of woe doth bear.
'Tis but a part of sorrow that we hear:
    Deep sounds make lesser noise than shallow fords,
    And sorrow ebbs, being blown with wind of words.

Her letter now is seal'd, and on it writ
'At Ardea to my lord with more than haste.'
The post attends, and she delivers it,
Charging the sour-fac'd groom to hie as fast
As lagging fowls before the northern blast;
    Speed more than speed but dull and slow she
        deems:
    Extremity still urgeth such extremes.

The homely villain cur'sies to her low,
And blushing on her with a steadfast eye,
Receives the scroll without or yea or no,
And forth with bashful innocence doth hie;
But they whose guilt within their bosoms lie,
    Imagine every eye beholds their blame,
    For Lucrece thought he blush'd to see her shame:

When, silly groom! God wot, it was defect
Of spirit, life and bold audacity;
Such harmless creatures have a true respect
To talk in deeds, while others saucily
Promise more speed, but do it leisurely.
    Even so this pattern of the worn-out age
    Pawn'd honest looks, but us'd no words to gage.

His kindled duty kindled her mistrust,
That two red fires in both their faces blazed;
She thought he blush'd, as knowing Tarquin's lust,
And blushing with him, wistly on him gazed.
Her earnest eye did make him more amazed;
    The more she saw the blood his cheeks replenish,
    The more she thought he spied in her some
        blemish.

But long she thinks till he return again,
And yet the duteous vassal scarce is gone;
The weary time she cannot entertain,
For now 'tis stale to sigh, to weep and groan:
So woe hath wearied woe, moan tired moan,
    That she her plaints a little while doth stay,
    Pausing for means to mourn some newer way.

At last she calls to mind where hangs a piece
Of skilful painting, made for Priam's Troy,
Before the which is drawn the power of Greece,
For Helen's rape the city to destroy,
Threat'ning cloud-kissing Ilion with annoy;
    Which the conceited painter drew so proud,
    As heaven, it seem'd, to kiss the turrets bow'd.

A thousand lamentable objects there,
In scorn of nature, art gave lifeless life:
Many a dry drop seem'd a weeping tear,
Shed for the slaughter'd husband by the wife;
The red blood reek'd to show the painter's strife,
    And dying eyes gleam'd forth their ashy lights,
    Like dying coals burnt out in tedious nights.

There might you see the labouring pioner
Begrim'd with sweat and smeared all with dust;
And from the towers of Troy there would appear
The very eyes of men through loop-holes thrust,
Gazing upon the Greeks with little lust:
    Such sweet observance in this work was had,
    That one might see those far-off eyes look sad.

In great commanders grace and majesty
You might behold, triumphing in their faces,
In youth, quick bearing and dexterity;
And here and there the painter interlaces
Pale cowards marching on with trembling paces,
    Which heartless peasants did so well resemble,
    That one would swear he saw them quake and
        tremble.

In Ajax and Ulysses, O what art
Of physiognomy might one behold!
The face of either cipher'd either's heart;
Their face their manners most expressly told.
In Ajax' eyes blunt rage and rigour roll'd,
    But the mild glance that sly Ulysses lent
    Show'd deep regard and smiling government.

There pleading might you see grave Nestor stand,
As 'twere encouraging the Greeks to fight,
Making such sober action with his hand
That it beguil'd attention, charm'd the sight;
In speech it seem'd his beard all silver white
    Wagg'd up and down, and from his lips did fly
    Thin winding breath which purl'd up to the sky.

About him were a press of gaping faces,
Which seem'd to swallow up his sound advice,
All jointly list'ning, but with several graces,
As if some mermaid did their ears entice, –
Some high, some low, the painter was so nice:
    The scalps of many almost hid behind,
    To jump up higher seem'd, to mock the mind.

Here one man's hand lean'd on another's head,
His nose being shadowed by his neighbour's ear;
Here one being throng'd bears back, all boll'n and
    red;
Another smother'd seems to pelt and swear:
And in their rage such signs of rage they bear
    As but for loss of Nestor's golden words,
    It seem'd they would debate with angry swords.

1325
1330
1335
1340
1345
1350
1355
1360
1365
1370
1375
1380
1385
1390
1395
1400
1405
1410
1415
1420

For much imaginary work was there, –
Conceit deceitful, so compact, so kind,
That for Achilles' image stood his spear
1425 Gripp'd in an armed hand; himself behind
Was left unseen, save to the eye of mind:
    A hand, a foot, a face, a leg, a head
    Stood for the whole to be imagined.

And from the walls of strong besieged Troy,
When their brave hope, bold Hector, march'd to
1430   field,
Stood many Trojan mothers sharing joy
To see their youthful sons bright weapons wield;
And to their hope they such odd action yield
    That through their light joy seemed to appear,
1435   Like bright things stain'd, a kind of heavy fear.

And from the strond of Dardan where they fought,
To Simois' reedy banks the red blood ran,
Whose waves to imitate the battle sought
With swelling ridges, and their ranks began
1440 To break upon the galled shore, and than
    Retire again, till meeting greater ranks
    They join, and shoot their foam at Simois' banks.

To this well-painted piece is Lucrece come,
To find a face where all distress is stell'd.
1445 Many she sees where cares have carved some,
But none where all distress and dolour dwell'd,
Till she despairing Hecuba beheld,
    Staring on Priam's wounds with her old eyes,
    Which bleeding under Pyrrhus' proud foot lies.

1450 In her the painter had anatomiz'd
Time's ruin, beauty's wrack, and grim care's reign;
Her cheeks with chops and wrinkles were disguis'd:
Of what she was no semblance did remain.
Her blue blood chang'd to black in every vein,
    Wanting the spring that those shrunk pipes had
1455   fed,
    Show'd life imprison'd in a body dead.

On this sad shadow Lucrece spends her eyes,
And shapes her sorrow to the beldam's woes,
Who nothing wants to answer her but cries
1460 And bitter words to ban her cruel foes;
The painter was no god to lend her those,
    And therefore Lucrece swears he did her wrong,
    To give her so much grief, and not a tongue.

'Poor instrument,' quoth she, 'without a sound,
1465 I'll tune thy woes with my lamenting tongue,
And drop sweet balm in Priam's painted wound,
And rail on Pyrrhus that hath done him wrong,
And with my tears quench Troy that burns so long,
    And with my knife scratch out the angry eyes
1470   Of all the Greeks that are thine enemies.

'Show me the strumpet that began this stir,
That with my nails her beauty I may tear!
Thy heat of lust, fond Paris, did incur
This load of wrath that burning Troy doth bear;
Thy eye kindled the fire that burneth here, 1475
    And here in Troy, for trespass of thine eye,
    The sire, the son, the dame and daughter die.

'Why should the private pleasure of some one
Become the public plague of many moe?
Let sin alone committed, light alone 1480
Upon his head that hath transgressed so;
Let guiltless souls be freed from guilty woe:
    For one's offence why should so many fall,
    To plague a private sin in general?

'Lo here weeps Hecuba, here Priam dies, 1485
Here manly Hector faints, here Troilus swounds;
Here friend by friend in bloody channel lies,
And friend to friend gives unadvised wounds;
And one man's lust these many lives confounds;
    Had doting Priam check'd his son's desire, 1490
    Troy had been bright with fame and not with
      fire.'

Here feelingly she weeps Troy's painted woes,
For sorrow, like a heavy hanging bell
Once set on ringing, with his own weight goes;
Then little strength rings out the doleful knell. 1495
So Lucrece set a-work, sad tales doth tell
    To pencill'd pensiveness and colour'd sorrow:
    She lends them words, and she their looks doth
      borrow.

She throws her eyes about the painting round,
And who she finds forlorn, she doth lament. 1500
At last she sees a wretched image bound,
That piteous looks to Phrygian shepherds lent;
His face though full of cares, yet show'd content.
    Onward to Troy with the blunt swains he goes,
    So mild that patience seem'd to scorn his woes. 1505

In him the painter labour'd with his skill
To hide deceit and give the harmless show
An humble gait, calm looks, eyes wailing still,
A brow unbent that seem'd to welcome woe,
Cheeks neither red nor pale, but mingled so 1510
    That blushing red no guilty instance gave,
    Nor ashy pale the fear that false hearts have.

But like a constant and confirmed devil,
He entertain'd a show so seeming just,
And therein so ensconc'd his secret evil, 1515
That jealousy itself could not mistrust
False creeping craft and perjury should thrust
    Into so bright a day such black-fac'd storms,
    Or blot with hell-born sin such saint-like forms.

1520 The well-skill'd workman this mild image drew
For perjur'd Sinon, whose enchanting story
The credulous old Priam after slew;
Whose words like wildfire burnt the shining glory
Of rich-built Ilion, that the skies were sorry,
1525   And little stars shot from their fixed places,
    When their glass fell, wherein they view'd their
      faces.

This picture she advisedly perus'd,
And chid the painter for his wondrous skill,
Saying some shape in Sinon's was abus'd:
1530 So fair a form lodg'd not a mind so ill.
And still on him she gaz'd, and gazing still,
    Such signs of truth in his plain face she spied,
    That she concludes the picture was belied.

'It cannot be,' quoth she, 'that so much guile,' –
1535 She would have said, – 'can lurk in such a look.'
But Tarquin's shape came in her mind the while,
And from her tongue 'can lurk' from 'cannot' took:
'It cannot be' she in that sense forsook,
    And turn'd it thus: 'It cannot be, I find,
1540   But such a face should bear a wicked mind.

'For even as subtle Sinon here is painted,
So sober sad, so weary and so mild, –
As if with grief or travail he had fainted, –
To me came Tarquin armed to beguild
1545 With outward honesty, but yet defil'd
    With inward vice. As Priam him did cherish,
    So did I Tarquin, – so my Troy did perish.

'Look, look how list'ning Priam wets his eyes,
To see those borrow'd tears that Sinon sheds!
1550 Priam, why art thou old and yet not wise?
For every tear he falls a Trojan bleeds.
His eye drops fire, no water thence proceeds:
    Those round clear pearls of his that move thy pity
    Are balls of quenchless fire to burn thy city.

1555 'Such devils steal effects from lightless hell,
For Sinon in his fire doth quake with cold;
And in that cold hot-burning fire doth dwell.
These contraries such unity do hold,
Only to flatter fools and make them bold;
1560   So Priam's trust false Sinon's tears doth flatter,
    That he finds means to burn his Troy with water.'

Here all enrag'd, such passion her assails,
That patience is quite beaten from her breast.
She tears the senseless Sinon with her nails,
1565 Comparing him to that unhappy guest
Whose deed hath made herself herself detest.
    At last she smilingly with this gives o'er:
    'Fool, fool,' quoth she, 'his wounds will not be sore.'

Thus ebbs and flows the current of her sorrow,
And time doth weary time with her complaining. 1570
She looks for night, and then she longs for morrow,
And both she thinks too long with her remaining.
Short time seems long in sorrow's sharp sustaining:
    Though woe be heavy, yet it seldom sleeps,
    And they that watch see time how slow it creeps. 1575

Which all this time hath overslipp'd her thought,
That she with painted images hath spent,
Being from the feeling of her own grief brought
By deep surmise of others' detriment,
Losing her woes in shows of discontent. 1580
    It easeth some, though none it ever cured,
    To think their dolour others have endured.

But now the mindful messenger come back
Brings home his lord and other company;
Who finds his Lucrece clad in mourning black, 1585
And round about her tear-distained eye
Blue circles stream'd, like rainbows in the sky:
    Those water-galls in her dim element
    Foretell new storms to those already spent.

Which when her sad beholding husband saw, 1590
Amazedly in her sad face he stares;
Her eyes though sod in tears, look'd red and raw,
Her lively colour kill'd with deadly cares.
He hath no power to ask her how she fares;
    Both stood like old acquaintance in a trance, 1595
    Met far from home, wond'ring each other's
      chance.

At last he takes her by the bloodless hand,
And thus begins: 'What uncouth ill event
Hath thee befall'n, that thou dost trembling stand?
Sweet love, what spite hath thy fair colour spent? 1600
Why art thou thus attir'd in discontent?
    Unmask, dear dear, this moody heaviness,
    And tell thy grief, that we may give redress.'

Three times with sighs she gives her sorrow fire,
Ere once she can discharge one word of woe. 1605
At length address'd to answer his desire,
She modestly prepares to let them know
Her honour is ta'en prisoner by the foe;
    While Collatine and his consorted lords
    With sad attention long to hear her words. 1610

And now this pale swan in her wat'ry nest
Begins the sad dirge of her certain ending:
'Few words,' quoth she, 'shall fit the trespass best,
Where no excuse can give the fault amending.
In me moe woes than words are now depending; 1615
    And my laments would be drawn out too long,
    To tell them all with one poor tired tongue.

'Then be this all the task it hath to say:
Dear husband, in the interest of thy bed
1620 A stranger came, and on that pillow lay
Where thou wast wont to rest thy weary head;
And what wrong else may be imagined
    By foul enforcement might be done to me,
    From that, alas, thy Lucrece is not free.

1625 'For in the dreadful dead of dark midnight,
With shining falchion in my chamber came
A creeping creature with a flaming light,
And softly cried "Awake, thou Roman dame,
And entertain my love; else lasting shame
1630   On thee and thine this night I will inflict,
    If thou my love's desire do contradict.

' "For some hard-favour'd groom of thine," quoth he,
"Unless thou yoke thy liking to my will,
I'll murder straight, and then I'll slaughter thee,
1635 And swear I found you where you did fulfil
The loathsome act of lust, and so did kill
    The lechers in their deed: this act will be
    My fame, and thy perpetual infamy."

'With this I did begin to start and cry,
1640 And then against my heart he set his sword,
Swearing, unless I took all patiently,
I should not live to speak another word.
So should my shame still rest upon record,
    And never be forgot in mighty Rome
1645   Th'adulterate death of Lucrece and her groom.

'Mine enemy was strong, my poor self weak,
And far the weaker with so strong a fear.
My bloody judge forbod my tongue to speak;
No rightful plea might plead for justice there.
1650 His scarlet lust came evidence to swear
    That my poor beauty had purloin'd his eyes;
    And when the judge is robb'd, the prisoner dies.

'O teach me how to make mine own excuse,
Or at the least, this refuge let me find:
1655 Though my gross blood be stain'd with this abuse,
Immaculate and spotless is my mind;
That was not forc'd, that never was inclin'd
    To accessory yieldings, but still pure
    Doth in her poison'd closet yet endure.'

1660 Lo here the hopeless merchant of this loss,
With head declin'd and voice damm'd up with woe,
With sad set eyes and wretched arms across,
From lips new-waxen pale begins to blow
The grief away that stops his answer so;
1665   But wretched as he is, he strives in vain:
    What he breathes out his breath drinks up again.

As through an arch the violent roaring tide
Outruns the eye that doth behold his haste,
Yet in the eddy boundeth in his pride
Back to the strait that forc'd him on so fast,   1670
In rage sent out, recall'd in rage being past:
    Even so his sighs, his sorrows make a saw,
    To push grief on and back the same grief draw.

Which speechless woe of his poor she attendeth,
And his untimely frenzy thus awaketh: 1675
'Dear lord, thy sorrow to my sorrow lendeth
Another power; no flood by raining slaketh;
My woe too sensible thy passion maketh
    More feeling-painful. Let it then suffice
    To drown one woe, one pair of weeping eyes.   1680

'And for my sake, when I might charm thee so,
For she that was thy Lucrece, now attend me:
Be suddenly revenged on my foe, –
Thine, mine, his own. Suppose thou dost defend me
From what is past: the help that thou shalt lend me   1685
    Comes all too late, yet let the traitor die,
    For sparing justice feeds iniquity.

'But ere I name him, you fair lords,' quoth she,
Speaking to those that came with Collatine,
'Shall plight your honourable faiths to me,   1690
With swift pursuit to 'venge this wrong of mine;
For 'tis a meritorious fair design
    To chase injustice with revengeful arms:
    Knights by their oaths should right poor ladies'
        harms.'

At this request, with noble disposition   1695
Each present lord began to promise aid,
As bound in knighthood to her imposition,
Longing to hear the hateful foe bewray'd;
But she that yet her sad task hath not said,
    The protestation stops. 'O speak,' quoth she: 1700
    'How may this forced stain be wip'd from me?

'What is the quality of my offence,
Being constrain'd with dreadful circumstance?
May my pure mind with the foul act dispense,
My low-declined honour to advance?   1705
May any terms acquit me from this chance?
    The poisoned fountain clears itself again,
    And why not I from this compelled stain?'

With this they all at once began to say,
Her body's stain her mind untainted clears,   1710
While with a joyless smile she turns away
The face, that map which deep impression bears
Of hard misfortune, carv'd in it with tears.
    'No, no,' quoth she, 'no dame hereafter living
    By my excuse shall claim excuse's giving.'   1715

Here with a sigh as if her heart would break,
She throws forth Tarquin's name. 'He, he,' she says,
But more than 'he' her poor tongue could not speak;
Till after many accents and delays,
1720　　Untimely breathings, sick and short assays,
　　　　She utters this: 'He, he, fair lords, 'tis he,
　　　　That guides this hand to give this wound to me.'

Even here she sheathed in her harmless breast
A harmful knife, that thence her soul unsheathed;
1725　That blow did bail it from the deep unrest
Of that polluted prison where it breathed.
Her contrite sighs unto the clouds bequeathed
　　　　Her winged sprite, and through her wounds doth
　　　　　　fly
　　　　Life's lasting date from cancell'd destiny.

1730　Stone-still, astonish'd with this deadly deed,
Stood Collatine and all his lordly crew,
Till Lucrece' father that beholds her bleed,
Himself on her self-slaughter'd body threw,
And from the purple fountain Brutus drew
1735　　The murd'rous knife, and as it left the place,
　　　　Her blood in poor revenge held it in chase.

And bubbling from her breast, it doth divide
In two slow rivers, that the crimson blood
Circles her body in on every side,
1740　Who like a late-sack'd island vastly stood
Bare and unpeopled in this fearful flood.
　　　　Some of her blood still pure and red remain'd,
　　　　And some look'd black, and that false Tarquin
　　　　　　stain'd.

About the mourning and congealed face
1745　Of that black blood a watery rigol goes,
Which seems to weep upon the tainted place;
And ever since, as pitying Lucrece' woes,
Corrupted blood some watery token shows,
　　　　And blood untainted still doth red abide,
1750　　Blushing at that which is so putrified.

'Daughter, dear daughter,' old Lucretius cries,
'That life was mine which thou hast here deprived;
If in the child the father's image lies,
Where shall I live now Lucrece is unlived?
1755　Thou wast not to this end from me derived:
　　　　If children predecease progenitors,
　　　　We are their offspring, and they none of ours.

'Poor broken glass, I often did behold
In thy sweet semblance my old age new-born;
1760　But now that fair fresh mirror, dim and old,
Shows me a bare-bon'd death by time outworn.
O from thy cheeks my image thou hast torn,
　　　　And shiver'd all the beauty of my glass,
　　　　That I no more can see what once I was.

'O time, cease thou thy course and last no longer,　　1765
If they surcease to be that should survive!
Shall rotten death make conquest of the stronger,
And leave the falt'ring feeble souls alive?
The old bees die, the young possess their hive;
　　　　Then live, sweet Lucrece, live again and see　　1770
　　　　Thy father die, and not thy father thee!'

By this, starts Collatine as from a dream,
And bids Lucretius give his sorrow place;
And then in key-cold Lucrece' bleeding stream
He falls, and bathes the pale fear in his face,　　1775
And counterfeits to die with her a space;
　　　　Till manly shame bids him possess his breath,
　　　　And live to be revenged on her death.

The deep vexation of his inward soul
Hath serv'd a dumb arrest upon his tongue;　　1780
Who, mad that sorrow should his use control
Or keep him from heart-easing words so long,
Begins to talk; but through his lips do throng
　　　　Weak words, so thick come in his poor heart's aid
　　　　That no man could distinguish what he said.　　1785

Yet sometime 'Tarquin' was pronounced plain,
But through his teeth, as if the name he tore.
This windy tempest, till it blow up rain,
Held back his sorrow's tide, to make it more.
At last it rains, and busy winds give o'er;　　1790
　　　　Then son and father weep with equal strife
　　　　Who should weep most, for daughter or for wife.

Then one doth call her his, the other his,
Yet neither may possess the claim they lay.
The father says, 'She's mine.' 'O mine she is,'　　1795
Replies her husband, 'do not take away
My sorrow's interest; let no mourner say
　　　　He weeps for her, for she was only mine,
　　　　And only must be wail'd by Collatine.'

'O,' quoth Lucretius, 'I did give that life　　1800
Which she too early and too late hath spill'd.'
'Woe, woe,' quoth Collatine, 'she was my wife;
I ow'd her, and 'tis mine that she hath kill'd.'
'My daughter' and 'my wife' with clamours fill'd
　　　　The dispers'd air, who holding Lucrece' life　　1805
　　　　Answer'd their cries, 'my daughter' and 'my
　　　　　　wife'.

Brutus, who pluck'd the knife from Lucrece' side,
Seeing such emulation in their woe,
Began to clothe his wit in state and pride,
Burying in Lucrece' wound his folly's show.　　1810
He with the Romans was esteemed so
　　　　As silly jeering idiots are with kings,
　　　　For sportive words and utt'ring foolish things.

But now he throws that shallow habit by,
1815 Wherein deep policy did him disguise,
And arm'd his long-hid wits advisedly,
To check the tears in Collatinus' eyes.
'Thou wronged lord of Rome,' quoth he, 'arise!
    Let my unsounded self, suppos'd a fool,
1820   Now set thy long-experienc'd wit to school.

'Why Collatine, is woe the cure for woe?
Do wounds help wounds, or grief help grievous
    deeds?
Is it revenge to give thyself a blow
For his foul act by whom thy fair wife bleeds?
1825 Such childish humour from weak minds proceeds;
    Thy wretched wife mistook the matter so,
    To slay herself that should have slain her foe.

'Courageous Roman, do not steep thy heart
In such relenting dew of lamentations;
1830 But kneel with me and help to bear thy part
To rouse our Roman gods with invocations,
That they will suffer these abominations, –
    Since Rome herself in them doth stand
        disgraced, –
    By our strong arms from forth her fair streets
        chased.

'Now by that Capitol that we adore, 1835
And by this chaste blood so unjustly stained,
By heaven's fair sun that breeds the fat earth's store,
By all our country rights in Rome maintained,
And by chaste Lucrece' soul that late complained
    Her wrongs to us, and by this bloody knife, 1840
    We will revenge the death of this true wife.'

This said, he strook his hand upon his breast,
And kiss'd the fatal knife to end his vow;
And to his protestation urg'd the rest,
Who wond'ring at him, did his words allow. 1845
Then jointly to the ground their knees they bow,
    And that deep vow which Brutus made before,
    He doth again repeat, and that they swore.

When they had sworn to this advised doom,
They did conclude to bear dead Lucrece thence, 1850
To show her bleeding body thorough Rome,
And so to publish Tarquin's foul offence;
Which being done with speedy diligence,
    The Romans plausibly did give consent
    To Tarquin's everlasting banishment. 1855

The Passionate Pilgrim

1

When my love swears that she is made of truth,
I do believe her, though I know she lies,
That she might think me some untutor'd youth,
Unskilful in the world's false forgeries.
Thus vainly thinking that she thinks me young,
Although I know my years be past the best,
I smiling credit her false-speaking tongue,
Outfacing faults in love with love's ill rest.
But wherefore says my love that she is young?
And wherefore say not I that I am old?
O, love's best habit's in a soothing tongue,
And age, in love, loves not to have years told.
    Therefore I'll lie with love, and love with me,
    Since that our faults in love thus smother'd be.

2

Two loves I have, of comfort and despair,
That like two spirits do suggest me still;
My better angel is a man, right fair,
My worser spirit a woman, colour'd ill.
To win me soon to hell, my female evil
Tempteth my better angel from my side,
And would corrupt my saint to be a devil,
Wooing his purity with her fair pride.
And whether that my angel be turn'd fiend,
Suspect I may, yet not directly tell;
For being both to me, both to each, friend,
I guess one angel in another's hell:
    The truth I shall not know, but live in doubt,
    Till my bad angel fire my good one out.

3

Did not the heavenly rhetoric of thine eye,
'Gainst whom the world could not hold argument,
Persuade my heart to this false perjury?
Vows for thee broke deserve not punishment.
A woman I forswore; but I will prove,
Thou being a goddess, I forswore not thee:
My vow was earthly, thou a heavenly love;
Thy grace being gain'd cures all disgrace in me.
My vow was breath, and breath a vapour is;
Then thou, fair sun that on this earth doth shine,
Exhal'st this vapour vow. In thee it is;
If broken then, it is no fault of mine.
    If by me broke, what fool is not so wise
    To break an oath, to win a paradise?

4

Sweet Cytherea, sitting by a brook
With young Adonis, lovely, fresh and green,
Did court the lad with many a lovely look,
Such looks as none could look but beauty's queen.
She told him stories to delight his ear;
She show'd him favours to allure his eye;
To win his heart, she touch'd him here and there;
Touches so soft still conquer chastity.
But whether unripe years did want conceit,
Or he refus'd to take her figur'd proffer,
The tender nibbler would not touch the bait,
But smile and jest at every gentle offer.
    Then fell she on her back, fair queen, and toward:
    He rose and ran away; ah fool too froward!

5

If love make me forsworn, how shall I swear to love?
O never faith could hold, if not to beauty vowed.
Though to myself forsworn, to thee I'll constant
    prove:
Those thoughts, to me like oaks, to thee like osiers
    bowed.
Study his bias leaves, and makes his book thine eyes,
Where all those pleasures live that art can
    comprehend.
If knowledge be the mark, to know thee shall suffice:
Well learned is that tongue that well can thee
    commend,
All ignorant that soul that sees thee without wonder;
Which is to me some praise, that I thy parts admire.
Thine eye love's lightning seems, thy voice his
    dreadful thunder,
Which, not to anger bent, is music and sweet fire.
    Celestial as thou art, O do not love that wrong,
    To sing heaven's praise with such an earthly
        tongue.

6

Scarce had the sun dried up the dewy morn,
And scarce the herd gone to the hedge for shade,
When Cytherea, all in love forlorn,
A longing tarriance for Adonis made
Under an osier growing by a brook,
A brook where Adon us'd to cool his spleen;
Hot was the day, she hotter that did look
For his approach, that often there had been.
Anon he comes, and throws his mantle by,
And stood stark naked on the brook's green brim:
The sun look'd on the world with glorious eye,
Yet not so wistly as this queen on him.
    He spying her, bounc'd in; whereas he stood,
    'O Jove,' quoth she, 'why was not I a flood?'

7

Fair is my love, but not so fair as fickle,
Mild as a dove, but neither true nor trusty,
Brighter than glass, and yet, as glass is, brittle,
Softer than wax, and yet as iron, rusty:
    A lily pale, with damask dye to grace her,
    None fairer, nor none falser to deface her.

Her lips to mine how often hath she joined,
Between each kiss her oaths of true love swearing!
How many tales to please me hath she coined,
Dreading my love, the loss whereof still fearing!
    Yet in the midst of all her pure protestings,
    Her faith, her oaths, her tears and all were
        jestings.

She burnt with love, as straw with fire flameth;
She burnt out love, as soon as straw out-burneth.
She fram'd the love, and yet she foil'd the framing;
She bade love last, and yet she fell a-turning.
    Was this a lover, or a lecher whether?
    Bad in the best, though excellent in neither.

8

If music and sweet poetry agree,
As they must needs, the sister and the brother,
Then must the love be great 'twixt thee and me,
Because thou lov'st the one and I the other.
Dowland to thee is dear, whose heavenly touch
Upon the lute, doth ravish human sense;
Spenser to me, whose deep conceit is such
As passing all conceit, needs no defence.
Thou lov'st to hear the sweet melodious sound
That Phoebus' lute, the queen of music, makes;
And I in deep delight am chiefly drown'd
Whenas himself to singing he betakes.
    One god is god of both, as poets feign;
    One knight loves both, and both in thee remain.

9

Fair was the morn, when the fair queen of love,
.   .   .   .
.   .   .   .
Paler for sorrow than her milk-white dove,
For Adon's sake, a youngster proud and wild;
Her stand she takes upon a steep-up hill;
Anon Adonis comes with horn and hounds.
She silly queen, with more than love's good will,
Forbade the boy he should not pass those grounds.
'Once,' quoth she, 'did I see a fair sweet youth
Here in these brakes deep-wounded with a boar,
Deep in the thigh, a spectacle of ruth!
See in my thigh,' quoth she, 'here was the sore!'
    She showed hers, he saw more wounds than one,
    And blushing fled, and left her all alone.

10

Sweet rose, fair flower, untimely pluck'd, soon vaded,
Pluck'd in the bud and vaded in the spring!
Bright orient pearl, alack too timely shaded!
Fair creature kill'd too soon by death's sharp sting!
    Like a green plum that hangs upon a tree,
    And falls, through wind, before the fall should be.

I weep for thee, and yet no cause I have,
For why thou lefts me nothing in thy will;
And yet thou lefts me more than I did crave,
For why I craved nothing of thee still.
    O yes, dear friend, I pardon crave of thee:
    Thy discontent thou didst bequeath to me.

11

Venus with Adonis sitting by her
Under a myrtle shade began to woo him;
She told the youngling how god Mars did try her,
And as he fell to her, she fell to him.
'Even thus,' quoth she, 'the warlike god embrac'd
        me,'
And then she clipp'd Adonis in her arms.
'Even thus,' quoth she, 'the warlike god unlac'd
        me,'
As if the boy should use like loving charms.
'Even thus,' quoth she, 'he seized on my lips,'
And with her lips on his did act the seizure;
And as she fetched breath, away he skips,
And would not take her meaning nor her pleasure.
    Ah, that I had my lady at this bay,
    To kiss and clip me till I run away!

12

Crabbed age and youth cannot live together:
Youth is full of pleasance, age is full of care;
Youth like summer morn, age like winter weather;
Youth like summer brave, age like winter bare.
Youth is full of sport, age's breath is short;
    Youth is nimble, age is lame;
Youth is hot and bold, age is weak and cold;
    Youth is wild and age is tame.
Age, I do abhor thee; youth, I do adore thee:
    O my love, my love is young!
Age, I do defy thee. O sweet shepherd, hie thee,
    For methinks thou stays too long.

13

Beauty is but a vain and doubtful good,
A shining gloss that vadeth suddenly,
A flower that dies when first it 'gins to bud,
A brittle glass that's broken presently:
    A doubtful good, a gloss, a glass, a flower,
    Lost, vaded, broken, dead within an hour.

And as goods lost are seld or never found,
As vaded gloss no rubbing will refresh,
As flowers dead lie withered on the ground,
As broken glass no cement can redress:
    So beauty blemish'd once, for ever lost,
    In spite of physic, painting, pain and cost.

14

Good night, good rest: ah, neither be my share!
She bade good night that kept my rest away,
And daff'd me to a cabin hang'd with care,
To descant on the doubts of my decay.
    'Farewell,' quoth she, 'and come again
        tomorrow;'
    Fare well I could not, for I supp'd with sorrow.

Yet at my parting sweetly did she smile,
In scorn or friendship, nill I conster whether:
'T may be she joy'd to jest at my exile,
'T may be again to make me wander thither:
    'Wander,' a word for shadows like myself,
    As take the pain, but cannot pluck the pelf.

Lord, how mine eyes throw gazes to the east!
My heart doth charge the watch; the morning rise
Doth cite each moving sense from idle rest.
Not daring trust the office of mine eyes,
    While Philomela sings, I sit and mark,
    And wish her lays were tuned like the lark.

For she doth welcome daylight with her ditty,
And drives away dark dreaming night.
The night so pack'd, I post unto my pretty;
Heart hath his hope and eyes their wished sight,
    Sorrow chang'd to solace, and solace mix'd with
        sorrow;
    For why, she sight, and bade me come to-morrow.

Were I with her, the night would post too soon,
But now are minutes added to the hours;
To spite me now, each minute seems a moon;
Yet not for me, shine sun to succour flowers!
    Pack night, peep day; good day, of night now
        borrow:
    Short night to night, and length thyself to
        morrow.

15

It was a lording's daughter, the fairest one of three,
That liked of her master as well as well might be,
Till looking on an Englishman, the fairest that eye
    could see,
    Her fancy fell a-turning.
Long was the combat doubtful, that love with love
    did fight,
To leave the master loveless, or kill the gallant knight;
To put in practice either, alas, it was a spite
    Unto the silly damsel!
But one must be refused; more mickle was the pain,
That nothing could be used to turn them both to gain,
For of the two the trusty knight was wounded with
    disdain:
    Alas, she could not help it!
Thus art with arms contending was victor of the day,
Which by a gift of learning did bear the maid away:
Then lullaby, the learned man hath got the lady gay;
    For now my song is ended.

16

On a day (alack the day)
Love, whose month was ever May,
Spied a blossom passing fair,
Playing in the wanton air.
Through the velvet leaves the wind
All unseen 'gan passage find,
That the lover, sick to death,
Wish'd himself the heaven's breath:
'Air,' quoth he, 'thy cheeks may blow;
Air, would I might triumph so!
But, alas, my hand hath sworn
Ne'er to pluck thee from thy throne:
Vow, alack, for youth unmeet,
Youth so apt to pluck a sweet!
 Thou for whom Jove would swear
Juno but an Ethiope were,
And deny himself for Jove,
Turning mortal for thy love.'

17

My flocks feed not, my ewes breed not,
My rams speed not, all is amiss:
Love is dying, faith's defying,
Heart's denying, causer of this.
All my merry jigs are quite forgot,
All my lady's love is lost, God wot:
Where her faith was firmly fix'd in love,
There a nay is plac'd without remove.
    One silly cross wrought all my loss:
    O frowning fortune, cursed fickle dame!
    For now I see inconstancy
    More in women than in men remain.

In black mourn I, all fears scorn I,
Love hath forlorn me, living in thrall.
Heart is bleeding, all help needing,
O cruel speeding, fraughted with gall!
My shepherd's pipe can sound no deal.
My wether's bell rings doleful knell;
My curtal dog that wont to have play'd
Plays not at all, but seems afraid.
    With sighs so deep procures to weep,
    In howling wise, to see my doleful plight.
    How sighs resound through heartless ground,
    Like a thousand vanquish'd men in bloody fight!

Clear wells spring not, sweet birds sing not,
Green plants bring not forth their dye;
Herds stands weeping, flocks all sleeping,
Nymphs back peeping fearfully.
All our pleasure known to us poor swains,
All our merry meetings on the plains,
All our evening sport from us is fled;
All our love is lost, for love is dead.
    Farewell, sweet love, thy like ne'er was
    For a sweet content, the cause of all my woe!
    Poor Corydon must live alone:
    Other help for him I see that there is none.

18

Whenas thine eye hath chose the dame,
And stall'd the deer that thou shouldst strike,
Let reason rule things worthy blame,
As well as fancy, partial might;
    Take counsel of some wiser head,
    Neither too young nor yet unwed.

And when thou com'st thy tale to tell,
Smooth not thy tongue with filed talk,
Lest she some subtle practice smell, –
A cripple soon can find a halt, –
    But plainly say thou lov'st her well,
    And set her person forth to sale.

And to her will frame all thy ways;
Spare not to spend, and chiefly there
Where thy desert may merit praise,
By ringing in thy lady's ear:
    The strongest castle, tower and town,
    The golden bullet beats it down.

Serve always with assured trust,
And in thy suit be humble true;
Unless thy lady prove unjust,
Press never thou to choose a new:
    When time shall serve, be thou not slack,
    To proffer, though she put thee back.

What though her frowning brows be bent?
Her cloudy looks will calm ere night,
And then too late she will repent,
That thus dissembled her delight;
    And twice desire, ere it be day,
    That which with scorn she put away.

What though she strive to try her strength,
And ban and brawl, and say thee nay?
Her feeble force will yield at length,
When craft hath taught her thus to say:
    'Had women been so strong as men,
    In faith, you had not had it then.'

The wiles and guiles that women work,
Dissembled with an outward show,
The tricks and toys that in them lurk,
The cock that treads them shall not know.
    Have you not heard it said full oft,
    A woman's nay doth stand for nought?

Think women still to strive with men,
To sin and never for to saint:
There is no heaven, by holy then,
When time with age shall them attaint.
    Were kisses all the joys in bed,
    One woman would another wed.

But soft, enough, – too much, – I fear
Lest that my mistress hear my song:
She will not stick to round me on th'ear,
To teach my tongue to be so long.
    Yet will she blush, here be it said,
    To hear her secrets so bewray'd.

19

Live with me and be my love,
And we will all the pleasures prove
That hills and valleys, dales and fields,
And all the craggy mountains yield.

There will we sit upon the rocks,
And see the shepherds feed their flocks,
By shallow rivers, by whose falls
Melodious birds sing madrigals.

There will I make thee a bed of roses,
With a thousand fragrant posies,
A cap of flowers, and a kirtle
Embroidered all with leaves of myrtle;

A belt of straw and ivy buds,
With coral clasps and amber studs:
And if these pleasures may thee move,
Then live with me and be my love.

LOVE'S ANSWER

If that the world and love were young,
And truth in every shepherd's tongue,
These pretty pleasures might me move
To live with thee and be thy love.

20

As it fell upon a day
In the merry month of May,
Sitting in a pleasant shade
Which a grove of myrtles made,
Beasts did leap and birds did sing,
Trees did grow and plants did spring;
Everything did banish moan,
Save the nightingale alone:
She, poor bird, as all forlorn,
Lean'd her breast up-till a thorn,
And there sung the dolefull'st ditty,
That to hear it was great pity.
'Fie, fie, fie,' now would she cry,
'Tereu, Tereu,' by and by;
That to hear her so complain,
Scarce I could from tears refrain,
For her griefs so lively shown
Made me think upon mine own.
Ah, thought I, thou mourn'st in vain!
None takes pity on thy pain.
Senseless trees they cannot hear thee,
Ruthless bears they will not cheer thee;
King Pandion he is dead,
All thy friends are lapp'd in lead,

All thy fellow birds do sing,
Careless of thy sorrowing.
Whilst as fickle fortune smiled,
Thou and I were both beguiled.
Every one that flatters thee
Is no friend in misery.
Words are easy, like the wind;
Faithful friends are hard to find.
Every man will be thy friend
Whilst thou hast wherewith to spend;
But if store of crowns be scant,
No man will supply thy want.
If that one be prodigal,
Bountiful they will him call,
And with such-like flattering:
'Pity but he were a king.'
If he be addict to vice,
Quickly him they will entice;
If to women he be bent,
They have at commandement.
But if fortune once do frown,
Then farewell his great renown:
They that fawn'd on him before,
Use his company no more.
He that is thy friend indeed,
He will help thee in thy need:
If thou sorrow, he will weep;
If thou wake, he cannot sleep:
Thus of every grief in heart
He with thee doth bear a part.
These are certain signs to know
Faithful friend from flatt'ring foe.

The Phoenix and Turtle

Let the bird of loudest lay
On the sole Arabian tree
Herald sad and trumpet be,
To whose sound chaste wings obey.

5 But thou shrieking harbinger,
Foul precurrer of the fiend,
Augur of the fever's end,
To this troop come thou not near.

From this session interdict
10 Every fowl of tyrant wing,
Save the eagle, feather'd king;
Keep the obsequy so strict.

Let the priest in surplice white,
That defunctive music can,
15 Be the death-divining swan,
Lest the requiem lack his right.

And thou treble-dated crow,
That thy sable gender mak'st
With the breath thou giv'st and tak'st,
20 'Mongst our mourners shalt thou go.

Here the anthem doth commence:
Love and constancy is dead;
Phoenix and the Turtle fled
In a mutual flame from hence.

25 So they lov'd, as love in twain
Had the essence but in one:
Two distincts, division none;
Number there in love was slain.

Hearts remote, yet not asunder;
30 Distance and no space was seen
'Twixt this Turtle and his queen:
But in them it were a wonder.

So between them love did shine
That the Turtle saw his right
35 Flaming in the Phoenix' sight;
Either was the other's mine.

Property was thus appalled
That the self was not the same:
Single nature's double name
Neither two nor one was called. 40

Reason, in itself confounded,
Saw division grow together,
To themselves yet either neither,
Simple were so well compounded:

That it cried, How true a twain 45
Seemeth this concordant one!
Love hath reason, reason none,
If what parts, can so remain.

Whereupon it made this Threne
To the Phoenix and the Dove, 50
Co-supremes and stars of love,
As Chorus to their tragic scene.

THRENOS

Beauty, truth and rarity,
Grace in all simplicity,
Here enclos'd, in cinders lie. 55

Death is now the Phoenix' nest,
And the Turtle's loyal breast
To eternity doth rest.

Leaving no posterity,
'Twas not their infirmity, 60
It was married chastity.

Truth may seem, but cannot be;
Beauty brag, but 'tis not she;
Truth and beauty buried be.

To this urn let those repair 65
That are either true or fair:
For these dead birds sigh a prayer.

All's Well That Ends Well

The only early text of *All's Well That Ends Well* is that of the 1623 Folio, in which it is the twelfth of the comedies, though it seems, judging from its tone and style, to have been written some twenty years earlier, probably about 1602-5. On 8 November 1623, along with fifteen other plays 'not formerly entered to other men', it was entered in the Stationers' Register to the Folio's principal publishers, Edward Blount and Isaac Jaggard. Neither in print nor on stage has the play enjoyed great popular success, no doubt because it lacks the joyful exuberance of many other comedies. Nonetheless it is a fascinating if disturbing play, a subtle and sober exploration of human desire and human aspirations to honour.

The story of the healing of the king and the satisfying of apparently impossible conditions by the young heroine is the stuff of folklore, but Shakespeare seems to have read it in William Painter's translation of the ninth story on the third day in Boccaccio's *Decameron*, first published in 1566 in his collection of translated *novelle*, *The Palace of Pleasure* (which was several times reprinted). The heroine, Giletta of Narbonne, cures the French king of a painful fistula and demands, as her reward, the hand of Beltramo, Count of Rossiglione. The Count flees this unwanted marriage, but Giletta finds him and 'by policy' gets pregnant by him, 'which known to her husband, he received her again, and afterwards he lived in great honour and felicity'.

Shakespeare follows this plot closely, but he has darkened its outlines and sharpened the social particularity of its characters. The callow, cowardly and ungenerous Bertram is hard to like, while Helena's single-minded pursuit of the unwilling Count is itself too insistent and self-regarding to be an unproblematic source of audience delight. The play ends well for Helena, who has got her man, and for Bertram, who will not now face the charges of murdering his wife and of seducing Diana; but the two stand together at the play's end in the knowledge that the process which has brought them there has also humiliated each. Shakespeare's distinctive additions to the story include his portrayal of the older generation, the Countess, the King, Lord Lafeu, perhaps also Lavatch, the dead Count's fool, and Diana's mother, the widow of Florence. Their beneficent support does much to win Helena a sympathy not always invited by her actions. The unmasking of Parolles – also a Shakespearean addition – reveals an unexpected humanity in the braggart sadly lacking in Bertram when he in turn is shown for what he truly is.

The ending is appropriately hedged with qualifications and conditionals: 'All yet seems well, and if it end so meet, / The bitter past, more welcome is the sweet.' The comedy has achieved the union of its lovers and the ordering of its society, as comedy must, but it has done so by questionable means, and the stability even of its subdued resolution is called into question by the King's offer to Diana: 'Choose thou thy husband and I'll pay thy dower.' The King's gesture can seem merely absurd – an invitation to the release of happy laughter at his inability to learn from experience – or, more disturbingly, it can be presented as a reassertion of the arbitrary power whose earlier exercise in imposing marriage on Bertram and Helena when both held back initiated the unhappiness only now, perhaps, resolved.

No wonder, then, that modern criticism has sought other terms than comedy to designate this play's genre. The label 'problem play' was first attached to it in 1896 by F.S. Boas, who recognized its kinship to *Measure for Measure* and *Troilus and Cressida*. These three plays, according to Boas, produced neither 'simple joy nor pain; we are excited, fascinated, perplexed, for the issues raised preclude a completely satisfactory outcome'. This is arguably the very source of the play's interest for us, as it complicates and holds up for criticism the wish-fulfilling logic of comedy itself. Helena desires to assure herself and us: 'All's well that ends well yet, / Though time seems so adverse and means unfit.' Even if the action 'ends well', the 'means unfit' by which it does so must challenge the comic claim. All is not automatically well that 'yet seems well', and dramatic actions that end well may be comic only in the most formal sense.

The Arden text is based on the 1623 First Folio.

KING	*of France*
DUKE	*of Florence*
BERTRAM	*Count of Rossillion*
LAFEW	*an old lord*
TWO LORDS, *the brothers* Dumaine	*French lords, later captains serving the Duke of Florence*
PAROLLES	*a follower of Bertram*
A French GENTLEMAN	
Rynaldo, *a* STEWARD	*to the Countess of Rossillion*
Lavatch, *a* CLOWN	*in her household*
PAGE	
MESSENGER	
COUNTESS	*of Rossillion, mother to Bertram*
HELENA	*an orphan protected by the Countess*
WIDOW Capilet	*of Florence*
DIANA	*daughter to the widow*
VIOLENTA	*neighbours and friends to the widow*
MARIANA	

Lords, Attendants, Soldiers etc., French and Florentine

All's Well That Ends Well

1.1 *Enter young* BERTRAM, *Count of Rossillion, his mother, the* COUNTESS, *and* HELENA, LORD LAFEW, *all in black.*

COUNTESS   In delivering my son from me, I bury a second husband.

BERTRAM   And I in going, madam, weep o'er my father's death anew; but I must attend his majesty's command, to whom I am now in ward, evermore in subjection.

LAFEW   You shall find of the king a husband, madam; you, sir, a father. He that so generally is at all times good must of necessity hold his virtue to you, whose worthiness would stir it up where it wanted, rather than lack it where there is such abundance.

COUNTESS   What hope is there of his majesty's amendment?

LAFEW   He hath abandon'd his physicians, madam; under whose practices he hath persecuted time with hope, and finds no other advantage in the process but only the losing of hope by time.

COUNTESS   This young gentlewoman had a father – O that 'had', how sad a passage 'tis! – whose skill was almost as great as his honesty; had it stretch'd so far, would have made nature immortal, and death should have play for lack of work. Would for the king's sake he were living! I think it would be the death of the king's disease.

LAFEW   How call'd you the man you speak of, madam?

COUNTESS   He was famous, sir, in his profession, and it was his great right to be so: Gerard de Narbon.

LAFEW   He was excellent indeed, madam; the king very lately spoke of him admiringly – and mourningly; he was skilful enough to have liv'd still, if knowledge could be set up against mortality.

BERTRAM   What is it, my good lord, the king languishes of?

LAFEW   A fistula, my lord.

BERTRAM   I heard not of it before.

LAFEW   I would it were not notorious. Was this gentlewoman the daughter of Gerard de Narbon?

COUNTESS   His sole child, my lord, and bequeathed to my overlooking. I have those hopes of her good that her education promises her dispositions she inherits – which makes fair gifts fairer; for where an unclean mind carries virtuous qualities, there commendations go with pity; they are virtues and traitors too. In her they are the better for their simpleness: she derives her honesty and achieves her goodness.

LAFEW   Your commendations, madam, get from her tears.

COUNTESS   'Tis the best brine a maiden can season her praise in. The remembrance of her father never approaches her heart but the tyranny of her sorrows takes all livelihood from her cheek. No more of this, Helena; go to, no more; lest it be rather thought you affect a sorrow than to have –

HELENA   I do affect a sorrow indeed, but I have it too.

LAFEW   Moderate lamentation is the right of the dead; excessive grief the enemy to the living.   55

COUNTESS   If the living be enemy to the grief, the excess makes it soon mortal.

BERTRAM   Madam, I desire your holy wishes.

LAFEW   How understand we that?

COUNTESS
  Be thou bless'd, Bertram, and succeed thy father   60
  In manners as in shape! Thy blood and virtue
  Contend for empire in thee, and thy goodness
  Share with thy birthright! Love all, trust a few,
  Do wrong to none. Be able for thine enemy
  Rather in power than use, and keep thy friend   65
  Under thy own life's key. Be check'd for silence,
  But never tax'd for speech. What heaven more will,
  That thee may furnish and my prayers pluck down,
  Fall on thy head! Farewell. My lord,
  'Tis an unseason'd courtier; good my lord,   70
  Advise him.

LAFEW   He cannot want the best
  That shall attend his love.

COUNTESS   Heaven bless him! Farewell, Bertram. *Exit.*

BERTRAM   The best wishes that can be forg'd in your thoughts be servants to you! [*to Helena*] Be comfort-   75
able to my mother, your mistress, and make much of her.

LAFEW   Farewell, pretty lady; you must hold the credit of your father.   *Exeunt Bertram and Lafew.*

HELENA   O, were that all! I think not on my father,   80
  And these great tears grace his remembrance more
  Than those I shed for him. What was he like?
  I have forgot him; my imagination
  Carries no favour in't but Bertram's.
  I am undone; there is no living, none,   85
  If Bertram be away; 'twere all one
  That I should love a bright particular star
  And think to wed it, he is so above me.
  In his bright radiance and collateral light
  Must I be comforted, not in his sphere.   90
  Th'ambition in my love thus plagues itself:
  The hind that would be mated by the lion
  Must die for love. 'Twas pretty, though a plague,
  To see him every hour; to sit and draw
  His arched brows, his hawking eye, his curls,   95
  In our heart's table – heart too capable
  Of every line and trick of his sweet favour.
  But now he's gone, and my idolatrous fancy
  Must sanctify his relics. Who comes here?

Enter PAROLLES.

  One that goes with him; I love him for his sake,   100
  And yet I know him a notorious liar,
  Think him a great way fool, solely a coward;
  Yet these fix'd evils sit so fit in him
  That they take place when virtue's steely bones
  Looks bleak i'th' cold wind; withal, full oft we see   105
  Cold wisdom waiting on superfluous folly.

PAROLLES   Save you, fair queen!

HELENA   And you, monarch!

PAROLLES   No.

110 HELENA   And no.

PAROLLES   Are you meditating on virginity?

HELENA   Ay. You have some stain of soldier in you; let me ask you a question. Man is enemy to virginity; how may we barricado it against him?

115 PAROLLES   Keep him out.

HELENA   But he assails; and our virginity, though valiant, in the defence yet is weak. Unfold to us some warlike resistance.

PAROLLES   There is none. Man setting down before you
120 will undermine you and blow you up.

HELENA   Bless our poor virginity from underminers and blowers-up! Is there no military policy how virgins might blow up men?

PAROLLES   Virginity being blown down man will
125 quicklier be blown up; marry, in blowing him down again, with the breach yourselves made you lose your city. It is not politic in the commonwealth of nature to preserve virginity. Loss of virginity is rational increase, and there was never virgin got till virginity
130 was first lost. That you were made of is mettle to make virgins. Virginity, by being once lost, may be ten times found; by being ever kept it is ever lost. 'Tis too cold a companion. Away with't!

HELENA   I will stand for't a little, though therefore I die
135 a virgin.

PAROLLES   There's little can be said in't; 'tis against the rule of nature. To speak on the part of virginity is to accuse your mothers, which is most infallible disobedience. He that hangs himself is a virgin;
140 virginity murthers itself, and should be buried in highways out of all sanctified limit, as a desperate offendress against nature. Virginity breeds mites, much like a cheese; consumes itself to the very paring, and so dies with feeding his own stomach. Besides,
145 virginity is peevish, proud, idle, made of self-love which is the most inhibited sin in the canon. Keep it not; you cannot choose but lose by't. Out with't! Within the year it will make itself two, which is a goodly increase, and the principal itself not much the
150 worse. Away with't!

HELENA   How might one do, sir, to lose it to her own liking?

PAROLLES   Let me see. Marry, ill, to like him that ne'er it likes. 'Tis a commodity will lose the gloss with lying;
155 the longer kept, the less worth. Off with't while 'tis vendible; answer the time of request. Virginity, like an old courtier, wears her cap out of fashion, richly suited but unsuitable, just like the brooch and the toothpick, which wear not now. Your date is better in your pie
160 and your porridge than in your cheek; and your virginity, your old virginity, is like one of our French wither'd pears: it looks ill, it eats drily; marry, 'tis a wither'd pear; it was formerly better; marry, yet 'tis a wither'd pear. Will you anything with it?

HELENA   Not my virginity; yet . . .   165
There shall your master have a thousand loves,
A mother, and a mistress, and a friend,
A phoenix, captain, and an enemy,
A guide, a goddess, and a sovereign,
A counsellor, a traitress, and a dear;   170
His humble ambition, proud humility,
His jarring-concord, and his discord-dulcet,
His faith, his sweet disaster; with a world
Of pretty, fond, adoptious christendoms
That blinking Cupid gossips. Now shall he –   175
I know not what he shall. God send him well!
The court's a learning-place, and he is one –

PAROLLES   What one, i'faith?

HELENA   That I wish well. 'Tis pity –

PAROLLES   What's pity?   180

HELENA   That wishing well had not a body in't
Which might be felt, that we, the poorer born,
Whose baser stars do shut us up in wishes,
Might with effects of them follow our friends,
And show what we alone must think, which never   185
Returns us thanks.

Enter Page.

PAGE   Monsieur Parolles, my lord calls for you.   *Exit.*

PAROLLES   Little Helen, farewell. If I can remember thee I will think of thee at court.

HELENA   Monsieur Parolles, you were born under a   190
charitable star.

PAROLLES   Under Mars, I.

HELENA   I especially think under Mars.

PAROLLES   Why under Mars?

HELENA   The wars hath so kept you under, that you   195
must needs be born under Mars.

PAROLLES   When he was predominant.

HELENA   When he was retrograde, I think rather.

PAROLLES   Why think you so?

HELENA   You go so much backward when you fight.   200

PAROLLES   That's for advantage.

HELENA   So is running away, when fear proposes the safety; but the composition that your valour and fear makes in you is a virtue of a good wing, and I like the wear well.   205

PAROLLES   I am so full of businesses I cannot answer thee acutely. I will return perfect courtier; in the which my instruction shall serve to naturalize thee, so thou wilt be capable of a courtier's counsel, and understand what advice shall thrust upon thee; else   210
thou diest in thine unthankfulness, and thine ignorance makes thee away. Farewell. When thou hast leisure, say thy prayers; when thou hast none, remember thy friends. Get thee a good husband, and use him as he uses thee. So, farewell.   *Exit.*   215

HELENA   Our remedies oft in ourselves do lie,
Which we ascribe to heaven; the fated sky
Gives us free scope; only doth backward pull
Our slow designs when we ourselves are dull.

220 What power is it which mounts my love so high,
That makes me see, and cannot feed mine eye?
The mightiest space in fortune nature brings
To join like likes, and kiss like native things.
Impossible be strange attempts to those
225 That weigh their pains in sense, and do suppose
What hath been cannot be. Who ever strove
To show her merit that did miss her love?
The king's disease – my project may deceive me,
But my intents are fix'd, and will not leave me.   *Exit.*

1.2 *Flourish cornets. Enter the* KING *of France with letters,*
and divers attendants.

KING   The Florentines and Senoys are by th'ears;
Have fought with equal fortune, and continue
A braving war.
1 LORD   So 'tis reported, sir.
KING   Nay, 'tis most credible. We here receive it
5 A certainty, vouch'd from our cousin Austria,
With caution that the Florentine will move us
For speedy aid; wherein our dearest friend
Prejudicates the business, and would seem
To have us make denial.
1 LORD   His love and wisdom,
10 Approv'd so to your majesty, may plead
For amplest credence.
KING   He hath arm'd our answer,
And Florence is denied before he comes;
Yet, for our gentlemen that mean to see
The Tuscan service, freely have they leave
To stand on either part.
2 LORD   It well may serve
A nursery to our gentry, who are sick
For breathing and exploit.
KING   What's he comes here?

Enter BERTRAM, LAFEW *and* PAROLLES.

1 LORD   It is the Count Rossillion, my good lord,
Young Bertram.
KING   Youth, thou bear'st thy father's face;
20 Frank nature, rather curious than in haste,
Hath well compos'd thee. Thy father's moral parts
Mayest thou inherit too! Welcome to Paris.
BERTRAM   My thanks and duty are your majesty's.
KING   I would I had that corporal soundness now,
25 As when thy father and myself in friendship
First tried our soldiership. He did look far
Into the service of the time, and was
Discipled of the bravest. He lasted long,
But on us both did haggish age steal on,
30 And wore us out of act. It much repairs me
To talk of your good father; in his youth
He had the wit which I can well observe
Today in our young lords; but they may jest
Till their own scorn return to them unnoted
35 Ere they can hide their levity in honour.

So like a courtier, contempt nor bitterness
Were in his pride or sharpness; if they were,
His equal had awak'd them, and his honour,
Clock to itself, knew the true minute when
40 Exception bid him speak, and at this time
His tongue obey'd his hand. Who were below him
He us'd as creatures of another place,
And bow'd his eminent top to their low ranks,
Making them proud of his humility
45 In their poor praise he humbled. Such a man
Might be a copy to these younger times;
Which, followed well, would demonstrate them now
But goers backward.
BERTRAM   His good remembrance, sir,
Lies richer in your thoughts than on his tomb;
50 So in approof lives not his epitaph
As in your royal speech.
KING   Would I were with him! He would always say –
Methinks I hear him now; his plausive words
He scatter'd not in ears, but grafted them
55 To grow there and to bear – 'Let me not live',
(This his good melancholy oft began
On the catastrophe and heel of pastime,
When it was out) 'Let me not live', quoth he,
'After my flame lacks oil, to be the snuff
60 Of younger spirits, whose apprehensive senses
All but new things disdain; whose judgments are
Mere fathers of their garments; whose constancies
Expire before their fashions'. This he wish'd.
I, after him, do after him wish too,
65 Since I nor wax nor honey can bring home,
I quickly were dissolved from my hive
To give some labourers room.
2 LORD   You're loved, sir;
They that least lend it you shall lack you first.
KING   I fill a place, I know't. How long is't, count,
70 Since the physician at your father's died?
He was much fam'd.
BERTRAM   Some six months since, my lord.
KING   If he were living I would try him yet –
Lend me an arm – the rest have worn me out
With several applications; nature and sickness
75 Debate it at their leisure. Welcome, count;
My son's no dearer.
BERTRAM   Thank your majesty.
Exeunt. Flourish.

1.3   *Enter* COUNTESS, Steward *and* Clown.

COUNTESS   I will now hear. What say you of this
gentlewoman?
STEWARD   Madam, the care I have had to even your
content I wish might be found in the calendar of my
5 past endeavours; for then we wound our modesty, and
make foul the clearness of our deservings, when of
ourselves we publish them.
COUNTESS   What does this knave here? get you gone,

93

sirrah. The complaints I have heard of you I do not all
believe; 'tis my slowness that I do not; for I know you
lack not folly to commit them and have ability enough
to make such knaveries yours.

CLOWN   'Tis not unknown to you, madam, I am a poor
fellow.

COUNTESS   Well, sir.

CLOWN   No, madam, 'tis not so well that I am poor,
though many of the rich are damn'd; but if I may have
your ladyship's good will to go to the world, Isbel the
woman and I will do as we may.

COUNTESS   Wilt thou needs be a beggar?

CLOWN   I do beg your good will in this case.

COUNTESS   In what case?

CLOWN   In Isbel's case and mine own. Service is no
heritage, and I think I shall never have the blessing of
God till I have issue a' my body; for they say barnes
are blessings.

COUNTESS   Tell me thy reason why thou wilt marry.

CLOWN   My poor body, madam, requires it; I am driven
on by the flesh, and he must needs go that the devil
drives.

COUNTESS   Is this all your worship's reason?

CLOWN   Faith, madam, I have other holy reasons, such
as they are.

COUNTESS   May the world know them?

CLOWN   I have been, madam, a wicked creature, as you
and all flesh and blood are, and indeed I do marry that
I may repent.

COUNTESS   Thy marriage, sooner than thy wickedness.

CLOWN   I am out a' friends, madam, and I hope to have
friends for my wife's sake.

COUNTESS   Such friends are thine enemies, knave.

CLOWN   Y'are shallow, madam, in great friends; for the
knaves come to do that for me which I am aweary of.
He that ears my land spares my team, and gives me
leave to in the crop; if I be his cuckold, he's my
drudge. He that comforts my wife is the cherisher of
my flesh and blood; he that cherishes my flesh and
blood loves my flesh and blood; he that loves my flesh
and blood is my friend; ergo, he that kisses my wife is
my friend. If men could be contented to be what they
are, there were no fear in marriage; for young Charbon
the puritan and old Poysam the papist, howsome'er
their hearts are sever'd in religion, their heads are both
one; they may jowl horns together like any deer i' th'
herd.

COUNTESS   Wilt thou ever be a foul-mouth'd and
calumnious knave?

CLOWN   A prophet I, madam; and I speak the truth the
next way:
        For I the ballad will repeat
            Which men full true shall find:
        Your marriage comes by destiny,
            Your cuckoo sings by kind.

COUNTESS   Get you gone, sir; I'll talk with you more anon.

STEWARD   May it please you, madam, that he bid Helen
come to you; of her I am to speak.

COUNTESS   Sirrah, tell my gentlewoman I would speak
with her – Helen I mean.

CLOWN   Was this fair face the cause, quoth she,
            Why the Grecians sacked Troy?
        Fond done, done fond,
            Was this King Priam's joy?
        With that she sighed as she stood,
        With that she sighed as she stood,
            And gave this sentence then:
        Among nine bad if one be good,
        Among nine bad if one be good,
            There's yet one good in ten.

COUNTESS   What, one good in ten? You corrupt the
song, sirrah.

CLOWN   One good woman in ten, madam, which is a
purifying a'th' song. Would God would serve the
world so all the year! We'd find no fault with the tithe-
woman if I were the parson. One in ten, quoth'a! And
we might have a good woman born but or every
blazing star or at an earthquake, 'twould mend the
lottery well; a man may draw his heart out ere 'a pluck
one.

COUNTESS   You'll be gone, sir knave, and do as I
command you?

CLOWN   That man should be at woman's command, and
yet no hurt done! Though honesty be no puritan, yet it
will do no hurt; it will wear the surplice of humility
over the black gown of a big heart. I am going, forsooth;
the business is for Helen to come hither.   *Exit.*

COUNTESS   Well, now.

STEWARD   I know, madam, you love your gentlewoman
entirely.

COUNTESS   Faith, I do. Her father bequeath'd her to me,
and she herself, without other advantage, may lawfully
make title to as much love as she finds; there is more
owing her than is paid, and more shall be paid her than
she'll demand.

STEWARD   Madam, I was very late more near her than I
think she wish'd me; alone she was, and did
communicate to herself her own words to her own
ears; she thought, I dare vow for her, they touch'd not
any stranger sense. Her matter was, she loved your
son. Fortune, she said, was no goddess, that had put
such difference betwixt their two estates; Love no god,
that would not extend his might only where qualities
were level; Diana no queen of virgins, that would
suffer her poor knight surpris'd without rescue in the
first assault or ransom afterward. This she deliver'd in
the most bitter touch of sorrow that ere I heard virgin
exclaim in, which I held my duty speedily to acquaint
you withal, sithence, in the loss that may happen, it
concerns you something to know it.

COUNTESS   You have discharg'd this honestly; keep it to
yourself. Many likelihoods inform'd me of this before,
which hung so tott'ring in the balance that I could
neither believe nor misdoubt. Pray you leave me; stall

this in your bosom; and I thank you for your honest
care. I will speak with you further anon. *Exit Steward.*

Enter HELENA.

125 COUNTESS   Even so it was with me when I was young;
If ever we are nature's, these are ours; this thorn
Doth to our rose of youth rightly belong;
Our blood to us, this to our blood is born:
It is the show and seal of nature's truth,
130 Where love's strong passion is impress'd in youth.
By our remembrances of days foregone,
Such were our faults, or then we thought them none.
Her eye is sick on't; I observe her now.
HELENA   What is your pleasure, madam?
COUNTESS   You know, Helen,
135 I am a mother to you.
HELENA   Mine honourable mistress.
COUNTESS   Nay, a mother.
Why not a mother? When I said 'a mother',
Methought you saw a serpent. What's in 'mother'
That you start at it? I say I am your mother,
140 And put you in the catalogue of those
That were enwombed mine. 'Tis often seen
Adoption strives with nature, and choice breeds
A native slip to us from foreign seeds.
You ne'er oppress'd me with a mother's groan,
145 Yet I express to you a mother's care.
God's mercy, maiden! does it curd thy blood
To say I am thy mother? what's the matter,
That this distempered messenger of wet,
The many-colour'd Iris, rounds thine eye?
– Why, that you are my daughter?
150 HELENA   That I am not.
COUNTESS   I say I am your mother.
HELENA   Pardon, madam;
The Count Rossillion cannot be my brother.
I am from humble, he from honoured name;
No note upon my parents, his all noble.
155 My master, my dear lord he is; and I
His servant live, and will his vassal die.
He must not be my brother.
COUNTESS   Nor I your mother?
HELENA
You are my mother, madam; would you were –
So that my lord your son were not my brother –
160 Indeed my mother! or were you both our mothers
I care no more for than I do for heaven,
So I were not his sister. Can't no other
But, I your daughter, he must be my brother?
COUNTESS
Yes, Helen, you might be my daughter-in-law.
165 God shield you mean it not! daughter and mother
So strive upon your pulse. What! pale again?
My fear hath catch'd your fondness; now I see
The myst'ry of your loneliness, and find
Your salt tears' head. Now to all sense 'tis gross:
170 You love my son. Invention is asham'd

Against the proclamation of thy passion
To say thou dost not. Therefore tell me true;
But tell me then, 'tis so; for, look, thy cheeks
Confess it t'one to th'other, and thine eyes
See it so grossly shown in thy behaviours   175
That in their kind they speak it; only sin
And hellish obstinacy tie thy tongue,
That truth should be suspected. Speak, is't so?
If it be so, you have wound a goodly clew;
If it be not, forswear't; howe'er, I charge thee,   180
As heaven shall work in me for thine avail,
To tell me truly.
HELENA   Good madam, pardon me.
COUNTESS   Do you love my son?
HELENA   Your pardon, noble mistress.
COUNTESS   Love you my son?
HELENA   Do not you love him, madam?
COUNTESS   Go not about; my love hath in't a bond   185
Whereof the world takes note. Come, come, disclose
The state of your affection, for your passions
Have to the full appeach'd.
HELENA   Then I confess,
Here on my knee, before high heaven and you,
That before you, and next unto high heaven,   190
I love your son.
My friends were poor, but honest; so's my love.
Be not offended, for it hurts not him
That he is lov'd of me; I follow him not
By any token of presumptuous suit,   195
Nor would I have him till I do deserve him;
Yet never know how that desert should be.
I know I love in vain, strive against hope;
Yet in this captious and inteemable sieve
I still pour in the waters of my love   200
And lack not to lose still. Thus, Indian-like,
Religious in mine error, I adore
The sun that looks upon his worshipper
But knows of him no more. My dearest madam,
Let not your hate encounter with my love,   205
For loving where you do; but if yourself,
Whose aged honour cites a virtuous youth,
Did ever, in so true a flame of liking,
Wish chastely and love dearly, that your Dian
Was both herself and love – O then, give pity   210
To her whose state is such that cannot choose
But lend and give where she is sure to lose;
That seeks not to find that her search implies,
But riddle-like lives sweetly where she dies!
COUNTESS
Had you not lately an intent – speak truly –   215
To go to Paris?
HELENA   Madam, I had.
COUNTESS   Wherefore? tell true.
HELENA   I will tell truth, by grace itself I swear.
You know my father left me some prescriptions
Of rare and prov'd effects, such as his reading
And manifest experience had collected   220

For general sovereignty; and that he will'd me
In heedfull'st reservation to bestow them,
As notes whose faculties inclusive were
More than they were in note. Amongst the rest
225   There is a remedy, approv'd, set down,
To cure the desperate languishings whereof
The king is render'd lost.
COUNTESS   This was your motive
For Paris was it? Speak.
HELENA   My lord your son made me to think of this;
230   Else Paris and the medicine and the king
Had from the conversation of my thoughts
Haply been absent then.
COUNTESS   But think you, Helen,
If you should tender your supposed aid,
He would receive it? He and his physicians
235   Are of a mind; he, that they cannot help him;
They, that they cannot help. How shall they credit
A poor unlearned virgin, when the schools,
Embowel'd of their doctrine, have left off
The danger to itself?
HELENA   There's something in't
240   More than my father's skill, which was the great'st
Of his profession, that his good receipt
Shall for my legacy be sanctified
By th' luckiest stars in heaven; and would your
        honour
But give me leave to try success, I'd venture
245   The well-lost life of mine on his grace's cure
By such a day, an hour.
COUNTESS   Dost thou believe't?
HELENA   Ay, madam, knowingly.
COUNTESS
Why, Helen, thou shalt have my leave and love,
Means and attendants, and my loving greetings
250   To those of mine in court. I'll stay at home
And pray God's blessing into thy attempt.
Be gone tomorrow; and be sure of this,
What I can help thee to, thou shalt not miss.   *Exeunt.*

2.1 *Enter the* KING *with divers young* Lords *taking leave
for the Florentine war;* BERTRAM *and* PAROLLES;
attendants. Flourish cornets.

KING   Farewell, young lords; these warlike principles
Do not throw from you; and you, my lords, farewell;
Share the advice betwixt you; if both gain all,
The gift doth stretch itself as 'tis receiv'd,
And is enough for both.
5   1 LORD   'Tis our hope, sir,
After well-ent'red soldiers, to return
And find your grace in health.
KING   No, no, it cannot be; and yet my heart
Will not confess he owes the malady
10   That doth my life besiege. Farewell, young lords.
Whether I live or die, be you the sons
Of worthy Frenchmen; let Higher Italy –
Those bated that inherit but the fall

Of the last monarchy – see that you come
Not to woo honour, but to wed it, when   15
The bravest questant shrinks: find what you seek,
That fame may cry you loud. I say farewell.
1 LORD   Health at your bidding serve your majesty!
KING   Those girls of Italy, take heed of them;
They say our French lack language to deny   20
If they demand; beware of being captives
Before you serve.
BOTH LORDS   Our hearts receive your warnings.
KING   Farewell. [*to some Lords*] Come hither to me.
        [*Retires.*]
1 LORD   O my sweet lord, that you will stay behind us!
PAROLLES   'Tis not his fault, the spark.
2 LORD   O, 'tis brave wars!   25
PAROLLES   Most admirable! I have seen those wars.
BERTRAM   I am commanded here, and kept a coil with
        'Too young', and 'The next year' and ' 'Tis too
        early'.
PAROLLES
And thy mind stand to't, boy, steal away bravely.
BERTRAM   I shall stay here the forehorse to a smock,   30
Creaking my shoes on the plain masonry,
Till honour be bought up, and no sword worn
But one to dance with. By heaven, I'll steal away!
1 LORD   There's honour in the theft.
PAROLLES   Commit it, count.
2 LORD   I am your accessary; and so farewell.   35
BERTRAM
I grow to you, and our parting is a tortur'd body.
1 LORD   Farewell, captain.
2 LORD   Sweet Monsieur Parolles!
PAROLLES   Noble heroes, my sword and yours are kin.
Good sparks and lustrous, a word, good metals. You   40
shall find in the regiment of the Spinii one Captain
Spurio, with his cicatrice, an emblem of war, here on
his sinister cheek; it was this very sword entrench'd it.
Say to him I live, and observe his reports for me.
1 LORD   We shall, noble captain.   *Exeunt Lords.*   45
PAROLLES   Mars dote on you for his novices! [*to
Bertram*] What will ye do?
BERTRAM   Stay the king.
PAROLLES   Use a more spacious ceremony to the noble
lords; you have restrain'd yourself within the list of too   50
cold an adieu. Be more expressive to them, for they
wear themselves in the cap of the time; there do
muster true gait, eat, speak, and move, under the
influence of the most receiv'd star; and though the
devil lead the measure, such are to be followed. After   55
them, and take a more dilated farewell.
BERTRAM   And I will do so.
PAROLLES   Worthy fellows, and like to prove most
sinewy sword-men.   *Exeunt Bertram and Parolles.*

        Enter LAFEW. *The* KING *comes forward.*

LAFEW [*kneeling*]
Pardon, my lord, for me and for my tidings.   60

KING   I'll fee thee to stand up.

LAFEW   Then here's a man stands that has brought his
    pardon.
    I would you had kneel'd, my lord, to ask me mercy,
    And that at my bidding you could so stand up.

KING   I would I had; so I had broke thy pate
    And ask'd thee mercy for't.

LAFEW   Good faith, across!
    But, my good lord, 'tis thus: will you be cur'd
    Of your infirmity?

KING   No.

LAFEW   O, will you eat
    No grapes, my royal fox? Yes, but you will
    My noble grapes, and if my royal fox
    Could reach them. I have seen a medicine
    That's able to breathe life into a stone,
    Quicken a rock, and make you dance canary
    With sprightly fire and motion; whose simple touch
    Is powerful to araise King Pippen, nay,
    To give great Charlemain a pen in's hand
    And write to her a love-line.

KING   What 'her' is this?

LAFEW   Why, Doctor She! My lord, there's one arriv'd,
    If you will see her. Now by my faith and honour,
    If seriously I may convey my thoughts
    In this my light deliverance, I have spoke
    With one that in her sex, her years, profession,
    Wisdom and constancy, hath amaz'd me more
    Than I dare blame my weakness. Will you see her,
    For that is her demand, and know her business?
    That done, laugh well at me.

KING   Now, good Lafew,
    Bring in the admiration that we with thee
    May spend our wonder too, or take off thine
    By wond'ring how thou took'st it.

LAFEW   Nay, I'll fit you,
    And not be all day neither. [*Lafew goes to the door.*]

KING   Thus he his special nothing ever prologues.

LAFEW   Nay, come your ways.

Enter HELENA.

KING   This haste hath wings indeed.

LAFEW   Nay, come your ways.
    This is his majesty; say your mind to him.
    A traitor you do look like, but such traitors
    His majesty seldom fears; I am Cressid's uncle
    That dare leave two together. Fare you well.   *Exit.*

KING   Now, fair one, does your business follow us?

HELENA   Ay, my good lord.
    Gerard de Narbon was my father,
    In what he did profess, well found.

KING   I knew him.

HELENA
    The rather will I spare my praises towards him;
    Knowing him is enough. On's bed of death
    Many receipts he gave me; chiefly one,
    Which, as the dearest issue of his practice,

And of his old experience th'only darling,
He bade me store up as a triple eye,
Safer than mine own two; more dear I have so,
And hearing your high majesty is touch'd
With that malignant cause, wherein the honour   110
Of my dear father's gift stands chief in power,
I come to tender it and my appliance,
With all bound humbleness.

KING   We thank you, maiden;
    But may not be so credulous of cure,
    When our most learned doctors leave us, and   115
    The congregated college have concluded
    That labouring art can never ransom nature
    From her inaidible estate. I say we must not
    So stain our judgment or corrupt our hope,
    To prostitute our past-cure malady   120
    To empirics, or to dissever so
    Our great self and our credit, to esteem
    A senseless help, when help past sense we deem.

HELENA   My duty then shall pay me for my pains.
    I will no more enforce mine office on you,   125
    Humbly entreating from your royal thoughts
    A modest one to bear me back again.

KING   I cannot give thee less, to be call'd grateful;
    Thou thought'st to help me, and such thanks I give
    As one near death to those that wish him live.   130
    But what at full I know, thou know'st no part;
    I knowing all my peril, thou no art.

HELENA   What I can do can do no hurt to try,
    Since you set up your rest 'gainst remedy.
    He that of greatest works is finisher   135
    Oft does them by the weakest minister.
    So holy writ in babes hath judgment shown,
    When judges have been babes. Great floods have flown
    From simple sources, and great seas have dried
    When miracles have by the great'st been denied.   140
    Oft expectation fails, and most oft there
    Where most it promises, and oft it hits
    Where hope is coldest and despair most fits.

KING   I must not hear thee. Fare thee well, kind maid.
    Thy pains, not us'd, must by thyself be paid;   145
    Proffers not took reap thanks for their reward.

HELENA   Inspired merit so by breath is barr'd.
    It is not so with Him that all things knows
    As 'tis with us that square our guess by shows;
    But most it is presumption in us when   150
    The help of heaven we count the act of men.
    Dear sir, to my endeavours give consent;
    Of heaven, not me, make an experiment.
    I am not an impostor, that proclaim
    Myself against the level of mine aim,   155
    But know I think, and think I know most sure,
    My art is not past power, nor you past cure.

KING   Art thou so confident? Within what space
    Hop'st thou my cure?

HELENA   The greatest Grace lending grace,
    Ere twice the horses of the sun shall bring   160

Their fiery coacher his diurnal ring,
Ere twice in murk and occidental damp
Moist Hesperus hath quench'd her sleepy lamp,
Or four and twenty times the pilot's glass
165   Hath told the thievish minutes how they pass,
What is infirm from your sound parts shall fly,
Health shall live free and sickness freely die.

KING Upon thy certainty and confidence
What dar'st thou venture?

HELENA   Tax of impudence,
170   A strumpet's boldness, a divulged shame,
Traduc'd by odious ballads; my maiden's name
Sear'd otherwise; ne worse of worst, extended
With vildest torture, let my life be ended.

KING Methinks in thee some blessed spirit doth speak
175   His powerful sound within an organ weak;
And what impossibility would slay
In common sense, sense saves another way.
Thy life is dear, for all that life can rate
Worth name of life in thee hath estimate:
180   Youth, beauty, wisdom, courage – all
That happiness and prime can happy call.
Thou this to hazard needs must intimate
Skill infinite, or monstrous desperate.
Sweet practiser, thy physic I will try,
185   That ministers thine own death if I die.

HELENA If I break time, or flinch in property
Of what I spoke, unpitied let me die,
And well deserv'd. Not helping, death's my fee;
But if I help, what do you promise me?

KING Make thy demand.
190 HELENA   But will you make it even?

KING Ay, by my sceptre and my hopes of heaven.

HELENA Then shalt thou give me with thy kingly hand
What husband in thy power I will command:
Exempted be from me the arrogance
195   To choose from forth the royal blood of France
My low and humble name to propagate
With any branch or image of thy state;
But such a one, thy vassal, whom I know
Is free for me to ask, thee to bestow.

200 KING Here is my hand; the premises observ'd,
Thy will by my performance shall be serv'd;
So make the choice of thy own time, for I,
Thy resolv'd patient, on thee still rely.
More should I question thee, and more I must,
205   Though more to know could not be more to trust:
From whence thou cam'st, how tended on; but rest,
Unquestion'd, welcome, and undoubted bless'd.
Give me some help here, ho! If thou proceed
As high as word, my deed shall match thy deed.

Flourish. Exeunt.

2.2   *Enter* COUNTESS *and* Clown.

COUNTESS Come on, sir; I shall now put you to the
height of your breeding.

CLOWN I will show myself highly fed and lowly taught.
I know my business is but to the court.

COUNTESS To the court! Why, what place make you   5
special, when you put off that with such contempt?
But to the court!

CLOWN Truly, madam, if God have lent a man any
manners he may easily put it off at court: he that
cannot make a leg, put off's cap, kiss his hand, and say   10
nothing, has neither leg, hands, lip, nor cap; and
indeed such a fellow, to say precisely, were not for the
court; but for me, I have an answer will serve all men.

COUNTESS Marry, that's a bountiful answer that fits all
questions.   15

CLOWN It is like a barber's chair that fits all buttocks:
the pin-buttock, the quatch-buttock, the brawn-
buttock, or any buttock.

COUNTESS Will your answer serve fit to all questions?

CLOWN As fit as ten groats is for the hand of an   20
attorney, as your French crown for your taffety punk,
as Tib's rush for Tom's forefinger, as a pancake for
Shrove Tuesday, a morris for May-day, as the nail to
his hole, the cuckold to his horn, as a scolding quean
to a wrangling knave, as the nun's lip to the friar's   25
mouth; nay, as the pudding to his skin.

COUNTESS Have you, I say, an answer of such fitness for
all questions?

CLOWN From below your duke to beneath your
constable, it will fit any question.   30

COUNTESS It must be an answer of most monstrous size
that must fit all demands.

CLOWN But a trifle neither, in good faith, if the learned
should speak truth of it. Here it is, and all that belongs
to't: ask me if I am a courtier; it shall do you no harm   35
to learn.

COUNTESS To be young again, if we could, I will be a
fool in question, hoping to be the wiser by your
answer. I pray you, sir, are you a courtier?

CLOWN O Lord, sir! There's a simple putting off. More,   40
more, a hundred of them.

COUNTESS Sir, I am a poor friend of yours that loves
you.

CLOWN O Lord, sir! Thick, thick; spare not me.

COUNTESS I think, sir, you can eat none of this homely   45
meat.

CLOWN O Lord, sir! Nay, put me to't, I warrant you.

COUNTESS You were lately whipp'd, sir, as I think.

CLOWN O Lord, sir! Spare not me.

COUNTESS Do you cry 'O Lord, sir!' at your whipping,   50
and 'spare not me'? Indeed your 'O Lord, sir!' is very
sequent to your whipping; you would answer very well
to a whipping, if you were but bound to't.

CLOWN
I ne'er had worse luck in my life in my 'O Lord, sir!'
I see things may serve long, but not serve ever.   55

COUNTESS I play the noble housewife with the time,
To entertain it so merrily with a fool.

CLOWN O Lord, sir! Why, there't serves well again.

COUNTESS

An end, sir! To your business: give Helen this,
And urge her to a present answer back.
Commend me to my kinsmen and my son.
This is not much.

CLOWN   Not much commendation to them?

COUNTESS

Not much employment for you. You understand me?

CLOWN   Most fruitfully. I am there before my legs.

COUNTESS   Haste you again.   *Exeunt.*

2.3   *Enter* BERTRAM, LAFEW *and* PAROLLES.

LAFEW   They say miracles are past; and we have our
philosophical persons to make modern and familiar,
things supernatural and causeless. Hence is it that we
make trifles of terrors, ensconcing ourselves into
seeming knowledge when we should submit ourselves
to an unknown fear.

PAROLLES   Why, 'tis the rarest argument of wonder that
hath shot out in our latter times.

BERTRAM   And so 'tis.

LAFEW   To be relinquish'd of the artists –

PAROLLES   So I say – both of Galen and Paracelsus.

LAFEW   Of all the learned and authentic Fellows –

PAROLLES   Right; so I say.

LAFEW   That gave him out incurable –

PAROLLES   Why, there 'tis; so say I too.

LAFEW   Not to be help'd.

PAROLLES   Right; as 'twere a man assur'd of a –

LAFEW   Uncertain life and sure death.

PAROLLES   Just. You say well. So would I have said.

LAFEW   I may truly say it is a novelty to the world.

PAROLLES   It is indeed; if you will have it in showing,
you shall read it in what-do-ye-call there.

LAFEW   [*reading*]   *A showing of a heavenly effect in an
earthly actor.*

PAROLLES   That's it; I would have said the very same.

LAFEW   Why, your dolphin is not lustier; fore me, I
speak in respect –

PAROLLES   Nay, 'tis strange, 'tis very strange; that is the
brief and the tedious of it; and he's of a most
facinerious spirit that will not acknowledge it to be
the –

LAFEW   Very hand of heaven.

PAROLLES   Ay, so I say.

LAFEW   In a most weak –

PAROLLES   And debile minister; great power, great
transcendence, which should indeed give us a further
use to be made than alone the recov'ry of the king, as
to be –

LAFEW   Generally thankful.

Enter KING, HELENA *and attendants.*

PAROLLES   I would have said it; you say well. Here
comes the king.

LAFEW   Lustique, as the Dutchman says. I'll like a maid
the better whilst I have a tooth in my head. Why, he's
able to lead her a coranto.

PAROLLES   *Mor du vinager!* Is not this Helen?   45

LAFEW   Fore God, I think so.

KING   Go, call before me all the lords in court.

Exit attendant.

Sit, my preserver, by thy patient's side,
And with this healthful hand, whose banish'd sense
Thou hast repeal'd, a second time receive   50
The confirmation of my promis'd gift,
Which but attends thy naming.

Enter three or four Lords.

Fair maid, send forth thine eye. This youthful parcel
Of noble bachelors stand at my bestowing,
O'er whom both sovereign power and father's voice   55
I have to use. Thy frank election make;
Thou hast power to choose, and they none to forsake.

HELENA   To each of you one fair and virtuous mistress
Fall, when love please! Marry, to each but one!

LAFEW   I'd give bay curtal and his furniture   60
My mouth no more were broken than these boys',
And writ as little beard.

KING   Peruse them well.
Not one of those but had a noble father.
[*She addresses her to a Lord.*]

HELENA   Gentlemen,
Heaven hath through me restor'd the king to health.   65

ALL   We understand it, and thank heaven for you.

HELENA   I am a simple maid, and therein wealthiest
That I protest I simply am a maid.
Please it your majesty, I have done already.
The blushes in my cheeks thus whisper me: 70
'We blush that thou should'st choose; but, be
refused,
Let the white death sit on thy cheek for ever,
We'll ne'er come there again.'

KING   Make choice, and see,
Who shuns thy love shuns all his love in me.

HELENA   Now, Dian, from thy altar do I fly,   75
And to imperial Love, that god most high
Do my sighs stream.
[*to First Lord*]   Sir, will you hear my suit?

1 LORD   And grant it.

HELENA   Thanks, sir; all the rest is mute.

LAFEW   I had rather be in this choice than throw ames-
ace for my life.   80

HELENA [*to Second Lord*]
The honour, sir, that flames in your fair eyes
Before I speak, too threat'ningly replies.
Love make your fortunes twenty times above
Her that so wishes, and her humble love!

2 LORD   No better, if you please.

HELENA   My wish receive,   85
Which great Love grant; and so I take my leave.

LAFEW Do all they deny her? And they were sons of
mine I'd have them whipp'd, or I would send them to
th' Turk to make eunuchs of.

HELENA [*to Third Lord*]
90   Be not afraid that I your hand should take;
I'll never do you wrong, for your own sake.
Blessing upon your vows, and in your bed
Find fairer fortune if you ever wed!

LAFEW These boys are boys of ice; they'll none have
95   her. Sure they are bastards to the English; the French
ne'er got 'em.

HELENA [*to Fourth Lord*]
You are too young, too happy, and too good,
To make yourself a son out of my blood.

4 LORD Fair one, I think not so.

100 LAFEW There's one grape yet. I am sure thy father
drunk wine; but if thou be'st not an ass, I am a youth
of fourteen; I have known thee already.

HELENA [*to Bertram*] I dare not say I take you, but I give
Me and my service, ever whilst I live,
105   Into your guiding power. This is the man.

KING
Why, then, young Bertram, take her; she's thy wife.

BERTRAM
My wife, my liege! I shall beseech your highness,
In such a business give me leave to use
The help of mine own eyes.

KING   Know'st thou not, Bertram,
What she has done for me?

110 BERTRAM   Yes, my good lord,
But never hope to know why I should marry her.

KING
Thou know'st she has rais'd me from my sickly bed.

BERTRAM But follows it, my lord, to bring me down
Must answer for your raising? I know her well:
115   She had her breeding at my father's charge –
A poor physician's daughter my wife! Disdain
Rather corrupt me ever!

KING   'Tis only title thou disdain'st in her, the which
I can build up. Strange is it that our bloods,
120   Of colour, weight, and heat, pour'd all together,
Would quite confound distinction, yet stands off
In differences so mighty. If she be
All that is virtuous, save what thou dislik'st –
A poor physician's daughter – thou dislik'st
125   Of virtue for the name. But do not so.
From lowest place when virtuous things proceed,
The place is dignified by th' doer's deed.
Where great additions swell's and virtue none,
It is a dropsied honour. Good alone
130   Is good, without a name; vileness is so:
The property by what it is should go,
Not by the title. She is young, wise, fair;
In these to nature she's immediate heir,
And these breed honour; that is honour's scorn
135   Which challenges itself as honour's born
And is not like the sire. Honours thrive

When rather from our acts we them derive
Than our foregoers. The mere word's a slave,
Debosh'd on every tomb, on every grave
A lying trophy, and as oft is dumb,   140
Where dust and damn'd oblivion is the tomb
Of honour'd bones indeed. What should be said?
If thou canst like this creature as a maid,
I can create the rest. Virtue and she
Is her own dower; honour and wealth from me.   145

BERTRAM I cannot love her nor will strive to do't.

KING
Thou wrong'st thyself if thou should'st strive to
choose.

HELENA
That you are well restor'd, my lord, I'm glad.
Let the rest go.

KING My honour's at the stake, which to defeat,   150
I must produce my power. Here, take her hand,
Proud, scornful boy, unworthy this good gift,
That dost in vile misprision shackle up
My love and her desert; that canst not dream
We, poising us in her defective scale,   155
Shall weigh thee to the beam; that wilt not know
It is in us to plant thine honour where
We please to have it grow. Check thy contempt;
Obey our will which travails in thy good;
Believe not thy disdain, but presently   160
Do thine own fortunes that obedient right
Which both thy duty owes and our power claims;
Or I will throw thee from my care for ever
Into the staggers and the careless lapse
Of youth and ignorance; both my revenge and hate   165
Loosing upon thee in the name of justice,
Without all terms of pity. Speak. Thine answer.

BERTRAM Pardon, my gracious lord; for I submit
My fancy to your eyes. When I consider
What great creation and what dole of honour   170
Flies where you bid it, I find that she, which late
Was in my nobler thoughts most base, is now
The praised of the king; who, so ennobled,
Is as 'twere born so.

KING   Take her by the hand
And tell her she is thine; to whom I promise   175
A counterpoise, if not to thy estate,
A balance more replete.

BERTRAM   I take her hand.

KING Good fortune and the favour of the king
Smile upon this contract; whose ceremony
Shall seem expedient on the now-born brief,   180
And be perform'd tonight. The solemn feast
Shall more attend upon the coming space,
Expecting absent friends. As thou lov'st her
Thy love's to me religious; else, does err.   *Exeunt.*

PAROLLES *and* LAFEW *stay behind, commenting of*
this wedding.

LAFEW Do you hear, monsieur? A word with you.   185

PAROLLES   Your pleasure, sir.

LAFEW   Your lord and master did well to make his recantation.

PAROLLES   Recantation! My lord! My master!

LAFEW   Ay. Is it not a language I speak?

PAROLLES   A most harsh one, and not to be understood without bloody succeeding. My master!

LAFEW   Are you companion to the Count Rossillion?

PAROLLES   To any Count; to all Counts; to what is man.

LAFEW   To what is Count's man; Count's master is of another style.

PAROLLES   You are too old, sir; let it satisfy you, you are too old.

LAFEW   I must tell thee, sirrah, I write man; to which title age cannot bring thee.

PAROLLES   What I dare too well do, I dare not do.

LAFEW   I did think thee for two ordinaries to be a pretty wise fellow; thou didst make tolerable vent of thy travel; it might pass. Yet the scarfs and the bannerets about thee did manifoldly dissuade me from believing thee a vessel of too great a burthen. I have now found thee; when I lose thee again I care not. Yet art thou good for nothing but taking up, and that thou'rt scarce worth.

PAROLLES   Hadst thou not the privilege of antiquity upon thee –

LAFEW   Do not plunge thyself too far in anger, lest thou hasten thy trial; which if – Lord have mercy on thee for a hen! So, my good window of lattice, fare thee well; thy casement I need not open, for I look through thee. Give me thy hand.

PAROLLES   My lord, you give me most egregious indignity.

LAFEW   Ay, with all my heart; and thou art worthy of it.

PAROLLES   I have not, my lord, deserv'd it.

LAFEW   Yes, good faith, ev'ry dram of it; and I will not bate thee a scruple.

PAROLLES   Well, I shall be wiser.

LAFEW   Ev'n as soon as thou canst; for thou hast to pull at a smack a' th' contrary. If ever thou be'st bound in thy scarf and beaten thou shall find what it is to be proud of thy bondage. I have a desire to hold my acquaintance with thee, or rather my knowledge, that I may say, in the default, 'He is a man I know'.

PAROLLES   My lord, you do me most insupportable vexation.

LAFEW   I would it were hell-pains for thy sake, and my poor doing eternal; for doing I am past, as I will by thee, in what motion age will give me leave.   *Exit.*

PAROLLES   Well, thou hast a son shall take this disgrace off me; scurvy, old, filthy, scurvy lord! Well, I must be patient; there is no fettering of authority. I'll beat him, by my life, if I can meet him with any convenience, and he were double and double a lord. I'll have no more pity of his age than I would have of – I'll beat him and if I could but meet him again.

Re-enter LAFEW.

LAFEW   Sirrah, your lord and master's married; there's news for you; you have a new mistress.

PAROLLES   I most unfeignedly beseech your lordship to make some reservation of your wrongs. He is my good lord; whom I serve above is my master.

LAFEW   Who? God?

PAROLLES   Ay, sir.

LAFEW   The devil it is that's thy master. Why dost thou garter up thy arms a' this fashion? Dost make hose of thy sleeves? Do other servants so? Thou wert best set thy lower part where thy nose stands. By mine honour, if I were but two hours younger I'd beat thee. Methink'st thou art a general offence and every man should beat thee. I think thou wast created for men to breathe themselves upon thee.

PAROLLES   This is hard and undeserved measure, my lord.

LAFEW   Go to, sir. You were beaten in Italy for picking a kernel out of a pomegranate. You are a vagabond and no true traveller. You are more saucy with lords and honourable personages than the commission of your birth and virtue gives you heraldry. You are not worth another word, else I'd call you knave. I leave you. *Exit.*

Re-enter BERTRAM.

PAROLLES   Good, very good; it is so then. Good, very good; let it be conceal'd awhile.

BERTRAM   Undone and forfeited to cares for ever!

PAROLLES   What's the matter, sweetheart?

BERTRAM
Although before the solemn priest I have sworn,
I will not bed her.

PAROLLES   What, what, sweetheart?

BERTRAM   O my Parolles, they have married me!
I'll to the Tuscan wars and never bed her.

PAROLLES   France is a dog-hole and it no more merits
The tread of a man's foot; to th' wars!

BERTRAM
There's letters from my mother; what th'import is
I know not yet.

PAROLLES
Ay, that would be known. To th' wars, my boy, to th' wars!
He wears his honour in a box unseen
That hugs his kicky-wicky here at home,
Spending his manly marrow in her arms,
Which should sustain the bound and high curvet
Of Mars's fiery steed. To other regions!
France is a stable; we that dwell in't jades.
Therefore to th' war!

BERTRAM   It shall be so. I'll send her to my house,
Acquaint my mother with my hate to her
And wherefore I am fled, write to the king
That which I durst not speak. His present gift
Shall furnish me to those Italian fields
Where noble fellows strike. Wars is no strife
To the dark house and the detested wife.

PAROLLES   Will this capriccio hold in thee, art sure?

BERTRAM   Go with me to my chamber and advise me.
I'll send her straight away. Tomorrow

295   I'll to the wars, she to her single sorrow.

PAROLLES
Why, these balls bound; there's noise in it. 'Tis hard:
A young man married is a man that's marr'd.
Therefore away, and leave her bravely; go.
The king has done you wrong; but hush 'tis so.

Exeunt.

2.4   *Enter* HELENA *and* Clown.

HELENA   My mother greets me kindly; is she well?

CLOWN   She is not well, but yet she has her health; she's
very merry, but yet she is not well. But thanks be given
she's very well and wants nothing i'th' world; but yet
5   she is not well.

HELENA   If she be very well what does she ail that she's
not very well?

CLOWN   Truly, she's very well indeed, but for two
things.

10   HELENA   What two things?

CLOWN   One, that she's not in heaven, whither God
send her quickly! The other, that she's in earth, from
whence God send her quickly!

Enter PAROLLES.

PAROLLES   Bless you, my fortunate lady.

15   HELENA   I hope, sir, I have your good will to have mine
own good fortune.

PAROLLES   You had my prayers to lead them on, and to
keep them on have them still. O, my knave! How does
my old lady?

20   CLOWN   So that you had her wrinkles and I her money,
I would she did as you say.

PAROLLES   Why, I say nothing.

CLOWN   Marry, you are the wiser man; for many a man's
tongue shakes out his master's undoing. To say
25   nothing, to do nothing, to know nothing, and to have
nothing, is to be a great part of your title, which is
within a very little of nothing.

PAROLLES   Away! Th'art a knave.

CLOWN   You should have said, sir, 'Before a knave th'art
30   a knave'; that's 'Before me, th'art a knave'. This had
been truth, sir.

PAROLLES   Go to, thou art a witty fool; I have found thee.

CLOWN   Did you find me in your self, sir, or were you
taught to find me? . . . The search, sir, was profitable;
35   and much fool may you find in you, even to the
world's pleasure and the increase of laughter.

PAROLLES   A good knave i'faith, and well fed.
Madam, my lord will go away tonight;
A very serious business calls on him.
40   The great prerogative and rite of love,
Which as your due time claims, he does acknowledge,
But puts it off to a compell'd restraint;

Whose want and whose delay is strew'd with sweets,
Which they distil now in the curbed time,
To make the coming hour o'erflow with joy   45
And pleasure drown the brim.

HELENA   What's his will else?

PAROLLES
That you will take your instant leave a'th' king,
And make this haste as your own good proceeding,
Strength'ned with what apology you think
May make it probable need.

HELENA   What more commands he?   50

PAROLLES   That, having this obtain'd, you presently
Attend his further pleasure.

HELENA   In everything I wait upon his will.

PAROLLES   I shall report it so.   *Exit.*

HELENA   I pray you. Come, sirrah.   *Exeunt.*

2.5   *Enter* LAFEW *and* BERTRAM.

LAFEW   But I hope your lordship thinks not him a soldier.

BERTRAM   Yes, my lord, and of very valiant approof.

LAFEW   You have it from his own deliverance.

BERTRAM   And by other warranted testimony.

LAFEW   Then my dial goes not true; I took this lark for   5
a bunting.

BERTRAM   I do assure you, my lord, he is very great in
knowledge, and accordingly valiant.

LAFEW   I have then sinn'd against his experience and
transgress'd against his valour; and my state that way   10
is dangerous, since I cannot yet find in my heart to
repent. Here he comes. I pray you make us friends; I
will pursue the amity.

Enter PAROLLES.

PAROLLES [*to Bertram*]   These things shall be done, sir.

LAFEW   Pray you, 'sir', who's his tailor?   15

PAROLLES   Sir!

LAFEW   O, I know him well. Ay, 'sir', he, sir, 's a good
workman, a very good tailor.

BERTRAM [*aside to Parolles*]   Is she gone to the king?

PAROLLES   She is.   20

BERTRAM   Will she away tonight?

PAROLLES   As you'll have her.

BERTRAM   I have writ my letters, casketed my treasure,
Given order for our horses; and tonight,
When I should take possession of the bride,   25
End ere I do begin.

LAFEW [*aside*]   A good traveller is something at the latter
end of a dinner, but one that lies three thirds and uses
a known truth to pass a thousand nothings with,
should be once heard and thrice beaten. [*aloud*] God   30
save you, captain!

BERTRAM   Is there any unkindness between my lord and
you, monsieur?

PAROLLES   I know not how I have deserved to run into
my lord's displeasure.   35

LAFEW   You have made shift to run into't, boots and

spurs and all, like him that leap'd into the custard; and
out of it you'll run again rather than suffer question
for your residence.

BERTRAM   It may be you have mistaken him, my lord.

LAFEW   And shall do so ever, though I took him at's
prayers. Fare you well, my lord, and believe this of me:
there can be no kernel in this light nut; the soul of this
man is his clothes. Trust him not in matter of heavy
consequence; I have kept of them tame, and know
their natures. Farewell, monsieur; I have spoken better
of you than you have or will to deserve at my hand; but
we must do good against evil.   *Exit.*

PAROLLES   An idle lord, I swear.

BERTRAM   I think not so.

PAROLLES   Why, do you not know him?

BERTRAM   Yes, I do know him well; and common speech
Gives him a worthy pass. Here comes my clog.

Enter HELENA.

HELENA   I have, sir, as I was commanded from you,
Spoke with the king, and have procur'd his leave
For present parting; only he desires
Some private speech with you.

BERTRAM   I shall obey his will.
You must not marvel, Helen, at my course,
Which holds not colour with the time, nor does
The ministration and required office
On my particular. Prepar'd I was not
For such a business; therefore am I found
So much unsettled. This drives me to entreat you
That presently you take your way for home,
And rather muse than ask why I entreat you;
For my respects are better than they seem,
And my appointments have in them a need
Greater than shows itself at the first view
To you that know them not. This to my mother.
[*giving a letter*]
'Twill be two days ere I shall see you, so
I leave you to your wisdom.

HELENA   Sir, I can nothing say
But that I am your most obedient servant.

BERTRAM   Come, come; no more of that.

HELENA   And ever shall
With true observance seek to eke out that
Wherein toward me my homely stars have fail'd
To equal my great fortune.

BERTRAM   Let that go.
My haste is very great. Farewell. Hie home.

HELENA   Pray sir, your pardon.

BERTRAM   Well, what would you say?

HELENA   I am not worthy of the wealth I owe,
Nor dare I say 'tis mine – and yet it is;
But, like a timorous thief, most fain would steal
What law does vouch mine own.

BERTRAM   What would you have?

HELENA
Something, and scarce so much; nothing indeed.

I would not tell you what I would, my lord.
Faith, yes: 85
Strangers and foes do sunder and not kiss.

BERTRAM   I pray you, stay not, but in haste to horse.

HELENA   I shall not break your bidding, good my lord.
Where are my other men? Monsieur, farewell.   *Exit.*

BERTRAM
Go thou toward home, where I will never come   90
Whilst I can shake my sword or hear the drum.
Away, and for our flight.

PAROLLES   Bravely. Coragio!   *Exeunt.*

3.1   *Flourish. Enter the* DUKE *of Florence, the two
French* Lords, *with a troop of soldiers.*

DUKE   So that from point to point now have you heard
The fundamental reasons of this war,
Whose great decision hath much blood let forth,
And more thirsts after.

1 LORD   Holy seems the quarrel
Upon your Grace's part; black and fearful   5
On the opposer.

DUKE   Therefore we marvel much our cousin France
Would in so just a business shut his bosom
Against our borrowing prayers.

2 LORD   Good my lord,
The reasons of our state I cannot yield,   10
But like a common and an outward man
That the great figure of a council frames
By self-unable motion; therefore dare not
Say what I think of it, since I have found
Myself in my incertain grounds to fail   15
As often as I guess'd.

DUKE   Be it his pleasure.

1 LORD   But I am sure the younger of our nature
That surfeit on their ease will day by day
Come here for physic.

DUKE   Welcome shall they be,
And all the honours that can fly from us   20
Shall on them settle. You know your places well;
When better fall, for your avails they fell.
Tomorrow to the field.   *Flourish. Exeunt.*

3.2   *Enter* COUNTESS *and* Clown.

COUNTESS   It hath happen'd all as I would have had it,
save that he comes not along with her.

CLOWN   By my troth, I take my young lord to be a very
melancholy man.

COUNTESS   By what observance, I pray you?   5

CLOWN   Why, he will look upon his boot and sing; mend
the ruff and sing; ask questions and sing; pick his teeth
and sing. I know a man that had this trick of
melancholy sold a goodly manor for a song.

COUNTESS   Let me see what he writes, and when he   10
means to come. [*Reads the letter.*]

CLOWN   I have no mind to Isbel since I was at court. Our
old lings and our Isbels a'th' country are nothing like

your old ling and your Isbels a'th' court. The brains of
my Cupid's knock'd out, and I begin to love as an old
man loves money, with no stomach.

COUNTESS   What have we here?

CLOWN   E'en that you have there.   *Exit.*

COUNTESS [*Reads.*]   *I have sent you a daughter-in-law;*
she hath recovered the king and undone me. I have wedded
her, not bedded her, and sworn to make the 'not' eternal.
You shall hear I am run away; know it before the report
come. If there be breadth enough in the world I will hold
a long distance. My duty to you. Your unfortunate son,
                                        BERTRAM.

This is not well, rash and unbridled boy,
To fly the favours of so good a king,
To pluck his indignation on thy head
By the misprizing of a maid too virtuous
For the contempt of empire.

Re-enter Clown.

CLOWN   O madam, yonder is heavy news within,
between two soldiers and my young lady.

COUNTESS   What is the matter?

CLOWN   Nay, there is some comfort in the news, some
comfort; your son will not be kill'd so soon as I
thought he would.

COUNTESS   Why should he be kill'd?

CLOWN   So say I, madam – if he run away, as I hear he
does; the danger is in standing to't; that's the loss of
men, though it be the getting of children. Here they
come will tell you more. For my part, I only hear your
son was run away.   *Exit.*

Enter HELENA *and the two French* Lords.

1 LORD   Save you, good madam.

HELENA   Madam, my lord is gone, for ever gone.

2 LORD   Do not say so.

COUNTESS   Think upon patience. Pray you,
      gentlemen –
I have felt so many quirks of joy and grief
That the first face of neither on the start
Can woman me unto't. Where is my son, I pray you?

2 LORD
Madam, he's gone to serve the Duke of Florence;
We met him thitherward, for thence we came,
And, after some dispatch in hand at court,
Thither we bend again.

HELENA
Look on his letter, madam; here's my passport:
[*Reads.*] *When thou canst get the ring upon my finger,*
which never shall come off, and show me a child begotten
of thy body that I am father to, then call me husband; but
in such a 'then' I write a 'never'.
This is a dreadful sentence.

COUNTESS   Brought you this letter, gentlemen?

1 LORD   Ay, madam; and for the contents' sake are sorry
for our pains.

COUNTESS   I prithee, lady, have a better cheer.

If thou engrossest all the griefs are thine
Thou robb'st me of a moiety. He was my son,
But I do wash his name out of my blood
And thou art all my child. Towards Florence is he?

2 LORD   Ay, madam.

COUNTESS   And to be a soldier?

2 LORD   Such is his noble purpose; and, believe't,
The duke will lay upon him all the honour
That good convenience claims.

COUNTESS   Return you thither?

1 LORD   Ay, madam, with the swiftest wing of speed.

HELENA [*Reads.*]   *Till I have no wife I have nothing in*
      France.
'Tis bitter.

COUNTESS   Find you that there?

HELENA   Ay, madam.

1 LORD   'Tis but the boldness of his hand, haply, which
his heart was not consenting to.

COUNTESS   Nothing in France until he have no wife!
There's nothing here that is too good for him
But only she, and she deserves a lord
That twenty such rude boys might tend upon
And call her, hourly, mistress. Who was with him?

1 LORD   A servant only, and a gentleman which I have
sometime known.

COUNTESS   Parolles, was it not?

1 LORD   Ay, my good lady, he.

COUNTESS   A very tainted fellow, and full of wickedness;
My son corrupts a well-derived nature
With his inducement.

1 LORD   Indeed, good lady,
The fellow has a deal of that too much,
Which holds him much to have.

COUNTESS   Y'are welcome, gentlemen.
I will entreat you, when you see my son,
To tell him that his sword can never win
The honour that he loses; more I'll entreat you
Written to bear along.

2 LORD   We serve you, madam,
In that and all your worthiest affairs.

COUNTESS   Not so, but as we change our courtesies.
Will you draw near?   *Exeunt Countess and Lords.*

HELENA   'Till I have no wife I have nothing in
      France.'
Nothing in France until he has no wife!
Thou shalt have none, Rossillion, none in France;
Then hast thou all again. Poor lord, is't I
That chase thee from thy country, and expose
Those tender limbs of thine to the event
Of the none-sparing war? And is it I
That drive thee from the sportive court, where thou
Wast shot at with fair eyes, to be the mark
Of smoky muskets? O you leaden messengers,
That ride upon the violent speed of fire,
Fly with false aim; move the still-piecing air
That sings with piercing; do not touch my lord.
Whoever shoots at him, I set him there;

Whoever charges on his forward breast,
I am the caitiff that do hold him to't;
15 And though I kill him not, I am the cause
His death was so effected. Better 'twere
I met the ravin lion when he roar'd
With sharp constraint of hunger; better 'twere
That all the miseries which nature owes
20 Were mine at once. No; come thou home, Rossillion,
Whence honour but of danger wins a scar,
As oft it loses all; I will be gone;
My being here it is that holds thee hence.
Shall I stay here to do't? No, no, although
25 The air of paradise did fan the house
And angels offic'd all. I will be gone,
That pitiful rumour may report my flight
To consolate thine ear. Come, night; end, day;
For with the dark, poor thief, I'll steal away.   *Exit.*

3.3 *Flourish. Enter the* DUKE *of Florence,* BERTRAM,
       drum and trumpets, soldiers, PAROLLES.

DUKE   The general of our horse thou art, and we,
       Great in our hope, lay our best love and credence
       Upon thy promising fortune.
BERTRAM   Sir, it is
       A charge too heavy for my strength; but yet
5   We'll strive to bear it for your worthy sake
       To th'extreme edge of hazard.
DUKE   Then go thou forth;
       And fortune play upon thy prosperous helm
       As thy auspicious mistress!
BERTRAM   This very day,
       Great Mars, I put myself into thy file;
10   Make me but like my thoughts and I shall prove
       A lover of thy drum, hater of love.   *Exeunt omnes.*

3.4   *Enter* COUNTESS *and* Steward.

COUNTESS Alas! and would you take the letter of her?
       Might you not know she would do as she has done
       By sending me a letter? Read it again.
STEWARD [*Reads.*]
       I am Saint Jaques' pilgrim, thither gone.
5   *Ambitious love hath so in me offended*
       That barefoot plod I the cold ground upon,
       With sainted vow my faults to have amended.
       Write, write, that from the bloody course of war
       My dearest master, your dear son, may hie.
10   *Bless him at home in peace, whilst I from far*
       His name with zealous fervour sanctify.
       His taken labours bid him me forgive;
       I, his despiteful Juno, sent him forth
       From courtly friends, with camping foes to live
15   *Where death and danger dogs the heels of worth.*
       He is too good and fair for death and me;
       Whom I myself embrace to set him free.
COUNTESS
       Ah, what sharp stings are in her mildest words!

Rynaldo, you did never lack advice so much
As letting her pass so; had I spoke with her,   20
I could have well diverted her intents,
Which thus she hath prevented.
STEWARD   Pardon me, madam;
       If I had given you this at overnight
       She might have been o'erta'en; and yet she writes
       Pursuit would be but vain.
COUNTESS   What angel shall   25
       Bless this unworthy husband? He cannot thrive,
       Unless her prayers, whom heaven delights to hear
       And loves to grant, reprieve him from the wrath
       Of greatest justice. Write, write, Rynaldo,
       To this unworthy husband of his wife;   30
       Let every word weigh heavy of her worth
       That he does weigh too light; my greatest grief,
       Though little he do feel it, set down sharply.
       Dispatch the most convenient messenger.
       When haply he shall hear that she is gone,   35
       He will return; and hope I may that she,
       Hearing so much, will speed her foot again,
       Led hither by pure love. Which of them both
       Is dearest to me I have no skill in sense
       To make distinction. Provide this messenger.   40
       My heart is heavy and mine age is weak;
       Grief would have tears and sorrow bids me speak.
                                        Exeunt.

3.5 *A tucket afar off. Enter old* Widow *of Florence,*
       her daughter DIANA, VIOLENTA *and* MARIANA, *with*
                    other citizens.

WIDOW   Nay, come; for if they do approach the city, we
       shall lose all the sight.
DIANA   They say the French count has done most
       honourable service.
WIDOW   It is reported that he has taken their great'st   5
       commander, and that with his own hand he slew the
       duke's brother. [*Tucket.*] We have lost our labour; they
       are gone a contrary way. Hark! You may know by their
       trumpets.
MARIANA   Come, let's return again and suffice ourselves   10
       with the report of it. Well, Diana, take heed of this
       French earl; the honour of a maid is her name, and no
       legacy is so rich as honesty.
WIDOW   I have told my neighbour how you have been
       solicited by a gentleman his companion.   15
MARIANA   I know that knave, hang him! one Parolles; a
       filthy officer he is in those suggestions for the young
       earl. Beware of them, Diana: their promises,
       enticements, oaths, tokens, and all these engines of
       lust, are not the things they go under; many a maid   20
       hath been seduced by them; and the misery is,
       example, that so terrible shows in the wrack of
       maidenhood, cannot for all that dissuade succession,
       but that they are limed with the twigs that threatens
       them. I hope I need not to advise you further; but I   25

hope your own grace will keep you where you are,
though there were no further danger known but the
modesty which is so lost.

DIANA   You shall not need to fear me.

Enter HELENA.

30   WIDOW   I hope so. Look, here comes a pilgrim. I know
she will lie at my house; thither they send one another.
I'll question her: God save you, pilgrim! Whither are
bound?

HELENA   To Saint Jaques le Grand.
35   Where do the palmers lodge, I do beseech you?

WIDOW   At the Saint Francis here beside the port.

HELENA   Is this the way?   [*A march afar.*]

WIDOW   Ay, marry, is't. Hark you, they come this way.
If you will tarry, holy pilgrim
40   But till the troops come by
I will conduct you where you shall be lodg'd;
The rather for I think I know your hostess
As ample as myself.

HELENA   Is it yourself?

WIDOW   If you shall please so, pilgrim.

45   HELENA   I thank you and will stay upon your leisure.

WIDOW   You came, I think, from France?

HELENA   I did so.

WIDOW   Here you shall see a countryman of yours
That has done worthy service.

HELENA   His name, I pray you.

DIANA   The Count Rossillion. Know you such a one?

50   HELENA   But by the ear, that hears most nobly of him;
His face I know not.

DIANA   Whatsome'er he is,
He's bravely taken here. He stole from France,
As 'tis reported, for the king had married him
Against his liking. Think you it is so?

55   HELENA   Ay, surely, mere the truth; I know his lady.

DIANA   There is a gentleman that serves the count
Reports but coarsely of her.

HELENA   What's his name?

DIANA   Monsieur Parolles.

HELENA   O, I believe with him,
In argument of praise or to the worth
60   Of the great count himself, she is too mean
To have her name repeated; all her deserving
Is a reserved honesty, and that
I have not heard examin'd.

DIANA   Alas, poor lady!
'Tis a hard bondage to become the wife
65   Of a detesting lord.

WIDOW   I warrant, good creature, wheresoe'er she is,
Her heart weighs sadly. This young maid might do
her
A shrewd turn if she pleas'd.

HELENA   How do you mean?
Maybe the amorous count solicits her
In the unlawful purpose?

70   WIDOW   He does indeed,

And brokes with all that can in such a suit
Corrupt the tender honour of a maid;
But she is arm'd for him and keeps her guard
In honestest defence.

Drum and colours. Enter BERTRAM, PAROLLES *and the
whole army.*

MARIANA   The gods forbid else!

WIDOW   So, now they come.   75
That is Antonio, the duke's eldest son;
That Escalus.

HELENA   Which is the Frenchman?

DIANA   He –
That with the plume; 'tis a most gallant fellow.
I would he lov'd his wife; if he were honester
He were much goodlier. Is't not a handsome
gentleman?   80

HELENA   I like him well.

DIANA
'Tis pity he is not honest. Yond's that same knave
That leads him to these places. Were I his lady
I would poison that vile rascal.

HELENA   Which is he?

DIANA
That jackanapes with scarfs. Why is he melancholy?   85

HELENA   Perchance he's hurt i'th' battle.

PAROLLES   Lose our drum! Well!

MARIANA   He's shrewdly vex'd at something. Look, he
has spied us.

WIDOW   Marry, hang you!   90

MARIANA   And your curtsy, for a ring-carrier!
Exeunt Bertram, Parolles and the army.

WIDOW
The troop is past. Come, pilgrim, I will bring you
Where you shall host; of enjoin'd penitents
There's four or five, to Great Saint Jaques bound,
Already at my house.

HELENA   I humbly thank you.   95
Please it this matron and this gentle maid
To eat with us tonight; the charge and thanking
Shall be for me; and, to requite you further,
I will bestow some precepts of this virgin,
Worthy the note.

BOTH   We'll take your offer kindly. *Exeunt.*   100

3.6   *Enter* BERTRAM *and the two French* Lords.

1 LORD   Nay, good my lord, put him to't; let him have
his way.

2 LORD   If your lordship find him not a hilding, hold me
no more in your respect.

1 LORD   On my life, my lord, a bubble.   5

BERTRAM   Do you think I am so far deceived in him?

1 LORD   Believe it, my lord, in mine own direct
knowledge, without any malice, but to speak of him as
my kinsman, he's a most notable coward, an infinite
and endless liar, an hourly promise-breaker, the owner   10

of no one good quality worthy your lordship's entertainment.

2 LORD   It were fit you knew him; lest, reposing too far in
his virtue, which he hath not, he might at some great
and trusty business in a main danger fail you.

BERTRAM   I would I knew in what particular action to
try him.

2 LORD   None better than to let him fetch off his drum,
which you hear him so confidently undertake to do.

1 LORD   I, with a troop of Florentines, will suddenly
surprise him; such I will have whom I am sure he
knows not from the enemy. We will bind and
hoodwink him so, that he shall suppose no other but
that he is carried into the leaguer of the adversaries
when we bring him to our own tents. Be but your
lordship present at his examination; if he do not for
the promise of his life, and in the highest compulsion
of base fear, offer to betray you and deliver all the
intelligence in his power against you, and that with the
divine forfeit of his soul upon oath, never trust my
judgment in anything.

2 LORD   O, for the love of laughter, let him fetch his
drum; he says he has a stratagem for't. When your
lordship sees the bottom of his success in't, and to
what metal this counterfeit lump of ore will be melted,
if you give him not John Drum's entertainment your
inclining cannot be removed. Here he comes.

Enter PAROLLES.

1 LORD   O, for the love of laughter, hinder not the
honour of his design; let him fetch off his drum in any
hand.

BERTRAM   How now, monsieur! This drum sticks sorely
in your disposition.

2 LORD   A pox on't! let it go; 'tis but a drum.

PAROLLES   But a drum! Is't but a drum? A drum so lost!
There was excellent command: to charge in with our
horse upon our own wings and to rend our own
soldiers!

2 LORD   That was not to be blam'd in the command of
the service; it was a disaster of war that Caesar himself
could not have prevented if he had been there to
command.

BERTRAM   Well, we cannot greatly condemn our
success; some dishonour we had in the loss of that
drum, but it is not to be recovered.

PAROLLES   It might have been recovered.

BERTRAM   It might; but it is not now.

PAROLLES   It is to be recovered. But that the merit of
service is seldom attributed to the true and exact
performer, I would have that drum or another, or *hic
jacet*.

BERTRAM   Why, if you have a stomach, to't, monsieur! If
you think your mystery in stratagem can bring this
instrument of honour again into his native quarter, be
magnanimious in the enterprise and go on; I will grace
the attempt for a worthy exploit; if you speed well in it

the duke shall both speak of it and extend to you what
further becomes his greatness, even to the utmost
syllable of your worthiness.

PAROLLES   By the hand of a soldier, I will undertake it.

BERTRAM   But you must not now slumber in it.   70

PAROLLES   I'll about it this evening; and I will presently
pen down my dilemmas, encourage myself in my
certainty, put myself into my mortal preparation; and
by midnight look to hear further from me.

BERTRAM   May I be bold to acquaint his grace you are   75
gone about it?

PAROLLES   I know not what the success will be, my lord,
but the attempt I vow.

BERTRAM   I know th'art valiant; and to the possibility of
thy soldiership will subscribe for thee. Farewell.   80

PAROLLES   I love not many words.   *Exit.*

1 LORD   No more than a fish loves water. Is not this a
strange fellow, my lord, that so confidently seems to
undertake this business, which he knows is not to be
done; damns himself to do, and dares better be damn'd   85
than to do't.

2 LORD   You do not know him, my lord, as we do; certain
it is that he will steal himself into a man's favour and
for a week escape a great deal of discoveries, but when
you find him out you have him ever after.   90

BERTRAM   Why, do you think he will make no deed at all
of this that so seriously he does address himself unto?

1 LORD   None in the world; but return with an invention,
and clap upon you two or three probable lies; but we
have almost emboss'd him; you shall see his fall tonight;   95
for indeed he is not for your lordship's respect.

2 LORD   We'll make you some sport with the fox ere we
case him; he was first smok'd by the old Lord Lafew;
when his disguise and he is parted tell me what a sprat
you shall find him; which you shall see this very night.   100

1 LORD   I must go look my twigs. He shall be caught.

BERTRAM   Your brother, he shall go along with me.

1 LORD   As't please your lordship. I'll leave you.   *Exit.*

BERTRAM
Now will I lead you to the house and show you
The lass I spoke of.

2 LORD   But you say she's honest.   105

BERTRAM
That's all the fault. I spoke with her but once
And found her wondrous cold, but I sent to her
By this same coxcomb that we have i'th' wind
Tokens and letters which she did re-send
And this is all I have done. She's a fair creature;   110
Will you go see her?

2 LORD   With all my heart, my lord.

                                                Exeunt.

3.7   *Enter* HELENA *and* Widow.

HELENA   If you misdoubt me that I am not she,
I know not how I shall assure you further
But I shall lose the grounds I work upon.

WIDOW   Though my estate be fall'n, I was well born,
5   Nothing acquainted with these businesses,
          And would not put my reputation now
          In any staining act.
HELENA   Nor would I wish you.
          First give me trust the count he is my husband,
          And what to your sworn counsel I have spoken
10   Is so from word to word; and then you cannot,
          By the good aid that I of you shall borrow,
          Err in bestowing it.
WIDOW   I should believe you,
          For you have show'd me that which well approves
          Y'are great in fortune.
HELENA   Take this purse of gold,
15   And let me buy your friendly help thus far,
          Which I will over-pay, and pay again
          When I have found it. The count he woos your
              daughter,
          Lays down his wanton siege before her beauty,
          Resolv'd to carry her; let her in fine consent
20   As we'll direct her how 'tis best to bear it.
          Now his important blood will naught deny
          That she'll demand; a ring the county wears
          That downward hath succeeded in his house
          From son to son some four or five descents
25   Since the first father wore it. This ring he holds
          In most rich choice; yet, in his idle fire,
          To buy his will it would not seem too dear,
          Howe'er repented after.
WIDOW   Now I see
          The bottom of your purpose.
30   HELENA   You see it lawful then; it is no more
          But that your daughter, ere she seems as won,
          Desires this ring; appoints him an encounter;
          In fine, delivers me to fill the time,
          Herself most chastely absent. After,
35   To marry her I'll add three thousand crowns
          To what is pass'd already.
WIDOW   I have yielded.
          Instruct my daughter how she shall persever
          That time and place with this deceit so lawful
          May prove coherent. Every night he comes
40   With musics of all sorts, and songs compos'd
          To her unworthiness; it nothing steads us
          To chide him from our eaves, for he persists
          As if his life lay on't.
HELENA   Why then tonight
          Let us assay our plot; which, if it speed,
45   Is wicked meaning in a lawful deed,
          And lawful meaning in a lawful act,
          Where both not sin, and yet a sinful fact.
          But let's about it.   *Exeunt.*

4.1   *Enter first French* Lord, *with five or six*
              other soldiers in ambush.

1 LORD   He can come no other way but by this hedge-

corner. When you sally upon him speak what terrible
language you will; though you understand it not
yourselves, no matter; for we must not seem to
understand him, unless some one among us, whom we
must produce for an interpreter.   5
1 SOLDIER   Good captain, let me be th'interpreter.
1 LORD   Art not acquainted with him? Knows he not thy
voice?
1 SOLDIER   No sir, I warrant you.   10
1 LORD   But what linsey-woolsey hast thou to speak to
us again?
1 SOLDIER   E'en such as you speak to me.
1 LORD   He must think us some band of strangers i'th'
adversary's entertainment. Now he hath a smack of all   15
neighbouring languages; therefore we must every one
be a man of his own fancy, not to know what we speak
one to another; so we seem to know is to know straight
our purpose – choughs' language: gabble enough and
good enough. As for you, interpreter, you must seem   20
very politic. But couch, ho! Here he comes to beguile
two hours in a sleep, and then to return and swear the
lies he forges.

                    Enter PAROLLES.

PAROLLES   Ten a'clock. Within these three hours 'twill be
time enough to go home. What shall I say I have done?   25
It must be a very plausive invention that carries it. They
begin to smoke me, and disgraces have of late knock'd
too often at my door. I find my tongue is too foolhardy,
but my heart hath the fear of Mars before it and of his
creatures, not daring the reports of my tongue.   30
1 LORD   This is the first truth that e'er thine own tongue
was guilty of.
PAROLLES   What the devil should move me to undertake
the recovery of this drum, being not ignorant of the
impossibility, and knowing I had no such purpose? I   35
must give myself some hurts, and say I got them in
exploit; yet slight ones will not carry it. They will say,
'Came you off with so little?' And great ones I dare not
give; wherefore, what's the instance? Tongue, I must
put you into a butter-woman's mouth, and buy myself   40
another of Bajazeth's mule if you prattle me into these
perils.
1 LORD   Is it possible he should know what he is, and be
that he is?
PAROLLES   I would the cutting of my garments would   45
serve the turn, or the breaking of my Spanish sword.
1 LORD   We cannot afford you so.
PAROLLES   Or the baring of my beard, and to say it was
in stratagem.
1 LORD   'Twould not do.   50
PAROLLES   Or to drown my clothes and say I was
stripp'd.
1 LORD   Hardly serve.
PAROLLES   Though I swore I leap'd from the window of
the citadel –   55
1 LORD   How deep?

PAROLLES   Thirty fadom.

1 LORD   Three great oaths would scarce make that be
believed.

PAROLLES   I would I had any drum of the enemy's; I
would swear I recover'd it.

1 LORD   You shall hear one anon.

PAROLLES   A drum now of the enemy's –
                              [*Alarum within.*]

1 LORD   *Throca movousus, cargo, cargo, cargo.*

ALL   *Cargo, cargo, cargo, villianda par corbo, cargo.*
[*They seize him.*]

PAROLLES   O, ransom, ransom! [*They blindfold him.*] Do
not hide mine eyes.

1 SOLDIER   *Boskos thromuldo boskos.*

PAROLLES   I know you are the Muskos' regiment,
And I shall lose my life for want of language.
If there be here German, or Dane, Low Dutch,
Italian, or French, let him speak to me,
I'll discover that which shall undo the Florentine.

1 SOLDIER   *Boskos vauvado.* I understand thee, and can
speak thy tongue. *Kerelybonto.* Sir, betake thee to thy
faith, for seventeen poniards are at thy bosom.

PAROLLES   O!

1 SOLDIER   O, pray, pray, pray! *Manka revania dulche.*

1 LORD   *Oscorbidulchos volivorco.*

1 SOLDIER   The general is content to spare thee yet,
And, hoodwink'd as thou art, will lead thee on
To gather from thee. Haply thou may'st inform
Something to save thy life.

PAROLLES   O, let me live,
And all the secrets of our camp I'll show,
Their force, their purposes; nay, I'll speak that
Which you will wonder at.

1 SOLDIER   But wilt thou faithfully?

PAROLLES   If I do not, damn me.

1 SOLDIER   *Acordo linta.*
Come on; thou art granted space.
                              Exit with Parolles guarded.
                              [*A short alarum within*]

1 LORD   Go tell the Count Rossillion and my brother
We have caught the woodcock and will keep him
    muffled
Till we do hear from them.

2 SOLDIER   Captain, I will.

1 LORD   'A will betray us all unto ourselves:
Inform on that.

2 SOLDIER   So I will, sir.

1 LORD   Till then I'll keep him dark and safely lock'd.
                              Exeunt.

4.2   *Enter* BERTRAM *and the maid called* DIANA.

BERTRAM
They told me that your name was Fontybell.

DIANA   No, my good lord, Diana.

BERTRAM   Titled goddess;
And worth it, with addition! But, fair soul,
In your fine frame hath love no quality?
If the quick fire of youth light not your mind
You are no maiden but a monument.
When you are dead you should be such a one
As you are now; for you are cold and stern,
And now you should be as your mother was
When your sweet self was got.

DIANA   She then was honest.

BERTRAM   So should you be.

DIANA   No.
My mother did but duty; such, my lord,
As you owe to your wife.

BERTRAM   No more a' that!
I prithee do not strive against my vows;
I was compell'd to her, but I love thee
By love's own sweet constraint, and will for ever
Do thee all rights of service.

DIANA   Ay, so you serve us
Till we serve you; but when you have our roses,
You barely leave our thorns to prick ourselves,
And mock us with our bareness.

BERTRAM   How have I sworn!

DIANA   'Tis not the many oaths that makes the truth,
But the plain single vow that is vow'd true.
What is not holy, that we swear not by,
But take the high'st to witness; then, pray you, tell me:
If I should swear by Jove's great attributes
I lov'd you dearly, would you believe my oaths
When I did love you ill? This has no holding,
To swear by Him whom I protest to love
That I will work against Him. Therefore your oaths
Are words, and poor conditions but unseal'd –
At least in my opinion.

BERTRAM   Change it, change it.
Be not so holy-cruel; love is holy;
And my integrity ne'er knew the crafts
That you do charge men with. Stand no more off,
But give thyself unto my sick desires,
Who then recovers. Say thou art mine, and ever
My love as it begins shall so persever.

DIANA   I see that men make rope's in such a scarre,
That we'll forsake ourselves. Give me that ring.

BERTRAM   I'll lend it thee, my dear, but have no power
To give it from me.

DIANA   Will you not, my lord?

BERTRAM   It is an honour 'longing to our house,
Bequeathed down from many ancestors,
Which were the greatest obloquy i'th' world
In me to lose.

DIANA   Mine honour's such a ring;
My chastity's the jewel of our house,
Bequeathed down from many ancestors,
Which were the greatest obloquy i'th' world
In me to lose. Thus your own proper wisdom
Brings in the champion Honour on my part
Against your vain assault.

BERTRAM   Here, take my ring;

My house, mine honour, yea, my life be thine,
And I'll be bid by thee.
DIANA   When midnight comes, knock at my chamber
        window;
55   I'll order take my mother shall not hear.
        Now will I charge you in the band of truth,
        When you have conquer'd my yet maiden bed,
        Remain there but an hour, nor speak to me.
        My reasons are most strong and you shall know them
60   When back again this ring shall be deliver'd;
        And on your finger in the night I'll put
        Another ring, that what in time proceeds
        May token to the future our past deeds
        Adieu till then; then, fail not. You have won
65   A wife of me, though there my hope be done.
BERTRAM
        A heaven on earth I have won by wooing thee.   *Exit.*
DIANA
        For which live long to thank both Heaven and me!
        You may so in the end.
        My mother told me just how he would woo
70   As if she sat in's heart. She says all men
        Have the like oaths. He had sworn to marry me
        When his wife's dead; therefore I'll lie with him
        When I am buried. Since Frenchmen are so braid,
        Marry that will, I live and die a maid.
75   Only, in this disguise, I think't no sin
        To cozen him that would unjustly win.   *Exit.*

4.3   *Enter the two French Lords, and some two or*
           three soldiers.

1 LORD   You have not given him his mother's letter?
2 LORD   I have deliv'red it an hour since; there is
          something in't that stings his nature, for on the
          reading it he chang'd almost into another man.
5   1 LORD   He has much worthy blame laid upon him for
          shaking off so good a wife and so sweet a lady.
     2 LORD   Especially he hath incurred the everlasting
          displeasure of the king, who had even tun'd his bounty
          to sing happiness to him. I will tell you a thing, but
10   you shall let it dwell darkly with you.
     1 LORD   When you have spoken it 'tis dead, and I am the
          grave of it.
     2 LORD   He hath perverted a young gentlewoman here in
          Florence, of a most chaste renown, and this night he
15   fleshes his will in the spoil of her honour; he hath
          given her his monumental ring, and thinks himself
          made in the unchaste composition.
     1 LORD   Now, God delay our rebellion! As we are
          ourselves, what things are we!
20   2 LORD   Merely our own traitors. And as in the
          common course of all treasons we still see them reveal
          themselves till they attain to their abhorr'd ends; so he
          that in this action contrives against his own nobility, in
          his proper stream o'erflows himself.
25   1 LORD   Is it not meant damnable in us to be trumpeters
          of our unlawful intents? We shall not then have his

company tonight?
2 LORD   Not till after midnight, for he is dieted to his
          hour.
1 LORD   That approaches apace. I would gladly have   30
          him see his company anatomiz'd, that he might take a
          measure of his own judgments wherein so curiously he
          had set this counterfeit.
2 LORD   We will not meddle with him till he come, for
          his presence must be the whip of the other.   35
1 LORD   In the meantime, what hear you of these wars?
2 LORD   I hear there is an overture of peace.
1 LORD   Nay, I assure you, a peace concluded.
2 LORD   What will Count Rossillion do then? Will he
          travel higher, or return again into France?   40
1 LORD   I perceive by this demand you are not
          altogether of his council.
2 LORD   Let it be forbid, sir! So should I be a great deal
          of his act.
1 LORD   Sir, his wife some two months since fled from   45
          his house. Her pretence is a pilgrimage to Saint Jaques
          le Grand; which holy undertaking with most austere
          sanctimony she accomplish'd; and there residing, the
          tenderness of her nature became as a prey to her grief;
          in fine, made a groan of her last breath, and now she   50
          sings in heaven.
2 LORD   How is this justified?
1 LORD   The stronger part of it by her own letters,
          which makes her story true even to the point of her
          death. Her death itself, which could not be her office   55
          to say is come, was faithfully confirm'd by the rector
          of the place.
2 LORD   Hath the count all this intelligence?
1 LORD   Ay, and the particular confirmations, point
          from point, to the full arming of the verity.   60
2 LORD   I am heartily sorry that he'll be glad of this.
1 LORD   How mightily sometimes we make us comforts
          of our losses!
2 LORD   And how mightily some other times we drown
          our gain in tears! The great dignity that his valour   65
          hath here acquir'd for him shall at home be
          encount'red with a shame as ample.
1 LORD   The web of our life is of a mingled yarn, good
          and ill together; our virtues would be proud if our
          faults whipp'd them not, and our crimes would   70
          despair if they were not cherish'd by our virtues.

                    Enter a Messenger.

How now? Where's your master?
MESSENGER   He met the duke in the street, sir, of whom
          he hath taken a solemn leave: his lordship will next
          morning for France. The duke hath offered him   75
          letters of commendations to the king.
2 LORD   They shall be no more than needful there if they
          were more than they can commend.

                    Enter BERTRAM.

1 LORD   They cannot be too sweet for the king's tartness.

Here's his lordship now. How now, my lord? Is't not
after midnight?

BERTRAM   I have tonight dispatch'd sixteen businesses a
month's length apiece. By an abstract of success: I
have congied with the duke, done my adieu with his
nearest, buried a wife, mourn'd for her, writ to my lady
mother I am returning, entertain'd my convoy, and
between these main parcels of dispatch effected many
nicer needs; the last was the greatest, but that I have
not ended yet.

2 LORD   If the business be of any difficulty, and this
morning your departure hence, it requires haste of
your lordship.

BERTRAM   I mean, the business is not ended, as fearing
to hear of it hereafter. But shall we have this dialogue
between the Fool and the Soldier? Come, bring forth
this counterfeit module has deceiv'd me like a double-
meaning prophesier.

2 LORD   Bring him forth.   *Exeunt soldiers.*
Has sat i'th' stocks all night, poor gallant knave.

BERTRAM   No matter. His heels have deserv'd it in
usurping his spurs so long. How does he carry
himself?

2 LORD   I have told your lordship already: the stocks
carry him. But to answer you as you would be
understood: he weeps like a wench that had shed her
milk; he hath confess'd himself to Morgan, whom he
supposes to be a friar, from the time of his
remembrance to this very instant disaster of his setting
i'th' stocks. And what think you he hath confess'd?

BERTRAM   Nothing of me, has 'a?

2 LORD   His confession is taken, and it shall be read to
his face; if your lordship be in't, as I believe you are,
you must have the patience to hear it.

Re-enter soldiers and PAROLLES, *with first* Soldier
as his interpreter.

BERTRAM   A plague upon him! muffled! He can say
nothing of me.

1 LORD   [*aside to Bertram*]   Hush, hush! Hoodman
comes. [*aloud*] *Portotartarossa.*

1 SOLDIER   He calls for the tortures. What will you say
without 'em?

PAROLLES   I will confess what I know without
constraint. If ye pinch me like a pasty I can say no
more.

1 SOLDIER   *Bosko chimurcho.*

1 LORD   *Boblibindo chicurmurco.*

1 SOLDIER   You are a merciful general. Our general bids
you answer to what I shall ask you out of a note.

PAROLLES   And truly, as I hope to live.

1 SOLDIER   [*Reads.*]   *First, demand of him, how many horse
the duke is strong.* What say you to that?

PAROLLES   Five or six thousand; but very weak and
unserviceable: the troops are all scattered and the
commanders very poor rogues, upon my reputation
and credit – and as I hope to live.

1 SOLDIER   Shall I set down your answer so?

PAROLLES   Do. I'll take the sacrament on't, how and
which way you will.

BERTRAM   All's one to him. What a past-saving slave is
this!

1 LORD   Y'are deceiv'd, my lord; this is Monsieur
Parolles, the gallant militarist – that was his own
phrase – that had the whole theoric of war in the knot
of his scarf, and the practice in the chape of his dagger.

2 LORD   I will never trust a man again for keeping his
sword clean, nor believe he can have everything in him
by wearing his apparel neatly.

1 SOLDIER   Well, that's set down.

PAROLLES   'Five or six thousand horse' I said – I will say
true – 'or thereabouts' set down, for I'll speak truth.

1 LORD   He's very near the truth in this.

BERTRAM   But I con him no thanks for't, in the nature
he delivers it.

PAROLLES   'Poor rogues' I pray you say.

1 SOLDIER   Well, that's set down.

PAROLLES   I humbly thank you, sir; a truth's a truth; the
rogues are marvellous poor.

1 SOLDIER   [*Reads.*]   *Demand of him of what strength they
are a-foot.* What say you to that?

PAROLLES   By my troth, sir, if I were to live this present
hour, I will tell true. Let me see: Spurio, a hundred
and fifty; Sebastian, so many; Corambus, so many;
Jaques, so many; Guiltian, Cosmo, Lodowick, and
Gratii, two hundred fifty each; mine own company,
Chitopher, Vaumond, Bentii, two hundred fifty each;
so that the muster-file, rotten and sound, upon my life,
amounts not to fifteen thousand poll; half of the which
dare not shake the snow from off their cassocks lest
they shake themselves to pieces.

BERTRAM   What shall be done to him?

1 LORD   Nothing but let him have thanks. Demand of
him my condition, and what credit I have with the
duke.

1 SOLDIER   Well, that's set down. [*Reads.*] *You shall
demand of him whether one Captain Dumaine be i'th'
camp, a Frenchman; what his reputation is with the duke,
what his valour, honesty and expertness in wars; or
whether he thinks it were not possible with well-weighing
sums of gold to corrupt him to a revolt.* What say you to
this? What do you know of it?

PAROLLES   I beseech you, let me answer to the particular
of the inter'gatories. Demand them singly.

1 SOLDIER   Do you know this Captain Dumaine?

PAROLLES   I know him: 'a was a botcher's prentice in
Paris, from whence he was whipp'd for getting the
shrieve's fool with child, a dumb innocent that could
not say him nay.

BERTRAM   Nay, by your leave, hold your hands – though
I know his brains are forfeit to the next tile that falls.

1 SOLDIER   Well, is this captain in the Duke of
Florence's camp?

PAROLLES   Upon my knowledge he is, and lousy.

1 LORD   Nay, look not so upon me; we shall hear of your lordship anon.

1 SOLDIER   What is his reputation with the duke?

PAROLLES   The duke knows him for no other but a poor officer of mine, and writ to me this other day to turn him out a'th' band. I think I have his letter in my pocket.

1 SOLDIER   Marry, we'll search.

PAROLLES   In good sadness, I do not know; either it is there or it is upon a file, with the duke's other letters, in my tent.

1 SOLDIER   Here 'tis; here's a paper; shall I read it to you?

PAROLLES   I do not know if it be it or no.

BERTRAM   Our interpreter does it well.

1 LORD   Excellently.

1 SOLDIER [*Reads.*]   *Dian, the count's a fool, and full of gold.*

PAROLLES   That is not the duke's letter, sir; that is an advertisement to a proper maid in Florence, one Diana, to take heed of the allurement of one Count Rossillion, a foolish idle boy, but for all that very ruttish. I pray you, sir, put it up again.

1 SOLDIER   Nay, I'll read it first by your favour.

PAROLLES   My meaning in't, I protest, was very honest in the behalf of the maid; for I knew the young count to be a dangerous and lascivious boy, who is a whale to virginity, and devours up all the fry it finds.

BERTRAM   Damnable both-sides rogue!

1 SOLDIER [*Reads.*]

    When he swears oaths, bid him drop gold, and take it;
    After he scores he never pays the score.
    Half-won is match well made; match, and well make it;
    He ne'er pays after-debts; take it before.
    And say a soldier, Dian, told thee this:
    Men are to mell with, boys are not to kiss;
    For count of this, the count's a fool, I know it,
    Who pays before, but not when he does owe it.
      Thine, as he vow'd to thee in thine ear,
                           PAROLLES.

BERTRAM   He shall be whipp'd through the army, with his rhyme in's forehead.

2 LORD   This is your devoted friend, sir, the manifold linguist, and the armipotent soldier.

BERTRAM   I could endure anything before but a cat, and now he's a cat to me.

1 SOLDIER   I perceive, sir, by the general's looks, we shall be fain to hang you.

PAROLLES   My life, sir, in any case! Not that I am afraid to die, but that, my offences being many, I would repent out the remainder of nature. Let me live, sir, in a dungeon, i'th' stocks, or anywhere, so I may live.

1 SOLDIER   We'll see what may be done, so you confess freely. Therefore once more to this Captain Dumaine: you have answer'd to his reputation with the duke and to his valour; what is his honesty?

PAROLLES   He will steal, sir, an egg out of a cloister; for rapes and ravishments he parallels Nessus. He professes not keeping of oaths; in breaking 'em he is stronger than Hercules. He will lie, sir, with such volubility that you would think truth were a fool; drunkenness is his best virtue, for he will be swine-drunk, and in his sleep he does little harm, save to his bedclothes about him; but they know his conditions and lay him in straw. I have but little more to say, sir, of his honesty: he has everything that an honest man should not have; what an honest man should have, he has nothing.

1 LORD   I begin to love him for this.

BERTRAM   For this description of thine honesty? A pox upon him! for me, he's more and more a cat.

1 SOLDIER   What say you to his expertness in war?

PAROLLES   Faith, sir, has led the drum before the English tragedians – to belie him I will not – and more of his soldiership I know not, except in that country he had the honour to be the officer at a place there called Mile-end, to instruct for the doubling of files. I would do the man what honour I can, but of this I am not certain.

1 LORD   He hath out-villain'd villainy so far that the rarity redeems him.

BERTRAM   A pox on him! He's a cat still.

1 SOLDIER   His qualities being at this poor price, I need not to ask you if gold will corrupt him to revolt.

PAROLLES   Sir, for a cardecue he will sell the fee-simple of his salvation, the inheritance of it, and cut th'entail from all remainders, and a perpetual succession for it perpetually.

1 SOLDIER   What's his brother, the other Captain Dumaine?

2 LORD   Why does he ask him of me?

1 SOLDIER   What's he?

PAROLLES   E'en a crow a'th' same nest; not altogether so great as the first in goodness, but greater a great deal in evil. He excels his brother for a coward, yet his brother is reputed one of the best that is. In a retreat he outruns any lackey; marry, in coming on he has the cramp.

1 SOLDIER   If your life be saved will you undertake to betray the Florentine?

PAROLLES   Ay, and the captain of his horse, Count Rossillion.

1 SOLDIER   I'll whisper with the general and know his pleasure.

PAROLLES   I'll no more drumming. A plague of all drums! Only to seem to deserve well, and to beguile the supposition of that lascivious young boy, the count, have I run into this danger; yet who would have suspected an ambush where I was taken?

1 SOLDIER   There is no remedy, sir, but you must die. The general says you that have so traitorously discover'd the secrets of your army, and made such pestiferous reports of men very nobly held, can serve the world for no honest use; therefore you must die. Come, headsman, off with his head.

PAROLLES   O Lord, sir, let me live, or let me see my death!

305   1 SOLDIER   That shall you, and take your leave of all your friends. [*unmuffling him*] So; look about you; know you any here?

BERTRAM   Good morrow, noble captain.

310   2 LORD   God bless you, Captain Parolles.

1 LORD   God save you, noble captain.

2 LORD   Captain, what greeting will you to my Lord Lafew? I am for France.

1 LORD   Good captain, will you give me a copy of the sonnet you writ to Diana in behalf of the Count Rossillion. And I were not a very coward I'd compel it of you; but fare you well.   *Exeunt Bertram and Lords.*

315

1 SOLDIER   You are undone, captain – all but your scarf; that has a knot on't yet.

PAROLLES   Who cannot be crush'd with a plot?

320   1 SOLDIER   If you could find out a country where but women were that had received so much shame you might begin an impudent nation. Fare ye well, sir. I am for France too; we shall speak of you there.   *Exeunt Soldiers.*

PAROLLES   Yet am I thankful. If my heart were great

325   'Twould burst at this. Captain I'll be no more,
But I will eat and drink and sleep as soft
As captain shall. Simply the thing I am
Shall make me live. Who knows himself a braggart,
Let him fear this; for it will come to pass

330   That every braggart shall be found an ass.
Rust, sword; cool, blushes; and Parolles live
Safest in shame; being fool'd, by fool'ry thrive.
There's place and means for every man alive.
I'll after them.   *Exit.*

4.4   *Enter* HELENA, Widow *and* DIANA.

HELENA
That you may well perceive I have not wrong'd you
One of the greatest in the Christian world
Shall be my surety; fore whose throne 'tis needful,
Ere I can perfect mine intents, to kneel.

5   Time was, I did him a desired office,
Dear almost as his life; which gratitude
Through flinty Tartar's bosom would peep forth
And answer thanks. I duly am inform'd
His grace is at Marcellus, to which place

10   We have convenient convoy. You must know
I am supposed dead. The army breaking,
My husband hies him home, where, heaven aiding,
And by the leave of my good lord the king,
We'll be before our welcome.

WIDOW   Gentle madam,

15   You never had a servant to whose trust
Your business was more welcome.

HELENA   Nor you, mistress,
Ever a friend whose thoughts more truly labour
To recompense your love. Doubt not but heaven

Hath brought me up to be your daughter's dower,
As it hath fated her to be my motive   20
And helper to a husband. But, O strange men!
That can such sweet use make of what they hate,
When saucy trusting of the cozen'd thoughts
Defiles the pitchy night; so lust doth play
With what it loathes for that which is away.   25
But more of this hereafter. You, Diana,
Under my poor instructions yet must suffer
Something in my behalf.

DIANA   Let death and honesty
Go with your impositions, I am yours,
Upon your will to suffer.

HELENA   Yet, I pray you;   30
But with the word: 'the time will bring on summer' –
When briars shall have leaves as well as thorns
And be as sweet as sharp. We must away;
Our wagon is prepar'd, and time revives us.
All's well that ends well; still the fine's the crown.   35
Whate'er the course, the end is the renown.   *Exeunt.*

4.5   *Enter* Clown, COUNTESS *and* LAFEW.

LAFEW   No, no, no, your son was misled with a snipp'd-taffeta fellow there, whose villainous saffron would have made all the unbak'd and doughy youth of a nation in his colour. Your daughter-in-law had been alive at this hour, and your son here at home, more   5
advanc'd by the king than by that red-tail'd humble-bee I speak of.

COUNTESS   I would I had not known him; it was the death of the most virtuous gentlewoman that ever nature had praise for creating. If she had partaken of   10
my flesh and cost me the dearest groans of a mother I could not have owed her a more rooted love.

LAFEW   'Twas a good lady; 'twas a good lady. We may pick a thousand sallets ere we light on such another herb.

CLOWN   Indeed, sir, she was the sweet-marjoram of the   15
sallet, or, rather, the herb of grace.

LAFEW   They are not herbs, you knave; they are nose-herbs.

CLOWN   I am no great Nabuchadnezzar, sir; I have not much skill in grass.   20

LAFEW   Whether dost thou profess thyself – a knave or a fool?

CLOWN   A fool, sir, at a woman's service, and a knave at a man's.

LAFEW   Your distinction?   25

CLOWN   I would cozen the man of his wife and do his service.

LAFEW   So you were a knave at his service indeed.

CLOWN   And I would give his wife my bauble, sir, to do her service.   30

LAFEW   I will subscribe for thee; thou art both knave and fool.

CLOWN   At your service.

LAFEW   No, no, no.

CLOWN   Why, sir, if I cannot serve you I can serve as great a prince as you are. 35

LAFEW   Who's that? a Frenchman?

CLOWN   Faith, sir, 'a has an English name; but his fisnomy is more hotter in France than there.

LAFEW   What prince is that? 40

CLOWN   The black prince, sir, alias the prince of darkness, alias the devil.

LAFEW   Hold thee, there's my purse. I give thee not this to suggest thee from thy master thou talk'st of; serve him still. 45

CLOWN   I am a woodland fellow, sir, that always loved a great fire, and the master I speak of ever keeps a good fire; but sure he is the prince of the world; let his nobility remain in's court, I am for the house with the narrow gate, which I take to be too little for pomp to enter; some that humble themselves may, but the many will be too chill and tender, and they'll be for the flow'ry way that leads to the broad gate and the great fire. 50

LAFEW   Go thy ways; I begin to be aweary of thee; and I tell thee so before, because I would not fall out with thee. Go thy ways; let my horses be well look'd to, without any tricks. 55

CLOWN   If I put any tricks upon 'em, sir, they shall be jades' tricks, which are their own right by the law of nature.   *Exit.* 60

LAFEW   A shrewd knave and an unhappy.

COUNTESS   So 'a is. My lord that's gone made himself much sport out of him; by his authority he remains here, which he thinks is a patent for his sauciness; and indeed he has no pace, but runs where he will. 65

LAFEW   I like him well; 'tis not amiss. And I was about to tell you, since I heard of the good lady's death and that my lord your son was upon his return home, I moved the king my master to speak in the behalf of my daughter; which, in the minority of them both, his majesty out of a self-gracious remembrance did first propose. His highness hath promis'd me to do it; and to stop up the displeasure he hath conceived against your son there is no fitter matter. How does your ladyship like it? 70 75

COUNTESS   With very much content, my lord, and I wish it happily effected.

LAFEW   His highness comes post from Marcellus, of as able body as when he number'd thirty. 'A will be here tomorrow, or I am deceiv'd by him that in such intelligence hath seldom fail'd. 80

COUNTESS   It rejoices me that I hope I shall see him ere I die. I have letters that my son will be here tonight. I shall beseech your lordship to remain with me till they meet together. 85

LAFEW   Madam, I was thinking with what manners I might safely be admitted.

COUNTESS   You need but plead your honourable privilege. 90

LAFEW   Lady, of that I have made a bold charter; but, I thank my God, it holds yet.

Re-enter Clown.

CLOWN   O madam, yonder's my lord your son with a patch of velvet on's face; whether there be a scar under't or no, the velvet knows; but 'tis a goodly patch of velvet. His left cheek is a cheek of two pile and a half, but his right cheek is worn bare. 95

LAFEW   A scar nobly got, or a noble scar, is a good liv'ry of honour; so belike is that.

CLOWN   But it is your carbonado'd face. 100

LAFEW   Let us go see your son, I pray you. I long to talk with the young noble soldier.

CLOWN   Faith, there's a dozen of 'em with delicate fine hats, and most courteous feathers which bow the head and nod at every man.   *Exeunt.* 105

5.1   *Enter* HELENA, Widow *and* DIANA, *with two attendants.*

HELENA   But this exceeding posting day and night
Must wear your spirits low. We cannot help it;
But since you have made the days and nights as one
To wear your gentle limbs in my affairs,
Be bold you do so grow in my requital 5
As nothing can unroot you.

Enter a Gentleman, *a stranger.*

                              In happy time!
This man may help me to his majesty's ear,
If he would spend his power. God save you, sir!

GENTLEMAN   And you.

HELENA   Sir, I have seen you in the court of France. 10

GENTLEMAN   I have been sometimes there.

HELENA   I do presume, sir, that you are not fall'n
From the report that goes upon your goodness,
And therefore, goaded with most sharp occasions
Which lay nice manners by, I put you to 15
The use of your own virtues, for the which
I shall continue thankful.

GENTLEMAN   What's your will?

HELENA   That it will please you
To give this poor petition to the king,
And aid me with that store of power you have 20
To come into his presence.

GENTLEMAN   The king's not here.

HELENA   Not here, sir?

GENTLEMAN   Not indeed.
He hence remov'd last night, and with more haste
Than is his use.

WIDOW   Lord, how we lose our pains!

HELENA   All's well that ends well yet, 25
Though time seem so adverse and means unfit.
I do beseech you, whither is he gone?

GENTLEMAN   Marry, as I take it, to Rossillion;
Whither I am going.

HELENA   I do beseech you, sir,
30   Since you are like to see the king before me,
      Commend the paper to his gracious hand,
      Which I presume shall render you no blame,
      But rather make you thank your pains for it.
      I will come after you with what good speed
      Our means will make us means.
35 GENTLEMAN   This I'll do for you.
HELENA
      And you shall find yourself to be well thank'd,
      Whate'er falls more. We must to horse again.
      Go, go, provide.   *Exeunt.*

5.2   *Enter* Clown *and* PAROLLES.

PAROLLES   Good Master Lavatch, give my Lord Lafew
    this letter; I have ere now, sir, been better known to
    you, when I have held familiarity with fresher clothes;
    but I am now, sir, muddied in Fortune's mood, and
5   smell somewhat strong of her strong displeasure.
CLOWN   Truly, Fortune's displeasure is but sluttish if it
    smell so strongly as thou speak'st of. I will henceforth
    eat no fish of Fortune's butt'ring. Prithee, allow the
    wind.
10 PAROLLES   Nay, you need not to stop your nose, sir. I
    spake but by a metaphor.
CLOWN   Indeed, sir, if your metaphor stink I will stop
    my nose, or against any man's metaphor. Prithee, get
    thee further.
15 PAROLLES   Pray you, sir, deliver me this paper.
CLOWN   Foh! Prithee stand away. A paper from
    Fortune's close-stool, to give to a nobleman! Look,
    here he comes himself.

               Enter LAFEW.

      Here is a pur of Fortune's, sir, or of Fortune's cat, but
20   not a musk-cat, that has fall'n into the unclean
      fishpond of her displeasure and, as he says, is muddied
      withal. Pray you, sir, use the carp as you may, for he
      looks like a poor, decayed, ingenious, foolish, rascally
      knave. I do pity his distress in my similes of comfort,
25   and leave him to your lordship.   *Exit.*
PAROLLES   My lord, I am a man whom Fortune hath
    cruelly scratch'd.
LAFEW   And what would you have me to do? 'Tis too
    late to pare her nails now. Wherein have you played
30   the knave with Fortune that she should scratch you,
    who of herself is a good lady and would not have
    knaves thrive long under her? There's a cardecue for
    you. Let the justices make you and Fortune friends; I
    am for other business.
35 PAROLLES   I beseech your honour to hear me one single
    word.
LAFEW   You beg a single penny more. Come, you shall
    ha't; save your word.
PAROLLES   My name, my good lord, is Parolles.
40 LAFEW   You beg more than 'word' then. Cox my
    passion! Give me your hand. How does your drum?

PAROLLES   O my good lord, you were the first that found
    me.
LAFEW   Was I, in sooth? And I was the first that lost
    thee.   45
PAROLLES   It lies in you, my lord, to bring me in some
    grace, for you did bring me out.
LAFEW   Out upon thee, knave! dost thou put upon me at
    once both the office of God and the devil? One brings
    thee in Grace and the other brings thee out. [*Trumpets*   50
    sound.] The king's coming; I know by his trumpets.
    Sirrah, inquire further after me. I had talk of you last
    night; though you are a fool and a knave you shall eat.
    Go to; follow.
PAROLLES   I praise God for you.   *Exeunt.*   55

5.3   *Flourish. Enter* KING, COUNTESS, LAFEW,
        the two French Lords, *with attendants.*

KING   We lost a jewel of her, and our esteem
       Was made much poorer by it; but your son,
       As mad in folly, lack'd the sense to know
       Her estimation home.
COUNTESS   'Tis past, my liege,
       And I beseech your majesty to make it   5
       Natural rebellion done i'th' blade of youth,
       When oil and fire, too strong for reason's force,
       O'erbears it and burns on.
KING   My honour'd lady,
       I have forgiven and forgotten all,
       Though my revenges were high bent upon him   10
       And watch'd the time to shoot.
LAFEW   This I must say –
       But first I beg my pardon – the young lord
       Did to his majesty, his mother and his lady
       Offence of mighty note, but to himself
       The greatest wrong of all. He lost a wife   15
       Whose beauty did astonish the survey
       Of richest eyes; whose words all ears took captive;
       Whose dear perfection hearts that scorn'd to serve
       Humbly call'd mistress.
KING   Praising what is lost
       Makes the remembrance dear. Well, call him hither;   20
       We are reconcil'd, and the first view shall kill
       All repetition. Let him not ask our pardon;
       The nature of his great offence is dead,
       And deeper than oblivion we do bury
       Th'incensing relics of it. Let him approach   25
       A stranger, no offender; and inform him
       So 'tis our will he should.
GENTLEMAN   I shall, my liege.   *Exit.*
KING
       What says he to your daughter? Have you spoke?
LAFEW All that he is hath reference to your highness.
KING   Then shall we have a match. I have letters sent me   30
       That sets him high in fame.

               Enter BERTRAM.

LAFEW   He looks well on't.

KING   I am not a day of season,
    For thou may'st see a sunshine and a hail
    In me at once. But to the brightest beams
35   Distracted clouds give way; so stand thou forth;
    The time is fair again.
BERTRAM   My high-repented blames
    Dear sovereign, pardon to me.
KING   All is whole.
    Not one word more of the consumed time;
    Let's take the instant by the forward top;
40   For we are old, and on our quick'st decrees
    Th'inaudible and noiseless foot of time
    Steals ere we can effect them. You remember
    The daughter of this lord?
BERTRAM   Admiringly, my liege. At first
45   I stuck my choice upon her, ere my heart
    Durst make too bold a herald of my tongue;
    Where, the impression of mine eye infixing,
    Contempt his scornful perspective did lend me,
    Which warp'd the line of every other favour,
50   Scorn'd a fair colour or express'd it stol'n,
    Extended or contracted all proportions
    To a most hideous object. Thence it came
    That she whom all men prais'd, and whom myself
    Since I have lost, have lov'd, was in mine eye
    The dust that did offend it.
55 KING   Well excus'd.
    That thou didst love her, strikes some scores away
    From the great compt; but love that comes too late,
    Like a remorseful pardon slowly carried,
    To the great sender turns a sour offence,
60   Crying, 'That's good that's gone'. Our rash faults
    Make trivial price of serious things we have,
    Not knowing them until we know their grave.
    Oft our displeasures, to ourselves unjust,
    Destroy our friends and after weep their dust;
65   Our own love waking cries to see what's done,
    While shameful hate sleeps out the afternoon.
    Be this sweet Helen's knell, and now forget her.
    Send forth your amorous token for fair Maudlin.
    The main consents are had, and here we'll stay
70   To see our widower's second marriage-day.
COUNTESS
    Which better than the first, O dear heaven, bless!
    Or, ere they meet, in me, O nature, cesse!
LAFEW   Come on, my son, in whom my house's name
    Must be digested; give a favour from you
75   To sparkle in the spirits of my daughter,
    That she may quickly come. [*Bertram gives a ring.*]
                By my old beard
    And ev'ry hair that's on't, Helen that's dead
    Was a sweet creature; such a ring as this,
    The last that e'er I took her leave at court,
    I saw upon her finger.
80 BERTRAM   Hers it was not.
KING   Now pray you let me see it; for mine eye,
    While I was speaking, oft was fasten'd to't.

This ring was mine, and when I gave it Helen
    I bade her, if her fortunes ever stood
    Necessitied to help, that by this token   85
    I would relieve her. Had you that craft to reave her
    Of what should stead her most?
BERTRAM   My gracious sovereign,
    Howe'er it pleases you to take it so,
    The ring was never hers.
COUNTESS   Son, on my life,
    I have seen her wear it, and she reckon'd it   90
    At her life's rate.
LAFEW   I am sure I saw her wear it.
BERTRAM   You are deceiv'd, my lord; she never saw it.
    In Florence was it from a casement thrown me,
    Wrapp'd in a paper which contain'd the name
    Of her that threw it. Noble she was, and thought   95
    I stood ingag'd; but when I had subscrib'd
    To mine own fortune, and inform'd her fully
    I could not answer in that course of honour
    As she had made the overture, she ceas'd
    In heavy satisfaction, and would never   100
    Receive the ring again.
KING   Plutus himself,
    That knows the tinct and multiplying med'cine,
    Hath not in nature's mystery more science
    Than I have in this ring. 'Twas mine, 'twas Helen's,
    Whoever gave it you; then if you know   105
    That you are well acquainted with yourself,
    Confess 'twas hers, and by what rough enforcement
    You got it from her. She call'd the saints to surety
    That she would never put it from her finger
    Unless she gave it to yourself in bed,   110
    Where you have never come, or sent it us
    Upon her great disaster.
BERTRAM   She never saw it.
KING   Thou speak'st it falsely, as I love mine honour,
    And mak'st conjectural fears to come into me
    Which I would fain shut out. If it should prove   115
    That thou art so inhuman – 'twill not prove so,
    And yet I know not; thou didst hate her deadly,
    And she is dead; which nothing but to close
    Her eyes myself could win me to believe,
    More than to see this ring. Take him away.   120
    My fore-past proofs, howe'er the matter fall,
    Shall tax my fears of little vanity,
    Having vainly fear'd too little. Away with him.
    We'll sift this matter further.
BERTRAM   If you shall prove
    This ring was ever hers, you shall as easy   125
    Prove that I husbanded her bed in Florence,
    Where yet she never was.   *Exit, guarded.*
KING   I am wrapp'd in dismal thinkings.

Enter the Gentleman *stranger.*

GENTLEMAN   Gracious sovereign,
    Whether I have been to blame or no, I know not:
    Here's a petition from a Florentine   130

Who hath for four or five removes come short
To tender it herself. I undertook it,
Vanquish'd thereto by the fair grace and speech
Of the poor suppliant, who, by this, I know,
135 Is here attending; her business looks in her
With an importing visage, and she told me,
In a sweet verbal brief, it did concern
Your highness with herself.
KING [*Reads the letter.*] *Upon his many protestations to*
140 *marry me when his wife was dead, I blush to say it, he won*
me. Now is the Count Rossillion a widower; his vows are
forfeited to me and my honour's paid to him. He stole
from Florence, taking no leave, and I follow him to his
country for justice. Grant it me, O king! In you it best
145 *lies; otherwise a seducer flourishes, and a poor maid is*
undone.

          DIANA CAPILET.

LAFEW I will buy me a son-in-law in a fair, and toll for
  this. I'll none of him.
150 KING The heavens have thought well on thee, Lafew,
To bring forth this discov'ry. Seek these suitors.
Go speedily, and bring again the count.
         Exeunt attendants.
I am afear'd the life of Helen, lady,
Was foully snatch'd.
COUNTESS   Now justice on the doers!

    Re-enter BERTRAM *guarded.*

155 KING I wonder, sir, since wives are monsters to you,
And that you fly them as you swear them lordship,
Yet you desire to marry.

    Enter Widow *and* DIANA.

        What woman's that?
DIANA I am, my lord, a wretched Florentine,
Derived from the ancient Capilet;
160 My suit, as I do understand, you know,
And therefore know how far I may be pitied.
WIDOW I am her mother, sir, whose age and honour
Both suffer under this complaint we bring,
And both shall cease, without your remedy.
165 KING Come hither, count; do you know these women?
BERTRAM My lord, I neither can nor will deny
But that I know them. Do they charge me further?
DIANA Why do you look so strange upon your wife?
BERTRAM She's none of mine, my lord.
DIANA   If you shall marry
170 You give away this hand and that is mine,
You give away heaven's vows and those are mine,
You give away myself which is known mine;
For I by vow am so embodied yours
That she which marries you must marry me –
175 Either both or none.
LAFEW
Your reputation comes too short for my daughter;
You are no husband for her.

BERTRAM
My lord, this is a fond and desp'rate creature
Whom sometime I have laugh'd with. Let your
  highness
Lay a more noble thought upon mine honour   180
Than for to think that I would sink it here.
KING
Sir, for my thoughts, you have them ill to friend
Till your deeds gain them; fairer prove your honour
Than in my thought it lies!
DIANA   Good my lord,
Ask him upon his oath if he does think   185
He had not my virginity.
KING What say'st thou to her?
BERTRAM   She's impudent, my lord,
And was a common gamester to the camp.
DIANA He does me wrong, my lord; if I were so
He might have bought me at a common price. 190
Do not believe him. O behold this ring
Whose high respect and rich validity
Did lack a parallel; yet for all that
He gave it to a commoner a'th' camp –
If I be one.
COUNTESS He blushes and 'tis hit.   195
Of six preceding ancestors, that gem
Conferr'd by testament to th' sequent issue,
Hath it been owed and worn. This is his wife:
That ring's a thousand proofs.
KING   Methought you said
You saw one here in court could witness it.   200
DIANA I did, my lord, but loath am to produce
So bad an instrument; his name's Parolles.
LAFEW I saw the man today, if man he be.
KING
Find him and bring him hither. *Exit an attendant.*
BERTRAM   What of him?
He's quoted for a most perfidious slave   205
With all the spots a'th' world tax'd and debosh'd,
Whose nature sickens but to speak a truth.
Am I or that or this for what he'll utter,
That will speak anything?
KING   She hath that ring of yours.
BERTRAM I think she has. Certain it is I lik'd her 210
And boarded her i'th' wanton way of youth.
She knew her distance and did angle for me,
Madding my eagerness with her restraint,
As all impediments in fancy's course
Are motives of more fancy; and in fine   215
Her inf'nite cunning with her modern grace
Subdu'd me to her rate; she got the ring,
And I had that which any inferior might
At market-price have bought.
DIANA   I must be patient.
You that have turn'd off a first so noble wife 220
May justly diet me. I pray you yet –
Since you lack virtue I will lose a husband –
Send for your ring, I will return it home,

And give me mine again.

BERTRAM   I have it not.

KING   What ring was yours, I pray you?

225   DIANA   Sir, much like

The same upon your finger.

KING   Know you this ring? This ring was his of late.

DIANA   And this was it I gave him, being abed.

KING   The story then goes false you threw it him

Out of a casement?

230   DIANA   I have spoke the truth.

Enter PAROLLES.

BERTRAM   My lord, I do confess the ring was hers.

KING   You boggle shrewdly; every feather starts you.

Is this the man you speak of?

DIANA   Ay, my lord.

KING   Tell me, sirrah – but tell me true I charge you,

235   Not fearing the displeasure of your master,

Which on your just proceeding I'll keep off –

By him and by this woman here what know you?

PAROLLES   So please your majesty, my master hath been

an honourable gentleman. Tricks he hath had in him,

240   which gentlemen have.

KING   Come, come, to th' purpose. Did he love this

woman?

PAROLLES   Faith, sir, he did love her; but how?

KING   How, I pray you?

245   PAROLLES   He did love her, sir, as a gentleman loves a

woman.

KING   How is that?

PAROLLES   He lov'd her, sir, and lov'd her not.

KING   As thou art a knave and no knave. What an

250   equivocal companion is this!

PAROLLES   I am a poor man, and at your majesty's

command.

LAFEW   He's a good drum, my lord, but a naughty

orator.

255   DIANA   Do you know he promis'd me marriage?

PAROLLES   Faith, I know more than I'll speak.

KING   But wilt thou not speak all thou know'st?

PAROLLES   Yes, so please your majesty. I did go between

them as I said; but more than that, he loved her, for

260   indeed he was mad for her and talk'd of Satan and of

Limbo and of furies and I know not what; yet I was in

that credit with them at that time that I knew of their

going to bed and of other motions, as promising her

marriage and things which would derive me ill will to

265   speak of; therefore I will not speak what I know.

KING   Thou hast spoken all already, unless thou canst

say they are married; but thou art too fine in thy

evidence; therefore, stand aside.

This ring you say was yours?

DIANA   Ay, my good lord.

270   KING   Where did you buy it? Or who gave it you?

DIANA   It was not given me, nor I did not buy it.

KING   Who lent it you?

DIANA   It was not lent me neither.

KING   Where did you find it then?

DIANA   I found it not.

KING   If it were yours by none of all these ways

How could you give it him?

DIANA   I never gave it him.   275

LAFEW   This woman's an easy glove, my lord; she goes

off and on at pleasure.

KING   This ring was mine; I gave it his first wife.

DIANA   It might be yours or hers for ought I know.

KING   Take her away. I do not like her now.   280

To prison with her. And away with him.

Unless thou tell'st me where thou hadst this ring

Thou diest within this hour.

DIANA   I'll never tell you.

KING   Take her away.

DIANA   I'll put in bail, my liege.

KING   I think thee now some common customer.   285

DIANA   By Jove, if ever I knew man 'twas you.

KING   Wherefore hast thou accus'd him all this while?

DIANA   Because he's guilty and he is not guilty.

He knows I am no maid, and he'll swear to't;

I'll swear I am a maid and he knows not.   290

Great king, I am no strumpet; by my life

I am either maid or else this old man's wife.

KING   She does abuse our ears. To prison with her.

DIANA   Good mother, fetch my bail. Stay, royal sir;

Exit Widow.

The jeweller that owes the ring is sent for   295

And he shall surety me. But for this lord

Who hath abus'd me as he knows himself –

Though yet he never harm'd me – here I quit him.

He knows himself my bed he hath defil'd;

And at that time he got his wife with child.   300

Dead though she be she feels her young one kick.

So there's my riddle: one that's dead is quick,

And now behold the meaning.

Re-enter Widow *with* HELENA.

KING   Is there no exorcist

Beguiles the truer office of mine eyes?

Is't real that I see?

HELENA   No, my good lord;   305

'Tis but the shadow of a wife you see;

The name and not the thing.

BERTRAM   Both, both. O pardon!

HELENA   O my good lord, when I was like this maid

I found you wondrous kind. There is your ring,

And, look you, here's your letter. This it says: 310

When from my finger you can get this ring

And is by me with child, etc. This is done;

Will you be mine now you are doubly won?

BERTRAM

If she, my liege, can make me know this clearly

I'll love her dearly, ever, ever dearly.   315

HELENA   If it appear not plain and prove untrue

Deadly divorce step between me and you!

O my dear mother, do I see you living?

LAFEW　Mine eyes smell onions; I shall weep anon. [*to*
320　　*Parolles*] Good Tom Drum, lend me a handkercher.
　　So, I thank thee. Wait on me home, I'll make sport
　　with thee. Let thy curtsies alone, they are scurvy ones.
KING　Let us from point to point this story know
　　To make the even truth in pleasure flow.
325　[*to Diana*] If thou beest yet a fresh uncropped flower
　　Choose thou thy husband and I'll pay thy dower;
　　For I can guess that by thy honest aid
　　Thou kept'st a wife herself, thyself a maid.
　　Of that and all the progress more and less
330　Resolvedly more leisure shall express.

All yet seems well, and if it end so meet,
The bitter past, more welcome is the sweet.

[*Flourish.*]

EPILOGUE

The king's a beggar, now the play is done;
All is well ended if this suit be won,
That you express content; which we will pay
With strife to please you, day exceeding day.
Ours be your patience then and yours our parts;　5
Your gentle hands lend us and take our hearts.

Exeunt omnes.

Antony and Cleopatra

Antony and Cleopatra was first published in the Folio of 1623, as the tenth of the tragedies. Along with 'The booke of Pericles prynce of Tyre', it had previously been entered by Edward Blount in the Stationers' Register on 20 May 1608. Both Barnabe Barnes's *The Devil's Charter* (performed at Court on 2 February 1607) and Samuel Daniel's 'newly altered' fourth edition of his tragedy *Cleopatra* (published in 1607) show knowledge of Shakespeare's play. It was therefore probably completed sometime in 1606, roughly contemporaneously with the writing of *Macbeth* and shortly before *Coriolanus*.

The story of the tragic love affair was, of course, well known; literary references go back as far as Virgil and Horace, and Chaucer includes Cleopatra in his *Legend of Good Women*. Shakespeare almost certainly knew several Renaissance versions of the story, most notably the Countess of Pembroke's tragedy *Antonius* (1592), adapted from Robert Garnier's *Marc Antoine*, and Daniel's *Cleopatra*, first published in 1594 and dedicated to the Countess of Pembroke. However, he depended mainly upon 'The Life of Marcus Antonius' in Plutarch's *Lives of the Noble Grecians and Romans*, translated from Greek into French by Jacques Amyot, from French into English by Thomas North, and published in London in 1579. Shakespeare often follows North's Plutarch closely – verbal borrowings are frequent – but he shapes the story to his own purposes, as the action constantly shifts location, ranging quickly back and forth across the Mediterranean.

Rome and Egypt are not merely the geographical poles of the action, but become powerful symbols of competing emotional and ethical values. Rome is a world of measure, Egypt of excess; Rome of pragmatism, Egypt of passion; Rome of political ambition, Egypt of emotional desire. Even stylistically the differences are marked: Roman speech is 'Attic', spare and direct; Egyptian speech is 'Asiatic', ornate and sensuous. However, the competing values are not wholly consistent, nor do they admit of easy judgements. If Roman values, judged on their own terms, appear disciplined and high-minded, by Egyptian standards they seem cold and inhuman; similarly, Egyptian values, judged on Egyptian terms as generous and life-affirming, by Roman standards appear self-indulgent and irresponsible. The play never allows an audience a secure and stable moral vantage-point from which to judge the action or the characters, giving us instead multiple perspectives and inviting constant reassessment of our responses.

Even death partakes at once of tragic loss and of a paradoxical victory and transcendence. Plutarch's Antony seeks his own death in despair, 'sith spiteful fortune hath taken from thee the only joy thou hadst'; Shakespeare's Antony rather seeks death, to be reunited with his queen: 'I will o'ertake thee, Cleopatra, and / Weep for my pardon.' Antony would be 'A bridegroom in [his] death', and Cleopatra dies with a final magnificent claim to Antony, 'Husband, I come!' For them, at least, love does overcome death. From Cleopatra's viewpoint indeed ''Tis paltry to be Caesar'. But, of course, Caesar survives to become Emperor of the world, and Rome will not 'in Tiber melt'.

The moral contents of the play are projected in a succession of scenes, many of them brief, which exploit to the full the fluid staging practices of early Jacobean theatres. The proscenium stages and the realistic props and scenery which developed after 1660 ensured that Shakespeare's play was superseded for a century or more by John Dryden's neoclassical rewriting of the story as *All for Love, or the World Well Lost* (1678). When *Antony and Cleopatra* returned to the theatres of the nineteenth and early twentieth centuries, productions became ever more opulent and operatic. Spectacle disrupted the play's own dramatic structure, and critics and reviewers regularly decried its apparent lack of unity. Simply set and played with the staccato rhythms marked by the text, the play has achieved notable, though infrequent, success on the modern stage, its principle of construction clear and effective, its moral design complex and compelling.

The Arden text is based on the 1623 First Folio.

Mark ANTONY ⎫
Octavius CAESAR ⎬ *triumvirs*
LEPIDUS ⎭
CLEOPATRA　　　*Queen of Egypt*
Sextus Pompeius *or* POMPEY　　*rebel against the triumvirs*
DEMETRIUS ⎫
PHILO
Domitius ENOBARBUS
VENTIDIUS
SILIUS ⎬ *followers of Antony*
EROS
CANIDIUS
SCARUS
DERCETUS
A Schoolmaster, Antony's AMBASSADOR ⎭
OCTAVIA　　*sister of Octavius Caesar*
MAECENAS ⎫
AGRIPPA
TAURUS
DOLABELLA ⎬ *followers of Caesar*
THIDIAS
GALLUS
PROCULEIUS ⎭
CHARMIAN ⎫
IRAS
ALEXAS
MARDIAN, *a eunuch* ⎬ *attendants on Cleopatra*
DIOMEDES
SELEUCUS ⎭
MENAS ⎫
MENECRATES ⎬ *followers of Pompey*
VARRIUS ⎭
MESSENGERS
SOOTHSAYER
SERVANTS　　*of Pompey*
BOY SINGER
CAPTAIN　　*in Antony's army*
SENTRIES *and* GUARDS
CLOWN

Eunuchs, Attendants, Captains, Soldiers, Servants

Antony and Cleopatra

1.1   *Enter* DEMETRIUS *and* PHILO.

PHILO   Nay, but this dotage of our general's
O'erflows the measure. Those his goodly eyes,
That o'er the files and musters of the war
Have glowed like plated Mars, now bend, now turn
The office and devotion of their view
Upon a tawny front. His captain's heart,
Which in the scuffles of great fights hath burst
The buckles on his breast, reneges all temper
And is become the bellows and the fan
To cool a gipsy's lust.

Flourish. Enter ANTONY, CLEOPATRA, *her ladies*
CHARMIAN *and* IRAS, *the train, with eunuchs fanning her.*

                    Look where they come!
Take but good note, and you shall see in him
The triple pillar of the world transformed
Into a strumpet's fool. Behold and see.

CLEOPATRA   If it be love indeed, tell me how much.

ANTONY
There's beggary in the love that can be reckoned.

CLEOPATRA   I'll set a bourn how far to be beloved.

ANTONY
Then must thou needs find out new heaven, new
earth.

Enter a Messenger.

MESSENGER   News, my good lord, from Rome.

ANTONY   Grates me! The sum.

CLEOPATRA   Nay, hear them, Antony.
Fulvia perchance is angry, or who knows
If the scarce-bearded Caesar have not sent
His powerful mandate to you: 'Do this, or this;
Take in that kingdom and enfranchise that.
Perform't, or else we damn thee.'

ANTONY   How, my love?

CLEOPATRA   Perchance? Nay, and most like.
You must not stay here longer; your dismission
Is come from Caesar; therefore hear it, Antony.
Where's Fulvia's process? – Caesar's, I would say.
Both?
Call in the messengers! As I am Egypt's Queen,
Thou blushest, Antony, and that blood of thine
Is Caesar's homager; else so thy cheek pays shame
When shrill-tongued Fulvia scolds. The messengers!

ANTONY   Let Rome in Tiber melt, and the wide arch
Of the ranged empire fall! Here is my space!
Kingdoms are clay! Our dungy earth alike
Feeds beast as man. The nobleness of life
Is to do thus, when such a mutual pair
And such a twain can do't, in which I bind,
On pain of punishment, the world to weet
We stand up peerless.

CLEOPATRA   Excellent falsehood!
Why did he marry Fulvia and not love her?
I'll seem the fool I am not. Antony

Will be himself.

ANTONY   But stirred by Cleopatra.
Now, for the love of Love and her soft hours,
Let's not confound the time with conference harsh.
There's not a minute of our lives should stretch
Without some pleasure now. What sport tonight?

CLEOPATRA   Hear the ambassadors.

ANTONY   Fie, wrangling queen,
Whom everything becomes – to chide, to laugh,
To weep; whose every passion fully strives
To make itself, in thee, fair and admired!
No messenger but thine, and all alone
Tonight we'll wander through the streets and note
The qualities of people. Come, my queen!
Last night you did desire it. [*to the Messenger*] Speak
not to us.

Exeunt Antony and Cleopatra with the train.

DEMETRIUS   Is Caesar with Antonius prized so slight?

PHILO   Sir, sometimes, when he is not Antony,
He comes too short of that great property
Which still should go with Antony.

DEMETRIUS   I am full sorry
That he approves the common liar who
Thus speaks of him at Rome, but I will hope
Of better deeds tomorrow. Rest you happy!   *Exeunt.*

1.2   *Enter* ENOBARBUS *and other Roman officers,*
a Soothsayer, CHARMIAN, IRAS, MARDIAN *the Eunuch*
and ALEXAS.

CHARMIAN   Lord Alexas, sweet Alexas, most anything
Alexas, almost most absolute Alexas, where's the
soothsayer that you praised so to th' Queen? O, that I
knew this husband which you say must charge his
horns with garlands!

ALEXAS   Soothsayer!

SOOTHSAYER   Your will?

CHARMIAN   Is this the man? Is't you, sir, that know
things?

SOOTHSAYER   In nature's infinite book of secrecy
A little I can read.

ALEXAS   Show him your hand.

ENOBARBUS
Bring in the banquet quickly; wine enough
Cleopatra's health to drink.

Enter servants with wine and other refreshments and
exeunt.

CHARMIAN [*Gives her hand to the Soothsayer.*]   Good sir,
give me good fortune.

SOOTHSAYER   I make not, but foresee.

CHARMIAN   Pray then, foresee me one.

SOOTHSAYER   You shall be yet far fairer than you are.

CHARMIAN   He means in flesh.

IRAS   No, you shall paint when you are old.

CHARMIAN   Wrinkles forbid!

ALEXAS   Vex not his prescience. Be attentive.

CHARMIAN   Hush!
SOOTHSAYER   You shall be more beloving than beloved.
25 CHARMIAN   I had rather heat my liver with drinking.
ALEXAS   Nay, hear him.
CHARMIAN   Good now, some excellent fortune! Let
me be married to three kings in a forenoon and widow
them all. Let me have a child at fifty to whom Herod
30 of Jewry may do homage. Find me to marry me with
Octavius Caesar and companion me with my mistress.
SOOTHSAYER
You shall outlive the lady whom you serve.
CHARMIAN   O, excellent! I love long life better than figs.
SOOTHSAYER
You have seen and proved a fairer former fortune
35 Than that which is to approach.
CHARMIAN   Then belike my children shall have no names.
Prithee, how many boys and wenches must I have?
SOOTHSAYER   If every of your wishes had a womb,
And fertile every wish, a million.
40 CHARMIAN   Out, fool! I forgive thee for a witch.
ALEXAS   You think none but your sheets are privy to
your wishes.
CHARMIAN   Nay, come, tell Iras hers.
ALEXAS   We'll know all our fortunes.
45 ENOBARBUS   Mine, and most of our fortunes tonight,
shall be drunk to bed.
IRAS   [*Holds out her hand.*]   There's a palm presages
chastity, if nothing else.
CHARMIAN   E'en as the o'erflowing Nilus presageth
50 famine.
IRAS   Go, you wild bedfellow, you cannot soothsay!
CHARMIAN   Nay, if an oily palm be not a fruitful
prognostication, I cannot scratch mine ear. Prithee,
tell her but a workaday fortune.
55 SOOTHSAYER   Your fortunes are alike.
IRAS   But how? But how? Give me particulars!
SOOTHSAYER   I have said.
IRAS   Am I not an inch of fortune better than she?
CHARMIAN   Well, if you were but an inch of fortune
60 better than I, where would you choose it?
IRAS   Not in my husband's nose.
CHARMIAN   Our worser thoughts heavens mend! Alexas
– come, his fortune, his fortune! O, let him marry a
woman that cannot go, sweet Isis I beseech thee, and
65 let her die too, and give him a worse, and let worse
follow worse, till the worst of all follow him laughing
to his grave, fiftyfold a cuckold! Good Isis, hear me
this prayer, though thou deny me a matter of more
weight; good Isis, I beseech thee!
70 IRAS   Amen. Dear goddess, hear that prayer of the
people! For as it is a heartbreaking to see a handsome
man loose-wived, so it is a deadly sorrow to behold a
foul knave uncuckolded. Therefore, dear Isis, keep
decorum and fortune him accordingly!
75 CHARMIAN   Amen.
ALEXAS   Lo now, if it lay in their hands to make me a
cuckold, they would make themselves whores, but
they'd do't.

Enter CLEOPATRA.

ENOBARBUS   Hush, here comes Antony.
CHARMIAN   Not he, the Queen.   80
CLEOPATRA   Saw you my lord?
ENOBARBUS   No, lady.
CLEOPATRA   Was he not here?
CHARMIAN   No, madam.
CLEOPATRA
He was disposed to mirth, but on the sudden   85
A Roman thought hath struck him. Enobarbus!
ENOBARBUS   Madam?
CLEOPATRA
Seek him and bring him hither.   *Exit Enobarbus.*
                          Where's Alexas?
ALEXAS   Here, at your service. My lord approaches.

Enter ANTONY *with a* Messenger.

CLEOPATRA   We will not look upon him. Go with us.   90
            Exeunt all but Antony and Messenger.
MESSENGER   Fulvia thy wife first came into the field.
ANTONY   Against my brother Lucius?
MESSENGER   Ay,
But soon that war had end, and the time's state
Made friends of them, jointing their force 'gainst
   Caesar,   95
Whose better issue in the war from Italy
Upon the first encounter drave them.
ANTONY   Well, what worst?
MESSENGER   The nature of bad news infects the teller.
ANTONY   When it concerns the fool or coward. On!   100
Things that are past are done with me. 'Tis thus:
Who tells me true, though in his tale lie death,
I hear him as he flattered.
MESSENGER   Labienus –
This is stiff news – hath with his Parthian force
Extended Asia. From Euphrates   105
His conquering banner shook, from Syria
To Lydia, and to Ionia,
Whilst –
ANTONY   'Antony', thou wouldst say –
MESSENGER   O, my lord!
ANTONY
Speak to me home; mince not the general tongue;
Name Cleopatra as she is called in Rome;   110
Rail thou in Fulvia's phrase, and taunt my faults
With such full licence as both truth and malice
Have power to utter. Oh, then we bring forth weeds
When our quick minds lie still, and our ills told us
Is as our earing. Fare thee well awhile.   115
MESSENGER   At your noble pleasure.   *Exit Messenger.*

Enter another Messenger.

ANTONY   From Sicyon how the news? Speak there!

2 MESSENGER   The man from Sicyon –
ANTONY   Is there such a one?
2 MESSENGER   He stays upon your will.
ANTONY   Let him appear.
Exit Second Messenger.

120 These strong Egyptian fetters I must break,
Or lose myself in dotage.

Enter another Messenger *with a letter.*

What are you?
MESSENGER   Fulvia thy wife is dead.
ANTONY   Where died she?
3 MESSENGER   In Sicyon.
125 Her length of sickness, with what else more serious
Importeth thee to know, this bears.
[*Gives him the letter.*]
ANTONY   Forbear me.
Exit Third Messenger.
There's a great spirit gone! Thus did I desire it.
What our contempts doth often hurl from us
We wish it ours again. The present pleasure,
130 By revolution lowering, does become
The opposite of itself. She's good, being gone.
The hand could pluck her back that shoved her on.
I must from this enchanting queen break off.
Ten thousand harms, more than the ills I know,
135 My idleness doth hatch. How now, Enobarbus!

Enter ENOBARBUS.

ENOBARBUS   What's your pleasure, sir?
ANTONY   I must with haste from hence.
ENOBARBUS   Why then we kill all our women. We see
how mortal an unkindness is to them. If they suffer
140 our departure, death's the word.
ANTONY   I must be gone.
ENOBARBUS   Under a compelling occasion let women
die. It were pity to cast them away for nothing,
though between them and a great cause they should be
145 esteemed nothing. Cleopatra, catching but the least
noise of this, dies instantly. I have seen her die twenty
times upon far poorer moment. I do think there is
mettle in death which commits some loving act upon
her, she hath such a celerity in dying.
150 ANTONY   She is cunning past man's thought.
ENOBARBUS   Alack, sir, no; her passions are made of
nothing but the finest part of pure love. We cannot call
her winds and waters sighs and tears; they are
greater storms and tempests than almanacs can report.
155 This cannot be cunning in her. If it be, she makes a
shower of rain as well as Jove.
ANTONY   Would I had never seen her!
ENOBARBUS   O, sir, you had then left unseen a wonderful
piece of work, which not to have been blest withal
160 would have discredited your travel.
ANTONY   Fulvia is dead.
ENOBARBUS   Sir?
ANTONY   Fulvia is dead.

ENOBARBUS   Fulvia?
ANTONY   Dead.   165
ENOBARBUS   Why, sir, give the gods a thankful sacrifice.
When it pleaseth their deities to take the wife of a man
from him, it shows to man the tailors of the earth;
comforting therein, that when old robes are worn out,
there are members to make new. If there were no more   170
women but Fulvia, then had you indeed a cut, and the
case to be lamented. This grief is crowned with
consolation: your old smock brings forth a new
petticoat, and indeed the tears live in an onion that
should water this sorrow.   175
ANTONY   The business she hath broached in the state
Cannot endure my absence.
ENOBARBUS   And the business you have broached here
cannot be without you, especially that of Cleopatra's,
which wholly depends on your abode.   180
ANTONY   No more light answers. Let our officers
Have notice what we purpose. I shall break
The cause of our expedience to the Queen
And get her leave to part. For not alone
The death of Fulvia, with more urgent touches,   185
Do strongly speak to us, but the letters too
Of many our contriving friends in Rome
Petition us at home. Sextus Pompeius
Hath given the dare to Caesar and commands
The empire of the sea. Our slippery people,   190
Whose love is never linked to the deserver
Till his deserts are past, begin to throw
Pompey the Great and all his dignities
Upon his son, who, high in name and power,
Higher than both in blood and life, stands up   195
For the main soldier; whose quality going on,
The sides o'th' world may danger. Much is breeding
Which, like the courser's hair, hath yet but life
And not a serpent's poison. Say our pleasure,
To such whose place is under us, requires   200
Our quick remove from hence.
ENOBARBUS   I shall do't.   *Exeunt.*

1.3   *Enter* CLEOPATRA, CHARMIAN, ALEXAS *and* IRAS.

CLEOPATRA   Where is he?
CHARMIAN   I did not see him since.
CLEOPATRA [*to Alexas*]
See where he is, who's with him, what he does.
I did not send you. If you find him sad,
Say I am dancing; if in mirth, report   5
That I am sudden sick. Quick, and return.
Exit Alexas.
CHARMIAN
Madam, methinks if you did love him dearly,
You do not hold the method to enforce
The like from him.
CLEOPATRA   What should I do I do not?
CHARMIAN
In each thing give him way; cross him in nothing.   10

CLEOPATRA
  Thou teachest like a fool: the way to lose him.

CHARMIAN   Tempt him not so too far; I wish, forbear.
  In time we hate that which we often fear.

Enter ANTONY.

  But here comes Antony.

CLEOPATRA   I am sick and sullen.

15 ANTONY   I am sorry to give breathing to my purpose –

CLEOPATRA   Help me away, dear Charmian! I shall fall!
  It cannot be thus long; the sides of nature
  Will not sustain it.

ANTONY   Now, my dearest queen –

CLEOPATRA   Pray you, stand farther from me!

ANTONY   What's the matter?

CLEOPATRA
20   I know by that same eye there's some good news.
  What, says the married woman you may go?
  Would she had never given you leave to come!
  Let her not say 'tis I that keep you here.
  I have no power upon you; hers you are.

ANTONY   The gods best know –

25 CLEOPATRA   O, never was there queen
  So mightily betrayed! Yet at the first
  I saw the treasons planted.

ANTONY   Cleopatra –

CLEOPATRA
  Why should I think you can be mine and true –
  Though you in swearing shake the throned gods –
30   Who have been false to Fulvia? Riotous madness,
  To be entangled with those mouth-made vows
  Which break themselves in swearing!

ANTONY   Most sweet queen –

CLEOPATRA
  Nay, pray you seek no colour for your going,
  But bid farewell and go. When you sued staying,
35   Then was the time for words; no going then.
  Eternity was in our lips and eyes,
  Bliss in our brows' bent; none our parts so poor
  But was a race of heaven. They are so still,
  Or thou, the greatest soldier of the world,
  Art turned the greatest liar.

40 ANTONY   How now, lady?

CLEOPATRA
  I would I had thy inches! Thou shouldst know
  There were a heart in Egypt!

ANTONY   Hear me, queen.
  The strong necessity of time commands
  Our services awhile, but my full heart
45   Remains in use with you. Our Italy
  Shines o'er with civil swords; Sextus Pompeius
  Makes his approaches to the port of Rome;
  Equality of two domestic powers
  Breed scrupulous faction; the hated, grown to
    strength,
50   Are newly grown to love; the condemned Pompey,
  Rich in his father's honour, creeps apace

Into the hearts of such as have not thrived
Upon the present state, whose numbers threaten;
And quietness, grown sick of rest, would purge
By any desperate change. My more particular,   55
And that which most with you should safe my going,
Is Fulvia's death.

CLEOPATRA
  Though age from folly could not give me freedom,
  It does from childishness. Can Fulvia die?

ANTONY   She's dead, my queen. [*Gives her the letters.*]   60
  Look here, and at thy sovereign leisure read
  The garboils she awaked. At the last, best,
  See when and where she died.

CLEOPATRA   O most false love!
  Where be the sacred vials thou shouldst fill
  With sorrowful water? Now I see, I see,   65
  In Fulvia's death how mine received shall be.

ANTONY   Quarrel no more, but be prepared to know
  The purposes I bear; which are, or cease,
  As you shall give th'advice. By the fire
  That quickens Nilus' slime, I go from hence   70
  Thy soldier, servant, making peace or war
  As thou affects.

CLEOPATRA   Cut my lace, Charmian, come!
  But let it be; I am quickly ill and well –
  So Antony loves.

ANTONY   My precious queen, forbear,
  And give true evidence to his love, which stands   75
  An honourable trial.

CLEOPATRA   So Fulvia told me.
  I prithee, turn aside and weep for her,
  Then bid adieu to me, and say the tears
  Belong to Egypt. Good now, play one scene
  Of excellent dissembling, and let it look   80
  Like perfect honour.

ANTONY   You'll heat my blood. No more.

CLEOPATRA   You can do better yet, but this is meetly.

ANTONY   Now by my sword –

CLEOPATRA   And target. Still he mends,
  But this is not the best. Look, prithee, Charmian,
  How this Herculean Roman does become   85
  The carriage of his chafe.

ANTONY   I'll leave you, lady.

CLEOPATRA   Courteous lord, one word:
  Sir, you and I must part, but that's not it;
  Sir, you and I have loved, but there's not it;   90
  That you know well. Something it is I would –
  Oh, my oblivion is a very Antony,
  And I am all forgotten!

ANTONY   But that your royalty
  Holds idleness your subject, I should take you
  For idleness itself.

CLEOPATRA   'Tis sweating labour   95
  To bear such idleness so near the heart
  As Cleopatra this. But, sir, forgive me,
  Since my becomings kill me when they do not
  Eye well to you. Your honour calls you hence;

100 Therefore be deaf to my unpitied folly,
And all the gods go with you! Upon your sword
Sit laurel victory, and smooth success
Be strewed before your feet!
ANTONY   Let us go. Come.
105 Our separation so abides and flies
That thou, residing here, goes yet with me,
And I, hence fleeting, here remain with thee.
Away!   *Exeunt.*

1.4   *Enter* OCTAVIUS CAESAR *reading a letter,*
            LEPIDUS *and their train.*

CAESAR   You may see, Lepidus, and henceforth know,
It is not Caesar's natural vice to hate
Our great competitor. From Alexandria
This is the news: he fishes, drinks, and wastes
5 The lamps of night in revel; is not more manlike
Than Cleopatra, nor the Queen of Ptolemy
More womanly than he; hardly gave audience, or
Vouchsafed to think he had partners. You shall find
     there
A man who is the abstract of all faults
That all men follow.
10 LEPIDUS   I must not think there are
Evils enough to darken all his goodness.
His faults, in him, seem as the spots of heaven,
More fiery by night's blackness; hereditary
Rather than purchased; what he cannot change
15 Than what he chooses.
CAESAR   You are too indulgent. Let's grant it is not
Amiss to tumble on the bed of Ptolemy,
To give a kingdom for a mirth, to sit
And keep the turn of tippling with a slave,
20 To reel the streets at noon, and stand the buffet
With knaves that smells of sweat. Say this becomes
     him –
As his composure must be rare indeed
Whom these things cannot blemish – yet must
     Antony
No way excuse his foils, when we do bear
25 So great weight in his lightness. If he filled
His vacancy with his voluptuousness,
Full surfeits and the dryness of his bones
Call on him for't. But to confound such time
That drums him from his sport, and speaks as loud
30 As his own state and ours, 'tis to be chid
As we rate boys who, being mature in knowledge,
Pawn their experience to their present pleasure
And so rebel to judgement.

Enter a Messenger.

LEPIDUS   Here's more news.
MESSENGER
Thy biddings have been done, and every hour,
35 Most noble Caesar, shalt thou have report
How 'tis abroad. Pompey is strong at sea,

And it appears he is beloved of those
That only have feared Caesar. To the ports
The discontents repair, and men's reports
Give him much wronged.
CAESAR   I should have known no less.   40
It hath been taught us from the primal state
That he which is was wished until he were,
And the ebbed man, ne'er loved till ne'er worth love,
Comes deared by being lacked. This common body,
Like to a vagabond flag upon the stream,   45
Goes to and back, lackeying the varying tide,
To rot itself with motion.

Enter another Messenger.

2 MESSENGER   Caesar, I bring thee word
Menecrates and Menas, famous pirates,
Makes the sea serve them, which they ear and wound   50
With keels of every kind. Many hot inroads
They make in Italy – the borders maritime
Lack blood to think on't – and flush youth revolt.
No vessel can peep forth but 'tis as soon
Taken as seen; for Pompey's name strikes more   55
Than could his war resisted.
CAESAR   Antony,
Leave thy lascivious wassails! When thou once
Was beaten from Modena, where thou slew'st
Hirtius and Pansa, consuls, at thy heel
Did famine follow, whom thou fought'st against,   60
Though daintily brought up, with patience more
Than savages could suffer. Thou didst drink
The stale of horses and the gilded puddle
Which beasts would cough at. Thy palate then did
     deign
The roughest berry on the rudest hedge.   65
Yea, like the stag when snow the pasture sheets,
The barks of trees thou browsed. On the Alps,
It is reported, thou didst eat strange flesh
Which some did die to look on. And all this –
It wounds thine honour that I speak it now –   70
Was borne so like a soldier that thy cheek
So much as lanked not.
LEPIDUS   'Tis pity of him.
CAESAR   Let his shames quickly
Drive him to Rome. 'Tis time we twain
Did show ourselves i'th' field, and to that end   75
Assemble we immediate council. Pompey
Thrives in our idleness.
LEPIDUS   Tomorrow, Caesar,
I shall be furnished to inform you rightly
Both what by sea and land I can be able
To front this present time.
CAESAR   Till which encounter,   80
It is my business too. Farewell.
LEPIDUS
Farewell, my lord. What you shall know meantime
Of stirs abroad, I shall beseech you, sir,
To let me be partaker.

CAESAR   Doubt not, sir.

85   I knew it for my bond.   *Exeunt by different doors.*

1.5   *Enter* CLEOPATRA, CHARMIAN, IRAS *and* MARDIAN.

CLEOPATRA   Charmian!

CHARMIAN   Madam?

CLEOPATRA [*Yawns.*]   Ha, ha.
   Give me to drink mandragora.

CHARMIAN   Why, madam?

CLEOPATRA
5   That I might sleep out this great gap of time
     My Antony is away.

CHARMIAN   You think of him too much.

CLEOPATRA   O, 'tis treason!

CHARMIAN   Madam, I trust not so.

CLEOPATRA   Thou, eunuch Mardian!

MARDIAN   What's your highness' pleasure?

CLEOPATRA
10   Not now to hear thee sing. I take no pleasure
     In aught an eunuch has. 'Tis well for thee
     That, being unseminared, thy freer thoughts
     May not fly forth of Egypt. Hast thou affections?

MARDIAN   Yes, gracious madam.

15   CLEOPATRA   Indeed?

MARDIAN   Not in deed, madam, for I can do nothing
     But what indeed is honest to be done.
     Yet have I fierce affections, and think
     What Venus did with Mars.

CLEOPATRA   O, Charmian,
20   Where think'st thou he is now? Stands he, or sits he?
     Or does he walk? Or is he on his horse?
     O happy horse, to bear the weight of Antony!
     Do bravely, horse, for wot'st thou whom thou
          mov'st?
     The demi-Atlas of this earth, the arm
25   And burgonet of men! He's speaking now,
     Or murmuring 'Where's my serpent of old Nile?'
     For so he calls me. Now I feed myself
     With most delicious poison. Think on me
     That am with Phoebus' amorous pinches black
30   And wrinkled deep in time? Broad-fronted Caesar,
     When thou wast here above the ground, I was
     A morsel for a monarch; and great Pompey
     Would stand and make his eyes grow in my brow;
     There would he anchor his aspect, and die
35   With looking on his life.

                    Enter ALEXAS *from Antony.*

ALEXAS   Sovereign of Egypt, hail!

CLEOPATRA   How much unlike art thou Mark Antony!
     Yet, coming from him, that great medicine hath
     With his tinct gilded thee.
40   How goes it with my brave Mark Antony?

ALEXAS   Last thing he did, dear queen,
     He kissed – the last of many doubled kisses –
     This orient pearl. His speech sticks in my heart.

CLEOPATRA   Mine ear must pluck it thence.

ALEXAS   'Good friend,' quoth he,
45   'Say the firm Roman to great Egypt sends
     This treasure of an oyster, at whose foot,
     To mend this petty present, I will piece
     Her opulent throne with kingdoms. All the East,
     Say thou, shall call her mistress.' So he nodded
50   And soberly did mount an arm-gaunt steed
     Who neighed so high that what I would have spoke
     Was beastly dumbed by him.

CLEOPATRA   What, was he sad or merry?

ALEXAS
     Like to the time o'th' year between the extremes
55   Of hot and cold, he was nor sad nor merry.

CLEOPATRA   O well-divided disposition! Note him,
     Note him, good Charmian, 'tis the man; but note
          him!
     He was not sad, for he would shine on those
     That make their looks by his; he was not merry,
60   Which seemed to tell them his remembrance lay
     In Egypt with his joy; but between both.
     O heavenly mingle! Be'st thou sad or merry,
     The violence of either thee becomes,
     So does it no man else. Met'st thou my posts?

ALEXAS   Ay, madam, twenty several messengers.
65   Why do you send so thick?

CLEOPATRA   Who's born that day
     When I forget to send to Antony
     Shall die a beggar. Ink and paper, Charmian!
     Welcome, my good Alexas! Did I, Charmian,
     Ever love Caesar so?

CHARMIAN   O that brave Caesar!

70   CLEOPATRA   Be choked with such another emphasis!
     Say, 'the brave Antony'.

CHARMIAN   The valiant Caesar!

CLEOPATRA   By Isis, I will give thee bloody teeth
     If thou with Caesar paragon again
     My man of men!

CHARMIAN   By your most gracious pardon,
75   I sing but after you.

CLEOPATRA   My salad days,
     When I was green in judgement, cold in blood,
     To say as I said then. But come, away,
     Get me ink and paper!
     He shall have every day a several greeting
80   Or I'll unpeople Egypt!   *Exeunt.*

2.1   *Enter* POMPEY, MENECRATES *and* MENAS *in*
                        warlike manner.

POMPEY   If the great gods be just, they shall assist
     The deeds of justest men.

MENECRATES   Know, worthy Pompey,
     That what they do delay they not deny.

POMPEY   Whiles we are suitors to their throne, decays
     The thing we sue for.

MENECRATES   We, ignorant of ourselves,
5   Beg often our own harms, which the wise powers

Deny us for our good; so find we profit
By losing of our prayers.
POMPEY　　　　　　　　I shall do well.
The people love me, and the sea is mine;
My powers are crescent, and my auguring hope
Says it will come to th' full. Mark Antony
In Egypt sits at dinner, and will make
No wars without doors; Caesar gets money where
He loses hearts; Lepidus flatters both,
Of both is flattered; but he neither loves,
Nor either cares for him.
MENAS　　　　　　　Caesar and Lepidus
Are in the field. A mighty strength they carry.
POMPEY　Where have you this? 'Tis false.
MENAS　　　　　　　　　From Silvius, sir.
POMPEY
He dreams. I know they are in Rome together,
Looking for Antony. But all the charms of love,
Salt Cleopatra, soften thy waned lip!
Let witchcraft join with beauty, lust with both;
Tie up the libertine in a field of feasts;
Keep his brain fuming. Epicurean cooks
Sharpen with cloyless sauce his appetite
That sleep and feeding may prorogue his honour
Even till a Lethe'd dullness –

Enter VARRIUS.

　　　　　　　　　　How now, Varrius?
VARRIUS　This is most certain that I shall deliver:
Mark Antony is every hour in Rome
Expected. Since he went from Egypt 'tis
A space for farther travel.
POMPEY　I could have given less matter
A better ear. Menas, I did not think
This amorous surfeiter would have donned his helm
For such a petty war. His soldiership
Is twice the other twain. But let us rear
The higher our opinion, that our stirring
Can from the lap of Egypt's widow pluck
The ne'er-lust-wearied Antony.
MENAS　　　　　　　　I cannot hope
Caesar and Antony shall well greet together.
His wife that's dead did trespasses to Caesar;
His brother warred upon him, although I think
Not moved by Antony.
POMPEY　　　　　　I know not, Menas,
How lesser enmities may give way to greater.
Were't not that we stand up against them all,
'Twere pregnant they should square between
　　themselves,
For they have entertained cause enough
To draw their swords. But how the fear of us
May cement their divisions, and bind up
The petty difference, we yet not know.
Be't as our gods will have't! It only stands
Our lives upon to use our strongest hands.
Come, Menas.　　　　　　　　　　*Exeunt.*

2.2　　*Enter* ENOBARBUS *and* LEPIDUS.

LEPIDUS　Good Enobarbus, 'tis a worthy deed,
And shall become you well, to entreat your captain
To soft and gentle speech.
ENOBARBUS　　　　　I shall entreat him
To answer like himself. If Caesar move him,
Let Antony look over Caesar's head　　　　5
And speak as loud as Mars. By Jupiter,
Were I the wearer of Antonio's beard,
I would not shave't today!
LEPIDUS　　　　　　'Tis not a time
For private stomaching.
ENOBARBUS　　　　Every time
Serves for the matter that is then born in't.　10
LEPIDUS
But small to greater matters must give way.
ENOBARBUS　Not if the small come first.
LEPIDUS　　　　　　Your speech is passion;
But pray you stir no embers up. Here comes
The noble Antony.

Enter ANTONY *and* VENTIDIUS.

ENOBARBUS　　　　And yonder Caesar.

Enter CAESAR, MAECENAS *and* AGRIPPA.

ANTONY　If we compose well here, to Parthia.　15
Hark, Ventidius.
CAESAR　I do not know, Maecenas. Ask Agrippa.
LEPIDUS　Noble friends,
That which combined us was most great, and let not
A leaner action rend us. What's amiss,　　20
May it be gently heard. When we debate
Our trivial difference loud, we do commit
Murder in healing wounds. Then, noble partners,
The rather for I earnestly beseech,
Touch you the sourest points with sweetest terms,　25
Nor curstness grow to th' matter.
ANTONY　　　　　　'Tis spoken well.
Were we before our armies, and to fight,
I should do thus.　　　　　[*Flourish.*]
CAESAR　Welcome to Rome.
ANTONY　Thank you.　　　　　　30
CAESAR　Sit.
ANTONY　Sit, sir.
CAESAR　Nay then. [*Caesar sits, then Antony.*]
ANTONY　I learn you take things ill which are not so,
Or being, concern you not.
CAESAR　　　　　　I must be laughed at　35
If, or for nothing or a little, I
Should say myself offended, and with you
Chiefly i'th' world; more laughed at that I should
Once name you derogately when to sound your name
It not concerned me.
ANTONY　　　　　My being in Egypt, Caesar,　40
What was't to you?

CAESAR   No more than my residing here at Rome
    Might be to you in Egypt. Yet if you there
    Did practise on my state, your being in Egypt
    Might be my question.

45   ANTONY   How intend you, 'practised'?
CAESAR   You may be pleased to catch at mine intent
    By what did here befall me. Your wife and brother
    Made wars upon me, and their contestation
    Was theme for you; you were the word of war.
ANTONY
50   You do mistake your business. My brother never
    Did urge me in his act. I did enquire it,
    And have my learning from some true reports
    That drew their swords with you. Did he not rather
    Discredit my authority with yours,
55   And make the wars alike against my stomach,
    Having alike your cause? Of this my letters
    Before did satisfy you. If you'll patch a quarrel,
    As matter whole you have to make it with,
    It must not be with this.
CAESAR   You praise yourself
60   By laying defects of judgement to me, but
    You patched up your excuses.
ANTONY   Not so, not so!
    I know you could not lack – I am certain on't –
    Very necessity of this thought, that I,
    Your partner in the cause 'gainst which he fought,
65   Could not with graceful eyes attend those wars
    Which fronted mine own peace. As for my wife,
    I would you had her spirit in such another.
    The third o'th' world is yours, which with a snaffle
    You may pace easy, but not such a wife.
70   ENOBARBUS   Would we had all such wives, that the men
    might go to wars with the women!
ANTONY   So much uncurbable, her garboils, Caesar,
    Made out of her impatience – which not wanted
    Shrewdness of policy too – I grieving grant
75   Did you too much disquiet. For that, you must
    But say I could not help it.
CAESAR   I wrote to you
    When rioting in Alexandria. You
    Did pocket up my letters, and with taunts
    Did gibe my missive out of audience.
ANTONY   Sir,
80   He fell upon me ere admitted, then.
    Three kings I had newly feasted, and did want
    Of what I was i'th' morning. But next day
    I told him of myself, which was as much
    As to have asked him pardon. Let this fellow
85   Be nothing of our strife; if we contend,
    Out of our question wipe him.
CAESAR   You have broken
    The article of your oath, which you shall never
    Have tongue to charge me with.
LEPIDUS   Soft, Caesar!
90   ANTONY   No, Lepidus, let him speak.
    The honour is sacred which he talks on now,

Supposing that I lacked it. But on, Caesar:
    'The article of my oath –'
CAESAR
    To lend me arms and aid when I required them,
    The which you both denied.
ANTONY   Neglected, rather;   95
    And then when poisoned hours had bound me up
    From mine own knowledge. As nearly as I may
    I'll play the penitent to you, but mine honesty
    Shall not make poor my greatness, nor my power
    Work without it. Truth is that Fulvia,   100
    To have me out of Egypt, made wars here,
    For which myself, the ignorant motive, do
    So far ask pardon as befits mine honour
    To stoop in such a case.
LEPIDUS   'Tis noble spoken.
MAECENAS   If it might please you to enforce no further   105
    The griefs between ye; to forget them quite
    Were to remember that the present need
    Speaks to atone you.
LEPIDUS   Worthily spoken, Maecenas.
ENOBARBUS   Or, if you borrow one another's love for the
    instant, you may, when you hear no more words of   110
    Pompey, return it again. You shall have time to
    wrangle in when you have nothing else to do.
ANTONY   Thou art a soldier only. Speak no more.
ENOBARBUS   That truth should be silent, I had almost
    forgot.   115
ANTONY
    You wrong this presence; therefore speak no more.
ENOBARBUS   Go to, then! Your considerate stone.
CAESAR   I do not much dislike the matter but
    The manner of his speech; for't cannot be
    We shall remain in friendship, our conditions   120
    So differing in their acts. Yet, if I knew
    What hoop should hold us staunch, from edge to
      edge
    O'th' world I would pursue it.
AGRIPPA   Give me leave, Caesar.
CAESAR   Speak, Agrippa.
AGRIPPA   Thou hast a sister by the mother's side,   125
    Admired Octavia. Great Mark Antony
    Is now a widower.
CAESAR   Say not so, Agrippa.
    If Cleopatra heard you, your reproof
    Were well deserved of rashness.
ANTONY   I am not married, Caesar. Let me hear   130
    Agrippa further speak.
AGRIPPA   To hold you in perpetual amity,
    To make you brothers, and to knit your hearts
    With an unslipping knot, take Antony
    Octavia to his wife; whose beauty claims   135
    No worse a husband than the best of men;
    Whose virtue and whose general graces speak
    That which none else can utter. By this marriage
    All little jealousies which now seem great,
    And all great fears which now import their dangers   140

Would then be nothing. Truths would be tales,
Where now half-tales be truths. Her love to both
Would each to other, and all loves to both
Draw after her. Pardon what I have spoke,
For 'tis a studied, not a present thought,
By duty ruminated.
ANTONY   Will Caesar speak?
CAESAR Not till he hears how Antony is touched
With what is spoke already.
ANTONY What power is in Agrippa,
If I would say, 'Agrippa, be it so',
To make this good?
CAESAR   The power of Caesar, and
His power unto Octavia.
ANTONY   May I never,
To this good purpose that so fairly shows,
Dream of impediment! Let me have thy hand.
Further this act of grace, and from this hour
The heart of brothers govern in our loves
And sway our great designs!
CAESAR   There's my hand.
[*They clasp hands.*]
A sister I bequeath you, whom no brother
Did ever love so dearly. Let her live
To join our kingdoms and our hearts; and never
Fly off our loves again!
LEPIDUS   Happily, amen!
ANTONY
I did not think to draw my sword 'gainst Pompey,
For he hath laid strange courtesies and great
Of late upon me. I must thank him, only
Lest my remembrance suffer ill report;
At heel of that, defy him.
LEPIDUS   Time calls upon's.
Of us must Pompey presently be sought
Or else he seeks out us.
ANTONY Where lies he?
CAESAR About the Mount Misena.
ANTONY What is his strength by land?
CAESAR Great and increasing, but by sea
He is an absolute master.
ANTONY   So is the fame.
Would we had spoke together! Haste we for it.
Yet, ere we put ourselves in arms, dispatch we
The business we have talked of.
CAESAR   With most gladness,
And do invite you to my sister's view,
Whither straight I'll lead you.
ANTONY Let us, Lepidus, not lack your company.
LEPIDUS Noble Antony, not sickness should detain me.
Flourish. Exeunt all except Enobarbus, Agrippa, Maecenas.
MAECENAS Welcome from Egypt, sir.
ENOBARBUS Half the heart of Caesar, worthy Maecenas!
My honourable friend, Agrippa!
AGRIPPA Good Enobarbus!
MAECENAS We have cause to be glad that matters are
so well digested. You stayed well by't in Egypt.

ENOBARBUS Ay, sir, we did sleep day out of countenance
and made the night light with drinking.
MAECENAS Eight wild boars roasted whole at a
breakfast, and but twelve persons there. Is this true?
ENOBARBUS This was but as a fly by an eagle. We had
much more monstrous matter of feast, which worthily
deserved noting.
MAECENAS She's a most triumphant lady, if report be
square to her.
ENOBARBUS When she first met Mark Antony, she
pursed up his heart upon the river of Cydnus.
AGRIPPA There she appeared indeed! Or my reporter
devised well for her.
ENOBARBUS I will tell you.
The barge she sat in, like a burnished throne,
Burned on the water; the poop was beaten gold;
Purple the sails, and so perfumed that
The winds were love-sick with them; the oars were
    silver,
Which to the tune of flutes kept stroke, and made
The water which they beat to follow faster,
As amorous of their strokes. For her own person,
It beggared all description: she did lie
In her pavilion, cloth-of-gold of tissue,
O'erpicturing that Venus where we see
The fancy outwork nature. On each side her
Stood pretty dimpled boys, like smiling cupids,
With divers-coloured fans, whose wind did seem
To glow the delicate cheeks which they did cool,
And what they undid did.
AGRIPPA   O, rare for Antony!
ENOBARBUS Her gentlewomen, like the Nereides,
So many mermaids, tended her i'th' eyes,
And made their bends adornings. At the helm
A seeming mermaid steers. The silken tackle
Swell with the touches of those flower-soft hands
That yarely frame the office. From the barge
A strange invisible perfume hits the sense
Of the adjacent wharfs. The city cast
Her people out upon her, and Antony,
Enthroned i'th' market-place, did sit alone,
Whistling to th'air, which, but for vacancy,
Had gone to gaze on Cleopatra, too,
And made a gap in nature.
AGRIPPA   Rare Egyptian!
ENOBARBUS Upon her landing, Antony sent to her;
Invited her to supper. She replied
It should be better he became her guest,
Which she entreated. Our courteous Antony,
Whom ne'er the word of 'No' woman heard speak,
Being barbered ten times o'er, goes to the feast,
And, for his ordinary, pays his heart
For what his eyes eat only.
AGRIPPA   Royal wench!
She made great Caesar lay his sword to bed.
He ploughed her, and she cropped.
ENOBARBUS   I saw her once

Hop forty paces through the public street
240 And, having lost her breath, she spoke and panted,
That she did make defect perfection,
And, breathless, pour breath forth.
MAECENAS   Now Antony must leave her utterly.
ENOBARBUS   Never! He will not.
245 Age cannot wither her, nor custom stale
Her infinite variety. Other women cloy
The appetites they feed, but she makes hungry
Where most she satisfies; for vilest things
Become themselves in her, that the holy priests
250 Bless her when she is riggish.
MAECENAS   If beauty, wisdom, modesty can settle
The heart of Antony, Octavia is
A blessed lottery to him.
AGRIPPA   Let us go.
Good Enobarbus, make yourself my guest
Whilst you abide here.
255 ENOBARBUS   Humbly, sir, I thank you.
                                            Exeunt.

2.3   *Enter* ANTONY, CAESAR; OCTAVIA *between them.*

ANTONY
The world and my great office will sometimes
Divide me from your bosom.
OCTAVIA   All which time
Before the gods my knee shall bow my prayers
To them for you.
ANTONY   Good night, sir. My Octavia,
5 Read not my blemishes in the world's report.
I have not kept my square, but that to come
Shall all be done by th' rule. Good night, dear lady.
OCTAVIA   Good night, sir.
CAESAR   Good night.   *Exeunt Caesar and Octavia.*

                Enter Soothsayer.

10 ANTONY   Now, sirrah! You do wish yourself in Egypt?
SOOTHSAYER
Would I had never come from thence, nor you
      thither!
ANTONY   If you can, your reason?
SOOTHSAYER
I see it in my motion; have it not in my tongue.
But yet hie you to Egypt again.
ANTONY   Say to me,
15 Whose fortunes shall rise higher, Caesar's or mine?
SOOTHSAYER   Caesar's.
Therefore, O Antony, stay not by his side.
Thy daemon – that thy spirit which keeps thee – is
Noble, courageous, high unmatchable,
20 Where Caesar's is not. But near him, thy angel
Becomes afeard, as being o'erpowered; therefore
Make space enough between you.
ANTONY   Speak this no more.
SOOTHSAYER
To none but thee; no more but when to thee.

If thou dost play with him at any game,
Thou art sure to lose; and of that natural luck   25
He beats thee 'gainst the odds. Thy lustre thickens
When he shines by. I say again, thy spirit
Is all afraid to govern thee near him;
But, he away, 'tis noble.
ANTONY   Get thee gone.
Say to Ventidius I would speak with him.   30
                                Exit Soothsayer.
He shall to Parthia. Be it art or hap,
He hath spoken true. The very dice obey him,
And in our sports my better cunning faints
Under his chance. If we draw lots, he speeds;
His cocks do win the battle still of mine   35
When it is all to naught, and his quails ever
Beat mine, inhooped, at odds. I will to Egypt;
And though I make this marriage for my peace,
I'th' East my pleasure lies.

            Enter VENTIDIUS.

                    O come, Ventidius.
You must to Parthia. Your commission's ready.   40
Follow me and receive't.   *Exeunt.*

2.4   *Enter* LEPIDUS, MAECENAS *and* AGRIPPA.

LEPIDUS
Trouble yourselves no further. Pray you hasten
Your generals after.
AGRIPPA   Sir, Mark Antony
Will e'en but kiss Octavia, and we'll follow.
LEPIDUS   Till I shall see you in your soldiers' dress,
Which will become you both, farewell.
MAECENAS   We shall,   5
As I conceive the journey, be at the Mount
Before you, Lepidus.
LEPIDUS   Your way is shorter;
My purposes do draw me much about.
You'll win two days upon me.
MAECENAS, AGRIPPA   Sir, good success!   10
LEPIDUS   Farewell.   *Exeunt.*

2.5   *Enter* CLEOPATRA, CHARMIAN, IRAS *and* ALEXAS.

CLEOPATRA   Give me some music – music, moody food
Of us that trade in love.
ALL   The music, ho!

            Enter MARDIAN *the Eunuch.*

CLEOPATRA
Let it alone. Let's to billiards. Come, Charmian.
CHARMIAN   My arm is sore. Best play with Mardian.
CLEOPATRA   As well a woman with an eunuch played   5
As with a woman. Come, you'll play with me, sir?
MARDIAN   As well as I can, madam.
CLEOPATRA
And when good will is showed, though't come too
      short,

The actor may plead pardon. I'll none now.
Give me mine angle; we'll to th' river. There,
My music playing far off, I will betray
Tawny-finned fishes. My bended hook shall pierce
Their slimy jaws, and, as I draw them up,
I'll think them every one an Antony,
And say 'Ah, ha! You're caught!'

CHARMIAN　　　　　　　　　　'Twas merry when
You wagered on your angling; when your diver
Did hang a salt fish on his hook, which he
With fervency drew up.

CLEOPATRA　　　　　　That time? O times!
I laughed him out of patience, and that night
I laughed him into patience, and next morn,
Ere the ninth hour, I drunk him to his bed,
Then put my tires and mantles on him, whilst
I wore his sword Philippan.

Enter a Messenger.

　　　　　　　　　　Oh, from Italy!
Ram thou thy fruitful tidings in mine ears,
That long time have been barren!

MESSENGER　　　　　　　Madam, madam –

CLEOPATRA　Antonio's dead! If thou say so, villain,
Thou kill'st thy mistress; but well and free,
If thou so yield him, there is gold, and here
My bluest veins to kiss, a hand that kings
Have lipped, and trembled, kissing.

MESSENGER　First, madam, he is well.

CLEOPATRA　　　　　　　Why, there's more gold.
But sirrah, mark, we use
To say the dead are well. Bring it to that,
The gold I give thee will I melt and pour
Down thy ill-uttering throat.

MESSENGER　　　　　　Good madam, hear me.

CLEOPATRA　Well, go to, I will.
But there's no goodness in thy face if Antony
Be free and healthful. So tart a favour
To trumpet such good tidings! If not well,
Thou shouldst come like a Fury crowned with
　　snakes,
Not like a formal man.

MESSENGER　　　　　Will't please you hear me?

CLEOPATRA
I have a mind to strike thee ere thou speak'st.
Yet if thou say Antony lives, is well,
Or friends with Caesar, or not captive to him,
I'll set thee in a shower of gold and hail
Rich pearls upon thee.

MESSENGER　　　　　Madam, he's well.

CLEOPATRA　　　　　　　　Well said!

MESSENGER　And friends with Caesar.

CLEOPATRA　　　　　　Thou'rt an honest man!

MESSENGER
Caesar and he are greater friends than ever.

CLEOPATRA　Make thee a fortune from me!

MESSENGER　　　　　　But yet, madam –

CLEOPATRA　I do not like 'But yet'. It does allay　50
The good precedence. Fie upon 'But yet'!
'But yet' is as a gaoler to bring forth
Some monstrous malefactor. Prithee, friend,
Pour out the pack of matter to mine ear,
The good and bad together. He's friends with Caesar,　55
In state of health, thou sayst, and, thou sayst, free.

MESSENGER　Free, madam? No. I made no such report.
He's bound unto Octavia.

CLEOPATRA　　　　　　　For what good turn?

MESSENGER　For the best turn i'th' bed.

CLEOPATRA　　　　　　　I am pale, Charmian.

MESSENGER　Madam, he's married to Octavia.　60

CLEOPATRA　The most infectious pestilence upon thee!
[*Strikes him down.*]

MESSENGER　Good madam, patience!

CLEOPATRA　　　　　　　　What say you?
[*Strikes him.*]　　　　　　　　　　Hence,
Horrible villain, or I'll spurn thine eyes
Like balls before me! I'll unhair thy head!
[*She hales him up and down.*]
Thou shalt be whipped with wire and stewed in brine,　65
Smarting in lingering pickle!

MESSENGER　　　　　　Gracious madam,
I that do bring the news made not the match.

CLEOPATRA　Say 'tis not so, a province I will give thee,
And make thy fortunes proud. The blow thou hadst
Shall make thy peace for moving me to rage,　70
And I will boot thee with what gift beside
Thy modesty can beg.

MESSENGER　　　　　He's married, madam.

CLEOPATRA　Rogue, thou hast lived too long!
[*Draws a knife.*]

MESSENGER　　　　　　Nay then, I'll run.
What mean you, madam? I have made no fault. *Exit.*

CHARMIAN
Good madam, keep yourself within yourself.　75
The man is innocent.

CLEOPATRA
Some innocents 'scape not the thunderbolt.
Melt Egypt into Nile, and kindly creatures
Turn all to serpents! Call the slave again!
Though I am mad, I will not bite him. Call!　80

CHARMIAN　He is afeard to come.

CLEOPATRA　　　　　　　I will not hurt him.
　　　　　　　　　　Exit Charmian.
These hands do lack nobility that they strike
A meaner than myself, since I myself
Have given myself the cause.

Enter the Messenger *again with* CHARMIAN.

　　　　　　　　　Come hither, sir.
Though it be honest, it is never good　85
To bring bad news. Give to a gracious message
An host of tongues, but let ill tidings tell
Themselves when they be felt.

MESSENGER　　　　　I have done my duty.

CLEOPATRA   Is he married?

90   I cannot hate thee worser than I do
      If thou again say 'Yes'.
MESSENGER   He's married, madam.
CLEOPATRA
      The gods confound thee! Dost thou hold there still?
MESSENGER   Should I lie, madam?
CLEOPATRA   Oh, I would thou didst,
      So half my Egypt were submerged and made
95   A cistern for scaled snakes! Go, get thee hence!
      Hadst thou Narcissus in thy face, to me
      Thou wouldst appear most ugly. He is married?
MESSENGER   I crave your highness' pardon.
CLEOPATRA   He is married?
MESSENGER
      Take no offence that I would not offend you.
100   To punish me for what you make me do
      Seems much unequal. He's married to Octavia.
CLEOPATRA
      Oh, that his fault should make a knave of thee
      That act not what thou'rt sure of! Get thee hence!
      The merchandise which thou hast brought from
            Rome
105   Are all too dear for me. Lie they upon thy hand
      And be undone by 'em.   *Exit Messenger.*
CHARMIAN   Good your highness, patience.
CLEOPATRA
      In praising Antony, I have dispraised Caesar.
CHARMIAN   Many times, madam.
CLEOPATRA   I am paid for't now.
      Lead me from hence;
110   I faint! O Iras, Charmian! 'Tis no matter.
      Go to the fellow, good Alexas, bid him
      Report the feature of Octavia, her years,
      Her inclination; let him not leave out
      The colour of her hair. Bring me word quickly.
                                    Exit Alexas.
115   Let him for ever go! Let him not, Charmian.
      Though he be painted one way like a Gorgon,
      The other way's a Mars. [*to Iras*] Bid you Alexas
      Bring me word how tall she is. Pity me, Charmian,
      But do not speak to me. Lead me to my chamber.
                                    Exeunt.

2.6   *Flourish. Enter* POMPEY *and* MENAS *at one door
       with drum and trumpet; at anothe*r CAESAR, LEPIDUS,
    ANTONY, ENOBARBUS, MAECENAS, AGRIPPA, *with soldiers
                        marching.*

POMPEY   Your hostages I have, so have you mine,
      And we shall talk before we fight.
CAESAR   Most meet
      That first we come to words, and therefore have we
      Our written purposes before us sent,
5   Which if thou hast considered, let us know
      If 'twill tie up thy discontented sword
      And carry back to Sicily much tall youth

That else must perish here.
POMPEY   To you all three,
      The senators alone of this great world,
      Chief factors for the gods: I do not know   10
      Wherefore my father should revengers want,
      Having a son and friends, since Julius Caesar,
      Who at Philippi the good Brutus ghosted,
      There saw you labouring for him. What was't
      That moved pale Cassius to conspire? And what   15
      Made the all-honoured, honest Roman, Brutus,
      With the armed rest, courtiers of beauteous freedom,
      To drench the Capitol, but that they would
      Have one man but a man? And that is it
      Hath made me rig my navy, at whose burden   20
      The angered ocean foams, with which I meant
      To scourge th'ingratitude that despiteful Rome
      Cast on my noble father.
CAESAR   Take your time.
ANTONY
      Thou canst not fear us, Pompey, with thy sails.
      We'll speak with thee at sea. At land thou know'st 25
      How much we do o'ercount thee.
POMPEY   At land indeed
      Thou dost o'ercount me of my father's house;
      But since the cuckoo builds not for himself,
      Remain in't as thou mayst.
LEPIDUS   Be pleased to tell us –
      For this is from the present – how you take   30
      The offers we have sent you.
CAESAR   There's the point.
ANTONY   Which do not be entreated to, but weigh
      What it is worth embraced.
CAESAR   And what may follow
      To try a larger fortune.
POMPEY   You have made me offer
      Of Sicily, Sardinia; and I must   35
      Rid all the sea of pirates; then to send
      Measures of wheat to Rome. This 'greed upon,
      To part with unhacked edges, and bear back
      Our targes undinted.
CAESAR, ANTONY, LEPIDUS
                      That's our offer.
POMPEY   Know, then,
      I came before you here a man prepared   40
      To take this offer, but Mark Antony
      Put me to some impatience. Though I lose
      The praise of it by telling, you must know
      When Caesar and your brother were at blows,
      Your mother came to Sicily and did find   45
      Her welcome friendly.
ANTONY   I have heard it, Pompey,
      And am well studied for a liberal thanks
      Which I do owe you.
POMPEY   Let me have your hand.
      [*They shake hands.*]
      I did not think, sir, to have met you here.

ANTONY
 The beds i'th' East are soft; and thanks to you
 That called me timelier than my purpose hither,
 For I have gained by't.
CAESAR   Since I saw you last,
 There is a change upon you.
POMPEY   Well, I know not
 What counts harsh Fortune casts upon my face,
 But in my bosom shall she never come
 To make my heart her vassal.
LEPIDUS   Well met here!
POMPEY
 I hope so, Lepidus. Thus we are agreed.
 I crave our composition may be written
 And sealed between us.
CAESAR   That's the next to do.
POMPEY We'll feast each other ere we part, and let's
 Draw lots who shall begin.
ANTONY   That will I, Pompey.
POMPEY No, Antony, take the lot.
 But, first or last, your fine Egyptian cookery
 Shall have the fame. I have heard that Julius Caesar
 Grew fat with feasting there.
ANTONY   You have heard much.
POMPEY I have fair meanings, sir.
ANTONY   And fair words to them.
POMPEY Then so much have I heard.
 And I have heard Apollodorus carried –
ENOBARBUS No more of that! He did so.
POMPEY   What, I pray you?
ENOBARBUS A certain queen to Caesar in a mattress.
POMPEY I know thee now. How far'st thou, soldier?
ENOBARBUS   Well;
 And well am like to do, for I perceive
 Four feasts are toward.
POMPEY   Let me shake thy hand.
 [*They shake hands.*]
 I never hated thee. I have seen thee fight
 When I have envied thy behaviour.
ENOBARBUS   Sir,
 I never loved you much, but I ha' praised ye
 When you have well deserved ten times as much
 As I have said you did.
POMPEY   Enjoy thy plainness;
 It nothing ill becomes thee.
 Aboard my galley I invite you all.
 Will you lead, lords?
CAESAR, ANTONY, LEPIDUS Show's the way, sir.
POMPEY   Come.
     Exeunt all but Enobarbus and Menas.
MENAS [*aside*] Thy father, Pompey, would ne'er have
 made this treaty. [*to Enobarbus*] You and I have known,
 sir.
ENOBARBUS At sea, I think.
MENAS We have, sir.
ENOBARBUS You have done well by water.
MENAS And you by land.

ENOBARBUS I will praise any man that will praise me,
 though it cannot be denied what I have done by land. 90
MENAS Nor what I have done by water.
ENOBARBUS Yes, something you can deny for your own
 safety: you have been a great thief by sea.
MENAS And you by land.
ENOBARBUS There I deny my land service. But give me 95
 your hand, Menas! [*They shake hands.*] If our eyes had
 authority, here they might take two thieves kissing.
MENAS All men's faces are true, whatsome'er their
 hands are.
ENOBARBUS But there is never a fair woman has a true 100
 face.
MENAS No slander. They steal hearts.
ENOBARBUS We came hither to fight with you.
MENAS For my part, I am sorry it is turned to a
 drinking. Pompey doth this day laugh away his 105
 fortune.
ENOBARBUS If he do, sure he cannot weep't back again.
MENAS You've said, sir. We looked not for Mark Antony
 here. Pray you, is he married to Cleopatra?
ENOBARBUS Caesar's sister is called Octavia. 110
MENAS True, sir. She was the wife of Caius Marcellus.
ENOBARBUS But she is now the wife of Marcus Antonius.
MENAS Pray ye, sir?
ENOBARBUS 'Tis true.
MENAS Then is Caesar and he for ever knit together. 115
ENOBARBUS If I were bound to divine of this unity, I
 would not prophesy so.
MENAS I think the policy of that purpose made more in
 the marriage than the love of the parties.
ENOBARBUS I think so too. But you shall find the band 120
 that seems to tie their friendship together will be the
 very strangler of their amity. Octavia is of a holy, cold
 and still conversation.
MENAS Who would not have his wife so?
ENOBARBUS Not he that himself is not so; which is 125
 Mark Antony. He will to his Egyptian dish again.
 Then shall the sighs of Octavia blow the fire up in
 Caesar, and, as I said before, that which is the strength
 of their amity shall prove the immediate author of
 their variance. Antony will use his affection where it 130
 is. He married but his occasion here.
MENAS And thus it may be. Come, sir, will you aboard?
 I have a health for you.
ENOBARBUS I shall take it, sir. We have used our throats
 in Egypt. 135
MENAS Come, let's away.   *Exeunt.*

2.7 *Music plays. Enter two or three* Servants *with a*
        banquet.

1 SERVANT Here they'll be man. Some o' their plants are
 ill-rooted already; the least wind i'th' world will blow
 them down.
2 SERVANT Lepidus is high-coloured.
1 SERVANT They have made him drink alms-drink. 5

2 SERVANT As they pinch one another by the disposition, he cries out 'No more', reconciles them to his entreaty, and himself to th' drink.

1 SERVANT But it raises the greater war between him and his discretion.

2 SERVANT Why, this it is to have a name in great men's fellowship. I had as lief have a reed that will do me no service as a partisan I could not heave.

1 SERVANT To be called into a huge sphere and not to be seen to move in't, are the holes where eyes should be, which pitifully disaster the cheeks.

A sennet sounded. Enter CAESAR, ANTONY, POMPEY, LEPIDUS, AGRIPPA, MAECENAS, ENOBARBUS, MENAS *with other captains and a* Boy Singer.

ANTONY
Thus do they, sir: they take the flow o'th' Nile
By certain scales i'th' pyramid. They know
By th'height, the lowness, or the mean, if dearth
Or foison follow. The higher Nilus swells,
The more it promises. As it ebbs, the seedsman
Upon the slime and ooze scatters his grain,
And shortly comes to harvest.

LEPIDUS You've strange serpents there?

ANTONY Ay, Lepidus.

LEPIDUS Your serpent of Egypt is bred, now, of your mud by the operation of your sun; so is your crocodile.

ANTONY They are so.

POMPEY Sit, and some wine! A health to Lepidus!
[They sit and drink.]

LEPIDUS I am not so well as I should be, but I'll ne'er out.

ENOBARBUS *[aside]* Not till you have slept. I fear me you'll be in till then.

LEPIDUS Nay, certainly, I have heard the Ptolemies' pyramises are very goodly things. Without contradiction I have heard that.

MENAS *[aside to Pompey]* Pompey, a word.

POMPEY *[aside to Menas]* Say in mine ear what is't.

MENAS *[Whispers in his ear.]*
Forsake thy seat, I do beseech thee, captain,
And hear me speak a word.

POMPEY *[aside to Menas]*
Forbear me till anon. – This wine for Lepidus!

LEPIDUS What manner o' thing is your crocodile?

ANTONY It is shaped, sir, like itself, and it is as broad as it hath breadth. It is just so high as it is, and moves with it own organs. It lives by that which nourisheth it, and the elements once out of it, it transmigrates.

LEPIDUS What colour is it of?

ANTONY Of it own colour too.

LEPIDUS 'Tis a strange serpent.

ANTONY 'Tis so, and the tears of it are wet.

CAESAR Will this description satisfy him?

ANTONY With the health that Pompey gives him, else he is a very epicure. *[Menas whispers again.]*

POMPEY *[aside to Menas]*
Go hang, sir, hang! Tell me of that? Away!
Do as I bid you. – Where's this cup I called for?

MENAS *[aside to Pompey]*
If for the sake of merit thou wilt hear me,
Rise from thy stool.

POMPEY *[aside to Menas]*
I think thou'rt mad. The matter?
[Rises and walks aside with Menas.]

MENAS I have ever held my cap off to thy fortunes.

POMPEY
Thou hast served me with much faith. What's else to say? –
Be jolly, lords.

ANTONY These quicksands, Lepidus,
Keep off them, for you sink.

MENAS Wilt thou be lord of all the world?

POMPEY What sayst thou?

MENAS Wilt thou be lord of the whole world?
That's twice.

POMPEY How should that be?

MENAS But entertain it,
And, though thou think me poor, I am the man
Will give thee all the world.

POMPEY Hast thou drunk well?

MENAS No, Pompey, I have kept me from the cup.
Thou art, if thou dar'st be, the earthly Jove,
Whate'er the ocean pales or sky inclips
Is thine, if thou wilt ha't.

POMPEY Show me which way.

MENAS These three world-sharers, these competitors,
Are in thy vessel. Let me cut the cable,
And when we are put off, fall to their throats.
All then is thine.

POMPEY Ah, this thou shouldst have done
And not have spoke on't. In me 'tis villainy;
In thee't had been good service. Thou must know
'Tis not my profit that does lead mine honour;
Mine honour, it. Repent that e'er thy tongue
Hath so betrayed thine act. Being done unknown,
I should have found it afterwards well done,
But must condemn it now. Desist and drink.
[Returns to the others.]

MENAS *[aside]* For this,
I'll never follow thy palled fortunes more.
Who seeks and will not take, when once 'tis offered,
Shall never find it more.

POMPEY This health to Lepidus!

ANTONY
Bear him ashore. I'll pledge it for him, Pompey.

ENOBARBUS Here's to thee, Menas!

MENAS Enobarbus, welcome!

POMPEY
Fill till the cup be hid.

ENOBARBUS There's a strong fellow, Menas.
[Points to the attendant who carries off Lepidus.]

MENAS Why?

ENOBARBUS
0   'A bears the third part of the world, man. Seest not?
MENAS
     The third part then he is drunk. Would it were all,
     That it might go on wheels!
ENOBARBUS   Drink thou! Increase the reels!
MENAS   Come!
95   POMPEY   This is not yet an Alexandrian feast.
ANTONY   It ripens towards it. Strike the vessels, ho!
     Here's to Caesar!
CAESAR   I could well forbear't.
     It's monstrous labour when I wash my brain
     And it grows fouler.
ANTONY   Be a child o'th' time.
100 CAESAR   'Possess it', I'll make answer.
     But I had rather fast from all, four days,
     Than drink so much in one.
ENOBARBUS [*to Antony*]   Ha, my brave emperor,
     Shall we dance now the Egyptian Bacchanals
     And celebrate our drink?
POMPEY   Let's ha't, good soldier.
105 ANTONY   Come, let's all take hands
     Till that the conquering wine hath steeped our sense
     In soft and delicate Lethe.
ENOBARBUS   All take hands.
     Make battery to our ears with the loud music,
     The while I'll place you; then the boy shall sing.
110 The holding every man shall beat as loud
     As his strong sides can volley.
          [*Music plays. Enobarbus places them hand in hand.*]

               The Song.
BOY   Come, thou monarch of the vine,
     Plumpy Bacchus with pink eyne!
     In thy vats our cares be drowned;
115   With thy grapes our hairs be crowned.
ALL   Cup us till the world go round!
            Cup us till the world go round!
CAESAR
     What would you more? Pompey, good night. Good
          brother,
     Let me request you off. Our graver business
120 Frowns at this levity. Gentle lords, let's part.
     You see we have burnt our cheeks. Strong Enobarb
     Is weaker than the wine, and mine own tongue
     Splits what it speaks. The wild disguise hath almost
     Anticked us all. What needs more words? Good
          night.
125 Good Antony, your hand.
POMPEY   I'll try you on the shore.
ANTONY   And shall, sir. Give's your hand.
POMPEY   O, Antony, you have my father's house.
     But what? We are friends! Come down into the boat.
ENOBARBUS   Take heed you fall not.
          Exeunt all but Enobarbus and Menas.
130   Menas, I'll not on shore.

MENAS
     No, to my cabin! These drums, these trumpets,
          flutes! What!
     Let Neptune hear we bid a loud farewell
     To these great fellows. Sound and be hanged! Sound
          out!   [*Sound a flourish with drums.*]
ENOBARBUS   Hoo, says 'a! There's my cap!
     [*Flings his cap in the air.*]
MENAS   Hoo! Noble captain, come!   *Exeunt.*   135

3.1   *Enter* VENTIDIUS *as it were in triumph, with*
     SILIUS *and other Romans, officers and soldiers, the dead*
               body of Pacorus borne before him.

VENTIDIUS
     Now, darting Parthia, art thou struck, and now
     Pleased Fortune does of Marcus Crassus' death
     Make me revenger. Bear the King's son's body
     Before our army. Thy Pacorus, Orodes,
     Pays this for Marcus Crassus.
SILIUS   Noble Ventidius,   5
     Whilst yet with Parthian blood thy sword is warm,
     The fugitive Parthians follow. Spur through Media,
     Mesopotamia, and the shelters whither
     The routed fly. So thy grand captain Antony
     Shall set thee on triumphant chariots and   10
     Put garlands on thy head.
VENTIDIUS   O Silius, Silius,
     I have done enough. A lower place, note well,
     May make too great an act. For learn this, Silius:
     Better to leave undone than, by our deed,
     Acquire too high a fame when him we serve's away.   15
     Caesar and Antony have ever won
     More in their officer than person. Sossius,
     One of my place in Syria, his lieutenant,
     For quick accumulation of renown,
     Which he achieved by th' minute, lost his favour.   20
     Who does i'th' wars more than his captain can,
     Becomes his captain's captain; and ambition,
     The soldier's virtue, rather makes choice of loss
     Than gain which darkens him.
     I could do more to do Antonius good,   25
     But 'twould offend him, and in his offence
     Should my performance perish.
SILIUS
     Thou hast, Ventidius, that
     Without the which a soldier and his sword
     Grants scarce distinction. Thou wilt write to Antony?   30
VENTIDIUS   I'll humbly signify what in his name,
     That magical word of war, we have effected;
     How, with his banners and his well-paid ranks,
     The ne'er-yet-beaten horse of Parthia
     We have jaded out o'th' field.
SILIUS   Where is he now?   35
VENTIDIUS
     He purposeth to Athens, whither, with what haste

137

The weight we must convey with's will permit,
We shall appear before him. On there! Pass along!

Exeunt.

3.2   *Enter* AGRIPPA *at one door,* ENOBARBUS *at another.*

AGRIPPA   What, are the brothers parted?
ENOBARBUS
They have dispatched with Pompey; he is gone.
The other three are sealing. Octavia weeps
To part from Rome; Caesar is sad, and Lepidus
5   Since Pompey's feast, as Menas says, is troubled
With the green-sickness.
AGRIPPA   'Tis a noble Lepidus.
ENOBARBUS   A very fine one. O, how he loves Caesar!
AGRIPPA   Nay, but how dearly he adores Mark Antony!
ENOBARBUS   Caesar? Why he's the Jupiter of men!
10   AGRIPPA   What's Antony? The god of Jupiter!
ENOBARBUS   Spake you of Caesar? Hoo! The nonpareil!
AGRIPPA   O Antony! O thou Arabian bird!
ENOBARBUS
Would you praise Caesar, say 'Caesar'. Go no further.
AGRIPPA
Indeed, he plied them both with excellent praises.
ENOBARBUS
15   But he loves Caesar best. Yet he loves Antony.
Hoo! Hearts, tongues, figures, scribes, bards, poets,
cannot
Think, speak, cast, write, sing, number – hoo! –
His love to Antony! But as for Caesar,
Kneel down, kneel down, and wonder!
AGRIPPA   Both he loves.
ENOBARBUS
They are his shards and he their beetle.

[*Trumpet within.*]
20   So,
This is to horse. Adieu, noble Agrippa.
AGRIPPA   Good fortune, worthy soldier, and farewell.

Enter CAESAR, ANTONY, LEPIDUS *and* OCTAVIA.

ANTONY   No further, sir.
CAESAR   You take from me a great part of myself.
25   Use me well in't. Sister, prove such a wife
As my thoughts make thee, and as my farthest bond
Shall pass on thy approof. Most noble Antony,
Let not the piece of virtue which is set
Betwixt us, as the cement of our love
30   To keep it builded, be the ram to batter
The fortress of it. For better might we
Have loved without this mean, if on both parts
This be not cherished.
ANTONY   Make me not offended
In your distrust.
CAESAR   I have said.
ANTONY   You shall not find,
35   Though you be therein curious, the least cause
For what you seem to fear. So the gods keep you,

And make the hearts of Romans serve your ends.
We will here part.
CAESAR   Farewell, my dearest sister, fare thee well.
The elements be kind to thee, and make   40
Thy spirits all of comfort! Fare thee well.
OCTAVIA   My noble brother! [*She weeps.*]
ANTONY   The April's in her eyes; it is love's spring
And these the showers to bring it on. Be cheerful.
OCTAVIA   Sir, look well to my husband's house, and –   45
CAESAR   What, Octavia?
OCTAVIA   I'll tell you in your ear.
[*She whispers to Caesar.*]
ANTONY   Her tongue will not obey her heart, nor can
Her heart inform her tongue – the swan's-down
feather
That stands upon the swell at full of tide,
And neither way inclines.   50
ENOBARBUS [*aside to Agrippa*]
Will Caesar weep?
AGRIPPA [*aside to Enobarbus*]   He has a cloud in's face.
ENOBARBUS [*aside to Agrippa*]
He were the worse for that were he a horse;
So is he, being a man.
AGRIPPA [*aside to Enobarbus*]   Why, Enobarbus,
When Antony found Julius Caesar dead,
He cried almost to roaring, and he wept   55
When at Philippi he found Brutus slain.
ENOBARBUS [*aside to Agrippa*]
That year, indeed, he was troubled with a rheum.
What willingly he did confound he wailed,
Believe't, till I wept too.
CAESAR   No, sweet Octavia,
You shall hear from me still. The time shall not   60
Outgo my thinking on you.
ANTONY   Come, sir, come,
I'll wrestle with you in my strength of love.
Look, here I have you [*embracing him*];
thus I let you go,
And give you to the gods.
CAESAR   Adieu. Be happy!
LEPIDUS   Let all the number of the stars give light   65
To thy fair way!
CAESAR   Farewell, farewell! [*Kisses Octavia.*]
ANTONY   Farewell!
Trumpets sound. Exeunt.

3.3   *Enter* CLEOPATRA, CHARMIAN, IRAS *and* ALEXAS.

CLEOPATRA   Where is the fellow?
ALEXAS   Half afeard to come.
CLEOPATRA
Go to, go to.

Enter the Messenger *as before.*

Come hither, sir.
ALEXAS   Good majesty,
Herod of Jewry dare not look upon you

But when you are well pleased.
CLEOPATRA   That Herod's head
    I'll have! But how, when Antony is gone,
    Through whom I might command it? – Come thou
        near.
MESSENGER   Most gracious majesty!
CLEOPATRA   Didst thou behold
    Octavia?
MESSENGER   Ay, dread queen.
CLEOPATRA   Where?
MESSENGER   Madam, in Rome.
    I looked her in the face, and saw her led
    Between her brother and Mark Antony.
CLEOPATRA   Is she as tall as me?
MESSENGER   She is not, madam.
CLEOPATRA
    Didst hear her speak? Is she shrill-tongued or low?
MESSENGER
    Madam, I heard her speak; she is low-voiced.
CLEOPATRA
    That's not so good. He cannot like her long.
CHARMIAN   Like her? O Isis! 'Tis impossible.
CLEOPATRA
    I think so, Charmian. Dull of tongue and dwarfish.
    What majesty is in her gait? Remember,
    If e'er thou look'dst on majesty.
MESSENGER   She creeps.
    Her motion and her station are as one.
    She shows a body rather than a life,
    A statue than a breather.
CLEOPATRA   Is this certain?
MESSENGER
    Or I have no observance.
CHARMIAN   Three in Egypt
    Cannot make better note.
CLEOPATRA   He's very knowing;
    I do perceiv't. There's nothing in her yet.
    The fellow has good judgement.
CHARMIAN   Excellent.
CLEOPATRA   Guess at her years, I prithee.
MESSENGER   Madam,
    She was a widow –
CLEOPATRA   Widow? Charmian, hark!
MESSENGER   And I do think she's thirty.
CLEOPATRA
    Bear'st thou her face in mind? Is't long or round?
MESSENGER   Round, even to faultiness.
CLEOPATRA
    For the most part, too, they are foolish that are so.
    Her hair, what colour?
MESSENGER   Brown, madam, and her forehead
    As low as she would wish it.
CLEOPATRA   There's gold for thee.
    Thou must not take my former sharpness ill.
    I will employ thee back again; I find thee
    Most fit for business. Go, make thee ready;
    Our letters are prepared.   *Exit Messenger.*

CHARMIAN   A proper man.
CLEOPATRA   Indeed, he is so. I repent me much
    That so I harried him. Why methinks, by him,
    This creature's no such thing.
CHARMIAN   Nothing, madam.   40
CLEOPATRA
    The man hath seen some majesty, and should know.
CHARMIAN   Hath he seen majesty? Isis else defend,
    And serving you so long!
CLEOPATRA
    I have one thing more to ask him yet, good
        Charmian.
    But 'tis no matter; thou shalt bring him to me   45
    Where I will write. All may be well enough.
CHARMIAN   I warrant you, madam.   *Exeunt.*

3.4   *Enter* ANTONY *and* OCTAVIA.

ANTONY   Nay, nay, Octavia, not only that.
    That were excusable – that, and thousands more
    Of semblable import – but he hath waged
    New wars 'gainst Pompey; made his will, and read it
    To public ear;   5
    Spoke scantly of me; when perforce he could not
    But pay me terms of honour, cold and sickly
    He vented them; most narrow measure lent me;
    When the best hint was given him, he not took't,
    Or did it from his teeth.
OCTAVIA   O, my good lord,   10
    Believe not all, or if you must believe,
    Stomach not all. A more unhappy lady,
    If this division chance, ne'er stood between,
    Praying for both parts.
    The good gods will mock me presently   15
    When I shall pray 'O, bless my lord and husband!';
    Undo that prayer by crying out as loud
    'O, bless my brother!' Husband win, win brother,
    Prays and destroys the prayer; no midway
    'Twixt these extremes at all.
ANTONY   Gentle Octavia,   20
    Let your best love draw to that point which seeks
    Best to preserve it. If I lose mine honour,
    I lose myself; better I were not yours
    Than yours so branchless. But, as you requested,
    Yourself shall go between's. The meantime, lady,   25
    I'll raise the preparation of a war
    Shall stain your brother. Make your soonest haste,
    So your desires are yours.
OCTAVIA   Thanks to my lord.
    The Jove of power make me, most weak, most weak,
    Your reconciler! Wars 'twixt you twain would be   30
    As if the world should cleave, and that slain men
    Should solder up the rift.
ANTONY   When it appears to you where this begins,
    Turn your displeasure that way, for our faults
    Can never be so equal that your love   35
    Can equally move with them. Provide your going;

139

Choose your own company, and command what cost
Your heart has mind to. *Exeunt.*

Enter ENOBARBUS *and* EROS, *meeting*.

ENOBARBUS   How now, friend Eros?

EROS   There's strange news come, sir.

ENOBARBUS   What, man?

EROS   Caesar and Lepidus have made wars upon
5   Pompey.

ENOBARBUS   This is old. What is the success?

EROS   Caesar, having made use of him in the wars 'gainst
Pompey, presently denied him rivality; would not let
him partake in the glory of the action, and, not resting
10   here, accuses him of letters he had formerly wrote to
Pompey; upon his own appeal, seizes him. So the poor
third is up, till death enlarge his confine.

ENOBARBUS
Then, world, thou hast a pair of chaps, no more,
And throw between them all the food thou hast,
15   They'll grind the one the other. Where's Antony?

EROS   He's walking in the garden, thus, and spurns
The rush that lies before him; cries, 'Fool Lepidus!',
And threats the throat of that his officer
That murdered Pompey.

ENOBARBUS   Our great navy's rigged.

20   EROS   For Italy and Caesar. More, Domitius:
My lord desires you presently. My news
I might have told hereafter.

ENOBARBUS   'Twill be naught,
But let it be. Bring me to Antony.

EROS   Come, sir. *Exeunt.*

Enter AGRIPPA, MAECENAS *and* CAESAR.

CAESAR
Contemning Rome, he has done all this, and more
In Alexandria. Here's the manner of't:
I'th' market-place, on a tribunal silvered,
Cleopatra and himself in chairs of gold
5   Were publicly enthroned. At the feet sat
Caesarion, whom they call my father's son,
And all the unlawful issue that their lust
Since then hath made between them. Unto her
He gave the stablishment of Egypt; made her
10   Of lower Syria, Cyprus, Lydia,
Absolute Queen.

MAECENAS   This in the public eye?

CAESAR   I'th' common showplace where they exercise.
His sons he there proclaimed the kings of kings:
Great Media, Parthia and Armenia
15   He gave to Alexander; to Ptolemy he assigned
Syria, Cilicia and Phoenicia. She
In th'habiliments of the goddess Isis
That day appeared, and oft before gave audience,
As 'tis reported, so.

20   MAECENAS   Let Rome be thus informed.

AGRIPPA   Who, queasy with his insolence already,
Will their good thoughts call from him.

CAESAR   The people knows it, and have now received
His accusations.

AGRIPPA   Who does he accuse?

CAESAR   Caesar; and that having in Sicily   25
Sextus Pompeius spoiled, we had not rated him
His part o'th' isle. Then does he say he lent me
Some shipping, unrestored. Lastly, he frets
That Lepidus of the triumvirate
Should be deposed and, being, that we detain   30
All his revenue.

AGRIPPA   Sir, this should be answered.

CAESAR
'Tis done already, and the messenger gone.
I have told him Lepidus was grown too cruel,
That he his high authority abused
And did deserve his change. For what I have
      conquered,   35
I grant him part; but then in his Armenia
And other of his conquered kingdoms, I
Demand the like.

MAECENAS   He'll never yield to that.

CAESAR   Nor must not then be yielded to in this.

Enter OCTAVIA *with her train.*

OCTAVIA
Hail, Caesar, and my lord! Hail, most dear Caesar!   40

CAESAR   That ever I should call thee castaway!

OCTAVIA
You have not called me so, nor have you cause.

CAESAR
Why have you stolen upon us thus? You come not
Like Caesar's sister. The wife of Antony
Should have an army for an usher, and   45
The neighs of horse to tell of her approach
Long ere she did appear. The trees by th' way
Should have borne men, and expectation fainted,
Longing for what it had not. Nay, the dust
Should have ascended to the roof of heaven,   50
Raised by your populous troops. But you are come
A market maid to Rome, and have prevented
The ostentation of our love which, left unshown,
Is often left unloved. We should have met you
By sea and land, supplying every stage   55
With an augmented greeting.

OCTAVIA   Good my lord,
To come thus was I not constrained, but did it
On my free will. My lord, Mark Antony,
Hearing that you prepared for war, acquainted
My grieved ear withal, whereon I begged   60
His pardon for return.

CAESAR   Which soon he granted,
Being an abstract 'tween his lust and him.

OCTAVIA   Do not say so, my lord.

CAESAR   I have eyes upon him,
And his affairs come to me on the wind.
Where is he now?

OCTAVIA   My lord, in Athens.

CAESAR   No,
My most wrongèd sister. Cleopatra hath
Nodded him to her. He hath given his empire
Up to a whore, who now are levying
The kings o'th' earth for war. He hath assembled
Bocchus the King of Libya, Archelaus
Of Cappadocia, Philadelphos King
Of Paphlagonia, the Thracian King Adallas,
King Manchus of Arabia, King of Pont,
Herod of Jewry, Mithridates King
Of Comagene, Polemon and Amyntas,
The Kings of Mede and Lycaonia,
With a more larger list of sceptres.

OCTAVIA   Ay me, most wretched,
That have my heart parted betwixt two friends
That does afflict each other!

CAESAR   Welcome hither.
Your letters did withhold our breaking forth
Till we perceived both how you were wrong led
And we in negligent danger. Cheer your heart.
Be you not troubled with the time, which drives
O'er your content these strong necessities,
But let determined things to destiny
Hold unbewailed their way. Welcome to Rome,
Nothing more dear to me! You are abused
Beyond the mark of thought, and the high gods,
To do you justice, makes his ministers
Of us and those that love you. Best of comfort,
And ever welcome to us.

AGRIPPA   Welcome, lady.

MAECENAS   Welcome, dear madam.
Each heart in Rome does love and pity you.
Only th'adulterous Antony, most large
In his abominations, turns you off
And gives his potent regiment to a trull
That noises it against us.

OCTAVIA   Is it so, sir?

CAESAR   Most certain. Sister, welcome. Pray you
Be ever known to patience. My dear'st sister! *Exeunt.*

3.7   *Enter* CLEOPATRA *and* ENOBARBUS.

CLEOPATRA   I will be even with thee, doubt it not.

ENOBARBUS   But why, why, why?

CLEOPATRA
Thou hast forspoke my being in these wars
And say'st it is not fit.

ENOBARBUS   Well, is it, is it?

CLEOPATRA
Is't not denounced against us? Why should not we
Be there in person?

ENOBARBUS   Well, I could reply
If we should serve with horse and mares together,
The horse were merely lost. The mares would bear
A soldier and his horse.

CLEOPATRA   What is't you say?

ENOBARBUS   Your presence needs must puzzle Antony,   10
Take from his heart, take from his brain, from's time
What should not then be spared. He is already
Traduced for levity, and 'tis said in Rome
That Photinus, an eunuch and your maids
Manage this war.

CLEOPATRA   Sink Rome, and their tongues rot   15
That speak against us! A charge we bear i'th' war,
And, as the president of my kingdom, will
Appear there for a man. Speak not against it!
I will not stay behind.

Enter ANTONY *and* CANIDIUS.

ENOBARBUS   Nay, I have done.
Here comes the Emperor.

ANTONY   Is it not strange, Canidius,   20
That from Tarentum and Brundusium
He could so quickly cut the Ionian sea
And take in Toryne? You have heard on't, sweet?

CLEOPATRA   Celerity is never more admired
Than by the negligent.

ANTONY   A good rebuke,   25
Which might have well becomed the best of men,
To taunt at slackness. Canidius, we
Will fight with him by sea.

CLEOPATRA   By sea – what else?

CANIDIUS   Why will my lord do so?

ANTONY   For that he dares us to't.

ENOBARBUS   So hath my lord dared him to single fight.   30

CANIDIUS   Ay, and to wage this battle at Pharsalia,
Where Caesar fought with Pompey. But these offers,
Which serve not for his vantage, he shakes off,
And so should you.

ENOBARBUS   Your ships are not well manned,
Your mariners are muleteers, reapers, people   35
Engrossed by swift impress. In Caesar's fleet
Are those that often have 'gainst Pompey fought;
Their ships are yare, yours heavy. No disgrace
Shall fall you for refusing him at sea,
Being prepared for land.

ANTONY   By sea, by sea.   40

ENOBARBUS   Most worthy sir, you therein throw away
The absolute soldiership you have by land;
Distract your army, which doth most consist
Of war-marked footmen; leave unexecuted
Your own renowned knowledge; quite forgo   45
The way which promises assurance; and
Give up yourself merely to chance and hazard
From firm security.

ANTONY   I'll fight at sea.

CLEOPATRA   I have sixty sails, Caesar none better.

ANTONY   Our overplus of shipping will we burn,   50
And with the rest full-manned, from th'head of
   Actium
Beat th'approaching Caesar. But if we fail,
We then can do't at land.

Enter a Messenger.

              Thy business?
MESSENGER   The news is true, my lord; he is descried.
55   Caesar has taken Toryne.
ANTONY   Can he be there in person? 'Tis impossible;
    Strange that his power should be. Canidius,
    Our nineteen legions thou shalt hold by land
    And our twelve thousand horse. We'll to our ship.
    Away, my Thetis!

Enter a Soldier.

60   How now, worthy soldier?
SOLDIER   O noble Emperor, do not fight by sea.
    Trust not to rotten planks. Do you misdoubt
    This sword and these my wounds? Let th'Egyptians
    And the Phoenicians go a-ducking; we
65   Have used to conquer standing on the earth
    And fighting foot to foot.
ANTONY   Well, well, away!
    Exeunt Antony, Cleopatra and Enobarbus.
SOLDIER   By Hercules, I think I am i'th' right.
CANIDIUS
    Soldier, thou art. But his whole action grows
    Not in the power on't. So our leader's led,
    And we are women's men.
70 SOLDIER   You keep by land
    The legions and the horse whole, do you not?
CANIDIUS   Marcus Octavius, Marcus Justeius,
    Publicola and Caelius are for sea,
    But we keep whole by land. This speed of Caesar's
    Carries beyond belief.
75 SOLDIER   While he was yet in Rome,
    His power went out in such distractions as
    Beguiled all spies.
CANIDIUS   Who's his lieutenant, hear you?
SOLDIER   They say one Taurus.
CANIDIUS   Well I know the man.

Enter a Messenger.

MESSENGER   The Emperor calls Canidius.
CANIDIUS
80   With news the time's in labour, and throws forth
    Each minute some.   *Exeunt.*

3.8 *Enter* CAESAR *and* TAURUS *with his army, marching.*

CAESAR   Taurus!
TAURUS   My lord?
CAESAR
    Strike not by land; keep whole; provoke not battle
    Till we have done at sea. Do not exceed
    The prescript of this scroll. [*Gives him a scroll.*]
5   Our fortune lies
    Upon this jump.   *Exeunt.*

3.9   *Enter* ANTONY *and* ENOBARBUS.

ANTONY   Set we our squadrons on yond side o'th' hill

    In eye of Caesar's battle, from which place
    We may the number of the ships behold
    And so proceed accordingly.   *Exeunt.*

3.10 CANIDIUS *marcheth with his land army one way over the stage, and* TAURUS, *the lieutenant of Caesar, the other way. After their going in, is heard the noise of a sea fight.*

Alarum. Enter ENOBARBUS.

ENOBARBUS
    Naught, naught, all naught! I can behold no longer!
    Th'Antoniad, the Egyptian admiral,
    With all their sixty, fly and turn the rudder.
    To see't mine eyes are blasted.

Enter SCARUS.

SCARUS   Gods and goddesses!
    All the whole synod of them!
ENOBARBUS   What's thy passion?   5
SCARUS   The greater cantle of the world is lost
    With very ignorance. We have kissed away
    Kingdoms and provinces.
ENOBARBUS   How appears the fight?
SCARUS   On our side, like the tokened pestilence
    Where death is sure. Yon ribaudred nag of Egypt – 10
    Whom leprosy o'ertake! – i'th' midst o'th' fight
    When vantage like a pair of twins appeared
    Both as the same – or, rather, ours the elder –
    The breeze upon her, like a cow in June,
    Hoists sails and flies.   15
ENOBARBUS   That I beheld.
    Mine eyes did sicken at the sight and could not
    Endure a further view.
SCARUS   She once being loofed,
    The noble ruin of her magic, Antony,
    Claps on his sea-wing and, like a doting mallard, 20
    Leaving the fight in height, flies after her.
    I never saw an action of such shame.
    Experience, manhood, honour, ne'er before
    Did violate so itself.
ENOBARBUS   Alack, alack!

Enter CANIDIUS.

CANIDIUS   Our fortune on the sea is out of breath 25
    And sinks most lamentably. Had our general
    Been what he knew – himself – it had gone well.
    Oh, he has given example for our flight
    Most grossly by his own!
ENOBARBUS   Ay, are you thereabouts?
    Why then, good night indeed. 30
CANIDIUS   Toward Peloponnesus are they fled.
SCARUS   'Tis easy to't, and there I will attend
    What further comes.
CANIDIUS   To Caesar will I render
    My legions and my horse. Six kings already
    Show me the way of yielding.

ENOBARBUS   I'll yet follow
  The wounded chance of Antony, though my reason
  Sits in the wind against me.

> *Exit at one door Canidius,*
> *at the other Scarus and Enobarbus.*

3.11   *Enter* ANTONY *with attendants.*

ANTONY
  Hark! The land bids me tread no more upon't;
  It is ashamed to bear me. Friends, come hither.
  I am so lated in the world that I
  Have lost my way for ever. I have a ship
  Laden with gold. Take that, divide it. Fly
  And make your peace with Caesar.
ALL   Fly? Not we.
ANTONY
  I have fled myself and have instructed cowards
  To run and show their shoulders. Friends, be gone.
  I have myself resolved upon a course
  Which has no need of you. Be gone.
  My treasure's in the harbour. Take it. O,
  I followed that I blush to look upon.
  My very hairs do mutiny, for the white
  Reprove the brown for rashness, and they them
  For fear and doting. Friends, be gone. You shall
  Have letters from me to some friends that will
  Sweep your way for you. Pray you, look not sad
  Nor make replies of loathness; take the hint
  Which my despair proclaims. Let that be left
  Which leaves itself. To the sea-side straightway.
  I will possess you of that ship and treasure.
  Leave me, I pray, a little – pray you, now;
  Nay, do so; for indeed I have lost command;
  Therefore, I pray you. I'll see you by and by.

> *Exeunt attendants. Antony sits down.*

Enter CLEOPATRA *led by* CHARMIAN, IRAS *and* EROS.

EROS   Nay, gentle madam, to him! Comfort him.
IRAS   Do, most dear queen.
CHARMIAN   Do? Why, what else?
CLEOPATRA   Let me sit down. O, Juno!
ANTONY   No, no, no, no, no!
EROS   See you here, sir?
ANTONY   O fie, fie, fie!
CHARMIAN   Madam!
IRAS   Madam! O, good empress!
EROS   Sir, sir!
ANTONY   Yes, my lord, yes. He at Philippi kept
  His sword e'en like a dancer, while I struck
  The lean and wrinkled Cassius, and 'twas I
  That the mad Brutus ended. He alone
  Dealt on lieutenantry, and no practice had
  In the brave squares of war. Yet now – no matter.
CLEOPATRA   Ah, stand by.
EROS   The Queen, my lord! The Queen!
IRAS   Go to him, madam; speak to him.

He is unqualitied with very shame.
CLEOPATRA   Well then, sustain me. O!
EROS   Most noble sir, arise. The Queen approaches.
  Her head's declined, and death will seize her but
  Your comfort makes the rescue.
ANTONY   I have offended reputation,
  A most unnoble swerving.
EROS   Sir, the Queen!
ANTONY   O, whither hast thou led me, Egypt? See
  How I convey my shame out of thine eyes
  By looking back what I have left behind
  'Stroyed in dishonour.
CLEOPATRA   O, my lord, my lord,
  Forgive my fearful sails! I little thought
  You would have followed.
ANTONY   Egypt, thou knewst too well
  My heart was to thy rudder tied by th' strings
  And thou shouldst tow me after. O'er my spirit
  Thy full supremacy thou knewst, and that
  Thy beck might from the bidding of the gods
  Command me.
CLEOPATRA   O, my pardon!
ANTONY   Now I must
  To the young man send humble treaties; dodge
  And palter in the shifts of lowness, who
  With half the bulk o'th' world played as I pleased,
  Making and marring fortunes. You did know
  How much you were my conqueror, and that
  My sword, made weak by my affection, would
  Obey it on all cause.
CLEOPATRA   Pardon, pardon!
ANTONY   Fall not a tear, I say; one of them rates
  All that is won and lost. Give me a kiss. [*They kiss.*]
  Even this repays me.
  We sent our schoolmaster. Is a come back?
  Love, I am full of lead. Some wine
  Within there and our viands! Fortune knows
  We scorn her most when most she offers blows.

> *Exeunt.*

3.12   *Enter* CAESAR, AGRIPPA, DOLABELLA *and*
            THIDIAS *with others.*

CAESAR   Let him appear that's come from Antony.
  Know you him?
DOLABELLA   Caesar, 'tis his schoolmaster;
  An argument that he is plucked, when hither
  He sends so poor a pinion of his wing,
  Which had superfluous kings for messengers
  Not many moons gone by.

Enter Ambassador *from Antony.*

CAESAR   Approach, and speak.
AMBASSADOR   Such as I am, I come from Antony.
  I was of late as petty to his ends
  As is the morn-dew on the myrtle leaf
  To his grand sea.

CAESAR   Be't so. Declare thine office.

AMBASSADOR   Lord of his fortunes he salutes thee, and
   Requires to live in Egypt; which not granted,
   He lessens his requests and to thee sues
   To let him breathe between the heavens and earth,
   A private man in Athens. This for him.
   Next, Cleopatra does confess thy greatness,
   Submits her to thy might, and of thee craves
   The circle of the Ptolemies for her heirs,
   Now hazarded to thy grace.

CAESAR   For Antony,
   I have no ears to his request. The Queen
   Of audience nor desire shall fail, so she
   From Egypt drive her all-disgraced friend
   Or take his life there. This if she perform,
   She shall not sue unheard. So to them both.

AMBASSADOR   Fortune pursue thee!

CAESAR   Bring him through the bands.
                Exit Ambassador, attended.

   [*to Thidias*]
   To try thy eloquence now 'tis time. Dispatch.
   From Antony win Cleopatra; promise,
   And in our name, what she requires; add more,
   From thine invention, offers. Women are not
   In their best fortunes strong, but want will perjure
   The ne'er-touch'd vestal. Try thy cunning, Thidias;
   Make thine own edict for thy pains, which we
   Will answer as a law.

THIDIAS   Caesar, I go.

CAESAR   Observe how Antony becomes his flaw,
   And what thou think'st his very action speaks
   In every power that moves.

THIDIAS   Caesar, I shall.   *Exeunt.*

3.13   *Enter* CLEOPATRA, ENOBARBUS, CHARMIAN *and*
                     IRAS.

CLEOPATRA   What shall we do, Enobarbus?

ENOBARBUS   Think, and die.

CLEOPATRA   Is Antony or we in fault for this?

ENOBARBUS   Antony only, that would make his will
   Lord of his reason. What though you fled
   From that great face of war, whose several ranges
   Frighted each other? Why should he follow?
   The itch of his affection should not then
   Have nicked his captainship, at such a point,
   When half to half the world opposed, he being
   The mered question. 'Twas a shame no less
   Than was his loss, to course your flying flags
   And leave his navy gazing.

CLEOPATRA   Prithee, peace.

       Enter the Ambassador *with* ANTONY.

ANTONY   Is that his answer?

AMBASSADOR   Ay, my lord.

ANTONY   The Queen shall then have courtesy, so she
   Will yield us up.

AMBASSADOR   He says so.

ANTONY   Let her know't.
   To the boy Caesar send this grizzled head,
   And he will fill thy wishes to the brim
   With principalities.

CLEOPATRA   That head, my lord?

ANTONY   To him again! Tell him he wears the rose
   Of youth upon him, from which the world should
     note
   Something particular. His coin, ships, legions,
   May be a coward's, whose ministers would prevail
   Under the service of a child as soon
   As i'th' command of Caesar. I dare him therefore
   To lay his gay caparisons apart
   And answer me declined, sword against sword,
   Ourselves alone. I'll write it. Follow me.
          Exeunt Antony and Ambassador.

ENOBARBUS [*aside*]
   Yes, like enough high-battled Caesar will
   Unstate his happiness, and be staged to th' show
   Against a sworder! I see men's judgements are
   A parcel of their fortunes, and things outward
   Do draw the inward quality after them
   To suffer all alike. That he should dream,
   Knowing all measures, the full Caesar will
   Answer his emptiness! Caesar, thou hast subdued
   His judgement too.

            Enter a Servant.

SERVANT   A messenger from Caesar.

CLEOPATRA
   What, no more ceremony? See, my women,
   Against the blown rose they may stop their nose
   That kneeled unto the buds. Admit him, sir.
                Exit Servant.

ENOBARBUS [*aside*]
   Mine honesty and I begin to square.
   The loyalty well held to fools does make
   Our faith mere folly. Yet he that can endure
   To follow with allegiance a fallen lord
   Does conquer him that did his master conquer,
   And earns a place i'th' story.

             Enter THIDIAS.

CLEOPATRA   Caesar's will?

THIDIAS   Hear it apart.

CLEOPATRA   None but friends. Say boldly.

THIDIAS   So haply are they friends to Antony.

ENOBARBUS   He needs as many, sir, as Caesar has,
   Or needs not us. If Caesar please, our master
   Will leap to be his friend. For us, you know,
   Whose he is we are, and that is Caesar's.

THIDIAS   So.
   Thus then, thou most renowned: Caesar entreats
   Not to consider in what case thou stand'st
   Further than he is Caesar.

CLEOPATRA   Go on; right royal.

THIDIAS   He knows that you embrace not Antony
  As you did love, but as you feared him.
CLEOPATRA   O!
THIDIAS   The scars upon your honour, therefore, he
  Does pity as constrained blemishes,
  Not as deserved.
CLEOPATRA   He is a god and knows
  What is most right. Mine honour was not yielded
  But conquered merely.
ENOBARBUS [*aside*]
  To be sure of that, I will ask Antony.
  Sir, sir, thou art so leaky
  That we must leave thee to thy sinking, for
  Thy dearest quit thee.   *Exit Enobarbus.*
THIDIAS   Shall I say to Caesar
  What you require of him? For he partly begs
  To be desired to give. It much would please him
  That of his fortunes you should make a staff
  To lean upon. But it would warm his spirits
  To hear from me you had left Antony
  And put yourself under his shroud,
  The universal landlord.
CLEOPATRA   What's your name?
THIDIAS   My name is Thidias.
CLEOPATRA   Most kind messenger,
  Say to great Caesar this in deputation:
  I kiss his conqu'ring hand. Tell him I am prompt
  To lay my crown at's feet, and there to kneel
  Till from his all-obeying breath I hear
  The doom of Egypt.
THIDIAS   'Tis your noblest course.
  Wisdom and fortune combating together,
  If that the former dare but what it can,
  No chance may shake it. Give me grace to lay
  My duty on your hand.
CLEOPATRA [*Offers him her hand.*]
  Your Caesar's father oft,
  When he hath mused of taking kingdoms in,
  Bestowed his lips on that unworthy place
  As it rained kisses.

          Enter ANTONY *and* ENOBARBUS.

ANTONY   Favours? By Jove that thunders!
  What art thou, fellow?
THIDIAS   One that but performs
  The bidding of the fullest man and worthiest
  To have command obeyed.
ENOBARBUS [*aside*]   You will be whipped.
ANTONY [*Calls for servants.*]
  Approach there! – Ah, you kite! – Now, gods and
    devils,
  Authority melts from me. Of late when I cried 'Ho!',
  Like boys unto a muss, kings would start forth
  And cry 'Your will?'

          Enter servants.

          Have you no ears? I am

Antony yet. Take hence the jack and whip him!
ENOBARBUS [*aside*]
  'Tis better playing with a lion's whelp
  Than with an old one dying.
ANTONY   Moon and stars!
  Whip him! Were't twenty of the greatest tributaries
  That do acknowledge Caesar, should I find them
  So saucy with the hand of she here – what's her
    name
  Since she was Cleopatra? Whip him, fellows,
  Till like a boy you see him cringe his face
  And whine aloud for mercy. Take him hence!
THIDIAS   Mark Antony –
ANTONY   Tug him away! Being whipped,
  Bring him again. The jack of Caesar's shall
  Bear us an errand to him.

          Exeunt servants with Thidias.

  You were half blasted ere I knew you. Ha?
  Have I my pillow left unpressed in Rome,
  Forborne the getting of a lawful race,
  And by a gem of women, to be abused
  By one that looks on feeders?
CLEOPATRA   Good my lord –
ANTONY   You have been a boggler ever.
  But when we in our viciousness grow hard –
  O, misery on't! – the wise gods seel our eyes,
  In our own filth drop our clear judgements, make us
  Adore our errors, laugh at's while we strut
  To our confusion.
CLEOPATRA   O, is't come to this?
ANTONY   I found you as a morsel, cold upon
  Dead Caesar's trencher – nay, you were a fragment
  Of Gnaeus Pompey's, besides what hotter hours,
  Unregistered in vulgar fame, you have
  Luxuriously picked out. For I am sure,
  Though you can guess what temperance should be,
  You know not what it is.
CLEOPATRA   Wherefore is this?
ANTONY   To let a fellow that will take rewards
  And say 'God quit you!' be familiar with
  My playfellow, your hand, this kingly seal
  And plighter of high hearts! O that I were
  Upon the hill of Basan, to outroar
  The horned herd! For I have savage cause,
  And to proclaim it civilly were like
  A haltered neck which does the hangman thank
  For being yare about him.

          Enter a Servant *with* THIDIAS.

                Is he whipped?
SERVANT   Soundly, my lord.
ANTONY   Cried he? And begged 'a pardon?
SERVANT   He did ask favour.
ANTONY [*to Thidias*]
  If that thy father live, let him repent
  Thou wast not made his daughter; and be thou sorry
  To follow Caesar in his triumph, since

Thou hast been whipped for following him. Henceforth

The white hand of a lady fever thee;

Shake thou to look on't. Get thee back to Caesar;

145 Tell him thy entertainment. Look thou say

He makes me angry with him. For he seems

Proud and disdainful, harping on what I am,

Not what he knew I was. He makes me angry,

And at this time most easy 'tis to do't,

150 When my good stars that were my former guides

Have empty left their orbs and shot their fires

Into th'abysm of hell. If he mislike

My speech and what is done, tell him he has

Hipparchus, my enfranched bondman, whom

155 He may at pleasure whip or hang or torture,

As he shall like to quit me. Urge it thou.

Hence with thy stripes! Be gone!

Exit Thidias with Servant.

CLEOPATRA   Have you done yet?

ANTONY   Alack, our terrene moon is now eclipsed

And it portends alone the fall of Antony.

160 CLEOPATRA   I must stay his time.

ANTONY   To flatter Caesar would you mingle eyes

With one that ties his points?

CLEOPATRA   Not know me yet?

ANTONY   Cold-hearted toward me?

CLEOPATRA   Ah, dear, if I be so,

From my cold heart let heaven engender hail

165 And poison it in the source, and the first stone

Drop in my neck; as it determines, so

Dissolve my life! The next Caesarion smite,

Till by degrees the memory of my womb,

Together with my brave Egyptians all,

170 By the discandying of this pelleted storm

Lie graveless, till the flies and gnats of Nile

Have buried them for prey!

ANTONY   I am satisfied.

Caesar sets down in Alexandria, where

I will oppose his fate. Our force by land

175 Hath nobly held; our severed navy too

Have knit again, and fleet, threat'ning most sea-like.

Where hast thou been, my heart? Dost thou hear,
    lady?

If from the field I shall return once more

To kiss these lips, I will appear in blood.

180 I and my sword will earn our chronicle.

There's hope in't yet.

CLEOPATRA   That's my brave lord!

ANTONY   I will be treble-sinewed, hearted, breathed,

And fight maliciously. For when mine hours

185 Were nice and lucky, men did ransom lives

Of me for jests. But now, I'll set my teeth

And send to darkness all that stop me. Come,

Let's have one other gaudy night. Call to me

All my sad captains. Fill our bowls once more.

Let's mock the midnight bell.

190 CLEOPATRA   It is my birthday.

I had thought t'have held it poor, but since my lord

Is Antony again, I will be Cleopatra.

ANTONY   We will yet do well.

CLEOPATRA [*to Charmian and Iras*]

Call all his noble captains to my lord!

ANTONY

Do so, we'll speak to them; and tonight I'll force   195

The wine peep through their scars. Come on, my
    queen,

There's sap in't yet! The next time I do fight

I'll make Death love me, for I will contend

Even with his pestilent scythe.

Exeunt all but Enobarbus.

ENOBARBUS

Now he'll outstare the lightning. To be furious   200

Is to be frighted out of fear, and in that mood

The dove will peck the estridge; and I see still

A diminution in our captain's brain

Restores his heart. When valour preys on reason,

It eats the sword it fights with. I will seek   205

Some way to leave him.   *Exit.*

4.1   *Enter* CAESAR, AGRIPPA *and* MAECENAS, *with his
    army, Caesar reading a letter.*

CAESAR   He calls me boy, and chides as he had power

To beat me out of Egypt. My messenger

He hath whipped with rods; dares me to personal
    combat,

Caesar to Antony. Let the old ruffian know

I have many other ways to die; meantime   5

Laugh at his challenge.

MAECENAS   Caesar must think,

When one so great begins to rage, he's hunted

Even to falling. Give him no breath, but now

Make boot of his distraction. Never anger   10

Made good guard for itself.

CAESAR   Let our best heads

Know that tomorrow the last of many battles

We mean to fight. Within our files there are,

Of those that served Mark Antony but late,

Enough to fetch him in. See it done,   15

And feast the army. We have store to do't

And they have earned the waste. Poor Antony!

Exeunt.

4.2   *Enter* ANTONY, CLEOPATRA, ENOBARBUS,
    CHARMIAN, IRAS, ALEXAS *with others.*

ANTONY   He will not fight with me, Domitius?

ENOBARBUS   No.

ANTONY   Why should he not?

ENOBARBUS

He thinks, being twenty times of better fortune,

He is twenty men to one.

ANTONY   Tomorrow, soldier,

By sea and land I'll fight. Or I will live,   5

Or bathe my dying honour in the blood

Shall make it live again. Woo't thou fight well?
ENOBARBUS   I'll strike, and cry 'Take all!'
ANTONY   Well said! Come on!
Call forth my household servants.   *Exit Alexas.*
                                   Let's tonight
Be bounteous at our meal.

Enter three or four servitors.

10   Give me thy hand.
Thou hast been rightly honest; so hast thou,
Thou, and thou, and thou. You have served me well
And kings have been your fellows.
CLEOPATRA *[aside to Enobarbus]*   What means this?
ENOBARBUS *[aside to Cleopatra]*
'Tis one of those odd tricks which sorrow shoots
Out of the mind.
15 ANTONY   And thou art honest too.
I wish I could be made so many men,
And all of you clapped up together in
An Antony, that I might do you service
So good as you have done.
ALL THE SERVANTS   The gods forbid!
20 ANTONY   Well, my good fellows, wait on me tonight;
Scant not my cups, and make as much of me
As when mine empire was your fellow too
And suffered my command.
CLEOPATRA *[aside to Enobarbus]* What does he mean?
ENOBARBUS *[aside to Cleopatra]*
To make his followers weep.
ANTONY   Tend me tonight.
25 May be it is the period of your duty.
Haply you shall not see me more, or if,
A mangled shadow. Perchance tomorrow
You'll serve another master. I look on you
As one that takes his leave. Mine honest friends,
30 I turn you not away, but, like a master
Married to your good service, stay till death.
Tend me tonight two hours – I ask no more –
And the gods yield you for't!
ENOBARBUS   What mean you, sir,
To give them this discomfort? Look, they weep,
35 And I, an ass, am onion-eyed. For shame!
Transform us not to women!
ANTONY   Ho, ho, ho!
Now the witch take me if I meant it thus!
Grace grow where those drops fall! My hearty
    friends,
You take me in too dolorous a sense,
40 For I spake to you for your comfort, did desire you
To burn this night with torches. Know, my hearts,
I hope well of tomorrow, and will lead you
Where rather I'll expect victorious life
Than death and honour. Let's to supper, come,
45 And drown consideration.   *Exeunt.*

4.3   *Enter through one door,* First Soldier *and his*
          Company, through the other door, Second Soldier.

1 SOLDIER   Brother, good night. Tomorrow is the day.
2 SOLDIER   It will determine one way. Fare you well.
    Heard you of nothing strange about the streets?
1 SOLDIER   Nothing. What news?
2 SOLDIER   Belike 'tis but a rumour. Good night to you.   5
1 SOLDIER   Well sir, good night.

Other Soldiers *enter and join Second Soldier.*

2 SOLDIER   Soldiers, have careful watch.
3 SOLDIER   And you. Good night, good night.
    [They place themselves in every corner of the stage.]
2 SOLDIER   Here we. And if tomorrow
    Our navy thrive, I have an absolute hope   10
    Our landmen will stand up.
1 SOLDIER   'Tis a brave army and full of purpose –
          [Music of the hautboys is under the stage.]
2 SOLDIER   Peace! What noise?
1 SOLDIER   List, list!
2 SOLDIER   Hark!   15
1 SOLDIER   Music i'th' air.
3 SOLDIER   Under the earth.
4 SOLDIER   It signs well, does it not?
3 SOLDIER   No.
1 SOLDIER   Peace, I say! What should this mean?   20
2 SOLDIER   'Tis the god Hercules whom Antony loved
    Now leaves him.
1 SOLDIER   Walk. Let's see if other watchmen
    Do hear what we do.
2 SOLDIER   How now, masters? *[Speak together.]*
ALL   How now? How now? Do you hear this?   25
1 SOLDIER   Ay. Is't not strange?
3 SOLDIER   Do you hear, masters? Do you hear?
1 SOLDIER   Follow the noise so far as we have quarter.
    Let's see how it will give off.
ALL   Content. 'Tis strange.
                                   Exeunt.

4.4   *Enter* ANTONY *and* CLEOPATRA *with* CHARMIAN
          and others.

ANTONY   Eros! Mine armour, Eros!
CLEOPATRA   Sleep a little.
ANTONY
No, my chuck. Eros! Come, mine armour, Eros!

Enter EROS *with armour.*

Come, good fellow, put thine iron on.
If fortune be not ours today, it is
Because we brave her. Come!
CLEOPATRA   Nay, I'll help too.   5
    What's this for?
ANTONY   Ah, let be, let be! Thou art
    The armourer of my heart. False, false! This, this!
CLEOPATRA   Sooth, la, I'll help. Thus it must be.

ANTONY   Well, well!
   We shall thrive now. Seest thou, my good fellow?
   Go put on thy defences.

10   EROS   Briefly, sir.

CLEOPATRA   Is not this buckled well?

ANTONY   Rarely, rarely!
   He that unbuckles this, till we do please
   To doff't for our repose, shall hear a storm.
   Thou fumblest, Eros, and my queen's a squire
15   More tight at this than thou. Dispatch. O love,
   That thou couldst see my wars today and knew'st
   The royal occupation, thou shouldst see
   A workman in't.

Enter an armed Soldier.

           Good morrow to thee! Welcome!
   Thou look'st like him that knows a warlike charge.
20   To business that we love we rise betime
   And go to't with delight.

SOLDIER   A thousand, sir,
   Early though't be, have on their riveted trim
   And at the port expect you.

               [*Shout. Trumpets flourish.*]

Enter Captains *and* Soldiers.

CAPTAIN   The morn is fair. Good morrow, General!

ALL THE SOLDIERS   Good morrow, General!

25   ANTONY   'Tis well blown, lads!
   This morning, like the spirit of a youth
   That means to be of note, begins betimes.
   [*to Cleopatra*] So, so. Come, give me that. This way.
     Well said.
   Fare thee well, dame. Whate'er becomes of me,
30   This is a soldier's kiss. [*Kisses her.*] Rebukable
   And worthy shameful check it were, to stand
   On more mechanic compliment. I'll leave thee
   Now like a man of steel. – You that will fight,
   Follow me close, I'll bring you to't. Adieu.

        Exeunt all but Cleopatra and Charmian

CHARMIAN   Please you retire to your chamber?

35   CLEOPATRA   Lead me.
   He goes forth gallantly. That he and Caesar might
   Determine this great war in single fight!
   Then Antony – but now –. Well, on.   *Exeunt.*

4.5   *Trumpets sound. Enter* ANTONY *and* EROS, *a*
            Soldier *meeting them.*

SOLDIER   The gods make this a happy day to Antony!

ANTONY
   Would thou and those thy scars had once prevailed
   To make me fight at land!

SOLDIER   Hadst thou done so,
   The kings that have revolted and the soldier
   That has this morning left thee would have still
5   Followed thy heels.

ANTONY   Who's gone this morning?

SOLDIER   Who?
   One ever near thee. Call for Enobarbus,
   He shall not hear thee, or from Caesar's camp
   Say 'I am none of thine.'

ANTONY   What sayest thou?

SOLDIER   Sir,
   He is with Caesar.

EROS   Sir, his chests and treasure   10
   He has not with him.

ANTONY   Is he gone?

SOLDIER   Most certain.

ANTONY   Go, Eros, send his treasure after. Do it.
   Detain no jot, I charge thee. Write to him –
   I will subscribe – gentle adieus and greetings.
   Say that I wish he never find more cause   15
   To change a master. O, my fortunes have
   Corrupted honest men! Dispatch. – Enobarbus!

                     Exeunt.

4.6   *Flourish. Enter* AGRIPPA, CAESAR, *with* ENOBARBUS
                 and DOLABELLA.

CAESAR   Go forth, Agrippa, and begin the fight.
   Our will is Antony be took alive.
   Make it so known.

AGRIPPA   Caesar, I shall.   *Exit.*

CAESAR   The time of universal peace is near.   5
   Prove this a prosp'rous day, the three-nooked world
   Shall bear the olive freely.

Enter a Messenger.

MESSENGER   Antony
   Is come into the field.

CAESAR   Go charge Agrippa
   Plant those that have revolted in the van
   That Antony may seem to spend his fury   10
   Upon himself.   *Exeunt all but Enobarbus.*

ENOBARBUS   Alexas did revolt and went to Jewry on
   Affairs of Antony; there did dissuade
   Great Herod to incline himself to Caesar
   And leave his master Antony. For this pains   15
   Caesar hath hanged him. Canidius and the rest
   That fell away have entertainment but
   No honourable trust. I have done ill,
   Of which I do accuse myself so sorely
   That I will joy no more.   20

Enter a Soldier *of Caesar's.*

SOLDIER   Enobarbus, Antony
   Hath after thee sent all thy treasure, with
   His bounty overplus. The messenger
   Came on my guard, and at thy tent is now
   Unloading of his mules.

ENOBARBUS   I give it you.

SOLDIER   Mock not, Enobarbus.   25
   I tell you true. Best you safed the bringer
   Out of the host. I must attend mine office

Or would have done't myself. Your emperor
Continues still a Jove.   *Exit.*   30
ENOBARBUS   I am alone the villain of the earth,
   And feel I am so most. O Antony,
   Thou mine of bounty, how wouldst thou have paid
   My better service, when my turpitude
   Thou dost so crown with gold! This blows my heart.   35
   If swift thought break it not, a swifter mean
   Shall outstrike thought, but thought will do't, I feel.
   I fight against thee? No, I will go seek
   Some ditch wherein to die; the foul'st best fits
   My latter part of life.   *Exit.*   40

4.7   *Alarum. Drums and trumpets. Enter* AGRIPPA
and others.

AGRIPPA   Retire! We have engaged ourselves too far.
   Caesar himself has work, and our oppression
   Exceeds what we expected.   *Exeunt.*

Alarums. Enter ANTONY, *and* SCARUS *wounded.*

SCARUS   O, my brave emperor, this is fought indeed!
   Had we done so at first, we had droven them home   5
   With clouts about their heads.
ANTONY   Thou bleed'st apace.
SCARUS   I had a wound here that was like a T
   But now 'tis made an H.   [*Sound retreat far off.*]
ANTONY   They do retire.
SCARUS   We'll beat 'em into bench-holes. I have yet
   Room for six scotches more.   10

Enter EROS.

EROS   They're beaten, sir, and our advantage serves
   For a fair victory.
SCARUS   Let us score their backs
   And snatch 'em up as we take hares – behind!
   'Tis sport to maul a runner.
ANTONY   I will reward thee
   Once for thy sprightly comfort, and tenfold   15
   For thy good valour. Come thee on!
SCARUS   I'll halt after.   *Exeunt.*

4.8   *Alarum. Enter* ANTONY *again in a march;* SCARUS
with others.

ANTONY
   We have beat him to his camp. Run one before
   And let the Queen know of our gests.   *Exit a Soldier.*
                      Tomorrow,
   Before the sun shall see's, we'll spill the blood
   That has today escaped. I thank you all,
   For doughty-handed are you, and have fought   5
   Not as you served the cause, but as't had been
   Each man's like mine. You have shown all Hectors.
   Enter the city; clip your wives, your friends;
   Tell them your feats, whilst they with joyful tears
   Wash the congealment from your wounds, and kiss   10
   The honoured gashes whole.

Enter CLEOPATRA.

[*to Scarus*]   Give me thy hand.
   To this great fairy I'll commend thy acts,
   Make her thanks bless thee.
[*to Cleopatra*]   O thou day o'th' world,
   Chain mine armed neck! Leap thou, attire and all,
   Through proof of harness to my heart, and there   15
   Ride on the pants triumphing! [*They embrace.*]
CLEOPATRA   Lord of lords!
   O infinite virtue! Com'st thou smiling from
   The world's great snare uncaught?
ANTONY   My nightingale,
   We have beat them to their beds. What, girl! Though grey
   Do something mingle with our younger brown, yet have we   20
   A brain that nourishes our nerves and can
   Get goal for goal of youth. Behold this man.
   Commend unto his lips thy favouring hand.
   [*She offers Scarus her hand.*]
   Kiss it, my warrior. He hath fought today
   As if a god in hate of mankind had   25
   Destroyed in such a shape.
CLEOPATRA   I'll give thee, friend,
   An armour all of gold. It was a king's.
ANTONY   He has deserved it, were it carbuncled
   Like holy Phoebus' car. Give me thy hand.
   Through Alexandria make a jolly march;   30
   Bear our hacked targets like the men that owe them.
   Had our great palace the capacity
   To camp this host, we all would sup together
   And drink carouses to the next day's fate
   Which promises royal peril. Trumpeters,   35
   With brazen din blast you the city's ear;
   Make mingle with our rattling taborins
   That heaven and earth may strike their sounds together,
   Applauding our approach.   *Trumpets sound. Exeunt.*

4.9   *Enter a* Sentry *and his Company of* Watch.
ENOBARBUS *follows.*

SENTRY   If we be not relieved within this hour,
   We must return to th' court of guard. The night
   Is shiny, and they say we shall embattle
   By th' second hour i'th' morn.
1 WATCH   This last day was a shrewd one to's.   5
ENOBARBUS   O bear me witness, night –
2 WATCH   What man is this?
1 WATCH   Stand close and list him. [*They stand aside.*]
ENOBARBUS   Be witness to me, O thou blessed moon,
   When men revolted shall upon record   10
   Bear hateful memory, poor Enobarbus did
   Before thy face repent.
SENTRY   Enobarbus?
2 WATCH   Peace! Hark further.

15 ENOBARBUS O sovereign mistress of true melancholy,
    The poisonous damp of night disponge upon me,
    That life, a very rebel to my will,
    May hang no longer on me. Throw my heart
    Against the flint and hardness of my fault,
20   Which, being dried with grief, will break to powder
    And finish all foul thoughts. O Antony,
    Nobler than my revolt is infamous,
    Forgive me in thine own particular,
    But let the world rank me in register
25   A master-leaver and a fugitive.
    O Antony! O Antony! [*He sinks down.*]
1 WATCH Let's speak to him.
SENTRY Let's hear him, for the things he speaks may
    concern Caesar.
30 2 WATCH Let's do so. But he sleeps.
SENTRY Swoons rather, for so bad a prayer as his was
    never yet for sleep.
1 WATCH Go we to him.
2 WATCH Awake sir! Awake! Speak to us!
35 1 WATCH Hear you, sir?
SENTRY The hand of death hath raught him. Hark!
    [*Drums afar off.*]   The drums
    Demurely wake the sleepers. Let us bear him
    To th' court of guard. He is of note. Our hour
    Is fully out.
40 2 WATCH Come on, then. He may recover yet.
                 Exeunt with the body.

4.10 *Enter* ANTONY *and* SCARUS *with their army.*

ANTONY Their preparation is today by sea;
    We please them not by land.
SCARUS   For both, my lord.
ANTONY
    I would they'd fight i'th' fire or i'th' air;
    We'd fight there too. But this it is: our foot
5   Upon the hills adjoining to the city
    Shall stay with us – order for sea is given;
    They have put forth the haven –
    Where their appointment we may best discover
    And look on their endeavour.   *Exeunt.*

4.11   *Enter* CAESAR *and his army.*

CAESAR But being charged we will be still by land,
    Which, as I take't, we shall, for his best force
    Is forth to man his galleys. To the vales,
    And hold our best advantage.   *Exeunt.*

4.12   *Alarum afar off, as at a sea fight. Enter*
        ANTONY *and* SCARUS.

ANTONY
    Yet they are not joined. Where yond pine does stand
    I shall discover all. I'll bring thee word
    Straight how 'tis like to go.   *Exit.*
SCARUS   Swallows have built

In Cleopatra's sails their nests. The augurs
Say they know not, they cannot tell; look grimly,   5
And dare not speak their knowledge. Antony
Is valiant and dejected, and by starts
His fretted fortunes give him hope and fear
Of what he has and has not.

            Enter ANTONY.

ANTONY   All is lost!
    This foul Egyptian hath betrayed me.   10
    My fleet hath yielded to the foe, and yonder
    They cast their caps up and carouse together
    Like friends long lost. Triple-turned whore! 'Tis
        thou
    Hast sold me to this novice, and my heart
    Makes only wars on thee. Bid them all fly!   15
    For when I am revenged upon my charm,
    I have done all. Bid them all fly! Be gone!
                 Exit Scarus.
    O sun, thy uprise shall I see no more.
    Fortune and Antony part here; even here
    Do we shake hands. All come to this! The hearts   20
    That spanieled me at heels, to whom I gave
    Their wishes, do discandy, melt their sweets
    On blossoming Caesar, and this pine is barked
    That overtopped them all. Betrayed I am.
    O this false soul of Egypt! This grave charm   25
    Whose eye becked forth my wars and called them
        home,
    Whose bosom was my crownet, my chief end,
    Like a right gipsy hath at fast and loose
    Beguiled me to the very heart of loss.
    What, Eros, Eros!

            Enter CLEOPATRA.

          Ah, thou spell! Avaunt!   30
CLEOPATRA Why is my lord enraged against his love?
ANTONY Vanish, or I shall give thee thy deserving
    And blemish Caesar's triumph. Let him take thee
    And hoist thee up to the shouting plebeians!
    Follow his chariot like the greatest spot   35
    Of all thy sex; most monster-like be shown
    For poor'st diminutives, for dolts, and let
    Patient Octavia plough thy visage up
    With her prepared nails!   *Exit Cleopatra.*
          'Tis well thou'rt gone
    If it be well to live. But better 'twere   40
    Thou fell'st into my fury, for one death
    Might have prevented many. Eros, ho!
    The shirt of Nessus is upon me. Teach me
    Alcides, thou mine ancestor, thy rage;
    Let me lodge Lichas on the horns o'th' moon,   45
    And with those hands that grasped the heaviest club
    Subdue my worthiest self. The witch shall die.
    To the young Roman boy she hath sold me, and I fall
    Under this plot. She dies for't. Eros, ho!   *Exit.*

4.13 *Enter* CLEOPATRA, CHARMIAN, IRAS, MARDIAN.

CLEOPATRA   Help me, my women! O, he's more mad
 Than Telamon for his shield; the boar of Thessaly
 Was never so embossed.
CHARMIAN   To th' monument!
 There lock yourself and send him word you are dead.
 The soul and body rive not more in parting
 Than greatness going off.
CLEOPATRA   To th' monument!
 Mardian, go tell him I have slain myself.
 Say that the last I spoke was 'Antony',
 And word it, prithee, piteously. Hence, Mardian,
 And bring me how he takes my death. To th'
  monument!   *Exeunt.*

4.14   *Enter* ANTONY *and* EROS.

ANTONY   Eros, thou yet behold'st me?
EROS   Ay, noble lord.
ANTONY   Sometime we see a cloud that's dragonish,
 A vapour sometime like a bear or lion,
 A towered citadel, a pendent rock,
 A forked mountain, or blue promontory
 With trees upon't that nod unto the world
 And mock our eyes with air. Thou hast seen these
  signs?
 They are black vesper's pageants.
EROS   Ay, my lord.
ANTONY
 That which is now a horse, even with a thought
 The rack dislimns and makes it indistinct
 As water is in water.
EROS   It does, my lord.
ANTONY   My good knave Eros, now thy captain is
 Even such a body. Here I am Antony,
 Yet cannot hold this visible shape, my knave.
 I made these wars for Egypt, and the Queen –
 Whose heart I thought I had, for she had mine,
 Which, whilst it was mine, had annexed unto't
 A million more, now lost – she, Eros, has
 Packed cards with Caesar, and false-played my glory
 Unto an enemy's triumph.
 Nay, weep not, gentle Eros. There is left us
 Ourselves to end ourselves.

     Enter MARDIAN.

     O thy vile lady!
 She has robbed me of my sword.
MARDIAN   No, Antony,
 My mistress loved thee and her fortunes mingled
 With thine entirely.
ANTONY   Hence, saucy eunuch! Peace!
 She hath betrayed me and shall die the death.
MARDIAN   Death of one person can be paid but once,
 And that she has discharged. What thou wouldst do
 Is done unto thy hand. The last she spake
 Was 'Antony! Most noble Antony!'

 Then, in the midst, a tearing groan did break
 The name of Antony; it was divided
 Between her heart and lips. She rendered life,
 Thy name so buried in her.
ANTONY   Dead, then?
MARDIAN   Dead.
ANTONY   Unarm, Eros. The long day's task is done 35
 And we must sleep.
 [*to Mardian*] That thou depart'st hence safe
 Does pay thy labour richly. Go. *Exit Mardian.*
 Off! Pluck off! [*Eros unarms him.*]
 The sevenfold shield of Ajax cannot keep
 The battery from my heart. O, cleave, my sides! 40
 Heart, once be stronger than thy continent;
 Crack thy frail case! Apace, Eros, apace!
 No more a soldier; bruised pieces go;
 You have been nobly borne. From me awhile.

        Exit Eros.

 I will o'ertake thee, Cleopatra, and 45
 Weep for my pardon. So it must be, for now
 All length is torture; since the torch is out,
 Lie down and stray no farther. Now all labour
 Mars what it does – yea, very force entangles
 Itself with strength. Seal then, and all is done. 50
 Eros! – I come, my queen. – Eros! – Stay for me.
 Where souls do couch on flowers we'll hand in hand
 And with our sprightly port make the ghosts gaze.
 Dido and her Aeneas shall want troops,
 And all the haunt be ours. Come Eros! Eros! 55

     Enter EROS.

EROS   What would my lord?
ANTONY   Since Cleopatra died,
 I have lived in such dishonour that the gods
 Detest my baseness. I, that with my sword
 Quartered the world and o'er green Neptune's back
 With ships made cities, condemn myself to lack 60
 The courage of a woman; less noble mind
 Than she which, by her death, our Caesar tells
 'I am conqueror of myself.' Thou art sworn, Eros,
 That when the exigent should come – which now
 Is come indeed – when I should see behind me 65
 Th'inevitable prosecution of
 Disgrace and horror, that on my command
 Thou then wouldst kill me. Do't. The time is come.
 Thou strik'st not me; 'tis Caesar thou defeat'st.
 Put colour in thy cheek.
EROS   The gods withhold me! 70
 Shall I do that which all the Parthian darts,
 Though enemy, lost aim and could not?
ANTONY   Eros,
 Wouldst thou be windowed in great Rome and see
 Thy master thus with pleached arms, bending down
 His corrigible neck, his face subdued 75
 To penetrative shame, whilst the wheeled seat
 Of fortunate Caesar, drawn before him, branded
 His baseness that ensued?

EROS   I would not see't.

ANTONY

   Come, then! For with a wound I must be cured.
80 Draw that thy honest sword which thou hast worn
   Most useful for thy country.

EROS   O sir, pardon me!

ANTONY

   When I did make thee free, swor'st thou not then
   To do this when I bade thee? Do it at once,
   Or thy precedent services are all
85 But accidents unpurposed. Draw, and come!

EROS   Turn from me then that noble countenance
   Wherein the worship of the whole world lies.

ANTONY [*Turns from him.*]   Lo thee!

EROS   My sword is drawn.

ANTONY   Then let it do at once
   The thing why thou hast drawn it.

90 EROS   My dear master,
   My captain and my emperor, let me say,
   Before I strike this bloody stroke, farewell.

ANTONY   'Tis said, man, and farewell.

EROS   Farewell, great chief. Shall I strike now?

ANTONY   Now, Eros.

EROS   Why, there then! [*Kills himself.*]
95   Thus I do escape the sorrow
   Of Antony's death.

ANTONY   Thrice nobler than myself!
   Thou teachest me, O valiant Eros, what
   I should and thou couldst not! My queen and Eros
   Have by their brave instruction got upon me
100 A nobleness in record. But I will be
   A bridegroom in my death and run into't
   As to a lover's bed. Come then! And, Eros,
   Thy master dies thy scholar. To do thus
   [*Falls on his sword.*]
   I learned of thee. How? Not dead? Not dead?
   The guard, ho! O, dispatch me.

   Enter a Company of the Guard, *one of them* DERCETUS.

105 1 GUARD   What's the noise?

ANTONY

   I have done my work ill, friends. O make an end
   Of what I have begun.

2 GUARD   The star is fallen.

1 GUARD   And time is at his period.

ALL THE GUARD   Alas and woe!

ANTONY   Let him that loves me strike me dead.

1 GUARD   Not I!

110 2 GUARD   Nor I!

3 GUARD   Nor any one!

   Exeunt all the Guard but Dercetus.

DERCETUS

   Thy death and fortunes bid thy followers fly.
   This sword but shown to Caesar with this tidings
   Shall enter me with him. [*Takes up Antony's sword.*]

   Enter DIOMEDES.

DIOMEDES   Where's Antony?   115

DERCETUS   There, Diomed, there!

DIOMEDES   Lives he? Wilt thou not answer, man?

   Exit Dercetus with the sword of Antony.

ANTONY

   Art thou there, Diomed? Draw thy sword and give
      me
   Sufficing strokes for death.

DIOMEDES   Most absolute lord,
   My mistress Cleopatra sent me to thee.   120

ANTONY   When did she send thee?

DIOMEDES   Now, my lord.

ANTONY   Where is she?

DIOMEDES

   Locked in her monument. She had a prophesying
      fear
   Of what hath come to pass, for when she saw –
   Which never shall be found – you did suspect
   She had disposed with Caesar, and that your rage 125
   Would not be purged, she sent you word she was
      dead,
   But fearing since how it might work, hath sent
   Me to proclaim the truth, and I am come,
   I dread, too late.

ANTONY

   Too late, good Diomed. Call my guard, I prithee. 130

DIOMEDES

   What ho! The Emperor's guard! The guard, what ho!
   Come, your lord calls!

   Enter four or five of the Guard *of Antony.*

ANTONY

   Bear me, good friends, where Cleopatra bides.
   'Tis the last service that I shall command you.

1 GUARD

   Woe, woe are we, sir! You may not live to wear   135
   All your true followers out.

ALL THE GUARD   Most heavy day!

ANTONY

   Nay, good my fellows, do not please sharp fate
   To grace it with your sorrows. Bid that welcome
   Which comes to punish us, and we punish it,
   Seeming to bear it lightly. Take me up.   140
   I have led you oft; carry me now, good friends,
   And have my thanks for all.

   Exeunt, bearing Antony and Eros.

4.15   *Enter* CLEOPATRA *and her maids aloft, with*
                  CHARMIAN *and* IRAS.

CLEOPATRA   O Charmian, I will never go from hence.

CHARMIAN   Be comforted, dear madam.

CLEOPATRA   No, I will not.
   All strange and terrible events are welcome,
   But comforts we despise. Our size of sorrow,

5   Proportioned to our cause, must be as great
        As that which makes it.

              Enter DIOMEDES *below.*

                How now? Is he dead?
DIOMEDES His death's upon him, but not dead.
        Look out o'th' other side your monument;
        His guard have brought him thither.

        Enter below ANTONY *borne by the* Guard.

10   CLEOPATRA O sun,
        Burn the great sphere thou mov'st in! Darkling stand
        The varying shore o'th' world! O Antony,
        Antony, Antony! Help, Charmian! Help, Iras, help!
        Help, friends below! Let's draw him hither.
    ANTONY   Peace!
15   Not Caesar's valour hath o'erthrown Antony,
        But Antony's hath triumphed on itself.
    CLEOPATRA So it should be that none but Antony
        Should conquer Antony, but woe 'tis so.
    ANTONY I am dying, Egypt, dying. Only
20   I here importune death awhile until
        Of many thousand kisses the poor last
        I lay upon thy lips.
    CLEOPATRA   I dare not, dear.
        Dear my lord, pardon. I dare not
        Lest I be taken. Not th'imperious show
25   Of the full-fortuned Caesar ever shall
        Be brooched with me. If knife, drugs, serpents, have
        Edge, sting or operation, I am safe.
        Your wife Octavia, with her modest eyes
        And still conclusion, shall acquire no honour
30   Demuring upon me. But come, come Antony –
        Help me, my women – we must draw thee up.
        Assist, good friends! [*They begin lifting.*]
    ANTONY   O quick, or I am gone!
    CLEOPATRA
        Here's sport indeed! How heavy weighs my lord!
        Our strength is all gone into heaviness;
35   That makes the weight. Had I great Juno's power,
        The strong-winged Mercury should fetch thee up
        And set thee by Jove's side. Yet come a little;
        Wishers were ever fools. O come, come, come,
        [*They heave Antony aloft to Cleopatra.*]
        And welcome, welcome! Die when thou hast lived;
40   Quicken with kissing. Had my lips that power,
        Thus would I wear them out. [*Kisses him.*]
    ALL THE GUARD Ah, heavy sight!
    ANTONY I am dying, Egypt, dying.
        Give me some wine and let me speak a little –
45   CLEOPATRA No, let me speak, and let me rail so high
        That the false huswife Fortune break her wheel,
        Provoked by my offence –
    ANTONY   One word, sweet queen:
        Of Caesar seek your honour with your safety. O!
    CLEOPATRA They do not go together.
    ANTONY   Gentle, hear me.

        None about Caesar trust but Proculeius.   50
    CLEOPATRA My resolution and my hands I'll trust;
        None about Caesar.
    ANTONY The miserable change now at my end,
        Lament nor sorrow at, but please your thoughts
        In feeding them with those my former fortunes   55
        Wherein I lived the greatest prince o'th' world,
        The noblest; and do now not basely die,
        Not cowardly put off my helmet to
        My countryman; a Roman by a Roman
        Valiantly vanquished. Now my spirit is going;   60
        I can no more.
    CLEOPATRA   Noblest of men, woo't die?
        Hast thou no care of me? Shall I abide
        In this dull world, which in thy absence is
        No better than a sty? O see, my women,
        The crown o'th' earth doth melt. My lord!   65
        [*Antony dies.*]
        O withered is the garland of the war,
        The soldier's pole is fallen; young boys and girls
        Are level now with men; the odds is gone
        And there is nothing left remarkable
        Beneath the visiting moon. [*She faints.*]
    CHARMIAN   O quietness, lady!   70
    IRAS She's dead too, our sovereign.
    CHARMIAN Lady!
    IRAS Madam!
    CHARMIAN O madam, madam, madam!
    IRAS Royal Egypt! Empress! [*Cleopatra stirs.*]   75
    CHARMIAN Peace, peace, Iras.
    CLEOPATRA
        No more but e'en a woman, and commanded
        By such poor passion as the maid that milks
        And does the meanest chares. It were for me
        To throw my sceptre at the injurious gods   80
        To tell them that this world did equal theirs
        Till they had stolen our jewel. All's but naught;
        Patience is sottish, and impatience does
        Become a dog that's mad. Then is it sin
        To rush into the secret house of death   85
        Ere death dare come to us? How do you, women?
        What, what, good cheer! Why, how now, Charmian?
        My noble girls! Ah, women, women! Look,
        Our lamp is spent, it's out. Good sirs, take heart.
        We'll bury him, and then what's brave, what's noble, 90
        Let's do't after the high Roman fashion
        And make death proud to take us. Come, away.
        This case of that huge spirit now is cold.
        Ah, women, women! Come, we have no friend
        But resolution and the briefest end.   95
          Exeunt, bearing off Antony's body.

5.1 *Enter* CAESAR *with his Council of War:* AGRIPPA,
      DOLABELLA, MAECENAS, PROCULEIUS, GALLUS.

    CAESAR Go to him, Dolabella, bid him yield.
        Being so frustrate, tell him, he mocks

The pauses that he makes.
DOLABELLA   Caesar, I shall.   *Exit.*

Enter DERCETUS *with the sword of Antony.*

CAESAR
    Wherefore is that? And what art thou that dar'st
    Appear thus to us?
5 DERCETUS   I am called Dercetus.
    Mark Antony I served, who best was worthy
    Best to be served. Whilst he stood up and spoke
    He was my master, and I wore my life
    To spend upon his haters. If thou please
10   To take me to thee, as I was to him
    I'll be to Caesar. If thou pleasest not,
    I yield thee up my life.
CAESAR   What is't thou say'st?
DERCETUS   I say, O Caesar, Antony is dead.
CAESAR   The breaking of so great a thing should make
15   A greater crack. The round world
    Should have shook lions into civil streets
    And citizens to their dens. The death of Antony
    Is not a single doom; in the name lay
    A moiety of the world.
DERCETUS   He is dead, Caesar,
20   Not by a public minister of justice,
    Nor by a hired knife, but that self hand
    Which writ his honour in the acts it did
    Hath, with the courage which the heart did lend it,
    Splitted the heart. This is his sword;
25   I robbed his wound of it. Behold it stained
    With his most noble blood.
CAESAR [*Points to the sword.*]   Look you, sad friends.
    The gods rebuke me, but it is tidings
    To wash the eyes of kings.
AGRIPPA   And strange it is
    That nature must compel us to lament
    Our most persisted deeds.
30 MAECENAS   His taints and honours
    Waged equal with him.
AGRIPPA   A rarer spirit never
    Did steer humanity; but you gods will give us
    Some faults to make us men. Caesar is touched.
MAECENAS
    When such a spacious mirror's set before him,
    He needs must see himself.
35 CAESAR   O Antony,
    I have followed thee to this; but we do launch
    Diseases in our bodies. I must perforce
    Have shown to thee such a declining day
    Or look on thine. We could not stall together
40   In the whole world. But yet let me lament
    With tears as sovereign as the blood of hearts
    That thou, my brother, my competitor
    In top of all design, my mate in empire,
    Friend and companion in the front of war,
45   The arm of mine own body, and the heart
    Where mine his thoughts did kindle, that our stars,

Unreconciliable, should divide
Our equalness to this. Hear me, good friends –

Enter an Egyptian.

But I will tell you at some meeter season.
The business of this man looks out of him;   50
We'll hear him what he says. Whence are you?
EGYPTIAN
A poor Egyptian yet. The Queen, my mistress,
Confined in all she has, her monument,
Of thy intents desires instruction,
That she preparedly may frame herself   55
To th' way she's forced to.
CAESAR   Bid her have good heart.
She soon shall know of us, by some of ours,
How honourable and how kindly we
Determine for her. For Caesar cannot lean
To be ungentle.
EGYPTIAN   So the gods preserve thee!   *Exit.* 60
CAESAR   Come hither, Proculeius. Go and say
We purpose her no shame. Give her what comforts
The quality of her passion shall require,
Lest, in her greatness, by some mortal stroke
She do defeat us. For her life in Rome   65
Would be eternal in our triumph. Go,
And with your speediest bring us what she says
And how you find of her.
PROCULEIUS   Caesar, I shall.
CAESAR   Gallus, go you along.
         Exeunt Proculeius and Gallus.
         Where's Dolabella
To second Proculeius?
ALL BUT CAESAR   Dolabella!   70
CAESAR   Let him alone, for I remember now
How he's employed. He shall in time be ready.
Go with me to my tent, where you shall see
How hardly I was drawn into this war,
How calm and gentle I proceeded still   75
In all my writings. Go with me and see
What I can show in this.   *Exeunt.*

5.2   *Enter* CLEOPATRA, CHARMIAN *and* IRAS.

CLEOPATRA   My desolation does begin to make
A better life. 'Tis paltry to be Caesar.
Not being Fortune, he's but Fortune's knave,
A minister of her will. And it is great
To do that thing that ends all other deeds,   5
Which shackles accidents and bolts up change,
Which sleeps and never palates more the dung,
The beggar's nurse and Caesar's.

Enter PROCULEIUS.

PROCULEIUS
Caesar sends greeting to the Queen of Egypt,
And bids thee study on what fair demands   10
Thou mean'st to have him grant thee.

CLEOPATRA   What's thy name?
PROCULEIUS   My name is Proculeius.
CLEOPATRA   Antony
  Did tell me of you, bade me trust you, but
  I do not greatly care to be deceived
  That have no use for trusting. If your master
  Would have a queen his beggar, you must tell him
  That majesty, to keep decorum, must
  No less beg than a kingdom. If he please
  To give me conquered Egypt for my son,
  He gives me so much of mine own as I
  Will kneel to him with thanks.
PROCULEIUS   Be of good cheer.
  You're fallen into a princely hand; fear nothing.
  Make your full reference freely to my lord,
  Who is so full of grace that it flows over
  On all that need. Let me report to him
  Your sweet dependency, and you shall find
  A conqueror that will pray in aid for kindness
  Where he for grace is kneeled to.
CLEOPATRA   Pray you tell him
  I am his fortune's vassal and I send him
  The greatness he has got. I hourly learn
  A doctrine of obedience, and would gladly
  Look him i'th' face.
PROCULEIUS   This I'll report, dear lady.
  Have comfort, for I know your plight is pitied
  Of him that caused it.

Enter GALLUS *and Roman soldiers.*

[*to the soldiers*] You see how easily she may be
    surprised.
  Guard her till Caesar come.
IRAS   Royal queen!
CHARMIAN   O Cleopatra, thou art taken, queen!
CLEOPATRA   Quick, quick, good hands.
  [*Draws a dagger.*]
PROCULEIUS   Hold, worthy lady, hold!
  [*Disarms her.*]
  Do not yourself such wrong, who are in this
  Relieved, but not betrayed.
CLEOPATRA   What, of death too,
  That rids our dogs of languish?
PROCULEIUS   Cleopatra,
  Do not abuse my master's bounty by
  Th'undoing of yourself. Let the world see
  His nobleness well acted, which your death
  Will never let come forth.
CLEOPATRA   Where art thou, Death?
  Come hither, come! Come, come and take a queen
  Worth many babes and beggars!
PROCULEIUS   O temperance, lady!
CLEOPATRA   Sir, I will eat no meat; I'll not drink, sir;
  If idle talk will once be necessary,
  I'll not sleep neither. This mortal house I'll ruin,
  Do Caesar what he can. Know, sir, that I

Will not wait pinioned at your master's court,
Nor once be chastised with the sober eye
Of dull Octavia. Shall they hoist me up
And show me to the shouting varletry   55
Of censuring Rome? Rather a ditch in Egypt
Be gentle grave unto me! Rather on Nilus' mud
Lay me stark naked, and let the water-flies
Blow me into abhorring! Rather make
My country's high pyramides my gibbet   60
And hang me up in chains!
PROCULEIUS   You do extend
  These thoughts of horror further than you shall
  Find cause in Caesar.

Enter DOLABELLA.

DOLABELLA   Proculeius,
  What thou hast done thy master Caesar knows,
  And he hath sent for thee. For the Queen,   65
  I'll take her to my guard.
PROCULEIUS   So, Dolabella,
  It shall content me best. Be gentle to her.
  [*to Cleopatra*] To Caesar I will speak what you shall
    please,
  If you'll employ me to him.
CLEOPATRA   Say I would die.
      Exit Proculeius with Gallus and soldiers.
DOLABELLA
  Most noble empress, you have heard of me?   70
CLEOPATRA   I cannot tell.
DOLABELLA   Assuredly you know me.
CLEOPATRA
  No matter, sir, what I have heard or known.
  You laugh when boys or women tell their dreams;
  Is't not your trick?
DOLABELLA   I understand not, madam.
CLEOPATRA   I dreamt there was an emperor Antony.   75
  O, such another sleep, that I might see
  But such another man!
DOLABELLA   If it might please ye –
CLEOPATRA
  His face was as the heavens, and therein stuck
  A sun and moon which kept their course and lighted
  The little O, the earth.
DOLABELLA   Most sovereign creature –   80
CLEOPATRA   His legs bestrid the ocean; his reared arm
  Crested the world; his voice was propertied
  As all the tuned spheres, and that to friends;
  But when he meant to quail and shake the orb,
  He was as rattling thunder. For his bounty,   85
  There was no winter in't; an autumn it was
  That grew the more by reaping. His delights
  Were dolphin-like: they showed his back above
  The element they lived in. In his livery
  Walked crowns and crownets; realms and islands
    were   90
  As plates dropped from his pocket.

DOLABELLA   Cleopatra –

CLEOPATRA
   Think you there was or might be such a man
   As this I dreamt of?

DOLABELLA   Gentle madam, no.

CLEOPATRA   You lie up to the hearing of the gods!
95   But if there be nor ever were one such,
   It's past the size of dreaming. Nature wants stuff
   To vie strange forms with fancy; yet t'imagine
   An Antony were nature's piece 'gainst fancy,
   Condemning shadows quite.

DOLABELLA   Hear me, good madam.
100   Your loss is as yourself, great, and you bear it
   As answering to the weight. Would I might never
   O'ertake pursued success, but I do feel,
   By the rebound of yours, a grief that smites
   My very heart at root.

CLEOPATRA   I thank you, sir.
105   Know you what Caesar means to do with me?

DOLABELLA
   I am loath to tell you what I would you knew.

CLEOPATRA   Nay, pray you, sir.

DOLABELLA   Though he be honourable –

CLEOPATRA   He'll lead me, then, in triumph.

DOLABELLA   Madam, he will. I know't.

Flourish. Enter. PROCULEIUS, CAESAR, GALLUS,
MAECENAS *and others of his train.*

110   ALL   Make way there! Caesar!

CAESAR   Which is the Queen of Egypt?

DOLABELLA   It is the Emperor, madam.
   [*Cleopatra kneels.*]

CAESAR   Arise! You shall not kneel.
   I pray you rise. Rise, Egypt.

CLEOPATRA   Sir, the gods
115   Will have it thus. My master and my lord
   I must obey. [*She stands.*]

CAESAR   Take to you no hard thoughts.
   The record of what injuries you did us,
   Though written in our flesh, we shall remember
   As things but done by chance.

CLEOPATRA   Sole sir o'th' world,
120   I cannot project mine own cause so well
   To make it clear, but do confess I have
   Been laden with like frailties which before
   Have often shamed our sex.

CAESAR   Cleopatra, know
   We will extenuate rather than enforce.
125   If you apply yourself to our intents,
   Which towards you are most gentle, you shall find
   A benefit in this change; but if you seek
   To lay on me a cruelty by taking
   Antony's course, you shall bereave yourself
130   Of my good purposes, and put your children
   To that destruction which I'll guard them from
   If thereon you rely. I'll take my leave.

CLEOPATRA
   And may through all the world! 'Tis yours, and we,
   Your scutcheons and your signs of conquest, shall
   Hang in what place you please. Here, my good lord. 135
   [*Hands him a paper.*]

CAESAR   You shall advise me in all for Cleopatra.

CLEOPATRA   This is the brief of money, plate and jewels
   I am possessed of. 'Tis exactly valued,
   Not petty things admitted. Where's Seleucus?

Enter SELEUCUS.

SELEUCUS   Here, madam. 140

CLEOPATRA
   This is my treasurer. Let him speak, my lord,
   Upon his peril, that I have reserved
   To myself nothing. Speak the truth, Seleucus.

SELEUCUS   Madam,
   I had rather seel my lips than to my peril 145
   Speak that which is not.

CLEOPATRA   What have I kept back?

SELEUCUS
   Enough to purchase what you have made known.

CAESAR   Nay, blush not, Cleopatra. I approve
   Your wisdom in the deed.

CLEOPATRA   See, Caesar! O behold
   How pomp is followed! Mine will now be yours 150
   And, should we shift estates, yours would be mine.
   The ingratitude of this Seleucus does
   Even make me wild. O slave, of no more trust
   Than love that's hired! What, go'st thou back?
      Thou shalt
   Go back, I warrant thee! But I'll catch thine eyes 155
   Though they had wings! Slave! Soulless villain! Dog!
   O rarely base!

CAESAR   Good queen, let us entreat you.

CLEOPATRA
   O Caesar, what a wounding shame is this,
   That – thou vouchsafing here to visit me,
   Doing the honour of thy lordliness 160
   To one so meek – that mine own servant should
   Parcel the sum of my disgraces by
   Addition of his envy! Say, good Caesar,
   That I some lady trifles have reserved,
   Immoment toys, things of such dignity 165
   As we greet modern friends withal; and say
   Some nobler token I have kept apart
   For Livia and Octavia, to induce
   Their mediation, must I be unfolded
   With one that I have bred? The gods! It smites me 170
   Beneath the fall I have. [*to Seleucus*] Prithee go hence,
   Or I shall show the cinders of my spirits
   Through th'ashes of my chance. Wert thou a man,
   Thou wouldst have mercy on me.

CAESAR   Forbear, Seleucus.
                 Exit Seleucus.

CLEOPATRA
   Be it known that we, the greatest, are misthought 175

For things that others do, and when we fall,
We answer others' merits in our name,
Are therefore to be pitied.
CAESAR　　　　　　　　　Cleopatra,
Not what you have reserved nor what acknowledged
180　Put we i'th' roll of conquest. Still be't yours;
Bestow it at your pleasure, and believe
Caesar's no merchant to make prize with you
Of things that merchants sold. Therefore be cheered;
Make not your thoughts your prisons. No, dear
　　queen,
185　For we intend so to dispose you as
Yourself shall give us counsel. Feed and sleep.
Our care and pity is so much upon you
That we remain your friend; and so, adieu.
CLEOPATRA　My master and my lord!
CAESAR　　　　　　　　　Not so. Adieu.
　　　　　Flourish. Exeunt Caesar and his train.
CLEOPATRA
190　He words me, girls, he words me, that I should not
Be noble to myself. But hark thee, Charmian.
[*Whispers to Charmian.*]
CHARMIAN　Finish, good lady. The bright day is done
And we are for the dark.
CLEOPATRA　　　　　Hie thee again.
I have spoke already and it is provided.
Go put it to the haste.
195　CHARMIAN　　　　　Madam, I will.

　　　　　Enter DOLABELLA.

DOLABELLA　Where's the Queen?
CHARMIAN　　　　　Behold, sir.　　*Exit.*
CLEOPATRA　　　　　　　Dolabella!
DOLABELLA
Madam, as thereto sworn by your command,
Which my love makes religion to obey,
I tell you this: Caesar through Syria
200　Intends his journey, and within three days
You with your children will he send before.
Make your best use of this. I have performed
Your pleasure and my promise.
CLEOPATRA　　　　　Dolabella,
I shall remain your debtor.
DOLABELLA　　　　　I, your servant.
205　Adieu, good queen. I must attend on Caesar.
CLEOPATRA　Farewell and thanks.　*Exit Dolabella.*
　　　　　Now, Iras, what think'st thou?
Thou an Egyptian puppet shall be shown
In Rome as well as I. Mechanic slaves
With greasy aprons, rules and hammers shall
210　Uplift us to the view. In their thick breaths,
Rank of gross diet, shall we be enclouded
And forced to drink their vapour.
IRAS　　　　　　　The gods forbid!
CLEOPATRA　Nay, 'tis most certain, Iras. Saucy lictors
Will catch at us like strumpets, and scald rhymers
215　Ballad us out o'tune. The quick comedians

Extemporally will stage us and present
Our Alexandrian revels; Antony
Shall be brought drunken forth; and I shall see
Some squeaking Cleopatra boy my greatness
I'th' posture of a whore.
IRAS　　　　　　　O the good gods!　　220
CLEOPATRA　Nay, that's certain.
IRAS　I'll never see't, for I am sure my nails
Are stronger than mine eyes!
CLEOPATRA　　　　　Why, that's the way
To fool their preparation and to conquer
Their most absurd intents.

　　　　　Enter CHARMIAN.

　　　　　　　　Now, Charmian!　　225
Show me, my women, like a queen. Go fetch
My best attires. I am again for Cydnus
To meet Mark Antony. Sirrah Iras, go.
Now, noble Charmian, we'll dispatch indeed,
And when thou hast done this chare, I'll give thee
　　leave　　230
To play till doomsday. Bring our crown and all.
　　　　　　　　Exit Iras.
　　　　　　　　[*a noise within*]
Wherefore's this noise?

　　　　　Enter a Guardsman.

GUARDSMAN　　　　　Here is a rural fellow
That will not be denied your highness' presence.
He brings you figs.
CLEOPATRA　Let him come in.　　*Exit Guardsman.*
　　　　　　　What poor an instrument　　235
May do a noble deed! He brings me liberty.
My resolution's placed, and I have nothing
Of woman in me. Now from head to foot
I am marble-constant. Now the fleeting moon
No planet is of mine.

　　　　　Enter Guardsman *and* Clown *with a basket.*

GUARDSMAN　　　　　This is the man.　　240
CLEOPATRA　Avoid, and leave him.　*Exit Guardsman.*
Hast thou the pretty worm of Nilus there
That kills and pains not?
CLOWN　Truly, I have him; but I would not be the party
that should desire you to touch him, for his biting is　　245
immortal. Those that do die of it do seldom or never
recover.
CLEOPATRA　Remember'st thou any that have died on't?
CLOWN　Very many; men and women too. I heard of one
of them no longer than yesterday – a very honest　　250
woman, but something given to lie, as a woman should
not do but in the way of honesty – how she died of the
biting of it, what pain she felt. Truly, she makes a very
good report o'th' worm; but he that will believe all
that they say shall never be saved by half that they do.　　255
But this is most falliable, the worm's an odd worm.
CLEOPATRA　Get thee hence. Farewell.

CLOWN   I wish you all joy of the worm.
[*Sets down his basket.*]

CLEOPATRA   Farewell.

260   CLOWN   You must think this, look you, that the worm
will do his kind.

CLEOPATRA   Ay, ay. Farewell.

CLOWN   Look you, the worm is not to be trusted but in
the keeping of wise people; for, indeed, there is no

265   goodness in the worm.

CLEOPATRA   Take thou no care; it shall be heeded.

CLOWN   Very good. Give it nothing, I pray you, for it is
not worth the feeding.

CLEOPATRA   Will it eat me?

270   CLOWN   You must not think I am so simple but I know
the devil himself will not eat a woman. I know that a
woman is a dish for the gods if the devil dress her not.
But truly, these same whoreson devils do the gods
great harm in their women, for in every ten that they

275   make, the devils mar five.

CLEOPATRA   Well, get thee gone. Farewell.

CLOWN   Yes, forsooth. I wish you joy o'th' worm. *Exit.*

Enter IRAS *with a robe, crown and other jewels.*

CLEOPATRA
Give me my robe. Put on my crown. I have
Immortal longings in me. Now no more

280   The juice of Egypt's grape shall moist this lip.
[*The women dress her.*]
Yare, yare, good Iras! Quick! Methinks I hear
Antony call. I see him rouse himself
To praise my noble act. I hear him mock
The luck of Caesar, which the gods give men

285   To excuse their after wrath. Husband, I come!
Now to that name my courage prove my title!
I am fire and air; my other elements
I give to baser life. So, have you done?
Come, then, and take the last warmth of my lips.

290   Farewell, kind Charmian. Iras, long farewell.
[*Kisses them. Iras falls and dies.*]
Have I the aspic in my lips? Dost fall?
If thou and nature can so gently part,
The stroke of death is as a lover's pinch
Which hurts and is desired. Dost thou lie still?

295   If thus thou vanishest, thou tell'st the world
It is not worth leave-taking.

CHARMIAN
Dissolve, thick cloud, and rain, that I may say
The gods themselves do weep!

CLEOPATRA   This proves me base.
If she first meet the curled Antony,

300   He'll make demand of her, and spend that kiss
Which is my heaven to have.
[*to the asp; applying it to her breast*]
                                    Come, thou mortal wretch,
With thy sharp teeth this knot intrinsicate
Of life at once untie. Poor venomous fool,
Be angry and dispatch. O, couldst thou speak,

That I might hear thee call great Caesar ass   305
Unpolicied!

CHARMIAN   O eastern star!

CLEOPATRA   Peace, peace!
Dost thou not see my baby at my breast
That sucks the nurse asleep?

CHARMIAN   O break! O break!

CLEOPATRA   As sweet as balm, as soft as air, as gentle –
O Antony! – Nay, I will take thee too.   310
[*Applies another asp to her arm.*]
What should I stay – [*Dies.*]

CHARMIAN   In this vile world? So fare thee well.
Now boast thee, Death, in thy possession lies
A lass unparalleled. Downy windows, close,
And golden Phoebus, never be beheld   315
Of eyes again so royal! Your crown's awry;
I'll mend it, and then play.

Enter the GUARD, *rustling in.*

1 GUARD   Where's the Queen?

CHARMIAN   Speak softly. Wake her not.

1 GUARD   Caesar hath sent –

CHARMIAN   Too slow a messenger.
[*Applies an asp.*]
O come apace! Dispatch! I partly feel thee.   320

1 GUARD
Approach ho! All's not well. Caesar's beguiled.

2 GUARD
There's Dolabella sent from Caesar. Call him.
                                    Exit a Guardsman.

1 GUARD
What work is here, Charmian? Is this well done?

CHARMIAN   It is well done, and fitting for a princess
Descended of so many royal kings.   325
Ah, soldier! [*Charmian dies.*]

Enter DOLABELLA.

DOLABELLA   How goes it here?

2 GUARD   All dead.

DOLABELLA   Caesar, thy thoughts
Touch their effects in this. Thyself art coming
To see performed the dreaded act which thou
So sought'st to hinder.   330

Enter CAESAR *and all his train, marching.*

ALL BUT CAESAR   A way there! A way for Caesar!

DOLABELLA   O sir, you are too sure an augurer:
That you did fear is done.

CAESAR   Bravest at the last,
She levelled at our purposes and, being royal,
Took her own way. The manner of their deaths?   335
I do not see them bleed.

DOLABELLA   Who was last with them?

1 GUARD
A simple countryman that brought her figs.
This was his basket.

CAESAR   Poisoned, then.

1 GUARD   O Caesar,
    This Charmian lived but now; she stood and spake.
40   I found her trimming up the diadem
    On her dead mistress. Tremblingly she stood,
    And on the sudden dropped.
CAESAR   O noble weakness!
    If they had swallowed poison, 'twould appear
    By external swelling; but she looks like sleep,
45   As she would catch another Antony
    In her strong toil of grace.
DOLABELLA   Here on her breast
    There is a vent of blood, and something blown;
    The like is on her arm.
1 GUARD   This is an aspic's trail, and these fig leaves
50   Have slime upon them such as th'aspic leaves
    Upon the caves of Nile.

CAESAR   Most probable
    That so she died, for her physician tells me
    She hath pursued conclusions infinite
    Of easy ways to die. Take up her bed,
    And bear her women from the monument.   355
    She shall be buried by her Antony.
    No grave upon the earth shall clip in it
    A pair so famous. High events as these
    Strike those that make them, and their story is
    No less in pity than his glory which   360
    Brought them to be lamented. Our army shall
    In solemn show attend this funeral,
    And then to Rome. Come, Dolabella, see
    High order in this great solemnity.
        Exeunt omnes, the soldiers bearing the dead bodies.

As You Like It

As You Like It seems to have been written about 1599, though it was first published in the Folio of 1623, where it is the tenth of the comedies. The list of Shakespeare's comedies in Francis Meres's *Palladis Tamia*, published in 1598, omits this play, but it was listed in the Stationers' Register on 4 August 1600 as one of four of 'My lord chamberlain's men's plays' that were ordered 'to be stayed' from publication. It is, therefore, roughly contemporaneous with *Much Ado About Nothing*.

The play is based on Thomas Lodge's popular prose romance, *Rosalynde: Euphues' Golden Legacy* (1590), and indeed Lodge's breezy presentation of his tale 'to the Gentleman readers' – 'if you like it, so' – may well have suggested the title of Shakespeare's play. Lodge's story of Rosader and Rosalynde, itself based on the fourteenth-century *Tale of Gamelyn*, provides virtually all the elements of the plot of Shakespeare's play.

Lodge's novel is one of many late Elizabethan examples of pastoral, a literary mode with classical precedents reaching back to the Greek writer Theocritus, but which in Elizabethan England became a fashionable form seemingly celebrating the virtues of simplicity but doing so in an extravagantly artificial manner. Lodge never criticizes the artificiality of his pastoral tale, but Shakespeare, in giving prominence to the love affair of Rosalind and Orlando (Lodge's Rosader), lessening the sensationalism of Lodge's plot and adding to his cast of characters, provides alternative views of Lodge's idealized story, exposing its artificiality to ironies and revealing the realities that conventions, both literary and social, obscure and, in some cases, ameliorate.

The most important of the play's counter-voices are Touchstone and Jaques, each similarly sceptical of the idealizing imagination. For the clown, Touchstone, the absurdities he encounters are occasions genially to expose the inconsistencies of the human heart, while for Jaques they become hard evidence for his own cynicism and melancholy. Touchstone indeed marries, joining, with Audrey, the parade of couples marching two by two at the end, but Jaques insistently remains outside the magic circle, going off to join the penitent Duke Frederick, though not before offering the couples his own surprisingly benevolent wishes.

The similarity of Jaques's blessings to Hymen's suggests the play's complex focus. Characters are redeemed and reunited in the Forest of Arden, but there is no magic in the forest. The natural is no more held up as an ideal than is the artificial, the country no more free from criticism than the court. The happy end that the play provides is made possible not by qualities inhering in a locale but by an enduring quality of human goodness, most apparent perhaps in Rosalind's resilience and creativity, but also evident in Celia, Orlando, Old Adam, Duke Senior and all who come to recognize the natural bonds of humankind.

As You Like It may well have been an early play performed in the Globe Theatre in 1599. Jaques's 'All the world's a stage' would have resonated wittily in the new theatre, which allegedly bore a motto from Petronius: *totus mundus agit histrionem*. Indeed, such self-consciousness is marked throughout; Jaques' fears that characters will speak in 'blank verse' call attention to the theatre poetry, just as Rosalind's male disguise and subsequent female 'pretence' (to say nothing of her line in the epilogue, 'If I were a woman . . .') foreground the theatre's convention of boys acting female parts.

For all the play's awareness of itself as theatre, there is no record of an early performance (only a later tradition that it was performed by the King's Men at Wilton in December 1603), and it was not until the mid-eighteenth century that the play became popular on stage, its attractive roles for women certainly part of its new appeal. On the modern stage it has been regularly played, its paradoxical combination of innocence and cynicism, of romanticism and realism, making it a popular comedy able to speak both to our knowledge and to our dreams.

The Arden text is based on the 1623 First Folio.

DUKE SENIOR	*living in exile*
DUKE FREDERICK	*his brother and usurper of his dominions*
LE BEAU	*a courtier attending on Frederick*
CHARLES	*Duke Frederick's wrestler*
TOUCHSTONE	*a fool at the Duke's court*
OLIVER	
ORLANDO	*sons of Sir Rowland de Boys*
JAQUES	
DENNIS	*servants to Oliver*
ADAM	
AMIENS	*lords attending on the banished Duke*
JAQUES	
CORIN	*shepherds in the Forest of Arden*
SILVIUS	
WILLIAM	*a country fellow*
SIR OLIVER Martext	*vicar of a country parish*
ROSALIND	*daughter to Duke Senior*
CELIA	*daughter to Duke Frederick*
PHEBE	*a shepherdess*
AUDREY	*a goat-herd*
HYMEN	

Lords attending on the Dukes, with Pages and other Attendants

1.1 *Enter* ORLANDO *and* ADAM.

ORLANDO As I remember, Adam, it was upon this fashion bequeathed me by will but poor a thousand crowns, and, as thou sayst, charged my brother on his blessing to breed me well; and there begins my sadness. My brother Jaques he keeps at school, and report speaks goldenly of his profit: for my part, he keeps me rustically at home, or, to speak more properly, stays me here at home unkept; for call you that keeping for a gentleman of my birth, that differs not from the stalling of an ox? His horses are bred better; for besides that they are fair with their feeding, they are taught their manage, and to that end riders dearly hired: but I, his brother, gain nothing under him but growth, for the which his animals on his dunghills are as much bound to him as I. Besides this nothing that he so plentifully gives me, the something that nature gave me his countenance seems to take from me. He lets me feed with his hinds, bars me the place of a brother, and, as much as in him lies, mines my gentility with my education. This is it, Adam, that grieves me, and the spirit of my father, which I think is within me, begins to mutiny against this servitude. I will no longer endure it, though yet I know no wise remedy how to avoid it.

ADAM Yonder comes my master, your brother.

Enter OLIVER.

ORLANDO Go apart Adam, and thou shalt hear how he will shake me up.

OLIVER Now sir, what make you here?

ORLANDO Nothing. I am not taught to make anything.

OLIVER What mar you then sir?

ORLANDO Marry sir, I am helping you to mar that which God made, a poor unworthy brother of yours, with idleness.

OLIVER Marry sir, be better employed, and be naught awhile.

ORLANDO Shall I keep your hogs and eat husks with them? What prodigal portion have I spent that I should come to such penury?

OLIVER Know you where you are sir?

ORLANDO O sir, very well: here in your orchard.

OLIVER Know you before whom sir?

ORLANDO Ay, better than him I am before knows me. I know you are my eldest brother, and in the gentle condition of blood you should so know me. The courtesy of nations allows you my better, in that you are the first-born, but the same tradition takes not away my blood, were there twenty brothers betwixt us. I have as much of my father in me as you, albeit I confess your coming before me is nearer to his reverence.

OLIVER [*striking him*] What, boy!

ORLANDO [*putting a wrestler's grip on him*] Come, come, elder brother, you are too young in this.

OLIVER Wilt thou lay hands on me villain?

ORLANDO I am no villain. I am the youngest son of Sir Rowland de Boys: he was my father, and he is thrice a villain that says such a father begot villains. Wert thou not my brother, I would not take this hand from thy throat till this other had pulled out thy tongue for saying so. Thou hast railed on thyself.

ADAM Sweet masters be patient. For your father's remembrance, be at accord.

OLIVER Let me go I say.

ORLANDO I will not till I please: you shall hear me. My father charged you in his will to give me good education: you have trained me like a peasant, obscuring and hiding from me all gentleman-like qualities. The spirit of my father grows strong in me, and I will no longer endure it. Therefore allow me such exercises as may become a gentleman, or give me the poor allottery my father left me by testament; with that I will go buy my fortunes.

OLIVER And what wilt thou do? Beg when that is spent? Well sir, get you in. I will not long be troubled with you; you shall have some part of your will. I pray you leave me.

ORLANDO I will no further offend you than becomes me for my good.

OLIVER Get you with him, you old dog.

ADAM Is old dog my reward? Most true, I have lost my teeth in your service. God be with my old master! – he would not have spoke such a word.

Exeunt Orlando and Adam.

OLIVER Is it even so? Begin you to grow upon me? I will physic your rankness, and yet give no thousand crowns neither. Holla Dennis!

Enter DENNIS.

DENNIS Calls your worship?

OLIVER Was not Charles the Duke's wrestler here to speak with me?

DENNIS So please you, he is here at the door and importunes access to you.

OLIVER Call him in.   *Exit Dennis.*
'Twill be a good way. And tomorrow the wrestling is.

Enter CHARLES.

CHARLES Good morrow to your worship.

OLIVER Good Monsieur Charles! What's the new news at the new court?

CHARLES There's no news at the court sir, but the old news. That is, the old Duke is banished by his younger brother the new Duke, and three or four loving lords have put themselves into voluntary exile with him, whose lands and revenues enrich the new Duke, therefore he gives them good leave to wander.

OLIVER Can you tell if Rosalind the Duke's daughter be banished with her father?

CHARLES O no; for the Duke's daughter her cousin so loves her, being ever from their cradles bred together, that she would have followed her exile, or have died to stay behind her. She is at the court, and no less beloved of her uncle than his own daughter, and never two ladies loved as they do.

110 OLIVER   Where will the old Duke live?

CHARLES   They say he is already in the Forest of Arden, and a many merry men with him; and there they live like the old Robin Hood of England. They say many young gentlemen flock to him every day, and fleet the
115 time carelessly as they did in the golden world.

OLIVER   What, you wrestle tomorrow before the new Duke?

CHARLES   Marry do I sir. And I came to acquaint you with a matter. I am given, sir, secretly to understand
120 that your younger brother Orlando hath a disposition to come in disguised against me to try a fall. Tomorrow, sir, I wrestle for my credit, and he that escapes me without some broken limb shall acquit him well. Your brother is but young and tender, and for
125 your love I would be loath to foil him, as I must for my own honour if he come in. Therefore out of my love to you, I came hither to acquaint you withal, that either you might stay him from his intendment, or brook such disgrace well as he shall run into, in that it is a
130 thing of his own search, and altogether against my will.

OLIVER   Charles, I thank thee for thy love to me, which thou shalt find I will most kindly requite. I had myself notice of my brother's purpose herein, and have by
135 underhand means laboured to dissuade him from it; but he is resolute. I'll tell thee Charles, it is the stubbornest young fellow of France, full of ambition, an envious emulator of every man's good parts, a secret and villainous contriver against me his natural
140 brother. Therefore use thy discretion; I had as lief thou didst break his neck as his finger. And thou wert best look to't; for if thou dost him any slight disgrace, or if he do not mightily grace himself on thee, he will practise against thee by poison, entrap thee by some
145 treacherous device, and never leave thee till he hath ta'en thy life by some indirect means or other. For I assure thee – and almost with tears I speak it – there is not one so young and so villainous this day living. I speak but brotherly of him, but should I anatomize
150 him to thee as he is, I must blush and weep, and thou must look pale and wonder.

CHARLES   I am heartily glad I came hither to you. If he come tomorrow, I'll give him his payment. If ever he go alone again, I'll never wrestle for prize more. And
155 so God keep your worship.

OLIVER   Farewell good Charles.   *Exit Charles.*
Now will I stir this gamester. I hope I shall see an end of him; for my soul – yet I know not why – hates nothing more than he. Yet he's gentle, never schooled
160 and yet learned, full of noble device, of all sorts enchantingly beloved, and indeed so much in the heart of the world, and especially of my own people, who

best know him, that I am altogether misprised. But it shall not be so long; this wrestler shall clear all. Nothing remains but that I kindle the boy thither, 165 which now I'll go about.   *Exit.*

1.2   *Enter* ROSALIND *and* CELIA.

CELIA   I pray thee Rosalind, sweet my coz, be merry.

ROSALIND   Dear Celia, I show more mirth than I am mistress of, and would you yet I were merrier? Unless you could teach me to forget a banished father, you must not learn me how to remember any extraordinary 5 pleasure.

CELIA   Herein I see thou lov'st me not with the full weight that I love thee. If my uncle thy banished father had banished thy uncle the Duke my father, so thou hadst been still with me, I could have taught my love 10 to take thy father for mine; so wouldst thou, if the truth of thy love to me were so righteously tempered as mine is to thee.

ROSALIND   Well, I will forget the condition of my estate, to rejoice in yours. 15

CELIA   You know my father hath no child but I, nor none is like to have; and truly when he dies, thou shalt be his heir; for what he hath taken away from thy father perforce, I will render thee again in affection. By mine honour I will, and when I break that oath, let 20 me turn monster. Therefore my sweet Rose, my dear Rose, be merry.

ROSALIND   From henceforth I will, coz, and devise sports. Let me see, what think you of falling in love?

CELIA   Marry I prithee do, to make sport withal. But 25 love no man in good earnest, nor no further in sport neither, than with safety of a pure blush thou mayst in honour come off again.

ROSALIND   What shall be our sport then?

CELIA   Let us sit and mock the good hussif Fortune 30 from her wheel, that her gifts may henceforth be bestowed equally.

ROSALIND   I would we could do so; for her benefits are mightily misplaced, and the bountiful blind woman doth most mistake in her gifts to women. 35

CELIA   'Tis true, for those that she makes fair, she scarce makes honest; and those that she makes honest, she makes very ill-favouredly.

ROSALIND   Nay now thou goest from Fortune's office to Nature's; Fortune reigns in gifts of the world, not in 40 the lineaments of Nature.

CELIA   No? When Nature hath made a fair creature, may she not by Fortune fall into the fire? Though Nature hath given us wit to flout at Fortune, hath not Fortune sent in this fool to cut off the argument? 45

Enter TOUCHSTONE.

ROSALIND   Indeed, there is Fortune too hard for Nature, when Fortune makes Nature's natural the cutter-off of Nature's wit.

CELIA   Peradventure this is not Fortune's work neither, but Nature's, who perceiveth our natural wits too dull to reason of such goddesses, and hath sent this natural for our whetstone; for always the dullness of the fool is the whetstone of the wits. How now Wit, whither wander you?

TOUCHSTONE   Mistress, you must come away to your father.

CELIA   Were you made the messenger?

TOUCHSTONE   No by mine honour, but I was bid to come for you.

CELIA   Where learned you that oath, fool?

TOUCHSTONE   Of a certain knight, that swore by his honour they were good pancakes, and swore by his honour the mustard was naught. Now I'll stand to it, the pancakes were naught and the mustard was good, and yet was not the knight forsworn.

CELIA   How prove you that in the great heap of your knowledge?

ROSALIND   Ay marry, now unmuzzle your wisdom.

TOUCHSTONE   Stand you both forth now: stroke your chins, and swear by your beards that I am a knave.

CELIA   By our beards, if we had them, thou art.

TOUCHSTONE   By my knavery, if I had it, then I were. But if you swear by that that is not, you are not forsworn. No more was this knight, swearing by his honour, for he never had any; or if he had, he had sworn it away before ever he saw those pancakes or that mustard.

CELIA   Prithee, who is't that thou mean'st?

TOUCHSTONE   One that old Frederick your father loves.

CELIA   My father's love is enough to honour him. Enough, speak no more of him; you'll be whipped for taxation one of these days.

TOUCHSTONE   The more pity that fools may not speak wisely what wisemen do foolishly.

CELIA   By my troth thou sayest true. For since the little wit that fools have was silenced, the little foolery that wisemen have makes a great show. Here comes Monsieur Le Beau.

Enter LE BEAU.

ROSALIND   With his mouth full of news.

CELIA   Which he will put on us, as pigeons feed their young.

ROSALIND   Then shall we be news-crammed.

CELIA   All the better; we shall be the more marketable. *Bonjour* Monsieur Le Beau. What's the news?

LE BEAU   Fair Princess, you have lost much good sport.

CELIA   Sport? Of what colour?

LE BEAU   What colour madam? How shall I answer you?

ROSALIND   As wit and fortune will.

TOUCHSTONE   Or as the Destinies decrees.

CELIA   Well said! That was laid on with a trowel.

TOUCHSTONE   Nay, if I keep not my rank –

ROSALIND   Thou losest thy old smell.

LE BEAU   You amaze me ladies. I would have told you of good wrestling, which you have lost the sight of.

ROSALIND   Yet tell us the manner of the wrestling.   105

LE BEAU   I will tell you the beginning, and if it please your ladyships, you may see the end, for the best is yet to do, and here where you are they are coming to perform it.

CELIA   Well, the beginning that is dead and buried.   110

LE BEAU   There comes an old man, and his three sons –

CELIA   I could match this beginning with an old tale.

LE BEAU   Three proper young men, of excellent growth and presence –

ROSALIND   With bills on their necks: 'Be it known unto   115
all men by these presents' –

LE BEAU   The eldest of the three wrestled with **Charles** the Duke's wrestler, which Charles in a moment threw him and broke three of his ribs, that there is little hope of life in him. So he served the second, and so the   120 third. Yonder they lie, the poor old man their father making such pitiful dole over them that all the beholders take his part with weeping.

ROSALIND   Alas!

TOUCHSTONE   But what is the sport monsieur, that the   125
ladies have lost?

LE BEAU   Why this that I speak of.

TOUCHSTONE   Thus men may grow wiser every day. It is the first time that ever I heard breaking of ribs was sport for ladies.   130

CELIA   Or I, I promise thee.

ROSALIND   But is there any else longs to see this broken music in his sides? Is there yet another dotes upon ribbreaking? Shall we see this wrestling, cousin?

LE BEAU   You must if you stay here, for here is the place   135 appointed for the wrestling, and they are ready to perform it.

CELIA   Yonder sure they are coming. Let us now stay and see it.

Flourish. Enter DUKE FREDERICK, *lords,*
ORLANDO, CHARLES *and attendants.*

DUKE FREDERICK   Come on. Since the youth will not be   140 entreated, his own peril on his forwardness.

ROSALIND   Is yonder the man?

LE BEAU   Even he, madam.

ROSALIND   Alas, he is too young. Yet he looks successfully.

DUKE FREDERICK   How now daughter and cousin? Are   145 you crept hither to see the wrestling?

ROSALIND   Ay my liege, so please you give us leave.

DUKE FREDERICK   You will take little delight in it, I can tell you, there is such odds in the man. In pity of the challenger's youth, I would fain dissuade him, but he   150 will not be entreated. Speak to him ladies; see if you can move him.

CELIA   Call him hither, good Monsieur Le Beau.

DUKE FREDERICK   Do so. I'll not be by.

LE BEAU   Monsieur the challenger, the Princess calls for   155 you.

ORLANDO   I attend them with all respect and duty.

ROSALIND   Young man, have you challenged Charles the
wrestler?

160 ORLANDO   No fair Princess: he is the general challenger.
I come but in as others do, to try with him the strength
of my youth.

CELIA   Young gentleman, your spirits are too bold for
your years. You have seen cruel proof of this man's
165 strength; if you saw yourself with your eyes or knew
yourself with your judgement, the fear of your
adventure would counsel you to a more equal
enterprise. We pray you for your own sake to embrace
your own safety and give over this attempt.

170 ROSALIND   Do young sir; your reputation shall not
therefore be misprized: we will make it our suit to the
Duke that the wrestling might not go forward.

ORLANDO   I beseech you, punish me not with your hard
thoughts, wherein I confess me much guilty to deny so
175 fair and excellent ladies anything. But let your fair eyes
and gentle wishes go with me to my trial; wherein if I
be foiled, there is but one shamed that was never
gracious; if killed, but one dead that is willing to be so.
I shall do my friends no wrong, for I have none to
180 lament me; the world no injury, for in it I have
nothing; only in the world I fill up a place which may
be better supplied when I have made it empty.

ROSALIND   The little strength that I have, I would it
were with you.

185 CELIA   And mine to eke out hers.

ROSALIND   Fare you well. Pray heaven I be deceived in
you!

CELIA   Your heart's desires be with you!

CHARLES   Come, where is this young gallant that is so
190 desirous to lie with his mother earth?

ORLANDO   Ready sir, but his will hath in it a more
modest working.

DUKE FREDERICK   You shall try but one fall.

CHARLES   No, I warrant your Grace you shall not
195 entreat him to a second, that have so mightily
persuaded him from a first.

ORLANDO   You mean to mock me after: you should not
have mocked me before. But come your ways.

ROSALIND   Now Hercules be thy speed, young man!

200 CELIA   I would I were invisible, to catch the strong
fellow by the leg. [*They wrestle.*]

ROSALIND   O excellent young man!

CELIA   If I had a thunderbolt in mine eye, I can tell who
should down. [*Shout. Charles is thrown.*]

205 DUKE FREDERICK   No more, no more.

ORLANDO   Yes, I beseech your Grace, I am not yet well
breathed.

DUKE FREDERICK   How dost thou Charles?

LE BEAU   He cannot speak my lord.

210 DUKE FREDERICK   Bear him away.
                              Charles is borne out.

What is thy name, young man?

ORLANDO
Orlando my liege, the youngest son of Sir Rowland
de Boys.

DUKE FREDERICK
I would thou hadst been son to some man else.
The world esteem'd thy father honourable,
But I did find him still mine enemy.   215
Thou should'st have better pleas'd me with this deed,
Hadst thou descended from another house.
But fare thee well, thou art a gallant youth –
I would thou hadst told me of another father.
                         Exeunt Duke, Le Beau and train.

CELIA   Were I my father, coz, would I do this?   220

ORLANDO   I am more proud to be Sir Rowland's son,
His youngest son, and would not change that calling
To be adopted heir to Frederick.

ROSALIND   My father lov'd Sir Rowland as his soul,
And all the world was of my father's mind.   225
Had I before known this young man his son,
I should have given him tears unto entreaties,
Ere he should thus have ventur'd.

CELIA   Gentle cousin,
Let us go thank him and encourage him.
My father's rough and envious disposition   230
Sticks me at heart. Sir, you have well deserv'd.
If you do keep your promises in love
But justly, as you have exceeded all promise,
Your mistress shall be happy.

ROSALIND [*giving him a chain from her neck*]
Gentleman,   235
Wear this for me; one out of suits with fortune,
That could give more but that her hand lacks means.
Shall we go coz?

CELIA   Ay. Fare you well, fair gentleman.

ORLANDO   Can I not say, 'I thank you'? My better parts
Are all thrown down, and that which here stands up   240
Is but a quintain, a mere lifeless block.

ROSALIND
He calls us back. My pride fell with my fortunes;
I'll ask him what he would. Did you call sir?
Sir, you have wrestled well, and overthrown
More than your enemies.

CELIA   Will you go coz?   245

ROSALIND   Have with you. Fare you well.
                         Exeunt Rosalind and Celia.

ORLANDO
What passion hangs these weights upon my tongue?
I cannot speak to her, yet she urg'd conference.

                      Enter LE BEAU.

O poor Orlando, thou art overthrown!
Or Charles, or something weaker masters thee.   250

LE BEAU   Good sir, I do in friendship counsel you
To leave this place. Albeit you have deserv'd
High commendation, true applause, and love,
Yet such is now the Duke's condition
That he misconsters all that you have done.   255

The Duke is humorous; what he is indeed
More suits you to conceive than I to speak of.

ORLANDO I thank you sir; and pray you tell me this,
Which of the two was daughter of the Duke
260   That here was at the wrestling?

LE BEAU Neither his daughter, if we judge by manners,
But yet indeed the taller is his daughter.
The other is daughter to the banish'd Duke,
And here detain'd by her usurping uncle
265   To keep his daughter company, whose loves
Are dearer than the natural bond of sisters.
But I can tell you that of late this Duke
Hath ta'en displeasure 'gainst his gentle niece,
Grounded upon no other argument
270   But that the people praise her for her virtues,
And pity her for her good father's sake;
And on my life his malice 'gainst the lady
Will suddenly break forth. Sir, fare you well.
Hereafter, in a better world than this,
275   I shall desire more love and knowledge of you.

ORLANDO I rest much bounden to you. Fare you well.

Exit Le Beau.

Thus must I from the smoke into the smother,
From tyrant Duke unto a tyrant brother.
But heavenly Rosalind!   *Exit.*

1.3   *Enter* CELIA *and* ROSALIND.

CELIA Why cousin, why Rosalind! Cupid have mercy,
not a word?

ROSALIND Not one to throw at a dog.

CELIA No, thy words are too precious to be cast away
5   upon curs. Throw some of them at me; come lame me
with reasons.

ROSALIND Then there were two cousins laid up, when
the one should be lamed with reasons and the other
mad without any.

10   CELIA But is all this for your father?

ROSALIND No, some of it is for my child's father. O how
full of briers is this working-day world!

CELIA They are but burs, cousin, thrown upon thee in
holiday foolery; if we walk not in the trodden paths
15   our very petticoats will catch them.

ROSALIND I could shake them off my coat: these burs
are in my heart.

CELIA Hem them away.

ROSALIND I would try, if I could cry hem and have him.

20   CELIA Come, come, wrestle with thy affections.

ROSALIND O they take the part of a better wrestler than
myself.

CELIA O a good wish upon you! You will cry in time, in
despite of a fall. But turning these jests out of service,
25   let us talk in good earnest. Is it possible, on such a
sudden, you should fall into so strong a liking with old
Sir Rowland's youngest son?

ROSALIND The Duke my father loved his father dearly.

CELIA Doth it therefore ensue that you should love his

son dearly? By this kind of chase, I should hate him,   30
for my father hated his father dearly; yet I hate not
Orlando.

ROSALIND No faith, hate him not, for my sake.

CELIA Why should I not? Doth he not deserve well?

ROSALIND Let me love him for that, and do you love   35
him because I do. Look, here comes the Duke.

Enter DUKE FREDERICK *with lords.*

CELIA With his eyes full of anger.

DUKE FREDERICK
Mistress, dispatch you with your safest haste
And get you from our court.

ROSALIND   Me uncle?

DUKE FREDERICK   You cousin.
Within these ten days if that thou be'st found   40
So near our public court as twenty miles,
Thou diest for it.

ROSALIND   I do beseech your Grace,
Let me the knowledge of my fault bear with me.
If with myself I hold intelligence,
Or have acquaintance with mine own desires,   45
If that I do not dream, or be not frantic,
As I do trust I am not, then dear uncle,
Never so much as in a thought unborn
Did I offend your Highness.

DUKE FREDERICK   Thus do all traitors.
If their purgation did consist in words,   50
They are as innocent as grace itself.
Let it suffice thee that I trust thee not.

ROSALIND Yet your mistrust cannot make me a traitor.
Tell me whereon the likelihood depends.

DUKE FREDERICK
Thou art thy father's daughter, there's enough.   55

ROSALIND
So was I when your Highness took his dukedom,
So was I when your Highness banish'd him.
Treason is not inherited, my lord,
Or if we did derive it from our friends,
What's that to me? My father was no traitor.   60
Then good my liege, mistake me not so much
To think my poverty is treacherous.

CELIA Dear sovereign, hear me speak.

DUKE FREDERICK
Ay Celia, we stay'd her for your sake,
Else had she with her father rang'd along.   65

CELIA I did not then entreat to have her stay;
It was your pleasure and your own remorse.
I was too young that time to value her,
But now I know her. If she be a traitor,
Why so am I. We still have slept together,   70
Rose at an instant, learn'd, play'd, eat together,
And whereso'er we went, like Juno's swans,
Still we went coupled and inseparable.

DUKE FREDERICK
She is too subtle for thee, and her smoothness,
Her very silence, and her patience   75

Speak to the people and they pity her.
Thou art a fool; she robs thee of thy name,
And thou wilt show more bright and seem more
    virtuous
When she is gone. Then open not thy lips.
80 Firm and irrevocable is my doom
Which I have pass'd upon her; she is banish'd.
CELIA   Pronounce that sentence then on me, my liege.
I cannot live out of her company.
DUKE FREDERICK
You are a fool. You, niece, provide yourself.
85 If you outstay the time, upon mine honour,
And in the greatness of my word, you die.
                Exeunt Duke Frederick and train.
CELIA   O my poor Rosalind, whither wilt thou go?
Wilt thou change fathers? I will give thee mine.
I charge thee be not thou more griev'd than I am.
ROSALIND   I have more cause.
90 CELIA   Thou hast not, cousin.
Prithee be cheerful. Know'st thou not the Duke
Hath banish'd me his daughter?
ROSALIND   That he hath not.
CELIA   No, hath not? Rosalind lacks then the love
Which teacheth thee that thou and I am one.
95 Shall we be sunder'd? Shall we part, sweet girl?
No, let my father seek another heir.
Therefore devise with me how we may fly,
Whither to go and what to bear with us,
And do not seek to take your change upon you,
100 To bear your griefs yourself and leave me out.
For by this heaven, now at our sorrows pale,
Say what thou canst, I'll go along with thee.
ROSALIND   Why, whither shall we go?
CELIA   To seek my uncle in the Forest of Arden.
105 ROSALIND   Alas, what danger will it be to us,
Maids as we are, to travel forth so far?
Beauty provoketh thieves sooner than gold.
CELIA   I'll put myself in poor and mean attire,
And with a kind of umber smirch my face;
110 The like do you. So shall we pass along
And never stir assailants.
ROSALIND   Were it not better,
Because that I am more than common tall,
That I did suit me all points like a man?
A gallant curtle-axe upon my thigh,
115 A boar-spear in my hand, and in my heart,
Lie there what hidden woman's fear there will,
We'll have a swashing and a martial outside,
As many other mannish cowards have
That do outface it with their semblances.
120 CELIA   What shall I call thee when thou art a man?
ROSALIND
I'll have no worse a name than Jove's own page,
And therefore look you call me Ganymede.
But what will you be call'd?
CELIA   Something that hath a reference to my state.
125 No longer Celia, but Aliena.

ROSALIND   But cousin, what if we assay'd to steal
The clownish fool out of your father's court?
Would he not be a comfort to our travel?
CELIA   He'll go along o'er the wide world with me;
130 Leave me alone to woo him. Let's away,
And get our jewels and our wealth together,
Devise the fittest time and safest way
To hide us from pursuit that will be made
After my flight. Now go we in content
135 To liberty, and not to banishment.   *Exeunt.*

2.1   *Enter* DUKE SENIOR, AMIENS *and two or three*
           Lords *like foresters.*

DUKE SENIOR   Now my co-mates and brothers in exile,
Hath not old custom made this life more sweet
Than that of painted pomp? Are not these woods
More free from peril than the envious court?
5 Here feel we not the penalty of Adam,
The seasons' difference, as the icy fang
And churlish chiding of the winter's wind,
Which when it bites and blows upon my body
Even till I shrink with cold, I smile, and say
10 'This is no flattery. These are counsellors
That feelingly persuade me what I am'.
Sweet are the uses of adversity,
Which like the toad, ugly and venomous,
Wears yet a precious jewel in his head;
15 And this our life, exempt from public haunt,
Finds tongues in trees, books in the running brooks,
Sermons in stones, and good in everything.
AMIENS   I would not change it. Happy is your Grace,
That can translate the stubbornness of fortune
20 Into so quiet and so sweet a style.
DUKE SENIOR   Come, shall we go and kill us venison?
And yet it irks me the poor dappled fools,
Being native burghers of this desert city,
Should in their own confines with forked heads
Have their round haunches gor'd.
25 1 LORD   Indeed my lord,
The melancholy Jaques grieves at that,
And in that kind swears you do more usurp
Than doth your brother that hath banish'd you.
To-day my Lord of Amiens and myself
30 Did steal behind him as he lay along
Under an oak, whose antique root peeps out
Upon the brook that brawls along this wood,
To the which place a poor sequester'd stag,
That from the hunter's aim had ta'en a hurt,
35 Did come to languish; and indeed my lord,
The wretched animal heav'd forth such groans
That their discharge did stretch his leathern coat
Almost to bursting, and the big round tears
Cours'd one another down his innocent nose
40 In piteous chase; and thus the hairy fool,
Much marked of the melancholy Jaques,
Stood on th'extremest verge of the swift brook,

Augmenting it with tears.

DUKE SENIOR   But what said Jaques?
Did he not moralize this spectacle?

45 1 LORD   O yes, into a thousand similes.
First, for his weeping into the needless stream,
'Poor deer', quoth he, 'thou mak'st a testament
As worldlings do, giving thy sum of more
To that which had too much.' Then being there
        alone,
50 Left and abandon'd of his velvet friend,
''Tis right', quoth he, 'thus misery doth part
The flux of company.' Anon a careless herd,
Full of the pasture, jumps along by him
And never stays to greet him. 'Ay', quoth Jaques,
55 'Sweep on you fat and greasy citizens,
'Tis just the fashion. Wherefore do you look
Upon that poor and broken bankrupt there?'
Thus most invectively he pierceth through
The body of country, city, court,
60 Yea, and of this our life, swearing that we
Are mere usurpers, tyrants, and what's worse,
To fright the animals and to kill them up
In their assign'd and native dwelling-place.

DUKE SENIOR
And did you leave him in this contemplation?
65 2 LORD   We did my lord, weeping and commenting
Upon the sobbing deer.

DUKE SENIOR   Show me the place:
I love to cope him in these sullen fits,
For then he's full of matter.
1 LORD   I'll bring you to him straight.   *Exeunt.*

2.2   *Enter* DUKE FREDERICK *with* Lords.

DUKE FREDERICK
Can it be possible that no man saw them?
It cannot be; some villains of my court
Are of consent and sufferance in this.
1 LORD   I cannot hear of any that did see her.
5 The ladies her attendants of her chamber
Saw her abed, and in the morning early,
They found the bed untreasur'd of their mistress.
2 LORD   My lord, the roynish clown, at whom so oft
Your Grace was wont to laugh, is also missing.
10 Hisperia, the princess' gentlewoman,
Confesses that she secretly o'erheard
Your daughter and her cousin much commend
The parts and graces of the wrestler
That did but lately foil the sinewy Charles,
15 And she believes wherever they are gone
That youth is surely in their company.

DUKE FREDERICK
Send to his brother. Fetch that gallant hither.
If he be absent, bring his brother to me;
I'll make him find him. Do this suddenly;
20 And let not search and inquisition quail
To bring again these foolish runaways.   *Exeunt.*

2.3   *Enter* ORLANDO *and* ADAM, *meeting.*

ORLANDO   Who's there?
ADAM   What my young master? O my gentle master,
O my sweet master, O you memory
Of old Sir Rowland! Why, what make you here?
Why are you virtuous? Why do people love you?   5
And wherefore are you gentle, strong, and valiant?
Why would you be so fond to overcome
The bonny prizer of the humorous Duke?
Your praise is come too swiftly home before you.
Know you not master, to some kind of men,   10
Their graces serve them but as enemies?
No more do yours. Your virtues, gentle master,
Are sanctified and holy traitors to you.
O what a world is this, when what is comely
Envenoms him that bears it!   15
ORLANDO   Why, what's the matter?
ADAM   O unhappy youth,
Come not within these doors; within this roof
The enemy of all your graces lives.
Your brother, no, no brother, yet the son –
Yet not the son, I will not call him son –   20
Of him I was about to call his father,
Hath heard your praises, and this night he means
To burn the lodging where you use to lie,
And you within it. If he fail of that,
He will have other means to cut you off.   25
I overheard him, and his practices.
This is no place: this house is but a butchery.
Abhor it, fear it, do not enter it.
ORLANDO
Why whither Adam would'st thou have me go?
ADAM   No matter whither, so you come not here.   30
ORLANDO
What, wouldst thou have me go and beg my food,
Or with a base and boist'rous sword enforce
A thievish living on the common road?
This I must do, or know not what to do;
Yet this I will not do, do how I can.   35
I rather will subject me to the malice
Of a diverted blood and bloody brother.
ADAM   But do not so. I have five hundred crowns,
The thrifty hire I sav'd under your father,
Which I did store to be my foster-nurse,   40
When service should in my old limbs lie lame,
And unregarded age in corners thrown.
Take that, and He that doth the ravens feed,
Yea providently caters for the sparrow,
Be comfort to my age. Here is the gold,   45
All this I give you. Let me be your servant.
Though I look old, yet I am strong and lusty;
For in my youth I never did apply
Hot and rebellious liquors in my blood,
Nor did not with unbashful forehead woo   50
The means of weakness and debility.
Therefore my age is as a lusty winter,

Frosty, but kindly. Let me go with you,
I'll do the service of a younger man
55   In all your business and necessities.
ORLANDO   O good old man, how well in thee appears
The constant service of the antique world,
When service sweat for duty, not for meed.
Thou art not for the fashion of these times,
60   Where none will sweat but for promotion,
And having that, do choke their service up
Even with the having; it is not so with thee.
But poor old man, thou prun'st a rotten tree,
That cannot so much as a blossom yield,
65   In lieu of all thy pains and husbandry.
But come thy ways, we'll go along together,
And ere we have thy youthful wages spent,
We'll light upon some settled low content.
ADAM   Master go on, and I will follow thee
70   To the last gasp with truth and loyalty.
From seventeen years, till now almost fourscore
Here lived I, but now live here no more.
At seventeen years, many their fortunes seek
But at fourscore, it is too late a week;
75   Yet fortune cannot recompense me better
Than to die well, and not my master's debtor.

                                         Exeunt.

2.4   *Enter* ROSALIND *as* Ganymede, CELIA *as*
              Aliena *and* TOUCHSTONE.

ROSALIND   O Jupiter, how weary are my spirits!
TOUCHSTONE   I care not for my spirits, if my legs were
    not weary.
ROSALIND   I could find in my heart to disgrace my
5   man's apparel and to cry like a woman. But I must
comfort the weaker vessel, as doublet and hose ought
to show itself courageous to petticoat; therefore
courage, good Aliena.
CELIA   I pray you bear with me. I cannot go no further.
10   TOUCHSTONE   For my part, I had rather bear with you
than bear you; yet I should bear no cross if I did bear
you, for I think you have no money in your purse.
ROSALIND   Well, this is the Forest of Arden.
TOUCHSTONE   Ay, now am I in Arden, the more fool I;
15   when I was at home I was in a better place, but
travellers must be content.
ROSALIND   Ay, be so, good Touchstone.

              Enter CORIN *and* SILVIUS.

Look you, who comes here,
A young man and an old in solemn talk.
20   CORIN   That is the way to make her scorn you still.
SILVIUS   O Corin, that thou knew'st how I do love her!
CORIN   I partly guess; for I have lov'd ere now.
SILVIUS   No Corin, being old, thou canst not guess,
Though in thy youth thou wast as true a lover
25   As ever sigh'd upon a midnight pillow.
But if thy love were ever like to mine,

As sure I think did never man love so,
How many actions most ridiculous
Hast thou been drawn to by thy fantasy?
CORIN   Into a thousand that I have forgotten.   30
SILVIUS   O thou didst then never love so heartily.
If thou remember'st not the slightest folly
That ever love did make thee run into,
Thou hast not lov'd.
Or if thou hast not sat as I do now,   35
Wearying thy hearer in thy mistress' praise,
Thou hast not lov'd.
Or if thou hast not broke from company
Abruptly as my passion now makes me,
Thou hast not lov'd.   40
O Phebe, Phebe, Phebe!   *Exit.*
ROSALIND
Alas, poor shepherd, searching of thy wound,
I have by hard adventure found mine own.
TOUCHSTONE   And I mine. I remember when I was in
love I broke my sword upon a stone, and bid him take   45
that for coming a-night to Jane Smile; and I remember
the kissing of her batler, and the cow's dugs that her
pretty chopt hands had milked; and I remember the
wooing of a peascod instead of her, from whom I took
two cods, and giving her them again, said with   50
weeping tears, 'Wear these for my sake'. We that are
true lovers run into strange capers; but as all is mortal
in nature, so is all nature in love mortal in folly.
ROSALIND   Thou speak'st wiser than thou art ware of.
TOUCHSTONE   Nay, I shall ne'er be ware of my own wit,   55
till I break my shins against it.
ROSALIND   Jove, Jove! this shepherd's passion
Is much upon my fashion.
TOUCHSTONE   And mine, but it grows something stale
with me.   60
CELIA   I pray you, one of you question yond man, if he
for gold will give us any food. I faint almost to death.
TOUCHSTONE   Holla, you clown!
ROSALIND   Peace fool, he's not thy kinsman.
CORIN   Who calls?   65
TOUCHSTONE   Your betters sir.
CORIN   Else are they very wretched.
ROSALIND   Peace, I say. Good even to you friend.
CORIN   And to you gentle sir, and to you all.
ROSALIND   I prithee shepherd, if that love or gold   70
Can in this desert place buy entertainment,
Bring us where we may rest ourselves and feed.
Here's a young maid with travel much oppress'd,
And faints for succour.
CORIN   Fair sir, I pity her,
And wish, for her sake more than for mine own,   75
My fortunes were more able to relieve her;
But I am shepherd to another man,
And do not shear the fleeces that I graze.
My master is of churlish disposition,
And little recks to find the way to heaven   80
By doing deeds of hospitality.

Besides, his cote, his flocks, and bounds of feed
Are now on sale, and at our sheepcote now
By reason of his absence there is nothing
That you will feed on. But what is, come see,   85
And in my voice most welcome shall you be.

ROSALIND
What is he that shall buy his flock and pasture?

CORIN
That young swain that you saw here but erewhile,
That little cares for buying anything.

ROSALIND   I pray thee, if it stand with honesty,   90
Buy thou the cottage, pasture, and the flock,
And thou shalt have to pay for it of us.

CELIA   And we will mend thy wages. I like this place,
And willingly could waste my time in it.

CORIN   Assuredly the thing is to be sold.   95
Go with me; if you like upon report
The soil, the profit, and this kind of life,
I will your very faithful feeder be,
And buy it with your gold right suddenly.   *Exeunt.*

2.5   *Enter* AMIENS, JAQUES *and others.*

AMIENS [*Sings.*]
Under the greenwood tree,
Who loves to lie with me,
And turn his merry note
Unto the sweet bird's throat,
Come hither, come hither, come hither.   5
Here shall he see
No enemy,
But winter and rough weather.

JAQUES   More, more, I prithee more.

AMIENS   It will make you melancholy, Monsieur Jaques.   10

JAQUES   I thank it. More, I prithee more. I can suck
melancholy out of a song, as a weasel sucks eggs.
More, I prithee more.

AMIENS   My voice is ragged, I know I cannot please you.

JAQUES   I do not desire you to please me, I do desire you   15
to sing. Come, more, another stanzo. Call you 'em
stanzos?

AMIENS   What you will Monsieur Jaques.

JAQUES   Nay, I care not for their names, they owe me
nothing. Will you sing?   20

AMIENS   More at your request than to please myself.

JAQUES   Well then, if ever I thank any man, I'll thank
you; but that they call compliment is like th'encounter
of two dog-apes. And when a man thanks me heartily,
methinks I have given him a penny and he renders me   25
the beggarly thanks. Come sing; and you that will not,
hold your tongues.

AMIENS   Well, I'll end the song. Sirs, cover the while:
the Duke will drink under this tree. He hath been all
this day to look you.   30

JAQUES   And I have been all this day to avoid him. He is
too disputable for my company. I think of as many
matters as he, but I give heaven thanks and make no
boast of them. Come, warble, come.

AMIENS [*Sings.*]
Who doth ambition shun,   35
And loves to live i'th' sun,
Seeking the food he eats,
And pleas'd with what he gets,

ALL   Come hither, come hither, come hither.
Here shall he see   40
No enemy,
But winter and rough weather.

JAQUES   I'll give you a verse to this note, that I made
yesterday in despite of my invention.

AMIENS   And I'll sing it.   45

JAQUES   Thus it goes.
If it do come to pass
That any man turn ass,
Leaving his wealth and ease,
A stubborn will to please,   50
Ducdame, ducdame, ducdame,
Here shall he see
Gross fools as he,
And if he will come to me.

AMIENS   What's that 'ducdame'?   55

JAQUES   'Tis a Greek invocation, to call fools into a
circle. I'll go sleep if I can; if I cannot, I'll rail against
all the first-born of Egypt.

AMIENS   And I'll go seek the Duke; his banquet is
prepared.   *Exeunt.*   60

2.6   *Enter* ORLANDO *and* ADAM.

ADAM   Dear master, I can go no further. O I die for food.
Here lie I down, and measure out my grave. Farewell
kind master.

ORLANDO   Why how now Adam? No greater heart in
thee? Live a little, comfort a little, cheer thyself a little.   5
If this uncouth forest yield anything savage, I will
either be food for it, or bring it for food to thee. Thy
conceit is nearer death than thy powers. For my sake
be comfortable; hold death awhile at the arm's end. I
will here be with thee presently, and if I bring thee not   10
something to eat, I will give thee leave to die; but if
thou diest before I come, thou art a mocker of my
labour. Well said! Thou lookst cheerly, and I'll be with
thee quickly. Yet thou liest in the bleak air. Come, I
will bear thee to some shelter and thou shalt not die for   15
lack of a dinner, if there live any thing in this desert.
Cheerly good Adam.   *Exeunt.*

2.7   *Enter* DUKE SENIOR, AMIENS
and Lords, *like outlaws.*

DUKE SENIOR   I think he be transform'd into a beast,
For I can nowhere find him like a man.

1 LORD   My lord, he is but even now gone hence.
Here was he merry, hearing of a song.

DUKE SENIOR   If he, compact of jars, grow musical,   5
We shall have shortly discord in the spheres.
Go seek him, tell him I would speak with him.

1 LORD   He saves my labour by his own approach.

Enter JAQUES.

DUKE SENIOR
10 Why how now monsieur? What a life is this,
    That your poor friends must woo your company?
    What, you look merrily?
JAQUES   A fool, a fool! I met a fool i'th' forest,
    A motley fool: a miserable world!
    As I do live by food, I met a fool,
15 Who laid him down and bask'd him in the sun,
    And rail'd on Lady Fortune in good terms,
    In good set terms, and yet a motley fool.
    'Good morrow, fool', quoth I. 'No, sir,' quoth he,
    'Call me not fool, till heaven hath sent me fortune'.
20 And then he drew a dial from his poke,
    And looking on it, with lack-lustre eye,
    Says, very wisely, 'It is ten o'clock.
    Thus we may see', quoth he, 'how the world wags:
    'Tis but an hour ago since it was nine,
25 And after one hour more 'twill be eleven;
    And so from hour to hour, we ripe, and ripe,
    And then from hour to hour, we rot, and rot,
    And thereby hangs a tale.' When I did hear
    The motley fool thus moral on the time,
30 My lungs began to crow like chanticleer,
    That fools should be so deep-contemplative;
    And I did laugh, sans intermission,
    An hour by his dial. O noble fool!
    A worthy fool! Motley's the only wear.
35 DUKE SENIOR   What fool is this?
JAQUES   O worthy fool! One that hath been a courtier
    And says, if ladies be but young and fair,
    They have the gift to know it. And in his brain,
    Which is as dry as the remainder biscuit
40 After a voyage, he hath strange places cramm'd
    With observation, the which he vents
    In mangled forms. O that I were a fool!
    I am ambitious for a motley coat.
DUKE SENIOR   Thou shalt have one.
JAQUES   It is my only suit,
45 Provided that you weed your better judgements
    Of all opinion that grows rank in them
    That I am wise. I must have liberty
    Withal, as large a charter as the wind,
    To blow on whom I please, for so fools have;
50 And they that are most galled with my folly,
    They most must laugh. And why sir must they so?
    The why is plain as way to parish church.
    He that a fool doth very wisely hit
    Doth very foolishly, although he smart,
55 Not to seem senseless of the bob. If not,
    The wiseman's folly is anatomiz'd
    Even by the squand'ring glances of the fool.
    Invest me in my motley. Give me leave
    To speak my mind, and I will through and through
60 Cleanse the foul body of th'infected world,

If they will patiently receive my medicine.
DUKE SENIOR
    Fie on thee! I can tell what thou wouldst do.
JAQUES   What, for a counter, would I do but good?
DUKE SENIOR
    Most mischievous foul sin, in chiding sin.
65 For thou thyself hast been a libertine,
    As sensual as the brutish sting itself,
    And all th'embossed sores and headed evils
    That thou with licence of free foot hast caught
    Wouldst thou disgorge into the general world.
70 JAQUES   Why who cries out on pride,
    That can therein tax any private party?
    Doth it not flow as hugely as the sea,
    Till that the weary very means do ebb?
    What woman in the city do I name,
75 When that I say the city-woman bears
    The cost of princes on unworthy shoulders?
    Who can come in and say that I mean her,
    When such a one as she, such is her neighbour?
    Or what is he of basest function,
80 That says his bravery is not on my cost,
    Thinking that I mean him, but therein suits
    His folly to the mettle of my speech?
    There then! How then? What then? Let me see
      wherein
    My tongue hath wrong'd him: if it do him right,
85 Then he hath wrong'd himself; if he be free,
    Why then my taxing like a wild-goose flies
    Unclaim'd of any man. But who comes here?

Enter ORLANDO *with sword drawn.*

ORLANDO   Forbear, and eat no more.
JAQUES   Why, I have eat none yet.
90 ORLANDO   Nor shalt not till necessity be served.
JAQUES   Of what kind should this cock come of?
DUKE SENIOR
    Art thou thus bolden'd man by thy distress?
    Or else a rude despiser of good manners,
    That in civility thou seem'st so empty?
ORLANDO
95 You touch'd my vein at first: the thorny point
    Of bare distress hath ta'en from me the show
    Of smooth civility. Yet am I inland bred,
    And know some nurture. But forbear, I say,
    He dies that touches any of this fruit,
100 Till I and my affairs are answered.
JAQUES
    And you will not be answered with reason, I must
      die.
DUKE SENIOR
    What would you have? Your gentleness shall force,
    More than your force move us to gentleness.
ORLANDO   I almost die for food, and let me have it.
DUKE SENIOR
105 Sit down and feed, and welcome to our table.
ORLANDO   Speak you so gently? Pardon me, I pray you.

I thought that all things had been savage here,
And therefore put I on the countenance
Of stern commandment. But whate'er you are
110　That in this desert inaccessible
Under the shade of melancholy boughs,
Lose and neglect the creeping hours of time;
If ever you have look'd on better days;
If ever been where bells have knoll'd to church;
115　If ever sat at any good man's feast;
If ever from your eyelids wip'd a tear,
And know what 'tis to pity and be pitied,
Let gentleness my strong enforcement be;
In the which hope, I blush, and hide my sword.
120　DUKE SENIOR　　True is it that we have seen better days,
And have with holy bell been knoll'd to church,
And sat at good men's feasts, and wip'd our eyes
Of drops that sacred pity hath engender'd;
And therefore sit you down in gentleness,
125　And take upon command what help we have
That to your wanting may be minister'd.
ORLANDO　　Then but forbear your food a little while,
Whiles, like a doe, I go to find my fawn,
And give it food. There is an old poor man,
130　Who after me hath many a weary step
Limp'd in pure love; till he be first suffic'd,
Oppress'd with two weak evils, age and hunger,
I will not touch a bit.
DUKE SENIOR　　　　　　Go find him out,
And we will nothing waste till you return.
ORLANDO
135　I thank ye, and be blest for your good comfort.　*Exit.*
DUKE SENIOR
Thou seest, we are not all alone unhappy:
This wide and universal theatre
Presents more woeful pageants than the scene
Wherein we play in.
JAQUES　　　　　　All the world's a stage,
140　And all the men and women merely players.
They have their exits and their entrances,
And one man in his time plays many parts,
His acts being seven ages. At first the infant,
Mewling and puking in the nurse's arms.
145　Then, the whining school-boy with his satchel
And shining morning face, creeping like snail
Unwillingly to school. And then the lover,
Sighing like furnace, with a woeful ballad
Made to his mistress' eyebrow. Then, a soldier,
150　Full of strange oaths, and bearded like the pard,
Jealous in honour, sudden, and quick in quarrel,
Seeking the bubble reputation
Even in the cannon's mouth. And then, the justice,
In fair round belly, with good capon lin'd,
155　With eyes severe, and beard of formal cut,
Full of wise saws, and modern instances,
And so he plays his part. The sixth age shifts
Into the lean and slipper'd pantaloon,
With spectacles on nose, and pouch on side,

His youthful hose well sav'd, a world too wide　160
For his shrunk shank, and his big manly voice,
Turning again toward childish treble, pipes
And whistles in his sound. Last scene of all,
That ends this strange eventful history,
Is second childishness and mere oblivion,　165
Sans teeth, sans eyes, sans taste, sans everything.

Enter ORLANDO *with* ADAM.

DUKE SENIOR
Welcome. Set down your venerable burden,
And let him feed.
ORLANDO　I thank you most for him.
ADAM　　　　　　　　　　　So had you need,
I scarce can speak to thank you for myself.　170
DUKE SENIOR　Welcome, fall to. I will not trouble you
As yet to question you about your fortunes.
Give us some music, and good cousin, sing.
AMIENS [*Sings.*]
Blow, blow, thou winter wind,
Thou art not so unkind　175
As man's ingratitude.
Thy tooth is not so keen,
Because thou art not seen,
Although thy breath be rude.
Heigh-ho, sing heigh-ho, unto the green holly　180
Most friendship is feigning, most loving mere folly.
Then heigh-ho, the holly,
This life is most jolly.

Freeze, freeze, thou bitter sky,
That dost not bite so nigh　185
As benefits forgot.
Though thou the waters warp,
Thy sting is not so sharp,
As friend remember'd not.
Heigh-ho, sing heigh-ho, unto the green holly,　190
Most friendship is feigning, most loving mere folly.
Then heigh-ho the holly,
This life is most jolly.
DUKE SENIOR
If that you were the good Sir Rowland's son,
As you have whisper'd faithfully you were,　195
And as mine eye doth his effigies witness
Most truly limn'd and living in your face,
Be truly welcome hither. I am the duke
That lov'd your father. The residue of your fortune,
Go to my cave and tell me. Good old man,　200
Thou art right welcome as thy master is.
Support him by the arm. Give me your hand
And let me all your fortunes understand.　*Exeunt.*

3.1　　　　*Enter* DUKE, *lords and* OLIVER.

DUKE FREDERICK
Not see him since? Sir, sir, that cannot be.
But were I not the better part made mercy,
I should not seek an absent argument

5 Of my revenge, thou present. But look to it:
   Find out thy brother whereso'er he is;
   Seek him with candle: bring him dead or living
   Within this twelvmonth, or turn thou no more
   To seek a living in our territory.
   Thy lands and all things that thou dost call thine,
10 Worth seizure, do we seize into our hands,
   Till thou canst quit thee by thy brother's mouth
   Of what we think against thee.

OLIVER   O that your Highness knew my heart in this!
   I never lov'd my brother in my life.

DUKE FREDERICK
15 More villain thou. Well, push him out of doors,
   And let my officers of such a nature
   Make an extent upon his house and lands.
   Do this expediently, and turn him going.   *Exeunt.*

3.2   *Enter* ORLANDO *with a paper.*

ORLANDO   Hang there my verse, in witness of my love,
   And thou thrice-crowned queen of night, survey
   With thy chaste eye, from thy pale sphere above,
   Thy huntress' name, that my full life doth sway.
5 O Rosalind, these trees shall be my books,
   And in their barks my thoughts I'll character,
   That every eye which in this forest looks,
   Shall see thy virtue witness'd everywhere.
   Run, run Orlando, carve on every tree
10 The fair, the chaste, and unexpressive she.   *Exit.*

Enter CORIN *and* TOUCHSTONE.

CORIN   And how like you this shepherd's life, Master Touchstone?

TOUCHSTONE   Truly shepherd, in respect of itself, it is a good life; but in respect that it is a shepherd's life, it is naught. In respect that it is solitary, I like it very well; but in respect that it is private, it is a very vile life. Now in respect it is in the fields, it pleaseth me well; but in respect it is not in the court, it is tedious. As it is a spare life, look you, it fits my humour well; but as there is no more plenty in it, it goes much against my stomach. Hast any philosophy in thee, shepherd?

CORIN   No more but that I know the more one sickens the worse at ease he is; and that he that wants money, means, and content is without three good friends; that the property of rain is to wet and fire to burn; that good pasture makes fat sheep; and that a great cause of the night is lack of the sun; that he that hath learned no wit by nature nor art may complain of good breeding or comes of a very dull kindred.

TOUCHSTONE   Such a one is a natural philosopher. Wast ever in court, shepherd?

CORIN   No truly.

TOUCHSTONE   Then thou art damned.

CORIN   Nay, I hope.

TOUCHSTONE   Truly thou art damned, like an ill-roasted egg, all on one side.

CORIN   For not being at court? Your reason.

TOUCHSTONE   Why, if thou never wast at court, thou never saw'st good manners; if thou never saw'st good manners, then thy manners must be wicked, and wickedness is sin, and sin is damnation. Thou art in a parlous state, shepherd.

CORIN   Not a whit, Touchstone. Those that are good manners at the court are as ridiculous in the country as the behaviour of the country is most mockable at the court. You told me you salute not at the court, but you kiss your hands: that courtesy would be uncleanly if courtiers were shepherds.

TOUCHSTONE   Instance, briefly; come, instance.

CORIN   Why we are still handling our ewes, and their fells you know are greasy.

TOUCHSTONE   Why, do not your courtier's hands sweat? And is not the grease of a mutton as wholesome as the sweat of a man? Shallow, shallow. A better instance I say. Come.

CORIN   Besides, our hands are hard.

TOUCHSTONE   Your lips will feel them the sooner. Shallow again. A more sounder instance, come.

CORIN   And they are often tarred over with the surgery of our sheep; and would you have us kiss tar? The courtier's hands are perfumed with civet.

TOUCHSTONE   Most shallow man! Thou worms-meat in respect of a good piece of flesh indeed! Learn of the wise and perpend. Civet is of a baser birth than tar, the very uncleanly flux of a cat. Mend the instance, shepherd.

CORIN   You have too courtly a wit for me, I'll rest.

TOUCHSTONE   Wilt thou rest damned? God help thee, shallow man! God make incision in thee, thou art raw!

CORIN   Sir, I am a true labourer: I earn that I eat, get that I wear; owe no man hate, envy no man's happiness; glad of other men's good, content with my harm; and the greatest of my pride is to see my ewes graze and my lambs suck.

TOUCHSTONE   That is another simple sin in you, to bring the ewes and the rams together, and to offer to get your living by the copulation of cattle; to be bawd to a bell-wether, and to betray a she-lamb of a twelvemonth to a crooked-pated old cuckoldly ram, out of all reasonable match. If thou beest not damned for this, the devil himself will have no shepherds. I cannot see else how thou shouldst 'scape.

CORIN   Here comes young Master Ganymede, my new mistress's brother.

Enter ROSALIND *with a paper, reading.*

ROSALIND
From the east to western Inde,
No jewel is like Rosalind.
Her worth being mounted on the wind,
Through all the world bears Rosalind.
All the pictures fairest lin'd

90   *Are but black to Rosalind.*
       Let no face be kept in mind
       But the fair of Rosalind.

TOUCHSTONE I'll rhyme you so, eight years together;
dinners and suppers and sleeping-hours excepted. It
95 is the right butter-women's rank to market.

ROSALIND Out fool!

TOUCHSTONE For a taste.
       If a hart do lack a hind,
       Let him seek out Rosalind.
100   *If the cat will after kind,*
       So be sure will Rosalind.
       Winter'd garments must be lin'd,
       So must slender Rosalind.
       They that reap must sheaf and bind,
105   *Then to cart with Rosalind.*
       Sweetest nut hath sourest rind,
       Such a nut is Rosalind.
       He that sweetest rose will find
       Must find love's prick, and Rosalind.
110 This is the very false gallop of verses; why do you
infect yourself with them?

ROSALIND Peace you dull fool! I found them on a tree.

TOUCHSTONE Truly the tree yields bad fruit.

ROSALIND I'll graff it with you, and then I shall graff it
115 with a medlar. Then it will be the earliest fruit i'th'
country; for you'll be rotten ere you be half ripe, and
that's the right virtue of the medlar.

TOUCHSTONE You have said; but whether wisely or no,
let the forest judge.

120 ROSALIND Peace! Here comes my sister, reading. Stand
aside.

      Enter CELIA *with a writing.*

CELIA [*Reads.*]
       Why should this desert be,
       For it is unpeopled? No.
       Tongues I'll hang on every tree,
125   *That shall civil sayings show.*
       Some, how brief the life of man
       Runs his erring pilgrimage,
       That the stretching of a span
       Buckles in his sum of age.
130   *Some of violated vows,*
       'Twixt the souls of friend and friend.
       But upon the fairest boughs,
       Or at every sentence end,
       Will I Rosalinda write,
135   *Teaching all that read to know*
       The quintessence of every sprite
       Heaven would in little show.
       Therefore Heaven Nature charg'd
       That one body should be fill'd
140   *With all graces wide-enlarg'd.*
       Nature presently distill'd
       Helen's cheek, but not her heart,

       Cleopatra's majesty,
       Atalanta's better part,
       Sad Lucretia's modesty. 145
       Thus Rosalind of many parts
       By heavenly synod was devis'd,
       Of many faces, eyes, and hearts,
       To have the touches dearest priz'd.
       Heaven would that she these gifts should have, 150
       And I to live and die her slave.

ROSALIND O most gentle Jupiter, what tedious homily
of love have you wearied your parishioners withal, and
never cried, 'Have patience good people!'

CELIA How now? Back-friends! Shepherd, go off a 155
little. Go with him sirrah.

TOUCHSTONE Come shepherd, let us make an
honourable retreat, though not with bag and baggage,
yet with scrip and scrippage.   *Exit with Corin.*

CELIA Didst thou hear these verses? 160

ROSALIND O yes, I heard them all, and more too, for
some of them had in them more feet than the verses
would bear.

CELIA That's no matter: the feet might bear the verses.

ROSALIND Ay, but the feet were lame, and could not 165
bear themselves without the verse, and therefore stood
lamely in the verse.

CELIA But didst thou hear without wondering how thy
name should be hanged and carved upon these
trees? 170

ROSALIND I was seven of the nine days out of the
wonder before you came; for look here what I found
on a palm-tree. I was never so berhymed since
Pythagoras' time that I was an Irish rat, which I can
hardly remember. 175

CELIA Trow you who hath done this?

ROSALIND Is it a man?

CELIA And a chain, that you once wore, about his neck.
Change you colour?

ROSALIND I prithee who? 180

CELIA O Lord, Lord! It is a hard matter for friends to
meet; but mountains may be remov'd with
earthquakes, and so encounter.

ROSALIND Nay, but who is it?

CELIA Is it possible? 185

ROSALIND Nay, I prithee now, with most petitionary
vehemence, tell me who it is.

CELIA O wonderful, wonderful! And most wonderful
wonderful! And yet again wonderful! And after that
out of all whooping. 190

ROSALIND Good my complexion! Dost thou think
though I am caparisoned like a man I have a doublet
and hose in my disposition? One inch of delay more is
a South Sea of discovery. I prithee tell me who is it
quickly, and speak apace. I would thou couldst 195
stammer, that thou mightst pour this concealed man
out of thy mouth, as wine comes out of a narrow-
mouthed bottle; either too much at once or none at all.

200 I prithee take the cork out of thy mouth, that I may
     drink thy tidings.

CELIA   So you may put a man in your belly.

ROSALIND   Is he of God's making? What manner of
     man? Is his head worth a hat? Or his chin worth a
     beard?

205 CELIA   Nay, he hath but a little beard.

ROSALIND   Why God will send more, if the man will be
     thankful. Let me stay the growth of his beard, if thou
     delay me not the knowledge of his chin.

CELIA   It is young Orlando, that tripped up the
210 wrestler's heels and your heart, both in an instant.

ROSALIND   Nay, but the devil take mocking. Speak sad
     brow and true maid.

CELIA   I'faith, coz, 'tis he.

ROSALIND   Orlando?

215 CELIA   Orlando.

ROSALIND   Alas the day, what shall I do with my doublet
     and hose? What did he when thou saw'st him? What
     said he? How looked he? Wherein went he? What
     makes he here? Did he ask for me? Where remains he?
220 How parted he with thee? And when shalt thou see
     him again? Answer me in one word.

CELIA   You must borrow me Gargantua's mouth first.
     'Tis a word too great for any mouth of this age's size.
     To say ay and no to these particulars is more than to
225 answer in a catechism.

ROSALIND   But doth he know that I am in this forest,
     and in man's apparel? Looks he as freshly as he did the
     day he wrestled?

CELIA   It is as easy to count atomies as to resolve the
230 propositions of a lover. But take a taste of my finding
     him, and relish it with good observance. I found him
     under a tree like a dropped acorn.

ROSALIND   It may well be called Jove's tree, when it
     drops such fruit.

235 CELIA   Give me audience, good madam.

ROSALIND   Proceed.

CELIA   There lay he stretched along like a wounded
     knight.

ROSALIND   Though it be pity to see such a sight, it well
240 becomes the ground.

CELIA   Cry holla to the tongue, I prithee; it curvets
     unseasonably. He was furnished like a hunter.

ROSALIND   O ominous! he comes to kill my heart!

CELIA   I would sing my song without a burden. Thou
245 bringest me out of tune.

ROSALIND   Do you not know I am a woman? When I
     think, I must speak. Sweet, say on.

CELIA   You bring me out. Soft! comes he not here?

Enter ORLANDO *and* JAQUES.

ROSALIND   'Tis he. Slink by and note him.

250 JAQUES   I thank you for your company, but good faith, I
     had as lief have been myself alone.

ORLANDO   And so had I: but yet for fashion sake I thank
     you too, for your society.

JAQUES   God buy you: let's meet as little as we can.

ORLANDO   I do desire we may be better strangers.   255

JAQUES   I pray you mar no more trees with writing
     lovesongs in their barks.

ORLANDO   I pray you mar no more of my verses with
     reading them ill-favouredly.

JAQUES   Rosalind is your love's name?   260

ORLANDO   Yes, just.

JAQUES   I do not like her name.

ORLANDO   There was no thought of pleasing you when
     she was christened.

JAQUES   What stature is she of?   265

ORLANDO   Just as high as my heart.

JAQUES   You are full of pretty answers. Have you not
     been acquainted with goldsmiths' wives, and conned
     them out of rings?

ORLANDO   Not so; but I answer you right painted cloth,   270
     from whence you have studied your questions.

JAQUES   You have a nimble wit; I think 'twas made of
     Atalanta's heels. Will you sit down with me and we
     two will rail against our mistress the world and all our
     misery?   275

ORLANDO   I will chide no breather in the world but
     myself, against whom I know most faults.

JAQUES   The worst fault you have is to be in love.

ORLANDO   'Tis a fault I will not change for your best
     virtue. I am weary of you.   280

JAQUES   By my troth, I was seeking for a fool when I
     found you.

ORLANDO   He is drowned in the brook. Look but in and
     you shall see him.

JAQUES   There I shall see mine own figure.   285

ORLANDO   Which I take to be either a fool, or a cipher.

JAQUES   I'll tarry no longer with you. Farewell good
     Signior Love.

ORLANDO   I am glad of your departure. Adieu good
     Monsieur Melancholy.   *Exit Jaques.*   290

ROSALIND [*aside to Celia*]   I will speak to him like a saucy
     lackey and under that habit play the knave with him. –
     Do you hear, forester?

ORLANDO   Very well. What would you?

ROSALIND   I pray you, what is't o'clock?   295

ORLANDO   You should ask me what time o' day; there's
     no clock in the forest.

ROSALIND   Then there is no true lover in the forest, else
     sighing every minute and groaning every hour would
     detect the lazy foot of Time, as well as a clock.   300

ORLANDO   And why not the swift foot of Time? Had not
     that been as proper?

ROSALIND   By no means sir. Time travels in divers paces
     with divers persons. I'll tell you who Time ambles
     withal, who Time trots withal, who Time gallops   305
     withal, and who he stands still withal.

ORLANDO   I prithee, who doth he trot withal?

ROSALIND   Marry he trots hard with a young maid,
     between the contract of her marriage and the day it is
     solemnized. If the interim be but a se'nnight, Time's   310

pace is so hard that it seems the length of seven year.

ORLANDO   Who ambles Time withal?

ROSALIND   With a priest that lacks Latin, and a rich man
that hath not the gout, for the one sleeps easily
because he cannot study, and the other lives merrily
because he feels no pain; the one lacking the burden
of lean and wasteful learning; the other knowing no
burden of heavy tedious penury. These Time ambles
withal.

ORLANDO   Who doth he gallop withal?

ROSALIND   With a thief to the gallows; for though he go
as softly as foot can fall, he thinks himself too soon
there.

ORLANDO   Who stays it still withal?

ROSALIND   With lawyers in the vacation; for they sleep
between term and term, and then they perceive not
how Time moves.

ORLANDO   Where dwell you pretty youth?

ROSALIND   With this shepherdess my sister; here in the
skirts of the forest, like fringe upon a petticoat.

ORLANDO   Are you native of this place?

ROSALIND   As the cony that you see dwell where she is
kindled.

ORLANDO   Your accent is something finer than you
could purchase in so removed a dwelling.

ROSALIND   I have been told so of many. But indeed, an
old religious uncle of mine taught me to speak, who
was in his youth an inland man, one that knew
courtship too well, for there he fell in love. I have
heard him read many lectures against it, and I thank
God I am not a woman, to be touched with so many
giddy offences as he hath generally taxed their whole
sex withal.

ORLANDO   Can you remember any of the principal evils
that he laid to the charge of women?

ROSALIND   There were none principal: they were all like
one another as half-pence are, every one fault seeming
monstrous, till his fellow-fault came to match it.

ORLANDO   I prithee recount some of them.

ROSALIND   No; I will not cast away my physic but on
those that are sick. There is a man haunts the forest
that abuses our young plants with carving 'Rosalind'
on their barks; hangs odes upon hawthorns and elegies
on brambles; all, forsooth, deifying the name of
Rosalind. If I could meet that fancy-monger, I would
give him some good counsel, for he seems to have the
quotidian of love upon him.

ORLANDO   I am he that is so love-shaked. I pray you tell
me your remedy.

ROSALIND   There is none of my uncle's marks upon you.
He taught me how to know a man in love; in which
cage of rushes I am sure you are not prisoner.

ORLANDO   What were his marks?

ROSALIND   A lean cheek, which you have not; a blue eye
and sunken, which you have not; an unquestionable
spirit, which you have not; a beard neglected, which
you have not – but I pardon you for that, for simply

your having in beard is a younger brother's revenue.
Then your hose should be ungartered, your bonnet
unbanded, your sleeve unbuttoned, your shoe untied,
and everything about you demonstrating a careless
desolation. But you are no such man: you are rather
point-device in your accoutrements, as loving yourself
than seeming the lover of any other.

ORLANDO   Fair youth, I would I could make thee believe
I love.

ROSALIND   Me believe it! You may as soon make her that
you love believe it, which I warrant she is apter to do
than to confess she does. That is one of the points in
the which women still give the lie to their consciences.
But in good sooth, are you he that hangs the verses on
the trees, wherein Rosalind is so admired?

ORLANDO   I swear to thee youth, by the white hand of
Rosalind, I am that he, that unfortunate he.

ROSALIND   But are you so much in love as your rhymes
speak?

ORLANDO   Neither rhyme nor reason can express how
much.

ROSALIND   Love is merely a madness, and I tell you,
deserves as well a dark house and a whip as madmen
do; and the reason why they are not so punished and
cured is that the lunacy is so ordinary that the
whippers are in love too. Yet I profess curing it by
counsel.

ORLANDO   Did you ever cure any so?

ROSALIND   Yes, one, and in this manner. He was to
imagine me his love, his mistress; and I set him every
day to woo me. At which time would I, being but a
moonish youth, grieve, be effeminate, changeable,
longing and liking, proud, fantastical, apish, shallow,
inconstant, full of tears, full of smiles, for every
passion something and for no passion truly
anything, as boys and women are for the most part
cattle of this colour; would now like him, now loathe
him; then entertain him, then forswear him; now weep
for him, then spit at him; that I drave my suitor from
his mad humour of love to a living humour of
madness, which was, to forswear the full stream of the
world and to live in a nook merely monastic. And thus
I cured him, and this way will I take upon me to wash
your liver as clean as a sound sheep's heart, that there
shall not be one spot of love in't.

ORLANDO   I would not be cured, youth.

ROSALIND   I would cure you, if you would but call me
Rosalind and come every day to my cote and woo me.

ORLANDO   Now by the faith of my love, I will. Tell me
where it is.

ROSALIND   Go with me to it, and I'll show it you; and by
the way, you shall tell me where in the forest you live.
Will you go?

ORLANDO   With all my heart, good youth.

ROSALIND   Nay, you must call me Rosalind. Come sister,
will you go?   *Exeunt.*

3.3 *Enter* TOUCHSTONE, AUDREY *and* JAQUES *behind.*

TOUCHSTONE   Come apace good Audrey. I will fetch up your goats, Audrey. And how Audrey, am I the man yet? Doth my simple feature content you?

AUDREY   Your features? Lord warrant us! What features?

TOUCHSTONE   I am here with thee and thy goats, as the most capricious poet, honest Ovid, was among the Goths.

JAQUES [*aside*]   O knowledge ill-inhabited, worse than Jove in a thatched house!

TOUCHSTONE   When a man's verses cannot be understood, nor a man's good wit seconded with the forward child, understanding, it strikes a man more dead than a great reckoning in a little room. Truly, I would the gods had made thee poetical.

AUDREY   I do not know what 'poetical' is. Is it honest in deed and word? Is it a true thing?

TOUCHSTONE   No truly; for the truest poetry is the most feigning, and lovers are given to poetry; and what they swear in poetry may be said as lovers they do feign.

AUDREY   Do you wish then that the gods had made me poetical?

TOUCHSTONE   I do truly. For thou swear'st to me thou art honest. Now if thou wert a poet, I might have some hope thou didst feign.

AUDREY   Would you not have me honest?

TOUCHSTONE   No truly, unless thou wert hard-favoured; for honesty coupled to beauty is to have honey a sauce to sugar.

JAQUES [*aside*]   A material fool!

AUDREY   Well, I am not fair, and therefore I pray the gods make me honest.

TOUCHSTONE   Truly, and to cast away honesty upon a foul slut were to put good meat into an unclean dish.

AUDREY   I am not a slut, though I thank the gods I am foul.

TOUCHSTONE   Well, praised be the gods for thy foulness; sluttishness may come hereafter. But be it as it may be, I will marry thee; and to that end I have been with Sir Oliver Martext, the vicar of the next village, who hath promised to meet me in this place of the forest and to couple us.

JAQUES [*aside*]   I would fain see this meeting.

AUDREY   Well, the gods give us joy!

TOUCHSTONE   Amen. A man may, if he were of a fearful heart, stagger in this attempt; for here we have no temple but the wood, no assembly but horn-beasts. But what though? Courage! As horns are odious, they are necessary. It is said, many a man knows no end of his goods. Right. Many a man has good horns and knows no end of them. Well, that is the dowry of his wife, 'tis none of his own getting. Horns? Even so. Poor men alone? No, no. The noblest deer hath them as huge as the rascal. Is the single man therefore blessed? No. As a walled town is more worthier than a village, so is the forehead of a married man more honourable than the bare brow of a bachelor; and by how much defence is better than no skill, by so much is a horn more precious than to want. Here comes Sir Oliver.

Enter SIR OLIVER MARTEXT.

Sir Oliver Martext, you are well met. Will you dispatch us here under this tree or shall we go with you to your chapel?

SIR OLIVER   Is there none here to give the woman?

TOUCHSTONE   I will not take her on gift of any man.

SIR OLIVER   Truly she must be given, or the marriage is not lawful.

JAQUES [*advancing*]   Proceed, proceed. I'll give her.

TOUCHSTONE   Good even, good Master What-ye-call't. How do you sir? You are very well met. God 'ild you for your last company. I am very glad to see you. Even a toy in hand here sir. Nay, pray be covered.

JAQUES   Will you be married, Motley?

TOUCHSTONE   As the ox hath his bow sir, the horse his curb, and the falcon her bells, so man hath his desires, and as pigeons bill, so wedlock would be nibbling.

JAQUES   And will you, being a man of your breeding, be married under a bush like a beggar? Get you to church, and have a good priest that can tell you what marriage is. This fellow will but join you together as they join wainscot; then one of you will prove a shrunk panel, and like green timber, warp, warp.

TOUCHSTONE [*aside*]   I am not in the mind but I were better to be married of him than of another, for he is not like to marry me well; and not being well married, it will be a good excuse for me hereafter to leave my wife.

JAQUES   Go thou with me, and let me counsel thee.

TOUCHSTONE   Come sweet Audrey, We must be married or we must live in bawdry. Farewell good Master Oliver. Not –

      O sweet Oliver,
      O brave Oliver,
   Leave me not behind thee:

but –

         Wind away,
      Be gone, I say,
   I will not to wedding with thee.
            Exeunt Jaques, Touchstone and Audrey.

SIR OLIVER   'Tis no matter. Ne'er a fantastical knave of them all shall flout me out of my calling.   *Exit.*

3.4   *Enter* ROSALIND *and* CELIA.

ROSALIND   Never talk to me, I will weep.

CELIA   Do I prithee, but yet have the grace to consider that tears do not become a man.

ROSALIND   But have I not cause to weep?

CELIA   As good cause as one would desire, therefore weep.

ROSALIND   His very hair is of the dissembling colour.

CELIA Something browner than Judas's. Marry his
  kisses are Judas's own children.

ROSALIND I'faith his hair is of a good colour.

CELIA An excellent colour. Your chestnut was ever the
  only colour.

ROSALIND And his kissing is as full of sanctity as the
  touch of holy bread.

CELIA He hath bought a pair of cast lips of Diana. A
  nun of winter's sisterhood kisses not more
  religiously, the very ice of chastity is in them.

ROSALIND But why did he swear he would come this
  morning and comes not?

CELIA Nay certainly there is no truth in him.

ROSALIND Do you think so?

CELIA Yes, I think he is not a pick-purse nor a horse-
  stealer, but for his verity in love, I do think him as
  concave as a covered goblet or a worm-eaten nut.

ROSALIND Not true in love?

CELIA Yes, when he is in, but I think he is not in.

ROSALIND You have heard him swear downright he was.

CELIA 'Was' is not 'is'; besides, the oath of a lover is no
  stronger than the word of a tapster. They are both
  the confirmer of false reckonings. He attends here in
  the forest on the Duke your father.

ROSALIND I met the Duke yesterday and had much
  question with him. He asked me of what parentage I
  was: I told him of as good as he, so he laughed and let
  me go. But what talk we of fathers, when there is such
  a man as Orlando?

CELIA O that's a brave man! He writes brave verses,
  speaks brave words, swears brave oaths, and breaks
  them bravely, quite traverse, athwart the heart of his
  lover, as a puisny tilter that spurs his horse but on
  one side breaks his staff like a noble goose. But all's
  brave that youth mounts and folly guides. Who
  comes here?

Enter CORIN.

CORIN Mistress and master, you have oft enquir'd
  After the shepherd that complain'd of love,
  Who you saw sitting by me on the turf
  Praising the proud disdainful shepherdess
  That was his mistress.

CELIA   Well, and what of him?

CORIN If you will see a pageant truly play'd
  Between the pale complexion of true love
  And the red glow of scorn and proud disdain,
  Go hence a little, and I shall conduct you
  If you will mark it.

ROSALIND   O come, let us remove.
  The sight of lovers feedeth those in love.
  Bring us to this sight, and you shall say
  I'll prove a busy actor in their play.   *Exeunt.*

3.5   *Enter* SILVIUS *and* PHEBE.

SILVIUS Sweet Phebe do not scorn me, do not Phebe.

Say that you love me not, but say not so
In bitterness. The common executioner,
Whose heart th'accustom'd sight of death makes
  hard,
Falls not the axe upon the humbled neck   5
But first begs pardon. Will you sterner be
Than he that dies and lives by bloody drops?

Enter ROSALIND, CELIA *and* CORIN *behind.*

PHEBE I would not be thy executioner;
  I fly thee, for I would not injure thee.
  Thou tell'st me there is murder in mine eye: 10
  'Tis pretty, sure, and very probable,
  That eyes, that are the frail'st and softest things,
  Who shut their coward gates on atomies,
  Should be call'd tyrants, butchers, murderers.
  Now I do frown on thee with all my heart,   15
  And if mine eyes can wound, now let them kill thee.
  Now counterfeit to swoon: why now fall down,
  Or if thou canst not, O for shame, for shame,
  Lie not, to say mine eyes are murderers.
  Now show the wound mine eye hath made in thee.   20
  Scratch thee but with a pin, and there remains
  Some scar of it; lean upon a rush,
  The cicatrice and capable impressure
  Thy palm some moment keeps; but now mine eyes,
  Which I have darted at thee, hurt thee not,   25
  Nor, I am sure, there is no force in eyes
  That can do hurt.

SILVIUS   O dear Phebe,
  If ever, as that ever may be near,
  You meet in some fresh cheek the power of fancy,
  Then shall you know the wounds invisible   30
  That love's keen arrows make.

PHEBE   But till that time
  Come not thou near me; and when that time comes,
  Afflict me with thy mocks, pity me not,
  As till that time I shall not pity thee.

ROSALIND [*advancing*]
  And why I pray you? Who might be your mother,   35
  That you insult, exult, and all at once,
  Over the wretched? What though you have no beauty –
  As by my faith I see no more in you
  Than without candle may go dark to bed –
  Must you be therefore proud and pitiless?   40
  Why what means this? Why do you look on me?
  I see no more in you than in the ordinary
  Of Nature's sale-work. 'Od's my little life,
  I think she means to tangle my eyes too!
  No faith proud mistress, hope not after it.   45
  'Tis not your inky brows, your black silk hair,
  Your bugle eyeballs, nor your cheek of cream
  That can entame my spirits to your worship.
  You foolish shepherd, wherefore do you follow her
  Like foggy South puffing with wind and rain?   50
  You are a thousand times a properer man
  Than she a woman. 'Tis such fools as you

That makes the world full of ill-favour'd children.
'Tis not her glass but you that flatters her,
55 And out of you she sees herself more proper
Than any of her lineaments can show her.
But mistress, know yourself. Down on your knees
And thank heaven, fasting, for a good man's love;
For I must tell you friendly in your ear,
60 Sell when you can, you are not for all markets.
Cry the man mercy, love him, take his offer;
Foul is most foul, being foul to be a scoffer.
So take her to thee shepherd. Fare you well.
PHEBE   Sweet youth, I pray you chide a year together.
65 I had rather hear you chide than this man woo.
ROSALIND [*to Phebe*] He's fallen in love with your
foulness, [*to Silvius*] and she'll fall in love with my
anger. If it be so, as fast as she answers thee with
frowning looks, I'll sauce her with bitter words.
70 [*to Phebe*] Why look you so upon me?
PHEBE   For no ill will I bear you.
ROSALIND   I pray you do not fall in love with me,
For I am falser than vows made in wine.
Besides, I like you not. If you will know my house,
75 'Tis at the tuft of olives here hard by.
Will you go sister? Shepherd, ply her hard.
Come sister. Shepherdess, look on him better
And be not proud; though all the world could see,
None could be so abus'd in sight as he.
80 Come, to our flock.
                              Exeunt Rosalind, Celia and Corin.
PHEBE   Dead shepherd, now I find thy saw of might,
'Who ever lov'd that lov'd not at first sight?'
SILVIUS   Sweet Phebe!
PHEBE   Hah? What say'st thou, Silvius?
SILVIUS   Sweet Phebe pity me.
85 PHEBE   Why I am sorry for thee gentle Silvius.
SILVIUS   Wherever sorrow is, relief would be.
If you do sorrow at my grief in love,
By giving love, your sorrow and my grief
Were both extermined.
90 PHEBE   Thou hast my love. Is not that neighbourly?
SILVIUS   I would have you.
PHEBE   Why that were covetousness.
Silvius, the time was that I hated thee;
And yet it is not that I bear thee love,
But since that thou canst talk of love so well,
95 Thy company, which erst was irksome to me,
I will endure; and I'll employ thee too.
But do not look for further recompense
Than thine own gladness that thou art employ'd.
SILVIUS   So holy and so perfect is my love,
100 And I in such a poverty of grace,
That I shall think it a most plenteous crop
To glean the broken ears after the man
That the main harvest reaps. Loose now and then
A scatter'd smile, and that I'll live upon.
PHEBE
105 Know'st thou the youth that spoke to me erewhile?

SILVIUS   Not very well, but I have met him oft,
And he hath bought the cottage and the bounds
That the old carlot once was master of.
PHEBE   Think not I love him, though I ask for him.
'Tis but a peevish boy – yet he talks well –   110
But what care I for words? Yet words do well
When he that speaks them pleases those that hear.
It is a pretty youth – not very pretty –
But sure he's proud, and yet his pride becomes him.
He'll make a proper man. The best thing in him   115
Is his complexion; and faster than his tongue
Did make offence, his eye did heal it up.
He is not very tall, yet for his years he's tall.
His leg is but so so; and yet 'tis well.
There was a pretty redness in his lip,   120
A little riper and more lusty red
Than that mix'd in his cheek; 'twas just the
    difference
Betwixt the constant red and mingled damask.
There be some women Silvius, had they mark'd him
In parcels as I did, would have gone near   125
To fall in love with him: but for my part
I love him not, nor hate him not; and yet
I have more cause to hate him than to love him.
For what had he to do to chide at me?
He said mine eyes were black, and my hair black,   130
And now I am remember'd, scorn'd at me.
I marvel why I answer'd not again.
But that's all one. Omittance is no quittance.
I'll write to him a very taunting letter,
And thou shalt bear it, wilt thou Silvius?   135
SILVIUS   Phebe, with all my heart.
PHEBE   I'll write it straight.
The matter's in my head, and in my heart.
I will be bitter with him and passing short.
Go with me Silvius.   *Exeunt.*

4.1   *Enter* ROSALIND, CELIA *and* JAQUES.

JAQUES   I prithee, pretty youth, let me be better
acquainted with thee.
ROSALIND   They say you are a melancholy fellow.
JAQUES   I am so. I do love it better than laughing.
ROSALIND   Those that are in extremity of either are   5
abominable fellows, and betray themselves to every
modern censure, worse than drunkards.
JAQUES   Why, 'tis good to be sad and say nothing.
ROSALIND   Why then 'tis good to be a post.
JAQUES   I have neither the scholar's melancholy, which   10
is emulation; nor the musician's, which is fantastical;
nor the courtier's, which is proud; nor the soldier's,
which is ambitious; nor the lawyer's, which is politic;
nor the lady's, which is nice; nor the lover's, which is
all these; but it is a melancholy of mine own,   15
compounded of many simples, extracted from many
objects, and indeed the sundry contemplation of my
travels, in which my often rumination wraps me in a
most humorous sadness.

ROSALIND   A traveller! By my faith, you have great reason to be sad. I fear you have sold your own lands to see other men's. Then to have seen much and to have nothing is to have rich eyes and poor hands.

JAQUES   Yes, I have gained my experience.

Enter ORLANDO.

ROSALIND   And your experience makes you sad. I had rather have a fool to make me merry than experience to make me sad, and to travel for it too!

ORLANDO   Good day and happiness, dear Rosalind.

JAQUES   Nay then God buy you, and you talk in blank verse!

ROSALIND   Farewell Monsieur Traveller. Look you lisp, and wear strange suits; disable all the benefits of your own country; be out of love with your nativity, and almost chide God for making you that countenance you are; or I will scarce think you have swam in a gondola.   *Exit Jaques.*
Why how now Orlando, where have you been all this while? You a lover! And you serve me such another trick, never come in my sight more.

ORLANDO   My fair Rosalind, I come within an hour of my promise.

ROSALIND   Break an hour's promise in love! He that will divide a minute into a thousand parts, and break but a part of the thousand part of a minute in the affairs of love, it may be said of him that Cupid hath clapped him o'th' shoulder, but I'll warrant him heart-whole.

ORLANDO   Pardon me dear Rosalind.

ROSALIND   Nay, and you be so tardy, come no more in my sight. I had as lief be wooed of a snail.

ORLANDO   Of a snail?

ROSALIND   Ay, of a snail. For though he comes slowly, he carries his house on his head; a better jointure I think than you make a woman. Besides, he brings his destiny with him.

ORLANDO   What's that?

ROSALIND   Why horns – which such as you are fain to be beholding to your wives for: but he comes armed in his fortune, and prevents the slander of his wife.

ORLANDO   Virtue is no horn-maker; and my Rosalind is virtuous.

ROSALIND   And I am your Rosalind.

CELIA   It pleases him to call you so: but he hath a Rosalind of a better leer than you.

ROSALIND   Come, woo me, woo me; for now I am in a holiday humour and like enough to consent. What would you say to me now, and I were your very very Rosalind?

ORLANDO   I would kiss before I spoke.

ROSALIND   Nay, you were better speak first, and when you were gravelled for lack of matter, you might take occasion to kiss. Very good orators when they are out, they will spit, and for lovers lacking – God warr'nt us! – matter, the cleanliest shift is to kiss.

ORLANDO   How if the kiss be denied?

ROSALIND   Then she puts you to entreaty, and there begins new matter.

ORLANDO   Who could be out, being before his beloved mistress?

ROSALIND   Marry that should you, if I were your mistress, or I should think my honesty ranker than my wit.

ORLANDO   What, of my suit?

ROSALIND   Not out of your apparel, and yet out of your suit. Am not I your Rosalind?

ORLANDO   I take some joy to say you are, because I would be talking of her.

ROSALIND   Well, in her person, I say I will not have you.

ORLANDO   Then in mine own person, I die.

ROSALIND   No, faith, die by attorney. The poor world is almost six thousand years old, and in all this time there was not any man died in his own person, videlicet, in a love-cause. Troilus had his brains dashed out with a Grecian club, yet he did what he could to die before, and he is one of the patterns of love. Leander, he would have lived many a fair year though Hero had turned nun, if it had not been for a hot mid summer night; for, good youth, he went but forth to wash him in the Hellespont, and being taken with the cramp, was drowned, and the foolish chroniclers of that age found it was Hero of Sestos. But these are all lies: men have died from time to time and worms have eaten them, but not for love.

ORLANDO   I would not have my right Rosalind of this mind, for I protest her frown might kill me.

ROSALIND   By this hand, it will not kill a fly. But come, now I will be your Rosalind in a more coming-on disposition; and ask me what you will, I will grant it.

ORLANDO   Then love me Rosalind.

ROSALIND   Yes faith will I, Fridays and Saturdays and all.

ORLANDO   And wilt thou have me?

ROSALIND   Ay, and twenty such.

ORLANDO   What sayest thou?

ROSALIND   Are you not good?

ORLANDO   I hope so.

ROSALIND   Why then, can one desire too much of a good thing? Come sister, you shall be the priest and marry us. Give me your hand Orlando. What do you say sister?

ORLANDO   Pray thee marry us.

CELIA   I cannot say the words.

ROSALIND   You must begin, 'Will you Orlando – '

CELIA   Go to. Will you Orlando have to wife this Rosalind?

ORLANDO   I will.

ROSALIND   Ay, but when?

ORLANDO   Why now, as fast as she can marry us.

ROSALIND   Then you must say 'I take thee Rosalind for wife.'

ORLANDO   I take thee Rosalind for wife.

ROSALIND   I might ask you for your commission; but I

do take thee Orlando for my husband. There's a girl goes before the priest, and certainly a woman's thought runs before her actions.

135 ORLANDO So do all thoughts, they are winged.

ROSALIND Now tell me how long you would have her, after you have possessed her?

ORLANDO For ever, and a day.

ROSALIND Say a day, without the ever. No, no, Orlando, 140 men are April when they woo, December when they wed. Maids are May when they are maids, but the sky changes when they are wives. I will be more jealous of thee than a Barbary cock-pigeon over his hen, more clamorous than a parrot against rain, more new-145 fangled than an ape, more giddy in my desires than a monkey. I will weep for nothing, like Diana in the fountain, and I will do that when you are disposed to be merry. I will laugh like a hyen, and that when thou art inclined to sleep.

150 ORLANDO But will my Rosalind do so?

ROSALIND By my life, she will do as I do.

ORLANDO O but she is wise.

ROSALIND Or else she could not have the wit to do this. The wiser, the waywarder. Make the doors upon a 155 woman's wit, and it will out at the casement; shut that, and 'twill out at the keyhole; stop that, 'twill fly with the smoke out at the chimney.

ORLANDO A man that had a wife with such a wit, he might say, 'Wit, whither wilt?'

160 ROSALIND Nay, you might keep that check for it, till you met your wife's wit going to your neighbour's bed.

ORLANDO And what wit could wit have to excuse that?

ROSALIND Marry to say she came to seek you there. You shall never take her without her answer, unless you 165 take her without her tongue. O that woman that cannot make her fault her husband's occasion, let her never nurse her child herself, for she will breed it like a fool.

ORLANDO For these two hours Rosalind, I will leave 170 thee.

ROSALIND Alas, dear love, I cannot lack thee two hours.

ORLANDO I must attend the Duke at dinner. By two o'clock I will be with thee again.

ROSALIND Ay, go your ways, go your ways. I knew what 175 you would prove. My friends told me as much, and I thought no less. That flattering tongue of yours won me. 'Tis but one cast away, and so, come death! Two o'clock is your hour?

ORLANDO Ay, sweet Rosalind.

180 ROSALIND By my troth, and in good earnest, and so God mend me, and by all pretty oaths that are not dangerous, if you break one jot of your promise, or come one minute behind your hour, I will think you the most pathetical break-promise, and the most 185 hollow lover, and the most unworthy of her you call Rosalind, that may be chosen out of the gross band of the unfaithful: therefore beware my censure and keep your promise.

ORLANDO With no less religion than if thou wert indeed 190 my Rosalind. So adieu.

ROSALIND Well, Time is the old justice that examines all such offenders, and let Time try. Adieu.

Exit Orlando.

CELIA You have simply misused our sex in your love-prate. We must have your doublet and hose plucked 195 over your head, and show the world what the bird hath done to her own nest.

ROSALIND O coz, coz, coz, my pretty little coz, that thou didst know how many fathom deep I am in love! But it cannot be sounded. My affection hath an 200 unknown bottom, like the Bay of Portugal.

CELIA Or rather bottomless, that as fast as you pour affection in, it runs out.

ROSALIND No. That same wicked bastard of Venus, that was begot of thought, conceived of spleen and born of 205 madness, that blind rascally boy that abuses everyone's eyes because his own are out, let him be judge how deep I am in love. I'll tell thee Aliena, I cannot be out of the sight of Orlando. I'll go find a shadow and sigh till he come.

CELIA And I'll sleep. *Exeunt.* 210

4.2 *Enter* JAQUES *and* Lords, *like foresters.*

JAQUES Which is he that killed the deer?

1 LORD Sir, it was I.

JAQUES Let's present him to the Duke like a Roman conqueror; and it would do well to set the deer's horns upon his head for a branch of victory. Have you no 5 song, forester, for this purpose?

2 LORD Yes sir.

JAQUES Sing it. 'Tis no matter how it be in tune, so it make noise enough.

[*Given a note, they sing.*]

LORDS What shall he have that kill'd the deer? 10
His leather skin and horns to wear.
Then sing him home. The rest shall bear
This burden.
Take thou no scorn to wear the horn,
It was a crest ere thou wast born. 15
Thy father's father wore it,
And thy father bore it.
The horn, the horn, the lusty horn,
Is not a thing to laugh to scorn. *Exeunt.*

4.3 *Enter* ROSALIND *and* CELIA.

ROSALIND How say you now, is it not past two o'clock? And here much Orlando!

CELIA I warrant you, with pure love and troubled brain, he hath ta'en his bow and arrows, and is gone forth to sleep. Look who comes here. 5

Enter SILVIUS.

SILVIUS My errand is to you, fair youth.

My gentle Phebe did bid me give you this.
I know not the contents, but as I guess
By the stern brow and waspish action
Which she did use as she was writing of it,
It bears an angry tenour. Pardon me.
I am but as a guiltless messenger.

ROSALIND   Patience herself would startle at this letter,
And play the swaggerer. Bear this, bear all.
She says I am not fair, that I lack manners.
She calls me proud, and that she could not love me,
Were man as rare as phoenix. 'Od's my will,
Her love is not the hare that I do hunt;
Why writes she so to me? Well shepherd, well,
This is a letter of your own device.

SILVIUS   No, I protest, I know not the contents,
Phebe did write it.

ROSALIND   Come, come, you are a fool,
And turn'd into the extremity of love.
I saw her hand. She has a leathern hand,
A freestone-colour'd hand. I verily did think
That her old gloves were on, but 'twas her hands.
She has a hussif's hand. But that's no matter.
I say she never did invent this letter.
This is a man's invention, and his hand.

SILVIUS   Sure it is hers.

ROSALIND   Why, 'tis a boisterous and a cruel style,
A style for challengers. Why, she defies me,
Like Turk to Christian. Women's gentle brain
Could not drop forth such giant-rude invention,
Such Ethiop words, blacker in their effect
Than in their countenance. Will you hear the letter?

SILVIUS   So please you, for I never heard it yet;
Yet heard too much of Phebe's cruelty.

ROSALIND
She Phebes me. Mark how the tyrant writes.
[*Reads.*] *Art thou god to shepherd turn'd,*
        That a maiden's heart hath burn'd?
Can a woman rail thus?

SILVIUS   Call you this railing?

ROSALIND
[*Reads.*] *Why, thy godhead laid apart,*
        Warr'st thou with a woman's heart?
Did you ever hear such railing?
        Whiles the eye of man did woo me,
        That could do no vengeance to me.
Meaning me a beast.
        If the scorn of your bright eyne
        Have power to raise such love in mine,
        Alack, in me, what strange effect
        Would they work in mild aspect?
        Whiles you chid me, I did love;
        How then might your prayers move?
        He that brings this love to thee
        Little knows this love in me;
        And by him seal up thy mind,
        Whether that thy youth and kind
        Will the faithful offer take

        Of me and all that I can make,
        Or else by him my love deny,
        And then I'll study how to die.

SILVIUS   Call you this chiding?

CELIA   Alas poor shepherd!   65

ROSALIND   Do you pity him? No, he deserves no pity.
Wilt thou love such a woman? What, to make thee an
instrument and play false strains upon thee? Not to
be endured! Well, go your way to her, for I see love
hath made thee a tame snake, and say this to her: that   70
if she love me, I charge her to love thee. If she will not,
I will never have her, unless thou entreat for her. If you
be a true lover, hence, and not a word; for here comes
more company.   *Exit Silvius.*

Enter OLIVER.

OLIVER
Good morrow, fair ones. Pray you, if you know,   75
Where in the purlieus of this forest stands
A sheep-cote fenc'd about with olive-trees?

CELIA
West of this place, down in the neighbour bottom.
The rank of osiers by the murmuring stream
Left on your right hand, brings you to the place.   80
But at this hour the house doth keep itself,
There's none within.

OLIVER   If that an eye may profit by a tongue,
Then should I know you by description,
Such garments and such years. 'The boy is fair,   85
Of female favour, and bestows himself
Like a ripe sister. The woman low,
And browner than her brother.' Are not you
The owner of the house I did enquire for?

CELIA   It is no boast, being ask'd, to say we are.   90

OLIVER   Orlando doth commend him to you both,
And to that youth he calls his Rosalind
He sends this bloody napkin. Are you he?

ROSALIND   I am. What must we understand by this?

OLIVER   Some of my shame, if you will know of me   95
What man I am, and how, and why, and where
This handkerchief was stain'd.

CELIA   I pray you tell it.

OLIVER
When last the young Orlando parted from you,
He left a promise to return again
Within an hour; and pacing through the forest,   100
Chewing the food of sweet and bitter fancy,
Lo what befell! He threw his eye aside,
And mark what object did present itself.
Under an old oak, whose boughs were moss'd with
        age
And high top bald with dry antiquity,   105
A wretched ragged man, o'ergrown with hair,
Lay sleeping on his back. About his neck
A green and gilded snake had wreath'd itself,
Who with her head, nimble in threats, approach'd
The opening of his mouth. But suddenly   110

Seeing Orlando, it unlink'd itself,
And with indented glides did slip away
Into a bush, under which bush's shade
A lioness, with udders all drawn dry,
115   Lay couching head on ground, with catlike watch
When that the sleeping man should stir; for 'tis
The royal disposition of that beast
To prey on nothing that doth seem as dead.
This seen, Orlando did approach the man,
120   And found it was his brother, his elder brother.
CELIA   O I have heard him speak of that same brother,
And he did render him the most unnatural
That liv'd amongst men.
OLIVER   And well he might so do,
For well I know he was unnatural.
125   ROSALIND   But to Orlando. Did he leave him there,
Food to the suck'd and hungry lioness?
OLIVER   Twice did he turn his back, and purpos'd so.
But kindness, nobler ever than revenge,
And nature, stronger than his just occasion,
130   Made him give battle to the lioness,
Who quickly fell before him; in which hurtling
From miserable slumber I awak'd.
CELIA   Are you his brother?
ROSALIND   Was't you he rescu'd?
CELIA   Was't you that did so oft contrive to kill him?
135   OLIVER   'Twas I. But 'tis not I. I do not shame
To tell you what I was, since my conversion
So sweetly tastes, being the thing I am.
ROSALIND   But for the bloody napkin.
OLIVER   By and by.
When from the first to last betwixt us two
140   Tears our recountments had most kindly bath'd –
As how I came into that desert place –
In brief, he led me to the gentle Duke,
Who gave me fresh array and entertainment,
Committing me unto my brother's love,
145   Who led me instantly unto his cave,
There stripp'd himself, and here upon his arm
The lioness had torn some flesh away,
Which all this while had bled; and now he fainted,
And cried in fainting upon Rosalind.
150   Brief, I recover'd him, bound up his wound,
And after some small space, being strong at heart,
He sent me hither, stranger as I am,
To tell this story, that you might excuse
His broken promise, and to give this napkin,
155   Dy'd in his blood, unto the shepherd youth
That he in sport doth call his Rosalind.
[*Rosalind faints.*]
CELIA   Why how now Ganymede! Sweet Ganymede!
OLIVER   Many will swoon when they do look on blood.
CELIA   There is more in it. Cousin Ganymede!
160   OLIVER   Look, he recovers.
ROSALIND   I would I were at home.
CELIA   We'll lead you thither. I pray you, will you take
him by the arm?

OLIVER   Be of good cheer, youth. You a man! You lack a
man's heart.   165
ROSALIND   I do so, I confess it. Ah, sirrah, a body would
think this was well counterfeited. I pray you tell your
brother how well I counterfeited. Heigh-ho!
OLIVER   This was not counterfeit, there is too great
testimony in your complexion that it was a passion of   170
earnest.
ROSALIND   Counterfeit, I assure you.
OLIVER   Well then, take a good heart, and counterfeit to
be a man.
ROSALIND   So I do. But i'faith, I should have been a   175
woman by right.
CELIA   Come, you look paler and paler. Pray you draw
homewards. Good sir, go with us.
OLIVER   That will I. For I must bear answer back how
you excuse my brother, Rosalind.   180
ROSALIND   I shall devise something. But I pray you
commend my counterfeiting to him. Will you go?
Exeunt.

5.1   *Enter* TOUCHSTONE *and* AUDREY.

TOUCHSTONE   We shall find a time, Audrey. Patience
gentle Audrey.
AUDREY   Faith the priest was good enough, for all the
old gentleman's saying.
TOUCHSTONE   A most wicked Sir Oliver, Audrey, a most   5
vile Martext. But Audrey, there is a youth here in the
forest lays claim to you.
AUDREY   Ay, I know who 'tis. He hath no interest in me
in the world. Here comes the man you mean.

Enter WILLIAM.

TOUCHSTONE   It is meat and drink to me to see a clown.   10
By my troth, we that have good wits have much to
answer for: we shall be flouting: we cannot hold.
WILLIAM   Good ev'n Audrey.
AUDREY   God ye good ev'n William.
WILLIAM   And good ev'n to you sir.   15
TOUCHSTONE   Good ev'n gentle friend. Cover thy head,
cover thy head. Nay prithee be covered. How old are
you friend?
WILLIAM   Five and twenty sir.
TOUCHSTONE   A ripe age. Is thy name William?   20
WILLIAM   William, sir.
TOUCHSTONE   A fair name. Was't born i'th' forest here?
WILLIAM   Ay sir, I thank God.
TOUCHSTONE   'Thank God.' A good answer. Art rich?
WILLIAM   Faith sir, so so.   25
TOUCHSTONE   'So so' is good, very good, very excellent
good. And yet it is not, it is but so so. Art thou wise?
WILLIAM   Ay sir, I have a pretty wit.
TOUCHSTONE   Why, thou sayest well. I do now
remember a saying: 'The fool doth think he is wise,   30
but the wiseman knows himself to be a fool'. The
heathen philosopher, when he had a desire to eat a

grape, would open his lips when he put it into his mouth, meaning thereby that grapes were made to eat and lips to open. You do love this maid?

WILLIAM   I do sir.

TOUCHSTONE   Give me your hand. Art thou learned?

WILLIAM   No sir.

TOUCHSTONE   Then learn this of me. To have is to have: for it is a figure in rhetoric that drink, being poured out of a cup into a glass, by filling the one doth empty the other. For all your writers do consent that *ipse* is he. Now you are not *ipse,* for I am he.

WILLIAM   Which he sir?

TOUCHSTONE   He sir that must marry this woman. Therefore you clown, abandon – which is in the vulgar leave – the society – which in the boorish is company – of this female – which in the common is woman. Which together is, abandon the society of this female, or clown thou perishest; or to thy better understanding, diest; or, to wit, I kill thee, make thee away, translate thy life into death, thy liberty into bondage. I will deal in poison with thee, or in bastinado, or in steel. I will bandy with thee in faction; I will o'er-run thee with policy; I will kill thee a hundred and fifty ways. Therefore tremble and depart.

AUDREY   Do, good William.

WILLIAM   God rest you merry, sir.   *Exit.*

Enter CORIN.

CORIN   Our master and mistress seeks you. Come away, away.

TOUCHSTONE   Trip Audrey, trip Audrey. I attend, I attend.   *Exeunt.*

5.2   *Enter* ORLANDO *and* OLIVER.

ORLANDO   Is't possible, that on so little acquaintance you should like her? That but seeing, you should love her? And loving woo? And wooing, she should grant? And will you persever to enjoy her?

OLIVER   Neither call the giddiness of it in question, the poverty of her, the small acquaintance, my sudden wooing, nor her sudden consenting. But say with me, I love Aliena; say with her that she loves me; consent with both, that we may enjoy each other. It shall be to your good; for my father's house and all the revenue that was old Sir Rowland's will I estate upon you, and here live and die a shepherd.

ORLANDO   You have my consent. Let your wedding be tomorrow. Thither will I invite the Duke and all's contented followers. Go you and prepare Aliena; for look you, here comes my Rosalind.

Enter ROSALIND.

ROSALIND   God save you brother.

OLIVER   And you fair sister.   *Exit.*

ROSALIND   O my dear Orlando, how it grieves me to see thee wear thy heart in a scarf!

ORLANDO   It is my arm.

ROSALIND   I thought thy heart had been wounded with the claws of a lion.

ORLANDO   Wounded it is, but with the eyes of a lady.

ROSALIND   Did your brother tell you how I counterfeited to swoon, when he showed me your handkerchief?

ORLANDO   Ay, and greater wonders than that.

ROSALIND   O, I know where you are. Nay, 'tis true. There was never anything so sudden, but the fight of two rams, and Caesar's thrasonical brag of I came, saw, and overcame. For your brother and my sister no sooner met, but they looked; no sooner looked, but they loved; no sooner loved, but they sighed; no sooner sighed, but they asked one another the reason; no sooner knew the reason, but they sought the remedy. And in these degrees have they made a pair of stairs to marriage, which they will climb incontinent, or else be incontinent before marriage. They are in the very wrath of love, and they will together. Clubs cannot part them.

ORLANDO   They shall be married tomorrow, and I will bid the Duke to the nuptial. But O, how bitter a thing it is to look into happiness through another man's eyes! By so much the more shall I tomorrow be at the height of heart-heaviness, by how much I shall think my brother happy in having what he wishes for.

ROSALIND   Why then tomorrow I cannot serve your turn for Rosalind?

ORLANDO   I can live no longer by thinking.

ROSALIND   I will weary you then no longer with idle talking. Know of me then – for now I speak to some purpose – that I know you are a gentleman of good conceit. I speak not this that you should bear a good opinion of my knowledge, insomuch I say I know you are; neither do I labour for a greater esteem than may in some little measure draw a belief from you to do yourself good, and not to grace me. Believe then, if you please, that I can do strange things. I have since I was three year old conversed with a magician, most profound in his art and yet not damnable. If you do love Rosalind so near the heart as your gesture cries it out, when your brother marries Aliena, shall you marry her. I know into what straits of fortune she is driven, and it is not impossible to me, if it appear not inconvenient to you, to set her before your eyes tomorrow, human as she is, and without any danger.

ORLANDO   Speak'st thou in sober meanings?

ROSALIND   By my life I do, which I tender dearly, though I say I am a magician. Therefore put you in your best array, bid your friends; for if you will be married tomorrow, you shall; and to Rosalind if you will. Look, here comes a lover of mine, and a lover of hers.

Enter SILVIUS *and* PHEBE.

75 PHEBE   Youth, you have done me much ungentleness,
       To show the letter that I writ to you.
    ROSALIND   I care not if I have. It is my study
       To seem despiteful and ungentle to you.
       You are there follow'd by a faithful shepherd,
80   Look upon him, love him. He worships you.
    PHEBE   Good shepherd, tell this youth what 'tis to love.
    SILVIUS   It is to be all made of sighs and tears,
       And so am I for Phebe.
    PHEBE   And I for Ganymede.
85 ORLANDO   And I for Rosalind.
    ROSALIND   And I for no woman.
    SILVIUS   It is to be all made of faith and service,
       And so am I for Phebe.
    PHEBE   And I for Ganymede.
90 ORLANDO   And I for Rosalind.
    ROSALIND   And I for no woman.
    SILVIUS   It is to be all made of fantasy,
       All made of passion and all made of wishes,
       All adoration, duty and observance,
95   All humbleness, all patience and impatience,
       All purity, all trial, all observance;
       And so am I for Phebe.
    PHEBE   And so am I for Ganymede.
    ORLANDO   And so am I for Rosalind.
100 ROSALIND   And so am I for no woman.
    PHEBE [*to Rosalind*]   If this be so, why blame you me to
       love you?
    SILVIUS [*to Phebe*]   If this be so, why blame you me to
       love you?
105 ORLANDO   If this be so, why blame you me to love you?
    ROSALIND   Who do you speak to 'Why blame you me to
       love you?'?
    ORLANDO   To her that is not here, nor doth not hear.
    ROSALIND   Pray you no more of this, 'tis like the howling
110   of Irish wolves against the moon. [*to Silvius*] I will
       help you if I can. [*to Phebe*] I would love you if I
       could. Tomorrow meet me all together.   [*to Phebe*] I
       will marry you, if ever I marry woman, and I'll be
       married tomorrow. [*to Orlando*] I will satisfy you, if
115   ever I satisfied man, and you shall be married
       tomorrow. [*to Silvius*] I will content you, if what
       pleases you contents you, and you shall be married
       tomorrow. [*to Orlando*] As you love Rosalind meet.
       [*to Silvius*] As you love Phebe meet. And as I love no
120   woman, I'll meet. So fare you well. I have left you
       commands.
    SILVIUS   I'll not fail, if I live.
    PHEBE   Nor I.
    ORLANDO   Nor I.   *Exeunt.*

5.3   *Enter* TOUCHSTONE *and* AUDREY.

    TOUCHSTONE   Tomorrow is the joyful day, Audrey.
       Tomorrow will we be married.

AUDREY   I do desire it with all my heart; and I hope it is
    no dishonest desire, to desire to be a woman of the
    world. Here come two of the banished Duke's pages.   5

Enter two Pages.

1 PAGE   Well met honest gentleman.
TOUCHSTONE   By my troth well met. Come, sit, sit, and
    a song.
2 PAGE   We are for you. Sit i'th' middle.
1 PAGE   Shall we clap into't roundly, without hawking or   10
    spitting or saying we are hoarse, which are the only
    prologues to a bad voice?
2 PAGE   I'faith, i'faith, and both in a tune like two gipsies
    on a horse.
    [*They sing.*]

       It was a lover and his lass,   15
          With a hey and a ho and a hey nonino,
       That o'er the green corn-field did pass,
          In spring-time, the only pretty ring-time,
       When birds do sing, hey ding a ding, ding,
       Sweet lovers love the spring.   20

       Between the acres of the rye,
          With a hey and a ho and a hey nonino,
       These pretty country-folks would lie,
          In spring-time, the only pretty ring-time,
       When birds do sing, hey ding a ding, ding,   25
       Sweet lovers love the spring.

       This carol they began that hour,
          With a hey and a ho and a hey nonino,
       How that a life was but a flower,
          In spring-time, the only pretty ring-time,   30
       When birds do sing, hey ding a ding, ding,
       Sweet lovers love the spring.

       And therefore take the present time,
          With a hey and a ho and a hey nonino,
       For love is crowned with the prime,   35
          In spring-time, the only pretty ring-time,
       When birds do sing, hey ding a ding, ding,
       Sweet lovers love the spring.

TOUCHSTONE   Truly young gentlemen, though there
    was no great matter in the ditty, yet the note was very   40
    untuneable.
1 PAGE   You are deceived sir. We kept time, we lost not
    our time.
TOUCHSTONE   By my troth yes. I count it but time lost
    to hear such a foolish song. God buy you, and God   45
    mend your voices. Come Audrey.   *Exeunt.*

5.4   *Enter* DUKE SENIOR, AMIENS, JAQUES,
          ORLANDO, OLIVER *and* CELIA.

DUKE SENIOR   Dost thou believe, Orlando, that the boy
    Can do all this that he hath promised?
ORLANDO
    I sometimes do believe, and sometimes do not,

As those that fear they hope, and know they fear.

Enter ROSALIND, SILVIUS *and* PHEBE.

ROSALIND
Patience once more, whiles our compact is urg'd.
You say, if I bring in your Rosalind,
You will bestow her on Orlando here?

DUKE SENIOR
That would I, had I kingdoms to give with her.

ROSALIND
And you say you will have her, when I bring her?

ORLANDO   That would I, were I of all kingdoms king.

ROSALIND   You say you'll marry me, if I be willing?

PHEBE   That will I, should I die the hour after.

ROSALIND   But if you do refuse to marry me,
You'll give yourself to this most faithful shepherd?

PHEBE   So is the bargain.

ROSALIND   You say that you'll have Phebe if she will?

SILVIUS
Though to have her and death were both one thing.

ROSALIND
I have promis'd to make all this matter even.
Keep you your word, O Duke, to give your daughter,
You yours, Orlando, to receive his daughter;
Keep you your word Phebe, that you'll marry me,
Or else refusing me to wed this shepherd.
Keep your word Silvius, that you'll marry her
If she refuse me; and from hence I go
To makes these doubts all even.

Exeunt Rosalind and Celia.

DUKE SENIOR   I do remember in this shepherd boy
Some lively touches of my daughter's favour.

ORLANDO   My lord, the first time that I ever saw him,
Methought he was a brother to your daughter.
But my good lord, this boy is forest-born,
And hath been tutored in the rudiments
Of many desperate studies, by his uncle,
Whom he reports to be a great magician,
Obscured in the circle of this forest.

JAQUES   There is sure another flood toward, and these
couples are coming to the ark. Here comes a pair of very
strange beasts, which in all tongues are called fools.

Enter TOUCHSTONE *and* AUDREY.

TOUCHSTONE   Salutation and greeting to you all.

JAQUES   Good my lord, bid him welcome. This is the
motley-minded gentleman that I have so often met in
the forest. He hath been a courtier he swears.

TOUCHSTONE   If any man doubt that, let him put me to
my purgation. I have trod a measure, I have flattered a
lady, I have been politic with my friend, smooth with
mine enemy, I have undone three tailors, I have had
four quarrels, and like to have fought one.

JAQUES   And how was that ta'en up?

TOUCHSTONE   Faith we met, and found the quarrel was
upon the seventh cause.

JAQUES   How seventh cause? Good my lord, like this   50
fellow.

DUKE SENIOR   I like him very well.

TOUCHSTONE   God 'ild you sir, I desire you of the like.
I press in here, sir, amongst the rest of the country
copulatives, to swear and to forswear, according as   55
marriage binds and blood breaks. A poor virgin sir, an
ill-favoured thing sir, but mine own; a poor humour of
mine sir, to take that that no man else will. Rich
honesty dwells like a miser sir, in a poor house, as your
pearl in your foul oyster.   60

DUKE SENIOR   By my faith, he is very swift and
sententious.

TOUCHSTONE   According to the fool's bolt sir, and such
dulcet diseases.

JAQUES   But for the seventh cause. How did you find the   65
quarrel on the seventh cause?

TOUCHSTONE   Upon a lie seven times removed. (Bear
your body more seeming, Audrey.) As thus sir. I did
dislike the cut of a certain courtier's beard; he sent me
word, if I said his beard was not well cut, he was in the   70
mind it was; this is called the Retort Courteous. If I
sent him word again, it was not well cut, he would
send me word he cut it to please himself; this is called
the Quip Modest. If again it was not well cut, he
disabled my judgement; this is called the Reply   75
Churlish. If again it was not well cut, he would answer
I spake not true; this is called the Reproof Valiant. If
again it was not well cut, he would say, I lie; this is
called the Countercheck Quarrelsome. And so to the
Lie Circumstantial and the Lie Direct.   80

JAQUES   And how oft did you say his beard was not well
cut?

TOUCHSTONE   I durst go no further than the Lie
Circumstantial, nor he durst not give me the Lie
Direct. And so we measured swords and parted.   85

JAQUES   Can you nominate in order now the degrees of
the lie?

TOUCHSTONE   O sir, we quarrel in print, by the book; as
you have books for good manners. I will name you the
degrees. The first, the Retort Courteous; the   90
second, the Quip Modest; the third, the Reply
Churlish; the fourth, the Reproof Valiant; the fifth,
the Countercheck Quarrelsome; the sixth, the Lie
with Circumstance; the seventh, the Lie Direct. All
these you may avoid but the Lie Direct; and you may   95
avoid that too, with an If. I knew when seven justices
could not take up a quarrel, but when the parties were
met themselves, one of them thought but of an If, as,
'If you said so, then I said so'. And they shook hands
and swore brothers. Your If is the only peacemaker: 100
much virtue in If.

JAQUES   Is not this a rare fellow my Lord? He's as good
at anything, and yet a fool.

DUKE SENIOR   He uses his folly like a stalking-horse, and
under the presentation of that he shoots his wit.   105

Enter HYMEN, ROSALIND *and* CELIA. *Still music.*

HYMEN   Then is there mirth in heaven,
When earthly things made even
Atone together.
Good Duke receive thy daughter,
110   Hymen from heaven brought her,
Yea brought her hither,
That thou mightst join her hand with his
Whose heart within his bosom is.

ROSALIND [*to the Duke*]
To you I give myself, for I am yours.
115   [*to Orlando*] To you I give myself, for I am yours.

DUKE SENIOR
If there be truth in sight, you are my daughter.

ORLANDO
If there be truth in sight, you are my Rosalind.

PHEBE   If sight and shape be true,
Why then my love adieu.

120   ROSALIND   I'll have no father, if you be not he.
I'll have no husband, if you be not he.
Nor ne'er wed woman, if you be not she.

HYMEN   Peace ho! I bar confusion.
'Tis I must make conclusion
125   Of these most strange events.
Here's eight that must take hands
To join in Hymen's bands,
If truth holds true contents.
You and you no cross shall part.
130   You and you are heart in heart.
You to his love must accord,
Or have a woman to your lord.
You and you are sure together,
As the winter to foul weather.
135   Whiles a wedlock hymn we sing,
Feed yourselves with questioning,
That reason wonder may diminish
How thus we met, and these things finish.

Song.
Wedding is great Juno's crown,
140   O blessed bond of board and bed.
'Tis Hymen peoples every town;
High wedlock then be honoured.
Honour, high honour and renown
To Hymen, god of every town.

DUKE SENIOR
145   O my dear niece, welcome thou art to me,
Even daughter welcome, in no less degree.

PHEBE [*to Silvius*]
I will not eat my word; now thou art mine,
Thy faith my fancy to thee doth combine.

Enter JACQUES DE BOYS.

JAQUES DE BOYS
Let me have audience for a word or two.
150   I am the second son of old Sir Rowland

That bring these tidings to this fair assembly.
Duke Frederick hearing how that every day
Men of great worth resorted to this forest,
Address'd a mighty power, which were on foot
In his own conduct, purposely to take   155
His brother here, and put him to the sword.
And to the skirts of this wild wood he came,
Where, meeting with an old religious man,
After some question with him, was converted
Both from his enterprise and from the world,   160
His crown bequeathing to his banish'd brother,
And all their lands restor'd to them again
That were with him exil'd. This to be true,
I do engage my life.

DUKE SENIOR   Welcome young man.
Thou offer'st fairly to thy brothers' wedding;   165
To one his lands withheld, and to the other
A land itself at large, a potent dukedom.
First, in this forest, let us do those ends
That here were well begun and well begot:
And after, every of this happy number   170
That have endur'd shrewd days and nights with us,
Shall share the good of our returned fortune,
According to the measure of their states.
Meantime forget this new-fall'n dignity,
And fall into our rustic revelry.   175
Play music, and you brides and bridegrooms all,
With measure heap'd in joy, to th'measures fall.

JAQUES   Sir, by your patience. If I heard you rightly,
The Duke hath put on a religious life,
And thrown into neglect the pompous court?   180

JAQUES DE BOYS   He hath.

JAQUES   To him will I. Out of these convertites,
There is much matter to be heard and learn'd.
[*to Duke Senior*] You to your former honour I
    bequeath,
Your patience and your virtue well deserve it.   185
[*to Orlando*] You to a love that your true faith doth
    merit:
[*to Oliver*] You to your land and love and great allies:
[*to Silvius*] You to a long and well-deserved bed:
[*to Touchstone*] And you to wrangling, for thy loving
    voyage
Is but for two months victuall'd. So to your
    pleasures.   190
I am for other than for dancing measures.

DUKE SENIOR   Stay, Jaques, stay.

JAQUES   To see no pastime, I. What you would have
I'll stay to know at your abandon'd cave.   *Exit.*

DUKE SENIOR
Proceed, proceed. We will begin these rites,   195
As we do trust they'll end, in true delights.
                        A dance, after which Rosalind
                        is left alone to speak the Epilogue.

ROSALIND   It is not the fashion to see the lady the
epilogue; but it is no more unhandsome than to see the
lord the prologue. If it be true that good wine needs no

bush, 'tis true that a good play needs no epilogue. Yet to good wine they do use good bushes; and good plays prove the better by the help of good epilogues. What a case am I in then, that am neither a good epilogue, nor cannot insinuate with you in the behalf of a good play? I am not furnished like a beggar, therefore to beg will not become me. My way is to conjure you, and I'll begin with the women. I charge you, O women, for the love you bear to men, to like as much of this play as please you. And I charge you, O men, for the love you bear to women – as I perceive by your simpering none of you hates them – that between you and the women the play may please. If I were a woman, I would kiss as many of you as had beards that pleased me, complexions that liked me, and breaths that I defied not. And I am sure, as many as have good beards, or good faces, or sweet breaths, will for my kind offer, when I make curtsy, bid me farewell.   *Exit.*

The Comedy of Errors

First published in the Folio of 1623 as the fifth of the comedies, *The Comedy of Errors* was nonetheless among Shakespeare's earliest plays, and seems, on grounds both of its style and of topical references in it, to belong to the early 1590s. Its first recorded performance was on 28 December 1594, during the Christmas revels at Gray's Inn. On this occasion it replaced the evening's 'intended' performance, cancelled after the festivities got out of hand, following which 'it was thought good not to offer anything of account, save dancing and revelling with gentlewomen; and after such sports, a Comedy of Errors (like to Plautus his *Menechmus*) was played by the players'.

The reference is almost certainly to Shakespeare's play, which is clearly based on Plautus' *Menaechmi*, a lively farce of twins separated in their youth, who now find themselves both in Epidamnum, where one has been raised by a merchant. The twins are constantly mistaken for one another, to the dismay of the citizens and the bewilderment of the brothers themselves. Only when they are seen together at the end is the cause of the confusions made clear; they are then reunited and propose to return together to Syracuse, home of the visiting brother, and start their lives anew. The twin from Epidamnum finally prepares to sell all his property – including his shrewish wife.

Shakespeare outdoes Plautus and multiplies the potential confusions by giving his twin brothers twin servants, likewise separated in infancy. He also borrows from another play by Plautus, *Amphitruo*, for 3.1, where Adriana excludes her husband from his own house while dining with Antipholus of Syracuse, whom she has mistaken for him. Shakespeare shifts his action from Epidamnum to Ephesus, famous for its Temple of Diana, but also well known to his audience from St Paul's journey to the city (Acts 19) and his Epistle to the Ephesians. This location imports Christian values into Plautus' action and contributes to the emotional and psychological gravity that finds its full voice in the family reunions at the end and in the quashing of the death sentence on Egeon, both so different in spirit from the cynicism of the ending of the *Menaechmi*.

The Comedy of Errors is Shakespeare's shortest play, only some 1700 lines long. In common only with *The Tempest*, it observes the neoclassical unities of time and place, conventions which help to suspend the audience's disbelief in the implausible situation for the brief hour and a half of performance. In one view a set piece, a self-conscious experiment in writing Roman comedy, adolescent in some regards, in another *The Comedy of Errors* anticipates themes and techniques which Shakespeare would develop and deepen in the mature comedies and later romances. Its affinities with *Twelfth Night* and *Pericles* are particularly marked.

In its own terms, *The Comedy of Errors* is a highly satisfying play and a reliable crowd-pleaser. Its theatrical effectiveness, a late nineteenth-century discovery, depended upon recovering the staging practices of the Elizabethan theatre. In the eighteenth and earlier nineteenth centuries the play was thought too indecorous and inconsequential to be played without adaptation, and Thomas Hull's version, called simply *The Twins*, with added songs and an intensified love interest, largely displaced it from the stage. In 1895 William Poel, with his Elizabethan Stage Society, returned the play once more to Gray's Inn, where he attempted exactly to reproduce the fluid staging of its original performances. Shakespeare's play was recognized as a potential theatrical success and returned to the repertory. Today it is a popular play, regularly revived and often inventively staged. Its comic ingenuity and energy make it accessible and attractive to audiences, who are often surprised to find behind the slapstick comedy of situation a more complex and sustaining story, as broken families are knit together in an action that can indeed seem, as it does for Antipholus of Syracuse, enchanted.

The Arden text is based on the 1623 First Folio.

Solinus, DUKE *of Ephesus*

EGEON — *a merchant of Syracuse*

ANTIPHOLUS OF EPHESUS
ANTIPHOLUS OF SYRACUSE } *twin brothers, and sons of Egeon and Emilia*

DROMIO OF EPHESUS
DROMIO OF SYRACUSE } *twin brothers, and servants to the Antipholus twins*

BALTHASAR — *a merchant*

ANGELO — *a goldsmith*

Doctor PINCH — *a schoolmaster*

FIRST MERCHANT

SECOND MERCHANT

Emilia, ABBESS *of Ephesus* — *and Egeon's wife*

ADRIANA — *wife of Antipholus of Ephesus*

LUCIANA — *her sister*

LUCE — *her maid*

COURTESAN

Jailor, Officers, Headsman and other Attendants

The Comedy of Errors

Enter SOLINUS *the* DUKE *of Ephesus, with*
       EGEON *the merchant of Syracuse,* Jailor
              and other attendants.

EGEON   Proceed, Solinus, to procure my fall,
  And by the doom of death end woes and all.
DUKE   Merchant of Syracusa, plead no more.
  I am not partial to infringe our laws;
  The enmity and discord which of late
  Sprung from the rancorous outrage of your Duke
  To merchants, our well-dealing countrymen,
  Who, wanting guilders to redeem their lives,
  Have seal'd his rigorous statutes with their bloods,
  Excludes all pity from our threat'ning looks;
  For since the mortal and intestine jars
  'Twixt thy seditious countrymen and us,
  It hath in solemn synods been decreed,
  Both by the Syracusians and ourselves,
  To admit no traffic to our adverse towns;
  Nay more, if any born at Ephesus
  Be seen at Syracusian marts and fairs;
  Again, if any Syracusian born
  Come to the bay of Ephesus, he dies,
  His goods confiscate to the Duke's dispose,
  Unless a thousand marks be levied
  To quit the penalty and to ransom him.
  Thy substance, valued at the highest rate,
  Cannot amount unto a hundred marks;
  Therefore by law thou art condemn'd to die.
EGEON
  Yet this my comfort; when your words are done,
  My woes end likewise with the evening sun.
DUKE   Well, Syracusian; say in brief the cause
  Why thou departedst from thy native home,
  And for what cause thou cam'st to Ephesus.
EGEON   A heavier task could not have been impos'd,
  Than I to speak my griefs unspeakable;
  Yet that the world may witness that my end
  Was wrought by nature, not by vile offence,
  I'll utter what my sorrow gives me leave.
  In Syracusa was I born, and wed
  Unto a woman happy but for me,
  And by me, – had not our hap been bad.
  With her I liv'd in joy; our wealth increas'd
  By prosperous voyages I often made
  To Epidamnum, till my factor's death,
  And the great care of goods at random left,
  Drew me from kind embracements of my spouse;
  From whom my absence was not six months old
  Before herself (almost at fainting under
  The pleasing punishment that women bear)
  Had made provision for her following me,
  And soon, and safe, arrived where I was.
  There had she not been long, but she became
  A joyful mother of two goodly sons,
  And, which was strange, the one so like the other,
  As could not be distinguish'd but by names.

That very hour, and in the self-same inn,
A mean woman was delivered
Of such a burden male, twins both alike;   55
Those, for their parents were exceeding poor,
I bought, and brought up to attend my sons.
My wife, not meanly proud of two such boys,
Made daily motions for our home return;
Unwilling I agreed; alas, too soon   60
We came aboard.
A league from Epidamnum had we sail'd
Before the always-wind-obeying deep
Gave any tragic instance of our harm,
But longer did we not retain much hope;   65
For what obscured light the heavens did grant,
Did but convey unto our fearful minds
A doubtful warrant of immediate death,
Which though myself would gladly have embrac'd,
Yet the incessant weepings of my wife,   70
Weeping before for what she saw must come,
And piteous plainings of the pretty babes,
That mourn'd for fashion, ignorant what to fear,
Forc'd me to seek delays for them and me,
And this it was (for other means was none):   75
The sailors sought for safety by our boat,
And left the ship, then sinking-ripe, to us.
My wife, more careful for the latter-born,
Had fasten'd him unto a small spare mast,
Such as sea-faring men provide for storms;   80
To him one of the other twins was bound,
Whilst I had been like heedful of the other.
The children thus dispos'd, my wife and I,
Fixing our eyes on whom our care was fix'd,
Fasten'd ourselves at either end the mast,   85
And floating straight, obedient to the stream,
Was carried towards Corinth, as we thought.
At length the sun, gazing upon the earth,
Dispers'd those vapours that offended us,
And by the benefit of his wished light   90
The seas wax'd calm, and we discovered
Two ships from far, making amain to us,
Of Corinth that, of Epidaurus this,
But ere they came – O, let me say no more;
Gather the sequel by that went before.   95
DUKE   Nay forward, old man, do not break off so,
  For we may pity, though not pardon thee.
EGEON   O, had the gods done so, I had not now
  Worthily term'd them merciless to us:
  For ere the ships could meet by twice five leagues,   100
  We were encounter'd by a mighty rock,
  Which being violently borne upon,
  Our helpful ship was splitted in the midst;
  So that in this unjust divorce of us,
  Fortune had left to both of us alike   105
  What to delight in, what to sorrow for;
  Her part, poor soul, seeming as burdened
  With lesser weight, but not with lesser woe,
  Was carried with more speed before the wind,

110 And in our sight they three were taken up
By fishermen of Corinth, as we thought.
At length another ship had seiz'd on us,
And knowing whom it was their hap to save,
Gave healthful welcome to their ship-wrack'd guests,
115 And would have reft the fishers of their prey,
Had not their bark been very slow of sail;
And therefore homeward did they bend their course.
Thus have you heard me sever'd from my bliss,
That by misfortunes was my life prolong'd
120 To tell sad stories of my own mishaps.
DUKE   And for the sake of them thou sorrowest for,
Do me the favour to dilate at full
What have befall'n of them and thee till now.
EGEON   My youngest boy, and yet my eldest care,
125 At eighteen years became inquisitive
After his brother, and importun'd me
That his attendant, so his case was like,
Reft of his brother, but retain'd his name,
Might bear him company in the quest of him;
130 Whom whilst I labour'd of a love to see,
I hazarded the loss of whom I lov'd.
Five summers have I spent in farthest Greece,
Roaming clean through the bounds of Asia,
And coasting homeward came to Ephesus,
135 Hopeless to find, yet loth to leave unsought
Or that or any place that harbours men:
But here must end the story of my life,
And happy were I in my timely death,
Could all my travels warrant me they live.
140 DUKE   Hapless Egeon, whom the fates have mark'd
To bear the extremity of dire mishap;
Now trust me, were it not against our laws,
Against my crown, my oath, my dignity,
Which princes, would they, may not disannul,
145 My soul should sue as advocate for thee;
But though thou art adjudged to the death,
And passed sentence may not be recall'd
But to our honour's great disparagement,
Yet will I favour thee in what I can;
150 Therefore, merchant, I'll limit thee this day
To seek thy health by beneficial help;
Try all the friends thou hast in Ephesus,
Beg thou, or borrow, to make up the sum,
And live; if no, then thou art doom'd to die.
155 Jailor, take him to thy custody.
JAILOR   I will, my lord.
EGEON   Hopeless and helpless doth Egeon wend,
But to procrastinate his lifeless end.   *Exeunt.*

1.2   *Enter* ANTIPHOLUS OF SYRACUSE,
         First Merchant *and* DROMIO.

1 MERCHANT
Therefore give out you are of Epidamnum,
Lest that your goods too soon be confiscate;
This very day a Syracusian merchant

Is apprehended for arrival here,
And not being able to buy out his life,   5
According to the statute of the town
Dies ere the weary sun set in the west.
There is your money that I had to keep.
ANTIPHOLUS S.
Go, bear it to the Centaur, where we host,
And stay there, Dromio, till I come to thee;   10
Within this hour it will be dinner time;
Till that I'll view the manners of the town,
Peruse the traders, gaze upon the buildings,
And then return and sleep within mine inn,
For with long travel I am stiff and weary.   15
Get thee away.
DROMIO S.   Many a man would take you at your word,
And go indeed, having so good a mean.   *Exit.*
ANTIPHOLUS S.   A trusty villain, sir, that very oft,
When I am dull with care and melancholy,   20
Lightens my humour with his merry jests.
What, will you walk with me about the town,
And then go to my inn and dine with me?
1 MERCHANT   I am invited, sir, to certain merchants,
Of whom I hope to make much benefit.   25
I crave your pardon; soon at five o'clock,
Please you, I'll meet with you upon the mart,
And afterward consort you till bed-time;
My present business calls me from you now.
ANTIPHOLUS S.   Farewell till then: I will go lose myself,   30
And wander up and down to view the city.
1 MERCHANT
Sir, I commend you to your own content.   *Exit.*
ANTIPHOLUS S.
He that commends me to mine own content
Commends me to the thing I cannot get.
I to the world am like a drop of water   35
That in the ocean seeks another drop,
Who, falling there to find his fellow forth,
(Unseen, inquisitive) confounds himself.
So I, to find a mother and a brother,
In quest of them, unhappy, lose myself.   40

         Enter DROMIO OF EPHESUS.

Here comes the almanac of my true date:
What now? How chance thou art return'd so soon?
DROMIO E.
Return'd so soon? rather approach'd too late;
The capon burns, the pig falls from the spit;
The clock hath strucken twelve upon the bell;   45
My mistress made it one upon my cheek;
She is so hot because the meat is cold;
The meat is cold because you come not home;
You come not home because you have no stomach;
You have no stomach having broke your fast;   50
But we that know what 'tis to fast and pray,
Are penitent for your default to-day.
ANTIPHOLUS S.
Stop in your wind, sir, tell me this I pray:

Where have you left the money that I gave you?

DROMIO E.   O, sixpence that I had o' Wednesday last,
To pay the saddler for my mistress' crupper:
The saddler had it, sir, I kept it not.

ANTIPHOLUS S.   I am not in a sportive humour now:
Tell me, and dally not, where is the money?
We being strangers here, how dar'st thou trust
So great a charge from thine own custody?

DROMIO E.   I pray you jest, sir, as you sit at dinner:
I from my mistress come to you in post;
If I return I shall be post indeed,
For she will scour your fault upon my pate.
Methinks your maw, like mine, should be your clock,
And strike you home without a messenger.

ANTIPHOLUS S.
Come Dromio, come, these jests are out of season,
Reserve them till a merrier hour than this;
Where is the gold I gave in charge to thee?

DROMIO E.   To me, sir? why, you gave no gold to me.

ANTIPHOLUS S.
Come on, sir knave, have done your foolishness,
And tell me how thou hast dispos'd thy charge.

DROMIO E.
My charge was but to fetch you from the mart
Home to your house, the Phoenix, sir, to dinner;
My mistress and her sister stays for you.

ANTIPHOLUS S.   Now as I am a Christian, answer me
In what safe place you have bestow'd my money,
Or I shall break that merry sconce of yours
That stands on tricks when I am undispos'd;
Where is the thousand marks thou hadst of me?

DROMIO E.   I have some marks of yours upon my pate;
Some of my mistress' marks upon my shoulders;
But not a thousand marks between you both.
If I should pay your worship those again,
Perchance you will not bear them patiently.

ANTIPHOLUS S.
Thy mistress' marks? what mistress, slave, hast thou?

DROMIO E.
Your worship's wife, my mistress at the Phoenix;
She that doth fast till you come home to dinner,
And prays that you will hie you home to dinner.

ANTIPHOLUS S.
What, wilt thou flout me thus unto my face
Being forbid? There, take you that, sir knave.

DROMIO E.
What mean you, sir? for God's sake hold your hands.
Nay, and you will not, sir, I'll take my heels.   *Exit.*

ANTIPHOLUS S.   Upon my life, by some device or other
The villain is o'er-raught of all my money.
They say this town is full of cozenage,
As nimble jugglers that deceive the eye,
Dark-working sorcerers that change the mind,
Soul-killing witches that deform the body,
Disguised cheaters, prating mountebanks,
And many such-like liberties of sin:
If it prove so, I will be gone the sooner.

I'll to the Centaur to go seek this slave;
I greatly fear my money is not safe.   *Exit.*   105

2.1   *Enter* ADRIANA, *wife to Antipholus of Ephesus,*
with LUCIANA, *her sister.*

ADRIANA   Neither my husband nor the slave return'd,
That in such haste I sent to seek his master?
Sure, Luciana, it is two o'clock.

LUCIANA   Perhaps some merchant hath invited him,
And from the mart he's somewhere gone to dinner.   5
Good sister let us dine, and never fret;
A man is master of his liberty;
Time is their master, and when they see time,
They'll go or come; if so, be patient, sister.

ADRIANA   Why should their liberty than ours be more?   10

LUCIANA   Because their business still lies out o'door.

ADRIANA   Look, when I serve him so, he takes it ill.

LUCIANA   O, know he is the bridle of your will.

ADRIANA   There's none but asses will be bridled so.

LUCIANA   Why, headstrong liberty is lash'd with woe.   15
There's nothing situate under heaven's eye
But hath his bound in earth, in sea, in sky.
The beasts, the fishes, and the winged fowls
Are their males' subjects, and at their controls;
Man, more divine, the master of all these,   20
Lord of the wide world and wild wat'ry seas,
Indued with intellectual sense and souls,
Of more pre-eminence than fish and fowls,
Are masters to their females, and their lords:
Then let your will attend on their accords.   25

ADRIANA   This servitude makes you to keep unwed.

LUCIANA   Not this, but troubles of the marriage bed.

ADRIANA
But were you wedded you would bear some sway.

LUCIANA   Ere I learn love, I'll practise to obey.

ADRIANA
How if your husband start some other where?   30

LUCIANA   Till he come home again I would forbear.

ADRIANA
Patience unmov'd! no marvel though she pause;
They can be meek that have no other cause.
A wretched soul bruis'd with adversity,
We bid be quiet when we hear it cry;   35
But were we burden'd with like weight of pain,
As much, or more, we should ourselves complain:
So thou that hast no unkind mate to grieve thee,
With urging helpless patience would relieve me;
But if thou live to see like right bereft,   40
This fool-begg'd patience in thee will be left.

LUCIANA   Well, I will marry one day but to try.
Here comes your man, now is your husband nigh.

Enter DROMIO OF EPHESUS.

ADRIANA   Say, is your tardy master now at hand?

DROMIO E.   Nay, he's at two hands with me, and that my   45
two ears can witness.

195

ADRIANA   Say, didst thou speak with him? knowst thou
  his mind?
DROMIO E.   Ay, ay, he told his mind upon mine ear,
50 Beshrew his hand, I scarce could understand it.
LUCIANA   Spake he so doubtfully, thou couldst not feel
  his meaning?
DROMIO E.   Nay, he struck so plainly I could too well feel
  his blows; and withal so doubtfully, that I could scarce
55 understand them.
ADRIANA   But say, I prithee, is he coming home?
  It seems he hath great care to please his wife.
DROMIO E.
  Why, mistress, sure my master is horn-mad.
ADRIANA   Horn-mad, thou villain?
DROMIO E.   I mean not cuckold-mad,
60 But sure he is stark mad.
  When I desir'd him to come home to dinner,
  He ask'd me for a thousand marks in gold;
  ' 'Tis dinner-time', quoth I; 'my gold,' quoth he;
  'Your meat will burn', quoth I; 'my gold', quoth he,
65 'Will you come?', quoth I; 'my gold', quoth he,
  'Where is the thousand marks I gave thee, villain?'
  'The pig', quoth I, 'is burn'd'; 'my gold', quoth he;
  'My mistress, sir . . .', quoth I; 'hang up thy mistress;
  I know not thy mistress, out on thy mistress . . .'
70 LUCIANA   Quoth who?
DROMIO E.   Quoth my master;
  'I know', quoth he, 'no house, no wife, no mistress',
  So that my errand due unto my tongue,
  I thank him, I bare home upon my shoulders;
75 For in conclusion, he did beat me there.
ADRIANA
  Go back again, thou slave, and fetch him home.
DROMIO E.   Go back again, and be new beaten home?
  For God's sake, send some other messenger.
ADRIANA   Back slave, or I will break thy pate across.
DROMIO E.
80 And he will bless that cross with other beating;
  Between you I shall have a holy head.
ADRIANA
  Hence, prating peasant, fetch thy master home.
DROMIO E.   Am I so round with you, as you with me,
  That like a football you do spurn me thus?
85 You spurn me hence, and he will spurn me hither;
  If I last in this service you must case me in leather.
                                               Exit.
LUCIANA   Fie, how impatience loureth in your face.
ADRIANA   His company must do his minions grace,
  Whilst I at home starve for a merry look.
90 Hath homely age th'alluring beauty took
  From my poor cheek? then he hath wasted it.
  Are my discourses dull? barren my wit?
  If voluble and sharp discourse be marr'd,
  Unkindness blunts it more than marble hard.
95 Do their gay vestments his affections bait?
  That's not my fault, he's master of my state.

What ruins are in me that can be found
By him not ruin'd? Then is he the ground
Of my defeatures; my decayed fair
A sunny look of his would soon repair;   100
But, too unruly deer, he breaks the pale
And feeds from home; poor I am but his stale.
LUCIANA   Self-harming jealousy! fie, beat it hence.
ADRIANA
Unfeeling fools can with such wrongs dispense;
I know his eye doth homage otherwhere,   105
Or else what lets it but he would be here?
Sister, you know he promis'd me a chain;
Would that alone a toy he would detain,
So he would keep fair quarter with his bed:
I see the jewel best enamelled   110
Will lose his beauty: yet the gold bides still
That others touch, and often touching will
Wear gold, and no man that hath a name
By falsehood and corruption doth it shame.
Since that my beauty cannot please his eye,   115
I'll weep what's left away, and weeping die.
LUCIANA   How many fond fools serve mad jealousy?
                                              Exeunt.

2.2   *Enter* ANTIPHOLUS OF SYRACUSE.

ANTIPHOLUS S.   The gold I gave to Dromio is laid up
  Safe at the Centaur, and the heedful slave
  Is wander'd forth in care to seek me out
  By computation and mine host's report.
  I could not speak with Dromio since at first   5
  I sent him from the mart; see, here he comes.

                Enter DROMIO OF SYRACUSE.

  How now, sir, is your merry humour alter'd?
  As you love strokes, so jest with me again.
  You know no Centaur? you receiv'd no gold?
  Your mistress sent to have me home to dinner?   10
  My house was at the Phoenix? Wast thou mad
  That thus so madly thou didst answer me?
DROMIO S.
  What answer, sir? when spake I such a word?
ANTIPHOLUS S.
  Even now, even here, not half an hour since.
DROMIO S.   I did not see you since you sent me hence, 15
  Home to the Centaur with the gold you gave me.
ANTIPHOLUS S.
  Villain, thou didst deny the gold's receipt,
  And told'st me of a mistress and a dinner,
  For which I hope thou felt'st I was displeas'd.
DROMIO S.   I am glad to see you in this merry vein;   20
  What means this jest; I pray you master, tell me?
ANTIPHOLUS S.
  Yea, dost thou jeer and flout me in the teeth?
  Think'st thou I jest? hold, take thou that, and that.
  [*Beats Dromio.*]

DROMIO S.
  Hold sir, for God's sake; now your jest is earnest,
  Upon what bargain do you give it me?

ANTIPHOLUS S.   Because that I familiarly sometimes
  Do use you for my fool, and chat with you,
  Your sauciness will jest upon my love,
  And make a common of my serious hours;
  When the sun shines let foolish gnats make sport,
  But creep in crannies when he hides his beams.
  If you will jest with me, know my aspect,
  And fashion your demeanour to my looks,
  Or I will beat this method in your sconce.

DROMIO S.   Sconce call you it? so you would leave
  battering, I had rather have it a head; and you use
  these blows long, I must get a sconce for my head, and
  insconce it too, or else I shall seek my wit in my
  shoulders; but I pray, sir, why am I beaten?

ANTIPHOLUS S.   Dost thou not know?

DROMIO S.   Nothing, sir, but that I am beaten.

ANTIPHOLUS S.   Shall I tell you why?

DROMIO S.   Ay, sir, and wherefore; for they say, every
  why hath a wherefore.

ANTIPHOLUS S.   Why, first, for flouting me, and then
  wherefore, for urging it the second time to me.

DROMIO S.
  Was there ever any man thus beaten out of season,
  When in the why and the wherefore is neither rhyme
    nor reason.
  Well, sir, I thank you.

ANTIPHOLUS S.   Thank me, sir, for what?

DROMIO S.   Marry, sir, for this something that you gave
  me for nothing.

ANTIPHOLUS S.   I'll make you amends next, to give you
  nothing for something. But say, sir, is it dinner-time?

DROMIO S.   No, sir, I think the meat wants that I have.

ANTIPHOLUS S.   In good time, sir; what's that?

DROMIO S.   Basting.

ANTIPHOLUS S.   Well, sir, then 'twill be dry.

DROMIO S.   If it be, sir, I pray you eat none of it.

ANTIPHOLUS S.   Your reason?

DROMIO S.   Lest it make you choleric, and purchase me
  another dry basting.

ANTIPHOLUS S.   Well, sir, learn to jest in good time;
  there's a time for all things.

DROMIO S.   I durst have denied that before you were so
  choleric.

ANTIPHOLUS S.   By what rule, sir?

DROMIO S.   Marry, sir, by a rule as plain as the plain bald
  pate of Father Time himself.

ANTIPHOLUS S.   Let's hear it.

DROMIO S.   There's no time for a man to recover his hair
  that grows bald by nature.

ANTIPHOLUS S.   May he not do it by fine and recovery?

DROMIO S.   Yes, to pay a fine for a periwig, and recover
  the lost hair of another man.

ANTIPHOLUS S.   Why is Time such a niggard of hair,
  being (as it is) so plentiful an excrement?

DROMIO S.   Because it is a blessing that he bestows on
  beasts, and what he hath scanted men in hair, he hath
  given them in wit.

ANTIPHOLUS S.   Why, but there's many a man hath more
  hair than wit.

DROMIO S.   Not a man of those but he hath the wit to
  lose his hair.

ANTIPHOLUS S.   Why, thou didst conclude hairy men
  plain dealers without wit.

DROMIO S.   The plainer dealer, the sooner lost; yet he
  loseth it in a kind of jollity.

ANTIPHOLUS S.   For what reason?

DROMIO S.   For two, and sound ones too.

ANTIPHOLUS S.   Nay, not sound, I pray you.

DROMIO S.   Sure ones, then.

ANTIPHOLUS S.   Nay, not sure in a thing falsing.

DROMIO S.   Certain ones then.

ANTIPHOLUS S.   Name them.

DROMIO S.   The one, to save the money that he spends in
  tiring; the other, that at dinner they should not drop in
  his porridge.

ANTIPHOLUS S.   You would all this time have proved,
  there is no time for all things.

DROMIO S.   Marry, and did, sir: namely, e'en no time to
  recover hair lost by nature.

ANTIPHOLUS S.   But your reason was not substantial,
  why there is no time to recover.

DROMIO S.   This I mend it: Time himself is bald, and
  therefore to the world's end will have bald followers.

ANTIPHOLUS S.   I knew 'twould be a bald conclusion;
  but soft, who wafts us yonder?

Enter ADRIANA *and* LUCIANA.

ADRIANA   Ay, ay, Antipholus, look strange and frown,
  Some other mistress hath thy sweet aspects;
  I am not Adriana, nor thy wife.
  The time was once when thou unurg'd wouldst vow
  That never words were music to thine ear,
  That never object pleasing in thine eye,
  That never touch well welcome to thy hand,
  That never meat sweet-savour'd in thy taste,
  Unless I spake, or look'd, or touch'd, or carv'd to
    thee.
  How comes it now, my husband, O, how comes it,
  That thou art then estranged from thyself? –
  Thyself I call it, being strange to me,
  That undividable, incorporate,
  Am better than thy dear self's better part.
  Ah, do not tear away thyself from me;
  For know, my love, as easy mayst thou fall
  A drop of water in the breaking gulf,
  And take unmingled thence that drop again
  Without addition or diminishing,
  As take from me thyself, and not me too.
  How dearly would it touch thee to the quick,

197

130   Shouldst thou but hear I were licentious?
       And that this body, consecrate to thee,
       By ruffian lust should be contaminate?
       Wouldst thou not spit at me, and spurn at me,
       And hurl the name of husband in my face,
135   And tear the stain'd skin off my harlot brow,
       And from my false hand cut the wedding-ring,
       And break it with a deep-divorcing vow?
       I know thou canst; and therefore, see thou do it!
       I am possess'd with an adulterate blot,
140   My blood is mingled with the crime of lust;
       For if we two be one, and thou play false,
       I do digest the poison of thy flesh,
       Being strumpeted by thy contagion.
       Keep then fair league and truce with thy true bed,
145   I live unstain'd, thou undishonoured.
    ANTIPHOLUS S.
       Plead you to me fair dame? I know you not.
       In Ephesus I am but two hours old,
       As strange unto your town as to your talk,
       Who, every word by all my wit being scann'd,
150   Wants wit in all one word to understand.
    LUCIANA
       Fie, brother, how the world is chang'd with you.
       When were you wont to use my sister thus?
       She sent for you by Dromio home to dinner.
    ANTIPHOLUS S.   By Dromio?
155 DROMIO S.   By me?
    ADRIANA
       By thee, and this thou didst return from him,
       That he did buffet thee, and in his blows
       Denied my house for his, me for his wife.
    ANTIPHOLUS S.
       Did you converse, sir, with this gentlewoman?
160   What is the course and drift of your compact?
    DROMIO S.   I, sir? I never saw her till this time.
    ANTIPHOLUS S.
       Villain, thou liest, for even her very words
       Didst thou deliver to me on the mart.
    DROMIO S.   I never spake with her in all my life.
    ANTIPHOLUS S.
165   How can she thus then call us by our names? –
       Unless it be by inspiration.
    ADRIANA   How ill agrees it with your gravity
       To counterfeit thus grossly with your slave,
       Abetting him to thwart me in my mood;
170   Be it my wrong, you are from me exempt,
       But wrong not that wrong with a more contempt.
       Come, I will fasten on this sleeve of thine;
       Thou art an elm, my husband, I a vine,
       Whose weakness married to thy stronger state,
175   Makes me with thy strength to communicate:
       If aught possess thee from me, it is dross,
       Usurping ivy, briar, or idle moss,
       Who all for want of pruning, with intrusion,
       Infect thy sap, and live on thy confusion.

    ANTIPHOLUS S. [*aside*]
       To me she speaks, she moves me for her theme;   180
       What, was I married to her in my dream?
       Or sleep I now, and think I hear all this?
       What error drives our eyes and ears amiss?
       Until I know this sure uncertainty,
       I'll entertain the offer'd fallacy.   185
    LUCIANA
       Dromio, go bid the servants spread for dinner.
    DROMIO S.   O for my beads; I cross me for a sinner.
       This is the fairy land; O spite of spites,
       We talk with goblins, elves and sprites;
       If we obey them not, this will ensue –   190
       They'll suck our breath, or pinch us black and blue.
    LUCIANA
       Why prat'st thou to thy self and answer'st not?
       Dromio, thou drone, thou snail, thou slug, thou sot.
    DROMIO S.   I am transformed, master, am I not?
    ANTIPHOLUS S.   I think thou art in mind, and so am I. 195
    DROMIO S.   Nay, master, both in mind and in my shape.
    ANTIPHOLUS S.   Thou hast thine own form.
    DROMIO S.   No, I am an ape.
    LUCIANA   If thou art chang'd to aught, 'tis to an ass.
    DROMIO S.   'Tis true, she rides me, and I long for grass;
       'Tis so, I am an ass, else it could never be   200
       But I should know her as well as she knows me.
    ADRIANA   Come, come, no longer will I be a fool,
       To put the finger in the eye and weep
       Whilst man and master laughs my woes to scorn.
       Come, sir, to dinner; Dromio, keep the gate.   205
       Husband, I'll dine above with you to-day,
       And shrive you of a thousand idle pranks.
       Sirrah, if any ask you for your master,
       Say he dines forth, and let no creature enter.
       Come, sister; Dromio, play the porter well.   210
    ANTIPHOLUS S. [*aside*]
       Am I in earth, in heaven, or in hell?
       Sleeping or waking, mad or well advis'd?
       Known unto these, and to myself disguis'd,
       I'll say as they say, and persever so,
       And in this mist at all adventures go.   215
    DROMIO S.   Master, shall I be porter at the gate?
    ADRIANA   Ay, and let none enter, lest I break your pate.
    LUCIANA   Come, come, Antipholus, we dine too late.
                                              Exeunt.

3.1 *Enter* ANTIPHOLUS OF EPHESUS, *his man* DROMIO,
       ANGELO *the goldsmith and* BALTHASAR *the merchant.*

    ANTIPHOLUS E.
       Good signior Angelo, you must excuse us all,
       My wife is shrewish when I keep not hours;
       Say that I linger'd with you at your shop
       To see the making of her carcanet,
       And that to-morrow you will bring it home.   5
       But here's a villain that would face me down
       He met me on the mart, and that I beat him,

And charg'd him with a thousand marks in gold,
And that I did deny my wife and house;
Thou drunkard, thou, what didst thou mean by this?

DROMIO E.
Say what you will, sir, but I know what I know;
That you beat me at the mart I have your hand to
show.
If the skin were parchment and the blows you gave
were ink,
Your own hand-writing would tell you what I think.

ANTIPHOLUS E.   I think thou art an ass.

DROMIO E.   Marry, so it doth appear
By the wrongs I suffer and the blows I bear;
I should kick, being kick'd, and being at that pass,
You would keep from my heels, and beware of an ass.

ANTIPHOLUS E.
You're sad, signior Balthazar; pray God our cheer
May answer my good will, and your good welcome
here.

BALTHASAR
I hold your dainties cheap, sir, and your welcome dear.

ANTIPHOLUS E.
O signior Balthazar, either at flesh or fish
A table full of welcome makes scarce one dainty dish.

BALTHASAR
Good meat, sir, is common; that every churl affords.

ANTIPHOLUS E.
And welcome more common, for that's nothing but
words.

BALTHASAR
Small cheer and great welcome makes a merry feast.

ANTIPHOLUS E.
Ay, to a niggardly host, and more sparing guest;
But though my cates be mean, take them in good part;
Better cheer may you have, but not with better heart.
But soft, my door is lock'd; go bid them let us in.

DROMIO E.
Maud, Bridget, Marian, Cicely, Gillian, Ginn!

DROMIO S. [*within*]
Mome, malthorse, capon, coxcomb, idiot, patch,
Either get thee from the door or sit down at the hatch:
Dost thou conjure for wenches, that thou call'st for
such store
When one is too many? Go, get thee from the door.

DROMIO E.
What patch is made our porter? my master stays in
the street.

DROMIO S.
Let him walk from whence he came, lest he catch
cold on's feet.

ANTIPHOLUS E.
Who talks within there? ho, open the door.

DROMIO S.
Right, sir, I'll tell you when, and you'll tell me
wherefore.

ANTIPHOLUS E.
Wherefore? for my dinner; I have not din'd to-day.

DROMIO S.
Nor to-day here you must not; come again when you
may.

ANTIPHOLUS E.
What art thou that keep'st me out from the house
I owe?

DROMIO S.
The porter for this time, sir, and my name is Dromio.

DROMIO E.
O villain, thou hast stol'n both mine office and my
name;
The one ne'er got me credit, the other mickle blame;   45
If thou hadst been Dromio to-day in my place,
Thou wouldst have chang'd thy office for an aim, or
thy name for an ass.

Enter LUCE, *concealed from Antipholus of Ephesus
and his companions.*

LUCE
What a coil is there, Dromio? who are those at the
gate?

DROMIO E.   Let my master in, Luce.

LUCE   Faith, no, he comes too late,
And so tell your master.

DROMIO E.   O Lord, I must laugh;   50
Have at you with a proverb – shall I set in my staff?

LUCE
Have at you with another, that's – when? can you
tell?

DROMIO S.
If thy name be called Luce, Luce thou hast answer'd
him well.

ANTIPHOLUS E.
Do you hear, you minion, you'll let us in I trow?

LUCE   I thought to have ask'd you.

DROMIO S.   And you said, no.   55

DROMIO E.
So come, help, well struck, there was blow for blow.

ANTIPHOLUS E.   Thou baggage, let me in.

LUCE   Can you tell for whose sake?

DROMIO E.   Master, knock the door hard.

LUCE   Let him knock till it ache.

ANTIPHOLUS E.
You'll cry for this, minion, if I beat the door down.

LUCE
What needs all that, and a pair of stocks in the town?   60

Enter ADRIANA *to Luce.*

ADRIANA
Who is that at the door that keeps all this noise?

DROMIO S.
By my troth, your town is troubled with unruly boys.

ANTIPHOLUS E.
Are you there, wife? you might have come before.

ADRIANA
Your wife, sir knave? go, get you from the door.
                                        Exit with Luce.

DROMIO E.

65   If you went in pain, master, this knave would go sore.

ANGELO

Here is neither cheer, sir, nor welcome; we would
        fain have either.

BALTHASAR

In debating which was best, we shall part with
        neither.

DROMIO E.

They stand at the door, master; bid them welcome
        hither.

ANTIPHOLUS E.

There is something in the wind that we cannot
        get in.

DROMIO E.

70   You would say so, master, if your garments were thin.
        Your cake here is warm within; you stand here in the
                cold;
        It would make a man mad as a buck to be so bought
                and sold.

ANTIPHOLUS E.

Go fetch me something, I'll break ope the gate.

DROMIO S.

Break any breaking here and I'll break your knave's
        pate.

DROMIO E.

A man may break a word with you, sir, and words are
75   but wind;
        Ay, and break it in your face, so he break it not
                behind.

DROMIO S.

It seems thou want'st breaking; out upon thee, hind.

DROMIO E.

Here's too much 'out upon thee'; I pray thee let
        me in.

DROMIO S.

Ay, when fowls have no feathers, and fish have no fin.

ANTIPHOLUS E.

80   Well, I'll break in; go, borrow me a crow.

DROMIO E.

A crow without feather; master, mean you so?
        For a fish without a fin, there's a fowl without a
                feather;
        If a crow help us in, sirrah, we'll pluck a crow
                together.

ANTIPHOLUS E.

Go, get thee gone; fetch me an iron crow.

BALTHASAR   Have patience, sir, O, let it not be so;
85   Herein you war against your reputation,
        And draw within the compass of suspect
        Th'unviolated honour of your wife.
        Once this, – your long experience of her wisdom,
90   Her sober virtue, years and modesty,
        Plead on her part some cause to you unknown;
        And doubt not, sir, but she will well excuse
        Why at this time the doors are made against you.
        Be rul'd by me, depart in patience,

And let us to the Tiger all to dinner,   95
And about evening, come yourself alone
To know the reason of this strange restraint.
If by strong hand you offer to break in
Now in the stirring passage of the day,
A vulgar comment will be made of it;   100
And that supposed by the common rout
Against your yet ungalled estimation,
That may with foul intrusion enter in,
And dwell upon your grave when you are dead;
For slander lives upon succession,   105
For e'er hous'd where it gets possession.

ANTIPHOLUS E.

You have prevail'd, I will depart in quiet,
And in despite of mirth mean to be merry.
I know a wench of excellent discourse,
Pretty and witty; wild and yet, too, gentle;   110
There will we dine. This woman that I mean,
My wife (but I protest, without desert)
Hath oftentimes upbraided me withal;
To her will we to dinner; [*to Angelo*] get you home
And fetch the chain, by this I know 'tis made;   115
Bring it, I pray you, to the Porpentine,
For there's the house – that chain will I bestow
(Be it for nothing but to spite my wife)
Upon mine hostess there – good sir, make haste.
Since mine own doors refuse to entertain me,   120
I'll knock elsewhere, to see if they'll disdain me.

ANGELO   I'll meet you at that place some hour hence.

ANTIPHOLUS E.

Do so; this jest shall cost me some expense.   *Exeunt.*

3.2 *Enter* LUCIANA, *with* ANTIPHOLUS OF SYRACUSE.

LUCIANA   And may it be that you have quite forgot
        A husband's office? shall, Antipholus,
        Even in the spring of love, thy love-springs rot?
        Shall love in building grow so ruinous?
        If you did wed my sister for her wealth,   5
        Then for her wealth's sake use her with more
                kindness;
        Or if you like elsewhere, do it by stealth,
        Muffle your false love with some show of blindness.
        Let not my sister read it in your eye;
        Be not thy tongue thy own shame's orator;   10
        Look sweet, speak fair, become disloyalty;
        Apparel vice like virtue's harbinger;
        Bear a fair presence, though your heart be tainted;
        Teach sin the carriage of a holy saint,
        Be secret false; what need she be acquainted?   15
        What simple thief brags of his own attaint?
        'Tis double wrong to truant with your bed,
        And let her read it in thy looks at board;
        Shame hath a bastard fame, well managed;
        Ill deeds is doubled with an evil word.   20
        Alas, poor women, make us but believe
        (Being compact of credit) that you love us;

Though others have the arm, show us the sleeve;
We in your motion turn, and you may move us.
Then, gentle brother, get you in again;
Comfort my sister, cheer her, call her wife;
'Tis holy sport to be a little vain
When the sweet breath of flattery conquers strife.

ANTIPHOLUS S.
  Sweet mistress, what your name is else I know not,
  Nor by what wonder you do hit of mine;
  Less in your knowledge and your grace you show not
  Than our earth's wonder, more than earth divine.
  Teach me, dear creature, how to think and speak;
  Lay open to my earthy gross conceit,
  Smother'd in errors, feeble, shallow, weak,
  The folded meaning of your words' deceit.
  Against my soul's pure truth, why labour you
  To make it wander in an unknown field?
  Are you a god? would you create me new?
  Transform me then, and to your power I'll yield.
  But if that I am I, then well I know
  Your weeping sister is no wife of mine,
  Nor to her bed no homage do I owe;
  Far more, far more to you do I decline;
  O, train me not, sweet mermaid, with thy note
  To drown me in thy sister's flood of tears;
  Sing, siren, for thyself, and I will dote;
  Spread o'er the silver waves thy golden hairs,
  And as a bed I'll take thee, and there lie,
  And in that glorious supposition think
  He gains by death that hath such means to die;
  Let love, being light, be drowned if she sink.

LUCIANA   What, are you mad that you do reason so?

ANTIPHOLUS S.
  Not mad, but mated, how I do not know.

LUCIANA   It is a fault that springeth from your eye.

ANTIPHOLUS S.
  For gazing on your beams, fair sun, being by.

LUCIANA
  Gaze where you should, and that will clear your
    sight.

ANTIPHOLUS S.
  As good to wink, sweet love, as look on night.

LUCIANA   Why call you me love? Call my sister so.

ANTIPHOLUS S.   Thy sister's sister.

LUCIANA   That's my sister.

ANTIPHOLUS S.   No,
  It is thyself, mine own self's better part,
  Mine eye's clear eye, my dear heart's dearer heart,
  My food, my fortune, and my sweet hope's aim,
  My sole earth's heaven, and my heaven's claim.

LUCIANA   All this my sister is, or else should be.

ANTIPHOLUS S.   Call thyself sister, sweet, for I am thee;
  Thee will I love, and with thee lead my life;
  Thou hast no husband yet, nor I no wife –
  Give me thy hand.

LUCIANA   O, soft, sir, hold you still;
  I'll fetch my sister to get her good will.   *Exit.*

Enter DROMIO OF SYRACUSE.

ANTIPHOLUS S.   Why, how now Dromio, where run'st
  thou so fast?

DROMIO S.   Do you know me sir? Am I Dromio? Am I
  your man? Am I myself?

ANTIPHOLUS S.   Thou art Dromio, thou art my man,   75
  thou art thyself.

DROMIO S.   I am an ass, I am a woman's man, and besides
  myself.

ANTIPHOLUS S.   What woman's man? and how besides
  thyself?   80

DROMIO S.   Marry, sir, besides myself, I am due to a
  woman, one that claims me, one that haunts me, one
  that will have me.

ANTIPHOLUS S.   What claim lays she to thee?

DROMIO S.   Marry sir, such claim as you would lay to   85
  your horse; and she would have me as a beast, not that
  I being a beast she would have me, but that she being
  a very beastly creature lays claim to me.

ANTIPHOLUS S.   What is she?

DROMIO S.   A very reverend body; ay, such a one as a   90
  man may not speak of, without he say 'sir-reverence';
  I have but lean luck in the match, and yet is she a
  wondrous fat marriage.

ANTIPHOLUS S.   How dost thou mean, a fat marriage?

DROMIO S.   Marry, sir, she's the kitchen wench, and all   95
  grease, and I know not what use to put her to but to
  make a lamp of her, and run from her by her own light.
  I warrant her rags and the tallow in them will burn a
  Poland winter; if she lives till doomsday she'll burn a
  week longer than the whole world.   100

ANTIPHOLUS S.   What complexion is she of?

DROMIO S.   Swart like my shoe, but her face nothing like
  so clean kept; for why? she sweats, a man may go over-
  shoes in the grime of it.

ANTIPHOLUS S.   That's a fault that water will mend.   105

DROMIO S.   No sir, 'tis in grain; Noah's flood could not
  do it.

ANTIPHOLUS S.   What's her name?

DROMIO S.   Nell, sir; but her name and three quarters,
  that's an ell and threequarters, will not measure her   110
  from hip to hip.

ANTIPHOLUS S.   Then she bears some breadth?

DROMIO S.   No longer from head to foot than from hip
  to hip; she is spherical, like a globe; I could find out
  countries in her.   115

ANTIPHOLUS S.   In what part of her body stands Ireland?

DROMIO S.   Marry, sir, in her buttocks; I found it out by
  the bogs.

ANTIPHOLUS S.   Where Scotland?

DROMIO S.   I found it by the barrenness, hard in the   120
  palm of the hand.

ANTIPHOLUS S.   Where France?

DROMIO S.   In her forehead, armed and reverted, making
  war against her heir.

ANTIPHOLUS S.   Where England?   125

DROMIO S.   I looked for the chalky cliffs, but I could find
no whiteness in them. But I guess it stood in her chin,
by the salt rheum that ran between France and it.

ANTIPHOLUS S.   Where Spain?

130 DROMIO S.   Faith, I saw it not; but I felt it hot in her
breath.

ANTIPHOLUS S.   Where America, the Indies?

DROMIO S.   O, sir, upon her nose, all o'er-embellished
with rubies, carbuncles, sapphires, declining their rich
135 aspect to the hot breath of Spain, who sent whole
armadoes of carracks to be ballast at her nose.

ANTIPHOLUS S.   Where stood Belgia, the Netherlands?

DROMIO S.   O, sir, I did not look so low. To conclude, this
drudge or diviner laid claim to me, called me Dromio,
140 swore I was assured to her, told me what privy marks
I had about me, as the mark of my shoulder, the mole
in my neck, the great wart on my left arm, that I,
amazed, ran from her as a witch.
And I think if my breast had not been made of faith,
and my heart of steel,
She had transform'd me to a curtal dog, and made
145 me turn i'th' wheel.

ANTIPHOLUS S.
Go, hie thee presently, post to the road;
And if the wind blow any way from shore
I will not harbour in this town to-night.
If any bark put forth, come to the mart,
150 Where I will walk till thou return to me;
If everyone knows us and we know none,
'Tis time I think to trudge, pack and be gone.

DROMIO S.   As from a bear a man would run for life,
So fly I from her that would be my wife.   *Exit.*

ANTIPHOLUS S.
155 There's none but witches do inhabit here,
And therefore 'tis high time that I were hence;
She that doth call me husband, even my soul
Doth for a wife abhor. But her fair sister,
Possess'd with such a gentle sovereign grace,
160 Of such enchanting presence and discourse,
Hath almost made me traitor to myself;
But lest myself be guilty to self-wrong,
I'll stop mine ears against the mermaid's song.

Enter ANGELO *with the chain.*

ANGELO   Master Antipholus.

ANTIPHOLUS S.   Ay, that's my name.

165 ANGELO   I know it well, sir; lo, here's the chain;
I thought to have ta'en you at the Porpentine,
The chain unfinish'd made me stay thus long.

ANTIPHOLUS S.
What is your will that I shall do with this?

ANGELO
What please yourself, sir; I have made it for you.

170 ANTIPHOLUS S.   Made it for me, sir? I bespoke it not.

ANGELO
Not once, nor twice, but twenty times you have.
Go home with it, and please your wife withal,

And soon at supper-time I'll visit you,
And then receive my money for the chain.

ANTIPHOLUS S.   I pray you, sir, receive the money now,   175
For fear you ne'er see chain nor money more.

ANGELO   You are a merry man, sir; fare you well.   *Exit.*

ANTIPHOLUS S.
What I should think of this I cannot tell;
But this I think, there's no man is so vain
That would refuse so fair an offer'd chain.   180
I see a man here needs not live by shifts
When in the streets he meets such golden gifts.
I'll to the mart, and there for Dromio stay;
If any ship put out, then straight, away.   *Exit.*

4.1   *Enter* Second Merchant, *the goldsmith* ANGELO
and an Officer.

2 MERCHANT
You know since Pentecost the sum is due,
And since I have not much importun'd you,
Nor now I had not, but that I am bound
To Persia, and want guilders for my voyage;
Therefore make present satisfaction,   5
Or I'll attach you by this officer.

ANGELO   Even just the sum that I do owe to you
Is growing to me by Antipholus,
And in the instant that I met with you
He had of me a chain; at five o'clock   10
I shall receive the money for the same.
Pleaseth you walk with me down to his house,
I will discharge my bond, and thank you too.

Enter ANTIPHOLUS OF EPHESUS *and* DROMIO
from the Courtesan's.

OFFICER
That labour may you save; see where he comes.

ANTIPHOLUS E.
While I go to the goldsmith's house, go thou   15
And buy a rope's end; that will I bestow
Among my wife and her confederates
For locking me out of my doors by day –
But soft, I see the goldsmith; get thee gone,
Buy thou a rope and bring it home to me.   20

DROMIO E.
I buy a thousand pound a year, I buy a rope!   *Exit.*

ANTIPHOLUS E.
A man is well holp up that trusts to you;
I promised your presence and the chain,
But neither chain nor goldsmith came to me.
Belike you thought our love would last too long   25
If it were chain'd together, and therefore came not.

ANGELO   Saving your merry humour, here's the note
How much your chain weighs to the utmost carrat,
The fineness of the gold, and chargeful fashion,
Which doth amount to three odd ducats more   30
Than I stand debted to this gentleman;
I pray you see him presently discharg'd,

For he is bound to sea and stays but for it.

ANTIPHOLUS E.

I am not furnish'd with the present money;
Besides, I have some business in the town;
Good signior, take the stranger to my house,
And with you take the chain, and bid my wife
Disburse the sum on the receipt thereof;
Perchance I will be there as soon as you.

ANGELO   Then you will bring the chain to her yourself.

ANTIPHOLUS E.

No, bear it with you, lest I come not time enough.

ANGELO   Well sir, I will. Have you the chain about you?

ANTIPHOLUS E.

And if I have not, sir, I hope you have,
Or else you may return without your money.

ANGELO   Nay, come, I pray you, sir, give me the chain;
Both wind and tide stays for this gentleman,
And I, to blame, have held him here too long.

ANTIPHOLUS E.

Good Lord! You use this dalliance to excuse
Your breach of promise to the Porpentine;
I should have chid you for not bringing it,
But like a shrew you first begin to brawl.

2 MERCHANT

The hour steals on; I pray you, sir, dispatch.

ANGELO   You hear how he importunes me; the chain!

ANTIPHOLUS E.

Why, give it to my wife and fetch your money.

ANGELO

Come, come, you know I gave it you even now.
Either send the chain or send me by some token.

ANTIPHOLUS E.

Fie, now you run this humour out of breath;
Come, where's the chain? I pray you let me see it.

2 MERCHANT   My business cannot brook this dalliance;
Good sir, say whe'er you'll answer me or no;
If not, I'll leave him to the officer.

ANTIPHOLUS E.

I answer you? What should I answer you?

ANGELO   The money that you owe me for the chain.

ANTIPHOLUS E.   I owe you none, till I receive the chain.

ANGELO   You know I gave it you half an hour since.

ANTIPHOLUS E.

You gave me none; you wrong me much to say so.

ANGELO   You wrong me more, sir, in denying it.
Consider how it stands upon my credit.

2 MERCHANT   Well, officer, arrest him at my suit.

OFFICER   I do,
And charge you in the duke's name to obey me.

ANGELO   This touches me in reputation;
Either consent to pay this sum for me,
Or I attach you by this officer.

ANTIPHOLUS E.   Consent to pay thee that I never had?
Arrest me, foolish fellow, if thou dar'st.

ANGELO   Here is thy fee, arrest him officer.
I would not spare my brother in this case
If he should scorn me so apparently.

OFFICER   I do arrest you, sir; you hear the suit.   80

ANTIPHOLUS E.   I do obey thee, till I give thee bail.
But sirrah, you shall buy this sport as dear
As all the metal in your shop will answer.

ANGELO   Sir, sir, I shall have law in Ephesus,
To your notorious shame, I doubt it not.   85

Enter DROMIO OF SYRACUSE *from the bay.*

DROMIO S.   Master, there's a bark of Epidamnum
That stays but till her owner comes aboard,
And then she bears away. Our fraughtage, sir,
I have convey'd aboard, and I have bought
The oil, the balsamum and aqua-vitae.   90
The ship is in her trim, the merry wind
Blows fair from land; they stay for nought at all
But for their owner, master, and yourself.

ANTIPHOLUS E.

How now? a madman? Why, thou peevish sheep,
What ship of Epidamnum stays for me?   95

DROMIO S.   A ship you sent me to, to hire waftage.

ANTIPHOLUS E.

Thou drunken slave, I sent thee for a rope,
And told thee to what purpose and what end.

DROMIO S.   You sent me for a rope's end, sir, as soon;
You sent me to the bay, sir, for a bark.   100

ANTIPHOLUS E.

I will debate this matter at more leisure,
And teach your ears to list me with more heed.
To Adriana, villain, hie thee straight:
Give her this key, and tell her in the desk
That's cover'd o'er with Turkish tapestry,   105
There is a purse of ducats; let her send it.
Tell her I am arrested in the street,
And that shall bail me; hie thee slave, be gone;
On, officer, to prison, till it come.

Exeunt all but Dromio.

DROMIO S.   To Adriana, – that is where we din'd,   110
Where Dowsabel did claim me for her husband;
She is too big I hope for me to compass.
Thither I must, although against my will;
For servants must their masters' minds fulfil.   *Exit.*

4.2   *Enter* ADRIANA *and* LUCIANA.

ADRIANA   Ah, Luciana, did he tempt thee so?
Might'st thou perceive austerely in his eye
That he did plead in earnest, yea or no?
Look'd he or red or pale, or sad or merrily?
What observation mad'st thou in this case,   5
Of his heart's meteors tilting in his face?

LUCIANA   First he denied you had in him no right.

ADRIANA

He meant he did me none; the more my spite.

LUCIANA   Then swore he that he was a stranger here.

ADRIANA

And true he swore, though yet forsworn he were.   10

LUCIANA   Then pleaded I for you.

ADRIANA   And what said he?

LUCIANA   That love I begg'd for you, he begg'd of me.

ADRIANA   With what persuasion did he tempt thy love?

LUCIANA

   With words that in an honest suit might move:

15   First he did praise my beauty, then my speech.

ADRIANA   Did'st speak him fair?

LUCIANA   Have patience, I beseech.

ADRIANA

   I cannot, nor I will not hold me still.

   My tongue, though not my heart, shall have his will.

   He is deformed, crooked, old and sere,

20   Ill-fac'd, worse bodied, shapeless everywhere;

   Vicious, ungentle, foolish, blunt, unkind,

   Stigmatical in making, worse in mind.

LUCIANA   Who would be jealous then of such a one?

   No evil lost is wail'd when it is gone.

25 ADRIANA   Ah, but I think him better than I say,

   And yet would herein others' eyes were worse:

   Far from her nest the lapwing cries away;

   My heart prays for him, though my tongue do curse.

Enter DROMIO OF SYRACUSE.

DROMIO S.

   Here, go: the desk; the purse; sweat now, make haste.

LUCIANA   How hast thou lost thy breath?

30 DROMIO S.   By running fast.

ADRIANA   Where is thy master, Dromio? is he well?

DROMIO S.   No, he's in Tartar limbo, worse than hell.

   A devil in an everlasting garment hath him,

   One whose hard heart is button'd up with steel;

35   A fiend, a fury, pitiless and rough,

   A wolf, nay worse, a fellow all in buff;

   A back-friend, a shoulder-clapper, one that

     countermands

   The passages of alleys, creeks and narrow lands;

   A hound that runs counter, and yet draws dry-foot

     well,

   One that, before the judgment, carries poor souls to

40   hell.

ADRIANA   Why, man, what is the matter?

DROMIO S.

   I do not know the matter; he is 'rested on the case.

ADRIANA   What, is he arrested? tell me at whose suit?

DROMIO S.

   I know not at whose suit he is arrested well;

   But is in a suit of buff which 'rested him, that can I

45   tell:

   Will you send him, mistress, redemption, the money

     in his desk?

ADRIANA   Go, fetch it, sister; this I wonder at,

                                 Exit Luciana.

   That he unknown to me should be in debt.

   Tell me, was he arrested on a band?

50 DROMIO S.   Not on a band, but on a stronger thing;

   A chain, a chain, do you not hear it ring?

ADRIANA   What, the chain?

DROMIO S.   No, no, the bell, 'tis time

   that I were gone,

   It was two ere I left him, and now the clock strikes

   one.

ADRIANA   The hours come back; that did I never hear.

DROMIO S.

   O yes, if any hour meet a sergeant, 'a turns back for

   very fear.   55

ADRIANA

   As if time were in debt; how fondly dost thou reason.

DROMIO S.

   Time is a very bankrupt, and owes more than he's

     worth to season.

   Nay, he's a thief too; have you not heard men say

   That time comes stealing on by night and day?

   If 'a be in debt and theft, and a sergeant in the way,   60

   Hath he not reason to turn back an hour in a day?

Enter LUCIANA *with the money.*

ADRIANA

   Go, Dromio, there's the money, bear it straight,

   And bring thy master home immediately.

   Come, sister, I am press'd down with conceit;

   Conceit, my comfort and my injury.   *Exeunt.*   65

4.3   *Enter* ANTIPHOLUS OF SYRACUSE.

ANTIPHOLUS S.

   There's not a man I meet but doth salute me

   As if I were their well-acquainted friend,

   And every one doth call me by my name:

   Some tender money to me, some invite me,

   Some other give me thanks for kindnesses,   5

   Some offer me commodities to buy.

   Even now a tailor call'd me in his shop,

   And show'd me silks that he had bought for me,

   And therewithal took measure of my body.

   Sure these are but imaginary wiles,   10

   And Lapland sorcerers inhabit here.

Enter DROMIO OF SYRACUSE.

DROMIO S.   Master, here's the gold you sent me for: what, have you got the picture of old Adam new-apparelled?

ANTIPHOLUS S.   What gold is this? What Adam dost   15 thou mean?

DROMIO S.   Not that Adam that kept the paradise, but that Adam that keeps the prison; he that goes in the calf's-skin that was killed for the prodigal; he that came behind you, sir, like an evil angel, and bid you   20 forsake your liberty.

ANTIPHOLUS S.   I understand thee not.

DROMIO S.   No? why, 'tis a plain case; he that went like a bass-viol in a case of leather; the man, sir, that when gentlemen are tired gives them a sob, and rests them;   25 he, sir, that takes pity on decayed men and gives them

suits of durance; he that sets up his rest to do more
exploits with his mace than a morris-pike.

ANTIPHOLUS S.   What, thou mean'st an officer?

DROMIO S.   Ay, sir, the sergeant of the band; he that
brings any man to answer it that breaks his band; one
that thinks a man always going to bed, and says, 'God
give you good rest'.

ANTIPHOLUS S.   Well, sir, there rest in your foolery. Is
there any ship puts forth to-night? may we be gone?

DROMIO S.   Why, sir, I brought you word an hour since,
that the bark *Expedition* put forth tonight, and then
were you hindered by the sergeant to tarry for the hoy
Delay. Here are the angels that you sent for to deliver
you.

ANTIPHOLUS S.   The fellow is distract, and so am I,
And here we wander in illusions –
Some blessed power deliver us from hence!

Enter a Courtesan.

COURTESAN   Well met, well met, master Antipholus;
I see, sir, you have found the goldsmith now;
Is that the chain you promis'd me to-day?

ANTIPHOLUS S.
Satan avoid, I charge thee tempt me not.

DROMIO S.   Master, is this mistress Satan?

ANTIPHOLUS S.   It is the devil.

DROMIO S.   Nay, she is worse, she is the devil's dam; and
here she comes in the habit of a light wench, and
thereof comes that the wenches say 'God damn me',
that's as much as to say, 'God make me a light wench'.
It is written, they appear to men like angels of light;
light is an effect of fire, and fire will burn; ergo, light
wenches will burn; come not near her.

COURTESAN
Your man and you are marvellous merry, sir.
Will you go with me? we'll mend our dinner here.

DROMIO S.   Master, if you do, expect spoon-meat, or
bespeak a long spoon.

ANTIPHOLUS S.   Why, Dromio?

DROMIO S.   Marry, he must have a long spoon that must
eat with the devil.

ANTIPHOLUS S.
Avoid then, fiend, what tell'st thou me of supping?
Thou art, as you are all, a sorceress:
I conjure thee to leave me and be gone.

COURTESAN
Give me the ring of mine you had at dinner,
Or for my diamond the chain you promis'd,
And I'll be gone, sir, and not trouble you.

DROMIO S.   Some devils ask but the parings of one's nail,
a rush, a hair, a drop of blood, a pin, a nut, a cherry-
stone; but she, more covetous, would have a chain.
Master, be wise; and if you give it her, the devil will
shake her chain and fright us with it.

COURTESAN   I pray you, sir, my ring, or else the chain;
I hope you do not mean to cheat me so?

ANTIPHOLUS S.
Avaunt, thou witch. Come, Dromio, let us go.

DROMIO S.
Fly pride, says the peacock; mistress, that you know.
Exeunt Antipholus and Dromio.

COURTESAN   Now out of doubt Antipholus is mad,
Else would he never so demean himself;   80
A ring he hath of mine worth forty ducats,
And for the same he promis'd me a chain;
Both one and other he denies me now.
The reason that I gather he is mad,
Besides this present instance of his rage,   85
Is a mad tale he told to-day at dinner
Of his own doors being shut against his entrance.
Belike his wife, acquainted with his fits,
On purpose shut the doors against his way –
My way is now to hie home to his house,   90
And tell his wife that, being lunatic,
He rush'd into my house and took perforce
My ring away. This course I fittest choose,
For forty ducats is too much to lose.   *Exit.*

4.4 *Enter* ANTIPHOLUS OF EPHESUS *with the* Officer.

ANTIPHOLUS E.
Fear me not, man, I will not break away.
I'll give thee ere I leave thee so much money
To warrant thee as I am 'rested for.
My wife is in a wayward mood to-day,
And will not lightly trust the messenger   5
That I should be attach'd in Ephesus;
I tell you 'twill sound harshly in her ears.

Enter DROMIO OF EPHESUS *with a rope's end.*

Here comes my man, I think he brings the money.
How now, sir? have you that I sent you for?

DROMIO E.   Here's that, I warrant you, will pay them all.   10

ANTIPHOLUS E.   But where's the money?

DROMIO E.   Why, sir, I gave the money for the rope.

ANTIPHOLUS E.   Five hundred ducats, villain, for a rope?

DROMIO E.   I'll serve you, sir, five hundred at the rate.

ANTIPHOLUS E.   To what end did I bid thee hie thee   15
home?

DROMIO E.   To a rope's end, sir, and to that end am I
return'd.

ANTIPHOLUS E.   And to that end, sir, I will welcome you.
[*Beats Dromio.*]

OFFICER   Good sir, be patient.   20

DROMIO E.   Nay, 'tis for me to be patient, I am in
adversity.

OFFICER   Good now, hold thy tongue.

DROMIO E.   Nay, rather persuade him to hold his hands.

ANTIPHOLUS E.   Thou whoreson, senseless villain.   25

DROMIO E.   I would I were senseless, sir, that I might not
feel your blows.

ANTIPHOLUS E.   Thou art sensible in nothing but blows,
and so is an ass.

DROMIO E.   I am an ass indeed; you may prove it by my
long ears. I have served him from the hour of my
nativity to this instant, and have nothing at his hands
for my service but blows. When I am cold, he heats me
with beating; when I am warm he cools me with
beating; I am waked with it when I sleep, raised with
it when I sit, driven out of doors with it when I go
from home, welcomed home with it when I return,
nay, I bear it on my shoulders as a beggar wont her
brat; and I think when he hath lamed me, I shall beg
with it from door to door.

Enter ADRIANA, LUCIANA, Courtesan
and a schoolmaster, called PINCH.

ANTIPHOLUS E.   Come, go along, my wife is coming
yonder.
DROMIO E.   Mistress, *respice finem*, respect your end, or
rather, to prophesy like the parrot, beware the rope's
end.
ANTIPHOLUS E.   Wilt thou still talk? [*Beats Dromio.*]
COURTESAN
How say you now? Is not your husband mad?
ADRIANA   His incivility confirms no less.
Good Doctor Pinch, you are a conjurer;
Establish him in his true sense again,
And I will please you what you will demand.
LUCIANA   Alas, how fiery, and how sharp he looks.
COURTESAN   Mark how he trembles in his ecstasy.
PINCH   Give me your hand, and let me feel your pulse.
ANTIPHOLUS E.
There is my hand, and let it feel your ear.
[*He strikes Pinch.*]
PINCH   I charge thee, Satan, hous'd within this man,
To yield possession to my holy prayers,
And to thy state of darkness hie thee straight;
I conjure thee by all the saints in heaven.
ANTIPHOLUS E.
Peace, doting wizard, peace; I am not mad.
ADRIANA   O that thou wert not, poor distressed soul.
ANTIPHOLUS E.
You minion, you, are these your customers?
Did this companion with the saffron face
Revel and feast it at my house to-day,
Whilst upon me the guilty doors were shut,
And I denied to enter in my house?
ADRIANA
O husband, God doth know you din'd at home,
Where would you had remain'd until this time,
Free from these slanders and this open shame.
ANTIPHOLUS E.
Din'd at home?
[*to Dromio*]   Thou villain, what sayest thou?
DROMIO E.   Sir, sooth to say, you did not dine at home.
ANTIPHOLUS E.
Were not my doors lock'd up, and I shut out?
DROMIO E.
Perdy, your doors were lock'd, and you shut out.

ANTIPHOLUS E.
And did she not herself revile me there?
DROMIO E.   Sans fable, she herself revil'd you there.
ANTIPHOLUS E.
Did not her kitchen-maid rail, taunt and scorn me?
DROMIO E.
Certes she did, the kitchen-vestal scorn'd you.
ANTIPHOLUS E.
And did not I in rage depart from thence?
DROMIO E.   In verity you did; my bones bears witness.
That since have felt the vigour of his rage.
ADRIANA   Is't good to soothe him in these contraries?
PINCH   It is no shame; the fellow finds his vein,
And yielding to him, humours well his frenzy.
ANTIPHOLUS E.
Thou hast suborn'd the goldsmith to arrest me.
ADRIANA   Alas, I sent you money to redeem you
By Dromio here, who came in haste for it.
DROMIO E.
Money by me? Heart and good will you might,
But surely, master, not a rag of money.
ANTIPHOLUS E.
Went'st not thou to her for a purse of ducats?
ADRIANA   He came to me and I deliver'd it.
LUCIANA   And I am witness with her that she did.
DROMIO E.   God and the rope-maker bear me witness
That I was sent for nothing but a rope.
PINCH   Mistress, both man and master is possess'd,
I know it by their pale and deadly looks;
They must be bound and laid in some dark room.
ANTIPHOLUS E.
Say, wherefore didst thou lock me forth to-day,
And why dost thou deny the bag of gold?
ADRIANA   I did not, gentle husband, lock thee forth.
DROMIO E.   And gentle master, I receiv'd no gold;
But I confess, sir, that we were lock'd out.
ADRIANA
Dissembling villain, thou speak'st false in both.
ANTIPHOLUS E.
Dissembling harlot, thou art false in all,
And art confederate with a damned pack
To make a loathsome abject scorn of me;
But with these nails I'll pluck out these false eyes
That would behold in me this shameful sport.
ADRIANA
O bind him, bind him, let him not come near me.
[*Enter three or four and offer to bind him; he strives.*]
PINCH   More company; the fiend is strong within him.
LUCIANA   Ay me, poor man, how pale and wan he looks.
ANTIPHOLUS E.
What, will you murder me? Thou jailor, thou,
I am thy prisoner; wilt thou suffer them
To make a rescue?
OFFICER   Masters, let him go;
He is my prisoner and you shall not have him.
PINCH   Go bind this man, for he is frantic too.
ADRIANA   What wilt thou do, thou peevish officer?

Hast thou delight to see a wretched man
Do outrage and displeasure to himself?
OFFICER   He is my prisoner; if I let him go
20   The debt he owes will be requir'd of me.
ADRIANA   I will discharge thee ere I go from thee;
Bear me forthwith unto his creditor,
And knowing how the debt grows, I will pay it.
Good master doctor, see him safe convey'd
25   Home to my house; O most unhappy day!
ANTIPHOLUS E.   O most unhappy strumpet!
DROMIO E.   Master, I am here enter'd in bond for you.
ANTIPHOLUS E.   Out on thee villain, wherefore dost thou
mad me?
30   DROMIO E.   Will you be bound for nothing? Be mad,
good master; cry 'the devil'.
LUCIANA   God help, poor souls, how idly do they talk!
ADRIANA   Go, bear him hence; sister, go you with me.
Say now, whose suit is he arrested at?
Exeunt Pinch and his assistants carrying
off Antipholus and Dromio of Ephesus.
35   OFFICER   One Angelo, a goldsmith; do you know him?
ADRIANA   I know the man; what is the sum he owes?
OFFICER   Two hundred ducats.
ADRIANA   Say, how grows it due?
OFFICER   Due for a chain your husband had of him.
ADRIANA
He did bespeak a chain for me, but had it not.
140   COURTESAN   When as your husband all in rage to-day
Came to my house and took away my ring,
The ring I saw upon his finger now,
Straight after did I meet him with a chain.
ADRIANA   It may be so, but I did never see it.
145   Come, jailor, bring me where the goldsmith is;
I long to know the truth hereof at large.

Enter ANTIPHOLUS *and* DROMIO OF SYRACUSE
with rapiers drawn.

LUCIANA   God for thy mercy, they are loose again!
ADRIANA
And come with naked swords; let's call more help
To have them bound again.
OFFICER   Away, they'll kill us!
They run all out, as fast as may be, frighted.
ANTIPHOLUS S.
150   I see these witches are afraid of swords.
DROMIO S.
She that would be your wife now ran from you.
ANTIPHOLUS S.
Come to the Centaur, fetch our stuff from thence;
I long that we were safe and sound aboard.
DROMIO S.   Faith, stay here this night, they will surely
155   do us no harm; you saw they speak us fair, give us
gold. Methinks they are such a gentle nation, that but
for the mountain of mad flesh that claims marriage of
me, I could find in my heart to stay here still and turn
witch.

ANTIPHOLUS S.   I will not stay to-night for all the town;   160
Therefore away, to get our stuff aboard.   *Exeunt.*

5.1   *Enter* Second Merchant
and ANGELO *the goldsmith.*

ANGELO   I am sorry, sir, that I have hinder'd you,
But I protest he had the chain of me,
Though most dishonestly he doth deny it.
2 MERCHANT
How is the man esteem'd here in the city?
ANGELO   Of very reverend reputation, sir,   5
Of credit infinite, highly belov'd,
Second to none that lives here in the city;
His word might bear my wealth at any time.
2 MERCHANT   Speak softly; yonder, as I think, he walks.

Enter ANTIPHOLUS *and* DROMIO OF SYRACUSE *again.*

ANGELO   'Tis so; and that self chain about his neck   10
Which he forswore most monstrously to have.
Good sir, draw near to me; I'll speak to him.
Signior Antipholus, I wonder much
That you would put me to this shame and trouble,
And not without some scandal to yourself,   15
With circumstance and oaths so to deny
This chain, which now you wear so openly.
Beside the charge, the shame, imprisonment,
You have done wrong to this my honest friend,
Who, but for staying on our controversy,   20
Had hoisted sail and put to sea to-day.
This chain you had of me, can you deny it?
ANTIPHOLUS S.   I think I had; I never did deny it.
ANGELO   Yes, that you did, sir, and forswore it too.
ANTIPHOLUS S.
Who heard me to deny it or forswear it?   25
2 MERCHANT
These ears of mine thou know'st did hear thee.
Fie on thee, wretch, 'tis pity that thou liv'st
To walk where any honest men resort.
ANTIPHOLUS S.   Thou art a villain to impeach me thus;
I'll prove mine honour and mine honesty   30
Against thee presently, if thou dar'st stand.
2 MERCHANT   I dare, and do defy thee for a villain.

They draw. Enter ADRIANA, LUCIANA,
Courtesan *and others.*

ADRIANA
Hold, hurt him not for God's sake, he is mad;
Some get within him, take his sword away;
Bind Dromio too, and bear them to my house.   35
DROMIO S.
Run master, run, for God's sake take a house;
This is some priory; in, or we are spoil'd.
Exeunt Antipholus and Dromio to the priory.

Enter EMILIA, *the Lady Abbess.*

ABBESS   Be quiet, people; wherefore throng you hither?

ADRIANA   To fetch my poor distracted husband hence;
40   Let us come in, that we may bind him fast
       And bear him home for his recovery.
ANGELO   I knew he was not in his perfect wits.
2 MERCHANT   I am sorry now that I did draw on him.
ABBESS   How long hath this possession held the man?
45   ADRIANA   This week he hath been heavy, sour, sad,
       And much, much different from the man he was;
       But till this afternoon his passion
       Ne'er brake into extremity of rage.
ABBESS   Hath he not lost much wealth by wrack of sea?
50   Buried some dear friend? Hath not else his eye
       Stray'd his affection in unlawful love,
       A sin prevailing much in youthful men,
       Who give their eyes the liberty of gazing?
       Which of these sorrows is he subject to?
55   ADRIANA   To none of these, except it be the last,
       Namely, some love that drew him oft from home.
ABBESS   You should for that have reprehended him.
ADRIANA   Why, so I did.
ABBESS   Ay, but not rough enough.
ADRIANA   As roughly as my modesty would let me.
ABBESS   Haply in private.
60   ADRIANA   And in assemblies too.
ABBESS   Ay, but not enough.
ADRIANA   It was the copy of our conference;
       In bed he slept not for my urging it,
       At board he fed not for my urging it;
65   Alone, it was the subject of my theme;
       In company I often glanc'd at it;
       Still did I tell him it was vile and bad.
ABBESS   And thereof came it that the man was mad.
       The venom clamours of a jealous woman
70   Poisons more deadly than a mad dog's tooth.
       It seems his sleeps were hinder'd by thy railing,
       And thereof comes it that his head is light.
       Thou say'st his meat was sauc'd with thy
         upbraidings;
       Unquiet meals make ill digestions;
75   Thereof the raging fire of fever bred,
       And what's a fever but a fit of madness?
       Thou sayest his sports were hinder'd by thy brawls;
       Sweet recreation barr'd, what doth ensue
       But moody and dull melancholy,
80   Kinsman to grim and comfortless despair,
       And at her heels a huge infectious troop
       Of pale distemperatures and foes to life?
       In food, in sport and life-preserving rest
       To be disturb'd, would mad or man or beast;
85   The consequence is then, thy jealous fits
       Hath scar'd thy husband from the use of wits.
LUCIANA   She never reprehended him but mildly,
       When he demean'd himself rough, rude and wildly;
       Why bear you these rebukes and answer not?
90   ADRIANA   She did betray me to mine own reproof.
       Good people, enter and lay hold on him.

ABBESS   No, not a creature enters in my house.
ADRIANA
       Then let your servants bring my husband forth.
ABBESS   Neither. He took this place for sanctuary,
       And it shall privilege him from your hands   95
       Till I have brought him to his wits again,
       Or lose my labour in assaying it.
ADRIANA   I will attend my husband, be his nurse,
       Diet his sickness, for it is my office,
       And will have no attorney but myself,   100
       And therefore let me have him home with me.
ABBESS   Be patient, for I will not let him stir
       Till I have us'd the approved means I have,
       With wholesome syrups, drugs and holy prayers,
       To make of him a formal man again.   105
       It is a branch and parcel of mine oath,
       A charitable duty of my order;
       Therefore depart, and leave him here with me.
ADRIANA   I will not hence and leave my husband here:
       And ill it doth beseem your holiness   110
       To separate the husband and the wife.
ABBESS   Be quiet and depart, thou shalt not have him.
                                                Exit.
LUCIANA   Complain unto the duke of this indignity.
ADRIANA   Come, go, I will fall prostrate at his feet,
       And never rise until my tears and prayers   115
       Have won his grace to come in person hither,
       And take perforce my husband from the abbess.
2 MERCHANT   By this I think the dial points at five;
       Anon I'm sure the Duke himself in person
       Comes this way to the melancholy vale,   120
       The place of death and sorry execution
       Behind the ditches of the abbey here.
ANGELO   Upon what cause?
2 MERCHANT   To see a reverend Syracusian merchant,
       Who put unluckily into this bay,   125
       Against the laws and statutes of this town,
       Beheaded publicly for his offence.
ANGELO
       See where they come; we will behold his death.
LUCIANA   Kneel to the Duke before he pass the abbey.

Enter SOLINUS *the* DUKE *of Ephesus, and* EGEON *the
merchant of Syracuse barehead, with the headsman
and other officers.*

DUKE   Yet once again proclaim it publicly,   130
       If any friend will pay the sum for him,
       He shall not die, so much we tender him.
ADRIANA   Justice, most sacred duke, against the abbess.
DUKE   She is a virtuous and a reverend lady,
       It cannot be that she hath done thee wrong.   135
ADRIANA
       May it please your grace, Antipholus my husband,
       Who I made lord of me and all I had
       At your important letters, this ill day
       A most outrageous fit of madness took him;

That desp'rately he hurried through the street,   140
With him his bondman, all as mad as he,
Doing displeasure to the citizens
By rushing in their houses; bearing thence
Rings, jewels, any thing his rage did like.
Once did I get him bound, and sent him home,   145
Whilst to take order for the wrongs I went,
That here and there his fury had committed;
Anon, I wot not by what strong escape,
He broke from those that had the guard of him,
And with his mad attendant and himself,   150
Each one with ireful passion, with drawn swords
Met us again, and madly bent on us,
Chas'd us away; till raising of more aid
We came again to bind them. Then they fled
Into this abbey, whither we pursu'd them,   155
And here the abbess shuts the gates on us,
And will not suffer us to fetch him out,
Nor send him forth that we may bear him hence.
Therefore, most gracious duke, with thy command
Let him be brought forth, and borne hence for help.   160

DUKE   Long since thy husband serv'd me in my wars,
And I to thee engag'd a prince's word,
When thou didst make him master of thy bed,
To do him all the grace and good I could.
Go some of you, knock at the abbey gate,   165
And bid the lady abbess come to me.
I will determine this before I stir.

Enter a Messenger.

MESSENGER
O mistress, mistress, shift and save yourself;
My master and his man are both broke loose,
Beaten the maids a-row, and bound the doctor,   170
Whose beard they have sing'd off with brands of fire,
And ever as it blaz'd, they threw on him
Great pails of puddled mire to quench the hair;
My master preaches patience to him, and the while
His man with scissors nicks him like a fool;   175
And sure (unless you send some present help)
Between them they will kill the conjurer.

ADRIANA   Peace, fool, thy master and his man are here,
And that is false thou dost report to us.

MESSENGER   Mistress, upon my life I tell you true,   180
I have not breath'd almost since I did see it.
He cries for you, and vows if he can take you
To scorch your face and to disfigure you.
[*cry within*]
Hark, hark, I hear him, mistress – fly, be gone.

DUKE
Come, stand by me, fear nothing; guard with   185
    halberds.

ADRIANA   Ay me, it is my husband; witness you
That he is borne about invisible;
Even now we hous'd him in the abbey here,
And now he's there, past thought of human reason.

Enter ANTIPHOLUS *and* DROMIO OF EPHESUS.

ANTIPHOLUS E.
Justice, most gracious Duke, O, grant me justice,   190
Even for the service that long since I did thee
When I bestrid thee in the wars, and took
Deep scars to save thy life; even for the blood
That then I lost for thee, now grant me justice.

EGEON   Unless the fear of death doth make me dote,   195
I see my son Antipholus and Dromio.

ANTIPHOLUS E.
Justice, sweet prince, against that woman there –
She whom thou gav'st to me to be my wife;
That hath abused and dishonour'd me,
Even in the strength and height of injury.   200
Beyond imagination is the wrong
That she this day hath shameless thrown on me.

DUKE   Discover how, and thou shalt find me just.

ANTIPHOLUS E.
This day, great duke, she shut the doors upon me
While she with harlots feasted in my house.   205

DUKE   A grievous fault: say, woman, didst thou so?

ADRIANA   No, my good lord. Myself, he, and my sister
To-day did dine together; so befall my soul
As this is false he burdens me withal.

LUCIANA   Ne'er may I look on day, nor sleep on night,   210
But she tells to your highness simple truth.

ANGELO [*aside*]
O perjur'd woman! They are both forsworn,
In this the madman justly chargeth them.

ANTIPHOLUS E.
My liege, I am advised what I say,
Neither disturb'd with the effect of wine,   215
Nor heady-rash, provok'd with raging ire,
Albeit my wrongs might make one wiser mad.
This woman lock'd me out this day from dinner;
That goldsmith there, were he not pack'd with her,
Could witness it; for he was with me then,   220
Who parted with me to go fetch a chain,
Promising to bring it to the Porpentine,
Where Balthasar and I did dine together.
Our dinner done, and he not coming thither,
I went to seek him. In the street I met him,   225
And in his company that gentleman.
There did this perjur'd goldsmith swear me down
That I this day of him receiv'd the chain,
Which, God he knows, I saw not. For the which
He did arrest me with an officer;   230
I did obey, and sent my peasant home
For certain ducats; he with none return'd.
Then fairly I bespoke the officer
To go in person with me to my house.
By th'way we met   235
My wife, her sister, and a rabble more
Of vile confederates; along with them
They brought one Pinch, a hungry lean-fac'd villain;
A mere anatomy, a mountebank,

240 A thread-bare juggler and a fortune-teller,
A needy-hollow-ey'd-sharp-looking-wretch;
A living dead man. This pernicious slave
Forsooth took on him as a conjurer,
And gazing in mine eyes, feeling my pulse,
245 And with no-face (as 'twere) out-facing me,
Cries out, I was possess'd. Then all together
They fell upon me, bound me, bore me thence,
And in a dark and dankish vault at home
There left me and my man, both bound together,
250 Till gnawing with my teeth my bonds in sunder,
I gain'd my freedom; and immediately
Ran hither to your grace, whom I beseech
To give me ample satisfaction
For these deep shames and great indignities.
ANGELO
255 My lord, in truth, thus far I witness with him,
That he din'd not at home, but was lock'd out.
DUKE   But had he such a chain of thee, or no?
ANGELO   He had, my lord, and when he ran in here
These people saw the chain about his neck.
2 MERCHANT
260 Besides, I will be sworn these ears of mine
Heard you confess you had the chain of him,
After you first forswore it on the mart,
And thereupon I drew my sword on you;
And then you fled into this abbey here,
265 From whence I think you are come by miracle.
ANTIPHOLUS E.
I never came within these abbey walls,
Nor ever didst thou draw thy sword on me;
I never saw the chain, so help me heaven;
And this is false you burden me withal.
270 DUKE   Why, what an intricate impeach is this?
I think you all have drunk of Circe's cup:
If here you hous'd him, here he would have been;
If he were mad, he would not plead so coldly.
You say he din'd at home, the goldsmith here
275 Denies that saying. Sirrah, what say you?
DROMIO E.
Sir, he din'd with her there, at the Porpentine.
COURTESAN
He did, and from my finger snatch'd that ring.
ANTIPHOLUS E.
'Tis true, my liege, this ring I had of her.
DUKE   Saw'st thou him enter at the abbey here?
280 COURTESAN   As sure, my liege, as I do see your grace.
DUKE   Why, this is strange: go, call the abbess hither.
I think you are all mated, or stark mad.
                              Exit one to the Abbess.
EGEON   Most mighty duke, vouchsafe me speak a word;
Haply I see a friend will save my life,
285 And pay the sum that may deliver me.
DUKE   Speak freely, Syracusian, what thou wilt.
EGEON   Is not your name, sir, call'd Antipholus?
And is not that your bondman Dromio?

DROMIO E.
Within this hour I was his bondman, sir,
But he, I thank him, gnaw'd in two my cords;   290
Now I am Dromio, and his man, unbound.
EGEON   I am sure you both of you remember me.
DROMIO E.   Ourselves we do remember, sir, by you.
For lately we were bound as you are now.
You are not Pinch's patient, are you sir?   295
EGEON
Why look you strange on me? you know me well.
ANTIPHOLUS E.
I never saw you in my life till now.
EGEON
O! grief hath chang'd me since you saw me last,
And careful hours with time's deformed hand
Have written strange defeatures in my face;   300
But tell me yet, dost thou not know my voice?
ANTIPHOLUS E.   Neither.
EGEON   Dromio, nor thou?
DROMIO E.   No, trust me sir, nor I.
EGEON   I am sure thou dost?
DROMIO E.   Ay sir, but I am sure I do not, and   305
whatsoever a man denies, you are bound to believe
him.
EGEON   Not know my voice? O time's extremity,
Hast thou so crack'd and splitted my poor tongue
In seven short years, that here my only son   310
Knows not my feeble key of untun'd cares?
Though now this grained face of mine be hid
In sap-consuming winter's drizzled snow,
And all the conduits of my blood froze up,
Yet hath my night of life some memory;   315
My wasting lamps some fading glimmer left;
My dull deaf ears a little use to hear –
All these old witnesses, I cannot err,
Tell me thou art my son Antipholus.
ANTIPHOLUS E.   I never saw my father in my life.   320
EGEON   But seven years since, in Syracusa, boy,
Thou know'st we parted, but perhaps, my son,
Thou sham'st to acknowledge me in misery.
ANTIPHOLUS E.
The duke, and all that know me in the city,
Can witness with me that it is not so.   325
I ne'er saw Syracusa in my life.
DUKE   I tell thee Syracusian, twenty years
Have I been patron to Antipholus,
During which time he ne'er saw Syracusa.
I see thy age and dangers make thee dote.   330

Enter EMILIA *the* ABBESS *with* ANTIPHOLUS *and*
DROMIO OF SYRACUSE.

ABBESS
Most mighty duke, behold a man much wrong'd.
[*All gather to see them.*]
ADRIANA   I see two husbands, or mine eyes deceive me.
DUKE   One of these men is *genius* to the other;

And so of these, which is the natural man,
And which the spirit? Who deciphers them?   35

DROMIO S.   I, sir, am Dromio, command him away.

DROMIO E.   I, sir, am Dromio, pray let me stay.

ANTIPHOLUS S.   Egeon art thou not? or else his ghost.

DROMIO S.
O, my old master, who hath bound him here?

ABBESS   Whoever bound him, I will loose his bonds,   40
And gain a husband by his liberty.
Speak old Egeon, if thou be'st the man
That hadst a wife once call'd Emilia,
That bore thee at a burden two fair sons?
O, if thou be'st the same Egeon, speak –   45
And speak unto the same Emilia.

DUKE   Why, here begins his morning story right:
These two Antipholus', these two so like,
And these two Dromios, one in semblance,
Besides her urging of her wrack at sea.   50
These are the parents to these children,
Which accidentally are met together.

EGEON   If I dream not, thou art Emilia;
If thou art she, tell me, where is that son
That floated with thee on the fatal raft?   55

ABBESS   By men of Epidamnum, he and I
And the twin Dromio, all were taken up;
But by and by, rude fishermen of Corinth
By force took Dromio and my son from them,
And me they left with those of Epidamnum.   60
What then became of them I cannot tell;
I, to this fortune that you see me in.

DUKE   Antipholus, thou cam'st from Corinth first.

ANTIPHOLUS S.   No, sir, not I, I came from Syracuse.

DUKE   Stay, stand apart, I know not which is which.   65

ANTIPHOLUS E.
I came from Corinth, my most gracious lord.

DROMIO E.   And I with him.

ANTIPHOLUS E.
Brought to this town by that most famous warrior,
Duke Menaphon, your most renowned uncle.

ADRIANA   Which of you two did dine with me to-day?   70

ANTIPHOLUS S.   I, gentle mistress.

ADRIANA   And are you not my husband?

ANTIPHOLUS E.   No, I say nay to that.

ANTIPHOLUS S.   And so do I, yet did she call me so;
And this fair gentlewoman, her sister here,
Did call me brother.

[*to Luciana*]   What I told you then,   75
I hope I shall have leisure to make good,
If this be not a dream I see and hear.

ANGELO   That is the chain, sir, which you had of me.

ANTIPHOLUS S.   I think it be, sir, I deny it not.

ANTIPHOLUS E.
And you, sir, for this chain arrested me.   80

ANGELO   I think I did, sir, I deny it not.

ADRIANA   I sent you money, sir, to be your bail
By Dromio, but I think he brought it not.

DROMIO E.   No, none by me.

ANTIPHOLUS S.
This purse of ducats I receiv'd from you,   385
And Dromio my man did bring them me.
I see we still did meet each other's man,
And I was ta'en for him, and he for me,
And thereupon these errors are arose.

ANTIPHOLUS E.
These ducats pawn I for my father here.   390

DUKE   It shall not need, thy father hath his life.

COURTESAN   Sir, I must have that diamond from you.

ANTIPHOLUS E.
There, take it, and much thanks for my good cheer.

ABBESS   Renowned duke, vouchsafe to take the pains
To go with us into the abbey here,   395
And hear at large discoursed all our fortunes;
And all that are assembled in this place,
That by this sympathised one day's error
Have suffer'd wrong, go, keep us company.
And we shall make full satisfaction.   400
Thirty-three years have I but gone in travail
Of you, my sons, and till this present hour
My heavy burden ne'er delivered.
The duke, my husband, and my children both,
And you, the calendars of their nativity,   405
Go to a gossips' feast, and joy with me,
After so long grief, such felicity.

DUKE   With all my heart, I'll gossip at this feast.
                    Exeunt; the two Dromios and two brothers
                                  Antipholus remain behind.

DROMIO S.
Master, shall I fetch your stuff from shipboard?

ANTIPHOLUS E.
Dromio, what stuff of mine hast thou embark'd?   410

DROMIO S.
Your goods that lay at host, sir, in the Centaur.

ANTIPHOLUS S.
He speaks to me; I am your master, Dromio.
Come, go with us, we'll look to that anon;
Embrace thy brother there, rejoice with him.
                    Exeunt the two Antipholuses together.

DROMIO S.   There is a fat friend at your master's house,   415
That kitchen'd me for you to-day at dinner;
She now shall be my sister, not my wife.

DROMIO E.
Methinks you are my glass, and not my brother:
I see by you I am a sweet-fac'd youth;
Will you walk in to see their gossiping?   420

DROMIO S.   Not I, sir, you are my elder.

DROMIO E.   That's a question, how shall we try it?

DROMIO S.
We'll draw cuts for the senior; till then, lead thou
    first.

DROMIO E.   Nay then, thus:
We came into the world like brother and brother,   425
And now let's go hand in hand, not one before
    another.   *Exeunt.*

Coriolanus

Coriolanus was first published in the Folio of 1623 as the first of the tragedies. On stylistic grounds it is usually dated about 1608, and possible topical references seem to confirm that date. The citizens' anger over the shortage of corn may well refer to the corn riots of 1607 in the Midlands (which would have lent immediacy to the 'sedition at Rome' described by Plutarch as partly motivated 'by reason of famine'), and 'the coal of fire upon the ice' may allude to the great frost in the winter of 1607-8 when the Thames froze and, according to a contemporary pamphlet, entrepreneurial Londoners were 'ready with pans of coals to warm your fingers'.

The main source of the play is Plutarch's 'Life of Caius Martius Coriolanus' in his *Lives of the Noble Grecians and Romans* which Shakespeare read in the English translation by Thomas North (1579). Plutarch's 'Life' is a straightforward biography, beginning with Caius Martius' ancestry and ending with his death. Shakespeare found in Plutarch all the necessary details for his play, but he imposed, as always, a different shape and emphasis to suit his dramatic vision, and amplified the roles of Menenius, Aufidius and Volumnia to bear greater significance. By contrast with the astonishing variety and amplitude of its immediate predecessor *Antony and Cleopatra*, also based on Plutarch, *Coriolanus* is sober and austere, its main character no 'mine of bounty' like Antony but arrogant and rigid, even in his virtue 'too noble for the world'.

Shakespeare exploits the conflict between Coriolanus and the people of Rome, but not as a simple opposition of the noble individual and the 'multiplying swarm'. Coriolanus is, indeed, a man of integrity, but if he is too honest to fawn before the populace for its support, he is also proud and contemptuous, caring little for Rome's citizens, 'the mutable, rank-scented meinie', and finally willing to sacrifice the city itself to satisfy his honour. Conversely, the people, who rightly resent his aristocratic disdain and precociously declare that 'the people are the city', are themselves fickle and easily manipulated by the tribunes. Perhaps, as Coleridge suggested, the play 'illustrates the wonderful philosophic impartiality in Shakespeare's politics'; certainly its political sympathies are multiple and complex.

While *Coriolanus* marks a further stage in Shakespeare's exploration of Rome and *romanitas*, it focuses on an earlier moment in Roman history than either *Antony and Cleopatra* or its predecessor, *Julius Caesar*. Between them *Coriolanus* and *Julius Caesar* virtually define the historical limits of the Roman Republic. Caius Martius' victory at Corioli, from which he earned his surname, was won in 439 BC, almost four hundred years before the murder of Julius Caesar in the Forum (44 BC), one of the events which led to the foundation of the Roman Empire under Augustus (Shakespeare's Octavius Caesar).

The early republic portrayed in *Coriolanus* would, however, certainly have been of interest to many in Shakespeare's audiences, who would have found in the struggle between an elected government, dependent for its authority upon the will of the people, and a polity still overseen by traditional aristocratic privilege, a powerful image of political strains just beginning to be articulated in the political discourses of Jacobean England.

But the play is also the play of a tragic individual, noble but flawed, his strengths and weaknesses inextricably entangled. Not only are his virtues more fit for war than for peace; his nobility too easily degenerates into an isolating pride and a withering contempt for others: 'You speak o'th' people / As if you were a god to punish, not / A man of their infirmity.' But he is indeed a man of their infirmity, whose very drive to excel is born of a human need and vulnerability he fears to acknowledge. His self-chosen isolation, his wish that he could be, however improbably, 'author of himself', is revealed to be a terrible compensation for the world of relatedness he would, but at last cannot, deny. In his last Roman play Shakespeare joins the personal and the political in a bleak vision of both the city and its greatest hero tragically self-divided.

The role of Coriolanus has been memorably played by leading actors from John Philip Kemble to Laurence Olivier, but in performance the part of his mother, Volumnia, whose victory over her son is the play's major climax, is of almost equal significance. The play's complex embodiment of its political debates has led to its propagandist use in support of all political positions from monarchist to communist: performances of it have been known to provoke civil unrest and even riots.

The Arden text is based on the 1623 First Folio.

Caius MARTIUS	afterwards Caius Martius Coriolanus
Titus LARTIUS	} generals against the Volscians
COMINIUS	
MENENIUS Agrippa	friend to Coriolanus
SICINIUS Velutus	} tribunes of the people
Junius BRUTUS	
YOUNG MARTIUS	son to Coriolanus
A Roman HERALD	
Nicanor, a ROMAN	
Tullus AUFIDIUS	general of the Volscians
LIEUTENANT to Aufidius	
CONSPIRATORS with Aufidius	
Adrian, a VOLSCIAN	
CITIZEN of Antium	
Two Volscian WATCHMEN	
VOLUMNIA	mother to Coriolanus
VIRGILIA	wife to Coriolanus
VALERIA	friend to Virgilia
GENTLEWOMAN	attending on Virgilia

Roman and Volscian Senators, Patricians, Aediles, Lictors, Soldiers, Citizens, Messengers, Servants to Aufidius and other Attendants.

Coriolanus

1.1   *Enter a company of mutinous* Citizens,
with staves, clubs and other weapons.

1 CITIZEN   Before we proceed any further, hear me
speak.

ALL   Speak, speak.

1 CITIZEN   You are all resolved rather to die than to
famish?

ALL   Resolved, resolved.

1 CITIZEN   First, you know Caius Martius is chief enemy
to the people.

ALL   We know't, we know't.

1 CITIZEN   Let us kill him, and we'll have corn at our
own price. Is't a verdict?

ALL   No more talking on't; let it be done. Away, away!

2 CITIZEN   One word, good citizens.

1 CITIZEN   We are accounted poor citizens, the patricians
good. What authority surfeits on would relieve us. If
they would yield us but the superfluity while it were
wholesome, we might guess they relieved us
humanely; but they think we are too dear: the leanness
that afflicts us, the object of our misery, is as an
inventory to particularise their abundance; our
sufferance is a gain to them. Let us revenge this with
our pikes, ere we become rakes. For the gods know, I
speak this in hunger for bread, not in thirst for
revenge.

2 CITIZEN   Would you proceed especially against Caius
Martius?

ALL   Against him first. He's a very dog to the
commonalty.

2 CITIZEN   Consider you what services he has done for
his country?

1 CITIZEN   Very well, and could be content to give him
good report for't, but that he pays himself with being
proud.

2 CITIZEN   Nay, but speak not maliciously.

1 CITIZEN   I say unto you, what he hath done famously,
he did it to that end: though soft-conscienced men can
be content to say it was for his country, he did it to
please his mother, and to be partly proud, which he is,
even to the altitude of his virtue.

2 CITIZEN   What he cannot help in his nature, you
account a vice in him. You must in no way say he is
covetous.

1 CITIZEN   If I must not, I need not be barren of
accusations. He hath faults, with surplus, to tire in
repetition. [*shouts within*] What shouts are these? The
other side o'th' city is risen: why stay we prating here?
To th' Capitol!

ALL   Come, come.

1 CITIZEN   Soft, who comes here?

Enter MENENIUS AGRIPPA.

2 CITIZEN   Worthy Menenius Agrippa, one that hath
always loved the people.

1 CITIZEN   He's one honest enough, would all the rest
were so!

MENENIUS   What work's, my countrymen, in hand?
Where go you
With bats and clubs? The matter? Speak, I pray you.   55

1 CITIZEN   Our business is not unknown to th' Senate;
they have had inkling this fortnight what we intend to
do, which now we'll show 'em in deeds. They say poor
suitors have strong breaths: they shall know we have
strong arms too.   60

MENENIUS
Why masters, my good friends, mine honest
neighbours,
Will you undo yourselves?

1 CITIZEN   We cannot, sir, we are undone already.

MENENIUS   I tell you, friends, most charitable care
Have the patricians of you. For your wants,   65
Your suffering in this dearth, you may as well
Strike at the heaven with your staves, as lift them
Against the Roman state, whose course will on
The way it takes, cracking ten thousand curbs
Of more strong link asunder than can ever   70
Appear in your impediment. For the dearth,
The gods, not the patricians, make it, and
Your knees to them, not arms, must help. Alack,
You are transported by calamity
Thither where more attends you; and you slander   75
The helms o'th' state, who care for you like fathers,
When you curse them as enemies.

1 CITIZEN   Care for us? True indeed! They ne'er cared
for us yet. Suffer us to famish, and their store-houses
crammed with grain; make edicts for usury, to support   80
usurers; repeal daily any wholesome act established
against the rich, and provide more piercing statutes
daily, to chain up and restrain the poor. If the wars eat
us not up, they will; and there's all the love they bear
us.   85

MENENIUS   Either you must
Confess yourselves wondrous malicious,
Or be accus'd of folly. I shall tell you
A pretty tale; it may be you have heard it,
But since it serves my purpose, I will venture   90
To stale't a little more.

1 CITIZEN   Well, I'll hear it, sir; yet you must not think
to fob off our disgrace with a tale; but, and't please
you, deliver.

MENENIUS
There was a time, when all the body's members   95
Rebell'd against the belly; thus accus'd it:
That only like a gulf it did remain
I'th' midst o'th' body, idle and unactive,
Still cupboarding the viand, never bearing
Like labour with the rest, where th'other instruments   100
Did see, and hear, devise, instruct, walk, feel,
And, mutually participate, did minister
Unto the appetite and affection common
Of the whole body. The belly answer'd –

1 CITIZEN   Well, sir, what answer made the belly?   105

MENENIUS   Sir, I shall tell you. With a kind of smile,

Which ne'er came from the lungs, but even thus –
For look you, I may make the belly smile,
As well as speak – it tauntingly replied
To th' discontented members, the mutinous parts   110
That envied his receipt; even so most fitly,
As you malign our senators, for that
They are not such as you.
1 CITIZEN   Your belly's answer – what?
The kingly crown'd head, the vigilant eye,   115
The counsellor heart, the arm our soldier,
Our steed the leg, the tongue our trumpeter,
With other muniments and petty helps
In this our fabric, if that they –
MENENIUS   What then?
'Fore me, this fellow speaks! What then? What then?
1 CITIZEN   Should by the cormorant belly be restrain'd,   120
Who is the sink o'th' body –
MENENIUS   Well, what then?
1 CITIZEN   The former agents, if they did complain,
What could the belly answer?
MENENIUS   I will tell you,
If you'll bestow a small (of what you have little)
Patience awhile, you'st hear the belly's answer.   125
1 CITIZEN   Y'are long about it.
MENENIUS   Note me this, good friend;
Your most grave belly was deliberate,
Not rash like his accusers, and thus answer'd:
'True is it, my incorporate friends,' quoth he,
'That I receive the general food at first   130
Which you do live upon; and fit it is,
Because I am the store-house and the shop
Of the whole body. But, if you do remember,
I send it through the rivers of your blood
Even to the court, the heart, to th' seat o'th' brain;   135
And through the cranks and offices of man,
The strongest nerves and small inferior veins
From me receive that natural competency
Whereby they live. And though that all at once,
You, my good friends,' – this says the belly, mark
me –   140
1 CITIZEN   Ay, sir; well, well.
MENENIUS   'Though all at once cannot
See what I do deliver out to each,
Yet I can make my audit up, that all
From me do back receive the flour of all,
And leave me but the bran.' What say you to't?   145
1 CITIZEN   It was an answer. How apply you this?
MENENIUS   The senators of Rome are this good belly,
And you the mutinous members: for examine
Their counsels and their cares, digest things rightly
Touching the weal o'th' common, you shall find   150
No public benefit which you receive
But it proceeds or comes from them to you,
And no way from yourselves. What do you think,
You, the great toe of this assembly?
1 CITIZEN   I the great toe? Why the great toe?   155

MENENIUS
For that being one o'th' lowest, basest, poorest
Of this most wise rebellion, thou goest foremost:
Thou rascal, that art worst in blood to run,
Lead'st first to win some vantage.
But make you ready your stiff bats and clubs;   160
Rome and her rats are at the point of battle;
The one side must have bale.

Enter CAIUS MARTIUS.

        Hail, noble Martius.
MARTIUS
Thanks. What's the matter, you dissentious rogues
That, rubbing the poor itch of your opinion,
Make yourselves scabs?
1 CITIZEN   We have ever your good word.   165
MARTIUS
He that will give good words to thee, will flatter
Beneath abhorring. What would you have, you curs,
That like nor peace nor war? The one affrights you,
The other makes you proud. He that trusts to you,
Where he should find you lions, finds you hares;   170
Where foxes, geese: you are no surer, no,
Than is the coal of fire upon the ice,
Or hailstone in the sun. Your virtue is,
To make him worthy whose offence subdues him,
And curse that justice did it. Who deserves
greatness,   175
Deserves your hate; and your affections are
A sick man's appetite, who desires most that
Which would increase his evil. He that depends
Upon your favours, swims with fins of lead,
And hews down oaks with rushes. Hang ye! Trust ye?   180
With every minute you do change a mind,
And call him noble that was now your hate,
Him vile that was your garland. What's the matter,
That in these several places of the city,
You cry against the noble Senate, who   185
(Under the gods) keep you in awe, which else
Would feed on one another? What's their seeking?
MENENIUS
For corn at their own rates, whereof they say
The city is well stor'd.
MARTIUS   Hang 'em! They say!
They'll sit by th' fire, and presume to know   190
What's done i'th' Capitol: who's like to rise,
Who thrives, and who declines; side factions, and
give out
Conjectural marriages; making parties strong,
And feebling such as stand not in their liking
Below their cobbled shoes. They say there's grain
enough?   195
Would the nobility lay aside their ruth,
And let me use my sword, I'd make a quarry
With thousands of these quarter'd slaves, as high
As I could pick my lance.

MENENIUS
Nay, these are almost thoroughly persuaded;
For though abundantly they lack discretion,
Yet are they passing cowardly. But I beseech you,
What says the other troop?

MARTIUS   They are dissolv'd. Hang 'em!
They said they were an-hungry, sigh'd forth
          proverbs –
That hunger broke stone walls; that dogs must eat;
That meat was made for mouths; that the gods sent
          not
Corn for the rich men only. With these shreds
They vented their complainings, which being
          answer'd
And a petition granted them, a strange one,
To break the heart of generosity
And make bold power look pale, they threw their
          caps
As they would hang them on the horns o'th' moon,
Shouting their emulation.

MENENIUS   What is granted them?

MARTIUS
Five tribunes to defend their vulgar wisdoms,
Of their own choice. One's Junius Brutus,
Sicinius Velutus, and I know not. 'Sdeath,
The rabble should have first unroof'd the city
Ere so prevail'd with me; it will in time
Win upon power, and throw forth greater themes
For insurrection's arguing.

MENENIUS   This is strange.

MARTIUS   Go get you home, you fragments!

Enter a Messenger *hastily.*

MESSENGER   Where's Caius Martius?

MARTIUS   Here; what's the matter?

MESSENGER   The news is, sir, the Volsces are in arms.

MARTIUS
I am glad on't; then we shall ha' means to vent
Our musty superfluity. See, our best elders.

Enter SICINIUS VELUTUS, JUNIUS BRUTUS; COMINIUS,
TITUS LARTIUS, *with other* Senators.

1 SENATOR
Martius, 'tis true, that you have lately told us,
The Volsces are in arms.

MARTIUS   They have a leader,
Tullus Aufidius, that will put you to't.
I sin in envying his nobility;
And were I anything but what I am,
I would wish me only he.

COMINIUS   You have fought together!

MARTIUS   Were half to half the world by th'ears, and he
Upon my party, I'd revolt to make
Only my wars with him. He is a lion
That I am proud to hunt.

1 SENATOR   Then, worthy Martius,
Attend upon Cominius to these wars.

COMINIUS   It is your former promise.

MARTIUS   Sir, it is,
And I am constant. Titus Lartius, thou
Shalt see me once more strike at Tullus' face.
What, art thou stiff? Standst out?

LARTIUS   No, Caius Martius,
I'll lean upon one crutch, and fight with t'other,
Ere stay behind this business.

MENENIUS   Oh, true-bred!

1 SENATOR   Your company to th' Capitol, where I know
Our greatest friends attend us.

LARTIUS [*to Cominius*]   Lead you on.
[*to Martius*] Follow Cominius, we must follow you,
Right worthy you priority.

COMINIUS   Noble Martius.

1 SENATOR [*to the Citizens*]
Hence to your homes, be gone!

MARTIUS   Nay, let them follow.
The Volsces have much corn: take these rats thither,
To gnaw their garners. Worshipful mutiners,
Your valour puts well forth: pray follow.   *Exeunt.*
[*Citizens steal away. Sicinius and Brutus remain.*]

SICINIUS   Was ever man so proud as is this Martius?

BRUTUS   He has no equal.

SICINIUS
When we were chosen tribunes for the people –

BRUTUS   Mark'd you his lip and eyes?

SICINIUS   Nay, but his taunts.

BRUTUS
Being mov'd, he will not spare to gird the gods.

SICINIUS   Bemock the modest moon.

BRUTUS   The present wars devour him! He is grown
Too proud to be so valiant.

SICINIUS   Such a nature,
Tickled with good success, disdains the shadow
Which he treads on at noon. But I do wonder
His insolence can brook to be commanded
Under Cominius!

BRUTUS   Fame, at the which he aims,
In whom already he's well grac'd, cannot
Better be held, nor more attain'd than by
A place below the first: for what miscarries
Shall be the general's fault, though he perform
To th'utmost of a man, and giddy censure
Will then cry out of Martius, 'Oh, if he
Had borne the business!'

SICINIUS   Besides, if things go well,
Opinion, that so sticks on Martius, shall
Of his demerits rob Cominius.

BRUTUS   Come.
Half all Cominius' honours are to Martius,
Though Martius earn'd them not; and all his faults
To Martius shall be honours, though indeed
In aught he merit not.

SICINIUS   Let's hence, and hear
How the dispatch is made; and in what fashion,
More than his singularity, he goes

Upon this present action.

BRUTUS   Let's along.   *Exeunt.*

1.2   *Enter* TULLUS AUFIDIUS *with* Senators *of Corioles.*

1 SENATOR   So, your opinion is, Aufidius,
That they of Rome are enter'd in our counsels,
And know how we proceed.

AUFIDIUS   Is it not yours?
What ever have been thought on in this state
5   That could be brought to bodily act, ere Rome
Had circumvention? 'Tis not four days gone
Since I heard thence; these are the words – I think
I have the letter here – yes, here it is:
'They have press'd a power, but it is not known
10   Whether for east or west. The dearth is great,
The people mutinous; and it is rumour'd,
Cominius, Martius your old enemy
(Who is of Rome worse hated than of you)
And Titus Lartius, a most valiant Roman,
15   These three lead on this preparation
Whither 'tis bent: most likely 'tis for you.
Consider of it.'

1 SENATOR   Our army's in the field.
We never yet made doubt but Rome was ready
To answer us.

AUFIDIUS   Nor did you think it folly
20   To keep your great pretences veil'd, till when
They needs must show themselves, which in the
       hatching,
It seem'd, appear'd to Rome. By the discovery
We shall be shorten'd in our aim, which was
To take in many towns, ere, almost, Rome
Should know we were afoot.

25   2 SENATOR   Noble Aufidius,
Take your commission, hie you to your bands;
Let us alone to guard Corioles.
If they set down before's, for the remove
Bring up your army; but I think you'll find
Th'have not prepar'd for us.

30   AUFIDIUS   Oh, doubt not that,
I speak from certainties. Nay more,
Some parcels of their power are forth already
And only hitherward. I leave your honours.
If we and Caius Martius chance to meet,
35   'Tis sworn between us, we shall ever strike
Till one can do no more.

ALL   The gods assist you!

AUFIDIUS   And keep your honours safe!

1 SENATOR   Farewell.

SECOND SENATOR   Farewell.

ALL   Farewell.   *Exeunt.*

1.3   *Enter* VOLUMNIA *and* VIRGILIA, *mother and wife to*
MARTIUS. *They set them down on two low stools and sew.*

VOLUMNIA   I pray you, daughter, sing, or express
yourself in a more comfortable sort. If my son were my

husband I should freelier rejoice in that absence
wherein he won honour, than in the embracements of
his bed, where he would show most love. When yet he 5
was but tender-bodied, and the only son of my womb;
when youth with comeliness plucked all gaze his
way; when for a day of kings' entreaties, a mother
should not sell him an hour from her beholding; I,
considering how honour would become such a 10
person – that it was no better than picture-like to hang
by th'wall, if renown made it not stir – was pleased
to let him seek danger where he was like to find
fame. To a cruel war I sent him, from whence he
returned, his brows bound with oak. I tell thee, 15
daughter, I sprang not more in joy at first hearing he
was a man-child, than now in first seeing he had
proved himself a man.

VIRGILIA   But had he died in the business, madam, how
then? 20

VOLUMNIA   Then his good report should have been my
son, I therein would have found issue. Hear me
profess sincerely: had I a dozen sons, each in my love
alike, and none less dear than thine and my good
Martius, I had rather had eleven die nobly for their 25
country, than one voluptuously surfeit out of action.

Enter a Gentlewoman.

GENTLEWOMAN
Madam, the Lady Valeria is come to visit you.

VIRGILIA   Beseech you give me leave to retire myself.

VOLUMNIA   Indeed you shall not.
Methinks I hear hither your husband's drum; 30
See him pluck Aufidius down by th'hair,
As children from a bear, the Volsces shunning him.
Methinks I see him stamp thus, and call thus:
'Come on you cowards, you were got in fear
Though you were born in Rome.' His bloody brow 35
With his mail'd hand then wiping, forth he goes
Like to a harvest man that's task'd to mow
Or all, or lose his hire.

VIRGILIA   His bloody brow? O Jupiter, no blood!

VOLUMNIA   Away you fool! it more becomes a man 40
Than gilt his trophy. The breasts of Hecuba
When she did suckle Hector, look'd not lovelier
Than Hector's forehead when it spit forth blood
At Grecian sword contemning. Tell Valeria
We are fit to bid her welcome.   *Exit Gentlewoman.* 45

VIRGILIA   Heavens bless my lord from fell Aufidius!

VOLUMNIA   He'll beat Aufidius' head below his knee,
And tread upon his neck.

Enter VALERIA *with an usher, and a gentlewoman.*

VALERIA   My ladies both, good day to you.

VOLUMNIA   Sweet madam. 50

VIRGILIA   I am glad to see your ladyship.

VALERIA   How do you both? You are manifest
housekeepers. What are you sewing here? A fine spot,
in good faith. How does your little son?

VIRGILIA I thank your ladyship; well, good madam.

VOLUMNIA He had rather see the swords and hear a drum, than look upon his schoolmaster.

VALERIA O'my word, the father's son! I'll swear 'tis a very pretty boy. O'my troth, I looked upon him o' Wednesday half an hour together: 'has such a confirmed countenance. I saw him run after a gilded butterfly, and when he caught it, he let it go again, and after it again, and over and over he comes, and up again, catched it again; or whether his fall enraged him, or how 'twas, he did so set his teeth and tear it. Oh, I warrant how he mammocked it!

VOLUMNIA One on's father's moods.

VALERIA Indeed, la, 'tis a noble child.

VIRGILIA A crack, madam.

VALERIA Come, lay aside your stitchery, I must have you play the idle huswife with me this afternoon.

VIRGILIA No, good madam, I will not out of doors.

VALERIA Not out of doors?

VOLUMNIA She shall, she shall.

VIRGILIA Indeed no, by your patience; I'll not over the threshold till my lord return from the wars.

VALERIA Fie, you confine yourself most unreasonably. Come, you must go visit the good lady that lies in.

VIRGILIA I will wish her speedy strength, and visit her with my prayers; but I cannot go thither.

VOLUMNIA Why, I pray you?

VIRGILIA 'Tis not to save labour, nor that I want love.

VALERIA You would be another Penelope; yet they say, all the yarn she spun in Ulysses' absence did but fill Ithaca full of moths. Come, I would your cambric were sensible as your finger, that you might leave pricking it for pity. Come, you shall go with us.

VIRGILIA No, good madam, pardon me; indeed I will not forth.

VALERIA In truth, la, go with me, and I'll tell you excellent news of your husband.

VIRGILIA Oh, good madam, there can be none yet.

VALERIA Verily I do not jest with you. There came news from him last night.

VIRGILIA Indeed, madam?

VALERIA In earnest, it's true; I heard a senator speak it. Thus it is: the Volsces have an army forth, against whom Cominius the general is gone, with one part of our Roman power. Your lord and Titus Lartius are set down before their city Corioles; they nothing doubt prevailing, and to make it brief wars. This is true on mine honour, and so, I pray, go with us.

VIRGILIA Give me excuse, good madam, I will obey you in everything hereafter.

VOLUMNIA Let her alone, lady; as she is now, she will but disease our better mirth.

VALERIA In troth, I think she would. Fare you well then. Come, good sweet lady. Prithee, Virgilia, turn thy solemness out o'door, and go along with us.

VIRGILIA No, at a word, madam; indeed I must not. I wish you much mirth.   110

VALERIA Well then, farewell.   *Exeunt.*

1.4 *Enter* MARTIUS, TITUS LARTIUS, *with drum and colours, with captains and soldiers, as before the city Corioles. To them a* Messenger.

MARTIUS Yonder comes news. A wager they have met.

LARTIUS My horse to yours, no.

MARTIUS   'Tis done.

LARTIUS   Agreed.

MARTIUS Say, has our general met the enemy?

MESSENGER

They lie in view, but have not spoke as yet.

LARTIUS So, the good horse is mine.

MARTIUS   I'll buy him of you.   5

LARTIUS

No, I'll nor sell nor give him: lend you him I will
For half a hundred years. Summon the town.

MARTIUS How far off lie these armies?

MESSENGER   Within this mile and half.

MARTIUS

Then shall we hear their 'larum, and they ours.
Now Mars, I prithee make us quick in work,   10
That we with smoking swords may march from
    hence
To help our fielded friends. Come, blow thy blast.

They sound a parley. Enter two Senators *with others, on the walls of Corioles.*

Tullus Aufidius, is he within your walls?

1 SENATOR

No, nor a man that fears you less than he;
That's lesser than a little.   [*Drum afar off.*]
                    Hark, our drums   15
Are bringing forth our youth. We'll break our walls
Rather than they shall pound us up; our gates,
Which yet seem shut, we have but pinn'd with
    rushes;
They'll open of themselves. Hark you, far off!
                    [*Alarum far off.*]
There is Aufidius. List what work he makes   20
Amongst your cloven army.

MARTIUS   Oh, they are at it!

LARTIUS Their noise be our instruction. Ladders ho!

Enter the army of the Volsces.

MARTIUS They fear us not, but issue forth their city.
Now put your shields before your hearts, and fight
With hearts more proof than shields. Advance, brave
    Titus.   25
They do disdain us much beyond our thoughts,
Which makes me sweat with wrath. Come on, my
    fellows:
He that retires, I'll take him for a Volsce,

And he shall feel mine edge.
[*Alarum. The Romans are beat back to their trenches.*]

Enter MARTIUS, *cursing.*

30   MARTIUS   All the contagion of the south light on you,
             You shames of Rome! You herd of – boils and plagues
             Plaster you o'er, that you may be abhorr'd
             Farther than seen, and one infect another
             Against the wind a mile! You souls of geese,
35   That bear the shapes of men, how have you run
             From slaves that apes would beat! Pluto and hell!
             All hurt behind, backs red, and faces pale
             With flight and agued fear! Mend and charge home,
             Or, by the fires of heaven, I'll leave the foe
40   And make my wars on you. Look to't. Come on;
             If you'll stand fast, we'll beat them to their wives,
             As they us to our trenches. Follow me!
             [*Another alarum, and Martius follows them to the gates.*]
             So, now the gates are ope. Now prove good seconds!
             'Tis for the followers Fortune widens them,
45   Not for the fliers. Mark me, and do the like!
             [*Enters the gates.*]
1 SOLDIER   Foolhardiness! not I.
2 SOLDIER   Nor I.
             [*Martius is shut in.*]
1 SOLDIER   See, they have shut him in.
                                    [*Alarum continues.*]
ALL   To th' pot, I warrant him.

Enter TITUS LARTIUS.

LARTIUS   What is become of Martius?
ALL   Slain, sir, doubtless.
1 SOLDIER   Following the fliers at the very heels,
50   With them he enters; who, upon the sudden,
             Clapp'd to their gates; he is himself alone,
             To answer all the city.
LARTIUS   Oh noble fellow!
             Who sensibly outdares his senseless sword,
             And when it bows, stand'st up. Thou art left,
               Martius:
55   A carbuncle entire, as big as thou art,
             Were not so rich a jewel. Thou wast a soldier
             Even to Cato's wish, not fierce and terrible
             Only in strokes, but with thy grim looks and
             The thunder-like percussion of thy sounds
60   Thou mad'st thine enemies shake, as if the world
             Were feverous and did tremble.

Enter MARTIUS, *bleeding, assaulted by the enemy.*

1 SOLDIER   Look sir!
LARTIUS   Oh, 'tis Martius!
             Let's fetch him off, or make remain alike.
             [*They fight, and all enter the city.*]

1.5   *Enter certain* Romans, *with spoils.*

1 ROMAN   This will I carry to Rome.

2 ROMAN   And I this.
3 ROMAN   A murrain on't! I took this for silver.   *Exeunt.*
                        [*Alarum continues still afar off.*]

Enter MARTIUS *and* TITUS LARTIUS *with a trumpet.*

MARTIUS
   See here these movers, that do prize their hours
   At a crack'd drachma! Cushions, leaden spoons,   5
   Irons of a doit, doublets that hangmen would
   Bury with those that wore them, these base slaves,
   Ere yet the fight be done, pack up. Down with them!
   And hark, what noise the general makes! To him!
   There is the man of my soul's hate, Aufidius,   10
   Piercing our Romans. Then, valiant Titus, take
   Convenient numbers to make good the city,
   Whilst I, with those that have the spirit, will haste
   To help Cominius.
LARTIUS   Worthy sir, thou bleed'st;
   Thy exercise hath been too violent   15
   For a second course of fight.
MARTIUS   Sir, praise me not;
   My work hath yet not warm'd me. Fare you well.
   The blood I drop is rather physical
   Than dangerous to me. To Aufidius thus
   I will appear and fight.
LARTIUS   Now the fair goddess, Fortune,   20
   Fall deep in love with thee, and her great charms
   Misguide thy opposers' swords! Bold gentleman,
   Prosperity be thy page!
MARTIUS   Thy friend no less
   Than those she placeth highest! So farewell.
LARTIUS
   Thou worthiest Martius!   *Exit Martius.*   25
   Go sound thy trumpet in the market-place;
   Call thither all the officers o'th'town,
   Where they shall know our mind. Away.   *Exeunt.*

1.6   *Enter* COMINIUS, *as it were in retire, with soldiers.*

COMINIUS
   Breathe you, my friends; well fought; we are come off
   Like Romans, neither foolish in our stands
   Nor cowardly in retire. Believe me, sirs,
   We shall be charg'd again. Whiles we have struck,
   By interims and conveying gusts we have heard   5
   The charges of our friends. The Roman gods
   Lead their successes as we wish our own,
   That both our powers, with smiling fronts
     encount'ring,
   May give you thankful sacrifice.

Enter a Messenger.

                          Thy news?
MESSENGER   The citizens of Corioles have issued,   10
   And given to Lartius and to Martius battle.
   I saw our party to their trenches driven,
   And then I came away.

COMINIUS   Though thou speak'st truth,
 Methinks thou speak'st not well. How long is't since?
MESSENGER Above an hour, my lord.
COMINIUS
 'Tis not a mile; briefly we heard their drums.
 How could'st thou in a mile confound an hour,
 And bring thy news so late?
MESSENGER   Spies of the Volsces
 Held me in chase, that I was forc'd to wheel
 Three or four miles about; else had I, sir,
 Half an hour since brought my report.

      Enter MARTIUS.

COMINIUS   Who's yonder,
 That does appear as he were flay'd? O Gods,
 He has the stamp of Martius, and I have
 Beforetime seen him thus.
MARTIUS   Come I too late?
COMINIUS
 The shepherd knows not thunder from a tabor,
 More than I know the sound of Martius' tongue
 From every meaner man.
MARTIUS   Come I too late?
COMINIUS Ay, if you come not in the blood of others,
 But mantled in your own.
MARTIUS   Oh! let me clip ye
 In arms as sound as when I woo'd; in heart
 As merry as when our nuptial day was done,
 And tapers burn'd to bedward.
COMINIUS   Flower of warriors,
 How is't with Titus Lartius?
MARTIUS As with a man busied about decrees:
 Condemning some to death, and some to exile,
 Ransoming him, or pitying, threat'ning th'other;
 Holding Corioles in the name of Rome,
 Even like a fawning greyhound in the leash,
 To let him slip at will.
COMINIUS   Where is that slave
 Which told me they had beat you to your trenches?
 Where is he? Call him hither.
MARTIUS   Let him alone,
 He did inform the truth; but for our gentlemen,
 The common file – a plague! tribunes for them! –
 The mouse ne'er shunn'd the cat as they did budge
 From rascals worse than they.
COMINIUS   But how prevail'd you?
MARTIUS Will the time serve to tell? I do not think.
 Where is the enemy? Are you lords o'th' field?
 If not, why cease you till you are so?
COMINIUS Martius, we have at disadvantage fought,
 And did retire to win our purpose.
MARTIUS
 How lies their battle? Know you on which side
 They have plac'd their men of trust?
COMINIUS   As I guess, Martius,

 Their bands i'th' vaward are the Antiates
 Of their best trust: o'er them Aufidius,
 Their very heart of hope.
MARTIUS   I do beseech you, 55
 By all the battles wherein we have fought,
 By th' blood we have shed together, by th' vows
 We have made to endure friends, that you directly
 Set me against Aufidius and his Antiates;
 And that you not delay the present, but, 60
 Filling the air with swords advanc'd and darts,
 We prove this very hour.
COMINIUS   Though I could wish
 You were conducted to a gentle bath,
 And balms applied to you, yet dare I never
 Deny your asking. Take your choice of those 65
 That best can aid your action.
MARTIUS   Those are they
 That most are willing. If any such be here –
 As it were sin to doubt – that love this painting
 Wherein you see me smear'd; if any fear
 Lesser his person than an ill report; 70
 If any think brave death outweighs bad life,
 And that his country's dearer than himself;
 Let him alone, or so many so minded,
 Wave thus to express his disposition,
 And follow Martius. 75
 [*They all shout and wave their swords.*]
ALL O me alone! Make you a sword of me!
 [*They take him up in their arms, and cast up their caps.*]
MARTIUS If these shows be not outward, which of you
 But is four Volsces? None of you but is
 Able to bear against the great Aufidius
 A shield as hard as his. A certain number 80
 (Though thanks to all) must I select from all: the rest
 Shall bear the business in some other fight,
 As cause will be obey'd. Please you to march,
 And I shall quickly draw out my command,
 Which men are best inclin'd.
COMINIUS   March on, my fellows: 85
 Make good this ostentation, and you shall
 Divide in all with us.   *Exeunt.*

1.7 TITUS LARTIUS, *having set a guard upon Corioles,*
going with drum and trumpet toward Cominius and Caius
Martius, enters with a Lieutenant, *other soldiers*
and a scout.

LARTIUS So, let the ports be guarded; keep your duties
 As I have set them down. If I do send, dispatch
 Those centuries to our aid; the rest will serve
 For a short holding: if we lose the field,
 We cannot keep the town.
LIEUTENANT   Fear not our care, sir. 5
LARTIUS Hence; and shut your gates upon's.
 Our guider, come; to the Roman camp conduct us.
            Exeunt.

Alarum as in battle.
Enter MARTIUS *and* AUFIDIUS *at several doors.*

MARTIUS
I'll fight with none but thee, for I do hate thee
Worse than a promise-breaker.
AUFIDIUS   We hate alike:
Not Afric owns a serpent I abhor
More than thy fame and envy. Fix thy foot.
5 MARTIUS Let the first budger die the other's slave,
And the gods doom him after!
AUFIDIUS   If I fly, Martius,
Holloa me like a hare.
MARTIUS   Within these three hours, Tullus,
Alone I fought in your Corioles walls,
And made what work I pleas'd: 'tis not my blood
10 Wherein thou seest me mask'd. For thy revenge,
Wrench up thy power to th'highest.
AUFIDIUS   Wert thou the Hector
That was the whip of your bragg'd progeny,
Thou shouldst not 'scape me here.
[*Here they fight, and certain Volsces come in the aid of
Aufidius. Martius fights till they be driven in breathless.*]
Officious, and not valiant, you have sham'd me
15 In your condemned seconds.   *Exeunt.*

1.9 *Flourish. Alarum. A retreat is sounded.*
Enter at one door, COMINIUS, *with the Romans;
at another door,* MARTIUS, *with his arm in a scarf.*

COMINIUS If I should tell thee o'er this thy day's work,
Thou't not believe thy deeds; but I'll report it,
Where senators shall mingle tears with smiles,
Where great patricians shall attend, and shrug,
5 I'th'end admire; where ladies shall be frighted,
And, gladly quak'd, hear more; where the dull
tribunes,
That with the fusty plebeians hate thine honours,
Shall say against their hearts, 'We thank the gods
Our Rome hath such a soldier.'
10 Yet cam'st thou to a morsel of this feast,
Having fully din'd before.

Enter TITUS LARTIUS, *with his power, from the pursuit.*

LARTIUS   O general,
Here is the steed, we the caparison:
Hadst thou beheld –
MARTIUS   Pray now, no more. My mother,
Who has a charter to extol her blood,
15 When she does praise me, grieves me. I have done
As you have done, that's what I can; induc'd
As you have been, that's for my country.
He that has but effected his good will
Hath overta'en mine act.
COMINIUS   You shall not be
20 The grave of your deserving; Rome must know
The value of her own. 'Twere a concealment
Worse than a theft, no less than a traducement,

To hide your doings, and to silence that
Which, to the spire and top of praises vouch'd,
Would seem but modest. Therefore I beseech you –   25
In sign of what you are, not to reward
What you have done – before our army hear me.
MARTIUS
I have some wounds upon me, and they smart
To hear themselves remember'd.
COMINIUS   Should they not,
Well might they fester 'gainst ingratitude,   30
And tent themselves with death. Of all the horses –
Whereof we have ta'en good, and good store – of all
The treasure in this field achiev'd and city,
We render you the tenth; to be ta'en forth,
Before the common distribution, at   35
Your only choice.
MARTIUS   I thank you, general;
But cannot make my heart consent to take
A bribe to pay my sword: I do refuse it,
And stand upon my common part with those
That have beheld the doing.   40
[*A long flourish. They all cry, 'Martius! Martius!', cast
up their caps and lances. Cominius and Lartius stand
bare.*]
May these same instruments, which you profane,
Never sound more! When drums and trumpets shall
I'th' field prove flatterers, let courts and cities be
Made all of false-fac'd soothing! When steel grows
Soft as the parasite's silk, let him be made   45
An ovator for th' wars! No more, I say!
For that I have not wash'd my nose that bled,
Or foil'd some debile wretch, which without note
Here's many else have done, you shout me forth
In acclamations hyperbolical,   50
As if I lov'd my little should be dieted
In praises sauc'd with lies.
COMINIUS   Too modest are you,
More cruel to your good report than grateful
To us that give you truly. By your patience,
If 'gainst yourself you be incens'd, we'll put you   55
(Like one that means his proper harm) in manacles,
Then reason safely with you. Therefore be it known,
As to us, to all the world, that Caius Martius
Wears this war's garland: in token of the which,
My noble steed, known to the camp, I give him,   60
With all his trim belonging; and from this time,
For what he did before Corioles, call him,
With all th'applause and clamour of the host,
Martius Caius Coriolanus!
Bear th'addition nobly ever!   65
[*Flourish. Trumpets sound, and drums.*]
ALL Martius Caius Coriolanus!
CORIOLANUS   I will go wash;
And when my face is fair, you shall perceive
Whether I blush or no: howbeit, I thank you.
I mean to stride your steed, and at all times
To undercrest your good addition,   70

To th' fairness of my power.

COMINIUS   So, to our tent;
    Where, ere we do repose us, we will write
    To Rome of our success. You, Titus Lartius,
    Must to Corioles back: send us to Rome
    The best, with whom we may articulate
    For their own good and ours.

LARTIUS   I shall, my lord.

CORIOLANUS
    The gods begin to mock me: I, that now
    Refus'd most princely gifts, am bound to beg
    Of my lord general.

COMINIUS   Take't, 'tis yours. What is't?

CORIOLANUS   I sometime lay here in Corioles,
    At a poor man's house: he us'd me kindly.
    He cried to me. I saw him prisoner.
    But then Aufidius was within my view,
    And wrath o'erwhelm'd my pity. I request you
    To give my poor host freedom.

COMINIUS   Oh well begg'd!
    Were he the butcher of my son, he should
    Be free as is the wind. Deliver him, Titus.

LARTIUS   Martius, his name?

CORIOLANUS   By Jupiter, forgot!
    I am weary, yea, my memory is tired;
    Have we no wine here?

COMINIUS   Go we to our tent.
    The blood upon your visage dries, 'tis time
    It should be look'd to. Come.   *Exeunt.*

1.10 *A flourish. Cornets. Enter* TULLUS AUFIDIUS,
        bloody, with two or three Soldiers.

AUFIDIUS   The town is ta'en!

1 SOLDIER   'Twill be deliver'd back on good condition.

AUFIDIUS   Condition!
    I would I were a Roman, for I cannot,
    Being a Volsce, be that I am. Condition?
    What good condition can a treaty find
    I'th' part that is at mercy? Five times, Martius,
    I have fought with thee; so often hast thou beat me;
    And wouldst do so, I think, should we encounter
    As often as we eat. By th'elements,
    If e'er again I meet him beard to beard,
    He's mine, or I am his. Mine emulation
    Hath not that honour in't it had: for where
    I thought to crush him in an equal force,
    True sword to sword, I'll potch at him some way,
    Or wrath or craft may get him.

1 SOLDIER   He's the devil.

AUFIDIUS
    Bolder, though not so subtle. My valour's poison'd
    With only suff'ring stain by him: for him
    Shall fly out of itself. Nor sleep, nor sanctuary,
    Being nakèd, sick; nor fane, nor Capitol,
    The prayers of priests, nor times of sacrifice –
    Embarquements all of fury – shall lift up

Their rotten privilege and custom 'gainst
    My hate to Martius. Where I find him, were it
    At home, upon my brother's guard, even there,   25
    Against the hospitable canon, would I
    Wash my fierce hand in's heart. Go you to th' city;
    Learn how 'tis held, and what they are that must
    Be hostages for Rome.

1 SOLDIER   Will not you go?

AUFIDIUS
    I am attended at the cypress grove. I pray you –   30
    'Tis south the city mills – bring me word thither
    How the world goes, that to the pace of it
    I may spur on my journey.

1 SOLDIER   I shall, sir.   *Exeunt.*

2.1 *Enter* MENENIUS *with the two tribunes of the people,*
        SICINIUS *and* BRUTUS.

MENENIUS   The augurer tells me we shall have news
    tonight.

BRUTUS   Good or bad?

MENENIUS   Not according to the prayer of the people,
    for they love not Martius.   5

SICINIUS   Nature teaches beasts to know their friends.

MENENIUS   Pray you, who does the wolf love?

SICINIUS   The lamb.

MENENIUS   Ay, to devour him, as the hungry plebeians
    would the noble Martius.   10

BRUTUS   He's a lamb indeed, that baes like a bear.

MENENIUS   He's a bear indeed, that lives like a lamb.
    You two are old men: tell me one thing that I shall ask
    you.

BOTH   Well, sir.   15

MENENIUS   In what enormity is Martius poor in, that
    you two have not in abundance?

BRUTUS   He's poor in no one fault, but stored with all.

SICINIUS   Especially in pride.

BRUTUS   And topping all others in boasting.   20

MENENIUS   This is strange now. Do you two know how
    you are censured here in the city, I mean of us o'th'
    right-hand file? Do you?

BOTH   Why, how are we censured?

MENENIUS   Because you talk of pride now – will you not   25
    be angry?

BOTH   Well, well, sir, well.

MENENIUS   Why, 'tis no great matter; for a very little
    thief of occasion will rob you of a great deal of
    patience. Give your dispositions the reins, and be   30
    angry at your pleasures; at the least, if you take it as a
    pleasure to you in being so. You blame Martius for
    being proud.

BRUTUS   We do it not alone, sir.

MENENIUS   I know you can do very little alone, for your   35
    helps are many, or else your actions would grow
    wondrous single: your abilities are too infant-like for
    doing much alone. You talk of pride. O that you could
    turn your eyes toward the napes of your necks, and

40 make but an interior survey of your good selves. O that
you could!

BOTH   What then, sir?

MENENIUS   Why, then you should discover a brace of
unmeriting, proud, violent, testy magistrates (alias
45 fools) as any in Rome.

SICINIUS   Menenius, you are known well enough too.

MENENIUS   I am known to be a humorous patrician, and
one that loves a cup of hot wine, with not a drop of
allaying Tiber in't; said to be something imperfect in
50 favouring the first complaint, hasty and tinder-like
upon too trivial motion; one that converses more with
the buttock of the night than with the forehead of the
morning. What I think, I utter, and spend my malice
in my breath. Meeting two such wealsmen as you are
55 – I cannot call you Lycurguses – if the drink you give
me touch my palate adversely, I make a crooked face at
it. I can say, your worships have delivered the matter
well, when I find the ass in compound with the major
part of your syllables. And though I must be content
60 to bear with those that say you are reverend grave
men, yet they lie deadly that tell you have good faces.
If you see this in the map of my microcosm, follows it
that I am known well enough too? What harm can
your bisson conspectuities glean out of this character,
65 if I be known well enough too?

BRUTUS   Come, sir, come, we know you well enough.

MENENIUS   You know neither me, yourselves, nor any
thing. You are ambitious for poor knaves' caps and
legs: you wear out a good wholesome forenoon in
70 hearing a cause between an orange-wife and a faucet-
seller, and then rejourn the controversy of threepence
to a second day of audience. When you are hearing a
matter between party and party, if you chance to be
pinched with the colic, you make faces like mummers,
75 set up the bloody flag against all patience, and, in
roaring for a chamber-pot, dismiss the controversy
bleeding, the more entangled by your hearing. All
the peace you make in their cause is calling both the
parties knaves. You are a pair of strange ones.

80 BRUTUS   Come, come, you are well understood to be a
perfecter giber for the table than a necessary bencher
in the Capitol.

MENENIUS   Our very priests must become mockers, if
they shall encounter such ridiculous subjects as you
85 are. When you speak best unto the purpose, it is not
worth the wagging of your beards; and your beards
deserve not so honourable a grave as to stuff a
botcher's cushion, or to be entombed in an ass's pack-
saddle. Yet you must be saying Martius is proud: who,
90 in a cheap estimation, is worth all your predecessors
since Deucalion, though peradventure some of the
best of 'em were hereditary hangmen. God-den to
your worships. More of your conversation would
infect my brain, being the herdsmen of the beastly
95 plebeians. I will be bold to take my leave of you.

[*Brutus and Sicinius aside.*]

Enter VOLUMNIA, VIRGILIA *and* VALERIA.

How now, my as fair as noble ladies – and the moon,
were she earthly, no nobler – whither do you follow
your eyes so fast?

VOLUMNIA   Honourable Menenius, my boy Martius
approaches; for the love of Juno, let's go. 100

MENENIUS   Ha? Martius coming home?

VOLUMNIA   Ay, worthy Menenius, and with most
prosperous approbation.

MENENIUS   Take my cap, Jupiter, and I thank thee. Hoo!
Martius coming home? 105

VIRGILIA, VALERIA   Nay, 'tis true.

VOLUMNIA   Look, here's a letter from him; the state
hath another, his wife another; and I think there's one
at home for you.

MENENIUS   I will make my very house reel tonight. A 110
letter for me?

VIRGILIA   Yes, certain, there's a letter for you; I saw't.

MENENIUS   A letter for me! It gives me an estate of seven
years' health; in which time I will make a lip at the
physician. The most sovereign prescription in Galen 115
is but empiricutic, and, to this preservative, of no
better report than a horse-drench. Is he not
wounded? He was wont to come home wounded.

VIRGILIA   Oh no, no, no.

VOLUMNIA   Oh, he is wounded; I thank the gods for't. 120

MENENIUS   So do I too, if it be not too much. Brings a
victory in his pocket? The wounds become him.

VOLUMNIA   On's brows: Menenius, he comes the third
time home with the oaken garland.

MENENIUS   Has he disciplined Aufidius soundly? 125

VOLUMNIA   Titus Lartius writes, they fought together,
but Aufidius got off.

MENENIUS   And 'twas time for him too, I'll warrant him
that: and he had stayed by him, I would not have been
so 'fidiussed for all the chests in Corioles and the gold 130
that's in them. Is the senate possessed of this?

VOLUMNIA   Good ladies, let's go. Yes, yes, yes. The
senate has letters from the general, wherein he gives
my son the whole name of the war: he hath in this
action outdone his former deeds doubly. 135

VALERIA   In troth, there's wondrous things spoke of
him.

MENENIUS   Wondrous! Ay, I warrant you, and not
without his true purchasing.

VIRGILIA   The gods grant them true. 140

VOLUMNIA   True? pow, waw!

MENENIUS   True? I'll be sworn they are true. Where is
he wounded? [*to the tribunes*] God save your good
worships! Martius is coming home: he has more
cause to be proud. [*to Volumnia*] Where is he 145
wounded?

VOLUMNIA   I'th' shoulder, and i'th' left arm: there will
be large cicatrices to show the people when he shall
stand for his place. He received in the repulse of
Tarquin seven hurts i'th' body. 150

MENENIUS   One i'th' neck, and two i'th' thigh – there's
   nine that I know.
VOLUMNIA   He had, before this last expedition, twenty-
   five wounds upon him.
MENENIUS   Now it's twenty-seven: every gash was an   55
   enemy's grave. [*A shout and flourish.*] Hark, the
   trumpets!
VOLUMNIA   These are the ushers of Martius: before him
   he carries noise, and behind him he leaves tears:
   Death, that dark spirit, in's nervy arm doth lie,   60
   Which, being advanc'd, declines, and then men die.

   A sennet. Trumpets sound. Enter COMINIUS *the General,*
   and TITUS LARTIUS: *between them* CORIOLANUS,
   crowned with an oaken garland; with captains
   and soldiers, and a Herald.

HERALD   Know, Rome, that all alone Martius did fight
   Within Corioles gates: where he hath won,
   With fame, a name to Martius Caius. These
   In honour follows Coriolanus.   65
   Welcome to Rome, renowned Coriolanus!
                                        [*Sound flourish.*]
ALL   Welcome to Rome, renowned Coriolanus!
CORIOLANUS   No more of this; it does offend my heart.
   Pray now, no more.
COMINIUS   Look, sir, your mother.
CORIOLANUS   Oh!
   You have, I know, petition'd all the gods   70
   For my prosperity. [*Kneels.*]
VOLUMNIA   Nay, my good soldier, up;
   My gentle Martius, worthy Caius, and
   By deed-achieving honour newly nam'd –
   What is it? – Coriolanus, must I call thee?
   But oh, thy wife –
CORIOLANUS   My gracious silence, hail!   75
   Wouldst thou have laugh'd had I come coffin'd home,
   That weep'st to see me triumph? Ah, my dear,
   Such eyes the widows in Corioles wear,
   And mothers that lack sons.
MENENIUS   Now the gods crown thee!
CORIOLANUS   And live you yet?
   [*to Valeria*]   O my sweet lady, pardon.   80
VOLUMNIA
   I know not where to turn: O welcome home!
   And welcome, general; and y'are welcome all.
MENENIUS
   A hundred thousand welcomes. I could weep,
   And I could laugh, I am light and heavy. Welcome!
   A curse begnaw at very root on's heart,   85
   That is not glad to see thee! You are three
   That Rome should dote on: yet, by the faith of men,
   We have some old crabtrees here at home that will
      not
   Be grafted to your relish. Yet welcome, warriors!
   We call a nettle but a nettle, and   90
   The faults of fools but folly.
COMINIUS   Ever right.

CORIOLANUS   Menenius, ever, ever.
HERALD   Give way there, and go on.
CORIOLANUS [*to Volumnia and Virgilia*]
   Your hand, and yours!
   Ere in our own house I do shade my head,   195
   The good patricians must be visited,
   From whom I have receiv'd not only greetings,
   But with them change of honours.
VOLUMNIA   I have liv'd
   To see inherited my very wishes,
   And the buildings of my fancy: only   200
   There's one thing wanting, which I doubt not but
   Our Rome will cast upon thee.
CORIOLANUS   Know, good mother,
   I had rather be their servant in my way
   Than sway with them in theirs.
COMINIUS   On, to the Capitol.
       Flourish. Cornets. Exeunt in state, as before.
   [*Brutus and Sicinius come forward.*]
BRUTUS
   All tongues speak of him, and the bleared sights   205
   Are spectacled to see him. Your prattling nurse
   Into a rapture lets her baby cry
   While she chats him. The kitchen malkin pins
   Her richest lockram 'bout her reechy neck,
   Clamb'ring the walls to eye him; stalls, bulks,
      windows,   210
   Are smother'd up, leads fill'd and ridges hors'd
   With variable complexions, all agreeing
   In earnestness to see him. Seld-shown flamens
   Do press among the popular throngs, and puff
   To win a vulgar station. Our veil'd dames   215
   Commit the war of white and damask in
   Their nicely gauded cheeks, to th'wanton spoil
   Of Phoebus' burning kisses. Such a pother,
   As if that whatsoever god who leads him
   Were slily crept into his human powers,   220
   And gave him graceful posture.
SICINIUS   On the sudden,
   I warrant him consul.
BRUTUS   Then our office may,
   During his power, go sleep.
SICINIUS   He cannot temp'rately transport his honours
   From where he should begin and end, but will   225
   Lose those he hath won.
BRUTUS   In that there's comfort.
SICINIUS   Doubt not
   The commoners, for whom we stand, but they
   Upon their ancient malice will forget
   With the least cause these his new honours; which
   That he will give them make I as little question   230
   As he is proud to do't.
BRUTUS   I heard him swear,
   Were he to stand for consul, never would he
   Appear i'th' market-place, nor on him put
   The napless vesture of humility;
   Nor showing (as the manner is) his wounds   235

To th' people, beg their stinking breaths.
SICINIUS   'Tis right.
BRUTUS   It was his word. Oh, he would miss it rather
          Than carry it but by the suit of the gentry to him
          And the desire of the nobles.
SICINIUS   I wish no better
240   Than have him hold that purpose, and to put it
          In execution.
BRUTUS   'Tis most like he will.
SICINIUS   It shall be to him then, as our good wills,
          A sure destruction.
BRUTUS   So it must fall out
245   To him; or our authority's for an end;
          We must suggest the people in what hatred
          He still hath held them: that to's power he would
          Have made them mules, silenc'd their pleaders, and
          Dispropertied their freedoms; holding them,
          In human action and capacity,
250   Of no more soul nor fitness for the world
          Than camels in their war, who have their provand
          Only for bearing burthens, and sore blows
          For sinking under them.
SICINIUS   This (as you say) suggested
          At some time when his soaring insolence
255   Shall touch the people – which time shall not want,
          If he be put upon't, and that's as easy
          As to set dogs on sheep – will be his fire
          To kindle their dry stubble; and their blaze
          Shall darken him for ever.

                      Enter a Messenger.

BRUTUS   What's the matter?
MESSENGER
260   You are sent for to the Capitol. 'Tis thought
          That Martius shall be consul.
          I have seen the dumb men throng to see him, and
          The blind to hear him speak. Matrons flung gloves,
          Ladies and maids their scarfs and handkerchers,
265   Upon him as he pass'd; the nobles bended
          As to Jove's statue, and the commons made
          A shower and thunder with their caps and shouts:
          I never saw the like.
BRUTUS   Let's to the Capitol,
          And carry with us ears and eyes for th' time,
          But hearts for the event.
270 SICINIUS   Have with you.   *Exeunt.*

2.2   *Enter two* Officers, *to lay cushions,*
                 as it were in the Capitol.

1 OFFICER   Come, come, they are almost here. How
          many stand for consulships?
2 OFFICER   Three, they say; but 'tis thought of everyone
          Coriolanus will carry it.
5 1 OFFICER   That's a brave fellow; but he's vengeance
          proud, and loves not the common people.
2 OFFICER   'Faith, there hath been many great men that

have flattered the people, who ne'er loved them; and
there be many that they have loved, they know not
wherefore: so that if they love they know not why, they   10
hate upon no better a ground. Therefore, for
Coriolanus neither to care whether they love or hate
him manifests the true knowledge he has in their
disposition, and out of his noble carelessness lets them
plainly see't.   15
1 OFFICER   If he did not care whether he had their love
or no, he waved indifferently 'twixt doing them
neither good nor harm; but he seeks their hate with
greater devotion than they can render it him, and
leaves nothing undone that may fully discover him   20
their opposite. Now to seem to affect the malice and
displeasure of the people is as bad as that which he
dislikes, to flatter them for their love.
2 OFFICER   He hath deserved worthily of his country;
and his ascent is not by such easy degrees as those   25
who, having been supple and courteous to the
people, bonneted, without any further deed to have
them at all into their estimation and report; but he
hath so planted his honours in their eyes and his
actions in their hearts, that for their tongues to be   30
silent and not confess so much were a kind of
ingrateful injury. To report otherwise were a malice
that, giving itself the lie, would pluck reproof and
rebuke from every ear that heard it.
1 OFFICER   No more of him; he's a worthy man: make   35
way, they are coming.

A sennet. Enter the patricians, and the tribunes of the
people, lictors before them; CORIOLANUS, MENENIUS,
     COMINIUS *the Consul.* SICINIUS *and* BRUTUS
     take their places by themselves; Coriolanus stands.

MENENIUS   Having determin'd of the Volsces, and
          To send for Titus Lartius, it remains,
          As the main point of this our after-meeting,
          To gratify his noble service that   40
          Hath thus stood for his country. Therefore, please
              you,
          Most reverend and grave elders, to desire
          The present consul, and last general
          In our well-found successes, to report
          A little of that worthy work perform'd   45
          By Martius Caius Coriolanus, whom
          We met here, both to thank and to remember,
          With honours like himself. [*Coriolanus sits.*]
1 SENATOR   Speak, good Cominius.
          Leave nothing out for length, and make us think
          Rather our state's defective for requital   50
          Than we to stretch it out.
          [*to the tribunes*]   Masters o'th' people,
          We do request your kindest ears, and after
          Your loving motion toward the common body,
          To yield what passes here.
SICINIUS   We are convented
          Upon a pleasing treaty, and have hearts   55

Inclinable to honour and advance
The theme of our assembly.
BRUTUS   Which the rather
  We shall be bless'd to do, if he remember
  A kinder value of the people than
  He hath hereto priz'd them at.
MENENIUS   That's off, that's off!
  I would you rather had been silent. Please you
  To hear Cominius speak?
BRUTUS   Most willingly;
  But yet my caution was more pertinent
  Than the rebuke you give it.
MENENIUS   He loves your people,
  But tie him not to be their bedfellow.
  Worthy Cominius, speak.
  [*Coriolanus rises, and offers to go away.*]
                        Nay, keep your place.
1 SENATOR   Sit, Coriolanus: never shame to hear
  What you have nobly done.
CORIOLANUS   Your honours' pardon:
  I had rather have my wounds to heal again
  Than hear say how I got them.
BRUTUS   Sir, I hope
  My words disbench'd you not?
CORIOLANUS   No, sir; yet oft,
  When blows have made me stay, I fled from words.
  You sooth'd not, therefore hurt not: but your people,
  I love them as they weigh –
MENENIUS   Pray now, sit down.
CORIOLANUS
  I had rather have one scratch my head i'th' sun
  When the alarum were struck, than idly sit
  To hear my nothings monster'd.   *Exit Coriolanus.*
MENENIUS   Masters of the people,
  Your multiplying spawn how can he flatter –
  That's thousand to one good one – when you now
      see
  He had rather venture all his limbs for honour
  Than one on's ears to hear it? Proceed, Cominius.
COMINIUS   I shall lack voice: the deeds of Coriolanus
  Should not be utter'd feebly. It is held
  That valour is the chiefest virtue and
  Most dignifies the haver: if it be,
  The man I speak of cannot in the world
  Be singly counter-pois'd. At sixteen years,
  When Tarquin made a head for Rome, he fought
  Beyond the mark of others; our then dictator,
  Whom with all praise I point at, saw him fight,
  When with his Amazonian chin he drove
  The bristled lips before him; he bestrid
  An o'erpress'd Roman, and i'th' consul's view
  Slew three opposers; Tarquin's self he met
  And struck him on his knee. In that day's feats,
  When he might act the woman in the scene,
  He prov'd best man i'th' field, and for his meed
  Was brow-bound with the oak. His pupil age
  Man-enter'd thus, he waxed like a sea,

And in the brunt of seventeen battles since   100
He lurch'd all swords of the garland. For this last,
Before and in Corioles, let me say
I cannot speak him home. He stopp'd the fliers,
And by his rare example made the coward
Turn terror into sport; as weeds before   105
A vessel under sail, so men obey'd
And fell below his stem: his sword, death's stamp,
Where it did mark, it took; from face to foot
He was a thing of blood, whose every motion
Was tim'd with dying cries: alone he enter'd   110
The mortal gate of th' city, which he painted
With shunless destiny, aidless came off,
And with a sudden reinforcement struck
Corioles like a planet. Now all's his;
When by and by the din of war gan pierce   115
His ready sense, then straight his doubled spirit
Requicken'd what in flesh was fatigate,
And to the battle came he, where he did
Run reeking o'er the lives of men, as if
'Twere a perpetual spoil; and till we call'd   120
Both field and city ours, he never stood
To ease his breast with panting.
MENENIUS   Worthy man.
1 SENATOR
  He cannot but with measure fit the honours
  Which we devise him.
COMINIUS   Our spoils he kick'd at,
  And look'd upon things precious as they were   125
  The common muck of the world. He covets less
  Than misery itself would give, rewards
  His deeds with doing them, and is content
  To spend the time to end it.
MENENIUS   He's right noble.
  Let him be call'd for.
1 SENATOR   Call Coriolanus.   130
OFFICER   He doth appear.

            Enter CORIOLANUS.

MENENIUS   The senate, Coriolanus, are well pleas'd
  To make thee consul.
CORIOLANUS   I do owe them still
  My life and services.
MENENIUS   It then remains
  That you do speak to the people.
CORIOLANUS   I do beseech you,   135
  Let me o'erleap that custom; for I cannot
  Put on the gown, stand naked, and entreat them
  For my wounds' sake to give their suffrage. Please
      you
  That I may pass this doing.
SICINIUS   Sir, the people
  Must have their voices; neither will they bate   140
  One jot of ceremony.
MENENIUS   Put them not to't.
  Pray you go fit you to the custom and
  Take to you, as your predecessors have,

Your honour with your form.

CORIOLANUS   It is a part

145 That I shall blush in acting, and might well
     Be taken from the people.

BRUTUS [*to Sicinius*]   Mark you that.

CORIOLANUS   To brag unto them, thus I did, and thus,
     Show them th'unaching scars which I should hide,
     As if I had receiv'd them for the hire
     Of their breath only!

150 MENENIUS   Do not stand upon't.
     We recommend to you, tribunes of the people,
     Our purpose to them; and to our noble consul
     Wish we all joy and honour.

SENATORS   To Coriolanus come all joy and honour!

                              Flourish cornets. Then exeunt.
     [*Sicinius and Brutus remain.*]

155 BRUTUS   You see how he intends to use the people.

SICINIUS
     May they perceive's intent! He will require them
     As if he did contemn what he requested
     Should be in them to give.

BRUTUS   Come, we'll inform them
     Of our proceedings here; on th' market-place

160 I know they do attend us.   *Exeunt.*

2.3   *Enter seven or eight* Citizens.

1 CITIZEN   Once, if he do require our voices, we ought
     not to deny him.

2 CITIZEN   We may, sir, if we will.

3 CITIZEN   We have power in ourselves to do it, but it is
5   a power that we have no power to do. For, if he show
     us his wounds and tell us his deeds, we are to put our
     tongues into those wounds and speak for them. So if
     he tell us his noble deeds, we must also tell him our
     noble acceptance of them. Ingratitude is monstrous,
10   and for the multitude to be ingrateful, were to make a
     monster of the multitude; of the which we being
     members, should bring ourselves to be monstrous
     members.

1 CITIZEN   And to make us no better thought of, a little
15   help will serve: for once we stood up about the corn,
     he himself stuck not to call us the many-headed
     multitude.

3 CITIZEN   We have been called so of many; not that our
     heads are some brown, some black, some abram, some
20   bald, but that our wits are so diversely coloured; and
     truly I think, if all our wits were to issue out of one
     skull, they would fly east, west, north, south, and their
     consent of one direct way should be at once to all the
     points o'th' compass.

25   2 CITIZEN   Think you so? Which way do you judge my
     wit would fly?

3 CITIZEN   Nay, your wit will not so soon out as another
     man's will; 'tis strongly wedged up in a blockhead: but
     if it were at liberty, 'twould, sure, southward.

30   2 CITIZEN   Why that way?

3 CITIZEN   To lose itself in a fog, where, being three
     parts melted away with rotten dews, the fourth would
     return for conscience' sake, to help to get thee a wife.

2 CITIZEN   You are never without your tricks; you may,
     you may.   35

3 CITIZEN   Are you all resolved to give your voices? But
     that's no matter, the greater part carries it. I say, if he
     would incline to the people, there was never a worthier
     man.

Enter CORIOLANUS *in a gown of humility, with* MENENIUS.

     Here he comes, and in the gown of humility: mark his   40
     behaviour. We are not to stay all together, but to come
     by him where he stands, by ones, by twos and by
     threes. He's to make his requests by particulars,
     wherein every one of us has a single honour, in giving
     him our own voices with our own tongues: therefore   45
     follow me, and I'll direct you how you shall go by him.

ALL   Content, content.   *Exeunt citizens.*

MENENIUS
     O sir, you are not right. Have you not known
     The worthiest men have done't?

CORIOLANUS   What must I say? –
     'I pray, sir,' – Plague upon't! I cannot bring   50
     My tongue to such a pace. 'Look, sir, my wounds!
     I got them in my country's service, when
     Some certain of your brethren roar'd and ran
     From th' noise of our own drums.'

MENENIUS   O me, the gods!
     You must not speak of that; you must desire them   55
     To think upon you.

CORIOLANUS   Think upon me? Hang 'em!
     I would they would forget me, like the virtues
     Which our divines lose by 'em.

MENENIUS   You'll mar all.
     I'll leave you. Pray you, speak to 'em, I pray you,
     In wholesome manner.   *Exit.*

Enter three of the Citizens.

CORIOLANUS   Bid them wash their faces,   60
     And keep their teeth clean. So, here comes a brace.
     You know the cause, sir, of my standing here?

3 CITIZEN   We do, sir; tell us what hath brought you to't.

CORIOLANUS   Mine own desert.

2 CITIZEN   Your own desert?   65

CORIOLANUS   Ay, but not mine own desire.

3 CITIZEN   How, not your own desire?

CORIOLANUS   No, sir, 'twas never my desire yet to
     trouble the poor with begging.

3 CITIZEN   You must think, if we give you anything, we   70
     hope to gain by you.

CORIOLANUS   Well then, I pray, your price o'th'
     consulship?

1 CITIZEN   The price is, to ask it kindly.

CORIOLANUS   Kindly, sir, I pray let me ha't. I have   75
     wounds to show you, which shall be yours in private.
     Your good voice, sir. What say you?

2 CITIZEN   You shall ha't, worthy sir.

CORIOLANUS   A match, sir. There's in all two worthy voices begged. I have your alms: adieu!

3 CITIZEN   But this is something odd.

2 CITIZEN   And 'twere to give again – but 'tis no matter.

Exeunt the three Citizens.

Enter two other Citizens.

CORIOLANUS   Pray you now, if it may stand with the tune of your voices that I may be consul, I have here the customary gown.

4 CITIZEN   You have deserved nobly of your country, and you have not deserved nobly.

CORIOLANUS   Your enigma?

4 CITIZEN   You have been a scourge to her enemies, you have been a rod to her friends; you have not indeed loved the common people.

CORIOLANUS   You should account me the more virtuous, that I have not been common in my love. I will, sir, flatter my sworn brother the people, to earn a dearer estimation of them; 'tis a condition they account gentle; and since the wisdom of their choice is rather to have my hat than my heart, I will practise the insinuating nod, and be off to them most counterfeitly; that is, sir, I will counterfeit the bewitchment of some popular man, and give it bountiful to the desirers. Therefore, beseech you, I may be consul.

5 CITIZEN   We hope to find you our friend, and therefore give you our voices heartily.

4 CITIZEN   You have received many wounds for your country.

CORIOLANUS   I will not seal your knowledge with showing them. I will make much of your voices, and so trouble you no farther.

BOTH   The gods give you joy, sir, heartily.

Exeunt the two Citizens.

CORIOLANUS   Most sweet voices!
Better it is to die, better to starve,
Than crave the hire which first we do deserve.
Why in this wolvish toge should I stand here,
To beg of Hob and Dick that does appear
Their needless vouches? Custom calls me to't.
What custom wills, in all things should we do't,
The dust on antique time would lie unswept
And mountainous error be too highly heap'd
For truth to o'erpeer. Rather than fool it so,
Let the high office and the honour go
To one that would do thus. I am half through,
The one part suffer'd, the other will I do.

Enter three Citizens *more.*

Here come moe voices.
Your voices! For your voices I have fought,
Watch'd for your voices; for your voices, bear
Of wounds two dozen odd; battles thrice six
I have seen and heard of; for your voices have

Done many things, some less, some more: your voices!
Indeed I would be consul.

6 CITIZEN   He has done nobly, and cannot go without any honest man's voice.

7 CITIZEN   Therefore let him be consul. The gods give him joy, and make him good friend to the people!

ALL   Amen, amen. God save thee, noble consul!

Exeunt the three Citizens.

CORIOLANUS   Worthy voices!

Enter MENENIUS, *with* BRUTUS *and* SICINIUS.

MENENIUS
You have stood your limitation, and the tribunes
Endue you with the people's voice; remains
That, in th'official marks invested, you
Anon do meet the senate.

CORIOLANUS   Is this done?

SICINIUS   The custom of request you have discharg'd.
The people do admit you, and are summon'd
To meet anon upon your approbation.

CORIOLANUS   Where? At the senate-house?

SICINIUS   There, Coriolanus.

CORIOLANUS   May I change these garments?

SICINIUS   You may, sir.

CORIOLANUS
That I'll straight do; and knowing myself again,
Repair to th' senate-house.

MENENIUS   I'll keep you company. Will you along?

BRUTUS   We stay here for the people.

SICINIUS   Fare you well.

Exeunt Coriolanus and Menenius.

He has it now; and by his looks, methinks
'Tis warm at's heart.

BRUTUS   With a proud heart he wore
His humble weeds. Will you dismiss the people?

Enter the Plebeians.

SICINIUS
How now, my masters, have you chose this man?

1 CITIZEN   He has our voices, sir.

BRUTUS   We pray the gods he may deserve your loves.

2 CITIZEN   Amen, sir. To my poor unworthy notice,
He mock'd us when he begg'd our voices.

3 CITIZEN   Certainly,
He flouted us downright.

1 CITIZEN
No, 'tis his kind of speech; he did not mock us.

2 CITIZEN   Not one amongst us, save yourself, but says
He us'd us scornfully: he should have show'd us
His marks of merit, wounds receiv'd for's country.

SICINIUS   Why, so he did, I am sure.

ALL   No, no; no man saw 'em.

3 CITIZEN
He said he had wounds which he could show in private;
And with his hat, thus waving it in scorn,

'I would be consul,' says he; 'aged custom,
But by your voices, will not so permit me:
Your voices therefore.' When we granted that,
Here was, 'I thank you for your voices, thank you;
Your most sweet voices: now you have left your
170   voices,
I have no further with you.' Was not this mockery?

SICINIUS Why either were you ignorant to see't,
Or, seeing it, of such childish friendliness
To yield your voices?

BRUTUS   Could you not have told him
175 As you were lesson'd: when he had no power,
But was a petty servant to the state,
He was your enemy, ever spake against
Your liberties and the charters that you bear
I'th' body of the weal; and now arriving
180 A place of potency and sway o'th' state,
If he should still malignantly remain
Fast foe to th' plebeii, your voices might
Be curses to yourselves? You should have said
That, as his worthy deeds did claim no less
185 Than what he stood for, so his gracious nature
Would think upon you for your voices, and
Translate his malice towards you into love,
Standing your friendly lord.

SICINIUS   Thus to have said,
As you were fore-advis'd, had touch'd his spirit
190 And tried his inclination: from him pluck'd
Either his gracious promise, which you might
As cause had call'd you up, have held him to;
Or else it would have gall'd his surly nature
Which easily endures not article
195 Tying him to aught; so putting him to rage,
You should have ta'en th'advantage of his choler,
And pass'd him unelected.

BRUTUS   Did you perceive
He did solicit you in free contempt
When he did need your loves; and do you think
200 That his contempt shall not be bruising to you
When he hath power to crush? Why, had your bodies
No heart among you? Or had you tongues to cry
Against the rectorship of judgement?

SICINIUS   Have you,
Ere now, denied the asker, and now again,
205 Of him that did not ask but mock, bestow
Your sued-for tongues?

3 CITIZEN He's not confirm'd: we may deny him yet.

2 CITIZEN And will deny him!
I'll have five hundred voices of that sound.

1 CITIZEN
210 I twice five hundred, and their friends to piece 'em.

BRUTUS Get you hence instantly, and tell those friends
They have chose a consul that will from them take
Their liberties, make them of no more voice
Than dogs that are as often beat for barking

As therefore kept to do so.

SICINIUS   Let them assemble;   215
And, on a safer judgement, all revoke
Your ignorant election. Enforce his pride
And his old hate unto you. Besides, forget not
With what contempt he wore the humble weed,
How in his suit he scorn'd you; but your loves,   220
Thinking upon his services, took from you
Th'apprehension of his present portance,
Which most gibingly, ungravely, he did fashion
After the inveterate hate he bears you.

BRUTUS   Lay
A fault on us, your tribunes: that we labour'd,   225
No impediment between, but that you must
Cast your election on him.

SICINIUS   Say you chose him
More after our commandment than as guided
By your own true affections; and that your minds
Pre-occupied with what you rather must do,   230
Than what you should, made you against the grain
To voice him consul. Lay the fault on us.

BRUTUS Ay, spare us not. Say we read lectures to you,
How youngly he began to serve his country,
How long continued, and what stock he springs of –   235
The noble house o'th' Martians: from whence came
That Ancus Martius, Numa's daughter's son,
Who after great Hostilius here was king;
Of the same house Publius and Quintus were,
That our best water brought by conduits hither;   240
And Censorinus that was so surnam'd
And nobly named so, twice being censor,
Was his great ancestor.

SICINIUS   One thus descended,
That hath beside well in his person wrought,
To be set high in place, we did commend   245
To your remembrances; but you have found,
Scaling his present bearing with his past,
That he's your fixed enemy, and revoke
Your sudden approbation.

BRUTUS   Say you ne'er had done't –
Harp on that still – but by our putting on;   250
And presently, when you have drawn your number,
Repair to th' Capitol.

ALL   We will so: almost all
Repent in their election.   *Exeunt Plebeians.*

BRUTUS   Let them go on;
This mutiny were better put in hazard
Than stay, past doubt, for greater.   255
If, as his nature is, he fall in rage
With their refusal, both observe and answer
The vantage of his anger.

SICINIUS   To th' Capitol, come:
We will be there before the stream o'th'people;
And this shall seem, as partly 'tis, their own,   260
Which we have goaded onward.   *Exeunt.*

3.1   *Cornets. Enter* CORIOLANUS, MENENIUS,
all the gentry. COMINIUS, TITUS LARTIUS
and other Senators.

CORIOLANUS
  Tullus Aufidius then had made new head?
LARTIUS
  He had, my lord; and that it was which caus'd
  Our swifter composition.
CORIOLANUS   So then the Volsces stand but as at first,
  Ready when time shall prompt them to make road
  Upon's again.
COMINIUS   They are worn, lord consul, so,
  That we shall hardly in our ages see
  Their banners wave again.
CORIOLANUS   Saw you Aufidius?
LARTIUS   On safeguard he came to me, and did curse
  Against the Volsces for they had so vilely
  Yielded the town: he is retir'd to Antium.
CORIOLANUS   Spoke he of me?
LARTIUS   He did, my lord.
CORIOLANUS   How? What?
LARTIUS   How often he had met you, sword to sword;
  That of all things upon the earth he hated
  Your person most; that he would pawn his fortunes
  To hopeless restitution, so he might
  Be call'd your vanquisher.
CORIOLANUS   At Antium lives he?
LARTIUS   At Antium.
CORIOLANUS   I wish I had a cause to seek him there,
  To oppose his hatred fully. Welcome home.

          Enter SICINIUS *and* BRUTUS.

  Behold, these are the tribunes of the people,
  The tongues o'th' common mouth. I do despise
      them:
  For they do prank them in authority,
  Against all noble sufferance.
SICINIUS   Pass no further.
CORIOLANUS   Ha! what is that?
BRUTUS   It will be dangerous to go on. No further.
CORIOLANUS   What makes this change?
MENENIUS   The matter?
COMINIUS
  Hath he not pass'd the noble and the common?
BRUTUS   Cominius, no.
CORIOLANUS   Have I had children's voices?
1 SENATOR
  Tribunes, give way: he shall to th' market-place.
BRUTUS   The people are incens'd against him.
SICINIUS   Stop,
  Or all will fall in broil.
CORIOLANUS   Are these your herd?
  Must these have voices, that can yield them now
  And straight disclaim their tongues? What are your
      offices?
  You being their mouths, why rule you not their
      teeth?

  Have you not set them on?
MENENIUS   Be calm, be calm.
CORIOLANUS   It is a purpos'd thing, and grows by plot,
  To curb the will of the nobility:
  Suffer't, and live with such as cannot rule,   40
  Nor ever will be rul'd.
BRUTUS   Call't not a plot.
  The people cry you mock'd them; and of late,
  When corn was given them gratis, you repin'd,
  Scandal'd the suppliants for the people, call'd them
  Time-pleasers, flatterers, foes to nobleness.   45
CORIOLANUS   Why, this was known before.
BRUTUS   Not to them all.
CORIOLANUS   Have you inform'd them sithence?
BRUTUS   How! I inform them!
COMINIUS   You are like to do such business.
BRUTUS   Not unlike
  Each way to better yours.
CORIOLANUS
  Why then should I be consul? By yond clouds,   50
  Let me deserve so ill as you, and make me
  Your fellow tribune.
SICINIUS   You show too much of that
  For which the people stir. If you will pass
  To where you are bound, you must inquire your way,
  Which you are out of, with a gentler spirit,   55
  Or never be so noble as a consul,
  Nor yoke with him for tribune.
MENENIUS   Let's be calm.
COMINIUS
  The people are abus'd; set on. This palt'ring
  Becomes not Rome; nor has Coriolanus
  Deserv'd this so dishonour'd rub, laid falsely   60
  I'th' plain way of his merit.
CORIOLANUS   Tell me of corn!
  This was my speech, and I will speak't again.
MENENIUS   Not now, not now.
1 SENATOR   Not in this heat, sir, now.
CORIOLANUS   Now as I live, I will. My nobler friends,
  I crave their pardons.   65
  For the mutable, rank-scented meinie, let them
  Regard me as I do not flatter, and
  Therein behold themselves. I say again,
  In soothing them, we nourish 'gainst our senate
  The cockle of rebellion, insolence, sedition,   70
  Which we ourselves have plough'd for, sow'd and
      scatter'd,
  By mingling them with us, the honour'd number
  Who lack not virtue, no, nor power, but that
  Which they have given to beggars.
MENENIUS   Well, no more.
1 SENATOR   No more words, we beseech you.
CORIOLANUS   How? no more!   75
  As for my country I have shed my blood,
  Not fearing outward force, so shall my lungs
  Coin words till their decay, against those measles
  Which we disdain should tetter us, yet sought

The very way to catch them.

BRUTUS   You speak o'th' people
80 As if you were a god to punish, not
A man of their infirmity.

SICINIUS   'Twere well
We let the people know't.

MENENIUS   What, what? His choler?

CORIOLANUS   Choler!
85 Were I as patient as the midnight sleep,
By Jove, 'twould be my mind!

SICINIUS   It is a mind
That shall remain a poison where it is,
Not poison any further.

CORIOLANUS   Shall remain!
Hear you this Triton of the minnows? Mark you
His absolute 'shall'?

COMINIUS   'Twas from the canon.

90 CORIOLANUS   'Shall!'
O good but most unwise patricians: why,
You grave but reckless senators, have you thus
Given Hydra here to choose an officer,
That with his peremptory 'shall', being but
95 The horn and noise o'th' monster's, wants not spirit
To say he'll turn your current in a ditch
And make your channel his? If he have power,
Then vail your ignorance; if none, awake
Your dangerous lenity. If you are learn'd
100 Be not as common fools; if you are not,
Let them have cushions by you. You are plebeians
If they be senators; and they are no less
When, both your voices blended, the great'st taste
Most palates theirs. They choose their magistrate,
105 And such a one as he, who puts his 'shall',
His popular 'shall', against a graver bench
Than ever frown'd in Greece. By Jove himself,
It makes the consuls base; and my soul aches
To know, when two authorities are up,
110 Neither supreme, how soon confusion
May enter 'twixt the gap of both, and take
The one by th'other.

COMINIUS   Well, on to th' market place.

CORIOLANUS   Whoever gave that counsel, to give forth
The corn o'th' storehouse gratis, as 'twas us'd
Sometime in Greece –

MENENIUS   Well, well, no more of that.

115 CORIOLANUS
Though there the people had more absolute power –
I say they nourish'd disobedience, fed
The ruin of the state.

BRUTUS   Why shall the people give
One that speaks thus their voice?

CORIOLANUS   I'll give my reasons
120 More worthier than their voices. They know the corn
Was not our recompense, resting well assur'd
They ne'er did service for't; being press'd to the war,
Even when the navel of the state was touch'd,
They would not thread the gates: this kind of service

Did not deserve corn gratis. Being i'th' war,   125
Their mutinies and revolts, wherein they show'd
Most valour, spoke not for them. Th'accusation
Which they have often made against the senate,
All cause unborn, could never be the native
Of our so frank donation. Well, what then?   130
How shall this bosom multiplied digest
The senate's courtesy? Let deeds express
What's like to be their words, 'We did request it,
We are the greater poll, and in true fear
They gave us our demands.' Thus we debase   135
The nature of our seats, and make the rabble
Call our cares fears; which will in time
Break ope the locks o'th' senate, and bring in
The crows to peck the eagles.

MENENIUS   Come, enough.

BRUTUS   Enough, with over-measure.

CORIOLANUS   No, take more!   140
What may be sworn by, both divine and human,
Seal what I end withal! This double worship,
Where one part does disdain with cause, the other
Insult without all reason: where gentry, title, wisdom,
Cannot conclude but by the yea and no   145
Of general ignorance, it must omit
Real necessities, and give way the while
To unstable slightness. Purpose so barr'd, it follows
Nothing is done to purpose. Therefore beseech you –
You that will be less fearful than discreet,   150
That love the fundamental part of state
More than you doubt the change on't; that prefer
A noble life before a long, and wish
To jump a body with a dangerous physic
That's sure of death without it – at once pluck out   155
The multitudinous tongue: let them not lick
The sweet which is their poison. Your dishonour
Mangles true judgement, and bereaves the state
Of that integrity which should becom't,
Not having the power to do the good it would   160
For th'ill which doth control't.

BRUTUS   'Has said enough.

SICINIUS   'Has spoken like a traitor, and shall answer
As traitors do.

CORIOLANUS   Thou wretch, despite o'erwhelm thee!
What should the people do with these bald tribunes?   165
On whom depending, their obedience fails
To th'greater bench. In a rebellion,
When what's not meet, but what must be, was law,
Then were they chosen. In a better hour,
Let what is meet be said it must be meet,   170
And throw their power i'th' dust.

BRUTUS   Manifest treason!

SICINIUS   This a consul? No!

BRUTUS   The aediles, ho!

Enter an Aedile.

Let him be apprehended.

SICINIUS   Go call the people;   *Exit Aedile*

in whose name myself
75   Attach thee as a traitorous innovator,
    A foe to th' public weal. Obey I charge thee,
    And follow to thine answer.
CORIOLANUS   Hence, old goat!
ALL PATRICIANS   We'll surety him.
COMINIUS   Aged sir, hands off.
CORIOLANUS
    Hence rotten thing! or I shall shake thy bones
    Out of thy garments.
80 SICINIUS   Help, ye citizens!

      Enter a rabble of Plebeians *with the Aediles.*

MENENIUS   On both sides more respect.
SICINIUS
    Here's he that would take from you all your power.
BRUTUS   Seize him, aediles!
ALL PLEBEIANS   Down with him! Down with him!
85 2 SENATOR   Weapons, weapons, weapons!
    [They all bustle about Coriolanus.]
ALL   Tribunes! Patricians! Citizens! What ho!
    Sicinius! Brutus! Coriolanus! Citizens!
    Peace, peace, peace! Stay! Hold! Peace!
MENENIUS   What is about to be? I am out of breath;
90   Confusion's near, I cannot speak. You, tribunes
    To th' people! Coriolanus, patience!
    Speak, good Sicinius!
SICINIUS   Hear me, people. Peace!
ALL PLEBEIANS
    Let's hear our tribune. Peace! Speak, speak, speak!
95 SICINIUS   You are at point to lose your liberties:
    Martius would have all from you, Martius
    Whom late you have nam'd for consul.
MENENIUS   Fie, fie, fie!
    This is the way to kindle, not to quench.
2 SENATOR   To unbuild the city and to lay all flat.
SICINIUS   What is the city but the people?
ALL PLEBEIANS   True,
200   The people are the city.
BRUTUS   By the consent of all we were establish'd
    The people's magistrates.
ALL PLEBEIANS   You so remain.
MENENIUS   And so are like to do.
COMINIUS   That is the way to lay the city flat,
205   To bring the roof to the foundation,
    And bury all which yet distinctly ranges
    In heaps and piles of ruin.
SICINIUS   This deserves death.
BRUTUS   Or let us stand to our authority
    Or let us lose it: we do here pronounce,
210   Upon the part o'th' people, in whose power
    We were elected theirs, Martius is worthy
    Of present death.
SICINIUS   Therefore lay hold of him.
    Bear him to th' rock Tarpeian, and from thence
    Into destruction cast him.
BRUTUS   Aediles, seize him!

ALL PLEBEIANS   Yield, Martius, yield!
MENENIUS   Hear me one word.   215
    Beseech you, tribunes, hear me but a word.
AEDILE   Peace, peace!
MENENIUS
    Be that you seem, truly your country's friend,
    And temp'rately proceed to what you would
    Thus violently redress.
BRUTUS   Sir, those cold ways,   220
    That seem like prudent helps, are very poisonous
    Where the disease is violent. Lay hands upon him,
    And bear him to the rock.
    [Coriolanus draws his sword.]
CORIOLANUS   No, I'll die here.
    There's some among you have beheld me fighting:
    Come, try upon yourselves what you have seen me!   225
MENENIUS
    Down with that sword! Tribunes, withdraw awhile.
BRUTUS   Lay hands upon him.
MENENIUS   Help Martius, help!
    You that be noble, help him, young and old!
ALL PLEBEIANS   Down with him, down with him!
    In this mutiny, the tribunes, the aediles and the people
                    are beat in and exeunt.
MENENIUS   Go, get you to your house: be gone, away!   230
    All will be naught else.
2 SENATOR   Get you gone.
CORIOLANUS   Stand fast.
    We have as many friends as enemies.
MENENIUS   Shall it be put to that?
1 SENATOR   The gods forbid.
    I prithee, noble friend, home to thy house:
    Leave us to cure this cause.
MENENIUS   For 'tis a sore upon us   235
    You cannot tent yourself: be gone, beseech you.
COMINIUS   Come, sir, along with us.
CORIOLANUS
    I would they were barbarians – as they are,
    Though in Rome litter'd; not Romans – as they are
      not,
    Though calv'd i'th' porch o'th' Capitol.
MENENIUS   Be gone!   240
    Put not your worthy rage into your tongue.
    One time will owe another.
CORIOLANUS   On fair ground
    I could beat forty of them.
MENENIUS   I could myself
    Take up a brace o'th' best of them; yea, the two
      tribunes.
COMINIUS   But now 'tis odds beyond arithmetic;   245
    And manhood is call'd foolery when it stands
    Against a falling fabric. Will you hence
    Before the tag return? Whose rage doth rend
    Like interrupted waters, and o'erbear
    What they are us'd to bear.
MENENIUS   Pray you be gone.   250
    I'll try whether my old wit be in request

With those that have but little: this must be patch'd
With cloth of any colour.

COMINIUS   Nay, come away.

Exeunt Coriolanus and Cominius, and others.

PATRICIAN   This man has marr'd his fortune.

255 MENENIUS   His nature is too noble for the world:
He would not flatter Neptune for his trident,
Or Jove for's power to thunder. His heart's his
      mouth:
What his breast forges, that his tongue must vent;
And being angry, does forget that ever

260 He heard the name of death.   [*A noise within.*]
Here's goodly work!

PATRICIAN   I would they were abed!

MENENIUS
I would they were in Tiber! What the vengeance,
Could he not speak 'em fair?

Enter BRUTUS *and* SICINIUS *with the rabble again.*

SICINIUS   Where is this viper
That would depopulate the city and
Be every man himself?

265 MENENIUS   You worthy tribunes –

SICINIUS   He shall be thrown down the Tarpeian rock
With rigorous hands: he hath resisted law,
And therefore law shall scorn him further trial
Than the severity of the public power,
Which he so sets at naught.

270 1 CITIZEN   He shall well know
The noble tribunes are the people's mouths
And we their hands.

ALL PLEBEIANS   He shall, sure on't.

MENENIUS   Sir, sir!

SICINIUS   Peace!

MENENIUS
Do not cry havoc where you should but hunt
With modest warrant.

275 SICINIUS   Sir, how comes't that you
Have help to make this rescue?

MENENIUS   Hear me speak!
As I do know the consul's worthiness,
So can I name his faults.

SICINIUS   Consul! What consul?

MENENIUS   The consul Coriolanus.

BRUTUS   He consul!

280 ALL PLEBEIANS   No, no, no, no, no.

MENENIUS
If, by the tribunes' leave, and yours, good people,
I may be heard, I would crave a word or two,
The which shall turn you to no further harm
Than so much loss of time.

SICINIUS   Speak briefly then:

285 For we are peremptory to dispatch
This viperous traitor. To eject him hence
Were but our danger, and to keep him here
Our certain death. Therefore it is decreed
He dies tonight.

MENENIUS   Now the good gods forbid
That our renowned Rome, whose gratitude   290
Towards her deserved children is enroll'd
In Jove's own book, like an unnatural dam
Should now eat up her own!

SICINIUS   He's a disease that must be cut away.

MENENIUS   Oh, he's a limb that has but a disease: 295
Mortal, to cut it off; to cure it, easy.
What has he done to Rome that's worthy death?
Killing our enemies, the blood he hath lost
(Which I dare vouch, is more than that he hath
By many an ounce) he dropp'd it for his country;   300
And what is left, to lose it by his country
Were to us all that do't and suffer it
A brand to th'end o'th' world.

SICINIUS   This is clean kam.

BRUTUS   Merely awry. When he did love his country,
It honour'd him.

SICINIUS   The service of the foot,   305
Being once gangren'd, is not then respected
For what before it was.

BRUTUS   We'll hear no more:
Pursue him to his house, and pluck him thence,
Lest his infection, being of catching nature,
Spread further.

MENENIUS   One word more, one word.   310
This tiger-footed rage, when it shall find
The harm of unscann'd swiftness will, too late,
Tie leaden pounds to's heels. Proceed by process,
Lest parties, as he is belov'd, break out
And sack great Rome with Romans.

BRUTUS   If it were so!   315

SICINIUS   What do ye talk?
Have we not had a taste of his obedience?
Our aediles smote? ourselves resisted? Come.

MENENIUS   Consider this: he has been bred i'th' wars
Since a could draw a sword, and is ill school'd   320
In bolted language; meal and bran together
He throws without distinction. Give me leave,
I'll go to him, and undertake to bring him
Where he shall answer by a lawful form –
In peace – to his utmost peril.

1 SENATOR   Noble tribunes,   325
It is the humane way. The other course
Will prove too bloody, and the end of it
Unknown to the beginning.

SICINIUS   Noble Menenius,
Be you then as the people's officer.
Masters, lay down your weapons.

BRUTUS   Go not home.   330

SICINIUS
Meet on the market-place: we'll attend to you there,
Where, if you bring not Martius, we'll proceed
In our first way.

MENENIUS   I'll bring him to you.
[*to the Senators*] Let me desire your company. He
      must come,

Or what is worst will follow.

35 1 SENATOR   Pray you, let's to him.

Exeunt.

3.2   *Enter* CORIOLANUS *with* Nobles.

CORIOLANUS

Let them pull all about mine ears, present me
Death on the wheel, or at wild horses' heels,
Or pile ten hills on the Tarpeian rock,
That the precipitation might down stretch
Below the beam of sight: yet will I still
Be thus to them.

Enter VOLUMNIA.

PATRICIAN   You do the nobler.

CORIOLANUS   I muse my mother
Does not approve me further, who was wont
To call them woollen vassals, things created
10 To buy and sell with groats, to show bare heads
In congregations, to yawn, be still, and wonder,
When one but of my ordinance stood up
To speak of peace or war. I talk of you.
Why did you wish me milder? Would you have me
15 False to my nature? Rather say I play
The man I am.

VOLUMNIA   O sir, sir, sir.
I would have had you put your power well on
Before you had worn it out.

CORIOLANUS   Let go.

VOLUMNIA

You might have been enough the man you are,
20 With striving less to be so: lesser had been
The thwartings of your dispositions, if
You had not show'd them how ye were dispos'd,
Ere they lack'd power to cross you.

CORIOLANUS   Let them hang.

VOLUMNIA   Ay, and burn too.

Enter MENENIUS *with the* Senators.

MENENIUS

Come, come, you have been too rough, something too
25   rough.
You must return and mend it.

1 SENATOR   There's no remedy,
Unless by not so doing, our good city
Cleave in the midst, and perish.

VOLUMNIA   Pray be counsell'd;
I have a heart as little apt as yours,
30 But yet a brain that leads my use of anger
To better vantage.

MENENIUS   Well said, noble woman.
Before he should thus stoop to th' herd, but that
The violent fit o'th' time craves it as physic
For the whole state, I would put mine armour on,
Which I can scarcely bear.

35 CORIOLANUS   What must I do?

MENENIUS   Return to th' tribunes.

CORIOLANUS   Well, what then? what then?

MENENIUS   Repent what you have spoke.

CORIOLANUS   For them? I cannot do it to the gods,
Must I then do't to them?

VOLUMNIA   You are too absolute.
Though therein you can never be too noble,   40
But when extremities speak. I have heard you say,
Honour and policy, like unsever'd friends,
I'th' war do grow together: grant that, and tell me,
In peace what each of them by th'other lose
That they combine not there.

CORIOLANUS   Tush, tush!

MENENIUS   A good demand.   45

VOLUMNIA   If it be honour in your wars to seem
The same you are not, which, for your best ends
You adopt your policy, how is it less or worse
That it shall hold companionship in peace
With honour, as in war, since that to both   50
It stands in like request?

CORIOLANUS   Why force you this?

VOLUMNIA   Because that now it lies you on to speak
To th' people; not by your own instruction,
Nor by th'matter which your heart prompts you,
But with such words that are but roted in   55
Your tongue, though but bastards and syllables
Of no allowance to your bosom's truth.
Now, this no more dishonours you at all,
Than to take in a town with gentle words
Which else would put you to your fortune and   60
The hazard of much blood.
I would dissemble with my nature where
My fortunes and my friends at stake requir'd
I should do so in honour. I am in this
Your wife, your son, these senators, the nobles;   65
And you will rather show our general louts
How you can frown, than spend a fawn upon 'em
For the inheritance of their loves and safeguard
Of what that want might ruin.

MENENIUS   Noble lady!
Come, go with us; speak fair; you may salve so   70
Not what is dangerous present, but the loss
Of what is past.

VOLUMNIA   I prithee now, my son,
Go to them, with this bonnet in thy hand,
And thus far having stretch'd it – here be with
    them –
Thy knee bussing the stones – for in such business   75
Action is eloquence, and the eyes of th'ignorant
More learned than the ears – waving thy head,
Which often, thus, correcting thy stout heart,
Now humble as the ripest mulberry
That will not hold the handling; or say to them,   80
Thou art their soldier, and being bred in broils,
Hast not the soft way which, thou dost confess,
Were fit for thee to use, as they to claim,
In asking their good loves; but thou wilt frame

85   Thyself, forsooth, hereafter theirs, so far
      As thou hast power and person.
MENENIUS   This but done,
      Even as she speaks, why, their hearts were yours:
      For they have pardons, being ask'd, as free
      As words to little purpose.
VOLUMNIA   Prithee now,
90   Go, and be rul'd; although I know thou hadst rather
      Follow thine enemy in a fiery gulf
      Than flatter him in a bower.

                    Enter COMINIUS.

                              Here is Cominius.
COMINIUS
      I have been i'th' market place; and, sir, 'tis fit
      You make strong party, or defend yourself
95   By calmness or by absence. All's in anger.
MENENIUS   Only fair speech.
COMINIUS   I think 'twill serve, if he
      Can thereto frame his spirit.
VOLUMNIA   He must, and will:
      Prithee now, say you will, and go about it.
CORIOLANUS
      Must I go show them my unbarb'd sconce? Must I
100   With my base tongue give to my noble heart
      A lie that it must bear? Well, I will do't:
      Yet were there but this single plot to lose,
      This mould of Martius, they to dust should grind it
      And throw't against the wind. To th' market-place!
105   You have put me now to such a part which never
      I shall discharge to th' life.
COMINIUS   Come, come, we'll prompt you.
VOLUMNIA   I prithee now, sweet son, as thou hast said
      My praises made thee first a soldier, so,
      To have my praise for this, perform a part
      Thou hast not done before.
110   CORIOLANUS   Well, I must do't.
      Away my disposition, and possess me
      Some harlot's spirit! My throat of war be turn'd,
      Which choired with my drum, into a pipe
      Small as an eunuch, or the virgin voice
115   That babies lull asleep! The smiles of knaves
      Tent in my cheeks, and schoolboys' tears take up
      The glasses of my sight! A beggar's tongue
      Make motion through my lips, and my arm'd knees
      Who bow'd but in my stirrup, bend like his
120   That hath receiv'd an alms! I will not do't,
      Lest I surcease to honour mine own truth,
      And by my body's action teach my mind
      A most inherent baseness.
VOLUMNIA   At thy choice then:
      To beg of thee it is my more dishonour
125   Than thou of them. Come all to ruin; let
      Thy mother rather feel thy pride than fear
      Thy dangerous stoutness, for I mock at death
      With as big heart as thou. Do as thou list.
      Thy valiantness was mine, thou suck'st it from me,

      But owe thy pride thyself.
CORIOLANUS   Pray be content.   130
      Mother, I am going to the market-place:
      Chide me no more. I'll mountebank their loves,
      Cog their hearts from them, and come home belov'd
      Of all the trades in Rome. Look, I am going.
      Commend me to my wife. I'll return consul,   135
      Or never trust to what my tongue can do
      I'th'way of flattery further.
VOLUMNIA   Do your will.   *Exit.*
COMINIUS
      Away! The tribunes do attend you: arm yourself
      To answer mildly; for they are prepar'd
      With accusations, as I hear, more strong   140
      Than are upon you yet.
CORIOLANUS   The word is 'mildly'. Pray you, let us go.
      Let them accuse me by invention: I
      Will answer in mine honour.
MENENIUS   Ay, but mildly.
CORIOLANUS   Well, mildly be it then. Mildly!   145
                                    Exeunt.

3.3   *Enter* SICINIUS *and* BRUTUS.

BRUTUS   In this point charge him home, that he affects
      Tyrannical power. If he evade us there,
      Enforce him with his envy to the people,
      And that the spoil got on the Antiates
      Was ne'er distributed.

                    Enter an Aedile.

                              What, will he come?   5
AEDILE   He's coming.
BRUTUS   How accompanied?
AEDILE   With old Menenius, and those senators
      That always favour'd him.
SICINIUS   Have you a catalogue
      Of all the voices that we have procur'd,
      Set down by th' poll?
AEDILE   I have: 'tis ready.   10
SICINIUS   Have you collected them by tribes?
AEDILE   I have.
SICINIUS   Assemble presently the people hither:
      And when they hear me say, 'It shall be so
      I'th' right and strength o'th' commons,' be it either
      For death, for fine, or banishment, then let them   15
      If I say fine, cry 'Fine', if death, cry 'Death',
      Insisting on the old prerogative
      And power i'th' truth o'th' cause.
AEDILE   I shall inform them.
BRUTUS   And when such time they have begun to cry,
      Let them not cease, but with a din confus'd   20
      Enforce the present execution
      Of what we chance to sentence.
AEDILE   Very well.
SICINIUS   Make them be strong, and ready for this hint
      When we shall hap to give't them.

BRUTUS   Go about it.
                                         Exit Aedile.
25 Put him to choler straight; he hath been us'd
    Ever to conquer, and to have his worth
    Of contradiction. Being once chaf'd, he cannot
    Be rein'd again to temperance; then he speaks
    What's in his heart, and that is there which looks
    With us to break his neck.
30 SICINIUS   Well, here he comes.

              Enter CORIOLANUS, MENENIUS
              and COMINIUS, *with others.*

MENENIUS   Calmly, I do beseech you.
CORIOLANUS
    Ay, as an hostler, that for th' poorest piece
    Will bear the knave by th' volume. Th'honour'd gods
    Keep Rome in safety, and the chairs of justice
35 Supplied with worthy men, plant love among's,
    Throng our large temples with the shows of peace
    And not our streets with war.
1 SENATOR   Amen, amen.
MENENIUS   A noble wish.

              Enter the Aedile *with the* Plebeians.

SICINIUS   Draw near, ye people.
40 AEDILE   List to your tribunes. Audience! Peace, I say!
CORIOLANUS   First, hear me speak!
BOTH TRIBUNES   Well, say. Peace, ho!
CORIOLANUS
    Shall I be charg'd no further than this present?
    Must all determine here?
SICINIUS   I do demand,
    If you submit you to the people's voices,
45 Allow their officers, and are content
    To suffer lawful censure for such faults
    As shall be prov'd upon you.
CORIOLANUS   I am content.
MENENIUS   Lo, citizens, he says he is content.
    The warlike service he has done, consider: think
50 Upon the wounds his body bears, which show
    Like graves i'th' holy churchyard.
CORIOLANUS   Scratches with briers,
    Scars to move laughter only.
MENENIUS   Consider further,
    That when he speaks not like a citizen,
    You find him like a soldier. Do not take
55 His rougher accents for malicious sounds,
    But, as I say, such as become a soldier,
    Rather than envy you.
COMINIUS   Well, well, no more.
CORIOLANUS   What is the matter,
    That being pass'd for consul with full voice,
60 I am so dishonour'd that the very hour
    You take it off again?
SICINIUS   Answer to us.
CORIOLANUS   Say then: 'tis true, I ought so.

SICINIUS
    We charge you, that you have contriv'd to take
    From Rome all season'd office, and to wind
    Yourself into a power tyrannical;   65
    For which you are a traitor to the people.
CORIOLANUS   How! Traitor?
MENENIUS   Nay, temperately: your promise!
CORIOLANUS
    The fires i'th' lowest hell fold in the people!
    Call me their traitor! Thou injurious tribune!
    Within thine eyes sat twenty thousand deaths,   70
    In thy hands clutch'd as many millions, in
    Thy lying tongue both numbers, I would say
    'Thou liest' unto thee, with a voice as free
    As I do pray the gods.
SICINIUS   Mark you this, people?
ALL PLEBEIANS   To th' rock, to th' rock with him.   75
SICINIUS   Peace!
    We need not put new matter to his charge.
    What you have seen him do, and heard him speak,
    Beating your officers, cursing yourselves,
    Opposing laws with strokes, and here defying   80
    Those whose great power must try him – even this,
    So criminal and in such capital kind,
    Deserves th'extremest death.
BRUTUS   But since he hath
    Serv'd well for Rome –
CORIOLANUS   What do you prate of service?
BRUTUS   I talk of that, that know it.
CORIOLANUS   You?   85
MENENIUS
    Is this the promise that you made your mother?
COMINIUS   Know, I pray you –
CORIOLANUS   I'll know no further.
    Let them pronounce the steep Tarpeian death,
    Vagabond exile, flaying, pent to linger
    But with a grain a day, I would not buy   90
    Their mercy at the price of one fair word,
    Nor check my courage for what they can give,
    To have't with saying, 'Good morrow'.
SICINIUS   For that he has,
    As much as in him lies, from time to time
    Envied against the people, seeking means   95
    To pluck away their power, as now at last
    Given hostile strokes, and that not in the presence
    Of dreaded justice, but on the ministers
    That doth distribute it – in the name o'th' people,
    And in the power of us the tribunes, we,   100
    Ev'n from this instant, banish him our city,
    In peril of precipitation
    From off the rock Tarpeian, never more
    To enter our Rome gates. I'th' people's name,
    I say it shall be so.   105
ALL PLEBEIANS
    It shall be so, it shall be so! Let him away!
    He's banish'd, and it shall be so!

COMINIUS
Hear me, my masters, and my common friends!

SICINIUS   He's sentenc'd: no more hearing.

COMINIUS   Let me speak.
110   I have been consul, and can show for Rome
Her enemies' marks upon me. I do love
My country's good with a respect more tender,
More holy and profound, than mine own life,
My dear wife's estimate, her womb's increase
115   And treasure of my loins: then if I would
Speak that –

SICINIUS   We know your drift. Speak what?

BRUTUS   There's no more to be said but he is banish'd,
As enemy to the people and his country.
It shall be so!

ALL PLEBEIANS   It shall be so, it shall be so!

CORIOLANUS
120   You common cry of curs! whose breath I hate
As reek o'th' rotten fens, whose loves I prize
As the dead carcasses of unburied men
That do corrupt my air: I banish you!
And here remain with your uncertainty!
125   Let every feeble rumour shake your hearts!
Your enemies, with nodding of their plumes,
Fan you into despair! Have the power still
To banish your defenders, till at length
Your ignorance – which finds not till it feels,
130   Making but reservation of yourselves,
Still your own foes – deliver you as most
Abated captives to some nation
That won you without blows! Despising
For you the city, thus I turn my back.
135   There is a world elsewhere!

Exeunt Coriolanus, Cominius, Menenius with the other
senators and patricians.

AEDILE   The people's enemy is gone, is gone!

ALL PLEBEIANS
Our enemy is banish'd! He is gone! Hoo! hoo!
[*They all shout, and throw up their caps.*]

SICINIUS   Go see him out at gates, and follow him
As he hath follow'd you, with all despite.
Give him deserv'd vexation. Let a guard
140   Attend us through the city.

ALL PLEBEIANS
Come, come, let's see him out at gates! Come!
The gods preserve our noble tribunes! Come!

Exeunt.

4.1   *Enter* CORIOLANUS, VOLUMNIA, VIRGILIA,
MENENIUS, COMINIUS, *with the young nobility of Rome.*

CORIOLANUS
Come, leave your tears. A brief farewell! The beast
With many heads butts me away. Nay, mother,
Where is your ancient courage? You were us'd
To say, extremities was the trier of spirits;
5   That common chances common men could bear,

That when the sea was calm all boats alike
Show'd mastership in floating; fortune's blows,
When most struck home, being gentle wounded, craves
A noble cunning. You were us'd to load me
With precepts that would make invincible   10
The heart that conn'd them.

VIRGILIA   O heavens! O heavens!

CORIOLANUS   Nay, I prithee woman.

VOLUMNIA
Now the red pestilence strike all trades in Rome,
And occupations perish!

CORIOLANUS   What, what, what!
I shall be lov'd when I am lack'd. Nay, mother,   15
Resume that spirit when you were wont to say,
If you had been the wife of Hercules,
Six of his labours you'd have done, and sav'd
Your husband so much sweat. Cominius,
Droop not: adieu. Farewell, my wife, my mother: 20
I'll do well yet. Thou old and true Menenius,
Thy tears are salter than a younger man's,
And venomous to thine eyes. My sometime general,
I have seen thee stern, and thou hast oft beheld
Heart-hard'ning spectacles; tell these sad women,   25
'Tis fond to wail inevitable strokes,
As 'tis to laugh at 'em. My mother, you wot well
My hazards still have been your solace; and
Believ't not lightly, though I go alone,
Like to a lonely dragon that his fen   30
Makes fear'd and talk'd of more than seen, your son
Will or exceed the common, or be caught
With cautelous baits and practice.

VOLUMNIA   My first son,
Whither wilt thou go? Take good Cominius
With thee awhile; determine on some course   35
More than a wild exposture to each chance
That starts i'th' way before thee.

VIRGILIA   O the gods!

COMINIUS   I'll follow thee a month, devise with thee
Where thou shalt rest, that thou mayst hear of us
And we of thee. So if the time thrust forth   40
A cause for thy repeal, we shall not send
O'er the vast world to seek a single man
And lose advantage, which doth ever cool
I'th' absence of the needer.

CORIOLANUS   Fare ye well.
Thou hast years upon thee, and thou art too full   45
Of the wars' surfeits to go rove with one
That's yet unbruis'd: bring me but out at gate.
Come, my sweet wife, my dearest mother, and
My friends of noble touch: when I am forth,
Bid me farewell, and smile. I pray you, come: 50
While I remain above the ground you shall
Hear from me still, and never of me aught
But what is like me formerly.

MENENIUS   That's worthily

As any ear can hear. Come, let's not weep.
If I could shake off but one seven years
From these old arms and legs, by the good gods
I'd with thee every foot.

CORIOLANUS   Give me thy hand.
Come.   *Exeunt.*

4.2   *Enter the two tribunes,* SICINIUS *and* BRUTUS,
             with the Aedile.

SICINIUS
Bid them all home; he's gone, and we'll no further.
The nobility are vex'd, whom we see have sided
In his behalf.

BRUTUS   Now we have shown our power,
Let us seem humbler after it is done
Than when it was a-doing.

SICINIUS   Bid them home.
Say their great enemy is gone and they
Stand in their ancient strength.

BRUTUS   Dismiss them home.
                     Exit Aedile.
Here comes his mother.

     Enter VOLUMNIA, VIRGILIA *and* MENENIUS.

SICINIUS   Let's not meet her.
BRUTUS   Why?
SICINIUS   They say she's mad.
BRUTUS   They have ta'en note of us: keep on your way.
VOLUMNIA
Oh, y'are well met: the hoarded plague o'th' gods
Requite your love!

MENENIUS   Peace, peace, be not so loud.
VOLUMNIA
If that I could for weeping, you should hear –
Nay, and you shall hear some.
[*to Brutus*]   Will you be gone?
[*to Sicinius*] You shall stay too.

VIRGILIA   I would I had the power
To say so to my husband.

SICINIUS   Are you mankind?
VOLUMNIA   Ay, fool; is that a shame? Note but this fool.
Was not a man my father? Hadst thou foxship
To banish him that struck more blows for Rome
Than thou hast spoken words?

SICINIUS   Oh blessed heavens!
VOLUMNIA
Moe noble blows than ever thou wise words;
And for Rome's good. I'll tell thee what – yet go!
Nay, but thou shalt stay too: I would my son
Were in Arabia, and thy tribe before him,
His good sword in his hand.

SICINIUS   What then?
VIRGILIA   What then!
VOLUMNIA   He'd make an end of thy posterity,
Bastards and all.
Good man, the wounds that he does bear for Rome!

MENENIUS   Come, come, peace!
SICINIUS   I would he had continued to his country
As he began, and not unknit himself
The noble knot he made.

BRUTUS   I would he had.
VOLUMNIA
'I would he had!' 'Twas you incens'd the rabble:
Cats, that can judge as fitly of his worth
As I can of those mysteries which heaven
Will not have earth to know.

BRUTUS   Pray let's go.
VOLUMNIA   Now, pray sir, get you gone.
You have done a brave deed. Ere you go, hear this:
As far as doth the Capitol exceed
The meanest house in Rome, so far my son –
This lady's husband here, this, do you see? –
Whom you have banish'd, does exceed you all.

BRUTUS   Well, well, we'll leave you.
SICINIUS   Why stay we to be baited
With one that wants her wits?   *Exeunt tribunes.*
VOLUMNIA   Take my prayers with you.
I would the gods had nothing else to do
But to confirm my curses! Could I meet 'em
But once a day, it would unclog my heart
Of what lies heavy to't.

MENENIUS   You have told them home,
And, by my troth, you have cause. You'll sup with
me?

VOLUMNIA   Anger's my meat: I sup upon myself
And so shall starve with feeding. Come, let's go.
Leave this faint puling, and lament as I do,
In anger, Juno-like. Come, come, come!
          Exeunt Volumnia and Virgilia.
MENENIUS   Fie, fie, fie!   *Exit.*

4.3   *Enter a* Roman *and a* Volsce.

NICANOR   I know you well, sir, and you know me: your
name I think is Adrian.
ADRIAN   It is so, sir; truly I have forgot you.
NICANOR   I am a Roman; and my services are, as you are,
against 'em. Know you me yet?
ADRIAN   Nicanor? No?
NICANOR   The same, sir.
ADRIAN   You had more beard when I last saw you, but
your favour is well appeared by your tongue. What's
the news in Rome? I have a note from the Volscian
state to find you out there; you have well saved me a
day's journey.
NICANOR   There hath been in Rome strange
insurrections: the people against the senators,
patricians and nobles.
ADRIAN   Hath been! Is it ended then? Our state thinks
not so; they are in a most warlike preparation, and
hope to come upon them in the heat of their
division.
NICANOR   The main blaze of it is past, but a small thing

would make it flame again. For the nobles receive so to heart the banishment of that worthy Coriolanus, that they are in a ripe aptness to take all power from the people, and to pluck from them their tribunes for ever. This lies glowing, I can tell you, and is almost 25 mature for the violent breaking out.

ADRIAN   Coriolanus banished?

NICANOR   Banished, sir.

ADRIAN   You will be welcome with this intelligence, 30 Nicanor.

NICANOR   The day serves well for them now. I have heard it said, the fittest time to corrupt a man's wife is when she's fallen out with her husband. Your noble Tullus Aufidius will appear well in these wars, his 35 great opposer, Coriolanus, being now in no request of his country.

ADRIAN   He cannot choose. I am most fortunate, thus accidentally to encounter you. You have ended my business, and I will merrily accompany you home.

NICANOR   I shall between this and supper tell you most 40 strange things from Rome, all tending to the good of their adversaries. Have you an army ready, say you?

ADRIAN   A most royal one: the centurions and their charges distinctly billeted, already in th'entertainment, and to be on foot at an hour's 45 warning.

NICANOR   I am joyful to hear of their readiness, and am the man, I think, that shall set them in present action. So, sir, heartily well met, and most glad of your 50 company.

ADRIAN   You take my part from me, sir: I have the most cause to be glad of yours.

NICANOR   Well, let us go together.   *Exeunt.*

4.4   *Enter* CORIOLANUS *in mean apparel,*
                    disguised and muffled.

CORIOLANUS   A goodly city is this Antium. City,
'Tis I that made thy widows: many an heir
Of these fair edifices 'fore my wars
Have I heard groan, and drop. Then know me not;
5 Lest that thy wives with spits, and boys with stones,
In puny battle slay me.

              Enter a Citizen.

            Save you, sir.

CITIZEN   And you.

CORIOLANUS   Direct me, if it be your will,
Where great Aufidius lies. Is he in Antium?

CITIZEN   He is, and feasts the nobles of the state
At his house this night.

10 CORIOLANUS   Which is his house, beseech you?

CITIZEN   This, here before you.

CORIOLANUS   Thank you, sir. Farewell.
                                 Exit Citizen.
O world, thy slippery turns! Friends now fast sworn,
Whose double bosoms seems to wear one heart,

Whose hours, whose bed, whose meal and exercise
Are still together, who twin, as 'twere, in love   15
Unseparable, shall within this hour,
On a dissension of a doit, break out
To bitterest enmity: so fellest foes,
Whose passions and whose plots have broke their
     sleep
To take the one the other, by some chance,   20
Some trick not worth an egg, shall grow dear friends
And interjoin their issues. So with me:
My birthplace hate I, and my love's upon
This enemy town. I'll enter: if he slay me
He does fair justice; if he give me way,   25
I'll do his country service.   *Exit.*

4.5   *Music plays. Enter a* Servingman.

1 SERVINGMAN   Wine, wine, wine! What service is here!
I think our fellows are asleep.   *Exit.*

              Enter another Servingman.

2 SERVINGMAN   Where's Cotus? My master calls for
him. Cotus!   *Exit.*

              Enter CORIOLANUS.

CORIOLANUS
A goodly house: the feast smells well, but I   5
Appear not like a guest.

              Enter the First Servingman.

1 SERVINGMAN   What would you have, friend? Whence
are you? Here's no place for you: pray, go to the door!
                                          Exit.

CORIOLANUS
I have deserv'd no better entertainment
In being Coriolanus.   10

              Enter Second Servingman.

2 SERVINGMAN   Whence are you sir? Has the porter his
eyes in his head, that he gives entrance to such
companions? Pray, get you out.

CORIOLANUS   Away!

2 SERVINGMAN   Away? Get you away!   15

CORIOLANUS   Now th'art troublesome.

2 SERVINGMAN   Are you so brave! I'll have you talked
with anon.

              Enter Third Servingman. *The* First *meets him.*

3 SERVINGMAN   What fellow's this?

1 SERVINGMAN   A strange one as ever I looked on. I   20
cannot get him out o'th' house. Prithee call my master
to him. [*Retires.*]

3 SERVINGMAN   What have you to do here, fellow? Pray
you, avoid the house.

CORIOLANUS   Let me but stand; I will not hurt your   25
hearth.

3 SERVINGMAN   What are you?

CORIOLANUS   A gentleman.

3 SERVINGMAN   A marv'llous poor one.

CORIOLANUS   True, so I am.

3 SERVINGMAN   Pray you, poor gentleman, take up some
other station. Here's no place for you; pray you,
avoid. Come.

CORIOLANUS   Follow your function, go, and batten on
cold bits. [*Pushes him away from him.*]

3 SERVINGMAN   What, you will not? Prithee, tell my
master what a strange guest he has here.

2 SERVINGMAN   And I shall.   *Exit Second Servingman.*

3 SERVINGMAN   Where dwell'st thou?

CORIOLANUS   Under the canopy.

3 SERVINGMAN   Under the canopy?

CORIOLANUS   Ay.

3 SERVINGMAN   Where's that?

CORIOLANUS   I'th' city of kites and crows.

3 SERVINGMAN   I'th' city of kites and crows? What an ass
it is! Then thou dwell'st with daws too?

CORIOLANUS   No, I serve not thy master.

3 SERVINGMAN   How, sir! Do you meddle with my
master?

CORIOLANUS   Ay; 'tis an honester service than to meddle
with thy mistress. Thou prat'st, and prat'st. Serve
with thy trencher: hence! [*Beats him away.*]
        Exit Third Servingman.

Enter AUFIDIUS *with the* Second Servingman.

AUFIDIUS   Where is this fellow?

2 SERVINGMAN   Here sir; I'd have beaten him like a dog,
but for disturbing the lords within.   [*Retires.*]

AUFIDIUS
Whence com'st thou? What wouldst thou? thy name?
Why speak'st not? Speak, man: what's thy name?

CORIOLANUS [*unmuffling*]   If, Tullus,
Not yet thou know'st me, and, seeing me, dost not
Think me for the man I am, necessity
Commands me name myself.

AUFIDIUS   What is thy name?
                [*Servants retire.*]

CORIOLANUS   A name unmusical to the Volscians' ears,
And harsh in sound to thine.

AUFIDIUS   Say, what's thy name?
Thou hast a grim appearance, and thy face
Bears a command in't. Though thy tackle's torn,
Thou show'st a noble vessel. What's thy name?

CORIOLANUS
Prepare thy brow to frown: know'st thou me yet?

AUFIDIUS   I know thee not! Thy name?

CORIOLANUS
My name is Caius Martius, who hath done
To thee particularly, and to all the Volsces,
Great hurt and mischief: thereto witness may
My surname, Coriolanus. The painful service,
The extreme dangers, and the drops of blood
Shed for my thankless country, are requited
But with that surname: a good memory

And witness of the malice and displeasure   75
Which thou should'st bear me. Only that name
    remains.
The cruelty and envy of the people,
Permitted by our dastard nobles, who
Have all forsook me, hath devour'd the rest;
And suffer'd me by th' voice of slaves to be   80
Whoop'd out of Rome. Now this extremity
Hath brought me to thy hearth, not out of hope
(Mistake me not) to save my life: for if
I had fear'd death, of all the men i'th' world
I would have 'voided thee; but in mere spite   85
To be full quit of those my banishers,
Stand I before thee here. Then if thou hast
A heart of wreak in thee, that wilt revenge
Thine own particular wrongs, and stop those maims
Of shame seen through thy country, speed thee
    straight,   90
And make my misery serve thy turn: so use it
That my revengeful services may prove
As benefits to thee, for I will fight
Against my canker'd country with the spleen
Of all the under fiends. But if so be   95
Thou dar'st not this, and that to prove more fortunes
Th'art tir'd, then, in a word, I also am
Longer to live most weary, and present
My throat to thee and to thy ancient malice;
Which not to cut would show thee but a fool,   100
Since I have ever follow'd thee with hate,
Drawn tuns of blood out of thy country's breast,
And cannot live but to thy shame, unless
It be to do thee service.

AUFIDIUS   O Martius, Martius!
Each word thou hast spoke hath weeded from my
    heart   105
A root of ancient envy. If Jupiter
Should from yond cloud speak divine things
And say ' 'Tis true', I'd not believe them more
Than thee, all-noble Martius. Let me twine
Mine arms about that body, where against   110
My grained ash an hundred times hath broke,
And scarr'd the moon with splinters. Here I clip
The anvil of my sword, and do contest
As hotly and as nobly with thy love
As ever in ambitious strength I did   115
Contend against thy valour. Know thou first,
I lov'd the maid I married; never man
Sigh'd truer breath; but that I see thee here,
Thou noble thing, more dances my rapt heart
Than when I first my wedded mistress saw   120
Bestride my threshold. Why, thou Mars! I tell thee
We have a power on foot; and I had purpose
Once more to hew thy target from thy brawn,
Or lose mine arm for't. Thou hast beat me out
Twelve several times, and I have nightly since   125
Dreamt of encounters 'twixt thyself and me –
We have been down together in my sleep,

Unbuckling helms, fisting each other's throat –
130   And wak'd half dead with nothing. Worthy Martius,
Had we no other quarrel else to Rome, but that
Thou art thence banish'd, we would muster all
From twelve to seventy, and pouring war
Into the bowels of ungrateful Rome,
Like a bold flood o'erbear't. O come, go in,
135   And take our friendly senators by'th' hands
Who now are here, taking their leaves of me
Who am prepar'd against your territories,
Though not for Rome itself.

CORIOLANUS   You bless me, gods!

AUFIDIUS
Therefore, most absolute sir, if thou wilt have
140   The leading of thine own revenges, take
Th'one half of my commission, and set down
As best thou art experienc'd, since thou know'st
Thy country's strength and weakness, thine own
       ways:
Whether to knock against the gates of Rome,
145   Or rudely visit them in parts remote,
To fright them, ere destroy. But come in.
Let me commend thee first to those that shall
Say yea to thy desires. A thousand welcomes!
And more a friend than e'er an enemy –
Yet, Martius, that was much! Your hand: most
150   welcome!   *Exeunt Coriolanus and Aufidius.*
[*The two Servingmen come forward.*]

1 SERVINGMAN   Here's a strange alteration!

2 SERVINGMAN   By my hand, I had thought to have
strucken him with a cudgel; and yet my mind gave
me his clothes made a false report of him.

155   1 SERVINGMAN   What an arm he has! He turned me
about with his finger and his thumb, as one would set
up a top.

2 SERVINGMAN   Nay, I knew by his face that there was
something in him. He had, sir, a kind of face,
160   methought – I cannot tell how to term it.

1 SERVINGMAN   He had so, looking as it were – would I
were hanged, but I thought there was more in him
than I could think.

2 SERVINGMAN   So did I, I'll be sworn. He is simply the
165   rarest man i'th' world.

1 SERVINGMAN   I think he is: but a greater soldier than
he, you wot on.

2 SERVINGMAN   Who? my master?

1 SERVINGMAN   Nay, it's no matter for that.

170   2 SERVINGMAN   Worth six on him.

1 SERVINGMAN   Nay, not so neither: but I take him to be
the greater soldier.

2 SERVINGMAN   Faith, look you, one cannot tell how to
say that: for the defence of a town our general is
175   excellent.

1 SERVINGMAN   Ay, and for an assault too.

Enter the Third Servingman.

3 SERVINGMAN   O slaves, I can tell you news, news you
rascals.

1, 2 SERVINGMEN   What, what, what? Let's partake.

180   3 SERVINGMAN   I would not be a Roman of all nations; I
had as lief be a condemned man.

1, 2 SERVINGMEN   Wherefore? Wherefore?

3 SERVINGMAN   Why, here's he that was wont to thwack
our general, Caius Martius.

185   1 SERVINGMAN   Why do you say 'thwack our general'?

3 SERVINGMAN   I do not say 'thwack our general'; but he
was always good enough for him.

2 SERVINGMAN   Come, we are fellows and friends: he was
ever too hard for him; I have heard him say so
190   himself.

1 SERVINGMAN   He was too hard for him directly, to say
the truth on't: before Corioles he scotched him and
notched him like a carbonado.

2 SERVINGMAN   And he had been cannibally given, he
195   might have broiled and eaten him too.

1 SERVINGMAN   But more of thy news.

3 SERVINGMAN   Why, he is so made on here within as if
he were son and heir to Mars; set at upper end o'th'
table; no question asked him by any of the senators but
200   they stand bald before him. Our general himself
makes a mistress of him, sanctifies himself with's
hand, and turns up the white o'th' eye to his
discourse. But the bottom of the news is, our general
is cut i'th' middle, and but one half of what he was
205   yesterday; for the other has half, by the entreaty and
grant of the whole table. He'll go, he says, and sowl the
porter of Rome gates by th'ears. He will mow all down
before him, and leave his passage polled.

2 SERVINGMAN   And he's as like to do't as any man I can
210   imagine.

3 SERVINGMAN   Do't? He will do't: for look you, sir, he
has as many friends as enemies; which friends, sir, as it
were, durst not, look you sir, show themselves, as we
term it, his friends, whilst he's in directitude.

215   1 SERVINGMAN   Directitude! What's that?

3 SERVINGMAN   But when they shall see, sir, his crest up
again, and the man in blood, they will out of their
burrows, like conies after rain, and revel all with
him.

220   1 SERVINGMAN   But when goes this forward?

3 SERVINGMAN   Tomorrow, today, presently; you shall
have the drum struck up this afternoon. 'Tis as it were
a parcel of their feast, and to be executed ere they wipe
their lips.

225   2 SERVINGMAN   Why, then we shall have a stirring world
again. This peace is nothing but to rust iron, increase
tailors, and breed ballad-makers.

1 SERVINGMAN   Let me have war, say I. It exceeds peace
as far as day does night: it's sprightly walking, audible,
230   and full of vent. Peace is a very apoplexy, lethargy;
mulled, deaf, sleepy, insensible; a getter of more
bastard children than war's a destroyer of
men.

2 SERVINGMAN 'Tis so, and as wars, in some sort, may
    be said to be a ravisher, so it cannot be denied but
    peace is a great maker of cuckolds.

1 SERVINGMAN Ay, and it makes men hate one another.

3 SERVINGMAN Reason: because they then less need one
    another. The wars for my money. I hope to see
    Romans as cheap as Volscians. They are rising, they
    are rising.

1, 2 SERVINGMEN In, in, in, in!   *Exeunt.*

4.6 *Enter the two tribunes,* SICINIUS *and* BRUTUS.

SICINIUS
  We hear not of him, neither need we fear him;
  His remedies are tame i'th' present peace
  And quietness of the people, which before
  Were in wild hurry. Here do we make his friends
  Blush that the world goes well; who rather had,
  Though they themselves did suffer by't, behold
  Dissentious numbers pest'ring streets, than see
  Our tradesmen singing in their shops and going
  About their functions friendly.

BRUTUS We stood to't in good time.

Enter MENENIUS.

                    Is this Menenius?

SICINIUS 'Tis he, 'tis he. Oh, he is grown most kind
  Of late. Hail, sir!

MENENIUS   Hail to you both!

SICINIUS Your Coriolanus is not much miss'd
  But with his friends: the commonwealth doth stand,
  And so would do, were he more angry at it.

MENENIUS
  All's well, and might have been much better if
  He could have temporiz'd.

SICINIUS   Where is he, hear you?

MENENIUS
  Nay, I hear nothing. His mother and his wife
  Hear nothing from him.

Enter three or four Citizens.

ALL The gods preserve you both!

SICINIUS   Good den, our neighbours.

BRUTUS Good den to you all, good den to you all.

1 CITIZEN
  Ourselves, our wives, and children, on our knees
  Are bound to pray for you both.

SICINIUS   Live, and thrive!

BRUTUS
  Farewell, kind neighbours. We wish'd Coriolanus
  Had lov'd you as we did.

ALL   Now the gods keep you!

BOTH TRIBUNES Farewell, farewell. *Exeunt Citizens.*

SICINIUS This is a happier and more comely time
  Than when those fellows ran about the streets
  Crying confusion.

BRUTUS   Caius Martius was

  A worthy officer i'th' war, but insolent,
  O'ercome with pride, ambitious past all thinking,
  Self-loving.

SICINIUS   And affecting one sole throne,
  Without assistance.

MENENIUS   I think not so.

SICINIUS We should by this, to all our lamentation,
  If he had gone forth consul, found it so.

BRUTUS
  The gods have well prevented it, and Rome
  Sits safe and still without him.

Enter an Aedile.

AEDILE   Worthy tribunes,
  There is a slave whom we have put in prison,
  Reports the Volsces with two several powers
  Are enter'd in the Roman territories,
  And with the deepest malice of the war,
  Destroy what lies before 'em.

MENENIUS   'Tis Aufidius,
  Who, hearing of our Martius' banishment,
  Thrusts forth his horns again into the world,
  Which were inshell'd when Martius stood for Rome,
  And durst not once peep out.

SICINIUS   Come, what talk you
  Of Martius?

BRUTUS Go see this rumourer whipp'd. It cannot be
  The Volsces dare break with us.

MENENIUS   Cannot be?
  We have record that very well it can,
  And three examples of the like hath been
  Within my age. But reason with the fellow
  Before you punish him, where he heard this,
  Lest you shall chance to whip your information,
  And beat the messenger who bids beware
  Of what is to be dreaded.

SICINIUS   Tell not me.
  I know this cannot be.

BRUTUS   Not possible.

Enter a Messenger.

MESSENGER The nobles in great earnestness are going
  All to the senate-house. Some news is coming
  That turns their countenances.

SICINIUS   'Tis this slave –
  Go whip him 'fore the people's eyes – his raising,
  Nothing but his report.

MESSENGER   Yes, worthy sir,
  The slave's report is seconded; and more,
  More fearful, is deliver'd.

SICINIUS   What more fearful?

MESSENGER It is spoke freely out of many mouths,
  How probable I do not know, that Martius,
  Join'd with Aufidius, leads a power 'gainst Rome,
  And vows revenge as spacious as between
  The young'st and oldest thing.

SICINIUS   This is most likely!

BRUTUS Rais'd only that the weaker sort may wish 70
  Good Martius home again.

SICINIUS   The very trick on't.

MENENIUS   This is unlikely:
  He and Aufidius can no more atone
  Than violent'st contrariety.

Enter a Second Messenger.

2 MESSENGER   You are sent for to the senate. 75
  A fearful army, led by Caius Martius,
  Associated with Aufidius, rages
  Upon our territories, and have already
  O'erborne their way, consum'd with fire, and took
  What lay before them. 80

Enter COMINIUS.

COMINIUS
  O, you have made good work.

MENENIUS   What news? What news?

COMINIUS
  You have holp to ravish your own daughters, and
  To melt the city leads upon your pates,
  To see your wives dishonour'd to your noses –

MENENIUS   What's the news? What's the news? 85

COMINIUS   Your temples burned in their cement, and
  Your franchises, whereon you stood, confin'd
  Into an auger's bore.

MENENIUS   Pray now, your news? –
  You have made fair work, I fear me. – Pray, your
    news?
  If Martius should be join'd wi'th' Volscians –

COMINIUS   If! 90
  He is their god. He leads them like a thing
  Made by some other deity than nature,
  That shapes man better; and they follow him
  Against us brats, with no less confidence
  Than boys pursuing summer butterflies, 95
  Or butchers killing flies.

MENENIUS   You have made good work,
  You, and your apron-men; you that stood so much
  Upon the voice of occupation and
  The breath of garlic-eaters!

COMINIUS   He'll shake your Rome about your ears.

MENENIUS   As Hercules 100
  Did shake down mellow fruit. You have made fair
    work!

BRUTUS   But is this true, sir?

COMINIUS   Ay, and you'll look pale
  Before you find it other. All the regions
  Do smilingly revolt, and who resists
  Are mock'd for valiant ignorance, 105
  And perish constant fools. Who is't can blame him?
  Your enemies and his find something in him.

MENENIUS   We are all undone unless
  The noble man have mercy.

COMINIUS   Who shall ask it?
  The tribunes cannot do't for shame; the people 110

Deserve such pity of him as the wolf
Does of the shepherds. For his best friends, if they
Should say, 'Be good to Rome', they charg'd him
  even
As those should do that had deserv'd his hate,
And therein show'd like enemies.

MENENIUS   'Tis true! 115
If he were putting to my house the brand
That should consume it, I have not the face
To say, 'Beseech you, cease'. You have made fair
  hands,
You and your crafts! You have crafted fair!

COMINIUS   You have brought
A trembling upon Rome, such as was never 120
S'incapable of help.

BOTH TRIBUNES   Say not we brought it.

MENENIUS
How? Was't we? We lov'd him, but, like beasts
And cowardly nobles, gave way unto your clusters,
Who did hoot him out o'th' city.

COMINIUS   But I fear
They'll roar him in again. Tullus Aufidius, 125
The second name of men, obeys his points
As if he were his officer. Desperation
Is all the policy, strength and defence,
That Rome can make against them.

Enter a troop of Citizens.

MENENIUS   Here come the clusters.
And is Aufidius with him? You are they 130
That made the air unwholesome when you cast
Your stinking greasy caps in hooting at
Coriolanus' exile. Now he's coming,
And not a hair upon a soldier's head
Which will not prove a whip. As many coxcombs 135
As you threw caps up will he tumble down,
And pay you for your voices. 'Tis no matter,
If he could burn us all into one coal,
We have deserv'd it.

CITIZENS   Faith, we hear fearful news.

1 CITIZEN   For mine own part, 140
When I said banish him, I said 'twas pity.

2 CITIZEN   And so did I.

3 CITIZEN And so did I; and, to say the truth, so did very
  many of us. That we did we did for the best, and
  though we willingly consented to his banishment, yet 145
  it was against our will.

COMINIUS   Y'are goodly things, you voices.

MENENIUS   You have made good work,
You and your cry. Shall's to the Capitol?

COMINIUS   O, ay, what else?

Exeunt Cominius and Menenius.

SICINIUS   Go masters, get you home; be not dismay'd; 150
  These are a side that would be glad to have
  This true which they so seem to fear. Go home,
  And show no sign of fear.

1 CITIZEN   The gods be good to us! Come, masters, let's

home. I ever said we were i'th' wrong when we
banished him.

2 CITIZEN   So did we all. But come, let's home.

Exeunt Citizens.

BRUTUS   I do not like this news.

SICINIUS   Nor I.

BRUTUS   Let's to the Capitol. Would half my wealth
    Would buy this for a lie!

SICINIUS   Pray let's go.   *Exeunt.*

4.7   *Enter* AUFIDIUS *with his* Lieutenant.

AUFIDIUS   Do they still fly to th'Roman?

LIEUTENANT
    I do not know what witchcraft's in him, but
    Your soldiers use him as the grace 'fore meat,
    Their talk at table and their thanks at end;
    And you are darken'd in this action, sir,
    Even by your own.

AUFIDIUS   I cannot help it now,
    Unless, by using means, I lame the foot
    Of our design. He bears himself more proudlier
    Even to my person than I thought he would
    When first I did embrace him. Yet his nature
    In that's no changeling, and I must excuse
    What cannot be amended.

LIEUTENANT   Yet I wish, sir,
    I mean for your particular, you had not
    Join'd in commission with him; but either
    Have borne the action of yourself, or else
    To him had left it solely.

AUFIDIUS   I understand thee well, and be thou sure
    When he shall come to his account, he knows not
    What I can urge against him. Although it seems,
    And so he thinks, and is no less apparent
    To th' vulgar eye, that he bears all things fairly
    And shows good husbandry for the Volscian state,
    Fights dragon-like, and does achieve as soon
    As draw his sword: yet he hath left undone
    That which shall break his neck or hazard mine
    Whene'er we come to our account.

LIEUTENANT
    Sir, I beseech you, think you he'll carry Rome?

AUFIDIUS   All places yields to him ere he sits down,
    And the nobility of Rome are his.
    The senators and patricians love him too;
    The tribunes are no soldiers, and their people
    Will be as rash in the repeal as hasty
    To expel him thence. I think he'll be to Rome
    As is the osprey to the fish, who takes it
    By sovereignty of nature. First, he was
    A noble servant to them, but he could not
    Carry his honours even. Whether 'twas pride,
    Which out of daily fortune ever taints
    The happy man; whether defect of judgement,
    To fail in the disposing of those chances
    Which he was lord of; or whether nature,
    Not to be other than one thing, not moving
    From th' casque to th' cushion, but commanding
      peace
    Even with the same austerity and garb
    As he controll'd the war; but one of these –
    As he hath spices of them all, not all,
    For I dare so far free him – made him fear'd,
    So hated, and so banish'd: but he has a merit
    To choke it in the utt'rance. So our virtues
    Lie in th'interpretation of the time,
    And power, unto itself most commendable,
    Hath not a tomb so evident as a chair
    T'extol what it hath done.
    One fire drives out one fire; one nail, one nail;
    Rights by rights falter, strengths by strengths do fail.
    Come, let's away. When, Caius, Rome is thine,
    Thou art poor'st of all: then shortly art thou mine.

Exeunt.

5.1   *Enter* MENENIUS, COMINIUS; SICINIUS, BRUTUS
(the two tribunes), with others.

MENENIUS   No, I'll not go: you hear what he hath said
    Which was sometime his general, who lov'd him
    In a most dear particular. He call'd me father:
    But what o' that? Go you that banish'd him;
    A mile before his tent fall down, and knee
    The way into his mercy. Nay, if he coy'd
    To hear Cominius speak, I'll keep at home.

COMINIUS   He would not seem to know me.

MENENIUS   Do you hear?

COMINIUS   Yet one time he did call me by my name.
    I urg'd our old acquaintance, and the drops
    That we have bled together. 'Coriolanus'
    He would not answer to; forbad all names:
    He was a kind of nothing, titleless,
    Till he had forg'd himself a name o'th' fire
    Of burning Rome.

MENENIUS   Why, so: you have made good work!
    A pair of tribunes that have wrack'd for Rome
    To make coals cheap: a noble memory!

COMINIUS   I minded him how royal 'twas to pardon
    When it was less expected. He replied
    It was a bare petition of a state
    To one whom they had punish'd.

MENENIUS   Very well.
    Could he say less?

COMINIUS   I offer'd to awaken his regard
    For's private friends. His answer to me was
    He could not stay to pick them in a pile
    Of noisome musty chaff. He said 'twas folly,
    For one poor grain or two, to leave unburnt
    And still to nose th'offence.

MENENIUS   For one poor grain or two?
    I am one of those; his mother, wife, his child,
    And this brave fellow too: we are the grains,
    You are the musty chaff, and you are smelt

Above the moon. We must be burnt for you.

SICINIUS   Nay, pray be patient. If you refuse your aid
    In this so never-needed help, yet do not
35 Upbraid's with our distress. But sure, if you
    Would be your country's pleader, your good tongue
    More than the instant army we can make,
    Might stop our countryman.

MENENIUS   No, I'll not meddle.

SICINIUS   Pray you go to him.

MENENIUS   What should I do?

40 BRUTUS   Only make trial what your love can do
    For Rome, towards Martius.

MENENIUS   Well, and say that Martius
    Return me, as Cominius is return'd,
    Unheard; what then?
    But as a discontented friend, grief-shot
    With his unkindness? Say't be so?

45 SICINIUS   Yet your good will
    Must have that thanks from Rome after the measure
    As you intended well.

MENENIUS   I'll undertake't.
    I think he'll hear me. Yet to bite his lip
    And hum at good Cominius, much unhearts me.
50 He was not taken well; he had not din'd:
    The veins unfill'd, our blood is cold, and then
    We pout upon the morning, are unapt
    To give or to forgive; but when we have stuff'd
    These pipes and these conveyances of our blood
55 With wine and feeding, we have suppler souls
    Than in our priest-like fasts. Therefore I'll watch
        him
    Till he be dieted to my request,
    And then I'll set upon him.

BRUTUS   You know the very road into his kindness,
    And cannot lose your way.

60 MENENIUS   Good faith, I'll prove him,
    Speed how it will. I shall ere long have knowledge
    Of my success.   *Exit.*

COMINIUS   He'll never hear him.

SICINIUS   Not?

COMINIUS   I tell you, he does sit in gold, his eye
    Red as 'twould burn Rome; and his injury
65 The gaoler to his pity. I kneel'd before him:
    'Twas very faintly he said 'Rise', dismiss'd me
    Thus, with his speechless hand. What he would do
    He sent in writing after me: what he would not,
    Bound with an oath to yield to his conditions:
70 So that all hope is vain,
    Unless his noble mother and his wife,
    Who, as I hear, mean to solicit him
    For mercy to his country. Therefore let's hence,
    And with our fair entreaties haste them on.   *Exeunt.*

5.2   *Enter* MENENIUS *to the* Watch *or guard.*

1 WATCH   Stay! Whence are you?

2 WATCH   Stand, and go back!

MENENIUS
    You guard like men; 'tis well. But, by your leave,
    I am an officer of state, and come
    To speak with Coriolanus.

1 WATCH   From whence?

MENENIUS   From Rome.

1 WATCH
    You may not pass; you must return: our general   5
    Will no more hear from thence.

2 WATCH
    You'll see your Rome embrac'd with fire before
    You'll speak with Coriolanus.

MENENIUS   Good my friends,
    If you have heard your general talk of Rome
    And of his friends there, it is lots to blanks   10
    My name hath touch'd your ears: it is Menenius.

1 WATCH
    Be it so, go back: the virtue of your name
    Is not here passable.

MENENIUS   I tell thee, fellow,
    Thy general is my lover. I have been
    The book of his good acts whence men have read   15
    His fame unparallel'd, haply amplified;
    For I have ever verified my friends,
    Of whom he's chief, with all the size that verity
    Would without lapsing suffer. Nay, sometimes,
    Like to a bowl upon a subtle ground,   20
    I have tumbled past the throw, and in his praise
    Have almost stamp'd the leasing. Therefore, fellow,
    I must have leave to pass.

1 WATCH   Faith, sir, if you had told as many lies in his
    behalf as you have uttered words in your own, you   25
    should not pass here; no, though it were as virtuous to
    lie as to live chastely. Therefore go back.

MENENIUS   Prithee, fellow, remember my name is
    Menenius, always factionary on the party of your
    general.   30

2 WATCH   Howsoever you have been his liar, as you say
    you have, I am one that, telling true under him, must
    say you cannot pass. Therefore go back.

MENENIUS   Has he dined, canst thou tell? For I would
    not speak with him till after dinner.   35

1 WATCH   You are a Roman, are you?

MENENIUS   I am as thy general is.

1 WATCH   Then you should hate Rome, as he does.
    Can you, when you have pushed out your gates the
    very defender of them, and, in a violent popular   40
    ignorance, given your enemy your shield, think to
    front his revenges with the easy groans of old women,
    the virginal palms of your daughters, or with the
    palsied intercession of such a decayed dotant as you
    seem to be? Can you think to blow out the intended   45
    fire your city is ready to flame in, with such weak
    breath as this? No, you are deceived; therefore back
    to Rome, and prepare for your execution. You are
    condemned; our general has sworn you out of reprieve
    and pardon.   50

MENENIUS   Sirrah, if thy captain knew I were here, he
would use me with estimation.

1 WATCH   Come, my captain knows you not.

MENENIUS   I mean thy general.

1 WATCH   My general cares not for you. Back, I say, go:
lest I let forth your half-pint of blood. Back, that's the
utmost of your having. Back!

MENENIUS   Nay, but fellow, fellow –

Enter CORIOLANUS *with* AUFIDIUS.

CORIOLANUS   What's the matter?

MENENIUS   Now, you companion, I'll say an errand for
you; you shall know now that I am in estimation; you
shall perceive that a Jack guardant cannot office me
from my son Coriolanus. Guess but by my
entertainment with him, if thou stand'st not i'th' state
of hanging, or of some death more long in
spectatorship and crueller in suffering. Behold now
presently, and swound for what's to come upon thee.
[*to Coriolanus*] The glorious gods sit in hourly synod
about thy particular prosperity, and love thee no worse
than thy old father Menenius does! O my son, my son,
thou art preparing fire for us: look thee, here's water
to quench it. I was hardly moved to come to thee, but
being assured none but myself could move thee, I have
been blown out of your gates with sighs, and conjure
thee to pardon Rome and thy petitionary countrymen.
The good gods assuage thy wrath, and turn the dregs
of it upon this varlet here – this, who, like a block, hath
denied my access to thee.

CORIOLANUS   Away!

MENENIUS   How! Away?

CORIOLANUS
Wife, mother, child, I know not. My affairs
Are servanted to others. Though I owe
My revenge properly, my remission lies
In Volscian breasts. That we have been familiar,
Ingrate forgetfulness shall poison rather
Than pity note how much. Therefore be gone.
Mine ears against your suits are stronger than
Your gates against my force. Yet, for I lov'd thee,
Take this along; I writ it for thy sake,
And would have sent it. [*Gives him a letter.*]
                              Another word, Menenius,
I will not hear thee speak. This man, Aufidius,
Was my belov'd in Rome: yet thou behold'st.

AUFIDIUS   You keep a constant temper.

Exeunt Coriolanus and Aufidius.
[*The Watch and Menenius remain.*]

1 WATCH   Now, sir, is your name Menenius?

2 WATCH   'Tis a spell, you see, of much power. You know
the way home again.

1 WATCH   Do you hear how we are shent for keeping
your greatness back?

2 WATCH   What cause do you think I have to swound?

MENENIUS   I neither care for th' world nor your general.

For such things as you, I can scarce think there's any,
y'are so slight. He that hath a will to die by himself,
fears it not from another: let your general do his worst.
For you, be that you are, long; and your misery
increase with your age! I say to you, as I was said to,
Away!   *Exit.*   105

1 WATCH   A noble fellow, I warrant him.

2 WATCH   The worthy fellow is our general: he's the
rock, the oak not to be wind-shaken.   *Exeunt.*

5.3   *Enter* CORIOLANUS *and* AUFIDIUS *with others.*

CORIOLANUS
We will before the walls of Rome tomorrow
Set down our host. My partner in this action,
You must report to th' Volscian lords how plainly
I have borne this business.

AUFIDIUS   Only their ends
You have respected, stopp'd your ears against   5
The general suit of Rome: never admitted
A private whisper, no, not with such friends
That thought them sure of you.

CORIOLANUS   This last old man,
Whom with a crack'd heart I have sent to Rome,
Lov'd me above the measure of a father,   10
Nay, godded me indeed. Their latest refuge
Was to send him; for whose old love I have
(Though I show'd sourly to him) once more offer'd
The first conditions, which they did refuse
And cannot now accept, to grace him only   15
That thought he could do more. A very little
I have yielded to. Fresh embassies and suits,
Nor from the state nor private friends, hereafter
Will I lend ear to. [*Shout within.*]
                              Ha! what shout is this?
Shall I be tempted to infringe my vow   20
In the same time 'tis made? I will not.

Enter VIRGILIA, VOLUMNIA, VALERIA,
YOUNG MARTIUS, *with attendants.*

My wife comes foremost; then the honour'd mould
Wherein this trunk was fram'd, and in her hand
The grandchild to her blood. But out, affection!
All bond and privilege of nature break!   25
Let it be virtuous to be obstinate.
What is that curtsy worth? or those doves' eyes,
Which can make gods forsworn? I melt, and am not
Of stronger earth than others. My mother bows,
As if Olympus to a molehill should   30
In supplication nod; and my young boy
Hath an aspect of intercession which
Great nature cries, 'Deny not'. Let the Volsces
Plough Rome and harrow Italy; I'll never
Be such a gosling to obey instinct, but stand   35
As if a man were author of himself
And knew no other kin.

VIRGILIA   My lord and husband!

CORIOLANUS

These eyes are not the same I wore in Rome.

VIRGILIA   The sorrow that delivers us thus chang'd
Makes you think so.

40   CORIOLANUS   Like a dull actor now
I have forgot my part and I am out,
Even to a full disgrace. Best of my flesh,
Forgive my tyranny; but do not say,
For that 'Forgive our Romans'. O, a kiss
45   Long as my exile, sweet as my revenge!
Now by the jealous queen of heaven, that kiss
I carried from thee, dear; and my true lip
Hath virgin'd it e'er since. You gods! I prate,
And the most noble mother of the world
50   Leave unsaluted. Sink, my knee, i'th' earth: [*Kneels.*]
Of thy deep duty more impression show
Than that of common sons.

VOLUMNIA   Oh, stand up bless'd!
Whilst, with no softer cushion than the flint,
I kneel before thee, and unproperly
55   Show duty as mistaken all this while
Between the child and parent. [*Kneels.*]

CORIOLANUS   What's this?
Your knees to me? to your corrected son?
Then let the pebbles on the hungry beach
Fillip the stars. Then let the mutinous winds
60   Strike the proud cedars 'gainst the fiery sun,
Murd'ring impossibility, to make
What cannot be, slight work!

VOLUMNIA   Thou art my warrior:
I holp to frame thee. Do you know this lady?

CORIOLANUS   The noble sister of Publicola,
65   The moon of Rome, chaste as the icicle
That's curdied by the frost from purest snow
And hangs on Dian's temple! Dear Valeria!

VOLUMNIA   This is a poor epitome of yours,
Which by th'interpretation of full time
70   May show like all yourself.

CORIOLANUS   The god of soldiers,
With the consent of supreme Jove, inform
Thy thoughts with nobleness, that thou mayst prove
To shame unvulnerable, and stick i'th' wars
Like a great sea-mark standing every flaw
And saving those that eye thee!

75   VOLUMNIA   Your knee, sirrah.

CORIOLANUS   That's my brave boy!

VOLUMNIA   Even he, your wife, this lady and myself
Are suitors to you.

CORIOLANUS   I beseech you, peace!
Or, if you'd ask, remember this before:
80   The thing I have forsworn to grant may never
Be held by you denials. Do not bid me
Dismiss my soldiers, or capitulate
Again with Rome's mechanics. Tell me not
Wherein I seem unnatural. Desire not
85   T'allay my rages and revenges with

Your colder reasons.

VOLUMNIA   Oh, no more, no more!
You have said you will not grant us anything:
For we have nothing else to ask but that
Which you deny already. Yet we will ask,
That if you fail in our request, the blame   90
May hang upon your hardness: therefore hear us.

CORIOLANUS

Aufidius, and you Volsces, mark; for we'll
Hear nought from Rome in private. Your request?

VOLUMNIA

Should we be silent and not speak, our raiment
And state of bodies would bewray what life   95
We have led since thy exile. Think with thyself
How more unfortunate than all living women
Are we come hither; since that thy sight, which
    should
Make our eyes flow with joy, hearts dance with
    comforts,
Constrains them weep, and shake with fear and
    sorrow,   100
Making the mother, wife and child to see
The son, the husband and the father, tearing
His country's bowels out. And to poor we
Thine enmity's most capital. Thou barr'st us
Our prayers to the gods, which is a comfort   105
That all but we enjoy; for how can we,
Alas! how can we for our country pray,
Whereto we are bound, together with thy victory,
Whereto we are bound? Alack, or we must lose
The country, our dear nurse, or else thy person,   110
Our comfort in the country. We must find
An evident calamity, though we had
Our wish, which side should win: for either thou
Must as a foreign recreant be led
With manacles through our streets, or else   115
Triumphantly tread on thy country's ruin,
And bear the palm for having bravely shed
Thy wife and children's blood. For myself, son,
I purpose not to wait on fortune till
These wars determine. If I cannot persuade thee   120
Rather to show a noble grace to both parts,
Than seek the end of one, thou shalt no sooner
March to assault thy country than to tread –
Trust to't, thou shalt not – on thy mother's womb
That brought thee to this world.

VIRGILIA   Ay, and mine,   125
That brought you forth this boy to keep your name
Living to time.

YOUNG MARTIUS   A shall not tread on me.
I'll run away till I am bigger, but then I'll fight.

CORIOLANUS   Not of a woman's tenderness to be,   130
Requires nor child nor woman's face to see.
I have sat too long. [*rising*]

VOLUMNIA   Nay, go not from us thus.
If it were so that our request did tend
To save the Romans, thereby to destroy   135

The Volsces whom you serve, you might condemn us
As poisonous of your honour. No, our suit
Is that you reconcile them: while the Volsces
May say, 'This mercy we have show'd', the Romans,
40 'This we receiv'd'; and each in either side
Give the all-hail to thee, and cry, 'Be bless'd
For making up this peace!' Thou know'st, great son,
The end of war's uncertain, but this certain,
That if thou conquer Rome, the benefit
45 Which thou shalt thereby reap is such a name
Whose repetition will be dogg'd with curses,
Whose chronicle thus writ: 'The man was noble,
But with his last attempt he wip'd it out,
Destroy'd his country, and his name remains
50 To th'insuing age abhorr'd.' Speak to me, son:
Thou has affected the fine strains of honour,
To imitate the graces of the gods,
To tear with thunder the wide cheeks o'th' air,
And yet to charge thy sulphur with a bolt
55 That should but rive an oak. Why dost not speak?
Think'st thou it honourable for a noble man
Still to remember wrongs? Daughter, speak you:
He cares not for your weeping. Speak thou, boy:
Perhaps thy childishness will move him more
60 Than can our reasons. There's no man in the world
More bound to's mother, yet here he lets me prate
Like one i'th' stocks. Thou hast never in thy life
Show'd thy dear mother any courtesy,
When she, poor hen, fond of no second brood,
65 Has cluck'd thee to the wars, and safely home,
Loaden with honour. Say my request's unjust,
And spurn me back; but if it be not so,
Thou art not honest, and the gods will plague thee
That thou restrain'st from me the duty which
70 To a mother's part belongs. He turns away.
Down ladies: let us shame him with our knees.
To his surname Coriolanus longs more pride
Than pity to our prayers. Down! an end:
This is the last. So, we will home to Rome
75 And die among our neighbours. Nay, behold's,
This boy that cannot tell what he would have,
But kneels, and holds up hands for fellowship,
Does reason our petition with more strength
Than thou hast to deny't. Come, let us go:
80 This fellow had a Volscian to his mother;
His wife is in Corioles, and his child
Like him by chance. Yet give us our dispatch:
I am husht until our city be afire,
And then I'll speak a little.

CORIOLANUS [*Holds her by the hand silent.*]
85   O mother, mother!
What have you done? Behold, the heavens do ope,
The gods look down, and this unnatural scene
They laugh at. O my mother, mother! O!
You have won a happy victory to Rome;
90 But for your son, believe it, O, believe it,
Most dangerously you have with him prevail'd,

If not most mortal to him. But let it come.
Aufidius, though I cannot make true wars,
I'll frame convenient peace. Now, good Aufidius,
Were you in my stead, would you have heard   195
A mother less? or granted less, Aufidius?
AUFIDIUS   I was mov'd withal.
CORIOLANUS   I dare be sworn you were:
And sir, it is no little thing to make
Mine eyes to sweat compassion. But, good sir,   200
What peace you'll make, advise me. For my part,
I'll not to Rome, I'll back with you; and pray you,
Stand to me in this cause. O mother! wife!
AUFIDIUS [*aside*]
I am glad thou hast set thy mercy and thy honour
At difference in thee. Out of that I'll work   205
Myself a former fortune.
CORIOLANUS [*to Volumnia, Virgilia, etc.*] Ay, by and by;
But we will drink together; and you shall bear
A better witness back than words, which we,
On like conditions, will have counterseal'd.   210
Come, enter with us. Ladies, you deserve
To have a temple built you. All the swords
In Italy and her confederate arms
Could not have made this peace.   *Exeunt.*

5.4   *Enter* MENENIUS *and* SICINIUS.

MENENIUS   See you yond coign o'th' Capitol, yond
    cornerstone?
SICINIUS   Why, what of that?
MENENIUS   If it be possible for you to displace it with
    your little finger, there is some hope the ladies of   5
    Rome, especially his mother, may prevail with him.
    But I say there is no hope in't; our throats are
    sentenced and stay upon execution.
SICINIUS   Is't possible that so short a time can alter the
    condition of a man?   10
MENENIUS   There is differency between a grub and a
    butterfly; yet your butterfly was a grub. This Martius
    is grown from man to dragon: he has wings: he's more
    than a creeping thing.
SICINIUS   He loved his mother dearly.   15
MENENIUS   So did he me; and he no more remembers
    his mother now than an eight-year-old horse. The
    tartness of his face sours ripe grapes. When he walks,
    he moves like an engine and the ground shrinks before
    his treading. He is able to pierce a corslet with his   20
    eye, talks like a knell, and his hum is a battery. He sits
    in his state as a thing made for Alexander. What he
    bids be done is finished with his bidding. He wants
    nothing of a god but eternity, and a heaven to throne
    in.   25
SICINIUS   Yes, mercy, if you report him truly.
MENENIUS   I paint him in the character. Mark what
    mercy his mother shall bring from him. There is no
    more mercy in him than there is milk in a male tiger;
    that shall our poor city find; and all this is long of you.   30

SICINIUS   The gods be good unto us.

MENENIUS   No, in such a case the gods will not be good
unto us. When we banished him, we respected not
them; and, he returning to break our necks, they
35   respect not us.

Enter a Messenger.

MESSENGER
Sir, if you'd save your life, fly to your house.
The plebeians have got your fellow-tribune,
And hale him up and down, all swearing, if
The Roman ladies bring not comfort home,
They'll give him death by inches.

Enter another Messenger.

40   SICINIUS   What's the news?
2 MESSENGER
Good news, good news! The ladies have prevail'd,
The Volscians are dislodg'd, and Martius gone.
                                      Exeunt attendants.
A merrier day did never yet greet Rome,
No, not th'expulsion of the Tarquins.
SICINIUS   Friend,
45   Art thou certain this is true? Is't most certain?
2 MESSENGER   As certain as I know the sun is fire.
Where have you lurk'd that you make doubt of it?
Ne'er through an arch so hurried the blown tide
As the recomforted through th'gates. Why, hark you!
                [Trumpets, hautboys, drums beat, all together.]
50   The trumpets, sackbuts, psalteries and fifes,
Tabors and cymbals and the shouting Romans
Make the sun dance. Hark you! *[A shout within.]*
MENENIUS   This is good news.
I will go meet the ladies. This Volumnia
Is worth of consuls, senators, patricians,
55   A city full; of tribunes such as you,
A sea and land full. You have pray'd well today.
This morning for ten thousand of your throats
I'd not have given a doit. Hark, how they joy!
                [Sound still with the shouts.]
SICINIUS
First, the gods bless you for your tidings; next
Accept my thankfulness.
60   2 MESSENGER   Sir, we have all
Great cause to give great thanks.
SICINIUS   They are near the city?
2 MESSENGER   Almost at point to enter.
SICINIUS   We'll meet them,
And help the joy.   *Exeunt.*

5.5   *Enter two* Senators, *with the ladies* VOLUMNIA,
VIRGILIA *and* VALERIA, *passing over the stage,
with other lords.*

1 SENATOR
Behold our patroness, the life of Rome!
Call all your tribes together, praise the gods,

And make triumphant fires. Strew flowers before
them;
Unshout the noise that banish'd Martius;
Repeal him with the welcome of his mother: 5
Cry, 'Welcome, ladies, welcome!'
ALL   Welcome, ladies,
Welcome!
                A flourish with drums and trumpets. Exeunt.

5.6   *Enter* TULLUS AUFIDIUS, *with attendants.*

AUFIDIUS   Go tell the lords o'th' city I am here.
Deliver them this paper. Having read it,
Bid them repair to th'market-place, where I,
Even in theirs and in the commons' ears,
Will vouch the truth of it. Him I accuse   5
The city ports by this hath enter'd, and
Intends t'appear before the people, hoping
To purge himself with words. Dispatch.
                                      Exeunt attendants.

Enter three or four Conspirators *of Aufidius's faction.*

Most welcome.
1 CONSPIRATOR   How is it with our general?
AUFIDIUS   Even so   10
As with a man by his own alms empoison'd,
And with his charity slain.
2 CONSPIRATOR   Most noble sir,
If you do hold the same intent wherein
You wish'd us parties, we'll deliver you
Of your great danger.
AUFIDIUS   Sir, I cannot tell.   15
We must proceed as we do find the people.
3 CONSPIRATOR
The people will remain uncertain whilst
'Twixt you there's difference; but the fall of either
Makes the survivor heir of all.
AUFIDIUS   I know it,
And my pretext to strike at him admits   20
A good construction. I rais'd him, and I pawn'd
Mine honour for his truth; who being so heighten'd,
He water'd his new plants with dews of flattery,
Seducing so my friends; and to this end
He bow'd his nature, never known before   25
But to be rough, unswayable and free.
3 CONSPIRATOR   Sir, his stoutness
When he did stand for consul, which he lost
By lack of stooping –
AUFIDIUS   That I would have spoke of.
Being banish'd for't, he came unto my hearth,   30
Presented to my knife his throat; I took him,
Made him joint-servant with me, gave him way
In all his own desires; nay, let him choose
Out of my files, his projects to accomplish,
My best and freshest men; serv'd his designments   35
In mine own person; holp to reap the fame
Which he did end all his; and took some pride

To do myself this wrong: till at the last
I seem'd his follower, not partner, and
He wag'd me with his countenance, as if
I had been mercenary.
1 CONSPIRATOR   So he did, my lord.
The army marvell'd at it, and in the last,
When he had carried Rome, and that we look'd
For no less spoil than glory –
AUFIDIUS   There was it:
For which my sinews shall be stretch'd upon him;
At a few drops of women's rheum, which are
As cheap as lies, he sold the blood and labour
Of our great action. Therefore shall he die,
And I'll renew me in his fall. But hark!
          [*Drums and trumpets sound,*
          with great shouts of the people.]
1 CONSPIRATOR
Your native town you enter'd like a post,
And had no welcomes home; but he returns
Splitting the air with noise.
2 CONSPIRATOR   And patient fools,
Whose children he hath slain, their base throats tear
With giving him glory.
3 CONSPIRATOR   Therefore, at your vantage,
Ere he express himself or move the people
With what he would say, let him feel your sword,
Which we will second. When he lies along,
After your way his tale pronounc'd shall bury
His reasons with his body.
AUFIDIUS   Say no more.
Here come the lords.

Enter the Lords *of the city.*

ALL LORDS   You are most welcome home.
AUFIDIUS   I have not deserv'd it.
But, worthy lords, have you with heed perus'd
What I have written to you?
ALL LORDS   We have.
1 LORD   And grieve to hear't.
What faults he made before the last, I think
Might have found easy fines; but there to end
Where he was to begin, and give away
The benefit of our levies, answering us
With our own charge, making a treaty where
There was a yielding: this admits no excuse.
AUFIDIUS
He approaches: you shall hear him.

Enter CORIOLANUS *marching with drum and colours,*
the Commoners *being with him.*

CORIOLANUS   Hail lords, I am return'd your soldier,
No more infected with my country's love
Than when I parted hence, but still subsisting
Under your great command. You are to know
That prosperously I have attempted, and
With bloody passage led your wars even to
The gates of Rome. Our spoils we have brought
home
Doth more than counterpoise a full third part
The charges of the action. We have made peace
With no less honour to the Antiates   80
Than shame to th' Romans; and we here deliver,
Subscrib'd by th' consuls and patricians,
Together with the seal o'th' senate, what
We have compounded on.
AUFIDIUS   Read it not, noble lords;
But tell the traitor in the highest degree   85
He hath abus'd your powers.
CORIOLANUS   Traitor? How now!
AUFIDIUS   Ay, traitor, Martius!
CORIOLANUS   Martius!
AUFIDIUS   Ay, Martius, Caius Martius! Dost thou think
I'll grace thee with that robbery, thy stol'n name
Coriolanus, in Corioles?   90
You lords and heads o'th' state, perfidiously
He has betray'd your business, and given up,
For certain drops of salt, your city Rome,
I say 'your city', to his wife and mother;
Breaking his oath and resolution, like   95
A twist of rotten silk, never admitting
Counsel o'th' war: but at his nurse's tears
He whin'd and roar'd away your victory,
That pages blush'd at him, and men of heart
Look'd wond'ring each at others.
CORIOLANUS   Hear'st thou, Mars?   100
AUFIDIUS   Name not the god, thou boy of tears!
CORIOLANUS   Ha!
AUFIDIUS   No more.
CORIOLANUS
Measureless liar, thou hast made my heart
Too great for what contains it. 'Boy'! O slave!
Pardon me, lords, 'tis the first time that ever   105
I was forc'd to scold. Your judgements, my grave
   lords,
Must give this cur the lie; and his own notion,
Who wears my stripes impress'd upon him, that
Must bear my beating to his grave, shall join
To thrust the lie unto him.
1 LORD   Peace, both, and hear me speak.   110
CORIOLANUS   Cut me to pieces, Volsces, men and lads,
Stain all your edges on me. Boy! False hound!
If you have writ your annals true, 'tis there,
That like an eagle in a dove-cote, I
Flutter'd your Volscians in Corioles.   115
Alone I did it. Boy!
AUFIDIUS   Why, noble lords,
Will you be put in mind of his blind fortune,
Which was your shame, by this unholy braggart,
'Fore your own eyes and ears?
ALL CONSPIRATORS   Let him die for't.
ALL PEOPLE   Tear him to pieces! Do it presently! He   120
killed my son! My daughter! He killed my cousin
Marcus! He killed my father!
2 LORD   Peace, ho! no outrage, peace!

The man is noble, and his fame folds in
This orb o'th' earth. His last offences to us
Shall have judicious hearing. Stand, Aufidius,
And trouble not the peace.
CORIOLANUS   O that I had him,
With six Aufidiuses, or more, his tribe,
To use my lawful sword.
AUFIDIUS   Insolent villian!
ALL CONSPIRATORS   Kill, kill, kill, kill, kill him!
      [*The Conspirators draw, and kill Martius, who falls;
      Aufidius stands on him.*]
LORDS   Hold, hold, hold, hold!
AUFIDIUS   My noble masters, hear me speak.
1 LORD   O Tullus!
2 LORD
      Thou hast done a deed whereat valour will weep.
3 LORD   Tread not upon him. Masters all, be quiet!
      Put up your swords.
AUFIDIUS
      My lords, when you shall know (as in this rage,
      Provok'd by him, you cannot) the great danger
      Which this man's life did owe you, you'll rejoice

That he is thus cut off. Please it your honours
To call me to your senate, I'll deliver
Myself your loyal servant or endure
Your heaviest censure.
1 LORD   Bear from hence his body,
And mourn you for him. Let him be regarded
As the most noble corse that ever herald
Did follow to his urn.
2 LORD   His own impatience
Takes from Aufidius a great part of blame.
Let's make the best of it.
AUFIDIUS   My rage is gone,
And I am struck with sorrow. Take him up.
Help, three o'th' chiefest soldiers. I'll be one.
Beat thou the drum that it speak mournfully;
Trail your steel pikes. Though in this city he
Hath widow'd and unchilded many a one,
Which to this hour bewail the injury,
Yet he shall have a noble memory.
Assist.   *Exeunt, bearing the body of Martius.*
                              A dead march sounded.

Cymbeline

Cymbeline is one of the eighteen plays never printed in Shakespeare's lifetime and first published in the Folio of 1623. On the basis of style and structure, scholars date it about 1610. In 1611, Simon Forman recorded in a commonplace book an account of the plot of 'Cymbalin', among several plays he saw at the Globe between April and September, when he died.

Cymbeline is unexpectedly placed in the Folio as the last of the tragedies. Though today the play's affinities with the other late romances, *Pericles*, *The Winter's Tale* and *The Tempest*, are unmistakable, the Folio editors either struggled to determine the play's genre or were aware that 'tragedy with a happy ending' was recognized by some critics. It is certainly a play in which two central characters die, ghosts appear, Jupiter throws thunderbolts and descends riding upon an eagle, and it lacks overtly comic characters. Dr Johnson's impatience with its anachronistic mixing of the Rome of the first century BC with sixteenth-century Europe and his notorious reference to the plot's 'unresisting imbecility' reflect his own, and his age's, lack of sympathy with romantic fictions.

The very incongruities that Johnson scorned are arguably the essence of the play's vision. The bewildering series of reversals and revelations that permits the play's three plots to come together in a marvellous conclusion is the apt denouement of what Granville Barker, with fuller sympathy, called the play's 'sophisticated artlessness'. In part this is, no doubt, a reflection of a new literary fashion for Italianate tragicomedy represented by such plays as Beaumont and Fletcher's popular *Philaster* (1609); but Shakespeare's use of this experimental form and dramaturgy imbues it with a power that is uniquely his own. Each of the play's three plot lines – that of Imogen's love and Posthumus' jealousy, that of Cymbeline's long-lost sons and that of Britain's challenge to the power of Rome – while very different in tone, even perhaps in genre, enacts the same archetypal pattern of innocence-fall-redemption; and each proves the truth of Caius Lucius' claim: 'Some falls are means the happier to arise.'

Each originates in Cymbeline's own misvaluing of a relationship, so that Posthumus and Belarius are exiled from the court, Imogen is threatened with Cloten's courtship and Britain is isolated from the wider community of the Roman world. In each plot characters move from error to truth, from scepticism to faith, from hatred to love; and each plot, from the individual regeneration of Posthumus, to the royal family reunion and the international reconciliation of Britain and Rome, describes an ever more inclusive circle of harmony.

In the final scene, all comes together. Cymbeline, the least informed figure on stage, faces one discovery after another (one critic counts twenty-five), but all the others also acquire knowledge that redeems the tragic potentialities of the play, and everything of value is restored. Confusion and loss are replaced by clarity and gain; families and nations are reunited and at peace. The comic order, as the soothsayer says of his vision, 'at this instant / Is full accomplished'. And if here we hear an echo of Christ's *'consummatum est'*, perhaps it is because the achievement of harmony in the play serves in some measure as a secular analogue to the 'rarer action' of salvation history. It can hardly be coincidental that the best known fact about the early British king Cymbeline was that he ruled at the moment of the Incarnation.

On 1 January 1634, the play was performed at court for Charles I, and it was 'well liked by the king'. From the Restoration onwards, *Cymbeline* has remained a play better liked in the theatre than in the study. Distressed by inadequate productions of *Cymbeline* he had seen, George Bernard Shaw notoriously altered the last act. His *Cymbeline Refinished* (1937) eliminates Jupiter descending on his holy eagle, cuts out the heroic actions of Guiderius and Arviragus, and in general recreates the characters and relationships in the manner of Ibsen. His aim was partly critical of what, in his habitual vein of Bardoclastic provocation, he called the 'tedious . . . sentimentality' of the fifth act, but his more serious challenge was to theatre companies to have the courage to stage the full text of it, including Posthumus' vision. He offered his rewriting as an alternative only to the truncated texts, not the full one.

The Arden text is based on the 1623 First Folio.

CYMBELINE	*King of Britain*
CLOTEN	*son to the Queen by a former husband*
POSTHUMUS Leonatus	*a gentleman, husband to Imogen*
BELARIUS	*a banished lord, disguised under the name of Morgan*
GUIDERIUS	*son to Cymbeline, disguised under the name of Polydore, supposed son to Morgan*
ARVIRAGUS	*son to Cymbeline, disguised under the name of Cadwal, supposed son to Morgan*
PHILARIO	*friend to Posthumus, Italian*
IACHIMO	*friend to Philario, Italian*
Caius LUCIUS	*general of the Roman forces*
PISANIO	*servant to Posthumus*
CORNELIUS	*a physician*
Philarmonus, *a* SOOTHSAYER	
Roman CAPTAIN	
Two British CAPTAINS	
FRENCHMAN	*friend to Philario*
TWO LORDS	*of Cymbeline's Court*
TWO GENTLEMEN	*of the same*
TWO GAOLERS	
QUEEN	*wife to Cymbeline*
IMOGEN	*daughter to Cymbeline by a former Queen*
Helen, *a* LADY	*attending on Imogen*

SICILIUS Leonatus
MOTHER
FIRST BROTHER } *apparitions*
SECOND BROTHER
JUPITER

Lords, Ladies, Roman Senators, Tribunes, a Dutchman, a Spaniard, Musicians, Officers, Captains, Soldiers, Messengers and other Attendants.

Cymbeline

1.1   *Enter two* Gentlemen.

1 GENTLEMAN

> You do not meet a man but frowns: our bloods
> No more obey the heavens than our courtiers
> Still seem as does the king's.

2 GENTLEMAN   But what's the matter?

1 GENTLEMAN

> His daughter, and the heir of's kingdom (whom
> He purpos'd to his wife's sole son – a widow
> That late he married) hath referr'd herself
> Unto a poor but worthy gentleman. She's wedded,
> Her husband banish'd; she imprison'd, all
> Is outward sorrow, though I think the king
> Be touch'd at very heart.

2 GENTLEMAN   None but the king?

1 GENTLEMAN

> He that hath lost her too: so is the queen,
> That most desir'd the match. But not a courtier,
> Although they wear their faces to the bent
> Of the king's looks, hath a heart that is not
> Glad at the thing they scowl at.

2 GENTLEMAN   And why so?

1 GENTLEMAN

> He that hath miss'd the princess is a thing
> Too bad for bad report: and he that hath her
> (I mean, that married her, alack good man,
> And therefore banish'd) is a creature such
> As, to seek through the regions of the earth
> For one his like; there would be something failing
> In him that should compare. I do not think
> So fair an outward, and such stuff within
> Endows a man, but he.

2 GENTLEMAN   You speak him far.

1 GENTLEMAN

> I do extend him, sir, within himself,
> Crush him together, rather than unfold
> His measure duly.

2 GENTLEMAN   What's his name and birth?

1 GENTLEMAN

> I cannot delve him to the root: his father
> Was call'd Sicilius, who did join his honour
> Against the Romans with Cassibelan,
> But had his titles by Tenantius, whom
> He served with glory and admired success:
> So gain'd the sur-addition Leonatus:
> And had (besides this gentleman in question)
> Two other sons, who in the wars o'th' time
> Died with their swords in hand. For which their
>   father,
> Then old, and fond of issue, took such sorrow
> That he quit being; and his gentle lady,
> Big of this gentleman (our theme) deceas'd
> As he was born. The king he takes the babe
> To his protection, calls him Posthumus Leonatus,
> Breeds him, and makes him of his bed-chamber,
> Puts to him all the learnings that his time

> Could make him the receiver of, which he took,
> As we do air, fast as 'twas minister'd,   45
> And in's spring became a harvest: liv'd in court
> (Which rare it is to do) most prais'd, most lov'd;
> A sample to the youngest, to th' more mature
> A glass that feated them, and to the graver
> A child that guided dotards. To his mistress,   50
> (For whom he now is banish'd) her own price
> Proclaims how she esteem'd him; and his virtue
> By her election may be truly read
> What kind of man he is.

2 GENTLEMAN   I honour him,

> Even out of your report. But pray you tell me,   55
> Is she sole child to th' king?

1 GENTLEMAN   His only child.

> He had two sons (if this be worth your hearing,
> Mark it) the eldest of them at three years old,
> I' th' swathing-clothes the other, from their nursery
> Were stol'n; and to this hour no guess in knowledge   60
> Which way they went.

2 GENTLEMAN   How long is this ago?

1 GENTLEMAN   Some twenty years.

2 GENTLEMAN

> That a king's children should be so convey'd,
> So slackly guarded, and the search so slow
> That could not trace them!

1 GENTLEMAN   Howsoe'er 'tis strange,   65

> Or that the negligence may well be laugh'd at,
> Yet is it true, sir.

2 GENTLEMAN   I do well believe you.

1 GENTLEMAN

> We must forbear. Here comes the gentleman,
> The queen, and princess.   *Exeunt.*

1.2   *Enter the* QUEEN, POSTHUMUS *and* IMOGEN.

QUEEN   No, be assur'd you shall not find me, daughter,
> After the slander of most stepmothers,
> Evil-ey'd unto you. You're my prisoner, but
> Your gaoler shall deliver you the keys
> That lock up your restraint. For you Posthumus,   5
> So soon as I can win th'offended king,
> I will be known your advocate: marry, yet
> The fire of rage is in him, and 'twere good
> You lean'd unto his sentence, with what patience
> Your wisdom may inform you.

POSTHUMUS   Please your highness,   10
> I will from hence to-day.

QUEEN   You know the peril.
> I'll fetch a turn about the garden, pitying
> The pangs of barr'd affections, though the king
> Hath charg'd you should not speak together.   *Exit.*

IMOGEN   O
> Dissembling courtesy! How fine this tyrant   15
> Can tickle where she wounds! My dearest husband,
> I something fear my father's wrath, but nothing
> (Always reserv'd my holy duty) what

His rage can do on me. You must be gone,
And I shall here abide the hourly shot
Of angry eyes: not comforted to live,
But that there is this jewel in the world
That I may see again.

POSTHUMUS   My queen, my mistress:
O lady, weep no more, lest I give cause
To be suspected of more tenderness
Than doth become a man. I will remain
The loyal'st husband that did e'er plight troth.
My residence in Rome, at one Philario's,
Who to my father was a friend, to me
Known but by letter; thither write, my queen,
And with mine eyes I'll drink the words you send,
Though ink be made of gall.

Re-enter QUEEN.

QUEEN   Be brief, I pray you:
If the king come, I shall incur I know not
How much of his displeasure:
[*aside*]   yet I'll move him
To walk this way: I never do him wrong
But he does buy my injuries, to be friends:
Pays dear for my offences.   *Exit.*

POSTHUMUS   Should we be taking leave
As long a term as yet we have to live,
The loathness to depart would grow. Adieu!

IMOGEN   Nay, stay a little:
Were you but riding forth to air yourself,
Such parting were too petty. Look here, love;
This diamond was my mother's; take it, heart;
But keep it till you woo another wife,
When Imogen is dead.

POSTHUMUS   How, how? Another?
You gentle gods, give me but this I have,
And sear up my embracements from a next
With bonds of death! Remain, remain thou here,
[*putting on the ring*]
While sense can keep it on: And sweetest, fairest,
As I my poor self did exchange for you
To your so infinite loss; so in our trifles
I still win of you. For my sake wear this,
It is a manacle of love, I'll place it
Upon this fairest prisoner.
[*putting a bracelet on her arm*]

IMOGEN   O the gods!
When shall we see again?

Enter CYMBELINE *and lords.*

POSTHUMUS   Alack, the king!

CYMBELINE
Thou basest thing, avoid hence, from my sight!
If after this command thou fraught the court
With thy unworthiness, thou diest. Away!
Thou'rt poison to my blood.

POSTHUMUS   The gods protect you,
And bless the good remainders of the court!

I am gone.   *Exit.*

IMOGEN   There cannot be a pinch in death
More sharp than this is.

CYMBELINE   O disloyal thing,
That shouldst repair my youth, thou heap'st
A year's age on me!

IMOGEN   I beseech you sir,
Harm not yourself with your vexation,
I am senseless of your wrath; a touch more rare
Subdues all pangs, all fears.

CYMBELINE   Past grace? obedience?

IMOGEN   Past hope, and in despair, that way past grace.

CYMBELINE
That mightst have had the sole son of my queen!

IMOGEN   O blessed, that I might not! I chose an eagle,
And did avoid a puttock.

CYMBELINE
Thou took'st a beggar, wouldst have made my throne
A seat for baseness.

IMOGEN   No, I rather added
A lustre to it.

CYMBELINE   O thou vile one!

IMOGEN   Sir,
It is your fault that I have lov'd Posthumus:
You bred him as my playfellow, and he is
A man worth any woman: overbuys me
Almost the sum he pays.

CYMBELINE   What? Art thou mad?

IMOGEN   Almost, sir: heaven restore me! Would I were
A neat-herd's daughter, and my Leonatus
Our neighbour-shepherd's son!

CYMBELINE   Thou foolish thing! –

Re-enter QUEEN.

They were again together: you have done
Not after our command. Away with her,
And pen her up.

QUEEN   Beseech your patience. Peace
Dear lady daughter, peace! – Sweet sovereign,
Leave us to ourselves, and make yourself some comfort
Out of your best advice.

CYMBELINE   Nay, let her languish
A drop of blood a day, and being aged
Die of this folly.   *Exeunt Cymbeline and lords.*

QUEEN   Fie! you must give way.

Enter PISANIO.

Here is your servant. How now, sir? What news?

PISANIO   My Lord your son drew on my master.

QUEEN   Ha?
No harm I trust is done?

PISANIO   There might have been,
But that my master rather play'd than fought,
And had no help of anger: they were parted
By gentlemen at hand.

QUEEN   I am very glad on't.

IMOGEN
    Your son's my father's friend, he takes his part
    To draw upon an exile. O brave sir!
    I would they were in Afric both together,
    Myself by with a needle, that I might prick
    The goer-back. Why came you from your master?
PISANIO   On his command: he would not suffer me
    To bring him to the haven: left these notes
    Of what commands I should be subject to,
    When't pleased you to employ me.
QUEEN   This hath been
    Your faithful servant: I dare lay mine honour
    He will remain so.
PISANIO   I humbly thank your highness
QUEEN   Pray, walk awhile.
IMOGEN
    About some half-hour hence, pray you, speak with
      me;
    You shall (at least) go see my lord aboard.
    For this time leave me.   *Exeunt.*

1.3   *Enter* CLOTEN *and two* Lords.

1 LORD   Sir, I would advise you to shift a shirt; the
violence of action hath made you reek as a sacrifice:
where air comes out, air comes in: there's none abroad
so wholesome as that you vent.
CLOTEN   If my shirt were bloody, then to shift it. Have I
hurt him?
2 LORD [*aside*]   No, faith: not so much as his patience.
1 LORD   Hurt him? his body's a passable carcass, if he be
not hurt. It is a throughfare for steel, if it be not hurt.
2 LORD [*aside*]   His steel was in debt, it went o'th'
backside the town.
CLOTEN   The villain would not stand me.
2 LORD [*aside*]   No, but he fled forward still, toward your
face.
1 LORD   Stand you? You have land enough of your own:
but he added to your having, gave you some ground.
2 LORD [*aside*]   As many inches as you have oceans.
Puppies!
CLOTEN   I would they had not come between us.
2 LORD [*aside*]   So would I, till you had measur'd how
long a fool you were upon the ground.
CLOTEN   And that she should love this fellow, and refuse
me!
2 LORD [*aside*]   If it be a sin to make a true election, she
is damn'd.
1 LORD   Sir, as I told you always, her beauty and her
brain go not together. She's a good sign, but I have
seen small reflection of her wit.
2 LORD [*aside*]   She shines not upon fools, lest the
reflection should hurt her.
CLOTEN   Come, I'll to my chamber. Would there had
been some hurt done!
2 LORD [*aside*]   I wish not so, unless it had been the fall
of an ass, which is no great hurt.

CLOTEN   You'll go with us?   35
1 LORD   I'll attend your lordship.
CLOTEN   Nay come, let's go together
2 LORD   Well my lord.   *Exeunt.*

1.4   *Enter* IMOGEN *and* PISANIO.

IMOGEN
    I would thou grew'st unto the shores o'th' haven,
    And question'dst every sail: if he should write,
    And I not have it, 'twere a paper lost
    As offer'd mercy is. What was the last
    That he spake to thee?
PISANIO   It was, his queen, his queen!   5
IMOGEN   Then wav'd his handkerchief?
PISANIO   And kiss'd it, madam.
IMOGEN   Senseless linen, happier therein than I!
    And that was all?
PISANIO   No, madam: for so long
    As he could make me with this eye, or ear,
    Distinguish him from others, he did keep   10
    The deck, with glove, or hat, or handkerchief,
    Still waving, as the fits and stirs of's mind
    Could best express how slow his soul sail'd on,
    How swift his ship.
IMOGEN   Thou shouldst have made him
    As little as a crow, or less, ere left   15
    To after-eye him.
PISANIO   Madam, so I did.
IMOGEN
    I would have broke mine eye-strings, crack'd them,
      but
    To look upon him, till the diminution
    Of space had pointed him sharp as my needle:
    Nay, followed him, till he had melted from   20
    The smallness of a gnat, to air: and then
    Have turn'd mine eye, and wept. But, good Pisanio,
    When shall we hear from him?
PISANIO   Be assur'd, madam,
    With his next vantage.
IMOGEN   I did not take my leave of him, but had   25
    Most pretty things to say: ere I could tell him
    How I would think on him at certain hours,
    Such thoughts, and such: or I could make him swear
    The shes of Italy should not betray
    Mine interest, and his honour; or have charg'd him,   30
    At the sixth hour of morn, at noon, at midnight,
    T'encounter me with orisons, for then
    I am in heaven for him; or ere I could
    Give him that parting kiss, which I had set
    Betwixt two charming words, comes in my father,   35
    And like the tyrannous breathing of the north,
    Shakes all our buds from growing.

                Enter a Lady.

LADY   The queen, madam,
    Desires your highness' company.

IMOGEN

Those things I bid you do, get them dispatch'd. –
I will attend the queen.

40 **PISANIO**   Madam, I shall.   *Exeunt.*

1.5   *Enter* PHILARIO, IACHIMO, *a* Frenchman, *a*
Dutchman and a Spaniard.

IACHIMO   Believe it sir, I have seen him in Britain; he
was then of a crescent note, expected to prove so
worthy as since he hath been allowed the name of. But
I could then have look'd on him without the help of
5   admiration, though the catalogue of his endowments
had been tabled by his side and I to peruse him by
items.

PHILARIO   You speak of him when he was less furnish'd
than now he is with that which makes him both
10 without and within.

FRENCHMAN   I have seen him in France: we had very
many there could behold the sun with as firm eyes as
he.

IACHIMO   This matter of marrying his king's daughter,
15 wherein he must be weighed rather by her value than
his own, words him (I doubt not) a great deal from the
matter.

FRENCHMAN   And then his banishment.

IACHIMO   Ay, and the approbation of those that weep
20 this lamentable divorce under her colours are
wonderfully to extend him; be it but to fortify her
judgement, which else an easy battery might lay flat,
for taking a beggar without less quality. But how
comes it he is to sojourn with you? how creeps
25 acquaintance?

PHILARIO   His father and I were soldiers together, to
whom I have been often bound for no less than my life.
– Here comes the Briton. Let him be so entertained
amongst you as suits, with gentlemen of your
30 knowing, to a stranger of his quality.

Enter POSTHUMUS.

I beseech you all be better known to this gentleman,
whom I commend to you as a noble friend of mine.
How worthy he is I will leave to appear hereafter,
rather than story him in his own hearing.

35 FRENCHMAN   Sir, we have known together in Orleans.

POSTHUMUS   Since when I have been debtor to you for
courtesies which I will be ever to pay, and yet pay still.

FRENCHMAN   Sir, you o'er-rate my poor kindness: I was
glad I did atone my countryman and you: it had been
40 pity you should have been put together, with so mortal
a purpose as then each bore, upon importance of so
slight and trivial a nature.

POSTHUMUS   By your pardon, sir, I was then a young
traveller, rather shunn'd to go even with what I heard
45 than in my every action to be guided by others'
experiences: but upon my mended judgement (if I
offend not to say it is mended) my quarrel was not
altogether slight.

FRENCHMAN   Faith yes, to be put to the arbitrement of
swords, and by such two, that would by all likelihood   50
have confounded one the other, or have fallen both.

IACHIMO   Can we with manners ask what was the
difference?

FRENCHMAN   Safely, I think: 'twas a contention in
public, which may (without contradiction) suffer the   55
report. It was much like an argument that fell out last
night, where each of us fell in praise of our country
mistresses; this gentleman at that time vouching (and
upon warrant of bloody affirmation) his to be more
fair, virtuous, wise, chaste, constant, qualified and less 60
attemptable than any the rarest of our ladies in France.

IACHIMO   That lady is not now living; or this
gentleman's opinion, by this, worn out.

POSTHUMUS   She holds her virtue still, and I my mind.

IACHIMO   You must not so far prefer her 'fore ours of   65
Italy.

POSTHUMUS   Being so far provok'd as I was in France, I
would abate her nothing, though I profess myself her
adorer, not her friend.

IACHIMO   As fair, and as good – a kind of hand-in-hand   70
comparison – had been something too fair, and too
good for any lady in Britany. If she went before others
I have seen, as that diamond of yours outlustres many
I have beheld, I could not believe she excelled many:
but I have not seen the most precious diamond that is,   75
nor you the lady.

POSTHUMUS   I prais'd her as I rated her: so do I my
stone.

IACHIMO   What do you esteem it at?

POSTHUMUS   More than the world enjoys.   80

IACHIMO   Either your unparagon'd mistress is dead, or
she's outpriz'd by a trifle.

POSTHUMUS   You are mistaken: the one may be sold or
given, or if there were wealth enough for the purchase,
or merit for the gift. The other is not a thing for sale,   85
and only the gift of the gods.

IACHIMO   Which the gods have given you?

POSTHUMUS   Which by their graces I will keep.

IACHIMO   You may wear her in title yours: but you know
strange fowl light upon neighbouring ponds. Your   90
ring may be stolen too: so your brace of unprizable
estimations, the one is but frail and the other casual; a
cunning thief, or a (that way) accomplished courtier,
would hazard the winning both of first and last.

POSTHUMUS   Your Italy contains none so accomplish'd   95
a courtier to convince the honour of my mistress, if
in the holding or loss of that, you term her frail: I do
nothing doubt you have store of thieves; notwithstanding, I fear not my ring.

PHILARIO   Let us leave here, gentlemen.   100

POSTHUMUS   Sir, with all my heart. This worthy signior,
I thank him, makes no stranger of me; we are familiar
at first.

IACHIMO   With five times so much conversation, I
should get ground of your fair mistress; make her go   105

back, even to the yielding, had I admittance, and
opportunity to friend.

POSTHUMUS   No, no.

IACHIMO   I dare thereupon pawn the moiety of my
estate, to your ring, which in my opinion o'ervalues it
something: but I make my wager rather against your
confidence than her reputation. And to bar your
offence herein too, I durst attempt it against any lady
in the world.

POSTHUMUS   You are a great deal abus'd in too bold a
persuasion, and I doubt not you sustain what you're
worthy of by your attempt.

IACHIMO   What's that?

POSTHUMUS   A repulse: though your attempt (as you
call it) deserve more; a punishment too.

PHILARIO   Gentlemen, enough of this, it came in too
suddenly, let it die as it was born, and I pray you be
better acquainted.

IACHIMO   Would I had put my estate and my
neighbour's on th'approbation of what I have spoke!

POSTHUMUS   What lady would you choose to assail?

IACHIMO   Yours, whom in constancy you think stands so
safe. I will lay you ten thousand ducats to your ring,
that, commend me to the court where your lady is,
with no more advantage than the opportunity of a
second conference, and I will bring from thence that
honour of hers, which you imagine so reserv'd.

POSTHUMUS   I will wage against your gold, gold to it:
my ring I hold dear as my finger, 'tis part of it.

IACHIMO   You are a friend, and therein the wiser. If you
buy ladies' flesh at a million a dram, you cannot
preserve it from tainting; but I see you have some
religion in you, that you fear.

POSTHUMUS   This is but a custom in your tongue: you
bear a graver purpose I hope.

IACHIMO   I am the master of my speeches, and would
undergo what's spoken, I swear.

POSTHUMUS   Will you? I shall but lend my diamond till
your return: let there be covenants drawn between's.
My mistress exceeds in goodness the hugeness of your
unworthy thinking. I dare you to this match: here's
my ring.

PHILARIO   I will have it no lay.

IACHIMO   By the gods, it is one. If I bring you no
sufficient testimony that I have enjoy'd the dearest
bodily part of your mistress, my ten thousand ducats
are yours, so is your diamond too: if I come off, and
leave her in such honour as you have trust in, she your
jewel, this your jewel, and my gold are yours: provided
I have your commendation for my more free
entertainment.

POSTHUMUS   I embrace these conditions, let us have
articles betwixt us. Only, thus far you shall answer: if
you make your voyage upon her, and give me directly
to understand you have prevail'd, I am no further your
enemy; she is not worth our debate. If she remain
unseduc'd, you not making it appear otherwise, for

your ill opinion, and th'assault you have made to her
chastity, you shall answer me with your sword.

IACHIMO   Your hand, a covenant: we will have these   165
things set down by lawful counsel, and straight away
for Britain, lest the bargain should catch cold and
starve. I will fetch my gold, and have our two wagers
recorded.

POSTHUMUS   Agreed.   *Exeunt Posthumus and Iachimo.*   170

FRENCHMAN   Will this hold, think you?

PHILARIO   Signior Iachimo will not from it. Pray let us
follow 'em.   *Exeunt.*

1.6   *Enter* QUEEN, Ladies *and* CORNELIUS.

QUEEN
   Whiles yet the dew's on ground, gather those
      flowers;
   Make haste. Who has the note of them?

1 LADY   I, madam.

QUEEN   Dispatch.   *Exeunt Ladies.*
   Now master doctor, have you brought those drugs?

CORNELIUS
   Pleaseth your highness, ay: here they are, madam: 5
   [*presenting a small box*]
   But I beseech your grace, without offence,
   (My conscience bids me ask) wherefore you have
   Commanded of me these most poisonous
      compounds,
   Which are the movers of a languishing death:
   But though slow, deadly.

QUEEN   I wonder, doctor,   10
   Thou ask'st me such a question. Have I not been
   Thy pupil long? Hast thou not learn'd me how
   To make perfumes? Distil? Preserve? Yea so,
   That our great king himself doth woo me oft
   For my confections? Having thus far proceeded   15
   (Unless thou think'st me devilish) is't not meet
   That I did amplify my judgement in
   Other conclusions? I will try the forces
   Of these thy compounds on such creatures as
   We count not worth the hanging (but none human)   20
   To try the vigour of them, and apply
   Allayments to their act, and by them gather
   Their several virtues, and effects.

CORNELIUS   Your highness
   Shall from this practice but make hard your heart:
   Besides, the seeing these effects will be   25
   Both noisome and infectious.

QUEEN   O, content thee.

   Enter PISANIO.

   [*aside*] Here comes a flattering rascal, upon him
   Will I first work: he's for his master,
   And enemy to my son. How now, Pisanio?
   Doctor, your service for this time is ended,   30
   Take your own way.

CORNELIUS [*aside*]   I do suspect you, madam;

But you shall do no harm.

QUEEN [*to Pisanio*]   Hark thee, a word.

CORNELIUS [*aside*]

    I do not like her. She doth think she has
    Strange ling'ring poisons: I do know her spirit;
35   And will not trust one of her malice with
    A drug of such damn'd nature. Those she has
    Will stupefy and dull the sense awhile;
    Which first (perchance) she'll prove on cats and
        dogs,
    Then afterward up higher: but there is
40   No danger in what show of death it makes,
    More than the locking up the spirits a time,
    To be more fresh, reviving. She is fool'd
    With a most false effect: and I the truer,
    So to be false with her.

QUEEN   No further service, doctor,
    Until I send for thee.

45 CORNELIUS   I humbly take my leave.   *Exit.*

QUEEN

    Weeps she still, say'st thou? Dost thou think in time
    She will not quench, and let instructions enter
    Where folly now possesses? Do thou work:
    When thou shalt bring me word she loves my son,
50   I'll tell thee on the instant, thou art then
    As great as is thy master: greater, for
    His fortunes all lie speechless, and his name
    Is at last gasp. Return he cannot, nor
    Continue where he is: to shift his being
55   Is to exchange one misery with another,
    And every day that comes comes to decay
    A day's work in him. What shalt thou expect,
    To be depender on a thing that leans?
    Who cannot be new built, nor has no friends,
    So much as but to prop him?
    [*The Queen drops the box. Pisanio takes it up.*]
60   Thou tak'st up
    Thou know'st not what: but take it for thy labour:
    It is a thing I made, which hath the king
    Five times redeem'd from death. I do not know
    What is more cordial. Nay, I prithee take it;
65   It is an earnest of a farther good
    That I mean to thee. Tell thy mistress how
    The case stands with her: do't, as from thyself;
    Think what a chance thou changest on; but think
    Thou hast thy mistress still, to boot, my son,
70   Who shall take notice of thee. I'll move the king
    To any shape of thy preferment, such
    As thou'lt desire: and then myself, I chiefly,
    That set thee on to this desert, am bound
    To load thy merit richly. Call my women:
    Think on my words.   *Exit Pisanio.*
75   A sly and constant knave.
    Not to be shak'd: the agent for his master,
    And the remembrancer of her to hold
    The hand-fast to her lord. I have given him that,
    Which if he take, shall quite unpeople her

    Of liegers for her sweet: and which she after,   80
    Except she bend her humour, shall be assur'd
    To taste of too.

        Re-enter PISANIO *and* Ladies.

           So, so: well done, well done:
    The violets, cowslips, and the primroses
    Bear to my closet. Fare thee well, Pisanio;
    Think on my words.   *Exeunt Queen and Ladies.*

PISANIO   And shall do: 85
    But when to my good lord I prove untrue,
    I'll choke myself: there's all I'll do for you.   *Exit.*

1.7   *Enter* IMOGEN *alone.*

IMOGEN   A father cruel, and a step-dame false,
    A foolish suitor to a wedded lady,
    That hath her husband banish'd: – O, that husband,
    My supreme crown of grief! and those repeated
    Vexations of it! Had I been thief-stolen,   5
    As my two brothers, happy: but most miserable
    Is the desire that's glorious. Bless'd be those,
    How mean soe'er, that have their honest wills,
    Which seasons comfort. – Who may this be? Fie!

        Enter PISANIO *and* IACHIMO.

PISANIO   Madam, a noble gentleman of Rome,   10
    Comes from my lord with letters.

IACHIMO   Change you, madam:
    The worthy Leonatus is in safety,
    And greets your highness dearly. [*Presents a letter.*]

IMOGEN   Thanks, good sir:
    You're kindly welcome.

IACHIMO [*aside*]
    All of her that is out of door most rich!   15
    If she be furnish'd with a mind so rare,
    She is alone th'Arabian bird; and I
    Have lost the wager. Boldness be my friend!
    Arm me, Audacity, from head to foot,
    Or like the Parthian I shall flying fight;   20
    Rather, directly fly.

IMOGEN [*Reads.*]   *He is one of the noblest note, to whose*
    kindnesses I am infinitely tied. Reflect upon him accord-
    ingly, as you value your trust –

                    LEONATUS.   25
    So far I read aloud.
    But even the very middle of my heart
    Is warm'd by th' rest, and takes it thankfully.
    You are as welcome, worthy sir, as I
    Have words to bid you, and shall find it so   30
    In all that I can do.

IACHIMO   Thanks, fairest lady. –
    What! are men mad? Hath nature given them eyes
    To see this vaulted arch, and the rich crop
    Of sea and land, which can distinguish 'twixt
    The fiery orbs above, and the twinn'd stones   35
    Upon the number'd beach, and can we not
    Partition make with spectacles so precious

'Twixt fair, and foul?

IMOGEN   What makes your admiration?

IACHIMO   It cannot be i'th' eye: for apes and monkeys,
'Twixt two such shes, would chatter this way, and
Contemn with mows the other. Nor i'the judgement:
For idiots in this case of favour, would
Be wisely definite: nor i'th' appetite.
Sluttery, to such neat excellence oppos'd,
Should make desire vomit emptiness,
Not so allur'd to feed.

IMOGEN   What is the matter, trow?

IACHIMO   The cloyed will –
That satiate yet unsatisfied desire, that tub
Both fill'd and running-ravening first the lamb,
Longs after for the garbage.

IMOGEN   What, dear sir,
Thus raps you? Are you well?

IACHIMO   Thanks madam, well:
[*to Pisanio*] Beseech you sir,
Desire my man's abode where I did leave him:
He's strange and peevish.

PISANIO   I was going, sir,
To give him welcome.   *Exit.*

IMOGEN
Continues well my lord? His health, beseech you?

IACHIMO   Well, madam.

IMOGEN   Is he disposed to mirth? I hope he is.

IACHIMO   Exceeding pleasant: none a stranger there,
So merry and so gamesome: he is call'd
The Briton reveller.

IMOGEN   When he was here
He did incline to sadness, and oft-times
Not knowing why.

IACHIMO   I never saw him sad.
There is a Frenchman his companion, one
An eminent monsieur, that, it seems, much loves
A Gallian girl at home. He furnaces
The thick sighs from him; whiles the jolly Briton
(Your lord, I mean) laughs from's free lungs: cries 'O,
Can my sides hold, to think that man, who knows
By history, report, or his own proof,
What woman is, yea what she cannot choose
But must be, will's free hours languish for
Assured bondage?'

IMOGEN   Will my lord say so?

IACHIMO
Ay, madam, with his eyes in flood with laughter:
It is a recreation to be by
And hear him mock the Frenchman: but heavens
    know
Some men are much to blame.

IMOGEN   Not he, I hope.

IACHIMO
Not he: but yet heaven's bounty towards him might
Be us'd more thankfully. In himself 'tis much;
In you, which I account his, beyond all talents,
Whilst I am bound to wonder, I am bound

To pity too.

IMOGEN   What do you pity, sir?

IACHIMO   Two creatures heartily.

IMOGEN   Am I one, sir?
You look on me: what wrack discern you in me
Deserves your pity?

IACHIMO   Lamentable! What   85
To hide me from the radiant sun, and solace
I' th' dungeon by a snuff?

IMOGEN   I pray you, sir,
Deliver with more openness your answers
To my demands. Why do you pity me?

IACHIMO   That others do   90
(I was about to say) enjoy your – But
It is an office of the gods to venge it,
Not mine to speak on't.

IMOGEN   You do seem to know
Something of me, or what concerns me; pray you,
Since doubting things go ill often hurts more   95
Than to be sure they do – for certainties
Either are past remedies; or timely knowing,
The remedy then born – discover to me
What both you spur and stop.

IACHIMO   Had I this cheek
To bathe my lips upon: this hand, whose touch   100
(Whose every touch) would force the feeler's soul
To th'oath of loyalty: this object, which
Takes prisoner the wild motion of mine eye,
Firing it only here; should I (damn'd then)
Slaver with lips as common as the stairs   105
That mount the Capitol: join gripes, with hands
Made hard with hourly falsehood (falsehood, as
With labour): then by-peeping in an eye
Base and illustrous as the smoky light
That's fed with stinking tallow: it were fit   110
That all the plagues of hell should at one time
Encounter such revolt.

IMOGEN   My lord, I fear,
Has forgot Britain.

IACHIMO   And himself. Not I,
Inclin'd to this intelligence, pronounce
The beggary of his change: but 'tis your graces   115
That from my mutest conscience to my tongue
Charms this report out.

IMOGEN   Let me hear no more.

IACHIMO
O dearest soul: your cause doth strike my heart
With pity that doth make me sick! A lady
So fair, and fasten'd to an empery   120
Would make the great'st king double, to be partner'd
With tomboys hir'd with that self exhibition
Which your own coffers yield! with diseas'd ventures,
That play with all infirmities for gold
Which rottenness can lend Nature! Such boil'd stuff   125
As well might poison poison! Be reveng'd,
Or she that bore you was no queen, and you
Recoil from your great stock.

IMOGEN   Reveng'd!

How should I be reveng'd? If this be true,
130 (As I have such a heart that both mine ears
Must not in haste abuse) if it be true,
How should I be reveng'd?
IACHIMO   Should he make me
Live like Diana's priest, betwixt cold sheets,
Whiles he is vaulting variable ramps,
135 In your despite, upon your purse – Revenge it.
I dedicate myself to your sweet pleasure,
More noble than that runagate to your bed,
And will continue fast to your affection,
Still close as sure.
IMOGEN   What ho, Pisanio!
140 IACHIMO   Let me my service tender on your lips.
IMOGEN   Away, I do condemn mine ears, that have
So long attended thee. If thou wert honourable,
Thou wouldst have told this tale for virtue, not
For such an end thou seek'st, as base, as strange.
145 Thou wrong'st a gentleman, who is as far
From thy report as thou from honour, and
Solicits here a lady that disdains
Thee, and the devil alike. What ho, Pisanio!
The king my father shall be made acquainted
150 Of thy assault: if he shall think it fit
A saucy stranger in his court to mart
As in a Romish stew, and to expound
His beastly mind to us, he hath a court
He little cares for, and a daughter who
155 He not respects at all. What ho, Pisanio!
IACHIMO   O happy Leonatus! I may say:
The credit that thy lady hath of thee
Deserves thy trust, and thy most perfect goodness
Her assur'd credit. Blessed live you long!
160 A lady to the worthiest sir that ever
Country call'd his; and you, his mistress, only
For the most worthiest fit. Give me your pardon.
I have spoke this to know if your affiance
Were deeply rooted, and shall make your lord
165 That which he is, new o'er: and he is one
The truest manner'd: such a holy witch
That he enchants societies into him:
Half all men's hearts are his.
IMOGEN   You make amends.
IACHIMO   He sits 'mongst men like a descended god;
170 He hath a kind of honour sets him off,
More than a mortal seeming. Be not angry,
Most mighty princess, that I have adventur'd
To try your taking of a false report, which hath
Honour'd with confirmation your great judgement
175 In the election of a sir so rare,
Which you know cannot err. The love I bear him
Made me to fan you thus, but the gods made you
(Unlike all others) chaffless. Pray, your pardon.
IMOGEN
All's well, sir: take my power i'th' court for yours.
180 IACHIMO   My humble thanks. I had almost forgot
T'entreat your grace, but in a small request,

And yet of moment too, for it concerns:
Your lord, myself, and other noble friends
Are partners in the business.
IMOGEN   Pray, what is't?
IACHIMO   Some dozen Romans of us, and your lord   185
(The best feather of our wing) have mingled sums
To buy a present for the emperor:
Which I (the factor for the rest) have done
In France: 'tis plate of rare device, and jewels
Of rich and exquisite form, their values great,   190
And I am something curious, being strange,
To have them in safe stowage: may it please you
To take them in protection?
IMOGEN   Willingly:
And pawn mine honour for their safety, since
My lord hath interest in them; I will keep them   195
In my bedchamber.
IACHIMO   They are in a trunk
Attended by my men: I will make bold
To send them to you, only for this night:
I must abroad to-morrow.
IMOGEN   O, no, no.
IACHIMO   Yes, I beseech: or I shall short my word   200
By length'ning my return. From Gallia
I cross'd the seas on purpose and on promise
To see your grace.
IMOGEN   I thank you for your pains:
But not away to-morrow!
IACHIMO   O, I must madam.
Therefore I shall beseech you, if you please   205
To greet your lord with writing, do't to-night:
I have outstood my time, which is material
To th' tender of our present.
IMOGEN   I will write.
Send your trunk to me, it shall safe be kept,
And truly yielded you: you're very welcome. *Exeunt.*   210

2.1   *Enter* CLOTEN *and two* Lords.

CLOTEN   Was there ever man had such luck? When I
kissed the jack upon an upcast, to be hit away! I had a
hundred pound on't: and then a whoreson jackanapes
must take me up for swearing, as if I borrowed mine
oaths of him, and might not spend them at my   5
pleasure.
1 LORD   What got he by that? You have broke his pate
with your bowl.
2 LORD [*aside*]   If his wit had been like him that broke it,
it would have run all out.   10
CLOTEN   When a gentleman is dispos'd to swear, it is not
for any standers-by to curtail his oaths. Ha?
2 LORD   No, my lord; [*aside*] nor crop the ears of them.
CLOTEN   Whoreson dog! I gave him satisfaction! Would
he had been one of my rank!   15
2 LORD [*aside*]   To have smelt like a fool.
CLOTEN   I am not vex'd more at any thing in th'earth: a
pox on't! I had rather not be so noble as I am: they dare

not fight with me, because of the queen my mother:
every Jack-slave hath his bellyful of fighting, and I
must go up and down like a cock, that nobody can
match.

2 LORD [*aside*] You are cock and capon too, and you
crow, cock, with your comb on.

CLOTEN Sayest thou?

2 LORD It is not fit your lordship should undertake
every companion that you give offence to.

CLOTEN No, I know that: but it is fit I should commit
offence to my inferiors.

2 LORD Ay, it is fit for your lordship only.

CLOTEN Why, so I say.

1 LORD Did you hear of a stranger that's come to court
to-night?

CLOTEN A stranger, and I know not on't?

2 LORD [*aside*] He's a strange fellow himself, and
knows it not.

1 LORD There's an Italian come, and 'tis thought one of
Leonatus' friends.

CLOTEN Leonatus? A banished rascal; and he's another,
whatsoever he be. Who told you of this stranger?

1 LORD One of your lordship's pages.

CLOTEN Is it fit I went to look upon him? Is there no
derogation in't?

2 LORD You cannot derogate, my lord.

CLOTEN Not easily, I think.

2 LORD [*aside*] You are a fool granted, therefore your
issues being foolish do not derogate.

CLOTEN Come, I'll go see this Italian: what I have lost
to-day at bowls I'll win to-night of him. Come: go.

2 LORD I'll attend your lordship.

Exeunt Cloten and First Lord.

That such a crafty devil as is his mother
Should yield the world this ass! a woman that
Bears all down with her brain, and this her son
Cannot take two from twenty, for his heart,
And leave eighteen. Alas poor princess,
Thou divine Imogen, what thou endur'st,
Betwixt a father by thy step-dame govern'd,
A mother hourly coining plots, a wooer
More hateful than the foul expulsion is
Of thy dear husband, than that horrid act
Of the divorce, he'ld make. The heavens hold firm
The walls of thy dear honour, keep unshak'd
That temple, thy fair mind, that thou mayst stand,
T'enjoy thy banish'd lord and this great land! *Exit.*

2.2   *Enter* IMOGEN *in her bed, and a* Lady.

IMOGEN Who's there? my woman Helen?

LADY   Please you, madam.

IMOGEN What hour is it?

LADY   Almost midnight, madam.

IMOGEN
I have read three hours then: mine eyes are weak,
Fold down the leaf where I have left: to bed.

Take not away the taper, leave it burning: 5
And if thou canst awake by four o'th' clock,
I prithee call me. Sleep hath seiz'd me wholly.
                                              Exit Lady.
To your protection I commend me, gods,
From fairies and the tempters of the night,
Guard me, beseech ye!   10
[*Sleeps. Iachimo comes from the trunk.*]

IACHIMO
The crickets sing, and man's o'er-labour'd sense
Repairs itself by rest. Our Tarquin thus
Did softly press the rushes, ere he waken'd
The chastity he wounded. Cytherea,
How bravely thou becom'st thy bed! fresh lily!   15
And whiter than the sheets! That I might touch!
But kiss, one kiss! Rubies unparagon'd,
How dearly they do't: 'tis her breathing that
Perfumes the chamber thus: the flame o'th' taper
Bows toward her, and would under-peep her lids,   20
To see th'enclosed lights, now canopied
Under these windows, white and azure lac'd
With blue of heaven's own tinct. But my design.
To note the chamber: I will write all down:
Such, and such pictures: there the window, such   25
Th'adornment of her bed; the arras, figures,
Why, such, and such; and the contents o'th' story.
Ah, but some natural notes about her body
Above ten thousand meaner moveables
Would testify, t'enrich mine inventory.   30
O sleep, thou ape of death, lie dull upon her,
And be her sense but as a monument,
Thus in a chapel lying. Come off, come off;
[*taking off her bracelet*]
As slippery as the Gordian knot was hard.
'Tis mine, and this will witness outwardly,   35
As strongly as the conscience does within,
To th' madding of her lord. On her left breast
A mole cinque-spotted: like the crimson drops
I'th' bottom of a cowslip. Here's a voucher,
Stronger than ever law could make; this secret   40
Will force him think I have pick'd the lock, and ta'en
The treasure of her honour. No more: to what end?
Why should I write this down, that's riveted,
Screw'd to my memory? She hath been reading late,
The tale of Tereus, here the leaf's turn'd down   45
Where Philomel gave up. I have enough:
To th' trunk again, and shut the spring of it.
Swift, swift, you dragons of the night, that dawning
May bare the raven's eye! I lodge in fear;
Though this a heavenly angel, hell is here.   50
                                          [*Clock strikes.*]
One, two, three: time, time!
[*Goes into the trunk. The scene closes.*]

2.3   *Enter* CLOTEN *and* Lords.

1 LORD Your lordship is the most patient man in loss,

the most coldest that ever turn'd up ace.

CLOTEN   It would make any man cold to lose.

1 LORD   But not every man patient after the noble
temper of your lordship. You are most hot and furious
when you win.

CLOTEN   Winning will put any man into courage. If I
could get this foolish Imogen, I should have gold
enough. It's almost morning, is't not?

1 LORD   Day, my lord.

CLOTEN   I would this music would come: I am advised
to give her music a mornings, they say it will
penetrate.

Enter Musicians.

Come on, tune: if you can penetrate her with your
fingering, so: we'll try with tongue too: if none will do,
let her remain: but I'll never give o'er. First, a very
excellent good-conceited thing; after, a wonderful
sweet air, with admirable rich words to it, and then let
her consider.

SONG

Hark, hark, the lark at heaven's gate sings,
   And Phoebus gins arise,
His steeds to water at those springs
   On chalic'd flowers that lies;
And winking Mary-buds begin to ope their golden
   eyes;
With every thing that pretty is, my lady sweet arise:
   Arise, arise!

CLOTEN   So get you gone: if this penetrate, I will
consider your music the better: if it do not, it is a vice
in her ears, which horse-hairs, and calves'-guts, nor
the voice of unpaved eunuch to boot, can never
amend.   *Exeunt musicians.*

2 LORD   Here comes the king.

CLOTEN   I am glad I was up so late, for that's the reason
I was up so early: he cannot choose but take this
service I have done fatherly.

Enter CYMBELINE and QUEEN.

Good morrow to your majesty, and to my gracious
mother.

CYMBELINE
Attend you here the door of our stern daughter?
Will she not forth?

CLOTEN   I have assail'd her with musics, but she
vouchsafes no notice.

CYMBELINE   The exile of her minion is too new,
She hath not yet forgot him, some more time
Must wear the print of his remembrance on't,
And then she's yours.

QUEEN   You are most bound to th' king,
Who lets go by no vantages that may
Prefer you to his daughter: frame yourself
To orderly solicits, and be friended

With aptness of the season: make denials
Increase your services: so seem, as if
You were inspir'd to do those duties which
You tender to her: that you in all obey her,
Save when command to your dismission tends,
And therein you are senseless.

CLOTEN   Senseless? not so.

Enter a Messenger.

MESSENGER
So like you, sir, ambassadors from Rome;
The one is Caius Lucius.

CYMBELINE   A worthy fellow,
Albeit he comes on angry purpose now;
But that's no fault of his: we must receive him
According to the honour of his sender,
And towards himself, his goodness forespent on us,
We must extend our notice. Our dear son,
When you have given good morning to your mistress,
Attend the queen and us; we will have need
T'employ you towards this Roman. Come, our
   queen.   *Exeunt all but Cloten.*

CLOTEN   If she be up, I'll speak with her: if not,
Let her lie still, and dream. By your leave, ho!
[*Knocks.*]
I know her women are about her: what
If I do line one of their hands? 'Tis gold
Which buys admittance (oft it doth) yea, and makes
Diana's rangers false themselves, yield up
Their deer to th' stand o'th' stealer: and 'tis gold
Which makes the true-man kill'd, and saves the thief:
Nay, sometime hangs both thief, and true-man: what
Can it not do, and undo? I will make
One of her women lawyer to me, for
I yet not understand the case myself.
By your leave. [*Knocks.*]

Enter a Lady.

LADY   Who's there that knocks?

CLOTEN   A gentleman.

LADY   No more?

CLOTEN   Yes, and a gentlewoman's son.

LADY   That's more
Than some whose tailors are as dear as yours
Can justly boast of. What's your lordship's pleasure?

CLOTEN   Your lady's person, is she ready?

LADY   Ay,
To keep her chamber.

CLOTEN   There is gold for you,
Sell me your good report.

LADY   How, my good name? or to report of you
What I shall think is good? The princess!   *Exit Lady.*

Enter IMOGEN.

CLOTEN   Good morrow, fairest: sister, your sweet hand.

IMOGEN   Good morrow, sir. You lay out too much pains
For purchasing but trouble: the thanks I give

Is telling you that I am poor of thanks,
And scarce can spare them.

CLOTEN   Still I swear I love you.

IMOGEN   If you but said so, 'twere as deep with me:
If you swear still, your recompense is still
That I regard it not.

CLOTEN   This is no answer.

IMOGEN   But that you shall not say I yield being silent,
I would not speak. I pray you spare me: 'faith
I shall unfold equal discourtesy
To your best kindness: one of your great knowing
Should learn (being taught) forbearance.

CLOTEN   To leave you in your madness, 'twere my sin,
I will not.

IMOGEN   Fools are not mad folks.

CLOTEN   Do you call me fool?

IMOGEN   As I am mad I do:
If you'll be patient, I'll no more be mad,
That cures us both. I am much sorry, sir,
You put me to forget a lady's manners,
By being so verbal: and learn now, for all,
That I, which know my heart, do here pronounce,
By th' very truth of it, I care not for you,
And am so near the lack of charity.
(To accuse myself) I hate you: which I had rather
You felt than make't my boast.

CLOTEN   You sin against
Obedience, which you owe your father; for
The contract you pretend with that base wretch,
One bred of alms, and foster'd with cold dishes,
With scraps o'th' court, it is no contract, none;
And though it be allow'd in meaner parties
(Yet who than he more mean?) to knit their souls
(On whom there is no more dependency
But brats and beggary) in self-figur'd knot,
Yet you are curb'd from that enlargement, by
The consequence o'th' crown, and must not foil
The precious note of it; with a base slave,
A hiding for a livery, a squire's cloth,
A pantler; not so eminent.

IMOGEN   Profane fellow,
Wert thou the son of Jupiter, and no more
But what thou art besides, thou wert too base
To be his groom: thou wert dignified enough,
Even to the point of envy, if 'twere made
Comparative for your virtues to be styled
The under-hangman of his kingdom; and hated
For being preferr'd so well.

CLOTEN   The south-fog rot him!

IMOGEN
He never can meet more mischance than come
To be but nam'd of thee. His mean'st garment,
That ever hath but clipp'd his body, is dearer
In my respect, than all the hairs above thee,
Were they all made such men. How now, Pisanio!

Enter PISANIO.

CLOTEN   'His garment!' Now, the devil –

IMOGEN   To Dorothy my woman hie thee presently.

CLOTEN   'His garment!'

IMOGEN   I am sprited with a fool,   140
Frighted, and anger'd worse. Go bid my woman
Search for a jewel, that too casually
Hath left mine arm: it was thy master's. 'Shrew me,
If I would lose it for a revenue
Of any king's in Europe! I do think   145
I saw't this morning: confident I am.
Last night 'twas on mine arm; I kiss'd it:
I hope it be not gone to tell my lord
That I kiss aught but he.

PISANIO   'Twill not be lost.

IMOGEN   I hope so: go and search.   *Exit Pisanio.*

CLOTEN   You have abus'd me: 150
'His meanest garment!'

IMOGEN   Ay, I said so, sir:
If you will make't an action, call witness to't.

CLOTEN   I will inform your father.

IMOGEN   Your mother too:
She's my good lady; and will conceive, I hope,
But the worst of me. So I leave you, sir,   155
To th' worst of discontent.   *Exit.*

CLOTEN   I'll be reveng'd:
'His mean'st garment!' Well.   *Exit.*

2.4   *Enter* POSTHUMUS *and* PHILARIO.

POSTHUMUS   Fear it not, sir: I would I were so sure
To win the king as I am bold her honour
Will remain hers.

PHILARIO   What means do you make to him?

POSTHUMUS   Not any: but abide the change of time,
Quake in the present winter's state, and wish   5
That warmer days would come: in these fear'd hopes,
I barely gratify your love; they failing,
I must die much your debtor.

PHILARIO   Your very goodness, and your company,
O'erpays all I can do. By this, your king   10
Hath heard of great Augustus: Caius Lucius
Will do's commission throughly. And I think
He'll grant the tribute: send th'arrearages,
Or look upon our Romans, whose remembrance
Is yet fresh in their grief.

POSTHUMUS   I do believe   15
(Statist though I am none, nor like to be)
That this will prove a war; and you shall hear
The legion now in Gallia sooner landed
In our not-fearing Britain than have tidings
Of any penny tribute paid. Our countrymen   20
Are men more order'd than when Julius Caesar
Smil'd at their lack of skill, but found their courage
Worthy his frowning at. Their discipline,
(Now wing-led with their courages) will make known
To their approvers they are people such   25
That mend upon the world.

Enter IACHIMO.

PHILARIO   See! Iachimo!
POSTHUMUS
  The swiftest harts have posted you by land;
  And winds of all the corners kiss'd your sails,
  To make your vessel nimble.
PHILARIO   Welcome, sir.
30 POSTHUMUS   I hope the briefness of your answer made
  The speediness of your return.
IACHIMO   Your lady,
  Is one the fairest that I have look'd upon –
POSTHUMUS
  And therewithal the best, or let her beauty
  Look through a casement to allure false hearts,
  And be false with them.
35 IACHIMO   Here are letters for you.
POSTHUMUS   Their tenour good, I trust.
IACHIMO   'Tis very like.
POSTHUMUS   Was Caius Lucius in the Britain court
  When you were there?
IACHIMO   He was expected then,
  But not approach'd.
POSTHUMUS   All is well yet.
40 Sparkles this stone as it was wont, or is't not
  Too dull for your good wearing?
IACHIMO   If I have lost it,
  I should have lost the worth of it in gold –
  I'll make a journey twice as far, t'enjoy
  A second night of such sweet shortness which
45 Was mine in Britain; for the ring is won.
POSTHUMUS   The stone's too hard to come by.
IACHIMO   Not a whit,
  Your lady being so easy.
POSTHUMUS   Make not, sir,
  Your loss your sport: I hope you know that we
  Must not continue friends.
IACHIMO   Good sir, we must
50 If you keep covenant. Had I not brought
  The knowledge of your mistress home, I grant
  We were to question farther; but I now
  Profess myself the winner of her honour,
  Together with your ring; and not the wronger
55 Of her or you, having proceeded but
  By both your wills.
POSTHUMUS   If you can make't apparent
  That you have tasted her in bed, my hand
  And ring is yours. If not, the foul opinion
  You had of her pure honour gains, or loses,
60 Your sword, or mine, or masterless leave both
  To who shall find them.
IACHIMO   Sir, my circumstances,
  Being so near the truth, as I will make them,
  Must first induce you to believe; whose strength
  I will confirm with oath, which I doubt not
65 You'll give me leave to spare, when you shall find
  You need it not.

POSTHUMUS   Proceed.
IACHIMO   First, her bedchamber,
  (Where I confess I slept not, but profess
  Had that was well worth watching) it was hang'd
  With tapestry of silk and silver, the story
70 Proud Cleopatra, when she met her Roman,
  And Cydnus swell'd above the banks, or for
  The press of boats, or pride. A piece of work
  So bravely done, so rich, that it did strive
  In workmanship and value; which I wonder'd
75 Could be so rarely and exactly wrought,
  Since the true life on't was –
POSTHUMUS   This is true:
  And this you might have heard of here, by me,
  Or by some other.
IACHIMO   More particulars
  Must justify my knowledge.
POSTHUMUS   So they must,
  Or do your honour injury.
IACHIMO   The chimney
80 Is south the chamber, and the chimney-piece,
  Chaste Dian, bathing: never saw I figures
  So likely to report themselves; the cutter
  Was as another Nature, dumb; outwent her,
  Motion and breath left out.
POSTHUMUS   This is a thing
85 Which you might from relation likewise reap,
  Being, as it is, much spoke of.
IACHIMO   The roof o'th' chamber
  With golden cherubins is fretted. Her andirons
  (I had forgot them) were two winking Cupids
  Of silver, each on one foot standing, nicely
90 Depending on their brands.
POSTHUMUS   This is her honour!
  Let it be granted you have seen all this (and praise
  Be given to your remembrance) the description
  Of what is in her chamber nothing saves
  The wager you have laid.
IACHIMO   Then, if you can
95 [*showing the bracelet*]
  Be pale, I beg but leave to air this jewel: see!
  And now 'tis up again: it must be married
  To that your diamond, I'll keep them.
POSTHUMUS   Jove! –
  Once more let me behold it: is it that
  Which I left with her?
IACHIMO   Sir (I thank her) that!
100 She stripp'd it from her arm: I see her yet:
  Her pretty action did outsell her gift,
  And yet enrich'd it too: she gave it me,
  And said she priz'd it once.
POSTHUMUS   May be she pluck'd it off
  To send it me.
IACHIMO   She writes so to you? Doth she?
105 POSTHUMUS   O, no, no, no, 'tis true. Here, take this too;
  [*Gives the ring.*]
  It is a basilisk unto mine eye,

Kills me to look on't. Let there be no honour
Where there is beauty: truth, where semblance: love,
Where there's another man. The vows of women
Of no more bondage be to where they are made
Than they are to their virtues, which is nothing.
O, above measure false!

PHILARIO   Have patience, sir,
And take your ring again, 'tis not yet won:
It may be probable she lost it: or
Who knows if one of her women, being corrupted,
Hath stol'n it from her?

POSTHUMUS   Very true,
And so, I hope, he came by't. Back my ring,
Render me some corporal sign about her
More evident than this: for this was stol'n.

IACHIMO   By Jupiter, I had it from her arm.

POSTHUMUS
Hark you, he swears: by Jupiter he swears.
'Tis true, nay, keep the ring, 'tis true: I am sure
She would not lose it: her attendants are
All sworn, and honourable: – they induc'd to steal it?
And by a stranger? No, he hath enjoy'd her:
The cognizance of her incontinency
Is this: she hath bought the name of whore, thus
   dearly.
There, take thy hire, and all the fiends of hell
Divide themselves between you!

PHILARIO   Sir, be patient:
This is not strong enough to be believed
Of one persuaded well of.

POSTHUMUS   Never talk on't:
She hath been colted by him.

IACHIMO   If you seek
For further satisfying, under her breast
(Worthy her pressing) lies a mole, right proud
Of that most delicate lodging. By my life,
I kiss'd it, and it gave me present hunger
To feed again, though full. You do remember
This stain upon her?

POSTHUMUS   Ay, and it doth confirm
Another stain, as big as hell can hold,
Were there no more but it.

IACHIMO   Will you hear more?

POSTHUMUS
Spare your arithmetic, never count the turns:
Once, and a million!

IACHIMO   I'll be sworn –

POSTHUMUS   No swearing:
If you will swear you have not done't you lie,
And I will kill thee if thou dost deny
Thou'st made me cuckold.

IACHIMO   I'll deny nothing.

POSTHUMUS
O, that I had her here, to tear her limb-meal!
I will go there and do't, i'th' court, before
Her father. I'll do something –   *Exit.*

PHILARIO   Quite besides

The government of patience! You have won: 150
Let's follow him, and pervert the present wrath
He hath against himself.

IACHIMO   With all my heart.   *Exeunt.*

Re-enter POSTHUMUS.

POSTHUMUS   Is there no way for men to be, but women
Must be half-workers? We are all bastards,
And that most venerable man, which I   155
Did call my father, was I know not where
When I was stamp'd. Some coiner with his tools
Made me a counterfeit: yet my mother seem'd
The Dian of that time: so doth my wife
The nonpareil of this. O vengeance, vengeance!   160
Me of my lawful pleasure she restrain'd,
And pray'd me oft forbearance: did it with
A pudency so rosy, the sweet view on't
Might well have warm'd old Saturn; that I thought
   her
As chaste as unsunn'd snow. O, all the devils!   165
This yellow Iachimo, in an hour, was't not?
Or less; at first? Perchance he spoke not, but
Like a full-acorn'd boar, a German one,
Cried 'O!' and mounted; found no opposition
But what he look'd for should oppose and she   170
Should from encounter guard. Could I find out
The woman's part in me – for there's no motion
That tends to vice in man, but I affirm
It is the woman's part: be it lying, note it,
The woman's: flattering, hers; deceiving, hers: 175
Lust, and rank thoughts, hers, hers: revenges, hers:
Ambitions, covetings, change of prides, disdain,
Nice longing, slanders, mutability;
All faults that name, nay, that hell knows, why, hers
In part, or all: but rather all. For even to vice 180
They are not constant, but are changing still;
One vice, but of a minute old, for one
Not half so old as that. I'll write against them,
Detest them, curse them: yet 'tis greater skill
In a true hate, to pray they have their will: 185
The very devils cannot plague them better.   *Exit.*

3.1   *Enter in state,* CYMBELINE, QUEEN,
           CLOTEN *and* Lords *at one door, and
           at another,* CAIUS LUCIUS *and attendants.*

CYMBELINE
Now say, what would Augustus Caesar with us?

LUCIUS   When Julius Caesar, (whose remembrance yet
Lives in men's eyes, and will to ears and tongues
Be theme and hearing ever) was in this Britain
And conquer'd it, Cassibelan, thine uncle,   5
(Famous in Caesar's praises, no whit less
Than in his feats deserving it) for him,
And his succession, granted Rome a tribute,
Yearly three thousand pounds; which (by thee) lately
Is left untender'd.

10   QUEEN   And, to kill the marvel,
     Shall be so ever.
     CLOTEN   There be many Caesars ere such another
     Julius: Britain's a world by itself, and we will nothing
     pay for wearing our own noses.

15   QUEEN   That opportunity,
     Which then they had to take from's, to resume
     We have again. Remember, sir, my liege,
     The kings your ancestors, together with
     The natural bravery of your isle, which stands

20   As Neptune's park, ribb'd and pal'd in
     With rocks unscaleable and roaring waters,
     With sands that will not bear your enemies' boats,
     But suck them up to th' topmast. A kind of conquest
     Caesar made here, but made not here his brag

25   Of 'Came, and saw, and overcame:' with shame
     (The first that ever touch'd him) he was carried
     From off our coast, twice beaten: and his shipping
     (Poor ignorant baubles!) on our terrible seas,
     Like egg-shells mov'd upon their surges, crack'd

30   As easily 'gainst our rocks. For joy whereof
     The fam'd Cassibelan, who was once at point
     (O giglot fortune!) to master Caesar's sword,
     Made Lud's town with rejoicing-fires bright,
     And Britons strut with courage.

35   CLOTEN   Come, there's no more tribute to be paid: our
     kingdom is stronger than it was at that time: and (as I
     said) there is no moe such Caesars, other of them may
     have crook'd noses, but to owe such straight arms,
     none.

40   CYMBELINE   Son, let your mother end.
     CLOTEN   We have yet many among us can gripe as hard
     as Cassibelan: I do not say I am one: but I have a hand.
     Why tribute? Why should we pay tribute? If Caesar
     can hide the sun from us with a blanket, or put the

45   moon in his pocket, we will pay him tribute for light:
     else, sir, no more tribute, pray you now.
     CYMBELINE   You must know,
     Till the injurious Romans did extort
     This tribute from us, we were free. Caesar's
     ambition,

50   Which swell'd so much that it did almost stretch
     The sides o'th' world, against all colour here
     Did put the yoke upon's: which to shake off
     Becomes a warlike people, whom we reckon
     Ourselves to be.
     CLOTEN AND LORDS   We do.
     CYMBELINE   Say then to Caesar,

55   Our ancestor was that Mulmutius which
     Ordain'd our laws, whose use the sword of Caesar
     Hath too much mangled; whose repair, and franchise,
     Shall (by the power we hold) be our good deed,
     Though Rome be therefore angry. Mulmutius made
      our laws,

60   Who was the first of Britain which did put
     His brows within a golden crown, and call'd
     Himself a king.

LUCIUS   I am sorry, Cymbeline,
   That I am to pronounce Augustus Caesar
   (Caesar, that hath moe kings his servants than
   Thyself domestic officers) thine enemy: 65
   Receive it from me, then. War and confusion
   In Caesar's name pronounce I 'gainst thee: look
   For fury, not to be resisted. Thus defied,
   I thank thee for myself.
CYMBELINE   Thou art welcome, Caius.
   Thy Caesar knighted me; my youth I spent   70
   Much under him; of him I gather'd honour,
   Which he to seek of me again, perforce,
   Behoves me keep at utterance. I am perfect
   That the Pannonians and Dalmatians for
   Their liberties are now in arms: a precedent   75
   Which not to read would show the Britons cold:
   So Caesar shall not find them.
LUCIUS   Let proof speak.
CLOTEN   His majesty bids you welcome. Make pastime
   with us a day or two, or longer: if you seek us
   afterwards in other terms, you shall find us in our salt- 80
   water girdle: if you beat us out of it, it is yours: if you
   fall in the adventure, our crows shall fare the better for
   you: and there's an end.
LUCIUS   So, sir.
CYMBELINE
   I know your master's pleasure, and he mine: 85
   All the remain is 'Welcome'.   *Exeunt.*

3.2   *Enter* PISANIO, *with a letter.*

PISANIO   How? of adultery? Wherefore write you not
   What monster's her accuser? Leonatus!
   O master, what a strange infection
   Is fall'n into thy ear! What false Italian
   (As poisonous tongu'd as handed) hath prevail'd   5
   On thy too ready hearing? Disloyal? No.
   She's punish'd for her truth; and undergoes,
   More goddess-like than wife-like, such assaults
   As would take in some virtue. O my master,
   Thy mind to her is now as low as were   10
   Thy fortunes. How? that I should murder her,
   Upon the love and truth and vows which I
   Have made to thy command? I, her? Her blood?
   If it be so to do good service, never
   Let me be counted serviceable. How look I,   15
   That I should seem to lack humanity
   So much as this fact comes to? [*reading*]
              Do't: the letter
   That I have sent her by her own command
   Shall give thee opportunity. O damn'd paper!
   Black as the ink that's on thee! Senseless bauble,   20
   Art thou a feodary for this act, and look'st
   So virgin-like without? Lo, here she comes.
   I am ignorant in what I am commanded.

           Enter IMOGEN.

IMOGEN   How now, Pisanio?

PISANIO   Madam, here is a letter from my lord.

IMOGEN   Who? thy lord? that is my lord Leonatus!
O, learn'd indeed were that astronomer
That knew the stars as I his characters;
He'd lay the future open. You good gods,
Let what is here contain'd relish of love,
Of my lord's health, of his content: yet not
That we two are asunder; let that grieve him;
Some griefs are med'cinable, that is one of them,
For it doth physic love: of his content,
All but in that! Good wax, thy leave: blest be
You bees that make these locks of counsel! Lovers
And men in dangerous bonds pray not alike:
Though forfeiters you cast in prison, yet
You clasp young Cupid's tables. Good news, gods!
[*Reads.*] *Justice, and your father's wrath (should he take
me in his dominion) could not be so cruel to me, as you (O
the dearest of creatures) would even renew me with your
eyes. Take notice that I am in Cambria at Milford-Haven:
what your own love will out of this advise you, follow. So
he wishes you all happiness, that remains loyal to his vow,
and your increasing in love.*
                                             LEONATUS POSTHUMUS.
O, for a horse with wings! Hear'st thou, Pisanio?
He is at Milford-Haven: read, and tell me
How far 'tis thither. If one of mean affairs
May plod it in a week, why may not I
Glide thither in a day? Then, true Pisanio,
Who long'st, like me, to see thy lord; who long'st
(O let me bate) but not like me: yet long'st
But in a fainter kind. O, not like me:
For mine's beyond beyond: say, and speak thick,
(Love's counsellor should fill the bores of hearing,
To th'smothering of the sense) how far it is
To this same blessed Milford. And by th' way
Tell me how Wales was made so happy as
T'inherit such a haven. But, first of all,
How we may steal from hence: and for the gap
That we shall make in time, from our hence-going
And our return, to excuse: but first, how get hence.
Why should excuse be born or ere begot?
We'll talk of that hereafter. Prithee speak,
How many score of miles may we well rid
'Twixt hour, and hour?

PISANIO   One score 'twixt sun and sun,
Madam's enough for you: and too much too.

IMOGEN   Why, one that rode to's execution, man,
Could never go so slow: I have heard of riding
         wagers,
Where horses have been nimbler than the sands
That run i'th' clock's behalf. But this is foolery:
Go, bid my woman feign a sickness, say
She'll home to her father; and provide me presently
A riding-suit; no costlier than would fit
A franklin's housewife.

PISANIO   Madam, you're best consider.

IMOGEN   I see before me, man: nor here, nor here,
Nor what ensues, but have a fog in them,
That I cannot look through. Away, I prithee,   80
Do as I bid thee: there's no more to say:
Accessible is none but Milford way.   *Exeunt.*

3.3   *Enter* BELARIUS, GUIDERIUS *and* ARVIRAGUS.

BELARIUS   A goodly day not to keep house with such
Whose roof's as low as ours! Stoop, boys: this gate
Instructs you how t'adore the heavens; and bows you
To a morning's holy office. The gates of monarchs
Are arch'd so high that giants may jet through   5
And keep their impious turbans on, without
Good morrow to the sun. Hail, thou fair heaven!
We house i'th' rock, yet use thee not so hardly
As prouder livers do.

GUIDERIUS   Hail, heaven!

ARVIRAGUS   Hail, heaven!

BELARIUS
Now for our mountain sport, up to yond hill!   10
Your legs are young: I'll tread these flats. Consider,
When you above perceive me like a crow,
That it is place which lessens and sets off,
And you may then revolve what tales I have told you
Of courts, of princes; of the tricks in war.   15
This service is not service, so being done,
But being so allow'd. To apprehend thus,
Draws us a profit from all things we see:
And often, to our comfort, shall we find
The sharded beetle in a safer hold   20
Than is the full-wing'd eagle. O, this life
Is nobler than attending for a check:
Richer than doing nothing for a robe,
Prouder than rustling in unpaid-for silk:
Such gain the cap of him that makes him fine,   25
Yet keeps his book uncross'd: no life to ours.

GUIDERIUS
Out of your proof you speak: we poor unfledg'd,
Have never wing'd from view o'th' nest; nor know
         not
What air's from home. Haply this life is best
(If quiet life be best) sweeter to you   30
That have a sharper known, well corresponding
With your stiff age; but unto us it is
A cell of ignorance, travelling a-bed,
A prison, or a debtor that not dares
To stride a limit.

ARVIRAGUS   What should we speak of   35
When we are old as you? When we shall hear
The rain and wind beat dark December? How
In this our pinching cave shall we discourse
The freezing hours away? We have seen nothing:
We are beastly: subtle as the fox for prey,   40
Like warlike as the wolf for what we eat:
Our valour is to chase what flies: our cage
We make a quire, as doth the prison'd bird,

And sing our bondage freely.

BELARIUS   How you speak!

45   Did you but know the city's usuries,
And felt them knowingly: the art o'th' court,
As hard to leave as keep: whose top to climb
Is certain falling: or so slipp'ry that
The fear's as bad as falling: the toil o'th' war,
50   A pain that only seems to seek out danger
I'th' name of fame and honour, which dies i'th'
      search,
And hath as oft a sland'rous epitaph
As record of fair act. Nay, many times,
Doth ill deserve by doing well: what's worse,
55   Must court'sy at the censure. O boys, this story
The world may read in me: my body's mark'd
With Roman swords; and my report was once
First, with the best of note. Cymbeline lov'd me,
And when a soldier was the theme, my name
60   Was not far off: then was I as a tree
Whose boughs did bend with fruit. But in one night,
A storm, or robbery (call it what you will)
Shook down my mellow hangings, nay, my leaves,
And left me bare to weather.

GUIDERIUS   Uncertain favour!

BELARIUS
65   My fault being nothing (as I have told you oft)
But that two villains, whose false oaths prevail'd
Before my perfect honour, swore to Cymbeline
I was confederate with the Romans: so
Follow'd my banishment, and this twenty years
70   This rock, and these demesnes, have been my world,
Where I have liv'd at honest freedom, paid
More pious debts to heaven than in all
The fore-end of my time. But up to th' mountains!
This is not hunter's language; he that strikes
75   The venison first shall be the lord o'th' feast,
To him the other two shall minister,
And we will fear no poison, which attends
In place of greater state. I'll meet you in the valleys.
                     Exeunt Guiderius and Arviragus.
How hard it is to hide the sparks of Nature!
80   These boys know little they are sons to th' king,
Nor Cymbeline dreams that they are alive.
They think they are mine, and though train'd up
      thus meanly,
I'th' cave wherein they bow, their thoughts do hit
The roofs of palaces, and Nature prompts them
85   In simple and low things to prince it, much
Beyond the trick of others. This Polydore,
The heir of Cymbeline and Britain, who
The king his father call'd Guiderius, – Jove!
When on my three-foot stool I sit, and tell
90   The warlike feats I have done, his spirits fly out
Into my story: say 'Thus mine enemy fell,
And thus I set my foot on's neck,' even then
The princely blood flows in his cheek, he sweats,
Strains his young nerves, and puts himself in posture

That acts my words. The younger brother, Cadwal,   95
Once Arviragus, in as like a figure
Strikes life into my speech, and shows much more
His own conceiving. Hark, the game is rous'd!
O Cymbeline, heaven and my conscience knows
Thou didst unjustly banish me: whereon,   100
At three and two years old, I stole these babes,
Thinking to bar thee of succession as
Thou refts me of my lands. Euriphile,
Thou wast their nurse, they took thee for their
      mother,
And every day do honour to her grave: 105
Myself, Belarius, that am Morgan call'd,
They take for natural father. The game is up.   *Exit.*

3.4   *Enter* PISANIO *and* IMOGEN.

IMOGEN
Thou told'st me when we came from horse, the place
Was near at hand: ne'er long'd my mother so
To see me first, as I have now – Pisanio! man!
Where is Posthumus? What is in thy mind
That makes thee stare thus? Wherefore breaks that
      sigh   5
From th'inward of thee? One but painted thus
Would be interpreted a thing perplex'd
Beyond self-explication. Put thyself
Into a haviour of less fear, ere wildness
Vanquish my staider senses. What's the matter?   10
Why tender'st thou that paper to me, with
A look untender? If't be summer news,
Smile to't before: if winterly, thou need'st
But keep that count'nance still. My husband's hand?
That drug-damn'd Italy hath out-craftied him,   15
And he's at some hard point. Speak, man, thy tongue
May take off some extremity, which to read
Would be even mortal to me.

PISANIO   Please you read;
And you shall find me (wretched man) a thing
The most disdain'd of fortune.   20

IMOGEN [*Reads.*]   *Thy mistress, Pisanio, hath played the*
strumpet in my bed: the testimonies whereof lie bleeding in
me. I speak not out of weak surmises, but from proof as
strong as my grief, and as certain as I expect my revenge.
That part thou, Pisanio, must act for me, if thy faith be not   25
tainted with the breach of hers; let thine own hands take
away her life: I shall give thee opportunity at Milford-
Haven: she hath my letter for the purpose: where, if thou
fear to strike, and to make me certain it is done, thou art
the pandar to her dishonour, and equally to me disloyal.   30

PISANIO
What shall I need to draw my sword? the paper
Hath cut her throat already. No, 'tis slander,
Whose edge is sharper than the sword, whose tongue
Outvenoms all the worms of Nile, whose breath
Rides on the posting winds, and doth belie   35
All corners of the world. Kings, queens, and states,

Maids, matrons, nay, the secrets of the grave
This viperous slander enters. What cheer, madam?
IMOGEN   False to his bed? What is it to be false?
40   To lie in watch there, and to think on him?
To weep 'twixt clock and clock? If sleep charge
          Nature,
To break it with a fearful dream of him,
And cry myself awake? That's false to's bed, is it?
PISANIO   Alas, good lady!
45   IMOGEN   I false? Thy conscience witness: Iachimo,
Thou didst accuse him of incontinency;
Thou then look'dst like a villain: now, methinks,
Thy favour's good enough. Some jay of Italy
(Whose mother was her painting) hath betray'd him:
50   Poor I am stale, a garment out of fashion,
And, for I am richer than to hang by th' walls,
I must be ripp'd: – to pieces with me! – O,
Men's vows are women's traitors! All good seeming,
By thy revolt, O husband, shall be thought
55   Put on for villainy; not born where't grows,
But worn a bait for ladies.
PISANIO   Good madam, hear me.
IMOGEN
True honest men, being heard like false Aeneas,
Were in his time thought false: and Sinon's weeping
60   Did scandal many a holy tear, took pity
From most true wretchedness: so thou, Posthumus
Wilt lay the leaven on all proper men;
Goodly and gallant shall be false and perjur'd
From thy great fail. Come fellow, be thou honest
Do thou thy master's bidding. When thou see'st him,
65   A little witness my obedience. Look,
I draw the sword myself, take it, and hit
The innocent mansion of my love, my heart:
Fear not, 'tis empty of all things, but grief:
Thy master is not there, who was indeed
70   The riches of it. Do his bidding, strike.
Thou mayst be valiant in a better cause;
But now thou seem'st a coward.
PISANIO   Hence, vile instrument!
Thou shalt not damn my hand.
IMOGEN   Why, I must die:
And if I do not by thy hand, thou art
75   No servant of thy master's. Against self-slaughter
There is a prohibition so divine
That cravens my weak hand. Come, here's my heart,
(Something's afore't, – soft, soft! we'll no defence)
Obedient as the scabbard. What is here?
80   The scriptures of the loyal Leonatus,
All turn'd to heresy? Away, away,
Corrupters of my faith! you shall no more
Be stomachers to my heart: thus may poor fools
Believe false teachers: though those that are betray'd
85   Do feel the treason sharply, yet the traitor
Stands in worse case of woe.
And thou, Posthumus, thou that didst set up
My disobedience 'gainst the king my father,

And make me put into contempt the suits
Of princely fellows, shalt hereafter find   90
It is no act of common passage, but
A strain of rareness: and I grieve myself
To think, when thou shalt be disedg'd by her
That now thou tirest on, how thy memory
Will then be pang'd by me. Prithee, dispatch: 95
The lamb entreats the butcher. Where's thy knife?
Thou art too slow to do thy master's bidding
When I desire it too.
PISANIO   O gracious lady:
Since I received command to do this business
I have not slept one wink.
IMOGEN   Do't, and to bed then.   100
PISANIO   I'll wake mine eye-balls out first.
IMOGEN   Wherefore then
Didst undertake it? Why hast thou abus'd
So many miles, with a pretence? This place?
Mine action, and thine own? Our horses' labour?
The time inviting thee? The perturb'd court   105
For my being absent? whereunto I never
Purpose return. Why hast thou gone so far,
To be unbent when thou hast ta'en thy stand,
Th'elected deer before thee?
PISANIO   But to win time
To lose so bad employment, in the which   110
I have consider'd of a course: good lady,
Hear me with patience.
IMOGEN   Talk thy tongue weary, speak:
I have heard I am a strumpet, and mine ear,
Therein false struck, can take no greater wound,
Nor tent, to bottom that. But speak.
PISANIO   Then, madam,   115
I thought you would not back again.
IMOGEN   Most like,
Bringing me here to kill me.
PISANIO   Not so, neither:
But if I were as wise as honest, then
My purpose would prove well: it cannot be
But that my master is abus'd: some villain,   120
Ay, and singular in his art, hath done you both
This cursed injury.
IMOGEN   Some Roman courtezan?
PISANIO   No, on my life:
I'll give but notice you are dead, and send him
Some bloody sign of it. For 'tis commanded   125
I should do so: you shall be miss'd at court,
And that will well confirm it.
IMOGEN   Why, good fellow,
What shall I do the while? Where bide? How live?
Or in my life what comfort, when I am
Dead to my husband?
PISANIO   If you'll back to th' court –   130
IMOGEN   No court, no father, nor no more ado
With that harsh, noble, simple nothing,
That Cloten, whose love-suit hath been to me

As fearful as a siege.
PISANIO   If not at court,
  Then not in Britain must you bide.
135 IMOGEN   Where then?
  Hath Britain all the sun that shines? Day? Night?
  Are they not but in Britain? I'th' world's volume
  Our Britain seems as of it, but not in't:
  In a great pool, a swan's nest: prithee think
  There's livers out of Britain.
140 PISANIO   I am most glad
  You think of other place: th'ambassador,
  Lucius the Roman, comes to Milford-Haven
  To-morrow. Now, if you could wear a mind
  Dark, as your fortune is, and but disguise
145 That which, t'appear itself, must not yet be
  But by self-danger, you should tread a course
  Pretty, and full of view; yea, haply, near
  The residence of Posthumus; so nigh (at least)
  That though his actions were not visible, yet
150 Report should render him hourly to your ear
  As truly as he moves.
IMOGEN   O, for such means,
  Though peril to my modesty, not death on't,
  I would adventure!
PISANIO   Well then, here's the point:
  You must forget to be a woman: change
155 Command into obedience: fear, and niceness
  (The handmaids of all women, or, more truly,
  Woman it pretty self) into a waggish courage,
  Ready in gibes, quick-answer'd, saucy, and
  As quarrelous as the weasel: nay, you must
160 Forget that rarest treasure of your cheek,
  Exposing it (but, O, the harder heart!)
  Alack, no remedy) to the greedy touch
  Of common-kissing Titan: and forget
  Your laboursome and dainty trims, wherein
  You made great Juno angry.
165 IMOGEN   Nay, be brief:
  I see into thy end, and am almost
  A man already.
PISANIO   First, make yourself but like one.
  Fore-thinking this, I have already fit
  ('Tis in my cloak-bag) doublet, hat, hose, all
170 That answer to them: would you, in their serving
  (And with what imitation you can borrow
  From youth of such a season) 'fore noble Lucius
  Present yourself, desire his service: tell him
  Wherein you're happy; which will make him know,
175 If that his head have ear in music, doubtless
  With joy he will embrace you: for he's honourable,
  And, doubling that, most holy. Your means abroad:
  You have me, rich, and I will never fail
  Beginning, nor supplyment.
IMOGEN   Thou art all the comfort
180 The gods will diet me with. Prithee away,
  There's more to be consider'd: but we'll even
  All that good time will give us. This attempt

I am soldier to, and will abide it with
  A prince's courage. Away, I prithee.
PISANIO   Well, madam, we must take a short farewell,   185
  Lest being miss'd, I be suspected of
  Your carriage from the court. My noble mistress,
  Here is a box, I had it from the queen,
  What's in't is precious: if you are sick at sea,
  Or stomach-qualm'd at land, a dram of this   190
  Will drive away distemper. To some shade,
  And fit you to your manhood: may the gods
  Direct you to the best!
IMOGEN   Amen: I thank thee.
Exeunt severally.

3.5   *Enter* CYMBELINE, QUEEN, CLOTEN, LUCIUS
and lords.

CYMBELINE   Thus far, and so farewell.
LUCIUS   Thanks, royal sir:
  My emperor hath wrote, I must from hence,
  And am right sorry that I must report ye
  My master's enemy.
CYMBELINE   Our subjects, sir,
  Will not endure his yoke; and for ourself   5
  To show less sovereignty than they, must needs
  Appear unkinglike.
LUCIUS   So, sir: I desire of you
  A conduct over land, to Milford-Haven.
  Madam, all joy befal your grace, and you!
CYMBELINE
  My lords, you are appointed for that office: 10
  The due of honour in no point omit.
  So farewell, noble Lucius.
LUCIUS   Your hand, my lord.
CLOTEN   Receive it friendly: but from this time forth
  I wear it as your enemy.
LUCIUS   Sir, the event
  Is yet to name the winner. Fare you well.   15
CYMBELINE
  Leave not the worthy Lucius, good my lords,
  Till he have cross'd the Severn. Happiness!
Exeunt Lucius and lords.
QUEEN   He goes hence frowning: but it honours us
  That we have given him cause.
CLOTEN   'Tis all the better,
  Your valiant Britons have their wishes in it.   20
CYMBELINE   Lucius hath wrote already to the emperor
  How it goes here. It fits us therefore ripely
  Our chariots and our horsemen be in readiness:
  The powers that he already hath in Gallia
  Will soon be drawn to head, from whence he moves   25
  His war for Britain.
QUEEN   'Tis not sleepy business,
  But must be look'd to speedily, and strongly.
CYMBELINE   Our expectation that it would be thus
  Hath made us forward. But, my gentle queen,
  Where is our daughter? She hath not appear'd   30

Before the Roman, nor to us hath tender'd
The duty of the day. She looks us like
A thing more made of malice than of duty,
We have noted it. Call her before us, for
We have been too slight in sufferance.

Exit an Attendant.

QUEEN   Royal sir,
Since the exile of Posthumus, most retir'd
Hath her life been: the cure whereof, my lord,
'Tis time must do. Beseech your majesty,
Forbear sharp speeches to her. She's a lady
So tender of rebukes that words are strokes,
And strokes death to her.

Re-enter Attendant.

CYMBELINE   Where is she, sir? How
Can her contempt be answer'd?

ATTENDANT   Please you, sir,
Her chambers are all lock'd, and there's no answer
That will be given to th' loud of noise we make.

QUEEN   My lord, when last I went to visit her,
She pray'd me to excuse her keeping close,
Whereto constrain'd by her infirmity,
She should that duty leave unpaid to you
Which daily she was bound to proffer: this
She wish'd me to make known: but our great court
Made me to blame in memory.

CYMBELINE   Her doors lock'd?
Not seen of late? Grant heavens, that which I fear
Prove false!   *Exit.*

QUEEN   Son, I say, follow the king.

CLOTEN   That man of hers, Pisanio, her old servant,
I have not seen these two days.

QUEEN   Go, look after:

Exit Cloten.

Pisanio, thou that stand'st so for Posthumus –
He hath a drug of mine: I pray his absence
Proceed by swallowing that. For he believes
It is a thing most precious. But for her,
Where is she gone? Haply, despair hath seiz'd her:
Or, wing'd with fervour of her love, she's flown
To her desir'd Posthumus: gone she is,
To death, or to dishonour, and my end
Can make good use of either. She being down,
I have the placing of the British crown.

Re-enter CLOTEN.

How now, my son?

CLOTEN   'Tis certain she is fled:
Go in and cheer the king, he rages, none
Dare come about him.

QUEEN [*aside*]   All the better: may
This night forestall him of the coming day!   *Exit.*

CLOTEN   I love, and hate her: for she's fair and royal,
And that she hath all courtly parts more exquisite
Than lady, ladies, woman, from every one
The best she hath, and she of all compounded

Outsells them all. I love her therefore, but   75
Disdaining me, and throwing favours on
The low Posthumus, slanders so her judgement
That what's else rare is chok'd: and in that point
I will conclude to hate her, nay indeed,
To be reveng'd upon her. For, when fools   80
Shall –

Enter PISANIO.

            Who is here? What, are you packing, sirrah?
Come hither: ah, you precious pandar! Villain,
Where is thy lady? In a word, or else
Thou art straightway with the fiends.

PISANIO   O, good my lord!

CLOTEN   Where is thy lady? or, by Jupiter –   85
I will not ask again. Close villain,
I'll have this secret from thy heart, or rip
Thy heart to find it. Is she with Posthumus?
From whose so many weights of baseness cannot
A dram of worth be drawn.

PISANIO   Alas, my lord,   90
How can she be with him? When was she miss'd?
He is in Rome.

CLOTEN   Where is she, sir? Come nearer:
No farther halting: satisfy me home,
What is become of her?

PISANIO   O, my all-worthy lord!

CLOTEN   All-worthy villain!   95
Discover where thy mistress is, at once,
At the next word: no more of 'worthy lord!'
Speak, or thy silence on the instant is
Thy condemnation and thy death.

PISANIO   Then, sir:
This paper is the history of my knowledge   100
Touching her flight. [*presenting a letter*]

CLOTEN   Let's see't: I will pursue her
Even to Augustus' throne.

PISANIO [*aside*]   Or this, or perish.
She's far enough, and what he learns by this
May prove his travel, not her danger.

CLOTEN   Hum!

PISANIO [*aside*]
I'll write to my lord she's dead: O Imogen,   105
Safe mayst thou wander, safe return again!

CLOTEN   Sirrah, is this letter true?

PISANIO   Sir, as I think.

CLOTEN   It is Posthumus' hand, I know't. Sirrah, if thou
wouldst not be a villain, but do me true service,   110
undergo those employments wherein I should have
cause to use thee with a serious industry, that is,
what villainy soe'er I bid thee do, to perform it,
directly and truly, I would think thee an honest man:
thou shouldst neither want my means for thy relief,   115
nor my voice for thy preferment.

PISANIO   Well, my good lord.

CLOTEN   Wilt thou serve me? For since patiently and
constantly thou hast stuck to the bare fortune of that

120 beggar Posthumus, thou canst not in the course of
gratitude but be a diligent follower of mine. Wilt
thou serve me?
PISANIO   Sir, I will.
CLOTEN   Give me thy hand, here's my purse. Hast any
125 of thy late master's garments in thy possession?
PISANIO   I have my lord, at my lodging the same suit he
wore when he took leave of my lady and mistress.
CLOTEN   The first service thou dost me, fetch that suit
hither, let it be thy first service, go.
130 PISANIO   I shall, my lord.   *Exit.*
CLOTEN   Meet thee at Milford-Haven! (I forgot to ask
him one thing, I'll remember't anon) even there, thou
villain Posthumus, will I kill thee. I would these
garments were come. She said upon a time (the
135 bitterness of it I now belch from my heart) that she
held the very garment of Posthumus in more respect
than my noble and natural person; together with the
adornment of my qualities. With that suit upon my
back, will I ravish her: first kill him, and in her eyes;
140 there shall she see my valour, which will then be a
torment to her contempt. He on the ground, my
speech of insultment ended on his dead body, and
when my lust hath dined (which, as I say, to vex her I
will execute in the clothes that she so prais'd) to the
145 court I'll knock her back, foot her home again. She
hath despis'd me rejoicingly, and I'll be merry in my
revenge.

Re-enter PISANIO, *with the clothes.*

Be those the garments?
PISANIO   Ay, my noble lord.
150 CLOTEN   How long is't since she went to Milford-
Haven?
PISANIO   She can scarce be there yet.
CLOTEN   Bring this apparel to my chamber, that is the
second thing that I have commanded thee. The third
155 is, that thou wilt be a voluntary mute to my design. Be
but duteous, and true preferment shall tender itself to
thee. My revenge is now at Milford: would I had wings
to follow it! Come, and be true.   *Exit.*
PISANIO   Thou bid'st me to my loss: for true to thee
160 Were to prove false, which I will never be,
To him that is most true. To Milford go,
And find not her whom thou pursuest. Flow, flow,
You heavenly blessings, on her! This fool's speed
Be cross'd with slowness; labour be his meed!   *Exit.*

3.6   *Enter* IMOGEN, *in boy's clothes.*

IMOGEN   I see a man's life is a tedious one,
I have tir'd myself: and for two nights together
Have made the ground my bed. I should be sick,
But that my resolution helps me: Milford,
5 When from the mountain-top Pisanio show'd thee,
Thou was within a ken. O Jove! I think
Foundations fly the wretched: such, I mean,
Where they should be reliev'd. Two beggars told me

I could not miss my way. Will poor folks lie,
That have afflictions on them, knowing 'tis   10
A punishment, or trial? Yes; no wonder,
When rich ones scarce tell true. To lapse in fulness
Is sorer than to lie for need: and falsehood
Is worse in kings than beggars. My dear lord,
Thou art one o'th' false ones! Now I think on thee, 15
My hunger's gone; but even before, I was
At point to sink, for food. – But what is this?
Here is a path to't: 'tis some savage hold:
I were best not call; I dare not call: yet famine,
Ere clean it o'erthrow Nature, makes it valiant.   20
Plenty and peace breeds cowards: hardness ever
Of hardiness is mother. Ho! who's here?
If any thing that's civil, speak: if savage,
Take, or lend. Ho! No answer? Then I'll enter.
Best draw my sword; and if mine enemy   25
But fear the sword like me, he'll scarcely look on't.
Such a foe, good heavens!   *Exit, to the cave.*

3.7   *Enter* BELARIUS, GUIDERIUS *and* ARVIRAGUS.

BELARIUS
You, Polydore, have prov'd best woodman, and
Are master of the feast: Cadwal and I
Will play the cook and servant, 'tis our match:
The sweat and industry would dry and die,
But for the end it works to. Come, our stomachs   5
Will make what's homely savoury: weariness
Can snore upon the flint, when resty sloth
Finds the down-pillow hard. Now peace be here,
Poor house, that keep'st thyself!
GUIDERIUS   I am throughly weary.
ARVIRAGUS   I am weak with toil, yet strong in appetite. 10
GUIDERIUS
There is cold meat i'th' cave, we'll browse on that,
Whilst what we have kill'd be cook'd.
BELARIUS [*looking into the cave*]   Stay, come not in:
But that it eats our victuals, I should think
Here were a fairy.
GUIDERIUS   What's the matter, sir?
BELARIUS   By Jupiter, an angel! or, if not,   15
An earthly paragon! Behold divineness
No elder than a boy!

Enter IMOGEN.

IMOGEN   Good masters, harm me not:
Before I enter'd here, I call'd, and thought
To have begg'd or bought what I have took: good
troth,   20
I have stol'n nought, nor would not, though I had
found
Gold strew'd i'th' floor. Here's money for my meat,
I would have left it on the board, so soon
As I had made my meal; and parted
With pray'rs for the provider.
GUIDERIUS   Money, youth?   25
ARVIRAGUS   All gold and silver rather turn to dirt,

As 'tis no better reckon'd, but of those
Who worship dirty gods.

IMOGEN   I see you're angry:
Know, if you kill me for my fault, I should
Have died had I not made it.

30 BELARIUS   Whither bound?

IMOGEN   To Milford-Haven.

BELARIUS   What's your name?

IMOGEN   Fidele, sir: I have a kinsman who
Is bound for Italy; he embark'd at Milford;
35 To whom being going, almost spent with hunger,
I am fall'n in this offence.

BELARIUS   Prithee, fair youth,
Think us no churls: nor measure our good minds
By this rude place we live in. Well encounter'd!
'Tis almost night, you shall have better cheer
40 Ere you depart; and thanks to stay and eat it:
Boys, bid him welcome.

GUIDERIUS   Were you a woman, youth,
I should woo hard, but be your groom in honesty:
I bid for you as I do buy.

ARVIRAGUS   I'll make't my comfort
He is a man, I'll love him as my brother:
45 And such a welcome as I'd give to him
(After long absence) such is yours. Most welcome!
Be sprightly, for you fall 'mongst friends.

IMOGEN   'Mongst friends?
If brothers: [aside] would it had been so, that they
Had been my father's sons, then had my prize
50 Been less, and so more equal ballasting
To thee, Posthumus.

BELARIUS   He wrings at some distress.

GUIDERIUS   Would I could free't!

ARVIRAGUS   Or I, whate'er it be,
What pain it cost, what danger! Gods!

BELARIUS [whispering]   Hark, boys.

IMOGEN   Great men,
55 That had a court no bigger than this cave,
That did attend themselves, and had the virtue
Which their own conscience seal'd them, laying by
That nothing-gift of differing multitudes,
Could not out-peer these twain. Pardon me, gods!
60 I'ld change my sex to be companion with them,
Since Leonatus false.

BELARIUS   It shall be so:
Boys, we'll go dress our hunt. Fair youth, come in;
Discourse is heavy, fasting: when we have supp'd
We'll mannerly demand thee of thy story,
So far as thou wilt speak it.

65 GUIDERIUS   Pray, draw near.

ARVIRAGUS
The night to th'owl and morn to th' lark less
welcome.

IMOGEN   Thanks, sir.

ARVIRAGUS   I pray, draw near.   *Exeunt.*

3.8   *Enter two* Senators *and* Tribunes.

1 SENATOR
This is the tenour of the emperor's writ;
That since the common men are now in action
'Gainst the Pannonians and Dalmatians,
And that the legions now in Gallia are
Full weak to undertake our wars against   5
The fall'n-off Britons, that we do incite
The gentry to this business. He creates
Lucius proconsul: and to you the tribunes,
For this immediate levy, he commands
His absolute commission. Long live Caesar!   10

1 TRIBUNE   Is Lucius general of the forces?

2 SENATOR   Ay.

1 TRIBUNE   Remaining now in Gallia?

1 SENATOR   With those legions
Which I have spoke of, whereunto your levy
Must be supplyant: the words of your commission
Will tie you to the numbers and the time   15
Of their despatch.

1 TRIBUNE   We will discharge our duty.
Exeunt.

4.1   *Enter* CLOTEN *alone.*

CLOTEN   I am near to th' place where they should meet,
if Pisanio have mapp'd it truly. How fit his garments
serve me! Why should his mistress who was made by
him that made the tailor, not be fit too? The rather
(saving reverence of the word) for 'tis said a woman's   5
fitness comes by fits. Therein I must play the
workman, I dare speak it to myself, for it is not vainglory for a man and his glass to confer in his own
chamber; I mean, the lines of my body are as well
drawn as his; no less young, more strong, not beneath   10
him in fortunes, beyond him in the advantage of the
time, above him in birth, alike conversant in general
services, and more remarkable in single oppositions;
yet this imperseverant thing loves him in my despite.
What mortality is! Posthumus, thy head (which now is   15
growing upon thy shoulders) shall within this hour
be off, thy mistress enforced, thy garments cut to
pieces before thy face: and all this done, spurn her
home to her father, who may (haply) be a little angry
for my so rough usage: but my mother, having power   20
of his testiness, shall turn all into my commendations.
My horse is tied up safe, out, sword, and to a sore
purpose! Fortune, put them into my hand! This is the
very description of their meeting-place, and the fellow
dares not deceive me.   *Exit.*   25

4.2   *Enter* BELARIUS, GUIDERIUS, ARVIRAGUS
and IMOGEN *from the cave.*

BELARIUS [to Imogen]
You are not well: remain here in the cave,
We'll come to you after hunting.

ARVIRAGUS [to Imogen]   Brother, stay here:

Are we not brothers?

IMOGEN   So man and man should be;
But clay and clay differs in dignity,
Whose dust is both alike. I am very sick.

GUIDERIUS   Go you to hunting, I'll abide with him.

IMOGEN   So sick I am not, yet I am not well:
But not so citizen a wanton as
To seem to die ere sick: so please you, leave me,
Stick to your journal course: the breach of custom
Is breach of all. I am ill, but your being by me
Cannot amend me. Society is no comfort
To one not sociable: I am not very sick,
Since I can reason of it: pray you, trust me here,
I'll rob none but myself, and let me die,
Stealing so poorly.

GUIDERIUS   I love thee: I have spoke it,
How much the quantity, the weight as much,
As I do love my father.

BELARIUS   What? How? How?

ARVIRAGUS   If it be sin to say so, sir, I yoke me
In my good brother's fault: I know not why
I love this youth, and I have heard you say,
Love's reason's without reason. The bier at door,
And a demand who is't shall die, I'd say
'My father, not this youth.'

BELARIUS [*aside*]   O noble strain!
O worthiness of nature! breed of greatness!
Cowards father cowards, and base things sire base;
Nature hath meal, and bran; contempt, and grace.
I'm not their father, yet who this should be,
Doth miracle itself, lov'd before me. –
'Tis the ninth hour o' th' morn.

ARVIRAGUS   Brother, farewell.

IMOGEN   I wish ye sport.

ARVIRAGUS   You health. – So please you, sir.

IMOGEN [*aside*]
These are kind creatures. Gods, what lies I have
    heard!
Our courtiers say all's savage but at court;
Experience, O, thou disprov'st report!
Th'emperious seas breed monsters; for the dish
Poor tributary rivers as sweet fish:
I am sick still, heart-sick; Pisanio,
I'll now taste of thy drug.

GUIDERIUS   I could not stir him:
He said he was gentle, but unfortunate;
Dishonestly afflicted, but yet honest.

ARVIRAGUS   Thus did he answer me: yet said, hereafter
I might know more.

BELARIUS   To th' field, to th' field!
We'll leave you for this time, go in, and rest.

ARVIRAGUS   We'll not be long away.

BELARIUS   Pray be not sick,
For you must be our housewife.

IMOGEN   Well, or ill,
I am bound to you.

BELARIUS   And shalt be ever.

Exit Imogen, to the cave.

This youth, howe'er distress'd, appears he hath had
Good ancestors.

ARVIRAGUS   How angel-like he sings!

GUIDERIUS
But his neat cookery! he cut our roots in characters,
And sauced our broths, as Juno had been sick,
And he her dieter.

ARVIRAGUS   Nobly he yokes
A smiling with a sigh; as if the sigh
Was that it was, for not being such a smile;
The smile mocking the sigh, that it would fly
From so divine a temple, to commix
With winds that sailors rail at.

GUIDERIUS   I do note
That grief and patience, rooted in them both,
Mingle their spurs together.

ARVIRAGUS   Grow, patience!
And let the stinking-elder, grief, untwine
His perishing root, with the increasing vine!

BELARIUS
It is great morning. Come, away! – who's there?

Enter CLOTEN.

CLOTEN   I cannot find those runagates, that villain
Hath mock'd me. I am faint.

BELARIUS   'Those runagates!'
Means he not us? I partly know him, 'tis
Cloten, the son o'th' queen. I fear some ambush:
I saw him not these many years, and yet
I know 'tis he: we are held as outlaws: hence!

GUIDERIUS   He is but one: you, and my brother search
What companies are near: pray you, away,
Let me alone with him.

Exeunt Belarius and Arviragus.

CLOTEN   Soft, what are you
That fly me thus? Some villain mountaineers?
I have heard of such. What slave art thou?

GUIDERIUS   A thing
More slavish did I ne'er than answering
A slave without a knock.

CLOTEN   Thou art a robber,
A law-breaker, a villain: yield thee, thief.

GUIDERIUS
To who? to thee? What art thou? Have not I
An arm as big as thine? a heart as big?
Thy words I grant are bigger: for I wear not
My dagger in my mouth. Say what thou art:
Why I should yield to thee.

CLOTEN   Thou villain base,
Know'st me not by my clothes?

GUIDERIUS   No, nor thy tailor, rascal,
Who is thy grandfather: he made those clothes,
Which (as it seems) make thee.

CLOTEN   Thou precious varlet,
My tailor made them not.

GUIDERIUS   Hence then, and thank
The man that gave them thee. Thou art some fool,

I am loath to beat thee.

CLOTEN   Thou injurious thief,
Hear but my name, and tremble.

GUIDERIUS   What's thy name?

CLOTEN   Cloten, thou villain.

GUIDERIUS   Cloten, thou double villain, be thy name,
I cannot tremble at it, were it Toad, or Adder,
    Spider,
'Twould move me sooner.

CLOTEN   To thy further fear,
Nay, to thy mere confusion, thou shalt know
I am son to th' queen.

GUIDERIUS   I am sorry for't: not seeming
So worthy as thy birth.

CLOTEN   Art not afeard?

GUIDERIUS
Those that I reverence, those I fear: the wise:
At fools I laugh: not fear them.

CLOTEN   Die the death:
When I have slain thee with my proper hand,
I'll follow those that even now fled hence:
And on the gates of Lud's town set your heads:
Yield, rustic mountaineer.   *Exeunt, fighting.*

Re-enter BELARIUS *and* ARVIRAGUS.

BELARIUS   No company's abroad?

ARVIRAGUS
None in the world: you did mistake him sure.

BELARIUS   I cannot tell: long is it since I saw him,
But time hath nothing blurr'd those lines of favour
Which then he wore: the snatches in his voice,
And burst of speaking were as his: I am absolute
'Twas very Cloten.

ARVIRAGUS   In this place we left them;
I wish my brother make good time with him,
You say he is so fell.

BELARIUS   Being scarce made up,
I mean, to man, he had not apprehension
Of roaring terrors: for defect of judgement
Is oft the cause of fear. But see, thy brother.

Re-enter GUIDERIUS *with Cloten's head.*

GUIDERIUS   This Cloten was a fool, an empty purse,
There was no money in't: not Hercules
Could have knock'd out his brains, for he had none:
Yet I not doing this, the fool had borne
My head, as I do his.

BELARIUS   What hast thou done?

GUIDERIUS
I am perfect what: cut off one Cloten's head,
Son to the queen (after his own report),
Who call'd me traitor, mountaineer, and swore,
With his own single hand he'ld take us in,
Displace our heads where (thank the gods!) they
    grow,
And set them on Lud's town.

BELARIUS   We are all undone.

GUIDERIUS   Why, worthy father, what have we to lose,
But that he swore to take, our lives? The law
Protects not us, then why should we be tender,
To let an arrogant piece of flesh threat us,
Play judge, and executioner, all himself,
For we do fear the law? What company
Discover you abroad?

BELARIUS   No single soul
Can we set eye on; but in all safe reason
He must have some attendants. Though his honour
Was nothing but mutation, ay, and that
From one bad thing to worse, not frenzy, not
Absolute madness could so far have rav'd,
To bring him here alone: although perhaps
It may be heard at court that such as we
Cave here, hunt here, are outlaws, and in time
May make some stronger head, the which he hearing
(As it is like him) might break out, and swear
He'ld fetch us in, yet is't not probable
To come alone, either he so undertaking,
Or they so suffering: then on good ground we fear,
If we do fear this body hath a tail
More perilous than the head.

ARVIRAGUS   Let ordinance
Come as the gods foresay it: howsoe'er,
My brother hath done well.

BELARIUS   I had no mind
To hunt this day: the boy Fidele's sickness
Did make my way long forth.

GUIDERIUS   With his own sword,
Which he did wave against my throat, I have ta'en
His head from him: I'll throw't into the creek
Behind our rock, and let it to the sea,
And tell the fishes he's the queen's son, Cloten,
That's all I reck.   *Exit.*

BELARIUS   I fear 'twill be reveng'd:
Would, Polydore, thou hadst not done't: though
    valour
Becomes thee well enough.

ARVIRAGUS   Would I had done't:
So the revenge alone pursued me! Polydore,
I love thee brotherly, but envy much
Thou hast robb'd me of this deed: I would revenges,
That possible strength might meet, would seek us
    through
And put us to our answer.

BELARIUS   Well, 'tis done:
We'll hunt no more to-day, nor seek for danger
Where there's no profit. I prithee, to our rock,
You and Fidele play the cooks: I'll stay
Till hasty Polydore return, and bring him
To dinner presently.

ARVIRAGUS   Poor sick Fidele!
I'll willingly to him; to gain his colour
I'ld let a parish of such Clotens blood,
And praise myself for charity.   *Exit.*

BELARIUS   O thou goddess,

170 Thou divine Nature; thou thyself thou blazon'st
In these two princely boys: they are as gentle
As zephyrs blowing below the violet,
Not wagging his sweet head; and yet, as rough,
(Their royal blood enchaf'd) as the rud'st wind
175 That by the top doth take the mountain pine
And make him stoop to th' vale. 'Tis wonder
That an invisible instinct should frame them
To royalty unlearn'd, honour untaught,
Civility not seen from other, valour
180 That wildly grows in them, but yields a crop
As if it had been sow'd. Yet still it's strange
What Cloten's being here to us portends,
Or what his death will bring us.

Re-enter GUIDERIUS.

GUIDERIUS   Where's my brother?
I have sent Cloten's clotpoll down the stream,
185 In embassy to his mother; his body's hostage
For his return.   [*Solemn music.*]
BELARIUS   My ingenious instrument
(Hark, Polydore) it sounds: but what occasion
Hath Cadwal now to give it motion? Hark!
GUIDERIUS
Is he at home?
BELARIUS   He went hence even now.
GUIDERIUS
What does he mean? Since death of my dear'st
190   mother
It did not speak before. All solemn things
Should answer solemn accidents. The matter?
Triumphs for nothing, and lamenting toys,
Is jollity for apes, and grief for boys.
Is Cadwal mad?

Re-enter ARVIRAGUS *with* IMOGEN, *dead, bearing*
her in his arms.

195 BELARIUS   Look, here he comes,
And brings the dire occasion in his arms
Of what we blame him for!
ARVIRAGUS   The bird is dead
That we have made so much on. I had rather
Have skipp'd from sixteen years of age to sixty:
200 To have turn'd my leaping time into a crutch,
Than have seen this.
GUIDERIUS   O sweetest, fairest lily:
My brother wears thee not the one half so well
As when thou grew'st thyself.
BELARIUS   O melancholy,
Who ever yet could sound thy bottom, find
205 The ooze, to show what coast thy sluggish care
Might'st easil'est harbour in? Thou blessed thing,
Jove knows what man thou mightst have made: but I,
Thou diedst a most rare boy, of melancholy.
How found you him?
ARVIRAGUS   Stark, as you see:
210 Thus smiling, as some fly had tickled slumber,

Not as death's dart, being laugh'd at: his right cheek
Reposing on a cushion.
GUIDERIUS   Where?
ARVIRAGUS   O'th' floor;
His arms thus leagu'd, I thought he slept, and put
My clouted brogues from off my feet, whose
      rudeness
Answer'd my steps too loud.
GUIDERIUS   Why, he but sleeps: 215
If he be gone, he'll make his grave a bed:
With female fairies will his tomb be haunted,
And worms will not come to thee.
ARVIRAGUS   With fairest flowers
Whilst summer lasts, and I live here, Fidele,
I'll sweeten thy sad grave: thou shalt not lack   220
The flower that's like thy face, pale primrose, nor
The azur'd harebell, like thy veins: no, nor
The leaf of eglantine, whom not to slander,
Out-sweet'ned not thy breath: the ruddock would
With charitable bill (O bill, sore shaming   225
Those rich-left heirs, that let their fathers lie
Without a monument!) bring thee all this;
Yea, and furr'd moss besides. When flowers are none,
To winter-ground thy corse –
GUIDERIUS   Prithee, have done,
And do not play in wench-like words with that   230
Which is so serious. Let us bury him,
And not protract with admiration what
Is now due debt. To th' grave!
ARVIRAGUS   Say, where shall's lay him?
GUIDERIUS   By good Euriphile, our mother.
ARVIRAGUS   Be't so:
And let us, Polydore, though now our voices   235
Have got the mannish crack, sing him to th' ground,
As once to our mother: use like note and words,
Save that Euriphile must be Fidele.
GUIDERIUS   Cadwal,
I cannot sing: I'll weep, and word it with thee;   240
For notes of sorrow out of tune are worse
Than priests and fanes that lie.
ARVIRAGUS   We'll speak it then.
BELARIUS
Great griefs, I see, med'cine the less; for Cloten
Is quite forgot. He was a queen's son, boys,
And though he came our enemy, remember,   245
He was paid for that: though mean and mighty,
      rotting
Together, have one dust, yet reverence
(That angel of the world) doth make distinction
Of place 'tween high, and low. Our foe was princely,
And though you took his life, as being our foe,   250
Yet bury him, as a prince.
GUIDERIUS   Pray you, fetch him hither,
Thersites' body is as good as Ajax',
When neither are alive.
ARVIRAGUS   If you'll go fetch him,
We'll say our song the whilst. – Brother, begin.
                                            Exit Belarius.

GUIDERIUS
255   Nay, Cadwal, we must lay his head to the east,
            My father hath a reason for't.
ARVIRAGUS   'Tis true.
GUIDERIUS Come on then, and remove him.
ARVIRAGUS   So, – Begin.

                              Song.

GUIDERIUS Fear no more the heat o'th' sun,
                  Nor the furious winter's rages,
260   Thou thy worldly task has done,
                  Home art gone and ta'en thy wages.
            Golden lads and girls all must,
            As chimney-sweepers, come to dust.

ARVIRAGUS Fear no more the frown o'th' great,
265   Thou art past the tyrant's stroke,
            Care no more to clothe and eat,
                  To thee the reed is as the oak:
            The sceptre, learning, physic, must
            All follow this and come to dust.

270 GUIDERIUS Fear no more the lightning-flash.
    ARVIRAGUS   Nor th'all-dreaded thunder-stone.
    GUIDERIUS Fear not slander, censure rash.
    ARVIRAGUS   Thou hast finish'd joy and moan.
    BOTH   All lovers young, all lovers must
275   Consign to thee and come to dust.

    GUIDERIUS No exorciser harm thee!
    ARVIRAGUS Nor no witchcraft charm thee!
    GUIDERIUS Ghost unlaid forbear thee!
    ARVIRAGUS Nothing ill come near thee!
280 BOTH   Quiet consummation have,
               And renowned be thy grave!

        Re-enter BELARIUS *with the body of Cloten.*

GUIDERIUS
    We have done our obsequies: come, lay him down.
BELARIUS
    Here's a few flowers, but 'bout midnight more:
    The herbs that have on them cold dew o'th' night
285 Are strewings fitt'st for graves: upon their faces.
    You were as flowers, now wither'd: even so
    These herblets shall, which we upon you strew.
    Come on, away, apart upon our knees:
    The ground that gave them first has them again:
290 Their pleasures here are past, so is their pain.
        Exeunt Belarius, Guiderius and Arviragus.
IMOGEN [*awakes*]
    Yes sir, to Milford-Haven, which is the way?
    I thank you: by yond bush? pray, how far thither?
    'Ods pittikins: can it be six mile yet?
    I have gone all night: faith, I'll lie down and sleep.
295 But, soft! no bedfellow! O gods and goddesses!
    [*seeing the body of Cloten*]
    These flowers are like the pleasures of the world;
    This bloody man, the care on't. I hope I dream:

    For so I thought I was a cave-keeper,
    And cook to honest creatures. But 'tis not so:
    'Twas but a bolt of nothing, shot at nothing,   300
    Which the brain makes of fumes. Our very eyes
    Are sometimes like our judgements, blind. Good
        faith,
    I tremble still with fear: but if there be
    Yet left in heaven as small a drop of pity
    As a wren's eye, fear'd gods, a part of it!   305
    The dream's here still: even when I wake it is
    Without me, as within me: not imagin'd, felt.
    A headless man? The garments of Posthumus?
    I know the shape of's leg: this is his hand:
    His foot Mercurial: his Martial thigh: 310
    The brawns of Hercules: but his Jovial face –
    Murder in heaven! How – ? 'Tis gone. Pisanio,
    All curses madded Hecuba gave the Greeks,
    And mine to boot, be darted on thee! Thou,
    Conspir'd with that irregulous devil, Cloten,   315
    Hast here cut off my lord. To write, and read
    Be henceforth treacherous! Damn'd Pisanio
    Hath with his forged letters (damn'd Pisanio)
    From this most bravest vessel of the world
    Struck the main-top! O Posthumus, alas,   320
    Where is thy head? where's that? Ay me! where's
        that?
    Pisanio might have kill'd thee at the heart,
    And left this head on. How should this be, Pisanio?
    'Tis he, and Cloten: malice and lucre in them
    Have laid this woe here. O, 'tis pregnant, pregnant!   325
    The drug he gave me, which he said was precious
    And cordial to me, have I not found it
    Murd'rous to th' senses? That confirms it home:
    This is Pisanio's deed, and Cloten – O!
    Give colour to my pale cheek with thy blood,   330
    That we the horrider may seem to those
    Which chance to find us. O, my lord! my lord!
    [*Falls on the body.*]

        Enter LUCIUS, Captains *and a* Soothsayer.

CAPTAIN   To them, the legions garrison'd in Gallia
    After your will have cross'd the sea, attending
    You here at Milford-Haven, with your ships: 335
    They are in readiness.
LUCIUS   But what from Rome?
CAPTAIN   The senate hath stirr'd up the confiners
    And gentlemen of Italy, most willing spirits,
    That promise noble service: and they come
    Under the conduct of bold Iachimo,   340
    Siena's brother.
LUCIUS   When expect you them?
CAPTAIN   With the next benefit o'th' wind.
LUCIUS   This forwardness
    Makes our hopes fair. Command our present
        numbers
    Be muster'd; bid the captains look to't. Now sir,
    What have you dream'd of late of this war's purpose?   345

SOOTHSAYER
    Last night the very gods show'd me a vision
    (I fast, and pray'd for their intelligence) thus:
    I saw Jove's bird, the Roman eagle, wing'd
    From the spongy south to this part of the west,
350   There vanish'd in the sunbeams, which portends
    (Unless my sins abuse my divination)
    Success to th' Roman host.
LUCIUS   Dream often so,
    And never false. Soft ho, what trunk is here?
    Without his top? The ruin speaks that sometime
355   It was a worthy building. How? a page?
    Or dead, or sleeping on him? But dead rather:
    For nature doth abhor to make his bed
    With the defunct, or sleep upon the dead.
    Let's see the boy's face.
CAPTAIN   He's alive, my lord.
LUCIUS
360   He'll then instruct us of this body. Young one,
    Inform us of thy fortunes, for it seems
    They crave to be demanded. Who is this
    Thou mak'st thy bloody pillow? Or who was he
    That (otherwise than noble Nature did)
365   Hath alter'd that good picture? What's thy interest
    In this sad wreck? How came't? Who is't?
    What art thou?
IMOGEN   I am nothing; or if not,
    Nothing to be were better. This was my master,
    A very valiant Briton, and a good,
370   That here by mountaineers lies slain. Alas!
    There is no more such masters: I may wander
    From east to occident, cry out for service,
    Try many, all good: serve truly: never
    Find such another master.
LUCIUS   'Lack, good youth!
375   Thou mov'st no less with thy complaining than
    Thy master in bleeding: say his name, good friend.
IMOGEN
    Richard du Champ: [*aside*] if I do lie, and do
    No harm by it, though the gods hear, I hope
    They'll pardon it. Say you, sir?
LUCIUS   Thy name?
IMOGEN   Fidele, sir.
LUCIUS
380   Thou dost approve thyself the very same:
    Thy name well fits thy faith; thy faith thy name:
    Wilt take thy chance with me? I will not say
    Thou shalt be so well master'd, but be sure
    No less belov'd. The Roman emperor's letters
385   Sent by a consul to me should not sooner
    Than thine own worth prefer thee: go with me.
IMOGEN   I'll follow, sir. But first, an't please the gods,
    I'll hide my master from the flies, as deep
    As these poor pickaxes can dig: and when
    With wild wood-leaves and weeds I ha' strew'd his
390   grave
    And on it said a century of prayers

    (Such as I can) twice o'er, I'll weep and sigh,
    And leaving so his service, follow you,
    So please you entertain me.
LUCIUS   Ay, good youth;
    And rather father thee than master thee.   395
    My friends,
    The boy hath taught us manly duties: let us
    Find out the prettiest daisied plot we can,
    And make him with our pikes and partisans
    A grave: come, arm him. Boy, he is preferr'd   400
    By thee to us, and he shall be interr'd
    As soldiers can. Be cheerful, wipe thine eyes:
    Some falls are means the happier to arise.   *Exeunt.*

4.3 *Enter* CYMBELINE, Lords, PISANIO *and attendants.*

CYMBELINE
    Again: and bring me word how 'tis with her.
                   Exit an attendant.
    A fever with the absence of her son;
    A madness, of which her life's in danger: heavens,
    How deeply you at once do touch me! Imogen,
    The great part of my comfort gone: my queen   5
    Upon a desperate bed, and in a time
    When fearful wars point at me: her son gone,
    So needful for this present. It strikes me, past
    The hope of comfort. But for thee, fellow,
    Who needs must know of her departure, and   10
    Dost seem so ignorant, we'll enforce it from thee
    By a sharp torture.
PISANIO   Sir, my life is yours,
    I humbly set it at your will: but, for my mistress,
    I nothing know where she remains: why gone,
    Nor when she purposes return. Beseech your
      highness,   15
    Hold me your loyal servant.
1 LORD   Good my liege,
    The day that she was missing, he was here:
    I dare be bound he's true, and shall perform
    All parts of his subjection loyally. For Cloten,
    There wants no diligence in seeking him,   20
    And will no doubt be found.
CYMBELINE   The time is troublesome:
    [*to Pisanio*] We'll slip you for a season, but our
      jealousy
    Does yet depend.
1 LORD   So please your majesty,
    The Roman legions, all from Gallia drawn,
    Are landed on your coast, with a supply   25
    Of Roman gentlemen, by the Senate sent.
CYMBELINE   Now for the counsel of my son and queen,
    I am amaz'd with matter.
1 LORD   Good my liege,
    Your preparation can affront no less
    Than what you hear of. Come more, for more you're
      ready: 30
    The want is but to put those powers in motion

That long to move.

CYMBELINE   I thank you: let's withdraw
And meet the time, as it seeks us. We fear not
What can from Italy annoy us, but
35   We grieve at chances here. Away!

Exeunt Cymbeline, Lords and attendants.

PISANIO   I heard no letter from my master since
I wrote him Imogen was slain. 'Tis strange:
Nor hear I from my mistress, who did promise
To yield me often tidings. Neither know I
40   What is betid to Cloten, but remain
Perplex'd in all. The heavens still must work.
Wherein I am false, I am honest; not true, to be true.
These present wars shall find I love my country,
Even to the note o'th' king, or I'll fall in them:
45   All other doubts, by time let them be clear'd,
Fortune brings in some boats that are not steer'd.

Exit.

4.4   *Enter* BELARIUS, GUIDERIUS *and* ARVIRAGUS.

GUIDERIUS   The noise is round about us.

BELARIUS   Let us from it.

ARVIRAGUS   What pleasure, sir, we find in life, to lock it
From action and adventure.

GUIDERIUS   Nay, what hope
Have we in hiding us? This way, the Romans
5   Must or for Britons slay us or receive us
For barbarous and unnatural revolts
During their use, and slay us after.

BELARIUS   Sons,
We'll higher to the mountains, there secure us.
To the king's party there's no going: newness
10   Of Cloten's death (we being not known, not muster'd
Among the bands) may drive us to a render
Where we have liv'd, and so extort from's that
Which we have done, whose answer would be death
Drawn on with torture.

GUIDERIUS   This is, sir, a doubt
15   In such a time nothing becoming you,
Nor satisfying us.

ARVIRAGUS   It is not likely
That when they hear their Roman horses neigh,
Behold their quarter'd fires; have both their eyes
20   And ears so cloy'd importantly as now,
That they will waste their time upon our note,
To know from whence we are.

BELARIUS   O, I am known
Of many in the army: many years
(Though Cloten then but young) you see, not wore
    him
From my remembrance. And besides, the king
25   Hath not deserv'd my service nor your loves,
Who find in my exile the want of breeding,
The certainty of this hard life, aye hopeless
To have the courtesy your cradle promis'd,
But to be still hot Summer's tanlings, and

The shrinking slaves of Winter.

GUIDERIUS   Than be so,   30
Better to cease to be. Pray, sir, to th'army:
I and my brother are not known; yourself
So out of thought, and thereto so o'ergrown,
Cannot be question'd.

ARVIRAGUS   By this sun that shines
I'll thither: what thing is't that I never   35
Did see man die, scarce ever look'd on blood,
But that of coward hares, hot goats, and venison!
Never bestrid a horse, save one that had
A rider like myself, who ne'er wore rowel,
Nor iron on his heel! I am ashamed   40
To look upon the holy sun, to have
The benefit of his blest beams, remaining
So long a poor unknown.

GUIDERIUS   By heavens, I'll go,
If you will bless me, sir, and give me leave,
I'll take the better care: but if you will not,   45
The hazard therefore due fall on me by
The hands of Romans!

ARVIRAGUS   So say I, amen.

BELARIUS   No reason I (since of your lives you set
So slight a valuation) should reserve
My crack'd one to more care. Have with you, boys!   50
If in your country wars you chance to die,
That is my bed too, lads, and there I'll lie.
Lead, lead. The time seems long, their blood thinks
    scorn
Till it fly out and show them princes born.   *Exeunt.*

5.1   *Enter* POSTHUMUS *alone.*

POSTHUMUS
Yea, bloody cloth, I'll keep thee: for I wish'd
Thou shouldst be colour'd thus. You married ones,
If each of you should take this course, how many
Must murder wives much better than themselves
For wrying but a little? O Pisanio,   5
Every good servant does not all commands:
No bond, but to do just ones. Gods, if you
Should have ta'en vengeance on my faults, I never
Had liv'd to put on this: so had you saved
The noble Imogen, to repent, and struck   10
Me, wretch, more worth your vengeance. But alack,
You snatch some hence for little faults; that's love,
To have them fall no more: you some permit
To second ills with ills, each elder worse,
And make them dread it, to the doers' thrift.   15
But Imogen is your own, do your best wills,
And make me blest to obey. I am brought hither
Among th'Italian gentry, and to fight
Against my lady's kingdom: 'tis enough
That, Britain, I have kill'd thy mistress: peace,   20
I'll give no wound to thee: therefore, good heavens,
Hear patiently my purpose. I'll disrobe me
Of these Italian weeds, and suit myself

25 As does a Briton peasant: so I'll fight
Against the part I come with: so I'll die
For thee, O Imogen, even for whom my life
Is, every breath, a death: and thus, unknown,
Pitied, nor hated, to the face of peril
30 Myself I'll dedicate. Let me make men know
More valour in me than my habits show.
Gods, put the strength o'th' Leonati in me!
To shame the guise o'th' world, I will begin,
The fashion less without, and more within.   *Exit.*

5.2 *Enter* LUCIUS, IACHIMO *and the Roman army
at one door: and the Briton Army at another:*
LEONATUS POSTHUMUS *following, like a poor
soldier. They march over, and go out. Then enter
again, in skirmish,* IACHIMO *and* POSTHUMUS: *he
vanquisheth and disarmeth Iachimo, and then
leaves him.*

IACHIMO   The heaviness and guilt within my bosom
Takes off my manhood: I have belied a lady,
The princess of this country; and the air on't
Revengingly enfeebles me, or could this carl,
5 A very drudge of Nature's, have subdued me
In my profession? Knighthoods and honours, borne
As I wear mine, are titles but of scorn.
If that thy gentry, Britain, go before
This lout, as he exceeds our lords, the odds
10 Is that we scarce are men and you are gods.   *Exit.*

*The battle continues, the Britons fly, Cymbeline is taken:
then enter to his rescue,* BELARIUS,
GUIDERIUS *and* ARVIRAGUS.

BELARIUS
Stand, stand, We have th'advantage of the ground;
The lane is guarded: nothing routs us but
The villainy of our fears.
GUIDERIUS, ARVIRAGUS   Stand, stand, and fight!

Re-enter POSTHUMUS, *and seconds the Britons. They rescue
Cymbeline and exeunt. Then re-enter* LUCIUS, IACHIMO
and IMOGEN.

LUCIUS   Away, boy, from the troops, and save thyself:
15 For friends kill friends, and the disorder's such
As war were hoodwink'd.
IACHIMO   'Tis their fresh supplies.
LUCIUS   It is a day turn'd strangely: or betimes
Let's re-inforce, or fly.   *Exeunt.*

5.3   *Enter* POSTHUMUS *and a Briton Lord.*

LORD   Cam'st thou from where they made the stand?
POSTHUMUS   I did,
Though you it seems come from the fliers.
LORD   I did.
POSTHUMUS   No blame be to you, sir, for all was lost,
But that the heavens fought: the king himself
5 Of his wings destitute, the army broken,

And but the backs of Britons seen; all flying
Through a strait lane; the enemy full-hearted,
Lolling the tongue with slaught'ring, having work
More plentiful than tools to do't, struck down
Some mortally, some slightly touch'd, some falling   10
Merely through fear, that the strait pass was damm'd
With dead men, hurt behind, and cowards living
To die with length'ned shame.
LORD   Where was this lane?
POSTHUMUS
Close by the battle, ditch'd, and wall'd with turf –
Which gave advantage to an ancient soldier,   15
(An honest one, I warrant) who deserv'd
So long a breeding as his white beard came to,
In doing this for's country. Athwart the lane,
He, with two striplings (lads more like to run
The country base than to commit such slaughter,   20
With faces fit for masks, or rather fairer
Than those for preservation cas'd, or shame)
Made good the passage, cried to those that fled,
'Our Britain's harts die flying, not our men:
To darkness fleet souls that fly backwards; stand,   25
Or we are Romans, and will give you that
Like beasts which you shun beastly, and may save
But to look back in frown: stand, stand!' These three,
Three thousand confident, in act as many, –
For three performers are the file when all   30
The rest do nothing, – with this word 'Stand, stand,'
Accommodated by the place, more charming,
With their own nobleness, which could have turn'd
A distaff to a lance, gilded pale looks;
Part shame, part spirit renew'd, that some, turn'd
coward   35
But by example (O, a sin in war,
Damn'd in the first beginners) 'gan to look
The way that they did, and to grin like lions
Upon the pikes o'th' hunters. Then began
A stop i'th' chaser; a retire: anon   40
A rout, confusion thick: forthwith they fly
Chickens, the way which they stoop'd eagles: slaves,
The strides they victors made: and now our cowards
Like fragments in hard voyages became
The life o'th' need: having found the back-door
open   45
Of the unguarded hearts, heavens, how they wound!
Some slain before, some dying, some their friends
O'er-borne i'th' former wave, ten chas'd by one,
Are now each one the slaughter-man of twenty:
Those that would die, or ere resist, are grown   50
The mortal bugs o'th' field.
LORD   This was strange chance:
A narrow lane, an old man, and two boys.
POSTHUMUS   Nay, do not wonder at it: you are made
Rather to wonder at the things you hear
Than to work any. Will you rhyme upon't,   55
And vent it for a mock'ry? Here is one:
Two boys, an old man twice a boy, a lane,

Preserv'd the Britons, was the Romans' bane.

LORD
    Nay, be not angry, sir.

POSTHUMUS   'Lack, to what end?
    Who dares not stand his foe, I'll be his friend: 160
    For if he'll do as he is made to do,
    I know he'll quickly fly my friendship too.
    You have put me into rhyme.

LORD   Farewell, you're angry.
                          Exit.

POSTHUMUS
    Still going? This is a lord! O noble misery, 165
    To be i'th' field, and ask 'what news?' of me!
    To-day how many would have given their honours
    To have sav'd their carcasses? Took heel to do't,
    And yet died too! I, in mine own woe charm'd,
    Could not find death where I did hear him groan, 170
    Nor feel him where he struck. Being an ugly
        monster,
    'Tis strange he hides him in fresh cups, soft beds,
    Sweet words; or hath moe ministers than we
    That draw his knives i'th' war. Well, I will find him:
    For being now a favourer to the Briton, 175
    No more a Briton, I have resumed again
    The part I came in. Fight I will no more,
    But yield me to the veriest hind that shall
    Once touch my shoulder. Great the slaughter is
    Here made by th' Roman; great the answer be 180
    Britons must take. For me, my ransom's death:
    On either side I come to spend my breath,
    Which neither here I'll keep nor bear again,
    But end it by some means for Imogen.

        Enter two British Captains *and soldiers.*

1 CAPTAIN   Great Jupiter be prais'd, Lucius is taken: 185
    'Tis thought the old man, and his sons, were angels.
2 CAPTAIN   There was a fourth man, in a silly habit,
    That gave th'affront with them.
1 CAPTAIN   So 'tis reported:
    But none of 'em can be found. Stand! who's there?
POSTHUMUS   A Roman, 190
    Who had not now been drooping here if seconds
    Had answer'd him.
2 CAPTAIN   Lay hands on him: a dog,
    A leg of Rome shall not return to tell
    What crows have peck'd them here: he brags his
        service
    As if he were of note: bring him to th' king.

    Enter CYMBELINE, BELARIUS, GUIDERIUS, ARVIRAGUS,
      PISANIO *and Roman captives. The captains present*
    Posthumus *to Cymbeline, who delivers him over to a Gaoler.*
                          Exeunt.

5.4   *Enter* POSTHUMUS *and two* Gaolers.

1 GAOLER
    You shall not now be stol'n, you have locks upon you:

So graze, as you find pasture.

2 GAOLER   Ay, or a stomach.
                        Exeunt Gaolers.

POSTHUMUS
    Most welcome bondage; for thou art a way,
    I think to liberty: yet am I better
    Than one that's sick o'th' gout, since he had rather 5
    Groan so in perpetuity than be cur'd
    By th' sure physician, Death; who is the key
    T'unbar these locks. My conscience, thou art fetter'd
    More than my shanks and wrists: you good gods, give
        me
    The penitent instrument to pick that bolt, 10
    Then free for ever. Is't enough I am sorry?
    So children temporal fathers do appease;
    Gods are more full of mercy. Must I repent,
    I cannot do it better than in gyves,
    Desir'd more than constrain'd: to satisfy, 15
    If of my freedom 'tis the mainport, take
    No stricter render of me than my all.
    I know you are more clement than vile men,
    Who of their broken debtors take a third,
    A sixth, a tenth, letting them thrive again 20
    On their abatement; that's not my desire.
    For Imogen's dear life take mine, and though
    'Tis not so dear, yet 'tis a life; you coin'd it:
    'Tween man and man they weigh not every stamp;
    Though light, take pieces for the figure's sake: 25
    You rather, mine being yours: and so, great powers,
    If you will take this audit, take this life,
    And cancel these cold bonds. O Imogen,
    I'll speak to thee in silence. [*Sleeps.*]

    Solemn music. Enter, as in an apparition, SICILIUS
    LEONATUS, *father to Posthumus, an old man, attired like a*
    warrior, leading in his hand an ancient matron, his wife,
    and Mother *to Posthumus, with music before them. Then,*
    after other music, follow the two young Leonati, Brothers
    to Posthumus, with wounds as they died in the wars. They
    circle Posthumus round as he lies sleeping.

SICILIUS   No more thou thunder-master show 30
            thy spite on mortal flies:
    With Mars fall out, with Juno chide,
            that thy adulteries
    Rates and revenges.

    Hath my poor boy done aught but well, 35
            whose face I never saw?
    I died whilst in the womb he stay'd,
            attending Nature's law:
    Whose father then (as men report
            thou orphans' father art) 40
    Thou shouldst have been, and shielded him
            from this earth-vexing smart.

MOTHER   Lucina lent not me her aid,
            but took me in my throes,
    That from me was Posthumus ript, 45

came crying 'mongst his foes,
    A thing of pity!

SICILIUS   Great nature, like his ancestry,
    moulded the stuff so fair,
50   That he deserved the praise o'th' world,
    as great Sicilius' heir.

1 BROTHER
    When once he was mature for man,
    in Britain where was he
    That could stand up his parallel,
55   or fruitful object be
    In eye of Imogen, that best
    could deem his dignity?

MOTHER   With marriage wherefore was he mock'd
    to be exil'd, and thrown
60   From Leonati seat, and cast
    from her his dearest one,
    Sweet Imogen?

SICILIUS   Why did you suffer Iachimo,
    slight thing of Italy,
65   To taint his nobler heart and brain
    with needless jealousy;
    And to become the geck and scorn
    o'th' other's villainy?

2 BROTHER
    For this, from stiller seats we came,
70   our parents and us twain,
    That striking in our country's cause
    fell bravely and were slain,
    Our fealty, and Tenantius' right,
    with honour to maintain.

1 BROTHER
75   Like hardiment Posthumus hath
    to Cymbeline perform'd:
    Then, Jupiter, thou king of gods
    why hast thou thus adjourn'd
    The graces for his merits due,
80   being all to dolours turn'd?

SICILIUS   Thy crystal window ope; look out;
    no longer exercise
    Upon a valiant race thy harsh
    and potent injuries.

85 MOTHER   Since, Jupiter, our son is good,
    take off his miseries.

SICILIUS   Peep through thy marble mansion, help,
    or we poor ghosts will cry
    To th' shining synod of the rest
90   against thy deity.

BROTHERS
    Help, Jupiter, or we appeal,
    and from thy justice fly.

JUPITER *descends in thunder and lightning, sitting upon an*
eagle: he throws a thunderbolt. The Ghosts fall on their
knees.

JUPITER
    No more, you petty spirits of region low,
    Offend our hearing: hush! How dare you ghosts
    Accuse the thunderer, whose bolt (you know)   95
    Sky-planted, batters all rebelling coasts?
    Poor shadows of Elysium, hence, and rest
    Upon your never-withering banks of flowers:
    Be not with mortal accidents opprest,
    No care of yours it is, you know 'tis ours.   100
    Whom best I love I cross; to make my gift,
    The more delay'd, delighted. Be content,
    Your low-laid son our godhead will uplift:
    His comforts thrive, his trials well are spent:
    Our Jovial star reign'd at his birth, and in   105
    Our temple was he married. Rise, and fade.
    He shall be lord of lady Imogen,
    And happier much by his affliction made.
    This tablet lay upon his breast, wherein
    Our pleasure his full fortune doth confine,   110
    And so away: no farther with your din
    Express impatience, lest you stir up mine.
    Mount, eagle, to my palace crystalline.   *Ascends.*

SICILIUS
    He came in thunder; his celestial breath
    Was sulphurous to smell: the holy eagle   115
    Stoop'd, as to foot us: his ascension is
    More sweet than our blest fields: his royal bird
    Prunes the immortal wing, and cloys his beak,
    As when his god is pleased.

ALL   Thanks, Jupiter!

SICILIUS
    The marble pavement closes, he is enter'd   120
    His radiant roof. Away! and to be blest
    Let us with care perform his great behest.
    The Ghosts vanish.

POSTHUMUS [*waking*]
    Sleep, thou hast been a grandsire, and begot
    A father to me: and thou hast created
    A mother, and two brothers: but, O scorn!   125
    Gone! they went hence so soon as they were born:
    And so I am awake. Poor wretches, that depend
    On greatness' favour, dream as I have done,
    Wake, and find nothing. But, alas, I swerve:
    Many dream not to find, neither deserve,   130
    And yet are steep'd in favours; so am I,
    That have this golden chance, and know not why.
    What fairies haunt this ground? A book? O rare one,
    Be not, as is our fangled world, a garment
    Nobler than that it covers. Let thy effects   135
    So follow, to be most unlike our courtiers,
    As good as promise.
    [*Reads.*] *When as a lion's whelp shall, to himself*
unknown, without seeking find, and be embrac'd by a

*piece of tender air: and when from a stately cedar shall be
lopp'd branches, which, being dead many years, shall
after revive, be jointed to the old stock, and freshly grow,
then shall Posthumus end his miseries, Britain be
fortunate, and flourish in peace and plenty.*
'Tis still a dream: or else such stuff as madmen
Tongue, and brain not: either both, or nothing,
Or senseless speaking, or a speaking such
As sense cannot untie. Be what it is,
The action of my life is like it, which
I'll keep, if but for sympathy.

Re-enter Gaolers.

1 GAOLER   Come, sir, are you ready for death?

POSTHUMUS   Over-roasted rather: ready long ago.

1 GAOLER   Hanging is the word, sir: if you be ready for
that, you are well cook'd.

POSTHUMUS   So, if I prove a good repast to the
spectators, the dish pays the shot.

1 GAOLER   A heavy reckoning for you sir: but the
comfort is you shall be called to no more payments,
fear no more tavern-bills, which are often the sadness
of parting, as the procuring of mirth: you come in faint
for want of meat, depart reeling with too much drink:
sorry that you have paid too much, and sorry that you
are paid too much: purse and brain, both empty: the
brain the heavier for being too light; the purse too
light, being drawn of heaviness. O, of this
contradiction you shall now be quit. O, the charity of
a penny cord! it sums up thousands in a trice: you have
no true debitor and creditor but it: of what's past, is,
and to come, the discharge: your neck, sir, is pen,
book, and counters; so the acquittance follows.

POSTHUMUS   I am merrier to die than thou art to live.

1 GAOLER   Indeed sir, he that sleeps feels ńot the
toothache: but a man that were to sleep your sleep, and
a hangman to help him to bed, I think he would
change places with his officer: for, look you, sir, you
know not which way you shall go.

POSTHUMUS   Yes, indeed do I, fellow.

1 GAOLER   Your death has eyes in's head then: I have not
seen him so pictur'd: you must either be directed by
some that take upon them to know, or to take upon
yourself that which I am sure you do not know, or
jump the after-inquiry on your own peril: and how
you shall speed in your journey's end, I think you'll
never return to tell on.

POSTHUMUS   I tell thee, fellow, there are none want eyes
to direct them the way I am going, but such as wink,
and will not use them.

1 GAOLER   What an infinite mock is this, that a man
should have the best use of eyes to see the way of
blindness! I am sure hanging's the way of winking.

Enter a Messenger.

MESSENGER   Knock off his manacles, bring your
prisoner to the king.

POSTHUMUS   Thou bring'st good news, I am call'd to be
made free.

1 GAOLER   I'll be hang'd then.

POSTHUMUS   Thou shalt be then freer than a gaoler; no
bolts for the dead.   *Exeunt all but First Gaoler.*

1 GAOLER   Unless a man would marry a gallows, and
beget young gibbets, I never saw one so prone: yet, on
my conscience, there are verier knaves desire to live,
for all he be a Roman; and there be some of them too,
that die against their wills; so should I, if I were one. I
would we were all of one mind, and one mind good: O,
there were desolation of gaolers and gallowses! I speak
against my present profit, but my wish hath a
preferment in't.   *Exit.*

5.5   Enter CYMBELINE, BELARIUS, GUIDERIUS,
ARVIRAGUS, PISANIO, *lords, officers and attendants.*

CYMBELINE
Stand by my side, you whom the gods have made
Preservers of my throne: woe is my heart,
That the poor soldier that so richly fought,
Whose rags sham'd gilded arms, whose naked breast
Stepp'd before targes of proof, cannot be found:
He shall be happy that can find him, if
Our grace can make him so.

BELARIUS   I never saw
Such noble fury in so poor a thing;
Such precious deeds in one that promised nought
But beggary and poor looks.

CYMBELINE   No tidings of him?

PISANIO
He hath been search'd among the dead and living;
But no trace of him.

CYMBELINE   To my grief, I am
The heir of his reward,
[*to Belarius, Guiderius and Arviragus*]
                    which I will add
To you, the liver, heart, and brain of Britain,
By whom (I grant) she lives. 'Tis now the time
To ask of whence you are. Report it.

BELARIUS   Sir,
In Cambria are we born, and gentlemen:
Further to boast were neither true nor modest,
Unless I add we are honest.

CYMBELINE   Bow your knees:
Arise my knights o'th' battle, I create you
Companions to our person, and will fit you
With dignities becoming your estates.

Enter CORNELIUS *and* Ladies.

There's business in these faces; why so sadly
Greet you our victory? you look like Romans,
And not o'th' court of Britain.

CORNELIUS   Hail, great king!
To sour your happiness, I must report
The queen is dead.

CYMBELINE   Who worse than a physician

Would this report become? But I consider,
By med'cine life may be prolong'd, yet death
30   Will seize the doctor too. How ended she?
CORNELIUS   With horror, madly dying, like her life,
Which (being cruel to the world) concluded
Most cruel to herself. What she confess'd
I will report, so please you. These her women
35   Can trip me, if I err, who with wet cheeks
Were present when she finish'd.
CYMBELINE   Prithee say.
CORNELIUS
First, she confess'd she never lov'd you: only
Affected greatness got by you: not you:
Married your royalty, was wife to your place:
Abhorr'd your person.
40 CYMBELINE   She alone knew this:
And but she spoke it dying, I would not
Believe her lips in opening it. Proceed.
CORNELIUS
Your daughter, whom she bore in hand to love
With such integrity, she did confess
45   Was as a scorpion to her sight, whose life
(But that her flight prevented it) she had
Ta'en off by poison.
CYMBELINE   O most delicate fiend!
Who is't can read a woman? Is there more?
CORNELIUS
More, sir, and worse. She did confess she had
50   For you a mortal mineral, which, being took,
Should by the minute feed on life and ling'ring
By inches waste you. In which time, she purpos'd
By watching, weeping, tendance, kissing, to
O'ercome you with her show; and in time
55   (When she had fitted you with her craft) to work
Her son into th'adoption of the crown:
But, failing of her end by his strange absence,
Grew shameless-desperate, open'd (in despite
Of heaven and men) her purposes: repented
60   The evils she hatch'd were not effected: so
Despairing died.
CYMBELINE   Heard you all this, her women?
LADIES   We did, so please your highness.
CYMBELINE   Mine eyes
Were not in fault, for she was beautiful:
Mine ears that heard her flattery, nor my heart
That thought her like her seeming. It had been
65   vicious
To have mistrusted her: yet, O my daughter,
That it was folly in me, thou mayst say,
And prove it in thy feeling. Heaven mend all!

Enter LUCIUS, IACHIMO, *the* Soothsayer *and other Roman*
prisoners, guarded; POSTHUMUS *behind, and* IMOGEN.

Thou com'st not, Caius, now for tribute; that
70   The Britons have raz'd out, though with the loss
Of many a bold one: whose kinsmen have made suit
That their good souls may be appeas'd with slaughter

Of you their captives, which ourself have granted:
So think of your estate.
LUCIUS   Consider, sir, the chance of war, the day   75
Was yours by accident: had it gone with us,
We should not, when the blood was cool, have
    threaten'd
Our prisoners with the sword. But since the gods
Will have it thus, that nothing but our lives
May be call'd ransom, let it come: sufficeth   80
A Roman with a Roman's heart can suffer:
Augustus lives to think on't: and so much
For my peculiar care. This one thing only
I will entreat, my boy (a Briton born)
Let him be ransom'd: never master had   85
A page so kind, so duteous, diligent,
So tender over his occasions, true,
So feat, so nurse-like: let his virtue join
With my request, which I'll make bold your highness
Cannot deny: he hath done no Briton harm,   90
Though he have serv'd a Roman. Save him, sir,
And spare no blood beside.
CYMBELINE   I have surely seen him:
His favour is familiar to me. Boy,
Thou hast look'd thyself into my grace,
And art mine own. I know not why, wherefore,   95
To say, live boy: ne'er thank thy master, live;
And ask of Cymbeline what boon thou wilt,
Fitting my bounty, and thy state, I'll give it:
Yea, though thou do demand a prisoner,
The noblest ta'en.
IMOGEN   I humbly thank your highness.   100
LUCIUS   I do not bid thee beg my life, good lad,
And yet I know thou wilt.
IMOGEN   No, no alack,
There's other work in hand: I see a thing
Bitter to me as death: your life, good master,
Must shuffle for itself.
LUCIUS   The boy disdains me,   105
He leaves me, scorns me: briefly die their joys
That place them on the truth of girls and boys.
Why stands he so perplex'd?
CYMBELINE   What wouldst thou, boy?
I love thee more and more: think more and more
What's best to ask. Know'st him thou look'st on?
    speak,   110
Wilt have him live? Is he thy kin? thy friend?
IMOGEN   He is a Roman, no more kin to me
Than I to your highness, who being born your vassal,
Am something nearer.
CYMBELINE   Wherefore ey'st him so?
IMOGEN   I'll tell you, sir, in private, if you please   115
To give me hearing.
CYMBELINE   Ay, with all my heart,
And lend my best attention. What's thy name?
IMOGEN   Fidele, sir.
CYMBELINE   Thou'rt my good youth: my page
I'll be thy master: walk with me: speak freely.

[*Cymbeline and Imogen walk aside.*]

BELARIUS   Is not this boy reviv'd from death?

ARVIRAGUS   One sand another
20   Not more resembles that sweet rosy lad,
  Who died, and was Fidele! What think you?

GUIDERIUS   The same dead thing alive.

BELARIUS
  Peace, peace, see further: he eyes us not, forbear;
25   Creatures may be alike: were't he, I am sure
  He would have spoke to us.

GUIDERIUS   But we see him dead.

BELARIUS   Be silent: let's see further.

PISANIO [*aside*]   It is my mistress:
  Since she is living, let the time run on,
  To good, or bad.

[*Cymbeline and Imogen come forward.*]

CYMBELINE   Come, stand thou by our side,
  Make thy demand aloud.

30 [*to Iachimo*]   Sir, step you forth,
  Give answer to this boy, and do it freely,
  Or, by our greatness and the grace of it
  (Which is our honour) bitter torture shall
  Winnow the truth from falsehood. On, speak to him.

35 IMOGEN   My boon is, that this gentleman may render
  Of whom he had this ring.

POSTHUMUS [*aside*]   What's that to him?

CYMBELINE   That diamond upon your finger, say
  How came it yours?

IACHIMO   Thou'lt torture me to leave unspoken that
  Which, to be spoke, would torture thee.

40 CYMBELINE   How? me?

IACHIMO   I am glad to be constrain'd to utter that
  Which torments me to conceal. By villainy
  I got this ring; 'twas Leonatus' jewel,
  Whom thou didst banish: and – which more may
    grieve thee,
45   As it doth me, – a nobler sir ne'er lived
  'Twixt sky and ground. Wilt thou hear more, my
    lord?

CYMBELINE   All that belongs to this.

IACHIMO   That paragon, thy daughter,
  For whom my heart drops blood, and my false spirits
  Quail to remember – Give me leave; I faint.

CYMBELINE
50   My daughter? what of her? Renew thy strength:
  I had rather thou shouldst live, while Nature will,
  Than die ere I hear more: strive, man, and speak.

IACHIMO   Upon a time, unhappy was the clock
  That struck the hour: it was in Rome, accurst
55   The mansion where: 'twas at a feast, O, would
  Our viands had been poison'd (or at least
  Those which I heaved to head) the good Posthumus
  (What should I say? he was too good to be
  Where ill men were, and was the best of all
60   Amongst the rar'st of good ones) sitting sadly,
  Hearing us praise our loves of Italy
  For beauty, that made barren the swell'd boast

  Of him that best could speak: for feature, laming
  The shrine of Venus, or straight-pight Minerva,
165   Postures, beyond brief Nature. For condition,
  A shop of all the qualities that man
  Loves woman for, besides that hook of wiving,
  Fairness, which strikes the eye.

CYMBELINE   I stand on fire.
  Come to the matter.

IACHIMO   All too soon I shall,
170   Unless thou wouldst grieve quickly. This Posthumus,
  Most like a noble lord in love and one
  That had a royal lover, took his hint,
  And (not dispraising whom we prais'd, therein
  He was as calm as virtue) he began
  His mistress' picture, which, by his tongue, being
    made,
175   And then a mind put in't, either our brags
  Were crak'd of kitchen-trulls, or his description
  Prov'd us unspeaking sots.

CYMBELINE   Nay, nay, to th' purpose.

IACHIMO   Your daughter's chastity (there it begins) –
  He spoke of her, as Dian had hot dreams,
180   And she alone were cold: whereat I, wretch,
  Made scruple of his praise, and wager'd with him
  Pieces of gold, 'gainst this (which he then wore
  Upon his honour'd finger) to attain
  In suit the place of's bed, and win this ring
185   By hers and mine adultery: he, true knight,
  No lesser of her honour confident
  Than I did truly find her, stakes this ring,
  And would so, had it been a carbuncle
  Of Phoebus' wheel; and might so safely, had it
190   Been all the worth of's car. Away to Britain
  Post I in this design: well may you, sir,
  Remember me at court, where I was taught
  Of your chaste daughter the wide difference
  'Twixt amorous and villainous. Being thus quench'd
195   Of hope, not longing, mine Italian brain
  Gan in your duller Britain operate
  Most vilely: for my vantage, excellent.
  And to be brief, my practice so prevail'd,
  That I return'd with simular proof enough
200   To make the noble Leonatus mad,
  By wounding his belief in her renown,
  With tokens thus, and thus: averring notes
  Of chamber-hanging, pictures, this her bracelet
205   (O cunning, how I got it!) nay, some marks
  Of secret on her person, that he could not
  But think her bond of chastity quite crak'd,
  I having ta'en the forfeit. Whereupon –
  Methinks I see him now –

POSTHUMUS [*advancing*]   Ay, so thou dost
210   Italian fiend! Ay me, most credulous fool,
  Egregious murderer, thief, any thing
  That's due to all the villains past, in being,
  To come. O, give me cord, or knife, or poison
  Some upright justicer! Thou, king, send out

215 For torturers ingenious: it is I
    That all th' abhorred things o'th' earth amend
    By being worse than they. I am Posthumus,
    That kill'd thy daughter: villain-like, I lie;
    That caus'd a lesser villain than myself,
220 A sacrilegious thief, to do't. The temple
    Of Virtue was she; yea, and she herself.
    Spit, and throw stones, cast mire upon me, set
    The dogs o'th' street to bay me: every villain
    Be call'd Posthumus Leonatus, and
225 Be villainy less than 'twas. O Imogen!
    My queen, my life, my wife, O Imogen,
    Imogen, Imogen!
    IMOGEN   Peace, my lord, hear, hear –
    POSTHUMUS
    Shall's have a play of this? Thou scornful page,
    There lie thy part. [*Striking her: she falls.*]
    PISANIO   O, gentlemen, help!
230 Mine and your mistress: O, my lord Posthumus!
    You ne'er kill'd Imogen till now. Help, help!
    Mine honour'd lady!
    CYMBELINE   Does the world go round?
    POSTHUMUS   How comes these staggers on me?
    PISANIO   Wake, my mistress!
    CYMBELINE
    If this be so, the gods do mean to strike me
    To death with mortal joy.
235 PISANIO   How fares my mistress?
    IMOGEN   O, get thee from my sight,
    Thou gav'st me poison: dangerous fellow, hence!
    Breathe not where princes are.
    CYMBELINE   The tune of Imogen!
    PISANIO   Lady,
240 The gods throw stones of sulphur on me, if
    That box I gave you was not thought by me
    A precious thing: I had it from the queen.
    CYMBELINE   New matter still.
    IMOGEN   It poison'd me.
    CORNELIUS   O gods!
    I left out one thing which the queen confess'd,
245 Which must approve thee honest. 'If Pisanio
    Have,' said she, 'given his mistress that confection
    Which I gave him for cordial, she is serv'd
    As I would serve a rat.'
    CYMBELINE   What's this, Cornelius?
    CORNELIUS   The queen, sir, very oft importun'd me
250 To temper poisons for her, still pretending
    The satisfaction of her knowledge only
    In killing creatures vile, as cats and dogs
    Of no esteem. I, dreading that her purpose
    Was of more danger, did compound for her
255 A certain stuff, which being ta'en would cease
    The present power of life, but in short time
    All offices of nature should again
    Do their due functions. Have you ta'en of it?
    IMOGEN   Most like I did, for I was dead.
    BELARIUS   My boys,

There was our error.
GUIDERIUS   This is sure Fidele.   260
IMOGEN
    Why did you throw your wedded lady from you?
    Think that you are upon a rock, and now
    Throw me again. [*embracing him*]
POSTHUMUS   Hang there like fruit, my soul,
    Till the tree die.
CYMBELINE   How now, my flesh, my child?
    What, mak'st thou me a dullard in this act?   265
    Wilt thou not speak to me?
IMOGEN [*kneeling*]   Your blessing, sir.
BELARIUS [*to Guiderius and Arviragus*]
    Though you did love this youth, I blame ye not,
    You had a motive for't.
CYMBELINE   My tears that fall
    Prove holy water on thee; Imogen,
    Thy mother's dead.
IMOGEN   I am sorry for't, my lord.   270
CYMBELINE   O, she was naught; and long of her it was
    That we meet here so strangely: but her son
    Is gone, we know not how, nor where.
PISANIO   My lord,
    Now fear is from me, I'll speak troth. Lord Cloten,
    Upon my lady's missing, came to me   275
    With his sword drawn, foam'd at the mouth, and
        swore,
    If I discover'd not which way she was gone,
    It was my instant death. By accident,
    I had a feigned letter of my master's
    Then in my pocket, which directed him   280
    To seek her on the mountains near to Milford;
    Where, in a frenzy, in my master's garments,
    (Which he enforc'd from me) away he posts
    With unchaste purpose, and with oath to violate
    My lady's honour: what became of him   285
    I further know not.
GUIDERIUS   Let me end the story:
    I slew him there.
CYMBELINE   Marry, the gods forfend!
    I would not thy good deeds should from my lips
    Pluck a hard sentence: prithee, valiant youth,
    Deny't again.
GUIDERIUS   I have spoke it, and I did it.   290
CYMBELINE   He was a prince.
GUIDERIUS   A most incivil one. The wrongs he did me
    Were nothing prince-like; for he did provoke me
    With language that would make me spurn the sea,
    If it could so roar to me. I cut off's head,   295
    And am right glad he is not standing here
    To tell this tale of mine.
CYMBELINE   I am sorrow for thee:
    By thine own tongue thou art condemn'd, and must
    Endure our law: thou'rt dead.
IMOGEN   That headless man
    I thought had been my lord.
CYMBELINE   Bind the offender,   300

And take him from our presence.

BELARIUS   Stay, sir king.
    This man is better than the man he slew,
    As well descended as thyself, and hath
    More of thee merited than a band of Clotens
    Had ever scar for. [*to the guard*] Let his arms alone,
    They were not born for bondage.

CYMBELINE   Why, old soldier:
    Wilt thou undo the worth thou art unpaid for
    By tasting of our wrath? How of descent
    As good as we?

ARVIRAGUS   In that he spake too far.

CYMBELINE   And thou shalt die for't.

BELARIUS   We will die all three,
    But I will prove that two on's are as good
    As I have given out him. My sons, I must
    For mine own part unfold a dangerous speech,
    Though haply well for you.

ARVIRAGUS   Your danger's ours.

GUIDERIUS   And our good his.

BELARIUS   Have at it then, by leave:
    Thou hadst, great king, a subject, who
    Was call'd Belarius. –

CYMBELINE   What of him? he is a banish'd traitor.

BELARIUS   He it is that hath
    Assum'd this age: indeed a banish'd man,
    I know not how a traitor.

CYMBELINE   Take him hence,
    The whole world shall not save him.

BELARIUS   Not too hot;
    First pay me for the nursing of thy sons,
    And let it be confiscate all, so soon
    As I have receiv'd it.

CYMBELINE   Nursing of my sons?

BELARIUS   I am too blunt, and saucy: here's my knee:
    Ere I arise I will prefer my sons;
    Then spare not the old father. Mighty sir,
    These two young gentlemen that call me father
    And think they are my sons, are none of mine;
    They are the issue of your loins, my liege,
    And blood of your begetting.

CYMBELINE   How? my issue?

BELARIUS
    So sure as you your father's. I (old Morgan)
    Am that Belarius, whom you sometime banish'd:
    Your pleasure was my ne'er-offence, my punishment
    Itself, and all my treason: that I suffer'd,
    Was all the harm I did. These gentle princes
    (For such and so they are) these twenty years
    Have I train'd up; those arts they have; as I
    Could put into them. My breeding was, sir, as
    Your highness knows. Their nurse, Euriphile,
    (Whom for the theft I wedded) stole these children
    Upon my banishment: I mov'd her to't,
    Having receiv'd the punishment before
    For that which I did then. Beaten for loyalty
    Excited me to treason. Their dear loss,

The more of you 'twas felt, the more it shap'd
    Unto my end of stealing them. But gracious sir,
    Here are your sons again, and I must lose
    Two of the sweet'st companions in the world.
    The benediction of these covering heavens
    Fall on their heads like dew, for they are worthy
    To inlay heaven with stars.

CYMBELINE   Thou weep'st, and speak'st:
    The service that you three have done is more
    Unlike than this thou tell'st. I lost my children:
    If these be they, I know not how to wish
    A pair of worthier sons.

BELARIUS   Be pleas'd awhile;
    This gentleman, whom I call Polydore,
    Most worthy prince, as yours, is true Guiderius:
    This gentleman, my Cadwal, Arviragus
    Your younger princely son, he, sir, was lapp'd
    In a most curious mantle, wrought by th' hand
    Of his queen mother, which for more probation
    I can with ease produce.

CYMBELINE   Guiderius had
    Upon his neck a mole, a sanguine star;
    It is a mark of wonder.

BELARIUS   This is he,
    Who hath upon him still that natural stamp:
    It was wise Nature's end, in the donation
    To be his evidence now.

CYMBELINE   O, what am I?
    A mother to the birth of three? Ne'er mother
    Rejoic'd deliverance more. Blest pray you be,
    That, after this strange starting from your orbs,
    You may reign in them now! O Imogen,
    Thou hast lost by this a kingdom.

IMOGEN   No, my lord;
    I have got two worlds by't. O my gentle brothers,
    Have we thus met? O, never say hereafter
    But I am truest speaker. You call'd me brother,
    When I was but your sister: I you brothers,
    When ye were so indeed.

CYMBELINE   Did you e'er meet?

ARVIRAGUS   Ay, my good lord.

GUIDERIUS   And at first meeting lov'd,
    Continu'd so, until we thought he died.

CORNELIUS   By the queen's dram she swallow'd.

CYMBELINE   O rare instinct!
    When shall I hear all through? This fierce
        abridgement
    Hath to it circumstantial branches, which
    Distinction should be rich in. Where? how liv'd you?
    And when came you to serve our Roman captive?
    How parted with your brothers? how first met them?
    Why fled you from the court? and whither? These,
    And your three motives to the battle, with
    I know not how much more, should be demanded
    And all the other by-dependances,
    From chance to chance. But nor the time nor place
    Will serve our long inter'gatories. See,

Posthumus anchors upon Imogen;
And she (like harmless lightning) throws her eye
On him: her brothers, me: her master hitting
Each object with a joy: the counterchange
Is severally in all. Let's quit this ground,
And smoke the temple with our sacrifices.
[*to Belarius*] Thou art my brother; so we'll hold thee
    ever.

IMOGEN   You are my father too, and did relieve me,
To see this gracious season.

CYMBELINE   All o'erjoy'd,
Save these in bonds, let them be joyful too,
For they shall taste our comfort.

IMOGEN   My good master,
I will yet do you service.

LUCIUS   Happy be you!

CYMBELINE   The forlorn soldier that so nobly fought,
He would have well becom'd this place, and grac'd
The thankings of a king.

POSTHUMUS   I am, sir,
The soldier that did company these three
In poor beseeming: 'twas a fitment for
The purpose I then follow'd. That I was he,
Speak, Iachimo: I had you down, and might
Have made you finish.

IACHIMO [*kneels*]   I am down again:
But now my heavy conscience sinks my knee,
As then your force did. Take that life, beseech you,
Which I so often owe: but your ring first,
And here the bracelet of the truest princess
That ever swore her faith.

POSTHUMUS   Kneel not to me:
The power that I have on you, is to spare you:
The malice towards you, to forgive you. Live
And deal with others better.

CYMBELINE   Nobly doom'd!
We'll learn our freeness of a son-in-law:
Pardon's the word to all.

ARVIRAGUS   You holp us, sir,
As you did mean indeed to be our brother;
Joy'd are we that you are.

POSTHUMUS
Your servant, princes. Good my lord of Rome,
Call forth your soothsayer: as I slept, methought
Great Jupiter, upon his eagle back'd,
Appear'd to me, with other spritely shows
Of mine own kindred. When I wak'd, I found
This label on my bosom; whose containing
Is so from sense in hardness, that I can
Make no collection of it. Let him show
His skill in the construction.

LUCIUS   Philarmonus!

SOOTHSAYER   Here, my good lord.

LUCIUS   Read, and declare the meaning.

SOOTHSAYER [*Reads.*]   *When as a lion's whelp shall, to*

himself unknown, without seeking find, and be
embrac'd by a piece of tender air: and when from a
stately cedar shall be lopp'd branches, which, being
dead many years, shall after revive, be jointed to the
old stock, and freshly grow, then shall Posthumus end
his miseries, Britain be fortunate, and flourish in peace
and plenty.

Thou, Leonatus, art the lion's whelp,
The fit and apt construction of thy name,
Being *Leo-natus*, doth impart so much:
[*to Cymbeline*] The piece of tender air, thy virtuous
    daughter,
Which we call *mollis aer*; and *mollis aer*
We term it *mulier*: which *mulier* I divine
Is this most constant wife, who even now,
Answering the letter of the oracle,
Unknown to you, unsought, were clipp'd about
With this most tender air.

CYMBELINE   This hath some seeming.

SOOTHSAYER   The lofty cedar, royal Cymbeline,
Personates thee: and thy lopp'd branches point
Thy two sons forth: who, by Belarius stol'n,
For many years thought dead, are now reviv'd,
To the majestic cedar join'd; whose issue
Promises Britain peace and plenty.

CYMBELINE   Well,
My peace we will begin: and Caius Lucius,
Although the victor, we submit to Caesar,
And to the Roman empire; promising
To pay our wonted tribute, from the which
We were dissuaded by our wicked queen,
Whom heavens in justice both on her, and hers,
Have laid most heavy hand.

SOOTHSAYER   The fingers of the powers above do tune
The harmony of this peace. The vision,
Which I made known to Lucius ere the stroke
Of yet this scarce-cold battle, at this instant
Is full accomplish'd. For the Roman eagle,
From south to west on wing soaring aloft,
Lessen'd herself and in the beams o'the sun
So vanish'd; which foreshadow'd our princely eagle,
Th'imperial Caesar, should again unite
His favour with the radiant Cymbeline,
Which shines here in the west.

CYMBELINE   Laud we the gods,
And let our crooked smokes climb to their nostrils
From our blest altars. Publish we this peace
To all our subjects. Set we forward: let
A Roman, and a British ensign wave
Friendly together: so through Lud's town march,
And in the temple of great Jupiter
Our peace we'll ratify: seal it with feasts.
Set on there! Never was a war did cease
(Ere bloody hands were wash'd) with such a peace.
                          Exeunt.

395
400
405
410
415
420
425
430
435
440
445
450
455
460
465
470
475
480
485

Hamlet

A short play called *The Tragical History of Hamlet, Prince of Denmark* was printed in 1603. It was ascribed to William Shakespeare on its title-page which also claimed that it had been 'divers times acted by his Highness' servants in the city of London, as also in the two universities of Cambridge and Oxford and elsewhere'; this text is known as the First Quarto (Q1). Soon another version appeared, variously dated 1604 or 1605, claiming on its title-page to be 'newly imprinted and enlarged to almost as much again as it was, according to the true and perfect copy'; this text is known as the Second Quarto (Q2). Its claim as to length is more or less accurate, and it is also a much more careful and coherent text than Q1, which has generally been dismissed as a 'bad' quarto, an unreliable version put together from the memories of actors or reporters. Finally, yet a third text (F) appeared in the First Folio in 1623, very like Q2 in many ways, but lacking around 230 lines that are in Q2 and adding around 70 lines of its own; it also has numerous minor verbal variants, some of which seem to be corrections but others of which are substitutions or errors.

Scholars have accepted both Q2 and F as authorial versions, with recent opinion inclining towards seeing F as Shakespeare's revision of Q2. The most significant of F's 'cuts' is the omission of the whole of 4.4 after the first 8 lines, including Hamlet's last soliloquy, but there are other major omissions in 1.1, 1.4, 3.4, 4.7 and 5.2. Most editions of *Hamlet* virtually ignore Q1 but include all the lines from both Q2 and F, providing a composite or 'conflated' text. Some recent editions bracket the Q2-only lines, or even consign them to an appendix.

The play is usually dated around 1600, just after *Julius Caesar*, whose story is mentioned in 1.1, 3.2 and 5.1. Shakespeare's Brutus in some ways prefigures his Hamlet and presumably the same actor, Richard Burbage, played both roles. Shakespeare's previous tragedies at this point were *Titus Andronicus* and *Romeo and Juliet*, both of which share *Hamlet*'s revenge theme; he went on to write *Othello*, *King Lear* and *Macbeth* over the next six years. *Hamlet* was an immediate and enduring success. Its story derives ultimately from a twelfth-century history of Denmark written in Latin by Saxo Grammaticus, but Shakespeare also seems to have used a 1580 French version by François de Belleforest and a lost play on the topic, now referred to as the *Ur-Hamlet*, and probably written by Thomas Kyd, whose *Spanish Tragedy* has many features in common with *Hamlet*.

Hamlet has a relatively unbroken history of performance, not only in England but virtually throughout the world; there have been over fifty films based on it. It was heavily cut in the Restoration but not, like most of the other plays, radically adapted or rewritten. Nevertheless it has of course inspired many spin-offs, sequels, prequels and parodies. The title-role has always attracted and challenged actors (including a large number of women). The play is endlessly quoted, and some key moments – the appearance of the Ghost on the battlements, the man in black holding a skull, the drowning of Ophelia – are instantly recognizable from countless illustrations. The character of the hero has been taken as representative of the spirit of entire countries, particularly Germany and Russia, while its political situation has been seen to parallel that in countries as different as Romania and South Africa.

Generally hailed until very recently as Shakespeare's 'greatest play', *Hamlet* is still performed and studied more often than its only rival, *King Lear*. The annual bibliographies published by the American journal *Shakespeare Quarterly* show that around 400 items (editions, translations, books and essays) appear on *Hamlet* every year, as compared with around 200 on *Lear*. It remains to be seen whether a mid-twentieth-century shift in taste towards *Lear* will be sustained or whether *Hamlet* will reassert its pre-eminence.

The Arden text is based primarily on the 1604–5 Second Quarto, but also draws on the 1623 First Folio and includes the Folio-only passages.

HAMLET	*Prince of Denmark*
KING Claudius	*King of Denmark, Hamlet's uncle*
GHOST	*of the late king, Hamlet's father*
QUEEN Gertrude	*the Queen, Hamlet's mother, now wife of Claudius*
POLONIUS	*councillor of State*
LAERTES	*Polonius' son*
OPHELIA	*Polonius' daughter*
HORATIO	*friend and confidant of Hamlet*
ROSENCRANTZ GUILDENSTERN	*courtiers, former schoolfellows of Hamlet*
FORTINBRAS	*Prince of Norway*
VOLTEMAND CORNELIUS	*Danish councillors, ambassadors to Norway*
MARCELLUS BARNARDO FRANCISCO	*members of the King's guard*
OSRIC	*a foppish courtier*
REYNALDO	*a servant of Polonius*
Players	
GENTLEMAN	*of the court*
PRIEST	
GRAVE-DIGGER	
The OTHER *grave-digger*	
CAPTAIN	*in Fortinbras' army*
English Ambassadors	

Lords, Ladies, Soldiers, Sailors, Messengers and Attendants

1.1 *Enter* BARNARDO *and* FRANCISCO, *two sentinels.*

BARNARDO   Who's there?

FRANCISCO
    Nay, answer me. Stand and unfold yourself.

BARNARDO   Long live the King!

FRANCISCO   Barnardo?

BARNARDO   He.

FRANCISCO   You come most carefully upon your hour.

BARNARDO
    'Tis now struck twelve. Get thee to bed, Francisco.

FRANCISCO
    For this relief much thanks. 'Tis bitter cold,
    And I am sick at heart.

BARNARDO   Have you had quiet guard?

FRANCISCO   Not a mouse stirring.

BARNARDO   Well, good night.
    If you do meet Horatio and Marcellus,
    The rivals of my watch, bid them make haste.

FRANCISCO   I think I hear them.

Enter HORATIO *and* MARCELLUS.

                        Stand, ho! Who is there?

HORATIO   Friends to this ground.

MARCELLUS   And liegemen to the Dane.

FRANCISCO   Give you good night.

MARCELLUS
    O, farewell honest soldier, who hath reliev'd you?

FRANCISCO
    Barnardo hath my place. Give you good night.   *Exit.*

MARCELLUS   Holla, Barnardo!

BARNARDO   Say, what, is Horatio there?

HORATIO   A piece of him.

BARNARDO
    Welcome, Horatio. Welcome, good Marcellus.

HORATIO   What, has this thing appear'd again tonight?

BARNARDO   I have seen nothing.

MARCELLUS   Horatio says 'tis but our fantasy,
    And will not let belief take hold of him,
    Touching this dreaded sight twice seen of us.
    Therefore I have entreated him along
    With us to watch the minutes of this night,
    That if again this apparition come,
    He may approve our eyes and speak to it.

HORATIO   Tush, tush, 'twill not appear.

BARNARDO   Sit down awhile,
    And let us once again assail your ears,
    That are so fortified against our story,
    What we have two nights seen.

HORATIO   Well, sit we down.
    And let us hear Barnardo speak of this.

BARNARDO   Last night of all,
    When yond same star that's westward from the pole,
    Had made his course t'illume that part of heaven
    Where now it burns, Marcellus and myself,
    The bell then beating one –

Enter Ghost.

MARCELLUS
    Peace, break thee off. Look where it comes again.

BARNARDO
    In the same figure like the King that's dead.

MARCELLUS
    Thou art a scholar, speak to it, Horatio.   45

BARNARDO
    Looks a not like the King? Mark it, Horatio.

HORATIO
    Most like. It harrows me with fear and wonder.

BARNARDO
    It would be spoke to.

MARCELLUS   Question it, Horatio.

HORATIO
    What art thou that usurp'st this time of night,
    Together with that fair and warlike form   50
    In which the majesty of buried Denmark
    Did sometimes march? By heaven, I charge thee
        speak.

MARCELLUS   It is offended.

BARNARDO   See, it stalks away.

HORATIO   Stay, speak, speak, I charge thee speak.
                                        Exit Ghost.

MARCELLUS   'Tis gone and will not answer.   55

BARNARDO
    How now, Horatio? You tremble and look pale.
    Is not this something more than fantasy?
    What think you on't?

HORATIO
    Before my God, I might not this believe
    Without the sensible and true avouch   60
    Of mine own eyes.

MARCELLUS   Is it not like the King?

HORATIO   As thou art to thyself.
    Such was the very armour he had on
    When he th'ambitious Norway combated.
    So frown'd he once, when in an angry parle   65
    He smote the sledded Polacks on the ice.
    'Tis strange.

MARCELLUS
    Thus twice before, and jump at this dead hour,
    With martial stalk hath he gone by our watch.

HORATIO
    In what particular thought to work I know not,   70
    But in the gross and scope of my opinion,
    This bodes some strange eruption to our state.

MARCELLUS
    Good now, sit down, and tell me, he that knows,
    Why this same strict and most observant watch
    So nightly toils the subject of the land,   75
    And why such daily cast of brazen cannon
    And foreign mart for implements of war,
    Why such impress of shipwrights, whose sore task
    Does not divide the Sunday from the week.
    What might be toward that this sweaty haste   80
    Doth make the night joint-labourer with the day,
    Who is't that can inform me?

HORATIO   That can I.
    At least the whisper goes so: our last King,
    Whose image even but now appear'd to us,
85   Was as you know by Fortinbras of Norway,
    Thereto prick'd on by a most emulate pride,
    Dar'd to the combat; in which our valiant Hamlet
    (For so this side of our known world esteem'd him)
    Did slay this Fortinbras, who by a seal'd compact
90   Well ratified by law and heraldry
    Did forfeit, with his life, all those his lands
    Which he stood seiz'd of to the conqueror;
    Against the which a moiety competent
    Was gaged by our King, which had return'd
95   To the inheritance of Fortinbras,
    Had he been vanquisher; as, by the same cov'nant
    And carriage of the article design'd,
    His fell to Hamlet. Now, sir, young Fortinbras,
    Of unimproved mettle, hot and full,
100   Hath in the skirts of Norway here and there
    Shark'd up a list of lawless resolutes
    For food and diet to some enterprise
    That hath a stomach in't, which is no other,
    As it doth well appear unto our state,
105   But to recover of us by strong hand
    And terms compulsatory those foresaid lands
    So by his father lost. And this, I take it,
    Is the main motive of our preparations,
    The source of this our watch, and the chief head
110   Of this post-haste and rummage in the land.
    BARNARDO   I think it be no other but e'en so.
    Well may it sort that this portentous figure
    Comes armed through our watch so like the King
    That was and is the question of these wars.
115 HORATIO   A mote it is to trouble the mind's eye.
    In the most high and palmy state of Rome,
    A little ere the mightiest Julius fell,
    The graves stood tenantless and the sheeted dead
    Did squeak and gibber in the Roman streets;
120   As stars with trains of fire and dews of blood,
    Disasters in the sun; and the moist star,
    Upon whose influence Neptune's empire stands,
    Was sick almost to doomsday with eclipse.
    And even the like precurse of fear'd events,
125   As harbingers preceding still the fates
    And prologue to the omen coming on,
    Have heaven and earth together demonstrated
    Unto our climatures and countrymen.

Enter Ghost.

    But soft, behold. Lo, where it comes again.
    I'll cross it though it blast me. [*Ghost spreads its arms.*]
130   Stay, illusion:
    If thou hast any sound or use of voice,
    Speak to me.
    If there be any good thing to be done
    That may to thee do ease, and grace to me,
135   Speak to me;

    If thou art privy to thy country's fate,
    Which, happily, foreknowing may avoid,
    O speak;
    Or if thou hast uphoarded in thy life
    Extorted treasure in the womb of earth,   140
    For which they say your spirits oft walk in death,
    Speak of it, stay and speak.
    [*The cock crows.*]   Stop it, Marcellus.
MARCELLUS   Shall I strike at it with my partisan?
HORATIO   Do if it will not stand.
BARNARDO   'Tis here.   145
HORATIO   'Tis here.   *Exit Ghost.*
MARCELLUS   'Tis gone.
    We do it wrong, being so majestical,
    To offer it the show of violence,
    For it is as the air, invulnerable,   150
    And our vain blows malicious mockery.
BARNARDO   It was about to speak when the cock crew.
HORATIO   And then it started like a guilty thing
    Upon a fearful summons. I have heard
    The cock, that is the trumpet to the morn,   155
    Doth with his lofty and shrill-sounding throat
    Awake the god of day, and at his warning,
    Whether in sea or fire, in earth or air,
    Th'extravagant and erring spirit hies
    To his confine; and of the truth herein   160
    This present object made probation.
MARCELLUS   It faded on the crowing of the cock.
    Some say that ever 'gainst that season comes
    Wherein our Saviour's birth is celebrated,
    This bird of dawning singeth all night long;   165
    And then, they say, no spirit dare stir abroad,
    The nights are wholesome, then no planets strike,
    No fairy takes, nor witch hath power to charm,
    So hallow'd and so gracious is that time.
HORATIO   So have I heard and do in part believe it.   170
    But look, the morn in russet mantle clad
    Walks o'er the dew of yon high eastward hill.
    Break we our watch up, and by my advice
    Let us impart what we have seen tonight
    Unto young Hamlet; for upon my life   175
    This spirit, dumb to us, will speak to him.
    Do you consent we shall acquaint him with it
    As needful in our loves, fitting our duty?
MARCELLUS
    Let's do't, I pray, and I this morning know
    Where we shall find him most convenient.   *Exeunt.* 180

1.2   *Flourish. Enter Claudius* KING *of Denmark,*
   Gertrude the QUEEN, *Council, including* VOLTEMAND,
   CORNELIUS, POLONIUS *and his son* LAERTES, HAMLET
        dressed in black, with others.

KING   Though yet of Hamlet our dear brother's death
    The memory be green, and that it us befitted
    To bear our hearts in grief, and our whole kingdom
    To be contracted in one brow of woe,

Yet so far hath discretion fought with nature
That we with wisest sorrow think on him
Together with remembrance of ourselves.
Therefore our sometime sister, now our queen,
Th'imperial jointress to this warlike state,
Have we, as 'twere with a defeated joy,
With an auspicious and a dropping eye,
With mirth in funeral and with dirge in marriage,
In equal scale weighing delight and dole,
Taken to wife. Nor have we herein barr'd
Your better wisdoms, which have freely gone
With this affair along. For all, our thanks.
Now follows that you know young Fortinbras,
Holding a weak supposal of our worth,
Or thinking by our late dear brother's death
Our state to be disjoint and out of frame,
Colleagued with this dream of his advantage,
He hath not fail'd to pester us with message
Importing the surrender of those lands
Lost by his father, with all bonds of law,
To our most valiant brother. So much for him.
Now for ourself, and for this time of meeting,
Thus much the business is: we have here writ
To Norway, uncle of young Fortinbras –
Who, impotent and bedrid, scarcely hears
Of this his nephew's purpose – to suppress
His further gait herein, in that the levies,
The lists, and full proportions are all made
Out of his subject; and we here dispatch
You, good Cornelius, and you, Voltemand,
For bearers of this greeting to old Norway,
Giving to you no further personal power
To business with the King more than the scope
Of these dilated articles allow.
Farewell, and let your haste commend your duty.

CORNELIUS, VOLTEMAND
  In that, and all things, will we show our duty.

KING   We doubt it nothing. Heartily farewell.

                    Exeunt Voltemand and Cornelius.
  And now, Laertes, what's the news with you?
  You told us of some suit: what is't, Laertes?
  You cannot speak of reason to the Dane
  And lose your voice. What wouldst thou beg,
    Laertes,
  That shall not be my offer, not thy asking?
  The head is not more native to the heart,
  The hand more instrumental to the mouth,
  Than is the throne of Denmark to thy father.
  What wouldst thou have, Laertes?

LAERTES   My dread lord,
  Your leave and favour to return to France,
  From whence though willingly I came to Denmark
  To show my duty in your coronation,
  Yet now I must confess, that duty done,
  My thoughts and wishes bend again toward France
  And bow them to your gracious leave and pardon.

KING
  Have you your father's leave? What says Polonius?

POLONIUS
  He hath, my lord, wrung from me my slow leave
  By laboursome petition, and at last
  Upon his will I seal'd my hard consent.   60
  I do beseech you give him leave to go.

KING   Take thy fair hour, Laertes, time be thine,
  And thy best graces spend it at thy will.
  But now, my cousin Hamlet, and my son –

HAMLET   A little more than kin, and less than kind.   65

KING   How is it that the clouds still hang on you?

HAMLET   Not so, my lord, I am too much in the sun.

QUEEN   Good Hamlet, cast thy nighted colour off,
  And let thine eye look like a friend on Denmark.
  Do not for ever with thy vailed lids   70
  Seek for thy noble father in the dust.
  Thou know'st 'tis common: all that lives must die,
  Passing through nature to eternity.

HAMLET   Ay, madam, it is common.

QUEEN   If it be,
  Why seems it so particular with thee?   75

HAMLET
  Seems, madam? Nay, it is. I know not 'seems'.
  'Tis not alone my inky cloak, good mother,
  Nor customary suits of solemn black,
  Nor windy suspiration of forc'd breath,
  No, nor the fruitful river in the eye,   80
  Nor the dejected haviour of the visage,
  Together with all forms, moods, shapes of grief,
  That can denote me truly. These indeed seem,
  For they are actions that a man might play;
  But I have that within which passes show,   85
  These but the trappings and the suits of woe.

KING
  'Tis sweet and commendable in your nature, Hamlet,
  To give these mourning duties to your father,
  But you must know your father lost a father,
  That father lost, lost his – and the survivor bound   90
  In filial obligation for some term
  To do obsequious sorrow. But to persever
  In obstinate condolement is a course
  Of impious stubbornness, 'tis unmanly grief,
  It shows a will most incorrect to heaven,   95
  A heart unfortified, a mind impatient,
  An understanding simple and unschool'd;
  For what we know must be, and is as common
  As any the most vulgar thing to sense –
  Why should we in our peevish opposition   100
  Take it to heart? Fie, 'tis a fault to heaven,
  A fault against the dead, a fault to nature,
  To reason most absurd, whose common theme
  Is death of fathers, and who still hath cried
  From the first corse till he that died today,   105
  'This must be so'. We pray you throw to earth
  This unprevailing woe, and think of us
  As of a father; for let the world take note

You are the most immediate to our throne,
110   And with no less nobility of love
Than that which dearest father bears his son
Do I impart toward you. For your intent
In going back to school in Wittenberg,
It is most retrograde to our desire,
115   And we beseech you bend you to remain
Here in the cheer and comfort of our eye,
Our chiefest courtier, cousin, and our son.
QUEEN   Let not thy mother lose her prayers, Hamlet.
I pray thee stay with us, go not to Wittenberg.
120   HAMLET   I shall in all my best obey you, madam.
KING   Why, 'tis a loving and a fair reply.
Be as ourself in Denmark. Madam, come.
This gentle and unforc'd accord of Hamlet
Sits smiling to my heart; in grace whereof
125   No jocund health that Denmark drinks today
But the great cannon to the clouds shall tell,
And the King's rouse the heaven shall bruit again,
Re-speaking earthly thunder. Come away.
                    Flourish. Exeunt all but Hamlet.
HAMLET   O that this too too sullied flesh would melt,
130   Thaw and resolve itself into a dew,
Or that the Everlasting had not fix'd
His canon 'gainst self-slaughter. O God! God!
How weary, stale, flat, and unprofitable
Seem to me all the uses of this world!
135   Fie on't, ah fie, 'tis an unweeded garden
That grows to seed; things rank and gross in nature
Possess it merely. That it should come to this!
But two months dead – nay, not so much, not two –
So excellent a king, that was to this
140   Hyperion to a satyr, so loving to my mother
That he might not beteem the winds of heaven
Visit her face too roughly. Heaven and earth,
Must I remember? Why, she would hang on him
As if increase of appetite had grown
145   By what it fed on; and yet within a month –
Let me not think on't – Frailty, thy name is
          woman –
A little month, or ere those shoes were old
With which she follow'd my poor father's body,
Like Niobe, all tears – why, she –
150   O God, a beast that wants discourse of reason
Would have mourn'd longer – married with my
          uncle,
My father's brother – but no more like my father
Than I to Hercules. Within a month,
Ere yet the salt of most unrighteous tears
155   Had left the flushing in her galled eyes,
She married – O most wicked speed! To post
With such dexterity to incestuous sheets!
It is not, nor it cannot come to good.
But break, my heart, for I must hold my tongue.

          Enter HORATIO, MARCELLUS *and* BARNARDO.

HORATIO   Hail to your lordship.

HAMLET   I am glad to see you well.   160
Horatio, or I do forget myself.
HORATIO
The same, my lord, and your poor servant ever.
HAMLET
Sir, my good friend, I'll change that name with you.
And what make you from Wittenberg, Horatio? –
Marcellus.   165
MARCELLUS   My good lord.
HAMLET
I am very glad to see you. –
[*to Barnardo*]   Good even, sir. –
But what in faith make you from Wittenberg?
HORATIO   A truant disposition, good my lord.
HAMLET   I would not hear your enemy say so,   170
Nor shall you do my ear that violence
To make it truster of your own report
Against yourself. I know you are no truant.
But what is your affair in Elsinore?
We'll teach you to drink deep ere you depart.   175
HORATIO   My lord, I came to see your father's funeral.
HAMLET   I prithee do not mock me, fellow-student.
I think it was to see my mother's wedding.
HORATIO   Indeed, my lord, it follow'd hard upon.
HAMLET
Thrift, thrift, Horatio. The funeral bak'd meats   180
Did coldly furnish forth the marriage tables.
Would I had met my dearest foe in heaven
Or ever I had seen that day, Horatio.
My father – methinks I see my father –
HORATIO   Where, my lord?
HAMLET   In my mind's eye, Horatio.   185
HORATIO   I saw him once; a was a goodly king.
HAMLET   'A was a man, take him for all in all:
I shall not look upon his like again.
HORATIO   My lord, I think I saw him yesternight.
HAMLET   Saw? Who?
HORATIO   My lord, the king your father.   190
HAMLET   The king my father?
HORATIO   Season your admiration for a while
With an attent ear till I may deliver
Upon the witness of these gentlemen
This marvel to you.
HAMLET   For God's love let me hear!   195
HORATIO   Two nights together had these gentlemen,
Marcellus and Barnardo, on their watch
In the dead waste and middle of the night
Been thus encounter'd: a figure like your father
Armed at point exactly, cap-à-pie,   200
Appears before them, and with solemn march
Goes slow and stately by them; thrice he walk'd
By their oppress'd and fear-surprised eyes
Within his truncheon's length, whilst they, distill'd
Almost to jelly with the act of fear,   205
Stand dumb and speak not to him. This to me
In dreadful secrecy impart they did,
And I with them the third night kept the watch,

Where, as they had deliver'd, both in time,
Form of the thing, each word made true and good,
The apparition comes. I knew your father;
These hands are not more like.

HAMLET   But where was this?

MARCELLUS
My lord, upon the platform where we watch.

HAMLET   Did you not speak to it?

HORATIO   My lord, I did,
But answer made it none. Yet once methought
It lifted up it head and did address
Itself to motion like as it would speak.
But even then the morning cock crew loud,
And at the sound it shrunk in haste away
And vanish'd from our sight.

HAMLET   'Tis very strange.

HORATIO   As I do live, my honour'd lord, 'tis true;
And we did think it writ down in our duty
To let you know of it.

HAMLET   Indeed, sirs; but this troubles me.
Hold you the watch tonight?

ALL   We do, my lord.

HAMLET   Arm'd, say you?

ALL   Arm'd, my lord.

HAMLET   From top to toe?

ALL   My lord, from head to foot.

HAMLET   Then saw you not his face?

HORATIO   O yes, my lord, he wore his beaver up.

HAMLET   What look'd he, frowningly?

HORATIO   A countenance more in sorrow than in anger.

HAMLET   Pale, or red?

HORATIO   Nay, very pale.

HAMLET   And fix'd his eyes upon you?

HORATIO   Most constantly.

HAMLET   I would I had been there.

HORATIO   It would have much amaz'd you.

HAMLET   Very like.
Stay'd it long?

HORATIO
While one with moderate haste might tell a hundred.

MARCELLUS, BARNARDO   Longer, longer.

HORATIO   Not when I saw't.

HAMLET   His beard was grizzled, no?

HORATIO   It was as I have seen it in his life,
A sable silver'd.

HAMLET   I will watch tonight.
Perchance 'twill walk again.

HORATIO   I war'nt it will.

HAMLET   If it assume my noble father's person,
I'll speak to it though hell itself should gape
And bid me hold my peace. I pray you all,
If you have hitherto conceal'd this sight,
Let it be tenable in your silence still;
And whatsomever else shall hap tonight,
Give it an understanding but no tongue.
I will requite your loves. So fare you well.
Upon the platform 'twixt eleven and twelve

I'll visit you.

ALL   Our duty to your honour.

HAMLET   Your loves, as mine to you. Farewell.
          Exeunt Horatio, Marcellus and Barnardo.
My father's spirit – in arms! All is not well.   255
I doubt some foul play. Would the night were come.
Till then sit still, my soul. Foul deeds will rise,
Though all the earth o'erwhelm them, to men's eyes.
                          Exit.

1.3   *Enter* LAERTES AND OPHELIA, *his sister.*

LAERTES   My necessaries are embark'd. Farewell.
And sister, as the winds give benefit
And convoy is assistant, do not sleep,
But let me hear from you.

OPHELIA   Do you doubt that?

LAERTES   For Hamlet, and the trifling of his favour,   5
Hold it a fashion and a toy in blood,
A violet in the youth of primy nature,
Forward, not permanent, sweet, not lasting,
The perfume and suppliance of a minute,
No more.

OPHELIA   No more but so?

LAERTES   Think it no more.   10
For nature crescent does not grow alone
In thews and bulk, but as this temple waxes,
The inward service of the mind and soul
Grows wide withal. Perhaps he loves you now,
And now no soil nor cautel doth besmirch   15
The virtue of his will; but you must fear,
His greatness weigh'd, his will is not his own.
For he himself is subject to his birth:
He may not, as unvalu'd persons do,
Carve for himself, for on his choice depends   20
The sanity and health of this whole state;
And therefore must his choice be circumscrib'd
Unto the voice and yielding of that body
Whereof he is the head. Then if he says he loves you,
It fits your wisdom so far to believe it   25
As he in his particular act and place
May give his saying deed; which is no further
Than the main voice of Denmark goes withal.
Then weigh what loss your honour may sustain
If with too credent ear you list his songs,   30
Or lose your heart, or your chaste treasure open
To his unmaster'd importunity.
Fear it, Ophelia, fear it, my dear sister,
And keep you in the rear of your affection
Out of the shot and danger of desire.   35
The chariest maid is prodigal enough
If she unmask her beauty to the moon.
Virtue itself scapes not calumnious strokes.
The canker galls the infants of the spring
Too oft before their buttons be disclos'd,   40
And in the morn and liquid dew of youth
Contagious blastments are most imminent.

Be wary then: best safety lies in fear.
Youth to itself rebels, though none else near.

45 OPHELIA   I shall th'effect of this good lesson keep
As watchman to my heart. But good my brother,
Do not as some ungracious pastors do,
Show me the steep and thorny way to heaven,
Whiles like a puff'd and reckless libertine
50 Himself the primrose path of dalliance treads,
And recks not his own rede.

LAERTES   O fear me not.
I stay too long.

Enter POLONIUS.

But here my father comes.
A double blessing is a double grace:
Occasion smiles upon a second leave.

POLONIUS
55 Yet here, Laertes? Aboard, aboard for shame.
The wind sits in the shoulder of your sail,
And you are stay'd for. There, my blessing with thee.
And these few precepts in thy memory
Look thou character. Give thy thoughts no tongue,
60 Nor any unproportion'd thought his act.
Be thou familiar, but by no means vulgar;
Those friends thou hast, and their adoption tried,
Grapple them unto thy soul with hoops of steel,
But do not dull thy palm with entertainment
65 Of each new-hatch'd, unfledg'd courage. Beware
Of entrance to a quarrel, but being in,
Bear't that th'opposed may beware of thee.
Give every man thy ear, but few thy voice;
Take each man's censure, but reserve thy judgment.
70 Costly thy habit as thy purse can buy,
But not express'd in fancy; rich, not gaudy;
For the apparel oft proclaims the man,
And they in France of the best rank and station
Are of a most select and generous chief in that.
75 Neither a borrower nor a lender be,
For loan oft loses both itself and friend,
And borrowing dulls the edge of husbandry.
This above all: to thine own self be true,
And it must follow as the night the day
80 Thou canst not then be false to any man.
Farewell, my blessing season this in thee.

LAERTES   Most humbly do I take my leave, my lord.

POLONIUS
The time invests you; go, your servants tend.

LAERTES   Farewell, Ophelia, and remember well
What I have said to you.

OPHELIA   'Tis in my memory lock'd,
85 And you yourself shall keep the key of it.

LAERTES   Farewell.   *Exit.*

POLONIUS   What is't, Ophelia, he hath said to you?

OPHELIA
So please you, something touching the Lord Hamlet.

90 POLONIUS   Marry, well bethought.
'Tis told me he hath very oft of late

Given private time to you, and you yourself
Have of your audience been most free and bounteous.
If it be so – as so 'tis put on me,
And that in way of caution – I must tell you   95
You do not understand yourself so clearly
As it behoves my daughter and your honour.
What is between you? Give me up the truth.

OPHELIA   He hath, my lord, of late made many tenders
Of his affection to me.   100

POLONIUS   Affection? Pooh, you speak like a green girl,
Unsifted in such perilous circumstance.
Do you believe his tenders, as you call them?

OPHELIA   I do not know, my lord, what I should think.

POLONIUS
Marry, I will teach you. Think yourself a baby   105
That you have ta'en these tenders for true pay
Which are not sterling. Tender yourself more dearly
Or – not to crack the wind of the poor phrase,
Running it thus – you'll tender me a fool.

OPHELIA   My lord, he hath importun'd me with love   110
In honourable fashion.

POLONIUS   Ay, fashion you may call it. Go to, go to.

OPHELIA
And hath given countenance to his speech, my lord,
With almost all the holy vows of heaven.

POLONIUS   Ay, springes to catch woodcocks. I do know,   115
When the blood burns, how prodigal the soul
Lends the tongue vows. These blazes, daughter,
Giving more light than heat, extinct in both
Even in their promise as it is a-making,
You must not take for fire. From this time   120
Be something scanter of your maiden presence,
Set your entreatments at a higher rate
Than a command to parley. For Lord Hamlet,
Believe so much in him that he is young,
And with a larger tether may he walk_   125
Than may be given you. In few, Ophelia,
Do not believe his vows; for they are brokers
Not of that dye which their investments show,
But mere implorators of unholy suits,
Breathing like sanctified and pious bawds   130
The better to beguile. This is for all.
I would not, in plain terms, from this time forth
Have you so slander any moment leisure
As to give words or talk with the Lord Hamlet.
Look to't, I charge you. Come your ways.   135

OPHELIA   I shall obey, my lord.   *Exeunt.*

1.4   *Enter* HAMLET, HORATIO *and* MARCELLUS.

HAMLET   The air bites shrewdly, it is very cold.

HORATIO   It is a nipping and an eager air.

HAMLET   What hour now?

HORATIO   I think it lacks of twelve.

MARCELLUS   No, it is struck.

HORATIO   Indeed? I heard it not.
It then draws near the season   5

Wherein the spirit held his wont to walk.
[*A flourish of trumpets, and two pieces
of ordnance go off.*]
What does this mean, my lord?

HAMLET
The King doth wake tonight and takes his rouse,
Keeps wassail, and the swagg'ring upspring reels;
And as he drains his draughts of Rhenish down,
The kettle-drum and trumpet thus bray out
The triumph of his pledge.

HORATIO   Is it a custom?

HAMLET   Ay marry is't,
But to my mind, though I am native here
And to the manner born, it is a custom
More honour'd in the breach than the observance.
This heavy-headed revel east and west
Makes us traduc'd and tax'd of other nations –
They clepe us drunkards, and with swinish phrase
Soil our addition; and indeed it takes
From our achievements, though perform'd at height,
The pith and marrow of our attribute.
So, oft it chances in particular men
That for some vicious mole of nature in them,
As in their birth, wherein they are not guilty
(Since nature cannot choose his origin),
By their o'ergrowth of some complexion,
Oft breaking down the pales and forts of reason,
Or by some habit, that too much o'erleavens
The form of plausive manners – that these men,
Carrying, I say, the stamp of one defect,
Being Nature's livery or Fortune's star,
His virtues else, be they as pure as grace,
As infinite as man may undergo,
Shall in the general censure take corruption
From that particular fault. The dram of evil
Doth all the noble substance often dout
To his own scandal.

Enter Ghost.

HORATIO   Look, my lord, it comes.

HAMLET   Angels and ministers of grace defend us!
Be thou a spirit of health or goblin damn'd,
Bring with thee airs from heaven or blasts from hell,
Be thy intents wicked or charitable,
Thou com'st in such a questionable shape
That I will speak to thee. I'll call thee Hamlet,
King, father, royal Dane. O answer me.
Let me not burst in ignorance, but tell
Why thy canoniz'd bones, hearsed in death,
Have burst their cerements, why the sepulchre
Wherein we saw thee quietly inurn'd
Hath op'd his ponderous and marble jaws
To cast thee up again. What may this mean,
That thou, dead corse, again in complete steel
Revisits thus the glimpses of the moon,
Making night hideous and we fools of nature
So horridly to shake our disposition

With thoughts beyond the reaches of our souls?
Say why is this? Wherefore? What should we do?
[*Ghost beckons.*]

HORATIO   It beckons you to go away with it,
As if it some impartment did desire
To you alone.

MARCELLUS   Look with what courteous action   60
It waves you to a more removed ground.
But do not go with it.

HORATIO   No, by no means.

HAMLET   It will not speak. Then I will follow it.

HORATIO   Do not, my lord.

HAMLET   Why, what should be the fear?
I do not set my life at a pin's fee,   65
And for my soul, what can it do to that,
Being a thing immortal as itself?
It waves me forth again. I'll follow it.

HORATIO
What if it tempt you toward the flood, my lord,
Or to the dreadful summit of the cliff   70
That beetles o'er his base into the sea,
And there assume some other horrible form
Which might deprive your sovereignty of reason
And draw you into madness? Think of it.
The very place puts toys of desperation,   75
Without more motive, into every brain
That looks so many fathoms to the sea
And hears it roar beneath.

HAMLET   It waves me still.
Go on, I'll follow thee.

MARCELLUS   You shall not go, my lord.

HAMLET   Hold off your hands.   80

HORATIO   Be rul'd; you shall not go.

HAMLET   My fate cries out
And makes each petty artire in this body
As hardy as the Nemean lion's nerve.
Still am I call'd. Unhand me, gentlemen.
By heaven, I'll make a ghost of him that lets me.   85
I say away. – Go on, I'll follow thee.
Exeunt Ghost and Hamlet.

HORATIO   He waxes desperate with imagination.

MARCELLUS   Let's follow. 'Tis not fit thus to obey him.

HORATIO   Have after. To what issue will this come?

MARCELLUS
Something is rotten in the state of Denmark.   90

HORATIO   Heaven will direct it.

MARCELLUS   Nay, let's follow him.
Exeunt.

1.5   *Enter* Ghost *and* HAMLET.

HAMLET
Whither wilt thou lead me? Speak, I'll go no further.

GHOST   Mark me.

HAMLET   I will.

GHOST   My hour is almost come
When I to sulph'rous and tormenting flames

Must render up myself.

HAMLET   Alas, poor ghost.

5   GHOST   Pity me not, but lend thy serious hearing
To what I shall unfold.

HAMLET   Speak, I am bound to hear.

GHOST   So art thou to revenge when thou shalt hear.

HAMLET   What?

GHOST   I am thy father's spirit,

10 Doom'd for a certain term to walk the night,
And for the day confin'd to fast in fires,
Till the foul crimes done in my days of nature
Are burnt and purg'd away. But that I am forbid
To tell the secrets of my prison-house,

15 I could a tale unfold whose lightest word
Would harrow up thy soul, freeze thy young blood,
Make thy two eyes like stars start from their spheres,
Thy knotted and combined locks to part,
And each particular hair to stand an end

20 Like quills upon the fretful porpentine.
But this eternal blazon must not be
To ears of flesh and blood. List, list, O list!
If thou didst ever thy dear father love –

HAMLET   O God!

25 GHOST   Revenge his foul and most unnatural murder.

HAMLET   Murder!

GHOST   Murder most foul, as in the best it is,
But this most foul, strange and unnatural.

HAMLET

Haste me to know't, that I with wings as swift

30 As meditation or the thoughts of love
May sweep to my revenge.

GHOST   I find thee apt.
And duller shouldst thou be than the fat weed
That roots itself in ease on Lethe wharf,
Wouldst thou not stir in this. Now, Hamlet, hear.

35 'Tis given out that, sleeping in my orchard,
A serpent stung me – so the whole ear of Denmark
Is by a forged process of my death
Rankly abus'd – but know, thou noble youth,
The serpent that did sting thy father's life

40 Now wears his crown.

HAMLET   O my prophetic soul! My uncle!

GHOST   Ay, that incestuous, that adulterate beast,
With witchcraft of his wit, with traitorous gifts –
O wicked wit, and gifts that have the power

45 So to seduce! – won to his shameful lust
The will of my most seeming-virtuous queen.
O Hamlet, what a falling off was there,
From me, whose love was of that dignity
That it went hand in hand even with the vow

50 I made to her in marriage, and to decline
Upon a wretch whose natural gifts were poor
To those of mine.
But virtue, as it never will be mov'd,
Though lewdness court it in a shape of heaven,

55 So lust, though to a radiant angel link'd,
Will sate itself in a celestial bed

And prey on garbage.
But soft, methinks I scent the morning air:
Brief let me be. Sleeping within my orchard,
My custom always of the afternoon,   60
Upon my secure hour thy uncle stole
With juice of cursed hebenon in a vial,
And in the porches of my ears did pour
The leperous distilment, whose effect
Holds such an enmity with blood of man   65
That swift as quicksilver it courses through
The natural gates and alleys of the body,
And with a sudden vigour it doth posset
And curd, like eager droppings into milk,
The thin and wholesome blood. So did it mine,   70
And a most instant tetter bark'd about,
Most lazar-like, with vile and loathsome crust
All my smooth body.
Thus was I, sleeping, by a brother's hand
Of life, of crown, of queen at once dispatch'd,   75
Cut off even in the blossoms of my sin,
Unhousel'd, disappointed, unanel'd,
No reck'ning made, but sent to my account
With all my imperfections on my head.
O horrible! O horrible! most horrible!   80
If thou has nature in thee, bear it not,
Let not the royal bed of Denmark be
A couch for luxury and damned incest.
But howsomever thou pursuest this act,
Taint not thy mind nor let thy soul contrive   85
Against thy mother aught. Leave her to heaven,
And to those thorns that in her bosom lodge
To prick and sting her. Fare thee well at once:
The glow-worm shows the matin to be near
And gins to pale his uneffectual fire.   90
Adieu, adieu, adieu. Remember me.   *Exit.*

HAMLET   O all you host of heaven! O earth! What else?
And shall I couple hell? O fie! Hold, hold, my heart,
And you, my sinews, grow not instant old,
But bear me stiffly up. Remember thee?   95
Ay, thou poor ghost, whiles memory holds a seat
In this distracted globe. Remember thee?
Yea, from the table of my memory
I'll wipe away all trivial fond records,
All saws of books, all forms, all pressures past   100
That youth and observation copied there,
And thy commandment all alone shall live
Within the book and volume of my brain,
Unmix'd with baser matter. Yes, by heaven!
O most pernicious woman!   105
O villain, villain, smiling damned villain!
My tables. Meet it is I set it down
That one may smile, and smile, and be a villain –
At least I am sure it may be so in Denmark. [*Writes.*]
So, uncle, there you are. Now to my word.   110
It is 'Adieu, adieu, remember me.'
I have sworn't.

Enter HORATIO *and* MARCELLUS *calling.*

HORATIO   My lord, my lord.

MARCELLUS   Lord Hamlet.

15   HORATIO   Heavens secure him.

HAMLET [*aside*]   So be it.

MARCELLUS   Hillo, ho, ho, my lord.

HAMLET   Hillo, ho, ho, boy. Come, bird, come.

MARCELLUS   How is't, my noble lord?

20   HORATIO   What news, my lord?

HAMLET   O, wonderful!

HORATIO   Good my lord, tell it.

HAMLET   No, you will reveal it.

HORATIO   Not I, my lord, by heaven.

25   MARCELLUS   Nor I, my lord.

HAMLET

How say you then, would heart of man once think
   it –
But you'll be secret?

HORATIO, MARCELLUS   Ay, by heaven.

HAMLET

There's never a villain dwelling in all Denmark
30   But he's an arrant knave.

HORATIO

There needs no ghost, my lord, come from the grave
To tell us this.

HAMLET   Why, right, you are in the right.
And so without more circumstance at all
I hold it fit that we shake hands and part,
135   You as your business and desire shall point you –
For every man hath business and desire,
Such as it is – and for my own poor part,
I will go pray.

HORATIO

These are but wild and whirling words, my lord.

140   HAMLET   I am sorry they offend you, heartily –
Yes faith, heartily.

HORATIO   There's no offence, my lord.

HAMLET   Yes by Saint Patrick but there is, Horatio,
And much offence too. Touching this vision here,
It is an honest ghost, that let me tell you.
145   For your desire to know what is between us,
O'ermaster't as you may. And now, good friends,
As you are friends, scholars, and soldiers,
Give me one poor request.

HORATIO   What is't, my lord? We will.

HAMLET

Never make known what you have seen tonight.

150   HORATIO, MARCELLUS   My lord, we will not.

HAMLET   Nay, but swear't.

HORATIO   In faith, my lord, not I.

MARCELLUS   Nor I, my lord, in faith.

HAMLET   Upon my sword.

155   MARCELLUS   We have sworn, my lord, already.

HAMLET   Indeed, upon my sword, indeed.

GHOST [*Cries under the stage.*]   Swear.

HAMLET

Ah ha, boy, say'st thou so? Art thou there,
   truepenny?
Come on, you hear this fellow in the cellarage.
Consent to swear.

HORATIO   Propose the oath, my lord.   160

HAMLET   Never to speak of this that you have seen.
Swear by my sword.

GHOST   Swear. [*They swear.*]

HAMLET   *Hic et ubique?* Then we'll shift our ground.
Come hither, gentlemen,   165
And lay your hands again upon my sword.
Swear by my sword
Never to speak of this that you have heard.

GHOST   Swear by his sword. [*They swear.*]

HAMLET

Well said, old mole. Canst work i'th' earth so fast?   170
A worthy pioner! Once more remove, good friends.

HORATIO

O day and night, but this is wondrous strange.

HAMLET

And therefore as a stranger give it welcome.
There are more things in heaven and earth, Horatio,
Than are dreamt of in your philosophy.   175
But come,
Here, as before, never, so help you mercy,
How strange or odd some'er I bear myself –
As I perchance hereafter shall think meet
To put an antic disposition on –   180
That you, at such time seeing me, never shall,
With arms encumber'd thus, or this head-shake,
Or by pronouncing of some doubtful phrase,
As 'Well, we know', or 'We could and if we would',
Or 'If we list to speak', or 'There be and if they
   might',   185
Or such ambiguous giving out, to note
That you know aught of me – this do swear,
So grace and mercy at your most need help you.

GHOST   Swear. [*They swear.*]

HAMLET   Rest, rest, perturbed spirit. So, gentlemen,   190
With all my love I do commend me to you;
And what so poor a man as Hamlet is
May do t'express his love and friending to you,
God willing, shall not lack. Let us go in together.
And still your fingers on your lips, I pray.   195
The time is out of joint. O cursed spite,
That ever I was born to set it right.
Nay, come, let's go together.   *Exeunt.*

2.1   *Enter old* POLONIUS, *with his man* REYNALDO.

POLONIUS

Give him this money and these notes, Reynaldo.

REYNALDO   I will, my lord.

POLONIUS

You shall do marvellous wisely, good Reynaldo,

Before you visit him, to make inquire
Of his behaviour.

5 REYNALDO   My lord, I did intend it.
POLONIUS

Marry, well said, very well said. Look you, sir,
Inquire me first what Danskers are in Paris,
And how, and who, what means, and where they
    keep,
What company, at what expense; and finding
10 By this encompassment and drift of question
That they do know my son, come you more nearer
Than your particular demands will touch it.
Take you as 'twere some distant knowledge of him,
As thus, 'I know his father, and his friends,
15 And in part him' – do you mark this, Reynaldo?

REYNALDO   Ay, very well, my lord.
POLONIUS

'And in part him. But', you may say, 'not well;
But if't be he I mean, he's very wild,
Addicted so and so' – and there put on him
20 What forgeries you please – marry, none so rank
As may dishonour him – take heed of that –
But, sir, such wanton, wild, and usual slips
As are companions noted and most known
To youth and liberty.

REYNALDO   As gaming, my lord?
25 POLONIUS   Ay, or drinking, fencing, swearing,
Quarrelling, drabbing – you may go so far.

REYNALDO   My lord, that would dishonour him.
POLONIUS

'Faith no, as you may season it in the charge.
You must not put another scandal on him,
30 That he is open to incontinency –
That's not my meaning; but breathe his faults so
    quaintly
That they may seem the taints of liberty,
The flash and outbreak of a fiery mind,
A savageness in unreclaimed blood,
35 Of general assault.

REYNALDO   But my good lord –
POLONIUS   Wherefore should you do this?

REYNALDO   Ay, my lord, I would know that.
POLONIUS   Marry, sir, here's my drift,
And I believe it is a fetch of warrant.
40 You laying these slight sullies on my son,
As 'twere a thing a little soil'd i'th' working,
Mark you,
Your party in converse, him you would sound,
Having ever seen in the prenominate crimes
45 The youth you breathe of guilty, be assur'd
He closes with you in this consequence:
'Good sir', or so, or 'friend', or 'gentleman',
According to the phrase or the addition
Of man and country.

REYNALDO   Very good, my lord.
50 POLONIUS   And then, sir, does a this – a does – what was

I about to say? By the mass, I was about to say
something. Where did I leave?

REYNALDO   At 'closes in the consequence'.
POLONIUS   At 'closes in the consequence', ay, marry.
He closes thus: 'I know the gentleman,   55
I saw him yesterday', or 'th'other day',
Or then, or then, with such or such, 'and as you say,
There was a gaming', 'there o'ertook in's rouse',
'There falling out at tennis', or perchance
'I saw him enter such a house of sale' –   60
Videlicet a brothel, or so forth.
See you now,
Your bait of falsehood takes this carp of truth;
And thus do we of wisdom and of reach,
With windlasses and with assays of bias,   65
By indirections find directions out.
So by my former lecture and advice
Shall you my son. You have me, have you not?

REYNALDO   My lord, I have.
POLONIUS   God buy ye, fare ye well.

REYNALDO   Good my lord.   70
POLONIUS   Observe his inclination in yourself.

REYNALDO   I shall, my lord.
POLONIUS   And let him ply his music.

REYNALDO   Well, my lord.   *Exit*.

Enter OPHELIA.

POLONIUS
Farewell. How now, Ophelia, what's the matter?

OPHELIA
O my lord, my lord, I have been so affrighted.   75

POLONIUS   With what, i'th' name of God?

OPHELIA   My lord, as I was sewing in my closet,
Lord Hamlet, with his doublet all unbrac'd,
No hat upon his head, his stockings foul'd,
Ungarter'd and down-gyved to his ankle,   80
Pale as his shirt, his knees knocking each other,
And with a look so piteous in purport
As if he had been loosed out of hell
To speak of horrors, he comes before me.

POLONIUS   Mad for thy love?

OPHELIA   My lord, I do not know,   85
But truly I do fear it.

POLONIUS   What said he?

OPHELIA
He took me by the wrist and held me hard.
Then goes he to the length of all his arm,
And with his other hand thus o'er his brow
He falls to such perusal of my face   90
As a would draw it. Long stay'd he so.
At last, a little shaking of mine arm,
And thrice his head thus waving up and down,
He rais'd a sigh so piteous and profound
As it did seem to shatter all his bulk   95
And end his being. That done, he lets me go,
And with his head over his shoulder turn'd

302

He seem'd to find his way without his eyes,
For out o' doors he went without their helps,
And to the last bended their light on me.
POLONIUS   Come, go with me, I will go seek the King.
This is the very ecstasy of love,
Whose violent property fordoes itself
And leads the will to desperate undertakings
As oft as any passion under heaven
That does afflict our natures. I am sorry –
What, have you given him any hard words of late?
OPHELIA   No, my good lord, but as you did command,
I did repel his letters and denied
His access to me.
POLONIUS   That hath made him mad.
I am sorry that with better heed and judgment
I had not quoted him. I fear'd he did but trifle
And meant to wrack thee. But beshrew my jealousy!
By heaven, it is as proper to our age
To cast beyond ourselves in our opinions
As it is common for the younger sort
To lack discretion. Come, go we to the King.
This must be known, which, being kept close, might
    move
More grief to hide than hate to utter love.
Come.   *Exeunt.*

2.2   *Flourish. Enter* KING *and* QUEEN, ROSENCRANTZ
           and GUILDENSTERN, *with attendants.*

KING   Welcome, dear Rosencrantz and Guildenstern.
Moreover that we much did long to see you,
The need we have to use you did provoke
Our hasty sending. Something have you heard
Of Hamlet's transformation – so I call it,
Sith nor th'exterior nor the inward man
Resembles that it was. What it should be,
More than his father's death, that thus hath put him
So much from th'understanding of himself
I cannot dream of. I entreat you both
That, being of so young days brought up with him,
And sith so neighbour'd to his youth and haviour,
That you vouchsafe your rest here in our court
Some little time, so by your companies
To draw him on to pleasures and to gather,
So much as from occasion you may glean,
Whether aught to us unknown afflicts him thus
That, open'd, lies within our remedy.
QUEEN   Good gentlemen, he hath much talk'd of you,
And sure I am, two men there is not living
To whom he more adheres. If it will please you
To show us so much gentry and good will
As to expend your time with us awhile
For the supply and profit of our hope,
Your visitation shall receive such thanks
As fits a king's remembrance.
ROSENCRANTZ   Both your Majesties
Might, by the sovereign power you have of us,

Put your dread pleasures more into command
Than to entreaty.
GUILDENSTERN   But we both obey,
And here give up ourselves in the full bent
To lay our service freely at your feet
To be commanded.
KING   Thanks, Rosencrantz and gentle Guildenstern.
QUEEN   Thanks, Guildenstern and gentle Rosencrantz.
And I beseech you instantly to visit
My too much changed son. Go, some of you,
And bring these gentlemen where Hamlet is.
GUILDENSTERN
Heavens make our presence and our practices
Pleasant and helpful to him.
QUEEN   Ay, amen.
Exeunt Rosencrantz and Guildenstern and an attendant.

Enter POLONIUS.

POLONIUS
Th'ambassadors from Norway, my good lord,
Are joyfully return'd.
KING   Thou still hast been the father of good news.
POLONIUS   Have I, my lord? I assure my good liege
I hold my duty as I hold my soul,
Both to my God and to my gracious King;
And I do think – or else this brain of mine
Hunts not the trail of policy so sure
As it hath us'd to do – that I have found
The very cause of Hamlet's lunacy.
KING   O speak of that: that do I long to hear.
POLONIUS   Give first admittance to th'ambassadors.
My news shall be the fruit to that great feast.
KING   Thyself do grace to them and bring them in.
                                                          Exit Polonius.
He tells me, my dear Gertrude, he hath found
The head and source of all your son's distemper.
QUEEN   I doubt it is no other but the main,
His father's death and our o'er-hasty marriage.
KING   Well, we shall sift him.

Enter POLONIUS, VOLTEMAND *and* CORNELIUS.

                                      Welcome, my good friends.
Say, Voltemand, what from our brother Norway?
VOLTEMAND
Most fair return of greetings and desires.
Upon our first, he sent out to suppress
His nephew's levies, which to him appear'd
To be a preparation 'gainst the Polack;
But better look'd into, he truly found
It was against your Highness; whereat griev'd
That so his sickness, age, and impotence
Was falsely borne in hand, sends out arrests
On Fortinbras; which he, in brief, obeys,
Receives rebuke from Norway, and, in fine,
Makes vow before his uncle never more
To give th'assay of arms against your Majesty:
Whereon old Norway, overcome with joy,

Gives him three thousand crowns in annual fee
And his commission to employ those soldiers
75 So levied, as before, against the Polack,
With an entreaty, herein further shown,
[*Gives a paper.*]
That it might please you to give quiet pass
Through your dominions for this enterprise
On such regards of safety and allowance
As therein are set down.
80 KING   It likes us well;
And at our more consider'd time we'll read,
Answer, and think upon this business.
Meantime, we thank you for your well-took labour.
Go to your rest, at night we'll feast together.
Most welcome home.
                          Exeunt Voltemand and Cornelius.
85 POLONIUS   This business is well ended.
My liege and madam, to expostulate
What majesty should be, what duty is,
Why day is day, night night, and time is time,
Were nothing but to waste night, day, and time.
90 Therefore, since brevity is the soul of wit,
And tediousness the limbs and outward flourishes,
I will be brief. Your noble son is mad.
Mad call I it, for to define true madness,
What is't but to be nothing else but mad?
But let that go.
95 QUEEN   More matter with less art.
POLONIUS   Madam, I swear I use no art at all.
That he is mad 'tis true; 'tis true 'tis pity;
And pity 'tis 'tis true. A foolish figure –
But farewell it, for I will use no art.
100 Mad let us grant him then. And now remains
That we find out the cause of this effect,
Or rather say the cause of this defect,
For this effect defective comes by cause.
Thus it remains; and the remainder thus:
105 Perpend,
I have a daughter – have while she is mine –
Who in her duty and obedience, mark,
Hath given me this. Now gather and surmise.
[*Reads.*] *To the celestial and my soul's idol, the most*
110 *beautified Ophelia* – That's an ill phrase, a vile phrase,
'beautified' is a vile phrase. But you shall hear – *these;*
in her excellent white bosom, these, etc.
QUEEN   Came this from Hamlet to her?
POLONIUS   Good madam, stay awhile, I will be faithful.
115   *Doubt thou the stars are fire,*
               Doubt that the sun doth move,
               Doubt truth to be a liar,
               But never doubt I love.
O dear Ophelia, I am ill at these numbers. I have not art
120 *to reckon my groans. But that I love thee best, O most*
best, believe it. Adieu.
               Thine evermore, most dear lady, whilst this
               machine is to him,   Hamlet.

This in obedience hath my daughter shown me,
And, more above, hath his solicitings,   125
As they fell out by time, by means, and place,
All given to mine ear.
KING   But how hath she receiv'd his love?
POLONIUS   What do you think of me?
KING   As of a man faithful and honourable.   130
POLONIUS
I would fain prove so. But what might you think,
When I had seen this hot love on the wing –
As I perceiv'd it, I must tell you that,
Before my daughter told me – what might you
Or my dear Majesty your queen here think,   135
If I had play'd the desk or table-book,
Or given my heart a winking mute and dumb,
Or look'd upon this love with idle sight –
What might you think? No, I went round to work,
And my young mistress thus I did bespeak: 140
'Lord Hamlet is a prince out of thy star.
This must not be.' And then I prescripts gave her,
That she should lock herself from his resort,
Admit no messengers, receive no tokens;
Which done, she took the fruits of my advice,   145
And he, repelled – a short tale to make –
Fell into a sadness, then into a fast,
Thence to a watch, thence into a weakness,
Thence to a lightness, and, by this declension,
Into the madness wherein now he raves   150
And all we mourn for.
KING   Do you think 'tis this?
QUEEN   It may be; very like.
POLONIUS
Hath there been such a time – I would fain know that
                                                                                –
That I have positively said ''Tis so',
When it prov'd otherwise?
KING   Not that I know.   155
POLONIUS   Take this from this if this be otherwise.
[*Points to his head and shoulder.*]
If circumstances lead me, I will find
Where truth is hid, though it were hid indeed
Within the centre.
KING   How may we try it further?
POLONIUS
You know sometimes he walks four hours together   160
Here in the lobby.
QUEEN   So he does indeed.
POLONIUS
At such a time I'll loose my daughter to him.
Be you and I behind an arras then,
Mark the encounter. If he love her not,
And be not from his reason fall'n thereon,   165
Let me be no assistant for a state,
But keep a farm and carters.
KING   We will try it.

                    Enter HAMLET, *reading on a book.*

QUEEN
But look where sadly the poor wretch comes reading.

POLONIUS   Away, I do beseech you both, away.
170   I'll board him presently. O give me leave.

Exeunt King and Queen and attendants.
How does my good Lord Hamlet?

HAMLET   Well, God-a-mercy.

POLONIUS   Do you know me, my lord?

HAMLET   Excellent well. You are a fishmonger.

175   POLONIUS   Not I, my lord.

HAMLET   Then I would you were so honest a man.

POLONIUS   Honest, my lord?

HAMLET   Ay sir. To be honest, as this world goes, is to
be one man picked out of ten thousand.

180   POLONIUS   That's very true, my lord.

HAMLET   For if the sun breed maggots in a dead dog,
being a good kissing carrion – Have you a daughter?

POLONIUS   I have, my lord.

HAMLET   Let her not walk i'th' sun. Conception is a
185   blessing, but as your daughter may conceive – friend,
look to't.

POLONIUS [*aside*]   How say you by that? Still harping on
my daughter. Yet he knew me not at first; a said I was
a fishmonger. A is far gone. And truly in my youth I
190   suffered much extremity for love, very near this. I'll
speak to him again. – What do you read, my lord?

HAMLET   Words, words, words.

POLONIUS   What is the matter, my lord?

HAMLET   Between who?

195   POLONIUS   I mean the matter that you read, my lord.

HAMLET   Slanders, sir. For the satirical rogue says here
that old men have gray beards, that their faces are
wrinkled, their eyes purging thick amber and plum-
tree gum, and that they have a plentiful lack of wit,
200   together with most weak hams – all which, sir,
though I most powerfully and potently believe, yet I
hold it not honesty to have it thus set down. For
yourself, sir, shall grow old as I am – if like a crab you
could go backward.

205   POLONIUS [*aside*]   Though this be madness, yet there is
method in't. – Will you walk out of the air, my lord?

HAMLET   Into my grave?

POLONIUS   Indeed, that's out of the air. – [*aside*] How
pregnant sometimes his replies are – a happiness that
210   often madness hits on, which reason and sanity could
not so prosperously be delivered of. I will leave him
and suddenly contrive the means of meeting between
him and my daughter. – My lord, I will take my leave
of you.

215   HAMLET   You cannot, sir, take from me anything that I
will not more willingly part withal – except my life,
except my life, except my life.

POLONIUS   Fare you well, my lord.

HAMLET   These tedious old fools.

Enter ROSENCRANTZ *and* GUILDENSTERN.

20   POLONIUS   You go to seek the Lord Hamlet. There he is.

ROSENCRANTZ   God save you, sir.   *Exit Polonius.*

GUILDENSTERN   My honoured lord.

ROSENCRANTZ   My most dear lord.

HAMLET   My excellent good friends. How dost thou,
Guildenstern? Ah, Rosencrantz. Good lads, how do   225
you both?

ROSENCRANTZ   As the indifferent children of the earth.

GUILDENSTERN   Happy in that we are not over-happy:
on Fortune's cap we are not the very button.

HAMLET   Nor the soles of her shoe?   230

ROSENCRANTZ   Neither, my lord.

HAMLET   Then you live about her waist, or in the
middle of her favours?

GUILDENSTERN   Faith, her privates we.

HAMLET   In the secret parts of Fortune? O most true,   235
she is a strumpet. What news?

ROSENCRANTZ   None, my lord, but the world's grown
honest.

HAMLET   Then is doomsday near. But your news is not
true. Let me question more in particular. What have   240
you, my good friends, deserved at the hands of
Fortune that she sends you to prison hither?

GUILDENSTERN   Prison, my lord?

HAMLET   Denmark's a prison.

ROSENCRANTZ   Then is the world one.   245

HAMLET   A goodly one, in which there are many
confines, wards, and dungeons, Denmark being one
o'th' worst.

ROSENCRANTZ   We think not so, my lord.

HAMLET   Why, then 'tis none to you; for there is nothing   250
either good or bad but thinking makes it so. To me it
is a prison.

ROSENCRANTZ   Why, then your ambition makes it one:
'tis too narrow for your mind.

HAMLET   O God, I could be bounded in a nutshell and   255
count myself a king of infinite space – were it not that
I have bad dreams.

GUILDENSTERN   Which dreams indeed are ambition; for
the very substance of the ambitious is merely the
shadow of a dream.   260

HAMLET   A dream itself is but a shadow.

ROSENCRANTZ   Truly, and I hold ambition of so airy and
light a quality that it is but a shadow's shadow.

HAMLET   Then are our beggars bodies, and our
monarchs and outstretched heroes the beggars'   265
shadows. Shall we to th' court? For by my fay, I cannot
reason.

ROSENCRANTZ, GUILDENSTERN   We'll wait upon you.

HAMLET   No such matter. I will not sort you with the
rest of my servants; for, to speak to you like an honest   270
man, I am most dreadfully attended. But in the beaten
way of friendship, what make you at Elsinore?

ROSENCRANTZ   To visit you, my lord, no other occasion.

HAMLET   Beggar that I am, I am even poor in thanks,
but I thank you. And sure, dear friends, my thanks are   275
too dear a halfpenny. Were you not sent for? Is it your
own inclining? Is it a free visitation? Come, come, deal

justly with me. Come, come. Nay, speak.

GUILDENSTERN   What should we say, my lord?

280 HAMLET   Anything but to th' purpose. You were sent
for, and there is a kind of confession in your looks,
which your modesties have not craft enough to colour.
I know the good King and Queen have sent for you.

ROSENCRANTZ   To what end, my lord?

285 HAMLET   That, you must teach me. But let me conjure
you, by the rights of our fellowship, by the consonancy
of our youth, by the obligation of our ever-preserved
love, and by what more dear a better proposer can
charge you withal, be even and direct with me
290 whether you were sent for or no.

ROSENCRANTZ [*aside to Guildenstern*]   What say you?

HAMLET   Nay, then I have an eye of you. If you love me,
hold not off.

GUILDENSTERN   My lord, we were sent for.

295 HAMLET   I will tell you why; so shall my anticipation
prevent your discovery, and your secrecy to the King
and Queen moult no feather. I have of late, but
wherefore I know not, lost all my mirth, forgone all
custom of exercises; and indeed it goes so heavily with
300 my disposition that this goodly frame the earth seems
to me a sterile promontory, this most excellent canopy
the air, look you, this brave o'erhanging firmament,
this majestical roof fretted with golden fire, why, it
appeareth nothing to me but a foul and pestilent
305 congregation of vapours. What piece of work is a man,
how noble in reason, how infinite in faculties, in form
and moving how express and admirable, in action how
like an angel, in apprehension how like a god: the
beauty of the world, the paragon of animals – and yet,
310 to me, what is this quintessence of dust? Man delights
not me – nor woman neither, though by your smiling
you seem to say so.

ROSENCRANTZ   My lord, there was no such stuff in my
thoughts.

315 HAMLET   Why did ye laugh then, when I said man
delights not me?

ROSENCRANTZ   To think, my lord, if you delight not in
man, what Lenten entertainment the players shall
receive from you. We coted them on the way, and
320 hither are they coming to offer you service.

HAMLET   He that plays the king shall be welcome – his
Majesty shall have tribute on me, the adventurous
knight shall use his foil and target, the lover shall not
sigh gratis, the humorous man shall end his part in
325 peace, the clown shall make those laugh whose lungs
are tickle a'th' sear, and the lady shall say her mind
freely – or the blank verse shall halt for't. What
players are they?

ROSENCRANTZ   Even those you were wont to take such
330 delight in, the tragedians of the city.

HAMLET   How chances it they travel? Their residence,
both in reputation and profit, was better both ways.

ROSENCRANTZ   I think their inhibition comes by the
means of the late innovation.

HAMLET   Do they hold the same estimation they did   335
when I was in the city? Are they so followed?

ROSENCRANTZ   No, indeed are they not.

HAMLET   How comes it? Do they grow rusty?

ROSENCRANTZ   Nay, their endeavour keeps in the
wonted pace; but there is, sir, an eyrie of children,   340
little eyases, that cry out on the top of question, and
are most tyrannically clapped for't. These are now the
fashion, and so berattle the common stages – so they
call them – that many wearing rapiers are afraid of
goose-quills and dare scarce come thither.   345

HAMLET   What, are they children? Who maintains 'em?
How are they escotted? Will they pursue the quality
no longer than they can sing? Will they not say
afterwards, if they should grow themselves to common
players – as it is most like, if their means are no   350
better – their writers do them wrong to make them
exclaim against their own succession?

ROSENCRANTZ   Faith, there has been much to do on
both sides; and the nation holds it no sin to tar them
to controversy. There was for a while no money bid for   355
argument unless the poet and the player went to cuffs
in the question.

HAMLET   Is't possible?

GUILDENSTERN   O, there has been much throwing about
of brains.   360

HAMLET   Do the boys carry it away?

ROSENCRANTZ   Ay, that they do, my lord, Hercules and
his load too.

HAMLET   It is not very strange; for my uncle is King of
Denmark, and those that would make mouths at him   365
while my father lived give twenty, forty, fifty, a
hundred ducats apiece for his picture in little.
'Sblood, there is something in this more than
natural, if philosophy could find it out.

[*A flourish of trumpets.*]

GUILDENSTERN   There are the players.   370

HAMLET   Gentlemen, you are welcome to Elsinore. Your
hands, come then. Th'appurtenance of welcome is
fashion and ceremony. Let me comply with you in this
garb – lest my extent to the players, which I tell you
must show fairly outwards, should more appear like   375
entertainment than yours. You are welcome. But my
uncle-father and aunt-mother are deceived.

GUILDENSTERN   In what, my dear lord?

HAMLET   I am but mad north-north-west. When the
wind is southerly, I know a hawk from a handsaw.   380

Enter POLONIUS.

POLONIUS   Well be with you, gentlemen.

HAMLET   Hark you, Guildenstern, and you too – at each
ear a hearer. That great baby you see there is not yet
out of his swaddling-clouts.

ROSENCRANTZ   Happily he is the second time come to   385
them, for they say an old man is twice a child.

HAMLET   I will prophesy he comes to tell me of the
players. Mark it. – You say right, sir, a Monday

morning, 'twas then indeed.

POLONIUS   My lord, I have news to tell you.

HAMLET   My lord, I have news to tell you. When
   Roscius was an actor in Rome –

POLONIUS   The actors are come hither, my lord.

HAMLET   Buzz, buzz.

POLONIUS   Upon my honour –

HAMLET   Then came each actor on his ass –

POLONIUS   The best actors in the world, either for
   tragedy, comedy, history, pastoral, pastoral-comical,
   historical-pastoral, tragical-historical, tragical comical
   historical-pastoral, scene individable, or poem unlimited. Seneca cannot be too heavy, nor Plautus too
   light. For the law of writ, and the liberty, these are
   the only men.

HAMLET   O Jephthah, judge of Israel, what a treasure
   hadst thou!

POLONIUS   What a treasure had he, my lord?

HAMLET   Why,
         One fair daughter and no more,
         The which he loved passing well.

POLONIUS [*aside*]   Still on my daughter.

HAMLET   Am I not i'th' right, old Jephthah?

POLONIUS   If you call me Jephthah, my lord, I have a
   daughter that I love passing well.

HAMLET   Nay, that follows not.

POLONIUS   What follows then, my lord?

HAMLET   Why,
         As by lot God wot,
   and then, you know,
         It came to pass, as most like it was.
   The first row of the pious chanson will show you
   more, for look where my abridgement comes.

Enter the Players.

You are welcome, masters. Welcome, all. – I am glad to
see thee well. – Welcome, good friends. – O, old
friend, why, thy face is valanced since I saw thee last.
Com'st thou to beard me in Denmark? – What, my
young lady and mistress! By'r lady, your ladyship is
nearer to heaven than when I saw you last by the
altitude of a chopine. Pray God your voice, like a
piece of uncurrent gold, be not cracked within the
ring. – Masters, you are all welcome. We'll e'en to't
like French falconers, fly at anything we see. We'll
have a speech straight. Come, give us a taste of your
quality. Come, a passionate speech.

1 PLAYER   What speech, my good lord?

HAMLET   I heard thee speak me a speech once, but it was
   never acted, or if it was, not above once – for the play,
   I remember, pleased not the million, 'twas caviare to
   the general. But it was, as I received it – and others,
   whose judgments in such matters cried in the top of
   mine – an excellent play, well digested in the scenes,
   set down with as much modesty as cunning. I
   remember one said there were no sallets in the lines to
   make the matter savoury, nor no matter in the phrase

that might indict the author of affection, but called it
an honest method, as wholesome as sweet, and by very
much more handsome than fine. One speech in't I
chiefly loved – 'twas Aeneas' tale to Dido – and
thereabout of it especially when he speaks of Priam's
slaughter. If it live in your memory, begin at this line –
let me see, let me see –
The rugged Pyrrhus, like th'Hyrcanian beast –
'Tis not so. It begins with Pyrrhus –
The rugged Pyrrhus, he whose sable arms,
Black as his purpose, did the night resemble
When he lay couched in the ominous horse,
Hath now this dread and black complexion smear'd
With heraldry more dismal. Head to foot
Now is he total gules, horridly trick'd
With blood of fathers, mothers, daughters, sons,
Bak'd and impasted with the parching streets,
That lend a tyrannous and a damned light
To their lord's murder. Roasted in wrath and fire,
And thus o'ersized with coagulate gore,
With eyes like carbuncles, the hellish Pyrrhus
Old grandsire Priam seeks.
So proceed you.

POLONIUS   'Fore God, my lord, well spoken, with good
   accent and good discretion.

1 PLAYER   *Anon he finds him,*
Striking too short at Greeks. His antique sword,
Rebellious to his arm, lies where it falls,
Repugnant to command. Unequal match'd,
Pyrrhus at Priam drives, in rage strikes wide;
But with the whiff and wind of his fell sword
Th'unnerved father falls. Then senseless Ilium,
Seeming to feel this blow, with flaming top
Stoops to his base, and with a hideous crash
Takes prisoner Pyrrhus' ear. For lo, his sword,
Which was declining on the milky head
Of reverend Priam, seem'd i'th' air to stick;
So, as a painted tyrant, Pyrrhus stood,
And like a neutral to his will and matter,
Did nothing.
But as we often see against some storm
A silence in the heavens, the rack stand still,
The bold winds speechless, and the orb below
As hush as death, anon the dreadful thunder
Doth rend the region; so after Pyrrhus' pause
Aroused vengeance sets him new awork,
And never did the Cyclops' hammers fall
On Mars's armour, forg'd for proof eterne,
With less remorse than Pyrrhus' bleeding sword
Now falls on Priam.
Out, out, thou strumpet Fortune! All you gods
In general synod take away her power,
Break all the spokes and fellies from her wheel,
And bowl the round nave down the hill of heaven
As low as to the fiends.

POLONIUS   This is too long.

HAMLET   It shall to the barber's with your beard. –

Prithee say on. He's for a jig or a tale of bawdry, or he
sleeps. Say on, come to Hecuba.

1 PLAYER
    But who – ah, woe! – had seen the mobbled queen –

HAMLET 'The mobbled queen'.

505 POLONIUS That's good.

1 PLAYER
    Run barefoot up and down, threat'ning the flames
    With bisson rheum, a clout upon that head
    Where late the diadem stood, and, for a robe,
    About her lank and all o'erteemed loins
510   *A blanket, in th'alarm of fear caught up –*
    Who this had seen, with tongue in venom steep'd,
    'Gainst Fortune's state would treason have pronounc'd.
    But if the gods themselves did see her then,
    When she saw Pyrrhus make malicious sport
515   *In mincing with his sword her husband's limbs,*
    The instant burst of clamour that she made,
    Unless things mortal move them not at all,
    Would have made milch the burning eyes of heaven
    And passion in the gods.

520 POLONIUS Look whe'er he has not turned his colour
and has tears in's eyes. Prithee no more.

HAMLET 'Tis well. I'll have thee speak out the rest of
this soon. – Good my lord, will you see the players
well bestowed? Do you hear, let them be well used, for
525 they are the abstract and brief chronicles of the time.
After your death you were better have a bad epitaph
than their ill report while you live.

POLONIUS My lord, I will use them according to their
desert.

530 HAMLET God's bodkin, man, much better. Use every
man after his desert, and who shall scape whipping?
Use them after your own honour and dignity: the less
they deserve, the more merit is in your bounty. Take
them in.

535 POLONIUS Come, sirs.

HAMLET Follow him, friends. We'll hear a play
tomorrow. [*to First Player*] Dost thou hear me, old
friend? Can you play *The Murder of Gonzago*?

1 PLAYER Ay, my lord.

540 HAMLET We'll ha't tomorrow night. You could for a
need study a speech of some dozen or sixteen lines,
which I would set down and insert in't, could you not?

1 PLAYER Ay, my lord.

HAMLET Very well. [*to all the Players*] Follow that lord,
545 and look you mock him not.
                      Exeunt Polonius and Players.
[*to Rosencrantz and Guildenstern*] My good friends, I'll
leave you till night. You are welcome to Elsinore.

ROSENCRANTZ Good my lord.
                  Exeunt Rosencrantz and Guildenstern.

HAMLET Ay, so, God buy to you. Now I am alone.
550   O what a rogue and peasant slave am I!
    Is it not monstrous that this player here,
    But in a fiction, in a dream of passion,

Could force his soul so to his own conceit
That from her working all his visage wann'd,
Tears in his eyes, distraction in his aspect,   555
A broken voice, and his whole function suiting
With forms to his conceit? And all for nothing!
For Hecuba!
What's Hecuba to him, or he to her,
That he should weep for her? What would he do   560
Had he the motive and the cue for passion
That I have? He would drown the stage with tears,
And cleave the general ear with horrid speech,
Make mad the guilty and appal the free,
Confound the ignorant, and amaze indeed   565
The very faculties of eyes and ears.
Yet I,
A dull and muddy-mettled rascal, peak
Like John-a-dreams, unpregnant of my cause,
And can say nothing – no, not for a king,   570
Upon whose property and most dear life
A damn'd defeat was made. Am I a coward?
Who calls me villain, breaks my pate across,
Plucks off my beard and blows it in my face,
Tweaks me by the nose, gives me the lie i'th' throat 575
As deep as to the lungs – who does me this?
Ha!
'Swounds, I should take it: for it cannot be
But I am pigeon-liver'd and lack gall
To make oppression bitter, or ere this   580
I should ha' fatted all the region kites
With this slave's offal. Bloody, bawdy villain!
Remorseless, treacherous, lecherous, kindless villain!
Why, what an ass am I! This is most brave,
That I, the son of a dear father murder'd,   585
Prompted to my revenge by heaven and hell,
Must like a whore unpack my heart with words
And fall a-cursing like a very drab,
A scullion! Fie upon't! Foh!
About, my brains. Hum – I have heard   590
That guilty creatures sitting at a play
Have, by the very cunning of the scene,
Been struck so to the soul that presently
They have proclaim'd their malefactions.
For murder, though it have no tongue, will speak   595
With most miraculous organ. I'll have these players
Play something like the murder of my father
Before mine uncle. I'll observe his looks;
I'll tent him to the quick. If a do blench,
I know my course. The spirit that I have seen   600
May be a devil, and the devil hath power
T'assume a pleasing shape, yea, and perhaps,
Out of my weakness and my melancholy,
As he is very potent with such spirits,
Abuses me to damn me. I'll have grounds   605
More relative than this. The play's the thing
Wherein I'll catch the conscience of the King. *Exit.*

3.1   *Enter* KING, QUEEN, POLONIUS, OPHELIA,   *Exit Queen.*
                ROSENCRANTZ, GUILDENSTERN.

KING   And can you by no drift of conference
        Get from him why he puts on this confusion,
        Grating so harshly all his days of quiet
        With turbulent and dangerous lunacy?

ROSENCRANTZ
        He does confess he feels himself distracted,   5
        But from what cause a will by no means speak.

GUILDENSTERN
        Nor do we find him forward to be sounded,
        But with a crafty madness keeps aloof
        When we would bring him on to some confession
        Of his true state.

QUEEN   Did he receive you well?   10

ROSENCRANTZ   Most like a gentleman.

GUILDENSTERN
        But with much forcing of his disposition.

ROSENCRANTZ
        Niggard of question, but of our demands
        Most free in his reply.

QUEEN   Did you assay him
        To any pastime?   15

ROSENCRANTZ
        Madam, it so fell out that certain players
        We o'erraught on the way. Of these we told him,
        And there did seem in him a kind of joy
        To hear of it. They are here about the court,
        And, as I think, they have already order   20
        This night to play before him.

POLONIUS   'Tis most true,
        And he beseech'd me to entreat your Majesties
        To hear and see the matter.

KING   With all my heart; and it doth much content me
        To hear him so inclin'd.   25
        Good gentlemen, give him a further edge,
        And drive his purpose into these delights.

ROSENCRANTZ   We shall, my lord.
                Exeunt Rosencrantz and Guildenstern.

KING   Sweet Gertrude, leave us too,
        For we have closely sent for Hamlet hither
        That he, as 'twere by accident, may here   30
        Affront Ophelia.
        Her father and myself, lawful espials,
        We'll so bestow ourselves that, seeing unseen,
        We may of their encounter frankly judge,
        And gather by him, as he is behav'd,   35
        If't be th'affliction of his love or no
        That thus he suffers for.

QUEEN   I shall obey you.
        And for your part, Ophelia, I do wish
        That your good beauties be the happy cause
        Of Hamlet's wildness; so shall I hope your virtues   40
        Will bring him to his wonted way again,
        To both your honours.

OPHELIA   Madam, I wish it may.

POLONIUS
        Ophelia, walk you here. – Gracious, so please you,
        We will bestow ourselves. – Read on this book,
        That show of such an exercise may colour   45
        Your loneliness. – We are oft to blame in this,
        'Tis too much prov'd, that with devotion's visage
        And pious action we do sugar o'er
        The devil himself.

KING [*aside*]   O 'tis too true.
        How smart a lash that speech doth give my
          conscience.   50
        The harlot's cheek, beautied with plast'ring art,
        Is not more ugly to the thing that helps it
        Than is my deed to my most painted word.
        O heavy burden!

POLONIUS
        I hear him coming. Let's withdraw, my lord.   55
                Exeunt King and Polonius.

                Enter HAMLET.

HAMLET   To be, or not to be, that is the question:
        Whether 'tis nobler in the mind to suffer
        The slings and arrows of outrageous fortune,
        Or to take arms against a sea of troubles
        And by opposing end them. To die – to sleep,   60
        No more; and by a sleep to say we end
        The heart-ache and the thousand natural shocks
        That flesh is heir to: 'tis a consummation
        Devoutly to be wish'd. To die, to sleep;
        To sleep, perchance to dream – ay, there's the rub: 65
        For in that sleep of death what dreams may come,
        When we have shuffled off this mortal coil,
        Must give us pause – there's the respect
        That makes calamity of so long life.
        For who would bear the whips and scorns of time,   70
        Th'oppressor's wrong, the proud man's contumely,
        The pangs of dispriz'd love, the law's delay,
        The insolence of office, and the spurns
        That patient merit of th'unworthy takes,
        When he himself might his quietus make   75
        With a bare bodkin? Who would fardels bear,
        To grunt and sweat under a weary life,
        But that the dread of something after death,
        The undiscover'd country, from whose bourn
        No traveller returns, puzzles the will,   80
        And makes us rather bear those ills we have
        Than fly to others that we know not of?
        Thus conscience does make cowards of us all,
        And thus the native hue of resolution
        Is sicklied o'er with the pale cast of thought,   85
        And enterprises of great pitch and moment
        With this regard their currents turn awry
        And lose the name of action. Soft you now,
        The fair Ophelia! Nymph, in thy orisons
        Be all my sins remember'd.

OPHELIA   Good my lord,   90

How does your honour for this many a day?

HAMLET   I humbly thank you, well.

OPHELIA   My lord, I have remembrances of yours
That I have longed long to redeliver.
I pray you now receive them.

95   HAMLET   No, not I.
I never gave you aught.

OPHELIA
My honour'd lord, you know right well you did,
And with them words of so sweet breath compos'd
As made the things more rich. Their perfume lost,
100   Take these again; for to the noble mind
Rich gifts wax poor when givers prove unkind.
There, my lord.

HAMLET   Ha, ha! Are you honest?

OPHELIA   My lord?

105   HAMLET   Are you fair?

OPHELIA   What means your lordship?

HAMLET   That if you be honest and fair, your honesty
should admit no discourse to your beauty.

OPHELIA   Could beauty, my lord, have better commerce
110   than with honesty?

HAMLET   Ay, truly, for the power of beauty will sooner
transform honesty from what it is to a bawd than the
force of honesty can translate beauty into his likeness.
This was sometime a paradox, but now the time gives
115   it proof. I did love you once.

OPHELIA   Indeed, my lord, you made me believe so.

HAMLET   You should not have believed me; for virtue
cannot so inoculate our old stock but we shall relish of
it. I loved you not.

120   OPHELIA   I was the more deceived.

HAMLET   Get thee to a nunnery. Why, wouldst thou be a
breeder of sinners? I am myself indifferent honest,
but yet I could accuse me of such things that it were
better my mother had not borne me. I am very
125   proud, revengeful, ambitious, with more offences at
my beck than I have thoughts to put them in,
imagination to give them shape, or time to act them in.
What should such fellows as I do crawling between
earth and heaven? We are arrant knaves all, believe
130   none of us. Go thy ways to a nunnery. Where's your
father?

OPHELIA   At home, my lord.

HAMLET   Let the doors be shut upon him, that he may
play the fool nowhere but in's own house. Farewell.

135   OPHELIA   O help him, you sweet heavens.

HAMLET   If thou dost marry, I'll give thee this plague for
thy dowry: be thou as chaste as ice, as pure as snow,
thou shalt not escape calumny. Get thee to a nunnery,
farewell. Or if thou wilt needs marry, marry a fool; for
140   wise men know well enough what monsters you make
of them. To a nunnery, go – and quickly too. Farewell.

OPHELIA   Heavenly powers, restore him.

HAMLET   I have heard of your paintings well enough.
God hath given you one face and you make yourselves
145   another. You jig and amble, and you lisp, you

nickname God's creatures, and make your wantonness
your ignorance. Go to, I'll no more on't, it hath made
me mad. I say we will have no mo marriage. Those
that are married already – all but one – shall live; the
rest shall keep as they are. To a nunnery, go.   *Exit*.   150

OPHELIA   O, what a noble mind is here o'erthrown!
The courtier's, soldier's, scholar's, eye, tongue,
    sword,
Th'expectancy and rose of the fair state,
The glass of fashion and the mould of form,
Th'observ'd of all observers, quite, quite down!   155
And I, of ladies most deject and wretched,
That suck'd the honey of his music vows,
Now see that noble and most sovereign reason
Like sweet bells jangled out of tune and harsh,
That unmatch'd form and feature of blown youth   160
Blasted with ecstasy. O woe is me
T'have seen what I have seen, see what I see.

Enter KING *and* POLONIUS.

KING   Love? His affections do not that way tend,
Nor what he spake, though it lack'd form a little,
Was not like madness. There's something in his soul   165
O'er which his melancholy sits on brood,
And I do doubt the hatch and the disclose
Will be some danger; which for to prevent,
I have in quick determination
Thus set it down: he shall with speed to England   170
For the demand of our neglected tribute.
Haply the seas and countries different,
With variable objects, shall expel
This something settled matter in his heart,
Whereon his brains still beating puts him thus   175
From fashion of himself. What think you on't?

POLONIUS   It shall do well. But yet do I believe
The origin and commencement of his grief
Sprung from neglected love. How now, Ophelia?
You need not tell us what Lord Hamlet said,   180
We heard it all. My lord, do as you please,
But if you hold it fit, after the play
Let his queen-mother all alone entreat him
To show his grief, let her be round with him,
And I'll be plac'd, so please you, in the ear   185
Of all their conference. If she find him not,
To England send him; or confine him where
Your wisdom best shall think.

KING   It shall be so.
Madness in great ones must not unwatch'd go.

Exeunt.

3.2   *Enter* HAMLET *and three of the* Players.

HAMLET   Speak the speech, I pray you, as I pronounced
it to you, trippingly on the tongue; but if you mouth it
as many of your players do, I had as lief the town-crier
spoke my lines. Nor do not saw the air too much with
your hand, thus, but use all gently; for in the very   5

torrent, tempest, and, as I may say, whirlwind of your passion, you must acquire and beget a temperance that may give it smoothness. O, it offends me to the soul to hear a robustious periwig-pated fellow tear a passion to tatters, to very rags, to split the ears of the groundlings, who for the most part are capable of nothing but inexplicable dumb-shows and noise. I would have such a fellow whipped for o'erdoing Termagant. It out-Herods Herod. Pray you avoid it.

1 PLAYER   I warrant your honour.

HAMLET   Be not too tame neither, but let your own discretion be your tutor. Suit the action to the word, the word to the action, with this special observance, that you o'erstep not the modesty of nature. For anything so o'erdone is from the purpose of playing, whose end, both at the first and now, was and is to hold as 'twere the mirror up to nature; to show virtue her feature, scorn her own image, and the very age and body of the time his form and pressure. Now this overdone or come tardy off, though it makes the unskilful laugh, cannot but make the judicious grieve, the censure of the which one must in your allowance o'erweigh a whole theatre of others. O, there be players that I have seen play – and heard others praise, and that highly – not to speak it profanely, that neither having th'accent of Christians, nor the gait of Christian, pagan, nor man, have so strutted and bellowed that I have thought some of Nature's journeymen had made men, and not made them well, they imitated humanity so abominably.

1 PLAYER   I hope we have reformed that indifferently with us.

HAMLET   O reform it altogether. And let those that play your clowns speak no more than is set down for them – for there be of them that will themselves laugh, to set on some quantity of barren spectators to laugh too, though in the meantime some necessary question of the play be then to be considered. That's villainous, and shows a most pitiful ambition in the fool that uses it. Go make you ready.   *Exeunt Players.*

Enter POLONIUS, ROSENCRANTZ *and* GUILDENSTERN.

How now, my lord? Will the King hear this piece of work?

POLONIUS   And the Queen too, and that presently.

HAMLET   Bid the players make haste.   *Exit Polonius.*
Will you two help to hasten them?

ROSENCRANTZ   Ay, my lord.
                    Exeunt Rosencrantz and Guildenstern.

HAMLET   What ho, Horatio!

Enter HORATIO.

HORATIO   Here, sweet lord, at your service.

HAMLET   Horatio, thou art e'en as just a man
As e'er my conversation cop'd withal.

HORATIO   O my dear lord.

HAMLET   Nay, do not think I flatter,
For what advancement may I hope from thee
That no revenue hast but thy good spirits
To feed and clothe thee? Why should the poor be
    flatter'd?   60
No, let the candied tongue lick absurd pomp,
And crook the pregnant hinges of the knee
Where thrift may follow fawning. Dost thou hear?
Since my dear soul was mistress of her choice,
And could of men distinguish her election,   65
Sh'ath seal'd thee for herself; for thou hast been
As one, in suff'ring all, that suffers nothing,
A man that Fortune's buffets and rewards
Hast ta'en with equal thanks; and blest are those
Whose blood and judgment are so well commeddled   70
That they are not a pipe for Fortune's finger
To sound what stop she please. Give me that man
That is not passion's slave, and I will wear him
In my heart's core, ay, in my heart of heart,
As I do thee. Something too much of this.   75
There is a play tonight before the King:
One scene of it comes near the circumstance
Which I have told thee of my father's death.
I prithee, when thou seest that act afoot,
Even with the very comment of thy soul   80
Observe my uncle. If his occulted guilt
Do not itself unkennel in one speech,
It is a damned ghost that we have seen,
And my imaginations are as foul
As Vulcan's stithy. Give him heedful note;   85
For I mine eyes will rivet to his face,
And after we will both our judgments join
In censure of his seeming.

HORATIO   Well, my lord.
If a steal aught the whilst this play is playing
And scape detecting, I will pay the theft.   90

Enter trumpets and kettle-drums and sound a flourish.

HAMLET   They are coming to the play. I must be idle.
Get you a place.

Enter KING, QUEEN, POLONIUS, OPHELIA, ROSENCRANTZ,
GUILDENSTERN *and other lords attendant, with the King's
guard carrying torches.*

KING   How fares our cousin Hamlet?

HAMLET   Excellent, i'faith, of the chameleon's dish. I
eat the air, promise-crammed. You cannot feed capons   95
so.

KING   I have nothing with this answer, Hamlet. These
words are not mine.

HAMLET   No, nor mine now. – [*to Polonius*] My lord, you
played once i'th' university, you say?   100

POLONIUS   That did I, my lord, and was accounted a
good actor.

HAMLET   What did you enact?

POLONIUS   I did enact Julius Caesar. I was killed i'th'
Capitol. Brutus killed me.   105

HAMLET   It was a brute part of him to kill so capital a calf there. Be the players ready?

ROSENCRANTZ   Ay, my lord, they stay upon your patience.

QUEEN   Come hither, my dear Hamlet, sit by me.   110

HAMLET   No, good mother, here's metal more attractive. [*Turns to Ophelia.*]

POLONIUS [*aside to the King*]   O ho! do you mark that?

HAMLET [*lying down at Ophelia's feet*]   Lady, shall I lie in your lap?

OPHELIA   No, my lord.   115

HAMLET   I mean, my head upon your lap.

OPHELIA   Ay, my lord.

HAMLET   Do you think I meant country matters?

OPHELIA   I think nothing, my lord.

HAMLET   That's a fair thought to lie between maids' legs.   120

OPHELIA   What is, my lord?

HAMLET   Nothing.

OPHELIA   You are merry, my lord.

HAMLET   Who, I?   125

OPHELIA   Ay, my lord.

HAMLET   O God, your only jig-maker. What should a man do but be merry? For look you how cheerfully my mother looks and my father died within's two hours.

OPHELIA   Nay, 'tis twice two months, my lord.   130

HAMLET   So long? Nay then, let the devil wear black, for I'll have a suit of sables. O heavens, die two months ago and not forgotten yet! Then there's hope a great man's memory may outlive his life half a year. But by'r lady a must build churches then, or else shall a suffer not thinking on, with the hobby-horse, whose epitaph is 'For O, for O, the hobby-horse is forgot'.   135

[*The trumpets sound. A dumb-show follows.*]

Enter a KING *and a* QUEEN, *the Queen embracing him and he her. She kneels, and makes show of protestation unto him. He takes her up, and declines his head upon her neck. He lies him down upon a bank of flowers. She, seeing him asleep, leaves him. Anon comes in another* Man, *takes off his crown, kisses it, pours poison in the sleeper's ears, and leaves him. The* QUEEN *returns, finds the King dead, makes passionate action. The* Poisoner *with some three or four comes in again. They seem to condole with her. The dead body is carried away. The Poisoner woos the Queen with gifts. She seems harsh awhile, but in the end accepts his love.*

Exeunt.

OPHELIA   What means this, my lord?

HAMLET   Marry, this is miching malicho. It means mischief.   140

OPHELIA   Belike this show imports the argument of the play.

Enter PROLOGUE.

HAMLET   We shall know by this fellow. The players cannot keep counsel: they'll tell all.

OPHELIA   Will a tell us what this show meant?   145

HAMLET   Ay, or any show that you will show him. Be not you ashamed to show, he'll not shame to tell you what it means.

OPHELIA   You are naught, you are naught. I'll mark the play.   150

PROLOGUE   *For us and for our tragedy,*
     Here stooping to your clemency,
     We beg your hearing patiently.   *Exit.*

HAMLET   Is this a prologue, or the posy of a ring?

OPHELIA   'Tis brief, my lord.   155

HAMLET   As woman's love.

Enter the PLAYER KING *and* QUEEN.

PLAYER KING
   Full thirty times hath Phoebus' cart gone round
   Neptune's salt wash and Tellus' orbed ground,
   And thirty dozen moons with borrow'd sheen
   About the world have times twelve thirties been   160
   Since love our hearts and Hymen did our hands
   Unite commutual in most sacred bands.

PLAYER QUEEN   *So many journeys may the sun and moon*
   Make us again count o'er ere love be done.
   But woe is me, you are so sick of late,   165
   So far from cheer and from your former state,
   That I distrust you. Yet though I distrust,
   Discomfort you, my lord, it nothing must;
   For women's fear and love hold quantity,
   In neither aught, or in extremity.   170
   Now what my love is, proof hath made you know,
   And as my love is siz'd, my fear is so.
   Where love is great, the littlest doubts are fear;
   Where little fears grow great, great love grows there.

PLAYER KING
   Faith, I must leave thee, love, and shortly too: 175
   My operant powers their functions leave to do;
   And thou shalt live in this fair world behind,
   Honour'd, belov'd; and haply one as kind
   For husband shalt thou —

PLAYER QUEEN   *O confound the rest.*
   Such love must needs be treason in my breast.   180
   In second husband let me be accurst;
   None wed the second but who kill'd the first.

HAMLET [*aside*]   That's wormwood.

PLAYER QUEEN   *The instances that second marriage move*
   Are base respects of thrift, but none of love.   185
   A second time I kill my husband dead,
   When second husband kisses me in bed.

PLAYER KING   *I do believe you think what now you speak;*
   But what we do determine, oft we break.
   Purpose is but the slave to memory,   190
   Of violent birth but poor validity,
   Which now, the fruit unripe, sticks on the tree,
   But fall unshaken when they mellow be.
   Most necessary 'tis that we forget
   To pay ourselves what to ourselves is debt.   195
   What to ourselves in passion we propose,
   The passion ending, doth the purpose lose.

The violence of either grief or joy
Their own enactures with themselves destroy.
Where joy most revels grief doth most lament;
Grief joys, joy grieves, on slender accident.
This world is not for aye, nor 'tis not strange
That even our loves should with our fortunes change,
For 'tis a question left us yet to prove,
Whether love lead fortune or else fortune love.
The great man down, you mark his favourite flies;
The poor advanc'd makes friends of enemies;
And hitherto doth love on fortune tend:
For who not needs shall never lack a friend,
And who in want a hollow friend doth try
Directly seasons him his enemy.
But orderly to end where I begun,
Our wills and fates do so contrary run
That our devices still are overthrown:
Our thoughts are ours, their ends none of our own.
So think thou wilt no second husband wed,
But die thy thoughts when thy first lord is dead.

PLAYER QUEEN
Nor earth to me give food, nor heaven light,
Sport and repose lock from me day and night,
To desperation turn my trust and hope,
An anchor's cheer in prison be my scope,
Each opposite, that blanks the face of joy,
Meet what I would have well and it destroy,
Both here and hence pursue me lasting strife,
If, once a widow, ever I be a wife.

HAMLET   If she should break it now.

PLAYER KING
'Tis deeply sworn. Sweet, leave me here awhile.
My spirits grow dull, and fain I would beguile
The tedious day with sleep.

PLAYER QUEEN   *Sleep rock thy brain,*
And never come mischance between us twain.
[*He sleeps.*]   *Exit.*

HAMLET   Madam, how like you this play?

QUEEN   The lady doth protest too much, methinks.

HAMLET   O, but she'll keep her word.

KING   Have you heard the argument? Is there no offence in't?

HAMLET   No, no, they do but jest – poison in jest. No offence i'th' world.

KING   What do you call the play?

HAMLET   *The Mousetrap* – marry, how tropically! This play is the image of a murder done in Vienna – Gonzago is the Duke's name, his wife Baptista – you shall see anon. 'Tis a knavish piece of work, but what o' that? Your Majesty, and we that have free souls, it touches us not. Let the galled jade wince, our withers are unwrung.

Enter LUCIANUS.

This is one Lucianus, nephew to the King.

OPHELIA   You are as good as a chorus, my lord.

HAMLET   I could interpret between you and your love if I could see the puppets dallying.

OPHELIA   You are keen, my lord, you are keen.   250

HAMLET   It would cost you a groaning to take off my edge.

OPHELIA   Still better, and worse.

HAMLET   So you mis-take your husbands. – Begin, murderer. Leave thy damnable faces and begin. Come,   255
the croaking raven doth bellow for revenge.

LUCIANUS
Thoughts black, hands apt, drugs fit, and time agreeing,
Confederate season, else no creature seeing,
Thou mixture rank, of midnight weeds collected,
With Hecate's ban thrice blasted, thrice infected,   260
Thy natural magic and dire property
On wholesome life usurps immediately.
[*Pours the poison in the sleeper's ears.*]

HAMLET   A poisons him i'th' garden for his estate. His name's Gonzago. The story is extant, and written in very choice Italian. You shall see anon how the   265
murderer gets the love of Gonzago's wife.

OPHELIA   The King rises.

HAMLET   What, frighted with false fire?

QUEEN   How fares my lord?

POLONIUS   Give o'er the play.   270

KING   Give me some light. Away.

POLONIUS   Lights, lights, lights.

                    Exeunt all but Hamlet and Horatio.

HAMLET
Why, let the strucken deer go weep,
*   The hart ungalled play;*
For some must watch while some must sleep,   275
*   Thus runs the world away.*
Would not this, sir, and a forest of feathers, if the rest of my fortunes turn Turk with me, with Provincial roses on my razed shoes, get me a fellowship in a cry of players?   280

HORATIO   Half a share.

HAMLET   A whole one, I.
For thou dost know, O Damon dear,
*   This realm dismantled was*
Of Jove himself, and now reigns here   285
*   A very, very – pajock.*

HORATIO   You might have rhymed.

HAMLET   O good Horatio, I'll take the ghost's word for a thousand pound. Didst perceive?

HORATIO   Very well, my lord.   290

HAMLET   Upon the talk of the poisoning?

HORATIO   I did very well note him.

HAMLET   Ah ha! Come, some music; come, the recorders.
For if the King like not the comedy,
Why then, belike he likes it not, perdie.   295
Come, some music.

Enter ROSENCRANTZ *and* GUILDENSTERN.

GUILDENSTERN   Good my lord, vouchsafe me a word with you.

HAMLET   Sir, a whole history.

GUILDENSTERN   The King, sir –
HAMLET   Ay, sir, what of him?
GUILDENSTERN   Is in his retirement marvellous distempered.
HAMLET   With drink, sir?
GUILDENSTERN   No, my lord, with choler.
HAMLET   Your wisdom should show itself more richer to signify this to the doctor, for for me to put him to his purgation would perhaps plunge him into more choler.
GUILDENSTERN   Good my lord, put your discourse into some frame, and start not so wildly from my affair.
HAMLET   I am tame, sir. Pronounce.
GUILDENSTERN   The Queen your mother, in most great affliction of spirit, hath sent me to you.
HAMLET   You are welcome.
GUILDENSTERN   Nay, good my lord, this courtesy is not of the right breed. If it shall please you to make me a wholesome answer, I will do your mother's commandment; if not, your pardon and my return shall be the end of my business.
HAMLET   Sir, I cannot.
ROSENCRANTZ   What, my lord?
HAMLET   Make you a wholesome answer. My wit's diseased. But sir, such answer as I can make, you shall command – or rather, as you say, my mother. Therefore no more, but to the matter. My mother, you say –
ROSENCRANTZ   Then thus she says: your behaviour hath struck her into amazement and admiration.
HAMLET   O wonderful son, that can so stonish a mother! But is there no sequel at the heels of this mother's admiration? Impart.
ROSENCRANTZ   She desires to speak with you in her closet ere you go to bed.
HAMLET   We shall obey, were she ten times our mother. Have you any further trade with us?
ROSENCRANTZ   My lord, you once did love me.
HAMLET   And do still, by these pickers and stealers.
ROSENCRANTZ   Good my lord, what is your cause of distemper? You do surely bar the door upon your own liberty if you deny your griefs to your friend.
HAMLET   Sir, I lack advancement.
ROSENCRANTZ   How can that be, when you have the voice of the King himself for your succession in Denmark?
HAMLET   Ay, sir, but while the grass grows – the proverb is something musty.

Enter the Players *with recorders.*

O, the recorders. Let me see one. – To withdraw with you, why do you go about to recover the wind of me, as if you would drive me into a toil?
GUILDENSTERN   O my lord, if my duty be too bold, my love is too unmannerly.
HAMLET   I do not well understand that. Will you play upon this pipe?

GUILDENSTERN   My lord, I cannot.
HAMLET   I pray you.
GUILDENSTERN   Believe me, I cannot.
HAMLET   I do beseech you.
GUILDENSTERN   I know no touch of it, my lord.
HAMLET   It is as easy as lying. Govern these ventages with your fingers and thumb, give it breath with your mouth, and it will discourse most eloquent music. Look you, these are the stops.
GUILDENSTERN   But these cannot I command to any utterance of harmony. I have not the skill.
HAMLET   Why, look you now, how unworthy a thing you make of me. You would play upon me, you would seem to know my stops, you would pluck out the heart of my mystery, you would sound me from my lowest note to the top of my compass; and there is much music, excellent voice, in this little organ, yet cannot you make it speak. 'Sblood, do you think I am easier to be played on than a pipe? Call me what instrument you will, though you fret me, you cannot play upon me.

Enter POLONIUS.

God bless you, sir.
POLONIUS   My lord, the Queen would speak with you, and presently.
HAMLET   Do you see yonder cloud that's almost in shape of a camel?
POLONIUS   By th' mass and 'tis – like a camel indeed.
HAMLET   Methinks it is like a weasel.
POLONIUS   It is backed like a weasel.
HAMLET   Or like a whale.
POLONIUS   Very like a whale.
HAMLET   Then I will come to my mother by and by. – [*aside*] They fool me to the top of my bent. – I will come by and by.
POLONIUS   I will say so.   *Exit.*
HAMLET   'By and by' is easily said. – Leave me, friends.
                                   Exeunt all but Hamlet.
'Tis now the very witching time of night,
When churchyards yawn and hell itself breathes out
Contagion to this world. Now could I drink hot blood,
And do such bitter business as the day
Would quake to look on. Soft, now to my mother.
O heart, lose not thy nature. Let not ever
The soul of Nero enter this firm bosom;
Let me be cruel, not unnatural.
I will speak daggers to her, but use none.
My tongue and soul in this be hypocrites:
How in my words somever she be shent,
To give them seals never my soul consent.   *Exit.*

3.3 *Enter* KING, ROSENCRANTZ *and* GUILDENSTERN.

KING   I like him not, nor stands it safe with us
To let his madness range. Therefore prepare you.
I your commission will forthwith dispatch,

And he to England shall along with you.
The terms of our estate may not endure
Hazard so near us as doth hourly grow
Out of his brows.
GUILDENSTERN   We will ourselves provide.
Most holy and religious fear it is
To keep those many many bodies safe
That live and feed upon your Majesty.
ROSENCRANTZ   The single and peculiar life is bound
With all the strength and armour of the mind
To keep itself from noyance; but much more
That spirit upon whose weal depends and rests
The lives of many. The cess of majesty
Dies not alone, but like a gulf doth draw
What's near it with it. Or it is a massy wheel
Fix'd on the summit of the highest mount,
To whose huge spokes ten thousand lesser things
Are mortis'd and adjoin'd, which when it falls,
Each small annexment, petty consequence,
Attends the boist'rous ruin. Never alone
Did the King sigh, but with a general groan.
KING   Arm you, I pray you, to this speedy voyage,
For we will fetters put about this fear
Which now goes too free-footed.
ROSENCRANTZ   We will haste us.
                              Exeunt Rosencrantz and Guildenstern.

                    Enter POLONIUS.

POLONIUS   My lord, he's going to his mother's closet.
Behind the arras I'll convey myself
To hear the process. I'll warrant she'll tax him home,
And as you said – and wisely was it said –
'Tis meet that some more audience than a mother,
Since nature makes them partial, should o'erhear
The speech of vantage. Fare you well, my liege.
I'll call upon you ere you go to bed,
And tell you what I know.
KING   Thanks, dear my lord.
                              Exit Polonius.

O, my offence is rank, it smells to heaven;
It hath the primal eldest curse upon't –
A brother's murder. Pray can I not,
Though inclination be as sharp as will,
My stronger guilt defeats my strong intent,
And, like a man to double business bound,
I stand in pause where I shall first begin,
And both neglect. What if this cursed hand
Were thicker than itself with brother's blood,
Is there not rain enough in the sweet heavens
To wash it white as snow? Whereto serves mercy
But to confront the visage of offence?
And what's in prayer but this twofold force,
To be forestalled ere we come to fall
Or pardon'd being down? Then I'll look up.
My fault is past – but O, what form of prayer
Can serve my turn? 'Forgive me my foul murder?'
That cannot be, since I am still possess'd

Of those effects for which I did the murder –
My crown, mine own ambition, and my queen.   55
May one be pardon'd and retain th'offence?
In the corrupted currents of this world
Offence's gilded hand may shove by justice,
And oft 'tis seen the wicked prize itself
Buys out the law. But 'tis not so above: 60
There is no shuffling, there the action lies
In his true nature, and we ourselves compell'd
Even to the teeth and forehead of our faults
To give in evidence. What then? What rests?
Try what repentance can. What can it not?   65
Yet what can it, when one cannot repent?
O wretched state! O bosom black as death!
O limed soul, that struggling to be free
Art more engag'd! Help, angels! Make assay.
Bow, stubborn knees; and heart with strings of steel,   70
Be soft as sinews of the new-born babe.
All may be well. [*He kneels.*]

                    Enter HAMLET.

HAMLET   Now might I do it pat, now a is a-praying.
And now I'll do't. [*Draws his sword.*]
                    And so a goes to heaven;
And so am I reveng'd. That would be scann'd: 75
A villain kills my father, and for that
I, his sole son, do this same villain send
To heaven.
Why, this is hire and salary, not revenge.
A took my father grossly, full of bread,   80
With all his crimes broad blown, as flush as May;
And how his audit stands who knows save heaven?
But in our circumstance and course of thought
'Tis heavy with him. And am I then reveng'd,
To take him in the purging of his soul,   85
When he is fit and season'd for his passage?
No.
Up, sword, and know thou a more horrid hent:
When he is drunk asleep, or in his rage,
Or in th'incestuous pleasure of his bed,   90
At game a-swearing, or about some act
That has no relish of salvation in't,
Then trip him, that his heels may kick at heaven
And that his soul may be as damn'd and black
As hell, whereto it goes. My mother stays.   95
This physic but prolongs thy sickly days.   *Exit.*
KING   My words fly up, my thoughts remain below.
Words without thoughts never to heaven go.   *Exit.*

3.4   *Enter* QUEEN *and* POLONIUS.

POLONIUS
A will come straight. Look you lay home to him,
Tell him his pranks have been too broad to bear with
And that your Grace hath screen'd and stood
          between
Much heat and him. I'll silence me even here.

Pray you be round.

5   QUEEN   I'll war'nt you, fear me not.
      Withdraw, I hear him coming.
      [*Polonius hides behind the arras.*]

              Enter HAMLET.

      HAMLET   Now mother, what's the matter?
      QUEEN   Hamlet, thou hast thy father much offended.
      HAMLET   Mother, you have my father much offended.
10   QUEEN   Come, come, you answer with an idle tongue.
      HAMLET   Go, go, you question with a wicked tongue.
      QUEEN   Why, how now, Hamlet?
      HAMLET   What's the matter now?
      QUEEN   Have you forgot me?
      HAMLET   No, by the rood, not so.
      You are the Queen, your husband's brother's wife,
15   And, would it were not so, you are my mother.
      QUEEN   Nay, then I'll set those to you that can speak.
      HAMLET
      Come, come, and sit you down, you shall not budge.
      You go not till I set you up a glass
      Where you may see the inmost part of you.
20   QUEEN   What wilt thou do? Thou wilt not murder me?
      Help, ho!
      POLONIUS [*behind the arras*]   What ho! Help!
      HAMLET   How now? A rat! Dead for a ducat, dead.
      [*Thrusts his rapier through the arras.*]
      POLONIUS [*behind*]   O, I am slain.
      QUEEN   O me, what hast thou done?
25   HAMLET   Nay, I know not.
      Is it the King?
      [*Lifts up the arras and discovers Polonius, dead.*]
      QUEEN   O what a rash and bloody deed is this!
      HAMLET   A bloody deed. Almost as bad, good mother,
      As kill a king and marry with his brother.
      QUEEN   As kill a king?
30   HAMLET   Ay, lady, it was my word. –
      Thou wretched, rash, intruding fool, farewell.
      I took thee for thy better. Take thy fortune:
      Thou find'st to be too busy is some danger. –
      Leave wringing of your hands. Peace, sit you down,
35   And let me wring your heart; for so I shall
      If it be made of penetrable stuff,
      If damned custom have not braz'd it so,
      That it be proof and bulwark against sense.
      QUEEN
      What have I done, that thou dar'st wag thy tongue
      In noise so rude against me?
40   HAMLET   Such an act
      That blurs the grace and blush of modesty,
      Calls virtue hypocrite, takes off the rose
      From the fair forehead of an innocent love
      And sets a blister there, makes marriage vows
45   As false as dicers' oaths – O, such a deed
      As from the body of contraction plucks
      The very soul, and sweet religion makes
      A rhapsody of words. Heaven's face does glow

O'er this solidity and compound mass
With tristful visage, as against the doom,   50
Is thought-sick at the act.
QUEEN   Ay me, what act
      That roars so loud and thunders in the index?
HAMLET   Look here upon this picture, and on this,
      The counterfeit presentment of two brothers.
      See what a grace was seated on this brow,   55
      Hyperion's curls, the front of Jove himself,
      An eye like Mars to threaten and command,
      A station like the herald Mercury
      New-lighted on a heaven-kissing hill,
      A combination and a form indeed   60
      Where every god did seem to set his seal
      To give the world assurance of a man.
      This was your husband. Look you now what follows.
      Here is your husband, like a mildew'd ear
      Blasting his wholesome brother. Have you eyes?   65
      Could you on this fair mountain leave to feed
      And batten on this moor? Ha, have you eyes?
      You cannot call it love; for at your age
      The heyday in the blood is tame, it's humble,
      And waits upon the judgment, and what judgment   70
      Would step from this to this? Sense sure you have,
      Else could you not have motion; but sure that sense
      Is apoplex'd, for madness would not err
      Nor sense to ecstasy was ne'er so thrall'd
      But it reserv'd some quantity of choice   75
      To serve in such a difference. What devil was't
      That thus hath cozen'd you at hoodman-blind?
      Eyes without feeling, feeling without sight,
      Ears without hands or eyes, smelling sans all,
      Or but a sickly part of one true sense   80
      Could not so mope. O shame, where is thy blush?
      Rebellious hell,
      If thou canst mutine in a matron's bones,
      To flaming youth let virtue be as wax
      And melt in her own fire; proclaim no shame   85
      When the compulsive ardour gives the charge,
      Since frost itself as actively doth burn
      And reason panders will.
QUEEN   O Hamlet, speak no more.
      Thou turn'st my eyes into my very soul,
      And there I see such black and grained spots   90
      As will not leave their tinct.
HAMLET   Nay, but to live
      In the rank sweat of an enseamed bed,
      Stew'd in corruption, honeying and making love
      Over the nasty sty!
QUEEN   O speak to me no more.
      These words like daggers enter in my ears.   95
      No more, sweet Hamlet.
HAMLET   A murderer and a villain,
      A slave that is not twentieth part the tithe
      Of your precedent lord, a vice of kings,
      A cutpurse of the empire and the rule,
      That from a shelf the precious diadem stole   100

And put it in his pocket –

QUEEN   No more.

HAMLET   A king of shreds and patches –

Enter GHOST.

Save me and hover o'er me with your wings,
You heavenly guards! What would your gracious
    figure?

QUEEN   Alas, he's mad.

HAMLET   Do you not come your tardy son to chide,
That, laps'd in time and passion, lets go by
Th'important acting of your dread command?
O say.

GHOST   Do not forget. This visitation
Is but to whet thy almost blunted purpose.
But look, amazement on thy mother sits.
O step between her and her fighting soul.
Conceit in weakest bodies strongest works.
Speak to her, Hamlet.

HAMLET   How is it with you, lady?

QUEEN   Alas, how is't with you,
That you do bend your eye on vacancy,
And with th'incorporal air do hold discourse?
Forth at your eyes your spirits wildly peep,
And, as the sleeping soldiers in th'alarm,
Your bedded hair, like life in excrements,
Start up and stand an end. O gentle son,
Upon the heat and flame of thy distemper
Sprinkle cool patience. Whereon do you look?

HAMLET
On him, on him. Look you how pale he glares.
His form and cause conjoin'd, preaching to stones,
Would make them capable. – Do not look upon me,
Lest with this piteous action you convert
My stern effects. Then what I have to do
Will want true colour – tears perchance for blood.

QUEEN   To whom do you speak this?

HAMLET   Do you see nothing there?

QUEEN   Nothing at all; yet all that is I see.

HAMLET   Nor did you nothing hear?

QUEEN   No, nothing but ourselves.

HAMLET   Why, look you there, look how it steals away.
My father, in his habit as he liv'd!
Look where he goes even now out at the portal.

Exit Ghost.

QUEEN   This is the very coinage of your brain.
This bodiless creation ecstasy
Is very cunning in.

HAMLET
My pulse as yours doth temperately keep time,
And makes as healthful music. It is not madness
That I have utter'd. Bring me to the test,
And I the matter will re-word, which madness
Would gambol from. Mother, for love of grace,
Lay not that flattering unction to your soul,
That not your trespass but my madness speaks.

It will but skin and film the ulcerous place,
Whiles rank corruption, mining all within,   150
Infects unseen. Confess yourself to heaven,
Repent what's past, avoid what is to come;
And do not spread the compost on the weeds
To make them ranker. Forgive me this my virtue;
For in the fatness of these pursy times   155
Virtue itself of vice must pardon beg,
Yea, curb and woo for leave to do him good.

QUEEN   O Hamlet, thou hast cleft my heart in twain.

HAMLET   O throw away the worser part of it
And live the purer with the other half.   160
Good night. But go not to my uncle's bed.
Assume a virtue if you have it not.
That monster, custom, who all sense doth eat
Of habits evil, is angel yet in this,
That to the use of actions fair and good   165
He likewise gives a frock or livery
That aptly is put on. Refrain tonight,
And that shall lend a kind of easiness
To the next abstinence, the next more easy;
For use almost can change the stamp of nature,   170
And either lodge the devil or throw him out
With wondrous potency. Once more, good night,
And when you are desirous to be blest,
I'll blessing beg of you. For this same lord
I do repent; but heaven hath pleas'd it so,   175
To punish me with this and this with me,
That I must be their scourge and minister.
I will bestow him, and will answer well
The death I gave him. So, again, good night.
I must be cruel only to be kind.   180
This bad begins, and worse remains behind.
One word more, good lady.

QUEEN   What shall I do?

HAMLET   Not this, by no means, that I bid you do:
Let the bloat King tempt you again to bed,
Pinch wanton on your cheek, call you his mouse,   185
And let him, for a pair of reechy kisses,
Or paddling in your neck with his damn'd fingers,
Make you to ravel all this matter out
That I essentially am not in madness,
But mad in craft. 'Twere good you let him know,   190
For who that's but a queen, fair, sober, wise,
Would from a paddock, from a bat, a gib,
Such dear concernings hide? Who would do so?
No, in despite of sense and secrecy,
Unpeg the basket on the house's top,   195
Let the birds fly, and like the famous ape,
To try conclusions, in the basket creep,
And break your own neck down.

QUEEN   Be thou assur'd, if words be made of breath,
And breath of life, I have no life to breathe   200
What thou hast said to me.

HAMLET   I must to England, you know that?

QUEEN   Alack,

I had forgot. 'Tis so concluded on.

HAMLET
There's letters seal'd, and my two schoolfellows,
205   Whom I will trust as I will adders fang'd –
They bear the mandate, they must sweep my way
And marshal me to knavery. Let it work;
For 'tis the sport to have the enginer
Hoist with his own petard, and't shall go hard
210   But I will delve one yard below their mines
And blow them at the moon. O, 'tis most sweet
When in one line two crafts directly meet.
This man shall set me packing.
I'll lug the guts into the neighbour room.
215   Mother, good night indeed. This counsellor
Is now most still, most secret, and most grave,
Who was in life a foolish prating knave.
Come, sir, to draw toward an end with you.
Good night, mother.
         Exit lugging in Polonius. The Queen remains.

4.1   *To the* QUEEN, *enter* KING, *with* ROSENCRANTZ
         and GUILDENSTERN.

KING
There's matter in these sighs, these profound heaves,
You must translate. 'Tis fit we understand them.
Where is your son?
QUEEN   Bestow this place on us a little while.
         Exeunt Rosencrantz and Guildenstern.
5   Ah, mine own lord, what have I seen tonight!
KING   What, Gertrude, how does Hamlet?
QUEEN   Mad as the sea and wind when both contend
Which is the mightier. In his lawless fit,
Behind the arras hearing something stir,
10   Whips out his rapier, cries 'A rat, a rat',
And in this brainish apprehension kills
The unseen good old man.
KING   O heavy deed!
It had been so with us had we been there.
His liberty is full of threats to all –
15   To you yourself, to us, to everyone.
Alas, how shall this bloody deed be answer'd?
It will be laid to us, whose providence
Should have kept short, restrain'd, and out of haunt
This mad young man. But so much was our love,
20   We would not understand what was most fit,
But like the owner of a foul disease,
To keep it from divulging, let it feed
Even on the pith of life. Where is he gone?
QUEEN   To draw apart the body he hath kill'd,
25   O'er whom – his very madness, like some ore
Among a mineral of metals base,
Shows itself pure – a weeps for what is done.
KING   O Gertrude, come away.
The sun no sooner shall the mountains touch
30   But we will ship him hence; and this vile deed
We must with all our majesty and skill

Both countenance and excuse. – Ho, Guildenstern!

       Enter ROSENCRANTZ *and* GUILDENSTERN.

Friends both, go join you with some further aid.
Hamlet in madness hath Polonius slain,
And from his mother's closet hath he dragg'd him.   35
Go seek him out – speak fair – and bring the body
Into the chapel. I pray you haste in this.
      Exeunt Rosencrantz and Guildenstern.
Come, Gertrude, we'll call up our wisest friends,
And let them know both what we mean to do
And what's untimely done. So envious slander,   40
Whose whisper o'er the world's diameter,
As level as the cannon to his blank,
Transports his poison'd shot, may miss our name
And hit the woundless air. O come away,
My soul is full of discord and dismay.   *Exeunt.*   45

4.2   *Enter* HAMLET.

HAMLET   Safely stowed. [*calling within*] But soft, what
noise? Who calls on Hamlet? O, here they come.

    Enter ROSENCRANTZ, GUILDENSTERN *and others.*

ROSENCRANTZ   What have you done, my lord, with the
dead body?
HAMLET   Compounded it with dust, whereto 'tis kin.   5
ROSENCRANTZ   Tell us where 'tis, that we may take it
thence and bear it to the chapel.
HAMLET   Do not believe it.
ROSENCRANTZ   Believe what?
HAMLET   That I can keep your counsel and not mine   10
own. Besides, to be demanded of a sponge – what
replication should be made by the son of a king?
ROSENCRANTZ   Take you me for a sponge, my lord?
HAMLET   Ay, sir, that soaks up the King's countenance,
his rewards, his authorities. But such officers do the   15
King best service in the end: he keeps them, like an
ape, in the corner of his jaw – first mouthed, to be last
swallowed. When he needs what you have gleaned, it
is but squeezing you and, sponge, you shall be dry
again.   20
ROSENCRANTZ   I understand you not, my lord.
HAMLET   I am glad of it. A knavish speech sleeps in a
foolish ear.
ROSENCRANTZ   My lord, you must tell us where the
body is and go with us to the King.   25
HAMLET   The body is with the King, but the King is not
with the body. The King is a thing –
GUILDENSTERN   A thing, my lord?
HAMLET   Of nothing. Bring me to him.   *Exeunt.*

4.3   *Enter* KING *and two or three lords.*

KING   I have sent to seek him and to find the body.
How dangerous is it that this man goes loose!
Yet must not we put the strong law on him:

He's lov'd of the distracted multitude,
Who like not in their judgment but their eyes,
And where 'tis so, th'offender's scourge is weigh'd,
But never the offence. To bear all smooth and even,
This sudden sending him away must seem
Deliberate pause. Diseases desperate grown
By desperate appliance are reliev'd,
Or not at all.

Enter ROSENCRANTZ, GUILDENSTERN *and others.*

        How now, what hath befall'n?
ROSENCRANTZ
Where the dead body is bestow'd, my lord,
We cannot get from him.
KING   But where is he?
ROSENCRANTZ
Without, my lord, guarded, to know your pleasure.
KING   Bring him before us.
ROSENCRANTZ   Ho! Bring in the lord.

Enter HAMLET *with guards.*

KING   Now, Hamlet, where's Polonius?
HAMLET   At supper.
KING   At supper? Where?
HAMLET   Not where he eats, but where a is eaten. A
  certain convocation of politic worms are e'en at him.
  Your worm is your only emperor for diet: we fat all
  creatures else to fat us, and we fat ourselves for
  maggots. Your fat king and your lean beggar is but
  variable service – two dishes, but to one table.
  That's the end.
KING   Alas, alas.
HAMLET   A man may fish with the worm that hath eat of
  a king, and eat of the fish that hath fed of that worm.
KING   What dost thou mean by this?
HAMLET   Nothing but to show you how a king may go a
  progress through the guts of a beggar.
KING   Where is Polonius?
HAMLET   In heaven. Send thither to see. If your
  messenger find him not there, seek him i'th' other
  place yourself. But if indeed you find him not within
  this month, you shall nose him as you go up the stairs
  into the lobby.
KING [*to some attendants*]   Go seek him there.
HAMLET   A will stay till you come.   *Exeunt attendants.*
KING   Hamlet, this deed, for thine especial safety –
  Which we do tender, as we dearly grieve
  For that which thou hast done – must send thee
    hence
  With fiery quickness. Therefore prepare thyself.
  The bark is ready, and the wind at help,
  Th'associates tend, and everything is bent
  For England.
HAMLET   For England?
KING   Ay, Hamlet.
HAMLET   Good.
KING   So is it, if thou knew'st our purposes.

HAMLET   I see a cherub that sees them. But come, for
  England. Farewell, dear mother.
KING   Thy loving father, Hamlet.
HAMLET   My mother. Father and mother is man and
  wife, man and wife is one flesh; so my mother. Come,   55
  for England.   *Exit.*
KING
Follow him at foot. Tempt him with speed aboard,
Delay it not – I'll have him hence tonight.
Away, for everything is seal'd and done
That else leans on th'affair. Pray you make haste.   60
                         Exeunt all but the King.
And England, if my love thou hold'st at aught –
As my great power thereof may give thee sense,
Since yet thy cicatrice looks raw and red
After the Danish sword, and thy free awe
Pays homage to us – thou mayst not coldly set   65
Our sovereign process, which imports at full,
By letters conguring to that effect,
The present death of Hamlet. Do it, England;
For like the hectic in my blood he rages,
And thou must cure me. Till I know 'tis done,   70
Howe'er my haps, my joys were ne'er begun.   *Exit.*

4.4   *Enter* FORTINBRAS *with his army
              marching over the stage.*

FORTINBRAS
Go, captain, from me greet the Danish king.
Tell him that by his licence Fortinbras
Craves the conveyance of a promis'd march
Over his kingdom. You know the rendezvous.
If that his Majesty would aught with us,   5
We shall express our duty in his eye;
And let him know so.
CAPTAIN   I will do't, my lord.
FORTINBRAS   Go softly on.   *Exeunt all but the Captain.*

Enter HAMLET, ROSENCRANTZ, GUILDENSTERN
            and others.

HAMLET   Good sir, whose powers are these?
CAPTAIN   They are of Norway, sir.   10
HAMLET   How purpos'd, sir, I pray you?
CAPTAIN   Against some part of Poland.
HAMLET   Who commands them, sir?
CAPTAIN   The nephew to old Norway, Fortinbras.
HAMLET   Goes it against the main of Poland, sir,   15
Or for some frontier?
CAPTAIN   Truly to speak, and with no addition,
We go to gain a little patch of ground
That hath in it no profit but the name.
To pay five ducats – five – I would not farm it;   20
Nor will it yield to Norway or the Pole
A ranker rate should it be sold in fee.
HAMLET   Why, then the Polack never will defend it.
CAPTAIN   Yes, it is already garrison'd.
HAMLET
Two thousand souls and twenty thousand ducats   25

Will not debate the question of this straw!
This is th'impostume of much wealth and peace,
That inward breaks, and shows no cause without
Why the man dies. I humbly thank you, sir.
CAPTAIN   God buy you, sir.   *Exit.*
30   ROSENCRANTZ   Will't please you go, my lord?
HAMLET   I'll be with you straight. Go a little before.
                                        Exeunt all but Hamlet.
How all occasions do inform against me,
And spur my dull revenge. What is a man
If his chief good and market of his time
35   Be but to sleep and feed? A beast, no more.
Sure he that made us with such large discourse,
Looking before and after, gave us not
That capability and godlike reason
To fust in us unus'd. Now whether it be
40   Bestial oblivion, or some craven scruple
Of thinking too precisely on th'event –
A thought which, quarter'd, hath but one part
     wisdom
And ever three parts coward – I do not know
Why yet I live to say this thing's to do,
45   Sith I have cause, and will, and strength, and means
To do't. Examples gross as earth exhort me,
Witness this army of such mass and charge,
Led by a delicate and tender prince,
Whose spirit, with divine ambition puff'd,
50   Makes mouths at the invisible event,
Exposing what is mortal and unsure
To all that fortune, death, and danger dare,
Even for an eggshell. Rightly to be great
Is not to stir without great argument,
55   But greatly to find quarrel in a straw
When honour's at the stake. How stand I then,
That have a father kill'd, a mother stain'd,
Excitements of my reason and my blood,
And let all sleep, while to my shame I see
60   The imminent death of twenty thousand men
That, for a fantasy and trick of fame,
Go to their graves like beds, fight for a plot
Whereon the numbers cannot try the cause,
Which is not tomb enough and continent
65   To hide the slain? O, from this time forth
My thoughts be bloody or be nothing worth.   *Exit.*

4.5   *Enter* QUEEN, HORATIO *and a* Gentleman.

QUEEN   I will not speak with her.
GENTLEMAN   She is importunate,
   Indeed distract. Her mood will needs be pitied.
QUEEN   What would she have?
GENTLEMAN
   She speaks much of her father, says she hears
   There's tricks i'th' world, and hems, and beats her
        heart,
5   Spurns enviously at straws, speaks things in doubt
   That carry but half sense. Her speech is nothing,

Yet the unshaped use of it doth move
The hearers to collection. They aim at it,
And botch the words up fit to their own thoughts,   10
Which, as her winks and nods and gestures yield
     them,
Indeed would make one think there might be
     thought,
Though nothing sure, yet much unhappily.
HORATIO
   'Twere good she were spoken with, for she may strew
   Dangerous conjectures in ill-breeding minds.   15
QUEEN   Let her come in.   *Exit Gentleman.*
   [*aside*] To my sick soul, as sin's true nature is,
   Each toy seems prologue to some great amiss.
   So full of artless jealousy is guilt,
   It spills itself in fearing to be spilt.   20

                    Enter OPHELIA.

OPHELIA   Where is the beauteous Majesty of Denmark?
QUEEN   How now, Ophelia?
OPHELIA [*Sings.*]
          How should I your true love know
               From another one?
          By his cockle hat and staff   25
               And his sandal shoon.
QUEEN   Alas, sweet lady, what imports this song?
OPHELIA   Say you? Nay, pray you mark.
   [*Sings.*]   He is dead and gone, lady,
               He is dead and gone,   30
          At his head a grass-green turf,
               At his heels a stone.
   O ho!
QUEEN   Nay, but Ophelia –
OPHELIA   Pray you mark.   35
   [*Sings.*]
          White his shroud as the mountain snow –

                    Enter KING.

QUEEN   Alas, look here, my lord.
OPHELIA [*Sings.*]
               Larded with sweet flowers
          Which bewept to the grave did not go
               With true-love showers.   40
KING   How do you, pretty lady?
OPHELIA   Well, good dild you. They say the owl was a
   baker's daughter. Lord, we know what we are, but
   know not what we may be. God be at your table.
KING   Conceit upon her father.   45
OPHELIA   Pray let's have no words of this, but when they
   ask you what it means, say you this.
   [*Sings.*] Tomorrow is Saint Valentine's day,
          All in the morning betime,
          And I a maid at your window,   50
               To be your Valentine.
       Then up he rose, and donn'd his clo'es,
          And dupp'd the chamber door,
          Let in the maid that out a maid

Never departed more.

KING Pretty Ophelia –

OPHELIA Indeed, without an oath, I'll make an end on't.

Sings. By Gis and by Saint Charity,
  Alack and fie for shame,
 Young men will do't if they come to't –
  By Cock, they are to blame.
 Quoth she, 'Before you tumbled me,
  You promis'd me to wed.'
He answers,

Sings. 'So would I a done, by yonder sun,
  And thou hadst not come to my bed.'

KING How long hath she been thus?

OPHELIA I hope all will be well. We must be patient. But
I cannot choose but weep to think they would lay
him i'th' cold ground. My brother shall know of it.
And so I thank you for your good counsel. Come, my
coach. Good night, ladies, good night. Sweet ladies,
good night, good night.   *Exit.*

KING Follow her close; give her good watch, I pray you.
                    Exit Horatio.

O, this is the poison of deep grief: it springs
All from her father's death. And now behold –
O Gertrude, Gertrude,
When sorrows come, they come not single spies,
But in battalions. First, her father slain;
Next, your son gone, and he most violent author
Of his own just remove; the people muddied,
Thick and unwholesome in their thoughts and
  whispers
For good Polonius' death – and we have done but
  greenly
In hugger-mugger to inter him; poor Ophelia
Divided from herself and her fair judgment,
Without the which we are pictures, or mere beasts;
Last, and as much containing as all these,
Her brother is in secret come from France,
Feeds on this wonder, keeps himself in clouds,
And wants not buzzers to infect his ear
With pestilent speeches of his father's death,
Wherein necessity, of matter beggar'd,
Will nothing stick our person to arraign
In ear and ear. O my dear Gertrude, this,
Like to a murd'ring-piece, in many places
Gives me superfluous death. [*A noise within.*]
                    Attend!
Where is my Switzers? Let them guard the door.

Enter a Messenger.

What is the matter?

MESSENGER   Save yourself, my lord.
The ocean, overpeering of his list,
Eats not the flats with more impetuous haste
Than young Laertes, in a riotous head,
O'erbears your officers. The rabble call him lord,
And, as the world were now but to begin,
Antiquity forgot, custom not known –

The ratifiers and props of every word –   105
They cry, 'Choose we! Laertes shall be king.'
Caps, hands, and tongues applaud it to the clouds,
'Laertes shall be king, Laertes king.'

QUEEN How cheerfully on the false trail they cry.
O, this is counter, you false Danish dogs.   110
[*A noise within.*]

KING The doors are broke.

Enter LAERTES *with* Followers.

LAERTES
Where is this king? – Sirs, stand you all without.

FOLLOWERS No, let's come in.

LAERTES   I pray you give me leave.

FOLLOWERS We will, we will.

LAERTES I thank you. Keep the door. *Exeunt Followers.*
                    O thou vile king,   115
Give me my father.

QUEEN [*holding him*] Calmly, good Laertes.

LAERTES
That drop of blood that's calm proclaims me bastard,
Cries cuckold to my father, brands the harlot
Even here between the chaste unsmirched brow
Of my true mother.

KING   What is the cause, Laertes,   120
That thy rebellion looks so giant-like? –
Let him go, Gertrude. Do not fear our person.
There's such divinity doth hedge a king
That treason can but peep to what it would,
Acts little of his will. – Tell me, Laertes,   125
Why thou art thus incens'd. – Let him go,
  Gertrude. –
Speak, man.

LAERTES Where is my father?

KING   Dead.

QUEEN   But not by him.

KING Let him demand his fill.

LAERTES How came he dead? I'll not be juggled with. 130
To hell, allegiance! Vows to the blackest devil!
Conscience and grace, to the profoundest pit!
I dare damnation. To this point I stand,
That both the worlds I give to negligence,
Let come what comes, only I'll be reveng'd   135
Most throughly for my father.

KING   Who shall stay you?

LAERTES My will, not all the world's.
And for my means, I'll husband them so well,
They shall go far with little.

KING   Good Laertes,
If you desire to know the certainty   140
Of your dear father, is't writ in your revenge
That, swoopstake, you will draw both friend and foe,
Winner and loser?

LAERTES None but his enemies.

KING   Will you know them then?

LAERTES
To his good friends thus wide I'll ope my arms,   145

And, like the kind life-rend'ring pelican,
Repast them with my blood.
KING   Why, now you speak
  Like a good child and a true gentleman.
  That I am guiltless of your father's death
150 And am most sensibly in grief for it,
  It shall as level to your judgment 'pear
  As day does to your eye.
  [*A noise within. Ophelia is heard singing.*]
                Let her come in.
LAERTES   How now, what noise is that?

             Enter OPHELIA.

  O heat, dry up my brains. Tears seven times salt
155 Burn out the sense and virtue of mine eye.
  By heaven, thy madness shall be paid with weight
  Till our scale turn the beam. O rose of May!
  Dear maid – kind sister – sweet Ophelia –
  O heavens, is't possible a young maid's wits
160 Should be as mortal as an old man's life?
  Nature is fine in love, and where 'tis fine
  It sends some precious instance of itself
  After the thing it loves.
OPHELIA [*Sings.*]
          They bore him bare-fac'd on the bier,
165   And in his grave rain'd many a tear –
  Fare you well, my dove.
LAERTES
  Hadst thou thy wits and didst persuade revenge,
  It could not move thus.
OPHELIA   You must sing *A-down a-down*, and you *Call*
170 *him a-down-a.* O, how the wheel becomes it! It is the
  false steward that stole his master's daughter.
LAERTES   This nothing's more than matter.
OPHELIA   There's rosemary, that's for remembrance –
  pray you, love, remember. And there is pansies, that's
175 for thoughts.
LAERTES   A document in madness: thoughts and
  remembrance fitted.
OPHELIA   There's fennel for you, and columbines.
  There's rue for you. And here's some for me. We may
180 call it herb of grace a Sundays. You must wear your
  rue with a difference. There's a daisy. I would give you
  some violets, but they withered all when my father
  died. They say a made a good end.
  [*Sings.*] For bonny sweet Robin is all my joy.
185 LAERTES   Thought and affliction, passion, hell itself
  She turns to favour and to prettiness.
OPHELIA [*Sings.*]
          And will 'a not come again?
          And will 'a not come again?
            No, no, he is dead,
190   Go to thy death-bed,
          He never will come again.

          His beard was as white as snow,
          All flaxen was his poll.

          He is gone, he is gone,
          And we cast away moan.   195
          God a mercy on his soul.
  And of all Christian souls. God buy you.   *Exit.*
LAERTES   Do you see this, O God?
KING   Laertes, I must commune with your grief,
  Or you deny me right. Go but apart,   200
  Make choice of whom your wisest friends you will,
  And they shall hear and judge 'twixt you and me.
  If by direct or by collateral hand
  They find us touch'd, we will our kingdom give,
  Our crown, our life, and all that we call ours   205
  To you in satisfaction; but if not,
  Be you content to lend your patience to us,
  And we shall jointly labour with your soul
  To give it due content.
LAERTES   Let this be so.
  His means of death, his obscure funeral –   210
  No trophy, sword, nor hatchment o'er his bones,
  No noble rite, nor formal ostentation –
  Cry to be heard, as 'twere from heaven to earth,
  That I must call't in question.
KING   So you shall.
  And where th'offence is, let the great axe fall.   215
  I pray you go with me.   *Exeunt.*

4.6   *Enter* HORATIO *and a* Servant.

HORATIO   What are they that would speak with me?
SERVANT   Seafaring men, sir. They say they have letters
  for you.
HORATIO   Let them come in.   *Exit Servant.*
  I do not know from what part of the world   5
  I should be greeted, if not from Lord Hamlet.

             Enter Sailors.

1 SAILOR   God bless you, sir.
HORATIO   Let him bless thee too.
1 SAILOR   A shall, sir, and please him. There's a letter for
  you, sir. It came from th'ambassador that was bound   10
  for England – if your name be Horatio, as I am let to
  know it is.
HORATIO [*Reads the letter.*]   *Horatio, when thou shalt have*
  overlooked this, give these fellows some means to the King.
  They have letters for him. Ere we were two days old at   15
  sea, a pirate of very warlike appointment gave us chase.
  Finding ourselves too slow of sail, we put on a compelled
  valour, and in the grapple I boarded them. On the instant
  they got clear of our ship, so I alone became their prisoner.
  They have dealt with me like thieves of mercy. But they   20
  knew what they did: I am to do a turn for them. Let the
  King have the letters I have sent, and repair thou to me
  with as much speed as thou wouldest fly death. I have
  words to speak in thine ear will make thee dumb; yet are
  they much too light for the bore of the matter. These good   25
  fellows will bring thee where I am. Rosencrantz and
  Guildenstern hold their course for England; of them I

have much to tell thee. Farewell.

He that thou knowest thine,
Hamlet.

Come, I will give you way for these your letters,
And do't the speedier that you may direct me
To him from whom you brought them.   *Exeunt.*

4.7   *Enter* KING *and* LAERTES.

KING   Now must your conscience my acquittance seal,
And you must put me in your heart for friend,
Sith you have heard, and with a knowing ear,
That he which hath your noble father slain
Pursu'd my life.

LAERTES   It well appears. But tell me
Why you proceeded not against these feats,
So crimeful and so capital in nature,
As by your safety, wisdom, all things else
You mainly were stirr'd up.

KING   O, for two special reasons,
Which may to you perhaps seem much unsinew'd,
But yet to me th'are strong. The Queen his mother
Lives almost by his looks, and for myself –
My virtue or my plague, be it either which –
She is so conjunctive to my life and soul
That, as the star moves not but in his sphere,
I could not but by her. The other motive
Why to a public count I might not go
Is the great love the general gender bear him,
Who, dipping all his faults in their affection,
Work like the spring that turneth wood to stone,
Convert his gyves to graces; so that my arrows,
Too slightly timber'd for so loud a wind,
Would have reverted to my bow again,
But not where I had aim'd them.

LAERTES   And so have I a noble father lost,
A sister driven into desp'rate terms,
Whose worth, if praises may go back again,
Stood challenger on mount of all the age
For her perfections. But my revenge will come.

KING
Break not your sleeps for that. You must not think
That we are made of stuff so flat and dull
That we can let our beard be shook with danger
And think it pastime. You shortly shall hear more.
I lov'd your father, and we love ourself,
And that, I hope, will teach you to imagine –

Enter a Messenger *with letters.*

MESSENGER   These to your Majesty, this to the Queen.
KING   From Hamlet! Who brought them?
MESSENGER   Sailors, my lord, they say. I saw them not.
They were given me by Claudio. He receiv'd them
Of him that brought them.

KING   Laertes, you shall hear them. –
Leave us.   *Exit Messenger.*
[*Reads.*]   *High and mighty, you shall know I am set*

naked on your kingdom. Tomorrow shall I beg leave to see
your kingly eyes, when I shall, first asking your pardon,
thereunto recount the occasion of my sudden and more   45
strange return.

Hamlet.

What should this mean? Are all the rest come back?
Or is it some abuse, and no such thing?

LAERTES   Know you the hand?
KING   'Tis Hamlet's character.   50
'Naked' –
And in a postscript here he says 'Alone'.
Can you devise me?

LAERTES   I am lost in it, my lord. But let him come.
It warms the very sickness in my heart   55
That I shall live and tell him to his teeth,
'Thus diest thou'.

KING   If it be so, Laertes –
As how should it be so, how otherwise? –
Will you be rul'd by me?

LAERTES   Ay, my lord,
So you will not o'errule me to a peace.   60

KING   To thine own peace. If he be now return'd,
As checking at his voyage, and that he means
No more to undertake it, I will work him
To an exploit, now ripe in my device,
Under the which he shall not choose but fall;   65
And for his death no wind of blame shall breathe,
But even his mother shall uncharge the practice
And call it accident.

LAERTES   My lord, I will be rul'd,
The rather if you could devise it so
That I might be the organ.

KING   It falls right.   70
You have been talk'd of since your travel much,
And that in Hamlet's hearing, for a quality
Wherein they say you shine. Your sum of parts
Did not together pluck such envy from him
As did that one, and that, in my regard,   75
Of the unworthiest siege.

LAERTES   What part is that, my lord?

KING   A very ribbon in the cap of youth –
Yet needful too, for youth no less becomes
The light and careless livery that it wears
Than settled age his sables and his weeds   80
Importing health and graveness. Two months since
Here was a gentleman of Normandy –
I have seen myself, and serv'd against, the French,
And they can well on horseback, but this gallant
Had witchcraft in't. He grew unto his seat,   85
And to such wondrous doing brought his horse
As had he been incorps'd and demi-natur'd
With the brave beast. So far he topp'd my thought
That I in forgery of shapes and tricks
Come short of what he did.

LAERTES   A Norman was't?   90

KING   A Norman.
LAERTES   Upon my life, Lamord.

KING　　　　　　　　　　　The very same.

LAERTES　I know him well. He is the brooch indeed
　And gem of all the nation.

95　KING　He made confession of you,
　And gave you such a masterly report
　For art and exercise in your defence,
　And for your rapier most especial,
　That he cried out 'twould be a sight indeed
100　If one could match you. The scrimers of their nation
　He swore had neither motion, guard, nor eye,
　If you oppos'd them. Sir, this report of his
　Did Hamlet so envenom with his envy
　That he could nothing do but wish and beg
105　Your sudden coming o'er to play with you.
　Now out of this –

LAERTES　　　　　　What out of this, my lord?

KING　Laertes, was your father dear to you?
　Or are you like the painting of a sorrow,
　A face without a heart?

LAERTES　　　　　　Why ask you this?

110　KING　Not that I think you did not love your father,
　But that I know love is begun by time,
　And that I see, in passages of proof,
　Time qualifies the spark and fire of it.
　There lives within the very flame of love
115　A kind of wick or snuff that will abate it;
　And nothing is at a like goodness still,
　For goodness, growing to a pleurisy,
　Dies in his own too-much. That we would do,
　We should do when we would: for this 'would'
　　changes
120　And hath abatements and delays as many
　As there are tongues, are hands, are accidents,
　And then this 'should' is like a spendthrift sigh
　That hurts by easing. But to the quick of th'ulcer:
　Hamlet comes back; what would you undertake
125　To show yourself in deed your father's son
　More than in words?

LAERTES　　　　　　To cut his throat i'th' church.

KING　No place indeed should murder sanctuarize;
　Revenge should have no bounds. But good Laertes,
　Will you do this, keep close within your chamber:
130　Hamlet, return'd, shall know you are come home;
　We'll put on those shall praise your excellence,
　And set a double varnish on the fame
　The Frenchman gave you, bring you, in fine,
　　together,
　And wager o'er your heads. He, being remiss,
135　Most generous, and free from all contriving,
　Will not peruse the foils, so that with ease –
　Or with a little shuffling – you may choose
　A sword unbated, and in a pass of practice
　Requite him for your father.

LAERTES　　　　　　I will do't.
140　And for that purpose, I'll anoint my sword.
　I bought an unction of a mountebank
　So mortal that but dip a knife in it,

Where it draws blood, no cataplasm so rare,
Collected from all simples that have virtue
Under the moon, can save the thing from death　　145
That is but scratch'd withal. I'll touch my point
With this contagion, that if I gall him slightly,
It may be death.

KING　　　　　Let's further think of this,
　Weigh what convenience both of time and means
　May fit us to our shape. If this should fail,　　150
　And that our drift look through our bad
　　performance,
　'Twere better not essay'd. Therefore this project
　Should have a back or second that might hold
　If this did blast in proof. Soft, let me see.
　We'll make a solemn wager on your cunnings –　　155
　I ha't!
　When in your motion you are hot and dry –
　As make your bouts more violent to that end –
　And that he calls for drink, I'll have prepar'd him
　A chalice for the nonce, whereon but sipping,　　160
　If he by chance escape your venom'd stuck,
　Our purpose may hold there. But stay, what noise?

Enter QUEEN.

QUEEN　One woe doth tread upon another's heel,
　So fast they follow. Your sister's drown'd, Laertes.

LAERTES　Drown'd? O, where?　　165

QUEEN　There is a willow grows askant the brook
　That shows his hoary leaves in the glassy stream.
　Therewith fantastic garlands did she make
　Of crow-flowers, nettles, daisies, and long purples,
　That liberal shepherds give a grosser name,　　170
　But our cold maids do dead men's fingers call them.
　There on the pendent boughs her crownet weeds
　Clamb'ring to hang, an envious sliver broke,
　When down her weedy trophies and herself
　Fell in the weeping brook. Her clothes spread wide,　　175
　And mermaid-like awhile they bore her up,
　Which time she chanted snatches of old lauds,
　As one incapable of her own distress,
　Or like a creature native and indued
　Unto that element. But long it could not be　　180
　Till that her garments, heavy with their drink,
　Pull'd the poor wretch from her melodious lay
　To muddy death.

LAERTES　　　　　Alas, then she is drown'd.

QUEEN　Drown'd, drown'd.

LAERTES　Too much of water hast thou, poor Ophelia,　　185
　And therefore I forbid my tears. But yet
　It is our trick; nature her custom holds,
　Let shame say what it will. [*Weeps.*]
　　　　　　　　When these are gone,
　The woman will be out. Adieu, my lord,
　I have a speech o' fire that fain would blaze　　190
　But that this folly douts it.　　　　　*Exit*

KING　　　　　Let's follow, Gertrude.
　How much I had to do to calm his rage.

Now fear I this will give it start again.
Therefore let's follow.   *Exeunt.*

5.1   *Enter two clowns – the* Gravedigger *and* Another.

GRAVEDIGGER   Is she to be buried in Christian burial,
when she wilfully seeks her own salvation?

OTHER   I tell thee she is, therefore make her grave
straight. The crowner hath sat on her and finds it
Christian burial.

GRAVEDIGGER   How can that be, unless she drowned
herself in her own defence?

OTHER   Why, 'tis found so.

GRAVEDIGGER   It must be *se offendendo,* it cannot be else.
For here lies the point: if I drown myself wittingly, it
argues an act, and an act hath three branches – it is to
act, to do, to perform; argal, she drowned herself
wittingly.

OTHER   Nay, but hear you, Goodman Delver –

GRAVEDIGGER   Give me leave. Here lies the water –
good. Here stands the man – good. If the man go to
this water and drown himself, it is, will he nill he, he
goes, mark you that. But if the water come to him and
drown him, he drowns not himself. Argal, he that is
not guilty of his own death shortens not his own life.

OTHER   But is this law?

GRAVEDIGGER   Ay, marry is't, crowner's quest law.

OTHER   Will you ha' the truth an't? If this had not been
a gentlewoman, she should have been buried out o'
Christian burial.

GRAVEDIGGER   Why, there thou say'st. And the more
pity that great folk should have countenance in this
world to drown or hang themselves more than their
even-Christen. Come, my spade. There is no ancient
gentlemen but gardeners, ditchers, and grave-makers
– they hold up Adam's profession. [*He digs.*]

OTHER   Was he a gentleman?

GRAVEDIGGER   A was the first that ever bore arms.

OTHER   Why, he had none.

GRAVEDIGGER   What, art a heathen? How dost thou
understand the Scripture? The Scripture says Adam
digged. Could he dig without arms? I'll put another
question to thee. If thou answerest me not to the
purpose, confess thyself –

OTHER   Go to.

GRAVEDIGGER   What is he that builds stronger than
either the mason, the shipwright, or the carpenter?

OTHER   The gallows-maker, for that frame outlives a
thousand tenants.

GRAVEDIGGER   I like thy wit well in good faith, the
gallows does well. But how does it well? It does well to
those that do ill. Now, thou dost ill to say the gallows
is built stronger than the church; argal, the gallows
may do well to thee. To't again, come.

OTHER   Who builds stronger than a mason, a
shipwright, or a carpenter?

GRAVEDIGGER   Ay, tell me that and unyoke.

OTHER   Marry, now I can tell.

GRAVEDIGGER   To't.

OTHER   Mass, I cannot tell.

GRAVEDIGGER   Cudgel thy brains no more about it, for
your dull ass will not mend his pace with beating. And
when you are asked this question next, say 'A grave-
maker'. The houses he makes lasts till doomsday. Go,
get thee to Yaughan; fetch me a stoup of liquor.
                                    Exit the other clown.

[*The Gravedigger continues digging.*]

[*Sings.*]   In youth when I did love, did love,
               Methought it was very sweet:
            To contract – O – the time for – a – my behove,
            O methought there – a – was nothing – a – meet.

While he is singing, enter HAMLET *and* HORATIO.

HAMLET   Has this fellow no feeling of his business a
sings in grave-making?

HORATIO   Custom hath made it in him a property of
easiness.

HAMLET   'Tis e'en so, the hand of little employment
hath the daintier sense.

GRAVEDIGGER [*Sings.*]
               But age with his stealing steps
                  Hath claw'd me in his clutch,
               And hath shipp'd me intil the land,
                  As if I had never been such.

[*He throws up a skull.*]

HAMLET   That skull had a tongue in it, and could sing
once. How the knave jowls it to th' ground, as if 'twere
Cain's jawbone, that did the first murder. This
might be the pate of a politician which this ass now
o'er-offices, one that would circumvent God, might
it not?

HORATIO   It might, my lord.

HAMLET   Or of a courtier, which could say, 'Good
morrow, sweet lord. How dost thou, sweet lord?' This
might be my Lord Such-a-one, that praised my Lord
Such-a-one's horse when a meant to beg it, might it
not?

HORATIO   Ay, my lord.

HAMLET   Why, e'en so, and now my Lady Worm's,
chopless, and knocked about the mazard with a
sexton's spade. Here's fine revolution and we had the
trick to see't. Did these bones cost no more the
breeding but to play at loggets with 'em? Mine ache to
think on't.

GRAVEDIGGER [*Sings.*]
               A pickaxe and a spade, a spade,
                  For and a shrouding-sheet,
               O a pit of clay for to be made
                  For such a guest is meet.

[*Throws up another skull.*]

HAMLET   There's another. Why, may not that be the
skull of a lawyer? Where be his quiddities now, his
quillities, his cases, his tenures, and his tricks? Why
does he suffer this mad knave now to knock him about
the sconce with a dirty shovel, and will not tell him of

his action of battery? Hum, this fellow might be in's
time a great buyer of land, with his statutes, his
recognizances, his fines, his double vouchers, his
recoveries. Is this the fine of his fines and the
recovery of his recoveries, to have his fine pate full of
fine dirt? Will his vouchers vouch him no more of
his purchases, and double ones too, than the length
and breadth of a pair of indentures? The very
conveyances of his lands will scarcely lie in this box,
and must th'inheritor himself have no more, ha?

HORATIO   Not a jot more, my lord.

HAMLET   Is not parchment made of sheepskins?

HORATIO   Ay, my lord, and of calveskins too.

HAMLET   They are sheep and calves which seek out
assurance in that. I will speak to this fellow. – Whose
grave's this, sirrah?

GRAVEDIGGER   Mine, sir.

[*Sings.*]   O a pit of clay for to be made –

HAMLET   I think it be thine indeed, for thou liest in't.

GRAVEDIGGER   You lie out on't, sir, and therefore 'tis not
yours. For my part, I do not lie in't, yet it is mine.

HAMLET   Thou dost lie in't, to be in't and say 'tis thine.
'Tis for the dead, not for the quick: therefore thou
liest.

GRAVEDIGGER   'Tis a quick lie, sir, 'twill away again
from me to you.

HAMLET   What man dost thou dig it for?

GRAVEDIGGER   For no man, sir.

HAMLET   What woman then?

GRAVEDIGGER   For none neither.

HAMLET   Who is to be buried in't?

GRAVEDIGGER   One that was a woman, sir; but rest her
soul, she's dead.

HAMLET   How absolute the knave is. We must speak by
the card or equivocation will undo us. By the Lord,
Horatio, this three years I have took note of it, the age
is grown so picked that the toe of the peasant comes so
near the heel of the courtier he galls his kibe. – How
long hast thou been grave-maker?

GRAVEDIGGER   Of all the days i'th' year I came to't that
day that our last King Hamlet o'ercame Fortinbras.

HAMLET   How long is that since?

GRAVEDIGGER   Cannot you tell that? Every fool can tell
that. It was that very day that young Hamlet was born
– he that is mad and sent into England.

HAMLET   Ay, marry. Why was he sent into England?

GRAVEDIGGER   Why, because a was mad. A shall
recover his wits there. Or if a do not, 'tis no great
matter there.

HAMLET   Why?

GRAVEDIGGER   'Twill not be seen in him there. There
the men are as mad as he.

HAMLET   How came he mad?

GRAVEDIGGER   Very strangely, they say.

HAMLET   How 'strangely'?

GRAVEDIGGER   Faith, e'en with losing his wits.

HAMLET   Upon what ground?

GRAVEDIGGER   Why, here in Denmark. I have been
sexton here, man and boy, thirty years.

HAMLET   How long will a man lie i'th' earth ere he rot?

GRAVEDIGGER   Faith, if a be not rotten before a die – as
we have many pocky corses nowadays that will
scarce hold the laying in – a will last you some eight
year or nine year. A tanner will last you nine year.

HAMLET   Why he more than another?

GRAVEDIGGER   Why, sir, his hide is so tanned with his
trade that a will keep out water a great while, and your
water is a sore decayer of your whoreson dead body.
Here's a skull now hath lien you i'th' earth three and
twenty years.

HAMLET   Whose was it?

GRAVEDIGGER   A whoreson mad fellow's it was. Whose
do you think it was?

HAMLET   Nay, I know not.

GRAVEDIGGER   A pestilence on him for a mad rogue! A
poured a flagon of Rhenish on my head once. This
same skull, sir, was Yorick's skull, the King's jester.

HAMLET   This? [*Takes the skull.*]

GRAVEDIGGER   E'en that.

HAMLET   Alas, poor Yorick. I knew him, Horatio, a
fellow of infinite jest, of most excellent fancy. He hath
bore me on his back a thousand times, and now – how
abhorred in my imagination it is. My gorge rises at it.
Here hung those lips that I have kissed I know not
how oft. Where be your gibes now, your gambols,
your songs, your flashes of merriment, that were
wont to set the table on a roar? Not one now to mock
your own grinning? Quite chop-fallen? Now get you
to my lady's chamber and tell her, let her paint an
inch thick, to this favour she must come. Make her
laugh at that. – Prithee, Horatio, tell me one thing.

HORATIO   What's that, my lord?

HAMLET   Dost thou think Alexander looked o' this
fashion i'th' earth?

HORATIO   E'en so.

HAMLET   And smelt so? Pah! [*Puts down the skull.*]

HORATIO   E'en so, my lord.

HAMLET   To what base uses we may return, Horatio!
Why, may not imagination trace the noble dust of
Alexander till a find it stopping a bung-hole?

HORATIO   'Twere to consider too curiously to consider
so.

HAMLET   No, faith, not a jot, but to follow him thither
with modesty enough, and likelihood to lead it.
Alexander died, Alexander was buried, Alexander
returneth to dust, the dust is earth, of earth we make
loam, and why of that loam whereto he was converted
might they not stop a beer-barrel?
Imperious Caesar, dead and turn'd to clay,
Might stop a hole to keep the wind away.
O that that earth which kept the world in awe
Should patch a wall t'expel the winter's flaw.
But soft, but soft awhile. Here comes the King,
The Queen, the courtiers.

Enter bearers with a coffin, a Priest, KING, QUEEN, LAERTES, *lords attendant.*

                        Who is this they follow?
And with such maimed rites? This doth betoken
The corse they follow did with desp'rate hand
Fordo it own life. 'Twas of some estate.

220   Couch we awhile and mark.

LAERTES   What ceremony else?

HAMLET   That is Laertes, a very noble youth. Mark.

LAERTES   What ceremony else?

PRIEST   Her obsequies have been as far enlarg'd

225   As we have warranty. Her death was doubtful;
And but that great command o'ersways the order,
She should in ground unsanctified been lodg'd
Till the last trumpet: for charitable prayers
Shards, flints, and pebbles should be thrown on her.

230   Yet here she is allow'd her virgin crants,
Her maiden strewments, and the bringing home
Of bell and burial.

LAERTES   Must there no more be done?

PRIEST   No more be done.
We should profane the service of the dead

235   To sing sage requiem and such rest to her
As to peace-parted souls.

LAERTES   Lay her i'th' earth,
And from her fair and unpolluted flesh
May violets spring. I tell thee, churlish priest,
A minist'ring angel shall my sister be
When thou liest howling.

240 HAMLET   What, the fair Ophelia!

QUEEN [*scattering flowers*]
Sweets to the sweet. Farewell.
I hop'd thou shouldst have been my Hamlet's wife:
I thought thy bride-bed to have deck'd, sweet maid,
And not have strew'd thy grave.

LAERTES   O, treble woe

245   Fall ten times treble on that cursed head
Whose wicked deed thy most ingenious sense
Depriv'd thee of. – Hold off the earth awhile,
Till I have caught her once more in mine arms.
[*Leaps in the grave.*]
Now pile your dust upon the quick and dead,

250   Till of this flat a mountain you have made
T'o'ertop old Pelion or the skyish head
Of blue Olympus.

HAMLET   What is he whose grief
Bears such an emphasis, whose phrase of sorrow
Conjures the wand'ring stars and makes them stand

255   Like wonder-wounded hearers? This is I,
Hamlet the Dane.

LAERTES [*grappling with him*]
The devil take thy soul!

HAMLET   Thou pray'st not well.
I prithee take thy fingers from my throat,
For though I am not splenative and rash,

260   Yet have I in me something dangerous,
Which let thy wiseness fear. Hold off thy hand.

KING   Pluck them asunder.

QUEEN   Hamlet! Hamlet!

ALL   Gentlemen!

HORATIO   Good my lord, be quiet.   265

HAMLET   Why, I will fight with him upon this theme
Until my eyelids will no longer wag.

QUEEN   O my son, what theme?

HAMLET   I lov'd Ophelia. Forty thousand brothers
Could not with all their quantity of love   270
Make up my sum. What wilt thou do for her?

KING   O, he is mad, Laertes.

QUEEN   For love of God forbear him.

HAMLET   'Swounds, show me what thou't do.
Woo't weep, woo't fight, woo't fast, woo't tear
    thyself,   275
Woo't drink up eisel, eat a crocodile?
I'll do't. Dost come here to whine,
To outface me with leaping in her grave?
Be buried quick with her, and so will I.
And if thou prate of mountains, let them throw   280
Millions of acres on us, till our ground,
Singeing his pate against the burning zone,
Make Ossa like a wart. Nay, and thou'lt mouth,
I'll rant as well as thou.

QUEEN   This is mere madness,
And thus awhile the fit will work on him.   285
Anon, as patient as the female dove
When that her golden couplets are disclos'd,
His silence will sit drooping.

HAMLET   Hear you, sir,
What is the reason that you use me thus?
I lov'd you ever. But it is no matter.   290
Let Hercules himself do what he may,
The cat will mew, and dog will have his day.   *Exit.*

KING   I pray thee, good Horatio, wait upon him.
                          Exit Horatio.

[*to Laertes*] Strengthen your patience in our last
    night's speech:
We'll put the matter to the present push. –   295
Good Gertrude, set some watch over your son.
This grave shall have a living monument.
An hour of quiet shortly shall we see;
Till then in patience our proceeding be.   *Exeunt.*

5.2   *Enter* HAMLET *and* HORATIO.

HAMLET
So much for this, sir. Now shall you see the other.
You do remember all the circumstance?

HORATIO   Remember it, my lord!

HAMLET   Sir, in my heart there was a kind of fighting
That would not let me sleep. Methought I lay   5
Worse than the mutines in the bilboes. Rashly –
And prais'd be rashness for it: let us know
Our indiscretion sometime serves us well
When our deep plots do pall; and that should learn
    us
There's a divinity that shapes our ends,   10

Rough-hew them how we will –

HORATIO   That is most certain.

HAMLET   Up from my cabin,
My sea-gown scarf'd about me, in the dark
Grop'd I to find out them, had my desire,
15 Finger'd their packet, and in fine withdrew
To mine own room again, making so bold,
My fears forgetting manners, to unseal
Their grand commission; where I found, Horatio –
Ah, royal knavery! – an exact command,
20 Larded with many several sorts of reasons
Importing Denmark's health, and England's too,
With ho! such bugs and goblins in my life,
That on the supervise, no leisure bated,
No, not to stay the grinding of the axe,
My head should be struck off.

25 HORATIO   Is't possible?

HAMLET
Here's the commission, read it at more leisure.
But wilt thou hear now how I did proceed?

HORATIO   I beseech you.

HAMLET   Being thus benetted round with villainies –
30 Or I could make a prologue to my brains,
They had begun the play – I sat me down,
Devis'd a new commission, wrote it fair –
I once did hold it, as our statists do,
A baseness to write fair, and labour'd much
35 How to forget that learning, but, sir, now
It did me yeoman's service. Wilt thou know
Th'effect of what I wrote?

HORATIO   Ay, good my lord.

HAMLET   An earnest conjuration from the King,
As England was his faithful tributary,
40 As love between them like the palm might flourish,
As peace should still her wheaten garland wear
And stand a comma 'tween their amities,
And many such-like 'as'es of great charge,
That on the view and knowing of these contents,
45 Without debatement further more or less,
He should those bearers put to sudden death,
Not shriving-time allow'd.

HORATIO   How was this seal'd?

HAMLET   Why, even in that was heaven ordinant.
I had my father's signet in my purse,
50 Which was the model of that Danish seal,
Folded the writ up in the form of th'other,
Subscrib'd it, gave't th'impression, plac'd it safely,
The changeling never known. Now the next day
Was our sea-fight, and what to this was sequent
55 Thou knowest already.

HORATIO   So Guildenstern and Rosencrantz go to't.

HAMLET
Why, man, they did make love to this employment.
They are not near my conscience, their defeat
Does by their own insinuation grow.
60 'Tis dangerous when the baser nature comes
Between the pass and fell incensed points

Of mighty opposites.

HORATIO   Why, what a king is this!

HAMLET
Does it not, think thee, stand me now upon –
He that hath kill'd my king and whor'd my mother,
65 Popp'd in between th'election and my hopes,
Thrown out his angle for my proper life
And with such coz'nage – is't not perfect conscience
To quit him with this arm? And is't not to be damn'd
To let this canker of our nature come
70 In further evil?

HORATIO
It must be shortly known to him from England
What is the issue of the business there.

HAMLET   It will be short. The interim is mine.
And a man's life's no more than to say 'one'.
75 But I am very sorry, good Horatio,
That to Laertes I forgot myself;
For by the image of my cause I see
The portraiture of his. I'll court his favours.
But sure the bravery of his grief did put me
Into a tow'ring passion.

HORATIO   Peace, who comes here? 80

Enter OSRIC, *a courtier.*

OSRIC   Your Lordship is right welcome back to
Denmark.

HAMLET   I humbly thank you sir. – Dost know this
waterfly?

HORATIO   No, my good lord. 85

HAMLET   Thy state is the more gracious, for 'tis a vice to
know him. He hath much land and fertile. Let a
beast be lord of beasts and his crib shall stand at the
king's mess. 'Tis a chuff, but, as I say, spacious in the
possession of dirt. 90

OSRIC   Sweet lord, if your lordship were at leisure, I
should impart a thing to you from his Majesty.

HAMLET   I will receive it, sir, with all diligence of spirit.
Your bonnet to his right use: 'tis for the head.

OSRIC   I thank your lordship, it is very hot. 95

HAMLET   No, believe me, 'tis very cold, the wind is
northerly.

OSRIC   It is indifferent cold, my lord, indeed.

HAMLET   But yet methinks it is very sultry and hot for
my complexion. 100

OSRIC   Exceedingly, my lord, it is very sultry – as 'twere
– I cannot tell how. My lord, his Majesty bade me
signify to you that a has laid a great wager on your
head. Sir, this is the matter –

HAMLET [*signing to him to put on his hat*]   I beseech you 105
remember –

OSRIC   Nay, good my lord, for my ease, in good faith. Sir,
here is newly come to court Laertes – believe me, an
absolute gentleman, full of most excellent differences,
of very soft society and great showing. Indeed, to 110
speak feelingly of him, he is the card or calendar of
gentry; for you shall find in him the continent of what

part a gentleman would see.

HAMLET Sir, his definement suffers no perdition in
you, though I know to divide him inventorially would
dozy th'arithmetic of memory, and yet but yaw
neither, in respect of his quick sail. But, in the verity
of extolment, I take him to be a soul of great article
and his infusion of such dearth and rareness as, to
make true diction of him, his semblable is his mirror
and who else would trace him his umbrage, nothing
more.

OSRIC Your lordship speaks most infallibly of him.

HAMLET The concernancy, sir? Why do we wrap the
gentleman in our more rawer breath?

OSRIC Sir?

HORATIO Is't not possible to understand in another
tongue? You will to't, sir, really.

HAMLET What imports the nomination of this
gentleman?

OSRIC Of Laertes?

HORATIO His purse is empty already, all's golden words
are spent.

HAMLET Of him, sir.

OSRIC I know you are not ignorant –

HAMLET I would you did, sir. Yet in faith if you did, it
would not much approve me. Well, sir?

OSRIC You are not ignorant of what excellence Laertes
is –

HAMLET I dare not confess that, lest I should compare
with him in excellence; but to know a man well were to
know himself.

OSRIC I mean, sir, for his weapon; but in the imputation
laid on him, by them in his meed, he's unfellowed.

HAMLET What's his weapon?

OSRIC Rapier and dagger.

HAMLET That's two of his weapons. But well.

OSRIC The King, sir, hath wagered with him six
Barbary horses, against the which he has impawned, as
I take it, six French rapiers and poniards, with their
assigns, as girdle, hanger, and so. Three of the
carriages, in faith, are very dear to fancy, very
responsive to the hilts, most delicate carriages, and of
very liberal conceit.

HAMLET What call you the carriages?

HORATIO I knew you must be edified by the margin ere
you had done.

OSRIC The carriages, sir, are the hangers.

HAMLET The phrase would be more german to the
matter if we could carry a cannon by our sides – I
would it might be hangers till then. But on. Six
Barbary horses against six French swords, their
assigns, and three liberal-conceited carriages – that's
the French bet against the Danish. Why is this –
impawned, as you call it?

OSRIC The King, sir, hath laid, sir, that in a dozen
passes between yourself and him he shall not exceed
you three hits; he hath laid on twelve for nine. And it
would come to immediate trial if your lordship would
vouchsafe the answer.

HAMLET How if I answer no?

OSRIC I mean, my lord, the opposition of your person in
trial.

HAMLET Sir, I will walk here in the hall. If it please his
Majesty, it is the breathing time of day with me. Let
the foils be brought, the gentleman willing, and the
King hold his purpose, I will win for him and I can; if
not, I will gain nothing but my shame and the odd hits.

OSRIC Shall I deliver you so?

HAMLET To this effect, sir, after what flourish your
nature will.

OSRIC I commend my duty to your lordship.

HAMLET Yours.   *Exit Osric.*
A does well to commend it himself, there are no
tongues else for's turn.

HORATIO This lapwing runs away with the shell on his
head.

HAMLET A did comply with his dug before a sucked it.
Thus has he – and many more of the same bevy that I
know the drossy age dotes on – only got the tune of
the time and, out of an habit of encounter, a kind of
yeasty collection, which carries them through and
through the most fanned and winnowed opinions;
and do but blow them to their trial, the bubbles are
out.

Enter a Lord.

LORD My lord, his Majesty commended him to you by
young Osric, who brings back to him that you attend
him in the hall. He sends to know if your pleasure hold
to play with Laertes or that you will take longer time.

HAMLET I am constant to my purposes, they follow the
King's pleasure. If his fitness speaks, mine is ready.
Now or whensoever, provided I be so able as now.

LORD The King and Queen and all are coming down.

HAMLET In happy time.

LORD The Queen desires you to use some gentle
entertainment to Laertes before you fall to play.

HAMLET She well instructs me.   *Exit Lord.*

HORATIO You will lose, my lord.

HAMLET I do not think so. Since he went into France, I
have been in continual practice. I shall win at the odds.
Thou wouldst not think how ill all's here about my
heart; but it is no matter.

HORATIO Nay, good my lord.

HAMLET It is but foolery, but it is such a kind of
gaingiving as would perhaps trouble a woman.

HORATIO If your mind dislike anything, obey it. I will
forestall their repair hither and say you are not fit.

HAMLET Not a whit. We defy augury. There is special
providence in the fall of a sparrow. If it be now, 'tis not
to come; if it be not to come, it will be now; if it be not
now, yet it will come. The readiness is all. Since no
man, of aught he leaves, knows aught, what is't to leave
betimes? Let be.

A table prepared. Trumpets, drums and officers with cushions. Enter KING, QUEEN, LAERTES, OSRIC *and all the state, and attendants with foils and daggers.*

KING
Come, Hamlet, come, and take this hand from me.
                    [*Puts Laertes's hand into Hamlet's.*]

HAMLET

225 Give me your pardon, sir. I have done you wrong;
But pardon't as you are a gentleman.
This presence knows, and you must needs have
        heard,
How I am punish'd with a sore distraction.
What I have done
230 That might your nature, honour, and exception
Roughly awake, I here proclaim was madness.
Was't Hamlet wrong'd Laertes? Never Hamlet.
If Hamlet from himself be ta'en away,
And when he's not himself does wrong Laertes,
235 Then Hamlet does it not, Hamlet denies it.
Who does it then? His madness. If't be so,
Hamlet is of the faction that is wrong'd;
His madness is poor Hamlet's enemy.
Sir, in this audience,
240 Let my disclaiming from a purpos'd evil
Free me so far in your most generous thoughts
That I have shot my arrow o'er the house
And hurt my brother.

LAERTES   I am satisfied in nature,
Whose motive in this case should stir me most
245 To my revenge; but in my terms of honour
I stand aloof, and will no reconcilement
Till by some elder masters of known honour
I have a voice and precedent of peace
To keep my name ungor'd. But till that time
250 I do receive your offer'd love like love
And will not wrong it.

HAMLET   I embrace it freely,
And will this brothers' wager frankly play. —
Give us the foils.

LAERTES   Come, one for me.

255 HAMLET   I'll be your foil, Laertes. In mine ignorance
Your skill shall like a star i'th' darkest night
Stick fiery off indeed.

LAERTES   You mock me, sir.

HAMLET   No, by this hand.

KING
Give them the foils, young Osric. Cousin Hamlet,
You know the wager?

260 HAMLET   Very well, my lord.
Your Grace has laid the odds o'th' weaker side.

KING   I do not fear it. I have seen you both,
But since he is better'd, we have therefore odds.

LAERTES   This is too heavy. Let me see another.

HAMLET
265 This likes me well. These foils have all a length?

OSRIC   Ay, my good lord. [*They prepare to play.*]

Enter servants with flagons of wine.

KING   Set me the stoups of wine upon that table.
If Hamlet give the first or second hit,
Or quit in answer of the third exchange,
Let all the battlements their ordnance fire: 270
The King shall drink to Hamlet's better breath,
And in the cup an union shall he throw
Richer than that which four successive kings
In Denmark's crown have worn – give me the cups –
And let the kettle to the trumpet speak,   275
The trumpet to the cannoneer without,
The cannons to the heavens, the heaven to earth,
'Now the King drinks to Hamlet.' Come, begin.
And you, the judges, bear a wary eye.

HAMLET   Come on, sir.   280

LAERTES   Come, my lord. [*They play.*]

HAMLET   One.

LAERTES   No.

HAMLET   Judgment.

OSRIC   A hit, a very palpable hit.   285

LAERTES   Well, again.

KING   Stay, give me drink. Hamlet this pearl is thine.
Here's to thy health.
                    [*Drums; trumpets; and shot goes off.*]
                    Give him the cup.

HAMLET   I'll play this bout first. Set it by awhile. Come.
[*They play again.*] Another hit. What say you?   290

LAERTES   I do confess't.

KING   Our son shall win.

QUEEN   He's fat and scant of breath.
Here, Hamlet, take my napkin, rub thy brows.
The Queen carouses to thy fortune, Hamlet.

HAMLET   Good madam.   295

KING   Gertrude, do not drink.

QUEEN   I will, my lord, I pray you pardon me.
[*She drinks and offers the cup to Hamlet.*]

KING [*aside*]   It is the poison'd cup. It is too late.

HAMLET   I dare not drink yet, madam – by and by.

QUEEN   Come, let me wipe thy face.   300

LAERTES   My lord, I'll hit him now.

KING   I do not think't.

LAERTES [*aside*]
And yet it is almost against my conscience.

HAMLET   Come for the third, Laertes. You do but dally.
I pray you pass with your best violence.
I am afeard you make a wanton of me.   305

LAERTES   Say you so? Come on. [*They play.*]

OSRIC   Nothing neither way.

LAERTES   Have at you now.
[*Laertes wounds Hamlet; then, in scuffling, they change rapiers.*]

KING   Part them; they are incensed.

HAMLET   Nay, come again.   310
[*He wounds Laertes. The Queen falls.*]

OSRIC   Look to the Queen there, ho!

HORATIO
  They bleed on both sides. How is it, my lord?
OSRIC   How is't, Laertes?
LAERTES
  Why, as a woodcock to mine own springe, Osric.
315 I am justly kill'd with mine own treachery.
HAMLET
  How does the Queen?
KING   She swoons to see them bleed.
QUEEN
  No, no, the drink, the drink! O my dear Hamlet!
  The drink, the drink! I am poison'd. [*Dies.*]
HAMLET   O villainy! Ho! Let the door be lock'd.
320 Treachery! Seek it out.   *Exit Osric.*
LAERTES   It is here, Hamlet. Hamlet, thou art slain.
  No medicine in the world can do thee good;
  In thee there is not half an hour's life.
  The treacherous instrument is in thy hand,
325 Unbated and envenom'd. The foul practice
  Hath turn'd itself on me. Lo, here I lie,
  Never to rise again. Thy mother's poison'd.
  I can no more. The King – the King's to blame.
HAMLET
  The point envenom'd too! Then, venom, to thy
    work. [*Wounds the King.*]
330 ALL   Treason! treason!
KING   O yet defend me, friends. I am but hurt.
HAMLET
  Here, thou incestuous, murd'rous, damned Dane,
  Drink off this potion. Is thy union here?
  Follow my mother. [*King dies.*]
335 LAERTES   He is justly serv'd.
  It is a poison temper'd by himself.
  Exchange forgiveness with me, noble Hamlet.
  Mine and my father's death come not upon thee,
  Nor thine on me. [*Dies.*]
HAMLET   Heaven make thee free of it. I follow thee.
340 I am dead, Horatio. Wretched Queen, adieu.
  You that look pale and tremble at this chance,
  That are but mutes or audience to this act,
  Had I but time – as this fell sergeant, Death,
  Is strict in his arrest – O, I could tell you –
345 But let it be. Horatio, I am dead,
  Thou livest. Report me and my cause aright
  To the unsatisfied.
HORATIO   Never believe it.
  I am more an antique Roman than a Dane.
  Here's yet some liquor left.
HAMLET   As th'art a man
350 Give me the cup. Let go, by Heaven I'll ha't.
  O God, Horatio, what a wounded name,
  Things standing thus unknown, shall I leave behind
    me.
  If thou didst ever hold me in thy heart,
  Absent thee from felicity awhile,
355 And in this harsh world draw thy breath in pain
  To tell my story.   [*A march afar off and shot within.*]
  What warlike noise is this?

Enter OSRIC.

OSRIC
  Young Fortinbras, with conquest come from Poland,
  To the ambassadors of England gives
  This warlike volley.
HAMLET
  O, I die, Horatio.
  The potent poison quite o'ercrows my spirit.   360
  I cannot live to hear the news from England,
  But I do prophesy th'election lights
  On Fortinbras. He has my dying voice.
  So tell him, with th'occurrents more and less
  Which have solicited – the rest is silence. [*Dies.*]   365
HORATIO
  Now cracks a noble heart. Good night, sweet prince,
  And flights of angels sing thee to thy rest.
                    [*March within.*]
  Why does the drum come hither?

Enter FORTINBRAS, *and the English* Ambassadors, *and
    soldiers with drum and colours.*

FORTINBRAS   Where is this sight?
HORATIO   What is it you would see?
  If aught of woe or wonder, cease your search.   370
FORTINBRAS
  This quarry cries on havoc. O proud Death,
  What feast is toward in thine eternal cell,
  That thou so many princes at a shot
  So bloodily hast struck?
1 AMBASSADOR   The sight is dismal;
  And our affairs from England come too late.   375
  The ears are senseless that should give us hearing
  To tell him his commandment is fulfill'd,
  That Rosencrantz and Guildenstern are dead.
  Where should we have our thanks?
HORATIO   Not from his mouth,
  Had it th'ability of life to thank you.   380
  He never gave commandment for their death.
  But since, so jump upon this bloody question,
  You from the Polack wars and you from England
  Are here arriv'd, give order that these bodies
  High on a stage be placed to the view,   385
  And let me speak to th'yet unknowing world
  How these things came about. So shall you hear
  Of carnal, bloody, and unnatural acts,
  Of accidental judgments, casual slaughters,
  Of deaths put on by cunning and forc'd cause,   390
  And, in this upshot, purposes mistook
  Fall'n on th'inventors' heads. All this can I
  Truly deliver.
FORTINBRAS   Let us haste to hear it,
  And call the noblest to the audience.
  For me, with sorrow I embrace my fortune.   395
  I have some rights of memory in this kingdom,
  Which now to claim my vantage doth invite me.
HORATIO   Of that I shall have also cause to speak,

And from his mouth whose voice will draw on more.
400   But let this same be presently perform'd
Even while men's minds are wild, lest more
   mischance
On plots and errors happen.
FORTINBRAS   Let four captains
Bear Hamlet like a soldier to the stage,
For he was likely, had he been put on,

To have prov'd most royal; and for his passage,   405
The soldier's music and the rite of war
Speak loudly for him.
Take up the bodies. Such a sight as this
Becomes the field, but here shows much amiss.
Go, bid the soldiers shoot.   410
      Exeunt marching, bearing off the bodies, after which a
                        peal of ordnance is shot off.

Julius Caesar

Julius Caesar seems to have been one of the first plays to be performed in the new Globe Theatre in the summer or autumn of 1599: Thomas Platter, a Swiss doctor who was in London from 18 September to 20 October, recorded having seen a performance of 'the tragedy of the first Emperor Julius' on 21 September which was in all probability Shakespeare's play. It is unlikely to have been written earlier since it is not included in the list of plays given by Francis Meres in *Palladis Tamia* (1598), but allusions to it begin to appear in 1600, indicating that it was a popular and influential work. It was not published, however, until it was included in the First Folio in 1623, as the fifth of the tragedies, in an unusually accurate text based apparently on a very clear manuscript, formerly thought to be authorial but now assumed to be a good scribal copy.

While today *Julius Caesar* tends to be categorized as a 'classical tragedy' or a 'Roman play', and discussed in relation to later plays of this kind such as *Antony and Cleopatra* and *Coriolanus*, its immediate context in Shakespeare's career as a dramatist gives it equally strong links with *Henry V* and *Hamlet*. By 1599 Shakespeare had written only two 'straight' tragedies, *Titus Andronicus* and *Romeo and Juliet*, though some of the English history plays had been printed with the word 'tragedy' on their title-pages. He seems to have been reading and thinking about Julius Caesar when he wrote *Henry V* (also generally dated 1599) since in the Chorus to act 5 he compares the triumphant return of Henry to England to the greeting of 'conquering Caesar' by the senators and plebeians of 'antique Rome' – the material of the opening scene of this play. A further link is provided by Fluellen's comparison of Henry and Alexander in 4.7 of *Henry V*: Shakespeare read about Alexander in Thomas North's translation of Plutarch's *Lives of the Noble Grecians and Romans*, where Alexander is paired with Julius Caesar in Plutarch's system of providing parallel Greek and Roman biographies. Shakespeare, who used Plutarch extensively in *Julius Caesar*, seems to suggest that Henry V could be added as a third, English example of a great military leader.

As *Henry V* looks forward to *Julius Caesar*, the latter play looks forward to *Hamlet*. The difficulty Brutus faces in arriving at his decision to kill Caesar can be compared with Hamlet's dilemma over killing Claudius, and the way Brutus describes the 'interim' between 'the acting of a dreadful thing / And the first motion' in 2.1 is if anything more accurate about Hamlet's situation than it is about his own. The 'sheeted dead' squeaking and gibbering in the Roman streets 'A little ere the mightiest Julius fell' are remembered in the first scene of *Hamlet*, and Polonius recalls acting the part of Caesar in 3.2.

While *Hamlet* quickly became a personal tragedy, with many of its political passages cut in performance, the theatrical and critical history of *Julius Caesar* has seen debate centred on its main political issue: were the conspirators justified in killing Caesar? The question was familiar to educated people in Elizabethan England as a stock topic for debate or 'disputation' in schools and universities. In the theatre, where it has been one of the most frequently performed of Shakespeare's plays, there has been a long tradition of presenting Brutus as a sympathetic hero and endorsing his republican sympathies; critics, and especially editors of the play, have been more inclined to find fault with him and to view the murder of Caesar as a crime or even 'sacrilege'. Many twentieth-century productions since Orson Welles's sensational 1937 New York version (subtitled 'Death of a Dictator') have modernized and simplified the play's politics by presenting Caesar as a Fascist leader like Hitler or Mussolini.

The Arden text is based on the 1623 First Folio.

Julius CAESAR

OCTAVIUS Caesar
Marcus ANTONIUS
M. Æmilius LEPIDUS
} *triumvirs after the death of Julius Caesar*

CICERO
PUBLIUS
POPILIUS Lena
} *senators*

Marcus BRUTUS

CASSIUS
VASCA
TREBONIUS
LIGARIUS
DECIUS Brutus,
METELLUS Cimber
} *conspirators against Julius Caesar*

CINNA

FLAVIUS *and* MARULLUS — *tribunes*

ARTEMIDORUS — *a sophist of Cnidos*

SOOTHSAYER

CINNA — *a poet*

Another POET

LUCILIUS, TITINIUS, MESSALA, Young CATO
and VOLUMNIUS
} *friends to Brutus and Cassius*

VARRO, CLITUS, CLAUDIS, STRATO, LUCIUS, DARDANIUS — *servants or officers to Brutus*

PINDARUS — *servant to Cassius*

COBBLER, CARPENTER *and other* PLEBEIANS

SERVANTS — *to Caesar; to Antony; to Octavius*

CALPHURNIA — *wife to Caesar*

PORTIA — *wife to Brutus*

GHOST *of Caesar*

Senators, Guards, Attendants, etc.

Julius Caesar

1.1   *Enter* FLAVIUS, MARULLUS *and*
        certain Commoners *over the stage.*

FLAVIUS
  Hence! home, you idle creatures, get you home:
  Is this a holiday? What, know you not,
  Being mechanical, you ought not walk
  Upon a labouring day without the sign
  Of your profession? Speak, what trade art thou?
CARPENTER   Why, sir, a carpenter.
MARULLUS   Where is thy leather apron, and thy rule?
  What dost thou with thy best apparel on?
  You, sir, what trade are you?
COBBLER   Truly, sir, in respect of a fine workman, I am
  but, as you would say, a cobbler.
MARULLUS
  But what trade art thou? Answer me directly.
COBBLER   A trade, sir, that I hope I may use with a safe
  conscience; which is, indeed, sir, a mender of bad
  soles.
MARULLUS
  What trade, thou knave? thou naughty knave, what
    trade?
COBBLER   Nay, I beseech you, sir, be not out with me:
  yet, if you be out, sir, I can mend you.
MARULLUS
  What meanest thou by that? Mend me, thou saucy
    fellow?
COBBLER   Why, sir, cobble you.
FLAVIUS   Thou art a cobbler, art thou?
COBBLER   Truly, sir, all that I live by is with the awl: I
  meddle with no tradesman's matters, nor women's
  matters; but withal I am, indeed, sir, a surgeon to old
  shoes: when they are in great danger I recover them.
  As proper men as ever trod upon neat's leather have
  gone upon my handiwork.
FLAVIUS   But wherefore art not in thy shop to-day?
  Why dost thou lead these men about the streets?
COBBLER   Truly, sir, to wear out their shoes, to get
  myself into more work. But indeed, sir, we make
  holiday to see Caesar, and to rejoice in his triumph.
MARULLUS
  Wherefore rejoice? What conquest brings he home?
  What tributaries follow him to Rome,
  To grace in captive bonds his chariot wheels?
  You blocks, you stones, you worse than senseless
    things!
  O you hard hearts, you cruel men of Rome,
  Knew you not Pompey? Many a time and oft
  Have you climb'd up to walls and battlements,
  To towers and windows, yea, to chimney-tops,
  Your infants in your arms, and there have sat
  The livelong day, with patient expectation,
  To see great Pompey pass the streets of Rome:
  And when you saw his chariot but appear,
  Have you not made an universal shout,
  That Tiber trembled underneath her banks
  To hear the replication of your sounds

Made in her concave shores?
And do you now put on your best attire?
And do you now cull out a holiday?   50
And do you now strew flowers in his way,
That comes in triumph over Pompey's blood?
Be gone!
Run to your houses, fall upon your knees,
Pray to the gods to intermit the plague   55
That needs must light on this ingratitude.
FLAVIUS   Go, go, good countrymen, and for this fault
  Assemble all the poor men of your sort;
  Draw them to Tiber banks, and weep your tears
  Into the channel, till the lowest stream   60
  Do kiss the most exalted shores of all.
                     Exeunt all the Commoners.
  See where their basest mettle be not mov'd;
  They vanish tongue-tied in their guiltiness.
  Go you down that way towards the Capitol;
  This way will I. Disrobe the images,   65
  If you do find them deck'd with ceremonies.
MARULLUS   May we do so?
  You know it is the feast of Lupercal.
FLAVIUS   It is no matter; let no images
  Be hung with Caesar's trophies. I'll about   70
  And drive away the vulgar from the streets;
  So do you too, where you perceive them thick.
  These growing feathers pluck'd from Caesar's wing
  Will make him fly an ordinary pitch,
  Who else would soar above the view of men   75
  And keep us all in servile fearfulness.   *Exeunt.*

1.2   *Enter* CAESAR, ANTONY *for the course,*
    CALPHURNIA, PORTIA, DECIUS, CICERO, BRUTUS,
    CASSIUS, CASCA, *a* Soothsayer, *and a great crowd;*
    after them MARULLUS *and* FLAVIUS.

CAESAR   Calphurnia.
CASCA   Peace, ho! Caesar speaks.
CAESAR   Calphurnia.
CALPHURNIA   Here, my lord.
CAESAR   Stand you directly in Antonius' way
  When he doth run his course. Antonius.
ANTONY   Caesar, my lord?   5
CAESAR   Forget not, in your speed, Antonius,
  To touch Calphurnia; for our elders say,
  The barren, touched in this holy chase,
  Shake off their sterile curse.
ANTONY   I shall remember:
  When Caesar says, 'Do this,' it is perform'd.   10
CAESAR   Set on, and leave no ceremony out.
SOOTHSAYER   Caesar!
CAESAR   Ha! Who calls?
CASCA   Bid every noise be still; peace yet again!
CAESAR   Who is it in the press that calls on me?   15
  I hear a tongue shriller than all the music
  Cry 'Caesar!' Speak. Caesar is turn'd to hear.
SOOTHSAYER   Beware the ides of March.
CAESAR   What man is that?

BRUTUS
   A soothsayer bids you beware the ides of March.

20 CAESAR   Set him before me; let me see his face.

CASSIUS
   Fellow, come from the throng; look upon Caesar.

CAESAR
   What say'st thou to me now? Speak once again.

SOOTHSAYER   Beware the ides of March.

CAESAR   He is a dreamer. Let us leave him. Pass.
         Sennet. Exeunt. Brutus and Cassius remain.

25 CASSIUS   Will you go see the order of the course?

BRUTUS   Not I.

CASSIUS   I pray you, do.

BRUTUS   I am not gamesome: I do lack some part
   Of that quick spirit that is in Antony.
   Let me not hinder, Cassius, your desires;
30   I'll leave you.

CASSIUS   Brutus, I do observe you now of late:
   I have not from your eyes that gentleness
   And show of love as I was wont to have.
   You bear too stubborn and too strange a hand
   Over your friend that loves you.

35 BRUTUS   Cassius,
   Be not deceiv'd: if I have veil'd my look,
   I turn the trouble of my countenance
   Merely upon myself. Vexed I am
   Of late with passions of some difference,
40   Conceptions only proper to myself,
   Which give some soil, perhaps, to my behaviours;
   But let not therefore my good friends be griev'd
   (Among which number, Cassius, be you one)
   Nor construe any further my neglect,
45   Than that poor Brutus, with himself at war,
   Forgets the shows of love to other men.

CASSIUS
   Then, Brutus, I have much mistook your passion;
   By means whereof this breast of mine hath buried
   Thoughts of great value, worthy cogitations.
50   Tell me, good Brutus, can you see your face?

BRUTUS   No, Cassius; for the eye sees not itself
   But by reflection, by some other things.

CASSIUS   'Tis just;
   And it is very much lamented, Brutus,
55   That you have no such mirrors as will turn
   Your hidden worthiness into your eye,
   That you might see your shadow. I have heard,
   Where many of the best respect in Rome
   (Except immortal Caesar), speaking of Brutus,
60   And groaning underneath this age's yoke,
   Have wish'd that noble Brutus had his eyes.

BRUTUS
   Into what dangers would you lead me, Cassius,
   That you would have me seek into myself
   For that which is not in me?

65 CASSIUS   Therefore, good Brutus, be prepar'd to hear;
   And since you know you cannot see yourself
   So well as by reflection, I, your glass,

   Will modestly discover to yourself
   That of yourself which you yet know not of.
   And be not jealous on me, gentle Brutus: 70
   Were I a common laughter, or did use
   To stale with ordinary oaths my love
   To every new protester; if you know
   That I do fawn on men and hug them hard,
   And after scandal them; or if you know   75
   That I profess myself in banqueting
   To all the rout, then hold me dangerous.
                   [Flourish and shout.]

BRUTUS
   What means this shouting? I do fear the people
   Choose Caesar for their king.

CASSIUS   Ay, do you fear it?
   Then must I think you would not have it so.   80

BRUTUS   I would not, Cassius; yet I love him well.
   But wherefore do you hold me here so long?
   What is it that you would impart to me?
   If it be aught toward the general good,
   Set honour in one eye, and death i'th' other,   85
   And I will look on both indifferently;
   For let the gods so speed me as I love
   The name of honour more than I fear death.

CASSIUS   I know that virtue to be in you, Brutus,
   As well as I do know your outward favour.   90
   Well, honour is the subject of my story.
   I cannot tell what you and other men
   Think of this life; but for my single self,
   I had as lief not be as live to be
   In awe of such a thing as I myself.   95
   I was born free as Caesar; so were you;
   We both have fed as well, and we can both
   Endure the winter's cold as well as he:
   For once, upon a raw and gusty day,
   The troubled Tiber chafing with her shores,   100
   Caesar said to me, 'Dar'st thou, Cassius, now
   Leap in with me into this angry flood,
   And swim to yonder point?' Upon the word,
   Accoutred as I was, I plunged in
   And bade him follow; so indeed he did.   105
   The torrent roar'd, and we did buffet it
   With lusty sinews, throwing it aside
   And stemming it with hearts of controversy.
   But ere we could arrive the point propos'd,
   Caesar cried, 'Help me, Cassius, or I sink.'   110
   I, as Aeneas, our great ancestor,
   Did from the flames of Troy upon his shoulder
   The old Anchises bear, so from the waves of Tiber
   Did I the tired Caesar. And this man
   Is now become a god, and Cassius is   115
   A wretched creature, and must bend his body
   If Caesar carelessly but nod on him.
   He had a fever when he was in Spain,
   And when the fit was on him, I did mark
   How he did shake; 'tis true, this god did shake;   120
   His coward lips did from their colour fly,

And that same eye whose bend doth awe the world
Did lose his lustre; I did hear him groan;
Ay, and that tongue of his, that bade the Romans
125 Mark him and write his speeches in their books,
Alas, it cried, 'Give me some drink, Titinius,'
As a sick girl. Ye gods, it doth amaze me
A man of such a feeble temper should
So get the start of the majestic world,
And bear the palm alone.   *[Shout. Flourish.]*
130 BRUTUS   Another general shout?
I do believe that these applauses are
For some new honours that are heap'd on Caesar.
CASSIUS   Why, man, he doth bestride the narrow world
Like a Colossus, and we petty men
135 Walk under his huge legs, and peep about
To find ourselves dishonourable graves.
Men at some time are masters of their fates:
The fault, dear Brutus, is not in our stars,
But in ourselves, that we are underlings.
140 Brutus and Caesar: what should be in that 'Caesar'?
Why should that name be sounded more than yours?
Write them together, yours is as fair a name;
Sound them, it doth become the mouth as well;
Weigh them, it is as heavy; conjure with 'em,
145 'Brutus' will start a spirit as soon as 'Caesar'.
Now in the names of all the gods at once,
Upon what meat doth this our Caesar feed,
That he is grown so great? Age, thou art sham'd!
Rome, thou hast lost the breed of noble bloods!
150 When went there by an age, since the great flood,
But it was fam'd with more than with one man?
When could they say, till now, that talk'd of Rome,
That her wide walks encompass'd but one man?
Now is it Rome indeed, and room enough,
155 When there is in it but one only man.
O, you and I have heard our fathers say,
There was a Brutus once that would have brook'd
Th' eternal devil to keep his state in Rome
As easily as a king.
160 BRUTUS   That you do love me, I am nothing jealous;
What you would work me to, I have some aim:
How I have thought of this, and of these times,
I shall recount hereafter. For this present,
I would not (so with love I might entreat you)
165 Be any further mov'd. What you have said
I will consider; what you have to say
I will with patience hear, and find a time
Both meet to hear and answer such high things.
Till then, my noble friend, chew upon this:
170 Brutus had rather be a villager
Than to repute himself a son of Rome
Under these hard conditions as this time
Is like to lay upon us.
CASSIUS   I am glad
That my weak words have struck but thus much show
175 Of fire from Brutus.

Enter CAESAR *and his train.*

BRUTUS   The games are done and Caesar is returning.
CASSIUS   As they pass by, pluck Casca by the sleeve,
And he will (after his sour fashion) tell you
What hath proceeded worthy note to-day.
180 BRUTUS   I will do so. But look you, Cassius,
The angry spot doth glow on Caesar's brow,
And all the rest look like a chidden train:
Calphurnia's cheek is pale, and Cicero
Looks with such ferret and such fiery eyes
185 As we have seen him in the Capitol,
Being cross'd in conference by some senators.
CASSIUS   Casca will tell us what the matter is.
CAESAR   Antonius.
ANTONY   Caesar?
CAESAR   Let me have men about me that are fat,
190 Sleek-headed men, and such as sleep a-nights.
Yond Cassius has a lean and hungry look;
He thinks too much: such men are dangerous.
ANTONY   Fear him not, Caesar, he's not dangerous.
He is a noble Roman, and well given.
195 CAESAR   Would he were fatter! But I fear him not:
Yet if my name were liable to fear,
I do not know the man I should avoid
So soon as that spare Cassius. He reads much,
He is a great observer, and he looks
200 Quite through the deeds of men. He loves no plays,
As thou dost, Antony; he hears no music.
Seldom he smiles, and smiles in such a sort
As if he mock'd himself, and scorn'd his spirit
That could be mov'd to smile at any thing.
205 Such men as he be never at heart's ease
Whiles they behold a greater than themselves,
And therefore are they very dangerous.
I rather tell thee what is to be fear'd
Than what I fear; for always I am Caesar.
210 Come on my right hand, for this ear is deaf,
And tell me truly what thou think'st of him.
         Sennet. Exeunt Caesar and his train.
CASCA
You pull'd me by the cloak. Would you speak with
  me?
BRUTUS
Ay, Casca. Tell us what hath chanc'd to-day,
That Caesar looks so sad.
215 CASCA   Why, you were with him, were you not?
BRUTUS   I should not then ask Casca what had chanc'd.
CASCA   Why, there was a crown offer'd him; and, being
offer'd him, he put it by with the back of his hand,
thus; and then the people fell a-shouting.
220 BRUTUS   What was the second noise for?
CASCA   Why, for that too.
CASSIUS   They shouted thrice: what was the last cry for?
CASCA   Why, for that too.
BRUTUS   Was the crown offer'd him thrice?
225 CASCA   Ay, marry, was't, and he put it by thrice, every

time gentler than other; and at every putting-by mine honest neighbours shouted.

CASSIUS   Who offered him the crown?

CASCA   Why, Antony.

230   BRUTUS   Tell us the manner of it, gentle Casca.

CASCA   I can as well be hang'd as tell the manner of it: it was mere foolery; I did not mark it. I saw Mark Antony offer him a crown; yet 'twas not a crown neither, 'twas one of these coronets; and, as I told

235   you, he put it by once; but for all that, to my thinking, he would fain have had it. Then he offered it to him again; then he put it by again; but to my thinking, he was very loath to lay his fingers off it. And then he offered it the third time. He put it the third time by;

240   and still as he refus'd it, the rabblement hooted, and clapp'd their chopt hands, and threw up their sweaty night-caps, and uttered such a deal of stinking breath because Caesar refus'd the crown, that it had, almost, choked Caesar; for he swounded, and fell down at it.

245   And for mine own part, I durst not laugh, for fear of opening my lips and receiving the bad air.

CASSIUS   But soft, I pray you; what, did Caesar swound?

CASCA   He fell down in the market-place, and foam'd at mouth, and was speechless.

250   BRUTUS   'Tis very like; he hath the falling-sickness.

CASSIUS   No, Caesar hath it not; but you, and I, And honest Casca, we have the falling-sickness.

CASCA   I know not what you mean by that, but I am sure Caesar fell down. If the tag-rag people did not clap

255   him and hiss him, according as he pleas'd and displeas'd them, as they use to do the players in the theatre, I am no true man.

BRUTUS   What said he when he came unto himself?

CASCA   Marry, before he fell down, when he perceiv'd

260   the common herd was glad he refus'd the crown, he pluck'd me ope his doublet, and offer'd them his throat to cut. And I had been a man of any occupation, if I would not have taken him at a word, I would I might go to hell among the rogues. And so he fell.

265   When he came to himself again, he said, if he had done or said anything amiss, he desir'd their worships to think it was his infirmity. Three or four wenches, where I stood, cried, 'Alas, good soul,' and forgave him with all their hearts; but there's no heed

270   to be taken of them; if Caesar had stabb'd their mothers, they would have done no less.

BRUTUS   And after that, he came thus sad away?

CASCA   Ay.

CASSIUS   Did Cicero say anything?

275   CASCA   Ay, he spoke Greek.

CASSIUS   To what effect?

CASCA   Nay, and I tell you that, I'll ne'er look you i'th' face again. But those that understood him smil'd at one another, and shook their heads; but for mine own

280   part, it was Greek to me. I could tell you more news too: Marullus and Flavius, for pulling scarfs off Caesar's images, are put to silence. Fare you well.

There was more foolery yet, if I could remember it.

CASSIUS   Will you sup with me to-night, Casca?

CASCA   No, I am promis'd forth.   285

CASSIUS   Will you dine with me to-morrow?

CASCA   Ay, if I be alive, and your mind hold, and your dinner worth the eating.

CASSIUS   Good. I will expect you.

CASCA   Do so. Farewell, both.   *Exit.*   290

BRUTUS   What a blunt fellow is this grown to be! He was quick mettle when he went to school.

CASSIUS   So is he now in execution Of any bold or noble enterprise, However he puts on this tardy form.   295 This rudeness is a sauce to his good wit, Which gives men stomach to disgest his words With better appetite.

BRUTUS   And so it is. For this time I will leave you. To-morrow, if you please to speak with me,   300 I will come home to you; or if you will, Come home to me, and I will wait for you.

CASSIUS   I will do so: till then, think of the world.

Exit Brutus.

Well, Brutus, thou art noble; yet I see Thy honourable mettle may be wrought   305 From that it is dispos'd: therefore 'tis meet That noble minds keep ever with their likes; For who so firm that cannot be seduc'd? Caesar doth bear me hard; but he loves Brutus. If I were Brutus now, and he were Cassius,   310 He should not humour me. I will this night, In several hands, in at his windows throw, As if they came from several citizens, Writings, all tending to the great opinion That Rome holds of his name; wherein obscurely   315 Caesar's ambition shall be glanced at. And after this, let Caesar seat him sure, For we will shake him, or worse days endure.   *Exit.*

1.3   *Thunder and lightning. Enter* CASCA *and* CICERO, *meeting.*

CICERO   Good even, Casca: brought you Caesar home? Why are you breathless? and why stare you so?

CASCA   Are you not mov'd, when all the sway of earth Shakes like a thing unfirm? O Cicero, I have seen tempests, when the scolding winds   5 Have riv'd the knotty oaks; and I have seen Th' ambitious ocean swell and rage and foam, To be exalted with the threat'ning clouds: But never till to-night, never till now, Did I go through a tempest dropping fire.   10 Either there is a civil strife in heaven, Or else the world, too saucy with the gods, Incenses them to send destruction.

CICERO   Why, saw you any thing more wonderful?

CASCA   A common slave, you know him well by sight,   15 Held up his left hand, which did flame and burn

Like twenty torches join'd; and yet his hand,
Not sensible of fire, remain'd unscorch'd.
Besides (I ha' not since put up my sword)
20 Against the Capitol I met a lion,
Who glaz'd upon me, and went surly by,
Without annoying me. And there were drawn
Upon a heap a hundred ghastly women,
Transformed with their fear, who swore they saw
25 Men, all in fire, walk up and down the streets.
And yesterday the bird of night did sit,
Even at noon-day, upon the market-place,
Hooting and shrieking. When these prodigies
Do so conjointly meet, let not men say,
30 'These are their reasons, they are natural';
For I believe, they are portentous things
Unto the climate that they point upon.
CICERO   Indeed, it is a strange-disposed time:
But men may construe things, after their fashion,
35 Clean from the purpose of the things themselves.
Comes Caesar to the Capitol to-morrow?
CASCA   He doth; for he did bid Antonius
Send word to you he would be there to-morrow.
CICERO   Good night then, Casca: this disturbed sky
40 Is not to walk in.
CASCA   Farewell, Cicero.   *Exit Cicero.*

Enter CASSIUS.

CASSIUS   Who's there?
CASCA   A Roman.
CASSIUS   Casca, by your voice.
CASCA   Your ear is good. Cassius, what night is this!
CASSIUS   A very pleasing night to honest men.
CASCA   Who ever knew the heavens menace so?
CASSIUS
45   Those that have known the earth so full of faults.
For my part, I have walk'd about the streets,
Submitting me unto the perilous night,
And, thus unbraced, Casca, as you see,
Have bar'd my bosom to the thunder-stone;
50 And when the cross blue lightning seem'd to open
The breast of heaven, I did present myself
Even in the aim and very flash of it.
CASCA
But wherefore did you so much tempt the heavens?
It is the part of men to fear and tremble
55 When the most mighty gods by tokens send
Such dreadful heralds to astonish us.
CASSIUS   You are dull, Casca, and those sparks of life
That should be in a Roman you do want,
Or else you use not. You look pale, and gaze,
60 And put on fear, and cast yourself in wonder,
To see the strange impatience of the heavens;
But if you would consider the true cause
Why all these fires, why all these gliding ghosts,
Why birds and beasts from quality and kind,
65 Why old men, fools, and children calculate,
Why all these things change from their ordinance,
Their natures, and pre-formed faculties,
To monstrous quality, why, you shall find
That heaven hath infus'd them with these spirits
70 To make them instruments of fear and warning
Unto some monstrous state.
Now could I, Casca, name to thee a man
Most like this dreadful night,
That thunders, lightens, opens graves, and roars
75 As doth the lion in the Capitol;
A man no mightier than thyself, or me,
In personal action, yet prodigious grown,
And fearful, as these strange eruptions are.
CASCA   'Tis Caesar that you mean, is it not, Cassius?
CASSIUS   Let it be who it is: for Romans now
80 Have thews and limbs like to their ancestors;
But, woe the while! our fathers' minds are dead,
And we are govern'd with our mothers' spirits;
Our yoke and sufferance show us womanish.
CASCA   Indeed, they say the senators to-morrow
85 Mean to establish Caesar as a king;
And he shall wear his crown by sea and land,
In every place, save here in Italy.
CASSIUS   I know where I will wear this dagger then;
Cassius from bondage will deliver Cassius:
90 Therein, ye gods, you make the weak most strong;
Therein, ye gods, you tyrants do defeat.
Nor stony tower, nor walls of beaten brass,
Nor airless dungeon, nor strong links of iron,
Can be retentive to the strength of spirit;
95 But life, being weary of these worldly bars,
Never lacks power to dismiss itself.
If I know this, know all the world besides,
That part of tyranny that I do bear
I can shake off at pleasure.   [*Thunder still.*]
CASCA   So can I:
100 So every bondman in his own hand bears
The power to cancel his captivity.
CASSIUS   And why should Caesar be a tyrant then?
Poor man! I know he would not be a wolf,
But that he sees the Romans are but sheep;
105 He were no lion, were not Romans hinds.
Those that with haste will make a mighty fire
Begin it with weak straws. What trash is Rome,
What rubbish, and what offal, when it serves
For the base matter to illuminate
110 So vile a thing as Caesar! But, O grief,
Where hast thou led me? I, perhaps, speak this
Before a willing bondman; then I know
My answer must be made. But I am arm'd,
And dangers are to me indifferent.
115 CASCA   You speak to Casca, and to such a man
That is no fleering tell-tale. Hold, my hand:
Be factious for redress of all these griefs,
And I will set this foot of mine as far
As who goes furthest.
CASSIUS   There's a bargain made.
120 Now know you, Casca, I have mov'd already

339

Some certain of the noblest-minded Romans
To undergo with me an enterprise
Of honourable-dangerous consequence;
125   And I do know, by this they stay for me
In Pompey's porch: for now, this fearful night,
There is no stir or walking in the streets;
And the complexion of the element
In favour's like the work we have in hand,
130   Most bloody, fiery, and most terrible.

Enter CINNA.

CASCA   Stand close awhile, for here comes one in haste.
CASSIUS   'Tis Cinna. I do know him by his gait.
He is a friend. Cinna, where haste you so?
CINNA   To find out you. Who's that? Metellus Cimber?
135   CASSIUS   No, it is Casca, one incorporate
To our attempts. Am I not stay'd for, Cinna?
CINNA   I am glad on't. What a fearful night is this!
There's two or three of us have seen strange sights.
CASSIUS   Am I not stay'd for? Tell me.
CINNA   Yes, you are.
140   O Cassius, if you could
But win the noble Brutus to our party –
CASSIUS   Be you content. Good Cinna, take this paper,
And look you lay it in the praetor's chair,
Where Brutus may but find it; and throw this
145   In at his window; set this up with wax
Upon old Brutus' statue: all this done,
Repair to Pompey's porch, where you shall find us.
Is Decius Brutus and Trebonius there?
CINNA   All but Metellus Cimber, and he's gone
150   To seek you at your house. Well, I will hie,
And so bestow these papers as you bade me.
CASSIUS   That done, repair to Pompey's theatre.
                                          Exit Cinna.

Come, Casca, you and I will yet ere day
See Brutus at his house: three parts of him
155   Is ours already, and the man entire
Upon the next encounter yields him ours.
CASCA   O, he sits high in all the people's hearts:
And that which would appear offence in us,
His countenance, like richest alchemy,
160   Will change to virtue and to worthiness.
CASSIUS   Him and his worth and our great need of him
You have right well conceited. Let us go,
For it is after midnight; and ere day
We will awake him and be sure of him.   *Exeunt.*

2.1   *Enter* BRUTUS *in his orchard.*

BRUTUS   What, Lucius, ho!
I cannot, by the progress of the stars,
Give guess how near to day. Lucius, I say!
I would it were my fault to sleep so soundly.
5   When, Lucius, when? Awake, I say! What, Lucius!

Enter LUCIUS.

LUCIUS   Call'd you, my lord?

BRUTUS   Get me a taper in my study, Lucius:
When it is lighted, come and call me here.
LUCIUS   I will, my lord.   *Exit.*
BRUTUS   It must be by his death: and for my part,   10
I know no personal cause to spurn at him,
But for the general. He would be crown'd:
How that might change his nature, there's the
    question.
It is the bright day that brings forth the adder,
And that craves wary walking. Crown him? – that; –   15
And then, I grant, we put a sting in him,
That at his will he may do danger with.
Th'abuse of greatness is when it disjoins
Remorse from power; and, to speak truth of Caesar,
I have not known when his affections sway'd   20
More than his reason. But 'tis a common proof,
That lowliness is young ambition's ladder,
Whereto the climber-upward turns his face;
But when he once attains the upmost round,
He then unto the ladder turns his back,   25
Looks in the clouds, scorning the base degrees
By which he did ascend. So Caesar may;
Then lest he may, prevent. And since the quarrel
Will bear no colour for the thing he is,
Fashion it thus: that what he is, augmented,   30
Would run to these and these extremities;
And therefore think him as a serpent's egg,
Which, hatch'd, would, as his kind, grow
    mischievous,
And kill him in the shell.

Enter LUCIUS.

LUCIUS   The taper burneth in your closet, sir.   35
Searching the window for a flint, I found
This paper, thus seal'd up; and I am sure
It did not lie there when I went to bed.
[*Gives him the letter.*]
BRUTUS   Get you to bed again; it is not day.
Is not to-morrow, boy, the ides of March?   40
LUCIUS   I know not, sir.
BRUTUS   Look in the calendar, and bring me word.
LUCIUS   I will, sir.   *Exit.*
BRUTUS   The exhalations whizzing in the air
Give so much light that I may read by them.   45
[*Opens the letter, and reads.*]
Brutus, thou sleep'st; awake, and see thyself.
Shall Rome, etc. Speak, strike, redress!
'Brutus, thou sleep'st; awake!'
Such instigations have been often dropp'd
Where I have took them up.   50
'Shall Rome, etc.' Thus must I piece it out:
Shall Rome stand under one man's awe? What,
    Rome?
My ancestors did from the streets of Rome
The Tarquin drive, when he was call'd a king.
'Speak, strike, redress!' Am I entreated   55
To speak, and strike? O Rome, I make thee promise,

If the redress will follow, thou receivest
Thy full petition at the hand of Brutus.

Enter LUCIUS.

LUCIUS   Sir, March is wasted fifteen days.
    [*Knock within.*]
BRUTUS   'Tis good. Go to the gate; somebody knocks.
                                                    Exit Lucius.

Since Cassius first did whet me against Caesar,
I have not slept.
Between the acting of a dreadful thing
And the first motion, all the interim is
Like a phantasma, or a hideous dream:
The genius and the mortal instruments
Are then in council; and the state of man,
Like to a little kingdom, suffers then
The nature of an insurrection.

Enter LUCIUS.

LUCIUS   Sir, 'tis your brother Cassius at the door,
Who doth desire to see you.
BRUTUS   Is he alone?
LUCIUS   No, sir, there are moe with him.
BRUTUS   Do you know them?
LUCIUS   No, sir, their hats are pluck'd about their ears,
And half their faces buried in their cloaks,
That by no means I may discover them
By any mark of favour.
BRUTUS   Let 'em enter.   *Exit Lucius.*
They are the faction. O conspiracy,
Sham'st thou to show thy dangerous brow by night,
When evils are most free? O, then by day
Where wilt thou find a cavern dark enough
To mask thy monstrous visage? Seek none,
    conspiracy;
Hide it in smiles and affability:
For if thou path, thy native semblance on,
Not Erebus itself were dim enough
To hide thee from prevention.

Enter the conspirators, CASSIUS, CASCA, DECIUS,
CINNA, METELLUS CIMBER *and* TREBONIUS.

CASSIUS   I think we are too bold upon your rest:
Good morrow, Brutus. Do we trouble you?
BRUTUS   I have been up this hour, awake all night.
Know I these men that come along with you?
CASSIUS   Yes, every man of them; and no man here
But honours you; and every one doth wish
You had but that opinion of yourself
Which every noble Roman bears of you.
This is Trebonius.
BRUTUS   He is welcome hither.
CASSIUS   This, Decius Brutus.
BRUTUS   He is welcome too.
CASSIUS
This, Casca; this, Cinna; and this, Metellus Cimber.

BRUTUS   They are all welcome.
What watchful cares do interpose themselves
Betwixt your eyes and night?
CASSIUS   Shall I entreat a word? [*They whisper.*]   100
DECIUS
Here lies the east: doth not the day break here?
CASCA   No.
CINNA   O, pardon, sir, it doth; and yon grey lines
That fret the clouds are messengers of day.
CASCA   You shall confess that you are both deceiv'd.   105
Here, as I point my sword, the sun arises,
Which is a great way growing on the south,
Weighing the youthful season of the year.
Some two months hence, up higher toward the north
He first presents his fire; and the high east   110
Stands, as the Capitol, directly here.
BRUTUS   Give me your hands all over, one by one.
CASSIUS   And let us swear our resolution.
BRUTUS   No, not an oath. If not the face of men,
The sufferance of our souls, the time's abuse –   115
If these be motives weak, break off betimes,
And every man hence to his idle bed.
So let high-sighted tyranny range on,
Till each man drop by lottery. But if these,
As I am sure they do, bear fire enough   120
To kindle cowards and to steel with valour
The melting spirits of women, then, countrymen,
What need we any spur but our own cause
To prick us to redress? what other bond
Than secret Romans, that have spoke the word,   125
And will not palter? and what other oath
Than honesty to honesty engag'd,
That this shall be, or we will fall for it?
Swear priests and cowards, and men cautelous,
Old feeble carrions, and such suffering souls   130
That welcome wrongs; unto bad causes swear
Such creatures as men doubt; but do not stain
The even virtue of our enterprise,
Nor th'insuppressive mettle of our spirits,
To think that or our cause or our performance   135
Did need an oath; when every drop of blood
That every Roman bears, and nobly bears,
Is guilty of a several bastardy,
If he do break the smallest particle
Of any promise that hath pass'd from him.   140
CASSIUS   But what of Cicero? Shall we sound him?
I think he will stand very strong with us.
CASCA   Let us not leave him out.
CINNA   No, by no means.
METELLUS   O, let us have him, for his silver hairs
Will purchase us a good opinion,   145
And buy men's voices to commend our deeds.
It shall be said his judgment rul'd our hands;
Our youths and wildness shall no whit appear,
But all be buried in his gravity.
BRUTUS   O, name him not; let us not break with him;   150

For he will never follow any thing
That other men begin.
CASSIUS   Then leave him out.
CASCA   Indeed he is not fit.
DECIUS   Shall no man else be touch'd but only Caesar?
155 CASSIUS   Decius, well urg'd. I think it is not meet,
Mark Antony, so well belov'd of Caesar,
Should outlive Caesar: we shall find of him
A shrewd contriver; and you know, his means,
If he improve them, may well stretch so far
160 As to annoy us all; which to prevent,
Let Antony and Caesar fall together.
BRUTUS
Our course will seem too bloody, Caius Cassius,
To cut the head off and then hack the limbs,
Like wrath in death and envy afterwards;
165 For Antony is but a limb of Caesar.
Let's be sacrificers, but not butchers, Caius.
We all stand up against the spirit of Caesar,
And in the spirit of men there is no blood.
O, that we then could come by Caesar's spirit,
170 And not dismember Caesar! But, alas,
Caesar must bleed for it. And, gentle friends,
Let's kill him boldly, but not wrathfully;
Let's carve him as a dish fit for the gods,
Not hew him as a carcass fit for hounds.
175 And let our hearts, as subtle masters do,
Stir up their servants to an act of rage,
And after seem to chide 'em. This shall make
Our purpose necessary, and not envious;
Which so appearing to the common eyes,
180 We shall be call'd purgers, not murderers.
And for Mark Antony, think not of him;
For he can do no more than Caesar's arm
When Caesar's head is off.
CASSIUS   Yet I fear him;
For in the ingrafted love he bears to Caesar –
185 BRUTUS   Alas, good Cassius, do not think of him:
If he love Caesar, all that he can do
Is to himself: take thought, and die for Caesar.
And that were much he should; for he is given
To sports, to wildness, and much company.
190 TREBONIUS   There is no fear in him; let him not die;
For he will live, and laugh at this hereafter.
[*Clock strikes.*]
BRUTUS   Peace! count the clock.
CASSIUS   The clock hath stricken three.
TREBONIUS   'Tis time to part.
CASSIUS   But it is doubtful yet
Whether Caesar will come forth to-day or no;
195 For he is superstitious grown of late,
Quite from the main opinion he held once
Of fantasy, of dreams, and ceremonies.
It may be these apparent prodigies,
The unaccustom'd terror of this night,
200 And the persuasion of his augurers,
May hold him from the Capitol to-day.

DECIUS   Never fear that: if he be so resolv'd,
I can o'ersway him; for he loves to hear
That unicorns may be betray'd with trees,
And bears with glasses, elephants with holes,   205
Lions with toils, and men with flatterers;
But when I tell him he hates flatterers,
He says he does, being then most flattered.
Let me work;
For I can give his humour the true bent,   210
And I will bring him to the Capitol.
CASSIUS   Nay, we will all of us be there to fetch him.
BRUTUS   By the eighth hour: is that the uttermost?
CINNA   Be that the uttermost, and fail not then.
METELLUS   Caius Ligarius doth bear Caesar hard,   215
Who rated him for speaking well of Pompey;
I wonder none of you have thought of him.
BRUTUS   Now, good Metellus, go along by him:
He loves me well, and I have given him reasons;
Send him but hither, and I'll fashion him.   220
CASSIUS
The morning comes upon 's: we'll leave you, Brutus.
And, friends, disperse yourselves; but all remember
What you have said, and show yourselves true
Romans.
BRUTUS   Good gentlemen, look fresh and merrily.
Let not our looks put on our purposes,   225
But bear it as our Roman actors do,
With untir'd spirits and formal constancy.
And so good morrow to you every one.
                    Exeunt. Brutus remains.
Boy! Lucius! Fast asleep? It is no matter;
Enjoy the honey-heavy dew of slumber: 230
Thou hast no figures nor no fantasies
Which busy care draws in the brains of men;
Therefore thou sleep'st so sound.

                    Enter PORTIA.

PORTIA   Brutus, my lord.
BRUTUS
Portia, what mean you? Wherefore rise you now?
It is not for your health thus to commit   235
Your weak condition to the raw cold morning.
PORTIA
Nor for yours neither. Y' have ungently, Brutus,
Stole from my bed; and yesternight at supper
You suddenly arose, and walk'd about,
Musing, and sighing, with your arms across;   240
And when I ask'd you what the matter was,
You star'd upon me with ungentle looks.
I urg'd you further; then you scratch'd your head,
And too impatiently stamp'd with your foot;
Yet I insisted, yet you answer'd not,   245
But with an angry wafture of your hand
Gave sign for me to leave you. So I did,
Fearing to strengthen that impatience
Which seem'd too much enkindled, and withal
Hoping it was but an effect of humour,   250

Which sometime hath his hour with every man.
It will not let you eat, nor talk, nor sleep;
And could it work so much upon your shape
As it hath much prevail'd on your condition,
55   I should not know you Brutus. Dear my lord,
Make me acquainted with your cause of grief.
BRUTUS   I am not well in health, and that is all.
PORTIA   Brutus is wise, and, were he not in health,
He would embrace the means to come by it.
60 BRUTUS   Why, so I do. Good Portia, go to bed.
PORTIA   Is Brutus sick, and is it physical
To walk unbraced and suck up the humours
Of the dank morning? What, is Brutus sick?
And will he steal out of his wholesome bed
65 To dare the vile contagion of the night,
And tempt the rheumy and unpurged air
To add unto his sickness? No, my Brutus;
You have some sick offence within your mind,
Which, by the right and virtue of my place,
70 I ought to know of; and, upon my knees,
I charm you, by my once commended beauty,
By all your vows of love, and that great vow
Which did incorporate and make us one,
That you unfold to me, your self, your half,
75 Why you are heavy, and what men to-night
Have had resort to you; for here have been
Some six or seven, who did hide their faces
Even from darkness.
BRUTUS   Kneel not, gentle Portia.
PORTIA   I should not need, if you were gentle Brutus.
80 Within the bond of marriage, tell me, Brutus,
Is it excepted I should know no secrets
That appertain to you? Am I your self
But, as it were, in sort or limitation,
To keep with you at meals, comfort your bed,
85 And talk to you sometimes? Dwell I but in the
    suburbs
Of your good pleasure? If it be no more,
Portia is Brutus' harlot, not his wife.
BRUTUS   You are my true and honourable wife,
As dear to me as are the ruddy drops
90 That visit my sad heart.
PORTIA
If this were true, then should I know this secret.
I grant I am a woman; but withal
A woman that Lord Brutus took to wife;
I grant I am a woman; but withal
95 A woman well reputed, Cato's daughter.
Think you I am no stronger than my sex,
Being so father'd, and so husbanded?
Tell me your counsels, I will not disclose 'em.
I have made strong proof of my constancy,
100 Giving myself a voluntary wound
Here, in the thigh: can I bear that with patience,
And not my husband's secrets?

BRUTUS   O ye gods,
Render me worthy of this noble wife! [*Knock.*]
Hark, hark! one knocks. Portia, go in awhile;
And by and by thy bosom shall partake   305
The secrets of my heart.
All my engagements I will construe to thee,
All the charactery of my sad brows.
Leave me with haste.   *Exit Portia.*

Enter LUCIUS *and* CAIUS LIGARIUS.

             Lucius, who's that knocks?
LUCIUS   Here is a sick man that would speak with you.   310
BRUTUS   Caius Ligarius, that Metellus spake of.
Boy, stand aside. Caius Ligarius, how?
LIGARIUS
Vouchsafe good morrow from a feeble tongue.
BRUTUS
O, what a time have you chose out, brave Caius,
To wear a kerchief! Would you were not sick!   315
LIGARIUS   I am not sick if Brutus have in hand
Any exploit worthy the name of honour.
BRUTUS   Such an exploit have I in hand, Ligarius,
Had you a healthful ear to hear of it.
LIGARIUS   By all the gods that Romans bow before,   320
I here discard my sickness. Soul of Rome!
Brave son, deriv'd from honourable loins!
Thou, like an exorcist, hast conjur'd up
My mortified spirit. Now bid me run,
And I will strive with things impossible,   325
Yea, get the better of them. What's to do?
BRUTUS
A piece of work that will make sick men whole.
LIGARIUS
But are not some whole that we must make sick?
BRUTUS   That must we also. What it is, my Caius,
I shall unfold to thee, as we are going   330
To whom it must be done.
LIGARIUS   Set on your foot,
And with a heart new-fir'd I follow you,
To do I know not what; but it sufficeth
That Brutus leads me on.   [*Thunder.*]
BRUTUS   Follow me then.   *Exeunt.*

2.2   *Thunder and lightning. Enter* JULIUS CAESAR
          in his night-gown.

CAESAR
Nor heaven nor earth have been at peace to-night:
Thrice hath Calphurnia in her sleep cried out,
'Help, ho! they murther Caesar!' Who's within?

Enter a Servant.

SERVANT   My lord?
CAESAR   Go bid the priests do present sacrifice,   5
And bring me their opinions of success.
SERVANT   I will, my lord.   *Exit.*

Enter CALPHURNIA.

CALPHURNIA

What mean you, Caesar? Think you to walk forth?
You shall not stir out of your house to-day.

CAESAR

10 Caesar shall forth. The things that threaten'd me
Ne'er look'd but on my back; when they shall see
The face of Caesar, they are vanished.

CALPHURNIA

Caesar, I never stood on ceremonies,
Yet now they fright me. There is one within,
15 Besides the things that we have heard and seen,
Recounts most horrid sights seen by the watch.
A lioness hath whelped in the streets,
And graves have yawn'd and yielded up their dead;
Fierce fiery warriors fight upon the clouds
20 In ranks and squadrons and right form of war,
Which drizzled blood upon the Capitol;
The noise of battle hurtled in the air,
Horses did neigh, and dying men did groan,
And ghosts did shriek and squeal about the streets.
25 O Caesar, these things are beyond all use,
And I do fear them.

CAESAR   What can be avoided
Whose end is purpos'd by the mighty gods?
Yet Caesar shall go forth; for these predictions
Are to the world in general as to Caesar.

CALPHURNIA

30 When beggars die, there are no comets seen;
The heavens themselves blaze forth the death of
princes.

CAESAR   Cowards die many times before their deaths;
The valiant never taste of death but once.
Of all the wonders that I yet have heard,
35 It seems to me most strange that men should fear,
Seeing that death, a necessary end,
Will come when it will come.

Enter a Servant.

                            What say the augurers?

SERVANT   They would not have you to stir forth to-day.
Plucking the entrails of an offering forth,
40 They could not find a heart within the beast.

CAESAR   The gods do this in shame of cowardice:
Caesar should be a beast without a heart
If he should stay at home to-day for fear.
No, Caesar shall not. Danger knows full well
45 That Caesar is more dangerous than he.
We are two lions litter'd in one day,
And I the elder and more terrible,
And Caesar shall go forth.

CALPHURNIA   Alas, my lord,
Your wisdom is consum'd in confidence.
50 Do not go forth to-day: call it my fear
That keeps you in the house, and not your own.
We'll send Mark Antony to the Senate House,

And he shall say you are not well to-day.
Let me upon my knee prevail in this.

CAESAR   Mark Antony shall say I am not well,   55
And for thy humour I will stay at home.

Enter DECIUS.

Here's Decius Brutus; he shall tell them so.

DECIUS   Caesar, all hail! Good morrow, worthy Caesar.
I come to fetch you to the Senate House.

CAESAR   And you are come in very happy time   60
To bear my greeting to the senators,
And tell them that I will not come to-day:
Cannot, is false; and that I dare not, falser;
I will not come to-day. Tell them so, Decius.

CALPHURNIA   Say he is sick.

CAESAR   Shall Caesar send a lie?   65
Have I in conquest stretch'd mine arm so far,
To be afeard to tell greybeards the truth?
Decius, go tell them Caesar will not come.

DECIUS   Most mighty Caesar, let me know some cause,
Lest I be laugh'd at when I tell them so.   70

CAESAR   The cause is in my will: I will not come;
That is enough to satisfy the Senate.
But for your private satisfaction,
Because I love you, I will let you know:
Calphurnia here, my wife, stays me at home.   75
She dreamt to-night she saw my statue,
Which like a fountain with an hundred spouts
Did run pure blood; and many lusty Romans
Came smiling, and did bathe their hands in it.
And these does she apply for warnings and portents   80
And evils imminent; and on her knee
Hath begg'd that I will stay at home to-day.

DECIUS   This dream is all amiss interpreted;
It was a vision fair and fortunate:
Your statue spouting blood in many pipes,   85
In which so many smiling Romans bath'd,
Signifies that from you great Rome shall suck
Reviving blood, and that great men shall press
For tinctures, stains, relics, and cognizance.
This by Calphurnia's dream is signified.   90

CAESAR   And this way have you well expounded it.

DECIUS   I have, when you have heard what I can say:
And know it now. The Senate have concluded
To give this day a crown to mighty Caesar.
If you shall send them word you will not come,   95
Their minds may change. Besides, it were a mock
Apt to be render'd for some one to say,
'Break up the Senate till another time,
When Caesar's wife shall meet with better dreams.'
If Caesar hide himself, shall they not whisper,   100
'Lo, Caesar is afraid'?
Pardon me, Caesar; for my dear dear love
To your proceeding bids me tell you this,
And reason to my love is liable.

CAESAR

How foolish do your fears seem now, Calphurnia!   105

I am ashamed I did yield to them.
Give me my robe, for I will go.

Enter BRUTUS, CAIUS LIGARIUS, METELLUS, CASCA,
TREBONIUS, CINNA *and* PUBLIUS.

And look where Publius is come to fetch me.
PUBLIUS   Good morrow, Caesar.
CAESAR   Welcome, Publius.
10   What, Brutus, are you stirr'd so early too?
Good morrow, Casca. Caius Ligarius,
Caesar was ne'er so much your enemy
As that same ague which hath made you lean.
What is't a clock?
BRUTUS   Caesar, 'tis strucken eight.
15   CAESAR   I thank you for your pains and courtesy.

Enter ANTONY

See! Antony, that revels long a-nights,
Is notwithstanding up. Good morrow, Antony.
ANTONY   So to most noble Caesar.
CAESAR   Bid them prepare within.
I am to blame to be thus waited for.
20   Now, Cinna; now, Metellus; what, Trebonius:
I have an hour's talk in store for you;
Remember that you call on me to-day:
Be near me, that I may remember you.
TREBONIUS   Caesar, I will: [*aside*] and so near will I be,
25   That your best friends shall wish I had been further.
CAESAR
Good friends, go in, and taste some wine with me;
And we, like friends, will straightway go together.
BRUTUS [*aside*]
That every like is not the same, O Caesar!
The heart of Brutus earns to think upon.   *Exeunt.*

2.3   *Enter* ARTEMIDORUS *reading a paper.*

ARTEMIDORUS   *Caesar, beware of Brutus; take heed of*
Cassius; come not near Casca; have an eye to Cinna;
trust not Trebonius; mark well Metellus Cimber; Decius
Brutus loves thee not; thou hast wrong'd Caius Ligarius.
There is but one mind in all these men, and it is bent
against Caesar. If thou beest not immortal, look about
you: security gives way to conspiracy. The mighty gods
defend thee! Thy lover,

ARTEMIDORUS.

Here will I stand till Caesar pass along,
And as a suitor will I give him this.
My heart laments that virtue cannot live
Out of the teeth of emulation.
If thou read this, O Caesar, thou may'st live;
If not, the Fates with traitors do contrive.   *Exit.*

2.4   *Enter* PORTIA *and* LUCIUS.

PORTIA   I prithee, boy, run to the Senate House.
Stay not to answer me, but get thee gone.

Why dost thou stay?
LUCIUS   To know my errand, madam.
PORTIA   I would have had thee there and here again
Ere I can tell thee what thou should'st do there.   5
O constancy, be strong upon my side;
Set a huge mountain 'tween my heart and tongue!
I have a man's mind, but a woman's might.
How hard it is for women to keep counsel!
Art thou here yet?
LUCIUS   Madam, what should I do?   10
Run to the Capitol, and nothing else?
And so return to you, and nothing else?
PORTIA   Yes, bring me word, boy, if thy lord look well,
For he went sickly forth; and take good note
What Caesar doth, what suitors press to him.   15
Hark, boy, what noise is that?
LUCIUS   I hear none, madam.
PORTIA   Prithee, listen well.
I heard a bustling rumour, like a fray,
And the wind brings it from the Capitol.
LUCIUS   Sooth, madam, I hear nothing.   20

Enter the Soothsayer.

PORTIA
Come hither, fellow. Which way hast thou been?
SOOTHSAYER   At mine own house, good lady.
PORTIA   What is't a clock?
SOOTHSAYER   About the ninth hour, lady.
PORTIA   Is Caesar yet gone to the Capitol?
SOOTHSAYER   Madam, not yet. I go to take my stand,   25
To see him pass on to the Capitol.
PORTIA   Thou hast some suit to Caesar, hast thou not?
SOOTHSAYER   That I have, lady, if it will please Caesar
To be so good to Caesar as to hear me:
I shall beseech him to befriend himself.   30
PORTIA
Why, know'st thou any harm's intended towards
    him?
SOOTHSAYER
None that I know will be, much that I fear may
    chance.
Good morrow to you. Here the street is narrow.
The throng that follows Caesar at the heels,
Of senators, of praetors, common suitors,   35
Will crowd a feeble man almost to death:
I'll get me to a place more void, and there
Speak to great Caesar as he comes along.   *Exit.*
PORTIA   I must go in. Ay me, how weak a thing
The heart of woman is! O Brutus,   40
The heavens speed thee in thine enterprise!
[*aside*] Sure, the boy heard me. Brutus hath a suit
That Caesar will not grant. [*aside*] O, I grow faint.
Run, Lucius, and commend me to my lord;
Say I am merry; come to me again,   45
And bring me word what he doth say to thee.
                              Exeunt severally.

3.1 *Flourish. Enter* CAESAR, BRUTUS, CASSIUS,
CASCA, DECIUS, METELLUS CIMBER, TREBONIUS,
CINNA, ANTONY, LEPIDUS, ARTEMIDORUS,
PUBLIUS, POPILIUS *and the* Soothsayer.

CAESAR The ides of March are come.

SOOTHSAYER Ay, Caesar, but not gone.

ARTEMIDORUS Hail, Caesar! Read this schedule.

DECIUS Trebonius doth desire you to o'er-read,
At your best leisure, this his humble suit.

ARTEMIDORUS
O Caesar, read mine first; for mine's a suit
That touches Caesar nearer. Read it, great Caesar.

CAESAR What touches us ourself shall be last serv'd.

ARTEMIDORUS Delay not, Caesar. Read it instantly.

CAESAR What, is the fellow mad?

PUBLIUS   Sirrah, give place.

CASSIUS What, urge you your petitions in the street?
Come to the Capitol.

CAESAR, and the rest, enter the Senate.

POPILIUS I wish your enterprise to-day may thrive.

CASSIUS What enterprise, Popilius?

POPILIUS   Fare you well.
[*Leaves him and joins Caesar.*]

BRUTUS What said Popilius Lena?

CASSIUS He wish'd to-day our enterprise might thrive.
I fear our purpose is discovered.

BRUTUS Look how he makes to Caesar: mark him.

CASSIUS Casca, be sudden, for we fear prevention.
Brutus, what shall be done? If this be known,
Cassius or Caesar never shall turn back,
For I will slay myself.

BRUTUS   Cassius, be constant:
Popilius Lena speaks not of our purposes;
For look, he smiles, and Caesar doth not change.

CASSIUS
Trebonius knows his time; for look you, Brutus,
He draws Mark Antony out of the way.
                        Exeunt Antony and Trebonius.

DECIUS Where is Metellus Cimber? Let him go,
And presently prefer his suit to Caesar.

BRUTUS He is address'd. Press near and second him.

CINNA Casca, you are the first that rears your hand.

CAESAR Are we all ready? What is now amiss
That Caesar and his senate must redress?

METELLUS
Most high, most mighty, and most puissant Caesar,
Metellus Cimber throws before thy seat
An humble heart, – [*kneeling*]

CAESAR   I must prevent thee, Cimber.
These couchings and these lowly courtesies
Might fire the blood of ordinary men,
And turn pre-ordinance and first decree
Into the law of children. Be not fond,
To think that Caesar bears such rebel blood
That will be thaw'd from the true quality
With that which melteth fools – I mean sweet words,

Low-crooked curtsies, and base spaniel fawning.
Thy brother by decree is banished:
If thou dost bend and pray and fawn for him,
I spurn thee like a cur out of my way.
Know, Caesar doth not wrong, nor without cause
Will he be satisfied.

METELLUS
Is there no voice more worthy than my own,
To sound more sweetly in great Caesar's ear
For the repealing of my banish'd brother?

BRUTUS I kiss thy hand, but not in flattery, Caesar,
Desiring thee that Publius Cimber may
Have an immediate freedom of repeal.

CAESAR What, Brutus?

CASSIUS   Pardon, Caesar; Caesar, pardon:
As low as to thy foot doth Cassius fall,
To beg enfranchisement for Publius Cimber.

CAESAR I could be well mov'd, if I were as you;
If I could pray to move, prayers would move me;
But I am constant as the northern star,
Of whose true-fix'd and resting quality
There is no fellow in the firmament.
The skies are painted with unnumber'd sparks,
They are all fire, and every one doth shine;
But there's but one in all doth hold his place.
So in the world: 'tis furnish'd well with men,
And men are flesh and blood, and apprehensive;
Yet in the number I do know but one
That unassailable holds on his rank,
Unshak'd of motion; and that I am he,
Let me a little show it, even in this,
That I was constant Cimber should be banish'd,
And constant do remain to keep him so.

CINNA O Caesar –

CAESAR   Hence! Wilt thou lift up Olympus?

DECIUS Great Caesar –

CAESAR   Doth not Brutus bootless kneel?

CASCA Speak hands for me! [*They stab Caesar.*]

CAESAR *Et tu, Brute?* – Then fall Caesar! [*Dies.*]

CINNA Liberty! Freedom! Tyranny is dead!
Run hence, proclaim, cry it about the streets.

CASSIUS Some to the common pulpits, and cry out,
'Liberty, freedom, and enfranchisement!'

BRUTUS People and senators, be not affrighted.
Fly not; stand still; ambition's debt is paid.

CASCA Go to the pulpit, Brutus.

DECIUS   And Cassius too.

BRUTUS Where's Publius?

CINNA Here, quite confounded with this mutiny.

METELLUS
Stand fast together, lest some friend of Caesar's
Should chance –

BRUTUS Talk not of standing. Publius, good cheer;
There is no harm intended to your person,
Nor to no Roman else. So tell them, Publius.

CASSIUS And leave us, Publius, lest that the people,
Rushing on us, should do your age some mischief.

BRUTUS   Do so; and let no man abide this deed
But we the doers.

Enter TREBONIUS.

CASSIUS   Where is Antony?

TREBONIUS   Fled to his house amaz'd.
Men, wives, and children stare, cry out, and run,
As it were doomsday.

BRUTUS   Fates, we will know your pleasures.
That we shall die, we know; 'tis but the time
And drawing days out, that men stand upon.

CASCA   Why, he that cuts off twenty years of life
Cuts off so many years of fearing death.

BRUTUS   Grant that, and then is death a benefit:
So are we Caesar's friends, that have abridg'd
His time of fearing death. Stoop, Romans, stoop,
And let us bathe our hands in Caesar's blood
Up to the elbows, and besmear our swords:
Then walk we forth, even to the market-place,
And waving our red weapons o'er our heads,
Let's all cry, 'Peace, freedom, and liberty!'

CASSIUS   Stoop then, and wash. How many ages hence
Shall this our lofty scene be acted over,
In states unborn, and accents yet unknown!

BRUTUS   How many times shall Caesar bleed in sport,
That now on Pompey's basis lies along,
No worthier than the dust!

CASSIUS   So oft as that shall be,
So often shall the knot of us be call'd
The men that gave their country liberty.

DECIUS   What, shall we forth?

CASSIUS   Ay, every man away.
Brutus shall lead, and we will grace his heels
With the most boldest and best hearts of Rome.

Enter a Servant.

BRUTUS   Soft, who comes here? A friend of Antony's.

SERVANT   Thus, Brutus, did my master bid me kneel;
Thus did Mark Antony bid me fall down;
And, being prostrate, thus he bade me say:
Brutus is noble, wise, valiant, and honest;
Caesar was mighty, bold, royal, and loving:
Say I love Brutus, and I honour him;
Say I fear'd Caesar, honour'd him, and lov'd him.
If Brutus will vouchsafe that Antony
May safely come to him, and be resolv'd
How Caesar hath deserv'd to lie in death,
Mark Antony shall not love Caesar dead
So well as Brutus living; but will follow
The fortunes and affairs of noble Brutus
Thorough the hazards of this untrod state,
With all true faith. So says my master Antony.

BRUTUS   Thy master is a wise and valiant Roman;
I never thought him worse.
Tell him, so please him come unto this place,
He shall be satisfied; and, by my honour,
Depart untouch'd.

SERVANT   I'll fetch him presently.

Exit Servant.

BRUTUS   I know that we shall have him well to friend.

CASSIUS   I wish we may: but yet have I a mind
That fears him much; and my misgiving still   145
Falls shrewdly to the purpose.

Enter ANTONY.

BRUTUS
But here comes Antony. Welcome, Mark Antony.

ANTONY   O mighty Caesar! dost thou lie so low?
Are all thy conquests, glories, triumphs, spoils,
Shrunk to this little measure? Fare thee well.   150
I know not, gentlemen, what you intend,
Who else must be let blood, who else is rank:
If I myself, there is no hour so fit
As Caesar's death's hour; nor no instrument
Of half that worth as those your swords, made rich   155
With the most noble blood of all this world.
I do beseech ye, if you bear me hard,
Now, whilst your purpled hands do reek and smoke,
Fulfil your pleasure. Live a thousand years,
I shall not find myself so apt to die;   160
No place will please me so, no mean of death,
As here by Caesar, and by you cut off,
The choice and master spirits of this age.

BRUTUS   O Antony, beg not your death of us.
Though now we must appear bloody and cruel,   165
As by our hands and this our present act
You see we do, yet see you but our hands
And this the bleeding business they have done.
Our hearts you see not; they are pitiful;
And pity to the general wrong of Rome –   170
As fire drives out fire, so pity pity –
Hath done this deed on Caesar. For your part,
To you our swords have leaden points, Mark Antony:
Our arms in strength of malice, and our hearts
Of brothers' temper, do receive you in   175
With all kind love, good thoughts, and reverence.

CASSIUS   Your voice shall be as strong as any man's
In the disposing of new dignities.

BRUTUS   Only be patient till we have appeas'd
The multitude, beside themselves with fear,   180
And then we will deliver you the cause
Why I, that did love Caesar when I struck him,
Have thus proceeded.

ANTONY   I doubt not of your wisdom.
Let each man render me his bloody hand.
First, Marcus Brutus, will I shake with you;   185
Next, Caius Cassius, do I take your hand;
Now, Decius Brutus, yours; now yours, Metellus;
Yours, Cinna; and, my valiant Casca, yours;
Though last, not least in love, yours, good Trebonius.
Gentlemen all – alas, what shall I say?   190
My credit now stands on such slippery ground,
That one of two bad ways you must conceit me,
Either a coward, or a flatterer.

That I did love thee, Caesar, O, 'tis true!
195   If then thy spirit look upon us now,
Shall it not grieve thee dearer than thy death,
To see thy Antony making his peace,
Shaking the bloody fingers of thy foes,
Most noble, in the presence of thy corse?
200   Had I as many eyes as thou hast wounds,
Weeping as fast as they stream forth thy blood,
It would become me better than to close
In terms of friendship with thine enemies.
Pardon me, Julius! Here wast thou bay'd, brave hart;
205   Here didst thou fall; and here thy hunters stand,
Sign'd in thy spoil, and crimson'd in thy lethe.
O world, thou wast the forest to this hart;
And this indeed, O world, the heart of thee.
How like a deer, strucken by many princes,
210   Dost thou here lie!
CASSIUS   Mark Antony –
ANTONY   Pardon me, Caius Cassius:
The enemies of Caesar shall say this;
Then, in a friend, it is cold modesty.
CASSIUS   I blame you not for praising Caesar so;
215   But what compact mean you to have with us?
Will you be prick'd in number of our friends,
Or shall we on, and not depend on you?
ANTONY   Therefore I took your hands, but was indeed
Sway'd from the point by looking down on Caesar.
220   Friends am I with you all, and love you all,
Upon this hope, that you shall give me reasons
Why, and wherein, Caesar was dangerous.
BRUTUS   Or else were this a savage spectacle.
Our reasons are so full of good regard,
225   That were you, Antony, the son of Caesar,
You should be satisfied.
ANTONY   That's all I seek;
And am moreover suitor that I may
Produce his body to the market-place,
And in the pulpit, as becomes a friend,
230   Speak in the order of his funeral.
BRUTUS   You shall, Mark Antony.
CASSIUS   Brutus, a word with you.
[*aside*] You know not what you do. Do not consent
That Antony speak in his funeral.
Know you how much the people may be mov'd
By that which he will utter?
235 BRUTUS   By your pardon:
I will myself into the pulpit first,
And show the reason of our Caesar's death.
What Antony shall speak, I will protest
He speaks by leave and by permission:
240   And that we are contented Caesar shall
Have all true rites and lawful ceremonies,
It shall advantage more than do us wrong.
CASSIUS   I know not what may fall; I like it not.
BRUTUS   Mark Antony, here, take you Caesar's body.
245   You shall not in your funeral speech blame us,
But speak all good you can devise of Caesar,

And say you do't by our permission;
Else shall you not have any hand at all
About his funeral. And you shall speak
In the same pulpit whereto I am going,   250
After my speech is ended.
ANTONY   Be it so;
I do desire no more.
BRUTUS   Prepare the body, then, and follow us.
             Exeunt. Antony remains.
ANTONY   O, pardon me, thou bleeding piece of earth,
That I am meek and gentle with these butchers.   255
Thou art the ruins of the noblest man
That ever lived in the tide of times.
Woe to the hand that shed this costly blood!
Over thy wounds now do I prophesy
(Which like dumb mouths do ope their ruby lips,   260
To beg the voice and utterance of my tongue),
A curse shall light upon the limbs of men;
Domestic fury and fierce civil strife
Shall cumber all the parts of Italy;
Blood and destruction shall be so in use,   265
And dreadful objects so familiar,
That mothers shall but smile when they behold
Their infants quartered with the hands of war,
All pity chok'd with custom of fell deeds;
And Caesar's spirit, ranging for revenge,   270
With Ate by his side come hot from hell,
Shall in these confines with a monarch's voice
Cry havoc and let slip the dogs of war,
That this foul deed shall smell above the earth
With carrion men, groaning for burial.   275

        Enter Octavius' Servant.

You serve Octavius Caesar, do you not?
SERVANT   I do, Mark Antony.
ANTONY   Caesar did write for him to come to Rome.
SERVANT   He did receive his letters, and is coming,
And bid me say to you by word of mouth –   280
O Caesar!
ANTONY   Thy heart is big; get thee apart and weep.
Passion, I see, is catching, for mine eyes,
Seeing those beads of sorrow stand in thine,
Began to water. Is thy master coming?   285
SERVANT
He lies to-night within seven leagues of Rome.
ANTONY
Post back with speed, and tell him what hath
    chanc'd.
Here is a mourning Rome, a dangerous Rome,
No Rome of safety for Octavius yet.
Hie hence and tell him so. Yet stay awhile;   290
Thou shalt not back till I have borne this corse
Into the market-place; there shall I try,
In my oration, how the people take
The cruel issue of these bloody men;
According to the which thou shalt discourse   295
To young Octavius of the state of things.

Lend me your hand.   *Exeunt.*

3.2   *Enter* BRUTUS *and goes into the pulpit,*
          and CASSIUS, *with the* Plebeians.

PLEBEIANS   We will be satisfied: let us be satisfied.
BRUTUS
      Then follow me, and give me audience, friends.
      Cassius, go you into the other street,
      And part the numbers.
5   Those that will hear me speak, let 'em stay here;
      Those that will follow Cassius, go with him;
      And public reasons shall be rendered
      Of Caesar's death.
1 PLEBEIAN   I will hear Brutus speak.
2 PLEBEIAN
      I will hear Cassius, and compare their reasons,
10   When severally we hear them rendered.
                  Exit Cassius, with some of the Plebeians.
3 PLEBEIAN   The noble Brutus is ascended: silence!
BRUTUS   Be patient till the last.
      Romans, countrymen, and lovers, hear me for my
      cause, and be silent, that you may hear. Believe me for
15   mine honour, and have respect to mine honour, that
      you may believe. Censure me in your wisdom, and
      awake your senses, that you may the better judge. If
      there be any in this assembly, any dear friend of
      Caesar's, to him I say that Brutus' love to Caesar was
20   no less than his. If then that friend demand why
      Brutus rose against Caesar, this is my answer: Not that
      I loved Caesar less, but that I loved Rome more. Had
      you rather Caesar were living, and die all slaves, than
      that Caesar were dead, to live all free men? As Caesar
25   loved me, I weep for him; as he was fortunate, I rejoice
      at it; as he was valiant, I honour him; but, as he was
      ambitious, I slew him. There is tears, for his love; joy,
      for his fortune; honour, for his valour; and death, for
      his ambition. Who is here so base, that would be a
30   bondman? If any, speak; for him have I offended. Who
      is here so rude, that would not be a Roman? If any,
      speak; for him have I offended. Who is here so vile,
      that will not love his country? If any, speak; for him
      have I offended. I pause for a reply.
35 ALL   None, Brutus, none.
BRUTUS   Then none have I offended. I have done no
      more to Caesar than you shall do to Brutus. The
      question of his death is enroll'd in the Capitol; his
      glory not extenuated, wherein he was worthy; nor his
40   offences enforc'd, for which he suffered death.

      Enter MARK ANTONY *and others, with Caesar's body.*

      Here comes his body, mourned by Mark Antony, who,
      though he had no hand in his death, shall receive the
      benefit of his dying, a place in the commonwealth, as
      which of you shall not? With this I depart, that, as I
45   slew my best lover for the good of Rome, I have the
      same dagger for myself, when it shall please my
      country to need my death.

ALL   Live, Brutus! live! live!
1 PLEBEIAN
      Bring him with triumph home unto his house.
2 PLEBEIAN
      Give him a statue with his ancestors.   50
3 PLEBEIAN   Let him be Caesar.
4 PLEBEIAN   Caesar's better parts
      Shall be crown'd in Brutus.
1 PLEBEIAN
      We'll bring him to his house with shouts and
         clamours.
BRUTUS   My countrymen –
2 PLEBEIAN   Peace! Silence! Brutus speaks.
1 PLEBEIAN   Peace, ho!   55
BRUTUS   Good countrymen, let me depart alone,
      And, for my sake, stay here with Antony.
      Do grace to Caesar's corpse, and grace his speech
      Tending to Caesar's glories, which Mark Antony,
      By our permission, is allow'd to make.   60
      I do entreat you, not a man depart,
      Save I alone, till Antony have spoke.   *Exit.*
1 PLEBEIAN   Stay, ho! and let us hear Mark Antony.
3 PLEBEIAN   Let him go up into the public chair.
      We'll hear him. Noble Antony, go up.   65
ANTONY   For Brutus' sake, I am beholding to you.
4 PLEBEIAN   What does he say of Brutus?
3 PLEBEIAN   He says, for Brutus' sake
      He finds himself beholding to us all.
4 PLEBEIAN
      'Twere best he speak no harm of Brutus here!
1 PLEBEIAN   This Caesar was a tyrant.
3 PLEBEIAN   Nay, that's certain.   70
      We are blest that Rome is rid of him.
2 PLEBEIAN   Peace! let us hear what Antony can say.
ANTONY   You gentle Romans, –
ALL   Peace, ho! let us hear him.
ANTONY
      Friends, Romans, countrymen, lend me your ears;
      I come to bury Caesar, not to praise him.   75
      The evil that men do lives after them,
      The good is oft interred with their bones;
      So let it be with Caesar. The noble Brutus
      Hath told you Caesar was ambitious.
      If it were so, it was a grievous fault,   80
      And grievously hath Caesar answer'd it.
      Here, under leave of Brutus and the rest,
      (For Brutus is an honourable man,
      So are they all, all honourable men)
      Come I to speak in Caesar's funeral.   85
      He was my friend, faithful and just to me;
      But Brutus says he was ambitious,
      And Brutus is an honourable man.
      He hath brought many captives home to Rome,
      Whose ransoms did the general coffers fill: 90
      Did this in Caesar seem ambitious?
      When that the poor have cried, Caesar hath wept;
      Ambition should be made of sterner stuff:

95   Yet Brutus says he was ambitious,
And Brutus is an honourable man.
You all did see that on the Lupercal
I thrice presented him a kingly crown,
Which he did thrice refuse. Was this ambition?
Yet Brutus says he was ambitious,
100 And sure he is an honourable man.
I speak not to disprove what Brutus spoke,
But here I am to speak what I do know.
You all did love him once, not without cause;
What cause withholds you then to mourn for him?
105 O judgment, thou art fled to brutish beasts,
And men have lost their reason. Bear with me.
My heart is in the coffin there with Caesar,
And I must pause till it come back to me.
1 PLEBEIAN
Methinks there is much reason in his sayings.
110 2 PLEBEIAN   If thou consider rightly of the matter,
Caesar has had great wrong.
3 PLEBEIAN   Has he, masters?
I fear there will a worse come in his place.
4 PLEBEIAN
Mark'd ye his words? He would not take the crown;
Therefore 'tis certain he was not ambitious.
115 1 PLEBEIAN   If it be found so, some will dear abide it.
2 PLEBEIAN
Poor soul! His eyes are red as fire with weeping.
3 PLEBEIAN
There's not a nobler man in Rome than Antony.
4 PLEBEIAN   Now mark him; he begins again to speak.
ANTONY   But yesterday the word of Caesar might
120 Have stood against the world; now lies he there,
And none so poor to do him reverence.
O masters! if I were dispos'd to stir
Your hearts and minds to mutiny and rage,
I should do Brutus wrong, and Cassius wrong,
125 Who, you all know, are honourable men.
I will not do them wrong; I rather choose
To wrong the dead, to wrong myself and you,
Than I will wrong such honourable men.
But here's a parchment with the seal of Caesar;
130 I found it in his closet; 'tis his will.
Let but the commons hear this testament,
Which, pardon me, I do not mean to read,
And they would go and kiss dead Caesar's wounds,
And dip their napkins in his sacred blood,
135 Yea, beg a hair of him for memory,
And, dying, mention it within their wills,
Bequeathing it as a rich legacy
Unto their issue.
4 PLEBEIAN   We'll hear the will. Read it, Mark Antony.
140 ALL   The will, the will! We will hear Caesar's will!
ANTONY
Have patience, gentle friends; I must not read it.
It is not meet you know how Caesar lov'd you.
You are not wood, you are not stones, but men;
And being men, hearing the will of Caesar,

145 It will inflame you, it will make you mad.
'Tis good you know not that you are his heirs;
For if you should, O, what would come of it?
4 PLEBEIAN   Read the will! We'll hear it, Antony!
You shall read us the will, Caesar's will!
150 ANTONY   Will you be patient? Will you stay awhile?
I have o'ershot myself to tell you of it.
I fear I wrong the honourable men
Whose daggers have stabb'd Caesar; I do fear it.
4 PLEBEIAN   They were traitors. Honourable men!
155 ALL   The will! – The testament!
2 PLEBEIAN   They were villains, murderers! The will!
Read the will!
ANTONY   You will compel me then to read the will?
Then make a ring about the corpse of Caesar,
160 And let me show you him that made the will.
Shall I descend? and will you give me leave?
ALL   Come down.
2 PLEBEIAN   Descend. [*Antony comes down.*]
3 PLEBEIAN   You shall have leave.
165 4 PLEBEIAN   A ring! Stand round.
1 PLEBEIAN
Stand from the hearse! stand from the body!
2 PLEBEIAN   Room for Antony, most noble Antony!
ANTONY   Nay, press not so upon me; stand far off.
ALL   Stand back! Room! Bear back!
170 ANTONY   If you have tears, prepare to shed them now.
You all do know this mantle. I remember
The first time ever Caesar put it on;
'Twas on a summer's evening in his tent,
That day he overcame the Nervii.
175 Look, in this place ran Cassius' dagger through:
See what a rent the envious Casca made:
Through this the well-beloved Brutus stabb'd;
And as he pluck'd his cursed steel away,
Mark how the blood of Caesar follow'd it,
180 As rushing out of doors, to be resolv'd
If Brutus so unkindly knock'd or no;
For Brutus, as you know, was Caesar's angel.
Judge, O you gods, how dearly Caesar lov'd him.
This was the most unkindest cut of all;
185 For when the noble Caesar saw him stab,
Ingratitude, more strong than traitors' arms,
Quite vanquish'd him: then burst his mighty heart;
And in his mantle muffling up his face,
Even at the base of Pompey's statue
190 (Which all the while ran blood) great Caesar fell.
O, what a fall was there, my countrymen!
Then I, and you, and all of us fell down,
Whilst bloody treason flourish'd over us.
O, now you weep, and I perceive you feel
195 The dint of pity. These are gracious drops.
Kind souls, what weep you when you but behold
Our Caesar's vesture wounded? Look you here!
Here is himself, marr'd, as you see, with traitors.
1 PLEBEIAN   O piteous spectacle!
200 2 PLEBEIAN   O noble Caesar!

3 PLEBEIAN   O woeful day!

4 PLEBEIAN   O traitors! villains!

1 PLEBEIAN   O most bloody sight!

2 PLEBEIAN   We will be revenged.

ALL   Revenge! – About! – Seek! – Burn! – Fire! – Kill!
   – Slay! – Let not a traitor live.

ANTONY   Stay, countrymen.

1 PLEBEIAN   Peace there! Hear the noble Antony.

2 PLEBEIAN   We'll hear him, we'll follow him, we'll die
   with him.

ANTONY
   Good friends, sweet friends, let me not stir you up
   To such a sudden flood of mutiny.
   They that have done this deed are honourable.
   What private griefs they have, alas, I know not,
   That made them do it. They are wise and
      honourable,
   And will, no doubt, with reasons answer you.
   I come not, friends, to steal away your hearts.
   I am no orator, as Brutus is,
   But (as you know me all) a plain blunt man,
   That love my friend; and that they know full well
   That gave me public leave to speak of him.
   For I have neither wit, nor words, nor worth,
   Action, nor utterance, nor the power of speech
   To stir men's blood; I only speak right on.
   I tell you that which you yourselves do know,
   Show you sweet Caesar's wounds, poor poor dumb
      mouths,
   And bid them speak for me. But were I Brutus,
   And Brutus Antony, there were an Antony
   Would ruffle up your spirits, and put a tongue
   In every wound of Caesar that should move
   The stones of Rome to rise and mutiny.

ALL   We'll mutiny.

1 PLEBEIAN   We'll burn the house of Brutus.

3 PLEBEIAN   Away then! Come, seek the conspirators.

ANTONY   Yet hear me, countrymen. Yet hear me speak.

ALL   Peace, ho! – Hear Antony, most noble Antony.

ANTONY
   Why, friends, you go to do you know not what.
   Wherein hath Caesar thus deserv'd your loves?
   Alas! you know not: I must tell you then.
   You have forgot the will I told you of.

ALL
   Most true. – The will! – Let's stay and hear the will.

ANTONY   Here is the will, and under Caesar's seal.
   To every Roman citizen he gives,
   To every several man, seventy-five drachmas.

2 PLEBEIAN
   Most noble Caesar! We'll revenge his death.

3 PLEBEIAN   O royal Caesar!

ANTONY   Hear me with patience.

ALL   Peace, ho!

ANTONY   Moreover, he hath left you all his walks,
   His private arbours, and new-planted orchards,
   On this side Tiber; he hath left them you,

   And to your heirs for ever: common pleasures,
   To walk abroad and recreate yourselves.
   Here was a Caesar! when comes such another?

1 PLEBEIAN   Never, never! Come, away, away!
   We'll burn his body in the holy place,
   And with the brands fire the traitors' houses.
   Take up the body.

2 PLEBEIAN   Go fetch fire.

3 PLEBEIAN   Pluck down benches.

4 PLEBEIAN   Pluck down forms, windows, any thing.

            Exeunt Plebeians with the body.

ANTONY   Now let it work. Mischief, thou art afoot,
   Take thou what course thou wilt! How now, fellow?

            Enter Servant.

SERVANT   Sir, Octavius is already come to Rome.

ANTONY   Where is he?

SERVANT   He and Lepidus are at Caesar's house.

ANTONY   And thither will I straight to visit him.
   He comes upon a wish. Fortune is merry,
   And in this mood will give us any thing.

SERVANT   I heard him say Brutus and Cassius
   Are rid like madmen through the gates of Rome.

ANTONY   Belike they had some notice of the people,
   How I had mov'd them. Bring me to Octavius.

            Exeunt.

3.3   *Enter* CINNA *the Poet, and after him the* Plebeians.

CINNA   I dreamt to-night that I did feast with Caesar,
   And things unluckily charge my fantasy.
   I have no will to wander forth of doors,
   Yet something leads me forth.

1 PLEBEIAN   What is your name?

2 PLEBEIAN   Whither are you going?

3 PLEBEIAN   Where do you dwell?

4 PLEBEIAN   Are you a married man or a bachelor?

2 PLEBEIAN   Answer every man directly.

1 PLEBEIAN   Ay, and briefly.

4 PLEBEIAN   Ay, and wisely.

3 PLEBEIAN   Ay, and truly, you were best.

CINNA   What is my name? Whither am I going? Where
   do I dwell? Am I a married man or a bachelor? Then,
   to answer every man directly and briefly, wisely and
   truly: wisely I say, I am a bachelor.

2 PLEBEIAN   That's as much as to say they are fools that
   marry. You'll bear me a bang for that, I fear. Proceed,
   directly.

CINNA   Directly, I am going to Caesar's funeral.

1 PLEBEIAN   As a friend or an enemy?

CINNA   As a friend.

2 PLEBEIAN   The matter is answered directly.

4 PLEBEIAN   For your dwelling, briefly.

CINNA   Briefly, I dwell by the Capitol.

3 PLEBEIAN   Your name, sir, truly.

CINNA   Truly, my name is Cinna.

1 PLEBEIAN   Tear him to pieces! He's a conspirator.

CINNA   I am Cinna the poet, I am Cinna the poet.

30   4 PLEBEIAN   Tear him for his bad verses, tear him for his
bad verses.

CINNA   I am not Cinna the conspirator.

1 PLEBEIAN   It is no matter, his name's Cinna; pluck
but his name out of his heart, and turn him going.

35   3 PLEBEIAN   Tear him, tear him! Come, brands, ho!
firebrands! To Brutus', to Cassius'; burn all! Some to
Decius' house, and some to Casca's; some to Ligarius'.
Away! go!

Exeunt all the Plebeians, dragging off Cinna.

4.1   *Enter* ANTONY, OCTAVIUS *and* LEPIDUS.

ANTONY
These many then shall die; their names are prick'd.

OCTAVIUS
Your brother too must die; consent you, Lepidus?

LEPIDUS   I do consent –

OCTAVIUS   Prick him down, Antony.

LEPIDUS   Upon condition Publius shall not live,

5   Who is your sister's son, Mark Antony.

ANTONY
He shall not live. Look, with a spot I damn him.
But, Lepidus, go you to Caesar's house;
Fetch the will hither, and we shall determine
How to cut off some charge in legacies.

10   LEPIDUS   What, shall I find you here?

OCTAVIUS   Or here or at the Capitol.   *Exit Lepidus.*

ANTONY   This is a slight unmeritable man,
Meet to be sent on errands. Is it fit,
The three-fold world divided, he should stand
One of the three to share it?

15   OCTAVIUS   So you thought him,
And took his voice who should be prick'd to die
In our black sentence and proscription.

ANTONY   Octavius, I have seen more days than you;
And though we lay these honours on this man,

20   To ease ourselves of divers sland'rous loads,
He shall but bear them as the ass bears gold,
To groan and sweat under the business,
Either led or driven, as we point the way;
And having brought our treasure where we will,

25   Then take we down his load, and turn him off,
Like to the empty ass, to shake his ears,
And graze in commons.

OCTAVIUS   You may do your will;
But he's a tried and valiant soldier.

ANTONY   So is my horse, Octavius, and for that

30   I do appoint him store of provender.
It is a creature that I teach to fight,
To wind, to stop, to run directly on,
His corporal motion govern'd by my spirit.
And, in some taste, is Lepidus but so:

35   He must be taught, and train'd, and bid go forth:
A barren-spirited fellow; one that feeds
On objects, arts, and imitations,

Which, out of use and stal'd by other men,
Begin his fashion. Do not talk of him
But as a property. And now, Octavius,   40
Listen great things. Brutus and Cassius
Are levying powers; we must straight make head.
Therefore let our alliance be combin'd,
Our best friends made, our means stretch'd;
And let us presently go sit in council,   45
How covert matters may be best disclos'd,
And open perils surest answered.

OCTAVIUS   Let us do so: for we are at the stake,
And bay'd about with many enemies;
And some that smile have in their hearts, I fear,   50
Millions of mischiefs.   *Exeunt.*

4.2   *Drum. Enter* BRUTUS, LUCILIUS, LUCIUS *and
the army.* TITINIUS *and* PINDARUS *meet them.*

BRUTUS   Stand ho!

LUCILIUS   Give the word, ho! and stand.

BRUTUS   What now, Lucilius, is Cassius near?

LUCILIUS   He is at hand, and Pindarus is come
To do you salutation from his master.   5

BRUTUS   He greets me well. Your master, Pindarus,
In his own change, or by ill officers,
Hath given me some worthy cause to wish
Things done undone; but if he be at hand,
I shall be satisfied.

PINDARUS   I do not doubt   10
But that my noble master will appear
Such as he is, full of regard and honour.

BRUTUS   He is not doubted. A word, Lucilius;
How he receiv'd you, let me be resolv'd.

LUCILIUS   With courtesy and with respect enough,   15
But not with such familiar instances,
Nor with such free and friendly conference,
As he hath us'd of old.

BRUTUS   Thou hast describ'd
A hot friend cooling. Ever note, Lucilius,
When love begins to sicken and decay   20
It useth an enforced ceremony.
There are no tricks in plain and simple faith;
But hollow men, like horses hot at hand,
Make gallant show and promise of their mettle;
[*Low march within.*]
But when they should endure the bloody spur,   25
They fall their crests, and like deceitful jades
Sink in the trial. Comes his army on?

LUCILIUS
They mean this night in Sardis to be quarter'd;
The greater part, the horse in general,
Are come with Cassius.

Enter CASSIUS *and his* Powers.

BRUTUS   Hark! he is arriv'd.   30
March gently on to meet him.

CASSIUS   Stand ho!

BRUTUS   Stand ho! Speak the word along.

1 SOLDIER   Stand!

2 SOLDIER   Stand!

3 SOLDIER   Stand!

CASSIUS   Most noble brother, you have done me wrong.

BRUTUS   Judge me, you gods; wrong I mine enemies?
And if not so, how should I wrong a brother?

CASSIUS
Brutus, this sober form of yours hides wrongs;
And when you do them –

BRUTUS   Cassius, be content.
Speak your griefs softly; I do know you well.
Before the eyes of both our armies here,
Which should perceive nothing but love from us,
Let us not wrangle. Bid them move away;
Then in my tent, Cassius, enlarge your griefs,
And I will give you audience.

CASSIUS   Pindarus,
Bid our commanders lead their charges off
A little from this ground.

BRUTUS   Lucius, do you the like; and let no man
Come to our tent till we have done our conference.
Lucilius and Titinius guard our door.   *Exeunt Powers.*

4.3   BRUTUS *and* CASSIUS *remain.*

CASSIUS
That you have wrong'd me doth appear in this:
You have condemn'd and noted Lucius Pella
For taking bribes here of the Sardians;
Wherein my letters, praying on his side,
Because I knew the man, was slighted off.

BRUTUS   You wrong'd yourself to write in such a case.

CASSIUS   In such a time as this it is not meet
That every nice offence should bear his comment.

BRUTUS   Let me tell you, Cassius, you yourself
Are much condemn'd to have an itching palm,
To sell and mart your offices for gold
To undeservers.

CASSIUS   I an itching palm!
You know that you are Brutus that speaks this,
Or, by the gods, this speech were else your last.

BRUTUS   The name of Cassius honours this corruption,
And chastisement doth therefore hide his head.

CASSIUS   Chastisement!

BRUTUS
Remember March, the ides of March remember.
Did not great Julius bleed for justice' sake?
What villain touch'd his body, that did stab,
And not for justice? What, shall one of us,
That struck the foremost man of all this world
But for supporting robbers, shall we now
Contaminate our fingers with base bribes,
And sell the mighty space of our large honours
For so much trash as may be grasped thus?
I had rather be a dog, and bay the moon,
Than such a Roman.

CASSIUS   Brutus, bait not me;
I'll not endure it. You forget yourself,
To hedge me in. I am a soldier, I,   30
Older in practice, abler than yourself
To make conditions.

BRUTUS   Go to! you are not, Cassius.

CASSIUS   I am.

BRUTUS   I say you are not.

CASSIUS   Urge me no more, I shall forget myself;   35
Have mind upon your health; tempt me no farther.

BRUTUS   Away, slight man!

CASSIUS   Is't possible?

BRUTUS   Hear me, for I will speak.
Must I give way and room to your rash choler?
Shall I be frighted when a madman stares?   40

CASSIUS   O ye gods, ye gods! Must I endure all this?

BRUTUS
All this? ay, more: fret till your proud heart break;
Go show your slaves how choleric you are,
And make your bondmen tremble. Must I budge?
Must I observe you? Must I stand and crouch   45
Under your testy humour? By the gods,
You shall digest the venom of your spleen,
Though it do split you; for, from this day forth,
I'll use you for my mirth, yea, for my laughter,
When you are waspish.

CASSIUS   Is it come to this?   50

BRUTUS   You say you are a better soldier:
Let it appear so; make your vaunting true,
And it shall please me well. For mine own part,
I shall be glad to learn of noble men.

CASSIUS
You wrong me every way; you wrong me, Brutus.   55
I said, an elder soldier, not a better:
Did I say better?

BRUTUS   If you did, I care not.

CASSIUS
When Caesar liv'd, he durst not thus have mov'd me.

BRUTUS
Peace, peace! you durst not so have tempted him.

CASSIUS   I durst not?   60

BRUTUS   No.

CASSIUS   What? durst not tempt him?

BRUTUS   For your life you durst not.

CASSIUS   Do not presume too much upon my love.
I may do that I shall be sorry for.

BRUTUS   You have done that you should be sorry for.   65
There is no terror, Cassius, in your threats;
For I am arm'd so strong in honesty
That they pass by me as the idle wind,
Which I respect not. I did send to you
For certain sums of gold, which you denied me;   70
For I can raise no money by vile means:
By heaven, I had rather coin my heart,
And drop my blood for drachmas, than to wring
From the hard hands of peasants their vile trash
By any indirection. I did send   75

To you for gold to pay my legions,
Which you denied me: was that done like Cassius?
Should I have answer'd Caius Cassius so?
When Marcus Brutus grows so covetous,
80 To lock such rascal counters from his friends,
Be ready, gods, with all your thunderbolts,
Dash him to pieces!
CASSIUS   I denied you not.
BRUTUS   You did.
CASSIUS   I did not. He was but a fool
    That brought my answer back. Brutus hath riv'd my
        heart.
85 A friend should bear his friend's infirmities;
    But Brutus makes mine greater than they are.
BRUTUS   I do not, till you practise them on me.
CASSIUS   You love me not.
BRUTUS   I do not like your faults.
CASSIUS   A friendly eye could never see such faults.
90 BRUTUS   A flatterer's would not, though they do appear
    As huge as high Olympus.
CASSIUS   Come, Antony, and young Octavius, come,
    Revenge yourselves alone on Cassius,
    For Cassius is aweary of the world:
95 Hated by one he loves; brav'd by his brother;
    Check'd like a bondman; all his faults observ'd,
    Set in a note-book, learn'd, and conn'd by rote,
    To cast into my teeth. O, I could weep
    My spirit from mine eyes! There is my dagger,
100 And here my naked breast; within, a heart
    Dearer than Pluto's mine, richer than gold:
    If that thou be'st a Roman, take it forth.
    I, that denied thee gold, will give my heart:
    Strike, as thou didst at Caesar; for I know,
    When thou didst hate him worst, thou lov'dst him
105   better
    Than ever thou lov'dst Cassius.
BRUTUS   Sheathe your dagger.
    Be angry when you will, it shall have scope;
    Do what you will, dishonour shall be humour.
    O Cassius, you are yoked with a lamb
110 That carries anger as the flint bears fire,
    Who, much enforced, shows a hasty spark,
    And straight is cold again.
CASSIUS   Hath Cassius liv'd
    To be but mirth and laughter to his Brutus,
    When grief and blood ill-temper'd vexeth him?
115 BRUTUS   When I spoke that, I was ill-temper'd too.
CASSIUS   Do you confess so much? Give me your hand.
BRUTUS   And my heart too.
CASSIUS   O Brutus!
BRUTUS   What's the matter?
CASSIUS   Have not you love enough to bear with me,
    When that rash humour which my mother gave me
    Makes me forgetful?
120 BRUTUS   Yes, Cassius; and from henceforth
    When you are over-earnest with your Brutus,
    He'll think your mother chides, and leave you so.

Enter a Poet, *followed by* LUCILIUS,
TITINIUS *and* LUCIUS.

POET   Let me go in to see the generals.
    There is some grudge between 'em; 'tis not meet
    They be alone.   125
LUCILIUS   You shall not come to them.
POET   Nothing but death shall stay me.
CASSIUS   How now? What's the matter?
POET   For shame, you generals! What do you mean?
    Love, and be friends, as two such men should be;   130
    For I have seen more years, I'm sure, than ye.
CASSIUS   Ha, ha! how vildly doth this cynic rhyme!
BRUTUS   Get you hence, sirrah! Saucy fellow, hence!
CASSIUS   Bear with him, Brutus; 'tis his fashion.
BRUTUS   I'll know his humour, when he knows his
      time.   135
    What should the wars do with these jigging fools?
    Companion, hence!
CASSIUS   Away, away, be gone!   *Exit Poet.*
BRUTUS   Lucilius and Titinius, bid the commanders
    Prepare to lodge their companies to-night.
CASSIUS   And come yourselves, and bring Messala with
      you   140
    Immediately to us.   *Exeunt Lucilius and Titinius.*
BRUTUS   Lucius, a bowl of wine.
                                          Exit Lucius.
CASSIUS   I did not think you could have been so angry.
BRUTUS   O Cassius, I am sick of many griefs.
CASSIUS   Of your philosophy you make no use,
    If you give place to accidental evils.   145
BRUTUS   No man bears sorrow better. Portia is dead.
CASSIUS   Ha? Portia?
BRUTUS   She is dead.
CASSIUS   How 'scap'd I killing, when I cross'd you so?
    O insupportable and touching loss!   150
    Upon what sickness?
BRUTUS   Impatient of my absence,
    And grief that young Octavius with Mark Antony
    Have made themselves so strong; for with her death
    That tidings came. With this she fell distract,
    And, her attendants absent, swallow'd fire.   155
CASSIUS   And died so?
BRUTUS   Even so.
CASSIUS   O ye immortal gods!

Enter LUCIUS *with wine and tapers.*

BRUTUS   Speak no more of her. Give me a bowl of wine.
    In this I bury all unkindness, Cassius. [*Drinks.*]
CASSIUS   My heart is thirsty for that noble pledge.
    Fill, Lucius, till the wine o'erswell the cup.   160
    I cannot drink too much of Brutus' love.   *Exit Lucius.*

Enter TITINIUS *and* MESSALA.

BRUTUS   Come in, Titinius. Welcome, good Messala.
    Now sit we close about this taper here,
    And call in question our necessities.
CASSIUS   Portia, art thou gone?

BRUTUS   No more, I pray you.
   Messala, I have here received letters,
   That young Octavius and Mark Antony
   Come down upon us with a mighty power,
   Bending their expedition toward Philippi.

MESSALA   Myself have letters of the self-same tenor.

BRUTUS   With what addition?

MESSALA   That by proscription and bills of outlawry
   Octavius, Antony, and Lepidus
   Have put to death an hundred senators.

BRUTUS   Therein our letters do not well agree.
   Mine speak of seventy senators that died
   By their proscriptions, Cicero being one.

CASSIUS   Cicero one?

MESSALA   Cicero is dead,
   And by that order of proscription.
   Had you your letters from your wife, my lord?

BRUTUS   No, Messala.

MESSALA   Nor nothing in your letters writ of her?

BRUTUS   Nothing, Messala.

MESSALA   That, methinks, is strange.

BRUTUS   Why ask you? Hear you aught of her in yours?

MESSALA   No, my lord.

BRUTUS   Now as you are a Roman, tell me true.

MESSALA   Then like a Roman bear the truth I tell;
   For certain she is dead, and by strange manner.

BRUTUS   Why, farewell, Portia. We must die, Messala.
   With meditating that she must die once,
   I have the patience to endure it now.

MESSALA
   Even so great men great losses should endure.

CASSIUS   I have as much of this in art as you,
   But yet my nature could not bear it so.

BRUTUS   Well, to our work alive. What do you think.
   Of marching to Philippi presently?

CASSIUS   I do not think it good.

BRUTUS   Your reason?

CASSIUS   This it is:
   'Tis better that the enemy seek us;
   So shall he waste his means, weary his soldiers,
   Doing himself offence, whilst we, lying still,
   Are full of rest, defence, and nimbleness.

BRUTUS
   Good reasons must of force give place to better.
   The people 'twixt Philippi and this ground
   Do stand but in a forc'd affection;
   For they have grudg'd us contribution.
   The enemy, marching along by them,
   By them shall make a fuller number up,
   Come on refresh'd, new-added, and encourag'd;
   From which advantage shall we cut him off
   If at Philippi we do face him there,
   These people at our back.

CASSIUS   Hear me, good brother.

BRUTUS   Under your pardon. You must note beside
   That we have tried the utmost of our friends,

   Our legions are brim-full, our cause is ripe.
   The enemy increaseth every day;   215
   We, at the height, are ready to decline.
   There is a tide in the affairs of men,
   Which, taken at the flood, leads on to fortune;
   Omitted, all the voyage of their life
   Is bound in shallows and in miseries.   220
   On such a full sea are we now afloat,
   And we must take the current when it serves,
   Or lose our ventures.

CASSIUS   Then, with your will, go on;
   We'll along ourselves, and meet them at Philippi.

BRUTUS   The deep of night is crept upon our talk,   225
   And nature must obey necessity,
   Which we will niggard with a little rest.
   There is no more to say?

CASSIUS   No more. Good night.
   Early to-morrow will we rise, and hence.

BRUTUS   Lucius!

Enter LUCIUS.

       My gown.   *Exit Lucius.*
            Farewell, good Messala.   230
   Good night, Titinius. Noble, noble Cassius,
   Good night, and good repose.

CASSIUS   O my dear brother,
   This was an ill beginning of the night.
   Never come such division 'tween our souls!
   Let it not, Brutus.

Enter LUCIUS, *with the gown.*

BRUTUS   Every thing is well.   235

CASSIUS   Good night, my lord.

BRUTUS   Good night, good brother.

TITINIUS, MESSALA   Good night, Lord Brutus.

BRUTUS   Farewell, every one.
       Exeunt Cassius, Titinius and Messala.
   Give me the gown. Where is thy instrument?

LUCIUS   Here in the tent.

BRUTUS   What, thou speak'st drowsily?
   Poor knave, I blame thee not; thou art o'er-watch'd.   240
   Call Claudius and some other of my men;
   I'll have them sleep on cushions in my tent.

LUCIUS   Varro and Claudius!

Enter VARRO *and* CLAUDIUS.

VARRO   Calls my lord?

BRUTUS   I pray you, sirs, lie in my tent and sleep.   245
   It may be I shall raise you by and by
   On business to my brother Cassius.

VARRO
   So please you, we will stand and watch your pleasure.

BRUTUS   I will not have it so; lie down, good sirs;
   It may be I shall otherwise bethink me.   250
   [*Varro and Claudius lie down.*]
   Look, Lucius, here's the book I sought for so;

I put it in the pocket of my gown.

LUCIUS   I was sure your lordship did not give it me.

BRUTUS   Bear with me, good boy, I am much forgetful.

255   Canst thou hold up thy heavy eyes awhile,
And touch thy instrument a strain or two?

LUCIUS   Ay, my lord, an't please you.

BRUTUS   It does, my boy.
I trouble thee too much, but thou art willing.

LUCIUS   It is my duty, sir.

260   BRUTUS   I should not urge thy duty past thy might;
I know young bloods look for a time of rest.

LUCIUS   I have slept, my lord, already.

BRUTUS   It was well done, and thou shalt sleep again;
I will not hold thee long. If I do live,

265   I will be good to thee.   [*Music, and a song.*]
This is a sleepy tune: O murd'rous slumber!
Layest thou thy leaden mace upon my boy,
That plays thee music? Gentle knave, good night;
I will not do thee so much wrong to wake thee.

270   If thou dost nod, thou break'st thy instrument;
I'll take it from thee; and, good boy, good night.
Let me see, let me see; is not the leaf turn'd down
Where I left reading? Here it is, I think.

Enter the Ghost *of Caesar.*

How ill this taper burns! Ha! who comes here?

275   I think it is the weakness of mine eyes
That shapes this monstrous apparition.
It comes upon me. Art thou any thing?
Art thou some god, some angel, or some devil,
That mak'st my blood cold, and my hair to stare?

280   Speak to me what thou art.

GHOST   Thy evil spirit, Brutus.

BRUTUS   Why com'st thou?

GHOST   To tell thee thou shalt see me at Philippi.

BRUTUS   Well; then I shall see thee again?

GHOST   Ay, at Philippi.

285   BRUTUS   Why, I will see thee at Philippi then.

Exit Ghost.

Now I have taken heart thou vanishest.
Ill spirit, I would hold more talk with thee.
Boy! Lucius! Varro! Claudius! Sirs, awake!
Claudius!

290   LUCIUS   The strings, my lord, are false.

BRUTUS   He thinks he still is at his instrument.
Lucius, awake!

LUCIUS   My lord?

BRUTUS
Didst thou dream, Lucius, that thou so criedst out?

295   LUCIUS   My lord, I do not know that I did cry.

BRUTUS   Yes, that thou didst. Didst see anything?

LUCIUS   Nothing, my lord.

BRUTUS   Sleep again, Lucius. Sirrah Claudius!
Fellow thou, awake!

VARRO   My lord?

CLAUDIUS   My lord?

300   BRUTUS   Why did you so cry out, sirs, in your sleep?

BOTH   Did we, my lord?

BRUTUS   Ay. Saw you any thing?

VARRO   No, my lord, I saw nothing.

CLAUDIUS   Nor I, my lord.

BRUTUS   Go and commend me to my brother Cassius.
Bid him set on his powers betimes before,
And we will follow.

BOTH   It shall be done, my lord. *Exeunt.*   305

5.1   *Enter* OCTAVIUS, ANTONY *and their army.*

OCTAVIUS   Now, Antony, our hopes are answered.
You said the enemy would not come down,
But keep the hills and upper regions.
It proves not so; their battles are at hand;
They mean to warn us at Philippi here,   5
Answering before we do demand of them.

ANTONY   Tut, I am in their bosoms, and I know
Wherefore they do it. They could be content
To visit other places, and come down
With fearful bravery, thinking by this face   10
To fasten in our thoughts that they have courage;
But 'tis not so.

Enter a Messenger.

MESSENGER   Prepare you, generals.
The enemy comes on in gallant show;
Their bloody sign of battle is hung out,
And something to be done immediately.   15

ANTONY   Octavius, lead your battle softly on
Upon the left hand of the even field.

OCTAVIUS   Upon the right hand I. Keep thou the left.

ANTONY   Why do you cross me in this exigent?

OCTAVIUS   I do not cross you; but I will do so. [*March.*]   20

Drum. Enter BRUTUS, CASSIUS *and their army;*
LUCILIUS, TITINIUS, MESSALA *and others.*

BRUTUS   They stand, and would have parley.

CASSIUS   Stand fast, Titinius; we must out and talk.

OCTAVIUS   Mark Antony, shall we give sign of battle?

ANTONY   No, Caesar, we will answer on their charge.
Make forth; the generals would have some words.   25

OCTAVIUS   Stir not until the signal.

BRUTUS   Words before blows: is it so, countrymen?

OCTAVIUS   Not that we love words better, as you do.

BRUTUS
Good words are better than bad strokes, Octavius.

ANTONY
In your bad strokes, Brutus, you give good words;   30
Witness the hole you made in Caesar's heart,
Crying, 'Long live! hail, Caesar!'

CASSIUS   Antony,
The posture of your blows are yet unknown;
But for your words, they rob the Hybla bees,
And leave them honeyless.

ANTONY   Not stingless too.   35

BRUTUS   O yes, and soundless too;
For you have stol'n their buzzing, Antony,

And very wisely threat before you sting.

ANTONY

 Villains! you did not so when your vile daggers

 Hack'd one another in the sides of Caesar:

 You show'd your teeth like apes, and fawn'd like

  hounds,

 And bow'd like bondmen, kissing Caesar's feet;

 Whilst damned Casca, like a cur, behind

 Struck Caesar on the neck. O you flatterers!

CASSIUS Flatterers? Now, Brutus, thank yourself.

 This tongue had not offended so to-day,

 If Cassius might have rul'd.

OCTAVIUS

 Come, come, the cause. If arguing make us sweat,

 The proof of it will turn to redder drops.

 Look,

 I draw a sword against conspirators.

 When think you that the sword goes up again?

 Never, till Caesar's three and thirty wounds

 Be well aveng'd; or till another Caesar

 Have added slaughter to the sword of traitors.

BRUTUS Caesar, thou canst not die by traitors' hands,

 Unless thou bring'st them with thee.

OCTAVIUS   So I hope.

 I was not born to die on Brutus' sword.

BRUTUS O, if thou wert the noblest of thy strain,

 Young man, thou could'st not die more honourable.

CASSIUS

 A peevish school-boy, worthless of such honour,

 Join'd with a masker and a reveller.

ANTONY Old Cassius still!

OCTAVIUS   Come, Antony; away!

 Defiance, traitors, hurl we in your teeth.

 If you dare fight to-day, come to the field;

 If not, when you have stomachs.

      Exeunt Octavius, Antony and army.

CASSIUS

 Why now, blow wind, swell billow, and swim bark!

 The storm is up, and all is on the hazard.

BRUTUS Ho, Lucilius, hark, a word with you.

LUCILIUS [*standing forth*] My lord?

 [*Brutus and Lucilius talk apart.*]

CASSIUS Messala.

MESSALA [*standing forth*] What says my general?

CASSIUS   Messala,

 This is my birth-day; as this very day

 Was Cassius born. Give me thy hand, Messala:

 Be thou my witness that against my will

 (As Pompey was) am I compell'd to set

 Upon one battle all our liberties.

 You know that I held Epicurus strong,

 And his opinion; now I change my mind,

 And partly credit things that do presage.

 Coming from Sardis, on our former ensign

 Two mighty eagles fell, and there they perch'd,

 Gorging and feeding from our soldiers' hands,

Who to Philippi here consorted us.

This morning are they fled away and gone,

And in their steads do ravens, crows, and kites 85

Fly o'er our heads, and downward look on us,

As we were sickly prey; their shadows seem

A canopy most fatal, under which

Our army lies, ready to give up the ghost.

MESSALA Believe not so.

CASSIUS   I but believe it partly, 90

 For I am fresh of spirit, and resolv'd

 To meet all perils very constantly.

BRUTUS Even so, Lucilius.

CASSIUS   Now, most noble Brutus,

 The gods to-day stand friendly, that we may,

 Lovers in peace, lead on our days to age! 95

 But since the affairs of men rests still incertain,

 Let's reason with the worst that may befall.

 If we do lose this battle, then is this

 The very last time we shall speak together:

 What are you then determined to do? 100

BRUTUS Even by the rule of that philosophy

 By which I did blame Cato for the death

 Which he did give himself, I know not how,

 But I do find it cowardly and vile,

 For fear of what might fall, so to prevent 105

 The time of life, arming myself with patience

 To stay the providence of some high powers

 That govern us below.

CASSIUS   Then, if we lose this battle,

 You are contented to be led in triumph

 Thorough the streets of Rome? 110

BRUTUS No, Cassius, no: think not, thou noble Roman,

 That ever Brutus will go bound to Rome;

 He bears too great a mind. But this same day

 Must end that work the ides of March begun;

 And whether we shall meet again I know not. 115

 Therefore our everlasting farewell take.

 For ever, and for ever, farewell, Cassius.

 If we do meet again, why, we shall smile;

 If not, why then this parting was well made.

CASSIUS For ever, and for ever, farewell, Brutus. 120

 If we do meet again, we'll smile indeed;

 If not, 'tis true this parting was well made.

BRUTUS Why then, lead on. O, that a man might know

 The end of this day's business ere it come!

 But it sufficeth that the day will end, 125

 And then the end is known. Come, ho! away! *Exeunt.*

5.2 *Alarum. Enter* BRUTUS *and* MESSALA.

BRUTUS Ride, ride, Messala, ride, and give these bills

 Unto the legions on the other side. [*Loud alarum.*]

 Let them set on at once, for I perceive

 But cold demeanour in Octavius' wing,

 And sudden push gives them the overthrow. 5

 Ride, ride, Messala; let them all come down. *Exeunt.*

5.3   *Alarums. Enter* CASSIUS *and* TITINIUS.

CASSIUS   O, look, Titinius, look, the villains fly.
     Myself have to mine own turn'd enemy:
     This ensign here of mine was turning back;
     I slew the coward, and did take it from him.

5   TITINIUS   O Cassius, Brutus gave the word too early,
     Who, having some advantage on Octavius,
     Took it too eagerly; his soldiers fell to spoil,
     Whilst we by Antony are all enclos'd.

               Enter PINDARUS.

PINDARUS   Fly further off, my lord, fly further off!
10   Mark Antony is in your tents, my lord.
     Fly, therefore, noble Cassius, fly far off!
CASSIUS   This hill is far enough. Look, look, Titinius!
     Are those my tents where I perceive the fire?
TITINIUS   They are, my lord.
CASSIUS   Titinius, if thou lov'st me,
15   Mount thou my horse, and hide thy spurs in him,
     Till he have brought thee up to yonder troops
     And here again, that I may rest assur'd
     Whether yond troops are friend or enemy.
TITINIUS   I will be here again, even with a thought.
                                  Exit.

20   CASSIUS   Go, Pindarus, get higher on that hill;
     My sight was ever thick. Regard Titinius,
     And tell me what thou not'st about the field.
                            Exit Pindarus.
     This day I breathed first. Time is come round,
     And where I did begin, there shall I end.
25   My life is run his compass. Sirrah, what news?
PINDARUS [*above*]   O my lord!
CASSIUS   What news?
PINDARUS   Titinius is enclosed round about
     With horsemen, that make to him on the spur,
30   Yet he spurs on. Now they are almost on him.
     Now, Titinius! now some light. O, he lights too!
     He's ta'en!   [*Shout.*]
            And, hark! they shout for joy.
CASSIUS   Come down; behold no more.
     O, coward that I am, to live so long,
35   To see my best friend ta'en before my face!

          Enter PINDARUS *from above.*

     Come hither, sirrah.
     In Parthia did I take thee prisoner;
     And then I swore thee, saving of thy life,
     That whatsoever I did bid thee do,
     Thou shouldst attempt it. Come now, keep thine
40   oath.
     Now be a freeman; and with this good sword,
     That ran through Caesar's bowels, search this bosom.
     Stand not to answer. Here, take thou the hilts,
     And when my face is cover'd, as 'tis now,
45   Guide thou the sword. – Caesar, thou art reveng'd,
     Even with the sword that kill'd thee. [*Dies.*]

PINDARUS   So, I am free; yet would not so have been,
     Durst I have done my will. O Cassius!
     Far from this country Pindarus shall run,
     Where never Roman shall take note of him.   *Exit.*   50

          Enter TITINIUS *and* MESSALA.

MESSALA   It is but change, Titinius; for Octavius
     Is overthrown by noble Brutus' power,
     As Cassius' legions are by Antony.
TITINIUS   These tidings will well comfort Cassius.
MESSALA   Where did you leave him?
TITINIUS   All disconsolate,   55
     With Pindarus his bondman, on this hill.
MESSALA   Is not that he that lies upon the ground?
TITINIUS   He lies not like the living. O my heart!
MESSALA   Is not that he?
TITINIUS   No, this was he, Messala,
     But Cassius is no more. O setting sun,   60
     As in thy red rays thou dost sink to night,
     So in his red blood Cassius' day is set.
     The sun of Rome is set. Our day is gone;
     Clouds, dews, and dangers come; our deeds are done.
     Mistrust of my success hath done this deed.   65
MESSALA
     Mistrust of good success hath done this deed.
     O hateful Error, Melancholy's child,
     Why dost thou show to the apt thoughts of men
     The things that are not? O Error, soon conceiv'd,
     Thou never com'st unto a happy birth,   70
     But kill'st the mother that engender'd thee.
TITINIUS   What, Pindarus! Where art thou, Pindarus?
MESSALA   Seek him, Titinius, whilst I go to meet
     The noble Brutus, thrusting this report
     Into his ears. I may say thrusting it;   75
     For piercing steel and darts envenomed
     Shall be as welcome to the ears of Brutus
     As tidings of this sight.
TITINIUS   Hie you, Messala,
     And I will seek for Pindarus the while.   *Exit Messala.*
     Why didst thou send me forth, brave Cassius?   80
     Did I not meet thy friends, and did not they
     Put on my brows this wreath of victory,
     And bid me give it thee? Didst thou not hear their
       shouts?
     Alas, thou hast misconstrued every thing.
     But hold thee, take this garland on thy brow;   85
     Thy Brutus bid me give it thee, and I
     Will do his bidding. Brutus, come apace,
     And see how I regarded Caius Cassius.
     By your leave, gods. This is a Roman's part:
     Come, Cassius' sword, and find Titinius' heart.   90
     [*Dies.*]

     Alarum. Enter BRUTUS, MESSALA, YOUNG CATO,
         STRATO, VOLUMNIUS *and* LUCILIUS.

BRUTUS   Where, where, Messala, doth his body lie?
MESSALA   Lo, yonder, and Titinius mourning it.

BRUTUS   Titinius' face is upward.
CATO   He is slain.
BRUTUS   O Julius Caesar, thou art mighty yet!
    Thy spirit walks abroad, and turns our swords
    In our own proper entrails.   [*Low alarums.*]
CATO   Brave Titinius!
    Look where he have not crown'd dead Cassius.
BRUTUS   Are yet two Romans living such as these?
    The last of all the Romans, fare thee well!
    It is impossible that ever Rome
    Should breed thy fellow. Friends, I owe moe tears
    To this dead man than you shall see me pay.
    I shall find time, Cassius, I shall find time.
    Come therefore, and to Thasos send his body.
    His funerals shall not be in our camp,
    Lest it discomfort us. Lucilius, come;
    And come, young Cato; let us to the field.
    Labeo and Flavius, set our battles on.
    'Tis three a clock; and, Romans, yet ere night
    We shall try fortune in a second fight.   *Exeunt.*

5.4   *Alarum. Enter* BRUTUS, MESSALA,
        YOUNG CATO, LUCILIUS *and* FLAVIUS.

BRUTUS   Yet, countrymen, O, yet hold up your heads!
                                        Exit.
CATO   What bastard doth not? Who will go with me?
    I will proclaim my name about the field.
    I am the son of Marcus Cato, ho!
    A foe to tyrants, and my country's friend.
    I am the son of Marcus Cato, ho!

        Enter Soldiers, *and fight.*

LUCILIUS   And I am Brutus, Marcus Brutus, I!
    Brutus, my country's friend; know me for Brutus!
    O young and noble Cato, art thou down?
    Why, now thou diest as bravely as Titinius,
    And mayst be honour'd, being Cato's son.
1 SOLDIER   Yield, or thou diest.
LUCILIUS   Only I yield to die:
    There is so much that thou wilt kill me straight:
    Kill Brutus, and be honour'd in his death.
1 SOLDIER   We must not. A noble prisoner!

        Enter ANTONY.

2 SOLDIER   Room, ho! Tell Antony, Brutus is ta'en.
1 SOLDIER   I'll tell the news. Here comes the general.
    Brutus is ta'en, Brutus is ta'en, my lord.
ANTONY   Where is he?
LUCILIUS   Safe, Antony; Brutus is safe enough.
    I dare assure thee that no enemy
    Shall ever take alive the noble Brutus.
    The gods defend him from so great a shame!
    When you do find him, or alive or dead,
    He will be found like Brutus, like himself.
ANTONY
    This is not Brutus, friend; but, I assure you,

A prize no less in worth. Keep this man safe;
    Give him all kindness. I had rather have
    Such men my friends than enemies. Go on,
    And see where Brutus be alive or dead;   30
    And bring us word unto Octavius' tent
    How every thing is chanc'd.   *Exeunt.*

5.5   *Enter* BRUTUS, DARDANIUS, CLITUS,
        STRATO *and* VOLUMNIUS.

BRUTUS
    Come, poor remains of friends, rest on this rock.
CLITUS   Statilius show'd the torch-light; but, my lord,
    He came not back; he is or ta'en or slain.
BRUTUS
    Sit thee down, Clitus. Slaying is the word;
    It is a deed in fashion. Hark thee, Clitus. [*Whispers.*]   5
CLITUS   What, I, my lord? No, not for all the world.
BRUTUS   Peace then. No words.
CLITUS   I'll rather kill myself.
BRUTUS   Hark thee, Dardanius. [*Whispers.*]
DARDANIUS   Shall I do such a deed?
CLITUS   O Dardanius!
DARDANIUS   O Clitus!   10
CLITUS   What ill request did Brutus make to thee?
DARDANIUS   To kill him, Clitus. Look, he meditates.
CLITUS   Now is that noble vessel full of grief,
    That it runs over even at his eyes.
BRUTUS   Come hither, good Volumnius: list a word.   15
VOLUMNIUS   What says my lord?
BRUTUS   Why, this, Volumnius:
    The ghost of Caesar hath appear'd to me
    Two several times by night: at Sardis once,
    And this last night, here in Philippi fields.
    I know my hour is come.
VOLUMNIUS   Not so, my lord.   20
BRUTUS   Nay, I am sure it is, Volumnius.
    Thou seest the world, Volumnius, how it goes:
    Our enemies have beat us to the pit.   [*Low alarums.*]
    It is more worthy to leap in ourselves
    Than tarry till they push us. Good Volumnius,   25
    Thou know'st that we two went to school together:
    Even for that our love of old, I prithee
    Hold thou my sword-hilts, whilst I run on it.
VOLUMNIUS   That's not an office for a friend, my lord.
                                        [*Alarum still.*]
CLITUS   Fly, fly, my lord, there is no tarrying here.   30
BRUTUS
    Farewell to you; and you; and you, Volumnius.
    Strato, thou hast been all this while asleep;
    Farewell to thee too, Strato. – Countrymen,
    My heart doth joy that yet in all my life
    I found no man but he was true to me.   35
    I shall have glory by this losing day
    More than Octavius and Mark Antony
    By this vile conquest shall attain unto.
    So fare you well at once; for Brutus' tongue

40   Hath almost ended his life's history.
      Night hangs upon mine eyes; my bones would rest,
      That have but labour'd to attain this hour.
                          [*Alarum. Cry within, 'Fly, fly, fly!'*]
      CLITUS   Fly, my lord, fly!
      BRUTUS   Hence! I will follow.
                Exeunt Clitus, Dardanius and Volumnius.
      I prithee, Strato, stay thou by thy lord.
45   Thou art a fellow of a good respect;
      Thy life hath had some smatch of honour in it.
      Hold then my sword, and turn away thy face,
      While I do run upon it. Wilt thou, Strato?
      STRATO
      Give me your hand first. Fare you well, my lord.
50   BRUTUS   Farewell, good Strato. – Caesar, now be still;
      I kill'd not thee with half so good a will. [*Dies.*]

      Alarum. Retreat. Enter ANTONY, OCTAVIUS, MESSALA,
                  LUCILIUS *and the army.*

      OCTAVIUS   What man is that?
      MESSALA
      My master's man. Strato, where is thy master?
      STRATO   Free from the bondage you are in, Messala.
55   The conquerors can but make a fire of him;
      For Brutus only overcame himself,
      And no man else hath honour by his death.

      LUCILIUS
      So Brutus should be found. I thank thee, Brutus,
      That thou hast prov'd Lucilius' saying true.
      OCTAVIUS   All that serv'd Brutus, I will entertain them.   60
      Fellow, wilt thou bestow thy time with me?
      STRATO   Ay, if Messala will prefer me to you.
      OCTAVIUS   Do so, good Messala.
      MESSALA   How died my master, Strato?
      STRATO   I held the sword, and he did run on it.   65
      MESSALA   Octavius, then take him to follow thee,
      That did the latest service to my master.
      ANTONY
      This was the noblest Roman of them all.
      All the conspirators save only he
      Did that they did in envy of great Caesar;   70
      He only, in a general honest thought
      And common good to all, made one of them.
      His life was gentle, and the elements
      So mix'd in him, that Nature might stand up
      And say to all the world, 'This was a man!'   75
      OCTAVIUS   According to his virtue let us use him,
      With all respect and rites of burial.
      Within my tent his bones to-night shall lie,
      Most like a soldier, order'd honourably.
      So call the field to rest, and let's away,   80
      To part the glories of this happy day.   *Exeunt omnes.*

King Henry IV, Part 1

King Henry IV, Part 1 was from the first both a theatrical and a literary success, as popular in the bookstalls as on stage. Entered in the Stationers' Register on 25 February 1598, as 'The historye of Henry the iiijth' (it was not until the 1623 Folio that the play was published as *The First Part of King Henry the Fourth*), the play quickly became a best seller. Two editions appeared in 1598 (the first surviving only in a single sheet, now in the Folger Shakespeare Library), and seven more editions were published before 1640, making it not only Shakespeare's most frequently reprinted play before the Interregnum but also one of the most popular of all printed plays in the period. In the theatre also it continuously thrived, though early references to specific performances are few.

Probably first performed in 1597, it held the stage throughout the seventeenth century. In a commendatory poem to Shakespeare's *Poems* (1640), Leonard Digges noted that, while Ben Jonson's plays no longer draw an audience large enough to cover the costs of production, 'let but Falstaff come, / Hal, Poins, the rest, you scarce shall have a room, / All is so pestered'.

Much of the play's popularity is no doubt due to the appeal of Falstaff. Indeed, in the seventeenth century there are more references to the fat knight than to any other dramatic character, though he first appeared on stage with the name 'Sir John Oldcastle'. A well-known fifteenth-century Lollard who had been burned as a heretic, Oldcastle emerged a century later as a celebrated precursor of the Protestant martyrs. Shakespeare's irreverent treatment of the historical figure seems to have offended William Brooke, Lord Cobham, who held his title in descent from Oldcastle's wife. Brooke was Queen Elizabeth's Lord Chamberlain from August 1596 to his death on 5 March 1597, and he seems to have insisted on the change of name. It has even been suggested that publication of the play was required to prove that Shakespeare and his acting company had complied with the Lord Chamberlain's demand.

By whatever name, however, the irrepressible knight has long delighted readers and audiences, offering a vital alternative to the sober world of political consideration over which Henry IV rules. The two men stand as opposing father figures for Prince Henry, one fat and full of life, the other 'portly' only in his power, each in turn drawing the commitment of the Prince who must, as history dictates, finally reject revel for responsibility and accept his destiny to rule. There is a third vector in the play, however, that further complicates his choice: the chivalric energies of the rebel Hotspur that lead Henry IV to wish this son of Northumberland his child instead of Hal. But on the battlefield at Shrewsbury the Prince displays both heroism and magnanimity, proving himself a worthy successor and putting to rest fears either that the irresponsible tavern world has claimed him or that he is only the self-regarding son of a calculating father.

The play, of course, is a 'history' and appears as the third of ten such in the catalogue of the 1623 Folio, but though it concerns the reign of a historical English king and is largely based upon Holinshed's *Chronicles*, it is hardly faithful to the historical record. Not only does it select, restructure and change that history (for example, Hotspur was in fact three years older than the King rather than the Prince's contemporary), but it mixes in completely invented material, that very tavern world that threatens to keep the Prince from his fate. It is precisely this that has made the play so continuously popular: that it is more than its historical plot. It mingles kings and clowns, history and comedy, challenging the exclusive logic of the aristocratic, political action with its rich variety and demotic energy.

The Arden text is based on the two Quartos of 1598.

KING Henry the Fourth
Henry, PRINCE of Wales
Lord John of LANCASTER } *sons to the King*
Earl of WESTMORELAND
Sir Walter BLUNT
Thomas Percy, Earl of WORCESTER
Henry Percy, Earl of NORTHUMBERLAND
Henry Percy, *surnamed* HOTSPUR   *his son*
Edmund MORTIMER, Earl of March.
Archibald, Earl of DOUGLAS
Owen GLENDOWER
Sir Richard VERNON
Richard Scroop, ARCHBISHOP of York
Sir John FALSTAFF
POINS
PETO
BARDOLPH
GADSHILL
LADY PERCY   *wife to Hotspur, and sister to Mortimer*
LADY MORTIMER   *daughter to Glendower, and wife to Mortimer*
Mistress Quickly, HOSTESS   *of the Boar's Head in Eastcheap*

Lords, Officers, Sheriff, Vintner, Chamberlain, Drawers, two Carriers, Ostler, Messengers, Travellers and Attendants.

King Henry IV, Part 1

Enter the KING, LORD JOHN OF LANCASTER,
EARL OF WESTMORELAND, SIR WALTER BLUNT,
with others.

KING   So shaken as we are, so wan with care,
Find we a time for frighted peace to pant,
And breathe short-winded accents of new broils
To be commenc'd in stronds afar remote:
No more the thirsty entrance of this soil   5
Shall daub her lips with her own children's blood,
No more shall trenching war channel her fields,
Nor bruise her flow'rets with the armed hoofs
Of hostile paces: those opposed eyes,
Which, like the meteors of a troubled heaven,   10
All of one nature, of one substance bred,
Did lately meet in the intestine shock
And furious close of civil butchery,
Shall now, in mutual well-beseeming ranks,
March all one way, and be no more oppos'd   15
Against acquaintance, kindred, and allies.
The edge of war, like an ill-sheathed knife,
No more shall cut his master. Therefore, friends,
As far as to the sepulchre of Christ –
Whose soldier now, under whose blessed cross   20
We are impressed and engag'd to fight –
Forthwith a power of English shall we levy,
Whose arms were moulded in their mothers' womb
To chase these pagans in those holy fields
Over whose acres walk'd those blessed feet   25
Which fourteen hundred years ago were nail'd
For our advantage on the bitter cross.
But this our purpose now is twelve month old,
And bootless 'tis to tell you we will go;
Therefor we meet not now. Then let me hear   30
Of you, my gentle cousin Westmoreland,
What yesternight our Council did decree
In forwarding this dear expedience.

WESTMORELAND
My liege, this haste was hot in question,
And many limits of the charge set down   35
But yesternight, when all athwart there came
A post from Wales, loaden with heavy news,
Whose worst was that the noble Mortimer,
Leading the men of Herefordshire to fight
Against the irregular and wild Glendower,   40
Was by the rude hands of that Welshman taken,
A thousand of his people butchered,
Upon whose dead corpse there was such misuse,
Such beastly shameless transformation,
By those Welshwomen done, as may not be   45
Without much shame retold or spoken of.

KING   It seems then that the tidings of this broil
Brake off our business for the Holy Land.

WESTMORELAND
This match'd with other did, my gracious lord,
For more uneven and unwelcome news   50
Came from the north, and thus it did import:
On Holy-rood day, the gallant Hotspur there,

Young Harry Percy, and brave Archibald,
That ever valiant and approved Scot,
At Holmedon met, where they did spend   55
A sad and bloody hour;
As by discharge of their artillery,
And shape of likelihood, the news was told;
For he that brought them, in the very heat
And pride of their contention did take horse,   60
Uncertain of the issue any way.

KING   Here is a dear, a true industrious friend,
Sir Walter Blunt, new lighted from his horse,
Stain'd with the variation of each soil
Betwixt that Holmedon and this seat of ours;   65
And he hath brought us smooth and welcome news.
The Earl of Douglas is discomfited;
Ten thousand bold Scots, two and twenty knights,
Balk'd in their own blood, did Sir Walter see
On Holmedon's plains; of prisoners Hotspur took   70
Mordake, Earl of Fife and eldest son
To beaten Douglas, and the Earl of Athol,
Of Murray, Angus, and Menteith:
And is not this an honourable spoil?
A gallant prize? ha, cousin, is it not?

WESTMORELAND   In faith,   75
It is a conquest for a prince to boast of.

KING
Yea, there thou mak'st me sad, and mak'st me sin
In envy that my Lord Northumberland
Should be the father to so blest a son;
A son who is the theme of honour's tongue,   80
Amongst a grove the very straightest plant,
Who is sweet Fortune's minion and her pride;
Whilst I by looking on the praise of him
See riot and dishonour stain the brow
Of my young Harry. O that it could be prov'd   85
That some night-tripping fairy had exchang'd
In cradle-clothes our children where they lay,
And call'd mine Percy, his Plantagenet!
Then would I have his Harry, and he mine:
But let him from my thoughts. What think you, coz, 90
Of this young Percy's pride? The prisoners
Which he in this adventure hath surpris'd
To his own use he keeps, and sends me word
I shall have none but Mordake, Earl of Fife.

WESTMORELAND
This is his uncle's teaching, this is Worcester,   95
Malevolent to you in all aspects,
Which makes him prune himself, and bristle up
The crest of youth against your dignity.

KING   But I have sent for him to answer this;
And for this cause awhile we must neglect   100
Our holy purpose to Jerusalem.
Cousin, on Wednesday next our Council we
Will hold at Windsor, so inform the lords:
But come yourself with speed to us again,
For more is to be said and to be done   105
Than out of anger can be uttered.

WESTMORELAND   I will, my liege.   *Exeunt.*

1.2   *Enter* PRINCE OF WALES *and* SIR JOHN FALSTAFF.

FALSTAFF   Now, Hal, what time of day is it, lad?

PRINCE   Thou art so fat-witted with drinking of old
sack, and unbuttoning thee after supper, and sleeping
upon benches after noon, that thou hast forgotten to
demand that truly which thou wouldst truly know.
What a devil hast thou to do with the time of the day?
Unless hours were cups of sack, and minutes capons,
and clocks the tongues of bawds, and dials the signs of
leaping-houses, and the blessed sun himself a fair hot
wench in flame-coloured taffeta, I see no reason why
thou shouldst be so superfluous to demand the time of
the day.

FALSTAFF   Indeed, you come near me now, Hal, for we
that take purses go by the moon and the seven stars,
and not 'by Phoebus, he, that wand'ring knight so
fair': and I prithee sweet wag, when thou art king, as
God save thy Grace – Majesty I should say, for grace
thou wilt have none –

PRINCE   What, none?

FALSTAFF   No, by my troth, not so much as will serve to
be prologue to an egg and butter.

PRINCE   Well, how then? Come, roundly, roundly.

FALSTAFF   Marry then sweet wag, when thou art king let
not us that are squires of the night's body be called
thieves of the day's beauty: let us be Diana's foresters,
gentlemen of the shade, minions of the moon; and let
men say we be men of good government, being
governed as the sea is, by our noble and chaste
mistress the moon, under whose countenance we steal.

PRINCE   Thou sayest well, and it holds well too, for the
fortune of us that are the moon's men doth ebb and
flow like the sea, being governed as the sea is, by the
moon – as for proof now, a purse of gold most
resolutely snatched on Monday night, and most
dissolutely spent on Tuesday morning, got with
swearing 'Lay by!', and spent with crying 'Bring in!',
now in as low an ebb as the foot of the ladder, and by
and by in as high a flow as the ridge of the gallows.

FALSTAFF   By the Lord thou say'st true, lad; and is not
my hostess of the tavern a most sweet wench?

PRINCE   As the honey of Hybla, my old lad of the castle;
and is not a buff jerkin a most sweet robe of durance?

FALSTAFF   How now, how now, mad wag? What, in thy
quips and thy quiddities? What a plague have I to do
with a buff jerkin?

PRINCE   Why, what a pox have I to do with my hostess of
the tavern?

FALSTAFF   Well, thou hast called her to a reckoning
many a time and oft.

PRINCE   Did I ever call for thee to pay thy part?

FALSTAFF   No, I'll give thee thy due, thou hast paid all
there.

PRINCE   Yea, and elsewhere, so far as my coin would
stretch, and where it would not I have used my credit.

FALSTAFF   Yea, and so used it that were it not here
apparent that thou art heir apparent – But I prithee
sweet wag, shall there be gallows standing in England
when thou art king? and resolution thus fubbed as it is
with the rusty curb of old father Antic the law? Do not
thou when thou art king hang a thief.

PRINCE   No, thou shalt.

FALSTAFF   Shall I? O rare! By the Lord, I'll be a brave
judge!

PRINCE   Thou judgest false already, I mean thou shalt
have the hanging of the thieves, and so become a rare
hangman.

FALSTAFF   Well, Hal, well; and in some sort it jumps
with my humour, as well as waiting in the court, I can
tell you.

PRINCE   For obtaining of suits?

FALSTAFF   Yea, for obtaining of suits, whereof the
hangman hath no lean wardrobe. 'Sblood, I am as
melancholy as a gib cat, or a lugged bear.

PRINCE   Or an old lion, or a lover's lute.

FALSTAFF   Yea, or the drone of a Lincolnshire bagpipe.

PRINCE   What sayest thou to a hare, or the melancholy of
Moor-ditch?

FALSTAFF   Thou hast the most unsavoury similes, and
art indeed the most comparative rascalliest sweet
young prince. But Hal, I prithee trouble me no more
with vanity. I would to God thou and I knew where a
commodity of good names were to be bought: an old
lord of the Council rated me the other day in the street
about you, sir, but I marked him not, and yet he talked
very wisely, but I regarded him not, and yet he talked
wisely, and in the street too.

PRINCE   Thou didst well, for wisdom cries out in the
streets and no man regards it.

FALSTAFF   O, thou hast damnable iteration, and art
indeed able to corrupt a saint: thou hast done much
harm upon me, Hal, God forgive thee for it: before I
knew thee, Hal, I knew nothing, and now am I, if a
man should speak truly, little better than one of the
wicked. I must give over this life, and I will give it
over: by the Lord, and I do not I am a villain, I'll be
damned for never a king's son in Christendom.

PRINCE   Where shall we take a purse tomorrow, Jack?

FALSTAFF   'Zounds, where thou wilt, lad, I'll make one;
an I do not, call me villain and baffle me.

PRINCE   I see a good amendment of life in thee, from
praying to purse-taking.

FALSTAFF   Why, Hal, 'tis my vocation, Hal, 'tis no sin
for a man to labour in his vocation.

Enter POINS.

Poins! – Now shall we know if Gadshill have set a
match. O, if men were to be saved by merit, what hole
in hell were hot enough for him? This is the most
omnipotent villain that ever cried 'Stand!' to a true
man.

PRINCE   Good morrow, Ned.

POINS   Good morrow, sweet Hal. What says Monsieur
110   Remorse? What says Sir John Sack – and Sugar? Jack!
how agrees the devil and thee about thy soul, that thou
soldest him on Good Friday last, for a cup of Madeira
and a cold capon's leg?

PRINCE   Sir John stands to his word, the devil shall have
115   his bargain, for he was never yet a breaker of proverbs:
he will give the devil his due.

POINS   Then art thou damned for keeping thy word with
the devil.

PRINCE   Else he had been damned for cozening the
120   devil.

POINS   But my lads, my lads, tomorrow morning, by
four o'clock early at Gad's Hill, there are pilgrims
going to Canterbury with rich offerings, and traders
riding to London with fat purses. I have vizards for
125   you all; you have horses for yourselves. Gadshill lies
tonight in Rochester, I have bespoke supper tomorrow
night in Eastcheap: we may do it as secure as sleep. If
you will go, I will stuff your purses full of crowns: if
130   you will not, tarry at home and be hanged.

FALSTAFF   Hear ye, Yedward, if I tarry at home and go
not, I'll hang you for going.

POINS   You will, chops?

FALSTAFF   Hal, wilt thou make one?

135   PRINCE   Who, I rob? I a thief? Not I, by my faith.

FALSTAFF   There's neither honesty, manhood, nor good
fellowship in thee, nor thou cam'st not of the blood
royal, if thou darest not stand for ten shillings.

PRINCE   Well then, once in my days I'll be a madcap.

140   FALSTAFF   Why, that's well said.

PRINCE   Well, come what will, I'll tarry at home.

FALSTAFF   By the Lord, I'll be a traitor then, when thou
art king.

PRINCE   I care not.

145   POINS   Sir John, I prithee leave the Prince and me alone:
I will lay him down such reasons for this adventure
that he shall go.

FALSTAFF   Well, God give thee the spirit of persuasion,
and him the ears of profiting, that what thou speakest
150   may move, and what he hears may be believed, that the
true prince may (for recreation sake) prove a false
thief, for the poor abuses of the time want
countenance. Farewell, you shall find me in Eastcheap.

155   PRINCE   Farewell, the latter spring! Farewell, All-hallown
summer!   *Exit Falstaff.*

POINS   Now, my good sweet honey lord, ride with us
tomorrow. I have a jest to execute that I cannot
manage alone. Falstaff, Bardolph, Peto, and Gadshill
160   shall rob those men that we have already waylaid –
yourself and I will not be there: and when they have
the booty, if you and I do not rob them, cut this head
off from my shoulders.

PRINCE   How shall we part with them in setting forth?

165   POINS   Why, we will set forth before or after them, and
appoint them a place of meeting, wherein it is at our
pleasure to fail; and then will they adventure upon the
exploit themselves, which they shall have no sooner
achieved but we'll set upon them.

PRINCE   Yea, but 'tis like that they will know us by our   170
horses, by our habits, and by every other appointment
to be ourselves.

POINS   Tut, our horses they shall not see, I'll tie them in
the wood; our vizards we will change after we leave
them; and sirrah, I have cases of buckram for the   175
nonce, to immask our noted outward garments.

PRINCE   Yea, but I doubt they will be too hard for us.

POINS   Well, for two of them, I know them to be as true-
bred cowards as ever turned back; and for the third, if
he fight longer than he sees reason, I'll forswear arms.   180
The virtue of this jest will be the incomprehensible
lies that this same fat rogue will tell us when we meet
at supper, how thirty at least he fought with, what
wards, what blows, what extremities he endured; and
in the reproof of this lives the jest.   185

PRINCE   Well, I'll go with thee; provide us all things
necessary, and meet me tomorrow night in Eastcheap;
there I'll sup. Farewell.

POINS   Farewell, my lord.   *Exit.*

PRINCE   I know you all, and will awhile uphold   190
The unyok'd humour of your idleness.
Yet herein will I imitate the sun,
Who doth permit the base contagious clouds
To smother up his beauty from the world,
That, when he please again to be himself,   195
Being wanted he may be more wonder'd at
By breaking through the foul and ugly mists
Of vapours that did seem to strangle him.
If all the year were playing holidays,
To sport would be as tedious as to work;   200
But when they seldom come, they wish'd-for come,
And nothing pleaseth but rare accidents:
So when this loose behaviour I throw off,
And pay the debt I never promised,
By how much better than my word I am,   205
By so much shall I falsify men's hopes;
And like bright metal on a sullen ground,
My reformation, glitt'ring o'er my fault,
Shall show more goodly, and attract more eyes
Than that which hath no foil to set it off.   210
I'll so offend, to make offence a skill,
Redeeming time when men think least I will.   *Exit.*

1.3   *Enter the* KING, NORTHUMBERLAND,
WORCESTER, HOTSPUR, SIR WALTER BLUNT,
with others.

KING   My blood hath been too cold and temperate,
Unapt to stir at these indignities,
And you have found me – for accordingly
You tread upon my patience: but be sure
I will from henceforth rather be myself,   5

Mighty, and to be fear'd, than my condition,
Which hath been smooth as oil, soft as young down,
And therefore lost that title of respect
Which the proud soul ne'er pays but to the proud.

WORCESTER

10 Our house, my sovereign liege, little deserves
The scourge of greatness to be us'd on it,
And that same greatness too which our own hands
Have holp to make so portly.

NORTHUMBERLAND   My lord, –

KING Worcester, get thee gone, for I do see
15 Danger and disobedience in thine eye:
O sir, your presence is too bold and peremptory,
And majesty might never yet endure
The moody frontier of a servant brow.
You have good leave to leave us; when we need
20 Your use and counsel we shall send for you.

Exit Worcester.

[*to Northumberland*] You were about to speak.

NORTHUMBERLAND   Yea, my good lord.
Those prisoners in your Highness' name demanded,
Which Harry Percy here at Holmedon took,
Were, as he says, not with such strength deny'd
25 As is deliver'd to your Majesty.
Either envy therefore, or misprision,
Is guilty of this fault, and not my son.

HOTSPUR My liege, I did deny no prisoners,
But I remember, when the fight was done,
30 When I was dry with rage, and extreme toil,
Breathless and faint, leaning upon my sword,
Came there a certain lord, neat and trimly dress'd,
Fresh as a bridegroom, and his chin new reap'd
Show'd like a stubble-land at harvest-home.
35 He was perfumed like a milliner,
And 'twixt his finger and his thumb he held
A pouncet-box, which ever and anon
He gave his nose, and took't away again –
Who therewith angry, when it next came there,
40 Took it in snuff – and still he smil'd and talk'd:
And as the soldiers bore dead bodies by,
He call'd them untaught knaves, unmannerly,
To bring a slovenly unhandsome corse
Betwixt the wind and his nobility.
45 With many holiday and lady terms
He question'd me, amongst the rest demanded
My prisoners in your Majesty's behalf.
I then, all smarting with my wounds being cold,
To be so pester'd with a popinjay,
50 Out of my grief and my impatience
Answer'd neglectingly, I know not what,
He should, or he should not, for he made me mad
To see him shine so brisk, and smell so sweet,
And talk so like a waiting-gentlewoman
Of guns, and drums, and wounds, God save the
55   mark!
And telling me the sovereignest thing on earth

Was parmacity for an inward bruise,
And that it was great pity, so it was,
This villainous saltpetre should be digg'd
Out of the bowels of the harmless earth,   60
Which many a good tall fellow had destroy'd
So cowardly, and but for these vile guns
He would himself have been a soldier.
This bald unjointed chat of his, my lord,
I answer'd indirectly, as I said,   65
And I beseech you, let not his report
Come current for an accusation
Betwixt my love and your high Majesty.

BLUNT The circumstance consider'd, good my lord,
Whate'er Lord Harry Percy then had said   70
To such a person, and in such a place,
At such a time, with all the rest retold,
May reasonably die, and never rise
To do him wrong, or any way impeach
What then he said, so he unsay it now.   75

KING Why, yet he doth deny his prisoners,
But with proviso and exception,
That we at our own charge shall ransom straight
His brother-in-law, the foolish Mortimer,
Who, on my soul, hath wilfully betray'd   80
The lives of those that he did lead to fight
Against that great magician, damn'd Glendower,
Whose daughter, as we hear, the Earl of March
Hath lately marry'd: shall our coffers then
Be empty'd to redeem a traitor home?   85
Shall we buy treason, and indent with fears
When they have lost and forfeited themselves?
No, on the barren mountains let him starve;
For I shall never hold that man my friend
Whose tongue shall ask me for one penny cost   90
To ransom home revolted Mortimer.

HOTSPUR Revolted Mortimer!
He never did fall off, my sovereign liege,
But by the chance of war: to prove that true
Needs no more but one tongue for all those wounds, 95
Those mouthed wounds, which valiantly he took,
When on the gentle Severn's sedgy bank,
In single opposition hand to hand,
He did confound the best part of an hour
In changing hardiment with great Glendower.   100
Three times they breath'd, and three times did they
   drink
Upon agreement of swift Severn's flood,
Who then affrighted with their bloody looks
Ran fearfully among the trembling reeds,
And hid his crisp head in the hollow bank,   105
Bloodstained with these valiant combatants.
Never did bare and rotten policy
Colour her working with such deadly wounds,
Nor never could the noble Mortimer
Receive so many, and all willingly: 110
Then let not him be slander'd with revolt.

KING Thou dost belie him, Percy, thou dost belie him,
He never did encounter with Glendower:
I tell thee, he durst as well have met the devil alone
115 As Owen Glendower for an enemy.
Art thou not asham'd? But sirrah, henceforth
Let me not hear you speak of Mortimer:
Send me your prisoners with the speediest means,
Or you shall hear in such a kind from me
120 As will displease you. My Lord Northumberland:
We license your departure with your son.
Send us your prisoners, or you will hear of it.

Exit King, with Blunt and train.

HOTSPUR And if the devil come and roar for them
I will not send them: I will after straight
125 And tell him so, for I will ease my heart,
Albeit I make a hazard of my head.
NORTHUMBERLAND
What, drunk with choler? Stay, and pause awhile,
Here comes your uncle.

Re-enter WORCESTER.

HOTSPUR   Speak of Mortimer?
'Zounds, I will speak of him, and let my soul
130 Want mercy if I do not join with him:
Yea, on his part I'll empty all these veins,
And shed my dear blood, drop by drop in the dust,
But I will lift the down-trod Mortimer
As high in the air as this unthankful King,
135 As this ingrate and canker'd Bolingbroke.
NORTHUMBERLAND
Brother, the King hath made your nephew mad.
WORCESTER Who struck this heat up after I was gone?
HOTSPUR He will forsooth have all my prisoners,
And when I urg'd the ransom once again
140 Of my wife's brother, then his cheek look'd pale,
And on my face he turn'd an eye of death,
Trembling even at the name of Mortimer.
WORCESTER
I cannot blame him: was not he proclaim'd,
By Richard that dead is, the next of blood?
145 NORTHUMBERLAND He was, I heard the proclamation:
And then it was, when the unhappy King
(Whose wrongs in us God pardon!) did set forth
Upon his Irish expedition;
From whence he, intercepted, did return
150 To be depos'd, and shortly murdered.
WORCESTER
And for whose death we in the world's wide mouth
Live scandaliz'd and foully spoken of.
HOTSPUR But soft, I pray you, did King Richard then
Proclaim my brother Edmund Mortimer
Heir to the crown?
155 NORTHUMBERLAND He did, myself did hear it.
HOTSPUR Nay, then I cannot blame his cousin King,
That wish'd him on the barren mountains starve.
But shall it be that you that set the crown
Upon the head of this forgetful man,

And for his sake wear the detested blot 160
Of murderous subornation – shall it be
That you a world of curses undergo,
Being the agents, or base second means,
The cords, the ladder, or the hangman rather?
– O, pardon me, that I descend so low, 165
To show the line and the predicament
Wherein you range under this subtle King!
Shall it for shame be spoken in these days,
Or fill up chronicles in time to come,
That men of your nobility and power 170
Did gage them both in an unjust behalf
(As both of you, God pardon it, have done)
To put down Richard, that sweet lovely rose,
And plant this thorn, this canker Bolingbroke?
And shall it in more shame be further spoken, 175
That you are fool'd, discarded, and shook off
By him for whom these shames ye underwent?
No, yet time serves wherein you may redeem
Your banish'd honours, and restore yourselves
Into the good thoughts of the world again: 180
Revenge the jeering and disdain'd contempt
Of this proud King, who studies day and night
To answer all the debt he owes to you,
Even with the bloody payment of your deaths:
Therefore, I say –
WORCESTER   Peace, cousin, say no more. 185
And now I will unclasp a secret book,
And to your quick-conceiving discontents
I'll read you matter deep and dangerous,
As full of peril and adventurous spirit
As to o'er-walk a current roaring loud 190
On the unsteadfast footing of a spear.
HOTSPUR If he fall in, good night, or sink, or swim!
Send danger from the east unto the west,
So honour cross it from the north to south,
And let them grapple: O, the blood more stirs 195
To rouse a lion than to start a hare!
NORTHUMBERLAND Imagination of some great exploit
Drives him beyond the bounds of patience.
HOTSPUR By heaven, methinks it were an easy leap
To pluck bright honour from the pale-fac'd moon, 200
Or dive into the bottom of the deep,
Where fathom-line could never touch the ground,
And pluck up drowned honour by the locks,
So he that doth redeem her thence might wear
Without corrival all her dignities: 205
But out upon this half-fac'd fellowship!
WORCESTER He apprehends a world of figures here,
But not the form of what he should attend:
Good cousin, give me audience for a while.
HOTSPUR I cry you mercy.
WORCESTER   Those same noble Scots 210
That are your prisoners –
HOTSPUR   I'll keep them all;
By God he shall not have a Scot of them,
No, if a Scot would save his soul he shall not.

I'll keep them, by this hand!

WORCESTER   You start away,
215   And lend no ear unto my purposes:
        Those prisoners you shall keep –
HOTSPUR   Nay, I will: that's flat!
        He said he would not ransom Mortimer,
        Forbade my tongue to speak of Mortimer,
        But I will find him when he lies asleep,
220   And in his ear I'll holla 'Mortimer!'
        Nay, I'll have a starling shall be taught to speak
        Nothing but 'Mortimer', and give it him
        To keep his anger still in motion.
WORCESTER   Hear you, cousin, a word.
225 HOTSPUR   All studies here I solemnly defy,
        Save how to gall and pinch this Bolingbroke:
        And that same sword-and-buckler Prince of Wales,
        But that I think his father loves him not,
        And would be glad he met with some mischance –
230   I would have him poison'd with a pot of ale!
WORCESTER   Farewell, kinsman: I'll talk to you
        When you are better temper'd to attend.
NORTHUMBERLAND
        Why, what a wasp-stung and impatient fool
        Art thou to break into this woman's mood,
235   Tying thine ear to no tongue but thine own!
HOTSPUR
        Why, look you, I am whipp'd and scourg'd with rods,
        Nettled, and stung with pismires, when I hear
        Of this vile politician Bolingbroke.
        In Richard's time – what do you call the place?
240   A plague upon it, it is in Gloucestershire –
        'Twas where the mad-cap Duke his uncle kept,
        His uncle York – where I first bow'd my knee
        Unto this king of smiles, this Bolingbroke,
        'Sblood, when you and he came back from
            Ravenspurgh.
245 NORTHUMBERLAND   At Berkeley castle.
HOTSPUR   You say true.
        Why, what a candy deal of courtesy
        This fawning greyhound then did proffer me!
        'Look when his infant fortune came to age',
250   And 'gentle Harry Percy', and 'kind cousin':
        O, the devil take such cozeners! – God forgive me!
        Good uncle, tell your tale; I have done.
WORCESTER   Nay, if you have not, to it again,
        We will stay your leisure.
HOTSPUR   I have done, i'faith.
WORCESTER
255   Then once more to your Scottish prisoners;
        Deliver them up without their ransom straight,
        And make the Douglas' son your only mean
        For powers in Scotland, which, for divers reasons
        Which I shall send you written, be assur'd
        Will easily be granted. –
260   [*to Northumberland*]   You, my lord,
        Your son in Scotland being thus employ'd,
        Shall secretly into the bosom creep

        Of that same noble prelate well-belov'd,
        The Archbishop.
HOTSPUR   Of York, is it not?
WORCESTER   True, who bears hard
        His brother's death at Bristow, the Lord Scroop.   265
        I speak not this in estimation,
        As what I think might be, but what I know
        Is ruminated, plotted, and set down,
        And only stays but to behold the face
        Of that occasion that shall bring it on.   270
HOTSPUR   I smell it. Upon my life it will do well!
NORTHUMBERLAND
        Before the game is afoot thou still let'st slip.
HOTSPUR   Why, it cannot choose but be a noble plot;
        And then the power of Scotland, and of York,
        To join with Mortimer, ha?
WORCESTER   And so they shall.   275
HOTSPUR   In faith it is exceedingly well aim'd.
WORCESTER   And 'tis no little reason bids us speed,
        To save our heads by raising of a head;
        For, bear ourselves as even as we can,
        The King will always think him in our debt,   280
        And think we think ourselves unsatisfy'd,
        Till he hath found a time to pay us home:
        And see already how he doth begin
        To make us strangers to his looks of love.
HOTSPUR   He does, he does, we'll be reveng'd on him.   285
WORCESTER   Cousin, farewell. No further go in this
        Than I by letters shall direct your course.
        When time is ripe, which will be suddenly,
        I'll steal to Glendower, and Lord Mortimer,
        Where you, and Douglas, and our powers at once,   290
        As I will fashion it, shall happily meet,
        To bear our fortunes in our own strong arms,
        Which now we hold at much uncertainty.
NORTHUMBERLAND
        Farewell, good brother; we shall thrive, I trust.
HOTSPUR   Uncle, adieu: O, let the hours be short,   295
        Till fields, and blows, and groans applaud our sport!
                                    Exeunt.

2.1   *Enter a* Carrier, *with a lantern in his hand.*

1 CARRIER   Heigh-ho! An it be not four by the day I'll be
        hanged; Charles' wain is over the new chimney, and
        yet our horse not packed. What, ostler!
OSTLER [*within*]   Anon, anon.
1 CARRIER   I prithee, Tom, beat Cut's saddle, put a few   5
        flocks in the point; poor jade is wrung in the withers
        out of all cess.

                    Enter another Carrier.

2 CARRIER   Peas and beans are as dank here as a dog, and
        that is the next way to give poor jades the bots: this
        house is turned upside down since Robin Ostler died.   10
1 CARRIER   Poor fellow never joyed since the price of oats
        rose, it was the death of him.

2 CARRIER   I think this be the most villainous house in all London road for fleas, I am stung like a tench.

1 CARRIER   Like a tench! By the mass, there is ne'er a king christen could be better bit than I have been since the first cock.

2 CARRIER   Why, they will allow us ne'er a jordan, and then we leak in your chimney, and your chamber-lye breeds fleas like a loach.

1 CARRIER   What, ostler! Come away, and be hanged, come away!

2 CARRIER   I have a gammon of bacon, and two razes of ginger, to be delivered as far as Charing Cross.

1 CARRIER   God's body! The turkeys in my pannier are quite starved. What, ostler! A plague on thee, hast thou never an eye in thy head? canst not hear? And 'twere not as good deed as drink to break the pate on thee, I am a very villain. Come, and be hanged! Hast no faith in thee?

Enter GADSHILL.

GADSHILL   Good morrow, carriers, what's o'clock?

1 CARRIER   I think it be two o'clock.

GADSHILL   I prithee lend me thy lantern, to see my gelding in the stable.

1 CARRIER   Nay, by God, soft! I know a trick worth two of that, i'faith.

GADSHILL   I pray thee lend me thine.

2 CARRIER   Ay, when? Canst tell? Lend me thy lantern, quoth he! Marry I'll see thee hanged first.

GADSHILL   Sirrah carrier, what time do you mean to come to London?

2 CARRIER   Time enough to go to bed with a candle, I warrant thee; come, neighbour Mugs, we'll call up the gentlemen, they will along with company, for they have great charge.   *Exeunt Carriers.*

GADSHILL   What ho! Chamberlain!

Enter CHAMBERLAIN.

CHAMBERLAIN   'At hand, quoth pick-purse.'

GADSHILL   That's even as fair as 'At hand, quoth the chamberlain': for thou variest no more from picking of purses than giving direction doth from labouring; thou layest the plot how.

CHAMBERLAIN   Good morrow, master Gadshill. It holds current that I told you yesternight: there's a franklin in the Wild of Kent hath brought three hundred marks with him in gold, I heard him tell it to one of his company last night at supper, a kind of auditor, one that hath abundance of charge too, God knows what; they are up already, and call for eggs and butter – they will away presently.

GADSHILL   Sirrah, if they meet not with Saint Nicholas' clerks, I'll give thee this neck.

CHAMBERLAIN   No, I'll none of it, I pray thee keep that for the hangman, for I know thou worshippest Saint Nicholas, as truly as a man of falsehood may.

GADSHILL   What talkest thou to me of the hangman? If I hang, I'll make a fat pair of gallows: for if I hang, old Sir John hangs with me, and thou knowest he is no starveling. Tut, there are other Troyans that thou dream'st not of, the which for sport sake are content to do the profession some grace, that would (if matters should be looked into) for their own credit sake make all whole. I am joined with no foot-landrakers, no long-staff sixpenny strikers, none of these mad mustachio purple-hued maltworms, but with nobility and tranquillity, burgomasters and great onyers, such as can hold in, such as will strike sooner than speak, and speak sooner than drink, and drink sooner than pray – and yet, 'zounds, I lie, for they pray continually to their saint the commonwealth, or rather not pray to her, but prey on her, for they ride up and down on her, and make her their boots.

CHAMBERLAIN   What, the commonwealth their boots? Will she hold out water in foul way?

GADSHILL   She will, she will, justice hath liquored her: we steal as in a castle, cock-sure: we have the receipt of fern-seed, we walk invisible.

CHAMBERLAIN   Nay, by my faith, I think you are more beholding to the night than to fern-seed for your walking invisible.

GADSHILL   Give me thy hand, thou shalt have a share in our purchase, as I am a true man.

CHAMBERLAIN   Nay, rather let me have it, as you are a false thief.

GADSHILL   Go to, *homo* is a common name to all men: bid the ostler bring my gelding out of the stable. Farewell, you muddy knave.   *Exeunt.*

2.2   *Enter* PRINCE, POINS *and* PETO.

POINS   Come, shelter, shelter! I have removed Falstaff's horse, and he frets like a gummed velvet.

PRINCE   Stand close! [*They retire.*]

Enter FALSTAFF.

FALSTAFF   Poins! Poins, and be hanged! Poins!

PRINCE [*coming forward*]   Peace, ye fat-kidneyed rascal, what a brawling dost thou keep!

FALSTAFF   Where's Poins, Hal?

PRINCE   He is walked up to the top of the hill; I'll go seek him. [*Retires.*]

FALSTAFF   I am accursed to rob in that thief's company; the rascal hath removed my horse and tied him I know not where. If I travel but four foot by the squier further afoot, I shall break my wind. Well, I doubt not but to die a fair death for all this, if I scape hanging for killing that rogue. I have forsworn his company hourly any time this two and twenty years, and yet I am bewitched with the rogue's company. If the rascal have not given me medicines to make me love him, I'll be hanged. It could not be else, I have drunk medicines. Poins! Hal! A plague upon you both! Bardolph! Peto! I'll starve ere I'll rob a foot further – and 'twere not as

good a deed as drink to turn true man, and to leave
these rogues, I am the veriest varlet that ever chewed
with a tooth; eight yards of uneven ground is
threescore and ten miles afoot with me, and the stony-
25   hearted villains know it well enough. A plague upon it
when thieves cannot be true one to another!
[*They whistle.*] Whew! A plague upon you all, give me
my horse, you rogues, give me my horse and be
30   hanged!

PRINCE [*coming forward*]   Peace, ye fat guts, lie down, lay
thine ear close to the ground, and list if thou canst
hear the tread of travellers.

FALSTAFF   Have you any levers to lift me up again, being
35   down? 'Sblood, I'll not bear my own flesh so far afoot
again for all the coin in thy father's exchequer. What a
plague mean ye to colt me thus?

PRINCE   Thou liest, thou art not colted, thou art
uncolted.

40   FALSTAFF   I prithee good Prince Hal, help me to my
horse, good king's son.

PRINCE   Out, ye rogue, shall I be your ostler?

FALSTAFF   Hang thyself in thine own heir-apparent
garters! If I be ta'en, I'll peach for this: and I have not
45   ballads made on you all, and sung to filthy tunes, let a
cup of sack be my poison – when a jest is so forward,
and afoot too! I hate it.

Enter GADSHILL *and* BARDOLPH.

GADSHILL   Stand!

FALSTAFF   So I do, against my will.

50   POINS   O, 'tis our setter, I know his voice. [*coming
forward with Peto*] Bardolph, what news?

BARDOLPH   Case ye, case ye, on with your vizards,
there's money of the King's coming down the hill, 'tis
going to the King's exchequer.

55   FALSTAFF   You lie, ye rogue, 'tis going to the King's
tavern.

GADSHILL   There's enough to make us all.

FALSTAFF   To be hanged.

PRINCE   Sirs, you four shall front them in the narrow
60   lane: Ned Poins and I will walk lower – if they scape
from your encounter, then they light on us.

PETO   How many be there of them?

GADSHILL   Some eight or ten.

FALSTAFF   'Zounds, will they not rob us?

65   PRINCE   What, a coward, Sir John Paunch?

FALSTAFF   Indeed, I am not John of Gaunt your
grandfather, but yet no coward, Hal.

PRINCE   Well, we leave that to the proof.

POINS   Sirrah Jack, thy horse stands behind the hedge;
70   when thou need'st him, there thou shalt find him.
Farewell, and stand fast.

FALSTAFF   Now cannot I strike him, if I should be
hanged.

PRINCE   Ned, where are our disguises?

75   POINS   Here, hard by, stand close.

Exeunt Prince and Poins.

FALSTAFF   Now, my masters, happy man be his dole, say
I – every man to his business.

Enter the Travellers.

1 TRAVELLER   Come, neighbour, the boy shall lead our
horses down the hill; we'll walk afoot awhile and ease
80   our legs.

THIEVES   Stand!

2 TRAVELLER   Jesus bless us!

FALSTAFF   Strike, down with them, cut the villains'
throats! Ah, whoreson caterpillars, bacon-fed knaves,
85   they hate us youth! Down with them, fleece them!

1 TRAVELLER   O, we are undone, both we and ours for
ever!

FALSTAFF   Hang ye, gorbellied knaves, are ye undone?
No, ye fat chuffs, I would your store were here! On,
90   bacons, on! What, ye knaves! young men must live.
You are grandjurors, are ye? We'll jure ye, faith.
[*Here they rob them and bind them.*]   *Exeunt.*

Re-enter the PRINCE *and* POINS, *disguised.*

PRINCE   The thieves have bound the true men; now
could thou and I rob the thieves, and go merrily to
London, it would be argument for a week, laughter for
95   a month, and a good jest for ever.

POINS   Stand close, I hear them coming. [*They retire.*]

Enter the Thieves *again.*

FALSTAFF   Come, my masters, let us share, and then to
horse before day; and the Prince and Poins be not two
arrant cowards there's no equity stirring; there's no
100   more valour in that Poins than in a wild duck.
[*As they are sharing the* PRINCE *and* POINS *set upon
them.*]

PRINCE   Your money!

POINS   Villains!

*They all run away, and Falstaff after a blow or two
runs away too, leaving the booty behind them.*

PRINCE   Got with much ease. Now merrily to horse:
The thieves are all scatter'd and possess'd with fear
105   So strongly that they dare not meet each other;
Each takes his fellow for an officer!
Away, good Ned – Falstaff sweats to death,
And lards the lean earth as he walks along.
Were't not for laughing I should pity him.

110   POINS   How the fat rogue roared.   *Exeunt.*

2.3   *Enter* HOTSPUR *alone, reading a letter.*

HOTSPUR   *But, for mine own part, my lord, I could be well
contented to be there, in respect of the love I bear your
house.* He could be contented: why is he not then? In
respect of the love he bears our house: he shows in
5   this, he loves his own barn better than he loves our
house. Let me see some more. *The purpose you
undertake is dangerous* – Why, that's certain; 'tis
dangerous to take a cold, to sleep, to drink; but I tell

you, my lord fool, out of this nettle, danger, we pluck
this flower, safety. *The purpose you undertake is*
dangerous, the friends you have named uncertain, the time
itself unsorted, and your whole plot too light, for the
counterpoise of so great an opposition. Say you so, say
you so? I say unto you again, you are a shallow
cowardly hind, and you lie: what a lack-brain is this!
By the Lord, our plot is a good plot, as ever was laid,
our friends true and constant: a good plot, good
friends, and full of expectation: an excellent plot, very
good friends; what a frosty-spirited rogue is this! Why,
my Lord of York commends the plot, and the general
course of the action. 'Zounds, and I were now by this
rascal I could brain him with his lady's fan. Is there
not my father, my uncle, and myself? Lord Edmund
Mortimer, my Lord of York, and Owen Glendower? Is
there not besides the Douglas? Have I not all their
letters to meet me in arms by the ninth of the next
month, and are they not some of them set forward
already? What a pagan rascal is this, an infidel! Ha!
You shall see now in very sincerity of fear and cold
heart will he to the King, and lay open all our
proceedings! O, I could divide myself, and go to
buffets, for moving such a dish of skim milk with so
honourable an action! Hang him, let him tell the King,
we are prepared: I will set forward tonight.

Enter LADY PERCY.

How now, Kate? I must leave you within these two
hours.

LADY PERCY   O my good lord, why are you thus alone?
For what offence have I this fortnight been
A banish'd woman from my Harry's bed?
Tell me, sweet lord, what is't that takes from thee
Thy stomach, pleasure, and thy golden sleep?
Why dost thou bend thine eyes upon the earth,
And start so often when thou sit'st alone?
Why hast thou lost the fresh blood in thy cheeks,
And given my treasures and my rights of thee
To thick-ey'd musing, and curst melancholy?
In thy faint slumbers I by thee have watch'd,
And heard thee murmur tales of iron wars,
Speak terms of manage to thy bounding steed,
Cry 'Courage! To the field!' And thou hast talk'd
Of sallies, and retires, of trenches, tents,
Of palisadoes, frontiers, parapets,
Of basilisks, of cannon, culverin,
Of prisoners' ransom, and of soldiers slain,
And all the currents of a heady fight.
Thy spirit within thee hath been so at war,
And thus hath so bestirr'd thee in thy sleep,
That beads of sweat have stood upon thy brow
Like bubbles in a late-disturbed stream,
And in thy face strange motions have appear'd,
Such as we see when men restrain their breath
On some great sudden hest. O, what portents are
these?

Some heavy business hath my lord in hand,
And I must know it, else he loves me not.
HOTSPUR   What ho!

Enter a Servant.

                    Is Gilliams with the packet gone?
SERVANT   He is, my lord, an hour ago.
HOTSPUR
Hath Butler brought those horses from the sheriff?
SERVANT   One horse, my lord, he brought even now.
HOTSPUR   What horse? A roan, a crop-ear is it not?
SERVANT   It is, my lord.
HOTSPUR   That roan shall be my throne.
Well, I will back him straight: O Esperance!
Bid Butler lead him forth into the park.

Exit Servant.

LADY PERCY   But hear you, my lord.
HOTSPUR   What say'st thou, my lady?
LADY PERCY   What is it carries you away?
HOTSPUR   Why, my horse, my love, my horse.
LADY PERCY   Out, you mad-headed ape!
A weasel hath not such a deal of spleen
As you are toss'd with. In faith,
I'll know your business, Harry, that I will;
I fear my brother Mortimer doth stir
About his title, and hath sent for you
To line his enterprise. But if you go –
HOTSPUR   So far afoot I shall be weary, love.
LADY PERCY   Come, come, you paraquito, answer me
Directly unto this question that I ask;
In faith, I'll break thy little finger, Harry,
And if thou wilt not tell me all things true.
HOTSPUR   Away,
Away, you trifler! Love! I love thee not,
I care not for thee, Kate; this is no world
To play with mammets, and to tilt with lips;
We must have bloody noses, and crack'd crowns,
And pass them current too. God's me! my horse!
What say'st thou, Kate? What wouldst thou have
with me?
LADY PERCY   Do you not love me? Do you not indeed?
Well, do not then, for since you love me not
I will not love myself. Do you not love me?
Nay, tell me if you speak in jest or no.
HOTSPUR   Come, wilt thou see me ride?
And when I am a-horseback I will swear
I love thee infinitely. But hark you, Kate,
I must not have you henceforth question me
Whither I go, nor reason whereabout:
Whither I must, I must; and, to conclude,
This evening must I leave you, gentle Kate.
I know you wise, but yet no farther wise
Than Harry Percy's wife; constant you are,
But yet a woman; and for secrecy
No lady closer, for I well believe
Thou wilt not utter what thou dost not know;
And so far will I trust thee, gentle Kate.

LADY PERCY   How? so far?

HOTSPUR   Not an inch further. But hark you, Kate,

115   Whither I go, thither shall you go too:

Today will I set forth, tomorrow you.

Will this content you, Kate?

LADY PERCY   It must, of force.

Exeunt.

2.4   *Enter* PRINCE *and* POINS.

PRINCE   Ned, prithee come out of that fat room, and lend me thy hand to laugh a little.

POINS   Where hast been, Hal?

PRINCE   With three or four loggerheads, amongst three
5   or fourscore hogsheads. I have sounded the very basestring of humility. Sirrah, I am sworn brother to a leash of drawers, and can call them all by their christen names, as Tom, Dick, and Francis. They take it already upon their salvation, that though I be but
10   Prince of Wales, yet I am the king of courtesy, and tell me flatly I am no proud Jack like Falstaff, but a Corinthian, a lad of mettle, a good boy (by the Lord, so they call me!), and when I am King of England I shall command all the good lads in Eastcheap. They
15   call drinking deep 'dyeing scarlet', and when you breathe in your watering they cry 'Hem!' and bid you 'Play it off!' To conclude, I am so good a proficient in one quarter of an hour that I can drink with any tinker in his own language during my life. I tell thee, Ned,
20   thou hast lost much honour that thou wert not with me in this action; but, sweet Ned – to sweeten which name of Ned I give thee this pennyworth of sugar, clapped even now into my hand by an underskinker, one that never spake other English in his life than
25   'Eight shillings and sixpence', and 'You are welcome', with this shrill addition, 'Anon, anon, sir! Score a pint of bastard in the Half-moon', or so. But Ned, to drive away the time till Falstaff come: – I prithee do thou stand in some by-room, while I question my puny
30   drawer to what end he gave me the sugar, and do thou never leave calling 'Francis!', that his tale to me may be nothing but 'Anon'. Step aside, and I'll show thee a precedent. [*Poins retires.*]

POINS [*within*]   Francis!

35   PRINCE   Thou art perfect.

POINS [*within*]   Francis!

Enter FRANCIS, *a drawer.*

FRANCIS   Anon, anon, sir. Look down into the Pomgarnet, Ralph.

PRINCE   Come hither, Francis.

40   FRANCIS   My lord?

PRINCE   How long hast thou to serve, Francis?

FRANCIS   Forsooth, five years, and as much as to –

POINS [*within*]   Francis!

FRANCIS   Anon, anon, sir.

45   PRINCE   Five year! By'r lady, a long lease for the clinking

of pewter; but Francis, darest thou be so valiant as to play the coward with thy indenture, and show it a fair pair of heels, and run from it?

FRANCIS   O Lord, sir, I'll be sworn upon all the books in
England, I could find in my heart –   50

POINS [*within*]   Francis!

FRANCIS   Anon, sir.

PRINCE   How old art thou, Francis?

FRANCIS   Let me see, about Michaelmas next I shall
be –   55

POINS [*within*]   Francis!

FRANCIS   Anon, sir – pray stay a little, my lord.

PRINCE   Nay but hark you, Francis, for the sugar thou gavest me, 'twas a pennyworth, was't not?

FRANCIS   O Lord, I would it had been two!   60

PRINCE   I will give thee for it a thousand pound – ask me when thou wilt, and thou shalt have it.

POINS [*within*]   Francis!

FRANCIS   Anon, anon.

PRINCE   Anon, Francis? No, Francis, but tomorrow,   65
Francis; or, Francis, a-Thursday; or indeed, Francis, when thou wilt. But Francis!

FRANCIS   My lord?

PRINCE   Wilt thou rob this leathern-jerkin, crystal-button, not-pated, agate-ring, puke-stocking, caddis-   70
garter, smooth-tongue Spanish pouch?

FRANCIS   O Lord, sir, who do you mean?

PRINCE   Why then your brown bastard is your only drink: for look you, Francis, your white canvas doublet will sully. In Barbary, sir, it cannot come to so much.   75

FRANCIS   What, sir?

POINS [*within*]   Francis!

PRINCE   Away, you rogue, dost thou not hear them call?
[*Here they both call him; the Drawer stands amazed, not knowing which way to go.*]

Enter Vintner.

VINTNER   What, stand'st thou still and hear'st such a calling? Look to the guests within.   *Exit Francis.*   80
My lord, old Sir John with half-a-dozen more are at the door – shall I let them in?

PRINCE   Let them alone awhile, and then open the door.

Exit Vintner.

Poins!

Re-enter POINS.

POINS   Anon, anon, sir.   85

PRINCE   Sirrah, Falstaff and the rest of the thieves are at the door; shall we be merry?

POINS   As merry as crickets, my lad; but hark ye, what cunning match have you made with this jest of the drawer: come, what's the issue?   90

PRINCE   I am now of all humours that have showed themselves humours since the old days of goodman Adam to the pupil age of this present twelve o'clock at midnight.

Re-enter FRANCIS.

What's o'clock, Francis?

FRANCIS Anon, anon, sir.   *Exit.*

PRINCE   That ever this fellow should have fewer words
than a parrot, and yet the son of a woman! His
industry is up-stairs and down-stairs, his eloquence
the parcel of a reckoning. I am not yet of Percy's mind,
the Hotspur of the north, he that kills me some six or
seven dozen of Scots at a breakfast, washes his hands,
and says to his wife, 'Fie upon this quiet life, I want
work'. 'O my sweet Harry', says she, 'how many hast
thou killed today?' 'Give my roan horse a drench', says
he, and answers, 'Some fourteen', an hour after; 'a
trifle, a trifle'. I prithee call in Falstaff; I'll play Percy,
and that damned brawn shall play Dame Mortimer his
wife. *Rivo!* says the drunkard: call in Ribs, call in
Tallow.

Enter FALSTAFF, GADSHILL, BARDOLPH *and* PETO;
followed by FRANCIS, *with wine.*

POINS   Welcome, Jack, where hast thou been?

FALSTAFF   A plague of all cowards, I say, and a
vengeance too, marry and amen! Give me a cup of
sack, boy. Ere I lead this life long, I'll sew nether-
stocks, and mend them and foot them too. A plague of
all cowards! Give me a cup of sack, rogue; is there no
virtue extant? [*He drinketh.*]

PRINCE   Didst thou never see Titan kiss a dish of butter
(pitiful-hearted Titan!), that melted at the sweet tale
of the sun's? If thou didst, then behold that
compound.

FALSTAFF   You rogue, here's lime in this sack too: there
is nothing but roguery to be found in villainous man,
yet a coward is worse than a cup of sack with lime in
it. A villainous coward! Go thy ways, old Jack, die
when thou wilt – if manhood, good manhood, be not
forgot upon the face of the earth, then am I a shotten
herring: there lives not three good men unhanged in
England, and one of them is fat, and grows old, God
help the while, a bad world I say. I would I were a
weaver; I could sing psalms, or anything. A plague of
all cowards, I say still.

PRINCE   How now, wool-sack, what mutter you?

FALSTAFF   A king's son! If I do not beat thee out of thy
kingdom with a dagger of lath, and drive all thy
subjects afore thee like a flock of wild geese, I'll never
wear hair on my face more. You, Prince of Wales!

PRINCE   Why, you whoreson round man, what's the
matter?

FALSTAFF   Are not you a coward? Answer me to that –
and Poins there?

POINS   'Zounds, ye fat paunch, and ye call me coward by
the Lord I'll stab thee.

FALSTAFF   I call thee coward? I'll see thee damned ere I
call thee coward, but I would give a thousand pound I
could run as fast as thou canst. You are straight

enough in the shoulders, you care not who sees your
back: call you that backing of your friends? A plague
upon such backing, give me them that will face me!
Give me a cup of sack: I am a rogue if I drunk today.   150

PRINCE   O villain! Thy lips are scarce wiped since thou
drunk'st last.

FALSTAFF   All is one for that. [*He drinketh.*] A plague
of all cowards, still say I.

PRINCE   What's the matter?   155

FALSTAFF   What's the matter? There be four of us here
have ta'en a thousand pound this day morning.

PRINCE   Where is it, Jack, where is it?

FALSTAFF   Where is it? Taken from us it is: a hundred
upon poor four of us.   160

PRINCE   What, a hundred, man?

FALSTAFF   I am a rogue if I were not at half-sword with
a dozen of them two hours together. I have scaped by
miracle. I am eight times thrust through the doublet,
four through the hose, my buckler cut through and   165
through, my sword hacked like a handsaw – *ecce
signum!* I never dealt better since I was a man: all
would not do. A plague of all cowards! Let them speak
– if they speak more or less than truth, they are
villains, and the sons of darkness.   170

PRINCE   Speak, sirs, how was it?

GADSHILL   We four set upon some dozen –

FALSTAFF   Sixteen at least, my lord.

GADSHILL   And bound them.

PETO   No, no, they were not bound.   175

FALSTAFF   You rogue, they were bound, every man of
them, or I am a Jew else: an Ebrew Jew.

GADSHILL   As we were sharing, some six or seven fresh
men set upon us –

FALSTAFF   And unbound the rest, and then come in the   180
other.

PRINCE   What, fought you with them all?

FALSTAFF   All? I know not what you call all, but if I
fought not with fifty of them I am a bunch of radish:
if there were not two or three and fifty upon poor old   185
Jack, then am I no two-legg'd creature.

PRINCE   Pray God you have not murdered some of them.

FALSTAFF   Nay, that's past praying for, I have peppered
two of them. Two I am sure I have paid, two rogues in
buckram suits. I tell thee what, Hal, if I tell thee a lie,   190
spit in my face, call me horse. Thou knowest my old
ward – here I lay, and thus I bore my point. Four
rogues in buckram let drive at me –

PRINCE   What, four? Thou saidst but two even now.

FALSTAFF   Four, Hal, I told thee four.   195

POINS   Ay, ay, he said four.

FALSTAFF   These four came all afront, and mainly thrust
at me; I made me no more ado, but took all their seven
points in my target, thus!

PRINCE   Seven? Why, there were but four even now.   200

FALSTAFF   In buckram?

POINS   Ay, four, in buckram suits.

FALSTAFF   Seven, by these hilts, or I am a villain else.

PRINCE   Prithee let him alone, we shall have more anon.

205   FALSTAFF   Dost thou hear me, Hal?

PRINCE   Ay, and mark thee too, Jack.

FALSTAFF   Do so, for it is worth the listening to. These nine in buckram that I told thee of –

PRINCE   So, two more already.

210   FALSTAFF   Their points being broken –

POINS   Down fell their hose.

FALSTAFF   Began to give me ground; but I followed me close, came in, foot and hand, and, with a thought, seven of the eleven I paid.

215   PRINCE   O monstrous! Eleven buckram men grown out of two!

FALSTAFF   But as the devil would have it, three misbegotten knaves in Kendal green came at my back and let drive at me, for it was so dark, Hal, that thou couldst not see thy hand.

220   PRINCE   These lies are like their father that begets them, gross as a mountain, open, palpable. Why, thou clay-brained guts, thou knotty-pated fool, thou whoreson obscene greasy tallow-catch, –

225   FALSTAFF   What, art thou mad? art thou mad? Is not the truth the truth?

PRINCE   Why, how couldst thou know these men in Kendal green when it was so dark thou couldst not see thy hand? Come, tell us your reason. What sayest thou

230   to this?

POINS   Come, your reason, Jack, your reason.

FALSTAFF   What, upon compulsion? 'Zounds, and I were at the strappado, or all the racks in the world, I would not tell you on compulsion. Give you a reason

235   on compulsion? If reasons were as plentiful as blackberries, I would give no man a reason upon compulsion, I.

PRINCE   I'll be no longer guilty of this sin. This sanguine coward, this bed-presser, this horse-back-breaker, this

240   huge hill of flesh, –

FALSTAFF   'Sblood, you starveling, you eel-skin, you dried neat's-tongue, you bull's-pizzle, you stock-fish – O for breath to utter what is like thee! – you tailor's-yard, you sheath, you bow-case, you vile standing

245   tuck!

PRINCE   Well, breathe awhile, and then to it again, and when thou hast tired thyself in base comparisons hear me speak but this.

POINS   Mark, Jack.

250   PRINCE   We two saw you four set on four, and bound them and were masters of their wealth – mark now how a plain tale shall put you down. Then did we two set on you four, and, with a word, out-faced you from your prize, and have it, yea, and can show it you here

255   in the house: and Falstaff you carried your guts away as nimbly, with as quick dexterity, and roared for mercy, and still run and roared, as ever I heard bull-calf. What a slave art thou to hack thy sword as thou hast done, and then say it was in fight! What trick,

260   what device, what starting-hole canst thou now find out, to hide thee from this open and apparent shame?

POINS   Come, let's hear, Jack, what trick hast thou now?

FALSTAFF   By the Lord, I knew ye as well as he that made ye. Why, hear you, my masters, was it for me to kill the heir-apparent? should I turn upon the true   265 prince? Why, thou knowest I am as valiant as Hercules: but beware instinct – the lion will not touch the true prince; instinct is a great matter. I was now a coward on instinct: I shall think the better of myself, and thee, during my life – I for a valiant lion, and thou   270 for a true prince. But by the Lord, lads, I am glad you have the money. Hostess, clap to the doors! Watch tonight, pray tomorrow! – Gallants, lads, boys, hearts of gold, all the titles of good fellowship come to you! What, shall we be merry, shall we have a play   275 extempore?

PRINCE   Content, and the argument shall be thy running away.

FALSTAFF   Ah, no more of that, Hal, and thou lovest me.

Enter Hostess.

HOSTESS   O Jesu, my lord the Prince!   280

PRINCE   How now, my lady the hostess, what say'st thou to me?

HOSTESS   Marry, my lord, there is a nobleman of the court at door would speak with you: he says he comes from your father.   285

PRINCE   Give him as much as will make him a royal man, and send him back again to my mother.

FALSTAFF   What manner of man is he?

HOSTESS   An old man.

FALSTAFF   What doth gravity out of his bed at   290 midnight? Shall I give him his answer?

PRINCE   Prithee do, Jack.

FALSTAFF   Faith, and I'll send him packing.   *Exit.*

PRINCE   Now, sirs: by'r lady, you fought fair, so did you, Peto, so did you, Bardolph; you are lions too, you ran   295 away upon instinct, you will not touch the true prince, no, fie!

BARDOLPH   Faith, I ran when I saw others run.

PRINCE   Faith, tell me now in earnest, how came Falstaff's sword so hacked?   300

PETO   Why, he hacked it with his dagger, and said he would swear truth out of England but he would make you believe it was done in fight, and persuaded us to do the like.

BARDOLPH   Yea, and to tickle our noses with spear-grass,   305 to make them bleed, and then to beslubber our garments with it, and swear it was the blood of true men. I did that I did not this seven year before, I blushed to hear his monstrous devices.

PRINCE   O villain, thou stolest a cup of sack eighteen   310 years ago, and wert taken with the manner, and ever since thou hast blushed extempore. Thou hadst fire and sword on thy side, and yet thou ran'st away – what instinct hadst thou for it?

BARDOLPH   My lord, do you see these meteors? do you behold these exhalations?

PRINCE   I do.

BARDOLPH   What think you they portend?

PRINCE   Hot livers, and cold purses.

BARDOLPH   Choler, my lord, if rightly taken.

PRINCE   No, if rightly taken, halter.

Re-enter FALSTAFF.

Here comes lean Jack, here comes bare-bone. How now, my sweet creature of bombast, how long is't ago, Jack, since thou sawest thine own knee?

FALSTAFF   My own knee? When I was about thy years, Hal, I was not an eagle's talon in the waist, I could have crept into any alderman's thumb-ring: a plague of sighing and grief, it blows a man up like a bladder. There's villainous news abroad: here was Sir John Bracy from your father; you must to the court in the morning. That same mad fellow of the north, Percy, and he of Wales that gave Amamon the bastinado, and made Lucifer cuckold, and swore the devil his true liegeman upon the cross of a Welsh hook – what a plague call you him?

POINS   O, Glendower.

FALSTAFF   Owen, Owen, the same; and his son-in-law Mortimer, and old Northumberland, and that sprightly Scot of Scots, Douglas, that runs a-horseback up a hill perpendicular –

PRINCE   He that rides at high speed, and with his pistol kills a sparrow flying.

FALSTAFF   You have hit it.

PRINCE   So did he never the sparrow.

FALSTAFF   Well, that rascal hath good mettle in him, he will not run.

PRINCE   Why, what a rascal art thou then, to praise him so for running!

FALSTAFF   A-horseback, ye cuckoo, but afoot he will not budge a foot.

PRINCE   Yes, Jack, upon instinct.

FALSTAFF   I grant ye, upon instinct: well, he is there too, and one Mordake, and a thousand blue-caps more. Worcester is stolen away tonight; thy father's beard is turned white with the news; you may buy land now as cheap as stinking mackerel.

PRINCE   Why then, it is like if there come a hot June, and this civil buffeting hold, we shall buy maidenheads as they buy hob-nails, by the hundreds.

FALSTAFF   By the mass, lad, thou sayest true, it is like we shall have good trading that way. But tell me, Hal, art not thou horrible afeard? Thou being heir apparent, could the world pick thee out three such enemies again, as that fiend Douglas, that spirit Percy, and that devil Glendower? Art thou not horribly afraid? Doth not thy blood thrill at it?

PRINCE   Not a whit, i'faith, I lack some of thy instinct.

FALSTAFF   Well, thou wilt be horribly chid tomorrow when thou comest to thy father; if thou love me practise an answer.

PRINCE   Do thou stand for my father and examine me upon the particulars of my life.

FALSTAFF   Shall I? Content! This chair shall be my state, this dagger my sceptre, and this cushion my crown.

PRINCE   Thy state is taken for a joint-stool, thy golden sceptre for a leaden dagger, and thy precious rich crown for a pitiful bald crown.

FALSTAFF   Well, and the fire of grace be not quite out of thee, now shalt thou be moved. Give me a cup of sack to make my eyes look red, that it may be thought I have wept, for I must speak in passion, and I will do it in King Cambyses' vein.

PRINCE   Well, here is my leg.

FALSTAFF   And here is my speech. Stand aside, nobility.

HOSTESS   O Jesu, this is excellent sport, i'faith.

FALSTAFF
Weep not, sweet Queen, for trickling tears are vain.

HOSTESS   O the Father, how he holds his countenance!

FALSTAFF
For God's sake, lords, convey my tristful Queen,
For tears do stop the floodgates of her eyes.

HOSTESS   O Jesu, he doth it as like one of these harlotry players as ever I see!

FALSTAFF   Peace, good pint-pot, peace, good tickle-brain. – Harry, I do not only marvel where thou spendest thy time, but also how thou art accompanied. For though the camomile, the more it is trodden on the faster it grows, yet youth, the more it is wasted the sooner it wears. That thou art my son I have partly thy mother's word, partly my own opinion, but chiefly a villainous trick of thine eye, and a foolish hanging of thy nether lip, that doth warrant me. If then thou be son to me, here lies the point – why, being son to me, art thou so pointed at? Shall the blessed sun of heaven prove a micher, and eat blackberries? A question not to be asked. Shall the son of England prove a thief, and take purses? A question to be asked. There is a thing, Harry, which thou hast often heard of, and it is known to many in our land by the name of pitch. This pitch (as ancient writers do report) doth defile, so doth the company thou keepest: for, Harry, now I do not speak to thee in drink, but in tears; not in pleasure, but in passion; not in words only, but in woes also. And yet there is a virtuous man whom I have often noted in thy company, but I know not his name.

PRINCE   What manner of man, and it like your Majesty?

FALSTAFF   A goodly portly man, i'faith, and a corpulent; of a cheerful look, a pleasing eye, and a most noble carriage; and, as I think, his age some fifty, or by'r lady inclining to threescore; and now I remember me, his name is Falstaff. If that man should be lewdly given, he deceiveth me; for, Harry, I see virtue in his looks. If then the tree may be known by the fruit, as the fruit by the tree, then peremptorily I speak it, there is virtue in that Falstaff; him keep with, the rest banish. And tell me now, thou naughty varlet, tell me where hast thou been this month?

PRINCE   Dost thou speak like a king? Do thou stand for me, and I'll play my father.

FALSTAFF   Depose me? If thou dost it half so gravely, so majestically, both in word and matter, hang me up by the heels for a rabbit-sucker, or a poulter's hare.

PRINCE   Well, here I am set.

FALSTAFF   And here I stand. Judge, my masters.

PRINCE   Now, Harry, whence come you?

FALSTAFF   My noble lord, from Eastcheap.

PRINCE   The complaints I hear of thee are grievous.

FALSTAFF   'Sblood, my lord, they are false: nay, I'll tickle ye for a young prince, i'faith.

PRINCE   Swearest thou, ungracious boy? Henceforth ne'er look on me. Thou art violently carried away from grace, there is a devil haunts thee in the likeness of an old fat man, a tun of man is thy companion. Why dost thou converse with that trunk of humours, that bolting-hutch of beastliness, that swollen parcel of dropsies, that huge bombard of sack, that stuffed cloak-bag of guts, that roasted Manningtree ox with the pudding in his belly, that reverend vice, that grey iniquity, that father ruffian, that vanity in years? Wherein is he good, but to taste sack and drink it? wherein neat and cleanly, but to carve a capon and eat it? wherein cunning, but in craft? wherein crafty, but in villainy? wherein villainous, but in all things? wherein worthy, but in nothing?

FALSTAFF   I would your Grace would take me with you: whom means your Grace?

PRINCE   That villainous abominable misleader of youth, Falstaff, that old white-bearded Satan.

FALSTAFF   My lord, the man I know.

PRINCE   I know thou dost.

FALSTAFF   But to say I know more harm in him than in myself were to say more than I know. That he is old, the more the pity, his white hairs do witness it, but that he is, saving your reverence, a whoremaster, that I utterly deny. If sack and sugar be a fault, God help the wicked! If to be old and merry be a sin, then many an old host that I know is damned: if to be fat be to be hated, then Pharaoh's lean kine are to be loved. No, my good lord; banish Peto, banish Bardolph, banish Poins – but for sweet Jack Falstaff, kind Jack Falstaff, true Jack Falstaff, valiant Jack Falstaff, and therefore more valiant, being as he is old Jack Falstaff, banish not him thy Harry's company, banish not him thy Harry's company, banish plump Jack, and banish all the world.

PRINCE   I do, I will.

[*A knocking heard.*]

Exeunt Hostess, Francis and Bardolph.

Re-enter BARDOLPH, *running.*

BARDOLPH   O my lord, my lord, the sheriff with a most monstrous watch is at the door.

FALSTAFF   Out, ye rogue! Play out the play! I have much to say in the behalf of that Falstaff.

Re-enter the Hostess.

HOSTESS   O Jesu, my lord, my lord!

PRINCE   Heigh, heigh, the devil rides upon a fiddle-stick, what's the matter?

HOSTESS   The sheriff and all the watch are at the door; they are come to search the house. Shall I let them in?

FALSTAFF   Dost thou hear, Hal? Never call a true piece of gold a counterfeit: thou art essentially made without seeming so.

PRINCE   And thou a natural coward without instinct.

FALSTAFF   I deny your major. If you will deny the sheriff, so; if not, let him enter. If I become not a cart as well as another man, a plague on my bringing up! I hope I shall as soon be strangled with a halter as another.

PRINCE   Go hide thee behind the arras, the rest walk up above. Now, my masters, for a true face, and good conscience.

FALSTAFF   Both which I have had, but their date is out, and therefore I'll hide me.

Exeunt all but the Prince and Peto.

PRINCE   Call in the sheriff.

Enter Sheriff *and the* Carrier.

Now, master sheriff, what is your will with me?

SHERIFF   First, pardon me, my lord. A hue and cry
Hath follow'd certain men unto this house.

PRINCE   What men?

SHERIFF   One of them is well known, my gracious lord,
A gross fat man.

1 CARRIER   As fat as butter.

PRINCE   The man I do assure you is not here,
For I myself at this time have employ'd him:
And sheriff, I will engage my word to thee,
That I will by tomorrow dinner-time
Send him to answer thee, or any man,
For anything he shall be charg'd withal;
And so let me entreat you leave the house.

SHERIFF   I will, my lord: there are two gentlemen
Have in this robbery lost three hundred marks.

PRINCE   It may be so: if he have robb'd these men
He shall be answerable; and so, farewell.

SHERIFF   Good night, my noble lord.

PRINCE   I think it is good morrow, is it not?

SHERIFF   Indeed, my lord, I think it be two o'clock.

Exit, with Carrier.

PRINCE   This oily rascal is known as well as Paul's: go call him forth.

PETO   Falstaff! – Fast asleep behind the arras, and snorting like a horse.

PRINCE   Hark how hard he fetches breath – search his
pockets. [*He searcheth his pockets, and findeth certain
papers.*] What hast thou found?

PETO   Nothing but papers, my lord.

PRINCE   Let's see what they be, read them.

PETO [*Reads.*]

Item a capon . . .	2s. 2d.	
Item sauce . . .	4d.	
Item sack two gallons . .	5s. 8d.	
Item anchovies and sack after supper	2s. 6d.	
Item bread . . .	ob.	

PRINCE   O monstrous! but one halfpennyworth of bread
to this intolerable deal of sack? What there is else keep
close, we'll read it at more advantage. There let him
sleep till day; I'll to the court in the morning. We must
all to the wars, and thy place shall be honourable. I'll
procure this fat rogue a charge of foot, and I know his
death will be a march of twelve score. The money shall
be paid back again with advantage. Be with me
betimes in the morning; and so, good morrow, Peto.

PETO   Good morrow, good my lord.   *Exeunt.*

3.1   *Enter* HOTSPUR, WORCESTER,
               LORD MORTIMER, OWEN GLENDOWER.

MORTIMER   These promises are fair, the parties sure,
And our induction full of prosperous hope.

HOTSPUR
Lord Mortimer, and cousin Glendower, will you sit
    down?
And uncle Worcester. A plague upon it!
I have forgot the map.

GLENDOWER   No, here it is:
Sit, cousin Percy, sit, good cousin Hotspur;
For by that name as oft as Lancaster doth speak of
    you
His cheek looks pale, and with a rising sigh
He wisheth you in heaven.

HOTSPUR   And you in hell,
As oft as he hears Owen Glendower spoke of.

GLENDOWER   I cannot blame him; at my nativity
The front of heaven was full of fiery shapes,
Of burning cressets, and at my birth
The frame and huge foundation of the earth
Shak'd like a coward.

HOTSPUR   Why, so it would have done
At the same season if your mother's cat
Had but kitten'd, though yourself had never been
    born.

GLENDOWER
I say the earth did shake when I was born.

HOTSPUR   And I say the earth was not of my mind,
If you suppose as fearing you it shook.

GLENDOWER
The heavens were all on fire, the earth did tremble –

HOTSPUR
O, then the earth shook to see the heavens on fire,
And not in fear of your nativity.

Diseased nature oftentimes breaks forth
In strange eruptions, oft the teeming earth
Is with a kind of colic pinch'd and vex'd
By the imprisoning of unruly wind
Within her womb, which for enlargement striving
Shakes the old beldam earth, and topples down
Steeples and moss-grown towers. At your birth
Our grandam earth, having this distemp'rature,
In passion shook.

GLENDOWER   Cousin, of many men
I do not bear these crossings; give me leave
To tell you once again that at my birth
The front of heaven was full of fiery shapes,
The goats ran from the mountains, and the herds
Were strangely clamorous to the frighted fields.
These signs have mark'd me extraordinary,
And all the courses of my life do show
I am not in the roll of common men.
Where is he living, clipp'd in with the sea
That chides the banks of England, Scotland, Wales,
Which calls me pupil or hath read to me?
And bring him out that is but woman's son
Can trace me in the tedious ways of art,
And hold me pace in deep experiments.

HOTSPUR   I think there's no man speaks better Welsh:
I'll to dinner.

MORTIMER
Peace, cousin Percy, you will make him mad.

GLENDOWER   I can call spirits from the vasty deep.

HOTSPUR   Why, so can I, or so can any man,
But will they come when you do call for them?

GLENDOWER
Why, I can teach you, cousin, to command the devil.

HOTSPUR
And I can teach thee, coz, to shame the devil,
By telling truth; tell truth, and shame the devil.
If thou have power to raise him, bring him hither,
And I'll be sworn I have power to shame him hence:
O, while you live, tell truth, and shame the devil!

MORTIMER
Come, come, no more of this unprofitable chat.

GLENDOWER
Three times hath Henry Bolingbroke made head
Against my power, thrice from the banks of Wye
And sandy-bottom'd Severn have I sent him
Bootless home, and weather-beaten back.

HOTSPUR
Home without boots, and in foul weather too!
How scapes he agues, in the devil's name?

GLENDOWER
Come, here is the map, shall we divide our right
According to our threefold order ta'en?

MORTIMER   The Archdeacon hath divided it
Into three limits very equally:
England, from Trent and Severn hitherto,
By south and east is to my part assign'd:
All westward, Wales beyond the Severn shore,

And all the fertile land within that bound,
To Owen Glendower: and, dear coz, to you
75 The remnant northward lying off from Trent.
And our indentures tripartite are drawn,
Which being sealed interchangeably,
(A business that this night may execute)
Tomorrow, cousin Percy, you and I
80 And my good Lord of Worcester will set forth
To meet your father and the Scottish power,
As is appointed us, at Shrewsbury.
My father Glendower is not ready yet,
Nor shall we need his help these fourteen days.
[*to Glendower*] Within that space you may have drawn
85   together
Your tenants, friends, and neighbouring gentlemen.

GLENDOWER
A shorter time shall send me to you, lords,
And in my conduct shall your ladies come,
From whom you now must steal and take no leave,
90 For there will be a world of water shed
Upon the parting of your wives and you.

HOTSPUR
Methinks my moiety, north from Burton here,
In quantity equals not one of yours:
See how this river comes me cranking in,
95 And cuts me from the best of all my land
A huge half-moon, a monstrous cantle out.
I'll have the current in this place damm'd up,
And here the smug and silver Trent shall run
In a new channel fair and evenly;
100 It shall not wind with such a deep indent,
To rob me of so rich a bottom here.

GLENDOWER
Not wind? It shall, it must – you see it doth.

MORTIMER   Yea,
But mark how he bears his course, and runs me up
105 With like advantage on the other side,
Gelding the opposed continent as much
As on the other side it takes from you.

WORCESTER
Yea, but a little charge will trench him here,
And on this north side win this cape of land,
110 And then he runs straight and even.

HOTSPUR   I'll have it so, a little charge will do it.

GLENDOWER   I'll not have it alter'd.

HOTSPUR   Will not you?

GLENDOWER   No, nor you shall not.

HOTSPUR   Who shall say me nay?

GLENDOWER   Why, that will I.

HOTSPUR
115 Let me not understand you then, speak it in Welsh.

GLENDOWER   I can speak English, lord, as well as you,
For I was train'd up in the English court,
Where being but young I framed to the harp
Many an English ditty lovely well,
120 And gave the tongue a helpful ornament –
A virtue that was never seen in you.

HOTSPUR   Marry and I am glad of it with all my heart!
I had rather be a kitten and cry 'mew'
Than one of these same metre ballad-mongers;
125 I had rather hear a brazen canstick turn'd,
Or a dry wheel grate on the axle-tree,
And that would set my teeth nothing on edge,
Nothing so much as mincing poetry –
'Tis like the forc'd gait of a shuffling nag.

GLENDOWER   Come, you shall have Trent turn'd. 130

HOTSPUR   I do not care, I'll give thrice so much land
To any well-deserving friend:
But in the way of bargain, mark ye me,
I'll cavil on the ninth part of a hair.
Are the indentures drawn? Shall we be gone? 135

GLENDOWER
The moon shines fair, you may away by night:
I'll haste the writer, and withal
Break with your wives of your departure hence.
I am afraid my daughter will run mad,
So much she doteth on her Mortimer.   *Exit.* 140

MORTIMER   Fie, cousin Percy, how you cross my father!

HOTSPUR   I cannot choose; sometime he angers me
With telling me of the moldwarp and the ant,
Of the dreamer Merlin and his prophecies,
And of a dragon and a finless fish, 145
A clip-wing'd griffin and a moulten raven,
A couching lion and a ramping cat,
And such a deal of skimble-skamble stuff
As puts me from my faith. I tell you what –
He held me last night at least nine hours 150
In reckoning up the several devils' names
That were his lackeys: I cried 'Hum', and 'Well, go
    to!'
But mark'd him not a word. O, he is as tedious
As a tired horse, a railing wife,
Worse than a smoky house. I had rather live 155
With cheese and garlic in a windmill, far,
Than feed on cates and have him talk to me
In any summer house in Christendom.

MORTIMER   In faith, he is a worthy gentleman,
Exceedingly well read, and profited 160
In strange concealments, valiant as a lion,
And wondrous affable, and as bountiful
As mines of India. Shall I tell you, cousin?
He holds your temper in a high respect
And curbs himself even of his natural scope 165
When you come 'cross his humour, faith he does:
I warrant you that man is not alive
Might so have tempted him as you have done
Without the taste of danger and reproof:
But do not use it oft, let me entreat you. 170

WORCESTER
In faith, my lord, you are too wilful-blame,
And since your coming hither have done enough
To put him quite besides his patience;
You must needs learn, lord, to amend this fault.
Though sometimes it show greatness, courage, blood, 175

– And that's the dearest grace it renders you –
Yet oftentimes it doth present harsh rage,
Defect of manners, want of government,
Pride, haughtiness, opinion, and disdain,
The least of which haunting a nobleman
Loseth men's hearts and leaves behind a stain
Upon the beauty of all parts besides,
Beguiling them of commendation.

HOTSPUR
Well, I am school'd – good manners be your speed!
Here come our wives, and let us take our leave.

Re-enter GLENDOWER *with the* Ladies.

MORTIMER   This is the deadly spite that angers me,
My wife can speak no English, I no Welsh.

GLENDOWER
My daughter weeps, she'll not part with you,
She'll be a soldier too, she'll to the wars.

MORTIMER
Good father, tell her that she and my aunt Percy
Shall follow in your conduct speedily.
[*Glendower speaks to her in Welsh, and she answers him
in the same.*]

GLENDOWER
She is desperate here, a peevish, self-willed harlotry,
one that no persuasion can do good upon.
[*The lady speaks in Welsh.*]

MORTIMER   I understand thy looks, that pretty Welsh
Which thou pourest down from these swelling
    heavens
I am too perfect in, and but for shame
In such a parley should I answer thee.
[*The lady speaks again in Welsh.*]
I understand thy kisses, and thou mine,
And that's a feeling disputation,
But I will never be a truant, love,
Till I have learnt thy language, for thy tongue
Makes Welsh as sweet as ditties highly penn'd,
Sung by a fair queen in a summer's bow'r
With ravishing division to her lute.

GLENDOWER   Nay, if you melt, then will she run mad.
[*The lady speaks again in Welsh.*]

MORTIMER   O, I am ignorance itself in this!

GLENDOWER
She bids you on the wanton rushes lay you down,
And rest your gentle head upon her lap,
And she will sing the song that pleaseth you,
And on your eyelids crown the god of sleep,
Charming your blood with pleasing heaviness,
Making such difference 'twixt wake and sleep
As is the difference betwixt day and night,
The hour before the heavenly-harness'd team
Begins his golden progress in the east.

MORTIMER   With all my heart I'll sit and hear her sing,
By that time will our book I think be drawn.

GLENDOWER
Do so, and those musicians that shall play to you

Hang in the air a thousand leagues from hence,
And straight they shall be here: sit, and attend.   220

HOTSPUR   Come, Kate, thou art perfect in lying down:
Come, quick, quick, that I may lay my head in thy
    lap.

LADY PERCY   Go, ye giddy goose.   [*The music plays.*]

HOTSPUR   Now I perceive the devil understands Welsh,
And 'tis no marvel he is so humorous,   225
By'r lady, he is a good musician.

LADY PERCY   Then should you be nothing but musical,
For you are altogether govern'd by humours.
Lie still, ye thief, and hear the lady sing in Welsh.

HOTSPUR
I had rather hear Lady my brach howl in Irish.   230

LADY PERCY   Wouldst thou have thy head broken?

HOTSPUR   No.

LADY PERCY   Then be still.

HOTSPUR   Neither, 'tis a woman's fault.

LADY PERCY   Now God help thee!   235

HOTSPUR   To the Welsh lady's bed.

LADY PERCY   What's that?

HOTSPUR   Peace, she sings.
             [*Here the lady sings a Welsh song.*]
Come, Kate, I'll have your song too.

LADY PERCY   Not mine, in good sooth.   240

HOTSPUR   Not yours, in good sooth! Heart, you swear
like a comfit-maker's wife – 'Not you, in good sooth!',
and 'As true as I live!', and 'As God shall mend me!',
and 'As sure as day!' –
And givest such sarcenet surety for thy oaths   245
As if thou never walk'st further than Finsbury.
Swear me, Kate, like a lady as thou art,
A good mouth-filling oath, and leave 'In sooth',
And such protest of pepper-gingerbread,
To velvet-guards, and Sunday citizens.   250
Come, sing.

LADY PERCY   I will not sing.

HOTSPUR   'Tis the next way to turn tailor, or be
redbreast teacher. And the indentures be drawn I'll
away within these two hours; and so come in when ye   255
will.   *Exit.*

GLENDOWER
Come, come, Lord Mortimer, you are as slow
As hot Lord Percy is on fire to go:
By this our book is drawn – we'll but seal,
And then to horse immediately.

MORTIMER   With all my heart.   260
                                          Exeunt.

3.2   *Enter the* KING, PRINCE OF WALES *and others.*

KING   Lords, give us leave; the Prince of Wales and I
Must have some private conference: but be near at
    hand,
For we shall presently have need of you.
                                 Exeunt lords.
I know not whether God will have it so

5 For some displeasing service I have done,
That in his secret doom out of my blood
He'll breed revengement and a scourge for me;
But thou dost in thy passages of life
Make me believe that thou art only mark'd
10 For the hot vengeance and the rod of heaven,
To punish my mistreadings. Tell me else
Could such inordinate and low desires,
Such poor, such bare, such lewd, such mean
    attempts,
Such barren pleasures, rude society,
15 As thou art match'd withal, and grafted to,
Accompany the greatness of thy blood,
And hold their level with thy princely heart?

PRINCE So please your Majesty, I would I could
Quit all offences with as clear excuse
20 As well as I am doubtless I can purge
Myself of many I am charg'd withal:
Yet such extenuation let me beg
As, in reproof of many tales devis'd,
Which oft the ear of greatness needs must hear,
25 By smiling pickthanks, and base newsmongers,
I may for some things true, wherein my youth
Hath faulty wander'd and irregular,
Find pardon on my true submission.

KING God pardon thee! Yet let me wonder, Harry,
30 At thy affections, which do hold a wing
Quite from the flight of all thy ancestors.
Thy place in Council thou hast rudely lost,
Which by thy younger brother is supply'd,
And art almost an alien to the hearts
35 Of all the court and princes of my blood:
The hope and expectation of thy time
Is ruin'd, and the soul of every man
Prophetically do forethink thy fall.
Had I so lavish of my presence been,
40 So common-hackney'd in the eyes of men,
So stale and cheap to vulgar company,
Opinion, that did help me to the crown,
Had still kept loyal to possession,
And left me in reputeless banishment,
45 A fellow of no mark nor likelihood.
By being seldom seen, I could not stir
But like a comet I was wonder'd at,
That men would tell their children, 'This is he!'
Others would say, 'Where, which is Bolingbroke?'
50 And then I stole all courtesy from heaven,
And dress'd myself in such humility
That I did pluck allegiance from men's hearts,
Loud shouts and salutations from their mouths,
Even in the presence of the crowned King.
55 Thus did I keep my person fresh and new,
My presence, like a robe pontifical,
Ne'er seen but wonder'd at, and so my state,
Seldom, but sumptuous, show'd like a feast,
And wan by rareness such solemnity.
60 The skipping King, he ambled up and down,

With shallow jesters, and rash bavin wits,
Soon kindled and soon burnt, carded his state,
Mingled his royalty with cap'ring fools,
Had his great name profaned with their scorns,
And gave his countenance against his name 65
To laugh at gibing boys, and stand the push
Of every beardless vain comparative,
Grew a companion to the common streets,
Enfeoff'd himself to popularity,
That, being daily swallow'd by men's eyes, 70
They surfeited with honey, and began
To loathe the taste of sweetness, whereof a little
More than a little is by much too much.
So, when he had occasion to be seen,
He was but as the cuckoo is in June, 75
Heard, not regarded; seen, but with such eyes
As, sick and blunted with community,
Afford no extraordinary gaze,
Such as is bent on sun-like majesty
When it shines seldom in admiring eyes, 80
But rather drows'd and hung their eyelids down,
Slept in his face, and render'd such aspect
As cloudy men use to their adversaries,
Being with his presence glutted, gorg'd, and full.
And in that very line, Harry, standest thou, 85
For thou hast lost thy princely privilege
With vile participation. Not an eye
But is a-weary of thy common sight,
Save mine, which hath desir'd to see thee more,
Which now doth that I would not have it do, 90
Make blind itself with foolish tenderness.

PRINCE I shall hereafter, my thrice gracious lord,
Be more myself.

KING   For all the world
As thou art to this hour was Richard then
When I from France set foot at Ravenspurgh, 95
And even as I was then is Percy now.
Now by my sceptre, and my soul to boot,
He hath more worthy interest to the state
Than thou the shadow of succession.
For of no right, nor colour like to right, 100
He doth fill fields with harness in the realm,
Turns head against the lion's armed jaws,
And being no more in debt to years than thou
Leads ancient lords and reverend bishops on
To bloody battles, and to bruising arms. 105
What never-dying honour hath he got
Against renowned Douglas! whose high deeds,
Whose hot incursions and great name in arms,
Holds from all soldiers chief majority
And military title capital 110
Through all the kingdoms that acknowledge Christ.
Thrice hath this Hotspur, Mars in swathling clothes,
This infant warrior, in his enterprises
Discomfited great Douglas, ta'en him once,
Enlarged him, and made a friend of him, 115
To fill the mouth of deep defiance up,

And shake the peace and safety of our throne.
And what say you to this? Percy, Northumberland,
The Archbishop's Grace of York, Douglas,
   Mortimer,
20 Capitulate against us and are up.
But wherefore do I tell these news to thee?
Why, Harry, do I tell thee of my foes,
Which art my nearest and dearest enemy?
Thou that art like enough, through vassal fear,
25 Base inclination, and the start of spleen,
To fight against me under Percy's pay,
To dog his heels, and curtsy at his frowns,
To show how much thou art degenerate.
PRINCE   Do not think so, you shall not find it so;
30 And God forgive them that so much have sway'd
Your Majesty's good thoughts away from me!
I will redeem all this on Percy's head,
And in the closing of some glorious day
Be bold to tell you that I am your son,
35 When I will wear a garment all of blood,
And stain my favours in a bloody mask,
Which, wash'd away, shall scour my shame with it;
And that shall be the day, whene'er it lights,
That this same child of honour and renown,
40 This gallant Hotspur, this all-praised knight,
And your unthought-of Harry chance to meet.
For every honour sitting on his helm,
Would they were multitudes, and on my head
My shames redoubled! For the time will come
45 That I shall make this northern youth exchange
His glorious deeds for my indignities.
Percy is but my factor, good my lord,
To engross up glorious deeds on my behalf,
And I will call him to so strict account
50 That he shall render every glory up,
Yea, even the slightest worship of his time,
Or I will tear the reckoning from his heart.
This in the name of God I promise here,
The which if He be pleas'd I shall perform,
55 I do beseech your Majesty may salve
The long-grown wounds of my intemperance:
If not, the end of life cancels all bands,
And I will die a hundred thousand deaths
Ere break the smallest parcel of this vow.
60 KING   A hundred thousand rebels die in this –
Thou shalt have charge and sovereign trust herein.

Enter BLUNT.

How now, good Blunt? Thy looks are full of speed.
BLUNT   So hath the business that I come to speak of.
Lord Mortimer of Scotland hath sent word
65 That Douglas and the English rebels met
The eleventh of this month at Shrewsbury.
A mighty and a fearful head they are,
If promises be kept on every hand,
As ever offer'd foul play in a state.

KING   The Earl of Westmoreland set forth today,   170
With him my son, Lord John of Lancaster,
For this advertisement is five days old.
On Wednesday next, Harry, you shall set forward,
On Thursday we ourselves will march.
Our meeting is Bridgnorth, and, Harry, you   175
Shall march through Gloucestershire, by which
   account,
Our business valued, some twelve days hence
Our general forces at Bridgnorth shall meet.
Our hands are full of business, let's away,
Advantage feeds him fat while men delay.   *Exeunt.*   180

3.3   *Enter* FALSTAFF *and* BARDOLPH.

FALSTAFF   Bardolph, am I not fallen away vilely since
this last action? Do I not bate? Do I not dwindle? Why,
my skin hangs about me like an old lady's loose gown.
I am withered like an old apple-john. Well, I'll repent,
and that suddenly, while I am in some liking; I shall be   5
out of heart shortly, and then I shall have no strength
to repent. And I have not forgotten what the inside of
a church is made of, I am a peppercorn, a brewer's
horse: the inside of a church! Company, villainous
company, hath been the spoil of me.   10
BARDOLPH   Sir John, you are so fretful you cannot live
long.
FALSTAFF   Why, there is it: come, sing me a bawdy song,
make me merry. I was as virtuously given as a
gentleman need to be; virtuous enough; swore little;   15
diced not above seven times – a week; went to a
bawdy-house not above once in a quarter – of an hour;
paid money that I borrowed – three or four times;
lived well, and in good compass; and now I live out of
all order, out of all compass.   20
BARDOLPH   Why, you are so fat, Sir John, that you must
needs be out of all compass, out of all reasonable
compass, Sir John.
FALSTAFF   Do thou amend thy face, and I'll amend my
life: thou art our admiral, thou bearest the lantern in   25
the poop, but 'tis in the nose of thee: thou art the
Knight of the Burning Lamp.
BARDOLPH   Why, Sir John, my face does you no harm.
FALSTAFF   No, I'll be sworn, I make as good use of it as
many a man doth of a death's-head, or a *memento mori*.   30
I never see thy face but I think upon hell-fire, and
Dives that lived in purple: for there he is in his robes,
burning, burning. If thou wert any way given to
virtue, I would swear by thy face: my oath should be
'By this fire, that's God's angel!' But thou art   35
altogether given over; and wert indeed, but for the
light in thy face, the son of utter darkness. When thou
ran'st up Gad's Hill in the night to catch my horse, if
I did not think thou hadst been an *ignis fatuus*, or a ball
of wildfire, there's no purchase in money. O, thou art   40
a perpetual triumph, an everlasting bonfire-light!
Thou hast saved me a thousand marks in links and

45 torches, walking with thee in the night betwixt tavern and tavern: but the sack that thou hast drunk me would have bought me lights as good cheap at the dearest chandler's in Europe. I have maintained that salamander of yours with fire any time this two and thirty years, God reward me for it!

BARDOLPH   'Sblood, I would my face were in your belly!

50 FALSTAFF   God-a-mercy! so should I be sure to be heartburnt.

Enter Hostess.

How now, dame Partlet the hen, have you enquired yet who picked my pocket?

HOSTESS   Why, Sir John, what do you think, Sir John, do you think I keep thieves in my house? I have searched, I have enquired, so has my husband, man by man, boy by boy, servant by servant – the tithe of a hair was never lost in my house before.

FALSTAFF   Ye lie, hostess: Bardolph was shaved and lost many a hair, and I'll be sworn my pocket was picked: go to, you are a woman, go.

HOSTESS   Who, I? No, I defy thee: God's light, I was never called so in mine own house before.

FALSTAFF   Go to, I know you well enough.

65 HOSTESS   No, Sir John, you do not know me, Sir John, I know you, Sir John, you owe me money, Sir John, and now you pick a quarrel to beguile me of it. I bought you a dozen of shirts to your back.

FALSTAFF   Dowlas, filthy dowlas. I have given them away to bakers' wives; they have made bolters of them.

HOSTESS   Now as I am a true woman, holland of eight shillings an ell! You owe money here besides, Sir John, for your diet, and by-drinkings, and money lent you, four and twenty pound.

75 FALSTAFF   He had his part of it, let him pay.

HOSTESS   He? Alas, he is poor, he hath nothing.

FALSTAFF   How? Poor? Look upon his face. What call you rich? Let them coin his nose, let them coin his cheeks, I'll not pay a denier. What, will you make a younker of me? Shall I not take mine ease in mine inn but I shall have my pocket picked? I have lost a seal-ring of my grandfather's worth forty mark.

HOSTESS   O Jesu, I have heard the Prince tell him, I know not how oft, that that ring was copper.

85 FALSTAFF   How? the Prince is a Jack, a sneak-up. 'Sblood, and he were here I would cudgel him like a dog if he would say so.

Enter the PRINCE *marching, with* PETO, *and* FALSTAFF *meets him, playing upon his truncheon like a fife.*

How now, lad? Is the wind in that door, i'faith, must we all march?

90 BARDOLPH   Yea, two and two, Newgate fashion.

HOSTESS   My lord, I pray you hear me.

PRINCE   What say'st thou, Mistress Quickly? How doth thy husband? I love him well, he is an honest man.

HOSTESS   Good my lord, hear me.

FALSTAFF   Prithee let her alone, and list to me.   95

PRINCE   What say'st thou, Jack?

FALSTAFF   The other night I fell asleep here, behind the arras, and had my pocket picked: this house is turned bawdy-house, they pick pockets.

PRINCE   What didst thou lose, Jack?   100

FALSTAFF   Wilt thou believe me, Hal, three or four bonds of forty pound apiece, and a seal-ring of my grandfather's.

PRINCE   A trifle, some eightpenny matter.

HOSTESS   So I told him, my lord, and I said I heard your   105
Grace say so: and, my lord, he speaks most vilely of you, like a foul-mouthed man as he is, and said he would cudgel you.

PRINCE   What! he did not?

HOSTESS   There's neither faith, truth, nor womanhood   110
in me else.

FALSTAFF   There's no more faith in thee than in a stewed prune, nor no more truth in thee than in a drawn fox – and for womanhood, Maid Marian may be the deputy's wife of the ward to thee. Go, you thing,   115
go!

HOSTESS   Say, what thing, what thing?

FALSTAFF   What thing? Why, a thing to thank God on.

HOSTESS   I am no thing to thank God on, I would thou shouldst know it, I am an honest man's wife, and   120
setting thy knighthood aside, thou art a knave to call me so.

FALSTAFF   Setting thy womanhood aside, thou art a beast to say otherwise.

HOSTESS   Say, what beast, thou knave, thou?   125

FALSTAFF   What beast? Why, an otter.

PRINCE   An otter, Sir John? Why an otter?

FALSTAFF   Why? She's neither fish nor flesh, a man knows not where to have her.

HOSTESS   Thou art an unjust man in saying so, thou or   130
any man knows where to have me, thou knave, thou.

PRINCE   Thou say'st true, hostess, and he slanders thee most grossly.

HOSTESS   So he doth you, my lord, and said this other day you ought him a thousand pound.   135

PRINCE   Sirrah, do I owe you a thousand pound?

FALSTAFF   A thousand pound, Hal? A million, thy love is worth a million, thou owest me thy love.

HOSTESS   Nay, my lord, he called you Jack, and said he would cudgel you.   140

FALSTAFF   Did I, Bardolph?

BARDOLPH   Indeed, Sir John, you said so.

FALSTAFF   Yea, if he said my ring was copper.

PRINCE   I say 'tis copper, darest thou be as good as thy word now?   145

FALSTAFF   Why, Hal, thou knowest as thou art but man I dare, but as thou art prince, I fear thee as I fear the roaring of the lion's whelp.

PRINCE   And why not as the lion?

FALSTAFF   The King himself is to be feared as the lion:
dost thou think I'll fear thee as I fear thy father? Nay,
and I do, I pray God my girdle break.

PRINCE   O, if it should, how would thy guts fall about
thy knees! But sirrah, there's no room for faith, truth,
nor honesty in this bosom of thine; it is all filled up
with guts and midriff. Charge an honest woman with
picking thy pocket? Why, thou whoreson impudent
embossed rascal, if there were anything in thy pocket
but tavern reckonings, memorandums of bawdy-
houses, and one poor pennyworth of sugar-candy to
make thee long-winded, if thy pocket were enriched
with any other injuries but these, I am a villain: and yet
you will stand to it, you will not pocket up wrong! Art
thou not ashamed?

FALSTAFF   Dost thou hear, Hal? Thou knowest in the
state of innocency Adam fell, and what should poor
Jack Falstaff do in the days of villainy? Thou seest I
have more flesh than another man, and therefore more
frailty. You confess then, you picked my pocket?

PRINCE   It appears so by the story.

FALSTAFF   Hostess, I forgive thee, go make ready
breakfast, love thy husband, look to thy servants,
cherish thy guests, thou shalt find me tractable to any
honest reason, thou seest I am pacified still, nay
prithee be gone.   *Exit Hostess.*
Now, Hal, to the news at court: for the robbery, lad,
how is that answered?

PRINCE   O my sweet beef, I must still be good angel to
thee – the money is paid back again.

FALSTAFF   O, I do not like that paying back, 'tis a double
labour.

PRINCE   I am good friends with my father and may do
anything.

FALSTAFF   Rob me the exchequer the first thing thou
dost, and do it with unwashed hands too.

BARDOLPH   Do, my lord.

PRINCE   I have procured thee, Jack, a charge of foot.

FALSTAFF   I would it had been of horse. Where shall I
find one that can steal well? O for a fine thief of the age
of two and twenty or thereabouts: I am heinously
unprovided. Well, God be thanked for these rebels,
they offend none but the virtuous; I laud them, I
praise them.

PRINCE   Bardolph!

BARDOLPH   My Lord?

PRINCE   Go bear this letter to Lord John of Lancaster,
To my brother John, this to my Lord of
     Westmoreland.   *Exit Bardolph.*
Go, Peto, to horse, to horse, for thou and I
Have thirty miles to ride yet ere dinner-time.
                                              Exit Peto.
Jack, meet me tomorrow in the Temple hall
At two o'clock in the afternoon:
There shalt thou know thy charge, and there receive
Money and order for their furniture.
The land is burning, Percy stands on high,

And either we or they must lower lie.   *Exit.*   205

FALSTAFF
Rare words! Brave world! Hostess, my breakfast,
   come!
O, I could wish this tavern were my drum.   *Exit.*

4.1   *Enter* HOTSPUR, WORCESTER *and* DOUGLAS.

HOTSPUR   Well said, my noble Scot! If speaking truth
In this fine age were not thought flattery,
Such attribution should the Douglas have
As not a soldier of this season's stamp
Should go so general current through the world.   5
By God, I cannot flatter, I do defy
The tongues of soothers, but a braver place
In my heart's love hath no man than yourself:
Nay, task me to my word, approve me, lord.

DOUGLAS   Thou art the king of honour: 10
No man so potent breathes upon the ground
But I will beard him.

HOTSPUR   Do so, and 'tis well.

Enter a Messenger, *with letters.*

What letters hast thou there? – I can but thank you.

MESSENGER   These letters come from your father.

HOTSPUR
Letters from him? Why comes he not himself?   15

MESSENGER
He cannot come, my lord, he is grievous sick.

HOTSPUR   'Zounds, how has he the leisure to be sick
In such a justling time? Who leads his power?
Under whose government come they along?

MESSENGER   His letters bear his mind, not I, my lord.   20

WORCESTER   I prithee tell me, doth he keep his bed?

MESSENGER   He did, my lord, four days ere I set forth,
And at the time of my departure thence
He was much fear'd by his physicians.

WORCESTER
I would the state of time had first been whole   25
Ere he by sickness had been visited:
His health was never better worth than now.

HOTSPUR
Sick now? Droop now? This sickness doth infect
The very life-blood of our enterprise;
'Tis catching hither, even to our camp.   30
He writes me here that inward sickness,
And that his friends by deputation could not
So soon be drawn, nor did he think it meet
To lay so dangerous and dear a trust
On any soul remov'd but on his own.   35
Yet doth he give us bold advertisement
That with our small conjunction we should on,
To see how fortune is dispos'd to us;
For, as he writes, there is no quailing now,
Because the King is certainly possess'd   40
Of all our purposes. What say you to it?

WORCESTER   Your father's sickness is a maim to us.

HOTSPUR   A perilous gash, a very limb lopp'd off –

And yet, in faith, it is not! His present want
45   Seems more than we shall find it. Were it good
      To set the exact wealth of all our states
      All at one cast? to set so rich a main
      On the nice hazard of one doubtful hour?
      It were not good, for therein should we read
50   The very bottom and the soul of hope,
      The very list, the very utmost bound
      Of all our fortunes.
      DOUGLAS   Faith, and so we should, where now remains
      A sweet reversion – we may boldly spend
55   Upon the hope of what is to come in.
      A comfort of retirement lives in this.
      HOTSPUR   A rendezvous, a home to fly unto,
      If that the devil and mischance look big
      Upon the maidenhead of our affairs.
      WORCESTER
60   But yet I would your father had been here:
      The quality and hair of our attempt
      Brooks no division; it will be thought,
      By some that know not why he is away,
      That wisdom, loyalty, and mere dislike
65   Of our proceedings kept the Earl from hence;
      And think how such an apprehension
      May turn the tide of fearful faction,
      And breed a kind of question in our cause:
      For well you know we of the off'ring side
70   Must keep aloof from strict arbitrement,
      And stop all sight-holes, every loop from whence
      The eye of reason may pry in upon us:
      This absence of your father's draws a curtain
      That shows the ignorant a kind of fear
      Before not dreamt of.
75   HOTSPUR   You strain too far.
      I rather of his absence make this use:
      It lends a lustre and more great opinion,
      A larger dare to our great enterprise,
      Than if the Earl were here; for men must think
80   If we without his help can make a head
      To push against a kingdom, with his help
      We shall o'erturn it topsy-turvy down.
      Yet all goes well, yet all our joints are whole.
      DOUGLAS   As heart can think: there is not such a word
85   Spoke of in Scotland as this term of fear.

Enter SIR RICHARD VERNON.

      HOTSPUR   My cousin Vernon! Welcome, by my soul!
      VERNON   Pray God my news be worth a welcome, lord.
      The Earl of Westmoreland seven thousand strong
      Is marching hitherwards, with him Prince John.
      HOTSPUR   No harm, what more?
90   VERNON   And further, I have learn'd,
      The King himself in person is set forth,
      Or hitherwards intended speedily,
      With strong and mighty preparation.
      HOTSPUR   He shall be welcome too: where is his son,
95   The nimble-footed madcap Prince of Wales,

And his comrades that daft the world aside
And bid it pass?
VERNON   All furnish'd, all in arms;
      All plum'd like estridges that with the wind
      Bated, like eagles having lately bath'd,
      Glittering in golden coats like images,   100
      As full of spirit as the month of May,
      And gorgeous as the sun at midsummer;
      Wanton as youthful goats, wild as young bulls.
      I saw young Harry with his beaver on,
      His cushes on his thighs, gallantly arm'd,   105
      Rise from the ground like feather'd Mercury,
      And vaulted with such ease into his seat
      As if an angel dropp'd down from the clouds
      To turn and wind a fiery Pegasus,
      And witch the world with noble horsemanship.   110
HOTSPUR
      No more, no more! Worse than the sun in March,
      This praise doth nourish agues. Let them come!
      They come like sacrifices in their trim,
      And to the fire-ey'd maid of smoky war
      All hot and bleeding will we offer them: 115
      The mailed Mars shall on his altar sit
      Up to the ears in blood. I am on fire
      To hear this rich reprisal is so nigh,
      And yet not ours! Come, let me taste my horse,
      Who is to bear me like a thunderbolt   120
      Against the bosom of the Prince of Wales.
      Harry to Harry shall, hot horse to horse,
      Meet and ne'er part till one drop down a corse.
      O that Glendower were come!
VERNON   There is more news:
      I learn'd in Worcester as I rode along   125
      He cannot draw his power this fourteen days.
      DOUGLAS   That's the worst tidings that I hear of yet.
      WORCESTER   Ay, by my faith, that bears a frosty sound.
      HOTSPUR
      What may the King's whole battle reach unto?
      VERNON   To thirty thousand.
      HOTSPUR   Forty let it be: 130
      My father and Glendower being both away,
      The powers of us may serve so great a day.
      Come, let us take a muster speedily –
      Doomsday is near; die all, die merrily.
      DOUGLAS   Talk not of dying, I am out of fear   135
      Of death or death's hand for this one half year.
                                            Exeunt.

4.2   *Enter* FALSTAFF *and* BARDOLPH.

FALSTAFF   Bardolph, get thee before to Coventry; fill me
      a bottle of sack. Our soldiers shall march through;
      we'll to Sutton Co'fil' tonight.
BARDOLPH   Will you give me money, captain?
FALSTAFF   Lay out, lay out.   5
BARDOLPH   This bottle makes an angel.
FALSTAFF   And if it do, take it for thy labour – and if it

make twenty, take them all, I'll answer the coinage.
Bid my lieutenant Peto meet me at town's end.

BARDOLPH   I will, captain: farewell.   *Exit.*

FALSTAFF   If I be not ashamed of my soldiers, I am a
soused gurnet; I have misused the King's press
damnably. I have got in exchange of a hundred and
fifty soldiers three hundred and odd pounds. I press
me none but good householders, yeomen's sons,
inquire me out contracted bachelors, such as had been
asked twice on the banns, such a commodity of warm
slaves as had as lief hear the devil as a drum, such as
fear the report of a caliver worse than a struck fowl or
a hurt wild duck. I pressed me none but such toasts-
and-butter, with hearts in their bellies no bigger than
pins' heads, and they have bought out their services;
and now my whole charge consists of ancients,
corporals, lieutenants, gentlemen of companies – slaves
as ragged as Lazarus in the painted cloth, where the
glutton's dogs licked his sores: and such as indeed
were never soldiers, but discarded unjust servingmen,
younger sons to younger brothers, revolted tapsters,
and ostlers trade-fallen, the cankers of a calm world
and a long peace, ten times more dishonourable-
ragged than an old fazed ancient; and such have I to
fill up the rooms of them as have bought out their
services, that you would think that I had a hundred
and fifty tattered prodigals lately come from swine-
keeping, from eating draff and husks. A mad fellow
met me on the way, and told me I had unloaded all the
gibbets and pressed the dead bodies. No eye hath seen
such scarecrows. I'll not march through Coventry
with them, that's flat: nay, and the villains march wide
betwixt the legs as if they had gyves on, for indeed I
had the most of them out of prison. There's not a shirt
and a half in all my company, and the half shirt is two
napkins tacked together and thrown over the
shoulders like a herald's coat without sleeves; and the
shirt to say the truth stolen from my host at Saint
Albans, or the red-nose innkeeper of Daventry. But
that's all one, they'll find linen enough on every hedge.

Enter the PRINCE *and the* LORD OF WESTMORELAND.

PRINCE   How now, blown Jack? How now, quilt?

FALSTAFF   What, Hal! How now, mad wag? What a devil
dost thou in Warwickshire? My good Lord of
Westmoreland, I cry you mercy, I thought your
honour had already been at Shrewsbury.

WESTMORELAND   Faith, Sir John, 'tis more than time
that I were there, and you too, but my powers are there
already; the King I can tell you looks for us all, we
must away all night.

FALSTAFF   Tut, never fear me, I am as vigilant as a cat to
steal cream.

PRINCE   I think, to steal cream indeed, for thy theft hath
already made thee butter; but tell me, Jack, whose
fellows are these that come after?

FALSTAFF   Mine, Hal, mine.

PRINCE   I did never see such pitiful rascals.

FALSTAFF   Tut, tut, good enough to toss, food for
powder, food for powder, they'll fill a pit as well as   65
better; tush, man, mortal men, mortal men.

WESTMORELAND   Ay, but, Sir John, methinks they are
exceeding poor and bare, too beggarly.

FALSTAFF   Faith, for their poverty I know not where
they had that; and for their bareness I am sure they   70
never learned that of me.

PRINCE   No, I'll be sworn, unless you call three fingers
in the ribs bare. But sirrah, make haste; Percy is
already in the field.   *Exit.*

FALSTAFF   What, is the King encamped?   75

WESTMORELAND   He is, Sir John, I fear we shall stay too
long.   *Exit.*

FALSTAFF   Well,
To the latter end of a fray, and the beginning of a
      feast
Fits a dull fighter and a keen guest.   *Exit.*   80

4.3   *Enter* HOTSPUR, WORCESTER,
                          DOUGLAS, VERNON.

HOTSPUR   We'll fight with him tonight.
WORCESTER   It may not be.
DOUGLAS   You give him then advantage.
VERNON   Not a whit.
HOTSPUR   Why say you so, looks he not for supply?
VERNON   So do we.
HOTSPUR   His is certain, ours is doubtful.
WORCESTER   Good cousin, be advis'd, stir not tonight.   5
VERNON   Do not, my lord.
DOUGLAS   You do not counsel well.
   You speak it out of fear and cold heart.
VERNON   Do me no slander, Douglas; by my life,
   And I dare well maintain it with my life,
   If well-respected honour bid me on,   10
   I hold as little counsel with weak fear
   As you, my lord, or any Scot that this day lives;
   Let it be seen tomorrow in the battle
   Which of us fears.
DOUGLAS   Yea, or tonight.
VERNON   Content.
HOTSPUR   Tonight, say I.   15
VERNON   Come, come, it may not be. I wonder much,
   Being men of such great leading as you are,
   That you foresee not what impediments
   Drag back our expedition: certain horse
   Of my cousin Vernon's are not yet come up,   20
   Your uncle Worcester's horse came but today,
   And now their pride and mettle is asleep,
   Their courage with hard labour tame and dull,
   That not a horse is half the half himself.
HOTSPUR   So are the horses of the enemy   25
   In general journey-bated and brought low.
   The better part of ours are full of rest.
WORCESTER   The number of the King exceedeth ours:
   For God's sake, cousin, stay till all come in.

[*The trumpet sounds a parley.*]

Enter SIR WALTER BLUNT.

30 BLUNT   I come with gracious offers from the King,
If you vouchsafe me hearing and respect.
HOTSPUR
Welcome, Sir Walter Blunt: and would to God
You were of our determination!
Some of us love you well, and even those some
35 Envy your great deservings and good name,
Because you are not of our quality,
But stand against us like an enemy.
BLUNT   And God defend but still I should stand so,
So long as out of limit and true rule
40 You stand against anointed majesty.
But to my charge. The King hath sent to know
The nature of your griefs, and whereupon
You conjure from the breast of civil peace
Such bold hostility, teaching his duteous land
45 Audacious cruelty. If that the King
Have any way your good deserts forgot,
Which he confesseth to be manifold,
He bids you name your griefs, and with all speed
You shall have your desires with interest
50 And pardon absolute for yourself, and these
Herein misled by your suggestion.
HOTSPUR
The King is kind, and well we know the King
Knows at what time to promise, when to pay:
My father, and my uncle, and myself
55 Did give him that same royalty he wears,
And when he was not six and twenty strong,
Sick in the world's regard, wretched and low,
A poor unminded outlaw sneaking home,
My father gave him welcome to the shore:
60 And when he heard him swear and vow to God
He came but to be Duke of Lancaster,
To sue his livery, and beg his peace
With tears of innocency, and terms of zeal,
My father, in kind heart and pity mov'd,
65 Swore him assistance, and perform'd it too.
Now when the lords and barons of the realm
Perceiv'd Northumberland did lean to him,
The more and less came in with cap and knee,
Met him in boroughs, cities, villages,
70 Attended him on bridges, stood in lanes,
Laid gifts before him, proffer'd him their oaths,
Gave him their heirs as pages, follow'd him
Even at the heels in golden multitudes.
He presently, as greatness knows itself,
75 Steps me a little higher than his vow
Made to my father while his blood was poor
Upon the naked shore at Ravenspurgh;
And now forsooth takes on him to reform
Some certain edicts and some strait decrees
80 That lie too heavy on the commonwealth;
Cries out upon abuses, seems to weep

Over his country's wrongs; and by this face,
This seeming brow of justice, did he win
The hearts of all that he did angle for;
Proceeded further – cut me off the heads   85
Of all the favourites that the absent King
In deputation left behind him here,
When he was personal in the Irish war.
BLUNT   Tut, I came not to hear this.
HOTSPUR   Then to the point.
In short time after he depos'd the King,   90
Soon after that depriv'd him of his life,
And in the neck of that task'd the whole state;
To make that worse, suffer'd his kinsman March
(Who is, if every owner were well plac'd,
Indeed his King) to be engag'd in Wales,   95
There without ransom to lie forfeited;
Disgrac'd me in my happy victories,
Sought to entrap me by intelligence,
Rated mine uncle from the Council-board,
In rage dismiss'd my father from the court,   100
Broke oath on oath, committed wrong on wrong,
And in conclusion drove us to seek out
This head of safety, and withal to pry
Into his title, the which we find
Too indirect for long continuance.   105
BLUNT   Shall I return this answer to the King?
HOTSPUR   Not so, Sir Walter. We'll withdraw awhile.
Go to the King, and let there be impawn'd
Some surety for a safe return again,
And in the morning early shall mine uncle   110
Bring him our purposes – and so, farewell.
BLUNT   I would you would accept of grace and love.
HOTSPUR   And may be so we shall.
BLUNT   Pray God you do.
Exeunt.

4.4   *Enter the* ARCHBISHOP OF YORK
and SIR MICHAEL.

ARCHBISHOP
Hie, good Sir Michael, bear this sealed brief
With winged haste to the lord marshal,
This to my cousin Scroop, and all the rest
To whom they are directed. If you knew
How much they do import you would make haste.   5
SIR MICHAEL   My good lord,
I guess their tenor.
ARCHBISHOP   Like enough you do.
Tomorrow, good Sir Michael, is a day
Wherein the fortune of ten thousand men
Must bide the touch; for, sir, at Shrewsbury,   10
As I am truly given to understand,
The King with mighty and quick-raised power
Meets with Lord Harry: and I fear, Sir Michael,
What with the sickness of Northumberland,
Whose power was in the first proportion,   15
And what with Owen Glendower's absence thence,

Who with them was a rated sinew too,
And comes not in, o'er-rul'd by prophecies,
I fear the power of Percy is too weak
20 To wage an instant trial with the King.
SIR MICHAEL   Why, my good lord, you need not fear,
There is Douglas, and Lord Mortimer.
ARCHBISHOP   No, Mortimer is not there.
SIR MICHAEL
But there is Mordake, Vernon, Lord Harry Percy,
25 And there is my Lord of Worcester, and a head
Of gallant warriors, noble gentlemen.
ARCHBISHOP
And so there is: but yet the King hath drawn
The special head of all the land together:
The Prince of Wales, Lord John of Lancaster,
30 The noble Westmoreland, and warlike Blunt,
And many mo corrivals and dear men
Of estimation and command in arms.
SIR MICHAEL
Doubt not, my lord, they shall be well oppos'd.
ARCHBISHOP   I hope no less, yet needful 'tis to fear;
35 And to prevent the worst, Sir Michael, speed.
For if Lord Percy thrive not, ere the King
Dismiss his power he means to visit us,
For he hath heard of our confederacy,
And 'tis but wisdom to make strong against him:
40 Therefore make haste – I must go write again
To other friends; and so, farewell, Sir Michael.
                                          Exeunt.

5.1   *Enter the* KING, PRINCE OF WALES,
                LORD JOHN OF LANCASTER,
                SIR WALTER BLUNT, FALSTAFF.

KING   How bloodily the sun begins to peer
Above yon bulky hill! The day looks pale
At his distemp'rature.
PRINCE   The southern wind
5 Doth play the trumpet to his purposes,
And by his hollow whistling in the leaves
Foretells a tempest and a blust'ring day.
KING   Then with the losers let it sympathise,
For nothing can seem foul to those that win.
                          [*The trumpet sounds.*]

        Enter WORCESTER *and* VERNON.

How now, my Lord of Worcester! 'tis not well
10 That you and I should meet upon such terms
As now we meet. You have deceiv'd our trust,
And made us doff our easy robes of peace
To crush our old limbs in ungentle steel:
This is not well, my lord, this is not well.
15 What say you to it? Will you again unknit
This churlish knot of all-abhorred war,
And move in that obedient orb again
Where you did give a fair and natural light,
And be no more an exhal'd meteor,
20 A prodigy of fear, and a portent

Of broached mischief to the unborn times?
WORCESTER   Hear me, my liege:
For mine own part I could be well content
To entertain the lag end of my life
With quiet hours. For I protest   25
I have not sought the day of this dislike.
KING   You have not sought it? How comes it, then?
FALSTAFF   Rebellion lay in his way, and he found it.
PRINCE   Peace, chewet, peace!
WORCESTER   It pleas'd your Majesty to turn your looks   30
Of favour from myself, and all our house,
And yet I must remember you, my lord,
We were the first and dearest of your friends;
For you my staff of office did I break
In Richard's time, and posted day and night   35
To meet you on the way, and kiss your hand,
When yet you were in place and in account
Nothing so strong and fortunate as I.
It was myself, my brother, and his son,
That brought you home, and boldly did outdare   40
The dangers of the time. You swore to us,
And you did swear that oath at Doncaster,
That you did nothing purpose 'gainst the state,
Nor claim no further than your new-fall'n right,
The seat of Gaunt, dukedom of Lancaster.   45
To this we swore our aid: but in short space
It rain'd down fortune show'ring on your head,
And such a flood of greatness fell on you,
What with our help, what with the absent King,
What with the injuries of a wanton time,   50
The seeming sufferances that you had borne,
And the contrarious winds that held the King
So long in his unlucky Irish wars
That all in England did repute him dead:
And from this swarm of fair advantages   55
You took occasion to be quickly woo'd
To gripe the general sway into your hand,
Forgot your oath to us at Doncaster,
And being fed by us, you us'd us so
As that ungentle gull the cuckoo's bird   60
Useth the sparrow – did oppress our nest,
Grew by our feeding to so great a bulk
That even our love durst not come near your sight
For fear of swallowing; but with nimble wing
We were enforc'd for safety sake to fly   65
Out of your sight, and raise this present head,
Whereby we stand opposed by such means
As you yourself have forg'd against yourself,
By unkind usage, dangerous countenance,
And violation of all faith and troth   70
Sworn to us in your younger enterprise.
KING   These things indeed you have articulate,
Proclaim'd at market crosses, read in churches,
To face the garment of rebellion
With some fine colour that may please the eye   75
Of fickle changelings and poor discontents,
Which gape and rub the elbow at the news

Of hurlyburly innovation;
And never yet did insurrection want
80   Such water-colours to impaint his cause,
Nor moody beggars starving for a time
Of pellmell havoc and confusion.
PRINCE   In both your armies there is many a soul
Shall pay full dearly for this encounter
85   If once they join in trial. Tell your nephew,
The Prince of Wales doth join with all the world
In praise of Henry Percy: by my hopes,
This present enterprise set off his head,
I do not think a braver gentleman,
90   More active-valiant or more valiant-young,
More daring or more bold, is now alive
To grace this latter age with noble deeds.
For my part, I may speak it to my shame,
I have a truant been to chivalry,
95   And so I hear he doth account me too;
Yet this before my father's majesty –
I am content that he shall take the odds
Of his great name and estimation,
And will, to save the blood on either side,
100   Try fortune with him in a single fight.
KING
And, Prince of Wales, so dare we venture thee,
Albeit, considerations infinite
Do make against it: no, good Worcester, no,
We love our people well, even those we love
105   That are misled upon your cousin's part,
And will they take the offer of our grace,
Both he, and they, and you, yea, every man
Shall be my friend again, and I'll be his:
So tell your cousin, and bring me word
110   What he will do. But if he will not yield,
Rebuke and dread correction wait on us,
And they shall do their office. So, be gone;
We will not now be troubled with reply:
We offer fair, take it advisedly.
                    Exit Worcester, with Vernon.
115   PRINCE   It will not be accepted, on my life;
The Douglas and the Hotspur both together
Are confident against the world in arms.
KING   Hence, therefore, every leader to his charge;
For on their answer will we set on them,
120   And God befriend us as our cause is just!
                    Exeunt all but the Prince and Falstaff.
FALSTAFF   Hal, if thou see me down in the battle and
bestride me, so; 'Tis a point of friendship.
PRINCE   Nothing but a Colossus can do thee that
friendship. Say thy prayers, and farewell.
125   FALSTAFF   I would 'twere bed-time, Hal, and all well.
PRINCE   Why, thou owest God a death.   *Exit.*
FALSTAFF   'Tis not due yet, I would be loath to pay him
before his day – what need I be so forward with him
that calls not on me? Well, 'tis no matter, honour
130   pricks me on. Yea, but how if honour prick me off
when I come on, how then? Can honour set to a leg?

No. Or an arm? No. Or take away the grief of a wound?
No. Honour hath no skill in surgery then? No. What is
honour? A word. What is in that word honour? What
is that honour? Air. A trim reckoning! Who hath it?   135
He that died a-Wednesday. Doth he feel it? No. Doth
he hear it? No. 'Tis insensible, then? Yea, to the dead.
But will it not live with the living? No. Why?
Detraction will not suffer it. Therefore I'll none of it.
Honour is a mere scutcheon – and so ends my   140
catechism.   *Exit.*

5.2   *Enter* WORCESTER *and* SIR RICHARD VERNON.

WORCESTER
O no, my nephew must not know, Sir Richard,
The liberal and kind offer of the King.
VERNON   'Twere best he did.
WORCESTER   Then are we all undone.
It is not possible, it cannot be,
The King should keep his word in loving us;   5
He will suspect us still, and find a time
To punish this offence in other faults:
Supposition all our lives shall be stuck full of eyes,
For treason is but trusted like the fox,
Who, never so tame, so cherish'd and lock'd up,   10
Will have a wild trick of his ancestors.
Look how we can, or sad or merrily,
Interpretation will misquote our looks,
And we shall feed like oxen at a stall,
The better cherish'd still the nearer death.   15
My nephew's trespass may be well forgot,
It hath the excuse of youth and heat of blood,
And an adopted name of privilege –
A hare-brain'd Hotspur, govern'd by a spleen:
All his offences live upon my head   20
And on his father's. We did train him on,
And, his corruption being ta'en from us,
We as the spring of all shall pay for all:
Therefore, good cousin, let not Harry know
In any case the offer of the King.   25
VERNON   Deliver what you will; I'll say 'tis so.
Here comes your cousin.

                    Enter HOTSPUR *and* DOUGLAS.

HOTSPUR   My uncle is return'd;
Deliver up my Lord of Westmoreland.
Uncle, what news?
WORCESTER   The King will bid you battle presently.   30
DOUGLAS   Defy him by the Lord of Westmoreland.
HOTSPUR   Lord Douglas, go you and tell him so.
DOUGLAS   Marry, and shall, and very willingly.   *Exit.*
WORCESTER   There is no seeming mercy in the King.
HOTSPUR   Did you beg any? God forbid!   35
WORCESTER   I told him gently of our grievances,
Of his oath-breaking; which he mended thus,
By now forswearing that he is forsworn:
He calls us rebels, traitors, and will scourge
With haughty arms this hateful name in us.   40

Re-enter DOUGLAS.

DOUGLAS   Arm, gentlemen, to arms! for I have thrown
  A brave defiance in King Henry's teeth,
  And Westmoreland that was engag'd did bear it,
  Which cannot choose but bring him quickly on.

WORCESTER

45   The Prince of Wales stepp'd forth before the King,
  And, nephew, challeng'd you to single fight.

HOTSPUR   O, would the quarrel lay upon our heads,
  And that no man might draw short breath today
  But I and Harry Monmouth! Tell me, tell me,
50   How show'd his tasking? Seem'd it in contempt?

VERNON   No, by my soul, I never in my life
  Did hear a challenge urg'd more modestly,
  Unless a brother should a brother dare
  To gentle exercise and proof of arms.
55   He gave you all the duties of a man,
  Trimm'd up your praises with a princely tongue,
  Spoke your deservings like a chronicle,
  Making you ever better than his praise
  By still dispraising praise valu'd with you,
60   And, which became him like a prince indeed,
  He made a blushing cital of himself,
  And chid his truant youth with such a grace
  As if he master'd there a double spirit
  Of teaching and of learning instantly.
65   There did he pause: but let me tell the world –
  If he outlive the envy of this day,
  England did never owe so sweet a hope
  So much misconstru'd in his wantonness.

HOTSPUR   Cousin, I think thou art enamoured
70   On his follies: never did I hear
  Of any prince so wild a liberty.
  But be he as he will, yet once ere night
  I will embrace him with a soldier's arm,
  That he shall shrink under my courtesy.
75   Arm, arm with speed! And fellows, soldiers, friends,
  Better consider what you have to do
  Than I that have not well the gift of tongue
  Can lift your blood up with persuasion.

Enter a Messenger.

MESSENGER   My lord, here are letters for you.
80   HOTSPUR   I cannot read them now.
  O gentlemen, the time of life is short!
  To spend that shortness basely were too long
  If life did ride upon a dial's point,
  Still ending at the arrival of an hour.
85   And if we live, we live to tread on kings,
  If die, brave death when princes die with us!
  Now, for our consciences, the arms are fair
  When the intent of bearing them is just.

Enter another Messenger.

MESSENGER
  My lord, prepare, the King comes on apace.
90   HOTSPUR   I thank him that he cuts me from my tale,

  For I profess not talking: only this –
  Let each man do his best; and here draw I
  A sword whose temper I intend to stain
  With the best blood that I can meet withal
  In the adventure of this perilous day.   95
  Now, Esperance! Percy! and set on,
  Sound all the lofty instruments of war,
  And by that music let us all embrace,
  For, heaven to earth, some of us never shall
  A second time do such a courtesy.   100
      Here they embrace, the trumpets sound, exeunt.

5.3   *The* KING *enters with his power. Alarum*
      to the battle. Then enter DOUGLAS *and*
      SIR WALTER BLUNT, *disguised as the King.*

BLUNT   What is thy name that in the battle thus
  Thou crossest me? What honour dost thou seek
  Upon my head?

DOUGLAS   Know then my name is Douglas,
  And I do haunt thee in the battle thus
  Because some tell me that thou art a king.   5

BLUNT   They tell thee true.

DOUGLAS
  The Lord of Stafford dear today hath bought
  Thy likeness, for instead of thee, King Harry,
  This sword hath ended him: so shall it thee
  Unless thou yield thee as my prisoner.   10

BLUNT   I was not born a yielder, thou proud Scot,
  And thou shalt find a king that will revenge
  Lord Stafford's death.
  [*They fight. Douglas kills Blunt.*]

Then enter HOTSPUR.

HOTSPUR
  O Douglas, hadst thou fought at Holmedon thus
  I never had triumph'd upon a Scot.   15

DOUGLAS
  All's done, all's won: here breathless lies the King.

HOTSPUR   Where?

DOUGLAS   Here.

HOTSPUR
  This, Douglas? No, I know this face full well,
  A gallant knight he was, his name was Blunt,
  Semblably furnish'd like the King himself.   20

DOUGLAS   A fool go with thy soul, whither it goes!
  A borrow'd title hast thou bought too dear.
  Why didst thou tell me that thou wert a king?

HOTSPUR   The King hath many marching in his coats.   25

DOUGLAS   Now, by my sword, I will kill all his coats;
  I'll murder all his wardrobe, piece by piece,
  Until I meet the King.

HOTSPUR   Up and away!
  Our soldiers stand full fairly for the day.   *Exeunt.*

Alarum. Enter FALSTAFF *alone.*

FALSTAFF   Though I could scape shot-free at London, I   30
fear the shot here, here's no scoring but upon the pate.

Soft! who are you? Sir Walter Blunt – there's honour
for you! Here's no vanity! I am as hot as molten lead,
and as heavy too: God keep lead out of me, I need no
more weight than mine own bowels. I have led my
35 ragamuffins where they are peppered; there's not
three of my hundred and fifty left alive, and they are
for the town's end, to beg during life. But who comes
here?

Enter the PRINCE.

PRINCE
40 What, stands thou idle here? Lend me thy sword:
Many a nobleman lies stark and stiff
Under the hoofs of vaunting enemies,
whose deaths are yet unrevenged. I prithee lend me
thy sword.
45 FALSTAFF   O Hal, I prithee give me leave to breathe
awhile – Turk Gregory never did such deeds in arms
as I have done this day; I have paid Percy, I have made
him sure.
PRINCE   He is indeed, and living to kill thee:
50 I prithee lend me thy sword.
FALSTAFF   Nay, before God, Hal, if Percy be alive thou
gets not my sword, but take my pistol if thou wilt.
PRINCE   Give it me: what, is it in the case?
FALSTAFF   Ay, Hal, 'tis hot, 'tis hot; there's that will sack
55 a city. [*The Prince draws it out, and finds it to be a bottle
of sack.*]
PRINCE   What, is it a time to jest and dally now? [*He
throws the bottle at him.*]   *Exit.*
FALSTAFF   Well, if Percy be alive, I'll pierce him. If he
do come in my way, so: if he do not, if I come in his
willingly, let him make a carbonado of me. I like not
60 such grinning honour as Sir Walter hath. Give me life,
which if I can save, so: if not, honour comes unlooked
for, and there's an end.   *Exit.*

5.4   *Alarum. Excursions. Enter the* KING,
the PRINCE, LORD JOHN OF LANCASTER,
EARL OF WESTMORELAND.

KING
I prithee, Harry, withdraw thyself, thou bleed'st too
much.
Lord John of Lancaster, go you with him.
LANCASTER   Not I, my lord, unless I did bleed too.
PRINCE   I beseech your Majesty, make up,
5 Lest your retirement do amaze your friends.
KING   I will do so. My Lord of Westmoreland,
Lead him to his tent.
WESTMORELAND
Come, my lord, I'll lead you to your tent.
PRINCE   Lead me, my lord? I do not need your help,
10 And God forbid a shallow scratch should drive
The Prince of Wales from such a field as this,
Where stain'd nobility lies trodden on,
And rebels' arms triumph in massacres!

LANCASTER
We breathe too long: come, cousin Westmoreland,
Our duty this way lies: for God's sake, come.   15
Exeunt Lancaster and Westmoreland.
PRINCE   By God, thou hast deceiv'd me, Lancaster,
I did not think thee lord of such a spirit:
Before, I lov'd thee as a brother, John,
But now I do respect thee as my soul.
KING   I saw him hold Lord Percy at the point   20
With lustier maintenance than I did look for
Of such an ungrown warrior.
PRINCE   O, this boy
Lends mettle to us all!   *Exit.*

Enter DOUGLAS.

DOUGLAS
Another king! They grow like Hydra's heads:
I am the Douglas, fatal to all those   25
That wear those colours on them. What art thou
That counterfeit'st the person of a king?
KING
The King himself, who, Douglas, grieves at heart
So many of his shadows thou hast met,
And not the very King. I have two boys   30
Seek Percy and thyself about the field,
But seeing thou fall'st on me so luckily
I will assay thee, and defend thyself.
DOUGLAS   I fear thou art another counterfeit,
And yet, in faith, thou bearest thee like a king;   35
But mine I am sure thou art, whoe'er thou be,
And thus I win thee.
[*They fight, the King being in danger.*]

Re-enter PRINCE.

PRINCE   Hold up thy head, vile Scot, or thou art like
Never to hold it up again! The spirits
Of valiant Shirley, Stafford, Blunt are in my arms.   40
It is the Prince of Wales that threatens thee,
Who never promiseth but he means to pay.
[*They fight.*]   *Douglas flieth.*
Cheerly, my lord, how fares your grace?
Sir Nicholas Gawsey hath for succour sent,
And so hath Clifton – I'll to Clifton straight.   45
KING   Stay and breathe a while:
Thou hast redeem'd thy lost opinion,
And show'd thou mak'st some tender of my life,
In this fair rescue thou hast brought to me.
PRINCE   O God, they did me too much injury   50
That ever said I hearken'd for your death.
If it were so, I might have let alone
The insulting hand of Douglas over you,
Which would have been as speedy in your end
As all the poisonous potions in the world,   55
And sav'd the treacherous labour of your son.
KING
Make up to Clifton, I'll to Sir Nicholas Gawsey.
                    Exit.

Enter HOTSPUR.

HOTSPUR   If I mistake not, thou art Harry Monmouth.
PRINCE   Thou speak'st as if I would deny my name.
HOTSPUR   My name is Harry Percy.
PRINCE   Why then I see
    A very valiant rebel of the name.
    I am the Prince of Wales, and think not, Percy,
    To share with me in glory any more:
    Two stars keep not their motion in one sphere,
    Nor can one England brook a double reign
    Of Harry Percy and the Prince of Wales.
HOTSPUR   Nor shall it, Harry, for the hour is come
    To end the one of us, and would to God
    Thy name in arms were now as great as mine!
PRINCE   I'll make it greater ere I part from thee,
    And all the budding honours on thy crest
    I'll crop to make a garland for my head.
HOTSPUR   I can no longer brook thy vanities.
    [*They fight.*]

Enter FALSTAFF.

FALSTAFF   Well said, Hal! To it, Hal! Nay, you shall find
    no boy's play here, I can tell you.

Re-enter DOUGLAS; *he fighteth with Falstaff,*
who falls down as if he were dead. Exit Douglas.
The Prince mortally wounds Hotspur.

HOTSPUR   O Harry, thou hast robb'd me of my youth!
    I better brook the loss of brittle life
    Than those proud titles thou hast won of me;
    They wound my thoughts worse than thy sword my
        flesh:
    But thoughts, the slaves of life, and life, time's fool,
    And time, that takes survey of all the world,
    Must have a stop. O, I could prophesy,
    But that the earthy and cold hand of death
    Lies on my tongue: no, Percy, thou art dust,
    And food for – [*Dies.*]
PRINCE
    For worms, brave Percy. Fare thee well, great heart!
    Ill-weav'd ambition, how much art thou shrunk!
    When that this body did contain a spirit,
    A kingdom for it was too small a bound;
    But now two paces of the vilest earth
    Is room enough. This earth that bears thee dead
    Bears not alive so stout a gentleman.
    If thou wert sensible of courtesy
    I should not make so dear a show of zeal;
    But let my favours hide thy mangled face,
    And even in thy behalf I'll thank myself
    For doing these fair rites of tenderness.
    Adieu, and take thy praise with thee to heaven!
    Thy ignominy sleep with thee in the grave,
    But not remember'd in thy epitaph!
    [*He spieth Falstaff on the ground.*]
    What, old acquaintance, could not all this flesh

Keep in a little life? Poor Jack, farewell!
I could have better spar'd a better man:
O, I should have a heavy miss of thee
If I were much in love with vanity: 105
Death hath not struck so fat a deer today,
Though many dearer, in this bloody fray.
Embowell'd will I see thee by and by,
Till then in blood by noble Percy lie.   *Exit.*
[*Falstaff riseth up.*]
FALSTAFF   Embowelled? If thou embowel me today, I'll   110
give you leave to powder me and eat me too tomorrow.
'Sblood, 'twas time to counterfeit, or that hot
termagant Scot had paid me, scot and lot too.
Counterfeit? I lie, I am no counterfeit: to die is to be a
counterfeit, for he is but the counterfeit of a man, who   115
hath not the life of a man: but to counterfeit dying,
when a man thereby liveth, is to be no counterfeit, but
the true and perfect image of life indeed. The better
part of valour is discretion, in the which better part I
have saved my life. 'Zounds, I am afraid of this   120
gunpowder Percy, though he be dead; how if he should
counterfeit too and rise? By my faith, I am afraid he
would prove the better counterfeit; therefore I'll make
him sure, yea, and I'll swear I killed him. Why may not
he rise as well as I? Nothing confutes me but eyes, and   125
nobody sees me: therefore, sirrah [*stabbing him*], with
a new wound in your thigh, come you along with me.
[*He takes up Hotspur on his back.*]

Re-enter PRINCE *and*
LORD JOHN OF LANCASTER.

PRINCE
    Come, brother John, full bravely hast thou flesh'd
    Thy maiden sword.
LANCASTER   But soft, whom have we here?
    Did you not tell me this fat man was dead?   130
PRINCE
    I did, I saw him dead,
    Breathless and bleeding on the ground. Art thou
        alive?
    Or is it fantasy that plays upon our eyesight?
    I prithee speak, we will not trust our eyes
    Without our ears: thou art not what thou seem'st.   135
FALSTAFF   No, that's certain, I am not a double-man:
    but if I be not Jack Falstaff, then am I a Jack: there is
    Percy [*throwing the body down*]! If your father will do
    me any honour, so: if not, let him kill the next Percy
    himself. I look to be either earl or duke, I can assure   140
    you.
PRINCE   Why, Percy I kill'd myself, and saw thee dead.
FALSTAFF   Didst thou? Lord, Lord, how this world is
    given to lying! I grant you I was down, and out of
    breath, and so was he, but we rose both at an instant,   145
    and fought a long hour by Shrewsbury clock. If I may
    be believed, so: if not, let them that should reward
    valour bear the sin upon their own heads. I'll take it

150   upon my death, I gave him this wound in the thigh; if
the man were alive, and would deny it, 'zounds, I
would make him eat a piece of my sword.

LANCASTER   This is the strangest tale that ever I heard.

PRINCE   This is the strangest fellow, brother John.
Come, bring your luggage nobly on your back.
155   [*aside to Falstaff*] For my part, if a lie may do thee
       grace,
I'll gild it with the happiest terms I have.
                       [*A retreat is sounded.*]
The trumpet sounds retreat, the day is ours.
Come, brother, let us to the highest of the field,
To see what friends are living, who are dead.
             Exeunt Prince of Wales and Lancaster.

160   FALSTAFF   I'll follow, as they say, for reward. He that
rewards me, God reward him! If I do grow great, I'll
grow less, for I'll purge, and leave sack, and live
cleanly as a nobleman should do.
                    Exit, bearing off the body.

5.5   *The trumpets sound. Enter the* KING,
         PRINCE, LORD JOHN OF LANCASTER,
      EARL OF WESTMORELAND, *with* WORCESTER
           and VERNON *prisoners.*

KING   Thus ever did rebellion find rebuke.
Ill-spirited Worcester, did not we send grace,
Pardon, and terms of love to all of you?
And wouldst thou turn our offers contrary?
5   Misuse the tenor of thy kinsman's trust?
Three knights upon our party slain today,
A noble earl and many a creature else,
Had been alive this hour,
If like a Christian thou hadst truly borne
10   Betwixt our armies true intelligence.

WORCESTER   What I have done my safety urg'd me to;
And I embrace this fortune patiently,
Since not to be avoided it falls on me.

KING   Bear Worcester to the death, and Vernon too:
Other offenders we will pause upon.   15
           Exeunt Worcester and Vernon, guarded.
How goes the field?

PRINCE   The noble Scot, Lord Douglas, when he saw
The fortune of the day quite turn'd from him,
The noble Percy slain, and all his men
Upon the foot of fear, fled with the rest,   20
And falling from a hill, he was so bruis'd
That the pursuers took him. At my tent
The Douglas is; and I beseech your Grace
I may dispose of him.

KING   With all my heart.

PRINCE   Then, brother John of Lancaster, to you   25
This honourable bounty shall belong;
Go to the Douglas and deliver him
Up to his pleasure, ransomless and free:
His valours shown upon our crests today
Have taught us how to cherish such high deeds,   30
Even in the bosom of our adversaries.

LANCASTER   I thank your Grace for this high courtesy,
Which I shall give away immediately.

KING   Then this remains, that we divide our power:
You, son John, and my cousin Westmoreland,   35
Towards York shall bend you with your dearest speed
To meet Northumberland and the prelate Scroop,
Who, as we hear, are busily in arms:
Myself and you, son Harry, will towards Wales,
To fight with Glendower and the Earl of March.   40
Rebellion in this land shall lose his sway,
Meeting the check of such another day,
And since this business so fair is done,
Let us not leave till all our own be won.   *Exeunt.*

King Henry IV, Part 2

'The second parte of the history of kinge HENRY the iiijth with the humours of Sir JOHN FFALLSTAFF' was entered in the Stationers' Register on 23 August 1600, and a Quarto was published that year, printed by Valentine Simmes. One scene, 3.1, in which King Henry makes his belated first appearance, was accidently omitted. To insert it Simmes set four new leaves, which not only include the missing scene but reprint the surrounding lines from the end of 2.4 and the beginning of 3.2. The two states of the 1600 Quarto, with or without 3.1, mark the only appearance of the play in print before the 1623 Folio, a surprising fact given the extraordinary popularity of *King Henry IV, Part 1*.

The Quarto text serves as the primary authority for most modern editions. The Folio, however, includes eight substantial passages absent from the Quarto, and seems in other places authoritatively to correct and add to the earlier text, so it too must be taken into account by editors. In other particulars, however, the Folio seems further from Shakespeare's own hand than the Quarto, regularizing its colloquialisms and purging the text of most of its oaths and profanities.

The play was written soon after *King Henry IV, Part 1*, probably early in 1598, but more as a sequel than as the second half of a single ten-act dramatic entity. Had two plays been clearly in his mind from the outset, Shakespeare would no doubt have parcelled out the historical material more evenly. Though *Part 2* brings the action forward to King Henry's death and Hal's accession to the throne, the play does more than merely complete the history of the reign. Shakespeare echoes the structure of the earlier play, transposing it into a darker key. *Part 2* also ignores various aspects of the plot of *Part 1*, even forgetting the reconciliation of father and son that ends the earlier play.

Yet if the trajectory of the action is the same in each play, dividing interest between the King and Prince, the rebels and Falstaff, the history in *Part 2* is more troubled and troubling. The climactic battles of each play, while structurally analogous, starkly establish the plays' different tones. *Part 1*'s glorious victory at Shrewsbury, where Hal magnificently proves himself a worthy successor, is paralleled by the betrayal at Gaultree Forest, where Prince John of Lancaster displays not the chivalric magnanimity of Hal but a prudential cynicism all too appropriate to the dispiriting world of this play.

Hal does not even appear on stage until 2.2, and his first line is telling: 'Before God, I am exceeding weary.' Even Falstaff is here more tired and cynical than in *Part 1*, his actions meaner, his wit less agile. Though his presence is still engaging, he shows the marks of the disease that infects the play world. He first enters worrying about the doctor's report about his urine sample, and his own diagnosis is that he suffers from 'consumption of the purse'.

Falstaff in this play is no longer a father figure for Hal; indeed the two are rarely together on stage, and the play's most notorious moment is the fat knight's public rejection. Falstaff eagerly anticipates the crowning of his erstwhile tavern friend as King, but the 'Hal' he knew is no more. The once wayward Prince is now King of England, and coldly tells Falstaff: 'Presume not that I am the thing I was.' The newly crowned Henry V has no choice but to repudiate the dissolute knight, but audiences inevitably feel that the new King gives up some of his humanity in so fully taking on his necessary public role. It is here, in the way in which Henry performs the rejection, in the degree of evident regret, in the extent to which he realizes what he has lost and what he has become, that productions of this complex and unsettling play reveal their moral focus.

Though never as popular on stage as its predecessor, *Part 2* has a distinguished performance history. It was one of the plays performed at Court in the winter of 1612-13 to celebrate the wedding of Princess Elizabeth and the Elector Palatine. After the Restoration it continued to be played, but often in adaptations that emphasized the role of Falstaff, or in conflations of the two parts. Such conflations go back at least as far as 1622-3, when Sir Edward Dering prepared one for his own private theatricals, but the tradition survives into the twentieth century, as in Orson Welles's film *Chimes at Midnight* (1966) and an extraordinary production of *Enrico IV* by the Colletivo di Parma, first staged in Italy in 1982 and brought to London the following year.

The Arden text is based on the 1600 Quarto, supplemented by the 1623 First Folio.

RUMOUR	*the presenter*
KING Henry the Fourth	
PRINCE Henry	*afterwards crowned King Henry the Fifth*
Prince John of LANCASTER	
Humphrey, Duke of GLOUCESTER	*sons to Henry the Fourth, and brethren to Henry the Fifth*
Thomas, Duke of CLARENCE	
Henry Percy, Earl of NORTHUMBERLAND	
The ARCHBISHOP of York	
Lord MOWBRAY	
Lord HASTINGS	*opposites against King Henry the Fourth*
LORD BARDOLPH	
TRAVERS	
MORTON	
Sir John COLEVILE	
Earl of WARWICK	
Earl of WESTMORELAND	
Earl of SURREY	
Sir John BLUNT	*of the King's party*
GOWER	
HARCOURT	
The Lord CHIEF JUSTICE	
SERVANT *of the Lord Chief Justice*	
POINS	
Sir John FALSTAFF	
BARDOLPH	*irregular humourists*
PISTOL	
PETO	
Falstaff's PAGE	
Robert SHALLOW	*both country Justices*
SILENCE	
DAVY	*servant to Shallow*
FANG *and* SNARE	*two sergeants*
Ralph MOULDY	
Simon SHADOW	
Thomas WART	*country soldiers*
Francis FEEBLE	
Peter BULLCALF	
LADY NORTHUMBERLAND	*Northumberland's wife*
LADY PERCY	*Percy's widow*
HOSTESS Quickly	
DOLL Tearsheet	
Speaker of the EPILOGUE	
FRANCIS *and other* DRAWERS	

Beadles and other Officers, Grooms, Porter, Messenger, Soldiers, Lords, Musicians, Attendants

King Henry IV, Part 2

INDUCTION

Enter RUMOUR *painted full of tongues.*

RUMOUR Open your ears; for which of you will stop
  The vent of hearing when loud Rumour speaks?
  I, from the Orient to the drooping West,
  Making the wind my post-horse, still unfold
  The acts commenced on this ball of earth.
  Upon my tongues continual slanders ride,
  The which in every language I pronounce,
  Stuffing the ears of men with false reports.
  I speak of peace, while covert enmity
  Under the smile of safety wounds the world;
  And who but Rumour, who but only I,
  Make fearful musters, and prepar'd defence,
  Whiles the big year, swoln with some other grief,
  Is thought with child by the stern tyrant War,
  And no such matter? Rumour is a pipe
  Blown by surmises, jealousies, conjectures,
  And of so easy and so plain a stop
  That the blunt monster with uncounted heads,
  The still-discordant wav'ring multitude,
  Can play upon it. But what need I thus
  My well-known body to anatomize
  Among my household? Why is Rumour here?
  I run before King Harry's victory,
  Who in a bloody field by Shrewsbury
  Hath beaten down young Hotspur and his troops,
  Quenching the flame of bold rebellion
  Even with the rebels' blood. But what mean I
  To speak so true at first? My office is
  To noise abroad that Harry Monmouth fell
  Under the wrath of noble Hotspur's sword,
  And that the King before the Douglas' rage
  Stoop'd his anointed head as low as death.
  This have I rumour'd through the peasant towns
  Between that royal field of Shrewsbury
  And this worm-eaten hold of ragged stone,
  Where Hotspur's father, old Northumberland,
  Lies crafty-sick. The posts come tiring on,
  And not a man of them brings other news
  Than they have learnt of me. From Rumour's tongues
  They bring smooth comforts false, worse than true
    wrongs.   *Exit.*

1.1   *Enter* LORD BARDOLPH.

LORD BARDOLPH Who keeps the gate here, ho?

Enter the Porter.

                              Where is the Earl?
PORTER What shall I say you are?
LORD BARDOLPH   Tell thou the Earl
  That the Lord Bardolph doth attend him here.
PORTER His lordship is walk'd forth into the orchard.
  Please it your honour knock but at the gate,
  And he himself will answer.

Enter NORTHUMBERLAND.

LORD BARDOLPH   Here comes the Earl.
                              Exit Porter.
NORTHUMBERLAND
  What news, Lord Bardolph? Every minute now
  Should be the father of some stratagem.
  The times are wild; contention, like a horse
  Full of high feeding, madly hath broke loose,   10
  And bears down all before him.
LORD BARDOLPH   Noble Earl,
  I bring you certain news from Shrewsbury.
NORTHUMBERLAND Good, and God will!
LORD BARDOLPH   As good as heart can wish.
  The King is almost wounded to the death;
  And, in the fortune of my lord your son,   15
  Prince Harry slain outright; and both the Blunts
  Kill'd by the hand of Douglas; young Prince John
  And Westmoreland and Stafford fled the field;
  And Harry Monmouth's brawn, the hulk Sir John,
  Is prisoner to your son. O, such a day,   20
  So fought, so follow'd, and so fairly won,
  Came not till now to dignify the times
  Since Caesar's fortunes!
NORTHUMBERLAND   How is this deriv'd?
  Saw you the field? Came you from Shrewsbury?
LORD BARDOLPH
  I spake with one, my lord, that came from thence,   25
  A gentleman well bred, and of good name,
  That freely render'd me these news for true.
NORTHUMBERLAND
  Here comes my servant Travers whom I sent
  On Tuesday last to listen after news.

Enter TRAVERS.

LORD BARDOLPH My lord, I over-rode him on the way, 30
  And he is furnish'd with no certainties
  More than he haply may retail from me.
NORTHUMBERLAND
  Now, Travers, what good tidings comes with you?
TRAVERS My lord, Sir John Umfrevile turn'd me back
  With joyful tidings, and, being better hors'd,   35
  Out-rode me. After him came spurring hard
  A gentleman almost forspent with speed,
  That stopp'd by me to breathe his bloodied horse.
  He ask'd the way to Chester, and of him
  I did demand what news from Shrewsbury.   40
  He told me that rebellion had ill luck,
  And that young Harry Percy's spur was cold.
  With that he gave his able horse the head,
  And bending forward struck his armed heels
  Against the panting sides of his poor jade   45
  Up to the rowel-head; and starting so
  He seem'd in running to devour the way,
  Staying no longer question.
NORTHUMBERLAND   Ha? Again!
  Said he young Harry Percy's spur was cold?

50 Of Hotspur, Coldspur? that rebellion
    Had met ill luck?
LORD BARDOLPH　　My lord, I'll tell you what:
    If my young lord your son have not the day,
    Upon mine honour, for a silken point
    I'll give my barony, never talk of it.
NORTHUMBERLAND
55 Why should that gentleman that rode by Travers
    Give then such instances of loss?
LORD BARDOLPH　　　　　　Who, he?
    He was some hilding fellow that had stol'n
    The horse he rode on, and, upon my life,
    Spoke at a venture. Look, here comes more news.

                Enter MORTON.

NORTHUMBERLAND
60 Yea, this man's brow, like to a title-leaf,
    Foretells the nature of a tragic volume.
    So looks the strond whereon the imperious flood
    Hath left a witness'd usurpation.
    Say, Morton, didst thou come from Shrewsbury?
65 MORTON　I ran from Shrewsbury, my noble lord,
    Where hateful death put on his ugliest mask
    To fright our party.
NORTHUMBERLAND　　How doth my son, and brother?
    Thou tremblest, and the whiteness in thy cheek
    Is apter than thy tongue to tell thy errand.
70 Even such a man, so faint, so spiritless,
    So dull, so dead in look, so woe-begone,
    Drew Priam's curtain in the dead of night,
    And would have told him half his Troy was burnt:
    But Priam found the fire ere he his tongue,
75 And I my Percy's death ere thou report'st it.
    This thou wouldst say, 'Your son did thus and thus;
    Your brother thus; so fought the noble Douglas' –
    Stopping my greedy ear with their bold deeds:
    But in the end, to stop my ear indeed,
80 Thou hast a sigh to blow away this praise,
    Ending with 'Brother, son, and all are dead'.
MORTON
    Douglas is living, and your brother, yet;
    But, for my lord your son –
NORTHUMBERLAND　　　　　Why, he is dead.
    See what a ready tongue suspicion hath!
85 He that but fears the thing he would not know
    Hath by instinct knowledge from others' eyes
    That what he fear'd is chanced. Yet speak, Morton;
    Tell thou an earl his divination lies,
    And I will take it as a sweet disgrace,
90 And make thee rich for doing me such wrong.
MORTON　You are too great to be by me gainsaid,
    Your spirit is too true, your fears too certain.
NORTHUMBERLAND
    Yet, for all this, say not that Percy's dead.
    I see a strange confession in thine eye:
95 Thou shak'st thy head, and hold'st it fear or sin
    To speak a truth. If he be slain, say so:

    The tongue offends not that reports his death;
    And he doth sin that doth belie the dead,
    Not he which says the dead is not alive.
100 Yet the first bringer of unwelcome news
    Hath but a losing office, and his tongue
    Sounds ever after as a sullen bell,
    Remember'd tolling a departing friend.
LORD BARDOLPH
    I cannot think, my lord, your son is dead.
105 MORTON　I am sorry I should force you to believe
    That which I would to God I had not seen;
    But these mine eyes saw him in bloody state,
    Rend'ring faint quittance, wearied, and out-breath'd,
    To Harry Monmouth, whose swift wrath beat down
110 The never-daunted Percy to the earth,
    From whence with life he never more sprung up.
    In few, his death, whose spirit lent a fire
    Even to the dullest peasant in his camp,
    Being bruited once, took fire and heat away
115 From the best-temper'd courage in his troops:
    For from his metal was his party steel'd,
    Which once in him abated, all the rest
    Turn'd on themselves, like dull and heavy lead:
    And as the thing that's heavy in itself
120 Upon enforcement flies with greatest speed,
    So did our men, heavy in Hotspur's loss,
    Lend to this weight such lightness with their fear
    That arrows fled not swifter toward their aim
    Than did our soldiers, aiming at their safety,
125 Fly from the field. Then was that noble Worcester
    Too soon ta'en prisoner, and that furious Scot,
    The bloody Douglas, whose well-labouring sword
    Had three times slain th'appearance of the King,
    Gan vail his stomach, and did grace the shame
130 Of those that turn'd their backs, and in his flight,
    Stumbling in fear, was took. The sum of all
    Is that the King hath won, and hath sent out
    A speedy power to encounter you, my lord,
    Under the conduct of young Lancaster
135 And Westmoreland. This is the news at full.
NORTHUMBERLAND
    For this I shall have time enough to mourn.
    In poison there is physic; and these news,
    Having been well, that would have made me sick,
    Being sick, have in some measure made me well.
140 And as the wretch whose fever-weaken'd joints,
    Like strengthless hinges, buckle under life,
    Impatient of his fit, breaks like a fire
    Out of his keeper's arms, even so my limbs,
    Weaken'd with grief, being now enrag'd with grief,
    Are thrice themselves. Hence, therefore, thou nice
        crutch!
145 A scaly gauntlet now with joints of steel
    Must glove this hand: and hence, thou sickly coif!
    Thou art a guard too wanton for the head
    Which princes, flesh'd with conquest, aim to hit.
150 Now bind my brows with iron, and approach

The ragged'st hour that time and spite dare bring
To frown upon th'enrag'd Northumberland!
Let heaven kiss earth! Now let not Nature's hand
Keep the wild flood confin'd! Let order die!
155 And let this world no longer be a stage
To feed contention in a ling'ring act;
But let one spirit of the first-born Cain
Reign in all bosoms, that, each heart being set
On bloody courses, the rude scene may end,
160 And darkness be the burier of the dead!

LORD BARDOLPH
This strained passion doth you wrong, my lord.

MORTON
Sweet earl, divorce not wisdom from your honour;
The lives of all your loving complices
Lean on your health; the which, if you give o'er
165 To stormy passion, must perforce decay.
You cast th'event of war, my noble lord,
And summ'd the account of chance, before you said
'Let us make head'. It was your presurmise
That in the dole of blows your son might drop.
170 You knew he walk'd o'er perils, on an edge,
More likely to fall in than to get o'er.
You were advis'd his flesh was capable
Of wounds and scars, and that his forward spirit
Would lift him where most trade of danger rang'd.
175 Yet did you say 'Go forth'; and none of this,
Though strongly apprehended, could restrain
The stiff-borne action. What hath then befall'n,
Or what hath this bold enterprise brought forth,
More than that being which was like to be?

180 LORD BARDOLPH We all that are engaged to this loss
Knew that we ventur'd on such dangerous seas
That if we wrought out life 'twas ten to one;
And yet we ventur'd for the gain propos'd,
Chok'd the respect of likely peril fear'd,
185 And since we are o'erset, venture again.
Come, we will all put forth, body and goods.

MORTON
'Tis more than time. And, my most noble lord,
I hear for certain, and dare speak the truth,
The gentle Archbishop of York is up
190 With well-appointed pow'rs. He is a man
Who with a double surety binds his followers.
My lord your son had only but the corpse,
But shadows and the shows of men, to fight;
For that same word 'rebellion' did divide
195 The action of their bodies from their souls,
And they did fight with queasiness, constrain'd,
As men drink potions, that their weapons only
Seem'd on our side; but, for their spirits and souls,
This word 'rebellion' – it had froze them up,
200 As fish are in a pond. But now the Bishop
Turns insurrection to religion;
Suppos'd sincere and holy in his thoughts,
He's follow'd both with body and with mind,
And doth enlarge his rising with the blood

Of fair King Richard, scrap'd from Pomfret stones; 205
Derives from heaven his quarrel and his cause;
Tells them he doth bestride a bleeding land,
Gasping for life under great Bolingbroke;
And more and less do flock to follow him.

NORTHUMBERLAND
I knew of this before, but, to speak truth, 210
This present grief had wip'd it from my mind.
Go in with me, and counsel every man
The aptest way for safety and revenge:
Get posts and letters, and make friends with speed:
Never so few, and never yet more need. *Exeunt.* 215

1.2 *Enter* SIR JOHN FALSTAFF, *with his* Page
bearing his sword and buckler.

FALSTAFF Sirrah, you giant, what says the doctor to my
water?

PAGE He said, sir, the water itself was a good healthy
water; but, for the party that owed it, he might have
moe diseases than he knew for. 5

FALSTAFF Men of all sorts take a pride to gird at me.
The brain of this foolish-compounded clay, man, is
not able to invent anything that intends to laughter
more than I invent, or is invented on me; I am not only
witty in myself, but the cause that wit is in other men. 10
I do here walk before thee like a sow that hath
overwhelmed all her litter but one. If the Prince put
thee into my service for any other reason than to set
me off, why then I have no judgment. Thou whoreson
mandrake, thou art fitter to be worn in my cap than to 15
wait at my heels. I was never manned with an agate till
now, but I will inset you, neither in gold nor silver, but
in vile apparel, and send you back again to your master
for a jewel, – the juvenal the Prince your master,
whose chin is not yet fledge. I will sooner have a beard 20
grow in the palm of my hand than he shall get one off
his cheek; and yet he will not stick to say his face is a
face-royal. God may finish it when He will, 'tis not a
hair amiss yet. He may keep it still at a face-royal, for
a barber shall never earn sixpence out of it. And yet 25
he'll be crowing as if he had writ man ever since his
father was a bachelor. He may keep his own grace, but
he's almost out of mine, I can assure him. What said
Master Dommelton about the satin for my short cloak
and my slops? 30

PAGE He said, sir, you should procure him better
assurance than Bardolph: he would not take his bond
and yours, he liked not the security.

FALSTAFF Let him be damned like the glutton! Pray
God his tongue be hotter! A whoreson Achitophel! 35
A rascally yea-forsooth knave, to bear a gentleman in
hand, and then stand upon security! The whoreson
smooth-pates do now wear nothing but high shoes and
bunches of keys at their girdles; and if a man is
through with them in honest taking up, then they 40
must stand upon security. I had as lief they would put

ratsbane in my mouth as offer to stop it with security.
I looked a should have sent me two and twenty yards
of satin, as I am a true knight, and he sends me
45 'security'! Well, he may sleep in security, for he hath
the horn of abundance, and the lightness of his wife
shines through it; and yet cannot he see, though he
have his own lanthorn to light him. Where's
Bardolph?

50 PAGE   He's gone into Smithfield to buy your worship a
horse.

FALSTAFF   I bought him in Paul's, and he'll buy me a
horse in Smithfield. And I could get me but a wife in
the stews, I were manned, horsed, and wived.

Enter Lord Chief Justice *and* Servant.

55 PAGE   Sir, here comes the nobleman that committed the
Prince for striking him about Bardolph.

FALSTAFF   Wait close, I will not see him.

CHIEF JUSTICE   What's he that goes there?

SERVANT   Falstaff, and't please your lordship.

60 CHIEF JUSTICE   He that was in question for the robbery?

SERVANT   He, my lord: but he hath since done good
service at Shrewsbury, and, as I hear, is now going
with some charge to the Lord John of Lancaster.

CHIEF JUSTICE   What, to York? Call him back again.

65 SERVANT   Sir John Falstaff!

FALSTAFF   Boy, tell him I am deaf.

PAGE   You must speak louder, my master is deaf.

CHIEF JUSTICE   I am sure he is, to the hearing of
anything good. Go pluck him by the elbow, I must
70 speak with him.

SERVANT   Sir John!

FALSTAFF   What! A young knave, and begging! Is there
not wars? Is there not employment? Doth not the
King lack subjects? Do not the rebels need soldiers?
75 Though it be a shame to be on any side but one, it is
worse shame to beg than to be on the worst side, were
it worse than the name of rebellion can tell how to
make it.

SERVANT   You mistake me, sir.

80 FALSTAFF   Why, sir, did I say you were an honest man?
Setting my knighthood and my soldiership aside, I had
lied in my throat if I had said so.

SERVANT   I pray you, sir, then set your knighthood and
your soldiership aside, and give me leave to tell you
85 you lie in your throat, if you say I am any other than
an honest man.

FALSTAFF   I give thee leave to tell me so? I lay aside that
which grows to me? If thou get'st any leave of me,
hang me. If thou tak'st leave, thou wert better be
90 hanged. You hunt counter. Hence! Avaunt!

SERVANT   Sir, my lord would speak with you.

CHIEF JUSTICE   Sir John Falstaff, a word with you.

FALSTAFF   My good lord! God give your lordship good
time of day. I am glad to see your lordship abroad, I
95 heard say your lordship was sick. I hope your lordship
goes abroad by advice; your lordship, though not clean

past your youth, have yet some smack of age in you,
some relish of the saltness of time; and I most humbly
beseech your lordship to have a reverend care of your
health.   100

CHIEF JUSTICE   Sir John, I sent for you before your
expedition to Shrewsbury.

FALSTAFF   And't please your lordship, I hear his
Majesty is returned with some discomfort from Wales.

CHIEF JUSTICE   I talk not of his Majesty. You would not   105
come when I sent for you.

FALSTAFF   And I hear, moreover, his Highness is fallen
into this same whoreson apoplexy.

CHIEF JUSTICE   Well, God mend him! I pray you let me
speak with you.   110

FALSTAFF   This apoplexy, as I take it, is a kind of
lethargy, and't please your lordship, a kind of sleeping
in the blood, a whoreson tingling.

CHIEF JUSTICE   What tell you me of it? Be it as it is.

FALSTAFF   It hath it original from much grief, from   115
study, and perturbation of the brain; I have read the
cause of his effects in Galen, it is a kind of deafness.

CHIEF JUSTICE   I think you are fallen into the disease, for
you hear not what I say to you.

FALSTAFF   Very well, my lord, very well. Rather, and't   120
please you, it is the disease of not listening, the malady
of not marking, that I am troubled withal.

CHIEF JUSTICE   To punish you by the heels would
amend the attention of your ears, and I care not if I do
become your physician.   125

FALSTAFF   I am as poor as Job, my lord, but not so
patient. Your lordship may minister the potion of
imprisonment to me in respect of poverty; but how I
should be your patient to follow your prescriptions,
the wise may make some dram of a scruple, or indeed   130
a scruple itself.

CHIEF JUSTICE   I sent for you when there were matters
against you for your life, to come speak with me.

FALSTAFF   As I was then advised by my learned counsel
in the laws of this land-service, I did not come.   135

CHIEF JUSTICE   Well, the truth is, Sir John, you live in
great infamy.

FALSTAFF   He that buckles himself in my belt cannot
live in less.

CHIEF JUSTICE   Your means are very slender, and your   140
waste is great.

FALSTAFF   I would it were otherwise, I would my means
were greater and my waist slenderer.

CHIEF JUSTICE   You have misled the youthful Prince.

FALSTAFF   The young Prince hath misled me. I am the   145
fellow with the great belly, and he my dog.

CHIEF JUSTICE   Well, I am loath to gall a new-healed
wound. Your day's service at Shrewsbury hath a little
gilded over your night's exploit on Gad's Hill. You
may thank th'unquiet time for your quiet o'er-posting   150
that action.

FALSTAFF   My lord! –

CHIEF JUSTICE   But since all is well, keep it so: wake not

a sleeping wolf.

155 FALSTAFF To wake a wolf is as bad as smell a fox.

CHIEF JUSTICE What! You are as a candle, the better part burnt out.

FALSTAFF A wassail candle, my lord, all tallow – if I did say of wax, my growth would approve the truth.

160 CHIEF JUSTICE There is not a white hair in your face but should have his effect of gravity.

FALSTAFF His effect of gravy, gravy, gravy.

CHIEF JUSTICE You follow the young Prince up and down, like his ill angel.

165 FALSTAFF Not so, my lord, your ill angel is light, but I hope he that looks upon me will take me without weighing. And yet in some respects, I grant, I cannot go. I cannot tell – virtue is of so little regard in these costermongers' times that true valour is turned

170 bearherd; pregnancy is made a tapster, and his quick wit wasted in giving reckonings; all the other gifts appertinent to man, as the malice of this age shapes them, are not worth a gooseberry. You that are old consider not the capacities of us that are young; you do

175 measure the heat of our livers with the bitterness of your galls; and we that are in the vaward of our youth, I must confess, are wags too.

CHIEF JUSTICE Do you set down your name in the scroll of youth, that are written down old with all the

180 characters of age? Have you not a moist eye, a dry hand, a yellow cheek, a white beard, a decreasing leg, an increasing belly? Is not your voice broken, your wind short, your chin double, your wit single, and every part about you blasted with antiquity? And will

185 you yet call yourself young? Fie, fie, fie, Sir John!

FALSTAFF My lord, I was born about three of the clock in the afternoon, with a white head, and something a round belly. For my voice, I have lost it with hallooing, and singing of anthems. To approve my youth further,

190 I will not: the truth is, I am only old in judgment and understanding; and he that will caper with me for a thousand marks, let him lend me the money, and have at him! For the box of the ear that the Prince gave you, he gave it like a rude prince, and you took it like a

195 sensible lord. I have checked him for it, and the young lion repents – [*aside*] marry, not in ashes and sackcloth, but in new silk and old sack.

CHIEF JUSTICE Well, God send the Prince a better companion!

200 FALSTAFF God send the companion a better prince! I cannot rid my hands of him.

CHIEF JUSTICE Well, the King hath severed you and Prince Harry: I hear you are going with Lord John of Lancaster, against the Archbishop and the Earl of

205 Northumberland.

FALSTAFF Yea, I thank your pretty sweet wit for it. But look you pray, all you that kiss my lady Peace at home, that our armies join not in a hot day; for, by the Lord, I take but two shirts out with me, and I mean not to

210 sweat extraordinarily. If it be a hot day, and I brandish anything but a bottle, I would I might never spit white again. There is not a dangerous action can peep out his head but I am thrust upon it. Well, I cannot last ever; but it was alway yet the trick of our English

215 nation, if they have a good thing, to make it too common. If ye will needs say I am an old man, you should give me rest. I would to God my name were not so terrible to the enemy as it is – I were better to be eaten to death with a rust than to be scoured to

220 nothing with perpetual motion.

CHIEF JUSTICE Well, be honest, be honest, and God bless your expedition!

FALSTAFF Will your lordship lend me a thousand pound to furnish me forth?

225 CHIEF JUSTICE Not a penny, not a penny; you are too impatient to bear crosses. Fare you well: commend me to my cousin Westmoreland.

Exeunt Lord Chief Justice and Servant.

FALSTAFF If I do, fillip me with a three-man beetle. A man can no more separate age and covetousness than a can part young limbs and lechery: but the gout galls

230 the one, and the pox pinches the other; and so both the degrees prevent my curses. Boy!

PAGE Sir?

FALSTAFF What money is in my purse?

PAGE Seven groats and two pence.

235 FALSTAFF I can get no remedy against this consumption of the purse; borrowing only lingers and lingers it out, but the disease is incurable. Go bear this letter to my Lord of Lancaster; this to the Prince; this to the Earl of Westmoreland; – and this to old mistress Ursula,

240 whom I have weekly sworn to marry since I perceived the first white hair of my chin. About it; you know where to find me. *Exit Page.*

A pox of this gout! or a gout of this pox! for the one or the other plays the rogue with my great toe. 'Tis no

245 matter if I do halt; I have the wars for my colour, and my pension shall seem the more reasonable. A good wit will make use of anything; I will turn diseases to commodity. *Exit.*

1.3 *Enter the* Archbishop, THOMAS MOWBRAY *the Earl Marshal, the Lords* HASTINGS *and* BARDOLPH.

ARCHBISHOP
Thus have you heard our cause, and known our
    means,
And, my most noble friends, I pray you all
Speak plainly your opinions of our hopes:
And first, Lord Marshal, what say you to it?

MOWBRAY I well allow the occasion of our arms, 5
But gladly would be better satisfied
How in our means we should advance ourselves
To look with forehead bold and big enough
Upon the power and puissance of the King.

HASTINGS Our present musters grow upon the file 10

To five and twenty thousand men of choice;
And our supplies live largely in the hope
Of great Northumberland, whose bosom burns
With an incensed fire of injuries.

LORD BARDOLPH
15   The question then, Lord Hastings, standeth thus –
Whether our present five and twenty thousand
May hold up head without Northumberland.

HASTINGS   With him we may.

LORD BARDOLPH   Yea, marry, there's the point:
But if without him we be thought too feeble
20   My judgment is, we should not step too far
Till we had his assistance by the hand;
For in a theme so bloody-fac'd as this
Conjecture, expectation, and surmise
Of aids incertain should not be admitted.

25   ARCHBISHOP   'Tis very true, Lord Bardolph, for indeed
It was young Hotspur's case at Shrewsbury.

LORD BARDOLPH
It was, my lord; who lin'd himself with hope,
Eating the air and promise of supply,
Flatt'ring himself in project of a power
30   Much smaller than the smallest of his thoughts,
And so, with great imagination
Proper to madmen, led his powers to death,
And winking leap'd into destruction.

HASTINGS   But, by your leave, it never yet did hurt
35   To lay down likelihoods and forms of hope.

LORD BARDOLPH   Yes, if this present quality of war –
Indeed the instant action, a cause on foot –
Lives so in hope, as in an early spring
We see th'appearing buds; which to prove fruit
40   Hope gives not so much warrant, as despair
That frosts will bite them. When we mean to build,
We first survey the plot, then draw the model,
And when we see the figure of the house,
Then must we rate the cost of the erection,
45   Which if we find outweighs ability,
What do we then but draw anew the model
In fewer offices, or at least desist
To build at all? Much more, in this great work –
Which is almost to pluck a kingdom down
50   And set another up – should we survey
The plot of situation and the model,
Consent upon a sure foundation,
Question surveyors, know our own estate,
How able such a work to undergo,
55   To weigh against his opposite; or else
We fortify in paper and in figures,
Using the names of men instead of men,
Like one that draws the model of an house
Beyond his power to build it, who, half-through,
60   Gives o'er, and leaves his part-created cost
A naked subject to the weeping clouds,
And waste for churlish winter's tyranny.

HASTINGS
Grant that our hopes, yet likely of fair birth,

Should be still-born, and that we now possess'd
The utmost man of expectation,   65
I think we are a body strong enough,
Even as we are, to equal with the King.

LORD BARDOLPH
What, is the King but five and twenty thousand?

HASTINGS
To us no more; nay, not so much, Lord Bardolph;
For his divisions, as the times do brawl,   70
Are in three heads: one power against the French;
And one against Glendower; perforce a third
Must take up us. So is the unfirm King
In three divided, and his coffers sound
With hollow poverty and emptiness.   75

ARCHBISHOP
That he should draw his several strengths together
And come against us in full puissance
Need not be dreaded.

HASTINGS   If he should do so,
He leaves his back unarm'd, the French and Welsh
Baying him at the heels: never fear that.   80

LORD BARDOLPH
Who is it like should lead his forces hither?

HASTINGS   The Duke of Lancaster, and Westmoreland;
Against the Welsh, himself and Harry Monmouth;
But who is substituted 'gainst the French
I have no certain notice.

ARCHBISHOP   Let us on,   85
And publish the occasion of our arms.
The commonwealth is sick of their own choice;
Their over-greedy love hath surfeited.
An habitation giddy and unsure
Hath he that buildeth on the vulgar heart.   90
O thou fond many, with what loud applause
Didst thou beat heaven with blessing Bolingbroke,
Before he was what thou wouldst have him be!
And being now trimm'd in thine own desires,
Thou, beastly feeder, art so full of him,   95
That thou provok'st thyself to cast him up.
So, so, thou common dog, didst thou disgorge
Thy glutton bosom of the royal Richard;
And now thou wouldst eat thy dead vomit up,
And howl'st to find it. What trust is in these times? 100
They that, when Richard liv'd, would have him die
Are now become enamour'd on his grave.
Thou that threw'st dust upon his goodly head,
When through proud London he came sighing on
After th'admired heels of Bolingbroke,   105
Cry'st now, 'O earth, yield us that King again,
And take thou this!' O thoughts of men accurs'd!
Past and to come seems best; things present, worst.

MOWBRAY   Shall we go draw our numbers and set on?

HASTINGS
We are time's subjects, and time bids be gone.   110

                                        Exeunt.

2.1   *Enter* Hostess, *with two officers,*
            FANG *with her and* SNARE *following.*

HOSTESS   Master Fang, have you entered the action?

FANG   It is entered.

HOSTESS   Where's your yeoman? Is't a lusty yeoman? Will a stand to't?

FANG   Sirrah – Where's Snare?

HOSTESS   O Lord, ay! Good Master Snare.

SNARE   Here, here.

FANG   Snare, we must arrest Sir John Falstaff.

HOSTESS   Yea, good Master Snare, I have entered him and all.

SNARE   It may chance cost some of us our lives, for he will stab.

HOSTESS   Alas the day, take heed of him – he stabbed me in mine own house, most beastly in good faith. A cares not what mischief he does, if his weapon be out; he will foin like any devil, he will spare neither man, woman, nor child.

FANG   If I can close with him, I care not for his thrust.

HOSTESS   No, nor I neither; I'll be at your elbow.

FANG   And I but fist him once, and a come but within my vice, –

HOSTESS   I am undone by his going, I warrant you, he's an infinitive thing upon my score. Good Master Fang, hold him sure; good Master Snare, let him not 'scape. A comes continuantly to Pie Corner – saving your manhoods – to buy a saddle, and he is indited to dinner to the Lubber's Head in Lumbert Street to Master Smooth's the silkman. I pray you, since my exion is entered, and my case so openly known to the world, let him be brought in to his answer. A hundred mark is a long one for a poor lone woman to bear, and I have borne, and borne, and borne, and have been fubbed off, and fubbed off, and fubbed off, from this day to that day, that it is a shame to be thought on. There is no honesty in such dealing, unless a woman should be made an ass, and a beast, to bear every knave's wrong.

Enter FALSTAFF, BARDOLPH *and* Page.

Yonder he comes, and that arrant malmsey-nose knave Bardolph with him. Do your offices, do your offices, Master Fang and Master Snare, do me, do me, do me your offices.

FALSTAFF   How now, whose mare's dead? What's the matter?

FANG   Sir John, I arrest you at the suit of Mistress Quickly.

FALSTAFF   Away, varlets! Draw, Bardolph! Cut me off the villain's head! Throw the quean in the channel!

HOSTESS   Throw me in the channel? I'll throw thee in the channel. Wilt thou, wilt thou, thou bastardly rogue? Murder! Murder! Ah, thou honeysuckle villain, wilt thou kill God's officers and the King's? Ah, thou honeyseed rogue! thou art a honeyseed, a man queller, and a woman queller.

FALSTAFF   Keep them off, Bardolph!

FANG   A rescue! A rescue!   55

HOSTESS   Good people, bring a rescue or two. Thou wot, wot thou, thou wot, wot ta? Do, do, thou rogue! Do, thou hempseed!

PAGE   Away, you scullion! you rampallian! you fustilarian! I'll tickle your catastrophe!   60

Enter Lord Chief Justice *and his men.*

CHIEF JUSTICE   What is the matter? Keep the peace here, ho!

HOSTESS   Good my lord, be good to me, I beseech you stand to me.

CHIEF JUSTICE
How now, Sir John? What are you brawling here?   65
Doth this become your place, your time, and business?
You should have been well on your way to York.
Stand from him, fellow, wherefore hang'st thou upon him?

HOSTESS   O my most worshipful lord, and't please your Grace, I am a poor widow of Eastcheap, and he is   70
arrested at my suit.

CHIEF JUSTICE   For what sum?

HOSTESS   It is more than for some, my lord, it is for all I have. He hath eaten me out of house and home, he hath put all my substance into that fat belly of his: but   75
I will have some of it out again, or I will ride thee a-nights like the mare.

FALSTAFF   I think I am as like to ride the mare if I have any vantage of ground to get up.

CHIEF JUSTICE   How comes this, Sir John? Fie! what   80
man of good temper would endure this tempest of exclamation? Are you not ashamed to enforce a poor widow to so rough a course to come by her own?

FALSTAFF   What is the gross sum that I owe thee?

HOSTESS   Marry, if thou wert an honest man, thyself   85
and the money too. Thou didst swear to me upon a parcelgilt goblet, sitting in my Dolphin chamber, at the round table, by a sea-coal fire, upon Wednesday in Wheeson week, when the Prince broke thy head for liking his father to a singing-man of Windsor – thou   90
didst swear to me then, as I was washing thy wound, to marry me, and make me my lady thy wife. Canst thou deny it? Did not goodwife Keech the butcher's wife come in then and call me gossip Quickly? – coming in to borrow a mess of vinegar, telling us she   95
had a good dish of prawns, whereby thou didst desire to eat some, whereby I told thee they were ill for a green wound? And didst thou not, when she was gone downstairs, desire me to be no more so familiarity with such poor people, saying that ere long they should call   100
me madam? And didst thou not kiss me, and bid me fetch thee thirty shillings? I put thee now to thy book oath, deny it if thou canst.

FALSTAFF   My lord, this is a poor mad soul, and she says up and down the town that her eldest son is like you.   105

She hath been in good case, and the truth is, poverty hath distracted her. But for these foolish officers, I beseech you I may have redress against them.

CHIEF JUSTICE   Sir John, Sir John, I am well acquainted with your manner of wrenching the true cause the false way. It is not a confident brow, nor the throng of words that come with such more than impudent sauciness from you, can thrust me from a level consideration. You have, as it appears to me, practised upon the easy-yielding spirit of this woman, and made her serve your uses both in purse and in person.

HOSTESS   Yea, in truth, my lord.

CHIEF JUSTICE   Pray thee, peace. Pay her the debt you owe her, and unpay the villainy you have done with her; the one you may do with sterling money, and the other with current repentance.

FALSTAFF   My lord, I will not undergo this sneap without reply. You call honourable boldness impudent sauciness; if a man will make curtsy and say nothing, he is virtuous. No, my lord, my humble duty remembered, I will not be your suitor. I say to you I do desire deliverance from these officers, being upon hasty employment in the King's affairs.

CHIEF JUSTICE   You speak as having power to do wrong; but answer in th'effect of your reputation, and satisfy the poor woman.

FALSTAFF   Come hither, hostess. [*Takes her aside.*]

Enter GOWER.

CHIEF JUSTICE   Now, Master Gower, what news?

GOWER   The King, my lord, and Harry Prince of Wales Are near at hand: the rest the paper tells.
[*Gives a letter.*]

FALSTAFF   As I am a gentleman!

HOSTESS   Faith, you said so before.

FALSTAFF   As I am a gentleman! Come, no more words of it.

HOSTESS   By this heavenly ground I tread on, I must be fain to pawn both my plate and the tapestry of my dining-chambers.

FALSTAFF   Glasses, glasses, is the only drinking; and for thy walls, a pretty slight drollery, or the story of the Prodigal, or the German hunting, in waterwork, is worth a thousand of these bed-hangers and these fly-bitten tapestries. Let it be ten pound if thou canst. Come, and 'twere not for thy humours, there's not a better wench in England. Go, wash thy face, and draw the action. Come, thou must not be in this humour with me, dost not know me? Come, come, I know thou wast set on to this.

HOSTESS   Pray thee, Sir John, let it be but twenty nobles; i'faith, I am loath to pawn my plate, so God save me, la!

FALSTAFF   Let it alone, I'll make other shift: you'll be a fool still.

HOSTESS   Well, you shall have it, though I pawn my gown. I hope you'll come to supper. You'll pay me all together?

FALSTAFF   Will I live? [*to Bardolph*] Go, with her, with her! Hook on, hook on!

HOSTESS   Will you have Doll Tearsheet meet you at supper?

FALSTAFF   No more words, let's have her.
Exeunt Hostess, Fang, Snare, Bardolph and Page.

CHIEF JUSTICE   I have heard better news.

FALSTAFF   What's the news, my lord?

CHIEF JUSTICE   Where lay the King tonight?

GOWER   At Basingstoke, my lord.

FALSTAFF   I hope, my lord, all's well. What is the news, my lord?

CHIEF JUSTICE   Come all his forces back?

GOWER   No, fifteen hundred foot, five hundred horse
Are march'd up to my Lord of Lancaster,
Against Northumberland and the Archbishop.

FALSTAFF   Comes the King back from Wales, my noble lord?

CHIEF JUSTICE   You shall have letters of me presently. Come, go along with me, good Master Gower.

FALSTAFF   My lord!

CHIEF JUSTICE   What's the matter?

FALSTAFF   Master Gower, shall I entreat you with me to dinner?

GOWER   I must wait upon my good lord here, I thank you, good Sir John.

CHIEF JUSTICE   Sir John, you loiter here too long, being you are to take soldiers up in counties as you go.

FALSTAFF   Will you sup with me, Master Gower?

CHIEF JUSTICE   What foolish master taught you these manners, Sir John?

FALSTAFF   Master Gower, if they become me not, he was a fool that taught them me. This is the right fencing grace, my lord; tap for tap, and so part fair.

CHIEF JUSTICE   Now the Lord lighten thee, thou art a great fool.   *Exeunt.*

2.2   *Enter* PRINCE HENRY *and* POINS.

PRINCE   Before God, I am exceeding weary.

POINS   Is't come to that? I had thought weariness durst not have attached one of so high blood.

PRINCE   Faith, it does me, though it discolours the complexion of my greatness to acknowledge it. Doth it not show vilely in me to desire small beer?

POINS   Why, a prince should not be so loosely studied as to remember so weak a composition.

PRINCE   Belike then my appetite was not princely got, for, by my troth, I do now remember the poor creature small beer. But indeed, these humble considerations make me out of love with my greatness. What a disgrace is it to me to remember thy name! or to know thy face tomorrow! or to take note how many pair of silk stockings thou hast – viz. these, and those that were thy peach-coloured ones! or to bear the inventory

of thy shirts – as, one for superfluity, and another
for use! But that the tennis-court keeper knows
better than I, for it is a low ebb of linen with thee
when thou keepest not racket there; as thou hast not
done a great while, because the rest of thy low
countries have made a shift to eat up thy holland. And
God knows whether those that bawl out the ruins of
thy linen shall inherit his kingdom: but the midwives
say the children are not in the fault; whereupon
the world increases, and kindreds are mightily
strengthened.

POINS   How ill it follows, after you have laboured so
hard, you should talk so idly! Tell me, how many good
young princes would do so, their fathers being so sick
as yours at this time is.

PRINCE   Shall I tell thee one thing, Poins?

POINS   Yes, faith, and let it be an excellent good thing.

PRINCE   It shall serve, among wits of no higher breeding
than thine.

POINS   Go to, I stand the push of your one thing that you
will tell.

PRINCE   Marry, I tell thee it is not meet that I should be
sad now my father is sick; albeit I could tell to thee, as
to one it pleases me for fault of a better to call my
friend, I could be sad, and sad indeed too.

POINS   Very hardly, upon such a subject.

PRINCE   By this hand, thou thinkest me as far in the
devil's book as thou and Falstaff, for obduracy and
persistency. Let the end try the man. But I tell thee,
my heart bleeds inwardly that my father is so sick; and
keeping such vile company as thou art hath in reason
taken from me all ostentation of sorrow.

POINS   The reason?

PRINCE   What wouldst thou think of me if I should
weep?

POINS   I would think thee a most princely hypocrite.

PRINCE   It would be every man's thought; and thou art a
blessed fellow, to think as every man thinks. Never a
man's thought in the world keeps the roadway better
than thine: every man would think me an hypocrite
indeed. And what accites your most worshipful
thought to think so?

POINS   Why, because you have been so lewd, and so
much engraffed to Falstaff.

PRINCE   And to thee.

POINS   By this light, I am well spoke on; I can hear it
with mine own ears. The worst that they can say of me
is that I am a second brother, and that I am a proper
fellow of my hands, and those two things I confess I
cannot help. By the mass, here comes Bardolph.

Enter BARDOLPH *and* Page.

PRINCE   And the boy that I gave Falstaff – a had him
from me Christian, and look if the fat villain have not
transformed him ape.

BARDOLPH   God save your Grace!

PRINCE   And yours, most noble Bardolph!

POINS   [*to Bardolph*]   Come, you virtuous ass, you
bashful fool, must you be blushing? Wherefore blush
you now? What a maidenly man-at-arms are you
become! Is't such a matter to get a pottle-pot's   75
maidenhead?

PAGE   A calls me e'en now, my lord, through a red
lattice, and I could discern no part of his face from the
window. At last I spied his eyes, and methought he had
made two holes in the ale-wife's new petticoat, and so   80
peeped through.

PRINCE   Has not the boy profited?

BARDOLPH   Away, you whoreson upright rabbit, away!

PAGE   Away, you rascally Althaea's dream, away!

PRINCE   Instruct us, boy; what dream, boy?   85

PAGE   Marry, my lord, Althaea dreamt she was delivered
of a firebrand; and therefore I call him her dream.

PRINCE   A crown's-worth of good interpretation! There
'tis, boy.

POINS   O, that this blossom could be kept from cankers!   90
Well, there is sixpence to preserve thee.

BARDOLPH   And you do not make him be hanged among
you, the gallows shall have wrong.

PRINCE   And how doth thy master, Bardolph?

BARDOLPH   Well, my lord. He heard of your Grace's   95
coming to town – there's a letter for you.

POINS   Delivered with good respect. And how doth the
martlemas your master?

BARDOLPH   In bodily health, sir.

POINS   Marry, the immortal part needs a physician, but   100
that moves not him; though that be sick, it dies not.

PRINCE   I do allow this wen to be as familiar with me as
my dog, and he holds his place, for look you how he
writes – [*Reads.*] *John Falstaff, Knight.*

POINS   Every man must know that, as oft as he has   105
occasion to name himself: even like those that are kin
to the King, for they never prick their finger but they
say, 'There's some of the King's blood spilt'. 'How
comes that?' says he that takes upon him not to
conceive. The answer is as ready as a borrower's cap –   110
'I am the King's poor cousin, sir'.

PRINCE   Nay, they will be kin to us, or they will fetch it
from Japhet. But the letter: – *Sir John Falstaff, Knight,
to the son of the King nearest his father, Harry Prince of
Wales, greeting.*   115

POINS   Why, this is a certificate!

PRINCE   Peace! *I will imitate the honourable Romans in
brevity.*

POINS   He sure means brevity in breath, short-winded.

PRINCE   *I commend me to thee, I commend thee, and I leave*   120
*thee. Be not too familiar with Poins, for he misuses thy
favours so much that he swears thou art to marry his sister
Nell. Repent at idle times as thou mayst, and so, farewell.*
   *Thine by yea and no – which is as much as to say, as
thou usest him – Jack Falstaff with my familiars, John*   125
*with my brothers and sisters, and Sir John with all
Europe.*

POINS   My lord, I'll steep this letter in sack and make

him eat it.

130 PRINCE   That's to make him eat twenty of his words. But do you use me thus, Ned? Must I marry your sister?

POINS   God send the wench no worse fortune! But I never said so.

135 PRINCE   Well, thus we play the fools with the time, and the spirits of the wise sit in the clouds and mock us. Is your master here in London?

BARDOLPH   Yea, my lord.

PRINCE   Where sups he? Doth the old boar feed in the old frank?

140

BARDOLPH   At the old place, my lord, in Eastcheap.

PRINCE   What company?

PAGE   Ephesians, my lord, of the old church.

PRINCE   Sup any women with him?

145 PAGE   None, my lord, but old Mistress Quickly, and Mistress Doll Tearsheet.

PRINCE   What pagan may that be?

PAGE   A proper gentlewoman, sir, and a kinswoman of my master's.

150 PRINCE   Even such kin as the parish heifers are to the town bull. Shall we steal upon them, Ned, at supper?

POINS   I am your shadow, my lord, I'll follow you.

PRINCE   Sirrah, you boy, and Bardolph, no word to your master that I am yet come to town – there's for your silence.

155

BARDOLPH   I have no tongue, sir.

PAGE   And for mine, sir, I will govern it.

PRINCE   Fare you well; go.

Exeunt Bardolph and Page.

160 This Doll Tearsheet should be some road.

POINS   I warrant you, as common as the way between Saint Albans and London.

PRINCE   How might we see Falstaff bestow himself tonight in his true colours, and not ourselves be seen?

165 POINS   Put on two leathern jerkins and aprons, and wait upon him at his table as drawers.

PRINCE   From a god to a bull? A heavy descension! It was Jove's case. From a prince to a prentice? A low transformation, that shall be mine, for in everything the purpose must weigh with the folly. Follow me, Ned.   *Exeunt.*

170

2.3   *Enter* NORTHUMBERLAND,
            LADY NORTHUMBERLAND *and* LADY PERCY.

NORTHUMBERLAND

I pray thee, loving wife and gentle daughter,
Give even way unto my rough affairs;
Put not you on the visage of the times
And be like them to Percy troublesome.

LADY NORTHUMBERLAND

5   I have given over, I will speak no more.
Do what you will, your wisdom be your guide.

NORTHUMBERLAND

Alas, sweet wife, my honour is at pawn,

And, but my going, nothing can redeem it.

LADY PERCY

O yet, for God's sake, go not to these wars!
The time was, father, that you broke your word   10
When you were more endear'd to it than now;
When your own Percy, when my heart's dear Harry,
Threw many a northward look to see his father
Bring up his powers; but he did long in vain.
Who then persuaded you to stay at home?   15
There were two honours lost, yours and your son's.
For yours, the God of heaven brighten it!
For his, it stuck upon him as the sun
In the grey vault of heaven, and by his light
Did all the chivalry of England move   20
To do brave acts. He was indeed the glass
Wherein the noble youth did dress themselves.
He had no legs that practis'd not his gait;
And speaking thick, which nature made his blemish,
Became the accents of the valiant;   25
For those that could speak low and tardily
Would turn their own perfection to abuse,
To seem like him. So that in speech, in gait,
In diet, in affections of delight,
In military rules, humours of blood,   30
He was the mark and glass, copy and book,
That fashion'd others. And him – O wondrous him!
O miracle of men! – him did you leave,
Second to none, unseconded by you,
To look upon the hideous god of war   35
In disadvantage, to abide a field
Where nothing but the sound of Hotspur's name
Did seem defensible: so you left him.
Never, O never, do his ghost the wrong
To hold your honour more precise and nice   40
With others than with him! Let them alone.
The Marshal and the Archbishop are strong:
Had my sweet Harry had but half their numbers,
Today might I, hanging on Hotspur's neck,
Have talk'd of Monmouth's grave.

NORTHUMBERLAND   Beshrew your heart,   45
Fair daughter, you do draw my spirits from me
With new lamenting ancient oversights.
But I must go and meet with danger there,
Or it will seek me in another place,
And find me worse provided.

LADY NORTHUMBERLAND   O, fly to Scotland,   50
Till that the nobles and the armed commons
Have of their puissance made a little taste.

LADY PERCY

If they get ground and vantage of the King,
Then join you with them like a rib of steel,
To make strength stronger: but, for all our loves,   55
First let them try themselves. So did your son;
He was so suffer'd; so came I a widow,
And never shall have length of life enough
To rain upon remembrance with mine eyes,
That it may grow and sprout as high as heaven   60

For recordation to my noble husband.

NORTHUMBERLAND
Come, come, go in with me. 'Tis with my mind
As with the tide swell'd up unto his height,
That makes a still-stand, running neither way.
Fain would I go to meet the Archbishop,
But many thousand reasons hold me back.
I will resolve for Scotland. There am I,
Till time and vantage crave my company.   *Exeunt.*

2.4   *Enter two* Drawers, FRANCIS *and another.*

FRANCIS
What the devil hast thou brought there – apple-johns?
Thou knowest Sir John cannot endure an apple-john.

2 DRAWER   Mass, thou sayst true. The Prince once set a
dish of apple-johns before him, and told him there
were five more Sir Johns; and, putting off his hat, said,
'I will now take my leave of these six dry, round, old,
withered knights'. It angered him to the heart; but he
hath forgot that.

FRANCIS   Why then, cover, and set them down, and see
if thou canst find out Sneak's noise. Mistress
Tearsheet would fain hear some music.

Enter Third Drawer.

3 DRAWER   Dispatch! The room where they supped is
too hot, they'll come in straight.

FRANCIS   Sirrah, here will be the Prince and Master
Poins anon, and they will put on two of our jerkins and
aprons, and Sir John must not know of it; Bardolph
hath brought word.

3 DRAWER   By the mass, here will be old utis; it will be an
excellent stratagem.

2 DRAWER   I'll see if I can find out Sneak.

Exit with Third Drawer.

Enter Hostess *and* DOLL TEARSHEET.

HOSTESS   I'faith, sweetheart, methinks now you are in
an excellent good temperality. Your pulsidge beats as
extraordinarily as heart would desire, and your colour
I warrant you is as red as any rose, in good truth, la!
But i'faith you have drunk too much canaries, and
that's a marvellous searching wine, and it perfumes
the blood ere one can say, 'What's this?' How do you
now?

DOLL   Better than I was – hem!

HOSTESS
Why, that's well said – a good heart's worth gold.
Lo, here comes Sir John.

Enter FALSTAFF, *singing.*

FALSTAFF
'When Arthur first in court' – Empty the jordan.
Exit Francis.
– 'And was a worthy king' – How now, Mistress Doll?

HOSTESS   Sick of a calm, yea, good faith.

FALSTAFF   So is all her sect; and they be once in a calm   35
they are sick.

DOLL   A pox damn you, you muddy rascal, is that all the
comfort you give me?

FALSTAFF   You make fat rascals, Mistress Doll.

DOLL   I make them? Gluttony and diseases make them,   40
I make them not.

FALSTAFF   If the cook help to make the gluttony, you
help to make the diseases, Doll; we catch of you, Doll,
we catch of you; grant that, my poor virtue, grant that.

DOLL   Yea, joy, our chains and our jewels.   45

FALSTAFF   'Your brooches, pearls, and ouches' – for to
serve bravely is to come halting off, you know; to come
off the breach, with his pike bent bravely; and to
surgery bravely; to venture upon the charged
chambers bravely; –   50

DOLL   Hang yourself, you muddy conger, hang
yourself!

HOSTESS   By my troth, this is the old fashion; you two
never meet but you fall to some discord. You are both
i' good truth as rheumatic as two dry toasts, you   55
cannot one bear with another's confirmities. What the
goodyear! one must bear, [*to Doll*] and that must be
you – you are the weaker vessel, as they say, the
emptier vessel.

DOLL   Can a weak empty vessel bear such a huge   60
full hogshead? There's a whole merchant's venture
of Bordeaux stuff in him; you have not seen a
hulk better stuffed in the hold. Come, I'll be friends
with thee, Jack, thou art going to the wars, and
whether I shall ever see thee again or no there is   65
nobody cares.

Enter Drawer.

DRAWER   Sir, Ancient Pistol's below, and would speak
with you.

DOLL   Hang him, swaggering rascal, let him not
come hither: it is the foul-mouth'dst rogue in   70
England.

HOSTESS   If he swagger, let him not come here. No, by
my faith! I must live among my neighbours, I'll no
swaggerers. I am in good name and fame with the very
best. Shut the door, there comes no swaggerers here. I   75
have not lived all this while to have swaggering now.
Shut the door I pray you.

FALSTAFF   Dost thou hear, hostess?

HOSTESS   Pray ye pacify yourself, Sir John, there comes
no swaggerers here.   80

FALSTAFF   Dost thou hear? It is mine ancient.

HOSTESS   Tilly-fally, Sir John, ne'er tell me: and your
ancient swagger, a comes not in my doors. I was before
Master Tisick the debuty t'other day, and, as he said
to me – 'twas no longer ago than Wednesday last, i'   85
good faith – 'Neighbour Quickly,' says he – Master
Dumb our minister was by then – 'Neighbour
Quickly,' says he, 'receive those that are civil, for', said
he, 'you are in an ill name' – now a said so, I can tell

90 whereupon. 'For', says he, 'you are an honest woman, and well thought on, therefore take heed what guests you receive; receive', says he, 'no swaggering companions': there comes none here. You would bless you to hear what he said. No, I'll no swaggerers.

95 FALSTAFF He's no swaggerer, hostess, a tame cheater, i'faith, you may stroke him as gently as a puppy greyhound. He'll not swagger with a Barbary hen, if her feathers turn back in any show of resistance. Call him up, drawer.   *Exit Drawer.*

100 HOSTESS Cheater, call you him? I will bar no honest man my house, nor no cheater, but I do not love swaggering, by my troth, I am the worse when one says 'swagger'. Feel, masters, how I shake, look you, I warrant you.

105 DOLL So you do, hostess.

HOSTESS Do I? Yea, in very truth do I, and 'twere an aspen leaf. I cannot abide swaggerers.

Enter Ancient PISTOL, BARDOLPH *and* Page.

PISTOL God save you, Sir John!

FALSTAFF Welcome, Ancient Pistol! Here, Pistol, I
110 charge you with a cup of sack; do you discharge upon mine hostess.

PISTOL I will discharge upon her, Sir John, with two bullets.

FALSTAFF She is pistol-proof, sir; you shall not hardly
115 offend her.

HOSTESS Come, I'll drink no proofs, nor no bullets; I'll drink no more than will do me good, for no man's pleasure, I.

PISTOL Then to you, Mistress Dorothy! I will charge
120 you.

DOLL Charge me? I scorn you, scurvy companion. What, you poor, base, rascally, cheating, lack-linen mate! Away, you mouldy rogue, away! I am meat for your master.

125 PISTOL I know you, Mistress Dorothy.

DOLL Away, you cutpurse rascal, you filthy bung, away! By this wine, I'll thrust my knife in your mouldy chaps and you play the saucy cuttle with me. Away, you bottle-ale rascal, you basket-hilt stale juggler, you!
130 Since when, I pray you, sir? God's light, with two points on your shoulder? Much!

PISTOL God let me not live, but I will murder your ruff for this.

FALSTAFF No more, Pistol! I would not have you go off
135 here. Discharge yourself of our company, Pistol.

HOSTESS

No, good Captain Pistol, not here, sweet captain.

DOLL Captain! Thou abominable damned cheater, art thou not ashamed to be called captain? And captains were of my mind, they would truncheon you out, for
140 taking their names upon you before you have earned them. You a captain? You slave! For what? For tearing a poor whore's ruff in a bawdy-house? He a captain? Hang him, rogue, he lives upon mouldy stewed prunes and dried cakes. A captain? God's light, these villains
145 will make the word as odious as the word 'occupy', which was an excellent good word before it was ill sorted: therefore captains had need look to't.

BARDOLPH Pray thee go down, good ancient.

FALSTAFF Hark thee hither, Mistress Doll.

PISTOL Not I! I tell thee what, Corporal Bardolph, I
150 could tear her! I'll be revenged of her.

PAGE Pray thee go down.

PISTOL I'll see her damned first! To Pluto's damnèd lake, by this hand, to th'infernal deep, with Erebus and tortures vile also! Hold hook and line, say I!
155 Down, down, dogs! Down, faitors! Have we not Hiren here? [*Draws his sword.*]

HOSTESS Good Captain Peesel, be quiet, 'tis very late i' faith; I beseek you now, aggravate your choler.
160

PISTOL

These be good humours indeed! Shall pack-horses,
And hollow pamper'd jades of Asia,
Which cannot go but thirty mile a day,
Compare with Caesars and with Cannibals,
And Troyant Greeks? Nay, rather damn them with   165
King Cerberus, and let the welkin roar!
Shall we fall foul for toys?

HOSTESS By my troth, captain, these are very bitter words.

BARDOLPH Be gone, good ancient, this will grow to a   170
brawl anon.

PISTOL Die men like dogs! Give crowns like pins! Have we not Hiren here?

HOSTESS O' my word, captain, there's none such here. What the goodyear, do you think I would deny her?   175
For God's sake be quiet.

PISTOL Then feed and be fat, my fair Calipolis!
Come, give's some sack.
Si fortune me tormente sperato me contento.
Fear we broadsides? No, let the fiend give fire!   180
Give me some sack; and sweetheart, lie thou there!
[*Lays down his sword.*]
Come we to full points here? And are etceteras
nothings?

FALSTAFF Pistol, I would be quiet.

PISTOL Sweet knight, I kiss thy neaf. What! we have
seen the seven stars.   185

DOLL For God's sake, thrust him downstairs, I cannot endure such a fustian rascal.

PISTOL Thrust him downstairs? Know we not Galloway nags?

FALSTAFF Quoit him down, Bardolph, like a shove-   190
groat shilling. Nay, and a do nothing but speak nothing, a shall be nothing here.

BARDOLPH Come, get you downstairs.

PISTOL What! shall we have incision? shall we imbrue?
[*Snatches up his sword.*]
Then death rock me asleep, abridge my doleful days!   195
Why then let grievous, ghastly, gaping wounds

Untwind the Sisters Three! Come, Atropos, I say!

HOSTESS Here's goodly stuff toward!

FALSTAFF Give me my rapier, boy.

DOLL I pray thee, Jack, I pray thee do not draw.

FALSTAFF [*drawing*] Get you downstairs.

HOSTESS Here's a goodly tumult! I'll forswear keeping house afore I'll be in these tirrits and frights! [*Falstaff thrusts at Pistol.*] So! Murder, I warrant now! Alas, alas, put up your naked weapons, put up your naked weapons.   *Exit Bardolph, driving Pistol out.*

DOLL I pray thee, Jack, be quiet, the rascal's gone. Ah, you whoreson little valiant villain, you!

HOSTESS Are you not hurt i'th' groin? Methought a made a shrewd thrust at your belly.

Enter BARDOLPH.

FALSTAFF Have you turned him out a-doors?

BARDOLPH Yea, sir, the rascal's drunk. You have hurt him, sir, i'th' shoulder.

FALSTAFF A rascal, to brave me!

DOLL Ah, you sweet little rogue, you! Alas, poor ape, how thou sweat'st! Come, let me wipe thy face. Come on, you whoreson chops! Ah, rogue, i'faith, I love thee. Thou art as valorous as Hector of Troy, worth five of Agamemnon, and ten times better than the Nine Worthies. Ah, villain!

FALSTAFF A rascally slave! I will toss the rogue in a blanket.

DOLL Do, and thou dar'st for thy heart. And thou dost, I'll canvass thee between a pair of sheets.

Enter musicians.

PAGE The music is come, sir.

FALSTAFF Let them play. Play, sirs!   [*Music.*]
Sit on my knee, Doll. A rascal bragging slave! The rogue fled from me like quicksilver.

DOLL I'faith, and thou followedst him like a church. Thou whoreson little tidy Bartholomew boar-pig, when wilt thou leave fighting a-days, and foining a-nights, and begin to patch up thine old body for heaven?

Enter, behind, the PRINCE *and* POINS *disguised as drawers.*

FALSTAFF Peace, good Doll, do not speak like a death's-head, do not bid me remember mine end.

DOLL Sirrah, what humour's the Prince of?

FALSTAFF A good shallow young fellow; a would have made a good pantler, a would ha' chipped bread well.

DOLL They say Poins has a good wit.

FALSTAFF He a good wit? Hang him, baboon! His wit's as thick as Tewkesbury mustard; there's no more conceit in him than is in a mallet.

DOLL Why does the Prince love him so, then?

FALSTAFF Because their legs are both of a bigness, and a plays at quoits well, and eats conger and fennel, and drinks off candles' ends for flap-dragons, and rides the wild mare with the boys, and jumps upon joint-stools, and swears with a good grace, and wears his boots very smooth like unto the sign of the Leg, and breeds no bate with telling of discreet stories, and such other gambol faculties a has that show a weak mind and an able body, for the which the Prince admits him: for the Prince himself is such another, the weight of a hair will turn the scales between their avoirdupois.

PRINCE Would not this nave of a wheel have his ears cut off?

POINS Let's beat him before his whore.

PRINCE Look whe'er the withered elder hath not his poll clawed like a parrot.

POINS Is it not strange that desire should so many years outlive performance?

FALSTAFF Kiss me, Doll.

PRINCE Saturn and Venus this year in conjunction! What says th'almanac to that?

POINS And look whether the fiery Trigon his man be not lisping to his master's old tables, his note-book, his counsel-keeper.

FALSTAFF Thou dost give me flattering busses.

DOLL By my troth, I kiss thee with a most constant heart.

FALSTAFF I am old, I am old.

DOLL I love thee better than I love e'er a scurvy young boy of them all.

FALSTAFF What stuff wilt have a kirtle of? I shall receive money a-Thursday, shalt have a cap tomorrow. A merry song! Come, it grows late, we'll to bed. Thou't forget me when I am gone.

DOLL By my troth, thou't set me a-weeping and thou sayst so. Prove that ever I dress myself handsome till thy return, – Well, hearken a'th' end.

FALSTAFF Some sack, Francis.

PRINCE }
POINS } [*coming forward*] Anon, anon, sir.

FALSTAFF Ha! A bastard son of the King's? And art not thou Poins his brother?

PRINCE Why, thou globe of sinful continents, what a life dost thou lead!

FALSTAFF A better than thou – I am a gentleman, thou art a drawer.

PRINCE Very true, sir, and I come to draw you out by the ears.

HOSTESS O the Lord preserve thy good Grace! By my troth, welcome to London! Now the Lord bless that sweet face of thine! O Jesu, are you come from Wales?

FALSTAFF Thou whoreson mad compound of majesty, by this light flesh and corrupt blood [*leaning his hand upon Doll*], thou art welcome.

DOLL How! You fat fool, I scorn you.

POINS My lord, he will drive you out of your revenge and turn all to a merriment, if you take not the heat.

PRINCE You whoreson candle-mine you, how vilely did you speak of me even now, before this honest, virtuous, civil gentlewoman!

HOSTESS   God's blessing of your good heart! and so she is, by my troth.

305 FALSTAFF   Didst thou hear me?

PRINCE   Yea, and you knew me, as you did when you ran away by Gad's Hill; you knew I was at your back, and spoke it on purpose to try my patience.

FALSTAFF   No, no, no, not so; I did not think thou wast
310 within hearing.

PRINCE   I shall drive you then to confess the wilful abuse, and then I know how to handle you.

FALSTAFF   No abuse, Hal, o'mine honour, no abuse.

PRINCE   Not? – to dispraise me, and call me pantler, and
315 bread-chipper, and I know not what?

FALSTAFF   No abuse, Hal.

POINS   No abuse?

FALSTAFF   No abuse, Ned, i'th' world, honest Ned, none. I dispraised him before the wicked [*Turns to the*
320 *Prince.*] that the wicked might not fall in love with thee: in which doing, I have done the part of a careful friend and a true subject, and thy father is to give me thanks for it. No abuse, Hal; none, Ned, none; no, faith, boys, none.

325 PRINCE   See now whether pure fear and entire cowardice doth not make thee wrong this virtuous gentlewoman to close with us. Is she of the wicked? Is thine hostess here of the wicked? Or is thy boy of the wicked? Or honest Bardolph, whose zeal burns in his nose, of the
330 wicked?

POINS   Answer, thou dead elm, answer.

FALSTAFF   The fiend hath pricked down Bardolph irrecoverable, and his face is Lucifer's privy-kitchen, where he doth nothing but roast malt-worms. For the
335 boy, there is a good angel about him, but the devil attends him too.

PRINCE   For the women?

FALSTAFF   For one of them, she's in hell already, and burns poor souls. For th'other, I owe her money, and
340 whether she be damned for that I know not.

HOSTESS   No, I warrant you.

FALSTAFF   No, I think thou art not, I think thou art quit for that. Marry, there is another indictment upon thee, for suffering flesh to be eaten in thy house, contrary to
345 the law, for the which I think thou wilt howl.

HOSTESS   All vict'lers do so. What's a joint of mutton or two in a whole Lent?

PRINCE   You, gentlewoman, –

DOLL   What says your Grace?

350 FALSTAFF   His Grace says that which his flesh rebels against. [*Peto knocks at door.*]

HOSTESS   Who knocks so loud at door? Look to th' door there, Francis.

Enter PETO.

PRINCE   Peto, how now, what news?

355 PETO   The King your father is at Westminster, And there are twenty weak and wearied posts

Come from the north; and as I came along
I met and overtook a dozen captains,
Bareheaded, sweating, knocking at the taverns,
And asking every one for Sir John Falstaff. 360

PRINCE   By heaven, Poins, I feel me much to blame,
So idly to profane the precious time,
When tempest of commotion, like the south
Borne with black vapour, doth begin to melt
And drop upon our bare unarmed heads. 365
Give me my sword and cloak. Falstaff, good night.

Exeunt Prince and Poins.

FALSTAFF   Now comes in the sweetest morsel of the night, and we must hence and leave it unpicked.

Knocking within. Exit Bardolph.

More knocking at the door?

Enter BARDOLPH.

How now, what's the matter? 370

BARDOLPH   You must away to court, sir, presently. A dozen captains stay at door for you.

FALSTAFF   [*to the Page*] Pay the musicians, sirrah. Farewell, hostess; farewell, Doll. You see, my good wenches, how men of merit are sought after; the 375 undeserver may sleep, when the man of action is called on. Farewell, good wenches: if I be not sent away post, I will see you again ere I go.

DOLL   I cannot speak; if my heart be not ready to burst – Well, sweet Jack, have a care of thyself. 380

FALSTAFF   Farewell, farewell.

Exit with Bardolph, Peto, Page and musicians.

HOSTESS   Well, fare thee well. I have known thee these twenty-nine years, come peascod-time, but an honester and truer-hearted man – Well, fare thee well.

BARDOLPH [*at the door*]   Mistress Tearsheet! 385

HOSTESS   What's the matter?

BARDOLPH   Bid Mistress Tearsheet come to my master.

HOSTESS   O, run Doll, run; run good Doll; come. She comes blubbered. [*to Doll*] Yea, will you come, Doll?

Exeunt.

3.1   *Enter the* KING *in his nightgown, with a page.*

KING   Go call the Earls of Surrey and of Warwick;
But ere they come, bid them o'er-read these letters
And well consider of them. Make good speed.

Exit page.

How many thousand of my poorest subjects
Are at this hour asleep! O sleep, O gentle sleep, 5
Nature's soft nurse, how have I frighted thee,
That thou no more wilt weigh my eyelids down,
And steep my senses in forgetfulness?
Why rather, sleep, liest thou in smoky cribs,
Upon uneasy pallets stretching thee, 10
And husht with buzzing night-flies to thy slumber,
Than in the perfum'd chambers of the great,
Under the canopies of costly state,
And lull'd with sound of sweetest melody?

O thou dull god, why li'st thou with the vile
In loathsome beds, and leav'st the kingly couch
A watch-case, or a common 'larum-bell?
Wilt thou upon the high and giddy mast
Seal up the ship-boy's eyes, and rock his brains
In cradle of the rude imperious surge,
And in the visitation of the winds,
Who take the ruffian billows by the top,
Curling their monstrous heads, and hanging them
With deafing clamour in the slippery clouds,
That with the hurly death itself awakes?
Canst thou, O partial sleep, give thy repose
To the wet sea-boy in an hour so rude,
And in the calmest and most stillest night,
With all appliances and means to boot,
Deny it to a King? Then happy low, lie down!
Uneasy lies the head that wears a crown.

Enter WARWICK *and* SURREY.

WARWICK   Many good morrows to your Majesty!
KING   Is it good morrow, lords?
WARWICK   'Tis one o'clock, and past.
KING   Why then, good morrow to you all, my lords.
    Have you read o'er the letters that I sent you?
WARWICK   We have, my liege.
KING   Then you perceive the body of our kingdom
    How foul it is, what rank diseases grow,
    And with what danger, near the heart of it.
WARWICK   It is but as a body yet distemper'd,
    Which to his former strength may be restor'd
    With good advice and little medicine.
    My Lord Northumberland will soon be cool'd.
KING   O God, that one might read the book of fate,
    And see the revolution of the times
    Make mountains level, and the continent,
    Weary of solid firmness, melt itself
    Into the sea, and other times to see
    The beachy girdle of the ocean
    Too wide for Neptune's hips; how chance's mocks
    And changes fill the cup of alteration
    With divers liquors! O, if this were seen,
    The happiest youth, viewing his progress through,
    What perils past, what crosses to ensue,
    Would shut the book and sit him down and die.
    'Tis not ten years gone,
    Since Richard and Northumberland, great friends,
    Did feast together, and in two years after
    Were they at wars. It is but eight years since,
    This Percy was the man nearest my soul;
    Who like a brother toil'd in my affairs,
    And laid his love and life under my foot;
    Yea, for my sake, even to the eyes of Richard
    Gave him defiance. But which of you was by –
    [*to Warwick*] You, cousin Nevil, as I may remember –
    When Richard, with his eye brimful of tears,
    Then check'd and rated by Northumberland,
    Did speak these words, now prov'd a prophecy?

'Northumberland, thou ladder by the which   70
My cousin Bolingbroke ascends my throne'
(Though then, God knows, I had no such intent
But that necessity so bow'd the state
That I and greatness were compell'd to kiss)
'The time shall come' – thus did he follow it –   75
'The time will come, that foul sin, gathering head,
Shall break into corruption' – so went on,
Foretelling this same time's condition,
And the division of our amity.
WARWICK   There is a history in all men's lives   80
    Figuring the nature of the times deceas'd;
    The which observ'd, a man may prophesy,
    With a near aim, of the main chance of things
    As yet not come to life, who in their seeds
    And weak beginnings lie intreasured.   85
    Such things become the hatch and brood of time;
    And by the necessary form of this
    King Richard might create a perfect guess
    That great Northumberland, then false to him,
    Would of that seed grow to a greater falseness,   90
    Which should not find a ground to root upon
    Unless on you.
KING   Are these things then necessities?
    Then let us meet them like necessities;
    And that same word even now cries out on us.
    They say the Bishop and Northumberland   95
    Are fifty thousand strong.
WARWICK   It cannot be, my lord.
    Rumour doth double, like the voice and echo,
    The numbers of the feared. Please it your Grace
    To go to bed: upon my soul, my lord,
    The powers that you already have sent forth   100
    Shall bring this prize in very easily.
    To comfort you the more, I have receiv'd
    A certain instance that Glendower is dead.
    Your Majesty hath been this fortnight ill,
    And these unseason'd hours perforce must add   105
    Unto your sickness.
KING   I will take your counsel.
    And were these inward wars once out of hand,
    We would, dear lords, unto the Holy Land.   *Exeunt.*

3.2   *Enter* Justice SHALLOW *and* Justice SILENCE,
        with MOULDY, SHADOW, WART, FEEBLE, BULLCALF
            and servants, behind.

SHALLOW   Come on, come on, come on: give me your
    hand, sir, give me your hand, sir; an early stirrer, by
    the rood! And how doth my good cousin Silence?
SILENCE   Good morrow, good cousin Shallow.
SHALLOW   And how doth my cousin your bedfellow?   5
    and your fairest daughter and mine, my god-daughter
    Ellen?
SILENCE   Alas, a black woosel, cousin Shallow!
SHALLOW   By yea and no, sir: I dare say my cousin
    William is become a good scholar; he is at Oxford still,   10
    is he not?

SILENCE   Indeed, sir, to my cost.

SHALLOW   A must then to the Inns o'Court shortly: I was once of Clement's Inn, where I think they will talk of mad Shallow yet.

SILENCE   You were called 'lusty Shallow' then, cousin.

SHALLOW   By the mass, I was called anything, and I would have done anything indeed too, and roundly too. There was I, and little John Doit of Staffordshire, and black George Barnes, and Francis Pickbone, and Will Squele, a Cotsole man – you had not four such swinge-bucklers in all the Inns o'Court again; and I may say to you, we knew where the bona-robas were, and had the best of them all at commandment. Then was Jack Falstaff, now Sir John, a boy, and page to Thomas Mowbray, Duke of Norfolk.

SILENCE   This Sir John, cousin, that comes hither anon about soldiers?

SHALLOW   The same Sir John, the very same. I see him break Scoggin's head at the court gate, when a was a crack, not thus high; and the very same day did I fight with one Samson Stockfish a fruiterer, behind Gray's Inn. Jesu, Jesu, the mad days that I have spent! And to see how many of my old acquaintance are dead!

SILENCE   We shall all follow, cousin.

SHALLOW   Certain, 'tis certain, very sure, very sure. Death, as the Psalmist saith, is certain to all, all shall die. How a good yoke of bullocks at Stamford fair?

SILENCE   By my troth, I was not there.

SHALLOW   Death is certain. Is old Double of your town living yet?

SILENCE   Dead, sir.

SHALLOW   Jesu, Jesu, dead! A drew a good bow, and dead! A shot a fine shoot. John a Gaunt loved him well, and betted much money on his head. Dead! A would have clapped i'th' clout at twelve score, and carried you a forehand shaft a fourteen and fourteen and a half, that it would have done a man's heart good to see. How a score of ewes now?

SILENCE   Thereafter as they be; a score of good ewes may be worth ten pounds.

SHALLOW   And is old Double dead?

SILENCE   Here come two of Sir John Falstaff's men, as I think.

Enter BARDOLPH *and one with him.*

SHALLOW   Good morrow, honest gentlemen.

BARDOLPH   I beseech you, which is Justice Shallow?

SHALLOW   I am Robert Shallow, sir, a poor esquire of this county, and one of the King's justices of the peace. What is your good pleasure with me?

BARDOLPH   My captain, sir, commends him to you, my captain Sir John Falstaff, a tall gentleman, by heaven, and a most gallant leader.

SHALLOW   He greets me well, sir; I knew him a good backsword man. How doth the good knight? May I ask how my lady his wife doth?

BARDOLPH   Sir, pardon: a soldier is better accommodated than with a wife.

SHALLOW   It is well said, in faith, sir, and it is well said indeed, too. 'Better accommodated'! It is good, yea indeed is it; good phrases are surely, and ever were, very commendable. 'Accommodated' – it comes of 'accommodo'; very good, a good phrase.

BARDOLPH   Pardon, sir, I have heard the word – phrase call you it? By this day, I know not the phrase, but I will maintain the word with my sword to be a soldier-like word, and a word of exceeding good command, by heaven. Accommodated: that is, when a man is, as they say, accommodated, or when a man is being whereby a may be thought to be accommodated; which is an excellent thing.

SHALLOW   It is very just.

Enter FALSTAFF.

Look, here comes good Sir John. Give me your good hand, give me your worship's good hand. By my troth, you like well, and bear your years very well. Welcome, good Sir John.

FALSTAFF   I am glad to see you well, good Master Robert Shallow. Master Surecard, as I think?

SHALLOW   No, Sir John, it is my cousin Silence, in commission with me.

FALSTAFF   Good Master Silence, it well befits you should be of the peace.

SILENCE   Your good worship is welcome.

FALSTAFF   Fie, this is hot weather, gentlemen. Have you provided me here half a dozen sufficient men?

SHALLOW   Marry have we, sir. Will you sit?

FALSTAFF   Let me see them, I beseech you.

SHALLOW   Where's the roll? where's the roll? where's the roll? Let me see, let me see, let me see. So, so, so, so, so, so, so. Yea, marry, sir: Rafe Mouldy! Let them appear as I call; let them do so, let them do so. Let me see; where is Mouldy?

MOULDY   Here, and't please you.

SHALLOW   What think you, Sir John? A good-limbed fellow, young, strong, and of good friends.

FALSTAFF   Is thy name Mouldy?

MOULDY   Yea, and't please you.

FALSTAFF   'Tis the more time thou wert used.

SHALLOW   Ha, ha, ha! most excellent, i'faith, things that are mouldy lack use: very singular good, in faith, well said, Sir John, very well said.

FALSTAFF   Prick him.

MOULDY   I was pricked well enough before, and you could have let me alone. My old dame will be undone now for one to do her husbandry and her drudgery. You need not to have pricked me, there are other men fitter to go out than I.

FALSTAFF   Go to; peace, Mouldy; you shall go, Mouldy; it is time you were spent.

MOULDY Spent?

SHALLOW Peace, fellow, peace – stand aside; know you where you are? For th'other, Sir John – let me see: Simon Shadow!

FALSTAFF Yea, marry, let me have him to sit under. He's like to be a cold soldier.

SHALLOW Where's Shadow?

SHADOW Here, sir.

FALSTAFF Shadow, whose son art thou?

SHADOW My mother's son, sir.

FALSTAFF Thy mother's son! Like enough, and thy father's shadow. So the son of the female is the shadow of the male; it is often so indeed – but much of the father's substance!

SHALLOW Do you like him, Sir John?

FALSTAFF Shadow will serve for summer. Prick him, for we have a number of shadows fill up the muster-book.

SHALLOW Thomas Wart!

FALSTAFF Where's he?

WART Here, sir.

FALSTAFF Is thy name Wart?

WART Yea, sir.

FALSTAFF Thou art a very ragged Wart.

SHALLOW Shall I prick him, Sir John?

FALSTAFF It were superfluous, for his apparel is built upon his back, and the whole frame stands upon pins: prick him no more.

SHALLOW Ha, ha, ha! you can do it, sir, you can do it, I commend you well. Francis Feeble!

FEEBLE Here, sir.

FALSTAFF What trade art thou, Feeble?

FEEBLE A woman's tailor, sir.

SHALLOW Shall I prick him, sir?

FALSTAFF You may; but if he had been a man's tailor he'd ha' pricked you. Wilt thou make as many holes in an enemy's battle as thou hast done in a woman's petticoat?

FEEBLE I will do my good will, sir, you can have no more.

FALSTAFF Well said, good woman's tailor! Well said, courageous Feeble! Thou wilt be as valiant as the wrathful dove, or most magnanimous mouse. Prick the woman's tailor: well, Master Shallow; deep, Master Shallow.

FEEBLE I would Wart might have gone, sir.

FALSTAFF I would thou wert a man's tailor, that thou mightst mend him and make him fit to go. I cannot put him to a private soldier, that is the leader of so many thousands. Let that suffice, most forcible Feeble.

FEEBLE It shall suffice, sir.

FALSTAFF I am bound to thee, reverend Feeble. Who is next?

SHALLOW Peter Bullcalf o'th' green!

FALSTAFF Yea, marry, let's see Bullcalf.

BULLCALF Here, sir.

FALSTAFF Fore God, a likely fellow! Come, prick me Bullcalf till he roar again.

BULLCALF O Lord, good my lord captain –

FALSTAFF What, dost thou roar before thou art pricked?

BULLCALF O Lord, sir, I am a diseased man.

FALSTAFF What disease hast thou?   180

BULLCALF A whoreson cold, sir, a cough, sir, which I caught with ringing in the King's affairs upon his coronation day, sir.

FALSTAFF Come, thou shalt go to the wars in a gown; we will have away thy cold, and I will take such order   185 that thy friends shall ring for thee. Is here all?

SHALLOW Here is two more called than your number; you must have but four here, sir: and so, I pray you, go in with me to dinner.

FALSTAFF Come, I will go drink with you, but I cannot   190 tarry dinner. I am glad to see you, by my troth, Master Shallow.

SHALLOW O, Sir John, do you remember since we lay all night in the Windmill in Saint George's Field?

FALSTAFF No more of that, good Master Shallow, no   195 more of that.

SHALLOW Ha, 'twas a merry night! And is Jane Nightwork alive?

FALSTAFF She lives, Master Shallow.

SHALLOW She never could away with me.   200

FALSTAFF Never, never; she would always say she could not abide Master Shallow.

SHALLOW By the mass, I could anger her to th'heart. She was then a bona-roba. Doth she hold her own well?   205

FALSTAFF Old, old, Master Shallow.

SHALLOW Nay, she must be old, she cannot choose but be old, certain she's old, and had Robin Nightwork by old Nightwork before I came to Clement's Inn.

SILENCE That's fifty-five year ago.   210

SHALLOW Ha, cousin Silence, that thou hadst seen that that this knight and I have seen! Ha, Sir John, said I well?

FALSTAFF We have heard the chimes at midnight, Master Shallow.   215

SHALLOW That we have, that we have, that we have; in faith, Sir John, we have; our watchword was 'Hem, boys!' – Come, let's to dinner; come, let's to dinner. Jesus, the days that we have seen! Come, come.

Exeunt Falstaff, Shallow and Silence.

BULLCALF Good Master Corporate Bardolph, stand my   220 friend; and here's four Harry ten shillings in French crowns for you. In very truth, sir, I had as lief be hanged, sir, as go. And yet for mine own part, sir, I do not care; but rather because I am unwilling, and, for mine own part, have a desire to stay with my friends;   225 else, sir, I did not care, for mine own part, so much.

BARDOLPH Go to, stand aside.

MOULDY And, good Master Corporal Captain, for my old dame's sake stand my friend. She has nobody to do anything about her when I am gone, and she is old and   230 cannot help herself. You shall have forty, sir.

BARDOLPH Go to, stand aside.

FEEBLE   By my troth I care not, a man can die but once, we owe God a death. I'll ne'er bear a base mind – and't
235   be my destiny, so; and't be not, so. No man's too good to serve's prince, and let it go which way it will, he that dies this year is quit for the next.

BARDOLPH   Well said, th'art a good fellow.

FEEBLE   Faith, I'll bear no base mind.

Enter FALSTAFF *and the* Justices.

240   FALSTAFF   Come, sir, which men shall I have?

SHALLOW   Four of which you please.

BARDOLPH   Sir, a word with you. I have three pound to free Mouldy and Bullcalf.

FALSTAFF   Go to, well.

245   SHALLOW   Come, Sir John, which four will you have?

FALSTAFF   Do you choose for me.

SHALLOW   Marry then, Mouldy, Bullcalf, Feeble, and Shadow.

FALSTAFF   Mouldy and Bullcalf: for you, Mouldy, stay
250   at home till you are past service; and for your part, Bullcalf, grow till you come unto it. I will none of you.

SHALLOW   Sir John, Sir John, do not yourself wrong, they are your likeliest men, and I would have you served with the best.

255   FALSTAFF   Will you tell me, Master Shallow, how to choose a man? Care I for the limb, the thews, the stature, bulk, and big assemblance of a man? Give me the spirit, Master Shallow. Here's Wart; you see what a ragged appearance it is – a shall charge you, and
260   discharge you, with the motion of a pewterer's hammer, come off and on swifter than he that gibbets on the brewer's bucket. And this same half-faced fellow Shadow; give me this man, he presents no mark to the enemy – the foeman may with as great aim level
265   at the edge of a penknife. And for a retreat, how swiftly will this Feeble the woman's tailor run off! O, give me the spare men, and spare me the great ones. Put me a caliver into Wart's hand, Bardolph.

BARDOLPH   Hold, Wart, traverse – thas! thas! thas!

270   FALSTAFF   Come, manage me your caliver. So, very well! Go to, very good! Exceeding good! O, give me always a little, lean, old, chopt, bald shot. Well said, i' faith, Wart, th'art a good scab. Hold, there's a tester for thee.

SHALLOW   He is not his craft's master, he doth not do it
275   right. I remember at Mile-End Green, when I lay at Clement's Inn – I was then Sir Dagonet in Arthur's show – there was a little quiver fellow, and a would manage you his piece thus, and a would about, and about, and come you in, and come you in. 'Rah, tah,
280   tah', would a say; 'Bounce', would a say; and away again would a go, and again would a come: I shall ne'er see such a fellow.

FALSTAFF   These fellows will do well, Master Shallow. God keep you, Master Silence: I will not use many
285   words with you. Fare you well, gentlemen both; I thank you. I must a dozen mile tonight. Bardolph, give the soldiers coats.

SHALLOW   Sir John, the Lord bless you! God prosper your affairs! God send us peace! At your return, visit
290   our house, let our old acquaintance be renewed. Peradventure I will with ye to the court.

FALSTAFF   Fore God, I would you would, Master Shallow.

SHALLOW   Go to, I have spoke at a word. God keep you!

FALSTAFF   Fare you well, gentle gentlemen.   295

Exeunt Justices.

On Bardolph, lead the men away.

Exeunt Bardolph and recruits.

As I return, I will fetch off these justices. I do see the bottom of Justice Shallow. Lord, Lord, how subject we old men are to this vice of lying! This same starved
300   justice hath done nothing but prate to me of the wildness of his youth, and the feats he hath done about Turnbull Street, and every third word a lie, duer paid to the hearer than the Turk's tribute. I do remember him at Clement's Inn, like a man made after supper of
305   a cheese-paring. When a was naked, he was for all the world like a forked radish, with a head fantastically carved upon it with a knife. A was so forlorn, that his dimensions to any thick sight were invisible; a was the very genius of famine, yet lecherous as a monkey, and
310   the whores called him mandrake. A came ever in the rearward of the fashion, and sung those tunes to the overscutched housewives that he heard the carmen whistle, and sware they were his fancies or his good-nights. And now is this Vice's dagger become a squire,
315   and talks as familiarly of John a Gaunt as if he had been sworn brother to him, and I'll be sworn a ne'er saw him but once in the tilt-yard, and then he burst his head for crowding among the marshal's men. I saw it and told John a Gaunt he beat his own name, for you
320   might have thrust him and all his apparel into an eel-skin – the case of a treble hautboy was a mansion for him, a court; and now has he land and beefs. Well, I'll be acquainted with him if I return, and't shall go hard but I'll make him a philosopher's two stones to me. If
325   the young dace be a bait for the old pike, I see no reason in the law of nature but I may snap at him: let time shape, and there an end.   *Exit.*

4.1   *Enter the* Archbishop, MOWBRAY,
HASTINGS *and others.*

ARCHBISHOP   What is this forest call'd?

HASTINGS
'Tis Gaultree Forest, and't shall please your Grace.

ARCHBISHOP
Here stand, my lords, and send discoverers forth
To know the numbers of our enemies.

HASTINGS   We have sent forth already.

ARCHBISHOP   'Tis well done.   5
My friends and brethren in these great affairs,
I must acquaint you that I have receiv'd
New-dated letters from Northumberland,

Their cold intent, tenor, and substance, thus:
10 Here doth he wish his person, with such powers
As might hold sortance with his quality,
The which he could not levy; whereupon
He is retir'd to ripe his growing fortunes
To Scotland, and concludes in hearty prayers
15 That your attempts may overlive the hazard
And fearful meeting of their opposite.
MOWBRAY
Thus do the hopes we have in him touch ground
And dash themselves to pieces.

Enter Messenger.

HASTINGS   Now, what news?
MESSENGER   West of this forest, scarcely off a mile,
20 In goodly form comes on the enemy,
And, by the ground they hide, I judge their number
Upon or near the rate of thirty thousand.
MOWBRAY   The just proportion that we gave them out.
Let us sway on and face them in the field.

Enter WESTMORELAND.

ARCHBISHOP
25 What well-appointed leader fronts us here?
MOWBRAY   I think it is my Lord of Westmoreland.
WESTMORELAND
Health and fair greeting from our general,
The Prince, Lord John and Duke of Lancaster.
ARCHBISHOP
Say on, my Lord of Westmoreland, in peace,
What doth concern your coming.
30 WESTMORELAND   Then, my lord,
Unto your Grace do I in chief address
The substance of my speech. If that rebellion
Came like itself, in base and abject routs,
Led on by bloody youth, guarded with rags,
35 And countenanc'd by boys and beggary;
I say, if damn'd commotion so appear'd
In his true, native, and most proper shape,
You, reverend father, and these noble lords
Had not been here to dress the ugly form
40 Of base and bloody insurrection
With your fair honours. You, Lord Archbishop,
Whose see is by a civil peace maintain'd,
Whose beard the silver hand of peace hath touch'd,
Whose learning and good letters peace hath tutor'd,
45 Whose white investments figure innocence,
The dove and very blessed spirit of peace,
Wherefore do you so ill translate yourself
Out of the speech of peace that bears such grace
Into the harsh and boist'rous tongue of war;
50 Turning your books to graves, your ink to blood,
Your pens to lances, and your tongue divine
To a loud trumpet and a point of war?
ARCHBISHOP
Wherefore do I this? so the question stands.
Briefly, to this end: we are all diseas'd,

And with our surfeiting, and wanton hours,   55
Have brought ourselves into a burning fever,
And we must bleed for it; of which disease
Our late King Richard being infected died.
But, my most noble Lord of Westmoreland,
I take not on me here as a physician,   60
Nor do I as an enemy to peace
Troop in the throngs of military men,
But rather show awhile like fearful war
To diet rank minds sick of happiness,
And purge th' obstructions which begin to stop   65
Our very veins of life. Hear me more plainly.
I have in equal balance justly weigh'd
What wrongs our arms may do, what wrongs we
    suffer,
And find our griefs heavier than our offences.
We see which way the stream of time doth run,   70
And are enforc'd from our most quiet there
By the rough torrent of occasion,
And have the summary of all our griefs,
When time shall serve, to show in articles,
Which long ere this we offer'd to the King   75
And might by no suit gain our audience.
When we are wrong'd, and would unfold our griefs,
We are denied access unto his person,
Even by those men that most have done us wrong.
The dangers of the days but newly gone,   80
Whose memory is written on the earth
With yet-appearing blood, and the examples
Of every minute's instance, present now,
Hath put us in these ill-beseeming arms,
Not to break peace, or any branch of it,   85
But to establish here a peace indeed,
Concurring both in name and quality.
WESTMORELAND
Whenever yet was your appeal denied?
Wherein have you been galled by the King?
What peer hath been suborn'd to grate on you,   90
That you should seal this lawless bloody book
Of forg'd rebellion with a seal divine,
And consecrate commotion's bitter edge?
ARCHBISHOP   My brother general, the commonwealth,
To brother born an household cruelty,   95
I make my quarrel in particular.
WESTMORELAND   There is no need of any such redress,
Or if there were, it not belongs to you.
MOWBRAY   Why not to him in part, and to us all
That feel the bruises of the days before,   100
And suffer the condition of these times
To lay a heavy and unequal hand
Upon our honours?
WESTMORELAND   O, my good Lord Mowbray,
Construe the times to their necessities,
And you shall say, indeed, it is the time,   105
And not the King, that doth you injuries.
Yet for your part, it not appears to me
Either from the King or in the present time

That you should have an inch of any ground
110 To build a grief on: were you not restor'd
To all the Duke of Norfolk's signories,
Your noble and right well-remember'd father's?
MOWBRAY What thing, in honour, had my father lost,
That need to be reviv'd and breath'd in me?
115 The King that lov'd him, as the state stood then,
Was force perforce compell'd to banish him,
And then that Henry Bolingbroke and he,
Being mounted and both roused in their seats,
Their neighing coursers daring of the spur,
120 Their armed staves in charge, their beavers down,
Their eyes of fire sparkling through sights of steel,
And the loud trumpet blowing them together,
Then, then, when there was nothing could have
       stay'd
My father from the breast of Bolingbroke,
125 O, when the King did throw his warder down,
His own life hung upon the staff he threw;
Then threw he down himself and all their lives
That by indictment and by dint of sword
Have since miscarried under Bolingbroke.
WESTMORELAND
130 You speak, Lord Mowbray, now you know not what.
The Earl of Hereford was reputed then
In England the most valiant gentleman.
Who knows on whom Fortune would then have
       smil'd?
But if your father had been victor there,
135 He ne'er had borne it out of Coventry;
For all the country, in a general voice,
Cried hate upon him; and all their prayers and love
Were set on Hereford, whom they doted on,
And bless'd, and grac'd, indeed more than the King.
140 But this is mere digression from my purpose.
Here come I from our princely general
To know your griefs, to tell you from his Grace
That he will give you audience; and wherein
It shall appear that your demands are just,
145 You shall enjoy them, everything set off
That might so much as think you enemies.
MOWBRAY But he hath forc'd us to compel this offer,
And it proceeds from policy, not love.
WESTMORELAND Mowbray, you overween to take it so.
150 This offer comes from mercy, not from fear;
For lo, within a ken our army lies,
Upon mine honour, all too confident
To give admittance to a thought of fear.
Our battle is more full of names than yours,
155 Our men more perfect in the use of arms,
Our armour all as strong, our cause the best;
Then reason will our hearts should be as good.
Say you not then, our offer is compell'd.
MOWBRAY Well, by my will we shall admit no parley.
WESTMORELAND
160 That argues but the shame of your offence:
A rotten case abides no handling.

HASTINGS Hath the Prince John a full commission,
In very ample virtue of his father,
To hear, and absolutely to determine,
Of what conditions we shall stand upon? 165
WESTMORELAND
That is intended in the general's name:
I muse you make so slight a question.
ARCHBISHOP
Then take, my Lord of Westmoreland, this schedule,
For this contains our general grievances.
Each several article herein redress'd, 170
All members of our cause, both here and hence,
That are ensinew'd to this action
Acquitted by a true substantial form
And present execution of our wills –
To us and to our purposes confin'd 175
We come within our aweful banks again,
And knit our powers to the arm of peace.
WESTMORELAND
This will I show the general. Please you, lords,
In sight of both our battles we may meet,
And either end in peace – which God so frame! – 180
Or to the place of diff'rence call the swords
Which must decide it.
ARCHBISHOP   My lord, we will do so.
                              Exit Westmoreland.
MOWBRAY There is a thing within my bosom tells me
That no conditions of our peace can stand.
HASTINGS Fear you not that: if we can make our peace 185
Upon such large terms, and so absolute,
As our conditions shall consist upon,
Our peace shall stand as firm as rocky mountains.
MOWBRAY Yea, but our valuation shall be such
That every slight and false-derived cause, 190
Yea, every idle, nice, and wanton reason,
Shall to the King taste of this action;
That were our royal faiths martyrs in love,
We shall be winnow'd with so rough a wind
That even our corn shall seem as light as chaff 195
And good from bad find no partition.
ARCHBISHOP
No, no, my lord, note this: the King is weary
Of dainty and such picking grievances;
For he hath found, to end one doubt by death
Revives two greater in the heirs of life: 200
And therefore will he wipe his tables clean,
And keep no tell-tale to his memory
That may repeat and history his loss
To new remembrance. For full well he knows
He cannot so precisely weed this land 205
As his misdoubts present occasion.
His foes are so enrooted with his friends
That plucking to unfix an enemy
He doth unfasten so and shake a friend.
So that this land, like an offensive wife 210
That hath enrag'd him on to offer strokes,
As he is striking, holds his infant up,

And hangs resolv'd correction in the arm
That was uprear'd to execution.
HASTINGS   Besides, the King hath wasted all his rods
On late offenders, that he now doth lack
The very instruments of chastisement;
So that his power, like to a fangless lion,
May offer, but not hold.
ARCHBISHOP   'Tis very true:
And therefore be assur'd, my good Lord Marshal,
If we do now make our atonement well,
Our peace will, like a broken limb united,
Grow stronger for the breaking.
MOWBRAY   Be it so.
Here is return'd my Lord of Westmoreland.

Enter WESTMORELAND.

WESTMORELAND
The Prince is here at hand. Pleaseth your lordship
To meet his Grace just distance 'tween our armies.
MOWBRAY
Your Grace of York, in God's name then set forward.
YORK   Before! and greet his Grace. – My lord, we come.
[*They go forward.*]

4.2 *Enter* PRINCE JOHN OF LANCASTER *and his army.*

LANCASTER
You are well encounter'd here, my cousin Mowbray;
Good day to you, gentle Lord Archbishop;
And so to you, Lord Hastings, and to all.
My Lord of York, it better show'd with you
When that your flock, assembled by the bell,
Encircled you to hear with reverence
Your exposition on the holy text
Than now to see you here an iron man,
Cheering a rout of rebels with your drum,
Turning the word to sword, and life to death.
That man that sits within a monarch's heart,
And ripens in the sunshine of his favour,
Would he abuse the countenance of the king,
Alack, what mischiefs might he set abroach
In shadow of such greatness! With you, Lord Bishop,
It is even so. Who hath not heard it spoken
How deep you were within the books of God,
To us the speaker in his parliament,
To us th'imagin'd voice of God himself,
The very opener and intelligencer
Between the grace, the sanctities of heaven,
And our dull workings? O, who shall believe
But you misuse the reverence of your place,
Employ the countenance and grace of heav'n
As a false favourite doth his prince's name,
In deeds dishonourable? You have ta'en up,
Under the counterfeited zeal of God,
The subjects of his substitute, my father,
And both against the peace of heaven and him
Have here up-swarm'd them.
ARCHBISHOP   Good my Lord of Lancaster,

I am not here against your father's peace;
But, as I told my Lord of Westmoreland,
The time misorder'd doth, in common sense,
Crowd us and crush us to this monstrous form
To hold our safety up. I sent your Grace   35
The parcels and particulars of our grief,
The which hath been with scorn shov'd from the
   court,
Whereon this Hydra son of war is born,
Whose dangerous eyes may well be charm'd asleep
With grant of our most just and right desires,   40
And true obedience, of this madness cur'd,
Stoop tamely to the foot of majesty.
MOWBRAY   If not, we ready are to try our fortunes
To the last man.
HASTINGS   And though we here fall down,
We have supplies to second our attempt: 45
If they miscarry, theirs shall second them;
And so success of mischief shall be born,
And heir from heir shall hold this quarrel up
Whiles England shall have generation.
LANCASTER
You are too shallow, Hastings, much too shallow,   50
To sound the bottom of the after-times.
WESTMORELAND
Pleaseth your Grace to answer them directly
How far forth you do like their articles.
LANCASTER   I like them all, and do allow them well,
And swear here, by the honour of my blood,   55
My father's purposes have been mistook,
And some about him have too lavishly
Wrested his meaning and authority.
My lord, these griefs shall be with speed redress'd;
Upon my soul they shall. If this may please you,   60
Discharge your powers unto their several counties,
As we will ours; and here between the armies
Let's drink together friendly and embrace,
That all their eyes may bear those tokens home
Of our restored love and amity.   65
ARCHBISHOP
I take your princely word for these redresses.
LANCASTER   I give it you, and will maintain my word;
And thereupon I drink unto your Grace.
HASTINGS   Go, captain, and deliver to the army
This news of peace. Let them have pay, and part.   70
I know it will well please them. Hie thee, captain.
                                                              Exit officer.
ARCHBISHOP   To you, my noble Lord of Westmoreland.
WESTMORELAND
I pledge your Grace; and if you knew what pains
I have bestow'd to breed this present peace
You would drink freely; but my love to ye   75
Shall show itself more openly hereafter.
ARCHBISHOP   I do not doubt you.
WESTMORELAND   I am glad of it.
Health to my lord and gentle cousin, Mowbray.
MOWBRAY   You wish me health in very happy season,

80   For I am on the sudden something ill.
ARCHBISHOP   Against ill chances men are ever merry,
     But heaviness foreruns the good event.
WESTMORELAND
     Therefore be merry, coz, since sudden sorrow
     Serves to say thus, 'Some good thing comes
          tomorrow'.
85 ARCHBISHOP   Believe me, I am passing light in spirit.
MOWBRAY
     So much the worse, if your own rule be true.
     [Shouts within.]
LANCASTER
     The word of peace is render'd. Hark how they shout!
MOWBRAY   This had been cheerful after victory.
ARCHBISHOP   A peace is of the nature of a conquest,
90   For then both parties nobly are subdu'd,
     And neither party loser.
LANCASTER   Go, my lord,
     And let our army be discharged too.
                              Exit Westmoreland.
     And, good my lord, so please you, let our trains
     March by us, that we may peruse the men
     We should have cop'd withal.
95 ARCHBISHOP   Go, good Lord Hastings,
     And, ere they be dismiss'd, let them march by.
                              Exit Hastings.
LANCASTER   I trust, lords, we shall lie tonight together.

               Enter WESTMORELAND.

     Now, cousin, wherefore stands our army still?
WESTMORELAND
     The leaders, having charge from you to stand,
100   Will not go off until they hear you speak.
LANCASTER   They know their duties.

                  Enter HASTINGS.

HASTINGS   My lord, our army is dispers'd already.
     Like youthful steers unyok'd they take their courses
     East, west, north, south; or, like a school broke up,
105   Each hurries toward his home and sporting-place.
WESTMORELAND
     Good tidings, my Lord Hastings; for the which
     I do arrest thee, traitor, of high treason;
     And you, Lord Archbishop, and you, Lord Mowbray,
     Of capital treason I attach you both.
110 MOWBRAY   Is this proceeding just and honourable?
WESTMORELAND   Is your assembly so?
ARCHBISHOP   Will you thus break your faith?
LANCASTER   I pawn'd thee none.
     I promis'd you redress of these same grievances
     Whereof you did complain; which, by mine honour,
115   I will perform with a most Christian care.
     But, for you rebels, look to taste the due
     Meet for rebellion and such acts as yours.
     Most shallowly did you these arms commence,
     Fondly brought here, and foolishly sent hence.
120   Strike up our drums, pursue the scatter'd stray:

     God, and not we, hath safely fought today.
     Some guard these traitors to the block of death,
     Treason's true bed and yielder-up of breath.   Exeunt.

4.3   Alarum. Excursions. Enter FALSTAFF
              and COLEVILE, meeting.

FALSTAFF   What's your name, sir? Of what condition are
     you, and of what place?
COLEVILE   I am a knight, sir, and my name is Colevile of
     the Dale.
FALSTAFF   Well then, Colevile is your name, a knight is   5
     your degree, and your place the Dale. Colevile shall be
     still your name, a traitor your degree, and the dungeon
     your place – a place deep enough; so shall you be still
     Colevile of the Dale.
COLEVILE   Are not you Sir John Falstaff?   10
FALSTAFF   As good a man as he, sir, whoe'er I am. Do ye
     yield, sir, or shall I sweat for you? If I do sweat, they
     are the drops of thy lovers, and they weep for thy
     death; therefore rouse up fear and trembling, and do
     observance to my mercy.   15
COLEVILE   [Kneels.]   I think you are Sir John Falstaff,
     and in that thought yield me.
FALSTAFF   I have a whole school of tongues in this belly
     of mine, and not a tongue of them all speaks any other
     word but my name. And I had but a belly of any   20
     indifferency, I were simply the most active fellow in
     Europe: my womb, my womb, my womb undoes me.
     Here comes our general.

Retreat sounded. Enter PRINCE JOHN, WESTMORELAND,
              BLUNT and others.

LANCASTER   The heat is past; follow no further now.
     Call in the powers, good cousin Westmoreland.   25
                              Exit Westmoreland.
     Now Falstaff, where have you been all this while?
     When everything is ended, then you come.
     These tardy tricks of yours will, on my life,
     One time or other break some gallows' back.
FALSTAFF   I would be sorry, my lord, but it should be   30
     thus. I never knew yet but rebuke and check was the
     reward of valour. Do you think me a swallow, an arrow,
     or a bullet? Have I in my poor and old motion the
     expedition of thought? I have speeded hither with the
     very extremest inch of possibility; I have foundered   35
     nine score and odd posts; and here, travel-tainted as I
     am, have in my pure and immaculate valour taken Sir
     John Colevile of the Dale, a most furious knight and
     valorous enemy. But what of that? He saw me, and
     yielded; that I may justly say, with the hook-nosed   40
     fellow of Rome, three words, 'I came, saw, and
     overcame'.
LANCASTER   It was more of his courtesy than your
     deserving.
FALSTAFF   I know not: here he is, and here I yield him;   45
     and I beseech your Grace, let it be booked with the

rest of this day's deeds, or by the Lord I will have it in a particular ballad else, with mine own picture on the top on't, Colevile kissing my foot: to the which course if I be enforced, if you do not all show like gilt twopences to me, and I in the clear sky of fame o'ershine you as much as the full moon doth the cinders of the element, which show like pins' heads to her, believe not the word of the noble. Therefore let me have right, and let desert mount.

LANCASTER Thine's too heavy to mount.

FALSTAFF Let it shine, then.

LANCASTER Thine's too thick to shine.

FALSTAFF Let it do something, my good lord, that may do me good, and call it what you will.

LANCASTER Is thy name Colevile?

COLEVILE   It is, my lord.

LANCASTER A famous rebel art thou, Colevile.

FALSTAFF And a famous true subject took him.

COLEVILE I am, my lord, but as my betters are
That led me hither. Had they been rul'd by me,
You should have won them dearer than you have.

FALSTAFF I know not how they sold themselves, but thou like a kind fellow gavest thyself away gratis, and I thank thee for thee.

Enter WESTMORELAND.

LANCASTER Now, have you left pursuit?

WESTMORELAND Retreat is made and execution stay'd.

LANCASTER Send Colevile with his confederates
To York, to present execution.
Blunt, lead him hence, and see you guard him sure.

Exit Blunt with Colevile, guarded.

And now dispatch we toward the court, my lords;
I hear the King my father is sore sick.
Our news shall go before us to his Majesty,
Which, cousin, you shall bear to comfort him,
And we with sober speed will follow you.

FALSTAFF My lord, I beseech you give me leave to go
Through Gloucestershire, and when you come to
court
Stand my good lord, pray, in your good report.

LANCASTER Fare you well, Falstaff. I, in my condition,
Shall better speak of you than you deserve.

Exit, with all but Falstaff.

FALSTAFF I would you had but the wit, 'twere better than your dukedom. Good faith, this same young sober-blooded boy doth not love me, nor a man cannot make him laugh; but that's no marvel, he drinks no wine. There's never none of these demure boys come to any proof; for thin drink doth so over-cool their blood, and making many fish meals, that they fall into a kind of male green-sickness; and then when they marry they get wenches. They are generally fools and cowards – which some of us should be too, but for inflammation. A good sherris-sack hath a twofold operation in it. It ascends me into the brain, dries me there all the foolish and dull and crudy vapours which environ it, makes it apprehensive, quick, forgetive, full of nimble, fiery, and delectable shapes, which delivered o'er to the voice, the tongue, which is the birth, becomes excellent wit. The second property of your excellent sherris is the warming of the blood, which before, cold and settled, left the liver white and pale, which is the badge of pusillanimity and cowardice; but the sherris warms it, and makes it course from the inwards to the parts' extremes. It illumineth the face, which, as a beacon, gives warning to all the rest of this little kingdom, man, to arm; and then the vital commoners, and inland petty spirits, muster me all to their captain, the heart; who, great and puffed up with this retinue, doth any deed of courage; and this valour comes of sherris. So that skill in the weapon is nothing without sack, for that sets it a-work, and learning a mere hoard of gold kept by a devil, till sack commences it and sets it in act and use. Hereof comes it that Prince Harry is valiant; for the cold blood he did naturally inherit of his father he hath like lean, sterile, and bare land manured, husbanded, and tilled, with excellent endeavour of drinking good and good store of fertile sherris, that he is become very hot and valiant. If I had a thousand sons, the first human principle I would teach them should be to forswear thin potations, and to addict themselves to sack.

Enter BARDOLPH.

How now, Bardolph?

BARDOLPH The army is discharged all and gone.

FALSTAFF Let them go. I'll through Gloucestershire, and there will I visit Master Robert Shallow, Esquire. I have him already tempering between my finger and my thumb, and shortly will I seal with him. Come away.   *Exeunt.*

4.4 *Enter the* KING, *carried in a chair,* WARWICK,
THOMAS DUKE OF CLARENCE, HUMPHREY
DUKE OF GLOUCESTER *and others.*

KING Now, lords, if God doth give successful end
To this debate that bleedeth at our doors,
We will our youth lead on to higher fields,
And draw no swords but what are sanctified.
Our navy is address'd, our power collected,
Our substitutes in absence well invested,
And every thing lies level to our wish;
Only we want a little personal strength,
And pause us till these rebels now afoot
Come underneath the yoke of government.

WARWICK Both which we doubt not but your Majesty
Shall soon enjoy.

KING   Humphrey, my son of Gloucester,
Where is the Prince your brother?

GLOUCESTER
I think he's gone to hunt, my lord, at Windsor.

KING   And how accompanied?

15 GLOUCESTER   I do not know, my lord.

KING   Is not his brother Thomas of Clarence with him?

GLOUCESTER   No, my good lord, he is in presence here.

CLARENCE   What would my lord and father?

KING   Nothing but well to thee, Thomas of Clarence.
How chance thou art not with the Prince thy
20   brother?
He loves thee, and thou dost neglect him, Thomas.
Thou hast a better place in his affection
Than all thy brothers: cherish it, my boy,
And noble offices thou mayst effect
25 Of mediation, after I am dead,
Between his greatness and thy other brethren.
Therefore omit him not, blunt not his love,
Nor lose the good advantage of his grace
By seeming cold, or careless of his will;
30 For he is gracious, if he be observ'd,
He hath a tear for pity, and a hand
Open as day for melting charity:
Yet notwithstanding, being incens'd, he's flint,
As humorous as winter, and as sudden
35 As flaws congealed in the spring of day.
His temper therefore must be well observ'd.
Chide him for faults, and do it reverently,
When you perceive his blood inclin'd to mirth;
But being moody, give him time and scope,
40 Till that his passions, like a whale on ground,
Confound themselves with working. Learn this,
        Thomas,
And thou shalt prove a shelter to thy friends,
A hoop óf gold to bind thy brothers in,
That the united vessel of their blood,
45 Mingled with venom of suggestion –
As force perforce the age will pour it in –
Shall never leak, though it do work as strong
As aconitum or rash gunpowder.

CLARENCE   I shall observe him with all care and love.

KING
50 Why art thou not at Windsor with him, Thomas?

CLARENCE   He is not there today, he dines in London.

KING   And how accompanied? Canst thou tell that?

CLARENCE
With Poins, and other his continual followers.

KING   Most subject is the fattest soil to weeds,
55 And he, the noble image of my youth,
Is overspread with them; therefore my grief
Stretches itself beyond the hour of death.
The blood weeps from my heart when I do shape
In forms imaginary th'unguided days
60 And rotten times that you shall look upon
When I am sleeping with my ancestors.
For when his headstrong riot hath no curb,
When rage and hot blood are his counsellors,
When means and lavish manners meet together,
65 O, with what wings shall his affections fly
Towards fronting peril and oppos'd decay!

WARWICK
My gracious lord, you look beyond him quite.
The Prince but studies his companions
Like a strange tongue, wherein, to gain the language,
'Tis needful that the most immodest word   70
Be look'd upon and learnt; which once attain'd,
Your Highness knows, comes to no further use
But to be known and hated. So, like gross terms,
The Prince will, in the perfectness of time,
Cast off his followers, and their memory   75
Shall as a pattern or a measure live
By which his Grace must mete the lives of other,
Turning past evils to advantages.

KING   'Tis seldom when the bee doth leave her comb
In the dead carrion.

Enter WESTMORELAND.

                        Who's here? Westmoreland?   80

WESTMORELAND
Health to my sovereign, and new happiness
Added to that that I am to deliver!
Prince John your son doth kiss your Grace's hand:
Mowbray, the Bishop Scroop, Hastings and all
Are brought to the correction of your law.   85
There is not now a rebel's sword unsheath'd,
But Peace puts forth her olive everywhere.
The manner how this action hath been borne
Here at more leisure may your Highness read,
With every course in his particular.   90

KING   O Westmoreland, thou art a summer bird,
Which ever in the haunch of winter sings
The lifting up of day.

Enter HARCOURT.

                        Look, here's more news.

HARCOURT   From enemies heaven keep your Majesty;
And when they stand against you, may they fall   95
As those that I am come to tell you of!
The Earl Northumberland, and the Lord Bardolph,
With a great power of English and of Scots,
Are by the shrieve of Yorkshire overthrown.
The manner and true order of the fight   100
This packet, please it you, contains at large.

KING
And wherefore should these good news make me
        sick?
Will Fortune never come with both hands full,
But write her fair words still in foulest letters?
She either gives a stomach, and no food –   105
Such are the poor, in health; or else a feast
And takes away the stomach – such are the rich
That have abundance and enjoy it not.
I should rejoice now at this happy news,
And now my sight fails, and my brain is giddy.   110
O me! come near me, now I am much ill.

GLOUCESTER   Comfort, your Majesty!

CLARENCE   O my royal father!

WESTMORELAND

My sovereign lord, cheer up yourself, look up.

WARWICK

Be patient, Princes; you do know these fits
Are with his Highness very ordinary.
Stand from him, give him air; he'll straight be well.

CLARENCE

No, no, he cannot long hold out these pangs.
Th'incessant care and labour of his mind
Hath wrought the mure that should confine it in
So thin that life looks through and will break out.

GLOUCESTER

The people fear me, for they do observe
Unfather'd heirs and loathly births of nature.
The seasons change their manners, as the year
Had found some months asleep and leap'd them over.

CLARENCE

The river hath thrice flow'd, no ebb between,
And the old folk, time's doting chronicles,
Say it did so a little time before
That our great-grandsire Edward sick'd and died.

WARWICK　Speak lower, Princes, for the King recovers.

GLOUCESTER　This apoplexy will certain be his end.

KING　I pray you take me up, and bear me hence
Into some other chamber: softly, pray.

4.5　*They take the* KING *up and lay him on a bed.*

KING　Let there be no noise made, my gentle friends,
Unless some dull and favourable hand
Will whisper music to my weary spirit.

WARWICK　Call for the music in the other room.

KING　Set me the crown upon my pillow here.

CLARENCE　His eye is hollow, and he changes much.

WARWICK　Less noise, less noise!

Enter PRINCE HENRY.

PRINCE　　　　　　　Who saw the Duke of Clarence?

CLARENCE　I am here, brother, full of heaviness.

PRINCE　How now, rain within doors, and none abroad?
How doth the King?

GLOUCESTER　Exceeding ill.

PRINCE　　　　　　　Heard he the good news yet?
Tell it him.

GLOUCESTER　He alter'd much upon the hearing it.

PRINCE

If he be sick with joy, he'll recover without physic.

WARWICK

Not so much noise, my lords. Sweet Prince, speak
low;
The King your father is dispos'd to sleep.

CLARENCE　Let us withdraw into the other room.

WARWICK　Will't please your Grace to go along with us?

PRINCE　No, I will sit and watch here by the King.

Exeunt all but the Prince.

Why doth the crown lie there upon his pillow,
Being so troublesome a bedfellow?

O polish'd perturbation! golden care!
That keep'st the ports of slumber open wide
To many a watchful night! Sleep with it now:
Yet not so sound, and half so deeply sweet,　25
As he whose brow with homely biggen bound
Snores out the watch of night. O majesty!
When thou dost pinch thy bearer, thou dost sit
Like a rich armour worn in heat of day,
That scald'st with safety. By his gates of breath　30
There lies a downy feather which stirs not:
Did he suspire, that light and weightless down
Perforce must move. My gracious lord! My father!
This sleep is sound indeed; this is a sleep
That from this golden rigol hath divorc'd　35
So many English kings. Thy due from me
Is tears and heavy sorrows of the blood,
Which nature, love, and filial tenderness
Shall, O dear father, pay thee plenteously.
My due from thee is this imperial crown,　40
Which, as immediate from thy place and blood,
Derives itself to me. [*putting it on his head*]
　　　　　　Lo where it sits,
Which God shall guard; and put the world's whole
strength
Into one giant arm, it shall not force
This lineal honour from me. This from thee　45
Will I to mine leave, as 'tis left to me.　　　*Exit.*

KING　Warwick! Gloucester! Clarence!

Enter WARWICK, GLOUCESTER, CLARENCE *and the rest.*

CLARENCE　Doth the King call?

WARWICK

What would your Majesty? How fares your Grace?

KING　Why did you leave me here alone, my lords?　50

CLARENCE

We left the Prince my brother here, my liege,
Who undertook to sit and watch by you.

KING

The Prince of Wales? Where is he? Let me see him.
He is not here.

WARWICK　This door is open, he is gone this way.　55

GLOUCESTER

He came not through the chamber where we stay'd.

KING

Where is the crown? Who took it from my pillow?

WARWICK　When we withdrew, my liege, we left it here.

KING　The Prince hath ta'en it hence. Go seek him out.
Is he so hasty that he doth suppose　60
My sleep my death?
Find him, my Lord of Warwick, chide him hither.

Exit Warwick.

This part of his conjoins with my disease,
And helps to end me. See, sons, what things you are,
How quickly nature falls into revolt　65
When gold becomes her object!
For this the foolish over-careful fathers
Have broke their sleep with thoughts,

Their brains with care, their bones with industry;
For this they have engrossed and pil'd up
The canker'd heaps of strange-achieved gold;
For this they have been thoughtful to invest
Their sons with arts and martial exercises;
When, like the bee, tolling from every flower
The virtuous sweets,
Our thighs pack'd with wax, our mouths with honey,
We bring it to the hive; and like the bees
Are murder'd for our pains. This bitter taste
Yields his engrossments to the ending father.

Enter WARWICK.

Now where is he that will not stay so long
Till his friend sickness have determin'd me?

WARWICK
My lord, I found the Prince in the next room,
Washing with kindly tears his gentle cheeks,
With such a deep demeanour in great sorrow,
That tyranny, which never quaff'd but blood,
Would, by beholding him, have wash'd his knife
With gentle eye-drops. He is coming hither.

KING   But wherefore did he take away the crown?

Enter PRINCE HENRY.

Lo where he comes. Come hither to me, Harry.
Depart the chamber, leave us here alone.

Exeunt Warwick and the rest.

PRINCE   I never thought to hear you speak again.
KING   Thy wish was father, Harry, to that thought;
I stay too long by thee, I weary thee.
Dost thou so hunger for mine empty chair
That thou wilt needs invest thee with my honours
Before thy hour be ripe? O foolish youth!
Thou seek'st the greatness that will overwhelm thee.
Stay but a little, for my cloud of dignity
Is held from falling with so weak a wind
That it will quickly drop; my day is dim.
Thou hast stol'n that which after some few hours
Were thine without offence, and at my death
Thou hast seal'd up my expectation.
Thy life did manifest thou lov'dst me not,
And thou wilt have me die assur'd of it.
Thou hid'st a thousand daggers in thy thoughts,
Which thou hast whetted on thy stony heart,
To stab at half an hour of my life.
What, canst thou not forbear me half an hour?
Then get thee gone, and dig my grave thyself,
And bid the merry bells ring to thine ear
That thou art crowned, not that I am dead.
Let all the tears that should bedew my hearse
Be drops of balm to sanctify thy head,
Only compound me with forgotten dust.
Give that which gave thee life unto the worms;
Pluck down my officers; break my decrees;
For now a time is come to mock at form –
Harry the fifth is crown'd! Up, vanity!

Down, royal state! All you sage counsellors, hence!
And to the English court assemble now
From every region, apes of idleness!
Now, neighbour confines, purge you of your scum!
Have you a ruffian that will swear, drink, dance,
Revel the night, rob, murder, and commit
The oldest sins the newest kind of ways?
Be happy, he will trouble you no more.
England shall double gild his treble guilt,
England shall give him office, honour, might:
For the fifth Harry from curb'd licence plucks
The muzzle of restraint, and the wild dog
Shall flesh his tooth on every innocent.
O my poor kingdom, sick with civil blows!
When that my care could not withhold thy riots,
What wilt thou do when riot is thy care?
O, thou wilt be a wilderness again,
Peopled with wolves, thy old inhabitants!

PRINCE [*Kneels.*]
O, pardon me, my liege! But for my tears,
The moist impediments unto my speech,
I had forestall'd this dear and deep rebuke,
Ere you with grief had spoke and I had heard
The course of it so far. There is your crown;
And He that wears the crown immortally
Long guard it yours! If I affect it more
Than as your honour and as your renown,
Let me no more from this obedience rise,
Which my most inward true and duteous spirit
Teacheth this prostrate and exterior bending.
God witness with me, when I here came in,
And found no course of breath within your Majesty,
How cold it struck my heart! If I do feign,
O, let me in my present wildness die,
And never live to show th'incredulous world
The noble change that I have purposed!
Coming to look on you, thinking you dead,
And dead almost, my liege, to think you were,
I spake unto this crown as having sense,
And thus upbraided it: 'The care on thee depending
Hath fed upon the body of my father;
Therefore thou best of gold art worst of gold.
Other, less fine in carat, is more precious,
Preserving life in med'cine potable;
But thou, most fine, most honour'd, most renown'd,
Hast eat thy bearer up'. Thus, my most royal liege,
Accusing it, I put it on my head,
To try with it, as with an enemy
That had before my face murder'd my father,
The quarrel of a true inheritor.
But if it did infect my blood with joy,
Or swell my thoughts to any strain of pride,
If any rebel or vain spirit of mine
Did with the least affection of a welcome
Give entertainment to the might of it,
Let God for ever keep it from my head,
And make me as the poorest vassal is,

That doth with awe and terror kneel to it!
KING   O my son,
    God put it in thy mind to take it hence,
    That thou mightst win the more thy father's love,
180 Pleading so wisely in excuse of it!
    Come hither, Harry, sit thou by my bed,
    And hear, I think, the very latest counsel
    That ever I shall breathe. God knows, my son,
    By what by-paths and indirect crook'd ways
185 I met this crown, and I myself know well
    How troublesome it sat upon my head.
    To thee it shall descend with better quiet,
    Better opinion, better confirmation,
    For all the soil of the achievement goes
190 With me into the earth. It seem'd in me
    But as an honour snatch'd with boist'rous hand,
    And I had many living to upbraid
    My gain of it by their assistances,
    Which daily grew to quarrel and to bloodshed,
195 Wounding supposed peace. All these bold fears
    Thou seest with peril I have answered;
    For all my reign hath been but as a scene
    Acting that argument. And now my death
    Changes the mood, for what in me was purchas'd
200 Falls upon thee in a more fairer sort;
    So thou the garland wear'st successively.
    Yet though thou stand'st more sure than I could do,
    Thou art not firm enough, since griefs are green;
    And all my friends, which thou must make thy
        friends,
205 Have but their stings and teeth newly ta'en out;
    By whose fell working I was first advanc'd,
    And by whose power I well might lodge a fear
    To be again displac'd; which to avoid,
    I cut them off, and had a purpose now
210 To lead out many to the Holy Land,
    Lest rest and lying still might make them look
    Too near unto my state. Therefore, my Harry,
    Be it thy course to busy giddy minds
    With foreign quarrels, that action hence borne out
215 May waste the memory of the former days.
    More would I, but my lungs are wasted so
    That strength of speech is utterly denied me.
    How I came by the crown, O God forgive,
    And grant it may with thee in true peace live!
220 PRINCE   My gracious liege,
    You won it, wore it, kept it, gave it me;
    Then plain and right must my possession be,
    Which I with more than with a common pain
    'Gainst all the world will rightfully maintain.

Enter PRINCE JOHN OF LANCASTER, WARWICK *and others.*

225 KING   Look, look, here comes my John of Lancaster.
LANCASTER
    Health, peace, and happiness to my royal father!
KING
    Thou bring'st me happiness and peace, son John,

But health, alack, with youthful wings is flown
From this bare wither'd trunk. Upon thy sight
My worldly business makes a period.   230
Where is my Lord of Warwick?
LANCASTER   My Lord of Warwick!
KING   Doth any name particular belong
    Unto the lodging where I first did swoon?
WARWICK   'Tis call'd Jerusalem, my noble lord.
KING   Laud be to God! Even there my life must end. 235
    It hath been prophesied to me, many years,
    I should not die but in Jerusalem,
    Which vainly I suppos'd the Holy Land.
    But bear me to that chamber; there I'll lie;
    In that Jerusalem shall Harry die.   *Exeunt.* 240

5.1   *Enter* SHALLOW, FALSTAFF,
                      BARDOLPH *and page.*

SHALLOW   By cock and pie, sir, you shall not away
    tonight. What, Davy, I say!
FALSTAFF   You must excuse me, Master Robert Shallow.
SHALLOW   I will not excuse you, you shall not be
    excused, excuses shall not be admitted, there is no   5
    excuse shall serve, you shall not be excused. Why,
    Davy!

                  Enter DAVY.

DAVY   Here, sir.
SHALLOW   Davy, Davy, Davy, Davy; let me see, Davy; let
    me see, Davy; let me see – yea, marry, William cook, 10
    bid him come hither. Sir John, you shall not be
    excused.
DAVY   Marry, sir, thus: those precepts cannot be
    served; and again, sir – shall we sow the hade land
    with wheat?   15
SHALLOW   With red wheat, Davy. But for William cook
    – are there no young pigeons?
DAVY   Yes, sir. Here is now the smith's note for shoeing
    and plough-irons.
SHALLOW   Let it be cast and paid. Sir John, you shall not 20
    be excused.
DAVY   Now, sir, a new link to the bucket must needs be
    had; and sir, do you mean to stop any of William's
    wages, about the sack he lost the other day at Hinckley
    fair?   25
SHALLOW   A shall answer it. Some pigeons, Davy, a
    couple of short-legged hens, a joint of mutton, and any
    pretty little tiny kickshaws, tell William cook.
DAVY   Doth the man of war stay all night, sir?
SHALLOW   Yea, Davy, I will use him well: a friend i'th'   30
    court is better than a penny in purse. Use his men
    well, Davy, for they are arrant knaves, and will
    backbite.
DAVY   No worse than they are backbitten, sir, for they
    have marvellous foul linen.   35
SHALLOW   Well conceited, Davy – about thy business,
    Davy.

DAVY   I beseech you, sir, to countenance William Visor
of Woncot against Clement Perkes a'th' Hill.

40 SHALLOW   There is many complaints, Davy, against that
Visor; that Visor is an arrant knave, on my knowledge.

DAVY   I grant your worship that he is a knave, sir: but yet
God forbid, sir, but a knave should have some
countenance at his friend's request. An honest man,

45 sir, is able to speak for himself, when a knave is not. I
have served your worship truly, sir, this eight years;
and if I cannot once or twice in a quarter bear out a
knave against an honest man, I have but a very little
credit with your worship. The knave is mine honest

50 friend, sir, therefore I beseech your worship let him be
countenanced.

SHALLOW   Go to; I say he shall have no wrong. Look
about, Davy.   *Exit Davy.*

Where are you, Sir John? Come, come, come, off with

55 your boots. Give me your hand, Master Bardolph.

BARDOLPH   I am glad to see your worship.

SHALLOW   I thank thee with all my heart, kind Master
Bardolph; and [*to the page*] welcome, my tall fellow.
Come, Sir John.

60 FALSTAFF   I'll follow you, good Master Robert Shallow.
                                                    Exit Shallow.

Bardolph, look to our horses.
                                     Exeunt Bardolph and page.

If I were sawed into quantities, I should make four
dozen of such bearded hermits' staves as Master
Shallow. It is a wonderful thing to see the semblable

65 coherence of his men's spirits and his. They, by
observing of him, do bear themselves like foolish
justices; he, by conversing with them, is turned into a
justice-like servingman. Their spirits are so married in
conjunction, with the participation of society, that

70 they flock together in consent, like so many wild geese.
If I had a suit to Master Shallow, I would humour his
men with the imputation of being near their master: if
to his men, I would curry with Master Shallow that no
man could better command his servants. It is certain

75 that either wise bearing or ignorant carriage is caught,
as men take diseases, one of another; therefore let men
take heed of their company. I will devise matter
enough out of this Shallow to keep Prince Harry in
continual laughter the wearing out of six fashions,

80 which is four terms, or two actions, and a shall laugh
without intervallums. O, it is much that a lie with a
slight oath, and a jest with a sad brow, will do with a
fellow that never had the ache in his shoulders! O, you
shall see him laugh till his face be like a wet cloak ill

85 laid up!

SHALLOW [*within*]   Sir John!

FALSTAFF   I come, Master Shallow, I come, Master
Shallow.   *Exit.*

5.2   *Enter* WARWICK *and the*
                LORD CHIEF JUSTICE, *meeting.*

WARWICK
How now, my Lord Chief Justice, whither away?

CHIEF JUSTICE   How doth the King?

WARWICK   Exceeding well: his cares are now all ended.

CHIEF JUSTICE   I hope, not dead.

WARWICK   He's walk'd the way of nature,
And to our purposes he lives no more.   5

CHIEF JUSTICE
I would his Majesty had call'd me with him.
The service that I truly did his life
Hath left me open to all injuries.

WARWICK
Indeed I think the young King loves you not.

CHIEF JUSTICE   I know he doth not, and do arm myself   10
To welcome the condition of the time,
Which cannot look more hideously upon me
Than I have drawn it in my fantasy.

       Enter PRINCE JOHN OF LANCASTER, CLARENCE,
                  GLOUCESTER *and others.*

WARWICK   Here come the heavy issue of dead Harry.
O that the living Harry had the temper   15
Of he, the worst of these three gentlemen!
How many nobles then should hold their places
That must strike sail to spirits of vile sort!

CHIEF JUSTICE   O God, I fear all will be overturn'd.

LANCASTER
Good morrow, cousin Warwick, good morrow.   20

GLOUCESTER, CLARENCE   Good morrow, cousin.

LANCASTER   We meet like men that had forgot to
speak.

WARWICK   We do remember, but our argument
Is all too heavy to admit much talk.

LANCASTER
Well, peace be with him that hath made us heavy!   25

CHIEF JUSTICE   Peace be with us, lest we be heavier!

GLOUCESTER
O good my lord, you have lost a friend indeed;
And I dare swear you borrow not that face
Of seeming sorrow – it is sure your own.

LANCASTER
Though no man be assur'd what grace to find,   30
You stand in coldest expectation.
I am the sorrier; would 'twere otherwise.

CLARENCE
Well, you must now speak Sir John Falstaff fair,
Which swims against your stream of quality.

CHIEF JUSTICE
Sweet Princes, what I did I did in honour,   35
Led by th'impartial conduct of my soul.
And never shall you see that I will beg
A ragged and forestall'd remission.
If truth and upright innocency fail me,
I'll to the King my master that is dead,   40
And tell him who hath sent me after him.

WARWICK   Here comes the Prince.

Enter KING HENRY THE FIFTH, *attended.*

CHIEF JUSTICE
Good morrow, and God save your Majesty!
KING   This new and gorgeous garment, majesty,
Sits not so easy on me as you think.
Brothers, you mix your sadness with some fear.
This is the English, not the Turkish court;
Not Amurath an Amurath succeeds,
But Harry Harry. Yet be sad, good brothers,
For by my faith it very well becomes you.
Sorrow so royally in you appears
That I will deeply put the fashion on,
And wear it in my heart. Why then, be sad;
But entertain no more of it, good brothers,
Than a joint burden laid upon us all.
For me, by heaven, I bid you be assur'd,
I'll be your father and your brother too;
Let me but bear your love, I'll bear your cares.
Yet weep that Harry's dead, and so will I;
But Harry lives, that shall convert those tears
By number into hours of happiness.
PRINCES   We hope no otherwise from your Majesty.
KING   You all look strangely on me – and you most;
You are, I think, assur'd I love you not.
CHIEF JUSTICE   I am assur'd, if I be measur'd rightly,
Your Majesty hath no just cause to hate me.
KING   No?
How might a prince of my great hopes forget
So great indignities you laid upon me?
What! rate, rebuke, and roughly send to prison
Th'immediate heir of England? Was this easy?
May this be wash'd in Lethe and forgotten?
CHIEF JUSTICE
I then did use the person of your father;
The image of his power lay then in me;
And in th'administration of his law,
Whiles I was busy for the commonwealth,
Your Highness pleased to forget my place,
The majesty and power of law and justice,
The image of the King whom I presented,
And struck me in my very seat of judgment;
Whereon, as an offender to your father,
I gave bold way to my authority
And did commit you. If the deed were ill,
Be you contented, wearing now the garland,
To have a son set your decrees at naught?
To pluck down justice from your aweful bench?
To trip the course of law, and blunt the sword
That guards the peace and safety of your person?
Nay more, to spurn at your most royal image,
And mock your workings in a second body?
Question your royal thoughts, make the case yours,
Be now the father, and propose a son,
Hear your own dignity so much profan'd,
See your most dreadful laws so loosely slighted,
Behold yourself so by a son disdain'd:
And then imagine me taking your part,

And in your power soft silencing your son.
After this cold considerance sentence me;
And, as you are a king, speak in your state
What I have done that misbecame my place,   100
My person, or my liege's sovereignty.
KING   You are right, Justice, and you weigh this well.
Therefore still bear the balance and the sword;
And I do wish your honours may increase
Till you do live to see a son of mine   105
Offend you and obey you, as I did.
So shall I live to speak my father's words:
'Happy am I, that have a man so bold
That dares do justice on my proper son;
And not less happy, having such a son   110
That would deliver up his greatness so
Into the hands of justice.' You did commit me:
For which I do commit into your hand
Th'unstained sword that you have us'd to bear,
With this remembrance – that you use the same   115
With the like bold, just, and impartial spirit
As you have done 'gainst me. There is my hand.
You shall be as a father to my youth,
My voice shall sound as you do prompt mine ear,
And I will stoop and humble my intents   120
To your well-practis'd wise directions.
And Princes all, believe me, I beseech you,
My father is gone wild into his grave,
For in his tomb lie my affections;
And with his spirits sadly I survive   125
To mock the expectation of the world,
To frustrate prophecies, and to raze out
Rotten opinion, who hath writ me down
After my seeming. The tide of blood in me
Hath proudly flow'd in vanity till now.   130
Now doth it turn, and ebb back to the sea,
Where it shall mingle with the state of floods,
And flow henceforth in formal majesty.
Now call we our high court of parliament,
And let us choose such limbs of noble counsel   135
That the great body of our state may go
In equal rank with the best-govern'd nation;
That war, or peace, or both at once, may be
As things acquainted and familiar to us;
In which you, father, shall have foremost hand.   140
Our coronation done, we will accite,
As I before remember'd, all our state:
And, God consigning to my good intents,
No prince nor peer shall have just cause to say,
God shorten Harry's happy life one day!   *Exeunt.*   145

5.3   *Enter* FALSTAFF, SHALLOW, SILENCE, DAVY,
BARDOLPH *and page.*

SHALLOW   Nay, you shall see my orchard, where, in an
arbour, we will eat a last year's pippin of mine own
graffing, with a dish of caraways, and so forth – come,
cousin Silence – and then to bed.
FALSTAFF   Fore God, you have here a goodly dwelling,   5

and a rich.

SHALLOW   Barren, barren, barren; beggars all, beggars
all, Sir John – marry, good air. Spread, Davy, spread,
Davy, well said, Davy.

10 FALSTAFF   This Davy serves you for good uses; he is
your serving-man, and your husband.

SHALLOW   A good varlet, a good varlet, a very good
varlet, Sir John – by the mass, I have drunk too much
sack at supper – a good varlet. Now sit down, now sit
15 down – come, cousin.

SILENCE   Ah, sirrah! quoth-a, we shall
[*Sings.*]
        Do nothing but eat, and make good cheer,
        And praise God for the merry year,
        When flesh is cheap and females dear,
20   And lusty lads roam here and there,
            So merrily,
        And ever among so merrily.

FALSTAFF   There's a merry heart, good Master Silence!
I'll give you a health for that anon.

25 SHALLOW   Give Master Bardolph some wine, Davy.

DAVY   Sweet sir, sit – I'll be with you anon – Most sweet
sir, sit; master page, good master page, sit. Proface!
What you want in meat, we'll have in drink; but you
must bear; the heart's all.   *Exit.*

30 SALLOW   Be merry, Master Bardolph, and my little
soldier there, be merry.

SILENCE [*Sings.*]
        Be merry, be merry, my wife has all,
        For women are shrews, both short and tall.
        'Tis merry in hall, when beards wags all,
        And welcome merry Shrove-tide! Be
35   merry, be merry.

FALSTAFF   I did not think Master Silence had been a
man of this mettle.

SILENCE   Who, I? I have been merry twice and once ere
now.

Enter DAVY.

40 DAVY [*to Bardolph*]   There's a dish of leather-coats for
you.

SHALLOW   Davy!

DAVY   Your worship? I'll be with you straight. [*to
Bardolph*]   A cup of wine, sir?

SILENCE [*Sings.*]
45   A cup of wine that's brisk and fine,
        And drink unto thee, leman mine,
        And a merry heart lives long-a.

FALSTAFF   Well said, Master Silence.

SILENCE   And we shall be merry, now comes in the sweet
50 o'th' night.

FALSTAFF   Health and long life to you, Master Silence.

SILENCE [*Sings.*]
        Fill the cup, and let it come,
        I'll pledge you a mile to th' bottom.

SHALLOW   Honest Bardolph, welcome! If thou want'st
55 anything, and wilt not call, beshrew thy heart. [*to the*

page] Welcome, my little tiny thief, and welcome
indeed, too! I'll drink to Master Bardolph, and to all
the cabileros about London.

DAVY   I hope to see London once ere I die.

60 BARDOLPH   And I might see you there, Davy, –

SHALLOW   By the mass, you'll crack a quart together –
ha! will you not, Master Bardolph?

BARDOLPH   Yea, sir, in a pottle-pot.

SHALLOW   By God's liggens, I thank thee; the knave will
65 stick by thee, I can assure thee that. A will not out, a;
'tis true bred!

BARDOLPH   And I'll stick by him, sir.

SHALLOW   Why, there spoke a king. Lack nothing!
Be merry! [*One knocks at door.*] Look who's at door
70 there, ho! Who knocks?   *Exit Davy.*

FALSTAFF [*to Silence, seeing him take off a bumper*]   Why,
now you have done me right.

SILENCE [*Sings.*]   Do me right,
                And dub me knight:
                Samingo.   75

Is't not so?

FALSTAFF   'Tis so.

SILENCE   Is't so? Why then, say an old man can do
somewhat.

Enter DAVY.

80 DAVY   And't please your worship, there's one Pistol
come from the court with news.

FALSTAFF   From the court? Let him come in.

Enter PISTOL.

How now, Pistol?

PISTOL   Sir John, God save you!

FALSTAFF   What wind blew you hither, Pistol?   85

PISTOL   Not the ill wind which blows no man to good.
Sweet knight, thou art now one of the greatest men in
this realm.

SILENCE   By'r lady, I think a be, but goodman Puff of
Barson.   90

PISTOL   Puff?
Puff i' thy teeth, most recreant coward base!
Sir John, I am thy Pistol and thy friend,
And helter-skelter have I rode to thee,
And tidings do I bring, and lucky joys,   95
And golden times, and happy news of price.

FALSTAFF   I pray thee now, deliver them like a man of
this world.

PISTOL   A foutre for the world and worldlings base!
I speak of Africa and golden joys.   100

FALSTAFF
O base Assyrian knight, what is thy news?
Let King Cophetua know the truth thereof.

SILENCE [*Sings.*]   And Robin Hood, Scarlet, and John.

PISTOL   Shall dunghill curs confront the Helicons?
And shall good news be baffled?   105
Then, Pistol, lay thy head in Furies' lap.

SHALLOW   Honest gentleman, I know not your breeding.

PISTOL   Why then, lament therefor.

SHALLOW   Give me pardon, sir; if, sir, you come with news from the court, I take it there's but two ways, either to utter them or conceal them. I am, sir, under the King, in some authority.

PISTOL   Under which king, Besonian? Speak, or die.

SHALLOW   Under King Harry.

PISTOL   Harry the Fourth, or Fifth?

SHALLOW   Harry the Fourth.

PISTOL   A foutre for thine office!
Sir John, thy tender lambkin now is King;
Harry the Fifth's the man: I speak the truth.
When Pistol lies, do this, and fig me, like
The bragging Spaniard.

FALSTAFF   What, is the old King dead?

PISTOL   As nail in door! The things I speak are just.

FALSTAFF   Away, Bardolph, saddle my horse. Master Robert Shallow, choose what office thou wilt in the land, 'tis thine. Pistol, I will double-charge thee with dignities.

BARDOLPH   O joyful day!
I would not take a knighthood for my fortune.

PISTOL   What, I do bring good news?

FALSTAFF   Carry Master Silence to bed. Master Shallow, my Lord Shallow – be what thou wilt; I am Fortune's steward! Get on thy boots, we'll ride all night. O sweet Pistol! Away, Bardolph!

Exit Bardolph.

Come, Pistol, utter more to me; and withal devise something to do thyself good. Boot, boot, Master Shallow! I know the young King is sick for me. Let us take any man's horses – the laws of England are at my commandment. Blessed are they that have been my friends, and woe to my Lord Chief Justice!

PISTOL   Let vultures vile seize on his lungs also!
'Where is the life that late I led?' say they:
Why, here it is; welcome these pleasant days! *Exeunt.*

5.4   *Enter* Beadles, *dragging in* HOSTESS QUICKLY *and* DOLL TEARSHEET.

HOSTESS   No, thou arrant knave! I would to God that I might die, that I might have thee hanged. Thou hast drawn my shoulder out of joint.

1 BEADLE   The constables have delivered her over to me, and she shall have whipping-cheer enough, I warrant her; there hath been a man or two lately killed about her.

DOLL   Nut-hook, nut-hook, you lie! Come on, I'll tell thee what, thou damned tripe-visaged rascal, and the child I go with do miscarry, thou wert better thou hadst struck thy mother, thou paper-faced villain.

HOSTESS   O the Lord, that Sir John were come! He would make this a bloody day to somebody. But I pray God the fruit of her womb miscarry!

1 BEADLE   If it do, you shall have a dozen of cushions again; you have but eleven now. Come, I charge you both, go with me, for the man is dead that you and Pistol beat amongst you.

DOLL   I'll tell you what, you thin man in a censer, I will have you as soundly swinged for this – you blue-bottle rogue, you filthy famished correctioner, if you be not swinged I'll forswear half-kirtles.

1 BEADLE   Come, come, you she knight-errant, come!

HOSTESS   O God, that right should thus overcome might! Well, of sufferance comes ease.

DOLL   Come, you rogue, come, bring me to a justice.

HOSTESS   Ay, come, you starved bloodhound.

DOLL   Goodman death, goodman bones!

HOSTESS   Thou atomy, thou!

DOLL   Come, you thin thing, come, you rascal!

1 BEADLE   Very well.   *Exeunt.*

5.5   *Enter three* Grooms, *strewers of rushes.*

1 GROOM   More rushes, more rushes!

2 GROOM   The trumpets have sounded twice.

3 GROOM   'Twill be two o'clock ere they come from the coronation. Dispatch, dispatch.   *Exeunt.*

Trumpets sound, and the KING *and his train pass over the stage: after them enter* FALSTAFF, SHALLOW, PISTOL, BARDOLPH *and the page.*

FALSTAFF   Stand here by me, Master Robert Shallow, I will make the King do you grace. I will leer upon him as a comes by, and do but mark the countenance that he will give me.

PISTOL   God bless thy lungs, good knight!

FALSTAFF   Come here, Pistol, stand behind me. [*to Shallow*] O, if I had had time to have made new liveries, I would have bestowed the thousand pound I borrowed of you. But 'tis no matter, this poor show doth better, this doth infer the zeal I had to see him.

SHALLOW   It doth so.

FALSTAFF   It shows my earnestness of affection –

SHALLOW   It doth so.

FALSTAFF   My devotion –

SHALLOW   It doth, it doth, it doth.

FALSTAFF   As it were, to ride day and night, and not to deliberate, not to remember, not to have patience to shift me –

SHALLOW   It is best, certain.

FALSTAFF   But to stand stained with travel, and sweating with desire to see him, thinking of nothing else, putting all affairs else in oblivion, as if there were nothing else to be done but to see him.

PISTOL   'Tis *semper idem*, for *obsque hoc nihil est;* 'tis all in every part.

SHALLOW   'Tis so, indeed.

PISTOL   My knight, I will inflame thy noble liver,
And make thee rage.
Thy Doll, and Helen of thy noble thoughts,
Is in base durance and contagious prison,
Hal'd thither

By most mechanical and dirty hand.
Rouse up Revenge from ebon den with fell Alecto's
      snake,
For Doll is in. Pistol speaks naught but truth.

FALSTAFF   I will deliver her. [*Shouts within.*]
                              [*The trumpets sound.*]

PISTOL
40   There roar'd the sea, and trumpet-clangor sounds.

Enter the KING *and his train, the*
Lord Chief Justice *among them.*

FALSTAFF
God save thy Grace, King Hal, my royal Hal!
PISTOL
The heavens thee guard and keep, most royal imp of
      fame!
FALSTAFF   God save thee, my sweet boy!
KING   My Lord Chief Justice, speak to that vain man.
CHIEF JUSTICE
45   Have you your wits? Know you what 'tis you speak?
FALSTAFF
My King! My Jove! I speak to thee, my heart!
KING   I know thee not, old man. Fall to thy prayers.
How ill white hairs becomes a fool and jester!
I have long dreamt of such a kind of man,
50   So surfeit-swell'd, so old, and so profane;
But being awak'd I do despise my dream.
Make less thy body hence, and more thy grace;
Leave gormandizing; know the grave doth gape
For thee thrice wider than for other men.
55   Reply not to me with a fool-born jest;
Presume not that I am the thing I was;
For God doth know, so shall the world perceive,
That I have turn'd away my former self;
So will I those that kept me company.
60   When thou dost hear I am as I have been,
Approach me, and thou shalt be as thou wast,
The tutor and the feeder of my riots.
Till then I banish thee, on pain of death,
As I have done the rest of my misleaders,
65   Not to come near our person by ten mile.
For competence of life I will allow you,
That lack of means enforce you not to evils;
And as we hear you do reform yourselves,
We will, according to your strengths and qualities,
Give you advancement.
70   [*to the Lord Chief Justice*] Be it your charge, my lord,
To see perform'd the tenor of my word.
Set on.   *Exit King with his train.*
FALSTAFF   Master Shallow, I owe you a thousand
      pound.
75 SHALLOW   Yea, marry, Sir John, which I beseech you to
      let me have home with me.
FALSTAFF   That can hardly be, Master Shallow. Do not
      you grieve at this; I shall be sent for in private to him.
      Look you, he must seem thus to the world. Fear not
80   your advancements; I will be the man yet that shall

make you great.
SHALLOW   I cannot perceive how, unless you give me
      your doublet, and stuff me out with straw. I beseech
      you, good Sir John, let me have five hundred of my
      thousand.   85
FALSTAFF   Sir, I will be as good as my word. This that
      you heard was but a colour.
SHALLOW   A colour that I fear you will die in, Sir John.
FALSTAFF   Fear no colours. Go with me to dinner.
      Come, Lieutenant Pistol; come, Bardolph. I shall be   90
      sent for soon at night.

Enter the Lord Chief Justice *and*
PRINCE JOHN, *with officers.*

CHIEF JUSTICE   Go carry Sir John Falstaff to the Fleet;
Take all his company along with him.
FALSTAFF   My lord, my lord, –
CHIEF JUSTICE
I cannot now speak: I will hear you soon.   95
Take them away.
PISTOL   *Si fortuna me tormenta, spero me contenta.*
          Exeunt all but Prince John and the Chief Justice.
LANCASTER   I like this fair proceeding of the King's.
He hath intent his wonted followers
Shall all be very well provided for,   100
But all are banish'd till their conversations
Appear more wise and modest to the world.
CHIEF JUSTICE   And so they are.
LANCASTER
The King hath call'd his parliament, my lord.
CHIEF JUSTICE   He hath.   105
LANCASTER   I will lay odds that, ere this year expire,
We bear our civil swords and native fire
As far as France. I heard a bird so sing,
Whose music, to my thinking, pleas'd the King.
Come, will you hence?   *Exeunt.*   110

EPILOGUE

First, my fear; then, my curtsy; last, my speech.
    My fear, is your displeasure; my curtsy, my duty;
and my speech, to beg your pardons. If you look for a
good speech now, you undo me, for what I have to say
is of mine own making; and what indeed I should say   5
will, I doubt, prove mine own marring. But to the
purpose, and so to the venture. Be it known to you, as
it is very well, I was lately here in the end of a
displeasing play, to pray your patience for it, and to
promise you a better. I meant indeed to pay you with   10
this; which if like an ill venture it come unluckily
home, I break, and you, my gentle creditors, lose. Here
I promised you I would be, and here I commit my
body to your mercies. Bate me some, and I will pay
you some, and, as most debtors do, promise you   15
infinitely: and so I kneel down before you – but,
indeed, to pray for the Queen.
    If my tongue cannot entreat you to acquit me, will

you command me to use my legs? And yet that were but light payment, to dance out of your debt. But a good conscience will make any possible satisfaction, and so would I. All the gentlewomen here have forgiven me: if the gentlemen will not, then the gentlemen do not agree with the gentlewomen, which was never seen before in such an assembly.

One word more, I beseech you. If you be not too much cloyed with fat meat, our humble author will continue the story, with Sir John in it, and make you merry with fair Katharine of France; where, for anything I know, Falstaff shall die of a sweat, unless already a be killed with your hard opinions; for Oldcastle died martyr, and this is not the man. My tongue is weary; when my legs are too, I will bid you good night. 30

King Henry V

King Henry V was first published in 1600 as *The Cronicle History of Henry the fift*. The printed play is about half the length of the one that would appear as the fifth of the histories in the Folio in 1623, lacking the choruses and omitting many passages and three entire scenes (1.1, 3.1 and 4.2). Possibly it is a 'reported' text, compiled by some process of recollection, probably by actors in a production; perhaps one based on a script abridged for performance on tour. The Folio text derives not from this early Quarto but from a manuscript, just possibly one in Shakespeare's own hand. Thus it serves as the basis of all modern editions, though the Quarto may well reflect an early staging of the play.

Apparently written about 1599, *King Henry V* could have been the first play performed at the Globe. The Chorus's apology for the limited resources of the 'wooden O' in which the action must be performed is perhaps an ironic reference to the fine new playhouse that had opened that year. The play contains Shakespeare's only unquestionable reference to a current event, which allows us to date it with some precision. Speaking of King Henry's triumphant re-entry into London after Agincourt, the Chorus compares the excitement that greets Henry to the enthusiastic response that would occur 'Were now the General of our gracious Empress, / As in good time he may, from Ireland coming, / Bringing rebellion broached on his sword'. These lines probably refer to the Earl of Essex, who had been sent by Elizabeth to Ireland in late March of 1599 to put down the rebellion led by Hugh O'Neill. Essex, however, failed in his charge and returned to London in late September. He was put under house arrest for leaving his command and was tried and sentenced in June of 1600. If the Chorus's lines are indeed a reference to Essex, the play must have been acted between March and September of 1599, between his optimistic departure and the ignominy of his return.

Essex's adventure could not have provided the impetus for the play itself, which is the foreseen conclusion of Hal's *Bildungsspiel* in the two parts of *King Henry IV*, though Henry V is the charismatic national hero that Essex aspired to be. Shakespeare's play can indeed be seen as an examination of the claims of heroic achievement, imparting a mythic shape and significance to the history of Henry's reign by organizing the historical material he found in Holinshed's *Chronicles* (1587) along the lines mapped out earlier by Edward Hall in his chronicle with the heading 'The Victorious Reign of King Henry V'. Henry leads a band of brave and loyal soldiers against a much larger force of arrogant Frenchmen, and the astounding victory at Agincourt confirms England's military and moral superiority. If this does not exactly conform to the facts of history, it does conform to the poetic logic of giant killing.

But if the play allows us to see and enjoy the great military and political achievements of Henry, it enables us also to see their costs. Shakespeare allows alternative angles of vision to the heroic. While the Chorus speaks the language of heroic idealization, the comic plot that parallels and comments on the historical action shows us a world of baser motive. The very structure of the play depends upon such ironic contrasts; the promises of the Chorus introducing each act are inevitably frustrated by the action that follows, as when at the beginning we are told that we shall see the confrontation of 'two mighty monarchies' but see instead the political manoeuvrings of worldly churchmen urging the French war to avoid a confiscatory bill.

The lustre of the celebrated war will certainly be tarnished if it is seen to be motivated not by a principled desire to regain lost rights but by the self-interest of a Church desperate to retain its wealth. Indeed, it is precisely by allowing an audience to see the uncertain genesis of the famous victories that Shakespeare begins his exploration of the necessarily imperfect man who must play the King. Performances on stage and on the screen have not always wished to see this qualification of Henry's heroic achievements; Laurence Olivier's film version, completed during World War II, understandably ignored all the play's darker tones. But Shakespeare's play, though not cynical about heroic action, is always aware of the matrix of human falliblity in which it is grounded. 'The king is a good king', as Pistol says, 'but it must be as it may'.

The Arden text is based on the 1623 First Folio.

CHORUS
KING Henry the Fifth
Duke of CLARENCE
Duke of BEDFORD } his brothers
Duke of GLOUCESTER
Duke of EXETER   his uncle
Duke of YORK
Earl of HUNTINGDON
Earl of SALISBURY
Earl of WARWICK
Earl of WESTMORLAND
Richard, Earl of CAMBRIDGE
Henry, Lord SCROOP *of Masham* } conspirators against the King
Sir Thomas GREY
Archbishop of CANTERBURY
Bishop of ELY
Sir Thomas ERPINGHAM
Captain FLUELLEN
Captain GOWER } officers in the King's army
Captain JAMY
Captain MACMORRIS
John BATES
Alexander COURT } soldiers in the King's army
Michael WILLIAMS
An English Herald
BARDOLPH
NYM } associates of Sir John Falstaff
PISTOL
BOY   *Falstaff's page*
Nell, HOSTESS   *of an Eastcheap tavern, formerly Mistress Quickly, now married to Pistol*

Charles the Sixth, *the* FRENCH KING
QUEEN ISABEL   *the French Queen*
Louis, *the* DAUPHIN   *their son*
Princess KATHERINE   *their daughter*
ALICE   *a lady attending on Princess Katherine*
Duke of BERRY
Duke of BOURBON
Duke of BRITAIN
Duke of BURGUNDY
Duke of ORLEANS
Charles Delabreth, *the* CONSTABLE   *of France*
Earl of GRANDPRÉ
Lord RAMBURES
GOVERNOR   *of Harfleur*
MONTJOY   *the French herald*
Two French Ambassadors *to the King of England*
Monsier Le Fer, *a* FRENCH SOLDIER
A French Messenger

Attendants, Lords, Soldiers, Citizens of Harfleur

430

King Henry V

PROLOGUE

Enter CHORUS.

CHORUS   O for a muse of fire, that would ascend
　　The brightest heaven of invention,
　　A kingdom for a stage, princes to act,
　　And monarchs to behold the swelling scene!
　　Then should the warlike Harry, like himself,
　　Assume the port of Mars, and at his heels,
　　Leashed in like hounds, should famine, sword and
　　　fire
　　Crouch for employment. But pardon, gentles all,
　　The flat unraised spirits that hath dared
　　On this unworthy scaffold to bring forth
　　So great an object. Can this cockpit hold
　　The vasty fields of France? Or may we cram
　　Within this wooden O the very casques
　　That did affright the air at Agincourt?
　　O pardon, since a crooked figure may
　　Attest in little place a million,
　　And let us, ciphers to this great account,
　　On your imaginary forces work.
　　Suppose within the girdle of these walls
　　Are now confined two mighty monarchies,
　　Whose high upreared and abutting fronts
　　The perilous narrow ocean parts asunder.
　　Piece out our imperfections with your thoughts.
　　Into a thousand parts divide one man
　　And make imaginary puissance.
　　Think, when we talk of horses, that you see them
　　Printing their proud hoofs i'th' receiving earth.
　　For 'tis your thoughts that now must deck our kings,
　　Carry them here and there, jumping o'er times,
　　Turning th'accomplishment of many years
　　Into an hour-glass: for the which supply,
　　Admit me Chorus to this history,
　　Who prologue-like your humble patience pray,
　　Gently to hear, kindly to judge our play.　　　*Exit.*

1.1　　*Enter the* Archbishop of CANTERBURY *and*
　　　　　the Bishop of ELY.

CANTERBURY
　　My lord, I'll tell you, that self bill is urged
　　Which in th'eleventh year of the last king's reign
　　Was like and had indeed against us passed
　　But that the scambling and unquiet time
　　Did push it out of farther question.
ELY　　But how, my lord, shall we resist it now?
CANTERBURY
　　It must be thought on. If it pass against us
　　We lose the better half of our possession:
　　For all the temporal lands which men devout
　　By testament have given to the Church
　　Would they strip from us, being valued thus:
　　As much as would maintain, to the King's honour,
　　Full fifteen earls and fifteen hundred knights,

　　Six thousand and two hundred good esquires,
　　And to relief of lazars and weak age,　　　　　15
　　Of indigent faint souls past corporal toil,
　　A hundred almshouses right well supplied,
　　And to the coffers of the King beside,
　　A thousand pounds by th' year. Thus runs the bill.
ELY　　This would drink deep.
CANTERBURY　　　　　　　'Twould drink the cup and all.　20
ELY　　But what prevention?
CANTERBURY　　The King is full of grace and fair regard.
ELY　　And a true lover of the holy Church.
CANTERBURY
　　The courses of his youth promised it not.
　　The breath no sooner left his father's body　　25
　　But that his wildness, mortified in him,
　　Seemed to die too; yea, at that very moment,
　　Consideration like an angel came
　　And whipped th'offending Adam out of him,
　　Leaving his body as a paradise　　　　　　　30
　　T'envelop and contain celestial spirits.
　　Never was such a sudden scholar made,
　　Never came reformation in a flood
　　With such a heady currence scouring faults,
　　Nor never Hydra-headed wilfulness　　　　　35
　　So soon did lose his seat, and all at once,
　　As in this king.
ELY　　　　　　　We are blessed in the change.
CANTERBURY　　Hear him but reason in divinity
　　And, all-admiring, with an inward wish
　　You would desire the King were made a prelate.　40
　　Hear him debate of commonwealth affairs,
　　You would say it hath been all in all his study.
　　List his discourse of war, and you shall hear
　　A fearful battle rendered you in music.
　　Turn him to any cause of policy,　　　　　　45
　　The Gordian knot of it he will unloose,
　　Familiar as his garter, that when he speaks,
　　The air, a chartered libertine, is still,
　　And the mute wonder lurketh in men's ears
　　To steal his sweet and honeyed sentences.　　50
　　So that the art and practic part of life
　　Must be the mistress to this theoric:
　　Which is a wonder how his grace should glean it,
　　Since his addiction was to courses vain,
　　His companies unlettered, rude, and shallow,　55
　　His hours filled up with riots, banquets, sports,
　　And never noted in him any study,
　　Any retirement, any sequestration
　　From open haunts and popularity.
ELY　　The strawberry grows underneath the nettle,　60
　　And wholesome berries thrive and ripen best
　　Neighboured by fruit of baser quality.
　　And so the Prince obscured his contemplation
　　Under the veil of wildness, which, no doubt,
　　Grew like the summer grass, fastest by night,　65
　　Unseen, yet crescive in his faculty.
CANTERBURY　　It must be so, for miracles are ceased,

And therefore we must needs admit the means
How things are perfected.

ELY   But my good lord,
70   How now for mitigation of this bill
Urged by the Commons? Doth his majesty
Incline to it, or no?

CANTERBURY   He seems indifferent,
Or rather swaying more upon our part
Than cherishing th'exhibitors against us.
75   For I have made an offer to his majesty,
Upon our spiritual convocation,
And in regard of causes now in hand
Which I have opened to his grace at large,
As touching France, to give a greater sum
80   Than ever at one time the clergy yet
Did to his predecessors part withal.

ELY   How did this offer seem received, my lord?

CANTERBURY   With good acceptance of his majesty,
Save that there was not time enough to hear,
85   As I perceived his grace would fain have done,
The severals and unhidden passages
Of his true titles to some certain dukedoms,
And generally to the crown and seat of France,
Derived from Edward, his great-grandfather.

90   ELY   What was th'impediment that broke this off?

CANTERBURY
The French ambassador upon that instant
Craved audience, and the hour I think is come
To give him hearing. Is it four o'clock?

ELY   It is.

95   CANTERBURY   Then go we in, to know his embassy,
Which I could with a ready guess declare
Before the Frenchman speak a word of it.

ELY   I'll wait upon you, and I long to hear it.   *Exeunt.*

1.2   *Enter the* KING, GLOUCESTER, BEDFORD,
CLARENCE, WARWICK, WESTMORLAND *and*
EXETER *and attendants.*

KING   Where is my gracious lord of Canterbury?

EXETER   Not here in presence.

KING   Send for him, good uncle.
Exit an attendant.

WESTMORLAND
Shall we call in th'ambassador, my liege?

KING   Not yet, my cousin: we would be resolved,
5   Before we hear him, of some things of weight
That task our thoughts concerning us and France.

Enter the Archbishop of CANTERBURY *and*
the Bishop of ELY.

CANTERBURY
God and his angels guard your sacred throne
And make you long become it!

KING   Sure, we thank you.
My learned lord, we pray you to proceed
10   And justly and religiously unfold

Why the law Salic that they have in France
Or should or should not bar us in our claim.
And God forbid, my dear and faithful lord,
That you should fashion, wrest or bow your reading
Or nicely charge your understanding soul   15
With opening titles miscreate, whose right
Suits not in native colours with the truth.
For God doth know how many now in health
Shall drop their blood in approbation
Of what your reverence shall incite us to.   20
Therefore take heed how you impawn our person,
How you awake our sleeping sword of war:
We charge you in the name of God take heed.
For never two such kingdoms did contend
Without much fall of blood, whose guiltless drops   25
Are every one a woe, a sore complaint
'Gainst him whose wrongs gives edge unto the
    swords
That makes such waste in brief mortality.
Under this conjuration speak, my lord,
For we will hear, note, and believe in heart   30
That what you speak is in your conscience washed
As pure as sin with baptism.

CANTERBURY
Then hear me, gracious sovereign, and you peers
That owe your selves, your lives and services
To this imperial throne. There is no bar   35
To make against your highness' claim to France
But this which they produce from Pharamond:
In terram Salicam mulieres ne succedant,
'No woman shall succeed in Salic land':
Which Salic land the French unjustly gloze   40
To be the realm of France, and Pharamond
The founder of this law and female bar.
Yet their own authors faithfully affirm
That the land Salic is in Germany,
Between the floods of Sala and of Elbe,   45
Where Charles the Great, having subdued the
    Saxons,
There left behind and settled certain French,
Who, holding in disdain the German women
For some dishonest manners of their life,
Established then this law, to wit, no female   50
Should be inheritrix in Salic land;
Which Salic (as I said, 'twixt Elbe and Sala)
Is at this day in Germany called Meissen.
Then doth it well appear the Salic law
Was not devised for the realm of France.   55
Nor did the French possess the Salic land
Until four hundred one-and-twenty years
After defunction of King Pharamond,
Idly supposed the founder of this law,
Who died within the year of our redemption   60
Four hundred twenty-six, and Charles the Great
Subdued the Saxons and did seat the French
Beyond the river Sala in the year
Eight hundred five. Besides, their writers say,

65 King Pepin, which deposed Childeric,
Did as heir general, being descended
Of Blithild, which was daughter to King Clothair,
Make claim and title to the crown of France.
Hugh Capet also, who usurped the crown
70 Of Charles the Duke of Lorraine, sole heir male
Of the true line and stock of Charles the Great,
To fine his title with some shows of truth,
Though in pure truth it was corrupt and naught,
Conveyed himself as heir to th' Lady Lingard,
75 Daughter to Charlemagne, who was the son
To Louis the Emperor, and Louis the son
Of Charles the Great. Also King Louis the Ninth,
Who was sole heir to the usurper Capet,
Could not keep quiet in his conscience,
80 Wearing the crown of France, till satisfied
That fair Queen Isabel, his grandmother,
Was lineal of the Lady Ermengard,
Daughter to Charles the foresaid Duke of Lorraine,
By the which marriage the line of Charles the Great
85 Was reunited to the crown of France.
So that, as clear as is the summer's sun,
King Pepin's title, and Hugh Capet's claim,
King Louis his satisfaction, all appear
To hold in right and title of the female.
90 So do the kings of France unto this day,
Howbeit they would hold up this Salic law
To bar your highness claiming from the female,
And rather choose to hide them in a net
Than amply to embare their crooked titles
95 Usurped from you and your progenitors.
KING
May I with right and conscience make this claim?
CANTERBURY   The sin upon my head, dread sovereign:
For in the Book of Numbers is it writ,
'When the man dies, let the inheritance
100 Descend unto the daughter.' Gracious lord,
Stand for your own, unwind your bloody flag,
Look back into your mighty ancestors.
Go, my dread lord, to your great-grandsire's tomb,
From whom you claim; invoke his warlike spirit,
105 And your great-uncle's, Edward the Black Prince,
Who on the French ground played a tragedy,
Making defeat on the full power of France,
Whiles his most mighty father on a hill
Stood smiling to behold his lion's whelp
110 Forage in blood of French nobility.
O noble English, that could entertain
With half their forces the full pride of France
And let another half stand laughing by,
All out of work and cold for action!
115 ELY   Awake remembrance of these valiant dead,
And with your puissant arm renew their feats.
You are their heir, you sit upon their throne,
The blood and courage that renowned them
Runs in your veins, and my thrice-puissant liege
120 Is in the very May-morn of his youth,

Ripe for exploits and mighty enterprises.
EXETER   Your brother kings and monarchs of the earth
Do all expect that you should rouse yourself
As did the former lions of your blood.
WESTMORLAND
They know your grace hath cause, and means, and
might; 125
So doth your highness. Never king of England
Had nobles richer and more loyal subjects,
Whose hearts have left their bodies here in England
And lie pavilioned in the fields of France.
CANTERBURY   O let their bodies follow, my dear liege, 130
With blood and sword and fire to win your right;
In aid whereof we of the spirituality
Will raise your highness such a mighty sum
As never did the clergy at one time
Bring in to any of your ancestors. 135
KING   We must not only arm t'invade the French,
But lay down our proportions to defend
Against the Scot, who will make road upon us
With all advantages.
CANTERBURY
They of those marches, gracious sovereign, 140
Shall be a wall sufficient to defend
Our inland from the pilfering borderers.
KING   We do not mean the coursing snatchers only,
But fear the main intendment of the Scot,
Who hath been still a giddy neighbour to us. 145
For you shall read that my great-grandfather
Never went with his forces into France
But that the Scot on his unfurnished kingdom
Came pouring like the tide into a breach,
With ample and brim fullness of his force, 150
Galling the gleaned land with hot assays,
Girding with grievous siege castles and towns,
That England, being empty of defence,
Hath shook and trembled at th'ill neighbourhood.
CANTERBURY   She hath been then more feared than
harmed, my liege. 155
For hear her but exampled by herself:
When all her chivalry hath been in France
And she a mourning widow of her nobles,
She hath herself not only well defended
But taken and impounded as a stray 160
The King of Scots, whom she did send to France,
To fill King Edward's fame with prisoner kings
And make her chronicle as rich with praise
As is the ooze and bottom of the sea
With sunken wrack and sumless treasuries. 165
WESTMORLAND   But there's a saying very old and true,
If that you will France win,
Then with Scotland first begin.
For once the eagle England being in prey,
To her unguarded nest the weasel Scot 170
Comes sneaking and so sucks her princely eggs,
Playing the mouse in absence of the cat,
To 'tame and havoc more than she can eat.

EXETER   It follows then the cat must stay at home;
175   Yet that is but a crushed necessity,
      Since we have locks to safeguard necessaries
      And pretty traps to catch the petty thieves.
      While that the armed hand doth fight abroad
      Th'advised head defends itself at home.
180   For government, though high and low and lower
      Put into parts, doth keep in one concent,
      Congreeing in a full and natural close
      Like music.
         CANTERBURY   True. Therefore doth heaven divide
      The state of man in diverse functions,
185   Setting endeavour in continual motion,
      To which is fixed, as an aim or butt,
      Obedience. For so work the honey-bees,
      Creatures that by a rule in nature teach
      The act of order to a peopled kingdom.
190   They have a king and officers of sorts,
      Where some like magistrates correct at home,
      Others like merchants venture trade abroad,
      Others like soldiers, armed in their stings,
      Make boot upon the summer's velvet buds,
195   Which pillage they with merry march bring home
      To the tent-royal of their emperor,
      Who busied in his majesty surveys
      The singing masons building roofs of gold,
      The civil citizens kneading up the honey,
200   The poor mechanic porters crowding in
      Their heavy burdens at his narrow gate,
      The sad-eyed justice, with his surly hum,
      Delivering o'er to executors pale
      The lazy yawning drone. I this infer,
205   That many things having full reference
      To one consent may work contrariously,
      As many arrows loosed several ways
      Come to one mark,
      As many several ways meet in one town,
210   As many fresh streams meet in one salt sea,
      As many lines close in the dial's centre.
      So may a thousand actions once afoot
      End in one purpose and be all well borne
      Without defeat. Therefore to France, my liege.
215   Divide your happy England into four,
      Whereof take you one quarter into France
      And you withal shall make all Gallia shake.
      If we with thrice such powers left at home
      Cannot defend our own doors from the dog,
220   Let us be worried and our nation lose
      The name of hardiness and policy.
         KING   Call in the messengers sent from the Dauphin.
                                    Exeunt some attendants.
      Now are we well resolved; and by God's help
      And yours, the noble sinews of our power,
225   France being ours, we'll bend it to our awe
      Or break it all to pieces. Or there we'll sit,
      Ruling in large and ample empery
      O'er France and all her almost kingly dukedoms,

      Or lay these bones in an unworthy urn,
      Tombless, with no remembrance over them.   230
      Either our history shall with full mouth
      Speak freely of our acts, or else our grave
      Like Turkish mute shall have a tongueless mouth,
      Not worshipped with a waxen epitaph.

                Enter Ambassadors *of France, with*
                   attendants carrying a tun.

      Now are we well prepared to know the pleasure   235
      Of our fair cousin Dauphin; for we hear
      Your greeting is from him, not from the King.
   AMBASSADOR
      May't please your majesty to give us leave
      Freely to render what we have in charge,
      Or shall we sparingly show you far off   240
      The Dauphin's meaning and our embassy?
   KING   We are no tyrant but a Christian king,
      Unto whose grace our passion is as subject
      As are our wretches fettered in our prisons:
      Therefore with frank and with uncurbed plainness 245
      Tell us the Dauphin's mind.
   AMBASSADOR   Thus then, in few.
      Your highness lately sending into France
      Did claim some certain dukedoms in the right
      Of your great predecessor King Edward the Third.
      In answer of which claim the Prince our master   250
      Says that you savour too much of your youth
      And bids you be advised. There's naught in France
      That can be with a nimble galliard won;
      You cannot revel into dukedoms there.
      He therefore sends you, meeter for your spirit,   255
      This tun of treasure, and in lieu of this
      Desires you let the dukedoms that you claim
      Hear no more of you. This the Dauphin speaks.
   KING   What treasure, uncle?
   EXETER   Tennis-balls, my liege.
   KING   We are glad the Dauphin is so pleasant with us. 260
      His present and your pains we thank you for.
      When we have matched our rackets to these balls
      We will in France, by God's grace, play a set
      Shall strike his father's crown into the hazard.
      Tell him he hath made a match with such a wrangler 265
      That all the courts of France shall be disturbed
      With chases. And we understand him well,
      How he comes o'er us with our wilder days,
      Not measuring what use we made of them.
      We never valued this poor seat of England,   270
      And therefore living hence did give ourself
      To barbarous licence, as 'tis ever common
      That men are merriest when they are from home.
      But tell the Dauphin I will keep my state,
      Be like a king and show my sail of greatness,   275
      When I do rouse me in my throne of France.
      For that have I laid by my majesty
      And plodded like a man for working-days,
      But I will rise there with so full a glory

That I will dazzle all the eyes of France,   80
Yea, strike the Dauphin blind to look on us.
And tell the pleasant Prince this mock of his
Hath turned his balls to gun-stones, and his soul
Shall stand sore charged for the wasteful vengeance
That shall fly with them; for many a thousand   85
    widows
Shall this his mock mock out of their dear husbands,
Mock mothers from their sons, mock castles down,
And some are yet ungotten and unborn
That shall have cause to curse the Dauphin's scorn.
But this lies all within the will of God,   90
To whom I do appeal, and in whose name
Tell you the Dauphin I am coming on
To venge me as I may, and to put forth
My rightful hand in a well-hallowed cause.
So get you hence in peace. And tell the Dauphin   95
His jest will savour but of shallow wit
When thousands weep more than did laugh at it. –
Convey them with safe conduct. – Fare you well.

                Exeunt Ambassadors and attendants.

EXETER   This was a merry message.
KING   We hope to make the sender blush at it.   100
  Therefore, my lords, omit no happy hour
  That may give furtherance to our expedition,
  For we have now no thought in us but France,
  Save those to God that run before our business.
  Therefore let our proportions for these wars   105
  Be soon collected and all things thought upon
  That may with reasonable swiftness add
  More feathers to our wings, for, God before,
  We'll chide this Dauphin at his father's door.
  Therefore let every man now task his thought,   110
  That this fair action may on foot be brought.

                      Flourish. Exeunt.

2.0   *Enter* CHORUS.

CHORUS   Now all the youth of England are on fire,
  And silken dalliance in the wardrobe lies.
  Now thrive the armourers, and honour's thought
  Reigns solely in the breast of every man.
  They sell the pasture now to buy the horse,
  Following the mirror of all Christian kings
  With winged heels, as English Mercuries.
  For now sits expectation in the air
  And hides a sword from hilts unto the point
  With crowns imperial, crowns and coronets,   10
  Promised to Harry and his followers.
  The French, advised by good intelligence
  Of this most dreadful preparation,
  Shake in their fear, and with pale policy
  Seek to divert the English purposes.   15
  O England, model to thy inward greatness,
  Like little body with a mighty heart,
  What mightst thou do, that honour would thee do,
  Were all thy children kind and natural!

But see, thy fault France hath in thee found out,   20
A nest of hollow bosoms, which he fills
With treacherous crowns; and three corrupted men,
One, Richard Earl of Cambridge, and the second,
Henry Lord Scroop of Masham, and the third,
Sir Thomas Grey, knight, of Northumberland,   25
Have, for the gilt of France, – O guilt indeed! –
Confirmed conspiracy with fearful France,
And by their hands this grace of kings must die,
If hell and treason hold their promises,
Ere he take ship for France, and in Southampton.   30
Linger your patience on and well digest
Th'abuse of distance, and we'll force our play.
The sum is paid, the traitors are agreed,
The King is set from London, and the scene
Is now transported, gentles, to Southampton.   35
There is the playhouse now, there must you sit,
And thence to France shall we convey you safe
And bring you back, charming the narrow seas
To give you gentle pass; for if we may,
We'll not offend one stomach with our play.   40
But till the King come forth and not till then
Unto Southampton do we shift our scene.   *Exit.*

2.1   *Enter* Corporal NYM *and*
             Lieutenant BARDOLPH, *meeting.*

BARDOLPH   Well met, Corporal Nym.
NYM   Good morrow, Lieutenant Bardolph.
BARDOLPH
  What, are Ancient Pistol and you friends yet?
NYM   For my part I care not. I say little; but when time
  shall serve there shall be smiles; but that shall be as it   5
  may. I dare not fight, but I will wink and hold out mine
  iron. It is a simple one, but what though? It will toast
  cheese, and it will endure cold as another man's sword
  will, and there's an end.
BARDOLPH   I will bestow a breakfast to make you   10
  friends, and we'll be all three sworn brothers to
  France. Let't be so, good Corporal Nym.
NYM   Faith, I will live so long as I may, that's the certain
  of it, and when I cannot live any longer, I will do as I
  may. That is my rest, that is the rendezvous of it.   15
BARDOLPH   It is certain, Corporal, that he is married to
  Nell Quickly, and certainly she did you wrong, for you
  were troth-plight to her.
NYM   I cannot tell. Things must be as they may. Men
  may sleep, and they may have their throats about them   20
  at that time, and some say knives have edges. It must
  be as it may. Though patience be a tired mare, yet she
  will plod. There must be conclusions. Well, I cannot
  tell.

             Enter PISTOL *and* Hostess.

BARDOLPH   Here comes Ancient Pistol and his wife.   25
  Good Corporal, be patient here.
NYM   How now, mine host Pistol?

PISTOL   Base tyke, call'st thou me host?
Now by this hand I swear I scorn the term;
30 Nor shall my Nell keep lodgers.
HOSTESS   No, by my troth, not long. For we cannot
lodge and board a dozen or fourteen gentlewomen that
live honestly by the prick of their needles but it will be
thought we keep a bawdy-house straight. [*Nym draws
35 his sword.*] O well-a-day, Lady, if he be not drawn!
Now we shall see wilful adultery and murder
committed. [*Pistol draws his sword.*]
BARDOLPH
Good Lieutenant, good Corporal, offer nothing here.
NYM   Pish!
40 PISTOL   Pish for thee, Iceland dog, thou prick-eared cur
of Iceland!
HOSTESS   Good Corporal Nym, show thy valour and
put up your sword. [*Nym and Pistol sheathe their
swords.*]
NYM   [*to Pistol*]   Will you shog off? I would have you
45 *solus.*
PISTOL   *Solus,* egregious dog? O viper vile!
The *solus* in thy most marvailous face,
The *solus* in thy teeth, and in thy throat,
And in thy hateful lungs, yea, in thy maw, perdy,
50 And, which is worse, within thy nasty mouth!
I do retort the *solus* in thy bowels,
For I can take, and Pistol's cock is up,
And flashing fire will follow.
NYM   I am not Barbason, you cannot conjure me. I have
55 an humour to knock you indifferently well. If you
grow foul with me, Pistol, I will scour you with my
rapier, as I may, in fair terms. If you would walk off, I
would prick your guts a little, in good terms, as I may,
and that's the humour of it.
60 PISTOL   O braggart vile and damned furious wight,
The grave doth gape, and doting death is near;
Therefore exhale. [*Pistol and Nym draw their swords.*]
BARDOLPH [*Draws his sword.*]   Hear me, hear me what I
say. He that strikes the first stroke, I'll run him up to
65 the hilts, as I am a soldier.
PISTOL   An oath of mickle might, and fury shall abate.
[*All sheathe their swords.*]
Give me thy fist, thy fore-foot to me give.
Thy spirits are most tall.
NYM   I will cut thy throat one time or other, in fair
70 terms, that is the humour of it.
PISTOL   'Couple a gorge'!
That is the word. I thee defy again.
O hound of Crete, think'st thou my spouse to get?
No, to the spital go,
75 And from the powdering-tub of infamy
Fetch forth the lazar kite of Cressid's kind,
Doll Tearsheet she by name, and her espouse.
I have and I will hold the quondam Quickly
For the only she; and *pauca,* there's enough.
80 Go to.

Enter the Boy.

BOY   Mine host Pistol, you must come to my master, and
you, hostess. He is very sick and would to bed. Good
Bardolph, put thy face between his sheets and do the
office of a warming-pan. Faith, he's very ill.
BARDOLPH   Away, you rogue!   85
HOSTESS   By my troth, he'll yield the crow a pudding
one of these days. The King has killed his heart. Good
husband, come home presently.
Exeunt Hostess and Boy.
BARDOLPH   Come, shall I make you two friends? We
must to France together. Why the devil should we   90
keep knives to cut one another's throats?
PISTOL
Let floods o'erswell and fiends for food howl on!
NYM   You'll pay me the eight shillings I won of you at
betting?
PISTOL   Base is the slave that pays.   95
NYM   That now I will have; that's the humour of it.
PISTOL   As manhood shall compound: push home! [*Pistol
and Nym draw their swords.*]
BARDOLPH [*Draws his sword.*]   By this sword, he that
makes the first thrust, I'll kill him. By this sword, I
will.   100
PISTOL
Sword is an oath, and oaths must have their course.
[*He sheathes his sword.*]
BARDOLPH   Corporal Nym, an thou wilt be friends, be
friends. An thou wilt not, why then, be enemies with
me too. Prithee, put up.
NYM   I shall have my eight shillings?   105
PISTOL   A noble shalt thou have, and present pay,
And liquor likewise will I give to thee,
And friendship shall combine and brotherhood.
I'll live by Nym and Nym shall live by me.
Is not this just? For I shall sutler be   110
Unto the camp, and profits will accrue.
Give me thy hand.
NYM   I shall have my noble?
PISTOL   In cash, most justly paid.
NYM   Well, then, that's the humour of't. [*Nym and   115
Bardolph sheathe their swords. Pistol and Nym shake
hands.*]

Enter Hostess.

HOSTESS   As ever you come of women, come in quickly
to Sir John. Ah, poor heart, he is so shaked of a
burning quotidian tertian that it is most lamentable to
behold. Sweet men, come to him.   *Exit.*
NYM   The King hath run bad humours on the knight,   120
that's the even of it.
PISTOL   Nym, thou hast spoke the right;
His heart is fracted and corroborate.
NYM   The King is a good king, but it must be as it
may. He passes some humours and careers.   125

PISTOL   Let us condole the knight, for, lambkins, we will
live.   *Exeunt.*

2.2   *Enter* EXETER, BEDFORD *and* WESTMORLAND.

BEDFORD
   'Fore God, his grace is bold to trust these traitors.
EXETER   They shall be apprehended by and by.
WESTMORLAND
   How smooth and even they do bear themselves,
   As if allegiance in their bosoms sat,
   Crowned with faith and constant loyalty!   5
BEDFORD   The King hath note of all that they intend,
   By interception, which they dream not of.
EXETER   Nay, but the man that was his bedfellow,
   Whom he hath dulled and cloyed with gracious
      favours,
   That he should for a foreign purse so sell   10
   His sovereign's life to death and treachery!

      Sound trumpets. Enter the KING, SCROOP,
      CAMBRIDGE *and* GREY, *lords and soldiers.*

KING   Now sits the wind fair, and we will aboard. –
   My lord of Cambridge, and my kind lord of Masham,
   And you, my gentle knight, give me your thoughts:
   Think you not that the powers we bear with us   15
   Will cut their passage through the force of France,
   Doing the execution and the act
   For which we have in head assembled them?
SCROOP   No doubt, my liege, if each man do his best.
KING   I doubt not that, since we are well persuaded   20
   We carry not a heart with us from hence
   That grows not in a fair consent with ours,
   Nor leave not one behind that doth not wish
   Success and conquest to attend on us.
CAMBRIDGE
   Never was monarch better feared and loved   25
   Than is your majesty; there's not, I think, a subject
   That sits in heart-grief and uneasiness
   Under the sweet shade of your government.
GREY   True: those that were your father's enemies
   Have steeped their galls in honey and do serve you   30
   With hearts create of duty and of zeal.
KING   We therefore have great cause of thankfulness,
   And shall forget the office of our hand
   Sooner than quittance of desert and merit
   According to their weight and worthiness.   35
SCROOP   So service shall with steeled sinews toil,
   And labour shall refresh itself with hope
   To do your grace incessant services.
KING   We judge no less. – Uncle of Exeter,
   Enlarge the man committed yesterday   40
   That railed against our person. We consider
   It was excess of wine that set him on,
   And on his more advice we pardon him.
SCROOP   That's mercy, but too much security.
   Let him be punished, sovereign, lest example   45

Breed, by his sufferance, more of such a kind.
KING   O let us yet be merciful.
CAMBRIDGE   So may your highness, and yet punish too.
GREY   Sir,
   You show great mercy if you give him life,   50
   After the taste of much correction.
KING   Alas, your too much love and care of me
   Are heavy orisons 'gainst this poor wretch.
   If little faults proceeding on distemper
   Shall not be winked at, how shall we stretch our eye   55
   When capital crimes, chewed, swallowed, and
      digested,
   Appear before us? – We'll yet enlarge that man,
   Though Cambridge, Scroop and Grey, in their dear
      care
   And tender preservation of our person,
   Would have him punished. And now to our French
      causes.   60
   Who are the late commissioners?
CAMBRIDGE   I one, my lord;
   Your highness bade me ask for it today.
SCROOP   So did you me, my liege.
GREY   And me, my royal sovereign.   65
KING   [*Gives papers.*]
   Then, Richard Earl of Cambridge, there is yours;
   There yours, Lord Scroop of Masham; and, sir
      knight,
   Grey of Northumberland, this same is yours:
   Read them, and know I know your worthiness. –
   My lord of Westmorland and uncle Exeter,   70
   We will aboard tonight. – Why, how now, gentlemen!
   What see you in those papers, that you lose
   So much complexion? – Look ye how they change!
   Their cheeks are paper. – Why, what read you there,
   That hath so cowarded and chased your blood   75
   Out of appearance?
   [*Cambridge, Scroop and Grey fall upon their knees.*]
CAMBRIDGE   I do confess my fault
   And do submit me to your highness' mercy.
GREY, SCROOP   To which we all appeal.
KING   The mercy that was quick in us but late
   By your own counsel is suppressed and killed: 80
   You must not dare, for shame, to talk of mercy,
   For your own reasons turn into your bosoms
   As dogs upon their masters, worrying you. –
   See you, my princes and my noble peers,
   These English monsters! My lord of Cambridge
      here,   85
   You know how apt our love was to accord
   To furnish him with all appertinents
   Belonging to his honour; and this man
   Hath for a few light crowns lightly conspired
   And sworn unto the practices of France   90
   To kill us here in Hampton. To the which
   This knight, no less for bounty bound to us
   Than Cambridge is, hath likewise sworn. – But oh,
   What shall I say to thee, Lord Scroop, thou cruel,

95   Ingrateful, savage and inhuman creature,
      Thou that didst bear the key of all my counsels,
      That knewst the very bottom of my soul,
      That almost mightst have coined me into gold
      Wouldst thou have practised on me for thy use?
100   May it be possible that foreign hire
      Could out of thee extract one spark of evil
      That might annoy my finger? 'Tis so strange
      That though the truth of it stands off as gross
      As black on white, my eye will scarcely see it.
105   Treason and murder ever kept together,
      As two yoke-devils sworn to either's purpose,
      Working so grossly in a natural cause
      That admiration did not whoop at them.
      But thou, 'gainst all proportion, didst bring in
110   Wonder to wait on treason and on murder;
      And whatsoever cunning fiend it was
      That wrought upon thee so preposterously
      Hath got the voice in hell for excellence.
      All other devils that suggest by treasons
115   Do botch and bungle up damnation
      With patches, colours and with forms being fetched
      From glistering semblances of piety;
      But he that tempered thee, bade thee stand up,
      Gave thee no instance why thou shouldst do treason
120   Unless to dub thee with the name of traitor.
      If that same demon that hath gulled thee thus
      Should with his lion-gait walk the whole world,
      He might return to vasty Tartar back
      And tell the legions 'I can never win
125   A soul so easy as that Englishman's.'
      O how hast thou with jealousy infected
      The sweetness of affiance! Show men dutiful?
      Why, so didst thou. Seem they grave and learned?
      Why, so didst thou. Come they of noble family?
130   Why, so didst thou. Seem they religious?
      Why, so didst thou. Or are they spare in diet,
      Free from gross passion or of mirth or anger,
      Constant in spirit, not swerving with the blood,
      Garnished and decked in modest complement,
135   Not working with the eye without the ear,
      And but in purged judgement trusting neither?
      Such and so finely boulted didst thou seem:
      And thus thy fall hath left a kind of blot
      To mark the full-fraught man and best endued
140   With some suspicion. I will weep for thee,
      For this revolt of thine, methinks, is like
      Another fall of man. – Their faults are open.
      Arrest them to the answer of the law,
      And God acquit them of their practices!
      [*Cambridge, Scroop and Grey rise.*]
145   EXETER   I arrest thee of high treason, by the name of
      Richard Earl of Cambridge.
      I arrest thee of high treason, by the name of Henry
      Lord Scroop of Masham.
      I arrest thee of high treason, by the name of Thomas
150   Grey, knight, of Northumberland.

SCROOP   Our purposes God justly hath discovered,
      And I repent my fault more than my death,
      Which I beseech your highness to forgive,
      Although my body pay the price of it.
CAMBRIDGE   For me, the gold of France did not seduce,   155
      Although I did admit it as a motive
      The sooner to effect what I intended.
      But God be thanked for prevention,
      Which I in sufferance heartily will rejoice,
      Beseeching God and you to pardon me.   160
GREY   Never did faithful subject more rejoice
      At the discovery of most dangerous treason
      Than I do at this hour joy o'er myself,
      Prevented from a damned enterprise.
      My fault, but not my body, pardon, sovereign.   165
KING   God quit you in his mercy! Hear your sentence.
      You have conspired against our royal person,
      Joined with an enemy proclaimed and fixed,
      And from his coffers
      Received the golden earnest of our death;   170
      Wherein you would have sold your king to slaughter,
      His princes and his peers to servitude,
      His subjects to oppression and contempt,
      And his whole kingdom into desolation.
      Touching our person seek we no revenge,   175
      But we our kingdom's safety must so tender,
      Whose ruin you have sought, that to her laws
      We do deliver you. Get ye therefore hence,
      Poor miserable wretches, to your death,
      The taste whereof God of his mercy give   180
      You patience to endure, and true repentance
      Of all your dear offences! – Bear them hence.
            Exeunt Cambridge, Scroop and Grey, guarded.
      Now, lords, for France; the enterprise whereof
      Shall be to you as us, like glorious.
      We doubt not of a fair and lucky war,   185
      Since God so graciously hath brought to light
      This dangerous treason lurking in our way
      To hinder our beginnings. We doubt not now
      But every rub is smoothed on our way.
      Then forth, dear countrymen. Let us deliver   190
      Our puissance into the hand of God,
      Putting it straight in expedition.
      Cheerly to sea; the signs of war advance.
      No king of England, if not king of France!
            Flourish. Exeunt.

2.3   *Enter* PISTOL, NYM, BARDOLPH, Boy *and* Hostess.

HOSTESS   Prithee, honey-sweet husband, let me bring
      thee to Staines.
PISTOL   No; for my manly heart doth earn.
      Bardolph, be blithe. Nym, rouse thy vaunting veins.
      Boy, bristle thy courage up;   5
      For Falstaff he is dead, and we must earn therefore.
BARDOLPH   Would I were with him, wheresome'er he is,
      either in heaven or in hell!

HOSTESS   Nay, sure, he's not in hell; he's in Arthur's bosom, if ever man went to Arthur's bosom. 'A made a finer end, and went away an it had been any christom child. 'A parted even just between twelve and one, even at the turning o'th' tide. For after I saw him fumble with the sheets and play wi'th' flowers, and smile upon his fingers' ends, I knew there was but one way; for his nose was as sharp as a pen, and 'a babbled of green fields. 'How now, Sir John?' quoth I, 'what, man! be o' good cheer.' So 'a cried out 'God, God, God!' three or four times. Now I, to comfort him, bid him 'a should not think of God; I hoped there was no need to trouble himself with any such thoughts yet. So 'a bade me lay more clothes on his feet. I put my hand into the bed and felt them, and they were as cold as any stone. Then I felt to his knees, and so up'ard and up'ard, and all was as cold as any stone.

NYM   They say he cried out of sack.

HOSTESS   Ay, that 'a did.

BARDOLPH   And of women.

HOSTESS   Nay, that 'a did not.

BOY   Yes, that 'a did, and said they were devils incarnate.

HOSTESS   'A could never abide carnation, 'twas a colour he never liked.

BOY   'A said once the devil would have him about women.

HOSTESS   'A did in some sort, indeed, handle women; but then he was rheumatic and talked of the Whore of Babylon.

BOY   Do you not remember 'a saw a flea stick upon Bardolph's nose and 'a said it was a black soul burning in hell-fire?

BARDOLPH   Well, the fuel is gone that maintained that fire; that's all the riches I got in his service.

NYM   Shall we shog? The King will be gone from Southampton.

PISTOL   Come, let's away. – My love, give me thy lips.
    [*Kisses her.*]
Look to my chattels and my moveables.
Let senses rule. The word is 'Pitch and pay'.
Trust none;
For oaths are straws, men's faiths are wafer-cakes,
And Holdfast is the only dog, my duck;
Therefore *Caveto* be thy counsellor.
Go, clear thy crystals. – Yoke-fellows in arms,
Let us to France, like horse-leeches, my boys,
To suck, to suck, the very blood to suck!

BOY   And that's but unwholesome food, they say.

PISTOL   Touch her soft mouth, and march.

BARDOLPH   Farewell, hostess. [*Kisses her.*]

NYM   I cannot kiss, that is the humour of it; but adieu.

PISTOL   Let housewifery appear; keep close, I thee command.

HOSTESS   Farewell. Adieu.   *Exeunt.*

2.4   *Flourish. Enter the* FRENCH KING, *the* DAUPHIN, *the* Constable *and the Dukes of Berry and Britain.*

FRENCH KING
Thus comes the English with full power upon us,
And more than carefully it us concerns
To answer royally in our defences.
Therefore the Dukes of Berry and of Britain,
Of Brabant and of Orleans, shall make forth,   5
And you, Prince Dauphin, with all swift dispatch,
To line and new repair our towns of war
With men of courage and with means defendant,
For England his approaches makes as fierce
As waters to the sucking of a gulf.   10
It fits us then to be as provident
As fear may teach us, out of late examples
Left by the fatal and neglected English
Upon our fields.

DAUPHIN   My most redoubted father,
It is most meet we arm us 'gainst the foe,   15
For peace itself should not so dull a kingdom,
Though war nor no known quarrel were in question,
But that defences, musters, preparations,
Should be maintained, assembled, and collected,
As were a war in expectation.   20
Therefore, I say, 'tis meet we all go forth
To view the sick and feeble parts of France.
And let us do it with no show of fear,
No, with no more than if we heard that England
Were busied with a Whitsun morris-dance.   25
For, my good liege, she is so idly kinged,
Her sceptre so fantastically borne
By a vain, giddy, shallow, humorous youth,
That fear attends her not.

CONSTABLE   O peace, Prince Dauphin!
You are too much mistaken in this king.   30
Question your grace the late ambassadors,
With what great state he heard their embassy,
How well supplied with noble counsellors,
How modest in exception, and withal
How terrible in constant resolution,   35
And you shall find his vanities forespent
Were but the outside of the Roman Brutus,
Covering discretion with a coat of folly,
As gardeners do with ordure hide those roots
That shall first spring and be most delicate.   40

DAUPHIN   Well, 'tis not so, my lord High Constable;
But though we think it so, it is no matter.
In cases of defence 'tis best to weigh
The enemy more mighty than he seems.
So the proportions of defence are filled,   45
Which, of a weak and niggardly projection,
Doth like a miser spoil his coat with scanting
A little cloth.

FRENCH KING   Think we King Harry strong;
    And, princes, look you strongly arm to meet him.
50   The kindred of him hath been fleshed upon us,
    And he is bred out of that bloody strain
    That haunted us in our familiar paths.
    Witness our too much memorable shame
    When Cressy battle fatally was struck,
55   And all our princes captived, by the hand
    Of that black name, Edward, Black Prince of Wales;
    Whiles that his mountain sire, on mountain standing
    Up in the air, crowned with the golden sun,
    Saw his heroical seed, and smiled to see him,
60   Mangle the work of nature and deface
    The patterns that by God and by French fathers
    Had twenty years been made. This is a stem
    Of that victorious stock, and let us fear
    The native mightiness and fate of him.

Enter a Messenger.

MESSENGER
65   Ambassadors from Harry, King of England,
    Do crave admittance to your majesty.
FRENCH KING
    We'll give them present audience. Go and bring
        them.   *Exit Messenger.*
    You see this chase is hotly followed, friends.
DAUPHIN   Turn head and stop pursuit, for coward dogs
70   Most spend their mouths when what they seem to
        threaten
    Runs far before them. Good my sovereign,
    Take up the English short and let them know
    Of what a monarchy you are the head.
    Self-love, my liege, is not so vile a sin
    As self-neglecting.

Enter EXETER, *with attendants.*

75 FRENCH KING   From our brother England?
EXETER   From him, and thus he greets your majesty:
    He wills you, in the name of God Almighty,
    That you divest yourself and lay apart
    The borrowed glories that by gift of heaven,
80   By law of nature and of nations, longs
    To him and to his heirs, namely the crown
    And all wide-stretched honours that pertain
    By custom and the ordinance of times
    Unto the crown of France. That you may know
85   'Tis no sinister nor no awkward claim,
    Picked from the worm-holes of long-vanished days,
    Nor from the dust of old oblivion raked,
    He sends you this most memorable line,
    In every branch truly demonstrative,
90   Willing you overlook this pedigree.
    And when you find him evenly derived
    From his most famed of famous ancestors,
    Edward the Third, he bids you then resign
    Your crown and kingdom indirectly held
95   From him the native and true challenger.

[*Gives the French King a paper.*]

FRENCH KING   Or else what follows?
EXETER   Bloody constraint; for if you hide the crown
    Even in your heart, there will he rake for it.
    Therefore in fierce tempest is he coming,
    In thunder and in earthquake, like a Jove,   100
    That if requiring fail, he will compel.
    And bids you, in the bowels of the Lord,
    Deliver up the crown and to take mercy
    On the poor souls for whom this hungry war
    Opens his vasty jaws; and on your head   105
    Turning the widows' tears, the orphans' cries,
    The dead men's blood, the pining maidens' groans,
    For husbands, fathers and betrothed lovers
    That shall be swallowed in this controversy.
    This is his claim, his threatening, and my message –   110
    Unless the Dauphin be in presence here,
    To whom expressly I bring greeting too.
FRENCH KING   For us, we will consider of this further.
    Tomorrow shall you bear our full intent
    Back to our brother England.
DAUPHIN   For the Dauphin,   115
    I stand here for him. What to him from England?
EXETER   Scorn and defiance, slight regard, contempt,
    And anything that may not misbecome
    The mighty sender, doth he prize you at.
    Thus says my king: an if your father's highness   120
    Do not, in grant of all demands at large,
    Sweeten the bitter mock you sent his majesty,
    He'll call you to so hot an answer for it
    That caves and womby vaultages of France
    Shall chide your trespass and return your mock   125
    In second accent of his ordinance.
DAUPHIN   Say if my father render fair return
    It is against my will, for I desire
    Nothing but odds with England. To that end,
    As matching to his youth and vanity,   130
    I did present him with the Paris-balls.
EXETER   He'll make your Paris Louvre shake for it,
    Were it the mistress-court of mighty Europe.
    And be assured you'll find a difference,
    As we his subjects have in wonder found,   135
    Between the promise of his greener days
    And these he masters now. Now he weighs time
    Even to the utmost grain. That you shall read
    In your own losses, if he stay in France.
FRENCH KING
    Tomorrow shall you know our mind at full. [*Flourish.*]   140
EXETER   Dispatch us with all speed, lest that our king
    Come here himself to question our delay,
    For he is footed in this land already.
FRENCH KING
    You shall be soon dispatched with fair conditions.
    A night is but small breath and little pause   145
    To answer matters of this consequence.
                              Flourish. Exeunt.

3.0   *Enter* CHORUS.

CHORUS   Thus with imagined wing our swift scene flies
    In motion of no less celerity
    Than that of thought. Suppose that you have seen
    The well-appointed King at Hampton pier
    Embark his royalty, and his brave fleet
    With silken streamers the young Phoebus fanning.
    Play with your fancies, and in them behold
    Upon the hempen tackle ship-boys climbing;
    Hear the shrill whistle which doth order give
    To sounds confused; behold the threaden sails,
    Borne with th'invisible and creeping wind,
    Draw the huge bottoms through the furrowed sea,
    Breasting the lofty surge. O do but think
    You stand upon the rivage and behold
    A city on th'inconstant billows dancing,
    For so appears this fleet majestical,
    Holding due course to Harfleur. Follow, follow!
    Grapple your minds to sternage of this navy,
    And leave your England as dead midnight still,
    Guarded with grandsires, babies and old women,
    Either past or not arrived to pith and puissance.
    For who is he, whose chin is but enriched
    With one appearing hair, that will not follow
    These culled and choice-drawn cavaliers to France?
    Work, work your thoughts, and therein see a siege;
    Behold the ordnance on their carriages,
    With fatal mouths gaping on girded Harfleur.
    Suppose th'ambassador from the French comes back,
    Tells Harry that the King doth offer him
    Katherine his daughter and with her, to dowry,
    Some petty and unprofitable dukedoms.
    The offer likes not; and the nimble gunner
    With linstock now the devilish cannon touches,
                   [*Alarum, and chambers go off.*]
    And down goes all before them. Still be kind,
    And eke out our performance with your mind. *Exit.*

3.1   *Alarum. Enter soldiers with scaling-ladders at*
      Harfleur. Enter the KING, EXETER, BEDFORD *and*
                 GLOUCESTER.

KING

    Once more unto the breach, dear friends, once more,
    Or close the wall up with our English dead.
    In peace there's nothing so becomes a man
    As modest stillness and humility;
    But when the blast of war blows in our ears,
    Then imitate the action of the tiger:
    Stiffen the sinews, conjure up the blood,
    Disguise fair nature with hard-favoured rage.
    Then lend the eye a terrible aspect;
    Let it pry through the portage of the head
    Like the brass cannon; let the brow o'erwhelm it
    As fearfully as doth a galled rock
    O'erhang and jutty his confounded base,
    Swilled with the wild and wasteful ocean.

    Now set the teeth and stretch the nostril wide,
    Hold hard the breath and bend up every spirit
    To his full height. On, on, you noble English,
    Whose blood is fet from fathers of war-proof,
    Fathers that like so many Alexanders
    Have in these parts from morn till even fought,
    And sheathed their swords for lack of argument.
    Dishonour not your mothers; now attest
    That those whom you called fathers did beget you.
    Be copy now to men of grosser blood
    And teach them how to war. And you, good yeomen,
    Whose limbs were made in England, show us here
    The mettle of your pasture; let us swear
    That you are worth your breeding – which I doubt
      not,
    For there is none of you so mean and base
    That hath not noble lustre in your eyes.
    I see you stand like greyhounds in the slips,
    Straining upon the start. The game's afoot.
    Follow your spirit, and upon this charge
    Cry 'God for Harry! England and Saint George!'
               Exeunt. Alarum, and chambers go off.

3.2   *Enter* NYM, BARDOLPH, PISTOL *and* Boy.

BARDOLPH   On, on, on, on, on, to the breach, to the
    breach!

NYM   Pray thee, Corporal, stay; the knocks are too hot,
    and for mine own part I have not a case of lives. The
    humour of it is too hot, that is the very plain-song of
    it.

PISTOL   The plain-song is most just, for humours do
    abound.
    Knocks go and come, God's vassals drop and die,
             And sword and shield
               In bloody field
             Doth win immortal fame.

BOY   Would I were in an alehouse in London! I would
    give all my fame for a pot of ale and safety.

PISTOL   And I.
             If wishes would prevail with me
             My purpose should not fail with me,
             But thither would I hie.

BOY   As duly –
             But not as truly –
             As bird doth sing on bough

               Enter FLUELLEN.

FLUELLEN [*Beats them.*]
    Up to the breach, you dogs! Avaunt, you cullions!

PISTOL   Be merciful, great duke, to men of mould!
    Abate thy rage, abate thy manly rage,
    Abate thy rage, great duke!
    Good bawcock, bate thy rage! Use lenity, sweet
    chuck!

NYM   These be good humours! Your honour runs bad
    humours!   *Exeunt all but Boy.*

BOY   As young as I am, I have observed these three swashers. I am boy to them all three, but all they three, though they would serve me, could not be man to me, for indeed three such antics do not amount to a man. For Bardolph, he is white-livered and red-faced, by the means whereof 'a faces it out but fights not. For Pistol, he hath a killing tongue and a quiet sword, by the means whereof a breaks words and keeps whole weapons. For Nym, he hath heard that men of few words are the best men, and therefore he scorns to say his prayers lest 'a should be thought a coward: but his few bad words are matched with as few good deeds, for 'a never broke any man's head but his own, and that was against a post when he was drunk. They will steal anything, and call it purchase. Bardolph stole a lute-case, bore it twelve leagues, and sold it for three-halfpence. Nym and Bardolph are sworn brothers in filching, and in Calais they stole a fire-shovel. I knew by that piece of service the men would carry coals. They would have me as familiar with men's pockets as their gloves or their handkerchiefs, which makes much against my manhood if I should take from another's pocket to put into mine, for it is plain pocketing up of wrongs. I must leave them and seek some better service; their villainy goes against my weak stomach, and therefore I must cast it up.   *Exit.*

Enter GOWER *and* FLUELLEN, *meeting.*

GOWER   Captain Fluellen, you must come presently to the mines; the Duke of Gloucester would speak with you.

FLUELLEN   To the mines? Tell you the Duke it is not so good to come to the mines; for, look you, the mines is not according to the disciplines of the wars; the concavities of it is not sufficient; for, look you, th'athversary, you may discuss unto the Duke, look you, is digt himself four yard under the countermines. By Cheshu, I think 'a will plow up all, if there is not better directions.

GOWER   The Duke of Gloucester, to whom the order of the siege is given, is altogether directed by an Irishman, a very valiant gentleman, i'faith.

FLUELLEN   It is Captain Macmorris, is it not?

GOWER   I think it be.

FLUELLEN   By Cheshu, he is an ass, as any is in the world. I will verify as much in his beard. He has no more directions in the true disciplines of the wars, look you, of the Roman disciplines, than is a puppy-dog.

Enter MACMORRIS *and* JAMY.

GOWER   Here 'a comes, and the Scots captain, Captain Jamy, with him.

FLUELLEN   Captain Jamy is a marvellous falorous gentleman, that is certain, and of great expedition and knowledge in th'anchient wars, upon my particular knowledge of his directions. By Cheshu, he will maintain his argument as well as any military man in the world, in the disciplines of the pristine wars of the Romans.

JAMY   I say guid day, Captain Fluellen.

FLUELLEN   God-den to your worship, good Captain James.

GOWER   How now, Captain Macmorris, have you quit the mines? Have the pioneers given o'er?

MACMORRIS   By Chrish, la, 'tish ill done; the work ish give over, the trompet sound the retreat. By my hand I swear, and my father's soul, the work ish ill done; it ish give over. I would have blowed up the town, so Chrish save me, la, in an hour. Oh, 'tish ill done, 'tish ill done; by my hand, 'tish ill done!

FLUELLEN   Captain Macmorris, I beseech you now, will you vouchsafe me, look you, a few disputations with you as partly touching or concerning the disciplines of the wars, the Roman wars, in the way of argument, look you, and friendly communication? Partly to satisfy my opinion, and partly for the satisfaction, look you, of my mind, as touching the direction of the military discipline, that is the point.

JAMY   It sall be vara guid, guid feith, guid captains baith, and I sall quit you, with guid leave, as I may pick occasion; that sall I, marry.

MACMORRIS   It is no time to discourse, so Chrish save me. The day is hot, and the weather, and the wars, and the King, and the Dukes. It is no time to discourse, the town is besieched, and the trumpet call us to the breach, and we talk, and, be Chrish, do nothing. 'Tis shame for us all, so God sa' me, 'tis shame to stand still, it is shame, by my hand; and there is throats to be cut, and works to be done, and there ish nothing done, so Chrish sa' me, la!

JAMY   By the mess, ere these eyes of mine take themselves to slumber I'll dae guid service, or I'll lig i'th' grund for it. I owe God a death, and I'll pay't as valorously as I may, that sall I surely do, that is the breff and the long. Marry, I wad full fain heard some question 'tween you twa.

FLUELLEN   Captain Macmorris, I think, look you, under your correction, there is not many of your nation –

MACMORRIS   Of my nation? What ish my nation? Ish a villain, and a bastard, and a knave, and a rascal? What ish my nation? Who talks of my nation?

FLUELLEN   Look you, if you take the matter otherwise than is meant, Captain Macmorris, peradventure I shall think you do not use me with that affability as in discretion you ought to use me, look you, being as good a man as yourself, both in the disciplines of war, and in the derivation of my birth, and in other particularities.

MACMORRIS   I do not know you so good a man as myself. So Chrish save me, I will cut off your head.

GOWER   Gentlemen both, you will mistake each other.

JAMY   Ah, that's a foul fault.   [*A parley is sounded.*]

GOWER   The town sounds a parley.

FLUELLEN Captain Macmorris, when there is more
better opportunity to be required, look you, I will be
so bold as to tell you I know the disciplines of war, and
there is an end.   *Exeunt.*

3.3   *The* Governor *and others upon the walls.*
Enter the KING *and all his train before the gates.*

KING   How yet resolves the Governor of the town?
This is the latest parle we will admit.
Therefore to our best mercy give yourselves,
Or like to men proud of destruction
Defy us to our worst; for, as I am a soldier,
A name that in my thoughts becomes me best,
If I begin the battery once again,
I will not leave the half-achieved Harfleur
Till in her ashes she lie buried.
The gates of mercy shall be all shut up,
And the fleshed soldier, rough and hard of heart,
In liberty of bloody hand shall range
With conscience wide as hell, mowing like grass
Your fresh fair virgins and your flowering infants.
What is it then to me if impious war,
Arrayed in flames like to the prince of fiends,
Do with his smirched complexion all fell feats
Enlinked to waste and desolation?
What is't to me, when you yourselves are cause,
If your pure maidens fall into the hand
Of hot and forcing violation?
What rein can hold licentious wickedness
When down the hill he holds his fierce career?
We may as bootless spend our vain command
Upon th'enraged soldiers in their spoil
As send precepts to the leviathan
To come ashore. Therefore, you men of Harfleur,
Take pity of your town and of your people
Whiles yet my soldiers are in my command,
Whiles yet the cool and temperate wind of grace
O'erblows the filthy and contagious clouds
Of heady murder, spoil and villainy.
If not, why, in a moment look to see
The blind and bloody soldier with foul hand
Defile the locks of your shrill-shrieking daughters,
Your fathers taken by the silver beards,
And their most reverend heads dashed to the walls,
Your naked infants spitted upon pikes,
Whiles the mad mothers with their howls confused
Do break the clouds, as did the wives of Jewry
At Herod's bloody-hunting slaughtermen.
What say you? Will you yield and this avoid?
Or, guilty in defence, be thus destroyed?
GOVERNOR   Our expectation hath this day an end.
The Dauphin, whom of succours we entreated,
Returns us that his powers are yet not ready
To raise so great a siege. Therefore, dread King,
We yield our town and lives to thy soft mercy.
Enter our gates, dispose of us and ours,
For we no longer are defensible.
KING   Open your gates.   *Exit Governor.*
Come, uncle Exeter,
Go you and enter Harfleur; there remain
And fortify it strongly 'gainst the French.
Use mercy to them all. For us, dear uncle,
The winter coming on and sickness growing
Upon our soldiers, we will retire to Calais.
Tonight in Harfleur will we be your guest;
Tomorrow for the march are we addressed.
                          [*Flourish, and enter the town.*]

3.4   *Enter* KATHERINE *and* ALICE, *an old gentlewoman.*

KATHERINE   *Alice, tu as été en Angleterre, et tu bien parles
le langage.*
ALICE   *Un peu, madame.*
KATHERINE   *Je te prie m'enseigner; il faut que j'apprenne à
parler. Comment appelez-vous la main en anglais?*
ALICE   *La main, elle est appelée* de hand.
KATHERINE   De hand. *Et les doigts?*
ALICE   *Les doigts? Ma foi, j'oublie les doigts, mais je me
souviendrai. Les doigts, je pense qu'ils sont appelés* de
fingres; *oui,* de fingres.
KATHERINE   *La main,* de hand; *les doigts,* de fingres. *Je
pense que je suis le bon écolier. J'ai gagné deux mots
d'anglais vitement. Comment appelez-vous les ongles?*
ALICE   *Les ongles, nous les appelons* de nails.
KATHERINE   De nails. *Écoutez; dites-moi si je parle
bien:* de hand, de fingres, *et* de nails.
ALICE   *C'est bien dit, madame; il est fort bon anglais.*
KATHERINE   *Dites-moi l'anglais pour le bras.*
ALICE   De arm, *madame.*
KATHERINE   *Et le coude?*
ALICE   D'elbow.
KATHERINE   D'elbow. *Je m'en fais la répétition de tous les
mots que vous m'avez appris dès à présent.*
ALICE   *Il est trop difficile, madame, comme je pense.*
KATHERINE   *Excusez-moi, Alice. Écoutez:* d' hand, de
fingres, de nails, de arm, de bilbow.
ALICE   D'elbow, *madame.*
KATHERINE   *O Seigneur Dieu, je m'en oublie!* D'elbow.
Comment appelez-vous le col?
ALICE   De nick, *madame.*
KATHERINE   De nick. *Et le menton?*
ALICE   De chin.
KATHERINE   De sin. *Le col,* de nick; *le menton,* de sin.
ALICE   *Oui. Sauf votre honneur, en vérité, vous prononcez
les mots aussi droit que les natifs d'Angleterre.*
KATHERINE   *Je ne doute point d'apprendre, par la grâce de
Dieu, et en peu de temps.*
ALICE   *N'avez-vous déjà oublié ce que je vous ai enseigné?*
KATHERINE   *Non, je le réciterai à vous promptement:*
d'hand, de fingres, de mails, –
ALICE   De nails, *madame.*
KATHERINE   De nails, de arm, de ilbow –
ALICE   *Sauf votre honneur,* d'elbow.
KATHERINE   *Ainsi dis-je,* d'elbow – de nick, *et* de sin.

45 *Comment appelez-vous le pied et la robe?*

ALICE   De foot, *madame, et* de coun.

KATHERINE   De foot, *et* de coun? *O Seigneur Dieu, ils sont les mots de son mauvais, corruptible, gros, et impudique, et non pour les dames d'honneur d'user. Je ne voudrais*

50 *prononcer ces mots devant les seigneurs de France pour tout le monde. Foh!* De foot *et* de coun! *Néanmoins, je réciterai une autre fois ma leçon ensemble:* d' hand, de fingres, de nails, d'arm, d'elbow, de nick, de sin, de foot, de coun.

55 ALICE   *Excellent, madame!*

KATHERINE   *C'est assez pour une fois. Allons-nous à dîner.*
                                                              Exeunt.

3.5   *Enter the* KING *of France, the* DAUPHIN,
              the DUKE OF BRITAIN, *the* Constable *of France*
                            and others.

FRENCH KING
  'Tis certain he hath passed the river Somme.

CONSTABLE   An if he be not fought withal, my lord,
  Let us not live in France; let us quit all
  And give our vineyards to a barbarous people.

5 DAUPHIN   *O Dieu vivant!* Shall a few sprays of us,
  The emptying of our fathers' luxury,
  Our scions, put in wild and savage stock,
  Spirt up so suddenly into the clouds
  And overlook their grafters?

BRITAIN
10 Normans, but bastard Normans, Norman bastards!
  Mort de ma vie, if they march along
  Unfought withal, but I will sell my dukedom
  To buy a slobbery and a dirty farm
  In that nook-shotten isle of Albion.

CONSTABLE
15 *Dieu de batailles*, where have they this mettle?
  Is not their climate foggy, raw and dull,
  On whom, as in despite, the sun looks pale,
  Killing their fruit with frowns? Can sodden water,
  A drench for sur-reined jades, their barley-broth,
20 Decoct their cold blood to such valiant heat?
  And shall our quick blood, spirited with wine,
  Seem frosty? O, for honour of our land,
  Let us not hang like roping icicles
  Upon our houses' thatch, whiles a more frosty people
25 Sweat drops of gallant youth in our rich fields!
  Poor we may call them in their native lords.

DAUPHIN   By faith and honour,
  Our madams mock at us and plainly say
  Our mettle is bred out, and they will give
30 Their bodies to the lust of English youth,
  To new-store France with bastard warriors.

BRITAIN   They bid us to the English dancing-schools
  And teach lavoltas high and swift corantos,
  Saying our grace is only in our heels,
35 And that we are most lofty runaways.

FRENCH KING
  Where is Montjoy the herald? Speed him hence:
  Let him greet England with our sharp defiance.
  Up, princes, and with spirit of honour edged
  More sharper than your swords hie to the field.
40 Charles Delabreth, High Constable of France,
  You Dukes of Orleans, Bourbon and of Berry,
  Alençon, Brabant, Bar and Burgundy,
  Jaques Chatillon, Rambures, Vaudemont,
  Beaumont, Grandpré, Roussi and Fauconbridge,
45 Foix, Lestrelles, Boucicault and Charolais,
  High dukes, great princes, barons, lords and knights,
  For your great seats now quit you of great shames.
  Bar Harry England, that sweeps through our land
  With pennons painted in the blood of Harfleur.
50 Rush on his host as doth the melted snow
  Upon the valleys, whose low vassal seat
  The Alps doth spit and void his rheum upon.
  Go down upon him, you have power enough,
  And in a captive chariot into Rouen
  Bring him our prisoner.

CONSTABLE   This becomes the great.
55
  Sorry am I his numbers are so few,
  His soldiers sick and famished in their march,
  For I am sure when he shall see our army
  He'll drop his heart into the sink of fear
60 And for achievement offer us his ransom.

FRENCH KING
  Therefore, Lord Constable, haste on Montjoy,
  And let him say to England that we send
  To know what willing ransom he will give. –
  Prince Dauphin, you shall stay with us in Rouen.

DAUPHIN   Not so, I do beseech your majesty.
65
FRENCH KING
  Be patient, for you shall remain with us. –
  Now forth, Lord Constable and princes all,
  And quickly bring us word of England's fall. *Exeunt.*

3.6   *Enter the English and Welsh captains* GOWER
                   and FLUELLEN, *meeting.*

GOWER   How now, Captain Fluellen, come you from the
  bridge?

FLUELLEN   I assure you there is very excellent services
  committed at the bridge.

GOWER   Is the Duke of Exeter safe?   5

FLUELLEN   The Duke of Exeter is as magnanimous as
  Agamemnon, and a man that I love and honour with
  my soul, and my heart, and my duty, and my life, and
  my living, and my uttermost power. He is not, God be
  praised and blessed, any hurt in the world, but keeps   10
  the bridge most valiantly, with excellent discipline.
  There is an anchient lieutenant there at the pridge, I
  think in my very conscience he is as valiant a man as
  Mark Antony, and he is a man of no estimation in the
  world, but I did see him do as gallant service –   15

GOWER What do you call him?

FLUELLEN He is called Anchient Pistol.

GOWER I know him not.

Enter PISTOL.

FLUELLEN Here is the man.

PISTOL Captain, I thee beseech to do me favours.
The Duke of Exeter doth love thee well.

FLUELLEN
Ay, I praise God, and I have merited some love at his
hands.

PISTOL Bardolph, a soldier firm and sound of heart,
Of buxom valour, hath, by cruel fate
And giddy Fortune's furious fickle wheel,
That goddess blind
That stands upon the rolling restless stone –

FLUELLEN By your patience, Anchient Pistol. Fortune
is painted blind, with a muffler afore her eyes, to
signify to you that Fortune is blind; and she is painted
also with a wheel, to signify to you, which is the moral
of it, that she is turning, and inconstant, and
mutability, and variation; and her foot, look you, is
fixed upon a spherical stone, which rolls, and rolls,
and rolls. In good truth, the poet makes a most
excellent description of it: Fortune is an excellent
moral.

PISTOL Fortune is Bardolph's foe, and frowns on him,
For he hath stolen a pax,
And hanged must 'a be, a damned death!
Let gallows gape for dog, let man go free,
And let not hemp his windpipe suffocate!
But Exeter hath given the doom of death
For pax of little price.
Therefore go speak – the Duke will hear thy voice –
And let not Bardolph's vital thread be cut
With edge of penny cord and vile reproach.
Speak, Captain, for his life, and I will thee requite.

FLUELLEN Anchient Pistol, I do partly understand your
meaning.

PISTOL Why then, rejoice therefor.

FLUELLEN Certainly, Anchient, it is not a thing to
rejoice at; for if, look you, he were my brother, I would
desire the Duke to use his good pleasure and put him
to execution; for discipline ought to be used.

PISTOL
Die and be damned, and *fico* for thy friendship!

FLUELLEN It is well.

PISTOL The fig of Spain!   *Exit.*

FLUELLEN Very good.

GOWER Why, this is an arrant counterfeit rascal, I
remember him now – a bawd, a cutpurse.

FLUELLEN I'll assure you 'a uttered as prave words at
the pridge as you shall see in a summer's day. But it is
very well; what he has spoke to me, that is well, I
warrant you, when time is serve.

GOWER Why, 'tis a gull, a fool, a rogue, that now and
then goes to the wars to grace himself at his return

into London under the form of a soldier. And such
fellows are perfect in the great commanders' names,
and they will learn you by rote where services were
done, at such and such a sconce, at such a breach, at
such a convoy; who came off bravely, who was shot,
who disgraced, what terms the enemy stood on. And
this they con perfectly in the phrase of war, which
they trick up with new-tuned oaths; and what a beard
of the General's cut and a horrid suit of the camp will
do among foaming bottles and ale-washed wits is
wonderful to be thought on. But you must learn to
know such slanders of the age, or else you may be
marvellously mistook.

FLUELLEN I tell you what, Captain Gower: I do
perceive he is not the man that he would gladly make
show to the world he is. If I find a hole in his coat, I
will tell him my mind.   [*Drum within.*]
Hark you, the King is coming, and I must speak with
him from the pridge.

*Drum and colours. Enter the KING and GLOUCESTER
and his poor soldiers.*

God pless your majesty!

KING
How now, Fluellen, cam'st thou from the bridge?

FLUELLEN Ay, so please your majesty. The Duke of
Exeter has very gallantly maintained the pridge; the
French is gone off, look you, and there is gallant and
most prave passages. Marry, th'athversary was have
possession of the pridge, but he is enforced to retire,
and the Duke of Exeter is master of the pridge. I can
tell your majesty, the Duke is a prave man.

KING What men have you lost, Fluellen?

FLUELLEN The perdition of th'athversary hath been
very great, reasonable great. Marry, for my part, I
think the Duke hath lost never a man, but one that is
like to be executed for robbing a church, one
Bardolph, if your majesty know the man. His face is all
bubuncles, and whelks, and knobs, and flames o' fire,
and his lips blows at his nose, and it is like a coal of
fire, sometimes plue and sometimes red; but his nose
is executed, and his fire's out.

KING We would have all such offenders so cut off; and
we give express charge that in our marches through
the country there be nothing compelled from the
villages, nothing taken but paid for, none of the
French upbraided or abused in disdainful language;
for when lenity and cruelty play for a kingdom, the
gentler gamester is the soonest winner.

Tucket. Enter MONTJOY.

MONTJOY You know me by my habit.

KING Well then, I know thee: what shall I know of thee?

MONTJOY My master's mind.

KING Unfold it.

MONTJOY Thus says my king: 'Say thou to Harry of
England, though we seemed dead, we did but sleep.

120 Advantage is a better soldier than rashness. Tell him we could have rebuked him at Harfleur, but that we thought not good to bruise an injury till it were full ripe. Now we speak upon our cue, and our voice is imperial. England shall repent his folly, see his

125 weakness, and admire our sufferance. Bid him therefore consider of his ransom, which must proportion the losses we have borne, the subjects we have lost, the disgrace we have digested, which in weight to reanswer, his pettiness would bow under.

130 For our losses, his exchequer is too poor; for th'effusion of our blood, the muster of his kingdom too faint a number; and for our disgrace, his own person kneeling at our feet but a weak and worthless satisfaction. To this add defiance, and tell him, for

135 conclusion, he hath betrayed his followers, whose condemnation is pronounced.' So far my king and master, so much my office.

KING   What is thy name? I know thy quality.

MONTJOY   Montjoy.

140 KING   Thou dost thy office fairly. Turn thee back,
And tell thy king I do not seek him now,
But could be willing to march on to Calais
Without impeachment; for, to say the sooth,
Though 'tis no wisdom to confess so much

145 Unto an enemy of craft and vantage,
My people are with sickness much enfeebled,
My numbers lessened, and those few I have
Almost no better than so many French;
Who when they were in health, I tell thee, herald,

150 I thought upon one pair of English legs
Did march three Frenchmen. Yet forgive me, God,
That I do brag thus! This your air of France
Hath blown that vice in me. I must repent.
Go therefore, tell thy master here I am.

155 My ransom is this frail and worthless trunk,
My army but a weak and sickly guard.
Yet, God before, tell him we will come on,
Though France himself and such another neighbour
Stand in our way. [*Gives a purse.*]
                        There's for thy labour, Montjoy.

160 Go, bid thy master well advise himself.
If we may pass, we will; if we be hindered,
We shall your tawny ground with your red blood
Discolour. And so, Montjoy, fare you well.
The sum of all our answer is but this:

165 We would not seek a battle as we are,
Nor as we are, we say, we will not shun it:
So tell your master.

MONTJOY   I shall deliver so. Thanks to your highness.
                                                    Exit.

GLOUCESTER   I hope they will not come upon us now.

170 KING   We are in God's hand, brother, not in theirs. –
March to the bridge. – It now draws toward night.
Beyond the river we'll encamp ourselves,
And on tomorrow bid them march away.   *Exeunt.*

3.7   *Enter the* Constable *of France,*
the LORD RAMBURES, ORLEANS *and*
the DAUPHIN, *with others.*

CONSTABLE   Tut, I have the best armour of the world. Would it were day!

ORLEANS   You have an excellent armour; but let my horse have his due.

CONSTABLE   It is the best horse of Europe.   5

ORLEANS   Will it never be morning?

DAUPHIN   My lord of Orleans and my lord High Constable, you talk of horse and armour?

ORLEANS   You are as well provided of both as any prince in the world.   10

DAUPHIN   What a long night is this! I will not change my horse with any that treads but on four pasterns. Ch'ha! He bounds from the earth as if his entrails were hairs – *le cheval volant*, the Pegasus, *qui a les narines de feu!* When I bestride him, I soar, I am a hawk. He trots the   15 air. The earth sings when he touches it; the basest horn of his hoof is more musical than the pipe of Hermes.

ORLEANS   He's of the colour of the nutmeg.

DAUPHIN   And of the heat of the ginger. It is a beast for   20 Perseus; he is pure air and fire, and the dull elements of earth and water never appear in him but only in patient stillness while his rider mounts him. He is indeed a horse, and all other jades you may call beasts.

CONSTABLE   Indeed, my lord, it is a most absolute and   25 excellent horse.

DAUPHIN   It is the prince of palfreys; his neigh is like the bidding of a monarch, and his countenance enforces homage.

ORLEANS   No more, cousin.   30

DAUPHIN   Nay, the man hath no wit that cannot, from the rising of the lark to the lodging of the lamb, vary deserved praise on my palfrey. It is a theme as fluent as the sea. Turn the sands into eloquent tongues and my horse is argument for them all. 'Tis a subject for a   35 sovereign to reason on, and for a sovereign's sovereign to ride on, and for the world, familiar to us and unknown, to lay apart their particular functions and wonder at him. I once writ a sonnet in his praise and began thus: 'Wonder of nature!'   40

ORLEANS   I have heard a sonnet begin so to one's mistress.

DAUPHIN   Then did they imitate that which I composed to my courser, for my horse is my mistress.

ORLEANS   Your mistress bears well.   45

DAUPHIN   Me well, which is the prescript praise and perfection of a good and particular mistress.

CONSTABLE   Nay, for methought yesterday your mistress shrewdly shook your back.

DAUPHIN   So perhaps did yours.   50

CONSTABLE   Mine was not bridled.

DAUPHIN   O then belike she was old and gentle, and you rode like a kern of Ireland, your French hose off and in your strait strossers.

CONSTABLE You have good judgement in horse-manship. 55

DAUPHIN Be warned by me then: they that ride so, and ride not warily, fall into foul bogs. I had rather have my horse to my mistress.

CONSTABLE I had as lief have my mistress a jade. 60

DAUPHIN I tell thee, Constable, my mistress wears his own hair.

CONSTABLE I could make as true a boast as that if I had a sow to my mistress.

DAUPHIN '*Le chien est retourné à son propre vomissement, et la truie lavée au bourbier.*' Thou mak'st use of anything. 65

CONSTABLE Yet do I not use my horse for my mistress, or any such proverb so little kin to the purpose.

RAMBURES My Lord Constable, the armour that I saw in your tent tonight, are those stars or suns upon it? 70

CONSTABLE Stars, my lord.

DAUPHIN Some of them will fall tomorrow, I hope.

CONSTABLE And yet my sky shall not want.

DAUPHIN That may be, for you bear a many superfluously, and 'twere more honour some were away. 75

CONSTABLE Even as your horse bears your praises, who would trot as well were some of your brags dismounted. 80

DAUPHIN Would I were able to load him with his desert! Will it never be day? I will trot tomorrow a mile, and my way shall be paved with English faces.

CONSTABLE I will not say so, for fear I should be faced out of my way. But I would it were morning, for I would fain be about the ears of the English. 85

RAMBURES Who will go to hazard with me for twenty prisoners?

CONSTABLE You must first go yourself to hazard ere you have them. 90

DAUPHIN 'Tis midnight; I'll go arm myself. *Exit.*

ORLEANS The Dauphin longs for morning.

RAMBURES He longs to eat the English.

CONSTABLE I think he will eat all he kills.

ORLEANS By the white hand of my lady, he's a gallant prince. 95

CONSTABLE Swear by her foot, that she may tread out the oath.

ORLEANS He is simply the most active gentleman of France. 100

CONSTABLE Doing is activity, and he will still be doing.

ORLEANS He never did harm that I heard of.

CONSTABLE Nor will do none tomorrow; he will keep that good name still.

ORLEANS I know him to be valiant. 105

CONSTABLE I was told that by one that knows him better than you.

ORLEANS What's he?

CONSTABLE Marry, he told me so himself, and he said he cared not who knew it. 110

ORLEANS He needs not, it is no hidden virtue in him.

CONSTABLE By my faith, sir, but it is: never anybody saw it but his lackey. 'Tis a hooded valour, and when it appears it will bate.

ORLEANS 'Ill will never said well.' 115

CONSTABLE I will cap that proverb with 'There is flattery in friendship.'

ORLEANS And I will take up that with 'Give the devil his due.'

CONSTABLE Well placed: there stands your friend for the devil. Have at the very eye of that proverb with 'A pox of the devil.' 120

ORLEANS You are the better at proverbs by how much 'A fool's bolt is soon shot.'

CONSTABLE You have shot over. 125

ORLEANS 'Tis not the first time you were overshot.

Enter a Messenger.

MESSENGER My lord High Constable, the English lie within fifteen hundred paces of your tents.

CONSTABLE Who hath measured the ground?

MESSENGER The Lord Grandpré. 130

CONSTABLE A valiant and most expert gentleman.

Exit Messenger.

Would it were day! Alas, poor Harry of England! He longs not for the dawning as we do.

ORLEANS What a wretched and peevish fellow is this King of England, to mope with his fat-brained followers so far out of his knowledge! 135

CONSTABLE If the English had any apprehension they would run away.

ORLEANS That they lack, for if their heads had any intellectual armour they could never wear such heavy headpieces. 140

RAMBURES That island of England breeds very valiant creatures: their mastiffs are of unmatchable courage.

ORLEANS Foolish curs, that run winking into the mouth of a Russian bear and have their heads crushed like rotten apples. You may as well say that's a valiant flea that dare eat his breakfast on the lip of a lion. 145

CONSTABLE Just, just; and the men do sympathize with the mastiffs in robustious and rough coming on, leaving their wits with their wives. And then give them great meals of beef and iron and steel, they will eat like wolves and fight like devils. 150

ORLEANS Ay, but these English are shrewdly out of beef.

CONSTABLE Then shall we find tomorrow they have only stomachs to eat and none to fight. Now is it time to arm; come, shall we about it? 155

ORLEANS It is now two o'clock; but, let me see, by ten We shall have each a hundred Englishmen. *Exeunt.*

4.0 *Enter* CHORUS.

CHORUS Now entertain conjecture of a time
When creeping murmur and the poring dark
Fills the wide vessel of the universe.

From camp to camp through the foul womb of night
The hum of either army stilly sounds,
5 That the fixed sentinels almost receive
The secret whispers of each other's watch.
Fire answers fire, and through their paly flames
Each battle sees the other's umbered face.
10 Steed threatens steed, in high and boastful neighs
Piercing the night's dull ear; and from the tents
The armourers accomplishing the knights,
With busy hammers closing rivets up,
Give dreadful note of preparation.
15 The country cocks do crow, the clocks do toll,
And the third hour of drowsy morning name.
Proud of their numbers and secure in soul,
The confident and over-lusty French
Do the low-rated English play at dice,
20 And chide the cripple tardy-gaited night
Who like a foul and ugly witch doth limp
So tediously away. The poor condemned English,
Like sacrifices, by their watchful fires
Sit patiently and inly ruminate
25 The morning's danger; and their gesture sad,
Investing lank-lean cheeks and war-torn coats,
Presenteth them unto the gazing moon
So many horrid ghosts. O now, who will behold
The royal captain of this ruined band
30 Walking from watch to watch, from tent to tent,
Let him cry 'Praise and glory on his head!'
For forth he goes and visits all his host,
Bids them good morrow with a modest smile,
And calls them brothers, friends and countrymen.
35 Upon his royal face there is no note
How dread an army hath enrounded him,
Nor doth he dedicate one jot of colour
Unto the weary and all-watched night,
But freshly looks and overbears attaint
40 With cheerful semblance and sweet majesty,
That every wretch, pining and pale before,
Beholding him plucks comfort from his looks.
A largess universal, like the sun,
His liberal eye doth give to every one,
45 Thawing cold fear, that mean and gentle all
Behold, as may unworthiness define,
A little touch of Harry in the night.
And so our scene must to the battle fly,
Where – oh for pity! – we shall much disgrace
50 With four or five most vile and ragged foils
Right ill-disposed in brawl ridiculous
The name of Agincourt. Yet sit and see,
Minding true things by what their mockeries be.

Exit.

4.1   *Enter the* KING *and* GLOUCESTER,
                    meeting BEDFORD.

KING   Gloucester, 'tis true that we are in great danger;
The greater therefore should our courage be. –

Good morrow, brother Bedford. God Almighty!
There is some soul of goodness in things evil,
5 Would men observingly distil it out:
For our bad neighbour makes us early stirrers,
Which is both healthful and good husbandry.
Besides, they are our outward consciences
And preachers to us all, admonishing
10 That we should dress us fairly for our end.
Thus may we gather honey from the weed
And make a moral of the devil himself.

Enter ERPINGHAM.

Good morrow, old Sir Thomas Erpingham.
A good soft pillow for that good white head
15 Were better than a churlish turf of France.
ERPINGHAM
Not so, my liege, this lodging likes me better,
Since I may say 'Now lie I like a king.'
KING   'Tis good for men to love their present pains
Upon example: so the spirit is eased,
20 And when the mind is quickened, out of doubt
The organs, though defunct and dead before,
Break up their drowsy grave and newly move
With casted slough and fresh legerity.
Lend me thy cloak, Sir Thomas. – Brothers both,
25 Commend me to the princes in our camp;
Do my good morrow to them, and anon
Desire them all to my pavilion.
GLOUCESTER   We shall, my liege.
ERPINGHAM   Shall I attend your grace?
KING   No, my good knight;
30 Go with my brothers to my lords of England.
I and my bosom must debate awhile,
And then I would no other company.
ERPINGHAM
The Lord in heaven bless thee, noble Harry!
Exeunt all but the King.
KING   God-a-mercy, old heart, thou speak'st cheerfully.

Enter PISTOL.

PISTOL   Che vous là?   35
KING   A friend.
PISTOL   Discuss unto me, art thou officer,
Or art thou base, common and popular?
KING   I am a gentleman of a company.
PISTOL   Trail'st thou the puissant pike?   40
KING   Even so. What are you?
PISTOL   As good a gentleman as the Emperor.
KING   Then you are a better than the King.
PISTOL   The King's a bawcock and a heart of gold,
A lad of life, an imp of Fame,   45
Of parents good, of fist most valiant.
I kiss his dirty shoe, and from heart-string
I love the lovely bully. What is thy name?
KING   Harry le Roy.
PISTOL   Le Roy?   50
A Cornish name: art thou of Cornish crew?

KING   No, I am a Welshman.

PISTOL   Know'st thou Fluellen?

KING   Yes.

PISTOL   Tell him I'll knock his leek about his pate
Upon Saint Davy's day.

KING   Do not you wear your dagger in your cap that day,
lest he knock that about yours.

PISTOL   Art thou his friend?

KING   And his kinsman too.

PISTOL   The *fico* for thee then!

KING   I thank you. God be with you!

PISTOL   My name is Pistol called.   *Exit.*

KING   It sorts well with your fierceness.

Enter FLUELLEN *and* GOWER, *separately.*

GOWER   Captain Fluellen!

FLUELLEN   'So! In the name of Jesu Christ, speak fewer.
It is the greatest admiration in the universal world
when the true and anchient prerogatifs and laws of the
wars is not kept. If you would take the pains but to
examine the wars of Pompey the Great you shall find,
I warrant you, that there is no tiddle-taddle nor
pibble-pabble in Pompey's camp. I warrant you, you
shall find the ceremonies of the wars, and the cares of
it, and the forms of it, and the sobriety of it, and the
modesty of it, to be otherwise.

GOWER   Why, the enemy is loud; you hear him all night.

FLUELLEN   If the enemy is an ass and a fool and a
prating coxcomb, is it meet, think you, that we should
also, look you, be an ass and a fool and a prating
coxcomb, in your own conscience now?

GOWER   I will speak lower.

FLUELLEN   I pray you and beseech you that you will.
Exeunt Gower and Fluellen.

KING   Though it appear a little out of fashion,
There is much care and valour in this Welshman.

Enter three soldiers, JOHN BATES, ALEXANDER COURT
and MICHAEL WILLIAMS.

COURT   Brother John Bates, is not that the morning
which breaks yonder?

BATES   I think it be; but we have no great cause to desire
the approach of day.

WILLIAMS   We see yonder the beginning of the day, but
I think we shall never see the end of it. – Who goes
there?

KING   A friend.

WILLIAMS   Under what captain serve you?

KING   Under Sir Thomas Erpingham.

WILLIAMS   A good old commander and a most kind
gentleman. I pray you, what thinks he of our estate?

KING   Even as men wrecked upon a sand, that look to be
washed off the next tide.

BATES   He hath not told his thought to the King?

KING   No, nor it is not meet he should. For though I
speak it to you, I think the King is but a man, as I am:
the violet smells to him as it doth to me; the element

shows to him as it doth to me; all his senses have but
human conditions; his ceremonies laid by, in his
nakedness he appears but a man; and though his   105
affections are higher mounted than ours, yet when
they stoop they stoop with the like wing. Therefore
when he sees reason of fears as we do, his fears, out of
doubt, be of the same relish as ours are. Yet, in reason,
no man should possess him with any appearance of   110
fear, lest he, by showing it, should dishearten his army.

BATES   He may show what outward courage he will, but
I believe, as cold a night as 'tis, he could wish himself
in Thames up to the neck; and so I would he were, and
I by him, at all adventures, so we were quit here.   115

KING   By my troth, I will speak my conscience of the
King. I think he would not wish himself anywhere but
where he is.

BATES   Then I would he were here alone; so should he
be sure to be ransomed, and a many poor men's lives   120
saved.

KING   I dare say you love him not so ill to wish him here
alone, howsoever you speak this to feel other men's
minds. Methinks I could not die anywhere so
contented as in the King's company, his cause being   125
just and his quarrel honourable.

WILLIAMS   That's more than we know.

BATES   Ay, or more than we should seek after, for we
know enough if we know we are the King's subjects. If
his cause be wrong, our obedience to the King wipes   130
the crime of it out of us.

WILLIAMS   But if the cause be not good, the King
himself hath a heavy reckoning to make when all those
legs and arms and heads chopped off in a battle shall
join together at the latter day and cry all 'We died at   135
such a place', some swearing, some crying for a
surgeon, some upon their wives left poor behind
them, some upon the debts they owe, some upon their
children rawly left. I am afeard there are few die well
that die in a battle, for how can they charitably dispose   140
of anything when blood is their argument? Now if
these men do not die well it will be a black matter for
the King, that led them to it, who to disobey were
against all proportion of subjection.

KING   So if a son that is by his father sent about   145
merchandise do sinfully miscarry upon the sea, the
imputation of his wickedness, by your rule, should be
imposed upon his father that sent him; or if a servant,
under his master's command transporting a sum of
money, be assailed by robbers and die in many   150
irreconciled iniquities, you may call the business of
the master the author of the servant's damnation. But
this is not so: the King is not bound to answer the
particular endings of his soldiers, the father of his son,
nor the master of his servant; for they purpose not   155
their death when they purpose their services. Besides,
there is no king, be his cause never so spotless, if it
come to the arbitrement of swords, can try it out with
all unspotted soldiers. Some, peradventure, have on

160 them the guilt of premeditated and contrived murder, some of beguiling virgins with the broken seals of perjury, some, making the wars their bulwark, that have before gored the gentle bosom of peace with pillage and robbery. Now if these men have defeated
165 the law and outrun native punishment, though they can outstrip men, they have no wings to fly from God. War is his beadle, war is his vengeance; so that here men are punished for before breach of the King's laws in now the King's quarrel. Where they feared the
170 death they have borne life away, and where they would be safe they perish. Then if they die unprovided, no more is the King guilty of their damnation than he was before guilty of those impieties for the which they are now visited. Every subject's duty is the King's, but
175 every subject's soul is his own. Therefore should every soldier in the wars do as every sick man in his bed, wash every mote out of his conscience; and dying so, death is to him advantage; or not dying, the time was blessedly lost wherein such preparation was gained;
180 and in him that escapes, it were not sin to think that, making God so free an offer, he let him outlive that day to see his greatness and to teach others how they should prepare.

WILLIAMS 'Tis certain, every man that dies ill, the ill
185 upon his own head; the King is not to answer it.

BATES I do not desire he should answer for me, and yet I determine to fight lustily for him.

KING I myself heard the King say he would not be ransomed.

190 WILLIAMS Ay, he said so to make us fight cheerfully; but when our throats are cut he may be ransomed and we ne'er the wiser.

KING If I live to see it, I will never trust his word after.

WILLIAMS You pay him then! That's a perilous shot out
195 of an elder-gun that a poor and a private displeasure can do against a monarch. You may as well go about to turn the sun to ice with fanning in his face with a peacock's feather. You'll never trust his word after! Come, 'tis a foolish saying.

200 KING Your reproof is something too round; I should be angry with you if the time were convenient.

WILLIAMS Let it be a quarrel between us, if you live.

KING I embrace it.

WILLIAMS How shall I know thee again?

205 KING Give me any gage of thine and I will wear it in my bonnet. Then if ever thou dar'st acknowledge it I will make it my quarrel.

WILLIAMS Here's my glove. Give me another of thine.

KING There. [*They exchange gloves.*]

210 WILLIAMS This will I also wear in my cap. If ever thou come to me and say after tomorrow 'This is my glove', by this hand I will take thee a box on the ear.

KING If ever I live to see it I will challenge it.

WILLIAMS Thou dar'st as well be hanged.

215 KING Well, I will do it, though I take thee in the King's company.

WILLIAMS Keep thy word. Fare thee well.

BATES Be friends, you English fools, be friends! We have French quarrels enough, if you could tell how to
220 reckon.

KING Indeed, the French may lay twenty French crowns to one they will beat us, for they bear them on their shoulders, but it is no English treason to cut French crowns, and tomorrow the King himself will
225 be a clipper.   *Exeunt soldiers.*

Upon the King! 'Let us our lives, our souls,
Our debts, our careful wives,
Our children and our sins lay on the King!'
We must bear all. O hard condition,
230 Twin-born with greatness, subject to the breath
Of every fool whose sense no more can feel
But his own wringing! What infinite heart's ease
Must kings neglect that private men enjoy!
And what have kings that privates have not too,
235 Save ceremony, save general ceremony?
And what art thou, thou idol ceremony?
What kind of god art thou, that suffer'st more
Of mortal griefs than do thy worshippers?
What are thy rents, what are thy comings-in?
240 O ceremony, show me but thy worth!
What is thy soul, O adoration?
Art thou aught else but place, degree and form,
Creating awe and fear in other men,
Wherein thou art less happy, being feared,
245 Than they in fearing?
What drink'st thou oft, instead of homage sweet,
But poisoned flattery? O be sick, great greatness,
And bid thy ceremony give thee cure!
Think'st thou the fiery fever will go out
250 With titles blown from adulation?
Will it give place to flexure and low bending?
Canst thou, when thou command'st the beggar's
    knee,
Command the health of it? No, thou proud dream
That play'st so subtly with a king's repose,
255 I am a king that find thee, and I know
'Tis not the balm, the sceptre and the ball,
The sword, the mace, the crown imperial,
The intertissued robe of gold and pearl,
The farced title running 'fore the king,
260 The throne he sits on, nor the tide of pomp
That beats upon the high shore of this world,
No, not all these, thrice-gorgeous ceremony,
Not all these, laid in bed majestical,
Can sleep so soundly as the wretched slave,
265 Who with a body filled and vacant mind
Gets him to rest, crammed with distressful bread:
Never sees horrid night, the child of hell,
But like a lackey from the rise to set
Sweats in the eye of Phoebus, and all night
270 Sleeps in Elysium; next day after dawn
Doth rise and help Hyperion to his horse,
And follows so the ever-running year

With profitable labour to his grave.
And but for ceremony such a wretch,
275 Winding up days with toil and nights with sleep,
Had the fore-hand and vantage of a king.
The slave, a member of the country's peace,
Enjoys it, but in gross brain little wots
What watch the King keeps to maintain the peace,
280 Whose hours the peasant best advantages.

Enter ERPINGHAM.

ERPINGHAM
My lord, your nobles, jealous of your absence,
Seek through your camp to find you.
KING   Good old knight,
Collect them all together at my tent.
I'll be before thee.
ERPINGHAM   I shall do't, my lord.   *Exit.*
KING [*Kneels.*]
285 O God of battles, steel my soldiers' hearts;
Possess them not with fear. Take from them now
The sense of reckoning, if th'opposed numbers
Pluck their hearts from them. Not today, O Lord,
O not today, think not upon the fault
290 My father made in compassing the crown.
I Richard's body have interred new,
And on it have bestowed more contrite tears
Than from it issued forced drops of blood.
Five hundred poor I have in yearly pay,
295 Who twice a day their withered hands hold up
Toward heaven to pardon blood; and I have built
Two chantries, where the sad and solemn priests
Sing still for Richard's soul. More will I do,
Though all that I can do is nothing worth,
300 Since that my penitence comes after all,
Imploring pardon.
GLOUCESTER [*within*]   My liege!
KING [*Rises.*]   My brother Gloucester's voice?

Enter GLOUCESTER.

I know thy errand, I will go with thee.
The day, my friends and all things stay for me.

Exeunt.

4.2   *Enter the* DAUPHIN, ORLEANS *and* RAMBURES.

ORLEANS   The sun doth gild our armour; up, my lords!
DAUPHIN   *Monte à cheval!* My horse, *varlet laquais*, ha!
ORLEANS   O brave spirit!
DAUPHIN   *Via, les eaux et terre!*
ORLEANS   *Rien puis? L'air et feu?*
DAUPHIN   *Cieux*, cousin Orleans!

Enter Constable.

DAUPHIN   Now, my lord Constable!
CONSTABLE
Hark, how our steeds for present service neigh!
DAUPHIN
Mount them and make incision in their hides,

That their hot blood may spin in English eyes
And dout them with superfluous courage, ha!   10
RAMBURES
What, will you have them weep our horses' blood?
How shall we then behold their natural tears?

Enter Messenger.

MESSENGER
The English are embattled, you French peers.   *Exit.*
CONSTABLE
To horse, you gallant princes, straight to horse!
Do but behold yon poor and starved band,   15
And your fair show shall suck away their souls,
Leaving them but the shales and husks of men.
There is not work enough for all our hands,
Scarce blood enough in all their sickly veins
To give each naked curtle-axe a stain   20
That our French gallants shall today draw out
And sheathe for lack of sport. Let us but blow on
    them,
The vapour of our valour will o'erturn them.
'Tis positive 'gainst all exceptions, lords,
That our superfluous lackeys and our peasants   25
Who in unnecessary action swarm
About our squares of battle were enough
To purge this field of such a hilding foe,
Though we upon this mountain's basis by
Took stand for idle speculation: 30
But that our honours must not. What's to say?
A very little little let us do,
And all is done. Then let the trumpets sound
The tucket sonance and the note to mount,
For our approach shall so much dare the field   35
That England shall couch down in fear and yield.

Enter GRANDPRÉ.

GRANDPRÉ
Why do you stay so long, my lords of France?
Yon island carrions, desperate of their bones,
Ill-favouredly become the morning field.
Their ragged curtains poorly are let loose,   40
And our air shakes them passing scornfully.
Big Mars seems bankrupt in their beggared host
And faintly through a rusty beaver peeps.
The horsemen sit like fixed candlesticks
With torch-staves in their hand, and their poor jades 45
Lob down their heads, drooping the hides and hips,
The gum down-roping from their pale-dead eyes,
And in their palled dull mouths the gimmaled bit
Lies foul with chewed grass, still and motionless.
And their executors, the knavish crows,   50
Fly o'er them all, impatient for their hour.
Description cannot suit itself in words
To demonstrate the life of such a battle
In life so lifeless as it shows itself.
CONSTABLE
They have said their prayers, and they stay for death. 55

DAUPHIN

    Shall we go send them dinners and fresh suits
    And give their fasting horses provender,
    And after fight with them?

CONSTABLE   I stay but for my guidon. To the field!

60   I will the banner from a trumpet take
    And use it for my haste. Come, come away!
    The sun is high and we outwear the day.   *Exeunt.*

4.3   *Enter* GLOUCESTER, BEDFORD, EXETER,
    ERPINGHAM *with all his host,* SALISBURY *and*
    WESTMORLAND.

GLOUCESTER   Where is the King?

BEDFORD

    The King himself is rode to view their battle.

WESTMORLAND

    Of fighting men they have full threescore thousand.

EXETER   There's five to one; besides, they all are fresh.

SALISBURY

5   God's arm strike with us! 'Tis a fearful odds.
    God bye you, princes all; I'll to my charge.
    If we no more meet till we meet in heaven,
    Then joyfully, my noble lord of Bedford,
    My dear lord Gloucester, and my good lord Exeter,

10   And my kind kinsman, warriors all, adieu.

BEDFORD

    Farewell, good Salisbury, and good luck go with thee.

EXETER   Farewell, kind lord. Fight valiantly today.
    And yet I do thee wrong to mind thee of it,
    For thou art framed of the firm truth of valour.
                        Exit Salisbury.

15 BEDFORD   He is as full of valour as of kindness,
    Princely in both.

              Enter the KING.

WESTMORLAND   O that we now had here
    But one ten thousand of those men in England
    That do no work today!

KING   What's he that wishes so?
    My cousin Westmorland? No, my fair cousin:

20   If we are marked to die, we are enough
    To do our country loss, and if to live,
    The fewer men, the greater share of honour.
    God's will, I pray thee wish not one man more.
    By Jove, I am not covetous for gold,

25   Nor care I who doth feed upon my cost;
    It earns me not if men my garments wear:
    Such outward things dwell not in my desires.
    But if it be a sin to covet honour
    I am the most offending soul alive.

30   No, faith, my coz, wish not a man from England.
    God's peace, I would not lose so great an honour
    As one man more, methinks, would share from me,
    For the best hope I have. O do not wish one more!
    Rather proclaim it, Westmorland, through my host,

35   That he which hath no stomach to this fight,
    Let him depart; his passport shall be made

    And crowns for convoy put into his purse.
    We would not die in that man's company
    That fears his fellowship to die with us.
    This day is called the feast of Crispian.   40
    He that outlives this day and comes safe home
    Will stand a-tiptoe when this day is named
    And rouse him at the name of Crispian.
    He that shall see this day and live old age
    Will yearly on the vigil feast his neighbours,   45
    And say 'Tomorrow is Saint Crispian.'
    Then will he strip his sleeve and show his scars,
    And say 'These wounds I had on Crispin's day.'
    Old men forget; yet all shall be forgot
    But he'll remember, with advantages,   50
    What feats he did that day. Then shall our names,
    Familiar in his mouth as household words,
    Harry the King, Bedford and Exeter,
    Warwick and Talbot, Salisbury and Gloucester,
    Be in their flowing cups freshly remembered.   55
    This story shall the good man teach his son,
    And Crispin Crispian shall ne'er go by
    From this day to the ending of the world
    But we in it shall be remembered,
    We few, we happy few, we band of brothers.   60
    For he today that sheds his blood with me
    Shall be my brother; be he ne'er so vile,
    This day shall gentle his condition.
    And gentlemen in England now abed
    Shall think themselves accursed they were not here,   65
    And hold their manhoods cheap whiles any speaks
    That fought with us upon Saint Crispin's day.

              Enter SALISBURY.

SALISBURY

    My sovereign lord, bestow yourself with speed.
    The French are bravely in their battles set
    And will with all expedience charge on us.   70

KING   All things are ready, if our minds be so.

WESTMORLAND

    Perish the man whose mind is backward now!

KING

    Thou dost not wish more help from England, coz?

WESTMORLAND

    God's will, my liege, would you and I alone,
    Without more help, could fight this royal battle!   75

KING

    Why, now thou hast unwished five thousand men,
    Which likes me better than to wish us one.
    You know your places. God be with you all!

         Tucket. Enter MONTJOY.

MONTJOY

    Once more I come to know of thee, King Harry,
    If for thy ransom thou wilt now compound,   80
    Before thy most assured overthrow:
    For certainly thou art so near the gulf
    Thou needs must be englutted. Besides, in mercy,

The Constable desires thee thou wilt mind
Thy followers of repentance, that their souls
May make a peaceful and a sweet retire
From off these fields where, wretches, their poor
    bodies
Must lie and fester.
KING   Who hath sent thee now?
MONTJOY   The Constable of France.
KING   I pray thee bear my former answer back:
Bid them achieve me and then sell my bones.
Good God, why should they mock poor fellows thus?
The man that once did sell the lion's skin
While the beast lived, was killed with hunting him.
A many of our bodies shall no doubt
Find native graves, upon the which, I trust,
Shall witness live in brass of this day's work.
And those that leave their valiant bones in France,
Dying like men, though buried in your dunghills,
They shall be famed, for there the sun shall greet
    them,
And draw their honours reeking up to heaven,
Leaving their earthly parts to choke your clime,
The smell whereof shall breed a plague in France.
Mark then abounding valour in our English,
That being dead, like to the bullets crazing,
Break out into a second course of mischief,
Killing in relapse of mortality.
Let me speak proudly. Tell the Constable
We are but warriors for the working-day;
Our gayness and our gilt are all besmirched
With rainy marching in the painful field.
There's not a piece of feather in our host
(Good argument, I hope, we will not fly),
And time hath worn us into slovenry.
But by the mass, our hearts are in the trim,
And my poor soldiers tell me yet ere night
They'll be in fresher robes, or they will pluck
The gay new coats o'er the French soldiers' heads
And turn them out of service. If they do this,
As, if God please, they shall, my ransom then
Will soon be levied. Herald, save thou thy labour:
Come thou no more for ransom, gentle herald.
They shall have none, I swear, but these my joints,
Which if they have as I will leave 'em them
Shall yield them little, tell the Constable.
MONTJOY   I shall, King Harry. And so fare thee well:
Thou never shalt hear herald any more.   *Exit.*
KING
I fear thou wilt once more come again for a ransom.

Enter YORK.

YORK   My lord, most humbly on my knee I beg
The leading of the vaward.
KING
Take it, brave York. – Now, soldiers, march away,
And how thou pleasest, God, dispose the day!
                                Exeunt.

4.4   *Alarum. Excursions. Enter* PISTOL,
           FRENCH SOLDIER *and* Boy.

PISTOL   Yield, cur!
FRENCH SOLDIER   *Je pense que vous êtes le gentilhomme*
de bonne qualité.
PISTOL   *Qualité?* 'Caleno custore me'!
Art thou a gentleman? What is thy name? Discuss.   5
FRENCH SOLDIER   *O Seigneur Dieu!*
PISTOL   O Signieur Dew should be a gentleman. –
Perpend my words, O Signieur Dew, and mark:
O Signieur Dew, thou diest on point of fox,
Except, O Signieur, thou do give to me   10
Egregious ransom.
FRENCH SOLDIER *O prenez miséricorde! Ayez pitié de moi!*
PISTOL   Moy shall not serve, I will have forty moys,
Or I will fetch thy rim out at thy throat
In drops of crimson blood.   15
FRENCH SOLDIER
Est-il impossible d'échapper la force de ton bras?
PISTOL   Brass, cur?
Thou damned and luxurious mountain goat,
Offer'st me brass?
FRENCH SOLDIER   *O pardonnez-moi!*   20
PISTOL   Say'st thou me so? Is that a ton of moys?
Come hither, boy;
Ask me this slave in French what is his name.
BOY   *Écoutez. Comment êtes-vous appelé?*
FRENCH SOLDIER   *Monsieur le Fer.*   25
BOY   He says his name is Master Fer.
PISTOL   Master Fer? I'll fer him, and firk him, and ferret
him. Discuss the same in French unto him.
BOY   I do not know the French for fer, and ferret and
firk.   30
PISTOL   Bid him prepare, for I will cut his throat.
FRENCH SOLDIER   *Que dit-il, monsieur?*
BOY   *Il me commande à vous dire que vous faites vous prêt,*
car ce soldat ici est disposé tout à cette heure de couper
votre gorge.   35
PISTOL   Owy, cuppele gorge, permafoy,
Peasant, unless thou give me crowns, brave crowns;
Or mangled shalt thou be by this my sword.
FRENCH SOLDIER   *O je vous supplie pour l'amour de Dieu*
me pardonner! Je suis le gentilhomme de bonne maison: 40
gardez ma vie, et je vous donnerai deux cents écus.
PISTOL   What are his words?
BOY   He prays you to save his life: he is a gentleman of a
good house, and for his ransom he will give you two
hundred crowns.   45
PISTOL   Tell him
My fury shall abate, and I the crowns will take.
FRENCH SOLDIER   *Petit monsieur, que dit-il?*
BOY   *Encore qu'il est contre son jurement de pardonner*
aucun prisonnier, néanmoins, pour les écus que vous lui ici   50
promettez, il est content à vous donner la liberté, le
franchisement.
FRENCH SOLDIER [*to Pistol*]   *Sur mes genoux je vous donne*

55 *mille remerciements, et je m'estime heureux que j'ai tombé
entre les mains d'un chevalier, comme je pense, le plus
brave, vaillant et très distingué seigneur d'Angleterre.*

PISTOL Expound unto me, boy.

BOY He gives you upon his knees a thousand thanks,
and he esteems himself happy that he hath fallen into
60 the hands of one, as he thinks, the most brave,
valorous and thrice-worthy *seigneur* of England.

PISTOL As I suck blood, I will some mercy show.
Follow me.

BOY *Suivez-vous le grand capitaine.*

Exeunt Pistol and French Soldier.

65 I did never know so full a voice issue from so empty a
heart; but the saying is true, 'The empty vessel makes
the greatest sound.' Bardolph and Nym had ten times
more valour than this roaring devil i'th' old play, that
every vice may pare his nails with a wooden dagger,
70 and they are both hanged, and so would this be if he
durst steal anything adventurously. I must stay with
the lackeys with the luggage of our camp; the French
might have a good prey of us if he knew of it, for there
is none to guard it but boys. *Exit.*

4.5 *Enter* Constable, ORLEANS, BOURBON,
the DAUPHIN *and* RAMBURES.

CONSTABLE *O diable!*

ORLEANS *O Seigneur! Le jour est perdu, tout est perdu!*

DAUPHIN *Mort de ma vie,* all is confounded, all!
Mortal reproach and everlasting shame
5 Sits mocking in our plumes. *O méchante Fortune!*
[*A short alarum.*]
Do not run away.

CONSTABLE Why, all our ranks are broke.

DAUPHIN O perdurable shame! Let's stab ourselves.
Be these the wretches that we played at dice for?

ORLEANS Is this the king we sent to for his ransom?

BOURBON
10 Shame, and eternal shame, nothing but shame!
Let us die instant. Once more back again,
And he that will not follow Bourbon now,
Let him go home and with his cap in hand
Like a base pandar hold the chamber-door
15 Whilst by a slave no gentler than my dog
His fairest daughter is contaminated.

CONSTABLE
Disorder, that hath spoiled us, friend us now!
Let us on heaps go offer up our lives.

ORLEANS We are enough yet living in the field
20 To smother up the English in our throngs
If any order might be thought upon.

BOURBON The devil take order now! I'll to the throng.
Let life be short, else shame will be too long. *Exeunt.*

4.6 *Alarum. Enter the* KING *and his train, with prisoners.*

KING Well have we done, thrice-valiant countrymen,
But all's not done: yet keep the French the field.

Exeunt soldiers and prisoners.

Enter EXETER.

EXETER
The Duke of York commends him to your majesty.

KING Lives he, good uncle? Thrice within this hour
I saw him down, thrice up again and fighting; 5
From helmet to the spur all blood he was.

EXETER In which array, brave soldier, doth he lie,
Larding the plain; and by his bloody side,
Yoke-fellow to his honour-owing wounds,
The noble Earl of Suffolk also lies. 10
Suffolk first died, and York, all haggled over,
Comes to him, where in gore he lay insteeped,
And takes him by the beard, kisses the gashes
That bloodily did yawn upon his face.
He cries aloud 'Tarry, my cousin Suffolk! 15
My soul shall thine keep company to heaven.
Tarry, sweet soul, for mine, then fly abreast,
As in this glorious and well-foughten field
We kept together in our chivalry.'
Upon these words I came and cheered him up; 20
He smiled me in the face, raught me his hand,
And with a feeble gripe says 'Dear my lord,
Commend my service to my sovereign.'
So did he turn, and over Suffolk's neck
He threw his wounded arm and kissed his lips, 25
And so, espoused to death, with blood he sealed
A testament of noble-ending love.
The pretty and sweet manner of it forced
Those waters from me which I would have stopped,
But I had not so much of man in me, 30
And all my mother came into mine eyes
And gave me up to tears.

KING   I blame you not,
For hearing this I must perforce compound
With my full eyes, or they will issue too. [*Alarum.*]
But hark, what new alarum is this same? 35
The French have reinforced their scattered men.
Then every soldier kill his prisoners!
Give the word through. *Exeunt.*

4.7 *Enter* FLUELLEN *and* GOWER.

FLUELLEN Kill the poys and the luggage! 'Tis expressly
against the law of arms. 'Tis as arrant a piece of
knavery, mark you now, as can be offert, in your
conscience now, is it not?

GOWER 'Tis certain there's not a boy left alive, and the 5
cowardly rascals that ran from the battle ha' done this
slaughter. Besides, they have burned and carried away
all that was in the King's tent, wherefore the King
most worthily hath caused every soldier to cut his
prisoner's throat. O, 'tis a gallant king! 10

FLUELLEN Ay, he was porn at Monmouth, Captain
Gower. What call you the town's name where
Alexander the Pig was born?

GOWER   Alexander the Great.

15 FLUELLEN   Why, I pray you, is not pig great? The pig, or the great, or the mighty, or the huge, or the magnanimous, are all one reckonings, save the phrase is a little variations.

20 GOWER   I think Alexander the Great was born in Macedon: his father was called Philip of Macedon, as I take it.

FLUELLEN   I think it is in Macedon where Alexander is porn. I tell you, Captain, if you look in the maps of the world, I warrant you shall find, in the comparisons
25 between Macedon and Monmouth, that the situations, look you, is both alike. There is a river in Macedon, and there is also moreover a river at Monmouth. It is called Wye at Monmouth, but it is out of my prains what is the name of the other river;
30 but 'tis all one, 'tis alike as my fingers is to my fingers, and there is salmons in both. If you mark Alexander's life well, Harry of Monmouth's life is come after it indifferent well, for there is figures in all things. Alexander, God knows, and you know, in his rages,
35 and his furies, and his wraths, and his cholers, and his moods, and his displeasures, and his indignations, and also being a little intoxicate in his prains, did in his ales and his angers, look you, kill his best friend Clytus.

GOWER   Our king is not like him in that: he never killed
40 any of his friends.

FLUELLEN   It is not well done, mark you now, to take the tales out of my mouth ere it is made an end and finished. I speak but in the figures and comparisons of it. As Alexander killed his friend Clytus, being in his
45 ales and his cups, so also Harry Monmouth, being in his right wits and his good judgements, turned away the fat knight with the great-belly doublet: he was full of jests, and gipes, and knaveries, and mocks; I have forgot his name.

50 GOWER   Sir John Falstaff.

FLUELLEN   That is he. I'll tell you, there is good men porn at Monmouth.

GOWER   Here comes his majesty.

Alarum. Enter KING HARRY *with* BOURBON *as his prisoner,*
WARWICK, GLOUCESTER, EXETER, *a herald and others,*
with prisoners. Flourish.

KING   I was not angry since I came to France
55 Until this instant. Take a trumpet, herald;
Ride thou unto the horsemen on yon hill.
If they will fight with us bid them come down,
Or void the field: they do offend our sight.
If they'll do neither, we will come to them
60 And make them skirr away as swift as stones
Enforced from the old Assyrian slings.
Besides, we'll cut the throats of those we have,
And not a man of them that we shall take
Shall taste our mercy. Go and tell them so.

Enter MONTJOY.

EXETER
Here comes the herald of the French, my liege.   65
GLOUCESTER
His eyes are humbler than they used to be.
KING
How now, what means this, herald? Know'st thou not
That I have fined these bones of mine for ransom?
Com'st thou again for ransom?
MONTJOY   No, great King:
I come to thee for charitable licence   70
That we may wander o'er this bloody field
To look our dead and then to bury them;
To sort our nobles from our common men.
For many of our princes – woe the while! –
Lie drowned and soaked in mercenary blood;   75
So do our vulgar drench their peasant limbs
In blood of princes; and their wounded steeds
Fret fetlock-deep in gore and with wild rage
Yerk out their armed heels at their dead masters,
Killing them twice. O give us leave, great King,   80
To view the field in safety and dispose
Of their dead bodies.
KING   I tell thee truly, herald,
I know not if the day be ours or no,
For yet a many of your horsemen peer
And gallop o'er the field.
MONTJOY   The day is yours.   85
KING   Praised be God, and not our strength, for it!
What is this castle called that stands hard by?
MONTJOY   They call it Agincourt.
KING   Then call we this the field of Agincourt,
Fought on the day of Crispin Crispian.   90
FLUELLEN   Your grandfather of famous memory, an't please your majesty, and your great-uncle Edward the Plack Prince of Wales, as I have read in the chronicles, fought a most prave pattle here in France.
KING   They did, Fluellen.   95
FLUELLEN   Your majesty says very true. If your majesty is remembered of it, the Welshmen did good service in a garden where leeks did grow, wearing leeks in their Monmouth caps, which your majesty know to this hour is an honourable badge of the service; and I do   100
believe your majesty takes no scorn to wear the leek upon Saint Tavy's day.
KING   I wear it for a memorable honour,
For I am Welsh, you know, good countryman.
FLUELLEN   All the water in Wye cannot wash your   105
majesty's Welsh plood out of your pody, I can tell you that. God pless it and preserve it, as long as it pleases his grace, and his majesty too!
KING   Thanks, good my countryman.
FLUELLEN   By Jeshu, I am your majesty's countryman, I   110
care not who know it. I will confess it to all the world: I need not to be ashamed of your majesty, praised be God, so long as your majesty is an honest man.
KING   God keep me so!

Enter WILLIAMS.

Our herald go with him:
115 Bring me just notice of the numbers dead
On both our parts.

Exeunt Montjoy, Gower and the English herald.

Call yonder fellow hither.

EXETER   Soldier, you must come to the King.

KING   Soldier, why wear'st thou that glove in thy cap?

WILLIAMS   An't please your majesty, 'tis the gage of one
120   that I should fight withal, if he be alive.

KING   An Englishman?

WILLIAMS   An't please your majesty, a rascal that
    swaggered with me last night, who if 'a live and ever
    dare to challenge this glove, I have sworn to take him
125   a box o'th' ear; or if I can see my glove in his cap,
    which he swore as he was a soldier he would wear if 'a
    lived, I will strike it out soundly.

KING   What think you, Captain Fluellen, is it fit this
    soldier keep his oath?

130 FLUELLEN   He is a craven and a villain else, an't please
    your majesty, in my conscience.

KING   It may be his enemy is a gentleman of great sort,
    quite from the answer of his degree.

FLUELLEN   Though he be as good a gentleman as the
135   devil is, as Lucifer and Belzebub himself, it is
    necessary, look your grace, that he keep his vow and
    his oath. If he be perjured, see you now, his reputation
    is as arrant a villain and a jack-sauce as ever his black
    shoe trod upon God's ground and his earth, in my
140   conscience, la!

KING   Then keep thy vow, sirrah, when thou meet'st the
    fellow.

WILLIAMS   So I will, my liege, as I live.

KING   Who serv'st thou under?

145 WILLIAMS   Under Captain Gower, my liege.

FLUELLEN   Gower is a good captain, and is good
    knowledge and literature in the wars.

KING   Call him hither to me, soldier.

WILLIAMS   I will, my liege.   *Exit.*

150 KING   Here, Fluellen, wear thou this favour for me and
    stick it in thy cap. When Alençon and myself were
    down together I plucked this glove from his helm. If
    any man challenge this he is a friend to Alençon and
    an enemy to our person. If thou encounter any such,
155   apprehend him, an thou dost me love.

FLUELLEN   Your grace does me as great honours as can
    be desired in the hearts of his subjects. I would fain see
    the man that has but two legs that shall find himself
    aggriefed at this glove, that is all; I would fain but see
160   it once, an't please God of his grace that I might.

KING   Know'st thou Gower?

FLUELLEN   He is my dear friend, an't please you.

KING   Pray thee go seek him and bring him to my tent.

FLUELLEN   I will fetch him.   *Exit.*

165 KING   My lord of Warwick and my brother Gloucester,
    Follow Fluellen closely at the heels.

The glove which I have given him for a favour
May haply purchase him a box o'th' ear;
It is the soldier's. I by bargain should
Wear it myself. Follow, good cousin Warwick.   170
If that the soldier strike him – as I judge
By his blunt bearing he will keep his word –
Some sudden mischief may arise of it,
For I do know Fluellen valiant
And, touched with choler, hot as gunpowder,   175
And quickly will return an injury.
Follow, and see there be no harm between them. –
Go you with me, uncle of Exeter.   *Exeunt.*

4.8   *Enter* GOWER *and* WILLIAMS.

WILLIAMS   I warrant it is to knight you, Captain.

Enter FLUELLEN.

FLUELLEN   God's will and his pleasure, Captain, I
    beseech you now, come apace to the King: there is
    more good toward you, peradventure, than is in your
    knowledge to dream of.   5

WILLIAMS   Sir, know you this glove?

FLUELLEN   Know the glove? I know the glove is a glove.

WILLIAMS   I know this, and thus I challenge it.

[*Strikes him.*]

FLUELLEN   'Sblood, an arrant traitor as any's in the
    universal world, or in France, or in England!   10

GOWER   How now, sir, you villain!

WILLIAMS   Do you think I'll be forsworn?

FLUELLEN   Stand away, Captain Gower: I will give
    treason his payment into plows, I warrant you.

WILLIAMS   I am no traitor.   15

FLUELLEN   That's a lie in thy throat.

Enter soldiers.

I charge you in his majesty's name apprehend him,
he's a friend of the Duke Alençon's.

Enter WARWICK *and* GLOUCESTER.

WARWICK   How now, how now, what's the matter?

FLUELLEN   My lord of Warwick, here is, praised be God   20
    for it, a most contagious treason come to light, look
    you, as you shall desire in a summer's day.

Enter the KING *and* EXETER.

Here is his majesty.

KING   How now, what's the matter?

FLUELLEN   My liege, here is a villain and a traitor that,   25
    look your grace, has struck the glove which your
    majesty is take out of the helmet of Alençon.

WILLIAMS   My liege, this was my glove, here is the
    fellow of it; and he that I gave it to in change promised
    to wear it in his cap; I promised to strike him if he did.   30
    I met this man with my glove in his cap, and I have
    been as good as my word.

FLUELLEN   Your majesty hear now, saving your

majesty's manhood, what an arrant, rascally, beggarly, lousy knave it is. I hope your majesty is pear me testimony, and witness, and avouchment that this is the glove of Alençon that your majesty is give me, in your conscience now.

KING Give me thy glove, soldier. Look, here is the fellow of it.
'Twas I indeed thou promised'st to strike,
And thou hast given me most bitter terms.

FLUELLEN An't please your majesty, let his neck answer for it, if there is any martial law in the world.

KING How canst thou make me satisfaction?

WILLIAMS All offences, my lord, come from the heart: never came any from mine that might offend your majesty.

KING It was our self thou didst abuse.

WILLIAMS Your majesty came not like your self: you appeared to me but as a common man – witness the night, your garments, your lowliness; and what your highness suffered under that shape, I beseech you take it for your own fault and not mine, for had you been as I took you for, I made no offence; therefore I beseech your highness pardon me. [*Kneels.*]

KING [*Raises him.*]
Here, uncle Exeter, fill this glove with crowns
And give it to this fellow. – Keep it, fellow,
And wear it for an honour in thy cap
Till I do challenge it. – Give him the crowns. –
And Captain, you must needs be friends with him.

FLUELLEN By this day and this light, the fellow has mettle enough in his belly. – Hold, there is twelve pence for you, and I pray you to serve God, and keep you out of prawls and prabbles, and quarrels and dissensions, and I warrant you it is the better for you.

WILLIAMS I will none of your money.

FLUELLEN It is with a good will. I can tell you, it will serve you to mend your shoes. Come, wherefore should you be so pashful? Your shoes is not so good. 'Tis a good shilling, I warrant you, or I will change it.

Enter Herald.

KING Now, herald, are the dead numbered?

HERALD
Here is the number of the slaughtered French.
[*Gives the King a paper.*]

KING What prisoners of good sort are taken, uncle?

EXETER
Charles, Duke of Orleans, nephew to the King;
John, Duke of Bourbon, and Lord Boucicault.
Of other lords and barons, knights and squires,
Full fifteen hundred, besides common men.

KING This note doth tell me of ten thousand French
That in the field lie slain. Of princes in this number
And nobles bearing banners, there lie dead
One hundred twenty-six. Added to these,
Of knights, esquires and gallant gentlemen,
Eight thousand and four hundred, of the which

Five hundred were but yesterday dubbed knights.   85
So that in these ten thousand they have lost
There are but sixteen hundred mercenaries;
The rest are princes, barons, lords, knights, squires
And gentlemen of blood and quality.
The names of those their nobles that lie dead: 90
Charles Delabreth, High Constable of France;
Jaques of Chatillon, Admiral of France;
The Master of the Crossbows, Lord Rambures;
Great Master of France, the brave Sir Guichard
  Dauphin;
John, Duke of Alençon; Anthony, Duke of Brabant,   95
The brother to the Duke of Burgundy;
And Edward, Duke of Bar: of lusty earls,
Grandpré and Roussi, Fauconbridge and Foix,
Beaumont and Marle, Vaudemont and Lestrelles.
Here was a royal fellowship of death.   100
Where is the number of our English dead?
[*Herald gives him another paper.*]
Edward the Duke of York; the Earl of Suffolk;
Sir Richard Keighley; Davy Gam, esquire;
None else of name, and of all other men
But five-and-twenty. O God, thy arm was here;   105
And not to us but to thy arm alone
Ascribe we all. When, without stratagem,
But in plain shock and even play of battle,
Was ever known so great and little loss
On one part and on th'other? Take it, God,   110
For it is none but thine.

EXETER   'Tis wonderful.

KING Come, go we in procession to the village,
And be it death proclaimed through our host
To boast of this, or take that praise from God
Which is his only.   115

FLUELLEN Is it not lawful, an't please your majesty, to tell how many is killed?

KING Yes, Captain, but with this acknowledgement,
That God fought for us.

FLUELLEN Yes, in my conscience, he did us great good.   120

KING Do we all holy rites.
Let there be sung *Non nobis* and *Te Deum*,
The dead with charity enclosed in clay,
And then to Calais, and to England then,
Where ne'er from France arrived more happy men.   125
                              Exeunt.

5.0   *Enter* CHORUS.

CHORUS
Vouchsafe to those that have not read the story
That I may prompt them; and of such as have,
I humbly pray them to admit th'excuse
Of time, of numbers and due course of things
Which cannot in their huge and proper life   5
Be here presented. Now we bear the King
Toward Calais: grant him there; there seen,
Heave him away upon your winged thoughts

Athwart the sea. Behold, the English beach
10 Pales in the flood with men, with wives and boys,
Whose shouts and claps outvoice the deep-mouthed
      sea,
Which like a mighty whiffler 'fore the King
Seems to prepare his way. So let him land,
And solemnly see him set on to London.
15 So swift a pace hath thought that even now
You may imagine him upon Blackheath,
Where that his lords desire him to have borne
His bruised helmet and his bended sword
Before him through the city. He forbids it,
20 Being free from vainness and self-glorious pride,
Giving full trophy, signal and ostent
Quite from himself to God. But now behold,
In the quick forge and working-house of thought,
How London doth pour out her citizens.
25 The Mayor and all his brethren in best sort,
Like to the senators of th'antique Rome
With the plebeians swarming at their heels,
Go forth and fetch their conquering Caesar in;
As, by a lower but as loving likelihood,
30 Were now the General of our gracious Empress,
As in good time he may, from Ireland coming,
Bringing rebellion broached on his sword,
How many would the peaceful city quit
To welcome him! Much more, and much more cause,
35 Did they this Harry. Now in London place him.
As yet the lamentation of the French
Invites the King of England's stay at home.
The Emperor's coming in behalf of France,
To order peace between them and omit
40 All the occurrences, whatever chanced,
Till Harry's back return again to France.
There must we bring him; and myself have played
The interim, by remembering you 'tis past.
Then brook abridgement and your eyes advance
45 After your thoughts straight back again to France.

                                       Exit.

5.1   *Enter* FLUELLEN *and* GOWER.

GOWER   Nay, that's right. But why wear you your leek
today? Saint Davy's day is past.
FLUELLEN   There is occasions and causes why and
wherefore in all things. I will tell you ass my friend,
5   Captain Gower. The rascally, scald, beggarly, lousy,
pragging knave Pistol, which you and yourself and all
the world know to be no petter than a fellow, look you
now, of no merits, he is come to me and prings me
pread and salt yesterday, look you, and bid me eat my
10   leek. It was in a place where I could not breed no
contention with him, but I will be so bold as to wear it
in my cap till I see him once again, and then I will tell
him a little piece of my desires.

                   Enter PISTOL.

GOWER   Why, here he comes, swelling like a turkey-
cock.
FLUELLEN   'Tis no matter for his swellings nor his
turkey-cocks. – God pless you, Anchient Pistol, you
scurvy, lousy knave, God pless you!
PISTOL
     Ha, art thou bedlam? Dost thou thirst, base Trojan,
     To have me fold up Parca's fatal web?
     Hence! I am qualmish at the smell of leek.
FLUELLEN   I peseech you heartily, scurvy, lousy knave,
at my desires, and my requests, and my petitions, to
eat, look you, this leek. Because, look you, you do not
love it, nor your affections and your appetites and your
digestions does not agree with it, I would desire you to
eat it.
PISTOL   Not for Cadwallader and all his goats.
FLUELLEN [*Strikes him with a cudgel.*]   There is one goat
for you. Will you be so good, scald knave, as eat it?
PISTOL   Base Trojan, thou shalt die.
FLUELLEN   You say very true, scald knave, when God's
will is. I will desire you to live in the meantime and eat
your victuals. [*Strikes him.*] Come, there is sauce for it.
You called me yesterday mountain-squire, but I will
make you today a squire of low degree. I pray you, fall
to; if you can mock a leek you can eat a leek.
GOWER   Enough, Captain, you have astonished him.
FLUELLEN   I say I will make him eat some part of my
leek, or I will peat his pate four days. – Bite, I pray
you; it is good for your green wound and your ploody
coxcomb.
PISTOL   Must I bite?
FLUELLEN   Yes, certainly, and out of doubt and out of
question too, and ambiguities.
PISTOL   By this leek, I will most horribly revenge –
[*Fluellen threatens him.*] I eat and eat – I swear –
FLUELLEN   Eat, I pray you. Will you have some more
sauce to your leek? There is not enough leek to swear
by.
PISTOL   Quiet thy cudgel, thou dost see I eat.
FLUELLEN   Much good do you, scald knave, heartily.
Nay, pray you, throw none away; the skin is good for
your broken coxcomb. When you take occasions to see
leeks hereafter, I pray you mock at 'em, that is all.
PISTOL   Good.
FLUELLEN   Ay, leeks is good. Hold you, there is a groat
to heal your pate.
PISTOL   Me a groat?
FLUELLEN   Yes, verily and in truth, you shall take it, or
I have another leek in my pocket which you shall eat.
PISTOL   I take thy groat in earnest of revenge.
FLUELLEN   If I owe you anything, I will pay you in
cudgels: you shall be a woodmonger, and buy nothing
of me but cudgels. God bye you, and keep you, and
heal your pate.   *Exit.*
PISTOL   All hell shall stir for this.
GOWER   Go, go, you are a counterfeit cowardly knave.

Will you mock at an ancient tradition, begun upon an
honourable respect and worn as a memorable trophy
of predeceased valour, and dare not avouch in your
deeds any of your words? I have seen you gleeking and
galling at this gentleman twice or thrice. You thought
because he could not speak English in the native garb
he could not therefore handle an English cudgel. You
find it otherwise, and henceforth let a Welsh
correction teach you a good English condition. Fare ye
well.   *Exit.*

PISTOL   Doth Fortune play the huswife with me now?
   News have I that my Nell is dead i'th' spital
   Of malady of France,
   And there my rendezvous is quite cut off.
   Old I do wax, and from my weary limbs
   Honour is cudgelled. Well, bawd I'll turn,
   And something lean to cutpurse of quick hand.
   To England will I steal, and there I'll steal;
   And patches will I get unto these cudgelled scars,
   And swear I got them in the Gallia wars.   *Exit.*

5.2   *Enter at one door* KING HENRY, EXETER,
      BEDFORD, WARWICK *and other lords* (GLOUCESTER,
      WESTMORLAND, CLARENCE *and* HUNTINGDON).
          At another, QUEEN ISABEL,
      the FRENCH KING, KATHERINE, ALICE,
      the DUKE OF BURGUNDY, *and other French.*

KING   Peace to this meeting, wherefore we are met.
   Unto our brother France and to our sister
   Health and fair time of day; joy and good wishes
   To our most fair and princely cousin Katherine;
   And, as a branch and member of this royalty,
   By whom this great assembly is contrived,
   We do salute you, Duke of Burgundy;
   And, princes French and peers, health to you all.
FRENCH KING   Right joyous are we to behold your face,
   Most worthy brother England; fairly met.
   So are you, princes English, every one.
QUEEN ISABEL   So happy be the issue, brother England,
   Of this good day and of this gracious meeting,
   As we are now glad to behold your eyes,
   Your eyes which hitherto have borne in them
   Against the French that met them in their bent
   The fatal balls of murdering basilisks.
   The venom of such looks we fairly hope
   Have lost their quality, and that this day
   Shall change all griefs and quarrels into love.
KING   To cry amen to that, thus we appear.
QUEEN ISABEL   You English princes all, I do salute you.
BURGUNDY   My duty to you both, on equal love,
   Great Kings of France and England. That I have
         laboured
   With all my wits, my pains and strong endeavours,
   To bring your most imperial majesties
   Unto this bar and royal interview
   Your mightiness on both parts best can witness.

Since then my office hath so far prevailed
That face to face and royal eye to eye   30
You have congreeted, let it not disgrace me
If I demand before this royal view
What rub or what impediment there is
Why that the naked, poor and mangled peace,
Dear nurse of arts, plenties and joyful births,   35
Should not in this best garden of the world,
Our fertile France, put up her lovely visage?
Alas, she hath from France too long been chased,
And all her husbandry doth lie on heaps,
Corrupting in it own fertility.   40
Her vine, the merry cheerer of the heart,
Unpruned dies; her hedges even-pleached,
Like prisoners wildly overgrown with hair,
Put forth disordered twigs; her fallow leas
The darnel, hemlock and rank fumitory   45
Doth root upon, while that the coulter rusts
That should deracinate such savagery.
The even mead, that erst brought sweetly forth
The freckled cowslip, burnet and green clover,
Wanting the scythe, all uncorrected, rank,   50
Conceives by idleness, and nothing teems
But hateful docks, rough thistles, kecksies, burrs,
Losing both beauty and utility.
And as our vineyards, fallows, meads and hedges,
Defective in their natures, grow to wildness,   55
Even so our houses and our selves and children
Have lost, or do not learn for want of time,
The sciences that should become our country,
But grow like savages, as soldiers will
That nothing do but meditate on blood,   60
To swearing and stern looks, diffused attire,
And everything that seems unnatural.
Which to reduce into our former favour
You are assembled; and my speech entreats
That I may know the let why gentle peace   65
Should not expel these inconveniences
And bless us with her former qualities.
KING   If, Duke of Burgundy, you would the peace
   Whose want gives growth to th'imperfections
   Which you have cited, you must buy that peace   70
   With full accord to all our just demands,
   Whose tenors and particular effects
   You have, enscheduled briefly, in your hands.
BURGUNDY   The King hath heard them, to the which
      as yet
   There is no answer made.
KING   Well then, the peace   75
   Which you before so urged lies in his answer.
FRENCH KING   I have but with a cursitory eye
   O'er-glanced the articles. Pleaseth your grace
   To appoint some of your council presently
   To sit with us once more, with better heed   80
   To re-survey them, we will suddenly
   Pass our accept and peremptory answer.

KING   Brother, we shall. – Go, uncle Exeter,
And brother Clarence, and you, brother Gloucester,
85   Warwick and Huntingdon, go with the King,
And take with you free power to ratify,
Augment or alter, as your wisdoms best
Shall see advantageable for our dignity,
Anything in or out of our demands,
90   And we'll consign thereto. – Will you, fair sister,
Go with the princes, or stay here with us?

QUEEN ISABEL
Our gracious brother, I will go with them.
Haply a woman's voice may do some good
When articles too nicely urged be stood on.

95   KING   Yet leave our cousin Katherine here with us:
She is our capital demand, comprised
Within the fore-rank of our articles.

QUEEN ISABEL   She hath good leave.
            Exeunt all but King and Katherine and Alice.

KING   Fair Katherine, and most fair,
Will you vouchsafe to teach a soldier terms
100   Such as will enter at a lady's ear
And plead his love-suit to her gentle heart?

KATHERINE   Your majesty shall mock at me; I cannot
speak your England.

KING   O fair Katherine, if you will love me soundly with
105   your French heart I will be glad to hear you confess it
brokenly with your English tongue. Do you like me,
Kate?

KATHERINE   *Pardonnez-moi*, I cannot tell vat is 'like me'.

KING   An angel is like you, Kate, and you are like an
110   angel.

KATHERINE   *Que dit-il, que je suis semblable à les anges?*

ALICE   *Oui, vraiment, sauf votre grâce, ainsi dit-il.*

KING   I said so, dear Katherine, and I must not blush to
affirm it.

115   KATHERINE   *O bon Dieu, les langues des hommes sont
pleines de tromperies!*

KING   What says she, fair one? That the tongues of men
are full of deceits?

ALICE   *Oui*, dat de tongues of de mans is be full of
120   deceits: dat is de Princess.

KING   The Princess is the better Englishwoman. I'faith,
Kate, my wooing is fit for thy understanding. I am
glad thou canst speak no better English, for if thou
couldst thou wouldst find me such a plain king that
125   thou wouldst think I had sold my farm to buy my
crown. I know no ways to mince it in love but directly
to say 'I love you.' Then if you urge me farther than to
say 'Do you in faith?', I wear out my suit. Give me
your answer, i'faith do, and so clap hands and a
130   bargain. How say you, lady?

KATHERINE   *Sauf votre honneur*, me understand vell.

KING   Marry, if you would put me to verses or to dance
for your sake, Kate, why, you undid me: for the one I
have neither words nor measure, and for the other I
135   have no strength in measure, yet a reasonable measure
in strength. If I could win a lady at leapfrog, or by
vaulting into my saddle with my armour on my back,
under the correction of bragging be it spoken, I should
quickly leap into a wife. Or if I might buffet for my
love or bound my horse for her favours, I could lay on   140
like a butcher and sit like a jackanapes, never off. But
before God, Kate, I cannot look greenly nor gasp out
my eloquence, nor I have no cunning in protestation,
only downright oaths, which I never use till urged, nor
never break for urging. If thou canst love a fellow of   145
this temper, Kate, whose face is not worth
sunburning, that never looks in his glass for love of
anything he sees there, let thine eye be thy cook. I
speak to thee plain soldier. If thou canst love me for
this, take me; if not, to say to thee that I shall die is   150
true; but for thy love, by the Lord, no; yet I love thee
too. And while thou liv'st, dear Kate, take a fellow of
plain and uncoined constancy, for he perforce must do
thee right, because he hath not the gift to woo in other
places; for these fellows of infinite tongue, that can   155
rhyme themselves into ladies' favours, they do always
reason themselves out again. What, a speaker is but a
prater, a rhyme is but a ballad. A good leg will fall, a
straight back will stoop, a black beard will turn white,
a curled pate will grow bald, a fair face will wither, a   160
full eye will wax hollow; but a good heart, Kate, is the
sun and the moon, or rather the sun and not the moon,
for it shines bright and never changes, but keeps his
course truly. If thou would have such a one, take me;
and take me, take a soldier; take a soldier, take a king.   165
And what sayst thou then to my love? Speak, my fair,
and fairly, I pray thee.

KATHERINE   Is it possible dat I sould love de enemy of
France?

KING   No, it is not possible you should love the enemy of   170
France, Kate: but in loving me you should love the
friend of France; for I love France so well that I will
not part with a village of it; I will have it all mine: and
Kate, when France is mine, and I am yours, then yours
is France, and you are mine.   175

KATHERINE   I cannot tell vat is dat.

KING   No, Kate? I will tell thee in French, which I am
sure will hang upon my tongue like a new-married
wife about her husband's neck, hardly to be shook off.
Je, quand j'ai le possession de France, et quand vous avez   180
le possession de moi – let me see, what then? Saint Denis
be my speed! – *donc votre est France, et vous êtes mienne.*
It is as easy for me, Kate, to conquer the kingdom as
to speak so much more French. I shall never move thee
in French, unless it be to laugh at me.   185

KATHERINE   *Sauf votre honneur, le français que vous
parlez, il est meilleur que l'anglais lequel je parle.*

KING   No, faith, is't not, Kate; but thy speaking of my
tongue, and I thine, most truly-falsely, must needs be
granted to be much at one. But Kate, dost thou   190
understand thus much English? 'Canst thou love me?'

KATHERINE   I cannot tell.

KING   Can any of your neighbours tell, Kate? I'll ask

them. Come, I know thou lovest me, and at night, when you come into your closet, you'll question this gentlewoman about me; and I know, Kate, you will to her dispraise those parts in me that you love with your heart: but, good Kate, mock me mercifully, the rather, gentle Princess, because I love thee cruelly. If ever thou be'st mine, Kate, as I have a saving faith within me tells me thou shalt, I get thee with scambling, and thou must therefore needs prove a good soldier-breeder. Shall not thou and I, between Saint Denis and Saint George, compound a boy, half French, half English, that shall go to Constantinople and take the Turk by the beard? Shall we not? What sayst thou, my fair flower-de-luce?

KATHERINE   I do not know dat.

KING   No, 'tis hereafter to know, but now to promise: do but now promise, Kate, you will endeavour for your French part of such a boy, and for my English moiety take the word of a king and a bachelor. How answer you, *la plus belle Katherine du monde, mon très cher et divin déesse?*

KATHERINE   Your majesty 'ave *fausse* French enough to deceive de most *sage demoiselle* dat is *en France.*

KING   Now fie upon my false French! By mine honour, in true English, I love thee, Kate: by which honour I dare not swear thou lovest me, yet my blood begins to flatter me that thou dost, notwithstanding the poor and untempering effect of my visage. Now beshrew my father's ambition! He was thinking of civil wars when he got me: therefore was I created with a stubborn outside, with an aspect of iron, that when I come to woo ladies I fright them. But in faith, Kate, the elder I wax the better I shall appear. My comfort is that old age, that ill layer-up of beauty, can do no more spoil upon my face. Thou hast me, if thou hast me, at the worst; and thou shalt wear me, if thou wear me, better and better. And therefore tell me, most fair Katherine, will you have me? Put off your maiden blushes, avouch the thoughts of your heart with the looks of an empress, take me by the hand, and say 'Harry of England, I am thine': which word thou shalt no sooner bless mine ear withal but I will tell thee aloud 'England is thine, Ireland is thine, France is thine, and Henry Plantagenet is thine', who, though I speak it before his face, if he be not fellow with the best king, thou shalt find the best king of good fellows. Come, your answer in broken music, for thy voice is music and thy English broken. Therefore, queen of all, Katherine, break thy mind to me in broken English: wilt thou have me?

KATHERINE   Dat is as it sall please *le roi mon père.*

KING   Nay, it will please him well, Kate; it shall please him, Kate.

KATHERINE   Den it sall also content me.

KING   Upon that I kiss your hand, and I call you my Queen.

KATHERINE   *Laissez, mon seigneur, laissez, laissez! Ma foi, je ne veux point que vous abaissiez votre grandeur en baisant la main d'une de votre seigneurie indigne serviteur. Excusez-moi, je vous supplie, mon très-puissant seigneur.*

KING   Then I will kiss your lips, Kate.

KATHERINE   *Les dames et demoiselles pour être baisées devant leurs noces, il n'est pas la coutume de France.*

KING   Madam my interpreter, what says she?

ALICE   Dat it is not de fashion *pour les* ladies of France – I cannot tell vat is *baiser en* Anglish.

KING   To kiss.

ALICE   Your majesty *entend* bettre *que moi.*

KING   It is not a fashion for the maids in France to kiss before they are married, would she say?

ALICE   *Oui, vraiment.*

KING   O Kate, nice customs curtsy to great kings. Dear Kate, you and I cannot be confined within the weak list of a country's fashion. We are the makers of manners, Kate, and the liberty that follows our places stops the mouth of all find-faults, as I will do yours for upholding the nice fashion of your country in denying me a kiss: therefore patiently, and yielding – [*Kisses her.*]   You have witchcraft in your lips, Kate: there is more eloquence in a sugar touch of them than in the tongues of the French Council, and they should sooner persuade Harry of England than a general petition of monarchs. Here comes your father.

Enter the French power *and the* English lords.

BURGUNDY   God save your majesty! My royal cousin, Teach you our Princess English?

KING   I would have her learn, my fair cousin, how perfectly I love her, and that is good English.

BURGUNDY   Is she not apt?

KING   Our tongue is rough, coz, and my condition is not smooth, so that having neither the voice nor the heart of flattery about me I cannot so conjure up the spirit of love in her that he will appear in his true likeness.

BURGUNDY   Pardon the frankness of my mirth if I answer you for that. If you would conjure in her, you must make a circle; if conjure up love in her in his true likeness, he must appear naked and blind. Can you blame her then, being a maid yet rosed over with the virgin crimson of modesty, if she deny the appearance of a naked blind boy in her naked seeing self? It were, my lord, a hard condition for a maid to consign to.

KING   Yet they do wink and yield, as love is blind and enforces.

BURGUNDY   They are then excused, my lord, when they see not what they do.

KING   Then good my lord, teach your cousin to consent winking.

BURGUNDY   I will wink on her to consent, my lord, if you will teach her to know my meaning. For maids well summered and warm kept are like flies at Bartholomew-tide, blind, though they have their eyes; and then they will endure handling, which before

461

would not abide looking on.

KING   This moral ties me over to time and a hot
summer; and so I shall catch the fly, your cousin, in
the latter end, and she must be blind too.

310   BURGUNDY   As love is, my lord, before that it loves.

KING   It is so: and you may some of you thank love for
my blindness, who cannot see many a fair French city
for one fair French maid that stands in my way.

FRENCH KING   Yes, my lord, you see them perspectively,
315   the cities turned into a maid; for they are all girdled
with maiden walls that no war hath entered.

KING   Shall Kate be my wife?

FRENCH KING   So please you.

KING   I am content, so the maiden cities you talk of may
320   wait on her: so the maid that stood in the way for my
wish shall show me the way to my will.

FRENCH KING   We have consented to all terms of reason.

KING   Is't so, my lords of England?

WESTMORLAND   The King hath granted every article:
325   His daughter first, and in the sequel all,
According to their firm proposed natures.

EXETER   Only he hath not yet subscribed this, where
your majesty demands that the King of France, having
any occasion to write for matter of grant, shall name
330   your highness in this form and with this addition:
[*Reads.*] in French, *Notre très cher fils Henri, roi
d'Angleterre, héritier de France*; and thus in Latin,
*Praeclarissimus filius noster Henricus, rex Angliae et
haeres Franciae.*

335   FRENCH KING   Nor this I have not, brother, so denied
But your request shall make me let it pass.

KING   I pray you then, in love and dear alliance,
Let that one article rank with the rest,
And thereupon give me your daughter.

FRENCH KING
340   Take her, fair son, and from her blood raise up
Issue to me, that the contending kingdoms
Of France and England, whose very shores look pale
With envy of each other's happiness,
May cease their hatred, and this dear conjunction
345   Plant neighbourhood and Christian-like accord

In their sweet bosoms, that never war advance
His bleeding sword 'twixt England and fair France.

LORDS   Amen.

KING   Now welcome, Kate, and bear me witness all
That here I kiss her as my sovereign queen.   350
[*Kisses her.*]   [*Flourish.*]

QUEEN ISABEL   God, the best maker of all marriages,
Combine your hearts in one, your realms in one!
As man and wife, being two, are one in love,
So be there 'twixt your kingdoms such a spousal
That never may ill office or fell jealousy,   355
Which troubles oft the bed of blessed marriage,
Thrust in between the paction of these kingdoms
To make divorce of their incorporate league;
That English may as French, French Englishmen,
Receive each other. God speak this amen.   360

ALL   Amen.

KING   Prepare we for our marriage; on which day,
My lord of Burgundy, we'll take your oath,
And all the peers', for surety of our leagues.
Then shall I swear to Kate, and you to me,   365
And may our oaths well kept and prosperous be!
                      Sennet. Exeunt.

EPILOGUE

Enter CHORUS.

CHORUS   Thus far, with rough and all-unable pen,
Our bending author hath pursued the story,
In little room confining mighty men,
Mangling by starts the full course of their glory.
Small time, but in that small most greatly lived   5
This star of England. Fortune made his sword
By which the world's best garden he achieved,
And of it left his son imperial lord.
Henry the Sixth, in infant bands crowned King
Of France and England, did this king succeed,   10
Whose state so many had the managing
That they lost France and made his England bleed,
Which oft our stage hath shown; and for their sake
In your fair minds let this acceptance take.   *Exit.*

King Henry VI, Part 1

First published as the sixth of the histories in the Folio of 1623, *King Henry VI, Part 1* may have been written as early as 1589: more certainly it was ready for the stage by 1592. A play entitled 'harey the vj' was performed at the Rose on 3 March 1592 by Lord Strange's Men, and it is usually assumed that it was this play. Later that year, Thomas Nashe remarked upon the play's extraordinary appeal, writing of how 'the brave *Talbot* (the terror of the French)' triumphed in the theatre, where 'ten thousand spectators at least (at several times) . . . imagine they behold him fresh bleeding'.

For all its early success, since 1734, when Lewis Theobald asserted that it was not 'entirely of his writing', scholars have wondered if the play was solely the product of Shakespeare's pen and many still believe that it was a collaboration – as were so many Elizabethan plays – written by Shakespeare with Nashe and two other dramatists, perhaps Robert Greene and George Peele. Andrew Cairncross, the Arden editor, however, argued energetically for Shakespeare's sole authorship of the play, and certainly Heminges and Condell, who included it in the Folio, seem to have regarded it as his. In any case, the question of authorship can make little difference to our sense of the work.

The three plays on Henry VI are the first of the history plays which, along with *King Richard III*, treat the end of the Plantagenet dynasty. The political and military achievements of Henry V are undone by the civil dissension that follows his death, as his son, who succeeded as a nine-month-old infant, proves unable to unify the country. *King Henry VI, Part 1* moves from the funeral of Henry V in 1422 to the impending marriage of Henry VI to Margaret of Anjou, covering some twenty-three years (actually the play covers more than thirty, as the death of Talbot took place only in 1453, eight years after the last event in the play), proceeding episodically across time and space to tell its tale of England weakened by disunity and faction at home.

As Nashe's comment reveals, the play's most powerful source of appeal was the character of Talbot, the 'terror of the French', an exemplary hero, who stands as an ideal of physical and moral excellence. His very name inspires his men. 'A Talbot! A Talbot!', they cry, rushing 'into the bowels of the battle'. His rigid commitment to chivalric values, however, prevents him from fleeing the battlefield in a lost cause, prematurely depriving England of its greatest hero and also of Talbot's only son (another of Shakespeare's changes of history; in fact Talbot was succeeded as Earl of Shrewsbury by a surviving son, also named John). Thus, though the play ends with an English triumph, the nation is weakened and made vulnerable, not only by Talbot's death but by the political faction that was its direct cause.

The play's other memorable character is Joan of Arc. She is Talbot's chief rival, heroine of the French, though in English eyes she is no holy maid but something monstrous, at once erotic and demonic. That she is French, but also that she is an assertive and powerful woman, marks her as unnatural; her presence is thoroughly discredited, identified entirely with its challenge to English virtue – though the history plays' readiness to demonize all women of action perhaps suggests that it is as much an insecure masculinity that is at risk.

Henry VI himself is of strangely little dramatic consequence in the play. He does not appear on stage until 3.1 – no doubt this is, in part, because he was less than one year old when the action begins – but the virtual absence from this play of the King whose name it bears is arguably its most telling dramatic point, unmistakable evidence of the power vacuum that the squabbling factions each seeks to fill.

The play was an early success on stage, performed at least fifteen times in 1592 alone, but it has been seldom staged since. A performance at Stratford in 1889 advertised itself as the first since Shakespeare's time, and modern audiences rarely have an opportunity to see it whole. If seen at all, it is often as a much reduced element in adaptations and conflations of the three parts of *King Henry VI*, as in John Barton's two-part *Wars of the Roses* (1963), or in the two-part adaptation by Charles Wood for the Royal Shakespeare Company's trilogy of *The Plantagenets* in 1988. In 1977, however, Terry Hands did direct the three parts in sequence without conflation or heavy cutting, with Alan Howard as the King, memorably charting his growth across the three plays from timid childhood to disillusioned and defeated maturity.

The Arden text is based on the 1623 First Folio.

THE HOUSES OF YORK AND LANCASTER

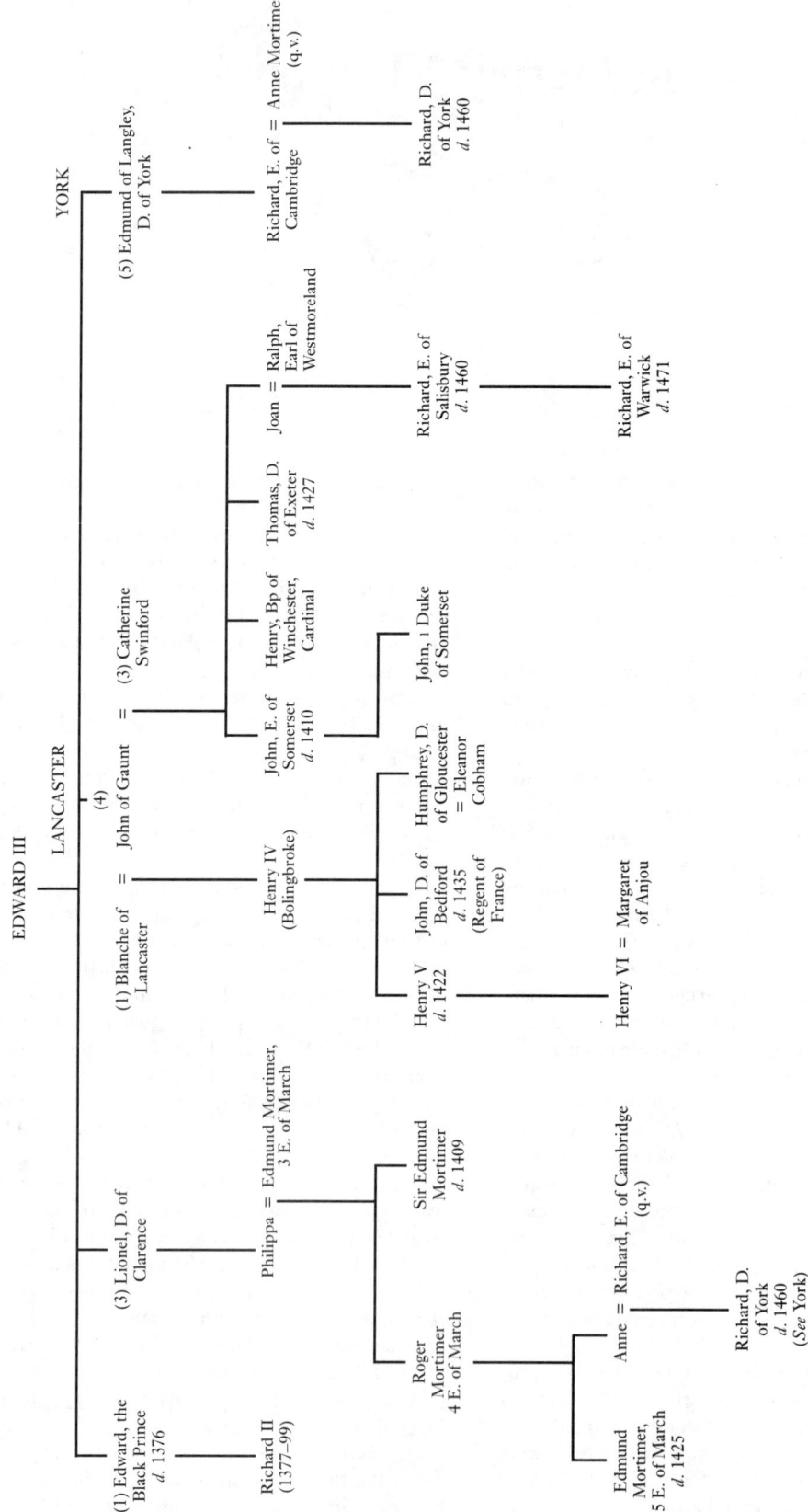

KING HENRY the Sixth
Duke of GLOUCESTER — *uncle to the King, and Protector*
Duke of BEDFORD — *uncle to the King, and Regent of France*
Duke of EXETER — *great-uncle to the King*
Bishop of WINCHESTER — *great-uncle to the King, and afterwards Cardinal*
Duke of SOMERSET
Richard PLANTAGENET — *afterwards Duke of York*
Earl of WARWICK
Earl of SALISBURY
Earl of SUFFOLK
Lord TALBOT — *afterwards Earl of Shrewsbury*
JOHN Talbot — *his son*
Edmund MORTIMER — *Earl of March*
Sir John FALSTAFF
Sir William LUCY
Sir William GLANSDALE
Sir Thomas GARGRAVE
MAYOR of London
WOODVILLE — *Lieutenant of the Tower*
VERNON — *of the White-Rose or York faction*
BASSET — *of the Red-Rose or Lancaster faction*
LAWYER
Mortimer's KEEPERS
Papal LEGATE
Two Ambassadors
CHARLES — *Dauphin, and afterwards King of France*
REIGNIER — *Duke of Anjou, and titular King of Naples*
Duke of BURGUNDY
Duke of ALENÇON
BASTARD of Orleans
Governor of Paris
MASTER-GUNNER *of Orleans, and his* BOY
GENERAL — *of the French forces in Bordeaux*
A French SERGEANT
PORTER
An old SHEPHERD — *father to Joan la Pucelle*
MARGARET — *daughter to Reignier, afterwards married to King Henry*
COUNTESS of Auvergne
Joan la PUCELLE — *commonly called Joan of Aire*

Lords, Warders of the Tower, Heralds, Officers, Soldiers, Messengers, and Attendants

Fiends appearing to Joan la Pucelle

King Henry VI, Part 1

1.1 *Dead March. Enter the funeral of*
King Henry the Fifth, attended on by the DUKE OF
BEDFORD, *Regent of France; the* DUKE OF GLOUCESTER,
Protector; the DUKE OF EXETER, *the* EARL OF WARWICK,
the Bishop of WINCHESTER *and the* DUKE OF SOMERSET.

BEDFORD
  Hung be the heavens with black, yield day to night!
  Comets, importing change of times and states,
  Brandish your crystal tresses in the sky,
  And with them scourge the bad revolting stars,
5 That have consented unto Henry's death –
  Henry the Fifth, too famous to live long!
  England ne'er lost a king of so much worth.
GLOUCESTER England ne'er had a king until his time.
  Virtue he had, deserving to command:
10 His brandish'd sword did blind men with his beams:
  His arms spread wider than a dragon's wings:
  His sparkling eyes, replete with wrathful fire,
  More dazzled and drove back his enemies
  Than mid-day sun fierce bent against their faces.
15 What should I say? His deeds exceed all speech:
  He ne'er lift up his hand but conquered.
EXETER
  We mourn in black: why mourn we not in blood?
  Henry is dead and never shall revive.
  Upon a wooden coffin we attend;
20 And Death's dishonourable victory
  We with our stately presence glorify,
  Like captives bound to a triumphant car.
  What! shall we curse the planets of mishap
  That plotted thus our glory's overthrow?
25 Or shall we think the subtle-witted French
  Conjurers and sorcerers, that, afraid of him,
  By magic verses have contriv'd his end?
WINCHESTER
  He was a king bless'd of the King of kings.
  Unto the French the dreadful judgment-day
30 So dreadful will not be as was his sight.
  The battles of the Lord of Hosts he fought;
  The Church's prayers made him so prosperous.
GLOUCESTER
  The Church! Where is it? Had not churchmen
    pray'd,
  His thread of life had not so soon decay'd.
35 None do you like but an effeminate prince,
  Whom like a school-boy you may overawe.
WINCHESTER
  Gloucester, whate'er we like, thou art Protector,
  And lookest to command the Prince and realm.
  Thy wife is proud; she holdeth thee in awe
40 More than God or religious churchmen may.
GLOUCESTER
  Name not religion, for thou lov'st the flesh,
  And ne'er throughout the year to church thou go'st
  Except it be to pray against thy foes.
BEDFORD
  Cease, cease these jars, and rest your minds in peace;

  Let's to the altar; heralds, wait on us.   *Exit funeral.* 45
  Instead of gold, we'll offer up our arms,
  Since arms avail not; now that Henry's dead,
  Posterity, await for wretched years,
  When at their mothers' moist eyes babes shall suck, 50
  Our isle be made a nourish of salt tears,
  And none but women left to wail the dead.
  Henry the Fifth, thy ghost I invocate:
  Prosper this realm, keep it from civil broils,
  Combat with adverse planets in the heavens.
  A far more glorious star thy soul will make 55
  Than Julius Caesar or bright –

        Enter a Messenger.

MESSENGER   My honourable lords, health to you all!
  Sad tidings bring I to you out of France,
  Of loss, of slaughter, and discomfiture:
  Guienne, Champaigne, Rheims, Rouen, Orleans, 60
  Paris, Guysors, Poictiers, are all quite lost.
BEDFORD
  What say'st thou, man! Before dead Henry's corse
  Speak softly, or the loss of those great towns
  Will make him burst his lead and rise from death.
GLOUCESTER   Is Paris lost? Is Rouen yielded up? 65
  If Henry were recall'd to life again,
  These news would cause him once more yield the
    ghost.
EXETER   How were they lost? What treachery was us'd?
MESSENGER
  No treachery, but want of men and money.
  Amongst the soldiers this is muttered – 70
  That here you maintain several factions:
  And whilst a field should be dispatch'd and fought,
  You are disputing of your generals;
  One would have lingering wars, with little cost;
  Another would fly swift, but wanteth wings; 75
  A third thinks, without expense at all,
  By guileful fair words peace may be obtain'd.
  Awake, awake, English nobility!
  Let not sloth dim your honours new-begot.
  Cropp'd are the flower-de-luces in your arms; 80
  Of England's coat one half is cut away.   *Exit.*
EXETER   Were our tears wanting to this funeral,
  These tidings would call forth her flowing tides.
BEDFORD
  Me they concern; Regent I am of France:
  Give me my steeled coat: I'll fight for France. 85
  Away with these disgraceful wailing robes!
  Wounds will I lend the French instead of eyes,
  To weep their intermissive miseries.

        Enter to them another Messenger.

2 MESSENGER
  Lords, view these letters full of bad mischance.
  France is revolted from the English quite, 90
  Except some petty towns of no import:
  The Dauphin Charles is crowned king in Rheims:

The Bastard of Orleans with him is join'd:
Reignier, Duke of Anjou, doth take his part:
95 The Duke of Alençon flieth to his side.   *Exit.*
EXETER   The Dauphin crowned king! All fly to him!
O, whither shall we fly from this reproach?
GLOUCESTER
We will not fly but to our enemies' throats.
Bedford, if thou be slack, I'll fight it out.
BEDFORD
100 Gloucester, why doubt'st thou of my forwardness?
An army have I muster'd in my thoughts,
Wherewith already France is overrun.

Enter another Messenger.

3 MESSENGER   My gracious lords, to add to your laments,
Wherewith you now bedew King Henry's hearse,
105 I must inform you of a dismal fight
Betwixt the stout Lord Talbot and the French.
WINCHESTER   What! Wherein Talbot overcame, is't so?
3 MESSENGER
O no: wherein Lord Talbot was o'erthrown:
The circumstance I'll tell you more at large.
110 The tenth of August last this dreadful lord,
Retiring from the siege of Orleans,
Having scarce full six thousand in his troop,
By three and twenty thousand of the French
Was round encompassed and set upon.
115 No leisure had he to enrank his men;
He wanted pikes to set before his archers;
Instead whereof sharp stakes pluck'd out of hedges
They pitched in the ground confusedly
To keep the horsemen off from breaking in.
120 More than three hours the fight continued;
Where valiant Talbot, above human thought,
Enacted wonders with his sword and lance:
Hundreds he sent to hell, and none durst stand him;
Here, there, and everywhere, enrag'd he flew:
125 The French exclaim'd the devil was in arms;
All the whole army stood agaz'd on him.
His soldiers, spying his undaunted spirit,
'A Talbot! a Talbot!' cried out amain,
And rush'd into the bowels of the battle.
130 Here had the conquest fully been seal'd up
If Sir John Falstaff had not play'd the coward.
He, being in the vaward, plac'd behind
With purpose to relieve and follow them,
Cowardly fled, not having struck one stroke.
135 Hence grew the general wrack and massacre:
Enclosed were they with their enemies;
A base Walloon, to win the Dauphin's grace,
Thrust Talbot with a spear into the back,
Whom all France, with their chief assembled
strength,
140 Durst not presume to look once in the face.
BEDFORD   Is Talbot slain? Then I will slay myself,
For living idly here, in pomp and ease,
Whilst such a worthy leader, wanting aid,

Unto his dastard foemen is betray'd.
3 MESSENGER   O no, he lives, but is took prisoner,   145
And Lord Scales with him, and Lord Hungerford;
Most of the rest slaughter'd, or took likewise.
BEDFORD   His ransom there is none but I shall pay:
I'll hale the Dauphin headlong from his throne;
His crown shall be the ransom of my friend;   150
Four of their lords I'll change for one of ours.
Farewell, my masters; to my task will I;
Bonfires in France forthwith I am to make
To keep our great Saint George's feast withal.
Ten thousand soldiers with me I will take,   155
Whose bloody deeds shall make all Europe quake.
3 MESSENGER   So had you need; 'fore Orleans besieg'd
The English army is grown weak and faint;
The Earl of Salisbury craveth supply
And hardly keeps his men from mutiny,   160
Since they, so few, watch such a multitude.   *Exit.*
EXETER
Remember, lords, your oaths to Henry sworn,
Either to quell the Dauphin utterly,
Or bring him in obedience to your yoke.
BEDFORD   I do remember it, and here take my leave   165
To go about my preparation.   *Exit.*
GLOUCESTER   I'll to the Tower with all the haste I can
To view th'artillery and munition;
And then I will proclaim young Henry king.   *Exit.*
EXETER   To Eltham will I, where the young King is,   170
Being ordain'd his special governor;
And for his safety there I'll best devise   *Exit.*
WINCHESTER
Each hath his place and function to attend:
I am left out; for me nothing remains;
But long I will not be Jack out of office.   175
The King from Eltham I intend to steal,
And sit at chiefest stern of public weal.   *Exit.*

1.2   *Sound a flourish. Enter* CHARLES, ALENÇON
and REIGNIER, *marching with drum and soldiers.*

CHARLES   Mars his true moving, even as in the heavens
So in the earth, to this day is not known.
Late did he shine upon the English side;
Now we are victors, upon us he smiles.
What towns of any moment but we have?   5
At pleasure here we lie near Orleans,
The whiles the famish'd English, like pale ghosts,
Faintly besiege us one hour in a month.
ALENÇON
They want their porridge and their fat bull-beeves:
Either they must be dieted like mules   10
And have their provender tied to their mouths,
Or piteous they will look, like drowned mice.
REIGNIER   Let's raise the siege: why live we idly here?
Talbot is taken, whom we wont to fear;
Remaineth none but mad-brain'd Salisbury,   15
And he may well in fretting spend his gall –

Nor men nor money hath he to make war.
CHARLES   Sound, sound alarum; we will rush on them.
Now for the honour of the forlorn French!
20   Him I forgive my death that killeth me
When he sees me go back one foot or fly.   *Exeunt.*

Here alarum; they are beaten back by the English
with great loss.

Enter CHARLES, ALENÇON *and* REIGNIER.

CHARLES   Who ever saw the like? What men have I!
Dogs! cowards! dastards! I would ne'er have fled
But that they left me 'midst my enemies.
25   REIGNIER   Salisbury is a desperate homicide;
He fighteth as one weary of his life:
The other lords, like lions wanting food,
Do rush upon us as their hungry prey.
ALENÇON   Froissart, a countryman of ours, records
30   England all Olivers and Rolands bred
During the time Edward the Third did reign.
More truly now may this be verified;
For none but Samsons and Goliases
It sendeth forth to skirmish. One to ten!
35   Lean raw-bon'd rascals! Who would e'er suppose
They had such courage and audacity?
CHARLES
Let's leave this town; for they are hare-brain'd slaves,
And hunger will enforce them be more eager:
Of old I know them; rather with their teeth
40   The walls they'll tear down than forsake the siege.
REIGNIER   I think by some odd gimmers or device
Their arms are set, like clocks, still to strike on;
Else ne'er could they hold out so as they do:
By my consent, we'll even let them alone.
45   ALENÇON   Be it so.

Enter the BASTARD OF ORLEANS.

BASTARD
Where's the Prince Dauphin? I have news for him.
CHARLES   Bastard of Orleans, thrice welcome to us.
BASTARD
Methinks your looks are sad, your cheer appall'd.
Hath the late overthrow wrought this offence?
50   Be not dismay'd, for succour is at hand:
A holy maid hither with me I bring,
Which, by a vision sent to her from heaven,
Ordained is to raise this tedious siege
And drive the English forth the bounds of France.
55   The spirit of deep prophecy she hath,
Exceeding the nine sibyls of old Rome:
What's past and what's to come she can descry.
Speak, shall I call her in? Believe my words,
For they are certain and unfallible.
CHARLES   Go call her in.   *Exit Bastard.*
60   But first, to try her skill,
Reignier, stand thou as Dauphin in my place;
Question her proudly; let thy looks be stern;
By this means shall we sound what skill she hath.

Enter the BASTARD OF ORLEANS *with* JOAN LA PUCELLE.

REIGNIER
Fair maid, is't thou wilt do these wondrous feats?
PUCELLE   Reignier, is't thou that thinkest to beguile me?   65
Where is the Dauphin? Come, come from behind;
I know thee well, though never seen before.
Be not amaz'd, there's nothing hid from me.
In private will I talk with thee apart:
Stand back, you lords, and give us leave awhile.   70
REIGNIER   She takes upon her bravely at first dash.
PUCELLE
Dauphin, I am by birth a shepherd's daughter,
My wit untrain'd in any kind of art.
Heaven and our Lady gracious hath it pleas'd
To shine on my contemptible estate.   75
Lo, whilst I waited on my tender lambs,
And to sun's parching heat display'd my cheeks,
God's Mother deigned to appear to me,
And in a vision full of majesty
Will'd me to leave my base vocation   80
And free my country from calamity:
Her aid she promis'd, and assur'd success.
In complete glory she reveal'd herself;
And, whereas I was black and swart before,
With those clear rays which she infus'd on me   85
That beauty am I blest with you may see.
Ask me what question thou canst possible,
And I will answer unpremeditated:
My courage try by combat, if thou dar'st,
And thou shalt find that I exceed my sex.   90
Resolve on this; thou shalt be fortunate
If thou receive me for thy warlike mate.
CHARLES
Thou hast astonish'd me with thy high terms.
Only this proof I'll of thy valour make –
In single combat thou shalt buckle with me;   95
And if thou vanquishest, thy words are true;
Otherwise I renounce all confidence.
PUCELLE   I am prepar'd: here is my keen-edg'd sword,
Deck'd with five flower-de-luces on each side,
The which at Touraine, in Saint Katherine's Church,   100
Out of a great deal of old iron I chose forth.
CHARLES
Then come, o' God's name; I fear no woman.
PUCELLE   And while I live I'll ne'er fly from a man.
[*Here they fight, and Joan la Pucelle overcomes.*]
CHARLES   Stay, stay thy hands; thou art an Amazon,
And fightest with the sword of Deborah.   105
PUCELLE
Christ's Mother helps me, else I were too weak.
CHARLES
Whoe'er helps thee, 'tis thou that must help me.
Impatiently I burn with thy desire;
My heart and hands thou hast at once subdu'd.
Excellent Pucelle, if thy name be so,   110
Let me thy servant and not sovereign be:

'Tis the French Dauphin sueth to thee thus.
PUCELLE   I must not yield to any rites of love,
 For my profession's sacred from above:
 When I have chased all thy foes from hence,   115
 Then will I think upon a recompense.
CHARLES
 Meantime look gracious on thy prostrate thrall.
REIGNIER   My lord, methinks, is very long in talk.
ALENÇON
 Doubtless he shrives this woman to her smock;
 Else ne'er could he so long protract his speech.   120
REIGNIER
 Shall we disturb him, since he keeps no mean?
ALENÇON
 He may mean more than we poor men do know;
 These women are shrewd tempters with their
  tongues.
REIGNIER
 My lord, where are you? What devise you on?
 Shall we give over Orleans, or no?   125
PUCELLE   Why, no, I say: distrustful recreants!
 Fight till the last gasp; I will be your guard.
CHARLES   What she says I'll confirm; we'll fight it out.
PUCELLE   Assign'd am I to be the English scourge.
 This night the siege assuredly I'll raise: 130
 Expect Saint Martin's summer, halcyon's days,
 Since I have entered into these wars.
 Glory is like a circle in the water,
 Which never ceaseth to enlarge itself
 Till by broad spreading it disperse to nought.   135
 With Henry's death the English circle ends;
 Dispersed are the glories it included.
 Now am I like that proud insulting ship
 Which Caesar and his fortune bare at once.
CHARLES   Was Mahomet inspired with a dove?   140
 Thou with an eagle art inspired then.
 Helen, the mother of great Constantine,
 Nor yet Saint Philip's daughters, were like thee.
 Bright star of Venus, fall'n down on the earth,
 How may I reverent worship thee enough?   145
ALENÇON   Leave off delays, and let us raise the siege.
REIGNIER
 Woman, do what thou canst to save our honours;
 Drive them from Orleans, and be immortaliz'd.
CHARLES   Presently we'll try: come, let's away about it:
 No prophet will I trust if she prove false.   *Exeunt.*   150

1.3 *Enter the* DUKE OF GLOUCESTER, *with his*
    Serving-men, *in blue coats.*

GLOUCESTER   I am come to survey the Tower this day;
 Since Henry's death, I fear, there is conveyance.
 Where be these warders that they wait not here?
 Open the gates; 'tis Gloucester that calls.
1 WARDER [*within*]
 Who's there that knocketh so imperiously?
1 SERVANT   It is the noble Duke of Gloucester.

2 WARDER [*within*]
 Whoe'er he be, you may not be let in.
1 SERVANT   Villains, answer you so the Lord Protector?
1 WARDER [*within*]
 The Lord protect him! so we answer him:
 We do no otherwise than we are will'd.   10
GLOUCESTER
 Who willed you, or whose will stands but mine?
 There's none Protector of the realm but I.
 Break up the gates, I'll be your warrantize.
 Shall I be flouted thus by dunghill grooms?
 [*Gloucester's men rush at the Tower gates, and*
 Woodville the Lieutenant speaks within.]
WOODVILLE [*within*]
 What noise is this? What traitors have we here?   15
GLOUCESTER   Lieutenant, is it you whose voice I hear?
 Open the gates; here's Gloucester that would enter.
WOODVILLE [*within*]
 Have patience, noble Duke; I may not open;
 The Cardinal of Winchester forbids:
 From him I have express commandment   20
 That thou nor none of thine shall be let in.
GLOUCESTER
 Faint-hearted Woodville, prizest him 'fore me?
 Arrogant Winchester, that haughty prelate
 Whom Henry, our late sovereign, ne'er could brook!
 Thou art no friend to God, or to the King.   25
 Open the gates, or I'll shut thee out shortly.
SERVING-MEN   Open the gates unto the Lord Protector;
 We'll burst them open, if that you come not quickly.

Enter to the Protector at the Tower gates WINCHESTER
and his men in tawny coats.

WINCHESTER
 How now, ambitious Humphrey! What means this?
GLOUCESTER
 Peel'd priest, dost thou command me be shut out?   30
WINCHESTER   I do, thou most usurping proditor,
 And not Protector, of the King or realm.
GLOUCESTER   Stand back, thou manifest conspirator,
 Thou that contrived'st to murder our dead lord;
 Thou that giv'st whores indulgences to sin: 35
 I'll canvas thee in thy broad cardinal's hat,
 If thou proceed in this thy insolence.
WINCHESTER
 Nay, stand thou back; I will not budge a foot:
 This be Damascus, be thou cursed Cain,
 To slay thy brother Abel, if thou wilt.   40
GLOUCESTER
 I will not slay thee, but I'll drive thee back.
 Thy scarlet robes, as a child's bearing-cloth,
 I'll use to carry thee out of this place.
WINCHESTER
 Do what thou dar'st, I beard thee to thy face.
GLOUCESTER
 What! am I dar'd and bearded to my face?   45
 Draw, men, for all this privileged place –

Blue coats to tawny. Priest, beware your beard;
I mean to tug it, and to cuff you soundly.
Under my feet I'll stamp thy cardinal's hat;
In spite of Pope or dignities of church,
Here by the cheeks I'll drag thee up and down.

WINCHESTER
Gloucester, thou'lt answer this before the Pope.

GLOUCESTER　Winchester goose! I cry, 'A rope! a rope!'
Now beat them hence; why do you let them stay?
Thee I'll chase hence, thou wolf in sheep's array.
Out, tawny coats! Out, scarlet hypocrite!

Here GLOUCESTER's *men beat out the Cardinal's men,*
and enter in the hurly-burly the Mayor of London
and his officers.

MAYOR
Fie, lords! that you, being supreme magistrates,
Thus contumeliously should break the peace!

GLOUCESTER
Peace, Mayor! thou know'st little of my wrongs:
Here's Beaufort, that regards nor God nor King,
Hath here distrain'd the Tower to his use.

WINCHESTER　Here's Gloucester, a foe to citizens,
One that still motions war, and never peace,
O'ercharging your free purses with large fines;
That seeks to overthrow religion,
Because he is Protector of the realm,
And would have armour here out of the Tower,
To crown himself King and suppress the Prince.

GLOUCESTER
I will not answer thee with words, but blows.
[*Here they skirmish again.*]

MAYOR　Nought rests for me in this tumultous strife
But to make open proclamation.
Come, officer, as loud as e'er thou canst. [*Cry.*]

OFFICER　All manner of men, assembled here in arms
this day, against God's peace and the King's, we
charge and command you, in his Highness' name, to
repair to your several dwelling-places; and not to wear,
handle, or use any sword, weapon, or dagger,
henceforward, upon pain of death.

GLOUCESTER　Cardinal, I'll be no breaker of the law;
But we shall meet and break our minds at large.

WINCHESTER
Gloucester, we will meet, to thy cost, be sure;
Thy heart-blood I will have for this day's work.

MAYOR　I'll call for clubs if you will not away.
This Cardinal's more haughty than the devil.

GLOUCESTER
Mayor, farewell: thou dost but what thou may'st.

WINCHESTER　Abominable Gloucester, guard thy head,
For I intend to have it ere't be long.
Exeunt, severally, Gloucester *and* Winchester,
with their serving-men.

MAYOR　See the coast clear'd, and then we will depart.
Good God, these nobles should such stomachs bear!

I myself fight not once in forty year.　　　*Exeunt.*　90

1.4　*Enter the* Master-Gunner *of Orleans and his* Boy.

MASTER-GUNNER
Sirrah, thou know'st how Orleans is besieg'd,
And how the English have the suburbs won.

BOY　Father, I know; and oft have shot at them,
Howe'er unfortunate I miss'd my aim.

MASTER-GUNNER
But now thou shalt not. Be thou rul'd by me:　5
Chief master-gunner am I of this town;
Something I must do to procure me grace.
The Prince' espials have informed me
How the English, in the suburbs close intrench'd,
Wont, through a secret grate of iron bars　10
In yonder tower, to overpeer the city,
And thence discover how with most advantage
They may vex us with shot or with assault.
To intercept this inconvenience,
A piece of ordnance 'gainst it I have plac'd　15
And even these three days watch'd if I could see
　them.
Now do thou watch, for I can stay no longer.
If thou spy'st any, run and bring me word;
And thou shalt find me at the Governor's.　*Exit.*

BOY　Father, I warrant you; take you no care;　20
I'll never trouble you if I may spy them.　*Exit.*

Enter SALISBURY *and* TALBOT *on the turrets, with*
SIR WILLIAM GLANSDALE, SIR THOMAS GARGRAVE
and others.

SALISBURY　Talbot, my life, my joy, again return'd!
How wert thou handled, being prisoner?
Or by what means gots thou to be releas'd?
Discourse, I prithee, on this turret's top.　25

TALBOT　The Earl of Bedford had a prisoner,
Call'd the brave Lord Ponton de Santrailles;
For him I was exchang'd and ransomed.
But with a baser man of arms by far
Once in contempt they would have barter'd me:　30
Which I disdaining scorn'd, and craved death
Rather than I would be so vile-esteem'd.
In fine, redeem'd I was as I desir'd.
But O! the treacherous Falstaff wounds my heart,
Whom with my bare fists I would execute　35
If I now had him brought into my power.

SALISBURY
Yet tell'st thou not how thou wert entertain'd.

TALBOT
With scoffs and scorns and contumelious taunts.
In open market-place produc'd they me
To be a public spectacle to all;　40
Here, said they, is the Terror of the French,
The scarecrow that affrights our children so.
Then broke I from the officers that led me,
And with my nails digg'd stones out of the ground

To hurl at the beholders of my shame.
My grisly countenance made others fly;
None durst come near for fear of sudden death.
In iron walls they deem'd me not secure;
So great fear of my name 'mongst them were spread
That they suppos'd I could rend bars of steel
And spurn in pieces posts of adamant.
Wherefore a guard of chosen shot I had,
That walk'd about me every minute-while;
And if I did but stir out of my bed,
Ready they were to shoot me to the heart.

Enter the Boy *with a linstock, and exit.*

SALISBURY   I grieve to hear what torments you endur'd;
But we will be reveng'd sufficiently.
Now it is supper-time in Orleans:
Here, through this grate, I count each one
And view the Frenchmen how they fortify:
Let us look in; the sight will much delight thee.
Sir Thomas Gargrave, and Sir William Glansdale,
Let me have your express opinions
Where is best place to make our battery next.
GARGRAVE
I think at the North Gate, for there stands lords.
GLANSDALE   And I here, at the bulwark of the bridge.
TALBOT   For aught I see, this city must be famish'd,
Or with light skirmishes enfeebled.
[*Here they shoot, and Salisbury and Gargrave fall down.*]
SALISBURY
O Lord, have mercy on us, wretched sinners!
GARGRAVE   O Lord, have mercy on me, woeful man!
TALBOT
What chance is this that suddenly hath cross'd us?
Speak, Salisbury; at least, if thou canst speak:
How far'st thou, mirror of all martial men?
One of thy eyes and thy cheek's side struck off!
Accursed tower! accursed fatal hand
That hath contriv'd this woeful tragedy!
In thirteen battles Salisbury o'ercame;
Henry the Fifth he first train'd to the wars;
Whilst any trump did sound, or drum struck up,
His sword did ne'er leave striking in the field.
Yet liv'st thou, Salisbury? Though thy speech doth
   fail,
One eye thou hast to look to heaven for grace;
The sun with one eye vieweth all the world.
Heaven, be thou gracious to none alive,
If Salisbury want mercy at thy hands!
Sir Thomas Gargrave, hast thou any life?
Speak unto Talbot; nay, look up to him.
Bear hence his body; I'll help to bury it.
Exeunt some with the body of Gargrave.
Salisbury, cheer thy spirit with this comfort,
Thou shalt not die whiles –
He beckons with his hand and smiles on me,
As who should say, 'When I am dead and gone,

Remember to avenge me on the French.'
Plantagenet, I will; and, Nero-like,
Play on the lute, beholding the towns burn.
Wretched shall France be only in my name.   95
[*Here an alarum, and it thunders and lightens.*]
What stir is this? What tumult's in the heavens?
Whence cometh this alarum, and the noise?

Enter a Messenger.

MESSENGER
My lord, my lord, the French have gather'd head:
The Dauphin, with one Joan de Pucelle join'd,   100
A holy prophetess new risen up,
Is come with a great power to raise the siege.
[*Here Salisbury lifts himself up, and groans.*]
TALBOT   Hear, hear how dying Salisbury doth groan;
It irks his heart he cannot be reveng'd.
Frenchmen, I'll be a Salisbury to you.   105
Puzzel or Pucelle, dolphin or dogfish,
Your hearts I'll stamp out with my horse's heels
And make a quagmire of your mingled brains.
Convey we Salisbury into his tent,
And then try what these dastard Frenchmen dare.   110
Alarum. Exeunt with the body of Salisbury.

1.5 *Here an alarum again, and* TALBOT *pursueth the*
DAUPHIN, *and driveth him: then enter* JOAN LA PUCELLE,
driving Englishmen before her, and exit after them.
Then enter TALBOT.

TALBOT
Where is my strength, my valour, and my force?
Our English troops retire, I cannot stay them;
A woman clad in armour chaseth them.

Enter LA PUCELLE.

Here, here she comes. I'll have a bout with thee;
Devil or devil's dam, I'll conjure thee: 5
Blood will I draw on thee, thou art a witch,
And straightway give thy soul to him thou serv'st.
PUCELLE
Come, come, 'tis only I that must disgrace thee.
[*Here they fight.*]
TALBOT   Heavens, can you suffer hell so to prevail?
My breast I'll burst with straining of my courage,   10
And from my shoulders crack my arms asunder,
But I will chastise this high-minded strumpet.
[*They fight again.*]
PUCELLE   Talbot, farewell; thy hour is not yet come:
I must go victual Orleans forthwith.
[*A short alarum: then enter the town with soldiers.*]
O'ertake me if thou canst: I scorn thy strength.   15
Go, go, cheer up thy hunger-starved men;
Help Salisbury to make his testament:
This day is ours, as many more shall be.   *Exit.*
TALBOT   My thoughts are whirled like a potter's wheel;
I know not where I am, nor what I do: 20

A witch by fear, not force, like Hannibal,
Drives back our troops and conquers as she lists:
So bees with smoke, and doves with noisome stench,
Are from their hives and houses driven away.
25 They call'd us, for our fierceness, English dogs;
Now like to whelps we crying run away.
[*A short alarum.*]

Hark, countrymen! either renew the fight,
Or tear the lions out of England's coat;
Renounce your style, give sheep in lions' stead:
30 Sheep run not half so treacherous from the wolf,
Or horse or oxen from the leopard,
As you fly from your oft-subdued slaves.
[*Alarum. Here another skirmish.*]

It will not be: retire into your trenches:
You all consented unto Salisbury's death,
35 For none would strike a stroke in his revenge.
Pucelle is enter'd into Orleans
In spite of us or aught that we could do.
O, would I were to die with Salisbury!
The shame hereof will make me hide my head.
Exit Talbot. Alarum; retreat.

1.6 *Flourish. Enter on the walls* LA PUCELLE,
CHARLES, REIGNIER, ALENÇON *and soldiers.*

PUCELLE Advance our waving colours on the walls;
Rescu'd is Orleans from the English.
Thus Joan de Pucelle hath perform'd her word.
CHARLES Divinest creature, Astraea's daughter,
5 How shall I honour thee for this success?
Thy promises are like Adonis' gardens,
That one day bloom'd, and fruitful were the next.
France, triumph in thy glorious prophetess!
Recover'd is the town of Orleans:
10 More blessed hap did ne'er befall our state.
REIGNIER
Why ring not bells aloud throughout the town?
Dauphin, command the citizens make bonfires
And feast and banquet in the open streets
To celebrate the joy that God hath given us.
15 ALENÇON All France will be replete with mirth and joy
When they shall hear how we have play'd the men.
CHARLES 'Tis Joan, not we, by whom the day is won;
For which I will divide my crown with her,
And all the priests and friars in my realm
20 Shall in procession sing her endless praise.
A statelier pyramis to her I'll rear
Than Rhodope's of Memphis ever was;
In memory of her, when she is dead,
Her ashes, in an urn more precious
25 Than the rich jewel-coffer of Darius,
Transported shall be at high festivals
Before the kings and queens of France.
No longer on Saint Denis will we cry,
But Joan de Pucelle shall be France's saint.
30 Come in, and let us banquet royally
After this golden day of victory. *Flourish. Exeunt.*

2.1 *Enter, on the walls, a French* Sergeant
of a Band, with two Sentinels.

SERGEANT Sirs, take your places and be vigilant;
If any noise or soldier you perceive
Near to the walls, by some apparent sign
Let us have knowledge at the court of guard.
1 SENTINEL Sergeant, you shall. *Exit Sergeant.*
Thus are poor servitors, 5
When others sleep upon their quiet beds,
Constrain'd to watch in darkness, rain, and cold.

Enter TALBOT, BEDFORD, BURGUNDY *and forces,*
with scaling-ladders.

TALBOT Lord Regent, and redoubted Burgundy,
By whose approach the regions of Artois,
Walloon, and Picardy, are friends to us, 10
This happy night the Frenchmen are secure,
Having all day carous'd and banqueted,
Embrace we then this opportunity,
As fitting best to quittance their deceit,
Contriv'd by art and baleful sorcery. 15
BEDFORD
Coward of France, how much he wrongs his fame,
Despairing of his own arm's fortitude,
To join with witches and the help of hell!
BURGUNDY Traitors have never other company.
But what's that Pucelle whom they term so pure? 20
TALBOT A maid, they say.
BEDFORD A maid! and be so martial!
BURGUNDY
Pray God she prove not masculine ere long,
If underneath the standard of the French
She carry armour as she hath begun.
TALBOT
Well, let them practise and converse with spirits; 25
God is our fortress, in whose conquering name
Let us resolve to scale their flinty bulwarks.
BEDFORD Ascend, brave Talbot; we will follow thee.
TALBOT Not all together; better far, I guess,
That we do make our entrance several ways, 30
That if it chance the one of us do fall,
The other yet may rise against their force.
BEDFORD Agreed; I'll to yon corner.
BURGUNDY And I to this.
TALBOT
And here will Talbot mount, or make his grave.
Now, Salisbury, for thee and for the right 35
Of English Henry, shall this night appear
How much in duty I am bound to both.
1, 2 SENTINEL Arm! arm! the enemy doth make assault.
[*Cry,* 'Saint George' 'A Talbot!']
The English scale the walls, and exeunt.

The French leap over the walls in their shirts. Enter,
several ways, the BASTARD OF ORLEANS, ALENÇON,
REIGNIER, *half ready and half unready.*

ALENÇON How now, my lords? What, all unready so?

BASTARD   Unready! Ay, and glad we 'scap'd so well.

REIGNIER
'Twas time, I trow, to wake and leave our beds,
Hearing alarums at our chamber-doors.

ALENÇON   Of all exploits since first I follow'd arms
Ne'er heard I of a warlike enterprise
More venturous or desperate than this.

BASTARD   I think this Talbot be a fiend of hell.

REIGNIER   If not of hell, the heavens, sure, favour him.

ALENÇON
Here cometh Charles: I marvel how he sped.

Enter CHARLES *and* LA PUCELLE.

BASTARD   Tut! holy Joan was his defensive guard.

CHARLES   Is this thy cunning, thou deceitful dame?
Didst thou at first, to flatter us withal,
Make us partakers of a little gain,
That now our loss might be ten times so much?

PUCELLE
Wherefore is Charles impatient with his friend?
At all times will you have my power alike?
Sleeping or waking, must I still prevail,
Or will you blame and lay the fault on me?
Improvident soldiers! had your watch been good
This sudden mischief never could have fallen.

CHARLES   Duke of Alençon, this was your default,
That, being captain of the watch to-night,
Did look no better to that weighty charge.

ALENÇON   Had all your quarters been as safely kept
As that whereof I had the government,
We had not been thus shamefully surpris'd.

BASTARD   Mine was secure.

REIGNIER   And so was mine, my lord.

CHARLES   And for myself, most part of all this night,
Within her quarter and mine own precinct
I was employ'd in passing to and fro
About relieving of the sentinels.
Then how or which way should they first break in?

PUCELLE   Question, my lords, no further of the case,
How or which way; 'tis sure they found some place
But weakly guarded, where the breach was made.
And now there rests no other shift but this:
To gather our soldiers, scatter'd and dispers'd,
And lay new platforms to endamage them.

Alarum. Enter an English Soldier, *crying,* 'A Talbot!
A Talbot!' *They fly, leaving their clothes behind.*

SOLDIER   I'll be so bold to take what they have left.
The cry of 'Talbot' serves me for a sword;
For I have loaden me with many spoils,
Using no other weapon but his name.   *Exit.*

2.2   *Enter* TALBOT, BEDFORD, BURGUNDY, *a*
Captain *and others.*

BEDFORD   The day begins to break, and night is fled,
Whose pitchy mantle over-veil'd the earth.

Here sound retreat and cease our hot pursuit.
                    [*Retreat sounded.*]

TALBOT   Bring forth the body of old Salisbury,
And here advance it in the market-place,
The middle centre of this cursed town.

Dead march. Enter with the body of Salisbury.

Now have I paid my vow unto his soul;
For every drop of blood was drawn from him
There hath at least five Frenchmen died to-night.
And that hereafter ages may behold
What ruin happen'd in revenge of him,
Within their chiefest temple I'll erect
A tomb, wherein his corpse shall be interr'd;
Upon the which, that every one may read,
Shall be engrav'd the sack of Orleans,
The treacherous manner of his mournful death,
And what a terror he had been to France.
                    Exit funeral.

But, lords, in all our bloody massacre,
I muse we met not with the Dauphin's Grace,
His new-come champion, virtuous Joan of Aire,
Nor any of his false confederates.

BEDFORD
'Tis thought, Lord Talbot, when the fight began,
Rous'd on the sudden from their drowsy beds,
They did amongst the troops of armed men
Leap o'er the walls for refuge in the field.

BURGUNDY   Myself, as far as I could well discern
For smoke and dusky vapours of the night,
Am sure I scar'd the Dauphin and his trull,
When arm in arm they both came swiftly running,
Like to a pair of loving turtle-doves
That could not live asunder day or night.
After that things are set in order here,
We'll follow them with all the power we have.

Enter a Messenger.

MESSENGER
All hail, my lords! Which of this princely train
Call ye the warlike Talbot, for his acts
So much applauded through the realm of France?

TALBOT
Here is the Talbot: who would speak with him?

MESSENGER   The virtuous lady, Countess of Auvergne,
With modesty admiring thy renown,
By me entreats, great lord, thou would'st vouchsafe
To visit her poor castle where she lies,
That she may boast she hath beheld the man
Whose glory fills the world with loud report.

BURGUNDY   Is it even so? Nay, then I see our wars
Will turn unto a peaceful comic sport,
When ladies crave to be encounter'd with.
You may not, my lord, despise her gentle suit.

TALBOT   Ne'er trust me then; for when a world of men
Could not prevail with all their oratory,
Yet hath a woman's kindness over-rul'd;

And therefore tell her I return great thanks
And in submission will attend on her.
Will not your honours bear me company?

BEDFORD   No, truly, it is more than manners will;
55   And I have heard it said unbidden guests
Are often welcomest when they are gone.

TALBOT   Well then, alone, since there's no remedy,
I mean to prove this lady's courtesy.
Come hither, Captain. [*Whispers.*]
                              You perceive my mind?

60   CAPTAIN   I do, my Lord, and mean accordingly.
                                                        Exeunt.

2.3   *Enter the* COUNTESS *and her* Porter.

COUNTESS   Porter, remember what I gave in charge;
And when you have done so, bring the keys to me.

PORTER   Madam, I will.   *Exit.*

COUNTESS   The plot is laid; if all things fall out right,
5   I shall as famous be by this exploit,
As Scythian Tomyris by Cyrus' death.
Great is the rumour of this dreadful knight,
And his achievements of no less account.
Fain would mine eyes be witness with mine ears
10   To give their censure of these rare reports.

Enter Messenger *and* TALBOT.

MESSENGER   According as your ladyship desir'd,
By message crav'd, so is Lord Talbot come.

COUNTESS   And he is welcome. What! is this the man?

MESSENGER   Madam, it is.

COUNTESS   Is this the Scourge of France?
15   Is this the Talbot, so much fear'd abroad
That with his name the mothers still their babes?
I see report is fabulous and false:
I thought I should have seen some Hercules,
A second Hector, for his grim aspect
20   And large proportion of his strong-knit limbs.
Alas, this is a child, a silly dwarf!
It cannot be this weak and writhled shrimp
Should strike such terror to his enemies.

TALBOT   Madam, I have been bold to trouble you;
25   But since your ladyship is not at leisure,
I'll sort some other time to visit you. [*going*]

COUNTESS
What means he now? Go ask him whither he goes.

MESSENGER   Stay, my Lord Talbot, for my lady craves
To know the cause of your abrupt departure.

30   TALBOT   Marry, for that she's in a wrong belief,
I go to certify her Talbot's here.

Enter Porter *with keys.*

COUNTESS   If thou be he, then art thou prisoner.

TALBOT   Prisoner! To whom?

COUNTESS   To me, blood-thirsty lord;
And for that cause I train'd thee to my house.
35   Long time thy shadow hath been thrall to me,

For in my gallery thy picture hangs;
But now the substance shall endure the like,
And I will chain these legs and arms of thine,
That hast by tyranny these many years
40   Wasted our country, slain our citizens,
And sent our sons and husbands captivate.

TALBOT   Ha, ha, ha!

COUNTESS
Laughest thou, wretch? Thy mirth shall turn to
   moan.

TALBOT   I laugh to see your ladyship so fond
45   To think that you have aught but Talbot's shadow
Whereon to practise your severity.

COUNTESS   Why, art not thou the man?

TALBOT   I am indeed.

COUNTESS   Then have I substance too.

TALBOT   No, no, I am but shadow of myself:
50   You are deceiv'd, my substance is not here;
For what you see is but the smallest part
And least proportion of humanity:
I tell you, madam, were the whole frame here,
It is of such a spacious lofty pitch
55   Your roof were not sufficient to contain't.

COUNTESS   This is a riddling merchant for the nonce;
He will be here, and yet he is not here:
How can these contrarieties agree?

TALBOT   That will I show you presently.
   [*Winds his horn; drums strike up; a peal of ordnance.*]

Enter soldiers.

How say you, madam? Are you now persuaded
60   That Talbot is but shadow of himself?
These are his substance, sinews, arms, and strength,
With which he yoketh your rebellious necks,
Razeth your cities, and subverts your towns,
And in a moment makes them desolate.
65
COUNTESS   Victorious Talbot, pardon my abuse;
I find thou art no less than fame hath bruited,
And more than may be gather'd by thy shape.
Let my presumption not provoke thy wrath,
For I am sorry that with reverence
70   I did not entertain thee as thou art.

TALBOT   Be not dismay'd, fair lady, nor misconster
The mind of Talbot as you did mistake
The outward composition of his body.
What you have done hath not offended me;
75   Nor other satisfaction do I crave
But only, with your patience, that we may
Taste of your wine and see what cates you have,
For soldiers' stomachs always serve them well.

COUNTESS   With all my heart, and think me honoured
80   To feast so great a warrior in my house.   *Exeunt.*

2.4   *Enter the Earls of* SOMERSET, SUFFOLK *and*
             WARWICK; RICHARD PLANTAGENET, VERNON
                         and another Lawyer.

PLANTAGENET
   Great lords and gentlemen, what means this silence?
   Dare no man answer in a case of truth?
SUFFOLK   Within the Temple Hall we were too loud;
   The garden here is more convenient.
PLANTAGENET
   Then say at once if I maintain'd the truth;
   Or else was wrangling Somerset in th'error?
SUFFOLK   Faith, I have been a truant in the law
   And never yet could frame my will to it;
   And therefore frame the law unto my will.
SOMERSET
   Judge you, my Lord of Warwick, then, between us.
WARWICK
   Between two hawks, which flies the higher pitch;
   Between two dogs, which hath the deeper mouth;
   Between two blades, which bears the better temper;
   Between two horses, which doth bear him best;
   Between two girls, which hath the merriest eye –
   I have perhaps some shallow spirit of judgment;
   But in these nice sharp quillets of the law,
   Good faith, I am no wiser than a daw.
PLANTAGENET
   Tut, tut, here is a mannerly forbearance:
   The truth appears so naked on my side
   That any purblind eye may find it out.
SOMERSET   And on my side it is so well apparell'd,
   So clear, so shining, and so evident,
   That it will glimmer through a blind man's eye.
PLANTAGENET
   Since you are tongue-tied and so loath to speak,
   In dumb significants proclaim your thoughts:
   Let him that is a true-born gentleman
   And stands upon the honour of his birth,
   If he suppose that I have pleaded truth,
   From off this brier pluck a white rose with me.
SOMERSET   Let him that is no coward nor no flatterer,
   But dare maintain the party of the truth,
   Pluck a red rose from off this thorn with me.
WARWICK   I love no colours; and without all colour
   Of base insinuating flattery
   I pluck this white rose with Plantagenet.
SUFFOLK   I pluck this red rose with young Somerset,
   And say withal I think he held the right.
VERNON   Stay, lords and gentlemen, and pluck no more
   Till you conclude that he upon whose side
   The fewest roses from the tree are cropp'd
   Shall yield the other in the right opinion.
SOMERSET   Good Master Vernon, it is well objected:
   If I have fewest, I subscribe in silence.
PLANTAGENET   And I.
VERNON   Then for the truth and plainness of the case,
   I pluck this pale and maiden blossom here,
   Giving my verdict on the white rose side.
SOMERSET   Prick not your finger as you pluck it off,
   Lest, bleeding, you do paint the white rose red,
   And fall on my side so against your will.

VERNON   If I, my lord, for my opinion bleed,
   Opinion shall be surgeon to my hurt
   And keep me on the side where still I am.
SOMERSET   Well, well, come on: who else?   55
LAWYER   Unless my study and my books be false,
   [*to Somerset*]
   The argument you held was wrong in law;
   In sign whereof I pluck a white rose too.
PLANTAGENET
   Now, Somerset, where is your argument?
SOMERSET   Here in my scabbard, meditating that   60
   Shall dye your white rose in a bloody red.
PLANTAGENET
   Meantime your cheeks do counterfeit our roses;
   For pale they look with fear, as witnessing
   The truth on our side.
SOMERSET   No, Plantagenet,
   'Tis not for fear, but anger that thy cheeks   65
   Blush for pure shame to counterfeit our roses,
   And yet thy tongue will not confess thy error.
PLANTAGENET   Hath not thy rose a canker, Somerset?
SOMERSET   Hath not thy rose a thorn, Plantagenet?
PLANTAGENET
   Ay, sharp and piercing, to maintain his truth;   70
   Whiles thy consuming canker eats his falsehood.
SOMERSET
   Well, I'll find friends to wear my bleeding roses,
   That shall maintain what I have said is true,
   Where false Plantagenet dare not be seen.
PLANTAGENET
   Now, by this maiden blossom in my hand,   75
   I scorn thee and thy fashion, peevish boy.
SUFFOLK   Turn not thy scorns this way, Plantagenet.
PLANTAGENET
   Proud Pole, I will, and scorn both him and thee.
SUFFOLK   I'll turn my part thereof into thy throat.
SOMERSET   Away, away, good William de la Pole!   80
   We grace the yeoman by conversing with him.
WARWICK
   Now, by God's will, thou wrong'st him, Somerset;
   His grandfather was Lionel Duke of Clarence,
   Third son to the third Edward, King of England:
   Spring crestless yeomen from so deep a root?   85
PLANTAGENET   He bears him on the place's privilege,
   Or durst not for his craven heart say thus.
SOMERSET
   By Him that made me, I'll maintain my words
   On any plot of ground in Christendom.
   Was not thy father, Richard Earl of Cambridge,   90
   For treason headed in our late king's days?
   And by his treason stand'st not thou attainted,
   Corrupted, and exempt from ancient gentry?
   His trespass yet lives guilty in thy blood;
   And, till thou be restor'd, thou art a yeoman.   95
PLANTAGENET   My father was attached, not attainted,
   Condemn'd to die for treason, but no traitor;
   And that I'll prove on better men than Somerset,

Were growing time once ripen'd to my will.
For your partaker Pole, and you yourself,
100   I'll note you in my book of memory,
To scourge you for this apprehension:
Look to it well, and say you are well warn'd.
SOMERSET   Ah, thou shalt find us ready for thee still;
And know us by these colours for thy foes,
105   For these my friends in spite of thee shall wear.
PLANTAGENET
And, by my soul, this pale and angry rose,
As cognizance of my blood-drinking hate,
Will I for ever, and my faction, wear,
Until it wither with me to my grave,
110   Or flourish to the height of my degree.
SUFFOLK
Go forward, and be chok'd with thy ambition!
And so farewell until I meet thee next.   *Exit.*
SOMERSET
Have with thee, Pole. Farewell, ambitious Richard.
                                       Exit.
PLANTAGENET
How I am brav'd and must perforce endure it!
115   WARWICK   This blot that they object against your house
Shall be wip'd out in the next Parliament,
Call'd for the truce of Winchester and Gloucester;
And if thou be not then created York,
I will not live to be accounted Warwick.
120   Meantime, in signal of my love to thee,
Against proud Somerset and William Pole,
Will I upon thy party wear this rose.
And here I prophesy: this brawl to-day,
Grown to this faction in the Temple Garden,
125   Shall send between the Red Rose and the White
A thousand souls to death and deadly night.
PLANTAGENET
Good Master Vernon, I am bound to you,
That you on my behalf would pluck a flower.
VERNON   In your behalf still will I wear the same.
130   LAWYER   And so will I.
PLANTAGENET   Thanks, gentlemen.
Come, let us four to dinner. I dare say
This quarrel will drink blood another day.   *Exeunt.*

2.5 *Enter* MORTIMER, *brought in a chair, and* Gaolers.

MORTIMER   Kind keepers of my weak decaying age,
Let dying Mortimer here rest himself.
Even like a man new haled from the rack,
So fare my limbs with long imprisonment;
And these grey locks, the pursuivants of Death,
5   Nestor-like aged in an age of care,
Argue the end of Edmund Mortimer.
These eyes, like lamps whose wasting oil is spent,
Wax dim, as drawing to their exigent;
Weak shoulders, overborne with burdening grief,
10   And pithless arms, like to a wither'd vine
That droops his sapless branches to the ground.

Yet are these feet, whose strengthless stay is numb,
Unable to support this lump of clay,
Swift-winged with desire to get a grave,
As witting I no other comfort have.   15
But tell me, keeper, will my nephew come?
1 KEEPER
Richard Plantagenet, my lord, will come:
We sent unto the Temple, unto his chamber,
And answer was return'd that he will come.
MORTIMER   Enough: my soul shall then be satisfied.   20
Poor gentleman! his wrong doth equal mine.
Since Henry Monmouth first began to reign,
Before whose glory I was great in arms,
This loathsome sequestration have I had;
And even since then hath Richard been obscur'd,   25
Depriv'd of honour and inheritance.
But now the arbitrator of despairs,
Just Death, kind umpire of men's miseries,
With sweet enlargement doth dismiss me hence.
I would his troubles likewise were expir'd,   30
That so he might recover what was lost.

Enter RICHARD PLANTAGENET.

1 KEEPER
My lord, your loving nephew now is come.
MORTIMER   Richard Plantagenet, my friend, is come?
PLANTAGENET   Ay, noble uncle, thus ignobly us'd,
Your nephew, late despised Richard, comes.   35
MORTIMER   Direct mine arms I may embrace his neck
And in his bosom spend my latter gasp.
O, tell me when my lips do touch his cheeks,
That I may kindly give one fainting kiss.
And now declare, sweet stem from York's great stock,   40
Why did'st thou say of late thou wert despis'd?
PLANTAGENET
First, lean thine aged back against mine arm,
And, in that ease, I'll tell thee my disease.
This day, in argument upon a case,
Some words there grew 'twixt Somerset and me;   45
Among which terms he us'd his lavish tongue
And did upbraid me with my father's death;
Which obloquy set bars before my tongue,
Else with the like I had requited him.
Therefore, good uncle, for my father's sake,   50
In honour of a true Plantagenet,
And for alliance' sake, declare the cause
My father, Earl of Cambridge, lost his head.
MORTIMER
That cause, fair nephew, that imprison'd me
And hath detain'd me all my flowering youth   55
Within a loathsome dungeon, there to pine,
Was cursed instrument of his decease.
PLANTAGENET
Discover more at large what cause that was,
For I am ignorant and cannot guess.
MORTIMER   I will, if that my fading breath permit   60

And death approach not ere my tale be done.
Henry the Fourth, grandfather to this king,
Depos'd his nephew Richard, Edward's son,
The first-begotten, and the lawful heir   65
Of Edward king, the third of that descent;
During whose reign the Percies of the north,
Finding his usurpation most unjust,
Endeavour'd my advancement to the throne.
The reason mov'd these warlike lords to this   70
Was, for that – young King Richard thus remov'd,
Leaving no heir begotten of his body –
I was the next by birth and parentage;
For by my mother I derived am
From Lionel Duke of Clarence, the third son   75
To King Edward the Third; whereas he
From John of Gaunt doth bring his pedigree
Being but fourth of that heroic line.
But mark: as in this haughty great attempt
They laboured to plant the rightful heir,   80
I lost my liberty, and they their lives.
Long after this, when Henry the Fifth,
Succeeding his father Bolingbroke, did reign,
Thy father, Earl of Cambridge then, deriv'd
From famous Edmund Langley, Duke of York,   85
Marrying my sister, that thy mother was,
Again, in pity of my hard distress,
Levied an army, weening to redeem
And have install'd me in the diadem;
But, as the rest, so fell that noble earl,   90
And was beheaded. Thus the Mortimers,
In whom the title rested, were suppress'd.

PLANTAGENET
Of which, my lord, your honour is the last.

MORTIMER   True; and thou seest that I no issue have,
And that my fainting words do warrant death.   95
Thou art my heir; the rest I wish thee gather:
But yet be wary in thy studious care.

PLANTAGENET
Thy grave admonishments prevail with me;
But yet methinks my father's execution
Was nothing less than bloody tyranny.   100

MORTIMER   With silence, nephew, be thou politic;
Strong-fixed is the house of Lancaster,
And like a mountain, not to be remov'd.
But now thy uncle is removing hence,
As princes do their courts when they are cloy'd 105
With long continuance in a settled place.

PLANTAGENET
O uncle, would some part of my young years
Might but redeem the passing of your age!

MORTIMER
Thou dost then wrong me, as that slaughterer doth,
Which giveth many wounds when one will kill.   110
Mourn not, except thou sorrow for my good;
Only give order for my funeral.
And so farewell; and fair befall thy hopes,

And prosperous be thy life in peace and war! [*Dies.*]

PLANTAGENET
And peace, no war, befall thy parting soul!   115
In prison hast thou spent a pilgrimage,
And like a hermit overpass'd thy days.
Well, I will lock his counsel in my breast;
And what I do imagine, let that rest.
Keepers, convey him hence; and I myself   120
Will see his burial better than his life.
       Exeunt Gaolers, bearing out the body of Mortimer.
Here dies the dusky torch of Mortimer,
Chok'd with ambition of the meaner sort;
And for those wrongs, those bitter injuries,
Which Somerset hath offer'd to my house,   125
I doubt not but with honour to redress;
And therefore haste I to the Parliament,
Either to be restored to my blood,
Or make mine ill th' advantage of my good.   *Exit.*

3.1   *Flourish. Enter* KING, EXETER, GLOUCESTER,
      WINCHESTER, WARWICK, SOMERSET, SUFFOLK,
      RICHARD PLANTAGENET. GLOUCESTER *offers to
      put up a bill;* WINCHESTER *snatches it, tears it.*

WINCHESTER
Com'st thou with deep-premeditated lines,
With written pamphlets studiously devis'd,
Humphrey of Gloucester? If thou canst accuse
Or aught intend'st to lay unto my charge,
Do it without invention, suddenly;   5
As I with sudden and extemporal speech
Purpose to answer what thou canst object.

GLOUCESTER
Presumptuous priest, this place commands my
      patience,
Or thou shouldst find thou hast dishonour'd me.
Think not, although in writing I preferr'd   10
The manner of thy vile outrageous crimes,
That therefore I have forg'd, or am not able
Verbatim to rehearse my method penn'd.
No, prelate; such is thy audacious wickedness,
Thy lewd, pestiferous, and dissentious pranks,   15
As very infants prattle of thy pride.
Thou art a most pernicious usurer,
Froward by nature, enemy to peace;
Lascivious, wanton, more than well beseems
A man of thy profession and degree;   20
And for thy treachery, what's more manifest,
In that thou laid'st a trap to take my life,
As well at London Bridge as at the Tower?
Beside, I fear me, if thy thoughts were sifted,
The King, thy sovereign, is not quite exempt   25
From envious malice of thy swelling heart.

WINCHESTER
Gloucester, I do defy thee. Lords, vouchsafe
To give me hearing what I shall reply.

If covetous, ambitious, or perverse,
30 As he will have me, how am I so poor?
Or how haps it I seek not to advance
Or raise myself, but keep my wonted calling?
And for dissension, who preferreth peace
More than I do? – except I be provok'd.
35 No, my good lords, it is not that offends;
It is not that that hath incens'd the Duke;
It is because no one should sway but he,
No one but he should be about the King;
And that engenders thunder in his breast
40 And makes him roar these accusations forth.
But he shall know I am as good –
GLOUCESTER   As good!
Thou bastard of my grandfather!
WINCHESTER   Ay, lordly sir; for what are you, I pray,
But one imperious in another's throne?
45 GLOUCESTER   Am I not Protector, saucy priest?
WINCHESTER   And am not I a prelate of the church?
GLOUCESTER   Yes, as an outlaw in a castle keeps,
And useth it – to patronage his theft.
WINCHESTER   Unreverent Gloucester!
GLOUCESTER   Thou art reverend
50 Touching thy spiritual function, not thy life.
WINCHESTER   Rome shall remedy this.
GLOUCESTER   Roam thither then.
WARWICK [*to Winchester*]
My lord, it were your duty to forbear.
SOMERSET   Ay, so the bishop be not overborne.
Methinks my lord should be religious,
55 And know the office that belongs to such.
WARWICK   Methinks his lordship should be humbler;
It fitteth not a prelate so to plead.
SOMERSET   Yes, when his holy state is touch'd so near.
WARWICK   State holy or unhallow'd, what of that?
60 Is not his Grace Protector to the King?
PLANTAGENET [*aside*]
Plantagenet, I see, must hold his tongue,
Lest it be said, 'Speak, sirrah, when you should;
Must your bold verdict enter talk with lords?'
Else would I have a fling at Winchester.
65 KING HENRY   Uncles of Gloucester and of Winchester,
The special watchmen of our English weal,
I would prevail, if prayers might prevail,
To join your hearts in love and amity.
O, what a scandal is it to our crown
70 That two such noble peers as ye should jar!
Believe me, lords, my tender years can tell
Civil dissension is a viperous worm
That gnaws the bowels of the commonwealth.
[*A noise within:* 'Down with the tawny-coats!']
What tumult's this?
WARWICK   An uproar, I dare warrant,
75 Begun through malice of the Bishop's men.
[*A noise again:* 'Stones! Stones!']

Enter Mayor.

MAYOR   O, my good lords, and virtuous Henry,
Pity the city of London, pity us!
The Bishop and the Duke of Gloucester's men,
Forbidden late to carry any weapon,
Have fill'd their pockets full of pebble stones   80
And, banding themselves in contrary parts,
Do pelt so fast at one another's pate
That many have their giddy brains knock'd out:
Our windows are broke down in every street,
And we for fear compell'd to shut our shops.   85

Enter Serving-men *in skirmish with bloody pates.*

KING HENRY   We charge you, on allegiance to ourself,
To hold your slaughtering hands and keep the peace.
Pray, uncle Gloucester, mitigate this strife.
1 SERVANT   Nay, if we be forbidden stones, we'll fall to
it with our teeth.   90
2 SERVANT   Do what ye dare, we are as resolute.
[*Skirmish again.*]
GLOUCESTER
You of my household, leave this peevish broil,
And set this unaccustom'd fight aside.
3 SERVANT   My lord, we know your Grace to be a man
Just and upright, and, for your royal birth,   95
Inferior to none but to his Majesty;
And ere that we will suffer such a prince,
So kind a father of the commonweal,
To be disgraced by an inkhorn mate,
We and our wives and children all will fight   100
And have our bodies slaughter'd by thy foes.
1 SERVANT   Ay, and the very parings of our nails
Shall pitch a field when we are dead. [*Begin again.*]
GLOUCESTER   Stay, stay, I say!
And if you love me, as you say you do,
Let me persuade you to forbear awhile.   105
KING HENRY   O, how this discord doth afflict my soul!
Can you, my Lord of Winchester, behold
My sighs and tears, and will not once relent?
Who should be pitiful, if you be not?
Or who should study to prefer a peace   110
If holy churchmen take delight in broils?
WARWICK   My Lord Protector, yield; yield, Winchester;
Except you mean with obstinate repulse
To slay your sovereign and destroy the realm.
You see what mischief, and what murder too,   115
Hath been enacted through your enmity;
Then be at peace, except ye thirst for blood.
WINCHESTER   He shall submit, or I will never yield.
GLOUCESTER
Compassion on the King commands me stoop,
Or I would see his heart out, ere the priest   120
Should ever get that privilege of me.
WARWICK   Behold, my Lord of Winchester, the Duke
Hath banish'd moody discontented fury,
As by his smoothed brows it doth appear:

125 Why look you still so stern and tragical?

GLOUCESTER Here, Winchester, I offer thee my hand.

KING HENRY

Fie, uncle Beaufort! I have heard you preach

That malice was a great and grievous sin;

And will you not maintain the thing you teach,

130 But prove a chief offender in the same?

WARWICK Sweet King! The Bishop hath a kindly gird.

For shame, my Lord of Winchester, relent!

What, shall a child instruct you what to do?

WINCHESTER

Well, Duke of Gloucester, I will yield to thee;

135 Love for thy love and hand for hand I give.

GLOUCESTER [*aside*]

Ay, but, I fear me, with a hollow heart. –

See here, my friends and loving countrymen,

This token serveth for a flag of truce

Betwixt ourselves and all our followers:

140 So help me God, as I dissemble not!

WINCHESTER [*aside*]

So help me God, as I intend it not!

KING HENRY O loving uncle, kind Duke of Gloucester,

How joyful am I made by this contract!

Away, my masters! trouble us no more,

145 But join in friendship, as your lords have done.

3 SERVANT Content; I'll to the surgeon's.

1 SERVANT And so will I.

2 SERVANT And I will see what physic the tavern affords.

Exeunt Serving-men, Mayor, etc.

WARWICK Accept this scroll, most gracious sovereign,

150 Which in the right of Richard Plantagenet

We do exhibit to your Majesty.

GLOUCESTER

Well urg'd, my Lord of Warwick; for, sweet prince,

And if your Grace mark every circumstance,

You have great reason to do Richard right,

155 Especially for those occasions

At Eltham Place I told your Majesty.

KING HENRY And those occasions, uncle, were of force;

Therefore, my loving lords, our pleasure is

That Richard be restored to his blood.

160 WARWICK Let Richard be restored to his blood;

So shall his father's wrongs be recompens'd.

WINCHESTER As will the rest, so willeth Winchester.

KING HENRY If Richard will be true, not that alone

But all the whole inheritance I give

165 That doth belong unto the house of York,

From whence you spring by lineal descent.

PLANTAGENET Thy humble servant vows obedience

And humble service till the point of death.

KING HENRY

Stoop then and set your knee against my foot;

170 And in reguerdon of that duty done

I girt thee with the valiant sword of York:

Rise, Richard, like a true Plantagenet,

And rise created princely Duke of York.

PLANTAGENET

And so thrive Richard as thy foes may fall!

175 And as my duty springs, so perish they

That grudge one thought against your Majesty!

ALL Welcome, high Prince, the mighty Duke of York!

SOMERSET [*aside*]

Perish, base Prince, ignoble Duke of York!

GLOUCESTER Now will it best avail your Majesty

180 To cross the seas and to be crown'd in France.

The presence of a king engenders love

Amongst his subjects and his loyal friends,

As it disanimates his enemies.

KING HENRY

When Gloucester says the word, King Henry goes;

185 For friendly counsel cuts off many foes.

GLOUCESTER Your ships already are in readiness.

Sennet. Flourish. Exeunt all but Exeter.

EXETER Ay, we may march in England, or in France,

Not seeing what is likely to ensue.

This late dissension grown betwixt the peers

190 Burns under feigned ashes of forg'd love,

And will at last break out into a flame;

As fester'd members rot but by degree

Till bones and flesh and sinews fall away,

So will this base and envious discord breed.

195 And now I fear that fatal prophecy

Which in the time of Henry nam'd the Fifth

Was in the mouth of every sucking babe:

That Henry born at Monmouth should win all,

And Henry born at Windsor should lose all:

200 Which is so plain that Exeter doth wish

His days may finish ere that hapless time. *Exit.*

3.2 *Enter* LA PUCELLE *disguised, with four* Soldiers
with sacks upon their backs.

PUCELLE These are the city gates, the gates of Rouen,

Through which our policy must make a breach.

Take heed, be wary how you place your words;

Talk like the vulgar sort of market men

5 That come to gather money for their corn.

If we have entrance, as I hope we shall,

And that we find the slothful watch but weak,

I'll by a sign give notice to our friends,

That Charles the Dauphin may encounter them.

1 SOLDIER Our sacks shall be a mean to sack the city, 10

And we be lords and rulers over Rouen;

Therefore we'll knock. [*knock*]

WATCH [*within*] *Qui la?*

PUCELLE *Paysans, la pauvre gens de France:*

Poor market folks that come to sell their corn. 15

WATCH [*Opens the gate.*]

Enter, go in; the market bell is rung.

PUCELLE

Now, Rouen, I'll shake thy bulwarks to the ground.

Exeunt.

Enter CHARLES, *the* BASTARD OF ORLEANS,
ALENÇON, REIGNIER *and forces.*

CHARLES   Saint Denis bless this happy stratagem,
And once again we'll sleep secure in Rouen.
20 BASTARD   Here enter'd Pucelle and her practisants;
Now she is there, how will she specify
Here is the best and safest passage in?
REIGNIER   By thrusting out a torch from yonder tower,
Which once discern'd shows that her meaning is:
25 No way to that, for weakness, which she enter'd.

Enter LA PUCELLE *on the top, thrusting out a torch
burning.*

PUCELLE   Behold, this is the happy wedding torch
That joineth Rouen unto her countrymen,
But burning fatal to the Talbonites.   *Exit.*
BASTARD   See, noble Charles, the beacon of our friend,
30 The burning torch, in yonder turret stands.
CHARLES   Now shine it like a comet of revenge,
A prophet to the fall of all our foes!
REIGNIER   Defer no time, delays have dangerous ends;
Enter and cry 'The Dauphin!' presently,
35 And then do execution on the watch.   *Exeunt.*

An alarum. Enter TALBOT *in an excursion.*

TALBOT
France, thou shalt rue this treason with thy tears,
If Talbot but survive thy treachery.
Pucelle, that witch, that damned sorceress,
Hath wrought this hellish mischief unawares,
40 That hardly we escap'd the pride of France.   *Exit.*

An alarum: excursions. BEDFORD *brought in sick
in a chair.*
Enter TALBOT *and* BURGUNDY *without: within,*
LA PUCELLE, CHARLES, BASTARD, ALENÇON *and*
REIGNIER, *on the walls.*

PUCELLE
Good morrow, gallants! Want ye corn for bread?
I think the Duke of Burgundy will fast
Before he'll buy again at such a rate.
'Twas full of darnel: do you like the taste?
BURGUNDY
45 Scoff on, vile fiend and shameless courtezan!
I trust ere long to choke thee with thine own,
And make thee curse the harvest of that corn.
CHARLES
Your Grace may starve, perhaps, before that time.
BEDFORD
O, let no words, but deeds, revenge this treason!
PUCELLE
50 What will you do, good grey-beard? Break a lance
And run a tilt at Death within a chair?
TALBOT   Foul fiend of France and hag of all despite,
Encompass'd with thy lustful paramours,
Becomes it thee to taunt his valiant age

And twit with cowardice a man half dead?   55
Damsel, I'll have a bout with you again,
Or else let Talbot perish with this shame.
PUCELLE   Are ye so hot? Yet, Pucelle, hold thy peace;
If Talbot do but thunder, rain will follow.
[*The English whisper together in council.*]
God speed the parliament! Who shall be the
    Speaker?   60
TALBOT   Dare ye come forth and meet us in the field?
PUCELLE   Belike your lordship takes us then for fools,
To try if that our own be ours or no.
TALBOT   I speak not to that railing Hecate,
But unto thee, Alençon, and the rest;   65
Will ye, like soldiers, come and fight it out?
ALENÇON   Signior, no.
TALBOT   Signior, hang! Base muleteers of France!
Like peasant foot-boys do they keep the walls,
And dare not take up arms like gentlemen.   70
JOAN LA PUCELLE
Captains, away, let's get us from the walls,
For Talbot means no goodness by his looks.
God b'uy, my lord; we came to tell you but
That we are here.   *Exeunt from the walls.*
TALBOT   And there will we be too, ere it be long,   75
Or else reproach be Talbot's greatest fame!
Vow, Burgundy, by honour of thy house,
Prick'd on by public wrongs sustain'd in France,
Either to get the town again or die;
And I, as sure as English Henry lives,   80
And as his father here was conqueror,
As sure as in this late-betrayed town
Great Coeur-de-lion's heart was buried –
So sure I swear to get the town or die.
BURGUNDY   My vows are equal partners with thy vows.   85
TALBOT   But, ere we go, regard this dying prince,
The valiant Duke of Bedford. Come, my lord,
We will bestow you in some better place,
Fitter for sickness and for crazy age.
BEDFORD   Lord Talbot, do not so dishonour me;   90
Here will I sit, before the walls of Rouen,
And will be partner of your weal or woe.
BURGUNDY
Courageous Bedford, let us now persuade you.
BEDFORD   Not to be gone from hence; for once I read
That stout Pendragon in his litter sick   95
Came to the field and vanquished his foes.
Methinks I should revive the soldiers' hearts,
Because I ever found them as myself.
TALBOT   Undaunted spirit in a dying breast!
Then be it so: heavens keep old Bedford safe!   100
And now no more ado, brave Burgundy,
But gather we our forces out of hand,
And set upon our boasting enemy.
          Exeunt all but Bedford and attendants.

An alarum: excursions. Enter SIR JOHN FALSTAFF
and a Captain.

CAPTAIN   Whither away, John Falstaff, in such haste?

FALSTAFF   Whither away? To save myself by flight:
We are like to have the overthrow again.

CAPTAIN   What! Will you fly, and leave Lord Talbot?

FALSTAFF   Ay,
All the Talbots in the world, to save my life.   *Exit.*

CAPTAIN   Cowardly knight! ill fortune follow thee!
                                                          Exit.

Retreat: excursions. La Pucelle, Alençon and Charles fly.

BEDFORD   Now, quiet soul, depart when heaven please,
For I have seen our enemies' overthrow.
What is the trust or strength of foolish man?
They that of late were daring with their scoffs
Are glad and fain by flight to save themselves.
                Bedford dies, and is carried in by two in his chair.

An alarum. Enter TALBOT, BURGUNDY *and the rest.*

TALBOT   Lost, and recover'd in a day again!
This is a double honour, Burgundy:
Let heavens have glory for this victory!

BURGUNDY   Warlike and martial Talbot, Burgundy
Enshrines thee in his heart, and there erects
Thy noble deeds as valour's monuments.

TALBOT
Thanks, gentle Duke. But where is Pucelle now?
I think her old familiar is asleep.
Now where's the Bastard's braves, and Charles his
     gleeks?
What, all amort? Rouen hangs her head for grief
That such a valiant company are fled.
Now will we take some order in the town,
Placing therein some expert officers,
And then depart to Paris to the King,
For there young Henry with his nobles lie.

BURGUNDY
What wills Lord Talbot pleaseth Burgundy.

TALBOT   But yet, before we go, let's not forget
The noble Duke of Bedford, late deceas'd,
But see his exequies fulfill'd in Rouen:
A braver soldier never couched lance,
A gentler heart did never sway in court;
But kings and mightiest potentates must die,
For that's the end of human misery.   *Exeunt.*

3.3   *Enter* CHARLES, *the* BASTARD OF ORLEANS,
         ALENÇON, LA PUCELLE *and forces.*

PUCELLE   Dismay not, Princes, at this accident,
Nor grieve that Rouen is so recovered:
Care is no cure, but rather corrosive,
For things that are not to be remedied.
Let frantic Talbot triumph for a while
And like a peacock sweep along his tail;
We'll pull his plumes and take away his train,
If Dauphin and the rest will be but rul'd.

CHARLES   We have been guided by thee hitherto,
And of thy cunning had no diffidence;

One sudden foil shall never breed distrust.

BASTARD   Search out thy wit for secret policies,
And we will make thee famous through the world.

ALENÇON   We'll set thy statue in some holy place,
And have thee reverenc'd like a blessed saint.
Employ thee, then, sweet virgin, for our good.

PUCELLE   Then thus it must be; this doth Joan devise:
By fair persuasions, mix'd with sugar'd words,
We will entice the Duke of Burgundy
To leave the Talbot and to follow us.

CHARLES   Ay, marry, sweeting, if we could do that,
France were no place for Henry's warriors;
Nor should that nation boast it so with us,
But be extirped from our provinces.

ALENÇON
For ever should they be expuls'd from France,
And not have title of an earldom here.

PUCELLE
Your honours shall perceive how I will work
To bring this matter to the wished end.
                                [Drum sounds afar off.]
Hark! by the sound of drum you may perceive
Their powers are marching unto Paris-ward.
                                [Here sound an English march.]
There goes the Talbot, with his colours spread,
And all the troops of English after him.
                                [French march.]
Now in the rearward comes the Duke and his:
Fortune in favour makes him lag behind.
Summon a parley; we will talk with him.
                                [Trumpets sound a parley.]

CHARLES   A parley with the Duke of Burgundy!

Enter BURGUNDY.

BURGUNDY   Who craves a parley with the Burgundy?

PUCELLE
The princely Charles of France, thy countryman.

BURGUNDY
What say'st thou, Charles? for I am marching hence.

CHARLES
Speak, Pucelle, and enchant him with thy words.

PUCELLE   Brave Burgundy, undoubted hope of France,
Stay, let thy humble handmaid speak to thee.

BURGUNDY   Speak on, but be not over-tedious.

PUCELLE   Look on thy country, look on fertile France,
And see the cities and the towns defac'd
By wasting ruin of the cruel foe;
As looks the mother on her lowly babe
When death doth close his tender dying eyes,
See, see the pining malady of France;
Behold the wounds, the most unnatural wounds
Which thou thyself hast given her woeful breast.
O, turn thy edged sword another way;
Strike those that hurt, and hurt not those that help!
One drop of blood drawn from thy country's bosom
Should grieve thee more than streams of foreign
     gore.

Return thee therefore with a flood of tears,
And wash away thy country's stained spots.
BURGUNDY [*aside*]
    Either she hath bewitch'd me with her words,
    Or nature makes me suddenly relent.
PUCELLE
60   Besides, all French and France exclaims on thee,
    Doubting thy birth and lawful progeny.
    Who join'st thou with but with a lordly nation
    That will not trust thee but for profit's sake?
    When Talbot hath set footing once in France,
65   And fashion'd thee that instrument of ill,
    Who then but English Henry will be lord,
    And thou be thrust out like a fugitive?
    Call we to mind, and mark but this for proof:
    Was not the Duke of Orleans thy foe?
70   And was he not in England prisoner?
    But when they heard he was thine enemy
    They set him free without his ransom paid,
    In spite of Burgundy and all his friends.
    See then, thou fight'st against thy countrymen,
75   And join'st with them will be thy slaughter-men.
    Come, come, return; return, thou wandering lord;
    Charles and the rest will take thee in their arms.
BURGUNDY [*aside*]
    I am vanquished; these haughty words of hers
    Have batter'd me like roaring cannon-shot
80   And made me almost yield upon my knees. –
    Forgive me, country, and sweet countrymen!
    And, lords, accept this hearty kind embrace.
    My forces and my power of men are yours.
    So farewell, Talbot; I'll no longer trust thee.
PUCELLE   Done like a Frenchman! [*aside*]
85   – turn and turn again.
CHARLES
    Welcome, brave Duke! thy friendship makes us fresh.
BASTARD   And doth beget new courage in our breasts.
ALENÇON   Pucelle hath bravely play'd her part in this,
    And doth deserve a coronet of gold.
90 CHARLES   Now let us on, my lords, and join our powers,
    And seek how we may prejudice the foe.   *Exeunt.*

3.4   *Enter the* KING, GLOUCESTER, WINCHESTER,
    YORK, SUFFOLK, SOMERSET, WARWICK, EXETER,
VERNON *and* BASSET. *To them, with his soldiers,* TALBOT.

TALBOT   My gracious Prince, and honourable peers,
    Hearing of your arrival in this realm,
    I have awhile given truce unto my wars
    To do my duty to my sovereign:
5   In sign whereof, this arm, that hath reclaim'd
    To your obedience fifty fortresses,
    Twelve cities, and seven walled towns of strength,
    Beside five hundred prisoners of esteem,
    Lets fall his sword before your Highness' feet;
10   And with submissive loyalty of heart
    Ascribes the glory of his conquest got
    First to my God, and next unto your Grace. [*Kneels.*]

KING HENRY   Is this the Talbot, uncle Gloucester,
    That hath so long been resident in France?
GLOUCESTER   Yes, if it please your Majesty, my liege.   15
KING HENRY
    Welcome, brave captain and victorious lord!
    When I was young, as yet I am not old,
    I do remember how my father said
    A stouter champion never handled sword.
    Long since we were resolved of your truth,   20
    Your faithful service, and your toil in war;
    Yet never have you tasted our reward,
    Or been reguerdon'd with so much as thanks,
    Because till now we never saw your face.
    Therefore stand up; and for these good deserts   25
    We here create you Earl of Shrewsbury;
    And in our coronation take your place.
        Sennet. Flourish. Exeunt all but Vernon and Basset.
VERNON   Now, sir, to you that were so hot at sea,
    Disgracing of these colours that I wear
    In honour of my noble Lord of York,   30
    Dar'st thou maintain the former words thou spak'st?
BASSET   Yes, sir, as well as you dare patronage
    The envious barking of your saucy tongue
    Against my lord the Duke of Somerset.
VERNON   Sirrah, thy lord I honour as he is.   35
BASSET   Why, what is he? As good a man as York!
VERNON   Hark ye, not so: in witness take ye that.
    [*Strikes him.*]
BASSET   Villain, thou knowest the law of arms is such
    That whoso draws a sword, 'tis present death,
    Or else this blow should broach thy dearest blood.   40
    But I'll unto his Majesty, and crave
    I may have liberty to venge this wrong;
    When thou shalt see I'll meet thee to thy cost.
VERNON   Well, miscreant, I'll be there as soon as you;
    And, after, meet you sooner than you would.   *Exeunt.*   45

4.1   *Enter the* KING, GLOUCESTER, WINCHESTER,
    YORK, SUFFOLK, SOMERSET, WARWICK, TALBOT,
    EXETER, *the Governor of Paris and others.*

GLOUCESTER
    Lord Bishop, set the crown upon his head.
WINCHESTER
    God save King Henry, of that name the sixth!
GLOUCESTER   Now, Governor of Paris, take your oath,
    [*Governor kneels.*]
    That you elect no other king but him;
    Esteem none friends but such as are his friends,   5
    And none your foes but such as shall pretend
    Malicious practices against his state:
    This shall ye do, so help you righteous God!
        Exeunt Governor and his train.

        Enter SIR JOHN FALSTAFF.

FALSTAFF
    My gracious sovereign, as I rode from Calais,
    To haste unto your coronation,   10

A letter was deliver'd to my hands,
Writ to your Grace from th' Duke of Burgundy.
TALBOT   Shame to the Duke of Burgundy and thee!
I vow'd, base knight, when I did meet thee next,
To tear the Garter from thy craven's leg,   15
[*Plucks it off.*]
Which I have done, because unworthily
Thou wast installed in that high degree.
Pardon me, princely Henry, and the rest:
This dastard, at the battle of Patay,
When but in all I was six thousand strong,   20
And that the French were almost ten to one,
Before we met or that a stroke was given,
Like to a trusty squire did run away;
In which assault we lost twelve hundred men;
Myself and divers gentlemen beside   25
Were there surpris'd and taken prisoners.
Then judge, great lords, if I have done amiss,
Or whether that such cowards ought to wear
This ornament of knighthood, yea or no?
GLOUCESTER   To say the truth, this fact was infamous,   30
And ill-beseeming any common man,
Much more a knight, a captain, and a leader.
TALBOT   When first this Order was ordain'd, my lords,
Knights of the Garter were of noble birth,
Valiant and virtuous, full of haughty courage,   35
Such as were grown to credit by the wars;
Not fearing death nor shrinking for distress,
But always resolute in most extremes.
He then that is not furnish'd in this sort
Doth but usurp the sacred name of knight,   40
Profaning this most honourable Order,
And should, if I were worthy to be judge,
Be quite degraded, like a hedge-born swain
That doth presume to boast of gentle blood.
KING HENRY
Stain to thy countrymen, thou hear'st thy doom!   45
Be packing, therefore, thou that wast a knight;
Henceforth we banish thee on pain of death.
                    Exit Falstaff.
And now, my Lord Protector, view the letter
Sent from our uncle, Duke of Burgundy.
GLOUCESTER
What means his Grace, that he hath chang'd his
    style?   50
No more but plain and bluntly 'To the King'!
Hath he forgot he is his sovereign?
Or doth this churlish superscription
Pretend some alteration in good-will?
What's here? [*Reads.*] 'I have, upon especial cause,   55
Mov'd with compassion of my country's wrack,
Together with the pitiful complaints
Of such as your oppression feeds upon,
Forsaken your pernicious faction
And join'd with Charles, the rightful King of
    France.'
O monstrous treachery! Can this be so —

That in alliance, amity, and oaths,
There should be found such false dissembling guile?
KING HENRY   What! doth my uncle Burgundy revolt?
GLOUCESTER
He doth, my lord, and is become your foe.   65
KING HENRY   Is that the worst this letter doth contain?
GLOUCESTER
It is the worst, and all, my lord, he writes.
KING HENRY
Why then Lord Talbot there shall talk with him
And give him chastisement for this abuse.
My lord, how say you, are you not content?   70
TALBOT
Content, my liege! Yes, but that I am prevented,
I should have begg'd I might have been employ'd.
KING HENRY
Then gather strength and march unto him straight;
Let him perceive how ill we brook his treason,
And what offence it is to flout his friends.   75
TALBOT   I go, my lord, in heart desiring still
You may behold confusion of your foes.   *Exit.*

Enter VERNON *and* BASSET.

VERNON   Grant me the combat, gracious sovereign.
BASSET   And me, my lord, grant me the combat too.
YORK   This is my servant: hear him, noble Prince.   80
SOMERSET   And this is mine: sweet Henry, favour him.
KING HENRY
Be patient, lords, and give them leave to speak.
Say, gentlemen, what makes you thus exclaim,
And wherefore crave you combat, or with whom?
VERNON
With him, my lord, for he hath done me wrong.   85
BASSET   And I with him, for he hath done me wrong.
KING HENRY
What is that wrong whereof you both complain?
First let me know, and then I'll answer you.
BASSET   Crossing the sea from England into France,
This fellow here, with envious carping tongue,   90
Upbraided me about the rose I wear,
Saying the sanguine colour of the leaves
Did represent my master's blushing cheeks
When stubbornly he did repugn the truth
About a certain question in the law,   95
Argu'd betwixt the Duke of York and him;
With other vile and ignominious terms:
In confutation of which rude approach,
And in defence of my lord's worthiness,
I crave the benefit of law of arms.   100
VERNON   And that is my petition, noble lord;
For though he seem with forged quaint conceit
To set a gloss upon his bold intent,
Yet know, my lord, I was provok'd by him,
And he first took exceptions at this badge,   105
Pronouncing that the paleness of this flower
Bewray'd the faintness of my master's heart.
YORK   Will not this malice, Somerset, be left?

SOMERSET
    Your private grudge, my Lord of York, will out,
110   Though ne'er so cunningly you smother it.
KING HENRY
    Good Lord, what madness rules in brainsick men,
    When for so slight and frivolous a cause
    Such factious emulations shall arise!
    Good cousins both, of York and Somerset,
115   Quiet yourselves, I pray, and be at peace.
YORK   Let this dissension first be tried by fight,
    And then your Highness shall command a peace.
SOMERSET   The quarrel toucheth none but us alone;
    Betwixt ourselves let us decide it then.
120 YORK   There is my pledge; accept it, Somerset.
    VERNON   Nay, let it rest where it began at first.
    BASSET   Confirm it so, mine honourable lord.
GLOUCESTER
    Confirm it so! Confounded be your strife!
    And perish ye, with your audacious prate!
125   Presumptuous vassals, are you not asham'd
    With this immodest clamorous outrage
    To trouble and disturb the King and us?
    And you, my lords, methinks you do not well
    To bear with their perverse objections,
130   Much less to take occasion from their mouths
    To raise a mutiny betwixt yourselves:
    Let me persuade you take a better course.
EXETER
    It grieves his Highness; good my lords, be friends.
KING HENRY
    Come hither, you that would be combatants:
135   Henceforth I charge you, as you love our favour,
    Quite to forget this quarrel, and the cause.
    And you, my lords, remember where we are:
    In France, amongst a fickle wavering nation;
    If they perceive dissension in our looks,
140   And that within ourselves we disagree,
    How will their grudging stomachs be provok'd
    To wilful disobedience, and rebel!
    Beside, what infamy will there arise
    When foreign princes shall be certified
145   That for a toy, a thing of no regard,
    King Henry's peers and chief nobility
    Destroy'd themselves, and lost the realm of France!
    O, think upon the conquest of my father,
    My tender years, and let us not forgo
150   That for a trifle that was bought with blood!
    Let me be umpire in this doubtful strife.
    I see no reason if I wear this rose,
    [putting on a red rose]
    That any one should therefore be suspicious
    I more incline to Somerset than York:
155   Both are my kinsmen, and I love them both;
    As well may they upbraid me with my crown
    Because, forsooth, the King of Scots is crown'd.
    But your discretions better can persuade
    Than I am able to instruct or teach;

    And therefore, as we hither came in peace,   160
    So let us still continue peace and love.
    Cousin of York, we institute your Grace
    To be our Regent in the parts of France:
    And, good my Lord of Somerset, unite
    Your troops of horsemen with his bands of foot: 165
    And like true subjects, sons of your progenitors,
    Go cheerfully together and digest
    Your angry choler on your enemies.
    Ourself, my Lord Protector, and the rest,
    After some respite will return to Calais; 170
    From thence to England, where I hope ere long
    To be presented by your victories
    With Charles, Alençon, and that traiterous rout.
          Flourish. Exeunt all but York, Warwick,
                    Exeter and Vernon.
WARWICK   My Lord of York, I promise you the King
    Prettily, methought, did play the orator. 175
YORK   And so he did; but yet I like it not,
    In that he wears the badge of Somerset.
WARWICK   Tush, that was but his fancy; blame him not;
    I dare presume, sweet Prince, he thought no harm.
YORK   And if I wist he did – but let it rest; 180
    Other affairs must now be managed.
                  Exeunt all but Exeter.
EXETER
    Well didst thou, Richard, to suppress thy voice;
    For, had the passions of thy heart burst out,
    I fear we should have seen decipher'd there
    More rancorous spite, more furious raging broils, 185
    Than yet can be imagin'd or suppos'd.
    But howsoe'er, no simple man that sees
    This jarring discord of nobility,
    This shouldering of each other in the Court,
    This factious bandying of their favourites, 190
    But sees it doth presage some ill event.
    'Tis much when sceptres are in children's hands;
    But more when envy breeds unkind division:
    There comes the ruin, there begins confusion. *Exit.*

4.2   *Enter* TALBOT, *with trump and drum.*

TALBOT   Go to the gates of Bordeaux, trumpeter;
    Summon their general unto the wall.

    Trumpet sounds. Enter General *and others aloft.*

    English John Talbot, captains, calls you forth,
    Servant in arms to Harry King of England;
    And thus he would: Open your city gates, 5
    Be humble to us, call my sovereign yours
    And do him homage as obedient subjects,
    And I'll withdraw me and my bloody power;
    But if you frown upon this proffer'd peace,
    You tempt the fury of my three attendants, 10
    Lean Famine, quartering Steel, and climbing Fire,
    Who in a moment even with the earth
    Shall lay your stately and air-braving towers,

If you forsake the offer of their love.

15 GENERAL   Thou ominous and fearful owl of death,
Our nation's terror and their bloody scourge!
The period of thy tyranny approacheth.
On us thou canst not enter but by death;
For, I protest, we are well fortified,
20 And strong enough to issue out and fight.
If thou retire, the Dauphin, well appointed,
Stands with the snares of war to tangle thee;
On either hand thee there are squadrons pitch'd
To wall thee from the liberty of flight;
25 And no way canst thou turn thee for redress
But Death doth front thee with apparent spoil,
And pale Destruction meets thee in the face.
Ten thousand French have ta'en the sacrament
To rive their dangerous artillery
30 Upon no Christian soul but English Talbot.
Lo, there thou stand'st a breathing valiant man
Of an invincible unconquer'd spirit:
This is the latest glory of thy praise,
That I, thy enemy, due thee withal;
35 For ere the glass, that now begins to run,
Finish the process of his sandy hour,
These eyes, that see thee now well coloured,
Shall see thee wither'd, bloody, pale and dead.
                                         [*Drum afar off.*]
Hark! hark! the Dauphin's drum, a warning bell,
40 Sings heavy music to thy timorous soul,
And mine shall ring thy dire departure out.
                                 Exeunt General, etc.
TALBOT   He fables not; I hear the enemy.
Out, some light horsemen, and peruse their wings.
O, negligent and heedless discipline!
45 How are we park'd and bounded in a pale –
A little herd of England's timorous deer,
Maz'd with a yelping kennel of French curs!
If we be English deer, be then in blood;
Not rascal-like to fall down with a pinch,
50 But rather, moody-mad and desperate stags,
Turn on the bloody hounds with heads of steel
And make the cowards stand aloof at bay:
Sell every man his life as dear as mine,
And they shall find dear deer of us, my friends.
55 God and Saint George, Talbot and England's right,
Prosper our colours in this dangerous fight! *Exeunt.*

4.3   *Enter a* Messenger *that meets* YORK. *Enter*
        YORK *with trumpet, and many soldiers.*

YORK   Are not the speedy scouts return'd again
That dogg'd the mighty army of the Dauphin?
MESSENGER
They are return'd, my lord, and give it out
That he is march'd to Bordeaux with his power
To fight with Talbot; as he march'd along,
By your espials were discovered
Two mightier troops than that the Dauphin led,

Which join'd with him and made their march for
Bordeaux.   *Exit.*
YORK   A plague upon that villain Somerset
That thus delays my promised supply   10
Of horsemen that were levied for this siege!
Renowned Talbot doth expect my aid,
And I am louted by a traitor villain
And cannot help the noble chevalier.
God comfort him in this necessity!   15
If he miscarry, farewell wars in France.

                Enter SIR WILLIAM LUCY.

LUCY   Thou princely leader of our English strength,
Never so needful on the earth of France,
Spur to the rescue of the noble Talbot,
Who now is girdled with a waist of iron,   20
And hemm'd about with grim destruction.
To Bordeaux, warlike Duke! to Bordeaux, York!
Else farewell, Talbot, France, and England's honour.
YORK   O God, that Somerset, who in proud heart
Doth stop my cornets, were in Talbot's place! 25
So should we save a valiant gentleman
By forfeiting a traitor and a coward.
Mad ire and wrathful fury makes me weep
That thus we die while remiss traitors sleep.
LUCY   O, send some succour to the distress'd lord!   30
YORK   He dies, we lose; I break my warlike word;
We mourn, France smiles; we lose, they daily get –
All long of this vile traitor Somerset.
LUCY   Then God take mercy on brave Talbot's soul,
And on his son, young John, who two hours since 35
I met in travel toward his warlike father.
This seven years did not Talbot see his son;
And now they meet where both their lives are done.
YORK   Alas, what joy shall noble Talbot have
To bid his young son welcome to his grave?   40
Away, vexation almost stops my breath,
That sunder'd friends greet in the hour of death.
Lucy, farewell; no more my fortune can
But curse the cause I cannot aid the man.
Maine, Blois, Poictiers, and Tours, are won away, 45
Long all of Somerset and his delay.
                        Exit York, with his soldiers.
LUCY   Thus, while the vulture of sedition
Feeds in the bosom of such great commanders,
Sleeping neglection doth betray to loss
The conquest of our scarce-cold conqueror,   50
That ever-living man of memory,
Henry the Fifth. Whiles they each other cross,
Lives, honours, lands, and all, hurry to loss.

4.4   *Enter* SOMERSET, *with his army, a* Captain *of*
        TALBOT's *with him.*

SOMERSET   It is too late; I cannot send them now:
This expedition was by York and Talbot
Too rashly plotted: all our general force

Might with a sally of the very town
Be buckled with: the over-daring Talbot
Hath sullied all his gloss of former honour
By this unheedful, desperate, wild adventure:
York set him on to fight and die in shame
That, Talbot dead, great York might bear the name.

CAPTAIN   Here is Sir William Lucy, who with me
Set from our o'ermatch'd forces forth for aid.

SOMERSET
How now, Sir William! whither were you sent?

LUCY
Whither, my lord! From bought and sold Lord
   Talbot,
Who, ring'd about with bold adversity,
Cries out for noble York and Somerset
To beat assailing Death from his weak legions;
And whiles the honourable captain there
Drops bloody sweat from his war-wearied limbs,
And, in advantage lingering, looks for rescue,
You, his false hopes, the trust of England's honour,
Keep off aloof with worthless emulation.
Let not your private discord keep away
The levied succours that should lend him aid,
While he, renowned noble gentleman,
Yield up his life unto a world of odds.
Orleans the Bastard, Charles, Burgundy,
Alençon, Reignier, compass him about,
And Talbot perisheth by your default.

SOMERSET
York set him on; York should have sent him aid.

LUCY   And York as fast upon your Grace exclaims,
Swearing that you withhold his levied horse,
Collected for this expedition.

SOMERSET
York lies; he might have sent and had the horse:
I owe him little duty, and less love,
And take foul scorn to fawn on him by sending.

LUCY   The fraud of England, not the force of France,
Hath now entrapp'd the noble-minded Talbot:
Never to England shall he bear his life,
But dies betray'd to fortune by your strife.

SOMERSET
Come, go; I will dispatch the horsemen straight.
Within six hours they will be at his side.

LUCY   Too late comes rescue: he is ta'en or slain,
For fly he could not if he would have fled;
And fly would Talbot never though he might.

SOMERSET   If he be dead, brave Talbot, then, adieu!

LUCY   His fame lives in the world, his shame in you.

Exeunt.

4.5   *Enter* TALBOT *and his* Son.

TALBOT   O young John Talbot, I did send for thee
To tutor thee in stratagems of war,
That Talbot's name might be in thee reviv'd,

When sapless age and weak unable limbs
Should bring thy father to his drooping chair.
But – O malignant and ill-boding stars! –
Now thou art come unto a feast of death,
A terrible and unavoided danger;
Therefore, dear boy, mount on my swiftest horse,
And I'll direct thee how thou shalt escape
By sudden flight. Come, dally not, be gone.

JOHN   Is my name Talbot? and am I your son?
And shall I fly? O, if you love my mother,
Dishonour not her honourable name,
To make a bastard and a slave of me!
The world will say, he is not Talbot's blood
That basely fled when noble Talbot stood.

TALBOT   Fly, to revenge my death if I be slain.

JOHN   He that flies so will ne'er return again.

TALBOT   If we both stay, we both are sure to die.

JOHN   Then let me stay; and, father, do you fly.
Your loss is great, so your regard should be;
My worth unknown, no loss is known in me.
Upon my death the French can little boast;
In yours they will, in you all hopes are lost.
Flight cannot stain the honour you have won;
But mine it will, that no exploit have done.
You fled for vantage, every one will swear;
But if I bow, they'll say it was for fear.
There is no hope that ever I will stay
If the first hour I shrink and run away.
Here, on my knee, I beg mortality,
Rather than life preserv'd with infamy.

TALBOT   Shall all thy mother's hopes lie in one tomb?

JOHN   Ay, rather than I'll shame my mother's womb.

TALBOT   Upon my blessing, I command thee go.

JOHN   To fight I will, but not to fly the foe.

TALBOT   Part of thy father may be sav'd in thee.

JOHN   No part of him but will be sham'd in me.

TALBOT
Thou never hadst renown, nor canst not lose it.

JOHN   Yes, your renowned name: shall flight abuse it?

TALBOT
Thy father's charge shall clear thee from that stain.

JOHN   You cannot witness for me, being slain.
If death be so apparent, then both fly.

TALBOT   And leave my followers here to fight and die?
My age was never tainted with such shame.

JOHN   And shall my youth be guilty of such blame?
No more can I be sever'd from your side
Than can yourself yourself in twain divide.
Stay, go, do what you will, the like do I;
For live I will not, if my father die.

TALBOT   Then here I take my leave of thee, fair son,
Born to eclipse thy life this afternoon.
Come, side by side, together live and die,
And soul with soul from France to heaven fly.

Exeunt.

4.6 *Alarum: excursions, wherein Talbot's Son is hemmed about, and* TALBOT *rescues him.*

TALBOT

Saint George and victory! Fight, soldiers, fight:
The Regent hath with Talbot broke his word,
And left us to the rage of France his sword.
Where is John Talbot? Pause and take thy breath;
I gave thee life and rescu'd thee from death.   5

JOHN   O, twice my father, twice am I thy son!
The life thou gav'st me first was lost and done,
Till with thy warlike sword, despite of fate,
To my determin'd time thou gav'st new date.

TALBOT

When from the Dauphin's crest thy sword struck
    fire,   10
It warm'd thy father's heart with proud desire
Of bold-fac'd victory. Then leaden age,
Quicken'd with youthful spleen and warlike rage,
Beat down Alençon, Orleans, Burgundy,
And from the pride of Gallia rescu'd thee.   15
The ireful Bastard Orleans, that drew blood
From thee, my boy, and had the maidenhood
Of thy first fight, I soon encountered,
And, interchanging blows, I quickly shed
Some of his bastard blood, and in disgrace   20
Bespoke him thus: 'Contaminated, base,
And misbegotten blood I spill of thine,
Mean and right poor, for that pure blood of mine
Which thou didst force from Talbot, my brave boy'.
Here, purposing the Bastard to destroy,   25
Came in strong rescue. Speak, thy father's care,
Art thou not weary, John? How dost thou fare?
Wilt thou yet leave the battle, boy, and fly,
Now thou art seal'd the son of chivalry?
Fly, to revenge my death when I am dead;   30
The help of one stands me in little stead.
O, too much folly is it, well I wot,
To hazard all our lives in one small boat!
If I to-day die not with Frenchmen's rage,
To-morrow I shall die with mickle age: 35
By me they nothing gain and if I stay:
'Tis but the shortening of my life one day;
In thee thy mother dies, our household's name,
My death's revenge, thy youth, and England's fame:
All these and more we hazard by thy stay;   40
All these are sav'd if thou wilt fly away.

JOHN   The sword of Orleans hath not made me smart;
These words of yours draw life-blood from my heart.
On that advantage, bought with such a shame,
To save a paltry life and slay bright fame,   45
Before young Talbot from old Talbot fly,
The coward horse that bears me fall and die!
And like me to the peasant boys of France,
To be shame's scorn and subject of mischance!
Surely, by all the glory you have won,   50
And if I fly, I am not Talbot's son.

Then talk no more of flight, it is no boot;
If son to Talbot, die at Talbot's foot.

TALBOT   Then follow thou thy desperate sire of Crete,
Thou Icarus; thy life to me is sweet: 55
If thou wilt fight, fight by thy father's side,
And, commendable prov'd, let's die in pride. *Exeunt.*

4.7   *Alarum: excursions. Enter old* TALBOT *led
by a* Servant.

TALBOT   Where is my other life? Mine own is gone.
O, where's young Talbot? Where is valiant John?
Triumphant Death, smear'd with captivity,
Young Talbot's valour makes me smile at thee.
When he perceiv'd me shrink and on my knee,   5
His bloody sword he brandish'd over me,
And like a hungry lion did commence
Rough deeds of rage and stern impatience;
But when my angry guardant stood alone,
Tendering my ruin and assail'd of none,   10
Dizzy-ey'd fury and great rage of heart
Suddenly made him from my side to start
Into the clustering battle of the French;
And in that sea of blood my boy did drench
His over-mounting spirit; and there died   15
My Icarus, my blossom, in his pride.

Enter soldiers, bearing the body of JOHN TALBOT.

SERVANT   O my dear lord, lo where your son is borne!

TALBOT

Thou antic Death, which laugh'st us here to scorn,
Anon, from thy insulting tyranny,
Coupled in bonds of perpetuity,   20
Two Talbots winged through the lither sky,
In thy despite shall scape mortality.
O thou whose wounds become hard-favour'd Death,
Speak to thy father ere thou yield thy breath!
Brave Death by speaking, whether he will or no;   25
Imagine him a Frenchman and thy foe.
Poor boy! he smiles, methinks, as who should say,
Had Death been French, then Death had died to-day.
Come, come, and lay him in his father's arms:
My spirit can no longer bear these harms.   30
Soldiers, adieu! I have what I would have,
Now my old arms are young John Talbot's grave.
                                           Dies.

Enter CHARLES, ALENÇON, BURGUNDY, BASTARD
and LA PUCELLE.

CHARLES   Had York and Somerset brought rescue in,
We should have found a bloody day of this.

BASTARD

How the young whelp of Talbot's, raging-wood,   35
Did flesh his puny sword in Frenchmen's blood!

PUCELLE   Once I encounter'd him, and thus I said:
'Thou maiden youth, be vanquish'd by a maid;'
But with a proud majestical high scorn

He answer'd thus: 'Young Talbot was not born
To be the pillage of a giglot wench.'
So, rushing in the bowels of the French,
He left me proudly, as unworthy fight.

BURGUNDY
Doubtless he would have made a noble knight;
See where he lies inhearsed in the arms
Of the most bloody nurser of his harms.

BASTARD Hew them to pieces, hack their bones asunder,
Whose life was England's glory, Gallia's wonder.

CHARLES O no, forbear! For that which we have fled
During the life, let us not wrong it dead.

Enter SIR WILLIAM LUCY, *attended.*

LUCY Conduct me to the Dauphin's tent, to know
Who hath obtain'd the glory of the day.

CHARLES On what submissive message art thou sent?

LUCY Submission, Dauphin! 'Tis a mere French word:
We English warriors wot not what it means.
I come to know what prisoners thou hast ta'en
And to survey the bodies of the dead.

CHARLES For prisoners ask'st thou? Hell our prison is.
But tell me whom thou seek'st.

LUCY But where's the great Alcides of the field,
Valiant Lord Talbot, Earl of Shrewsbury,
Created for his rare success in arms
Great Earl of Washford, Waterford, and Valence,
Lord Talbot of Goodrig and Urchinfield,
Lord Strange of Blackmere, Lord Verdun of Alton,
Cromwell of Wingfield, Furnival of Sheffield,
The thrice victorious Lord of Falconbridge,
Knight of the noble Order of Saint George,
Worthy Saint Michael, and the Golden Fleece,
Great Marshal to Henry the Sixth
Of all his wars within the realm of France?

PUCELLE Here is a silly-stately style indeed!
The Turk, that two and fifty kingdoms hath,
Writes not so tedious a style as this.
Him that thou magnifiest with all these titles,
Stinking and fly-blown lies here at our feet.

LUCY Is Talbot slain – the Frenchmen's only Scourge,
Your kingdom's Terror and black Nemesis?
O, were mine eye-balls into bullets turn'd,
That I in rage might shoot them at your faces!
O that I could but call these dead to life!
It were enough to fright the realm of France.
Were but his picture left amongst you here,
It would amaze the proudest of you all.
Give me their bodies, that I bear them hence
And give them burial as beseems their worth.

PUCELLE I think this upstart is old Talbot's ghost,
He speaks with such a proud commanding spirit.
For God's sake, let him have them; to keep them
here,
They would but stink and putrefy the air.

CHARLES Go, take their bodies hence.

LUCY   I'll bear them hence;

But from their ashes shall be rear'd
A phoenix that shall make all France afeard.
Exeunt Lucy and attendants with the bodies.

CHARLES So we be rid, do with them what thou wilt.
And now to Paris in this conquering vein:
All will be ours now bloody Talbot's slain. *Exeunt.*

5.1 *Sennet. Enter* KING, GLOUCESTER *and* EXETER.

KING HENRY
Have you perus'd the letters from the Pope,
The Emperor, and the Earl of Armagnac?

GLOUCESTER I have, my lord; and their intent is this:
They humbly sue unto your Excellence
To have a godly peace concluded of
Between the realms of England and of France.

KING HENRY
How doth your Grace affect their motion?

GLOUCESTER
Well, my good lord, and as the only means
To stop effusion of our Christian blood
And stablish quietness on every side.

KING HENRY Ay, marry, uncle, for I always thought
It was both impious and unnatural
That such immanity and bloody strife
Should reign among professors of one faith.

GLOUCESTER Beside, my lord, the sooner to effect
And surer bind this knot of amity,
The Earl of Armagnac, near knit to Charles,
A man of great authority in France,
Proffers his only daughter to your Grace
In marriage, with a large and sumptuous dowry.

KING HENRY
Marriage, uncle! Alas, my years are young!
And fitter is my study and my books
Than wanton dalliance with a paramour.
Yet call th' ambassadors, and, as you please,
So let them have their answers every one:
I shall be well content with any choice
Tends to God's glory and my country's weal.

Enter WINCHESTER *in cardinal's habit, a* Legate
and two ambassadors.

EXETER What! is my Lord of Winchester install'd,
And call'd unto a cardinal's degree?
Then I perceive that will be verified
Henry the Fifth did sometime prophesy:
'If once he come to be a cardinal,
He'll make his cap co-equal with the crown.'

KING HENRY
My Lords Ambassadors, your several suits
Have been consider'd and debated on.
Your purpose is both good and reasonable;
And therefore are we certainly resolv'd
To draw conditions of a friendly peace,
Which by my Lord of Winchester we mean
Shall be transported presently to France.

GLOUCESTER
  And for the proffer of my lord your master,
  I have inform'd his Highness so at large,
  As, liking of the lady's virtuous gifts,
  Her beauty, and the value of her dower,
45 He doth intend she shall be England's Queen.
KING HENRY
  In argument and proof of which contract,
  Bear her this jewel, pledge of my affection,
  And so, my Lord Protector, see them guarded
  And safely brought to Dover; where, inshipp'd,
50 Commit them to the fortune of the sea.
          Exeunt all but Winchester and Legate.
WINCHESTER
  Stay, my Lord Legate; you shall first receive
  The sum of money which I promised
  Should be deliver'd to his Holiness
  For clothing me in these grave ornaments.
55 LEGATE   I will attend upon your lordship's leisure.
                          Exit.

WINCHESTER   Now Winchester will not submit, I trow,
  Or be inferior to the proudest peer.
  Humphrey of Gloucester, thou shalt well perceive
  That neither in birth nor for authority
60 The Bishop will be overborne by thee;
  I'll either make thee stoop and bend thy knee,
  Or sack this country with a mutiny.   *Exit.*

5.2 *Enter* CHARLES, BURGUNDY, ALENÇON, BASTARD,
        REIGNIER *and* LA PUCELLE.

CHARLES
  These news, my lords, may cheer our drooping
    spirits:
  'Tis said the stout Parisians do revolt
  And turn again unto the warlike French.
ALENÇON
  Then march to Paris, royal Charles of France,
5 And keep not back your powers in dalliance.
PUCELLE   Peace be amongst them, if they turn to us;
  Else ruin come within their palaces!

             Enter Scout.

SCOUT   Success unto our valiant general,
  And happiness to his accomplices!
CHARLES
10 What tidings send our scouts? I prithee speak.
SCOUT   The English army, that divided was
  Into two parties, is now conjoin'd in one,
  And means to give you battle presently.
CHARLES   Somewhat too sudden, sirs, the warning is;
15 But we will presently provide for them.
BURGUNDY   I trust the ghost of Talbot is not there:
  Now he is gone, my lord, you need not fear.
PUCELLE   Of all base passions, fear is most accurs'd.
  Command the conquest, Charles, it shall be thine:
20 Let Henry fret and all the world repine.

CHARLES   Then on, my lords; and France be fortunate.
                      Exeunt.

5.3   *Alarum: excursions. Enter* LA PUCELLE.

PUCELLE   The Regent conquers and the Frenchmen fly.
  Now help, ye charming spells and periapts;
  And ye choice spirits that admonish me,
  And give me signs of future accidents: [*Thunder.*]
  You speedy helpers that are substitutes   5
  Under the lordly monarch of the north,
  Appear and aid me in this enterprise!

          Enter fiends.

  This speed and quick appearance argues proof
  Of your accustom'd diligence to me.
  Now, ye familiar spirits that are cull'd   10
  Out of the powerful regions under earth,
  Help me this once, that France may get the field.
  [*They walk, and speak not.*]
  O, hold me not with silence over-long!
  Where I was wont to feed you with my blood,
  I'll lop a member off and give it you   15
  In earnest of a further benefit,
  So you do condescend to help me now.
  [*They hang their heads.*]
  No hope to have redress? My body shall
  Pay recompense if you will grant my suit.
  [*They shake their heads.*]
  Cannot my body nor blood-sacrifice   20
  Entreat you to your wonted furtherance?
  Then take my soul; my body, soul, and all,
  Before that England give the French the foil.
  [*They depart.*]
  See! they forsake me. Now the time is come
  That France must vail her lofty-plumed crest   25
  And let her head fall into England's lap.
  My ancient incantations are too weak,
  And hell too strong for me to buckle with:
  Now, France, thy glory droopeth to the dust.   *Exit.*

Excursions. BURGUNDY *and* YORK *fight hand to hand. The*
    French fly, leaving LA PUCELLE *in* YORK's *power.*

YORK   Damsel of France, I think I have you fast: 30
  Unchain your spirits now with spelling charms,
  And try if they can gain your liberty.
  A goodly prize, fit for the devil's grace!
  See how the ugly witch doth bend her brows,
  As if, with Circe, she would change my shape!   35
PUCELLE   Chang'd to a worser shape thou canst not be.
YORK   O, Charles the Dauphin is a proper man:
  No shape but his can please your dainty eye.
PUCELLE   A plaguing mischief light on Charles and thee!
  And may ye both be suddenly surpris'd   40
  By bloody hands, in sleeping on your beds!
YORK   Fell banning hag, enchantress, hold thy tongue!
PUCELLE   I prithee, give me leave to curse awhile.

YORK
   Curse, miscreant, when thou comest to the stake.
                               Exeunt.

Alarum. Enter SUFFOLK, *with* MARGARET *in his hand.*

45 SUFFOLK   Be what thou wilt, thou art my prisoner.
     [*Gazes on her.*]
   O fairest beauty, do not fear nor fly!
   For I will touch thee but with reverent hands,
   And lay them gently on thy tender side.
   I kiss these fingers for eternal peace.
50   Who art thou, say, that I may honour thee?
  MARGARET
   Margaret my name, and daughter to a king,
   The King of Naples – whosoe'er thou art.
  SUFFOLK   An earl I am, and Suffolk am I call'd.
   Be not offended, nature's miracle,
55   Thou art allotted to be ta'en by me:
   So doth the swan her downy cygnets save,
   Keeping them prisoner underneath her wings.
   Yet, if this servile usage once offend,
   Go and be free again as Suffolk's friend. [*She is going.*]
60   O, stay! – I have no power to let her pass;
   My hand would free her, but my heart says no.
   As plays the sun upon the glassy streams,
   Twinkling another counterfeited beam,
   So seems this gorgeous beauty to mine eyes.
65   Fain would I woo her, yet I dare not speak:
   I'll call for pen and ink, and write my mind.
   Fie, de la Pole! disable not thyself;
   Hast not a tongue? Is she not prisoner here?
   Wilt thou be daunted at a woman's sight?
70   Ay, beauty's princely majesty is such
   Confounds the tongue and makes the senses rough.
  MARGARET   Say, Earl of Suffolk, if thy name be so,
   What ransom must I pay before I pass?
   For I perceive I am thy prisoner.
75 SUFFOLK   How canst thou tell she will deny thy suit,
   Before thou make a trial of her love?
  MARGARET
   Why speak'st thou not? What ransom must I pay?
  SUFFOLK   She's beautiful, and therefore to be woo'd;
   She is a woman, therefore to be won.
80 MARGARET   Wilt thou accept of ransom, yea or no?
  SUFFOLK   Fond man, remember that thou hast a wife;
   Then how can Margaret be thy paramour?
  MARGARET
   'Twere best to leave him, for he will not hear.
  SUFFOLK   There all is marr'd; there lies a cooling card.
85 MARGARET   He talks at random; sure, the man is mad.
  SUFFOLK   And yet a dispensation may be had.
  MARGARET
   And yet I would that you would answer me.
  SUFFOLK   I'll win this Lady Margaret. For whom?
   Why, for my king! Tush, that's a wooden thing!
90 MARGARET   He talks of wood: it is some carpenter.
  SUFFOLK   Yet so my fancy may be satisfied,

And peace established between these realms.
But there remains a scruple in that too;
For though her father be the King of Naples,
Duke of Anjou and Maine, yet is he poor,   95
And our nobility will scorn the match.
MARGARET   Hear ye, captain, are you not at leisure?
SUFFOLK   It shall be so, disdain they ne'er so much;
  Henry is youthful, and will quickly yield. –
  Madam, I have a secret to reveal.   100
MARGARET
  What though I be enthrall'd? He seems a knight,
  And will not any way dishonour me.
SUFFOLK   Lady, vouchsafe to listen what I say.
MARGARET   Perhaps I shall be rescu'd by the French;
  And then I need not crave his courtesy.   105
SUFFOLK   Sweet madam, give me hearing in a cause –
MARGARET   Tush, women have been captivate ere now.
SUFFOLK   Lady, wherefore talk you so?
MARGARET   I cry you mercy, 'tis but *quid* for *quo.*
SUFFOLK   Say, gentle Princess, would you not suppose   110
  Your bondage happy, to be made a queen?
MARGARET   To be a queen in bondage is more vile
  Than is a slave in base servility;
  For princes should be free.
SUFFOLK   And so shall you,
  If happy England's royal king be free.   115
MARGARET   Why, what concerns his freedom unto me?
SUFFOLK   I'll undertake to make thee Henry's queen,
  To put a golden sceptre in thy hand
  And set a precious crown upon thy head,
  If thou wilt condescend to be my –
MARGARET   What?   120
SUFFOLK   His love.
MARGARET   I am unworthy to be Henry's wife.
SUFFOLK   No, gentle madam, I unworthy am
  To woo so fair a dame to be his wife,
  And have no portion in the choice myself.   125
  How say you, madam, are ye so content?
MARGARET   And if my father please, I am content.
SUFFOLK   Then call our captains and our colours forth!
  And, madam, at your father's castle walls
  We'll crave a parley, to confer with him.   130

    Sound a parley. Enter REIGNIER *on the walls.*

  See, Reignier, see, thy daughter prisoner!
REIGNIER   To whom?
SUFFOLK   To me.
REIGNIER   Suffolk, what remedy?
  I am a soldier, and unapt to weep
  Or to exclaim on fortune's fickleness.
SUFFOLK   Yes, there is remedy enough, my lord: 135
  Consent, and for thy honour give consent,
  Thy daughter shall be wedded to my king,
  Whom I with pain have woo'd and won thereto;
  And this her easy-held imprisonment
  Hath gain'd thy daughter princely liberty.   140
REIGNIER   Speaks Suffolk as he thinks?

SUFFOLK   Fair Margaret knows
   That Suffolk doth not flatter, face, or feign.
REIGNIER   Upon thy princely warrant I descend
   To give thee answer of thy just demand.
                                        Exit from the walls.

145   SUFFOLK   And here will I expect thy coming.

              Trumpets sound. Enter REIGNIER, *below.*

REIGNIER   Welcome, brave Earl, into our territories;
   Command in Anjou what your Honour please.
SUFFOLK   Thanks, Reignier, happy for so sweet a child,
   Fit to be made companion with a king.
150   What answer makes your Grace unto my suit?
REIGNIER   Since thou dost deign to woo her little worth
   To be the princely bride of such a lord,
   Upon condition I may quietly
   Enjoy mine own, the country Maine, and Anjou,
155   Free from oppression or the stroke of war,
   My daughter shall be Henry's, if he please.
SUFFOLK   That is her ransom; I deliver her;
   And these two counties I will undertake
   Your Grace shall well and quietly enjoy.
160   REIGNIER   And I again, in Henry's royal name,
   As deputy unto that gracious king,
   Give thee her hand for sign of plighted faith.
SUFFOLK   Reignier of France, I give thee kingly thanks,
   Because this is in traffic of a king.
165   [*aside*] And yet, methinks, I could be well content
   To be mine own attorney in this case.
   I'll over then to England with this news
   And make this marriage to be solemniz'd.
   So farewell, Reignier: set this diamond safe
170   In golden palaces, as it becomes.
REIGNIER   I do embrace thee, as I would embrace
   The Christian prince, King Henry, were he here.
MARGARET
   Farewell, my lord. Good wishes, praise, and prayers
   Shall Suffolk ever have of Margaret. [*She is going.*]
SUFFOLK
175   Farewell, sweet maid; but hark you, Margaret:
   No princely commendations to my king?
MARGARET   Such commendations as becomes a maid,
   A virgin, and his servant, say to him.
SUFFOLK   Words sweetly plac'd and modestly directed;
180   But, madam, I must trouble you again:
   No loving token to his Majesty?
MARGARET   Yes, my good lord; a pure unspotted heart,
   Never yet taint with love, I send the King.
SUFFOLK   And this withal. [*Kisses her.*]
185   MARGARET   That for thyself: I will not so presume
   To send such peevish tokens to a king.
                          Exeunt Reignier and Margaret.
SUFFOLK   O, wert thou for myself! But, Suffolk, stay;
   Thou may'st not wander in that labyrinth:
   There Minotaurs and ugly treasons lurk.
190   Solicit Henry with her wondrous praise.
   Bethink thee on her virtues that surmount,

   And natural graces that extinguish art;
   Repeat their semblance often on the seas,
   That, when thou com'st to kneel at Henry's feet,
   Thou may'st bereave him of his wits with wonder.   195
                                                  Exit.

5.4   *Enter* YORK, WARWICK *and others.*

YORK   Bring forth that sorceress condemn'd to burn.

      Enter LA PUCELLE *guarded, and a* Shepherd.

SHEPHERD
   Ah, Joan, this kills thy father's heart outright!
   Have I sought every country far and near,
   And, now it is my chance to find thee out,
   Must I behold thy timeless cruel death?   5
   Ah, Joan, sweet daughter, Joan I'll die with thee!
PUCELLE   Decrepit miser! base ignoble wretch!
   I am descended of a gentler blood:
   Thou art no father nor no friend of mine.
SHEPHERD
   Out, out! My lords, and please you, 'tis not so; 10
   I did beget her, all the parish knows:
   Her mother liveth yet, can testify
   She was the first fruit of my bachelorship.
WARWICK   Graceless, wilt thou deny thy parentage?
YORK   This argues what her kind of life hath been,   15
   Wicked and vile; and so her death concludes.
SHEPHERD   Fie, Joan, that thou wilt be so obstacle!
   God knows thou art a collop of my flesh;
   And for thy sake have I shed many a tear.
   Deny me not, I prithee, gentle Joan.   20
PUCELLE   Peasant, avaunt! You have suborn'd this man
   Of purpose to obscure my noble birth.
SHEPHERD   'Tis true, I gave a noble to the priest
   The morn that I was wedded to her mother.
   Kneel down and take my blessing, good my girl.   25
   Wilt thou not stoop? Now cursed be the time
   Of thy nativity! I would the milk
   Thy mother gave thee when thou suck'dst her breast
   Had been a little ratsbane for thy sake;
   Or else, when thou didst keep my lambs a-field, 30
   I wish some ravenous wolf had eaten thee.
   Dost thou deny thy father, cursed drab?
   O, burn her, burn her: hanging is too good.   *Exit.*
YORK   Take her away, for she hath liv'd too long,
   To fill the world with vicious qualities.   35
PUCELLE
   First let me tell you whom you have condemn'd:
   Not one begotten of a shepherd swain,
   But issued from the progeny of kings;
   Virtuous and holy, chosen from above,
   By inspiration of celestial grace,   40
   To work exceeding miracles on earth.
   I never had to do with wicked spirits;
   But you, that are polluted with your lusts,
   Stain'd with the guiltless blood of innocents,

45 Corrupt and tainted with a thousand vices,
Because you want the grace that others have,
You judge it straight a thing impossible
To compass wonders but by help of devils.
No, misconceived Joan of Aire hath been
50 A virgin from her tender infancy,
Chaste and immaculate in very thought;
Whose maiden blood, thus rigorously effus'd,
Will cry for vengeance at the gates of heaven.
YORK   Ay, ay; away with her to execution!
55 WARWICK   And hark ye, sirs; because she is a maid,
Spare for no faggots, let there be enow:
Place barrels of pitch upon the fatal stake,
That so her torture may be shortened.
PUCELLE   Will nothing turn your unrelenting hearts?
60 Then, Joan, discover thine infirmity
That warranteth by law to be thy privilege:
I am with child, ye bloody homicides;
Murder not then the fruit within my womb,
Although ye hale me to a violent death.
YORK
65 Now heaven forfend! The holy maid with child!
WARWICK   The greatest miracle that e'er ye wrought!
Is all your strict preciseness come to this?
YORK   She and the Dauphin have been juggling:
I did imagine what would be her refuge.
70 WARWICK   Well, go to; we will have no bastards live,
Especially since Charles must father it.
PUCELLE   You are deceiv'd; my child is none of his:
It was Alençon that enjoy'd my love.
YORK   Alençon, that notorious Machiavel!
75 It dies and if it had a thousand lives.
PUCELLE   O, give me leave, I have deluded you:
'Twas neither Charles, nor yet the Duke I nam'd,
But Reignier, King of Naples, that prevail'd.
WARWICK   A married man! that's most intolerable.
YORK
80 Why, here's a girl! I think she knows not well –
There were so many – whom she may accuse.
WARWICK   It's sign she hath been liberal and free.
YORK   And yet, forsooth, she is a virgin pure!
Strumpet, thy words condemn thy brat and thee:
85 Use no entreaty, for it is in vain.
PUCELLE
Then lead me hence, with whom I leave my curse:
May never glorious sun reflex his beams
Upon the country where you make abode;
But darkness and the gloomy shade of death
90 Environ you, till mischief and despair
Drive you to break your necks or hang yourselves!
Exit guarded.
YORK
Break thou in pieces and consume to ashes,
Thou foul accursed minister of hell!

Enter Cardinal BEAUFORT, *Bishop of* WINCHESTER, *attended.*

WINCHESTER   Lord Regent, I do greet your Excellence
With letters of commission from the King. 95
For know, my lords, the states of Christendom,
Mov'd with remorse of these outrageous broils,
Have earnestly implor'd a general peace
Betwixt our nation and the aspiring French;
And here at hand the Dauphin and his train 100
Approacheth to confer about the same.
YORK   Is all our travail turn'd to this effect?
After the slaughter of so many peers,
So many captains, gentlemen, and soldiers,
That in this quarrel have been overthrown 105
And sold their bodies for their country's benefit,
Shall we at last conclude effeminate peace?
Have we not lost most part of all the towns,
By treason, falsehood, and by treachery,
Our great progenitors had conquered? 110
O, Warwick, Warwick! I foresee with grief
The utter loss of all the realm of France.
WARWICK   Be patient, York: if we conclude a peace,
It shall be with such strict and several covenants
As little shall the Frenchmen gain thereby. 115

Enter CHARLES, ALENÇON, BASTARD, REIGNIER
and others.

CHARLES   Since, lords of England, it is thus agreed
That peaceful truce shall be proclaim'd in France,
We come to be informed by yourselves
What the conditions of that league must be.
YORK   Speak, Winchester, for boiling choler chokes 120
The hollow passage of my poison'd voice
By sight of these our baleful enemies.
WINCHESTER   Charles and the rest, it is enacted thus:
That, in regard King Henry gives consent,
Of mere compassion and of lenity, 125
To ease your country of distressful war,
And suffer you to breathe in fruitful peace,
You shall become true liegemen to his crown.
And, Charles, upon condition thou wilt swear
To pay him tribute and submit thyself, 130
Thou shalt be plac'd as viceroy under him,
And still enjoy thy regal dignity.
ALENÇON   Must he be then as shadow of himself?
Adorn his temples with a coronet,
And yet, in substance and authority, 135
Retain but privilege of a private man?
This proffer is absurd and reasonless.
CHARLES   'Tis known already that I am possess'd
With more than half the Gallian territories,
And therein reverenc'd for their lawful king: 140
Shall I, for lucre of the rest unvanquish'd,
Detract so much from that prerogative
As to be call'd but viceroy of the whole?
No, Lord Ambassador, I'll rather keep
That which I have than, coveting for more, 145
Be cast from possibility of all.
YORK   Insulting Charles! Hast thou by secret means

Us'd intercession to obtain a league,
And, now the matter grows to compromise,
Stand'st thou aloof upon comparison?
Either accept the title thou usurp'st,
Of benefit proceeding from our king
And not of any challenge of desert,
Or we will plague thee with incessant wars.

REIGNIER [*aside to Charles*]
My lord, you do not well in obstinacy
To cavil in the course of this contract;
If once it be neglected, ten to one
We shall not find like opportunity.

ALENÇON [*aside to Charles*]
To say the truth, it is your policy
To save your subjects from such massacre
And ruthless slaughters as are daily seen
By our proceeding in hostility;
And therefore take this compact of a truce,
Although you break it when your pleasure serves.

WARWICK
How say'st thou, Charles? shall our condition stand?

CHARLES   It shall; only reserv'd you claim no interest
In any of our towns of garrison.

YORK   Then swear allegiance to his Majesty:
As thou art knight, never to disobey
Nor be rebellious to the crown of England,
Thou, nor thy nobles, to the crown of England.
[*Charles and the rest give tokens of fealty.*]
So, now dismiss your army when ye please;
Hang up your ensigns, let your drums be still,
For here we entertain a solemn peace.   *Exeunt.*

5.5   *Enter* SUFFOLK *in conference with the* KING,
            GLOUCESTER *and* EXETER.

KING HENRY
Your wondrous rare description, noble Earl,
Of beauteous Margaret hath astonish'd me:
Her virtues graced with external gifts
Do breed love's settled passions in my heart:
And like as rigour of tempestuous gusts
Provokes the mightiest hulk against the tide,
So am I driven by breath of her renown
Either to suffer shipwreck, or arrive
Where I may have fruition of her love.

SUFFOLK   Tush, my good lord, this superficial tale
Is but a preface of her worthy praise;
The chief perfections of that lovely dame,
Had I sufficient skill to utter them,
Would make a volume of enticing lines,
Able to ravish any dull conceit;
And, which is more, she is not so divine,
So full replete with choice of all delights,
But with as humble lowliness of mind
She is content to be at your command;
Command, I mean, of virtuous chaste intents,
To love and honour Henry as her lord.

KING HENRY   And otherwise will Henry ne'er presume.
Therefore, my Lord Protector, give consent
That Margaret may be England's royal Queen.

GLOUCESTER   So should I give consent to flatter sin.
You know, my lord, your Highness is betroth'd
Unto another lady of esteem;
How shall we then dispense with that contract,
And not deface your honour with reproach.

SUFFOLK   As doth a ruler with unlawful oaths;
Or one that, at a triumph, having vow'd
To try his strength, forsaketh yet the lists
By reason of his adversary's odds:
A poor earl's daughter is unequal odds,
And therefore may be broke without offence.

GLOUCESTER
Why, what, I pray, is Margaret more than that?
Her father is no better than an earl,
Although in glorious titles he excel.

SUFFOLK   Yes, my lord, her father is a king,
The King of Naples and Jerusalem;
And of such great authority in France
As his alliance will confirm our peace,
And keep the Frenchmen in allegiance.

GLOUCESTER   And so the Earl of Armagnac may do,
Because he is near kinsman unto Charles.

EXETER
Beside, his wealth doth warrant a liberal dower,
Where Reignier sooner will receive than give.

SUFFOLK
A dower, my lords! Disgrace not so your king,
That he should be so abject, base, and poor,
To choose for wealth and not for perfect love.
Henry is able to enrich his queen,
And not to seek a queen to make him rich:
So worthless peasants bargain for their wives,
As market-men for oxen, sheep, or horse.
Marriage is a matter of more worth
Than to be dealt in by attorneyship;
Not whom we will, but whom his Grace affects,
Must be companion of his nuptial bed;
And therefore, lords, since he affects her most,
That most of all these reasons bindeth us
In our opinions she should be preferr'd.
For what is wedlock forced but a hell,
An age of discord and continual strife?
Whereas the contrary bringeth bliss,
And is a pattern of celestial peace.
Whom should we match with Henry, being a king,
But Margaret, that is daughter to a king?
Her peerless feature, joined with her birth,
Approves her fit for none but for a king;
Her valiant courage and undaunted spirit,
More than in women commonly is seen,
Will answer our hope in issue of a king;
For Henry, son unto a conqueror,
Is likely to beget more conquerors,
If with a lady of so high resolve

As is fair Margaret he be link'd in love.
Then yield, my lords; and here conclude with me
That Margaret shall be Queen, and none but she.
KING HENRY
  Whether it be through force of your report,
80 My noble Lord of Suffolk, or for that
My tender youth was never yet attaint
With any passion of inflaming love,
I cannot tell; but this I am assur'd,
I feel such sharp dissension in my breast,
85 Such fierce alarums both of hope and fear,
As I am sick with working of my thoughts.
Take therefore shipping; post, my lord, to France;
Agree to any covenants, and procure
That Lady Margaret do vouchsafe to come
90 To cross the seas to England and be crown'd
King Henry's faithful and anointed queen.
For your expenses and sufficient charge,

Among the people gather up a tenth.
Be gone, I say; for till you do return
I rest perplexed with a thousand cares. 95
And you, good uncle, banish all offence;
If you do censure me by what you were,
Not what you are, I know it will excuse
This sudden execution of my will.
And so conduct me where from company 100
I may revolve and ruminate my grief.   *Exit.*
GLOUCESTER   Ay, grief, I fear me, both at first and last.
    Exeunt Gloucester and Exeter.
SUFFOLK
  Thus Suffolk hath prevail'd; and thus he goes,
As did the youthful Paris once to Greece;
With hope to find the like event in love, 105
But prosper better than the Trojan did.
Margaret shall now be Queen, and rule the King;
But I will rule both her, the King, and realm.   *Exit.*

King Henry VI, Part 2

Before its appearance as the seventh of the histories in the Folio of 1623, a version of *King Henry VI, Part 2* was published in 1594 as *The First Part of the Contention betwixt the two famous Houses of York and Lancaster*. The 1594 Quarto was reprinted in 1600, and in 1619 this play and *King Henry VI, Part 3* (published in 1595 as *The true Tragedy of Richard Duke of York*) were combined and published as *The Whole Contention between the two Famous Houses, Lancaster and York*. These earliest printings of *Part 2* differ from the Folio text: they are shorter by about a third and seem to represent a reported version, put together probably by actors touring with the play. Thus they have little authority when compared with the fuller and better text available in the 1623 Folio, but they do provide, by virtue of their provenance, important evidence of early theatrical practice.

King Henry VI, Part 2, continues the history soon after it breaks off in *Part 1*, but with its own formal and thematic integrity. The play covers ten years of Henry's tumultuous reign, beginning with Margaret's coronation (which took place in May 1445, two years after the disgrace of Duke Humphrey's wife Eleanor, also included within the action) and continues to the Battle of St Albans (1455). France has now effectively been lost. The factionalism evident in *Part 1* finally bursts here into full-fledged civil war, and the aristocratic struggles for the throne have a demotic echo in the emergence of the popular unrest that explodes into Jack Cade's rebellion. Through it all, we can see the ominous emergence of one man able to impose his will on history, Richard Plantagenet, Duke of York.

Part 1 plays off England against France, Talbot against Joan, mighty opposites that work to define a model of English greatness, however vulnerable it is finally shown to be; *Part 2* confronts the stresses and tensions tearing at the fabric of the nation itself. This is a new world, no longer based on aristocratic honour and feudal obligation, but a world of appetite and ambition, a world in which neither Henry's piety nor Gloucester's virtue offers protection or relief.

Jack Cade's rebellion is perhaps a mere inset into the dismal story of aristocratic wrangles, but it is a telling episode. It can be seen as evidence of the dangerous unruliness of the rabble, a degrading comedy of misrule, but the rebels voice legitimate social concerns and aspirations. If the uprising seems finally a travesty of the desire for social justice, it is because their leader, Cade, is revealed as a pawn of York's ambitions and his pathetic mimic, rather than because the issues are themselves laughable.

Thirteen people die in *King Henry VI, Part 2*, none in easeful sleep. The language is of snakes, spiders and scorpions; bleeding heifers, slaughtered calves, innocent lambs threatened by wolves; butchers with axes and headless bodies on piles of dung. Not far beneath the veneer of courtly sophistication is a fierce and violent world that can no longer be ordered by the institutions and ceremonies designed to control the flux of reality. The fall of the good and innocent Humphrey, Duke of Gloucester, is at once symptom and at least partial cause of the lawlessness that reigns. His absence leaves the state without any effective force of social coherence. The idea of kingship itself is endlessly appealed to, but it is never a unifying centre for the country or the play; for the ambitious York it is only the object of his brazen will to power, and for the inept Henry it is a condition to be escaped: 'never subject longed to be a king / As I do long and wish to be a subject'.

Of the three parts of *King Henry VI*, Dr Johnson thought 'the second the best'. Certainly it is a powerful play, though one that modern audiences have had little chance to see. When played at all, it has usually been cut and adapted, as in John Barton's two-part *The Wars of the Roses* (1963), tailored from the three parts of *King Henry VI*, or in 1986 by the English Shakespeare Company and in 1988 by the Royal Shakespeare Company, both of whom also condensed the three plays into two. In 1977, however, Terry Hands directed all three plays in sequence at Stratford-upon-Avon, with Alan Howard playing the King. The stark staging and strong performances revealed the dramatic power of the plays and the darkness of their political understanding.

The Arden text is based on the 1623 First Folio.

KING Henry the Sixth
Humphrey, Duke of GLOUCESTER · *his uncle*
CARDINAL Beaufort · *Bishop of Winchester, great-uncle to the King*
Richard Plantagenet, Duke of YORK
EDWARD and RICHARD · *his sons*
Duke of SOMERSET
Duke of SUFFOLK
Duke of BUCKINGHAM
Lord CLIFFORD
YOUNG CLIFFORD · *his son*
Earl of SALISBURY
Earl of WARWICK · *his son*
Lord SCALES
Lord SAY
Sir Humphrey STAFFORD *and*
William Stafford, *his* BROTHER
Sir John STANLEY
VAUX
Matthew GOFFE
Walter WHITMORE
LIEUTENANT, MASTER *and Master's* MATE
Two GENTLEMEN · *prisoners with Suffolk*
John HUME *and* John SOUTHWELL · *priests*
Roger BOLINGBROKE · *a conjurer*
Thomas HORNER · *an armourer*
PETER · *his man*
CLERK · *of Chartham*
MAYOR of Saint Albans
SIMPCOX · *an impostor*
Jack CADE · *a rebel*
BEVIS, John HOLLAND, Dick the BUTCHER,
Smith the WEAVER, MICHAEL, *etc.* } *followers of Cade*
Alexander IDEN · *a Kentish gentleman*
Two MURDERERS

Margaret, QUEEN *to King Henry*
Eleanor Cobham, DUCHESS of Gloucester
MARGERY JOURDAIN · *a witch*
WIFE *to Simpcox*

Lords, Ladies and Attendants; Herald; Petitioners, Aldermen,
a Beadle, Sheriff and Officers; Citizens, Prentices, Falconers,
Guards, Soldiers, Messengers, etc.

A Spirit

King Henry VI, Part 2

1.1 *Flourish of trumpets: then hautboys. Enter the* KING, DUKE HUMPHREY, SALISBURY, WARWICK *and* BEAUFORT *on the one side; the* QUEEN, SUFFOLK, YORK, SOMERSET *and* BUCKINGHAM, *on the other.*

SUFFOLK   As by your high imperial Majesty
I had in charge at my depart for France,
As procurator to your Excellence,
To marry Princess Margaret for your Grace;
So, in the famous ancient city, Tours,
In presence of the Kings of France and Sicil,
The Dukes of Orleans, Calaber, Bretagne, and
    Alençon,
Seven earls, twelve barons, and twenty reverend
    bishops,
I have perform'd my task, and was espous'd:
And humbly now upon my bended knee,
In sight of England and her lordly peers,
Deliver up my title in the Queen
To your most gracious hands, that are the substance
Of that great shadow I did represent;
The happiest gift that ever marquess gave,
The fairest queen that ever king receiv'd.

KING   Suffolk, arise. Welcome, Queen Margaret:
I can express no kinder sign of love
Than this kind kiss. O Lord, that lends me life,
Lend me a heart replete with thankfulness!
For thou hast given me in this beauteous face
A world of earthly blessings to my soul,
If sympathy of love unite our thoughts.

QUEEN
Great King of England, and my gracious lord,
The mutual conference that my mind hath had
By day, by night, waking, and in my dreams,
In courtly company, or at my beads,
With you mine alderliefest sovereign,
Makes me the bolder to salute my king
With ruder terms, such as my wit affords,
And over joy of heart doth minister.

KING   Her sight did ravish, but her grace in speech,
Her words y-clad with wisdom's majesty,
Makes me from wond'ring fall to weeping joys,
Such is the fulness of my heart's content.
Lords, with one cheerful voice welcome my love.

ALL *[kneeling]*
Long live Queen Margaret, England's happiness!
                    [Flourish.]

QUEEN   We thank you all.

SUFFOLK
My Lord Protector, so it please your Grace,
Here are the articles of contracted peace
Between our sovereign and the French King Charles,
For eighteen months concluded by consent.

GLOUCESTER *[Reads.]*   *Imprimis, It is agreed between the
French King Charles, and William de la Pole,
Marquess of Suffolk, ambassador for Henry King of
England, That the said Henry shall espouse the Lady*
*Margaret, daughter unto Reignier King of Naples,
Sicilia, and Jerusalem, and crown her Queen of England,
ere the thirtieth of May next ensuing. Item, It is further
agreed between them, That the duchy of Anjou and the
county of Maine shall be releas'd and deliver'd to the
King her father –* [*Lets the paper fall.*]

KING   Uncle, how now!

GLOUCESTER   Pardon me, gracious lord;
Some sudden qualm hath struck me at the heart
And dimm'd mine eyes, that I can read no further.

KING   Uncle of Winchester, I pray read on.

CARDINAL   *Item, It is further agreed between them, That
the duchy of Anjou and the county of Maine shall be
releas'd and deliver'd to the King her father, and she sent
over of the King of England's own proper cost and
charges, without having any dowry.*

KING   They please us well.
Lord Marquess, kneel down: we here create thee
First Duke of Suffolk, and girt thee with the sword.
Cousin of York, we here discharge your Grace
From being Regent in the parts of France,
Till term of eighteen months be full expir'd.
Thanks, uncle Winchester, Gloucester, and York,
Buckingham, Somerset, Salisbury, and Warwick;
We thank you all for this great favour done,
In entertainment to my princely Queen.
Come, let us in, and with all speed provide
To see her coronation be perform'd.
            *Exeunt King, Queen and Suffolk. Gloucester
                            stays all the rest.*

GLOUCESTER
Brave peers of England, pillars of the state,
To you Duke Humphrey must unload his grief –
Your grief, the common grief of all the land.
What! did my brother Henry spend his youth,
His valour, coin, and people, in the wars?
Did he so often lodge in open field,
In winter's cold, and summer's parching heat,
To conquer France, his true inheritance?
And did my brother Bedford toil his wits,
To keep by policy what Henry got?
Have you yourselves, Somerset, Buckingham,
Brave York, Salisbury, and victorious Warwick,
Receiv'd deep scars in France and Normandy?
Or hath mine uncle Beaufort and myself,
With all the learned Council of the realm,
Studied so long, sat in the Council House
Early and late, debating to and fro
How France and Frenchmen might be kept in awe?
And had his highness in his infancy
Crowned in Paris, in despite of foes?
And shall these labours and these honours die?
Shall Henry's conquest, Bedford's vigilance,
Your deeds of war, and all our counsel die?
O peers of England! shameful is this league,
Fatal this marriage, cancelling your fame,

Blotting your names from books of memory,
100   Razing the characters of your renown,
Defacing monuments of conquer'd France,
Undoing all, as all had never been!

CARDINAL
Nephew, what means this passionate discourse,
This peroration with such circumstance?
105   For France, 'tis ours; and we will keep it still.

GLOUCESTER
Ay, uncle, we will keep it, if we can;
But now it is impossible we should.
Suffolk, the new-made duke that rules the roast,
Hath given the duchy of Anjou and Maine
110   Unto the poor King Reignier, whose large style
Agrees not with the leanness of his purse.

SALISBURY
Now, by the death of Him that died for all,
These counties were the keys of Normandy!
But wherefore weeps Warwick, my valiant son?

WARWICK
115   For grief that they are past recovery:
For, were there hope to conquer them again,
My sword should shed hot blood, mine eyes no tears.
Anjou and Maine! myself did win them both;
Those provinces these arms of mine did conquer:
120   And are the cities, that I got with wounds,
Deliver'd up again with peaceful words?
Mort Dieu!

YORK
For Suffolk's duke, may he be suffocate,
That dims the honour of this warlike isle!
125   France should have torn and rent my very heart
Before I would have yielded to this league.
I never read but England's kings have had
Large sums of gold and dowries with their wives;
And our King Henry gives away his own,
130   To match with her that brings no vantages.

GLOUCESTER
A proper jest, and never heard before,
That Suffolk should demand a whole fifteenth
For costs and charges in transporting her!
She should have stayed in France, and starv'd in
     France,
135   Before –

CARDINAL
My Lord of Gloucester, now ye grow too hot:
It was the pleasure of my lord the King.

GLOUCESTER
My Lord of Winchester, I know your mind:
'Tis not my speeches that you do mislike,
140   But 'tis my presence that doth trouble ye.
Rancour will out: proud prelate, in thy face
I see thy fury. If I longer stay
We shall begin our ancient bickerings.
Lordings, farewell; and say, when I am gone,
145   I prophesied France will be lost ere long.   *Exit.*

CARDINAL
So, there goes our Protector in a rage.
'Tis known to you he is mine enemy;
Nay, more, an enemy unto you all,
And no great friend, I fear me, to the King.
150   Consider, lords, he is the next of blood,
And heir apparent to the English crown:
Had Henry got an empire by his marriage,
And all the wealthy kingdoms of the west,
There's reason he should be displeas'd at it.
155   Look to it, lords; let not his smoothing words
Bewitch your hearts; be wise and circumspect.
What though the common people favour him,
Calling him 'Humphrey, the good Duke of
     Gloucester,'
Clapping their hands, and crying with loud voice
160   'Jesu maintain your royal Excellence!'
With 'God preserve the good Duke Humphrey!'
I fear me, lords, for all this flattering gloss,
He will be found a dangerous Protector.

BUCKINGHAM
Why should he then protect our sovereign,
165   He being of age to govern of himself?
Cousin of Somerset, join you with me,
And all together, with the Duke of Suffolk,
We'll quickly hoise Duke Humphrey from his seat.

CARDINAL
This weighty business will not brook delay;
170   I'll to the Duke of Suffolk presently.   *Exit.*

SOMERSET
Cousin of Buckingham, though Humphrey's pride
And greatness of his place be grief to us,
Yet let us watch the haughty Cardinal:
His insolence is more intolerable
175   Than all the princes' in the land beside:
If Gloucester be displac'd, he'll be Protector.

BUCKINGHAM
Or thou or I, Somerset, will be Protector,
Despite Duke Humphrey or the Cardinal.
           Exeunt Buckingham and Somerset.

SALISBURY
Pride went before, Ambition follows him.
180   While these do labour for their own preferment,
Behooves it us to labour for the realm.
I never saw but Humphrey, Duke of Gloucester,
Did bear him like a noble gentleman.
Oft have I seen the haughty Cardinal –
185   More like a soldier than a man o'th' church,
As stout and proud as he were lord of all –
Swear like a ruffian, and demean himself
Unlike the ruler of a commonweal.
Warwick, my son, the comfort of my age,
190   Thy deeds, thy plainness, and thy house-keeping,
Hath won the greatest favour of the commons,
Excepting none but good Duke Humphrey:
And, brother York, thy acts in Ireland,

In bringing them to civil discipline,
Thy late exploits done in the heart of France,
When thou wert Regent for our sovereign,
Have made thee fear'd and honour'd of the people.
The reverence of mine age, and Nevil's name,
Is of no little force, if I command.
Join we together for the public good,
In what we can, to bridle and suppress
The pride of Suffolk and the Cardinal,
With Somerset's and Buckingham's ambition;
And, as we may, cherish Duke Humphrey's deeds,
While they do tend the profit of the land.

WARWICK
So God help Warwick, as he loves the land,
And common profit of his country!

YORK
And so says York – [aside] for he hath greatest cause.

SALISBURY
Then let's make haste, and look unto the main.

WARWICK
Unto the main! O father, Maine is lost!
That Maine which by main force Warwick did win,
And would have kept so long as breath did last:
Main chance, father, you meant; but I meant Maine,
Which I will win from France, or else be slain.
                              Exeunt Warwick and Salisbury.

YORK   Anjou and Maine are given to the French;
Paris is lost; the state of Normandy
Stands on a tickle point now they are gone;
Suffolk concluded on the articles,
The peers agreed, and Henry was well pleas'd
To change two dukedoms for a duke's fair daughter.
I cannot blame them all: what is't to them?
'Tis thine they give away, and not their own.
Pirates may make cheap pennyworths of their pillage,
And purchase friends, and give to courtezans,
Still revelling like lords till all be gone;
While as the silly owner of the goods
Weeps over them, and wrings his hapless hands,
And shakes his head, and trembling stands aloof,
While all is shar'd and all is borne away,
Ready to starve, and dare not touch his own.
So York must sit and fret and bite his tongue
While his own lands are bargain'd for and sold.
Methinks the realms of England, France, and Ireland
Bear that proportion to my flesh and blood
As did the fatal brand Althaea burnt
Unto the prince's heart of Calydon.
Anjou and Maine both given unto the French!
Cold news for me, for I had hope of France,
Even as I have of fertile England's soil.
A day will come when York shall claim his own;
And therefore I will take the Nevils' parts
And make a show of love to proud Duke Humphrey,
And when I spy advantage, claim the crown,
For that's the golden mark I seek to hit.
Nor shall proud Lancaster usurp my right,

Nor hold the sceptre in his childish fist,
Nor wear the diadem upon his head,
Whose church-like humour fits not for a crown.
Then, York, be still awhile, till time do serve:
Watch thou, and wake when others be asleep,   250
To pry into the secrets of the state;
Till Henry surfeit in the joys of love,
With his new bride and England's dear-bought queen,
And Humphrey with the peers be fall'n at jars:
Then will I raise aloft the milk-white rose,   255
With whose sweet smell the air shall be perfum'd,
And in my standard bear the arms of York,
To grapple with the house of Lancaster;
And force perforce I'll make him yield the crown,
Whose bookish rule hath pull'd fair England down. 260
                                          Exit.

1.2 *Enter* DUKE HUMPHREY *and his wife* ELEANOR.

DUCHESS
Why droops my lord, like over-ripen'd corn,
Hanging the head at Ceres' plenteous load?
Why doth the great Duke Humphrey knit his brows,
As frowning at the favours of the world?
Why are thine eyes fix'd to the sullen earth,   5
Gazing on that which seems to dim thy sight?
What seest thou there? King Henry's diadem,
Enchas'd with all the honours of the world?
If so, gaze on, and grovel on thy face,
Until thy head be circled with the same.   10
Put forth thy hand, reach at the glorious gold.
What, is't too short? I'll lengthen it with mine;
And, having both together heav'd it up,
We'll both together lift our heads to heaven,
And never more abase our sight so low   15
As to vouchsafe one glance unto the ground.

GLOUCESTER
O Nell, sweet Nell, if thou dost love thy lord,
Banish the canker of ambitious thoughts!
And may that hour, when I imagine ill
Against my king and nephew, virtuous Henry,   20
Be my last breathing in this mortal world!
My troublous dreams this night doth make me sad.

DUCHESS
What dream'd my lord? Tell me, and I'll requite it
With sweet rehearsal of my morning's dream.

GLOUCESTER
Methought this staff, mine office-badge in court, 25
Was broke in twain; by whom I have forgot,
But, as I think, it was by th' Cardinal;
And on the pieces of the broken wand
Were plac'd the heads of Edmund Duke of Somerset,
And William de la Pole, first Duke of Suffolk.   30
This was my dream; what it doth bode, God knows.

DUCHESS
Tut! this was nothing but an argument,
That he that breaks a stick of Gloucester's grove

Shall lose his head for his presumption.
35   But list to me, my Humphrey, my sweet duke:
Methought I sat in seat of majesty
In the cathedral church of Westminster,
And in that chair where kings and queens are
            crown'd;
40   Where Henry and Dame Margaret kneel'd to me,
And on my head did set the diadem.

GLOUCESTER
Nay, Eleanor, then must I chide outright:
Presumptuous dame! ill-nurtur'd Eleanor!
Art thou not second woman in the realm,
And the Protector's wife, belov'd of him?
45   Hast thou not worldly pleasure at command,
Above the reach or compass of thy thought?
And wilt thou still be hammering treachery,
To tumble down thy husband and thyself
From top of Honour to Disgrace's feet?
50   Away from me, and let me hear no more!

DUCHESS
What, what, my lord! Are you so choleric
With Eleanor, for telling but her dream?
Next time I'll keep my dreams unto myself,
And not be check'd.

GLOUCESTER
55   Nay, be not angry; I am pleas'd again.

Enter a Messenger.

MESSENGER
My Lord Protector, 'tis his Highness' pleasure
You do prepare to ride unto Saint Albans,
Where as the King and Queen do mean to hawk.

GLOUCESTER
I go. Come, Nell, thou 'lt ride with us, I'm sure?
60   DUCHESS   Yes, my good lord, I'll follow presently.
                    Exeunt Gloucester and Messenger.
Follow I must; I cannot go before,
While Gloucester bears this base and humble mind.
Were I a man, a duke, and next of blood,
I would remove these tedious stumbling-blocks
65   And smooth my way upon their headless necks;
And, being a woman, I will not be slack
To play my part in Fortune's pageant.
Where are you there, Sir John? nay, fear not, man,
We are alone; here's none but thee and I.

Enter HUME.

70   HUME   Jesu preserve your royal Majesty!
DUCHESS
What say'st thou? Majesty! I am but Grace.
HUME
But, by the grace of God, and Hume's advice,
Your Grace's title shall be multiplied.
DUCHESS
What say'st thou, man? Hast thou as yet conferr'd
75   With Margery Jourdain, the witch of Eie,
With Bolingbroke, the cunning conjurer,

And will they undertake to do me good?
HUME
This they have promis'd me, to show your Highness
A spirit rais'd from depth of under ground,
That shall make answer to such questions   80
As by your Grace shall be propounded him.
DUCHESS
It is enough: I'll think upon the questions.
When from Saint Albans we do make return
We'll see these things effected to the full.
Here, Hume, take this reward; make merry, man,   85
With thy confederates in this weighty cause.   *Exit.*
HUME
Hume must make merry with the Duchess' gold;
Marry and shall. But how now, Sir John Hume!
Seal up your lips and give no words but mum:
The business asketh silent secrecy.   90
Dame Eleanor gives gold to bring the witch:
Gold cannot come amiss, were she a devil.
Yet have I gold flies from another coast:
I dare not say from the rich Cardinal
And from the great and new-made Duke of Suffolk;   95
Yet I do find it so: for, to be plain,
They, knowing Dame Eleanor's aspiring humour,
Have hired me to undermine the Duchess,
And buz these conjurations in her brain.
They say 'A crafty knave does need no broker';   100
Yet am I Suffolk and the Cardinal's broker.
Hume, if you take not heed, you shall go near
To call them both a pair of crafty knaves.
Well, so it stands; and thus, I fear, at last
Hume's knavery will be the Duchess' wrack,   105
And her attainture will be Humphrey's fall.
Sort how it will, I shall have gold for all.   *Exit.*

1.3 *Enter three or four* Petitioners, PETER, *the armourer's
man, being one.*

1 PETITIONER   My masters, let's stand close: my Lord
Protector will come this way by and by, and then we
may deliver our supplications in the quill.
2 PETITIONER   Marry, the Lord protect him, for he's a
good man, Jesu bless him!   5

Enter SUFFOLK *and* QUEEN.

PETER   Here a comes, methinks, and the Queen with
him. I'll be the first, sure.
2 PETITIONER   Come back, fool! this is the Duke of
Suffolk, and not my Lord Protector.
SUFFOLK   How now, fellow! would'st any thing with me?   10
1 PETITIONER   I pray, my lord, pardon me: I took ye for
my Lord Protector.
QUEEN [*Reads.*]   *To my Lord Protector!* Are your
supplications to his lordship? Let me see them: what
is thine?   15
1 PETITIONER   Mine is, and 't please your Grace, against
John Goodman, my Lord Cardinal's man, for keeping my

house, and lands, and wife, and all, from me.

SUFFOLK   Thy wife too! that's some wrong indeed.
What's yours? What's here! [*Reads.*] *Against the Duke
of Suffolk, for enclosing the commons of Long Melford.*
How now, sir knave!

2 PETITIONER   Alas! sir, I am but a poor petitioner of our
whole township.

PETER   Against my master, Thomas Horner, for saying
that the Duke of York was rightful heir to the crown.

QUEEN   What say'st thou? Did the Duke of York say he
was rightful heir to the crown?

PETER   That my master was? No, forsooth: my master
said that he was, and that the King was an usurer.

QUEEN   An usurper, thou wouldst say.

PETER   Ay, forsooth, an usurper.

SUFFOLK   Who is there?

Enter servant.

Take this fellow in, and send for his master with a
pursuivant presently. We'll hear more of your matter
before the King.   *Exit with Peter.*

QUEEN   And as for you, that love to be protected
Under the wings of our Protector's grace,
Begin your suits anew, and sue to him.
[*Tears the supplication.*]
Away, base cullions! Suffolk, let them go.

ALL   Come, let's be gone.   *Exeunt.*

QUEEN   My Lord of Suffolk, say, is this the guise,
Is this the fashions in the court of England?
Is this the government of Britain's isle,
And this the royalty of Albion's king?
What! shall King Henry be a pupil still
Under the surly Gloucester's governance?
Am I a queen in title and in style,
And must be made a subject to a duke?
I tell thee, Pole, when in the city Tours
Thou ran'st a tilt in honour of my love,
And stol'st away the ladies' hearts of France,
I thought King Henry had resembled thee
In courage, courtship, and proportion:
But all his mind is bent to holiness,
To number Ave-Maries on his beads;
His champions are the prophets and apostles,
His weapons holy saws of sacred writ,
His study is his tilt-yard, and his loves
Are brazen images of canoniz'd saints.
I would the college of the Cardinals
Would choose him Pope, and carry him to Rome,
And set the triple crown upon his head:
That were a state fit for his Holiness.

SUFFOLK   Madam, be patient; as I was cause
Your Highness came to England, so will I
In England work your Grace's full content.

QUEEN
Beside the haught Protector, have we Beaufort
The imperious churchman; Somerset, Buckingham,
And grumbling York; and not the least of these

But can do more in England than the King.

SUFFOLK
And he of these that can do most of all
Cannot do more in England than the Nevils:
Salisbury and Warwick are no simple peers.

QUEEN   Not all these lords do vex me half so much   75
As that proud dame, the Lord Protector's wife:
She sweeps it through the court with troops of ladies,
More like an empress than Duke Humphrey's wife.
Strangers in court do take her for the queen:
She bears a duke's revenues on her back,   80
And in her heart she scorns our poverty.
Shall I not live to be aveng'd on her?
Contemptuous base-born callet as she is,
She vaunted 'mongst her minions t'other day,
The very train of her worst wearing gown   85
Was better worth than all my father's lands,
Till Suffolk gave two dukedoms for his daughter.

SUFFOLK
Madam, myself have lim'd a bush for her,
And plac'd a quire of such enticing birds
That she will light to listen to their lays,   90
And never mount to trouble you again.
So, let her rest: and, madam, list to me;
For I am bold to counsel you in this:
Although we fancy not the Cardinal,
Yet must we join with him and with the lords   95
Till we have brought Duke Humphrey in disgrace.
As for the Duke of York, this late complaint
Will make but little for his benefit:
So, one by one, we'll weed them all at last,
And you yourself shall steer the happy helm.   100

Sound a sennet. Enter the KING, DUKE HUMPHREY OF
GLOUCESTER, *Cardinal* BEAUFORT, BUCKINGHAM,
YORK, SOMERSET, SALISBURY, WARWICK *and the*
DUCHESS OF GLOUCESTER.

KING   For my part, noble lords, I care not which;
Or Somerset or York, all's one to me.

YORK   If York have ill demean'd himself in France,
Then let him be denay'd the regentship.

SOMERSET   If Somerset be unworthy of the place,   105
Let York be regent; I will yield to him.

WARWICK   Whether your Grace be worthy, yea or no,
Dispute not that: York is the worthier.

CARDINAL
Ambitious Warwick, let thy betters speak.

WARWICK
The Cardinal's not my better in the field.   110

BUCKINGHAM
All in this presence are thy betters, Warwick.

WARWICK
Warwick may live to be the best of all.

SALISBURY
Peace, son! and show some reason, Buckingham,
Why Somerset should be preferr'd in this.

QUEEN   Because the king, forsooth, will have it so.   115

GLOUCESTER

Madam, the king is old enough himself
To give his censure. These are no women's matters.

QUEEN

If he be old enough, what needs your Grace
To be Protector of his Excellence?

GLOUCESTER

120   Madam, I am Protector of the realm,
And at his pleasure will resign my place.

SUFFOLK

Resign it then, and leave thine insolence.
Since thou wert king – as who is king but thou? –
The commonwealth hath daily run to wrack;
125   The Dauphin hath prevail'd beyond the seas;
And all the peers and nobles of the realm
Have been as bondmen to thy sovereignty.

CARDINAL

The commons hast thou rack'd; the clergy's bags
Are lank and lean with thy extortions.

SOMERSET

130   Thy sumptuous buildings and thy wife's attire
Have cost a mass of public treasury.

BUCKINGHAM   Thy cruelty in execution
Upon offenders hath exceeded law,
And left thee to the mercy of the law.

QUEEN   Thy sale of offices and towns in France,
135   If they were known, as the suspect is great,
Would make thee quickly hop without thy head.

Exit Gloucester.

[*The Queen drops her fan.*]
Give me my fan: what, minion! can ye not?
[*She gives the Duchess a box on the ear.*]
I cry you mercy, madam; was it you?

DUCHESS

140   Was't I! yea, I it was, proud Frenchwoman:
Could I come near your beauty with my nails
I'd set my ten commandments in your face.

KING

Sweet aunt, be quiet; 'twas against her will.

DUCHESS

Against her will, good King? Look to 't in time;
145   She'll hamper thee and dandle thee like a baby:
Though in this place most master wear no breeches,
She shall not strike Dame Eleanor unreveng'd.   *Exit.*

BUCKINGHAM

Lord Cardinal, I will follow Eleanor,
And listen after Humphrey, how he proceeds:
150   She's tickled now; her fury needs no spurs,
She'll gallop far enough to her destruction.   *Exit.*

Re-enter GLOUCESTER.

GLOUCESTER

Now, lords, my choler being over-blown
With walking once about the quadrangle,
I come to talk of commonwealth affairs.
155   As for your spiteful false objections,
Prove them, and I lie open to the law:

But God in mercy so deal with my soul
As I in duty love my king and country!
But to the matter that we have in hand.
I say, my Sovereign, York is meetest man   160
To be your Regent in the realm of France.

SUFFOLK

Before we make election, give me leave
To show some reason, of no little force,
That York is most unmeet of any man.

YORK

I'll tell thee, Suffolk, why I am unmeet: 165
First, for I cannot flatter thee in pride;
Next, if I be appointed for the place,
My Lord of Somerset will keep me here,
Without discharge, money, or furniture,
Till France be won into the Dauphin's hands.   170
Last time I danc'd attendance on his will
Till Paris was besieg'd, famish'd, and lost.

WARWICK   That can I witness; and a fouler fact
Did never traitor in the land commit.

SUFFOLK   Peace, headstrong Warwick!   175

WARWICK

Image of Pride, why should I hold my peace?

Enter HORNER *the armourer, and his man* PETER, *guarded.*

SUFFOLK

Because here is a man accus'd of treason:
Pray God the Duke of York excuse himself!

YORK

Doth any one accuse York for a traitor?

KING

What mean'st thou, Suffolk? Tell me, what are these?   180

SUFFOLK

Please it your Majesty, this is the man
That doth accuse his master of high treason.
His words were these: that Richard Duke of York
Was rightful heir unto the English crown,
And that your Majesty was an usurper.   185

KING   Say, man, were these thy words?

HORNER   And 't shall please your Majesty, I never said
nor thought any such matter: God is my witness, I am
falsely accus'd by the villain.

PETITIONER   By these ten bones, my lords, he did speak   190
them to me in the garret one night, as we were
scouring my Lord of York's armour.

YORK   Base dunghill villain, and mechanical,
I'll have thy head for this thy traitor's speech.
I do beseech your royal Majesty   195
Let him have all the rigour of the law.

HORNER   Alas! my lord, hang me if ever I spake the
words. My accuser is my prentice; and when I did
correct him for his fault the other day, he did vow
upon his knees he would be even with me: I have good   200
witness of this: therefore, I beseech your Majesty, do
not cast away an honest man for a villain's accusation.

KING   Uncle, what shall we say to this in law?

GLOUCESTER

205   This doom, my lord, if I may judge by case:
        Let Somerset be Regent o'er the French,
        Because in York this breeds suspicion;
        And let these have a day appointed them
        For single combat in convenient place;
        For he hath witness of his servant's malice.

KING

210   This is the law, and this Duke Humphrey's doom.

SOMERSET   I humbly thank your royal Majesty.

HORNER   And I accept the combat willingly.

PETITIONER   Alas! my lord, I cannot fight; for God's
        sake, pity my case! The spite of man prevaileth against
215   me. O Lord, have mercy upon me! I shall never be able
        to fight a blow. O Lord, my heart!

GLOUCESTER   Sirrah, or you must fight or else be hang'd.

KING   Away with them to prison; and the day
        Of combat be the last of the next month.
220   Come, Somerset, we'll see thee sent away.

                        Flourish. Exeunt.

1.4   *Enter* MARGERY JOURDAIN, HUME, SOUTHWELL *and*
                        BOLINGBROKE.

HUME   Come, my masters; the Duchess, I tell you,
        expects performance of your promises.

BOLINGBROKE   Master Hume, we are therefore
        provided: will her ladyship behold and hear our
5   exorcisms?

HUME   Ay, what else? Fear you not her courage.

BOLINGBROKE   I have heard her reported to be a woman
        of an invincible spirit: but it shall be convenient,
        Master Hume, that you be by her aloft, while we be
10   busy below; and so, I pray you, go, in God's name, and
        leave us.   *Exit Hume.*
        Mother Jourdain, be you prostrate, and grovel on the
        earth; John Southwell, read you; and let us to our
        work.

        Enter DUCHESS *aloft,* HUME *following.*

15 DUCHESS   Well said, my masters; and welcome all. To
        this gear, the sooner the better.

BOLINGBROKE

        Patience, good lady; wizards know their times:
        Deep night, dark night, the silent of the night,
        The time of night when Troy was set on fire,
20   The time when screech-owls cry, and ban-dogs howl,
        And spirits walk, and ghosts break up their graves;
        That time best fits the work we have in hand.
        Madam, sit you, and fear not: whom we raise
        We will make fast within a hallow'd verge.
        [*Here do the ceremonies belonging, and make the circle;
        Bolingbroke or Southwell reads,* Conjuro te, *etc. It
        thunders and lightens terribly; then the* Spirit *rises.*]

SPIRIT   *Adsum.*

MARGERY JOURDAIN   Asnath!
        By the eternal God, whose name and power
        Thou tremblest at, answer that I shall ask;

        For till thou speak thou shalt not pass from hence.

SPIRIT   Ask what thou wilt. That I had said and done!   30

BOLINGBROKE [*Reads.*]
        First, of the King, what shall of him become?

SPIRIT   The duke yet lives that Henry shall depose;
        But him outlive, and die a violent death.

        [*As the Spirit speaks, Southwell writes the answer.*]

BOLINGBROKE
        Tell me what fate awaits the Duke of Suffolk.

SPIRIT   By water shall he die and take his end.   35

BOLINGBROKE   *What shall betide the Duke of Somerset?*

SPIRIT   Let him shun castles:
        Safer shall he be upon the sandy plains
        Than where castles mounted stand.
        Have done, for more I hardly can endure.   40

BOLINGBROKE
        Descend to darkness and the burning lake:
        False fiend, avoid!   *Thunder and lightning. Exit Spirit.*

        Enter YORK *and* BUCKINGHAM, *with their guard, and
                        break in.*

YORK   Lay hands upon these traitors and their trash.
        Beldam, I think we watch'd you at an inch.
        What! madam, are you there? The king and
           commonweal
        Are deeply indebted for this piece of pains: 45
        My Lord Protector will, I doubt it not,
        See you well guerdon'd for these good deserts.

DUCHESS   Not half so bad as thine to England's king,
        Injurious Duke, that threatest where's no cause.   50

BUCKINGHAM
        True, madam, none at all. What call you this?
        Away with them! let them be clapp'd up close,
        And kept asunder. You, madam, shall with us:
        Stafford, take her to thee.

                Exeunt above Duchess and Hume, guarded.
        We'll see your trinkets here all forthcoming.   55
        All, away!

                Exeunt guard, with Southwell, Bolingbroke, etc.

YORK
        Lord Buckingham, methinks you watch'd her well:
        A pretty plot, well chosen to build upon!
        Now, pray, my lord, let's see the Devil's writ.
        What have we here? [*Reads.*]   60
        *The duke yet lives that Henry shall depose;
        But him outlive, and die a violent death.*
        Why, this is just *Aio te, Aeacida,
        Romanos vincere posse.* Well, to the rest:
        Tell me what fate awaits the Duke of Suffolk.   65
        By water shall he die and take his end.
        What shall betide the Duke of Somerset?
        Let him shun castles:
        Safer shall he be upon the sandy plains
        Than where castles mounted stand.   70
        Come, come, my lords, these oracles
        Are hardly attain'd, and hardly understood.
        The King is now in progress towards Saint Albans;

With him the husband of this lovely lady:
75   Thither goes these news as fast as horse can carry them:
A sorry breakfast for my Lord Protector.

BUCKINGHAM
Your Grace shall give me leave, my Lord of York,
To be the post, in hope of his reward.

YORK
At your pleasure, my good lord. Within there, ho!

Enter a servingman.

80   Invite my Lords of Salisbury and Warwick
To sup with me to-morrow night. Away!   *Exeunt.*

2.1   *Enter the* KING, QUEEN, GLOUCESTER, Cardinal
and SUFFOLK, *with falconers hallooing.*

QUEEN   Believe me, lords, for flying at the brook,
I saw not better sport these seven years' day:
Yet, by your leave, the wind was very high,
And, ten to one, old Joan had not gone out.
5   KING   But what a point, my lord, your falcon made,
And what a pitch she flew above the rest!
To see how God in all his creatures works!
Yea, man and birds are fain of climbing high.
SUFFOLK   No marvel, and it like your Majesty,
10   My Lord Protector's hawks do tower so well;
They know their master loves to be aloft,
And bears his thoughts above his falcon's pitch.
GLOUCESTER   My lord, 'tis but a base ignoble mind
That mounts no higher than a bird can soar.
15   CARDINAL   I thought as much; he'd be above the clouds.
GLOUCESTER
Ay, my lord Cardinal, how think you by that?
Were it not good your Grace could fly to heaven?
KING   The treasury of everlasting joy.
CARDINAL
Thy heaven is on earth; thine eyes and thoughts
20   Beat on a crown, the treasure of thy heart;
Pernicious Protector, dangerous peer,
That smooth'st it so with king and commonweal!
GLOUCESTER
What, Cardinal, is your Priesthood grown peremptory?
Tantaene animis coelestibus irae?
Churchmen so hot? Good uncle, can you dote,
25   To hide such malice with such holiness?
SUFFOLK   No malice, sir; no more than well becomes
So good a quarrel and so bad a peer.
GLOUCESTER   As who, my lord?
SUFFOLK   Why, as yourself, my lord;
An't like your lordly Lord-Protectorship.
30   GLOUCESTER
Why, Suffolk, England knows thine insolence.
QUEEN   And thy ambition, Gloucester.
KING   I prithee, peace,
Good queen, and whet not on these furious peers;
For blessed are the peacemakers on earth.
35   CARDINAL   Let me be blessed for the peace I make

Against this proud Protector with my sword!
GLOUCESTER [*aside to Cardinal*]
Faith, holy uncle, would 'twere come to that.
CARDINAL [*aside to Gloucester*]
Marry, when thou darest.
GLOUCESTER [*aside to Cardinal*]
                   Dare! I tell thee, priest,
Plantagenets could never brook the dare.
CARDINAL [*aside to Gloucester*]
I am Plantagenet as well as thou,   40
And son to John of Gaunt.
GLOUCESTER [*aside to Cardinal*]   In bastardy!
CARDINAL [*aside to Gloucester*]   I scorn thy words!
GLOUCESTER [*aside to Cardinal*]
Make up no factious numbers for the matter;
In thine own person answer thy abuse.
CARDINAL [*aside to Gloucester*]
Ay, where thou dar'st not peep: and if thou dar'st,   45
This evening on the east side of the grove.
KING   How now, my lords!
CARDINAL   Believe me, cousin Gloucester,
Had not your man put up the fowl so suddenly,
We had had more sport.
[*aside to Gloucester*]   Come with thy two-hand sword.
GLOUCESTER
True, uncle. [*aside to Cardinal*] Are ye advis'd? the east
    side of the grove.   50
CARDINAL [*aside to Gloucester*]   I am with you.
KING   Why, how now, uncle Gloucester!
GLOUCESTER
Talking of hawking; nothing else, my lord.
[*aside to Cardinal*]   Now, by God's mother, I'll shave
    your crown for this,
Or all my fence shall fail.
CARDINAL [*aside to Gloucester*]
                   Medice, teipsum –
Protector, see to't well, protect yourself.   55
KING
The winds grow high; so do your stomachs, lords.
How irksome is this music to my heart!
When such strings jar, what hope of harmony?
I pray, my lords, let me compound this strife.

Enter One, *crying* 'A miracle.'

GLOUCESTER
What means this noise? Fellow, what miracle   60
Dost thou proclaim?
ONE   A miracle! a miracle!
SUFFOLK
Come to the King and tell him what miracle.
ONE   Forsooth, a blind man at Saint Alban's shrine,
Within this half hour hath receiv'd his sight;
A man that ne'er saw in his life before.   65
KING   Now, God be prais'd, that to believing souls
Gives light in darkness, comfort in despair!

Enter the Mayor *of Saint Albans and his brethren, with
music, bearing the man,* SIMPCOX, *between two in a
chair; his* Wife *and townsmen following.*

CARDINAL
  Here comes the townsmen, on procession,
  To present your Highness with the man.
KING   Great is his comfort in this earthly vale,
  Although by sight his sin be multiplied.
GLOUCESTER
  Stand by, my masters; bring him near the King:
  His Highness' pleasure is to talk with him.
KING   Good fellow, tell us here the circumstance,
  That we for thee may glorify the Lord.
  What! hast thou been long blind, and now restor'd?
SIMPCOX   Born blind, and 't please your Grace.
WIFE   Ay, indeed, was he.
SUFFOLK   What woman is this?
WIFE   His wife, and 't like your worship.
GLOUCESTER
  Hadst thou been his mother, thou could'st have
    better told.
KING   Where wert thou born?
SIMPCOX
  At Berwick in the north, and 't like your Grace.
KING
  Poor soul! God's goodness hath been great to thee:
  Let never day nor night unhallow'd pass,
  But still remember what the Lord hath done.
QUEEN
  Tell me, good fellow, cam'st thou here by chance,
  Or of devotion, to this holy shrine?
SIMPCOX   God knows, of pure devotion; being call'd
  A hundred times and oft'ner, in my sleep,
  By good Saint Alban; who said, 'Simon, come;
  Come, offer at my shrine, and I will help thee.'
WIFE   Most true, forsooth; and many time and oft
  Myself have heard a voice to call him so.
CARDINAL   What! art thou lame?
SIMPCOX   Ay, God Almighty help me!
SUFFOLK   How cam'st thou so?
SIMPCOX   A fall off of a tree.
WIFE   A plum-tree, master.
GLOUCESTER   How long hast thou been blind?
SIMPCOX   O! born so, master.
GLOUCESTER   What! and would'st climb a tree?
SIMPCOX   But that in all my life, when I was a youth.
WIFE   Too true; and bought his climbing very dear.
GLOUCESTER
  'Mass, thou lov'd'st plums well, that would'st
    venture so.
SIMPCOX
  Alas! good master, my wife desir'd some damsons,
  And made me climb with danger of my life.
GLOUCESTER
  A subtle knave! But yet it shall not serve. –
  Let me see thine eyes: wink now: now open them.

In my opinion yet thou see'st not well.
SIMPCOX
  Yes, master, clear as day, I thank God and Saint Alban.
GLOUCESTER
  Say'st thou me so? What colour is this cloak of?
SIMPCOX   Red, master; red as blood.
GLOUCESTER
  Why, that's well said. What colour is my gown of?
SIMPCOX   Black, forsooth; coal-black as jet.
KING   Why then, thou know'st what colour jet is of?
SUFFOLK   And yet, I think, jet did he never see.
GLOUCESTER
  But cloaks and gowns before this day a many.
WIFE   Never, before this day, in all his life.
GLOUCESTER   Tell me, sirrah, what's my name?
SIMPCOX   Alas! master, I know not.
GLOUCESTER   What's his name?
SIMPCOX   I know not.
GLOUCESTER   Nor his?
SIMPCOX   No, indeed, master.
GLOUCESTER   What's thine own name?
SIMPCOX
  Saunder Simpcox, and if it please you, master.
GLOUCESTER
  Then Saunder, sit thou there, the lying'st knave
  In Christendom. If thou hadst been born blind,
  Thou might'st as well have known our names, as thus
  To name the several colours we do wear.
  Sight may distinguish of colours; but suddenly
  To nominate them all, it is impossible.
  Saint Alban here hath done a miracle;
  And would ye not think his cunning to be great,
  That could restore this cripple to his legs?
SIMPCOX   O master, that you could!
GLOUCESTER   My masters of Saint Albans, have you not
  A beadle in your town, and things call'd whips?
MAYOR   Yes, my lord.
GLOUCESTER   Send for one presently.
MAYOR   Sirrah, go fetch the beadle hither straight.
                        Exit an attendant.
GLOUCESTER   Now fetch me a stool hither by and by.
  Now, sirrah, if you mean to save yourself
  From whipping, leap me over this stool and run.
SIMPCOX
  Alas! master, I am not able to stand alone:
  You go about to torture me in vain.

        Enter a Beadle *with whips.*

GLOUCESTER
  Well, sirrah, we must have you find your legs.
  Whip him till he leap over that same stool.
BEADLE
  Come on, sirrah, off with your doublet, quickly.
SIMPCOX
  Alas! master, what shall I do? I am not able to stand.
*[After the Beadle hath hit him once, he leaps over the stool
and runs away; and they follow and cry, 'A miracle!']*

KING   O God! seest Thou this, and bearest so long?

QUEEN   It made me laugh to see the villain run.

GLOUCESTER

Follow the knave; and take this drab away.

150   WIFE   Alas! sir, we did it for pure need.

GLOUCESTER

Let them be whipp'd through every market-town,

Till they come to Berwick, from whence they came.

Exeunt Mayor, Beadle, Wife, etc.

CARDINAL

Duke Humphrey has done a miracle to-day.

SUFFOLK   True; made the lame to leap and fly away.

GLOUCESTER

155   But you have done more miracles than I;

You made in a day, my lord, whole towns to fly.

Enter BUCKINGHAM.

KING   What tidings with our cousin Buckingham?

BUCKINGHAM   Such as my heart doth tremble to unfold:

A sort of naughty persons, lewdly bent,

160   Under the countenance and confederacy

Of Lady Eleanor, the Protector's wife,

The ringleader and head of all this rout,

Have practis'd dangerously against your state,

Dealing with witches and with conjurers:

165   Whom we have apprehended in the fact;

Raising up wicked spirits from under ground,

Demanding of King Henry's life and death,

And other of your Highness' Privy Council,

As more at large your Grace shall understand.

CARDINAL

170   And so, my Lord Protector, by this means

Your lady is forthcoming yet at London.

This news, I think, hath turn'd your weapon's edge;

'Tis like, my lord, you will not keep your hour.

GLOUCESTER

Ambitious churchman, leave to afflict my heart:

175   Sorrow and grief have vanquish'd all my powers;

And, vanquish'd as I am, I yield to thee,

Or to the meanest groom.

KING   O God! what mischiefs work the wicked ones,

Heaping confusion on their own heads thereby!

180   QUEEN   Gloucester, see here the tainture of thy nest,

And look thyself be faultless, thou wert best.

GLOUCESTER

Madam, for myself, to heaven I do appeal,

How I have lov'd my King and commonweal;

And, for my wife, I know not how it stands.

185   Sorry I am to hear what I have heard:

Noble she is, but if she have forgot

Honour and virtue, and convers'd with such

As, like to pitch, defile nobility,

I banish her my bed and company,

190   And give her as a prey to law and shame,

That hath dishonour'd Gloucester's honest name.

KING   Well, for this night we will repose us here:

To-morrow toward London back again,

To look into this business thoroughly,

And call these foul offenders to their answers,   195

And poise the cause in Justice' equal scales,

Whose beam stands sure, whose rightful cause prevails.

Flourish. Exeunt.

2.2   *Enter* YORK, SALISBURY *and* WARWICK.

YORK   Now, my good Lords of Salisbury and Warwick,

Our simple supper ended, give me leave,

In this close walk, to satisfy myself,

In craving your opinion of my title,

Which is infallible, to England's crown.   5

SALISBURY   My lord, I long to hear it at full.

WARWICK   Sweet York, begin; and if thy claim be good,

The Nevils are thy subjects to command.

YORK   Edward the Third, my lords, had seven sons:

The first, Edward the Black Prince, Prince of Wales;   10

The second, William of Hatfield; and the third,

Lionel Duke of Clarence; next to whom

Was John of Gaunt, the Duke of Lancaster;

The fifth was Edmund Langley, Duke of York;

The sixth was Thomas of Woodstock, Duke of

     Gloucester;   15

William of Windsor was the seventh and last.

Edward the Black Prince died before his father,

And left behind him Richard, his only son,

Who, after Edward the Third's death, reign'd as king;

Till Henry Bolingbroke, Duke of Lancaster,   20

The eldest son and heir of John of Gaunt,

Crown'd by the name of Henry the Fourth,

Seiz'd on the realm, depos'd the rightful king,

Sent his poor Queen to France, from whence she came,

And him to Pomfret; where, as all you know,   25

Harmless Richard was murder'd traitorously.

WARWICK   Father, the duke of York hath told the truth;

Thus got the house of Lancaster the crown.

YORK

Which now they hold by force, and not by right;

For Richard, the first son's heir, being dead,   30

The issue of the next son should have reign'd.

SALISBURY

But William of Hatfield died without an heir.

YORK

The third son, Duke of Clarence, from whose line

I claim the crown, had issue Philippe, a daughter,

Who married Edmund Mortimer, Earl of March;   35

Edmund had issue, Roger, Earl of March;

Roger had issue, Edmund, Anne, and Eleanor.

SALISBURY   This Edmund, in the reign of Bolingbroke,

As I have read, laid claim unto the crown;

And, but for Owen Glendower, had been king,   40

Who kept him in captivity till he died.

But to the rest.

YORK   His eldest sister, Anne,

My mother, being heir unto the crown,
Married Richard, Earl of Cambridge, who was son
To Edmund Langley, Edward the Third's fifth son.
By her I claim the kingdom: she was heir
To Roger, Earl of March, who was the son
Of Edmund Mortimer, who married Philippe,
Sole daughter unto Lionel Duke of Clarence:
So, if the issue of the elder son
Succeed before the younger, I am king.

WARWICK
What plain proceedings is more plain than this?
Henry doth claim the crown from John of Gaunt,
The fourth son; York claims it from the third.
Till Lionel's issue fails, his should not reign:
It fails not yet, but flourishes in thee,
And in thy sons, fair slips of such a stock.
Then, father Salisbury, kneel we together,
And in this private plot be we the first
That shall salute our rightful sovereign
With honour of his birthright to the crown.

BOTH
Long live our sovereign Richard, England's king!

YORK We thank you, lords. But I am not your king
Till I be crown'd and that my sword be stain'd
With heart-blood of the house of Lancaster;
And that's not suddenly to be perform'd
But with advice and silent secrecy.
Do you as I do in these dangerous days,
Wink at the Duke of Suffolk's insolence,
At Beaufort's pride, at Somerset's ambition,
At Buckingham, and all the crew of them,
Till they have snar'd the shepherd of the flock,
That virtuous prince, the good Duke Humphrey:
'Tis that they seek; and they, in seeking that,
Shall find their deaths, if York can prophesy.

SALISBURY
My lord, break off; we know your mind at full.

WARWICK
My heart assures me that the Earl of Warwick
Shall one day make the Duke of York a king.

YORK And, Nevil, this I do assure myself:
Richard shall live to make the Earl of Warwick
The greatest man in England but the king.   *Exeunt.*

2.3   *Sound trumpets. Enter the* QUEEN,
GLOUCESTER, YORK, SUFFOLK *and* SALISBURY; *the*
Duchess of GLOUCESTER, MARGERY JOURDAIN,
SOUTHWELL, HUME *and* BOLINGBROKE, *under guard.*

KING
Stand forth, Dame Eleanor Cobham, Gloucester's wife.
In sight of God and us, your guilt is great;
Receive the sentence of the law for sins
Such as by God's book are adjudg'd to death.
You four, from hence to prison back again;
From thence unto the place of execution:

The witch in Smithfield shall be burn'd to ashes,
And you three shall be strangled on the gallows.
You, madam, for you are more nobly born,
Despoiled of your honour in your life,   10
Shall, after three days' open penance done,
Live in your country here in banishment,
With Sir John Stanley, in the Isle of Man.

DUCHESS
Welcome is banishment; welcome were my death.

GLOUCESTER
Eleanor, the law, thou seest, hath judged thee: 15
I cannot justify whom the law condemns.
          Exeunt Duchess and other prisoners, guarded.
Mine eyes are full of tears, my heart of grief.
Ah! Humphrey, this dishonour in thine age
Will bring thy head with sorrow to the grave.
I beseech your Majesty, give me leave to go;   20
Sorrow would solace and mine age would ease.

KING
Stay, Humphrey, Duke of Gloucester: ere thou go,
Give up thy staff: Henry will to himself
Protector be; and God shall be my hope,
My stay, my guide, and lantern to my feet.   25
And go in peace, Humphrey, no less belov'd
Than when thou wert Protector to thy King.

QUEEN I see no reason why a king of years
Should be to be protected like a child.
God and King Henry govern England's helm!   30
Give up your staff, sir, and the King his realm.

GLOUCESTER My staff? here, noble Henry, is my staff:
As willingly do I the same resign
As erst thy father Henry made it mine;
And even as willing at thy feet I leave it   35
As others would ambitiously receive it.
Farewell, good king! when I am dead and gone,
May honourable peace attend thy throne.   *Exit.*

QUEEN
Why, now is Henry King, and Margaret Queen;
And Humphrey Duke of Gloucester scarce himself,   40
That bears so shrewd a maim: two pulls at once;
His lady banish'd, and a limb lopp'd off;
This staff of honour raught: there let it stand,
Where it best fits to be, in Henry's hand.

SUFFOLK
Thus droops this lofty pine and hangs his sprays;   45
Thus Eleanor's pride dies in her youngest days.

YORK Lords, let him go. Please it your Majesty
This is the day appointed for the combat;
And ready are the appellant and defendant,
The armourer and his man, to enter the lists,   50
So please your Highness to behold the fight.

QUEEN Ay, good my lord; for purposely therefore
Left I the court to see this quarrel tried.

KING A God's name, see the lists and all things fit:
Here let them end it; and God defend the right!   55

YORK I never saw a fellow worse bested,

Or more afraid to fight, than is the appellant,
The servant of this armourer, my lords.

Enter, at one door, the Armourer, *and his* Neighbours
*drinking to him so much that he is drunk; and he enters
bearing his staff with a sand-bag fastened to it; a drum
before him: and at the other door, his man with a drum
and sand-bag, and* Prentices *drinking to him.*

1 NEIGHBOUR   Here, neighbour Horner, I drink to you in
a cup of sack: and fear not, neighbour, you shall do
well enough.
2 NEIGHBOUR   And here, neighbour, here's a cup of
charneco.
3 NEIGHBOUR   And here's a pot of good double beer,
neighbour: drink, and fear not your man.
HORNER   Let it come, i' faith, and I'll pledge you all; and
a fig for Peter!
1 PRENTICE   Here, Peter, I drink to thee; and be not
afeard.
2 PRENTICE   Be merry, Peter, and fear not thy master:
fight for credit of the prentices.
PETER   I thank you all: drink, and pray for me, I pray
you; for I think I have taken my last draught in this
world. Here, Robin, and if I die, I give thee my apron;
and, Will, thou shalt have my hammer: and here, Tom,
take all the money that I have. O Lord bless me, I pray
God, for I am never able to deal with my master, he
hath learnt so much fence already.
SALISBURY   Come, leave your drinking, and fall to blows.
Sirrah, what's thy name?
PETER   Peter, forsooth.
SALISBURY   Peter! what more?
PETER   Thump.
SALISBURY   Thump! Then see thou thump thy master
well.
HORNER   Masters, I am come hither, as it were, upon my
man's instigation, to prove him a knave, and myself an
honest man: and touching the Duke of York, I will
take my death I never meant him any ill, nor the King,
nor the Queen: and therefore, Peter, have at thee with
a downright blow.
YORK   Dispatch: this knave's tongue begins to double.
Sound, trumpets, alarum to the combatants.
[*Alarum. They fight, and Peter strikes him down.*]
HORNER   Hold, Peter, hold! I confess, I confess treason.
[*Dies.*]
YORK   Take away his weapon. Fellow, thank God, and
the good wine in thy master's way.
PETER [*kneeling*]   O God! have I overcome mine enemies
in this presence? O Peter! thou hast prevail'd in right.
KING   Go, take hence that traitor from our sight;
For by his death we do perceive his guilt:
And God in justice hath reveal'd to us
The truth and innocence of this poor fellow,
Which he had thought to have murder'd wrongfully.
Come, fellow, follow us for thy reward.
                                   Sound a flourish. Exeunt.

60

65

70

75

80

85

90

95

100

2.4   *Enter* GLOUCESTER *and his* Men, *in mourning cloaks.*

GLOUCESTER
Thus sometimes hath the brightest day a cloud;
And after summer evermore succeeds
Barren winter, with his wrathful nipping cold:
So cares and joys abound, as seasons fleet.
Sirs, what's o'clock?
SERVANT   Ten, my lord.   5
GLOUCESTER   Ten is the hour that was appointed me
To watch the coming of my punish'd duchess:
Uneath may she endure the flinty streets,
To tread them with her tender-feeling feet.
Sweet Nell, ill can thy noble mind abrook   10
The abject people gazing on thy face
With envious looks, laughing at thy shame,
That erst did follow thy proud chariot wheels
When thou didst ride in triumph through the streets.
But soft! I think she comes; and I'll prepare   15
My tear-stain'd eyes to see her miseries.

Enter the DUCHESS OF GLOUCESTER, *barefoot in a
white sheet, and a taper burning in her hand; with*
SIR JOHN STANLEY, *the* Sheriff *and officers.*

SERVANT
So please your Grace, we'll take her from the sheriff.
GLOUCESTER   No, stir not, for your lives; let her pass by.
DUCHESS   Come you, my lord, to see my open shame?
Now thou dost penance too. Look how they gaze!   20
See how the giddy multitude do point,
And nod their heads, and throw their eyes on thee!
Ah! Gloucester, hide thee from their hateful looks,
And, in thy closet pent up, rue my shame,
And ban thine enemies, both mine and thine.   25
GLOUCESTER   Be patient, gentle Nell; forget this grief.
DUCHESS   Ah! Gloucester, teach me to forget myself;
For whilst I think I am thy married wife,
And thou a prince, Protector of this land,
Methinks I should not thus be led along,   30
Mail'd up in shame, with papers on my back,
And follow'd with a rabble that rejoice
To see my tears and hear my deep-fet groans.
The ruthless flint doth cut my tender feet,
And when I start, the envious people laugh,   35
And bid me be advised how I tread.
Ah! Humphrey, can I bear this shameful yoke?
Trowest thou that e'er I'll look upon the world,
Or count them happy that enjoys the sun?
No; dark shall be my light, and night my day;   40
To think upon my pomp shall be my hell.
Sometime I'll say, I am Duke Humphrey's wife,
And he a prince and ruler of the land:
Yet so he rul'd, and such a prince he was,
As he stood by whilst I, his forlorn duchess,   45
Was made a wonder and a pointing-stock
To every idle rascal follower.
But be thou mild, and blush not at my shame,
Nor stir at nothing till the axe of death

Hang over thee, as sure it shortly will;
For Suffolk, he that can do all in all
With her that hateth thee, and hates us all,
And York, and impious Beaufort, that false priest,
Have all lim'd bushes to betray thy wings;
And, fly thou how thou canst, they'll tangle thee:
But fear not thou, until thy foot be snar'd,
Nor never seek prevention of thy foes.

GLOUCESTER   Ah! Nell, forbear: thou aimest all awry;
I must offend before I be attainted;
And had I twenty times so many foes,
And each of them had twenty times their power,
All these could not procure me any scathe,
So long as I am loyal, true, and crimeless.
Would'st have me rescue thee from this reproach?
Why, yet thy scandal were not wip'd away,
But I in danger for the breach of law.
Thy greatest help is quiet, gentle Nell:
I pray thee, sort thy heart to patience;
These few days' wonder will be quickly worn.

Enter a Herald.

HERALD
I summon your Grace to his Majesty's Parliament,
Holden at Bury the first of this next month.
GLOUCESTER
And my consent ne'er ask'd herein before!
This is close dealing. Well, I will be there.
Exit Herald.
My Nell, I take my leave: and, Master sheriff,
Let not her penance exceed the King's commission.
SHERIFF
And 't please your grace, here my commission stays,
And Sir John Stanley is appointed now
To take her with him to the Isle of Man.
GLOUCESTER
Must you, Sir John, protect my lady here?
STANLEY
So am I given in charge, may 't please your Grace.
GLOUCESTER   Entreat her not the worse in that I pray
You use her well. The world may laugh again;
And I may live to do you kindness if
You do it her: and so, Sir John, farewell.
DUCHESS   What! gone, my lord, and bid me not farewell.
GLOUCESTER
Witness my tears, I cannot stay to speak.
Exeunt Gloucester and his men.
DUCHESS
Art thou gone too? All comfort go with thee!
For none abides with me: my joy is death;
Death, at whose name I oft have been afeard,
Because I wish'd this world's eternity.
Stanley, I prithee, go, and take me hence;
I care not whither, for I beg no favour,
Only convey me where thou art commanded.
STANLEY   Why, madam, that is to the Isle of Man;
There to be us'd according to your state.

DUCHESS   That's bad enough, for I am but reproach:
And shall I then be us'd reproachfully?
STANLEY
Like to a duchess, and Duke Humphrey's lady:
According to that state you shall be us'd.
DUCHESS   Sheriff, farewell, and better than I fare,   100
Although thou hast been conduct of my shame.
SHERIFF   It is my office; and, madam, pardon me.
DUCHESS   Ay, ay, farewell; thy office is discharg'd.
Come, Stanley, shall we go?
STANLEY
Madam, your penance done, throw off this sheet,   105
And go we to attire you for our journey.
DUCHESS   My shame will not be shifted with my sheet:
No; it will hang upon my richest robes,
And show itself, attire me how I can.
Go, lead the way; I long to see my prison.   *Exeunt.*   110

3.1   *Sound a sennet. Enter* KING, QUEEN, Cardinal,
SUFFOLK, YORK, BUCKINGHAM, SALISBURY *and*
WARWICK, *to the Parliament.*

KING   I muse my Lord of Gloucester is not come:
'Tis not his wont to be the hindmost man,
Whate'er occasion keeps him from us now.
QUEEN   Can you not see, or will ye not observe
The strangeness of his alter'd countenance?   5
With what a majesty he bears himself,
How insolent of late he is become,
How proud, how peremptory, and unlike himself?
We know the time since he was mild and affable,
And if we did but glance a far-off look,   10
Immediately he was upon his knee,
That all the court admir'd him for submission:
But meet him now, and be it in the morn,
When every one will give the time of day,
He knits his brow and shows an angry eye,   15
And passeth by with stiff unbowed knee,
Disdaining duty that to us belongs.
Small curs are not regarded when they grin,
But great men tremble when the lion roars;
And Humphrey is no little man in England.   20
First note that he is near you in descent,
And should you fall, he is the next will mount.
Me seemeth then it is no policy,
Respecting what a rancorous mind he bears,
And his advantage following your decease,   25
That he should come about your royal person
Or be admitted to your Highness' Council.
By flattery hath he won the commons' hearts,
And when he please to make commotion,
'Tis to be fear'd they all will follow him.   30
Now 'tis the spring, and weeds are shallow-rooted;
Suffer them now, and they'll o'ergrow the garden,
And choke the herbs for want of husbandry.
The reverent care I bear unto my lord
Made me collect these dangers in the Duke.   35

If it be fond, call it a woman's fear;
Which fear if better reasons can supplant,
I will subscribe, and say I wrong'd the Duke.
My Lord of Suffolk, Buckingham, and York,

40   Reprove my allegation if you can;
Or else conclude my words effectual.

SUFFOLK   Well hath your Highness seen into this duke;
And had I first been put to speak my mind,
I think I should have told your Grace's tale.

45   The Duchess by his subornation,
Upon my life, began her devilish practices:
Or if he were not privy to those faults,
Yet, by reputing of his high descent,
As next the King he was successive heir,

50   And such high vaunts of his nobility,
Did instigate the bedlam brain-sick Duchess
By wicked means to frame our sovereign's fall.
Smooth runs the water where the brook is deep,
And in his simple show he harbours treason.

55   The fox barks not when he would steal the lamb:
No, no, my sovereign; Gloucester is a man
Unsounded yet, and full of deep deceit.

CARDINAL   Did he not, contrary to form of law,
Devise strange deaths for small offences done?

60 YORK   And did he not, in his Protectorship,
Levy great sums of money through the realm
For soldiers' pay in France, and never sent it?
By means whereof the towns each day revolted.

BUCKINGHAM
Tut! these are petty faults to faults unknown,
Which time will bring to light in smooth Duke

65   Humphrey.

KING   My lords, at once: the care you have of us,
To mow down thorns that would annoy our foot,
Is worthy praise; but, shall I speak my conscience,
Our kinsman Gloucester is as innocent

70   From meaning treason to our royal person,
As is the sucking lamb or harmless dove.
The duke is virtuous, mild, and too well given
To dream on evil, or to work my downfall.

QUEEN
Ah! what's more dangerous than this fond affiance?

75   Seems he a dove? His feathers are but borrow'd,
For he's disposed as the hateful raven:
Is he a lamb? His skin is surely lent him,
For he's inclin'd as is the ravenous wolves.
Who cannot steal a shape that means deceit?

80   Take heed, my lord; the welfare of us all
Hangs on the cutting short that fraudful man.

Enter SOMERSET.

SOMERSET   All health unto my gracious sovereign!

KING
Welcome, Lord Somerset. What news from France?

SOMERSET   That all your interest in those territories

85   Is utterly bereft you: all is lost.

KING
Cold news, Lord Somerset: but God's will be done!

YORK [*aside*]
Cold news for me; for I had hope of France
As firmly as I hope for fertile England.
Thus are my blossoms blasted in the bud,

90   And caterpillars eat my leaves away;
But I will remedy this gear ere long,
Or sell my title for a glorious grave.

Enter GLOUCESTER.

GLOUCESTER   All happiness unto my lord the King!
Pardon, my liege, that I have stay'd so long.

SUFFOLK
Nay, Gloucester, know that thou art come too soon,   95
Unless thou wert more loyal than thou art.
I do arrest thee of high treason here.

GLOUCESTER
Well, Suffolk's Duke, thou shalt not see me blush,
Nor change my countenance for this arrest:
A heart unspotted is not easily daunted.   100
The purest spring is not so free from mud
As I am clear from treason to my sovereign.
Who can accuse me? Wherein am I guilty?

YORK
'Tis thought, my lord, that you took bribes of
    France,
And, being Protector, stay'd the soldiers' pay;   105
By means whereof his Highness hath lost France.

GLOUCESTER
Is it but thought so? What are they that think it?
I never robb'd the soldiers of their pay,
Nor ever had one penny bribe from France.
So help me God, as I have watch'd the night,   110
Ay, night by night, in studying good for England!
That doit that e'er I wrested from the King,
Or any groat I hoarded to my use,
Be brought against me at my trial-day!
No; many a pound of mine own proper store,   115
Because I would not tax the needy commons,
Have I dispursed to the garrisons,
And never ask'd for restitution.

CARDINAL   It serves you well, my lord, to say so much.

GLOUCESTER
I say no more than truth, so help me God!   120

YORK   In your Protectorship you did devise
Strange tortures for offenders, never heard of,
That England was defam'd by tyranny.

GLOUCESTER
Why, 'tis well known that, whiles I was Protector,
Pity was all the fault that was in me;   125
For I should melt at an offender's tears,
And lowly words were ransom for their fault.
Unless it were a bloody murderer,
Or foul felonious thief that fleec'd poor passengers,
I never gave them condign punishment: 130

Murder indeed, that bloody sin, I tortur'd
Above the felon or what trespass else.

SUFFOLK

My lord, these faults are easy, quickly answer'd;
But mightier crimes are laid unto your charge,   35
Whereof you cannot easily purge yourself.
I do arrest you in his Highness' name;
And here commit to my Lord Cardinal
To keep, until your further time of trial.

KING   My Lord of Gloucester, 'tis my special hope
That you will clear yourself from all suspense: 40
My conscience tells me you are innocent.

GLOUCESTER

Ah! gracious lord, these days are dangerous.
Virtue is chok'd with foul Ambition,
And Charity chas'd hence by Rancour's hand;
Foul Subornation is predominant,   45
And Equity exil'd your Highness' land.
I know their complot is to have my life;
And if my death might make this island happy,
And prove the period of their tyranny,
I would expend it with all willingness.   50
But mine is made the prologue to their play;
For thousands more, that yet suspect no peril,
Will not conclude their plotted tragedy.
Beaufort's red sparkling eyes blab his heart's malice,
And Suffolk's cloudy brow his stormy hate;   55
Sharp Buckingham unburthens with his tongue
The envious load that lies upon his heart;
And dogged York, that reaches at the moon,
Whose overweening arm I have pluck'd back,
By false accuse doth level at my life.   60
And you, my sovereign lady, with the rest,
Causeless have laid disgraces on my head,
And with your best endeavour have stirr'd up
My liefest liege to be mine enemy.
Ay, all of you have laid your heads together –   65
Myself had notice of your conventicles –
And all to make away my guiltless life.
I shall not want false witness to condemn me,
Nor store of treasons to augment my guilt;
The ancient proverb will be well effected: 70
A staff is quickly found to beat a dog!

CARDINAL   My liege, his railing is intolerable.
If those that care to keep your royal person
From Treason's secret knife and traitors' rage
Be thus upbraided, chid, and rated at,   75
And the offender granted scope of speech,
'Twill make them cool in zeal unto your Grace.

SUFFOLK   Hath he not twit our sovereign lady here
With ignominious words, though clerkly couch'd,
As if she had suborned some to swear   80
False allegations to o'erthrow his state?

QUEEN   But I can give the loser leave to chide.

GLOUCESTER

Far truer spoke than meant: I lose, indeed;

Beshrew the winners, for they play'd me false!
And well such losers may have leave to speak.   185

BUCKINGHAM

He'll wrest the sense and hold us here all day.
Lord Cardinal, he is your prisoner.

CARDINAL

Sirs, take away the Duke, and guard him sure.

GLOUCESTER

Ah! thus King Henry throws away his crutch
Before his legs be firm to bear his body.   190
Thus is the shepherd beaten from thy side,
And wolves are gnarling who shall gnaw thee first.
Ah! that my fear were false; ah! that it were;
For, good King Henry, thy decay I fear.

Exit, guarded.

KING   My lords, what to your wisdoms seemeth best,   195
Do, or undo, as if ourself were here.

QUEEN

What! will your Highness leave the Parliament?

KING   Ay, Margaret; my heart is drown'd with grief,
Whose flood begins to flow within mine eyes,
My body round engirt with misery,   200
For what's more miserable than discontent?
Ah! uncle Humphrey, in thy face I see
The map of Honour, Truth, and Loyalty;
And yet, good Humphrey, is the hour to come
That e'er I prov'd thee false, or fear'd thy faith.   205
What low'ring star now envies thy estate,
That these great lords, and Margaret our Queen,
Do seek subversion of thy harmless life?
Thou never didst them wrong, nor no man wrong;
And as the butcher takes away the calf,   210
And binds the wretch, and beats it when it strains,
Bearing it to the bloody slaughter-house;
Even so, remorseless, have they borne him hence;
And as the dam runs lowing up and down,
Looking the way her harmless young one went,   215
And can do nought but wail her darling's loss;
Even so myself bewails good Gloucester's case
With sad unhelpful tears, and with dimm'd eyes
Look after him, and cannot do him good;
So mighty are his vowed enemies.   220
His fortunes I will weep; and 'twixt each groan
Say 'Who's a traitor? Gloucester he is none.'   *Exit.*

QUEEN

Free lords, cold snow melts with the sun's hot beams.
Henry my lord is cold in great affairs,
Too full of foolish pity; and Gloucester's show   225
Beguiles him as the mournful crocodile
With sorrow snares relenting passengers;
Or as the snake, roll'd in a flow'ring bank,
With shining checker'd slough, doth sting a child
That for the beauty thinks it excellent.   230
Believe me, lords, were none more wise than I,
And yet herein I judge mine own wit good,
This Gloucester should be quickly rid the world,

To rid us from the fear we have of him.

235 CARDINAL   That he should die is worthy policy;
But yet we want a colour for his death.
'Tis meet he be condemn'd by course of law.

SUFFOLK   But in my mind that were no policy:
The King will labour still to save his life;

240 The commons haply rise to save his life;
And yet we have but trivial argument,
More than mistrust, that shows him worthy death.

YORK   So that, by this, you would not have him die.

SUFFOLK   Ah! York, no man alive so fain as I.

245 YORK   'Tis York that hath more reason for his death.
But, my Lord Cardinal, and you, my Lord of Suffolk,
Say as you think, and speak it from your souls,
Were't not all one an empty eagle were set
To guard the chicken from a hungry kite,

250 As place Duke Humphrey for the king's Protector?

QUEEN   So the poor chicken should be sure of death.

SUFFOLK
Madam, 'tis true; and were't not madness then
To make the fox surveyor of the fold?
Who, being accus'd a crafty murderer,

255 His guilt should be but idly posted over
Because his purpose is not executed.
No; let him die, in that he is a fox,
By nature prov'd an enemy to the flock,
Before his chaps be stain'd with crimson blood,

260 As Humphrey, prov'd by treasons, to my liege.
And do not stand on quillets how to slay him:
Be it by gins, by snares, by subtlety,
Sleeping or waking, 'tis no matter how,
So he be dead; for that is good deceit

265 Which mates him first that first intends deceit.

QUEEN   Thrice-noble Suffolk, 'tis resolutely spoke.

SUFFOLK   Not resolute, except so much were done;
For things are often spoke and seldom meant:
But that my heart accordeth with my tongue,

270 Seeing the deed is meritorious,
And to preserve my sovereign from his foe,
Say but the word and I will be his priest.

CARDINAL
But I would have him dead, my Lord of Suffolk,
Ere you can take due orders for a priest:

275 Say you consent and censure well the deed,
And I'll provide his executioner;
I tender so the safety of my liege.

SUFFOLK   Here is my hand, the deed is worthy doing.

QUEEN   And so say I.

280 YORK   And I: and now we three have spoken it,
It skills not greatly who impugns our doom.

Enter a Post.

POST   Great lords, from Ireland am I come amain,
To signify that rebels there are up,
And put the Englishmen unto the sword.

285 Send succours, lords, and stop the rage betime,
Before the wound do grow uncurable;

For, being green, there is great hope of help.

CARDINAL
A breach that craves a quick expedient stop!
What counsel give you in this weighty cause?

YORK   That Somerset be sent as Regent thither. 290
'Tis meet that lucky ruler be employ'd;
Witness the fortune he hath had in France.

SOMERSET   If York, with all his far-fet policy,
Had been the Regent there instead of me,
He never would have stay'd in France so long. 295

YORK   No, not to lose it all, as thou hast done.
I rather would have lost my life betimes
Than bring a burden of dishonour home,
By staying there so long till all were lost.
Show me one scar character'd on thy skin: 300
Men's flesh preserv'd so whole do seldom win.

QUEEN   Nay then, this spark will prove a raging fire
If wind and fuel be brought to feed it with.
No more, good York; sweet Somerset, be still:
Thy fortune, York, hadst thou been Regent there, 305
Might happily have prov'd far worse than his.

YORK
What! worse than nought? Nay, then a shame take all!

SOMERSET   And in the number thee, that wishest shame.

CARDINAL   My Lord of York, try what your fortune is.
The uncivil kerns of Ireland are in arms 310
And temper clay with blood of Englishmen:
To Ireland will you lead a band of men,
Collected choicely, from each county some,
And try your hap against the Irishmen?

YORK   I will, my lord, so please his Majesty. 315

SUFFOLK   Why, our authority is his consent,
And what we do establish he confirms:
Then, noble York, take thou this task in hand.

YORK   I am content: provide me soldiers, lords,
Whiles I take order for mine own affairs. 320

SUFFOLK
A charge, Lord York, that I will see perform'd.
But now return we to the false Duke Humphrey.

CARDINAL   No more of him; for I will deal with him
That henceforth he shall trouble us no more.
And so break off; the day is almost spent. 325

SUFFOLK   Lord, you and I must talk of that event.

YORK   My Lord of Suffolk, within fourteen days
At Bristow I expect my soldiers;
For there I'll ship them all for Ireland.

SUFFOLK   I'll see it truly done, my Lord of York. 330

Exeunt all but York.

YORK   Now, York, or never, steel thy fearful thoughts,
And change misdoubt to resolution:
Be that thou hop'st to be, or what thou art
Resign to death; it is not worth th' enjoying.
Let pale-fac'd fear keep with the mean-born man, 335
And find no harbour in a royal heart.
Faster than spring-time showers comes thought on
  thought,
And not a thought but thinks on dignity.

My brain, more busy than the labouring spider,
Weaves tedious snares to trap mine enemies.
Well, nobles, well; 'tis politicly done,
To send me packing with an host of men:
I fear me you but warm the starved snake,
Who, cherish'd in your breasts, will sting your hearts.
'Twas men I lack'd, and you will give them me:
I take it kindly; yet be well assur'd
You put sharp weapons in a madman's hands.
Whiles I in Ireland nourish a mighty band,
I will stir up in England some black storm
Shall blow ten thousand souls to heaven, or hell;
And this fell tempest shall not cease to rage
Until the golden circuit on my head,
Like to the glorious sun's transparent beams,
Do calm the fury of this mad-bred flaw.
And, for a minister of my intent,
I have seduc'd a headstrong Kentishman,
John Cade of Ashford,
To make commotion, as full well he can,
Under the title of John Mortimer.
In Ireland have I seen this stubborn Cade
Oppose himself against a troop of kerns,
And fought so long, till that his thighs with darts
Were almost like a sharp-quill'd porpentine:
And, in the end being rescu'd, I have seen
Him caper upright like a wild Morisco,
Shaking the bloody darts as he his bells.
Full often, like a shag-hair'd crafty kern,
Hath he conversed with the enemy,
And undiscover'd come to me again,
And given me notice of their villanies.
This devil here shall be my substitute;
For that John Mortimer, which now is dead,
In face, in gait, in speech, he doth resemble:
By this I shall perceive the commons' mind,
How they affect the house and claim of York.
Say he be taken, rack'd, and tortured,
I know no pain they can inflict upon him
Will make him say I mov'd him to those arms.
Say that he thrive, as 'tis great like he will,
Why, then from Ireland come I with my strength,
And reap the harvest which that rascal sow'd;
For Humphrey being dead, as he shall be,
And Henry put apart, the next for me.   *Exit.*

3.2 *Enter two or three running over the stage, from the
murder of Duke Humphrey.*

1 MURDERER
    Run to my Lord of Suffolk; let him know
    We have dispatch'd the Duke, as he commanded.
2 MURDERER
    O, that it were to do! What have we done?
    Didst ever hear a man so penitent?

                    Enter SUFFOLK.

1 MURDERER   Here comes my Lord.
SUFFOLK   Now, sirs, have you dispatch'd this thing?
1 MURDERER   Ay, my good lord, he's dead.
SUFFOLK
    Why, that's well said. Go, get you to my house;
    I will reward you for this venturous deed.
    The King and all the peers are here at hand.   10
    Have you laid fair the bed? Is all things well,
    According as I gave directions?
1 MURDERER   'Tis handsome, my good lord.
SUFFOLK   Away! be gone.
                    Exeunt Murderers.

Sound trumpets. Enter the KING, *the* QUEEN, CARDINAL
    BEAUFORT, SOMERSET, *with attendants.*

KING   Go, call our uncle to our presence straight;
    Say we intend to try his Grace to-day,   15
    If he be guilty, as 'tis published.
SUFFOLK   I'll call him presently, my noble lord.   *Exit.*
KING   Lords, take your places; and, I pray you all,
    Proceed no straiter 'gainst our uncle Gloucester
    Than from true evidence, of good esteem,   20
    He be approv'd in practice culpable.
QUEEN   God forbid any malice should prevail
    That faultless may condemn a nobleman!
    Pray God he may acquit him of suspicion!
KING
    I thank thee, Meg; these words content me much.   25

                    Re-enter SUFFOLK.

    How now! why look'st thou pale? Why tremblest
        thou?
    Where is our uncle? What's the matter, Suffolk?
SUFFOLK
    Dead in his bed, my lord; Gloucester is dead.
QUEEN   Marry, God forfend!
CARDINAL
    God's secret judgment: I did dream to-night   30
    The Duke was dumb and could not speak a word.
    [*The King swoons.*]
QUEEN
    How fares my lord? Help, lords! The King is dead.
SOMERSET   Rear up his body; wring him by the nose.
QUEEN   Run, go, help, help! O, Henry, ope thine eyes!
SUFFOLK   He doth revive again: madam, be patient.   35
KING   O heavenly God!
QUEEN   How fares my gracious lord?
SUFFOLK
    Comfort, my sovereign! Gracious Henry, comfort!
KING   What, doth my Lord of Suffolk comfort me?
    Came he right now to sing a raven's note,
    Whose dismal tune bereft my vital powers,   40
    And thinks he that the chirping of a wren,
    By crying comfort from a hollow breast,
    Can chase away the first-conceived sound?

Hide not thy poison with such sug'red words;
45   Lay not thy hands on me; forbear, I say:
Their touch affrights me as a serpent's sting.
Thou baleful messenger, out of my sight!
Upon thy eye-balls murderous Tyranny
Sits in grim majesty to fright the world.
50   Look not upon me, for thine eyes are wounding:
Yet do not go away; come, basilisk,
And kill the innocent gazer with thy sight;
For in the shade of death I shall find joy,
In life but double death, now Gloucester's dead.
55   QUEEN   Why do you rate my Lord of Suffolk thus?
Although the Duke was enemy to him,
Yet he, most Christian-like, laments his death:
And for myself, foe as he was to me,
Might liquid tears or heart-offending groans
60   Or blood-consuming sighs recall his life,
I would be blind with weeping, sick with groans,
Look pale as primrose with blood-drinking sighs,
And all to have the noble Duke alive.
What know I how the world may deem of me?
65   For it is known we were but hollow friends:
It may be judg'd I made the Duke away:
So shall my name with Slander's tongue be wounded,
And princes' courts be fill'd with my reproach.
This get I by his death. Ay me, unhappy!
70   To be a queen, and crown'd with infamy!
KING   Ah! woe is me for Gloucester, wretched man.
QUEEN   Be woe for me, more wretched than he is.
What, dost thou turn away and hide thy face?
I am no loathsome leper; look on me.
75   What! art thou, like the adder, waxen deaf?
Be poisonous too, and kill thy forlorn Queen.
Is all thy comfort shut in Gloucester's tomb?
Why, then, Dame Margaret was ne'er thy joy:
Erect his statuë and worship it,
80   And make my image but an alehouse sign.
Was I for this nigh wreck'd upon the sea,
And twice by awkward wind from England's bank
Drove back again unto my native clime?
What boded this, but well forewarning wind
85   Did seem to say 'Seek not a scorpion's nest,
Nor set no footing on this unkind shore'?
What did I then, but curs'd the gentle gusts
And he that loos'd them forth their brazen caves;
And bid them blow towards England's blessed shore,
90   Or turn our stem upon a dreadful rock.
Yet Aeolus would not be a murderer,
But left that hateful office unto thee:
The pretty vaulting sea refus'd to drown me,
Knowing that thou wouldst have me drown'd on shore
95   With tears as salt as sea through thy unkindness:
The splitting rocks cower'd in the sinking sands,
And would not dash me with their ragged sides,
Because thy flinty heart, more hard than they,
Might in thy palace perish Margaret.

As far as I could ken thy chalky cliffs,   100
When from thy shore the tempest beat us back,
I stood upon the hatches in the storm,
And when the dusky sky began to rob
My earnest-gaping sight of thy land's view,
I took a costly jewel from my neck –   105
A heart it was, bound in with diamonds –
And threw it towards thy land. The sea receiv'd it,
And so I wish'd thy body might my heart:
And even with this I lost fair England's view,
And bid mine eyes be packing with my heart,   110
And call'd them blind and dusky spectacles
For losing ken of Albion's wished coast.
How often have I tempted Suffolk's tongue –
The agent of thy foul inconstancy –
To sit and witch me, as Ascanius did   115
When he to madding Dido would unfold
His father's acts, commenc'd in burning Troy!
Am I not witch'd like her? thou false like him?
Ay me! I can no more. Die, Margaret!
For Henry weeps that thou dost live so long.   120

Noise within. Enter WARWICK, SALISBURY *and many*
Commons.

WARWICK   It is reported, mighty sovereign,
That good Duke Humphrey traitorously is murder'd
By Suffolk and the Cardinal Beaufort's means.
The commons, like an angry hive of bees
That want their leader, scatter up and down,   125
And care not who they sting in his revenge.
Myself have calm'd their spleenful mutiny,
Until they hear the order of his death.
KING   That he is dead, good Warwick, 'tis too true;
But how he died God knows, not Henry.   130
Enter his chamber, view his breathless corpse,
And comment then upon his sudden death.
WARWICK   That shall I do, my liege. Stay, Salisbury,
With the rude multitude till I return.
Exeunt Warwick, and Salisbury with the Commons.
KING
O Thou that judgest all things, stay my thoughts –   135
My thoughts that labour to persuade my soul
Some violent hands were laid on Humphrey's life.
If my suspect be false, forgive me, God,
For judgment only doth belong to Thee.
Fain would I go to chafe his paly lips   140
With twenty thousand kisses, and to drain
Upon his face an ocean of salt tears,
To tell my love unto his dumb deaf trunk,
And with my fingers feel his hand unfeeling:
But all in vain are these mean obsequies,   145
[*Bed put forth.*]
And to survey his dead and earthy image
What were it but to make my sorrow greater?
[*Warwick draws the curtains, and shows Duke
Humphrey in his bed.*]

WARWICK
  Come hither, gracious sovereign, view this body.
KING   That is to see how deep my grave is made;
  For with his soul fled all my worldly solace,
  For, seeing him, I see my life in death.
WARWICK   As surely as my soul intends to live
  With that dread King that took our state upon Him
  To free us from his Father's wrathful curse,
  I do believe that violent hands were laid
  Upon the life of this thrice-famed duke.
SUFFOLK
  A dreadful oath, sworn with a solemn tongue!
  What instance gives Lord Warwick for his vow?
WARWICK   See how the blood is settled in his face.
  Oft have I seen a timely-parted ghost,
  Of ashy semblance, meagre, pale, and bloodless,
  Being all descended to the labouring heart;
  Who, in the conflict that it holds with death,
  Attracts the same for aidance 'gainst the enemy;
  Which with the heart there cools, and ne'er returneth
  To blush and beautify the cheek again.
  But see, his face is black and full of blood,
  His eye-balls further out than when he liv'd,
  Staring full ghastly like a strangled man;
  His hair uprear'd, his nostrils stretch'd with
      struggling;
  His hands abroad display'd, as one that grasp'd
  And tugg'd for life, and was by strength subdu'd.
  Look, on the sheets his hair, you see, is sticking;
  His well-proportion'd beard made rough and rugged,
  Like to the summer's corn by tempest lodg'd.
  It cannot be but he was murder'd here;
  The least of all these signs were probable.
SUFFOLK
  Why, Warwick, who should do the Duke to death?
  Myself and Beaufort had him in protection;
  And we, I hope, sir, are no murderers.
WARWICK
  But both of you were vow'd Duke Humphrey's foes,
  And you, forsooth, had the good Duke to keep:
  'Tis like you would not feast him like a friend,
  And 'tis well seen he found an enemy.
QUEEN   Then you, belike, suspect these noblemen
  As guilty of Duke Humphrey's timeless death.
WARWICK
  Who finds the heifer dead, and bleeding fresh,
  And sees fast by a butcher with an axe,
  But will suspect 'twas he that made the slaughter?
  Who finds the partridge in the puttock's nest,
  But may imagine how the bird was dead,
  Although the kite soar with unbloodied beak?
  Even so suspicious is this tragedy.
QUEEN
  Are you the butcher, Suffolk? Where's your knife?
  Is Beaufort termed a kite? Where are his talons?
SUFFOLK
  I wear no knife to slaughter sleeping men;

But here's a vengeful sword, rusted with ease,
That shall be scoured in his rancorous heart
That slanders me with murder's crimson badge.
Say, if thou dar'st, proud Lord of Warwickshire,   200
That I am faulty in Duke Humphrey's death.
                              Exeunt Cardinal and others.
WARWICK
  What dares not Warwick, if false Suffolk dare him?
QUEEN   He dares not calm his contumelious spirit,
  Nor cease to be an arrogant controller,
  Though Suffolk dare him twenty thousand times.   205
WARWICK   Madam, be still, with reverence may I say;
  For every word you speak in his behalf
  Is slander to your royal dignity.
SUFFOLK   Blunt-witted lord, ignoble in demeanour!
  If ever lady wrong'd her lord so much,   210
  Thy mother took into her blameful bed
  Some stern untutor'd churl, and noble stock
  Was graft with crab-tree slip, whose fruit thou art,
  And never of the Nevils' noble race.
WARWICK   But that the guilt of murder bucklers thee,   215
  And I should rob the deathsman of his fee,
  Quitting thee thereby of ten thousand shames,
  And that my sovereign's presence makes me mild,
  I would, false murd'rous coward, on thy knee
  Make thee beg pardon for thy passed speech,   220
  And say it was thy mother that thou meant'st;
  That thou thyself wast born in bastardy:
  And after all this fearful homage done,
  Give thee thy hire and send thy soul to hell,
  Pernicious blood-sucker of sleeping men!   225
SUFFOLK   Thou shalt be waking while I shed thy blood,
  If from this presence thou dar'st go with me.
WARWICK   Away even now, or I will drag thee hence:
  Unworthy though thou art, I'll cope with thee,
  And do some service to Duke Humphrey's ghost.   230
                              Exeunt Suffolk and Warwick.
KING
  What stronger breastplate than a heart untainted!
  Thrice is he arm'd that hath his quarrel just,
  And he but naked, though lock'd up in steel,
  Whose conscience with injustice is corrupted.
  [*a noise within*]
QUEEN   What noise is this?   235

Re-enter SUFFOLK *and* WARWICK, *with their weapons drawn.*

KING
  Why, how now, lords! your wrathful weapons drawn
  Here in our presence! Dare you be so bold?
  Why, what tumultuous clamour have we here?
SUFFOLK
  The trait'rous Warwick, with the men of Bury,
  Set all upon me, mighty sovereign.   240

                    Enter SALISBURY.

SALISBURY [*to the Commons entering*]
  Sirs, stand apart; the King shall know your mind.

Dread lord, the commons sends you word by me,
Unless false Suffolk straight be done to death,
Or banished fair England's territories,
They will by violence tear him from your palace   245
And torture him with grievous ling'ring death.
They say, by him the good Duke Humphrey died;
They say, in him they fear your Highness' death;
And mere instinct of love and loyalty,
Free from a stubborn opposite intent,   250
As being thought to contradict your liking,
Makes them thus forward in his banishment.
They say, in care of your most royal person,
That if your Highness should intend to sleep,
And charge that no man should disturb your rest,   255
In pain of your dislike or pain of death,
Yet, notwithstanding such a strait edict,
Were there a serpent seen, with forked tongue,
That slily glided towards your Majesty,
It were but necessary you were wak'd,   260
Lest, being suffer'd, in that harmful slumber,
The mortal worm might make the sleep eternal:
And therefore do they cry, though you forbid,
That they will guard you, whe'r you will or no,
From such fell serpents as false Suffolk is;   265
With whose envenomed and fatal sting,
Your loving uncle, twenty times his worth,
They say, is shamefully bereft of life.

COMMONS [*within*]
     An answer from the King, my Lord of Salisbury!

SUFFOLK
     'Tis like the commons, rude unpolish'd hinds,   270
     Could send such message to their sovereign;
     But you, my lord, were glad to be employ'd,
     To show how quaint an orator you are:
     But all the honour Salisbury hath won
     Is that he was the lord ambassador,   275
     Sent from a sort of tinkers to the King.

COMMONS [*within*]
     An answer from the King, or we will all break in!

KING   Go, Salisbury, and tell them all from me,
     I thank them for their tender loving care;
     And had I not been cited so by them,   280
     Yet did I purpose as they do entreat;
     For sure, my thoughts do hourly prophesy
     Mischance unto my state by Suffolk's means:
     And therefore, by His Majesty I swear,
     Whose far unworthy deputy I am,   285
     He shall not breathe infection in this air
     But three days longer, on the pain of death.

                              Exit Salisbury.

QUEEN   O Henry, let me plead for gentle Suffolk!

KING   Ungentle Queen, to call him gentle Suffolk!
     No more, I say; if thou dost plead for him   290
     Thou wilt but add increase unto my wrath.
     Had I but said, I would have kept my word;

But when I swear, it is irrevocable.
If after three days' space thou here be'st found
On any ground that I am ruler of,   295
The world shall not be ransom for thy life.
Come, Warwick, come, good Warwick, go with me;
I have great matters to impart to thee.

               Exeunt all but Queen and Suffolk.

QUEEN   Mischance and Sorrow go along with you!
     Heart's Discontent and sour Affliction   300
     Be playfellows to keep you company!
     There's two of you; the Devil make a third!
     And threefold Vengeance tend upon your steps!

SUFFOLK   Cease, gentle queen, these execrations,
     And let thy Suffolk take his heavy leave.   305

QUEEN   Fie, coward woman and soft-hearted wretch!
     Hast thou not spirit to curse thine enemy?

SUFFOLK
     A plague upon them! Wherefore should I curse them?
     Would curses kill, as doth the mandrake's groan,
     I would invent as bitter searching terms,   310
     As curst, as harsh, and horrible to hear,
     Deliver'd strongly through my fixed teeth,
     With full as many signs of deadly hate,
     As lean-fac'd Envy in her loathsome cave.
     My tongue should stumble in mine earnest words;   315
     Mine eyes should sparkle like the beaten flint;
     My hair be fix'd an end, as one distract;
     Ay, every joint should seem to curse and ban:
     And even now my burden'd heart would break
     Should I not curse them. Poison be their drink!   320
     Gall, worse than gall, the daintiest that they taste!
     Their sweetest shade a grove of cypress trees!
     Their chiefest prospect murd'ring basilisks!
     Their softest touch as smart as lizards' stings!
     Their music frightful as the serpent's hiss,   325
     And boding screech-owls make the consort full!
     All the foul terrors in dark-seated hell –

QUEEN   Enough, sweet Suffolk; thou torments thyself;
     And these dread curses, like the sun 'gainst glass,
     Or like an overcharged gun, recoil   330
     And turn the force of them upon thyself.

SUFFOLK   You bade me ban, and will you bid me leave?
     Now, by the ground that I am banish'd from,
     Well could I curse away a winter's night,
     Though standing naked on a mountain top,   335
     Where biting cold would never let grass grow,
     And think it but a minute spent in sport.

QUEEN
     O! let me entreat thee cease. Give me thy hand,
     That I may dew it with my mournful tears;
     Nor let the rain of heaven wet this place,   340
     To wash away my woeful monuments.
     O! could this kiss be printed in thy hand,
     That thou might'st think upon these by the seal,
     Through whom a thousand sighs are breath'd for thee.

So, get thee gone, that I may know my grief;
'Tis but surmis'd whiles thou art standing by,
As one that surfeits thinking on a want.
I will repeal thee, or, be well assur'd,
Adventure to be banished myself;
And banished I am, if but from thee.
Go; speak not to me; even now be gone.
O! go not yet. Even thus two friends condemn'd
Embrace and kiss and take ten thousand leaves,
Loather a hundred times to part than die.
Yet now farewell; and farewell life with thee.

SUFFOLK   Thus is poor Suffolk ten times banished,
Once by the King, and three times thrice by thee.
'Tis not the land I care for, wert thou thence;
A wilderness is populous enough,
So Suffolk had thy heavenly company:
For where thou art, there is the world itself,
With every several pleasure in the world,
And where thou art not, desolation.
I can no more. Live thou to joy thy life;
Myself to joy in nought but that thou liv'st.

Enter VAUX.

QUEEN
Whither goes Vaux so fast? What news, I prithee?
VAUX   To signify unto his Majesty
That Cardinal Beaufort is at point of death;
For suddenly a grievous sickness took him,
That makes him gasp, and stare, and catch the air,
Blaspheming God, and cursing men on earth.
Sometimes he talks as if Duke Humphrey's ghost
Were by his side; sometime he calls the King,
And whispers to his pillow, as to him,
The secrets of his overcharged soul:
And I am sent to tell his Majesty
That even now he cries aloud for him.

QUEEN   Go, tell this heavy message to the King.
Exit Vaux.

Ay me! What is this world! What news are these!
But wherefore grieve I at an hour's poor loss,
Omitting Suffolk's exile, my soul's treasure?
Why only, Suffolk, mourn I not for thee,
And with the southern clouds contend in tears,
Theirs for the earth's increase, mine for my sorrows?
Now get thee hence: the King, thou know'st, is coming;
If thou be found by me thou art but dead.

SUFFOLK   If I depart from thee I cannot live;
And in thy sight to die, what were it else
But like a pleasant slumber in thy lap?
Here could I breathe my soul into the air,
As mild and gentle as the cradle-babe
Dying with mother's dug between his lips;
Where, from thy sight, I should be raging mad,
And cry out for thee to close up mine eyes,
To have thee with thy lips to stop my mouth:

So should'st thou either turn my flying soul,
Or I should breathe it so into thy body,
And then it liv'd in sweet Elysium.
To die by thee were but to die in jest;
From thee to die were torture more than death.   400
O! let me stay, befall what may befall.

QUEEN   Though parting be a fretful corrosive,
It is applied to a deathful wound.
To France, sweet Suffolk! Let me hear from thee;
For wheresoe'er thou art in this world's globe,   405
I'll have an Iris that shall find thee out.
Away!

SUFFOLK   I go.

QUEEN   And take my heart with thee.
[*She kisses him.*]

SUFFOLK   A jewel, lock'd into the woefull'st cask
That ever did contain a thing of worth.
Even as a splitted bark so sunder we: 410
This way fall I to death.

QUEEN   This way for me.
Exeunt severally.

3.3   *Enter the* KING, SALISBURY, WARWICK, *to the*
Cardinal *in bed.*

KING
How fares my lord? Speak, Beaufort, to thy
sovereign.

CARDINAL
If thou be'st death, I'll give thee England's treasure,
Enough to purchase such another island,
So thou wilt let me live, and feel no pain.

KING   Ah, what a sign it is of evil life   5
Where death's approach is seen so terrible!

WARWICK   Beaufort, it is thy sovereign speaks to thee.

CARDINAL   Bring me unto my trial when you will.
Died he not in his bed? Where should he die?
Can I make men live whe'r they will or no?   10
O, torture me no more! I will confess.
Alive again? Then show me where he is:
I'll give a thousand pound to look upon him.
He hath no eyes, the dust hath blinded them.
Comb down his hair; look! look! it stands upright,   15
Like lime-twigs set to catch my winged soul.
Give me some drink; and bid the apothecary
Bring the strong poison that I bought of him.

KING   O thou eternal Mover of the heavens!
Look with a gentle eye upon this wretch;   20
O! beat away the busy meddling fiend
That lays strong siege unto this wretch's soul,
And from his bosom purge this black despair.

WARWICK
See how the pangs of death do make him grin!

SALISBURY   Disturb him not; let him pass peaceably.   25

KING   Peace to his soul! if God's good pleasure be.
Lord Cardinal, if thou think'st on heaven's bliss,

Hold up thy hand, make signal of thy hope.
He dies, and makes no sign. O God, forgive him!
30   WARWICK   So bad a death argues a monstrous life.
KING   Forbear to judge, for we are sinners all.
    Close up his eyes, and draw the curtain close;
    And let us all to meditation.   *Exeunt.*

4.1   *Alarum. Fight at sea. Ordnance goes off. Enter*
    a Lieutenant, a Master, a Master's Mate, WALTER
WHITMORE *and soldiers; with* SUFFOLK, *disguised, and two*
             Gentlemen, *prisoners.*

LIEUTENANT   The gaudy, blabbing, and remorseful day
    Is crept into the bosom of the sea,
    And now loud-howling wolves arouse the jades
    That drag the tragic melancholy night;
5   Who with their drowsy, slow, and flagging wings
    Clip dead men's graves, and from their misty jaws
    Breathe foul contagious darkness in the air.
    Therefore bring forth the soldiers of our prize,
    For whilst our pinnace anchors in the Downs
10   Here shall they make their ransom on the sand,
    Or with their blood stain this discolour'd shore.
    Master, this prisoner freely give I thee;
    And thou that art his mate make boot of this;
    The other, Walter Whitmore, is thy share.
1 GENTLEMAN
15   What is my ransom, master? let me know.
MASTER
    A thousand crowns, or else lay down your head.
MATE   And so much shall you give, or off goes yours.
LIEUTENANT
    What! think you much to pay two thousand crowns,
    And bear the name and port of gentlemen?
20   Cut both the villains' throats – for die you shall:
    The lives of those which we have lost in fight
    Be counterpois'd with such a petty sum!
1 GENTLEMAN
    I'll give it, sir; and therefore spare my life.
2 GENTLEMAN
    And so will I, and write home for it straight.
25   WHITMORE   I lost mine eye in laying the prize aboard,
    And therefore to revenge it shalt thou die;
    [*to Suffolk*] And so should these, if I might have my
    will.
LIEUTENANT   Be not so rash: take ransom; let him live.
SUFFOLK   Look on my George; I am a gentleman.
30   Rate me at what thou wilt, thou shalt be paid.
WHITMORE
    And so am I; my name is Walter Whitmore.
    How now! why starts thou? What doth thee affright?
SUFFOLK
    Thy name affrights me, in whose sound is death.
    A cunning man did calculate my birth,
35   And told me that by water I should die:
    Yet let not this make thee be bloody-minded;
    Thy name is Gualtier, being rightly sounded.

WHITMORE   Gualtier or Walter, which it is, I care not.
    Never yet did base dishonour blur our name
    But with our sword we wip'd away the blot;   40
    Therefore, when merchant-like I sell revenge,
    Broke be my sword, my arms torn and defac'd,
    And I proclaim'd a coward through the world!
SUFFOLK
    Stay, Whitmore, for thy prisoner is a prince,
    The Duke of Suffolk, William de la Pole.   45
WHITMORE   The Duke of Suffolk, muffled up in rags!
SUFFOLK   Ay, but these rags are no part of the Duke:
    Jove sometime went disguis'd, and why not I?
LIEUTENANT   But Jove was never slain, as thou shalt be.
SUFFOLK
    Obscure and lowly swain, King Henry's blood,   50
    The honourable blood of Lancaster,
    Must not be shed by such a jaded groom.
    Hast thou not kiss'd thy hand and held my stirrup?
    And bare-head plodded by my foot-cloth mule,
    And thought thee happy when I shook my head?   55
    How often hast thou waited at my cup,
    Fed from my trencher, kneel'd down at the board,
    When I have feasted with Queen Margaret?
    Remember it and let it make thee crest-fall'n,
    Ay, and allay this thy abortive pride,   60
    How in our voiding lobby hast thou stood
    And duly waited for my coming forth.
    This hand of mine hath writ in thy behalf,
    And therefore shall it charm thy riotous tongue.
WHITMORE
    Speak, Captain, shall I stab the forlorn swain?   65
LIEUTENANT
    First let my words stab him, as he hath me.
SUFFOLK
    Base slave, thy words are blunt, and so art thou.
LIEUTENANT
    Convey him hence, and on our long-boat's side
    Strike off his head.
SUFFOLK   Thou dar'st not for thine own.
LIEUTENANT   Poole!
SUFFOLK   Poole?
LIEUTENANT   Ay, kennel, puddle, sink, whose filth   70
    Troubles the silver spring where England drinks;
    Now will I dam up this thy yawning mouth
    For swallowing the treasure of the realm.
    Thy lips, that kiss'd the Queen, shall sweep the
       ground;
    And thou that smil'dst at good Duke Humphrey's
       death,   75
    Against the senseless winds shalt grin in vain,
    Who in contempt shall hiss at thee again:
    And wedded be thou to the hags of hell,
    For daring to affy a mighty lord
    Unto the daughter of a worthless king,   80
    Having neither subject, wealth, nor diadem.

By devilish policy art thou grown great,
And, like ambitious Sylla, overgorg'd
With gobbets of thy mother's bleeding heart.
By thee Anjou and Maine were sold to France,
The false revolting Normans thorough thee
Disdain to call us lord, and Picardy
Hath slain their governors, surpris'd our forts,
And sent the ragged soldiers wounded home.
The princely Warwick, and the Nevils all,
Whose dreadful swords were never drawn in vain,
As hating thee, are rising up in arms:
And now the house of York, thrust from the crown
By shameful murder of a guiltless king,
And lofty proud encroaching tyranny,
Burns with revenging fire; whose hopeful colours
Advance our half-fac'd sun, striving to shine,
Under the which is writ *Invitis nubibus.*
The commons here in Kent are up in arms;
And to conclude, reproach and beggary
Is crept into the palace of our King,
And all by thee. Away! convey him hence.
SUFFOLK   O! that I were a god, to shoot forth thunder
Upon these paltry, servile, abject drudges.
Small things make base men proud: this villain here,
Being captain of a pinnace, threatens more
Than Bargulus, the strong Illyrian pirate.
Drones suck not eagles' blood but rob bee-hives.
It is impossible that I should die
By such a lowly vassal as thyself.
Thy words move rage and not remorse in me.
LIEUTENANT   Ay, but my deeds shall stay thy fury soon.
SUFFOLK   I go of message from the Queen to France.
I charge thee waft me safely 'cross the Channel.
WHITMORE
Come, Suffolk, I must waft thee to thy death.
SUFFOLK   *Pene gelidus timor occupat artus:*
'Tis thee I fear.
WHITMORE
Thou shalt have cause to fear before I leave thee.
What! are ye daunted now? Now will ye stoop?
1 GENTLEMAN
My gracious lord, entreat him, speak him fair.
SUFFOLK   Suffolk's imperial tongue is stern and rough,
Us'd to command, untaught to plead for favour.
Far be it we should honour such as these
With humble suit: no, rather let my head
Stoop to the block than these knees bow to any
Save to the God of heaven, and to my king;
And sooner dance upon a bloody pole
Than stand uncover'd to the vulgar groom.
True nobility is exempt from fear:
More can I bear than you dare execute.
LIEUTENANT   Hale him away, and let him talk no more.
SUFFOLK   Come, soldiers, show what cruelty ye can,
That this my death may never be forgot.
Great men oft die by vile bezonians.
A Roman sworder and banditto slave

Murder'd sweet Tully; Brutus' bastard hand
Stabb'd Julius Caesar; savage islanders
Pompey the Great; and Suffolk dies by pirates.
Exeunt Whitmore and others with Suffolk.
LIEUTENANT
And as for these whose ransom we have set,
It is our pleasure one of them depart: 140
Therefore come you with us, and let him go.
Exeunt all but the First Gentleman.

Re-enter WHITMORE, *with Suffolk's body.*

WHITMORE   There let his head and lifeless body lie,
Until the Queen his mistress bury it.   *Exit.*
1 GENTLEMAN   O barbarous and bloody spectacle!
His body will I bear unto the King: 145
If he revenge it not, yet will his friends;
So will the Queen, that living held him dear.
Exit with the body.

4.2   *Enter* GEORGE BEVIS *and* JOHN HOLLAND.

BEVIS   Come, and get thee a sword, though made of a
lath: they have been up these two days.
HOLLAND   They have the more need to sleep now then.
BEVIS   I tell thee, Jack Cade the clothier means to dress
the commonwealth, and turn it, and set a new nap   5
upon it.
HOLLAND   So he had need, for 'tis threadbare. Well, I
say it was never merry world in England since
gentlemen came up.
BEVIS   O miserable age! Virtue is not regarded in handi-   10
craftsmen.
HOLLAND   The nobility think scorn to go in leather aprons.
BEVIS   Nay, more; the King's Council are no good workmen.
HOLLAND   True; and yet it is said, 'Labour in thy   15
vocation': which is as much to say as, 'Let the
magistrates be labouring men'; and therefore should
we be magistrates.
BEVIS   Thou hast hit it; for there's no better sign of a
brave mind than a hard hand.   20
HOLLAND   I see them! I see them! There's Best's son,
the tanner of Wingham, –
BEVIS   He shall have the skins of our enemies to make
dog's-leather of.
HOLLAND   And Dick the butcher, –   25
BEVIS   Then is Sin struck down like an ox, and
Iniquity's throat cut like a calf.
HOLLAND   And Smith the weaver, –
BEVIS   *Argo,* their thread of life is spun.
HOLLAND   Come, come; let's fall in with them.   30

Drum. Enter CADE, DICK BUTCHER, SMITH THE WEAVER
and a sawyer, with infinite numbers.

CADE   We John Cade, so term'd of our suppos'd father, –
BUTCHER   [*aside*]   Or rather, of stealing a cade of
herrings.

CADE   For our enemies shall fall before us, inspir'd with
35   the spirit of putting down kings and princes, –
        Command silence.
BUTCHER   Silence!
CADE   My father was a Mortimer, –
BUTCHER [*aside*]   He was an honest man, and a good
40   brick-layer.
CADE   My mother a Plantagenet, –
BUTCHER [*aside*]   I knew her well; she was a midwife.
CADE   My wife descended of the Lacies, –
BUTCHER [*aside*]   She was, indeed, a pedlar's daughter,
45   and sold many laces.
WEAVER [*aside*]   But not of late, not able to travel with
        her furr'd pack, she washes bucks here at home.
CADE   Therefore am I of an honourable house.
BUTCHER [*aside*]   Ay, by my faith, the field is
50   honourable, and there was he born, under a hedge; for
        his father had never a house but the cage.
CADE   Valiant I am.
WEAVER [*aside*]   A must needs, for beggary is valiant.
CADE   I am able to endure much.
55   BUTCHER [*aside*]   No question of that, for I have seen
        him whipp'd three market-days together.
CADE   I fear neither sword nor fire.
WEAVER [*aside*]   He need not fear the sword, for his coat
        is of proof.
60   BUTCHER [*aside*]   But methinks he should stand in fear
        of fire, being burnt i'th' hand for stealing of sheep.
CADE   Be brave then; for your captain is brave, and vows
        reformation. There shall be in England seven half-
        penny loaves sold for a penny; the three-hoop'd pot
65   shall have ten hoops; and I will make it felony to drink
        small beer. All the realm shall be in common, and in
        Cheapside shall my palfrey go to grass. And when I am
        king, as king I will be, –
ALL   God save your Majesty!
70   CADE   I thank you, good people – there shall be no
        money; all shall eat and drink on my score, and I will
        apparel them all in one livery, that they may agree like
        brothers, and worship me their lord.
BUTCHER   The first thing we do, let's kill all the lawyers.
75   CADE   Nay, that I mean to do. Is not this a lamentable
        thing, that of the skin of an innocent lamb should be
        made parchment? that parchment, being scribbled
        o'er, should undo a man? Some say the bee stings; but
        I say, 'tis the bee's wax, for I did but seal once to a
80   thing, and I was never mine own man since. How now!
        Who's there?

Enter some, bringing forward the CLERK *of Chartham.*

WEAVER   The clerk of Chartham: he can write and read
        and cast accompt.
CADE   O monstrous!
85   WEAVER   We took him setting of boys' copies.
CADE   Here's a villain!
WEAVER   H'as a book in his pocket with red letters in 't.
CADE   Nay, then he is a conjurer.

BUTCHER   Nay, he can make obligations, and write
        courthand.   90
CADE   I am sorry for 't. The man is a proper man, of
        mine honour; unless I find him guilty, he shall not die.
        Come hither, sirrah, I must examine thee. What is thy
        name?
CLERK   Emmanuel.   95
BUTCHER   They use to write it on the top of letters.
        'Twill go hard with you.
CADE   Let me alone. Dost thou use to write thy name?
        Or hast thou a mark to thyself, like an honest plain-
        dealing man?   100
CLERK   Sir, I thank God I have been so well brought up
        that I can write my name.
ALL   He hath confess'd: away with him! he's a villain
        and a traitor.
CADE   Away with him, I say: hang him with his pen and   105
        ink-horn about his neck.   *Exit one with the Clerk.*

Enter MICHAEL.

MICHAEL   Where's our general?
CADE   Here I am, thou particular fellow.
MICHAEL   Fly, fly, fly! Sir Humphrey Stafford and his
        brother are hard by, with the King's forces.   110
CADE   Stand, villain, stand, or I'll fell thee down. He
        shall be encount'red with a man as good as himself. He
        is but a knight, is a?
MICHAEL   No.
CADE   To equal him, I will make myself a knight   115
        presently. [*Kneels.*] Rise up Sir John Mortimer. [*Rises.*]
        Now have at him!

Enter SIR HUMPHREY STAFFORD, *and his* Brother, *with
drum and soldiers.*

STAFFORD
        Rebellious hinds, the filth and scum of Kent,
        Mark'd for the gallows, lay your weapons down;
        Home to your cottages, forsake this groom: 120
        The King is merciful, if you revolt.
BROTHER
        But angry, wrathful, and inclin'd to blood,
        If you go forward: therefore yield, or die.
CADE   As for these silken-coated slaves, I pass not:
        It is to you, good people, that I speak,   125
        Over whom, in time to come, I hope to reign;
        For I am rightful heir unto the crown.
STAFFORD   Villain! thy father was a plasterer;
        And thou thyself a shearman, art thou not?
CADE   And Adam was a gardener.
BROTHER   What of that?   130
CADE   Marry, this: Edmund Mortimer, Earl of March,
        Married the Duke of Clarence' daughter, did he not?
STAFFORD   Ay, sir.
CADE   By her he had two children at one birth.
BROTHER   That's false.   135
CADE   Ay, there's the question; but I say, 'tis true.
        The elder of them, being put to nurse,

Was by a beggar-woman stol'n away;
And, ignorant of his birth and parentage,
Became a bricklayer when he came to age:
His son am I; deny it if you can.

BUTCHER   Nay, 'tis too true; therefore he shall be king.

WEAVER   Sir, he made a chimney in my father's house,
and the bricks are alive at this day to testify; therefore
deny it not.

STAFFORD
And will you credit this base drudge's words,
That speaks he knows not what?

ALL   Ay, marry, will we; therefore get ye gone.

BROTHER
Jack Cade, the Duke of York hath taught you this.

CADE [*aside*]   He lies, for I invented it myself. – Go to,
sirrah, tell the King from me, that for his father's sake,
Henry the Fifth, in whose time boys went to span-
counter for French crowns, I am content he shall
reign; but I'll be Protector over him.

BUTCHER   And furthermore, we'll have the Lord Say's
head for selling the dukedom of Maine.

CADE   And good reason; for thereby is England main'd
and fain to go with a staff, but that my puissance holds
it up. Fellow kings, I tell you that that Lord Say hath
gelded the commonwealth and made it an eunuch; and
more than that, he can speak French; and therefore he
is a traitor.

STAFFORD   O gross and miserable ignorance!

CADE   Nay, answer if you can: the Frenchmen are our
enemies; go to then, I ask but this: can he that speaks
with the tongue of an enemy be a good counsellor, or no?

ALL   No, no; and therefore we'll have his head.

BROTHER   Well, seeing gentle words will not prevail,
Assail them with the army of the King.

STAFFORD   Herald, away; and throughout every town
Proclaim them traitors that are up with Cade;
That those which fly before the battle ends
May, even in their wives' and children's sight,
Be hang'd up for example at their doors.
And you that be the King's friends, follow me.
                    Exeunt the two Staffords and forces.

CADE   And you that love the commons, follow me.
Now show yourselves men; 'tis for liberty.
We will not leave one lord, one gentleman:
Spare none but such as go in clouted shoon,
For they are thrifty honest men, and such
As would, but that they dare not, take our parts.

BUTCHER   They are all in order, and march toward us.

CADE   But then are we in order when we are most out of
order. Come: march forward!   *Exeunt.*

4.3   *Alarums to the fight, wherein both the* Staffords *are
slain. Enter* CADE *and the rest.*

CADE   Where's Dick, the butcher of Ashford?

BUTCHER   Here, sir.

CADE   They fell before thee like sheep and oxen, and
thou behaved'st thyself as if thou hadst been in thine
own slaughter-house. Therefore thus will I reward
thee – the Lent shall be as long again as it is; thou shalt
have licence to kill for a hundred lacking one.

BUTCHER   I desire no more.

CADE   And, to speak truth, thou deserv'st no less. [*He
puts on Sir Humphrey's armour.*] This monument of
the victory will I bear; and the bodies shall be dragg'd
at my horse heels till I do come to London, where we
will have the mayor's sword borne before us.

BUTCHER   If we mean to thrive and do good, break open
the gaols and let out the prisoners.

CADE   Fear not that, I warrant thee. Come; let's march
towards London.   *Exeunt.*

4.4   *Enter the* KING *with a supplication, and the*
QUEEN *with Suffolk's head, the* DUKE OF BUCKINGHAM
and the LORD SAY.

QUEEN [*aside*]
Oft have I heard that grief softens the mind,
And makes it fearful and degenerate;
Think therefore on revenge, and cease to weep.
But who can cease to weep and look on this?
Here may his head lie on my throbbing breast;
But where's the body that I should embrace?

BUCKINGHAM   What answer makes your Grace to the
rebels' supplication?

KING   I'll send some holy bishop to entreat;
For God forbid so many simple souls
Should perish by the sword! And I myself,
Rather than bloody war shall cut them short,
Will parley with Jack Cade their general.
But stay, I'll read it over once again.

QUEEN [*aside*]
Ah! barbarous villains! hath this lovely face
Rul'd like a wandering planet over me,
And could it not enforce them to relent,
That were unworthy to behold the same?

KING
Lord Say, Jack Cade hath sworn to have thy head.

SAY   Ay, but I hope your Highness shall have his.

KING   How, madam! Still lamenting Suffolk's death?
I fear me, love, if that I had been dead,
Thou wouldest not have mourn'd so much for me.

QUEEN
My love; I should not mourn, but die for thee.

                    Enter a Messenger.

KING
How now! What news? Why com'st thou in such
haste?

1 MESSENGER
The rebels are in Southwark; fly, my lord!
Jack Cade proclaims himself Lord Mortimer,

Descended from the Duke of Clarence' house,
And calls your Grace usurper, openly
30 And vows to crown himself in Westminster.
His army is a ragged multitude
Of hinds and peasants, rude and merciless:
Sir Humphrey Stafford and his brother's death
Hath given them heart and courage to proceed.
35 All scholars, lawyers, courtiers, gentlemen,
They call false caterpillars, and intend their death.
KING   O graceless men! they know not what they do.
BUCKINGHAM   My gracious lord, retire to Killingworth,
Until a power be rais'd to put them down.
40 QUEEN   Ah, were the Duke of Suffolk now alive,
These Kentish rebels would be soon appeas'd!
KING   Lord Say, the traitors hateth thee,
Therefore away with us to Killingworth.
SAY   So might your Grace's person be in danger.
45 The sight of me is odious in their eyes;
And therefore in this city will I stay,
And live alone as secret as I may.

Enter another Messenger.

2 MESSENGER
Jack Cade hath almost gotten London Bridge;
The citizens fly and forsake their houses;
50 The rascal people, thirsting after prey,
Join with the traitor; and they jointly swear
To spoil the city and your royal court.
BUCKINGHAM
Then linger not, my lord; away! take horse.
KING
Come, Margaret: God, our hope, will succour us.
QUEEN [*aside*]
55 My hope is gone, now Suffolk is deceas'd.
KING
Farewell, my lord: trust not the Kentish rebels.
BUCKINGHAM   Trust nobody, for fear you be betray'd.
SAY   The trust I have is in mine innocence,
And therefore am I bold and resolute.   *Exeunt.*

4.5 *Enter* LORD SCALES *upon the Tower, walking.*
Then enter two or three Citizens *below.*

SCALES   How now! Is Jack Cade slain?
1 CITIZEN   No, my lord, nor likely to be slain; for they
have won the bridge, killing all those that withstand
them. The Lord Mayor craves aid of your Honour from
the Tower to defend the city from the rebels.
5 SCALES   Such aid as I can spare you shall command;
But I am troubled here with them myself;
The rebels have assay'd to win the Tower.
But get you to Smithfield and gather head,
And thither I will send you Matthew Goffe;
10 Fight for your king, your country, and your lives;
And so farewell, for I must hence again.   *Exeunt.*

4.6 *Enter* JACK CADE *and the rest, and strikes his staff on*
London Stone.

CADE   Now is Mortimer lord of this city. And here,
sitting upon London Stone, I charge and command
that, of the city's cost, the pissing-conduit run nothing
but claret wine this first year of our reign. And now
5 henceforward it shall be treason for any that calls me
other than Lord Mortimer.

Enter a Soldier, *running.*

SOLDIER   Jack Cade! Jack Cade!
CADE   Knock him down there [*They kill him.*]
BUTCHER   If this fellow be wise, he'll never call ye Jack
10 Cade more: I think he hath a very fair warning. My
lord, there's an army gathered together in Smithfield.
CADE   Come then, let's go fight with them. But first, go
and set London bridge afire, and, if you can, burn
down the Tower too. Come, let's away.   *Exeunt.*

4.7 *Alarums.* MATTHEW GOFFE *is slain, and all the rest.*
Then enter JACK CADE, *with his company.*

CADE   So, sirs. Now go some and pull down the Savoy;
others to the Inns of Court: down with them all.
BUTCHER   I have a suit unto your lordship.
CADE   Be it a lordship, thou shalt have it for that word.
5 BUTCHER   Only that the laws of England may come out
of your mouth.
HOLLAND [*aside*]   Mass, 'twill be sore law then; for he
was thrust in the mouth with a spear, and 'tis not
whole yet.
10 WEAVER [*aside*]   Nay, John, it will be stinking law; for his
breath stinks with eating toasted cheese.
CADE   I have thought upon it; it shall be so. Away! burn
all the records of the realm; my mouth shall be the
parliament of England.
15 HOLLAND [*aside*]   Then we are like to have biting
statutes, unless his teeth be pull'd out.
CADE   And henceforward all things shall be in common.

Enter a Messenger.

MESSENGER   My lord, a prize, a prize! here's the Lord
Say, which sold the towns in France; he that made us
20 pay one-and-twenty fifteens, and one shilling to the
pound, the last subsidy.

Enter GEORGE [BEVIS], *with the* Lord SAY.

CADE   Well, he shall be beheaded for it ten times. Ah,
thou say, thou serge, nay, thou buckram lord! now art
thou within point-blank of our jurisdiction regal.
25 What canst thou answer to my Majesty for giving up
of Normandy unto Mounsieur Basimecu, the
Dauphin of France? Be it known unto thee by these
presence, even the presence of Lord Mortimer, that I
am the besom that must sweep the court clean of such

filth as thou art. Thou hast most traitorously corrupted the youth of the realm in erecting a grammar-school; and whereas, before, our forefathers had no other books but the score and the tally, thou hast caus'd printing to be us'd; and contrary to the King his crown, and dignity, thou hast built a paper-mill. It will be prov'd to thy face that thou hast men about thee that usually talk of a noun, and a verb, and such abominable words as no Christian ear can endure to hear. Thou hast appointed justices of peace, to call poor men before them about matters they were not able to answer. Moreover, thou hast put them in prison; and because they could not read, thou hast hang'd them; when, indeed, only for that cause they have been most worthy to live. Thou dost ride in a foot-cloth, dost thou not?

SAY   What of that?

CADE   Marry, thou ought'st not to let thy horse wear a cloak, when honester men than thou go in their hose and doublets.

BUTCHER   And work in their shirt too; as myself, for example, that am a butcher.

SAY   You men of Kent –

BUTCHER   What say you of Kent?

SAY   Nothing but this: 'tis *bona terra, mala gens.*

CADE   Away with him! away with him! he speaks Latin.

SAY   Hear me but speak, and bear me where you will.
Kent, in the Commentaries Caesar writ,
Is term'd the civil'st place of all this isle:
Sweet is the country, because full of riches;
The people liberal, valiant, active, wealthy;
Which makes me hope you are not void of pity.
I sold not Maine, I lost not Normandy;
Yet, to recover them, would lose my life.
Justice with favour have I always done;
Prayers and tears have mov'd me, gifts could never.
When have I aught exacted at your hands,
But to maintain the King, the realm, and you?
Large gifts have I bestow'd on learned clerks,
Because my book preferr'd me to the King,
And seeing ignorance is the curse of God,
Knowledge the wing wherewith we fly to heaven,
Unless you be possess'd with devilish spirits,
You cannot but forbear to murder me:
This tongue hath parley'd unto foreign kings
For your behoof, –

CADE   Tut, when struck'st thou one blow in the field?

SAY   Great men have reaching hands: oft have I struck
Those that I never saw, and struck them dead.

GEORGE   O monstrous coward! What, to come behind folks!

SAY   These cheeks are pale with watching for your good.

CADE   Give him a box o'th' ear, and that will make 'em red again.

SAY   Long sitting, to determine poor men's causes,
Hath made me full of sickness and diseases.

CADE   Ye shall have a hempen caudle then, and pap with, a hatchet.

BUTCHER   Why dost thou quiver, man?

SAY   The palsy, and not fear, provokes me.

CADE   Nay, he nods at us; as who should say, 'I'll be even   90
with you': I'll see if his head will stand steadier on a pole or no. Take him away and behead him.

SAY   Tell me: wherein have I offended most?
Have I affected wealth or honour? speak.
Are my chests fill'd up with extorted gold?   95
Is my apparel sumptuous to behold?
Whom have I injur'd, that ye seek my death?
These hands are free from guiltless blood-shedding,
This breast from harbouring foul deceitful thoughts.
O! let me live.   100

CADE   [*aside*]   I feel remorse in myself with his words;
but I'll bridle it: he shall die, and it be but for pleading so well for his life. Away with him! he has a familiar under his tongue; he speaks not a God's name. Go, take him away, I say, and strike off his head presently;   105
and then break into his son-in-law's house, Sir James Cromer, and strike off his head, and bring them both upon two poles hither.

ALL   It shall be done.

SAY   Ah! countrymen, if when you make your prayers,   110
God should be so obdurate as yourselves, How would it fare with your departed souls? And therefore yet relent and save my life.

CADE   Away with him! and do as I command ye.

Exeunt one or two with the Lord Say.

The proudest peer in the realm shall not wear a head   115
on his shoulders, unless he pay me tribute; there shall not a maid be married, but she shall pay to me her maidenhead, ere they have it. Men shall hold of me in capite; and we charge and command that their wives be as free as heart can wish or tongue can tell.   120

BUTCHER   My lord, when shall we go to Cheapside and take up commodities upon our bills?

CADE   Marry, presently.

ALL   O! brave.

Enter one with the heads.

CADE   But is not this braver? Let them kiss one another;   125
for they loved well when they were alive. Now part them again, lest they consult about the giving up of some more towns in France. Soldiers, defer the spoil of the city until night; for with these borne before us, instead of maces, will we ride through the streets; and   130
at every corner have them kiss. Away!   *Exeunt.*

4.8   *Alarum and retreat. Enter again* CADE *and all his rabblement.*

CADE   Up Fish Street! down Saint Magnus' Corner! kill and knock down! throw them into Thames! [*Sound a parley.*] What noise is this I hear? Dare any be so bold to sound retreat or parley, when I command them kill?

Enter BUCKINGHAM *and* OLD CLIFFORD.

BUCKINGHAM
5   Ay, here they be that dare and will disturb thee:
       Know, Cade, we come ambassadors from the King
       Unto the commons, whom thou hast misled;
       And here pronounce free pardon to them all
       That will forsake thee and go home in peace.
10 CLIFFORD   What say ye, countrymen? Will ye relent
       And yield to mercy, whilst 'tis offer'd you,
       Or let a rebel lead you to your deaths?
       Who loves the King, and will embrace his pardon,
       Fling up his cap, and say 'God save his Majesty!'
15   Who hateth him, and honours not his father,
       Henry the Fifth, that made all France to quake,
       Shake he his weapon at us, and pass by.
    ALL   God save the King! God save the King!
    CADE   What! Buckingham and Clifford, are ye so brave?
20   And you, base peasants, do ye believe him? Will you
       needs be hang'd with your pardons about your necks?
       Hath my sword therefore broke through London
       gates, that you should leave me at the White Hart in
       Southwark? I thought ye would never have given out
25   these arms till you had recover'd your ancient
       freedom; but you are all recreants and dastards, and
       delight to live in slavery to the nobility. Let them
       break your backs with burdens, take your houses over
       your heads, ravish your wives and daughters before
30   your faces. For me, I will make shift for one, and so
       God's curse light upon you all!
    ALL   We'll follow Cade, we'll follow Cade!
    CLIFFORD   Is Cade the son of Henry the Fifth,
       That thus you do exclaim you'll go with him?
35   Will he conduct you through the heart of France,
       And make the meanest of you earls and dukes?
       Alas! he hath no home, no place to fly to;
       Nor knows he how to live but by the spoil,
       Unless by robbing of your friends and us.
40   Were't not a shame, that whilst you live at jar,
       The fearful French, whom you late vanquished,
       Should make a start o'er seas and vanquish you?
       Methinks already in this civil broil
       I see them lording it in London streets,
45   Crying 'Villiago!' unto all they meet.
       Better ten thousand base-born Cades miscarry
       Than you should stoop unto a Frenchman's mercy.
       To France, to France! and get what you have lost;
       Spare England, for it is your native coast.
50   Henry hath money, you are strong and manly;
       God on our side, doubt not of victory.
    ALL   A Clifford! a Clifford! we'll follow the King and
       Clifford.
    CADE [*aside*]   Was ever feather so lightly blown to and
55   fro as this multitude? The name of Henry the Fifth
       hales them to an hundred mischiefs, and makes them
       leave me desolate. I see them lay their heads together
       to surprise me. My sword make way for me, for here is

no staying. – In despite of the devils and hell, have
through the very midst of you! and heavens and   60
honour be witness, that no want of resolution in me,
but only my followers' base and ignominious treasons,
make me betake me to my heels.   *Exit.*
BUCKINGHAM
    What, is he fled? Go some, and follow him;
    And he that brings his head unto the King   65
    Shall have a thousand crowns for his reward.
                          Exeunt some of them.
    Follow me, soldiers: we'll devise a mean
    To reconcile you all unto the King.   *Exeunt.*

4.9 *Sound trumpets. Enter* KING, QUEEN *and* SOMERSET,
                    on the terrace.

KING   Was ever king that joy'd an earthly throne,
    And could command no more content than I?
    No sooner was I crept out of my cradle
    But I was made a king at nine months old;
    Was never subject long'd to be a king   5
    As I do long and wish to be a subject.

            Enter BUCKINGHAM *and* CLIFFORD.

BUCKINGHAM   Health and glad tidings to your Majesty!
KING   Why, Buckingham, is the traitor Cade surpris'd?
    Or is he but retir'd to make him strong?

    Enter multitudes, with halters about their necks.

CLIFFORD
    He is fled, my lord, and all his powers do yield,   10
    And humbly thus, with halters on their necks,
    Expect your Highness' doom, of life, or death.
KING   Then, heaven, set ope thy everlasting gates,
    To entertain my vows of thanks and praise!
    Soldiers, this day have you redeem'd your lives,   15
    And show'd how well you love your Prince and
        country:
    Continue still in this so good a mind,
    And Henry, though he be infortunate,
    Assure yourselves, will never be unkind:
    And so, with thanks and pardon to you all,   20
    I do dismiss you to your several countries.
ALL   God save the King! God save the King!

            Enter a Messenger.

MESSENGER   Please it your Grace to be advertised
    The Duke of York is newly come from Ireland,
    And with a puissant and a mighty power   25
    Of gallowglasses and stout kerns
    Is marching hitherward in proud array;
    And still proclaimeth, as he comes along,
    His arms are only to remove from thee
    The Duke of Somerset, whom he terms a traitor.   30
KING
    Thus stands my state, 'twixt Cade and York
        distress'd;

Like to a ship that, having scap'd a tempest,
Is straightway calm'd, and boarded with a pirate.
But now is Cade driven back, his men dispers'd,
And now is York in arms to second him.
I pray thee, Buckingham, go and meet him,
And ask him what's the reason of these arms.
Tell him I'll send Duke Edmund to the Tower,
And, Somerset, we will commit thee thither,
Until his army be dismiss'd from him.

SOMERSET   I'll yield, my lord, to prison willingly,
Or unto death, to do my country good.

KING   In any case, be not too rough in terms,
For he is fierce and cannot brook hard language.

BUCKINGHAM   I will, my lord; and doubt not so to deal
As all things shall redound unto your good.

KING   Come, wife, let's in, and learn to govern better;
For yet may England curse my wretched reign.

Flourish. Exeunt.

4.10   *Enter* CADE.

CADE   Fie on ambitions! fie on myself, that have a
sword, and yet am ready to famish! These five days
have I hid me in these woods and durst not peep out,
for all the country is laid for me; but now am I so
hungry, that if I might have a lease of my life for a
thousand years, I could stay no longer. Wherefore, on
a brick wall have I climb'd into this garden, to see if I
can eat grass, or pick a sallet another while, which is
not amiss to cool a man's stomach this hot weather.
And I think this word 'sallet' was born to do me good:
for many a time, but for a sallet, my brain-pan had
been cleft with a brown bill; and many a time, when I
have been dry and bravely marching, it hath serv'd me
instead of a quart-pot to drink in; and now the word
'sallet' must serve me to feed on.

Enter IDEN.

IDEN   Lord! who would live turmoiled in the court,
And may enjoy such quiet walks as these?
This small inheritance my father left me
Contenteth me, and worth a monarchy.
I seek not to wax great by others' waning,
Or gather wealth I care not with what envy:
Sufficeth, that I have maintains my state,
And sends the poor well pleased from my gate.

CADE   [*aside*]   Here's the lord of the soil come to seize me
for a stray, for entering his fee-simple without leave. –
Ah, villain, thou wilt betray me, and get a thousand
crowns of the King by carrying my head to him; but I'll
make thee eat iron like an ostrich, and swallow my
sword like a great pin, ere thou and I part.

IDEN   Why, rude companion, whatsoe'er thou be,
I know thee not; why then should I betray thee?

Is't not enough to break into my garden,
And like a thief to come to rob my grounds,
Climbing my walls in spite of me the owner,
But thou wilt brave me with these saucy terms?   35

CADE   Brave thee! ay, by the best blood that ever was
broach'd, and beard thee too. Look on me well: I have
eat no meat these five days; yet, come thou and thy five
men, and if I do not leave you all as dead as a door-nail,
I pray God I may never eat grass more.   40

IDEN   Nay, it shall ne'er be said, while England stands,
That Alexander Iden, esquire of Kent,
Took odds to combat a poor famish'd man.
Oppose thy steadfast-gazing eyes to mine,
See if thou canst outface me with thy looks: 45
Set limb to limb, and thou art far the lesser;
Thy hand is but a finger to my fist;
Thy leg a stick compared with this truncheon;
My foot shall fight with all the strength thou hast;
And if mine arm be heaved in the air   50
Thy grave is digg'd already in the earth.
As for words, whose greatness answers words,
Let this my sword report what speech forbears.

CADE   By my valour, the most complete champion that
ever I heard! Steel, if thou turn the edge, or cut not out 55
the burly-bon'd clown in chines of beef ere thou sleep
in thy sheath, I beseech God on my knees thou may'st
be turned to hobnails. [*Here they fight. Cade falls.*] O,
I am slain! Famine and no other hath slain me: let ten
thousand devils come against me, and give me but the   60
ten meals I have lost, and I'd defy them all. Wither,
garden; and be henceforth a burying-place to all that
do dwell in this house, because the unconquer'd soul
of Cade is fled.

IDEN
Is't Cade that I have slain, that monstrous traitor?   65
Sword, I will hallow thee for this thy deed,
And hang thee o'er my tomb when I am dead:
Ne'er shall this blood be wiped from thy point,
But thou shalt wear it as a herald's coat,
To emblaze the honour that thy master got.   70

CADE   Iden, farewell; and be proud of thy victory. Tell
Kent from me, she hath lost her best man, and exhort
all the world to be cowards; for I, that never fear'd any,
am vanquish'd by famine, not by valour. [*Dies.*]

IDEN
How much thou wrong'st me, heaven be my judge.   75
Die, damned wretch, the curse of her that bare thee!
And as I thrust thy body in with my sword,
So wish I I might thrust thy soul to hell.
Hence will I drag thee headlong by the heels
Unto a dunghill, which shall be thy grave,   80
And there cut off thy most ungracious head;
Which I will bear in triumph to the King,
Leaving thy trunk for crows to feed upon.   *Exit.*

5.1 *Enter* YORK *and his army of Irish, with drum and*
colours.

YORK   From Ireland thus comes York to claim his right,
  And pluck the crown from feeble Henry's head:
  Ring, bells, aloud; burn, bonfires, clear and bright,
  To entertain great England's lawful king.
5   Ah! sancta majestas, who'd not buy thee dear?
  Let them obey that knows not how to rule;
  This hand was made to handle nought but gold:
  I cannot give due action to my words,
  Except a sword or sceptre balance it.
10   A sceptre shall it have, have I a sword,
  On which I'll toss the fleur-de-luce of France.

Enter BUCKINGHAM.

  Whom have we here? Buckingham, to disturb me?
  The King hath sent him, sure: I must dissemble.
BUCKINGHAM
  York, if thou meanest well, I greet thee well.
YORK
15   Humphrey of Buckingham, I accept thy greeting.
  Art thou a messenger, or come of pleasure?
BUCKINGHAM
  A messenger from Henry, our dread liege,
  To know the reason of these arms in peace;
  Or why thou, being a subject, as I am,
20   Against thy oath and true allegiance sworn,
  Should raise so great a power without his leave,
  Or dare to bring thy force so near the court.
YORK [*aside*]   Scarce can I speak, my choler is so great:
  O, I could hew up rocks and fight with flint,
25   I am so angry at these abject terms;
  And now, like Ajax Telamonius,
  On sheep or oxen could I spend my fury.
  I am far better born than is the King,
  More like a king, more kingly in my thoughts;
30   But I must make fair weather yet awhile,
  Till Henry be more weak, and I more strong. –
  Buckingham, I prithee, pardon me,
  That I have given no answer all this while;
  My mind was troubled with deep melancholy.
35   The cause why I have brought this army hither
  Is to remove proud Somerset from the king,
  Seditious to his Grace and to the state.
BUCKINGHAM
  That is too much presumption on thy part:
  But if thy arms be to no other end,
40   The king hath yielded unto thy demand:
  The Duke of Somerset is in the Tower.
YORK   Upon thine honour, is he prisoner?
BUCKINGHAM   Upon mine honour, he is prisoner.
YORK   Then, Buckingham, I do dismiss my powers.
45   Soldiers, I thank you all; disperse yourselves:
  Meet me to-morrow in Saint George's Field,
  You shall have pay, and every thing you wish.

Exeunt soldiers.

  And let my sovereign, virtuous Henry,
  Command my eldest son, nay, all my sons,
50   As pledges of my fealty and love;
  I'll send them all as willing as I live:
  Lands, goods, horse, armour, any thing I have,
  Is his to use, so Somerset may die.
BUCKINGHAM   York, I commend this kind submission:
55   We twain will go into his Highness' tent.

Enter KING *and attendants.*

KING   Buckingham, doth York intend no harm to us,
  That thus he marcheth with thee arm in arm?
YORK   In all submission and humility
  York doth present himself unto your Highness.
KING   Then what intends these forces thou dost bring?   60
YORK   To heave the traitor Somerset from hence,
  And fight against that monstrous rebel, Cade,
  Who since I heard to be discomfited.

Enter IDEN, *with* Cade's *head.*

IDEN   If one so rude and of so mean condition
  May pass into the presence of a king,   65
  Lo! I present your Grace a traitor's head,
  The head of Cade, whom I in combat slew.
KING
  The head of Cade! Great God, how just art Thou!
  O, let me view his visage, being dead,
  That living wrought me such exceeding trouble.   70
  Tell me, my friend, art thou the man that slew him?
IDEN   I was, an't like your Majesty.
KING   How art thou call'd? And what is thy degree?
IDEN   Alexander Iden, that's my name;
  A poor esquire of Kent, that loves his king.   75
BUCKINGHAM
  So please it you, my lord, 'twere not amiss
  He were created knight for his good service.
KING   Iden, kneel down. [*He kneels.*] Rise up a knight.
  We give thee for reward a thousand marks;
  And will that thou henceforth attend on us.   80
IDEN   May Iden live to merit such a bounty,
  And never live but true unto his liege.

Enter QUEEN *and* SOMERSET.

KING
  See, Buckingham, Somerset comes with th' Queen:
  Go, bid her hide him quickly from the Duke.
QUEEN   For thousand Yorks he shall not hide his head,   85
  But boldly stand and front him to his face.
YORK   How now! is Somerset at liberty?
  Then, York, unloose thy long-imprison'd thoughts
  And let thy tongue be equal with thy heart.
  Shall I endure the sight of Somerset?   90
  False king! why hast thou broken faith with me,
  Knowing how hardly I can brook abuse?
  King did I call thee? No, thou art not king;
  Not fit to govern and rule multitudes,
  Which dar'st not, no, nor canst not rule a traitor.   95

That head of thine doth not become a crown;
Thy hand is made to grasp a palmer's staff,
And not to grace an awful princely sceptre.
That gold must round engirt these brows of mine,
Whose smile and frown, like to Achilles' spear,
Is able with the change to kill and cure.
Here is a hand to hold a sceptre up,
And with the same to act controlling laws.
Give place: by heaven, thou shalt rule no more
O'er him whom heaven created for thy ruler.

SOMERSET   O monstrous traitor! I arrest thee, York,
Of capital treason 'gainst the king and crown.
Obey, audacious traitor; kneel for grace.

YORK
Would'st have me kneel? First let me ask of these
If they can brook I bow a knee to man.
Sirrah, call in my sons to be my bail: *Exit attendant.*
I know ere they will have me go to ward,
They'll pawn their swords for my enfranchisement.

QUEEN   Call hither Clifford; bid him come amain,
To say if that the bastard boys of York
Shall be the surety for their traitor father.
                                                          Exit attendant.

YORK   O blood-bespotted Neapolitan,
Outcast of Naples, England's bloody scourge!
The sons of York, thy betters in their birth,
Shall be their father's bail; and bane to those
That for my surety will refuse the boys!

Enter EDWARD and RICHARD.

See where they come: I'll warrant they'll make it
   good.

Enter CLIFFORD and his Son.

QUEEN   And here comes Clifford, to deny their bail.

CLIFFORD
Health and all happiness to my lord the King!
[*Kneels.*]

YORK   I thank thee, Clifford: say, what news with thee?
Nay, do not fright us with an angry look:
We are thy sovereign, Clifford, kneel again;
For thy mistaking so, we pardon thee.

CLIFFORD   This is my King, York; I do not mistake;
But thou mistakes me much to think I do.
To Bedlam with him! Is the man grown mad!

KING   Ay, Clifford; a bedlam and ambitious humour
Makes him oppose himself against his king.

CLIFFORD   He is a traitor; let him to the Tower,
And chop away that factious pate of his.

QUEEN   He is arrested, but will not obey:
His sons, he says, shall give their words for him.

YORK   Will you not, sons?

EDWARD   Ay, noble father, if our words will serve.

RICHARD
And if words will not, then our weapons shall.

CLIFFORD   Why, what a brood of traitors have we here!

YORK   Look in a glass, and call thy image so;

I am thy king, and thou a false-heart traitor.
Call hither to the stake my two brave bears,
That with the very shaking of their chains   145
They may astonish these fell-lurking curs:
Bid Salisbury and Warwick come to me.

Enter the EARLS OF WARWICK and SALISBURY.

CLIFFORD
Are these thy bears? We'll bait thy bears to death,
And manacle the bear'ard in their chains,
If thou dar'st bring them to the baiting-place.   150

RICHARD   Oft have I seen a hot o'erweening cur
Run back and bite, because he was withheld;
Who, being suffer'd, with the bear's fell paw
Hath clapp'd his tail between his legs and cried:
And such a piece of service will you do,   155
If you oppose yourselves to match Lord Warwick.

CLIFFORD   Hence, heap of wrath, foul indigested lump,
As crooked in thy manners as thy shape!

YORK   Nay, we shall heat you thoroughly anon.

CLIFFORD
Take heed, lest by your heat you burn yourselves.   160

KING   Why, Warwick, hath thy knee forgot to bow?
Old Salisbury, shame to thy silver hair,
Thou mad misleader of thy brain-sick son!
What! wilt thou on thy death-bed play the ruffian,
And seek for sorrow with thy spectacles?   165
O! where is faith? O! where is loyalty?
If it be banish'd from the frosty head,
Where shall it find a harbour in the earth?
Wilt thou go dig a grave to find out war,
And shame thine honourable age with blood?   170
Why art thou old and want'st experience?
Or wherefore dost abuse it, if thou hast it?
For shame! in duty bend thy knee to me,
That bows unto the grave with mickle age.

SALISBURY   My lord, I have consider'd with myself   175
The title of this most renowned duke;
And in my conscience do repute his Grace
The rightful heir to England's royal seat.

KING   Hast thou not sworn allegiance unto me?

SALISBURY   I have.   180

KING
Canst thou dispense with heaven for such an oath?

SALISBURY   It is great sin to swear unto a sin,
But greater sin to keep a sinful oath.
Who can be bound by any solemn vow
To do a murd'rous deed, to rob a man,   185
To force a spotless virgin's chastity,
To reave the orphan of his patrimony,
To wring the widow from her custom'd right,
And have no other reason for this wrong
But that he was bound by a solemn oath?   190

QUEEN   A subtle traitor needs no sophister.

KING   Call Buckingham, and bid him arm himself.

YORK   Call Buckingham, and all the friends thou hast,
Both thou and they shall curse this fatal hour;

195   I am resolv'd for death or dignity.

CLIFFORD
    The first I warrant thee, if dreams prove true.

WARWICK
    Thou were best to go to bed and dream again,
    To keep thee from the tempest of the field.

CLIFFORD   I am resolv'd to bear a greater storm
200   Than any thou canst conjure up to-day;
    And that I'll write upon thy burgonet,
    Might I but know thee by thy housed badge.

WARWICK   Now, by my father's badge, old Nevil's crest,
    The rampant bear chain'd to the ragged staff,
205   This day I'll wear aloft my burgonet, –
    As on a mountain top the cedar shows
    That keeps his leaves in spite of any storm, –
    Even to affright thee with the view thereof.

CLIFFORD   And from thy burgonet I'll rend thy bear,
210   And tread it under foot with all contempt,
    Despite the bear'ard that protects the bear.

YOUNG CLIFFORD   And so to arms, victorious father,
    To quell the rebels and their complices.

RICHARD   Fie! charity for shame! speak not in spite,
215   For you shall sup with Jesu Christ to-night.

YOUNG CLIFFORD
    Foul stigmatic, that's more than thou canst tell.

RICHARD   If not in heaven, you'll surely sup in hell.
                            Exeunt severally.

5.2   *Alarums to the battle. Enter* WARWICK.

WARWICK   Clifford of Cumberland, 'tis Warwick calls:
    And if thou dost not hide thee from the bear,
    Now, when the angry trumpet sounds alarum,
    And dead men's cries do fill the empty air,
5   Clifford, I say, come forth and fight with me!
    Proud northern lord, Clifford of Cumberland,
    Warwick is hoarse with calling thee to arms.

Enter YORK.

    How now, my noble lord! what! all afoot?

YORK   The deadly-handed Clifford slew my steed;
10   But match to match I have encounter'd him,
    And made a prey for carrion kites and crows
    Even of the bonny beast he loved so well.

Enter CLIFFORD.

WARWICK   Of one or both of us the time is come.

YORK   Hold, Warwick! seek thee out some other chase,
15   For I myself must hunt this deer to death.

WARWICK
    Then, nobly, York; 'tis for a crown thou fight'st.
    As I intend, Clifford, to thrive to-day,
    It grieves my soul to leave thee unassail'd.   *Exit.*

CLIFFORD
    What seest thou in me, York? Why dost thou pause?

20 YORK   With thy brave bearing should I be in love,
    But that thou art so fast mine enemy.

CLIFFORD
    Nor should thy prowess want praise and esteem,
    But that 'tis shown ignobly and in treason.

YORK   So let it help me now against thy sword
    As I in justice and true right express it.   25

CLIFFORD   My soul and body on the action both!

YORK   A dreadful lay! Address thee instantly.

CLIFFORD   *La fin couronne les oeuvres.*
    [*They fight, and Clifford falls and dies.*]

YORK   Thus war hath given thee peace, for thou art still.
    Peace with his soul, heaven, if it be thy will!   *Exit.*   30

Enter YOUNG CLIFFORD.

YOUNG CLIFFORD
    Shame and confusion! all is on the rout:
    Fear frames disorder, and disorder wounds
    Where it should guard. O war, thou son of hell,
    Whom angry heavens do make their minister,
    Throw in the frozen bosoms of our part   35
    Hot coals of vengeance! Let no soldier fly.
    He that is truly dedicate to war
    Hath no self-love; nor he that loves himself
    Hath not essentially, but by circumstance,
    The name of valour.
    [*seeing his dead father*] O! let the vile world end,   40
    And the premised flames of the last day
    Knit earth and heaven together;
    Now let the general trumpet blow his blast,
    Particularities and petty sounds
    To cease! Wast thou ordain'd, dear father,   45
    To lose thy youth in peace, and to achieve
    The silver livery of advised age,
    And, in thy reverence and thy chair-days, thus
    To die in ruffian battle? Even at this sight
    My heart is turn'd to stone: and while 'tis mine   50
    It shall be stony. York not our old men spares;
    No more will I their babes: tears virginal
    Shall be to me even as the dew to fire;
    And beauty, that the tyrant oft reclaims,
    Shall to my flaming wrath be oil and flax.   55
    Henceforth I will not have to do with pity:
    Meet I an infant of the house of York,
    Into as many gobbets will I cut it
    As wild Medea young Absyrtus did:
    In cruelty will I seek out my fame.   60
    Come, thou new ruin of old Clifford's house:
    As did Aeneas old Anchises bear,
    So bear I thee upon my manly shoulders;
    But then Aeneas bare a living load,
    Nothing so heavy as these woes of mine.   65
                     Exit, bearing off his father.

Enter RICHARD *and* SOMERSET *to fight. Somerset is killed.*

RICHARD   So, lie thou there;
    For underneath an alehouse' paltry sign,
    The Castle in Saint Albans, Somerset
    Hath made the wizard famous in his death.

70 Sword, hold thy temper; heart, be wrathful still:
Priests pray for enemies, but princes kill.　　　*Exit.*

Fight. Excursions. Enter KING, QUEEN *and others.*

QUEEN　Away, my lord! you are slow: for shame, away!
KING
Can we outrun the heavens? Good Margaret, stay.
QUEEN
What are you made of? You'll nor fight nor fly;
75 Now is it manhood, wisdom, and defence,
To give the enemy way, and to secure us
By what we can, which can no more but fly.
　　　　　　　　　　　　　　[Alarum afar off.]
If you be ta'en, we then should see the bottom
Of all our fortunes; but if we haply scape, –
80 As well we may, if not through your neglect, –
We shall to London get, where you are lov'd,
And where this breach now in our fortunes made
May readily be stopp'd.

Re-enter YOUNG CLIFFORD.

YOUNG CLIFFORD
But that my heart's on future mischief set,
85 I would speak blasphemy ere bid you fly;
But fly you must; uncurable discomfit
Reigns in the hearts of all our present parts.
Away, for your relief! and we will live
To see their day and them our fortune give.
90 Away, my lord, away!　　　　　　*Exeunt.*

5.3 *Alarum. Retreat. Enter* YORK, RICHARD, WARWICK
and soldiers, with drum and colours.

YORK　Old Salisbury, who can report of him,
That winter lion, who in rage forgets
Aged contusions and all brush of time,
And, like a gallant in the brow of youth,

Repairs him with occasion? This happy day 5
Is not itself, nor have we won one foot,
If Salisbury be lost.
RICHARD　　　　　　My noble father,
Three times to-day I holp him to his horse,
Three times bestrid him; thrice I led him off,
Persuaded him from any further act: 10
But still, where danger was, still there I met him;
And like rich hangings in a homely house,
So was his will in his old feeble body.
But, noble as he is, look where he comes.

Enter SALISBURY.

SALISBURY
Now, by my sword, well hast thou fought to-day; 15
By the mass, so did we all. I thank you, Richard:
God knows how long it is I have to live;
And it hath pleas'd him that three times to-day
You have defended me from imminent death.
Well, lords, we have not got that which we have: 20
'Tis not enough our foes are this time fled,
Being opposites of such repairing nature.
YORK　I know our safety is to follow them;
For, as I hear, the King is fled to London,
To call a present court of Parliament: 25
Let us pursue him ere the writs go forth.
What says Lord Warwick? Shall we after them?
WARWICK　After them! Nay, before them, if we can.
Now, by my faith, lords, 'twas a glorious day:
Saint Albans battle, won by famous York, 30
Shall be eterniz'd in all age to come.
Sound drums and trumpets! and to London all:
And more such days as these to us befall!　　*Exeunt.*

King Henry VI, Part 3

The textual history of *King Henry VI, Part 3*, is much like that of *Part 2*, and indeed is intertwined with it. *Part 3* also exists in two versions: it was published as the eighth of the histories in the Folio of 1623, though in 1595 a shorter version had appeared in an octavo printing, entitled *The true Tragedy of Richard Duke of York, and the death of good King Henry the Sixth, with the whole contention between the two houses Lancaster and York*. This was reprinted in 1600, and in 1619 *Parts 2* and *3* were published together as *The Whole Contention between the two Famous Houses, Lancaster and York*. These early printings of *Part 3* appear to be based on a memorial text, one reconstructed by actors, possibly those playing Warwick and Clifford. The Folio text is verbally superior and about a third as long again as the earlier printings.

The play must have been written about 1590. In a pamphlet published in September 1592, the dying Robert Greene parodied a line from it (1.4.137) in an attack on Shakespeare as an 'upstart Crow, beautified with our feathers, that with his "tiger's heart wrapp'd in a player's hide", supposes he is as well able to bombast out a blank verse as the best of you'. Seemingly Greene objects that a mere actor and non-graduate like Shakespeare, who may well have performed in plays by Greene, would presume to compete with the dramatists, and he is bitter that Shakespeare has done so with such success. Whatever Greene's intent, his allusion provides a later limit for dating the play of the summer of 1592, when *A Groatsworth of Wit Purchased with a Million of Repentance* was written.

The play seems to have succeeded on stage, though its early theatrical history is obscure. The 1595 octavo tells us on the title-page that the play 'was sundry times acted by the Right Honourable the Earl of Pembroke his servants', and the Folio has 'Sinklo' and 'Humphrey' as the speech prefixes for the two keepers in 3.1. Almost certainly these are the names of the actors who played the roles, John Sincler and Humphrey Jeffes, both members of Pembroke's Men in the 1590s. Little is know of this company or of Shakespeare's relation to it beyond the fact that it was active in London in 1592, was disbanded on tour in the provinces in the late summer of 1593 and apparently had a few of Shakespeare's plays in its repertoire. Perhaps

the shortened text of *King Henry VI, Part 3* was even prepared for its tour in 1593.

The play itself continues the history of Henry's reign from the very point where *Part 2* ends, though like *Parts 1* and *2* it stands as an independent play, with its own structure and thematic concerns. It picks up the action in the aftermath of the Lancastrian defeat at St Albans (1455) and continues the history to the death of Henry and the confirmation of Edward IV as King in 1471. As the seventeen-year scope demands, history is condensed, events omitted, rearranged or fused together. Still, the broad outline follows the pattern Shakespeare found in the historical accounts of Edward Hall's *Union of the Two Noble and Illustre Families of Lancaster and York* (1548).

If in one sense *King Henry VI, Part 3* can be seen as a continuation of Shakespeare's dramatic meditation on the horrors of unchecked human appetite visible in the Wars of the Roses, in another it reveals a unique understanding of the tragedy that has befallen England. The object that has motivated the action is the crown, but here it is stripped of all dignity, a bone fought over by hungry dogs. The word 'crown' itself appears more often than in any other play, but rather than establishing its value, the repetition gradually erodes its meaning. The oscillations of rule, as power shifts back and forth from Henry to Edward, further evacuate what sacred authority might once have inhered in the crown. In this world, the pious Henry is clearly unsuited to rule, as he himself knows: the crown he seeks 'is call'd content'. This world demands harder men, and by the end the sinister figure of Richard of Gloucester emerges, the nightmare fulfilment of the play's deepest logic.

On the modern stage, the play has usually been seen in two-part conflations of the three plays, as in that by the Royal Shakespeare Company in 1988. In 1977, however, Terry Hands directed all three parts of *King Henry VI* in sequence at Stratford-upon-Avon, and in 1994 Katie Mitchell directed *Part 3* independently at the Other Place, Stratford-upon-Avon, in a brave production whose insistent religious motifs served powerfully to emphasize the viciousness of the struggle for the throne.

The Arden text is based on the 1623 First Folio.

KING HENRY the Sixth
Edward, PRINCE of Wales — *his son*
KING LEWIS the Eleventh — *of France*

Duke of SOMERSET
Duke of EXETER
Earl of OXFORD
Earl of NORTHUMBERLAND — *of King Henry's party*
Earl of WESTMORELAND
Lord CLIFFORD

Richard Plantagenet, Duke of YORK

EDWARD, Earl of March, *afterwards*
  KING EDWARD the Fourth
GEORGE, *afterwards* Duke of Clarence — *his sons*
RICHARD, *afterwards* Duke of Gloucester
Edmund, Earl of RUTLAND

Duke of NORFOLK
Marquess of MONTAGUE
Earl of WARWICK
Earl of Pembroke — *of the Duke of York's Party*
Lord FALCONBRIDGE
Lord HASTINGS
Lord Stafford

SIR JOHN Mortimer
Sir Hugh Mortimer — *uncles to the Duke of York*

HENRY, Earl of Richmond — *a youth*
Earl RIVERS — *brother to Lady Grey*
Sir William Stanley
Sir John MONTGOMERY
Sir John SOMERVILLE
TUTOR — *to Rutland*
MAYOR *of York*
LIEUTENANT — *of the Tower*
NOBLEMAN
TWO KEEPERS
HUNTSMAN
SON — *that has killed his father*
FATHER — *that has killed his son*
QUEEN MARGARET
LADY Elizabeth GREY — *afterwards Queen to Edward the Fourth*
BONA — *sister to the French Queen*

Soldiers, Attendants, Messengers, Watchmen, etc.

1.1 *Alarum. Enter the* DUKE OF YORK, EDWARD, RICHARD, NORFOLK, FALCONBRIDGE, WARWICK *and soldiers, with white roses in their hats.*

WARWICK   I wonder how the King escap'd our hands!

YORK   While we pursu'd the horsemen of the north,
He slily stole away and left his men:
Whereat the great Lord of Northumberland,
Whose war-like ears could never brook retreat,
Cheer'd up the drooping army; and himself,
Lord Clifford, and Lord Stafford, all abreast,
Charg'd our main battle's front, and breaking in
Were by the swords of common soldiers slain.

EDWARD   Lord Stafford's father, Duke of Buckingham,
Is either slain or wounded dangerous;
I cleft his beaver with a downright blow:
That this is true, father, behold his blood.

FALCONBRIDGE
And, brother, here's the Earl of Wiltshire's blood,
Whom I encounter'd as the battles join'd.

RICHARD
Speak thou for me, and tell them what I did.
[*throwing down the Duke of Somerset's head*]

YORK   Richard hath best deserv'd of all my sons.
But is your Grace dead, my Lord of Somerset?

NORFOLK   Such hap have all the line of John of Gaunt!

RICHARD   Thus do I hope to shake King Henry's head.

WARWICK   And so do I. Victorious Prince of York,
Before I see thee seated in that throne
Which now the house of Lancaster usurps,
I vow by heavens these eyes shall never close.
This is the palace of the fearful King,
And this the regal seat: possess it, York;
For this is thine and not King Henry's heirs'.

YORK   Assist me then, sweet Warwick, and I will;
For hither we have broken in by force.

NORFOLK   We'll all assist you; he that flies shall die.

YORK   Thanks, gentle Norfolk. Stay by me, my lords;
And, soldiers, stay and lodge by me this night.
[*They go up.*]

WARWICK
And when the King comes, offer him no violence,
Unless he seek to thrust you out perforce.

YORK   The Queen this day here holds her Parliament,
But little thinks we shall be of her Council:
By words or blows here let us win our right.

RICHARD   Arm'd as we are, let's stay within this house.

WARWICK   The bloody parliament shall this be call'd,
Unless Plantagenet, Duke of York, be king,
And bashful Henry be depos'd, whose cowardice
Hath made us by-words to our enemies.

YORK   Then leave me not, my lords; be resolute;
I mean to take possession of my right.

WARWICK
Neither the King, nor he that loves him best,
The proudest he that holds up Lancaster,
Dares stir a wing if Warwick shake his bells.

I'll plant Plantagenet, root him up who dares.
Resolve thee, Richard; claim the English crown.

Flourish. Enter KING HENRY, CLIFFORD, NORTHUMBERLAND, WESTMORELAND, EXETER *and the rest, with red roses in their hats.*

KING HENRY
My lords, look where the sturdy rebel sits,   50
Even in the chair of state! Belike he means,
Back'd by the power of Warwick, that false peer,
To aspire unto the crown and reign as king.
Earl of Northumberland, he slew thy father,
And thine, Lord Clifford; and you both have vow'd revenge   55
On him, his sons, his favourites, and his friends.

NORTHUMBERLAND
If I be not, heavens be reveng'd on me!

CLIFFORD
The hope thereof makes Clifford mourn in steel.

WESTMORELAND
What! shall we suffer this? Let's pluck him down:
My heart for anger burns: I cannot brook it.   60

KING HENRY   Be patient, gentle Earl of Westmoreland.

CLIFFORD   Patience is for poltroons, such as he:
He durst not sit there had your father liv'd.
My gracious lord, here in the parliament
Let us assail the family of York.   65

NORTHUMBERLAND
Well hast thou spoken, cousin: be it so.

KING HENRY   Ah, know you not the city favours them,
And they have troops of soldiers at their beck?

EXETER   But when the Duke is slain they'll quickly fly.

KING HENRY
Far be the thought of this from Henry's heart,   70
To make a shambles of the parliament-house!
Cousin of Exeter, frowns, words, and threats,
Shall be the war that Henry means to use.
Thou factious Duke of York, descend my throne,
And kneel for grace and mercy at my feet;   75
I am thy sovereign.

YORK   I am thine.

EXETER
For shame, come down: he made thee Duke of York.

YORK   'Twas mine inheritance, as the earldom was.

EXETER   Thy father was a traitor to the crown.

WARWICK   Exeter, thou art a traitor to the crown   80
In following this usurping Henry.

CLIFFORD
Whom should he follow but his natural king?

WARWICK
True, Clifford: that is Richard, Duke of York.

KING HENRY
And shall I stand, and thou sit in my throne?

YORK   It must and shall be so: content thyself.   85

WARWICK   Be Duke of Lancaster: let him be King.

WESTMORELAND
He is both King and Duke of Lancaster;

And that the Lord of Westmoreland shall maintain.

WARWICK   And Warwick shall disprove it. You forget
90 That we are those which chas'd you from the field
And slew your fathers, and with colours spread
March'd through the city to the palace gates.

NORTHUMBERLAND
Yes, Warwick, I remember it to my grief;
And, by his soul, thou and thy house shall rue it.

WESTMORELAND
95 Plantagenet, of thee and these thy sons,
Thy kinsmen and thy friends, I'll have more lives
Than drops of blood were in my father's veins.

CLIFFORD   Urge it no more; lest that, instead of words,
I send thee, Warwick, such a messenger
100 As shall revenge his death before I stir.

WARWICK
Poor Clifford, how I scorn his worthless threats!

YORK   Will you we show our title to the crown?
If not, our swords shall plead it in the field.

KING HENRY   What title hast thou, traitor, to the crown?
105 Thy father was, as thou art, Duke of York.
Thy grandsire, Roger Mortimer, Earl of March.
I am the son of Henry the Fifth,
Who made the Dauphin and the French to stoop,
And seiz'd upon their towns and provinces.

110 WARWICK   Talk not of France, sith thou hast lost it all.

KING HENRY   The Lord Protector lost it, and not I:
When I was crown'd I was but nine months old.

RICHARD
You are old enough now, and yet, methinks, you lose.
Father, tear the crown from the usurper's head.

115 EDWARD   Sweet father, do so; set it on your head.

FALCONBRIDGE
Good brother, as thou lov'st and honourest arms,
Let's fight it out and not stand cavilling thus.

RICHARD
Sound drums and trumpets, and the King will fly.

YORK   Sons, peace!

NORTHUMBERLAND
120 Peace thou, and give King Henry leave to speak.

WARWICK   Plantagenet shall speak first: hear him, lords;
And be you silent and attentive too,
For he that interrupts him shall not live.

KING HENRY
Plantagenet, why seek'st thou to depose me?
125 Are we not both Plantagenets by birth,
And from two brothers lineally descent?
Suppose by right and equity thou be king,
Think'st thou that I will leave my kingly throne,
Wherein my grandsire and my father sat?
130 No: first shall war unpeople this my realm;
Ay, and their colours, often borne in France,
And now in England to our heart's great sorrow,
Shall be my winding-sheet. Why faint you, lords?
My title's good, and better far than his.

135 WARWICK   Prove it, Henry, and thou shalt be king.

KING HENRY
Henry the Fourth by conquest got the crown.

YORK   'Twas by rebellion against his king.

KING HENRY [aside]
I know not what to say: my title's weak.
Tell me, may not a king adopt an heir?

YORK   What then?   140

KING HENRY   And if he may, then am I lawful king;
For Richard, in the view of many lords,
Resign'd the crown to Henry the Fourth,
Whose heir my father was, and I am his.

YORK   He rose against him, being his sovereign,   145
And made him to resign his crown perforce.

WARWICK   Suppose, my lords, he did it unconstrain'd,
Think you 'twere prejudicial to his crown?

EXETER   No: for he could not so resign his crown
But that the next heir should succeed and reign.   150

KING HENRY   Art thou against us, Duke of Exeter?

EXETER   His is the right, and therefore pardon me.

YORK   Why whisper you, my lords, and answer not?

EXETER   My conscience tells me he is lawful king.

KING HENRY [aside]
All will revolt from me, and turn to him.   155

NORTHUMBERLAND
Plantagenet, for all the claim thou lay'st,
Think not that Henry shall be so depos'd.

WARWICK   Depos'd he shall be in despite of all.

NORTHUMBERLAND
Thou art deceiv'd: 'tis not thy southern power,
Of Essex, Norfolk, Suffolk, nor of Kent,   160
Which makes thee thus presumptuous and proud,
Can set the Duke up in despite of me.

CLIFFORD   King Henry, be thy title right or wrong,
Lord Clifford vows to fight in thy defence:
May that ground gape and swallow me alive,   165
Where I shall kneel to him that slew my father!

KING HENRY
O Clifford, how thy words revive my heart!

YORK   Henry of Lancaster, resign thy crown.
What mutter you, or what conspire you, lords?

WARWICK   Do right unto this princely Duke of York,   170
Or I will fill the house with armed men,
And o'er the chair of state, where now he sits,
Write up his title with usurping blood.
[He stamps with his foot, and the soldiers show
themselves.]

KING HENRY
My Lord of Warwick, hear me but one word:
Let me for this my life-time reign as king.   175

YORK   Confirm the crown to me and to mine heirs,
And thou shalt reign in quiet whilst thou liv'st.

KING HENRY
Convey the soldiers hence, and then I will.

WARWICK   Captain, conduct them into Tuthill Fields.
                                        Exeunt soldiers.

KING HENRY   I am content: Richard Plantagenet,   180

Enjoy the kingdom after my decease.

CLIFFORD

What wrong is this unto the Prince your son!

WARWICK   What good is this to England and himself!

WESTMORELAND   Base, fearful, and despairing Henry!

CLIFFORD   How hast thou injur'd both thyself and us!

WESTMORELAND   I cannot stay to hear these articles.

NORTHUMBERLAND   Nor I.

CLIFFORD

Come, cousin, let us tell the Queen these news.

WESTMORELAND

Farewell, faint-hearted and degenerate king,

In whose cold blood no spark of honour bides.   *Exit.*

NORTHUMBERLAND

Be thou a prey unto the house of York,

And die in bands for this unmanly deed!   *Exit.*

CLIFFORD   In dreadful war may'st thou be overcome,

Or live in peace abandon'd and despis'd!   *Exit.*

WARWICK   Turn this way, Henry, and regard them not.

EXETER

They seek revenge and therefore will not yield.

KING HENRY   Ah! Exeter.

WARWICK   Why should you sigh, my lord?

KING HENRY

Not for myself, Lord Warwick, but my son,

Whom I unnaturally shall disinherit.

But be it as it may: [*to York*] I here entail

The crown to thee and to thine heirs for ever;

Conditionally that here thou take thine oath

To cease this civil war and, whilst I live,

To honour me as thy king and sovereign;

And neither by treason nor hostility

To seek to put me down and reign thyself.

YORK   This oath I willingly take and will perform.

[*coming from the throne*]

WARWICK

Long live King Henry! Plantagenet, embrace him.

KING HENRY

And long live thou and these thy forward sons!

YORK   Now York and Lancaster are reconcil'd.

EXETER

Accurs'd be he that seeks to make them foes!

[*Sennet. Here they come down.*]

YORK   Farewell, my gracious lord; I'll take my leave,

For I'll to Wakefield to my castle.   ·*Exit with his sons.*

WARWICK   And I'll keep London with my soldiers.

Exeunt.

NORFOLK   And I to Norfolk with my followers. *Exeunt.*

FALCONBRIDGE

And I unto the sea from whence I came.   *Exit.*

KING HENRY   And I with grief and sorrow to the court.

Enter QUEEN MARGARET *and the* PRINCE OF WALES.

EXETER

Here comes the Queen, whose looks bewray her
    anger:

I'll steal away.

KING HENRY   Exeter, so will I.

QUEEN MARGARET

Nay, go not from me; I will follow thee.   220

KING HENRY   Be patient, gentle Queen, and I will stay.

QUEEN MARGARET

Who can be patient in such extremes?

Ah! wretched man, would I had died a maid,

And never seen thee, never borne thee son,

Seeing thou hast prov'd so unnatural a father.   225

Hath he deserv'd to lose his birthright thus?

Hadst thou but lov'd him half so well as I,

Or felt that pain which I did for him once,

Or nourish'd him as I did with my blood,

Thou would'st have left thy dearest heart-blood
    there,   230

Rather than made that savage duke thine heir,

And disinherited thine only son.

PRINCE   Father, you cannot disinherit me:

If you be king, why should not I succeed?

KING HENRY

Pardon me, Margaret; pardon me, sweet son: 235

The Earl of Warwick and the Duke enforc'd me.

QUEEN MARGARET

Enforc'd thee! Art thou King, and wilt be forc'd?

I shame to hear thee speak. Ah! timorous wretch,

Thou hast undone thyself, thy son, and me;

And given unto the house of York such head   240

As thou shalt reign but by their sufferance.

To entail him and his heirs unto the crown,

What is it but to make thy sepulchre,

And creep into it far before thy time?

Warwick is Chancellor, Salisbury Lord of Calais;   245

Stern Falconbridge commands the narrow seas;

The Duke is made Protector of the realm;

And yet shalt thou be safe? Such safety finds

The trembling lamb environed with wolves.

Had I been there, which am a silly woman,   250

The soldiers should have toss'd me on their pikes

Before I would have granted to that act;

But thou prefer'st thy life before thine honour:

And seeing thou dost, I here divorce myself

Both from thy table, Henry, and thy bed,   255

Until that act of parliament be repeal'd

Whereby my son is disinherited.

The northern lords, that have forsworn thy colours,

Will follow mine, if once they see them spread;

And spread they shall be, to thy foul disgrace,   260

And utter ruin of the house of York.

Thus do I leave thee. Come, son, let's away;

Our army is ready; come, we'll after them.

KING HENRY   Stay, gentle Margaret, and hear me speak.

QUEEN MARGARET

Thou hast spoke too much already: get thee gone.   265

KING HENRY

Gentle son Edward, thou wilt stay with me?

QUEEN MARGARET   Ay, to be murder'd by his enemies.

PRINCE   When I return with victory from the field

I'll see your Grace: till then I'll follow her.

QUEEN MARGARET

270   Come, son, away; we may not linger thus.

               Exeunt Queen Margaret and the Prince.

KING HENRY

     Poor Queen! how love to me and to her son

     Hath made her break out into terms of rage.

     Reveng'd may she be on that hateful Duke,

     Whose haughty spirit, winged with desire,

275   Will cost my crown, and like an empty eagle

     Tire on the flesh of me and of my son!

     The loss of those three lords torments my heart:

     I'll write unto them and entreat them fair.

     Come, cousin; you shall be the messenger.

280   EXETER   And I, I hope, shall reconcile them all.

               Flourish. Exeunt.

1.2   *Enter* EDWARD, RICHARD *and* MONTAGUE.

RICHARD

     Brother, though I be youngest, give me leave.

EDWARD   No, I can better play the orator.

MONTAGUE   But I have reasons strong and forcible.

            Enter the DUKE OF YORK.

YORK   Why, how now, sons and brother! at a strife?

5   What is your quarrel? How began it first?

EDWARD   No quarrel, but a slight contention.

YORK   About what?

RICHARD

     About that which concerns your Grace and us –

     The crown of England, father, which is yours.

10   YORK   Mine, boy? Not till King Henry be dead.

RICHARD   Your right depends not on his life or death.

EDWARD   Now you are heir, therefore enjoy it now:

     By giving the house of Lancaster leave to breathe,

     It will outrun you, father, in the end.

15   YORK   I took an oath that he should quietly reign.

EDWARD   But for a kingdom any oath may be broken:

     I would break a thousand oaths to reign one year.

RICHARD

     No; God forbid your Grace should be forsworn.

YORK   I shall be, if I claim by open war.

RICHARD

20   I'll prove the contrary, if you'll hear me speak.

YORK   Thou canst not, son; it is impossible.

RICHARD   An oath is of no moment, being not took

     Before a true and lawful magistrate

     That hath authority over him that swears.

25   Henry had none, but did usurp the place;

     Then, seeing 'twas he that made you to depose,

     Your oath, my lord, is vain and frivolous.

     Therefore, to arms! And, father, do but think

     How sweet a thing it is to wear a crown,

30   Within whose circuit is Elysium

     And all that poets feign of bliss and joy.

     Why do we linger thus? I cannot rest

     Until the white rose that I wear be dy'd

     Even in the lukewarm blood of Henry's heart.

35   YORK   Richard, enough; I will be king, or die.

     Brother, thou shalt to London presently,

     And whet on Warwick to this enterprise.

     Thou, Richard, shalt to the Duke of Norfolk straight

     And tell him privily of our intent.

40   You, Edward, shall to Edmund Brook Lord Cobham,

     With whom the Kentishmen will willingly rise:

     In them I trust, for they are soldiers,

     Witty, courteous, liberal, full of spirit.

     While you are thus employ'd, what resteth more

45   But that I seek occasion how to rise,

     And yet the King not privy to my drift,

     Nor any of the house of Lancaster?

            Enter a Messenger.

     But stay: what news? Why com'st thou in such post?

MESSENGER

     The Queen with all the northern earls and lords

50   Intend here to besiege you in your castle.

     She is hard by with twenty thousand men;

     And therefore fortify your hold, my lord.

YORK

     Ay, with my sword. What! think'st thou that we fear

       them?

     Edward and Richard, you shall stay with me;

55   My brother Montague shall post to London.

     Let noble Warwick, Cobham, and the rest,

     Whom we have left protectors of the King,

     With powerful policy strengthen themselves,

     And trust not simple Henry nor his oaths.

60   MONTAGUE   Brother, I go; I'll win them, fear it not:

     And thus most humbly I do take my leave.   *Exit.*

       Enter SIR JOHN *and Sir Hugh Mortimer.*

YORK   Sir John and Sir Hugh Mortimer, mine uncles,

     You are come to Sandal in a happy hour;

     The army of the Queen mean to besiege us.

SIR JOHN

     She shall not need; we'll meet her in the field.

65   YORK   What, with five thousand men!

RICHARD   Ay, with five hundred, father, for a need.

     A woman's general; what should we fear?

             [A march afar off.]

EDWARD   I hear their drums: let's set our men in order,

70   And issue forth and bid them battle straight.

YORK   Five men to twenty! Though the odds be great,

     I doubt not, uncles, of our victory.

     Many a battle have I won in France,

     When as the enemy hath been ten to one:

75   Why should I not now have the like success? *Exeunt.*

1.3   *Alarums. Enter* RUTLAND *and his* Tutor.

RUTLAND   Ah, whither shall I fly to scape their hands?

     Ah, tutor, look where bloody Clifford comes!

Enter CLIFFORD *and soldiers.*

CLIFFORD
  Chaplain, away! thy priesthood saves thy life.
  As for the brat of this accursed duke,
  Whose father slew my father, he shall die.
TUTOR   And I, my lord, will bear him company.
CLIFFORD   Soldiers, away with him!
TUTOR   Ah, Clifford, murder not this innocent child,
  Lest thou be hated both of God and man.
                Exit, dragged off by soldiers.
CLIFFORD   How now! is he dead already? Or is it fear
  That makes him close his eyes? I'll open them.
RUTLAND   So looks the pent-up lion o'er the wretch
  That trembles under his devouring paws;
  And so he walks, insulting o'er his prey,
  And so he comes to rend his limbs in sunder.
  Ah, gentle Clifford, kill me with thy sword,
  And not with such a cruel threatening look.
  Sweet Clifford, hear me speak before I die:
  I am too mean a subject for thy wrath;
  Be thou reveng'd on men, and let me live.
CLIFFORD
  In vain thou speak'st, poor boy; my father's blood
  Hath stopp'd the passage where thy words should
    enter.
RUTLAND   Then let my father's blood open it again:
  He is a man, and, Clifford, cope with him.
CLIFFORD
  Had I thy brethren here, their lives and thine
  Were not revenge sufficient for me;
  No, if I digg'd up thy forefathers' graves
  And hung their rotten coffins up in chains,
  It could not slake mine ire nor ease my heart.
  The sight of any of the house of York
  Is as a Fury to torment my soul;
  And till I root out their accursed line
  And leave not one alive, I live in hell.
  Therefore – [*lifting his hand*]
RUTLAND   O, let me pray before I take my death!
  To thee I pray; sweet Clifford, pity me.
CLIFFORD   Such pity as my rapier's point affords.
RUTLAND
  I never did thee harm; why wilt thou slay me?
CLIFFORD   Thy father hath.
RUTLAND   But 'twas ere I was born.
  Thou hast one son; for his sake pity me,
  Lest in revenge thereof, sith God is just,
  He be as miserably slain as I.
  Ah, let me live in prison all my days,
  And when I give occasion of offence
  Then let me die, for now thou hast no cause.
CLIFFORD   Thy father slew my father; therefore die.
  [*Stabs him.*]
RUTLAND   *Di faciant laudis summa sit ista tuae!*
CLIFFORD   Plantagenet, I come, Plantagenet!
  And this thy son's blood cleaving to my blade

Shall rust upon my weapon, till thy blood,   50
Congeal'd with this, do make me wipe off both. *Exit.*

1.4   *Alarum. Enter* RICHARD, DUKE OF YORK.

YORK   The army of the Queen hath got the field:
  My uncles both are slain in rescuing me;
  And all my followers to the eager foe
  Turn back and fly, like ships before the wind,
  Or lambs pursu'd by hunger-starved wolves.   5
  My sons, God knows what hath bechanced them:
  But this I know, they have demean'd themselves
  Like men born to renown by life or death.
  Three times did Richard make a lane to me,
  And thrice cried 'Courage, father! fight it out!'   10
  And full as oft came Edward to my side
  With purple falchion, painted to the hilt
  In blood of those that had encounter'd him:
  And when the hardiest warriors did retire,
  Richard cried, 'Charge! and give no foot of ground!'   15
  Edward, 'A crown, or else a glorious tomb!
  A sceptre, or an earthly sepulchre!'
  With this we charg'd again: but out alas!
  We budg'd again; as I have seen a swan
  With bootless labour swim against the tide   20
  And spend her strength with over-matching waves.
              [*A short alarum within.*]
  Ah, hark! the fatal followers do pursue,
  And I am faint and cannot fly their fury;
  And were I strong I would not shun their fury.
  The sands are number'd that makes up my life;   25
  Here must I stay, and here my life must end.

Enter QUEEN MARGARET, CLIFFORD, NORTHUMBERLAND,
     the young PRINCE *and soldiers.*

  Come, bloody Clifford, rough Northumberland,
  I dare your quenchless fury to more rage:
  I am your butt, and I abide your shot.
NORTHUMBERLAND
  Yield to our mercy, proud Plantagenet.   30
CLIFFORD   Ay, to such mercy as his ruthless arm
  With downright payment show'd unto my father.
  Now Phaëthon hath tumbled from his car,
  And made an evening at the noontide prick.
YORK   My ashes, like the phoenix, may bring forth   35
  A bird that will revenge upon you all;
  And in that hope I throw mine eyes to heaven,
  Scorning whate'er you can afflict me with.
  Why come you not? What! multitudes, and fear?
CLIFFORD
  So cowards fight when they can fly no further;   40
  So doves do peck the falcon's piercing talons;
  So desperate thieves, all hopeless of their lives,
  Breathe out invectives 'gainst the officers.
YORK   O Clifford, but bethink thee once again,
  And in thy thought o'errun my former time;   45
  And, if thou canst for blushing, view this face,

And bite thy tongue that slanders him with
   cowardice
Whose frown hath made thee faint and fly ere this.
CLIFFORD   I will not bandy with thee word for word,
50   But buckle with thee blows twice two for one.
   [Draws.]
QUEEN MARGARET
   Hold, valiant Clifford; for a thousand causes
   I would prolong awhile the traitor's life.
   Wrath makes him deaf: speak thou, Northumberland.
NORTHUMBERLAND
   Hold, Clifford! do not honour him so much
55   To prick thy finger, though to wound his heart.
   What valour were it, when a cur doth grin,
   For one to thrust his hand between his teeth,
   When he might spurn him with his foot away?
   It is war's prize to take all vantages;
60   And ten to one is no impeach of valour.
   [They lay hands on York, who struggles.]
CLIFFORD   Ay, ay, so strives the woodcock with the gin.
NORTHUMBERLAND
   So doth the cony struggle in the net.
YORK   So triumph thieves upon their conquer'd booty;
   So true men yield, with robbers so o'er-match'd.
NORTHUMBERLAND
65   What would your Grace have done unto him now?
QUEEN MARGARET
   Brave warriors, Clifford and Northumberland,
   Come make him stand upon this molehill here,
   That raught at mountains with outstretched arms,
   Yet parted but the shadow with his hand.
70   What, was it you that would be England's king?
   Was't you that revell'd in our parliament
   And made a preachment of your high descent?
   Where are your mess of sons to back you now –
   The wanton Edward and the lusty George?
75   And where's that valiant crook-back prodigy,
   Dicky your boy, that with his grumbling voice
   Was wont to cheer his dad in mutinies?
   Or, with the rest, where is your darling Rutland?
   Look, York: I stain'd this napkin with the blood
80   That valiant Clifford with his rapier's point
   Made issue from the bosom of the boy;
   And if thine eyes can water for his death,
   I give thee this to dry thy cheeks withal.
   Alas, poor York! but that I hate thee deadly,
85   I should lament thy miserable state.
   I prithee grieve, to make me merry, York.
   What, hath thy fiery heart so parch'd thine entrails
   That not a tear can fall for Rutland's death?
   Why art thou patient, man? thou should'st be mad;
90   And I to make thee mad do mock thee thus.
   Stamp, rave, and fret, that I may sing and dance.
   Thou would'st be fee'd, I see, to make me sport;
   York cannot speak unless he wear a crown.
   A crown for York! and, lords, bow low to him:
95   Hold you his hands whilst I do set it on.

   [Putting a paper crown on his head]
   Ay, marry, sir, now looks he like a king!
   Ay, this is he that took King Henry's chair,
   And this is he was his adopted heir.
   But how is it that great Plantagenet
100   Is crown'd so soon and broke his solemn oath?
   As I bethink me, you should not be king
   Till our King Henry had shook hands with Death.
   And will you pale your head in Henry's glory,
   And rob his temples of the diadem,
105   Now in his life, against your holy oath?
   O, 'tis a fault too too unpardonable!
   Off with the crown, and, with the crown, his head;
   And, whilst we breathe, take time to do him dead.
CLIFFORD   That is my office, for my father's sake.
QUEEN MARGARET
110   Nay, stay; let's hear the orisons he makes.
YORK
   She-wolf of France, but worse than wolves of France,
   Whose tongue more poisons than the adder's tooth!
   How ill-beseeming is it in thy sex
   To triumph like an Amazonian trull
115   Upon their woes whom Fortune captivates!
   But that thy face is vizard-like, unchanging,
   Made impudent with use of evil deeds,
   I would assay, proud queen, to make thee blush.
   To tell thee whence thou cam'st, of whom deriv'd,
   Were shame enough to shame thee, wert not
     shameless.
120   Thy father bears the type of King of Naples,
   Of both the Sicils, and Jerusalem,
   Yet not so wealthy as an English yeoman.
   Hath that poor monarch taught thee to insult?
125   It needs not, nor it boots thee not, proud queen;
   Unless the adage must be verified,
   That beggars mounted run their horse to death.
   'Tis beauty that doth oft make women proud;
   But God he knows thy share thereof is small.
130   'Tis virtue that doth make them most admir'd;
   The contrary doth make thee wonder'd at.
   'Tis government that makes them seem divine;
   The want thereof makes thee abominable.
   Thou art as opposite to every good
135   As the Antipodes are unto us,
   Or as the south to the Septentrion.
   O tiger's heart wrapp'd in a woman's hide!
   How could'st thou drain the life-blood of the child,
   To bid the father wipe his eyes withal,
140   And yet be seen to bear a woman's face?
   Women are soft, mild, pitiful, and flexible;
   Thou stern, indurate, flinty, rough, remorseless.
   Bid'st thou me rage? Why, now thou hast thy wish.
   Would'st have me weep? Why, now thou hast thy
     will.
145   For raging wind blows up incessant showers,
   And when the rage allays, the rain begins.
   These tears are my sweet Rutland's obsequies,

And every drop cries vengeance for his death
'Gainst thee, fell Clifford, and thee, false French-
    woman.

NORTHUMBERLAND
50   Beshrew me, but his passion moves me so
  As hardly can I check my eyes from tears.

YORK   That face of his the hungry cannibals
  Would not have touch'd, would not have stain'd with
    blood;
  But you are more inhuman, more inexorable –
55   O, ten times more – than tigers of Hyrcania.
  See, ruthless queen, a hapless father's tears.
  This cloth thou dipp'd'st in blood of my sweet boy,
  And I with tears do wash the blood away.
  Keep thou the napkin, and go boast of this;
60   And if thou tell the heavy story right,
  Upon my soul, the hearers will shed tears;
  Yea, even my foes will shed fast-falling tears,
  And say 'Alas! it was a piteous deed.'
  There, take the crown, and with the crown my curse;
65   And in thy need such comfort come to thee
  As now I reap at thy too cruel hand!
  Hard-hearted Clifford, take me from the world:
  My soul to heaven, my blood upon your heads!

NORTHUMBERLAND
  Had he been slaughter-man to all my kin
70   I should not for my life but weep with him,
  To see how inly sorrow gripes his soul.

QUEEN MARGARET
  What, weeping-ripe, my lord Northumberland?
  Think but upon the wrong he did us all,
  And that will quickly dry thy melting tears.

CLIFFORD
75   Here's for my oath, here's for my father's death.
  [*stabbing him*]

QUEEN MARGARET
  And here's to right our gentle-hearted king.
  [*stabbing him*]

YORK   Open thy gate of mercy, gracious God!
  My soul flies through these wounds to seek out
    Thee. [*Dies.*]

QUEEN MARGARET
  Off with his head, and set it on York gates;
80   So York may overlook the town of York.

                            Flourish. Exeunt.

2.1   *A March. Enter* EDWARD, RICHARD *and*
                  their power.

EDWARD   I wonder how our princely father scap'd,
  Or whether he be scap'd away or no
  From Clifford's and Northumberland's pursuit.
  Had he been ta'en, we should have heard the news;
  Had he been slain, we should have heard the news;
  Or had he scap'd, methinks we should have heard
  The happy tidings of his good escape.
  How fares my brother? Why is he so sad?

RICHARD   I cannot joy until I be resolv'd
  Where our right valiant father is become.   10
  I saw him in the battle range about,
  And watch'd him how he singled Clifford forth.
  Methought he bore him in the thickest troop
  As doth a lion in a herd of neat;
  Or as a bear, encompass'd round with dogs,   15
  Who having pinch'd a few and made them cry,
  The rest stand all aloof and bark at him.
  So far'd our father with his enemies;
  So fled his enemies my warlike father:
  Methinks 'tis prize enough to be his son.   20
  See how the morning opes her golden gates,
  And takes her farewell of the glorious sun;
  How well resembles it the prime of youth,
  Trimm'd like a younker prancing to his love!
  [*Three suns appear in the air.*]

EDWARD   Dazzle mine eyes, or do I see three suns?   25

RICHARD   Three glorious suns, each one a perfect sun;
  Not separated with the racking clouds,
  But sever'd in a pale clear-shining sky.
  See, see! they join, embrace, and seem to kiss,
  As if they vow'd some league inviolable: 30
  Now are they but one lamp, one light, one sun.
  In this the heaven figures some event.

EDWARD
  'Tis wondrous strange, the like yet never heard of.
  I think it cites us, brother, to the field,
  That we, the sons of brave Plantagenet,   35
  Each one already blazing by our meeds,
  Should notwithstanding join our lights together,
  And over-shine the earth, as this the world.
  Whate'er it bodes, henceforward will I bear
  Upon my target three fair-shining suns.   40

RICHARD
  Nay, bear three daughters: by your leave I speak it,
  You love the breeder better than the male.

        Enter a Messenger, *blowing.*

  But what art thou, whose heavy looks foretell
  Some dreadful story hanging on thy tongue?

MESSENGER   Ah, one that was a woeful looker-on   45
  When as the noble Duke of York was slain,
  Your princely father and my loving lord!

EDWARD   O, speak no more, for I have heard too much.

RICHARD   Say how he died, for I will hear it all.

MESSENGER   Environed he was with many foes,   50
  And stood against them, as the hope of Troy
  Against the Greeks that would have enter'd Troy.
  But Hercules himself must yield to odds;
  And many strokes, though with a little axe,
  Hews down and fells the hardest-timber'd oak.   55
  By many hands your father was subdu'd;
  But only slaughter'd by the ireful arm
  Of unrelenting Clifford, and the Queen,
  Who crown'd the gracious Duke in high despite,
  Laugh'd in his face; and when with grief he wept,   60

The ruthless Queen gave him to dry his cheeks
A napkin steeped in the harmless blood
Of sweet young Rutland by rough Clifford slain:
And after many scorns, many foul taunts,
65 They took his head, and on the gates of York
They set the same; and there it doth remain,
The saddest spectacle that e'er I view'd.

EDWARD Sweet Duke of York, our prop to lean upon,
Now thou art gone, we have no staff, no stay.
70 O Clifford, boisterous Clifford! thou hast slain
The flower of Europe for his chivalry;
And treacherously hast thou vanquish'd him,
For hand to hand he would have vanquish'd thee.
Now my soul's palace is become a prison:
75 Ah, would she break from hence, that this my body
Might in the ground be closed up in rest!
For never henceforth shall I joy again;
Never, O never, shall I see more joy.

RICHARD I cannot weep, for all my body's moisture
80 Scarce serves to quench my furnace-burning heart;
Nor can my tongue unload my heart's great burden;
For self-same wind that I should speak withal
Is kindling coals that fires all my breast,
And burns me up with flames that tears would
quench.
85 To weep is to make less the depth of grief:
Tears then for babes; blows and revenge for me!
Richard, I bear thy name; I'll venge thy death,
Or die renowned by attempting it.

EDWARD
His name that valiant duke hath left with thee;
90 His dukedom and his chair with me is left.

RICHARD Nay, if thou be that princely eagle's bird,
Show thy descent by gazing 'gainst the sun:
For chair and dukedom, throne and kingdom say,
Either that is thine, or else thou wert not his.

March. Enter WARWICK, MARQUESS MONTAGUE
and their army.

WARWICK
95 How now, fair lords! What fare? What news abroad?

RICHARD Great Lord of Warwick, if we should recount
Our baleful news, and at each word's deliverance
Stab poniards in our flesh till all were told,
The words would add more anguish than the
wounds.
100 O valiant lord, the Duke of York is slain!

EDWARD O Warwick, Warwick! that Plantagenet
Which held thee dearly as his soul's redemption
Is by the stern Lord Clifford done to death.

WARWICK Ten days ago I drown'd these news in tears,
105 And now, to add more measure to your woes,
I come to tell you things sith then befall'n.
After the bloody fray at Wakefield fought,
Where your brave father breath'd his latest gasp,
Tidings, as swiftly as the posts could run,
110 Were brought me of your loss and his depart.

I, then in London, keeper of the King,
Muster'd my soldiers, gather'd flocks of friends,
And very well appointed, as I thought,
March'd toward St Albans to intercept the Queen,
115 Bearing the King in my behalf along;
For by my scouts I was advertised
That she was coming with a full intent
To dash our late decree in Parliament,
Touching King Henry's oath and your succession.
120 Short tale to make, we at St Albans met,
Our battles join'd, and both sides fiercely fought:
But whether 'twas the coldness of the King,
Who look'd full gently on his warlike Queen,
That robb'd my soldiers of their heated spleen;
125 Or whether 'twas report of her success;
Or more than common fear of Clifford's rigour,
Who thunders to his captives blood and death,
I cannot judge: but, to conclude with truth,
Their weapons like to lightning came and went;
130 Our soldiers', like the night-owl's lazy flight,
Or like an idle thresher with a flail,
Fell gently down, as if they struck their friends.
I cheer'd them up with justice of our cause,
With promise of high pay and great rewards:
135 But all in vain; they had no heart to fight,
And we in them no hope to win the day;
So that we fled: the King unto the Queen;
Lord George your brother, Norfolk and myself,
In haste, post-haste, are come to join with you;
140 For in the Marches here we heard you were,
Making another head to fight again.

EDWARD
Where is the Duke of Norfolk, gentle Warwick?
And when came George from Burgundy to England?

WARWICK
Some six miles off the Duke is with the soldiers;
145 And for your brother, he was lately sent
From your kind aunt, Duchess of Burgundy,
With aid of soldiers to this needful war.

RICHARD
'Twas odds, belike, when valiant Warwick fled:
Oft have I heard his praises in pursuit,
150 But ne'er till now his scandal of retire.

WARWICK
Nor now my scandal, Richard, dost thou hear;
For thou shalt know this strong right hand of mine
Can pluck the diadem from faint Henry's head,
And wring the awful sceptre from his fist,
155 Were he as famous and as bold in war
As he is fam'd for mildness, peace, and prayer.

RICHARD I know it well, Lord Warwick; blame me not:
'Tis love I bear thy glories makes me speak.
But in this troublous time what's to be done?
160 Shall we go throw away our coats of steel,
And wrap our bodies in black mourning gowns,
Numbering our Ave-Maries with our beads?
Or shall we on the helmets of our foes

Tell our devotion with revengeful arms?
If for the last, say ay, and to it, lords.

WARWICK
Why, therefore Warwick came to seek you out,
And therefore comes my brother Montague.
Attend me, lords. The proud insulting Queen,
With Clifford and the haught Northumberland,
And of their feather many moe proud birds,
Have wrought the easy-melting King like wax.
He sware consent to your succession,
His oath enrolled in the Parliament;
And now to London all the crew are gone,
To frustrate both his oath and what beside
May make against the house of Lancaster.
Their power, I think, is thirty thousand strong:
Now, if the help of Norfolk and myself,
With all the friends that thou, brave Earl of March,
Amongst the loving Welshmen canst procure,
Will but amount to five-and-twenty thousand,
Why, *Via!* to London will we march amain,
And once again bestride our foaming steeds,
And once again cry 'Charge upon our foes!'
But never once again turn back and fly.

RICHARD
Ay, now methinks I hear great Warwick speak.
Ne'er may he live to see a sunshine day,
That cries 'Retire', if Warwick bid him stay.

EDWARD   Lord Warwick, on thy shoulder will I lean;
And when thou fall'st – as God forbid the hour! –
Must Edward fall, which peril heaven forfend!

WARWICK   No longer Earl of March, but Duke of York:
The next degree is England's royal throne;
For King of England shalt thou be proclaim'd
In every borough as we pass along;
And he that throws not up his cap for joy
Shall for the fault make forfeit of his head.
King Edward, valiant Richard, Montague,
Stay we no longer, dreaming of renown,
But sound the trumpets, and about our task.

RICHARD
Then, Clifford, were thy heart as hard as steel,
As thou hast shown it flinty by thy deeds,
I come to pierce it, or to give thee mine.

EDWARD
Then strike up, drums! God and Saint George for us!

Enter a Messenger.

WARWICK   How now! what news?

MESSENGER
The Duke of Norfolk sends you word by me,
The Queen is coming with a puissant host;
And craves your company for speedy counsel.

WARWICK
Why then it sorts; brave warriors, let's away.   *Exeunt.*

2.2   *Flourish. Enter* KING HENRY, QUEEN MARGARET,
the PRINCE OF WALES, CLIFFORD *and* NORTHUMBERLAND,
with drum and trumpets.

QUEEN MARGARET
Welcome, my lord, to this brave town of York.
Yonder's the head of that arch-enemy
That sought to be encompass'd with your crown:
Doth not the object cheer your heart, my lord?

KING HENRY
Ay, as the rocks cheer them that fear their wrack: 5
To see this sight, it irks my very soul.
Withhold revenge, dear God! 'tis not my fault,
Nor wittingly have I infring'd my vow.

CLIFFORD   My gracious liege, this too much lenity
And harmful pity must be laid aside.   10
To whom do lions cast their gentle looks?
Not to the beast that would usurp their den.
Whose hand is that the forest bear doth lick?
Not his that spoils her young before her face.
Who scapes the lurking serpent's mortal sting?   15
Not he that sets his foot upon her back.
The smallest worm will turn being trodden on,
And doves will peck in safeguard of their brood.
Ambitious York did level at thy crown,
Thou smiling while he knit his angry brows: 20
He, but a duke, would have his son a king,
And raise his issue like a loving sire;
Thou, being a king, bless'd with a goodly son,
Didst yield consent to disinherit him,
Which argued thee a most unloving father.   25
Unreasonable creatures feed their young;
And though man's face be fearful to their eyes,
Yet, in protection of their tender ones,
Who hath not seen them, even with those wings
Which sometime they have us'd with fearful flight,   30
Make war with him that climb'd unto their nest,
Offering their own lives in their young's defence?
For shame, my liege, make them your precedent!
Were it not pity that this goodly boy
Should lose his birthright by his father's fault,   35
And long hereafter say unto his child,
'What my great-grandfather and grandsire got
My careless father fondly gave away'?
Ah, what a shame were this! Look on the boy;
And let his manly face, which promiseth   40
Successful fortune, steel thy melting heart
To hold thine own and leave thine own with him.

KING HENRY   Full well hath Clifford play'd the orator,
Inferring arguments of mighty force.
But, Clifford, tell me, didst thou never hear   45
That things evil got had ever bad success?
And happy always was it for that son
Whose father for his hoarding went to hell?
I'll leave my son my virtuous deeds behind;

50 And would my father had left me no more!
    For all the rest is held at such a rate
    As brings a thousand-fold more care to keep
    Than in possession any jot of pleasure.
    Ah, cousin York, would thy best friends did know
55 How it doth grieve me that thy head stands here!
QUEEN MARGARET
    My lord, cheer up your spirits; our foes are nigh,
    And this soft courage makes your followers faint.
    You promis'd knighthood to our forward son:
    Unsheathe your sword, and dub him presently.
60 Edward, kneel down.
KING HENRY   Edward Plantagenet, arise a knight;
    And learn this lesson: Draw thy sword in right.
PRINCE   My gracious father, by your kingly leave,
    I'll draw it as apparent to the crown,
65 And in that quarrel use it to the death.
CLIFFORD   Why, that is spoken like a toward prince.

          Enter a Messenger.

MESSENGER   Royal commanders, be in readiness;
    For with a band of thirty thousand men
    Comes Warwick, backing of the Duke of York;
70 And in the towns, as they do march along,
    Proclaims him king, and many fly to him.
    Darraign your battle, for they are at hand.
CLIFFORD
    I would your highness would depart the field:
    The Queen hath best success when you are absent.
QUEEN MARGARET
75 Ay, good my lord, and leave us to our fortune.
KING HENRY
    Why, that's my fortune too: therefore I'll stay.
NORTHUMBERLAND   Be it with resolution then to fight.
PRINCE   My royal father, cheer these noble lords,
    And hearten those that fight in your defence.
    Unsheathe your sword, good father: cry, 'Saint
80   George'.

    March. Enter EDWARD, GEORGE, RICHARD, WARWICK,
          NORFOLK, MONTAGUE *and soldiers.*

EDWARD
    Now, perjur'd Henry, wilt thou kneel for grace,
    And set thy diadem upon my head;
    Or bide the mortal fortune of the field?
QUEEN MARGARET
    Go rate thy minions, proud insulting boy!
85 Becomes it thee to be thus bold in terms
    Before thy sovereign and thy lawful king?
EDWARD   I am his king, and he should bow his knee:
    I was adopted heir by his consent:
    Since when his oath is broke; for, as I hear,
90 You that are king, though he do wear the crown,
    Have caus'd him by new Act of Parliament
    To blot out me, and put his own son in.
CLIFFORD   And reason too:
    Who should succeed the father but the son?

RICHARD   Are you there, butcher? O, I cannot speak!   95
CLIFFORD   Ay, Crook-back, here I stand to answer thee,
    Or any he, the proudest of thy sort.
RICHARD
    'Twas you that kill'd young Rutland, was it not?
CLIFFORD   Ay, and old York, and yet not satisfied.
RICHARD   For God's sake, lords, give signal to the fight.   100
WARWICK
    What say'st thou, Henry, wilt thou yield the crown?
QUEEN MARGARET
    Why, how now, long-tongu'd Warwick! dare you
        speak?
    When you and I met at St Albans last,
    Your legs did better service than your hands.
WARWICK
    Then 'twas my turn to flee, and now 'tis thine.   105
CLIFFORD   You said so much before, and yet you fled.
WARWICK
    'Twas not your valour, Clifford, drove me thence.
NORTHUMBERLAND
    No, nor your manhood that durst make you stay.
RICHARD   Northumberland, I hold thee reverently.
    Break off the parley; for scarce I can refrain   110
    The execution of my big-swoln heart
    Upon that Clifford, that cruel child-killer.
CLIFFORD   I slew thy father: call'st thou him a child?
RICHARD   Ay, like a dastard and a treacherous coward,
    As thou didst kill our tender brother Rutland;   115
    But ere sun set I'll make thee curse the deed.
KING HENRY
    Have done with words, my lords, and hear me speak.
QUEEN MARGARET
    Defy them then, or else hold close thy lips.
KING HENRY   I prithee give no limits to my tongue:
    I am a king, and privileg'd to speak.   120
CLIFFORD
    My liege, the wound that bred this meeting here
    Cannot be cur'd by words; therefore be still.
RICHARD   Then, executioner, unsheathe thy sword.
    By Him that made us all, I am resolv'd
    That Clifford's manhood lies upon his tongue.   125
EDWARD   Say, Henry, shall I have my right or no?
    A thousand men have broke their fasts to-day
    That ne'er shall dine unless thou yield the crown.
WARWICK   If thou deny, their blood upon thy head;
    For York in justice puts his armour on.   130
PRINCE   If that be right which Warwick says is right,
    There is no wrong, but every thing is right.
RICHARD   Whoever got thee, there thy mother stands;
    For well I wot thou hast thy mother's tongue.
QUEEN MARGARET
    But thou art neither like thy sire nor dam,   135
    But like a foul misshapen stigmatic,
    Mark'd by the Destinies to be avoided,
    As venom toads, or lizards' dreadful stings.
RICHARD   Iron of Naples, hid with English gilt,
    Whose father bears the title of a king   140

As if a channel should be call'd the sea –
Sham'st thou not, knowing whence thou art
 extraught,
To let thy tongue detect thy base-born heart?

EDWARD
45 A wisp of straw were worth a thousand crowns
    To make this shameless callet know herself.
    Helen of Greece was fairer far than thou,
    Although thy husband may be Menelaus;
    And ne'er was Agamemnon's brother wrong'd
50 By that false woman as this king by thee.
    His father revell'd in the heart of France,
    And tam'd the King, and made the Dauphin stoop;
    And had he match'd according to his state,
    He might have kept that glory to this day;
55 But when he took a beggar to his bed
    And grac'd thy poor sire with his bridal day,
    Even then that sunshine brew'd a shower for him
    That wash'd his father's fortunes forth of France
    And heap'd sedition on his crown at home.
    For what hath broach'd this tumult but thy pride?
60 Hadst thou been meek, our title still had slept;
    And we, in pity of the gentle King,
    Had slipp'd our claim until another age.

GEORGE
    But when we saw our sunshine made thy spring,
    And that thy summer bred us no increase,
65 We set the axe to thy usurping root;
    And though the edge have something hit ourselves,
    Yet know thou, since we have begun to strike,
    We'll never leave till we have hewn thee down,
    Or bath'd thy growing with our heated bloods.

70 EDWARD   And in this resolution I defy thee;
    Not willing any longer conference,
    Since thou deniest the gentle King to speak.
    Sound trumpets! let our bloody colours wave!
    And either victory, or else a grave.

75 QUEEN MARGARET   Stay, Edward.

EDWARD   No wrangling woman, we'll no longer stay:
    These words will cost ten thousand lives this day.
                                    Exeunt.

2.3   *Alarum. Excursions. Enter* WARWICK.

WARWICK   Forspent with toil, as runners with a race,
    I lay me down a little while to breathe;
    For strokes receiv'd, and many blows repaid,
    Have robb'd my strong-knit sinews of their strength,
    And spite of spite needs must I rest awhile.

            Enter EDWARD, *running.*

EDWARD
    Smile, gentle heaven, or strike, ungentle death;
    For this world frowns, and Edward's sun is clouded.

WARWICK
    How now, my lord! What hap? What hope of good?

            Enter GEORGE.

GEORGE   Our hap is loss, our hope but sad despair,
    Our ranks are broke, and ruin follows us.   10
    What counsel give you? Whither shall we fly?

EDWARD   Bootless is flight, they follow us with wings;
    And weak we are, and cannot shun pursuit.

            Enter RICHARD.

RICHARD
    Ah, Warwick, why hast thou withdrawn thyself?
    Thy brother's blood the thirsty earth hath drunk,   15
    Broach'd with the steely point of Clifford's lance;
    And in the very pangs of death he cried,
    Like to a dismal clangor heard from far,
    'Warwick, revenge! Brother, revenge my death!'
    So, underneath the belly of their steeds,   20
    That stain'd their fetlocks in his smoking blood,
    The noble gentleman gave up the ghost.

WARWICK
    Then let the earth be drunken with our blood;
    I'll kill my horse because I will not fly.
    Why stand we like soft-hearted women here,   25
    Wailing our losses, whiles the foe doth rage;
    And look upon, as if the tragedy
    Were play'd in jest by counterfeiting actors?
    Here on my knee I vow to God above
    I'll never pause again, never stand still,   30
    Till either death hath clos'd these eyes of mine,
    Or fortune given me measure of revenge.

EDWARD   O Warwick, I do bend my knee with thine;
    And in this vow do chain my soul to thine!
    And ere my knee rise from the earth's cold face,   35
    I throw my hands, mine eyes, my heart to Thee,
    Thou setter up and plucker down of kings,
    Beseeching Thee, if with Thy will it stands,
    That to my foes this body must be prey,
    Yet that Thy brazen gates of heaven may ope,   40
    And give sweet passage to my sinful soul!
    Now, lords, take leave until we meet again,
    Where'er it be, in heaven or in earth.

RICHARD
    Brother, give me thy hand; and, gentle Warwick,
    Let me embrace thee in my weary arms: 45
    I, that did never weep, now melt with woe
    That winter should cut off our spring-time so.

WARWICK
    Away, away! Once more, sweet lords, farewell.

GEORGE   Yet let us all together to our troops,
    And give them leave to fly that will not stay,   50
    And call them pillars that will stand to us;
    And if we thrive, promise them such rewards
    As victors wear at the Olympian games.
    This may plant courage in their quailing breasts;
    For yet is hope of life and victory.   55
    Forslow no longer; make we hence amain.   *Exeunt.*

2.4   *Excursions. Enter* RICHARD *and* CLIFFORD.

RICHARD   Now, Clifford, I have singled thee alone.
    Suppose this arm is for the Duke of York,
    And this for Rutland; both bound to revenge,
    Wert thou environ'd with a brazen wall.
CLIFFORD   Now, Richard, I am with thee here alone.
    This is the hand that stabb'd thy father York,
    And this the hand that slew thy brother Rutland;
    And here's the heart that triumphs in their death
    And cheers these hands, that slew thy sire and
      brother,
    To execute the like upon thyself;
    And so, have at thee!

     They fight. WARWICK *comes. Clifford flies.*

RICHARD   Nay, Warwick, single out some other chase;
    For I myself will hunt this wolf to death.   *Exeunt.*

2.5   *Alarum. Enter* KING HENRY *alone.*

KING HENRY
    This battle fares like to the morning's war,
    When dying clouds contend with growing light,
    What time the shepherd, blowing of his nails,
    Can neither call it perfect day nor night.
    Now sways it this way, like a mighty sea
    Forc'd by the tide to combat with the wind;
    Now sways it that way, like the self-same sea
    Forc'd to retire by fury of the wind.
    Sometime the flood prevails, and then the wind;
    Now one the better, then another best;
    Both tugging to be victors, breast to breast;
    Yet neither conqueror nor conquered.
    So is the equal poise of this fell war.
    Here on this molehill will I sit me down.
    To whom God will, there be the victory!
    For Margaret my queen, and Clifford too,
    Have chid me from the battle, swearing both
    They prosper best of all when I am thence.
    Would I were dead, if God's good will were so!
    For what is in this world but grief and woe?
    O God! methinks it were a happy life
    To be no better than a homely swain;
    To sit upon a hill, as I do now,
    To carve out dials quaintly, point by point,
    Thereby to see the minutes how they run –
    How many makes the hour full complete,
    How many hours brings about the day,
    How many days will finish up the year,
    How many years a mortal man may live.
    When this is known, then to divide the times –
    So many hours must I tend my flock;
    So many hours must I take my rest;
    So many hours must I contemplate;
    So many hours must I sport myself;
    So many days my ewes have been with young;
    So many weeks ere the poor fools will ean;

    So many years ere I shall shear the fleece:
    So minutes, hours, days, weeks, months, and years,
    Pass'd over to the end they were created,
    Would bring white hairs unto a quiet grave.
    Ah, what a life were this! how sweet! how lovely!
    Gives not the hawthorn bush a sweeter shade
    To shepherds looking on their silly sheep,
    Than doth a rich embroider'd canopy
    To kings that fear their subjects' treachery?
    O yes, it doth; a thousand-fold it doth.
    And to conclude, the shepherd's homely curds,
    His cold thin drink out of his leather bottle,
    His wonted sleep under a fresh tree's shade,
    All which secure and sweetly he enjoys,
    Is far beyond a prince's delicates –
    His viands sparkling in a golden cup,
    His body couched in a curious bed,
    When Care, Mistrust, and Treason waits on him.

     Alarum. Enter a Son *that hath kill'd his father, with*
              the body in his arms.

SON   Ill blows the wind that profits nobody.
    This man whom hand to hand I slew in fight
    May be possessed with some store of crowns;
    And I, that haply take them from him now,
    May yet ere night yield both my life and them
    To some man else, as this dead man doth me.
    Who's this? O God! it is my father's face,
    Whom in this conflict I unwares have kill'd.
    O heavy times, begetting such events!
    From London by the King was I press'd forth;
    My father, being the Earl of Warwick's man,
    Came on the part of York, press'd by his master;
    And I, who at his hands receiv'd my life,
    Have by my hands of life bereaved him.
    Pardon me, God, I knew not what I did:
    And pardon, father, for I knew not thee.
    My tears shall wipe away these bloody marks;
    And no more words till they have flow'd their fill.
KING HENRY   O piteous spectacle! O bloody times!
    Whilst lions war and battle for their dens,
    Poor harmless lambs abide their enmity.
    Weep, wretched man; I'll aid thee tear for tear;
    And let our hearts and eyes, like civil war,
    Be blind with tears, and break o'ercharg'd with grief.

     Enter a Father *that hath kill'd his son, with the*
              body in his arms.

FATHER   Thou that so stoutly hath resisted me,
    Give me thy gold, if thou hast any gold,
    For I have bought it with an hundred blows.
    But let me see: is this our foeman's face?
    Ah, no, no, no; it is mine only son!
    Ah, boy, if any life be left in thee,
    Throw up thine eye! see, see, what showers arise,
    Blown with the windy tempest of my heart
    Upon thy wounds, that kills mine eye and heart!

O, pity, God, this miserable age!
What stratagems, how fell, how butcherly,
Erroneous, mutinous, and unnatural,
This deadly quarrel daily doth beget!
O boy, thy father gave thee life too soon,
And hath bereft thee of thy life too late!

KING HENRY
  Woe above woe! grief more than common grief!
  O that my death would stay these ruthful deeds!
  O pity, pity, gentle heaven, pity!
  The red rose and the white are on his face,
  The fatal colours of our striving houses:
  The one his purple blood right well resembles;
  The other his pale cheeks, methinks, presenteth.
  Wither one rose, and let the other flourish!
  If you contend, a thousand lives must wither.

SON How will my mother for a father's death
Take on with me and ne'er be satisfied!

FATHER How will my wife for slaughter of my son
Shed seas of tears and ne'er be satisfied!

KING HENRY
  How will the country for these woeful chances
  Misthink the King and not be satisfied!

SON Was ever son so rued a father's death?

FATHER Was ever father so bemoan'd his son?

KING HENRY
  Was ever king so griev'd for subjects' woe?
  Much is your sorrow; mine, ten times so much.

SON I'll bear thee hence, where I may weep my fill.
                        Exit with the body.

FATHER
  These arms of mine shall be thy winding-sheet;
  My heart, sweet boy, shall be thy sepulchre,
  For from my heart thine image ne'er shall go.
  My sighing breast shall be thy funeral bell;
  And so obsequious will thy father be,
  Even for the loss of thee, having no more,
  As Priam was for all his valiant sons.
  I'll bear thee hence; and let them fight that will,
  For I have murder'd where I should not kill.
                        Exit with the body.

KING HENRY
  Sad-hearted men, much overgone with care,
  Here sits a king more woeful than you are.

Alarums. Excursions. Enter QUEEN MARGARET, *the*
PRINCE *and* EXETER.

PRINCE Fly, father, fly! for all your friends are fled,
And Warwick rages like a chafed bull.
Away! for death doth hold us in pursuit.

QUEEN MARGARET
  Mount you, my lord; towards Berwick post amain.
  Edward and Richard, like a brace of greyhounds
  Having the fearful-flying hare in sight,
  With fiery eyes sparkling for very wrath,
  And bloody steel grasp'd in their ireful hands,
  Are at our backs; and therefore hence amain.

EXETER Away! for vengeance comes along with them.
  Nay, stay not to expostulate; make speed,   135
  Or else come after: I'll away before.

KING HENRY
  Nay, take me with thee, good sweet Exeter:
  Not that I fear to stay, but love to go
  Whither the Queen intends. Forward; away! *Exeunt.*

2.6   *A loud alarum. Enter* CLIFFORD *wounded,*
with an arrow in his neck.

CLIFFORD Here burns my candle out; ay, here it dies,
  Which, whiles it lasted, gave King Henry light.
  Oh, Lancaster, I fear thy overthrow
  More than my body's parting with my soul.
  My love and fear glu'd many friends to thee;   5
  And, now I fall, thy tough commixture melts,
  Impairing Henry, strengthening misproud York.
  The common people swarm like summer flies;
  And whither fly the gnats but to the sun?
  And who shines now but Henry's enemies?   10
  O Phoebus, hadst thou never given consent
  That Phaëton should check thy fiery steeds,
  Thy burning car never had scorch'd the earth!
  And, Henry, hadst thou sway'd as kings should do,
  Or as thy father, and his father did,   15
  Giving no ground unto the house of York,
  They never then had sprung like summer flies;
  I, and ten thousand in this luckless realm
  Had left no mourning widows for our death;
  And thou this day hadst kept thy chair in peace.   20
  For what doth cherish weeds but gentle air?
  And what makes robbers bold but too much lenity?
  Bootless are plaints, and cureless are my wounds;
  No way to fly, nor strength to hold our flight:
  The foe is merciless and will not pity;   25
  For at their hands I have deserv'd no pity.
  The air hath got into my deadly wounds,
  And much effuse of blood doth make me faint.
  Come, York and Richard, Warwick and the rest;
  I stabb'd your fathers' bosoms: split my breast.   30
  [*He faints.*]

Alarum and retreat. Enter EDWARD, GEORGE, RICHARD,
MONTAGUE, WARWICK *and soldiers.*

EDWARD
  Now breathe we, lords: good fortune bids us pause
  And smooth the frowns of war with peaceful looks.
  Some troops pursue the bloody-minded Queen,
  That led calm Henry, though he were a king,
  As doth a sail, fill'd with a fretting gust,   35
  Command an argosy to stem the waves.
  But think you, lords, that Clifford fled with them?

WARWICK No, 'tis impossible he should escape;
  For, though before his face I speak the words,
  Your brother Richard mark'd him for the grave;   40
  And, wheresoe'er he be, he's surely dead.

[Clifford groans and dies.]

RICHARD
    Whose soul is that which takes her heavy leave?
    A deadly groan, like life and death's departing.
    See who it is.
EDWARD   And now the battle's ended,
45   If friend or foe, let him be gently us'd.
RICHARD   Revoke that doom of mercy, for 'tis Clifford,
    Who, not contented that he lopp'd the branch
    In hewing Rutland when his leaves put forth,
    But set his murdering knife unto the root
50   From whence that tender spray did sweetly spring –
    I mean our princely father, Duke of York.
WARWICK
    From off the gates of York fetch down the head,
    Your father's head, which Clifford placed there;
    Instead whereof let this supply the room;
55   Measure for measure must be answered.
EDWARD
    Bring forth that fatal screech-owl to our house,
    That nothing sung but death to us and ours:
    Now death shall stop his dismal threatening sound,
    And his ill-boding tongue no more shall speak.
60 WARWICK   I think his understanding is bereft.
    Speak, Clifford, dost thou know who speaks to thee?
    Dark cloudy death o'ershades his beams of life,
    And he nor sees, nor hears us, what we say.
RICHARD   O, would he did! and so, perhaps, he doth:
65   'Tis but his policy to counterfeit,
    Because he would avoid such bitter taunts
    Which in the time of death he gave our father.
GEORGE   If so thou think'st, vex him with eager words.
RICHARD   Clifford, ask mercy, and obtain no grace.
70 EDWARD   Clifford, repent in bootless penitence.
WARWICK   Clifford, devise excuses for thy faults.
GEORGE   While we devise fell tortures for thy faults.
RICHARD   Thou didst love York, and I am son to York.
EDWARD   Thou pitied'st Rutland, I will pity thee.
75 GEORGE   Where's Captain Margaret, to fence you now?
WARWICK
    They mock thee, Clifford; swear as thou wast wont.
RICHARD
    What, not an oath? Nay, then the world goes hard
    When Clifford cannot spare his friends an oath.
    I know by that he's dead; and, by my soul,
80   If this right hand would buy but two hours' life,
    That I in all despite might rail at him,
    This hand should chop it off, and with the issuing
       blood
    Stifle the villain whose unstaunched thirst
    York and young Rutland could not satisfy.
WARWICK
85   Ay, but he's dead. Off with the traitor's head,
    And rear it in the place your father's stands.
    And now to London with triumphant march,
    There to be crowned England's royal king;

    From whence shall Warwick cut the sea to France,
    And ask the Lady Bona for thy queen.   90
    So shalt thou sinew both these lands together;
    And, having France thy friend, thou shalt not dread
    The scatter'd foe that hopes to rise again;
    For though they cannot greatly sting to hurt,
    Yet look to have them buzz to offend thine ears.   95
    First will I see the coronation;
    And then to Brittany I'll cross the sea
    To effect this marriage, so it please my lord.
EDWARD   Even as thou wilt, sweet Warwick, let it be;
    For in thy shoulder do I build my seat,   100
    And never will I undertake the thing
    Wherein thy counsel and consent is wanting.
    Richard, I will create thee Duke of Gloucester;
    And George, of Clarence; Warwick, as ourself,
    Shall do and undo as him pleaseth best.   105
RICHARD
    Let me be Duke of Clarence, George of Gloucester,
    For Gloucester's dukedom is too ominous.
WARWICK   Tut, that's a foolish observation:
    Richard, be Duke of Gloucester. Now to London,
    To see these honours in possession.   *Exeunt.*   110

3.1   *Enter two* Keepers, *with cross-bows in their hands.*

1 KEEPER
    Under this thick-grown brake we'll shroud ourselves,
    For through this laund anon the deer will come;
    And in this covert will we make our stand,
    Culling the principal of all the deer.
2 KEEPER   I'll stay above the hill, so both may shoot.   5
1 KEEPER
    That cannot be; the noise of thy cross-bow
    Will scare the herd, and so my shoot is lost.
    Here stand we both, and aim we at the best;
    And, for the time shall not seem tedious,
    I'll tell thee what befell me on a day   10
    In this self place where now we mean to stand.
2 KEEPER
    Here comes a man; let's stay till he be past.

    Enter KING HENRY, *disguised, with a prayer-book.*

KING HENRY
    From Scotland am I stol'n, even of pure love,
    To greet mine own land with my wishful sight.
    No, Harry, Harry, 'tis no land of thine;   15
    Thy place is fill'd, thy sceptre wrung from thee,
    Thy balm wash'd off wherewith thou wast anointed:
    No bending knee will call thee Caesar now,
    No humble suitors press to speak for right,
    No, not a man comes for redress of thee: 20
    For how can I help them and not myself?
1 KEEPER
    Ay, here's a deer whose skin's a keeper's fee:
    This is the quondam king; let's seize upon him.
KING HENRY   Let me embrace thee, sour Adversity,

25 For wise men say it is the wisest course.

2 KEEPER
Why linger we? let us lay hands upon him.

1 KEEPER   Forbear awhile; we'll hear a little more.

KING HENRY
My queen and son are gone to France for aid;
And, as I hear, the great commanding Warwick
30 Is thither gone, to crave the French King's sister
To wife for Edward. If this news be true,
Poor queen and son, your labour is but lost;
For Warwick is a subtle orator
And Lewis a prince soon won with moving words.
35 By this account, then, Margaret may win him,
For she's a woman to be pitied much:
Her sighs will make a battery in his breast;
Her tears will pierce into a marble heart;
The tiger will be mild whiles she doth mourn;
40 And Nero will be tainted with remorse,
To hear and see her plaints, her brinish tears.
Ay, but she's come to beg, Warwick to give;
She on his left side craving aid for Henry:
He on his right, asking a wife for Edward.
45 She weeps, and says her Henry is depos'd:
He smiles, and says his Edward is install'd;
That she, poor wretch, for grief can speak no more;
Whiles Warwick tells his title, smooths the wrong,
Inferreth arguments of mighty strength,
50 And in conclusion wins the King from her
With promise of his sister, and what else,
To strengthen and support King Edward's place.
O Margaret, thus 'twill be; and thou, poor soul,
Art then forsaken, as thou went'st forlorn.

2 KEEPER
55 Say, what art thou that talk'st of kings and queens?

KING HENRY
More than I seem, and less than I was born to:
A man at least, for less I should not be;
And men may talk of kings, and why not I?

2 KEEPER   Ay, but thou talk'st as if thou wert a king.

60 KING HENRY   Why, so I am, in mind; and that's enough.

2 KEEPER   But if thou be a king, where is thy crown?

KING HENRY   My crown is in my heart, not on my head;
Not deck'd with diamonds and Indian stones,
Nor to be seen: my crown is call'd content;
65 A crown it is that seldom kings enjoy.

2 KEEPER
Well, if you be a king crown'd with content,
Your crown content, and you, must be contented
To go along with us; for, as we think,
You are the king King Edward hath depos'd;
70 And we his subjects, sworn in all allegiance,
Will apprehend you as his enemy.

KING HENRY
But did you never swear, and break an oath?

2 KEEPER   No, never such an oath; nor will not now.

KING HENRY
Where did you dwell when I was King of England?

2 KEEPER
Here in this country, where we now remain.   75

KING HENRY   I was anointed king at nine months old;
My father and my grandfather were kings,
And you were sworn true subjects unto me:
And tell me then, have you not broke your oaths?

1 KEEPER
No, we were subjects but while you were king.   80

KING HENRY   Why, am I dead? do I not breathe a man?
Ah, simple men, you know not what you sware.
Look, as I blow this feather from my face,
And as the air blows it to me again,
Obeying with my wind when I do blow,   85
And yielding to another when it blows,
Commanded always by the greater gust,
Such is the lightness of you common men.
But do not break your oaths; for of that sin
My mild entreaty shall not make you guilty.   90
Go where you will, the King shall be commanded;
And be you kings; command, and I'll obey.

1 KEEPER
We are true subjects to the king, King Edward.

KING HENRY   So would you be again to Henry,
If he were seated as King Edward is.   95

1 KEEPER
Therefore we charge you, in God's name, and the
    king's,
To go with us unto the officers.

KING HENRY
In God's name, lead; your king's name be obey'd:
And what God will, that let your king perform;
And what he will, I humbly yield unto.   *Exeunt.*   100

3.2   *Enter* KING EDWARD, RICHARD, DUKE OF
GLOUCESTER, GEORGE, DUKE OF CLARENCE
and LADY ELIZABETH GREY.

KING EDWARD
Brother of Gloucester, at St Albans field
This lady's husband, Sir John Grey, was slain,
His lands then seiz'd on by the conqueror.
Her suit is now to repossess those lands;
Which we in justice cannot well deny,   5
Because in quarrel of the house of York
The worthy gentleman did lose his life.

RICHARD
Your Highness shall do well to grant her suit;
It were dishonour to deny it her.

KING EDWARD
It were no less; but yet I'll make a pause.   10

RICHARD [*aside to George*]   Yea, is it so?
I see the lady hath a thing to grant,
Before the King will grant her humble suit.

GEORGE [*aside to Richard*]
He knows the game: how true he keeps the wind!

RICHARD [*aside to George*]   Silence!   15

KING EDWARD   Widow, we will consider of your suit;

And come some other time to know our mind.
LADY GREY   Right gracious lord, I cannot brook delay:
    May it please your Highness to resolve me now;
20   And what your pleasure is shall satisfy me.
RICHARD [*aside to George*]
    Ay, widow? then I'll warrant you all your lands,
    And if what pleases him shall pleasure you.
    Fight closer or, good faith, you'll catch a clap.
GEORGE [*aside to Richard*]
    I fear her not, unless she chance to fall.
RICHARD [*aside to George*]
25   Marry, Godsforbot! for he'll take vantages.
KING EDWARD
    How many children hast thou, widow, tell me.
GEORGE [*aside to Richard*]
    I think he means to beg a child of her.
RICHARD [*aside to George*]
    Nay, whip me then; he'll rather give her two.
LADY GREY   Three, my most gracious lord.
RICHARD [*aside*]
30   You shall have four, and you'll be rul'd by him.
KING EDWARD
    'Twere pity they should lose their father's lands.
LADY GREY   Be pitiful, dread lord, and grant it then.
KING EDWARD
    Lords, give us leave; I'll try this widow's wit.
RICHARD [*aside*]
    Ay, good leave have you; for you will have leave
35   Till youth take leave and leave you to the crutch.
    [*Richard and George retire.*]
KING EDWARD
    Now tell me, madam, do you love your children?
LADY GREY   Ay, full as dearly as I love myself.
KING EDWARD
    And would you not do much to do them good?
LADY GREY
    To do them good, I would sustain some harm.
KING EDWARD
40   Then get your husband's lands, to do them good.
LADY GREY   Therefore I came unto your Majesty.
KING EDWARD
    I'll tell you how these lands are to be got.
LADY GREY
    So shall you bind me to your Highness' service.
KING EDWARD
    What service wilt thou do me if I give them?
45   LADY GREY   What you command that rests in me to do.
KING EDWARD
    But you will take exceptions to my boon.
LADY GREY   No, gracious lord, except I cannot do it.
KING EDWARD
    Ay, but thou canst do what I mean to ask.
LADY GREY
    Why, then I will do what your Grace commands.
RICHARD [*aside to George*]
50   He plies her hard; and much rain wears the marble.

GEORGE [*aside to Richard*]
    As red as fire! Nay, then, her wax must melt.
LADY GREY
    Why stops my lord? Shall I not hear my task?
KING EDWARD   An easy task; 'tis but to love a king.
LADY GREY
    That's soon perform'd, because I am a subject.
KING EDWARD
    Why, then, thy husband's lands I freely give thee.   55
LADY GREY
    I take my leave with many thousand thanks.
RICHARD [*aside to George*]
    The match is made; she seals it with a curtsy.
KING EDWARD
    But stay thee – 'tis the fruits of love I mean.
LADY GREY   The fruits of love I mean, my loving liege.
KING EDWARD   Ay, but, I fear me, in another sense.   60
    What love think'st thou I sue so much to get?
LADY GREY
    My love till death, my humble thanks, my prayers;
    That love which virtue begs, and virtue grants.
KING EDWARD
    No, by my troth, I did not mean such love.
LADY GREY
    Why, then, you mean not as I thought you did.   65
KING EDWARD
    But now you partly may perceive my mind.
LADY GREY   My mind will never grant what I perceive
    Your Highness aims at, if I aim aright.
KING EDWARD   To tell thee plain, I aim to lie with thee.
LADY GREY   To tell you plain, I had rather lie in prison.   70
KING EDWARD
    Why, then thou shalt not have thy husband's lands.
LADY GREY
    Why, then mine honesty shall be my dower;
    For by that loss I will not purchase them.
KING EDWARD
    Therein thou wrong'st thy children mightily.
LADY GREY
    Herein your Highness wrongs both them and me;   75
    But, mighty lord, this merry inclination
    Accords not with the sadness of my suit:
    Please you dismiss me, either with ay or no.
KING EDWARD   Ay, if thou wilt say ay to my request;
    No, if thou dost say no to my demand.   80
LADY GREY   Then, no, my lord. My suit is at an end.
RICHARD [*aside to George*]
    The widow likes him not, she knits her brows.
GEORGE [*aside to Richard*]
    He is the bluntest wooer in Christendom.
KING EDWARD [*aside*]
    Her looks doth argue her replete with modesty;
    Her words doth show her wit incomparable;   85
    All her perfections challenge sovereignty:
    One way or other, she is for a king;
    And she shall be my love, or else my queen. –

Say that King Edward take thee for his queen?

LADY GREY
'Tis better said than done, my gracious lord:
I am a subject, fit to jest withal,
But far unfit to be a sovereign.

KING EDWARD
Sweet widow, by my state I swear to thee
I speak no more than what my soul intends;
And that is to enjoy thee for my love.

LADY GREY   And that is more than I will yield unto.
I know I am too mean to be your queen,
And yet too good to be your concubine.

KING EDWARD   You cavil, widow, I did mean my queen.

LADY GREY
'Twill grieve your Grace my sons should call you
        father.

KING EDWARD
No more than when my daughters call thee mother.
Thou art a widow, and thou hast some children;
And by God's mother, I, being but a bachelor,
Have other some. Why, 'tis a happy thing
To be the father unto many sons.
Answer no more, for thou shalt be my queen.

RICHARD [*aside to George*]
The ghostly father now hath done his shrift.

GEORGE [*aside to Richard*]
When he was made a shriver, 'twas for shift.

KING EDWARD
Brothers, you muse what chat we two have had.

RICHARD   The widow likes it not, for she looks vex'd.

KING EDWARD
You'd think it strange if I should marry her.

GEORGE   To who, my lord?

KING EDWARD   Why, Clarence, to myself.

RICHARD   That would be ten days' wonder at the least.

GEORGE   That's a day longer than a wonder lasts.

RICHARD   By so much is the wonder in extremes.

KING EDWARD
Well, jest on, brothers: I can tell you both
Her suit is granted for her husband's lands.

Enter a Nobleman.

NOBLEMAN   My gracious lord, Henry your foe is taken
And brought your prisoner to your palace gate.

KING EDWARD
See that he be convey'd unto the Tower:
And go we, brothers, to the man that took him,
To question of his apprehension.
Widow, go you along. Lords, use her honourably.
                   Exeunt all but Richard.

RICHARD   Ay, Edward will use women honourably.
Would he were wasted, marrow, bones, and all,
That from his loins no hopeful branch may spring,
To cross me from the golden time I look for!
And yet, between my soul's desire and me –
The lustful Edward's title buried –
Is Clarence, Henry, and his son young Edward,

And all the unlook'd for issue of their bodies,
To take their rooms ere I can plant myself –
A cold premeditation for my purpose!
Why then I do but dream on sovereignty;
Like one that stands upon a promontory   135
And spies a far-off shore where he would tread,
Wishing his foot were equal with his eye;
And chides the sea, that sunders him from thence,
Saying he'll lade it dry to have his way:
So do I wish the crown, being so far off;   140
And so I chide the means that keeps me from it;
And so I say I'll cut the causes off,
Flattering me with impossibilities.
My eye's too quick, my heart o'erweens too much,
Unless my hand and strength could equal them.   145
Well, say there is no kingdom then for Richard;
What other pleasure can the world afford?
I'll make my heaven in a lady's lap,
And deck my body in gay ornaments,
And 'witch sweet ladies with my words and looks.   150
O miserable thought! and more unlikely,
Than to accomplish twenty golden crowns.
Why, Love forswore me in my mother's womb:
And, for I should not deal in her soft laws,
She did corrupt frail Nature with some bribe,   155
To shrink mine arm up like a wither'd shrub;
To make an envious mountain on my back,
Where sits Deformity to mock my body;
To shape my legs of an unequal size;
To disproportion me in every part,   160
Like to a chaos, or unlick'd bear-whelp
That carries no impression like the dam.
And am I then a man to be belov'd?
O monstrous fault to harbour such a thought!
Then, since this earth affords no joy to me   165
But to command, to check, to o'erbear such
As are of better person than myself,
I'll make my heaven to dream upon the crown;
And, whiles I live, t'account this world but hell,
Until my misshap'd trunk that bears this head   170
Be round impaled with a glorious crown.
And yet I know not how to get the crown,
For many lives stand between me and home:
And I, – like one lost in a thorny wood,
That rents the thorns and is rent with the thorns,   175
Seeking a way, and straying from the way;
Not knowing how to find the open air,
But toiling desperately to find it out –
Torment myself to catch the English crown:
And from that torment I will free myself,   180
Or hew my way out with a bloody axe.
Why, I can smile, and murder whiles I smile,
And cry 'Content!' to that that grieves my heart,
And wet my cheeks with artificial tears,
And frame my face to all occasions.   185
I'll drown more sailors than the Mermaid shall;
I'll slay more gazers than the basilisk;

I'll play the orator as well as Nestor,
Deceive more slily than Ulysses could,
190 And, like a Sinon, take another Troy.
I can add colours to the chameleon,
Change shapes with Proteus for advantages,
And set the murderous Machiavel to school.
Can I do this, and cannot get a crown?
195 Tut! were it further off, I'll pluck it down.   *Exit.*

3.3 *Flourish. Enter* LEWIS *the French King, his sister*
BONA, *his Admiral, called Bourbon;* PRINCE EDWARD,
QUEEN MARGARET *and the* EARL OF OXFORD.
LEWIS *sits, and riseth up again.*

KING LEWIS   Fair Queen of England, worthy Margaret,
Sit down with us: it ill befits thy state
And birth that thou should'st stand while Lewis doth
sit.
QUEEN MARGARET
No, mighty King of France: now Margaret
5 Must strike her sail, and learn awhile to serve
Where kings command: I was, I must confess,
Great Albion's Queen in former golden days;
But now mischance hath trod my title down
And with dishonour laid me on the ground,
10 Where I must take like seat unto my fortune
And to my humble state conform myself.
KING LEWIS
Why, say, fair Queen, whence springs this deep
despair?
QUEEN MARGARET
From such a cause as fills mine eyes with tears
And stops my tongue, while heart is drown'd in
cares.
15 KING LEWIS   Whate'er it be, be thou still like thyself,
And sit thee by our side. [*Seats her by him.*]
Yield not thy neck
To Fortune's yoke, but let thy dauntless mind
Still ride in triumph over all mischance.
Be plain, Queen Margaret, and tell thy grief;
20 It shall be eas'd, if France can yield relief.
QUEEN MARGARET
Those gracious words revive my drooping thoughts
And give my tongue-tied sorrows leave to speak.
Now, therefore, be it known to noble Lewis
That Henry, sole possessor of my love,
25 Is, of a king, become a banish'd man,
And forc'd to live in Scotland a forlorn;
While proud ambitious Edward, Duke of York,
Usurps the regal title and the seat
Of England's true-anointed lawful King.
30 This is the cause that I, poor Margaret,
With this my son, Prince Edward, Henry's heir,
Am come to crave thy just and lawful aid;
And if thou fail us, all our hope is done.
Scotland hath will to help, but cannot help;
35 Our people and our peers are both misled,

Our treasure seiz'd, our soldiers put to flight,
And, as thou seest, ourselves in heavy plight.
KING LEWIS
Renowned Queen, with patience calm the storm,
While we bethink a means to break it off.
QUEEN MARGARET
The more we stay, the stronger grows our foe.   40
KING LEWIS   The more I stay, the more I'll succour thee.
QUEEN MARGARET
O, but impatience waiteth on true sorrow.
And see where comes the breeder of my sorrow.

Enter WARWICK.

KING LEWIS
What's he approacheth boldly to our presence?
QUEEN MARGARET
Our Earl of Warwick, Edward's greatest friend.   45
KING LEWIS
Welcome, brave Warwick! What brings thee to
France?
[*He descends. She ariseth.*]
QUEEN MARGARET
Ay, now begins a second storm to rise;
For this is he that moves both wind and tide.
WARWICK   From worthy Edward, King of Albion,
My lord and sovereign, and thy vowed friend,   50
I come, in kindness and unfeigned love,
First, to do greetings to thy royal person,
And then to crave a league of amity,
And lastly to confirm that amity
With nuptial knot, if thou vouchsafe to grant   55
That virtuous Lady Bona, thy fair sister,
To England's King in lawful marriage.
QUEEN MARGARET [*aside*]
If that go forward, Henry's hope is done.
WARWICK [*to Bona*]
And, gracious madam, in our king's behalf,
I am commanded, with your leave and favour,   60
Humbly to kiss your hand, and with my tongue
To tell the passion of my sovereign's heart;
Where Fame, late entering at his heedful ears,
Hath plac'd thy beauty's image and thy virtue.
QUEEN MARGARET
King Lewis and Lady Bona, hear me speak   65
Before you answer Warwick. His demand
Springs not from Edward's well-meant honest love,
But from Deceit, bred by Necessity;
For how can tyrants safely govern home
Unless abroad they purchase great alliance?   70
To prove him tyrant this reason may suffice,
That Henry liveth still; but were he dead,
Yet here Prince Edward stands, King Henry's son.
Look, therefore, Lewis, that by this league and
marriage
Thou draw not on thy danger and dishonour;   75
For though usurpers sway the rule awhile,
Yet heavens are just, and time suppresseth wrongs.

WARWICK   Injurious Margaret!
PRINCE   And why not Queen?
WARWICK   Because thy father Henry did usurp;
    And thou no more art prince than she is queen.
OXFORD
    Then Warwick disannuls great John of Gaunt,
    Which did subdue the greatest part of Spain;
    And after John of Gaunt, Henry the Fourth,
    Whose wisdom was a mirror to the wisest;
    And after that wise prince, Henry the Fifth,
    Who by his prowess conquered all France:
    From these our Henry lineally descends.
WARWICK
    Oxford, how haps it in this smooth discourse
    You told not how Henry the Sixth hath lost
    All that which Henry the Fifth had gotten?
    Methinks these peers of France should smile at that.
    But for the rest: you tell a pedigree
    Of threescore and two years – a silly time
    To make prescription for a kingdom's worth.
OXFORD
    Why, Warwick, canst thou speak against thy liege,
    Whom thou obeyed'st thirty and six years,
    And not bewray thy treason with a blush?
WARWICK   Can Oxford, that did ever fence the right,
    Now buckler falsehood with a pedigree?
    For shame! leave Henry, and call Edward king.
OXFORD   Call him my king by whose injurious doom
    My elder brother, the Lord Aubrey Vere,
    Was done to death? and more than so, my father,
    Even in the downfall of his mellow'd years,
    When Nature brought him to the door of Death?
    No, Warwick, no; while life upholds this arm,
    This arm upholds the house of Lancaster.
WARWICK   And I the house of York.
KING LEWIS
    Queen Margaret, Prince Edward, and Oxford,
    Vouchsafe at our request to stand aside,
    While I use further conference with Warwick.
    [*They stand aloof.*]
QUEEN MARGARET
    Heavens grant that Warwick's words bewitch him
      not!
KING LEWIS
    Now, Warwick, tell me, even upon thy conscience,
    Is Edward your true king? for I were loath
    To link with him that were not lawful chosen.
WARWICK   Thereon I pawn my credit and mine honour.
KING LEWIS   But is he gracious in the people's eye?
WARWICK   The more that Henry was unfortunate.
KING LEWIS   Then further: all dissembling set aside,
    Tell me for truth the measure of his love
    Unto our sister Bona.
WARWICK   Such it seems
    As may beseem a monarch like himself.
    Myself have often heard him say, and swear,
    That this his love was an eternal plant,

    Whereof the root was fix'd in Virtue's ground, 125
    The leaves and fruit maintain'd with Beauty's sun,
    Exempt from envy, but not from disdain,
    Unless the Lady Bona quite his pain.
KING LEWIS   Now, sister, let us hear your firm resolve.
BONA   Your grant, or your denial, shall be mine: 130
    [*to Warwick*] Yet I confess that often ere this day,
    When I have heard your king's desert recounted,
    Mine ear hath temper'd judgment to desire.
KING LEWIS
    Then, Warwick, thus: our sister shall be Edward's.
    And now forthwith shall articles be drawn 135
    Touching the jointure that your king must make,
    Which with her dowry shall be counterpois'd.
    Draw near, Queen Margaret, and be a witness
    That Bona shall be wife to the English king.
PRINCE   To Edward, but not to the English king. 140
QUEEN MARGARET
    Deceitful Warwick, it was thy device
    By this alliance to make void my suit:
    Before thy coming Lewis was Henry's friend.
KING LEWIS   And still is friend to him and Margaret:
    But if your title to the crown be weak, 145
    As may appear by Edward's good success,
    Then 'tis but reason that I be releas'd
    From giving aid which late I promised.
    Yet shall you have all kindness at my hand
    That your estate requires and mine can yield. 150
WARWICK   Henry now lives in Scotland, at his ease,
    Where having nothing, nothing can he lose.
    And as for you yourself, our quondam queen,
    You have a father able to maintain you,
    And better 'twere you troubled him than France. 155
QUEEN MARGARET
    Peace, impudent and shameless Warwick, peace,
    Proud setter up and puller down of kings!
    I will not hence till with my talk and tears,
    Both full of truth, I make King Lewis behold
    Thy sly conveyance and thy lord's false love; 160
    For both of you are birds of self-same feather.
        [*Post blowing a horn within.*]
KING LEWIS   Warwick, this is some post to us or thee.

        Enter the Post.

POST [*to Warwick*]
    My lord ambassador, these are for you,
    Sent from your brother, Marquess Montague;
    [*to Lewis*] These from our King unto your Majesty: 165
    [*to Margaret*] And, madam, these for you; from whom
      I know not. [*They all read their letters.*]
OXFORD   I like it well that our fair Queen and mistress
    Smiles at her news, while Warwick frowns at his.
PRINCE
    Nay, mark how Lewis stamps as he were nettled:
    I hope all's for the best. 170
KING LEWIS
    Warwick, what are thy news? and yours, fair Queen?

QUEEN MARGARET
    Mine, such as fill my heart with unhop'd joys.
WARWICK   Mine, full of sorrow and heart's discontent.
KING LEWIS
    What? has your king married the Lady Grey?
175   And now, to soothe your forgery and his,
    Sends me a paper to persuade me patience?
    Is this th'alliance that he seeks with France?
    Dare he presume to scorn us in this manner?
QUEEN MARGARET   I told your Majesty as much before:
180   This proveth Edward's love and Warwick's honesty.
WARWICK
    King Lewis, I here protest in sight of heaven,
    And by the hope I have of heavenly bliss,
    That I am clear from this misdeed of Edward's –
    No more my king, for he dishonours me,
185   But most himself, if he could see his shame.
    Did I forget that by the house of York
    My father came untimely to his death?
    Did I let pass th'abuse done to my niece?
    Did I impale him with the regal crown?
190   Did I put Henry from his native right?
    And am I guerdon'd at the last with shame?
    Shame on himself! for my desert is honour;
    And to repair my honour lost for him
    I here renounce him and return to Henry.
195   My noble Queen, let former grudges pass,
    And henceforth I am thy true servitor.
    I will revenge his wrong to Lady Bona,
    And replant Henry in his former state.
QUEEN MARGARET
    Warwick, these words have turn'd my hate to love;
200   And I forgive and quite forget old faults,
    And joy that thou becom'st King Henry's friend.
WARWICK   So much his friend, ay, his unfeigned friend,
    That if King Lewis vouchsafe to furnish us
    With some few bands of chosen soldiers,
205   I'll undertake to land them on our coast
    And force the tyrant from his seat by war.
    'Tis not his new-made bride shall succour him;
    And as for Clarence, as my letters tell me,
    He's very likely now to fall from him
210   For matching more for wanton lust than honour
    Or than for strength and safety of our country.
BONA   Dear brother, how shall Bona be reveng'd
    But by thy help to this distressed queen?
QUEEN MARGARET
    Renowned Prince, how shall poor Henry live
215   Unless thou rescue him from foul despair?
BONA   My quarrel and this English queen's are one.
WARWICK   And mine, fair Lady Bona, joins with yours.
KING LEWIS
    And mine with hers, and thine, and Margaret's.
    Therefore at last I firmly am resolv'd
220   You shall have aid.

QUEEN MARGARET
    Let me give humble thanks for all at once.
KING LEWIS
    Then, England's messenger, return in post
    And tell false Edward, thy supposed king,
    That Lewis of France is sending over maskers
    To revel it with him and his new bride.   225
    Thou seest what's past, go fear thy king withal.
BONA   Tell him, in hope he'll prove a widower shortly,
    I'll wear the willow garland for his sake.
QUEEN MARGARET
    Tell him my mourning weeds are laid aside,
    And I am ready to put armour on.   230
WARWICK
    Tell him from me that he hath done me wrong,
    And therefore I'll uncrown him ere't be long.
    There's thy reward; be gone.   *Exit Post.*
KING LEWIS   But, Warwick,
    Thou and Oxford, with five thousand men,
    Shall cross the seas and bid false Edward battle;   235
    And, as occasion serves, this noble Queen
    And Prince shall follow with a fresh supply.
    Yet, ere thou go, but answer me one doubt:
    What pledge have we of thy firm loyalty?
WARWICK   This shall assure my constant loyalty: 240
    That if our Queen and this young Prince agree,
    I'll join mine eldest daughter and my joy
    To him forthwith in holy wedlock's bands.
QUEEN MARGARET
    Yes, I agree, and thank you for your motion.
    Son Edward, she is fair and virtuous,   245
    Therefore delay not, give thy hand to Warwick;
    And with thy hand thy faith irrevocable
    That only Warwick's daughter shall be thine.
PRINCE   Yes, I accept her, for she well deserves it;
    And here, to pledge my vow, I give my hand.   250
    [*He gives his hand to Warwick.*]
KING LEWIS
    Why stay we now? These soldiers shall be levied,
    And thou, Lord Bourbon, our High Admiral,
    Shalt waft them over with our royal fleet.
    I long till Edward fall by war's mischance
    For mocking marriage with a dame of France.   255
                       Exeunt all but Warwick.
WARWICK   I came from Edward as ambassador,
    But I return his sworn and mortal foe:
    Matter of marriage was the charge he gave me,
    But dreadful war shall answer his demand.
    Had he none else to make a stale but me?   260
    Then none but I shall turn his jest to sorrow.
    I was the chief that rais'd him to the crown,
    And I'll be chief to bring him down again:
    Not that I pity Henry's misery,
    But seek revenge on Edward's mockery.   *Exit.*   265

4.1   *Enter* RICHARD, GEORGE, SOMERSET
and MONTAGUE.

RICHARD
    Now tell me, brother Clarence, what think you
    Of this new marriage with the Lady Grey?
    Hath not our brother made a worthy choice?
GEORGE   Alas, you know 'tis far from hence to France!
    How could he stay till Warwick made return?
SOMERSET
    My lords, forbear this talk; here comes the King.

Flourish. Enter KING EDWARD *attended;* LADY GREY, *as*
QUEEN; *Pembroke, Stafford,* HASTINGS *and others. Four
stand on one side and four on the other.*

RICHARD   And his well-chosen bride.
GEORGE   I mind to tell him plainly what I think.
KING EDWARD
    Now, brother of Clarence, how like you our choice,
    That you stand pensive, as half malcontent?
GEORGE
    As well as Lewis of France or the Earl of Warwick,
    Which are so weak of courage and in judgment
    That they'll take no offence at our abuse.
KING EDWARD
    Suppose they take offence without a cause;
    They are but Lewis and Warwick: I am Edward,
    Your King and Warwick's, and must have my will.
RICHARD
    And you shall have your will, because our King:
    Yet hasty marriage seldom proveth well.
KING EDWARD
    Yea, brother Richard, are you offended too?
RICHARD
    No, God forfend that I should wish them sever'd
    Whom God hath join'd: ay, and 'twere pity
    To sunder them that yoke so well together.
KING EDWARD
    Setting your scorns and your mislike aside,
    Tell me some reason why the Lady Grey
    Should not become my wife and England's Queen.
    And you too, Somerset and Montague,
    Speak freely what you think.
GEORGE   Then this is my opinion: that King Lewis
    Becomes your enemy for mocking him
    About the marriage of the Lady Bona.
RICHARD
    And Warwick, doing what you gave in charge,
    Is now dishonour'd by this marriage.
KING EDWARD
    What if both Lewis and Warwick be appeas'd
    By such invention as I can devise?
MONTAGUE
    Yet to have join'd with France in such alliance
    Would more have strengthen'd this our
       commonwealth

    'Gainst foreign storms than any home-bred marriage.
HASTINGS   Why, knows not Montague that of itself
    England is safe, if true within itself?
MONTAGUE   But the safer when 'tis back'd with France.   40
HASTINGS
    'Tis better using France than trusting France.
    Let us be back'd with God and with the seas
    Which he hath given for fence impregnable,
    And with their helps only defend ourselves:
    In them and in ourselves our safety lies.   45
GEORGE
    For this one speech Lord Hastings well deserves
    To have the heir of the Lord Hungerford.
KING EDWARD
    Ay, what of that? it was my will and grant;
    And for this once my will shall stand for law.
RICHARD
    And yet, methinks, your Grace hath not done well   50
    To give the heir and daughter of Lord Scales
    Unto the brother of your loving bride;
    She better would have fitted me, or Clarence:
    But in your bride you bury brotherhood.
GEORGE   Or else you would not have bestow'd the heir   55
    Of the Lord Bonville on your new wife's son,
    And leave your brothers to go speed elsewhere.
KING EDWARD   Alas, poor Clarence! is it for a wife
    That thou art malcontent? I will provide thee.
GEORGE
    In choosing for yourself you show'd your judgment,   60
    Which being shallow, you shall give me leave
    To play the broker in mine own behalf;
    And to that end I shortly mind to leave you.
KING EDWARD
    Leave me, or tarry, Edward will be King,
    And not be tied unto his brother's will.   65
QUEEN ELIZABETH
    My lords, before it pleas'd his Majesty
    To raise my state to title of a queen,
    Do me but right, and you must all confess
    That I was not ignoble of descent;
    And meaner than myself have had like fortune.   70
    But as this title honours me and mine,
    So your dislikes, to whom I would be pleasing,
    Doth cloud my joys with danger and with sorrow.
KING EDWARD
    My love, forbear to fawn upon their frowns:
    What danger or what sorrow can befall thee   75
    So long as Edward is thy constant friend
    And their true sovereign whom they must obey?
    Nay, whom they shall obey, and love thee too,
    Unless they seek for hatred at my hands;
    Which if they do, yet will I keep thee safe,   80
    And they shall feel the vengeance of my wrath.
RICHARD [*aside*]
    I hear, yet say not much, but think the more.

Enter a Post.

KING EDWARD

   Now, messenger, what letters or what news
   From France?

85   POST   My sovereign liege, no letters, and few words,
   But such as I, without your special pardon,
   Dare not relate.

KING EDWARD

   Go to, we pardon thee: therefore, in brief,
   Tell me their words as near as thou canst guess them.

90   What answer makes King Lewis unto our letters?

   POST   At my depart, these were his very words:
   'Go tell false Edward, thy supposed king,
   That Lewis of France is sending over maskers
   To revel it with him and his new bride.'

KING EDWARD

95   Is Lewis so brave? Belike he thinks me Henry.
   But what said Lady Bona to my marriage?

POST

   These were her words, utter'd with mild disdain:
   'Tell him, in hope he'll prove a widower shortly,
   I'll wear the willow garland for his sake.'

100 KING EDWARD   I blame not her; she could say little less;
   She had the wrong. But what said Henry's queen?
   For I have heard that she was there in place.

POST

   'Tell him,' quoth she, 'my mourning weeds are done,
   And I am ready to put armour on.'

105 KING EDWARD   Belike she minds to play the Amazon.
   But what said Warwick to these injuries?

POST   He, more incens'd against your Majesty
   Than all the rest, discharg'd me with these words:
   'Tell him from me that he hath done me wrong,

110   And therefore I'll uncrown him ere't be long.'

KING EDWARD

   Ha! durst the traitor breathe out so proud words?
   Well, I will arm me, being thus forewarn'd:
   They shall have wars and pay for their presumption.
   But say, is Warwick friends with Margaret?

POST

   Ay, gracious sovereign, they are so link'd in
115   friendship
   That young Prince Edward marries Warwick's
     daughter.

GEORGE

   Belike the elder; Clarence will have the younger.
   Now, brother king, farewell, and sit you fast,
   For I will hence to Warwick's other daughter;

120   That, though I want a kingdom, yet in marriage
   I may not prove inferior to yourself.
   You that love me and Warwick, follow me.

             Exit George, and Somerset follows.

RICHARD [*aside*]

   Not I: my thoughts aim at a further matter;
   I stay not for the love of Edward, but the crown.

KING EDWARD

125   Clarence and Somerset both gone to Warwick!

   Yet am I arm'd against the worst can happen,
   And haste is needful in this desperate case.
   Pembroke and Stafford, you in our behalf
   Go levy men and make prepare for war;
   They are already, or quickly will be, landed: 130
   Myself in person will straight follow you.

             Exeunt Pembroke and Stafford.

   But, ere I go, Hastings and Montague,
   Resolve my doubt. You twain, of all the rest,
   Are nearest to Warwick by blood and by alliance:
   Tell me if you love Warwick more than me.   135
   If it be so, then both depart to him;
   I rather wish you foes than hollow friends.
   But if you mind to hold your true obedience,
   Give me assurance with some friendly vow,
   That I may never have you in suspect.   140

MONTAGUE   So God help Montague as he proves true!

HASTINGS   And Hastings as he favours Edward's cause!

KING EDWARD

   Now, brother Richard, will you stand by us?

RICHARD   Ay, in despite of all that shall withstand you.

KING EDWARD   Why, so! then am I sure of victory.   145
   Now, therefore, let us hence, and lose no hour
   Till we meet Warwick with his foreign power.`

                    Exeunt.

4.2   *Enter* WARWICK *and* OXFORD *in England,*
               with French soldiers.

WARWICK   Trust me, my lord, all hitherto goes well;
   The common people by numbers swarm to us.

         Enter GEORGE *and* SOMERSET.

   But see where Somerset and Clarence comes.
   Speak suddenly, my lords: are we all friends?

GEORGE   Fear not that, my lord.   5

WARWICK

   Then, gentle Clarence, welcome unto Warwick;
   And welcome Somerset. I hold it cowardice
   To rest mistrustful where a noble heart
   Hath pawn'd an open hand in sign of love;
   Else might I think that Clarence, Edward's brother,   10
   Were but a feigned friend to our proceedings.
   But come, sweet Clarence; my daughter shall be
     thine.
   And now what rests but, in night's coverture,
   Thy brother being carelessly encamp'd,
   His soldiers lurking in the towns about,   15
   And but attended by a simple guard,
   We may surprise and take him at our pleasure?
   Our scouts have found the adventure very easy:
   That, as Ulysses and stout Diomede
   With sleight and manhood stole to Rhesus' tents,   20
   And brought from thence the Thracian fatal steeds,
   So we, well cover'd with the night's black mantle,
   At unawares may beat down Edward's guard,
   And seize himself – I say not, slaughter him,
   For I intend but only to surprise him.   25

You that will follow me to this attempt,
Applaud the name of Henry with your leader.
[*They all cry 'Henry!'*]
Why, then, let's on our way in silent sort,
For Warwick and his friends, God and St George!

Exeunt.

4.3 *Enter three* Watchmen *to guard the King's tent.*

1 WATCHMAN
Come on, my masters, each man take his stand:
The King by this is set him down to sleep.

2 WATCHMAN   What, will he not to bed?

1 WATCHMAN
Why, no; for he hath made a solemn vow
Never to lie and take his natural rest
Till Warwick or himself be quite suppress'd.

2 WATCHMAN
To-morrow then belike shall be the day,
If Warwick be so near as men report.

3 WATCHMAN
But say, I pray, what nobleman is that
That with the King here resteth in his tent?

1 WATCHMAN
'Tis the Lord Hastings, the King's chiefest friend.

3 WATCHMAN
O, is it so? But why commands the King
That his chief followers lodge in towns about him,
While he himself keeps in the cold field?

2 WATCHMAN
'Tis the more honour because more dangerous.

3 WATCHMAN
Ay, but give me worship and quietness;
I like it better than a dangerous honour.
If Warwick knew in what estate he stands,
'Tis to be doubted he would waken him.

1 WATCHMAN
Unless our halberds did shut up his passage.

2 WATCHMAN
Ay, wherefore else guard we his royal tent
But to defend his person from night-foes?

Enter WARWICK, GEORGE, OXFORD, SOMERSET *and*
French soldiers, silent all.

WARWICK
This is his tent; and see where stand his guard.
Courage, my masters! Honour now or never!
But follow me, and Edward shall be ours.

1 WATCHMAN   Who goes there?

2 WATCHMAN   Stay, or thou diest.

[*Warwick and the rest cry all, 'Warwick! Warwick!' and set*
upon the guard, who fly, crying, 'Arm! Arm!', Warwick
and the rest following them.]

The drum playing and the trumpet sounding, enter
WARWICK, SOMERSET *and the rest, bringing the* KING *out*
in his gown, sitting in a chair. RICHARD *and* HASTINGS
fly over the stage.

SOMERSET   What are they that fly there?

WARWICK   Richard and Hastings; let them go;
Here is the Duke.

KING EDWARD   Why, Warwick, when we parted,   30
Thou call'dst me King.

WARWICK   Ay, but the case is alter'd.
When you disgrac'd me in my embassade,
Then I degraded you from being King,
And come now to create you Duke of York.
Alas, how should you govern any kingdom   35
That know not how to use ambassadors,
Nor how to be contented with one wife,
Nor how to use your brothers brotherly,
Nor how to study for the people's welfare,
Nor how to shroud yourself from enemies?   40

KING EDWARD
Yea, brother of Clarence, art thou here too?
Nay, then I see that Edward needs must down.
Yet, Warwick, in despite of all mischance,
Of thee thyself and all thy complices,
Edward will always bear himself a king.   45
Though Fortune's malice overthrow my state,
My mind exceeds the compass of her wheel.

WARWICK
Then, for his mind, be Edward England's king;
[*Takes off his crown.*]
But Henry now shall wear the English crown
And be true King indeed; thou but the shadow. 50
My lord of Somerset, at my request,
See that forthwith Duke Edward be convey'd
Unto my brother, Archbishop of York.
When I have fought with Pembroke and his fellows,
I'll follow you, and come and tell what answer   55
Lewis and the Lady Bona send to him.
Now, for a while, farewell, good Duke of York.

KING EDWARD
What fates impose, that men must needs abide;
It boots not to resist both wind and tide.
They lead him out forcibly.

OXFORD   What now remains, my lords, for us to do   60
But march to London with our soldiers?

WARWICK   Ay, that's the first thing that we have to do,
To free King Henry from imprisonment
And see him seated in the regal throne.   *Exeunt.*

4.4   *Enter* QUEEN ELIZABETH *and* RIVERS.

RIVERS
Madam, what makes in you this sudden change?

QUEEN ELIZABETH
Why, brother Rivers, are you yet to learn
What late misfortune is befall'n King Edward?

RIVERS
What, loss of some pitch'd battle against Warwick?

QUEEN ELIZABETH
No, but the loss of his own royal person.   5

RIVERS   Then is my sovereign slain?

QUEEN ELIZABETH

    Ay, almost slain, for he is taken prisoner;

    Either betray'd by falsehood of his guard,

    Or by his foe surpris'd at unawares:

10   And, as I further have to understand,

    Is new committed to the Bishop of York,

    Fell Warwick's brother, and by that our foe.

RIVERS   These news, I must confess, are full of grief;

    Yet gracious madam, bear it as you may:

15   Warwick may lose that now hath won the day.

QUEEN ELIZABETH

    Till then, fair hope must hinder life's decay,

    And I the rather wean me from despair

    For love of Edward's offspring in my womb:

    This is it that makes me bridle passion

20   And bear with mildness my misfortune's cross,

    Ay, ay, for this I draw in many a tear

    And stop the rising of blood-sucking sighs,

    Lest with my sighs or tears I blast or drown

    King Edward's fruit, true heir to th' English crown.

25 RIVERS   But, madam, where is Warwick then become?

QUEEN ELIZABETH

    I am inform'd that he comes towards London

    To set the crown once more on Henry's head.

    Guess thou the rest: King Edward's friends must

        down.

    But to prevent the tyrant's violence –

30   For trust not him that hath once broken faith –

    I'll hence forthwith unto the sanctuary

    To save at least the heir of Edward's right.

    There shall I rest secure from force and fraud.

    Come, therefore, let us fly while we may fly:

35   If Warwick take us, we are sure to die.   *Exeunt.*

4.5   *Enter* RICHARD, LORD HASTINGS, *Sir William*
Stanley and others.

RICHARD

    Now, my Lord Hastings and Sir William Stanley

    Leave off to wonder why I drew you hither

    Into this chiefest thicket of the park.

    Thus stands the case: you know our King, my

        brother,

5   Is prisoner to the Bishop here, at whose hands

    He hath good usage and great liberty,

    And often but attended with weak guard

    Comes hunting this way to disport himself.

    I have advertis'd him by secret means

10   That if about this hour he make this way,

    Under the colour of his usual game,

    He shall here find his friends with horse and men

    To set him free from his captivity.

    Enter KING EDWARD *and a* Huntsman *with him.*

HUNTSMAN

    This way, my lord, for this way lies the game.

KING EDWARD

15   Nay, this way, man: see where the huntsmen stand.

    Now, brother of Gloucester, Hastings, and the rest,

    Stand you thus close to steal the Bishop's deer?

RICHARD   Brother, the time and case requireth haste;

    Your horse stands ready at the park corner.

KING EDWARD   But whither shall we then?

HASTINGS   To Lynn, my lord?   20

    And ship from thence to Flanders?

RICHARD

    Well guess'd, believe me; for that was my meaning.

KING EDWARD   Stanley, I will requite thy forwardness.

RICHARD   But wherefore stay we? 'tis no time to talk.

KING EDWARD

    Huntsman, what say'st thou? wilt thou go along?   25

HUNTSMAN   Better do so than tarry and be hang'd.

RICHARD   Come then, away; let's ha' no more ado.

KING EDWARD

    Bishop, farewell: shield thee from Warwick's frown,

    And pray that I may repossess the crown.   *Exeunt.*

4.6 *Flourish. Enter* KING HENRY, GEORGE, WARWICK,
SOMERSET, *young* RICHMOND, OXFORD, MONTAGUE
and Lieutenant *of the Tower.*

KING HENRY

    Master Lieutenant, now that God and friends

    Have shaken Edward from the regal seat

    And turn'd my captive state to liberty,

    My fear to hope, my sorrows unto joys,

    At our enlargement what are thy due fees?   5

LIEUTENANT

    Subjects may challenge nothing of their sovereigns;

    But, if an humble prayer may prevail,

    I then crave pardon of your Majesty.

KING HENRY

    For what, Lieutenant? For well using me?

    Nay, be thou sure, I'll well requite thy kindness,   10

    For that it made my prisonment a pleasure;

    Ay, such a pleasure as incaged birds

    Conceive when, after many moody thoughts,

    At last by notes of household harmony

    They quite forget their loss of liberty.   15

    But, Warwick, after God, thou set'st me free,

    And chiefly therefore I thank God and thee;

    He was the author, thou the instrument.

    Therefore, that I may conquer Fortune's spite

    By living low where Fortune cannot hurt me,   20

    And that the people of this blessed land

    May not be punish'd with my thwarting stars,

    Warwick, although my head still wear the crown,

    I here resign my government to thee,

    For thou are fortunate in all thy deeds.   25

WARWICK

    Your Grace hath still been fam'd for virtuous,

    And now may seem as wise as virtuous

    By spying and avoiding Fortune's malice,

    For few men rightly temper with the stars;

    Yet in this one thing let me blame your Grace,   30

    For choosing me when Clarence is in place.

GEORGE   No, Warwick, thou art worthy of the sway,
　To whom the heavens in thy nativity
　Adjudg'd an olive branch and laurel crown,
　As likely to be blest in peace and war;
　And therefore I yield thee my free consent.
WARWICK   And I choose Clarence only for Protector.
KING HENRY
　Warwick and Clarence, give me both your hands:
　Now join your hands, and with your hands your
　　hearts,
　That no dissension hinder government.
　I make you both Protectors of this land,
　While I myself will lead a private life
　And in devotion spend my latter days
　To sin's rebuke and my Creator's praise.
WARWICK
　What answers Clarence to his sovereign's will?
GEORGE   That he consents, if Warwick yield consent;
　For on thy fortune I repose myself.
WARWICK
　Why then, though loath, yet must I be content.
　We'll yoke together, like a double shadow
　To Henry's body, and supply his place;
　I mean, in bearing weight of government,
　While he enjoys the honour, and his ease.
　And, Clarence, now then it is more than needful
　Forthwith that Edward be pronounc'd a traitor
　And all his lands and goods be confiscate.
GEORGE
　What else? And that succession be determin'd.
WARWICK   Ay, therein Clarence shall not want his part.
KING HENRY   But with the first of all your chief affairs
　Let me entreat – for I command no more –
　That Margaret your Queen and my son Edward
　Be sent for to return from France with speed;
　For till I see them here, by doubtful fear
　My joy of liberty is half eclips'd.
GEORGE   It shall be done, my sovereign, with all speed.
KING HENRY
　My Lord of Somerset, what youth is that,
　Of whom you seem to have so tender care?
SOMERSET
　My liege, it is young Henry, Earl of Richmond.
KING HENRY
　Come hither, England's hope.
　[*Lays his hand on his head.*]   If secret powers
　Suggest but truth to my divining thoughts,
　This pretty lad will prove our country's bliss.
　His looks are full of peaceful majesty;
　His head by nature fram'd to wear a crown,
　His hand to wield a sceptre; and himself
　Likely in time to bless a regal throne.
　Make much of him, my lords, for this is he
　Must help you more than you are hurt by me.

　　　　　　　Enter a Post.

WARWICK   What news, my friend?

POST   That Edward is escaped from your brother
　And fled, as he hears since, to Burgundy.
WARWICK   Unsavoury news! But how made he escape?   80
POST
　He was convey'd by Richard, Duke of Gloucester
　And the Lord Hastings, who attended him
　In secret ambush on the forest side
　And from the Bishop's huntsmen rescu'd him;
　For hunting was his daily exercise.   85
WARWICK   My brother was too careless of his charge.
　But let us hence, my sovereign, to provide
　A salve for any sore that may betide.
　　　　Exeunt all but Somerset, Richmond and Oxford.
SOMERSET
　My lord, I like not of this flight of Edward's;
　For doubtless Burgundy will yield him help,   90
　And we shall have more wars before't be long.
　As Henry's late presaging prophecy
　Did glad my heart with hope of this young
　　Richmond,
　So doth my heart misgive me, in these conflicts,
　What may befall him to his harm and ours.   95
　Therefore, Lord Oxford, to prevent the worst,
　Forthwith we'll send him hence to Brittany,
　Till storms be past of civil enmity.
OXFORD   Ay, for if Edward repossess the crown,
　'Tis like that Richmond with the rest shall down.   100
SOMERSET   It shall be so: he shall to Brittany.
　Come, therefore, let's about it speedily.   *Exeunt.*

4.7   *Flourish. Enter* KING EDWARD, RICHARD,
　　　　　HASTINGS *and soldiers.*

KING EDWARD
　Now, brother Richard, Hastings, and the rest,
　Yet thus far Fortune maketh us amends,
　And says that once more I shall interchange
　My waned state for Henry's regal crown.
　Well have we pass'd and now repass'd the seas,   5
　And brought desired help from Burgundy;
　What then remains, we being thus arriv'd
　From Ravenspurgh haven before the gates of York,
　But that we enter, as into our dukedom?
RICHARD   The gates made fast! Brother, I like not this;   10
　For many men that stumble at the threshold
　Are well foretold that danger lurks within.
KING EDWARD
　Tush, man, abodements must not now affright us:
　By fair or foul means we must enter in,
　For hither will our friends repair to us.   15
HASTINGS
　My liege, I'll knock once more to summon them.

　Enter, on the walls, the Mayor *of York and his brethren.*

MAYOR   My lords, we were forewarned of your coming
　And shut the gates for safety of ourselves,
　For now we owe allegiance unto Henry.

KING EDWARD

20   But, Master Mayor, if Henry be your king,
    Yet Edward, at the least, is Duke of York.

MAYOR   True, my good lord, I know you for no less.

KING EDWARD

    Why, and I challenge nothing but my dukedom,
    As being well content with that alone.

RICHARD [*aside*]

25   But when the fox hath once got in his nose,
    He'll soon find means to make the body follow.

HASTINGS

    Why, Master Mayor, why stand you in a doubt?
    Open the gates; we are King Henry's friends.

MAYOR   Ay, say you so? the gates shall then be open'd.
                                 He descends.

30 RICHARD   A wise stout captain, and soon persuaded!

HASTINGS

    The good old man would fain that all were well
    So 'twere not 'long of him; but being enter'd,
    I doubt not, I, but we shall soon persuade
    Both him and all his brothers unto reason.

      Enter the Mayor *and two Aldermen, below.*

KING EDWARD

35   So, Master Mayor: these gates must not be shut
    But in the night or in the time of war.
    What! fear not, man, but yield me up the keys;
    [*Takes his keys.*]
    For Edward will defend the town and thee
    And all those friends that deign to follow me.

    March. Enter SIR JOHN MONTGOMERY, *with drum and*
                        soldiers.

40 RICHARD   Brother, this is Sir John Montgomery,
    Our trusty friend, unless I be deceiv'd.

KING EDWARD

    Welcome, Sir John! But why come you in arms?

MONTGOMERY

    To help King Edward in his time of storm,
    As every loyal subject ought to do.

KING EDWARD

45   Thanks, good Montgomery; but we now forget
    Our title to the crown, and only claim
    Our dukedom till God please to send the rest.

MONTGOMERY

    Then fare you well, for I will hence again:
    I came to serve a king and not a duke.

50   Drummer, strike up, and let us march away.
                      [*The drum begins to march.*]

KING EDWARD

    Nay, stay, Sir John, a while; and we'll debate
    By what safe means the crown may be recover'd.

MONTGOMERY

    What talk you of debating? In few words:
    If you'll not here proclaim yourself our King,
55   I'll leave you to your fortune and be gone
    To keep them back that come to succour you.

    Why shall we fight, if you pretend no title?

RICHARD

    Why, brother, wherefore stand you on nice points?
    Resolve yourself, and let us claim the crown.

KING EDWARD

    When we grow stronger, then we'll make our claim: 60
    Till then 'tis wisdom to conceal our meaning.

HASTINGS

    Away with scrupulous wit! Now arms must rule.

RICHARD

    And fearless minds climb soonest unto crowns.
    Brother, we will proclaim you out of hand;
    The bruit thereof will bring you many friends.   65

KING EDWARD   Then be it as you will; for 'tis my right,
    And Henry but usurps the diadem.

MONTGOMERY

    Ay, now my sovereign speaketh like himself,
    And now will I be Edward's champion.

HASTINGS

    Sound trumpet; Edward shall be here proclaim'd.   70
    Come, fellow soldier, make thou proclamation.
    [*Gives him a paper.*]   [*Flourish.*]

SOLDIER

    Edward the Fourth, by the grace of God, King of
    England and France, and Lord of Ireland, etc.

MONTGOMERY

    And whosoe'er gainsays King Edward's right,
    By this I challenge him to single fight.   75
    [*Throws down his gauntlet.*]

ALL   Long live Edward the Fourth!

KING EDWARD

    Thanks, brave Montgomery, and thanks unto you all:
    If Fortune serve me, I'll requite this kindness.
    Now for this night let's harbour here in York,
    And when the morning sun shall raise his car   80
    Above the border of this horizon
    We'll forward towards Warwick and his mates;
    For well I wot that Henry is no soldier.
    Ah, froward Clarence, how evil it beseems thee
    To flatter Henry and forsake thy brother!   85
    Yet, as we may, we'll meet both thee and Warwick.
    Come on, brave soldiers: doubt not of the day,
    And, that once gotten, doubt not of large pay.
                                Exeunt.

4.8   *Flourish. Enter* KING HENRY, WARWICK,
      MONTAGUE, GEORGE, OXFORD *and* EXETER.

WARWICK   What counsel, lords? Edward from Belgia,
    With hasty Germans and blunt Hollanders,
    Is pass'd in safety through the Narrow Seas,
    And with his troops doth march amain to London;
    And many giddy people flock to him.   5

KING HENRY   Let's levy men and beat him back again.

GEORGE   A little fire is quickly trodden out,
    Which, being suffer'd, rivers cannot quench.

WARWICK   In Warwickshire I have true-hearted friends,

10 Not mutinous in peace, yet bold in war;
Those will I muster up, and thou, son Clarence,
Shalt stir in Suffolk, Norfolk, and in Kent,
The knights and gentlemen to come with thee:
Thou, brother Montague, in Buckingham,
15 Northampton, and in Leicestershire, shalt find
Men well inclin'd to hear what thou command'st:
And thou, brave Oxford, wondrous well-belov'd
In Oxfordshire, shalt muster up thy friends.
My sovereign, with the loving citizens,
20 Like to his island girt in with the ocean,
Or modest Dian circled with her nymphs,
Shall rest in London till we come to him.
Fair lords, take leave and stand not to reply.
Farewell, my sovereign.

KING HENRY
25 Farewell, my Hector and my Troy's true hope.

GEORGE   In sign of truth, I kiss your Highness' hand.

KING HENRY
Well-minded Clarence, be thou fortunate.

MONTAGUE   Comfort, my lord; and so I take my leave.

OXFORD   And thus I seal my truth and bid adieu.

KING HENRY
30 Sweet Oxford, and my loving Montague,
And all at once, once more a happy farewell.

WARWICK   Farewell, sweet lords; let's meet at Coventry.
Exeunt all but King Henry and Exeter.

KING HENRY
Here at the palace will I rest a while.
Cousin of Exeter, what thinks your lordship?
35 Methinks the power that Edward hath in field
Should not be able to encounter mine.

EXETER   The doubt is that he will seduce the rest.

KING HENRY
That's not my fear; my meed hath got me fame:
I have not stopp'd mine ears to their demands,
40 Nor posted off their suits with slow delays;
My pity hath been balm to heal their wounds,
My mildness hath allay'd their swelling griefs,
My mercy dried their water-flowing tears;
I have not been desirous of their wealth,
45 Nor much oppress'd them with great subsidies,
Nor forward of revenge, though they much err'd.
Then why should they love Edward more than me?
No, Exeter, these graces challenge grace;
And, when the lion fawns upon the lamb,
50 The lamb will never cease to follow him.
[*Shout within, 'A York! A York!'*]

EXETER   Hark, hark, my lord! what shouts are these?

Enter KING EDWARD, RICHARD and soldiers.

KING EDWARD
Seize on the shame-fac'd Henry, bear him hence;
And once again proclaim us King of England.
You are the fount that makes small brooks to flow:
55 Now stops thy spring; my sea shall suck them dry,
And swell so much the higher by their ebb.

Hence with him to the Tower: let him not speak.
Exeunt some with King Henry.
And, lords, towards Coventry bend we our course,
Where peremptory Warwick now remains.
The sun shines hot; and if we use delay,   60
Cold biting winter mars our hop'd-for hay.

RICHARD   Away betimes, before his forces join,
And take the great-grown traitor unawares:
Brave warriors, march amain towards Coventry.
Exeunt.

5.1   *Enter* WARWICK, *the Mayor of Coventry, two
Messengers and others upon the walls.*

WARWICK
Where is the post that came from valiant Oxford?
How far hence is thy lord, mine honest fellow?

1 MESSENGER
By this at Dunsmore, marching hitherward.

WARWICK   How far off is our brother Montague?
Where is the post that came from Montague?   5

2 MESSENGER
By this at Daintry, with a puissant troop.

Enter SIR JOHN SOMERVILLE.

WARWICK   Say, Somerville, what says my loving son?
And by thy guess how nigh is Clarence now?

SOMERSET   At Southam I did leave him with his forces,
And do expect him here some two hours hence.   10
[*Drum heard.*]

WARWICK   Then Clarence is at hand; I hear his drum.

SOMERSET   It is not his, my lord; here Southam lies:
The drum your honour hears marcheth from
Warwick.

WARWICK
Who should that be? Belike, unlook'd for friends.

SOMERSET
They are at hand, and you shall quickly know.   15

March. Flourish. Enter EDWARD, RICHARD and soldiers.

KING EDWARD
Go, trumpet, to the walls and sound a parle.

RICHARD   See how the surly Warwick mans the wall.

WARWICK   O unbid spite! Is sportful Edward come?
Where slept our scouts or how are they seduc'd
That we could hear no news of his repair?   20

KING EDWARD
Now, Warwick, wilt thou ope the city gates,
Speak gentle words, and humbly bend thy knee,
Call Edward King, and at his hands beg mercy,
And he shall pardon thee these outrages?

WARWICK   Nay, rather, wilt thou draw thy forces hence,   25
Confess who set thee up and pluck'd thee down,
Call Warwick patron, and be penitent,
And thou shalt still remain – the Duke of York?

RICHARD
I thought at least he would have said the King;

30 Or did he make the jest against his will?
WARWICK   Is not a dukedom, sir, a goodly gift?
RICHARD   Ay, by my faith, for a poor earl to give;
　　I'll do thee service for so good a gift.
WARWICK
　　'Twas I that gave the kingdom to thy brother.
KING EDWARD
35 Why then 'tis mine, if but by Warwick's gift.
WARWICK   Thou art no Atlas for so great a weight;
　　And, weakling, Warwick takes his gift again;
　　And Henry is my King, Warwick his subject.
KING EDWARD
　　But Warwick's king is Edward's prisoner;
40 And, gallant Warwick, do but answer this:
　　What is the body when the head is off?
RICHARD   Alas, that Warwick had no more forecast,
　　But, whiles he thought to steal the single ten,
　　The king was slily finger'd from the deck!
45 You left poor Henry at the Bishop's palace,
　　And ten to one you'll meet him in the Tower.
KING EDWARD   'Tis even so: yet you are Warwick still.
RICHARD
　　Come, Warwick, take the time; kneel down, kneel
　　　down.
　　Nay, when? Strike now, or else the iron cools.
50 WARWICK   I had rather chop this hand off at a blow
　　And with the other fling it at thy face,
　　Than bear so low a sail to strike to thee.
KING EDWARD
　　Sail how thou canst, have wind and tide thy friend,
　　This hand, fast wound about thy coal-black hair,
55 Shall, whiles thy head is warm and new cut off,
　　Write in the dust this sentence with thy blood:
　　'Wind-changing Warwick now can change no more'.

Enter OXFORD, *with drum and colours.*

WARWICK
　　O cheerful colours! See where Oxford comes!
OXFORD   Oxford, Oxford, for Lancaster!
　　[*He and his forces enter the city.*]
60 RICHARD   The gates are open, let us enter too.
KING EDWARD   So other foes may set upon our backs.
　　Stand we in good array, for they no doubt
　　Will issue out again and bid us battle;
　　If not, the city being but of small defence,
65 We'll quickly rouse the traitors in the same.
WARWICK   O welcome, Oxford, for we want thy help.

Enter MONTAGUE, *with drum and colours.*

MONTAGUE   Montague, Montague, for Lancaster!
　　[*He and his forces enter the city.*]
RICHARD
　　Thou and thy brother both shall buy this treason
　　Even with the dearest blood your bodies bear.
KING EDWARD
70 The harder match'd, the greater victory:

My mind presageth happy gain and conquest.

Enter SOMERSET, *with drum and colours.*

SOMERSET   Somerset, Somerset, for Lancaster!
　　[*He and his forces enter the city.*]
RICHARD   Two of thy name, both Dukes of Somerset,
　　Have sold their lives unto the house of York,
　　And thou shalt be the third, and this sword hold. 75

Enter GEORGE, *with drum and colours.*

WARWICK
　　And lo, where George of Clarence sweeps along,
　　Of force enough to bid his brother battle;
　　With whom an upright zeal to right prevails
　　More than the nature of a brother's love.
GEORGE   Clarence, Clarence, for Lancaster! 80
KING EDWARD   *Et tu, Brute!* wilt thou stab Caesar too?
　　A parley, sirrah, to George of Clarence.
　　　　　[*Sound a parley. Richard and George whisper.*]
WARWICK
　　Come, Clarence, come; thou wilt if Warwick call.
　　[*George takes the red rose from his hat and throws it at
　　Warwick.*]
GEORGE
　　Father of Warwick, know you what this means?
　　Look, here I throw my infamy at thee: 85
　　I will not ruinate my father's house,
　　Who gave his blood to lime the stones together,
　　And set up Lancaster. Why, trowest thou, Warwick,
　　That Clarence is so harsh, so blunt, unnatural,
　　To bend the fatal instruments of war 90
　　Against his brother and his lawful King?
　　Perhaps thou wilt object my holy oath:
　　To keep that oath were more impiety
　　Than Jephthah's when he sacrific'd his daughter.
　　I am so sorry for my trespass made, 95
　　That, to deserve well at my brothers' hands,
　　I here proclaim myself thy mortal foe;
　　With resolution, wheresoe'er I meet thee –
　　As I will meet thee if thou stir abroad –
　　To plague thee for thy foul misleading me. 100
　　And so, proud-hearted Warwick, I defy thee,
　　And to my brother turn my blushing cheeks.
　　Pardon me, Edward, I will make amends:
　　And, Richard, do not frown upon my faults,
　　For I will henceforth be no more unconstant. 105
KING EDWARD
　　Now welcome more, and ten times more belov'd,
　　Than if thou never hadst deserv'd our hate.
RICHARD   Welcome, good Clarence; this is brother-like.
WARWICK   O passing traitor, perjur'd and unjust!
KING EDWARD
　　What, Warwick, wilt thou leave the town and fight? 110
　　Or shall we beat the stones about thine ears?
WARWICK   Alas, I am not coop'd here for defence!
　　I will away towards Barnet presently

And bid thee battle, Edward, if thou dar'st.

KING EDWARD

15   Yes, Warwick, Edward dares, and leads the way.
Lords, to the field; Saint George and victory!
          Exeunt. March. Warwick and his company follow.

5.2   *Alarum, and excursions. Enter* KING EDWARD,
          bringing forth WARWICK *wounded.*

KING EDWARD

So, lie thou there: die thou, and die our fear;
For Warwick was a bug that fear'd us all.
Now, Montague, sit fast; I seek for thee,
That Warwick's bones may keep thine company. *Exit.*

WARWICK   Ah, who is nigh? Come to me, friend or foe,
And tell me who is victor, York or Warwick?
Why ask I that my mangled body shows? –
My blood, my want of strength, my sick heart
     shows? –
That I must yield my body to the earth,
10   And, by my fall, the conquest to my foe.
Thus yields the cedar to the axe's edge
Whose arms gave shelter to the princely eagle,
Under whose shade the ramping lion slept,
Whose top branch over-peer'd Jove's spreading tree
15   And kept low shrubs from winter's powerful wind.
These eyes, that now are dimm'd with death's black
     veil,
Have been as piercing as the mid-day sun
To search the secret treasons of the world;
The wrinkles in my brows, now fill'd with blood,
20   Were liken'd oft to kingly sepulchres;
For who liv'd King but I could dig his grave?
And who durst smile when Warwick bent his brow?
Lo now my glory smear'd in dust and blood!
My parks, my walks, my manors that I had,
25   Even now forsake me; and of all my lands
Is nothing left me but my body's length.
Why, what is pomp, rule, reign, but earth and dust?
And live we how we can, yet die we must.

          Enter OXFORD *and* SOMERSET.

SOMERSET   Ah, Warwick, Warwick! wert thou as we are
30   We might recover all our loss again.
The Queen from France hath brought a puissant
     power.
Even now we heard the news. Ah, couldst thou fly!

WARWICK   Why then, I would not fly. Ah, Montague,
If thou be there, sweet brother, take my hand,
35   And with thy lips keep in my soul a while!
Thou lov'st me not; for, brother, if thou didst,
Thy tears would wash this cold congealed blood
That glues my lips and will not let me speak.
Come quickly, Montague, or I am dead.

SOMERSET

40   Ah, Warwick! Montague hath breath'd his last;
And to the latest gasp cried out for Warwick,

And said, 'Commend me to my valiant brother.'
And more he would have said; and more he spoke;
Which sounded like a cannon in a vault
That mought not be distinguish'd; but at last   45
I well might hear, deliver'd with a groan,
'O farewell, Warwick!'

WARWICK   Sweet rest his soul!
Fly, lords, and save yourselves, for Warwick bids
You all farewell, to meet in heaven. [*He dies.*]

OXFORD   Away, away, to meet the Queen's great power!   50
          Here they bear away his body. Exeunt.

5.3   *Flourish. Enter* KING EDWARD *in triumph, with*
          RICHARD, GEORGE *and the rest.*

KING EDWARD

Thus far our fortune keeps an upward course,
And we are grac'd with wreaths of victory:
But in the midst of this bright-shining day
I spy a black suspicious threatening cloud
That will encounter with our glorious sun   5
Ere he attain his easeful western bed –
I mean, my lord, those powers that the Queen
Hath rais'd in Gallia have arriv'd our coast,
And, as we hear, march on to fight with us.

GEORGE   A little gale will soon disperse that cloud   10
And blow it to the source from whence it came;
Thy very beams will dry those vapours up,
For every cloud engenders not a storm.

RICHARD   The Queen is valu'd thirty thousand strong,
And Somerset, with Oxford, fled to her: 15
If she have time to breathe, be well assur'd
Her faction will be full as strong as ours.

KING EDWARD   We are advertis'd by our loving friends
That they do hold their course toward Tewkesbury.
We, having now the best at Barnet field,   20
Will thither straight, for willingness rids way;
And as we march our strength will be augmented
In every county as we go along.
Strike up the drum; cry 'Courage!' and away. *Exeunt.*

5.4   *Flourish. March. Enter* QUEEN MARGARET,
          PRINCE EDWARD, SOMERSET, OXFORD *and soldiers.*

QUEEN MARGARET

Great lords, wise men ne'er sit and wail their loss,
But cheerly seek how to redress their harms.
What though the mast be now blown overboard,
The cable broke, the holding anchor lost,
And half our sailors swallow'd in the flood;   5
Yet lives our pilot still: is't meet that he
Should leave the helm and, like a fearful lad,
With tearful eyes add water to the sea
And give more strength to that which hath too much;
Whiles, in his moan, the ship splits on the rock,   10
Which industry and courage might have sav'd?
Ah, what a shame! ah, what a fault were this!
Say Warwick was our anchor; what of that?

And Montague our top-mast; what of him?
15 Our slaughter'd friends the tackles; what of these?
Why, is not Oxford here another anchor?
And Somerset another goodly mast?
The friends of France our shrouds and tacklings?
And, though unskilful, why not Ned and I
20 For once allow'd the skilful pilot's charge?
We will not from the helm to sit and weep,
But keep our course, though the rough wind say no,
From shelves and rocks that threaten us with wrack.
As good to chide the waves as speak them fair.
25 And what is Edward but a ruthless sea?
What Clarence but a quicksand of deceit?
And Richard but a ragged fatal rock?
All these the enemies to our poor bark.
Say you can swim – alas, 'tis but a while!
30 Tread on the sand – why, there you quickly sink:
Bestride the rock – the tide will wash you off,
Or else you famish; that's a threefold death.
This speak I, lords, to let you understand,
If case some one of you would fly from us,
35 That there's no hop'd-for mercy with the brothers
More than with ruthless waves, with sands, and
  rocks.
Why, courage then! what cannot be avoided
'Twere childish weakness to lament or fear.
PRINCE Methinks a woman of this valiant spirit
40 Should, if a coward heard her speak these words,
Infuse his breast with magnanimity
And make him, naked, foil a man at arms.
I speak not this as doubting any here;
For did I but suspect a fearful man,
45 He should have leave to go away betimes,
Lest in our need he might infect another
And make him of like spirit to himself.
If any such be here – as God forbid! –
Let him depart before we need his help.
50 OXFORD Women and children of so high a courage,
And warriors faint! why, 'twere perpetual shame.
O brave young Prince! thy famous grandfather
Doth live again in thee: long may'st thou live
To bear his image and renew his glories!
55 SOMERSET And he that will not fight for such a hope
Go home to bed and, like the owl by day,
If he arise, be mock'd and wonder'd at.
QUEEN MARGARET
 Thanks, gentle Somerset; sweet Oxford, thanks.
PRINCE And take his thanks that yet hath nothing else.

Enter a Messenger.

60 MESSENGER Prepare you, lords, for Edward is at hand
Ready to fight; therefore be resolute.
OXFORD I thought no less: it is his policy
To haste thus fast, to find us unprovided.
SOMERSET But he's deceiv'd; we are in readiness.
QUEEN MARGARET
65 This cheers my heart, to see your forwardness.

OXFORD
 Here pitch our battle; hence we will not budge.

Flourish, and march. Enter KING EDWARD, RICHARD,
  GEORGE *and soldiers.*

KING EDWARD
 Brave followers, yonder stands the thorny wood
 Which by the heavens' assistance and your strength
 Must by the roots be hewn up yet ere night.
 I need not add more fuel to your fire,   70
 For well I wot ye blaze to burn them out.
 Give signal to the fight, and to it, lords!
QUEEN MARGARET
 Lords, knights, and gentlemen, what I should say
 My tears gainsay; for every word I speak
 Ye see I drink the water of my eye.   75
 Therefore no more but this: Henry, your sovereign,
 Is prisoner to the foe, his state usurp'd,
 His realm a slaughter-house, his subjects slain,
 His statutes cancell'd, and his treasure spent;
 And yonder stands the wolf that makes this spoil. 80
 You fight in justice: then, in God's name, lords,
 Be valiant, and give signal to the fight.
    Alarum. Retreat. Excursions. Exeunt.

5.5 *Flourish. Enter* KING EDWARD, RICHARD,
GEORGE *and soldiers; with* QUEEN MARGARET, OXFORD
  and SOMERSET, *prisoners.*

KING EDWARD Now here a period of tumultuous broils.
 Away with Oxford to Hames Castle straight:
 For Somerset, off with his guilty head.
 Go, bear them hence; I will not hear them speak.
OXFORD For my part, I'll not trouble thee with words. 5
SOMERSET
 Nor I; but stoop with patience to my fortune.
    Exeunt Oxford and Somerset, guarded.
QUEEN MARGARET
 So part we sadly in this troublous world,
 To meet with joy in sweet Jerusalem.
KING EDWARD
 Is proclamation made that who finds Edward
 Shall have a high reward, and he his life? 10
RICHARD It is: and lo where youthful Edward comes.

Enter soldiers, with PRINCE EDWARD.

KING EDWARD
 Bring forth the gallant: let us hear him speak.
 What, can so young a thorn begin to prick?
 Edward, what satisfaction canst thou make
 For bearing arms, for stirring up my subjects, 15
 And all the trouble thou hast turn'd me to?
PRINCE Speak like a subject, proud ambitious York.
 Suppose that I am now my father's mouth;
 Resign thy chair, and where I stand kneel thou,
 Whilst I propose the self-same words to thee 20
 Which, traitor, thou would'st have me answer to.

QUEEN MARGARET

   Ah, that thy father had been so resolv'd!

RICHARD   That you might still have worn the petticoat

   And ne'er have stol'n the breech from Lancaster.

PRINCE   Let Aesop fable in a winter's night; 25

   His currish riddles sorts not with this place.

RICHARD   By heaven, brat, I'll plague ye for that word.

QUEEN MARGARET

   Ay, thou wast born to be a plague to men.

RICHARD   For God's sake, take away this captive scold.

PRINCE   Nay, take away this scolding crookback rather. 30

KING EDWARD

   Peace, wilful boy, or I will charm your tongue.

GEORGE   Untutor'd lad, thou art too malapert.

PRINCE   I know my duty; you are all undutiful:

   Lascivious Edward, and thou perjur'd George,

   And thou misshapen Dick, I tell ye all 35

   I am your better, traitors as ye are,

   And thou usurp'st my father's right and mine.

KING EDWARD

   Take that, the likeness of this railer here. [*Stabs him.*]

RICHARD   Sprawl'st thou? Take that to end thy agony.

   [*Stabs him.*]

GEORGE   And there's for twitting me with perjury. 40

   [*Stabs him.*]

QUEEN MARGARET   O, kill me too!

RICHARD   Marry, and shall.

   [*Offers to kill her.*]

KING EDWARD

   Hold, Richard, hold; for we have done too much.

RICHARD

   Why should she live to fill the world with words?

KING EDWARD

   What, doth she swoon? Use means for her recovery.

RICHARD   Clarence, excuse me to the King my brother: 45

   I'll hence to London on a serious matter:

   Ere ye come there, be sure to hear some news.

GEORGE   What? what?

RICHARD   The Tower! the Tower! I'll root them out.

   Exit.

QUEEN MARGARET

   O Ned, sweet Ned, speak to thy mother, boy!

   Canst thou not speak? O traitors! murderers! 50

   They that stabb'd Caesar shed no blood at all,

   Did not offend, nor were not worthy blame,

   If this foul deed were by to equal it.

   He was a man; this, in respect, a child;

   And men ne'er spend their fury on a child. 55

   What's worse than murderer, that I may name it?

   No, no, my heart will burst and if I speak;

   And I will speak, that so my heart may burst.

   Butchers and villains! bloody cannibals!

   How sweet a plant have you untimely cropp'd! 60

   You have no children, butchers; if you had,

   The thought of them would have stirr'd up remorse:

   But if you ever chance to have a child,

   Look in his youth to have him so cut off

   As, deathsmen, you have rid this sweet young prince! 65

KING EDWARD

   Away with her; go bear her hence perforce.

QUEEN MARGARET

   Nay, never bear me hence; dispatch me here:

   Here sheath thy sword; I'll pardon thee my death.

   What, wilt thou not? Then, Clarence, do it thou.

GEORGE   By heaven, I will not do thee so much ease. 70

QUEEN MARGARET

   Good Clarence, do; sweet Clarence, do thou do it.

GEORGE

   Didst thou not hear me swear I would not do it?

QUEEN MARGARET

   Ay, but thou usest to forswear thyself.

   'Twas sin before, but now 'tis charity.

   What! wilt thou not? Where is that devil's butcher? 75

   Richard, hard-favour'd Richard, where art thou,

   Thou art not here: murder is thy alms-deed;

   Petitioners for blood thou ne'er put'st back.

KING EDWARD   Away, I say; I charge ye bear her hence.

QUEEN MARGARET

   So come to you and yours as to this prince! 80

   Exit, led out forcibly.

KING EDWARD   Where's Richard gone?

GEORGE   To London all in post, and, as I guess,

   To make a bloody supper in the Tower.

KING EDWARD   He's sudden if a thing come in his head.

   Now march we hence: discharge the common sort 85

   With pay and thanks, and let's away to London

   And see our gentle Queen how well she fares:

   By this, I hope, she hath a son for me.   *Exeunt.*

5.6   *Enter* KING HENRY *and* RICHARD, *with the*
       lieutenant, on the walls.

RICHARD

   Good day, my lord. What, at your book so hard?

KING HENRY

   Ay, my good lord – my lord, I should say rather.

   'Tis sin to flatter; 'good' was little better:

   'Good Gloucester' and 'good devil' were alike,

   And both preposterous; therefore not 'good lord'. 5

RICHARD

   Sirrah, leave us to ourselves; we must confer.

   Exit lieutenant.

KING HENRY

   So flies the reckless shepherd from the wolf;

   So first the harmless sheep doth yield his fleece,

   And next his throat unto the butcher's knife.

   What scene of death hath Roscius now to act? 10

RICHARD   Suspicion always haunts the guilty mind;

   The thief doth fear each bush an officer.

KING HENRY   The bird that hath been limed in a bush

   With trembling wings misdoubteth every bush;

   And I, the hapless male to one sweet bird, 15

   Have now the fatal object in my eye

   Where my poor young was lim'd, was caught, and

      kill'd.

RICHARD   Why, what a peevish fool was that of Crete,
    That taught his son the office of a fowl!
20   And yet, for all his wings, the fool was drown'd.
KING HENRY   I, Daedalus; my poor boy, Icarus;
    Thy father, Minos, that denied our course;
    The sun that sear'd the wings of my sweet boy,
    Thy brother Edward; and thyself, the sea
25   Whose envious gulf did swallow up his life.
    Ah, kill me with thy weapon, not with words!
    My breast can better brook thy dagger's point
    Than can my ears that tragic history.
    But wherefore dost thou come? Is't for my life?
30 RICHARD   Think'st thou I am an executioner?
KING HENRY   A persecutor I am sure thou art:
    If murdering innocents be executing,
    Why then thou art an executioner.
RICHARD   Thy son I kill'd for his presumption.
KING HENRY
    Hadst thou been kill'd when first thou didst
35   presume,
    Thou hadst not liv'd to kill a son of mine.
    And thus I prophesy: that many a thousand
    Which now mistrust no parcel of my fear,
    And many an old man's sigh, and many a widow's,
40   And many an orphan's water-standing eye –
    Men for their sons', wives for their husbands',
    Orphans for their parents' timeless death –
    Shall rue the hour that ever thou wast born.
    The owl shriek'd at thy birth – an evil sign;
45   The night-crow cried, aboding luckless time;
    Dogs howl'd, and hideous tempests shook down
      trees;
    The raven rook'd her on the chimney's top,
    And chattering pies in dismal discords sung;
    Thy mother felt more than a mother's pain,
50   And yet brought forth less than a mother's hope,
    To wit, an indigest deformed lump,
    Not like the fruit of such a goodly tree.
    Teeth hadst thou in thy head when thou wast born,
    To signify thou cam'st to bite the world;
55   And if the rest be true which I have heard,
    Thou cam'st –
RICHARD   I'll hear no more: die, prophet, in thy speech.
    [*Stabs him.*]
    For this, amongst the rest, was I ordain'd.
KING HENRY   Ay, and for much more slaughter after this.
60   O God, forgive my sins and pardon thee! [*Dies.*]
RICHARD   What, will the aspiring blood of Lancaster
    Sink in the ground? I thought it would have
      mounted.
    See how my sword weeps for the poor King's death.
    O, may such purple tears be alway shed
65   From those that wish the downfall of our house!
    If any spark of life be yet remaining,
    Down, down to hell; and say I sent thee thither –
    [*Stabs him again.*]
    I that have neither pity, love, nor fear.

    Indeed 'tis true that Henry told me of:
    For I have often heard my mother say   70
    I came into the world with my legs forward.
    Had I not reason, think ye, to make haste
    And seek their ruin that usurp'd our right?
    The midwife wonder'd, and the women cried
    'O Jesu bless us, he is born with teeth!'   75
    And so I was, which plainly signified
    That I should snarl, and bite, and play the dog.
    Then, since the heavens have shap'd my body so,
    Let hell make crook'd my mind to answer it.
    I have no brother, I am like no brother;   80
    And this word 'love', which greybeards call divine,
    Be resident in men like one another,
    And not in me: I am myself alone.
    Clarence, beware; thou keep'st me from the light,
    But I will sort a pitchy day for thee;   85
    For I will buzz abroad such prophecies
    As Edward shall be fearful of his life;
    And then, to purge his fear, I'll be thy death.
    King Henry and the Prince his son are gone;
    Clarence, thy turn is next, and then the rest,   90
    Counting myself but bad till I be best.
    I'll throw thy body in another room,
    And triumph, Henry, in thy day of doom.
                  Exit, with the body.

5.7 *Flourish. Enter* KING EDWARD, QUEEN ELIZABETH,
    GEORGE, RICHARD, HASTINGS, *a nurse with the*
        young Prince and attendants.

KING EDWARD
    Once more we sit in England's royal throne,
    Repurchas'd with the blood of enemies.
    What valiant foemen, like to autumn's corn,
    Have we mow'd down in tops of all their pride!
    Three Dukes of Somerset, threefold renown'd   5
    For hardy and undoubted champions;
    Two Cliffords, as the father and the son;
    And two Northumberlands – two braver men
    Ne'er spurr'd their coursers at the trumpet's sound;
    With them, the two brave bears, Warwick and
      Montague,   10
    That in their chains fetter'd the kingly lion
    And made the forest tremble when they roar'd.
    Thus have we swept suspicion from our seat
    And made our footstool of security.
    Come hither, Bess, and let me kiss my boy.   15
    Young Ned, for thee thine uncles and myself
    Have in our armours watch'd the winter's night,
    Went all afoot in summer's scalding heat,
    That thou might'st repossess the crown in peace;
    And of our labours thou shalt reap the gain.   20
RICHARD [*aside*]
    I'll blast his harvest, and your head were laid;
    For yet I am not look'd on in the world.
    This shoulder was ordain'd so thick to heave,

25 And heave it shall some weight, or break my back:
Work thou the way, and that shall execute.

KING EDWARD
Clarence and Gloucester, love my lovely Queen;
And kiss your princely nephew, brothers both.

GEORGE   The duty that I owe unto your Majesty
I seal upon the lips of this sweet babe.

QUEEN ELIZABETH
30 Thanks, noble Clarence; worthy brother, thanks.

RICHARD
And, that I love the tree from whence thou sprang'st,
Witness the loving kiss I give the fruit.
[*aside*] To say the truth, so Judas kiss'd his master
And cried 'All hail!' when as he meant all harm.

KING EDWARD   Now am I seated as my soul delights,   35
Having my country's peace and brothers' loves.

GEORGE
What will your Grace have done with Margaret?
Reignier, her father, to the King of France
Hath pawn'd the Sicils and Jerusalem,
And hither have they sent it for her ransom.   40

KING EDWARD
Away with her and waft her hence to France.
And now what rests but that we spend the time
With stately triumphs, mirthful comic shows,
Such as befits the pleasure of the court?
Sound drums and trumpets! Farewell, sour annoy!   45
For here, I hope, begins our lasting joy.   *Exeunt.*

King Henry VIII

King Henry VIII, also known as *All is True*, can be dated with unusual precision because it was being performed at the Globe on 29 June 1613 when the firing of cannon set light to the thatched roof and the theatre was burnt to the ground – fortunately without loss of life or injury. Several contemporary accounts of the fire refer to *King Henry VIII* as a new play at the time, so scholars agree in dating it 1613, though some would put it back to the beginning of that year, arguing that it would have been appropriate for performance at Court during the wedding celebrations of James I's daughter Elizabeth and Frederick, the Elector Palatine. Shakespeare's company, the King's Men, did perform six of his plays as contributions to the festivities but there is no definite proof that *King Henry VIII* was one of them.

It was printed as the last of Shakespeare's English history plays in the First Folio in 1623, and its historical material derives in part from the chronicles of Raphael Holinshed and Edward Hall – sources Shakespeare had used for his earlier histories – but it was composed some fourteen years after *Henry V*, the latest in the sequence of nine history plays Shakespeare had written between 1590 and 1599, and in some ways it is a different kind of play, having as many affinities with the late tragicomedies or 'romances' such as *The Winter's Tale* and *The Tempest* as it has with the histories. It comes no nearer to a battlefield than a description of the ceremonial 'Field of the Cloth of Gold', where Henry VIII met Francis I to inaugurate a peace treaty between England and France; and it presents its main political events, which provide an implicit history of the Reformation, as a series of setpieces on the fall from greatness of some characters (the Duke of Buckingham, Katherine of Aragon, Cardinal Wolsey) and the rise of others (Anne Boleyn, Thomas Cranmer). It lacks conspiracy, political intrigue, revenge and even violent death – all standard ingredients of the earlier histories – and it ends with a celebration of the birth of the future Elizabeth I and a tribute to her supposedly even more glorious successor, James I. It imbues its historical events with a degree of myth or symbolism and manages to present Henry as a benign and rather detached monarch (not unlike Prospero), despite some darker hints.

Most editors and scholars believe that this play, like *Cardenio* (now lost) and *The Two Noble Kinsmen*, was a collaboration between Shakespeare and John Fletcher. All three plays date from the period 1612-13 when Shakespeare was scaling down his level of participation in the King's Men's activities; Fletcher succeeded him as the chief dramatist of the company, and seems to have preferred to work collaboratively, writing plays with Francis Beaumont and Philip Massinger as well as with Shakespeare. The scenes in the play generally attributed to Shakespeare are 1.1, 1.2, 2.3, 2.4, 3.2 to line 203 and 5.1. A minority of scholars, including the editor of the 1957 Arden edition of *King Henry VIII*, would give him a larger share or sole authorship.

The play was revived during the Restoration and remained popular in the eighteenth and nineteenth centuries, partly because of the opportunities it afforded for lavish spectacle and pageantry; it tends to be performed at times of coronation. The roles of Wolsey and Katherine came to dominate productions and were performed by leading actors from John Philip Kemble and his sister Sarah Siddons in 1806 to Henry Irving and Ellen Terry in 1892; much of the play used to be cut in order to focus attention on these roles. Twentieth-century productions have restored Henry to a central position and have aimed for a more thoughtful and serious reading of the play, finding ironies and contradictions in it as well as theatrical display.

The Arden text is based on the 1623 First Folio.

KING Henry VIII
Cardinal WOLSEY
Cardinal CAMPEIUS
CRANMER   *Archbishop of Canterbury*
GARDINER   *Bishop of Winchester*
Bishop of LINCOLN
Duke of BUCKINGHAM
Duke of NORFOLK
Duke of SUFFOLK
Duke of SURREY
Lord ABERGAVENNY
Lord SANDS (Sir Walter Sands)
Lord CHANCELLOR
Lord CHAMBERLAIN
Sir Henry GUILFORD
Sir Thomas LOVELL
Sir Nicholas VAUX
Sir Anthony DENNY
BRANDON
CROMWELL   *Wolsey's servant*
DOCTOR BUTTS
GRIFFITH   *Gentleman-Usher to Queen Katherine*
CAPUCHIUS   *Ambassador from Emperor Charles V*
THREE GENTLEMEN
GARTER King-at-Arms
SERGEANT-at-Arms
PORTER *and his* MAN
Door-KEEPER   *of the Council Chamber*
SECRETARY   *to Wolsey*
BOY   *page to Gardiner*
CRIER, MESSENGER, *and* SERVANT

Queen KATHERINE   *King Henry's wife, afterwards divorced*
ANNE Bullen   *her Maid of Honour, afterwards Queen*
OLD LADY   *Anne Bullen's friend*
PATIENCE   *Queen Katherine's woman*

Lords, Ladies, Bishops, Judges, Gentlemen and Priests;
Lord Mayor of London and Aldermen; Vergers, Scribes, Guards, Attendants,
Servants and Common People; Women attending upon Queen Katherine; Spirits

King Henry VIII

PROLOGUE

I come no more to make you laugh; things now
That bear a weighty and a serious brow,
Sad, high, and working, full of state and woe;
Such noble scenes as draw the eye to flow
We now present. Those that can pity, here
May (if they think it well) let fall a tear,
The subject will deserve it. Such as give
Their money out of hope they may believe,
May here find truth too. Those that come to see
Only a show or two, and so agree
The play may pass, if they be still and willing,
I'll undertake may see away their shilling.
Richly in two short hours. Only they
That come to hear a merry bawdy play,
A noise of targets, or to see a fellow
In a long motley coat guarded with yellow,
Will be deceiv'd: for gentle hearers, know
To rank our chosen truth with such a show
As fool and fight is, beside forfeiting
Our own brains and the opinion that we bring
To make that only true we now intend,
Will leave us never an understanding friend.
Therefore, for goodness' sake, and as you are known
The first and happiest hearers of the town,
Be sad, as we would make ye. Think ye see
The very persons of our noble story
As they were living: think you see them great,
And follow'd with the general throng, and sweat
Of thousand friends; then, in a moment, see
How soon this mightiness meets misery:
And if you can be merry then, I'll say
A man may weep upon his wedding day.

1.1 *Enter the* DUKE OF NORFOLK *at one door.*
At the other the DUKE OF BUCKINGHAM
and the LORD ABERGAVENNY.

BUCKINGHAM
Good morrow, and well met. How have ye done
Since last we saw in France?

NORFOLK   I thank your grace,
Healthful, and ever since a fresh admirer
Of what I saw there.

BUCKINGHAM   An untimely ague
Stayed me a prisoner in my chamber, when
Those suns of glory, those two lights of men
Met in the vale of Andren.

NORFOLK   'Twixt Guynes and Arde,
I was then present, saw them salute on horseback,
Beheld them when they lighted, how they clung
In their embracement as they grew together,
Which had they, what four thron'd ones could have
    weigh'd
Such a compounded one?

BUCKINGHAM   All the whole time
I was my chamber's prisoner.

NORFOLK   Then you lost
The view of earthly glory: men might say
Till this time pomp was single, but now married   15
To one above itself. Each following day
Became the next day's master, till the last
Made former wonders, its. To-day the French,
All clinquant all in gold, like heathen gods
Shone down the English; and to-morrow they   20
Made Britain India: every man that stood
Show'd like a mine. Their dwarfish pages were
As cherubins, all gilt: the madams too,
Not us'd to toil, did almost sweat to bear
The pride upon them, that their very labour   25
Was to them as a painting. Now this masque
Was cried incomparable; and th'ensuing night
Made it a fool and beggar. The two kings
Equal in lustre, were now best, now worst,
As presence did present them: him in eye   30
Still him in praise, and being present both,
'Twas said they saw but one, and no discerner
Durst wag his tongue in censure. When these suns
(For so they phrase 'em) by their heralds challeng'd
The noble spirits to arms, they did perform   35
Beyond thought's compass, that former fabulous
    story
Being now seen possible enough, got credit
That Bevis was believ'd.

BUCKINGHAM   O you go far.

NORFOLK   As I belong to worship, and affect
In honour honesty, the tract of ev'ry thing   40
Would by a good discourser lose some life
Which action's self was tongue to. All was royal;
To the disposing of it nought rebell'd,
Order gave each thing view: the office did
Distinctly his full function.

BUCKINGHAM   Who did guide,   45
I mean who set the body and the limbs
Of this great sport together, as you guess?

NORFOLK   One certes, that promises no element
In such a business.

BUCKINGHAM   I pray you who, my lord?

NORFOLK   All this was order'd by the good discretion   50
Of the right reverend Cardinal of York.

BUCKINGHAM
The devil speed him: no man's pie is freed
From his ambitious finger. What had he
To do in these fierce vanities? I wonder
That such a keech can with his very bulk   55
Take up the rays o'th' beneficial sun,
And keep it from the earth.

NORFOLK   Surely sir,
There's in him stuff that puts him to these ends;
For being not propp'd by ancestry, whose grace
Chalks successors their way, nor call'd upon   60
For high feats done to th' crown, neither allied
To eminent assistants, but spider-like,
Out of his self-drawing web, O, gives us note,

The force of his own merit makes his way,
65   A gift that heaven gives for him, which buys
A place next to the king.

ABERGAVENNY   I cannot tell
What heaven hath given him: let some graver eye
Pierce into that, but I can see his pride
70   Peep through each part of him: whence has he that?
If not from hell the devil is a niggard,
Or has given all before, and he begins
A new hell in himself.

BUCKINGHAM   Why the devil,
Upon this French going-out, took he upon him
(Without the privity o'th' king) t'appoint
75   Who should attend on him? He makes up the file
Of all the gentry; for the most part such
To whom as great a charge, as little honour
He meant to lay upon: and his own letter,
The honourable board of council, out
Must fetch him in he papers.

80 ABERGAVENNY   I do know
Kinsmen of mine, three at the least, that have
By this so sicken'd their estates that never
They shall abound as formerly.

BUCKINGHAM   O many
Have broke their backs with laying manors on 'em
85   For this great journey. What did this vanity
But minister communication of
A most poor issue?

NORFOLK   Grievingly I think,
The peace between the French and us not values
The cost that did conclude it.

BUCKINGHAM   Every man,
90   After the hideous storm that follow'd, was
A thing inspir'd, and, not consulting, broke
Into a general prophecy; that this tempest
Dashing the garment of this peace, aboded
The sudden breach on't.

NORFOLK   Which is budded out,
95   For France hath flaw'd the league, and hath attach'd
Our merchants' goods at Bordeaux.

ABERGAVENNY   Is it therefore
Th'ambassador is silenc'd?

NORFOLK   Marry is't.

ABERGAVENNY   A proper title of a peace, and purchas'd
At a superfluous rate.

BUCKINGHAM   Why, all this business
Our reverend Cardinal carried.

100 NORFOLK   Like it your grace,
The state takes notice of the private difference
Betwixt you and the Cardinal. I advise you
(And take it from a heart that wishes towards you
Honour and plenteous safety) that you read
105   The Cardinal's malice and his potency
Together; to consider further that,
What his high hatred would effect wants not
A minister in his power. You know his nature,
That he's revengeful, and I know his sword

Hath a sharp edge: it's long, and't may be said   110
It reaches far, and where 'twill not extend,
Thither he darts it. Bosom up my counsel,
You'll find it wholesome. Loe, where comes that rock
That I advise your shunning.

Enter Cardinal WOLSEY, *the purse borne before him,*
certain of the guard, and two secretaries with papers:
the Cardinal in his passage fixeth his eye on Buckingham,
and Buckingham on him, both full of disdain.

WOLSEY   The Duke of Buckingham's surveyor, ha?   115
Where's his examination?

1 SECRETARY   Here so please you.

WOLSEY   Is he in person ready?

1 SECRETARY   Ay, please your grace.

WOLSEY
Well, we shall then know more, and Buckingham
Shall lessen this big look.

            Exeunt Cardinal and his train.

BUCKINGHAM
This butcher's cur is venom-mouth'd, and I   120
Have not the power to muzzle him, therefore best
Not wake him in his slumber. A beggar's book
Outworths a noble's blood.

NORFOLK   What, are you chaf'd?
Ask God for temp'rance, that's th'appliance only
Which your disease requires.

BUCKINGHAM   I read in's looks   125
Matter against me, and his eye revil'd
Me as his abject object; at this instant
He bores me with some trick; he's gone to th' king:
I'll follow and out-stare him.

NORFOLK   Stay my lord,
And let your reason with your choler question   130
What 'tis you go about: to climb steep hills
Requires slow pace at first. Anger is like
A full hot horse, who being allow'd his way,
Self-mettle tires him: not a man in England
Can advise me like you; be to yourself   135
As you would to your friend.

BUCKINGHAM   I'll to the king,
And from a mouth of honour quite cry down
This Ipswich fellow's insolence; or proclaim
There's difference in no persons.

NORFOLK   Be advis'd;
Heat not a furnace for your foe so hot   140
That it do singe yourself. We may outrun
By violent swiftness that which we run at,
And lose by over-running: know you not
The fire that mounts the liquor till't run o'er
In seeming to augment it wastes it? be advis'd;   145
I say again there is no English soul
More stronger to direct you than yourself,
If with the sap of reason you would quench,
Or but allay the fire of passion.

BUCKINGHAM   Sir,
I am thankful to you, and I'll go along   150

By your prescription: but this top-proud fellow
(Whom from the flow of gall I name not, but
From sincere motions) by intelligence
And proofs as clear as founts in July when
155   We see each grain of gravel, I do know
To be corrupt and treasonous.
NORFOLK   Say not treasonous.
BUCKINGHAM
To th'king I'll say't, and make my vouch as strong
As shore of rock: attend. This holy fox,
Or wolf, or both (for he is equal rav'nous
160   As he is subtle, and as prone to mischief
As able to perform't), his mind and place
Infecting one another, yea reciprocally,
Only to show his pomp as well in France
As here at home, suggests the king our master
165   To this last costly treaty; th'interview
That swallowed so much treasure, and like a glass
Did break i'th' wrenching.
NORFOLK   Faith, and so it did.
BUCKINGHAM
Pray give me favour sir: this cunning cardinal
The articles o'th' combination drew
170   As himself pleas'd; and they were ratified
As he cried 'Thus let be', to as much end
As give a crutch to th' dead. But our court-cardinal
Has done this, and 'tis well; for worthy Wolsey
(Who cannot err) he did it. Now this follows
175   (Which as I take it, is a kind of puppy
To th' old dam treason), Charles the Emperor,
Under pretence to see the queen his aunt
(For 'twas indeed his colour, but he came
To whisper Wolsey), here makes visitation;
180   His fears were that the interview betwixt
England and France might through their amity
Breed him some prejudice, for from this league
Peep'd harms that menac'd him: privily
Deals with our cardinal, and as I trow
185   (Which I do well; for I am sure the emperor
Paid ere he promis'd, whereby his suit was granted
Ere it was ask'd) but when the way was made
And pav'd with gold, the emperor thus desir'd,
That he would please to alter the king's course
190   And break the foresaid peace. Let the king know
(As soon he shall by me) that thus the cardinal
Does buy and sell his honour as he pleases,
And for his own advantage.
NORFOLK   I am sorry
To hear this of him, and could wish he were
Something mistaken in't.
195   BUCKINGHAM   No, not a syllable:
I do pronounce him in that very shape
He shall appear in proof.

Enter BRANDON, *a* Sergeant-at-Arms *before him,
and two or three of the guard.*

BRANDON   Your office Sergeant; execute it.
SERGEANT   Sir,

My lord the Duke of Buckingham, and Earl
Of Hereford, Stafford and Northampton, I   200
Arrest thee of high treason, in the name
Of our most sovereign king.
BUCKINGHAM   Loe you, my lord,
The net has fall'n upon me; I shall perish
Under device and practice.
BRANDON   I am sorry
To see you ta'en from liberty, to look on   205
The business present. 'Tis his highness' pleasure
You shall to th' Tower.
BUCKINGHAM   It will help me nothing
To plead mine innocence, for that dye is on me
Which makes my whit'st part black. The will of
heav'n
Be done in this and all things: I obey.   210
O my lord Aberga'nny, fare you well.
BRANDON   Nay, he must bear you company.
[*To Abergavenny*]   The king
Is pleas'd you shall to th'Tower, till you know
How he determines further.
ABERGAVENNY   As the duke said,
The will of Heaven be done, and the king's pleasure   215
By me obey'd.
BRANDON   Here is a warrant from
The king t'attach Lord Montacute, and the bodies
Of the duke's confessor, John de la Car,
One Gilbert Perk, his chancellor –
BUCKINGHAM   So, so;
These are the limbs o'th'plot: no more I hope.   220
BRANDON   A monk o'th' Chartreux.
BUCKINGHAM   O, Nicholas Hopkins?
BRANDON   He.
BUCKINGHAM
My surveyor is false: the o'er-great cardinal
Hath show'd him gold; my life is spann'd already:
I am the shadow of poor Buckingham,
Whose figure even this instant cloud puts on   225
By dark'ning my clear sun. My lord, farewell. *Exeunt.*

1.2 *Cornets. Enter* KING HENRY, *leaning on the* Cardinal's
shoulder, the nobles, and SIR THOMAS LOVELL: *the
Cardinal places himself under the King's feet on his right
side. A secretary of the Cardinal's is in attendance.*

KING   My life itself, and the best heart of it,
Thanks you for this great care: I stood i'th' level
Of a full-charg'd confederacy, and give thanks
To you that chok'd it. Let be call'd before us
That gentleman of Buckingham's; in person   5
I'll hear him his confessions justify,
And point by point the treasons of his master
He shall again relate.

*A noise within crying room for the Queen, who is usher'd by
the Duke of Norfolk. Enter the* QUEEN, NORFOLK *and*
SUFFOLK: *she kneels. King riseth from his state, takes her
up, kisses and placeth her by him.*

KATHERINE   Nay, we must longer kneel; I am a suitor.

10   KING   Arise, and take place by us; half your suit
Never name to us; you have half our power,
The other moiety ere you ask is given;
Repeat your will and take it.

KATHERINE   Thank your majesty;
That you would love yourself, and in that love
15   Not unconsider'd leave your honour nor
The dignity of your office, is the point
Of my petition.

KING   Lady mine, proceed.

KATHERINE   I am solicited not by a few,
And those of true condition, that your subjects
20   Are in great grievance: there have been commissions
Sent down among 'em, which hath flaw'd the heart
Of all their loyalties; wherein, although
My good lord cardinal they vent reproaches
Most bitterly on you, as putter on
25   Of these exactions, yet the king, our master
Whose honour heaven shield from soil, – even he
escapes not
Language unmannerly, yea, such which breaks
The sides of loyalty, and almost appears
In loud rebellion.

NORFOLK   Not almost appears,
30   It doth appear; for, upon these taxations,
The clothiers all not able to maintain
The many to them longing, have put off
The spinsters, carders, fullers, weavers, who,
Unfit for other life, compell'd by hunger
35   And lack of other means, in desperate manner
Daring th' event to th' teeth, are all in uproar,
And danger serves among them.

KING   Taxation?
Wherein? and what taxation? my lord cardinal,
You that are blam'd for it alike with us,
Know you of this taxation?

40   WOLSEY   Please you sir,
I know but of a single part in aught
Pertains to th' state, and front but in that file
Where others tell steps with me.

KATHERINE   No, my lord,
You know no more than others; but you frame
Things that are known alike, which are not
45   wholesome
To those which would not know them, and yet must
Perforce be their acquaintance. These exactions
(Whereof my sovereign would have note) they are
Most pestilent to th' hearing, and to bear 'em
50   The back is sacrifice to th' load; they say
They are devis'd by you, or else you suffer
Too hard an exclamation.

KING   Still exaction:
The nature of it, in what kind let's know,
Is this exaction.

KATHERINE   I am much too venturous
55   In tempting of your patience, but am bolden'd

Under your promis'd pardon. The subjects' grief
Comes through commissions, which compels from
each
The sixth part of his substance, to be levied
Without delay; and the pretence for this
Is nam'd your wars in France: this makes bold
mouths,   60
Tongues spit their duties out, and cold hearts freeze
Allegiance in them; their curses now
Live where their prayers did; and it's come to pass
This tractable obedience is a slave
To each incensed will. I would your highness   65
Would give it quick consideration; for
There is no primer baseness.

KING   By my life,
This is against our pleasure.

WOLSEY   And for me,
I have no further gone in this than by
A single voice, and that not pass'd me but   70
By learned approbation of the judges: if I am
Traduc'd by ignorant tongues, which neither know
My faculties nor person, yet will be
The chronicles of my doing, let me say
'Tis but the fate of place, and the rough brake   75
That virtue must go through: we must not stint
Our necessary actions in the fear
To cope malicious censurers, which ever
As rav'nous fishes, do a vessel follow
That is new trimm'd, but benefit no further   80
Than vainly longing. What we oft do best,
By sick interpreters (once weak ones) is
Not ours or not allow'd; what worst, as oft
Hitting a grosser quality, is cried up
For our best act. If we shall stand still,   85
In fear our motion will be mock'd or carp'd at,
We should take root here, where we sit;
Or sit state-statues only.

KING   Things done well
And with a care exempt themselves from fear;
Things done without example, in their issue   90
Are to be fear'd. Have you a precedent
Of this commission? I believe, not any.
We must not rend our subjects from our laws
And stick them in our will. Sixth part of each?
A trembling contribution; why, we take   95
From every tree lop, bark and part o'th' timber,
And though we leave it with a root, thus hack'd,
The air will drink the sap. To every county
Where this is question'd, send our letters, with
Free pardon to each man that has denied   .   100
The force of this commission: pray look to't;
I put it to your care.

WOLSEY [*to the secretary*]   A word with you.
Let there be letters writ to every shire,
Of the king's grace and pardon. The grieved
commons
Hardly conceive of me: let it be nois'd   105

That through our intercession this revokement
And pardon comes: I shall anon advise you
Further in the proceeding.   *Exit secretary.*

Enter Surveyor.

KATHERINE   I am sorry that the Duke of Buckingham
  Is run in your displeasure.

KING   It grieves many:
  The gentleman is learn'd, and a most rare speaker,
  To nature none more bound; his training such
  That he may furnish and instruct great teachers,
  And never seek for aid out of himself: yet see,
  When these so noble benefits shall prove
  Not well dispos'd, the mind growing once corrupt,
  They turn to vicious forms, ten times more ugly
  Than ever they were fair. This man so complete,
  Who was enroll'd 'mongst wonders (and when we,
  Almost with ravish'd list'ning, could not find
  His hour of speech a minute) he, my lady,
  Hath into monstrous habits put the graces
  That once were his, and is become as black
  As if besmear'd in hell. Sit by us, you shall hear
  (This was his gentleman in trust) of him
  Things to strike honour sad. Bid him recount
  The fore-recited practices, whereof
  We cannot feel too little, hear too much.

WOLSEY
  Stand forth, and with bold spirit relate what you
  Most like a careful subject have collected
  Out of the Duke of Buckingham.

KING   Speak freely.

SURVEYOR   First, it was usual with him, every day
  It would infect his speech, that if the king
  Should without issue die, he'll carry it so
  To make the sceptre his. These very words
  I've heard him utter to his son-in-law,
  Lord Aberga'nny, to whom by oath he menac'd
  Revenge upon the cardinal.

WOLSEY   Please your highness note
  This dangerous conception in this point,
  Not friended by his wish to your high person;
  His will is most malignant, and it stretches
  Beyond you to your friends.

KATHERINE   My learn'd lord cardinal,
  Deliver all with charity.

KING   Speak on;
  How grounded he his title to the crown
  Upon our fail? to this point hast thou heard him
  At any time speak aught?

SURVEYOR   He was brought to this
  By a vain prophecy of Nicholas Henton.

KING   What was that Henton?

SURVEYOR   Sir, a Chartreux friar,
  His confessor, who fed him every minute
  With words of sovereignty.

KING   How know'st thou this?

SURVEYOR
  Not long before your highness sped to France,
  The duke being at the Rose, within the parish
  Saint Lawrence Poultney, did of me demand
  What was the speech among the Londoners
  Concerning the French journey. I replied,
  Men fear'd the French would prove perfidious,
  To the king's danger: presently the duke
  Said 'twas the fear indeed, and that he doubted
  'Twould prove the verity of certain words
  Spoke by a holy monk, that oft, says he,
  Hath sent to me, wishing me to permit
  John de la Car, my chaplain, a choice hour
  To hear from him a matter of some moment:
  Whom after under the confession's seal
  He solemnly had sworn, that what he spoke
  My chaplain to no creature living but
  To me should utter, with demure confidence
  This pausingly ensued: neither the king nor's heirs
  (Tell you the duke) shall prosper; bid him strive
  To [win] the love o'th'commonalty; the duke
  Shall govern England.

KATHERINE   If I know you well,
  You were the duke's surveyor, and lost your office
  On the complaint o'th' tenants; take good heed
  You charge not in your spleen a noble person
  And spoil your nobler soul; I say, take heed;
  Yes, heartily beseech you.

KING   Let him on:
  Go forward.

SURVEYOR   On my soul, I'll speak but truth.
  I told my lord the duke, by th'devil's illusions
  The monk might be deceived, and that 'twas
      dangerous
  For him to ruminate on this so far until
  It forg'd him some design, which being believ'd
  It was much like to do: he answer'd 'Tush,
  It can do me no damage'; adding further,
  That had the king in his last sickness fail'd,
  The cardinal's and Sir Thomas Lovell's heads
  Should have gone off.

KING   Ha? what, so rank? Ah, ha!
  There's mischief in this man; canst thou say further?

SURVEYOR   I can my liege.

KING   Proceed.

SURVEYOR   Being at Greenwich,
  After your highness had reproved the duke
  About Sir William Bulmer –

KING
  I remember of such a time, being my sworn servant,
  The duke retain'd him his. But on; what hence?

SURVEYOR
  'If' (quoth he) 'I for this had been committed,
  As to the Tower I thought, I would have play'd
  The part my father meant to act upon
  Th'usurper Richard, who being at Sal'sbury,
  Made suit to come in his presence; which if granted,

As he made semblance of his duty, would
Have put his knife into him.'
KING　　　　　　　　　　A giant traitor.
WOLSEY
Now madam, may his highness live in freedom,
And this man out of prison?
KATHERINE　　　　　　　　God mend all.
KING　There's something more would out of thee; what
　say'st?
SURVEYOR　After 'the duke his father', with the 'knife',
He stretch'd him, and with one hand on his dagger,
Another spread on's breast, mounting his eyes
He did discharge a horrible oath, whose tenour
Was, were he evil us'd, he would outgo
His father by as much as a performance
Does an irresolute purpose.
KING　　　　　　　　　There's his period,
To sheath his knife in us: he is attach'd,
Call him to present trial; if he may
Find mercy in the law, 'tis his; if none,
Let him not seek't of us. By day and night,
He's traitor to th' height!　　　　　*Exeunt*.

1.3　　*Enter* Lord Chamberlain *and* LORD SANDS.

CHAMBERLAIN
Is't possible the spells of France should juggle
Men into such strange mysteries?
SANDS　　　　　　　　　New customs,
Though they be never so ridiculous
(Nay, let 'em be unmanly) yet are follow'd.
CHAMBERLAIN　As far as I see, all the good our English
Have got by the late voyage is but merely
A fit or two o'th' face – but they are shrewd ones,
For when they hold 'em, you would swear directly
Their very noses had been counsellors
To Pepin or Clotharius, they keep state so.
SANDS
They have all new legs, and lame ones; one would
　take it,
That never see 'em pace before, the spavin,
A springhalt reign'd among 'em.
CHAMBERLAIN　　　　　　Death my lord,
Their clothes are after such a pagan cut to't
That sure th'have worn out Christendom: how now?
What news Sir Thomas Lovell?

　　　　Enter SIR THOMAS LOVELL.

LOVELL　　　　　　　　Faith my lord,
I hear of none but the new proclamation
That's clapp'd upon the Court-gate.
CHAMBERLAIN　　　　　　What is't for?
LOVELL　The reformation of our travell'd gallants,
That fill the court with quarrels, talk and tailors.
CHAMBERLAIN
I'm glad 'tis there; now I would pray our monsieurs
To think an English courtier may be wise,
And never see the Louvre.
LOVELL　　　　　　　They must either
(For so run the conditions) leave those remnants
Of fool and feather that they got in France,
With all their honourable points of ignorance
Pertaining thereunto, as fights and fireworks,
Abusing better men than they can be
Out of a foreign wisdom, renouncing clean
The faith they have in tennis and tall stockings,
Short blister'd breeches, and those types of travel,
And understand again like honest men,
Or pack to their old playfellows; there, I take it,
They may *cum privilegio* 'oui' away
The lag end of their lewdness, and be laugh'd at.
SANDS　'Tis time to give 'em physic, their diseases
Are grown so catching.
CHAMBERLAIN　　　　　What a loss our ladies
Will have of these trim vanities!
LOVELL　　　　　　　　Ay marry,
There will be woe indeed lords; the sly whoresons
Have got a speeding trick to lay down ladies.
A French song and a fiddle has no fellow.
SANDS　The devil fiddle 'em, I am glad they are going,
For sure there's no converting of 'em: now
An honest country lord as I am, beaten
A long time out of play, may bring his plain-song,
And have an hour of hearing, and by'r lady
Held current music too.
CHAMBERLAIN　　　　Well said Lord Sands,
Your colt's tooth is not cast yet?
SANDS　　　　　　　　No my lord,
Nor shall not while I have a stump.
CHAMBERLAIN　　　　　　Sir Thomas,
Whither were you a-going?
LOVELL　　　　　　　To the cardinal's;
Your lordship is a guest too.
CHAMBERLAIN　　　　　O, 'tis true;
This night he makes a supper, and a great one,
To many lords and ladies; there will be
The beauty of this kingdom, I'll assure you.
LOVELL
That churchman bears a bounteous mind indeed,
A hand as fruitful as the land that feeds us;
His dews fall everywhere.
CHAMBERLAIN　　　　　No doubt he's noble;
He had a black mouth that said other of him.
SANDS　He may my lord; 'has wherewithal: in him
Sparing would show a worse sin than ill doctrine;
Men of his way should be most liberal,
They are set here for examples.
CHAMBERLAIN　　　　　True, they are so;
But few now give so great ones. My barge stays;
Your lordship shall along: come, good Sir Thomas,
We shall be late else, which I would not be
For I was spoke to, with Sir Henry Guilford,
This night to be comptrollers.
SANDS　　　　　　　I am your lordship's.
　　　　　　　　　　　　Exeunt.

1.4 *Hautboys. A small table under a state for the Cardinal, a longer table for the guests. Then enter* ANNE BULLEN, *and divers other ladies and gentlemen, as guests at one door; at another door enter* SIR HENRY GUILFORD.

GUILFORD   Ladies, a general welcome from his grace
Salutes ye all; this night he dedicates
To fair content, and you: none here he hopes,
In all this noble bevy, has brought with her
One care abroad: he would have all as merry   5
As first, good company, good wine, good welcome
Can make good people.

Enter Lord Chamberlain, LORD SANDS *and* LOVELL.

                              O my lord, y'are tardy;
The very thought of this fair company
Clapp'd wings to me.
CHAMBERLAIN   You are young, Sir Harry Guilford.   10
SANDS   Sir Thomas Lovell, had the cardinal
But half my lay-thoughts in him, some of these
Should find a running banquet ere they rested,
I think would better please 'em: by my life,
They are a sweet society of fair ones.   15
LOVELL   O that your lordship were but now confessor
To one or two of these.
SANDS   I would I were,
They should find easy penance.
LOVELL   Faith, how easy?
SANDS   As easy as a down-bed would afford it.
CHAMBERLAIN
Sweet ladies, will it please you sit? Sir Harry
Place you that side, I'll take the charge of this: 20
His grace is ent'ring. Nay, you must not freeze,
Two women plac'd together makes cold weather:
My Lord Sands, you are one will keep 'em waking;
Pray sit between these ladies.
SANDS   By my faith,
And thank your lordship: by your leave sweet ladies,   25
If I chance to talk a little wild, forgive me;
I had it from my father.
ANNE   Was he mad sir?
SANDS   O very mad, exceeding mad, in love too;
But he would bite none; just as I do now,
He would kiss you twenty with a breath.
CHAMBERLAIN   Well said my lord.   30
So now y'are fairly seated: gentlemen,
The penance lies on you if these fair ladies
Pass away frowning.
SANDS   For my little cure
Let me alone.

Hautboys. Enter Cardinal WOLSEY *and takes his state.*

WOLSEY   Y'are welcome my fair guests; that noble lady   35
Or gentleman that is not freely merry
Is not my friend. This to confirm my welcome,
And to you all, good health. [*Drinks.*]
SANDS   Your grace is noble;

Let me have such a bowl may hold my thanks,
And save me so much talking.
WOLSEY   My Lord Sands,   40
I am beholding to you: cheer your neighbours:
Ladies, you are not merry; gentlemen,
Whose fault is this?
SANDS   The red wine first must rise
In their fair cheeks my lord, then we shall have 'em
Talk us to silence.
ANNE   You are a merry gamester   45
My Lord Sands.
SANDS   Yes, if I make my play:
Here's to your ladyship, and pledge it madam,
For 'tis to such a thing –
ANNE   You cannot show me.
              [*Drum and trumpet; chambers discharg'd.*]
SANDS   I told your grace they would talk anon.
WOLSEY   What's that?
CHAMBERLAIN   Look out there, some of ye.
                              Exit a servant.
WOLSEY   What warlike voice,   50
And to what end is this? Nay ladies, fear not;
By all the laws of war y'are privileg'd.

              Re-enter a Servant.

CHAMBERLAIN   How now, what is't?
SERVANT   A noble troop of strangers,
For so they seem; th'have left their barge and landed,
And hither make, as great ambassadors   55
From foreign princes.
WOLSEY   Good lord chamberlain,
Go, give 'em welcome; you can speak the French
    tongue;
And pray receive 'em nobly and conduct 'em
Into our presence, where this heaven of beauty
Shall shine at full upon them. Some attend him.   60
              Exit Chamberlain attended.
[*All rise, and tables remov'd.*]
You have now a broken banquet, but we'll mend it.
A good digestion to you all; and once more
I shower a welcome on ye: welcome all.

Hautboys. Enter KING *and others as masquers, habited like shepherds, usher'd by the* Lord Chamberlain. *They pass directly before the Cardinal, and gracefully salute him.*

A noble company: what are their pleasures?
CHAMBERLAIN
Because they speak no English, thus they pray'd   65
To tell your grace: that having heard by fame
Of this so noble and so fair assembly
This night to meet here, they could do no less
(Out of the great respect they bear to beauty)
But leave their flocks, and under your fair conduct   70
Crave leave to view these ladies, and entreat
An hour of revels with 'em.
WOLSEY   Say, Lord Chamberlain,

They have done my poor house grace; for which I
    pay 'em
    A thousand thanks and pray 'em take their pleasures.
    [*Choose ladies; King and Anne Bullen.*]

75   KING   The fairest hand I ever touch'd: O beauty,
    Till now I never knew thee.   [*Music; dance.*]
  WOLSEY   My lord.
  CHAMBERLAIN   Your grace?
  WOLSEY   Pray tell 'em thus much from me:
    There should be one amongst 'em, by his person,
    More worthy this place than myself; to whom
80   (If I but knew him) with my love and duty
    I would surrender it.
  CHAMBERLAIN   I will, my lord. [*whisper*]
  WOLSEY   What say they?
  CHAMBERLAIN   Such a one they all confess
    There is indeed, which they would have your grace
    Find out, and he will take it.
  WOLSEY   Let me see then,
85   By all your good leaves, gentlemen; here I'll make
    My royal choice.
  KING [*unmasking*]   Ye have found him Cardinal;
    You hold a fair assembly; you do well lord:
    You are a churchman, or I'll tell you cardinal,
    I should judge now unhappily.
  WOLSEY   I am glad
    Your grace is grown so pleasant.
90   KING   My Lord Chamberlain,
    Prithee come hither; what fair lady's that?
  CHAMBERLAIN
    An't please your grace, Sir Thomas Bullen's
      daughter,
    The Viscount Rochford, one of her highness'
      women.
  KING   By heaven she is a dainty one. Sweet heart,
95   I were unmannerly to take you out
    And not to kiss you. A health gentlemen,
    Let it go round.
  WOLSEY   Sir Thomas Lovell, is the banquet ready
    I'th'privy chamber?
  LOVELL   Yes my lord.
  WOLSEY   Your grace,
100   I fear, with dancing is a little heated.
  KING   I fear too much.
  WOLSEY   There's fresher air, my lord,
    In the next chamber.
  KING   Lead in your ladies ev'ry one: sweet partner,
    I must not yet forsake you. Let's be merry,
105   Good my lord cardinal: I have half a dozen healths
    To drink to these fair ladies, and a measure
    To lead 'em once again, and then let's dream
    Who's best in favour. Let the music knock it.
                      Exeunt with trumpets.

2.1   *Enter two gentlemen at several doors.*

1 GENTLEMAN   Whither away so fast?

2 GENTLEMAN   O, God save ye:
  Ev'n to the hall, to hear what shall become
  Of the great Duke of Buckingham.
1 GENTLEMAN   I'll save you
  That labour sir. All's now done but the ceremony
  Of bringing back the prisoner.
2 GENTLEMAN   Were you there?   5
1 GENTLEMAN   Yes indeed was I.
2 GENTLEMAN   Pray speak what has happen'd.
1 GENTLEMAN   You may guess quickly what.
2 GENTLEMAN   Is he found guilty?
1 GENTLEMAN   Yes truly is he, and condemn'd upon't.
2 GENTLEMAN   I am sorry for't.
1 GENTLEMAN   So are a number more.
2 GENTLEMAN   But pray, how pass'd it?   10
1 GENTLEMAN   I'll tell you in a little. The great duke
  Came to the bar; where to his accusations
  He pleaded still not guilty, and alleg'd
  Many sharp reasons to defeat the law.
  The king's attorney on the contrary   15
  Urg'd on the examinations, proofs, confessions
  Of divers witnesses, which the duke desir'd
  To have brought *viva voce* to his face;
  At which appear'd against him his surveyor,
  Sir Gilbert Perk his chancellor, and John Car,   20
  Confessor to him, with that devil monk,
  Hopkins, that made this mischief.
2 GENTLEMAN   That was he
  That fed him with his prophecies.
1 GENTLEMAN   The same;
  All these accus'd him strongly, which he fain
  Would have flung from him; but indeed he could not,   25
  And so his peers upon this evidence
  Have found him guilty of high treason. Much
  He spoke, and learnedly for life; but all
  Was either pitied in him or forgotten.
2 GENTLEMAN   After all this, how did he bear himself?   30
1 GENTLEMAN
  When he was brought again to th' bar, to hear
  His knell rung out, his judgment, he was stirr'd
  With such an agony, he sweat extremely,
  And something spoke in choler, ill and hasty:
  But he fell to himself again, and sweetly   35
  In all the rest show'd a most noble patience.
2 GENTLEMAN   I do not think he fears death.
1 GENTLEMAN   Sure he does not,
  He never was so womanish; the cause
  He may a little grieve at.
2 GENTLEMAN   Certainly
  The cardinal is the end of this.
1 GENTLEMAN   'Tis likely   40
  By all conjectures: first Kildare's attendure,
  Then deputy of Ireland, who remov'd,
  Earl Surrey was sent thither, and in haste too,
  Lest he should help his father.
2 GENTLEMAN   That trick of state
  Was a deep envious one.

1 GENTLEMAN   At his return
  No doubt he will requite it; this is noted
  (And generally) whoever the king favours,
  The card'nal instantly will find employment,
  And far enough from court too.

2 GENTLEMAN   All the commons
  Hate him perniciously, and o'my conscience
  Wish him ten faddom deep: this duke as much
  They love and dote on; call him bounteous
    Buckingham,
  The mirror of all courtesy –

Enter BUCKINGHAM *from his arraignment, tipstaves before*
him, the axe with the edge towards him, halberds on each
side, accompanied with SIR THOMAS LOVELL,
SIR NICHOLAS VAUX, SIR WALTER SANDS,
and common people, etc.

1 GENTLEMAN   Stay there sir,
  And see the noble ruin'd man you speak of.

2 GENTLEMAN
  Let's stand close and behold him.

BUCKINGHAM   All good people,
  You that thus far have come to pity me,
  Hear what I say, and then go home and lose me.
  I have this day receiv'd a traitor's judgment,
  And by that name must die; yet heaven bear witness,
  And if I have a conscience, let it sink me,
  Even as the axe falls, if I be not faithful.
  The law I bear no malice for my death,
  'T has done upon the premises but justice:
  But those that sought it I could wish more
    Christians:
  Be what they will, I heartily forgive 'em;
  Yet let 'em look they glory not in mischief,
  Nor build their evils on the graves of great men,
  For then my guiltless blood must cry against 'em.
  For further life in this world I ne'er hope,
  Nor will I sue, although the king have mercies
  More than I dare make faults. You few that lov'd me,
  And dare be bold to weep for Buckingham,
  His noble friends and fellows, whom to leave
  Is only bitter to him, only dying;
  Go with me like good angels to my end,
  And as the long divorce of steel falls on me,
  Make of your prayers one sweet sacrifice
  And lift my soul to heaven. Lead on a' God's name.

LOVELL   I do beseech your grace, for charity,
  If ever any malice in your heart
  Were hid against me, now to forgive me frankly.

BUCKINGHAM   Sir Thomas Lovell, I as free forgive you
  As I would be forgiven: I forgive all.
  There cannot be those numberless offences
  'Gainst me that I cannot take peace with: no black
    envy
  Shall make my grave. Commend me to his grace,
  And if he speaks of Buckingham, pray tell him
  You met him half in heaven: my vows and prayers

  Yet are the king's, and till my soul forsake
  Shall cry for blessings on him. May he live   90
  Longer than I have time to tell his years;
  Ever belov'd and loving may his rule be;
  And when old time shall lead him to his end,
  Goodness and he fill up one monument!

LOVELL   To th'water-side I must conduct your grace,   95
  Then give my charge up to Sir Nicholas Vaux,
  Who undertakes you to your end.

VAUX   Prepare there,
  The duke is coming: see the barge be ready,
  And fit it with such furniture as suits
  The greatness of his person.

BUCKINGHAM   Nay, Sir Nicholas,   100
  Let it alone; my state now will but mock me.
  When I came hither I was Lord High Constable
  And Duke of Buckingham: now poor Edward Bohun;
  Yet I am richer than my base accusers,
  That never knew what truth meant: I now seal it,   105
  And with that blood will make 'em one day groan
    for't.
  My noble father Henry of Buckingham,
  Who first rais'd head against usurping Richard,
  Flying for succour to his servant Banister,
  Being distress'd, was by that wretch betray'd,   110
  And without trial fell; God's peace be with him.
  Henry the Seventh succeeding, truly pitying
  My father's loss, like a most royal prince
  Restor'd me to my honours; and out of ruins
  Made my name once more noble. Now his son,   115
  Henry the Eighth, life, honour, name and all
  That made me happy, at one stroke has taken
  For ever from the world. I had my trial,
  And must needs say a noble one; which makes me
  A little happier than my wretched father: 120
  Yet thus far we are one in fortunes; both
  Fell by our servants, by those men we lov'd most:
  A most unnatural and faithless service.
  Heaven has an end in all; yet you that hear me,
  This from a dying man receive as certain: 125
  Where you are liberal of your loves and counsels,
  Be sure you be not loose; for those you make friends
  And give your hearts to, when they once perceive
  The least rub in your fortunes, fall away
  Like water from ye, never found again   130
  But where they mean to sink ye. All good people
  Pray for me; I must now forsake ye; the last hour
  Of my long weary life is come upon me:
  Farewell;
  And when you would say something that is sad,   135
  Speak how I fell. I have done, and God forgive me.
                  Exeunt Duke and train.

1 GENTLEMAN   O, this is full of pity; sir, it calls
  I fear, too many curses on their heads
  That were the authors.

2 GENTLEMAN   If the duke be guiltless,
  'Tis full of woe: yet I can give you inkling   140

Of an ensuing evil, if it fall,
Greater than this.

1 GENTLEMAN   Good angels keep it from us:
What may it be? you do not doubt my faith sir?

2 GENTLEMAN
This secret is so weighty, 'twill require
A strong faith to conceal it.

145   1 GENTLEMAN   Let me have it;
I do not talk much.

2 GENTLEMAN   I am confident;
You shall sir: did you not of late days hear
A buzzing of a separation
Between the king and Katherine?

1 GENTLEMAN   Yes, but it held not;

150   For when the king once heard it, out of anger
He sent command to the lord mayor straight
To stop the rumour, and allay those tongues
That durst disperse it.

2 GENTLEMAN   But that slander, sir,
Is found a truth now; for it grows again

155   Fresher than e'er it was, and held for certain
The king will venture at it. Either the cardinal,
Or some about him near, have, out of malice
To the good queen, possess'd him with a scruple
That will undo her: to confirm this too,

160   Cardinal Campeius is arriv'd, and lately,
As all think, for this business.

1 GENTLEMAN   'Tis the cardinal;
And merely to revenge him on the emperor,
For not bestowing on him at his asking
The archbishopric of Toledo, this is purpos'd.

2 GENTLEMAN

165   I think you have hit the mark; but is't not cruel
That she should feel the smart of this? The cardinal
Will have his will, and she must fall.

1 GENTLEMAN   'Tis woeful.
We are too open here to argue this;
Let's think in private more.   *Exeunt.*

2.2   *Enter* Lord Chamberlain, *reading this letter.*

CHAMBERLAIN   *My lord, the horses your lordship sent for,
with all the care I had, I saw well chosen, ridden and
furnish'd. They were young and handsome, and of the best
breed in the north. When they were ready to set out for*

5   *London, a man of my lord cardinal's, by commission and
main power took 'em from me, with this reason: his master
would be serv'd before a subject, if not before the king,
which stopp'd our mouths sir.*

I fear he will indeed; well, let him have them;

10   He will have all I think.

*Enter to the Lord Chamberlain,
the* DUKES OF NORFOLK *and* SUFFOLK.

NORFOLK   Well met my lord chamberlain.
CHAMBERLAIN   Good day to both your graces.
SUFFOLK   How is the king employ'd?

CHAMBERLAIN   I left him private,
Full of sad thoughts and troubles.

NORFOLK   What's the cause?

CHAMBERLAIN
It seems the marriage with his brother's wife   15
Has crept too near his conscience.

SUFFOLK [*aside*]   No, his conscience
Has crept too near another lady.

NORFOLK   'Tis so;
This is the cardinal's doing: the king-cardinal,
That blind priest, like the eldest son of fortune,
Turns what he list. The king will know him one day.   20

SUFFOLK
Pray God he do, he'll never know himself else.

NORFOLK   How holily he works in all his business,
And with what zeal! for now he has crack'd the
    league
Between us and the emperor (the queen's great
    nephew),
He dives into the king's soul, and there scatters   25
Dangers, doubts, wringing of the conscience,
Fears and despairs, and all these for his marriage:
And out of all these, to restore the king,
He counsels a divorce, a loss of her
That like a jewel has hung twenty years   30
About his neck, yet never lost her lustre;
Of her that loves him with that excellence
That angels love good men with; even of her
That when the greatest stroke of fortune falls
Will bless the king: and is not this course pious?   35

CHAMBERLAIN
Heaven keep me from such counsel: 'tis most true
These news are everywhere, every tongue speaks 'em,
And every true heart weeps for't. All that dare
Look into these affairs see this main end,
The French king's sister. Heaven will one day open   40
The king's eyes, that so long have slept upon
This bold bad man.

SUFFOLK   And free us from his slavery.

NORFOLK   We had need pray,
And heartily, for our deliverance,
Or this imperious man will work us all   45
From princes into pages: all men's honours
Lie like one lump before him, to be fashion'd
Into what pitch he please.

SUFFOLK   For me, my lords,
I love him not, nor fear him, there's my creed:
As I am made without him, so I'll stand,   50
If the king please; his curses and his blessings
Touch me alike, th'are breath I not believe in.
I knew him, and I know him: so I leave him
To him that made him proud, the Pope.

NORFOLK   Let's in,
And with some other business put the king   55
From these sad thoughts that work too much upon
    him:
My lord, you'll bear us company?

CHAMBERLAIN   Excuse me,
    The king has sent me otherwhere: besides,
    You'll find a most unfit time to disturb him:
    Health to your lordships.
60   NORFOLK   Thanks, my good lord chamberlain.
        Exit Lord Chamberlain, and the King draws
        the curtain and sits reading pensively.
SUFFOLK How sad he looks; sure he is much afflicted.
KING Who's there? Ha?
NORFOLK   Pray God he be not angry.
KING
    Who's there I say? How dare you thrust yourselves
    Into my private meditations?
65   Who am I? Ha?
NORFOLK A gracious king that pardons all offences,
    Malice ne'er meant: our breach of duty this way
    Is business of estate, in which we come
    To know your royal pleasure.
KING   Ye are too bold:
70   Go to; I'll make ye know your times of business:
    Is this an hour for temporal affairs? Ha?

    Enter WOLSEY *and* CAMPEIUS *with a commission.*

    Who's there? my good lord cardinal? O my Wolsey,
    The quiet of my wounded conscience;
    Thou art a cure fit for a king;
    [*to Campeius*]   you're welcome
75   Most learned reverend sir, into our kingdom;
    Use us and it:
    [*to Wolsey*]   my good lord, have great care
    I be not found a talker.
WOLSEY   Sir, you cannot;
    I would your grace would give us but an hour
    Of private conference.
KING [*to Norfolk and Suffolk*]   We are busy; go.
NORFOLK [*aside to Suffolk*]
    This priest has no pride in him?
SUFFOLK [*aside to Norfolk*]   Not to speak of:
    I would not be so sick though for his place;
    But this cannot continue.
NORFOLK [*aside to Suffolk*]   If it do,
    I'll venture one; have at him!
SUFFOLK [*aside to Norfolk*]   I another.
        Exeunt Norfolk and Suffolk.
WOLSEY Your grace has given a precedent of wisdom
    Above all princes, in committing freely
    Your scruple to the voice of Christendom:
    Who can be angry now? what envy reach you?
    The Spaniard tied by blood and favour to her,
    Must now confess, if they have any goodness,
    The trial just and noble. All the clerks
    (I mean the learned ones in Christian kingdoms)
    Have their free voices: Rome, the nurse of judgment,
    Invited by your noble self, hath sent
    One general tongue unto us; this good man,
    This just and learned priest, Cardinal Campeius,
    Whom once more I present unto your highness.

KING
    And once more in mine arms I bid him welcome,
    And thank the holy conclave for their loves;
    They have sent me such a man I would have wish'd
    for.
CAMPEIUS
    Your grace must needs deserve all strangers' loves,   100
    You are so noble: to your highness' hand
    I tender my commission; by whose virtue,
    The court of Rome commanding, you my lord
    Cardinal of York, are join'd with me their servant
    In the unpartial judging of this business.   105
KING Two equal men: the queen shall be acquainted
    Forthwith for what you come. Where's Gardiner?
WOLSEY I know your majesty has always lov'd her
    So dear in heart, not to deny her that
    A woman of less place might ask by law,   110
    Scholars allow'd freely to argue for her.
KING Ay, and the best she shall have; and my favour
    To him that does best, God forbid else: Cardinal,
    Prithee call Gardiner to me, my new secretary.
    I find him a fit fellow.   115

    Enter GARDINER.

WOLSEY [*aside to Gardiner*]
    Give me your hand: much joy and favour to you;
    You are the king's now.
GARDINER [*aside to Wolsey*]   But to be commanded
    For ever by your grace, whose hand has rais'd me.
KING Come hither Gardiner. [*Walks and whispers.*]
CAMPEIUS My lord of York, was not one Doctor Pace   120
    In this man's place before him?
WOLSEY   Yes, he was.
CAMPEIUS Was he not held a learned man?
WOLSEY   Yes surely.
CAMPEIUS
    Believe me, there's an ill opinion spread then,
    Even of yourself, lord cardinal.
WOLSEY   How? of me?
CAMPEIUS They will not stick to say you envied him,   125
    And fearing he would rise (he was so virtuous)
    Kept him a foreign man still, which so griev'd him
    That he ran mad and died.
WOLSEY   Heav'n's peace be with him:
    That's Christian care enough; for living murmurers
    There's places of rebuke. He was a fool,   130
    For he would needs be virtuous. That good fellow,
    If I command him follows my appointment,
    I will have none so near else. Learn this brother,
    We live not to be grip'd by meaner persons.
KING Deliver this with modesty to th' queen.   135
        Exit Gardiner.
    The most convenient place that I can think of
    For such receipt of learning is Black-Friars:
    There ye shall meet about this weighty business.
    My Wolsey, see it furnish'd; O my lord,
    Would it not grieve an able man to leave   140

So sweet a bedfellow? But conscience, conscience;
O 'tis a tender place, and I must leave her.   *Exeunt.*

2.3   *Enter* ANNE BULLEN *and an* Old Lady.

ANNE
Not for that neither; here's the pang that pinches:
His highness having liv'd so long with her, and she
So good a lady that no tongue could ever
Pronounce dishonour of her (by my life,
5 She never knew harm-doing) – O, now after
So many courses of the sun enthroned,
Still growing in a majesty and pomp, the which
To leave a thousand-fold more bitter than
'Tis sweet at first t'acquire: after this process,
10 To give her the avaunt, it is a pity
Would move a monster!
OLD LADY   Hearts of most hard temper
Melt and lament for her.
ANNE   O God's will, much better
She ne'er had known pomp; though 't be temporal,
Yet if that quarrel, fortune, do divorce
15 It from the bearer, 'tis a sufferance panging
As soul and body's severing.
OLD LADY   Alas poor lady,
She's a stranger now again.
ANNE   So much the more
Must pity drop upon her: verily
I swear, 'tis better to be lowly born,
20 And range with humble livers in content,
Than to be perk'd up in a glist'ring grief
And wear a golden sorrow.
OLD LADY   Our content
Is our best having.
ANNE   By my troth and maidenhead,
I would not be a queen.
OLD LADY   Beshrew me, I would,
25 And venture maidenhead for't, and so would you,
For all this spice of your hypocrisy:
You that have so fair parts of woman on you,
Have too a woman's heart, which ever yet
Affected eminence, wealth, sovereignty;
30 Which, to say sooth, are blessings; and which gifts
(Saving your mincing) the capacity
Of your soft cheveril conscience would receive,
If you might please to stretch it.
ANNE   Nay, good troth.
OLD LADY
Yes troth and troth; you would not be a queen?
35 ANNE   No, not for all the riches under heaven.
OLD LADY
'Tis strange; a threepence bow'd would hire me
Old as I am, to queen it: but I pray you,
What think you of a duchess? Have you limbs
To bear that load of title?
ANNE   No in truth.
OLD LADY
40 Then you are weakly made; pluck off a little,

I would not be a young count in your way
For more than blushing comes to: if your back
Cannot vouchsafe this burthen, 'tis too weak
Ever to get a boy.
ANNE   How you do talk!
I swear again, I would not be a queen   45
For all the world.
OLD LADY   In faith, for little England
You'ld venture an emballing: I myself
Would for Carnarvonshire, although there long'd
No more to th' crown but that: lo, who comes here?

Enter Lord Chamberlain.

CHAMBERLAIN
Good morrow ladies; what were't worth to know   50
The secret of your conference?
ANNE   My good lord,
Not your demand; it values not your asking:
Our mistress' sorrows we were pitying.
CHAMBERLAIN   It was a gentle business, and becoming
The action of good women; there is hope   55
All will be well.
ANNE   Now I pray God, amen.
CHAMBERLAIN
You bear a gentle mind, and heav'nly blessings
Follow such creatures. That you may, fair lady,
Perceive I speak sincerely, and high note's
Ta'en of your many virtues, the king's majesty   60
Commends his good opinion of you, and
Does purpose honour to you no less flowing
Than Marchioness of Pembroke; to which title
A thousand pound a year, annual support,
Out of his grace he adds.
ANNE   I do not know   65
What kind of my obedience I should tender;
More than my all is nothing: nor my prayers
Are not words duly hallow'd, nor my wishes
More worth than empty vanities; yet prayers and
    wishes
Are all I can return. Beseech your lordship,   70
Vouchsafe to speak my thanks and my obedience,
As from a blushing handmaid, to his highness,
Whose health and royalty I pray for.
CHAMBERLAIN   Lady,
I shall not fail t'approve the fair conceit
The king hath of you. [*aside*] I have perus'd her well;   75
Beauty and honour in her are so mingled
That they have caught the king: and who knows yet
But from this lady may proceed a gem
To lighten all this isle. – I'll to the king,
And say I spoke with you.   *Exit Lord Chamberlain.*
ANNE   My honour'd lord.   80
OLD LADY   Why this it is: see, see,
I have been begging sixteen years in court
(Am yet a courtier beggarly) nor could
Come pat betwixt too early and too late
For any suit of pounds: and you (O fate!)   85

A very fresh fish here (fie, fie, fie upon
This compell'd fortune) have your mouth fill'd up
Before you open it.

ANNE   This is strange to me.

OLD LADY   How tastes it? Is it bitter? Forty pence, no:
There was a lady once ('tis an old story)
That would not be a queen, that would she not
For all the mud in Egypt; have you heard it?

ANNE   Come, you are pleasant.

OLD LADY   With your theme I could
O'ermount the lark: the Marchioness of Pembroke?
A thousand pounds a year, for pure respect?
No other obligation? by my life,
That promises moe thousands: honour's train
Is longer than his foreskirt; by this time
I know your back will bear a duchess. Say,
Are you not stronger than you were?

ANNE   Good lady,
Make yourself mirth with your particular fancy,
And leave me out on't. Would I had no being
If this salute my blood a jot; it faints me
To think what follows.
The queen is comfortless, and we forgetful
In our long absence: pray do not deliver
What here y'have heard to her.

OLD LADY   What do you think me? –

Exeunt.

2.4   [*Trumpets, sennet and cornets.*]

Enter two vergers with short silver wands; next them two
scribes in the habit of doctors; after them the Archbishop of
CANTERBURY *alone; after him the* Bishops of LINCOLN,
Ely, Rochester and St Asaph: next them, with some small
distance, follows a gentleman bearing the purse, with the great
seal and a cardinal's hat: then two priests, bearing each a
silver cross: then a Gentleman Usher *bare-headed,*
accompanied with a sergeant-at-arms bearing a silver mace:
then two gentlemen bearing two great silver pillars: after
them, side by side, the two Cardinals, *two noblemen, with the*
sword and mace. The KING *takes place under the cloth of*
state. The two cardinals sit under him as judges. The QUEEN
takes place some distance from the King. The bishops place
themselves on each side the court in manner of a consistory:
below them the scribes. The lords sit next the bishops. The rest
of the attendants stand in convenient order about the stage.

WOLSEY   Whilst our commission from Rome is read,
Let silence be commanded.

KING   What's the need?
It hath already publicly been read,
And on all sides th'authority allow'd;
You may then spare that time.

WOLSEY   Be't so; proceed.

SCRIBE   Say, Henry King of England, come into the
court.

CRIER   Henry King of England, etc.

SCRIBE   Say, Katherine Queen of England, come into
the court.   10

CRIER   Katherine Queen of England, etc.

[*The Queen makes no answer, rises out of her chair,*
goes about the court, comes to the King, and kneels at his
feet: then speaks.]

KATHERINE   Sir, I desire you do me right and justice,
And to bestow your pity on me; for
I am a most poor woman, and a stranger,
Born out of your dominions: having here   15
No judge indifferent, nor no more assurance
Of equal friendship and proceeding. Alas sir,
In what have I offended you? What cause
Hath my behaviour given to your displeasure,
That thus you should proceed to put me off,   20
And take your good grace from me? Heaven witness,
I have been to you a true and humble wife,
At all times to your will conformable,
Ever in fear to kindle your dislike,
Yea, subject to your countenance, glad or sorry   25
As I saw it inclin'd. When was the hour
I ever contradicted your desire
Or made it not mine too? Or which of your friends
Have I not strove to love, although I knew
He were mine enemy? What friend of mine,   30
That had to him deriv'd your anger, did I
Continue in my liking? nay, gave notice
He was from thence discharg'd? Sir, call to mind
That I have been your wife in this obedience
Upward of twenty years, and have been blest   35
With many children by you. If in the course
And process of this time you can report,
And prove it too, against mine honour aught,
My bond to wedlock, or my love and duty
Against your sacred person; in God's name   40
Turn me away, and let the foul'st contempt
Shut door upon me, and so give me up
To the sharp'st kind of justice. Please you, sir,
The king your father was reputed for
A prince most prudent, of an excellent   45
And unmatch'd wit and judgment: Ferdinand
My father, King of Spain, was reckon'd one
The wisest prince that there had reign'd by many
A year before. It is not to be question'd
That they had gather'd a wise council to them   50
Of every realm, that did debate this business,
Who deem'd our marriage lawful: wherefore I
humbly
Beseech you sir, to spare me till I may
Be by my friends in Spain advis'd, whose counsel
I will implore. If not, i'th' name of God   55
Your pleasure be fulfill'd.

WOLSEY   You have here lady
(And of your choice) these reverend fathers, men
Of singular integrity and learning,
Yea, the elect o'th' land, who are assembled

60 To plead your cause. It shall be therefore bootless
That longer you desire the court, as well
For your own quiet as to rectify
What is unsettled in the king.

CAMPEIUS   His grace
Hath spoken well and justly: therefore madam,
65 It's fit this royal session do proceed,
And that without delay their arguments
Be now produc'd and heard.

KATHERINE   Lord Cardinal,
To you I speak.

WOLSEY   Your pleasure, madam.

KATHERINE   Sir,
I am about to weep; but thinking that
70 We are a queen (or long have dream'd so) certain
The daughter of a king, my drops of tears
I'll turn to sparks of fire.

WOLSEY   Be patient yet.

KATHERINE   I will, when you are humble; nay before,
Or God will punish me. I do believe
75 (Induc'd by potent circumstances) that
You are mine enemy, and make my challenge
You shall not be my judge. For it is you
Have blown this coal betwixt my lord and me
(Which God's dew quench), therefore I say again
80 I utterly abhor; yea, from my soul
Refuse you for my judge, whom yet once more
I hold my most malicious foe, and think not
At all a friend to truth.

WOLSEY   I do profess
You speak not like yourself; who ever yet
85 Have stood to charity and display'd th'effects
Of disposition gentle, and of wisdom
O'ertopping woman's power. Madam, you do me
    wrong:
I have no spleen against you, nor injustice
For you or any: how far I have proceeded,
90 Or how far further shall, is warranted
By a commission from the consistory,
Yea, the whole consistory of Rome. You charge me
That I have blown this coal: I do deny it;
The king is present; if it be known to him
95 That I gainsay my deed, how may he wound,
And worthily, my falsehood, yea, as much
As you have done my truth. If he know
That I am free of your report, he knows
I am not of your wrong. Therefore in him
100 It lies to cure me, and the cure is to
Remove these thoughts from you: the which before
His highness shall speak in, I do beseech
You, gracious madam, to unthink your speaking
And to say so no more.

KATHERINE   My lord, my lord,
105 I am a simple woman, much too weak
T'oppose your cunning. Y'are meek and humble-
    mouth'd,
You sign your place and calling, in full seeming,

With meekness and humility: but your heart
Is cramm'd with arrogancy, spleen and pride.
110 You have by fortune, and his highness' favours,
Gone slightly o'er low steps, and now are mounted
Where powers are your retainers, and your words
(Domestics to you) serve your will as't please
Yourself pronounce their office. I must tell you,
115 You tender more your person's honour than
Your high profession spiritual; that again
I do refuse you for my judge, and here
Before you all, appeal unto the Pope,
To bring my whole cause 'fore his holiness
And to be judg'd by him.

[*She curtsies to the King, and offers to depart.*]

CAMPEIUS   The queen is obstinate,
120 Stubborn to justice, apt to accuse it, and
Disdainful to be tried by't; 'tis not well.
She's going away.

KING   Call her again.

CRIER
Katherine Queen of England, come into the court.
125

GENTLEMAN USHER   Madam, you are call'd back.

KATHERINE
What need you note it? pray you keep your way,
When you are call'd return. Now the Lord help,
They vex me past my patience. Pray you pass on;
130 I will not tarry; no, nor ever more
Upon this business my appearance make
In any of their courts. *Exit Queen, and her attendants.*

KING   Go thy ways Kate;
That man i'th' world who shall report he has
A better wife, let him in nought be trusted,
135 For speaking false in that; thou art alone
(If thy rare qualities, sweet gentleness,
Thy meekness saintlike, wife-like government,
Obeying in commanding, and thy parts
Sovereign and pious else, could speak thee out)
140 The queen of earthly queens: she's noble born,
And like her true nobility she has
Carried herself towards me.

WOLSEY   Most gracious sir,
In humblest manner I require your highness,
That it shall please you to declare in hearing
145 Of all these ears (for where I am robb'd and bound,
There must I be unloos'd, although not there
At once and fully satisfied) whether ever I
Did broach this business to your highness, or
Laid any scruple in your way which might
150 Induce you to the question on't; or ever
Have to you, but with thanks to God for such
A royal lady, spake one the least word that might
Be to the prejudice of her present state
Or touch of her good person?

KING   My lord cardinal
155 I do excuse you; yea, upon mine honour
I free you from't: you are not to be taught
That you have many enemies that know not

Why they are so, but like to village curs
Bark when their fellows do. By some of these
The queen is put in anger; y'are excus'd:
But will you be more justified? you ever
Have wish'd the sleeping of this business, never
   desir'd
It to be stirr'd, but oft have hinder'd, oft
The passages made toward it; on my honour,
I speak my good lord card'nal to this point,
And thus far clear him. Now what mov'd me to't,
I will be bold with time and your attention:
Then mark th'inducement: thus it came; give heed
   to't:
My conscience first receiv'd a tenderness,
Scruple and prick, on certain speeches utter'd
By th' Bishop of Bayonne, then French ambassador,
Who had been hither sent on the debating
A marriage 'twixt the Duke of Orleans and
Our daughter Mary: i'th' progress of this business,
Ere a determinate resolution, he
(I mean the Bishop) did require a respite,
Wherein he might the king his lord advertise
Whether our daughter were legitimate
Respecting this our marriage with the dowager,
Sometimes our brother's wife. This respite shook
The bosom of my conscience, enter'd me,
Yea, with a spitting power, and made to tremble
The region of my breast, which forc'd such way
That many maz'd considerings did throng
And press'd in with this caution. First, methought
I stood not in the smile of heaven, who had
Commanded nature, that my lady's womb,
If it conceiv'd a male-child by me, should
Do no more offices of life to't than
The grave does to th' dead: for her male issue
Or died where they were made, or shortly after
This world had air'd them. Hence I took a thought
This was a judgment on me, that my kingdom
(Well worthy the best heir o'th' world) should not
Be gladded in't by me. Then follows that
I weigh'd the danger which my realms stood in
By this my issue's fail, and that gave to me
Many a groaning throe: thus hulling in
The wild sea of my conscience, I did steer
Toward this remedy whereupon we are
Now present here together: that's to say,
I meant to rectify my conscience, which
I then did feel full sick, and yet not well,
By all the reverend fathers of the land
And doctors learn'd. First I began in private
With you my Lord of Lincoln; you remember
How under my oppression I did reek
When I first mov'd you.

LINCOLN   Very well my liege.

KING   I have spoke long, be pleas'd yourself to say
  How far you satisfied me.

LINCOLN   So please your highness,

The question did at first so stagger me,
Bearing a state of mighty moment in't
And consequence of dread, that I committed
The daring'st counsel which I had to doubt,
And did entreat your highness to this course   215
Which you are running here.

KING   I then mov'd you,
My Lord of Canterbury, and got your leave
To make this present summons: unsolicited
I left no reverend person in this court,
But by particular consent proceeded   220
Under your hands and seals; therefore go on,
For no dislike i'th' world against the person
Of the good Queen, but the sharp thorny points
Of my alleged reasons drives this forward:
Prove but our marriage lawful, by my life   225
And kingly dignity, we are contented
To wear our mortal state to come with her
(Katherine our Queen) before the primest creature
That's paragon'd o'th' world.

CAMPEIUS   So please your highness,
The queen being absent, 'tis a needful fitness   230
That we adjourn this court till further day;
Meanwhile must be an earnest motion
Made to the queen to call back her appeal
She intends unto his holiness.

KING [*aside*]   I may perceive
These cardinals trifle with me: I abhor   235
This dilatory sloth and tricks of Rome.
My learn'd and well-beloved servant Cranmer,
Prithee return; with thy approach, I know
My comfort comes along. – Break up the court;
I say set on.   *Exeunt, in manner as they enter'd.*

3.1   *Enter* QUEEN *and her women as at work.*

KATHERINE
Take thy lute wench, my soul grows sad with
   troubles.
Sing, and disperse 'em if thou canst: leave working.

                Song.

    Orpheus with his lute made trees,
    And the mountain tops that freeze,
      Bow themselves when he did sing: 5
    To his music plants and flowers
    Ever sprung, as sun and showers
      There had made a lasting spring.

    Every thing that heard him play,
    Even the billows of the sea,   10
      Hung their heads and then lay by:
    In sweet music is such art,
    Killing care and grief of heart
      Fall asleep, or hearing die.

            Enter a Gentleman.

KATHERINE   How now?   15

GENTLEMAN
  And't please your grace, the two great cardinals
  Wait in the presence.
KATHERINE   Would they speak with me?
GENTLEMAN   They will'd me say so madam.
KATHERINE   Pray their graces
  To come near: *Exit Gentleman.*
                what can be their business
20 With me, a poor weak woman, fall'n from favour?
  I do not like their coming; now I think on't,
  They should be good men, their affairs as righteous:
  But all hoods make not monks.

        Enter the two Cardinals, WOLSEY *and* CAMPEIUS.

WOLSEY   Peace to your highness.
KATHERINE
  Your graces find me here part of a housewife;
25 I would be all, against the worst may happen:
  What are your pleasures with me, reverent lords?
WOLSEY   May it please you noble madam, to withdraw
  Into your private chamber; we shall give you
  The full cause of our coming.
KATHERINE   Speak it here.
30 There's nothing I have done yet o' my conscience
  Deserves a corner; would all other women
  Could speak this with as free a soul as I do.
  My lords, I care not (so much I am happy
  Above a number) if my actions
35 Were tried by ev'ry tongue, ev'ry eye saw 'em,
  Envy and base opinion set against 'em,
  I know my life so even. If your business
  Seek me out, and that way I am wife in,
  Out with it boldly: truth loves open dealing.
WOLSEY
40 *Tanta est erga te mentis integritas Regina serenissima* –
KATHERINE   O good my lord, no latin;
  I am not such a truant since my coming
  As not to know the language I have liv'd in;
  A strange tongue makes my cause more strange,
      suspicious:
45 Pray speak in English; here are some will thank you,
  If you speak truth, for their poor mistress' sake;
  Believe me she has had much wrong. Lord cardinal,
  The willing'st sin I ever yet committed
  May be absolv'd in English.
WOLSEY   Noble lady,
50 I am sorry my integrity should breed
  (And service to his majesty and you)
  So deep suspicion where all faith was meant;
  We come not by the way of accusation,
  To taint that honour every good tongue blesses,
55 Nor to betray you any way to sorrow –
  You have too much, good lady: but to know
  How you stand minded in the weighty difference
  Between the king and you, and to deliver
  (Like free and honest men) our just opinions
  And comforts to your cause.

CAMPEIUS   Most honour'd madam,   60
  My lord of York, out of his noble nature,
  Zeal and obedience he still bore your grace,
  Forgetting (like a good man) your late censure
  Both of his truth and him (which was too far)
  Offers, as I do, in a sign of peace   65
  His service and his counsel.
KATHERINE [*aside*]   To betray me. –
  My lords, I thank you both for your good wills,
  Ye speak like honest men (pray God ye prove so)
  But how to make ye suddenly an answer
  In such a point of weight, so near mine honour   70
  (More near my life I fear) with my weak wit,
  And to such men of gravity and learning,
  In truth I know not. I was set at work
  Among my maids, full little (God knows) looking
  Either for such men or such business;   75
  For her sake that I have been (for I feel
  The last fit of my greatness) – good your graces
  Let me have time and counsel for my cause:
  Alas, I am a woman friendless, hopeless.
WOLSEY
  Madam, you wrong the king's love with these fears,   80
  Your hopes and friends are infinite.
KATHERINE   In England
  But little for my profit; can you think lords,
  That any Englishman dare give me counsel?
  Or be a known friend 'gainst his highness' pleasure
  (Though he be grown so desperate to be honest)   85
  And live a subject? Nay forsooth, my friends,
  They that must weigh out my afflictions,
  They that my trust must grow to, live not here;
  They are (as all my other comforts) far hence
  In mine own country, lords.
CAMPEIUS   I would your grace   90
  Would leave your griefs, and take my counsel.
KATHERINE   How sir?
CAMPEIUS
  Put your main cause into the king's protection,
  He's loving and most gracious. 'Twill be much
  Both for your honour better and your cause,
  For if the trial of the law o'ertake ye,   95
  You'll part away disgrac'd.
WOLSEY   He tells you rightly.
KATHERINE   Ye tell me what ye wish for both, my ruin:
  Is this your Christian counsel? Out upon ye.
  Heaven is above all yet; there sits a judge
  That no king can corrupt.
CAMPEIUS   Your rage mistakes us.   100
KATHERINE
  The more shame for ye; holy men I thought ye,
  Upon my soul two reverend cardinal virtues;
  But cardinal sins and hollow hearts I fear ye:
  Mend 'em for shame my lords. Is this your comfort?
  The cordial that ye bring a wretched lady,   105
  A woman lost among ye, laugh'd at, scorn'd?
  I will not wish ye half my miseries,

I have more charity. But say I warn'd ye;
Take heed, for heaven's sake take heed, lest at once
110   The burthen of my sorrows fall upon ye.
WOLSEY   Madam, this is a mere distraction;
You turn the good we offer into envy.
KATHERINE   Ye turn me into nothing. Woe upon ye,
And all such false professors. Would you have me
115   (If you have any justice, any pity,
If ye be anything but churchmen's habits)
Put my sick cause into his hands that hates me?
Alas, 'has banish'd me his bed already,
His love, too long ago. I am old my lords,
120   And all the fellowship I hold now with him
Is only my obedience. What can happen
To me, above this wretchedness? All your studies
Make me a curse like this.
CAMPEIUS   Your fears are worse.
KATHERINE
Have I liv'd thus long (let me speak myself,
125   Since virtue finds no friends) a wife, a true one?
A woman (I dare say without vainglory)
Never yet branded with suspicion?
Have I with all my full affections
Still met the king? lov'd him next heav'n? obey'd
    him?
130   Been (out of fondness) superstitious to him?
Almost forgot my prayers to content him?
And am I thus rewarded? 'tis not well, lords.
Bring me a constant woman to her husband,
One that ne'er dream'd a joy beyond his pleasure,
135   And to that woman (when she has done most)
Yet will I add an honour, a great patience.
WOLSEY
Madam, you wander from the good we aim at.
KATHERINE   My lord, I dare not make myself so guilty
To give up willingly that noble title
140   Your master wed me to: nothing but death
Shall e'er divorce my dignities.
WOLSEY   Pray hear me.
KATHERINE   Would I had never trod this English earth,
Or felt the flatteries that grow upon it:
Ye have angels' faces, but heaven knows your hearts.
145   What will become of me now, wretched lady?
I am the most unhappy woman living.
Alas poor wenches, where are now your fortunes?
Shipwrack'd upon a kingdom where no pity,
No friends, no hope, no kindred weep for me,
150   Almost no grave allow'd me: like the lily
That once was mistress of the field and flourish'd,
I'll hang my head and perish.
WOLSEY   If your grace
Could but be brought to know our ends are honest,
You'ld feel more comfort. Why should we, good lady,
155   Upon what cause wrong you? alas, our places,
The way of our profession is against it;
We are to cure such sorrows, not to sow 'em.
For goodness' sake consider what you do,
How you may hurt yourself, ay, utterly
Grow from the king's acquaintance by this carriage.   160
The hearts of princes kiss obedience,
So much they love it; but to stubborn spirits
They swell and grow as terrible as storms.
I know you have a gentle, noble temper,
A soul as even as a calm; pray think us   165
Those we profess, peace-makers, friends and
    servants.
CAMPEIUS
Madam you'll find it so: you wrong your virtues
With these weak women's fears. A noble spirit,
As yours was put into you, ever casts
Such doubts as false coin from it. The king loves
    you,   170
Beware you lose it not: for us (if you please
To trust us in your business) we are ready
To use our utmost studies in your service.
KATHERINE
Do what ye will, my lords; and pray forgive me;
If I have us'd myself unmannerly,   175
You know I am a woman, lacking wit
To make a seemly answer to such persons.
Pray do my service to his majesty;
He has my heart yet, and shall have my prayers
While I shall have my life. Come reverend fathers,   180
Bestow your counsels on me; she now begs
That little thought when she set footing here
She should have bought her dignities so dear. *Exeunt.*

3.2   *Enter the* DUKE OF NORFOLK,
         DUKE OF SUFFOLK, LORD SURREY
         and Lord Chamberlain.

NORFOLK   If you will now unite in your complaints
And force them with a constancy, the cardinal
Cannot stand under them. If you omit
The offer of this time, I cannot promise
But that you shall sustain moe new disgraces   5
With these you bear already.
SURREY   I am joyful
To meet the least occasion that may give me
Remembrance of my father-in-law, the duke,
To be reveng'd on him.
SUFFOLK   Which of the peers
Have uncontemn'd gone by him, or at least   10
Strangely neglected? When did he regard
The stamp of nobleness in any person
Out of himself?
CHAMBERLAIN   My lords, you speak your pleasures:
What he deserves of you and me I know;
What we can do to him (though now the time   15
Gives way to us) I much fear. If you cannot
Bar his access to th' king, never attempt
Any thing on him; for he hath a witchcraft
Over the king in's tongue.
NORFOLK   O fear him not,

His spell in that is out: the king hath found
Matter against him that for ever mars
The honey of his language. No, he's settled
(Not to come off) in his displeasure.

SURREY   Sir,
I should be glad to hear such news as this
Once every hour.

NORFOLK   Believe it, this is true.
In the divorce his contrary proceedings
Are all unfolded; wherein he appears
As I would wish mine enemy.

SURREY   How came
His practices to light?

SUFFOLK   Most strangely.

SURREY   O how? how?

SUFFOLK   The cardinal's letters to the Pope miscarried,
And came to th'eye o'th' king, wherein was read
How that the cardinal did entreat his holiness
To stay the judgement o'th' divorce; for if
It did take place, 'I do' (quoth he) 'perceive
My king is tangled in affection to
A creature of the queen's, Lady Anne Bullen'.

SURREY   Has the king this?

SUFFOLK   Believe it.

SURREY   Will this work?

CHAMBERLAIN
The king in this perceives him, how he coasts
And hedges his own way. But in this point
All his tricks founder, and he brings his physic
After his patient's death; the king already
Hath married the fair lady.

SURREY   Would he had.

SUFFOLK   May you be happy in your wish my lord,
For I profess you have it.

SURREY   Now all my joy
Trace the conjunction.

SUFFOLK   My amen to't.

NORFOLK   All men's.

SUFFOLK   There's order given for her coronation:
Marry this is yet but young, and may be left
To some ears unrecounted. But my lords
She is a gallant creature, and complete
In mind and feature. I persuade me, from her
Will fall some blessing to this land, which shall
In it be memoriz'd.

SURREY   But will the king
Digest this letter of the cardinal's?
The Lord forbid!

NORFOLK   Marry amen.

SUFFOLK   No, no;
There be moe wasps that buzz about his nose
Will make this sting the sooner. Cardinal Campeius
Is stolen away to Rome, hath ta'en no leave,
Has left the cause o'th' king unhandled, and
Is posted as the agent of our cardinal,
To second all his plot. I do assure you,
The king cried 'Ha' at this.

CHAMBERLAIN   Now God incense him
And let him cry 'Ha' louder.

NORFOLK   But my lord,
When returns Cranmer?

SUFFOLK   He is return'd in his opinions, which
Have satisfied the king for his divorce,
Together with all famous colleges
Almost in Christendom: shortly (I believe)
His second marriage shall be publish'd, and
Her coronation. Katherine no more
Shall be call'd queen, but princess dowager,
And widow to Prince Arthur.

NORFOLK   This same Cranmer's
A worthy fellow, and hath ta'en much pain
In the king's business.

SUFFOLK   He has, and we shall see him
For it an archbishop.

NORFOLK   So I hear.

SUFFOLK   'Tis so.

Enter WOLSEY *and* CROMWELL.

The cardinal.

NORFOLK   Observe, observe, he's moody.

WOLSEY   The packet Cromwell, gave't you the king?

CROMWELL   To his own hand, in's bedchamber.

WOLSEY   Look'd he
O'th' inside of the paper?

CROMWELL   Presently
He did unseal them, and the first he view'd,
He did it with a serious mind; a heed
Was in his countenance. You he bade
Attend him here this morning.

WOLSEY   Is he ready
To come abroad?

CROMWELL   I think by this he is.

WOLSEY   Leave me awhile.   *Exit Cromwell.*
[aside] It shall be to the Duchess of Alençon,
The French king's sister; he shall marry her.
Anne Bullen? no; I'll no Anne Bullens for him,
There's more in't than fair visage. Bullen?
No, we'll no Bullens: speedily I wish
To hear from Rome. The Marchioness of Pembroke?

NORFOLK   He's discontented.

SUFFOLK   May be he hears the king
Does whet his anger to him.

SURREY   Sharp enough
Lord for thy justice.

WOLSEY [aside]
The late queen's gentlewoman? a knight's daughter
To be her mistress' mistress? the queen's queen?
This candle burns not clear, 'tis I must snuff it,
Then out it goes. What though I know her virtuous
And well-deserving? yet I know her for
A spleeny Lutheran, and not wholesome to
Our cause, that she should lie i'th' bosom of
Our hard-rul'd king. Again, there is sprung up
An heretic, an arch-one, Cranmer, one

Hath crawl'd into the favour of the king
And is his oracle.

NORFOLK   He is vex'd at something.

Enter KING, *reading of a schedule, and* LOVELL.

SURREY
I would 'twere something that would fret the string,
The master-cord on's heart.

SUFFOLK   The king, the king!

KING   What piles of wealth hath he accumulated
To his own portion! and what expense by th' hour
Seems to flow from him! How i'th' name of thrift
Does he rake this together? Now my lords,
Saw you the cardinal?

NORFOLK   My lord, we have
Stood here observing him. Some strange commotion
Is in his brain; he bites his lip, and starts,
Stops on a sudden, looks upon the ground,
Then lays his finger on his temple; straight
Springs out into fast gait, then stops again,
Strikes his breast hard, and anon he casts
His eye against the moon: in most strange postures
We have seen him set himself.

KING   It may well be,
There is a mutiny in's mind. This morning
Papers of state he sent me, to peruse
As I required: and wot you what I found
There (on my conscience put unwittingly)
Forsooth an inventory, thus importing
The several parcels of his plate, his treasure,
Rich stuffs and ornaments of household, which
I find at such proud rate, that it out-speaks
Possession of a subject.

NORFOLK   It's heaven's will;
Some spirit put this paper in the packet
To bless your eye withal.

KING   If we did think
His contemplation were above the earth
And fix'd on spiritual object, he should still
Dwell in his musings, but I am afraid
His thinkings are below the moon, not worth
His serious considering.

[*King takes his seat, whispers Lovell, who goes to the Cardinal.*]

WOLSEY   Heaven forgive me.
Ever God bless your highness.

KING   Good my lord,
You are full of heavenly stuff, and bear the inventory
Of your best graces in your mind, the which
You were now running o'er: you have scarce time
To steal from spiritual leisure a brief span
To keep your earthly audit; sure in that
I deem you an ill husband, and am glad
To have you therein my companion.

WOLSEY   Sir,
For holy offices I have a time; a time
To think upon the part of business which

I bear i'th' state; and nature does require
Her times of preservation, which perforce
I her frail son, amongst my brethren mortal,
Must give my tendance to.

KING   You have said well.

WOLSEY   And ever may your highness yoke together   150
(As I will lend you cause) my doing well
With my well saying.

KING   'Tis well said again,
And 'tis a kind of good deed to say well,
And yet words are no deeds. My father lov'd you,
He said he did, and with his deed did crown   155
His word upon you. Since I had my office
I have kept you next my heart, have not alone
Employ'd you where high profits might come home,
But par'd my present havings to bestow
My bounties upon you.

WOLSEY [*aside*]   What should this mean?   160

SURREY [*aside*]   The Lord increase this business.

KING   Have I not made you
The prime man of the state? I pray you tell me,
If what I now pronounce you have found true:
And if you may confess it, say withal
If you are bound to us, or no. What say you?   165

WOLSEY   My sovereign, I confess your royal graces
Shower'd on me daily, have been more than could
My studied purposes requite, which went
Beyond all man's endeavours. My endeavours
Have ever come too short of my desires,   170
Yet fil'd with my abilities: mine own ends
Have been mine so, that ever more they pointed
To th'good of your most sacred person, and
The profit of the state. For your great graces
Heap'd upon me (poor undeserver) I   175
Can nothing render but allegiant thanks,
My prayers to heaven for you, my loyalty
Which ever has and ever shall be growing,
Till death, that winter, kill it.

KING   Fairly answer'd:
A loyal, and obedient subject is   180
Therein illustrated; the honour of it
Does pay the act of it, as i'th' contrary
The foulness is the punishment. I presume
That as my hand has open'd bounty to you,
My heart dropp'd love, my power rain'd honour, more   185
On you than any; so your hand and heart,
Your brain and every function of your power,
Should, notwithstanding that your bond of duty,
As 'twere in love's particular, be more
To me your friend, than any.

WOLSEY   I do profess   190
That for your highness' good I ever labour'd
More than mine own: that am, have, and will be
(Though all the world should crack their duty to you
And throw it from their soul, though perils did
Abound as thick as thought could make 'em, and   195

Appear in forms more horrid) yet my duty,
As doth a rock against the chiding flood,
Should the approach of this wild river break,
And stand unshaken yours.

KING   'Tis nobly spoken:
200   Take notice lords, he has a loyal breast,
For you have seen him open't. [*giving him papers*]
                      Read o'er this,
And after, this, and then to breakfast with
What appetite you have.

Exit King, frowning upon the Cardinal; the nobles
throng after him, smiling and whispering.

WOLSEY   What should this mean?
What sudden anger's this? How have I reap'd it?
205   He parted frowning from me, as if ruin
Leap'd from his eyes. So looks the chafed lion
Upon the daring huntsman that has gall'd him;
Then makes him nothing. I must read this paper;
I fear, the story of his anger. 'Tis so;
210   This paper has undone me: 'tis th'accompt
Of all that world of wealth I have drawn together
For mine own ends (indeed to gain the popedom
And fee my friends in Rome). O negligence!
Fit for a fool to fall by: what cross devil
215   Made me put this main secret in the packet
I sent the king? Is there no way to cure this?
No new device to beat this from his brains?
I know 'twill stir him strongly; yet I know
A way, if it take right, in spite of fortune
220   Will bring me off again. What's this? 'To th' Pope'?
The letter, as I live, with all the business
I writ to's holiness. Nay then, farewell:
I have touch'd the highest point of all my greatness,
And from that full meridian of my glory
225   I haste now to my setting. I shall fall
Like a bright exhalation in the evening,
And no man see me more.

Re-enter to Wolsey the DUKES OF NORFOLK *and* SUFFOLK,
the EARL OF SURREY *and the* Lord Chamberlain.

NORFOLK
Hear the king's pleasure Cardinal, who commands
   you
To render up the great seal presently
230   Into our hands, and to confine yourself
To Asher-house, my Lord of Winchester's,
Till you hear further from his highness.

WOLSEY   Stay:
Where's your commission lords? words cannot carry
Authority so weighty.

SUFFOLK   Who dare cross 'em,
235   Bearing the king's will from his mouth expressly?

WOLSEY   Till I find more than will or words to do it
(I mean your malice) know, officious lords,
I dare, and must deny it. Now I feel
Of what coarse metal ye are moulded, envy,
240   How eagerly ye follow my disgraces

As if it fed ye, and how sleek and wanton
Ye appear in every thing may bring my ruin!
Follow your envious courses, men of malice;
You have Christian warrant for 'em, and no doubt
In time will find their fit rewards. That seal   245
You ask with such a violence, the king
(Mine and your master) with his own hand gave me;
Bade me enjoy it, with the place and honours
During my life; and to confirm his goodness,
Tied it by letters patents. Now, who'll take it?   250

SURREY   The king that gave it.

WOLSEY   It must be himself then.

SURREY   Thou art a proud traitor, priest.

WOLSEY   Proud lord, thou liest:
Within these forty hours Surrey durst better
Have burnt that tongue than said so.

SURREY   Thy ambition,
Thou scarlet sin, robb'd this bewailing land   255
Of noble Buckingham, my father-in-law;
The heads of all thy brother-cardinals
(With thee and all thy best parts bound together)
Weigh'd not a hair of his. Plague of your policy;
You sent me deputy for Ireland,   260
Far from his succour, from the king, from all
That might have mercy on the fault thou gav'st him;
Whilst your great goodness, out of holy pity,
Absolv'd him with an axe.

WOLSEY   This, and all else
This talking lord can lay upon my credit,   265
I answer, is most false. The duke by law
Found his deserts. How innocent I was
From any private malice in his end,
His noble jury, and foul cause can witness.
If I lov'd many words, lord, I should tell you   270
You have as little honesty as honour,
That in the way of loyalty and truth
Toward the king, my ever royal master,
Dare mate a sounder man than Surrey can be,
And all that love his follies.

SURREY   By my soul,   275
Your long coat, priest, protects you, thou should'st
   feel
My sword i'th' life blood of thee else. My lords,
Can ye endure to hear this arrogance?
And from this fellow? If we live thus tamely,
To be thus jaded by a piece of scarlet,   280
Farewell nobility: let his grace go forward,
And dare us with his cap, like larks.

WOLSEY   All goodness
Is poison to thy stomach.

SURREY   Yes, that goodness
Of gleaming all the land's wealth into one,
Into your own hands, cardinal, by extortion;   285
The goodness of your intercepted packets
You writ to th' Pope against the king: your goodness,
Since you provoke me, shall be most notorious.
My Lord of Norfolk, as you are truly noble,

As you respect the common good, the state
Of our despis'd nobility, our issues
(Who if he live, will scarce be gentlemen)
Produce the grand sum of his sins, the articles
Collected from his life. I'll startle you
Worse than the sacring bell, when the brown wench
Lay kissing in your arms, lord cardinal.

WOLSEY
How much methinks, I could despise this man,
But that I am bound in charity against it.

NORFOLK
Those articles, my lord, are in the king's hand:
But thus much, they are foul ones.

WOLSEY   So much fairer
And spotless shall mine innocence arise,
When the king knows my truth.

SURREY   This cannot save you:
I thank my memory, I yet remember
Some of these articles, and out they shall.
Now, if you can blush, and cry 'guilty' cardinal,
You'll show a little honesty.

WOLSEY   Speak on sir,
I dare your worst objections: if I blush,
It is to see a nobleman want manners.

SURREY
I had rather want those than my head; have at you.
First, that without the king's assent or knowledge
You wrought to be a legate, by which power
You maim'd the jurisdiction of all bishops.

NORFOLK   Then, that in all you writ to Rome, or else
To foreign princes, *Ego et Rex meus*
Was still inscrib'd; in which you brought the king
To be your servant.

SUFFOLK   Then, that without the knowledge
Either of king or council, when you went
Ambassador to the emperor, you made bold
To carry into Flanders the great seal.

SURREY   Item, you sent a large commission
To Gregory de Cassado, to conclude
Without the king's will or the state's allowance,
A league between his highness and Ferrara.

SUFFOLK   That out of mere ambition, you have caus'd
Your holy hat to be stampt on the king's coin.

SURREY
Then, that you have sent innumerable substance
(By what means got, I leave to your own conscience)
To furnish Rome and to prepare the ways
You have for dignities, to the mere undoing
Of all the kingdom. Many more there are,
Which since they are of you, and odious,
I will not taint my mouth with.

CHAMBERLAIN   O my lord,
Press not a falling man too far; 'tis virtue:
His faults lie open to the laws, let them,
Not you, correct him. My heart weeps to see him
So little of his great self.

SURREY   I forgive him.

SUFFOLK   Lord cardinal, the king's further pleasure is,
Because all those things you have done of late
By your power legative within this kingdom
Fall into th'compass of a praemunire;   340
That therefore such a writ be sued against you,
To forfeit all your goods, lands, tenements,
Chattels and whatsoever, and to be
Out of the king's protection. This is my charge.

NORFOLK   And so we'll leave you to your meditations   345
How to live better. For your stubborn answer
About the giving back the great seal to us,
The king shall know it, and (no doubt) shall thank
      you.
So fare you well, my little good lord cardinal.
                              Exeunt all but Wolsey.

WOLSEY   So farewell, to the little good you bear me.   350
Farewell? a long farewell to all my greatness.
This is the state of man; to-day he puts forth
The tender leaves of hopes, to-morrow blossoms,
And bears his blushing honours thick upon him:
The third day comes a frost, a killing frost,   355
And when he thinks, good easy man, full surely
His greatness is a-ripening, nips his root,
And then he falls as I do. I have ventur'd
Like little wanton boys that swim on bladders,
This many summers in a sea of glory,   360
But far beyond my depth: my high-blown pride
At length broke under me, and now has left me,
Weary and old with service, to the mercy
Of a rude stream that must for ever hide me.
Vain pomp and glory of this world, I hate ye;   365
I feel my heart new open'd. O how wretched
Is that poor man that hangs on princes' favours!
There is betwixt that smile we would aspire to,
That sweet aspect of princes, and their ruin,
More pangs and fears than wars or women have;   370
And when he falls, he falls like Lucifer,
Never to hope again.

            Enter CROMWELL, *standing amazed.*

                        Why how now, Cromwell?
CROMWELL   I have no power to speak, sir.
WOLSEY   What, amaz'd
At my misfortunes? Can thy spirit wonder
A great man should decline? Nay, and you weep   375
I am fall'n indeed.
CROMWELL   How does your grace?
WOLSEY   Why well;
Never so truly happy, my good Cromwell;
I know myself now, and I feel within me
A peace above all earthly dignities,
A still and quiet conscience. The king has cur'd me,   380
I humbly thank his grace; and from these shoulders,
These ruin'd pillars, out of pity taken
A load would sink a navy, too much honour.
O 'tis a burden Cromwell, 'tis a burden
Too heavy for a man that hopes for heaven.   385

CROMWELL
  I am glad your grace has made that right use of it.
WOLSEY   I hope I have: I am able now, methinks,
  (Out of a fortitude of soul I feel)
  To endure more miseries, and greater far
390 Than my weak-hearted enemies dare offer.
  What news abroad?
CROMWELL   The heaviest and the worst
  Is your displeasure with the king.
WOLSEY   God bless him.
CROMWELL
  The next is, that Sir Thomas More is chosen
  Lord Chancellor in your place.
WOLSEY   That's somewhat sudden,
395 But he's a learned man. May he continue
  Long in his highness' favour, and do justice
  For truth's sake, and his conscience; that his bones,
  When he has run his course and sleeps in blessings,
  May have a tomb of orphans' tears wept on him.
  What more?
400 CROMWELL   That Cranmer is return'd with welcome;
  Install'd Lord Archbishop of Canterbury.
WOLSEY   That's news indeed.
CROMWELL   Last, that the Lady Anne,
  Whom the king hath in secrecy long married,
  This day was view'd in open as his queen,
405 Going to chapel; and the voice is now
  Only about her coronation.
WOLSEY
  There was the weight that pull'd me down. O
      Cromwell,
  The king has gone beyond me: all my glories
  In that one woman I have lost for ever.
410 No sun shall ever usher forth mine honours,
  Or gild again the noble troops that waited
  Upon my smiles. Go get thee from me Cromwell,
  I am a poor fall'n man, unworthy now
  To be thy lord and master. Seek the king
415 (That sun I pray may never set). I have told him
  What, and how true thou art; he will advance thee:
  Some little memory of me will stir him
  (I know his noble nature) not to let
  Thy hopeful service perish too. Good Cromwell
420 Neglect him not; make use now, and provide
  For thine own future safety.
CROMWELL   O my lord,
  Must I then leave you? must I needs forgo
  So good, so noble and so true a master?
  Bear witness, all that have not hearts of iron,
425 With what a sorrow Cromwell leaves his lord.
  The king shall have my service; but my prayers
  For ever and for ever shall be yours.
WOLSEY   Cromwell, I did not think to shed a tear
  In all my miseries; but thou hast forc'd me,
430 Out of thy honest truth, to play the woman.
  Let's dry our eyes; and thus far hear me Cromwell,
  And when I am forgotten, as I shall be,

And sleep in dull cold marble, where no mention
Of me more must be heard of, say I taught thee;
Say Wolsey, that once trod the ways of glory,   435
And sounded all the depths and shoals of honour,
Found thee a way (out of his wrack) to rise in,
A sure and safe one, though thy master miss'd it.
Mark but my fall, and that that ruin'd me:
Cromwell, I charge thee, fling away ambition,   440
By that sin fell the angels; how can man then,
The image of his maker, hope to win by it?
Love thyself last, cherish those hearts that hate thee;
Corruption wins not more than honesty.
Still in thy right hand carry gentle peace   445
To silence envious tongues. Be just, and fear not;
Let all the ends thou aim'st at be thy country's,
Thy God's and truth's: then if thou fall'st, O
    Cromwell,
Thou fall'st a blessed martyr.
Serve the king: and prithee lead me in: 450
There take an inventory of all I have,
To the last penny, 'tis the king's. My robe,
And my integrity to heaven, is all
I dare now call mine own. O Cromwell, Cromwell,
Had I but serv'd my God with half the zeal   455
I serv'd my king, he would not in mine age
Have left me naked to mine enemies.
CROMWELL   Good sir, have patience.
WOLSEY   So I have. Farewell
  The hopes of court, my hopes in heaven do dwell.
                                        Exeunt.

4.1   *Enter two* Gentlemen, *meeting one another.*

1 GENTLEMAN   Y'are well met once again.
2 GENTLEMAN   So are you.
1 GENTLEMAN
  You come to take your stand here, and behold
  The Lady Anne pass from her coronation?
2 GENTLEMAN
  'Tis all my business. At our last encounter
  The Duke of Buckingham came from his trial.   5
1 GENTLEMAN
  'Tis very true. But that time offer'd sorrow,
  This general joy.
2 GENTLEMAN   'Tis well: the citizens
  I am sure have shown at full their royal minds
  (As let 'em have their rights, they are ever forward)
  In celebration of this day with shows,   10
  Pageants and sights of honour.
1 GENTLEMAN   Never greater,
  Nor I'll assure you, better taken sir.
2 GENTLEMAN
  May I be bold to ask what that contains,
  That paper in your hand?
1 GENTLEMAN   Yes, 'tis the list
  Of those that claim their offices this day,   15
  By custom of the coronation.

The Duke of Suffolk is the first, and claims
To be high steward; next the Duke of Norfolk,
He to be earl marshal: you may read the rest.

2 GENTLEMAN
I thank you sir: had I not known those customs,
I should have been beholding to your paper:
But I beseech you, what's become of Katherine
The princess dowager? how goes her business?

1 GENTLEMAN
That I can tell you too. The Archbishop
Of Canterbury, accompanied with other
Learned and reverend fathers of his order,
Held a late court at Dunstable, six miles off
From Ampthill where the princess lay, to which
She was often cited by them, but appear'd not:
And to be short, for not-appearance, and
The king's late scruple, by the main assent
Of all these learned men, she was divorc'd
And the late marriage made of none effect:
Since which she was remov'd to Kimmalton,
Where she remains now sick.

2 GENTLEMAN   Alas good lady.
The trumpets sound: stand close, the queen is
    coming.   [*Hautboys.*]

The Order of the Coronation.

1. *A lively flourish of trumpets.*
2. *Then, two judges.*
3. *Lord Chancellor, with purse and mace before him.*
4. *Choristers singing. Music.*
5. *Mayor of London, bearing the mace. Then* Garter, *in his coat of arms, and on his head he wore a gilt copper crown.*
6. *Marquess Dorset, bearing a scepter of gold, on his head a demi-coronal of gold. With him, the* EARL OF SURREY, *bearing the rod of silver with the dove, crowned with an earl's coronet. Collars of Esses.*
7. DUKE OF SUFFOLK, *in his robe of Estate, his coronet on his head, bearing a long white wand, as High Steward. With him, the* DUKE OF NORFOLK, *with the rod of marshalship, a coronet on his head. Collars of Esses.*
8. *A canopy, born by four of the Cinque-ports, under it the* QUEEN, *in her robe; in her hair, richly adorned with pearl, crowned. On each side her, the Bishops of London and Winchester.*
9. *The old Duchess of Norfolk, in a coronal of gold, wrought with flowers, bearing the queen's train.*
10. *Certain ladies or countesses, with plain circlets of gold without flowers.*
    Exeunt, first passing over the stage in order and state, and then, a great flourish of trumpets.

2 GENTLEMAN   A royal train, believe me: these I know;
Who's that that bears the sceptre?

1 GENTLEMAN   Marquess Dorset,
And that the Earl of Surrey with the rod.

2 GENTLEMAN
A bold brave gentleman. That should be

The Duke of Suffolk.

1 GENTLEMAN   'Tis the same: high steward.

2 GENTLEMAN   And that my Lord of Norfolk?

1 GENTLEMAN   Yes.

2 GENTLEMAN [*looking on the Queen*]
                            Heaven bless thee!
Thou hast the sweetest face I ever look'd on.
Sir, as I have a soul, she is an angel;
Our king has all the Indies in his arms,   45
And more, and richer, when he strains that lady;
I cannot blame his conscience.

1 GENTLEMAN   They that bear
The cloth of honour over her, are four barons
Of the Cinque-ports.

2 GENTLEMAN
Those men are happy, and so are all are near her.   50
I take it, she that carries up the train
Is that old noble lady, Duchess of Norfolk.

1 GENTLEMAN   It is, and all the rest are countesses.

2 GENTLEMAN
Their coronets say so. These are stars indeed –

1 GENTLEMAN   And sometimes falling ones.

2 GENTLEMAN   No more of that.   55
The end of the procession leaves; the trumpets sound.

Enter a Third Gentleman.

1 GENTLEMAN
God save you sir. Where have you been broiling?

3 GENTLEMAN
Among the crowd i'th' abbey, where a finger
Could not be wedg'd in more: I am stifled
With the mere rankness of their joy.

2 GENTLEMAN   You saw
The ceremony?

3 GENTLEMAN   That I did.

1 GENTLEMAN   How was it?   60

3 GENTLEMAN   Well worth the seeing.

2 GENTLEMAN   Good sir, speak it to us.

3 GENTLEMAN   As well as I am able. The rich stream
Of lords and ladies, having brought the queen
To a prepar'd place in the choir, fell off
A distance from her; while her grace sat down   65
To rest a while, some half an hour or so,
In a rich chair of state, opposing freely
The beauty of her person to the people.
Believe me sir, she is the goodliest woman
That ever lay by man: which when the people   70
Had the full view of, such a noise arose
As the shrouds make at sea in a stiff tempest,
As loud, and to as many tunes. Hats, cloaks
(Doublets, I think) flew up, and had their faces
Been loose, this day they had been lost. Such joy   75
I never saw before. Great-bellied women,
That had not half a week to go, like rams
In the old time of war, would shake the press
And make 'em reel before 'em. No man living
Could say 'This is my wife' there, all were woven   80

591

So strangely in one piece.

2 GENTLEMAN   But what follow'd?

3 GENTLEMAN
At length her grace rose, and with modest paces
Came to the altar, where she kneel'd, and saintlike
Cast her fair eyes to heaven and pray'd devoutly:
85 Then rose again and bow'd her to the people;
When by the Archbishop of Canterbury
She had all the royal makings of a queen,
As holy oil, Edward Confessor's crown,
The rod, and bird of peace and all such emblems
90 Laid nobly on her: which perform'd, the choir
With all the choicest music of the kingdom
Together sung *Te Deum.* So she parted,
And with the same full state pac'd back again
To York-place, where the feast is held.

1 GENTLEMAN   Sir,
95 You must no more call it York-place, that's past;
For since the cardinal fell, that title's lost,
'Tis now the king's, and call'd Whitehall.

3 GENTLEMAN   I know it;
But 'tis so lately alter'd that the old name
Is fresh about me.

2 GENTLEMAN   What two reverend bishops
100 Were those that went on each side of the queen?

3 GENTLEMAN
Stokesley and Gardiner, the one of Winchester,
Newly preferr'd from the king's secretary;
The other, London.

2 GENTLEMAN   He of Winchester
Is held no great good lover of the archbishop's,
The virtuous Cranmer.

105 3 GENTLEMAN   All the land knows that:
However, yet there is no great breach; when it comes
Cranmer will find a friend will not shrink from him.

2 GENTLEMAN
Who may that be, I pray you?

3 GENTLEMAN   Thomas Cromwell,
A man in much esteem with th' king, and truly
110 A worthy friend. The king has made him master
O'th' jewel-house,
And one already of the privy council.

2 GENTLEMAN He will deserve more.

3 GENTLEMAN   Yes, without all doubt.
Come gentlemen, ye shall go my way,
115 Which is to th'court, and there ye shall be my guests:
Something I can command. As I walk thither
I'll tell ye more.

BOTH   You may command us, sir.   *Exeunt.*

4.2   *Enter* KATHERINE DOWAGER, *sick, led between*
GRIFFITH, *her gentleman usher, and* PATIENCE, *her*
woman.

GRIFFITH   How does your grace?

KATHERINE   O Griffith, sick to death:
My legs like loaden branches bow to th'earth,

Willing to leave their burthen: reach a chair;
So now, methinks, I feel a little ease.
Didst thou not tell me Griffith, as thou ledst me,   5
That the great child of honour, Cardinal Wolsey,
Was dead?

GRIFFITH   Yes madam; but I think your grace,
Out of the pain you suffer'd, gave no ear to't.

KATHERINE   Prithee good Griffith, tell me how he died.
If well, he stepp'd before me happily   10
For my example.

GRIFFITH   Well, the voice goes, madam,
For after the stout Earl Northumberland
Arrested him at York, and brought him forward
As a man sorely tainted, to his answer,
He fell sick suddenly, and grew so ill   15
He could not sit his mule.

KATHERINE   Alas poor man.

GRIFFITH
At last, with easy roads, he came to Leicester,
Lodg'd in the abbey, where the reverend abbot
With all his covent honourably receiv'd him;
To whom he gave these words: 'O father abbot,   20
An old man, broken with the storms of state,
Is come to lay his weary bones among ye:
Give him a little earth for charity'.
So went to bed, where eagerly his sickness
Pursued him still, and three nights after this,   25
About the hour of eight, which he himself
Foretold should be his last, full of repentance,
Continual meditations, tears and sorrows,
He gave his honours to the world again,
His blessed part to heaven, and slept in peace.   30

KATHERINE
So may he rest, his faults lie gently on him:
Yet thus far, Griffith, give me leave to speak him,
And yet with charity. He was a man
Of an unbounded stomach, ever ranking
Himself with princes; one that by suggestion   35
Tied all the kingdom; simony was fair play;
His own opinion was his law: i'th' presence
He would say untruths, and be ever double
Both in his words and meaning. He was never
(But where he meant to ruin) pitiful: 40
His promises were as he then was, mighty,
But his performance, as he is now, nothing:
Of his own body he was ill, and gave
The clergy ill example.

GRIFFITH   Noble madam,
Men's evil manners live in brass, their virtues   45
We write in water. May it please your highness
To hear me speak his good now?

KATHERINE   Yes good Griffith,
I were malicious else.

GRIFFITH   This cardinal,
Though from an humble stock, undoubtedly
Was fashion'd to much honour. From his cradle   50
He was a scholar, and a ripe and good one,

Exceeding wise, fair-spoken and persuading:
Lofty and sour to them that lov'd him not,
But to those men that sought him, sweet as summer.
55 And though he were unsatisfied in getting
(Which was a sin) yet in bestowing, madam,
He was most princely: ever witness for him
Those twins of learning that he rais'd in you,
Ipswich and Oxford; one of which fell with him,
60 Unwilling to outlive the good that did it,
The other (though unfinish'd) yet so famous,
So excellent in art, and still so rising,
That Christendom shall ever speak his virtue.
His overthrow heap'd happiness upon him,
65 For then, and not till then, he felt himself,
And found the blessedness of being little;
And to add greater honours to his age
Than man could give him, he died fearing God.

KATHERINE   After my death I wish no other herald,
70   No other speaker of my living actions
    To keep mine honour from corruption,
    But such an honest chronicler as Griffith.
    Whom I most hated living, thou hast made me,
    With thy religious truth and modesty,
75   Now in his ashes honour: peace be with him.
    Patience, be near me still, and set me lower;
    I have not long to trouble thee. Good Griffith,
    Cause the musicians play me that sad note
    I nam'd my knell, whilst I sit meditating
80   On that celestial harmony I go to.

                    [*Sad and solemn music.*]

GRIFFITH
    She is asleep: good wench, let's sit down quiet,
    For fear we wake her. Softly, gentle Patience.

                    The Vision.

[*Enter solemnly tripping one after another, six personages, clad in white robes, wearing on their heads garlands of bays, and golden vizards on their faces, branches of bays or palm in their hands. They first congee unto her, then dance: and at certain changes, the first two hold a spare garland over her head, at which the other four make reverend curtsies. Then the two that held the garland deliver the same to the other next two, who observe the same order in their changes, and holding the garland over her head. Which done, they deliver the same garland to the last two, who likewise observe the same order. At which (as it were by inspiration) she makes (in her sleep) signs of rejoicing, and holdeth up her hands to heaven. And so in their dancing vanish, carrying the garland with them. The music continues.*]

KATHERINE
    Spirits of peace, where are ye? are ye all gone?
    And leave me here in wretchedness behind ye?
GRIFFITH   Madam, we are here.
KATHERINE   It is not you I call for;
85   Saw ye none enter since I slept?
GRIFFITH   None, madam.

KATHERINE   No? Saw you not even now a blessed troop
    Invite me to a banquet, whose bright faces
    Cast thousand beams upon me, like the sun?
    They promis'd me eternal happiness,   90
    And brought me garlands, Griffith, which I feel
    I am not worthy yet to wear; I shall assuredly.
GRIFFITH   I am most joyful, madam, such good dreams
    Possess your fancy.
KATHERINE   Bid the music leave,
    They are harsh and heavy to me.   [*Music ceases.*]
PATIENCE   Do you note   95
    How much her grace is alter'd on the sudden?
    How long her face is drawn! how pale she looks,
    And of an earthy cold! Mark her eyes!
GRIFFITH   She is going wench; pray, pray.
PATIENCE   Heaven comfort her.

                    Enter a Messenger.

MESSENGER   And't like your grace –
KATHERINE   You are a saucy fellow,   100
    Deserve we no more reverence?
GRIFFITH   You are to blame,
    Knowing she will not lose her wonted greatness
    To use so rude behaviour. Go to, kneel.
MESSENGER
    I humbly do entreat your highness' pardon,
    My haste made me unmannerly. There is staying   105
    A gentleman, sent from the king, to see you.
KATHERINE
    Admit him entrance Griffith. But this fellow
    Let me ne'er see again.   *Exit Messenger.*

                    Enter LORD CAPUCHIUS.

                    If my sight fail not,
    You should be lord ambassador from the emperor,
    My royal nephew, and your name Capuchius.   110
CAPUCHIUS   Madam, the same: your servant.
KATHERINE   O my lord,
    The times and titles now are alter'd strangely
    With me, since first you knew me. But I pray you,
    What is your pleasure with me?
CAPUCHIUS   Noble lady,
    First mine own service to your grace, the next   115
    The king's request that I would visit you,
    Who grieves much for your weakness, and by me
    Sends you his princely commendations,
    And heartily entreats you take good comfort.
KATHERINE
    O my good lord, that comfort comes too late,   120
    'Tis like a pardon after execution;
    That gentle physic, given in time, had cur'd me;
    But now I am past all comforts here but prayers.
    How does his highness?
CAPUCHIUS   Madam, in good health.
KATHERINE   So may he ever do, and ever flourish,   125
    When I shall dwell with worms, and my poor name
    Banish'd the kingdom. Patience, is that letter

I caus'd you write yet sent away?

PATIENCE   No madam.

KATHERINE   Sir, I most humbly pray you to deliver
   This to my lord the king.

130   CAPUCHIUS   Most willing, madam.

KATHERINE
   In which I have commended to his goodness
   The model of our chaste loves, his young daughter
   (The dews of heaven fall thick in blessings on her)
   Beseeching him to give her virtuous breeding
135   (She is young and of a noble modest nature,
   I hope she will deserve well) and a little
   To love her for her mother's sake, that lov'd him,
   Heaven knows how dearly. My next poor petition
   Is that his noble grace would have some pity
140   Upon my wretched women, that so long
   Have follow'd both my fortunes faithfully,
   Of which there is not one, I dare avow
   (And now I should not lie) but will deserve
   For virtue and true beauty of the soul,
145   For honesty and decent carriage,
   A right good husband (let him be a noble),
   And sure those men are happy that shall have 'em.
   The last is for my men, they are the poorest
   (But poverty could never draw 'em from me),
150   That they may have their wages duly paid 'em,
   And something over to remember me by.
   If heaven had pleas'd to have given me longer life
   And able means, we had not parted thus.
   These are the whole contents, and good my lord,
155   By that you love the dearest in this world,
   As you wish Christian peace to souls departed,
   Stand these poor people's friend, and urge the king
   To do me this last right.

   CAPUCHIUS   By heaven I will,
   Or let me lose the fashion of a man.

160   KATHERINE   I thank you honest lord. Remember me
   In all humility unto his highness:
   Say his long trouble now is passing
   Out of this world. Tell him in death I bless'd him,
   For so I will; mine eyes grow dim. Farewell
165   My lord. Griffith farewell. Nay Patience,
   You must not leave me yet. I must to bed,
   Call in more women. When I am dead, good wench,
   Let me be us'd with honour; strew me over
   With maiden flowers, that all the world may know
170   I was a chaste wife to my grave: embalm me,
   Then lay me forth; although unqueen'd, yet like
   A queen, and daughter to a king inter me.
   I can no more.   *Exeunt leading Katherine.*

5.1   *Enter* GARDINER *Bishop of* WINCHESTER, *a* Page
   with a torch before him, met by SIR THOMAS LOVELL.

GARDINER   It's one a'clock boy, is't not?

BOY   It hath struck.

GARDINER   These should be hours for necessities,
   Not for delights; times to repair our nature

With comforting repose, and not for us
To waste these times. Good hour of night Sir
   Thomas: 5
Whither so late?

LOVELL   Came you from the king, my lord?

GARDINER   I did Sir Thomas, and left him at primero
   With the Duke of Suffolk.

LOVELL   I must to him too
   Before he go to bed. I'll take my leave.

GARDINER
   Not yet Sir Thomas Lovell: what's the matter?   10
   It seems you are in haste; and if there be
   No great offence belongs to't, give your friend
   Some touch of your late business: affairs that walk
   (As they say spirits do) at midnight, have
   In them a wilder nature than the business   15
   That seeks dispatch by day.

LOVELL   My lord, I love you,
   And durst commend a secret to your ear
   Much weightier than this work. The queen's in
      labour,
   They say in great extremity, and fear'd
   She'll with the labour end.

GARDINER   The fruit she goes with   20
   I pray for heartily, that it may find
   Good time, and live: but for the stock, Sir Thomas,
   I wish it grubb'd up now.

LOVELL   Methinks I could
   Cry the amen, and yet my conscience says
   She's a good creature, and sweet lady, does   25
   Deserve our better wishes.

GARDINER   But sir, sir,
   Hear me Sir Thomas, y'are a gentleman
   Of mine own way: I know you wise, religious,
   And let me tell you, it will ne'er be well,
   'Twill not Sir Thomas Lovell, take't of me,   30
   Till Cranmer, Cromwell, her two hands, and she
   Sleep in their graves.

LOVELL   Now sir, you speak of two
   The most remark'd i'th' kingdom: as for Cromwell,
   Beside that of the jewel-house, is made master
   O'th' rolls, and the king's secretary; further sir,   35
   Stands in the gap and trade of moe preferments,
   With which the time will load him. Th'archbishop
   Is the king's hand and tongue, and who dare speak
   One syllable against him?

GARDINER   Yes, yes, Sir Thomas,
   There are that dare, and I myself have ventur'd   40
   To speak my mind of him: and indeed this day,
   Sir (I may tell it you), I think I have
   Incens'd the lords o'th' council that he is
   (For so I know he is, they know he is)
   A most arch-heretic, a pestilence   45
   That does infect the land: with which they, mov'd,
   Have broken with the king, who hath so far
   Given ear to our complaint, of his great grace
   And princely care foreseeing those fell mischiefs

50 Our reasons laid before him, 'hath commanded
To-morrow morning to the council board
He be convented. He's a rank weed Sir Thomas,
And we must root him out. From your affairs
I hinder you too long: good night, Sir Thomas.

Exit Gardiner and Page.

LOVELL

55 Many good nights, my lord; I rest your servant.

Enter KING *and* SUFFOLK.

KING   Charles, I will play no more to-night,
My mind's not on't, you are too hard for me.
SUFFOLK   Sir, I did never win of you before.
KING   But little, Charles,
60 Nor shall not when my fancy's on my play.
Now Lovell, from the queen what is the news?
LOVELL   I could not personally deliver to her
What you commanded me, but by her woman
I sent your message, who return'd her thanks
65 In the great'st humbleness, and desir'd your highness
Most heartily to pray for her.
KING   What say'st thou? Ha?
To pray for her? what, is she crying out?
LOVELL
So said her woman, and that her suff'rance made
Almost each pang a death.
KING   Alas good lady.
70 SUFFOLK   God safely quit her of her burthen, and
With gentle travail, to the gladding of
Your highness with an heir.
KING   'Tis midnight Charles;
Prithee to bed, and in thy prayers remember
Th'estate of my poor queen. Leave me alone,
75 For I must think of that which company
Would not be friendly to.
SUFFOLK   I wish your highness
A quiet night, and my good mistress will
Remember in my prayers.
KING   Charles, good night.

Exit Suffolk.

Enter SIR ANTHONY DENNY.

Well sir, what follows?
80 DENNY   Sir, I have brought my lord the archbishop,
As you commanded me.
KING   Ha? Canterbury?
DENNY   Ay my good lord.
KING   'Tis true: where is he, Denny?
DENNY   He attends your highness' pleasure.
KING   Bring him to us.

Exit Denny.

LOVELL [*aside*]
This is about that which the bishop spake;
85 I am happily come hither.

Enter CRANMER *and* DENNY.

KING   Avoid the gallery. [*Lovell seems to stay.*]

Ha? I have said. Be gone.
What?   *Exeunt Lovell and Denny.*
CRANMER [*aside*]
I am fearful: wherefore frowns he thus?
'Tis his aspect of terror. All's not well.
KING   How now my lord? You do desire to know
Wherefore I sent for you.
CRANMER [*kneeling*]   It is my duty   90
T'attend your highness' pleasure.
KING   Pray you arise,
My good and gracious Lord of Canterbury:
Come, you and I must walk a turn together;
I have news to tell you. Come, come give me your
hand.
Ah my good lord, I grieve at what I speak,   95
And am right sorry to repeat what follows.
I have, and most unwillingly, of late
Heard many grievous, I do say my lord,
Grievous complaints of you; which being consider'd,
Have mov'd us and our council, that you shall   100
This morning come before us, where I know
You cannot with such freedom purge yourself,
But that till further trial in those charges
Which will require your answer, you must take
Your patience to you, and be well contented   105
To make your house our Tower: you, a brother of us
It fits we thus proceed, or else no witness
Would come against you.
CRANMER [*kneeling*]   I humbly thank your highness,
And am right glad to catch this good occasion
Most throughly to be winnow'd, where my chaff   110
And corn shall fly asunder. For I know
There's none stands under more calumnious tongues
Than I myself, poor man.
KING   Stand up, good Canterbury,
Thy truth and thy integrity is rooted
In us thy friend. Give me thy hand, stand up;   115
Prithee let's walk. Now by my holidame,
What manner of man are you? My lord, I look'd
You would have given me your petition, that
I should have ta'en some pains to bring together
Yourself and your accusers, and to have heard you   120
Without indurance further.
CRANMER   Most dread liege,
The good I stand on is my truth and honesty:
If they shall fail, I with mine enemies
Will triumph o'er my person, which I weigh not,
Being of those virtues vacant. I fear nothing   125
What can be said against me.
KING   Know you not
How your state stands i'th' world, with the whole
world?
Your enemies are many, and not small; their practices
Must bear the same proportion, and not ever
The justice and the truth o'th' question carries   130
The due o'th' verdict with it: at what ease
Might corrupt minds procure knaves as corrupt

To swear against you? such things have been done.
You are potently oppos'd, and with a malice
135   Of as great size. Ween you of better luck,
I mean in perjur'd witness, than your master,
Whose minister you are, whiles here he liv'd
Upon this naughty earth? Go to, go to,
You take a precipice for no leap of danger,
And woo your own destruction.

140   CRANMER   God and your majesty
Protect mine innocence, or I fall into
The trap is laid for me.
     KING   Be of good cheer,
They shall no more prevail than we give way to:
Keep comfort to you, and this morning see
145   You do appear before them. If they shall chance
In charging you with matters to commit you,
The best persuasions to the contrary
Fail not to use, and with what vehemency
Th'occasion shall instruct you. If entreaties
150   Will render you no remedy, this ring
Deliver them, and your appeal to us
There make before them. Look, the good man weeps:
He's honest on mine honour. God's blest mother,
I swear he is true-hearted, and a soul
155   None better in my kingdom. Get you gone,
And do as I have bid you.   *Exit Cranmer.*
                      He has strangled
His language in his tears.

Enter Old Lady; LOVELL *following.*

GENTLEMAN [*within*]   Come back: what mean you?
OLD LADY   I'll not come back, the tidings that I bring
Will make my boldness manners. Now good angels
160   Fly o'er thy royal head, and shade thy person
Under their blessed wings.
     KING   Now by thy looks
I guess thy message. Is the queen deliver'd?
Say ay, and of a boy.
     OLD LADY   Ay, ay my liege,
And of a lovely boy: the God of heaven
165   Both now and ever bless her: 'tis a girl
Promises boys hereafter. Sir, your queen
Desires your visitation, and to be
Acquainted with this stranger; 'tis as like you
As cherry is to cherry.
     KING   Lovell!
     LOVELL   Sir.
170   KING   Give her an hundred marks. I'll to the queen.
                           Exit King.

OLD LADY
An hundred marks? By this light, I'll ha' more.
An ordinary groom is for such payment.
I will have more, or scold it out of him.
Said I for this the girl was like to him?
I'll have more, or else unsay't; and now, while 'tis
175   hot,
I'll put it to the issue.   *Exeunt.*

5.2   *Enter* CRANMER, *Archbishop of* CANTERBURY;
pursuivants, pages, etc. are in attendance at the door.

CRANMER
I hope I am not too late, and yet the gentleman
That was sent to me from the council, pray'd me
To make great haste. All fast? What means this? Ho!
Who waits there? Sure you know me?

Enter Keeper.

KEEPER   Yes my Lord,
But yet I cannot help you.
CRANMER   Why?
KEEPER   Your grace   5
Must wait till you be call'd for.

Enter DOCTOR BUTTS.

CRANMER   So.
DOCTOR BUTTS [*aside*]
This is a piece of malice: I am glad
I came this way so happily. The king
Shall understand it presently.   *Exit Butts.*
CRANMER [*aside*]   'Tis Butts,
The king's physician; as he pass'd along   10
How earnestly he cast his eyes upon me:
Pray heaven he sound not my disgrace: for certain
This is of purpose laid by some that hate me
(God turn their hearts, I never sought their malice)
To quench mine honour; they would shame to make
    me   15
Wait else at door, a fellow-councillor,
'Mong boys, grooms and lackeys. But their pleasures
Must be fulfill'd, and I attend with patience.

Enter the KING *and* BUTTS *at a window above.*

DOCTOR BUTTS
I'll show your grace the strangest sight –
KING   What's that, Butts?
DOCTOR BUTTS
I think your highness saw this many a day.   20
KING   Body a' me; where is it?
DOCTOR BUTTS   There my lord:
The high promotion of his grace of Canterbury,
Who holds his state at door 'mongst pursuivants,
Pages and footboys.
KING   Ha? 'tis he indeed.
Is this the honour they do one another?   25
'Tis well there's one above 'em yet; I had thought
They had parted so much honesty among 'em,
At least good manners, as not thus to suffer
A man of his place, and so near our favour
To dance attendance on their lordships' pleasures,   30
And at the door too, like a post with packets:
By holy Mary, Butts, there's knavery;
Let 'em alone, and draw the curtain close:
We shall hear more anon.

596

A council-table brought in with chairs and stools, and placed under the state. Enter Lord Chancellor, *places himself at the upper end of the table, on the left hand; a seat being left void above him, as for Canterbury's seat.* DUKE OF SUFFOLK, DUKE OF NORFOLK, SURREY, *Lord Chamberlain,* GARDINER, *seat themselves in order on each side.* CROMWELL *at lower end, as secretary.*

CHANCELLOR   Speak to the business, master secretary;
    Why are we met in council?
CROMWELL   Please your honours,
    The chief cause concerns his grace of Canterbury.
GARDINER   Has he had knowledge of it?
CROMWELL   Yes.
NORFOLK   Who waits there?
KEEPER   Without, my noble lords?
GARDINER   Yes.
KEEPER   My lord archbishop;
    And has done half an hour to know your pleasures.
CHANCELLOR   Let him come in.
KEEPER   Your grace may enter now.
    [*Cranmer approaches the council-table.*]
CHANCELLOR   My good lord archbishop, I'm very sorry
    To sit here at this present and behold
    That chair stand empty: but we all are men,
    In our own natures frail, and capable
    Of our flesh; few are angels; out of which frailty
    And want of wisdom, you that best should teach us
    Have misdemean'd yourself, and not a little;
    Toward the king first, then his laws, in filling
    The whole realm by your teaching and your
        chaplains'
    (For so we are inform'd) with new opinions
    Divers and dangerous; which are heresies,
    And not reform'd, may prove pernicious.
GARDINER   Which reformation must be sudden too,
    My noble lords; for those that tame wild horses
    Pace 'em not in their hands to make 'em gentle,
    But stop their mouths with stubborn bits and spur
        'em,
    Till they obey the manage. If we suffer
    Out of our easiness and childish pity
    To one man's honour, this contagious sickness,
    Farewell all physic: and what follows then?
    Commotions, uproars, with a general taint
    Of the whole state, as of late days our neighbours,
    The upper Germany, can dearly witness,
    Yet freshly pitied in our memories.
CRANMER   My good lords; hitherto, in all the progress
    Both of my life and office, I have labour'd,
    And with no little study, that my teaching
    And the strong course of my authority,
    Might go one way, and safely; and the end
    Was ever to do well: nor is there living
    (I speak it with a single heart, my lords)
    A man that more detests, more stirs against,
    Both in his private conscience and his place,

Defacers of a public peace than I do:
    Pray heaven the king may never find a heart
    With less allegiance in it. Men that make
    Envy and crooked malice nourishment,
    Dare bite the best. I do beseech your lordships
    That in this case, of justice, my accusers,
    Be what they will, may stand forth face to face,
    And freely urge against me.
SUFFOLK   Nay, my lord,
    That cannot be; you are a councillor,
    And by that virtue no man dare accuse you.
GARDINER
    My lord, because we have business of more moment,
    We will be short with you. 'Tis his highness' pleasure
    And our consent, for better trial of you,
    From hence you be committed to the Tower,
    Where being but a private man again,
    You shall know many dare accuse you boldly,
    More than (I fear) you are provided for.
CRANMER
    Ah my good lord of Winchester: I thank you,
    You are always my good friend; if your will pass,
    I shall both find your lordship judge and juror,
    You are so merciful. I see your end,
    'Tis my undoing. Love and meekness, lord,
    Become a churchman better than ambition:
    Win straying souls with modesty again,
    Cast none away: that I shall clear myself,
    Lay all the weight ye can upon my patience,
    I make as little doubt as you do conscience
    In doing daily wrongs. I could say more,
    But reverence to your calling makes me modest.
GARDINER   My lord, my lord, you are a sectary,
    That's the plain truth; your painted gloss discovers
    To men that understand you, words and weakness.
CROMWELL   My lord of Winchester, y'are a little,
    By your good favour, too sharp; men so noble,
    However faulty, yet should find respect
    For what they have been: 'tis a cruelty
    To load a falling man.
GARDINER   Good master secretary,
    I cry your honour mercy; you may worst
    Of all this table say so.
CROMWELL   Why my lord?
GARDINER   Do not I know you for a favourer
    Of this new sect? ye are not sound.
CROMWELL   Not sound?
GARDINER   Not sound I say.
CROMWELL   Would you were half so honest;
    Men's prayers then would seek you, not their fears.
GARDINER   I shall remember this bold language.
CROMWELL   Do.
    Remember your bold life too.
CHANCELLOR   This is too much;
    Forbear for shame my lords.
GARDINER   I have done.
CROMWELL   And I.

CHANCELLOR
　　Then thus for you my lord, it stands agreed
　　I take it, by all voices; that forthwith
　　You be convey'd to th' Tower a prisoner,
　　There to remain till the king's further pleasure
125　Be known unto us; are you all agreed, lords?
ALL　We are.
CRANMER　　Is there no other way of mercy
　　But I must needs to th' Tower, my lords?
GARDINER　　　　　　　　What other
　　Would you expect? You are strangely troublesome:
　　Let some o'th' guard be ready there.

Enter the guard.

CRANMER　　　　　　　For me?
　　Must I go like a traitor thither?
130 GARDINER　　　　　　Receive him,
　　And see him safe i'th' Tower.
CRANMER　　　　　Stay good my lords,
　　I have a little yet to say. Look there my lords;
　　By virtue of that ring, I take my cause
　　Out of the gripes of cruel men, and give it
135　To a most noble judge, the king my master.
CHAMBERLAIN　This is the king's ring.
SURREY　　　　　　　'Tis no counterfeit.
SUFFOLK　'Tis the right ring, by heaven: I told ye all,
　　When we first put this dangerous stone a-rolling,
　　'Twould fall upon ourselves.
NORFOLK　　　　　Do you think my lords
140　The king will suffer but the little finger
　　Of this man to be vex'd?
CHAMBERLAIN　　　　'Tis now too certain;
　　How much more is his life in value with him?
　　Would I were fairly out on't.
CROMWELL　　　　　My mind gave me,
　　In seeking tales and informations
145　Against this man, whose honesty the devil
　　And his disciples only envy at,
　　Ye blew the fire that burns ye: now have at ye.

Enter KING *frowning on them, takes his seat.*

GARDINER
　　Dread sovereign, how much are we bound to heaven
　　In daily thanks, that gave us such a prince,
150　Not only good and wise, but most religious:
　　One that, in all obedience, makes the church
　　The chief aim of his honour, and to strengthen
　　That holy duty out of dear respect,
　　His royal self in judgement comes to hear
155　The cause betwixt her and this great offender.
KING　You were ever good at sudden commendations,
　　Bishop of Winchester. But know, I come not
　　To hear such flattery now, and in my presence
　　They are too thin and base to hide offences;
　　To me you cannot reach. You play the spaniel,
160　And think with wagging of your tongue to win me;
　　But whatsoe'er thou tak'st me for, I'm sure

Thou hast a cruel nature and a bloody.
[*to Cranmer*] Good man, sit down: now let me see the
　　proudest
He, that dares most, but wag his finger at thee,
By all that's holy, he had better starve　　165
Than but once think his place becomes thee not.
SURREY　May it please your grace –
KING　　　　　No sir, it does not please me;
　　I had thought I had had men of some understanding
　　And wisdom of my council; but I find none:　170
　　Was it discretion lords, to let this man,
　　This good man (few of you deserve that title)
　　This honest man, wait like a lousy footboy
　　At chamber-door? and one as great as you are?
　　Why, what a shame was this? Did my commission　175
　　Bid ye so far forget yourselves? I gave ye
　　Power as he was a councillor to try him,
　　Not as a groom: there's some of ye, I see,
　　More out of malice than integrity
　　Would try him to the utmost, had ye mean,　180
　　Which ye shall never have while I live.
CHANCELLOR　　　　　Thus far
　　My most dread sovereign, may it like your grace
　　To let my tongue excuse all. What was purpos'd
　　Concerning his imprisonment, was rather
　　(If there be faith in men) meant for his trial,　185
　　And fair purgation to the world than malice,
　　I'm sure, in me.
KING　　　Well, well my lords, respect him,
　　Take him and use him well; he's worthy of it.
　　I will say thus much for him, if a prince
　　May be beholding to a subject, I　190
　　Am for his love and service, so to him.
　　Make me no more ado, but all embrace him;
　　Be friends for shame my lords: my lord of
　　　　Canterbury,
　　I have a suit which you must not deny me;
　　That is, a fair young maid that yet wants baptism;　195
　　You must be godfather, and answer for her.
CRANMER　The greatest monarch now alive may glory
　　In such an honour: how may I deserve it,
　　That am a poor and humble subject to you?
KING　Come, come my lord, you'ld spare your spoons;　200
　　you shall have two noble partners with you; the old
　　duchess of Norfolk, and Lady Marquess Dorset; will
　　these please you?
　　Once more my lord of Winchester, I charge you
　　Embrace and love this man.
GARDINER　　　　With a true heart　205
　　And brother-love I do it.
CRANMER　　　　　And let heaven
　　Witness how dear I hold this confirmation.
KING
　　Good man, those joyful tears show thy true heart;
　　The common voice I see is verified
　　Of thee, which says thus: 'Do my lord of Canterbury　210
　　A shrewd turn, and he's your friend for ever'.

Come lords, we trifle time away: I long
To have this young one made a Christian.
As I have made ye one lords, one remain;
215 So I grow stronger, you more honour gain.   *Exeunt.*

5.3   *Noise and tumult within: enter* Porter
and his Man.

PORTER   You'll leave your noise anon ye rascals: do you
take the court for Parish-garden? ye rude slaves, leave
your gaping.

ONE [*within*]   Good master porter, I belong to th' larder.

5 PORTER   Belong to th' gallows, and be hang'd ye rogue;
is this a place to roar in? Fetch me a dozen crab-tree
staves, and strong ones; these are but switches to 'em:
I'll scratch your heads; you must be seeing
christenings? do you look for ale and cakes here, you
10 rude rascals?

MAN   Pray sir, be patient; 'tis as much impossible
(Unless we sweep 'em from the door with cannons)
To scatter 'em, as 'tis to make 'em sleep
On may-day morning, which will never be:
15 We may as well push against Paul's as stir 'em.

PORTER   How got they in, and be hang'd?

MAN   Alas I know not, how gets the tide in?
As much as one sound cudgel of four foot
(You see the poor remainder) could distribute,
I made no spare, sir.

20 PORTER   You did nothing, sir.

MAN   I am not Samson, nor Sir Guy, nor Colbrand,
To mow 'em down before me; but if I spar'd any
That had a head to hit, either young or old,
He or she, cuckold or cuckold-maker,
25 Let me ne'er hope to see a chine again,
And that I would not for a cow, God save her.

ONE [*within*]   Do you hear master porter?

PORTER
I shall be with you presently, good master puppy;
Keep the door close sirrah.

30 MAN   What would you have me do?

PORTER   What should you do, but knock 'em down by
th' dozens? Is this Moorfields to muster in? Or have
we some strange Indian with the great tool come to
court, the women so besiege us? Bless me, what a fry
35 of fornication is at door! On my Christian conscience
this one christening will beget a thousand, here will
be father, godfather, and all together.

MAN   The spoons will be the bigger sir: there is a fellow
somewhat near the door, he should be a brazier by his
40 face, for o' my conscience twenty of the dog-days now
reign in's nose; all that stand about him are under the
line, they need no other penance: that fire-drake did I
hit three times on the head, and three times was his
nose discharg'd against me; he stands there like a
45 mortar-piece to blow us. There was a haberdasher's
wife of small wit near him, that rail'd upon me till her
pink'd porringer fell off her head, for kindling such a

combustion in the state. I miss'd the meteor once, and
hit that woman, who cried out 'Clubs', when I might
see from far some forty truncheoners draw to her   50
succour, which were the hope o'th' Strand where she
was quarter'd; they fell on, I made good my place; at
length they came to th' broomstaff to me, I defied 'em
still, when suddenly a file of boys behind 'em, loose
shot, deliver'd such a shower of pebbles, that I was fain   55
to draw mine honour in and let 'em win the work; the
devil was amongst 'em I think surely.

PORTER   These are the youths that thunder at a
playhouse, and fight for bitten apples, that no
audience but the tribulation of Tower-hill, or the   60
limbs of Limehouse their dear brothers, are able to
endure. I have some of 'em in *Limbo Patrum*, and
there they are like to dance these three days; besides
the running banquet of two beadles that is to come.

Enter Lord Chamberlain.

CHAMBERLAIN
Mercy o' me; what a multitude are here!   65
They grow still too; from all parts they are coming,
As if we kept a fair here: where are these porters,
These lazy knaves? Y'have made a fine hand, fellows!
There's a trim rabble let in; are all these
Your faithful friends o'th' suburbs? We shall have   70
Great store of room no doubt, left for the ladies,
When they pass back from the christening.

PORTER   And't please your honour,
We are but men, and what so many may do,
Not being torn a-pieces, we have done:
An army cannot rule 'em.

CHAMBERLAIN   As I live,   75
If the king blame me for't, I'll lay ye all
By th' heels, and suddenly; and on your heads
Clap round fines for neglect: y'are lazy knaves,
And here ye lie baiting of bombards when
Ye should do service. Hark, the trumpets sound,   80
Th'are come already from the christening;
Go break among the press, and find a way out
To let the troop pass fairly, or I'll find
A Marshalsea shall hold ye play these two months.

PORTER   Make way there for the princess.

MAN   You great fellow,   85
Stand close up, or I'll make your head ache.

PORTER   You i'th' chamblet, get up o'th' rail,
I'll peck you o'er the pales else.   *Exeunt.*   5

5.4   *Enter trumpets sounding: then two aldermen,* Lord
Mayor, Garter, CRANMER, DUKE OF NORFOLK *with his
marshal's staff,* DUKE OF SUFFOLK, *two noblemen bearing
great standing bowls for the christening gifts: then four
noblemen bearing a canopy, under which the Duchess of
Norfolk, godmother, bearing the child richly habited in a
mantle, etc.; train borne by a lady: then follows the
Marchioness Dorset, the other godmother and ladies.
The troop pass once about the stage, and Garter speaks.*

GARTER Heaven, from thy endless goodness, send
prosperous life, long and ever happy, to the high and
mighty princess of England, Elizabeth.

Flourish. Enter KING *and guard.*

CRANMER [*kneeling*]
 And to your royal grace, and the good queen,
5 My noble partners and myself thus pray,
 All comfort, joy in this most gracious lady,
 Heaven ever laid up to make parents happy,
 May hourly fall upon ye.
KING   Thank you good lord archbishop:
 What is her name?
CRANMER   Elizabeth.
KING   Stand up lord;
 [*The king kisses the child.*]
10 With this kiss take my blessing: God protect thee,
 Into whose hand I give thy life.
CRANMER   Amen.
KING My noble gossips, y'have been too prodigal;
 I thank ye heartily: so shall this lady,
 When she has so much English.
CRANMER   Let me speak sir,
15 For heaven now bids me; and the words I utter,
 Let none think flattery, for they'll find 'em truth.
 This royal infant (heaven still move about her)
 Though in her cradle, yet now promises
 Upon this land a thousand thousand blessings,
20 Which time shall bring to ripeness: she shall be
 (But few now living can behold that goodness)
 A pattern to all princes living with her,
 And all that shall succeed: Saba was never
 More covetous of wisdom and fair virtue
25 Than this pure soul shall be. All princely graces
 That mould up such a mighty piece as this is,
 With all the virtues that attend the good,
 Shall still be doubled on her. Truth shall nurse her,
 Holy and heavenly thoughts still counsel her;
30 She shall be lov'd and fear'd: her own shall bless her;
 Her foes shake like a field of beaten corn,
 And hang their heads with sorrow: good grows with
  her;
 In her days every man shall eat in safety
 Under his own vine what he plants, and sing
35 The merry songs of peace to all his neighbours.
 God shall be truly known, and those about her
 From her shall read the perfect ways of honour,
 And by those claim their greatness, not by blood.
 Nor shall this peace sleep with her; but, as when
40 The bird of wonder dies, the maiden phoenix,
 Her ashes new create another heir
 As great in admiration as herself,
 So shall she leave her blessedness to one

 (When heaven shall call her from this cloud of
  darkness)
 Who from the sacred ashes of her honour   45
 Shall star-like rise, as great in fame as she was,
 And so stand fix'd. Peace, plenty, love, truth, terror,
 That were the servants to this chosen infant,
 Shall then be his, and like a vine grow to him;
 Wherever the bright sun of heaven shall shine, 50
 His honour and the greatness of his name
 Shall be, and make new nations. He shall flourish,
 And like a mountain cedar, reach his branches
 To all the plains about him: our children's children
 Shall see this, and bless heaven.
KING   Thou speakest wonders. 55
CRANMER She shall be, to the happiness of England,
 An aged princess; many days shall see her,
 And yet no day without a deed to crown it.
 Would I had known no more; but she must die,
 She must, the saints must have her; yet a virgin, 60
 A most unspotted lily shall she pass
 To th' ground, and all the world shall mourn her.
KING O lord archbishop,
 Thou hast made me now a man; never before
 This happy child did I get anything.   65
 This oracle of comfort has so pleas'd me,
 That when I am in heaven I shall desire
 To see what this child does, and praise my maker.
 I thank ye all. To you my good lord mayor,
 And your good brethren, I am much beholding: 70
 I have receiv'd much honour by your presence,
 And ye shall find me thankful. Lead the way lords,
 Ye must all see the queen, and she must thank ye,
 She will be sick else. This day, no man think
 'Has business at his house; for all shall stay: 75
 This little one shall make it Holy-day. *Exeunt.*

EPILOGUE

'Tis ten to one this play can never please
All that are here: some come to take their ease
And sleep an hour or two; but those we fear
W'have frighted with our trumpets, so 'tis clear
They'll say 'tis naught: others to hear the city 5
Abus'd extremely, and to cry 'That's witty',
Which we have not done neither; that I fear
All the expected good w'are like to hear
For this play at this time, is only in
The merciful construction of good women, 10
For such a one we show'd 'em: if they smile,
And say 'twill do, I know within a while
All the best men are ours; for 'tis ill hap
If they hold, when their ladies bid 'em clap.

King John

The date and sources of *King John* are difficult to determine with any certainty because of the intricate and disputed relationship between the Folio text of this play and that of a play called *The Troublesome Reign of King John* which was published anonymously as a quarto in 1591 and reprinted with an attribution to 'W. Sh.' in 1611. The many parallels between the works in plot and structure (though not in language) indicate either that one was a source for the other or that they both drew on the same common source; scholars have been unable to agree on these matters, though they do agree that the Folio play was probably written between 1590 and 1595. It uses material from John Foxe's *Acts and Monuments* (1583, often referred to as 'Foxe's Book of Martyrs') and the second edition of Holinshed's *Chronicles* (1587); it was listed amongst Shakespeare's 'tragedies' by Francis Meres in his *Palladis Tamia* in 1598.

King John stands outside the historical sequence of the two 'tetralogies' – the eight 'Richard' and 'Henry' plays covering the period of English history from the events leading up to the deposition of Richard II (1399) to the overthrow of Richard III at Bosworth (1485). The play accordingly appears as the first of the histories in the First Folio. John's reign was much earlier (1199-1216), and was mainly noted by Tudor historians for the monarch's defiance of the Pope, which allowed him to be seen as a proto-Protestant figure (the *Troublesome Reign* is rather more anti-Catholic than *King John*). The one event most English people associate with King John today – the signing of the *Magna Carta* – is not highlighted in Tudor accounts. A feature of Shakespeare's play is the focus on the Bastard, Philip Faulconbridge, an essentially fictional figure based on one fleeting reference in the chronicles who also appears in the *Troublesome Reign*. His engaging and often satirical commentary on morality, war and politics serves to expose the opportunism and cynicism of most of the other characters. Ironically, he seems better equipped to be king than either of the legitimate claimants, John and Arthur; Shakespeare in fact altered his sources to make both their claims weaker: by suggesting John rules by might rather than by right and by making Arthur younger than he really was.

There are no records of any pre-Restoration performances, but it was revived in the mid-eighteenth century and also adapted by Colley Cibber as *Papal Tyranny in the Reign of John* (1745). It had a reasonably steady stage history from the eighteenth to the early twentieth century and was traditionally seen as a good vehicle for actors because of the number of strong roles and the opportunities for big set-piece debates and confrontations. Despite his earlier cynicism, the Bastard's final speech has aroused patriotic fervour at times when the play's concern with foreign invasion has seemed topical.

During the nineteenth century in particular, *King John*'s popularity seems to have depended on some spectacular productions including large casts and elaborately detailed historical sets. These were also notable for the presence of star performers in the role of Constance, from Sarah Siddons to Sybil Thorndike. Like *King Richard III* it has four significant roles for women (Eleanor, Lady Faulconbridge and Blanche, as well as Constance); their roles as the mothers and wives of powerful men underline the play's concern with legitimacy and usurpation. The tolerant attitude taken to the adultery of Lady Faulconbridge is in marked contrast to Shakespeare's attitude elsewhere in the canon, as the positive representation of the Bastard contrasts with his portrayals of Don John in *Much Ado About Nothing* and Edmund in *King Lear*.

The Arden text is based on the 1623 First Folio.

LIST OF ROLES

KING JOHN	
PRINCE HENRY	*son to the king*
ARTHUR	*Duke of Brittany, nephew to the king*
The Earl of SALISBURY	
The Earl of PEMBROKE	
The Earl of ESSEX	
The Lord BIGOT	
ROBERT Faulconbridge	*son to Sir Robert Faulconbridge*
Philip the BASTARD	*his half-brother*
HUBERT	*a citizen of Angers*
James GURNEY	*servant to Lady Faulconbridge*
PETER *of Pomfret*	*a prophet*
KING PHILIP	*of France*
LEWIS	*the Dauphin*
Limoges, Duke of AUSTRIA	
MELUN	*a French lord*
CHATILLON	*ambassador from France to King John*
Cardinal PANDULPH	*the Pope's legate*
Queen ELEANOR	*mother to King John*
CONSTANCE	*mother to Arthur*
BLANCHE	*of Spain, niece to King John*
LADY FAULCONBRIDGE	*widow to Sir Robert Faulconbridge*

Lords, Sheriff, Heralds, Officers, Soldiers, Messengers and other Attendants

602

King John

1.1   *Enter* KING JOHN, QUEEN ELEANOR,
     PEMBROKE, ESSEX, SALISBURY *and attendants,*
     with them CHATILLON *of France.*

KING JOHN
     Now, say, Chatillon, what would France with us?
CHATILLON
     Thus, after greeting, speaks the King of France
     In my behaviour to the majesty,
     The borrow'd majesty, of England here.
ELEANOR   A strange beginning: 'borrow'd majesty'!   5
KING JOHN   Silence, good mother; hear the embassy.
CHATILLON   Philip of France, in right and true behalf
     Of thy deceased brother Geoffrey's son,
     Arthur Plantagenet, lays most lawful claim
     To this fair island and the territories: 10
     To Ireland, Poictiers, Anjou, Touraine, Maine,
     Desiring thee to lay aside the sword
     Which sways usurpingly these several titles,
     And put the same into young Arthur's hand,
     Thy nephew and right royal sovereign.   15
KING JOHN   What follows if we disallow of this?
CHATILLON
     The proud control of fierce and bloody war,
     To enforce these rights so forcibly withheld.
KING JOHN
     Here have we war for war and blood for blood,
     Controlment for controlment: so answer France.   20
CHATILLON
     Then take my king's defiance from my mouth,
     The farthest limit of my embassy.
KING JOHN   Bear mine to him, and so depart in peace.
     Be thou as lightning in the eyes of France,
     For, ere thou canst report, I will be there: 25
     The thunder of my cannon shall be heard.
     So, hence! Be thou the trumpet of our wrath
     And sullen presage of your own decay.
     An honourable conduct let him have:
     Pembroke, look to't. Farewell, Chatillon.   30
                 Exeunt Chatillon and Pembroke.
ELEANOR   What now, my son! have I not ever said
     How that ambitious Constance would not cease
     Till she had kindled France, and all the world,
     Upon the right and party of her son?
     This might have been prevented and made whole   35
     With very easy arguments of love,
     Which now the manage of two kingdoms must
     With fearful-bloody issue arbitrate.
KING JOHN   Our strong possession and our right for us.
ELEANOR
     Your strong possession much more than your right,   40
     Or else it must go wrong with you and me:
     So much my conscience whispers in your ear,
     Which none but heaven, and you, and I, shall hear.

                 Enter a sheriff.

ESSEX   My liege, here is the strangest controversy,

Come from the country to be judg'd by you,   45
That e'er I heard: shall I produce the men?
KING JOHN   Let them approach.
     Our abbeys and our priories shall pay
     This expeditious charge.

       Enter ROBERT FAULCONBRIDGE, *and* PHILIP,
           his Bastard *brother.*

               What men are you?
BASTARD   Your faithful subject I, a gentleman,   50
     Born in Northamptonshire, and eldest son,
     As I suppose, to Robert Faulconbridge,
     A soldier, by the honour-giving hand
     Of Coeur-de-lion knighted in the field.
KING JOHN   What art thou?   55
ROBERT
     The son and heir to that same Faulconbridge.
KING JOHN   Is that the elder, and art thou the heir?
     You came not of one mother then, it seems.
BASTARD   Most certain of one mother, mighty king;
     That is well known; and, as I think, one father: 60
     But for the certain knowledge of that truth
     I put you o'er to heaven and to my mother:
     Of that I doubt, as all men's children may.
ELEANOR
     Out on thee, rude man! thou dost shame thy mother
     And wound her honour with this diffidence.   65
BASTARD   I, madam? no, I have no reason for it;
     That is my brother's plea and none of mine;
     The which if he can prove, a pops me out
     At least from fair five hundred pound a year:
     Heaven guard my mother's honour, and my land!   70
KING JOHN
     A good blunt fellow. Why, being younger born,
     Doth he lay claim to thine inheritance?
BASTARD   I know not why – except to get the land –
     But once he slander'd me with bastardy:
     But whe'r I be as true begot or no,   75
     That still I lay upon my mother's head;
     But that I am as well begot, my liege –
     Fair fall the bones that took the pains for me! –
     Compare our faces and be judge yourself.
     If old Sir Robert did beget us both   80
     And were our father, and this son like him,
     O old Sir Robert, father, on my knee
     I give heaven thanks I was not like to thee!
KING JOHN
     Why, what a madcap hath heaven lent us here!
ELEANOR   He hath a trick of Coeur-de-lion's face;   85
     The accent of his tongue affecteth him.
     Do you not read some tokens of my son
     In the large composition of this man?
KING JOHN   Mine eye hath well examined his parts
     And finds them perfect Richard. Sirrah, speak,   90
     What doth move you to claim your brother's land?
BASTARD   Because he hath a half-face, like my father!
     With half that face would he have all my land:

A half-fac'd groat five hundred pound a year!

95 ROBERT   My gracious liege, when that my father liv'd,
Your brother did employ my father much –

BASTARD   Well sir, by this you cannot get my land:
Your tale must be how he employ'd my mother.

ROBERT   – And once dispatch'd him in an embassy
100 To Germany, there with the emperor
To treat of high affairs touching that time.
Th'advantage of his absence took the king
And in the mean time sojourn'd at my father's,
Where how he did prevail I shame to speak;
105 But truth is truth: large lengths of seas and shores
Between my father and my mother lay,
As I have heard my father speak himself,
When this same lusty gentleman was got.
Upon his death-bed he by will bequeath'd
110 His lands to me, and took it on his death
That this my mother's son was none of his;
And if he were, he came into the world
Full fourteen weeks before the course of time.
Then, good my liege, let me have what is mine,
115 My father's land, as was my father's will.

KING JOHN   Sirrah, your brother is legitimate;
Your father's wife did after wedlock bear him,
And if she did play false, the fault was hers;
Which fault lies on the hazards of all husbands
120 That marry wives. Tell me, how if my brother,
Who, as you say, took pains to get this son,
Had of your father claim'd this son for his?
In sooth, good friend, your father might have kept
This calf, bred from his cow, from all the world;
125 In sooth he might; then, if he were my brother's,
My brother might not claim him; nor your father,
Being none of his, refuse him: this concludes;
My mother's son did get your father's heir;
Your father's heir must have your father's land.

130 ROBERT   Shall then my father's will be of no force
To dispossess that child which is not his?

BASTARD   Of no more force to dispossess me, sir,
Than was his will to get me, as I think.

ELEANOR
Whether hadst thou rather be a Faulconbridge,
135 And like thy brother, to enjoy thy land,
Or the reputed son of Coeur-de-lion,
Lord of thy presence and no land beside?

BASTARD   Madam, and if my brother had my shape,
And I had his, Sir Robert's his like him;
140 And if my legs were two such riding-rods,
My arms such eel-skins stuff'd, my face so thin
That in mine ear I durst not stick a rose
Lest men should say 'Look, where three-farthings
goes!'
And, to his shape, were heir to all this land,
145 Would I might never stir from off this place,
I would give it every foot to have this face:
It would not be Sir Knob in any case.

ELEANOR
I like thee well: wilt thou forsake thy fortune,
Bequeath thy land to him and follow me?
I am a soldier and now bound to France.   150

BASTARD
Brother, take you my land, I'll take my chance.
Your face hath got five hundred pound a year,
Yet sell your face for five pence and 'tis dear.
Madam, I'll follow you unto the death.

ELEANOR   Nay, I would have you go before me thither.   155

BASTARD   Our country manners give our betters way.

KING JOHN   What is thy name?

BASTARD   Philip, my liege, so is my name begun;
Philip, good old Sir Robert's wive's eldest son.

KING JOHN
From henceforth bear his name whose form thou
bearest: 160
Kneel thou down Philip, but rise more great,
Arise Sir Richard, and Plantagenet.

BASTARD
Brother by th' mother's side, give me your hand:
My father gave me honour, yours gave land.
Now blessed be the hour, by night or day,   165
When I was got, Sir Robert was away!

ELEANOR   The very spirit of Plantagenet!
I am thy grandam, Richard; call me so.

BASTARD
Madam, by chance but not by truth; what though?
Something about, a little from the right,   170
In at the window, or else o'er the hatch:
Who dares not stir by day must walk by night,
And have is have, however men do catch.
Near or far off, well won is still well shot,
And I am I, howe'er I was begot.   175

KING JOHN
Go, Faulconbridge: now hast thou thy desire;
A landless knight makes thee a landed squire.
Come, madam, and come, Richard, we must speed
For France, for France, for it is more than need.

BASTARD   Brother, adieu: good fortune come to thee!   180
For thou wast got i'th' way of honesty.

Exeunt all but Bastard.

A foot of honour better than I was,
But many a many foot of land the worse.
Well, now can I make any Joan a lady.
'Good den, Sir Richard!' – 'God-a-mercy, fellow!' –   185
And if his name be George, I'll call him Peter;
For new-made honour doth forget men's names:
'Tis too respective and too sociable
For your conversion. Now your traveller,
He and his toothpick at my worship's mess,   190
And when my knightly stomach is suffic'd,
Why then I suck my teeth and catechize
My picked man of countries: 'My dear sir,' –
Thus, leaning on mine elbow, I begin,
'I shall beseech you,' – that is Question now;   195

And then comes Answer like an Absey book:
'O sir,' says Answer, 'at your best command;
At your employment; at your service, sir:'
'No, sir,' says Question, 'I, sweet sir, at yours:'
And so, ere Answer knows what Question would, 200
Saving in dialogue of compliment,
And talking of the Alps and Apennines,
The Pyrenean and the river Po,
It draws toward supper in conclusion so.
But this is worshipful society, 205
And fits the mounting spirit like myself;
For he is but a bastard to the time
That doth not smack of observation;
And so am I, whether I smoke or no.
And not alone in habit and device, 210
Exterior form, outward accoutrement,
But from the inward motion to deliver
Sweet, sweet, sweet poison for the age's tooth:
Which, though I will not practise to deceive,
Yet, to avoid deceit, I mean to learn; 215
For it shall strew the footsteps of my rising.
But who comes in such haste in riding-robes?
What woman-post is this? hath she no husband
That will take pains to blow a horn before her?

Enter LADY FAULCONBRIDGE *and* JAMES GURNEY.

O me! 'tis my mother. – How now, good lady? 220
What brings you here to court so hastily?
LADY FAULCONBRIDGE
Where is that slave, thy brother? where is he,
That holds in chase mine honour up and down?
BASTARD   My brother Robert? old Sir Robert's son?
Colbrand the giant, that same mighty man? 225
Is it Sir Robert's son that you seek so?
LADY FAULCONBRIDGE
Sir Robert's son! Ay, thou unreverend boy –
Sir Robert's son? – why scorn'st thou at Sir Robert?
He is Sir Robert's son, and so art thou.
BASTARD
James Gurney, wilt thou give us leave awhile? 230
GURNEY   Good leave, good Philip.
BASTARD   Philip? – sparrow! – James,
There's toys abroad: anon I'll tell thee more.
                                    Exit Gurney.
Madam, I was not old Sir Robert's son:
Sir Robert might have ate his part in me
Upon Good Friday and ne'er broke his fast: 235
Sir Robert could do – well, marry, to confess –
Could . . . get me? Sir Robert could not do it.
We know his handiwork: therefore, good mother,
To whom am I beholding for these limbs?
Sir Robert never holp to make this leg. 240
LADY FAULCONBRIDGE
Hast thou conspired with thy brother too,
That for thine own gain shouldst defend mine
        honour?
What means this scorn, thou most untoward knave?

BASTARD   Knight, knight, good mother, Basilisco-like:
What! I am dubb'd! I have it on my shoulder. 245
But, mother, I am not Sir Robert's son:
I have disclaim'd Sir Robert and my land;
Legitimation, name and all is gone.
Then, good my mother, let me know my father;
Some proper man, I hope: who was it, mother? 250
LADY FAULCONBRIDGE
Hast thou denied thyself a Faulconbridge?
BASTARD   As faithfully as I deny the devil.
LADY FAULCONBRIDGE
King Richard Coeur-de-lion was thy father:
By long and vehement suit I was seduc'd
To make room for him in my husband's bed. 255
Heaven, lay not my transgression to my charge
That art the issue of my dear offence,
Which was so strongly urg'd past my defence!
BASTARD   Now, by this light, were I to get again,
Madam, I would not wish a better father. 260
Some sins do bear their privilege on earth,
And so doth yours: your fault was not your folly.
Needs must you lay your heart at his dispose,
Subjected tribute to commanding love,
Against whose fury and unmatched force 265
The aweless lion could not wage the fight,
Nor keep his princely heart from Richard's hand.
He that perforce robs lions of their hearts
May easily win a woman's. Ay, my mother,
With all my heart I thank thee for my father! 270
Who lives and dares but say thou didst not well
When I was got, I'll send his soul to hell.
Come, lady, I will show thee to my kin;
And they shall say, when Richard me begot,
If thou hadst said him nay, it had been sin; 275
Who says it was, he lies: I say 'twas not!   *Exeunt.*

2.1   *Enter, on one side, the* Archduke of AUSTRIA,
and forces; on the other, PHILIP, *King of France, and forces,*
LEWIS, CONSTANCE, ARTHUR *and attendants.*

LEWIS   Before Angiers well met, brave Austria.
KING PHILIP   Arthur, that great forerunner of thy blood,
Richard, that robb'd the lion of his heart
And fought the holy wars in Palestine,
By this brave duke came early to his grave: 5
And for amends to his posterity
At our importance hither is he come,
To spread his colours, boy, in thy behalf,
And to rebuke the usurpation
Of thy unnatural uncle, English John: 10
Embrace him, love him, give him welcome hither.
ARTHUR
God shall forgive you Coeur-de-lion's death
The rather that you give his offspring life,
Shadowing their right under your wings of war:
I give you welcome with a powerless hand, 15
But with a heart full of unstained love:

605

Welcome before the gates of Angiers, duke.
LEWIS   Ah, noble boy, who would not do thee right?
AUSTRIA   Upon thy cheek lay I this zealous kiss,
20   As seal to this indenture of my love:
That to my home I will no more return,
Till Angiers and the right thou hast in France,
Together with that pale, that white-fac'd shore,
Whose foot spurns back the ocean's roaring tides
25   And coops from other lands her islanders,
Even till that England, hedg'd in with the main,
That water-walled bulwark, still secure
And confident from foreign purposes,
Even till that utmost corner of the west
30   Salute thee for her king; till then, fair boy,
Will I not think of home, but follow arms.
CONSTANCE
O, take his mother's thanks, a widow's thanks,
Till your strong hand shall help to give him strength
To make a more requital to your love!
AUSTRIA
35   The peace of heaven is theirs that lift their swords
In such a just and charitable war.
KING PHILIP   Well then, to work; our cannon shall be bent
Against the brows of this resisting town.
Call for our chiefest men of discipline,
40   To cull the plots of best advantages:
We'll lay before this town our royal bones,
Wade to the market-place in Frenchmen's blood,
But we will make it subject to this boy.
CONSTANCE   Stay for an answer to your embassy,
45   Lest unadvis'd you stain your swords with blood:
My Lord Chatillon may from England bring
That right in peace which here we urge in war,
And then we shall repent each drop of blood
That hot rash haste so indirectly shed.

Enter CHATILLON.

50   KING PHILIP   A wonder, lady! lo, upon thy wish,
Our messenger Chatillon is arriv'd!
What England says, say briefly, gentle lord;
We coldly pause for thee; Chatillon, speak.
CHATILLON
Then turn your forces from this paltry siege
55   And stir them up against a mightier task.
England, impatient of your just demands,
Hath put himself in arms: the adverse winds,
Whose leisure I have stay'd, have given him time
To land his legions all as soon as I;
60   His marches are expedient to this town,
His forces strong, his soldiers confident.
With him along is come the mother-queen,
An Ate, stirring him to blood and strife;
With her her niece, the Lady Blanche of Spain;
65   With them a bastard of the king's deceas'd,
And all th'unsettled humours of the land;
Rash, inconsiderate, fiery voluntaries,
With ladies' faces and fierce dragons' spleens,

Have sold their fortunes at their native homes,
Bearing their birthrights proudly on their backs,   70
To make a hazard of new fortunes here:
In brief, a braver choice of dauntless spirits
Than now the English bottoms have waft o'er
Did never float upon the swelling tide,
To do offence and scathe in Christendom.   75
                                    [*Drum beats.*]
The interruption of their churlish drums
Cuts off more circumstance: they are at hand,
To parley or to fight; therefore prepare.
KING PHILIP   How much unlook'd for is this expedition!
AUSTRIA   By how much unexpected, by so much   80
We must awake endeavour for defence,
For courage mounteth with occasion:
Let them be welcome then; we are prepar'd.

Enter KING JOHN, ELEANOR, BLANCHE, *the* Bastard,
lords and forces.

KING JOHN
Peace be to France, if France in peace permit
Our just and lineal entrance to our own;   85
If not, bleed France, and peace ascend to heaven,
Whiles we, God's wrathful agent, do correct
Their proud contempt that beats His peace to
   heaven.
KING PHILIP   Peace be to England, if that war return
From France to England, there to live in peace.   90
England we love; and for that England's sake
With burden of our armour here we sweat.
This toil of ours should be a work of thine;
But thou from loving England art so far,
That thou hast underwrought his lawful king,   95
Cut off the sequence of posterity,
Outfaced infant state, and done a rape
Upon the maiden virtue of the crown.
Look here upon thy brother Geoffrey's face;
These eyes, these brows, were moulded out of his: 100
This little abstract doth contain that large
Which died in Geoffrey: and the hand of time
Shall draw this brief into as huge a volume.
That Geoffrey was thy elder brother born,
And this his son; England was Geoffrey's right,   105
And this is Geoffrey's; in the name of God
How comes it then that thou art call'd a king,
When living blood doth in these temples beat,
Which owe the crown that thou o'ermasterest?
KING JOHN
From whom hast thou this great commission,
   France,   110
To draw my answer from thy articles?
KING PHILIP
From that supernal judge that stirs good thoughts
In any beast of strong authority
To look into the blots and stains of right.
That judge hath made me guardian to this boy: 115
Under whose warrant I impeach thy wrong

And by whose help I mean to chastise it.
KING JOHN   Alack, thou dost usurp authority.
KING PHILIP   Excuse it is to beat usurping down.
ELEANOR   Who is it thou dost call usurper, France?   20
CONSTANCE   Let me make answer: thy usurping son.
ELEANOR   Out, insolent! thy bastard shall be king,
    That thou mayst be a queen, and check the world!
CONSTANCE   My bed was ever to thy son as true
    As thine was to thy husband; and this boy   25
    Liker in feature to his father Geoffrey
    Than thou and John in manners; being as like
    As rain to water, or devil to his dam.
    My boy a bastard! By my soul, I think
    His father never was so true begot: 30
    It cannot be and if thou wert his mother.
ELEANOR
    There's a good mother, boy, that blots thy father.
CONSTANCE
    There's a good grandam, boy, that would blot thee.
AUSTRIA   Peace!
BASTARD   Hear the crier!
AUSTRIA   What the devil art thou?
BASTARD   One that will play the devil, sir, with you,   35
    And a may catch your hide and you alone:
    You are the hare of whom the proverb goes,
    Whose valour plucks dead lions by the beard.
    I'll smoke your skin-coat, and I catch you right;
    Sirrah, look to't; i'faith I will, i'faith.   40
BLANCHE   O, well did he become that lion's robe
    That did disrobe the lion of that robe!
BASTARD   It lies as sightly on the back of him
    As great Alcides' shoes upon an ass:
    But, ass, I'll take that burthen from your back,   45
    Or lay on that shall make your shoulders crack.
AUSTRIA   What cracker is this same that deafs our ears
    With this abundance of superfluous breath?
KING PHILIP
    Lewis, determine what we shall do straight.
LEWIS   Women and fools, break off your conference.   50
KING PHILIP   King John, this is the very sum of all:
    England and Ireland, Anjou, Touraine, Maine,
    In right of Arthur do I claim of thee.
    Wilt thou resign them and lay down thy arms?
KING JOHN   My life as soon: I do defy thee, France.   55
    Arthur of Britain, yield thee to my hand;
    And out of my dear love I'll give thee more
    Than e'er the coward hand of France can win:
    Submit thee, boy.
ELEANOR   Come to thy grandam, child.
CONSTANCE   Do, child, go to it grandam, child;   60
    Give grandam kingdom, and it grandam will
    Give it a plum, a cherry, and a fig:
    There's a good grandam.
ARTHUR   Good my mother, peace!
    I would that I were low laid in my grave:
    I am not worth this coil that's made for me.   65

ELEANOR
    His mother shames him so, poor boy, he weeps.
CONSTANCE
    Now shame upon you, whe'r she does or no!
    His grandam's wrongs, and not his mother's shames,
    Draws those heaven-moving pearls from his poor
      eyes,
    Which heaven shall take in nature of a fee;   170
    Ay, with these crystal beads heaven shall be brib'd
    To do him justice and revenge on you.
ELEANOR
    Thou monstrous slanderer of heaven and earth!
CONSTANCE
    Thou monstrous injurer of heaven and earth!
    Call not me slanderer; thou and thine usurp   175
    The dominations, royalties and rights
    Of this oppressed boy: this is thy eldest son's son,
    Infortunate in nothing but in thee:
    Thy sins are visited in this poor child;
    The canon of the law is laid on him,   180
    Being but the second generation
    Removed from thy sin-conceiving womb.
KING JOHN   Bedlam, have done.
CONSTANCE   I have but this to say,
    That he is not only plagued for her sin,
    But God hath made her sin and her the plague   185
    On this removed issue, plagued for her
    And with her plague; her sin his injury,
    Her injury the beadle to her sin,
    All punish'd in the person of this child,
    And all for her; a plague upon her!   190
ELEANOR   Thou unadvised scold, I can produce
    A will that bars the title of thy son.
CONSTANCE   Ay, who doubts that? a will! a wicked will;
    A woman's will; a cank'red grandam's will!
KING PHILIP   Peace, lady! pause, or be more temperate: 195
    It ill beseems this presence to cry aim
    To these ill-tuned repetitions.
    Some trumpet summon hither to the walls
    These men of Angiers: let us hear them speak
    Whose title they admit, Arthur's or John's.   200

    Trumpet sounds. Enter HUBERT *upon the walls.*

HUBERT   Who is it that hath warn'd us to the walls?
KING PHILIP   'Tis France, for England.
KING JOHN   England, for itself.
    You men of Angiers, and my loving subjects –
KING PHILIP
    You loving men of Angiers, Arthur's subjects,
    Our trumpet call'd you to this gentle parle –   205
KING JOHN   For our advantage; therefore hear us first.
    These flags of France, that are advanced here
    Before the eye and prospect of your town,
    Have hither march'd to your endamagement.
    The cannons have their bowels full of wrath,   210
    And ready mounted are they to spit forth
    Their iron indignation 'gainst your walls:

All preparation for a bloody siege
And merciless proceeding by these French
215   Comforts your city's eyes, your winking gates;
And but for our approach those sleeping stones,
That as a waist doth girdle you about,
By the compulsion of their ordinance
By this time from their fixed beds of lime
220   Had been dishabited, and wide havoc made
For bloody power to rush upon your peace.
But on the sight of us your lawful king,
Who painfully with much expedient march
Have brought a countercheck before your gates,
225   To save unscratch'd your city's threat'ned cheeks,
Behold, the French amaz'd vouchsafe a parle;
And now, instead of bullets wrapp'd in fire,
To make a shaking fever in your walls,
They shoot but calm words folded up in smoke,
230   To make a faithless error in your ears:
Which trust accordingly, kind citizens,
And let us in, your king, whose labour'd spirits
Forwearied in this action of swift speed
Craves harbourage within your city walls.
     KING PHILIP
235   When I have said, make answer to us both.
Lo, in this right hand, whose protection
Is most divinely vow'd upon the right
Of him it holds, stands young Plantagenet,
Son to the elder brother of this man,
240   And king o'er him and all that he enjoys:
For this down-trodden equity we tread
In warlike march these greens before your town,
Being no further enemy to you
Than the constraint of hospitable zeal
245   In the relief of this oppressed child
Religiously provokes. Be pleased then
To pay that duty which you truly owe
To him that owes it, namely this young prince:
And then our arms, like to a muzzled bear,
250   Save in aspect, hath all offence seal'd up;
Our cannons' malice vainly shall be spent
Against th' invulnerable clouds of heaven;
And with a blessed and unvex'd retire,
With unhack'd swords and helmets all unbruis'd,
255   We will bear home that lusty blood again
Which here we came to spout against your town,
And leave your children, wives and you in peace.
But if you fondly pass our proffer'd offer,
'Tis not the roundure of your old-fac'd walls
260   Can hide you from our messengers of war,
Though all these English and their discipline
Were harbour'd in their rude circumference.
Then tell us, shall your city call us lord,
In that behalf which we have challeng'd it?
265   Or shall we give the signal to our rage
And stalk in blood to our possession?
     HUBERT
In brief, we are the king of England's subjects:

For him, and in his right, we hold this town.
KING JOHN   Acknowledge then the king, and let me in.
HUBERT   That can we not; but he that proves the king,   270
To him will we prove loyal: till that time
Have we ramm'd up our gates against the world.
KING JOHN
Doth not the crown of England prove the king?
And if not that, I bring you witnesses,
Twice fifteen thousand hearts of England's breed –   275
BASTARD   Bastards and else.
KING JOHN   To verify our title with their lives.
KING PHILIP
As many and as well-born bloods as those –
BASTARD   Some bastards too.
KING PHILIP   Stand in his face to contradict his claim.   280
HUBERT   Till you compound whose right is worthiest,
We for the worthiest hold the right from both.
KING JOHN   Then God forgive the sin of all those souls
That to their everlasting residence,
Before the dew of evening fall, shall fleet,   285
In dreadful trial of our kingdom's king!
KING PHILIP   Amen, amen! Mount, chevaliers! to arms!
BASTARD
Saint George, that swindg'd the dragon, and e'er
     since
Sits on's horse-back at mine hostess' door,
Teach us some fence!
[*to Austria*]   Sirrah, were I at home,   290
At your den, sirrah, with your lioness,
I would set an ox-head to your lion's hide,
And make a monster of you.
AUSTRIA   Peace! no more.
BASTARD   O, tremble: for you hear the lion roar!
KING JOHN
Up higher to the plain; where we'll set forth   295
In best appointment all our regiments.
BASTARD   Speed then, to take advantage of the field.
KING PHILIP   It shall be so; and at the other hill
Command the rest to stand. God and our right!
     Exeunt, severally, the English and French kings, etc.

     Here, after excursions, enter the Herald of France,
         with trumpeters, to the gates.

FRENCH HERALD
You men of Angiers, open wide your gates,   300
And let young Arthur, Duke of Britain, in,
Who by the hand of France this day hath made
Much work for tears in many an English mother,
Whose sons lie scatter'd on the bleeding ground:
Many a widow's husband grovelling lies,   305
Coldly embracing the discolour'd earth;
And victory, with little loss, doth play
Upon the dancing banners of the French,
Who are at hand, triumphantly display'd,
To enter conquerors, and to proclaim   310
Arthur of Britain England's king, and yours.

Enter English Herald, *with trumpeter.*

ENGLISH HERALD

    Rejoice, you men of Angiers, ring your bells;
    King John, your king and England's, doth approach,
    Commander of this hot malicious day.
    Their armours, that march'd hence so silver-bright,   5
    Hither return all gilt with Frenchmen's blood;
    There stuck no plume in any English crest
    That is removed by a staff of France;
    Our colours do return in those same hands
    That did display them when we first march'd forth;   10
    And, like a jolly troop of huntsmen, come
    Our lusty English, all with purpled hands,
    Dyed in the dying slaughter of their foes:
    Open your gates and give the victors way.

HUBERT

    Heralds, from off our towers we might behold,   15
    From first to last, the onset and retire
    Of both your armies; whose equality
    By our best eyes cannot be censured:
    Blood hath bought blood and blows have answer'd
       blows;
    Strength match'd with strength, and power
       confronted power: 20
    Both are alike, and both alike we like.
    One must prove greatest: while they weigh so ever
    We hold our town for neither, yet for both.

Re-enter, on one side, KING JOHN, ELEANOR, BLANCHE,
the BASTARD, *lords and forces; on the other,*
KING PHILIP, LEWIS, AUSTRIA *and forces.*

KING JOHN

    France, hast thou yet more blood to cast away?
    Say, shall the current of our right roam on?   35
    Whose passage, vex'd with thy impediment,
    Shall leave his native channel and o'erswell,
    With course disturb'd, even thy confining shores,
    Unless thou let his silver water keep
    A peaceful progress to the ocean.   40

KING PHILIP

    England, thou hast not sav'd one drop of blood,
    In this hot trial, more than we of France;
    Rather, lost more. And by this hand I swear,
    That sways the earth this climate overlooks,
    Before we will lay down our just-borne arms,   45
    We'll put thee down 'gainst whom these arms we
       bear,
    Or add a royal number to the dead,
    Gracing the scroll that tells of this war's loss
    With slaughter coupled to the name of kings.

BASTARD   Ha, majesty! how high thy glory towers   50
    When the rich blood of kings is set on fire!
    O, now doth death line his dead chaps with steel;
    The swords of soldiers are his teeth, his fangs;
    And now he feasts, mousing the flesh of men,
    In undetermin'd differences of kings.   55

    Why stand these royal fronts amazed thus?
    Cry 'havoc!' kings; back to the stained field,
    You equal potents, fiery kindled spirits!
    Then let confusion of one part confirm
    The other's peace; till then, blows, blood, and death!   360

KING JOHN   Whose party do the townsmen yet admit?

KING PHILIP

    Speak, citizens, for England; who's your king?

HUBERT   The king of England, when we know the king.

KING PHILIP

    Know him in us, that here hold up his right.

KING JOHN   In us, that are our own great deputy,   365
    And bear possession of our person here,
    Lord of our presence, Angiers, and of you.

HUBERT   A greater power than we denies all this;
    And till it be undoubted, we do lock
    Our former scruple in our strong-barr'd gates: 370
    Kings of our fear, until our fears, resolv'd,
    Be by some certain king purg'd and depos'd.

BASTARD

    By heaven, these scroyles of Angiers flout you, kings,
    And stand securely on their battlements,
    As in a theatre, whence they gape and point   375
    At your industrious scenes and acts of death.
    Your royal presences be rul'd by me:
    Do like the mutines of Jerusalem,
    Be friends awhile and both conjointly bend
    Your sharpest deeds of malice on this town.   380
    By east and west let France and England mount
    Their battering cannon charged to the mouths,
    Till their soul-fearing clamours have brawl'd down
    The flinty ribs of this contemptuous city:
    I'd play incessantly upon these jades,   385
    Even till unfenced desolation
    Leave them as naked as the vulgar air.
    That done, dissever your united strengths,
    And part your mingled colours once again;
    Turn face to face and bloody point to point;   390
    Then, in a moment, fortune shall cull forth
    Out of one side her happy minion,
    To whom in favour she shall give the day,
    And kiss him with a glorious victory.
    How like you this wild counsel, mighty states?   395
    Smacks it not something of the policy?

KING JOHN

    Now, by the sky that hangs above our heads,
    I like it well. France, shall we knit our powers
    And lay this Angiers even with the ground;
    Then after fight who shall be king of it?   400

BASTARD   And if thou hast the mettle of a king,
    Being wrong'd as we are by this peevish town,
    Turn thou the mouth of thy artillery,
    As we will ours, against these saucy walls;
    And when that we have dash'd them to the ground,   405
    Why then defy each other, and pell-mell
    Make work upon ourselves, for heaven or hell.

KING PHILIP   Let it be so. Say, where will you assault?

KING JOHN   We from the west will send destruction
410   Into this city's bosom.
AUSTRIA   I from the north.
KING PHILIP   Our thunder from the south
    Shall rain their drift of bullets on this town.
BASTARD [*aside*]
    O prudent discipline! From north to south
    Austria and France shoot in each other's mouth:
415   I'll stir them to it. – Come, away, away!
HUBERT   Hear us, great kings: vouchsafe awhile to stay,
    And I shall show you peace and fair-fac'd league;
    Win you this city without stroke or wound;
    Rescue those breathing lives to die in beds,
420   That here come sacrifices for the field:
    Persever not, but hear me, mighty kings!
KING JOHN   Speak on, with favour; we are bent to hear.
HUBERT
    That daughter there of Spain, the Lady Blanche,
    Is near to England: look upon the years
425   Of Lewis the Dolphin and that lovely maid:
    If lusty love should go in quest of beauty,
    Where should he find it fairer than in Blanche?
    If zealous love should go in search of virtue,
    Where should he find it purer than in Blanche?
430   If love ambitious sought a match of birth,
    Whose veins bound richer blood than Lady Blanche?
    Such as she is, in beauty, virtue, birth,
    Is the young Dolphin every way complete:
    If not complete of, say he is not she;
435   And she again wants nothing, to name want,
    If want it be not that she is not he:
    He is the half part of a blessed man,
    Left to be finished by such as she;
    And she a fair divided excellence,
440   Whose fulness of perfection lies in him.
    O, two such silver currents, when they join,
    Do glorify the banks that bound them in;
    And two such shores, to two such streams made one,
    Two such controlling bounds shall you be, kings,
445   To these two princes, if you marry them.
    This union shall do more than battery can
    To our fast-closed gates; for at this match,
    With swifter spleen than powder can enforce,
    The mouth of passage shall we fling wide ope,
450   And give you entrance: but without this match
    The sea enraged is not half so deaf,
    Lions more confident, mountains and rocks
    More free from motion, no, not death himself
    In mortal fury half so peremptory,
    As we to keep this city.
455 BASTARD   Here's a stay
    That shakes the rotten carcass of old death
    Out of his rags! Here's a large mouth indeed,
    That spits forth death and mountains, rocks and seas,
    Talks as familiarly of roaring lions
460   As maids of thirteen do of puppy-dogs!
    What cannoneer begot this lusty blood?

He speaks plain cannon, fire, and smoke, and bounce;
He gives the bastinado with his tongue;
Our ears are cudgell'd; not a word of his
But buffets better than a fist of France.   465
Zounds! I was never so bethump'd with words
Since I first call'd my brother's father dad.
ELEANOR
    Son, list to this conjunction, make this match;
    Give with our niece a dowry large enough:
    For by this knot thou shalt so surely tie   470
    Thy now unsur'd assurance to the crown,
    That yon green boy shall have no sun to ripe
    The bloom that promiseth a mighty fruit.
    I see a yielding in the looks of France;
    Mark, how they whisper: urge them while their souls   475
    Are capable of this ambition,
    Lest zeal, now melted by the windy breath
    Of soft petitions, pity and remorse,
    Cool and congeal again to what it was.
HUBERT   Why answer not the double majesties   480
    This friendly treaty of our threat'ned town?
KING PHILIP
    Speak England first, that hath been forward first
    To speak unto this city: what say you?
KING JOHN   If that the Dolphin there, thy princely son,
    Can in this book of beauty read 'I love',   485
    Her dowry shall weigh equal with a queen:
    For Anjou, and fair Touraine, Maine, Poictiers,
    And all that we upon this side the sea –
    Except this city now by us besieg'd –
    Find liable to our crown and dignity,   490
    Shall gild her bridal bed, and make her rich
    In titles, honours and promotions,
    As she in beauty, education, blood,
    Holds hand with any princess of the world.
KING PHILIP
    What say'st thou, boy? look in the lady's face.   495
LEWIS   I do, my lord; and in her eye I find
    A wonder, or a wondrous miracle,
    The shadow of myself form'd in her eye;
    Which, being but the shadow of your son,
    Becomes a sun and makes your son a shadow: 500
    I do protest I never lov'd myself
    Till now infixed I beheld myself
    Drawn in the flattering table of her eye.
    [*Whispers with Blanche.*]
BASTARD [*aside*]
    Drawn in the flattering table of her eye!
    Hang'd in the frowning wrinkle of her brow!   505
    And quarter'd in her heart! he doth espy
    Himself love's traitor: this is pity now,
    That, hang'd and drawn and quarter'd, there should
        be
    In such a love so vile a lout as he!
BLANCHE [*to Lewis*]
    My uncle's will in this respect is mine: 510
    If he see aught in you that makes him like,

That any thing he sees, which moves his liking,
I can with ease translate it to my will;
Or if you will, to speak more properly,
I will enforce it eas'ly to my love.
Further I will not flatter you, my lord,
That all I see in you is worthy love,
Than this: that nothing do I see in you,
Though churlish thoughts themselves should be your
  judge,
That I can find should merit any hate.

KING JOHN
What say these young ones? What say you, my niece?

BLANCHE   That she is bound in honour still to do
What you in wisdom still vouchsafe to say.

KING JOHN
Speak then, prince Dolphin: can you love this lady?

LEWIS   Nay, ask me if I can refrain from love;
For I do love her most unfeignedly.

KING JOHN
Then do I give Volquessen, Touraine, Maine,
Poictiers, and Anjou, these five provinces,
With her to thee; and this addition more,
Full thirty thousand marks of English coin.
Philip of France, if thou be pleas'd withal,
Command thy son and daughter to join hands.

KING PHILIP
It likes us well; young princes, close your hands.

AUSTRIA   And your lips too; for I am well assur'd
That I did so when I was first assur'd.

KING PHILIP   Now, citizens of Angiers, ope your gates,
Let in that amity which you have made;
For at Saint Mary's chapel presently
The rites of marriage shall be solemniz'd.
Is not the Lady Constance in this troop?
I know she is not, for this match made up
Her presence would have interrupted much:
Where is she and her son? tell me, who knows.

LEWIS   She is sad and passionate at your highness' tent.

KING PHILIP
And, by my faith, this league that we have made
Will give her sadness very little cure.
Brother of England, how may we content
This widow lady? In her right we came;
Which we, God knows, have turn'd another way,
To our own vantage.

KING JOHN   We will heal up all;
For we'll create young Arthur Duke of Britain
And Earl of Richmond; and this rich fair town
We make him lord of. Call the Lady Constance;
Some speedy messenger bid her repair
To our solemnity: I trust we shall,
If not fill up the measure of her will,
Yet in some measure satisfy her so
That we shall stop her exclamation.
Go we, as well as haste will suffer us,
To this unlook'd for, unprepared pomp.

Exeunt all but the Bastard.

BASTARD   Mad world! mad kings! mad composition!
John, to stop Arthur's title in the whole,
Hath willingly departed with a part:
And France, whose armour conscience buckled on,
Whom zeal and charity brought to the field   565
As God's own soldier, rounded in the ear
With that same purpose-changer, that sly divel,
That broker, that still breaks the pate of faith,
That daily break-vow, he that wins of all,
Of kings, of beggars, old men, young men, maids,   570
Who, having no external thing to lose
But the word 'maid', cheats the poor maid of that,
That smooth-fac'd gentleman, tickling commodity,
Commodity, the bias of the world,
The world, who of itself is peised well,   575
Made to run even upon even ground,
Till this advantage, this vile drawing bias,
This sway of motion, this commodity,
Makes it take head from all indifferency,
From all direction, purpose, course, intent: 580
And this same bias, this commodity,
This bawd, this broker, this all-changing word,
Clapp'd on the outward eye of fickle France,
Hath drawn him from his own determin'd aid,
From a resolv'd and honourable war,   585
To a most base and vile-concluded peace.
And why rail I on this commodity?
But for because he hath not woo'd me yet:
Not that I have the power to clutch my hand,
When his fair angels would salute my palm;   590
But for my hand, as unattempted yet,
Like a poor beggar, raileth on the rich.
Well, whiles I am a beggar, I will rail
And say there is no sin but to be rich;
And being rich, my virtue then shall be   595
To say there is no vice but beggary.
Since kings break faith upon commodity,
Gain, be my lord, for I will worship thee!   *Exit.*

2.2   *Enter* CONSTANCE, ARTHUR *and* SALISBURY.

CONSTANCE
Gone to be married! gone to swear a peace!
False blood to false blood join'd! gone to be friends!
Shall Lewis have Blanche, and Blanche those
  provinces?
It is not so; thou hast misspoke, misheard;
Be well advis'd, tell o'er thy tale again.   5
It cannot be; thou dost but say 'tis so.
I trust I may not trust thee, for thy word
Is but the vain breath of a common man;
Believe me, I do not believe thee, man:
I have a king's oath to the contrary.   10
Thou shalt be punish'd for thus frighting me,
For I am sick and capable of fears,
Oppress'd with wrongs and therefore full of fears,
A widow, husbandless, subject to fears,

15 A woman, naturally born to fears;
And though thou now confess thou didst but jest
With my vex'd spirits I cannot take a truce,
But they will quake and tremble all this day.
What dost thou mean by shaking of thy head?
20 Why dost thou look so sadly on my son?
What means that hand upon that breast of thine?
Why holds thine eye that lamentable rheum,
Like a proud river peering o'er his bounds?
Be these sad signs confirmers of thy words?
25 Then speak again; not all thy former tale,
But this one word, whether thy tale be true.

SALISBURY As true as I believe you think them false
That give you cause to prove my saying true.

CONSTANCE O, if thou teach me to believe this sorrow,
30 Teach thou this sorrow how to make me die,
And let belief and life encounter so
As doth the fury of two desperate men
Which in the very meeting fall, and die.
Lewis marry Blanche! O boy, then where art thou?
35 France friend with England, what becomes of me?
Fellow, be gone: I cannot brook thy sight.
This news hath made thee a most ugly man.

SALISBURY What other harm have I, good lady, done,
But spoke the harm that is by others done?

40 CONSTANCE Which harm within itself so heinous is
As it makes harmful all that speak of it.

ARTHUR I do beseech you, madam, be content.

CONSTANCE
If thou, that bid'st me be content, wert grim,
Ugly, and sland'rous to thy mother's womb,
45 Full of unpleasing blots and sightless stains,
Lame, foolish, crooked, swart, prodigious,
Patch'd with foul moles and eye-offending marks,
I would not care, I then would be content,
For then I should not love thee: no, nor thou
50 Become thy great birth, nor deserve a crown.
But thou art fair, and at thy birth, dear boy,
Nature and fortune join'd to make thee great:
Of nature's gifts thou mayst with lilies boast
And with the half-blown rose. But fortune, O,
55 She is corrupted, chang'd and won from thee;
Sh' adulterates hourly with thine uncle John,
And with her golden hand hath pluck'd on France
To tread down fair respect of sovereignty,
And made his majesty the bawd to theirs.
60 France is a bawd to fortune and King John,
That strumpet fortune, that usurping John!
Tell me, thou fellow, is not France forsworn?
Envenom him with words, or get thee gone,
And leave those woes alone which I alone
Am bound to underbear!

65 SALISBURY   Pardon me, madam,
I may not go without you to the kings.

CONSTANCE
Thou mayst, thou shalt; I will not go with thee:
I will instruct my sorrows to be proud,

For grief is proud an't makes his owner stoop.
70 To me and to the state of my great grief
Let kings assemble; for my grief's so great
That no supporter but the huge firm earth
Can hold it up: here I and sorrows sit;
Here is my throne, bid kings come bow to it.
[*Throws herself on the ground.*]   *Exit Salisbury.*

3.1   CONSTANCE *and* ARTHUR, *seated. Enter*
KING JOHN, KING PHILIP, LEWIS, BLANCHE,
ELEANOR, *the* BASTARD, AUSTRIA, SALISBURY
and attendants.

KING PHILIP
'Tis true, fair daughter; and this blessed day
Ever in France shall be kept festival:
To solemnize this day the glorious sun
Stays in his course and plays the alchemist,
5 Turning with splendour of his precious eye
The meagre cloddy earth to glittering gold:
The yearly course that brings this day about
Shall never see it but a holy day.

CONSTANCE A wicked day, and not a holy day! [*rising*]
10 What hath this day deserv'd? what hath it done,
That it in golden letters should be set
Among the high tides in the calendar?
Nay, rather turn this day out of the week,
This day of shame, oppression, perjury.
15 Or, if it must stand still, let wives with child
Pray that their burthens may not fall this day,
Lest that their hopes prodigiously be cross'd:
But on this day let seamen fear no wrack;
No bargains break that are not this day made;
20 This day, all things begun come to ill end,
Yea, faith itself to hollow falsehood change!

KING PHILIP By heaven, lady, you shall have no cause
To curse the fair proceedings of this day:
Have I not pawn'd to you my majesty?

25 CONSTANCE You have beguil'd me with a counterfeit
Resembling majesty, which, being touch'd and tried,
Proves valueless: you are forsworn, forsworn!
You came in arms to spill mine enemies' blood,
But now in arms you strengthen it with yours.
30 The grappling vigour and rough frown of war
Is cold in amity, and painted peace,
And our oppression hath made up this league.
Arm, arm, you heavens, against these perjur'd kings!
A widow cries; be husband to me, heavens!
35 Let not the hours of this ungodly day
Wear out the day's in peace; but, ere sunset,
Set armed discord 'twixt these perjur'd kings!
Hear me, O, hear me!

AUSTRIA   Lady Constance, peace!

CONSTANCE War! war! no peace! peace is to me a war.
40 O Limoges! O Austria! thou dost shame
That bloody spoil: thou slave, thou wretch, thou
          coward!

Thou little valiant, great in villainy!
Thou ever strong upon the stronger side!
Thou fortune's champion, that dost never fight
But when her humorous ladyship is by
To teach thee safety! thou art perjur'd too,
And sooth'st up greatness. What a fool art thou,
A ramping fool, to brag, and stamp, and swear
Upon my party! Thou cold-blooded slave,
Hast thou not spoke like thunder on my side,
Been sworn my soldier, bidding me depend
Upon thy stars, thy fortune and thy strength,
And dost thou now fall over to my foes?
Thou wear a lion's hide! doff it for shame,
And hang a calve's-skin on those recreant limbs.

AUSTRIA
  O, that a man should speak those words to me!

BASTARD
  And hang a calve's-skin on those recreant limbs.

AUSTRIA Thou dar'st not say so, villain, for thy life.

BASTARD
  And hang a calve's-skin on those recreant limbs.

KING JOHN We like not this; thou dost forget thyself.

Enter PANDULPH.

KING PHILIP Here comes the holy legate of the pope.

PANDULPH Hail, you anointed deputies of heaven!
  To thee, King John, my holy errand is.
  I Pandulph, of fair Milan cardinal,
  And from Pope Innocent the legate here,
  Do in his name religiously demand
  Why thou against the church, our holy mother,
  So wilfully dost spurn; and force perforce
  Keep Stephen Langton, chosen archbishop
  Of Canterbury, from that holy see:
  This, in our foresaid holy father's name,
  Pope Innocent, I do demand of thee.

KING JOHN What earthy name to interrogatories
  Can taste the free breath of a sacred king?
  Thou canst not, cardinal, devise a name
  So slight, unworthy and ridiculous,
  To charge me to an answer, as the pope.
  Tell him this tale; and from the mouth of England
  Add thus much more, that no Italian priest
  Shall tithe or toll in our dominions;
  But as we, under God, are supreme head,
  So under Him that great supremacy,
  Where we do reign, we will alone uphold
  Without th' assistance of a mortal hand:
  So tell the pope, all reverence set apart
  To him and his usurp'd authority.

KING PHILIP
  Brother of England, you blaspheme in this.

KING JOHN
  Though you and all the kings of Christendom
  Are led so grossly by this meddling priest,
  Dreading the curse that money may buy out;
  And by the merit of vild gold, dross, dust,

Purchase corrupted pardon of a man,
Who in that sale sells pardon from himself;
Though you and all the rest so grossly led
This juggling witchcraft with revenue cherish,   95
Yet I alone, alone do me oppose
Against the pope, and count his friends my foes.

PANDULPH Then, by the lawful power that I have,
  Thou shalt stand curs'd and excommunicate:
  And blessed shall he be that doth revolt   100
  From his allegiance to an heretic;
  And meritorious shall that hand be call'd,
  Canonized and worshipp'd as a saint,
  That takes away by any secret course
  Thy hateful life.

CONSTANCE   O, lawful let it be   105
  That I have room with Rome to curse awhile!
  Good father cardinal, cry thou amen
  To my keen curses; for without my wrong
  There is no tongue hath power to curse him right.

PANDULPH
  There's law and warrant, lady, for my curse.   110

CONSTANCE
  And for mine too: when law can do no right
  Let it be lawful that law bar no wrong!
  Law cannot give my child his kingdom here,
  For he that holds his kingdom holds the law;
  Therefore, since law itself is perfect wrong,   115
  How can the law forbid my tongue to curse?

PANDULPH Philip of France, on peril of a curse,
  Let go the hand of that arch-heretic;
  And raise the power of France upon his head,
  Unless he do submit himself to Rome.   120

ELEANOR
  Look'st thou pale, France? do not let go thy hand.

CONSTANCE
  Look to that, devil, lest that France repent,
  And by disjoining hands, hell lose a soul.

AUSTRIA King Philip, listen to the cardinal.

BASTARD
  And hang a calve's-skin on his recreant limbs.   125

AUSTRIA Well, ruffian, I must pocket up these wrongs,
  Because –

BASTARD   Your breeches best may carry them.

KING JOHN Philip, what say'st thou to the cardinal?

CONSTANCE What should he say, but as the cardinal?

LEWIS Bethink you, father; for the difference   130
  Is purchase of a heavy curse from Rome,
  Or the light loss of England for a friend:
  Forgo the easier.

BLANCHE   That's the curse of Rome.

CONSTANCE
  O Lewis, stand fast! the devil tempts thee here
  In likeness of a new untrimmed bride.   135

BLANCHE
  The Lady Constance speaks not from her faith,
  But from her need.

CONSTANCE   O, if thou grant my need,

Which only lives but by the death of faith,
That need must needs infer this principle,
140 That faith would live again by death of need.
O then tread down my need, and faith mounts up:
Keep my need up, and faith is trodden down!
KING JOHN   The king is mov'd, and answers not to this.
CONSTANCE   O, be remov'd from him, and answer well!
145 AUSTRIA   Do so, King Philip; hang no more in doubt.
BASTARD
    Hang nothing but a calve's-skin, most sweet lout.
KING PHILIP   I am perplex'd, and know not what to say.
PANDULPH
    What canst thou say but will perplex thee more,
    If thou stand excommunicate and curs'd?
KING PHILIP
150   Good reverend father, make my person yours,
    And tell me how you would bestow yourself.
    This royal hand and mine are newly knit,
    And the conjunction of our inward souls –
    Married in league, coupled and link'd together
155   With all religious strength of sacred vows;
    The latest breath that gave the sound of words –
    Was deep-sworn faith, peace, amity, true love
    Between our kingdoms and our royal selves.
    And even before this truce, but new before,
160   No longer than we well could wash our hands
    To clap this royal bargain up of peace,
    Heaven knows, they were besmear'd and overstain'd
    With slaughter's pencil, where revenge did paint
    The fearful difference of incensed kings:
165   And shall these hands, so lately purg'd of blood,
    So newly join'd in love, so strong in both,
    Unyoke this seizure and this kind regreet?
    Play fast and loose with faith? so jest with heaven,
    Make such unconstant children of ourselves,
170   As now again to snatch our palm from palm,
    Unswear faith sworn, and on the marriage-bed
    Of smiling peace to march a bloody host,
    And make a riot on the gentle brow
    Of true sincerity? O, holy sir,
175   My reverend father, let it not be so!
    Out of your grace, devise, ordain, impose
    Some gentle order, and then we shall be blest
    To do your pleasure and continue friends.
PANDULPH   All form is formless, order orderless,
180   Save what is opposite to England's love.
    Therefore to arms! be champion of our church,
    Or let the church, our mother, breathe her curse,
    A mother's curse, on her revolting son.
    France, thou mayst hold a serpent by the tongue,
185   A cased lion by the mortal paw,
    A fasting tiger safer by the tooth,
    Than keep in peace that hand which thou dost hold.
KING PHILIP   I may disjoin my hand, but not my faith.
PANDULPH   So mak'st thou faith an enemy to faith,
190   And like a civil war set'st oath to oath,
    Thy tongue against thy tongue. O, let thy vow
First made to heaven, first be to heaven perform'd,
That is, to be the champion of our church.
What since thou swor'st is sworn against thyself
And may not be performed by thyself, 195
For that which thou hast sworn to do amiss
Is not amiss when it is truly done,
And being not done, where doing tends to ill,
The truth is then most done not doing it:
The better act of purposes mistook 200
Is to mistake again; though indirect,
Yet indirection thereby grows direct,
And falsehood falsehood cures, as fire cools fire
Within the scorched veins of one new-burn'd.
It is religion that doth make vows kept, 205
But thou hast sworn against religion:
By what thou swear'st against the thing thou
    swear'st,
And mak'st an oath the surety for thy truth!
Against an oath the truth thou art unsure
To swear – swears only not to be forsworn! – 210
Else what a mockery should it be to swear?
But thou dost swear only to be forsworn,
And most forsworn, to keep what thou dost swear.
Therefore thy later vows against thy first
Is in thyself rebellion to thyself; 215
And better conquest never canst thou make
Than arm thy constant and thy nobler parts
Against these giddy loose suggestions:
Upon which better part our prayers come in,
If thou vouchsafe them. But if not, then know 220
The peril of our curses light on thee
So heavy as thou shalt not shake them off,
But in despair die under their black weight.
AUSTRIA   Rebellion, flat rebellion!
BASTARD   Will't not be?
    Will not a calve's-skin stop that mouth of thine? 225
LEWIS   Father, to arms!
BLANCHE   Upon thy wedding-day?
    Against the blood that thou hast married?
    What, shall our feast be kept with slaughter'd men?
    Shall braying trumpets and loud churlish drums,
    Clamours of hell, be measures to our pomp? 230
    O husband, hear me! ay, alack, how new
    Is 'husband' in my mouth! even for that name,
    Which till this time my tongue did ne'er pronounce,
    Upon my knee I beg, go not to arms
    Against mine uncle.
CONSTANCE   O, upon my knee, 235
    Made hard with kneeling, I do pray to thee,
    Thou virtuous Dolphin, alter not the doom
    Forethought by heaven!
BLANCHE   Now shall I see thy love: what motive may
    Be stronger with thee than the name of wife? 240
CONSTANCE
    That which upholdeth him that thee upholds,
    His honour: O, thine honour, Lewis, thine honour!
LEWIS   I muse your majesty doth seem so cold,

When such profound respects do pull you on.
PANDULPH   I will denounce a curse upon his head.
KING PHILIP
  Thou shalt not need. England, I will fall from thee.
CONSTANCE   O fair return of banish'd majesty!
ELEANOR   O foul revolt of French inconstancy!
KING JOHN
  France, thou shalt rue this hour within this hour.
BASTARD
  Old time the clock-setter, that bald sexton time,
  Is it as he will? well then, France shall rue.
BLANCHE
  The sun's o'ercast with blood: fair day, adieu!
  Which is the side that I must go withal?
  I am with both: each army hath a hand;
  And in their rage, I having hold of both,
  They whirl asunder and dismember me.
  Husband, I cannot pray that thou mayst win;
  Uncle, I needs must pray that thou mayst lose;
  Father, I may not wish the fortune thine;
  Grandam, I will not wish thy wishes thrive:
  Whoever wins, on that side shall I lose;
  Assured loss before the match be play'd.
LEWIS   Lady, with me, with me thy fortune lies.
BLANCHE
  There where my fortune li'es, there my life dies.
KING JOHN   Cousin, go draw our puissance together.
                                    Exit Bastard.
  France, I am burn'd up with inflaming wrath;
  A rage whose heat hath this condition,
  That nothing can allay, nothing but blood,
  The blood, and dearest-valued blood, of France.
KING PHILIP
  Thy rage shall burn thee up, and thou shalt turn
  To ashes, ere our blood shall quench that fire:
  Look to thyself, thou art in jeopardy.
KING JOHN
  No more than he that threats. To arms let's hie!
                                      Exeunt.

3.2   *Alarums, excursions. Enter the* Bastard,
         with AUSTRIA's *head.*

BASTARD
  Now, by my life, this day grows wondrous hot;
  Some airy devil hovers in the sky,
  And pours down mischief. Austria's head lie there,

         Enter KING JOHN, ARTHUR *and* HUBERT.

  While Philip breathes.
KING JOHN   Hubert, keep this boy. Philip, make up:
  My mother is assailed in our tent,
  And ta'en, I fear.
BASTARD   My lord, I rescued her;
  Her highness is in safety, fear you not:
  But on, my liege; for very little pains
  Will bring this labour to an happy end.   *Exeunt.*

Alarums, excursions, retreat. Re-enter KING JOHN,
  ARTHUR, *the* Bastard, HUBERT, *with* ELEANOR
                  and lords.

KING JOHN [*to Eleanor*]
  So shall it be; your grace shall stay behind
  So strongly guarded. [*to Arthur*] Cousin, look not sad:
  Thy grandam loves thee; and thy uncle will
  As dear be to thee as thy father was.
ARTHUR   O, this will make my mother die with grief!   15
KING JOHN [*to the Bastard*]
  Cousin, away for England! haste before:
  And, ere our coming, see thou shake the bags
  Of hoarding abbots; imprison'd angels
  Set at liberty: the fat ribs of peace
  Must by the hungry now be fed upon: 20
  Use our commission in his utmost force.
BASTARD
  Bell, book, and candle shall not drive me back
  When gold and silver becks me to come on:
  I leave your highness. Grandam, I will pray –
  If ever I remember to be holy –   25
  For your fair safety; so, I kiss your hand.
ELEANOR   Farewell, gentle cousin.
KING JOHN   Coz, farewell.
                                    Exit Bastard.
ELEANOR   Come hither, little kinsman; hark, a word.
  [*She takes Arthur aside.*]
KING JOHN   Come hither, Hubert. O my gentle Hubert,
  We owe thee much! within this wall of flesh   30
  There is a soul counts thee her creditor,
  And with advantage means to pay thy love:
  And, my good friend, thy voluntary oath
  Lives in this bosom, dearly cherished.
  Give me thy hand. I had a thing to say,   35
  But I will fit it with some better tune.
  By heaven, Hubert, I am almost asham'd
  To say what good respect I have of thee.
HUBERT   I am much bounden to your majesty.
KING JOHN
  Good friend, thou hast no cause to say so yet,   40
  But thou shalt have; and creep time ne'er so slow,
  Yet it shall come for me to do thee good.
  I had a thing to say, but let it go:
  The sun is in the heaven, and the proud day,
  Attended with the pleasures of the world,   45
  Is all too wanton and too full of gauds
  To give me audience: if the midnight bell
  Did, with his iron tongue and brazen mouth,
  Sound on into the drowsy race of night;
  If this same were a churchyard where we stand,   50
  And thou possessed with a thousand wrongs;
  Or if that surly spirit, melancholy,
  Had bak'd thy blood and made it heavy, thick,
  Which else runs tickling up and down the veins,
  Making that idiot, laughter, keep men's eyes   55
  And strain their cheeks to idle merriment,

A passion hateful to my purposes;
Or if that thou couldst see me without eyes,
Hear me without thine ears, and make reply
60 Without a tongue, using conceit alone,
Without eyes, ears, and harmful sound of words;
Then, in despite of brooded watchful day,
I would into thy bosom pour my thoughts:
But, ah, I will not. Yet I love thee well;
65 And, by my troth, I think thou lov'st me well.
HUBERT   So well, that what you bid me undertake,
Though that my death were adjunct to my act,
By heaven, I would do it.
KING JOHN   Do not I know thou wouldst?
Good Hubert, Hubert, Hubert, throw thine eye
70 On yon young boy; I'll tell thee what, my friend,
He is a very serpent in my way;
And wheresoe'er this foot of mine doth tread,
He lies before me: dost thou understand me?
Thou art his keeper.
HUBERT   And I'll keep him so
75 That he shall not offend your majesty.
KING JOHN   Death.
HUBERT   My lord?
KING JOHN   A grave.
HUBERT   He shall not live.
KING JOHN   Enough.
I could be merry now. Hubert, I love thee.
Well, I'll not say what I intend for thee:
Remember. – Madam, fare you well:
80 I'll send those powers o'er to your majesty.
ELEANOR   My blessing go with thee!
KING JOHN   For England, cousin, go:
Hubert shall be your man, attend on you
With all true duty. On toward Calais, ho!   *Exeunt.*

3.3   *Enter* KING PHILIP, LEWIS, PANDULPH
and attendants.

KING PHILIP   So, by a roaring tempest on the flood,
A whole armado of convicted sail
Is scatter'd and disjoin'd from fellowship.
PANDULPH   Courage and comfort! all shall yet go well.
KING PHILIP
5 What can go well, when we have run so ill?
Are we not beaten? Is not Angiers lost?
Arthur ta'en prisoner? divers dear friends slain?
And bloody England into England gone,
O'erbearing interruption, spite of France?
10 LEWIS   What he hath won, that hath he fortified:
So hot a speed with such advice dispos'd,
Such temperate order in so fierce a cause,
Doth want example: who hath read or heard
Of any kindred action like to this?
KING PHILIP
15 Well could I bear that England had this praise
So we could find some pattern of our shame.

Enter CONSTANCE.

Look, who comes here! a grave unto a soul;
Holding th'eternal spirit, against her will,
In the vild prison of afflicted breath.
I prithee, lady, go away with me.   20
CONSTANCE
Lo! now – now see the issue of your peace!
KING PHILIP
Patience, good lady! comfort, gentle Constance!
CONSTANCE   No! – I defy all counsel, all redress,
But that which ends all counsel, true redress:
Death! death, O amiable, lovely death!   25
Thou odoriferous stench! sound rottenness!
Arise forth from the couch of lasting night,
Thou hate and terror to prosperity,
And I will kiss thy detestable bones
And put my eyeballs in thy vaulty brows,   30
And ring these fingers with thy household worms,
And stop this gap of breath with fulsome dust,
And be a carrion monster like thyself:
Come, grin on me, and I will think thou smil'st,
And buss thee as thy wife. Misery's love,   35
O, come to me!
KING PHILIP   O fair affliction, peace!
CONSTANCE   No, no, I will not, having breath to cry:
O, that my tongue were in the thunder's mouth!
Then with a passion would I shake the world;
And rouse from sleep that fell anatomy   40
Which cannot hear a lady's feeble voice,
Which scorns a modern invocation.
PANDULPH   Lady, you utter madness, and not sorrow.
CONSTANCE   Thou art holy to belie me so! –
I am not mad: this hair I tear is mine;   45
My name is Constance; I was Geoffrey's wife;
Young Arthur is my son, and he is lost!
I am not mad: I would to heaven I were!
For then 'tis like I should forget myself:
O, if I could, what grief should I forget!   50
Preach some philosophy to make me mad,
And thou shalt be canoniz'd, cardinal;
For, being not mad but sensible of grief,
My reasonable part produces reason
How I may be deliver'd of these woes,   55
And teaches me to kill or hang myself:
If I were mad, I should forget my son,
Or madly think a babe of clouts were he.
I am not mad; too well, too well I feel
The different plague of each calamity.   60
KING PHILIP   Bind up those tresses. O, what love I note
In the fair multitude of those her hairs!
Where but by chance a silver drop hath fall'n,
Even to that drop ten thousand wiry friends
Do glue themselves in sociable grief,   65
Like true, inseparable, faithful loves,
Sticking together in calamity.
CONSTANCE   To England, if you will.
KING PHILIP   Bind up your hairs.
CONSTANCE   Yes, that I will; and wherefore will I do it?

70   I tore them from their bonds and cried aloud,
'O that these hands could so redeem my son,
As they have given these hairs their liberty!'
But now I envy at their liberty,
And will again commit them to their bonds,
75   Because my poor child is a prisoner.
And, father cardinal, I have heard you say
That we shall see and know our friends in heaven:
If that be true, I shall see my boy again;
For since the birth of Cain, the first male child,
80   To him that did but yesterday suspire,
There was not such a gracious creature born.
But now will canker-sorrow eat my bud
And chase the native beauty from his cheek
And he will look as hollow as a ghost,
85   As dim and meagre as an ague's fit,
And so he'll die; and, rising so again,
When I shall meet him in the court of heaven
I shall not know him: therefore never, never
Must I behold my pretty Arthur more.
90   PANDULPH   You hold too heinous a respect of grief.
CONSTANCE   He talks to me that never had a son.
KING PHILIP   You are as fond of grief as of your child.
CONSTANCE
Grief fills the room up of my absent child,
Lies in his bed, walks up and down with me,
95   Puts on his pretty looks, repeats his words,
Remembers me of all his gracious parts,
Stuffs out his vacant garments with his form;
Then have I reason to be fond of grief?
Fare you well: had you such a loss as I
100   I could give better comfort than you do.
I will not keep this form upon my head,
When there is such disorder in my wit.
O Lord! my boy, my Arthur, my fair son!
My life, my joy, my food, my all the world!
105   My widow-comfort, and my sorrows' cure!   *Exit.*
KING PHILIP   I fear some outrage, and I'll follow her.
                                       Exit.
LEWIS   There's nothing in this world can make me joy:
Life is as tedious as a twice-told tale
Vexing the dull ear of a drowsy man;
110   And bitter shame hath spoil'd the sweet word's taste,
That it yields nought but shame and bitterness.
PANDULPH   Before the curing of a strong disease,
Even in the instant of repair and health,
The fit is strongest; evils that take leave,
115   On their departure most of all show evil.
What have you lost by losing of this day?
LEWIS   All days of glory, joy and happiness.
PANDULPH   If you had won it, certainly you had.
No, no; when fortune means to men most good
120   She looks upon them with a threat'ning eye.
'Tis strange to think how much King John hath lost
In this which he accounts so clearly won:
Are not you griev'd that Arthur is his prisoner?
LEWIS   As heartily as he is glad he hath him.

PANDULPH   Your mind is all as youthful as your blood.   125
Now hear me speak with a prophetic spirit;
For even the breath of what I mean to speak
Shall blow each dust, each straw, each little rub,
Out of the path which shall directly lead
Thy foot to England's throne; and therefore mark.   130
John hath seiz'd Arthur; and it cannot be
That, whiles warm life plays in that infant's veins,
The misplac'd John should entertain an hour,
One minute, nay, one quiet breath of rest.
A sceptre snatch'd with an unruly hand   135
Must be as boisterously maintain'd as gain'd;
And he that stands upon a slipp'ry place
Makes nice of no vild hold to stay him up:
That John may stand, then, Arthur needs must fall;
So be it, for it cannot but be so.   140
LEWIS   But what shall I gain by young Arthur's fall?
PANDULPH
You, in the right of Lady Blanche your wife,
May then make all the claim that Arthur did.
LEWIS   And lose it, life and all, as Arthur did.
PANDULPH
How green you are and fresh in this old world!   145
John lays you plots; the times conspire with you;
For he that steeps his safety in true blood
Shall find but bloody safety and untrue.
This act so evilly borne shall cool the hearts
Of all his people, and freeze up their zeal,   150
That none so small advantage shall step forth
To check his reign, but they will cherish it;
No natural exhalation in the sky,
No scope of nature, no distemper'd day,
No common wind, no customed event,   155
But they will pluck away his natural cause
And call them meteors, prodigies and signs,
Abortives, presages, and tongues of heaven,
Plainly denouncing vengeance upon John.
LEWIS   Maybe he will not touch young Arthur's life,   160
But hold himself safe in his prisonment.
PANDULPH   O, sir, when he shall hear of your approach,
If that young Arthur be not gone already,
Even at that news he dies; and then the hearts
Of all his people shall revolt from him,   165
And kiss the lips of unacquainted change,
And pick strong matter of revolt and wrath
Out of the bloody fingers' ends of John.
Methinks I see this hurly all on foot:
And, O, what better matter breeds for you   170
Than I have nam'd! The bastard Faulconbridge
Is now in England ransacking the church,
Offending charity: if but a dozen French
Were there in arms, they would be as a call
To train ten thousand English to their side,   175
Or as a little snow, tumbled about,
Anon becomes a mountain. O noble Dolphin,
Go with me to the king: 'tis wonderful
What may be wrought out of their discontent,

180 Now that their souls are topful of offence.
For England go; I will whet on the king.

LEWIS
Strong reasons makes strange actions. Let us go:
If you say ay, the king will not say no. *Exeunt.*

4.1 *Enter* HUBERT *and* Executioners.

HUBERT   Heat me these irons hot; and look thou stand
Within the arras: when I strike my foot
Upon the bosom of the ground, rush forth
And bind the boy which you shall find with me
Fast to the chair. Be heedful: hence, and watch.

5 1 EXECUTIONER
I hope your warrant will bear out the deed.

HUBERT   Uncleanly scruples! fear not you; look to't.
[*The Executioners withdraw.*]
Young lad, come forth; I have to say with you.

Enter ARTHUR.

ARTHUR   Good morrow, Hubert.

HUBERT   Good morrow, little prince.

ARTHUR   As little prince having so great a title
To be more prince, as may be. – You are sad.

10 HUBERT   Indeed, I have been merrier.

ARTHUR   Mercy on me!
Methinks nobody should be sad but I:
Yet, I remember, when I was in France,
Young gentlemen would be as sad as night,
Only for wantonness. By my christendom,

15 So I were out of prison and kept sheep,
I should be as merry as the day is long;
And so I would be here, but that I doubt
My uncle practises more harm to me.
He is afraid of me and I of him:

20 Is it my fault that I was Geoffrey's son?
No, indeed, is't not; and I would to heaven
I were your son, so you would love me, Hubert.

HUBERT [*aside*]   If I talk to him, with his innocent prate
He will awake my mercy, which lies dead:

25 Therefore I will be sudden and dispatch.

ARTHUR   Are you sick, Hubert? you look pale to-day.
In sooth, I would you were a little sick,
That I might sit all night and watch with you:
I warrant I love you more than you do me.

30 HUBERT [*aside*]
His words do take possession of my bosom.
Read here, young Arthur. [*showing a paper*]
[*aside*]   How now, foolish rheum!
Turning dispiteous torture out of door!
I must be brief, lest resolution drop

35 Out at mine eyes in tender womanish tears. –
Can you not read it? is it not fair writ?

ARTHUR   Too fairly, Hubert, for so foul effect:
Must you with hot irons burn out both mine eyes?

HUBERT   Young boy, I must.

ARTHUR   And will you?

40 HUBERT   And I will.

ARTHUR
Have you the heart? When your head did but ache,
I knit my handkercher about your brows,
The best I had, a princess wrought it me,
And I did never ask it you again;

45 And with my hand at midnight held your head,
And, like the watchful minutes to the hour,
Still and anon cheer'd up the heavy time,
Saying, 'What lack you?' and 'Where lies your grief?'
Or 'What good love may I perform for you?'

50 Many a poor man's son would have lien still
And ne'er have spoke a loving word to you;
But you at your sick-service had a prince.
Nay, you may think my love was crafty love,
And call it cunning: do, and if you will.

55 If heaven be pleas'd that you must use me ill,
Why then you must. Will you put out mine eyes?
These eyes that never did nor never shall
So much as frown on you.

HUBERT   I have sworn to do it;
And with hot irons must I burn them out.

60 ARTHUR   Ah, none but in this iron age would do it!
The iron of itself, though heat red-hot,
Approaching near these eyes, would drink my tears
And quench this fiery indignation
Even in the matter of mine innocence;

65 Nay, after that, consume away in rust,
But for containing fire to harm mine eye.
Are you more stubborn-hard than hammer'd iron?
And if an angel should have come to me
And told me Hubert should put out mine eyes,

70 I would not have believ'd him, – no tongue
But Hubert's.

HUBERT   Come forth! [*Stamps.*]
[*The Executioners come forth, with a cord, irons, etc.*]
                          Do as I bid you do.

ARTHUR   O, save me, Hubert, save me! my eyes are out
Even with the fierce looks of these bloody men.

HUBERT   Give me the iron, I say, and bind him here.

75 ARTHUR   Alas, what need you be so boist'rous-rough?
I will not struggle, I will stand stone-still.
For heaven sake, Hubert, let me not be bound!
Nay, hear me, Hubert, drive these men away,
And I will sit as quiet as a lamb;

80 I will not stir, nor winch, nor speak a word,
Nor look upon the iron angerly:
Thrust but these men away, and I'll forgive you
Whatever torment you do put me to.

HUBERT   Go, stand within; let me alone with him.

1 EXECUTIONER
I am best pleas'd to be from such a deed.

85 *Exeunt Executioners.*

ARTHUR   Alas, I then have chid away my friend!
He hath a stern look, but a gentle heart:

Let him come back, that his compassion may
Give life to yours.
HUBERT   Come, boy, prepare yourself.
ARTHUR   Is there no remedy?
HUBERT   None, but to lose your eyes.
ARTHUR
O heaven, that there were but a mote in yours,
A grain, a dust, a gnat, a wandering hair,
Any annoyance in that precious sense!
Then, feeling what small things are boisterous there,
Your vild intent must needs seem horrible.
HUBERT   Is this your promise? go to, hold your tongue.
ARTHUR   Hubert, the utterance of a brace of tongues.
Must needs want pleading for a pair of eyes:
Let me not hold my tongue, let me not, Hubert!
Or, Hubert, if you will, cut out my tongue,
So I may keep mine eyes: O, spare mine eyes,
Though to no use but still to look on you!
Lo, by my troth, the instrument is cold
And would not harm me.
HUBERT   I can heat it, boy.
ARTHUR   No, in good sooth; the fire is dead with grief,
Being create for comfort, to be us'd
In undeserv'd extremes; see else yourself:
There is no malice in this burning coal;
The breath of heaven hath blown his spirit out
And strew'd repentant ashes on his head.
HUBERT   But with my breath I can revive it, boy.
ARTHUR   And if you do, you will but make it blush
And glow with shame of your proceedings, Hubert:
Nay, it perchance will sparkle in your eyes;
And, like a dog that is compell'd to fight,
Snatch at his master that doth tarre him on.
All things that you should use to do me wrong
Deny their office: only you do lack
That mercy which fierce fire and iron extends –
Creatures of note for mercy lacking uses!
HUBERT   Well, see to live; I will not touch thine eye
For all the treasure that thine uncle owes:
Yet am I sworn and I did purpose, boy,
With this same very iron to burn them out.
ARTHUR   O, now you look like Hubert! all this while
You were disguis'd.
HUBERT   Peace; no more. Adieu.
Your uncle must not know but you are dead.
I'll fill these dogged spies with false reports:
And, pretty child, sleep doubtless and secure
That Hubert, for the wealth of all the world,
Will not offend thee.
ARTHUR   O heaven! I thank you, Hubert.
HUBERT   Silence; no more. Go closely in with me:
Much danger do I undergo for thee.   *Exeunt.*

4.2   *Enter* KING JOHN, PEMBROKE, SALISBURY
                    and other lords.

KING JOHN
Here once again we sit, once again crown'd,

And look'd upon, I hope, with cheerful eyes.
PEMBROKE
This 'once again', but that your highness pleas'd,
Was once superfluous: you were crown'd before,
And that high royalty was ne'er pluck'd off,   5
The faiths of men ne'er stained with revolt;
Fresh expectation troubled not the land
With any long'd-for change or better state.
SALISBURY
Therefore, to be possess'd with double pomp,
To guard a title that was rich before,   10
To gild refined gold, to paint the lily,
To throw a perfume on the violet,
To smooth the ice, or add another hue
Unto the rainbow, or with taper-light
To seek the beauteous eye of heaven to garnish,   15
Is wasteful and ridiculous excess.
PEMBROKE   But that your royal pleasure must be done,
This act is as an ancient tale new told,
And, in the last repeating, troublesome,
Being urged at a time unseasonable.   20
SALISBURY   In this the antique and well-noted face
Of plain old form is much disfigured;
And, like a shifted wind unto a sail,
It makes the course of thoughts to fetch about,
Startles and frights consideration,   25
Makes sound opinion sick and truth suspected,
For putting on so new a fashion'd robe.
PEMBROKE
When workmen strive to do better than well
They do confound their skill in covetousness;
And oftentimes excusing of a fault   30
Doth make the fault the worse by th'excuse:
As patches set upon a little breach
Discredit more in hiding of the fault
Than did the fault before it was so patch'd.
SALISBURY
To this effect, before you were new crown'd,   35
We breath'd our counsel: but it pleas'd your highness
To overbear it, and we are all well pleas'd,
Since all and every part of what we would
Doth make a stand at what your highness will.
KING JOHN   Some reasons of this double coronation   40
I have possess'd you with, and think them strong;
And more, more strong than lesser is my fear,
I shall indue you with: meantime but ask
What you would have reform'd that is not well,
And well shall you perceive how willingly   45
I will both hear and grant you your requests.
PEMBROKE   Then I, as one that am the tongue of these,
To sound the purposes of all their hearts,
Both for myself and them, but, chief of all,
Your safety, for the which, myself and them,   50
Bend their best studies, heartily request
Th'enfranchisement of Arthur: whose restraint
Doth move the murmuring lips of discontent
To break into this dangerous argument:

55 If what in rest you have in right you hold,
Why then your fears, which, as they say, attend
The steps of wrong, should move you to mew up
Your tender kinsman, and to choke his days
With barbarous ignorance, and deny his youth
60 The rich advantage of good exercise?
That the time's enemies may not have this
To grace occasions, let it be our suit
That you have bid us ask his liberty;
Which for our goods we do no further ask
65 Than whereupon our weal, on you depending,
Counts it your weal he have his liberty.

Enter HUBERT.

KING JOHN   Let it be so: I do commit his youth
To your direction. Hubert, what news with you?
[*taking him apart*]
PEMBROKE   This is the man should do the bloody deed:
70 He show'd his warrant to a friend of mine.
The image of a wicked heinous fault
Lives in his eye; that close aspect of his
Do show the mood of a much troubled breast;
And I do fearfully believe 'tis done,
75 What we so fear'd he had a charge to do.
SALISBURY   The colour of the king doth come and go
Between his purpose and his conscience,
Like heralds 'twixt two dreadful battles set:
His passion is so ripe, it needs must break.
80 PEMBROKE   And when it breaks, I fear will issue thence
The foul corruption of a sweet child's death.
KING JOHN   We cannot hold mortality's strong hand:
Good lords, although my will to give is living,
The suit which you demand is gone and dead:
85 He tells us Arthur is deceas'd to-night.
SALISBURY   Indeed we fear'd his sickness was past cure.
PEMBROKE
Indeed we heard how near his death he was,
Before the child himself felt he was sick:
This must be answer'd, either here or hence.
KING JOHN
90 Why do you bend such solemn brows on me?
Think you I bear the shears of destiny?
Have I commandment on the pulse of life?
SALISBURY   It is apparent foul-play; and 'tis shame
That greatness should so grossly offer it:
95 So thrive it in your game! and so, farewell.
PEMBROKE   Stay yet, Lord Salisbury; I'll go with thee,
And find th' inheritance of this poor child,
His little kingdom of a forced grave.
That blood which ow'd the breadth of all this isle
100 Three foot of it doth hold: bad world the while!
This must not be thus borne: this will break out
To all our sorrows, and ere long I doubt.
Exeunt Lords.
KING JOHN   They burn in indignation.

Enter a Messenger.

I repent:
There is no sure foundation set on blood,
No certain life achiev'd by others' death. 105
[*to the Messenger*] A fearful eye thou hast: where is
that blood
That I have seen inhabit in those cheeks?
So foul a sky clears not without a storm:
Pour down thy weather: how goes all in France?
MESSENGER
From France to England. Never such a power 110
For any foreign preparation
Was levied in the body of a land.
The copy of your speed is learn'd by them;
For when you should be told they do prepare
The tidings comes that they are all arriv'd. 115
KING JOHN   O, where hath our intelligence been drunk?
Where hath it slept? Where is my mother's care,
That such an army could be drawn in France,
And she not hear of it?
MESSENGER   My liege, her ear
Is stopp'd with dust: the first of April died 120
Your noble mother; and, as I hear, my lord,
The Lady Constance in a frenzy died
Three days before: but this from rumour's tongue
I idly heard; if true or false I know not.
KING JOHN   Withhold thy speed, dreadful occasion! 125
O, make a league with me, till I have pleas'd
My discontented peers! What! mother dead!
How wildly then walks my estate in France!
Under whose conduct came those powers of France
That thou for truth giv'st out are landed here? 130
MESSENGER   Under the Dolphin.

Enter the Bastard *and* PETER *of Pomfret.*

KING JOHN   Thou hast made me giddy
With these ill tidings. – Now, what says the world
To your proceedings? do not seek to stuff
My head with more ill news, for it is full.
BASTARD   But if you be afeard to hear the worst, 135
Then let the worst unheard fall on your head.
KING JOHN   Bear with me, cousin; for I was amaz'd
Under the tide: but now I breathe again
Aloft the flood, and can give audience
To any tongue, speak it of what it will. 140
BASTARD   How I have sped among the clergymen
The sums I have collected shall express.
But as I travaill'd hither through the land
I find the people strangely fantasied;
Possess'd with rumours, full of idle dreams, 145
Not knowing what they fear, but full of fear.
And here's a prophet, that I brought with me
From forth the streets of Pomfret, whom I found
With many hundreds treading on his heels;
To whom he sung, in rude harsh-sounding rhymes, 150
That, ere the next Ascension-day at noon,
Your highness should deliver up your crown.

KING JOHN
  Thou idle dreamer, wherefore didst thou so?
PETER Foreknowing that the truth will fall out so.
KING JOHN Hubert, away with him; imprison him:
  And on that day at noon, whereon he says
  I shall yield up my crown, let him be hang'd.
  Deliver him to safety, and return,
  For I must use thee.   *Exit Hubert with Peter.*
                O my gentle cousin,
  Hear'st thou the news abroad, who are arriv'd?
BASTARD
  The French, my lord: men's mouths are full of it.
  Besides, I met Lord Bigot and Lord Salisbury,
  With eyes as red as new-enkindled fire,
  And others more, going to seek the grave
  Of Arthur, whom they say is kill'd to-night
  On your suggestion.
KING JOHN   Gentle kinsman, go,
  And thrust thyself into their companies.
  I have a way to win their loves again;
  Bring them before me.
BASTARD   I will seek them out.
KING JOHN Nay, but make haste: the better foot before!
  O, let me have no subject enemies,
  When adverse foreigners affright my towns
  With dreadful pomp of stout invasion!
  Be Mercury, set feathers to thy heels,
  And fly like thought from them to me again.
BASTARD The spirit of the time shall teach me speed.
                                    Exit.
KING JOHN Spoke like a sprightful noble gentleman.
  Go after him; for he perhaps shall need
  Some messenger betwixt me and the peers;
  And be thou he.
MESSENGER With all my heart, my liege.   *Exit.*
KING JOHN My mother dead!

              Re-enter HUBERT.

HUBERT
  My lord, they say five moons were seen to-night:
  Four fixed, and the fift did whirl about
  The other four in wondrous motion.
KING JOHN Five moons?
HUBERT   Old men and beldams in the streets
  Do prophesy upon it dangerously:
  Young Arthur's death is common in their mouths:
  And when they talk of him, they shake their heads
  And whisper one another in the ear;
  And he that speaks doth gripe the hearer's wrist,
  Whilst he that hears makes fearful action,
  With wrinkled brows, with nods, with rolling eyes.
  I saw a smith stand with his hammer, thus,
  The whilst his iron did on the anvil cool,
  With open mouth swallowing a tailor's news;
  Who, with his shears and measure in his hand,
  Standing on slippers, which his nimble haste
  Had falsely thrust upon contrary feet,

  Told of a many thousand warlike French
  That were embattailed and rank'd in Kent: 200
  Another lean unwash'd artificer
  Cuts off his tale and talks of Arthur's death.
KING JOHN
  Why seek'st thou to possess me with these fears?
  Why urgest thou so oft young Arthur's death?
  Thy hand hath murd'red him: I had a mighty cause   205
  To wish him dead, but thou hadst none to kill him.
HUBERT
  No had, my lord! why, did you not provoke me?
KING JOHN It is the curse of kings to be attended
  By slaves that take their humours for a warrant
  To break within the bloody house of life,   210
  And on the winking of authority
  To understand a law, to know the meaning
  Of dangerous majesty, when perchance it frowns
  More upon humour than advis'd respect.
HUBERT Here is your hand and seal for what I did.   215
KING JOHN
  O, when the last accompt 'twixt heaven and earth
  Is to be made, then shall this hand and seal
  Witness against us to damnation!
  How oft the sight of means to do ill deeds
  Make deeds ill done! Hadst not thou been by,   220
  A fellow by the hand of nature mark'd,
  Quoted and sign'd to do a deed of shame,
  This murther had not come into my mind;
  But taking note of thy abhorr'd aspect,
  Finding thee fit for bloody villainy,   225
  Apt, liable to be employ'd in danger,
  I faintly broke with thee of Arthur's death;
  And thou, to be endeared to a king,
  Made it no conscience to destroy a prince.
HUBERT My lord –   230
KING JOHN
  Hadst thou but shook thy head or made a pause
  When I spake darkly what I purposed,
  Or turn'd an eye of doubt upon my face,
  As bid me tell my tale in express words,
  Deep shame had struck me dumb, made me break
        off,   235
  And those thy fears might have wrought fears in me:
  But thou didst understand me by my signs
  And didst in signs again parley with sin;
  Yea, without stop, didst let thy heart consent,
  And consequently thy rude hand to act   240
  The deed, which both our tongues held vild to name.
  Out of my sight, and never see me more!
  My nobles leave me, and my state is brav'd,
  Even at my gates, with ranks of foreign powers:
  Nay, in the body of this fleshly land,   245
  This kingdom, this confine of blood and breath,
  Hostility and civil tumult reigns
  Between my conscience and my cousin's death.
HUBERT Arm you against your other enemies,
  I'll make a peace between your soul and you.   250

Young Arthur is alive: this hand of mine
Is yet a maiden and an innocent hand,
Not painted with the crimson spots of blood.
Within this bosom never ent'red yet
255   The dreadful motion of a murderous thought;
And you have slander'd nature in my form,
Which, howsoever rude exteriorly,
Is yet the cover of a fairer mind
Than to be butcher of an innocent child.

KING JOHN
260   Doth Arthur live? O, haste thee to the peers,
Throw this report on their incensed rage,
And make them tame to their obedience!
Forgive the comment that my passion made
Upon thy feature; for my rage was blind,
265   And foul imaginary eyes of blood
Presented thee more hideous than thou art.
O, answer not, but to my closet bring
The angry lords with all expedient haste.
I conjure thee but slowly: run more fast!   *Exeunt.*

4.3   *Enter* ARTHUR, *on the walls.*

ARTHUR   The wall is high, and yet will I leap down:
Good ground, be pitiful and hurt me not!
There's few or none do know me: if they did,
This ship-boy's semblance hath disguis'd me quite.
5   I am afraid; and yet I'll venture it.
If I get down, and do not break my limbs,
I'll find a thousand shifts to get away:
As good to die and go, as die and stay.
[*He leaps, and lies momentarily in a trance.*]
O me! my uncle's spirit is in these stones:
10   Heaven take my soul, and England keep my bones!
[*Dies.*]

Enter PEMBROKE, SALISBURY *and* BIGOT.

SALISBURY
Lords, I will meet him at Saint Edmundsbury:
It is our safety, and we must embrace
This gentle offer of the perilous time.
PEMBROKE   Who brought that letter from the cardinal?
15 SALISBURY   The Count Melun, a noble lord of France;
Whose private with me of the Dolphin's love
Is much more general than these lines import.
BIGOT   To-morrow morning let us meet him then.
SALISBURY   Or rather then set forward; for 'twill be
20   Two long days' journey, lords, or ere we meet.

Enter the Bastard.

BASTARD
Once more to-day well met, distemper'd lords!
The king by me requests your presence straight.
SALISBURY   The king hath dispossess'd himself of us:
We will not line his thin bestained cloak
25   With our pure honours, nor attend the foot
That leaves the print of blood where'er it walks.

Return and tell him so: we know the worst.
BASTARD
Whate'er you think, good words, I think, were best.
SALISBURY
Our griefs, and not our manners, reason now.
BASTARD   But there is little reason in your grief;   30
Therefore 'twere reason you had manners now.
PEMBROKE   Sir, sir, impatience hath his privilege.
BASTARD
'Tis true, to hurt his master, no manners else.
SALISBURY
This is the prison.
[*seeing Arthur*]   What is he lies here?
PEMBROKE
O death, made proud with pure and princely beauty!   35
The earth had not a hole to hide this deed.
SALISBURY   Murther, as hating what himself hath done,
Doth lay it open to urge on revenge.
BIGOT   Or, when he doom'd this beauty to a grave,
Found it too precious-princely for a grave.   40
SALISBURY
Sir Richard, what think you? You have beheld.
Or have you read, or heard? or could you think,
Or do you almost think, although you see,
That you do see? could thought, without this object,
Form such another? This is the very top,   45
The heighth, the crest, or crest unto the crest,
Of murther's arms: this is the bloodiest shame,
The wildest savagery, the vildest stroke,
That ever wall-ey'd wrath or staring rage
Presented to the tears of soft remorse.   50
PEMBROKE   All murthers past do stand excus'd in this:
And this, so sole and so unmatchable,
Shall give a holiness, a purity,
To the yet unbegotten sin of times;
And prove a deadly bloodshed but a jest,   55
Exampled by this heinous spectacle.
BASTARD   It is a damned and a bloody work;
The graceless action of a heavy hand,
If that it be the work of any hand.
SALISBURY   If that it be the work of any hand!   60
We had a kind of light what would ensue:
It is the shameful work of Hubert's hand,
The practice and the purpose of the king:
From whose obedience I forbid my soul,
Kneeling before this ruin of sweet life,   65
And breathing to his breathless excellence
The incense of a vow, a holy vow,
Never to taste the pleasures of the world,
Never to be infected with delight,
Nor conversant with ease and idleness,   70
Till I have set a glory to this hand,
By giving it the worship of revenge.
PEMBROKE, BIGOT
Our souls religiously confirm thy words.

Enter HUBERT.

HUBERT   Lords, I am hot with haste in seeking you:
    Arthur doth live; the king hath sent for you.
SALISBURY   O, he is bold and blushes not at death.
    Avaunt, thou hateful villain, get thee gone!
HUBERT   I am no villain.
SALISBURY   Must I rob the law?
    [*drawing his sword*]
BASTARD   Your sword is bright, sir; put it up again.
SALISBURY   Not till I sheathe it in a murtherer's skin.
HUBERT   Stand back, Lord Salisbury, stand back, I say;
    By heaven, I think my sword's as sharp as yours.
    I would not have you, lord, forget yourself,
    Nor tempt the danger of my true defence;
    Lest I, by marking of your rage, forget
    Your worth, your greatness and nobility.
BIGOT   Out, dunghill! dar'st thou brave a nobleman?
HUBERT   Not for my life: but yet I dare defend
    My innocent life against an emperor.
SALISBURY   Thou art a murtherer.
HUBERT   Do not prove me so:
    Yet I am none. Whose tongue soe'er speaks false,
    Not truly speaks; who speaks not truly, lies.
PEMBROKE   Cut him to pieces!
BASTARD   Keep the peace, I say.
SALISBURY   Stand by, or I shall gall you, Faulconbridge.
BASTARD   Thou wert better gall the divel, Salisbury:
    If thou but frown on me, or stir thy foot,
    Or teach thy hasty spleen to do me shame,
    I'll strike thee dead. Put up thy sword betime –
    Or I'll so maul you and your toasting-iron
    That you shall think the divel is come from hell.
BIGOT   What wilt thou do, renowned Faulconbridge?
    Second a villain and a murtherer?
HUBERT   Lord Bigot, I am none.
BIGOT   Who kill'd this prince?
HUBERT   'Tis not an hour since I left him well:
    I honour'd him, I lov'd him, and will weep
    My date of life out for his sweet live's loss.
SALISBURY   Trust not those cunning waters of his eyes,
    For villainy is not without such rheum;
    And he, long traded in it, makes it seem
    Like rivers of remorse and innocency.
    Away with me, all you whose souls abhor
    Th'uncleanly savours of a slaughter-house;
    For I am stifled with this smell of sin.
BIGOT   Away toward Bury, to the Dolphin there!
PEMBROKE   There tell the king he may inquire us out.
                Exeunt Lords.

BASTARD
    Here's a good world! Knew you of this fair work?
    Beyond the infinite and boundless reach
    Of mercy, if thou didst this deed of death,
    Art thou damn'd, Hubert.
HUBERT   Do but hear me, sir –
BASTARD   Ha! I'll tell thee what;
    Thou'rt damn'd as black – nay, nothing is so black;
    Thou art more deep damn'd than Prince Lucifer:

There is not yet so ugly a fiend of hell
    As thou shalt be, if thou didst kill this child.
HUBERT   Upon my soul –
BASTARD   If thou didst but consent   125
    To this most cruel act, do but despair;
    And if thou want'st a cord, the smallest thread
    That ever spider twisted from her womb
    Will serve to strangle thee; a rush will be a beam
    To hang thee on; or wouldst thou drown thyself,   130
    Put but a little water in a spoon,
    And it shall be as all the ocean,
    Enough to stifle such a villain up.
    I do suspect thee very grievously.
HUBERT   If I in act, consent, or sin of thought,   135
    Be guilty of the stealing that sweet breath
    Which was embounded in this beauteous clay,
    Let hell want pains enough to torture me!
    I left him well.
BASTARD   Go, bear him in thine arms.
    I am amaz'd, methinks and lose my way   140
    Among the thorns and dangers of this world.
    How easy dost thou take all England up
    From forth this morsel of dead royalty!
    The life, the right and truth of all this realm
    Is fled to heaven; and England now is left   145
    To tug and scamble, and to part by th' teeth
    The unow'd interest of proud swelling state.
    Now for the bare-pick'd bone of majesty
    Doth dogged war bristle his angry crest
    And snarleth in the gentle eyes of peace: 150
    Now powers from home and discontents at home
    Meet in one line; and vast confusion waits,
    As doth a raven on a sick-fall'n beast,
    The imminent decay of wrested pomp.
    Now happy he whose cloak and ceinture can   155
    Hold out this tempest. Bear away that child
    And follow me with speed: I'll to the king.
    A thousand businesses are brief in hand,
    And heaven itself doth frown upon the land. *Exeunt.*

5.1   *Enter* KING JOHN, PANDULPH *and attendants.*

KING JOHN   Thus have I yielded up into your hand
    The circle of my glory. [*giving the crown*]
PANDULPH   Take again
    [*giving back the crown*]
    From this my hand, as holding of the pope,
    Your sovereign greatness and authority.
KING JOHN
    Now keep your holy word: go meet the French,   5
    And from his holiness use all your power
    To stop their marches 'fore we are inflam'd.
    Our discontented counties do revolt;
    Our people quarrel with obedience,
    Swearing allegiance and the love of soul   10
    To stranger blood, to foreign royalty.
    This inundation of mistemp'red humour

Rests by you only to be qualified:
Then pause not; for the present time's so sick
15 That present med'cine must be minist'red
Or overthrow incurable ensues.
PANDULPH   It was my breath that blew this tempest up,
Upon your stubborn usage of the pope;
But since you are a gentle convertite
20 My tongue shall hush again this storm of war,
And make fair weather in your blust'ring land.
On this Ascension-day, remember well,
Upon your oath of service to the pope,
Go I to make the French lay down their arms.   *Exit.*
25 KING JOHN   Is this Ascension-day? Did not the prophet
Say that before Ascension-day at noon
My crown I should give off? Even so I have:
I did suppose it should be on constraint;
But, heaven be thank'd, it is but voluntary.

Enter the Bastard.

BASTARD
30 All Kent hath yielded: nothing there holds out
But Dover Castle; London hath receiv'd,
Like a kind host, the Dolphin and his powers;
Your nobles will not hear you, but are gone
To offer service to your enemy;
35 And wild amazement hurries up and down
The little number of your doubtful friends.
KING JOHN   Would not my lords return to me again
After they heard young Arthur was alive?
BASTARD
They found him dead and cast into the streets,
40 An empty casket, where the jewel of life
By some damn'd hand was robb'd and ta'en away.
KING JOHN   That villain Hubert told me he did live.
BASTARD   So, on my soul, he did, for aught he knew.
But wherefore do you droop? why look you sad?
45 Be great in act, as you have been in thought;
Let not the world see fear and sad distrust
Govern the motion of a kingly eye!
Be stirring as the time, be fire with fire,
Threaten the threat'ner, and outface the brow
50 Of bragging horror: so shall inferior eyes,
That borrow their behaviours from the great,
Grow great by your example and put on
The dauntless spirit of resolution.
Away, and glister like the god of war
55 When he intendeth to become the field:
Show boldness and aspiring confidence!
What, shall they seek the lion in his den,
And fright him there? and make him tremble there?
O, let it not be said: forage, and run
60 To meet displeasure farther from the doors,
And grapple with him ere he come so nigh!
KING JOHN   The legate of the pope hath been with me,
And I have made a happy peace with him;
And he hath promis'd to dismiss the powers
Led by the Dolphin.

BASTARD   O inglorious league!   65
Shall we, upon the footing of our land,
Send fair-play orders and make comprimise,
Insinuation, parley and base truce
To arms invasive? shall a beardless boy,
A cock'red silken wanton, brave our fields,   70
And flesh his spirit in a warlike soil,
Mocking the air with colours idly spread,
And find no check? Let us, my liege, to arms!
Perchance the cardinal cannot make your peace;
Or if he do, let it at least be said   75
They saw we had a purpose of defence.
KING JOHN
Have thou the ordering of this present time.
BASTARD   Away, then, with good courage! yet, I know,
Our party may well meet a prouder foe.   *Exeunt.*

5.2   *Enter, in arms,* LEWIS, SALISBURY, MELUN,
                PEMBROKE, BIGOT *and soldiers.*

LEWIS   My Lord Melun, let this be copied out,
And keep it safe for our remembrance:
Return the precedent to these lords again;
That, having our fair order written down,
Both they and we, perusing o'er these notes,   5
May know wherefore we took the sacrament
And keep our faiths firm and inviolable.
SALISBURY   Upon our sides it never shall be broken.
And, noble Dolphin, albeit we swear
A voluntary zeal and an unurg'd faith   10
To your proceedings; yet believe me, prince,
I am not glad that such a sore of time
Should seek a plaster by contemn'd revolt,
And heal the inveterate canker of one wound
By making many. O, it grieves my soul,   15
That I must draw this metal from my side
To be a widow-maker! O, and there
Where honourable rescue and defence
Cries out upon the name of Salisbury!
But such is the infection of the time,   20
That, for the health and physic of our right,
We cannot deal but with the very hand
Of stern injustice and confused wrong.
And is't not pity, O my grieved friends,
That we, the sons and children of this isle,   25
Was born to see so sad an hour as this;
Wherein we step after a stranger, march
Upon her gentle bosom, and fill up
Her enemies' ranks – I must withdraw and weep
Upon the spot of this enforced cause –   30
To grace the gentry of a land remote,
And follow unacquainted colours here?
What, here? O nation, that thou couldst remove!
That Neptune's arms, who clippeth thee about,
Would bear thee from the knowledge of thyself –   35
And cripple thee – unto a pagan shore,
Where these two Christian armies might combine

The blood of malice in a vein of league,
And not to spend it so unneighbourly!

40 LEWIS   A noble temper dost thou show in this;
And great affections wrastling in thy bosom
Doth make an earthquake of nobility.
O, what a noble combat hast thou fought
Between compulsion and a brave respect!

45 Let me wipe off this honourable dew,
That silverly doth progress on thy cheeks:
My heart hath melted at a lady's tears,
Being an ordinary inundation;
But this effusion of such manly drops,

50 This shower, blown up by tempest of the soul,
Startles mine eyes, and makes me more amaz'd
Than had I seen the vaulty top of heaven
Figur'd quite o'er with burning meteors.
Lift up thy brow, renowned Salisbury,

55 And with a great heart heave away this storm:
Commend these waters to those baby eyes
That never saw the giant world enrag'd,
Nor met with fortune other than at feasts,
Full warm of blood, of mirth, of gossiping.

60 Come, come; for thou shalt thrust thy hand as deep
Into the purse of rich prosperity
As Lewis himself: so, nobles, shall you all,
That knit your sinews to the strength of mine.

Enter PANDULPH.

And even there, methinks, an angel spake:

65 Look, where the holy legate comes apace,
To give us warrant from the hand of heaven,
And on our actions set the name of right
With holy breath.

PANDULPH   Hail, noble prince of France!
The next is this: King John hath reconcil'd

70 Himself to Rome; his spirit is come in,
That so stood out against the holy church,
The great metropolis and see of Rome.
Therefore thy threat'ning colours now wind up,
And tame the savage spirit of wild war,

75 That, like a lion foster'd up at hand,
It may lie gently at the foot of peace,
And be no further harmful than in show.

LEWIS   Your grace shall pardon me, I will not back:
I am too high-born to be propertied,

80 To be a secondary at control,
Or useful serving-man and instrument
To any sovereign state throughout the world.
Your breath first kindled the dead coal of wars
Between this chastis'd kingdom and myself,

85 And brought in matter that should feed this fire;
And now 'tis far too huge to be blown out
With that same weak wind which enkindled it.
You taught me how to know the face of right,
Acquainted me with interest to this land,

90 Yea, thrust this enterprise into my heart;
And come ye now to tell me John hath made

His peace with Rome? What is that peace to me?
I, by the honour of my marriage-bed,
After young Arthur, claim this land for mine;
And, now it is half-conquer'd, must I back   95
Because that John hath made his peace with Rome?
Am I Rome's slave? What penny hath Rome borne,
What men provided, what munition sent,
To underprop this action? Is't not I
That undergo this charge? who else but I,   100
And such as to my claim are liable,
Sweat in this business and maintain this war?
Have I not heard these islanders shout out
'Vive le roi!' as I have bank'd their towns?
Have I not here the best cards for the game   105
To win this easy match play'd for a crown?
And shall I now give o'er the yielded set?
No, no, on my soul, it never shall be said.

PANDULPH   You look but on the outside of this work.

LEWIS   Outside or inside, I will not return   110
Till my attempt so much be glorified
As to my ample hope was promised
Before I drew this gallant head of war,
And cull'd these fiery spirits from the world,
To outlook conquest and to win renown   115
Even in the jaws of danger and of death.

                                   [*Trumpet sounds.*]
What lusty trumpet thus doth summon us?

Enter the Bastard, *attended.*

BASTARD   According to the fair-play of the world,
Let me have audience; I am sent to speak:
My holy lord of Milan, from the king   120
I come, to learn how you have dealt for him;
And, as you answer, I do know the scope
And warrant limited unto my tongue.

PANDULPH   The Dolphin is too wilful-opposite,
And will not temporize with my entreaties;   125
He flatly says he'll not lay down his arms.

BASTARD   By all the blood that ever fury breath'd,
The youth says well. Now hear our English king,
For thus his royalty doth speak in me:
He is prepar'd, and reason too he should –   130
This apish and unmannerly approach,
This harness'd masque and unadvised revel,
This unhair'd sauciness and boyish troops,
The king doth smile at; and is well prepar'd
To whip this dwarfish war, this pigmy arms,   135
From out the circle of his territories. –
That hand which had the strength, even at your door,
To cudgel you and make you take the hatch,
To dive like buckets in concealed wells,
To crouch in litter of your stable planks,   140
To lie like pawns lock'd up in chests and trunks,
To hug with swine, to seek sweet safety out
In vaults and prisons, and to thrill and shake
Even at the crying of your nation's crow,
Thinking this voice an armed Englishman;   145

Shall that victorious hand be feebled here,
That in your chambers gave you chastisement?
No: know the gallant monarch is in arms
And like an eagle o'er his aery towers,
150 To souse annoyance that comes near his nest.
And you degenerate, you ingrate revolts,
You bloody Neroes, ripping up the womb
Of your dear mother England, blush for shame:
For your own ladies and pale-visag'd maids
155 Like Amazons come tripping after drums,
Their thimbles into armed gauntlets change,
Their needl's to lances, and their gentle hearts
To fierce and bloody inclination.
LEWIS
There end thy brave, and turn thy face in peace;
160 We grant thou canst outscold us: fare thee well;
We hold our time too precious to be spent
With such a brabbler.
PANDULPH   Give me leave to speak.
BASTARD   No, I will speak.
LEWIS   We will attend to neither.
Strike up the drums; and let the tongue of war
165 Plead for our interest and our being here.
BASTARD
Indeed, your drums, being beaten, will cry out;
And so shall you, being beaten: do but start
An echo with the clamour of thy drum,
And even at hand a drum is ready brac'd
170 That shall reverberate all, as loud as thine:
Sound but another, and another shall
As loud as thine rattle the welkin's ear
And mock the deep-mouth'd thunder: for at hand –
Not trusting to this halting legate here,
175 Whom he hath us'd rather for sport than need –
Is warlike John; and in his forehead sits
A bare-ribb'd death, whose office is this day
To feast upon whole thousands of the French.
LEWIS   Strike up our drums, to find this danger out.
BASTARD
180 And thou shalt find it, Dolphin, do not doubt.
                                        Exeunt.

5.3   *Alarums. Enter* KING JOHN *and* HUBERT.

KING JOHN
How goes the day with us? O, tell me, Hubert.
HUBERT   Badly, I fear. How fares your majesty?
KING JOHN   This fever, that hath troubled me so long,
Lies heavy on me; O, my heart is sick!

Enter a Messenger.

MESSENGER
5 My lord, your valiant kinsman, Faulconbridge,
Desires your majesty to leave the field
And send him word by me which way you go.
KING JOHN
Tell him, toward Swinstead, to the abbey there.

MESSENGER   Be of good comfort; for the great supply
That was expected by the Dolphin here,   10
Are wrack'd three nights ago on Goodwin Sands.
This news was brought to Richard but even now:
The French fight coldly, and retire themselves.
KING JOHN   Ay me! this tyrant fever burns me up,
And will not let me welcome this good news.   15
Set on toward Swinstead; to my litter straight:
Weakness possesseth me, and I am faint.   *Exeunt.*

5.4   *Enter* SALISBURY, PEMBROKE *and* BIGOT.

SALISBURY
I did not think the king so stor'd with friends.
PEMBROKE   Up once again; put spirit in the French:
If they miscarry, we miscarry too.
SALISBURY   That misbegotten divel, Faulconbridge,
In spite of spite, alone upholds the day.   5
PEMBROKE
They say King John sore sick hath left the field.

Enter MELUN, *wounded.*

MELUN   Lead me to the revolts of England here.
SALISBURY   When we were happy we had other names.
PEMBROKE   It is the Count Melun.
SALISBURY   Wounded to death.
MELUN   Fly, noble English, you are bought and sold;   10
Unthread the rude eye of rebellion
And welcome home again discarded faith.
Seek out King John and fall before his feet;
For if the French be lords of this loud day
Lewis means to recompense the pains you take   15
By cutting off your heads: thus hath he sworn
And I with him, and many moe with me,
Upon the altar at Saint Edmundsbury;
Even on that altar where we swore to you
Dear amity and everlasting love.   20
SALISBURY   May this be possible? may this be true?
MELUN   Have I not hideous death within my view,
Retaining but a quantity of life,
Which bleeds away, even as a form of wax
Resolveth from his figure 'gainst the fire?   25
What in the world should make me now deceive,
Since I must lose the use of all deceit?
Why should I then be false, since it is true
That I must die here and live hence by truth?
I say again, if Lewis do win the day,   30
He is forsworn if e'er those eyes of yours
Behold another day break in the east:
But even this night, whose black contagious breath
Already smokes about the burning crest
Of the old, feeble and day-wearied sun,   35
Even this ill night, your breathing shall expire,
Paying the fine of rated treachery
Even with a treacherous fine of all your lives,
If Lewis by your assistance win the day.
Commend me to one Hubert with your king: 40

The love of him, and this respect besides,
For that my grandsire was an Englishman,
Awakes my conscience to confess all this.
In lieu whereof, I pray you, bear me hence
From forth the noise and rumour of the field,
Where I may think the remnant of my thoughts
In peace, and part this body and my soul
With contemplation and devout desires.
SALISBURY   We do believe thee; and beshrew my soul
But I do love the favour and the form
Of this most fair occasion, by the which
We will untread the steps of damned flight,
And like a bated and retired flood,
Leaving our rankness and irregular course,
Stoop low within those bounds we have o'erlook'd,
And calmly run on in obedience
Even to our ocean, to our great King John.
My arm shall give thee help to bear thee hence;
For I do see the cruel pangs of death
Right in thine eye. Away, my friends! New flight;
And happy newness, that intends old right!
Exeunt, leading off Melun.

5.5   *Enter LEWIS and his train.*

LEWIS   The sun of heaven methought was loath to set,
But stay'd and made the western welkin blush,
When English measure backward their own ground
In faint retire. O, bravely came we off,
When with a volley of our needless shot,
After such bloody toil, we bid good-night,
And wound our tott'ring colours clearly up,
Last in the field, and almost lords of it!

Enter a Messenger.

MESSENGER   Where is my prince, the Dolphin?
LEWIS   Here: what news?
MESSENGER
The Count Melun is slain; the English lords
By his persuasion are again fall'n off,
And your supply, which you have wish'd so long,
Are cast away and sunk on Goodwin Sands.
LEWIS   Ah, foul shrewd news! beshrew thy very heart!
I did not think to be so sad to-night
As this hath made me. Who was he that said
King John did fly an hour or two before
The stumbling night did part our weary powers?
MESSENGER   Whoever spoke it, it is true, my lord.
LEWIS   Well; keep good quarter and good care to-night:
The day shall not be up so soon as I,
To try the fair adventure of to-morrow.   *Exeunt.*

5.6   *Enter the BASTARD and HUBERT, severally.*

HUBERT
Who's there? speak, ho! speak quickly, or I shoot.
BASTARD   A friend. What art thou?
HUBERT   Of the part of England.

BASTARD   Whither dost thou go?
HUBERT
What's that to thee? [*pause*] Why, may not I demand
Of thine affairs as well as thou of mine?   5
BASTARD   Hubert, I think.
HUBERT   Thou hast a perfect thought:
I will upon all hazards well believe
Thou art my friend, that know'st my tongue so well.
Who art thou?
BASTARD   Who thou wilt: and if thou please
Thou mayst befriend me so much as to think   10
I come one way of the Plantagenets.
HUBERT
Unkind remembrance! thou and endless night
Have done me shame: brave soldier, pardon me,
That any accent breaking from thy tongue
Should 'scape the true acquaintance of mine ear.   15
BASTARD
Come, come; sans compliment, what news abroad?
HUBERT   Why, here walk I in the black brow of night,
To find you out.
BASTARD   Brief, then; and what's the news?
HUBERT   O, my sweet sir, news fitting to the night,
Black, fearful, comfortless and horrible.   20
BASTARD   Show me the very wound of this ill news:
I am no woman, I'll not swound at it.
HUBERT   The king, I fear, is poison'd by a monk:
I left him almost speechless; and broke out
To acquaint you with this evil, that you might   25
The better arm you to the sudden time,
Than if you had at leisure known of this.
BASTARD   How did he take it? who did taste to him?
HUBERT   A monk – I tell you, a resolved villain –
Whose bowels suddenly burst out: the king   30
Yet speaks and peradventure may recover.
BASTARD   Who didst thou leave to tend his majesty?
HUBERT
Why, know you not? the lords are all come back,
And brought Prince Henry in their company;
At whose request the king hath pardon'd them,   35
And they are all about his majesty.
BASTARD   Withhold thine indignation, mighty heaven,
And tempt us not to bear above our power!
I'll tell thee, Hubert, half my power this night,
Passing these flats, are taken by the tide;   40
These Lincoln Washes have devoured them;
Myself, well mounted, hardly have escap'd.
Away before: conduct me to the king;
I doubt he will be dead or ere I come.   *Exeunt.*

5.7   *Enter PRINCE HENRY, SALISBURY and BIGOT.*

PRINCE HENRY   It is too late: the life of all his blood
Is touch'd corruptibly, and his pure brain,
Which some suppose the soul's frail dwelling-house,
Doth by the idle comments that it makes
Foretell the ending of mortality.   5

Enter PEMBROKE.

PEMBROKE
His highness yet doth speak, and holds belief
That, being brought into the open air,
It would allay the burning quality
Of that fell poison which assaileth him.
PRINCE HENRY
10   Let him be brought into the orchard here.
Doth he still rage?   *Exit Bigot.*
PEMBROKE   He is more patient
Than when you left him; even now he sung.
PRINCE HENRY   O vanity of sickness! fierce extremes
In their continuance will not feel themselves.
15   Death, having prey'd upon the outward parts,
Leaves them invisible, and his siege is now
Against the mind, the which he pricks and wounds
With many legions of strange fantasies,
Which, in their throng and press to that last hold,
Confound themselves. 'Tis strange that death should
20   sing.
I am the cygnet to this pale faint swan
Who chants a doleful hymn to his own death
And from the organ-pipe of frailty sings
His soul and body to their lasting rest.
SALISBURY
25   Be of good comfort, prince; for you are born
To set a form upon that indigest
Which he hath left so shapeless and so rude.

*Enter attendants and BIGOT, bringing in KING JOHN
in a chair.*

KING JOHN   Ay, marry, now my soul hath elbow-room
It would not out at windows nor at doors.
30   There is so hot a summer in my bosom,
That all my bowels crumble up to dust:
I am a scribbled form, drawn with a pen
Upon a parchment, and against this fire
Do I shrink up.
PRINCE HENRY   How fares your majesty?
35 KING JOHN   Poison'd, ill fare; dead, forsook, cast off:
And none of you will bid the winter come
To thrust his icy fingers in my maw,
Nor let my kingdom's rivers take their course
Through my burn'd bosom, nor entreat the north
40   To make his bleak winds kiss my parched lips
And comfort me with cold. I do not ask you much,
I beg cold comfort; and you are so strait,
And so ingrateful, you deny me that.
PRINCE HENRY
O that there were some virtue in my tears
That might relieve you!
45 KING JOHN   The salt in them is hot.
Within me is a hell; and there the poison
Is as a fiend confin'd to tyrannize
On unreprievable condemned blood.

Enter the Bastard.

BASTARD   O, I am scalded with my violent motion,
And spleen of speed to see your majesty!   50
KING JOHN   O cousin, thou art come to set mine eye:
The tackle of my heart is crack'd and burn'd,
And all the shrouds wherewith my life should sail
Are turned to one thread, one little hair;
My heart hath one poor string to stay it by,   55
Which holds but till thy news be uttered;
And then all this thou seest is but a clod
And module of confounded royalty.
BASTARD   The Dolphin is preparing hitherward,
Where God He knows how we shall answer him;   60
For in a night the best part of my power,
As I upon advantage did remove,
Were in the Washes all unwarily
Devoured by the unexpected flood. [*The King dies.*]
SALISBURY
You breathe these dead news in as dead an ear.   65
My liege! my lord! – But now a king, now thus.
PRINCE HENRY
Even so must I run on, and even so stop.
What surety of the world, what hope, what stay,
When this was now a king, and now is clay?
BASTARD   Art thou gone so? I do but stay behind 70
To do the office for thee of revenge,
And then my soul shall wait on thee to heaven,
As it on earth hath been thy servant still.
Now, now, you stars that move in your right spheres,
Where be your powers? show now your mended
    faiths,   75
And instantly return with me again,
To push destruction and perpetual shame
Out of the weak door of our fainting land.
Straight let us seek, or straight we shall be sought;
The Dolphin rages at our very heels.   80
SALISBURY
It seems you know not, then, so much as we:
The Cardinal Pandulph is within at rest,
Who half an hour since came from the Dolphin,
And brings from him such offers of our peace
As we with honour and respect may take,   85
With purpose presently to leave this war.
BASTARD   He will the rather do it when he sees
Ourselves well sinew'd to our defence.
SALISBURY   Nay, 'tis in a manner done already,
For many carriages he hath dispatch'd   90
To the sea-side, and put his cause and quarrel
To the disposing of the cardinal:
With whom yourself, myself and other lords,
If you think meet, this afternoon will post
To consummate this business happily.   95
BASTARD   Let it be so: and you, my noble prince,
With other princes that may best be spar'd,
Shall wait upon your father's funeral.
PRINCE HENRY   At Worcester must his body be interr'd;
For so he will'd it.
BASTARD   Thither shall it then: 100

And happily may your sweet self put on
The lineal state and glory of the land!
To whom, with all submission, on my knee
I do bequeath my faithful services
And true subjection everlastingly.

SALISBURY   And the like tender of our love we make,
To rest without a spot for evermore.

PRINCE HENRY
I have a kind soul that would give thanks
And knows not how to do it but with tears.

BASTARD   O, let us pay the time but needful woe,   110
Since it hath been beforehand with our griefs.
This England never did, nor never shall,
Lie at the proud foot of a conqueror,
But when it first did help to wound itself.
Now these her princes are come home again   115
Come the three corners of the world in arms
And we shall shock them! Nought shall make us rue
If England to itself do rest but true!   *Exeunt.*

King Lear

King Lear was first printed in quarto format with the title *The History of King Lear* in 1608; a different text appeared in the First Folio, where it is the eighth of the tragedies, as *The Tragedy of King Lear* in 1623. There are in addition something like 850 verbal variants between the two texts, and several speeches are assigned to different speakers. The military action of acts 4 and 5 is handled differently, and there are minor changes in the characterization of Lear, Cordelia and Goneril, but the most striking change is in Edgar who is a stronger character in 1623 than in the 1608 version; Albany and Kent are weaker by comparison. Several recent scholars maintain that the 1608 text represents Shakespeare's first version of the play and the 1623 version represents his revision of it; they therefore reject the traditional editorial practice of combining the two texts into a single conflated version; some editions of the 'Complete Works' now print both texts of the play.

King Lear is usually dated 1604-5, putting it after *Hamlet* and *Othello* but before *Macbeth*. The 1608 Quarto title-page refers to a performance before King James at Whitehall on 24 December 1606 (see Fig. 9, p. 7). Shakespeare knew the Lear story from Raphael Holinshed's *Chronicles* (1587) and from the *Mirror for Magistrates* (1574) as well as from a brief version in Edmund Spenser's *Fairy Queen* (1590: book 2, canto 10). He also knew, and may have acted in, an anonymous play called *The True Chronicle History of King Leir and his three daughters* (usually referred to as *King Leir*), which was published in 1605 but probably written and first performed around 1590. He complicated the Lear story by inventing Lear's madness and by adding the parallel plot of Gloucester and his sons which derives from Philip Sidney's *Arcadia* (1590). He used Samuel Harsnett's *A Declaration of Egregious Popish Impostures* (1603) for building up the characterization of Edgar as Poor Tom.

Nahum Tate's Restoration adaptation of Shakespeare's play (1681) is notorious for providing a happy ending, with Lear and Gloucester still alive and Cordelia betrothed to Edgar, who has earlier saved her from being raped by Edmund. This version, which also omitted the Fool, was thought to be more acceptable by readers and audiences until the mid-nineteenth century, but since then admiration for Shakespeare's bleak play has increased to the point that many people would now see *King Lear* as his greatest tragedy, surpassing even *Hamlet*. Its social and political vision of 'the promised end...or image of that horror' has appealed to a world threatened by genocide and environmental or nuclear catastrophe, while at the personal and familial level the play's presentation of conflict between the generations ('age is unnecessary') speaks to societies where people are living longer and the elderly make up an increasing proportion of the population. Modern productions and films frequently evoke Samuel Beckett's *Endgame* (1957), turning it into a kind of prophecy of the disintegration of modern as well as Renaissance civilization.

King Lear has been interpreted more positively as a tragedy of Christian suffering and redemption, and as one which embraces radical socialism ('So distribution should undo excess, / And each man have enough'). However, despite the fact that a number of major characters are still alive at the end of the play and gestures are made towards 'sustaining' 'the gored state', the final impression is one of apocalyptic finality where an escape from suffering is all that can be hoped for.

Note on the text (see also Preface)

There are two texts of *King Lear*, the Quarto of 1608 and the First Folio of 1623. They differ in many ways, and any editor has to choose between variant readings. The text presented here relies mainly on the Folio text, which was probably revised by Shakespeare, perhaps with advice from his fellow-actors. However, the Quarto has about 300 lines that are not found in the Folio, and the Folio has about 110 lines that are not in the Quarto. Since all these appear to be authentically Shakespearean, they are included in the present text; but so that they can be readily identified, passages and words found only in the Quarto are marked by superscript Q, and passages or words found only in the Folio by superscript F at the beginning and end of them. Where no superscript Q or F occurs, square brackets indicate stage directions, or words in them, which have been added by the editor.

LEAR	*King of Britain*
GONERIL	*his eldest daughter*
REGAN	*his second daughter*
CORDELIA	*his youngest daughter*
Duke of ALBANY	*married to Goneril*
Duke of CORNWALL	*married to Regan*
King of FRANCE	
Duke of BURGUNDY	
Earl of GLOUCESTER	
EDGAR	*his elder son*
EDMUND	*his younger bastard son*
Earl of KENT	
FOOL	*attendant on Lear*
OSWALD	*Goneril's steward*
CURAN	*a follower of Gloucester*
OLD MAN	*Gloucester's tenant*

A Herald, a Captain, an Officer, a Doctor, Knights, Gentlemen, Attendants, Servants and Messengers

1.1 *Enter* KENT, GLOUCESTER *and* EDMUND.

KENT I thought the King had more affected the Duke of Albany than Cornwall.

GLOUCESTER It did always seem so to us: but now, in the division of the kingdom, it appears not which of the dukes he values most, for qualities are so weighed that curiosity in neither can make choice of either's moiety.

KENT Is not this your son, my lord?

GLOUCESTER His breeding, sir, hath been at my charge. I have so often blushed to acknowledge him that now I am brazed to't.

KENT I cannot conceive you.

GLOUCESTER Sir, this young fellow's mother could; whereupon she grew round-wombed, and had, indeed, sir, a son for her cradle ere she had a husband for her bed. Do you smell a fault?

KENT I cannot wish the fault undone, the issue of it being so proper.

GLOUCESTER But I have a son, sir, by order of law, some year elder than this, who yet is no dearer in my account. Though this knave came something saucily to the world before he was sent for, yet was his mother fair, there was good sport at his making, and the whoreson must be acknowledged. Do you know this noble gentleman, Edmund?

EDMUND No, my lord.

GLOUCESTER [*to Edmund*] My lord of Kent: remember him hereafter, as my honourable friend.

EDMUND My services to your lordship.

KENT I must love you, and sue to know you better.

EDMUND [*to Kent*] Sir, I shall study deserving.

GLOUCESTER He hath been out nine years, and away he shall again. The King is coming.

Sennet. Enter ᴼ*one bearing a coronet, then*ᴼ LEAR, CORNWALL, ALBANY, GONERIL, REGAN, CORDELIA *and attendants.*

LEAR
   Attend the lords of France and Burgundy, Gloucester.

GLOUCESTER I shall, my lord. ᶠ*Exit.*ᶠ

LEAR Meantime we shall express our darker purpose.
   ᶠGive meᶠ the map there. Know ᶠthatᶠ we have divided
   In three our kingdom; and 'tis our fast intent
   To shake all cares and business from our age,
   Conferring them on younger strengths, ᶠwhile we
   Unburdened crawl toward death. Our son of Cornwall,
   And you, our no less loving son of Albany,
   We have this hour a constant will to publish
   Our daughters' several dowers, that future strife
   May be prevented now.ᶠ
   The ᴼtwo greatᴼ princes, France and Burgundy,
   Great rivals in our youngest daughter's love,
   Long in our court have made their amorous sojourn,
   And here are to be answered. Tell me, my daughters –
   ᶠSince now we will divest us both of rule,
   Interest of territory, cares of state –ᶠ

Which of you shall we say doth love us most,
   That we our largest bounty may extend
   Where nature doth with merit challenge. – Goneril,
   Our eldest born, speak first.

GONERIL
   Sir, I ᴼdoᴼ love you more than word can wield the
      matter,   55
   Dearer than eyesight, space and liberty,
   Beyond what can be valued, rich or rare,
   No less than life, with grace, health, beauty, honour.
   As much as child e'er loved, or father found,
   A love that makes breath poor and speech unable,   60
   Beyond all manner of so much I love you.

CORDELIA [*aside*]
   What shall Cordelia speak? Love, and be silent.

LEAR Of all these bounds, even from this line to this,
   With shadowy forests ᶠand with champaigns riched,
   With plenteous riversᶠ and wide-skirted meads,   65
   We make thee lady. To thine and Albany's issues
   Be this perpetual. – What says our second daughter,
   Our dearest Regan, wife of Cornwall? ᴼSpeak.ᴼ

REGAN ᴼSirᴼ I am made of that self mettle as my sister,
   And prize me at her worth. In my true heart   70
   I find she names my very deed of love:
   Only she comes ᶠtooᶠ short, that I profess
   Myself an enemy to all other joys
   Which the most precious square of sense possesses,
   And find I am alone felicitate   75
   In your dear highness' love.

CORDELIA [*aside*]   Then poor Cordelia,
   And yet not so, since I am sure my love's
   More ponderous than my tongue.

LEAR To thee and thine hereditary ever
   Remain this ample third of our fair kingdom,   80
   No less in space, validity and pleasure
   Than that conferred on Goneril. – ᴼButᴼ now our joy,
   Although our last and least, to whose young love
   ᶠThe vines of France and milk of Burgundy
   Strive to be interested,ᶠ what can you say to draw   85
   A third more opulent than your sisters? ᶠSpeak.ᶠ

CORDELIA Nothing, my lord.

ᶠLEAR Nothing?

CORDELIA Nothing.ᶠ

LEAR
   ᴼHow,ᴼ nothing will come of nothing. Speak again.   90

CORDELIA Unhappy that I am, I cannot heave
   My heart into my mouth. I love your majesty
   According to my bond, no more nor less.

LEAR How, how, ᶠCordelia?ᶠ Mend your speech a little,
   Lest you may mar your fortunes.

CORDELIA   Good my lord,   95
   You have begot me, bred me, loved me. I
   Return those duties back as are right fit,
   Obey you, love you and most honour you.
   Why have my sisters husbands, if they say
   They love you all? Haply when I shall wed,   100
   That lord whose hand must take my plight shall carry

Half my love with him, half my care and duty.
Sure I shall never marry like my sisters
^QTo love my father all.^Q

105 LEAR But goes thy heart with this?

CORDELIA Ay, my good lord.

LEAR So young and so untender?

CORDELIA So young, my lord, and true.

LEAR

^QWell^Q, let it be so. Thy truth then be thy dower,

110 For by the sacred radiance of the sun,
The mysteries of Hecate and the night,
By all the operation of the orbs
From whom we do exist and cease to be,
Here I disclaim all my paternal care,

115 Propinquity and property of blood,
And as a stranger to my heart and me
Hold thee from this for ever. The barbarous Scythian,
Or he that makes his generation messes
To gorge his appetite, shall ^Fto my bosom^F

120 Be as well neighboured, pitied and relieved,
As thou my sometime daughter.

KENT   Good my liege –

LEAR Peace, Kent,
Come not between the dragon and his wrath!
I loved her most, and thought to set my rest
On her kind nursery.

125 [*to Cordelia*]   Hence and avoid my sight.
So be my grave my peace, as here I give
Her father's heart from her. Call France. Who stirs?
Call Burgundy.   [*Attendants rush off.*]
      Cornwall and Albany,
With my two daughters' dowers, digest this third.

130 Let pride, which she calls plainness, marry her.
I do invest you jointly with my power,
Pre-eminence and all the large effects
That troop with majesty. Ourself by monthly course,
With reservation of an hundred knights

135 By you to be sustained, shall our abode
Make with you by due turn; only we shall retain
The name, and all th'addition to a king: the sway,
Revenue, execution of the rest,
Beloved sons, be yours; which to confirm,
This coronet part between you.

140 KENT   Royal Lear,
Whom I have ever honoured as my king,
Loved as my father, as my master followed,
As my great patron thought on in my prayers –

LEAR

The bow is bent and drawn; make from the shaft.

145 KENT Let it fall rather, though the fork invade
The region of my heart: be Kent unmannerly
When Lear is mad. What wouldst thou do, old man?
Think'st thou that duty shall have dread to speak,
When power to flattery bows? To plainness honour's
bound

150 When majesty falls to folly. Reserve thy state,
And in thy best consideration check

This hideous rashness. Answer my life my judgement,
Thy youngest daughter does not love thee least,
Nor are those empty-hearted, whose low sounds
Reverb no hollowness.

LEAR   Kent, on thy life, no more. 155

KENT My life I never held but as ^Qa^Q pawn
To wage against thine enemies, ne'er fear to lose it,
Thy safety being ^Qthe^Q motive.

LEAR   Out of my sight!

KENT See better, Lear, and let me still remain
The true blank of thine eye. 160

LEAR Now by Apollo –

KENT   Now by Apollo, King,
Thou swear'st thy gods in vain.

LEAR   ^FO^F vassal! Miscreant!

^FALBANY, CORNWALL Dear sir, forbear!^F

KENT ^QDo,^Q kill thy physician, and thy fee bestow
Upon the foul disease. Revoke thy gift, 165
Or whilst I can vent clamour from my throat
I'll tell thee thou dost evil.

LEAR Hear me, ^Frecreant,^F on thine allegiance, hear me:
That thou hast sought to make us break our vows,
Which we durst never yet, and with strained pride 170
To come betwixt our sentences and our power,
Which nor our nature, nor our place can bear,
Our potency made good, take thy reward.
Five days we do allot thee for provision,
To shield thee from disasters of the world, 175
And on the sixth to turn thy hated back
Upon our kingdom. If on the next day following
Thy banished trunk be found in our dominions,
The moment is thy death. Away! By Jupiter,
This shall not be revoked. 180

KENT

^QWhy^Q, fare thee well, King, since thus thou wilt
 appear,
Freedom lives hence and banishment is here.
[*to Cordelia*] The gods to their dear shelter take thee,
 maid,
That justly think'st and hast most rightly said;
[*to Goneril and Regan*] And your large speeches may
 your deeds approve, 185
That good effects may spring from words of love.
Thus Kent, O princes, bids you all adieu;
He'll shape his old course in a country new. ^F*Exit.*^F

^F*Flourish.*^F *Enter* GLOUCESTER *with* FRANCE, *and*
BURGUNDY [*and*] ^F*attendants.*^F

CORNWALL Here's France and Burgundy, my noble lord.

LEAR My lord of Burgundy, 190
We first address toward you, who with this king
Hath rivalled for our daughter. What in the least
Will you require in present dower with her,
Or cease your quest of love?

BURGUNDY   ^FMost^F royal majesty,
I crave no more than hath your highness offered – 195
Nor will you tender less?

LEAR   Right noble Burgundy,
When she was dear to us, we did hold her so,
But now her price is fallen. Sir, there she stands:
If aught within that little-seeming substance,
Or all of it, with our displeasure pieced,
And nothing more, may fitly like your grace,
She's there, and she is yours.
BURGUNDY   I know no answer.
LEAR   ᵠSirᵠ, will you, with those infirmities she owes,
Unfriended, new adopted to our hate,
Dowered with our curse and strangered with our oath,
Take her or leave her?
BURGUNDY   Pardon me, royal sir;
Election makes not up in such conditions.
LEAR
Then leave her, sir, for, by the power that made me,
I tell you all her wealth. [*to France*] For you, great
    king,
I would not from your love make such a stray
To match you where I hate, therefore beseech you
T'avert your liking a more worthier way
Than on a wretch whom nature is ashamed
Almost t'acknowledge hers.
FRANCE   This is most strange,
That she who even but now was your ᵠbestᵠ object,
The argument of your praise, balm of your age,
The best, the dearest, should in this trice of time
Commit a thing so monstrous, to dismantle
So many folds of favour. Sure her offence
Must be of such unnatural degree
That monsters it, or your fore-vouched affection
Fall into taint, which to believe of her
Must be a faith that reason without miracle
Should never plant in me.
CORDELIA   I yet beseech your majesty,
If for I want that glib and oily art
To speak and purpose not – since what I well intend,
I'll do't before I speak – that you make known
It is no vicious blot, murder, or foulness,
No unchaste action or dishonoured step,
That hath deprived me of your grace and favour,
But even for want of that for which I am richer,
A still soliciting eye and such a tongue
That I am glad I have not – though not to have it
Hath lost me in your liking.
LEAR   ᵠGo to, go to,ᵠ better thou
Hadst not been born than not to have pleased me better.
FRANCE   Is it ᵠno moreᵠ but this? – a tardiness in nature,
Which often leaves the history unspoke
That it intends to do? My lord of Burgundy,
What say you to the lady? Love's not love
When it is mingled with regards that stands
Aloof from th'entire point. Will you have her?
She is herself a dowry.
BURGUNDY   Royal King,
Give but that portion which yourself proposed,
And here I take Cordelia by the hand,

Duchess of Burgundy.
LEAR   Nothing. I have sworn, ᶠI am firm.ᶠ
BURGUNDY [*to Cordelia*]
I am sorry then you have so lost a father
That you must lose a husband.
CORDELIA   Peace be with Burgundy.
Since that respect and fortunes are his love,
I shall not be his wife.
FRANCE   Fairest Cordelia, that art most rich being poor,
Most choice forsaken and most loved despised,
Thee and thy virtues here I seize upon,
Be it lawful I take up what's cast away.
Gods, gods! 'Tis strange that from their cold'st neglect
My love should kindle to inflamed respect.
Thy dowerless daughter, King, thrown to my chance,
Is queen of us, of ours and our fair France.
Not all the dukes of waterish Burgundy
Can buy this unprized, precious maid of me.
Bid them farewell, Cordelia, though unkind;
Thou losest here a better where to find.
LEAR   Thou hast her, France; let her be thine, for we
Have no such daughter, nor shall ever see
That face of hers again. Therefore, be gone,
Without our grace, our love, our benison.
Come, noble Burgundy.
         ᶠFlourish.ᶠ Exeunt ᵠLear and Burgundyᵠ [, *Cornwall,*
                  Albany, Gloucester, Edmund and attendants.]
FRANCE   Bid farewell to your sisters.
CORDELIA   The jewels of our father, with washed eyes
Cordelia leaves you. I know you what you are,
And like a sister am most loath to call
Your faults as they are named. Love well our father.
To your professed bosoms I commit him,
But yet, alas, stood I within his grace
I would prefer him to a better place.
So farewell to you both.
REGAN   Prescribe not us our duty.
GONERIL   Let your study
Be to content your lord, who hath received you
At fortune's alms. You have obedience scanted,
And well are worth the want that you have wanted.
CORDELIA
Time shall unfold what plighted cunning hides,
Who covert faults at last with shame derides.
Well may you prosper.
FRANCE   Come, ᶠmyᶠ fair Cordelia.
                    Exeunt France and Cordelia.
GONERIL   Sister, it is not ᵠaᵠ little I have to say of what
most nearly appertains to us both. I think our father
will hence tonight.
REGAN   That's most certain, and with you. Next month
with us.
GONERIL   You see how full of changes his age is. The
observation we have made of it hath ᵠnotᵠ been little.
He always loved our sister most, and with what poor
judgement he hath now cast her off appears too grossly.

190
195
200
210
215
220
225
230
235
240
245

250
255
260
265
270
275
280
285
290

REGAN 'Tis the infirmity of his age, yet he hath ever but
slenderly known himself.

GONERIL The best and soundest of his time hath been
but rash; then must we look from his age to receive not
alone the imperfections of long-engrafted condition,
but therewithal ^Fthe^F unruly waywardness that infirm
and choleric years bring with them.

REGAN Such unconstant starts are we like to have from
him as this of Kent's banishment.

GONERIL There is further compliment of leave-taking
between France and him. Pray ^Fyou^F let us hit
together. If our father carry authority with such
disposition as he bears, this last surrender of his will
but offend us.

REGAN We shall further think of it.

GONERIL We must do something, and i'the heat.

Exeunt.

1.2 *Enter* [EDMUND, *the*] *Bastard*[, *holding a letter*].

EDMUND Thou, Nature, art my goddess; to thy law
My services are bound. Wherefore should I
Stand in the plague of custom, and permit
The curiosity of nations to deprive me?
For that I am some twelve or fourteen moonshines
Lag of a brother? Why bastard? Wherefore base?
When my dimensions are as well compact,
My mind as generous and my shape as true
As honest madam's issue? Why brand they us
With base? With baseness, bastardy? ^FBase, base?^F
Who in the lusty stealth of nature take
More composition and fierce quality
Than doth within a dull stale tired bed
Go to the creating ^Qof^Q a whole tribe of fops
Got 'tween a sleep and wake. Well, then,
Legitimate Edgar, I must have your land.
Our father's love is to the bastard Edmund
As to the legitimate. ^FFine word, 'legitimate'!^F
Well, my legitimate, if this letter speed
And my invention thrive, Edmund the base
Shall top the legitimate. I grow, I prosper:
Now gods, stand up for bastards!

Enter GLOUCESTER.

GLOUCESTER
Kent banished thus? and France in choler parted?
And the King gone tonight? Prescribed his power,
Confined to exhibition? All this done
Upon the gad? – Edmund, how now, what news?

EDMUND [*Pockets the letter.*] So please your lordship, none.

GLOUCESTER Why so earnestly seek you to put up that
letter?

EDMUND I know no news, my lord.

GLOUCESTER What paper were you reading?

EDMUND Nothing, my lord.

GLOUCESTER No? What needed then that terrible
dispatch of it into your pocket? The quality of nothing
hath not such need to hide itself. Let's see. – Come, if
it be nothing, I shall not need spectacles.

EDMUND I beseech you, sir, pardon me. It is a letter
from my brother that I have not all o'er-read; ^Fand^F for
so much as I have perused, I find it not fit for your
o'er-looking.

GLOUCESTER Give me the letter, sir.

EDMUND I shall offend, either to detain or give it. The
contents, as in part I understand them, are too blame.

GLOUCESTER Let's see, let's see.

EDMUND I hope, for my brother's justification, he
wrote this but as an essay, or taste of my virtue.

GLOUCESTER [^FReads^F.] *This policy, ^Fand reverence^F of age,
makes the world bitter to the best of our times, keeps our
fortunes from us till our oldness cannot relish them. I begin
to find an idle and fond bondage in the oppression of aged
tyranny, who sways not as it hath power, but as it is
suffered. Come to me, that of this I may speak more. If our
father would sleep till I waked him, you should enjoy half
his revenue for ever and live the beloved of your brother.
Edgar.* Hum! Conspiracy! *Sleep till I wake him, you
should enjoy half his revenue* – My son Edgar, had he
a hand to write this? A heart and brain to breed it in?
When came this to you? Who brought it?

EDMUND It was not brought me, my lord, there's the
cunning of it. I found it thrown in at the casement of
my closet.

GLOUCESTER You know the character to be your
brother's?

EDMUND If the matter were good, my lord, I durst
swear it were his; but, in respect of that, I would fain
think it were not.

GLOUCESTER It is his?

EDMUND It is his hand, my lord; but I hope his heart is
not in the contents.

GLOUCESTER Has he never before sounded you in this
business?

EDMUND Never, my lord. But I have heard him oft
maintain it to be fit that, sons at perfect age and
fathers declined, the father should be as ward to the
son and the son manage his revenue.

GLOUCESTER O villain, villain! His very opinion in the
letter. Abhorred villain! Unnatural, detested, brutish
villain – worse than brutish! Go, sirrah, seek him. I'll
apprehend him. Abominable villain, where is he?

EDMUND I do not well know, my lord. If it shall please
you to suspend your indignation against my brother till
you can derive from him better testimony of his intent,
you should run a certain course; where, if you violently
proceed against him, mistaking his purpose, it would
make a great gap in your own honour and shake in
pieces the heart of his obedience. I dare pawn down my
life for him, ^Fthat^F he hath writ this to feel my affection
to your honour and to no other pretence of danger.

GLOUCESTER Think you so?

EDMUND If your honour judge it meet, I will place you
where you shall hear us confer of this and by an

auricular assurance have your satisfaction, and that without any further delay than this very evening.

GLOUCESTER He cannot be such a monster.

^QEDMUND Nor is not, sure.

GLOUCESTER To his father, that so tenderly and entirely loves him. Heaven and earth!^Q Edmund, seek him out. Wind me into him, I pray you: frame the business after your own wisdom. I would unstate myself to be in a due resolution.

EDMUND I will seek him, sir, presently, convey the business as I shall find means and acquaint you withal.

GLOUCESTER These late eclipses in the sun and moon portend no good to us. Though the wisdom of Nature can reason ^Fit^F thus and thus, yet nature finds itself scourged by the sequent effects. Love cools, friendship falls off, brothers divide: in cities, mutinies; in countries, discord; ^Fin^F palaces, treason; ^Fand^F the bond cracked 'twixt son and father. ^FThis villain of mine comes under the prediction – there's son against father. The King falls from bias of nature – there's father against child. We have seen the best of our time. Machinations, hollowness, treachery and all ruinous disorders follow us disquietly to our graves.^F Find out this villain, Edmund; it shall lose thee nothing. Do it carefully. – And the noble and true-hearted Kent banished, his offence honesty! ^F'Tis^F strange, ^Qstrange!^Q *^FExit.^F*

EDMUND This is the excellent foppery of the world, that when we are sick in fortune, often the surfeits of our own behaviour, we make guilty of our disasters the sun, the moon and ^Qthe^Q stars, as if we were villains on necessity, fools by heavenly compulsion, knaves, thieves and treachers by spherical predominance; drunkards, liars and adulterers by an enforced obedience of planetary influence; and all that we are evil in by a divine thrusting on. An admirable evasion of whoremaster man, to lay his goatish disposition on the charge of a star. My father compounded with my mother under the dragon's tail and my nativity was under Ursa Major, so that it follows I am rough and lecherous. ^QFut!^Q I should have been that I am had the maidenliest star in the firmament twinkled on my bastardizing.

Enter EDGAR.

Pat he comes, like the catastrophe of the old comedy. My cue is villainous melancholy, with a sigh like Tom o'Bedlam. – O, these eclipses do portend these divisions. ^FFa, sol, la, mi.^F

EDGAR How now, brother Edmund, what serious contemplation are you in?

EDMUND I am thinking, brother, of a prediction I read this other day, what should follow these eclipses.

EDGAR Do you busy yourself with that?

EDMUND I promise you, the effects he writes of succeed unhappily, ^Qas of unnaturalness between the child and the parent, death, dearth, dissolutions of ancient amities, divisions in state, menaces and maledictions against King and nobles, needless diffidences, banishment of friends, dissipation of cohorts, nuptial breaches and I know not what.

EDGAR How long have you been a sectary astronomical?

EDMUND Come, come,^Q when saw you my father last?

EDGAR ^QWhy,^Q the night gone by.

EDMUND Spake you with him?

EDGAR ^FAy,^F two hours together.

EDMUND Parted you in good terms? Found you no displeasure in him, by word nor countenance?

EDGAR None at all.

EDMUND Bethink yourself wherein you may have offended him, and at my entreaty forbear his presence until some little time hath qualified the heat of his displeasure; which at this instant so rageth in him that with the mischief of your person it would scarcely allay.

EDGAR Some villain hath done me wrong.

EDMUND That's my fear. ^FI pray you have a continent forbearance till the speed of his rage goes slower; and, as I say, retire with me to my lodging, from whence I will fitly bring you to hear my lord speak. Pray ye, go: there's my key. If you do stir abroad, go armed.

EDGAR Armed, brother?^F

EDMUND Brother, I advise you to the best, ^Qgo armed.^Q I am no honest man if there be any good meaning toward you. I have told you what I have seen and heard – but faintly; nothing like the image and horror of it. Pray you, away!

EDGAR Shall I hear from you anon?

EDMUND I do serve you in this business. *Exit Edgar.*
A credulous father and a brother noble,
Whose nature is so far from doing harms
That he suspects none – on whose foolish honesty
My practices ride easy. I see the business.
Let me, if not by birth, have lands by wit;
All with me's meet that I can fashion fit. *Exit.*

1.3 *Enter* GONERIL *and* [OSWALD, *her*] *steward.*

GONERIL Did my father strike my gentleman for chiding of his fool?

OSWALD Ay, madam.

GONERIL By day and night he wrongs me. Every hour
He flashes into one gross crime or other
That sets us all at odds. I'll not endure it.
His knights grow riotous and himself upbraids us
On every trifle. When he returns from hunting,
I will not speak with him; say I am sick.
If you come slack of former services
You shall do well; the fault of it I'll answer.
[Horns within.]

OSWALD He's coming, madam, I hear him.

GONERIL Put on what weary negligence you please,
You and your fellows; I'd have it come to question.
If he distaste it, let him to my sister,
Whose mind and mine I know in that are one,
^QNot to be overruled. Idle old man,

That still would manage those authorities
That he hath given away. Now by my life
20 Old fools are babes again and must be used
With checks as flatteries, when they are seen abused.^Q
Remember what I have said.

OSWALD   ^QVery^Q well, madam.

GONERIL
And let his knights have colder looks among you,
What grows of it no matter; advise your fellows so.
25 ^QI would breed from hence occasions, and I shall,
That I may speak.^Q I'll write straight to my sister
To hold my ^Qvery^Q course. ^QGo,^Q prepare for dinner.

Exeunt.

1.4   *Enter* KENT[, *disguised*].

KENT   If but as well I other accents borrow
That can my speech diffuse, my good intent
May carry through itself to that full issue
For which I razed my likeness. Now, banished Kent,
5 If thou canst serve where thou dost stand condemned
^FSo may it come^F thy master whom thou lov'st
Shall find thee full of labours.

^FHorns within.^F Enter LEAR *^Fand^F*
[*four or more* Knights *as*] *^Fattendants.^F*

LEAR   Let me not stay a jot for dinner; go, get it ready.
[*Exit First Knight.*]
[*to Kent*] How now, what art thou?
10 KENT   A man, sir.
LEAR   What dost thou profess? What wouldst thou with
us?
KENT   I do profess to be no less than I seem; to serve
him truly that will put me in trust, to love him that is
15 honest, to converse with him that is wise and says
little, to fear judgement, to fight when I cannot choose
– and to eat no fish.
LEAR   What art thou?
KENT   A very honest-hearted fellow, and as poor as the
20 King.
LEAR   If thou be'st as poor for a subject as he's for a king,
thou art poor enough. What wouldst thou?
KENT   Service.
LEAR   Who wouldst thou serve?
25 KENT   You.
LEAR   Dost thou know me, fellow?
KENT   No, sir; but you have that in your countenance
which I would fain call master.
LEAR   What's that?
30 KENT   Authority.
LEAR   What services canst ^Fthou^F do?
KENT   I can keep honest counsel, ride, run, mar a
curious tale in telling it and deliver a plain message
bluntly. That which ordinary men are fit for I am
35 qualified in, and the best of me is diligence.
LEAR   How old art thou?
KENT   Not so young, ^Fsir^F, to love a woman for singing,

nor so old to dote on her for anything. I have years on
my back forty-eight.
LEAR   Follow me, thou shalt serve me; if I like thee no   40
worse after dinner, I will not part from thee yet.
Dinner, ho, dinner! Where's my knave, my fool? Go
you and call my fool hither.   [*Exit Second Knight.*]

Enter OSWALD.

You, ^Fyou^F, sirrah, where's my daughter?
OSWALD   So please you –   ^FExit.^F   45
LEAR   What says the fellow there? Call the clotpoll back.
[*Exit Third Knight.*]
Where's my fool? Ho, I think the world's asleep.

Enter Third Knight.

How now, where's that mongrel?
3 KNIGHT   He says, my lord, your daughter is not well.
LEAR   Why came not the slave back to me when I called   50
him?
3 KNIGHT   Sir, he answered me in the roundest manner,
he would not.
LEAR   He would not?
3 KNIGHT   My lord, I know not what the matter is, but   55
to my judgement your highness is not entertained with
that ceremonious affection as you were wont. There's
a great abatement ^Fof kindness^F appears as well in the
general dependants as in the Duke himself also, and
your daughter.   60
LEAR   Ha? Sayst thou so?
3 KNIGHT   I beseech you pardon me, my lord, if I be
mistaken, for my duty cannot be silent when I think
your highness wronged.
LEAR   Thou but rememberest me of mine own   65
conception. I have perceived a most faint neglect of
late, which I have rather blamed as mine own jealous
curiosity than as a very pretence and purpose of
unkindness. I will look further into't. But where's my
fool? I have not seen him this two days.   70
3 KNIGHT   Since my young lady's going into France, sir,
the fool hath much pined away.
LEAR   No more of that, I have noted it ^Fwell^F. Go you
and tell my daughter I would speak with her.
[*Exit Third Knight.*]
Go you; call hither my fool.   [*Exit Fourth Knight.*]   75

^FEnter OSWALD.^F

O you, sir, you, come you hither, sir: who am I, sir?
OSWALD   My lady's father.
LEAR   My lady's father? My lord's knave, you whoreson
dog, you slave, you cur!
OSWALD   I am none of these, my lord, I beseech your   80
pardon.
LEAR   Do you bandy looks with me, you rascal?
[*Strikes him.*]
OSWALD   I'll not be strucken, my lord.
KENT   [*Trips him.*]   Nor tripped neither, you base
football player.   85

LEAR   I thank thee, fellow. Thou serv'st me and I'll love thee.

KENT   Come, sir, ᶠarise, away,ᶠ I'll teach you differences. Away, away; if you will measure your lubber's length again, tarry; but away, ᶠgo to,ᶠ have you wisdom? ᶠSo!ᶠ [*Pushes him out.*]

LEAR   Now, ᶠmyᶠ friendly knave, I thank thee. There's earnest of thy service. [*Gives him money.*]

Enter Fool.

FOOL   Let me hire him too; [*to Kent, holding out his cap*] here's my coxcomb.

LEAR   How now, my pretty knave, how dost thou?

FOOL [*to Kent*]   Sirrah, you were best take my coxcomb.

KENT   Why, fool?

FOOL   Why? For taking one's part that's out of favour. Nay, an thou canst not smile as the wind sits, thou'lt catch cold shortly. There, take my coxcomb. Why, this fellow has banished two on's daughters and did the third a blessing against his will – if thou follow him, thou must needs wear my coxcomb. [*to Lear*] How now, nuncle? Would I had two coxcombs and two daughters.

LEAR   Why, my boy?

FOOL   If I gave them all my living, I'd keep my coxcombs myself. There's mine; beg another of thy daughters.

LEAR   Take heed, sirrah, the whip.

FOOL   Truth's a dog ᵠthatᵠ must to kennel; he must be whipped out, when the Lady Brach may stand by the fire and stink.

LEAR   A pestilent gall to me.

FOOL   Sirrah, I'll teach thee a speech.

LEAR   Do.

FOOL   Mark it, nuncle:

    Have more than thou showest,
    Speak less than thou knowest,
    Lend less than thou owest,
    Ride more than thou goest,
    Learn more than thou trowest,
    Set less than thou throwest,
    Leave thy drink and thy whore
    And keep in-a-door,
    And thou shalt have more
    Than two tens to a score.

KENT   This is nothing, fool.

FOOL   Then ᶠ'tisᶠ like the breath of an unfee'd lawyer, you gave me nothing for't. [*to Lear*] Can you make no use of nothing, nuncle?

LEAR   Why no, boy; nothing can be made out of nothing.

FOOL [*to Kent*]   Prithee tell him, so much the rent of his land comes to; he will not believe a fool.

LEAR   A bitter fool.

FOOL   Dost ᶠthouᶠ know the difference, my boy, between a bitter fool and a sweet one?

LEAR   No, lad, teach me.

ᵠFOOL

That lord that counselled thee to give away thy land,
Come place him here by me; do thou for him stand.

The sweet and bitter fool will presently appear,
The one in motley here, the other found out there.   140

LEAR   Dost thou call me fool, boy?

FOOL   All thy other titles thou hast given away; that thou wast born with.

KENT   This is not altogether fool, my lord.

FOOL   No, faith, lords and great men will not let me; if I   145
had a monopoly out, they would have part on't; and ladies too, they will not let me have all the fool to myself, they'll be snatching.ᵠ Nuncle, give me an egg and I'll give thee two crowns.

LEAR   What two crowns shall they be?   150

FOOL   Why, after I have cut the egg i'the middle and eat up the meat, the two crowns of the egg. When thou clovest thy crown i'the middle and gav'st away both parts, thou bor'st thine ass on thy back o'er the dirt. Thou hadst little wit in thy bald crown when thou   155
gav'st thy golden one away. If I speak like myself in this, let him be whipped that first finds it so.
[*Sings.*] Fools had ne'er less grace in a year,
    For wise men are grown foppish,
    And know not how their wits to wear,   160
    Their manners are so apish.

LEAR   When were you wont to be so full of songs, sirrah?

FOOL   I have used it, nuncle, e'er since thou mad'st thy daughters thy mothers; for when thou gav'st them the rod and putt'st down thine own breeches,   165
[*Sings.*] Then they for sudden joy did weep
    And I for sorrow sung,
    That such a king should play bo-peep,
    And go the fools among.
Prithee, nuncle, keep a schoolmaster that can teach thy   170
fool to lie; I would fain learn to lie.

LEAR   An you lie, ᶠsirrah,ᶠ we'll have you whipped.

FOOL   I marvel what kin thou and thy daughters are. They'll have me whipped for speaking true, thou'lt have me whipped for lying, and sometimes I am   175
whipped for holding my peace. I had rather be any kind o'thing than a fool, and yet I would not be thee, nuncle. Thou hast pared thy wit o'both sides and left nothing i'the middle. Here comes one o'the parings.

Enter GONERIL.

LEAR

How now, daughter? What makes that frontlet on?   180
ᵠMethinksᵠ you are too much of late i'the frown.

FOOL   Thou wast a pretty fellow when thou hadst no need to care for her frowning. Now thou art an O without a figure; I am better than thou art now. I am a fool, thou art nothing. [*to Goneril*] Yes, forsooth, I will   185
hold my tongue; so your face bids me, though you say nothing. Mum, mum!
    He that keeps nor crust nor crumb,
    Weary of all, shall want some.
[*Points to Lear.*] That's a shelled peascod.   190

GONERIL   Not only, sir, this your all-licensed fool,
But other of your insolent retinue

Do hourly carp and quarrel, breaking forth
In rank and not to be endured riots. Sir,
195   I had thought by making this well known unto you
To have found a safe redress, but now grow fearful
By what yourself too late have spoke and done,
That you protect this course and put [F]it[F] on
By your allowance; which if you should, the fault
200   Would not scape censure, nor the redresses sleep,
Which in the tender of a wholesome weal
Might in their working do you that offence
Which else were shame, that then necessity
Will call discreet proceeding.
205   FOOL   For you know, nuncle,
The hedge-sparrow fed the cuckoo so long
That it's had it head bit off by it young.
So out went the candle and we were left darkling.
LEAR   Are you our daughter?
210   GONERIL   [Q]Come, sir,[Q]
I would you would make use of your good wisdom,
Whereof I know you are fraught, and put away
These dispositions, which of late transport you
From what you rightly are.
215   FOOL   May not an ass know when the cart draws the
horse? Whoop, Jug, I love thee.
LEAR
Does any here know me? [Q]Why[Q], this is not Lear.
Does Lear walk thus, speak thus? Where are his eyes?
Either his notion weakens, [Q]or[Q] his discernings are
220   lethargied – Ha! [Q]sleeping or[Q] waking? [Q]Sure[Q] 'tis not
so. Who is it that can tell me who I am?
[F]FOOL[F]   Lear's shadow.
[Q]LEAR   I would learn that, for by the marks of
sovereignty, knowledge and reason, I should be false
225   persuaded I had daughters.
FOOL   Which they will make an obedient father.[Q]
LEAR   Your name, fair gentlewoman?
GONERIL   This admiration, sir, is much o'the savour
Of other your new pranks. I do beseech you
230   [F]To[F] understand my purposes aright:
As you are old and reverend, should be wise.
Here do you keep a hundred knights and squires,
Men so disordered, so debauched and bold,
That this our court, infected with their manners,
235   Shows like a riotous inn. Epicurism and lust
Makes [F]it[F] more like a tavern or a brothel
Than a graced palace. The shame itself doth speak
For instant remedy. Be then desired,
By her that else will take the thing she begs,
240   A little to disquantity your train,
And the remainders that shall still depend
To be such men as may besort your age,
Which know themselves, and you.
LEAR   Darkness and devils!
Saddle my horses; call my train together.
245   Degenerate bastard, I'll not trouble thee:
Yet have I left a daughter.

GONERIL
You strike my people, and your disordered rabble
Make servants of their betters.

Enter ALBANY.

LEAR
Woe that too late repents! – [Q]O sir, are you come?[Q]
250   Is it your will? Speak, sir. – Prepare my horses.
                                          [*Exit a Knight.*]
Ingratitude, thou marble-hearted fiend,
More hideous when thou show'st thee in a child
Than the sea-monster.
[F]ALBANY   Pray, sir, be patient.
LEAR[F] [*to Goneril*]   Detested kite, thou liest.
255   My train are men of choice and rarest parts
That all particulars of duty know,
And in the most exact regard support
The worships of their name. O most small fault,
How ugly didst thou in Cordelia show,
260   Which like an engine wrenched my frame of nature
From the fixed place, drew from my heart all love
And added to the gall. O Lear, Lear[F], Lear[F]!
[*striking his head*] Beat at this gate that let thy folly in
And thy dear judgement out. Go, go, my people.
                [*Exeunt Kent, Knights and attendants.*]
265   ALBANY   My lord, I am guiltless as I am ignorant
[F]Of what hath moved you.[F]
LEAR   It may be so, my lord.
Hear, Nature, hear, dear goddess, [F]hear[F]:
Suspend thy purpose if thou didst intend
To make this creature fruitful.
270   Into her womb convey sterility,
Dry up in her the organs of increase,
And from her derogate body never spring
A babe to honour her. If she must teem,
Create her child of spleen, that it may live
275   And be a thwart disnatured torment to her.
Let it stamp wrinkles in her brow of youth,
With cadent tears fret channels in her cheeks,
Turn all her mother's pains and benefits
To laughter and contempt, that she may feel
280   How sharper than a serpent's tooth it is
To have a thankless child. Away, away!
                [F]Exeunt[F] [*Lear and Fool*].
ALBANY   Now gods that we adore, whereof comes this?
GONERIL   Never afflict yourself to know more of it,
But let his disposition have that scope
285   As dotage gives it.

[F]*Enter* LEAR[F], *followed by the* Fool.

LEAR   What, fifty of my followers at a clap?
Within a fortnight?
ALBANY   What's the matter, sir?
LEAR
I'll tell thee. [*to Goneril*] Life and death, I am ashamed
That thou hast power to shake my manhood thus,
290   That these hot tears, which break from me perforce,

Should make thee worth them. Blasts and fogs upon
  ᶠthee ᶠ!
Th'untented woundings of a father's curse
Pierce every sense about thee. Old fond eyes,
Beweep this cause again, I'll pluck ye out,
295 And cast you with the waters that you loose
To temper clay. ᵠYea, is't come to this?ᵠ
ᶠHa? Let it be so.ᶠ I have another daughter,
Who I am sure is kind and comfortable:
When she shall hear this of thee with her nails
300 She'll flay thy wolvish visage. Thou shalt find
That I'll resume the shape which thou dost think
I have cast off for ever. ᵠThou shalt, I warrant thee.ᵠ
                                             ᶠ*Exit*ᶠ.

GONERIL   Do you mark that, ᵠmy lordᵠ?
ALBANY   I cannot be so partial, Goneril,
  To the great love I bear you –
305 GONERIL   ᶠPray you, content.ᶠ
  ᵠCome, sir, no more.ᵠ ᶠWhat, Oswald, ho?ᶠ
  [*to the Fool*] You, ᶠsir,ᶠ more knave than fool, after
    your master.
FOOL   Nuncle Lear, nuncle Lear, tarry, ᵠandᵠ take the
  fool with ᶠthee:ᶠ
310   A fox when one has caught her,
            And such a daughter,
            Should sure to the slaughter,
            If my cap would buy a halter;
            So the fool follows after.   ᶠ*Exit*ᶠ.
GONERIL
315 ᶠThis man hath had good counsel – a hundred knights!
  'Tis politic, and safe, to let him keep
  At point a hundred knights! Yes, that on every dream,
  Each buzz, each fancy, each complaint, dislike,
  He may enguard his dotage with their powers
320 And hold our lives in mercy. Oswald, I say!
ALBANY   Well, you may fear too far.
GONERIL   Safer than trust too far.
  Let me still take away the harms I fear,
  Not fear still to be taken. I know his heart;
325 What he hath uttered I have writ my sister.
  If she sustain him and his hundred knights
  When I have showed th'unfitness –ᶠ

            ᶠ*Enter* OSWALD.ᶠ

ᵠOSWALD   Here, madam.ᵠ
GONERIL   ᶠHow now, Oswald?ᶠ What, have you writ
330   that letter to my sister?
OSWALD   Ay, madam.
GONERIL   Take you some company and away to horse.
  Inform her full of my particular fear,
  And thereto add such reasons of your own
335   As may compact it more. Get you gone,
  And hasten your return.   [*Exit Oswald.*]
            No, no, my lord,
  This milky gentleness and course of yours,
  Though I condemn not, yet, under pardon,
  You are much more attasked for want of wisdom

Than praised for harmful mildness.   340
ALBANY
  How far your eyes may pierce I cannot tell;
  Striving to better, oft we mar what's well.
GONERIL   Nay then –
ALBANY   Well, well, th'event.   *Exeunt.*

1.5   *Enter* LEAR, ᶠKENT[, *disguised,*] *and* Fool.ᶠ

LEAR [*to Kent*]   Go you before to Gloucester with these
  letters. Acquaint my daughter no further with
  anything you know than comes from her demand out
  of the letter. If your diligence be not speedy, I shall be
  there afore you.   5
KENT   I will not sleep, my lord, till I have delivered your
  letter.   *Exit.*
FOOL   If a man's brains were in's heels, were't not in
  danger of kibes?
LEAR   Ay, boy.   10
FOOL   Then I prithee be merry; thy wit shall not go
  slipshod.
LEAR   Ha, ha, ha.
FOOL   Shalt see thy other daughter will use thee kindly,
  for though she's as like this as a crab's like an apple, yet   15
  I can tell what I can tell.
LEAR   ᵠWhy,ᵠ what canst ᵠthouᵠ tell, ᵠmyᵠ boy?
FOOL   She will taste as like this as a crab does to a crab.
  Thou canst ᵠnotᵠ tell why one's nose stands i'the
  middle on's face?   20
LEAR   No.
FOOL   Why, to keep one's eyes of either side's nose, that
  what a man cannot smell out he may spy into.
LEAR   I did her wrong.
FOOL   Canst tell how an oyster makes his shell?   25
LEAR   No.
FOOL   Nor I neither; but I can tell why a snail has a house.
LEAR   Why?
FOOL   Why, to put's head in, not to give it away to his
  daughters and leave his horns without a case.   30
LEAR   I will forget my nature: so kind a father! Be my
  horses ready?
FOOL   Thy asses are gone about 'em. The reason why the
  seven stars are no more than seven is a pretty reason.
LEAR   Because they are not eight.   35
FOOL   Yes ᶠindeed,ᶠ thou wouldst make a good fool.
LEAR   To take't again perforce – monster ingratitude!
FOOL   If thou wert my fool, nuncle, I'd have thee beaten
  for being old before thy time.
LEAR   How's that?   40
FOOL   Thou shouldst not have been old till thou hadst
  been wise.
LEAR   O let me not be mad, ᶠnot madᶠ, sweet heaven! ᵠI
  would not be mad.ᵠ
  Keep me in temper, I would not be mad.   45

            [*Enter* a Gentleman.]

ᶠHow now,ᶠ are the horses ready?

GENTLEMAN   Ready, my lord.

LEAR   Come, boy.   ^Q*Exeunt*^Q [*Lear and Gentleman*].

FOOL

    She that's a maid now, and laughs at my departure,

50   Shall not be a maid long, unless things be cut shorter.

                            Exit.

2.1   *Enter* EDMUND *and* CURAN, *severally*.

EDMUND   Save thee, Curan.

CURAN   And you, sir. I have been with your father and
    given him notice that the Duke of Cornwall and
    ^FRegan^F his Duchess will be here with him this
5   night.

EDMUND   How comes that?

CURAN   Nay, I know not. You have heard of the news
    abroad? – I mean the whispered ones, for they are yet
    but ear-bussing arguments.

10 EDMUND   Not I; pray you, what are they?

CURAN   Have you heard of no likely wars toward 'twixt
    the ^Qtwo^Q dukes of Cornwall and Albany?

EDMUND   Not a word.

CURAN   You may ^Fdo^F then in time. Fare you well, sir.
                            ^F*Exit.*^F

15 EDMUND   The Duke be here tonight? The better – best!

    This weaves itself perforce into my business.

    My father hath set guard to take my brother,

    And I have one thing of a queasy question

    Which I must act. Briefness and fortune work!

20   Brother, a word; descend, brother, I say.

Enter EDGAR.

    My father watches; O ^Fsir^F, fly this place!

    Intelligence is given where you are hid:

    You have now the good advantage of the night.

    Have you not spoken 'gainst the Duke of Cornwall

        ^Qaught^Q? –

25   He's coming hither, now, i'the night, i'the haste,

    And Regan with him. Have you nothing said

    Upon his party 'gainst the Duke of Albany?

    Advise yourself.

EDGAR   I am sure on't, not a word.

EDMUND   I hear my father coming – pardon me;

30   In cunning I must draw my sword upon you.

    ^FDraw,^F seem to defend yourself; now quit you well.

    [*loudly*] Yield, come before my father! Light, ho, here!

    [*to Edgar*] Fly, brother, ^Qfly^Q! [*loudly*] Torches,

    torches! – [*to Edgar*] So farewell.   ^F*Exit Edgar.*^F

    Some blood drawn on me would beget opinion

    Of my more fierce endeavour. [*Cuts his arm.*]

35   I have seen drunkards

    Do more than this in sport. Father, father!

    Stop, stop, no help?

Enter GLOUCESTER ^F*and servants, with torches.*^F

GLOUCESTER   Now, Edmund, where's the villain?

EDMUND

    Here stood he in the dark, his sharp sword out,

    Mumbling of wicked charms, conjuring the moon

    To stand^Q's^Q auspicious mistress.

GLOUCESTER   But where is he?   40

EDMUND   Look, sir, I bleed.

GLOUCESTER   Where is the villain, Edmund?

EDMUND

    Fled this way, sir, when by no means he could –

GLOUCESTER [*to servants*]

    Pursue him, ^Fho!^F Go after!   [*Servants rush off.*]

               – 'By no means' what?

EDMUND   Persuade me to the murder of your lordship,

    But that I told him the revenging gods   45

    'Gainst parricides did all their thunders bend,

    Spoke with how manifold and strong a bond

    The child was bound to the father. Sir, in fine,

    Seeing how loathly opposite I stood

    To his unnatural purpose, in fell motion,   50

    With his prepared sword, he charges home

    My unprovided body, latched mine arm;

    But when he saw my best alarumed spirits,

    Bold in the quarrel's right, roused to th'encounter,   55

    Or whether ghasted by the noise I made,

    Full suddenly he fled.

GLOUCESTER   Let him fly far:

    Not in this land shall he remain uncaught,

    And found – dispatch! The noble Duke, my master,

    My worthy arch and patron, comes tonight;

    By his authority I will proclaim it,   60

    That he which finds him shall deserve our thanks,

    Bringing the murderous coward to the stake:

    He that conceals him, death!

EDMUND   When I dissuaded him from his intent,

    And found him pight to do it, with curst speech   65

    I threatened to discover him. He replied,

    'Thou unpossessing bastard, dost thou think,

    If I would stand against thee, would the reposal

    Of any trust, virtue or worth in thee

    Make thy words faithed? No, what I should deny,   70

    As this I would, ^Qay,^Q though thou didst produce

    My very character, I'd turn it all

    To thy suggestion, plot and damned practice;

    And thou must make a dullard of the world

    If they not thought the profits of my death   75

    Were very pregnant and potential spurs

    To make thee seek it.'   [^F*Tucket within.*^F]

GLOUCESTER   ^FO^F strange and fastened villain,

    Would he deny his letter, ^Fsaid he?^F ^QI never got him.^Q

    Hark, the Duke's trumpets; I know not why he comes.

    All ports I'll bar, the villain shall not scape;   80

    The Duke must grant me that. Besides, his picture

    I will send far and near, that all the kingdom

    May have ^Fdue^F note of him; and of my land,

    Loyal and natural boy, I'll work the means

    To make thee capable.   85

Enter CORNWALL, ^FREGAN *and attendants.*^F

CORNWALL
    How now, my noble friend? Since I came hither,
    Which I can call but now, I have heard strange news.
REGAN   If it be true, all vengeance comes too short
    Which can pursue th'offender. How dost, my lord?
GLOUCESTER
    ^FO^F madam, my old heart is cracked, it's cracked.
REGAN   What, did my father's godson seek your life?
    He whom my father named, your Edgar?
GLOUCESTER   O lady, lady, shame would have it hid.
REGAN
    Was he not companion with the riotous knights
    That tended upon my father?
GLOUCESTER   I know not, madam; 'tis too bad, too bad.
EDMUND   Yes, madam, he was ^Fof that consort^F.
REGAN   No marvel, then, though he were ill affected.
    'Tis they have put him on the old man's death,
    To have th'expense and waste of his revenues.
    I have this present evening from my sister
    Been well informed of them, and with such cautions
    That if they come to sojourn at my house
    I'll not be there.
CORNWALL   Nor I, assure thee, Regan.
    Edmund, I hear that you have shown your father
    A child-like office.
EDMUND   It was my duty, sir.
GLOUCESTER [*to Cornwall*]
    He did bewray his practice, and received
    This hurt you see, striving to apprehend him.
CORNWALL   Is he pursued?
GLOUCESTER   Ay, my good lord.
CORNWALL   If he be taken, he shall never more
    Be feared of doing harm, make your own purpose
    How in my strength you please. For you, Edmund,
    Whose virtue and obedience doth this instant
    So much commend itself, you shall be ours.
    Natures of such deep trust we shall much need;
    You we first seize on.
EDMUND   I shall serve you, ^Fsir^F, truly, however else.
GLOUCESTER   For him I thank your grace.
CORNWALL   You know not why we came to visit you?
REGAN   Thus out of season, threading dark-eyed night?
    Occasions, noble Gloucester, of some poise
    Wherein we must have use of your advice.
    Our father he hath writ, so hath our sister,
    Of differences, which I best thought it fit
    To answer from our home. The several messengers
    From hence attend dispatch. Our good old friend,
    Lay comforts to your bosom, and bestow
    Your needful counsel to our business,
    Which craves the instant use.
GLOUCESTER   I serve you, madam.
    Your graces are right welcome.   *Exeunt.* ^F*Flourish.*^F

2.2 *Enter* KENT[, *disguised,*] *and* OSWALD, ^F*severally.*^F

OSWALD   Good dawning to thee, friend. Art of this
    house?

KENT   Ay.
OSWALD   Where may we set our horses?
KENT   I'the mire.   5
OSWALD   Prithee, if thou lov'st me, tell me.
KENT   I love thee not.
OSWALD   Why then, I care not for thee.
KENT   If I had thee in Lipsbury pinfold, I would make
    thee care for me.   10
OSWALD   Why dost thou use me thus? I know thee not.
KENT   Fellow, I know thee.
OSWALD   What dost thou know me for?
KENT   A knave, a rascal, an eater of broken meats; a base,
    proud, shallow, beggarly, three-suited-hundred-pound,   15
    filthy, worsted-stocking knave; a lily-livered, action-
    taking ^Qknave, a^Q whoreson, glass-gazing, super-
    serviceable, finical rogue; one trunk-inheriting slave,
    one that wouldst be a bawd in way of good service and
    art nothing but the composition of a knave, beggar,   20
    coward, pander and the son and heir of a mongrel bitch;
    ^Fone^F whom I will beat into clamorous whining if thou
    deniest the least syllable of thy addition.
OSWALD   ^FWhy,^F what a monstrous fellow art thou, thus
    to rail on one that is neither known of thee, nor knows   25
    thee!
KENT   What a brazen-faced varlet art thou to deny thou
    knowest me? Is it two days ^Qago^Q since I tripped up thy
    heels and beat thee before the King? Draw, you rogue,
    for though it be night, ^Fyet^F the moon shines.   [*Draws*   30
    his sword.]   I'll make a sop o'the moonshine of you.
    ^QDraw^Q you whoreson cullionly barber-monger! Draw!
OSWALD   Away, I have nothing to do with thee.
KENT   Draw, you rascal! You come with letters against
    the King, and take Vanity the puppet's part against the   35
    royalty of her father. Draw, you rogue, or I'll so
    carbonado your shanks! – draw, you rascal, come your
    ways!
OSWALD   Help, ho! Murder, help!
KENT   Strike, you slave. Stand, rogue, stand you neat   40
    slave, strike! [*Beats him.*]
OSWALD   Help, ho! Murder, murder!

Enter EDMUND, ^Q*with his rapier drawn,*^Q CORNWALL,
    REGAN, GLOUCESTER [*and*] ^F*servants.*^F

EDMUND   How now, what's the matter? ^FPart!^F
KENT [*to Edmund*]   With you, goodman boy, if you
    please. Come, I'll flesh ye; come on, young master.   45
GLOUCESTER   Weapons? Arms? What's the matter here?
CORNWALL   Keep peace upon your lives: he dies that
    strikes again. What is the matter?
REGAN   The messengers from our sister and the King.
CORNWALL [*to Kent*]   What is your difference? Speak.   50
OSWALD   I am scarce in breath, my lord.
KENT   No marvel, you have so bestirred your valour,
    you cowardly rascal; nature disclaims in thee – a tailor
    made thee.
CORNWALL   Thou art a strange fellow – a tailor make a   55
    man?

KENT   ^QAy,^Q a tailor, sir; a stone-cutter or a painter could
not have made him so ill, though they had been but
two years o'the trade.

60 CORNWALL [*to Oswald*]   Speak yet: how grew your
quarrel?

OSWALD   This ancient ruffian, sir, whose life I have
spared at suit of his grey beard –

KENT   Thou whoreson zed, thou unnecessary letter! My
65 lord, if you will give me leave, I will tread this
unbolted villain into mortar and daub the wall of a
jakes with him. [*to Oswald*] Spare my grey beard, you
wagtail?

CORNWALL   Peace, sirrah. You beastly knave, know you
70 no reverence?

KENT   Yes, sir, but anger hath a privilege.

CORNWALL   Why art thou angry?

KENT   That such a slave as this should wear a sword,
Who wears no honesty. Such smiling rogues as these
75 Like rats oft bite the ^Fholy^F cords atwain
Which are too intrince t'unloose; smooth every passion
That in the natures of their lords rebel,
Bring oil to fire, snow to their colder moods,
Renege, affirm and turn their halcyon beaks
80 With every gale and vary of their masters,
Knowing naught, like dogs, but following.
[*to Oswald*] A plague upon your epileptic visage.
Smile you my speeches as I were a fool?
Goose, if I had you upon Sarum plain,
85 I'd drive ye cackling home to Camelot.

CORNWALL   What, art thou mad, old fellow?

GLOUCESTER   How fell you out, say that.

KENT   No contraries hold more antipathy
Than I and such a knave.

CORNWALL
90 Why dost thou call him knave? What is his fault?

KENT   His countenance likes me not.

CORNWALL
No more perchance does mine, nor his, nor hers.

KENT   Sir, 'tis my occupation to be plain:
I have seen better faces in my time
95 Than stands on any shoulder that I see
Before me at this instant.

CORNWALL   This is some fellow
Who, having been praised for bluntness, doth affect
A saucy roughness and constrains the garb
Quite from his nature. He cannot flatter, he;
100 An honest mind and plain, he must speak truth;
An they will take it, so; if not, he's plain.
These kind of knaves I know, which in this plainness
Harbour more craft and more corrupter ends
Than twenty silly-ducking observants
105 That stretch their duties nicely.

KENT   Sir, in good faith, ^Qor^Q in sincere verity,
Under th'allowance of your great aspect,
Whose influence, like the wreath of radiant fire
On flickering Phoebus' front –

CORNWALL   What mean'st ^Qthou^Q by this?

KENT   To go out of my dialect, which you discommend   110
so much. I know, sir, I am no flatterer. He that
beguiled you in a plain accent was a plain knave, which
for my part I will not be, though I should win your
displeasure to entreat me to't.

CORNWALL [*to Oswald*] What was th'offence you gave him?   115

OSWALD   I never gave him any.
It pleased the King his master very late
To strike at me upon his misconstruction,
When he, compact and flattering his displeasure,
Tripped me behind; being down, insulted, railed   120
And put upon him such a deal of man
That worthied him, got praises of the King
For him attempting who was self-subdued;
And in the fleshment of this dread exploit
Drew on me here again.

KENT   None of these rogues and cowards   125
But Ajax is their fool.

CORNWALL   Fetch forth the stocks, ^Qho^Q!
                          [*Exeunt one or two servants.*]
You stubborn, ancient knave, you reverend braggart,
We'll teach you.

KENT   ^FSir,^F I am too old to learn.
Call not your stocks for me; I serve the King,
On whose employment I was sent to you.   130
You shall do small respect, show too bold malice
Against the grace and person of my master,
Stocking his messenger.

CORNWALL   Fetch forth the stocks!
As I have life and honour, there shall he sit till noon.

REGAN
Till noon? Till night, my lord, and all night too.   135

KENT   Why, madam, if I were your father's dog
You should not use me so.

REGAN   Sir, being his knave, I will.
[^F*Stocks brought out.*^F]

CORNWALL   This is a fellow of the selfsame colour
Our sister speaks of. Come, bring away the stocks.

GLOUCESTER   Let me beseech your grace not to do so.   140
^QHis fault is much, and the good King, his master,
Will check him for't. Your purposed low correction
Is such as basest and contemnedst wretches
For pilferings and most common trespasses
Are punished with.^Q   145
The King, ^Fhis master, needs^F must take it ill
That he, so slightly valued in his messenger,
Should have him thus restrained.

CORNWALL   I'll answer that.

REGAN   My sister may receive it much more worse
To have her gentleman abused, assaulted,   150
^QFor following her affairs. Put in his legs.^Q
[*Kent is put in the stocks.*]

^FCORNWALL^F   Come, my ^Qgood^Q lord, away.
                          ^F*Exeunt*^F [*all but Gloucester and Kent*].

GLOUCESTER
I am sorry for thee, friend; 'tis the Duke's pleasure,
Whose disposition all the world well knows

Will not be rubbed nor stopped. I'll entreat for thee.

KENT

Pray ᵟyouᵟ do not, sir. I have watched and travelled
    hard.

Some time I shall sleep out, the rest I'll whistle.

A good man's fortune may grow out at heels.

Give you good morrow.

GLOUCESTER

The Duke's too blame in this; 'twill be ill taken.

ᶠ*Exit.*ᶠ

KENT   Good King, that must approve the common saw,

Thou out of heaven's benediction com'st

To the warm sun.

Approach, thou beacon to this under-globe,

That by thy comfortable beams I may

Peruse this letter. Nothing almost sees miracles

But misery. I know 'tis from Cordelia,

Who hath most fortunately been informed

Of my obscured course,

[*reading the letter*]   *and shall find time*

From this enormous state, seeking to give

Losses their remedies. All weary and o'erwatched,

Take vantage, heavy eyes, not to behold

This shameful lodging.

Fortune, good night: smile once more; turn thy wheel.

[ᵟ*Sleeps.*ᵟ]

Enter EDGAR.   [2.3]

EDGAR   I heard myself proclaimed,

And by the happy hollow of a tree

Escaped the hunt. No port is free, no place

That guard and most unusual vigilance

Does not attend my taking. While I may scape

I will preserve myself, and am bethought

To take the basest and most poorest shape

That ever penury in contempt of man

Brought near to beast. My face I'll grime with filth,

Blanket my loins, elf all my hair in knots

And with presented nakedness outface

The winds and persecutions of the sky.

The country gives me proof and precedent

Of Bedlam beggars, who, with roaring voices,

Strike in their numbed ᶠandᶠ mortified ᵟbareᵟ arms

Pins, wooden pricks, nails, sprigs of rosemary;

And with this horrible object, from low farms,

Poor pelting villages, sheepcotes and mills,

Sometime with lunatic bans, sometime with prayers,

Enforce their charity. Poor Turlygod, poor Tom,

That's something yet: Edgar I nothing am.   *Exit.*

Enter LEAR, ᶠ*Fool and a* Knight.ᶠ   [2.4]

LEAR

'Tis strange that they should so depart from home

And not send back my messenger.

KNIGHT   As I learned,

The night before there was no purpose ᶠin themᶠ

Of this remove.

KENT [*Wakes.*]   Hail to thee, noble master.

LEAR   Ha? Mak'st thou this shame thy pastime?

ᶠKENT   No, my lord.ᶠ   200

FOOL   Ha, ha, ᵟlookᵟ, he wears cruel garters. Horses are
    tied by the heads, dogs and bears by the neck, monkeys
    by the loins and men by the legs. When a man's
    overlusty at legs, then he wears wooden nether-stocks.

LEAR [*to Kent*]

What's he that hath so much thy place mistook   205

To set thee here?

KENT   It is both he and she,   [11]

Your son and daughter.

LEAR   No.

KENT   Yes.

LEAR   No, I say.   210

KENT   I say, yea.

ᵟLEAR   No, no, they would not.

KENT   Yes, they have.ᵟ

LEAR   By Jupiter, I swear no.

ᶠKENT   By Juno, I swear ay.

LEARᶠ   They durst not do't: 215

They could not, would not do't – 'tis worse than
    murder   [21]

To do upon respect such violent outrage.

Resolve me with all modest haste which way

Thou mightst deserve or they impose this usage,

Coming from us.   220

KENT   My lord, when at their home

I did commend your highness' letters to them,

Ere I was risen from the place that showed

My duty kneeling, came there a reeking post,

Stewed in his haste, half breathless, panting forth

From Goneril, his mistress, salutations;   225

Delivered letters, spite of intermission,   [31]

Which presently they read; on those contents

They summoned up their meiny, straight took horse,

Commanded me to follow and attend

The leisure of their answer, gave me cold looks;   230

And meeting here the other messenger,

Whose welcome I perceived had poisoned mine,

Being the very fellow which of late

Displayed so saucily against your highness,

Having more man than wit about me, drew.   235

He raised the house with loud and coward cries.   [41]

Your son and daughter found this trespass worth

The shame which here it suffers.

ᶠFOOL   Winter's not gone yet, if the wild geese fly that
    way.   240

        Fathers that wear rags
            Do make their children blind,
        But fathers that bear bags
            Shall see their children kind:
        Fortune, that arrant whore,   245
            Ne'er turns the key to the poor.   [51]

But for all this thou shalt have as many dolours for thy
daughters as thou canst tell in a year.ᶠ

LEAR   O, how this mother swells up toward my heart!

250 *Hysterica passio*, down, thou climbing sorrow,
Thy element's below. Where is this daughter?
KENT   With the Earl, sir, ᶠhereᶠ within.
LEAR   Follow me not; stay here.   ᶠExit.ᶠ
KNIGHT   Made you no more offence but what you speak of?
255 KENT   None. How chance the King comes with so small
[61]   a number?
FOOL   An thou hadst been set i'the stocks for that
       question, thou hadst well deserved it.
KENT   Why, fool?
260 FOOL   We'll set thee to school to an ant, to teach thee
       there's no labouring i'the winter. All that follow their
       noses are led by their eyes but blind men, and there's
       not a nose among twenty but can smell him that's
       stinking. Let go thy hold when a great wheel runs
265   down a hill lest it break thy neck with following ᵠitᵠ;
[71]   but the great one that goes upward, let him draw thee
       after. When a wise man gives thee better counsel give
       me mine again; I would have none but knaves follow it,
       since a fool gives it.
270   That sir which serves ᶠand seeksᶠ for gain,
               And follows but for form,
           Will pack when it begins to rain,
               And leave thee in the storm;
           But I will tarry, the fool will stay,
275   And let the wise man fly:
[81]   The knave turns fool that runs away,
               The fool no knave perdy.
KENT   Where learned you this, fool?
FOOL   Not i'the stocks, ᶠfool.ᶠ

Enter LEAR *and* GLOUCESTER

LEAR
       Deny to speak with me? They are sick, they are
280   weary,
       They ᶠhaveᶠ travelled all the night? – mere fetches
           ᵠayᵠ,
       The images of revolt and flying off.
       Fetch me a better answer.
GLOUCESTER   My dear lord,
       You know the fiery quality of the Duke,
285   How unremovable and fixed he is
[91]   In his own course.
LEAR   Vengeance, plague, death, confusion!
       Fiery? What quality? Why, Gloucester, Gloucester,
       I'd speak with the Duke of Cornwall and his wife.
ᶠGLOUCESTER
290   Well, my good lord, I have informed them so.
LEAR
       'Informed them'? Dost thou understand me, man?ᶠ
GLOUCESTER   Ay, my good lord.
LEAR
       The King would speak with Cornwall, the dear
           father
       Would with his daughter speak, commands – tends –
           service.
295   ᶠAre they informed of this? My breath and blood!

'Fiery'?ᶠ The fiery Duke, tell the hot Duke that
   ᵠLearᵠ –   [101]
No, but not yet, maybe he is not well;
Infirmity doth still neglect all office
Whereto our health is bound. We are not ourselves
When nature, being oppressed, commands the mind   300
To suffer with the body. I'll forbear,
And am fallen out with my more headier will
To take the indisposed and sickly fit
For the sound man.
[*Notices Kent.*]   Death on my state! Wherefore
Should he sit here? This act persuades me   305
That this remotion of the Duke and her   [111]
Is practice only. Give me my servant forth.
ᶠGoᶠ tell the Duke and's wife I'd speak with them,
Now, presently: bid them come forth and hear me,
Or at their chamber door I'll beat the drum   310
Till it cry sleep to death.
GLOUCESTER   I would have all well betwixt you. ᶠExit.ᶠ
LEAR   O ᶠme,ᶠ my heart! My ᶠrisingᶠ heart! ᶠBut down!
FOOL   Cry to it, nuncle, as the cockney did to the eels
       when she put 'em i'the paste alive: she knapped 'em 315
       o'the coxcombs with a stick, and cried 'Down,   [121]
       wantons, down!' 'Twas her brother that in pure
       kindness to his horse buttered his hay.

Enter CORNWALL, REGAN, ᶠGLOUCESTER [*and*] *servants.*ᶠ

LEAR   Good morrow to you both.
CORNWALL   Hail to your grace.
       [ᶠ*Kent here set at liberty.*ᶠ]
REGAN   I am glad to see your highness.   320
LEAR   Regan, I think you are. I know what reason
       I have to think so. If thou shouldst not be glad,
       I would divorce me from thy mother's tomb,
       Sepulchring an adultress. [*to Kent*] O, are you free?
       Some other time for that. – Beloved Regan,   325
       Thy sister's naught. O, Regan, she hath tied   [131]
       Sharp-toothed unkindness, like a vulture, here.
       [*Lays his hand on his heart.*]
       I can scarce speak to thee; thou'lt not believe
       With how depraved a quality – O, Regan!
REGAN   I pray ᶠyouᶠ, sir, take patience. I have hope   330
       You less know how to value her desert
       Than she to scant her duty.
ᶠLEAR   Say? how is that?
REGAN   I cannot think my sister in the least
       Would fail her obligation. If, sir, perchance
       She have restrained the riots of your followers,   335
       'Tis on such ground and to such wholesome end   [141]
       As clears her from all blame.ᶠ
LEAR   My curses on her.
REGAN   O, sir, you are old:
       Nature in you stands on the very verge
       Of her confine. You should be ruled and led   340
       By some discretion that discerns your state
       Better than you yourself. Therefore I pray ᶠyouᶠ
       That to our sister you do make return;

Say you have wronged her, ᵠsir.ᵠ

LEAR   Ask her forgiveness?

5   Do you ᶠbutᶠ mark how this becomes the house?

61]   [*Kneels.*] Dear daughter, I confess that I am old;
         Age is unnecessary. On my knees I beg
         That you'll vouchsafe me raiment, bed and food.

REGAN   Good sir, no more. These are unsightly tricks.
         Return you to my sister.

0   LEAR [*Rises.*]   Never, Regan:
         She hath abated me of half my train,
         Looked black upon me, struck me with her tongue
         Most serpent-like, upon the very heart.
         All the stored vengeances of heaven fall
5   On her ingrateful top! Strike her young bones,
         You taking airs, with lameness!

61]   CORNWALL   Fie, sir, fie!

ᶠLEARᶠ
         You nimble lightnings, dart your blinding flames
         Into her scornful eyes! Infect her beauty,
         You fen-sucked fogs, drawn by the powerful sun
         To fall and blister!

0   REGAN   O, the blest gods!
         So will you wish on me when the rash mood ᶠis on.ᶠ

LEAR   No, Regan, thou shalt never have my curse.
         Thy tender-hafted nature shall not give
         Thee o'er to harshness. Her eyes are fierce, but
            thine
5   Do comfort and not burn. 'Tis not in thee
71]   To grudge my pleasures, to cut off my train,
         To bandy hasty words, to scant my sizes
         And, in conclusion, to oppose the bolt
         Against my coming in. Thou better knowst
0   The offices of nature, bond of childhood,
         Effects of courtesy, dues of gratitude.
         Thy half o'the kingdom hast thou not forgot,
         Wherein I thee endowed.

REGAN   Good sir, to the purpose
                                    [ᶠ*Tucket within.*ᶠ]

LEAR   Who put my man i'the stocks?

Enter OSWALD.

CORNWALL   What trumpet's that?

5   REGAN   I know't, my sister's. This approves her letter
         That she would soon be here.

81]   [*to Oswald*]   Is your lady come?

LEAR   This is a slave whose easy borrowed pride
         Dwells in the fickle grace of her he follows.
         Out, varlet, from my sight!

CORNWALL   What means your grace?

Enter GONERIL.

LEAR
0   Who stocked my servant? Regan, I have good hope
         Thou didst not know on't. Who comes here? O
            heavens!
         If you do love old men, if your sweet sway
         Allow obedience, if ᶠyouᶠ yourselves are old,

Make it your cause. Send down, and take my part!

[*to Goneril*] Art not ashamed to look upon this beard?   385

O, Regan, will you take her by the hand?   [191]

GONERIL
         Why not by the hand, sir? How have I offended?
         All's not offence that indiscretion finds
         And dotage terms so.

LEAR   O sides, you are too tough!
         Will you yet hold? How came my man i'the stocks?   390

CORNWALL   I set him there, sir; but his own disorders
         Deserved much less advancement.

LEAR   You? Did you?

REGAN   I pray you, father, being weak, seem so.
         If till the expiration of your month
         You will return and sojourn with my sister,   395
         Dismissing half your train, come then to me.   [201]
         I am now from home and out of that provision
         Which shall be needful for your entertainment.

LEAR   Return to her? And fifty men dismissed?
         No! Rather I abjure all roofs and choose   400
         To wage against the enmity o'th' air –
         To be a comrade with the wolf and owl –
         Necessity's sharp pinch! Return with her?
         Why, the hot-blooded France, that dowerless took
         Our youngest born, I could as well be brought   405
         To knee his throne and squire-like pension beg,   [211]
         To keep base life afoot. Return with her?
         Persuade me rather to be slave and sumpter
         To this detested groom. [*Points at Oswald.*]

GONERIL   At your choice, sir.

LEAR
         ᵠNowᵠ I prithee, daughter, do not make me mad: 410
         I will not trouble thee, my child. Farewell:
         We'll no more meet, no more see one another.
         But yet thou art my flesh, my blood, my daughter,
         Or rather a disease that's in my flesh,
         Which I must needs call mine. Thou art a boil,   415
         A plague sore, or embossèd carbuncle   [221]
         In my corrupted blood. But I'll not chide thee:
         Let shame come when it will; I do not call it,
         I do not bid the thunder-bearer shoot,
         Nor tell tales of thee to high-judging Jove.   420
         Mend when thou canst, be better at thy leisure:
         I can be patient, I can stay with Regan,
         I and my hundred knights.

REGAN   Not altogether so, ᵠsirᵠ.
         I looked not for you yet, nor am provided
         For your fit welcome. Give ear, sir, to my sister;   425
         For those that mingle reason with your passion   [231]
         Must be content to think you ᵠareᵠ old, and so –
         But she knows what she does.

LEAR   Is this well spoken ᵠnowᵠ?

REGAN   I dare avouch it, sir. What, fifty followers?
         Is it not well? What should you need of more?   430
         Yea, or so many, sith that both charge and danger
         Speak 'gainst so great a number? How in one house
         Should many people, under two commands,

Hold amity? 'Tis hard, almost impossible.

GONERIL

435   Why might not you, my lord, receive attendance
[241]   From those that she calls servants or from mine?

REGAN

Why not, my lord? If then they chanced to slack ye
We could control them. If you will come to me –
For now I spy a danger – I entreat you

440   To bring but five and twenty: to no more
Will I give place or notice.

LEAR   I gave you all –

REGAN   And in good time you gave it.

LEAR   – Made you my guardians, my depositaries,
But kept a reservation to be followed

445   With such a number. What, must I come to you
[251]   With five and twenty? Regan, said you so?

REGAN   And speak't again, my lord: no more with me.

LEAR

Those wicked creatures yet do look well favoured
When others are more wicked; not being the worst
Stands in some rank of praise.

450   [*to Goneril*]   I'll go with thee;
Thy fifty yet doth double five and twenty,
And thou art twice her love.

GONERIL   Hear me, my lord:
What need you five and twenty? Ten? Or five?
To follow in a house where twice so many
Have a command to tend you?

455   REGAN   What need one?
[261]   LEAR   O, reason not the need! Our basest beggars
Are in the poorest thing superfluous;
Allow not nature more than nature needs,
Man's life is cheap as beast's. Thou art a lady;

460   If only to go warm were gorgeous,
Why, nature needs not what thou gorgeous wear'st,
Which scarcely keeps thee warm. But for true need –
You heavens, give me that patience, patience I need!
You see me here, you gods, a poor old man,

465   As full of grief as age, wretched in both:
[271]   If it be you that stirs these daughters' hearts
Against their father, fool me not so much
To bear it tamely; touch me with noble anger,
And let not women's weapons, water-drops,

470   Stain my man's cheeks. No, you unnatural hags,
I will have such revenges on you both
That all the world shall – I will do such things –
What they are yet I know not, but they shall be
The terrors of the earth! You think I'll weep,

475   No, I'll not weep.   [ᶠ*Storm and tempest.*ᶠ]
[281]   I have full cause of weeping, but this heart
Shall break into a hundred thousand flaws
Or e'er I'll weep. O fool, I shall go mad.
        Exeunt ᵠ*Lear, Gloucester, Kent, Fool*ᵠ [*and Knight*].

CORNWALL   Let us withdraw; 'twill be a storm.

480   REGAN   This house is little; the old man and's people
Cannot be well bestowed.

GONERIL   'Tis his own blame; hath put himself from rest

And must needs taste his folly.

REGAN   For his particular, I'll receive him gladly,
But not one follower.

GONERIL   So am I purposed.   485
Where is my lord of Gloucester?   [291]

                Enter GLOUCESTER.

CORNWALL
Followed the old man forth – he is returned.

GLOUCESTER   The King is in high rage.

ᶠCORNWALL   Whither is he going?

GLOUCESTER
He calls to horse,ᶠ but will I know not whither.   490

CORNWALL   'Tis best to give him way; he leads himself.

GONERIL [*to Gloucester*]
My lord, entreat him by no means to stay.

GLOUCESTER
Alack, the night comes on, and the high winds
Do sorely ruffle; for many miles about
There's scarce a bush.

REGAN   O sir, to wilful men   495
The injuries that they themselves procure   [301]
Must be their schoolmasters. Shut up your doors.
He is attended with a desperate train,
And what they may incense him to, being apt
To have his ear abused, wisdom bids fear.   500

CORNWALL
Shut up your doors, my lord; 'tis a wild night.
My Regan counsels well; come out o'the storm.
                                        Exeunt.

3.1   ᶠ*Storm still.*ᶠ *Enter* KENT[*, disguised,*]
                and a Knight, *severally.*

KENT   Who's there, besides foul weather?

KNIGHT   One minded like the weather, most unquietly.

KENT   I know you. Where's the King?

KNIGHT   Contending with the fretful elements;
Bids the wind blow the earth into the sea,   5
Or swell the curled waters 'bove the main,
That things might change, or cease; ᵠtears his white
        hair,
Which the impetuous blasts with eyeless rage
Catch in their fury and make nothing of,
Strives in his little world of man to outscorn   10
The to and fro conflicting wind and rain;
This night wherein the cub-drawn bear would couch,
The lion and the belly-pinched wolf
Keep their fur dry, unbonneted he runs,
And bids what will take all.ᵠ

KENT   But who is with him?   15

KNIGHT   None but the fool, who labours to outjest
His heart-struck injuries.

KENT   Sir, I do know you
And dare upon the warrant of my note
Commend a dear thing to you. There is division,
Although as yet the face of it is covered   20

With mutual cunning, 'twixt Albany and Cornwall,
ᶠWho have, as who have not that their great stars
Throned and set high, servants, who seem no less,
Which are to France the spies and speculations
Intelligent of our state – what hath been seen,
Either in snuffs and packings of the dukes,
Or the hard rein which both of them hath borne
Against the old kind King, or something deeper,
Whereof, perchance, these are but furnishings. –ᶠ
ᵠNow to you:
If on my credit you dare build so far
To make your speed to Dover, you shall find
Some that will thank you, making just report
Of how unnatural and bemadding sorrow
The King hath cause to plain.
I am a gentleman of blood and breeding,
And from some knowledge and assurance
Offer this office to you.ᵠ

KNIGHT   I will talk further with you.

KENT   No, do not.
For confirmation that I ᶠamᶠ much more
Than my out-wall, open this purse and take
What it contains. If you shall see Cordelia,
As fear not but you shall, show her this ring,
And she will tell you who your fellow is
That yet you do not know. Fie on this storm;
I will go seek the King.

KNIGHT   Give me your hand.
Have you no more to say?

KENT   Few words, but to effect
More than all yet: that when we have found the King,
ᶠIn which your painᶠ that way, I'll this,
He that first lights on him holla the other.   *Exeunt.*

3.2   ᶠ*Storm still.*ᶠ *Enter* LEAR *and* Fool.

LEAR   Blow winds and crack your cheeks! Rage, blow!
You cataracts and hurricanoes, spout
Till you have drenched our steeples, drowned the cocks!
You sulphurous and thought-executing fires,
Vaunt-couriers of oak-cleaving thunderbolts,
Singe my white head! And thou, all-shaking thunder,
Strike flat the thick rotundity o'the world,
Crack nature's moulds, all germens spill at once
That make ingrateful man!

FOOL   O, nuncle, court holy-water in a dry house is
better than this rain-water out o'door. Good nuncle,
in, ᵠandᵠ ask thy daughters blessing. Here's a night
pities neither wise men nor fools.

LEAR   Rumble thy bellyful! Spit fire, spout rain!
Nor rain, wind, thunder, fire are my daughters;
I tax not you, you elements, with unkindness.
I never gave you kingdom, called you children;
You owe me no subscription. ᵠWhyᵠ then, let fall
Your horrible pleasure. Here I stand your slave,
A poor, infirm, weak and despised old man.
But yet I call you servile ministers
That will with two pernicious daughters join

Your high-engendered battles 'gainst a head
So old and white as this. O ᶠho!ᶠ 'tis foul.

FOOL   He that has a house to put's head in has a good   25
headpiece:
The codpiece that will house
Before the head has any,
The head and he shall louse:
So beggars marry many.   30
The man that makes his toe
What he his heart should make,
Shall of a corn cry woe
And turn his sleep to wake.
For there was never yet fair woman but she made   35
mouths in a glass.

Enter KENT[, *disguised*].

LEAR   No, I will be the pattern of all patience,
I will say nothing.

KENT   Who's there?

FOOL   Marry, here's grace and a codpiece – that's a wise   40
man and a fool.

KENT [*to Lear*]
Alas, sir, are you here? Things that love night
Love not such nights as these. The wrathful skies
Gallow the very wanderers of the dark,
And make them keep their caves. Since I was man   45
Such sheets of fire, such bursts of horrid thunder,
Such groans of roaring wind and rain I never
Remember to have heard. Man's nature cannot carry
Th'affliction, nor the fear.

LEAR   Let the great gods
That keep this dreadful pudder o'er our heads   50
Find out their enemies now. Tremble, thou wretch,
That hast within thee undivulged crimes,
Unwhipped of justice. Hide thee, thou bloody hand,
Thou perjured, and thou simular of virtue
That art incestuous. Caitiff, to pieces shake,   55
That under covert and convenient seeming
Has practised on man's life. Close pent-up guilts
Rive your concealing continents and cry
These dreadful summoners grace. I am a man
More sinned against than sinning.

KENT   Alack, bareheaded?   60
Gracious my lord, hard by here is a hovel:
Some friendship will it lend you 'gainst the tempest.
Repose you there, while I to this hard house –
More harder than the stones whereof 'tis raised,
Which even but now, demanding after you,   65
Denied me to come in – return and force
Their scanted courtesy.

LEAR   My wits begin to turn.
[*to the Fool*] Come on, my boy. How dost my boy?
Art cold?
I am cold myself.
[*to Kent*]   Where is this straw, my fellow?
The art of our necessities is strange,   70
And can make vile things precious. Come; your
hovel.

[*to the Fool*] Poor fool and knave, I have one part in my heart
That's sorry yet for thee.

FOOL   He that has ᶠandᶠ a little tiny wit,
        With heigh-ho, the wind and the rain,
75   Must make content with his fortunes fit,
        Though the rain it raineth every day.

LEAR   True, ᵠmy goodᵠ boy.
[*to Kent*]   Come, bring us to this hovel.
                           [*Exeunt Lear and Kent.*]

ᶠFOOL   This is a brave night to cool a courtesan. I'll speak a prophecy ere I go:
80   When priests are more in word than matter,
        When brewers mar their malt with water,
        When nobles are their tailors' tutors,
        No heretics burned but wenches' suitors;
        When every case in law is right
85   No squire in debt, nor no poor knight;
        When slanders do not live in tongues,
        Nor cut-purses come not to throngs,
        When usurers tell their gold i'the field,
        And bawds and whores do churches build,
90   Then shall the realm of Albion
        Come to great confusion:
        Then comes the time, who lives to see't,
        That going shall be used with feet.
    This prophecy Merlin shall make, for I live before his
95   time.   *Exit.*ᶠ

3.3   *Enter* GLOUCESTER *and* EDMUND, ᵠ*with lights*ᵠ.

GLOUCESTER   Alack, alack, Edmund, I like not this unnatural dealing. When I desired their leave that I might pity him, they took from me the use of mine own house; charged me on pain of perpetual displeasure neither to speak of him, entreat for him, or
5   any way sustain him.

EDMUND   Most savage and unnatural.

GLOUCESTER   Go to, say you nothing. There is division between the dukes, and a worse matter than that: I
10   have received a letter this night – 'tis dangerous to be spoken – I have locked the letter in my closet. These injuries the King now bears will be revenged home. There is part of a power already footed; we must incline to the King. I will look him and privily relieve
15   him. Go you and maintain talk with the Duke, that my charity be not of him perceived. If he ask for me, I am ill and gone to bed. If I die for it – as no less is threatened me – the King my old master must be relieved. There is strange things toward, Edmund;
20   pray you, be careful.   *Exit.*

EDMUND   This courtesy, forbid thee, shall the Duke
    Instantly know and of that letter too.
    This seems a fair deserving and must draw me
    That which my father loses, no less than all.
25   The younger rises when the old doth fall.   *Exit.*

3.4   *Enter* LEAR, KENT[, *disguised,*] *and* Fool.

KENT   Here is the place, my lord: good my lord, enter;
    The tyranny of the open night's too rough
    For nature to endure.   [ᶠ*Storm still*.ᶠ]

LEAR   Let me alone.

KENT   Good my lord, enter ᶠhereᶠ.

LEAR   Wilt break my heart?

KENT
5   I had rather break mine own. Good my lord, enter.

LEAR
    Thou think'st 'tis much that this contentious storm
    Invades us to the skin: so 'tis to thee,
    But where the greater malady is fixed,
    The lesser is scarce felt. Thou'dst shun a bear,
10   But if thy flight lay toward the roaring sea,
    Thou'dst meet the bear i'the mouth. When the
        mind's free,
    The body's delicate: this tempest in my mind
    Doth from my senses take all feeling else,
    Save what beats there, filial ingratitude.
15   Is it not as this mouth should tear this hand
    For lifting food to't? But I will punish home;
    No, I will weep no more. ᶠIn such a night
    To shut me out? Pour on, I will endure.ᶠ
    In such a night as this? O, Regan, Goneril,
    Your old, kind father, whose frank heart gave ᵠyouᵠ
20   all –
    O, that way madness lies, let me shun that;
    No more of that.

KENT   Good my lord, enter ᶠhereᶠ.

LEAR   Prithee go in thyself, seek thine own ease.
    This tempest will not give me leave to ponder
25   On things would hurt me more. But I'll go in;
    [*to the Fool*] ᶠIn boy, go first. You houseless
        poverty –
    Nay, get thee in. I'll pray, and then I'll sleep.
                            *Exit*ᶠ [*Fool*].
    [*Kneels.*] Poor naked wretches, wheresoe'er you are,
    That bide the pelting of this pitiless storm,
30   How shall your houseless heads and unfed sides,
    Your looped and windowed raggedness, defend you
    From seasons such as these? O, I have ta'en
    Too little care of this. Take physic, pomp,
    Expose thyself to feel what wretches feel,
35   That thou mayst shake the superflux to them
    And show the heavens more just.

[*Enter* Fool, *as from the hovel.*]

ᶠEDGAR [*within*]   Fathom and half, fathom and half: Poor Tom!ᶠ

FOOL   Come not in here, nuncle, here's a spirit. Help
40   me, help me!

KENT   Give me thy hand. Who's there?

FOOL   A spirit, ᶠa spirit.ᶠ He says his name's Poor Tom.

KENT   What art thou that dost grumble there i'the straw? Come forth.

Enter EDGAR[, *disguised as Poor Tom*].

45 EDGAR Away, the foul fiend follows me. Through the
sharp hawthorn blows the �'s cold 's wind. ᶠHumh,ᶠ go
to thy ᴼcoldᴼ bed and warm thee.

LEAR Didst thou give all to thy ᵒtwoᵒ daughters? And
art thou come to this?

50 EDGAR Who gives anything to Poor Tom? Whom the
foul fiend hath led through fire and ᶠthrough flame,ᶠ
through ford and whirlpool, o'er bog and quagmire;
that hath laid knives under his pillow and halters in his
pew; set ratsbane by his porridge, made him proud of
55 heart, to ride on a bay trotting horse over four-inched
bridges, to course his own shadow for a traitor. Bless
thy five wits, Tom's a-cold. ᶠO do, de, do, de, do, de:ᶠ
bless thee from whirlwinds, star-blasting and taking.
Do Poor Tom some charity, whom the foul fiend
60 vexes. There could I have him now, and there, and
there again, ᶠand there.ᶠ   [ᶠ*Storm still.*ᶠ]

LEAR Have his daughters brought him to this pass?
Couldst thou save nothing? Wouldst thou give 'em all?

FOOL Nay, he reserved a blanket, else we had been all
65 shamed.

LEAR [*to Edgar*]
Now all the plagues that in the pendulous air
Hang fated o'er men's faults light on thy daughters.

KENT He hath no daughters, sir.

LEAR
Death, traitor! Nothing could have subdued nature
70 To such a lowness but his unkind daughters.
Is it the fashion that discarded fathers
Should have thus little mercy on their flesh?
Judicious punishment, 'twas this flesh begot
Those pelican daughters.

75 EDGAR   Pillicock sat on Pillicock hill,
Alow, alow, loo, loo!

FOOL This cold night will turn us all to fools and
madmen.

EDGAR Take heed o'the foul fiend; obey thy parents,
80 keep thy word justly, swear not, commit not with
man's sworn spouse, set not thy sweet-heart on proud
array. Tom's a-cold.

LEAR What hast thou been?

EDGAR A serving-man, proud in heart and mind, that
85 curled my hair, wore gloves in my cap, served the lust
of my mistress' heart and did the act of darkness with
her; swore as many oaths as I spake words and broke
them in the sweet face of heaven. One that slept in the
contriving of lust and waked to do it. Wine loved I
90 deeply, dice dearly; and, in woman, out-paramoured
the Turk: false of heart, light of ear, bloody of hand;
hog in sloth, fox in stealth, wolf in greediness, dog in
madness, lion in prey. Let not the creaking of shoes,
nor the rustling of silks, betray thy poor heart to
95 woman. Keep thy foot out of brothels, thy hand out of
plackets, thy pen from lenders' books, and defy the
foul fiend. Still through the hawthorn blows the cold

wind, says suum, mun, nonny, Dauphin my boy, ᵒmyᵒ
boy, *cessez!* Let him trot by.   [ᶠ*Storm still.*ᶠ]

LEAR ᵒWhyᵒ, thou wert better in a grave than to answer 100
with thy uncovered body this extremity of the skies. Is
man no more than this? Consider him well. Thou
ow'st the worm no silk, the beast no hide, the sheep no
wool, the cat no perfume. ᶠHa?ᶠ Here's three on's us
are sophisticated; thou art the thing itself. 105
Unaccommodated man is no more but such a poor,
bare, forked animal as thou art. Off, off, you lendings:
come, unbutton ᶠhereᶠ. [*Tearing at his clothes, he is
restrained by Kent and the Fool.*]

ᶠ*Enter* GLOUCESTER, *with a torch* .ᶠ

FOOL Prithee, nuncle, be contented; 'tis a naughty night
to swim in. Now a little fire in a wild field were like an 110
old lecher's heart, a small spark, all the rest on's body
cold: look, here comes a walking fire.

EDGAR This is the foul ᵒfiendᵒ Flibbertigibbet: he
begins at curfew and walks till the first cock; he gives
the web and the pin, squinies the eye and makes the 115
harelip; mildews the white wheat and hurts the poor
creature of earth.
          Swithold footed thrice the wold;
          He met the nightmare and her nine foal,
          Bid her alight and her troth plight, 120
          And aroint thee, witch, aroint thee.

KENT How fares your grace?

LEAR What's he?

KENT [*to Gloucester*] Who's there? What is't you seek?

GLOUCESTER What are you there? Your names? 125

EDGAR Poor Tom, that eats the swimming frog, the
toad, the tadpole, the wall-newt and the water – ; that
in the fury of his heart, when the foul fiend rages, eats
cow-dung for salads; swallows the old rat and the
ditch-dog; drinks the green mantle of the standing 130
pool; who is whipped from tithing to tithing and
stocked, punished and imprisoned – who hath ᵒhadᵒ
three suits to his back, six shirts to his body,
          Horse to ride and weapon to wear.
          But mice and rats and such small deer 135
          Have been Tom's food for seven long year.
Beware my follower. Peace Smulkin, peace, thou fiend.

GLOUCESTER
What, hath your grace no better company?

EDGAR The prince of darkness is a gentleman. Modo
he's called, and Mahu. 140

GLOUCESTER
Our flesh and blood, my lord, is grown so vile
That it doth hate what gets it.

EDGAR Poor Tom's a-cold.

GLOUCESTER [*to Lear*]
Go in with me. My duty cannot suffer
T'obey in all your daughters' hard commands. 145
Though their injunction be to bar my doors
And let this tyrannous night take hold upon you,
Yet have I ventured to come seek you out,

And bring you where both fire and food is ready.

150   LEAR   First let me talk with this philosopher:
      [*to Edgar*] What is the cause of thunder?
      KENT   Good my lord,
        Take his offer, go into the house.
      LEAR   I'll talk a word with this same learned Theban:
        What is your study?
155   EDGAR   How to prevent the fiend and to kill vermin.
      LEAR   Let me ask you one word in private.
      KENT [*to Gloucester*]
        Importune him ᶠonce moreᶠ to go, my lord;
        His wits begin t'unsettle.
      GLOUCESTER   Canst thou blame him?
                                  [ᶠ*Storm still.*ᶠ]
        His daughters seek his death. Ah, that good Kent,
160   He said it would be thus, poor banished man.
        Thou sayest the King grows mad; I'll tell thee, friend,
        I am almost mad myself. I had a son,
        Now outlawed from my blood; he sought my life,
        But lately, very late. I loved him, friend,
165   No father his son dearer. True to tell thee,
        The grief hath crazed my wits. What a night's this?
        [*to Lear*] I do beseech your grace.
      LEAR   O, cry you mercy, ᶠsir.ᶠ
      [*to Edgar*] Noble philosopher, your company.
      EDGAR   Tom's a-cold.
      GLOUCESTER
170   In, fellow, there, into the hovel; keep thee warm.
      LEAR   Come, let's in all.
      KENT   This way, my lord.
      LEAR   With him;
        I will keep still with my philosopher.
      KENT
        Good my lord, soothe him; let him take the fellow.
      GLOUCESTER   Take you him on.
175   KENT   Sirrah, come on; go along with us.
      LEAR   Come, good Athenian.
      GLOUCESTER   No words, no words; hush.
      EDGAR
        Childe Rowland to the dark tower came,
        His word was still 'Fie, foh and fum,
180   I smell the blood of a British man.'   ᶠ*Exeunt.*ᶠ

3.5   *Enter* CORNWALL *and* EDMUND.

      CORNWALL   I will have my revenge, ere I depart his house.
      EDMUND   How, my lord, I may be censured that nature
        thus gives way to loyalty something fears me to think
        of.
5   CORNWALL   I now perceive it was not altogether your
        brother's evil disposition made him seek his death, but
        a provoking merit set a-work by a reprovable badness
        in himself.
      EDMUND   How malicious is my fortune, that I must
10   repent to be just? This is the letter ᶠwhichᶠ he spoke
        of, which approves him an intelligent party to the
        advantages of France. O heavens! That this treason

were ᶠnotᶠ, or not I the detector.
      CORNWALL   Go with me to the Duchess.
      EDMUND   If the matter of this paper be certain, you have   15
        mighty business in hand.
      CORNWALL   True or false, it hath made thee Earl of
        Gloucester. Seek out where thy father is, that he may
        be ready for our apprehension.
      EDMUND [*aside*]   If I find him comforting the King, it   20
        will stuff his suspicion more fully. [*to Cornwall*] I will
        persever in my course of loyalty, though the conflict be
        sore between that and my blood.
      CORNWALL   I will lay trust upon thee and thou shalt find
        a dear father in my love.   *Exeunt.*   25

3.6   *Enter* KENT[, *disguised,*] *and* GLOUCESTER.

      GLOUCESTER   Here is better than the open air; take it
        thankfully. I will piece out the comfort with what
        addition I can. I will not be long from you.
      KENT   All the power of his wits have given way to ᶠhisᶠ
        impatience. The gods reward your kindness.   5
                                  Exit [*Gloucester*].

    Enter LEAR, EDGAR[, *disguised as Poor Tom,*] *and* Fool.

      EDGAR   Frateretto calls me, and tells me Nero is an
        angler in the lake of darkness. Pray, innocent, ᶠandᶠ
        beware the foul fiend.
      FOOL   Prithee, nuncle, tell me whether a madman be a
        gentleman or a yeoman?   10
      LEAR   A king, a king.
      ᶠFOOL   No, he's a yeoman that has a gentleman to his
        son; for he's a mad yeoman that sees his son a
        gentleman before him.
      LEARᶠ   To have a thousand with red burning spits   15
        Come hizzing in upon 'em!
      ᵠEDGAR   The foul fiend bites my back.
      FOOL   He's mad that trusts in the tameness of a wolf, a
        horse's health, a boy's love or a whore's oath.
      LEAR   It shall be done, I will arraign them straight.   20
      [*to Edgar*] Come, sit thou here, most learned justicer;
      [*to the Fool*] Thou sapient sir, sit here. No, you she-
      foxes –
      EDGAR   Look where she stands and glares! Want'st thou
        eyes at trial, madam?
                  Come o'er the bourn, Bessy, to me.   25
      FOOL   Her boat hath a leak,
                  And she must not speak
             Why she dares not come over to thee.
      EDGAR   The foul fiend haunts Poor Tom in the voice of
        a nightingale. Hoppedance cries in Tom's belly for   30
        two white herring. Croak not, black angel, I have no
        food for thee.
      KENT   How do you, sir? Stand you not so amazed.
        Will you lie down and rest upon the cushions?
      LEAR   I'll see their trial first. Bring in their evidence.   35
      [*to Edgar*] Thou robed man of justice, take thy place.
      [*to the Fool*] And thou, his yoke-fellow of equity,

Bench by his side. [*to Kent*] You are o'the commission;
Sit you too.

40 EDGAR   Let us deal justly.
    Sleepest or wakest thou, jolly shepherd?
      Thy sheep be in the corn;
    And for one blast of thy minikin mouth
      Thy sheep shall take no harm.
45 Purr, the cat is grey.

LEAR   Arraign her first, 'tis Goneril – I here take my
oath before this honourable assembly – kicked the
poor King her father.

FOOL   Come hither, mistress: is your name Goneril?

50 LEAR   She cannot deny it.

FOOL   Cry you mercy, I took you for a joint-stool.

LEAR
And here's another whose warped looks proclaim
What store her heart is made on. Stop her there!
Arms, arms, sword, fire, corruption in the place!
55 False justicer, why hast thou let her 'scape?^Q

EDGAR   Bless thy five wits.

KENT   O pity! Sir, where is the patience now
That you so oft have boasted to retain?

EDGAR [*aside*]
My tears begin to take his part so much
They mar my counterfeiting.

60 LEAR   The little dogs and all,
Trey, Blanch and Sweetheart, see, they bark at me.

EDGAR   Tom will throw his head at them: avaunt, you
curs!
    Be thy mouth or black or white,
65   Tooth that poisons if it bite;
    Mastiff, greyhound, mongrel grim,
    Hound or spaniel, brach or him,
    ^FOr^F bobtail tyke or trundle-tail,
    Tom will make him weep and wail;
70   For with throwing thus my head,
    Dogs leap the hatch and all are fled.
Do, de, de, de. ^F*Cessez!*^F Come, march to wakes and
fairs and market towns. Poor Tom, thy horn is dry.

LEAR   Then let them anatomize Regan; see what breeds
75 about her heart. Is there any cause in nature that make
these hard hearts? [*to Edgar*] You, sir, I entertain ^Qyou^Q
for one of my hundred; only I do not like the fashion
of your garments. You will say they are Persian
^Qattire^Q, but let them be changed.

80 KENT   Now, good my lord, lie here ^Fand rest^F awhile.

LEAR   Make no noise, make no noise, draw the curtains.
So, so, ^Qso^Q; we'll go to supper i'the morning ^Qso, so, so.^Q
[*He sleeps.*]

^FFOOL   And I'll go to bed at noon.^F

Enter GLOUCESTER.

GLOUCESTER
Come hither, friend; where is the King my master?

KENT
85 Here, sir, but trouble him not; his wits are gone.

GLOUCESTER
Good friend, I prithee take him in thy arms.
I have o'erheard a plot of death upon him.
There is a litter ready; lay him in't
And drive toward Dover, friend, where thou shalt
    meet
Both welcome and protection. Take up thy master: 90
If thou shouldst dally half an hour his life,
With thine and all that offer to defend him,
Stand in assured loss. Take up, take up,
And follow me, that will to some provision
Give thee quick conduct.

^QKENT   Oppressed nature sleeps. 95
This rest might yet have balmed thy broken sinews,
Which if convenience will not allow
Stand in hard cure. [*to the Fool*] Come, help to bear
    thy master;
Thou must not stay behind.^Q

GLOUCESTER   Come, come away!
    Exeunt [*all but Edgar;*
    Kent and the Fool supporting Lear].

^QEDGAR   When we our betters see bearing our woes, 100
We scarcely think our miseries our foes.
Who alone suffers, suffers most i'the mind,
Leaving free things and happy shows behind.
But then the mind much sufferance doth o'erskip,
When grief hath mates and bearing fellowship. 105
How light and portable my pain seems now,
When that which makes me bend makes the King
    bow,
He childed as I fathered. Tom, away;
Mark the high noises, and thyself bewray
When false opinion, whose wrong thoughts defile
    thee, 110
In thy just proof repeals and reconciles thee.
What will hap more tonight, safe 'scape the King.
Lurk, lurk!^Q   [*Exit.*]

3.7   *Enter* CORNWALL, REGAN, GONERIL, EDMUND
    ^F*and servants.*^F

CORNWALL [*to Goneril*]   Post speedily to my lord your
husband. Show him this letter: the army of France is
landed. [*to servants*] Seek out the traitor, Gloucester.

REGAN   Hang him instantly!   [*Some servants rush off.*]

GONERIL   Pluck out his eyes! 5

CORNWALL   Leave him to my displeasure. Edmund, keep
you our sister company; the revenges we are bound to
take upon your traitorous father are not fit for your
beholding. Advise the Duke where you are going to a
most festinate preparation; we are bound to the like. 10
Our posts shall be swift and intelligent betwixt us.
Farewell, dear sister; farewell, my lord of Gloucester.

Enter OSWALD.

How now, where's the King?

OSWALD

    My lord of Gloucester hath conveyed him hence.

15   Some five- or six-and-thirty of his knights,

    Hot questrists after him, met him at gate,

    Who with some other of the lord's dependants

    Are gone with him toward Dover, where they boast

    To have well-armed friends.

20   CORNWALL   Get horses for your mistress. [*Exit Oswald.*]

GONERIL   Farewell, sweet lord and sister.

CORNWALL

    Edmund, farewell.   *Exeunt* ᵠ*Goneril and Edmund*ᵠ.

    [*to servants*]   Go, seek the traitor Gloucester;

    Pinion him like a thief, bring him before us.

                          [*Servants leave.*]

    Though ᶠwellᶠ we may not pass upon his life

25   Without the form of justice, yet our power

    Shall do a courtesy to our wrath, which men

    May blame but not control. Who's there? The traitor?

          Enter GLOUCESTER, ᵠ*brought in*

            *by two or three*ᵠ ᶠ*Servants.*ᶠ

REGAN   Ingrateful fox, 'tis he.

CORNWALL   Bind fast his corky arms.

GLOUCESTER   What means your graces?

30   Good my friends, consider; you are my guests.

    Do me no foul play, friends.

CORNWALL   Bind him, I say –

    [*Servants bind his arms.*]

REGAN   Hard, hard. O, filthy traitor!

GLOUCESTER   Unmerciful lady as you are, I'm none.

CORNWALL

    To this chair bind him. [*to Gloucester*] Villain, thou

        shalt find – [*Regan plucks his beard.*]

35   GLOUCESTER   By the kind gods, 'tis most ignobly done

    To pluck me by the beard.

REGAN   So white, and such a traitor?

GLOUCESTER   Naughty lady,

    These hairs which thou dost ravish from my chin

    Will quicken and accuse thee. I am your host;

40   With robber's hands my hospitable favours

    You should not ruffle thus. What will you do?

CORNWALL

    Come, sir, what letters had you late from France?

REGAN   Be simple answered, for we know the truth.

CORNWALL

    And what confederacy have you with the traitors,

    Late footed in the kingdom?

45   REGAN   To whose hands

    You have sent the lunatic King. Speak.

GLOUCESTER   I have a letter guessingly set down

    Which came from one that's of a neutral heart,

    And not from one opposed.

CORNWALL   Cunning.

REGAN   And false.

CORNWALL   Where hast thou sent the King?

50   GLOUCESTER   To Dover.

REGAN

    Wherefore to Dover? Wast thou not charged at peril –

CORNWALL

    Wherefore to Dover? Let him ᵠfirstᵠ answer that.

GLOUCESTER

    I am tied to the stake and I must stand the course.

REGAN   Wherefore to Dover, ᵠsirᵠ?

GLOUCESTER   Because I would not see thy cruel nails   55

    Pluck out his poor old eyes; nor thy fierce sister

    In his anointed flesh stick boarish fangs.

    The sea, with such a storm as his bare head

    In hell-black night endured, would have buoyed up

    And quenched the stelled fires.   60

    Yet, poor old heart, he help the heavens to rain.

    If wolves had at thy gate howled that stern time,

    Thou shouldst have said, 'Good porter, turn the key,

    All cruels else subscribed'; but I shall see

    The winged vengeance overtake such children.   65

CORNWALL

    See't shalt thou never. Fellows, hold the chair;

    Upon these eyes of thine I'll set my foot.

GLOUCESTER   He that will think to live till he be old,

    Give me some help! – O cruel! O you gods!

REGAN   One side will mock another – th'other too.   70

CORNWALL   If you see vengeance –

1 SERVANT   Hold your hand, my lord.

    I have served ᶠyouᶠ ever since I was a child,

    But better service have I never done you

    Than now to bid you hold.

REGAN   How now, you dog?

1 SERVANT   If you did wear a beard upon your chin,   75

    I'd shake it on this quarrel. What do you mean?

CORNWALL   My villein? [*They*] ᵠ*draw and fight.*ᵠ

1 SERVANT

    Nay then, come on, and take the chance of anger.

    [*He wounds Cornwall.*]

REGAN [*to another Servant*]

    Give me thy sword. A peasant stand up thus?

    [ᵠ*She takes a sword and runs at him behind.*ᵠ ᶠ*Kills him.*ᶠ]

1 SERVANT

    O, I am slain. My lord, you have one eye left   80

    To see some mischief on him. O! [*He dies.*]

CORNWALL   Lest it see more, prevent it. Out, vile jelly,

    Where is thy lustre now?

GLOUCESTER

    All dark and comfortless? Where's my son Edmund?

    Edmund, enkindle all the sparks of nature   85

    To quit this horrid act.

REGAN   Out, ᶠtreacherousᶠ villain,

    Thou call'st on him that hates thee. It was he

    That made the overture of thy treasons to us,

    Who is too good to pity thee.

GLOUCESTER   O my follies! Then Edgar was abused?   90

    Kind gods, forgive me that and prosper him.

REGAN [*to a Servant*]

    Go, thrust him out at gates and let him smell

    His way to Dover. How is't, my lord? How look you?

CORNWALL   I have received a hurt. Follow me, lady.
   [*to Servants*] Turn out that eyeless villain. Throw
      this slave
   Upon the dunghill.
               Exeunt [*Servants*] ᶠ*with Gloucester*ᶠ [*and the body*].
                     Regan, I bleed apace;
   Untimely comes this hurt. Give me your arm.
                        Exeunt [*Cornwall and Regan*].
�ۊ2 SERVANT   I'll never care what wickedness I do
   If this man come to good.
3 SERVANT   If she live long
   And in the end meet the old course of death,
   Women will all turn monsters.
2 SERVANT
   Let's follow the old Earl and get the bedlam
   To lead him where he would. His roguish madness
   Allows itself to anything.
3 SERVANT
   Go thou: I'll fetch some flax and whites of eggs
   To apply to his bleeding face. Now heaven help him!
                              *Exeunt.*ᵠ

4.1   *Enter* EDGAR[, *disguised as Poor Tom*].

EDGAR   Yet better thus, and known to be contemned
   Than still contemned and flattered. To be worst,
   The lowest and most dejected thing of fortune,
   Stands still in esperance, lives not in fear.
   The lamentable change is from the best,
   The worst returns to laughter. ᶠWelcome then,
   Thou unsubstantial air that I embrace;
   The wretch that thou hast blown unto the worst
   Owes nothing to thy blasts.ᶠ

           Enter GLOUCESTER, *led by an* Old Man.

   ᶠButᶠ who comes here? My father, poorly led?
   World, world, O world!
   But that thy strange mutations make us hate thee,
   Life would not yield to age.
OLD MAN   O my good lord, I have been your tenant and
   your father's tenant these fourscore ᶠyearsᶠ –
GLOUCESTER
   Away, get thee away; good friend, be gone.
   Thy comforts can do me no good at all,
   Thee they may hurt.
OLD MAN   ᵠAlack, sir,ᵠ you cannot see your way.
GLOUCESTER
   I have no way, and therefore want no eyes:
   I stumbled when I saw. Full oft 'tis seen
   Our means secure us and our mere defects
   Prove our commodities. O dear son Edgar,
   The food of thy abused father's wrath,
   Might I but live to see thee in my touch,
   I'd say I had eyes again.
OLD MAN   How now? Who's there?
EDGAR [*aside*]
   O gods! Who is't can say 'I am at the worst'?

   I am worse than e'er I was.
OLD MAN [*to Gloucester*]   'Tis poor mad Tom.
EDGAR [*aside*]   And worse I may be yet; the worst is not
   So long as we can say 'This is the worst.'
OLD MAN [*to Edgar*]   Fellow, where goest?
GLOUCESTER   Is it a beggar-man?
OLD MAN   Madman, and beggar too.
GLOUCESTER
   He has some reason, else he could not beg.
   I'the last night's storm I such a fellow saw,
   Which made me think a man a worm. My son
   Came then into my mind, and yet my mind
   Was then scarce friends with him. I have heard more
      since:
   As flies to wanton boys are we to the gods,
   They kill us for their sport.
EDGAR [*aside*]   How should this be?
   Bad is the trade that must play fool to sorrow,
   Angering itself and others.
   [*to Gloucester*]   Bless thee, master.
GLOUCESTER   Is that the naked fellow?
OLD MAN   Ay, my lord.
GLOUCESTER
   ᵠThen prithee ᵠget thee away. If for my sake
   Thou wilt o'ertake us hence a mile or twain
   I'the way toward Dover, do it for ancient love,
   And bring some covering for this naked soul,
   Which I'll entreat to lead me.
OLD MAN   Alack, sir, he is mad.
GLOUCESTER
   'Tis the time's plague when madmen lead the blind.
   Do as I bid thee, or rather do thy pleasure;
   Above the rest, be gone.
OLD MAN   I'll bring him the best 'pparel that I have,
   Come on't what will.   ᶠ*Exit.*ᶠ
GLOUCESTER   Sirrah, naked fellow.
EDGAR
   Poor Tom's a-cold. [*aside*] I cannot daub it further –
GLOUCESTER   Come hither, fellow.
EDGAR [*aside*]
   ᶠAnd yet I must.ᶠ
   [*to Gloucester*]   Bless thy sweet eyes, they bleed.
GLOUCESTER   Knowst thou the way to Dover?
EDGAR   Both stile and gate, horseway and footpath. Poor
   Tom hath been scared out of his good wits. Bless thee,
   goodman's son, from the foul fiend. ᵠFive fiends have
   been in Poor Tom at once, of lust, as Obidicut;
   Hobbididence, prince of darkness; Mahu, of stealing;
   Modo, of murder; Flibbertigibbet, of mopping and
   mowing, who since possesses chambermaids and
   waiting-women. So, bless thee, master.ᵠ
GLOUCESTER
   Here, take this purse, thou whom the heaven's plagues
   Have humbled to all strokes. That I am wretched
   Makes thee the happier. Heavens deal so still!
   Let the superfluous and lust-dieted man
   That slaves your ordinance, that will not see

Because he does not feel, feel your power quickly:
So distribution should undo excess
And each man have enough. Dost thou know Dover?
75 EDGAR   Ay, master.
GLOUCESTER
There is a cliff whose high and bending head
Looks fearfully in the confined deep:
Bring me but to the very brim of it,
And I'll repair the misery thou dost bear
80 With something rich about me. From that place
I shall no leading need.
EDGAR   Give me thy arm,
Poor Tom shall lead thee.   ᶠ*Exeunt.*ᶠ

4.2   *Enter* GONERIL, EDMUND, [*followed by*] OSWALD.

GONERIL
Welcome, my lord. I marvel our mild husband
Not met us on the way.
[*to Oswald*]   Now, where's your master?
OSWALD   Madam, within; but never man so changed.
I told him of the army that was landed;
5 He smiled at it. I told him you were coming;
His answer was 'The worse.' Of Gloucester's treachery
And of the loyal service of his son,
When I informed him, then he called me sot,
And told me I had turned the wrong side out.
10 What most he should dislike seems pleasant to him,
What like, offensive.
GONERIL [*to Edmund*]   Then shall you go no further.
It is the cowish terror of his spirit,
That dares not undertake. He'll not feel wrongs
Which tie him to an answer. Our wishes on the way
15 May prove effects. Back, Edmund, to my brother;
Hasten his musters and conduct his powers.
I must change names at home and give the distaff
Into my husband's hands. This trusty servant
Shall pass between us. Ere long you are like to hear –
20 If you dare venture in your own behalf –
A mistress's command. Wear this.
[*She places a chain about his neck.*] Spare speech,
Decline your head. This kiss, if it durst speak,
Would stretch thy spirits up into the air.
Conceive, and fare thee well –
EDMUND   Yours in the ranks of death.   ᶠ*Exit.*ᶠ
25 GONERIL   – my most dear Gloucester.
ᶠO, the difference of man and man!ᶠ
To thee a woman's services are due;
A fool usurps my bed.
OSWALD   Madam, here comes my lord.   ᵠ*Exit.*ᵠ

ᶠ*Enter* ALBANY.ᶠ

GONERIL   I have been worth the whistling.
30 ALBANY   O Goneril,
You are not worth the dust which the rude wind
Blows in your face. ᵠI fear your disposition;
That nature which contemns its origin
Cannot be bordered certain in itself.

She that herself will sliver and disbranch   35
From her material sap perforce must wither,
And come to deadly use.
GONERIL   No more, the text is foolish.
ALBANY   Wisdom and goodness to the vile seem vile;
Filths savour but themselves. What have you done?   40
Tigers, not daughters, what have you performed?
A father, and a gracious aged man
Whose reverence even the head-lugged bear would lick,
Most barbarous, most degenerate, have you madded.
Could my good brother suffer you to do it?   45
A man, a prince, by him so benefitted?
If that the heavens do not their visible spirits
Send quickly down to tame these vile offences,
It will come:
Humanity must perforce prey on itself,   50
Like monsters of the deep.ᵠ
GONERIL   Milk-livered man,
That bear'st a cheek for blows, a head for wrongs,
Who hast not in thy brows an eye discerning
Thine honour from thy suffering; ᵠthat not knowst
Fools do those villains pity who are punished   55
Ere they have done their mischief. Where's thy drum?
France spreads his banners in our noiseless land;
With plumed helm thy state begins to threat,
Whilst thou, a moral fool, sits still and cries,
'Alack, why does he so?'ᵠ
ALBANY   See thyself, devil: 60
Proper deformity shows not in the fiend
So horrid as in woman.
GONERIL   O vain fool!
ᵠALBANY
Thou changed and self-covered thing, for shame
Be-monster not thy feature. Were't my fitness
To let these hands obey my blood,   65
They are apt enough to dislocate and tear
Thy flesh and bones. Howe'er thou art a fiend,
A woman's shape doth shield thee.
GONERIL   Marry, your manhood, mew! –ᵠ

Enter a Messenger.

ᵠALBANY   What news?ᵠ   70
MESSENGER
O my good lord, the Duke of Cornwall's dead,
Slain by his servant, going to put out
The other eye of Gloucester.
ALBANY   Gloucester's eyes?
MESSENGER
A servant that he bred, thrilled with remorse,
Opposed against the act, bending his sword   75
To his great master, who, thereat enraged,
Flew on him and amongst them felled him dead;
But not without that harmful stroke which since
Hath plucked him after.
ALBANY   This shows you are above,
You justicers, that these our nether crimes
So speedily can venge. But, O, poor Gloucester,   80

Lost he his other eye?
MESSENGER   Both, both, my lord.
  [*to Goneril*] This letter, madam, craves a speedy answer;
  'Tis from your sister.
GONERIL [*aside*]   One way I like this well;
  But being widow, and my Gloucester with her,   5
  May all the building in my fancy pluck
  Upon my hateful life. Another way
  The news is not so tart.
  [*to the Messenger*]   I'll read and answer.   ^Q^*Exit.*^Q^
ALBANY
  Where was his son when they did take his eyes?
MESSENGER   Come with my lady hither.
ALBANY   He is not here.   10
MESSENGER   No, my good lord; I met him back again.
ALBANY   Knows he the wickedness?
MESSENGER
  Ay, my good lord, 'twas he informed against him
  And quit the house on purpose that their punishment
  Might have the freer course.
ALBANY   Gloucester, I live   15
  To thank thee for the love thou showd'st the King
  And to revenge thine eyes. Come hither, friend,
  Tell me what more thou knowst.   *Exeunt.*

4.3   ^Q^*Enter* KENT[, *disguised,*] *and a* Gentleman.

KENT   Why the King of France is so suddenly gone
  back, know you no reason?
GENTLEMAN   Something he left imperfect in the state
  which since his coming forth is thought of, which
  imports to the kingdom so much fear and danger that   5
  his personal return was most required and necessary.
KENT   Who hath he left behind him General?
GENTLEMAN   The Marshal of France, Monsieur la Far.
KENT   Did your letters pierce the queen to any demonst-   10
  ration of grief?
GENTLEMAN
  Ay, sir. She took them, read them in my presence,
  And now and then an ample tear trilled down
  Her delicate cheek. It seemed she was a queen
  Over her passion, who, most rebel-like,
  Sought to be king o'er her.
KENT   O, then, it moved her?   15
GENTLEMAN   Not to a rage; patience and sorrow strove
  Who should express her goodliest. You have seen
  Sunshine and rain at once, her smiles and tears
  Were like a better way. Those happy smilets
  That played on her ripe lip seemed not to know   20
  What guests were in her eyes, which parted thence
  As pearls from diamonds dropped. In brief,
  Sorrow would be a rarity most beloved
  If all could so become it.
KENT   Made she no verbal question?   25
GENTLEMAN
  Faith, once or twice she heaved the name of father
  Pantingly forth as if it pressed her heart;

Cried 'Sisters, sisters, shame of ladies, sisters!
  Kent, father, sisters! What, i'the storm, i'the night?
  Let pity not be believed!' There she shook   30
  The holy water from her heavenly eyes,
  And clamour mastered her; then away she started,
  To deal with grief alone.
KENT   It is the stars,
  The stars above us govern our conditions,
  Else one self mate and make could not beget   35
  Such different issues. You spoke not with her since?
GENTLEMAN   No.
KENT   Was this before the King returned?
GENTLEMAN   No, since.
KENT   Well, sir, the poor distressed Lear's i'the town,
  Who sometime in his better tune remembers   40
  What we are come about, and by no means
  Will yield to see his daughter.
GENTLEMAN   Why, good sir?
KENT
  A sovereign shame so elbows him. His own unkindness
  That stripped her from his benediction, turned her
  To foreign casualties, gave her dear rights   45
  To his dog-hearted daughters, these things sting
  His mind so venomously that burning shame
  Detains him from Cordelia.
GENTLEMAN   Alack, poor gentleman.
KENT
  Of Albany's and Cornwall's powers you heard not?
GENTLEMAN   'Tis so; they are afoot.   50
KENT   Well, sir, I'll bring you to our master, Lear,
  And leave you to attend him. Some dear cause
  Will in concealment wrap me up awhile.
  When I am known aright, you shall not grieve,
  Lending me this acquaintance.   55
  I pray you, go along with me.   *Exeunt.*^Q^

4.4   *Enter* ^F^*with drum and colours*^F^ CORDELIA
            Gentleman, [*officer*] ^F^*and soldiers.*^F^

CORDELIA   Alack, 'tis he. Why, he was met even now
  As mad as the vexed sea, singing aloud,
  Crowned with rank fumiter and furrow-weeds,
  With burdocks, hemlock, nettles, cuckoo-flowers,
  Darnel and all the idle weeds that grow   5
  In our sustaining corn.
  [*to officer*]   A century send forth;
  Search every acre in the high-grown field
  And bring him to our eye. What can man's wisdom
  In the restoring his bereaved sense,
  He that helps him take all my outward worth.   10
                              [*Exit officer, with soldiers.*]
GENTLEMAN   There is means, madam.
  Our foster nurse of nature is repose,
  The which he lacks: that to provoke in him
  Are many simples operative, whose power
  Will close the eye of anguish.
CORDELIA   All blest secrets,   15

All you unpublished virtues of the earth,
Spring with my tears. Be aidant and remediate
In the good man's distress. Seek, seek for him,
Lest his ungoverned rage dissolve the life
That wants the means to lead it.

Enter Messenger.

20   MESSENGER   News, madam:
The British powers are marching hitherward.
CORDELIA   'Tis known before. Our preparation stands
In expectation of them. O dear father,
It is thy business that I go about;
25   Therefore great France
My mourning and important tears hath pitied.
No blown ambition doth our arms incite,
But love, dear love, and our aged father's right:
Soon may I hear and see him.   *Exeunt.*

4.5   *Enter* REGAN *and* OSWALD.

REGAN   But are my brother's powers set forth?
OSWALD   Ay, madam.
REGAN   Himself in person ᶠthereᶠ?
OSWALD   Madam, with much ado; your sister is the
5   better soldier.
REGAN   Lord Edmund spake not with your lord at home?
OSWALD   No, madam.
REGAN   What might import my sister's letter to him?
OSWALD   I know not, lady.
10   REGAN   Faith, he is posted hence on serious matter.
It was great ignorance, Gloucester's eyes being out,
To let him live. Where he arrives he moves
All hearts against us. Edmund, I think, is gone
In pity of his misery to dispatch
15   His nighted life; moreover to descry
The strength o'th' enemy.
OSWALD   I must needs after him, ᶠmadam,ᶠ with my letter.
REGAN
Our troops set forth tomorrow; stay with us.
The ways are dangerous.
OSWALD   I may not, madam;
20   My lady charged my duty in this business.
REGAN
Why should she write to Edmund? Might not you
Transport her purposes by word? Belike –
Some things, I know not what – I'll love thee much;
Let me unseal the letter.
OSWALD   Madam, I had rather –
25   REGAN   I know your lady does not love her husband,
I am sure of that; and at her late being here
She gave strange oeillades and most speaking looks
To noble Edmund. I know you are of her bosom.
OSWALD   I, madam?
30   REGAN   I speak in understanding; y'are, I know't.
Therefore I do advise you take this note.
My lord is dead; Edmund and I have talked,
And more convenient is he for my hand

Than for your lady's. You may gather more.
If you do find him, pray you give him this;   35
And when your mistress hears thus much from you,
I pray desire her call her wisdom to her.
So fare ᶠyouᶠ well.
If you do chance to hear of that blind traitor,
Preferment falls on him that cuts him off.   40
OSWALD
Would I could meet ᵠhimᵠ, madam, I should show
What party I do follow.
REGAN   Fare thee well.   *Exeunt.*

4.6   *Enter* GLOUCESTER *and* EDGAR[, *in peasant's
clothing and with a staff*].

GLOUCESTER
When shall I come to the top of that same hill?
EDGAR   You do climb up it now. Look how we labour.
GLOUCESTER   Methinks the ground is even.
EDGAR   Horrible steep.
Hark, do you hear the sea?
GLOUCESTER   No, truly.
EDGAR   Why then, your other senses grow imperfect   5
By your eyes' anguish.
GLOUCESTER   So may it be indeed.
Methinks thy voice is altered and thou speak'st
In better phrase and matter than thou didst.
EDGAR   You're much deceived; in nothing am I changed
But in my garments.
GLOUCESTER   Methinks you're better spoken.   10
EDGAR
Come on, sir, here's the place. Stand still: how
      fearful
And dizzy 'tis to cast one's eyes so low.
The crows and choughs that wing the midway air
Show scarce so gross as beetles. Half-way down
Hangs one that gathers samphire, dreadful trade;   15
Methinks he seems no bigger than his head.
The fishermen that walk upon the beach
Appear like mice, and yon tall anchoring barque
Diminished to her cock, her cock a buoy
Almost too small for sight. The murmuring surge   20
That on th'unnumbered idle pebble chafes,
Cannot be heard so high. I'll look no more,
Lest my brain turn and the deficient sight
Topple down headlong.
GLOUCESTER   Set me where you stand.
EDGAR   Give me your hand: you are now within a foot   25
Of th'extreme verge. For all beneath the moon
Would I not leap upright.
GLOUCESTER   Let go my hand.
Here, friend, 's another purse, in it a jewel
Well worth a poor man's taking. Fairies and gods
Prosper it with thee. Go thou further off;   30
Bid me farewell and let me hear thee going.
EDGAR   Now fare ye well, good sir.
GLOUCESTER   With all my heart.

EDGAR [*aside*]   Why I do trifle thus with his despair
Is done to cure it.
GLOUCESTER [^Q*He kneels*.^Q]   O you mighty gods,
This world I do renounce and in your sights
Shake patiently my great affliction off.
If I could bear it longer and not fall
To quarrel with your great opposeless wills,
My snuff and loathed part of nature should
Burn itself out. If Edgar live, O, bless ^Fhim^F!
Now, fellow, fare thee well. [^Q*He falls*.^Q]
EDGAR   Gone, sir; farewell.
[*aside*] And yet I know not how conceit may rob
The treasury of life when life itself
Yields to the theft. Had he been where he thought,
By this had thought been past.
[*to Gloucester*]   Alive or dead?
Ho, you, sir! ^FFriend,^F hear you, sir? Speak! –
[*aside*] Thus might he pass indeed. Yet he revives. –
What are you, sir?
GLOUCESTER   Away and let me die.
EDGAR
Hadst thou been aught but gossamer, feathers, air,
So many fathom down precipitating,
Thou'dst shivered like an egg; but thou dost breathe,
Hast heavy substance, bleed'st not, speak'st, art
      sound.
Ten masts at each make not the altitude
Which thou hast perpendicularly fell.
Thy life's a miracle. Speak yet again.
GLOUCESTER   But have I fallen, or no?
EDGAR   From the dread summit of this chalky bourn.
Look up a-height: the shrill-gorged lark so far
Cannot be seen or heard. Do but look up.
GLOUCESTER   Alack, I have no eyes.
Is wretchedness deprived that benefit
To end itself by death? 'Twas yet some comfort
When misery could beguile the tyrant's rage
And frustrate his proud will.
EDGAR   Give me your arm.
Up, so. How ^Fis't^F? Feel you your legs? You stand.
GLOUCESTER   Too well, too well.
EDGAR   This is above all strangeness.
Upon the crown o'the cliff what thing was that
Which parted from you?
GLOUCESTER   A poor unfortunate beggar.
EDGAR   As I stood here below methought his eyes
Were two full moons. He had a thousand noses,
Horns whelked and waved like the enraged sea.
It was some fiend. Therefore, thou happy father,
Think that the clearest gods, who make them
      honours
Of men's impossibilities, have preserved thee.
GLOUCESTER   I do remember now. Henceforth I'll bear
Affliction till it do cry out itself
'Enough, enough' and die. That thing you speak of,
I took it for a man. Often 'twould say
'The fiend, the fiend'; he led me to that place.

EDGAR   Bear free and patient thoughts.

Enter LEAR ^Q*mad*^Q[*, crowned with wild flowers*].

                                  But who comes here?   80
The safer sense will ne'er accommodate
His master thus.
LEAR   No, they cannot touch me for coining. I am the
King himself.
EDGAR   O thou side-piercing sight!   85
LEAR   Nature's above art in that respect. There's your
press-money. That fellow handles his bow like a crow-
keeper: draw me a clothier's yard. Look, look, a
mouse: peace, peace, this ^Fpiece of^F toasted cheese will
do't. There's my gauntlet, I'll prove it on a giant.   90
Bring up the brown bills. O well flown, bird, i'the
clout, i'the clout! Hewgh! Give the word.
EDGAR   Sweet marjoram.
LEAR   Pass.
GLOUCESTER   I know that voice.   95
LEAR   Ha! Goneril ^Fwith a white beard?^F They flattered
me like a dog and told me I had ^Fthe^F white hairs in my
beard ere the black ones were there. To say 'ay' and 'no'
to everything ^Fthat^F I said 'ay' and 'no' to was no good
divinity. When the rain came to wet me once and the   100
wind to make me chatter; when the thunder would not
peace at my bidding, there I found 'em, there I smelt
'em out. Go to, they are not men o'their words: they
told me I was everything; 'tis a lie, I am not ague-proof.
GLOUCESTER
The trick of that voice I do well remember: 105
Is't not the King?
LEAR   Ay, every inch a king.
When I do stare, see how the subject quakes.
I pardon that man's life. What was thy cause?
Adultery?
Thou shalt not die – die for adultery? No!   110
The wren goes to't and the small gilded fly
Does lecher in my sight. Let copulation thrive,
For Gloucester's bastard son was kinder to his father
Than were my daughters got 'tween the lawful sheets.
To't, luxury, pell-mell, for I lack soldiers.   115
Behold yon simp'ring dame,
Whose face between her forks presages snow,
That minces virtue and does shake the head
^FTo^F hear of pleasure's name –
The fitchew, nor the soiled horse, goes to't with a   120
more riotous appetite. Down from the waist they are
centaurs, though women all above. But to the girdle do
the gods inherit, beneath is all the fiend's: there's hell,
there's darkness, there is the sulphurous pit, burning,
scalding, stench, consumption! Fie, fie, fie! Pah, pah!   125
Give me an ounce of civet, good apothecary, ^Qto^Q
sweeten my imagination. There's money for thee.
GLOUCESTER   O, let me kiss that hand!
LEAR   Let me wipe it first, it smells of mortality.
GLOUCESTER
O ruined piece of nature, this great world   130

Shall so wear out to naught. Dost thou know me?

LEAR   I remember thine eyes well enough. Dost thou
squiny at me?

No, do thy worst, blind Cupid, I'll not love.

135 Read thou this challenge, mark ᶠbutᶠ the penning of it.

GLOUCESTER
Were all thy letters suns, I could not see ᵠoneᵠ.

EDGAR [*aside*]   I would not take this from report: it is,
And my heart breaks at it.

LEAR   Read.

140 GLOUCESTER   What? With the case of eyes?

LEAR   Oh ho, are you there with me? No eyes in your
head, nor no money in your purse? Your eyes are in a
heavy case, your purse in a light, yet you see how this
world goes.

145 GLOUCESTER   I see it feelingly.

LEAR   What, art mad? A man may see how this world
goes with no eyes. Look with thine ears. See how yon
justice rails upon yon simple thief. Hark in thine ear:
ᶠchange places andᶠ handy-dandy, which is the justice,
150 which is the thief? Thou hast seen a farmer's dog bark
at a beggar?

GLOUCESTER   Ay, sir.

LEAR   And the creature run from the cur – there thou
mightst behold the great image of authority: a dog's
155 obeyed in office.
Thou, rascal beadle, hold thy bloody hand;
Why dost thou lash that whore? Strip thine own back,
Thou hotly lusts to use her in that kind
For which thou whipp'st her. The usurer hangs the
cozener.
160 Through tattered clothes great vices do appear;
Robes and furred gowns hide all. ᶠPlate sin with gold,
And the strong lance of justice hurtless breaks;
Arm it in rags, a pigmy's straw does pierce it.
None does offend, none, I say none. I'll able 'em;
165 Take that of me, my friend, who have the power
To seal th'accuser's lips.ᶠ Get thee glass eyes,
And like a scurvy politician seem
To see the things thou dost not. Now, ᶠnow, now, now,ᶠ
pull off my boots; harder, harder, so.

170 EDGAR [*aside*]   O matter and impertinency mixed,
Reason in madness.

LEAR   If thou wilt weep my fortunes, take my eyes.
I know thee well enough, thy name is Gloucester.
Thou must be patient. We came crying hither:
175 Thou knowst the first time that we smell the air
We wawl and cry. I will preach to thee: mark ᵠmeᵠ.

GLOUCESTER   Alack, alack the day!

LEAR   When we are born we cry that we are come
To this great stage of fools. This a good block:
180 It were a delicate stratagem to shoe
A troop of horse with felt. ᶠI'll put it in proofᶠ
And when I have stolen upon these son-in-laws,
Then kill, kill, kill, kill, kill, kill!

Enter a Gentleman[, *and two attendants*].

GENTLEMAN   O, here he is: lay hand upon him. Sir,
Your most dear ᶠdaughter – ᶠ   185

LEAR   No rescue? What, a prisoner? I am even
The natural fool of fortune. Use me well,
You shall have ransom. Let me have surgeons,
I am cut to the brains.

GENTLEMAN   　　　　You shall have anything.

LEAR   No seconds? All myself?   190
Why, this would make a man ᶠa manᶠ of salt,
To use his eyes for garden water-pots.
ᵠAy, and laying autumn's dust.ᵠ

ᵠ²GENTLEMAN   　　　　　　Good sir.ᵠ²

ᵠLEARᵠ   I will die bravely, like a ᶠsmugᶠ bridegroom.
What? I will be jovial. Come, come,   195
I am a king, ᵠmyᵠ masters, know you that?

GENTLEMAN   You are a royal one and we obey you.

LEAR   Then there's life in't. Come, an you get it,
You shall get it by running. ᶠSa, sa, sa, sa.ᶠ

　　　　　　Exit ᵠrunningᵠ [, *followed by attendants*].

GENTLEMAN
A sight most pitiful in the meanest wretch,   200
Past speaking of in a king. Thou hast one daughter
Who redeems nature from the general curse
Which twain have brought her to.

EDGAR   　　　　　　　　Hail, gentle sir.

GENTLEMAN   Sir, speed you. What's your will?

EDGAR   　　　　　　　Do you hear aught,
ᶠSir,ᶠ of a battle toward?

GENTLEMAN   　　　　Most sure and vulgar.   205
Everyone hears that, which can distinguish sound.

EDGAR
But, by your favour, how near's the other army?

GENTLEMAN
Near, and on speedy foot. The main descry
Stands on the hourly thought.

EDGAR   　　　　　　　I thank you, sir.
That's all.   210

GENTLEMAN
Though that the queen on special cause is here
Her army is moved on.

EDGAR   　　　　　I thank you, sir
　　　　　　　　　　Exit [Gentleman].

GLOUCESTER
You ever gentle gods, take my breath from me;
Let not my worser spirit tempt me again
To die before you please.

EDGAR   　　　　　Well pray you, father.   215

GLOUCESTER   Now, good sir, what are you?

EDGAR
A most poor man, made tame to fortune's blows,
Who, by the art of known and feeling sorrows,
Am pregnant to good pity. Give me your hand;
I'll lead you to some biding.

GLOUCESTER   　　　　　Hearty thanks.   220
The bounty and the benison of heaven
To boot, to boot.

Enter OSWALD.

OSWALD   A proclaimed prize; most happy!
That eyeless head of thine was first framed flesh
To raise my fortunes! Thou old, unhappy traitor,
225 Briefly thyself remember. The sword is out
That must destroy thee.
GLOUCESTER   Now let thy friendly hand
Put strength enough to't.
OSWALD   Wherefore, bold peasant,
Dar'st thou support a published traitor? Hence,
Lest ᶠthatᶠ th' infection of his fortune take
230 Like hold on thee. Let go his arm.
EDGAR Ch'ill not let go, zir, without ᶠvurtherᶠ 'cagion.
OSWALD Let go, slave, or thou diest.
EDGAR Good gentleman, go your gait ᶠandᶠ let poor
volk pass. And 'ch'ud ha' been zwaggered out of my
235 life, 'twould not ha' been zo long ᶠas 'tisᶠ by a
vortnight. Nay, come not near th'old man; keep out,
che vor ye, or I'se try whether your costard or my
baton be the harder. Ch'ill be plain with you.
OSWALD Out, dunghill. [*Draws his sword.*] ᵠ*They fight.*ᵠ
240 EDGAR Ch'ill pick your teeth, zir. Come, no matter vor
your foins. [*Oswald falls.*]
OSWALD
Slave, thou hast slain me. Villain, take my purse.
If ever thou wilt thrive, bury my body,
And give the letters which thou find'st about me
245 To Edmund, Earl of Gloucester. Seek him out
Upon the English party. O untimely death, death!
[ᵠ*He dies.*ᵠ]
EDGAR I know thee well; a serviceable villain,
As duteous to the vices of thy mistress
As badness would desire.
GLOUCESTER   What, is he dead?
250 EDGAR Sit you down, father; rest you. –
Let's see these pockets: the letters that he speaks of
May be my friends. He's dead; I am only sorry
He had no other deathsman. Let us see:
Leave, gentle wax; and manners, blame us not.
255 To know our enemies' minds we rip their hearts,
Their papers is more lawful.
[ᶠ*Reads the letter.*ᶠ] *Let our reciprocal vows be*
remembered. You have many opportunities to cut him off.
If your will want not, time and place will be fruitfully
260 *offered. There is nothing done if he return the conqueror;*
then am I the prisoner, and his bed my gaol, from the
loathed warmth whereof, deliver me and supply the place
for your labour. Your (wife, so I would say) affectionate
servant ᵠ*and for you her own for venture.*ᵠ *Goneril.*
265 O indistinguished space of woman's will!
A plot upon her virtuous husband's life
And the exchange my brother. Here in the sands
Thee I'll rake up, the post unsanctified
Of murderous lechers; and in the mature time,
270 With this ungracious paper strike the sight
Of the death-practised duke. For him 'tis well

That of thy death and business I can tell.
[*Exit, dragging the body.*]
GLOUCESTER
The King is mad: how stiff is my vile sense,
That I stand up and have ingenious feeling
Of my huge sorrows? Better I were distract;   275
So should my thoughts be severed from my griefs,
And woes by wrong imaginations lose
The knowledge of themselves.   *Drum afar off.*

[*Enter* EDGAR.]

EDGAR   Give me your hand.
Far off methinks I hear the beaten drum.
Come, father, I'll bestow you with a friend.   *Exeunt.* 280

4.7 *Enter* CORDELIA, KENT[, *disguised,*] *and* **Gentleman.**

CORDELIA O thou good Kent, how shall I live and work
To match thy goodness? My life will be too short,
And every measure fail me.
KENT To be acknowledged, madam, is o'erpaid.
All my reports go with the modest truth,   5
Nor more, nor clipped, but so.
CORDELIA   Be better suited;
These weeds are memories of those worser hours.
I prithee put them off.
KENT   Pardon, dear madam;
Yet to be known shortens my made intent.
My boon I make it that you know me not   10
Till time and I think meet.
CORDELIA
Then be't so, my good lord.
[*to the Gentleman*]   How does the King?
GENTLEMAN Madam, sleeps still.
CORDELIA O you kind gods!
Cure this great breach in his abused nature;   15
Th'untuned and jarring senses, O, wind up
Of this child-changed father.
GENTLEMAN   So please your majesty,
That we may wake the King? He hath slept long.
CORDELIA
Be governed by your knowledge and proceed
I'the sway of your own will. Is he arrayed?   20

ᶠ*Enter* LEAR *in a chair carried by servants.*ᶠ

GENTLEMAN Ay, madam. In the heaviness of sleep
We put fresh garments on him.
Be by, good madam, when we do awake him.
I doubt ᵠnotᵠ of his temperance.
ᵠCORDELIA   Very well.
GENTLEMAN
Please you draw near; louder the music there.ᵠ   25
CORDELIA O my dear father, restoration hang
Thy medicine on my lips, and let this kiss
Repair those violent harms that my two sisters
Have in thy reverence made.
KENT   Kind and dear princess!

CORDELIA

    Had you not been their father, these white flakes   30
    Did challenge pity of them. Was this a face
    To be opposed against the warring winds?
    �QTo stand against the deep dread-bolted thunder,
    In the most terrible and nimble stroke
    Of quick cross-lightning? To watch, poor perdu,   35
    With this thin helm?Q Mine enemy's dog
    Though he had bit me should have stood that night
    Against my fire; and wast thou fain, poor father,
    To hovel thee with swine and rogues forlorn
    In short and musty straw? Alack, alack!   40
    'Tis wonder that thy life and wits at once
    Had not concluded all. He wakes; speak to him.

GENTLEMAN   Madam, do you; 'tis fittest.

CORDELIA

    How does my royal lord? How fares your majesty?

LEAR   You do me wrong to take me out o'the grave.   45
    Thou art a soul in bliss, but I am bound
    Upon a wheel of fire that mine own tears
    Do scald like molten lead.

CORDELIA   Sir, Fdo youF know me?

LEAR   You are a spirit, I know; where did you die?

CORDELIA   Still, still far wide.   50

GENTLEMAN   He's scarce awake; let him alone awhile.

LEAR

    Where have I been? Where am I? Fair daylight?
    I am mightily abused. I should ev'n die with pity
    To see another thus. I know not what to say.
    I will not swear these are my hands: let's see –   55
    I feel this pinprick. Would I were assured
    Of my condition.

CORDELIA [*Kneels.*]   O look upon me, sir,
    And hold your hands in benediction o'er me!
    [*She restrains him as he tries to kneel.*]
    QNo, sir,Q you must not kneel.

LEAR   Pray do not mock Fme.F
    I am a very foolish, fond old man,   60
    Fourscore and upward, Fnot an hour more nor less;F
    And to deal plainly,
    I fear I am not in my perfect mind.
    Methinks I should know you and know this man,
    Yet I am doubtful; for I am mainly ignorant   65
    What place this is and all the skill I have
    Remembers not these garments; nor I know not
    Where I did lodge last night. Do not laugh at me,
    For, as I am a man, I think this lady
    To be my child Cordelia.

CORDELIA   And so I am, FI am.F   70

LEAR   Be your tears wet? Yes, faith; I pray weep not.
    If you have poison for me, I will drink it.
    I know you do not love me, for your sisters
    Have, as I do remember, done me wrong.
    You have some cause, they have not.

CORDELIA   No cause, no cause.   75

LEAR   Am I in France?

KENT   In your own kingdom, sir.

LEAR   Do not abuse me.

GENTLEMAN

    Be comforted, good madam, the great rage
    You see is killed in him, Qand yet it is danger
    To make him even o'er the time he has lost.Q   80
    Desire him to go in. Trouble him no more
    Till further settling.

CORDELIA   Will't please your highness walk?

LEAR   You must bear with me. Pray Fyou Fnow, forget
    and forgive; I am old and foolish.
                       Exeunt. Q*Kent and the Gentleman remain.*Q

QGENTLEMAN   Holds it true, sir, that the Duke of   85
    Cornwall was so slain?

KENT   Most certain, sir.

GENTLEMAN   Who is conductor of his people?

KENT   As 'tis said, the bastard son of Gloucester.

GENTLEMAN   They say Edgar his banished son is with   90
    the Earl of Kent in Germany.

KENT   Report is changeable; 'tis time to look about. The
    powers of the kingdom approach apace.

GENTLEMAN   The arbitrement is like to be bloody. Fare
    you well, sir.   *Exit.*   95

KENT

    My point and period will be throughly wrought,
    Or well or ill as this day's battle's fought.   *Exit.*Q

5.1   *Enter* F*with drum and colours*F EDMUND, REGAN,
                  gentlemen and soldiers

EDMUND [*to a gentleman*]

    Know of the Duke if his last purpose hold,
    Or whether since he is advised by aught
    To change the course. He's full of alteration
    And self-reproving. Bring his constant pleasure.
                                 [*Exit gentleman.*]

REGAN   Our sister's man is certainly miscarried.   5

EDMUND   'Tis to be doubted, madam.

REGAN   Now, sweet lord,
    You know the goodness I intend upon you:
    Tell me but truly, but then speak the truth,
    Do you not love my sister?

EDMUND   In honoured love.

REGAN   But have you never found my brother's way   10
    To the forfended place?

QEDMUND   That thought abuses you.

REGAN   I am doubtful that you have been conjunct
    And bosomed with her, as far as we call hers.Q

EDMUND   No, by mine honour, madam.

REGAN   I never shall endure her. Dear my lord,   15
    Be not familiar with her.

EDMUND   Fear Qme Q not –

    Enter F*with drum and colours*F ALBANY, GONERIL
                [*and*] *soldiers.*

    She and the Duke her husband.

QGONERIL [*aside*]

    I had rather lose the battle than that sister

Should loosen him and me.^Q

20 ALBANY   Our very loving sister, well be-met.
Sir, this I heard: the King is come to his daughter,
With others whom the rigour of our state
Forced to cry out. ^QWhere I could not be honest
I never yet was valiant. For this business,
25 It touches us as France invades our land,
Not bolds the King, with others whom I fear
Most just and heavy causes make oppose.
EDMUND   Sir, you speak nobly.^Q
REGAN   Why is this reasoned?
GONERIL   Combine together 'gainst the enemy,
30 For these domestic and particular broils
Are not the question here.
ALBANY   Let's then determine with the ancient of war
on our proceeding.
^QEDMUND   I shall attend you presently at your tent.^Q
Exit.

35 REGAN   Sister, you'll go with us?
GONERIL   No.
REGAN   'Tis most convenient; pray ^Qyou^Q go with us.
GONERIL   O ho, I know the riddle. I will go.
Exeunt [*Edmund, Regan, Goneril and*] ^F*both the armies.*^F

[*As Albany is leaving,*] *enter* EDGAR[, *in peasant's clothing*].

EDGAR   If e'er your grace had speech with man so poor,
Hear me one word.
ALBANY [*to his soldiers*]   I'll overtake you.
40   [*to Edgar*]   Speak.
EDGAR   Before you fight the battle, ope this letter.
If you have victory, let the trumpet sound
For him that brought it. Wretched though I seem,
I can produce a champion that will prove
45 What is avouched there. If you miscarry,
Your business of the world hath so an end
^FAnd machination ceases.^F Fortune love you.
ALBANY   Stay till I have read the letter.
EDGAR   I was forbid it.
When time shall serve, let but the herald cry
50 And I'll appear again.   *Exit.*
ALBANY   Why, fare thee well. I will o'erlook thy paper.

Enter EDMUND.

EDMUND   The enemy's in view; draw up your powers.
[*Hands him a note.*] Here is the guess of their true
strength and forces,
By diligent discovery; but your haste
Is now urged on you.
55 ALBANY   We will greet the time.   *Exit.*
EDMUND   To both these sisters have I sworn my love,
Each jealous of the other as the stung
Are of the adder. Which of them shall I take?
Both? One? Or neither? Neither can be enjoyed
60 If both remain alive. To take the widow
Exasperates, makes mad her sister Goneril,
And hardly shall I carry out my side,
Her husband being alive. Now then, we'll use

His countenance for the battle, which being done,
Let her who would be rid of him devise   65
His speedy taking off. As for the mercy
Which he intends to Lear and to Cordelia,
The battle done, and they within our power,
Shall never see his pardon; for my state
Stands on me to defend, not to debate.   *Exit.*   70

5.2   *Alarum* ^F*within*^F. *Enter* ^F*with drum and colours*^F
LEAR, CORDELIA *and soldiers*[*. They pass*] *over the stage*
^F*and exeunt.*^F

Enter EDGAR[, *in peasant's clothing,*] *and* GLOUCESTER.

EDGAR   Here, father, take the shadow of this tree
For your good host. Pray that the right may thrive.
If ever I return to you again
I'll bring you comfort.
GLOUCESTER   Grace go with you, sir.
Exit [*Edgar*].

Alarum and retreat ^F*within. Enter* EDGAR.^F

EDGAR   Away, old man, give me thy hand, away!   5
King Lear hath lost, he and his daughter ta'en.
Give me thy hand; come on!
GLOUCESTER   No further, sir; a man may rot even here.
EDGAR   What, in ill thoughts again? Men must endure
Their going hence even as their coming hither.   10
Ripeness is all. Come on.
^FGLOUCESTER   And that's true too.
Exeunt.^F

5.3   *Enter* ^F*in conquest with drum and colours*^F
EDMUND, [*with*] LEAR *and* CORDELIA *as prisoners,*
^F*soldiers* [*and a*] Captain.^F

EDMUND   Some officers take them away – good guard,
Until their greater pleasures first be known
That are to censure them.
CORDELIA   We are not the first
Who with best meaning have incurred the worst.
For thee, oppressed King, I am cast down;   5
Myself could else outfrown false fortune's frown.
Shall we not see these daughters and these sisters?
LEAR   No, no, ^Fno, no^F. Come, let's away to prison;
We two alone will sing like birds i'the cage.
When thou dost ask me blessing I'll kneel down   10
And ask of thee forgiveness. So we'll live
And pray, and sing, and tell old tales, and laugh
At gilded butterflies, and hear poor rogues
Talk of court news; and we'll talk with them too –
Who loses and who wins, who's in, who's out –   15
And take upon's the mystery of things
As if we were God's spies. And we'll wear out
In a walled prison packs and sects of great ones
That ebb and flow by the moon.
EDMUND [*to soldiers*]   Take them away.
LEAR   Upon such sacrifices, my Cordelia,   20

The gods themselves throw incense. Have I caught
  thee? [*Embraces her.*]
He that parts us shall bring a brand from heaven,
And fire us hence like foxes. Wipe thine eyes;
The good ᶠyearsᶠ shall devour them, flesh and fell,
25   Ere they shall make us weep!
We'll see 'em starved first: come.
                    ᶠ*Exeunt*ᶠ [*Lear and Cordelia, guarded*].
EDMUND   Come hither, captain, hark:
Take thou this note. Go, follow them to prison.
One step I have advanced thee. If thou dost
30   As this instructs thee, thou dost make thy way
To noble fortunes. Know thou this, that men
Are as the time is; to be tender-minded
Does not become a sword. Thy great employment
Will not bear question: either say thou'lt do't,
  Or thrive by other means.
35 CAPTAIN   I'll do't, my lord.
EDMUND
About it and write 'happy' when thou'st done't.
Mark, I say, instantly; and carry it so
  As I have set it down.
ᵠCAPTAIN   I cannot draw a cart, nor eat dried oats.
40   If it be man's work, I'll do't.ᵠ   ᶠ*Exit.*ᶠ

ᶠ*Flourish.*ᶠ *Enter* ALBANY, GONERIL, REGAN [*and*] *soldiers*
[*with a trumpeter*].

ALBANY   Sir, you have showed today your valiant strain
And fortune led you well. You have the captives
Who were the opposites of this day's strife:
I do require them of you, so to use them
45   As we shall find their merits and our safety
  May equally determine.
EDMUND   Sir, I thought it fit
To send the old and miserable King
To some retention ᵠand appointed guard,ᵠ
Whose age had charms in it, whose title more,
50   To pluck the common bosom on his side,
And turn our impressed lances in our eyes
Which do command them. With him I sent the queen,
My reason all the same; and they are ready
Tomorrow, or at further space, t'appear
55   Where you shall hold your session. ᵠAt this time
We sweat and bleed; the friend hath lost his friend
And the best quarrels in the heat are cursed
By those that feel their sharpness.
The question of Cordelia and her father
  Requires a fitter place.ᵠ
60 ALBANY   Sir, by your patience,
I hold you but a subject of this war,
  Not as a brother.
REGAN   That's as we list to grace him.
Methinks our pleasure might have been demanded
Ere you had spoke so far. He led our powers,
65   Bore the commission of my place and person,
The which immediacy may well stand up
And call itself your brother.

GONERIL   Not so hot!
In his own grace he doth exalt himself
  More than in your addition.
REGAN   In my rights,
70   By me invested, he compeers the best.
ALBANY
  That were the most, if he should husband you.
REGAN   Jesters do oft prove prophets.
GONERIL   Holla, holla!
  That eye that told you so looked but asquint.
REGAN   Lady, I am not well, else I should answer
75   From a full-flowing stomach. [*to Edmund*] General,
Take thou my soldiers, prisoners, patrimony;
ᶠDispose of them, of me, the walls is thine.ᶠ
Witness the world, that I create thee here
  My lord and master.
GONERIL   Mean you to enjoy him ᵠthenᵠ?
80 ALBANY   The let-alone lies not in your good will.
EDMUND   Nor in thine, lord.
ALBANY   Half-blooded fellow, yes.
REGAN [*to Edmund*]
  Let the drum strike and prove my title thine.
ALBANY   Stay yet, hear reason: Edmund, I arrest thee
On capital treason, and in thine attaint
This gilded serpent. [*Points to Goneril.*]
85 [*to Regan*]   For your claim, fair sister,
I bar it in the interest of my wife:
'Tis she is sub-contracted to this lord
And I her husband contradict your banns:
If you will marry, make your love to me;
  My lady is bespoke.
90 ᶠGONERIL   An interlude!
ALBANYᶠ
Thou art armed, Gloucester. ᶠLet the trumpet
  sound.ᶠ
If none appear to prove upon thy person
Thy heinous, manifest and many treasons,
There is my pledge. [*Throws down his gauntlet.*]
          I'll make it on thy heart,
95   Ere I taste bread, thou art in nothing less
  Than I have here proclaimed thee.
REGAN   Sick, O, sick!
GONERIL [*aside*]   If not, I'll ne'er trust medicine.
EDMUND
There's my exchange. [*Throws down his gauntlet.*]
         What in the world he is
That names me traitor, villain-like he lies.
100   Call by the trumpet: he that dares approach,
On him, on you – who not? – I will maintain
  My truth and honour firmly.
ALBANY   A herald, ho!

ᶠ*Enter a* Herald.ᶠ

[*to Edmund*] Trust to thy single virtue, for thy
  soldiers,
All levied in my name, have in my name
Took their discharge.

REGAN   My sickness grows upon me.

ALBANY   She is not well; convey her to my tent.

                                   [*Exit Regan, supported.*]

  Come hither, herald; let the trumpet sound

  And read out this.   [^F*A trumpet sounds.*^F]

HERALD [^F*Reads.*^F]   *If any man of quality or degree within*

  the lists of the army will maintain upon Edmund,

  supposed Earl of Gloucester, that he is a manifold traitor,

  let him appear by the third sound of the trumpet. He is

  bold in his defence.   [^F*First trumpet.*^F]

  Again!   [^F*Second trumpet.*^F]

  Again!   [^F*Third trumpet.*^F]

                            [^F*Trumpet answers within.*^F]

              Enter EDGAR ^F*armed.*^F

ALBANY   Ask him his purposes, why he appears

  Upon this call o'the trumpet.

HERALD   What are you?

  Your name, your quality, and why you answer

  This present summons?

EDGAR   ^QO^Q know my name is lost,

  By treason's tooth bare-gnawn and canker-bit;

  Yet am I noble as the adversary

  I come to cope ^Qwithal^Q.

ALBANY   Which is that adversary?

EDGAR

  What's he that speaks for Edmund, Earl of

    Gloucester?

EDMUND   Himself. What sayst thou to him?

EDGAR   Draw thy sword,

  That if my speech offend a noble heart,

  Thy arm may do thee justice. Here is mine.

  [*Draws his sword.*]

  Behold: it is the privilege of mine honours,

  My oath and my profession. I protest,

  Maugre thy strength, youth, place and eminence,

  Despite thy victor sword and fire-new fortune,

  Thy valour and thy heart, thou art a traitor:

  False to thy gods, thy brother and thy father,

  Conspirant 'gainst this high illustrious prince,

  And from th'extremest upward of thy head

  To the descent and dust below thy foot

  A most toad-spotted traitor. Say thou no,

  This sword, this arm and my best spirits are bent

  To prove upon thy heart, whereto I speak,

  Thou liest.

EDMUND   In wisdom I should ask thy name,

  But since thy outside looks so fair and warlike,

  And that thy tongue some say of breeding breathes,

  ^FWhat safe and nicely I might well delay^F

  By rule of knighthood, I disdain and spurn.

  Back do I toss these treasons to thy head,

  With the hell-hated lie o'erwhelm thy heart,

  Which for they yet glance by and scarcely bruise,

  This sword of mine shall give them instant way,

  Where they shall rest for ever. Trumpets, speak.

  [^F*Alarums. Fight.*^F [*Edmund falls*].]

ALBANY [*to Edgar*]   Save him, save him!

GONERIL   This is ^Qmere^Q practice, Gloucester.

  By the law of war thou wast not bound to answer   150

  An unknown oppposite. Thou art not vanquished,

  But cozened and beguiled.

ALBANY   Shut your mouth, dame,

  Or with this paper shall I stop it.

  [*to Edmund*]   ^FHold, sir,^F

  Thou worse than any name, read thine own evil.

  [*to Goneril*] ^QNay^Q, no tearing, lady; I perceive you

    know it.   155

GONERIL   Say if I do, the laws are mine, not thine.

  Who can arraign me for't?   *Exit.*

ALBANY   Most monstrous! ^FO!^F

  [*to Edmund*] Knowst thou this paper?

EDMUND   Ask me not what I know.

ALBANY [*to an officer, who follows Goneril*]

  Go after her; she's desperate, govern her.

EDMUND

  What you have charged me with, that have I done,   160

  And more, much more; the time will bring it out.

  'Tis past and so am I. [*to Edgar*] But what art thou

  That hast this fortune on me? If thou'rt noble,

  I do forgive thee.

EDGAR   Let's exchange charity:

  I am no less in blood than thou art, Edmund;   165

  If more, the more thou'st wronged me.

  My name is Edgar and thy father's son.

  The gods are just and of our pleasant vices

  Make instruments to plague us:

  The dark and vicious place where thee he got   170

  Cost him his eyes.

EDMUND   Thou'st spoken ^Fright, 'tis^F true;

  The wheel is come full circle, I am here.

ALBANY [*to Edgar*]

  Methought thy very gait did prophesy

  A royal nobleness. I must embrace thee.

  Let sorrow split my heart if ever I   175

  Did hate thee or thy father.

EDGAR   Worthy prince, I know't.

ALBANY   Where have you hid yourself?

  How have you known the miseries of your father?

EDGAR   By nursing them, my lord. List a brief tale,   180

  And when 'tis told, O, that my heart would burst!

  The bloody proclamation to escape

  That followed me so near – O, our lives' sweetness,

  That we the pain of death would hourly die

  Rather than die at once! – taught me to shift   185

  Into a madman's rags, t'assume a semblance

  That very dogs disdained; and in this habit

  Met I my father with his bleeding rings,

  Their precious stones new lost; became his guide,

  Led him, begged for him, saved him from despair,   190

  Never – O fault! – revealed myself unto him

  Until some half-hour past, when I was armed,

  Not sure, though hoping of this good success.

  I asked his blessing and from first to last

195 Told him our pilgrimage. But his flawed heart,
　Alack, too weak the conflict to support,
　'Twixt two extremes of passion, joy and grief,
　Burst smilingly.
EDMUND　　　　　This speech of yours hath moved me,
　And shall perchance do good; but speak you on,
200　You look as you had something more to say.
ALBANY　If there be more, more woeful, hold it in,
　For I am almost ready to dissolve
　Hearing of this.
^QEDGAR　　　　　This would have seemed a period
　To such as love not sorrow, but another
205　To amplify too much would make much more
　And top extremity.
　Whilst I was big in clamour, came there in a man
　Who, having seen me in my worst estate,
　Shunned my abhorred society, but then finding
210　Who 'twas that so endured, with his strong arms,
　He fastened on my neck and bellowed out
　As he'd burst heaven, threw him on my father,
　Told the most piteous tale of Lear and him
　That ever ear received, which in recounting
215　His grief grew puissant and the strings of life
　Began to crack. Twice then the trumpets sounded
　And there I left him tranced.
ALBANY　　　　　But who was this?
EDGAR　Kent, sir, the banished Kent, who in disguise
　Followed his enemy king and did him service
220　Improper for a slave.^Q

Enter a Gentleman ^Q*with a bloody knife.*^Q

GENTLEMAN　Help, help, ^FO, help!^F
EDGAR　　　　　What kind of help?
^FALBANY　　　　　　　Speak, man.
EDGAR^F　What means this bloody knife?
GENTLEMAN　　　　　'Tis hot, it smokes,
　It came even from the heart of – ^FO, she's dead!^F
ALBANY　Who ^Fdead^F? Speak, man.
225 GENTLEMAN　Your lady, sir, your lady; and her sister
　By her is poisoned; she confesses it.
EDMUND　I was contracted to them both; all three
　Now marry in an instant.
EDGAR　　　　　Here comes Kent.

Enter KENT.

ALBANY　Produce the bodies, be they alive or dead.
　Goneril's and Regan's bodies brought out.
230　This judgement of the heavens that makes us tremble
　Touches us not with pity – O, is this he?
　The time will not allow the compliment
　Which very manners urges.
KENT　　　　　I am come
　To bid my King and master aye good night.
　Is he not here?
235 ALBANY　　　　　Great thing of us forgot!
　Speak, Edmund, where's the King? And where's
　　Cordelia?

Seest thou this object, Kent?
KENT　　　　　Alack, why thus?
EDMUND　Yet Edmund was beloved:
　The one the other poisoned for my sake,
　And after slew herself.
ALBANY　　　　　Even so; cover their faces. 240
EDMUND　I pant for life. Some good I mean to do,
　Despite of mine own nature. Quickly send –
　Be brief in it – to the castle, for my writ
　Is on the life of Lear and on Cordelia;
　Nay, send in time.
ALBANY　　　　　Run, run, O run. 245
EDGAR
　To who, my lord? Who has the office?
　[*to Edmund*]　　　　　Send
　Thy token of reprieve.
EDMUND
　Well thought on, take my sword; ^Qthe captain,^Q
　Give it the captain.
EDGAR [*to Gentleman*]　Haste thee for thy life.
　　　　　　　　　[*Exit Gentleman.*]
EDMUND　He hath commission from thy wife and me 250
　To hang Cordelia in the prison and
　To lay the blame upon her own despair,
　That she fordid herself.
ALBANY　The gods defend her. Bear him hence awhile.
　[*Edmund is carried off.*]

Enter LEAR *with* CORDELIA *in his arms* [*followed by the*
　　　　　　Gentleman].

LEAR
　Howl, howl, howl, ^Qhowl^Q! O, you are men of stones! 255
　Had I your tongues and eyes, I'd use them so
　That heaven's vault should crack: she's gone for ever.
　I know when one is dead and when one lives;
　She's dead as earth. [*He lays her down.*]
　　　　　　Lend me a looking-glass;
　If that her breath will mist or stain the stone, 260
　Why then she lives.
KENT　　　　　Is this the promised end?
EDGAR　Or image of that horror?
ALBANY　　　　　Fall, and cease.
LEAR　This feather stirs, she lives: if it be so,
　It is a chance which does redeem all sorrows
　That ever I have felt.
KENT　　　　　O, my good master! 265
LEAR　Prithee, away!
EDGAR　　　　　'Tis noble Kent, your friend.
LEAR　A plague upon you murderers, traitors all;
　I might have saved her; now she's gone for ever.
　Cordelia, Cordelia, stay a little. Ha?
　What is't thou sayst? Her voice was ever soft, 270
　Gentle and low, an excellent thing in woman.
　I killed the slave that was a-hanging thee.
GENTLEMAN　'Tis true, my lords, he did.
LEAR　　　　　Did I not, fellow?
　I have seen the day, with my good biting falchion

I would have made him skip. I am old now
And these same crosses spoil me.
[*to Kent*]   Who are you?
Mine eyes are not o'the best, I'll tell you straight.

KENT   If Fortune brag of two she loved and hated,
One of them we behold.

LEAR   ᶠThis is a dull sight:ᶠ are you not Kent?

KENT   The same;
Your servant Kent; where is your servant Caius?

LEAR   He's a good fellow, I can tell ᶠyouᶠ that;
He'll strike and quickly too. He's dead and rotten.

KENT   No, my good lord, I am the very man –

LEAR   I'll see that straight.

KENT   That from your first of difference and decay
Have followed your sad steps –

LEAR   You're welcome hither.

KENT
Nor no man else. All's cheerless, dark and deadly;
Your eldest daughters have fordone themselves
And desperately are dead.

LEAR   Ay, so I think.

ALBANY   He knows not what he says and vain is it
That we present us to him.

Enter a Messenger.

EDGAR   Very bootless.

MESSENGER [*to Albany*]   Edmund is dead, my lord.

ALBANY   That's but a trifle here.
You lords and noble friends, know our intent:
What comfort to this ᶠgreatᶠ decay may come
Shall be applied. For us, we will resign
During the life of this old majesty
To him our absolute power;
[*to Edgar and Kent*]   you to your rights,
With boot and such addition as your honours   300
Have more than merited. All friends shall taste
The wages of their virtue and all foes
The cup of their deservings. O, see, see!

LEAR   And my poor fool is hanged. No, no, ᶠnoᶠ life!
Why should a dog, a horse, a rat have life   305
And thou no breath at all? ᵠOᵠ thou'lt come no more,
Never, never, never, ᶠnever, never.ᶠ
[*to Edgar?*] Pray you undo this button. Thank you,
    sir. ᵠO, o, o, o.ᵠ
ᶠDo you see this? Look on her: look, her lips,
Look there, look there! [*He dies.*ᶠ]

EDGAR   He faints: my lord, my lord!   310

KENT   Break, heart, I prithee break.

EDGAR   Look up, my lord.

KENT
Vex not his ghost; O, let him pass. He hates him
That would upon the rack of this tough world
Stretch him out longer.

EDGAR   ᵠOᵠ he is gone indeed.

KENT   The wonder is he hath endured so long;   315
He but usurped his life.

ALBANY   Bear them from hence. Our present business
Is ᵠtoᵠ general woe.
[*to Edgar and Kent*] Friends of my soul, you twain,
Rule in this realm and the gored state sustain.

KENT   I have a journey, sir, shortly to go;   320
My master calls me, I must not say no.

EDGAR   The weight of this sad time we must obey,
Speak what we feel, not what we ought to say.
The oldest hath borne most; we that are young
Shall never see so much, nor live so long.   325
                    ᶠ*Exeunt with a dead march.*ᶠ

King Richard II

When this play first appeared in print in 1597 under the title *The Tragedy of King Richard the Second*, the episode showing Richard relinquishing his crown to Bolingbroke in 4.1 was omitted, as it was in subsequent editions until 1608. Scholars assume that this was because the deposition of a king was an inflammatory topic in Elizabethan England, and that the printed texts of the play (though not, apparently, the performances) were subject to political censorship. Such an assumption is supported by an anecdote recorded by William Lambarde in which Queen Elizabeth compared herself to Richard II, and by the incident in 1601 when the Earl of Essex paid for a special performance of a Richard II play, most likely Shakespeare's, on the eve of his abortive rebellion, presumably hoping it would incite people to assist him in deposing the Queen.

Despite the fact that one of the Globe shareholders described *King Richard II* in 1601 as 'so old and so long out of use that they should have small or no company at it', the play is usually dated around 1595, partly because it makes use of Samuel Daniel's *The Civil Wars*, of which the first four books were published that year. It must also have preceded the *King Henry IV* plays, which are dated 1596-7 on circumstantial evidence. The main source is Raphael Holinshed's account of the last two years of Richard's reign in his *Chronicles*, of which Shakespeare used the 1587 edition. He seems also to have consulted the translation of Froissart's Chronicles by John Bouchier, Lord Berners, and possibly the anonymous play *Woodstock* (c. 1592–3) which focuses on the murder of the Duke of Gloucester (called 'Woodstock' by John of Gaunt in *King Richard II* at 1.2.1).

While *King Richard II* is the first of Shakespeare's second tetralogy on English history, it goes back in time to the beginning of the events that led to the Wars of the Roses. In the first tetralogy, consisting of the three *King Henry VI* plays and *King Richard III*, Shakespeare had previously dramatized history from the death of Henry V through the long period of contention between the Houses of York and Lancaster to the death of Richard III and the establishment of the Tudor dynasty with the accession of Henry VII after the battle of Bosworth. The second tetralogy, consisting of *King Richard II*, the *King Henry IV* plays and *King Henry V*, forms a kind of extended prequel to the first by showing the deposition of Richard II and the usurpation of the throne by Henry Bolingbroke (who became Henry IV), Henry IV's problems with incipient rebellion, and his son Henry V's solution to the problem of unrest at home by taking his father's advice to 'busy giddy minds / With foreign quarrels' (*2 Henry IV* 4.5.213-14). As the final Chorus of *King Henry V* reminds us, this solution turns out to be a temporary one.

King Richard II seems to have been a popular play before the Civil War but ran into censorship problems during the Restoration and was little performed in the eighteenth century. In 1815 Edmund Kean reintroduced the play to the London stage, presenting Richard as a tragic hero rather than as an incompetent king, and interpretations of this kind, sometimes ending with the death of Richard, dominated the nineteenth century. As in the case of *Hamlet*, the twentieth century has broadly continued this focus on the psychology of the individual hero at the expense of the play's political issues.

The Arden text is based on the 1597 First Quarto, with the addition of the deposition scene (4.1.162–318) from the 1623 First Folio.

King RICHARD the Second
John of GAUNT, Duke of Lancaster — *uncle to the King*
Henry BOLINGBROKE, Duke of Hereford — *son to John of Gaunt, afterwards King Henry IV*
Thomas MOWBRAY, Duke of Norfolk
The DUCHESS of Gloucester — *widow to Thomas of Woodstock, Duke of Gloucester*
The Lord MARSHAL
The Duke of AUMERLE — *son to the Duke of York*
Two HERALDS
Sir Henry GREENE
Sir John BUSHY
Sir John BAGOT
Edmund of Langley, Duke of YORK — *uncle to the King*
Henry Percy, Earl of NORTHUMBERLAND
Lord ROSS
Lord WILLOUGHBY
Isabel, QUEEN — *to King Richard*
The Duke of York's SERVINGMAN
Harry PERCY — *surnamed Hotspur, son to the Earl of Northumberland*
Lord BERKELEY
The Earl of SALISBURY
A Welsh CAPTAIN
The Bishop of CARLISLE
Sir Stephen SCROOPE
Two LADIES — *attendant upon Queen Isabel*
GARDENER
His MAN
Lord FITZWATER
LORD
The Duke of SURREY
The ABBOT *of Westminster*
The DUCHESS OF YORK
Sir Piers EXTON
His SERVANT
GROOM — *of the stable to King Richard*
The KEEPER — *of the prison at Pomfret*

Guards, Soldiers and Servants

King Richard II

1.1   *Enter* KING RICHARD, JOHN OF GAUNT,
with other nobles and attendants.

RICHARD   Old John of Gaunt, time-honoured Lancaster,
Hast thou according to thy oath and band
Brought hither Henry Herford thy bold son,
Here to make good the boist'rous late appeal,
Which then our leisure would not let us hear,
Against the Duke of Norfolk, Thomas Mowbray?
GAUNT   I have, my liege.
RICHARD   Tell me, moreover, hast thou sounded him,
If he appeal the Duke on ancient malice,
Or worthily as a good subject should
On some known ground of treachery in him?
GAUNT   As near as I could sift him on that argument,
On some apparent danger seen in him,
Aim'd at your Highness, no inveterate malice.
RICHARD   Then call them to our presence; face to face,
And frowning brow to brow, ourselves will hear
The accuser and the accused freely speak.
High-stomach'd are they both and full of ire,
In rage, deaf as the sea, hasty as fire.

Enter BOLINGBROKE *and* MOWBRAY.

BOLINGBROKE   Many years of happy days befall
My gracious sovereign, my most loving liege!
MOWBRAY   Each day still better other's happiness
Until the heavens, envying earth's good hap,
Add an immortal title to your crown!
RICHARD   We thank you both, yet one but flatters us,
As well appeareth by the cause you come,
Namely, to appeal each other of high treason:
Cousin of Herford, what dost thou object
Against the Duke of Norfolk, Thomas Mowbray?
BOLINGBROKE
First – heaven be the record to my speech!
In the devotion of a subject's love,
Tend'ring the precious safety of my prince,
And free from other misbegotten hate,
Come I appellant to this princely presence.
Now Thomas Mowbray do I turn to thee,
And mark my greeting well; for what I speak
My body shall make good upon this earth,
Or my divine soul answer it in heaven.
Thou art a traitor and a miscreant,
Too good to be so, and too bad to live,
Since the more fair and crystal is the sky,
The uglier seem the clouds that in it fly;
Once more, the more to aggravate the note,
With a foul traitor's name stuff I thy throat,
And wish – so please my sovereign – ere I move,
What my tongue speaks my right drawn sword may
    prove.
MOWBRAY   Let not my cold words here accuse my zeal.
'Tis not the trial of a woman's war,
The bitter clamour of two eager tongues,
Can arbitrate this cause betwixt us twain;
The blood is hot that must be cool'd for this.

Yet can I not of such tame patience boast
As to be hush'd and nought at all to say.
First, the fair reverence of your Highness curbs me
From giving reins and spurs to my free speech,   55
Which else would post until it had return'd
These terms of treason doubled down his throat;
Setting aside his high blood's royalty,
And let him be no kinsman to my liege,
I do defy him, and I spit at him,   60
Call him a slanderous coward, and a villain,
Which to maintain I would allow him odds,
And meet him were I tied to run afoot
Even to the frozen ridges of the Alps,
Or any other ground inhabitable   65
Where ever Englishman durst set his foot.
Meantime, let this defend my loyalty –
By all my hopes most falsely doth he lie.
BOLINGBROKE
Pale trembling coward, there I throw my gage,
Disclaiming here the kindred of the king,   70
And lay aside my high blood's royalty,
Which fear, not reverence, makes thee to except.
If guilty dread have left thee so much strength
As to take up mine honour's pawn, then stoop.
By that, and all the rites of knighthood else,   75
Will I make good against thee, arm to arm,
What I have spoke, or thou canst worse devise.
MOWBRAY   I take it up; and by that sword I swear,
Which gently laid my knighthood on my shoulder,
I'll answer thee in any fair degree   80
Or chivalrous design of knightly trial;
And when I mount, alive may I not light,
If I be traitor or unjustly fight!
RICHARD
What doth our cousin lay to Mowbray's charge?
It must be great that can inherit us   85
So much as of a thought of ill in him.
BOLINGBROKE
Look what I speak, my life shall prove it true:
That Mowbray hath receiv'd eight thousand nobles
In name of lendings for your Highness' soldiers,
The which he hath detain'd for lewd imployments,   90
Like a false traitor, and injurious villain;
Besides I say, and will in battle prove,
Or here, or elsewhere to the furthest verge
That ever was survey'd by English eye,
That all the treasons for these eighteen years   95
Complotted and contrived in this land
Fetch from false Mowbray their first head and
    spring;
Further I say, and further will maintain
Upon his bad life to make all this good,
That he did plot the Duke of Gloucester's death,   100
Suggest his soon-believing adversaries,
And consequently, like a traitor coward,
Sluic'd out his innocent soul through streams of
    blood,

105 Which blood, like sacrificing Abel's, cries
Even from the tongueless caverns of the earth
To me for justice and rough chastisement;
And, by the glorious worth of my descent,
This arm shall do it, or this life be spent.
110 RICHARD   How high a pitch his resolution soars!
Thomas of Norfolk, what say'st thou to this?
MOWBRAY   O, let my sovereign turn away his face,
And bid his ears a little while be deaf,
Till I have told this slander of his blood
How God and good men hate so foul a liar.
115 RICHARD   Mowbray, impartial are our eyes and ears.
Were he my brother, nay, my kingdom's heir,
As he is but my father's brother's son,
Now by my sceptre's awe I make a vow,
Such neighbour nearness to our sacred blood
120 Should nothing privilege him nor partialize
The unstooping firmness of my upright soul.
He is our subject, Mowbray; so art thou:
Free speech and fearless I to thee allow.
MOWBRAY   Then, Bolingbroke, as low as to thy heart
125 Through the false passage of thy throat thou liest.
Three parts of that receipt I had for Callice
Disburs'd I duly to his Highness' soldiers;
The other part reserv'd I by consent,
For that my sovereign liege was in my debt
130 Upon remainder of a dear account
Since last I went to France to fetch his queen:
Now swallow down that lie. For Gloucester's death,
I slew him not, but to my own disgrace
Neglected my sworn duty in that case.
135 For you, my noble lord of Lancaster,
The honourable father to my foe,
Once did I lay an ambush for your life,
A trespass that doth vex my grieved soul;
But ere I last receiv'd the sacrament,
140 I did confess it, and exactly begg'd
Your grace's pardon, and I hope I had it.
This is my fault – as for the rest appeal'd,
It issues from the rancour of a villain,
A recreant and most degenerate traitor,
145 Which in myself I boldly will defend,
And interchangeably hurl down my gage
Upon this overweening traitor's foot,
To prove myself a loyal gentleman
Even in the best blood chamber'd in his bosom.
150 In haste whereof most heartily I pray
Your Highness to assign our trial day.
RICHARD   Wrath-kindled gentlemen, be rul'd by me,
Let's purge this choler without letting blood –
This we prescribe, though no physician;
155 Deep malice makes too deep incision.
Forget, forgive, conclude and be agreed:
Our doctors say this is no month to bleed.
Good uncle, let this end where it begun;
We'll calm the Duke of Norfolk, you your son.
160 GAUNT   To be a make-peace shall become my age.

Throw down, my son, the Duke of Norfolk's gage.
RICHARD   And, Norfolk, throw down his.
GAUNT   When, Harry, when?
Obedience bids I should not bid again.
RICHARD   Norfolk, throw down we bid, there is no boot.
MOWBRAY   Myself I throw, dread sovereign, at thy foot; 165
My life thou shalt command, but not my shame:
The one my duty owes, but my fair name,
Despite of death, that lives upon my grave,
To dark dishonour's use thou shalt not have.
I am disgrac'd, impeach'd, and baffl'd here, 170
Pierc'd to the soul with slander's venom'd spear,
The which no balm can cure but his heart-blood
Which breath'd this poison.
RICHARD   Rage must be withstood:
Give me his gage; lions make leopards tame.
MOWBRAY
Yea, but not change his spots. Take but my shame, 175
And I resign my gage. My dear dear lord,
The purest treasure mortal times afford
Is spotless reputation – that away,
Men are but gilded loam, or painted clay.
A jewel in a ten-times barr'd-up chest 180
Is a bold spirit in a loyal breast.
Mine honour is my life, both grow in one,
Take honour from me, and my life is done.
Then, dear my liege, mine honour let me try;
In that I live, and for that will I die. 185
RICHARD   Cousin, throw up your gage, do you begin.
BOLINGBROKE
O God defend my soul from such deep sin!
Shall I seem crest-fallen in my father's sight?
Or with pale beggar-fear impeach my height
Before this out-dar'd dastard? Ere my tongue 190
Shall wound my honour with such feeble wrong,
Or sound so base a parle, my teeth shall tear
The slavish motive of recanting fear,
And spit it bleeding in his high disgrace,
Where shame doth harbour, even in Mowbray's face. 195
RICHARD   We were not born to sue, but to command;
Which since we cannot do to make you friends,
Be ready, as your lives shall answer it,
At Coventry upon Saint Lambert's day.
There shall your swords and lances arbitrate 200
The swelling difference of your settled hate.
Since we cannot atone you, we shall see
Justice design the victor's chivalry.
Marshal, command our officers-at-arms
Be ready to direct these home alarms.   *Exeunt.* 205

1.2   *Enter* JOHN OF GAUNT *with the*
             DUCHESS OF GLOUCESTER.

GAUNT   Alas, the part I had in Woodstock's blood
Doth more solicit me than your exclaims
To stir against the butchers of his life;
But since correction lieth in those hands

Which made the fault that we cannot correct,
Put we our quarrel to the will of heaven,
Who, when they see the hours ripe on earth,
Will rain hot vengeance on offenders' heads.
DUCHESS   Finds brotherhood in thee no sharper spur?
Hath love in thy old blood no living fire?
Edward's seven sons, whereof thyself art one,
Were as seven vials of his sacred blood,
Or seven fair branches springing from one root.
Some of those seven are dried by nature's course,
Some of those branches by the Destinies cut;
But Thomas my dear lord, my life, my Gloucester,
One vial full of Edward's sacred blood,
One flourishing branch of his most royal root,
Is crack'd, and all the precious liquor spilt,
Is hack'd down, and his summer leaves all faded,
By envy's hand, and murder's bloody axe.
Ah, Gaunt, his blood was thine! that bed, that womb,
That mettle, that self mould, that fashioned thee
Made him a man; and though thou livest and
   breathest,
Yet art thou slain in him; thou dost consent
In some large measure to thy father's death
In that thou seest thy wretched brother die,
Who was the model of thy father's life.
Call it not patience, Gaunt, it is despair;
In suff'ring thus thy brother to be slaught'red,
Thou showest the naked pathway to thy life,
Teaching stern murder how to butcher thee.
That which in mean men we intitle patience
Is pale cold cowardice in noble breasts.
What shall I say? to safeguard thine own life,
The best way is to venge my Gloucester's death.
GAUNT   God's is the quarrel – for God's substitute,
His deputy anointed in His sight,
Hath caus'd his death; the which if wrongfully,
Let heaven revenge, for I may never lift
An angry arm against His minister.
DUCHESS   Where then, alas, may I complain myself?
GAUNT   To God, the widow's champion and defence.
DUCHESS   Why then, I will. Farewell, old Gaunt.
Thou goest to Coventry, there to behold
Our cousin Herford and fell Mowbray fight.
O, sit my husband's wrongs on Herford's spear,
That it may enter butcher Mowbray's breast!
Or if misfortune miss the first career,
Be Mowbray's sins so heavy in his bosom
That they may break his foaming courser's back
And throw the rider headlong in the lists,
A caitive recreant to my cousin Herford!
Farewell, old Gaunt; thy sometimes brother's wife
With her companion, grief, must end her life.
GAUNT   Sister, farewell; I must to Coventry,
As much good stay with thee as go with me!
DUCHESS
Yet one word more – grief boundeth where it falls,
Not with the empty hollowness, but weight.

I take my leave before I have begun,   60
For sorrow ends not when it seemeth done.
Commend me to thy brother Edmund York.
Lo, this is all – nay, yet depart not so,
Though this be all, do not so quickly go;
I shall remember more. Bid him – ah, what? –   65
With all good speed at Plashy visit me.
Alack, and what shall good old York there see
But empty lodgings and unfurnish'd walls,
Unpeopled offices, untrodden stones,
And what hear there for welcome but my groans?   70
Therefore commend me; let him not come there
To seek out sorrow that dwells everywhere.
Desolate, desolate, will I hence and die:
The last leave of thee takes my weeping eye. *Exeunt.*

1.3   *Enter* Lord Marshal *and the* DUKE AUMERLE.

MARSHAL   My Lord Aumerle, is Harry Herford arm'd?
AUMERLE   Yea, at all points, and longs to enter in.
MARSHAL   The Duke of Norfolk, sprightfully and bold,
Stays but the summons of the appellant's trumpet.
MARSHAL
Why then, the champions are prepar'd, and stay   5
For nothing but his Majesty's approach.

The trumpets sound and the KING *enters with his nobles;*
when they are set, enter MOWBRAY *in arms, defendant.*

RICHARD   Marshal, demand of yonder champion
The cause of his arrival here in arms,
Ask him his name, and orderly proceed
To swear him in the justice of his cause.   10
MARSHAL
In God's name and the king's, say who thou art,
And why thou comest thus knightly clad in arms,
Against what man thou com'st and what thy quarrel.
Speak truly on thy knighthood and thy oath,
As so defend thee heaven and thy valour!   15
MOWBRAY
My name is Thomas Mowbray, Duke of Norfolk,
Who hither come ingaged by my oath
(Which God defend a knight should violate!)
Both to defend my loyalty and truth
To God, my king, and my succeeding issue,   20
Against the Duke of Herford that appeals me,
And by the grace of God, and this mine arm,
To prove him, in defending of myself,
A traitor to my God, my king, and me –
And as I truly fight, defend me heaven!   25

The trumpets sound. Enter BOLINGBROKE, *appellant,*
in armour.

RICHARD   Marshal, demand of yonder knight in arms,
Both who he is, and why he cometh hither
Thus plated in habiliments of war;
And formally, according to our law,
Depose him in the justice of his cause.   30

MARSHAL
    What is thy name? and wherefore com'st thou hither
    Before King Richard in his royal lists?
    Against whom comest thou? and what's thy quarrel?
    Speak like a true knight, so defend thee heaven!

35 BOLINGBROKE   Harry of Herford, Lancaster and Derby
    Am I, who ready here do stand in arms
    To prove by God's grace, and my body's valour
    In lists, on Thomas Mowbray, Duke of Norfolk,
    That he's a traitor foul and dangerous,

40   To God of heaven, King Richard and to me –
    And as I truly fight, defend me heaven!

MARSHAL   On pain of death, no person be so bold
    Or daring-hardy as to touch the lists,
    Except the marshal and such officers

45   Appointed to direct these fair designs.

BOLINGBROKE
    Lord Marshal, let me kiss my sovereign's hand,
    And bow my knee before his Majesty;
    For Mowbray and myself are like two men
    That vow a long and weary pilgrimage;

50   Then let us take a ceremonious leave
    And loving farewell of our several friends.

MARSHAL
    The appellant in all duty greets your Highness,
    And craves to kiss your hand and take his leave.

RICHARD   We will descend and fold him in our arms.

55   Cousin of Herford, as thy cause is right,
    So be thy fortune in this royal fight!
    Farewell, my blood; which if to-day thou shed,
    Lament we may, but not revenge thee dead.

BOLINGBROKE   O, let no noble eye profane a tear

60   For me, if I be gor'd with Mowbray's spear!
    As confident as is the falcon's flight
    Against a bird, do I with Mowbray fight.
    My loving lord, I take my leave of you;
    Of you, my noble cousin, Lord Aumerle;

65   Not sick, although I have to do with death,
    But lusty, young, and cheerly drawing breath.
    Lo, as at English feasts, so I regreet
    The daintiest last, to make the end most sweet.
    O thou, the earthly author of my blood,

70   Whose youthful spirit in me regenerate
    Doth with a twofold vigour lift me up
    To reach at victory above my head,
    Add proof unto mine armour with thy prayers,
    And with thy blessings steel my lance's point,

75   That it may enter Mowbray's waxen coat,
    And furbish new the name of John a Gaunt,
    Even in the lusty haviour of his son.

GAUNT   God in thy good cause make thee prosperous,
    Be swift like lightning in the execution,

80   And let thy blows, doubly redoubled,
    Fall like amazing thunder on the casque
    Of thy adverse pernicious enemy!
    Rouse up thy youthful blood, be valiant and live.

BOLINGBROKE
    Mine innocence and Saint George to thrive!

85 MOWBRAY   However God or Fortune cast my lot,
    There lives or dies true to King Richard's throne,
    A loyal, just, and upright gentleman.
    Never did captive with a freer heart
    Cast off his chains of bondage, and embrace

90   His golden uncontroll'd enfranchisement,
    More than my dancing soul doth celebrate
    This feast of battle with mine adversary.
    Most mighty liege, and my companion peers,
    Take from my mouth the wish of happy years;

95   As gentle and as jocund as to jest
    Go I to fight: truth hath a quiet breast.

RICHARD   Farewell, my lord, securely I espy
    Virtue with valour couched in thine eye.
    Order the trial, Marshal, and begin.

100 MARSHAL   Harry of Herford, Lancaster and Derby,
    Receive thy lance, and God defend the right!

BOLINGBROKE   Strong as a tower in hope, I cry amen.

MARSHAL
    Go bear this lance to Thomas, Duke of Norfolk.

1 HERALD   Harry of Herford, Lancaster and Derby,
105   Stands here, for God, his sovereign, and himself,
    On pain to be found false and recreant,
    To prove the Duke of Norfolk, Thomas Mowbray,
    A traitor to his God, his king, and him,
    And dares him to set forward to the fight.

2 HERALD
    Here standeth Thomas Mowbray, Duke of Norfolk,
110   On pain to be found false and recreant,
    Both to defend himself, and to approve
    Henry of Herford, Lancaster and Derby,
    To God, his sovereign, and to him disloyal,
115   Courageously, and with a free desire,
    Attending but the signal to begin.

MARSHAL
    Sound trumpets, and set forward, combatants.
                        [A charge sounded.]
    Stay, the king hath thrown his warder down.

RICHARD
    Let them lay by their helmets and their spears,
120   And both return back to their chairs again.
    Withdraw with us, and let the trumpets sound,
    While we return these dukes what we decree.
                           [A long flourish]

    Draw near,
    And list what with our council we have done.
125   For that our kingdom's earth should not be soil'd
    With that dear blood which it hath fostered;
    And for our eyes do hate the dire aspect
    Of civil wounds plough'd up with neighbours' sword,
    And for we think the eagle-winged pride
130   Of sky-aspiring and ambitious thoughts,
    With rival-hating envy, set on you
    To wake our peace, which in our country's cradle
    Draws the sweet infant breath of gentle sleep;

Which so rous'd up with boist'rous untun'd drums,
With harsh-resounding trumpets' dreadful bray,
And grating shock of wrathful iron arms,
Might from our quiet confines fright fair peace,
And make us wade even in our kindred's blood –
Therefore we banish you our territories.
You, cousin Herford, upon pain of life,
Till twice five summers have enrich'd our fields,
Shall not regreet our fair dominions,
But tread the stranger paths or banishment.

BOLINGBROKE
You will be done; this must my comfort be,
That sun that warms you here, shall shine on me,
And those his golden beams to you here lent
Shall point on me and gild my banishment.

RICHARD   Norfolk, for thee remains a heavier doom,
Which I with some unwillingness pronounce.
The sly slow hours shall not determinate
The dateless limit of thy dear exile;
The hopeless word of 'never to return'
Breathe I against thee, upon pain of life.

MOWBRAY   A heavy sentence, my most sovereign liege,
And all unlook'd for from your Highness' mouth;
A dearer merit, not so deep a maim
As to be cast forth in the common air,
Have I deserved at your Highness' hands.
The language I have learnt these forty years,
My native English, now I must forgo,
And now my tongue's use is to me no more
Than an unstringed viol or a harp,
Or like a cunning instrument cas'd up –
Or being open, put into his hands
That knows no touch to tune the harmony.
Within my mouth you have engaol'd my tongue,
Doubly portcullis'd with my teeth and lips,
And dull unfeeling barren ignorance
Is made my gaoler to attend on me.
I am too old to fawn upon a nurse,
Too far in years to be a pupil now:
What is thy sentence then but speechless death,
Which robs my tongue from breathing native breath?

RICHARD   It boots thee not to be compassionate;
After our sentence plaining comes too late.

MOWBRAY
Then thus I turn me from my country's light,
To dwell in solemn shades of endless night.

RICHARD   Return again, and take an oath with thee.
Lay on our royal sword your banish'd hands,
Swear by the duty that you owe to God –
Our part therein we banish with yourselves –
To keep the oath that we administer:
You never shall, so help you truth and God,
Embrace each other's love in banishment,
Nor never look upon each other's face,
Nor never write, regreet, nor reconcile
This louring tempest of your home-bred hate,
Nor never by advised purpose meet

To plot, contrive, or complot any ill
'Gainst us, our state, our subjects, or our land.   190

BOLINGBROKE   I swear.

MOWBRAY   And I, to keep all this.

BOLINGBROKE   Norfolk, so far as to mine enemy:
By this time, had the king permitted us,
One of our souls had wand'red in the air,   195
Banish'd this frail sepulchre of our flesh,
As now our flesh is banish'd from this land –
Confess thy treasons ere thou fly the realm;
Since thou hast far to go, bear not along
The clogging burthen of a guilty soul.   200

MOWBRAY   No, Bolingbroke, if ever I were traitor,
My name be blotted from the book of life,
And I from heaven banish'd as from hence!
But what thou art, God, thou, and I do know,
And all too soon, I fear, the king shall rue.   205
Farewell, my liege. Now no way can I stray –
Save back to England all the world's my way.   *Exit.*

RICHARD   Uncle, even in the glasses of thine eyes
I see thy grieved heart. Thy sad aspect
Hath from the number of his banish'd years   210
Pluck'd four away.
[*to Bolingbroke*]   Six frozen winters spent,
Return with welcome home from banishment.

BOLINGBROKE   How long a time lies in one little word!
Four lagging winters and four wanton springs
End in a word: such is the breath of kings.   215

GAUNT   I thank my liege that in regard of me
He shortens four years of my son's exile,
But little vantage shall I reap thereby;
For ere the six years that he hath to spend
Can change their moons, and bring their times about,   220
My oil-dried lamp and time-bewasted light
Shall be extinct with age and endless night,
My inch of taper will be burnt and done,
And blindfold Death not let me see my son.

RICHARD   Why, uncle, thou hast many years to live.   225

GAUNT   But not a minute, king, that thou canst give:
Shorten my days thou canst with sullen sorrow,
And pluck nights from me, but not lend a morrow;
Thou canst help time to furrow me with age,
But stop no wrinkle in his pilgrimage;   230
Thy word is current with him for my death,
But dead, thy kingdom cannot buy my breath.

RICHARD   Thy son is banish'd upon good advice,
Whereto thy tongue a party-verdict gave:
Why at our justice seem'st thou then to lour?   235

GAUNT   Things sweet to taste prove in digestion sour.
You urg'd me as a judge, but I had rather
You would have bid me argue like a father.
O, had it been a stranger, not my child,
To smooth his fault I should have been more mild.   240
A partial slander sought I to avoid,
And in the sentence my own life destroy'd.
Alas, I look'd when some of you should say
I was too strict to make mine own away;

245 But you gave leave to my unwilling tongue
Against my will to do myself this wrong.
RICHARD   Cousin, farewell – and uncle, bid him so,
Six years we banish him and he shall go.
                    Flourish. Exeunt King Richard and train.
AUMERLE   Cousin, farewell; what presence must not
      know,
250 From where you do remain let paper show.
MARSHAL   My lord, no leave take I, for I will ride
As far as land will let me by your side.
GAUNT   O, to what purpose dost thou hoard thy words,
That thou returnest no greeting to thy friends?
255 BOLINGBROKE   I have too few to take my leave of you,
When the tongue's office should be prodigal
To breathe the abundant dolour of the heart.
GAUNT   Thy grief is but thy absence for a time.
BOLINGBROKE   Joy absent, grief is present for that time.
260 GAUNT   What is six winters? they are quickly gone –
BOLINGBROKE
To men in joy; but grief makes one hour ten.
GAUNT   Call it a travel that thou tak'st for pleasure.
BOLINGBROKE   My heart will sigh when I miscall it so,
Which finds it an inforced pilgrimage.
265 GAUNT   The sullen passage of thy weary steps
Esteem as foil wherein thou art to set
The precious jewel of thy home return.
BOLINGBROKE   Nay, rather, every tedious stride I make
Will but remember me what a deal of world
270 I wander from the jewels that I love.
Must I not serve a long apprenticehood
To foreign passages, and in the end,
Having my freedom, boast of nothing else
But that I was a journeyman to grief?
275 GAUNT   All places that the eye of heaven visits
Are to a wise man ports and happy havens.
Teach thy necessity to reason thus –
There is no virtue like necessity.
Think not the king did banish thee,
280 But thou the king. Woe doth the heavier sit
Where it perceives it is but faintly borne.
Go, say I sent thee forth to purchase honour,
And not the king exil'd thee; or suppose
Devouring pestilence hangs in our air,
285 And thou art flying to a fresher clime.
Look what thy soul holds dear, imagine it
To lie that way thou goest, not whence thou com'st.
Suppose the singing birds musicians,
The grass whereon thou tread'st the presence
      strew'd,
290 The flowers fair ladies, and thy steps no more
Than a delightful measure or a dance;
For gnarling sorrow hath less power to bite
The man that mocks at it and sets it light.
BOLINGBROKE   O, who can hold a fire in his hand
295 By thinking on the frosty Caucasus?
Or cloy the hungry edge of appetite
By bare imagination of a feast?

Or wallow naked in December snow
By thinking on fantastic summer's heat?
O no, the apprehension of the good   300
Gives but the greater feeling to the worse.
Fell sorrow's tooth doth never rankle more
Than when he bites, but lanceth not the sore.
GAUNT   Come, come, my son, I'll bring thee on thy way,
Had I thy youth and cause, I would not stay.   305
BOLINGBROKE
Then, England's ground, farewell; sweet soil, adieu,
My mother and my nurse that bears me yet!
Where'er I wander boast of this I can,
Though banish'd, yet a true-born Englishman.
                                        Exeunt.

1.4   *Enter the* KING *with* BAGOT *and* GREENE *at
        one door; and the* LORD AUMERLE *at another.*

RICHARD   We did observe. Cousin Aumerle,
How far brought you high Herford on his way?
AUMERLE   I brought high Herford, if you call him so,
But to the next highway, and there I left him.
RICHARD
And say, what store of parting tears were shed?   5
AUMERLE
Faith, none for me, except the north-east wind,
Which then blew bitterly against our faces,
Awak'd the sleeping rheum, and so by chance
Did grace our hollow parting with a tear.
RICHARD
What said our cousin when you parted with him?   10
AUMERLE   'Farewell' –
And, for my heart disdained that my tongue
Should so profane the word, that taught me craft
To counterfeit oppression of such grief
That words seem'd buried in my sorrow's grave.   15
Marry, would the word 'farewell' have length'ned
      hours
And added years to his short banishment,
He should have had a volume of farewells;
But since it would not, he had none of me.
RICHARD   He is our cousin, cousin, but 'tis doubt,   20
When time shall call him home from banishment,
Whether our kinsman come to see his friends.
Ourself and Bushy
Observ'd his courtship to the common people,
How he did seem to dive into their hearts   25
With humble and familiar courtesy;
What reverence he did throw away on slaves,
Wooing poor craftsmen with the craft of smiles
And patient underbearing of his fortune,
As 'twere to banish their affects with him.   30
Off goes his bonnet to an oyster-wench;
A brace of draymen bid God speed him well,
And had the tribute of his supple knee,
With 'Thanks, my countrymen, my loving friends' –
As were our England in reversion his,   35
And he our subjects' next degree in hope.

GREENE

    Well, he is gone; and with him go these thoughts.
    Now for the rebels which stand out in Ireland,
    Expedient manage must be made, my liege,
    Ere further leisure yield them further means
    For their advantage and your Highness' loss.

RICHARD   We will ourself in person to this war;
    And for our coffers, with too great a court
    And liberal largess, are grown somewhat light,
    We are inforc'd to farm our royal realm,
    The revenue whereof shall furnish us
    For our affairs in hand. If that come short,
    Our substitutes at home shall have blank charters,
    Whereto, when they shall know what men are rich,
    They shall subscribe them for large sums of gold,
    And send them after to supply our wants;
    For we will make for Ireland presently.

Enter BUSHY.

    Bushy, what news?

BUSHY   Old John of Gaunt is grievous sick, my lord,
    Suddenly taken, and hath sent post-haste
    To intreat your Majesty to visit him.

RICHARD   Where lies he?

BUSHY   At Ely House.

RICHARD   Now put it, God, in the physician's mind
    To help him to his grave immediately!
    The lining of his coffers shall make coats
    To deck our soldiers for these Irish wars.
    Come, gentlemen, let's all go visit him,
    Pray God we may make haste and come too late!

ALL   Amen.   *Exeunt.*

2.1   *Enter* JOHN OF GAUNT *sick, with the*
             DUKE OF YORK, *etc.*

GAUNT   Will the king come that I may breathe my last
    In wholesome counsel to his unstaid youth?

YORK

    Vex not yourself, nor strive not with your breath;
    For all in vain comes counsel to his ear.

GAUNT   O, but they say the tongues of dying men
    Inforce attention like deep harmony.
    Where words are scarce they are seldom spent in
       vain,
    For they breathe truth that breathe their words in
       pain.
    He that no more must say is listened more
    Than they whom youth and ease have taught to
       glose;
    More are men's ends mark'd than their lives before.
    The setting sun, and music at the close,
    As the last taste of sweets, is sweetest last,
    Writ in remembrance more than things long past:
    Though Richard my life's counsel would not hear,
    My death's sad tale may yet undeaf his ear.

YORK   No, it is stopp'd with other flattering sounds,

    As praises, of whose taste the wise are fond,
    Lascivious metres, to whose venom sound
    The open ear of youth doth always listen,   20
    Report of fashions in proud Italy,
    Whose manners still our tardy-apish nation
    Limps after in base imitation.
    Where doth the world thrust forth a vanity –
    So it be new, there's no respect how vile –   25
    That is not quickly buzz'd into his ears?
    Then all too late comes counsel to be heard,
    Where will doth mutiny with wit's regard.
    Direct not him whose way himself will choose:
    'Tis breath thou lack'st and that breath wilt thou
       lose.   30

GAUNT   Methinks I am a prophet new inspir'd,
    And thus expiring do foretell of him:
    His rash fierce blaze of riot cannot last.
    For violent fires soon burn out themselves;
    Small showers last long, but sudden storms are short;   35
    He tires betimes that spurs too fast betimes;
    With eager feeding food doth choke the feeder;
    Light vanity, insatiate cormorant,
    Consuming means, soon preys upon itself.
    This royal throne of kings, this scept'red isle,   40
    This earth of majesty, this seat of Mars,
    This other Eden, demi-paradise,
    This fortress built by Nature for herself
    Against infection and the hand of war,
    This happy breed of men, this little world,   45
    This precious stone set in the silver sea,
    Which serves it in the office of a wall,
    Or as a moat defensive to a house,
    Against the envy of less happier lands;
    This blessed plot, this earth, this realm, this
       England,   50
    This nurse, this teeming womb of royal kings,
    Fear'd by their breed, and famous by their birth,
    Renowned for their deeds as far from home,
    For Christian service and true chivalry,
    As is the sepulchre in stubborn Jewry   55
    Of the world's ransom, blessed Mary's son;
    This land of such dear souls, this dear dear land,
    Dear for her reputation through the world,
    Is now leas'd out – I die pronouncing it –
    Like to a tenement or pelting farm.   60
    England, bound in with the triumphant sea,
    Whose rocky shore beats back the envious siege
    Of wat'ry Neptune, is now bound in with shame,
    With inky blots and rotten parchment bonds;
    That England, that was wont to conquer others,   65
    Hath made a shameful conquest of itself.
    Ah, would the scandal vanish with my life,
    How happy then were my ensuing death!

Enter KING, QUEEN, AUMERLE, BUSHY, GREENE, BAGOT,
        ROSS *and* WILLOUGHBY.

YORK   The king is come, deal mildly with his youth,

70   For young hot colts being rein'd do rage the more.
QUEEN   How fares our noble uncle, Lancaster?
RICHARD
     What comfort, man? how is't with aged Gaunt?
GAUNT   O, how that name befits my composition!
     Old Gaunt indeed, and gaunt in being old.
75   Within me grief hath kept a tedious fast,
     And who abstains from meat that is not gaunt?
     For sleeping England long time have I watch'd,
     Watching breeds leanness, leanness is all gaunt.
     The pleasure that some fathers feed upon
80   Is my strict fast – I mean my children's looks,
     And therein fasting hast thou made me gaunt.
     Gaunt am I for the grave, gaunt as a grave,
     Whose hollow womb inherits nought but bones.
RICHARD   Can sick men play so nicely with their names?
85 GAUNT   No, misery makes sport to mock itself:
     Since thou dost seek to kill my name in me,
     I mock my name, great king, to flatter thee.
RICHARD   Should dying men flatter with those that live?
GAUNT   No, no, men living flatter those that die.
90 RICHARD   Thou now a-dying sayest thou flatterest me.
GAUNT   Oh no, thou diest, though I the sicker be.
RICHARD   I am in health, I breathe, and see thee ill.
GAUNT   Now He that made me knows I see thee ill,
     Ill in myself to see, and in thee, seeing ill.
95   Thy death-bed is no lesser than thy land,
     Wherein thou liest in reputation sick,
     And thou, too careless patient as thou art,
     Commit'st thy anointed body to the cure
     Of those physicians that first wounded thee:
100   A thousand flatterers sit within thy crown,
     Whose compass is no bigger than thy head,
     And yet, incaged in so small a verge,
     The waste is no whit lesser than thy land.
     O, had thy grandsire with a prophet's eye
105   Seen how his son's son should destroy his sons,
     From forth thy reach he would have laid thy shame,
     Deposing thee before thou wert possess'd,
     Which art possess'd now to depose thyself.
     Why, cousin, wert thou regent of the world,
110   It were a shame to let this land by lease;
     But for thy world enjoying but this land,
     Is it not more than shame to shame it so?
     Landlord of England art thou now, not king,
     Thy state of law is bondslave to the law,
     And thou –
115 RICHARD   A lunatic lean-witted fool,
     Presuming on an ague's privilege,
     Darest with thy frozen admonition
     Make pale our cheek, chasing the royal blood
     With fury from his native residence.
120   Now by my seat's right royal majesty,
     Wert thou not brother to great Edward's son,
     This tongue that runs so roundly in thy head
     Should run thy head from thy unreverent shoulders.
GAUNT   O, spare me not, my brother Edward's son,

     For that I was his father Edward's son;   125
     That blood already, like the pelican,
     Hast thou tapp'd out and drunkenly carous'd:
     My brother Gloucester, plain well-meaning soul,
     Whom fair befall in heaven 'mongst happy souls,
     May be a president and witness good   130
     That thou respect'st not spilling Edward's blood.
     Join with the present sickness that I have,
     And thy unkindness be like crooked age,
     To crop at once a too long withered flower.
     Live in thy shame, but die not shame with thee!   135
     These words hereafter thy tormentors be!
     Convey me to my bed, then to my grave –
     Love they to live that love and honour have.   *Exit.*
RICHARD   And let them die that age and sullens have,
     For both hast thou, and both become the grave.   140
YORK   I do beseech your Majesty, impute his words
     To wayward sickliness and age in him;
     He loves you, on my life, and holds you dear,
     As Harry Duke of Herford, were he here.
RICHARD   Right, you say true; as Herford's love, so his;   145
     As theirs, so mine; and all be as it is.

Enter NORTHUMBERLAND.

NORTHUMBERLAND
     My liege, old Gaunt commends him to your Majesty.
RICHARD   What says he?
NORTHUMBERLAND   Nay nothing, all is said:
     His tongue is now a stringless instrument;
     Words, life, and all, old Lancaster hath spent.   150
YORK   Be York the next that must be bankrout so!
     Though death be poor, it ends a mortal woe.
RICHARD   The ripest fruit first falls, and so doth he;
     His time is spent, our pilgrimage must be.
     So much for that. Now for our Irish wars: 155
     We must supplant those rough rug-headed kerns,
     Which live like venom where no venom else,
     But only they, have privilege to live.
     And for these great affairs do ask some charge,
     Towards our assistance we do seize to us   160
     The plate, coin, revenues, and moveables,
     Whereof our uncle Gaunt did stand possess'd.
YORK   How long shall I be patient? ah, how long
     Shall tender duty make me suffer wrong?
     Not Gloucester's death, nor Herford's banishment,   165
     Nor Gaunt's rebukes, nor England's private wrongs,
     Nor the prevention of poor Bolingbroke
     About his marriage, nor my own disgrace,
     Have ever made me sour my patient cheek,
     Or bend one wrinkle on my sovereign's face.   170
     I am the last of noble Edward's sons,
     Of whom thy father, Prince of Wales, was first.
     In war was never lion rag'd more fierce,
     In peace was never gentle lamb more mild,
     Than was that young and princely gentleman.   175
     His face thou hast, for even so look'd he,
     Accomplish'd with the number of thy hours;

But when he frown'd it was against the French,
And not against his friends; his noble hand
Did win what he did spend, and spent not that
Which his triumphant father's hand had won;
His hands were guilty of no kindred blood,
But bloody with the enemies of his kin.
O Richard! York is too far gone with grief,
Or else he never would compare between –

RICHARD   Why, uncle, what's the matter?

YORK   O my liege,
Pardon me, if you please; if not, I pleas'd
Not to be pardoned, am content withal.
Seek you to seize and gripe into your hands
The royalties and rights of banish'd Herford?
Is not Gaunt dead? and doth not Herford live?
Was not Gaunt just? and is not Harry true?
Did not the one deserve to have an heir?
Is not his heir a well-deserving son?
Take Herford's rights away, and take from time
His charters, and his customary rights;
Let not to-morrow then ensue to-day:
Be not thyself. For how art thou a king
But by fair sequence and succession?
Now afore God – God forbid I say true! –
If you do wrongfully seize Herford's rights,
Call in the letters patents that he hath
By his attorneys-general to sue
His livery, and deny his off'red homage,
You pluck a thousand dangers on your head,
You lose a thousand well-disposed hearts,
And prick my tender patience to those thoughts
Which honour and allegiance cannot think.

RICHARD   Think what you will, we seize into our hands
His plate, his goods, his money and his lands.

YORK   I'll not be by the while. My liege, farewell.
What will ensue hereof there's none can tell;
But by bad courses may be understood
That their events can never fall out good.   *Exit.*

RICHARD   Go, Bushy, to the Earl of Wiltshire straight,
Bid him repair to us to Ely House
To see this business. To-morrow next
We will for Ireland, and 'tis time, I trow.
And we create, in absence of ourself,
Our uncle York Lord Governor of England;
For he is just, and always loved us well.
Come on, our queen, to-morrow must we part;
Be merry, for our time of stay is short.
                    Exeunt King, Queen, Aumerle,
                    Bushy, Greene and Bagot.

NORTHUMBERLAND
Well, lords, the Duke of Lancaster is dead.

ROSS   And living too, for now his son is Duke.

WILLOUGHBY   Barely in title, not in revenues.

NORTHUMBERLAND
Richly in both, if justice had her right.

ROSS   My heart is great, but it must break with silence,
Ere't be disburdened with a liberal tongue.

NORTHUMBERLAND
Nay, speak thy mind, and let him ne'er speak more
That speaks thy words again to do thee harm.

WILLOUGHBY
Tends that that thou wouldst speak to the Duke of
    Herford?
If it be so, out with it boldly, man;
Quick is mine ear to hear of good towards him.

ROSS   No good at all that I can do for him,
Unless you call it good to pity him,
Bereft, and gelded of his patrimony.

NORTHUMBERLAND
Now afore God 'tis shame such wrongs are borne
In him, a royal prince, and many mo
Of noble blood in this declining land;
The king is not himself, but basely led
By flatterers; and what they will inform,
Merely in hate, 'gainst any of us all,
That will the king severely prosecute
'Gainst us, our lives, our children, and our heirs.

ROSS   The commons hath he pill'd with grievous taxes,
And quite lost their hearts. The nobles hath he fin'd
For ancient quarrels and quite lost their hearts.

WILLOUGHBY   And daily new exactions are devis'd.
As blanks, benevolences, and I wot not what –
But what a God's name doth become of this?

NORTHUMBERLAND
Wars hath not wasted it, for warr'd he hath not,
But basely yielded upon compromise
That which his ancestors achiev'd with blows;
More hath he spent in peace than they in wars.

ROSS   The Earl of Wiltshire hath the realm in farm.

WILLOUGHBY
The king's grown bankrout like a broken man.

NORTHUMBERLAND
Reproach and dissolution hangeth over him.

ROSS   He hath not money for these Irish wars,
His burthenous taxations notwithstanding,
But by the robbing of the banish'd Duke.

NORTHUMBERLAND
His noble kinsman – most degenerate king!
But, lords, we hear this fearful tempest sing,
Yet seek no shelter to avoid the storm;
We see the wind sit sore upon our sails,
And yet we strike not, but securely perish.

ROSS   We see the very wrack that we must suffer,
And unavoided is the danger now,
For suffering so the causes of our wrack.

NORTHUMBERLAND
Not so, even through the hollow eyes of death
I spy life peering; but I dare not say
How near the tidings of our comfort is.

WILLOUGHBY
Nay, let us share thy thoughts as thou dost ours.

ROSS   Be confident to speak, Northumberland:
We three are but thyself, and, speaking so,
Thy words are but as thoughts; therefore be bold.

NORTHUMBERLAND

    Then thus: I have from le Port Blanc,
    A bay in Brittaine, receiv'd intelligence
    That Harry Duke of Herford, Rainold Lord
      Cobham,
280   The son of Richard Earl of Arundel,
    That late broke from the Duke of Exeter,
    His brother, Archbishop late of Canterbury,
    Sir Thomas Erpingham, Sir John Ramston,
    Sir John Norbery, Sir Robert Waterton, and Francis
      Quoint –
285   All these well furnished by the Duke of Brittaine
    With eight tall ships, three thousand men of war,
    Are making hither with all due expedience,
    And shortly mean to touch our northern shore.
    Perhaps they had ere this, but that they stay
290   The first departing of the king for Ireland.
    If then we shall shake off our slavish yoke,
    Imp out our drooping country's broken wing,
    Redeem from broking pawn the blemish'd crown,
    Wipe off the dust that hides our sceptre's gilt,
295   And make high majesty look like itself,
    Away with me in post to Ravenspurgh;
    But if you faint, as fearing to do so,
    Stay, and be secret, and myself will go.

ROSS   To horse, to horse! urge doubts to them that fear.

WILLOUGHBY

300   Hold out my horse, and I will first be there.   *Exeunt.*

2.2   *Enter the* QUEEN, BUSHY *and* BAGOT.

BUSHY   Madam, your Majesty is too much sad.
    You promis'd, when you parted with the king,
    To lay aside life-harming heaviness,
    And entertain a cheerful disposition.
5   QUEEN   To please the king I did – to please myself
    I cannot do it; yet I know no cause
    Why I should welcome such a guest as grief,
    Save bidding farewell to so sweet a guest
    As my sweet Richard. Yet again methinks
10   Some unborn sorrow ripe in Fortune's womb
    Is coming towards me, and my inward soul
    With nothing trembles; at some thing it grieves,
    More than with parting from my lord the king.
BUSHY   Each substance of a grief hath twenty shadows,
15   Which shows like grief itself, but is not so.
    For sorrow's eye, glazed with blinding tears,
    Divides one thing entire to many objects,
    Like perspectives, which, rightly gaz'd upon,
    Show nothing but confusion; ey'd awry,
20   Distinguish form. So your sweet Majesty,
    Looking awry upon your lord's departure,
    Find shapes of grief more than himself to wail,
    Which, look'd on as it is, is nought but shadows
    Of what it is not; then, thrice-gracious queen,
25   More than your lord's departure weep not – more's
      not seen,

    Or if it be, 'tis with false sorrow's eye,
    Which, for things true, weeps things imaginary.
QUEEN   It may be so; but yet my inward soul
    Persuades me it is otherwise. Howe'er it be,
    I cannot but be sad; so heavy sad,   30
    As, though on thinking on no thought I think,
    Makes me with heavy nothing faint and shrink.
BUSHY   'Tis nothing but conceit, my gracious lady.
QUEEN   'Tis nothing less: conceit is still deriv'd
    From some forefather grief; mine is not so,   35
    For nothing hath begot my something grief,
    Or something hath the nothing that I grieve –
    'Tis in reversion that I do possess –
    But what it is that is not yet known what,
    I cannot name: 'tis nameless woe, I wot.   40

             Enter GREENE.

GREENE

    God save your Majesty! and well met, gentlemen.
    I hope the king is not yet shipp'd for Ireland.
QUEEN   Why hopest thou so? 'tis better hope he is,
    For his designs crave haste, his haste good hope.
    Then wherefore dost thou hope he is not shipp'd?   45
GREENE

    That he, our hope, might have retir'd his power,
    And driven into despair an enemy's hope,
    Who strongly hath set footing in this land:
    The banish'd Bolingbroke repeals himself,
    And with uplifted arms is safe arriv'd   50
    At Ravenspurgh.
QUEEN   Now God in heaven forbid!
GREENE   Ah, madam, 'tis too true; and that is worse,
    The lord Northumberland, his son young Henry
      Percy,
    The lords of Ross, Beaumond, and Willoughby,
    With all their powerful friends, are fled to him.   55
BUSHY   Why have you not proclaim'd Northumberland
    And all the rest revolted faction traitors?
GREENE   We have; whereupon the Earl of Worcester
    Hath broken his staff, resign'd his stewardship,
    And all the household servants fled with him   60
    To Bolingbroke.
QUEEN   So, Greene, thou art the midwife to my woe,
    And Bolingbroke my sorrow's dismal heir;
    Now hath my soul brought forth her prodigy,
    And I, a gasping new-deliver'd mother,   65
    Have woe to woe, sorrow to sorrow join'd.
BUSHY   Despair not, madam.
QUEEN   Who shall hinder me?
    I will despair, and be at enmity
    With cozening Hope – he is a flatterer,
    A parasite, a keeper-back of Death,   70
    Who gently would dissolve the bands of life,
    Which false Hope lingers in extremity.

             Enter YORK.

GREENE   Here comes the Duke of York.

QUEEN   With signs of war about his aged neck;
75   O, full of careful business are his looks!
             Uncle, for God's sake, speak comfortable words.
YORK   Should I do so, I should belie my thoughts;
             Comfort's in heaven, and we are on the earth,
             Where nothing lives but crosses, cares, and grief.
80   Your husband, he is gone to save far off,
             Whilst others come to make him lose at home.
             Here am I left to underprop his land,
             Who weak with age cannot support myself;
             Now comes the sick hour that his surfeit made,
85   Now shall he try his friends that flatter'd him.

Enter a Servant.

SERVANT   My lord, your son was gone before I came.
YORK   He was? why, so go all which way it will!
             The nobles they are fled, the commons cold,
             And will, I fear, revolt on Herford's side.
90   Sirrah, get thee to Plashy, to my sister Gloucester,
             Bid her send me presently a thousand pound.
             Hold, take my ring.
SERVANT   My lord, I had forgot to tell your lordship:
             To-day as I came by I called there –
95   But I shall grieve you to report the rest.
YORK   What is't, knave?
SERVANT   An hour before I came the Duchess died.
YORK   God for his mercy, what a tide of woes
             Comes rushing on this woeful land at once!
100   I know not what to do, I would to God,
             So my untruth had not provok'd him to it,
             The king had cut my head off with my brother's.
             What, are there no posts dispatch'd for Ireland?
             How shall we do for money for these wars?
105   Come, sister – cousin, I would say, pray pardon me.
             Go, fellow, get thee home, provide some carts
             And bring away the armour that is there.
                                                            Exit Servant.
             Gentlemen, will you go muster men?
             If I know how or which way to order these affairs,
110   Thus thrust disorderly into my hands,
             Never believe me. Both are my kinsmen:
             Th'one is my sovereign, whom both my oath
             And duty bids defend; th'other again
             Is my kinsman, whom the king hath wrong'd,
115   Whom conscience and my kindred bids to right.
             Well, somewhat we must do. Come, cousin,
             I'll dispose of you. Gentlemen, go muster up your
                 men,
             And meet me presently at Berkeley.
             I should to Plashy too,
120   But time will not permit. All is uneven,
             And everything is left at six and seven.
                                            Exeunt York and Queen.
BUSHY   The wind sits fair for news to go for Ireland,
             But none returns. For us to levy power
             Proportionable to the enemy
125   Is all unpossible.

GREENE   Besides, our nearness to the king in love
             Is near the hate of those love not the king.
BAGOT
             And that's the wavering commons, for their love
             Lies in their purses, and whoso empties them,
             By so much fills their hearts with deadly hate.   130
BUSHY   Wherein the king stands generally condemn'd.
BAGOT   If judgment lie in them, then so do we,
             Because we ever have been near the king.
GREENE
             Well, I will for refuge straight to Bristow castle,
             The Earl of Wiltshire is already there.   135
BUSHY   Thither will I with you; for little office
             The hateful commons will perform for us,
             Except like curs to tear us all to pieces.
             Will you go along with us?
BAGOT   No, I will to Ireland to his Majesty.   140
             Farewell. If heart's presages be not vain,
             We three here part that ne'er shall meet again.
BUSHY   That's as York thrives to beat back Bolingbroke.
GREENE   Alas, poor Duke! the task he undertakes
             Is numb'ring sands and drinking oceans dry;   145
             Where one on his side fights, thousands will fly.
             Farewell at once – for once, for all, and ever.
BUSHY   Well, we may meet again.
BAGOT   I fear me, never.
                                                            Exeunt.

2.3   *Enter* BOLINGBROKE *and* NORTHUMBERLAND.

BOLINGBROKE   How far is it, my lord, to Berkeley now?
NORTHUMBERLAND   Believe me, noble lord,
             I am a stranger here in Gloucestershire.
             These high wild hills and rough uneven ways
             Draws out our miles and makes them wearisome,   5
             And yet your fair discourse hath been as sugar,
             Making the hard way sweet and delectable.
             But I bethink me what a weary way
             From Ravenspurgh to Cotshall will be found
             In Ross and Willoughby, wanting your company,   10
             Which I protest hath very much beguil'd
             The tediousness and process of my travel.
             But theirs is sweet'ned with the hope to have
             The present benefit which I possess,
             And hope to joy is little less in joy   15
             Than hope enjoy'd. By this the weary lords
             Shall make their way seem short, as mine hath done
             By sight of what I have, your noble company.
BOLINGBROKE   Of much less value is my company
             Than your good words. But who comes here?   20

Enter HARRY PERCY.

NORTHUMBERLAND   It is my son, young Harry Percy,
             Sent from my brother Worcester, whencesoever.
             Harry, how fares your uncle?
PERCY
             I had thought, my lord, to have learn'd his health of
                 you.

NORTHUMBERLAND　Why, is he not with the queen? 25

PERCY　No, my good lord, he hath forsook the court,
　Broken his staff of office and dispers'd
　The household of the king.

NORTHUMBERLAND　　　　　　What was his reason?
　He was not so resolv'd when last we spake together.

PERCY　Because your lordship was proclaimed traitor. 30
　But he, my lord, is gone to Ravenspurgh
　To offer service to the Duke of Herford,
　And sent me over by Berkeley to discover
　What power the Duke of York had levied there,
　Then with directions to repair to Ravenspurgh. 35

NORTHUMBERLAND
　Have you forgot the Duke of Herford, boy?

PERCY　No, my good lord, for that is not forgot
　Which ne'er I did remember: to my knowledge,
　I never in my life did look on him.

NORTHUMBERLAND
　Then learn to know him now. This is the Duke. 40

PERCY　My gracious lord, I tender you my service,
　Such as it is, being tender, raw, and young,
　Which elder days shall ripen and confirm
　To more approved service and desert.

BOLINGBROKE　I thank thee, gentle Percy, and be sure 45
　I count myself in nothing else so happy
　As in a soul rememb'ring my good friends,
　And as my fortune ripens with thy love,
　It shall be still thy true love's recompense.
　My heart this covenant makes, my hand thus seals it. 50

NORTHUMBERLAND
　How far is it to Berkeley? and what stir
　Keeps good old York there with his men of war?

PERCY　There stands the castle by yon tuft of trees,
　Mann'd with three hundred men, as I have heard,
　And in it are the Lords of York, Berkeley, and
　　Seymour – 55
　None else of name and noble estimate.

Enter ROSS *and* WILLOUGHBY.

NORTHUMBERLAND
　Here come the Lords of Ross and Willoughby,
　Bloody with spurring, fiery-red with haste.

BOLINGBROKE
　Welcome, my lords; I wot your love pursues
　A banish'd traitor. All my treasury 60
　Is yet but unfelt thanks, which, more inrich'd,
　Shall be your love and labour's recompense.

ROSS　Your presence makes us rich, most noble lord.

WILLOUGHBY　And far surmounts our labour to attain it.

BOLINGBROKE
　Evermore thank's the exchequer of the poor, 65
　Which, till my infant fortune comes to years,
　Stands for my bounty. But who comes here?

Enter BERKELEY.

NORTHUMBERLAND
　It is my Lord of Berkeley, as I guess.

BERKELEY　My Lord of Herford, my message is to you.

BOLINGBROKE　My lord, my answer is – to Lancaster, 70
　And I am come to seek that name in England,
　And I must find that title in your tongue,
　Before I make reply to aught you say.

BERKELEY
　Mistake me not, my lord, 'tis not my meaning
　To race one title of your honour out. 75
　To you, my lord, I come, what lord you will,
　From the most gracious regent of this land,
　The Duke of York, to know what pricks you on
　To take advantage of the absent time,
　And fright our native peace with self-borne arms. 80

Enter YORK.

BOLINGBROKE
　I shall not need transport my words by you;
　Here comes his grace in person. My noble uncle!
　[*Kneels.*]

YORK　Show me thy humble heart, and not thy knee,
　Whose duty is deceivable and false.

BOLINGBROKE　My gracious uncle – 85

YORK
　Tut, tut! grace me no grace, nor uncle me no uncle,
　I am no traitor's uncle, and that word 'grace'
　In an ungracious mouth is but profane.
　Why have those banish'd and forbidden legs
　Dar'd once to touch a dust of England's ground? 90
　But then more 'why?' – why have they dar'd to
　　march
　So many miles upon her peaceful bosom,
　Frighting her pale-fac'd villages with war
　And ostentation of despised arms?
　Com'st thou because the anointed king is hence? 95
　Why, foolish boy, the king is left behind,
　And in my loyal bosom lies his power.
　Were I but now the lord of such hot youth,
　As when brave Gaunt, thy father, and myself,
　Rescued the Black Prince, that young Mars of men, 100
　From forth the ranks of many thousand French,
　O then how quickly should this arm of mine,
　Now prisoner to the palsy, chastise thee,
　And minister correction to thy fault!

BOLINGBROKE
　My gracious uncle, let me know my fault: 105
　On what condition stands it and wherein?

YORK　Even in condition of the worst degree –
　In gross rebellion and detested treason;
　Thou art a banish'd man, and here art come,
　Before the expiration of thy time, 110
　In braving arms against thy sovereign.

BOLINGBROKE
　As I was banish'd, I was banish'd Herford;
　But as I come, I come for Lancaster.
　And, noble uncle, I beseech your grace
　Look on my wrongs with an indifferent eye. 115
　You are my father, for methinks in you

I see old Gaunt alive. O then my father,
Will you permit that I shall stand condemn'd
A wandering vagabond, my rights and royalties   20
Pluck'd from my arms perforce, and given away
To upstart unthrifts? Wherefore was I born?
If that my cousin king be King in England,
It must be granted I am Duke of Lancaster.
You have a son, Aumerle, my noble cousin;
Had you first died, and he been thus trod down,   25
He should have found his uncle Gaunt a father
To rouse his wrongs and chase them to the bay.
I am denied to sue my livery here,
And yet my letters patents give me leave.
My father's goods are all distrain'd and sold,   30
And these, and all, are all amiss employ'd.
What would you have me do? I am a subject,
And I challenge law; attorneys are denied me,
And therefore personally I lay my claim
To my inheritance of free descent.   35

NORTHUMBERLAND
The noble Duke hath been too much abused.

ROSS   It stands your grace upon to do him right.

WILLOUGHBY
Base men by his endowments are made great.

YORK   My lords of England, let me tell you this:
I have had feeling of my cousin's wrongs,   40
And labour'd all I could to do him right.
But in this kind to come, in braving arms,
Be his own carver, and cut out his way,
To find out right with wrong – it may not be.
And you that do abet him in this kind   45
Cherish rebellion, and are rebels all.

NORTHUMBERLAND
The noble Duke hath sworn his coming is
But for his own; and for the right of that
We all have strongly sworn to give him aid.
And let him ne'er see joy that breaks that oath!   50

YORK   Well, well, I see the issue of these arms.
I cannot mend it, I must needs confess,
Because my power is weak and all ill left.
But if I could, by Him that gave me life,
I would attach you all, and make you stoop   55
Unto the sovereign mercy of the king;
But since I cannot, be it known unto you,
I do remain as neuter. So, fare you well,
Unless you please to enter in the castle,
And there repose you for this night.   160

BOLINGBROKE   An offer, uncle, that we will accept.
But we must win your grace to go with us
To Bristow castle, which they say is held
By Bushy, Bagot, and their complices,
The caterpillars of the commonwealth,   165
Which I have sworn to weed and pluck away.

YORK   It may be I will go with you; but yet I'll pause
For I am loath to break our country's laws.
Nor friends, nor foes, to me welcome you are.
Things past redress are now with me past care.   170
                                                    Exeunt.

2.4   *Enter* EARL OF SALISBURY *and a* Welsh Captain.

CAPTAIN
My Lord of Salisbury, we have stay'd ten days,
And hardly kept our countrymen together,
And yet we hear no tidings from the king;
Therefore we will disperse ourselves. Farewell.

SALISBURY   Stay yet another day, thou trusty Welshman: 5
The king reposeth all his confidence in thee.

CAPTAIN   'Tis thought the king is dead; we will not stay.
The bay-trees in our country are all wither'd,
And meteors fright the fixed stars of heaven,
The pale-fac'd moon looks bloody on the earth,   10
And lean-look'd prophets whisper fearful change,
Rich men look sad, and ruffians dance and leap –
The one in fear to lose what they enjoy,
The other to enjoy by rage and war.
These signs forerun the death or fall of kings.   15
Farewell: our countrymen are gone and fled,
As well assured Richard their king is dead.   *Exit.*

SALISBURY   Ah, Richard! with the eyes of heavy mind
I see thy glory like a shooting star
Fall to the base earth from the firmament.   20
Thy sun sets weeping in the lowly west,
Witnessing storms to come, woe, and unrest.
Thy friends are fled to wait upon thy foes,
And crossly to thy good all fortune goes.   *Exit.*

3.1   *Enter* BOLINGBROKE, YORK, NORTHUMBERLAND,
          with BUSHY *and* GREENE, *prisoners.*

BOLINGBROKE   Bring forth these men.
Bushy and Greene, I will not vex your souls,
Since presently your souls must part your bodies,
With too much urging your pernicious lives,
For 'twere no charity; yet, to wash your blood   5
From off my hands, here in the view of men
I will unfold some causes of your deaths:
You have misled a prince, a royal king,
A happy gentleman in blood and lineaments,
By you unhappied and disfigured clean;   10
You have in manner, with your sinful hours,
Made a divorce betwixt his queen and him,
Broke the possession of a royal bed,
And stain'd the beauty of a fair queen's cheeks
With tears, drawn from her eyes by your foul wrongs; 15
Myself – a prince by fortune of my birth,
Near to the king in blood, and near in love,
Till you did make him misinterpret me –
Have stoop'd my neck under your injuries,
And sigh'd my English breath in foreign clouds,   20
Eating the bitter bread of banishment,
Whilst you have fed upon my signories,
Dispark'd my parks and fell'd my forest woods,
From my own windows torn my household coat,
Rac'd out my imprese, leaving me no sign,   25
Save men's opinions and my living blood,
To show the world I am a gentleman.

This and much more, much more than twice all this,
Condemns you to the death. See them delivered over
To execution and the hand of death.
30 BUSHY   More welcome is the stroke of death to me
Than Bolingbroke to England. Lords, farewell.
GREENE   My comfort is, that heaven will take our souls,
And plague injustice with the pains of hell.
BOLINGBROKE
35 My lord Northumberland, see them dispatch'd.
                    Exeunt Northumberland and prisoners.
Uncle, you say the queen is at your house;
For God's sake fairly let her be intreated,
Tell her I send to her my kind commends;
Take special care my greetings be delivered.
40 YORK   A gentleman of mine I have dispatch'd
With letters of your love to her at large.
BOLINGBROKE   Thanks, gentle uncle. Come, lords, away,
To fight with Glendor and his complices:
A while to work, and after holiday.   *Exeunt.*

3.2   *Drums: flourish and colours.*
        Enter KING RICHARD, AUMERLE,
        the Bishop of CARLISLE *and soldiers.*

RICHARD   Barkloughly castle call they this at hand?
AUMERLE   Yea, my lord. How brooks your grace the air,
After your late tossing on the breaking seas?
RICHARD   Needs must I like it well: I weep for joy
5 To stand upon my kingdom once again.
Dear earth, I do salute thee with my hand,
Though rebels wound thee with their horses' hoofs.
As a long-parted mother with her child
Plays fondly with her tears and smiles in meeting,
10 So weeping, smiling, greet I thee, my earth,
And do thee favours with my royal hands;
Feed not thy sovereign's foe, my gentle earth,
Nor with thy sweets comfort his ravenous sense,
But let thy spiders that suck up thy venom
15 And heavy-gaited toads lie in their way,
Doing annoyance to the treacherous feet,
Which with usurping steps do trample thee;
Yield stinging nettles to mine enemies;
And when they from thy bosom pluck a flower,
20 Guard it, I pray thee, with a lurking adder,
Whose double tongue may with a mortal touch
Throw death upon thy sovereign's enemies.
Mock not my senseless conjuration, lords:
This earth shall have a feeling, and these stones
25 Prove armed soldiers ere her native king
Shall falter under foul rebellion's arms.
CARLISLE
Fear not, my lord. That Power that made you king
Hath power to keep you king in spite of all.
The means that heaven yields must be imbrac'd
30 And not neglected; else, heaven would,
And we will not; heavens offer, we refuse
The proffered means of succour and redress.

AUMERLE   He means, my lord, that we are too remiss;
Whilst Bolingbroke, through our security,
Grows strong and great in substance and in power.   35
RICHARD   Discomfortable cousin! know'st thou not
That when the searching eye of heaven is hid
Behind the globe and lights the lower world,
Then thieves and robbers range abroad unseen
In murthers and in outrage boldly here;   40
But when from under this terrestrial ball
He fires the proud tops of the eastern pines,
And darts his light through every guilty hole,
Then murthers, treasons, and detested sins,
The cloak of night being pluck'd from off their
    backs,   45
Stand bare and naked, trembling at themselves?
So when this thief, this traitor, Bolingbroke,
Who all this while hath revell'd in the night,
Whilst we were wand'ring with the Antipodes,
Shall see us rising in our throne the east,   50
His treasons will sit blushing in his face,
Not able to endure the sight of day,
But self-affrighted tremble at his sin.
Not all the water in the rough rude sea
Can wash the balm off from an anointed king;   55
The breath of worldly men cannot depose
The deputy elected by the Lord;
For every man that Bolingbroke hath press'd
To lift shrewd steel against our golden crown,
God for his Richard hath in heavenly pay   60
A glorious angel: then, if angels fight,
Weak men must fall, for heaven still guards the right.

        Enter SALISBURY.

Welcome, my lord: how far off lies your power?
SALISBURY   Nor near nor farther off, my gracious lord,
Than this weak arm; discomfort guides my tongue,   65
And bids me speak of nothing but despair.
One day too late, I fear me, noble lord,
Hath clouded all thy happy days on earth.
O, call back yesterday, bid time return,
And thou shalt have twelve thousand fighting men! 70
To-day, to-day, unhappy day too late,
O'erthrows thy joys, friends, fortune and thy state;
For all the Welshmen, hearing thou wert dead,
Are gone to Bolingbroke, dispers'd and fled.
AUMERLE
Comfort, my liege, why looks your grace so pale?   75
RICHARD   But now the blood of twenty thousand men
Did triumph in my face, and they are fled;
And till so much blood thither come again,
Have I not reason to look pale and dead?
All souls that will be safe, fly from my side,   80
For time hath set a blot upon my pride.
AUMERLE   Comfort, my liege, remember who you are.
RICHARD   I had forgot myself, am I not king?
Awake, thou coward majesty! thou sleepest.
Is not the king's name twenty thousand names?   85

Arm, arm, my name! a puny subject strikes
At thy great glory. Look not to the ground,
Ye favourites of a king, are we not high?
High be our thoughts. I know my uncle York
Hath power enough to serve our turn. But who
90   comes here?

Enter SCROOPE.

SCROOPE   More health and happiness betide my liege
Than can my care-tun'd tongue deliver him.
RICHARD   Mine ear is open and my heart prepar'd.
The worst is worldly loss thou canst unfold.
95 Say, is my kingdom lost? why, 'twas my care,
And what loss is it to be rid of care?
Strives Bolingbroke to be as great as we?
Greater he shall not be. If he serve God,
We'll serve Him too, and be his fellow so.
100 Revolt our subjects? that we cannot mend;
They break their faith to God as well as us.
Cry woe, destruction, ruin, and decay –
The worst is death, and death will have his day.
SCROOPE   Glad am I that your Highness is so arm'd
105 To bear the tidings of calamity.
Like an unseasonable stormy day,
Which makes the silver rivers drown their shores,
As if the world were all dissolv'd to tears,
So high above his limits swells the rage
110 Of Bolingbroke, covering your fearful land
With hard bright steel, and hearts harder than steel.
White-beards have arm'd their thin and hairless
   scalps
Against thy majesty; boys, with women's voices,
Strive to speak big, and clap their female joints
115 In stiff unwieldy arms against thy crown;
Thy very beadsmen learn to bend their bows
Of double-fatal yew against thy state;
Yea, distaff-women manage rusty bills
Against thy seat: both young and old rebel,
120 And all goes worse than I have power to tell.
RICHARD   Too well, too well thou tell'st tale so ill.
Where is the Earl of Wiltshire? where is Bagot?
What is become of Bushy? where is Greene?
That they have let the dangerous enemy
125 Measure our confines with such peaceful steps?
If we prevail, their heads shall pay for it:
I warrant they have made peace with Bolingbroke.
SCROOPE
Peace have they made with him indeed, my lord.
RICHARD
O villains, vipers, damn'd without redemption!
130 Dogs, easily won to fawn on any man!
Snakes, in my heart-blood warm'd, that sting my
   heart!
Three Judases, each one thrice worse than Judas!
Would they make peace? Terrible hell,
Make war upon their spotted souls for this!
135 SCROOPE   Sweet love, I see, changing his property,

Turns to the sourest and most deadly hate.
Again uncurse their souls; their peace is made
With heads and not with hands; those whom you
   curse
Have felt the worst of death's destroying wound,
And lie full low, grav'd in the hollow ground.   140
AUMERLE
Is Bushy, Greene, and the Earl of Wiltshire dead?
SCROOPE   Ay, all of them at Bristow lost their heads.
AUMERLE
Where is the Duke my father with his power?
RICHARD   No matter where – of comfort no man speak.
Let's talk of graves, of worms, and epitaphs,   145
Make dust our paper, and with rainy eyes
Write sorrow on the bosom of the earth.
Let's choose executors and talk of wills.
And yet not so – for what can we bequeath
Save our deposed bodies to the ground?   150
Our lands, our lives, and all, are Bolingbroke's,
And nothing can we call our own but death;
And that small model of the barren earth
Which serves as paste and cover to our bones.
For God's sake let us sit upon the ground   155
And tell sad stories of the death of kings:
How some have been depos'd, some slain in war,
Some haunted by the ghosts they have deposed,
Some poisoned by their wives, some sleeping kill'd,
All murthered – for within the hollow crown   160
That rounds the mortal temples of a king
Keeps Death his court, and there the antic sits,
Scoffing his state and grinning at his pomp,
Allowing him a breath, a little scene,
To monarchize, be fear'd, and kill with looks;   165
Infusing him with self and vain conceit,
As if this flesh which walls about our life
Were brass impregnable; and, humour'd thus,
Comes at the last, and with a little pin
Bores thorough his castle wall, and farewell king!   170
Cover your heads, and mock not flesh and blood
With solemn reverence; throw away respect,
Tradition, form, and ceremonious duty;
For you have but mistook me all this while.
I live with bread like you, feel want,   175
Taste grief, need friends – subjected thus,
How can you say to me, I am a king?
CARLISLE
My lord, wise men ne'er sit and wail their woes,
But presently prevent the ways to wail.
To fear the foe, since fear oppresseth strength,   180
Gives in your weakness strength unto your foe,
And so your follies fight against yourself.
Fear and be slain – no worse can come to fight;
And fight and die is death destroying death,
Where fearing dying pays death servile breath.   185
AUMERLE   My father hath a power; inquire of him,
And learn to make a body of a limb.

RICHARD

    Thou chid'st me well. Proud Bolingbroke, I come
    To change blows with thee for our day of doom.
190   This ague fit of fear is overblown;
    An easy task it is to win our own.
    Say, Scroope, where lies our uncle with his power?
    Speak sweetly, man, although thy looks be sour.
    SCROOPE   Men judge by the complexion of the sky
195   The state and inclination of the day;
    So may you by my dull and heavy eye:
    My tongue hath but a heavier tale to say.
    I play the torturer by small and small
    To lengthen out the worst that must be spoken:
200   Your uncle York is join'd with Bolingbroke,
    And all your northern castles yielded up,
    And all your southern gentlemen in arms
    Upon his party.
    RICHARD   Thou hast said enough.
    Beshrew thee, cousin, which didst lead me forth
205   [*to Aumerle*] Of that sweet way I was in to despair!
    What say you now? What comfort have we now?
    By heaven, I'll hate him everlastingly
    That bids me be of comfort any more.
    Go to Flint Castle, there I'll pine away –
210   A king, woe's slave, shall kingly woe obey.
    That power I have, discharge, and let them go
    To ear the land that hath some hope to grow,
    For I have none. Let no man speak again
    To alter this, for counsel is but vain.
    AUMERLE   My liege, one word.
215   RICHARD   He does me double wrong
    That wounds me with the flatteries of his tongue.
    Discharge my followers; let them hence away,
    From Richard's night, to Bolingbroke's fair day.
                           Exeunt.

3.3   *Enter, with drum and colours,* BOLINGBROKE,
       YORK, NORTHUMBERLAND, *attendants.*

BOLINGBROKE   So that by this intelligence we learn
    The Welshmen are dispers'd; and Salisbury
    Is gone to meet the king, who lately landed
    With some few private friends upon this coast.
NORTHUMBERLAND
5   The news is very fair and good, my lord;
    Richard not far from hence hath hid his head.
    YORK   It would beseem the Lord Northumberland
    To say 'King Richard'. Alack the heavy day,
    When such a sacred king should hide his head!
NORTHUMBERLAND
10   Your grace mistakes; only to be brief,
    Left I his title out.
    YORK   The time hath been,
    Would you have been so brief with him, he would
    Have been so brief with you to shorten you,
    For taking so the head, your whole head's length

BOLINGBROKE

    Mistake not, uncle, further than you should.   15
    YORK   Take not, good cousin, further than you should,
    Lest you mistake: the heavens are o'er our heads.
    BOLINGBROKE   I know it, uncle; and oppose not myself
    Against their will. But who comes here?

                    Enter PERCY.

    Welcome, Harry. What, will not this castle yield?   20
    PERCY   The castle royally is mann'd, my lord,
    Against thy entrance.
    BOLINGBROKE   Royally!
    Why, it contains no king?
    PERCY   Yes, my good lord,
    It doth contain a king; King Richard lies   25
    Within the limits of yon lime and stone;
    And with him are the Lord Aumerle, Lord Salisbury,
    Sir Stephen Scroope, besides a clergyman
    Of holy reverence; who, I cannot learn.
    NORTHUMBERLAND   O belike it is the Bishop of Carlisle.   30
    BOLINGBROKE   Noble lord,
    Go to the rude ribs of that ancient castle,
    Through brazen trumpet send the breath of parle
    Into his ruin'd ears, and thus deliver:
    Henry Bolingbroke   35
    On both his knees doth kiss King Richard's hand,
    And sends allegiance and true faith of heart
    To his most royal person; hither come
    Even at his feet to lay my arms and power,
    Provided that my banishment repeal'd   40
    And lands restor'd again be freely granted;
    If not, I'll use the advantage of my power
    And lay the summer's dust with showers of blood
    Rain'd from the wounds of slaughtered Englishmen –
    The which, how far off from the mind of
        Bolingbroke   45
    It is such crimson tempest should bedrench
    The fresh green lap of fair King Richard's land,
    My stooping duty tenderly shall show.
    Go, signify as much, while here we march
    Upon the grassy carpet of this plain.   50
    Let's march without the noise of threat'ning drum,
    That from this castle's tottered battlements
    Our fair appointments may be well perus'd.
    Methinks King Richard and myself should meet
    With no less terror than the elements   55
    Of fire and water, when their thund'ring shock
    At meeting tears the cloudy cheeks of heaven.
    Be he the fire, I'll be the yielding water;
    The rage be his, whilst on the earth I rain
    My waters – on the earth, and not on him.   60
    March on, and mark King Richard how he looks.

    Parle without, and answer within: then a flourish.
    Enter on the walls RICHARD, CARLISLE, AUMERLE,
             SCROOPE, SALISBURY.

See, see, King Richard doth himself appear,
As doth the blushing discontented sun
From out the fiery portal of the East,
When he perceives the envious clouds are bent
To dim his glory and to stain the track
Of his bright passage to the occident.
YORK   Yet looks he like a king. Behold, his eye,
As bright as is the eagle's, lightens forth
Controlling majesty; alack, alack for woe
That any harm should stain so fair a show!
RICHARD [*to Northumberland*]
We are amaz'd, and thus long have we stood
To watch the fearful bending of thy knee,
Because we thought ourself thy lawful king;
And if we be, how dare thy joints forget
To pay their awful duty to our presence?
If we be not, show us the hand of God
That hath dismiss'd us from our stewardship;
For well we know no hand of blood and bone
Can gripe the sacred handle of our sceptre,
Unless he do profane, steal, or usurp.
And though you think that all, as you have done,
Have torn their souls by turning them from us,
And we are barren and bereft of friends,
Yet know, my master, God omnipotent,
Is mustering in his clouds, on our behalf,
Armies of pestilence, and they shall strike
Your children yet unborn, and unbegot,
That lift your vassal hands against my head,
And threat the glory of my precious crown.
Tell Bolingbroke, for yon methinks he stands,
That every stride he makes upon my land
Is dangerous treason. He is come to open
The purple testament of bleeding war.
But ere the crown he looks for live in peace,
Ten thousand bloody crowns of mother's sons
Shall ill become the flower of England's face,
Change the complexion of her maid-pale peace
To scarlet indignation and bedew
Her pastures' grass with faithful English blood.
NORTHUMBERLAND
The King of Heaven forbid our lord the king
Should so with civil and uncivil arms
Be rush'd upon! Thy thrice noble cousin,
Harry Bolingbroke, doth humbly kiss thy hand,
And by the honourable tomb he swears,
That stands upon your royal grandsire's bones,
And by the royalties of both your bloods,
Currents that spring from one most gracious head,
And by the buried hand of warlike Gaunt,
And by the worth and hónour of himself,
Comprising all that may be sworn or said,
His coming hither hath no further scope
Than for his lineal royalties, and to beg
Infranchisement immediate on his knees,
Which on thy royal party granted once,
His glittering arms he will commend to rust,

His barbed steeds to stables, and his heart
To faithful service of your Majesty.
This, swears he as he is a prince and just;
And, as I am a gentleman, I credit him.   120
RICHARD
Northumberland, say thus the king returns:
His noble cousin is right welcome hither,
And all the number of his fair demands
Shall be accomplish'd without contradiction;
With all the gracious utterance that thou hast   125
Speak to his gentle hearing kind commends.
[*to Aumerle*] We do debase ourselves, cousin, do we
    not,
To look so poorly, and to speak so fair?
Shall we call back Northumberland and send
Defiance to the traitor, and so die?   130
AUMERLE
No, good my lord, let's fight with gentle words.
Till time lend friends, and friends their helpful
    swords.
RICHARD
O God! O God! that e'er this tongue of mine,
That laid the sentence of dread banishment
On yon proud man, should take it off again   135
With words of sooth! O that I were as great
As is my grief, or lesser than my name!
Or that I could forget what I have been!
Or not remember what I must be now!
Swell'st thou, proud heart? I'll give thee scope to
    beat,   140
Since foes have scope to beat both thee and me.
AUMERLE
Northumberland comes back from Bolingbroke.
RICHARD
What must the king do now? Must he submit?
The king shall do it. Must he be depos'd?
The king shall be contented. Must he lose   145
The name of king? a God's name, let it go.
I'll give my jewels for a set of beads;
My gorgeous palace for a hermitage;
My gay apparel for an almsman's gown;
My figur'd goblets for a dish of wood;   150
My sceptre for a palmer's walking staff;
My subjects for a pair of carved saints,
And my large kingdom for a little grave,
A little little grave, an obscure grave,
Or I'll be buried in the king's highway,   155
Some way of common trade, where subjects' feet
May hourly trample on their sovereign's head;
For on my heart they tread now whilst I live:
And buried once, why not upon my head?
Aumerle, thou weep'st (my tender-hearted cousin!), 160
We'll make foul weather with despised tears;
Our sighs and they shall lodge the summer corn,
And make a dearth in this revolting land.
Or shall we play the wantons with our woes,
And make some pretty match with shedding tears?   165

As thus to drop them still upon one place,
Till they have fretted us a pair of graves
Within the earth, and therein laid – there lies
Two kinsmen digg'd their graves with weeping eyes!
170   Would not this ill do well? Well, well, I see
I talk but idly, and you laugh at me.
Most mighty prince, my Lord Northumberland,
What says King Bolingbroke? Will his Majesty
Give Richard leave to live till Richard die?
175   You make a leg, and Bolingbroke says 'ay'.

NORTHUMBERLAND
My lord, in the base court he doth attend
To speak with you; may it please you to come down?

RICHARD   Down, down I come, like glist'ring Phaeton,
Wanting the manage of unruly jades.
180   In the base court? Base court, where kings grow base,
To come at traitors' calls, and do them grace!
In the base court? Come down? Down, court! down,
    king!
For night-owls shriek where mounting larks should
    sing.   *Exeunt from above.*

BOLINGBROKE   What says his Majesty?

NORTHUMBERLAND   Sorrow and grief of heart
185   Makes him speak fondly like a frantic man;
Yet he is come.

        Enter KING RICHARD *and his attendants below.*

BOLINGBROKE   Stand all apart,
And show fair duty to his Majesty. [*He kneels down.*]
My gracious lord.

RICHARD   Fair cousin, you debase your princely knee
190   To make the base earth proud with kissing it.
Me rather had my heart might feel your love,
Than my unpleased eye see your courtesy.
Up, cousin, up; your heart is up, I know,
195   Thus high at least, although your knee be low.

BOLINGBROKE
My gracious lord, I come but for mine own.

RICHARD   Your own is yours, and I am yours, and all.

BOLINGBROKE   So far be mine, my most redoubted lord,
As my true service shall deserve your love.

200 RICHARD   Well you deserve. They well deserve to have
That know the strong'st and surest way to get.
Uncle, give me your hands; nay, dry your eyes –
Tears show their love, but want their remedies.
Cousin, I am too young to be your father,
205   Though you are old enough to be my heir;
What you will have, I'll give, and willing too,
For do we must what force will have us do.
Set on towards London, cousin, is it so?

BOLINGBROKE   Yea, my good lord.

RICHARD   Then I must not say no.
                     Flourish. Exeunt.

3.4   *Enter the* QUEEN *and two* Ladies.

QUEEN   What sport shall we devise here in this garden,
To drive away the heavy thought of care?

LADY   Madam, we'll play at bowls.

QUEEN   'Twill make me think the world is full of rubs
And that my fortune runs against the bias.   5

LADY   Madam, we'll dance.

QUEEN   My legs can keep no measure in delight,
When my poor heart no measure keeps in grief:
Therefore no dancing, girl – some other sport.

LADY   Madam, we'll tell tales.   10

QUEEN   Of sorrow or of joy?

LADY   Of either, madam.

QUEEN   Of neither, girl.
For if of joy, being altogether wanting,
It doth remember me the more of sorrow;
Or if of grief, being altogether had,   15
It adds more sorrow to my want of joy;
For what I have I need not to repeat,
And what I want it boots not to complain.

LADY   Madam, I'll sing.

QUEEN   'Tis well that thou hast cause,
But thou shouldst please me better wouldst thou
    weep.   20

LADY   I could weep, madam, would it do you good.

QUEEN   And I could sing, would weeping do me good,
And never borrow any tear of thee.

        Enter a Gardener *and two* Servants.

But stay, here come the gardeners.
Let's step into the shadow of these trees.
My wretchedness unto a row of pins,   25
They'll talk of state, for everyone doth so
Against a change: woe is forerun with woe.

GARDENER
Go, bind thou up young dangling apricocks,
Which like unruly children make their sire   30
Stoop with oppression of their prodigal weight,
Give some supportance to the bending twigs.
Go thou, and like an executioner
Cut off the heads of too fast growing sprays,
That look too lofty in our commonwealth: 35
All must be even in our government.
You thus employed, I will go root away
The noisome weeds which without profit suck
The soil's fertility from wholesome flowers.

MAN   Why should we, in the compass of a pale,   40
Keep law and form and due proportion,
Showing, as in a model, our firm estate,
When our sea-walled garden, the whole land,
Is full of weeds, her fairest flowers chok'd up,
Her fruit-trees all unprun'd, her hedges ruin'd,   45
Her knots disordered, and her wholesome herbs
Swarming with caterpillars?

GARDENER   Hold thy peace –
He that hath suffered this disordered spring
Hath now himself met with the fall of leaf.
The weeds which his broad-spreading leaves did
    shelter,   50
That seem'd in eating him to hold him up,

Are pluck'd up root and all by Bolingbroke –
I mean the Earl of Wiltshire, Bushy, Greene.

MAN   What, are they dead?

GARDENER   They are; and Bolingbroke
Hath seiz'd the wasteful king. O, what pity is it
That he had not so trimm'd and dress'd his land
As we this garden! We at time of year
Do wound the bark, the skin of our fruit-trees,
Lest, being over-proud in sap and blood,
With too much riches it confound itself;
Had he done so to great and growing men,
They might have liv'd to bear, and he to taste
Their fruits of duty. Superfluous branches
We lop away, that bearing boughs may live;
Had he done so, himself had borne the crown,
Which waste of idle hours hath quite thrown down.

MAN   What, think you the king shall be deposed?

GARDENER   Depress'd he is already, and depos'd
'Tis doubt he will be. Letters came last night
To a dear friend of the good Duke of York's
That tell black tidings.

QUEEN
O, I am press'd to death through want of speaking!
Thou, old Adam's likeness set to dress this garden,
How dares thy harsh rude tongue sound this
     unpleasing news?
What Eve, what serpent, hath suggested thee
To make a second fall of cursed man?
Why dost thou say King Richard is depos'd?
Dar'st thou, thou little better thing than earth,
Divine his downfall? Say, where, when, and how
Cam'st thou by this ill tidings? Speak, thou wretch.

GARDENER   Pardon me, madam, little joy have I
To breathe this news, yet what I say is true.
King Richard he is in the mighty hold
Of Bolingbroke. Their fortunes both are weigh'd;
In your lord's scale is nothing but himself,
And some few vanities that make him light.
But in the balance of great Bolingbroke,
Besides himself, are all the English peers,
And with that odds he weighs King Richard down.
Post you to London and you'll find it so;
I speak no more than everyone doth know.

QUEEN   Nimble mischance, that art so light of foot,
Doth not thy embassage belong to me,
And am I last that knows it? O, thou thinkest
To serve me last that I may longest keep
Thy sorrow in my breast. Come, ladies, go
To meet at London London's king in woe.
What, was I born to this, that my sad look
Should grace the triumph of great Bolingbroke?
Gard'ner, for telling me these news of woe,
Pray God the plants thou graft'st may never grow.
                        Exeunt Queen and Ladies.

GARDENER
Poor queen, so that thy state might be no worse,
I would my skill were subject to thy curse.

Here did she fall a tear; here in this place
I'll set a bank of rue, sour herb of grace.   105
Rue, even for ruth, here shortly shall be seen,
In the remembrance of a weeping queen.   *Exeunt.*

4.1   *Enter as to the Parliament* BOLINGBROKE,
          AUMERLE, NORTHUMBERLAND, PERCY,
       FITZWATER, SURREY, *the* Bishop of CARLISLE,
     the Abbot of Westminster *and another* LORD, *herald,*
                officers and BAGOT.

BOLINGBROKE   Call forth Bagot.
Now, Bagot, freely speak thy mind –
What thou dost know of noble Gloucester's death,
Who wrought it with the king, and who perform'd
The bloody office of his timeless end.   5

BAGOT   Then set before my face the Lord Aumerle.

BOLINGBROKE
Cousin, stand forth, and look upon that man.

BAGOT   My Lord Aumerle, I know your daring tongue
Scorns to unsay what once it hath delivered.
In that dead time when Gloucester's death was
     plotted,   10
I heard you say 'Is not my arm of length,
That reacheth from the restful English court
As far as Callice, to mine uncle's head?'
Amongst much other talk that very time
I heard you say that you had rather refuse   15
The offer of an hundred thousand crowns
Than Bolingbroke's return to England –
Adding withal, how bless'd this would be,
In this your cousin's death.

AUMERLE   Princes and noble lords,
What answer shall I make to this base man?   20
Shall I so much dishonour my fair stars
On equal terms to give him chastisement?
Either I must, or have mine honour soil'd
With the attainder of his slanderous lips.
There is my gage, the manual seal of death,   25
That marks thee out for hell. I say thou liest,
And will maintain what thou hast said is false
In thy heart-blood, though being all too base
To stain the temper of my knightly sword.

BOLINGBROKE
Bagot, forbear, thou shalt not take it up.   30

AUMERLE   Excepting one, I would he were the best
In all this presence that hath mov'd me so.

FITZWATER   If that thy valour stand on sympathy,
There is my gage, Aumerle, in gage to thine;
By that fair sun which shows me where thou stand'st,   35
I heard thee say, and vauntingly thou spak'st it,
That thou wert cause of noble Gloucester's death.
If thou deniest it twenty times, thou liest;
And I will turn thy falsehood to thy heart,
Where it was forged, with my rapier's point.   40

AUMERLE   Thou dar'st not, coward, live to see that day.

FITZWATER   Now by my soul, I would it were this hour.

AUMERLE　Fitzwater, thou art damn'd to hell for this.

PERCY　Aumerle, thou liest, his honour is as true

45　　In this appeal as thou art all unjust;
　　And that thou art so, there I throw my gage,
　　To prove it on thee to the extremest point
　　Of mortal breathing. Seize it, if thou dar'st.

AUMERLE　And if I do not, may my hands rot off,

50　　And never brandish more revengeful steel
　　Over the glittering helmet of my foe!

ANOTHER LORD
　　I task the earth to the like, forsworn Aumerle,
　　And spur thee on with full as many lies
　　As may be hollowed in thy treacherous ear

55　　From sun to sun. There is my honour's pawn;
　　Ingage it to the trial if thou darest.

AUMERLE
　　Who sets me else? By heaven, I'll throw at all!
　　I have a thousand spirits in one breast
　　To answer twenty thousand such as you.

60　SURREY　My Lord Fitzwater, I do remember well
　　The very time Aumerle and you did talk.

FITZWATER　'Tis very true; you were in presence then,
　　And you can witness with me this is true.

SURREY　As false, by heaven, as heaven itself is true.

FITZWATER　Surrey, thou liest.

65　SURREY　　　　　　　　　　Dishonourable boy,
　　That lie shall lie so heavy on my sword
　　That it shall render vengeance and revenge
　　Till thou, the lie-giver, and that lie do lie
　　In earth as quiet as thy father's skull.

70　　In proof whereof there is my honour's pawn;
　　Ingage it to the trial if thou darest.

FITZWATER　How fondly dost thou spur a forward horse!
　　If I dare eat, or drink, or breathe, or live,
　　I dare meet Surrey in a wilderness,

75　　And spit upon him whilst I say he lies,
　　And lies, and lies. There is my bond of faith
　　To tie thee to my strong correction.
　　As I intend to thrive in this new world,
　　Aumerle is guilty of my true appeal.

80　　Besides, I heard the banished Norfolk say
　　That thou, Aumerle, did'st send two of thy men
　　To execute the noble Duke at Callice.

AUMERLE　Some honest Christian trust me with a gage,
　　That Norfolk lies – here do I throw down this,

85　　If he may be repeal'd to try his honour.

BOLINGBROKE
　　These differences shall all rest under gage
　　Till Norfolk be repeal'd – repeal'd he shall be,
　　And, though mine enemy, restor'd again
　　To all his lands and signories. When he's return'd,

90　　Against Aumerle we will inforce his trial.

CARLISLE　That honourable day shall ne'er be seen.
　　Many a time hath banish'd Norfolk fought
　　For Jesu Christ in glorious Christian field,
　　Streaming the ensign of the Christian cross

95　　Against black Pagans, Turks, and Saracens;

　　And, toil'd with works of war, retir'd himself
　　To Italy; and there at Venice gave
　　His body to that pleasant country's earth,
　　And his pure soul unto his captain Christ,
　　Under whose colours he had fought so long.　　100

BOLINGBROKE　Why, Bishop, is Norfolk dead?

CARLISLE　As surely as I live, my lord.

BOLINGBROKE
　　Sweet peace conduct his sweet soul to the bosom
　　Of good old Abraham! Lords appellants,
　　Your differences shall all rest under gage　　105
　　Till we assign you to your days of trial.

Enter YORK.

YORK　Great Duke of Lancaster, I come to thee
　　From plume-pluck'd Richard, who with willing soul
　　Adopts thee heir, and his high sceptre yields
　　To the possession of thy royal hand.　　110
　　Ascend his throne, descending now from him,
　　And long live Henry, fourth of that name!

BOLINGBROKE
　　In God's name, I'll ascend the regal throne.

CARLISLE　Marry, God forbid!
　　Worst in this royal presence may I speak,　　115
　　Yet best beseeming me to speak the truth.
　　Would God that any in this noble presence
　　Were enough noble to be upright judge
　　Of noble Richard! then true noblesse would
　　Learn him forbearance from so foul a wrong.　　120
　　What subject can give sentence on his king?
　　And who sits here that is not Richard's subject?
　　Thieves are not judg'd but they are by to hear,
　　Although apparent guilt be seen in them,
　　And shall the figure of God's majesty,　　125
　　His captain, steward, deputy elect,
　　Anointed, crowned, planted many years,
　　Be judg'd by subject and inferior breath,
　　And he himself not present? O forfend it, God,
　　That in Christian climate souls refin'd　　130
　　Should show so heinous, black, obscene a deed!
　　I speak to subjects, and a subject speaks,
　　Stirr'd up by God thus boldly for his king.
　　My Lord of Herford here, whom you call king,
　　Is a foul traitor to proud Herford's king,　　135
　　And if you crown him, let me prophesy –
　　The blood of English shall manure the ground,
　　And future ages groan for this foul act,
　　Peace shall go sleep with Turks and infidels,
　　And, in this seat of peace, tumultuous wars　　140
　　Shall kin with kin, and kind with kind, confound.
　　Disorder, horror, fear, and mutiny,
　　Shall here inhabit, and this land be call'd
　　The field of Golgotha and dead men's skulls –
　　O, if you raise this house against this house,　　145
　　It will the woefullest division prove
　　That ever fell upon this cursed earth.
　　Prevent it, resist it, let it not be so,

690

Lest child, child's children, cry against you woe.
NORTHUMBERLAND
150 Well have you argued, sir, and, for your pains,
Of capital treason we arrest you here.
My Lord of Westminster, be it your charge
To keep him safely till his day of trial.
May it please you, lords, to grant the commons' suit?
BOLINGBROKE
155 Fetch hither Richard, that in common view
He may surrender; so we shall proceed
Without suspicion.
YORK   I will be his conduct.   *Exit.*
BOLINGBROKE
Lords, you that here are under our arrest,
Procure your sureties for your days of answer.
160 Little are we beholding to your love,
And little look'd for at your helping hands.

Re-enter YORK, *with* RICHARD, *and officers
bearing the regalia.*

RICHARD   Alack, why am I sent for to a king
Before I have shook off the regal thoughts
Wherewith I reign'd? I hardly yet have learn'd
165 To insinuate, flatter, bow, and bend my knee.
Give sorrow leave awhile to tutor me
To this submission. Yet I well remember
The favours of these men. Were they not mine?
Did they not sometime cry 'All hail!' to me?
170 So Judas did to Christ. But he, in twelve,
Found truth in all but one; I, in twelve thousand,
    none.
God save the king! Will no man say amen?
Am I both priest and clerk? well then, amen.
God save the king! although I be not he;
175 And yet, amen, if heaven do think him me.
To do what service am I sent for hither?
YORK   To do that office of thine own good will
Which tired majesty did make thee offer:
The resignation of thy state and crown
180 To Henry Bolingbroke.
RICHARD
Give me the crown. Here, cousin, seize the crown.
Here, cousin,
On this side my hand, and on that side thine.
Now is this golden crown like a deep well
185 That owes two buckets, filling one another,
The emptier ever dancing in the air,
The other down, unseen, and full of water.
That bucket down and full of tears am I,
Drinking my griefs, whilst you mount up on high.
BOLINGBROKE
190 I thought you had been willing to resign.
RICHARD   My crown I am, but still my griefs are mine.
You may my glories and my state depose,
But not my griefs; still am I king of those.
BOLINGBROKE
Part of your cares you give me with your crown.

RICHARD   Your cares set up do not pluck my cares down. 195
My care is loss of care, by old care done;
Your care is gain of care, by new care won.
The cares I give, I have, though given away,
They 'tend the crown, yet still with me they stay.
BOLINGBROKE
Are you contented to resign the crown?   200
RICHARD   Ay, no; no, ay; for I must nothing be.
Therefore no 'no', for I resign to thee.
Now, mark me how I will undo myself.
I give this heavy weight from off my head,
And this unwieldy sceptre from my hand,   205
The pride of kingly sway from out my heart;
With mine own tears I wash away my balm,
With mine own hands I give away my crown,
With mine own tongue deny my sacred state,
With mine own breath release all duteous oaths;   210
All pomp and majesty I do forswear;
My manors, rents, revenues, I forgo;
My acts, decrees, and statutes I deny.
God pardon all oaths that are broke to me,
God keep all vows unbroke are made to thee!   215
Make me, that nothing have, with nothing griev'd,
And thou with all pleas'd, that hast all achiev'd.
Long may'st thou live in Richard's seat to sit,
And soon lie Richard in an earthy pit.
God save King Henry, unking'd Richard says,   220
And send him many years of sunshine days!
What more remains?
NORTHUMBERLAND   No more; but that you read
These accusations, and these grievous crimes
Committed by your person and your followers
Against the state and profit of this land;   225
That, by confessing them, the souls of men
May deem that you are worthily depos'd.
RICHARD   Must I do so? and must I ravel out
My weav'd-up follies? Gentle Northumberland,
If thy offences were upon record,   230
Would it not shame thee, in so fair a troop,
To read a lecture of them? If thou wouldst,
There shouldst thou find one heinous article,
Containing the deposing of a king,
And cracking the strong warrant of an oath,   235
Mark'd with a blot, damn'd in the book of heaven.
Nay, all of you, that stand and look upon me
Whilst that my wretchedness doth bait myself,
Though some of you, with Pilate, wash your hands,
Showing an outward pity – yet you Pilates   240
Have here deliver'd me to my sour cross,
And water cannot wash away your sin.
NORTHUMBERLAND
My lord, dispatch, read o'er these articles.
RICHARD   Mine eyes are full of tears, I cannot see.
And yet salt water blinds them not so much   245
But they can see a sort of traitors here.
Nay, if I turn mine eyes upon myself,
I find myself a traitor with the rest.

For I have given here my soul's consent
250 T'undeck the pompous body of a king;
Made glory base, and sovereignty a slave;
Proud majesty a subject, state a peasant.
NORTHUMBERLAND   My lord –
RICHARD   No lord of thine, thou haught insulting man;
255 Nor no man's lord. I have no name, no title;
No, not that name was given me at the font,
But 'tis usurp'd. Alack the heavy day,
That I have worn so many winters out,
And know not now what name to call myself!
260 O that I were a mockery king of snow,
Standing before the sun of Bolingbroke,
To melt myself away in water-drops!
Good king, great king, and yet not greatly good,
And if my word be sterling yet in England,
265 Let it command a mirror hither straight,
That it may show me what a face I have
Since it is bankrupt of his majesty.
BOLINGBROKE
Go some of you, and fetch a looking-glass.
                    Exit an attendant.
NORTHUMBERLAND
Read o'er this paper while the glass doth come.
270 RICHARD   Fiend, thou torments me ere I come to hell.
BOLINGBROKE
Urge it no more, my Lord Northumberland.
NORTHUMBERLAND
The commons will not then be satisfi'd.
RICHARD   They shall be satisfi'd. I'll read enough
When I do see the very book indeed
275 Where all my sins are writ, and that's myself.

Enter one with a glass.

Give me that glass, and therein will I read.
No deeper wrinkles yet? hath sorrow struck
So many blows upon this face of mine
And made no deeper wounds? O flatt'ring glass,
280 Like to my followers in prosperity,
Thou dost beguile me. Was this face the face
That every day under his household roof
Did keep ten thousand men? Was this the face
That like the sun did make beholders wink?
285 Is this the face which fac'd so many follies,
That was at last out-fac'd by Bolingbroke?
A brittle glory shineth in this face;
As brittle as the glory is the face,
[*Dashes the glass against the ground.*]
For there it is, crack'd in an hundred shivers.
290 Mark, silent king, the moral of this sport –
How soon my sorrow hath destroy'd my face.
BOLINGBROKE
The shadow of your sorrow hath destroy'd
The shadow of your face.
RICHARD   Say that again.
The shadow of my sorrow? ha! let's see –
295 'Tis very true, my grief lies all within,

And these external manners of lament
Are merely shadows to the unseen grief
That swells with silence in the tortur'd soul.
There lies the substance. And I thank thee, king,
For thy great bounty, that not only giv'st   300
Me cause to wail, but teachest me the way
How to lament the cause. I'll beg one boon,
And then be gone, and trouble you no more.
Shall I obtain it?
BOLINGBROKE   Name it, fair cousin.
RICHARD   Fair cousin! I am greater than a king;   305
For when I was a king, my flatterers
Were then but subjects; being now a subject,
I have a king here to my flatterer.
Being so great, I have no need to beg.
BOLINGBROKE   Yet ask.   310
RICHARD   And shall I have?
BOLINGBROKE   You shall.
RICHARD   Then give me leave to go.
BOLINGBROKE   Whither?
RICHARD
Whither you will, so I were from your sights.   315
BOLINGBROKE
Go some of you, convey him to the Tower.
RICHARD   O, good! Convey! Conveyers are you all,
That rise thus nimbly by a true king's fall.
                    Exeunt Richard and Guard.
BOLINGBROKE
On Wednesday next we solemnly set down
Our coronation. Lords, prepare yourselves.   320
          Exeunt all except the Bishop of Carlisle,
               the Abbot of Westminster and Aumerle.
ABBOT   A woeful pageant have we here beheld.
CARLISLE   The woe's to come; the children yet unborn
Shall feel this day as sharp to them as thorn.
AUMERLE   You holy clergymen, is there no plot
To rid the realm of this pernicious blot?   325
ABBOT   My lord,
Before I freely speak my mind herein,
You shall not only take the sacrament
To bury mine intents, but also to effect
Whatever I shall happen to devise.   330
I see your brows are full of discontent,
Your hearts of sorrow, and your eyes of tears.
Come home with me to supper; I will lay
A plot shall show us all a merry day.   *Exeunt*

5.1   *Enter the* QUEEN *with her attendants.*

QUEEN   This way the king will come; this is the way
To Julius Caesar's ill-erected tower,
To whose flint bosom my condemned lord
Is doom'd a prisoner by proud Bolingbroke.
Here let us rest, if this rebellious earth   5
Have any resting for her true king's queen.

Enter RICHARD *and guard.*

But soft, but see, or rather do not see,
My fair rose wither – yet look up, behold,
That you in pity may dissolve to dew,
And wash him fresh again with true-love tears.   10
Ah, thou, the model where old Troy did stand!
Thou map of honour, thou King Richard's tomb,
And not King Richard! Thou most beauteous inn,
Why should hard-favour'd grief be lodg'd in thee,
When triumph is become an alehouse guest?   15

RICHARD   Join not with grief, fair woman, do not so,
To make my end too sudden. Learn, good soul,
To think our former state a happy dream;
From which awak'd, the truth of what we are
Shows us but this. I am sworn brother, sweet,   20
To grim Necessity, and he and I
Will keep a league till death. Hie thee to France
And cloister thee in some religious house.
Our holy lives must win a new world's crown
Which our profane hours here have thrown down.   25

QUEEN   What, is my Richard both in shape and mind
Transform'd and weak'ned? hath Bolingbroke
      depos'd
Thine intellect? hath he been in thy heart?
The lion dying thrusteth forth his paw
And wounds the earth, if nothing else, with rage   30
To be o'erpow'r'd, and wilt thou, pupil-like,
Take the correction mildly, kiss the rod,
And fawn on rage with base humility,
Which art a lion and the king of beasts?

RICHARD   A king of beasts, indeed – if aught but beasts,   35
I had been still a happy king of men.
Good sometimes queen, prepare thee hence for
      France.
Think I am dead, and that even here thou takest,
As from my death-bed, thy last living leave.
In winter's tedious nights sit by the fire   40
With good old folks, and let them tell thee tales
Of woeful ages long ago betid;
And ere thou bid good night, to quite their griefs
Tell thou the lamentable tale of me,
And send the hearers weeping to their beds;   45
For why, the senseless brands will sympathize
The heavy accent of thy moving tongue,
And in compassion weep the fire out,
And some will mourn in ashes, some coal-black,
For the deposing of a rightful king.   50

Enter NORTHUMBERLAND.

NORTHUMBERLAND
My lord, the mind of Bolingbroke is chang'd;
You must to Pomfret, not unto the Tower.
And, madam, there is order ta'en for you:
With all swift speed you must away to France.

RICHARD   Northumberland, thou ladder wherewithal   55
The mounting Bolingbroke ascends my throne,
The time shall not be many hours of age
More than it is, ere foul sin gathering head

Shall break into corruption: thou shalt think,
Though he divide the realm and give thee half,   60
It is too little, helping him to all;
He shall think that thou, which knowest the way
To plant unrightful kings, wilt know again,
Being ne'er so little urg'd, another way
To pluck him headlong from the usurped throne.   65
The love of wicked men converts to fear,
That fear to hate, and hate turns one or both
To worthy danger and deserved death.

NORTHUMBERLAND
My guilt be on my head, and there an end.
Take leave and part, for you must part forthwith.   70

RICHARD   Doubly divorc'd! Bad men, you violate
A two-fold marriage – 'twixt my crown and me,
And then betwixt me and my married wife.
Let me unkiss the oath 'twixt thee and me;
And yet not so, for with a kiss 'twas made.   75
Part us, Northumberland: I towards the north,
Where shivering cold and sickness pines the clime;
My wife to France, from whence set forth in pomp,
She came adorned hither like sweet May,
Sent back like Hollowmas or short'st of day.   80

QUEEN   And must we be divided? must we part?

RICHARD
Ay, hand from hand, my love, and heart from heart.

QUEEN   Banish us both, and send the king with me.

NORTHUMBERLAND
That were some love, but little policy.

QUEEN   Then whither he goes, thither let me go.   85

RICHARD   So two, together weeping, make one woe.
Weep thou for me in France, I for thee here;
Better far off than, near, be ne'er the near.
Go count thy way with sighs; I mine with groans.

QUEEN   So longest way shall have the longest moans.   90

RICHARD
Twice for one step I'll groan, the way being short,
And piece the way out with a heavy heart.
Come, come, in wooing sorrow let's be brief,
Since, wedding it, there is such length in grief:
One kiss shall stop our mouths, and dumbly part;   95
Thus give I mine, and thus take I thy heart.

QUEEN   Give me mine own again; 'twere no good part
To take on me to keep and kill thy heart.
So, now I have mine own again, be gone,
That I may strive to kill it with a groan.   100

RICHARD   We make woe wanton with this fond delay.
Once more, adieu; the rest let sorrow say.   *Exeunt.*

5.2   *Enter* DUKE OF YORK *and the* DUCHESS.

DUCHESS OF YORK
My lord, you told me you would tell the rest,
When weeping made you break the story off,
Of our two cousins' coming into London.

YORK   Where did I leave?

DUCHESS OF YORK   At that sad stop, my lord,

5   Where rude misgoverned hands from windows' tops
     Threw dust and rubbish on King Richard's head.
YORK   Then, as I said, the Duke, great Bolingbroke,
     Mounted upon a hot and fiery steed
     Which his aspiring rider seem'd to know,
10   With slow but stately pace kept on his course,
     Whilst all tongues cried 'God save thee,
        Bolingbroke!'
     You would have thought the very windows spake,
     So many greedy looks of young and old
     Through casements darted their desiring eyes
15   Upon his visage; and that all the walls
     With painted imagery had said at once
     'Jesu preserve thee! Welcome, Bolingbroke!'
     Whilst he, from one side to the other turning,
     Bare-headed, lower than his proud steed's neck,
20   Bespake them thus, 'I thank you, countrymen'.
     And thus still doing, thus he pass'd along.
DUCHESS OF YORK
     Alack, poor Richard! where rode he the whilst?
YORK   As in a theatre the eyes of men,
     After a well-grac'd actor leaves the stage,
25   Are idly bent on him that enters next,
     Thinking his prattle to be tedious;
     Even so, or with much more contempt, men's eyes
     Did scowl on Richard. No man cried 'God save him!'
     No joyful tongue gave him his welcome home,
30   But dust was thrown upon his sacred head;
     Which with such gentle sorrow he shook off,
     His face still combating with tears and smiles,
     The badges of his grief and patience,
     That had not God for some strong purpose steel'd
35   The hearts of men, they must perforce have melted,
     And barbarism itself have pitied him.
     But heaven hath a hand in these events,
     To whose high will we bound our calm contents.
     To Bolingbroke are we sworn subjects now,
40   Whose state and honour I for aye allow.

                    Enter AUMERLE.

DUCHESS OF YORK   Here comes my son Aumerle.
YORK   Aumerle that was,
     But that is lost for being Richard's friend,
     And, madam, you must call him Rutland now.
     I am in parliament pledge for his truth
45   And lasting fealty to the new-made king.
DUCHESS OF YORK
     Welcome, my son. Who are the violets now
     That strew the green lap of the new-come spring?
AUMERLE   Madam, I know not, nor I greatly care not;
     God knows I had as lief be none as one.
50   YORK   Well, bear you well in this new spring of time,
     Lest you be cropp'd before you come to prime.
     What news from Oxford? Do these justs and
        triumphs hold?
AUMERLE   For aught I know, my lord, they do.
YORK   You will be there, I know.

AUMERLE   If God prevent it not, I purpose so.   55
YORK   What seal is that that hangs without thy bosom?
     Yea, look'st thou pale? Let me see the writing.
AUMERLE   My lord, 'tis nothing.
YORK   No matter, then, who see it.
     I will be satisfied; let me see the writing.
AUMERLE   I do beseech your grace to pardon me;   60
     It is a matter of small consequence,
     Which for some reasons I would not have seen.
YORK   Which for some reasons, sir, I mean to see.
     I fear, I fear –
DUCHESS OF YORK   What should you fear?
     'Tis nothing but some band that he is ent'red into   65
     For gay apparel 'gainst the triumph day.
YORK   Bound to himself? What doth he with a bond
     That he is bound to? Wife, thou art a fool.
     Boy, let me see the writing.
AUMERLE
     I do beseech you, pardon me; I may not show it.   70
YORK   I will be satisfied; let me see it, I say.
     [*He plucks it out of his bosom and reads it.*]
     Treason, foul treason! Villain! Traitor! Slave!
DUCHESS OF YORK   What is the matter, my lord?
YORK   Ho, who is within there? Saddle my horse!
     God for his mercy! What treachery is here!   75
DUCHESS OF YORK   Why, what is it, my lord?
YORK   Give me my boots, I say! Saddle my horse!
     Now by mine honour, by my life, by my troth,
     I will appeach the villain.
DUCHESS OF YORK   What is the matter?
YORK   Peace, foolish woman.   80
DUCHESS OF YORK
     I will not peace. What is the matter, Aumerle?
AUMERLE   Good mother, be content – it is no more
     Than my poor life must answer.
DUCHESS OF YORK   Thy life answer!
YORK   Bring me my boots: I will unto the king.

                His man enters with his boots.

DUCHESS OF YORK
     Strike him, Aumerle. Poor boy, thou art amaz'd.   85
     Hence, villain! never more come in my sight.
YORK   Give me my boots, I say.
DUCHESS OF YORK   Why, York, what wilt thou do?
     Wilt thou not hide the trespass of thine own?
     Have we more sons? Or are we like to have?   90
     Is not my teeming date drunk up with time?
     And wilt thou pluck my fair son from mine age
     And rob me of a happy mother's name?
     Is he not like thee? Is he not thine own?
YORK   Thou fond mad woman,   95
     Wilt thou conceal this dark conspiracy?
     A dozen of them here have ta'en the sacrament,
     And interchangeably set down their hands
     To kill the king at Oxford.
DUCHESS OF YORK   He shall be none;
     We'll keep him here, then what is that to him?   100

YORK   Away, fond woman! were he twenty times my son
  I would appeach him.
DUCHESS OF YORK   Had'st thou groan'd for him
  As I have done, thou wouldst be more pitiful.
  But now I know thy mind: thou dost suspect
  That I have been disloyal to thy bed,
  And that he is a bastard, not thy son.
  Sweet York, sweet husband, be not of that mind;
  He is as like thee as a man may be,
  Not like to me, or any of my kin,
  And yet I love him.
YORK   Make way, unruly woman! *Exit.*
DUCHESS OF YORK
  After, Aumerle! Mount thee upon his horse,
  Spur post, and get before him to the king,
  And beg thy pardon ere he do accuse thee.
  I'll not be long behind – though I be old,
  I doubt not but to ride as fast as York;
  And never will I rise up from the ground
  Till Bolingbroke have pardoned thee. Away, be gone.
                    Exeunt.

5.3   *Enter* BOLINGBROKE, PERCY *and other lords.*

BOLINGBROKE   Can no man tell me of my unthrifty son?
  'Tis full three months since I did see him last.
  If any plague hang over us, 'tis he.
  I would to God, my lords, he might be found.
  Inquire at London, 'mongst the taverns there,
  For there, they say, he daily doth frequent
  With unrestrained loose companions,
  Even such, they say, as stand in narrow lanes
  And beat our watch and rob our passengers,
  While he, young wanton, and effeminate boy,
  Takes on the point of honour to support
  So dissolute a crew.
PERCY   My lord, some two days since I saw the prince,
  And told him of those triumphs held at Oxford.
BOLINGBROKE   And what said the gallant?
PERCY   His answer was, he would unto the stews,
  And from the common'st creature pluck a glove,
  And wear it as a favour; and with that
  He would unhorse the lustiest challenger.
BOLINGBROKE   As dissolute as desperate! But yet
  Through both I see some sparks of better hope,
  Which elder years may happily bring forth.
  But who comes here?

    Enter AUMERLE, *amazed.*

AUMERLE   Where is the king?
BOLINGBROKE   What means
  Our cousin, that he stares and looks so wildly?
AUMERLE
  God save your grace! I do beseech your Majesty
  To have some conference with your grace alone.
BOLINGBROKE
  Withdraw yourselves, and leave us here alone.
              Exeunt Percy and lords.

What is the matter with our cousin now?
AUMERLE   For ever may my knees grow to the earth,
  My tongue cleave to my roof within my mouth,
  Unless a pardon ere I rise or speak.
BOLINGBROKE   Intended, or committed, was this fault?
  If on the first, how heinous e'er it be,
  To win thy after-love I pardon thee.
AUMERLE   Then give me leave that I may turn the key,
  That no man enter till my tale be done.
BOLINGBROKE   Have thy desire.
  [*The Duke of York knocks at the door and crieth.*]
YORK   My liege, beware; look to thyself;
  Thou hast a traitor in thy presence there.
BOLINGBROKE   I'll make thee safe. [*Draws his sword.*]
AUMERLE   Stay thy revengeful hand,
  Thou hast no cause to fear.
YORK   Open the door,
  Secure, foolhardy king. Shall I, for love,
  Speak treason to thy face? Open the door,
  Or I will break it open.

    Enter YORK.

BOLINGBROKE   Uncle, speak,
  Recover breath, tell us how near is danger
  That we may arm us to encounter it.
YORK   Peruse this writing here, and thou shalt know
  The treason that my haste forbids me show.
AUMERLE
  Remember, as thou read'st, thy promise pass'd;
  I do repent me, read not my name there,
  My heart is not confederate with my hand.
YORK   It was, villain, ere thy hand did set it down.
  I tore it from the traitor's bosom, king;
  Fear, and not love, begets his penitence.
  Forget to pity him, lest thy pity prove
  A serpent that will sting thee to the heart.
BOLINGBROKE   O heinous, strong, and bold conspiracy!
  O loyal father of a treacherous son!
  Thou sheer, immaculate and silver fountain,
  From whence this stream, through muddy passages,
  Hath held his current and defil'd himself,
  Thy overflow of good converts to bad;
  And thy abundant goodness shall excuse
  This deadly blot in thy digressing son.
YORK   So shall my virtue be his vice's bawd,
  And he shall spend mine honour with his shame,
  As thriftless sons their scraping fathers' gold.
  Mine honour lives when his dishonour dies,
  Or my sham'd life in his dishonour lies;
  Thou kill'st me in his life – giving him breath,
  The traitor lives, the true man's put to death.
DUCHESS OF YORK [*within*]
  What ho, my liege, for God's sake, let me in!
BOLINGBROKE
  What shrill-voic'd suppliant makes this eager cry?
DUCHESS OF YORK
  A woman, and thine aunt, great king, – 'tis I.

75   Speak with me, pity me, open the door,
      A beggar begs that never begg'd before.
      BOLINGBROKE
      Our scene is alt'red from a serious thing,
      And now chang'd to 'The Beggar and the King'.
      My dangerous cousin, let your mother in;
80   I know she's come to pray for your foul sin.
      YORK   If thou do pardon, whosoever pray,
      More sins for this forgiveness prosper may.
      This fest'red joint cut off, the rest rest sound;
      This, let alone, will all the rest confound.

                    Enter DUCHESS.

      DUCHESS OF YORK
85   O king, believe not this hard-hearted man!
      Love loving not itself none other can.
      YORK   Thou frantic woman, what dost thou make here?
      Shall thy old dugs once more a traitor rear?
      DUCHESS OF YORK
      Sweet York, be patient. Hear me, gentle liege.
      BOLINGBROKE   Rise up, good aunt.
90   DUCHESS OF YORK   Not yet, I thee beseech:
      For ever will I walk upon my knees,
      And never see day that the happy sees
      Till thou give joy – until thou bid me joy,
      By pardoning Rutland my transgressing boy.
95   AUMERLE   Unto my mother's prayers I bend my knee.
      YORK   Against them both my true joints bended be.
      Ill may'st thou thrive if thou grant any grace!
      DUCHESS OF YORK
      Pleads he in earnest? Look upon his face.
      His eyes do drop no tears, his prayers are in jest,
      His words come from his mouth, ours from our
100   breast;
      He prays but faintly and would be denied,
      We pray with heart and soul, and all beside;
      His weary joints would gladly rise, I know;
      Our knees still kneel till to the ground they grow;
105   His prayers are full of false hypocrisy,
      Ours of true zeal and deep integrity;
      Our prayers do outpray his – then let them have
      That mercy which true prayer ought to have.
      BOLINGBROKE   Good aunt, stand up.
      DUCHESS OF YORK   Nay, do not say 'stand up';
110   Say 'pardon' first, and afterwards 'stand up'.
      And if I were thy nurse, thy tongue to teach,
      'Pardon' should be the first word of thy speech.
      I never long'd to hear a word till now;
      Say 'pardon', king, let pity teach thee how;
115   The word is short, but not so short as sweet;
      No word like 'pardon' for kings' mouths so meet.
      YORK   Speak it in French, king, say 'pardonne moy'.
      DUCHESS OF YORK
      Dost thou teach pardon pardon to destroy?
      Ah, my sour husband, my hard-hearted lord,
120   That sets the word itself against the word!
      Speak 'pardon' as 'tis current in our land,

      The chopping French we do not understand.
      Thine eye begins to speak, set thy tongue there;
      Or in thy piteous heart plant thou thine ear,
      That, hearing how our plaints and prayers do pierce,   125
      Pity may move thee 'pardon' to rehearse.
      BOLINGBROKE   Good aunt, stand up.
      DUCHESS OF YORK   I do not sue to stand.
      Pardon is all the suit I have in hand.
      BOLINGBROKE   I pardon him, as God shall pardon me.
      DUCHESS OF YORK
      O happy vantage of a kneeling knee!   130
      Yet am I sick for fear – speak it again:
      Twice saying 'pardon' doth not pardon twain,
      But makes one pardon strong.
      BOLINGBROKE   With all my heart
      I pardon him.
      DUCHESS OF YORK   A god on earth thou art.
      BOLINGBROKE
      But for our trusty brother-in-law and the abbot,   135
      With all the rest of that consorted crew,
      Destruction straight shall dog them at the heels.
      Good uncle, help to order several powers
      To Oxford, or where'er these traitors are.
      They shall not live within this world, I swear,   140
      But I will have them, if I once know where.
      Uncle, farewell; and cousin too, adieu:
      Your mother well hath pray'd, and prove you true.
      DUCHESS OF YORK
      Come, my old son, I pray God make thee new.
                                            Exeunt.

5.4   *Enter* EXTON *and* Servants.

      EXTON
      Didst thou not mark the king, what words he spake?
      'Have I no friend will rid me of this living fear?'
      Was it not so?
      SERVANT   These were his very words.
      EXTON
      'Have I no friend?' quoth he. He spake it twice,
      And urg'd it twice together, did he not?   5
      SERVANT   He did.
      EXTON   And, speaking it, he wishtly look'd on me,
      As who should say 'I would thou wert the man
      That would divorce this terror from my heart',
      Meaning the king at Pomfret. Come, let's go.   10
      I am the king's friend, and will rid his foe.   *Exeunt.*

5.5   *Enter* RICHARD *alone.*

      RICHARD   I have been studying how I may compare
      This prison where I live unto the world;
      And, for because the world is populous
      And here is not a creature but myself,
      I cannot do it. Yet I'll hammer it out.   5
      My brain I'll prove the female to my soul,
      My soul the father, and these two beget
      A generation of still-breeding thoughts,

And these same thoughts people this little world,
In humours like the people of this world;
For no thought is contented. The better sort,
As thoughts of things divine, are intermix'd
With scruples, and do set the word itself
Against the word,
As thus: 'Come, little ones'; and then again,
'It is as hard to come as for a camel
To thread the postern of a small needle's eye'.
Thoughts tending to ambition, they do plot
Unlikely wonders: how these vain weak nails
May tear a passage thorough the flinty ribs
Of this hard world, my ragged prison walls;
And for they cannot, die in their own pride.
Thoughts tending to content flatter themselves
That they are not the first of fortune's slaves,
Nor shall not be the last – like silly beggars
Who, sitting in the stocks, refuge their shame,
That many have and others must sit there;
And in this thought they find a kind of ease,
Bearing their own misfortunes on the back
Of such as have before indur'd the like.
Thus play I in one person many people,
And none contented. Sometimes am I king,
Then treasons make me wish myself a beggar,
And so I am. Then crushing penury
Persuades me I was better when a king;
Then am I king'd again, and by and by
Think that I am unking'd by Bolingbroke,
And straight am nothing. But whate'er I be,
Nor I, nor any man that but man is,
With nothing shall be pleas'd, till he be eas'd
With being nothing.   [*The music plays.*]
        Music do I hear?
Ha, ha! keep time – how sour sweet music is
When time is broke and no proportion kept!
So is it in the music of men's lives.
And here have I the daintiness of ear
To check time broke in a disordered string;
But for the concord of my state and time,
Had not an ear to hear my true time broke:
I wasted time, and now doth time waste me;
For now hath time made me his numb'ring clock;
My thoughts are minutes, and with sighs they jar
Their watches on unto mine eyes, the outward
        watch,
Whereto my finger, like a dial's point,
Is pointing still, in cleansing them from tears.
Now sir, the sound that tells what hour it is
Are clamorous groans which strike upon my heart,
Which is the bell – so sighs, and tears, and groans,
Show minutes, times, and hours. But my time
Runs posting on in Bolingbroke's proud joy,
While I stand fooling here, his Jack of the clock.
This music mads me. Let it sound no more;
For though it have holp mad men to their wits,
In me it seems it will make wise men mad.

Yet blessing on his heart that gives it me,
For 'tis a sign of love; and love to Richard   65
Is a strange brooch in this all-hating world.

        Enter a Groom *of the stable.*

GROOM   Hail, royal prince!
RICHARD   Thanks, noble peer;
    The cheapest of us is ten groats too dear.
    What art thou? and how comest thou hither,
    Where no man never comes, but that sad dog   70
    That brings me food to make misfortune live?
GROOM   I was a poor groom of thy stable, king,
    When thou wert king; who, travelling towards York,
    With much ado at length have gotten leave
    To look upon my sometimes royal master's face.   75
    O, how it ern'd my heart when I beheld
    In London streets that coronation day
    When Bolingbroke rode on roan Barbary –
    That horse that thou so often hast bestrid,
    That horse that I so carefully have dress'd!   80
RICHARD   Rode he on Barbary? Tell me, gentle friend,
    How went he under him?
GROOM   So proudly as if he disdain'd the ground.
RICHARD   So proud that Bolingbroke was on his back!
    That jade hath eat bread from my royal hand;   85
    This hand hath made him proud with clapping him.
    Would he not stumble? would he not fall down,
    Since pride must have a fall, and break the neck
    Of that proud man that did usurp his back?
    Forgiveness, horse! why do I rail on thee,   90
    Since thou, created to be aw'd by man,
    Wast born to bear? I was not made a horse,
    And yet I bear a burthen like an ass,
    Spurr'd, gall'd, and tir'd by jauncing Bolingbroke.

        Enter One *to Richard with meat.*

KEEPER   Fellow, give place; here is no longer stay.   95
RICHARD   If thou love me, 'tis time thou wert away.
GROOM
    What my tongue dares not, that my heart shall say.
                                Exit Groom.
KEEPER   My lord, will't please you to fall to?
RICHARD   Taste of it first as thou art wont to do.
KEEPER   My lord, I dare not. Sir Pierce of Exton, who   100
    lately came from the king, commands the contrary.
RICHARD   The devil take Henry of Lancaster, and thee!
    Patience is stale, and I am weary of it.
    [*Strikes the Keeper.*]
KEEPER   Help, help, help!

        The Murderers *rush in.*

RICHARD
    How now! what means death in this rude assault?   105
    Villain, thy own hand yields thy death's instrument.
    Go thou and fill another room in hell.
    [*Here Exton strikes him down.*]
    That hand shall burn in never-quenching fire

That staggers thus my person. Exton, thy fierce
　　hand
Hath with the king's blood stain'd the king's own
110　　land.
Mount, mount, my soul! thy seat is up on high,
Whilst my gross flesh sinks downward, here to die.
[*Dies.*]

EXTON　　As full of valour as of royal blood.
Both have I spill'd; O would the deed were good!
115 For now the devil that told me I did well
Says that this deed is chronicled in hell.
This dead king to the living king I'll bear.
Take hence the rest, and give them burial here.
　　　　　　　　　　　　　　　　　　　　Exeunt.

5.6　　　*Flourish. Enter* BOLINGBROKE, YORK,
　　　　　　with other lords and attendants.

BOLINGBROKE
Kind uncle York, the latest news we hear,
Is that the rebels have consum'd with fire
Our town of Ciceter in Gloucestershire,
But whether they be ta'en or slain we hear not.

　　　　　　Enter NORTHUMBERLAND.

5 Welcome, my lord; what is the news?
NORTHUMBERLAND
First, to thy sacred state wish I all happiness.
The next news is, I have to London sent
The heads of Salisbury, Spencer, Blunt and Kent:
The manner of their taking may appear
10 At large discoursed in this paper here.
BOLINGBROKE
We thank thee, gentle Percy, for thy pains,
And to thy worth will add right worthy gains.

　　　　　　Enter FITZWATER.

FITZWATER
My lord, I have from Oxford sent to London
The heads of Broccas and Sir Bennet Seely,
15 Two of the dangerous consorted traitors
That sought at Oxford thy dire overthrow.

BOLINGBROKE　　Thy pains, Fitzwater, shall not be forgot;
Right noble is thy merit, well I wot.

　　　　Enter PERCY *and the* Bishop of CARLISLE.

PERCY　　The grand conspirator, Abbot of Westminster,
With clog of conscience and sour melancholy 20
Hath yielded up his body to the grave.
But here is Carlisle living, to abide
Thy kingly doom and sentence of his pride.
BOLINGBROKE　　Carlisle, this is your doom:
Choose out some secret place, some reverend room, 25
More than thou hast, and with it joy thy life.
So as thou liv'st in peace, die free from strife;
For though mine enemy thou hast ever been,
High sparks of honour in thee have I seen.

　　　　　Enter EXTON *with the coffin.*

EXTON　　Great king, within this coffin I present 30
Thy buried fear. Herein all breathless lies
The mightiest of thy greatest enemies,
Richard of Burdeaux, by me hither brought.
BOLINGBROKE
Exton, I thank thee not, for thou hast wrought
A deed of slander with thy fatal hand 35
Upon my head and all this famous land.
EXTON
From your own mouth, my lord, did I this deed
BOLINGBROKE
They love not poison that do poison need,
Nor do I thee. Though I did wish him dead,
I hate the murtherer, love him murthered. 40
The guilt of conscience take thou for thy labour,
But neither my good word nor princely favour;
With Cain go wander thorough shades of night,
And never show thy head by day nor light.
Lords, I protest my soul is full of woe 45
That blood should sprinkle me to make me grow.
Come mourn with me for what I do lament,
And put on sullen black incontinent.
I'll make a voyage to the Holy Land,
To wash this blood off from my guilty hand. 50
March sadly after; grace my mournings here
In weeping after this untimely bier.　　　　*Exeunt.*

King Richard III

King Richard III was an early bestseller. Published first in 1597 as *The Tragedy of King Richard the Third*, it was reprinted five times before it appeared as the ninth of the histories in the First Folio in 1623. The Folio text differs significantly from the Quartos, including about 230 lines absent from them and cutting about 50 that they do print. The relation between the Quarto and Folio texts is complex: roughnesses in the Quarto have suggested either that it is based on a reconstruction of the play by actors or that it derives from an incompletely revised authorial draft; the Folio made use of the third and sixth Quartos (1602, 1622), but corrected them from an independent manuscript of a more complete and tidier version. Modern editions tend to be based on the Folio, while adopting some readings from the Quarto text, but *Richard III* remains among the most perplexing of Shakespearean textual puzzles.

Richard III is the earliest English play to have had continuous success on stage from its first performance to the present day. Frequent references indicate its popularity in Shakespeare's time, when the title-role was taken by Richard Burbage. It was performed at Court on 16 November 1633. After the Restoration it retained its popularity, after 1700 in an adaptation by Colley Cibber, including lines from Shakespeare's other histories, which held the stage until Henry Irving restored Shakespeare's text for his 1877 production. Some of Cibber's 'improvements' endured (a few can still be heard in Laurence Olivier's 1955 film version).

The play's popularity derives from the outrageous wickedness of its title character. Richard is a star role irresistible to actors: always aware of his own impressive theatricality, he delights himself as much as the audience with his virtuosity and range. He plays the concerned brother, the good-natured uncle, the pious student, the passionate lover. This last is the most audacious, as the misshapen Richard sets out to seduce Lady Anne, whose husband and father-in-law he has murdered. After his success, he shares the audience's amazement: 'Was ever woman in this humour woo'd? / Was ever woman in this humour won?'

Shakespeare did not invent the character of the villainous Richard. About 1516, Sir Thomas More wrote an unfinished *History of Richard III*, which was appropriated by chroniclers and forms part of the account of Richard's reign in Edward Hall's *Union of the Two Noble and Illustre Families of Lancaster and York* (1548) and the *Chronicles* of Raphael Holinshed (1577, second edition 1587). Shakespeare dramatizes More's deformed villain, a monstrous tyrant with a self-dramatizing will to power. More provides much of the ironic action and commentary concerning Edward IV, Buckingham and Hastings, but the unhistorical roles of Queen Margaret (dead in exile before Richard became king) and Lady Anne (Richard's wife of many years and mother of his only son) are Shakespeare's invention.

Already in Shakespeare's time some questioned the accuracy of this portrait of Richard. In 1617 Sir William Cornwallis offered his paradoxical 'Praise of King Richard III', bemoaning the 'malicious credulity' of 'witty playmakers' who had unfairly denigrated the King's character and achievement. The effort to rehabilitate Richard continues today (including, in popular form, a fine detective novel, Josephine Tey's *The Daughter of Time*). His defenders insist – despite evidence dating from his own lifetime of suspicion that Richard had had his nephews murdered in the Tower – that the blackening of Richard's character is the result of a Tudor conspiracy designed to legitimize Henry VII's path to the throne. Some of the myth was undoubtedly so motivated: a coronation portrait of Richard shows no sign of his alleged deformity, which can be traced to a hostile early chronicler, and he was not implicated in the death of Clarence.

Shakespeare's acceptance of the legitimacy of Edward IV and his sons shows that he was no propagandist for the Tudors, though the play does confirm the providential vision of English history in which Henry Richmond's victory at Bosworth in 1485 (and his inauguration of the Tudor dynasty) is seen as divine deliverance of England from Richard's evil, which was itself punishment for the nation's sins. Far more important, though, for Shakespeare than these Tudor orthodoxies is the role of Richard himself, a charismatic villain who candidly shares his thoughts with us as he contrives and dominates the action.

The Arden text is based on the 1623 First Folio, with some readings from the 1597 First Quarto.

RICHARD, Duke of Gloucester, later KING RICHARD III

The Duke of CLARENCE — *his brother (later, his GHOST)*

Sir Robert BRAKENBURY — *Lieutenant of the Tower*

Lord HASTINGS — *the Lord Chamberlain (later, his GHOST)*

Lady ANNE — *widow of Edward, Prince of Wales (later, her GHOST)*

TRESSEL
BERKELEY — } *Gentlemen attending Lady Anne*

QUEEN ELIZABETH — *wife of King Edward IV*

Lord RIVERS — *her brother (later, his GHOST)*

Lord GREY — *her son (later, his GHOST)*

The Marquess of DORSET — *her son*

The Duke of BUCKINGHAM — *(later, his GHOST)*

STANLEY, Earl of Derby

QUEEN MARGARET — *widow of King Henry VI*

Sir William CATESBY

Two MURDERERS

The KEEPER *of the Tower*

KING EDWARD IV

Sir Richard RATCLIFFE

The DUCHESS of York — *mother of Richard, Edward IV, and Clarence*

BOY
GIRL — } *Clarence's children*

Three CITIZENS

ARCHBISHOP *of York*

Richard, the Duke of YORK — *younger son of King Edward IV (later, his GHOST)*

PRINCE Edward, Prince of Wales — *elder son of King Edward IV (later, his GHOST)*

Lord CARDINAL Bourchier — *Archbishop of Canterbury*

Lord MAYOR *of London*

HASTINGS, *a* PURSUIVANT

PRIEST

Sir Thomas VAUGHAN — *(later, his GHOST)*

The Bishop of ELY, *John Morton*

The Duke of NORFOLK

Lord LOVELL

SCRIVENER

Two Bishops (Shaa and Penker)

PAGE

Sir James TYRREL

Seven MESSENGERS

CHRISTOPHER Urswick — *a priest*

SHERIFF — *of Wiltshire*

The Earl of RICHMOND — *afterwards King Henry VII*

The Earl of OXFORD

Sir James BLUNT

Sir Walter HERBERT

The Earl of SURREY

Sir William BRANDON

GHOST OF EDWARD — *Prince of Wales, son of Henry VI*

GHOST OF KING HENRY VI

Guards, Halberdiers, Gentlemen, Lords, Citizens, Attendants, Soldiers

King Richard III

1.1 *Enter* RICHARD, DUKE OF GLOUCESTER, *alone.*

RICHARD   Now is the winter of our discontent
Made glorious summer by this son of York;
And all the clouds that lour'd upon our House
In the deep bosom of the ocean buried.
Now are our brows bound with victorious wreaths,
Our bruised arms hung up for monuments,
Our stern alarums chang'd to merry meetings,
Our dreadful marches to delightful measures.
Grim-visag'd War hath smooth'd his wrinkled front:
And now, instead of mounting barbed steeds
To fright the souls of fearful adversaries,
He capers nimbly in a lady's chamber,
To the lascivious pleasing of a lute.
But I, that am not shap'd for sportive tricks,
Nor made to court an amorous looking-glass;
I, that am rudely stamp'd, and want love's majesty
To strut before a wanton ambling nymph:
I, that am curtail'd of this fair proportion,
Cheated of feature by dissembling Nature,
Deform'd, unfinish'd, sent before my time
Into this breathing world scarce half made up –
And that so lamely and unfashionable
That dogs bark at me, as I halt by them –
Why, I, in this weak piping time of peace,
Have no delight to pass away the time,
Unless to spy my shadow in the sun,
And descant on mine own deformity.
And therefore, since I cannot prove a lover
To entertain these fair well-spoken days,
I am determined to prove a villain,
And hate the idle pleasures of these days.
Plots have I laid, inductions dangerous,
By drunken prophecies, libels, and dreams,
To set my brother Clarence and the King
In deadly hate, the one against the other:
And if King Edward be as true and just
As I am subtle, false, and treacherous,
This day should Clarence closely be mew'd up
About a prophecy, which says that 'G'
Of Edward's heirs the murderer shall be –
Dive, thoughts, down to my soul: here Clarence
    comes.

Enter CLARENCE *and* BRAKENBURY, *with a guard of men.*

Brother, good day; what means this armed guard
That waits upon your Grace?
CLARENCE   His Majesty,
Tend'ring my person's safety, hath appointed
This conduct to convey me to the Tower.
RICHARD   Upon what cause?
CLARENCE   Because my name is George.
RICHARD   Alack, my lord, that fault is none of yours:
He should for that commit your godfathers.
O, belike his Majesty hath some intent
That you should be new-christen'd in the Tower.

But what's the matter, Clarence, may I know?
CLARENCE   Yea, Richard, when I know: for I protest
As yet I do not. But, as I can learn,
He hearkens after prophecies and dreams,
And from the cross-row plucks the letter G;   55
And says a wizard told him that by 'G'
His issue disinherited should be.
And for my name of George begins with G.
It follows in his thought that I am he.
These, as I learn, and such like toys as these,   60
Have mov'd his Highness to commit me now.
RICHARD   Why, this it is, when men are rul'd by women:
'Tis not the King that sends you to the Tower;
My Lady Grey, his wife, Clarence, 'tis she
That tempers him to this extremity.   65
Was it not she, and that good man of worship,
Anthony Woodeville, her brother there,
That made him send Lord Hastings to the Tower,
From whence this present day he is deliver'd?
We are not safe, Clarence, we are not safe!   70
CLARENCE   By heaven, I think there is no man secure,
But the Queen's kindred, and night-walking heralds
That trudge betwixt the King and Mistress Shore.
Heard you not what an humble suppliant
Lord Hastings was to her, for his delivery?   75
RICHARD   Humbly complaining to her deity
Got my Lord Chamberlain his liberty.
I'll tell you what: I think it is our way,
If we will keep in favour with the King,
To be her men, and wear her livery.   80
The jealous o'er-worn widow and herself,
Since that our brother dubb'd them gentlewomen,
Are mighty gossips in our monarchy.
BRAKENBURY
I beseech your Graces both to pardon me:
His Majesty hath straitly given in charge   85
That no man shall have private conference –
Of what degree soever – with his brother.
RICHARD
Even so; and please your worship, Brakenbury,
You may partake of any thing we say.
We speak no treason, man: we say the King   90
Is wise and virtuous, and his noble Queen
Well struck in years, fair, and not jealous.
We say that Shore's wife hath a pretty foot,
A cherry lip, a bonny eye, a passing pleasing tongue,
And that the Queen's kindred are made gentlefolks.   95
How say you, sir? Can you deny all this?
BRAKENBURY
With this, my lord, myself have nought to do.
RICHARD
Naught with Mistress Shore? I tell thee, fellow,
He that doth naught with her (excepting one)
Were best to do it secretly, alone.   100
BRAKENBURY   What one, my lord?
RICHARD
Her husband, knave! Wouldst thou betray me?

BRAKENBURY

    I do beseech your Grace to pardon me, and withal

    Forbear your conference with the noble Duke.

CLARENCE

105   We know thy charge, Brakenbury, and will obey.

RICHARD   We are the Queen's abjects, and must obey.

    Brother, farewell. I will unto the King,

    And whatso'er you will employ me in –

    Were it to call King Edward's widow 'sister' –

110   I will perform it to enfranchise you.

    Meantime, this deep disgrace in brotherhood

    Touches me deeper than you can imagine.

    [*Embraces Clarence, weeping.*]

CLARENCE   I know it pleaseth neither of us well.

RICHARD   Well, your imprisonment shall not be long:

115   I will deliver you, or else lie for you.

    Meantime, have patience.

CLARENCE   I must, perforce. Farewell.

    Exeunt Clarence, Brakenbury and guard.

RICHARD

    Go, tread the path that thou shalt ne'er return;

    Simple, plain Clarence, I do love thee so

    That I will shortly send thy soul to Heaven –

120   If Heaven will take the present at our hands.

    But who comes here? The new-deliver'd Hastings?

        Enter LORD HASTINGS.

HASTINGS   Good time of day unto my gracious lord.

RICHARD   As much unto my good Lord Chamberlain:

    Well are you welcome to the open air.

125   How hath your lordship brook'd imprisonment?

HASTINGS

    With patience, noble lord, as prisoners must;

    But I shall live, my lord, to give them thanks

    That were the cause of my imprisonment.

RICHARD

    No doubt, no doubt; and so shall Clarence too:

130   For they that were your enemies are his,

    And have prevail'd as much on him, as you.

HASTINGS   More pity that the eagles should be mew'd,

    While kites and buzzards prey at liberty.

RICHARD   What news abroad?

135 HASTINGS   No news so bad abroad, as this at home:

    The King is sickly, weak and melancholy,

    And his physicians fear him mightily.

RICHARD   Now by Saint John, that news is bad indeed.

    O, he hath kept an evil diet long,

140   And over-much consum'd his royal person:

    'Tis very grievous to be thought upon.

    Where is he, in his bed?

HASTINGS   He is.

RICHARD   Go you before, and I will follow you.

         Exit Hastings.

145   He cannot live, I hope, and must not die

    Till George be pack'd with post-horse up to Heaven.

    I'll in to urge his hatred more to Clarence,

    With lies well-steel'd with weighty arguments;

    And if I fail not in my deep intent,

    Clarence hath not another day to live: 150

    Which done, God take King Edward to his mercy,

    And leave the world for me to bustle in.

    For then I'll marry Warwick's youngest daughter –

    What though I kill'd her husband and her father?

    The readiest way to make the wench amends   155

    Is to become her husband, and her father:

    The which will I, not all so much for love

    As for another secret close intent,

    By marrying her which I must reach unto.

    But yet I run before my horse to market: 160

    Clarence still breathes, Edward still lives and reigns;

    When they are gone, then must I count my gains.

         Exit.

1.2   *Enter the corse of Henry the Sixth with* Halberds

    to guard it, LADY ANNE *being the mourner, attended*

    by TRESSEL, BERKELEY *and other* Gentlemen.

ANNE   Set down, set down your honourable load

    (If honour may be shrouded in a hearse)

    Whilst I awhile obsequiously lament

    Th'untimely fall of virtuous Lancaster.

    Poor key-cold Figure of a holy king,   5

    Pale ashes of the House of Lancaster,

    Thou bloodless remnant of that royal blood:

    Be it lawful that I invocate thy ghost

    To hear the lamentations of poor Anne,

    Wife to thy Edward, to thy slaughter'd son,   10

    Stabb'd by the selfsame hand that made these

        wounds.

    Lo, in these windows that let forth thy life

    I pour the helpless balm of my poor eyes.

    O, cursed be the hand that made these holes;

    Cursed the heart that had the heart to do it;   15

    Cursed the blood that let this blood from hence.

    More direful hap betide that hated wretch

    That makes us wretched by the death of thee

    Than I can wish to adders, spiders, toads,

    Or any creeping venom'd thing that lives.   20

    If ever he have child, abortive be it:

    Prodigious, and untimely brought to light,

    Whose ugly and unnatural aspect

    May fright the hopeful mother at the view,

    And that be heir to his unhappiness.   25

    If ever he have wife, let her be made

    More miserable by the death of him

    Than I am made by my young lord, and thee.

    Come now towards Chertsey with your holy load,

    Taken from Paul's to be interred there;   30

    And still, as you are weary of the weight,

    Rest you, while I lament King Henry's corse.

        Enter RICHARD.

RICHARD   Stay, you that bear the corse, and set it down.

ANNE   What black magician conjures up this fiend

To stop devoted charitable deeds?

RICHARD   Villains! set down the corse or by Saint Paul

I'll make a corse of him that disobeys!

HALBERDIER

My lord, stand back and let the coffin pass.

RICHARD

Unmanner'd dog, stand thou when I command!

Advance thy halberd higher than my breast,

Or by Saint Paul I'll strike thee to my foot,

And spurn upon thee, beggar, for thy boldness.

ANNE   What, do you tremble? Are you all afraid?

Alas, I blame you not, for you are mortal,

And mortal eyes cannot endure the devil.

Avaunt, thou dreadful minister of hell!

Thou hadst but power over his mortal body:

His soul thou canst not have; therefore begone.

RICHARD   Sweet saint, for charity be not so curst.

ANNE

Foul devil, for God's sake hence, and trouble us not;

For thou hast made the happy earth thy hell,

Fill'd it with cursing cries and deep exclaims.

If thou delight to view thy heinous deeds,

Behold this pattern of thy butcheries.

O gentlemen! See, see dead Henry's wounds

Open their congeal'd mouths and bleed afresh.

Blush, blush, thou lump of foul deformity,

For 'tis thy presence that exhales this blood

From cold and empty veins where no blood dwells:

Thy deed inhuman and unnatural

Provokes this deluge most unnatural.

O God! which this blood mad'st, revenge his death;

O earth! which this blood drink'st, revenge his death;

Either heav'n with lightning strike the murderer

   dead,

Or earth gape open wide and eat him quick,

As thou dost swallow up this good King's blood

Which his hell-govern'd arm hath butchered.

RICHARD   Lady, you know no rules of charity,

Which renders good for bad, blessings for curses.

ANNE   Villain, thou know'st no law of God nor man.

No beast so fierce but knows some touch of pity.

RICHARD   But I know none, and therefore am no beast.

ANNE   O wonderful, when devils tell the truth!

RICHARD   More wonderful, when angels are so angry.

Vouchsafe, divine perfection of a woman,

Of these supposed crimes, to give me leave,

By circumstance, but to acquit myself.

ANNE   Vouchsafe, diffus'd infection of a man,

Of these known evils, but to give me leave,

By circumstance, t'accuse thy cursed self.

RICHARD

Fairer than tongue can name thee, let me have

Some patient leisure to excuse myself.

ANNE

Fouler than heart can think thee, thou canst make

No excuse current but to hang thyself.

RICHARD   By such despair I should accuse myself.

ANNE   And by despairing shalt thou stand excus'd

For doing worthy vengeance on thyself

That didst unworthy slaughter upon others.

RICHARD   Say that I slew them not?

ANNE   Then say they were not slain: 90

But dead they are, and, devilish slave, by thee.

RICHARD   I did not kill your husband.

ANNE   Why then he is alive.

RICHARD   Nay he is dead, and slain by Edward's hand.

ANNE

In thy foul throat thou liest: Queen Margaret saw   95

Thy murd'rous falchion smoking in his blood,

The which thou once didst bend against her breast,

But that thy brothers beat aside the point.

RICHARD   I was provoked by her sland'rous tongue,

That laid their guilt upon my guiltless shoulders.   100

ANNE   Thou wast provoked by thy bloody mind,

That never dream'st on aught but butcheries.

Didst thou not kill this King?

RICHARD   I grant ye, yea.

ANNE

Dost grant me, hedgehog! Then God grant me too

Thou mayst be damned for that wicked deed.   105

O he was gentle, mild, and virtuous.

RICHARD

The better for the King of Heaven that hath him.

ANNE   He is in Heaven, where thou shalt never come.

RICHARD

Let him thank me that holp to send him thither,

For he was fitter for that place than earth.   110

ANNE   And thou unfit for any place but hell.

RICHARD

Yes, one place else, if you will hear me name it.

ANNE   Some dungeon?

RICHARD   Your bed-chamber.

ANNE   Ill rest betide the chamber where thou liest.   115

RICHARD   So will it, madam, till I lie with you.

ANNE   I hope so!

RICHARD   I know so. But, gentle Lady Anne,

To leave this keen encounter of our wits,

And fall something into a slower method: 120

Is not the causer of the timeless deaths

Of these Plantagenets, Henry and Edward,

As blameful as the executioner?

ANNE   Thou wast the cause, and most accurs'd effect.

RICHARD   Your beauty was the cause of that effect: 125

Your beauty, that did haunt me in my sleep

To undertake the death of all the world,

So I might live one hour in your sweet bosom.

ANNE   If I thought that, I tell thee, homicide,

These nails should rend that beauty from my cheeks.   130

RICHARD

These eyes could not endure that beauty's wrack;

You should not blemish it if I stood by.

As all the world is cheered by the sun,

So I by that; it is my day, my life.

ANNE   Black night o'ershade thy day, and death thy life.   135

RICHARD
  Curse not thyself, fair creature; thou art both.
ANNE   I would I were, to be reveng'd on thee.
RICHARD   It is a quarrel most unnatural,
  To be reveng'd on him that loveth thee.
140   ANNE   It is a quarrel just and reasonable,
  To be reveng'd on him that kill'd my husband.
RICHARD   He that bereft thee, lady, of thy husband,
  Did it to help thee to a better husband.
ANNE   His better doth not breathe upon the earth.
145   RICHARD   He lives that loves thee better than he could.
ANNE   Name him.
RICHARD   Plantagenet.
ANNE   Why that was he.
RICHARD   The selfsame name, but one of better nature.
ANNE   Where is he?
RICHARD   Here. [*She spits at him.*]
               Why dost thou spit at me?
ANNE   Would it were mortal poison, for thy sake.
150   RICHARD   Never came poison from so sweet a place.
ANNE   Never hung poison on a fouler toad.
  Out of my sight! Thou dost infect mine eyes.
RICHARD   Thine eyes, sweet lady, have infected mine.
ANNE   Would they were basilisks, to strike thee dead.
155   RICHARD   I would they were, that I might die at once;
  For now they kill me with a living death.
  Those eyes of thine from mine have drawn salt tears,
  Sham'd their aspects with store of childish drops;
  These eyes, which never shed remorseful tear,
160   No, when my father York and Edward wept
  To hear the piteous moan that Rutland made
  When black-fac'd Clifford shook his sword at him;
  Nor when thy warlike father, like a child
  Told the sad story of my father's death,
165   And twenty times made pause to sob and weep,
  That all the standers-by had wet their cheeks
  Like trees bedash'd with rain. In that sad time
  My manly eyes did scorn an humble tear;
  And what these sorrows could not thence exhale,
  Thy beauty hath, and made them blind with
170   weeping.
  I never sued to friend nor enemy:
  My tongue could never learn sweet smoothing word;
  But now thy beauty is propos'd my fee,
  My proud heart sues, and prompts my tongue to
     speak. [*She looks scornfully at him.*]
175   Teach not thy lip such scorn; for it was made
  For kissing, lady, not for such contempt.
  If thy revengeful heart cannot forgive,
  Lo here I lend thee this sharp-pointed sword,
  Which if thou please to hide in this true breast,
180   And let the soul forth that adoreth thee,
  I lay it naked to the deadly stroke,
  And humbly beg the death upon my knee.
  [*Kneels; he lays his breast open, she offers at it with his*
  sword.]
  Nay, do not pause, for I did kill King Henry –

But 'twas thy beauty that provoked me.
Nay, now dispatch: 'twas I that stabb'd young
  Edward –   185
But 'twas thy heavenly face that set me on.
[*She falls the sword.*]
Take up the sword again, or take up me.
ANNE   Arise, dissembler; though I wish thy death,
[*He rises.*]
I will not be thy executioner.
RICHARD   Then bid me kill myself, and I will do it.   190
ANNE   I have already.
RICHARD   That was in thy rage:
  Speak it again, and even with the word,
  This hand, which for thy love did kill thy love,
  Shall for thy love kill a far truer love:
  To both their deaths shalt thou be accessary.   195
ANNE   I would I knew thy heart.
RICHARD   'Tis figur'd in my tongue.
ANNE   I fear me both are false.
RICHARD   Then never was man true.
ANNE   Well, well, put up your sword.   200
RICHARD   Say then my peace is made.
ANNE   That shalt thou know hereafter.
RICHARD   But shall I live in hope?
ANNE   All men, I hope, live so.
RICHARD   Vouchsafe to wear this ring.   205
ANNE   To take is not to give.
RICHARD   Look how my ring encompasseth thy finger:
  Even so thy breast encloseth my poor heart;
  Wear both of them, for both of them are thine.
  And if thy poor devoted servant may   210
  But beg one favour at thy gracious hand,
  Thou dost confirm his happiness for ever.
ANNE   What is it?
RICHARD
  That it may please you leave these sad designs
  To him that hath most cause to be a mourner,   215
  And presently repair to Crosby Place,
  Where, after I have solemnly interr'd
  At Chertsey Monastery this noble King,
  And wet his grave with my repentant tears,
  I will with all expedient duty see you.   220
  For divers unknown reasons, I beseech you
  Grant me this boon.
ANNE   With all my heart, and much it joys me too,
  To see you are become so penitent.
  Tressel and Berkeley, go along with me.   225
RICHARD   Bid me farewell.
ANNE   'Tis more than you deserve;
  But since you teach me how to flatter you,
  Imagine I have said farewell already.
          Exeunt Tressel and Berkeley with Anne.
RICHARD   Sirs, take up the corse.
GENTLEMAN   Towards Chertsey, noble lord?   230
RICHARD   No, to Whitefriars; there attend my coming.
          Exeunt Gentlemen and Halberds with corse.

Was ever woman in this humour woo'd?
Was ever woman in this humour won?
I'll have her, but I will not keep her long.
What, I that kill'd her husband and his father: 5
To take her in her heart's extremest hate,
With curses in her mouth, tears in her eyes,
The bleeding witness of her hatred by,
Having God, her conscience, and these bars against
    me –
And I, no friends to back my suit at all   10
But the plain devil and dissembling looks –
And yet to win her, all the world to nothing!
Ha!
Hath she forgot already that brave prince,
Edward, her lord, whom I, some three months since,   15
Stabb'd in my angry mood at Tewkesbury?
A sweeter and a lovelier gentleman,
Fram'd in the prodigality of Nature,
Young, valiant, wise, and no doubt right royal,
The spacious world cannot again afford.   20
And will she yet debase her eyes on me,
That cropp'd the golden prime of this sweet prince,
And made her widow to a woeful bed?
On me, whose all not equals Edward's moiety?
On me, that halts and am misshapen thus?   25
My dukedom to a beggarly denier,
I do mistake my person all this while!
Upon my life, she finds – although I cannot –
Myself to be a marvellous proper man.
I'll be at charges for a looking-glass,   30
And entertain a score or two of tailors
To study fashions to adorn my body:
Since I am crept in favour with myself,
I will maintain it with some little cost.
But first I'll turn yon fellow in his grave,   35
And then return, lamenting, to my love.
Shine out, fair sun, till I have bought a glass,
That I may see my shadow as I pass.   *Exit.*

1.3   *Enter* QUEEN ELIZABETH, LORD RIVERS,
      LORD GREY *and the* MARQUESS OF DORSET.

RIVERS
  Have patience, Madam, there's no doubt his Majesty
  Will soon recover his accustom'd health.
GREY   In that you brook it ill, it makes him worse;
  Therefore, for God's sake entertain good comfort,
  And cheer his Grace with quick and merry eyes.
ELIZABETH   If he were dead, what would betide on me?
GREY   No other harm but loss of such a lord.
ELIZABETH   The loss of such a lord includes all harms.
GREY   The heavens have bless'd you with a goodly son
  To be your comforter when he is gone.   10
ELIZABETH   Ah, he is young, and his minority
  Is put unto the trust of Richard Gloucester,
  A man that loves not me, nor none of you.
RIVERS   Is it concluded he shall be Protector?
ELIZABETH   It is determin'd, not concluded yet;   15

But so it must be, if the King miscarry.

    Enter BUCKINGHAM *and* STANLEY, EARL OF DERBY.

GREY   Here come the lords of Buckingham and Derby.
BUCKINGHAM
  Good time of day unto your royal Grace.
STANLEY
  God make your Majesty joyful, as you have been.
ELIZABETH
  The Countess Richmond, good my lord of Derby,   20
  To your good prayer will scarcely say Amen;
  Yet, Derby, notwithstanding she's your wife,
  And loves not me, be you, good lord, assur'd
  I hate not you for her proud arrogance.
STANLEY   I do beseech you, either not believe   25
  The envious slanders of her false accusers,
  Or if she be accus'd on true report,
  Bear with her weakness, which I think proceeds
  From wayward sickness, and no grounded malice.
RIVERS   Saw you the King today, my lord of Derby?   30
STANLEY   But now the Duke of Buckingham and I
  Are come from visiting his Majesty.
ELIZABETH   What likelihood of his amendment, lords?
BUCKINGHAM
  Madam, good hope; his Grace speaks cheerfully.
ELIZABETH
  God grant him health. Did you confer with him?   35
BUCKINGHAM
  Ay, madam; he desires to make atonement
  Between the Duke of Gloucester and your brothers,
  And between them and my Lord Chamberlain;
  And sent to warn them to his royal presence.
ELIZABETH
  Would all were well – but that will never be;   40
  I fear our happiness is at the height.

    Enter RICHARD *and* HASTINGS.

RICHARD   They do me wrong, and I will not endure it!
  Who is it that complains unto the King
  That I, forsooth, am stern, and love them not?
  By holy Paul, they love his Grace but lightly   45
  That fill his ears with such dissentious rumours.
  Because I cannot flatter, and look fair,
  Smile in men's faces, smooth, deceive and cog,
  Duck with French nods and apish courtesy,
  I must be held a rancorous enemy.   50
  Cannot a plain man live and think no harm,
  But thus his simple truth must be abus'd
  With silken, sly, insinuating Jacks?
GREY   To who in all this presence speaks your Grace?
RICHARD   To thee, that hast nor honesty nor grace.   55
  When have I injur'd thee? When done thee wrong?
  Or thee? Or thee? Or any of your faction?
  A plague upon you all! His royal Grace
  (Whom God preserve better than you would wish)
  Cannot be quiet scarce a breathing while   60
  But you must trouble him with lewd complaints.

ELIZABETH
  Brother of Gloucester, you mistake the matter:
  The King, on his own royal disposition,
  And not provok'd by any suitor else,
65 Aiming, belike, at your interior hatred,
  That in your outward action shows itself
  Against my children, brothers, and myself,
  Makes him to send, that he may learn the ground
  Of your ill will, and thereby to remove it.
70 RICHARD   I cannot tell; the world is grown so bad
  That wrens make prey where eagles dare not perch.
  Since every Jack became a gentleman
  There's many a gentle person made a jack.
ELIZABETH
  Come, come: we know your meaning, brother
    Gloucester.
75 You envy my advancement, and my friends'.
  God grant we never may have need of you.
RICHARD
  Meantime, God grants that we have need of you:
  Our brother is imprison'd by your means,
  Myself disgrac'd, and the nobility
80 Held in contempt, while great promotions
  Are daily given to ennoble those
  That scarce some two days since were worth a noble.
ELIZABETH
  By Him that rais'd me to this careful height
  From that contented hap which I enjoy'd,
85 I never did incense his Majesty
  Against the Duke of Clarence, but have been
  An earnest advocate to plead for him.
  My lord, you do me shameful injury,
  Falsely to draw me in these vile suspects.
90 RICHARD   You may deny that you were not the mean
  Of my Lord Hastings' late imprisonment.
  RIVERS   She may, my lord, for –
RICHARD
  She may, Lord Rivers; why, who knows not so?
  She may do more, sir, than denying that:
95 She may help you to many fair preferments,
  And then deny her aiding hand therein,
  And lay those honours on your high desert.
  What may she not? She may – ay, marry may she –
  RIVERS   What, marry may she?
100 RICHARD   What marry may she? Marry with a king;
  A bachelor, and a handsome stripling too:
  Iwis, your grandam had a worser match.
ELIZABETH
  My lord of Gloucester, I have too long borne
  Your blunt upbraidings and your bitter scoffs;
105 By heaven, I will acquaint his Majesty
  Of those gross taunts that oft I have endur'd.

        Enter old QUEEN MARGARET.

  I had rather be a country servant maid,
  Than a great queen, with this condition,
  To be so baited, scorn'd, and stormed at:

  Small joy have I in being England's queen.   110
MARGARET [*aside*]
  And lessen'd be that small, God I beseech Him:
  Thy honour, state, and seat is due to me.
RICHARD
  What, threat you me with telling of the King?
  Tell him, and spare not: look what I have said
  I will avouch't in presence of the King: 115
  I dare adventure to be sent to th' Tower;
  'Tis time to speak: my pains are quite forgot.
MARGARET [*aside*]
  Out, devil! I remember them too well:
  Thou kill'dst my husband Henry in the Tower,
  And Edward, my poor son, at Tewkesbury.   120
RICHARD
  Ere you were queen, ay, or your husband king,
  I was a pack-horse in his great affairs;
  A weeder-out of his proud adversaries;
  A liberal rewarder of his friends:
  To royalize his blood, I spent mine own.   125
MARGARET [*aside*]
  Ay, and much better blood than his, or thine.
RICHARD
  In all which time, you and your husband Grey
  Were factious for the House of Lancaster:
  And Rivers, so were you. Was not your husband
  In Margaret's battle at Saint Albans slain?   130
  Let me put in your minds, if you forget,
  What you have been ere this, and what you are;
  Withal, what I have been, and what I am.
MARGARET [*aside*]
  A murd'rous villain, and so still thou art.
RICHARD
  Poor Clarence did forsake his father Warwick,   135
  Ay, and forswore himself – which Jesu pardon –
MARGARET [*aside*]   Which God revenge.
RICHARD   To fight on Edward's party for the crown:
  And for his meed, poor lord, he is mew'd up.
  I would to God my heart were flint, like Edward's,   140
  Or Edward's soft and pitiful, like mine.
  I am too childish-foolish for this world.
MARGARET [*aside*]
  Hie thee to hell for shame, and leave this world,
  Thou cacodemon: there thy kingdom is.
RIVERS   My lord of Gloucester, in those busy days   145
  Which here you urge to prove us enemies,
  We follow'd then our lord, our sovereign king:
  So should we you, if you should be our king.
RICHARD   If I should be? I had rather be a pedlar!
  Far be it from my heart, the thought thereof.   150
ELIZABETH   As little joy, my lord, as you suppose
  You should enjoy, were you this country's king:
  As little joy you may suppose in me
  That I enjoy, being the Queen thereof.
MARGARET [*aside*]
  Ay, little joy enjoys the Queen thereof: 155
  For I am she, and altogether joyless.

I can no longer hold me patient! [*coming forward*]
Hear me, you wrangling pirates, that fall out
In sharing that which you have pill'd from me:
Which of you trembles not, that looks on me?
If not that I am Queen you bow like subjects,
Yet that by you depos'd you quake like rebels.
Ah, gentle villain! do not turn away.

RICHARD
Foul wrinkled witch, what mak'st thou in my sight?

MARGARET   But repetition of what thou hast marr'd:
That will I make, before I let thee go.

RICHARD   Wert thou not banished on pain of death?

MARGARET
I was, but I do find more pain in banishment
Than death can yield me here by my abode.
A husband and a son thou ow'st to me;
And thou a kingdom; all of you, allegiance.
This sorrow that I have by right is yours;
And all the pleasures you usurp are mine.

RICHARD   The curse my noble father laid on thee
When thou didst crown his warlike brows with paper,
And with thy scorns drew'st rivers from his eyes,
And then to dry them, gav'st the Duke a clout
Steep'd in the faultless blood of pretty Rutland –
His curses then, from bitterness of soul
Denounc'd against thee, are all fall'n upon thee,
And God, not we, hath plagu'd thy bloody deed.

ELIZABETH   So just is God, to right the innocent.

HASTINGS   O, 'twas the foulest deed to slay that babe,
And the most merciless, that e'er was heard of.

RIVERS
Tyrants themselves wept when it was reported.

DORSET   No man but prophesied revenge for it.

BUCKINGHAM
Northumberland, then present, wept to see it.

MARGARET
What? Were you snarling all before I came,
Ready to catch each other by the throat,
And turn you all your hatred now on me?
Did York's dread curse prevail so much with heaven
That Henry's death, my lovely Edward's death,
Their kingdom's loss, my woeful banishment,
Should all but answer for that peevish brat?
Can curses pierce the clouds and enter heaven?
Why then, give way, dull clouds, to my quick curses:
Though not by war, by surfeit die your King,
As ours by murder, to make him a king.
Edward thy son, that now is Prince of Wales,
For Edward my son, that was Prince of Wales,
Die in his youth, by like untimely violence.
Thyself, a queen, for me that was a queen,
Outlive thy glory like my wretched self:
Long may'st thou live to wail thy children's death,
And see another, as I see thee now,
Deck'd in thy rights, as thou art stall'd in mine;
Long die thy happy days before thy death,
And after many lengthen'd hours of grief,

Die neither mother, wife, nor England's Queen.
Rivers and Dorset, you were standers-by,   210
And so wast thou, Lord Hastings, when my son
Was stabb'd with bloody daggers. God, I pray Him,
That none of you may live his natural age,
But by some unlook'd accident cut off.

RICHARD
Have done thy charm, thou hateful wither'd hag.   215

MARGARET
And leave out thee? Stay, dog, for thou shalt hear me.
If heaven have any grievous plague in store
Exceeding those that I can wish upon thee,
O, let them keep it till thy sins be ripe,
And then hurl down their indignation   220
On thee, the troubler of the poor world's peace.
The worm of conscience still begnaw thy soul;
Thy friends suspect for traitors while thou liv'st,
And take deep traitors for thy dearest friends;
No sleep close up that deadly eye of thine,   225
Unless it be while some tormenting dream
Affrights thee with a hell of ugly devils.
Thou elvish-mark'd, abortive, rooting hog,
Thou that wast seal'd in thy nativity
The slave of Nature, and the son of hell;   230
Thou slander of thy heavy mother's womb,
Thou loathed issue of thy father's loins,
Thou rag of honour, thou detested –

RICHARD   Margaret!

MARGARET   Richard!

RICHARD   Ha?

MARGARET   I call thee not.

RICHARD   I cry thee mercy then, for I did think   235
That thou hadst call'd me all these bitter names.

MARGARET
Why so I did, but look'd for no reply.
O, let me make the period to my curse!

RICHARD   'Tis done by me, and ends in 'Margaret'.

ELIZABETH
Thus have you breath'd your curse against yourself. 240

MARGARET
Poor painted queen, vain flourish of my fortune:
Why strew'st thou sugar on that bottled spider,
Whose deadly web ensnareth thee about?
Fool, fool; thou whet'st a knife to kill thyself.
The day will come that thou shalt wish for me   245
To help thee curse this poisonous bunch-back'd toad.

HASTINGS   False-boding woman, end thy frantic curse,
Lest to thy harm thou move our patience.

MARGARET
Foul shame upon you, you have all mov'd mine.

RIVERS
Were you well serv'd, you would be taught your duty. 250

MARGARET
To serve me well, you all should do me duty:
Teach me to be your queen, and you my subjects.
O, serve me well, and teach yourselves that duty.

DORSET   Dispute not with her; she is lunatic.

MARGARET   Peace, Master Marquess: you are malapert;
    Your fire-new stamp of honour is scarce current.
    O, that your young nobility could judge
    What 'twere to lose it and be miserable.
    They that stand high have many blasts to shake
       them,
    And if they fall, they dash themselves to pieces.
RICHARD
    Good counsel, marry! Learn it, learn it, Marquess.
DORSET   It touches you, my lord, as much as me.
RICHARD   Ay, and much more; but I was born so high:
    Our aery buildeth in the cedar's top,
    And dallies with the wind, and scorns the sun.
MARGARET   And turns the sun to shade, alas, alas!
    Witness my son, now in the shade of death,
    Whose bright out-shining beams thy cloudy wrath
    Hath in eternal darkness folded up.
    Your aery buildeth in our aery's nest;
    O God, that seest it, do not suffer it:
    As it is won with blood, lost be it so.
BUCKINGHAM
    Peace, peace, for shame, if not for charity.
MARGARET   Urge neither charity nor shame to me:
    Uncharitably with me have you dealt,
    And shamefully my hopes by you are butcher'd.
    My charity is outrage, life my shame;
    And in that shame, still live my sorrows' rage.
BUCKINGHAM   Have done, have done!
MARGARET   O princely Buckingham, I'll kiss thy hand
    In sign of league and amity with thee:
    Now fair befall thee and thy noble House;
    Thy garments are not spotted with our blood,
    Nor thou within the compass of my curse.
BUCKINGHAM   Nor no-one here: for curses never pass
    The lips of those that breathe them in the air.
MARGARET
    I will not think but they ascend the sky,
    And there awake God's gentle sleeping peace.
    O Buckingham, take heed of yonder dog!
    Look when he fawns, he bites; and when he bites
    His venom tooth will rankle to the death.
    Have not to do with him; beware of him;
    Sin, death, and hell have set their marks on him,
    And all their ministers attend on him.
RICHARD   What doth she say, my lord of Buckingham?
BUCKINGHAM
    Nothing that I respect, my gracious lord.
MARGARET
    What, dost thou scorn me for my gentle counsel,
    And soothe the devil that I warn thee from?
    O, but remember this another day
    When he shall split thy very heart with sorrow,
    And say, poor Margaret was a prophetess.
    Live, each of you, the subjects to his hate,
    And he to yours, and all of you to God's.   *Exit.*
BUCKINGHAM
    My hair doth stand on end to hear her curses.

RIVERS   And so doth mine; I muse why she's at liberty.
RICHARD   I cannot blame her: by God's holy mother,
    She hath had too much wrong; and I repent
    My part thereof that I have done to her.
ELIZABETH   I never did her any, to my knowledge.
RICHARD   Yet you have all the vantage of her wrong.
    I was too hot to do somebody good
    That is too cold in thinking of it now;
    Marry, as for Clarence, he is well repaid:
    He is frank'd up to fatting for his pains.
    God pardon them that are the cause thereof.
RIVERS   A virtuous and a Christian-like conclusion,
    To pray for them that have done scathe to us.
RICHARD
    So do I ever – [*Speaks to himself.*] being well advis'd;
    For had I curs'd now, I had curs'd myself.

Enter CATESBY.

CATESBY   Madam, his Majesty doth call for you,
    And for your Grace, and you my gracious lords.
ELIZABETH
    Catesby, I come. Lords, will you go with me?
RIVERS   We wait upon your Grace.

Exeunt all but Richard.

RICHARD   I do the wrong, and first begin to brawl:
    The secret mischiefs that I set abroach
    I lay unto the grievous charge of others.
    Clarence, whom I, indeed, have cast in darkness,
    I do beweep to many simple gulls,
    Namely to Derby, Hastings, Buckingham;
    And tell them 'tis the Queen and her allies
    That stir the King against the Duke my brother.
    Now they believe it, and withal whet me
    To be reveng'd on Rivers, Dorset, Grey.
    But then I sigh, and, with a piece of Scripture,
    Tell them that God bids us do good for evil:
    And thus I clothe my naked villainy
    With odd old ends stol'n forth of Holy Writ,
    And seem a saint, when most I play the devil.

Enter two Murderers.

    But soft, here come my executioners.
    How now, my hardy, stout, resolved mates;
    Are you now going to dispatch this thing?
1 MURDERER
    We are, my lord, and come to have the warrant,
    That we may be admitted where he is.
RICHARD   Well thought upon; I have it here about me.
    When you have done, repair to Crosby Place –
    But sirs, be sudden in the execution,
    Withal obdurate: do not hear him plead;
    For Clarence is well-spoken, and perhaps
    May move your hearts to pity, if you mark him.
2 MURDERER
    Tut, tut, my lord: we will not stand to prate.
    Talkers are no good doers; be assur'd
    We go to use our hands, and not our tongues.

255
260
265
270
275
280
285
290
295
300

305
310
315
320
325
330
335
340
345
350

RICHARD
Your eyes drop millstones, when fools' eyes fall tears.
I like you, lads: about your business straight.
Go, go, dispatch.
355 BOTH   We will, my noble lord.   *Exeunt.*

1.4   *Enter* CLARENCE *and* Keeper.

KEEPER   Why looks your Grace so heavily today?
CLARENCE   O, I have pass'd a miserable night,
So full of fearful dreams, of ugly sights,
That, as I am a Christian faithful man,
5 I would not spend another such a night
Though 'twere to buy a world of happy days,
So full of dismal terror was the time.
KEEPER
What was your dream, my lord? I pray you tell me.
CLARENCE
Methoughts that I had broken from the Tower,
10 And was embark'd to cross to Burgundy;
And in my company my brother Gloucester,
Who from my cabin tempted me to walk
Upon the hatches: thence we look'd toward England,
And cited up a thousand heavy times,
15 During the wars of York and Lancaster,
That had befall'n us. As we pac'd along
Upon the giddy footing of the hatches,
Methought that Gloucester stumbled, and in falling,
Struck me (that thought to stay him) overboard,
20 Into the tumbling billows of the main.
O Lord! Methought what pain it was to drown:
What dreadful noise of waters in my ears;
What sights of ugly death within my eyes!
Methoughts I saw a thousand fearful wrecks;
25 Ten thousand men that fishes gnaw'd upon;
Wedges of gold, great anchors, heaps of pearl,
Inestimable stones, unvalu'd jewels,
All scatter'd in the bottom of the sea.
Some lay in dead men's skulls, and in the holes
30 Where eyes did once inhabit, there were crept –
As 'twere in scorn of eyes – reflecting gems,
That woo'd the slimy bottom of the deep,
And mock'd the dead bones that lay scatter'd by.
KEEPER   Had you such leisure in the time of death
35 To gaze upon these secrets of the deep?
CLARENCE   Methought I had; and often did I strive
To yield the ghost, but still the envious flood
Stopp'd in my soul, and would not let it forth
To find the empty, vast, and wand'ring air,
40 But smother'd it within my panting bulk,
Which almost burst to belch it in the sea.
KEEPER   Awak'd you not in this sore agony?
CLARENCE
No, no; my dream was lengthen'd after life.
O, then began the tempest to my soul:
45 I pass'd, methought, the melancholy flood,
With that sour ferryman which poets write of,

Unto the kingdom of perpetual night.
The first that there did greet my stranger-soul
Was my great father-in-law, renowned Warwick,
50 Who spake aloud, 'What scourge for perjury
Can this dark monarchy afford false Clarence?'
And so he vanish'd. Then came wand'ring by
A shadow like an angel, with bright hair
Dabbled in blood; and he shriek'd out aloud,
55 'Clarence is come: false, fleeting, perjur'd Clarence,
That stabb'd me in the field by Tewkesbury!
Seize on him, Furies! Take him unto torment!'
With that, methoughts, a legion of foul fiends
Environ'd me, and howled in mine ears
60 Such hideous cries, that with the very noise
I trembling wak'd, and for a season after
Could not believe but that I was in hell,
Such terrible impression made my dream.
KEEPER   No marvel, lord, though it affrighted you;
65 I am afraid, methinks, to hear you tell it.
CLARENCE
Ah, Keeper, Keeper, I have done these things,
That now give evidence against my soul,
For Edward's sake: and see how he requites me.
O God, if my deep prayers cannot appease Thee,
70 But Thou wilt be aveng'd on my misdeeds,
Yet execute Thy wrath in me alone;
O spare my guiltless wife and my poor children.
Keeper, I prithee sit by me awhile:
My soul is heavy, and I fain would sleep.
KEEPER
75 I will, my lord; God give your Grace good rest.

Enter BRAKENBURY *the lieutenant.*

BRAKENBURY
Sorrow breaks seasons and reposing hours,
Makes the night morning, and the noontide night.
Princes have but their titles for their glories,
An outward honour for an inward toil;
80 And for unfelt imaginations
They often feel a world of restless cares:
So that between their titles, and low name,
There's nothing differs but the outward fame.

Enter the two Murderers.

1 MURDERER   Ho, who's here?
BRAKENBURY
What would'st thou, fellow? And how cam'st thou
     hither?
85 2 MURDERER   I would speak with Clarence, and I came
hither on my legs.
BRAKENBURY   What, so brief?
1 MURDERER   'Tis better, sir, than to be tedious. Let
him see our commission, and talk no more.
90 [*Brakenbury reads.*]
BRAKENBURY   I am in this commanded to deliver
The noble Duke of Clarence to your hands.

I will not reason what is meant hereby,
Because I will be guiltless from the meaning.
There lies the Duke asleep; and there the keys.
I'll to the King, and signify to him
That thus I have resign'd to you my charge.

1 MURDERER
You may, sir; 'tis a point of wisdom. Fare you well.
       Exeunt Brakenbury and Keeper.

2 MURDERER What, shall I stab him as he sleeps?

1 MURDERER No: he'll say 'twas done cowardly, when he wakes.

2 MURDERER Why, he shall never wake until the great Judgement Day.

1 MURDERER Why, then he'll say we stabbed him sleeping.

2 MURDERER The urging of that word, 'Judgement', hath bred a kind of remorse in me.

1 MURDERER What, art thou afraid?

2 MURDERER Not to kill him – having a warrant – but to be damned for killing him, from the which no warrant can defend me.

1 MURDERER I thought thou hadst been resolute.

2 MURDERER So I am – to let him live.

1 MURDERER I'll back to the Duke of Gloucester, and tell him so.

2 MURDERER Nay, I prithee stay a little: I hope this passionate humour of mine will change. It was wont to hold me but while one tells twenty.

1 MURDERER How dost thou feel thyself now?

2 MURDERER Some certain dregs of conscience are yet within me.

1 MURDERER Remember our reward, when the deed's done.

2 MURDERER Zounds, he dies! I had forgot the reward.

1 MURDERER Where's thy conscience now?

2 MURDERER Oh, in the Duke of Gloucester's purse.

1 MURDERER When he opens his purse to give us our reward, thy conscience flies out?

2 MURDERER 'Tis no matter; let it go. There's few, or none, will entertain it.

1 MURDERER What if it come to thee again?

2 MURDERER I'll not meddle with it; it makes a man a coward. A man cannot steal but it accuseth him; a man cannot swear but it checks him; a man cannot lie with his neighbour's wife but it detects him. 'Tis a blushing, shamefaced spirit, that mutinies in a man's bosom. It fills a man full of obstacles; it made me once restore a purse of gold that by chance I found. It beggars any man that keeps it; it is turned out of towns and cities for a dangerous thing; and every man that means to live well endeavours to trust to himself, and live without it.

1 MURDERER Zounds, 'tis even now at my elbow, persuading me not to kill the Duke.

2 MURDERER Take the devil in thy mind, and believe him not: he would insinuate with thee but to make thee sigh.

1 MURDERER I am strong-framed; he cannot prevail with me.

2 MURDERER Spoke like a tall man that respects thy reputation! Come, shall we fall to work?

1 MURDERER Take him on the costard with the hilts of thy sword, and then throw him into the malmsey-butt in the next room.

2 MURDERER Oh excellent device! and make a sop of him.

1 MURDERER Soft, he wakes.

2 MURDERER Strike!

1 MURDERER No, we'll reason with him.

CLARENCE
Where art thou, Keeper? Give me a cup of wine.

2 MURDERER
You shall have wine enough, my lord, anon.

CLARENCE In God's name, what art thou?

2 MURDERER   A man, as you are.

CLARENCE But not as I am, royal.

1 MURDERER Nor you as we are, loyal.

CLARENCE
Thy voice is thunder, but thy looks are humble.

1 MURDERER
My voice is now the King's, my looks mine own.

CLARENCE
How darkly, and how deadly dost thou speak.
Your eyes do menace me; why look you pale?
Who sent you hither? Wherefore do you come?

BOTH To – to – to –

CLARENCE   To murder me?

BOTH   Ay, ay.

CLARENCE You scarcely have the hearts to tell me so,
And therefore cannot have the hearts to do it.
Wherein, my friends, have I offended you?

1 MURDERER Offended us you have not, but the King.

CLARENCE I shall be reconcil'd to him again.

2 MURDERER Never, my lord; therefore prepare to die.

CLARENCE Are you drawn forth among a world of men
To slay the innocent? What is my offence?
Where is the evidence that doth accuse me?
What lawful quest have giv'n their verdict up
Unto the frowning judge? Or who pronounc'd
The bitter sentence of poor Clarence' death?
Before I be convict by course of law,
To threaten me with death is most unlawful.
I charge you, as you hope to have redemption,
By Christ's dear blood, shed for our grievous sins,
That you depart and lay no hands on me:
The deed you undertake is damnable.

1 MURDERER What we will do, we do upon command.

2 MURDERER
And he that hath commanded is our King.

CLARENCE Erroneous vassals! The great King of kings
Hath in the table of His law commanded
That thou shalt do no murder. Will you then
Spurn at His edict, and fulfil a man's?
Take heed! For He holds vengeance in His hand

To hurl upon their heads that break His law.

2 MURDERER
And that same vengeance doth He hurl on thee,
For false forswearing, and for murder too:
Thou didst receive the sacrament to fight
In quarrel of the House of Lancaster.

1 MURDERER   And like a traitor to the name of God
Didst break that vow, and with thy treacherous blade
Unrip'st the bowels of thy sovereign's son.

2 MURDERER
Whom thou wast sworn to cherish and defend.

1 MURDERER
How canst thou urge God's dreadful law to us,
When thou hast broke it in such dear degree?

CLARENCE   Alas, for whose sake did I that ill deed?
For Edward, for my brother, for his sake.
He sends you not to murder me for this,
For in that sin he is as deep as I.
If God will be avenged for the deed,
O know you yet, He doth it publicly;
Take not the quarrel from His powerful arm.
He needs no indirect or lawless course
To cut off those that have offended Him.

1 MURDERER   Who made thee then a bloody minister,
When gallant-springing, brave Plantagenet,
That princely novice, was struck dead by thee?

CLARENCE   My brother's love, the devil, and my rage.

1 MURDERER
Thy brother's love, our duty, and thy faults
Provoke us hither now to slaughter thee.

CLARENCE   O, if you love my brother, hate not me:
I am his brother, and I love him well.
If you are hir'd for meed, go back again,
And I will send you to my brother Gloucester,
Who shall reward you better for my life
Than Edward will for tidings of my death.

2 MURDERER
You are deceiv'd: your brother Gloucester hates you.

CLARENCE   O no, he loves me, and he holds me dear;
Go you to him from me.

1 MURDERER   Ay, so we will.

CLARENCE
Tell him, when that our princely father York
Bless'd his three sons with his victorious arm,
And charg'd us from his soul to love each other,
He little thought of this divided friendship:
Bid Gloucester think of this, and he will weep.

1 MURDERER
Ay, millstones, as he lesson'd us to weep.

CLARENCE   O, do not slander him, for he is kind.

1 MURDERER   Right, as snow in harvest.
Come: you deceive yourself;
'Tis he that sends us to destroy you here.

CLARENCE   It cannot be: for he bewept my fortune,
And hugg'd me in his arms, and swore with sobs
That he would labour my delivery.

1 MURDERER   Why so he doth, when he delivers you

From this earth's thraldom to the joys of Heaven.   245

2 MURDERER
Make peace with God, for you must die, my lord.

CLARENCE   Have you that holy feeling in your souls
To counsel me to make my peace with God,
And are you yet to your own souls so blind
That you will war with God by murd'ring me?   250
O sirs, consider: they that set you on
To do this deed will hate you for the deed.

2 MURDERER   What shall we do?

CLARENCE   Relent, and save your souls.

1 MURDERER   Relent? No, 'tis cowardly and womanish.

CLARENCE   Not to relent is beastly, savage, devilish.   255
Which of you – if you were a prince's son,
Being pent from liberty as I am now –
If two such murderers as yourselves came to you,
Would not entreat for life? Ay, you would beg,
Were you in my distress.   260
[*to Second Murderer*] My friend, I spy some pity in
thy looks:
O, if thine eye be not a flatterer,
Come thou on my side, and entreat for me;
A begging prince, what beggar pities not?

2 MURDERER   Look behind you, my lord!   265

1 MURDERER   Take that! and that!
[*Stabs him.*]   If all this will not do,
I'll drown you in the malmsey-butt within.
Exit with body.

2 MURDERER
A bloody deed, and desperately dispatch'd.
How fain, like Pilate, would I wash my hands
Of this most grievous murder.   270

Enter First Murderer.

1 MURDERER   How now? What mean'st thou that
thou help'st me not?
By heavens, the Duke shall know how slack you have
been.

2 MURDERER
I would he knew that I had sav'd his brother.
Take thou the fee, and tell him what I say,
For I repent me that the Duke is slain.   *Exit.*   275

1 MURDERER   So do not I: go, coward as thou art.
Well, I'll go hide the body in some hole
Till that the Duke give order for his burial.
And when I have my meed, I will away:
For this will out, and then I must not stay.   *Exit.*   280

2.1   *Flourish. Enter* KING EDWARD *sick*,
QUEEN ELIZABETH, DORSET, RIVERS, HASTINGS,
BUCKINGHAM *and* GREY.

KING   Why, so: now have I done a good day's work:
You peers, continue this united league.
I every day expect an embassage
From my Redeemer, to redeem me hence;
And more in peace my soul shall part to Heaven   5

Since I have made my friends at peace on earth.
Rivers and Hastings, take each other's hand;
Dissemble not your hatred: swear your love.

RIVERS
By heaven, my soul is purg'd from grudging hate,
10　　And with my hand I seal my true heart's love.
HASTINGS　So thrive I, as I truly swear the like.
KING　Take heed you dally not before your King,
Lest He that is the supreme King of kings
Confound your hidden falsehood, and award
15　　Either of you to be the other's end.
HASTINGS　So prosper I, as I swear perfect love.
RIVERS　And I, as I love Hastings with my heart.
KING　Madam, yourself is not exempt from this;
Nor you, son Dorset; Buckingham, nor you:
20　　You have been factious, one against the other.
Wife, love Lord Hastings, let him kiss your hand:
And what you do, do it unfeignedly.

ELIZABETH
There, Hastings: I will never more remember
Our former hatred, so thrive I and mine.

KING
25　　Dorset, embrace him; Hastings, love lord Marquess.
DORSET　This interchange of love, I here protest,
Upon my part shall be inviolable.
HASTINGS　And so swear I. [*They embrace.*]
KING　Now, princely Buckingham, seal thou this league
30　　With thy embracements to my wife's allies,
And make me happy in your unity.

BUCKINGHAM
Whenever Buckingham doth turn his hate
Upon your Grace, but with all duteous love
Doth cherish you and yours, God punish me
35　　With hate in those where I expect most love.
When I have most need to employ a friend,
And most assured that he is a friend,
Deep, hollow, treacherous, and full of guile
Be he unto me: this do I beg of God,
40　　When I am cold in love to you or yours. [*Embrace.*]
KING　A pleasing cordial, princely Buckingham,
Is this thy vow unto my sickly heart.
There wanteth now our brother Gloucester here
To make the blessed period of this peace.

Enter RATCLIFFE *and* RICHARD.

45　　BUCKINGHAM　And in good time,
Here comes Sir Richard Ratcliffe and the Duke.
RICHARD
Good morrow to my sovereign King and Queen;
And princely peers, a happy time of day.
KING　Happy indeed, as we have spent the day;
50　　Gloucester, we have done deeds of charity,
Made peace of enmity, fair love of hate,
Between these swelling, wrong-incensed peers.
RICHARD　A blessed labour, my most sovereign lord.
Among this princely heap – if any here
55　　By false intelligence or wrong surmise

Hold me a foe –
If I unwittingly, or in my rage,
Have aught committed that is hardly borne
By any in this presence, I desire
To reconcile me to his friendly peace:　　60
'Tis death to me to be at enmity;
I hate it, and desire all good men's love.
First, madam, I entreat true peace of you,
Which I will purchase with my duteous service;
Of you, my noble cousin Buckingham,　　65
If ever any grudge were lodg'd between us;
Of you, Lord Rivers, and Lord Grey, of you,
That all without desert have frown'd on me:
Dukes, earls, lords, gentlemen: indeed of all.
I do not know that Englishmen alive　　70
With whom my soul is any jot at odds,
More than the infant that is born tonight –
I thank my God for my humility.
ELIZABETH　A holy day shall this be kept hereafter;
I would to God all strifes were well compounded.　　75
My sovereign lord, I do beseech your Highness
To take our brother Clarence to your grace.
RICHARD　Why, madam, have I offer'd love for this,
To be so flouted in this royal presence?
Who knows not that the gentle Duke is dead?　　80
[*They all start.*]
You do him injury to scorn his corse!
RIVERS　Who knows not he is dead! Who knows he is?
ELIZABETH　All-seeing heaven, what a world is this?
BUCKINGHAM　Look I so pale, Lord Dorset, as the rest?
DORSET　Ay, my good lord, and no man in the presence　　85
But his red colour hath forsook his cheeks.
KING　Is Clarence dead? The order was revers'd.
RICHARD　But he, poor man, by your first order died,
And that a winged Mercury did bear;
Some tardy cripple bore the countermand,　　90
That came too lag to see him buried.
God grant that some, less noble and less loyal,
Nearer in bloody thoughts, but not in blood,
Deserve not worse than wretched Clarence did,
And yet go current from suspicion.　　95

Enter STANLEY, EARL OF DERBY.

STANLEY　A boon, my sovereign, for my service done!
KING　I prithee peace; my soul is full of sorrow.
STANLEY　I will not rise unless your Highness hear me.
KING　Then say at once what is it thou demand'st.
STANLEY　The forfeit, Sovereign, of my servant's life.　　100
Who slew today a riotous gentleman
Lately attendant on the Duke of Norfolk.
KING　Have I a tongue to doom my brother's death,
And shall that tongue give pardon to a slave?
My brother kill'd no man: his fault was thought,　　105
And yet his punishment was bitter death.
Who sued to me for him? Who, in my wrath,
Kneel'd at my feet and bade me be advis'd?
Who spoke of brotherhood? Who spoke of love?

Who told me how the poor soul did forsake
The mighty Warwick, and did fight for me?
Who told me, in the field at Tewkesbury
When Oxford had me down, he rescued me
And said, 'Dear brother, live and be a king'?
Who told me, when we both lay in the field
Frozen almost to death, how he did lap me
Even in his garments, and did give himself,
All thin and naked, to the numb-cold night?
All this from my remembrance brutish wrath
Sinfully pluck'd, and not a man of you
Had so much grace to put it in my mind.
But when your carters or your waiting vassals
Have done a drunken slaughter, and defac'd
The precious image of our dear Redeemer,
You straight are on your knees for 'Pardon, pardon!'
And I, unjustly too, must grant it you.
But for my brother not a man would speak,
Nor I, ungracious, speak unto myself
For him, poor soul. The proudest of you all
Have been beholding to him in his life,
Yet none of you would once beg for his life.
O God, I fear Thy justice will take hold
On me, and you, and mine and yours for this.
Come, Hastings, help me to my closet.
Ah, poor Clarence!

                              Exeunt some with King and Queen.

RICHARD   This is the fruits of rashness: mark'd you not
How that the guilty kindred of the Queen
Look'd pale when they did hear of Clarence' death?
O, they did urge it still unto the King:
God will revenge it. Come, lords, will you go
To comfort Edward with our company.
BUCKINGHAM   We wait upon your Grace.   *Exeunt.*

2.2   *Enter the old* DUCHESS OF YORK, *with the two*
          Children *of Clarence.*

BOY   Good grandam tell us, is our father dead?
DUCHESS   No, boy.
GIRL   Why do you weep so oft, and beat your breast?
And cry 'O Clarence, my unhappy son'?
BOY   Why do you look on us, and shake your head,
And call us orphans, wretches, castaways,
If that our noble father were alive?
DUCHESS   My pretty cousins, you mistake me both:
I do lament the sickness of the King,
As loath to lose him; not your father's death:
It were lost sorrow to wail one that's lost.
BOY   Then you conclude, my grandam, he is dead:
The King mine uncle is to blame for it.
God will revenge it, whom I will importune
With earnest prayers, all to that effect.
GIRL   And so will I.
DUCHESS
Peace, children, peace: the King doth love you well.
Incapable and shallow innocents,

You cannot guess who caus'd your father's death.
BOY   Grandam, we can: for my good uncle Gloucester
Told me the King, provok'd to't by the Queen,
Devis'd impeachments to imprison him;
And when my uncle told me so he wept,
And pitied me, and kindly kiss'd my cheek;
Bade me rely on him as on my father,
And he would love me dearly as a child.
DUCHESS
Ah, that Deceit should steal such gentle shape,
And with a virtuous vizor hide deep Vice!
He is my son, ay, and herein my shame;
Yet from my dugs he drew not this deceit.
BOY   Think you my uncle did dissemble, grandam?
DUCHESS   Ay, boy.
BOY   I cannot think it. Hark, what noise is this?

          Enter QUEEN ELIZABETH *with her hair about her ears,*
                    RIVERS *and* DORSET *after her.*

ELIZABETH   Ah! who shall hinder me to wail and weep,
To chide my fortune, and torment myself?
I'll join with black despair against my soul
And to myself become an enemy.
DUCHESS   What means this scene of rude impatience?
ELIZABETH   To make an act of tragic violence:
Edward, my lord, thy son, our King, is dead.
Why grow the branches, when the root is gone?
Why wither not the leaves that want their sap?
If you will live, lament; if die, be brief,
That our swift-winged souls may catch the King's
Or like obedient subjects follow him
To his new kingdom of ne'er-changing night.
DUCHESS   Ah, so much interest have I in thy sorrow
As I had title in thy noble husband.
I have bewept a worthy husband's death,
And liv'd with looking on his images:
But now two mirrors of his princely semblance
Are crack'd in pieces by malignant death;
And I, for comfort, have but one false glass,
That grieves me when I see my shame in him.
Thou art a widow – yet thou art a mother,
And hast the comfort of thy children left;
But death hath snatch'd my husband from mine arms
And pluck'd two crutches from my feeble hands:
Clarence and Edward. O, what cause have I,
Thine being but a moiety of my moan,
To overgo thy woes and drown thy cries.
BOY   Ah, Aunt, you wept not for our father's death:
How can we aid you with our kindred tears?
GIRL   Our fatherless distress was left unmoan'd:
Your widow-dolour likewise be unwept.
ELIZABETH   Give me no help in lamentation:
I am not barren to bring forth complaints:
All springs reduce their currents to mine eyes,
That I, being govern'd by the watery moon,
May send forth plenteous tears to drown the world.
Ah, for my husband, for my dear lord Edward!

CHILDREN

    Ah, for our father, for our dear lord Clarence!

DUCHESS

    Alas for both, both mine Edward and Clarence!

ELIZABETH

    What stay had I but Edward, and he's gone.

CHILDREN

75   What stay had we but Clarence, and he's gone.

DUCHESS

    What stays had I but they, and they are gone.

ELIZABETH   Was never widow had so dear a loss.

CHILDREN   Were never orphans had so dear a loss.

DUCHESS   Was never mother had so dear a loss

80   Alas, I am the mother of these griefs:

    Their woes are parcell'd, mine is general.

    She for an Edward weeps, and so do I;

    I for a Clarence weep, so doth not she;

    These babes for Clarence weep, and so do I;

85   I for an Edward weep, so do not they.

    Alas, you three, on me, threefold distress'd,

    Pour all your tears: I am your sorrow's nurse.

    And I will pamper it with lamentation.

DORSET

    Comfort, dear mother: God is much displeas'd

90   That you take with unthankfulness His doing.

    In common worldly things, 'tis call'd ungrateful

    With dull unwillingness to repay a debt

    Which with more bounteous hand was kindly lent:

    Much more to be thus opposite with Heaven,

95   For it requires the royal debt it lent you.

RIVERS   Madam, bethink you, like a careful mother,

    Of the young prince your son: send straight for him;

    Let him be crown'd; in him your comfort lives.

    Drown desperate sorrow in dead Edward's grave,

100   And plant your joys in living Edward's throne.

Enter RICHARD, BUCKINGHAM, STANLEY, EARL OF DERBY,
HASTINGS *and* RATCLIFFE.

RICHARD   Sister, have comfort: all of us have cause

    To wail the dimming of our shining star,

    But none can help our harms by wailing them.

    Madam my mother, I do cry your mercy:

105   I did not see your Grace. Humbly on my knee

    I crave your blessing. [*Kneels.*]

DUCHESS

    God bless thee, and put meekness in thy breast;

    Love, charity, obedience, and true duty.

RICHARD   Amen;

    [*Rises: aside*]   and make me die a good old man –

110   That is the butt-end of a mother's blessing:

    I marvel that her Grace did leave it out.

BUCKINGHAM

    You cloudy princes and heart-sorrowing peers

    That bear this heavy mutual load of moan,

    Now cheer each other in each other's love.

115   Though we have spent our harvest of this king,

    We are to reap the harvest of his son.

    The broken rancour of your high-swoll'n hates,

    But lately splinted, knit, and join'd together

    Must gently be preserv'd, cherish'd, and kept.

    Meseemeth good, that with some little train,   120

    Forthwith from Ludlow the young Prince be fet

    Hither to London, to be crown'd our King.

RIVERS

    Why with some little train, my lord of Buckingham?

BUCKINGHAM   Marry, my lord, lest by a multitude

    The new-heal'd wound of malice should break out,   125

    Which would be so much the more dangerous

    By how much the estate is green and yet ungovern'd.

    Where every horse bears his commanding rein,

    And may direct his course as please himself,

    As well the fear of harm, as harm apparent,   130

    In my opinion, ought to be prevented.

RICHARD   I hope the King made peace with all of us,

    And the compact is firm and true in me.

RIVERS   And so in me, and so, I think, in all:

    Yet since it is but green, it should be put   135

    To no apparent likelihood of breach,

    Which haply by much company might be urg'd.

    Therefore I say with noble Buckingham

    That it is meet so few should fetch the Prince.

HASTINGS   And so say I.   140

RICHARD   Then be it so, and go we to determine

    Who they shall be that straight shall post to Ludlow.

    Madam, and you my sister, will you go

    To give you censures in this business?

ELIZABETH, DUCHESS   With all our hearts.   145

        Exeunt all but Buckingham and Richard.

BUCKINGHAM

    My lord, whoever journeys to the Prince,

    For God's sake let not us two stay at home:

    For by the way I'll sort occasion,

    As index to the story we late talk'd of,

    To part the Queen's proud kindred from the Prince.   150

RICHARD   My other self, my counsel's consistory,

    My oracle, my prophet, my dear cousin:

    I, as a child, will go by thy direction.

    Toward Ludlow then, for we'll not stay behind.

        Exeunt.

2.3   *Enter one* Citizen *at one door, and* Another
                   at the other.

1 CITIZEN

    Good morrow, neighbour: whither away so fast?

2 CITIZEN   I promise you, I scarcely know myself.

    Hear you the news abroad?

1 CITIZEN   Yes, that the King is dead.

2 CITIZEN   Ill news, by'rlady; seldom comes the better.

    I fear, I fear, 'twill prove a giddy world.   5

        Enter another Citizen.

3 CITIZEN   Neighbours, God speed.

1 CITIZEN   Give you good-morrow, sir.

3 CITIZEN

Doth the news hold of good King Edward's death?

2 CITIZEN   Ay, sir, it is too true, God help the while.

3 CITIZEN

Then, masters, look to see a troublous world.

1 CITIZEN

No, no; by God's good grace, his son shall reign.

3 CITIZEN   Woe to that land that's govern'd by a child.

2 CITIZEN   In him there is a hope of government,

Which, in his nonage, council under him,

And in his full and ripen'd years himself,

No doubt shall then, and till then, govern well.

1 CITIZEN   So stood the state when Henry the Sixth

Was crown'd in Paris but at nine months old.

3 CITIZEN

Stood the state so? No, no, good friends, God wot.

For then this land was famously enrich'd

With politic grave counsel; then the King

Had virtuous uncles to protect his Grace.

1 CITIZEN

Why, so hath this, both by his father and mother.

3 CITIZEN   Better it were they all came by his father,

Or by his father there were none at all:

For emulation who shall now be nearest

Will touch us all too near, if God prevent not.

O, full of danger is the Duke of Gloucester,

And the Queen's sons and brothers, haught and
    proud;

And were they to be rul'd, and not to rule,

This sickly land might solace as before.

1 CITIZEN

Come, come: we fear the worst; all will be well.

3 CITIZEN

When clouds are seen, wise men put on their cloaks;

When great leaves fall, then winter is at hand;

When the sun sets, who doth not look for night?

Untimely storms makes men expect a dearth.

All may be well; but if God sort it so

'Tis more than we deserve, or I expect.

2 CITIZEN   Truly, the hearts of men are full of fear:

You cannot reason almost with a man

That looks not heavily and full of dread.

3 CITIZEN   Before the days of change still is it so:

By a divine instinct men's minds mistrust

Ensuing danger, as by proof we see

The water swell before a boist'rous storm.

But leave it all to God. Whither away?

2 CITIZEN   Marry, we were sent for to the Justices.

3 CITIZEN   And so was I: I'll bear you company.

Exeunt.

2.4   *Enter* ARCHBISHOP *of York, the young* DUKE OF
YORK, QUEEN ELIZABETH *and the* DUCHESS OF YORK.

ARCHBISHOP

Last night, I hear, they lay at Stony Stratford,

And at Northampton they do rest tonight:

Tomorrow, or next day, they will be here.

DUCHESS   I long with all my heart to see the Prince;

I hope he is much grown since last I saw him.   5

ELIZABETH   But I hear no: they say my son of York

Has almost overta'en him in his growth.

YORK   Ay, mother, but I would not have it so.

DUCHESS   Why, my good cousin? It is good to grow.

YORK   Grandam, one night as we did sit at supper,   10

My uncle Rivers talk'd how I did grow

More than my brother. 'Ay,' quoth my uncle
    Gloucester,

'Small herbs have grace; great weeds do grow apace.'

And since, methinks I would not grow so fast,

Because sweet flowers are slow and weeds make
    haste.   15

DUCHESS

Good faith, good faith, the saying did not hold

In him that did object the same to thee!

He was the wretched'st thing when he was young,

So long a-growing, and so leisurely,

That if his rule were true, he should be gracious.   20

ARCHBISHOP

And so no doubt he is, my gracious madam.

DUCHESS   I hope he is, but yet let mothers doubt.

YORK   Now by my troth, if I had been remember'd,

I could have given my uncle's Grace a flout

To touch his growth nearer than he touch'd mine.   25

DUCHESS

How, my young York? I prithee let me hear it.

YORK   Marry, they say my uncle grew so fast

That he could gnaw a crust at two hours old:

'Twas full two years ere I could get a tooth.

Grandam, this would have been a biting jest!   30

DUCHESS   I prithee, pretty York, who told thee this?

YORK   Grandam, his nurse.

DUCHESS

His nurse? Why she was dead ere thou wast born.

YORK   If 'twere not she, I cannot tell who told me.

ELIZABETH   A parlous boy: go to, you are too shrewd.   35

DUCHESS   Good madam, be not angry with the child.

ELIZABETH   Pitchers have ears.

Enter a Messenger.

ARCHBISHOP   Here comes a messenger. What news?

MESSENGER

Such news, my lord, as grieves me to report.

ELIZABETH   How doth the Prince?

MESSENGER   Well, madam, and in health.   40

DUCHESS   What is thy news?

MESSENGER   Lord Rivers and Lord Grey

Are sent to Pomfret, and with them

Sir Thomas Vaughan, prisoners.

DUCHESS   Who hath committed them?

MESSENGER   The mighty Dukes,

Gloucester and Buckingham.

ARCHBISHOP   For what offence?   45

MESSENGER   The sum of all I can I have disclos'd:

Why or for what the nobles were committed
Is all unknown to me, my gracious lord.
50 ELIZABETH   Ay me! I see the ruin of my House:
The tiger now hath seiz'd the gentle hind;
Insulting tyranny begins to jut
Upon the innocent and aweless throne.
Welcome destruction, blood, and massacre;
I see, as in a map, the end of all.
55 DUCHESS   Accursed and unquiet wrangling days,
How many of you have mine eyes beheld!
My husband lost his life to get the crown,
And often up and down my sons were toss'd
For me to joy and weep their gain and loss;
60 And being seated, and domestic broils
Clean over-blown, themselves, the conquerors,
Make war upon themselves, brother to brother,
Blood to blood, self against self. O preposterous
And frantic outrage, end thy damned spleen,
65 Or let me die, to look on earth no more.
ELIZABETH   Come, come my boy: we will to sanctuary,
Madam, farewell.
DUCHESS   Stay, I will go with you.
ELIZABETH   You have no cause.
ARCHBISHOP   My gracious lady, go,
And thither bear your treasure and your goods.
70 For my part, I'll resign unto your Grace
The seal I keep; and so betide to me
As well I tender you and all of yours.
Go; I'll conduct you to the sanctuary.   *Exeunt.*

3.1 *The trumpets sound. Enter young* PRINCE EDWARD,
    the DUKES OF GLOUCESTER *and* BUCKINGHAM,
    LORD CARDINAL BOURCHIER, CATESBY, *with others.*

BUCKINGHAM
Welcome, sweet Prince, to London, to your chamber.
RICHARD
Welcome, dear cousin, my thoughts' sovereign.
The weary way hath made you melancholy.
PRINCE   No, uncle, but our crosses on the way
5 Have made it tedious, wearisome, and heavy;
I want more uncles here to welcome me.
RICHARD
Sweet Prince, the untainted virtue of your years
Hath not yet div'd into the world's deceit,
Nor more can you distinguish of a man
10 Than of his outward show, which – God He knows –
Seldom or never jumpeth with the heart:
Those uncles which you want were dangerous;
Your Grace attended to their sugar'd words,
But look'd not on the poison of their hearts.
God keep you from them, and from such false
15   friends!
PRINCE
God keep me from false friends – but they were
    none.

Enter Lord Mayor *with attendants.*

RICHARD
My Lord, the Mayor of London comes to greet you.
MAYOR
God bless your Grace with health and happy days!
PRINCE   I thank you, good my lord, and thank you all.
20 I thought my mother and my brother York
Would long ere this have met us on the way.
Fie, what a slug is Hastings, that he comes not
To tell us whether they will come or no.

Enter LORD HASTINGS.

BUCKINGHAM
And in good time, here comes the sweating lord.
PRINCE
25 Welcome, my lord. What, will our mother come?
HASTINGS   On what occasion God he knows, not I,
The Queen your mother and your brother York
Have taken sanctuary. The tender prince
Would fain have come with me to meet your Grace,
30 But by his mother was perforce withheld.
BUCKINGHAM   Fie, what an indirect and peevish course
Is this of hers! Lord Cardinal, will your Grace
Persuade the Queen to send the Duke of York
Unto his princely brother presently?
If she deny, Lord Hastings, go with him
35 And from her jealous arms pluck him perforce.
CARDINAL
My Lord of Buckingham, if my weak oratory
Can from his mother win the Duke of York,
Anon expect him here; but if she be obdurate
40 To mild entreaties, God in Heaven forbid
We should infringe the holy privilege
Of blessed sanctuary! Not for all this land
Would I be guilty of so deep a sin.
BUCKINGHAM   You are too senseless-obstinate, my lord,
45 Too ceremonious and traditional.
Weigh it but with the grossness of this age,
You break not sanctuary in seizing him;
The benefit thereof is always granted
To those whose dealings have deserv'd the place,
50 And those who have the wit to claim the place.
The prince hath neither claim'd it nor deserv'd it:
And therefore in mine opinion cannot have it;
Then taking him from thence that is not there,
You break no privilege nor charter there.
55 Oft have I heard of sanctuary men,
But sanctuary children, never till now.
CARDINAL
My lord, you shall o'er-rule my mind for once.
Come on, Lord Hastings, will you go with me?
HASTINGS   I go my lord.
PRINCE   Good lords, make all the speedy haste you may.
60   *Exeunt Cardinal and Hastings.*
Say, uncle Gloucester, if our brother come,
Where shall we sojourn till our coronation?
RICHARD   Where it seems best unto your royal self.
If I may counsel you, some day or two

65 Your Highness shall repose you at the Tower,
Then where you please and shall be thought most fit
For your best health and recreation.
PRINCE   I do not like the Tower, of any place.
Did Julius Caesar build that place, my lord?
BUCKINGHAM
70 He did, my gracious lord, begin that place,
Which since, succeeding ages have re-edified.
PRINCE   Is it upon record, or else reported
Successively from age to age, he built it?
BUCKINGHAM   Upon record, my gracious lord.
75 PRINCE   But say, my lord, it were not register'd,
Methinks the truth should live from age to age,
As 'twere retail'd to all posterity,
Even to the general all-ending day.
RICHARD [*aside*]
So wise so young, they say, do never live long.
80 PRINCE   What say you, uncle?
RICHARD   I say, without characters fame lives long.
[*aside*] Thus, like the formal Vice, Iniquity,
I moralize two meanings in one word.
PRINCE   That Julius Caesar was a famous man:
85 With what his valour did enrich his wit,
His wit set down to make his valour live;
Death makes no conquest of this conqueror,
For now he lives in fame, though not in life.
I'll tell you what, my cousin Buckingham.
90 BUCKINGHAM   What, my gracious lord?
PRINCE   And if I live until I be a man,
I'll win our ancient right in France again,
Or die a soldier, as I liv'd a king.
RICHARD   Short summers lightly have a forward spring.

Enter young DUKE OF YORK, HASTINGS, CARDINAL.

BUCKINGHAM
95 Now in good time here comes the Duke of York.
PRINCE   Richard of York: how fares our loving brother?
YORK   Well, my dread lord – so must I call you now.
PRINCE   Ay, brother, to our grief as it is yours;
Too late he died that might have kept that title,
100 Which by his death hath lost much majesty.
RICHARD   How fares our cousin, noble lord of York?
YORK   I thank you, gentle uncle. O my lord,
You said that idle weeds are fast in growth:
The Prince my brother hath outgrown me far!
RICHARD   He hath, my lord.
105 YORK   And therefore is he idle?
RICHARD   O my fair cousin, I must not say so!
YORK   Then he is more beholding to you than I.
RICHARD   He may command me as my sovereign,
But you have power in me as in a kinsman.
110 YORK   I pray you, uncle, give me this dagger.
RICHARD   My dagger, little cousin? With all my heart.
PRINCE   A beggar, brother?
YORK   Of my kind uncle, that I know will give,
And being but a toy, which is no grief to give.
115 RICHARD   A greater gift than that I'll give my cousin.

YORK   A greater gift? O, that's the sword to it.
RICHARD   Ay, gentle cousin, were it light enough.
YORK   O, then I see you will part but with light gifts;
In weightier things you'll say a beggar nay.
120 RICHARD   It is too heavy for your Grace to wear.
YORK   I weigh it lightly, were it heavier.
RICHARD
What, would you have my weapon, little lord?
YORK   I would, that I might thank you as you call me.
RICHARD   How?
125 YORK   Little.
PRINCE   My lord of York will still be cross in talk;
Uncle, your Grace knows how to bear with him.
YORK   You mean to bear me, not to bear with me;
Uncle, my brother mocks both you and me:
130 Because that I am little like an ape,
He thinks that you should bear me on your
    shoulders!
BUCKINGHAM
With what a sharp-provided wit he reasons:
To mitigate the scorn he gives his uncle
He prettily and aptly taunts himself.
135 So cunning and so young is wonderful!
RICHARD   My lord, will't please you pass along?
Myself and my good cousin Buckingham
Will to your mother, to entreat of her
To meet you at the Tower and welcome you.
140 YORK   What, will you go unto the Tower, my lord?
PRINCE   My Lord Protector needs will have it so.
YORK   I shall not sleep in quiet at the Tower.
RICHARD   Why, what should you fear?
YORK   Marry, my uncle Clarence' angry ghost:
145 My grandam told me he was murder'd there.
PRINCE   I fear no uncles dead.
RICHARD   Nor none that live, I hope?
PRINCE   And if they live, I hope I need not fear.
But come, my lord: with a heavy heart,
150 Thinking on them, go I unto the Tower.
*A Sennet. Exeunt Prince, York, Hastings, Dorset and all
    but Richard, Buckingham, and Catesby.*
BUCKINGHAM
Think you, my lord, this little prating York
Was not incensed by his subtle mother
To taunt and scorn you thus opprobriously?
RICHARD   No doubt, no doubt; O, 'tis a parlous boy,
155 Bold, quick, ingenious, forward, capable:
He is all the mother's, from the top to toe.
BUCKINGHAM
Well, let them rest. Come hither, Catesby:
Thou art sworn as deeply to effect what we intend
As closely to conceal what we impart;
160 Thou know'st our reasons, urg'd upon the way:
What think'st thou? Is it not an easy matter
To make William Lord Hastings of our mind
For the instalment of this noble Duke
In the seat royal of this famous isle?
165 CATESBY   He for his father's sake so loves the Prince

That he will not be won to aught against him.
BUCKINGHAM
　　What think'st thou then of Stanley? Will not he?
CATESBY　He will do all in all as Hastings doth.
BUCKINGHAM
　　Well, then, no more but this: go, gentle Catesby,
170　And as it were afar off, sound thou Lord Hastings
　　How he doth stand affected to our purpose,
　　And summon him tomorrow to the Tower
　　To sit about the coronation.
　　If thou dost find him tractable to us,
175　Encourage him, and tell him all our reasons;
　　If he be leaden, icy, cold, unwilling,
　　Be thou so too, and so break off the talk,
　　And give us notice of his inclination:
　　For we tomorrow hold divided Councils,
180　Wherein thyself shalt highly be employ'd.
RICHARD
　　Commend me to Lord William; tell him, Catesby,
　　His ancient knot of dangerous adversaries
　　Tomorrow are let blood at Pomfret castle,
　　And bid my lord for joy of this good news
185　Give Mistress Shore one gentle kiss the more.
BUCKINGHAM
　　Good Catesby, go effect this business soundly.
CATESBY　My good lords both, with all the heed I can.
RICHARD
　　Shall we hear from you, Catesby, ere we sleep?
CATESBY　You shall, my lord.
RICHARD
190　At Crosby Place, there shall you find us both.
　　　　　　　　　　　　　　　　　Exit Catesby.
BUCKINGHAM
　　Now, my lord, what shall we do if we perceive
　　Lord Hastings will not yield to our complots?
RICHARD
　　Chop off his head, man; somewhat will we do.
　　And look when I am king, claim thou of me
195　The earldom of Hereford, and all·the moveables
　　Whereof the King my brother was possess'd.
BUCKINGHAM
　　I'll claim that promise at your Grace's hand.
RICHARD
　　And look to have it yielded with all kindness.
　　Come, let us sup betimes, that afterwards
200　We may digest our complots in some form.　*Exeunt.*

3.2 *Enter a* Messenger *to the door of Lord Hastings.*

MESSENGER　My lord, my lord! [*Knocks.*]
HASTINGS [*within*]　Who knocks?
MESSENGER　One from the Lord Stanley.

　　　　　　　　Enter HASTINGS.

HASTINGS　What is't o'clock?
MESSENGER　　　　　　Upon the stroke of four.

HASTINGS
　　Cannot my Lord Stanley sleep these tedious nights?　5
MESSENGER　So it appears by that I have to say.
　　First, he commends him to your noble self.
HASTINGS　What then?
MESSENGER
　　Then certifies your lordship that this night
　　He dreamt the boar had razed off his helm;　　10
　　Besides, he says there are two Councils kept,
　　And that may be determin'd at the one
　　Which may make you and him to rue at th'other.
　　Therefore he sends to know your lordship's pleasure,
　　If you will presently take horse with him　　15
　　And with all speed post with him toward the north,
　　To shun the danger that his soul divines.
HASTINGS　Go, fellow, go: return unto thy lord;
　　Bid him not fear the separated Council:
　　His honour and myself are at the one,　　20
　　And at the other is my good friend Catesby,
　　Where nothing can proceed that toucheth us
　　Whereof I shall not have intelligence.
　　Tell him his fears are shallow, without instance;
　　And for his dreams, I wonder he's so simple　　25
　　To trust the mockery of unquiet slumbers.
　　To fly the boar before the boar pursues
　　Were to incense the boar to follow us,
　　And make pursuit where he did mean no chase.
　　Go, bid thy master rise, and come to me,　　30
　　And we will both together to the Tower,
　　Where he shall see the boar will use us kindly.
MESSENGER
　　I'll go, my lord, and tell him what you say.　*Exit.*

　　　　　　　　Enter CATESBY.

CATESBY　Many good morrows to my noble lord.
HASTINGS
　　Good morrow, Catesby; you are early stirring.　35
　　What news, what news in this our tott'ring state?
CATESBY　It is a reeling world indeed, my lord,
　　And I believe will never stand upright
　　Till Richard wear the garland of the realm.
HASTINGS
　　How, wear the garland? Dost thou mean the crown?　40
CATESBY　Ay, my good lord.
HASTINGS
　　I'll have this crown of mine cut from my shoulders
　　Before I'll see the crown so foul misplac'd.
　　But canst thou guess that he doth aim at it?
CATESBY　Ay, on my life, and hopes to find you forward　45
　　Upon his party for the gain thereof;
　　And thereupon he sends you this good news
　　That this same very day your enemies,
　　The kindred of the Queen, must die at Pomfret.
HASTINGS　Indeed, I am no mourner for that news,　50
　　Because they have been still my adversaries:
　　But that I'll give my voice on Richard's side

To bar my master's heirs in true descent,
God knows I will not do it, to the death.
CATESBY
God keep your lordship in that gracious mind.
HASTINGS
But I shall laugh at this a twelve-month hence,
That they which brought me in my master's hate,
I live to look upon their tragedy.
Well, Catesby, ere a fortnight make me older
I'll send some packing that yet think not on't.
CATESBY 'Tis a vile thing to die, my gracious lord,
When men are unprepar'd and look not for't.
HASTINGS
O, monstrous, monstrous! And so falls it out
With Rivers, Vaughan, Grey: and so 'twill do
With some men else that think themselves as safe
As thou and I, who as thou know'st are dear
To princely Richard and to Buckingham.
CATESBY
The Princes both make high account of you –
[*aside*] For they account his head upon the Bridge.
HASTINGS   I know they do, and I have well deserv'd it.

Enter STANLEY, EARL OF DERBY.

Come on, come on: where is your boar-spear, man?
Fear you the boar, and go so unprovided?
STANLEY
My lord, good morrow; good morrow, Catesby.
You may jest on, but by the holy Rood,
I do not like these several Councils, I.
HASTINGS   My lord, I hold my life as dear as you,
And never in my days, I do protest,
Was it so precious to me as 'tis now:
Think you, but that I know our state secure,
I would be so triumphant as I am?
STANLEY
The lords at Pomfret, when they rode from London,
Were jocund, and suppos'd their states were sure,
And they indeed had no cause to mistrust:
But yet you see how soon the day o'ercast.
This sudden stab of rancour I misdoubt;
Pray God, I say, I prove a needless coward.
What, shall we toward the Tower? The day is spent.
HASTINGS
Come, come: have with you. Wot you what, my lord?
Today the lords you talk'd of are beheaded.
STANLEY
They, for their truth, might better wear their heads
Than some that have accus'd them wear their hats.
But come, my lord, let's away.

Enter HASTINGS, *a Pursuivant.*

HASTINGS   Go on before; I'll talk with this good fellow.
Exeunt Stanley and Catesby.
Well met, Hastings; how goes the world with thee?
H. PURSUIVANT
The better that your lordship please to ask.

HASTINGS   I tell thee, man, 'tis better with me now
Than when I met thee last, where now we meet:
Then was I going prisoner to the Tower,
By the suggestion of the Queen's allies:
But now I tell thee – keep it to thyself –
This day those enemies are put to death,
And I in better state than e'er I was!
H. PURSUIVANT
God hold it to your honour's good content.
HASTINGS
Gramercy, Hastings: there, drink that for me.
[*Throws him his purse.*]
H. PURSUIVANT   I thank your honour.   *Exit.*

Enter a Priest.

PRIEST
Well met, my lord; I am glad to see your honour.
HASTINGS
I thank thee, good Sir John, with all my heart.
I am in your debt for your last exercise:
Come the next sabbath and I will content you.
[*He whispers in his ear.*]

Enter BUCKINGHAM.

PRIEST   I'll wait upon your lordship.   *Exit Priest.*
BUCKINGHAM
What, talking with a priest, Lord Chamberlain?
Your friends at Pomfret, they do need the priest;
Your honour hath no shriving work in hand!
HASTINGS   Good faith, and when I met this holy man,
The men you talk of came into my mind.
What, go you toward the Tower?
BUCKINGHAM
I do, my lord, but long I cannot stay there:
I shall return before your lordship thence.
HASTINGS   Nay, like enough, for I stay dinner there.
BUCKINGHAM [*aside*]
And supper too, although thou know'st it not.
Come, will you go?
HASTINGS   I'll wait upon your lordship.
Exeunt.

3.3   *Enter* SIR RICHARD RATCLIFFE, *with halberds,*
carrying the nobles, RIVERS, GREY *and* VAUGHAN,
to death at Pomfret.

RATCLIFFE   Come, bring forth the prisoners.
RIVERS   Sir Richard Ratcliffe, let me tell thee this:
Today shalt thou behold a subject die
For truth, for duty, and for loyalty.
GREY   God bless the Prince from all the pack of you!
A knot you are of damned bloodsuckers.
VAUGHAN
You live, that shall cry woe for this hereafter.
RATCLIFFE   Dispatch: the limit of your lives is out.
RIVERS   O Pomfret, Pomfret! O thou bloody prison,
Fatal and ominous to noble peers!

Within the guilty closure of thy walls
Richard the Second here was hack'd to death;
And for more slander to thy dismal seat,
We give to thee our guiltless blood to drink.

15 GREY Now Margaret's curse is fall'n upon our heads,
When she exclaim'd on Hastings, you, and I,
For standing by when Richard stabb'd her son.

RIVERS
Then curs'd she Richard, then curs'd she Buckingham,
Then curs'd she Hastings. O remember, God,

20 To hear her prayer for them, as now for us;
And for my sister and her princely sons,
Be satisfied, dear God, with our true blood,
Which – as thou know'st – unjustly must be spilt.

RATCLIFFE Make haste: the hour of death is expiate.

RIVERS
25 Come Grey, come Vaughan, let us here embrace.
Farewell, until we meet again in Heaven. *Exeunt.*

3.4 *Enter* BUCKINGHAM, STANLEY, EARL OF DERBY,
HASTINGS, *the* Bishop of ELY, NORFOLK, RATCLIFFE,
LOVELL, *with others, at a table.*

HASTINGS Now, noble peers, the cause why we are met
Is to determine of the coronation.
In God's name speak: when is the royal day?

BUCKINGHAM Is all things ready for the royal time?

5 STANLEY It is, and wants but nomination.

ELY Tomorrow, then, I judge a happy day.

BUCKINGHAM
Who knows the Lord Protector's mind herein?
Who is most inward with the noble Duke?

ELY
Your Grace, we think, should soonest know his mind.

BUCKINGHAM
10 We know each other's faces; for our hearts
He knows no more of mine than I of yours,
Or I of his, my lord, than you of mine.
Lord Hastings, you and he are near in love.

HASTINGS I thank his Grace, I know he loves me well;
15 But for his purpose in the coronation
I have not sounded him, nor he deliver'd
His gracious pleasure any way therein.
But you, my honourable lords, may name the time,
And in the Duke's behalf I'll give my voice,
20 Which I presume he'll take in gentle part.

Enter RICHARD.

ELY In happy time, here comes the Duke himself.

RICHARD
My noble lords and cousins all, good morrow:
I have been long a sleeper, but I trust
My absence doth neglect no great design
25 Which by my presence might have been concluded.

BUCKINGHAM
Had you not come upon your cue, my lord,
William Lord Hastings had pronounc'd your part –

I mean your voice for crowning of the King.

RICHARD
Than my Lord Hastings no man might be bolder:
His lordship knows me well, and loves me well.   30
My Lord of Ely, when I was last in Holborn
I saw good strawberries in your garden there;
I do beseech you, send for some of them.

ELY Marry, and will, my lord, with all my heart. *Exit.*

RICHARD Cousin of Buckingham, a word with you.   35
Catesby hath sounded Hastings in our business,
And finds the testy gentleman so hot
That he will lose his head ere give consent
His master's child (as worshipfully he terms it)
Shall lose the royalty of England's throne.   40

BUCKINGHAM
Withdraw yourself a while: I'll go with you.
Exeunt Richard and Buckingham.

STANLEY
We have not yet set down this day of triumph.
Tomorrow, in my judgement, is too sudden,
For I myself am not so well provided
As else I would be, were the day prolong'd.   45

Enter Bishop of ELY.

ELY Where is my lord the Duke of Gloucester?
I have sent for these strawberries.

HASTINGS
His Grace looks cheerfully and smooth today:
There's some conceit or other likes him well
When that he bids good morrow with such spirit.   50
I think there's never a man in Christendom
Can lesser hide his love or hate than he,
For by his face straight shall you know his heart.

STANLEY What of his heart perceive you in his face
By any livelihood he show'd today?   55

HASTINGS
Marry, that with no man here he is offended,
For were he, he had shown it in his looks.

STANLEY I pray God he be not, I say.

Enter RICHARD *and* BUCKINGHAM.

RICHARD I pray you all, tell me what they deserve
That do conspire my death with devilish plots   60
Of damned witchcraft, and that have prevail'd
Upon my body with their hellish charms?

HASTINGS The tender love I bear your Grace, my lord,
Makes me most forward in this princely presence,
To doom th'offenders, whatso'er they be: 65
I say, my lord, they have deserved death.

RICHARD Then be your eyes the witness of their evil.
See how I am bewitch'd! Behold, mine arm
Is like a blasted sapling wither'd up!
And this is Edward's wife, that monstrous witch,   70
Consorted with that harlot, strumpet Shore,
That by their witchcraft thus have marked me.

HASTINGS
If they have done this deed, my noble lord –

RICHARD If? Thou protector of this damned strumpet,
75   Talk'st thou to me of ifs! Thou art a traitor:
     Off with his head! Now by Saint Paul I swear
     I will not dine until I see the same.
     Lovell and Ratcliffe, look that it be done;
     The rest that love me, rise and follow me.
                    Exeunt all but Lovell and Ratcliffe
                         and the Lord Hastings.
80 HASTINGS Woe, woe for England; not a whit for me –
     For I, too fond, might have prevented this.
     Stanley did dream the boar did raze his helm,
     And I did scorn it and disdain to fly;
     Three times today my foot-cloth horse did stumble,
85   And started when he look'd upon the Tower,
     As loath to bear me to the slaughter-house.
     O, now I need the priest that spake to me;
     I now repent I told the pursuivant,
     As too triumphing, how mine enemies
90   Today at Pomfret bloodily were butcher'd,
     And I myself secure in grace and favour.
     O Margaret, Margaret, now thy heavy curse
     Is lighted on poor Hastings' wretched head.
RATCLIFFE
     Come, come, dispatch: the Duke would be at dinner;
95   Make a short shrift: he longs to see your head.
HASTINGS O momentary grace of mortal men,
     Which we more hunt for than the grace of God.
     Who builds his hope in air of your good looks
     Lives like a drunken sailor on a mast,
100 Ready with every nod to tumble down
     Into the fatal bowels of the deep.
LOVELL Come, come, dispatch: 'tis bootless to exclaim.
HASTINGS O bloody Richard! Miserable England,
     I prophesy the fearfull'st time to thee
105 That ever wretched age hath look'd upon.
     Come, lead me to the block: bear him my head.
     They smile at me who shortly shall be dead. *Exeunt.*

3.5   *Enter* RICHARD *and* BUCKINGHAM
           in rotten armour, marvellous ill-favoured.

RICHARD
     Come, cousin, canst thou quake and change thy colour,
     Murder thy breath in middle of a word,
     And then again begin, and stop again,
     As if thou were distraught and mad with terror?
BUCKINGHAM
     Tut, I can counterfeit the deep tragedian,
5   Speak, and look back, and pry on every side,
     Tremble and start at wagging of a straw,
     Intending deep suspicion. Ghastly looks
     Are at my service like enforced smiles,
     And both are ready in their offices
10   At any time to grace my stratagems.
     But what, is Catesby gone?

          Enter the Lord Mayor *and* CATESBY.

RICHARD He is, and see, he brings the Mayor along.
BUCKINGHAM Lord Mayor –
RICHARD Look to the draw-bridge there!   15
BUCKINGHAM Hark, a drum!
RICHARD Catesby, o'erlook the walls!   *Exit Catesby.*
BUCKINGHAM Lord Mayor, the reason we have sent –

    Enter LOVELL *and* RATCLIFFE, *with Hastings's head.*

RICHARD Look back! Defend thee, here are enemies!
BUCKINGHAM
     God and our innocence defend and guard us!   20
RICHARD
     Be patient, they are friends: Ratcliffe and Lovell.
LOVELL Here is the head of that ignoble traitor,
     The dangerous and unsuspected Hastings.
RICHARD So dear I lov'd the man that I must weep.
     I took him for the plainest harmless creature   25
     That breath'd upon the earth a Christian;
     Made him my book, wherein my soul recorded
     The history of all her secret thoughts.
     So smooth he daub'd his vice with show of virtue
     That, his apparent open guilt omitted –   30
     I mean his conversation with Shore's wife –
     He liv'd from all attainder of suspects.
BUCKINGHAM
     Well, well, he was the covert'st shelter'd traitor.
     Would you imagine, or almost believe,
     Were't not that by great preservation   35
     We live to tell it, that the subtle traitor
     This day had plotted, in the council-house,
     To murder me and my good lord of Gloucester?
MAYOR Had he done so?
RICHARD What, think you we are Turks or infidels?   40
     Or that we would, against the form of law,
     Proceed thus rashly in the villain's death,
     But that the extreme peril of the case,
     The peace of England, and our persons' safety,
     Enforc'd us to this execution.   45
MAYOR Now fair befall you! He deserv'd his death,
     And your good Graces both have well proceeded,
     To warn false traitors from the like attempts.
BUCKINGHAM I never look'd for better at his hands
     After he once fell in with Mistress Shore.   50
     Yet had we not determin'd he should die
     Until your lordship came to see his end –
     Which now the loving haste of these our friends,
     Something against our meanings, have prevented –
     Because, my lord, we would have had you heard   55
     The traitor speak, and timorously confess
     The manner and the purpose of his treasons,
     That you might well have signified the same
     Unto the citizens, who haply may
     Misconstrue us in him and wail his death.   60
MAYOR
     But, my good lord, your Graces' words shall serve
     As well as I had seen and heard him speak;
     And do not doubt, right noble princes both,

But I'll acquaint our duteous citizens
65   With all your just proceedings in this cause.
RICHARD
And to that end we wish'd your lordship here,
T' avoid the censures of the carping world.
BUCKINGHAM
Which, since you come too late of our intent,
Yet witness what you hear we did intend:
70   And so, my good Lord Mayor, we bid farewell.
                         Exit Lord Mayor.
RICHARD   Go after, after, cousin Buckingham:
The Mayor towards Guildhall hies him in all post.
There, at your meet'st advantage of the time,
Infer the bastardy of Edward's children;
75   Tell them how Edward put to death a citizen
Only for saying he would make his son
Heir to the Crown – meaning indeed his house,
Which by the sign thereof was termed so.
Moreover, urge his hateful luxury
80   And bestial appetite in change of lust,
Which stretch'd unto their servants, daughters,
     wives,
Even where his raging eye or savage heart
Without control lusted to make a prey.
Nay, for a need, thus far come near my person:
85   Tell them, when that my mother went with child
Of that insatiate Edward, noble York
My princely father then had wars in France,
And by true computation of the time
Found that the issue was not his-begot;
90   Which well appeared in his lineaments,
Being nothing like the noble Duke, my father –
Yet touch this sparingly, as 'twere far off;
Because, my lord, you know my mother lives.
BUCKINGHAM   Doubt not, my lord: I'll play the orator
95   As if the golden fee for which I plead
Were for myself; and so, my lord, adieu.
RICHARD
If you thrive well, bring them to Baynard's Castle,
Where you shall find me well accompanied
With reverend fathers and well-learned bishops.
100   BUCKINGHAM   I go, and towards three or four o'clock
Look for the news that the Guildhall affords.   *Exit.*
RICHARD   Go, Lovell, with all speed, to Doctor Shaa;
[*to Ratcliffe*] Go thou to Friar Penker; bid them both
Meet me within this hour at Baynard's Castle.
                  Exeunt Ratcliffe and Lovell.
Now will I go to take some privy order
105   To draw the brats of Clarence out of sight,
And to give notice that no manner person
Have, any time, recourse unto the Princes.   *Exit.*

3.6   *Enter a* Scrivener *with a paper in his hand.*

SCRIVENER
Here is the indictment of the good Lord Hastings,
Which in a set hand fairly is engross'd,

That it may be today read o'er in Paul's.
And mark how well the sequel hangs together:
Eleven hours I have spent to write it over,   5
For yesternight by Catesby was it sent me;
The precedent was full as long a-doing
And yet within these five hours Hastings liv'd,
Untainted, unexamin'd, free, at liberty.
Here's a good world the while! Who is so gross   10
That cannot see this palpable device?
Yet who's so bold but says he sees it not?
Bad is the world, and all will come to naught
When such ill-dealing must be seen in thought. *Exit.*

3.7   *Enter* RICHARD *and* BUCKINGHAM *at several doors.*

RICHARD   How now, how now? What say the citizens?
BUCKINGHAM   Now by the holy Mother of our Lord,
The citizens are mum, say not a word.
RICHARD
Touch'd you the bastardy of Edward's children?
BUCKINGHAM   I did, with his contract with Lady Lucy,   5
And his contract by deputy in France;
Th'unsatiate greediness of his desire,
And his enforcement of the city wives;
His tyranny for trifles; his own bastardy,
As being got, your father then in France,   10
And his resemblance, being not like the Duke.
Withal, I did infer your lineaments –
Being the right idea of your father,
Both in your form and nobleness of mind –
Laid open all your victories in Scotland,   15
Your discipline in war, wisdom in peace,
Your bounty, virtue, fair humility;
Indeed, left nothing fitting for your purpose
Untouch'd, or slightly handled in discourse.
And when mine oratory drew to an end,   20
I bid them that did love their country's good
Cry, 'God save Richard, England's royal King!'
RICHARD   And did they so?
BUCKINGHAM
No, so God help me: they spake not a word,
But like dumb statues or breathing stones   25
Star'd each on other, and look'd deadly pale.
Which when I saw, I reprehended them,
And ask'd the Mayor what meant this wilful silence.
His answer was, the people were not us'd
To be spoke to but by the Recorder.   30
Then he was urg'd to tell my tale again:
'Thus saith the Duke; thus hath the Duke inferr'd' –
But nothing spake in warrant from himself.
When he had done, some followers of mine own
At lower end of the hall, hurl'd up their caps,   35
And some ten voices cried 'God save King Richard!'
And thus I took the vantage of those few:
'Thanks gentle citizens and friends,' quoth I;
'This general applause and cheerful shout
Argues your wisdoms and your love to Richard.'   40

And even here brake off, and came away.

RICHARD
What, tongueless blocks were they? Would they not
    speak!
Will not the Mayor then and his brethren come?

BUCKINGHAM
The Mayor is here at hand. Intend some fear;
Be not you spoke with but by mighty suit.
And look you get a prayer-book in your hand,
And stand between two churchmen, good my lord:
For on that ground I'll build a holy descant.
And be not easily won to our requests:
Play the maid's part: still answer nay, and take it.

RICHARD   I go, and if you plead as well for them
As I can say nay to thee for myself,
No doubt we bring it to a happy issue.

BUCKINGHAM
Go, go up to the leads, the Lord Mayor knocks.
                                        Exit Richard.

Enter the Lord Mayor *and citizens.*

Welcome, my lord: I dance attendance here.
I think the Duke will not be spoke withal.

Enter CATESBY *above.*

Now, Catesby, what says your lord to my request?

CATESBY   He doth entreat your Grace, my noble lord,
To visit him tomorrow, or next day:
He is within, with two right reverend fathers,
Divinely bent to meditation;
And in no worldly suits would he be mov'd
To draw him from his holy exercise.

BUCKINGHAM
Return, good Catesby, to the gracious Duke;
Tell him myself, the Mayor and aldermen,
In deep designs, in matter of great moment,
No less importing than our general good,
Are come to have some conference with his Grace.

CATESBY   I'll signify so much unto him straight.   *Exit.*

BUCKINGHAM
Ah ha, my lord, this prince is not an Edward:
He is not lolling on a lewd love-bed,
But on his knees at meditation;
Not dallying with a brace of courtesans,
But meditating with two deep divines;
Not sleeping, to engross his idle body,
But praying, to enrich his watchful soul.
Happy were England, would this virtuous Prince
Take on his Grace the sovereignty thereof.
But sure I fear we shall not win him to it.

MAYOR
Marry, God defend his Grace should say us nay!

BUCKINGHAM   I fear he will.

Enter CATESBY.

                    Here Catesby comes again.
Now, Catesby, what says his Grace?

CATESBY   He wonders to what end you have assembled
Such troops of citizens to come to him,
His Grace not being warn'd thereof before.
He fears, my lord, you mean no good to him.

BUCKINGHAM   Sorry I am my noble cousin should
Suspect me that I mean no good to him.
By heaven, we come to him in perfect love:
And so once more return and tell his Grace.
                                        Exit Catesby.
When holy and devout religious men
Are at their beads, 'tis much to draw them thence,
So sweet is zealous contemplation.

Enter RICHARD *aloft, between two bishops with* CATESBY.

MAYOR
See where his Grace stands, 'tween two clergymen!

BUCKINGHAM
Two props of virtue for a Christian Prince,
To stay him from the fall of vanity;
And see, a book of prayer in his hand –
True ornaments to know a holy man.
Famous Plantagenet, most gracious Prince,
Lend favourable ear to our requests,
And pardon us the interruption
Of thy devotion and right Christian zeal.

RICHARD   My lord, there needs no such apology;
I do beseech your Grace to pardon me,
Who – earnest in the service of my God –
Deferr'd the visitation of my friends.
But leaving this, what is your Grace's pleasure?

BUCKINGHAM
Even that, I hope, which pleaseth God above,
And all good men of this ungovern'd isle.

RICHARD   I do suspect I have done some offence
That seems disgracious in the City's eye.
And that you come to reprehend my ignorance.

BUCKINGHAM
You have, my lord: would it might please your Grace
On our entreaties to emend your fault.

RICHARD   Else wherefore breathe I in a Christian land?

BUCKINGHAM
Know then, it is your fault that you resign
The supreme seat, the throne majestical,
The sceptred office of your ancestors,
Your state of fortune, and your due of birth,
The lineal glory of your royal House,
To the corruption of a blemish'd stock;
Whiles in the mildness of your sleepy thoughts –
Which here we waken to our country's good –
The noble isle doth want her proper limbs;
Her face defac'd with scars of infamy,
Her royal stock graft with ignoble plants,
And almost shoulder'd in the swallowing gulf
Of dark forgetfulness and deep oblivion;
Which to recure, we heartily solicit
Your gracious self to take on you the charge
And kingly government of this your land,

Not as Protector, steward, substitute,
Or lowly factor for another's gain,
But as successively from blood to blood,
135   Your right of birth, your empery, your own.
For this, consorted with the citizens –
Your very worshipful and loving friends,
And by their vehement instigation –
In this just cause come I to move your Grace.
140 RICHARD   I cannot tell if to depart in silence
Or bitterly to speak in your reproof
Best fitteth my degree or your condition.
If not to answer, you might haply think
Tongue-tied ambition, not replying, yielded
145   To bear the golden yoke of sovereignty
Which fondly you would here impose on me;
If to reprove you for this suit of yours,
So season'd with your faithful love to me,
Then, on the other side, I check'd my friends.
150   Therefore, to speak, and to avoid the first,
And then, in speaking, not to incur the last,
Definitively thus I answer you:
Your love deserves my thanks, but my desert
Unmeritable shuns your high request.
155   First, if all obstacles were cut away,
And that my path were even to the crown
As the ripe revenue and due of birth,
Yet so much is my poverty of spirit,
So mighty and so many my defects,
160   That I would rather hide me from my greatness –
Being a bark to brook no mighty sea –
Than in my greatness covet to be hid,
And in the vapour of my glory smother'd.
But, God be thank'd, there is no need of me –
165   And much I need, to help you, were there need.
The royal tree hath left us royal fruit,
Which, mellow'd by the stealing hours of time,
Will well become the seat of majesty,
And make, no doubt, us happy by his reign.
170   On him I lay that you would lay on me:
The right and fortune of his happy stars,
Which God defend that I should wring from him.
BUCKINGHAM
My lord, this argues conscience in your Grace;
But the respects thereof are nice and trivial,
175   All circumstances well considered.
You say that Edward is your brother's son:
So say we too – but not by Edward's wife.
For first was he contract to Lady Lucy
(Your mother lives a witness to his vow),
180   And afterward by substitute betroth'd
To Bona, sister to the King of France.
These both put off, a poor petitioner,
A care-craz'd mother to a many sons,
A beauty-waning and distressed widow,
185   Even in the afternoon of her best days
Made prize and purchase of his wanton eye,
Seduc'd the pitch and height of his degree

To base declension and loath'd bigamy.
By her, in his unlawful bed, he got
This Edward, whom our manners call the Prince.   190
More bitterly could I expostulate,
Save that for reverence to some alive
I give a sparing limit to my tongue.
Then, good my lord, take to your royal self
This proffer'd benefit of dignity: 195
If not to bless us and the land withal,
Yet to draw forth your noble ancestry
From the corruption of abusing times
Unto a lineal, true-derived course.
MAYOR   Do, good my lord: your citizens entreat you.   200
BUCKINGHAM
Refuse not, mighty lord, this proffer'd love.
CATESBY   O make them joyful; grant their lawful suit.
RICHARD   Alas, why would you heap this care on me?
I am unfit for state and majesty.
I do beseech you, take it not amiss;   205
I cannot, nor I will not, yield to you.
BUCKINGHAM   If you refuse it, as in love and zeal
Loath to despose the child, your brother's son –
As well we know your tenderness of heart,
And gentle, kind, effeminate remorse,   210
Which we have noted in you to your kindred,
And equally indeed to all estates –
Yet know, whe'er you accept our suit or no,
Your brother's son shall never reign our king,
But we will plant some other in the throne   215
To the disgrace and downfall of your House;
And with this resolution here we leave you.
Come, citizens; zounds, I'll entreat no more.
RICHARD   O, do not swear, my lord of Buckingham!
Exeunt Buckingham, Lord Mayor, and citizens.
CATESBY
Call him again, sweet Prince; accept their suit.   220
If you deny them, all the land will rue it.
RICHARD   Will you enforce me to a world of cares?
Call them again. I am not made of stones,
But penetrable to your kind entreaties,
Albeit against my conscience and my soul.   225

Enter BUCKINGHAM *and the rest.*

Cousin of Buckingham, and sage grave men,
Since you will buckle fortune on my back
To bear her burden whe'er I will or no,
I must have patience to endure the load.
But if black scandal, or foul-fac'd reproach,   230
Attend the sequel of your imposition,
Your mere enforcement shall acquittance me
From all the impure blots and stains thereof:
For God doth know, and you may partly see,
How far I am from the desire of this.   235
MAYOR   God bless your Grace: we see it, and will say it.
RICHARD   In saying so, you shall but say the truth.
BUCKINGHAM   Then I salute you with this royal title:
Long live Richard, England's worthy King!

40 ALL   Amen.

BUCKINGHAM

Tomorrow may it please you to be crown'd?

RICHARD   Even when you please, for you will have it so.

BUCKINGHAM

Tomorrow then we will attend your Grace;

And so most joyfully we take our leave.

45 RICHARD   Come, let us to our holy work again.

Farewell my cousin, farewell gentle friends.   *Exeunt.*

4.1 *Enter* QUEEN ELIZABETH, *the* DUCHESS OF YORK,
MARQUESS OF DORSET *at one door;* ANNE, DUCHESS OF
GLOUCESTER *at another door with Clarence's daughter.*

DUCHESS   Who meets us here? My niece Plantagenet

Led in the hand of her kind aunt of Gloucester:

Now, for my life, she's wandering to the Tower,

On pure heart's love, to greet the tender Prince.

Daughter, well met.

ANNE   God give your Graces both

A happy and a joyful time of day.

ELIZABETH

As much to you, good sister; whither away?

ANNE   No farther than the Tower, and as I guess,

Upon the like devotion as yourselves:

To gratulate the gentle Princes there.

ELIZABETH   Kind sister, thanks; we'll enter all together.

Enter BRAKENBURY.

And in good time, here the Lieutenant comes.

Master Lieutenant, pray you by your leave:

How doth the Prince and my young son of York?

BRAKENBURY

Right well, dear madam. By your patience,

I may not suffer you to visit them:

The King hath strictly charg'd the contrary.

ELIZABETH   The King! Who's that?

BRAKENBURY   I mean the Lord Protector.

ELIZABETH

The Lord protect him from that kingly title!

Hath he set bounds between their love and me?

I am their mother; who shall bar me from them?

DUCHESS   I am their father's mother: I will see them.

ANNE   Their aunt I am in law, in love their mother;

Then bring me to their sights. I'll bear thy blame,

And take thy office from thee, on my peril.

BRAKENBURY   No, madam, no: I may not leave it so.

I am bound by oath; and therefore pardon me.   *Exit.*

Enter STANLEY, EARL OF DERBY.

STANLEY   Let me but meet you, ladies, one hour hence,

And I'll salute your Grace of York as mother

And reverend looker-on of two fair queens.

[*to Anne*] Come, madam, you must straight to
Westminster,

There to be crowned Richard's royal queen.

ELIZABETH   Ah, cut my lace asunder

That my pent heart may have some scope to beat,

Or else I swoon with this dead-killing news.   35

ANNE   Despiteful tidings! O unpleasing news!

DORSET

Be of good cheer, mother: how fares your Grace?

ELIZABETH   O Dorset, speak not to me; get thee gone.

Death and destruction dogs thee at thy heels;

Thy mother's name is ominous to children.   40

If thou wilt outstrip death, go, cross the seas

And live with Richmond, from the reach of hell.

Go: hie thee, hie thee from this slaughter-house

Lest thou increase the number of the dead,

And make me die the thrall of Margaret's curse: 45

Nor mother, wife, nor England's counted Queen.

STANLEY

Full of wise care is this your counsel, madam.

[*to Dorset*] Take all the swift advantage of the hours;

You shall have letters from me to my son

In your behalf, to meet you on the way.   50

Be not ta'en tardy by unwise delay.

DUCHESS   O ill-dispersing wind of misery!

O my accursed womb, the bed of death!

A cockatrice hast thou hatch'd to the world

Whose unavoided eye is murderous.   55

STANLEY   Come madam, come: I in all haste was sent.

ANNE   And I with all unwillingness will go.

O would to God that the inclusive verge

Of golden metal that must round my brow

Were red-hot steel, to sear me to the brains.   60

Anointed let me be with deadly venom,

And die ere men can say 'God save the Queen'.

ELIZABETH   Go, go, poor soul; I envy not thy glory.

To feed my humour, wish thyself no harm.

ANNE   No? Why? When he that is my husband now   65

Came to me as I follow'd Henry's corse,

When scarce the blood was well wash'd from his
hands

Which issued from my other angel-husband,

And that dear saint which then I weeping follow'd;

O when, I say, I look'd on Richard's face   70

This was my wish: 'Be thou', quoth I, 'accurs'd

For making me, so young, so old a widow;

And when thou wed'st, let sorrow haunt thy bed;

And be thy wife – if any be so mad –

More miserable by the life of thee   75

Than thou hast made me by my dear lord's death'.

Lo, ere I can repeat this curse again,

Within so small a time, my woman's heart

Grossly grew captive to his honey words,

And prov'd the subject of mine own soul's curse,   80

Which hitherto hath held my eyes from rest;

For never yet one hour in his bed

Did I enjoy the golden dew of sleep,

But with his timorous dreams was still awak'd.

Besides, he hates me for my father Warwick,   85

And will, no doubt, shortly be rid of me.
ELIZABETH
    Poor heart, adieu; I pity thy complaining.
ANNE   No more than with my soul I mourn for yours.
DORSET   Farewell, thou woeful welcomer of glory.
90 ANNE   Adieu, poor soul, that tak'st thy leave of it.
DUCHESS [*to Dorset*]
    Go thou to Richmond, and good fortune guide thee;
    [*to Anne*] Go thou to Richard, and good angels tend
        thee;
    [*to Elizabeth*] Go thou to sanctuary, and good
        thoughts posess thee;
    I to my grave, where peace and rest lie with me.
95   Eighty odd years of sorrow have I seen,
    And each hour's joy wrack'd with a week of teen.
ELIZABETH   Stay, yet look back with me unto the Tower.
    Pity, you ancient stones, those tender babes
    Whom envy hath immur'd within your walls –
100   Rough cradle for such little pretty ones,
    Rude ragged nurse, old sullen playfellow
    For tender princes, use my babies well.
    So foolish sorrows bids your stones farewell. *Exeunt.*

4.2   *The trumpets sound a sennet. Enter* RICHARD
in pomp, crowned; BUCKINGHAM, CATESBY, RATCLIFFE,
        LOVELL *with other nobles and a* Page.

KING RICHARD   Stand all apart. Cousin of Buckingham!
BUCKINGHAM   My gracious sovereign!
KING RICHARD   Give me thy hand.
    [*Here he ascendeth the throne.*]   [*Sound trumpets.*]
                    Thus high, by thy advice
    And thy assistance is King Richard seated.
5   But shall we wear these glories for a day.
    Or shall they last, and we rejoice in them?
BUCKINGHAM   Still live they, and for ever let them last!
KING RICHARD
    Ah, Buckingham, now do I play the touch
    To try if thou be current gold indeed.
10   Young Edward lives – think now what I would speak.
BUCKINGHAM   Say on, my loving lord.
KING RICHARD
    Why, Buckingham, I say I would be King.
BUCKINGHAM
    Why so you are, my thrice-renowned lord.
KING RICHARD
    Ha, am I King? 'Tis so – but Edward lives.
BUCKINGHAM   True, noble Prince.
15 KING RICHARD   O bitter consequence,
    That Edward still should live – true noble prince!
    Cousin, thou wast not wont to be so dull.
    Shall I be plain? I wish the bastards dead,
    And I would have it suddenly perform'd.
20   What say'st thou now? Speak suddenly, be brief.
BUCKINGHAM   Your Grace may do your pleasure.
KING RICHARD
    Tut, tut, thou art all ice; thy kindness freezes.
    Say, have I thy consent that they shall die?

BUCKINGHAM
    Give me some little breath, some pause, dear lord,
    Before I positively speak in this;   25
    I will resolve you herein presently.   *Exit.*
CATESBY   The King is angry: see, he gnaws his lip.
KING RICHARD [*aside*]
    I will converse with iron-witted fools
    And unrespective boys; none are for me
    That look into me with considerate eyes.   30
    High-reaching Buckingham grows circumspect. –
    Boy!
PAGE   My lord?
KING RICHARD
    Know'st thou not any whom corrupting gold
    Will tempt unto a close exploit of death?   35
PAGE   I know a discontented gentleman,
    Whose humble means match not his haughty spirit;
    Gold were as good as twenty orators,
    And will, no doubt, tempt him to anything.
KING RICHARD   What is his name?
PAGE   His name, my lord, is Tyrrel.   40
KING RICHARD
    I partly know the man: go call him hither.   *Exit Page.*
    [*aside*] The deep-revolving, witty Buckingham
    No more shall be the neighbour to my counsels.
    Hath he so long held out with me, untir'd,
    And stops he now for breath! Well, be it so.   45

        Enter STANLEY, EARL OF DERBY.

    How now, Lord Stanley, what's the news?
STANLEY   Know, my loving lord,
    The Marquess Dorset, as I hear, is fled
    To Richmond in the parts where he abides.
KING RICHARD
    Come hither, Catesby. Rumour it abroad   50
    That Anne my wife is very grievous sick;
    I will take order for her keeping close.
    Enquire me out some mean poor gentleman,
    Whom I will marry straight to Clarence' daughter –
    The boy is foolish, and I fear not him.   55
    Look how thou dream'st! I say again, give out
    That Anne, my Queen, is sick and like to die.
    About it, for it stands me much upon
    To stop all hopes whose growth may damage me.
                            Exit Catesby.
    I must be married to my brother's daughter,   60
    Or else my kingdom stands on brittle glass.
    Murder her brothers, and then marry her –
    Uncertain way of gain! But I am in
    So far in blood that sin will pluck on sin;
    Tear-falling pity dwells not in this eye.   65

            Enter TYRREL.

    Is thy name Tyrrel?
TYRREL   James Tyrrel, and your most obedient subject.
KING RICHARD   Art thou indeed?
TYRREL   Prove me, my gracious lord.

KING RICHARD
  Dar'st thou resolve to kill a friend of mine?
TYRREL Please you; but I had rather kill two enemies.
KING RICHARD
  Why then thou hast it; two deep enemies,
  Foes to my rest, and my sweet sleep's disturbers,
  Are they that I would have thee deal upon.
  Tyrrel, I mean those bastards in the Tower.
TYRREL Let me have open means to come to them,
  And soon I'll rid you from the fear of them.
KING RICHARD
  Thou sing'st sweet music. Hark, come hither, Tyrrel:
  Go by this token. Rise, and lend thine ear.
  [*He whispers in his ear.*]
  There is no more but so: say it is done,
  And I will love thee, and prefer thee for it.
TYRREL I will dispatch it straight.   *Exit.*

          Enter BUCKINGHAM.

BUCKINGHAM My lord, I have consider'd in my mind
  The late request that you did sound me in.
KING RICHARD
  Well, let that rest. Dorset is fled to Richmond.
BUCKINGHAM I hear the news, my lord.
KING RICHARD
  Stanley, he is your wife's son. Well, look unto it.
BUCKINGHAM
  My lord, I claim the gift, my due by promise,
  For which your honour and your faith is pawn'd:
  Th'earldom of Hereford, and the moveables
  Which you have promised I shall possess.
KING RICHARD Stanley, look to your wife; if she convey
  Letters to Richmond, you shall answer it.
BUCKINGHAM
  What says your Highness to my just demand?
KING RICHARD I do remember me, Henry the Sixth
  Did prophesy that Richmond should be King,
  When Richmond was a little peevish boy.
  A king . . . perhaps . . . perhaps –
BUCKINGHAM   My lord!
KING RICHARD
  How chance the prophet could not, at that time,
  Have told me – I being by – that I should kill him?
BUCKINGHAM
  My lord, your promise for the earldom –
KING RICHARD Richmond! When last I was at Exeter,
  The Mayor in courtesy show'd me the castle,
  And call'd it Rougemont, at which name I started,
  Because a bard of Ireland told me once
  I should not live long after I saw 'Richmond'.
BUCKINGHAM My lord –
KING RICHARD Ay – what's o'clock?
BUCKINGHAM
  I am thus bold to put your Grace in mind
  Of what you promis'd me.
KING RICHARD Well, but what's o'clock?
BUCKINGHAM Upon the stroke of ten.

KING RICHARD Well, let it strike.
BUCKINGHAM Why let it strike?
KING RICHARD
  Because that like a jack thou keep'st the stroke
  Betwixt thy begging and my meditation.
  I am not in the giving vein today.
BUCKINGHAM
  May it please you to resolve me in my suit?
KING RICHARD Thou troublest me; I am not in vein.
          Exit followed by all save Buckingham.
BUCKINGHAM
  And is it thus? Repays he my deep service
  With such contempt? Made I him King for this?
  O let me think on Hastings, and be gone
  To Brecknock while my fearful head is on.   *Exit.*

4.3   *Enter* TYRREL.

TYRREL The tyrannous and bloody act is done;
  The most arch deed of piteous massacre
  That ever yet this land was guilty of.
  Dighton and Forrest, who I did suborn
  To do this piece of ruthless butchery –
  Albeit they were flesh'd villains, bloody dogs –
  Melted with tenderness and mild compassion,
  Wept like two children, in their deaths' sad story.
  'O thus', quoth Dighton, 'lay the gentle babes';
  'Thus, thus', quoth Forrest, 'girdling one another
  Within their alabaster innocent arms;
  Their lips were four red roses on a stalk,
  And in their summer beauty kiss'd each other.
  A book of prayers on their pillow lay,
  Which once', quoth Forrest, 'almost chang'd my
      mind.
  But O, the Devil –' There the villain stopp'd,
  When Dighton thus told on: 'We smothered
  The most replenished sweet work of Nature,
  That from the prime creation e'er she fram'd.'
  Hence both are gone with conscience and remorse
  They could not speak, and so I left them both
  To bear this tidings to the bloody King;

          Enter KING RICHARD.

  And here he comes. All health, my sovereign lord.
KING RICHARD Kind Tyrrel, am I happy in thy news?
TYRREL If to have done the thing you gave in charge
  Beget your happiness, be happy then,
  For it is done.
KING RICHARD But did'st thou see them dead?
TYRREL I did, my lord.
KING RICHARD   And buried, gentle Tyrrel?
TYRREL The chaplain of the Tower hath buried them,
  But where, to say the truth, I do not know.
KING RICHARD
  Come to me, Tyrrel, soon at after-supper,
  When thou shalt tell the process of their death.
  Meantime, but think how I may do thee good,

And be inheritor of thy desire.
Farewell till then.

35 TYRREL   I humbly take my leave.   *Exit.*

KING RICHARD
The son of Clarence have I pent up close;
His daughter meanly have I match'd in marriage;
The sons of Edward sleep in Abraham's bosom,
And Anne my wife hath bid this world good night.
40 Now, for I know the Breton Richmond aims
At young Elizabeth, my brother's daughter,
And by that knot looks proudly on the crown –
To her go I, a jolly thriving wooer.

Enter RATCLIFFE.

RATCLIFFE   My lord!
KING RICHARD
45 Good or bad news, that thou com'st in so bluntly?
RATCLIFFE
Bad news, my lord. Morton is fled to Richmond,
And Buckingham, back'd with the hardy Welshmen,
Is in the field, and still his power increaseth.
KING RICHARD
Ely with Richmond troubles me more near
50 Than Buckingham and his rash-levied strength.
Come: I have learn'd that fearful commenting
Is leaden servitor to dull delay;
Delay leads impotent and snail-pac'd beggary:
Then fiery expedition be my wing,
55 Jove's Mercury, and herald for a king.
Go muster men. My counsel is my shield.
We must be brief, when traitors brave the field.

Exeunt.

4.4   *Enter old* QUEEN MARGARET.

MARGARET   So now prosperity begins to mellow,
And drop into the rotten mouth of death.
Here in these confines slily have I lurk'd
To watch the waning of mine enemies.
5 A dire induction am I witness to,
And will to France, hoping the consequence
Will prove as bitter, black, and tragical.

Enter DUCHESS OF YORK *and* QUEEN ELIZABETH.

Withdraw thee, wretched Margaret: who comes here?
ELIZABETH   Ah, my poor Princes! Ah, my tender babes,
10 My unblow'd flowers, new-appearing sweets!
If yet your gentle souls fly in the air,
And be not fix'd in doom perpetual,
Hover about me with your airy wings,
And hear your mother's lamentation.
MARGARET [*aside*]
15 Hover about her; say that right for right
Hath dimm'd your infant morn to aged night.
DUCHESS   So many miseries have craz'd my voice
That my woe-wearied tongue is still and mute.
Edward Plantagenet, why art thou dead?

MARGARET [*aside*]   Plantagenet doth quit Plantagenet: 20
Edward, for Edward, pays a dying debt.
ELIZABETH
Wilt thou, O God, fly from such gentle lambs,
And throw them in the entrails of the wolf?
When didst Thou sleep when such a deed was done?
MARGARET [*aside*]
When holy Harry died, and my sweet son.   25
DUCHESS
Dead life, blind sight, poor mortal living ghost;
Woe's scene, world's shame, grave's due by life
    usurp'd;
Brief abstract and record of tedious days,
[*sitting*] Rest thy unrest on England's lawful earth,
Unlawfully made drunk with innocent blood.   30
ELIZABETH
Ah, that thou wouldst as soon afford a grave
As thou canst yield a melancholy seat,
Then would I hide my bones, not rest them here.
[*sitting*] Ah, who hath any cause to mourn but we?
MARGARET   If ancient sorrow be most reverend   35
Give mine the benefit of seigniory,
And let my griefs frown on the upper hand.
If sorrow can admit society,
Tell o'er your woes again by viewing mine.
I had an Edward, till a Richard kill'd him;   40
I had a husband, till a Richard kill'd him:
Thou hadst an Edward, till a Richard kill'd him;
Thou hadst a Richard, till a Richard kill'd him.
DUCHESS   I had a Richard too, and thou didst kill him;
I had a Rutland too: thou holp'st to kill him.   45
MARGARET
Thou hadst a Clarence too, and Richard kill'd him.
From forth the kennel of thy womb hath crept
A hell-hound that doth hunt us all to death:
That dog, that had his teeth before his eyes,
To worry lambs, and lap their gentle blood;   50
That excellent grand tyrant of the earth,
That reigns in galled eyes of weeping souls;
That foul defacer of God's handiwork
Thy womb let loose to chase us to our graves.
O upright, just, and true-disposing God!   55
How do I thank thee, that this carnal cur
Preys on the issue of his mother's body,
And makes her pew-fellow with others' moan.
DUCHESS   O, Harry's wife, triumph not in my woes.
God witness with me, I have wept for thine.   60
MARGARET   Bear with me: I am hungry for revenge,
And now I cloy me with beholding it.
Thy Edward he is dead, that kill'd my Edward;
Thy other Edward dead, to quit my Edward;
Young York, he is but boot, because both they   65
Match'd not the high perfection of my loss.
Thy Clarence he is dead, that stabb'd my Edward;
And the beholders of this frantic play,
Th'adulterate Hastings, Rivers, Vaughan, Grey,
Untimely smother'd in their dusky graves.   70

Richard yet lives, hell's black intelligencer,
Only reserv'd their factor to buy souls
And send them thither. But at hand, at hand
Ensues his piteous and unpitied end.
Earth gapes, hell burns, fiends roar, saints pray,
To have him suddenly convey'd from hence.
Cancel his bond of life, dear God I pray,
That I may live and say 'The dog is dead.'

ELIZABETH
O, thou didst prophesy the time would come
That I should wish for thee to help me curse
That bottled spider, that foul bunch-back'd toad.

MARGARET
I call'd thee then vain flourish of my fortune;
I call'd thee, then, poor shadow, painted queen,
The presentation of but what I was;
The flattering index of a direful pageant;
One heav'd a-high, to be hurl'd down below;
A mother only mock'd with two fair babes;
A dream of what thou wast; a garish flag
To be the aim of every dangerous shot;
A sign of dignity; a breath, a bubble;
A queen in jest, only to fill the scene.
Where is thy husband now? Where be thy brothers?
Where are thy two sons? Wherein dost thou joy?
Who sues, and kneels, and says 'God save the
    Queen'?
Where be the bending peers that flatter'd thee?
Where be the thronging troops that follow'd thee?
Decline all this, and see what now thou art:
For happy wife, a most distressed widow;
For joyful mother, one that wails the name;
For one being sued to, one that humbly sues;
For Queen, a very caitiff, crown'd with care;
For she that scorn'd at me, now scorn'd of me;
For she being fear'd of all, now fearing one;
For she commanding all, obey'd of none.
Thus hath the course of justice whirl'd about
And left thee but a very prey to time,
Having no more but thought of what thou wast
To torture thee the more, being what thou art.
Thou didst usurp my place, and dost thou not
Usurp the just proportion of my sorrow?
Now thy proud neck bears half my burden'd yoke,
From which even here I slip my weary head,
And leave the burden of it all on thee.
Farewell, York's wife, and Queen of sad mischance;
These English woes shall make me smile in France.

ELIZABETH   O thou, well skill'd in curses, stay awhile
And teach me how to curse mine enemies.

MARGARET
Forbear to sleep the nights, and fast the days;
Compare dead happiness with living woe;
Think that thy babes were sweeter than they were,
And he that slew them fouler than he is:
Bettering thy loss makes the bad-causer worse.
Revolving this will teach thee how to curse.

ELIZABETH
My words are dull: O quicken them with thine.

MARGARET
Thy woes will make them sharp and pierce like mine. 125
                                        Exit.

DUCHESS   Why should calamity be full of words?
ELIZABETH   Windy attorneys to their clients' woes,
    Airy succeeders of intestate joys,
    Poor breathing orators of miseries:
    Let them have scope, though what they will impart 130
    Help nothing else, yet do they ease the heart.
DUCHESS   If so, then be not tongue-tied; go with me
    And in the breath of bitter words let's smother
    My damned son, that thy two sweet sons smother'd.
    The trumpet sounds; be copious in exclaims. 135

Enter KING RICHARD *and his train including* CATESBY,
marching with drums and trumpets.

KING RICHARD   Who intercepts me in my expedition?
DUCHESS   O, she that might have intercepted thee –
    By strangling thee in her accursed womb –
    From all the slaughters, wretch, that thou hast done.
ELIZABETH
    Hid'st thou that forehead with a golden crown 140
    Where should be branded, if that right were right,
    The slaughter of the Prince that ow'd that crown,
    And the dire death of my poor sons and brothers?
    Tell me, thou villain-slave, where are my children?
DUCHESS
    Thou toad, thou toad, where is thy brother Clarence, 145
    And little Ned Plantagenet his son?
ELIZABETH   Where is the gentle Rivers, Vaughan, Grey?
DUCHESS   Where is kind Hastings?
KING RICHARD
    A flourish, trumpets! Strike alarum, drums!
    Let not the heavens hear these tell-tale women 150
    Rail on the Lord's anointed. Strike, I say!
                            [*Flourish; alarums.*]
    Either be patient and entreat me fair,
    Or with the clamorous report of war
    Thus will I drown your exclamations.
DUCHESS   Art thou my son? 155
KING RICHARD
    Ay, I thank God, my father, and yourself.
DUCHESS   Then patiently hear my impatience.
KING RICHARD
    Madam, I have a touch of your condition,
    That cannot brook the accent of reproof.
DUCHESS   O let me speak.
KING RICHARD   Do then, but I'll not hear. 160
DUCHESS   I will be mild and gentle in my words.
KING RICHARD
    And brief, good mother, for I am in haste.
DUCHESS   Art thou so hasty? I have stay'd for thee,
    God knows, in torment and in agony.
KING RICHARD   And came I not at last to comfort you? 165
DUCHESS   No, by the holy Rood, thou know'st it well:

Thou cam'st on earth to make the earth my hell.
A grievous burden was thy birth to me;
Tetchy and wayward was thy infancy;
Thy school-days frightful, desp'rate, wild, and
170   furious;
Thy prime of manhood daring, bold, and venturous;
Thy age confirm'd, proud, subtle, sly, and bloody:
More mild, but yet more harmful, kind in hatred.
What comfortable hour canst thou name
175   That ever grac'd me with thy company?

KING RICHARD
Faith, none but Humphrey Hower, that call'd your
     Grace
To breakfast once, forth of my company.
If I be so disgracious in your eye,
Let me march on and not offend you, madam.
Strike up the drum!

180 DUCHESS   I prithee, hear me speak.
KING RICHARD   You speak too bitterly.
DUCHESS   Hear me a word,
For I shall never speak to thee again.
KING RICHARD   So!
DUCHESS   Either thou wilt die by God's just ordinance
185   Ere from this war thou turn a conqueror,
Or I with grief and extreme age shall perish,
And nevermore behold thy face again.
Therefore, take with thee my most grievous curse,
Which in the day of battle tire thee more
190   Than all the complete armour that thou wear'st.
My prayers on the adverse party fight;
And there the little souls of Edward's children
Whisper the spirits of thine enemies
And promise them success and victory.
195   Bloody thou art; bloody will be thy end.
Shame serves thy life and doth thy death attend.
                                          Exit.

ELIZABETH
Though far more cause, yet much less spirit to curse
Abides in me, I say Amen to her.
KING RICHARD
Stay, madam: I must talk a word with you.
200 ELIZABETH   I have no more sons of the royal blood
For thee to slaughter. For my daughters, Richard,
They shall be praying nuns, not weeping queens,
And therefore level not to hit their lives.
KING RICHARD   You have a daughter call'd Elizabeth,
205   Virtuous and fair, royal and gracious.
ELIZABETH   And must she die for this? O let her live,
And I'll corrupt her manners, stain her beauty,
Slander myself as false to Edward's bed,
Throw over her the veil of infamy;
210   So she may live unscarr'd of bleeding slaughter
I will confess she was not Edward's daughter.
KING RICHARD
Wrong not her birth; she is a royal princess.
ELIZABETH   To save her life I'll say she is not so.
KING RICHARD   Her life is safest only in her birth.

ELIZABETH   And only in that safety died her brothers. 215
KING RICHARD
Lo, at their birth good stars were opposite.
ELIZABETH   No, to their lives ill friends were contrary.
KING RICHARD   All unavoided is the doom of destiny.
ELIZABETH   True, when avoided grace makes destiny.
My babes were destin'd to a fairer death, 220
If grace had blest thee with a fairer life.
KING RICHARD
You speak as if that I had slain my cousins.
ELIZABETH
Cousins indeed! And by their uncle cozen'd
Of comfort, kingdom, kindred, freedom, life:
Whose hand soever lanc'd their tender hearts, 225
Thy head, all indirectly, gave direction.
No doubt the murd'rous knife was dull and blunt
Till it was whetted on thy stone-hard heart
To revel in the entrails of my lambs.
But that still use of grief makes wild grief tame, 230
My tongue should to thy ears not name my boys
Till that my nails were anchor'd in thine eyes,
And I in such a desp'rate bay of death,
Like a poor bark of sails and tackling reft,
Rush all to pieces on thy rocky bosom. 235
KING RICHARD   Madam, so thrive I in my enterprise
And dangerous success of bloody wars,
As I intend more good to you and yours
Than ever you or yours by me were harm'd.
ELIZABETH
What good is cover'd with the face of heaven, 240
To be discover'd, that can do me good?
KING RICHARD
Th'advancement of your children, gentle lady.
ELIZABETH
Up to some scaffold, there to lose their heads.
KING RICHARD   Unto the dignity and height of fortune,
The high imperial type of this earth's glory! 245
ELIZABETH   Flatter my sorrow with report of it.
Tell me what state, what dignity, what honour,
Canst thou demise to any child of mine?
KING RICHARD   Even all I have – ay, and myself and all
Will I withal endow a child of thine; 250
So in the Lethe of thy angry soul
Thou drown the sad remembrance of those wrongs
Which thou supposest I have done to thee.
ELIZABETH
Be brief, lest that the process of thy kindness
Last longer telling than thy kindness' date. 255
KING RICHARD
Then know that from my soul I love thy daughter.
ELIZABETH
My daughter's mother thinks it with her soul.
KING RICHARD   What do you think?
ELIZABETH
That thou dost love my daughter from thy soul:
So from thy soul's love didst thou love her brothers, 260
And from my heart's love I do thank thee for it.

KING RICHARD

  Be not so hasty to confound my meaning:
  I mean that with my soul I love thy daughter,
  And do intend to make her Queen of England.

ELIZABETH

  Well then, who dost thou mean shall be her king?

KING RICHARD

  Even he that makes her Queen. Who else should be?

ELIZABETH What, thou?

KING RICHARD   Even so. How think you of it?

ELIZABETH How canst thou woo her?

KING RICHARD   That would I learn of you,
  As one being best acquainted with her humour.

ELIZABETH And wilt thou learn of me?

KING RICHARD   Madam, with all my heart!

ELIZABETH

  Send to her, by the man that slew her brothers,
  A pair of bleeding hearts; thereon engrave
  'Edward' and 'York'. Then haply will she weep;
  Therefore present to her – as sometimes Margaret
  Did to thy father, steep'd in Rutland's blood –
  A handkerchief: which, say to her, did drain
  The purple sap from her sweet brother's body,
  And bid her wipe her weeping eyes withal.
  If this inducement move her not to love,
  Send her a letter of thy noble deeds:
  Tell her thou mad'st away her uncle Clarence,
  Her uncle Rivers – ay, and for her sake
  Mad'st quick conveyance with her good aunt Anne.

KING RICHARD

  You mock me, madam; this is not the way
  To win your daughter!

ELIZABETH   There is no other way –
  Unless thou couldst put on some other shape,
  And not be Richard, that hath done all this.

KING RICHARD Say that I did all this for love of her?

ELIZABETH

  Nay, then indeed she cannot chose but hate thee,
  Having bought love with such a bloody spoil.

KING RICHARD

  Look what is done cannot be now amended:
  Men shall deal unadvisedly sometimes,
  Which after-hours gives leisure to repent.
  If I did take the kingdom from your sons,
  To make amends I'll give it to your daughter;
  If I have kill'd the issue of your womb,
  To quicken your increase, I will beget
  Mine issue of your blood upon your daughter.
  A grandam's name is little less in love
  Than is the doting title of a mother;
  They are as children but one step below;
  Even of your metal, of your very blood;
  Of all one pain, save for a night of groans
  Endur'd of her, for whom you bid like sorrow.
  Your children were vexation to your youth,
  But mine shall be a comfort to your age;
  The loss you have is but a son being King;

And by that loss your daughter is made Queen.
I cannot make you what amends I would:
Therefore accept such kindness as I can.   310
Dorset your son, that with a fearful soul
Leads discontented steps in foreign soil,
This fair alliance quickly shall call home
To high promotions and great dignity.
The King that calls your beauteous daughter wife, 315
Familiarly shall call thy Dorset brother;
Again shall you be mother to a king,
And all the ruins of distressful times
Repair'd with double riches of content.
What! We have many goodly days to see.   320
The liquid drops of tears that you have shed
Shall come again, transform'd to orient pearl,
Advantaging their loan with interest
Of ten times double gain of happiness.
Go then, my mother; to thy daughter go: 325
Make bold her bashful years with your experience;
Prepare her ears to hear a wooer's tale;
Put in her tender heart th'aspiring flame
Of golden sovereignty; acquaint the Princess
With the sweet, silent hours of marriage joys, 330
And when this arm of mine hath chastised
The petty rebel, dull-brain'd Buckingham,
Bound with triumphant garlands will I come
And lead thy daughter to a conqueror's bed;
To whom I will retail my conquest won,   335
And she shall be sole victoress, Caesar's Caesar.

ELIZABETH

  What were I best to say? Her father's brother
  Would be her lord? Or shall I say her uncle?
  Or he that slew her brothers and her uncles?
  Under what title shall I woo for thee,   340
  That God, the law, my honour, and her love
  Can make seem pleasing to her tender years?

KING RICHARD

  Infer fair England's peace by this alliance.

ELIZABETH

  Which she shall purchase with still-lasting war.

KING RICHARD

  Tell her the King, that may command, entreats. 345

ELIZABETH

  That, at her hands, which the King's King forbids.

KING RICHARD

  Say she shall be a high and mighty queen.

ELIZABETH To vail the title, as her mother doth.

KING RICHARD Say I will love her everlastingly.

ELIZABETH But how long shall that title 'ever' last? 350

KING RICHARD

  Sweetly in force, until her fair life's end.

ELIZABETH

  But how long fairly shall her sweet life last?

KING RICHARD

  As long as heaven and nature lengthens it.

ELIZABETH As long as hell and Richard likes of it.

KING RICHARD Say I, her sovereign, am her subject low. 355

ELIZABETH
    But she, your subject, loathes such sovereignty.
KING RICHARD   Be eloquent in my behalf to her.
ELIZABETH   An honest tale speeds best being plainly told.
KING RICHARD   Then plainly to her tell my loving tale.
360 ELIZABETH   Plain and not honest is too harsh a style.
KING RICHARD
    Your reasons are too shallow and too quick.
ELIZABETH   O no, my reasons are too deep and dead:
    Too deep and dead, poor infants, in their graves.
KING RICHARD
    Harp not on that string, madam; that is past.
ELIZABETH
365   Harp on it still shall I, till heart-strings break.
KING RICHARD
    Now by my George, my Garter, and my crown –
ELIZABETH
    Profan'd, dishonour'd, and the third usurp'd.
KING RICHARD   I swear –
ELIZABETH   By nothing, for this is no oath:
    Thy George, profan'd, hath lost his holy honour;
370 Thy Garter, blemish'd, pawn'd his knightly virtue;
    Thy crown, usurp'd, disgrac'd his kingly glory.
    If something thou wouldst swear to be believ'd,
    Swear then by something that thou hast not wrong'd.
KING RICHARD   Now, by the world –
ELIZABETH   'Tis full of thy foul wrongs.
KING RICHARD   My father's death –
375 ELIZABETH   Thy life hath it dishonour'd.
KING RICHARD   Then by my self –
ELIZABETH   Thy self is self-misus'd.
KING RICHARD   Why then, by God –
ELIZABETH   God's wrong is most of all:
    If thou didst fear to break an oath with Him,
    The unity the King my husband made
380 Thou hadst not broken, nor my brothers died;
    If thou hadst fear'd to break an oath by Him,
    Th'imperial metal circling now thy head
    Had grac'd the tender temples of my child,
    And both the Princes had been breathing here,
385 Which now – two tender bed-fellows for dust –
    Thy broken faith hath made the prey for worms.
    What can'st thou swear by now?
KING RICHARD   The time to come!
ELIZABETH
    That thou hast wronged in the time o'erpast:
    For I myself have many tears to wash
390 Hereafter time, for time past wrong'd by thee.
    The children live whose fathers thou hast
        slaughter'd:
    Ungovern'd youth, to wail it in their age;
    The parents live whose children thou hast butcher'd:
    Old barren plants, to wail it with their age.
395 Swear not by time to come, for that thou hast
    Misus'd, ere us'd, by times ill-us'd o'erpast.
KING RICHARD   As I intend to prosper and repent,
    So thrive I in my dangerous affairs

    Of hostile arms! Myself myself confound!
    God and fortune, bar me happy hours!   400
    Day, yield me not thy light, nor, night, thy rest!
    Be opposite, all planets of good luck,
    To my proceeding if with dear heart's love,
    Immaculate devotion, holy thoughts,
    I tender not thy beauteous, princely daughter.   405
    In her consists my happiness and thine;
    Without her follows to myself, and thee,
    Herself, the land, and many a Christian soul,
    Death, desolation, ruin, and decay.
    It cannot be avoided but by this;   410
    It will not be avoided but by this.
    Therefore, dear mother – I must call you so –
    Be the attorney of my love to her;
    Plead what I will be, not what I have been;
    Not my deserts, but what I will deserve.   415
    Urge the necessity and state of times,
    And be not peevish found in great designs.
ELIZABETH   Shall I be tempted of the devil thus?
KING RICHARD   Ay, if the devil tempt you to do good.
ELIZABETH   Shall I forget myself to be myself?   420
KING RICHARD
    Ay, if your self's remembrance wrong yourself.
ELIZABETH   Yet thou didst kill my children.
KING RICHARD
    But in your daughter's womb I bury them,
    Where, in that nest of spicery, they will breed
    Selves of themselves, to your recomforture.   425
ELIZABETH   Shall I go win my daughter to thy will?
KING RICHARD   And be a happy mother by the deed.
ELIZABETH   I go. Write to me very shortly,
    And you shall understand from me her mind.
KING RICHARD
    Bear her my true love's kiss; [Kisses her]
                          and so farewell.   430
                                        Exit Elizabeth
    Relenting fool, and shallow, changing woman!

                          Enter RATCLIFFE.

    How now, what news?
RATCLIFFE
    Most mighty sovereign, on the western coast
    Rideth a puissant navy; to our shores
    Throng many doubtful, hollow-hearted friends,   435
    Unarm'd, and unresolv'd to beat them back.
    'Tis thought that Richmond is their admiral;
    And there they hull, expecting but the aid
    Of Buckingham to welcome them ashore.
KING RICHARD
    Some light-foot friend post to the Duke of Norfolk.   440
    Ratcliffe, thyself – or Catesby – where is he?
CATESBY   Here, my good lord.
KING RICHARD   Catesby, fly to the Duke.
CATESBY   I will, my lord, with all convenient haste.
KING RICHARD
    Ratcliffe, come hither. Post to Salisbury.

732

When thou com'st thither –
[*to Catesby*]   Dull unmindful villain!
Why stay'st thou here and go'st not to the Duke?

CATESBY
First, mighty liege, tell me your Highness' pleasure,
What from your Grace I shall deliver to him.

KING RICHARD
O, true, good Catesby! Bid him levy straight
The greatest strength and power that he can make,
And meet me suddenly at Salisbury.

CATESBY   I go.   *Exit.*

RATCLIFFE
What, may it please you, shall I do at Salisbury?

KING RICHARD
Why, what wouldst thou do there before I go?

RATCLIFFE
Your Highness told me I should post before.

KING RICHARD   My mind is chang'd.

Enter STANLEY, EARL OF DERBY.

Stanley, what news with you?

STANLEY
None good, my liege, to please you with the hearing;
Nor none so bad but well may be reported.

KING RICHARD
Hoyday, a riddle! Neither good nor bad –
What need'st thou run so many miles about
When thou mayst tell thy tale the nearest way?
Once more, what news?

STANLEY   Richmond is on the seas.

KING RICHARD
There let him sink, and the seas on him –
White-liver'd runagate! What doth he there?

STANLEY   I know not, mighty sovereign, but by guess.

KING RICHARD   Well, as you guess?

STANLEY
Stirr'd up by Dorset, Buckingham, and Morton,
He makes for England, here to claim the crown.

KING RICHARD
Is the chair empty? Is the sword unsway'd?
Is the King dead? The empire unpossess'd?
What heir of York is there alive but we?
And who is England's King but great York's heir?
Then tell me, what makes he upon the seas!

STANLEY   Unless for that, my liege, I cannot guess.

KING RICHARD
Unless for that he comes to be your liege,
You cannot guess wherefore the Welshman comes.
Thou wilt revolt and fly to him, I fear.

STANLEY   No, my good lord; therefore mistrust me not.

KING RICHARD
Where is thy power then to beat him back?
Where be thy tenants and thy followers?
Are they not now upon the western shore,
Safe-conducting the rebels from their ships?

STANLEY
No, my good lord, my friends are in the north.

KING RICHARD
Cold friends to me! What do they in the north,
When they should serve their sovereign in the west?

STANLEY
They have not been commanded, mighty King.
Pleaseth your Majesty to give me leave,
I'll muster up my friends, and meet your Grace
Where and what time your Majesty shall please.

KING RICHARD
Ay, ay, thou wouldst be gone, to join with Richmond.
But I'll not trust thee.

STANLEY   Most mighty sovereign,
You have no cause to hold my friendship doubtful.
I never was, nor never will be, false.

KING RICHARD
Go then, and muster men – but leave behind
Your son George Stanley. Look your heart be firm,
Or else his head's assurance is but frail.

STANLEY   So deal with him as I prove true to you.
                                                    Exit.

Enter a Messenger.

1 MESSENGER
My gracious sovereign, now in Devonshire –
As I by friends am well advertised –
Sir Edward Courtney and the haughty prelate,
Bishop of Exeter, his elder brother,
With many more confederates, are in arms.

Enter another Messenger.

2 MESSENGER
In Kent, my liege, the Guilfords are in arms,
And every hour more competitors
Flock to the rebels, and their power grows strong.

Enter another Messenger.

3 MESSENGER
My lord, the army of great Buckingham –

KING RICHARD
Out on you, owls! Nothing but songs of death?
[*He striketh him.*]
There, take thou that, till thou bring better news.

3 MESSENGER
The news I have to tell your Majesty
Is, that by sudden floods and fall of waters,
Buckingham's army is dispers'd and scatter'd,
And he himself wander'd away alone,
No man knows whither.

KING RICHARD   I cry thee mercy;
There is my purse, to cure that blow of thine.
Hath any well-advised friend proclaim'd
Reward to him that brings the traitor in?

3 MESSENGER
Such proclamation hath been made, my lord.

Enter another Messenger.

4 MESSENGER
　　Sir Thomas Lovel and Lord Marquess Dorset
　　'Tis said, my liege, in Yorkshire are in arms;
520　　But this good comfort bring I to your Highness:
　　The Breton navy is dispers'd by tempest.
　　Richmond, in Dorsetshire, sent out a boat
　　Unto the shore, to ask those on the banks
　　If they were his assistants, yea or no? –
525　　Who answer'd him they came from Buckingham
　　Upon his party. He, mistrusting them,
　　Hois'd sail, and made his course again for Bretagne.
KING RICHARD
　　March on, march on, since we are up in arms:
　　If not to fight with foreign enemies,
530　　Yet to beat down these rebels here at home.

Enter CATESBY.

CATESBY　My liege, the Duke of Buckingham is taken:
　　That is the best news. That the Earl of Richmond
　　Is with a mighty power landed at Milford
　　Is colder tidings, yet they must be told.
KING RICHARD
535　　Away towards Salisbury! While we reason here
　　A royal battle might be won and lost.
　　Someone take order Buckingham be brought
　　To Salisbury; the rest march on with me.
　　　　　　　　　　　　　　Flourish. Exeunt.

4.5　　*Enter* STANLEY, EARL OF DERBY
　　　　and SIR CHRISTOPHER URSWICK.

STANLEY
　　Sir Christopher, tell Richmond this from me:
　　That in the sty of the most deadly boar
　　My son George Stanley is frank'd up in hold;
　　If I revolt, off goes young George's head;
5　　The fear of that holds off my present aid.
　　So get thee gone: commend me to thy lord;
　　Withal say that the Queen hath heartily consented
　　He should espouse Elizabeth her daughter.
　　But tell me, where is princely Richmond now?
CHRISTOPHER
10　　At Pembroke, or at Ha'rfordwest in Wales.
STANLEY　What men of name resort to him?
CHRISTOPHER　Sir Walter Herbert, a renowned soldier;
　　Sir Gilbert Talbot, Sir William Stanley,
　　Oxford, redoubted Pembroke, Sir James Blunt,
15　　And Rice ap Thomas, with a valiant crew,
　　And many other of great name and worth;
　　And towards London do they bend their power,
　　If by the way they be not fought withal.
STANLEY　Well, hie thee to thy lord; I kiss his hand.
20　　My letter will resolve him of my mind.
　　Farewell.　　　　　　　　　　　　　*Exeunt.*

5.1　　　　*Enter* Sheriff *with halberds,*
　　　　　　and BUCKINGHAM *led to execution.*

BUCKINGHAM
　　Will not King Richard let me speak with him?
SHERIFF　No, my good lord; therefore be patient.
BUCKINGHAM
　　Hastings, and Edward's children, Grey and Rivers,
　　Holy King Henry, and thy fair son Edward,
　　Vaughan, and all that have miscarried　　　　　5
　　By underhand, corrupted foul injustice –
　　If that your moody, discontented souls
　　Do through the clouds behold this present hour,
　　Even for revenge mock my destruction.
　　This is All-Souls' day, fellow, is it not?　　　10
SHERIFF　It is.
BUCKINGHAM
　　Why then, All-Souls' day is my body's doomsday.
　　This is the day which, in King Edward's time,
　　I wish'd might fall on me when I was found
　　False to his children and his wife's allies.　　15
　　This is the day wherein I wish'd to fall
　　By the false faith of him whom most I trusted.
　　This, this All-Souls' day to my fearful soul
　　Is the determin'd respite of my wrongs:
　　That high All-seer which I dallied with　　　20
　　Hath turn'd my feigned prayer on my head,
　　And given in earnest what I begg'd in jest.
　　Thus doth He force the swords of wicked men
　　To turn their own points in their masters' bosoms.
　　Thus Margaret's curse falls heavy on my neck:　25
　　'When he,' quoth she, 'shall split thy heart with
　　　　sorrow,
　　Remember Margaret was a prophetess!'
　　Come, lead me, officers, to the block of shame;
　　Wrong hath but wrong, and blame the due of blame.
　　　　　　　　　　　　　　Exit with officers.

5.2　　*Enter* RICHMOND, OXFORD, BLUNT, HERBERT
　　　　and others, with drum and colours.

RICHMOND
　　Fellows in arms, and my most loving friends,
　　Bruis'd underneath the yoke of tyranny;
　　Thus far into the bowels of the land
　　Have we march'd on without impediment;
　　And here receive we from our father Stanley　　5
　　Lines of fair comfort and encouragement.
　　The wretched, bloody, and usurping boar,
　　That spoil'd your summer fields and fruitful vines,
　　Swills your warm blood like wash, and makes his
　　　　trough
　　In your embowell'd bosoms – this foul swine　　10
　　Is now even in the centre of this isle,
　　Near to the town of Leicester, as we learn.
　　From Tamworth thither is but one day's march:
　　In God's name, cheerly on, courageous friends,

To reap the harvest of perpetual peace
By this one bloody trial of sharp war.
OXFORD   Every man's conscience is a thousand men,
To fight against this guilty homicide.
HERBERT   I doubt not but his friends will turn to us.
BLUNT
He hath no friends but what are friends for fear,
Which in his dearest need will fly from him.
RICHMOND
All for our vantage; then in God's name march.
True hope is swift, and flies with swallow's wings:
Kings it makes gods, and meaner creatures kings.
Exeunt.

5.3   *Enter* KING RICHARD *in arms, with* NORFOLK,
RATCLIFFE *and the* EARL OF SURREY, *with others.*

KING RICHARD
Here pitch our tent, even here in Bosworth field.
[*Richard's tent is raised, on one side of the stage.*]
My lord of Surrey, why look you so sad?
SURREY   My heart is ten times lighter than my looks.
KING RICHARD   My lord of Norfolk.
NORFOLK   Here, most gracious liege.
KING RICHARD
Norfolk, we must have knocks – ha, must we not?
NORFOLK   We must both give and take, my loving lord.
KING RICHARD
Up with my tent! Here will I lie tonight –
But where tomorrow? Well, all's one for that.
Who hath descried the number of the traitors?
NORFOLK   Six or seven thousand is their utmost power.
KING RICHARD   Why, our battalia trebles that account!
Besides, the King's name is a tower of strength
Which they upon the adverse faction want.
Up with the tent! Come, noble gentlemen,
Let us survey the vantage of the ground.
Call for some men of sound direction;
Let's lack no discipline, make no delay:
For, lords, tomorrow is a busy day!
[*The tent is now ready.*]   *Exeunt through one door.*

Enter through the other door RICHMOND, SIR WILLIAM
BRANDON, OXFORD, *and* HERBERT, BLUNT, *and others, who
pitch Richmond's tent on the other side of the stage.*

RICHMOND   The weary sun hath made a golden set,
And by the bright track of his fiery car
Gives token of a goodly day tomorrow.
Sir William Brandon, you shall bear my standard.
My lord of Oxford, you Sir William Brandon,
And you Sir Walter Herbert, stay with me;
The Earl of Pembroke keeps his regiment –
Good captain Blunt, bear my goodnight to him,
And by the second hour in the morning
Desire the Earl to see me in my tent.
Yet one thing more, good captain, do for me:
Where is Lord Stanley quarter'd, do you know?

BLUNT   Unless I have mista'en his colours much,
Which well I am assur'd I have not done,
His regiment lies half a mile at least
South from the mighty power of the King.
RICHMOND   If without peril it be possible,   35
Sweet Blunt, make some good means to speak with
him,
And give him from me this most needful note.
BLUNT   Upon my life, my lord, I'll undertake it;
And so God give you quiet rest tonight.
RICHMOND   Good night, good captain Blunt.   40
Exit Blunt.
Give me some ink and paper in my tent;
I'll draw the form and model of our battle;
Limit each leader to his several charge,
And part in just proportion our small power.
Come, gentlemen: 45
Let us consult upon tomorrow's business;
Into my tent: the dew is raw and cold.
Richmond, Brandon, Oxford and Herbert withdraw
into the tent. The others exeunt.

Enter KING RICHARD, RATCLIFFE, NORFOLK
and CATESBY *and attendant soldiers.*

KING RICHARD   What is't o'clock?
CATESBY   It's supper time, my lord: it's nine o'clock.
KING RICHARD
I will not sup tonight. Give me some ink and paper.   50
What, is my beaver easier than it was,
And all my armour laid into my tent?
CATESBY   It is, my liege, and all things are in readiness.
KING RICHARD   Good Norfolk, hie thee to thy charge;
Use careful watch; choose trusty sentinels.   55
NORFOLK   I go, my lord.
KING RICHARD
Stir with the lark tomorrow, gentle Norfolk.
NORFOLK   I warrant you, my lord.   *Exit.*
KING RICHARD   Catesby!
CATESBY   My lord?
KING RICHARD   Send out a pursuivant-at-arms   60
To Stanley's regiment. Bid him bring his power
Before sun-rising, lest his son George fall
Into the blind cave of eternal night.   *Exit Catesby.*
Fill me a bowl of wine. Give me a watch.
Saddle white Surrey for the field tomorrow;   65
Look that my staves be sound, and not too heavy.
Ratcliffe!
RATCLIFFE   My lord?
KING RICHARD
Saw'st thou the melancholy Lord Northumberland?
RATCLIFFE   Thomas the Earl of Surrey and himself,   70
Much about cockshut time, from troop to troop
Went through the army cheering up the soldiers.
KING RICHARD
So, I am satisfied. Give me a bowl of wine.
I have not that alacrity of spirit
Nor cheer of mind that I was wont to have.   75

Set it down. Is ink and paper ready?
RATCLIFFE   It is, my lord.
KING RICHARD   Bid my guard watch; leave me.
     Ratcliffe, about the mid of night come to my tent
     And help to arm me. Leave me, I say.
               Exit Ratcliffe. Richard withdraws into his tent;
                     attendant soldiers guard it.

    Enter STANLEY, EARL OF DERBY *to Richmond in his tent.*

80   STANLEY   Fortune and Victory sit on thy helm!
     RICHMOND   All comfort that the dark night can afford
     Be to thy person, noble father-in-law.
     Tell me, how fares our loving mother?
     STANLEY   I, by attorney, bless thee from thy mother,
85   Who prays continually for Richmond's good.
     So much for that. The silent hours steal on,
     And flaky darkness breaks within the East.
     In brief, for so the season bids us be,
     Prepare thy battle early in the morning,
90   And put thy fortune to the arbitrement
     Of bloody strokes and mortal-staring war.
     I, as I may – that which I would, I cannot –
     With best advantage will deceive the time,
     And aid thee in this doubtful shock of arms.
95   But on thy side I may not be too forward,
     Lest, being seen, thy brother, tender George,
     Be executed in his father's sight.
     Farewell; the leisure and the fearful time
     Cuts off the ceremonious vows of love
100   And ample interchange of sweet discourse
     Which so long sunder'd friends should dwell upon.
     God give us leisure for these rites of love.
     Once more adieu: be valiant, and speed well.
     RICHMOND   Good lords, conduct him to his regiment.
105   I'll strive, with troubled thoughts, to take a nap
     Lest leaden slumber peise me down tomorrow
     When I should mount with wings of victory.
     Once more, good night, kind lords and gentlemen.
         Exeunt Stanley with Brandon, Oxford, Herbert.
     [*Kneels.*] O Thou, whose captain I account myself,
110   Look on my forces with a gracious eye;
     Put in their hands Thy bruising irons of wrath
     That they may crush down, with a heavy fall,
     Th'usurping helmets of our adversaries;
     Make us Thy ministers of chastisement,
115   That we may praise Thee in the victory.
     To Thee I do commend my watchful soul
     Ere I let fall the windows of mine eyes:
     Sleeping and waking, O defend me still!
     [*Rises, withdraws into his tent, lies down and sleeps.*]

    Enter the ghost of young PRINCE EDWARD,
         son of Harry the Sixth.

     GHOST OF PRINCE EDWARD [*to King Richard*]
     Let me sit heavy on thy soul tomorrow.
120   Think how thou stab'st me in my prime of youth
     At Tewkesbury; despair therefore, and die.

[*to Richmond*]   Be cheerful, Richmond, for the
     wronged souls
     Of butcher'd princes fight in thy behalf;
     King Henry's issue, Richmond, comforts thee.   *Exit.*

    Enter the ghost of HENRY THE SIXTH.

GHOST OF HENRY [*to King Richard*]
     When I was mortal, my anointed body   125
     By thee was punched full of deadly holes.
     Think on the Tower and me: despair and die;
     Harry the Sixth bids thee despair and die!
     [*to Richmond*] Virtuous and holy, be thou conqueror:
     Harry, that prophesied thou shouldst be King,   130
     Doth comfort thee in thy sleep. Live and flourish!
                          Exit.

    Enter the ghost of CLARENCE.

GHOST OF CLARENCE [*to King Richard*]
     Let me sit heavy in thy soul tomorrow –
     I, that was wash'd to death with fulsome wine,
     Poor Clarence, by thy guile betray'd to death –
     Tomorrow in the battle think on me,   135
     And fall thy edgeless sword; despair and die.
     [*to Richmond*] Thou offspring of the House of
         Lancaster,
     The wronged heirs of York do pray for thee.
     Good angels guard thy battle; live and flourish.
                          Exit.

    Enter the ghosts of RIVERS, GREY *and* VAUGHAN.

GHOST OF RIVERS [*to King Richard*]
     Let me sit heavy in thy soul tomorrow,   140
     Rivers that died at Pomfret: despair and die.
GHOST OF GREY [*to King Richard*]
     Think upon Grey, and let thy soul despair.
GHOST OF VAUGHAN [*to King Richard*]
     Think upon Vaughan, and with guilty fear
     Let fall thy lance; despair and die.
ALL [*to Richmond*]
     Awake, and think our wrongs in Richard's bosom   145
     Will conquer him: awake, and win the day.   *Exeunt.*

    Enter the ghost of HASTINGS.

GHOST OF HASTINGS [*to King Richard*]
     Bloody and guilty, guiltily awake,
     And in a bloody battle end thy days.
     Think on Lord Hastings; despair and die.
     [*to Richmond*] Quiet, untroubled soul, awake, awake: 150
     Arm, fight, and conquer for fair England's sake.
                         Exit.

    Enter the ghosts of the two young PRINCES.

GHOSTS OF PRINCES EDWARD AND YORK
     [*to King Richard*]
     Dream on thy cousins, smother'd in the Tower:
     Let us be lead within thy bosom, Richard,
     And weigh thee down to ruin, shame, and death;

Thy nephews' souls bid thee despair and die.   55
[*to Richmond*] Sleep, Richmond, sleep in peace, and
    wake in joy;
Good angels guard thee from the boar's annoy.
Live, and beget a happy race of kings;
Edward's unhappy sons do bid thee flourish.
                                            Exeunt.

Enter the ghost of LADY ANNE, *his wife.*

GHOST OF ANNE [*to King Richard*]
Richard, thy wife, that wretched Anne, thy wife,   160
That never slept a quiet hour with thee,
Now fills thy sleep with perturbations.
Tomorrow in the battle think on me,
And fall thy edgeless sword: despair and die.
[*to Richmond*] Thou quiet soul, sleep thou a quiet   165
    sleep;
Dream of success and happy victory.
Thy adversary's wife doth pray for thee.   *Exit.*

Enter the ghost of BUCKINGHAM.

GHOST OF BUCKINGHAM [*to King Richard*]
The first was I that help'd thee to the crown;
The last was I that felt thy tyranny.
O, in the battle think of Buckingham,   170
And die in terror of thy guiltiness.
Dream on, dream on of bloody deeds and death;
Fainting, despair: despairing, yield thy breath.
[*to Richmond*] I died for hope ere I could lend thee
    aid,
But cheer thy heart, and be thou not dismay'd.   175
God and good angels fight on Richmond's side;
And Richard fall in height of all his pride.   *Exit.*
[*Richard starteth up out of a dream.*]
KING RICHARD
Give me another horse! Bind up my wounds!
Have mercy, Jesu! – Soft, I did but dream.
O coward conscience, how dost thou afflict me!   180
The lights burn blue; it is now dead midnight.
Cold fearful drops stand on my trembling flesh.
What do I fear? Myself? There's none else by;
Richard loves Richard, that is, I and I.
Is there a murderer here? No. Yes, I am!   185
Then fly. What, from myself? Great reason why,
Lest I revenge? What, myself upon myself?
Alack, I love myself. Wherefore? For any good
That I myself have done unto myself?
O no, alas, I rather hate myself   190
For hateful deeds committed by myself.
I am a villain – yet I lie, I am not!
Fool, of thyself speak well! Fool, do not flatter.
My conscience hath a thousand several tongues,
And every tongue brings in a several tale,   195
And every tale condemns me for a villain:
Perjury, perjury, in the highest degree;
Murder, stern murder, in the direst degree;
All several sins, all us'd in each degree,

Throng to the bar, crying all, 'Guilty, guilty!'   200
I shall despair. There is no creature loves me,
And if I die, no soul will pity me –
And wherefore should they, since that I myself
Find in myself no pity to myself?
Methought the souls of all that I had murder'd   205
Came to my tent, and every one did threat
Tomorrow's vengeance on the head of Richard.

Enter RATCLIFFE.

RATCLIFFE   My lord!
KING RICHARD   Zounds! Who is there?
RATCLIFFE
Ratcliffe, my lord; 'tis I. The early village cock   210
Hath twice done salutation to the morn;
Your friends are up and buckle on their armour.
KING RICHARD
O Ratcliffe, I have dream'd a fearful dream!
What thinkest thou – will our friends prove all true?
RATCLIFFE   No doubt, my lord.
KING RICHARD   O Ratcliffe, I fear, I fear!   215
RATCLIFFE
Nay, good my lord, be not afraid of shadows.
KING RICHARD   By the Apostle Paul, shadows tonight
Have struck more terror to the soul of Richard
Than can the substance of ten thousand soldiers,
Armed in proof, and led by shallow Richmond.   220
'Tis not yet near day; come, go with me:
Under our tents I'll play the eavesdropper
To see if any mean to shrink from me.
                        Exeunt Richard and Ratcliffe.

Enter the Lords *to* RICHMOND *sitting in his tent.*

LORDS   Good morrow, Richmond.
RICHMOND   Cry mercy, lords and watchful gentlemen,   225
That you have ta'en a tardy sluggard here.
1 LORD   How have you slept, my lord?
RICHMOND
The sweetest sleep and fairest-boding dreams
That ever enter'd in a drowsy head
Have I, since your departure, had, my lords.   230
Methought their souls whose bodies Richard
    murder'd
Came to my tent and cried on victory.
I promise you my soul is very jocund
In the remembrance of so fair a dream.
How far into the morning is it, lords?   235
1 LORD   Upon the stroke of four
RICHMOND
Why then 'tis time to arm and give direction.
[*Comes out from the tent.*]

His oration to his soldiers.

More than I have said, loving countrymen,
The leisure and enforcement of the time
Forbids to dwell upon. Yet remember this: 240
God, and our good cause, fight upon our side;

The prayers of holy saints and wronged souls,
Like high-rear'd bulwarks, stand before our faces.
Richard except, those whom we fight against
245   Had rather have us win than him they follow.
For what is he they follow? Truly, gentlemen,
A bloody tyrant and a homicide;
One rais'd in blood, and one in blood establish'd;
One that made means to come by what he hath,
And slaughter'd those that were the means to help
250   him;
A base foul stone, made precious by the foil
Of England's chair, where he is falsely set;
One that hath ever been God's enemy.
Then, if you fight against God's enemy,
255   God will, in justice, ward you as his soldiers;
If you do sweat to put a tyrant down,
You sleep in peace, the tyrant being slain;
If you do fight against your country's foes,
Your country's fat shall pay your pains the hire;
260   If you do fight in safeguard of your wives,
Your wives shall welcome home the conquerors;
If you do free your children from the sword,
Your children's children quits in it your age.
Then, in the name of God and all these rights,
265   Advance your standards, draw your willing swords!
For me, the ransom of my bold attempt
Shall be this cold corpse on the earth's cold face;
But if I thrive, the gain of my attempt
The least of you shall share his part thereof.
270   Sound, drums, and trumpets, boldly and cheerfully!
God, and Saint George! Richmond and victory!

Exeunt Richmond and his followers.

Enter KING RICHARD, RATCLIFFE *and soldiers.*

KING RICHARD
What said Northumberland, as touching Richmond?
RATCLIFFE   That he was never trained up in arms.
KING RICHARD
He said the truth. And what said Surrey then?
RATCLIFFE
275   He smil'd and said, 'The better for our purpose.'
KING RICHARD   He was in the right, and so indeed it is.
                                    [*The clock striketh.*]
Tell the clock there! Give me a calendar –
Who saw the sun today?
RATCLIFFE   Not I, my lord.
KING RICHARD
Then he disdains to shine, for by the book
280   He should have brav'd the east an hour ago.
A black day will it be to somebody.
Ratcliffe!
RATCLIFFE   My lord?
KING RICHARD   The sun will not be seen today!
The sky doth frown and lour upon our army:
285   I would these dewy tears were from the ground.
Not shine today? Why, what is that to me
More than to Richmond? For the self-same heaven

That frowns on me looks sadly upon him.

Enter NORFOLK.

NORFOLK
Arm, arm, my lord: the foe vaunts in the field!
KING RICHARD
Come, bustle, bustle! Caparison my horse.   290
[*Richard arms.*]
Call up Lord Stanley; bid him bring his power.
I will lead forth my soldiers to the plain,
And thus my battle shall be ordered:
My foreward shall be drawn out all in length,
Consisting equally of horse and foot;   295
Our archers shall be placed in the midst.
John, Duke of Norfolk, Thomas, Earl of Surrey
Shall have the leading of this foot and horse;
They thus directed, we will follow
In the main battle, whose puissance on either side   300
Shall be well winged with our chiefest horse.
This, and Saint George to boot! What think'st thou,
    Norfolk?
NORFOLK   A good direction, warlike sovereign.
[*He sheweth him a paper.*]
This I found on my tent this morning.
KING RICHARD [*reading*]
    Jockey of Norfolk, be not so bold: 305
    For Dickon thy master is bought and sold.
A thing devised by the enemy.
Go, gentlemen: every man unto his charge!
Let not our babbling dreams affright our souls;
Conscience is but a word that cowards use,   310
Devis'd at first to keep the strong in awe.
Our strong arms be our conscience, swords our law.
March on! Join bravely. Let us to it pell-mell –
If not to Heaven, then hand in hand to hell!

His oration to his army.

What shall I say, more than I have inferr'd?   315
Remember whom you are to cope withal:
A sort of vagabonds, rascals, and runaways;
A scum of Bretons and base lackey peasants,
Whom their o'er-cloyed country vomits forth
To desperate adventures and assur'd destruction.   320
You sleeping safe, they bring to you unrest;
You having lands, and bless'd with beauteous wives,
They would restrain the one, distain the other.
And who doth lead them but a paltry fellow,
Long kept in Bretagne at our brother's cost?   325
A milksop! One that never in his life
Felt so much cold as over-shoes in snow.
Let's whip these stragglers o'er the seas again,
Lash hence these overweening rags of France,
These famish'd beggars, weary of their lives –   330
Who, but for dreaming on this fond exploit,
For want of means, poor rats, had hang'd themselves.
If we be conquer'd, let men conquer us!
And not these bastard Bretons, whom our fathers

Have in their own land beaten, bobb'd, and thump'd,
And in record left them the heirs of shame.
Shall these enjoy our lands? Lie with our wives?
Ravish our daughters?   [*Drum afar off.*]
                        Hark, I hear their drum.
Fight, gentlemen of England! Fight, bold yeomen!
Draw, archers, draw your arrows to the head!
Spur your proud horses hard, and ride in blood!
Amaze the welkin with your broken staves!

                Enter a Messenger.

What says Lord Stanley? Will he bring his power?
MESSENGER   My lord, he doth deny to come.
KING RICHARD   Off with his son George's head!
NORFOLK   My lord, the enemy is past the marsh!
    After the battle let George Stanley die.
KING RICHARD
    A thousand hearts are great within my bosom.
    Advance, our standards! Set upon our foes!
    Our ancient word of courage, fair Saint George,
    Inspire us with the spleen of fiery dragons!
    Upon them! Victory sits on our helms.   *Exeunt.*

5.4   *Alarum. Excursions. Enter* NORFOLK
        and soldiers; then at the other door CATESBY.

CATESBY   Rescue! My lord of Norfolk, rescue, rescue!
    The King enacts more wonders than a man,
    Daring an opposite to every danger.
    His horse is slain, and all on foot he fights,
    Seeking for Richmond in the throat of death.
    Rescue, fair lord, or else the day is lost!
                        Exeunt Norfolk and soldiers.

            Alarums. Enter KING RICHARD.

KING RICHARD
    A horse! A horse! My kingdom for a horse!
CATESBY   Withdraw, my lord; I'll help you to a horse.
KING RICHARD   Slave! I have set my life upon a cast,
    And I will stand the hazard of the die.
    I think there be six Richmonds in the field:
    Five have I slain today instead of him.
    A horse! A horse! My kingdom for a horse!   *Exeunt.*

5.5   *Alarum. Enter* KING RICHARD *and* RICHMOND;
    they fight. Richard is slain, then, retreat being sounded,
        exit Richmond; Richard's body is carried off.
    Flourish. Enter RICHMOND, STANLEY, EARL OF DERBY
        bearing the crown, with other lords and soldiers.

RICHMOND
    God, and your arms, be prais'd, victorious friends:
    The day is ours; the bloody dog is dead.
STANLEY
    Courageous Richmond, well hast thou acquit thee!
    [*presenting the crown*]
    Lo, here, this long-usurped royalty
    From the dead temples of this bloody wretch   5
    Have I pluck'd off to grace thy brows withal.
    Wear it, enjoy it, and make much of it.
RICHMOND   Great God of Heaven, say Amen to all!
    But tell me, is young George Stanley living?
STANLEY   He is, my lord, and safe in Leicester town,   10
    Whither, if it please you, we may now withdraw us.
RICHMOND   What men of name are slain on either side?
STANLEY
    John, Duke of Norfolk; Walter, Lord Ferrers;
    Sir Robert Brakenbury, and Sir William Brandon.
RICHMOND   Inter their bodies as become their births.   15
    Proclaim a pardon to the soldiers fled
    That in submission will return to us;
    And then, as we have ta'en the sacrament,
    We will unite the white rose and the red.
    Smile, heaven, upon this fair conjunction,   20
    That long have frown'd upon their enmity.
    What traitor hears me and says not Amen?
    England hath long been mad, and scarr'd herself:
    The brother blindly shed the brother's blood;
    The father rashly slaughter'd his own son;   25
    The son, compell'd, been butcher to the sire.
    All this divided York and Lancaster –
    Divided, in their dire division.
    O now let Richmond and Elizabeth,
    The true succeeders of each royal House,   30
    By God's fair ordinance conjoin together,
    And let their heirs, God, if Thy will be so,
    Enrich the time to come with smooth-fac'd peace,
    With smiling plenty, and fair prosperous days.
    Abate the edge of traitors, gracious Lord,   35
    That would reduce these bloody days again,
    And make poor England weep in streams of blood.
    Let them not live to taste this land's increase,
    That would with treason wound this fair land's
        peace.
    Now civil wounds are stopp'd; peace lives again.   40
    That she may long live here, God say Amen.   *Exeunt*

Love's Labour's Lost

Love's Labour's Lost is generally labelled an 'early comedy' along with *The Two Gentlemen of Verona*, *The Taming of the Shrew* and *The Comedy of Errors*. The four plays show Shakespeare at the beginning of his career experimenting with a range of materials and moods including romantic intrigue, classical farce and traditional folktale. Unlike the other three plays in this category, *Love's Labour's Lost* does not have a readily identifiable narrative or dramatic source, though affinities have been discerned with both literary and real-life accounts of courtly activities. Its presentation of Rosaline as a 'dark' heroine has encouraged some readers to speculate on possible connections with the narrative recounted in Shakespeare's *Sonnets*. Somewhat blighted by its reputation as a 'topical' play, it is perhaps more often performed than studied today.

The 1598 First Quarto of the play is the earliest dramatic text to have 'by W. Shakespeare' on its title-page. *Love's Labour's Lost* is described as 'a pleasant conceited comedy' and we are informed that it was 'presented before her Highness this last Christmas'. The title-page further claims that the text is 'newly corrected and augmented', implying that it was written and performed somewhat earlier than 1598, and perhaps that a previous edition, now lost, had been published. It is listed by Francis Meres (along with the mysterious *Love's Labour's Won*) as one of Shakespeare's comedies in his *Palladis Tamia* (also 1598), but it is usually dated 1594-5, mainly on internal evidence. It was revived in 1604 for performance at Court before Queen Anne. Some inconsistencies in the narrative, confusion over characters' names and repetition of dialogue in this text seem to indicate that it was printed from Shakespeare's working manuscript. Two passages, at 4.3.292–313 and 5.2.810–15, are evidently rejected first drafts of lines which appear after them in revised form. They are accordingly enclosed in square brackets.

The phrase 'conceited comedy' is in this case an appropriate designation of a play whose verbal wit and ingenuity must have dazzled its original audiences and can occasionally baffle modern ones. Not only the supposedly sophisticated courtiers but also the lower-class characters play endlessly with language, achieving effects which can be brilliant, pedantic or bathetic, but are very frequently connected with obscenity. This has been one cause of the play's relative unpopularity, though recent productions have shown that it can work well on stage as a lively and quite acerbic courtship comedy. Some of the wordplay does seem to be topical – the play is self-conscious about what Moth refers to as 'a great feast of languages' (5.1.35) – but broader attempts to find historical models for the characters and situations are now widely discounted.

The play's title reflects its unconventional ending: in the short term at least the male lovers (with the surprising exception of Armado) have lost their labour in so far as they have not won the women. The closing songs are enigmatic, particularly in raising the threat of infidelity even before marriage is assured. A modern emphasis on the darker aspects of the play has taken more seriously such things as the breaking of vows, the cruelty of the courtiers to the amateur actors and the intrusion of death at the end. At the same time Berowne and Rosaline as sparring partners have appealed to actors and audiences as prototypes of Benedick and Beatrice in *Much Ado About Nothing*, and talented performers have proved that the comedy of Don Armado and Holofernes is still not past its sell-by date.

The Arden text is based on the 1598 First Quarto, supplemented by the 1623 First Folio.

KING Ferdinand — *of Navarre*

BEROWNE
LONGAVILLE } *lords attending on the King*
DUMAIN

BOYET } *lords attending the Princess of France*
MARCADE

Don Adriano de ARMADO — *a fantastical Spaniard*
Sir NATHANIEL — *a curate*
HOLOFERNES — *a schoolmaster*
DULL — *a constable*
COSTARD — *a clown*
MOTH — *page to Armado*
FORESTER
The PRINCESS *of France*

MARIA
KATHARINE } *ladies attending on the Princess*
ROSALINE

JAQUENETTA — *a country Wench*

Officers and others, Attendants on the King and Princess

Love's Labour's Lost

1.1 *Enter* FERDINAND, KING OF NAVARRE,
BEROWNE, LONGAVILLE *and* DUMAIN.

KING   Let fame, that all hunt after in their lives,
    Live register'd upon our brazen tombs,
    And then grace us in the disgrace of death;
    When, spite of cormorant devouring Time,
    Th'endeavour of this present breath may buy
    That honour which shall bate his scythe's keen edge,
    And make us heirs of all eternity.
    Therefore, brave conquerors – for so you are,
    That war against your own affections
    And the huge army of the world's desires –
    Our late edict shall strongly stand in force:
    Navarre shall be the wonder of the world;
    Our court shall be a little academe,
    Still and contemplative in living art.
    You three, Berowne, Dumain, and Longaville,
    Have sworn for three years' term to live with me,
    My fellow-scholars, and to keep those statutes
    That are recorded in this schedule here:
    Your oaths are pass'd; and now subscribe your
        names,
    That his own hand may strike his honour down
    That violates the smallest branch herein: –
    If you are arm'd to do, as sworn to do,
    Subscribe to your deep oaths, and keep it too.

LONGAVILLE   I am resolv'd; 'tis but a three years' fast:
    The mind shall banquet, though the body pine:
    Fat paunches have lean pates, and dainty bits
    Make rich the ribs, but bankrupt quite the wits.

DUMAIN   My loving lord, Dumain is mortified:
    The grosser manner of these world's delights
    He throws upon the gross world's baser slaves:
    To love, to wealth, to pomp, I pine and die;
    With all these living in philosophy.

BEROWNE   I can but say their protestation over;
    So much, dear liege, I have already sworn,
    That is, to live and study here three years.
    But there are other strict observances;
    As not to see a woman in that term,
    Which I hope well is not enrolled there:
    And one day in a week to touch no food,
    And but one meal on every day beside;
    The which I hope is not enrolled there:
    And then to sleep but three hours in the night,
    And not be seen to wink of all the day,
    When I was wont to think no harm all night,
    And make a dark night too of half the day,
    Which I hope well is not enrolled there.
    O, these are barren tasks, too hard to keep,
    Not to see ladies, study, fast, not sleep.

KING   Your oath is pass'd to pass away from these.

BEROWNE   Let me say no, my liege, an if you please.
    I only swore to study with your grace,
    And stay here in your court for three years space.

LONGAVILLE
    You swore to that, Berowne, and to the rest.

BEROWNE   By yea and nay, sir, then I swore in jest.
    What is the end of study, let me know?   55

KING
    Why, that to know which else we should not know.

BEROWNE
    Things hid and barr'd, you mean, from common
        sense?

KING   Ay, that is study's god-like recompense.

BEROWNE   Come on, then; I will swear to study so,
    To know the thing I am forbid to know;   60
    As thus, – to study where I well may dine,
    When I to feast expressly am forbid;
    Or study where to meet some mistress fine,
    When mistresses from common sense are hid;
    Or, having sworn too hard a keeping oath,   65
    Study to break it and not break my troth.
    If study's gain be thus, and this be so,
    Study knows that which yet it doth not know.
    Swear me to this, and I will ne'er say no.

KING   These be the stops that hinder study quite,   70
    And train our intellects to vain delight.

BEROWNE
    Why! all delights are vain, but that most vain,
    Which with pain purchas'd doth inherit pain:
    As, painfully to pore upon a book
    To seek the light of truth; while truth the while   75
    Doth falsely blind the eyesight of his look:
    Light seeking light doth light of light beguile:
    So, ere you find where light in darkness lies,
    Your light grows dark by losing of your eyes.
    Study me how to please the eye indeed,   80
    By fixing it upon a fairer eye,
    Who dazzling so, that eye shall be his heed,
    And give him light that it was blinded by.
    Study is like the heaven's glorious sun,
    That will not be deep-search'd with saucy looks;   85
    Small have continual plodders ever won,
    Save base authority from others' books.
    These earthly godfathers of heaven's lights,
    That give a name to every fixed star,
    Have no more profit of their shining nights   90
    Than those that walk and wot not what they are.
    Too much to know is to know nought but fame;
    And every godfather can give a name.

KING   How well he's read, to reason against reading!

DUMAIN   Proceeded well, to stop all good proceeding!   95

LONGAVILLE
    He weeds the corn, and still lets grow the weeding.

BEROWNE
    The spring is near, when green geese are a-breeding.

DUMAIN   How follows that?

BEROWNE   Fit in his place and time.

DUMAIN   In reason nothing.

BEROWNE   Something then in rhyme.

100 KING   Berowne is like an envious sneaping frost
That bites the first-born infants of the spring.

BEROWNE
Well, say I am; why should proud summer boast
Before the birds have any cause to sing?
Why should I joy in any abortive birth?

105 At Christmas I no more desire a rose
Than wish a snow in May's new-fangled shows;
But like of each thing that in season grows.
So you, to study now it is too late,
Climb o'er the house to unlock the little gate.

110 KING   Well, sit you out: go home, Berowne: adieu!

BEROWNE
No, my good lord; I have sworn to stay with you:
And though I have for barbarism spoke more
Than for that angel knowledge you can say,
Yet confident I'll keep what I have sworn,

115 And bide the penance of each three years' day.
Give me the paper; let me read the same;
And to the strict'st decrees I'll write my name.

KING   How well this yielding rescues thee from shame!

BEROWNE [*Reads.*]   *Item: that no woman shall come within*

120 *a mile of my court,* – Hath this been proclaimed?

LONGAVILLE   Four days ago.

BEROWNE
Let's see the penalty – *on pain of losing her tongue.*
Who devised this penalty?

LONGAVILLE   Marry, that did I.

125 BEROWNE   Sweet lord, and why?

LONGAVILLE
To fright them hence with that dread penalty.

BEROWNE   A dangerous law against gentility!
Item: if any man be seen to talk with a woman within the
term of three years, he shall endure such public shame as

130 *the rest of the court can possibly devise.*
This article, my liege, yourself must break;
For well you know here comes in embassy
The French king's daughter with yourself to speak –
A maid of grace and complete majesty –

135 About surrender up of Aquitaine
To her decrepit, sick, and bed-rid father:
Therefore this article is made in vain,
Or vainly comes th'admired princess hither.

KING   What say you, lords? why, this was quite forgot.

140 BEROWNE   So study evermore is overshot:
While it doth study to have what it would,
It doth forget to do the thing it should;
And when it hath the thing it hunteth most,
'Tis won as towns with fire, so won, so lost.

145 KING   We must of force dispense with this decree;
She must lie here on mere necessity.

BEROWNE   Necessity will make us all forsworn
Three thousand times within these three years'
     space;
For every man with his affects is born,

150 Not by might master'd, but by special grace.

If I break faith, this word shall speak for me,
I am forsworn on mere necessity.
So to the laws at large I write my name;
And he that breaks them in the least degree
Stands in attainder of eternal shame: 155
Suggestions are to other as to me;
But I believe, although I seem so loath,
I am the last that will last keep his oath.
But is there no quick recreation granted?

KING
Ay, that there is. Our court, you know, is haunted   160
With a refined traveller of Spain;
A man in all the world's new fashion planted,
That hath a mint of phrases in his brain;
One who the music of his own vain tongue
Doth ravish like enchanting harmony;   165
A man of complements, whom right and wrong
Have chose as umpire of their mutiny:
This child of fancy, that Armado hight,
For interim to our studies shall relate
In high-born words the worth of many a knight   170
From tawny Spain, lost in the world's debate.
How you delight, my lords, I know not, I;
But I protest I love to hear him lie,
And I will use him for my minstrelsy.

BEROWNE   Armado is a most illustrious wight,   175
A man of fire-new words, fashion's own knight.

LONGAVILLE
Costard the swain, and he, shall be our sport,
And so to study three years is but short.

Enter DULL *with a letter, and* COSTARD.

DULL   Which is the duke's own person?

BEROWNE   This, fellow. What would'st?   180

DULL   I myself reprehend his own person, for I am his
grace's farborough: but I would see his own person
in flesh and blood.

BEROWNE   This is he.

DULL   Signior Arm – Arm – commends you. There's   185
villany abroad: this letter will tell you more.

COSTARD   Sir, the contempts thereof are as touching me.

KING   A letter from the magnificent Armado.

BEROWNE   How low soever the matter, I hope in God for
high words.   190

LONGAVILLE   A high hope for a low heaven: God grant
us patience!

BEROWNE   To hear? or forbear hearing?

LONGAVILLE   To hear meekly, sir, and to laugh
moderately; or to forbear both.   195

BEROWNE   Well, sir, be it as the style shall give us cause
to climb in the merriness.

COSTARD   The matter is to me, sir, as concerning
Jaquenetta. The manner of it is, I was taken with the
manner.   200

BEROWNE   In what manner?

COSTARD   In manner and form following, sir; all those

three: I was seen with her in the manor-house, sitting
with her upon the form, and taken following her into
the park; which, put together, is in manner and form
following. Now, sir, for the manner, – it is the manner
of a man to speak to a woman; for the form, – in some
form.

BEROWNE   For the following, sir?

COSTARD   As it shall follow in my correction; and God
defend the right!

KING   Will you hear this letter with attention?

BEROWNE   As we would hear an oracle.

COSTARD   Such is the simplicity of man to hearken after
the flesh.

KING [*Reads.*] *Great deputy, the welkin's vicegerent, and
sole dominator of Navarre, my soul's earth's God, and
body's fostering patron.*

COSTARD   Not a word of Costard yet.

KING   *So it is,* –

COSTARD   It may be so; but if he say it is so, he is, in
telling true, but so.

KING   Peace!

COSTARD   Be to me and every man that dares not fight.

KING   No words!

COSTARD   Of other men's secrets, I beseech you.

KING   *So it is, besieged with sable-coloured melancholy, I
did commend the black oppressing humour to the most
wholesome physic of thy health-giving air; and, as I am a
gentleman, betook myself to walk. The time when? About
the sixth hour; when beasts most graze, birds best peck,
and men sit down to that nourishment which is called
supper: so much for the time when. Now for the ground
which? which, I mean, I walked upon: it is ycleped thy
park. Then for the place where? where, I mean, I did
encounter that obscene and most preposterous event, that
draweth from my snow-white pen the ebon-coloured ink,
which here thou viewest, beholdest, surveyest, or seest. But
to the place where: it standeth north-north-east and by
east from the west corner of thy curious-knotted garden:
there did I see that low-spirited swain, that base minnow
of thy mirth,* –

COSTARD   Me?

KING   *that unlettered small-knowing soul,* –

COSTARD   Me?

KING   *that shallow vassal,* –

COSTARD   Still me?

KING   *which, as I remember, hight Costard,* –

COSTARD   O! me.

KING   *sorted and consorted, contrary to thy established
proclaimed edict and continent canon, which with* – O!
with – but with this I passion to say wherewith, –

COSTARD   With a wench.

KING   *with a child of our grandmother Eve, a female; or,
for thy more sweet understanding, a woman. Him, I, as
my ever-esteemed duty pricks me on, have sent to thee, to
receive the meed of punishment, by thy sweet grace's
officer, Anthony Dull, a man of good repute, carriage,
bearing, and estimation.*

DULL   Me, an't shall please you; I am Anthony Dull.

KING   *For Jaquenetta – so is the weaker vessel called –
which I apprehended with the aforesaid swain, I keep her
as a vessel of thy law's fury; and shall, at the least of thy
sweet notice, bring her to trial. Thine in all compliments of
devoted and heart-burning heat of duty,*

            DON ADRIANO DE ARMADO.

BEROWNE   This is not so well as I looked for, but the best
that ever I heard.

KING   Ay, the best for the worst. But, sirrah, what say
you to this?

COSTARD   Sir, I confess the wench.

KING   Did you hear the proclamation?

COSTARD   I do confess much of the hearing it, but little
of the marking of it.

KING   It was proclaimed a year's imprisonment to be
taken with a wench.

COSTARD   I was taken with none, sir: I was taken with a
demsel.

KING   Well, it was proclaimed damsel.

COSTARD   This was no damsel neither, sir: she was a
virgin.

KING   It is so varied too, for it was proclaimed virgin.

COSTARD   If it were, I deny her virginity: I was taken
with a maid.

KING   This maid will not serve your turn, sir.

COSTARD   This maid will serve my turn, sir.

KING   Sir, I will pronounce your sentence: you shall fast
a week with bran and water.

COSTARD   I had rather pray a month with mutton and
porridge.

KING   And Don Armado shall be your keeper.
  My Lord Berowne, see him deliver'd o'er:
  And go we, lords, to put in practice that
  Which each to other hath so strongly sworn.

        Exeunt King, Longaville and Dumain.

BEROWNE   I'll lay my head to any good man's hat,
  These oaths and laws will prove an idle scorn.
  Sirrah, come on.

COSTARD   I suffer for the truth, sir: for true it is I was
taken with Jaquenetta, and Jaquenetta is a true girl;
and therefore welcome the sour cup of prosperity!
Affliction may one day smile again; and till then, sit
thee down, sorrow!   *Exeunt.*

1.2   *Enter* ARMADO *and* MOTH.

ARMADO   Boy, what sign is it when a man of great spirit
grows melancholy?

MOTH   A great sign, sir, that he will look sad.

ARMADO   Why! sadness is one and the self-same thing,
dear imp.

MOTH   No, no; O Lord, sir, no.

ARMADO   How canst thou part sadness and melancholy,
my tender juvenal?

MOTH   By a familiar demonstration of the working, my
tough Signor.

ARMADO   Why tough Signor? why tough Signor?

MOTH   Why tender juvenal? why tender juvenal?

ARMADO   I spoke it, tender juvenal, as a congruent
epitheton appertaining to thy young days, which we
may nominate tender.

MOTH   And I, tough Signor, as an appertinent title to
your old time, which we may name tough.

ARMADO   Pretty, and apt.

MOTH   How mean you, sir? I pretty, and my saying apt?
or I apt, and my saying pretty?

ARMADO   Thou pretty, because little.

MOTH   Little pretty, because little. Wherefore apt?

ARMADO   And therefore apt, because quick.

MOTH   Speak you this in my praise, master?

ARMADO   In thy condign praise.

MOTH   I will praise an eel with the same praise.

ARMADO   What! that an eel is ingenious?

MOTH   That an eel is quick.

ARMADO   I do say thou art quick in answers: thou heat'st
my blood.

MOTH   I am answered, sir.

ARMADO   I love not to be crossed.

MOTH [*aside*]   He speaks the mere contrary: crosses love
not him.

ARMADO   I have promised to study three years with the
duke.

MOTH   You may do it in an hour, sir.

ARMADO   Impossible.

MOTH   How many is one thrice told?

ARMADO   I am ill at reckoning; it fitteth the spirit of a
tapster.

MOTH   You are a gentleman and a gamester, sir.

ARMADO   I confess both: they are both the varnish of a
complete man.

MOTH   Then I am sure you know how much the gross
sum of deuce-ace amounts to.

ARMADO   It doth amount to one more than two.

MOTH   Which the base vulgar do call three.

ARMADO   True.

MOTH   Why, sir, is this such a piece of study? Now here
is three studied ere ye'll thrice wink; and how easy it is
to put years to the word three, and study three years
in two words, the dancing horse will tell you.

ARMADO   A most fine figure!

MOTH [*aside*]   To prove you a cipher.

ARMADO   I will hereupon confess I am in love; and as it
is base for a soldier to love, so am I in love with a base
wench. If drawing my sword against the humour of
affection would deliver me from the reprobate thought
of it, I would take Desire prisoner, and ransom him to
any French courtier for a new-devised courtesy. I
think scorn to sigh: methinks I should outswear
Cupid. Comfort me, boy. What great men have been
in love?

MOTH   Hercules, master.

ARMADO   Most sweet Hercules! More authority, dear
boy, name more; and, sweet my child, let them be men

of good repute and carriage.

MOTH   Samson, master: he was a man of good carriage,
great carriage, for he carried the town-gates on his
back like a porter; and he was in love.

ARMADO   O well-knit Samson! strong-jointed Samson! I
do excell thee in my rapier as much as thou didst me
in carrying gates. I am in love too. Who was Samson's
love, my dear Moth?

MOTH   A woman, master.

ARMADO   Of what complexion?

MOTH   Of all the four, or the three, or the two, or one of
the four.

ARMADO   Tell me precisely of what complexion.

MOTH   Of the sea-water green, sir.

ARMADO   Is that one of the four complexions?

MOTH   As I have read, sir; and the best of them too.

ARMADO   Green indeed is the colour of lovers; but to
have a love of that colour, methinks, Samson had small
reason for it. He surely affected her for her wit.

MOTH   It was so, sir, for she had a green wit.

ARMADO   My love is most immaculate white and red.

MOTH   Most maculate thoughts, master, are masked
under such colours.

ARMADO   Define, define, well-educated infant.

MOTH   My father's wit and my mother's tongue assist
me!

ARMADO   Sweet invocation of a child; most pretty and
pathetical!

MOTH   If she be made of white and red,
 Her faults will ne'er be known,
For blushing cheeks by faults are bred,
 And fears by pale white shown:
Then if she fear, or be to blame,
 By this you shall not know,
For still her cheeks possess the same
 Which native she doth owe.
A dangerous rhyme, master, against the reason of
white and red.

ARMADO   Is there not a ballad, boy, of the King and the
Beggar?

MOTH   The world was very guilty of such a ballad some
three ages since; but I think now 'tis not to be found;
or, if it were, it would neither serve for the writing nor
the tune.

ARMADO   I will have that subject newly writ o'er, that I
may example my digression by some mighty
precedent. Boy, I do love that country girl that I took
in the park with the rational hind Costard: she
deserves well.

MOTH [*aside*]   To be whipped; and yet a better love
than my master.

ARMADO   Sing, boy: my spirit grows heavy in love.

MOTH [*aside*]   And that's great marvel, loving a light
wench.

ARMADO   I say, sing.

MOTH   Forbear till this company be past.

Enter DULL, COSTARD *and* JAQUENETTA.

DULL   Sir, the duke's pleasure is that you keep Costard
safe: and you must suffer him to take no delight nor no
penance, but a' must fast three days a week. For this
damsel, I must keep her at the park; she is allowed for
the day-woman. Fare you well.

ARMADO   I do betray myself with blushing. Maid.

JAQUENETTA   Man.

ARMADO   I will visit thee at the lodge.

JAQUENETTA   That's hereby.

ARMADO   I know where it is situate.

JAQUENETTA   Lord, how wise you are!

ARMADO   I will tell thee wonders.

JAQUENETTA   With that face?

ARMADO   I love thee.

JAQUENETTA   So I heard you say.

ARMADO   And so farewell.

JAQUENETTA   Fair weather after you!

DULL   Come, Jaquenetta, away!

Exeunt Dull and Jaquenetta.

ARMADO   Villain, thou shalt fast for thy offences ere
thou be pardoned.

COSTARD   Well, sir, I hope when I do it I shall do it on a
full stomach.

ARMADO   Thou shalt be heavily punished.

COSTARD   I am more bound to you than your fellows, for
they are but lightly rewarded.

ARMADO   Take away this villain: shut him up.

MOTH   Come, you transgressing slave: away!

COSTARD   Let me not be pent up, sir; I will fast, being
loose.

MOTH   No, sir, that were fast and loose: thou shalt to
prison.

COSTARD   Well, if ever I do see the merry days of
desolation that I have seen, some shall see –

MOTH   What shall some see?

COSTARD   Nay, nothing, Master Moth, but what they
look upon. It is not for prisoners to be too silent in
their words, and therefore I will say nothing: I thank
God I have as little patience as another man, and
therefore I can be quiet.   *Exeunt Moth and Costard.*

ARMADO   I do affect the very ground, which is base,
where her shoe, which is baser, guided by her foot,
which is basest, doth tread. I shall be forsworn, which
is a great argument of falsehood, if I love. And how
can that be true love which is falsely attempted? Love
is a familiar; Love is a devil: there is no evil angel but
Love. Yet was Samson so tempted, and he had an
excellent strength; yet was Solomon so seduced, and
he had a very good wit. Cupid's butt-shaft is too hard
for Hercules' club, and therefore too much odds for a
Spaniard's rapier. The first and second cause will not
serve my turn; the passado he respects not, the duello
he regards not: his disgrace is to be called boy, but his
glory is to subdue men. Adieu, valour! rust, rapier! be
still, drum! for your manager is in love; yea, he loveth.

Assist me, some extemporal god of rhyme, for I am
sure I shall turn sonnet. Devise, wit; write, pen; for I
am for whole volumes in folio.   *Exit.*   180

2.1   *Enter the* PRINCESS *of France,*
MARIA, KATHARINE, ROSALINE, BOYET,
Lords *and other attendants.*

BOYET   Now, madam, summon up your dearest spirits:
Consider who the king your father sends,
To whom he sends, and what's his embassy:
Yourself, held precious in the world's esteem,
To parley with the sole inheritor   5
Of all perfections that a man may owe,
Matchless Navarre; the plea of no less weight
Than Aquitaine, a dowry for a queen.
Be now as prodigal of all dear grace
As Nature was in making graces dear   10
When she did starve the general world beside,
And prodigally gave them all to you.

PRINCESS
Good Lord Boyet, my beauty, though but mean,
Needs not the painted flourish of your praise:
Beauty is bought by judgment of the eye,   15
Not utter'd by base sale of chapmen's tongues.
I am less proud to hear you tell my worth
Than you much willing to be counted wise
In spending your wit in the praise of mine.
But now to task the tasker: good Boyet,   20
You are not ignorant all-telling fame
Doth noise abroad Navarre hath made a vow,
Till painful study shall outwear three years,
No woman may approach his silent court:
Therefore to's seemeth it a needful course,   25
Before we enter his forbidden gates,
To know his pleasure; and in that behalf,
Bold of your worthiness, we single you
As our best-moving fair solicitor.
Tell him the daughter of the King of France,   30
On serious business craving quick dispatch,
Importunes personal conference with his grace.
Haste, signify so much; while we attend,
Like humble-visag'd suitors, his high will.

BOYET   Proud of employment, willingly I go.   35

PRINCESS
All pride is willing pride, and yours is so. *Exit Boyet.*
Who are the votaries, my loving lords,
That are vow-fellows with this virtuous duke?

FIRST LORD   Lord Longaville is one.

PRINCESS   Know you the man?

MARIA   I know him, madam: at a marriage-feast,   40
Between Lord Perigort and the beauteous heir
Of Jaques Falconbridge, solemnized
In Normandy, saw I this Longaville:
A man of sovereign parts he is esteem'd,
Well fitted in arts, glorious in arms;   45
Nothing becomes him ill that he would well.

The only soil of his fair virtue's gloss,
If virtue's gloss will stain with any soil,
Is a sharp wit match'd with too blunt a will;
50 Whose edge hath power to cut, whose will still wills
It should none spare that come within his power.
PRINCESS Some merry mocking lord, belike; is't so?
MARIA They say so most that most his humours know.
PRINCESS Such short-liv'd wits do wither as they grow.
55 Who are the rest?
KATHARINE
The young Dumain, a well accomplish'd youth,
Of all that virtue love for virtue lov'd:
Most power to do most harm, least knowing ill,
For he hath wit to make an ill shape good,
60 And shape to win grace though he had no wit.
I saw him at the Duke Alençon's once;
And much too little of that good I saw
Is my report to his great worthiness.
ROSALINE Another of these students at that time
65 Was there with him, if I have heard a truth,
Berowne they call him; but a merrier man,
Within the limit of becoming mirth,
I never spent an hour's talk withal.
His eye begets occasion for his wit;
70 For every object that the one doth catch
The other turns to a mirth-moving jest,
Which his fair tongue (conceit's expositor)
Delivers in such apt and gracious words
That aged ears play truant at his tales,
75 And younger hearings are quite ravished;
So sweet and voluble is his discourse.
PRINCESS
God bless my ladies! are they all in love,
That every one her own hath garnished
With such bedecking ornaments of praise?
FIRST LORD Here comes Boyet.

Re-enter BOYET.

80 PRINCESS   Now, what admittance, lord?
BOYET Navarre had notice of your fair approach;
And he and his competitors in oath
Were all address'd to meet you, gentle lady,
Before I came. Marry, thus much I have learnt;
85 He rather means to lodge you in the field,
Like one that comes here to besiege his court,
Than seek a dispensation for his oath,
To let you enter his unpeopled house.
Here comes Navarre.

Enter KING, LONGAVILLE, DUMAIN, BEROWNE
and attendants.

90 KING Fair princess, welcome to the court of Navarre.
PRINCESS
Fair I give you back again; and welcome I have not yet:
the roof of this court is too high to be yours, and
welcome to the wide fields too base to be mine.

KING You shall be welcome, madam, to my court.
PRINCESS I will be welcome then: conduct me thither. 95
KING Hear me, dear lady; I have sworn an oath.
PRINCESS Our Lady help my lord! he'll be forsworn.
KING Not for the world, fair madam, by my will.
PRINCESS
Why, will shall break it will, and nothing else.
KING Your ladyship is ignorant what it is. 100
PRINCESS Were my lord so, his ignorance were wise,
Where now his knowledge must prove ignorance.
I hear your grace hath sworn out house-keeping:
'Tis deadly sin to keep that oath, my lord,
And sin to break it. 105
But pardon me, I am too sudden-bold:
To teach a teacher ill beseemeth me.
Vouchsafe to read the purpose of my coming,
And suddenly resolve me in my suit.
KING Madam, I will, if suddenly I may. 110
PRINCESS You will the sooner that I were away,
For you'll prove perjur'd if you make me stay.
BEROWNE Did not I dance with you in Brabant once?
ROSALINE Did not I dance with you in Brabant once?
BEROWNE I know you did. 115
ROSALINE
How needless was it then to ask the question!
BEROWNE You must not be so quick.
ROSALINE
'Tis long of you that spur me with such questions.
BEROWNE
Your wit's too hot, it speeds too fast, 'twill tire.
ROSALINE Not till it leave the rider in the mire. 120
BEROWNE What time o' day?
ROSALINE The hour that fools should ask.
BEROWNE Now fair befall your mask!
ROSALINE Fair fall the face it covers!
BEROWNE And send you many lovers! 125
ROSALINE Amen, so you be none.
BEROWNE Nay, then will I be gone.
KING Madam, your father here doth intimate
The payment of a hundred thousand crowns;
Being but the one half of an entire sum 130
Disbursed by my father in his wars.
But say that he, or we, as neither have,
Receiv'd that sum, yet there remains unpaid
A hundred thousand more; in surety of the which,
One part of Aquitaine is bound to us, 135
Although not valued to the money's worth.
If then the king your father will restore
But that one half of which is unsatisfied,
We will give up our right in Aquitaine,
And hold fair friendship with his majesty. 140
But that, it seems, he little purposeth,
For here he doth demand to have repaid
A hundred thousand crowns; and not demands
On payment of a hundred thousand crowns
To have his title live in Aquitaine; 145

Which we much rather had depart withal,
And have the money by our father lent,
Than Aquitaine, so gelded as it is.
Dear princess, were not his requests so far
50   From reason's yielding, your fair self should make
A yielding 'gainst some reason in my breast,
And go well satisfied to France again.
PRINCESS   You do the king my father too much wrong,
And wrong the reputation of your name,
55   In so unseeming to confess receipt
Of that which hath so faithfully been paid.
KING   I do protest I never heard of it;
And if you prove it I'll repay it back,
Or yield up Aquitaine.
PRINCESS   We arrest your word:
60   Boyet, you can produce acquittances
For such a sum from special officers
Of Charles his father.
KING   Satisfy me so.
BOYET   So please your grace, the packet is not come
Where that and other specialties are bound:
65   To-morrow you shall have a sight of them.
KING   It shall suffice me: at which interview
All liberal reason I will yield unto.
Meantime, receive such welcome at my hand
As honour, without breach of honour, may
70   Make tender of to thy true worthiness.
You may not come fair princess, within my gates;
But here without you shall be so receiv'd
As you shall deem your self lodg'd in my heart,
Though so denied fair harbour in my house.
175 Your own good thoughts excuse me, and farewell:
To-morrow shall we visit you again.
PRINCESS
Sweet health and fair desires consort your grace!
KING   Thy own wish wish I thee in every place!   *Exit.*
BEROWNE
Lady, I will commend you to mine own heart.
180 ROSALINE   Pray you do my commendations; I would be
glad to see it.
BEROWNE   I would you heard it groan.
ROSALINE   Is the fool sick?
BEROWNE   Sick at the heart.
185 ROSALINE   Alack! let it blood.
BEROWNE   Would that do it good?
ROSALINE   My physic says, ay.
BEROWNE   Will you prick't with your eye?
ROSALINE   No point, with my knife.
190 BEROWNE   Now God save thy life!
ROSALINE   And yours, from long living!
BEROWNE   I cannot stay thanksgiving. [*retiring*]
DUMAIN
Sir, I pray you, a word: what lady is that same?
BOYET   The heir of Alençon, Katharine her name.
195 DUMAIN   A gallant lady. Monsieur, fare you well.   *Exit.*
LONGAVILLE
I beseech you a word: what is she in the white?

BOYET
A woman sometimes, an you saw her in the light.
LONGAVILLE
Perchance light in the light. I desire her name.
BOYET
She hath but one for herself; to desire that were a
shame.
LONGAVILLE   Pray you, sir, whose daughter?   200
BOYET   Her mother's, I have heard.
LONGAVILLE   God's blessing on your beard!
BOYET   Good sir, be not offended.
She is an heir of Falconbridge.
LONGAVILLE   Nay, my choler is ended.   205
She is a most sweet lady.
BOYET   Not unlike, sir; that may be.   *Exit Longaville.*
BEROWNE   What's her name in the cap?
BOYET   Rosaline, by good hap.
BEROWNE   Is she wedded or no?   210
BOYET   To her will sir, or so.
BEROWNE   O you are welcome, sir. Adieu.
BOYET   Farewell to me, sir, and welcome to you.
                                                    Exit Berowne.
MARIA   That last is Berowne, the merry mad-cap lord:
Not a word with him but a jest.
BOYET   And every jest but a word.   215
PRINCESS
It was well done of you to take him at his word.
BOYET   I was as willing to grapple as he was to board.
KATHARINE   Two hot sheeps, marry!
BOYET   And wherefore not ships?
No sheep, sweet lamb, unless we feed on your lips.
KATHARINE
You sheep, and I pasture: shall that finish the jest?   220
BOYET   So you grant pasture for me.
KATHARINE   Not so, gentle beast:
My lips are no common, though several they be.
BOYET   Belonging to whom?
KATHARINE   To my fortunes and me.
PRINCESS
Good wits will be jangling; but, gentles, agree:
This civil war of wits were much better us'd   225
On Navarre and his book-men, for here 'tis abus'd.
BOYET   If my observation, which very seldom lies,
By the heart's still rhetoric disclosed with eyes
Deceive me not now, Navarre is infected.
PRINCESS   With what?   230
BOYET   With that which we lovers entitle affected.
PRINCESS   Your reason?
BOYET   Why, all his behaviours did make their retire
To the court of his eye, peeping thorough desire:
His heart, like an agate, with your print impress'd,   235
Proud with his form, in his eye pride express'd:
His tongue, all impatient to speak and not see,
Did stumble with haste in his eyesight to be;
All senses to that sense did make their repair,
To feel only looking on fairest of fair: 240
Methought all his senses were lock'd in his eye,

As jewels in crystal for some prince to buy;
Who, tend'ring their own worth from where they
     were glass'd,
Did point you to buy them, along as you pass'd:
His face's own margent did quote such amazes,
That all eyes saw his eyes enchanted with gazes.
I'll give you Aquitaine, and all that is his,
An you give him for my sake but one loving kiss.

PRINCESS   Come to our pavilion: Boyet is dispos'd.

BOYET
But to speak that in words which his eye hath
     disclos'd.
I only have made a mouth of his eye,
By adding a tongue which I know will not lie.

MARIA
Thou art an old love-monger, and speak'st skilfully.

KATHARINE
He is Cupid's grandfather and learns news of him.

ROSALINE
Then was Venus like her mother, for her father is but
     grim.

BOYET   Do you hear, my mad wenches?

MARIA   No.

BOYET   What then, do you see?

MARIA   Ay, our way to be gone.

BOYET   You are too hard for me.
                                        Exeunt.

3.1   *Enter* ARMADO *and* MOTH.

ARMADO   Warble, child: make passionate my sense of
     hearing.

MOTH [*Sings.*]   Concolinel.

ARMADO   Sweet air! Go, tenderness of years; take this
     key, give enlargement to the swain, bring him
     festinately hither; I must employ him in a letter to my
     love.

MOTH   Master, will you win your love with a French
     brawl?

ARMADO   How meanest thou? brawling in French?

MOTH   No, my complete master; but to jig off a tune at
     the tongue's end, canary to it with your feet, humour
     it with turning up your eyelids, sigh a note and sing a
     note, sometime through the throat as if you swallowed
     love with singing love, sometime through the nose, as
     if you snuffed up love by smelling love; with your hat
     penthouse-like o'er the shop of your eyes; with your
     arms crossed on your thin-belly doublet like a rabbit
     on a spit; or your hands in your pocket, like a man
     after the old painting; and keep not too long in one
     tune, but a snip and away. These are complements,
     these are humours, these betray nice wenches, that
     would be betrayed without these; and make them men
     of note (do you note, men?) that most are affected to
     these.

ARMADO   How hast thou purchased this experience?

MOTH   By my penny of observation.

ARMADO   But O, but O, –

MOTH   The hobby-horse is forgot.

ARMADO   Call'st thou my love hobby-horse?

MOTH   No, master; the hobby-horse is but a colt, [*aside*]
     – and your love perhaps a hackney. But have you
     forgot your love?

ARMADO   Almost I had.

MOTH   Negligent student! learn her by heart.

ARMADO   By heart, and in heart, boy.

MOTH   And out of heart, master: all those three I will
     prove.

ARMADO   What wilt thou prove?

MOTH   A man, if I live; and this, by, in, and without,
     upon the instant: by heart you love her, because your
     heart cannot come by her; in heart you love her,
     because your heart is in love with her; and out of heart
     you love her, being out of heart that you cannot enjoy
     her.

ARMADO   I am all these three.

MOTH   And three times as much more, and yet nothing
     at all.

ARMADO   Fetch hither the swain: he must carry me a
     letter.

MOTH   A message well sympathized: a horse to be
     ambassador for an ass.

ARMADO   Ha? ha? what sayest thou?

MOTH   Marry, sir, you must send the ass upon the horse,
     for he is very slow-gaited. But I go.

ARMADO   The way is but short: away!

MOTH   As swift as lead, sir.

ARMADO   The meaning, pretty ingenious?
Is not lead a metal heavy, dull, and slow?

MOTH   *Minime*, honest master; or rather, master, no.

ARMADO   I say lead is slow.

MOTH   You are too swift, sir, to say so:
Is that lead slow which is fir'd from a gun?

ARMADO   Sweet smoke of rhetoric!
He reputes me a cannon, and the bullet, that's he –
I shoot thee at the swain.

MOTH   Thump then, and I flee.   *Exit.*

ARMADO   A most acute juvenal; voluble and free of
     grace!
By thy favour, sweet welkin, I must sigh in thy face:
Most rude melancholy, valour gives thee place.
My herald is return'd.

          Re-enter MOTH *with* COSTARD.

MOTH   A wonder, master! here's a costard broken in a
     shin.

ARMADO   Some enigma, some riddle: come, thy l'envoy;
     begin.

COSTARD   No egma, no riddle, no l'envoy; no salve in
     the mail, sir. O, sir, plantain, a plain plantain! no
     l'envoy, no l'envoy: no salve, sir, but a plantain!

ARMADO   By virtue, thou enforcest laughter; thy silly
     thought my spleen; the heaving of my lungs provokes
     me to ridiculous smiling: O, pardon me, my stars!

Doth the inconsiderate take salve for l'envoy, and the
word l'envoy for a salve?

MOTH   Do the wise think them other? is not l'envoy a
salve?

ARMADO   No, page: it is an epilogue or discourse to
make plain

Some obscure precedence that hath tofore been sain.
I will example it:
       The fox, the ape, and the humble-bee,
       Were still at odds, being but three.
There's the moral: now the l'envoy.

MOTH   I will add the l'envoy. Say the moral again.

ARMADO   The fox, the ape, and the humble-bee,
       Were still at odds, being but three.

MOTH   Until the goose came out of door,
       And stay'd the odds by adding four.
Now will I begin your moral, and do you follow with
my l'envoy.
       The fox, the ape, and the humble-bee,
       Were still at odds, being but three.

ARMADO   Until the goose came out of door,
       Staying the odds by adding four.

MOTH   A good l'envoy, ending in the goose: would you
desire more?

COSTARD
The boy hath sold him a bargain, a goose, that's flat.
Sir, your pennyworth is good an your goose be fat.
To sell a bargain well is as cunning as fast and loose:
Let me see; a fat l'envoy; ay, that's a fat goose.

ARMADO
Come hither, come hither. How did this argument
   begin?

MOTH   By saying that a costard was broken in a shin.
Then call'd you for the l'envoy.

COSTARD
True, and I for a plantain: thus came your argument
   in;
Then the boy's fat l'envoy, the goose that you
   bought;
And he ended the market.

ARMADO   But tell me; how was there a costard broken in
a shin?

MOTH   I will tell you sensibly.

COSTARD   Thou hast no feeling of it, Moth: I will speak
that l'envoy.
      I, Costard, running out, that was safely within,
      Fell over the threshold and broke my shin.

ARMADO   We will talk no more of this matter.

COSTARD   Till there be more matter in the shin.

ARMADO   Sirrah Costard, I will enfranchise thee.

COSTARD   O! marry me to one Frances – I smell some
l'envoy, some goose in this.

ARMADO   By my sweet soul, I mean setting thee at
liberty, enfreedoming thy person: thou wert immured,
restrained, captivated, bound.

COSTARD   True, true, and now you will be my purgation
and let me loose.

ARMADO   I give thee thy liberty, set thee from durance;   130
and, in lieu thereof, impose on thee nothing but this:
bear this significant to the country maid Jaquenetta.
There is remuneration; for the best ward of mine
honour is rewarding my dependents. Moth, follow.
                           Exit.

MOTH   Like the sequel, I. Signior Costard, adieu.   135

COSTARD   My sweet ounce of man's flesh! my incony
Jew!   *Exit Moth.*
Now will I look to his remuneration. Remuneration!
O that's the Latin word for three farthings: three
farthings, remuneration. 'What's the price of this
inkle?' 'One penny': 'No, I'll give you a remuneration':   140
why, it carries it. Remuneration! why it is a fairer name
than French crown. I will never buy and sell out of this
word.

            Enter BEROWNE.

BEROWNE   O my good knave Costard! exceedingly well
met.   145

COSTARD   Pray you, sir, how much carnation ribbon
may a man buy for a remuneration?

BEROWNE   O what is a remuneration?

COSTARD   Marry, sir, halfpenny farthing.

BEROWNE   O! why then, three-farthing worth of silk.   150

COSTARD   I thank your worship. God be wi' you!

BEROWNE   O stay, slave! I must employ thee:
As thou wilt win my favour, good my knave,
Do one thing for me that I shall entreat.

COSTARD   When would you have it done, sir?   155

BEROWNE   O this afternoon.

COSTARD   Well, I will do it, sir. Fare you well.

BEROWNE   O thou knowest not what it is.

COSTARD   I shall know, sir, when I have done it.

BEROWNE   Why, villain, thou must know first.   160

COSTARD   I will come to your worship to-morrow
morning.

BEROWNE   It must be done this afternoon. Hark, slave, it
is but this:
The princess comes to hunt here in the park,   165
And in her train there is a gentle lady;
When tongues speak sweetly, then they name her
   name,
And Rosaline they call her: ask for her,
And to her white hand see thou do commend
This seal'd-up counsel. There's thy guerdon: go.   170

COSTARD
Gardon, O sweet gardon! better than remuneration;
a'leven-pence farthing better. Most sweet gardon! I
will do it, sir, in print. Gardon! Remuneration!   *Exit.*

BEROWNE   O! and I forsooth in love!
I, that have been love's whip;   175
A very beadle to a humorous sigh;
A critic, nay, a night-watch constable,
A domineering pedant o'er the boy,
Than whom no mortal so magnificent!
This wimpled, whining, purblind, wayward boy,   180

This signor junior, giant-dwarf, dan Cupid;
Regent of love rhymes, lord of folded arms,
The anointed sovereign of sighs and groans,
Liege of all loiterers and malcontents,
Dread prince of plackets, king of codpieces,   185
Sole imperator and great general
Of trotting paritors: O my little heart!
And I to be a corporal of his field,
And wear his colours like a tumbler's hoop!
What! I love! I sue! I seek a wife!   190
A woman that is like a German clock,
Still a-repairing, ever out of frame,
And never going aright, being a watch,
But being watch'd that it may still go right!
Nay to be perjur'd, which is worst of all;   195
And among three, to love the worst of all;
A whitely wanton with a velvet brow,
With two pitch-balls stuck in her face for eyes;
Ay and by heaven, one that will do the deed
Though Argus were her eunuch and her guard: 200
And I to sigh for her! to watch for her!
To pray for her! Go to; it is a plague
That Cupid will impose for my neglect
Of his almighty dreadful little might.
Well, I will love, write, sigh, pray, sue, and groan: 205
Some men must love my lady, and some Joan.   *Exit.*

4.1   *Enter the* PRINCESS, MARIA, KATHARINE,
ROSALINE, BOYET, *lords, attendants and a* Forester.

PRINCESS
Was that the king, that spurr'd his horse so hard
Against the steep-up rising of the hill?
FORESTER   I know not; but I think it was not he.
PRINCESS   Whoe'er a' was, a' show'd a mounting mind.
Well, lords, to-day we shall have our despatch;   5
On Saturday we will return to France.
Then, forester, my friend, where is the bush
That we must stand and play the murderer in?
FORESTER   Hereby, upon the edge of yonder coppice;
A stand where you may make the fairest shoot.   10
PRINCESS   I thank my beauty, I am fair that shoot,
And thereupon thou speak'st the fairest shoot.
FORESTER   Pardon me, madam, for I meant not so.
PRINCESS
What, what? first praise me, and again say no?
O short-liv'd pride! Not fair? alack for woe!   15
FORESTER   Yes, madam, fair.
PRINCESS   Nay, never paint me now:
Where fair is not, praise cannot mend the brow.
Here, good my glass, take this for telling true:
Fair payment for foul words is more than due.
FORESTER   Nothing but fair is that which you inherit. 20
PRINCESS   See, see! my beauty will be saved by merit.
O heresy in fair, fit for these days!
A giving hand, though foul, shall have fair praise.
But come, the bow: now mercy goes to kill,

And shooting well is then accounted ill.   25
Thus will I save my credit in the shoot:
Not wounding, pity would not let me do't;
If wounding, then it was to show my skill,
That more for praise than purpose meant to kill.
And out of question so it is sometimes,   30
Glory grows guilty of detested crimes,
When, for fame's sake, for praise, an outward part,
We bend to that the working of the heart;
As I for praise alone now seek to spill
The poor deer's blood, that my heart means no ill.   35
BOYET   Do not curst wives hold that self-sovereignty
Only for praise' sake, when they strive to be
Lords o'er their lords?
PRINCESS   Only for praise; and praise we may afford
To any lady that subdues a lord.   40

Enter COSTARD.

BOYET   Here comes a member of the commonwealth.
COSTARD   God dig-you-den all! Pray you, which is the
head lady?
PRINCESS   Thou shalt know her, fellow, by the rest that
have no heads.   45
COSTARD   Which is the greatest lady, the highest?
PRINCESS   The thickest and the tallest.
COSTARD
The thickest and the tallest! it is so; truth is truth.
An your waist, mistress, were as slender as my wit,
One o' these maids' girdles for your waist should be
fit.   50
Are not you the chief woman? you are the thickest
here.
PRINCESS   What's your will, sir? What's your will?
COSTARD
I have a letter from Monsieur Berowne to one Lady
Rosaline.
PRINCESS
O! thy letter, thy letter; he's a good friend of mine. 55
Stand aside, good bearer. Boyet, you can carve;
Break up this capon.
BOYET   I am bound to serve.
This letter is mistook; it importeth none here:
It is writ to Jaquenetta.
PRINCESS   We will read it, I swear.
Break the neck of the wax, and every one give ear.   60
BOYET [*Reads.*] *By heaven, that thou art fair, is most
infallible; true, that thou art beauteous; truth itself,
that thou art lovely. More fairer than fair, beautiful
than beauteous, truer than truth itself, have
commiseration on thy heroical vassal! The magnanimous* 65
*and most illustrate king Cophetua set eye upon the
pernicious and indubitate beggar Zenelophon, and he it
was that might rightly say,* veni, vidi, vici; *which to
annothanize in the vulgar (O base and obscure vulgar!)*
videlicet, *he came, saw, and overcame: he came, one;*   70
*saw, two; overcame, three. Who came? the king: why did
he come? to see: why did he see? to overcome. To whom*

came he? to the beggar: what saw he? the beggar: who overcame he? the beggar. The conclusion is victory: on whose side? the king's. The captive is enriched: on whose side? the beggar's. The catastrophe is a nuptial: on whose side? the king's; no, on both in one, or one in both. I am the king, for so stands the comparison; thou the beggar, for so witnesseth thy lowliness. Shall I command thy love? I may. Shall I enforce thy love? I could. Shall I entreat thy love? I will. What shalt thou exchange for rags? robes: for tittles? titles: for thyself? me. Thus, expecting thy reply, I profane my lips on thy foot, my eyes on thy picture, and my heart on thy every part.

> *Thine in the dearest design of industry,*
>   DON ADRIANO DE ARMADO.

Thus dost thou hear the Nemean lion roar
'Gainst thee, thou lamb, that standest as his prey;
Submissive fall his princely feet before,
And he from forage will incline to play.
But if thou strive, poor soul, what art thou then?
Food for his rage, repasture for his den.

PRINCESS
What plume of feathers is he that indited this letter?
What vane? what weathercock? did you ever hear better?

BOYET   I am much deceiv'd but I remember the style.

PRINCESS
Else your memory is bad, going o'er it erewhile.

BOYET
This Armado is a Spaniard, that keeps here in court;
A phantasime, a Monarcho, and one that makes sport
To the prince and his book-mates.

PRINCESS   Thou, fellow, a word.
Who gave thee this letter?

COSTARD   I told you; my lord.

PRINCESS   To whom should'st thou give it?

COSTARD   From my lord to my lady.

PRINCESS   From which lord to which lady?

COSTARD
From my lord Berowne, a good master of mine,
To a lady of France that he call'd Rosaline.

PRINCESS
Thou hast mistaken his letter. Come, lords, away.
Here, sweet, put up this: 'twill be thine another day.
                    Exeunt Princess and train.

BOYET   Who is the suitor? who is the suitor?

ROSALINE   Shall I teach you to know?

BOYET   Ay, my continent of beauty.

ROSALINE   Why, she that bears the bow.
Finely put off!

BOYET   My lady goes to kill horns; but if thou marry,
Hang me by the neck if horns that year miscarry.
Finely put on!

ROSALINE   Well, then I am the shooter.

BOYET   And who is your deer?

ROSALINE
If we choose by the horns, yourself come not near.

Finely put on, indeed!

MARIA
You still wrangle with her, Boyet, and she strikes at the brow.

BOYET
But she herself is hit lower: have I hit her now?

ROSALINE   Shall I come upon thee with an old saying, that was a man when King Pepin of France was a little boy, as touching the hit it?

BOYET   So I may answer thee with one as old, that was a woman when Queen Guinever of Britain was a little wench, as touching the hit it.

ROSALINE
Thou canst not hit it, hit it, hit it,
Thou canst not hit it, my good man.
                                        Exit.

BOYET   An I cannot, cannot, cannot,
An I cannot, another can.

COSTARD
By my troth, most pleasant: how both did fit it!

MARIA
A mark marvellous well shot, for they both did hit it.

BOYET
A mark! O! mark but that mark; a mark, says my lady.
Let the mark have a prick in't, to mete at, if it may be.

MARIA
Wide o'the bow-hand! i'faith, your hand is out.

COSTARD
Indeed, a' must shoot nearer, or he'll ne'er hit the clout.

BOYET
An if my hand be out, then belike your hand is in.

COSTARD
Then will she get the upshoot by cleaving the pin.

MARIA
Come, come, you talk greasily; your lips grow foul.

COSTARD
She's too hard for you at pricks, sir: challenge her to bowl.

BOYET
I fear too much rubbing. Good night, my good owl.
                    Exeunt Boyet, Maria and Katharine.

COSTARD   By my soul, a swain! a most simple clown!
Lord, Lord, how the ladies and I have put him down!
O'my troth, most sweet jests! most incony vulgar wit;
When it comes so smoothly off, so obscenely as it were, so fit.
Armado to th'one side, O! a most dainty man,
To see him walk before a lady, and to bear her fan!
To see him kiss his hand! and how most sweetly a' will swear!
And his page o't' other side, that handful of wit!
Ah! heavens, it is a most pathetical nit.
Sola, sola! [*Shout within.*]   *Exit Costard.*

4.2 *Enter* HOLOFERNES, SIR NATHANIEL *and* DULL.

NATHANIEL   Very reverend sport, truly: and done in the testimony of a good conscience.

HOLOFERNES   The deer was, as you know, *sanguis*, in blood; ripe as the pomewater, who now hangeth like a jewel in the ear of *coelo*, the sky, the welkin, the heaven; and anon falleth like a crab on the face of *terra*, the soil, the land, the earth.

NATHANIEL   Truly, Master Holofernes, the epithets are sweetly varied, like a scholar at the least: but, sir, I assure ye, it was a buck of the first head.

HOLOFERNES   Sir Nathaniel, *haud credo*.

DULL   'Twas not a *haud credo*, 'twas a pricket.

HOLOFERNES   Most barbarous intimation! yet a kind of insinuation, as it were *in via*, in way of explication; *facere*, as it were replication, or, rather, *ostentare*, to show, as it were, his inclination, – after his undressed, unpolished, uneducated, unpruned, untrained, or rather unlettered, or ratherest, unconfirmed fashion – to insert again my *haud credo* for a deer.

DULL   I said the deer was not a *haud credo;* 'twas a pricket.

HOLOFERNES   Twice-sod simplicity, *bis coctus!*
O! thou monster Ignorance, how deform'd dost thou look.

NATHANIEL
Sir, he hath never fed of the dainties that are bred in a book.
He hath not eat paper, as it were; he hath not drunk ink: his intellect is not replenished; he is only an animal, only sensible in the duller parts;
And such barren plants are set before us, that we thankful should be,
Which we of taste and feeling are, for those parts that do fructify in us more than he;
For as it would ill become me to be vain, indiscreet, or a fool,
So were there a patch set on learning, to see him in a school:
But, *omne bene*, say I; being of an old father's mind,
Many can brook the weather that love not the wind.

DULL
You two are book-men: can you tell me by your wit
What was a month old at Cain's birth, that's not five weeks old as yet?

HOLOFERNES
Dictynna, goodman Dull; Dictynna, goodman Dull.

DULL   What is Dictynna?

NATHANIEL   A title to Phoebe, to Luna, to the moon.

HOLOFERNES
The moon was a month old when Adam was no more;
And raught not to five weeks when he came to five-score.
The allusion holds in the exchange.

DULL   'Tis true indeed: the collusion holds in the exchange.

HOLOFERNES   God comfort thy capacity! I say the allusion holds in the exchange.

DULL   And I say the pollution holds in the exchange, for the moon is never but a month old; and I say beside that, 'twas a pricket that the princess killed.

HOLOFERNES   Sir Nathaniel, will you hear an extemporal epitaph on the death of the deer? and, to humour the ignorant, I have call'd the deer the princess killed, a pricket.

NATHANIEL   *Perge*, good Master Holofernes, *perge;* so it shall please you to abrogate scurrility.

HOLOFERNES   I will something affect the letter; for it argues facility.
The preyful princess pierc'd and prick'd a pretty pleasing pricket;
Some say a sore; but not a sore, till now made sore with shooting.
The dogs did yell; put 'ell to sore, then sorel jumps from thicket;
Or pricket sore, or else sore'll the people fall a-hooting.
If sore be sore, then 'ell to sore makes fifty sores – O – sorel!
Of one sore I an hundred make, by adding but one more l.

NATHANIEL   A rare talent!

DULL   If a talent be a claw, look how he claws him with a talent.

HOLOFERNES   This is a gift that I have, simple, simple; a foolish extravagant spirit, full of forms, figures, shapes, objects, ideas, apprehensions, motions, revolutions: these are begot in the ventricle of memory, nourished in the womb of *pia mater*, and delivered upon the mellowing of occasion. But the gift is good in those in whom it is acute, and I am thankful for it.

NATHANIEL   Sir, I praise the Lord for you, and so may my parishioners; for their sons are well tutored by you, and their daughters profit very greatly under you: you are a good member of the commonwealth.

HOLOFERNES   *Mehercle!* if their sons be ingenious, they shall want no instruction; if their daughters be capable, I will put it to them. But *vir sapit qui pauca loquitur*. A soul feminine saluteth us.

Enter JAQUENETTA *and* COSTARD.

JAQUENETTA   God give you good morrow, master Person.

HOLOFERNES   Master Person, *quasi* pierce-one. An if one should be pierced, which is the one?

COSTARD   Marry, master schoolmaster, he that is likest to a hogshead.

HOLOFERNES   Of piercing a hogshead! a good lustre of conceit in a turf of earth; fire enough for a flint, pearl enough for a swine: 'tis pretty; it is well.

JAQUENETTA   Good master Person, be so good as read me this letter: it was given me by Costard, and sent me from Don Armado: I beseech you, read it.

HOLOFERNES *Facile precor gelida quando pecus omne sub*
umbra Ruminat, and so forth. Ah! good old Mantuan.
I may speak of thee as the traveller doth of Venice:

> *Venetia, Venetia,*
>   *Chi non ti vede, non ti pretia.*

Old Mantuan! old Mantuan! who understandeth
thee not, loves thee not. *Ut, re, sol, la, mi, fa.* Under
pardon, sir, what are the contents? or, rather, as
Horace says in his – what, my soul! verses?

NATHANIEL Ay, sir, and very learned.

HOLOFERNES Let me hear a staff, a stanze, a verse: *lege,*
domine.

NATHANIEL

> If love make me forsworn, how shall I swear to love?
>   Ah! never faith could hold, if not to beauty vow'd;
> Though to myself forsworn, to thee I'll faithful
>   prove:
>   Those thoughts to me were oaks, to thee like osiers
>   bow'd.
> Study his bias leaves and makes his book thine eyes,
>   Where all those pleasures live that art would
>   comprehend.
> If knowledge be the mark, to know thee shall suffice;
>   Well learned is that tongue that well can thee
>   commend;
> All ignorant that soul that sees thee without wonder;
>   Which is to me some praise that I thy parts
>   admire.
> Thy eye Jove's lightning bears, thy voice his dreadful
>   thunder,
>   Which, not to anger bent, is music and sweet fire.
> Celestial as thou art, O! pardon love this wrong,
> That sings heaven's praise with such an earthly
>   tongue.

HOLOFERNES You find not the apostrophus, and so miss
the accent: let me supervise the canzonet. Here are
only numbers ratified; but, for the elegancy, facility,
and golden cadence of poesy, *caret.* Ovidius Naso was
the man: and why, indeed, *Naso,* but for smelling out
the odoriferous flowers of fancy, the jerks of
invention? *Imitari* is nothing; so doth the hound his
master, the ape his keeper, the tired horse his rider.
But, damosella virgin, was this directed to you?

JAQUENETTA Ay, sir, from one Monsieur Berowne, one
of the strange queen's lords.

HOLOFERNES I will overglance the superscript. 'To the
snow-white hand of the most beauteous Lady
Rosaline.' I will look again on the intellect of the letter,
for the nomination of the party writing to the person
written unto: 'Your ladyship's in all desired
employment, Berowne.' Sir Nathaniel, this Berowne
is one of the votaries with the king; and here he hath
framed a letter to a sequent of the stranger queen's,
which, accidentally, or by the way of progression,
hath miscarried. Trip and go, my sweet; deliver this
paper into the royal hand of the king; it may concern

much. Stay not thy compliment; I forgive thy duty:
adieu.

JAQUENETTA Good Costard, go with me. Sir, God save
your life!

COSTARD Have with thee, my girl.

Exeunt Costard and Jaquenetta.

NATHANIEL Sir, you have done this in the fear of God,
very religiously; and, as a certain father saith, –

HOLOFERNES Sir, tell not me of the father; I do fear
colourable colours. But to return to the verses: did
they please you, Sir Nathaniel?

NATHANIEL Marvellous well for the pen.

HOLOFERNES I do dine to-day at the father's of a certain
pupil of mine; where, if (before repast) it shall please
you to gratify the table with a grace, I will, on my
privilege I have with the parents of the foresaid child
or pupil, undertake your *ben venuto;* where I will
prove those verses to be very unlearned, neither
savouring of poetry, wit, nor invention. I beseech your
society.

NATHANIEL And thank you too; for society, saith the
text, is the happiness of life.

HOLOFERNES And, certes, the text most infallibly
concludes it. [*to Dull*] Sir, I do invite you too: you
shall not say me nay: *pauca verba.* Away! the gentles
are at their game, and we will to our recreation.

Exeunt.

4.3   *Enter* BEROWNE, *with a paper.*

BEROWNE The king he is hunting the deer; I am
coursing myself: they have pitched a toil; I am toiling
in a pitch, – pitch that defiles: defile! a foul word.
Well, set thee down, sorrow! for so they say the fool
said, and so say I, and I the fool: well proved, wit! By
the Lord, this love is as mad as Ajax: it kills sheep, it
kills me, I a sheep: well proved again o'my side! I will
not love; if I do, hang me; i'faith, I will not. O! but her
eye, – by this light, but for her eye, I would not love
her; yes, for her two eyes. Well, I do nothing in the
world but lie, and lie in my throat. By heaven, I do
love, and it hath taught me to rhyme, and to be
melancholy; and here is part of my rhyme, and here
my melancholy. Well, she hath one o'my sonnets
already: the clown bore it, the fool sent it, and the
lady hath it: sweet clown, sweeter fool, sweetest lady!
By the world, I would not care a pin if the other three
were in. Here comes one with a paper: God give him
grace to groan! [*Stands aside.*]

Enter the KING, *with a paper.*

KING Ay me!

BEROWNE Shot, by heaven! Proceed, sweet Cupid: thou
hast thumped him with thy bird-bolt under the left
pap. In faith, secrets!

KING [*Reads.*]

> So sweet a kiss the golden sun gives not

25   To those fresh morning drops upon the rose,
        As thy eye-beams when their fresh rays have smote
           The night of dew that on my cheeks down flows:
        Nor shines the silver moon one half so bright
           Through the transparent bosom of the deep,
30   As doth thy face through tears of mine give light
           Thou shin'st in every tear that I do weep:
        No drop but as a coach doth carry thee;
           So ridest thou triumphing in my woe.
        Do but behold the tears that swell in me,
35   And they thy glory through my grief will show:
        But do not love thyself; then thou will keep
        My tears for glasses, and still make me weep.
        O queen of queens! how far dost thou excel,
        No thought can think, nor tongue of mortal tell.

40   How shall she know my griefs? I'll drop the paper:
        Sweet leaves, shade folly. Who is he comes here?
        [*Steps aside.*]
        What, Longaville! and reading! listen, ear.

            Enter LONGAVILLE, *with several papers.*

BEROWNE   Now, in thy likeness, one more fool appear!
LONGAVILLE   Ay me! I am forsworn.
BEROWNE
45   Why, he comes in like a perjure, wearing papers.
KING   In love, I hope: sweet fellowship in shame!
BEROWNE   One drunkard loves another of the name.
LONGAVILLE   Am I the first that have been perjur'd so?
BEROWNE
        I could put thee in comfort: not by two that I know.
50   Thou mak'st the triumviry, the corner-cap of society,
        The shape of love's Tyburn, that hangs up simplicity.
LONGAVILLE
        I fear these stubborn lines lack power to move.
        O sweet Maria, empress of my love!
        These numbers will I tear, and write in prose.
BEROWNE
55   O! rhymes are guards on wanton Cupid's hose:
        Disfigure not his shop.
LONGAVILLE   This same shall go.
        [*Reads the sonnet.*]
        Did not the heavenly rhetoric of thine eye,
          'Gainst whom the world cannot hold argument,
        Persuade my heart to this false perjury?
60   Vows for thee broke deserve not punishment.
        A woman I forswore; but I will prove,
          Thou being a goddess, I forswore not thee:
        My vow was earthly, thou a heavenly love;
          Thy grace being gain'd cures all disgrace in me.
65   Vows are but breath, and breath a vapour is:
          Then thou, fair sun, which on my earth dost shine,
        Exhal'st this vapour-vow; in thee it is:
          If broken then, it is no fault of mine:
        If by me broke, what fool is not so wise
70   To lose an oath to win a paradise?
BEROWNE
        This is the liver vein, which makes flesh a deity;

A green goose a goddess; pure, pure idolatry.
God amend us, God amend! we are much out o'th'
   way.
LONGAVILLE
        By whom shall I send this? – Company! stay.
        [*Steps aside.*]
BEROWNE   All hid, all hid; an old infant play.   75
        Like a demi-god here sit I in the sky,
        And wretched fools' secrets heedfully o'er-eye.
        More sacks to the mill! O heavens! I have my wish:

            Enter DUMAIN, *with a paper.*

        Dumain transform'd: four woodcocks in a dish!
DUMAIN   O most divine Kate!   80
BEROWNE   O most profane coxcomb!
DUMAIN   By heaven, the wonder in a mortal eye!
BEROWNE   By earth, she is not, corporal; there you lie.
DUMAIN   Her amber hairs for foul have amber quoted.
BEROWNE   An amber-coloured raven was well noted.   85
DUMAIN   As upright as the cedar.
BEROWNE   Stoop, I say;
        Her shoulder is with child.
DUMAIN   As fair as day.
BEROWNE
        Ay, as some days; but then no sun must shine.
DUMAIN   O! that I had my wish.
LONGAVILLE   And I had mine!
KING   And I mine too, good Lord!   90
BEROWNE
        Amen, so I had mine. Is not that a good word?
DUMAIN   I would forget her; but a fever she
        Reigns in my blood, and will remember'd be.
BEROWNE   A fever in your blood! why, then incision
        Would let her out in saucers: sweet misprision!   95
DUMAIN   Once more I'll read the ode that I have writ.
BEROWNE   Once more I'll mark how love can vary wit.
DUMAIN [*Reads his sonnet.*]
        On a day, alack the day!
        Love, whose month is ever May,
        Spied a blossom passing fair   100
        Playing in the wanton air:
        Through the velvet leaves the wind,
        All unseen can passage find;
        That the lover, sick to death,
        Wish'd himself the heaven's breath.   105
        Air, quoth he, thy cheeks may blow;
        Air, would I might triumph so!
        But alack! my hand is sworn
        Ne'er to pluck thee from thy thorn:
        Vow, alack! for youth unmeet,   110
        Youth so apt to pluck a sweet.
        Do not call it sin in me,
        That I am forsworn for thee;
        Thou for whom Jove would swear
        Juno but an Ethiop were;   115
        And deny himself for Jove,
        Turning mortal for thy love.

This will I send, and something else more plain,
That shall express my true love's fasting pain.
120 O! would the king, Berowne, and Longaville,
Were lovers too. Ill, to example ill,
Would from my forehead wipe a perjur'd note;
For none offend where all alike do dote.
LONGAVILLE [*advancing*]
Dumain, thy love is far from charity,
125 That in love's grief desir'st society:
You may look pale, but I should blush, I know,
To be o'erheard and taken napping so.
KING [*advancing*]
Come, sir, you blush; as his your case is such;
You chide at him, offending twice as much:
130 You do not love Maria! Longaville
Did never sonnet for her sake compile,
Nor never lay his wreathed arms athwart
His loving bosom to keep down his heart.
I have been closely shrouded in this bush,
135 And mark'd you both, and for you both did blush.
I heard your guilty rhymes, observed your fashion,
Saw sighs reek from you, noted well your passion:
Ay me! says one: O Jove! the other cries;
One, her hairs were gold, crystal the other's eyes:
140 You would for paradise break faith and troth;
[*to Longaville*]
And Jove, for your love would infringe an oath.
[*to Dumain*]
What will Berowne say when that he shall hear
A faith infringed, which such zeal did swear?
How will he scorn! how will he spend his wit!
145 How will he triumph, leap, and laugh at it!
For all the wealth that ever I did see,
I would not have him know so much by me.
BEROWNE
Now step I forth to whip hypocrisy. [*advancing*]
Ah! good my liege, I pray thee, pardon me:
150 Good heart! what grace hast thou, thus to reprove
These worms for loving, that art most in love?
Your eyes do make no coaches; in your tears
There is no certain princess that appears:
You'll not be perjur'd, 'tis a hateful thing:
155 Tush! none but minstrels like of sonneting.
But are you not asham'd? nay, are you not,
All three of you, to be thus much o'ershot?
You found his mote; the king your mote did see;
But I a beam do find in each of three.
160 O! what a scene of foolery have I seen,
Of sighs, of groans, of sorrow, and of teen;
O! me with what strict patience have I sat,
To see a king transformed to a gnat;
To see a great Hercules whipping a gig,
165 And profound Solomon to tune a jig,
And Nestor play at push-pin with the boys,
And critic Timon laugh at idle toys!
Where lies thy grief? O! tell me, good Dumain,
And, gentle Longaville, where lies thy pain?

And where my liege's? all about the breast: 170
A caudle, ho!
KING   Too bitter is thy jest.
Are we betray'd thus to thy over-view?
BEROWNE   Not you by me, but I betray'd to you:
I, that am honest; I, that hold it sin
To break the vow I am engaged in;   175
I am betray'd, by keeping company
With moon-like men, men of inconstancy.
When shall you see me write a thing in rhyme?
Or groan for Joan? or spend a minute's time
In pruning me? When shall you hear that I   180
Will praise a hand, a foot, a face, an eye,
A gait, a state, a brow, a breast, a waist,
A leg, a limb – ?
KING   Soft! whither away so fast?
A true man or a thief that gallops so?
BEROWNE   I post from love; good lover, let me go.   185

Enter JAQUENETTA *and* COSTARD.

JAQUENETTA   God bless the king!
KING   What present hast thou there?
COSTARD   Some certain treason.
KING   What makes treason here?
COSTARD   Nay, it makes nothing, sir.
KING   If it mar nothing neither,
The treason and you go in peace away together.
JAQUENETTA
I beseech your grace, let this letter be read: 190
Our Person misdoubts it; 'twas treason, he said.
KING   Berowne, read it over.
[*Berowne reads the letter.*]
Where hadst thou it?
JAQUENETTA   Of Costard.
KING   Where hadst thou it?   195
COSTARD   Of Dun Adramadio, Dun Adramadio.
KING   How now! what is in you? why dost thou tear it?
BEROWNE
A toy, my liege, a toy: your grace needs not fear it.
LONGAVILLE
It did move him to passion, and therefore let's hear
it.
DUMAIN [*Gathers up the pieces.*]
It is Berowne's writing, and here is his name.   200
BEROWNE [*to Costard*]
Ah! you whoreson loggerhead, you were born to do
me shame.
Guilty, my lord, guilty! I confess, I confess.
KING   What?
BEROWNE   That you three fools lack'd me, fool, to
make up the mess;
He, he, and you, and you, my liege, and I,
Are pick-purses in love, and we deserve to die.   205
O! dismiss this audience, and I shall tell you more.
DUMAIN   Now the number is even.
BEROWNE   True, true; we are four.
Will these turtles be gone?

KING   Hence, Sirs; away!

COSTARD

     Walk aside the true folk, and let the traitors stay.

                   Exeunt Costard and Jaquenetta.

BEROWNE

210   Sweet lords, sweet lovers, O! let us embrace.

     As true we are as flesh and blood can be:

     The sea will ebb and flow, heaven show his face;

     Young blood doth not obey an old decree:

     We cannot cross the cause why we were born;

215   Therefore, of all hands must we be forsworn.

KING

     What! did these rent lines show some love of thine?

BEROWNE

     Did they? quoth you. Who sees the heavenly

       Rosaline,

     That, like a rude and savage man of Inde,

     At the first opening of the gorgeous east,

220   Bows not his vassal head, and strooken blind,

     Kisses the base ground with obedient breast?

     What peremptory eagle-sighted eye

     Dares look upon the heaven of her brow,

     That is not blinded by her majesty?

225   KING   What zeal, what fury hath inspir'd thee now?

     My love, her mistress, is a gracious moon;

     She an attending star, scarce seen a light.

   BEROWNE   My eyes are then no eyes, nor I Berowne:

     O! but for my love, day would turn to night.

230   Of all complexions the cull'd sovereignty

     Do meet, as at a fair, in her fair cheek;

     Where several worthies make one dignity,

     Where nothing wants that want itself doth seek.

     Lend me the flourish of all gentle tongues, –

235   Fie, painted rhetoric! O! she needs it not:

     To things of sale a seller's praise belongs;

     She passes praise; then praise too short doth blot.

     A wither'd hermit, five-score winters worn,

     Might shake off fifty, looking in her eye:

240   Beauty doth varnish age, as if new-born,

     And gives the crutch the cradle's infancy.

     O! 'tis the sun that maketh all things shine.

   KING   By heaven, thy love is black as ebony.

   BEROWNE   Is ebony like her? O wood divine!

245   A wife of such wood were felicity.

     O! who can give an oath? where is a book?

     That I may swear beauty doth beauty lack,

     If that she learn not of her eye to look:

     No face is fair that is not full so black.

250   KING   O paradox! Black is the badge of hell,

     The hue of dungeons and the school of night;

     And beauty's crest becomes the heavens well.

BEROWNE

     Devils soonest tempt, resembling spirits of light.

     O! if in black my lady's brows be deck'd,

255   It mourns that painting and usurping hair

     Should ravish doters with a false aspect;

     And therefore is she born to make black fair.

     Her favour turns the fashion of the days,

     For native blood is counted painting now:

     And therefore red, that would avoid dispraise,   260

     Paints itself black, to imitate her brow.

DUMAIN   To look like her are chimney-sweepers black.

LONGAVILLE

     And since her time are colliers counted bright.

KING   And Ethiops of their sweet complexion crack.

DUMAIN   Dark needs no candles now, for dark is light.   265

BEROWNE   Your mistresses dare never come in rain,

     For fear their colours should be wash'd away.

KING   'Twere good, yours did; for, sir, to tell you plain,

     I'll find a fairer face not wash'd to-day.

BEROWNE   I'll prove her fair, or talk till doomsday here.   270

KING   No devil will fright thee then so much as she.

DUMAIN   I never knew man hold vile stuff so dear.

LONGAVILLE

     Look, here's thy love: my foot and her face see.

     [*showing his shoe*]

BEROWNE   O! if the streets were paved with thine eyes,

     Her feet were much too dainty for such tread.   275

DUMAIN   O vile! then, as she goes, what upward lies

     The street should see as she walk'd overhead.

KING   But what of this? Are we not all in love?

BEROWNE

     O! nothing so sure; and thereby all forsworn.

KING

     Then leave this chat; and, good Berowne, now prove   280

     Our loving lawful, and our faith not torn.

DUMAIN   Ay, marry, there; some flattery for this evil.

LONGAVILLE   O! some authority how to proceed;

     Some tricks, some quillets, how to cheat the devil.

DUMAIN   Some salve for perjury.

BEROWNE   O! 'tis more than need.   285

     Have at you then, affection's men-at-arms:

     Consider what you first did swear unto,

     To fast, to study, and to see no woman;

     Flat treason 'gainst the kingly state of youth.

     Say, can you fast? your stomachs are too young,   290

     And abstinence engenders maladies.

     [And where that you have vow'd to study, lords,

     In that each of you have forsworn his book,

     Can you still dream and pore and thereon look?

     For when would you, my lord, or you, or you,   295

     Have found the ground of study's excellence

     Without the beauty of a woman's face?

     From women's eyes this doctrine I derive:

     They are the ground, the books, the academes,

     From whence doth spring the true Promethean fire.   300

     Why, universal plodding poisons up

     The nimble spirits in the arteries,

     As motion and long-during action tires

     The sinewy vigour of the traveller.

     Now, for not looking on a woman's face,   305

     You have in that forsworn the use of eyes,

     And study too, the causer of your vow;

     For where is any author in the world

Teaches such beauty as a woman's eye?
310 Learning is but an adjunct to ourself,
And where we are our learning likewise is:
Then when ourselves we see in ladies' eyes,
Do we not likewise see our learning there?]
O! we have made a vow to study, lords,
315 And in that vow we have forsworn our books:
For when would you, my liege, or you, or you,
In leaden contemplation have found out
Such fiery numbers as the prompting eyes
Of beauty's tutors have enrich'd you with?
320 Other slow arts entirely keep the brain,
And therefore, finding barren practisers,
Scarce show a harvest of their heavy toil;
But love, first learned in a lady's eyes,
Lives not alone immured in the brain,
325 But, with the motion of all elements,
Courses as swift as thought in every power,
And gives to every power a double power,
Above their functions and their offices.
It adds a precious seeing to the eye;
330 A lover's eyes will gaze an eagle blind;
A lover's ear will hear the lowest sound,
When the suspicious head of theft is stopp'd:
Love's feeling is more soft and sensible
Than are the tender horns of cockled snails:
335 Love's tongue proves dainty Bacchus gross in taste.
For valour, is not Love a Hercules,
Still climbing trees in the Hesperides?
Subtle as Sphinx; as sweet and musical
As bright Apollo's lute, strung with his hair;
340 And when Love speaks, the voice of all the gods
Make heaven drowsy with the harmony.
Never durst poet touch a pen to write
Until his ink were temper'd with Love's sighs;
O! then his lines would ravish savage ears,
345 And plant in tyrants mild humility.
From women's eyes this doctrine I derive:
They sparkle still the right Promethean fire;
They are the books, the arts, the academes,
That show, contain, and nourish all the world;
350 Else none at all in aught proves excellent.
Then fools you were these women to forswear,
Or, keeping what is sworn, you will prove fools.
For wisdom's sake, a word that all men love,
Or for love's sake, a word that loves all men,
355 Or for men's sake, the authors of these women,
Or women's sake, by whom we men are men,
Let us once lose our oaths to find ourselves,
Or else we lose ourselves to keep our oaths.
It is religion to be thus forsworn;
360 For charity itself fulfils the law;
And who can sever love from charity?
KING Saint Cupid, then! and, soldiers, to the field!
BEROWNE
Advance your standards, and upon them, lords!
Pell-mell, down with them! but be first advis'd,

In conflict that you get the sun of them.   365
LONGAVILLE Now to plain-dealing; lay these glozes by:
Shall we resolve to woo these girls of France?
KING And win them too: therefore let us devise
Some entertainment for them in their tents.
BEROWNE
First, from the park let us conduct them thither;   370
Then homeward every man attach the hand
Of his fair mistress: in the afternoon
We will with some strange pastime solace them,
Such as the shortness of the time can shape;
For revels, dances, masks, and merry hours,   375
Forerun fair Love, strewing her way with flowers.
KING Away, away! no time shall be omitted
That will be time, and may by us be fitted.
BEROWNE *Allons! allons!* Sow'd cockle reap'd no corn;
And justice always whirls in equal measure: 380
Light wenches may prove plagues to men forsworn;
If so, our copper buys no better treasure.   *Exeunt.*

5.1 *Enter* HOLOFERNES, SIR NATHANIEL *and* DULL.

HOLOFERNES *Satis quid sufficit.*
NATHANIEL I praise God for you, sir: your reasons at
dinner have been sharp and sententious; pleasant
without scurrility, witty without affection, audacious
without impudency, learned without opinion, and   5
strange without heresy. I did converse this quondam
day with a companion of the king's, who is intituled,
nominated, or called, Don Adriano de Armado.
HOLOFERNES *Novi hominem tanquam te*: his humour is
lofty, his discourse peremptory, his tongue filed, his   10
eye ambitious, his gait majestical, and his general
behaviour vain, ridiculous, and thrasonical. He is too
picked, too spruce, too affected, too odd, as it were,
too peregrinate, as I may call it.
NATHANIEL A most singular and choice epithet.   15
[*Draws out his table-book.*]
HOLOFERNES He draweth out the thread of his
verbosity finer than the staple of his argument. I abhor
such fanatical phantasimes, such insociable and point-
devise companions; such rackers of orthography, as to
speak dout, fine, when he should say doubt; det, when   20
he should pronounce debt, – d, e, b, t, not d, e, t; he
clepeth a calf, cauf; half, hauf; neighbour *vocatur*
nebour; neigh abbreviated ne. This is abhominable,
which he would call abominable, it insinuateth me of
insanie: *ne intelligis domine?* to make frantic, lunatic.   25
NATHANIEL *Laus Deo, bone intelligo.*
HOLOFERNES *Bone? Bon, fort bon*; Priscian a little
scratched: 'twill serve.

Enter ARMADO, MOTH *and* COSTARD.

NATHANIEL *Videsne quis venit?*
HOLOFERNES *Video, et gaudeo.*   30
ARMADO Chirrah!
HOLOFERNES *Quare* chirrah, not sirrah?

ARMADO   Men of peace, well encountered.

HOLOFERNES   Most military sir, salutation.

35 MOTH   They have been at a great feast of languages, and
stolen the scraps.

COSTARD   O, they have lived long on the alms-basket of
words. I marvel thy master hath not eaten thee for a
word; for thou art not so long by the head as
40 *honorificabilitudinitatibus:* thou art easier swallowed
than a flap-dragon.

MOTH   Peace! the peal begins.

ARMADO [*to Holofernes*]   Monsieur, are you not lettered?

MOTH   Yes, yes, he teaches boys the horn-book. What is
45 a, b, spelt backward with the horn on his head?

HOLOFERNES   Ba, *pueritia,* with a horn added.

MOTH   Ba! most silly sheep with a horn. You hear his
learning.

HOLOFERNES   *Quis, quis,* thou consonant?

50 MOTH   The last of the five vowels, if you repeat them; or
the fifth, if I.

HOLOFERNES   I will repeat them; a, e, i, –

MOTH   The sheep: the other two concludes it; o, u.

ARMADO   Now, by the salt wave of the Mediterraneum,
55 a sweet touch, a quick venue of wit! snip, snap, quick
and home! it rejoiceth my intellect; true wit!

MOTH   Offered by a child to an old man; which is wit-
old.

HOLOFERNES   What is the figure? what is the figure?

60 MOTH   Horns.

HOLOFERNES   Thou disputes like an infant: go, whip thy
gig.

MOTH   Lend me your horn to make one, and I will whip
about your infamy *manu cita.* A gig of a cuckold's
65 horn!

COSTARD   An I had but one penny in the world, thou
should'st have it to buy gingerbread. Hold, there is the
very remuneration I had of thy master, thou halfpenny
purse of wit, thou pigeon-egg of discretion. O, an
70 the heavens were so pleased that thou wert but my
bastard, what a joyful father wouldst thou make me.
Go to; thou hast it *ad dunghill,* at the fingers' ends, as
they say.

HOLOFERNES   O, I smell false Latin: dunghill for
75 *unguem.*

ARMADO   Arts-man, preambulate: we will be singled
from the barbarous. Do you not educate youth at the
charge-house on the top of the mountain?

HOLOFERNES   Or *mons,* the hill.

80 ARMADO   At your sweet pleasure, for the mountain.

HOLOFERNES   I do, sans question.

ARMADO   Sir, it is the king's most sweet pleasure and
affection to congratulate the princess at her pavilion in
the posteriors of this day, which the rude multitude
85 call the afternoon.

HOLOFERNES   The posterior of the day, most generous
sir, is liable, congruent, and measurable for the
afternoon: the word is well culled, chose; sweet and
apt, I do assure you, sir; I do assure.

ARMADO   Sir, the king is a noble gentleman, and my   90
familiar, I do assure ye, very good friend. For what is
inward between us, let it pass; (I do beseech thee,
remember thy courtesy – I beseech thee, apparel thy
head) and among other importunate and most serious
designs, and of great import indeed, too, but let that   95
pass; for I must tell thee, it will please his grace, by
the world, sometime to lean upon my poor shoulder,
and with his royal finger, thus, dally with my
excrement, with my mustachio: but, sweet heart, let
that pass. By the world, I recount no fable: some   100
certain special honours it pleaseth his greatness to
impart to Armado, a soldier, a man of travel, that
hath seen the world: but let that pass. The very all of
all is, but, sweet heart, I do implore secrecy, that the
king would have me present the princess, sweet   105
chuck, with some delightful ostentation, or show, or
pageant, or antic, or firework. Now, understanding
that the curate and your sweet self are good at such
eruptions and sudden breaking out of mirth, as it
were, I have acquainted you withal, to the end to crave   110
your assistance.

HOLOFERNES   Sir, you shall present before her the Nine
Worthies. Sir Nathaniel, as concerning some
entertainment of time, some show in the posterior of
this day, to be rendered by our assistance, the king's   115
command, and this most gallant, illustrate, and
learned gentleman, before the princess; I say, none so
fit as to present the Nine Worthies.

NATHANIEL   Where will you find men worthy enough to
present them?   120

HOLOFERNES   Joshua, yourself; myself and this gallant
gentleman, Judas Maccabaeus; this swain, because of
his great limb or joint, shall pass Pompey the Great;
the page, Hercules –

ARMADO   Pardon, sir; error: he is not quantity enough   125
for that Worthy's thumb: he is not so big as the end of
his club.

HOLOFERNES   Shall I have audience? he shall present
Hercules in minority: his enter and exit shall be
strangling a snake; and I will have an apology for   130
that purpose.

MOTH   An excellent device! so if any of the audience
hiss, you may cry 'Well done, Hercules! now thou
crushest the snake!' That is the way to make an
offence gracious, though few have the grace to do it.   135

ARMADO   For the rest of the Worthies?

HOLOFERNES   I will play three myself.

MOTH   Thrice-worthy gentleman!

ARMADO   Shall I tell you a thing?

HOLOFERNES   We attend.   140

ARMADO   We will have, if this fadge not, an antic. I
beseech you, follow.

HOLOFERNES   *Via,* goodman Dull! thou hast spoken no
word all this while.

DULL   Nor understand none neither, sir.   145

HOLOFERNES   *Allons!* we will employ thee.

DULL   I'll make one in a dance, or so; or I will play on
    the tabor to the Worthies, and let them dance the
    hay.
50 HOLOFERNES   Most dull, honest Dull. To our sport,
    away!   *Exeunt.*

5.2   *Enter the* PRINCESS, MARIA, KATHARINE
                       and ROSALINE.

PRINCESS   Sweet hearts, we shall be rich ere we depart,
    If fairings come thus plentifully in:
    A lady wall'd about with diamonds!
    Look you what I have from the loving king.
ROSALINE   Madam, came nothing else along with that?
PRINCESS   Nothing but this! yes; as much love in rhyme
    As would be cramm'd up in a sheet of paper,
    Writ o' both sides the leaf, margent and all,
    That he was fain to seal on Cupid's name.
ROSALINE   That was the way to make his godhead wax;
    For he hath been five thousand year a boy.
KATHARINE   Ay, and a shrewd unhappy gallows too.
ROSALINE
    You'll ne'er be friends with him: 'a kill'd your sister.
KATHARINE   He made her melancholy, sad, and heavy;
    And so she died: had she been light, like you,
    Of such a merry, nimble, stirring spirit,
    She might ha' been a grandam ere she died;
    And so may you, for a light heart lives long.
ROSALINE
    What's your dark meaning, mouse, of this light word?
KATHARINE   A light condition in a beauty dark.
ROSALINE
    We need more light to find your meaning out.
KATHARINE   You'll mar the light by taking it in snuff;
    Therefore I'll darkly end the argument.
ROSALINE   Look what you do, you do it still i'the dark.
KATHARINE   So do not you, for you are a light wench.
ROSALINE   Indeed I weigh not you, and therefore light.
KATHARINE
    You weigh me not? O! that's you care not for me.
ROSALINE   Great reason; for past care is still past cure.
PRINCESS   Well bandied both; a set of wit well play'd.
    But, Rosaline, you have a favour too:
    Who sent it? and what is it?
ROSALINE   I would you knew:
    An if my face were but as fair as yours,
    My favour were as great; be witness this.
    Nay, I have verses too, I thank Berowne:
    The numbers true; and, were the numbering too,
    I were the fairest goddess on the ground:
    I am compar'd to twenty thousand fairs.
    O! he hath drawn my picture in his letter.
PRINCESS   Any thing like?
ROSALINE   Much in the letters, nothing in the praise.
PRINCESS   Beauteous as ink; a good conclusion.
KATHARINE   Fair as a text B in a copy-book.
ROSALINE   Ware pencils, ho! let me not die your debtor,

My red dominical, my golden letter:
    O! that your face were not so full of O's.   45
PRINCESS   A pox of that jest! and I beshrew all shrows!
    But, Katharine, what was sent to you from fair
    Dumain?
KATHARINE   Madam, this glove.
PRINCESS   Did he not send you twain?
KATHARINE   Yes, madam; and moreover,
    Some thousand verses of a faithful lover;   50
    A huge translation of hypocrisy,
    Vilely compil'd, profound simplicity.
MARIA   This, and these pearls to me sent Longaville:
    The letter is too long by half a mile.
PRINCESS   I think no less. Dost thou not wish in heart   55
    The chain were longer and the letter short?
MARIA   Ay, or I would these hands might never part.
PRINCESS   We are wise girls to mock our lovers so.
ROSALINE
    They are worse fools to purchase mocking so.
    That same Berowne I'll torture ere I go.   60
    O! that I knew he were but in by the week.
    How I would make him fawn, and beg, and seek,
    And wait the season, and observe the times,
    And spend his prodigal wits in bootless rimes,
    And shape his service wholly to my hests   65
    And make him proud to make me proud that jests!
    So Pair-Taunt like would I o'ersway his state
    That he should be my fool, and I his fate.
PRINCESS
    None are so surely caught, when they are catch'd,
    As wit turn'd fool: folly, in wisdom hatch'd,   70
    Hath wisdom's warrant and the help of school
    And wit's own grace to grace a learned fool.
ROSALINE
    The blood of youth burns not with such excess
    As gravity's revolt to wantonness.
MARIA   Folly in fools bears not so strong a note   75
    As foolery in the wise, when wit doth dote;
    Since all the power thereof it doth apply
    To prove, by wit, worth in simplicity.

                    Enter BOYET.

PRINCESS   Here comes Boyet, and mirth is in his face.
BOYET
    O! I am stabb'd with laughter. Where's her grace?   80
PRINCESS   Thy news, Boyet?
BOYET   Prepare, madam, prepare!
    Arm, wenches, arm! encounters mounted are
    Against your peace: Love doth approach disguis'd,
    Armed in arguments; you'll be surpris'd:
    Muster your wits; stand in your own defence;   85
    Or hide your heads like cowards, and fly hence.
PRINCESS   Saint Denis to Saint Cupid! What are they
    That charge their breath against us? say, scout, say.
BOYET   Under the cool shade of a sycamore
    I thought to close mine eyes some half an hour,   90
    When, lo! to interrupt my purpos'd rest,

Towards that shade I might behold address
The king and his companions: warily
I stole into a neighbour thicket by,
95   And overheard what you shall overhear:
That, by and by, disguis'd they will be here.
Their herald is a pretty knavish page,
That well by heart hath conn'd his embassage:
Action and accent did they teach him there;
100 'Thus must thou speak, and thus thy body bear':
And ever and anon they made a doubt
Presence majestical would put him out;
'For,' quoth the king, 'an angel shalt thou see;
Yet fear not thou, but speak audaciously.'
105 The boy replied, 'An angel is not evil;
I should have fear'd her had she been a devil.'
With that all laugh'd and clapp'd him on the
     shoulder,
Making the bold wag by their praises bolder.
One rubb'd his elbow thus, and fleer'd, and swore
110 A better speech was never spoke before;
Another, with his finger and his thumb,
Cry'd '*Via!* we will do't, come what will come';
The third he caper'd, and cried, 'All goes well';
The fourth turn'd on the toe, and down he fell.
115 With that, they all did tumble on the ground,
With such a zealous laughter, so profound,
That in this spleen ridiculous appears,
To check their folly, passion's solemn tears.
PRINCESS   But what, but what, come they to visit us?
120 BOYET   They do, they do; and are apparell'd thus,
Like Muscovites, or Russians, as I guess.
Their purpose is to parle, to court and dance;
And every one his love-feat will advance
Unto his several mistress, which they'll know
125 By favours several which they did bestow.
PRINCESS   And will they so? the gallants shall be task'd;
For, ladies, we will every one be mask'd,
And not a man of them shall have the grace,
Despite of suit, to see a lady's face.
130 Hold, Rosaline, this favour thou shalt wear,
And then the king will court thee for his dear:
Hold, take thou this, my sweet, and give me thine,
So shall Berowne take me for Rosaline.
And change you favours too; so shall your loves
135 Woo contrary, deceiv'd by these removes.
ROSALINE
Come on, then; wear the favours most in sight.
KATHARINE   But in this changing what is your intent?
PRINCESS   The effect of my intent is to cross theirs:
They do it but in mockery merriment;
140 And mock for mock is only my intent.
Their several counsels they unbosom shall
To loves mistook, and so be mock'd withal
Upon the next occasion that we meet,
With visages display'd, to talk and greet.
145 ROSALINE   But shall we dance, if they desire us to't?
PRINCESS   No; to the death we will not move a foot:

Nor to their penn'd speech render we no grace;
But while 'tis spoke each turn away her face.
BOYET
Why, that contempt will kill the speaker's heart,
And quite divorce his memory from his part.   150
PRINCESS   Therefore I do it; and I make no doubt
The rest will ne'er come in, if he be out.
There's no such sport as sport by sport o'erthrown,
To make theirs ours and ours none but our own:
So shall we stay, mocking intended game,   155
And they, well mock'd, depart away with shame.
                              [*Sound trumpet.*]
BOYET
The trumpet sounds: be mask'd; the maskers come.

Enter blackamoors with music; MOTH *with a speech; the*
     KING *and the rest of the* lords *disguised*
          like Russians, and visored.

MOTH   All hail, the richest beauties on the earth!
BOYET   Beauties no richer than rich taffeta.
MOTH   A holy parcel of the fairest dames,   160
     [*The ladies turn their backs to him.*]
That ever turn'd their – backs – to mortal views!
BEROWNE   'Their eyes,' villain, 'their eyes.'
MOTH   That ever turn'd their eyes to mortal views!
     Out –
BOYET   True; 'out' indeed.   165
MOTH   Out of your favours, heavenly spirits, vouchsafe
     Not to behold –
BEROWNE   'Once to behold,' rogue.
MOTH   Once to behold with your sun-beamed eyes, –
     with your sun-beamed eyes –   170
BOYET   They will not answer to that epithet;
You were best call it 'daughter-beamed eyes.'
MOTH   They do not mark me, and that brings me out.
BEROWNE   Is this your perfectness? be gone, you rogue!
                              Exit Moth.
ROSALINE   What would these strangers? know their
     minds, Boyet.   175
If they do speak our language, 'tis our will
That some plain man recount their purposes:
Know what they would.
BOYET   What would you with the princess?
BEROWNE   Nothing but peace and gentle visitation.
ROSALINE   What would they, say they?   180
BOYET   Nothing but peace and gentle visitation.
ROSALINE
Why, that they have; and bid them so be gone.
BOYET   She says, you have it, and you may be gone.
KING   Say to her, we have measur'd many miles
To tread a measure with her on this grass.   185
BOYET   They say, that they have measur'd many a mile
To tread a measure with you on this grass.
ROSALINE   It is not so. Ask them how many inches
Is in one mile: if they have measur'd many,
The measure then of one is easily told.   190
BOYET   If, to come hither, you have measur'd miles,

And many miles, the princess bids you tell
How many inches doth fill up one mile.
BEROWNE Tell her we measure them by weary steps.
BOYET She hears herself.
95 ROSALINE   How many weary steps,
Of many weary miles you have o'ergone,
Are numbered in the travel of one mile?
BEROWNE We number nothing that we spend for you:
Our duty is so rich, so infinite,
200 That we may do it still without account.
Vouchsafe to show the sunshine of your face,
That we, like savages, may worship it.
ROSALINE My face is but a moon, and clouded too.
KING Blessed are clouds, to do as such clouds do!
205 Vouchsafe, bright moon, and these thy stars, to shine,
Those clouds remov'd, upon our watery eyne.
ROSALINE O vain petitioner! beg a greater matter;
Thou now requests but moonshine in the water.
KING
Then, in our measure do but vouchsafe one change.
210 Thou bidd'st me beg; this begging is not strange.
ROSALINE Play, music, then! nay, you must do it soon.
Not yet? – no dance: – thus change I like the moon.
KING
Will you not dance? How come you thus estranged?
ROSALINE
You took the moon at full, but now she's changed.
215 KING Yet still she is the moon, and I the man.
The music plays; vouchsafe some motion to it.
ROSALINE Our ears vouchsafe it.
KING   But your legs should do it.
ROSALINE
Since you are strangers, and come here by chance,
We'll not be nice: take hands: – we will not dance.
KING Why take we hands then?
220 ROSALINE   Only to part friends.
Court'sy, sweet hearts; and so the measure ends.
KING More measure of this measure: be not nice.
ROSALINE We can afford no more at such a price.
KING Price you yourselves: what buys your company?
ROSALINE Your absence only.
225 KING   That can never be.
ROSALINE Then cannot we be bought: and so adieu;
Twice to your visor, and half once to you!
KING If you deny to dance, lets hold more chat.
ROSALINE In private then.
KING   I am best pleased with that.
[*They converse apart.*]
BEROWNE
230 White-handed mistress, one sweet word with thee.
PRINCESS Honey, and milk, and sugar: there is three.
BEROWNE Nay then, two treys, an if you grow so nice,
Metheglin, wort, and malmsey: well run, dice!
There's half-a-dozen sweets.
PRINCESS   Seventh sweet, adieu.
235 Since you can cog, I'll play no more with you.
BEROWNE One word is secret.

PRINCESS   Let it not be sweet.
BEROWNE Thou griev'st my gall.
PRINCESS   Gall! bitter.
BEROWNE   Therefore meet.
[*They converse apart.*]
DUMAIN
Will you vouchsafe with me to change a word?
MARIA Name it.
DUMAIN   Fair lady, –
MARIA   Say you so? Fair lord, –
Take that for your fair lady.
DUMAIN   Please it you,   240
As much in private, and I'll bid adieu.
[*They converse apart.*]
KATHARINE
What! was your visor made without a tongue?
LONGAVILLE I know the reason, lady, why you ask.
KATHARINE O! for your reason; quickly, sir; I long.
LONGAVILLE
You have a double tongue within your mask,   245
And would afford my speechless visor half.
KATHARINE
Veal, quoth the Dutchman. Is not veal a calf?
LONGAVILLE A calf, fair lady!
KATHARINE   No, a fair lord calf.
LONGAVILLE Let's part the word.
KATHARINE   No, I'll not be your half:
Take all, and wean it: it may prove an ox.   250
LONGAVILLE
Look, how you butt yourself in these sharp mocks.
Will you give horns, chaste lady? do not so.
KATHARINE
Then die a calf, before your horns do grow.
LONGAVILLE One word in private with you ere I die.
KATHARINE
Bleat softly then; the butcher hears you cry.   255
[*They converse apart.*]
BOYET The tongues of mocking wenches are as keen
As is the razor's edge invisible,
Cutting a smaller hair than may be seen;
Above the sense of sense; so sensible
Seemeth their conference; their conceits have wings   260
Fleeter than arrows, bullets, wind, thought, swifter
things.
ROSALINE
Not one word more, my maids: break off, break off.
BEROWNE By heaven, all dry-beaten with pure scoff!
KING Farewell, mad wenches: you have simple wits.
PRINCESS Twenty adieus, my frozen Muscovites.   265
                    Exeunt lords and blackamoors.
Are these the breed of wits so wonder'd at?
BOYET
Tapers they are, with your sweet breaths puff'd out.
ROSALINE
Well-liking wits they have; gross, gross; fat, fat.
PRINCESS O poverty in wit, kingly-poor flout!
Will they not, think you, hang themselves to-night?   270

Or ever, but in visors, show their faces?
This pert Berowne was out of countenance quite.
ROSALINE   O, they were all in lamentable cases!
The king was weeping-ripe for a good word.
275 PRINCESS   Berowne did swear himself out of all suit.
MARIA   Dumain was at my service, and his sword:
No point, quoth I: my servant straight was mute.
KATHARINE
Lord Longaville said, I came o'er his heart;
And trow you what he call'd me?
PRINCESS   Qualm, perhaps.
KATHARINE   Yes, in good faith.
280 PRINCESS   Go, sickness as thou art!
ROSALINE
Well, better wits have worn plain statute-caps.
But will you hear? the king is my love sworn.
PRINCESS
And quick Berowne hath plighted faith to me.
KATHARINE   And Longaville was for my service born.
285 MARIA   Dumain is mine, as sure as bark on tree.
BOYET   Madam, and pretty mistresses, give ear.
Immediately they will again be here
In their own shapes; for it can never be
They will digest this harsh indignity.
PRINCESS   Will they return?
290 BOYET   They will, they will, God knows;
And leap for joy, though they are lame with blows:
Therefore change favours; and when they repair,
Blow like sweet roses in this summer air.
PRINCESS
How blow? how blow? speak to be understood.
295 BOYET   Fair ladies, mask'd, are roses in their bud:
Dismask'd, their damask sweet commixture shown,
Are angels vailing clouds, or roses blown.
PRINCESS   Avaunt, perplexity! What shall we do
If they return in their own shapes to woo?
300 ROSALINE   Good madam, if by me you'll be advis'd,
Let's mock them still, as well known as disguis'd.
Let us complain to them what fools were here,
Disguis'd like Muscovites, in shapeless gear;
And wonder what they were, and to what end
305 Their shallow shows and prologue vilely penn'd,
And their rough carriage so ridiculous,
Should be presented at our tent to us.
BOYET   Ladies, withdraw; the gallants are at hand.
PRINCESS   Whip to our tents, as roes run o'er the land.
Exeunt Princess, Rosaline, Katharine and Maria.

Re-enter the KING, BEROWNE, LONGAVILLE
and DUMAIN *in their proper habits.*

310 KING   Fair sir, God save you! Where's the princess?
BOYET   Gone to her tent. Please it your majesty,
Command me any service to her thither?
KING   That she vouchsafe me audience for one word.
BOYET   I will; and so will she, I know, my lord.   *Exit.*
315 BEROWNE   This fellow pecks up wit, as pigeons pease,
And utters it again when God doth please.

He is wit's pedlar, and retails his wares
At wakes, and wassails, meetings, markets, fairs;
And we that sell by gross, the Lord doth know,
Have not the grace to grace it with such show.   320
This gallant pins the wenches on his sleeve;
Had he been Adam, he had tempted Eve.
'A can carve too, and lisp: why, this is he
That kiss'd his hand away in courtesy;
This is the ape of form, monsieur the nice,   325
That, when he plays at tables, chides the dice
In honourable terms: nay, he can sing
A mean most meanly, and, in ushering,
Mend him who can: the ladies call him sweet;
The stairs, as he treads on them, kiss his feet.   330
This is the flower that smiles on every one,
To show his teeth as white as whale his bone;
And consciences, that will not die in debt,
Pay him the due of honey-tongu'd Boyet.
KING   A blister on his sweet tongue, with my heart,   335
That put Armado's page out of his part!

Re-enter the PRINCESS, *ushered by* BOYET; ROSALINE,
MARIA, KATHARINE *and attendants.*

BEROWNE
See where it comes! Behaviour, what wert thou
Till this madman show'd thee? and what art thou
   now?
KING   All hail, sweet madam, and fair time of day!
PRINCESS   Fair in all hail is foul, as I conceive.   340
KING   Construe my speeches better, if you may.
PRINCESS   Then wish me better: I will give you leave.
KING   We came to visit you, and purpose now
To lead you to our court: vouchsafe it then.
PRINCESS
This field shall hold me, and so hold your vow: 345
Nor God, nor I, delights in perjur'd men.
KING   Rebuke me not for that which you provoke:
The virtue of your eye must break my oath.
PRINCESS
You nickname virtue; vice you should have spoke;
For virtue's office never breaks men's troth.   350
Now, by my maiden honour, yet as pure
As the unsullied lily, I protest,
A world of torments though I should endure,
I would not yield to be your house's guest;
So much I hate a breaking cause to be   355
Of heavenly oaths, vow'd with integrity.
KING   O! you have liv'd in desolation here,
Unseen, unvisited, much to our shame.
PRINCESS   Not so, my lord; it is not so, I swear:
We have had pastimes here and pleasant game.   360
A mess of Russians left us but of late.
KING   How, madam! Russians!
PRINCESS   Ay, in truth, my lord;
Trim gallants, full of courtship and of state.
ROSALINE   Madam, speak true. It is not so, my lord:
My lady, to the manner of the days,   365

In courtesy gives undeserving praise.
We four, indeed, confronted were with four
In Russian habit: here they stay'd an hour,
And talk'd apace; and in that hour, my lord,
370 They did not bless us with one happy word.
I dare not call them fools; but this I think,
When they are thirsty, fools would fain have drink.
BEROWNE This jest is dry to me. My gentle sweet,
Your wit makes wise things foolish: when we greet,
375 With eyes best seeing, heaven's fiery eye,
By light we lose light: your capacity
Is of that nature that to your huge store
Wise things seem foolish and rich things but poor.
ROSALINE
This proves you wise and rich, for in my eye, –
380 BEROWNE I am a fool, and full of poverty.
ROSALINE But that you take what doth to you belong,
It were a fault to snatch words from my tongue.
BEROWNE O! I am yours, and all that I possess.
ROSALINE All the fool mine?
BEROWNE I cannot give you less.
385 ROSALINE Which of the visors was it that you wore?
BEROWNE
Where? when? what visor? why demand you this?
ROSALINE
There, then, that visor; that superfluous case
That hid the worse and show'd the better face.
KING
We were descried: they'll mock us now downright.
390 DUMAIN Let us confess, and turn it to a jest.
PRINCESS
Amaz'd, my lord? Why looks your highness sad?
ROSALINE
Help! hold his brows! he'll swoon. Why look you
pale?
Sea-sick, I think, coming from Muscovy.
BEROWNE
Thus pour the stars down plagues for perjury.
395 Can any face of brass hold longer out?
Here stand I, lady; dart thy skill at me;
Bruise me with scorn, confound me with a flout;
Thrust thy sharp wit quite through my ignorance;
Cut me to pieces with thy keen conceit;
400 And I will wish thee never more to dance,
Nor never more in Russian habit wait.
O! never will I trust to speeches penn'd,
Nor to the motion of a school-boy's tongue,
Nor never come in visor to my friend,
405 Nor woo in rhyme, like a blind harper's song,
Taffeta phrases, silken terms precise,
Three-pil'd hyperboles, spruce affection,
Figures pedantical; these summer flies
Have blown me full of maggot ostentation:
410 I do forswear them; and I here protest,
By this white glove (how white the hand, God
knows),
Henceforth my wooing mind shall be express'd

In russet yeas and honest kersey noes:
And, to begin: Wench, – so God help me, law! –
My love to thee is sound, sans crack or flaw. 415
ROSALINE Sans 'sans,' I pray you.
BEROWNE Yet I have a trick
Of the old rage: bear with me, I am sick;
I'll leave it by degrees. Soft! let us see:
Write 'Lord have mercy on us' on those three;
They are infected, in their hearts it lies; 420
They have the plague, and caught it of your eyes:
These lords are visited; you are not free,
For the Lord's tokens on you do I see.
PRINCESS
No, they are free that gave these tokens to us.
BEROWNE Our states are forfeit: seek not to undo us. 425
ROSALINE It is not so. For how can this be true,
That you stand forfeit, being those that sue?
BEROWNE Peace! for I will not have to do with you.
ROSALINE Nor shall not, if I do as I intend.
BEROWNE Speak for yourselves: my wit is at an end. 430
KING
Teach us, sweet madam, for our rude transgression
Some fair excuse.
PRINCESS The fairest is confession.
Were not you here, but even now, disguis'd?
KING Madam, I was.
PRINCESS And were you well advis'd?
KING I was, fair madam.
PRINCESS When you then were here, 435
What did you whisper in your lady's ear?
KING That more than all the world I did respect her.
PRINCESS
When she shall challenge this, you will reject her.
KING Upon mine honour, no.
PRINCESS Peace! peace! forbear:
Your oath once broke, you force not to forswear. 440
KING Despise me, when I break this oath of mine.
PRINCESS I will; and therefore keep it. Rosaline,
What did the Russian whisper in your ear?
ROSALINE Madam, he swore that he did hold me dear
As precious eyesight, and did value me 445
Above this world; adding thereto, moreover,
That he would wed me, or else die my lover.
PRINCESS God give thee joy of him! the noble lord
Most honourably doth uphold his word.
KING What mean you, madam? by my life, my troth, 450
I never swore this lady such an oath.
ROSALINE By heaven, you did; and to confirm it plain,
You gave me this: but take it, sir, again.
KING My faith and this the princess I did give:
I knew her by this jewel on her sleeve. 455
PRINCESS Pardon me, sir, this jewel did she wear;
And Lord Berowne, I thank him, is my dear.
What, will you have me, or your pearl again?
BEROWNE Neither of either; I remit both twain.
I see the trick on't: here was a consent, 460
Knowing aforehand of our merriment,

To dash it like a Christmas comedy.
Some carry-tale, some please-man, some slight zany,
Some mumble-news, some trencher-knight, some
    Dick,
465 That smiles his cheek in years, and knows the trick
To make my lady laugh when she's disposed,
Told our intents before; which once disclos'd,
The ladies did change favours, and then we,
Following the signs, woo'd but the sign of she.
470 Now, to our perjury to add more terror,
We are again forsworn, in will and error.
Much upon this 'tis: – and might not you;   [*to Boyet*]
Forestall our sport, to make us thus untrue?
Do not you know my lady's foot by the square
475 And laugh upon the apple of her eye?
And stand between her back, sir, and the fire,
Holding a trencher, jesting merrily?
You put our page out: go, you are allow'd;
Die when you will, a smock shall be your shroud.
480 You leer upon me, do you? there's an eye
Wounds like a leaden sword.
BOYET   Full merrily
Hath this brave manage, this career, been run.
BEROWNE   Lo! he is tilting straight. Peace! I have done.

Enter COSTARD.

Welcome, pure wit! thou part'st a fair fray.
485 COSTARD   O Lord, sir, they would know,
Whether the three Worthies shall come in or no.
BEROWNE   What, are there but three?
COSTARD   No, sir; but it is vara fine,
For every one pursents three.
BEROWNE   And three times thrice is nine.
COSTARD
Not so, sir; under correction, sir, I hope it is not so.
You cannot beg us, sir, I can assure you, sir; we know
490   what we know:
I hope, sir, three times thrice, sir, –
BEROWNE   Is not nine.
COSTARD
Under correction, sir, we know whereuntil it doth
    amount.
BEROWNE   By Jove, I always took three threes for nine.
COSTARD   O Lord, sir! it were pity you should get your
495   living by reckoning, sir.
BEROWNE   How much is it?
COSTARD   O Lord, sir! the parties themselves, the
actors, sir, will show whereuntil it doth amount: for
mine own part, I am, as they say, but to parfect one
500   man in one poor man, Pompion the Great, sir.
BEROWNE   Art thou one of the Worthies?
COSTARD   It pleased them to think me worthy of
Pompey the Great: for mine own part, I know not the
degree of the Worthy, but I am to stand for him.
505 BEROWNE   Go, bid them prepare.
COSTARD   We will turn it finely off, sir; we will take

some care.   *Exit.*
KING
Berowne, they will shame us; let them not approach.
BEROWNE
We are shame-proof, my lord; and 'tis some policy
To have one show worse than the king's and his
    company.   510
KING   I say they shall not come.
PRINCESS
Nay, my good lord, let me o'er-rule you now.
That sport best pleases that doth least know how.
Where zeal strives to content, and the contents
Dies in the zeal of that which it presents;   515
Their form confounded makes most form in mirth,
When great things labouring perish in their birth.
BEROWNE   A right description of our sport, my lord.

Enter ARMADO.

ARMADO   Anointed, I implore so much expense of thy
royal sweet breath as will utter a brace of words.   520
[*Converses with the King, and delivers a paper to him.*]
PRINCESS   Doth this man serve God?
BEROWNE   Why ask you?
PRINCESS   'A speaks not like a man of God's making.
ARMADO   That is all one, my fair, sweet, honey
monarch; for I protest, the schoolmaster is exceeding   525
fantastical; too, too vain; too, too vain: but we will put
it, as they say, to *fortuna de la guerra.* I wish you the
peace of mind, most royal couplement!   *Exit.*
KING   Here is like to be a good presence of Worthies. He
presents Hector of Troy; the swain, Pompey the   530
Great; the parish curate, Alexander; Armado's page,
Hercules; the pedant, Judas Maccabaeus.
And if these four Worthies in their first show thrive,
These four will change habits, and present the other
    five.
BEROWNE   There is five in the first show.   535
KING   You are deceived, 'tis not so.
BEROWNE   The pedant, the braggart, the hedge-priest,
the fool, and the boy: –
Abate throw at novum, and the whole world again
Cannot pick out five such, take each one in his vein.   540
KING
The ship is under sail, and here she comes amain.

Enter COSTARD *for Pompey.*

COSTARD   I Pompey am, –
BEROWNE   You lie, you are not he.
COSTARD   I Pompey am, –
BOYET   With libbard's head on knee.
BEROWNE
Well said, old mocker: I must needs be friends with
    thee.
COSTARD   I Pompey am, Pompey surnam'd the Big, –   545
DUMAIN   The Great.
COSTARD

It is 'Great,' sir; Pompey surnam'd the Great;
That oft in field, with targe and shield, did make my
    foe to sweat:
And travelling along this coast, I here am come by
    chance
And lay my arms before the legs of this sweet lass of
    France.
If your ladyship would say, 'Thanks, Pompey,' I had
    done.

PRINCESS   Great thanks, great Pompey.

COSTARD   'Tis not so much worth; but I hope I was
    perfect. I made a little fault in 'Great.'

BEROWNE   My hat to a halfpenny, Pompey proves the
best Worthy.

Enter SIR NATHANIEL *for Alexander.*

NATHANIEL
When in the world I liv'd, I was the world's
    commander;
By east, west, north, and south, I spread my
    conquering might:
My scrutcheon plain declares that I am Alisander, –

BOYET
Your nose says, no, you are not; for it stands too
    right.

BEROWNE
Your nose smells 'no,' in this, most tender-smelling
    knight.

PRINCESS
The conqueror is dismay'd. Proceed, good
    Alexander.

NATHANIEL
When in the world I liv'd, I was the world's
    Commander, –

BOYET   Most true; 'tis right: you were so, Alisander.

BEROWNE   Pompey the Great, –

COSTARD   Your servant, and Costard.

BEROWNE   Take away the conqueror, take away
Alisander.

COSTARD [*to Nathaniel*] O! sir, you have overthrown
Alisander the conqueror. You will be scraped out of
the painted cloth for this: your lion, that holds his
poll-axe sitting on a close-stool, will be given to Ajax:
he will be the ninth Worthy. A conqueror, and afeard
to speak! run away for shame, Alisander. [*Nathaniel
retires.*] There, an't shall please you: a foolish mild
man; an honest man, look you, and soon dashed! He is
a marvellous good neighbour, faith, and a very good
bowler; but, for Alisander, – alas! you see how 'tis, – a
little o'erparted. But there are Worthies a-coming will
speak their mind in some other sort.

PRINCESS   Stand aside, good Pompey.

Enter HOLOFERNES *for Judas, and* MOTH *for Hercules.*

HOLOFERNES   Great Hercules is presented by this imp,
Whose club kill'd Cerberus, that three-headed *canus*;
And, when he was a babe, a child, a shrimp,

Thus did he strangle serpents in his *manus*.
Quoniam he seemeth in minority,
Ergo I come with this apology.
Keep some state in thy exit, and vanish. *Moth retires.*
Judas I am, –   590

DUMAIN   A Judas!

HOLOFERNES   Not Iscariot, sir.
Judas I am, ycleped Maccabaeus.

DUMAIN   Judas Maccabaeus clipt is plain Judas.

BEROWNE
A kissing traitor. How, art thou prov'd Judas?   595

HOLOFERNES   Judas I am, –

DUMAIN   The more shame for you, Judas.

HOLOFERNES   What mean you, sir?

BOYET   To make Judas hang himself.

HOLOFERNES   Begin, sir; you are my elder.   600

BEROWNE   Well follow'd: Judas was hang'd on an elder.

HOLOFERNES   I will not be put out of countenance.

BEROWNE   Because thou hast no face.

HOLOFERNES   What is this?

BOYET   A cittern-head.   605

DUMAIN   The head of a bodkin.

BEROWNE   A death's face in a ring.

LONGAVILLE
The face of an old Roman coin, scarce seen.

BOYET   The pommel of Caesar's falchion.

DUMAIN   The carved bone face on a flask.   610

BEROWNE   Saint George's half-cheek in a brooch.

DUMAIN   Ay, and in a brooch of lead.

BEROWNE   Ay, and worn in the cap of a toothdrawer.
And now, forward; for we have put thee in coun-
tenance.   615

HOLOFERNES   You have put me out of countenance.

BEROWNE   False: we have given thee faces.

HOLOFERNES   But you have outfaced them all.

BEROWNE   An thou wert a lion, we would do so.

BOYET   Therefore, as he is, an ass, let him go.   620
And so adieu, sweet Jude! nay, why dost thou stay?

DUMAIN   For the latter end of his name.

BEROWNE
For the ass to the Jude? give it him: – Jud-as, away!

HOLOFERNES
This is not generous, not gentle, not humble.

BOYET
A light for Monsieur Judas! it grows dark, he may
    stumble.   *Holofernes retires.*   625

PRINCESS
Alas! poor Maccabaeus, how hath he been baited.

Enter ARMADO *for Hector.*

BEROWN   Hide thy head, Achilles: here comes Hector in
arms.

DUMAIN   Though my mocks come home by me, I will
now be merry.   630

KING   Hector was but a Troyan in respect of this.

BOYET   But is this Hector?

KING   I think Hector was not so clean-timbered.

	LONGAVILLE His leg is too big for Hector's.
635	DUMAIN More calf, certain.
	BOYET No; he is best indued in the small.
	BEROWNE This cannot be Hector.
	DUMAIN He's a god or a painter; for he makes faces.
640	ARMADO The armipotent Mars, of lances the almighty,
	Gave Hector a gift, –
	DUMAIN A gilt nutmeg.
	BEROWNE A lemon.
	LONGAVILLE Stuck with cloves.
	DUMAIN No, cloven.
645	ARMADO Peace!
	The armipotent Mars, of lances the almighty,
	Gave Hector a gift, the heir of Ilion;
	A man so breath'd that certain he would fight; yea
	From morn till night, out of his pavilion.
	I am that flower, –
	DUMAIN That mint.
650	LONGAVILLE That columbine.
	ARMADO Sweet Lord Longaville, rein thy tongue.
	LONGAVILLE I must rather give it the rein, for it runs
	against Hector.
	DUMAIN Ay, and Hector's a greyhound.
655	ARMADO The sweet war-man is dead and rotten; sweet
	chucks, beat not the bones of the buried; when he
	breathed, he was a man. But I will forward with my
	device. Sweet royalty, bestow on me the sense of
	hearing. [*Berowne steps forth.*]
660	PRINCESS Speak, brave Hector; we are much delighted.
	ARMADO I do adore thy sweet grace's slipper.
	BOYET Loves her by the foot.
	DUMAIN He may not by the yard.
	ARMADO This Hector far surmounted Hannibal, the
665	party is gone –
	COSTARD Fellow Hector, she is gone; she is two months
	on her way.
	ARMADO What meanest thou?
	COSTARD Faith, unless you play the honest Troyan, the
670	poor wench is cast away: she's quick; the child brags in
	her belly already: 'tis yours.
	ARMADO Dost thou infamonize me among potentates?
	Thou shalt die.
	COSTARD Then shall Hector be whipped for Jaquenetta
675	that is quick by him, and hanged for Pompey that is
	dead by him.
	DUMAIN Most rare Pompey!
	BOYET Renowned Pompey!
	BEROWNE Greater than great, great, great, great
680	Pompey! Pompey the Huge!
	DUMAIN Hector trembles.
	BEROWNE Pompey is moved. More Ates, more Ates! stir
	them on! stir them on!
	DUMAIN Hector will challenge him.
685	BEROWNE Ay, if 'a have no more man's blood in his belly
	than will sup a flea.
	ARMADO By the north pole, I do challenge thee.
	COSTARD I will not fight with a pole, like a northern

	man: I'll slash; I'll do it by the sword. I bepray you, let
690	me borrow my arms again.
	DUMAIN Room for the incensed Worthies!
	COSTARD I'll do it in my shirt.
	DUMAIN Most resolute Pompey!
695	MOTH Master, let me take you a button-hole lower. Do
	you not see Pompey is uncasing for the combat? What
	mean you? you will lose your reputation.
	ARMADO Gentlemen and soldiers, pardon me; I will not
	combat in my shirt.
700	DUMAIN You may not deny it; Pompey hath made the
	challenge.
	ARMADO Sweet bloods, I both may and will.
	BEROWNE What reason have you for't?
	ARMADO The naked truth of it is, I have no shirt. I go
	woolward for penance.
705	BOYET True, and it was enjoined him in Rome for want
	of linen; since when I'll be sworn he wore none but a
	dishclout of Jaquenetta's, and that 'a wears next his
	heart for a favour.

Enter MARCADE, *a messenger*.

	MARCADE God save you, madam!
	PRINCESS Welcome, Marcade,
710	But that thou interrupt'st our merriment.
	MARCADE I am sorry, madam; for the news I bring
	Is heavy in my tongue. The king your father –
	PRINCESS Dead, for my life!
	MARCADE Even so: my tale is told.
715	BEROWNE Worthies, away! The scene begins to cloud.
	ARMADO For mine own part, I breathe free breath. I
	have seen the day of wrong through the little hole of
	discretion, and I will right myself like a soldier.

Exeunt Worthies.

	KING How fares your majesty?
720	PRINCESS Boyet, prepare: I will away to-night.
	KING Madam, not so; I do beseech you, stay.
	PRINCESS Prepare, I say. I thank you, gracious lords,
	For all your fair endeavours; and entreat,
	Out of a new-sad soul, that you vouchsafe
725	In your rich wisdom to excuse or hide
	The liberal opposition of our spirits,
	If over-boldly we have borne ourselves
	In the converse of breath; your gentleness
	Was guilty of it. Farewell, worthy lord!
730	A heavy heart bears not a humble tongue.
	Excuse me so, coming too short of thanks
	For my great suit so easily obtain'd.
	KING The extreme parts of time extremely forms
	All causes to the purpose of his speed,
735	And often, at his very loose, decides
	That which long process could not arbitrate:
	And though the mourning brow of progeny
	Forbid the smiling courtesy of love
	The holy suit which fain it would convince;
740	Yet since love's argument was first on foot,
	Let not the cloud of sorrow justle it

From what it purpos'd; since, to wail friends lost
Is not by much so wholesome-profitable
As to rejoice at friends but newly found.

745 PRINCESS   I understand you not: my griefs are double.

BEROWNE
Honest plain words best pierce the ear of grief;
And by these badges understand the king.
For your fair sakes have we neglected time,
Play'd foul play with our oaths. Your beauty, ladies,
750 Hath much deform'd us, fashioning our humours
Even to the opposed end of our intents;
And what in us hath seem'd ridiculous, –
As love is full of unbefitting strains;
All wanton as a child, skipping and vain;
755 Form'd by the eye, and therefore, like the eye,
Full of strange shapes, of habits, and of forms,
Varying in subjects, as the eye doth roll
To every varied object in his glance:
Which party-coated presence of loose love
760 Put on by us, if, in your heavenly eyes,
Have misbecom'd our oaths and gravities,
Those heavenly eyes, that look into these faults,
Suggested us to make. Therefore, ladies,
Our love being yours, the error that love makes
765 Is likewise yours: we to ourselves prove false,
By being once false for ever to be true
To those that make us both, – fair ladies, you:
And even that falsehood, in itself a sin,
Thus purifies itself and turns to grace.

770 PRINCESS   We have receiv'd your letters full of love;
Your favours, the ambassadors of love;
And in our maiden council, rated them
At courtship, pleasant jest, and courtesy,
As bombast and as lining to the time.
775 But more devout than this in our respects
Have we not been; and therefore met your loves
In their own fashion, like a merriment.

DUMAIN
Our letters, madam, show'd much more than jest.

LONGAVILLE   So did our looks.

ROSALINE   We did not quote them so.

780 KING   Now, at the latest minute of the hour,
Grant us your loves.

PRINCESS   A time, methinks, too short
To make a world-without-end bargain in.
No, no, my lord, your grace is perjur'd much,
Full of dear guiltiness; and therefore this:
785 If for my love, as there is no such cause,
You will do aught, this shall you do for me:
Your oath I will not trust; but go with speed
To some forlorn and naked hermitage,
Remote from all the pleasures of the world;
790 There stay, until the twelve celestial signs
Have brought about the annual reckoning.
If this austere insociable life
Change not your offer made in heat of blood;
If frosts and fasts, hard lodging and thin weeds,

Nip not the gaudy blossoms of your love,   795
But that it bear this trial and last love;
Then at the expiration of the year,
Come challenge me, challenge me by these deserts,
And, by this virgin palm now kissing thine,
I will be thine; and, till that instant, shut   800
My woeful self up in a mourning house,
Raining the tears of lamentation
For the remembrance of my father's death.
If this thou do deny, let our hands part;
Neither intitled in the other's heart.   805

KING   If this, or more than this, I would deny,
To flatter up these powers of mine with rest,
The sudden hand of death close up mine eye!
Hence hermit, then – my heart is in thy breast.

[BEROWNE   And what to me, my love? and what to me?   810

ROSALINE   You must be purged to your sins are rack'd:
You are attaint with faults and perjury;
Therefore, if you my favour mean to get,
A twelvemonth shall you spend and never rest
But seek the weary beds of people sick.]   815

DUMAIN   But what to me, my love? but what to me?
A wife?

KATHARINE   A beard, fair health, and honesty;
With three-fold love I wish you all these three.

DUMAIN   O! shall I say, I thank you, gentle wife?

KATHARINE
Not so, my lord. A twelvemonth and a day   820
I'll mark no words that smooth-faced wooers say:
Come when the king doth to my lady come;
Then, if I have much love, I'll give you some.

DUMAIN   I'll serve thee true and faithfully till then.

KATHARINE   Yet swear not, lest you be forsworn again. 825

LONGAVILLE   What says Maria?

MARIA   At the twelvemonth's end
I'll change my black gown for a faithful friend.

LONGAVILLE
I'll stay with patience; but the time is long.

MARIA   The liker you; few taller are so young.

BEROWNE   Studies my lady? mistress, look on me.   830
Behold the window of my heart, mine eye,
What humble suit attends thy answer there;
Impose some service on me for thy love.

ROSALINE   Oft have I heard of you, my Lord Berowne,
Before I saw you, and the world's large tongue   835
Proclaims you for a man replete with mocks;
Full of comparisons and wounding flouts,
Which you on all estates will execute
That lie within the mercy of your wit:
To weed this wormwood from your fruitful brain,   840
And there withal to win me, if you please,
Without the which I am not to be won,
You shall this twelve month term from day to day,
Visit the speechless sick, and still converse
With groaning wretches; and your task shall be   845
With all the fierce endeavour of your wit
To enforce the pained impotent to smile.

BEROWNE
   To move wild laughter in the throat of death?
   It cannot be; it is impossible:
850   Mirth cannot move a soul in agony.
ROSALINE   Why, that's the way to choke a gibing spirit,
   Whose influence is begot of that loose grace
   Which shallow laughing hearers give to fools.
   A jest's prosperity lies in the ear
855   Of him that hears it, never in the tongue
   Of him that makes it: then, if sickly ears,
   Deaf'd with the clamours of their own dear groans,
   Will hear your idle scorns, continue then,
   And I will have you and that fault withal;
860   But if they will not, throw away that spirit,
   And I shall find you empty of that fault,
   Right joyful of your reformation.
BEROWNE   A twelvemonth! well, befall what will befall,
   I'll jest a twelvemonth in an hospital.
PRINCESS [*to the King*]
865   Ay, sweet my lord; and so I take my leave.
KING   No, madam; we will bring you on your way.
BEROWNE   Our wooing doth not end like an old play;
   Jack hath not Jill: these ladies' courtesy
   Might well have made our sport a comedy.
870 KING   Come, sir, it wants a twelvemonth and a day,
   And then 'twill end.
BEROWNE   That's too long for a play.

Re-enter ARMADO.

ARMADO   Sweet majesty, vouchsafe me, –
PRINCESS   Was not that Hector?
DUMAIN   The worthy knight of Troy.
875 ARMADO   I will kiss thy royal finger, and take leave. I am
   a votary; I have vowed to Jaquenetta to hold the
   plough for her sweet love three year. But, most
   esteemed greatness, will you hear the dialogue that the
   two learned men have compiled in praise of the owl
880   and the cuckoo? it should have followed in the end of
   our show.
KING   Call them forth quickly; we will do so.
ARMADO   Holla! approach.

Re-enter HOLOFERNES, NATHANIEL, MOTH,
COSTARD *and others.*

This side is *Hiems*, Winter, this *Ver*, the Spring: the
885   one maintained by the owl, the other by the cuckoo.
Ver, begin.

Song.

SPRING
   When daisies pied and violets blue
     And lady-smocks all silver-white
   And cuckoo-buds of yellow hue
     Do paint the meadows with delight. 890
   The cuckoo then, on every tree,
   Mocks married men; for thus sings he,
       Cuckoo;
   Cuckoo, cuckoo: O word of fear,
   Unpleasing to a married ear! 895

   When shepherds pipe on oaten straws,
     And merry larks are ploughman's clocks,
   When turtles tread, and rooks, and daws,
     And maidens bleach their summer smocks, 900
   The cuckoo then, on every tree,
   Mocks married men; for thus sings he,
       Cuckoo;
   Cuckoo, cuckoo; O word of fear,
   Unpleasing to a married ear!

WINTER
   When icicles hang by the wall, 905
     And Dick the shepherd blows his nail,
   And Tom bears logs into the hall,
     And milk comes frozen home in pail,
   When blood is nipp'd, and ways be foul,
   Then nightly sings the staring owl, 910
       Tu-whit;
   Tu-who, a merry note,
   While greasy Joan doth keel the pot.

   When all aloud the wind doth blow,
     And coughing drowns the parson's saw, 915
   And birds sit brooding in the snow,
     And Marian's nose looks red and raw,
   When roasted crabs hiss in the bowl,
   Then nightly sings the staring owl,
       Tu-whit; 920
   Tu-who, a merry note,
   While greasy Joan doth keel the pot.

The words of Mercury are harsh after the songs of
Apollo.   *Exeunt.*

Macbeth

Macbeth was first published as the sixth of the tragedies in the First Folio in 1623, but it is generally thought to have been written around 1606, quite early in the reign of James VI of Scotland, who succeeded to the English throne in 1603, becoming James I of England. Also in 1603, James became the patron of Shakespeare's acting company, who changed their name from the Lord Chamberlain's Men to the King's Men. In addition to its Scottish setting, the play has further links with the King, who traced his ancestry to Macbeth's fellow-thane Banquo, prided himself on his ability to cure the King's evil (as the English King is said to do in 4.3), and took an interest in witchcraft, having published a book on the topic, the *Daemonology*, in 1599. *Macbeth* seems to have been written after *Hamlet*, *Othello* and *King Lear*, but before *Antony and Cleopatra* and *Coriolanus*. Its concern with the murder of a king links it with history plays like *Richard II* as well as with *Hamlet*.

The text that was printed in the Folio is unusually short compared with the other tragedies and may have been cut for performance at some point between 1606 and 1623. It also contains some passages which have long been held to be interpolations from another hand: the passages in question are 3.5 and parts of 4.1. These passages involve Hecate, Queen of the Witches, who does not appear elsewhere, and they are written mainly in octosyllabic couplets rather than in iambic pentameter. They call for the performance of two songs: just the opening words are cited but the songs appear in full in a play called *The Witch* by Thomas Middleton, who is thought by many scholars to have been responsible for the interpolations. Some scholars today credit him as the 'adapter' of *Macbeth*.

Shakespeare's principal source was the Scottish section of Raphael Holinshed's *Chronicles* (1587), which he had used for his English history plays. In this case the accounts of the reigns of Duncan and Macbeth (covering the years 1034 to 1057) were used, together with an account of an earlier king, Duff, who was killed at Forres by his thane Donwald and his wife. Shakespeare compresses the time-scale of events and somewhat idealizes Duncan as a king. He also idealizes Banquo, who is Macbeth's co-conspirator in Holinshed; this is not surprising, since James I traced his ancestry to Banquo and Fleance. He follows up his experiment with the introduction of a comic character – the Fool – in *King Lear* by inventing the Porter, whose role derives ultimately from the medieval mystery plays which dramatized Christ's descent into Hell and featured comic devils as gatekeepers. The jokes about 'equivocation' in the Porter's monologue in 2.3 may be a topical reference to the post-Gunpowder Plot trial of the Jesuit Henry Garnet, who famously equivocated under interrogation.

The play has always been popular on the stage, though at the same time it has been regarded as unlucky in the theatre, where it is never named but always referred to superstitiously as 'the Scottish play'. William Davenant rewrote it in quasi-operatic mode in 1666 but David Garrick restored much of Shakespeare's text (though not the Porter) in 1744. Lady Macbeth is one of the best roles in Shakespearean tragedy for a mature actress, and many have triumphed in the part, from Sarah Siddons to Ellen Terry and Judi Dench. Nineteenth-century productions were often burdened with elaborately 'authentic' scenery and costumes, while simpler styles of staging in the twentieth century have often served to emphasize the claustrophobic intensity of the play and have substituted psychological for pictorial realism. Modern productions and films use special effects and lighting (or rather darkness) to create the atmosphere that must have been evoked by the language and sound effects alone in early daylight performances at the Globe.

The Arden text is based on the 1623 First Folio.

DUNCAN	*King of Scotland*
DONALBAIN MALCOLM	} *his sons*
MACBETH BANQUO	} *generals of the King's army*
MACDUFF LENOX ROSSE MENTETH ANGUS CATHNESS	} *noblemen of Scotland*
FLEANCE	*son to Banquo*
SIWARD	*Earl of Northumberland, general of the English forces*
YOUNG SIWARD	*his son*
SEYTON	*an officer attending on Macbeth*
BOY	*son to Macduff*
English DOCTOR	
Scottish DOCTOR	
SOLDIER	
PORTER	
OLD MAN	
LADY MACBETH	
LADY MACDUFF	
GENTLEWOMAN	*attending on Lady Macbeth*
HECATE	
THREE WITCHES	

Lords, Gentlemen, Officers, Soldiers, Murderers, Witches, Attendants and Messengers

The Ghost of Banquo and other Apparitions

Macbeth

1.1 *Thunder and lightning. Enter three* Witches.

1 WITCH   When shall we three meet again?
  In thunder, lightning, or in rain?
2 WITCH   When the hurlyburly's done,
  When the battle's lost and won.
5 3 WITCH   That will be ere the set of sun.
1 WITCH   Where the place?
2 WITCH   Upon the heath.
3 WITCH   There to meet with Macbeth.
1 WITCH   I come, Graymalkin!
2 WITCH   Paddock calls.
10 3 WITCH   Anon!
ALL   Fair is foul, and foul is fair:
  Hover through the fog and filthy air.   *Exeunt.*

1.2   *Alarum within. Enter* KING DUNCAN,
    MALCOLM, DONALBAIN, LENOX, *with*
    attendants, meeting a bleeding Captain.

DUNCAN   What bloody man is that? He can report,
  As seemeth by his plight, of the revolt
  The newest state.
MALCOLM   This is the Sergeant,
  Who, like a good and hardy soldier, fought
5 'Gainst my captivity. – Hail, brave friend!
  Say to the King the knowledge of the broil,
  As thou didst leave it.
CAPTAIN   Doubtful it stood;
  As two spent swimmers, that do cling together
  And choke their art. The merciless Macdonwald
10 (Worthy to be a rebel, for to that
  The multiplying villainies of nature
  Do swarm upon him) from the western isles
  Of Kernes and Gallowglasses is supplied;
  And Fortune, on his damned quarrel smiling,
15 Show'd like a rebel's whore: but all's too weak;
  For brave Macbeth (well he deserves that name),
  Disdaining Fortune, with his brandish'd steel,
  Which smok'd with bloody execution,
  Like Valour's minion, carv'd out his passage,
20 Till he fac'd the slave;
  Which ne'er shook hands, nor bade farewell to him,
  Till he unseam'd him from the nave to th' chops,
  And fix'd his head upon our battlements.
DUNCAN   O valiant cousin! worthy gentleman!
25 CAPTAIN   As whence the sun 'gins his reflection,
  Shipwracking storms and direful thunders break,
  So from that spring, whence comfort seem'd to come,
  Discomfort swells. Mark, King of Scotland, mark:
  No sooner justice had, with valour arm'd,
30 Compell'd these skipping Kernes to trust their heels,
  But the Norweyan Lord, surveying vantage,
  With furbish'd arms, and new supplies of men,
  Began a fresh assault.
DUNCAN   Dismay'd not this
  Our captains, Macbeth and Banquo?
CAPTAIN   Yes;

As sparrows eagles, or the hare the lion.   35
  If I say sooth, I must report they were
  As cannons overcharg'd with double cracks;
  So they
  Doubly redoubled strokes upon the foe:
  Except they meant to bathe in reeking wounds,   40
  Or memorize another Golgotha,
  I cannot tell –
  But I am faint, my gashes cry for help.
DUNCAN
  So well thy words become thee, as thy wounds:
  They smack of honour both. – Go, get him surgeons.   45
                    Exit Captain, attended.

            Enter ROSSE *and* ANGUS.

  Who comes here?
MALCOLM   The worthy Thane of Rosse.
LENOX
  What a haste looks through his eyes! So should he
    look
  That seems to speak things strange.
ROSSE   God save the King!
DUNCAN   Whence cam'st thou, worthy Thane?
ROSSE   From Fife, great King,
  Where the Norweyan banners flout the sky,   50
  And fan our people cold. Norway himself,
  With terrible numbers,
  Assisted by that most disloyal traitor,
  The Thane of Cawdor, began a dismal conflict;
  Till that Bellona's bridegroom, lapp'd in proof,   55
  Confronted him with self-comparisons,
  Point against point, rebellious arm 'gainst arm,
  Curbing his lavish spirit: and, to conclude,
  The victory fell on us; –
DUNCAN   Great happiness!
ROSSE   That now   60
  Sweno, the Norways' King, craves composition;
  Nor would we deign him burial of his men
  Till he disbursed at Saint Colme's Inch
  Ten thousand dollars to our general use.
DUNCAN   No more that Thane of Cawdor shall deceive   65
  Our bosom interest. – Go pronounce his present
    death,
  And with his former title greet Macbeth.
ROSSE   I'll see it done.
DUNCAN   What he hath lost, noble Macbeth hath won.
                    Exeunt.

1.3   *Thunder. Enter the three* Witches.

1 WITCH   Where hast thou been, Sister?
2 WITCH   Killing swine.
3 WITCH   Sister, where thou?
1 WITCH   A sailor's wife had chestnuts in her lap,
  And mounch'd, and mounch'd, and mounch'd: 'Give
    me,' quoth I: –   5
  'Aroynt thee, witch!' the rump-fed ronyon cries.

Her husband's to Aleppo gone, master o'th' *Tiger:*
But in a sieve I'll thither sail,
And like a rat without a tail;
10   I'll do, I'll do, and I'll do.
2 WITCH   I'll give thee a wind.
1 WITCH   Th'art kind.
3 WITCH   And I another.
1 WITCH   I myself have all the other;
15   And the very ports they blow,
All the quarters that they know
I'th' shipman's card.
I'll drain him dry as hay:
Sleep shall neither night nor day
20   Hang upon his penthouse lid;
He shall live a man forbid.
Weary sev'n-nights nine times nine,
Shall he dwindle, peak, and pine:
Though his bark cannot be lost,
25   Yet it shall be tempest-tost.
Look what I have.
2 WITCH   Show me, show me.
1 WITCH   Here I have a pilot's thumb,
Wrack'd, as homeward he did come.
                               [Drum within.]
30   3 WITCH   A drum! a drum!
Macbeth doth come.
ALL   The Weïrd Sisters, hand in hand,
Posters of the sea and land,
Thus do go about, about:
35   Thrice to thine, and thrice to mine,
And thrice again, to make up nine
Peace! – the charm's wound up.

            Enter MACBETH *and* BANQUO.

MACBETH   So foul and fair a day I have not seen.
BANQUO
How far is't call'd to Forres? – What are these,
40   So wither'd and so wild in their attire,
That look not like th'inhabitants o'th'earth,
And yet are on't? Live you? or are you aught
That man may question? You seem to understand
   me,
By each at once her choppy finger laying
45   Upon her skinny lips: you should be women,
And yet your beards forbid me to interpret
That you are so.
MACBETH   Speak, if you can: – what are you?
1 WITCH
All hail, Macbeth! hail to thee, Thane of Glamis!
2 WITCH
All hail, Macbeth! hail to thee, Thane of Cawdor!
3 WITCH
50   All hail, Macbeth! that shalt be King hereafter.
BANQUO   Good Sir, why do you start, and seem to fear
Things that do sound so fair? – I'th' name of truth,
Are ye fantastical, or that indeed
Which outwardly ye show? My noble partner

You greet with present grace, and great prediction   55
Of noble having, and of royal hope,
That he seems rapt withal: to me you speak not.
If you can look into the seeds of time,
And say which grain will grow, and which will not,
Speak then to me, who neither beg, nor fear,   60
Your favours nor your hate.
1 WITCH   Hail!
2 WITCH   Hail!
3 WITCH   Hail!
1 WITCH   Lesser than Macbeth, and greater.   65
2 WITCH   Not so happy, yet much happier.
3 WITCH   Thou shalt get kings, though thou be none:
So all hail, Macbeth and Banquo!
1 WITCH   Banquo and Macbeth, all hail!
MACBETH   Stay, you imperfect speakers, tell me more.   70
By Sinel's death I know I am Thane of Glamis;
But how of Cawdor? the Thane of Cawdor lives,
A prosperous gentleman; and to be King
Stands not within the prospect of belief,
No more than to be Cawdor. Say from whence   75
You owe this strange intelligence? or why
Upon this blasted heath you stop our way
With such prophetic greeting? – Speak, I charge you.
                                 Witches vanish.
BANQUO   The earth hath bubbles, as the water has,
And these are of them. – Whither are they vanish'd?   80
MACBETH   Into the air; and what seem'd corporal,
Melted as breath into the wind. Would they had
   stay'd!
BANQUO   Were such things here, as we do speak about,
Or have we eaten on the insane root,
That takes the reason prisoner?   85
MACBETH   Your children shall be kings.
BANQUO   You shall be King.
MACBETH   And Thane of Cawdor too; went it not so?
BANQUO   To th' selfsame tune, and words. Who's here?

            Enter ROSSE *and* ANGUS.

ROSSE   The King hath happily receiv'd, Macbeth,
The news of thy success; and when he reads   90
Thy personal venture in the rebels' fight,
His wonders and his praises do contend,
Which should be thine, or his: silenc'd with that,
In viewing o'er the rest o'th' selfsame day,
He finds thee in the stout Norweyan ranks,   95
Nothing afeard of what thyself didst make,
Strange images of death. As thick as hail,
Came post with post; and every one did bear
Thy praises in his kingdom's great defence,
And pour'd them down before him.
ANGUS   We are sent,   100
To give thee from our royal master thanks;
Only to herald thee into his sight,
Not pay thee.
ROSSE   And, for an earnest of a greater honour,
He bade me, from him, call thee Thane of Cawdor: 105

In which addition, hail, most worthy Thane,
For it is thine.
BANQUO   What! can the Devil speak true?
MACBETH
The Thane of Cawdor lives: why do you dress me
In borrow'd robes?
ANGUS   Who was Thane, lives yet;
110   But under heavy judgment bears that life
Which he deserves to lose. Whether he was combin'd
With those of Norway, or did line the rebel
With hidden help and vantage, or that with both
He labour'd in his country's wrack, I know not;
115   But treasons capital, confess'd and prov'd,
Have overthrown him.
MACBETH [aside]   Glamis, and Thane of Cawdor:
The greatest is behind.
[to Rosse and Angus]   Thanks for your pains. –
[to Banquo] Do you not hope your children shall be
    kings,
When those that gave the Thane of Cawdor to me
Promis'd no less to them?
120   BANQUO   That, trusted home,
Mighty yet enkindle you unto the crown,
Besides the Thane of Cawdor. But 'tis strange:
And oftentimes, to win us to our harm,
The instruments of Darkness tell us truths;
125   Win us with honest trifles, to betray's
In deepest consequence. –
Cousins, a word, I pray you.
MACBETH [aside]   Two truths are told,
As happy prologues to the swelling act
Of the imperial theme. – I thank you, gentlemen. –
130   [aside] This supernatural soliciting
Cannot be ill; cannot be good: –
If ill, why hath it given me earnest of success,
Commencing in a truth? I am Thane of Cawdor:
If good, why do I yield to that suggestion
135   Whose horrid image doth unfix my hair,
And make my seated heart knock at my ribs,
Against the use of nature? Present fears
Are less than horrible imaginings.
My thought, whose murther yet is but fantastical,
140   Shakes so my single state of man,
That function is smother'd in surmise,
And nothing is, but what is not.
BANQUO   Look, how our partner's rapt.
MACBETH [aside]   If Chance will have me King, why,
    Chance may crown me,
    Without my stir.
145   BANQUO   New honours come upon him,
Like our strange garments, cleave not to their mould,
But with the aid of use.
MACBETH [aside]   Come what come may,
Time and the hour runs through the roughest day.
BANQUO   Worthy Macbeth, we stay upon your leisure.
MACBETH
150   Give me your favour: my dull brain was wrought

With things forgotten. Kind gentlemen, your pains
Are register'd where every day I turn
The leaf to read them. – Let us toward the King. –
[to Banquo] Think upon what hath chanc'd; and at
    more time,
The Interim having weigh'd it, let us speak   155
Our free hearts each to other.
BANQUO   Very gladly.
MACBETH   Till then, enough. – Come, friends. *Exeunt.*

1.4   *Flourish. Enter* DUNCAN, MALCOLM,
          DONALBAIN, LENOX *and attendants.*

DUNCAN   Is execution done on Cawdor? Or not
Those in commission yet return'd?
MALCOLM   My Liege,
They are not yet come back; but I have spoke
With one that saw him die: who did report,
That very frankly he confess'd his treasons,   5
Implor'd your Highness' pardon, and set forth
A deep repentance. Nothing in his life
Became him like the leaving it: he died
As one that had been studied in his death,
To throw away the dearest thing he ow'd,   10
As 'twere a careless trifle.
DUNCAN   There's no art
To find the mind's construction in the face:
He was a gentleman on whom I built
An absolute trust –

     Enter MACBETH, BANQUO, ROSSE *and* ANGUS.

               O worthiest cousin!
The sin of my ingratitude even now   15
Was heavy on me. Thou art so far before,
That swiftest wing of recompense is slow
To overtake thee: would thou hadst less deserv'd,
That the proportion both of thanks and payment
Might have been mine! only I have left to say,   20
More is thy due than more than all can pay.
MACBETH   The service and the loyalty I owe,
In doing it, pays itself. Your Highness' part
Is to receive our duties: and our duties
Are to your throne and state, children and servants;   25
Which do but what they should, by doing everything
Safe toward your love and honour.
DUNCAN   Welcome hither:
I have begun to plant thee, and will labour
To make thee full of growing. – Noble Banquo,
That hast no less deserv'd, nor must be known   30
No less to have done so, let me infold thee,
And hold thee to my heart.
BANQUO   There if I grow,
The harvest is your own.
DUNCAN   My plenteous joys,
Wanton in fulness, seek to hide themselves
In drops of sorrow. – Sons, kinsmen, Thanes,   35
And you whose places are the nearest, know,
We will establish our estate upon

Our eldest, Malcolm; whom we name hereafter
The Prince of Cumberland: which honour must
40 Not unaccompanied invest him only,
But signs of nobleness, like stars, shall shine
On all deservers. – From hence to Inverness,
And bind us further to you.
MACBETH   The rest is labour, which is not us'd for you:
45 I'll be myself the harbinger, and make joyful
The hearing of my wife with your approach;
So, humbly take my leave.
DUNCAN   My worthy Cawdor!
MACBETH [*aside*]
The Prince of Cumberland! – That is a step
On which I must fall down, or else o'erleap,
50 For in my way it lies. Stars, hide your fires!
Let not light see my black and deep desires;
The eye wink at the hand; yet let that be,
Which the eye fears, when it is done, to see.   *Exit.*
DUNCAN   True, worthy Banquo: he is full so valiant,
55 And in his commendations I am fed;
It is a banquet to me. Let's after him,
Whose care is gone before to bid us welcome:
It is a peerless kinsman.   *Flourish. Exeunt.*

1.5   *Enter* LADY MACBETH, *reading a letter.*

LADY MACBETH   *They met me in the day of success; and I
have learn'd by the perfect'st report, they have more in
them than mortal knowledge. When I burn'd in desire to
question them further, they made themselves air, into
5 which they vanish'd. Whiles I stood rapt in the wonder of
it, came missives from the King, who all-hail'd me,
'Thane of Cawdor'; by which title, before, these Weïrd
Sisters saluted me, and referr'd me to the coming on of
time, with 'Hail, King that shalt be!' This have I thought
10 good to deliver thee (my dearest partner of greatness) that
thou might'st not lose the dues of rejoicing, by being
ignorant of what greatness is promis'd thee. Lay it to thy
heart, and farewell.*
Glamis thou art, and Cawdor; and shalt be
15 What thou art promis'd. – Yet do I fear thy nature:
It is too full o'th' milk of human kindness,
To catch the nearest way. Thou wouldst be great;
Art not without ambition, but without
The illness should attend it: what thou wouldst
highly,
20 That wouldst thou holily; wouldst not play false,
And yet wouldst wrongly win; thou'dst have, great
Glamis,
That which cries, 'Thus thou must do,' if thou have
it;
And that which rather thou dost fear to do,
Than wishest should be undone. Hie thee hither,
25 That I may pour my spirits in thine ear,
And chastise with the valour of my tongue
All that impedes thee from the golden round,
Which fate and metaphysical aid doth seem
To have thee crown'd withal.

Enter a Messenger.

What is your tidings?
MESSENGER   The King comes here to-night.
LADY MACBETH   Thou'rt mad to say it.   30
Is not thy master with him? who, were't so,
Would have inform'd for preparation.
MESSENGER
So please you, it is true: our Thane is coming;
One of my fellows had the speed of him,
Who, almost dead for breath, had scarcely more   35
Than would make up his message.
LADY MACBETH   Give him tending:
He brings great news.   *Exit Messenger.*
The raven himself is hoarse,
That croaks the fatal entrance of Duncan
Under my battlements. Come, you Spirits
That tend on mortal thoughts, unsex me here,   40
And fill me, from the crown to the toe, top-full
Of direst cruelty! make thick my blood,
Stop up th'access and passage to remorse;
That no compunctious visitings of Nature
Shake my fell purpose, nor keep peace between   45
Th'effect and it! Come to my woman's breasts,
And take my milk for gall, you murth'ring ministers,
Wherever in your sightless substances
You wait on Nature's mischief! Come, thick Night,
And pall thee in the dunnest smoke of Hell,   50
That my keen knife see not the wound it makes,
Nor Heaven peep through the blanket of the dark,
To cry, 'Hold, hold!'

Enter MACBETH

Great Glamis! worthy Cawdor!
Greater than both, by the all-hail hereafter!
Thy letters have transported me beyond   55
This ignorant present, and I feel now
The future in the instant.
MACBETH   My dearest love,
Duncan comes here to-night.
LADY MACBETH   And when goes hence?
MACBETH   To-morrow, as he purposes.
LADY MACBETH   O! never
Shall sun that morrow see!   60
Your face, my Thane, is as a book, where men
May read strange matters. To beguile the time,
Look like the time; bear welcome in your eye,
Your hand, your tongue: look like th'innocent flower,
But be the serpent under't. He that's coming   65
Must be provided for; and you shall put
This night's great business into my dispatch;
Which shall to all our nights and days to come
Give solely sovereign sway and masterdom.
MACBETH   We will speak further.
LADY MACBETH   Only look up clear;   70
To alter favour ever is to fear.
Leave all the rest to me.   *Exeunt.*

1.6 *Hautboys and torches. Enter* DUNCAN,
MALCOLM, DONALBAIN, BANQUO, LENOX,
MACDUFF, ROSSE, ANGUS *and attendants.*

DUNCAN   This castle hath a pleasant seat; the air
   Nimbly and sweetly recommends itself
   Unto our gentle senses.
BANQUO   This guest of summer,
   The temple-haunting martlet, does approve,
   By his loved mansionry, that the heaven's breath
   Smells wooingly here: no jutty, frieze,
   Buttress, nor coign of vantage, but this bird
   Hath made his pendent bed, and procreant cradle:
   Where they most breed and haunt, I have observ'd
   The air is delicate.

Enter LADY MACBETH.

DUNCAN   See, see! our honour'd hostess. –
   The love that follows us sometime is our trouble,
   Which still we thank as love. Herein I teach you,
   How you shall bid God 'ild us for your pains,
   And thank us for your trouble.
LADY MACBETH   All our service,
   In every point twice done, and then done double,
   Were poor and single business, to contend
   Against those honours deep and broad, wherewith
   Your Majesty loads our house: for those of old,
   And the late dignities heap'd up to them,
   We rest your hermits.
DUNCAN   Where's the Thane of Cawdor?
   We cours'd him at the heels, and had a purpose
   To be his purveyor: but he rides well;
   And his great love, sharp as his spur, hath holp him
   To his home before us. Fair and noble hostess,
   We are your guest to-night.
LADY MACBETH   Your servants ever
   Have theirs, themselves, and what is theirs, in compt,
   To make their audit at your Highness' pleasure,
   Still to return your own.
DUNCAN   Give me your hand;
   Conduct me to mine host: we love him highly,
   And shall continue our graces towards him.
   By your leave, hostess.   *Exeunt.*

1.7 *Hautboys and torches. Enter, and pass over the
stage, a sewer and divers servants with dishes
and service. Then enter* MACBETH.

MACBETH
   If it were done, when 'tis done, then 'twere well
   It were done quickly: if th'assassination
   Could trammel up the consequence, and catch
   With his surcease success; that but this blow
   Might be the be-all and the end-all – here,
   But here, upon this bank and shoal of time,
   We'd jump the life to come. – But in these cases,
   We still have judgment here; that we but teach
   Bloody instructions, which, being taught, return

To plague th'inventor: this even-handed Justice   10
Commends th'ingredience of our poison'd chalice
To our own lips. He's here in double trust:
First, as I am his kinsman and his subject,
Strong both against the deed; then, as his host,
Who should against his murtherer shut the door,   15
Not bear the knife myself. Besides, this Duncan
Hath borne his faculties so meek, hath been
So clear in his great office, that his virtues
Will plead like angels, trumpet-tongu'd, against
The deep damnation of his taking-off;   20
And Pity, like a naked new-born babe,
Striding the blast, or heaven's Cherubins, hors'd
Upon the sightless couriers of the air,
Shall blow the horrid deed in every eye,
That tears shall drown the wind. – I have no spur   25
To prick the sides of my intent, but only
Vaulting ambition, which o'erleaps itself
And falls on th'other –

Enter LADY MACBETH

           How now! what news?
LADY MACBETH
   He has almost supp'd. Why have you left the
     chamber?
MACBETH   Hath he ask'd for me?
LADY MACBETH   Know you not, he has?   30
MACBETH   We will proceed no further in this business:
   He hath honour'd me of late; and I have bought
   Golden opinions from all sorts of people,
   Which would be worn now in their newest gloss,
   Not cast aside so soon.
LADY MACBETH   Was the hope drunk,   35
   Wherein you dress'd yourself? Hath it slept since?
   And wakes it now, to look so green and pale
   At what it did so freely? From this time
   Such I account thy love. Art thou afeard
   To be the same in thine own act and valour,   40
   As thou art in desire? Would'st thou have that
   Which thou esteem'st the ornament of life,
   And live a coward in thine own esteem,
   Letting 'I dare not' wait upon 'I would,'
   Like the poor cat i'th'adage?
MACBETH   Pr'ythee, peace.   45
   I dare do all that may become a man;
   Who dares do more, is none.
LADY MACBETH   What beast was't then,
   That made you break this enterprise to me?
   When you durst do it, then you were a man;
   And, to be more than what you were, you would   50
   Be so much more the man. Nor time, nor place,
   Did then adhere, and yet you would make both:
   They have made themselves, and that their fitness
     now
   Does unmake you. I have given suck, and know
   How tender 'tis to love the babe that milks me: 55
   I would, while it was smiling in my face,

Have pluck'd my nipple from his boneless gums,
And dash'd the brains out, had I so sworn
As you have done to this.

MACBETH   If we should fail?

60 LADY MACBETH   We fail?
But screw your courage to the sticking-place,
And we'll not fail. When Duncan is asleep
(Whereto the rather shall his day's hard journey
Soundly invite him), his two chamberlains
65 Will I with wine and wassail so convince,
That memory, the warder of the brain,
Shall be a fume, and the receipt of reason
A limbeck only: when in swinish sleep
Their drenched natures lie, as in a death,
70 What cannot you and I perform upon
Th'unguarded Duncan? what not put upon
His spongy officers, who shall bear the guilt
Of our great quell?

MACBETH   Bring forth men-children only!
For thy undaunted mettle should compose
75 Nothing but males. Will it not be receiv'd,
When we have mark'd with blood those sleepy two
Of his own chamber, and us'd their very daggers,
That they have done't?

LADY MACBETH   Who dares receive it other,
As we shall make our griefs and clamour roar
Upon his death?

80 MACBETH   I am settled, and bend up
Each corporal agent to this terrible feat.
Away, and mock the time with fairest show:
False face must hide what the false heart doth know.
                                        Exeunt.

2.1   *Enter* BANQUO *and* FLEANCE,
                  with a torch before him.

BANQUO   How goes the night, boy?
FLEANCE
The moon is down; I have not heard the clock.
BANQUO   And she goes down at twelve.
FLEANCE   I take't, 'tis later, Sir.
BANQUO
Hold, take my sword. – There's husbandry in
    heaven;
5 Their candles are all out. – Take thee that too.
A heavy summons lies like lead upon me,
And yet I would not sleep: merciful Powers!
Restrain in me the cursed thoughts that nature
Gives way to in repose! – Give me my sword.

    Enter MACBETH, *and a servant with a torch.*

10 Who's there?
MACBETH   A friend.
BANQUO   What, Sir! not yet at rest? The King's a-bed:
He hath been in unusual pleasure, and
Sent forth great largess to your offices.
15 This diamond he greets your wife withal,
By the name of most kind hostess, and shut up

In measureless content.
MACBETH   Being unprepar'd,
Our will became the servant to defect,
Which else should free have wrought.
BANQUO   All's well.
I dreamt last night of the three Weïrd Sisters: 20
To you they have show'd some truth.
MACBETH   I think not of them:
Yet, when we can entreat an hour to serve,
We would spend it in some words upon that
    business,
If you would grant the time.
BANQUO   At your kind'st leisure.
MACBETH   If you shall cleave to my consent, when 'tis,   25
It shall make honour for you.
BANQUO   So I lose none
In seeking to augment it, but still keep
My bosom franchis'd, and allegiance clear,
I shall be counsell'd.
MACBETH   Good repose, the while!
BANQUO   Thanks, Sir: the like to you.   30
                Exeunt Banquo and Fleance.
MACBETH
Go, bid thy mistress, when my drink is ready,
She strike upon the bell. Get thee to bed. –
                                Exit servant.
Is this a dagger, which I see before me,
The handle toward my hand? Come, let me clutch
    thee: –
I have thee not, and yet I see thee still.   35
Art thou not, fatal vision, sensible
To feeling, as to sight? or art thou but
A dagger of the mind, a false creation,
Proceeding from the heat-oppressed brain?
I see thee yet, in form as palpable   40
As this which now I draw.
Thou marshall'st me the way that I was going;
And such an instrument I was to use. –
Mine eyes are made the fools o'th' other senses,
Or else worth all the rest: I see thee still;   45
And on thy blade, and dudgeon, gouts of blood,
Which was not so before. – There's no such thing.
It is the bloody business which informs
Thus to mine eyes. – Now o'er the one half-world
Nature seems dead, and wicked dreams abuse   50
The curtain'd sleep: Witchcraft celebrates
Pale Hecate's off'rings; and wither'd Murther,
Alarum'd by his sentinel, the wolf,
Whose howl's his watch, thus with his stealthy pace,
With Tarquin's ravishing strides, towards his design 55
Moves like a ghost. – Thou sure and firm-set earth,
Hear not my steps, which way they walk, for fear
Thy very stones prate of my where-about,
And take the present horror from the time,
Which now suits with it. – Whiles I threat, he lives: 60
Words to the heat of deeds too cold breath gives.
[*A bell rings.*]

I go, and it is done: the bell invites me.
Hear it not, Duncan; for it is a knell
That summons thee to Heaven, or to Hell.   *Exit.*

2.2   *Enter* LADY MACBETH.

LADY MACBETH
That which hath made them drunk hath made me
    bold:
What hath quench'd them hath given me fire. –
    Hark! – Peace!
It was the owl that shriek'd, the fatal bellman,
Which gives the stern'st good-night. He is about it.
The doors are open; and the surfeited grooms
Do mock their charge with snores: I have drugg'd
    their possets,
That Death and Nature do contend about them,
Whether they live, or die.

MACBETH [*within*]   Who's there? – what, ho!
LADY MACBETH   Alack! I am afraid they have awak'd,
And 'tis not done: – th'attempt and not the deed
Confounds us. – Hark! – I laid their daggers ready;
He could not miss 'em. – Had he not resembled
My father as he slept, I had done't. – My husband!

Enter MACBETH.

MACBETH
I have done the deed. – Didst thou not hear a noise?
LADY MACBETH
I heard the owl scream, and the crickets cry.
Did not you speak?
MACBETH   When?
LADY MACBETH   Now.
MACBETH   As I descended?
LADY MACBETH   Ay.
MACBETH   Hark!
Who lies i'th' second chamber?
LADY MACBETH   Donalbain.
MACBETH   This is a sorry sight.
LADY MACBETH   A foolish thought to say a sorry sight.
MACBETH
There's one did laugh in's sleep, and one cried,
    'Murther!'
That they did wake each other: I stood and heard
    them;
But they did say their prayers, and address'd them
Again to sleep.
LADY MACBETH   There are two lodg'd together.
MACBETH
One cried, 'God bless us!' and, 'Amen,' the other,
As they had seen me with these hangman's hands.
List'ning their fear, I could not say, 'Amen,'
When they did say, 'God bless us.'
LADY MACBETH   Consider it not so deeply.
MACBETH
But wherefore could not I pronounce 'Amen'?
I had most need of blessing, and 'Amen'

Stuck in my throat.
LADY MACBETH   These deeds must not be thought
After these ways: so, it will make us mad.
MACBETH
Methought, I heard a voice cry, 'Sleep no more!
Macbeth does murther Sleep,' – the innocent Sleep;   35
Sleep, that knits up the ravell'd sleave of care,
The death of each day's life, sore labour's bath,
Balm of hurt minds, great Nature's second course,
Chief nourisher in life's feast; –
LADY MACBETH   What do you mean?
MACBETH
Still it cried, 'Sleep no more!' to all the house: 40
'Glamis hath murther'd Sleep, and therefore Cawdor
Shall sleep no more, Macbeth shall sleep no more!'
LADY MACBETH
Who was it that thus cried? Why, worthy Thane,
You do unbend your noble strength, to think
So brainsickly of things. Go, get some water,   45
And wash this filthy witness from your hand. –
Why did you bring these daggers from the place?
They must lie there: go, carry them, and smear
The sleepy grooms with blood.
MACBETH   I'll go no more:
I am afraid to think what I have done;   50
Look on't again I dare not.
LADY MACBETH   Infirm of purpose!
Give me the daggers. The sleeping, and the dead,
Are but as pictures; 'tis the eye of childhood
That fears a painted devil. If he do bleed,
I'll gild the faces of the grooms withal,   55
For it must seem their guilt.   *Exit.*
[*Knocking within.*]
MACBETH   Whence is that knocking? –
How is't with me, when every noise appals me?
What hands are here? Ha! they pluck out mine eyes.
Will all great Neptune's ocean wash this blood
Clean from my hand? No, this my hand will rather   60
The multitudinous seas incarnadine,
Making the green one red.

Re-enter LADY MACBETH.

LADY MACBETH
My hands are of your colour; but I shame
To wear a heart so white. [*knock*] I hear a knocking
At the south entry: – retire we to our chamber.   65
A little water clears us of this deed:
How easy is it then! Your constancy
Hath left you unattended. –
[*knock*]   Hark! more knocking.
Get on your night-gown, lest occasion call us,
And show us to be watchers. – Be not lost   70
So poorly in your thoughts.
MACBETH
To know my deed, 'twere best not know myself.
[*knock*]

Wake Duncan with thy knocking: I would thou
     couldst!   *Exeunt.*

2.3   *Enter a* Porter.

[*knocking within*]

PORTER   Here's a knocking, indeed! If a man were Porter
     of Hell Gate, he should have old turning the key.
     [*knocking*] Knock, knock, knock. Who's there, i'th'
     name of Belzebub? – Here's a farmer, that hang'd
5   himself on th' expectation of plenty: come in, time-
     pleaser; have napkins enow about you; here you'll
     sweat for't. [*knocking*] Knock, knock. Who's there,
     i'th' other devil's name? – Faith, here's an equivocator,
     that could swear in both the scales against either scale;
10   who committed treason enough for God's sake, yet
     could not equivocate to heaven: O! come in,
     equivocator. [*knocking*] Knock, knock, knock. Who's
     there? – Faith, here's an English tailor come hither for
     stealing out of a French hose: come in, tailor; here you
15   may roast your goose. [*knocking*] Knock, knock. Never
     at quiet! What are you? – But this place is too cold for
     Hell. I'll devil-porter it no further: I had thought to
     have let in some of all professions, that go the primrose
     way to th'everlasting bonfire. [*knocking*] Anon, anon:
20   I pray you, remember the Porter. [*Opens the gate.*]

                Enter MACDUFF *and* LENOX.

MACDUFF   Was it so late, friend, ere you went to bed,
     That you do lie so late?
PORTER   Faith, Sir, we were carousing till the second
     cock; and drink, Sir, is a great provoker of three
25   things.
MACDUFF   What three things does drink especially
     provoke?
PORTER   Marry, Sir, nose-painting, sleep, and urine.
     Lechery, Sir, it provokes, and unprovokes: it provokes
30   the desire, but it takes away the performance.
     Therefore, much drink may be said to be an
     equivocator with lechery: it makes him, and it mars
     him; it sets him on, and it takes him off; it persuades
     him, and disheartens him; makes him stand to, and not
35   stand to: in conclusion, equivocates him in a sleep,
     and, giving him the lie, leaves him.
MACDUFF   I believe, drink gave thee the lie last night.
PORTER   That it did, Sir, i'the very throat on me: but I
     requited him for his lie; and (I think) being too strong
40   for him, though he took up my legs sometime, yet I
     made a shift to cast him.
MACDUFF   Is thy master stirring?

                Enter MACBETH.

     Our knocking has awak'd him; here he comes.
LENOX   Good morrow, noble Sir!
MACBETH   Good morrow, both!
MACDUFF   Is the King stirring, worthy Thane?
45   MACBETH   Not yet.

MACDUFF   He did command me to call timely on him:
     I have almost slipp'd the hour.
MACBETH   I'll bring you to him.
MACDUFF   I know, this is a joyful trouble to you;
     But yet 'tis one.
MACBETH   The labour we delight in physics pain.   50
     This is the door.
MACDUFF   I'll make so bold to call,
     For 'tis my limited service.   *Exit.*
LENOX   Goes the King hence to-day?
MACBETH   He does: – he did appoint so.
LENOX   The night has been unruly: where we lay,
     Our chimneys were blown down; and, as they say,   55
     Lamentings heard i'th' air; strange screams of death,
     And, prophesying with accents terrible
     Of dire combustion, and confus'd events,
     New hatch'd to th' woeful time, the obscure bird
     Clamour'd the livelong night: some say, the earth   60
     Was feverous, and did shake.
MACBETH   'Twas a rough night.
LENOX   My young remembrance cannot parallel
     A fellow to it.

                Re-enter MACDUFF.

MACDUFF   O horror! horror! horror!
     Tongue nor heart cannot conceive, nor name thee!
MACBETH, LENOX   What's the matter?   65
MACDUFF   Confusion now hath made his masterpiece!
     Most sacrilegious Murther hath broke ope
     The Lord's anointed Temple, and stole thence
     The life o'th' building!
MACBETH   What is't you say? the life?
LENOX   Mean you his Majesty?
MACDUFF
     Approach the chamber, and destroy your sight   70
     With a new Gorgon. – Do not bid me speak:
     See, and then speak yourselves. –
                Exeunt Macbeth and Lenox.
                        Awake! awake! –
     Ring the alarum-bell. – Murther, and treason!
     Banquo, and Donalbain! Malcolm, awake!
     Shake off this downy sleep, death's counterfeit,   75
     And look on death itself! – up, up, and see
     The great doom's image! – Malcolm! Banquo!
     As from your graves rise up, and walk like sprites,
     To countenance this horror!   [*Bell rings.*]

                Enter LADY MACBETH.

LADY MACBETH   What's the business,
     That such a hideous trumpet calls to parley   80
     The sleepers of the house? speak, speak!
MACDUFF   O gentle lady,
     'Tis not for you to hear what I can speak:
     The repetition, in a woman's ear,
     Would murther as it fell.

                Enter BANQUO.

                O Banquo! Banquo!
  Our royal master's murther'd!
LADY MACBETH   Woe, alas!
  What! in our house?
BANQUO   Too cruel, anywhere.
  Dear Duff, I pr'ythee, contradict thyself,
  And say, it is not so.

      Re-enter MACBETH *and* LENOX.

MACBETH   Had I but died an hour before this chance,
  I had liv'd a blessed time; for, from this instant,
  There's nothing serious in mortality;
  All is but toys: renown, and grace, is dead;
  The wine of life is drawn, and the mere lees
  Is left this vault to brag of.

      Enter MALCOLM *and* DONALBAIN.

DONALBAIN   What is amiss?
MACBETH   You are, and do not know't:
  The spring, the head, the fountain of your blood
  Is stopp'd; the very source of it is stopp'd.
MACDUFF   Your royal father's murther'd.
MALCOLM   O! by whom?
LENOX   Those of his chamber, as it seem'd, had done't:
  Their hands and faces were all badg'd with blood;
  So were their daggers, which, unwip'd, we found
  Upon their pillows: they star'd, and were distracted;
  No man's life was to be trusted with them.
MACBETH   O! yet I do repent me of my fury,
  That I did kill them.
MACDUFF   Wherefore did you so?
MACBETH
  Who can be wise, amaz'd, temperate and furious,
  Loyal and neutral, in a moment? No man:
  Th'expedition of my violent love
  Outrun the pauser, reason. – Here lay Duncan,
  His silver skin lac'd with his golden blood;
  And his gash'd stabs look'd like a breach in nature
  For ruin's wasteful entrance: there, the murtherers.
  Steep'd in the colours of their trade, their daggers
  Unmannerly breech'd with gore. Who could refrain,
  That had a heart to love, and in that heart
  Courage, to make's love known?
LADY MACBETH   Help me hence, ho!
MACDUFF Look to the Lady.
MALCOLM [*aside to Donalbain*]
  Why do we hold our tongues, that most may claim
  This argument for ours?
DONALBAIN [*aside to Malcolm*]   What should be spoken
  Here, where our fate, hid in an auger-hole,
  May rush, and seize us? Let's away:
  Our tears are not yet brew'd.
MALCOLM [*aside to Donalbain*]   Nor our strong sorrow
  Upon the foot of motion.
BANQUO   Look to the Lady: –
             Lady Macbeth is carried out.
  And when we have our naked frailties hid,

That suffer in exposure, let us meet,
  And question this most bloody piece of work,
  To know it further. Fears and scruples shake us:
  In the great hand of God I stand; and thence   130
  Against the undivulg'd pretence I fight
  Of treasonous malice.
MACDUFF   And so do I.
ALL   So all.
MACBETH   Let's briefly put on manly readiness,
  And meet i'th' hall together.
ALL   Well contented.
      Exeunt all but Malcolm and Donalbain.
MALCOLM
  What will you do? Let's not consort with them: 135
  To show an unfelt sorrow is an office
  Which the false man does easy. I'll to England.
DONALBAIN   To Ireland, I: our separated fortune
  Shall keep us both the safer; where we are,
  There's daggers in men's smiles: the near in blood,   140
  The nearer bloody.
MALCOLM   This murtherous shaft that's shot
  Hath not yet lighted, and our safest way
  Is to avoid the aim: therefore, to horse;
  And let us not be dainty of leave-taking,
  But shift away. There's warrant in that theft   145
  Which steals itself, when there's no mercy left.
                   Exeunt.

2.4   *Enter* ROSSE *and an* Old Man.

OLD MAN   Threescore and ten I can remember well;
  Within the volume of which time I have seen
  Hours dreadful, and things strange, but this sore
     night
  Hath trifled former knowings.
ROSSE   Ha, good Father,
  Thou seest the heavens, as troubled with man's act,   5
  Threatens his bloody stage: by th' clock 'tis day,
  And yet dark night strangles the travelling lamp.
  Is't night's predominance, or the day's shame,
  That darkness does the face of earth entomb,
  When living light should kiss it?
OLD MAN   'Tis unnatural,   10
  Even like the deed that's done. On Tuesday last,
  A falcon, towering in her pride of place,
  Was by a mousing owl hawk'd at, and kill'd.
ROSSE
  And Duncan's horses (a thing most strange and
     certain)
  Beauteous and swift, the minions of their race,   15
  Turn'd wild in nature, broke their stalls, flung out,
  Contending 'gainst obedience, as they would make
  War with mankind.
OLD MAN   'Tis said, they eat each other.
ROSSE They did so; to th'amazement of mine eyes,
  That look'd upon't.

      Enter MACDUFF.

20   Here comes the good Macduff.
How goes the world, Sir, now?
MACDUFF   Why, see you not?
ROSSE
Is't known, who did this more than bloody deed?
MACDUFF   Those that Macbeth hath slain.
ROSSE   Alas, the day!
What good could they pretend?
MACDUFF   They were suborn'd.
25   Malcolm, and Donalbain, the King's two sons,
Are stol'n away and fled; which puts upon them
Suspicion of the deed.
ROSSE   'Gainst nature still:
Thriftless Ambition, that will ravin up
Thine own life's means! – Then 'tis most like
30   The sovereignty will fall upon Macbeth.
MACDUFF   He is already nam'd, and gone to Scone
To be invested.
ROSSE   Where is Duncan's body?
MACDUFF   Carried to Colme-kill,
The sacred storehouse of his predecessors,
And guardian of their bones.
35 ROSSE   Will you to Scone?
MACDUFF   No cousin; I'll to Fife.
ROSSE   Well, I will thither.
MACDUFF
Well, may you see things well done there: – adieu! –
Lest our old robes sit easier than our new!
ROSSE   Farewell, Father.
40 OLD MAN   God's benison go with you; and with those
That would make good of bad, and friends of foes!
                                          Exeunt.

3.1   *Enter* BANQUO.

BANQUO   Thou hast it now, King, Cawdor, Glamis, all,
As the Weïrd Women promis'd; and, I fear,
Thou play'dst most foully for't; yet it was said,
It should not stand in thy posterity;
5   But that myself should be the root and father
Of many kings. If there come truth from them
(As upon thee, Macbeth, their speeches shine),
Why, by the verities on thee made good,
May they not be my oracles as well,
10   And set me up in hope? But, hush; no more.

Sennet sounded. Enter MACBETH *as King;*
LADY MACBETH *as Queen;* LENOX, ROSSE,
lords and attendants.

MACBETH   Here's our chief guest.
LADY MACBETH   If he had been forgotten,
It had been as a gap in our great feast,
And all-thing unbecoming.
MACBETH   To-night we hold a solemn supper, Sir,
And I'll request your presence.
15 BANQUO   Let your Highness
Command upon me, to the which my duties

Are with a most indissoluble tie
For ever knit.
MACBETH   Ride you this afternoon?
BANQUO   Ay, my good Lord.
MACBETH
We should have else desir'd your good advice   20
(Which still hath been both grave and prosperous)
In this day's council; but we'll take to-morrow.
Is't far you ride?
BANQUO   As far, my Lord, as will fill up the time
'Twixt this and supper: go not my horse the better, 25
I must become a borrower of the night,
For a dark hour, or twain.
MACBETH   Fail not our feast.
BANQUO   My Lord, I will not.
MACBETH   We hear, our bloody cousins are bestow'd
In England, and in Ireland; not confessing   30
Their cruel parricide, filling their hearers
With strange invention. But of that to-morrow,
When, therewithal, we shall have cause of State,
Craving us jointly. Hie you to horse: adieu,
Till you return at night. Goes Fleance with you? 35
BANQUO   Ay, my good Lord: our time does call upon's.
MACBETH   I wish your horses swift, and sure of foot;
And so I do commend you to their backs.
Farewell. –   *Exit Banquo.*
Let every man be master of his time   40
Till seven at night;
To make society the sweeter welcome,
We will keep ourself till supper-time alone:
While then, God be with you.
              Exeunt all except Macbeth and a Servant.
                        Sirrah, a word with you.
Attend those men our pleasure?
SERVANT   They are, my Lord,   45
Without the palace gate.
MACBETH   Bring them before us.
                                  Exit Servant.
To be thus is nothing, but to be safely thus:
Our fears in Banquo
Stick deep, and in his royalty of nature
Reigns that which would be fear'd: 'tis much he
    dares;   50
And, to that dauntless temper of his mind,
He hath a wisdom that doth guide his valour
To act in safety. There is none but he
Whose being I do fear: and under him
My Genius is rebuk'd; as, it is said,   55
Mark Antony's was by Caesar. He chid the Sisters,
When first they put the name of King upon me,
And bade them speak to him; then, prophet-like,
They hail'd him father to a line of kings:
Upon my head they plac'd a fruitless crown,   60
And put a barren sceptre in my gripe,
Thence to be wrench'd with an unlineal hand,
No son of mine succeeding. If't be so,
For Banquo's issue have I fil'd my mind;

For them the gracious Duncan have I murther'd;
Put rancours in the vessel of my peace,
Only for them; and mine eternal jewel
Given to the common Enemy of man,
To make them kings, the seed of Banquo kings!
Rather than so, come, fate, into the list,
And champion me to th'utterance! – Who's there? –

Re-enter Servant, *with two* Murderers.

Now, go to the door, and stay there till we call.
Exit Servant.

Was it not yesterday we spoke together?
1 MURDERER   It was, so please your Highness.
MACBETH   Well then, now
Have you consider'd of my speeches? – know
That it was he, in the times past, which held you
So under fortune, which you thought had been
Our innocent self? This I made good to you
In our last conference; pass'd in probation with you,
How you were borne in hand; how cross'd; the
    instruments;
Who wrought with them; and all things else, that
    might,
To half a soul, and to a notion craz'd,
Say, 'Thus did Banquo.'
1 MURDERER   You made it known to us.
MACBETH   I did so; and went further, which is now
Our point of second meeting. Do you find
Your patience so predominant in your nature,
That you can let this go? Are you so gospell'd,
To pray for this good man, and for his issue,
Whose heavy hand hath bow'd you to the grave,
And beggar'd yours for ever?
1 MURDERER   We are men, my Liege.
MACBETH   Ay, in the catalogue ye go for men;
As hounds, and greyhounds, mongrels, spaniels,
    curs,
Shoughs, water-rugs, and demi-wolves, are clept
All by the name of dogs: the valu'd file
Distinguishes the swift, the slow, the subtle,
The housekeeper, the hunter, every one
According to the gift which bounteous Nature
Hath in him clos'd; whereby he does receive
Particular addition, from the bill
That writes them all alike; and so of men.
Now, if you have a station in the file,
Not i'th' worst rank of manhood, say't;
And I will put that business in your bosoms,
Whose execution takes your enemy off,
Grapples you to the heart and love of us,
Who wear our health but sickly in his life,
Which in his death were perfect.
2 MURDERER   I am one, my Liege,
Whom the vile blows and buffets of the world
Hath so incens'd, that I am reckless what
I do, to spite the world.
1 MURDERER   And I another,

So weary with disasters, tugg'd with fortune,
That I would set my life on any chance,
To mend it, or be rid on't.
MACBETH   Both of you
Know, Banquo was your enemy.
2 MURDERER   True, my Lord.
MACBETH   So is he mine; and in such bloody distance,   115
That every minute of his being thrusts
Against my near'st of life: and though I could
With bare-fac'd power sweep him from my sight,
And bid my will avouch it, yet I must not,
For certain friends that are both his and mine,   120
Whose loves I may not drop, but wail his fall
Who I myself struck down: and thence it is
That I to your assistance do make love,
Masking the business from the common eye,
For sundry weighty reasons.
2 MURDERER   We shall, my Lord,   125
Perform what you command us.
1 MURDERER   Though our lives –
MACBETH
Your spirits shine through you. Within this hour, at
    most,
I will advise you where to plant yourselves,
Acquaint you with the perfect spy o'th' time,
The moment on't; for't must be done to-night,   130
And something from the palace; always thought,
That I require a clearness: and with him
(To leave no rubs nor botches in the work),
Fleance his son, that keeps him company,
Whose absence is no less material to me   135
Than is his father's, must embrace the fate
Of that dark hour. Resolve yourselves apart;
I'll come to you anon.
2 MURDERER   We are resolv'd, my Lord.
MACBETH   I'll call upon you straight: abide within. –
Exeunt Murderers.
It is concluded: Banquo, thy soul's flight,   140
If it find Heaven, must find it out to-night.   *Exit.*

3.2   *Enter* LADY MACBETH *and a* Servant.

LADY MACBETH   Is Banquo gone from court?
SERVANT   Ay, Madam, but returns again to-night.
LADY MACBETH
Say to the King, I would attend his leisure
For a few words.
SERVANT   Madam, I will.   *Exit.*
LADY MACBETH   Nought's had, all's spent,
Where our desire is got without content: 5
'Tis safer to be that which we destroy,
Than by destruction dwell in doubtful joy.

Enter MACBETH.

How now, my Lord? why do you keep alone,
Of sorriest fancies your companions making,
Using those thoughts, which should indeed have died   10

With them they think on? Things without all remedy
Should be without regard: what's done is done.
MACBETH   We have scorch'd the snake, not kill'd it:
She'll close, and be herself; whilst our poor malice
Remains in danger of her former tooth.
But let the frame of things disjoint, both the worlds
suffer,
Ere we will eat our meal in fear, and sleep
In the affliction of these terrible dreams,
That shake us nightly. Better be with the dead,
Whom we, to gain our peace, have sent to peace,
Than on the torture of the mind to lie
In restless ecstasy. Duncan is in his grave;
After life's fitful fever he sleeps well;
Treason has done his worst: nor steel, nor poison,
Malice domestic, foreign levy, nothing
Can touch him further!
LADY MACBETH   Come on:
Gentle my Lord, sleek o'er your rugged looks;
Be bright and jovial among your guests to-night.
MACBETH   So shall I, Love; and so, I pray, be you.
Let your remembrance apply to Banquo:
Present him eminence, both with eye and tongue:
Unsafe the while, that we
Must lave our honours in these flattering streams,
And make our faces vizards to our hearts,
Disguising what they are.
LADY MACBETH   You must leave this
MACBETH   O! full of scorpions is my mind, dear wife!
Thou know'st that Banquo, and his Fleance, lives.
LADY MACBETH
But in them Nature's copy's not eterne.
MACBETH   There's comfort yet; they are assailable:
Then be thou jocund. Ere the bat hath flown
His cloister'd flight; ere to black Hecate's summons
The shard-born beetle, with his drowsy hums,
Hath rung Night's yawning peal, there shall be done
A deed of dreadful note.
LADY MACBETH   What's to be done?
MACBETH
Be innocent of the knowledge, dearest chuck,
Till thou applaud the deed. Come, seeling Night,
Scarf up the tender eye of pitiful Day,
And, with thy bloody and invisible hand,
Cancel, and tear to pieces, that great bond
Which keeps me pale! – Light thickens; and the crow
Makes wing to th' rooky wood;
Good things of Day begin to droop and drowse,
Whiles Night's black agents to their preys do rouse.
Thou marvell'st at my words: but hold thee still;
Things bad begun make strong themselves by ill.
So, pr'ythee, go with me.   *Exeunt.*

3.3   *Enter three* Murderers.

1 MURDERER   But who did bid thee join with us?
3 MURDERER   Macbeth.

2 MURDERER
He needs not our mistrust; since he delivers
Our offices, and what we have to do,
To the direction just.
1 MURDERER   Then stand with us.
The west yet glimmers with some streaks of day;
Now spurs the lated traveller apace,
To gain the timely inn; and near approaches
The subject of our watch.
3 MURDERER   Hark! I hear horses.
BANQUO [*within*]   Give us a light there, ho!
2 MURDERER   Then 'tis he: the rest
That are within the note of expectation,
Already are i'th' court.
1 MURDERER   His horses go about.
3 MURDERER   Almost a mile; but he does usually,
So all men do, from hence to the palace gate
Make it their walk.

Enter BANQUO *and* FLEANCE, *with a torch.*

2 MURDERER   A light, a light!
3 MURDERER   'Tis he.
1 MURDERER   Stand to't.
BANQUO   It will be rain to-night.
1 MURDERER   Let it come down.
[*The First Murderer strikes out the light, while the others
assault Banquo.*]
BANQUO   O, treachery! Fly, good Fleance, fly, fly, fly!
Thou may'st revenge – O slave! [*Dies.*]
            Fleance escapes.
3 MURDERER   Who did strike out the light?
1 MURDERER   Was't not the way?
3 MURDERER   There's but one down: the son is fled.
2 MURDERER   We have lost
Best half of our affair.
1 MURDERER   Well, let's away,
And say how much is done.   *Exeunt.*

3.4   *A banquet prepared. Enter* MACBETH,
            LADY MACBETH, ROSSE, LENOX,
            Lords *and attendants.*

MACBETH
You know your own degrees, sit down: at first
And last, the hearty welcome.
LORDS   Thanks to your Majesty.
MACBETH   Ourself will mingle with society,
And play the humble host.
Our hostess keeps her state; but, in best time,
We will require her welcome.
LADY MACBETH
Pronounce it for me, Sir, to all our friends;
For my heart speaks, they are welcome.

Enter First Murderer, *to the door.*

MACBETH
See, they encounter thee with their hearts' thanks.

Both sides are even: here I'll sit i'th' midst.
Be large in mirth; anon, we'll drink a measure
The table round. [*Goes to door.*]
There's blood upon thy face.

1 MURDERER   'Tis Banquo's then.

MACBETH   'Tis better thee without, than he within.
Is he dispatch'd?

1 MURDERER   My Lord, his throat is cut;
That I did for him.

MACBETH   Thou art the best o'th' cut-throats;
Yet he's good that did the like for Fleance:
If thou didst it, thou art the nonpareil.

1 MURDERER   Most royal Sir . . . Fleance is scap'd.

MACBETH

Then comes my fit again: I had else been perfect;
Whole as the marble, founded as the rock,
As broad and general as the casing air:
But now, I am cabin'd, cribb'd, confin'd, bound in
To saucy doubts and fears. – But Banquo's safe?

1 MURDERER

Ay, my good Lord, safe in a ditch he bides,
With twenty trenched gashes on his head;
The least a death to nature.

MACBETH   Thanks for that. –
There the grown serpent lies; the worm, that's fled,
Hath nature that in time will venom breed,
No teeth for th' present. – Get thee gone; to-morrow
We'll hear ourselves again.   *Exit Murderer.*

LADY MACBETH   My royal Lord,
You do not give the cheer: the feast is sold,
That is not often vouch'd, while 'tis a-making,
'Tis given with welcome: to feed were best at home;
From thence, the sauce to meat is ceremony;
Meeting were bare without it.

MACBETH   Sweet remembrancer! –
Now, good digestion wait on appetite,
And health on both!

LENOX   May it please your Highness sit?

MACBETH

Here had we now our country's honour roof'd,
Were the grac'd person of our Banquo present;

The ghost of BANQUO *enters,
and sits in Macbeth's place.*

Who may I rather challenge for unkindness,
Than pity for mischance!

ROSSE   His absence, Sir,
Lays blame upon his promise. Please't your Highness
To grace us with your royal company?

MACBETH   The table's full.

LENOX   Here is a place reserv'd, Sir.

MACBETH   Where?

LENOX

Here, my good Lord. What is't that moves your
    Highness?

MACBETH   Which of you have done this?

LORDS   What, my good Lord?

MACBETH   Thou canst not say, I did it: never shake
Thy gory locks at me.

ROSSE   Gentlemen, rise; his Highness is not well.

LADY MACBETH

Sit, worthy friends. My Lord is often thus,
And hath been from his youth: pray you, keep seat;
The fit is momentary; upon a thought
He will again be well. If much you note him,
You shall offend him, and extend his passion;
Feed, and regard him not. – Are you a man?

MACBETH   Ay, and a bold one, that dare look on that
Which might appal the Devil.

LADY MACBETH   O proper stuff!
This is the very painting of your fear:
This is the air-drawn dagger, which, you said,
Led you to Duncan. O! these flaws and starts
(Impostors to true fear), would well become
A woman's story at a winter's fire,
Authoris'd by her grandam. Shame itself!
Why do you make such faces? When all's done,
You look but on a stool.

MACBETH   Pr'ythee, see there!
Behold! look! lo! how say you?
Why, what care I? If thou canst nod, speak too. –
If charnel-houses and our graves must send
Those that we bury, back, our monuments
Shall be the maws of kites.   *Ghost disappears.*

LADY MACBETH   What! quite unmann'd in folly?

MACBETH   If I stand here, I saw him.

LADY MACBETH   Fie! for shame!

MACBETH

Blood hath been shed ere now, i'th' olden time,
Ere humane statute purg'd the gentle weal;
Ay, and since too, murthers have been perform'd
Too terrible for the ear: the time has been,
That, when the brains were out, the man would die,
And there an end; but now, they rise again,
With twenty mortal murthers on their crowns,
And push us from our stools. This is more strange
Than such a murther is.

LADY MACBETH   My worthy Lord,
Your noble friends do lack you.

MACBETH   I do forget. –
Do not muse at me, my most worthy friends,
I have a strange infirmity, which is nothing
To those that know me. Come, love and health to all;
Then, I'll sit down. – Give me some wine: fill full: –
I drink to th' general joy o'th' whole table,
And to our dear friend Banquo, whom we miss;
Would he were here!

Re-enter ghost.

                To all, and him, we thirst,
And all to all.

LORDS   Our duties, and the pledge.

MACBETH

Avaunt! and quit my sight! let the earth hide thee!

785

Thy bones are marrowless, thy blood is cold;
Thou hast no speculation in those eyes,
Which thou dost glare with.

95 LADY MACBETH　　　　　　　Think of this, good Peers,
But as a thing of custom: 'tis no other;
Only it spoils the pleasure of the time.

MACBETH　What man dare, I dare:
Approach thou like the rugged Russian bear,
100 The arm'd rhinoceros, or th'Hyrcan tiger;
Take any shape but that, and my firm nerves
Shall never tremble: or, be alive again,
And dare me to the desert with thy sword;
If trembling I inhabit then, protest me
105 The baby of a girl. Hence, horrible shadow!
Unreal mock'ry, hence! –　　　　　*Ghost disappears.*
　　　　　　　　　Why, so; – being gone,
I am a man again. – Pray you, sit still.

LADY MACBETH
You have displac'd the mirth, broke the good meeting
With most admir'd disorder.

MACBETH　　　　　　　Can such things be,
110 And overcome us like a summer's cloud,
Without our special wonder? You make me strange
Even to the disposition that I owe,
When now I think you can behold such sights,
And keep the natural ruby of your cheeks,
When mine is blanch'd with fear.

115 ROSSE　　　　　　　What sights, my Lord?

LADY MACBETH
I pray you, speak not; he grows worse and worse;
Question enrages him. At once, good night: –
Stand not upon the order of your going,
But go at once.

LENOX　　　　Good night, and better health
Attend his Majesty!

120 LADY MACBETH　　　　A kind good night to all!
　　　　　　　Exeunt Lords and attendants.

MACBETH
It will have blood, they say: blood will have blood:
Stones have been known to move, and trees to speak;
Augures, and understood relations, have
By magot-pies, and choughs, and rooks, brought
　forth
125 The secret'st man of blood. – What is the night?

LADY MACBETH
Almost at odds with morning, which is which.

MACBETH
How say'st thou, that Macduff denies his person,
At our great bidding?

LADY MACBETH　　　　Did you send to him, Sir?

MACBETH　I heard it by the way; but I will send.
130 There's not a one of them, but in his house
I keep a servant fee'd. I will to-morrow
(And betimes I will) to the Weïrd Sisters:
More shall they speak; for now I am bent to know,
By the worst means, the worst. For mine own good,
135 All causes shall give way: I am in blood

Stepp'd in so far, that, should I wade no more,
Returning were as tedious as go o'er.
Strange things I have in head, that will to hand,
Which must be acted, ere they may be scann'd.

LADY MACBETH　You lack the season of all natures, sleep.　140

MACBETH
Come, we'll to sleep. My strange and self-abuse
Is the initiate fear, that wants hard use:
We are yet but young in deed.　　　　*Exeunt.*

3.5 *Thunder. Enter the three* Witches, *meeting* HECATE.

1 WITCH　Why, how now, Hecate? you look angerly.

HECATE　Have I not reason, beldams as you are,
Saucy, and overbold? How did you dare
To trade and traffic with Macbeth,
In riddles, and affairs of death;　　　　　5
And I, the mistress of your charms,
The close contriver of all harms,
Was never call'd to bear my part,
Or show the glory of our art?
And, which is worse, all you have done　　10
Hath been but for a wayward son,
Spiteful, and wrathful; who, as others do,
Loves for his own ends, not for you.
But make amends now: get you gone,
And at the pit of Acheron　　　　　15
Meet me i'th' morning: thither he
Will come to know his destiny.
Your vessels, and your spells, provide,
Your charms, and everything beside.
I am for th'air; this night I'll spend　　20
Unto a dismal and a fatal end:
Great business must be wrought ere noon.
Upon the corner of the moon
There hangs a vap'rous drop profound;
I'll catch it ere it come to ground:　　25
And that, distill'd by magic sleights,
Shall raise such artificial sprites,
As, by the strength of their illusion,
Shall draw him on to his confusion.
He shall spurn fate, scorn death, and bear　30
His hopes 'bove wisdom, grace, and fear;
And you all know, security
Is mortals' chiefest enemy.
　　　[*Song within:* 'Come away, come away,' *etc.*]
Hark! I am call'd: my little spirit, see,
Sits in a foggy cloud, and stays for me. *Exit.*　35

1 WITCH
Come, let's make haste: she'll soon be back again.
　　　　　　　　　　Exeunt.

3.6　　　　　*Enter* LENOX *and another* Lord.

LENOX　My former speeches have but hit your thoughts,
Which can interpret farther: only, I say,
Things have been strangely borne. The gracious
　Duncan

Was pitied of Macbeth: – marry, he was dead: –
5   And the right-valiant Banquo walk'd too late;
Whom, you may say (if't please you) Fleance kill'd,
For Fleance fled. Men must not walk too late.
Who cannot want the thought, how monstrous
It was for Malcolm, and for Donalbain,
10   To kill their gracious father? damned fact!
How it did grieve Macbeth! did he not straight,
In pious rage, the two delinquents tear,
That were the slaves of drink, and thralls of sleep?
Was not that nobly done? Ay, and wisely too;
15   For 'twould have anger'd any heart alive
To hear the men deny't. So that, I say,
He has borne all things well: and I do think,
That, had he Duncan's sons under his key
(As, and't please Heaven, he shall not), they should
   find
20   What 'twere to kill a father; so should Fleance.
But, peace! – for from broad words, and 'cause he
   fail'd
His presence at the tyrant's feast, I hear,
Macduff lives in disgrace. Sir, can you tell
Where he bestows himself?

LORD   The son of Duncan,
25   From whom this tyrant holds the due of birth,
Lives in the English court; and is receiv'd
Of the most pious Edward with such grace,
That the malevolence of fortune nothing
Takes from his high respect. Thither Macduff
30   Is gone to pray the holy King, upon his aid
To wake Northumberland, and warlike Siward;
That, by the help of these (with Him above
To ratify the work), we may again
Give to our tables meat, sleep to our nights,
35   Free from our feasts and banquets bloody knives,
Do faithful homage, and receive free honours,
All which we pine for now. And this report
Hath so exasperate the King, that he
Prepares for some attempt of war.

LENOX   Sent he to Macduff?
40   LORD   He did: and with an absolute 'Sir, not I,'
The cloudy messenger turns me his back,
And hums, as who should say, 'You'll rue the time
That clogs me with this answer.'

LENOX   And that well might
Advise him to a caution, t'hold what distance
45   His wisdom can provide. Some holy Angel
Fly to the court of England, and unfold
His message ere he come, that a swift blessing
May soon return to this our suffering country
Under a hand accurs'd!

LORD   I'll send my prayers with him.
Exeunt.

4.1   *Thunder. Enter the three* Witches.

1 WITCH   Thrice the brinded cat hath mew'd.
2 WITCH   Thrice, and once the hedge-pig whin'd.

3 WITCH   Harpier cries: – 'Tis time, 'tis time.
1 WITCH   Round about the cauldron go;
5   In the poison'd entrails throw. –
         Toad, that under cold stone
         Days and nights has thirty-one
         Swelter'd venom, sleeping got,
         Boil thou first i'th' charmed pot.
ALL   Double, double toil and trouble: 10
         Fire, burn; and, cauldron, bubble.
2 WITCH   Fillet of a fenny snake,
         In the cauldron boil and bake;
         Eye of newt, and toe of frog,
         Wool of bat, and tongue of dog,   15
         Adder's fork, and blind-worm's sting,
         Lizard's leg, and howlet's wing,
         For a charm of powerful trouble,
         Like a hell-broth boil and bubble.
ALL   Double, double toil and trouble: 20
         Fire, burn; and, cauldron, bubble.
3 WITCH   Scale of dragon, tooth of wolf;
         Witches' mummy; maw, and gulf,
         Of the ravin'd salt-sea shark;
         Root of hemlock, digg'd i'th' dark;   25
         Liver of blaspheming Jew;
         Gall of goat, and slips of yew,
         Sliver'd in the moon's eclipse;
         Nose of Turk, and Tartar's lips;
         Finger of birth-strangled babe,   30
         Ditch-deliver'd by a drab,
         Make the gruel thick and slab:
         Add thereto a tiger's chaudron,
         For th'ingredient of our cauldron.
ALL   Double, double toil and trouble: 35
         Fire, burn; and, cauldron, bubble.
2 WITCH   Cool it with a baboon's blood:
         Then the charm is firm and good.

Enter HECATE, *and the other three witches.*

HECATE   O, well done! I commend your pains,
         And every one shall share i'th' gains.   40
         And now about the cauldron sing,
         Like elves and fairies in a ring,
         Enchanting all that you put in.
            [*Music and a song, 'Black spirits,' etc.*]
            [*Exeunt Hecate and the three other witches.*]
2 WITCH   By the pricking of my thumbs,
         Something wicked this way comes. –   45
[*knocking*]
         Open, locks,
         Whoever knocks.

Enter MACBETH.

MACBETH
         How now, you secret, black, and midnight hags!
         What is't you do?
ALL   A deed without a name.
MACBETH   I conjure you, by that which you profess,   50

Howe'er you come to know it, answer me:
Though you untie the winds, and let them fight
Against the Churches; though the yesty waves
Confound and swallow navigation up;
Though bladed corn be lodg'd, and trees blown
    down;   55
Though castles topple on their warders' heads;
Though palaces, and pyramids, do slope
Their heads to their foundations; though the treasure
Of Nature's germens tumble all together,
Even till destruction sicken, answer me   60
To what I ask you.
1 WITCH   Speak.
2 WITCH   Demand.
3 WITCH   We'll answer.
1 WITCH
  Say, if thou'dst rather hear it from our mouths,
  Or from our masters?
MACBETH   Call 'em; let me see 'em.
1 WITCH   Pour in sow's blood, that hath eaten
          Her nine farrow; grease, that's sweaten   65
          From the murderer's gibbet, throw
          Into the flame.
ALL   Come, high, or low;
          Thyself and office deftly show.

Thunder. First Apparition, *an armed head.*

MACBETH   Tell me, thou unknown power, –
1 WITCH   He knows thy thought:
  Hear his speech, but say thou nought.   70
1 APPARITION
  Macbeth! Macbeth! Macbeth! beware Macduff;
  Beware the Thane of Fife. – Dismiss me. – Enough.
                        Descends.
MACBETH
  Whate'er thou art, for thy good caution, thanks:
  Thou hast harp'd my fear aright. – But one word
      more: –
1 WITCH   He will not be commanded. Here's another,   75
  More potent than the first.

Thunder. Second Apparition, *a bloody child.*

2 APPARITION   Macbeth! Macbeth! Macbeth! –
MACBETH   Had I three ears, I'd hear thee.
2 APPARITION
  Be bloody, bold, and resolute: laugh to scorn
  The power of man, for none of woman born   80
  Shall harm Macbeth.   *Descends.*
MACBETH
  Then live, Macduff: what need I fear of thee?
  But yet I'll make assurance double sure,
  And take a bond of Fate: thou shalt not live;
  That I may tell pale-hearted fear it lies,   85
  And sleep in spite of thunder. –

Thunder. Third Apparition, *a child crowned,*
with a tree in his hand.

                  What is this,
That rises like the issue of a king;
And wears upon his baby brow the round
And top of sovereignty?
ALL   Listen, but speak not to't.
3 APPARITION   Be lion-mettled, proud, and take no care   90
  Who chafes, who frets, or where conspirers are:
  Macbeth shall never vanquish'd be, until
  Great Birnam wood to high Dunsinane hill
  Shall come against him.   *Descends.*
MACBETH   That will never be:
  Who can impress the forest; bid the tree   95
  Unfix his earth-bound root? Sweet bodements! good!
  Rebellious dead, rise never, till the wood
  Of Birnam rise; and our high-plac'd Macbeth
  Shall live the lease of Nature, pay his breath
  To time, and mortal custom. – Yet my heart   100
  Throbs to know one thing: tell me (if your art
  Can tell so much), shall Banquo's issue ever
  Reign in this kingdom?
ALL   Seek to know no more.
MACBETH   I will be satisfied: deny me this,
  And an eternal curse fall on you! Let me know. –   105
  Why sinks that cauldron? and what noise is this?
                       [Hautboys.]
1 WITCH   Show!
2 WITCH   Show!
3 WITCH   Show!
ALL   Show his eyes, and grieve his heart;   110
     Come like shadows, so depart.

A show of eight kings, the last with a glass in his hand;
BANQUO *following.*

MACBETH
  Thou art too like the spirit of Banquo: down!
  Thy crown does sear mine eye-balls: – and thy hair,
  Thou other gold-bound brow, is like the first: –
  A third is like the former: – filthy hags!   115
  Why do you show me this? – A fourth? – Start, eyes!
  What! will the line stretch out to th'crack of doom?
  Another yet? – A seventh? – I'll see no more: –
  And yet the eighth appears, who bears a glass,
  Which shows me many more; and some I see,   120
  That two-fold balls and treble sceptres carry.
  Horrible sight! – Now, I see, 'tis true;
  For the blood-bolter'd Banquo smiles upon me,
  And points at them for his. – What! is this so?
1 WITCH   Ay, Sir, all this is so: – but why   125
          Stands Macbeth thus amazedly? –
          Come, sisters, cheer we up his sprites,
          And show the best of our delights.
          I'll charm the air to give a sound,
          While you perform your antic round;   130
          That this great King may kindly say,
          Our duties did his welcome pay.
          Music. The Witches dance, and vanish.

MACBETH

    Where are they? Gone? – Let this pernicious hour

    Stand aye accursed in the calendar! –

    Come in, without there!

Enter LENOX.

135   LENOX   What's your Grace's will?

LENOX   Saw you the Weïrd Sisters?

LENOX   No, my Lord.

MACBETH   Came they not by you?

LENOX   No, indeed, my Lord.

MACBETH   Infected be the air whereon they ride;

    And damn'd all those that trust them! – I did hear

140   The galloping of horse: who was't came by?

LENOX

    'Tis two or three, my Lord, that bring you word,

    Macduff is fled to England.

MACBETH   Fled to England?

LENOX   Ay, my good Lord.

MACBETH [*aside*]

    Time, thou anticipat'st my dread exploits:

145   The flighty purpose never is o'ertook,

    Unless the deed go with it. From this moment,

    The very firstlings of my heart shall be

    The firstlings of my hand. And even now,

    To crown my thoughts with acts, be it thought and done:

150   The castle of Macduff I will surprise;

    Seize upon Fife; give to th'edge o'th' sword

    His wife, his babes, and all unfortunate souls

    That trace him in his line. No boasting like a fool;

    This deed I'll do, before this purpose cool:

155   But no more sights! – Where are these gentlemen?

    Come, bring me where they are.   *Exeunt.*

4.2   *Enter* LADY MACDUFF, *her* Son *and* ROSSE.

LADY MACDUFF

    What had he done, to make him fly the land?

ROSSE   You must have patience, Madam.

LADY MACDUFF   He had none:

    His flight was madness: when our actions do not,

    Our fears do make us traitors.

ROSSE   You know not,

5   Whether it was his wisdom, or his fear.

LADY MACDUFF

    Wisdom! to leave his wife, to leave his babes,

    His mansion, and his titles, in a place

    From whence himself does fly? He loves us not:

    He wants the natural touch; for the poor wren,

10   The most diminitive of birds, will fight,

    Her young ones in her nest, against the owl.

    All is the fear, and nothing is the love;

    As little is the wisdom, where the flight

    So runs against all reason.

ROSSE   My dearest coz,

I pray you, school yourself: but, for your husband,   15

He is noble, wise, judicious, and best knows

The fits o'th' season. I dare not speak much further:

But cruel are the times, when we are traitors,

And do not know ourselves; when we hold rumour

From what we fear, yet know not what we fear,   20

But float upon a wild and violent sea

Each way, and move – I take my leave of you:

Shall not be long but I'll be here again.

Things at the worst will cease, or else climb upward

To what they were before. – My pretty cousin,   25

Blessing upon you!

LADY MACDUFF   Father'd he is, and yet he's fatherless.

ROSSE   I am so much a fool, should I stay longer,

    It would be my disgrace, and your discomfort:

    I take my leave at once.   *Exit.*

LADY MACDUFF   Sirrah, your father's dead: 30

    And what will you do now? How will you live?

SON   As birds do, mother.

LADY MACDUFF   What, with worms and flies?

SON   With what I get, I mean; and so do they.

LADY MACDUFF

    Poor bird! thou'dst never fear the net, nor lime,

    The pit-fall, nor the gin.

SON   Why should I, mother?   35

    Poor birds they are not set for.

    My father is not dead, for all your saying.

LADY MACDUFF

    Yes, he is dead: how wilt thou do for a father?

SON   Nay, how will you do for a husband?

LADY MACDUFF

    Why, I can buy me twenty at any market.   40

SON   Then you'll buy 'em to sell again.

LADY MACDUFF   Thou speak'st with all thy wit;

    And yet, i'faith, with wit enough for thee.

SON   Was my father a traitor, mother?

LADY MACDUFF   Ay, that he was.   45

SON   What is a traitor?

LADY MACDUFF   Why, one that swears and lies.

SON   And be all traitors that do so?

LADY MACDUFF   Every one that does so is a traitor, and

    must be hang'd.   50

SON   And must they all be hang'd that swear and lie?

LADY MACDUFF   Every one.

SON   Who must hang them?

LADY MACDUFF   Why, the honest men.

SON   Then the liars and swearers are fools; for there are   55

    liars and swearers enow to beat the honest men, and

    hang up them.

LADY MACDUFF   Now God help thee, poor monkey! But

    how wilt thou do for a father?

SON   If he were dead, you'd weep for him: if you would   60

    not, it were a good sign that I should quickly have a

    new father.

LADY MACDUFF   Poor prattler, how thou talk'st!

Enter a Messenger.

MESSENGER

  Bless you, fair dame! I am not to you known,

65   Though in your state of honour I am perfect.

  I doubt, some danger does approach you nearly:

  If you will take a homely man's advice,

  Be not found here; hence, with your little ones.

  To fright you thus, methinks, I am too savage;

70   To do worse to you were fell cruelty,

  Which is too nigh your person. Heaven preserve you!

  I dare abide no longer.   *Exit.*

LADY MACDUFF   Whither should I fly?

  I have done no harm. But I remember now

  I am in this earthly world, where, to do harm

75   Is often laudable; to do good, sometime

  Accounted dangerous folly: why then, alas!

  Do I put up that womanly defence,

  To say, I have done no harm? What are these faces!

Enter Murderers.

1 MURDERER   Where is your husband?

80 LADY MACDUFF   I hope, in no place so unsanctified,

  Where such as thou may'st find him.

1 MURDERER   He's a traitor.

SON   Thou liest, thou shag-hair'd villain!

1 MURDERER   What, you egg!

85   [*stabbing him*] Young fry of treachery!

SON   He has kill'd me, mother:

  Run away, I pray you! [*Dies.*]

Exit Lady Macduff, crying 'Murther!'
and pursued by the Murderers.

4.3   *Enter* MALCOLM *and* MACDUFF.

MALCOLM

  Let us seek out some desolate shade, and there

  Weep our sad bosoms empty.

MACDUFF   Let us rather

  Hold fast the mortal sword, and like good men

  Bestride our downfall birthdom. Each new morn,

5   New widows howl, new orphans cry; new sorrows

  Strike heaven on the face, that it resounds

  As if it felt with Scotland, and yell'd out

  Like syllable of dolour.

MALCOLM   What I believe, I'll wail;

  What know, believe; and what I can redress,

10   As I shall find the time to friend, I will.

  What you have spoke, it may be so, perchance.

  This tyrant, whose sole name blisters our tongues,

  Was once thought honest: you have lov'd him well;

  He hath not touch'd you yet. I am young; but something

  You may deserve of him through me, and wisdom

15   To offer up a weak, poor, innocent lamb,

  T'appease an angry god.

MACDUFF   I am not treacherous.

MALCOLM   But Macbeth is.

  A good and virtuous nature may recoil,

  In an imperial charge. But I shall crave your pardon: 20

  That which you are my thoughts cannot transpose:

  Angels are bright still, though the brightest fell:

  Though all things foul would wear the brows of grace,

  Yet Grace must still look so.

MACDUFF   I have lost my hopes.

MALCOLM

  Perchance even there where I did find my doubts. 25

  Why in that rawness left you wife and child

  (Those precious motives, those strong knots of love),

  Without leave-taking? – I pray you,

  Let not my jealousies be your dishonours,

  But mine own safeties: you may be rightly just, 30

  Whatever I shall think.

MACDUFF   Bleed, bleed, poor country!

  Great tyranny, lay thou thy basis sure,

  For goodness dare not check thee! wear thou thy wrongs;

  The title is affeer'd! – Fare thee well, Lord:

  I would not be the villain that thou think'st 35

  For the whole space that's in the tyrant's grasp,

  And the rich East to boot.

MALCOLM   Be not offended:

  I speak not as in absolute fear of you.

  I think our country sinks beneath the yoke;

  It weeps, it bleeds; and each new day a gash 40

  Is added to her wounds: I think, withal,

  There would be hands uplifted in my right;

  And here, from gracious England, have I offer

  Of goodly thousands: but, for all this,

  When I shall tread upon the tyrant's head, 45

  Or wear it on my sword, yet my poor country

  Shall have more vices than it had before,

  More suffer, and more sundry ways than ever,

  By him that shall succeed.

MACDUFF   What should he be?

MALCOLM   It is myself I mean; in whom I know 50

  All the particulars of vice so grafted,

  That, when they shall be open'd, black Macbeth

  Will seem as pure as snow; and the poor State

  Esteem him as a lamb, being compar'd

  With my confineless harms.

MACDUFF   Not in the legions 55

  Of horrid Hell can come a devil more damn'd

  In evils, to top Macbeth.

MALCOLM   I grant him bloody,

  Luxurious, avaricious, false, deceitful,

  Sudden, malicious, smacking of every sin

  That has a name; but there's no bottom, none, 60

  In my voluptuousness: your wives, your daughters,

  Your matrons, and your maids, could not fill up

  The cistern of my lust; and my desire

  All continent impediments would o'erbear,

  That did oppose my will: better Macbeth, 65

  Than such an one to reign.

MACDUFF   Boundless intemperance

In nature is a tyranny; it hath been
Th'untimely emptying of the happy throne,
And fall of many kings. But fear not yet
To take upon you what is yours: you may
Convey your pleasures in a spacious plenty,
And yet seem cold – the time you may so hoodwink:
We have willing dames enough; there cannot be
That vulture in you, to devour so many
As will to greatness dedicate themselves,
Finding it so inclin'd.

MALCOLM   With this, there grows
In my most ill-compos'd affection such
A staunchless avarice, that, were I King,
I should cut off the nobles for their lands;
Desire his jewels, and this other's house:
And my more-having would be as a sauce
To make me hunger more; that I should forge
Quarrels unjust against the good and loyal,
Destroying them for wealth.

MACDUFF   This avarice
Sticks deeper, grows with more pernicious root
Than summer-seeming lust; and it hath been
The sword of our slain kings: yet do not fear;
Scotland hath foisons to fill up your will,
Of your mere own. All these are portable,
With other graces weigh'd.

MALCOLM   But I have none: the king-becoming graces,
As Justice, Verity, Temp'rance, Stableness,
Bounty, Perseverance, Mercy, Lowliness,
Devotion, Patience, Courage, Fortitude,
I have no relish of them; but abound
In the division of each several crime,
Acting it many ways. Nay, had I power, I should
Pour the sweet milk of concord into Hell,
Uproar the universal peace, confound
All unity on earth.

MACDUFF   O Scotland! Scotland!

MALCOLM   If such a one be fit to govern, speak:
I am as I have spoken.

MACDUFF   Fit to govern?
No, not to live. – O nation miserable!
With an untitled tyrant bloody-scepter'd,
When shalt thou see thy wholesome days again,
Since that the truest issue of thy throne
By his own interdiction stands accus'd,
And does blaspheme his breed? Thy royal father
Was a most sainted King: the Queen, that bore thee,
Oft'ner upon her knees than on her feet,
Died every day she liv'd. Fare thee well!
These evils thou repeat'st upon thyself
Hath banish'd me from Scotland. – O my breast,
Thy hope ends here!

MALCOLM   Macduff, this noble passion,
Child of integrity, hath from my soul
Wip'd the black scruples, reconcil'd my thoughts
To thy good truth and honour. Devilish Macbeth
By many of these trains hath sought to win me

Into his power, and modest wisdom plucks me
From over-credulous haste: but God above   120
Deal between thee and me! for even now
I put myself to thy direction, and
Unspeak mine own detraction; here abjure
The taints and blames I laid upon myself,
For strangers to my nature. I am yet   125
Unknown to woman; never was forsworn;
Scarcely have coveted what was mine own;
At no time broke my faith: would not betray
The Devil to his fellow; and delight
No less in truth, than life: my first false speaking   130
Was this upon myself. What I am truly,
Is thine, and my poor country's, to command:
Whither, indeed, before thy here-approach,
Old Siward, with ten thousand warlike men,
Already at a point, was setting forth.   135
Now we'll together, and the chance of goodness
Be like our warranted quarrel. Why are you silent?

MACDUFF
Such welcome and unwelcome things at once,
'Tis hard to reconcile.

Enter a Doctor.

MALCOLM   Well, more anon.
Comes the King forth, I pray you?   140

DOCTOR   Aye, Sir; there are a crew of wretched souls,
That stay his cure: their malady convinces
The great assay of art; but at his touch,
Such sanctity hath Heaven given his hand,
They presently amend.

MALCOLM   I thank you, Doctor.   145

Exit Doctor.

MACDUFF   What's the disease he means?

MALCOLM   'Tis call'd the Evil:
A most miraculous work in this good King,
Which often, since my here-remain in England,
I have seen him do. How he solicits Heaven,
Himself best knows; but strangely-visited people,   150
All swoln and ulcerous, pitiful to the eye,
The mere despair of surgery, he cures;
Hanging a golden stamp about their necks,
Put on with holy prayers: and 'tis spoken,
To the succeeding royalty he leaves   155
The healing benediction. With this strange virtue,
He hath a heavenly gift of prophecy;
And sundry blessings hang about his throne,
That speak him full of grace.

Enter ROSSE.

MACDUFF   See, who comes here.

MALCOLM   My countryman; but yet I know him not.   160

MACDUFF   My ever-gentle cousin, welcome hither.

MALCOLM
I know him now. Good God, betimes remove
The means that makes us strangers!

ROSSE   Sir, amen.

MACDUFF   Stands Scotland where it did?

ROSSE   Alas, poor country!
165   Almost afraid to know itself. It cannot
       Be call'd our mother, but our grave; where nothing,
       But who knows nothing, is once seen to smile;
       Where sighs, and groans, and shrieks that rent the air
       Are made, not mark'd; where violent sorrow seems
170   A modern ecstasy: the dead man's knell
       Is there scarce ask'd for who; and good men's lives
       Expire before the flowers in their caps,
       Dying or ere they sicken.

MACDUFF   O relation,
       Too nice, and yet too true!

MALCOLM   What's the newest grief?
175   ROSSE   That of an hour's age doth hiss the speaker;
       Each minute teems a new one.

MACDUFF   How does my wife?

ROSSE   Why, well.

MACDUFF   And all my children?

ROSSE   Well too.

MACDUFF   The tyrant has not batter'd at their peace?

ROSSE
       No; they were well at peace, when I did leave 'em.

MACDUFF
180   Be not a niggard of your speech: how goes't?

ROSSE   When I came hither to transport the tidings,
       Which I have heavily borne, there ran a rumour
       Of many worthy fellows that were out;
       Which was to my belief witness'd the rather,
185   For that I saw the tyrant's power afoot.
       Now is the time of help. Your eye in Scotland
       Would create soldiers, make our women fight,
       To doff their dire distresses.

MALCOLM   Be't their comfort,
       We are coming thither. Gracious England hath
190   Lent us good Siward, and ten thousand men;
       An older, and a better soldier, none
       That Christendom gives out.

ROSSE   Would I could answer
       This comfort with the like! But I have words,
       That would be howl'd out in the desert air,
       Where hearing should not latch them.

195   MACDUFF   What concern they?
       The general cause? or is it a free-grief,
       Due to some single breast?

ROSSE   No mind that's honest
       But in it shares some woe, though the main part
       Pertains to you alone.

MACDUFF   If it be mine,
200   Keep it not from me; quickly let me have it.

ROSSE   Let not your ears despise my tongue for ever,
       Which shall possess them with the heaviest sound,
       That ever yet they heard.

MACDUFF   Humh! I guess at it.

ROSSE   Your castle is surpris'd; your wife, and babes,
205   Savagely slaughter'd: to relate the manner,
       Were, on the quarry of these murther'd deer,

To add the death of you.

MALCOLM   Merciful Heaven! –
       What, man! ne'er pull your hat upon your brows:
       Give sorrow words; the grief, that does not speak,
       Whispers the o'er-fraught heart, and bids it break.   210

MACDUFF   My children too?

ROSSE   Wife, children, servants, all
       That could be found.

MACDUFF   And I must be from thence!
       My wife kill'd too?

ROSSE   I have said.

MALCOLM   Be comforted:
       Let's make us med'cines of our great revenge,
       To cure this deadly grief.   215

MACDUFF   He has no children. – All my pretty ones?
       Did you say all? – O Hell-kite! – All?
       What, all my pretty chickens, and their dam,
       At one fell swoop?

MALCOLM   Dispute it like a man.

MACDUFF   I shall do so;   220
       But I must also feel it as a man:
       I cannot but remember such things were,
       That were most precious to me. – Did Heaven look
          on,
       And would not take their part? Sinful Macduff!
       They were all struck for thee. Naught that I am,   225
       Not for their own demerits, but for mine,
       Fell slaughter on their souls: Heaven rest them now!

MALCOLM
       Be this the whetstone of your sword: let grief
       Convert to anger; blunt not the heart, enrage it.

MACDUFF   O! I could play the woman with mine eyes,   230
       And braggart with my tongue. – But, gentle
          Heavens,
       Cut short all intermission; front to front,
       Bring thou this fiend of Scotland, and myself;
       Within my sword's length set him; if he 'scape,
       Heaven forgive him too!

MALCOLM   This tune goes manly.   235
       Come, go we to the King: our power is ready;
       Our lack is nothing but our leave. Macbeth
       Is ripe for shaking, and the Powers above
       Put on their instruments. Receive what cheer you
          may;
       The night is long that never finds the day.   *Exeunt.*   240

5.1   *Enter a* Doctor of Physic *and a*
                Waiting-Gentlewoman.

DOCTOR   I have two nights watch'd with you, but can
       perceive no truth in your report. When was it she last
       walk'd?

GENTLEWOMAN   Since his Majesty went into the field, I
       have seen her rise from her bed, throw her night-gown   5
       upon her, unlock her closet, take forth paper, fold it,
       write upon't, read it, afterwards seal it, and again
       return to bed; yet all this while in a most fast sleep.

DOCTOR A great perturbation in nature, to receive at once the benefit of sleep, and do the effects of watching! In this slumbery agitation, besides her walking and other actual performances, what, at any time, have you heard her say?

GENTLEWOMAN That, Sir, which I will not report after her.

DOCTOR You may, to me; and 'tis most meet you should.

GENTLEWOMAN Neither to you, nor any one; having no witness to confirm my speech.

Enter LADY MACBETH, *with a taper.*

Lo you! here she comes. This is her very guise; and, upon my life, fast asleep. Observe her: stand close.

DOCTOR How came she by that light?

GENTLEWOMAN Why, it stood by her: she has light by her continually; 'tis her command.

DOCTOR You see, her eyes are open.

GENTLEWOMAN Ay, but their sense are shut.

DOCTOR What is it she does now? Look, how she rubs her hands.

GENTLEWOMAN It is an accustom'd action with her, to seem thus washing her hands. I have known her continue in this a quarter of an hour.

LADY MACBETH Yet here's a spot.

DOCTOR Hark! she speaks. I will set down what comes from her, to satisfy my remembrance the more strongly.

LADY MACBETH Out, damned spot! out, I say! – One; two: why, then 'tis time to do't. – Hell is murky. – Fie, my Lord, fie! a soldier, and afeard? – What need we fear who knows it, when none can call our power to accompt? – Yet who would have thought the old man to have had so much blood in him?

DOCTOR Do you mark that?

LADY MACBETH The Thane of Fife had a wife: where is she now? – What, will these hands ne'er be clean? – No more o'that, my Lord, no more o'that: you mar all with this starting.

DOCTOR Go to, go to: you have known what you should not.

GENTLEWOMAN She has spoke what she should not, I am sure of that: Heaven knows what she has known.

LADY MACBETH Here's the smell of the blood still: all the perfumes of Arabia will not sweeten this little hand. Oh! oh! oh!

DOCTOR What a sigh is there! The heart is sorely charg'd.

GENTLEWOMAN I would not have such a heart in my bosom, for the dignity of the whole body.

DOCTOR Well, well, well.

GENTLEWOMAN Pray God it be, sir.

DOCTOR This disease is beyond my practice: yet I have known those which have walk'd in their sleep, who have died holily in their beds.

LADY MACBETH Wash your hands, put on your night-gown; look not so pale. – I tell you yet again, Banquo's buried: he cannot come out on's grave. 65

DOCTOR Even so?

LADY MACBETH To bed, to bed: there's knocking at the gate. Come, come, come, come, give me your hand. What's done cannot be undone. To bed, to bed, to bed.   *Exit.* 70

DOCTOR Will she go now to bed?

GENTLEWOMAN Directly.

DOCTOR Foul whisp'rings are abroad. Unnatural deeds
Do breed unnatural troubles: infected minds
To their deaf pillows will discharge their secrets. 75
More needs she the divine than the physician. –
God, God forgive us all! Look after her;
Remove from her the means of all annoyance,
And still keep eyes upon her. – So, good night:
My mind she has mated, and amaz'd my sight. 80
I think, but dare not speak.

GENTLEWOMAN   Good night, good Doctor.
                                                        Exeunt.

5.2   *Enter, with drums and colours,* MENTETH,
           CATHNESS, ANGUS, LENOX *and soldiers.*

MENTETH
The English power is near, led on by Malcolm,
His uncle Siward, and the good Macduff.
Revenges burn in them; for their dear causes
Would, to the bleeding and the grim alarm,
Excite the mortified man.

ANGUS   Near Birnam wood 5
Shall we well meet them: That way are they coming.

CATHNESS
Who knows if Donalbain be with his brother?

LENOX For certain, Sir, he is not. I have a file
Of all the gentry: there is Siward's son,
And many unrough youths, that even now 10
Protest their first of manhood.

MENTETH   What does the tyrant?

CATHNESS Great Dunsinane he strongly fortifies.
Some say he's mad; others, that lesser hate him,
Do call it valiant fury: but, for certain,
He cannot buckle his distemper'd cause 15
Within the belt of rule.

ANGUS   Now does he feel
His secret murthers sticking on his hands;
Now minutely revolts upbraid his faith-breach:
Those he commands move only in command,
Nothing in love: now does he feel his title 20
Hang loose about him, like a giant's robe
Upon a dwarfish thief.

MENTETH   Who then shall blame
His pester'd senses to recoil and start,
When all that is within him does condemn
Itself, for being there?

CATHNESS   Well; march we on, 25
To give obedience where 'tis truly ow'd:
Meet we the med'cine of the sickly weal;

And with him pour we, in our country's purge,
Each drop of us.

LENOX   Or so much as it needs
30   To dew the sovereign flower, and drown the weeds.
Make we our march towards Birnam.

Exeunt, marching.

5.3   *Enter* MACBETH, Doctor *and attendants.*

MACBETH   Bring me no more reports; let them fly all:
Till Birnam wood remove to Dunsinane,
I cannot taint with fear. What's the boy Malcolm?
Was he not born of woman? The spirits that know
5   All mortal consequence have pronounc'd me thus:
'Fear not, Macbeth; no man that's born of woman
Shall e'er have power upon thee.' – Then fly, false
     Thanes,
And mingle with the English epicures:
The mind I sway by, and the heart I bear,
10   Shall never sag with doubt, nor shake with fear.

Enter a Servant.

The devil damn thee black, thou cream-fac'd loon!
Where gott'st thou that goose look?

SERVANT   There is ten thousand –

MACBETH   Geese, villain?

SERVANT   Soldiers, Sir.

MACBETH   Go, prick thy face, and over-red thy fear,
15   Thou lily-liver'd boy. What soldiers, patch?
Death of thy soul! those linen cheeks of thine
Are counsellors to fear. What soldiers, whey-face?

SERVANT   The English force, so please you.

MACBETH   Take thy face hence.   *Exit Servant.*
                        – Seyton! – I am sick at heart,
20   When I behold – Seyton, I say! – This push
Will cheer me ever, or disseat me now.
I have liv'd long enough: my way of life
Is fall'n into the sere, the yellow leaf;
And that which should accompany old age,
25   As honour, love, obedience, troops of friends,
I must not look to have; but in their stead,
Curses, not loud, but deep, mouth-honour, breath,
Which the poor heart would fain deny, and dare not.
Seyton! –

Enter SEYTON.

SEYTON   What's your gracious pleasure?

30   MACBETH   What news more?

SEYTON
All is confirm'd, my Lord, which was reported.

MACBETH
I'll fight, till from my bones my flesh be hack'd.
Give me my armour.

SEYTON   'Tis not needed yet.

MACBETH   I'll put it on.
35   Send out moe horses, skirt the country round;
Hang those that talk of fear. Give me mine armour. –

How does your patient, Doctor?

DOCTOR   Not so sick, my Lord,
As she is troubled with thick-coming fancies,
That keep her from her rest.

MACBETH   Cure her of that:
40   Canst thou not minister to a mind diseas'd,
Pluck from the memory a rooted sorrow,
Raze out the written troubles of the brain,
And with some sweet oblivious antidote
Cleanse the stuff'd bosom of that perilous stuff
Which weighs upon the heart?

DOCTOR   Therein the patient   45
Must minister to himself.

MACBETH   Throw physic to the dogs; I'll none of it. –
Come, put mine armour on; give me my staff. –
Seyton, send out – Doctor, the Thanes fly from
     me. –
Come, sir, despatch. – If thou couldst, Doctor, cast   50
The water of my land, find her disease,
And purge it to a sound and pristine health,
I would applaud thee to the very echo,
That should applaud again. – Pull't off, I say. –
What rhubarb, cyme or what purgative drug,   55
Would scour these English hence? – Hear'st thou of
     them?

DOCTOR   Ay, my good Lord: your royal preparation
Makes us hear something.

MACBETH   Bring it after me. –
I will not be afraid of death and bane,
Till Birnam forest come to Dunsinane.   *Exit.*   60

DOCTOR [*aside*]
Were I from Dunsinane away and clear,
Profit again should hardly draw me here.   *Exeunt.*

5.4   *Enter, with drum and colours,* MALCOLM,
OLD SIWARD *and his son,* MACDUFF, MENTETH,
CATHNESS, ANGUS, LENOX, ROSSE *and* Soldiers,
marching.

MALCOLM   Cousins, I hope the days are near at hand,
That chambers will be safe.

MENTETH   We doubt it nothing.

SIWARD   What wood is this before us?

MENTETH   The wood of Birnam.

MALCOLM   Let every soldier hew him down a bough,
And bear't before him: thereby shall we shadow   5
The numbers of our host, and make discovery
Err in report of us.

SOLDIER   It shall be done.

SIWARD   We learn no other but the confident tyrant
Keeps still in Dunsinane, and will endure
Our setting down before't.

MALCOLM   'Tis his main hope;   10
For where there is advantage to be gone,
Both more and less have given him the revolt,
And none serve with him but constrained things,
Whose hearts are absent too.

MACDUFF   Let our just censures
15 Attend the true event, and put we on
 Industrious soldiership.
SIWARD   The time approaches,
 That will with due decision make us know
 What we shall say we have, and what we owe.
 Thoughts speculative their unsure hopes relate,
20 But certain issue strokes must arbitrate;
 Towards which advance the war. *Exeunt, marching.*

5.5 *Enter, with drum and colours,* MACBETH,
   SEYTON *and soldiers.*

MACBETH Hang out our banners on the outward walls;
 The cry is still, 'They come!' Our castle's strength
 Will laugh a siege to scorn: here let them lie,
 Till famine and the ague eat them up.
5 Were they not forc'd with those that should be ours,
 We might have met them dareful, beard to beard,
 And beat them backward home. What is that noise?
 [*a cry within, of women*]
SEYTON It is the cry of women, my good Lord. *Exit.*
MACBETH I have almost forgot the taste of fears.
10 The time has been, my senses would have cool'd
 To hear a night-shriek; and my fell of hair
 Would at a dismal treatise rouse, and stir,
 As life were in't. I have supp'd full with horrors:
 Direness, familiar to my slaughterous thoughts,
 Cannot once start me.

   Re-enter SEYTON.

15   Wherefore was that cry?
SEYTON The Queen, my Lord, is dead.
MACBETH She should have died hereafter:
 There would have been a time for such a word. –
 To-morrow, and to-morrow, and to-morrow,
20 Creeps in this petty pace from day to day,
 To the last syllable of recorded time;
 And all our yesterdays have lighted fools
 The way to dusty death. Out, out, brief candle!
 Life's but a walking shadow; a poor player,
25 That struts and frets his hour upon the stage,
 And then is heard no more: it is a tale
 Told by an idiot, full of sound and fury,
 Signifying nothing.

   Enter a Messenger.

 Thou com'st to use thy tongue; thy story quickly.
30 MESSENGER Gracious my Lord,
 I should report that which I say I saw,
 But know not how to do't.
MACBETH   Well, say, sir.
MESSENGER As I did stand my watch upon the hill,
 I look'd toward Birnam, and anon, methought,
 The wood began to move.
35 MACBETH   Liar, and slave!
MESSENGER Let me endure your wrath, if 't be not so.

Within this three mile may you see it coming;
 I say, a moving grove.
MACBETH   If thou speak'st false,
 Upon the next tree shalt thou hang alive,
 Till famine cling thee: if thy speech be sooth, 40
 I care not if thou dost for me as much. –
 I pull in resolution; and begin
 To doubt th'equivocation of the fiend,
 That lies like truth: 'Fear not, till Birnam wood
 Do come to Dunsinane'; – and now a wood 45
 Comes toward Dunsinane. – Arm, arm, and out! –
 If this which he avouches does appear,
 There is nor flying hence, nor tarrying here.
 I 'gin to be aweary of the sun,
 And wish th'estate o'th' world were now undone. – 50
 Ring the alarum bell! – Blow, wind! come, wrack!
 At least we'll die with harness on our back. *Exeunt.*

5.6 *Enter, with drum and colours,* MALCOLM,
  OLD SIWARD, MACDUFF, *etc., and their army,*
   with boughs.

MALCOLM
 Now, near enough: your leavy screens throw down,
 And show like those you are. – You, worthy uncle,
 Shall, with my cousin, your right noble son,
 Lead our first battle: worthy Macduff, and we,
 Shall take upon's what else remains to do, 5
 According to our order.
SIWARD   Fare you well. –
 Do we but find the tyrant's power to-night,
 Let us be beaten, if we cannot fight.
MACDUFF
 Make all our trumpets speak; give them all breath,
 Those clamorous harbingers of blood and death. 10
   Exeunt. Alarums continued.

5.7   *Enter* MACBETH.

MACBETH They have tied me to a stake: I cannot fly,
 But, bear-like, I must fight the course. – What's he,
 That was not born of woman? Such a one
 Am I to fear, or none.

   Enter YOUNG SIWARD.

YOUNG SIWARD What is thy name?
MACBETH   Thou'lt be afraid to hear it. 5
YOUNG SIWARD
 No; though thou call'st thyself a hotter name
 Than any is in hell.
MACBETH   My name's Macbeth.
YOUNG SIWARD
 The devil himself could not pronounce a title
 More hateful to mine ear.
MACBETH   No, nor more fearful.
YOUNG SIWARD
 Thou liest, abhorred tyrant: with my sword 10
 I'll prove the lie thou speak'st.

[They fight, and Young Siward is slain.]

MACBETH   Thou wast born of woman: –
But swords I smile at, weapons laugh to scorn,
Brandish'd by man that's of a woman born.   *Exit.*

Alarums. Enter MACDUFF.

MACDUFF

That way the noise is. – Tyrant, show thy face:
15   If thou be'st slain, and with no stroke of mine,
My wife and children's ghosts will haunt me still.
I cannot strike at wretched Kernes, whose arms
Are hir'd to bear their staves: either thou, Macbeth,
Or else my sword, with an unbatter'd edge,
20   I sheathe again undeeded. There thou shouldst be;
By this great clatter, one of greatest note
Seems bruited. Let me find him, Fortune!
And more I beg not.   *Exit. Alarum.*

Enter MALCOLM *and* OLD SIWARD.

SIWARD

This way, my Lord; – the castle's gently render'd:
25   The tyrant's people on both sides do fight;
The noble Thanes do bravely in the war.
The day almost itself professes yours,
And little is to do.
MALCOLM   We have met with foes
That strike beside us.
SIWARD   Enter, Sir, the castle.
                                    Exeunt. Alarum.

5.8   *Enter* MACBETH.

MACBETH   Why should I play the Roman fool, and die
On mine own sword? whiles I see lives, the gashes
Do better upon them.

Re-enter MACDUFF.

MACDUFF   Turn, Hell-hound, turn!
MACBETH   Of all men else I have avoided thee:
5   But get thee back, my soul is too much charg'd
With blood of thine already.
MACDUFF   I have no words;
My voice is in my sword: thou bloodier villain
Than terms can give thee out! *[They fight.]*
MACBETH   Thou losest labour:
As easy may'st thou the intrenchant air
10   With thy keen sword impress, as make me bleed:
Let fall thy blade on vulnerable crests;
I bear a charmed life; which must not yield
To one of woman born.
MACDUFF   Despair thy charm;
And let the Angel, whom thou still hast serv'd,
15   Tell thee, Macduff was from his mother's womb
Untimely ripp'd.
MACBETH   Accursed be that tongue that tells me so,
For it hath cow'd my better part of man:
And be these juggling fiends no more believ'd,

That palter with us in a double sense;   20
That keep the word of promise to our ear,
And break it to our hope. – I'll not fight with thee.
MACDUFF   Then yield thee, coward,
And live to be the show and gaze o'th' time:
We'll have thee, as our rarer monsters are,   25
Painted upon a pole, and underwrit,
'Here may you see the tyrant.'
MACBETH   I will not yield,
To kiss the ground before young Malcolm's feet,
And to be baited with the rabble's curse.
Though Birnam wood be come to Dunsinane,   30
And thou oppos'd, being of no woman born,
Yet I will try the last: before my body
I throw my warlike shield: lay on, Macduff;
And damn'd be him that first cries, 'Hold, enough!'
                    Exeunt, fighting. Alarums.
          Re-enter fighting, and Macbeth slain.

5.9   *Retreat. Flourish. Enter, with drum and colours,*
       MALCOLM, OLD SIWARD, ROSSE, *thanes and soldiers.*

MALCOLM

I would the friends we miss were safe arriv'd.
SIWARD   Some must go off; and yet, by these I see,
So great a day as this is cheaply bought.
MALCOLM   Macduff is missing, and your noble son.
ROSSE   Your son, my Lord, has paid a soldier's debt: 5
He only liv'd but till he was a man;
The which no sooner had his prowess confirm'd,
In the unshrinking station where he fought,
But like a man he died.
SIWARD   Then he is dead?
ROSSE

Ay, and brought off the field. Your cause of sorrow   10
Must not be measur'd by his worth, for then
It hath no end.
SIWARD   Had he his hurts before?
ROSSE   Ay, on the front.
SIWARD   Why then, God's soldier be he!
Had I as many sons as I have hairs,
I would not wish them to a fairer death: 15
And so, his knell is knoll'd.
MALCOLM   He's worth more sorrow,
And that I'll spend for him.
SIWARD   He's worth no more;
They say he parted well and paid his score:
And so, God be with him! – Here comes newer
     comfort.

Re-enter MACDUFF, *with Macbeth's head.*

MACDUFF

Hail, King! for so thou art. Behold, where stands   20
Th'usurper's cursed head: the time is free.
I see thee compass'd with thy kingdom's pearl,
That speak my salutation in their minds;
Whose voices I desire aloud with mine, –

Hail, King of Scotland!

25   ALL   Hail, King of Scotland!
                                                    [*Flourish.*]

MALCOLM   We shall not spend a large expense of time,
Before we reckon with your several loves,
And make us even with you. My Thanes and
    kinsmen,
Henceforth be Earls; the first that ever Scotland
30 In such an honour nam'd. What's more to do,
Which would be planted newly with the time, –
As calling home our exil'd friends abroad,

That fled the snares of watchful tyranny;
Producing forth the cruel ministers
Of this dead butcher, and his fiend-like Queen,   35
Who, as 'tis thought, by self and violent hands
Took off her life; – this, and what needful else
That calls upon us, by the grace of Grace,
We will perform in measure, time, and place.
So thanks to all at once, and to each one,   40
Whom we invite to see us crown'd at Scone.
                                        Flourish. Exeunt.

Measure for Measure

Measure for Measure was first printed in the First Folio in 1623 as the fourth of the comedies, but it was performed at the Court of James I on 26 December 1604; it had probably been written and acted at the Globe earlier that year. Possibly the first play Shakespeare wrote after the accession of James I, it deals with many moral and political issues discussed by James in his *Basilicon Doron* (1599, reprinted 1603). Composed later than most of the comedies and at a time when Shakespeare was turning increasingly to tragedy, it has been seen as having particular affinities with *All's Well That Ends Well*, with which it is sometimes classified as a 'problem comedy'. *All's Well* is difficult to date, but it shares with *Measure for Measure* a darker tone than the other comedies, a strong, outspoken (and for some, dislikeable) heroine, and a plot resolved by a 'bed-trick' – the substitution of one woman for another in bed.

Shakespeare's sources were Giraldi Cinthio and George Whetstone, both of whom wrote two versions of the story of the magistrate who demands sexual favours in return for mercy: Cinthio told the story first in his *Hecatommithi* (1565) and dramatized it as *Epitia* (1573); Whetstone wrote a two-part play *Promos and Cassandra* (1578) and a prose version in his *Heptameron of Civil Discourses* (1582). *Promos and Cassandra* seems to have been the main source, but Shakespeare also used the *Hecatommithi* for the source of *Othello* which was written close in time to *Measure for Measure*. In all the previous versions of the story the character who is the equivalent of Isabella does agree to have sex with the magistrate to save her brother's (or in some versions her husband's) life, but in none of them is she about to take vows as a nun; and Mariana is Shakespeare's invention, though the bed-trick was familiar from folklore and romance. The presence throughout of the disguised ruler is also Shakespeare's invention.

There are some anomalies and dislocations in the text which have been explained in various ways: some scholars have seen them as evidence of authorial revision, the Arden 2 editor ascribes them to oversights and changes of plan, while the editors of the Oxford *Complete Works* argue that the play was adapted after Shakespeare's death, most likely by Thomas Middleton, who may also have had a hand in *Macbeth* and a larger one in *Timon of Athens*. The passages affected are the opening of 1.2, where there is a noticeable inconsistency over Mistress Overdone's knowledge of Claudio's arrest, and the Duke's brief soliloquy at 4.1.60-5, which seems to have been transferred from his earlier speech at 3.2.179-82 in order to cover the conversation between Isabella and Mariana.

William Davenant adapted *Measure for Measure* in 1662 as *The Law Against Lovers*, a play which also took characters and situations from *Much Ado About Nothing*. Many people in the eighteenth and nineteenth centuries found its subject-matter distasteful and its conclusion arbitrary: Charlotte Lennox, for example, compared Shakespeare's version with Cinthio's and roundly condemned the former for altering the story for the worse and introducing 'low contrivance, absurd intrigue and improbable incidents . . . in order to bring about three or four weddings instead of one good beheading' (*Shakespeare Illustrated*, 1753). Coleridge called it 'a hateful work', and twentieth-century attempts to rehabilitate it by interpreting it as a Christian parable (with the Duke as 'power divine') have not convinced everyone. It has, however, appealed to modern performers and critics as a play about repressed desire and sexual decadence set, prophetically, in Freud's city of Vienna, and some powerful productions have emphasized the claustrophobia of its containment within the walls of convent, brothel and prison. In the theatre there is often a degree of suspense as to how Isabella will react to the Duke's proposal of marriage in the final scene: Shakespeare gives her no verbal response.

The Arden text is based on the 1623 Folio.

LIST OF ROLES

Vincentio, *the* DUKE	*of Vienna*
ANGELO	*the Deputy*
ESCALUS	*an ancient lord*
CLAUDIO	*a young gentleman*
LUCIO	*a fantastic*
Two other like GENTLEMEN	
PROVOST	
FRIAR Thomas *or* FRIAR PETER	
JUSTICE	
ELBOW	*a simple constable*
FROTH	*a foolish gentleman*
POMPEY	*servant to Mistress Overdone*
ABHORSON	*an executioner*
BARNARDINE	*a dissolute prisoner*
Varrius	*a gentleman, friend to the Duke*
ISABELLA	*sister to Claudio*
MARIANA	*betrothed to Angelo*
JULIET	*beloved of Claudio*
Francisca, *a* NUN	
MISTRESS OVERDONE	*a bawd*

Lords in attendance, Officers, Servants, Citizens and a Boy

Measure for Measure

1.1 *Enter* DUKE, ESCALUS, *lords and attendants.*

DUKE Escalus.

ESCALUS My lord.

DUKE Of government the properties to unfold
 Would seem in me t'affect speech and discourse,
5 Since I am put to know that your own science
 Exceeds, in that, the lists of all advice
 My strength can give you. Then no more remains
 But that, to your sufficiency, as your worth is able,
 And let them work. The nature of our people,
10 Our city's institutions, and the terms
 For common justice, y'are as pregnant in
 As art and practice hath enriched any
 That we remember. There is our commission,
 From which we would not have you warp. Call
  hither,
15 I say, bid come before us Angelo.   *Exit an attendant.*
 What figure of us, think you, he will bear?
 For you must know, we have with special soul
 Elected him our absence to supply;
 Lent him our terror, drest him with our love,
20 And given his deputation all the organs
 Of our own power. What think you of it?

ESCALUS If any in Vienna be of worth
 To undergo such ample grace and honour,
 It is Lord Angelo.

Enter ANGELO.

DUKE   Look where he comes.
25 ANGELO Always obedient to your Grace's will,
 I come to know your pleasure.

DUKE   Angelo:
 There is a kind of character in thy life
 That to th'observer doth thy history
 Fully unfold. Thyself and thy belongings
30 Are not thine own so proper as to waste
 Thyself upon thy virtues, they on thee.
 Heaven doth with us as we with torches do,
 Not light them for themselves; for if our virtues
 Did not go forth of us, 'twere all alike
35 As if we had them not. Spirits are not finely touch'd
 But to fine issues; nor nature never lends
 The smallest scruple of her excellence
 But, like a thrifty goddess, she determines
 Herself the glory of a creditor,
40 Both thanks and use. But I do bend my speech
 To one that can my part in him advertise:
 Hold therefore, Angelo.
 In our remove, be thou at full ourself.
 Mortality and mercy in Vienna
45 Live in thy tongue, and heart. Old Escalus,
 Though first in question, is thy secondary.
 Take thy commission.

ANGELO   Now, good my lord,
 Let there be some more test made of my metal,
 Before so noble and so great a figure
 Be stamp'd upon it.

DUKE   No more evasion. 50
 We have with a leaven'd and prepared choice
 Proceeded to you; therefore take your honours.
 Our haste from hence is of so quick condition
 That it prefers itself, and leaves unquestion'd
 Matters of needful value. We shall write to you, 55
 As time and our concernings shall importune,
 How it goes with us; and do look to know
 What doth befall you here. So, fare you well.
 To th'hopeful execution do I leave you
 Of your commissions.

ANGELO   Yet give leave, my lord, 60
 That we may bring you something on the way.

DUKE My haste may not admit it;
 Nor need you, on mine honour, have to do
 With any scruple. Your scope is as mine own,
 So to enforce or qualify the laws 65
 As to your soul seems good. Give me your hand;
 I'll privily away. I love the people,
 But do not like to stage me to their eyes:
 Though it do well, I do not relish well
 Their loud applause and *Aves* vehement; 70
 Nor do I think the man of safe discretion
 That does affect it. Once more, fare you well.

ANGELO The heavens give safety to your purposes!

ESCALUS Lead forth and bring you back in happiness!

DUKE I thank you; fare you well.   *Exit.* 75

ESCALUS I shall desire you, sir, to give me leave
 To have free speech with you; and it concerns me
 To look into the bottom of my place.
 A power I have, but of what strength and nature
 I am not yet instructed. 80

ANGELO 'Tis so with me. Let us withdraw together,
 And we may soon our satisfaction have
 Touching that point.

ESCALUS   I'll wait upon your honour.

                Exeunt.

1.2 *Enter* LUCIO *and two other* Gentlemen.

LUCIO If the Duke, with the other dukes, come not to
 composition with the King of Hungary, why then all
 the dukes fall upon the King.

1 GENTLEMAN Heaven grant us its peace, but not the
 King of Hungary's! 5

2 GENTLEMAN Amen.

LUCIO Thou conclud'st like the sanctimonious pirate,
 that went to sea with the Ten Commandments, but
 scrap'd one out of the table.

2 GENTLEMAN 'Thou shalt not steal'? 10

LUCIO Ay, that he raz'd.

1 GENTLEMAN Why, 'twas a commandment to command the captain and all the rest from their functions:
 they put forth to steal. There's not a soldier of us all
 that, in the thanksgiving before meat, do relish the 15
 petition well that prays for peace.

2 GENTLEMAN   I never heard any soldier dislike it.

LUCIO   I believe thee; for I think thou never wast where grace was said.

20   2 GENTLEMAN   No? A dozen times at least.

1 GENTLEMAN   What, in metre?

LUCIO   In any proportion, or in any language.

1 GENTLEMAN   I think, or in any religion.

25   LUCIO   Ay, why not? Grace is grace, despite of all controversy; as for example, thou thyself art a wicked villain, despite of all grace.

1 GENTLEMAN   Well, there went but a pair of shears between us.

30   LUCIO   I grant: as there may between the lists and the velvet. Thou art the list.

1 GENTLEMAN   And thou the velvet; thou art good velvet; thou'rt a three-piled piece, I warrant thee: I had as lief be a list of an English kersey, as be piled, as thou art pilled, for a French velvet. Do I speak

35   feelingly now?

LUCIO   I think thou dost: and indeed, with most painful feeling of thy speech. I will, out of thine own confession, learn to begin thy health; but whilst I live, forget to drink after thee.

40   1 GENTLEMAN   I think I have done myself wrong, have I not?

2 GENTLEMAN   Yes, that thou hast; whether thou art tainted or free.

Enter MISTRESS OVERDONE.

LUCIO   Behold, behold, where Madam Mitigation comes! I have purchased as many diseases under her

45   roof as come to –

2 GENTLEMAN   To what, I pray?

LUCIO   Judge.

2 GENTLEMAN   To three thousand dolours a year.

50   1 GENTLEMAN   Ay, and more.

LUCIO   A French crown more.

1 GENTLEMAN   Thou art always figuring diseases in me; but thou art full of error; I am sound.

LUCIO   Nay, not, as one would say, healthy: but so sound

55   as things that are hollow; thy bones are hollow; impiety has made a feast of thee.

1 GENTLEMAN   How now, which of your hips has the most profound sciatica?

MISTRESS OVERDONE   Well, well! There's one yonder

60   arrested and carried to prison, was worth five thousand of you all.

2 GENTLEMAN   Who's that, I prithee?

MISTRESS OVERDONE   Marry sir, that's Claudio; Signior Claudio.

65   1 GENTLEMAN   Claudio to prison? 'Tis not so.

MISTRESS OVERDONE   Nay, but I know 'tis so. I saw him arrested: saw him carried away: and which is more, within these three days his head to be chopped off.

LUCIO   But, after all this fooling, I would not have it so.

70   Art thou sure of this?

MISTRESS OVERDONE   I am too sure of it: and it is for getting Madam Julietta with child.

LUCIO   Believe me, this may be: he promised to meet me two hours since, and he was ever precise in promise-keeping.   75

2 GENTLEMAN   Besides, you know, it draws something near to the speech we had to such a purpose.

1 GENTLEMAN   But most of all agreeing with the proclamation.

LUCIO   Away! Let's go learn the truth of it.   80

Exeunt Lucio and Gentlemen.

MISTRESS OVERDONE   Thus, what with the war, what with the sweat, what with the gallows, and what with poverty, I am custom-shrunk.

Enter POMPEY.

How now? What's the news with you?

POMPEY   Yonder man is carried to prison.   85

MISTRESS OVERDONE   Well! What has he done?

POMPEY   A woman.

MISTRESS OVERDONE   But what's his offence?

POMPEY   Groping for trouts, in a peculiar river.

MISTRESS OVERDONE   What? Is there a maid with child   90
by him?

POMPEY   No: but there's a woman with maid by him. You have not heard of the proclamation, have you?

MISTRESS OVERDONE   What proclamation, man?

POMPEY   All houses in the suburbs of Vienna must be   95
plucked down.

MISTRESS OVERDONE   And what shall become of those in the city?

POMPEY   They shall stand for seed: they had gone down too, but that a wise burgher put in for them.   100

MISTRESS OVERDONE   But shall all our houses of resort in the suburbs be pulled down?

POMPEY   To the ground, mistress.

MISTRESS OVERDONE   Why, here's a change indeed in the commonwealth! What shall become of me?   105

POMPEY   Come: fear not you: good counsellors lack no clients: though you change your place, you need not change your trade: I'll be your tapster still; courage, there will be pity taken on you; you that have worn your eyes almost out in the service, you will be   110
considered.

MISTRESS OVERDONE   What's to do here, Thomas tapster? Let's withdraw!

POMPEY   Here comes Signior Claudio, led by the Provost to prison: and there's Madam Juliet.   115

Exeunt.

Enter Provost *and officers with* CLAUDIO *and* JULIET,
LUCIO *and the two gentlemen.*

CLAUDIO
Fellow, why dost thou show me thus to th' world?
Bear me to prison, where I am committed.

PROVOST   I do it not in evil disposition,
But from Lord Angelo by special charge.

CLAUDIO   Thus can the demi-god, Authority,   120

Make us pay down for our offence by weight.
The words of heaven; on whom it will, it will;
On whom it will not, so; yet still 'tis just.

LUCIO
Why, how now, Claudio? Whence comes this restraint?

CLAUDIO   From too much liberty, my Lucio. Liberty,
As surfeit, is the father of much fast;
So every scope by the immoderate use
Turns to restraint. Our natures do pursue,
Like rats that ravin down their proper bane,
A thirsty evil; and when we drink, we die.

LUCIO   If I could speak so wisely under an arrest, I
would send for certain of my creditors; and yet, to say
the truth, I had as lief have the foppery of freedom as
the morality of imprisonment. – What's thy offence,
Claudio?

CLAUDIO   What but to speak of would offend again.

LUCIO   What, is't murder?

CLAUDIO   No.

LUCIO   Lechery?

CLAUDIO   Call it so.

PROVOST   Away, sir; you must go.

CLAUDIO
One word, good friend: Lucio, a word with you.

LUCIO   A hundred – if they'll do you any good.
Is lechery so look'd after?

CLAUDIO   Thus stands it with me: upon a true contract
I got possession of Julietta's bed.
You know the lady; she is fast my wife,
Save that we do the denunciation lack
Of outward order. This we came not to
Only for propagation of a dower
Remaining in the coffer of her friends,
From whom we thought it meet to hide our love
Till time had made them for us. But it chances
The stealth of our most mutual entertainment
With character too gross is writ on Juliet.

LUCIO   With child, perhaps?

CLAUDIO   Unhappily, even so.
And the new deputy now for the Duke –
Whether it be the fault and glimpse of newness,
Of whether that the body public be
A horse whereon the governor doth ride,
Who, newly in the seat, that it may know
He can command, lets it straight feel the spur;
Whether the tyranny be in his place,
Or in his eminence that fills it up,
I stagger in – but this new governor
Awakes me all the enrolled penalties
Which have, like unscour'd armour, hung by th' wall
So long, that nineteen zodiacs have gone round,
And none of them been worn; and for a name
Now puts the drowsy and neglected act
Freshly on me: 'tis surely for a name.

LUCIO   I warrant it is: and thy head stands so tickle on
thy shoulders, that a milkmaid, if she be in love, may
sigh it off. Send after the Duke, and appeal to him.

CLAUDIO   I have done so, but he's not to be found.
I prithee, Lucio, do me this kind service:
This day my sister should the cloister enter,
And there receive her approbation.   175
Acquaint her with the danger of my state:
Implore her, in my voice, that she make friends
To the strict deputy: bid herself assay him.
I have great hope in that. For in her youth
There is a prone and speechless dialect   180
Such as move men; beside, she hath prosperous art
When she will play with reason and discourse,
And well she can persuade.

LUCIO   I pray she may: as well for the encouragement of
the like, which else would stand under grievous   185
imposition, as for the enjoying of thy life, who I would
be sorry should be thus foolishly lost at a game of tick-
tack. – I'll to her.

CLAUDIO   I thank you, good friend Lucio.

LUCIO   Within two hours.   190

CLAUDIO   Come, officer, away.   *Exeunt.*

1.3   *Enter* DUKE *and* FRIAR THOMAS.

DUKE   No. Holy father, throw away that thought;
Believe not that the dribbling dart of love
Can pierce a complete bosom. Why I desire thee
To give me secret harbour hath a purpose
More grave and wrinkled than the aims and ends   5
Of burning youth.

FRIAR   May your Grace speak of it?

DUKE   My holy sir, none better knows than you
How I have ever lov'd the life remov'd,
And held in idle price to haunt assemblies,
Where youth, and cost, witless bravery keeps.   10
I have deliver'd to Lord Angelo –
A man of stricture and firm abstinence –
My absolute power and place here in Vienna,
And he supposes me travell'd to Poland;
For so I have strew'd it in the common ear,   15
And so it is receiv'd. Now, pious sir,
You will demand of me, why I do this.

FRIAR   Gladly, my lord.

DUKE   We have strict statutes and most biting laws,
The needful bits and curbs to headstrong jades,   20
Which for this fourteen years we have let slip;
Even like an o'er-grown lion in a cave
That goes not out to prey. Now, as fond fathers,
Having bound up the threatening twigs of birch,
Only to stick it in their children's sight   25
For terror, not to use, in time the rod
Becomes more mock'd than fear'd: so our decrees,
Dead to infliction, to themselves are dead,
And Liberty plucks Justice by the nose,
The baby beats the nurse, and quite athwart   30
Goes all decorum.

FRIAR   It rested in your Grace
To unloose this tied-up justice when you pleas'd;

And it in you more dreadful would have seem'd
Than in Lord Angelo.
DUKE   I do fear, too dreadful.
35 Sith 'twas my fault to give the people scope,
'Twould be my tyranny to strike and gall them
For what I bid them do: for we bid this be done,
When evil deeds have their permissive pass,
And not the punishment. Therefore indeed, my
    father,
40 I have on Angelo impos'd the office;
Who may in th'ambush of my name strike home,
And yet my nature never in the fight
To do in slander. And to behold his sway,
I will, as 'twere a brother of your order,
45 Visit both prince and people. Therefore, I prithee,
Supply me with the habit, and instruct me
How I may formally in person bear
Like a true friar. Moe reasons for this action
At our more leisure shall I render you;
50 Only this one: Lord Angelo is precise;
Stands at a guard with Envy; scarce confesses
That his blood flows; or that his appetite
Is more to bread than stone. Hence shall we see
If power change purpose, what our seemers be.
                                        Exeunt.

1.4 *Enter* ISABELLA *and* FRANCISCA, *a* Nun.

ISABELLA   And have you nuns no farther privileges?
NUN   Are not these large enough?
ISABELLA   Yes, truly; I speak not as desiring more,
But rather wishing a more strict restraint
5 Upon the sisters stood, the votarists of Saint Clare.
LUCIO [*within*] Hoa! Peace be in this place!
ISABELLA   Who's that which calls?
NUN   It is a man's voice! Gentle Isabella,
Turn you the key, and know his business of him;
You may, I may not; you are yet unsworn:
10 When you have vow'd, you must not speak with men
But in the presence of the prioress;
Then, if you speak, you must not show your face;
Or if you show your face, you must not speak.
He calls again: I pray you, answer him.   *Retires.*
15 ISABELLA   Peace and prosperity! Who is't that calls?

Enter LUCIO.

LUCIO   Hail virgin, if you be – as those cheek-roses
Proclaim you are no less – can you so stead me
As bring me to the sight of Isabella,
A novice of this place, and the fair sister
20 To her unhappy brother Claudio?
ISABELLA   Why 'her unhappy brother'? Let me ask,
The rather for I now must make you know
I am that Isabella, and his sister.
LUCIO   Gentle and fair. Your brother kindly greets you.
25 Not to be weary with you, he's in prison.
ISABELLA   Woe me! For what?

LUCIO   For that which, if myself might be his judge,
He should receive his punishment in thanks:
He hath got his friend with child.
ISABELLA   Sir, make me not your story.
30 LUCIO   'Tis true.
I would not, though 'tis my familiar sin,
With maids to seem the lapwing, and to jest
Tongue far from heart, play with all virgins so.
I hold you as a thing enskied and sainted
35 By your renouncement, an immortal spirit,
And to be talk'd with in sincerity,
As with a saint.
ISABELLA   You do blaspheme the good, in mocking me.
LUCIO   Do not believe it. Fewness and truth; 'tis thus:
40 Your brother and his lover have embrac'd;
As those that feed grow full, as blossoming time
That from the seedness the bare fallow brings
To teeming foison, even so her plenteous womb
Expresseth his full tilth and husbandry.
ISABELLA
45 Someone with child by him? My cousin Juliet?
LUCIO   Is she your cousin?
ISABELLA
Adoptedly, as schoolmaids change their names
By vain though apt affection.
LUCIO   She it is.
ISABELLA   O, let him marry her!
LUCIO   This is the point.
50 The Duke is very strangely gone from hence;
Bore many gentlemen – myself being one –
In hand, and hope of action: but we do learn,
By those that know the very nerves of state,
His giving out were of an infinite distance
55 From his true-meant design. Upon his place,
And with full line of his authority,
Governs Lord Angelo; a man whose blood
Is very snow-broth; one who never feels
The wanton stings and motions of the sense;
60 But doth rebate and blunt his natural edge
With profits of the mind, study and fast.
He, to give fear to use and liberty,
Which have for long run by the hideous law
As mice by lions, hath pick'd out an act
65 Under whose heavy sense your brother's life
Falls into forfeit: he arrests him on it,
And follows close the rigour of the statute
To make him an example. All hope is gone,
Unless you have the grace by your fair prayer
70 To soften Angelo. And that's my pith of business
'Twixt you and your poor brother.
ISABELLA   Doth he so,
Seek his life?
LUCIO   Has censur'd him already;
And, as I hear, the Provost hath a warrant
For's execution.
75 ISABELLA   Alas, what poor ability's in me
To do him good!

LUCIO   Assay the power you have.
ISABELLA   My power? Alas, I doubt.
LUCIO   Our doubts are traitors,
  And makes us lose the good we oft might win
  By fearing to attempt. Go to Lord Angelo,
  And let him learn to know, when maidens sue,
  Men give like gods; but when they weep and kneel,
  All their petitions are as freely theirs
  As they themselves would owe them.
ISABELLA   I'll see what I can do.
LUCIO   But speedily.
ISABELLA   I will about it straight;
  No longer staying but to give the Mother
  Notice of my affair. I humbly thank you.
  Commend me to my brother: soon at night
  I'll send him certain word of my success.
LUCIO   I take my leave of you.
ISABELLA   Good sir, adieu.
                        Exeunt severally.

2.1   *Enter* ANGELO, ESCALUS *and servants, a Justice.*

ANGELO   We must not make a scarecrow of the law,
  Setting it up to fear the birds of prey,
  And let it keep one shape till custom make it
  Their perch, and not their terror.
ESCALUS   Ay, but yet
  Let us be keen, and rather cut a little,
  Than fall, and bruise to death. Alas, this gentleman,
  Whom I would save, had a most noble father.
  Let but your honour know –
  Whom I believe to be most strait in virtue –
  That in the working of your own affections,
  Had time coher'd with place, or place with wishing,
  Or that the resolute acting of your blood
  Could have attain'd th'effect of your own purpose,
  Whether you had not sometime in your life
  Err'd in this point, which now you censure him,
  And pull'd the law upon you.
ANGELO   'Tis one thing to be tempted, Escalus,
  Another thing to fall. I not deny
  The jury passing on the prisoner's life
  May in the sworn twelve have a thief, or two,
  Guiltier than him they try. What's open made to
      justice,
  That justice seizes. What knows the laws
  That thieves do pass on thieves? 'Tis very pregnant,
  The jewel that we find, we stoop and take't,
  Because we see it; but what we do not see,
  We tread upon, and never think of it.
  You may not so extenuate his offence
  For I have had such faults; but rather tell me,
  When I that censure him do so offend,
  Let mine own judgement pattern out my death,
  And nothing come in partial. Sir, he must die.

                Enter PROVOST.

ESCALUS   Be it as your wisdom will.
ANGELO   Where is the Provost?
PROVOST   Here, if it like your honour.
ANGELO   See that Claudio
  Be executed by nine tomorrow morning;
  Bring him his confessor, let him be prepar'd,
  For that's the utmost of his pilgrimage.
                        Exit Provost.
ESCALUS   Well, heaven forgive him; and forgive us all.
  Some rise by sin, and some by virtue fall.
  Some run from brakes of ice and answer none,
  And some condemned for a fault alone.

    Enter ELBOW *and officers with* FROTH *and* POMPEY.

ELBOW   Come, bring them away. If these be good people
  in a commonweal, that do nothing but use their abuses
  in common houses, I know no law. Bring them away.
ANGELO   How now sir, what's your name? And what's
  the matter?
ELBOW   If it please your honour, I am the poor Duke's
  constable, and my name is Elbow. I do lean upon
  justice, sir, and do bring in here before your good
  honour two notorious benefactors.
ANGELO   Benefactors? Well, what benefactors are they?
  Are they not malefactors?
ELBOW   If it please your honour, I know not well what
  they are. But precise villains they are, that I am sure
  of, and void of all profanation in the world, that good
  Christians ought to have.
ESCALUS [*to Angelo*]   This comes off well: here's a wise
  officer.
ANGELO   Go to. What quality are they of? Elbow is your
  name? Why dost thou not speak, Elbow?
POMPEY   He cannot, sir: he's out at elbow.
ANGELO   What are you, sir?
ELBOW   He, sir? A tapster, sir; parcel bawd; one that
  serves a bad woman; whose house, sir, was, as they say,
  plucked down in the suburbs; and now she professes a
  hot-house; which I think is a very ill house too.
ESCALUS   How know you that?
ELBOW   My wife, sir, whom I detest before heaven and
  your honour –
ESCALUS   How? Thy wife?
ELBOW   Ay, sir: whom I thank heaven is an honest
  woman –
ESCALUS   Dost thou detest her therefore?
ELBOW   I say, sir, I will detest myself also, as well as she,
  that this house, if it be not a bawd's house, it is pity of
  her life, for it is a naughty house.
ESCALUS   How dost thou know that, constable?
ELBOW   Marry, sir, by my wife, who, if she had been a
  woman cardinally given, might have been accused in
  fornication, adultery, and all uncleanliness there.
ESCALUS   By the woman's means?
ELBOW   Ay, sir, by Mistress Overdone's means; but as
  she spit in his face, so she defied him.
POMPEY   Sir, if it please your honour, this is not so.

ELBOW   Prove it before these varlets here, thou
85   honourable man, prove it.

ESCALUS [*to Angelo*]   Do you hear how he misplaces?

POMPEY   Sir, she came in great with child; and longing,
        saving your honours' reverence, for stewed prunes; sir,
        we had but two in the house, which at that very distant
90   time stood as it were in a fruit-dish, a dish of some
        three pence, your honours have seen such dishes, they
        are not china dishes, but very good dishes, –

ESCALUS   Go to, go to: no matter for the dish, sir.

POMPEY   No indeed, sir, not of a pin: you are therein in
95   the right: but to the point. As I say, this Mistress
        Elbow being, as I say, with child, and being great-
        bellied, and longing, as I said, for prunes; and having
        but two in the dish, as I said, Master Froth here, this
        very man, having eaten the rest, as I said, and, as I say,
100   paying for them very honestly; for, as you know,
        Master Froth, I could not give you three pence
        again –

FROTH   No, indeed.

POMPEY   Very well: you being then, if you be
105   remembered, cracking the stones of the foresaid
        prunes –

FROTH   Ay, so I did indeed.

POMPEY   Why, very well: I telling you then, if you be
        remembered, that such a one and such a one were past
110   cure of the thing you wot of, unless they kept very
        good diet, as I told you –

FROTH   All this is true.

POMPEY   Why, very well then –

ESCALUS   Come, you are a tedious fool. To the purpose:
115   what was done to Elbow's wife that he hath cause to
        complain of? Come me to what was done to her.

POMPEY   Sir, your honour cannot come to that yet.

ESCALUS   No, sir, nor I mean it not.

POMPEY   Sir, but you shall come to it, by your honour's
120   leave. And I beseech you, look into Master Froth here,
        sir; a man of fourscore pound a year; whose father died
        at Hallowmas – was't not at Hallowmas, Master
        Froth?

FROTH   All-hallond Eve.

125 POMPEY   Why, very well: I hope here be truths. He, sir,
        sitting, as I say, in a lower chair, sir – 'twas in the
        Bunch of Grapes, where indeed you have a delight to
        sit, have you not?

FROTH   I have so, because it is an open room, and good
130   for winter.

POMPEY   Why, very well then: I hope here be truths.

ANGELO   This will last out a night in Russia
        When nights are longest there. I'll take my leave,
        And leave you to the hearing of the cause;
135   Hoping you'll find good cause to whip them all.

ESCALUS   I think no less: good morrow to your lordship.
                                        Exit Angelo.
        Now, sir, come on. What was done to Elbow's wife,
        once more?

POMPEY   Once, sir? There was nothing done to her once.

ELBOW   I beseech you, sir, ask him what this man did to   140
        my wife.

POMPEY   I beseech your honour, ask me.

ESCALUS   Well, sir, what did this gentleman to her?

POMPEY   I beseech you, sir, look in this gentleman's face.
        Good Master Froth, look upon his honour; 'tis for a   145
        good purpose. – Doth your honour mark his face?

ESCALUS   Ay, sir, very well.

POMPEY   Nay, I beseech you, mark it well.

ESCALUS   Well, I do so.

POMPEY   Doth your honour see any harm in his face?   150

ESCALUS   Why, no.

POMPEY   I'll be supposed upon a book, his face is the
        worst thing about him. – Good, then: if his face be the
        worst thing about him, how could Master Froth do the
        constable's wife any harm? I would know that of your   155
        honour.

ESCALUS   He's in the right, constable; what say you to it?

ELBOW   First, and it like you, the house is a respected
        house; next, this is a respected fellow; and his mistress
        is a respected woman.   160

POMPEY   By this hand, sir, his wife is a more respected
        person than any of us all.

ELBOW   Varlet, thou liest! Thou liest, wicked varlet! The
        time is yet to come that she was ever respected with
        man, woman, or child.   165

POMPEY   Sir, she was respected with him, before he
        married with her.

ESCALUS   Which is the wiser here, Justice or Iniquity? Is
        this true?

ELBOW   O thou caitiff! O thou varlet! O thou wicked   170
        Hannibal! I respected with her, before I was married
        to her? If ever I was respected with her, or she with
        me, let not your worship think me the poor Duke's
        officer. Prove this, thou wicked Hannibal, or I'll have
        mine action of battery on thee.   175

ESCALUS   If he took you a box o'th' ear, you might have
        your action of slander too.

ELBOW   Marry, I thank your good worship for it. What
        is't your worship's pleasure I shall do with this wicked
        caitiff?   180

ESCALUS   Truly, officer, because he hath some offences
        in him that thou wouldst discover if thou couldst, let
        him continue in his courses till thou know'st what they
        are.

ELBOW   Marry, I thank your worship for it. – Thou   185
        seest, thou wicked varlet now, what's come upon thee.
        Thou art to continue now, thou varlet, thou art to
        continue.

ESCALUS   Where were you born, friend?

FROTH   Here in Vienna, sir.   190

ESCALUS   Are you of fourscore pounds a year?

FROTH   Yes, and 't please you, sir.

ESCALUS   So. [*to Pompey*] What trade are you of, sir?

POMPEY   A tapster, a poor widow's tapster.

ESCALUS   Your mistress' name?   195

POMPEY   Mistress Overdone.

ESCALUS   Hath she had any more than one husband?

POMPEY   Nine, sir; Overdone by the last.

ESCALUS   Nine! – Come hither to me, Master Froth. Master Froth, I would not have you acquainted with tapsters; they will draw you, Master Froth, and you will hang them. Get you gone, and let me hear no more of you.

FROTH   I thank your worship. For mine own part, I never come into any room in a tap-house, but I am drawn in.

ESCALUS   Well: no more of it, Master Froth: farewell.
Exit Froth.
Come you hither to me, Master tapster. What's your name, Master tapster?

POMPEY   Pompey.

ESCALUS   What else?

POMPEY   Bum, sir.

ESCALUS   Troth, and your bum is the greatest thing about you; so that, in the beastliest sense, you are Pompey the Great. Pompey, you are partly a bawd, Pompey, howsoever you colour it in being a tapster, are you not? Come, tell me true, it shall be the better for you.

POMPEY   Truly, sir, I am a poor fellow that would live.

ESCALUS   How would you live, Pompey? By being a bawd? What do you think of the trade, Pompey? Is it a lawful trade?

POMPEY   If the law would allow it, sir.

ESCALUS   But the law will not allow it, Pompey; nor it shall not be allowed in Vienna.

POMPEY   Does your worship mean to geld and splay all the youth of the city?

ESCALUS   No, Pompey.

POMPEY   Truly sir, in my poor opinion, they will to't then. If your worship will take order for the drabs and the knaves, you need not to fear the bawds.

ESCALUS   There is pretty orders beginning, I can tell you. It is but heading and hanging.

POMPEY   If you head and hang all that offend that way but for ten year together, you'll be glad to give out a commission for more heads: if this law hold in Vienna ten year, I'll rent the fairest house in it after three pence a bay. If you live to see this come to pass, say Pompey told you so.

ESCALUS   Thank you, good Pompey; and, in requital of your prophecy, hark you: I advise you, let me not find you before me again upon any complaint whatsoever; no, not for dwelling where you do. If I do, Pompey, I shall beat you to your tent, and prove a shrewd Caesar to you: in plain dealing, Pompey, I shall have you whipped. So for this time, Pompey, fare you well.

POMPEY   I thank your worship for your good counsel; [*aside*] but I shall follow it as the flesh and fortune shall better determine.
Whip me? No, no, let carman whip his jade;
The valiant heart's not whipt out of his trade.   *Exit.*

ESCALUS   Come hither to me, Master Elbow: come hither, Master constable. How long have you been in this place of constable?

ELBOW   Seven year and a half, sir.   255

ESCALUS   I thought, by the readiness in the office, you had continued in it some time. – You say seven years together?

ELBOW   And a half, sir.

ESCALUS   Alas, it hath been great pains to you: they do   260
you wrong to put you so oft upon't. Are there not men in your ward sufficient to serve it?

ELBOW   Faith, sir, few of any wit in such matters. As they are chosen, they are glad to choose me for them; I do it for some piece of money, and go through with   265
all.

ESCALUS   Look you bring me in the names of some six or seven, the most sufficient of your parish.

ELBOW   To your worship's house, sir?

ESCALUS   To my house. Fare you well.   *Exit Elbow.*   270
What's o'clock, think you?

JUSTICE   Eleven, sir.

ESCALUS   I pray you home to dinner with me.

JUSTICE   I humbly thank you.

ESCALUS   It grieves me for the death of Claudio,   275
But there's no remedy.

JUSTICE   Lord Angelo is severe.

ESCALUS   It is but needful.
Mercy is not itself, that oft looks so;
Pardon is still the nurse of second woe.
But yet, poor Claudio! There is no remedy.   280
Come, sir.   *Exeunt.*

2.2   *Enter* Provost *and a* Servant.

SERVANT
He's hearing of a cause: he will come straight;
I'll tell him of you.

PROVOST   Pray you, do.   *Exit Servant.*
                               I'll know
His pleasure, may be he will relent. Alas,
He hath but as offended in a dream;
All sects, all ages smack of this vice, and he   5
To die for't!

Enter ANGELO.

ANGELO   Now, what's the matter, Provost?

PROVOST   Is it your will Claudio shall die tomorrow?

ANGELO   Did I not tell thee yea? Hadst thou not order?
Why dost thou ask again?

PROVOST   Lest I might be too rash.
Under your good correction, I have seen   10
When, after execution, judgement hath
Repented o'er his doom.

ANGELO   Go to; let that be mine;
Do you your office, or give up your place,
And you shall well be spar'd.

PROVOST   I crave your honour's pardon.
What shall be done, sir, with the groaning Juliet?   15

She's very near her hour.

ANGELO   Dispose of her
To some more fitter place; and that with speed.

Enter Servant.

SERVANT   Here is the sister of the man condemn'd,
Desires access to you.

ANGELO   Hath he a sister?

20   PROVOST   Ay, my good lord, a very virtuous maid;
And to be shortly of a sisterhood,
If not already.

ANGELO   Well, let her be admitted.
                                        Exit Servant.

See you the fornicatress be remov'd;
Let her have needful, but not lavish means;
There shall be order for't.

Enter LUCIO *and* ISABELLA.

25   PROVOST   Save your honour! [*going*]

ANGELO   Stay a little while.
[*to Isabella*]   Y'are welcome: what's your will?

ISABELLA   I am a woeful suitor to your honour;
Please but your honour hear me.

ANGELO   Well: what's your suit?

ISABELLA   There is a vice that most I do abhor,

30   And most desire should meet the blow of justice;
For which I would not plead, but that I must;
For which I must not plead, but that I am
At war 'twixt will and will not.

ANGELO   Well: the matter?

ISABELLA   I have a brother is condemn'd to die;

35   I do beseech you, let it be his fault,
And not my brother.

PROVOST [*aside*]   Heaven give thee moving graces!

ANGELO   Condemn the fault, and not the actor of it?
Why, every fault's condemn'd ere it be done:
Mine were the very cipher of a function

40   To fine the faults, whose find stands in record,
And let go by the actor.

ISABELLA   O just but severe law!
I had a brother, then: heaven keep your honour.
[*going*]

LUCIO [*to Isabella*]
Give't not o'er so. – To him again, entreat him,
Kneel down before him, hang upon his gown;

45   You are too cold. If you should need a pin,
You could not with more tame a tongue desire it.
To him, I say.

ISABELLA   Must he needs die?

ANGELO   Maiden, no remedy.

ISABELLA   Yes: I do think that you might pardon him,

50   And neither heaven nor man grieve at the mercy.

ANGELO   I will not do't.

ISABELLA   But can you if you would?

ANGELO   Look what I will not, that I cannot do.

ISABELLA
But might you do't, and do the world no wrong,

If so your heart were touch'd with that remorse
As mine is to him?

ANGELO   He's sentenc'd, 'tis too late.   55

LUCIO [*to Isabella*]   You are too cold.

ISABELLA   Too late? Why, no. I that do speak a word
May call it again. – Well, believe this:
No ceremony that to great ones longs,
Not the king's crown, nor the deputed sword,   60
The marshal's truncheon, nor the judge's robe,
Become them with one half so good a grace
As mercy does.
If he had been as you, and you as he,
You would have slipp'd like him, but he like you   65
Would not have been so stern.

ANGELO   Pray you be gone.

ISABELLA   I would to heaven I had your potency,
And you were Isabel! Should it then be thus?
No; I would tell what 'twere to be a judge,
And what a prisoner.

LUCIO [*to Isabella*]   Ay, touch him: there's the vein.   70

ANGELO   Your brother is a forfeit of the law,
And you but waste your words.

ISABELLA   Alas, alas!
Why, all the souls that were, were forfeit once,
And He that might the vantage best have took
Found out the remedy. How would you be   75
If He, which is the top of judgement, should
But judge you as you are? O, think on that,
And mercy then will breathe within your lips,
Like man new made.

ANGELO   Be you content, fair maid;
It is the law, not I, condemn your brother;   80
Were he my kinsman, brother, or my son,
It should be thus with him. He must die tomorrow.

ISABELLA   Tomorrow? O, that's sudden.
Spare him, spare him!
He's not prepar'd for death. Even for our kitchens   85
We kill the fowl of season: shall we serve heaven
With less respect than we do minister
To our gross selves? Good, good my lord, bethink
   you:
Who is it that hath died for this offence?
There's many have committed it.

LUCIO [*to Isabella*]   Ay, well said.   90

ANGELO
The law hath not been dead, though it hath slept:
Those many had not dar'd to do that evil
If the first that did th'edict infringe
Had answer'd for his deed. Now 'tis awake,
Takes note of what is done, and like a prophet   95
Looks in a glass that shows what future evils,
Either new, or by remissness new conceiv'd,
And so in progress to be hatch'd and born,
Are now to have no successive degrees,
But ere they live, to end.

ISABELLA   Yet show some pity.   100

ANGELO   I show it most of all when I show justice;

For then I pity those I do not know,
Which a dismiss'd offence would after gall,
And do him right that, answering one foul wrong,
Lives not to act another. Be satisfied;
Your brother dies tomorrow; be content.

ISABELLA
So you must be the first that gives this sentence,
And he, that suffers. O, it is excellent
To have a giant's strength, but it is tyrannous
To use it like a giant.

LUCIO [*to Isabella*]   That's well said.

ISABELLA   Could great men thunder
As Jove himself does, Jove would ne'er be quiet,
For every pelting petty officer
Would use his heaven for thunder; nothing but
    thunder.
Merciful Heaven,
Thou rather with thy sharp and sulphurous bolt
Splits the unwedgeable and gnarled oak,
Than the soft myrtle. But man, proud man,
Dress'd in a little brief authority,
Most ignorant of what he's most assur'd –
His glassy essence – like an angry ape
Plays such fantastic tricks before high heaven
As makes the angels weep; who, with our spleens,
Would all themselves laugh mortal.

LUCIO [*to Isabella*]
O, to him, to him, wench! He will relent;
He's coming: I perceive't.

PROVOST [*aside*]   Pray heaven she win him.

ISABELLA   We cannot weigh our brother with ourself.
Great men may jest with saints: 'tis wit in them,
But in the less, foul profanation.

LUCIO [*to Isabella*]   Thou'rt i'th' right, girl; more o' that.

ISABELLA   That in the captain's but a choleric word,
Which in the soldier is flat blasphemy.

LUCIO [*to Isabella*]   Art avis'd o' that? More on't.

ANGELO   Why do you put these sayings upon me?

ISABELLA   Because authority, though it err like others,
Hath yet a kind of medicine in itself
That skins the vice o'th' top. Go to your bosom,
Knock there, and ask your heart what it doth know
That's like my brother's fault. If it confess
A natural guiltiness, such as is his,
Let it not sound a thought upon your tongue
Against my brother's life.

ANGELO [*aside*]   She speaks, and 'tis such sense
That my sense breeds with it. – Fare you well.
[*going*]

ISABELLA   Gentle my lord, turn back.

ANGELO   I will bethink me. Come again tomorrow.
[*going*]

ISABELLA
Hark, how I'll bribe you: good my lord, turn back.

ANGELO   How! Bribe me?

ISABELLA
Ay, with such gifts that heaven shall share with you.

LUCIO [*to Isabella*]   You had marr'd all else.

ISABELLA   Not with fond sickles of the tested gold,   150
Or stones, whose rate are either rich or poor
As fancy values them: but with true prayers,
That shall be up at heaven and enter there
Ere sunrise: prayers from preserved souls,
From fasting maids, whose minds are dedicate   155
To nothing temporal.

ANGELO   Well: come to me tomorrow.

LUCIO [*to Isabella*]   Go to: 'tis well; away.

ISABELLA   Heaven keep your honour safe.

ANGELO [*aside*]   Amen.
For I am that way going to temptation,
Where prayer's cross'd.

ISABELLA   At what hour tomorrow   160
Shall I attend your lordship?

ANGELO   At any time 'fore noon.

ISABELLA   Save your honour.   *Exeunt all but Angelo.*

ANGELO   From thee: even from thy virtue!
What's this? What's this? Is this her fault, or mine?
The tempter, or the tempted, who sins most, ha?
Not she; nor doth she tempt; but it is I   165
That, lying by the violet in the sun,
Do as the carrion does, not as the flower,
Corrupt with virtuous season. Can it be
That modesty may more betray our sense
Than woman's lightness? Having waste ground
    enough,   170
Shall we desire to raze the sanctuary
And pitch our evils there? O fie, fie, fie!
What dost thou, or what art thou, Angelo?
Dost thou desire her foully for those things
That make her good? O, let her brother live!   175
Thieves for their robbery have authority,
When judges steal themselves. What, do I love her,
That I desire to hear her speak again?
And feast upon her eyes? What is't I dream on?
O cunning enemy, that, to catch a saint,   180
With saints dost bait thy hook! Most dangerous
Is that temptation that doth goad us on
To sin in loving virtue. Never could the strumpet
With all her double vigour, art and nature,
Once stir my temper: but this virtuous maid   185
Subdues me quite. Ever till now
When men were fond, I smil'd, and wonder'd how.
                                        Exit.

2.3   *Enter severally* DUKE,
            disguised as a friar, and Provost.

DUKE   Hail to you, Provost – so I think you are.

PROVOST
I am the Provost. What's your will, good Friar?

DUKE   Bound by my charity, and my bless'd order,
I come to visit the afflicted spirits
Here in the prison. Do me the common right   5
To let me see them, and to make me know

I had rather give my body than my soul.
ANGELO   I talk not of your soul: our compell'd sins
Stand more for number than for accompt.
ISABELLA   How say you?
ANGELO   Nay, I'll not warrant that: for I can speak
Against the thing I say. Answer to this:
I – now the voice of the recorded law –
Pronounce a sentence on your brother's life:
Might there not be a charity in sin
To save this brother's life?
ISABELLA   Please you to do't,
I'll take it as a peril to my soul;
It is no sin at all, but charity.
ANGELO   Pleas'd you to do't, at peril of your soul,
Were equal poise of sin and charity.
ISABELLA   That I do beg his life, if it be sin,
Heaven let me bear it; you granting of my suit,
If that be sin, I'll make it my morn prayer
To have it added to the faults of mine,
And nothing of your answer.
ANGELO   Nay, but hear me;
Your sense pursues not mine: either you are ignorant,
Or seem so, crafty; and that's not good.
ISABELLA   Let me be ignorant, and in nothing good,
But graciously to know I am no better.
ANGELO   Thus wisdom wishes to appear most bright
When it doth tax itself: as these black masks
Proclaim an enciel'd beauty ten times louder
Than beauty could, display'd. But mark me;
To be received plain, I'll speak more gross.
Your brother is to die.
ISABELLA   So.
ANGELO   And his offence is so, as it appears,
Accountant to the law upon that pain.
ISABELLA   True.
ANGELO   Admit no other way to save his life –
As I subscribe not that, nor any other,
But in the loss of question – that you, his sister,
Finding yourself desir'd of such a person
Whose credit with the judge, or own great place,
Could fetch your brother from the manacles
Of the all-binding law; and that there were
No earthly mean to save him, but that either
You must lay down the treasures of your body
To this suppos'd, or else to let him suffer:
What would you do?
ISABELLA   As much for my poor brother as myself;
That is, were I under the terms of death,
Th'impression of keen whips I'd wear as rubies,
And strip myself to death as to a bed
That longing have been sick for, ere I'd yield
My body up to shame.
ANGELO   Then must your brother die.
ISABELLA   And 'twere the cheaper way.
Better it were a brother died at once,
Than that a sister, by redeeming him,
Should die for ever.

ANGELO   Were you not then as cruel as the sentence
That you have slander'd so?
ISABELLA   Ignomy in ransom and free pardon
Are of two houses: lawful mercy
Is nothing kin to foul redemption.
ANGELO   You seem'd of late to make the law a tyrant,
And rather prov'd the sliding of your brother
A merriment than a vice.
ISABELLA   O pardon me, my lord; it oft falls out
To have what we would have, we speak not what we
mean.
I something do excuse the thing I hate
For his advantage that I dearly love.
ANGELO   We are all frail.
ISABELLA   Else let my brother die,
If not a feodary but only he
Owe and succeed thy weakness.
ANGELO   Nay, women are frail too.
ISABELLA
Ay, as the glasses where they view themselves,
Which are as easy broke as they make forms.
Women? – Help, heaven! Men their creation mar
In profiting by them. Nay, call us ten times frail;
For we are soft as our complexions are,
And credulous to false prints.
ANGELO   I think it well;
And from this testimony of your own sex –
Since I suppose we are made to be no stronger
Than faults may shake our frames – let me be bold.
I do arrest your words. Be that you are,
That is, a woman; if you be more, you're none.
If you be one – as you are well express'd
By all external warrants – show it now,
By putting on the destin'd livery.
ISABELLA   I have no tongue but one; gentle my lord,
Let me entreat you speak the former language.
ANGELO   Plainly conceive, I love you.
ISABELLA   My brother did love Juliet,
And you tell me that he shall die for't.
ANGELO   He shall not, Isabel, if you give me love.
ISABELLA   I know your virtue hath a licence in't,
Which seems a little fouler than it is,
To pluck on others.
ANGELO   Believe me, on mine honour,
My words express my purpose.
ISABELLA   Ha? Little honour, to be much believ'd,
And most pernicious purpose! Seeming, seeming!
I will proclaim thee, Angelo, look for't.
Sign me a present pardon for my brother,
Or with an outstretch'd throat I'll tell the world
aloud
What man thou art.
ANGELO   Who will believe thee, Isabel?
My unsoil'd name, th'austereness of my life,
My vouch against you, and my place i'th' state
Will so your accusation overweigh,
That you shall stifle in your own report,

60

65

70

75

80

85

90

95

100

105

110

115

120

125

130

135

140

145

150

155

And smell of calumny. I have begun,
And now I give my sensual race the rein:
160 Fit thy consent to my sharp appetite;
Lay by all nicety and prolixious blushes
That banish what they sue for. Redeem thy brother
By yielding up thy body to my will;
Or else he must not only die the death,
165 But thy unkindness shall his death draw out
To ling'ring sufferance. Answer me tomorrow,
Or, by the affection that now guides me most,
I'll prove a tyrant to him. As for you,
Say what you can: my false o'erweighs your true.
                                                                    Exit.

170 ISABELLA To whom should I complain? Did I tell this,
Who would believe me? O perilous mouths,
That bear in them one and the self-same tongue
Either of condemnation or approof,
Bidding the law make curtsey to their will,
175 Hooking both right and wrong to th'appetite,
To follow as it draws! I'll to my brother.
Though he hath fall'n by prompture of the blood,
Yet hath he in him such a mind of honour,
That had he twenty heads to tender down
180 On twenty bloody blocks, he'd yield them up
Before his sister should her body stoop
To such abhorr'd pollution.
Then, Isabel live chaste, and brother, die:
More than our brother is our chastity.
185 I'll tell him yet of Angelo's request,
And fit his mind to death, for his soul's rest. *Exit.*

3.1 *Enter* DUKE, *disguised, and* Provost *with* CLAUDIO.

DUKE So then you hope of pardon from Lord Angelo?
CLAUDIO The miserable have no other medicine
But only hope:
I have hope to live, and am prepar'd to die.
5 DUKE Be absolute for death: either death or life
Shall thereby be the sweeter. Reason thus with life:
If I do lose thee, I do lose a thing
That none but fools would keep. A breath thou art,
Servile to all the skyey influences
10 That dost this habitation where thou keep'st
Hourly afflict. Merely, thou art Death's fool;
For him thou labour'st by thy flight to shun,
And yet run'st toward him still. Thou art not noble;
For all th'accommodations that thou bear'st
15 Are nurs'd by baseness. Thou'rt by no means valiant;
For thou dost fear the soft and tender fork
Of a poor worm. Thy best of rest is sleep;
And that thou oft provok'st, yet grossly fear'st
Thy death, which is no more. Thou art not thyself;
20 For thou exists on many a thousand grains
That issue out of dust. Happy thou art not;
For what thou hast not, still thou striv'st to get,
And what thou hast, forget'st. Thou art not certain;
For thy complexion shifts to strange effects
After the moon. If thou art rich, thou'rt poor; 25
For, like an ass whose back with ingots bows,
Thou bear'st thy heavy riches but a journey,
And Death unloads thee. Friend hast thou none;
For thine own bowels which do call thee sire,
The mere effusion of thy proper loins, 30
Do curse the gout, serpigo, and the rheum
For ending thee no sooner. Thou hast nor youth, nor
   age,
But as it were an after-dinner's sleep
Dreaming on both; for all thy blessed youth
Becomes as aged, and doth beg the alms 35
Of palsied eld: and when thou art old and rich,
Thou hast neither heat, affection, limb, nor beauty
To make thy riches pleasant. What's yet in this
That bears the name of life? Yet in this life
Lie hid moe thousand deaths; yet death we fear 40
That makes these odds all even.
CLAUDIO   I humbly thank you.
To sue to live, I find I seek to die,
And seeking death, find life. Let it come on.
ISABELLA [*within*]
What hoa! Peace here; grace and good company!
PROVOST
Who's there? Come in; the wish deserves a welcome. 45
DUKE Dear sir, ere long I'll visit you again.
CLAUDIO Most holy sir, I thank you.

                        Enter ISABELLA.

ISABELLA My business is a word or two with Claudio.
PROVOST
And very welcome. Look, signior, here's your sister.
DUKE Provost, a word with you. 50
PROVOST As many as you please.
DUKE Bring me to hear them speak, where I may be
conceal'd. [*Duke and Provost retire.*]
CLAUDIO Now, sister, what's the comfort?
ISABELLA Why,
As all comforts are: most good, most good indeed. 55
Lord Angelo, having affairs to heaven,
Intends you for his swift ambassador,
Where you shall be an everlasting leiger.
Therefore your best appointment make with speed;
Tomorrow you set on.
CLAUDIO   Is there no remedy? 60
ISABELLA None, but such remedy as, to save a head,
To cleave a heart in twain.
CLAUDIO   But is there any?
ISABELLA Yes, brother, you may live;
There is a devilish mercy in the judge,
If you'll implore it, that will free your life, 65
But fetter you till death.
CLAUDIO   Perpetual durance?
ISABELLA Ay, just, perpetual durance; a restraint,
Though all the world's vastidity you had,
To a determin'd scope.
CLAUDIO   But in what nature?

ISABELLA   In such a one as, you consenting to't,
    Would bark your honour from that trunk you bear,
    And leave you naked.
CLAUDIO   Let me know the point.
ISABELLA   O, I do fear thee, Claudio, and I quake
    Lest thou a feverous life shouldst entertain,
    And six or seven winters more respect
    Than a perpetual honour. Dar'st thou die?
    The sense of death is most in apprehension;
    And the poor beetle that we tread upon
    In corporal sufferance finds a pang as great
    As when a giant dies.
CLAUDIO   Why give you me this shame?
    Think you I can a resolution fetch
    From flowery tenderness? If I must die,
    I will encounter darkness as a bride
    And hug it in mine arms.
ISABELLA
    There spake my brother: there my father's grave
    Did utter forth a voice. Yes, thou must die.
    Thou art too noble to conserve a life
    In base appliances. This outward-sainted deputy,
    Whose settl'd visage and deliberate word
    Nips youth i'th' head and follies doth enew
    As falcon doth the fowl, is yet a devil:
    His filth within being cast, he would appear
    A pond as deep as hell.
CLAUDIO   The precise Angelo!
ISABELLA   O, 'tis the cunning livery of hell
    The damnedst body to invest and cover
    In precise guards! Dost thou think, Claudio,
    If I would yield him my virginity
    Thou mightst be freed?
CLAUDIO   O heavens, it cannot be!
ISABELLA
    Yes, he would give't thee, from this rank offence,
    So to offend him still. This night's the time
    That I should do what I abhor to name;
    Or else thou diest tomorrow.
CLAUDIO   Thou shalt not do't.
ISABELLA   O, were it but my life,
    I'd throw it down for your deliverance
    As frankly as a pin.
CLAUDIO   Thanks, dear Isabel.
ISABELLA   Be ready, Claudio, for your death tomorrow.
CLAUDIO   Yes. – Has he affections in him,
    That thus can make him bite the law by th'nose
    When he would force it? – Sure, it is no sin;
    Or of the deadly seven it is the least.
ISABELLA   Which is the least?
CLAUDIO   If it were damnable, he being so wise,
    Why would he for the momentary trick
    Be perdurably fin'd? – O Isabel!
ISABELLA   What says my brother?
CLAUDIO   Death is a fearful thing.
ISABELLA   And shamed life a hateful.
CLAUDIO   Ay, but to die, and go we know not where;

To lie in cold obstruction, and to rot;
This sensible warm motion to become
A kneaded clod; and the delighted spirit   120
To bath in fiery floods, or to reside
In thrilling region of thick-ribbed ice;
To be imprison'd in the viewless winds
And blown with restless violence round about
The pendent world: or to be worse than worst   125
Of those that lawless and incertain thought
Imagine howling, – 'tis too horrible.
The weariest and most loathed worldly life
That age, ache, penury and imprisonment
Can lay on nature, is a paradise   130
To what we fear of death.
ISABELLA   Alas, alas!
CLAUDIO   Sweet sister, let me live.
    What sin you do to save a brother's life,
    Nature dispenses with the deed so far
    That it becomes a virtue.
ISABELLA   O, you beast!   135
    O faithless coward! O dishonest wretch!
    Wilt thou be made a man out of my vice?
    Is't not a kind of incest, to take life
    From thine own sister's shame? What should I think?
    Heaven shield my mother play'd my father fair: 140
    For such a warped slip of wilderness
    Ne'er issued from his blood. Take my defiance,
    Die, perish! Might but my bending down
    Reprieve thee from thy fate, it should proceed.
    I'll pray a thousand prayers for thy death;   145
    No word to save thee.
CLAUDIO   Nay hear me, Isabel.
ISABELLA   O fie, fie, fie!
    Thy sin's not accidental, but a trade;
    Mercy to thee would prove itself a bawd;
    'Tis best that thou diest quickly. [*going*]
CLAUDIO   O hear me, Isabella.   150
DUKE [*advancing*]
    Vouchsafe a word, young sister, but one word.
ISABELLA   What is your will?
DUKE   Might you dispense with your leisure, I would by
    and by have some speech with you: the satisfaction I
    would require is likewise your own benefit.   155
ISABELLA   I have no superfluous leisure; my stay must
    be stolen out of other affairs: but I will attend you a
    while. [*Waits behind.*]
DUKE   Son, I have overheard what hath passed between
    you and your sister. Angelo had never the purpose to   160
    corrupt her; only he hath made an assay of her virtue,
    to practise his judgement with the disposition of
    natures. She, having the truth of honour in her, hath
    made him that gracious denial which he is most glad
    to receive. I am confessor to Angelo, and I know this   165
    to be true; therefore prepare yourself to death. Do not
    satisfy your resolution with hopes that are fallible;
    tomorrow you must die; go to your knees, and make
    ready.

CLAUDIO   Let me ask my sister pardon; I am so out of
170   love with life that I will sue to be rid of it.

DUKE   Hold you there: farewell. – [*Claudio retires.*]
Provost, a word with you.

PROVOST [*advancing*]   What's your will, father?

DUKE   That, now you are come, you will be gone. Leave
175   me a while with the maid; my mind promises with my
habit no loss shall touch her by my company.

PROVOST   In good time.

Exit with Claudio. Isabella comes forward.

DUKE   The hand that hath made you fair hath made you
180   good. The goodness that is cheap in beauty makes
beauty brief in goodness; but grace, being the soul of
your complexion, shall keep the body of it ever fair.
The assault that Angelo hath made to you, fortune
hath conveyed to my understanding; and, but that
185   frailty hath examples for his falling, I should wonder
at Angelo. How will you do to content this substitute,
and to save your brother?

ISABELLA   I am now going to resolve him. I had rather
my brother die by the law, than my son should be
190   unlawfully born. But O, how much is the good Duke
deceived in Angelo! If ever he return, and I can speak
to him, I will open my lips in vain, or discover his
government.

DUKE   That shall not be much amiss. Yet, as the matter
195   now stands, he will avoid your accusation – he made
trial of you only. Therefore fasten your ear on my
advisings, to the love I have in doing good; a remedy
presents itself. I do make myself believe that you may
most uprighteously do a poor wronged lady a merited
200   benefit; redeem your brother from the angry law; do
no stain to your own gracious person; and much please
the absent Duke, if peradventure he shall ever return
to have hearing of this business.

ISABELLA   Let me hear you speak farther. I have spirit to
205   do anything that appears not foul in the truth of my
spirit.

DUKE   Virtue is bold, and goodness never fearful. Have
you not heard speak of Mariana, the sister of
Frederick, the great soldier who miscarried at sea?

ISABELLA   I have heard of the lady, and good words went
210   with her name.

DUKE   She should this Angelo have married: was
affianced to her oath, and the nuptial appointed.
Between which time of the contract and limit of the
215   solemnity, her brother Frederick was wracked at sea,
having in that perished vessel the dowry of his sister.
But mark how heavily this befell to the poor
gentlewoman. There she lost a noble and renowned
brother, in his love toward her ever most kind and
220   natural; with him, the portion and sinew of her
fortune, her marriage dowry; with both, her
combinate husband, this well-seeming Angelo.

ISABELLA   Can this be so? Did Angelo so leave her?

DUKE   Left her in her tears, and dried not one of them
225   with his comfort: swallowed his vows whole,
pretending in her discoveries of dishonour: in few,
bestowed her on her own lamentation, which she yet
wears for his sake; and he, a marble to her tears, is
washed with them, but relents not.

ISABELLA   What a merit were it in death to take this poor
230   maid from the world! What corruption in this life, that
it will let this man live! But how out of this can she
avail?

DUKE   It is a rupture that you may easily heal: and the
cure of it not only saves your brother, but keeps you
235   from dishonour in doing it.

ISABELLA   Show me how, good father.

DUKE   This forenamed maid hath yet in her the
continuance of her first affection. His unjust
240   unkindness, that in all reason should have quenched
her love, hath, like an impediment in the current,
made it more violent and unruly. Go you to Angelo;
answer his requiring with a plausible obedience; agree
with his demands to the point. Only refer yourself to
245   this advantage: first, that your stay with him may not
be long; that the place may have all shadow and silence
in it; and the time answer to convenience. This being
granted in course, and now follows all. We shall advise
this wronged maid to stead up your appointment, go
250   in your place. If the encounter acknowledge itself
hereafter, it may compel him to her recompense; and
hear, by this is your brother saved, your honour
untainted, the poor Mariana advantaged, and the
corrupt deputy scaled. The maid will I frame, and
255   make fit for his attempt. If you think well to carry this
as you may, the doubleness of the benefit defends the
deceit from reproof. What think you of it?

ISABELLA   The image of it gives me content already, and
I trust it will grow to a most prosperous perfection.

DUKE   It lies much in your holding up. Haste you
260   speedily to Angelo; if for this night he entreat you to
his bed, give him promise of satisfaction. I will
presently to Saint Luke's; there at the moated grange
resides this dejected Mariana; at that place call upon
me; and dispatch with Angelo, that it may be quickly.
265

ISABELLA   I thank you for this comfort. Fare you well,
good father.   *Exit Isabella.*

3.2   *Enter* ELBOW *and officers with* POMPEY.

ELBOW   Nay, if there be no remedy for it, but that you
will needs buy and sell men and women like beasts, we
shall have all the world drink brown and white bastard.

DUKE   O heavens, what stuff is here!

POMPEY   'Twas never merry world since, of two usuries,   5
the merriest was put down, and the worser allowed by
order of law; a furred gown to keep him warm; and
furred with fox on lambskins too, to signify that craft,
being richer than innocency, stands for the facing.

ELBOW   Come your way, sir. – Bless you, good father   10
friar.

DUKE   And you, good brother father. What offence hath
this man made you, sir?

ELBOW   Marry, sir, he hath offended the law; and, sir, we
　　take him to be a thief too, sir: for we have found upon
　　him, sir, a strange pick-lock, which we have sent to the
　　deputy.

DUKE   Fie, sirrah, a bawd, a wicked bawd;
　　The evil that thou causest to be done,
　　That is thy means to live. Do thou but think
　　What 'tis to cram a maw or clothe a back
　　From such a filthy vice. Say to thyself,
　　From their abominable and beastly touches
　　I drink, I eat, array myself, and live.
　　Canst thou believe thy living is a life,
　　So stinkingly depending? Go mend, go mend.

POMPEY
　　Indeed it does stink in some sort, sir. But yet, sir,
　　would prove –

DUKE   Nay, if the devil have given thee proofs for sin,
　　Thou wilt prove his. Take him to prison, officer:
　　Correction and instruction must both work
　　Ere this rude beast will profit.

ELBOW   He must before the deputy, sir; he has given him
　　warning. The deputy cannot abide a whoremaster. If
　　he be a whoremonger and comes before him, he were
　　as good go a mile on his errand.

DUKE   That we were all, as some would seem to be,
　　From our faults, as faults from seeming, free!

ELBOW   His neck will come to your waist – a cord, sir.

Enter LUCIO.

POMPEY   I spy comfort, I cry bail! Here's a gentleman,
　　and a friend of mine.

LUCIO   How now, noble Pompey! What, at the wheels of
　　Caesar? Art thou led in triumph? What, is there none
　　of Pygmalion's images newly made woman to be had
　　now, for putting the hand in the pocket and extracting
　　clutched? What reply, ha? What say'st thou to this
　　tune, matter and method? Is't not drowned i'th' last
　　rain? Ha? What say'st thou, trot? Is the world as it was,
　　man? Which is the way? Is it sad, and few words? Or
　　how? The trick of it?

DUKE   Still thus, and thus: still worse!

LUCIO   How doth my dear morsel, thy mistress?
　　Procures she still, ha?

POMPEY   Troth, sir, she hath eaten up all her beef, and
　　she is herself in the tub.

LUCIO   Why, 'tis good: it is the right of it: it must be so.
　　Ever your fresh whore, and your powdered bawd; an
　　unshunned consequence; it must be so. Art going to
　　prison, Pompey?

POMPEY   Yes, faith, sir.

LUCIO   Why, 'tis not amiss, Pompey. Farewell: go, say I
　　sent thee thither. – For debt, Pompey, or how?

POMPEY   For being a bawd, for being a bawd.

LUCIO   Well, then, imprison him. If imprisonment be
　　the due of a bawd, why, 'tis his right. Bawd is he
　　doubtless, and of antiquity, too: bawd born. Farewell,
　　good Pompey. Commend me to the prison, Pompey;

you will turn good husband now, Pompey; you will
keep the house.

POMPEY   I hope, sir, your good worship will be my bail?   70

LUCIO   No, indeed will I not, Pompey; it is not the wear.
　　I will pray, Pompey, to increase your bondage; if you
　　take it not patiently, why, your mettle is the more!
　　Adieu, trusty Pompey. – Bless you, friar.

DUKE   And you.   75

LUCIO   Does Bridget paint still, Pompey? Ha?

ELBOW [*to Pompey*]   Come your ways, sir, come.

POMPEY   You will not bail me then, sir?

LUCIO   Then, Pompey, nor now. – What news abroad,
　　friar? What news?   80

ELBOW [*to Pompey*]   Come your ways, sir, come.

LUCIO   Go to kennel, Pompey, go.
　　　　　　　Exeunt Elbow and officers with Pompey.
　　What news, friar, of the Duke?

DUKE   I know none: can you tell me of any?

LUCIO   Some say he is with the Emperor of Russia; other   85
　　some, he is in Rome: but where is he, think you?

DUKE   I know not where: but wheresoever, I wish him
　　well.

LUCIO   It was a mad, fantastical trick of him to steal
　　from the state and usurp the beggary he was never   90
　　born to. Lord Angelo dukes it well in his absence: he
　　puts transgression to't.

DUKE   He does well in't.

LUCIO   A little more lenity to lechery would do no harm
　　in him. Something too crabbed that way, friar.   95

DUKE   It is too general a vice, and severity must cure it.

LUCIO   Yes, in good sooth, the vice is of a great kindred;
　　it is well allied; but it is impossible to extirp it quite,
　　friar, till eating and drinking be put down. – They say
　　this Angelo was not made by man and woman, after   100
　　this downright way of creation: is it true, think you?

DUKE   How should he be made, then?

LUCIO   Some report, a sea-maid spawned him. Some,
　　that he was begot between two stockfishes. But it is
　　certain that when he makes water, his urine is   105
　　congealed ice; that I know to be true. And he is a
　　motion ungenerative; that's infallible.

DUKE   You are pleasant, sir, and speak apace.

LUCIO   Why, what a ruthless thing is this in him, for the
　　rebellion of a codpiece to take away the life of a man!   110
　　Would the Duke that is absent have done this? Ere he
　　would have hanged a man for the getting a hundred
　　bastards, he would have paid for the nursing a
　　thousand. He had some feeling of the sport; he knew
　　the service; and that instructed him to mercy.   115

DUKE   I have never heard the absent Duke much
　　detected for women; he was not inclined that way.

LUCIO   O sir, you are deceived.

DUKE   'Tis not possible.

LUCIO   Who, not the Duke? Yes, your beggar of fifty;   120
　　and his use was to put a ducat in her clack-dish; the
　　Duke had crotchets in him. He would be drunk too,
　　that let me inform you.

DUKE   You do him wrong, surely.

125 LUCIO   Sir, I was an inward of his. A shy fellow was the Duke; and I believe I know the cause of his withdrawing.

DUKE   What, I prithee, might be the cause?

LUCIO   No, pardon: 'tis a secret must be locked within
130   the teeth and the lips. But this I can let you understand: the greater file of the subject held the Duke to be wise.

DUKE   Wise? Why, no question but he was.

LUCIO   A very superficial, ignorant, unweighing fellow –

135 DUKE   Either this is envy in you, folly, or mistaking. The very stream of his life, and the business he hath helmed, must upon a warranted need give him a better proclamation. Let him be but testimonied in his own bringings-forth, and he shall appear to the envious a
140   scholar, a statesman, and a soldier. Therefore you speak unskilfully: or, if your knowledge be more, it is much darkened in your malice.

LUCIO   Sir, I know him and I love him.

DUKE   Love talks with better knowledge, and knowledge
145   with dearer love.

LUCIO   Come, sir, I know what I know.

DUKE   I can hardly believe that, since you know not what you speak. But if ever the Duke return – as our prayers are he may – let me desire you to make your
150   answer before him. If it be honest you have spoke, you have courage to maintain it; I am bound to call upon you, and I pray you your name.

LUCIO   Sir, my name is Lucio, well known to the Duke.

DUKE   He shall know you better, sir, if I may live to
155   report you.

LUCIO   I fear you not.

DUKE   O, you hope the Duke will return no more; or you imagine me too unhurtful an opposite. But indeed, I can do you little harm. You'll forswear this
160   again?

LUCIO   I'll be hanged first. Thou art deceived in me, friar. But no more of this. – Canst thou tell if Claudio die tomorrow, or no?

DUKE   Why should he die, sir?

165 LUCIO   Why? For filling a bottle with a tun-dish. I would the Duke we talk of were returned again: this ungenitured agent will unpeople the province with continency. Sparrows must not build in his house-eaves, because they are lecherous. – The Duke yet
170   would have dark deeds darkly answered: he would never bring them to light: would he were returned! Marry, this Claudio is condemned for untrussing. – Farewell, good friar, I prithee pray for me. The Duke, I say to thee again, would eat mutton on Fridays. He's
175   now past it; yet, and I say to thee, he would mouth with a beggar though she smelt brown bread and garlic, say that I said so. Farewell.   *Exit.*

DUKE   No might nor greatness in mortality Can censure 'scape. Back-wounding calumny
180   The whitest virtue strikes. What king so strong

Can tie the gall up in the slanderous tongue? But who comes here?

Enter severally ESCALUS, Provost *and officers with* MISTRESS OVERDONE.

ESCALUS   Go, away with her to prison.

MISTRESS OVERDONE   Good my lord, be good to me. Your honour is accounted a merciful man. Good my   185 lord.

ESCALUS   Double and treble admonition, and still forfeit in the same kind! This would make mercy swear and play the tyrant.

PROVOST   A bawd of eleven years' continuance, may it   190 please your honour.

MISTRESS OVERDONE   My lord, this is one Lucio's information against me, Mistress Kate Keep-down was with child by him in the Duke's time, he promised her marriage. His child is a year and a quarter old   195 come Philip and Jacob. I have kept it myself; and see how he goes about to abuse me.

ESCALUS   That fellow is a fellow of much license. Let him be called before us. Away with her to prison. – Go to, no more words.   200

Exeunt officers with Mistress Overdone.

Provost, my brother Angelo will not be altered; Claudio must die tomorrow. Let him be furnished with divines, and have all charitable preparation. If my brother wrought by my pity, it should not be so with him.   205

PROVOST   So please you, this friar hath been with him, and advised him for th'entertainment of death.

ESCALUS   Good even, good father.

DUKE   Bliss and goodness on you!

ESCALUS   Of whence are you?   210

DUKE   Not of this country, though my chance is now To use it for my time. I am a brother Of gracious order, late come from the See In special business from his Holiness.

ESCALUS   What news abroad i'th' world?   215

DUKE   None, but that there is so great a fever on goodness that the dissolution of it must cure it. Novelty is only in request, and it is as dangerous to be aged in any kind of course as it is virtuous to be constant in any undertaking. There is scarce truth   220 enough alive to make societies secure; but security enough to make fellowships accurst. Much upon this riddle runs the wisdom of the world. This news is old enough, yet it is every day's news. I pray you, sir, of what disposition was the Duke?   225

ESCALUS   One that, above all other strifes, contended especially to know himself.

DUKE   What pleasure was he given to?

ESCALUS   Rather rejoicing to see another merry, than merry at anything which professed to make him   230 rejoice. A gentleman of all temperance. But leave we him to his events, with a prayer they may prove prosperous, and let me desire to know how you find

Claudio prepared. I am made to understand that you
have lent him visitation.

DUKE   He professes to have received no sinister measure
from his judge, but most willingly humbles himself to
the determination of justice. Yet had he framed to
himself, by the instruction of his frailty, many
deceiving promises of life, which I, by my good
leisure, have discredited to him; and now is he
resolved to die.

ESCALUS   You have paid the heavens your function, and
the prisoner the very debt of your calling. I have
laboured for the poor gentleman to the extremest
shore of my modesty, but my brother-justice have I
found so severe that he hath forced me to tell him he
is indeed Justice.

DUKE   If his own life answer the straitness of his
proceeding, it shall become him well: wherein if he
chance to fail, he hath sentenced himself.

ESCALUS   I am going to visit the prisoner; fare you well.

DUKE   Peace be with you.   *Exeunt Escalus and Provost.*
          He who the sword of heaven will bear
          Should be as holy as severe:
          Pattern in himself to know,
          Grace to stand, and virtue, go:
          More nor less to others paying
          Than by self-offences weighing.
          Shame to him whose cruel striking
          Kills for faults of his own liking!
          Twice treble shame on Angelo,
          To weed my vice, and let his grow!
          O, what may man within him hide,
          Though angel on the outward side!
          How may likeness made in crimes,
          Making practice on the times
          To draw with idle spiders' strings
          Most ponderous and substantial things!
          Craft against vice I must apply.
          With Angelo tonight shall lie
          His old betrothed, but despised:
          So disguise shall by th'disguised
          Pay with falsehood false exacting,
          And perform an old contracting.   *Exit.*

4.1   *Enter* MARIANA, *and a boy singing.*

               Song.

        Take, o take those lips away
          that so sweetly were forsworn,
        And those eyes, the break of day
          lights that do mislead the morn:
        But my kisses bring again,
                              bring again;
        Seals of love, but seal'd in vain,
                              seal'd in vain.

          Enter DUKE, *disguised.*

MARIANA
      Break off thy song, and haste thee quick away;
      Here comes a man of comfort, whose advice
      Hath often still'd my brawling discontent.   *Exit boy.*
      I cry you mercy, sir, and well could wish   10
      You had not found me here so musical.
      Let me excuse me, and believe me so;
      My mirth it much displeas'd, but pleas'd my woe.
DUKE   'Tis good; though music oft hath such a charm
      To make bad good, and good provoke to harm.   15
      I pray you tell me, hath anybody enquired for me here
      to-day? Much upon this time have I promised here to
      meet.
MARIANA   You have not been enquired after: I have
      sat here all day.   20

               Enter ISABELLA.

DUKE   I do constantly believe you: the time is come even
      now. I shall crave your forbearance a little; may be I
      will call upon you anon for some advantage to
      yourself.
MARIANA   I am always bound to you.   *Exit.*   25
DUKE [*to Isabella*]   Very well met, and well come.
      What is the news from this good deputy?
ISABELLA   He hath a garden circummur'd with brick,
      Whose western side is with a vineyard back'd;
      And to that vineyard is a planched gate,   30
      That makes his opening with this bigger key.
      This other doth command a little door
      Which from the vineyard to the garden leads;
      There have I made my promise
      Upon the heavy middle of the night   35
      To call upon him.
DUKE   But shall you on your knowledge find this way?
ISABELLA   I have ta'en a due and wary note upon't;
      With whispering and most guilty diligence,
      In action all of precept, he did show me   40
      The way twice o'er.
DUKE   Are there no other tokens
      Between you 'greed, concerning her observance?
ISABELLA   No; none, but only a repair i'th' dark;
      And that I have possess'd him my most stay
      Can be but brief: for I have made him know   45
      I have a servant comes with me along,
      That stays upon me; whose persuasion is
      I come about my brother.
DUKE   'Tis well borne up.
      I have not yet made known to Mariana
      A word of this. – What hoa, within! Come forth.   50

               Enter MARIANA.

      [*to Mariana*] I pray you be acquainted with this
          maid;
      She comes to do you good.
ISABELLA   I do desire the like.
DUKE   Do you persuade yourself that I respect you?

               817

MARIANA
    Good friar, I know you do, and so have found it.

55 DUKE   Take, then, this your companion by the hand,
    Who hath a story ready for your ear.
    I shall attend your leisure; but make haste,
    The vaporous night approaches.
MARIANA [*to Isabella*]   Will't please you walk aside?
             [*Mariana and Isabella withdraw.*]

60 DUKE   O place and greatness! Millions of false eyes
    Are stuck upon thee: volumes of report
    Run with these false, and most contrarious quest
    Upon thy doings: thousand escapes of wit
    Make thee the father of their idle dream
    And rack thee in their fancies.
             [*Mariana and Isabella return.*]
65   Welcome; how agreed?
ISABELLA   She'll take the enterprise upon her, father,
    If you advise it.
DUKE   It is not my consent,
    But my entreaty too.
ISABELLA   Little have you to say
    When you depart from him, but, soft and low,
    'Remember now my brother'.
70 MARIANA   Fear me not.
DUKE   Nor, gentle daughter, fear you not at all.
    He is your husband on a pre-contract:
    To bring you thus together 'tis no sin,
    Sith that the justice of your title to him
75   Doth flourish the deceit. – Come, let us go;
    Our corn's to reap, for yet our tithe's to sow. *Exeunt.*

4.2   *Enter* Provost *and* POMPEY.

PROVOST   Come hither, sirrah. Can you cut off a man's
    head?
POMPEY   If the man be a bachelor, sir, I can; but if he be
    a married man, he's his wife's head; and I can never
5   cut off a woman's head.
PROVOST   Come, sir, leave me your snatches, and yield
    me a direct answer. Tomorrow morning are to die
    Claudio and Barnardine. Here is in our prison a
    common executioner, who in his office lacks a helper;
10   if you will take it on you to assist him, it shall redeem
    you from your gyves: if not, you shall have your full
    time of imprisonment, and your deliverance with an
    unpitied whipping; for you have been a notorious
    bawd.
15 POMPEY   Sir, I have been an unlawful bawd time out of
    mind, but yet I will be content to be a lawful hangman.
    I would be glad to receive some instruction from my
    fellow-partner.
PROVOST   What hoa, Abhorson! Where's Abhorson
20   there?

          Enter ABHORSON.

ABHORSON   Do you call, sir?
PROVOST   Sirrah, here's a fellow will help you tomorrow

in your execution. If you think it meet, compound
with him by the year, and let him abide here with you;
if not, use him for the present, and dismiss him. He   25
cannot plead his estimation with you: he hath been a
bawd.
ABHORSON   A bawd, sir? Fie upon him, he will discredit
our mystery.
PROVOST   Go to, sir, you weigh equally: a feather will   30
turn the scale.   *Exit.*
POMPEY   Pray, sir, by your good favour – for surely, sir, a
good favour you have, but that you have a hanging look
– do you call, sir, your occupation a mystery?
ABHORSON   Ay, sir, a mystery.   35
POMPEY   Painting, sir, I have heard say, is a mystery; and
your whores, sir, being members of my occupation,
using painting, do prove my occupation a mystery. But
what mystery there should be in hanging, if I should
be hanged, I cannot imagine.   40
ABHORSON   Sir, it is a mystery.
POMPEY   Proof?
ABHORSON   Every true man's apparel fits your thief. If it
be too little for your thief, your true man thinks it big
enough. If it be too big for your thief, your thief thinks   45
it little enough. So every true man's apparel fits your
thief.

          Enter Provost.

PROVOST   Are you agreed?
POMPEY   Sir, I will serve him; for I do find your
hangman is a more penitent trade than your bawd; he   50
doth oftener ask forgiveness.
PROVOST   You, sirrah, provide your block and your axe
tomorrow four o'clock.
ABHORSON   Come on, bawd, I will instruct thee in my
trade. Follow.   55
POMPEY   I do desire to learn, sir; and I hope, if you have
occasion to use me for your own turn, you shall find
me yare. For truly, sir, for your kindness I owe you a
good turn.
PROVOST   Call hither Barnardine and Claudio.   60
             Exeunt Abhorson and Pompey.
    Th'one has my pity; not a jot the other,
    Being a murderer, though he were my brother.

          Enter CLAUDIO.

    Look, here's the warrant, Claudio, for thy death;
    'Tis now dead midnight, and by eight tomorrow
    Thou must be made immortal. Where's Barnardine?   65
CLAUDIO   As fast lock'd up in sleep as guiltless labour
    When it lies starkly in the traveller's bones.
    He will not wake.
PROVOST   Who can do good on him?
    Well, go; prepare yourself.
    [*knocking within*]   But hark, what noise?
    Heaven give your spirits comfort!   *Exit Claudio.*
    [*knocking*]   – By and by. –   70
    I hope it is some pardon or reprieve

For the most gentle Claudio.

Enter DUKE, *disguised.*

                    Welcome, father.
DUKE   The best and wholesom'st spirits of the night
    Envelop you, good Provost! Who call'd here of late?
75 PROVOST   None since the curfew rung.
DUKE   Not Isabel?
PROVOST   No.
DUKE   They will then, ere't be long.
PROVOST   What comfort is for Claudio?
DUKE   There's some in hope.
PROVOST   It is a bitter deputy.
DUKE   Not so, not so; his life is parallel'd
80   Even with the stroke and line of his great justice.
    He doth with holy abstinence subdue
    That in himself which he spurs on his power
    To qualify in others: were he meal'd with that
    Which he corrects, then were he tyrannous;
    But this being so, he's just.
    [*Knocking within. Provost goes to the door.*]
85   – Now are they come.
    This is a gentle provost; seldom when
    The steeled gaoler is the friend of men. [*knocking*]
    How now? What noise? That spirit's possess'd with
        haste
    That wounds th'unsisting postern with these strokes.
    [*Provost returns.*]
90 PROVOST   There must he stay until the officer
    Arise to let him in. He is call'd up.
DUKE   Have you no countermand for Claudio yet,
    But he must die tomorrow?
PROVOST   None, sir, none.
DUKE   As near the dawning, Provost, as it is,
    You shall hear more ere morning.
95 PROVOST   Happily
    You something know: yet I believe there comes
    No countermand. No such example have we.
    Besides, upon the very siege of justice
    Lord Angelo hath to the public ear
    Profess'd the contrary.

Enter a Messenger.

100   This is his lordship's man.
DUKE   And here comes Claudio's pardon.
MESSENGER   My lord hath sent you this note, and by me
    this further charge: that you swerve not from the
105   smallest article of it, neither in time, matter, or other
    circumstance. Good-morrow; for, as I take it, it is
    almost day.
PROVOST   I shall obey him.   *Exit Messenger.*
DUKE [*aside*]   This is his pardon, purchas'd by such sin
110   For which the pardoner himself is in.
    Hence hath offence his quick celerity,
    When it is borne in high authority.
    When vice makes mercy, mercy's so extended
    That for the fault's love is th'offender friended.

Now, sir, what news?
PROVOST   I told you: Lord Angelo, belike thinking me 115
    remiss in mine office, awakens me with this unwonted
    putting-on; methinks strangely, for he hath not used it
    before.
DUKE   Pray you, let's hear.
PROVOST [*Reads.*]   *Whatsoever you may hear to the* 120
    contrary, let Claudio be executed by four of the clock, and
    in the afternoon, Barnardine. For my better satisfaction,
    let me have Claudio's head sent me by five. Let this be
    duly performed, with a thought that more depends on it
    than we must yet deliver. Thus fail not to do your office, 125
    as you will answer it at your peril.
    What say you to this, sir?
DUKE   What is that Barnardine, who is to be executed in
    th'afternoon?
PROVOST   A Bohemian born, but here nursed up and 130
    bred; one that is a prisoner nine years old.
DUKE   How came it that the absent Duke had not either
    delivered him to his liberty, or executed him? I have
    heard it was ever his manner to do so.
PROVOST   His friends still wrought reprieves for him; 135
    and indeed, his fact till now in the government of
    Lord Angelo came not to an undoubtful proof.
DUKE   It is now apparent?
PROVOST   Most manifest, and not denied by himself.
DUKE   Hath he borne himself penitently in prison? How 140
    seems he to be touched?
PROVOST   A man that apprehends death no more
    dreadfully but as a drunken sleep; careless, reckless,
    and fearless of what's past, present, or to come:
    insensible of mortality, and desperately mortal. 145
DUKE   He wants advice.
PROVOST   He will hear none. He hath evermore had the
    liberty of the prison: give him leave to escape hence,
    he would not. Drunk many times a day, if not many
    days entirely drunk. We have very oft awaked him, as 150
    if to carry him to execution, and showed him a
    seeming warrant for it; it hath not moved him at all.
DUKE   More of him anon. There is written in your brow,
    Provost, honesty and constancy; if I read it not truly,
    my ancient skill beguiles me. But in the boldness of 155
    my cunning, I will lay myself in hazard. Claudio,
    whom here you have warrant to execute, is no greater
    forfeit to the law than Angelo who hath sentenced
    him. To make you understand this in a manifested
    effect, I crave but four days' respite: for the which, you 160
    are to do me both a present and a dangerous courtesy.
PROVOST   Pray sir, in what?
DUKE   In the delaying death.
PROVOST   Alack, how may I do it? Having the hour
    limited, and an express command under penalty to 165
    deliver his head in the view of Angelo? I may make my
    case as Claudio's to cross this in the smallest.
DUKE   By the vow of mine order, I warrant you, if my
    instructions may be your guide: let this Barnardine be
    this morning executed, and his head borne to Angelo. 170

PROVOST   Angelo hath seen them both, and will discover the favour.

DUKE   O, death's a great disguiser; and you may add to it. Shave the head, and tie the beard, and say it was the desire of the penitent to be so bared before his death: you know the course is common. If anything fall to you upon this, more than thanks and good fortune, by the saint whom I profess, I will plead against it with my life.

PROVOST   Pardon me, good father; it is against my oath.

DUKE   Were you sworn to the Duke, or to the Deputy?

PROVOST   To him, and to his substitutes.

DUKE   You will think you have made no offence if the Duke avouch the justice of your dealing?

PROVOST   But what likelihood is in that?

DUKE   Not a resemblance, but a certainty. Yet, since I see you fearful, that neither my coat, integrity, nor persuasion can with ease attempt you, I will go further than I meant, to pluck all fears out of you. Look you, sir, here is the hand and seal of the Duke: you know the character, I doubt not, and the signet is not strange to you?

PROVOST   I know them both.

DUKE   The contents of this is the return of the Duke: you shall anon over-read it at your pleasure, where you shall find within these two days he will be here. This is a thing that Angelo knows not; for he this very day receives letters of strange tenour, perchance of the Duke's death, perchance entering into some monastery; but, by chance, nothing of what is writ. Look, th'unfolding star calls up the shepherd. Put not yourself into amazement how these things should be; all difficulties are but easy when they are known. Call your executioner, and off with Barnardine's head. I will give him a present shrift, and advise him for a better place. Yet you are amazed; but this shall absolutely resolve you. Come away; it is almost clear dawn.   *Exeunt.*

4.3   *Enter* POMPEY.

POMPEY   I am as well acquainted here as I was in our house of profession: one would think it were Mistress Overdone's own house, for here be many of her old customers. First, here's young Master Rash; he's in for a commodity of brown paper and old ginger, nine score and seventeen pounds; of which he made five marks ready money: marry, then, ginger was not much in request, for the old women were all dead. Then is there here one Master Caper, at the suit of Master Three-pile the mercer, for some four suits of peach-coloured satin, which now peaches him a beggar. Then have we here young Dizie, and young Master Deep-vow, and Master Copperspur, and Master Starve-Lackey the rapier and dagger man, and young Drop-heir that killed lusty Pudding, and Master Forthright the tilter, and brave Master Shoe-tie the great traveller, and wild Half-can that stabbed pots, and I think forty more, all great doers in our trade, and are now 'for the Lord's sake'.

Enter ABHORSON.

ABHORSON   Sirrah, bring Barnardine hither.

POMPEY   Master Barnardine! You must rise and be hanged, Master Barnardine.

ABHORSON   What hoa, Barnardine!

BARNARDINE [*within*]   A pox o' your throats! Who makes that noise there? What are you?

POMPEY   Your friends, sir, the hangman. You must be so good, sir, to rise and be put to death.

BARNARDINE [*within*]   Away, you rogue, away; I am sleepy.

ABHORSON   Tell him he must awake, and that quickly too.

POMPEY   Pray, Master Barnardine, awake till you are executed, and sleep afterwards.

ABHORSON   Go in to him and fetch him out.

POMPEY   He is coming, sir, he is coming. I hear his straw rustle.

Enter BARNARDINE.

ABHORSON   Is the axe upon the block, sirrah?

POMPEY   Very ready, sir.

BARNARDINE   How now, Abhorson? What's the news with you?

ABHORSON   Truly, sir, I would desire you to clap into your prayers; for look you, the warrant's come.

BARNARDINE   You rogue, I have been drinking all night; I am not fitted for't.

POMPEY   O, the better, sir; for he that drinks all night, and is hanged betimes in the morning, may sleep the sounder all the next day.

Enter DUKE, *disguised.*

ABHORSON   Look you, sir, here comes your ghostly father. Do we jest now, think you?

DUKE   Sir, induced by my charity, and hearing how hastily you are to depart, I am come to advise you, comfort you, and pray with you.

BARNARDINE   Friar, not I. I have been drinking hard all night, and I will have more time to prepare me, or they shall beat out my brains with billets. I will not consent to die this day, that's certain.

DUKE   O sir, you must; and therefore I beseech you Look forward on the journey you shall go.

BARNARDINE   I swear I will not die today for any man's persuasion.

DUKE   But hear you –

BARNARDINE   Not a word. If you have anything to say to me, come to my ward: for thence will not I today.   *Exit.*

Enter Provost.

DUKE   Unfit to live or die! O gravel heart.

PROVOST   After him, fellows, bring him to the block!   55
                                                   Exeunt Abhorson and Pompey.
         Now sir, how do you find the prisoner?
DUKE   A creature unprepar'd, unmeet for death;
         And to transport him in the mind he is
         Were damnable.
PROVOST   Here in the prison, father,
         There died this morning of a cruel fever   70
         One Ragozine, a most notorious pirate,
         A man of Claudio's years; his beard and head
         Just of his colour. What if we do omit
         This reprobate till he were well inclin'd,
         And satisfy the deputy with the visage   75
         Of Ragozine, more like to Claudio?
DUKE   O, 'tis an accident that heaven provides.
         Dispatch it presently; the hour draws on
         Prefix'd by Angelo. See this be done,
         And sent according to command, whiles I   80
         Persuade this rude wretch willingly to die.
PROVOST   This shall be done, good father, presently.
         But Barnardine must die this afternoon;
         And how shall we continue Claudio,
         To save me from the danger that might come   85
         If he were known alive?
DUKE   Let this be done: put them in secret holds,
         Both Barnardine and Claudio.
         Ere twice the sun hath made his journal greeting
         To yonder generation, you shall find   90
         Your safety manifested.
PROVOST   I am your free dependant.
DUKE   Quick, dispatch, and send the head to Angelo.
                                                   Exit Provost.
         Now will I write letters to Angelo,
         The Provost, he shall bear them, whose contents
         Shall witness to him I am near at home;   95
         And that by great injunctions I am bound
         To enter publicly. Him I'll desire
         To meet me at the consecrated fount
         A league below the city; and from thence,
         By cold gradation and well-balanc'd form,   100
         We shall proceed with Angelo.

                         Enter Provost.

PROVOST   Here is the head; I'll carry it myself.
DUKE   Convenient is it. Make a swift return;
         For I would commune with you of such things
         That want no ear but yours.
PROVOST   I'll make all speed. *Exit.*   105
ISABELLA [*within*]   Peace, hoa, be here!
DUKE   The tongue of Isabel. She's come to know
         If yet her brother's pardon be come hither;
         But I will keep her ignorant of her good,
         To make her heavenly comforts of despair   110
         When it is least expected.

                         Enter ISABELLA.

ISABELLA   Hoa, by your leave!

DUKE
         Good morning to you, fair and gracious daughter.
ISABELLA   The better, given me by so holy a man.
         Hath yet the deputy sent my brother's pardon?
DUKE   He hath releas'd him, Isabel, – from the world.   115
         His head is off, and sent to Angelo.
ISABELLA   Nay, but it is not so!
DUKE   It is no other. Show your wisdom, daughter,
         In your close patience.
ISABELLA   O, I will to him and pluck out his eyes!   120
DUKE   You shall not be admitted to his sight.
ISABELLA   Unhappy Claudio! wretched Isabel!
         Injurious world! most damned Angelo!
DUKE   This nor hurts him, nor profits you a jot.
         Forbear it therefore; give your cause to heaven.   125
         Mark what I say, which you shall find
         By every syllable a faithful verity.
         The Duke comes home tomorrow; – nay, dry your
             eyes –
         One of our covent, and his confessor
         Gives me this instance. Already he hath carried   130
         Notice to Escalus and Angelo,
         Who do prepare to meet him at the gates
         There to give up their power. If you can pace your
             wisdom
         In that good path that I would wish it go,
         And you shall have your bosom on this wretch,   135
         Grace of the Duke, revenges to your heart,
         And general honour.
ISABELLA   I am directed by you.
DUKE   This letter then to Friar Peter give;
         'Tis that he sent me of the Duke's return.
         Say, by this token I desire his company   140
         At Mariana's house tonight. Her cause and yours
         I'll perfect him withal, and he shall bring you
         Before the Duke; and to the head of Angelo
         Accuse him home and home. For my poor self,
         I am combined by a sacred vow,   145
         And shall be absent. Wend you with this letter.
         Command these fretting waters from your eyes
         With a light heart; trust not my holy order,
         If I pervert your course. – Who's here?

                         Enter LUCIO.

LUCIO   Good even.
         Friar, where's the Provost?
DUKE   Not within, sir.   150
LUCIO   O pretty Isabella, I am pale at mine heart to see
         thine eyes so red: thou must be patient. – I am fain to
         dine and sup with water and bran: I dare not for my
         head fill my belly: one fruitful meal would set me to't.
         – But they say the Duke will be here tomorrow. By my   155
         troth, Isabel, I loved thy brother; if the old fantastical
         duke of dark corners had been at home, he had lived.
                                                   Exit Isabella.
DUKE   Sir, the Duke is marvellous little beholding to
         your reports; but the best is, he lives not in them.

160 LUCIO   Friar, thou knowest not the Duke so well as I do.
        He's a better woodman than thou tak'st him for.
      DUKE   Well! you'll answer this one day. Fare ye well.
        [*going*]
      LUCIO   Nay tarry, I'll go along with thee: I can tell thee
        pretty tales of the Duke.
165   DUKE   You have told me too many of him already, sir, if
        they be true: if not true, none were enough.
      LUCIO   I was once before him for getting a wench with
        child.
      DUKE   Did you such a thing?
170   LUCIO   Yes, marry, did I; but I was fain to forswear it;
        they would else have married me to the rotten medlar.
      DUKE   Sir, your company is fairer than honest; rest you
        well. [*going*]
      LUCIO   By my troth, I'll go with thee to the lane's end.
175   If bawdy talk offend you, we'll have very little of it.
        Nay, friar, I am a kind of burr, I shall stick.   *Exeunt.*

4.4   *Enter* ANGELO *and* ESCALUS.

ESCALUS   Every letter he hath writ hath disvouched
        other.
      ANGELO   In most uneven and distracted manner. His
        actions show much like to madness; pray heaven his
5   wisdom be not tainted. And why meet him at the gates
        and redeliver our authorities there?
      ESCALUS   I guess not.
      ANGELO   And why should we proclaim it in an hour
        before his entering, that if any crave redress of
10   injustice, they should exhibit their petitions in the
        street?
      ESCALUS   He shows his reason for that: to have a
        dispatch of complaints, and to deliver us from devices
        hereafter, which shall then have no power to stand
15   against us.
      ANGELO   Well, I beseech you, let it be proclaim'd
        Betimes i'th' morn: I'll call you at your house.
        Give notice to such men of sort and suit
        As are to meet him.
      ESCALUS   I shall, sir: fare you well.
20   ANGELO   Good night.   *Exit Escalus.*
        This deed unshapes me quite; makes me unpregnant
        And dull to all proceedings. A deflower'd maid;
        And by an eminent body, that enforc'd
        The law against it! But that her tender shame
25   Will not proclaim against her maiden loss,
        How might she tongue me! Yet reason dares her no,
        For my authority bears so credent bulk
        That no particular scandal once can touch,
        But it confounds the breather. He should have liv'd;
30   Save that his riotous youth, with dangerous sense,
        Might in the times to come have ta'en revenge
        By so receiving a dishonour'd life
        With ransom of such shame. Would yet he had lived.
        Alack, when once our grace we have forgot,
35   Nothing goes right; we would, and we would not.
                                              Exit.

4.5   *Enter* DUKE, *in his own habit, and* FRIAR PETER.

DUKE   These letters at fit time deliver me.
        The Provost knows our purpose and our plot;
        The matter being afoot, keep your instruction,
        And hold you ever to our special drift,
5   Though sometimes you do blench from this to that
        As cause doth minister. Go call at Flavius' house,
        And tell him where I stay. Give the like notice
        To Valencius, Rowland, and to Crassus,
        And bid them bring the trumpets to the gate:
        But send me Flavius first.
FRIAR PETER   It shall be speeded well.   10
                                        Exit Friar.

              Enter Varrius.

DUKE
        I thank thee, Varrius, thou hast made good haste.
        Come, we will walk. There's other of our friends
        Will greet us here anon. My gentle Varrius!   *Exeunt.*

4.6   *Enter* ISABELLA *and* MARIANA.

ISABELLA   To speak so indirectly I am loth;
        I would say the truth, but to accuse him so
        That is your part; yet I am advis'd to do it,
        He says, to veil full purpose.
MARIANA   Be rul'd by him.
ISABELLA   Besides, he tells me that, if peradventure   5
        He speak against me on the adverse side,
        I should not think it strange, for 'tis a physic
        That's bitter to sweet end.

              Enter FRIAR PETER.

MARIANA   I would Friar Peter –
ISABELLA   O peace, the friar is come.
FRIAR PETER
        Come, I have found you out a stand most fit,   10
        Where you may have such vantage on the Duke
        He shall not pass you. Twice have the trumpets
            sounded.
        The generous and gravest citizens
        Have hent the gates, and very near upon
        The Duke is ent'ring: therefore hence, away.   *Exeunt.*   15

5.1   *Enter at several doors* DUKE, *in his own habit,*
        Varrius, lords and attendants; ANGELO,
        ESCALUS, LUCIO *and citizens.*

DUKE   My very worthy cousin, fairly met.
        Our old and faithful friend, we are glad to see you.
ANGELO, ESCALUS
        Happy return be to your royal grace!
DUKE   Many and hearty thankings to you both.
        We have made enquiry of you, and we hear   5
        Such goodness of your justice that our soul
        Cannot but yield you forth to public thanks,
        Forerunning more requital.

ANGELO   You make my bonds still greater.

DUKE

10   O, but your desert speaks loud, and I should wrong it
    To lock it in the wards of covert bosom,
    When it deserves with characters of brass
    A forted residence 'gainst the tooth of time
    And razure of oblivion. Give we our hand,
15   And let the subject see, to make them know
    That outward courtesies would fain proclaim
    Favours that keep within. Come, Escalus,
    You must walk by us on our other hand;
    And good supporters are you.

Enter FRIAR PETER *and* ISABELLA.

FRIAR PETER

20   Now is your time: speak loud, and kneel before him.

ISABELLA   Justice, O royal Duke! Vail your regard
    Upon a wrong'd – I would fain have said, a maid.
    O worthy prince, dishonour not your eye
    By throwing it on any other object,
25   Till you have heard me in my true complaint,
    And given me justice! Justice! Justice! Justice!

DUKE

    Relate your wrongs. In what? By whom? Be brief.
    Here is Lord Angelo shall give you justice,
    Reveal yourself to him.

ISABELLA   O worthy Duke,
30   You bid me seek redemption of the devil.
    Hear me yourself: for that which I must speak
    Must either punish me, not being believ'd,
    Or wring redress from you.
    Hear me! O hear me, hear!

35 ANGELO   My lord, her wits I fear me are not firm.
    She hath been a suitor to me for her brother,
    Cut off by course of justice.

ISABELLA   By course of justice!

ANGELO   And she will speak most bitterly and strange.

ISABELLA   Most strange: but yet most truly will I speak.
40   That Angelo's forsworn, is it not strange?
    That Angelo's a murderer, is't not strange?
    That Angelo is an adulterous thief,
    An hypocrite, a virgin-violator,
    Is it not strange, and strange?

45 DUKE   Nay, it is ten times strange!

ISABELLA   It is not truer he is Angelo,
    Than this is all as true as it is strange;
    Nay, it is ten times true, for truth is truth
    To th'end of reck'ning.

DUKE   Away with her. Poor soul,
50   She speaks this in th'infirmity of sense.

ISABELLA   O Prince, I conjure thee, as thou believ'st
    There is another comfort than this world,
    That thou neglect me not with that opinion
    That I am touch'd with madness. Make not
        impossible
55   That which but seems unlike. 'Tis not impossible
    But one, the wicked'st caitiff on the ground,

    May seem as shy, as grave, as just, as absolute,
    As Angelo; even so may Angelo,
    In all his dressings, caracts, titles, forms,
60   Be an arch-villain. Believe it, royal Prince,
    If he be less, he's nothing; but he's more,
    Had I more name for badness.

DUKE   By mine honesty,
    If she be mad, as I believe no other,
    Her madness hath the oddest frame of sense,
65   Such a dependency of thing on thing,
    As e'er I heard in madness.

ISABELLA   O gracious Duke,
    Harp not on that; nor do not banish reason
    For inequality; but let your reason serve
    To make the truth appear where it seems hid,
    And hide the false seems true.

DUKE   Many that are not mad 70
    Have, sure, more lack of reason. What would you
      say?

ISABELLA   I am the sister of one Claudio,
    Condemn'd upon the act of fornication
    To lose his head; condemn'd by Angelo.
    I – in probation of a sisterhood – 75
    Was sent to by my brother; one Lucio
    As then the messenger.

LUCIO   That's I, and't like your Grace.
    I came to her from Claudio, and desir'd her
    To try her gracious fortune with Lord Angelo
    For her poor brother's pardon.

ISABELLA   That's he indeed. 80

DUKE *[to Lucio]*   You were not bid to speak.

LUCIO   No, my good lord,
    Nor wish'd to hold my peace.

DUKE   I wish you now, then;
    Pray you take note of it;
    And when you have a business for yourself,
    Pray heaven you then be perfect.

LUCIO   I warrant your honour. 85

DUKE   The warrant's for yourself: take heed to't.

ISABELLA   This gentleman told somewhat of my tale.

LUCIO   Right.

DUKE   It may be right, but you are i' the wrong
    To speak before your time. – Proceed.

ISABELLA   I went 90
    To this pernicious caitiff Deputy.

DUKE   That's somewhat madly spoken.

ISABELLA   Pardon it;
    The phrase is to the matter.

DUKE   Mended again. The matter: proceed.

ISABELLA   In brief, to set the needless process by – 95
    How I persuaded, how I pray'd and kneel'd,
    How he refell'd me, and how I replied
    (For this was of much length) – the vile conclusion
    I now begin with grief and shame to utter.
    He would not, but by gift of my chaste body 100
    To his concupiscible intemperate lust,
    Release my brother; and after much debatement,

My sisterly remorse confutes mine honour,
And I did yield to him. But the next morn betimes,
105 His purpose surfeiting, he sends a warrant
For my poor brother's head.
DUKE   This is most likely!
ISABELLA   O, that it were as like as it is true.
DUKE
By heaven, fond wretch, thou know'st not what thou
      speak'st,
Or else thou art suborn'd against his honour
110 In hateful practice. First, his integrity
Stands without blemish; next, it imports no reason
That with such vehemency he should pursue
Faults proper to himself. If he had so offended,
He would have weigh'd thy brother by himself,
115 And not have cut him off. Someone hath set you on:
Confess the truth, and say by whose advice
Thou cam'st here to complain.
ISABELLA   And is this all?
Then, O you blessed ministers above,
Keep me in patience, and with ripen'd time
120 Unfold the evil which is here wrapt up
In countenance! Heaven shield your Grace from woe,
As I, thus wrong'd, hence unbelieved go.
DUKE   I know you'd fain be gone. An officer!
To prison with her! [*Isabella is placed under guard.*]
                              Shall we thus permit
125 A blasting and a scandalous breath to fall
On him so near us? This needs must be a practice.
Who knew of your intent and coming hither?
ISABELLA   One that I would were here, Friar Lodowick.
                                        Exit guarded.
DUKE
A ghostly father, belike. – Who knows that Lodowick?
130 LUCIO   My lord, I know him. 'Tis a meddling friar;
I do not like the man; had he been lay, my lord,
For certain words he spake against your Grace
In your retirement, I had swing'd him soundly.
DUKE   Words against me! This' a good friar belike.
135 And to set on this wretched woman here
Against our substitute! Let this friar be found.
LUCIO   But yesternight, my lord, she and that friar,
I saw them at the prison: a saucy friar,
A very scurvy fellow.
FRIAR PETER   Bless'd be your royal Grace!
140 I have stood by, my lord, and I have heard
Your royal ear abus'd. First hath this woman
Most wrongfully accus'd your substitute,
Who is as free from touch or soil with her
As she from one ungot.
DUKE   We did believe no less.
145 Know you that Friar Lodowick that she speaks of?
FRIAR PETER   I know him for a man divine and holy,
Not scurvy, nor a temporary meddler,
As he's reported by this gentleman;
And, on my trust, a man that never yet
150 Did, as he vouches, misreport your Grace.

LUCIO   My lord, most villainously; believe it.
FRIAR PETER
Well, he in time may come to clear himself;
But at this instant he is sick, my lord:
Of a strange fever. Upon his mere request,
Being come to knowledge that there was complaint   155
Intended 'gainst Lord Angelo, came I hither,
To speak, as from his mouth, what he doth know
Is true and false; and what he with his oath
And all probation will make up full clear
Whensoever he's convented. First, for this woman,   160
To justify this worthy nobleman
So vulgarly and personally accus'd,
Her shall you hear disproved to her eyes,
Till she herself confess it.
DUKE   Good friar, let's hear it.
Do you not smile at this, Lord Angelo?   165
O heaven, the vanity of wretched fools!
Give us some seats. – Come, cousin Angelo,
In this I'll be impartial: be you judge
Of your own cause.

                Enter MARIANA, *veiled.*

                         Is this the witness, friar?
First, let her show her face, and after, speak.   170
MARIANA   Pardon, my lord; I will not show my face
Until my husband bid me.
DUKE   What, are you married?
MARIANA   No, my lord.
DUKE   Are you a maid?
MARIANA   No, my lord.   175
DUKE   A widow, then?
MARIANA   Neither, my lord.
DUKE   Why, you are nothing then: neither maid, widow,
nor wife!
LUCIO   My lord, she may be a punk; for many of them   180
are neither maid, widow nor wife.
DUKE   Silence that fellow! I would he had some cause to
prattle for himself.
LUCIO   Well, my lord.
MARIANA   My lord, I do confess I ne'er was married;   185
And I confess besides, I am no maid.
I have known my husband; yet my husband
Knows not that ever he knew me.
LUCIO
He was drunk then, my lord; it can be no better.
DUKE
For the benefit of silence, would thou wert so too.   190
LUCIO   Well, my lord.
DUKE   This is no witness for Lord Angelo.
MARIANA   Now I come to't, my lord.
She that accuses him of fornication
In self-same manner doth accuse my husband,   195
And charges him, my lord, with such a time
When I'll depose I had him in mine arms
With all th'effect of love.
ANGELO   Charges she moe than me?

MARIANA   Not that I know.

DUKE   No? You say your husband.

MARIANA   Why just, my lord, and that is Angelo,
Who thinks he knows that he ne'er knew my body,
But knows, he thinks, that he knows Isabel's.

ANGELO   This is a strange abuse. Let's see thy face.

MARIANA [*unveiling*]
My husband bids me; now I will unmask.
This is that face, thou cruel Angelo,
Which once thou swor'st was worth the looking on:
This is the hand which, with a vow'd contract,
Was fast belock'd in thine: this is the body
That took away the match from Isabel
And did supply thee at thy garden-house,
In her imagin'd person.

DUKE   Know you this woman?

LUCIO   Carnally, she says.

DUKE   Sirrah, no more!

LUCIO   Enough, my lord.

ANGELO   My lord, I must confess I know this woman;
And five years since, there was some speech of
    marriage
Betwixt myself and her; which was broke off,
Partly for that her promised proportions
Came short of composition; but in chief
For that her reputation was disvalu'd
In levity: since which time of five years
I never spake with her, saw her, nor heard from her,
Upon my faith and honour.

MARIANA   Noble Prince,
As there comes light from heaven, and words from
    breath,
As there is sense in truth, and truth in virtue,
I am affianc'd this man's wife, as strongly
As words could make up vows. And, my good lord,
But Tuesday night last gone, in's garden house,
He knew me as a wife. As this is true
Let me in safety raise me from my knees,
Or else for ever be confixed here,
A marble monument.

ANGELO   I did but smile till now:
Now, good my lord, give me the scope of justice.
My patience here is touch'd: I do perceive
These poor informal women are no more
But instruments of some more mightier member
That sets them on. Let me have way, my lord,
To find this practice out.

DUKE   Ay, with my heart;
And punish them to your height of pleasure.
Thou foolish friar, and thou pernicious woman,
Compact with her that's gone: think'st thou thy
    oaths,
Though they would swear down each particular
    saint,
Were testimonies against his worth and credit,
That's seal'd in approbation? You, Lord Escalus,
Sit with my cousin; lend him your kind pains

To find out this abuse, whence 'tis deriv'd.
There is another friar that set them on;
Let him be sent for.

FRIAR PETER
Would he were here, my lord; for he indeed
Hath set the women on to this complaint.   250
Your Provost knows the place where he abides,
And he may fetch him.

DUKE   Go, do it instantly.
                                Exit an attendant.
And you, my noble and well-warranted cousin,
Whom it concerns to hear this matter forth,
Do with your injuries as seems you best   255
In any chastisement. I for a while will leave you;
But stir not you till you have well determin'd
Upon these slanderers.

ESCALUS   My lord, we'll do it throughly.
                                Exit Duke.
Signior Lucio, did not you say you knew that Friar
Lodowick to be a dishonest person?   260

LUCIO   *Cucullus non facit monachum:* honest in nothing
but in his clothes, and one that hath spoke most
villainous speeches of the Duke.

ESCALUS   We shall entreat you to abide here till he come,
and enforce them against him. We shall find this friar   265
a notable fellow.

LUCIO   As any in Vienna, on my word!

ESCALUS   Call that same Isabel here once again; I would
speak with her.   *Exit an attendant.*
Pray you, my lord, give me leave to question; you shall   270
see how I'll handle her.

LUCIO   Not better than he, by her own report.

ESCALUS   Say you?

LUCIO   Marry, sir, I think if you handled her privately
she would sooner confess; perchance publicly she'll be   275
ashamed.

Enter at several doors Provost *with* DUKE, *in
disguise and hooded, and* ISABELLA *under guard.*

ESCALUS   I will go darkly to work with her.

LUCIO   That's the way; for women are light at midnight.

ESCALUS   Come on, mistress, here's a gentlewoman
denies all that you have said.   280

LUCIO   My lord, here comes the rascal I spoke of, here
with the Provost.

ESCALUS   In very good time. Speak not you to him till
we call upon you.

LUCIO   Mum.   285

ESCALUS   Come, sir: did you set these women on to
slander Lord Angelo? They have confess'd you did.

DUKE   'Tis false.

ESCALUS   How! Know you where you are?

DUKE   Respect to your great place; and let the devil   290
Be sometime honour'd for his burning throne.
Where is the Duke? 'Tis he should hear me speak.

ESCALUS
The Duke's in us; and we will hear you speak;

Look you speak justly.

295 DUKE   Boldly, at least. But O, poor souls,
Come you to seek the lamb here of the fox?
Good-night to your redress! Is the Duke gone?
Then is your cause gone too. The Duke's unjust
300 Thus to retort your manifest appeal,
And put your trial in the villain's mouth
Which here you come to accuse.

LUCIO   This is the rascal: this is he I spoke of.

ESCALUS   Why, thou unreverend and unhallow'd friar!
Is't not enough thou hast suborn'd these women
305 To accuse this worthy man, but in foul mouth,
And in the witness of his proper ear,
To call him villain? And then to glance from him
To th' Duke himself, to tax him with injustice?
Take him hence! To th' rack with him! – We'll touse you
310 Joint by joint, but we will know his purpose.
What! Unjust!

DUKE   Be not so hot: the Duke
Dare no more stretch this finger of mine than he
Dare rack his own. His subject am I not,
Nor here provincial. My business in this state
315 Made me a looker-on here in Vienna,
Where I have seen corruption boil and bubble
Till it o'errun the stew: laws for all faults,
But faults so countenanc'd that the strong statutes
Stand like the forfeits in a barber's shop,
As much in mock as mark.

320 ESCALUS   Slander to th' state!
Away with him to prison!

ANGELO
What can you vouch against him, Signior Lucio?
Is this the man that you did tell us of?

LUCIO   'Tis he, my lord. – Come hither, goodman
325 Baldpate, do you know me?

DUKE   I remember you, sir, by the sound of your voice;
I met you at the prison, in the absence of the Duke.

LUCIO   O, did you so? And do you remember what you
said of the Duke?

330 DUKE   Most notedly, sir.

LUCIO   Do you so, sir? And was the Duke a fleshmonger,
a fool, and a coward, as you then reported him to be?

DUKE   You must, sir, change persons with me, ere you
make that my report. You indeed spoke so of him, and
335 much more, much worse.

LUCIO   O, thou damnable fellow! Did not I pluck thee by
the nose for thy speeches?

DUKE   I protest, I love the Duke as I love myself.

ANGELO   Hark how the villain would close now, after his
340 treasonable abuses!

ESCALUS   Such a fellow is not to be talked withal. Away
with him to prison! Where is the Provost? Away with
him to prison! Lay bolts enough upon him: let him
speak no more. Away with those giglets too, and with
345 the other confederate companion!
[*The Provost lays hands on the Duke.*]

DUKE   Stay, sir, stay a while.

ANGELO   What, resists he? Help him, Lucio.

LUCIO   Come, sir! Come, sir! Come, sir! Foh, sir! Why,
you bald-pated, lying rascal! – You must be hooded,
350 must you? Show your knave's visage, with a pox to
you! Show your sheep-biting face, and be hanged an
hour! Will't not off?
[*Pulls off the friar's hood and discovers the Duke.*]

DUKE   Thou art the first knave that e'er mad'st a duke.
First, Provost, let me bail these gentle three.
355 [*to Lucio*] Sneak not away, sir, for the friar and you
Must have a word anon. – Lay hold on him.

LUCIO [*aside*]   This may prove worse than hanging.

DUKE [*to Escalus*]   What you have spoke, I pardon: sit
you down.
We'll borrow place of him.
[*to Angelo*]   Sir, by your leave.
360 Hast thou or word, or wit, or impudence,
That yet can do thee office? If thou hast,
Rely upon it till my tale be heard,
And hold no longer out.

ANGELO   O my dread lord,
I should be guiltier than my guiltiness
365 To think I can be undiscernible,
When I perceive your Grace, like power divine,
Hath looked upon my passes. Then, good prince,
No longer session hold upon my shame,
But let my trial be mine own confession.
370 Immediate sentence, then, and sequent death
Is all the grace I beg.

DUKE   Come hither, Mariana. –
Say: wast thou e'er contracted to this woman?

ANGELO   I was, my lord.

DUKE   Go, take her hence, and marry her instantly.
375 Do you the office, friar; which consummate,
Return him here again. Go with him, Provost.
Exeunt Angelo, Mariana, Friar Peter and Provost.

ESCALUS   My lord, I am more amaz'd at his dishonour
Than at the strangeness of it.

DUKE   Come hither, Isabel.
Your friar is now your prince. As I was then,
380 Advertising and holy to your business,
Not changing heart with habit, I am still
Attorney'd at your service.

ISABELLA   O, give me pardon,
That I, your vassal, have employ'd and pain'd
Your unknown sovereignty.

DUKE   You are pardon'd, Isabel.
385 And now, dear maid, be you as free to us.
Your brother's death, I know, sits at your heart:
And you may marvel why I obscur'd myself,
Labouring to save his life, and would not rather
Make rash remonstrance of my hidden power
390 Than let him so be lost. O most kind maid,
It was the swift celerity of his death,
Which I did think with slower foot came on,
That brain'd my purpose. But peace be with him.

That life is better life, past fearing death,
Than that which lives to fear. Make it your comfort,
So happy is your brother.
ISABELLA   I do, my lord.

Enter ANGELO, MARIANA, FRIAR PETER *and* Provost.

DUKE   For this new-married man approaching here,
Whose salt imagination yet hath wrong'd
Your well defended honour, you must pardon
For Mariana's sake: but as he adjudg'd your brother,
Being criminal in double violation
Of sacred chastity and of promise-breach
Thereon dependent, for your brother's life,
The very mercy of the law cries out
Most audible, even from his proper tongue:
'An Angelo for Claudio; death for death.
Haste still pays haste, and leisure answers leisure;
Like doth quit like, and Measure still for Measure.'
Then, Angelo, thy fault's thus manifested,
Which, though thou would'st deny, denies thee
    vantage.
We do condemn thee to the very block
Where Claudio stoop'd to death, and with like haste.
Away with him.
MARIANA   O my most gracious lord,
I hope you will not mock me with a husband.
DUKE   It is your husband mock'd you with a husband.
Consenting to the safeguard of your honour,
I thought your marriage fit: else imputation,
For that he knew you, might reproach your life,
And choke your good to come. For his possessions,
Although by confiscation they are ours,
We do instate and widow you with all,
To buy you a better husband.
MARIANA   O my dear lord,
I crave no other, nor no better man.
DUKE   Never crave him; we are definitive.
MARIANA   Gentle my liege –
DUKE   You do but lose your labour.
Away with him to death.
[*to Lucio*]   Now, sir, to you.
MARIANA [*kneeling*]
O my good lord – sweet Isabel, take my part;
Lend me your knees, and all my life to come
I'll lend you all my life to do you service.
DUKE   Against all sense you do importune her.
Should she kneel down in mercy of this fact,
Her brother's ghost his paved bed would break,
And take her hence in horror.
MARIANA   Isabel!
Sweet Isabel, do yet but kneel by me;
Hold up your hands, say nothing: I'll speak all.
They say best men are moulded out of faults,
And, for the most, become much more the better
For being a little bad. So may my husband.
O Isabel! Will you not lend a knee?
DUKE   He dies for Claudio's death.

ISABELLA [*kneeling*]   Most bounteous sir:
Look, if it please you, on this man condemn'd
As if my brother liv'd. I partly think
A due sincerity govern'd his deeds
Till he did look on me. Since it is so,
Let him not die. My brother had but justice,
In that he did the thing for which he died:
For Angelo,
His act did not o'ertake his bad intent,
And must be buried but as an intent
That perish'd by the way. Thoughts are no subjects;
Intents, but merely thoughts.
MARIANA   Merely, my lord.
DUKE   Your suit's unprofitable. Stand up, I say.
I have bethought me of another fault.
Provost, how came it Claudio was beheaded
At an unusual hour?
PROVOST   It was commanded so.
DUKE   Had you a special warrant for the deed?
PROVOST   No, my good lord: it was by private message.
DUKE   For which I do discharge you of your office.
Give up your keys.
PROVOST   Pardon me, noble lord;
I thought it was a fault, but knew it not;
Yet did repent me after more advice.
For testimony whereof, one in the prison
That should by private order else have died,
I have reserv'd alive.
DUKE   What's he?
PROVOST   His name is Barnardine.
DUKE   I would thou hadst done so by Claudio.
Go, fetch him hither, let me look upon him.
                                        Exit Provost.
ESCALUS   I am sorry one so learned and so wise
As you, Lord Angelo, have still appear'd,
Should slip so grossly, both in the heat of blood
And lack of temper'd judgement afterward.
ANGELO   I am sorry that such sorrow I procure,
And so deep sticks it in my penitent heart
That I crave death more willingly than mercy;
'Tis my deserving, and I do entreat it.

Enter Provost *with* BARNARDINE, CLAUDIO,
muffled, and JULIET.

DUKE   Which is that Barnardine?
PROVOST   This, my lord.
DUKE   There was a friar told me of this man.
Sirrah, thou art said to have a stubborn soul
That apprehends no further than this world,
And squar'st thy life according. Thou'rt condemn'd;
But, for those earthly faults, I quit them all,
And pray thee take this mercy to provide
For better times to come. Friar, advise him;
I leave him to your hand. – What muffl'd fellow's
    that?
PROVOST   This is another prisoner that I sav'd,
Who should have died when Claudio lost his head;

As like almost to Claudio as himself.
[*Unmuffles Claudio.*]
DUKE [*to Isabella*]
  If he be like your brother, for his sake
  Is he pardon'd; and for your lovely sake
  Give me your hand and say you will be mine.
490   He is my brother too: but fitter time for that.
  By this Lord Angelo perceives he's safe;
  Methinks I see a quickening in his eye.
  Well, Angelo, your evil quits you well.
  Look that you love your wife: her worth, worth
    yours.
495   I find an apt remission in myself.
  And yet here's one in place I cannot pardon.
  [*to Lucio*] You, sirrah, that knew me for a fool, a
    coward,
  One all of luxury, an ass, a madman:
  Wherein have I so deserv'd of you
500   That you extol me thus?
LUCIO   Faith, my lord, I spoke it but according to the
  trick: if you will hang me for it, you may: but I had
  rather it would please you I might be whipped.
DUKE   Whipp'd first, sir, and hang'd after.
505   Proclaim it, Provost, round about the city,
  If any woman wrong'd by this lewd fellow,
  – As I have heard him swear himself there's one
  Whom he begot with child – let her appear,
  And he shall marry her. The nuptial finish'd,

Let him be whipp'd and hang'd.   510
LUCIO   I beseech your Highness, do not marry me to a
  whore. Your Highness said even now, I made you a
  duke; good my lord, do not recompense me in making
  me a cuckold.
DUKE   Upon mine honour, thou shalt marry her.   515
  Thy slanders I forgive, and therewithal
  Remit thy other forfeits. – Take him to prison,
  And see our pleasure herein executed.
LUCIO   Marrying a punk, my lord, is pressing to death,
  Whipping, and hanging.
DUKE   Slandering a prince deserves it.   520
  She, Claudio, that you wrong'd, look you restore.
  Joy to you, Mariana; love her, Angelo:
  I have confess'd her, and I know her virtue.
  Thanks, good friend Escalus, for thy much goodness;
  There's more behind that is more gratulate.   525
  Thanks, Provost, for thy care and secrecy;
  We shall employ thee in a worthier place.
  Forgive him, Angelo, that brought you home
  The head of Ragozine for Claudio's:
  Th'offence pardons itself. Dear Isabel,   530
  I have a motion much imports your good;
  Whereto if you'll a willing ear incline,
  What's mine is yours, and what is yours is mine.
  So bring us to our palace, where we'll show
  What's yet behind that's meet you all should know.   535
        Exeunt omnes.

The Merchant of Venice

This play first appeared in print as a Quarto entitled *The Comical History of the Merchant of Venice* in 1600. An alternative early title seems to have been *The Jew of Venice*, focusing attention on Shylock, a role which has proved to be popular with actors but controversial with readers and audiences. *The Merchant of Venice* is one of the six comedies by Shakespeare listed by Francis Meres in his *Palladis Tamia* (1598), and it is generally thought to have been written between 1596 and 1597, after *Love's Labour's Lost* and *A Midsummer Night's Dream* but before *Much Ado About Nothing*, *As You Like It* and *Twelfth Night*. At much the same time Shakespeare was writing the *King Henry IV* plays, which also contain a character who threatens to upset their moral and aesthetic balance: Falstaff.

The main plot is very similar to one found in *Il Pecorone*, a fourteenth-century collection of stories first printed in Italian in 1598, in which a merchant called Ansaldo borrows money from a Jew on the surety of a pound of flesh so that his godson, Giannetto, can go to sea to seek his fortune. Instead, Giannetto courts and wins the Lady of Belmont, returning to find his god-father's life at risk. The Lady disguises herself as a lawyer, defeats the Jew, and begs her own ring from Giannetto as payment. Scholars assume that Shakespeare must have known an English version of this story, now lost, and that he (or the author of the lost version) added the story of the three caskets which is found in various medieval sources including John Gower's *Confessio Amantis* (late 1380s) and Giovanni Boccaccio's *Decameron* (1353). He was also influenced by Christopher Marlowe's play *The Jew of Malta* (c. 1591), in which the Jew's daughter elopes with a Christian. Officially, Jews had been expelled from England in the reign of Edward I, but if they conformed outwardly they were not persecuted. Officially, lending money for interest was condemned, but the Globe theatre was built on borrowed money and Shakespeare himself lent money as a business practice.

The 1600 Quarto claims that *The Merchant of Venice* had been 'divers times acted by the Lord Chamberlain his servants', Shakespeare's regular company, but there are no specific records of early performances apart from two at Court before James I in 1605. An adaptation by George Granville called *The Jew of Venice* displaced Shakespeare's version on the stage from 1701 until 1741, when Charles Macklin restored *The Merchant*. Edmund Kean, who first played Shylock in 1814, broke with the tradition of presenting him as a comic villain and made him a sympathetic and ultimately tragic figure – an interpretation which was followed by actors from Henry Irving to Laurence Olivier. While Shylock generally dominated the play, several actresses triumphed as Portia, including Sarah Siddons, Helen Faucit, Ellen Terry and Peggy Ashcroft. In the many books and essays on Shakespeare's heroines written by women in the nineteenth century (including Faucit's memoirs) Portia receives pride of place, and is held up as a demonstration that a woman can (at least in fiction) be an intellectual and a professional without losing her attractiveness to men.

The Merchant of Venice has become something of a problem play in the twentieth century; the systematic massacre of Jews in the holocaust has made it impossible for us to take the anti-semitism of the Christian characters lightly. Although many performers have aroused sympathy for Shylock, he cannot be sentimentalized beyond a certain point: he makes his claim for humanity ('Hath not a Jew eyes?' etc., in 3.1), but he does so as a sanction for vindictiveness and he remains a villain who seeks the life of his enemy. The play requires us to celebrate his defeat and to see his involuntary conversion as an opportunity for salvation.

The Arden text is based on the 1600 First Quarto.

The DUKE OF VENICE

The Prince of MOROCCO

The Prince of ARRAGON } *suitors to Portia*

ANTONIO *a Merchant of Venice*

BASSANIO *his friend, and suitor to Portia*

GRATIANO

SALERIO } *friends to Antonio and Bassanio*

SOLANIO

LORENZO *in love with Jessica*

SHYLOCK *a Jew*

TUBAL *a Jew his friend*

LAUNCELOT GOBBO *a clown, servant to Shylock*

Old GOBBO *father to Launcelot*

Leonardo, SERVANT *to Bassanio*

BALTHAZAR } *servants to Portia*

STEPHANO

PORTIA *an heiress, of Belmont*

NERISSA *her waiting-woman*

JESSICA *daughter to Shylock*

Magnificoes of Venice, Officers of the Court of Justice, a Gaoler, Servants and other Attendants

The Merchant of Venice

1.1 *Enter* ANTONIO, SALERIO *and* SOLANIO.

ANTONIO In sooth I know not why I am so sad,
  It wearies me, you say it wearies you;
  But how I caught it, found it, or came by it,
  What stuff 'tis made of, whereof it is born,
  I am to learn:
  And such a want-wit sadness makes of me,
  That I have much ado to know myself.
SALERIO Your mind is tossing on the ocean,
  There where your argosies with portly sail
  Like signiors and rich burghers on the flood,
  Or as it were the pageants of the sea,
  Do overpeer the petty traffickers
  That cur'sy to them (do them reverence)
  As they fly by them with their woven wings.
SOLANIO Believe me sir, had I such venture forth,
  The better part of my affections would
  Be with my hopes abroad. I should be still
  Plucking the grass to know where sits the wind,
  Piring in maps for ports, and piers and roads:
  And every object that might make me fear
  Misfortune to my ventures, out of doubt
  Would make me sad.
SALERIO   My wind cooling my broth,
  Would blow me to an ague when I thought
  What harm a wind too great might do at sea.
  I should not see the sandy hour-glass run
  But I should think of shallows and of flats,
  And see my wealthy Andrew dock'd in sand
  Vailing her high top lower than her ribs
  To kiss her burial; should I go to church
  And see the holy edifice of stone
  And not bethink me straight of dangerous rocks,
  Which touching but my gentle vessel's side
  Would scatter all her spices on the stream,
  Enrobe the roaring waters with my silks,
  And in a word, but even now worth this,
  And now worth nothing? Shall I have the thought
  To think on this, and shall I lack the thought
  That such a thing bechanc'd would make me sad?
  But tell not me, I know Antonio
  Is sad to think upon his merchandise.
ANTONIO Believe me no, I thank my fortune for it –
  My ventures are not in one bottom trusted,
  Nor to one place; nor is my whole estate
  Upon the fortune of this present year:
  Therefore my merchandise makes me not sad.
SOLANIO Why then you are in love.
ANTONIO   Fie, fie!
SOLANIO
  Not in love neither: then let us say you are sad
  Because you are not merry; and 'twere as easy
  For you to laugh and leap, and say you are merry
  Because you are not sad. Now by two-headed Janus,
  Nature hath fram'd strange fellows in her time:
  Some that will evermore peep through their eyes,

And laugh like parrots at a bagpiper:
And other of such vinegar aspect,
That they'll not show their teeth in way of smile   55
Though Nestor swear the jest be laughable.

Enter BASSANIO, LORENZO *and* GRATIANO.

Here comes Bassanio your most noble kinsman,
Gratiano, and Lorenzo. Fare ye well,
We leave you now with better company.
SALERIO I would have stay'd till I had made you merry,   60
  If worthier friends had not prevented me.
ANTONIO Your worth is very dear in my regard.
  I take it your own business calls on you,
  And you embrace th'occasion to depart.
SALERIO Good morrow my good lords.   65
BASSANIO
  Good signiors both when shall we laugh? say, when?
  You grow exceeding strange: must it be so?
SALERIO We'll make our leisures to attend on yours.
                    Exeunt Salerio and Solanio.
LORENZO
  My Lord Bassanio, since you have found Antonio
  We two will leave you, but at dinner-time   70
  I pray you have in mind where we must meet.
BASSANIO I will not fail you.
GRATIANO You look not well Signior Antonio,
  You have too much respect upon the world:
  They lose it that do buy it with much care, –   75
  Believe me you are marvellously chang'd.
ANTONIO I hold the world but as the world Gratiano,
  A stage, where every man must play a part,
  And mine a sad one.
GRATIANO   Let me play the fool,
  With mirth and laughter let old wrinkles come,   80
  And let my liver rather heat with wine
  Than my heart cool with mortifying groans.
  Why should a man whose blood is warm within,
  Sit like his grandsire, cut in alablaster?
  Sleep when he wakes? and creep into the jaundice   85
  By being peevish? I tell thee what Antonio,
  (I love thee, and 'tis my love that speaks):
  There are a sort of men whose visages
  Do cream and mantle like a standing pond,
  And do a wilful stillness entertain,   90
  With purpose to be dress'd in an opinion
  Of wisdom, gravity, profound conceit,
  As who should say, 'I am Sir Oracle,
  And when I ope my lips, let no dog bark.'
  O my Antonio, I do know of these   95
  That therefore only are reputed wise
  For saying nothing; when I am very sure
  If they should speak, would almost damn those ears
  Which (hearing them) would call their brothers
    fools, –
  I'll tell thee more of this another time.   100
  But fish not with this melancholy bait
  For this fool gudgeon, this opinion: –

Come good Lorenzo, – fare ye well a while,
I'll end my exhortation after dinner.

105 LORENZO   Well, we will leave you then till dinner-time.
I must be one of these same dumb wise men,
For Gratiano never lets me speak.

GRATIANO   Well keep me company but two years moe
Thou shalt not know the sound of thine own tongue.

110 ANTONIO   Fare you well, I'll grow a talker for this gear.

GRATIANO
Thanks i'faith, for silence is only commendable
In a neat's tongue dried, and a maid not vendible.
Exeunt Gratiano and Lorenzo.

ANTONIO   It is that anything now.

BASSANIO   Gratiano speaks an infinite deal of nothing
115 (more than any man in all Venice), his reasons are as
two grains of wheat hid in two bushels of chaff: you
shall seek all day ere you find them, and when you
have them, they are not worth the search.

ANTONIO   Well, tell me now what lady is the same
120 To whom you swore a secret pilgrimage –
That you to-day promis'd to tell me of?

BASSANIO   'Tis not unknown to you Antonio
How much I have disabled mine estate,
By something showing a more swelling port
125 Than my faint means would grant continuance:
Nor do I now make moan to be abridg'd
From such a noble rate, but my chief care
Is to come fairly off from the great debts
Wherein my time (something too prodigal)
130 Hath left me gag'd: to you Antonio
I owe the most in money and in love,
And from your love I have a warranty
To unburthen all my plots and purposes
How to get clear of all the debts I owe.

135 ANTONIO   I pray you good Bassanio let me know it,
And if it stand as you yourself still do,
Within the eye of honour, be assur'd
My purse, my person, my extremest means
Lie all unlock'd to your occasions.

BASSANIO
140 In my school-days, when I had lost one shaft,
I shot his fellow of the self-same flight
The self-same way, with more advised watch
To find the other forth, and by adventuring both,
I oft found both: I urge this childhood proof
145 Because what follows is pure innocence.
I owe you much, and (like a wilful youth)
That which I owe is lost, but if you please
To shoot another arrow that self way
Which you did shoot the first, I do not doubt,
150 (As I will watch the aim) or to find both,
Or bring your latter hazard back again,
And thankfully rest debtor for the first.

ANTONIO
You know me well, and herein spend but time
To wind about my love with circumstance,
155 And out of doubt you do me now more wrong

In making question of my uttermost
Than if you had made waste of all I have:
Then do but say to me what I should do
That in your knowledge may by me be done,
And I am prest unto it: therefore speak. 160

BASSANIO   In Belmont is a lady richly left,
And she is fair, and (fairer than that word),
Of wondrous virtues, – sometimes from her eyes
I did receive fair speechless messages:
Her name is Portia, nothing undervalu'd 165
To Cato's daughter, Brutus' Portia,
Nor is the wide world ignorant of her worth,
For the four winds blow in from every coast
Renowned suitors, and her sunny locks
Hang on her temples like a golden fleece, 170
Which makes her seat of Belmont Colchos' strond,
And many Jasons come in quest of her.
O my Antonio, had I but the means
To hold a rival place with one of them,
I have a mind presages me such thrift 175
That I should questionless be fortunate.

ANTONIO   Thou know'st that all my fortunes are at sea,
Neither have I money, nor commodity
To raise a present sum, therefore go forth
Try what my credit can in Venice do, – 180
That shall be rack'd even to the uttermost
To furnish thee to Belmont to fair Portia.
Go presently inquire (and so will I)
Where money is, and I no question make
To have it of my trust, or for my sake.   *Exeunt.* 185

1.2   *Enter* PORTIA *with her waiting-woman* NERISSA.

PORTIA   By my troth Nerissa, my little body is aweary of
this great world.

NERISSA   You would be (sweet madam), if your miseries
were in the same abundance as your good fortunes are:
and yet for aught I see, they are as sick that surfeit with 5
too much, as they that starve with nothing; it is no
mean happiness therefore to be seated in the mean, –
superfluity comes sooner by white hairs, but
competency lives longer.

PORTIA   Good sentences, and well pronounc'd. 10

NERISSA   They would be better if well followed.

PORTIA   If to do were as easy as to know what were good
to do, chapels had been churches, and poor men's
cottages princes' palaces, – it is a good divine that
follows his own instructions, – I can easier teach 15
twenty what were good to be done, than be one of the
twenty to follow mine own teaching: the brain may
devise laws for the blood, but a hot temper leaps o'er a
cold decree, – such a hare is madness the youth, to
skip o'er the meshes of good counsel the cripple; but 20
this reasoning is not in the fashion to choose me a
husband, – O me the word 'choose'! I may neither
choose who I would, nor refuse who I dislike, so is the
will of a living daughter curb'd by the will of a dead

father: is it not hard Nerissa, that I cannot choose one, nor refuse none?

NERISSA Your father was ever virtuous, and holy men at their death have good inspirations, – therefore the lott'ry that he hath devised in these three chests of gold, silver, and lead, whereof who chooses his meaning chooses you, will no doubt never be chosen by any rightly, but one who you shall rightly love. But what warmth is there in your affection towards any of these princely suitors that are already come?

PORTIA I pray thee over-name them, and as thou namest them, I will describe them, and according to my description level at my affection.

NERISSA First there is the Neapolitan prince.

PORTIA Ay that's a colt indeed, for he doth nothing but talk of his horse, and he makes it a great appropriation to his own good parts that he can shoe him himself: I am much afeard my lady his mother played false with a smith.

NERISSA Then is there the County Palatine.

PORTIA He doth nothing but frown (as who should say, 'and you will not have me, choose'), he hears merry tales and smiles not, (I fear he will prove the weeping philosopher when he grows old, being so full of unmannerly sadness in his youth), I had rather be married to a death's-head with a bone in his mouth, than to either of these: God defend me from these two.

NERISSA How say you by the French lord, Monsieur Le Bon?

PORTIA God made him, and therefore let him pass for a man, – in truth I know it is a sin to be a mocker, but he! why he hath a horse better than the Neapolitan's, a better bad habit of frowning than the Count Palatine, he is every man in no man, if a throstle sing, he falls straight a-cap'ring, he will fence with his own shadow. If I should marry him, I should marry twenty husbands: if he would despise me, I would forgive him, for if he love me to madness, I shall never requite him.

NERISSA What say you then to Falconbridge, the young baron of England?

PORTIA You know I say nothing to him, for he understands not me, nor I him: he hath neither Latin, French, nor Italian, and you will come into the court and swear that I have a poor pennyworth in the English: he is a proper man's picture, but alas! who can converse with a dumb-show? How oddly he is suited! I think he bought his doublet in Italy, his round hose in France, his bonnet in Germany, and his behaviour everywhere.

NERISSA What think you of the Scottish lord his neighbour?

PORTIA That he hath a neighbourly charity in him, for he borrowed a box of the ear of the Englishman, and swore he would pay him again when he was able: I think the Frenchman became his surety, and seal'd under for another. 80

NERISSA How like you the young German, the Duke of Saxony's nephew?

PORTIA Very vildly in the morning when he is sober, and most vildly in the afternoon when he is drunk: 85 when he is best, he is a little worse than a man, and when he is worst he is little better than a beast, – and the worst fall that ever fell, I hope I shall make shift to go without him.

NERISSA If he should offer to choose, and choose the 90 right casket, you should refuse to perform your father's will, if you should refuse to accept him.

PORTIA Therefore for fear of the worst, I pray thee set a deep glass of Rhenish wine on the contrary casket, for if the devil be within, and that temptation without, I 95 know he will choose it. I will do anything Nerissa ere I will be married to a sponge.

NERISSA You need not fear lady the having any of these lords, they have acquainted me with their determinations, which is indeed to return to their 100 home, and to trouble you with no more suit, unless you may be won by some other sort than your father's imposition, depending on the caskets.

PORTIA If I live to be as old as Sibylla, I will die as chaste as Diana, unless I be obtained by the manner of my 105 father's will: I am glad this parcel of wooers are so reasonable, for there is not one among them but I dote on his very absence: and I pray God grant them a fair departure.

NERISSA Do you not remember lady in your father's 110 time, a Venetian (a scholar and a soldier) that came hither in company of the Marquis of Montferrat?

PORTIA Yes, yes, it was Bassanio, as I think so was he call'd.

NERISSA True madam, he of all the men that ever my 115 foolish eyes look'd upon, was the best deserving a fair lady.

PORTIA I remember him well, and I remember him worthy of thy praise.

Enter a Servingman.

How now, what news? 120

SERVINGMAN The four strangers seek for you madam to take their leave: and there is a forerunner come from a fifth, the Prince of Morocco, who brings word the prince his master will be here to-night.

PORTIA If I could bid the fifth welcome with so good 125 heart as I can bid the other four farewell, I should be glad of his approach: if he have the condition of a saint, and the complexion of a devil, I had rather he should shrive me than wive me.

Come Nerissa, sirrah go before: 130
Whiles we shut the gate upon one wooer, another
knocks at the door.   *Exeunt.*

1.3   *Enter* BASSANIO *with* SHYLOCK *the Jew.*

SHYLOCK   Three thousand ducats, well.

BASSANIO   Ay sir, for three months.

SHYLOCK   For three months, well.

BASSANIO   For the which as I told you, Antonio shall be
bound.   5

SHYLOCK   Antonio shall become bound, well.

BASSANIO   May you stead me? Will you pleasure me?
Shall I know your answer?

SHYLOCK   Three thousand ducats for three months, and
Antonio bound.   10

BASSANIO   Your answer to that.

SHYLOCK   Antonio is a good man.

BASSANIO   Have you heard any imputation to the
contrary?

SHYLOCK   Ho no, no, no, no: my meaning in saying he is   15
a good man, is to have you understand me that he is
sufficient, – yet his means are in supposition: he hath
an argosy bound to Tripolis, another to the Indies, I
understand moreover upon the Rialto, he hath a third
at Mexico, a fourth for England, and other ventures he   20
hath squand'red abroad, – but ships are but boards,
sailors but men, there be land-rats, and water-rats,
water-thieves, and land-thieves, (I mean pirates), and
then there is the peril of waters, winds, and rocks: the
man is notwithstanding sufficient, – three thousand   25
ducats, – I think I may take his bond.

BASSANIO   Be assur'd you may.

SHYLOCK   I will be assur'd I may: and that I may be
assured, I will bethink me, – may I speak with
Antonio?   30

BASSANIO   If it please you to dine with us.

SHYLOCK   Yes, to smell pork, to eat of the habitation
which your prophet the Nazarite conjured the devil
into: I will buy with you, sell with you, talk with you,
walk with you, and so following: but I will not eat with   35
you, drink with you, nor pray with you. What news on
the Rialto? who is he comes here?

Enter ANTONIO.

BASSANIO   This is Signior Antonio.

SHYLOCK [*aside*]   How like a fawning publican he looks!
I hate him for he is a Christian: 40
But more, for that in low simplicity
He lends out money gratis, and brings down
The rate of usance here with us in Venice.
If I can catch him once upon the hip,
I will feed fat the ancient grudge I bear him.   45
He hates our sacred nation, and he rails
(Even there where merchants most do congregate)
On me, my bargains, and my well-won thrift,
Which he calls interest: cursed be my tribe
If I forgive him!   50

BASSANIO   Shylock, do you hear?

SHYLOCK   I am debating of my present store,
And by the near guess of my memory

I cannot instantly raise up the gross
Of full three thousand ducats: what of that?
Tubal (a wealthy Hebrew of my tribe)   55
Will furnish me; but soft! how many months
Do you desire?
[*to Antonio*]   Rest you fair good signior,
Your worship was the last man in our mouths.

ANTONIO   Shylock, albeit I neither lend nor borrow
By taking nor by giving of excess,   60
Yet to supply the ripe wants of my friend,
I'll break a custom:
[*to Bassanio*]   is he yet possess'd
How much ye would?

SHYLOCK   Ay, ay, three thousand ducats.

ANTONIO   And for three months.

SHYLOCK   I had forgot, – three months, –
[*to Bassanio*]   you told me so.   65
Well then, your bond: and let me see, – but hear you,
Me thoughts you said, you neither lend nor borrow
Upon advantage.

ANTONIO   I do never use it.

SHYLOCK   When Jacob graz'd his uncle Laban's sheep, –
This Jacob from our holy Abram was   70
(As his wise mother wrought in his behalf)
The third possessor: ay, he was the third.

ANTONIO   And what of him? did he take interest?

SHYLOCK   No, not take interest, not as you would say
Directly int'rest, – mark what Jacob did, –   75
When Laban and himself were compromis'd
That all the eanlings which were streak'd and pied
Should fall as Jacob's hire, the ewes being rank
In end of autumn turned to the rams,
And when the work of generation was   80
Between these woolly breeders in the act,
The skilful shepherd pill'd me certain wands,
And in the doing of the deed of kind
He stuck them up before the fulsome ewes,
Who then conceiving, did in eaning time   85
Fall parti-colour'd lambs, and those were Jacob's.
This was a way to thrive, and he was blest:
And thrift is blessing if men steal it not.

ANTONIO   This was a venture sir that Jacob serv'd for,
A thing not in his power to bring to pass,   90
But sway'd and fashion'd by the hand of heaven.
Was this inserted to make interest good?
Or is your gold and silver ewes and rams?

SHYLOCK   I cannot tell, I make it breed as fast, –
But note me signior.

ANTONIO   Mark you this Bassanio,   95
The devil can cite Scripture for his purpose, –
An evil soul producing holy witness
Is like a villain with a smiling cheek,
A goodly apple rotten at the heart.
O what a goodly outside falsehood hath!   100

SHYLOCK
Three thousand ducats, 'tis a good round sum.
Three months from twelve, then let me see the rate.

ANTONIO
  Well Shylock, shall we be beholding to you?

SHYLOCK   Signior Antonio, many a time and oft
  In the Rialto you have rated me
  About my moneys and my usances:
  Still have I borne it with a patient shrug,
  (For suff'rance is the badge of all our tribe)
  You call me misbeliever, cut-throat dog,
  And spet upon my Jewish gaberdine,
  And all for use of that which is mine own.
  Well then, it now appears you need my help:
  Go to then, you come to me, and you say,
  'Shylock, we would have moneys,' you say so:
  You that did void your rheum upon my beard,
  And foot me as you spurn a stranger cur
  Over your threshold, moneys is your suit.
  What should I say to you? Should I not say
  'Hath a dog money? is it possible
  A cur can lend three thousand ducats?' or
  Shall I bend low, and in a bondman's key
  With bated breath, and whisp'ring humbleness
  Say this:
  'Fair sir, you spet on me on Wednesday last,
  You spurn'd me such a day, another time
  You call'd me dog: and for these courtesies
  I'll lend you thus much moneys'?

ANTONIO   I am as like to call thee so again,
  To spet on thee again, to spurn thee too.
  If thou wilt lend this money, lend it not
  As to thy friends, for when did friendship take
  A breed for barren metal of his friend?
  But lend it rather to thine enemy,
  Who if he break, thou may'st with better face
  Exact the penalty.

SHYLOCK   Why look you how you storm!
  I would be friends with you, and have your love,
  Forget the shames that you have stain'd me with,
  Supply your present wants, and take no doit
  Of usance for my moneys, and you'll not hear me, –
  This is kind I offer.

BASSANIO   This were kindness.

SHYLOCK   This kindness will I show,
  Go with me to a notary, seal me there
  Your single bond, and (in a merry sport)
  If you repay me not on such a day
  In such a place, such sum or sums as are
  Express'd in the condition, let the forfeit
  Be nominated for an equal pound
  Of your fair flesh, to be cut off and taken
  In what part of your body pleaseth me.

ANTONIO   Content in faith, I'll seal to such a bond,
  And say there is much kindness in the Jew.

BASSANIO   You shall not seal to such a bond for me,
  I'll rather dwell in my necessity.

ANTONIO   Why fear not man, I will not forfeit it, –
  Within these two months, that's a month before
  This bond expires, I do expect return

Of thrice three times the value of this bond.

SHYLOCK   O father Abram, what these Christians are,   160
  Whose own hard dealings teaches them suspect
  The thoughts of others! Pray you tell me this, –
  If he should break his day what should I gain
  By the exaction of the forfeiture?
  A pound of man's flesh taken from a man,
  Is not so estimable, profitable neither   165
  As flesh of muttons, beefs, or goats, – I say
  To buy his favour, I extend this friendship, –
  If he will take it, so, – if not, adieu,
  And for my love I pray you wrong me not.

ANTONIO   Yes Shylock, I will seal unto this bond.   170

SHYLOCK   Then meet me forthwith at the notary's,
  Give him direction for this merry bond –
  And I will go and purse the ducats straight,
  See to my house left in the fearful guard
  Of an unthrifty knave: and presently   175
  I'll be with you.   *Exit.*

ANTONIO   Hie thee gentle Jew.
  The Hebrew will turn Christian, he grows kind.

BASSANIO   I like not fair terms, and a villain's mind.

ANTONIO   Come on, in this there can be no dismay,
  My ships come home a month before the day.   180
                                      Exeunt.

2.1   *Flourish cornets. Enter the* PRINCE OF
         MOROCCO *(a tawny Moor all in white), and three
         or four followers accordingly, with* PORTIA,
         NERISSA *and their train.*

MOROCCO   Mislike me not for my complexion,
  The shadowed livery of the burnish'd sun,
  To whom I am a neighbour, and near bred.
  Bring me the fairest creature northward born,
  Where Phoebus' fire scarce thaws the icicles,   5
  And let us make incision for your love,
  To prove whose blood is reddest, his or mine.
  I tell thee lady this aspect of mine
  Hath fear'd the valiant, – by my love I swear,
  The best-regarded virgins of our clime   10
  Have lov'd it too: I would not change this hue,
  Except to steal your thoughts my gentle queen.

PORTIA   In terms of choice I am not solely led
  By nice direction of a maiden's eyes:
  Besides, the lott'ry of my destiny   15
  Bars me the right of voluntary choosing:
  But if my father had not scanted me,
  And hedg'd me by his wit to yield myself
  His wife, who wins me by that means I told you,
  Your self (renowned prince) then stood as fair   20
  As any comer I have look'd on yet
  For my affection.

MOROCCO   Even for that I thank you,
  Therefore I pray you lead me to the caskets
  To try my fortune: by this scimitar
  That slew the Sophy, and a Persian prince   25

That won three fields of Sultan Solyman,
I would o'erstare the sternest eyes that look:
Outbrave the heart most daring on the earth:
Pluck the young sucking cubs from the she-bear,
30   Yea, mock the lion when a roars for prey
To win thee lady. But alas the while!
If Hercules and Lichas play at dice
Which is the better man, the greater throw
May turn by fortune from the weaker hand:
35   So is Alcides beaten by his rage,
And so may I, blind Fortune leading me,
Miss that which one unworthier may attain,
And die with grieving.
PORTIA   You must take your chance,
And either not attempt to choose at all,
40   Or swear before you choose, if you choose wrong
Never to speak to lady afterward
In way of marriage, – therefore be advis'd.
MOROCCO
Nor will not, – come bring me unto my chance.
PORTIA   First forward to the temple, after dinner
Your hazard shall be made.
45   MOROCCO   Good fortune then,
To make me blest or cursed'st among men!
Cornets. Exeunt.

2.2   *Enter* LAUNCELOT GOBBO *(the clown) alone.*

LAUNCELOT   Certainly, my conscience will serve me to
run from this Jew my master: the fiend is at mine
elbow, and tempts me, saying to me, 'Gobbo,
Launcelot Gobbo, good Launcelot,' or 'good Gobbo,'
5   or 'good Launcelot Gobbo, use your legs, take the
start, run away.' My conscience says 'No; take heed
honest Launcelot, take heed honest Gobbo,' or as
aforesaid 'honest Launcelot Gobbo, do not run, scorn
running with thy heels.' Well, the most courageous
10   fiend bids me pack, 'Fia!' says the fiend, 'away!' says
the fiend, 'for the heavens rouse up a brave mind' says
the fiend, 'and run.' Well, my conscience hanging
about the neck of my heart, says very wisely to me:
'My honest friend Launcelot' – being an honest man's
15   son, or rather an honest woman's son, for indeed my
father did something smack, something grow to; he
had a kind of taste; – well, my conscience says
'Launcelot budge not!' – 'Budge!' says the fiend, –
'Budge not!' says my conscience. 'Conscience' say I,
20   'you counsel well, – Fiend' say I, 'you counsel well,' –
to be rul'd by my conscience, I should stay with the
Jew my master, who (God bless the mark) is a kind of
devil; and to run away from the Jew I should be ruled
by the fiend, who (saving your reverence) is the devil
25   himself: certainly the Jew is the very devil incarnation,
and in my conscience, my conscience is but a kind of
hard conscience, to offer to counsel me to stay with the
Jew; the fiend gives the more friendly counsel: I will
run fiend, my heels are at your commandment, I will
30   run.

Enter OLD GOBBO *with a basket.*

GOBBO   Master young man, you I pray you, which is the
way to Master Jew's?
LAUNCELOT [*aside*]   O heavens! this is my true-begotten
father, who being more than sand-blind, high gravel-
blind, knows me not, – I will try confusions with him.   35
GOBBO   Master young gentleman, I pray you which is
the way to Master Jew's?
LAUNCELOT   Turn up on your right hand at the next
turning, but at the next turning of all on your left;
marry at the very next turning turn of no hand, but   40
turn down indirectly to the Jew's house.
GOBBO   Be God's sonties 'twill be a hard way to hit, –
can you tell me whether one Launcelot that dwells
with him, dwell with him or no?
LAUNCELOT   Talk you of young Master Launcelot?   45
[*aside*] Mark me now, now will I raise the waters; – talk
you of young Master Launcelot?
GOBBO   No 'master' sir, but a poor man's son, – his
father (though I say't) is an honest exceeding poor
man, and (God be thanked) well to live.   50
LAUNCELOT   Well, let his father be what a will, we talk
of young Master Launcelot.
GOBBO   Your worship's friend and Launcelot sir.
LAUNCELOT   But I pray you ergo old man, ergo I
beseech you, talk you of young Master Launcelot.   55
GOBBO   Of Launcelot an't please your mastership.
LAUNCELOT   Ergo Master Launcelot, – talk not of
Master Launcelot father, for the young gentleman
(according to fates and destinies, and such odd
sayings, the Sisters Three, and such branches of   60
learning), is indeed deceased, or as you would say in
plain terms, gone to heaven.
GOBBO   Marry God forbid! the boy was the very staff of
my age, my very prop.
LAUNCELOT [*aside*]   Do I look like a cudgel or a hovel-   65
post, a staff, or a prop? – Do you know me father?
GOBBO   Alack the day! I know you not young gentleman,
but I pray you tell me, is my boy (God rest his soul)
alive or dead?
LAUNCELOT   Do you not know me father?   70
GOBBO   Alack sir I am sand-blind, I know you not.
LAUNCELOT   Nay, indeed if you had your eyes you
might fail of the knowing me: it is a wise father that
knows his own child. Well, old man, I will tell you
news of your son, – [*Kneels.*] give me your blessing, –   75
truth will come to light, murder cannot be hid long, a
man's son may, but in the end truth will out.
GOBBO   Pray you sir stand up, I am sure you are not
Launcelot my boy.
LAUNCELOT   Pray you let's have no more fooling about   80
it, but give me your blessing: I am Launcelot your boy
that was, your son that is, your child that shall be.
GOBBO   I cannot think you are my son.
LAUNCELOT   I know not what I shall think of that: but I
am Launcelot the Jew's man, and I am sure Margery   85
your wife is my mother.

GOBBO Her name is Margery indeed, – I'll be sworn if thou be Launcelot, thou art mine own flesh and blood: Lord worshipp'd might he be, what a beard hast thou got! thou hast got more hair on thy chin, than Dobbin my fill-horse has on his tail.

LAUNCELOT It should seem then that Dobbin's tail grows backward. I am sure he had more hair of his tail than I have of my face when I last saw him.

GOBBO Lord how art thou chang'd! How dost thou and thy master agree? I have brought him a present; how 'gree you now?

LAUNCELOT Well, well, but for mine own part, as I have set up my rest to run away, so I will not rest till I have run some ground; my master's a very Jew, – give him a present? give him a halter! – I am famish'd in his service. You may tell every finger I have with my ribs: father I am glad you are come, give me your present to one Master Bassanio, who indeed gives rare new liveries, – if I serve not him, I will run as far as God has any ground. O rare fortune! here comes the man, to him father, for I am a Jew if I serve the Jew any longer.

Enter BASSANIO *with* LEONARDO *and*
a follower or two.

BASSANIO You may do so, but let it be so hasted that supper be ready at the farthest by five of the clock: see these letters delivered, put the liveries to making, and desire Gratiano to come anon to my lodging.
Exit one of his men.

LAUNCELOT To him father.

GOBBO God bless your worship.

BASSANIO Gramercy, wouldst thou aught with me?

GOBBO Here's my son sir, a poor boy.

LAUNCELOT Not a poor boy sir, but the rich Jew's man that would sir as my father shall specify.

GOBBO He hath a great infection sir, (as one would say) to serve.

LAUNCELOT Indeed the short and the long is, I serve the Jew, and have a desire as my father shall specify.

GOBBO His master and he (saving your worship's reverence) are scarce cater-cousins, –

LAUNCELOT To be brief, the very truth is, that the Jew having done me wrong, doth cause me as my father (being I hope an old man) shall frutify unto you.

GOBBO I have here a dish of doves that I would bestow upon you worship, and my suit is –

LAUNCELOT In very brief, the suit is impertinent to myself, as your worship shall know by this honest old man, and though I say it, though old man, yet (poor man) my father.

BASSANIO One speak for both, what would you?

LAUNCELOT Serve you sir.

GOBBO That is the very defect of the matter sir.

BASSANIO
I know thee well, thou hast obtain'd thy suit, –

Shylock thy master spoke with me this day,
And hath preferr'd thee, if it be preferment
To leave a rich Jew's service, to become   140
The follower of so poor a gentleman.

LAUNCELOT The old proverb is very well parted be tween my master Shylock and you sir, you have 'the grace of God' sir, and he hath 'enough'.

BASSANIO
Thou speak'st it well; go father with thy son –   145
Take leave of thy old master, and inquire
My lodging out, –
[*to his followers*] give him a livery
More guarded than his fellows': see it done.

LAUNCELOT Father in, – I cannot get a service, no! I have ne'er a tongue in my head: well, if any man in   150
Italy have a fairer table which doth offer to swear upon a book, I shall have good fortune; go to, here's a simple line of life, here's a small trifle of wives, – alas! fifteen wives is nothing, aleven widows and nine maids is a simple coming-in for one man, and then to scape   155
drowning thrice, and to be in peril of my life with the edge of a feather-bed, here are simple scapes: well, if Fortune be a woman she's a good wench for this gear: father come, I'll take my leave of the Jew in the twinkling.   *Exit with Old Gobbo.*   160

BASSANIO I pray thee good Leonardo think on this, –
These things being bought and orderly bestowed
Return in haste, for I do feast to-night
My best-esteem'd acquaintance, hie thee go.

LEONARDO My best endeavours shall be done herein.   165
[*He leaves Bassanio.*]

Enter GRATIANO.

GRATIANO Where's your master?
LEONARDO   Yonder sir he walks. *Exit.*
GRATIANO Signior Bassanio!
BASSANIO Gratiano!
GRATIANO I have suit to you.
BASSANIO   You have obtain'd it.
GRATIANO
You must not deny me, I must go with you to
Belmont.   170
BASSANIO
Why then you must – but hear thee Gratiano,
Thou art too wild, too rude, and bold of voice,
Parts that become thee happily enough,
And in such eyes as ours appear not faults –
But where thou art not known; – why there they
show   175
Something too liberal, – pray thee take pain
To allay with some cold drops of modesty
Thy skipping spirit, lest through thy wild behaviour
I be misconst'red in the place I go to,
And lose my hopes.
GRATIANO   Signior Bassanio, hear me, –   180
If I do not put on a sober habit,

Talk with respect, and swear but now and then,
Wear prayer-books in my pocket, look demurely,
Nay more, while grace is saying hood mine eyes
185 Thus with my hat, and sigh and say 'amen':
Use all the observance of civility
Like one well studied in a sad ostent
To please his grandam, never trust me more.
BASSANIO   Well, we shall see your bearing.
GRATIANO
190 Nay but I bar to-night, you shall not gauge me
By what we do to-night.
BASSANIO   No that were pity,
I would entreat you rather to put on
Your boldest suit of mirth, for we have friends
That purpose merriment: but fare you well,
195 I have some business.
GRATIANO   And I must to Lorenzo and the rest,
But we will visit you at supper-time.   *Exeunt.*

2.3   *Enter* JESSICA *and* LAUNCELOT *the clown.*

JESSICA   I am sorry thou wilt leave my father so,
Our house is hell, and thou (a merry devil)
Didst rob it of some taste of tediousness, –
But fare thee well, there is a ducat for thee,
5 And Launcelot, soon at supper shalt thou see
Lorenzo, who is thy new master's guest,
Give him this letter, – do it secretly, –
And so farewell: I would not have my father
See me in talk with thee.
10 LAUNCELOT   Adieu! tears exhibit my tongue, most
beautiful pagan, most sweet Jew! – if a Christian do
not play the knave and get thee, I am much deceived;
but adieu! these foolish drops do something drown my
manly spirit: adieu!   *Exit.*
15 JESSICA   Farewell good Launcelot.
Alack, what heinous sin is it in me
To be ashamed to be my father's child!
But though I am a daughter to his blood
I am not to his manners: O Lorenzo
20 If thou keep promise I shall end this strife,
Become a Christian and thy loving wife!   *Exit.*

2.4   *Enter* GRATIANO, LORENZO, SALERIO
and SOLANIO.

LORENZO   Nay, we will slink away in supper-time,
Disguise us at my lodging, and return
All in an hour.
GRATIANO   We have not made good preparation.
5 SALERIO   We have not spoke us yet of torch-bearers, –
SOLANIO   'Tis vile unless it may be quaintly ordered,
And better in my mind not undertook.
LORENZO
'Tis now but four of clock, we have two hours
To furnish us;

Enter LAUNCELOT, *with a letter.*

friend Launcelot what's the news?
LAUNCELOT   And it shall please you to break up this, it   10
shall seem to signify.
LORENZO   I know the hand, in faith 'tis a fair hand,
And whiter than the paper it writ on
Is the fair hand that writ.
GRATIANO   Love-news in faith.
LAUNCELOT   By your leave sir.   15
LORENZO   Whither goest thou?
LAUNCELOT
Marry sir to bid my old master the Jew to sup tonight
with my new master the Christian.
LORENZO   Hold here – take this, tell gentle Jessica
I will not fail her, – speak it privately. *Exit Launcelot.* 20
Go gentlemen,
Will you prepare you for this masque to-night?
I am provided of a torch-bearer.
SALERIO   Ay marry, I'll be gone about it straight.
SOLANIO   And so will I.
LORENZO   Meet me and Gratiano   25
At Gratiano's lodging some hour hence.
SALERIO   'Tis good we do so.

Exeunt Salerio and Solanio.

GRATIANO   Was not that letter from fair Jessica?
LORENZO   I must needs tell thee all, – she hath directed
How I shall take her from her father's house,   30
What gold and jewels she is furnish'd with,
What page's suit she hath in readiness, –
If e'er the Jew her father come to heaven,
It will be for his gentle daughter's sake,
And never dare misfortune cross her foot,   35
Unless she do it under this excuse,
That she is issue to a faithless Jew:
Come go with me, peruse this as thou goest, –
Fair Jessica shall be my torch-bearer.   *Exeunt.*

2.5   *Enter* SHYLOCK *the Jew and* LAUNCELOT
his man that was the clown.

SHYLOCK
Well, thou shalt see, thy eyes shall be thy judge,
The difference of old Shylock and Bassanio; –
What Jessica! – thou shalt not gormandize
As thou hast done with me: – what Jessica! –
And sleep, and snore, and rend apparel out.   5
Why Jessica I say!
LAUNCELOT   Why Jessica!
SHYLOCK   Who bids thee call? I do not bid thee call.
LAUNCELOT   Your worship was wont to tell me, I could
do nothing without bidding.

Enter JESSICA.

JESSICA   Call you? what is your will?   10
SHYLOCK   I am bid forth to supper Jessica,
There are my keys: – but wherefore should I go?
I am not bid for love, they flatter me,
But yet I'll go in hate, to feed upon

The prodigal Christian. Jessica my girl,
Look to my house, – I am right loath to go,
There is some ill a-brewing towards my rest,
For I did dream of money-bags to-night.

LAUNCELOT   I beseech you sir go, my young master doth
expect your reproach.

SHYLOCK   So do I his.

LAUNCELOT   And they have conspired together, – I will
not say you shall see a masque, but if you do, then it
was not for nothing that my nose fell a-bleeding on
Black-Monday last, at six o'clock i'th' morning, falling
out that year on Ash-Wednesday was four year in
th'afternoon.

SHYLOCK
What are there masques? Hear you me Jessica,
Lock up my doors, and when you hear the drum
And the vile squealing of the wry-neck'd fife
Clamber not you up to the casements then
Nor thrust your head into the public street
To gaze on Christian fools with varnish'd faces:
But stop my house's ears, I mean my casements,
Let not the sound of shallow fopp'ry enter
My sober house. By Jacob's staff I swear
I have no mind of feasting forth to-night:
But I will go: go you before me sirrah,
Say I will come.

LAUNCELOT   I will go before sir.
Mistress look out at window for all this, –

There will come a Christian by
Will be worth a Jewes eye.   *Exit.*

SHYLOCK
What says that fool of Hagar's offspring? ha?

JESSICA
His words were 'Farewell mistress,' nothing else.

SHYLOCK
The patch is kind enough, but a huge feeder,
Snail-slow in profit, and he sleeps by day
More than the wild-cat: drones hive not with me,
Therefore I part with him, and part with him
To one that I would have him help to waste
His borrowed purse. Well Jessica go in, –
Perhaps I will return immediately, –
Do as I bid you, shut doors after you,
Fast bind, fast find. –
A proverb never stale in thrifty mind.   *Exit.*

JESSICA   Farewell, – and if my fortune be not crost,
I have a father, you a daughter, lost.   *Exit.*

2.6   *Enter the masquers,* GRATIANO *and* SALERIO.

GRATIANO
This is the penthouse under which Lorenzo
Desired us to make stand.

SALERIO   His hour is almost past.

GRATIANO   And it is marvel he out-dwells his hour,
For lovers ever run before the clock.

SALERIO   O ten times faster Venus' pigeons fly

To seal love's bonds new-made, than they are wont
To keep obliged faith unforfeited!

GRATIANO   That ever holds: who riseth from a feast
With that keen appetite that he sits down?
Where is the horse that doth untread again   10
His tedious measures with the unbated fire
That he did pace them first? – all things that are,
Are with more spirit chased than enjoy'd.
How like a younger or a prodigal
The scarfed bark puts from her native bay –   15
Hugg'd and embraced by the strumpet wind!
How like the prodigal doth she return
With over-weather'd ribs and ragged sails –
Lean, rent, and beggar'd by the strumpet wind!

Enter LORENZO.

SALERIO   Here comes Lorenzo, more of this hereafter.   20

LORENZO
Sweet friends, your patience for my long abode
(Not I but my affairs have made you wait):
When you shall please to play the thieves for wives
I'll watch as long for you then: approach –
Here dwells my father Jew. How! who's within?   25

Enter JESSICA *above, in boy's clothes.*

JESSICA   Who are you? – tell me for more certainty,
Albeit I'll swear that I do know your tongue.

LORENZO   Lorenzo and thy love.

JESSICA   Lorenzo certain, and my love indeed,
For who love I so much? and now who knows   30
But you Lorenzo whether I am yours?

LORENZO
Heaven and thy thoughts are witness that thou art.

JESSICA   Here catch this casket, it is worth the pains.
I am glad 'tis night – you do not look on me, –
For I am much asham'd of my exchange: 35
But love is blind, and lovers cannot see
The pretty follies that themselves commit,
For if they could, Cupid himself would blush
To see me thus transformed to a boy.

LORENZO   Descend, for you must be my torch-bearer.   40

JESSICA   What, must I hold a candle to my shames? –
They in themselves (goodsooth) are too too light.
Why, 'tis an office of discovery (love),
And I should be obscur'd.

LORENZO   So are you (sweet)
Even in the lovely garnish of a boy.   45
But come at once,
For the close night doth play the runaway,
And we are stay'd for at Bassanio's feast.

JESSICA   I will make fast the doors and gild myself
With some moe ducats, and be with you straight. 50
                                     Exit above.

GRATIANO   Now (by my hood) a gentle, and no Jew.

LORENZO   Beshrew me but I love her heartily,
For she is wise, if I can judge of her,
And fair she is, if that mine eyes be true,

55 And true she is, as she hath prov'd herself:
And therefore like herself, wise, fair, and true,
Shall she be placed in my constant soul.

Enter JESSICA.

What, art thou come? – on gentlemen, away!
Our masquing mates by this time for us stay.
                    Exit with Jessica and Salerio;
                    Gratiano is about to follow them.

Enter ANTONIO.

60 ANTONIO   Who's there?
GRATIANO   Signior Antonio?
ANTONIO   Fie, fie Gratiano! where are all the rest?
'Tis nine o'clock, our friends all stay for you, –
No masque to-night, – the wind is come about –
65 Bassanio presently will go aboard, –
I have sent twenty out to seek for you.
GRATIANO   I am glad on't, – I desire no more delight
Than to be under sail, and gone to-night.   *Exeunt.*

2.7   *Flourish cornets. Enter* PORTIA *with*
           MOROCCO *and both their trains.*

PORTIA   Go, draw aside the curtains and discover
The several caskets to this noble prince:
Now make your choice.
MOROCCO
This first of gold, who this inscription bears,
5 *Who chooseth me, shall gain what many men desire.*
The second silver, which this promise carries,
Who chooseth me, shall get as much as he deserves.
This third, dull lead, with warning all as blunt,
Who chooseth me, must give and hazard all he hath,
10 How shall I know if I do choose the right?
PORTIA   The one of them contains my picture prince,
If you choose that, then I am yours withal.
MOROCCO   Some god direct my judgment! let me see,
I will survey th'inscriptions back again, –
15 What says this leaden casket?
Who chooseth me, must give and hazard all he hath,
Must give, – for what? for lead, hazard for lead!
This casket threatens – men that hazard all
Do it in hope of fair advantages:
20 A golden mind stoops not to shows of dross,
I'll then nor give nor hazard aught for lead.
What says the silver with her virgin hue?
Who chooseth me, shall get as much as he deserves.
As much as he deserves, – pause there Morocco,
25 And weigh thy value with an even hand, –
If thou be'st rated by thy estimation
Thou dost deserve enough, and yet enough
May not extend so far as to the lady:
And yet to be afeard of my deserving
30 Were but a weak disabling of myself.
As much as I deserve, – why that's the lady.
I do in birth deserve her, and in fortunes,

In graces, and in qualities of breeding:
But more than these, in love I do deserve, –
35 What if I stray'd no further, but chose here?
Let's see once more this saying grav'd in gold:
Who chooseth me shall gain what many men desire:
Why that's the lady, all the world desires her.
From the four corners of the earth they come
40 To kiss this shrine, this mortal breathing saint.
The Hyrcanian deserts, and the vasty wilds
Of wide Arabia are as throughfares now
For princes to come view fair Portia.
The watery kingdom, whose ambitious head
45 Spets in the face of heaven, is no bar
To stop the foreign spirits, but they come
As o'er a brook to see fair Portia.
One of these three contains her heavenly picture.
Is't like that lead contains her? – 'twere damnation
50 To think so base a thought, it were too gross
To rib her cerecloth in the obscure grave, –
Or shall I think in silver she's immur'd
Being ten times undervalued to try'd gold?
O sinful thought! never so rich a gem
55 Was set in worse than gold. They have in England
A coin that bears the figure of an angel
Stamp'd in gold, but that's insculp'd upon:
But here an angel in a golden bed
Lies all within. Deliver me the key:
60 Here do I choose, and thrive I as I may.
PORTIA   There take it prince, and if my form lie there
Then I am yours! [*He unlocks the golden casket.*]
MOROCCO   O hell! what have we here?
A carrion Death, within whose empty eye
There is a written scroll, – I'll read the writing.
[*Reads.*]
    All that glisters is not gold,   65
    Often have you heard that told, –
    Many a man his life hath sold
    But my outside to behold, –
    Gilded tombs do worms infold:
    Had you been as wise as bold,   70
    Young in limbs, in judgment old,
    Your answer had not been inscroll'd, –
    Fare you well, your suit is cold.
    Cold indeed and labour lost,
    Then farewell heat, and welcome frost: 75
Portia adieu! I have too griev'd a heart
To take a tedious leave: thus losers part.
                    Exit with his train.
PORTIA   A gentle riddance, – draw the curtains, go, –
Let all of his complexion choose me so.   *Exeunt.*

2.8   *Enter* SALERIO *and* SOLANIO.

SALERIO   Why man I saw Bassanio under sail,
With him is Gratiano gone along;
And in their ship I am sure Lorenzo is not.
SOLANIO   The villain Jew with outcries rais'd the duke,

5   Who went with him to search Bassanio's ship.

SALERIO   He came too late, the ship was under sail,
        But there the duke was given to understand
        That in a gondola were seen together
        Lorenzo and his amorous Jessica.
10   Besides, Antonio certified the duke
        They were not with Bassanio in his ship.

SOLANIO   I never heard a passion so confus'd,
        So strange, outrageous, and so variable
        As the dog Jew did utter in the streets, –
15   'My daughter! O my ducats! O my daughter!
        Fled with a Christian! O my Christian ducats!
        Justice, the law, my ducats, and my daughter!
        A sealed bag, two sealed bags of ducats,
        Of double ducats, stol'n from me by my daughter!
20   And jewels, two stones, two rich and precious stones,
        Stol'n by my daughter! Justice! – find the girl,
        She hath the stones upon her, and the ducats!'

SALERIO   Why all the boys in Venice follow him,
        Crying his stones, his daughter, and his ducats.

25 SOLANIO   Let good Antonio look he keep his day
        Or he shall pay for this.

SALERIO   Marry well rememb'red, –
        I reason'd with a Frenchman yesterday,
        Who told me, in the narrow seas that part
        The French and English, there miscarried
30   A vessel of our country richly fraught:
        I thought upon Antonio when he told me,
        And wish'd in silence that it were not his.

SOLANIO
        You were best to tell Antonio what you hear, –
        Yet do not suddenly, for it may grieve him.

35 SALERIO   A kinder gentleman treads not the earth, –
        I saw Bassanio and Antonio part,
        Bassanio told him he would make some speed
        Of his return: he answered, 'Do not so,
        Slubber not business for my sake Bassanio,
40   But stay the very riping of the time,
        And for the Jew's bond which he hath of me –
        Let it not enter in your mind of love:
        Be merry, and employ your chiefest thoughts
        To courtship, and such fair ostents of love
45   As shall conveniently become you there.'
        And even there (his eye being big with tears),
        Turning his face, he put his hand behind him,
        And with affection wondrous sensible
        He wrung Bassanio's hand, and so they parted.

50 SOLANIO   I think he only loves the world for him, –
        I pray thee let us go and find him out
        And quicken his embraced heaviness
        With some delight or other.

SALERIO   Do we so.   *Exeunt.*

2.9   *Enter* NERISSA *and a servitor.*

NERISSA
        Quick, quick I pray thee, draw the curtain straight, –

The Prince of Arragon hath ta'en his oath,
And comes to his election presently.

Flourish cornets. Enter the PRINCE OF ARRAGON,
his train, and PORTIA.

PORTIA   Behold, there stand the caskets noble prince,
        If you choose that wherein I am contain'd   5
        Straight shall our nuptial rites be solemniz'd:
        But if you fail, without more speech my lord
        You must be gone from hence immediately.

ARRAGON
        I am enjoin'd by oath to observe three things, –
        First, never to unfold to any one   10
        Which casket 'twas I chose; next, if I fail
        Of the right casket, never in my life
        To woo a maid in way of marriage:
        Lastly,
        If I do fail in fortune of my choice,   15
        Immediately to leave you, and be gone.

PORTIA   To these injunctions every one doth swear
        That comes to hazard for my worthless self.

ARRAGON   And so have I address'd me, – fortune now
        To my heart's hope! – gold, silver, and base lead.   20
        Who chooseth me, must give and hazard all he hath.
        You shall look fairer ere I give or hazard.
        What says the golden chest? ha! let me see,
        Who chooseth me, shall gain what many men desire,
        What many men desire, – that 'many' may be meant   25
        By the fool multitude that choose by show,
        Not learning more than the fond eye doth teach,
        Which pries not to th' interior, but like the martlet
        Builds in the weather on the outward wall,
        Even in the force and road of casualty.   30
        I will not choose what many men desire,
        Because I will not jump with common spirits,
        And rank me with the barbarous multitudes.
        Why then to thee (thou silver treasure house),
        Tell me once more what title thou dost bear;   35
        Who chooseth me shall get as much as he deserves,
        And well said too; for who shall go about
        To cozen Fortune, and be honourable
        Without the stamp of merit? – let none presume
        To wear an undeserved dignity: 40
        O that estates, degrees, and offices,
        Were not deriv'd corruptly, and that clear honour
        Were purchas'd by the merit of the wearer! –
        How many then should cover that stand bare!
        How many be commanded that command!   45
        How much low peasantry would then be gleaned
        From the true seed of honour! and how much honour
        Pick'd from the chaff and ruin of the times,
        To be new-varnish'd! – well, but to my choice.
        Who chooseth me shall get as much as he deserves, –   50
        I will assume desert; give me a key for this,
        And instantly unlock my fortunes here.
        [*He opens the silver casket.*]

PORTIA
　　Too long a pause for that which you find there.

ARRAGON　What's here? the portrait of a blinking idiot
55　　Presenting me a schedule! I will read it:
　　How much unlike art thou to Portia!
　　How much unlike my hopes and my deservings!
　　Who chooseth me, shall have as much as he deserves!
　　Did I deserve no more than a fool's head?
60　　Is that my prize? are my deserts no better?

PORTIA　To offend and judge are distinct offices,
　　And of opposed natures.

ARRAGON　　　　　　What is here?
　　The fire seven times tried this:
65　　*Seven times tried that judgment is,*
　　That did never choose amiss.
　　Some there be that shadows kiss,
　　Such have but a shadow's bliss:
　　There be fools alive (Iwis)
70　　*Silver'd o'er, and so was this.*
　　Take what wife you will to bed,
　　I will ever be your head:
　　So be gone, you are sped.
　　Still more fool I shall appear
75　　By the time I linger here, –
　　With one fool's head I came to woo,
　　But I go away with two.
　　Sweet adieu! I'll keep my oath,
　　Patiently to bear my wroth.

　　　　　　　　　Exit Arragon with his train.
80 PORTIA　Thus hath the candle sing'd the moth:
　　O these deliberate fools! when they do choose,
　　They have the wisdom by their wit to lose.

NERISSA　The ancient saying is no heresy,
　　Hanging and wiving goes by destiny.

PORTIA　Come draw the curtain Nerissa.

　　　　　　　　Enter Messenger.

85 MESSENGER　Where is my lady?

PORTIA　　　　　　Here, what would my lord?

MESSENGER　Madam, there is alighted at your gate
　　A young Venetian, one that comes before
　　To signify th'approaching of his lord,
90　　From whom he bringeth sensible regreets;
　　To wit, (besides commends and courteous breath)
　　Gifts of rich value; yet I have not seen
　　So likely an ambassador of love.
　　A day in April never came so sweet
95　　To show how costly summer was at hand,
　　As this fore-spurrer comes before his lord.

PORTIA　No more I pray thee, I am half afeard
　　Thou wilt say anon he is some kin to thee,
　　Thou spend'st such high-day wit in praising him:
100　　Come, come Nerissa, for I long to see
　　Quick Cupid's post that comes so mannerly.

NERISSA　Bassanio, Lord Love, if thy will it be! *Exeunt.*

3.1　　　　　*Enter* SOLANIO *and* SALERIO.

SOLANIO　Now what news on the Rialto?

SALERIO　Why yet it lives there uncheck'd, that Antonio
　　hath a ship of rich lading wrack'd on the narrow seas;
　　the Goodwins I think they call the place, a very
　　dangerous flat, and fatal, where the carcases of many a　5
　　tall ship lie buried, as they say, – if my gossip Report
　　be an honest woman of her word.

SOLANIO　I would she were as lying a gossip in that, as
　　ever knapp'd ginger, or made her neighbours believe
　　she wept for the death of a third husband: but it is　10
　　true, without any slips of prolixity, or crossing the
　　plain highway of talk, that the good Antonio, the
　　honest Antonio; – O that I had a title good enough to
　　keep his name company! –

SALERIO　Come, the full stop.　15

SOLANIO　Ha! what sayest thou? – why the end is, he
　　hath lost a ship.

SALERIO　I would it might prove the end of his losses.

SOLANIO　Let me say 'amen' betimes, lest the devil cross
　　my prayer, for here he comes in the likeness of a Jew.　20

　　　　　　　　Enter SHYLOCK.

　　How now Shylock! what news among the merchants?

SHYLOCK　You knew, none so well, none so well as you,
　　of my daughter's flight.

SALERIO　That's certain, – I (for my part) knew the tailor
　　that made the wings she flew withal.　25

SOLANIO　And Shylock (for his own part) knew the bird
　　was flidge, and then it is the complexion of them all to
　　leave the dam.

SHYLOCK　She is damn'd for it.

SALERIO　That's certain, if the devil may be her judge.　30

SHYLOCK　My own flesh and blood to rebel!

SOLANIO　Out upon it old carrion! rebels it at these
　　years?

SHYLOCK　I say my daughter is my flesh and my blood.

SALERIO　There is more difference between thy flesh　35
　　and hers, than between jet and ivory, more between
　　your bloods, than there is between red wine and
　　Rhenish: but tell us, do you hear whether Antonio
　　have had any loss at sea or no?

SHYLOCK　There I have another bad match, a bankrupt,　40
　　a prodigal, who dare scarce show his head on the
　　Rialto, a beggar that was us'd to come so smug upon
　　the mart: let him look to his bond! he was wont to call
　　me usurer, let him look to his bond! he was wont to
　　lend money for a Christian cur'sy, let him look to his　45
　　bond!

SALERIO　Why I am sure if he forfeit, thou wilt not take
　　his flesh, – what's that good for?

SHYLOCK　To bait fish withal, – if it will feed nothing
　　else, it will feed my revenge; he hath disgrac'd me, and　50
　　hind'red me half a million, laugh'd at my losses,
　　mock'd at my gains, scorned my nation, thwarted my
　　bargains, cooled my friends, heated mine enemies, –

and what's his reason? I am a Jew. Hath not a Jew eyes? hath not a Jew hands, organs, dimensions, senses, affections, passions? fed with the same food, hurt with the same weapons, subject to the same diseases, healed by the same means, warmed and cooled by the same winter and summer as a Christian is? – if you prick us do we not bleed? if you tickle us do we not laugh? if you poison us do we not die? and if you wrong us shall we not revenge? – if we are like you in the rest, we will resemble you in that. If a Jew wrong a Christian, what is his humility? revenge! If a Christian wrong a Jew, what should his sufferance be by Christian example? – why revenge! The villainy you teach me I will execute, and it shall go hard but I will better the instruction.

Enter a Servingman *from Antonio.*

SERVINGMAN   Gentlemen, my master Antonio is at his house, and desires to speak with you both.

SALERIO   We have been up and down to seek him.

Enter TUBAL.

SOLANIO   Here comes another of the tribe, – a third cannot be match'd, unless the devil himself turn Jew.
                Exeunt Solanio and Salerio with Servant.

SHYLOCK   How now Tubal! what news from Genoa? hast thou found my daughter?

TUBAL   I often came where I did hear of her, but cannot find her.

SHYLOCK   Why there, there, there, there! a diamond gone cost me two thousand ducats in Frankfort, – the curse never fell upon our nation till now, I never felt it till now, – two thousand ducats in that, and other precious, precious jewels; I would my daughter were dead at my foot, and the jewels in her ear: would she were hears'd at my foot, and the ducats in her coffin: – no news of them? why so! – and I know not what's spent in the search: why thou – loss upon loss! the thief gone with so much, and so much to find the thief, and no satisfaction, no revenge, nor no ill luck stirring but what lights o' my shoulders, no sighs but o' my breathing, no tears but o' my shedding.

TUBAL   Yes, other men have ill luck too, – Antonio (as I heard in Genoa) –

SHYLOCK   What, what, what? ill luck, ill luck?

TUBAL   – hath an argosy cast away coming from Tripolis.

SHYLOCK   I thank God, I thank God! is it true, is it true?

TUBAL   I spoke with some of the sailors that escaped the wrack.

SHYLOCK   I thank thee good Tubal, good news, good news: ha ha! heard in Genoa!

TUBAL   Your daughter spent in Genoa, as I heard, one night, fourscore ducats.

SHYLOCK   Thou stick'st a dagger in me, – I shall never see my gold again, – fourscore ducats at a sitting, fourscore ducats!

TUBAL   There came divers of Antonio's creditors in my company to Venice, that swear, he cannot choose but break. 105

SHYLOCK   I am very glad of it, – I'll plague him, I'll torture him, – I am glad of it.

TUBAL   One of them showed me a ring that he had of your daughter for a monkey. 110

SHYLOCK   Out upon her! – thou torturest me Tubal, – it was my turquoise, I had it of Leah when I was a bachelor: I would not have given it for a wilderness of monkeys. 115

TUBAL   But Antonio is certainly undone.

SHYLOCK   Nay, that's true, that's very true, – go Tubal, fee me an officer, bespeak him a fortnight before, – I will have the heart of him if he forfeit, for were he out of Venice I can make what merchandise I will: go 120 Tubal, and meet me at our synagogue, – go good Tubal, – at our synagogue Tubal.   *Exeunt.*

3.2   *Enter* BASSANIO, PORTIA, GRATIANO,
            NERISSA *and all their trains.*

PORTIA   I pray you tarry, pause a day or two
Before you hazard, for in choosing wrong
I lose your company; therefore forbear a while, –
There's something tells me (but it is not love)
I would not lose you, and you know yourself, 5
Hate counsels not in such a quality;
But lest you should not understand me well, –
And yet a maiden hath no tongue, but thought, –
I would detain you here some month or two
Before you venture for me. I could teach you 10
How to choose right, but then I am forsworn,
So will I never be, – so may you miss me, –
But if you do, you'll make me wish a sin,
That I had been forsworn. Beshrew your eyes,
They have o'erlook'd me and divided me, 15
One half of me is yours, the other half yours, –
Mine own I would say: but if mine then yours,
And so all yours; O these naughty times
Put bars between the owners and their rights!
And so though yours, not yours, – prove it so, 20
Let Fortune go to hell for it, not I.
I speak too long, but 'tis to peise the time,
To eche it, and to draw it out in length,
To stay you from election.

BASSANIO   Let me choose,
For as I am, I live upon the rack. 25

PORTIA   Upon the rack Bassanio? then confess
What treason there is mingled with your love.

BASSANIO   None but that ugly treason of mistrust,
Which makes me fear th'enjoying of my love, –
There may as well be amity and life 30
'Tween snow and fire, as treason and my love.

PORTIA   Ay, but I fear you speak upon the rack
Where men enforced do speak any thing.

BASSANIO Promise me life, and I'll confess the truth.

PORTIA Well then, confess and live.

35 BASSANIO   'Confess and love'
Had been the very sum of my confession:
O happy torment, when my torturer
Doth teach me answers for deliverance!
But let me to my fortune and the caskets.

40 PORTIA Away then! I am lock'd in one of them, –
If you do love me, you will find me out.
Nerissa and the rest, stand all aloof, –
Let music sound while he doth make his choice,
Then if he lose he makes a swan-like end,
45 Fading in music. That the comparison
May stand more proper, my eye shall be the stream
And wat'ry death-bed for him: – he may win,
And what is music then? Then music is
Even as the flourish, when true subiects bow
50 To a new-crowned monarch: such it is,
As are those dulcet sounds in break of day,
That creep into the dreaming bridegroom's ear,
And summon him to marriage. Now he goes
With no less presence, but with much more love
55 Than young Alcides, when he did redeem
The virgin tribute, paid by howling Troy
To the sea-monster: I stand for sacrifice,
The rest aloof are the Dardanian wives,
With bleared visages come forth to view
60 The issue of th'exploit: go Hercules!
Live thou, I live – with much much more dismay,
I view the fight, than thou that mak'st the fray.

A song to music the whilst Bassanio comments on the
caskets to himself.

Tell me where is Fancy bred,
Or in the heart, or in the head?
65 How begot, how nourished?
ALL Reply, reply.
It is engend'red in the eyes,
With gazing fed, and Fancy dies
In the cradle where it lies:
70 Let us all ring Fancy's knell.
I'll begin it. Ding, dong, bell.
ALL Ding, dong, bell.

BASSANIO
So may the outward shows be least themselves, –
The world is still deceiv'd with ornament –
75 In law, what plea so tainted and corrupt,
But being season'd with a gracious voice,
Obscures the show of evil? In religion,
What damned error but some sober brow
Will bless it, and approve it with a text,
80 Hiding the grossness with fair ornament?
There is no vice so simple, but assumes
Some mark of virtue on his outward parts;
How many cowards whose hearts are all as false
As stairs of sand, wear yet upon their chins

The beards of Hercules and frowning Mars, 85
Who inward search'd, have livers white as milk? –
And these assume but valour's excrement
To render them redoubted. Look on beauty,
And you shall see 'tis purchas'd by the weight,
Which therein works a miracle in nature, 90
Making them lightest that wear most of it:
So are those crisped snaky golden locks
Which make such wanton gambols with the wind
Upon supposed fairness, often known
To be the dowry of a second head, 95
The skull that bred them in the sepulchre.
Thus ornament is but the guiled shore
To a most dangerous sea: the beauteous scarf
Veiling an Indian beauty; in a word,
The seeming truth which cunning times put on 100
To entrap the wisest. Therefore thou gaudy gold,
Hard food for Midas, I will none of thee,
Nor none of thee thou pale and common drudge
'Tween man and man: but thou, thou meagre lead
Which rather threaten'st than dost promise aught, 105
Thy paleness moves me more than eloquence,
And here choose I, – joy be the consequence!

PORTIA [*aside*] How all the other passions fleet to air:
As doubtful thoughts, and rash-embrac'd despair,
And shudd'ring fear, and green-eyed jealousy. 110
O love be moderate, allay thy extasy,
In measure rain thy joy, scant this excess!
I feel too much thy blessing, make it less
For fear I surfeit.

BASSANIO   What find I here?
[*He opens the leaden casket.*]
Fair Portia's counterfeit! What demi-god 115
Hath come so near creation? move these eyes?
Or whether (riding on the balls of mine)
Seem they in motion? Here are sever'd lips
Parted with sugar breath, – so sweet a bar
Should sunder such sweet friends: here in her hairs 120
The painter plays the spider, and hath woven
A golden mesh t'entrap the hearts of men
Faster than gnats in cobwebs, – but her eyes!
How could he see to do them? having made one,
Methinks it should have power to steal both his 125
And leave itself unfurnish'd: yet look how far
The substance of my praise doth wrong this shadow
In underprizing it, so far this shadow
Doth limp behind the substance. Here's the scroll,
The continent and summary of my fortune. 130

You that choose not by the view
Chance as fair, and choose as true:
Since this fortune falls to you,
Be content, and seek no new.
If you be well pleas'd with this, 135
And hold your fortune for your bliss,
Turn you where your lady is,
And claim her with a loving kiss.

A gentle scroll: fair lady, by your leave,
I come by note to give, and to receive, –
Like one of two contending in a prize
That thinks he hath done well in people's eyes,
Hearing applause and universal shout,
Giddy in spirit, still gazing in a doubt
Whether those peals of praise be his or no,
So (thrice-fair lady) stand I even so,
As doubtful whether what I see be true,
Until confirm'd, sign'd, ratified by you.

PORTIA   You see me Lord Bassanio where I stand,
Such as I am; though for myself alone
I would not be ambitious in my wish
To wish myself much better, yet for you,
I would be trebled twenty times myself,
A thousand times more fair, ten thousand times more rich,
That only to stand high in your account,
I might in virtues, beauties, livings, friends
Exceed account: but the full sum of me
Is sum of something: which to term in gross,
Is an unlesson'd girl, unschool'd, unpractised,
Happy in this, she is not yet so old
But she may learn: happier than this,
She is not bred so dull but she can learn;
Happiest of all, is that her gentle spirit
Commits itself to yours to be directed,
As from her lord, her governor, her king.
Myself, and what is mine, to you and yours
Is now converted. But now I was the lord
Of this fair mansion, master of my servants,
Queen o'er myself: and even now, but now.
This house, these servants, and this same myself
Are yours, – my lord's! – I give them with this ring,
Which when you part from, lose, or give away,
Let it presage the ruin of your love,
And be my vantage to exclaim on you.

BASSANIO   Madam, you have bereft me of all words,
Only my blood speaks to you in my veins,
And there is such confusion in my powers,
As after some oration fairly spoke
By a beloved prince, there doth appear
Among the buzzing pleased multitude,
Where every something being blent together,
Turns to a wild of nothing, save of joy
Express'd, and not express'd: but when this ring
Parts from this finger, then parts life from hence, –
O then be bold to say Bassanio's dead!

NERISSA   My lord and lady, it is now our time
That have stood by and seen our wishes prosper,
To cry good joy, – good joy my lord and lady!

GRATIANO   My Lord Bassanio, and my gentle lady,
I wish you all the joy that you can wish:
For I am sure you can wish none from me:
And when your honours mean to solemnize
The bargain of your faith, I do beseech you
Even at that time I may be married too.

BASSANIO   With all my heart, so thou canst get a wife.

GRATIANO   I thank your lordship, you have got me one.
My eyes my lord can look as swift as yours:
You saw the mistress, I beheld the maid:
You lov'd, I lov'd – for intermission
No more pertains to me my lord than you;
Your fortune stood upon the caskets there,
And so did mine too as the matter falls:
For wooing here until I sweat again,
And swearing till my very roof was dry
With oaths of love, at last, (if promise last)
I got a promise of this fair one here
To have her love, provided that your fortune
Achiev'd her mistress.

PORTIA   Is this true Nerissa?

NERISSA   Madam it is, so you stand pleas'd withal.

BASSANIO   And do you Gratiano mean good faith?

GRATIANO   Yes – faith my lord.

BASSANIO
Our feast shall be much honoured in your marriage.

GRATIANO   We'll play with them the first boy for a thousand ducats.

NERISSA   What! and stake down?

GRATIANO
No, we shall ne'er win at that sport and stake down.
But who comes here? Lorenzo and his infidel!
What! and my old Venetian friend Salerio?

Enter LORENZO, JESSICA *and* SALERIO
(a messenger from Venice).

BASSANIO   Lorenzo and Salerio, welcome hither,
If that the youth of my new int'rest here
Have power to bid you welcome: – by your leave
I bid my very friends and countrymen
(Sweet Portia) welcome.

PORTIA   So do I my lord,
They are entirely welcome.

LORENZO   I thank your honour, – for my part my lord
My purpose was not to have seen you here,
But meeting with Salerio by the way
He did entreat me (past all saying nay)
To come with him along.

SALERIO   I did my lord,
And I have reason for it, – Signior Antonio
Commends him to you. [*Gives Bassanio a letter.*]

BASSANIO   Ere I ope his letter
I pray you tell me how my good friend doth.

SALERIO   Not sick my lord, unless it be in mind,
Nor well, unless in mind: his letter there
Will show you his estate. [*Bassanio opens the letter.*]

GRATIANO
Nerissa, cheer yond stranger, bid her welcome.
Your hand Salerio, – what's the news from Venice?
How doth that royal merchant good Antonio?
I know he will be glad of our success,

240 We are the Jasons, we have won the fleece.

SALERIO
  I would you had won the fleece that he hath lost.

PORTIA
  There are some shrewd contents in yond same paper
  That steals the colour from Bassanio's cheek, –
  Some dear friend dead, else nothing in the world
245   Could turn so much the constitution
  Of any constant man: what worse and worse?
  With leave Bassanio, I am half yourself,
  And I must freely have the half of anything
  That this same paper brings you.

BASSANIO   O sweet Portia,
250   Here are a few of the unpleasant'st words
  That ever blotted paper! Gentle lady
  When I did first impart my love to you,
  I freely told you all the wealth I had
  Ran in my veins, – I was a gentleman, –
255   And then I told you true: and yet dear lady
  Rating myself at nothing, you shall see
  How much I was a braggart, – when I told you
  My state was nothing, I should then have told you
  That I was worse than nothing; for indeed
260   I have engag'd myself to a dear friend,
  Engag'd my friend to his mere enemy
  To feed my means. Here is a letter lady,
  The paper as the body of my friend,
  And every word in it a gaping wound
265   Issuing life-blood. But is it true Salerio?
  Hath all his ventures fail'd? what not one hit?
  From Tripolis, from Mexico and England,
  From Lisbon, Barbary, and India,
  And not one vessel scape the dreadful touch
  Of merchant-marring rocks?

270 SALERIO   Not one my lord.
  Besides, it should appear, that if he had
  The present money to discharge the Jew,
  He would not take it: never did I know
  A creature that did bear the shape of man
275   So keen and greedy to confound a man.
  He plies the duke at morning and at night,
  And doth impeach the freedom of the state
  If they deny him justice. Twenty merchants,
  The duke himself, and the magnificoes
280   Of greatest port have all persuaded with him,
  But none can drive him from the envious plea
  Of forfeiture, of justice, and his bond.

JESSICA   When I was with him, I have heard him swear
  To Tubal and to Chus, his countrymen,
285   That he would rather have Antonio's flesh
  Than twenty times the value of the sum
  That he did owe him: and I know my lord,
  If law, authority, and power deny not,
  It will go hard with poor Antonio.

290 PORTIA   Is it your dear friend that is thus in trouble?

BASSANIO   The dearest friend to me, the kindest man,

  The best-condition'd and unwearied spirit
  In doing courtesies: and one in whom
  The ancient Roman honour more appears
  Than any that draws breath in Italy.   295

PORTIA   What sum owes he the Jew?

BASSANIO   For me three thousand ducats.

PORTIA   What no more?
  Pay him six thousand, and deface the bond:
  Double six thousand, and then treble that,
  Before a friend of this description   300
  Shall lose a hair through Bassanio's fault.
  First go with me to church, and call me wife,
  And then away to Venice to your friend:
  For never shall you lie by Portia's side
  With an unquiet soul. You shall have gold   305
  To pay the petty debt twenty times over.
  When it is paid, bring your true friend along, –
  My maid Nerissa, and myself meantime
  Will live as maids and widows; – come away!
  For you shall hence upon your wedding day: 310
  Bid your friends welcome, show a merry cheer, –
  Since you are dear bought, I will love you dear.
  But let me hear the letter of your friend.

BASSANIO [*Reads.*] *Sweet Bassanio, my ships have all*
  miscarried, my creditors grow cruel, my estate is very low,   315
  my bond to the Jew is forfeit, and (since in paying it, it is
  impossible I should live), all debts are clear'd between you
  and I, if I might but see you at my death: notwithstanding,
  use your pleasure, – if your love do not persuade you to
  come, let not my letter.   320

PORTIA   O love! – dispatch all business and be gone!

BASSANIO   Since I have your good leave to go away,
  I will make haste; but till I come again,
  No bed shall e'er be guilty of my stay,
  Nor rest be interposer 'twixt us twain.   *Exeunt.*   325

3.3   *Enter* SHYLOCK *the Jew,* SOLANIO,
             ANTONIO *and the gaoler.*

SHYLOCK   Gaoler, look to him, – tell not me of mercy, –
  This is the fool that lent out money gratis.
  Gaoler, look to him.

ANTONIO   Hear me yet good Shylock.

SHYLOCK
  I'll have my bond, speak not against my bond, –
  I have sworn an oath, that I will have my bond: 5
  Thou call'dst me dog before thou hadst a cause,
  But since I am a dog, beware my fangs, –
  The duke shall grant me justice, – I do wonder
  (Thou naughty gaoler) that thou art so fond
  To come abroad with him at his request.   10

ANTONIO   I pray thee hear me speak.

SHYLOCK   I'll have my bond. I will not hear thee speak,
  I'll have my bond, and therefore speak no more.
  I'll not be made a soft and dull-ey'd fool,
  To shake the head, relent, and sigh, and yield   15

To Christian intercessors: follow not, –
I'll have no speaking, I will have my bond.   *Exit.*
SOLANIO   It is the most impenetrable cur
  That ever kept with men.
ANTONIO   Let him alone,
  I'll follow him no more with bootless prayers.
  He seeks my life, his reason well I know;
  I oft deliver'd from his forfeitures
  Many that have at times made moan to me,
  Therefore he hates me.
SOLANIO   I am sure the duke
  Will never grant this forfeiture to hold.
ANTONIO   The duke cannot deny the course of law:
  For the commodity that strangers have
  With us in Venice, if it be denied,
  Will much impeach the justice of the state,
  Since that the trade and profit of the city
  Consisteth of all nations. Therefore go, –
  These griefs and losses have so bated me
  That I shall hardly spare a pound of flesh
  To-morrow, to my bloody creditor.
  Well gaoler, on, – pray God Bassanio come
  To see me pay his debt, and then I care not.   *Exeunt.*

3.4   *Enter* PORTIA, NERISSA, LORENZO, JESSICA
      and BALTHAZAR *(a man of Portia's).*

LORENZO
  Madam, although I speak it in your presence,
  You have a noble and a true conceit
  Of god-like amity, which appears most strongly
  In bearing thus the absence of your lord.
  But if you knew to whom you show this honour,
  How true a gentleman you send relief,
  How dear a lover of my lord your husband,
  I know you would be prouder of the work
  Than customary bounty can enforce you.
PORTIA   I never did repent for doing good,
  Nor shall not now: for in companions
  That do converse and waste the time together,
  Whose souls do bear an egall yoke of love,
  There must be needs a like proportion
  Of lineaments, of manners, and of spirit;
  Which makes me think that this Antonio
  Being the bosom lover of my lord,
  Must needs be like my lord. If it be so,
  How little is the cost I have bestowed
  In purchasing the semblance of my soul,
  From out the state of hellish cruelty! –
  This comes too near the praising of myself,
  Therefore no more of it: hear other things –
  Lorenzo I commit into your hands,
  The husbandry and manage of my house,
  Until my lord's return: for mine own part
  I have toward heaven breath'd a secret vow,
  To live in prayer and contemplation,
  Only attended by Nerissa here,

  Until her husband and my lord's return, –   30
  There is a monast'ry two miles off,
  And there we will abide. I do desire you
  Not to deny this imposition,
  The which my love and some necessity
  Now lays upon you.
LORENZO   Madam, with all my heart,   35
  I shall obey you in all fair commands.
PORTIA   My people do already know my mind,
  And will acknowledge you and Jessica
  In place of Lord Bassanio and myself.
  So fare you well till we shall meet again.   40
LORENZO   Fair thoughts and happy hours attend on you!
JESSICA   I wish your ladyship all heart's content.
PORTIA   I thank you for your wish, and am well pleas'd
  To wish it back on you: fare you well Jessica.
          Exeunt Jessica and Lorenzo.
  Now Balthazar,   45
  As I have ever found thee honest-true,
  So let me find thee still: take this same letter,
  And use thou all th'endeavour of a man
  In speed to Padua, see thou render this
  Into my cousin's hand (Doctor Bellario),   50
  And look what notes and garments he doth give thee, –
  Bring them (I pray thee) with imagin'd speed
  Unto the traject, to the common ferry
  Which trades to Venice; waste no time in words
  But get thee gone, – I shall be there before thee.   55
BALTHAZAR   Madam, I go with all convenient speed.
          Exit.
PORTIA   Come on Nerissa, I have work in hand
  That you yet know not of; we'll see our husbands
  Before they think of us!
NERISSA   Shall they see us?
PORTIA   They shall Nerissa: but in such a habit,   60
  That they shall think we are accomplished
  With that we lack; I'll hold thee any wager
  When we are both accoutered like young men,
  I'll prove the prettier fellow of the two,
  And wear my dagger with the braver grace,   65
  And speak between the change of man and boy,
  With a reed voice, and turn two mincing steps
  Into a manly stride; and speak of frays
  Like a fine bragging youth: and tell quaint lies
  How honourable ladies sought my love,   70
  Which I denying, they fell sick and died:
  I could not do withal: – then I'll repent,
  And wish for all that, that I had not kill'd them;
  And twenty of these puny lies I'll tell,
  That men shall swear I have discontinued school   75
  Above a twelvemonth: I have within my mind
  A thousand raw tricks of these bragging Jacks,
  Which I will practise.
NERISSA   Why, shall we turn to men?
PORTIA   Fie! what a question's that,
  If thou wert near a lewd interpreter!   80

But come, I'll tell thee all my whole device
When I am in my coach, which stays for us
At the park gate; and therefore haste away,
For we must measure twenty miles to-day.   *Exeunt.*

3.5   *Enter* LAUNCELOT *the clown and* JESSICA.

LAUNCELOT   Yes truly, for look you, the sins of the
father are to be laid upon the children, therefore (I
promise you), I fear you, – I was always plain with you,
and so now I speak my agitation of the matter:
5   therefore be o' good cheer, for truly I think you are
damn'd, – there is but one hope in it that can do you
any good, and that is but a kind of bastard hope
neither.

JESSICA   And what hope is that I pray thee?

10   LAUNCELOT   Marry, you may partly hope that your
father got you not, that you are not the Jew's daughter.

JESSICA   That were a kind of bastard hope indeed, – so
the sins of my mother should be visited upon me.

LAUNCELOT   Truly then I fear you are damn'd both by
15   father and mother: thus when I shun Scylla (your
father), I fall into Charybdis (your mother); well, you
are gone both ways.

JESSICA   I shall be sav'd by my husband, – he hath made
me a Christian!

20   LAUNCELOT   Truly the more to blame he, we were
Christians enow before, e'en as many as could well live
one by another: this making of Christians will raise the
price of hogs, – if we grow all to be pork-eaters, we
shall not shortly have a rasher on the coals for money.

Enter LORENZO.

25   JESSICA   I'll tell my husband (Launcelot) what you say,
– here he comes!

LORENZO   I shall grow jealous of you shortly Launcelot,
if you thus get my wife into corners!

JESSICA   Nay, you need not fear us Lorenzo, Launcelot
30   and I are out, – he tells me flatly there's no mercy for
me in heaven, because I am a Jew's daughter: and he
says you are no good member of the commonwealth,
for in converting Jews to Christians, you raise the
price of pork.

35   LORENZO   I shall answer that better to the
commonwealth than you can the getting up of the
negro's belly: the Moor is with child by you
Launcelot!

LAUNCELOT   It is much that the Moor should be more
40   than reason: but if she be less than an honest woman,
she is indeed more than I took her for.

LORENZO   How every fool can play upon the word! I
think the best grace of wit will shortly turn into
silence, and discourse grow commendable in none
45   only but parrots: go in sirrah, bid them prepare for
dinner!

LAUNCELOT   That is done sir, they have all stomachs!

LORENZO   Goodly Lord, what a wit-snapper are you!
then bid them prepare dinner!

LAUNCELOT   That is done too sir, only 'cover' is the   50
word.

LORENZO   Will you cover then sir?

LAUNCELOT   Not so sir neither, I know my duty.

LORENZO   Yet more quarrelling with occasion! wilt thou
show the whole wealth of thy wit in an instant? I pray   55
thee understand a plain man in his plain meaning: go
to thy fellows, bid them cover the table, serve in the
meat, and we will come in to dinner.

LAUNCELOT   For the table sir, it shall be serv'd in, – for
the meat sir, it shall be cover'd, – for your coming in to   60
dinner sir, why let it be as humours and conceits shall
govern.   *Exit.*

LORENZO   O dear discretion, how his words are suited!
The fool hath planted in his memory
An army of good words, and I do know   65
A many fools that stand in better place,
Garnish'd like him, that for a tricksy word
Defy the matter: how cheer'st thou Jessica?
And now (good sweet) say thy opinion,
How dost thou like the Lord Bassanio's wife?   70

JESSICA   Past all expressing, – it is very meet
The Lord Bassanio live an upright life
For having such a blessing in his lady,
He finds the joys of heaven here on earth,
And if on earth he do not merit it,   75
In reason he should never come to heaven!
Why, if two gods should play some heavenly match,
And on the wager lay two earthly women,
And Portia one, there must be something else
Pawn'd with the other, for the poor rude world   80
Hath not her fellow.

LORENZO   Even such a husband
Hast thou of me, as she is for a wife.

JESSICA   Nay, but ask my opinion too of that.

LORENZO   I will anon, – first let us go to dinner.

JESSICA   Nay, let me praise you while I have a stomach.   85

LORENZO   No pray thee, let it serve for table-talk,
Then howsome'er thou speak'st, 'mong other things
I shall digest it.

JESSICA   Well, I'll set you forth.   *Exeunt.*

4.1   *Enter the* DUKE, *the magnificoes*, ANTONIO,
BASSANIO *and* GRATIANO, SALERIO *and others.*

DUKE   What, is Antonio here?

ANTONIO   Ready, so please your grace!

DUKE   I am sorry for thee, – thou art come to answer
A stony adversary, an inhuman wretch,
Uncapable of pity, void, and empty   5
From any dram of mercy.

ANTONIO   I have heard
Your grace hath ta'en great pains to qualify
His rigorous course; but since he stands obdurate,

And that no lawful means can carry me
10 Out of his envy's reach, I do oppose
My patience to his fury, and am arm'd
To suffer with a quietness of spirit,
The very tyranny and rage of his.
DUKE   Go one and call the Jew into the court.
SALERIO
15 He is ready at the door, – he comes my lord.

Enter SHYLOCK.

DUKE   Make room, and let him stand before our face.
Shylock the world thinks, and I think so too,
That thou but leadest this fashion of thy malice
To the last hour of act, and then 'tis thought
20 Thou'lt show thy mercy and remorse more strange
Than is thy strange apparent cruelty;
And where thou now exacts the penalty,
Which is a pound of this poor merchant's flesh,
Thou wilt not only loose the forfeiture,
25 But touch'd with human gentleness and love,
Forgive a moiety of the principal,
Glancing an eye of pity on his losses
That have of late so huddled on his back,
Enow to press a royal merchant down,
30 And pluck commiseration of his state
From brassy bosoms and rough hearts of flint,
From stubborn Turks, and Tartars never train'd
To offices of tender courtesy:
We all expect a gentle answer Jew!
SHYLOCK
35 I have possess'd your grace of what I purpose,
And by our holy Sabbath have I sworn
To have the due and forfeit of my bond, –
If you deny it, let the danger light
Upon your charter and your city's freedom!
40 You'll ask me why I rather choose to have
A weight of carrion flesh, than to receive
Three thousand ducats: I'll not answer that!
But say it is my humour, – is it answer'd?
What if my house be troubled with a rat,
45 And I be pleas'd to give ten thousand ducats
To have it ban'd? what, are you answer'd yet?
Some men there are love not a gaping pig!
Some that are mad if they behold a cat!
And others when the bagpipe sings i'th' nose,
50 Cannot contain their urine – for affection
(Master of passion) sways it to the mood
Of what it likes or loathes, – now for your answer:
As there is no firm reason to be rend'red
Why he cannot abide a gaping pig,
55 Why he a harmless necessary cat,
Why he a woollen bagpipe, but of force
Must yield to such inevitable shame,
As to offend himself being offended:
So can I give no reason, nor I will not,
60 More than a lodg'd hate, and a certain loathing
I bear Antonio, that I follow thus

A losing suit against him! – are you answered?
BASSANIO   This is no answer thou unfeeling man,
To excuse the current of thy cruelty.
SHYLOCK
I am not bound to please thee with my answers!   65
BASSANIO   Do all men kill the things they do not love?
SHYLOCK   Hates any man the thing he would not kill?
BASSANIO   Every offence is not a hate at first!
SHYLOCK
What! wouldst thou have a serpent sting thee twice?
ANTONIO   I pray you think you question with the Jew, –   70
You may as well go stand upon the beach
And bid the main flood bate his usual height,
You may as well use question with the wolf,
Why he hath made the ewe bleak for the lamb:
You may as well forbid the mountain pines   75
To wag their high tops, and to make no noise
When they are fretten with the gusts of heaven:
You may as well do any thing most hard
As seek to soften that – than which what's harder? –
His Jewish heart! Therefore (I do beseech you)   80
Make no moe offers, use no farther means,
But with all brief and plain conveniency
Let me have judgment, and the Jew his will!
BASSANIO   For thy three thousand ducats here is six!
SHYLOCK   If every ducat in six thousand ducats   85
Were in six parts, and every part a ducat,
I would not draw them, I would have my bond!
DUKE   How shalt thou hope for mercy rend'ring none?
SHYLOCK   What judgment shall I dread doing no wrong?
You have among you many a purchas'd slave,   90
Which (like your asses, and your dogs and mules)
You use in abject and in slavish parts,
Because you bought them, – shall I say to you,
Let them be free, marry them to your heirs?
Why sweat they under burthens? let their beds   95
Be made as soft as yours, and let their palates
Be season'd with such viands? you will answer
'The slaves are ours,' – so do I answer you:
The pound of flesh which I demand of him
Is dearly bought, 'tis mine and I will have it: 100
If you deny me, fie upon your law!
There is no force in the decrees of Venice:
I stand for judgment, – answer, shall I have it?
DUKE   Upon my power I may dismiss this court,
Unless Bellario (a learned doctor,   105
Whom I have sent for to determine this)
Come here to-day.
SALERIO   My lord, here stays without
A messenger with letters from the doctor,
New come from Padua.
DUKE   Bring us the letters! call the messenger!   110
BASSANIO
Good cheer Antonio! what man, courage yet!
The Jew shall have my flesh, blood, bones and all,
Ere thou shalt lose for me one drop of blood.
ANTONIO   I am a tainted wether of the flock,

115   Meetest for death, – the weakest kind of fruit
        Drops earliest to the ground, and so let me;
        You cannot better be employ'd Bassanio,
        Than to live still and write mine epitaph.

        Enter NERISSA, *dressed like a lawyer's clerk.*

        DUKE   Came you from Padua from Bellario?
        NERISSA
120   From both, my lord. Bellario greets your grace.
        [*She presents a letter.*]
        BASSANIO   Why dost thou whet thy knife so earnestly?
        SHYLOCK
        To cut the forfeiture from that bankrupt there!
        GRATIANO   Not on thy sole: but on thy soul (harsh Jew)
        Thou mak'st thy knife keen: but no metal can, –
125   No, not the hangman's axe – bear half the keenness
        Of thy sharp envy: can no prayers pierce thee?
        SHYLOCK   No, none that thou hast wit enough to make.
        GRATIANO   O be thou damn'd, inexecrable dog!
        And for thy life let justice be accus'd;
130   Thou almost mak'st me waver in my faith,
        To hold opinion with Pythagoras,
        That souls of animals infuse themselves
        Into the trunks of men: thy currish spirit
        Govern'd a wolf, who hang'd for human slaughter –
135   Even from the gallows did his fell soul fleet,
        And whilst thou layest in thy unhallowed dam,
        Infus'd itself in thee: for thy desires
        Are wolvish, bloody, starv'd, and ravenous.
        SHYLOCK
        Till thou canst rail the seal from off my bond,
140   Thou but offend'st thy lungs to speak so loud:
        Repair thy wit good youth, or it will fall
        To cureless ruin. I stand here for law.
        DUKE   This letter from Bellario doth commend
        A young and learned doctor to our court:
        Where is he?
145   NERISSA   He attendeth here hard by
        To know your answer – whether you'll admit him.
        DUKE   With all my heart: some three or four of you
        Go give him courteous conduct to this place,
        Meantime the court shall hear Bellario's letter.
150   [*Reads.*] *Your grace shall understand, that at the
        receipt of your letter I am very sick, but in the instant
        that your messenger came, in loving visitation was with
        me a young doctor of Rome, his name is Balthazar: I
        acquainted him with the cause in controversy between the
155   Jew and Antonio the merchant, we turn'd o'er many
        books together, he is furnished with my opinion, which
        (bettered with his own learning, the greatness whereof I
        cannot enough commend), comes with him at my
        importunity, to fill up your grace's request in my stead. I
160   beseech you let his lack of years be no impediment to let
        him lack a reverend estimation, for I never knew so
        young a body with so old a head: I leave him to your
        gracious acceptance, whose trial shall better publish his
        commendation.*

        Enter PORTIA, *dressed like a doctor of laws.*

        You hear the learn'd Bellario what he writes,   165
        And here (I take it) is the doctor come.
        Give me your hand, – come you from old Bellario?
        PORTIA   I did my lord.
        DUKE   You are welcome, take your place:
        Are you acquainted with the difference
        That holds this present question in the court?   170
        PORTIA   I am informed throughly of the cause, –
        Which is the merchant here? and which the Jew?
        DUKE   Antonio and old Shylock, both stand forth.
        PORTIA   Is your name Shylock?
        SHYLOCK   Shylock is my name.
        PORTIA   Of a strange nature is the suit you follow,   175
        Yet in such rule, that the Venetian law
        Cannot impugn you as you do proceed.
        You stand within his danger, do you not?
        ANTONIO   Ay, so he says.
        PORTIA   Do you confess the bond?
        ANTONIO   I do.
        PORTIA   Then must the Jew be merciful.   180
        SHYLOCK   On what compulsion must I? tell me that.
        PORTIA   The quality of mercy is not strain'd,
        It droppeth as the gentle rain from heaven
        Upon the place beneath: it is twice blest,
        It blesseth him that gives, and him that takes,   185
        'Tis mightiest in the mightiest, it becomes
        The throned monarch better than his crown.
        His sceptre shows the force of temporal power,
        The attribute to awe and majesty,
        Wherein doth sit the dread and fear of kings: 190
        But mercy is above this sceptred sway,
        It is enthroned in the hearts of kings,
        It is an attribute to God himself;
        And earthly power doth then show likest God's
        When mercy seasons justice: therefore Jew,   195
        Though justice be thy plea, consider this,
        That in the course of justice, none of us
        Should see salvation: we do pray for mercy,
        And that same prayer, doth teach us all to render
        The deeds of mercy. I have spoke thus much   200
        To mitigate the justice of thy plea,
        Which if thou follow, this strict court of Venice
        Must needs give sentence 'gainst the merchant there.
        SHYLOCK   My deeds upon my head! I crave the law,
        The penalty and forfeit of my bond.   205
        PORTIA   Is he not able to discharge the money?
        BASSANIO   Yes, here I tender it for him in the court,
        Yea, twice the sum, – if that will not suffice,
        I will be bound to pay it ten times o'er
        On forfeit of my hands, my head, my heart, –   210
        If this will not suffice, it must appear
        That malice bears down truth. And I beseech you
        Wrest once the law to your authority, –
        To do a great right, do a little wrong, –
        And curb this cruel devil of his will.   215

850

PORTIA It must not be, there is no power in Venice
　Can alter a decree established:
　'Twill be recorded for a precedent,
　And many an error by the same example
220　Will rush into the state, – it cannot be.
　SHYLOCK A Daniel come to judgment: yea a Daniel!
　O wise young judge how I do honour thee!
　PORTIA I pray you let me look upon the bond.
　SHYLOCK Here 'tis most reverend doctor, here it is.
225　PORTIA Shylock there's thrice thy money off'red thee.
　SHYLOCK An oath, an oath, I have an oath in heaven, –
　Shall I lay perjury upon my soul?
　No not for Venice.
　PORTIA　　　　　Why this bond is forfeit,
　And lawfully by this the Jew may claim
230　A pound of flesh, to be by him cut off
　Nearest the merchant's heart: be merciful,
　Take thrice thy money, bid me tear the bond.
　SHYLOCK When it is paid, according to the tenour.
　It doth appear you are a worthy judge,
235　You know the law, your exposition
　Hath been most sound: I charge you by the law,
　Whereof you are a well-deserving pillar,
　Proceed to judgment: by my soul I swear,
　There is no power in the tongue of man
240　To alter me, – I stay here on my bond.
　ANTONIO Most heartily I do beseech the court
　To give the judgment.
　PORTIA　　　　　Why then thus it is, –
　You must prepare your bosom for his knife.
　SHYLOCK O noble judge! O excellent young man!
245　PORTIA For the intent and purpose of the law
　Hath full relation to the penalty,
　Which here appeareth due upon the bond.
　SHYLOCK 'Tis very true: O wise and upright judge,
　How much more elder art thou than thy looks!
　PORTIA Therefore lay bare your bosom.
250　SHYLOCK　　　　　Ay, his breast,
　So says the bond, doth it not noble judge?
　'Nearest his heart,' those are the very words.
　PORTIA It is so, – are there balance here to weigh
　The flesh?
　SHYLOCK I have them ready.
　PORTIA
255　Have by some surgeon Shylock on your charge,
　To stop his wounds, lest he do bleed to death.
　SHYLOCK Is it so nominated in the bond?
　PORTIA It is not so express'd, but what of that?
　'Twere good you do so much for charity.
260　SHYLOCK I cannot find it, 'tis not in the bond.
　PORTIA You merchant, have you any thing to say?
　ANTONIO But little; I am arm'd and well prepar'd, –
　Give me your hand Bassanio, fare you well,
　Grieve not that I am fall'n to this for you:
265　For herein Fortune shows herself more kind
　Than is her custom: it is still her use
　To let the wretched man outlive his wealth,

To view with hollow eye and wrinkled brow
An age of poverty: from which ling'ring penance
Of such misery doth she cut me off.　　270
Commend me to your honourable wife,
Tell her the process of Antonio's end,
Say how I lov'd you, speak me fair in death:
And when the tale is told, bid her be judge
Whether Bassanio had not once a love:　275
Repent but you that you shall lose your friend
And he repents not that he pays your debt.
For if the Jew do cut but deep enough,
I'll pay it instantly with all my heart.
BASSANIO Antonio, I am married to a wife　280
　Which is as dear to me as life itself,
　But life itself, my wife, and all the world,
　Are not with me esteem'd above thy life.
　I would lose all, ay sacrifice them all
　Here to this devil, to deliver you.　285
PORTIA Your wife would give you little thanks for that
　If she were by to hear you make the offer.
GRATIANO I have a wife who I protest I love, –
　I would she were in heaven, so she could
　Entreat some power to change this currish Jew.　290
NERISSA 'Tis well you offer it behind her back,
　The wish would make else an unquiet house.
SHYLOCK [aside]
　These be the Christian husbands! I have a daughter –
　Would any of the stock of Barrabas
　Had been her husband, rather than a Christian.　295
　We trifle time, I pray thee pursue sentence.
PORTIA A pound of that same merchant's flesh is thine,
　The court awards it, and the law doth give it.
SHYLOCK Most rightful judge!
PORTIA And you must cut this flesh from off his breast,　300
　The law allows it, and the court awards it.
SHYLOCK
Most learned judge! a sentence, come prepare.
PORTIA Tarry a little, there is something else, –
　This bond doth give thee here no jot of blood,
　The words expressly are 'a pound of flesh':　305
　Take then thy bond, take thou thy pound of flesh,
　But in the cutting it, if thou dost shed
　One drop of Christian blood, thy lands and goods
　Are (by the laws of Venice) confiscate
　Unto the state of Venice.
GRATIANO　　　　　O upright judge! –　310
　Mark Jew, – O learned judge!
SHYLOCK Is that the law?
PORTIA　　　　　Thyself shalt see the act:
　For as thou urgest justice, be assur'd
　Thou shalt have justice more than thou desir'st.
GRATIANO
　O learned judge! – mark Jew, a learned judge.　315
SHYLOCK I take this offer then, – pay the bond thrice
　And let the Christian go.
BASSANIO　　　　　Here is the money.
PORTIA Soft!

320 The Jew shall have all justice, – soft no haste!
He shall have nothing but the penalty.
GRATIANO   O Jew! an upright judge, a learned judge!
PORTIA   Therefore prepare thee to cut off the flesh, –
Shed thou no blood, nor cut thou less nor more
325 But just a pound of flesh: if thou tak'st more
Or less than a just pound, be it but so much
As makes it light or heavy in the substance,
Or the division of the twentieth part
Of one poor scruple, nay if the scale do turn
But in the estimation of a hair,
330 Thou diest, and all thy goods are confiscate.
GRATIANO   A second Daniel, a Daniel, Jew! –
Now infidel I have you on the hip.
PORTIA   Why doth the Jew pause? take thy forfeiture.
SHYLOCK   Give me my principal, and let me go.
335 BASSANIO   I have it ready for thee, here it is.
PORTIA   He hath refus'd it in the open court,
He shall have merely justice and his bond.
GRATIANO   A Daniel still say I, a second Daniel! –
I thank thee Jew for teaching me that word.
340 SHYLOCK   Shall I not have barely my principal?
PORTIA   Thou shalt have nothing but the forfeiture
To be so taken at thy peril Jew.
SHYLOCK   Why then the devil give him good of it:
I'll stay no longer question.
PORTIA   Tarry Jew,
345 The law hath yet another hold on you.
It is enacted in the laws of Venice,
If it be proved against an alien,
That by direct, or indirect attempts
He seek the life of any citizen,
350 The party 'gainst the which he doth contrive,
Shall seize one half his goods, the other half
Comes to the privy coffer of the state,
And the offender's life lies in the mercy
Of the Duke only, 'gainst all other voice.
355 In which predicament I say thou stand'st:
For it appears by manifest proceeding,
That indirectly, and directly too,
Thou hast contrived against the very life
Of the defendant: and thou hast incurr'd
360 The danger formerly by me rehears'd.
Down therefore, and beg mercy of the duke.
GRATIANO
Beg that thou may'st have leave to hang thyself, –
And yet thy wealth being forfeit to the state,
Thou hast not left the value of a cord,
365 Therefore thou must be hang'd at the state's charge.
DUKE   That thou shalt see the difference of our spirit
I pardon thee thy life before thou ask it:
For half thy wealth, it is Antonio's,
The other half comes to the general state,
370 Which humbleness may drive unto a fine.
PORTIA   Ay for the state, not for Antonio.
SHYLOCK   Nay, take my life and all, pardon not that, –

You take my house, when you do take the prop
That doth sustain my house: you take my life
375 When you do take the means whereby I live.
PORTIA   What mercy can you render him Antonio?
GRATIANO   A halter gratis, nothing else for Godsake!
ANTONIO   So please my lord the duke, and all the court,
To quit the fine for one half of his goods,
380 I am content: so he will let me have
The other half in use, to render it
Upon his death unto the gentleman
That lately stole his daughter.
Two things provided more, that for this favour
385 He presently become a Christian:
The other, that he do record a gift
(Here in the court) of all he dies possess'd
Unto his son Lorenzo and his daughter.
DUKE   He shall do this, or else I do recant
390 The pardon that I late pronounced here.
PORTIA   Art thou contented Jew? what dost thou say?
SHYLOCK   I am content.
PORTIA   Clerk, draw a deed of gift.
SHYLOCK   I pray you give me leave to go from hence,
I am not well, – send the deed after me,
And I will sign it.
DUKE   Get thee gone, but do it. 395
GRATIANO
In christ'ning shalt thou have two godfathers, –
Had I been judge, thou shouldst have had ten more,
To bring thee to the gallows, not to the font.
                                        Exit Shylock.
DUKE   Sir I entreat you home with me to dinner.
PORTIA   I humbly do desire your grace of pardon, 400
I must away this night toward Padua,
And it is meet I presently set forth.
DUKE   I am sorry that your leisure serves you not.
Antonio, gratify this gentleman,
For in my mind you are much bound to him. 405
                          Exit Duke and his train.
BASSANIO   Most worthy gentleman, I and my friend
Have by your wisdom been this day acquitted
Of grievous penalties, in lieu whereof,
Three thousand ducats due unto the Jew
We freely cope your courteous pains withal. 410
ANTONIO   And stand indebted over and above
In love and service to you evermore.
PORTIA   He is well paid that is well satisfied,
And I delivering you, am satisfied,
And therein do account myself well paid, – 415
My mind was never yet more mercenary.
I pray you know me when we meet again,
I wish you well, and so I take my leave.
BASSANIO
Dear sir, of force I must attempt you further, –
Take some remembrance of us as a tribute, 420
Not as a fee: grant me two things I pray you, –
Not to deny me, and to pardon me.

PORTIA
  You press me far, and therefore I will yield, –
  Give me your gloves, I'll wear them for your sake,
425 And (for your love) I'll take this ring from you, –
  Do not draw back your hand, I'll take no more,
  And you in love shall not deny me this!
BASSANIO
  This ring good sir? alas it is a trifle,
  I will not shame myself to give you this!
430 PORTIA   I will have nothing else but only this,
  And now methinks I have a mind to it!
BASSANIO
  There's more depends on this than on the value, –
  The dearest ring in Venice will I give you,
  And find it out by proclamation,
435 Only for this I pray you pardon me!
PORTIA   I see sir you are liberal in offers, –
  You taught me first to beg, and now methinks
  You teach me how a beggar should be answer'd.
BASSANIO   Good sir, this ring was given me by my wife,
440 And when she put it on, she made me vow
  That I should neither sell, nor give, nor lose it.
PORTIA
  That scuse serves many men to save their gifts, –
  And if your wife be not a mad-woman,
  And know how well I have deserv'd this ring,
445 She would not hold out enemy for ever
  For giving it to me: well, peace be with you!
                    Exeunt Portia and Nerissa.
ANTONIO   My Lord Bassanio, let him have the ring,
  Let his deservings and my love withal
  Be valued 'gainst your wife's commandement.
450 BASSANIO   Go Gratiano, run and overtake him,
  Give him the ring, and bring him if thou canst
  Unto Antonio's house, – away, make haste.
                    Exit Gratiano.

  Come, you and I will thither presently,
  And in the morning early will we both
455 Fly toward Belmont, – come Antonio.   *Exeunt.*

4.2   *Enter* PORTIA *and* NERISSA.

PORTIA
  Inquire the Jew's house out, give him this deed,
  And let him sign it, – we'll away to-night,
  And be a day before our husbands home:
  This deed will be well welcome to Lorenzo!

        Enter GRATIANO.

5 GRATIANO   Fair sir, you are well o'erta'en:
  My Lord Bassanio upon more advice,
  Hath sent you here this ring, and doth entreat
  Your company at dinner.
PORTIA   That cannot be;
  His ring I do accept most thankfully,
10 And so I pray you tell him: furthermore,
  I pray you show my youth old Shylock's house.

GRATIANO   That will I do.
NERISSA   Sir, I would speak with you:
  [*aside to Portia*] I'll see if I can get my husband's
    ring
  Which I did make him swear to keep for ever.
PORTIA
  Thou may'st I warrant, – we shall have old swearing   15
  That they did give the rings away to men;
  But we'll outface them, and outswear them too:
  Away, make haste! thou know'st where I will tarry.
NERISSA
  Come good sir, will you show me to this house?
                    Exeunt.

5.1   *Enter* LORENZO *and* JESSICA.

LORENZO
  The moon shines bright. In such a night as this,
  When the sweet wind did gently kiss the trees,
  And they did make no noise, in such a night
  Troilus methinks mounted the Trojan walls,
  And sigh'd his soul toward the Grecian tents   5
  Where Cressid lay that night.
JESSICA   In such a night
  Did Thisbe fearfully o'ertrip the dew,
  And saw the lion's shadow ere himself,
  And ran dismayed away.
LORENZO   In such a night
  Stood Dido with a willow in her hand   10
  Upon the wild sea banks, and waft her love
  To come again to Carthage.
JESSICA   In such a night
  Medea gathered the enchanted herbs
  That did renew old Aeson.
LORENZO   In such a night
  Did Jessica steal from the wealthy Jew,   15
  And with an unthrift love did run from Venice,
  As far as Belmont.
JESSICA   In such a night
  Did young Lorenzo swear he loved her well,
  Stealing her soul with many vows of faith,
  And ne'er a true one.
LORENZO   In such a night   20
  Did pretty Jessica (like a little shrew)
  Slander her love, and he forgave it her.
JESSICA   I would out-night you did nobody come:
  But hark, I hear the footing of a man.

        Enter STEPHANO (*a messenger*).

LORENZO   Who comes so fast in silence of the night?   25
STEPHANO   A friend!
LORENZO
  A friend! what friend? your name I pray you friend?
STEPHANO   Stephano is my name, and I bring word
  My mistress will before the break of day
  Be here at Belmont, – she doth stray about   30
  By holy crosses where she kneels and prays

For happy wedlock hours.

LORENZO   Who comes with her?

STEPHANO   None but a holy hermit and her maid:
I pray you is my master yet return'd?

LORENZO

35   He is not, nor we have not heard from him, –
But go we in (I pray thee Jessica),
And ceremoniously let us prepare
Some welcome for the mistress of the house.

Enter LAUNCELOT, *the clown.*

LAUNCELOT   Sola, sola! wo ha, ho! sola, sola!

40   LORENZO   Who calls?

LAUNCELOT   Sola! did you see Master Lorenzo?
Master Lorenzo, sola, sola!

LORENZO   Leave hollowing man, – here!

LAUNCELOT   Sola! where, where?

45   LORENZO   Here!

LAUNCELOT   Tell him there's a post come from my
master, with his horn full of good news, – my master
will be here ere morning.   *Exit.*

LORENZO

Sweet soul let's in, and there expect their coming.

50   And yet no matter: why should we go in?
My friend Stephano, signify (I pray you)
Within the house, your mistress is at hand,
And bring your music forth into the air.
                                      Exit Stephano.

How sweet the moonlight sleeps upon this bank!

55   Here will we sit, and let the sounds of music
Creep in our ears – soft stillness and the night
Become the touches of sweet harmony:
Sit Jessica, – look how the floor of heaven
Is thick inlaid with patens of bright gold,

60   There's not the smallest orb which thou behold'st
But in his motion like an angel sings,
Still quiring to the young-ey'd cherubins;
Such harmony is in immortal souls,
But whilst this muddy vesture of decay

65   Doth grossly close it in, we cannot hear it:

Enter musicians.

Come ho! and wake Diana with a hymn,
With sweetest touches pierce your mistress' ear,
And draw her home with music.   [*Music.*]

JESSICA   I am never merry when I hear sweet music.

70   LORENZO   The reason is your spirits are attentive:
For do but note a wild and wanton herd
Or race of youthful and unhandled colts
Fetching mad bounds, bellowing and neighing loud,
Which is the hot condition of their blood, –

75   If they but hear perchance a trumpet sound,
Or any air of music touch their ears,
You shall perceive them make a mutual stand,
Their savage eyes turn'd to a modest gaze,
By the sweet power of music: therefore the poet

Did feign that Orpheus drew trees, stones, and
floods,   80
Since naught so stockish, hard, and full of rage,
But music for the time doth change his nature, –
The man that hath no music in himself,
Nor is not moved with concord of sweet sounds,
Is fit for treasons, stratagems, and spoils,   85
The motions of his spirit are dull as night,
And his affections dark as Erebus:
Let no such man be trusted: – mark the music.

Enter PORTIA *and* NERISSA.

PORTIA   That light we see is burning in my hall:
How far that little candle throws his beams!   90
So shines a good deed in a naughty world.

NERISSA

When the moon shone we did not see the candle.

PORTIA   So doth the greater glory dim the less, –
A substitute shines brightly as a king
Until a king be by, and then his state   95
Empties itself, as doth an inland brook
Into the main of waters: – music – hark!

NERISSA   It is your music (madam) of the house.

PORTIA   Nothing is good (I see) without respect, –
Methinks it sounds much sweeter than by day.   100

NERISSA   Silence bestows that virtue on it madam.

PORTIA   The crow doth sing as sweetly as the lark
When neither is attended: and I think
The nightingale if she should sing by day
When every goose is cackling, would be thought   105
No better a musician than the wren!
How many things by season, season'd are
To their right praise, and true perfection!
Peace! – how the moon sleeps with Endymion,
And would not be awak'd!   [*Music ceases.*]

LORENZO   That is the voice,   110
Or I am much deceiv'd, of Portia.

PORTIA

He knows me as the blind man knows the cuckoo –
By the bad voice!

LORENZO   Dear lady welcome home!

PORTIA

We have bin praying for our husbands' welfare,
Which speed (we hope) the better for our words: 115
Are they return'd?

LORENZO   Madam, they are not yet:
But there is come a messenger before
To signify their coming.

PORTIA   Go in Nerissa.
Give order to my servants, that they take
No note at all of our being absent hence, –   120
Nor you Lorenzo, – Jessica nor you. [*A tucket sounds.*]

LORENZO

Your husband is at hand, I hear his trumpet, –
We are no tell-tales madam, fear you not.

PORTIA   This night methinks is but the daylight sick,

854

25   It looks a little paler, – 'tis a day,
     Such as the day is when the sun is hid.

          Enter BASSANIO, ANTONIO, GRATIANO
                and their followers.

BASSANIO   We should hold day with the Antipodes,
     If you would walk in absence of the sun.
PORTIA   Let me give light, but let me not be light,
30   For a light wife doth make a heavy husband,
     And never be Bassanio so for me, –
     But God sort all: you are welcome home my lord.
BASSANIO
     I thank you madam, – give welcome to my friend, –
     This is the man, this is Antonio,
35   To whom I am so infinitely bound.
PORTIA   You should in all sense be much bound to him,
     For (as I hear) he was much bound for you.
ANTONIO   No more than I am well acquitted of.
PORTIA   Sir, you are very welcome to our house:
40   It must appear in other ways than words,
     Therefore I scant this breathing courtesy.
GRATIANO [*to Nerissa*]
     By yonder moon I swear you do me wrong,
     In faith I gave it to the judge's clerk, –
     Would he were gelt that had it for my part,
45   Since you do take it (love) so much at heart.
PORTIA   A quarrel ho, already! what's the matter?
GRATIANO   About a hoop of gold, a paltry ring
     That she did give me, whose posy was
     For all the world like cutler's poetry
50   Upon a knife, 'Love me, and leave me not.'
NERISSA   What talk you of the posy or the value?
     You swore to me when I did give it you,
     That you would wear it till your hour of death,
     And that it should lie with you in your grave, –
55   Though not for me, yet for your vehement oaths,
     You should have been respective and have kept it.
     Gave it a judge's clerk! no – God's my judge –
     The clerk will ne'er wear hair on's face that had it.
GRATIANO   He will, and if he live to be a man.
60   NERISSA   Ay, if a woman live to be a man.
GRATIANO   Now (by this hand) I gave it to a youth,
     A kind of boy, a little scrubbed boy,
     No higher than thyself, the judge's clerk,
     A prating boy that begg'd it as a fee, –
65   I could not for my heart deny it him.
PORTIA
     You were to blame, – I must be plain with you, –
     To part so slightly with your wife's first gift,
     A thing stuck on with oaths upon your finger,
     And so riveted with faith unto your flesh.
70   I gave my love a ring, and made him swear
     Never to part with it, and here he stands:
     I dare be sworn for him he would not leave it,
     Nor pluck it from his finger, for the wealth
     That the world masters. Now in faith Gratiano
75   You give your wife too unkind a cause of grief,

     And 'twere to me I should be mad at it.
BASSANIO [*aside*]
     Why I were best to cut my left hand off,
     And swear I lost the ring defending it.
GRATIANO   My Lord Bassanio gave his ring away
     Unto the judge that begg'd it, and indeed   180
     Deserv'd it too: and then the boy (his clerk)
     That took some pains in writing, he begg'd mine,
     And neither man nor master would take aught
     But the two rings.
PORTIA   What ring gave you my lord?
     Not that (I hope) which you receiv'd of me.   185
BASSANIO   If I could add a lie unto a fault,
     I would deny it: but you see my finger
     Hath not the ring upon it, it is gone.
PORTIA   Even so void is your false heart of truth.
     By heaven I will ne'er come in your bed   190
     Until I see the ring!
NERISSA   Nor I in yours
     Till I again see mine!
BASSANIO   Sweet Portia,
     If you did know to whom I gave the ring,
     If you did know for whom I gave the ring,
     And would conceive for what I gave the ring,   195
     And how unwillingly I left the ring,
     When nought would be accepted but the ring,
     You would abate the strength of your displeasure.
PORTIA   If you had known the virtue of the ring,
     Or half her worthiness that gave the ring,   200
     Or your own honour to contain the ring,
     You would not then have parted with the ring:
     What man is there so much unreasonable
     (If you had pleas'd to have defended it
     With any terms of zeal): – wanted the modesty   205
     To urge the thing held as a ceremony?
     Nerissa teaches me what to believe, –
     I'll die for't, but some woman had the ring!
BASSANIO   No by my honour madam, by my soul
     No woman had it, but a civil doctor,   210
     Which did refuse three thousand ducats of me,
     And begg'd the ring, – the which I did deny him,
     And suffer'd him to go displeas'd away,
     Even he that had held up the very life
     Of my dear friend. What should I say sweet lady?   215
     I was enforc'd to send it after him,
     I was beset with shame and courtesy,
     My honour would not let ingratitude
     So much besmear it: pardon me good lady,
     For by these blessed candles of the night,   220
     Had you been there, I think you would have begg'd
     The ring of me to give the worthy doctor.
PORTIA
     Let not that doctor e'er come near my house –
     Since he hath got the jewel that I loved,
     And that which you did swear to keep for me,   225
     I will become as liberal as you,
     I'll not deny him any thing I have,

No, not my body, nor my husband's bed:
Know him I shall, I am well sure of it.
Lie not a night from home. Watch me like Argus, –
If you do not, if I be left alone,
Now by mine honour (which is yet mine own),
I'll have that doctor for my bedfellow.

NERISSA   And I his clerk: therefore be well advis'd
How you do leave me to mine own protection.

GRATIANO   Well do you so: let not me take him then,
For if I do, I'll mar the young clerk's pen.

ANTONIO   I am th'unhappy subject of these quarrels.

PORTIA
    Sir, grieve not you, – you are welcome notwithstanding.

BASSANIO   Portia, forgive me this enforced wrong,
And in the hearing of these many friends
I swear to thee, even by thine own fair eyes
Wherein I see myself –

PORTIA   Mark you but that!
In both my eyes he doubly sees himself:
In each eye one, – swear by your double self,
And there's an oath of credit.

BASSANIO   Nay, but hear me.
Pardon this fault, and by my soul I swear
I never more will break an oath with thee.

ANTONIO   I once did lend my body for his wealth,
Which but for him that had your husband's ring
Had quite miscarried. I dare be bound again,
My soul upon the forfeit, that your lord
Will never more break faith advisedly.

PORTIA   Then you shall be his surety: give him this,
And bid him keep it better than the other.

ANTONIO   Here Lord Bassanio, swear to keep this ring.

BASSANIO   By heaven it is the same I gave the doctor!

PORTIA   I had it of him: pardon me Bassanio,
For by this ring the doctor lay with me.

NERISSA   And pardon me my gentle Gratiano,
For that same scrubbed boy (the doctor's clerk)
In lieu of this, last night did lie with me.

GRATIANO   Why this is like the mending of highways
In summer where the ways are fair enough!
What, are we cuckolds ere we have deserv'd it?

PORTIA   Speak not so grossly, – you are all amaz'd;
Here is a letter, read it at your leisure, –
It comes from Padua from Bellario, –

There you shall find that Portia was the doctor,
Nerissa there her clerk. Lorenzo here
Shall witness I set forth as soon as you,
And even but now return'd: I have not yet
Enter'd my house. Antonio you are welcome,
And I have better news in store for you
Than you expect: unseal this letter soon,
There you shall find three of your argosies
Are richly come to harbour suddenly.
You shall not know by what strange accident
I chanced on this letter.

ANTONIO   I am dumb!

BASSANIO   Were you the doctor, and I knew you not?

GRATIANO
Were you the clerk that is to make me cuckold?

NERISSA   Ay, but the clerk that never means to do it,
Unless he live until he be a man.

BASSANIO   Sweet doctor, you shall be my bedfellow, –
When I am absent then lie with my wife.

ANTONIO   Sweet lady, you have given me life and living;
For here I read for certain that my ships
Are safely come to road.

PORTIA   How now Lorenzo?
My clerk hath some good comforts too for you.

NERISSA   Ay, and I'll give them him without a fee.
There do I give to you and Jessica
From the rich Jew, a special deed of gift
After his death, of all he dies possess'd of.

LORENZO   Fair ladies, you drop manna in the way
Of starved people.

PORTIA   It is almost morning,
And yet I am sure you are not satisfied
Of these events at full. Let us go in,
And charge us there upon inter'gatories,
And we will answer all things faithfully.

GRATIANO   Let it be so, – the first inter'gatory
That my Nerissa shall be sworn on, is,
Whether till the next night she had rather stay,
Or go to bed now (being two hours to day):
But were the day come, I should wish it dark
Till I were couching with the doctor's clerk.
Well, while I live, I'll fear no other thing
So sore, as keeping safe Nerissa's ring.   *Exeunt.*

The Merry Wives of Windsor

The Merry Wives of Windsor, despite the fact that it uses some characters from the *King Henry IV* plays which are set in the early fifteenth century, seems to come as close as Shakespeare ever gets to depicting his own contemporary society. The tavern scenes in the histories are moving in this direction, but in *Merry Wives* the political context has disappeared altogether and the result feels more like the 'city comedies' written by Shakespeare's contemporaries such as Jonson and Middleton than like his own usual style of romantic comedy with its more remote settings and upper-class characters. Shakespeare's only comedy set in England (if we exclude *Cymbeline* with its setting in Ancient Britain) is very much a bourgeois play, with 'Sir John' having to adapt to his provincial environment. The main theme is still courtship, and the plot has many precedents in folklore, but the tone is very different from Shakespeare's recent comedies, *Love's Labour's Lost*, *A Midsummer Night's Dream* and *The Merchant of Venice*, or the possibly contemporaneous *Much Ado About Nothing*. Although jokes about cuckolds are a standard element in many plays, it is unusual to find the jealous husband treated as the figure of fun he is here: in *Othello*, *The Winter's Tale* and *Cymbeline* Shakespeare treats him very differently. *Merry Wives* may date from 1597; if, however, as seems more probable, it was written in 1598–9, Shakespeare would have had a model in the comic Thorello in Ben Jonson's *Every Man in His Humour* (1598), a play he had acted in.

An early eighteenth-century story claims that Queen Elizabeth encouraged the composition of the play because she wanted to see 'Falstaff in love'; modern scholars still relate this story while questioning its veracity. Certainly *Merry Wives* seems to be an Elizabethan play, written after the *King Henry IV* plays (1596–8) and perhaps having a direct connection with the installation of George Carey, the Lord Chamberlain and patron of Shakespeare's company, as a Knight of the Garter in Windsor in 1597: the Garter ceremonies are referred to quite specifically in Mistress Quickly's speech at 5.5.56-77. If *Merry Wives* is to be related to the chronology of the histories, Falstaff's penury and the absence of Prince Hal might suggest the period of his disgrace between *King Henry IV, Part 2* and his death in *King Henry V*. Its tone is of course much lighter: despite Falstaff's attempts to win his way into the Wives' favours and their husbands' fortunes, we remain confident of the basic affability and good sense of most of the people of Windsor. Shakespeare does not seem to be aiming for strict consistency with the history plays: it is difficult, for example, to reconcile the Mistress Quickly here with the character in the *Henry IV* and *Henry V* plays.

The earliest published text of this play, the First Quarto of 1602 (Q1), is only about half the length of the version in the 1623 First Folio (F1) (where it is the third of the comedies), and has generally been dismissed as a 'bad' quarto, put together from memory by actors or reporters, and containing some echoes of *King Henry V*. The appearance of five further quartos during the seventeenth century (one based on Q1, the others on F1) attests to the popularity of the play. There are records of revivals in 1604, 1613, 1638, 1661 and 1667. *Merry Wives* continued to be popular in the eighteenth and nineteenth centuries, although it was often abridged in performance. It has been used as the basis for the libretti of at least nine operas including Giuseppe Verdi's *Falstaff* (1893) and Ralph Vaughan Williams's *Sir John in Love* (1929). Twentieth-century productions often revel in the particularity of the Windsor setting which allows them to celebrate a 'merry England' not otherwise notably associated with Shakespeare; the fact that the play was chosen for presentation at the Festival of Britain in 1951 testifies to this tendency.

The Arden edition is based on the 1623 First Folio.

Sir John FALSTAFF

FENTON — *a young gentleman*

SHALLOW — *a country Justice*

Abraham SLENDER — *Shallow's kinsman*

Frank FORD }
George PAGE } *citizens of Windsor*

WILLIAM Page — *a boy, son of Page and Mistress Page*

Sir Hugh EVANS — *a Welsh parson*

Doctor CAIUS — *a French physician*

HOST — *of the Garter Inn*

BARDOLPH }
PISTOL } *followers of Falstaff*
NYM }

ROBIN — *Falstaff's page*

Peter SIMPLE — *Slender's servant*

John RUGBY — *Caius' servant*

JOHN *and* ROBERT — *Ford's servants*

MISTRESS FORD (Alice)

MISTRESS PAGE (Margaret)

ANNE Page — *daughter of Page and Mistress Page*

Mistress QUICKLY — *Caius' servant*

Three or four Children *(dressed in the last act as fairies)*

1.1 *Enter* JUSTICE SHALLOW, SLENDER
and SIR HUGH EVANS.

SHALLOW   Sir Hugh, persuade me not: I will make a
Star Chamber matter of it. If he were twenty Sir John
Falstaffs, he shall not abuse Robert Shallow, Esquire.

SLENDER   In the county of Gloucester, Justice of Peace
and Coram.

SHALLOW   Ay, cousin Slender, and Custalorum.

SLENDER   Ay, and Ratolorum too; and a gentleman
born, Master Parson, who writes himself 'Armigero'
in any bill, warrant, quittance, or obligation –
'Armigero'.

SHALLOW   Ay, that I do, and have done any time these
three hundred years.

SLENDER   All his successors, gone before him, hath
done't, and all his ancestors, that come after him, may:
they may give the dozen white luces in their coat.

SHALLOW   It is an old coat.

EVANS   The dozen white louses do become an old coat
well; it agrees well, passant; it is a familiar beast to
man, and signifies love.

SHALLOW   The luce is the fresh fish; the salt fish is an
old coat.

SLENDER   I may quarter, coz.

SHALLOW   You may, by marrying.

EVANS   It is marring indeed, if he quarter it.

SHALLOW   Not a whit.

EVANS   Yes, per-lady: if he has a quarter of your coat,
there is but three skirts for yourself, in my simple
conjectures; but that is all one. If Sir John Falstaff
have committed disparagements unto you, I am of the
church and will be glad to do my benevolence, to make
atonements and compromises between you.

SHALLOW   The Council shall hear it; it is a riot.

EVANS   It is not meet the Council hear a riot: there is no
fear of Got in a riot. The Council, look you, shall
desire to hear the fear of Got, and not to hear a riot;
take your vizaments in that.

SHALLOW   Ha! O' my life, if I were young again, the
sword should end it.

EVANS   It is petter that friends is the sword, and end it;
and there is also another device in my prain, which
peradventure prings goot discretions with it. There is
Anne Page, which is daughter to Master Thomas
Page, which is pretty virginity.

SLENDER   Mistress Anne Page? She has brown hair, and
speaks small like a woman.

EVANS   It is that fery person for all the 'orld, as just as
you will desire; and seven hundred pounds of moneys,
and gold, and silver, is her grandsire upon his
death's-bed (Got deliver to a joyful resurrections!)
give, when she is able to overtake seventeen years
old. It were a goot motion if we leave our pribbles
and prabbles, and desire a marriage between Master
Abraham and Mistress Anne Page.

SLENDER   Did her grandsire leave her seven hundred
pound?

EVANS   Ay, and her father is make her a petter penny.

SHALLOW   I know the young gentlewoman; she has good
gifts.

EVANS   Seven hundred pounds, and possibilities, is goot
gifts.

SHALLOW   Well, let us see honest Master Page. Is
Falstaff there?

EVANS   Shall I tell you a lie? I do despise a liar as I do
despise one that is false, or as I despise one that is not
true. The knight Sir John is there; and I beseech you
be ruled by your well-willers. I will peat the door for
Master Page. [*knocks*] What hoa? Got pless your house
here!

PAGE [*within*]   Who's there?

Enter PAGE.

EVANS   Here is Got's plessing and your friend, and
Justice Shallow, and here young Master Slender,
that peradventures shall tell you another tale, if
matters grow to your likings.

PAGE   I am glad to see your worships well. I thank you
for my venison, Master Shallow.

SHALLOW   Master Page, I am glad to see you: much
good do it your good heart! I wished your venison
better; it was ill killed. How doth good Mistress Page?
And I thank you always with my heart, la, with my
heart.

PAGE   Sir, I thank you.

SHALLOW   Sir, I thank you; by yea and no I do.

PAGE   I am glad to see you, good Master Slender.

SLENDER   How does your fallow greyhound, sir? I heard
say he was outrun on Cotsall.

PAGE   It could not be judged, sir.

SLENDER   You'll not confess, you'll not confess.

SHALLOW   That he will not. 'Tis your fault, 'tis your
fault; 'tis a good dog.

PAGE   A cur, sir.

SHALLOW   Sir, he's a good dog, and a fair dog: can there
be more said? He is good and fair. Is Sir John Falstaff
here?

PAGE   Sir, he is within; and I would I could do a good
office between you.

EVANS   It is spoke as a Christians ought to speak.

SHALLOW   He hath wronged me, Master Page.

PAGE   Sir, he doth in some sort confess it.

SHALLOW   If it be confessed, it is not redressed: is not
that so, Master Page? He hath wronged me, indeed he
hath; at a word, he hath, believe me. Robert Shallow,
Esquire, saith he is wronged.

PAGE   Here comes Sir John.

Enter SIR JOHN FALSTAFF, BARDOLPH, NYM *and* PISTOL.

FALSTAFF   Now, Master Shallow, you'll complain of me
to the King?

SHALLOW   Knight, you have beaten my men, killed my
deer, and broke open my lodge.

FALSTAFF But not kissed your keeper's daughter?

SHALLOW Tut, a pin; this shall be answered.

FALSTAFF I will answer it straight: I have done all this.
110   That is now answered.

SHALLOW The Council shall know this.

FALSTAFF 'Twere better for you if it were known in
counsel: you'll be laughed at.

EVANS *Pauca verba*; Sir John, good worts.

115 FALSTAFF Good worts? Good cabbage! Slender, I broke
your head: what matter have you against me?

SLENDER Marry, sir, I have matter in my head against
you, and against your cony-catching rascals,
Bardolph, Nym, and Pistol.

120 BARDOLPH You Banbury cheese!

SLENDER Ay, it is no matter.

PISTOL How now, Mephostophilus?

SLENDER Ay, it is no matter.

NYM Slice, I say; *pauca, pauca*; slice, that's my humour!

125 SLENDER Where's Simple, my man? Can you tell,
cousin?

EVANS Peace, I pray you. Now let us understand: there
is three umpires in this matter, as I understand; that is,
Master Page (fidelicet Master Page); and there is
130 myself (fidelicet myself); and the three party is (lastly
and finally) mine host of the Garter.

PAGE We three to hear it and end it between them.

EVANS Fery goot; I will make a prief of it in my
notebook, and we will afterwards 'ork upon the cause
135 with as great discreetly as we can.

FALSTAFF Pistol!

PISTOL He hears with ears.

EVANS The tevil and his tam! What phrase is this, 'He
hears with ear'? Why, it is affectations.

140 FALSTAFF Pistol, did you pick Master Slender's purse?

SLENDER Ay, by these gloves, did he, or I would I might
never come in mine own great chamber again else, of
seven groats in mill-sixpences, and two Edward
shovel-boards that cost me two shilling and twopence
145 apiece of Yead Miller, by these gloves.

FALSTAFF Is this true, Pistol?

EVANS No, it is false, if it is a pick-purse.

PISTOL
Ha, thou mountain foreigner! Sir John and master
mine,
I combat challenge of this latten bilbo.
150 Word of denial in thy labras here!
Word of denial: froth and scum, thou liest!

SLENDER [*pointing at Nym*] By these gloves, then, 'twas
he.

NYM Be avised, sir, and pass good humours: I will say
155 'marry trap with you', if you run the nuthook's
humour on me; that is the very note of it.

SLENDER By this hat, then he in the red face had it; for
though I cannot remember what I did when you
made me drunk, yet I am not altogether an ass.

160 FALSTAFF What say you, Scarlet and John?

BARDOLPH Why, sir, for my part, I say the gentleman

had drunk himself out of his five sentences.

EVANS It is his 'five senses'. Fie, what the ignorance is!

BARDOLPH And being fap, sir, was, as they say,
cashiered; and so conclusions passed the careers.   165

SLENDER Ay, you spake in Latin then too; but 'tis no
matter. I'll ne'er be drunk whilst I live again, but in
honest, civil, godly company, for this trick: if I be
drunk, I'll be drunk with those that have the fear of
God, and not with drunken knaves.   170

EVANS So Got 'udge me, that is a virtuous mind.

FALSTAFF You hear all these matters denied, gentlemen; you hear it.

Enter ANNE PAGE, *with wine;*
then MISTRESS FORD *and* MISTRESS PAGE.

PAGE Nay, daughter, carry the wine in; we'll drink
within.   *Exit Anne Page.*   175

SLENDER O heaven, this is Mistress Anne Page.

PAGE How now, Mistress Ford?

FALSTAFF Mistress Ford, by my troth, you are very well
met: by your leave, good mistress. [*Kisses her.*]

PAGE Wife, bid these gentlemen welcome. Come, we   180
have a hot venison pasty to dinner; come, gentlemen,
I hope we shall drink down all unkindness.

Exeunt all except Slender.

SLENDER I had rather than forty shillings I had my book
of Songs and Sonnets here.

Enter SIMPLE.

How now, Simple, where have you been? I must wait   185
on myself, must I? You have not the book of Riddles
about you, have you?

SIMPLE Book of Riddles? Why, did you not lend it to
Alice Shortcake upon All-hallowmas last, a fortnight
afore Michaelmas?   190

Enter SHALLOW *and* EVANS.

SHALLOW Come, coz; come, coz; we stay for you. A
word with you, coz. Marry, this, coz: there is, as
'twere, a tender, a kind of tender, made afar off by Sir
Hugh here. Do you understand me?

SLENDER Ay, sir, you shall find me reasonable; if it be   195
so, I shall do that that is reason.

SHALLOW Nay, but understand me.

SLENDER So I do, sir.

EVANS Give ear to his motions. Master Slender, I will
description the matter to you, if you be capacity of it.   200

SLENDER Nay, I will do as my cousin Shallow says. I
pray you pardon me; he's a Justice of Peace in his
country, simple though I stand here.

EVANS But that is not the question: the question is
concerning your marriage.   205

SHALLOW Ay, there's the point, sir.

EVANS Marry, is it; the very point of it – to Mistress
Anne Page.

SLENDER Why, if it be so, I will marry her upon any
reasonable demands.   210

EVANS   But can you affection the 'oman? Let us command to know that of your mouth or of your lips; for divers philosophers hold that the lips is parcel of the mouth. Therefore, precisely, can you carry your good will to the maid?

15

SHALLOW   Cousin Abraham Slender, can you love her?

SLENDER   I hope, sir, I will do as it shall become one that would do reason.

EVANS   Nay, Got's lords, and His ladies! You must speak possable, if you can carry her your desires towards her.

20

SHALLOW   That you must. Will you, upon good dowry, marry her?

SLENDER   I will do a greater thing than that, upon your request, cousin, in any reason.

25

SHALLOW   Nay, conceive me, conceive me, sweet coz: what I do is to pleasure you, coz. Can you love the maid?

SLENDER   I will marry her, sir, at your request; but if there be no great love in the beginning, yet heaven may decrease it upon better acquaintance, when we are married and have more occasion to know one another. I hope upon familiarity will grow more content: but if you say 'Marry her', I will marry her; that I am freely dissolved, and dissolutely.

30

35

EVANS   It is a fery discretion answer; save the fall is in the 'ord 'dissolutely': the 'ort is, according to our meaning, 'resolutely'. His meaning is good.

SHALLOW   Ay, I think my cousin meant well.

40

SLENDER   Ay, or else I would I might be hanged, la!

SHALLOW   Here comes fair Mistress Anne.

Enter ANNE PAGE.

Would I were young for your sake, Mistress Anne!

ANNE   The dinner is on the table; my father desires your worships' company.

45

SHALLOW   I will wait on him, fair Mistress Anne.

EVANS   Od's plessed will, I will not be absence at the grace.   *Exeunt Shallow and Evans.*

ANNE   Will't please your worship to come in, sir?

SLENDER   No, I thank you, forsooth, heartily; I am very well.

50

ANNE   The dinner attends you, sir.

SLENDER   I am not a-hungry, I thank you, forsooth. [*to Simple*] Go, sirrah, for all you are my man, go wait upon my cousin Shallow.   *Exit Simple.*

A Justice of Peace sometime may be beholding to his friend for a man. I keep but three men and a boy yet, till my mother be dead: but what though, yet I live like a poor gentleman born.

55

ANNE   I may not go in without your worship: they will not sit till you come.

60

SLENDER   I'faith, I'll eat nothing; I thank you as much as though I did.

ANNE   I pray you, sir, walk in.

SLENDER   I had rather walk here, I thank you. I bruised my shin th'other day with playing at sword and dagger with a master of fence – three veneys for a dish of stewed prunes – and, by my troth, I cannot abide the smell of hot meat since. Why do your dogs bark so? Be there bears i'th' town?

265

ANNE   I think there are, sir; I heard them talked of.

270

SLENDER   I love the sport well, but I shall as soon quarrel at it as any man in England. You are afraid if you see the bear loose, are you not?

ANNE   Ay, indeed, sir.

SLENDER   That's meat and drink to me, now. I have seen Sackerson loose twenty times, and have taken him by the chain; but, I warrant you, the women have so cried and shrieked at it that it passed: but women, indeed, cannot abide 'em; they are very ill-favoured rough things.

275

280

Enter PAGE.

PAGE   Come, gentle Master Slender, come: we stay for you.

SLENDER   I'll eat nothing, I thank you, sir.

PAGE   By cock and pie, you shall not choose, sir: come, come.

285

SLENDER   Nay, pray you lead the way.

PAGE   Come on, sir.

SLENDER   Mistress Anne, yourself shall go first.

ANNE   Not I, sir; pray you keep on.

SLENDER   Truly, I will not go first; truly, la, I will not do you that wrong.

290

ANNE   I pray you, sir.

SLENDER   I'll rather be unmannerly than troublesome. You do yourself wrong, indeed, la!   *Exeunt.*

1.2   *Enter* EVANS *and* SIMPLE.

EVANS   Go your ways, and ask of Doctor Caius' house which is the way; and there dwells one Mistress Quickly, which is in the manner of his nurse; or his dry nurse; or his cook; or his laundry; his washer, and his wringer.

5

SIMPLE   Well, sir.

EVANS   Nay, it is petter yet. Give her this letter; for it is a 'oman that altogether's acquaintance with Mistress Anne Page; and the letter is to desire and require her to solicit your master's desires, to Mistress Anne Page. I pray you be gone. I will make an end of my dinner; there's pippins and cheese to come.   *Exeunt.*

10

1.3   *Enter* FALSTAFF, Host, BARDOLPH,
                   NYM, PISTOL *and* ROBIN.

FALSTAFF   Mine host of the Garter!

HOST   What says my bully rook? Speak scholarly and wisely.

FALSTAFF   Truly, mine host, I must turn away some of my followers.

5

HOST   Discard, bully Hercules, cashier: let them wag; trot, trot.

FALSTAFF   I sit at ten pounds a week.

HOST   Thou'rt an emperor, Caesar, Keiser, and Pheazar.
10 I will entertain Bardolph; he shall draw, he shall tap. Said I well, bully Hector?

FALSTAFF   Do so, good mine host.

HOST   I have spoke; let him follow. [*to Bardolph*] Let me see thee froth and lime. I am at a word; follow.   *Exit.*

FALSTAFF   Bardolph, follow him. A tapster is a good
15 trade; an old cloak makes a new jerkin; a withered servingman a fresh tapster. Go; adieu.

BARDOLPH   It is a life that I have desired: I will thrive.

PISTOL   O base Hungarian wight, wilt thou the spigot
20 wield?   *Exit Bardolph.*

NYM   He was gotten in drink: is not the humour conceited?

FALSTAFF   I am glad I am so acquit of this tinder-box: his thefts were too open; his filching was like an
25 unskilful singer, he kept not time.

NYM   The good humour is to steal at a minute's rest.

PISTOL   'Convey', the wise it call. 'Steal'! Foh, a fico for the phrase!

FALSTAFF   Well, sirs, I am almost out at heels.

30 PISTOL   Why, then, let kibes ensue.

FALSTAFF   There is no remedy: I must cony-catch; I must shift.

PISTOL   Young ravens must have food.

FALSTAFF   Which of you know Ford of this town?

35 PISTOL   I ken the wight: he is of substance good.

FALSTAFF   My honest lads, I will tell you what I am about.

PISTOL   Two yards, and more.

FALSTAFF   No quips now, Pistol. Indeed, I am in the
40 waist two yards about, but I am now about no waste: I am about thrift. Briefly, I do mean to make love to Ford's wife. I spy entertainment in her: she discourses, she carves, she gives the leer of invitation; I can construe the action of her familiar style, and the
45 hardest voice of her behaviour, to be Englished rightly, is, 'I am Sir John Falstaff's'.

PISTOL   He hath studied her will, and translated her will – out of honesty into English.

NYM   The anchor is deep: will that humour pass?

50 FALSTAFF   Now, the report goes she has all the rule of her husband's purse; he hath a legion of angels.

PISTOL   As many devils entertain; and to her, boy, say I.

NYM   The humour rises; it is good. Humour me the angels.

55 FALSTAFF   I have writ me here a letter to her; and here another to Page's wife, who even now gave me good eyes too, examined my parts with most judicious oeillades: sometimes the beam of her view gilded my foot, sometimes my portly belly.

60 PISTOL   Then did the sun on dunghill shine.

NYM   I thank thee for that humour.

FALSTAFF   O, she did so course o'er my exteriors with such a greedy intention that the appetite of her eye did seem to scorch me up like a burning-glass! Here's another letter to her; she bears the purse too: she is a 65 region in Guiana, all gold and bounty. I will be cheaters to them both, and they shall be exchequers to me: they shall be my East and West Indies, and I will trade to them both. Go bear thou this letter to Mistress Page; and thou this to Mistress Ford: we 70 will thrive, lads, we will thrive.

PISTOL   Shall I Sir Pandarus of Troy become,
And by my side wear steel? Then Lucifer take all!

NYM   I will run no base humour. Here, take the humour-letter; I will keep the haviour of reputation. 75

FALSTAFF   [*to Robin*]
Hold, sirrah, bear you these letters tightly;
Sail like my pinnace to these golden shores.
Rogues, hence, avaunt, vanish like hailstones; go;
Trudge; plod away i'th' hoof; seek shelter, pack!
Falstaff will learn the honour of the age; 80
French thrift, you rogues – myself and skirted page.
                              Exeunt Falstaff and Robin.

PISTOL
Let vultures gripe thy guts, for gourd and fullam holds,
And high and low beguiles the rich and poor;
Tester I'll have in pouch when thou shalt lack,
Base Phrygian Turk! 85

NYM   I have operations which be humours of revenge.

PISTOL   Wilt thou revenge?

NYM   By welkin and her star!

PISTOL   With wit or steel?

NYM   With both the humours, I: I will discuss the 90 humour of this love to Ford.

PISTOL   And I to Page shall eke unfold
              How Falstaff, varlet vile,
           His dove will prove, his gold will hold,
              And his soft couch defile. 95

NYM   My humour shall not cool: I will incense Ford to deal with poison; I will possess him with yellowness, for the revolt of mine is dangerous. That is my true humour.

PISTOL   Thou art the Mars of Malcontents. I second 100 thee; troop on.   *Exeunt.*

1.4   *Enter* MISTRESS QUICKLY *and* SIMPLE.

QUICKLY   What, John Rugby!

Enter RUGBY.

I pray thee go to the casement and see if you can see my master, Master Doctor Caius, coming. If he do, i'faith, and find anybody in the house, here will be an old abusing of God's patience and the King's English. 5

RUGBY   I'll go watch.

QUICKLY   Go; and we'll have a posset for 't soon at night, in faith, at the latter end of a sea-coal fire.
                                            Exit Rugby.

An honest, willing, kind fellow, as ever servant shall

come in house withal; and, I warrant you, no tell-tale nor no breed-bate. His worst fault is that he is given to prayer; he is something peevish that way; but nobody but has his fault; but let that pass. Peter Simple, you say your name is?

SIMPLE Ay, for fault of a better.

QUICKLY And Master Slender's your master?

SIMPLE Ay, forsooth.

QUICKLY Does he not wear a great round beard, like a glover's paring-knife?

SIMPLE No, forsooth: he hath but a little wee face, with a little yellow beard – a Cain-coloured beard.

QUICKLY A softly-sprighted man, is he not?

SIMPLE Ay, forsooth, but he is as tall a man of his hands as any is between this and his head: he hath fought with a warrener.

QUICKLY How say you? – O, I should remember him: does he not hold up his head, as it were, and strut in his gait?

SIMPLE Yes, indeed, does he.

QUICKLY Well, heaven send Anne Page no worse fortune! Tell Master Parson Evans I will do what I can for your master: Anne is a good girl, and I wish –

Enter RUGBY.

RUGBY Out, alas, here comes my master.

QUICKLY We shall all be shent. Run in here, good young man; go into this closet; he will not stay long. [*Simple steps into the closet.*] What, John Rugby! John! What, John, I say! Go, John, go enquire for my master: I doubt he be not well, that he comes not home. [*singing*] And down, down, adown-a, etc.

Enter DOCTOR CAIUS.

CAIUS Vat is you sing? I do not like des toys. Pray you go and vetch me in my closet *une boitine verde* – a box, a green-a box. Do intend vat I speak? A green-a box.

QUICKLY Ay, forsooth; I'll fetch it you. [*aside*] I am glad he went not in himself: if he had found the young man, he would have been horn-mad.

CAIUS *Fe, fe, fe, fe, ma foi, il fait fort chaud. Je m'en vais voir à la court la grande affaire.*

QUICKLY Is it this, sir?

CAIUS *Oui, mette le au mon pocket: dépêche*, quickly. Vere is dat knave Rugby?

QUICKLY What, John Rugby! John!

RUGBY Here, sir!

CAIUS You are John Rugby, and you are Jack Rugby. Come, take-a your rapier, and come after my heel to the court.

RUGBY 'Tis ready, sir, here in the porch.

CAIUS By my trot, I tarry too long. Od's me, *que ai je oublié?* Dere is some simples in my closet dat I vill not for the varld I shall leave behind.

QUICKLY Ay me, he'll find the young man there, and be mad!

CAIUS *O diable, diable!* Vat is in my closet? Villainy, *larron!* [*pulling Simple out*] Rugby, my rapier!

QUICKLY Good master, be content.

CAIUS Wherefore shall I be content-a?

QUICKLY The young man is an honest man.

CAIUS What shall de honest man do in my closet? Dere is no honest man dat shall come in my closet.

QUICKLY I beseech you, be not so phlegmatic. Hear the truth of it: he came of an errand to me from Parson Hugh.

CAIUS Vell?

SIMPLE Ay, forsooth; to desire her to –

QUICKLY Peace, I pray you.

CAIUS Peace-a your tongue. [*to Simple*] Speak-a your tale.

SIMPLE To desire this honest gentlewoman, your maid, to speak a good word to Mistress Anne Page for my master in the way of marriage.

QUICKLY This is all, indeed, la, but I'll ne'er put my finger in the fire, and need not.

CAIUS Sir Hugh send-a you? Rugby, ballow me some paper. Tarry you a little-a while. [*Writes.*]

QUICKLY [*aside to Simple*] I am glad he is so quiet: if he had been throughly moved, you should have heard him so loud and so melancholy. But notwithstanding, man, I'll do you your master what good I can; and the very yea and the no is, the French doctor, my master – I may call him my master, look you, for I keep his house; and I wash, wring, brew, bake, scour, dress meat and drink, make the beds, and do all myself –

SIMPLE [*aside to Quickly*] 'Tis a great charge to come under one body's hand.

QUICKLY [*aside to Simple*] Are you avised o' that? You shall find it a great charge; and to be up early and down late; but notwithstanding – to tell you in your ear; I would have no words of it – my master himself is in love with Mistress Anne Page; but notwithstanding that, I know Anne's mind – that's neither here nor there.

CAIUS You jack'nape, give-a this letter to Sir Hugh; by gar, it is a shallenge. I will cut his troat in de Park, and I will teach a scurvy jack-a-nape priest to meddle or make. You may be gone; it is not good you tarry here. By gar, I will cut all his two stones; by gar, he shall not have a stone to throw at his dog. *Exit Simple.*

QUICKLY Alas, he speaks but for his friend.

CAIUS It is no matter-a ver dat: do not you tell-a me dat I shall have Anne Page for myself? By gar, I vill kill de Jack-priest; and I have appointed mine host of de Jarteer to measure our weapon. By gar, I will myself have Anne Page.

QUICKLY Sir, the maid loves you, and all shall be well. We must give folks leave to prate: what the good year!

CAIUS Rugby, come to the court with me. – [*to Quickly*] By gar, if I have not Anne Page, I shall turn your head out of my door. – Follow my heels, Rugby.

QUICKLY   You shall have An –

Exeunt Caius and Rugby.

– fool's head of your own. No, I know Anne's mind for
120   that; never a woman in Windsor knows more of Anne's
mind than I do, nor can do more than I do with her, I
thank heaven.

FENTON [*within*]   Who's within there, hoa?

QUICKLY   Who's there, I trow? Come near the house, I
125   pray you.

Enter FENTON.

FENTON   How now, good woman, how dost thou?

QUICKLY   The better that it pleases your good worship
to ask.

FENTON   What news? How does pretty Mistress Anne?

130   QUICKLY   In truth, sir, and she is pretty, and honest, and
gentle, and one that is your friend – I can tell you that
by the way, I praise heaven for it.

FENTON   Shall I do any good, think'st thou? Shall I not
lose my suit?

135   QUICKLY   Troth, sir, all is in His hands above; but
notwithstanding, Master Fenton, I'll be sworn on a
book she loves you. Have not your worship a wart
above your eye?

FENTON   Yes, marry, have I; what of that?

140   QUICKLY   Well, thereby hangs a tale. Good faith, it is
such another Nan; but, I detest, an honest maid as
ever broke bread; we had an hour's talk of that wart –
I shall never laugh but in that maid's company! – but,
indeed, she is given too much to allicholy and musing;
145   but for you – well – go to.

FENTON   Well, I shall see her to-day. Hold, there's
money for thee: let me have thy voice in my behalf; if
thou seest her before me, commend me.

QUICKLY   Will I? I'faith, that we will; and I will tell your
150   worship more of the wart the next time we have
confidence; and of other wooers.

FENTON   Well, farewell; I am in great haste now.

QUICKLY   Farewell to your worship.   *Exit Fenton.*
Truly, an honest gentleman – but Anne loves him not;
155   for I know Anne's mind as well as another does. – Out
upon't, what have I forgot?   *Exit.*

2.1   *Enter* MISTRESS PAGE, *with a letter.*

MISTRESS PAGE   What, have I scaped love-letters in the
holiday-time of my beauty, and am I now a subject for
them? Let me see. [*Reads.*] *Ask me no reason why I love*
you, for though Love use Reason for his precisian, he
5   *admits him not for his counsellor. You are not young, no*
more am I; go to, then, there's sympathy. You are merry,
so am I; ha, ha, then, there's more sympathy. You love
sack, and so do I; would you desire better sympathy? Let
it suffice thee, Mistress Page – at the least, if the love of
soldier can suffice – that I love thee. I will not say pity me
10   *– 'tis not a soldier-like phrase – but I say, love me. By me,*
Thine own true knight,

By day or night,
Or any kind of light,
With all his might   15
For thee to fight,

John Falstaff.

What a Herod of Jewry is this? O wicked, wicked
world: one that is well-nigh worn to pieces with age
to show himself a young gallant! What an unweighed   20
behaviour hath this Flemish drunkard picked –
with the devil's name – out of my conversation, that
he dares in this manner assay me? Why, he hath not
been thrice in my company! What should I say to
him? I was then frugal of my mirth. Heaven forgive   25
me! Why, I'll exhibit a bill in the parliament for the
putting down of men. How shall I be revenged on
him? For revenged I will be, as sure as his guts are
made of puddings.

Enter MISTRESS FORD.

MISTRESS FORD   Mistress Page! Trust me, I was going to   30
your house.

MISTRESS PAGE   And, trust me, I was coming to you.
You look very ill.

MISTRESS FORD   Nay, I'll ne'er believe that; I have to
show to the contrary.   35

MISTRESS PAGE   Faith, but you do, in my mind.

MISTRESS FORD   Well, I do, then; yet, I say, I could show
you to the contrary. O Mistress Page, give me some
counsel!

MISTRESS PAGE   What's the matter, woman?   40

MISTRESS FORD   O woman, if it were not for one trifling
respect, I could come to such honour!

MISTRESS PAGE   Hang the trifle, woman, take the
honour. What is it? Dispense with trifles – what is it?

MISTRESS FORD   If I would but go to hell for an eternal   45
moment or so, I could be knighted.

MISTRESS PAGE   What? Thou liest! Sir Alice Ford?
These knights will hack; and so thou shouldst not alter
the article of thy gentry.

MISTRESS FORD   We burn daylight. Here, read, read;   50
perceive how I might be knighted. I shall think the
worse of fat men as long as I have an eye to make
difference of men's liking; and yet he would not swear,
praised women's modesty, and gave such orderly and
well-behaved reproof to all uncomeliness that I would   55
have sworn his disposition would have gone to the
truth of his words; but they do no more adhere and
keep place together than the hundred Psalms to the
tune of 'Greensleeves'. What tempest, I trow, threw
this whale, with so many tuns of oil in his belly,   60
ashore at Windsor? How shall I be revenged on him? I
think the best way were to entertain him with hope till
the wicked fire of lust have melted him in his own
grease. Did you ever hear the like?

MISTRESS PAGE   Letter for letter, but that the name of   65
Page and Ford differs! To thy great comfort in this
mystery of ill opinions, here's the twin-brother of

thy letter; but let thine inherit first, for I protest mine never shall. I warrant he hath a thousand of these letters, writ with blank space for different names – sure, more – and these are of the second edition. He will print them, out of doubt; for he cares not what he puts into the press, when he would put us two: I had rather be a giantess, and lie under Mount Pelion. Well, I will find you twenty lascivious turtles ere one chaste man.

MISTRESS FORD   Why, this is the very same: the very hand, the very words. What doth he think of us?

MISTRESS PAGE   Nay, I know not: it makes me almost ready to wrangle with mine own honesty. I'll entertain myself like one that I am not acquainted withal; for, sure, unless he know some strain in me that I know not myself, he would never have boarded me in this fury.

MISTRESS FORD   'Boarding' call you it? I'll be sure to keep him above deck.

MISTRESS PAGE   So will I: if he come under my hatches, I'll never to sea again. Let's be revenged on him: let's appoint him a meeting, give him a show of comfort in his suit, and lead him on with a fine-baited delay till he hath pawned his horses to mine host of the Garter.

MISTRESS FORD   Nay, I will consent to act any villainy against him that may not sully the chariness of our honesty. O that my husband saw this letter; it would give eternal food to his jealousy.

MISTRESS PAGE   Why, look where he comes; and my good man too. He's as far from jealousy as I am from giving him cause; and that, I hope, is an unmeasurable distance.

MISTRESS FORD   You are the happier woman.

MISTRESS PAGE   Let's consult together against this greasy knight. Come hither. [*They stand back.*]

Enter FORD, *with* PISTOL, *and* PAGE, *with* NYM.

FORD   Well, I hope it be not so.

PISTOL   Hope is a curtal dog in some affairs:
Sir John affects thy wife.

FORD   Why, sir, my wife is not young.

PISTOL
He woos both high and low, both rich and poor,
Both young and old, one with another, Ford;
He loves the gallimaufry: Ford, perpend.

FORD   Love my wife?

PISTOL   With liver burning hot. Prevent,
Or go thou, like Sir Actaeon he,
With Ringwood at thy heels.
O, odious is the name!

FORD   What name, sir?

PISTOL   The horn, I say. Farewell.
Take heed; have open eye; for thieves do foot by night:
Take heed, ere summer comes, or cuckoo-birds do sing.
– Away, Sir Corporal Nym! – Believe it, Page, he

speaks sense.   *Exit.*   120

FORD [*aside*]   I will be patient; I will find out this.

NYM [*to Page*]   And this is true; I like not the humour of lying. He hath wronged me in some humours. I should have borne the humoured letter to her; but I have a sword, and it shall bite upon my necessity. He loves your wife; there's the short and the long. My name is Corporal Nym; I speak, and I avouch; 'tis true: my name is Nym, and Falstaff loves your wife. Adieu. I love not the humour of bread and cheese. Adieu.   *Exit.*   130

PAGE   The 'humour' of it, quoth 'a! Here's a fellow frights English out of his wits.

FORD   I will seek out Falstaff.

PAGE   I never heard such a drawling, affecting rogue.

FORD   If I do find it – well.   135

PAGE   I will not believe such a Cataian, though the priest o'th' town commended him for a true man.

FORD   'Twas a good sensible fellow – well.

PAGE   How now, Meg?

MISTRESS PAGE *and* MISTRESS FORD *come forward.*

MISTRESS PAGE   Whither go you, George? Hark you.   140

MISTRESS FORD   How now, sweet Frank, why art thou melancholy?

FORD   I melancholy? I am not melancholy. Get you home, go.

MISTRESS FORD   Faith, thou hast some crotchets in thy head now. Will you go, Mistress Page?   145

MISTRESS PAGE   Have with you. You'll come to dinner, George? [*aside to Mistress Ford*] Look who comes yonder: she shall be our messenger to this paltry knight.   150

MISTRESS FORD [*aside to Mistress Page*]   Trust me, I thought on her: she'll fit it.

Enter MISTRESS QUICKLY.

MISTRESS PAGE   You are come to see my daughter Anne?

QUICKLY   Ay, forsooth; and, I pray, how does good Mistress Anne?   155

MISTRESS PAGE   Go in with us and see; we have an hour's talk with you.

Exeunt Mistress Page, Mistress Ford and Mistress Quickly.

PAGE   How now, Master Ford?

FORD   You heard what this knave told me, did you not?

PAGE   Yes; and you heard what the other told me?   160

FORD   Do you think there is truth in them?

PAGE   Hang 'em, slaves: I do not think the knight would offer it. But these that accuse him in his intent towards our wives are a yoke of his discarded men: very rogues, now they be out of service.   165

FORD   Were they his men?

PAGE   Marry, were they.

FORD   I like it never the better for that. Does he lie at the Garter?

PAGE   Ay, marry, does he. If he should intend this voyage toward my wife, I would turn her loose to   170 him, and what he gets more of her than sharp words, let it lie on my head.

FORD   I do not misdoubt my wife; but I would be loath to turn them together; a man may be too confident; I would have nothing lie on my head; I cannot be thus satisfied.

175

PAGE   Look where my ranting host of the Garter comes; there is either liquor in his pate or money in his purse when he looks so merrily.

180

Enter Host.

How now, mine host?

HOST   How now, bully rook? Thou'rt a gentleman. – Cavaliero Justice, I say!

Enter SHALLOW.

SHALLOW   I follow, mine host, I follow. Good even and twenty, good Master Page! Master Page, will you go with us? We have sport in hand.

185

HOST   Tell him, Cavaliero Justice; tell him, bully rook.

SHALLOW   Sir, there is a fray to be fought between Sir Hugh the Welsh priest and Caius the French doctor.

FORD   Good mine host o'th' Garter, a word with you.
       [drawing him aside]

190

HOST   What say'st thou, my bully rook?

SHALLOW *[to Page]*   Will you go with us to behold it? My merry host hath had the measuring of their weapons, and, I think, hath appointed them contrary places; for, believe me, I hear the parson is no jester. Hark, I will tell you what our sport shall be. *[They converse apart.]*

195

HOST   Hast thou no suit against my knight, my guest cavalier?

FORD   None, I protest; but I'll give you a pottle of burnt sack to give me recourse to him, and tell him my name is Brook – only for a jest.

200

HOST   My hand, bully; thou shalt have egress and regress – said I well? – and thy name shall be   Brook. It is a merry knight. – Will you go, Anheers?

SHALLOW   Have with you, mine host.

205

PAGE   I have heard the Frenchman hath good skill in his rapier.

SHALLOW   Tut, sir, I could have told you more. In these times you stand on distance, your passes, stoccadoes, and I know not what. 'Tis the heart, Master Page, 'tis here, 'tis here. I have seen the time, with my long sword I would have made you four tall fellows skip like rats.

210

HOST   Here, boys, here, here; shall we wag?

PAGE   Have with you. I had rather hear them scold than fight.   *Exeunt Host, Shallow and Page.*

215

FORD   Though Page be a secure fool, and stands so firmly on his wife's frailty, yet I cannot put off my opinion so easily: she was in his company at Page's house; and what they made there, I know not. Well, I will look further into't, and I have a disguise to sound Falstaff. If I find her honest, I lose not my labour; if she be otherwise, 'tis labour well bestowed.

220

                                                          Exit.

2.2   *Enter* FALSTAFF *and* PISTOL.

FALSTAFF   I will not lend thee a penny.

PISTOL   Why, then the world's mine oyster, which I with sword will open.

FALSTAFF   Not a penny. I have been content, sir, you should lay my countenance to pawn; I have grated upon my good friends for three reprieves for you and your coach-fellow Nym – or else you had looked through the grate, like a geminy of baboons; I am damned in hell for swearing to gentlemen my friends you were good soldiers and tall fellows; and when Mistress Bridget lost the handle of her fan, I took't upon mine honour thou hadst it not.

5

10

PISTOL   Didst not thou share? Hadst thou not fifteen pence?

FALSTAFF   Reason, you rogue, reason: think'st thou I'll endanger my soul gratis? At a word, hang no more about me; I am no gibbet for you. Go – a short knife and a throng! – to your manor of Pickt-hatch, go! You'll not bear a letter for me, you rogue? You stand upon your honour? Why, thou unconfinable baseness, it is as much as I can do to keep the terms of my honour precise: I, I, I myself sometimes, leaving the fear of heaven on the left hand, and hiding mine honour in my necessity, am fain to shuffle, to hedge, and to lurch; and yet you, rogue, will ensconce your rags, your cat-a-mountain looks, your red-lattice phrases, and your bold beating oaths, under the shelter of your honour! You will not do it, you?

15

20

25

PISTOL   I do relent: what would thou more of man?

Enter ROBIN.

ROBIN   Sir, here's a woman would speak with you.

30

FALSTAFF   Let her approach.

Enter MISTRESS QUICKLY.

QUICKLY   Give your worship good morrow.

FALSTAFF   Good morrow, goodwife.

QUICKLY   Not so, and't please your worship.

FALSTAFF   Good maid, then.

35

QUICKLY   I'll be sworn – as my mother was, the first hour I was born.

FALSTAFF   I do believe the swearer. What with me?

QUICKLY   Shall I vouchsafe your worship a word or two?

FALSTAFF   Two thousand, fair woman, and I'll vouchsafe thee the hearing.

40

QUICKLY   There is one Mistress Ford, sir – I pray come a little nearer this ways – I myself dwell with Master Doctor Caius –

FALSTAFF   Well, on; Mistress Ford, you say –

45

QUICKLY   Your worship says very true. – I pray your worship come a little nearer this ways.

FALSTAFF   I warrant thee, nobody hears. Mine own people, mine own people.

QUICKLY   Are they so? Heaven bless them, and make them his servants!

50

FALSTAFF   Well, Mistress Ford – what of her?

QUICKLY   Why, sir, she's a good creature. – Lord, Lord, your worship's a wanton! Well, heaven forgive you and all of us, I pray!

FALSTAFF   Mistress Ford; come, Mistress Ford.

QUICKLY   Marry, this is the short and the long of it; you have brought her into such a canaries as 'tis wonderful. The best courtier of them all, when the court lay at Windsor, could never have brought her to such a canary. Yet there has been knights, and lords, and gentlemen, with their coaches – I warrant you, coach after coach, letter after letter, gift after gift – smelling so sweetly, all musk, and so rushling, I warrant you, in silk and gold, and in such alligant terms, and in such wine and sugar of the best and the fairest, that would have won any woman's heart; and, I warrant you, they could never get an eyewink of her; I had myself twenty angels given me this morning; but I defy all angels – in any such sort, as they say – but in the way of honesty; and, I warrant you, they could never get her so much as sip on a cup with the proudest of them all, and yet there has been earls, nay, which is more, pensioners, but, I warrant you, all is one with her.

FALSTAFF   But what says she to me? Be brief, my good she-Mercury.

QUICKLY   Marry, she hath received your letter; for the which she thanks you a thousand times; and she gives you to notify that her husband will be absence from his house between ten and eleven.

FALSTAFF   Ten and eleven.

QUICKLY   Ay, forsooth; and then you may come and see the picture, she says, that you wot of; Master Ford, her husband, will be from home. Alas, the sweet woman leads an ill life with him: he's a very jealousy man; she leads a very frampold life with him, good heart.

FALSTAFF   Ten and eleven. Woman, commend me to her; I will not fail her.

QUICKLY   Why, you say well. But I have another messenger to your worship: Mistress Page hath her hearty commendations to you too; and let me tell you in your ear, she's as fartuous a civil modest wife, and one, I tell you, that will not miss you morning nor evening prayer, as any is in Windsor, whoe'er be the other; and she bade me tell your worship that her husband is seldom from home, but she hopes there will come a time. I never knew a woman so dote upon a man; surely, I think you have charms, la; yes, in truth.

FALSTAFF   Not I, I assure thee; setting the attraction of my good parts aside, I have no other charms.

QUICKLY   Blessing on your heart for't!

FALSTAFF   But I pray thee tell me this: has Ford's wife and Page's wife acquainted each other how they love me?

QUICKLY   That were a jest indeed! They have not so little grace, I hope; that were a trick indeed! But Mistress Page would desire you to send her your little page, of all loves: her husband has a marvellous infection to the little page; and, truly, Master Page is an honest man. Never a wife in Windsor leads a better life than she does; do what she will, say what she will, take all, pay all, go to bed when she list, rise when she list, all is as she will; and, truly, she deserves it; for if there be a kind woman in Windsor, she is one. You must send her your page, no remedy.

FALSTAFF   Why, I will.

QUICKLY   Nay, but do so, then, and, look you, he may come and go between you both; and in any case have a nay-word, that you may know one another's mind, and the boy never need to understand anything; for 'tis not good that children should know any wickedness: old folks, you know, have discretion, as they say, and know the world.

FALSTAFF   Fare thee well; commend me to them both. There's my purse; I am yet thy debtor. Boy, go along with this woman.   *Exeunt Mistress Quickly and Robin.* This news distracts me.

PISTOL   This punk is one of Cupid's carriers.
Clap on more sails, pursue; up with your fights;
Give fire; she is my prize, or ocean whelm them all!
Exit.

FALSTAFF   Say'st thou so, old Jack? Go thy ways; I'll make more of thy old body than I have done. Will they yet look after thee? Wilt thou, after the expense of so much money, be now a gainer? Good body, I thank thee. Let them say 'tis grossly done; so it be fairly done, no matter.

Enter BARDOLPH.

BARDOLPH   Sir John, there's one Master Brook below would fain speak with you, and be acquainted with you; and hath sent your worship a morning's draught of sack.

FALSTAFF   Brook is his name?

BARDOLPH   Ay, sir.

FALSTAFF   Call him in.   *Exit Bardolph.* Such Brooks are welcome to me, that o'erflows such liquor. Ah, ha, Mistress Ford and Mistress Page, have I encompassed you? Go to; via!

Enter BARDOLPH, *and* FORD *in disguise.*

FORD   Bless you, sir.

FALSTAFF   And you, sir. Would you speak with me?

FORD   I make bold to press with so little preparation upon you.

FALSTAFF   You're welcome. What's your will? – Give us leave, drawer.   *Exit Bardolph.*

FORD   Sir, I am a gentleman that have spent much; my name is Brook.

FALSTAFF   Good Master Brook, I desire more acquaintance of you.

FORD   Good Sir John, I sue for yours: not to charge you, for I must let you understand I think myself in better plight for a lender than you are – the which hath

something emboldened me to this unseasoned
intrusion; for they say, if money go before, all ways
do lie open.

165 FALSTAFF Money is a good soldier, sir, and will on.

FORD Troth, and I have a bag of money here troubles
me; if you will help to bear it, Sir John, take all, or
half, for easing me of the carriage.

FALSTAFF Sir, I know not how I may deserve to be your
170 porter.

FORD I will tell you, sir, if you will give me the hearing.

FALSTAFF Speak, good Master Brook, I shall be glad to
be your servant.

FORD Sir, I hear you are a scholar – I will be brief with
175 you – and you have been a man long known to me,
though I had never so good means as desire to make
myself acquainted with you. I shall discover a thing
to you, wherein I must very much lay open mine
own imperfection; but, good Sir John, as you have
180 one eye upon my follies, as you hear them unfolded,
turn another into the register of your own, that I may
pass with a reproof the easier, sith you yourself know
how easy it is to be such an offender.

FALSTAFF Very well, sir; proceed.

185 FORD There is a gentlewoman in this town – her
husband's name is Ford.

FALSTAFF Well, sir.

FORD I have long loved her and, I protest to you,
bestowed much on her; followed her with a doting
190 observance; engrossed opportunities to meet her; fee'd
every slight occasion that could but niggardly give me
sight of her; not only bought many presents to give
her, but have given largely to many to know what she
would have given: briefly, I have pursued her as love
195 hath pursued me; which hath been on the wing of all
occasions. But whatsoever I have merited, either in my
mind or in my means, meed I am sure I have received
none, unless experience be a jewel, that I have
purchased at an infinite rate and that hath taught me
200 to say this:

Love like a shadow flies when substance love pursues;
Pursuing that that flies, and flying what pursues.

FALSTAFF Have you received no promise of satisfaction
at her hands?

205 FORD Never.

FALSTAFF Have you importuned her to such a purpose?

FORD Never.

FALSTAFF Of what quality was your love, then?

FORD Like a fair house built on another man's ground,
210 so that I have lost my edifice by mistaking the place
where I erected it.

FALSTAFF To what purpose have you unfolded this to
me?

FORD When I have told you that, I have told you all.
215 Some say that though she appear honest to me, yet
in other places she enlargeth her mirth so far that
there is shrewd construction made of her. Now, Sir
John, here is the heart of my purpose: you are a

gentleman of excellent breeding, admirable discourse,
of great admittance, authentic in your place and 220
person, generally allowed for your many war-like,
court-like, and learned preparations.

FALSTAFF O sir!

FORD Believe it, for you know it. There is money; spend
it, spend it, spend more; spend all I have, only give 225
me so much of your time in exchange of it as to lay an
amiable siege to the honesty of this Ford's wife. Use
your art of wooing; win her to consent to you; if any
man may, you may as soon as any.

FALSTAFF Would it apply well to the vehemency of your 230
affection that I should win what you would enjoy?
Methinks you prescribe to yourself very preposterously.

FORD O, understand my drift: she dwells so securely on
the excellency of her honour that the folly of my soul 235
dares not present itself; she is too bright to be looked
against. Now, could I come to her with any detection
in my hand, my desires had instance and argument to
commend themselves; I could drive her then from the
ward of her purity, her reputation, her marriage-vow, 240
and a thousand other her defences which now are too
too strongly embattled against me. What say you to't,
Sir John?

FALSTAFF Master Brook, I will first make bold with
your money; next, give me your hand; and last, as I am 245
a gentleman, you shall, if you will, enjoy Ford's wife.

FORD O good sir!

FALSTAFF I say you shall.

FORD Want no money, Sir John; you shall want none.

FALSTAFF Want no Mistress Ford, Master Brook; you 250
shall want none. I shall be with her, I may tell you, by
her own appointment; even as you came in to me,
her assistant, or go-between, parted from me: I say I
shall be with her between ten and eleven; for at that
time the jealous rascally knave her husband will be 255
forth. Come you to me at night, you shall know how I
speed.

FORD I am blest in your acquaintance. Do you know
Ford, sir?

FALSTAFF Hang him, poor cuckoldly knave, I know him 260
not. Yet I wrong him to call him poor: they say the
jealous wittolly knave hath masses of money, for the
which his wife seems to me well-favoured. I will use
her as the key of the cuckoldly rogue's coffer, and
there's my harvest-home. 265

FORD I would you knew Ford, sir, that you might avoid
him if you saw him.

FALSTAFF Hang him, mechanical salt-butter rogue! I
will stare him out of his wits; I will awe him with my
cudgel: it shall hang like a meteor o'er the cuckold's 270
horns. Master Brook, thou shalt know I will
predominate over the peasant, and thou shalt lie with
his wife. Come to me soon at night. Ford's a knave,
and I will aggravate his style; thou, Master Brook,
shalt know him for knave and cuckold. Come to me 275

soon at night.   *Exit.*

FORD   What a damned Epicurean rascal is this? My
heart is ready to crack with impatience. Who says
this is improvident jealousy? My wife hath sent to
him, the hour is fixed, the match is made. Would any
man have thought this? See the hell of having a false
woman: my bed shall be abused, my coffers
ransacked, my reputation gnawn at, and I shall not
only receive this villainous wrong, but stand under
the adoption of abominable terms, and by him that
does me this wrong. Terms! Names! Amaimon sounds
well; Lucifer, well; Barbason, well: yet they are devils'
additions, the names of fiends. But cuckold? Wittol?
Cuckold! The devil himself hath not such a name.
Page is an ass, a secure ass: he will trust his wife, he
will not be jealous. I will rather trust a Fleming with
my butter, Parson Hugh the Welshman with my
cheese, an Irishman with my aqua-vitae bottle, or a
thief to walk my ambling gelding, than my wife with
herself. Then she plots, then she ruminates, then she
devises; and what they think in their hearts they may
effect, they will break their hearts but they will effect.
Heaven be praised for my jealousy! – Eleven o'clock
the hour: I will prevent this, detect my wife, be
revenged on Falstaff, and laugh at Page. I will about it;
better three hours too soon than a minute too late. Fie,
fie, fie; cuckold, cuckold, cuckold!   *Exit.*

2.3   *Enter* CAIUS *and* RUGBY.

CAIUS   Jack Rugby!
RUGBY   Sir?
CAIUS   Vat is the clock, Jack?
RUGBY   'Tis past the hour, sir, that Sir Hugh promised
to meet.
CAIUS   By gar, he has save his soul, dat he is no come; he
has pray his Pible well, dat he is no come; by gar, Jack
Rugby, he is dead already, if he be come.
RUGBY   He is wise, sir: he knew your worship would kill
him if he came.
CAIUS   By gar, de herring is no dead so as I vill kill him.
Take your rapier, Jack; I vill tell you how I vill kill him.
RUGBY   Alas, sir, I cannot fence.
CAIUS   Villainy, take your rapier.
RUGBY   Forbear; here's company.

Enter Host, SHALLOW, SLENDER *and* PAGE.

HOST   Bless thee, bully Doctor.
SHALLOW   Save you, Master Doctor Caius.
PAGE   Now, good Master Doctor.
SLENDER   Give you good morrow, sir.
CAIUS   Vat be all you, one, two, tree, four, come for?
HOST   To see thee fight, to see thee foin, to see thee
traverse, to see thee here, to see thee there, to see
thee pass thy punto, thy stock, thy reverse, thy
distance, thy montant. Is he dead, my Ethiopian? Is he
dead, my Francisco? Ha, bully? What says my

Aesculapius? My Galen? My heart of elder? Ha, is
he dead, bully stale? Is he dead?
CAIUS   By gar, he is de coward Jack priest of de vorld; he
is not show his face.
HOST   Thou art a Castalian-king-Urinal: Hector of
Greece, my boy!
CAIUS   I pray you bear witness that me have stay six or
seven, two, tree hours for him, and he is no come.
SHALLOW   He is the wiser man, Master Doctor: he is a
curer of souls, and you a curer of bodies; if you should
fight, you go against the hair of your professions. Is
it not true, Master Page?
PAGE   Master Shallow, you have yourself been a great
fighter, though now a man of peace.
SHALLOW   Bodykins, Master Page, though I now be old,
and of the Peace, if I see a sword out, my finger itches
to make one. Though we are justices, and doctors, and
churchmen, Master Page, we have some salt of our
youth in us; we are the sons of women, Master Page.
PAGE   'Tis true, Master Shallow.
SHALLOW   It will be found so, Master Page. Master
Doctor Caius, I am come to fetch you home. I am
sworn of the Peace; you have showed yourself a wise
physician, and Sir Hugh hath shown himself a wise
and patient churchman; you must go with me, Master
Doctor.
HOST   Pardon, guest Justice. – A word, Mounseur
Mockwater.
CAIUS   Mock-vater? Vat is dat?
HOST   Mock-water, in our English tongue, is valour,
bully.
CAIUS   By gar, then, I have as much mock-vater as de
Englishman. Scurvy Jack-dog priest! By gar, me vill
cut his ears.
HOST   He will clapper-claw thee tightly, bully.
CAIUS   Clapper-de-claw? Vat is dat?
HOST   That is, he will make thee amends.
CAIUS   By gar, me do look he shall clapper-de-claw me,
for, by gar, me vill have it.
HOST   And I will provoke him to't, or let him wag.
CAIUS   Me tank you for dat.
HOST   And, moreover, bully – [*to the others, aside*] But
first, Master guest, and Master Page, and eke
Cavaliero Slender, go you through the town to
Frogmore.
PAGE   Sir Hugh is there, is he?
HOST   He is there. See what humour he is in; and I will
bring the doctor about by the fields. Will it do well?
SHALLOW   We will do it.
PAGE, SHALLOW, SLENDER   Adieu, good Master Doctor.
Exeunt Page, Shallow and Slender.
CAIUS   By gar, me vill kill de priest, for he speak for a
jack-an-ape to Anne Page.
HOST   Let him die; sheathe thy impatience; throw cold
water on thy choler; go about the fields with me
through Frogmore, I will bring thee where Mistress
Anne Page is, at a farm-house a-feasting; and thou

shalt woo her. Cried game; said I well?

CAIUS   By gar, me dank you vor dat; by gar, I love you;
and I shall procure-a you de good guest: de earl, de
knight, de lords, de gentlemen, my patients.

HOST   For the which I will be thy adversary toward
Anne Page. Said I well?

CAIUS   By gar, 'tis good; vell said.

HOST   Let us wag, then.

CAIUS   Come at my heels, Jack Rugby.   *Exeunt.*

3.1   *Enter* EVANS *and* SIMPLE.

EVANS   I pray you now, good Master Slender's
servingman, and friend Simple by your name, which
way have you looked for Master Caius, that calls
himself Doctor of Physic?

SIMPLE   Marry, sir, the Pitty-ward, the Park-ward, every
way; Old Windsor way, and every way but the town
way.

EVANS   I most fehemently desire you you will also look
that way.

SIMPLE   I will, sir. [*going aside*]

EVANS   Pless my soul, how full of chollors I am, and
trempling of mind: I shall be glad if he have deceived
me. How melancholies I am! I will knog his urinals
about his knave's costard when I have good
opportunities for the 'ork. Pless my soul!
[*singing*] To shallow rivers, to whose falls
        Melodious birds sings madrigals;
        There will we make our peds of roses,
        And a thousand fragrant posies.
        To shallow –
Mercy on me! I have a great dispositions to cry. –
[*singing*] Melodious birds sing madrigals –
        Whenas I sat in Pabylon –
        And a thousand vagram posies.
        To shallow, etc.

SIMPLE   Yonder he is coming, this way, Sir Hugh.

EVANS   He's welcome. –
[*singing*] To shallow rivers, to whose falls –
Heaven prosper the right! – What weapons is he?

SIMPLE   No weapons, sir. There comes my master,
Master Shallow, and another gentleman; from
Frogmore, over the stile, this way.

EVANS   Pray you, give me my gown, or else keep it in
your arms.

Enter PAGE, SHALLOW *and* SLENDER.

SHALLOW   How now, Master Parson? Good morrow,
good Sir Hugh. Keep a gamester from the dice, and a
good student from his book, and it is wonderful.

SLENDER   Ah, sweet Anne Page!

PAGE   Save you, good Sir Hugh.

EVANS   Pless you from His mercy sake, all of you.

SHALLOW   What, the sword and the word? Do you study
them both, Master Parson?

PAGE   And youthful still, in your doublet and hose this
raw rheumatic day?

EVANS   There is reasons and causes for it.

PAGE   We are come to you to do a good office, Master
Parson.

EVANS   Fery well: what is it?

PAGE   Yonder is a most reverend gentleman, who, belike
having received wrong by some person, is at most
odds with his own gravity and patience that ever you
saw.

SHALLOW   I have lived fourscore years and upward; I
never heard a man of his place, gravity, and learning so
wide of his own respect.

EVANS   What is he?

PAGE   I think you know him: Master Doctor Caius, the
renowned French physician.

EVANS   Got's will and His passion of my heart, I had as
lief you would tell me of a mess of porridge.

PAGE   Why?

EVANS   He has no more knowledge in Hibocrates and
Galen, and he is a knave besides: a cowardly knave as
you would desires to be acquainted withal.

PAGE   I warrant you, he's the man should fight with
him.

SLENDER   O sweet Anne Page!

SHALLOW   It appears so by his weapons. Keep them
asunder; here comes Doctor Caius.

Enter Host, CAIUS *and* RUGBY

PAGE   Nay, good Master Parson, keep in your weapon.

SHALLOW   So do you, good Master Doctor.

HOST   Disarm them, and let them question; let them
keep their limbs whole, and hack our English.

CAIUS   I pray you let-a me speak a word with your ear.
Verefore vill you not meet-a me?

EVANS   [*aside to Caius*]   Pray you use your patience.
[*aloud*] In good time.

CAIUS   By gar, you are de coward; de Jack dog; John ape.

EVANS [*aside to Caius*]   Pray you let us not be laughing-
stocks to other men's humours; I desire you in
friendship, and I will one way or other make you
amends. [*aloud*] I will knog your urinal about your
knave's cogscomb.

CAIUS   *Diable*! Jack Rugby, mine host de Jarteer, have I
not stay for him to kill him? Have I not, at de place I
did appoint?

EVANS   As I am a Christians soul, now, look you, this is
the place appointed. I'll be judgement by mine host of
the Garter.

HOST   Peace, I say, Gallia and Gaul, French and Welsh,
soul-curer and body-curer.

CAIUS   Ay, dat is very good, excellant.

HOST   Peace, I say; hear mine host of the Garter. Am I
politic? Am I subtle? Am I a Machiavel? Shall I lose
my doctor? No, he gives me the potions and the
motions. Shall I lose my parson? My priest? My Sir
Hugh? No, he gives me the proverbs and the no-verbs.
Give me thy hand, terrestrial, so; give me thy hand,

celestial, so. Boys of art, I have deceived you both: I have directed you to wrong places; your hearts are mighty, your skins are whole, and let burnt sack be the issue. Come, lay their swords to pawn. Follow me, lads of peace; follow, follow, follow. *Exit.*

SHALLOW   Trust me, a mad host. Follow, gentlemen, follow.

SLENDER   O sweet Anne Page!

Exeunt Shallow, Slender and Page.

CAIUS   Ha, do I perceive dat? Have you make-a de sot of us, ha, ha?

EVANS   This is well; he has made us his vlouting-stog. I desire you that we may be friends; and let us knog our prains together to be revenge on this same scall, scurvy, cogging companion, the host of the Garter.

CAIUS   By gar, with all my heart. He promise to bring me where is Anne Page; by gar, he deceive me too.

EVANS   Well, I will smite his noddles. Pray you follow.

Exeunt.

3.2   *Enter* MISTRESS PAGE *following* ROBIN.

MISTRESS PAGE   Nay, keep your way, little gallant; you were wont to be a follower, but now you are a leader. Whether had you rather lead mine eyes, or eye your master's heels?

ROBIN   I had rather, forsooth, go before you like a man than follow him like a dwarf.

MISTRESS PAGE   O, you are a flattering boy: now I see you'll be a courtier.

Enter FORD.

FORD   Well met, Mistress Page. Whither go you?

MISTRESS PAGE   Truly, sir, to see your wife. Is she at home?

FORD   Ay, and as idle as she may hang together, for want of company. I think, if your husbands were dead, you two would marry.

MISTRESS PAGE   Be sure of that – two other husbands.

FORD   Where had you this pretty weathercock?

MISTRESS PAGE   I cannot tell what the dickens his name is my husband had him of. – What do you call your knight's name, sirrah?

ROBIN   Sir John Falstaff.

FORD   Sir John Falstaff?

MISTRESS PAGE   He, he; I can never hit on's name. There is such a league between my goodman and he! Is your wife at home indeed?

FORD   Indeed she is.

MISTRESS PAGE   By your leave, sir; I am sick till I see her.

Exeunt Mistress Page and Robin.

FORD   Has Page any brains? Hath he any eyes? Hath he any thinking? Sure, they sleep: he hath no use of them. Why, this boy will carry a letter twenty mile as easy as a cannon will shoot point-blank twelve score. He pieces out his wife's inclination; he gives her folly motion and advantage: and now she's going to my wife, and Falstaff's boy with her. A man may hear this shower sing in the wind. And Falstaff's boy with her! Good plots! They are laid; and our revolted wives share damnation together. Well, I will take him, then torture my wife, pluck the borrowed veil of modesty from the so-seeming Mistress Page, divulge Page himself for a secure and wilful Actaeon; and to these violent proceedings all my neighbours shall cry aim. [*clock strikes*] The clock gives me my cue, and my assurance bids me search: there I shall find Falstaff. I shall be rather praised for this than mocked, for it is as positive as the earth is firm that Falstaff is there. I will go.

Enter PAGE, SHALLOW, SLENDER,
Host, EVANS, CAIUS *and* RUGBY.

SHALLOW, PAGE, ETC.   Well met, Master Ford.

FORD [*aside*]   Trust me, a good knot. – [*aloud*] I have good cheer at home, and I pray you all go with me.

SHALLOW   I must excuse myself, Master Ford.

SLENDER   And so must I, sir: we have appointed to dine with Mistress Anne, and I would not break with her for more money than I'll speak of.

SHALLOW   We have lingered about a match between Anne Page and my cousin Slender, and this day we shall have our answer.

SLENDER   I hope I have your good will, father Page.

PAGE   You have, Master Slender, I stand wholly for you. But my wife, Master Doctor, is for you altogether.

CAIUS   Ay, be-gar, and de maid is love-a me: my nursh-a Quickly tell me so mush.

HOST   What say you to young Master Fenton? He capers, he dances, he has eyes of youth; he writes verses, he speaks holiday, he smells April and May. He will carry't, he will carry't; 'tis in his buttons he will carry't.

PAGE   Not by my consent, I promise you. The gentleman is of no having: he kept company with the wild Prince and Poins. He is of too high a region; he knows too much. No, he shall not knit a knot in his fortunes with the finger of my substance; if he take her, let him take her simply: the wealth I have waits on my consent, and my consent goes not that way.

FORD   I beseech you heartily, some of you go home with me to dinner; besides your cheer, you shall have sport: I will show you a monster. Master Doctor, you shall go; so shall you, Master Page, and you, Sir Hugh.

SHALLOW   Well, fare you well: we shall have the freer wooing at Master Page's. *Exeunt Shallow and Slender.*

CAIUS   Go home, John Rugby; I come anon.

Exit Rugby.

HOST   Farewell, my hearts; I will to my honest knight Falstaff, and drink canary with him. *Exit.*

FORD [*aside*]   I think I shall drink in pipe-wine first with him; I'll make him dance. – Will you go, gentles?

ALL   Have with you to see this monster. *Exeunt.*

3.3   *Enter* MISTRESS FORD *and* MISTRESS PAGE.

MISTRESS FORD   What, John! What, Robert!
MISTRESS PAGE   Quickly, quickly, is the buck-basket –
MISTRESS FORD   I warrant. What, Robin, I say!

Enter JOHN *and* ROBERT *with a basket.*

MISTRESS PAGE   Come, come, come.
5 MISTRESS FORD   Here, set it down.
MISTRESS PAGE   Give your men the charge; we must be
   brief.
MISTRESS FORD   Marry, as I told you before, John and
   Robert, be ready here hard by in the brew-house, and
10 when I suddenly call you, come forth, and, without
   any pause or staggering, take this basket on your
   shoulders. That done, trudge with it in all haste, and
   carry it among the whitsters in Datchet Mead, and
   there empty it in the muddy ditch close by the
15 Thames side.
MISTRESS PAGE   You will do it?
MISTRESS FORD   I ha' told them over and over; they lack
   no   direction. – Be gone, and come when you are
   called.   *Exeunt John and Robert.*
20 MISTRESS PAGE   Here comes little Robin.

Enter ROBIN.

MISTRESS FORD   How now, my eyas-musket, what news
   with you?
ROBIN   My master, Sir John, is come in at your back
   door, Mistress Ford, and requests your company.
25 MISTRESS PAGE   You little Jack-a-Lent, have you been
   true to us?
ROBIN   Ay, I'll be sworn. My master knows not of your
   being here, and hath threatened to put me into
   everlasting liberty if I tell you of it; for he swears
30 he'll turn me away.
MISTRESS PAGE   Thou'rt a good boy: this secrecy of
   thine shall be a tailor to thee, and shall make thee a
   new doublet and hose. – I'll go hide me.
MISTRESS FORD   Do so. – Go tell thy master I am alone.
                                          Exit Robin.
35 Mistress Page, remember you your cue.
MISTRESS PAGE   I warrant thee; if I do not act it, hiss me.
MISTRESS FORD   Go to, then: we'll use this unwholesome humidity, this gross watery pumpion; we'll teach
   him to know turtles from jays.   *Exit Mistress Page.*

Enter FALSTAFF.

40 FALSTAFF   Have I caught thee, my heavenly jewel? Why,
   now let me die, for I have lived long enough: this is the
   period of my ambition. O this blessed hour!
MISTRESS FORD   O sweet Sir John!
FALSTAFF   Mistress Ford, I cannot cog, I cannot prate,
45 Mistress Ford. Now shall I sin in my wish: I would
   thy husband were dead; I'll speak it before the best
   lord: I would make thee my lady.
MISTRESS FORD   I your lady, Sir John? Alas, I should be

a pitiful lady.
FALSTAFF   Let the court of France show me such   50
   another. I see how thine eye would emulate the
   diamond: thou hast the right arched beauty of the
   brow that becomes the ship-tire, the tire-valiant, or
   any tire of Venetian admittance.
MISTRESS FORD   A plain kerchief, Sir John: my brows   55
   become nothing else, nor that well neither.
FALSTAFF   Thou art a tyrant to say so; thou wouldst
   make an absolute courtier, and the firm fixture of thy
   foot would give an excellent motion to thy gait in a
   semicircled farthingale. I see what thou wert if   60
   Fortune (thy foe) were – not Nature – thy friend.
   Come, thou canst not hide it.
MISTRESS FORD   Believe me, there's no such thing in
   me.
FALSTAFF   What made me love thee? Let that persuade   65
   thee there's something extraordinary in thee. Come, I
   cannot cog and say thou art this and that, like a many
   of these lisping hawthorn-buds that come like women
   in men's apparel, and smell like Bucklersbury in
   simple time; I cannot; but I love thee, none but thee;   70
   and thou deserv'st it.
MISTRESS FORD   Do not betray me, sir. I fear you love
   Mistress Page.
FALSTAFF   Thou mightst as well say I love to walk by the
   Counter-gate, which is as hateful to me as the reek of   75
   a lime-kill.
MISTRESS FORD   Well, heaven knows how I love you, and
   you shall one day find it.
FALSTAFF   Keep in that mind: I'll deserve it.
MISTRESS FORD   Nay, I must tell you, so you do; or else   80
   I could not be in that mind.

Enter ROBIN.

ROBIN   Mistress Ford, Mistress Ford! Here's Mistress
   Page at the door, sweating and blowing, and looking
   wildly, and would needs speak with you presently.
FALSTAFF   She shall not see me: I will ensconce me   85
   behind the arras.
MISTRESS FORD   Pray you do so; she's a very tattling
   woman. [*Falstaff hides behind the arras.*]

Enter MISTRESS PAGE.

What's the matter? How now?
MISTRESS PAGE   O Mistress Ford, what have you done?   90
   You're shamed, you're overthrown, you're undone
   for ever!
MISTRESS FORD   What's the matter, good Mistress Page?
MISTRESS PAGE   O well-a-day, Mistress Ford, having an
   honest man to your husband, to give him such cause of   95
   suspicion!
MISTRESS FORD   What cause of suspicion?
MISTRESS PAGE   What cause of suspicion? Out upon
   you: how am I mistook in you!
MISTRESS FORD   Why, alas, what's the matter?   100
MISTRESS PAGE   Your husband's coming hither, woman,

with all the officers in Windsor, to search for a
gentleman that he says is here now in the house, by
your consent, to take an ill advantage of his absence.
You are undone.

105 MISTRESS FORD 'Tis not so, I hope.

MISTRESS PAGE Pray heaven it be not so, that you have
such a man here – but 'tis most certain your husband's
coming, with half Windsor at his heels, to search for
110 such a one, I come before to tell you. If you know
yourself clear, why, I am glad of it; but if you have a
friend here, convey, convey him out. Be not amazed,
call all your senses to you, defend your reputation, or
bid farewell to your good life for ever.

115 MISTRESS FORD What shall I do? There is a gentleman,
my dear friend; and I fear not mine own shame so
much as his peril. I had rather than a thousand
pound he were out of the house.

MISTRESS PAGE For shame, never stand 'you had rather'
120 and 'you had rather': your husband's here at hand!
Bethink you of some conveyance; in the house you
cannot hide him. O, how have you deceived me!
Look, here is a basket; if he be of any reasonable
stature, he may creep in here; and throw foul linen
125 upon him, as if it were going to bucking; or – it is
whiting-time – send him by your two men to
Datchet Mead.

MISTRESS FORD He's too big to go in there. What shall
I do?

130 FALSTAFF [*coming forward*] Let me see't, let me see't, O,
let me see't! I'll in, I'll in. Follow your friend's
counsel; I'll in.

MISTRESS PAGE What, Sir John Falstaff? – Are these
your letters, knight?

135 FALSTAFF I love thee; help me away. Let me creep in
here. I'll never –
[*Gets into the basket; they cover him with 'foul linen'.*]

MISTRESS PAGE Help to cover your master, boy. – Call
your men, Mistress Ford. – You dissembling knight!

MISTRESS FORD What, John! Robert! John!

Enter JOHN and ROBERT.

140 Go take up these clothes here quickly. Where's the
cowl-staff? Look, how you drumble! Carry them to
the laundress in Datchet Mead; quickly, come.

Enter FORD, PAGE, CAIUS and EVANS.

FORD Pray you come near: if I suspect without cause,
why then make sport at me; then let me be your jest, I
145 deserve it. – How now? Whither bear you this?

JOHN To the laundress, forsooth.

MISTRESS FORD Why, what have you to do whither they
bear it? You were best meddle with buck-washing!

FORD Buck? I would I could wash myself of the buck!
150 Buck, buck, buck! Ay, buck; I warrant you, buck;
and of the season too, it shall appear.
Exeunt John, Robert and Robin with the basket.
Gentlemen, I have dreamed to-night; I'll tell you my

dream. Here, here, here be my keys; ascend my
chambers; search, seek, find out. I'll warrant we'll
unkennel the fox. Let me stop this way first. [*locking* 155
the door] So, now uncape.

PAGE Good Master Ford, be contented; you wrong
yourself too much.

FORD True, Master Page. – Up, gentlemen, you shall
see sport anon; follow me, gentlemen. *Exit.* 160

EVANS This is fery fantastical humours and jealousies.

CAIUS By gar, 'tis no the fashion of France; it is not
jealous in France.

PAGE Nay, follow him, gentlemen; see the issue of his
search. *Exeunt Page, Caius and Evans.* 165

MISTRESS PAGE Is there not a double excellency in this?

MISTRESS FORD I know not which pleases me better,
that my husband is deceived, or Sir John.

MISTRESS PAGE What a taking was he in when your
husband asked who was in the basket! 170

MISTRESS FORD I am half afraid he will have need of
washing – so throwing him into the water will do him
a benefit.

MISTRESS PAGE Hang him, dishonest rascal! I would all
of the same strain were in the same distress. 175

MISTRESS FORD I think my husband hath some special
suspicion of Falstaff's being here, for I never saw him
so gross in his jealousy till now.

MISTRESS PAGE I will lay a plot to try that, and we will
yet have more tricks with Falstaff: his dissolute disease 180
will scarce obey this medicine.

MISTRESS FORD Shall we send that foolish carrion,
Mistress Quickly, to him, and excuse his throwing into
the water, and give him another hope, to betray him to
another punishment? 185

MISTRESS PAGE We will do it: let him be sent for
to-morrow eight o'clock to have amends.

Enter FORD, PAGE, CAIUS and EVANS.

FORD I cannot find him; maybe the knave bragged of
that he could not compass.

MISTRESS PAGE [*aside to Mistress Ford*] Heard you that? 190

MISTRESS FORD You use me well, Master Ford, do you?

FORD Ay, I do so.

MISTRESS FORD Heaven make you better than your
thoughts!

FORD Amen! 195

MISTRESS PAGE You do yourself mighty wrong, Master
Ford.

FORD Ay, ay; I must bear it.

EVANS If there be anypody in the house, and in the
chambers, and in the coffers, and in the presses, 200
heaven forgive my sins at the day of judgement!

CAIUS By gar, nor I too: there is nobodies.

PAGE Fie, fie, Master Ford, are you not ashamed? What
spirit, what devil suggests this imagination? I would
not ha' your distemper in this kind for the wealth of 205
Windsor Castle.

FORD 'Tis my fault, Master Page, I suffer for it.

EVANS   You suffer for a pad conscience. Your wife is as
honest a 'omans as I will desires among five
210   thousand, and five hundred too.

CAIUS   By gar, I see 'tis an honest woman.

FORD   Well, I promised you a dinner. Come, come, walk
in the Park. I pray you pardon me; I will hereafter
make known to you why I have done this. Come,
215   wife, come, Mistress Page, I pray you pardon me; pray
heartily pardon me.

PAGE   Let's go in, gentlemen – [*aside*] but, trust me, we'll
mock him. – I do invite you to-morrow morning   to
my house to breakfast; after, we'll a-birding   together
220   – I have a fine hawk for the bush. Shall it be so?

FORD   Anything.

EVANS   If there is one, I shall make two in the company.

CAIUS   If there be one or two, I shall make-a the turd.

FORD   Pray you go, Master Page.   *Exit, with Page.*

225   EVANS   I pray you now, remembrance to-morrow on the
lousy knave mine host.

CAIUS   Dat is good, by gar; with all my heart!

EVANS   A lousy knave, to have his gibes and his
mockeries!   *Exeunt.*

3.4   *Enter* FENTON *and* ANNE PAGE.

FENTON   I see I cannot get thy father's love;
Therefore no more turn me to him, sweet Nan.

ANNE   Alas, how then?

FENTON   Why, thou must be thyself.
He doth object I am too great of birth,
5   And that my state being gall'd with my expense,
I seek to heal it only by his wealth;
Besides these, other bars he lays before me –
My riots past, my wild societies –
And tells me 'tis a thing impossible
10   I should love thee but as a property.

ANNE   Maybe he tells you true.

FENTON   No, heaven so speed me in my time to come!
Albeit I will confess thy father's wealth
Was the first motive that I woo'd thee, Anne,
15   Yet, wooing thee, I found thee of more value
Than stamps in gold or sums in sealed bags;
And 'tis the very riches of thyself
That now I aim at.

ANNE   Gentle Master Fenton,
Yet seek my father's love; still seek it, sir.
20   If opportunity and humblest suit
Cannot attain it, why then – hark you hither!
[*They converse apart.*]

Enter SHALLOW, SLENDER *and* MISTRESS QUICKLY.

SHALLOW   Break their talk, Mistress Quickly. My
kinsman shall speak for himself.

SLENDER   I'll make a shaft or a bolt on't. 'Slid, 'tis but
25   venturing.

SHALLOW   Be not dismayed.

SLENDER   No, she shall not dismay me: I care not for
that, but that I am afeard.

QUICKLY   [*to Anne*]   Hark ye, Master Slender would
speak a word with you.   30

ANNE   I come to him. [*aside*] This is my father's choice.
O, what a world of vile ill-favour'd faults
Looks handsome in three hundred pounds a year!

QUICKLY   And how does good Master Fenton? Pray you,
a word with you.   35

SHALLOW   [*to Slender*]   She's coming; to her, coz. O boy,
thou hadst a father!

SLENDER   I had a father, Mistress Anne; my uncle can
tell you good jests of him. Pray you, uncle, tell
Mistress Anne the jest how my father stole two geese   40
out of a pen, good uncle.

SHALLOW   Mistress Anne, my cousin loves you.

SLENDER   Ay, that I do, as well as I love any woman in
Gloucestershire.

SHALLOW   He will maintain you like a gentlewoman.   45

SLENDER   Ay, that I will, come cut and long-tail, under
the degree of a squire.

SHALLOW   He will make you a hundred and fifty pounds
jointure.

ANNE   Good Master Shallow, let him woo for himself.   50

SHALLOW   Marry, I thank you for it; I thank you for that
good comfort. She calls you, coz; I'll leave you.

ANNE   Now, Master Slender.

SLENDER   Now, good Mistress Anne.

ANNE   What is your will?   55

SLENDER   My will? Od's heartlings, that's a pretty jest
indeed! I ne'er made my will yet, I thank heaven: I am
not such a sickly creature, I give heaven praise.

ANNE   I mean, Master Slender, what would you with
me?   60

SLENDER   Truly, for mine own part, I would little or
nothing with you. Your father and my uncle hath
made motions. If it be my luck, so; if not, happy man
be his dole! They can tell you how things go, better
than I can. You may ask your father; here he comes.   65

Enter PAGE *and* MISTRESS PAGE.

PAGE   Now, Master Slender; love him, daughter Anne. –
Why, how now, what does Master Fenton here?
You wrong me, sir, thus still to haunt my house.
I told you, sir, my daughter is disposed of.

FENTON   Nay, Master Page, be not impatient.   70

MISTRESS PAGE
Good Master Fenton, come not to my child.

PAGE   She is no match for you.

FENTON   Sir, will you hear me?

PAGE   No, good Master Fenton.
Come, Master Shallow; come, son Slender; in.
Knowing my mind, you wrong me, Master Fenton.   75
Exeunt Page, Shallow and Slender.

QUICKLY   Speak to Mistress Page.

FENTON

Good Mistress Page, for that I love your daughter
In such a righteous fashion as I do,
Perforce, against all checks, rebukes and manners,
80 I must advance the colours of my love,
And not retire. Let me have your good will.

ANNE   Good mother, do not marry me to yond fool.

MISTRESS PAGE

I mean it not; I seek you a better husband.

QUICKLY [*aside*]   That's my master, Master Doctor.

85 ANNE   Alas, I had rather be set quick i'th' earth, And
bowl'd to death with turnips!

MISTRESS PAGE

Come, trouble not yourself. Good Master Fenton,
I will not be your friend nor enemy.
My daughter will I question how she loves you,
90 And as I find her, so am I affected.
Till then, farewell, sir; she must needs go in;
Her father will be angry.

FENTON   Farewell, gentle mistress; farewell, Nan.

Exeunt Mistress Page and Anne.

QUICKLY   This is my doing now. 'Nay', said I, 'will you
95 cast away your child on a fool, and a physician? Look
on Master Fenton.' This is my doing.

FENTON   I thank thee; and I pray thee, once to-night
Give my sweet Nan this ring. There's for thy pains.

QUICKLY   Now heaven send thee good fortune!

Exit Fenton.

100 A kind heart he hath: a woman would run through fire
and water for such a kind heart. But yet I would my
master had Mistress Anne; or I would Master Slender
had her; or, in sooth, I would Master Fenton had her.
I will do what I can for them all three, for so I have
105 promised, and I'll be as good as my word, but
speciously for Master Fenton. Well, I must of another
errand to Sir John Falstaff from my two mistresses;
what a beast am I to slack it!   *Exit.*

3.5   *Enter* FALSTAFF.

FALSTAFF   Bardolph, I say!

Enter BARDOLPH.

BARDOLPH   Here, sir.

FALSTAFF   Go fetch me a quart of sack; put a toast in't.

Exit Bardolph.

5 Have I lived to be carried in a basket, like a barrow of
butcher's offal, and to be thrown in the Thames? Well,
if I be served such another trick, I'll have my brains
ta'en out and buttered, and give them to a dog for a
New Year's gift. The rogues slighted me into the river
with as little remorse as they would have drowned a
10 blind bitch's puppies, fifteen i'th' litter; and you may
know by my size that I have a kind of alacrity in
sinking: if the bottom were as deep as hell, I should
down. I had been drowned but that the shore was
shelvy and shallow – a death that I abhor: for the water

swells a man; and what a thing should I have been 15
when I had been swelled! I should have been a
mountain of mummy.

Enter BARDOLPH *with sack.*

BARDOLPH   Here's Mistress Quickly, sir, to speak with
you.

FALSTAFF   Come, let me pour in some sack to the 20
Thames water: for my belly's as cold as if I had
swallowed snowballs for pills to cool the reins. Call her
in.

BARDOLPH   Come in, woman!

Enter MISTRESS QUICKLY.

QUICKLY   By your leave; I cry you mercy. Give your 25
worship good morrow.

FALSTAFF   Take away these chalices. Go brew me a
pottle of sack finely.

BARDOLPH   With eggs, sir?

FALSTAFF   Simple of itself; I'll no pullet-sperm in my 30
brewage.   *Exit Bardolph.*
How now?

MISTRESS QUICKLY   Marry, sir, I come to your worship
from Mistress Ford.

FALSTAFF   Mistress Ford! I have had ford enough; I was 35
thrown into the ford; I have my belly full of ford.

QUICKLY   Alas the day, good heart, that was not her
fault! She does so take on with her men; they mistook
their erection.

FALSTAFF   So did I mine, to build upon a foolish 40
woman's promise.

QUICKLY   Well, she laments, sir, for it, that it would
yearn your heart to see it. Her husband goes this
morning a-birding; she desires you once more to come
to her, between eight and nine. I must carry her word 45
quickly; she'll make you amends, I warrant you.

FALSTAFF   Well, I will visit her; tell her so. And bid her
think what a man is; let her consider his frailty, and
then judge of my merit.

QUICKLY   I will tell her.   50

FALSTAFF   Do so. Between nine and ten, sayst thou?

QUICKLY   Eight and nine, sir.

FALSTAFF   Well, be gone; I will not miss her.

QUICKLY   Peace be with you, sir.   *Exit.*

FALSTAFF   I marvel I hear not of Master Brook; he sent 55
me word to stay within. I like his money well. – O,
here he comes.

Enter FORD *as* BROOK.

FORD   Bless you, sir!

FALSTAFF   Now, Master Brook, you come to know what
hath passed between me and Ford's wife?   60

FORD   That, indeed, Sir John, is my business.

FALSTAFF   Master Brook, I will not lie to you: I was at
her house the hour she appointed me.

FORD   And sped you, sir?

65 FALSTAFF   Very ill-favouredly, Master Brook.

FORD   How so, sir? Did she change her determination?

FALSTAFF   No, Master Brook, but the peaking cornuto
her husband, Master Brook, dwelling in a continual
larum of jealousy, comes me in the instant of our
70 encounter, after we had embraced, kissed, protested,
and, as it were, spoke the prologue of our comedy;
and at his heels a rabble of his companions, thither
provoked and instigated by his distemper, and,
forsooth, to search his house for his wife's love.

75 FORD   What, while you were there?

FALSTAFF   While I was there.

FORD   And did he search for you, and could not find
you?

FALSTAFF   You shall hear. As good luck would have it,
80 comes in one Mistress Page; gives intelligence of
Ford's approach; and, in her invention and Ford's
wife's distraction, they conveyed me into a buck-
basket –

FORD   A buck-basket?

85 FALSTAFF   Yes, a buck-basket! – rammed me in with foul
shirts and smocks, socks, foul stockings, greasy
napkins, that, Master Brook, there was the rankest
compound of villainous smell that ever offended
nostril.

90 FORD   And how long lay you there?

FALSTAFF   Nay, you shall hear, Master Brook, what I
have suffered to bring this woman to evil, for your
good. Being thus crammed in the basket, a couple of
Ford's knaves, his hinds, were called forth by their
95 mistress to carry me in the name of foul clothes to
Datchet Lane; they took me on their shoulders; met
the jealous knave their master in the door, who asked
them once or twice what they had in their basket. I
quaked for fear lest the lunatic knave would have
100 searched it; but fate, ordaining he should be a cuckold,
held his hand. Well, on went he for a search, and away
went I for foul clothes. But mark the sequel, Master
Brook: I suffered the pangs of three several deaths.
First, an intolerable fright, to be detected with a
105 jealous rotten bell-wether; next, to be compassed like
a good bilbo in the circumference of a peck, hilt to
point, heel to head; and then to be stopped in like a
strong distillation with stinking clothes that fretted in
their own grease – think of that – a man of my kidney
110 – think of that – that am as subject to heat as butter; a
man of continual dissolution and thaw: it was a miracle
to 'scape suffocation. And in the height of this bath,
when I was more than half stewed in grease, like a
Dutch dish, to be thrown into the Thames and cooled,
115 glowing hot, in that surge, like a horse-shoe – think of
that – hissing hot – think of that, Master Brook!

FORD   In good sadness, sir, I am sorry that for my sake
you have suffered all this. My suit, then, is desperate:
you'll undertake her no more?

120 FALSTAFF   Master Brook, I will be thrown into Etna, as

I have been into Thames, ere I will leave her thus. Her
husband is this morning gone a-birding; I have
received from her another embassy of meeting. 'Twixt
eight and nine is the hour, Master Brook.

FORD   'Tis past eight already, sir.   125

FALSTAFF   Is it? I will then address me to my
appointment. Come to me at your convenient leisure
and you shall know how I speed; and the conclusion
shall be crowned with your enjoying her. Adieu. You
shall have her, Master Brook; Master Brook, you shall   130
cuckold Ford.   *Exit.*

FORD   Hum! Ha! Is this a vision? Is this a dream? Do I
sleep? Master Ford, awake; awake, Master Ford:
there's a hole made in your best coat, Master Ford.
This 'tis to be married; this 'tis to have linen and   135
buck-baskets! Well, I will proclaim myself what I
am. I will now take the lecher; he is at my house; he
cannot 'scape me; 'tis impossible he should; he cannot
creep into a halfpenny purse, nor into a pepper-box;
but, lest the devil that guides him should aid him, I   140
will search impossible places. Though what I am I
cannot avoid, yet to be what I would not shall not
make me tame: if I have horns to make one mad, let
the proverb go with me – I'll be horn-mad.   *Exit.*

4.1   *Enter* MISTRESS PAGE,
              MISTRESS QUICKLY *and* WILLIAM.

MISTRESS PAGE   Is he at Master Ford's already, think'st
thou?

QUICKLY   Sure he is by this, or will be presently; but
truly he is very courageous mad about his throwing
into the water. Mistress Ford desires you to come   5
suddenly.

MISTRESS PAGE   I'll be with her by and by: I'll but bring
my young man here to school. Look, where his master
comes; 'tis a playing-day, I see.

              Enter EVANS.

How now, Sir Hugh, no school to-day?   10

EVANS   No; Master Slender is let the boys leave to play.

QUICKLY   Blessing of his heart!

MISTRESS PAGE   Sir Hugh, my husband says my son
profits nothing in the world at his book. I pray you,
ask him some questions in his accidence.   15

EVANS   Come hither, William. Hold up your head;
come.

MISTRESS PAGE   Come on, sirrah, hold up your head.
Answer your master, be not afraid.

EVANS   William, how many numbers is in nouns?   20

WILLIAM PAGE   Two.

QUICKLY   Truly I thought there had been one number
more, because they say 'Od's nouns'.

EVANS   Peace your tattlings! What is 'fair', William?

WILLIAM PAGE   *Pulcher.*   25

QUICKLY   Polecats? There are fairer things than
polecats, sure.

EVANS　You are a very simplicity 'oman: I pray you, peace. – What is *lapis*, William?

30　WILLIAM PAGE　A stone.

EVANS　And what is 'a stone', William?

WILLIAM PAGE　A pebble.

EVANS　No, it is *lapis*: I pray you remember in your prain.

WILLIAM PAGE　*Lapis*.

35　EVANS　That is a good William. What is he, William, that does lend articles?

WILLIAM PAGE　Articles are borrowed of the pronoun, and be thus declined: *Singulariter nominativo hic, haec, hoc.*

EVANS　*Nominativo hig, hag, hog.* Pray you mark: *genitivo*

40　*huius.* Well, what is your accusative case?

WILLIAM PAGE　*Accusativo hinc.*

EVANS　I pray you have your remembrance, child: *accusativo hing, hang, hog.*

QUICKLY　'Hang-hog' is Latin for bacon, I warrant you.

45　EVANS　Leave your prabbles, 'oman. – What is the focative case, William?

WILLIAM PAGE　*O – vocativo, O.*

EVANS　Remember, William: focative is *caret.*

QUICKLY　And that's a good root.

50　EVANS　'Oman, forbear.

MISTRESS PAGE　Peace.

EVANS　What is your genitive case plural, William?

WILLIAM PAGE　Genitive case?

EVANS　Ay.

55　WILLIAM PAGE　Genitive *horum, harum, horum.*

QUICKLY　Vengeance of Ginny's case; fie on her! Never name her, child, if she be a whore.

EVANS　For shame, 'oman.

QUICKLY　You do ill to teach the child such words. – He

60　teaches him to hick and to hack, which they'll do fast enough of themselves, and to call 'horum' – fie upon you!

EVANS　'Oman, art thou lunatics? Hast thou no understandings for thy cases, and the numbers of the

65　genders? Thou art as foolish Christian creatures as I would desires.

MISTRESS PAGE　[*to Quickly*]　Prithee hold thy peace.

EVANS　Show me now, William, some declensions of your pronouns.

70　WILLIAM PAGE　Forsooth, I have forgot.

EVANS　It is *qui, quae, quod*: if you forget your *quies*, your *quaes*, and your *quods*, you must be preeches. Go your ways, and play; go.

MISTRESS PAGE　He is a better scholar than I thought

75　he was.

EVANS　He is a good sprag memory. Farewell, Mistress Page.

MISTRESS PAGE　Adieu, good Sir Hugh.　　　*Exit Evans.*
Get you home, boy. Come, we stay too long.　*Exeunt.*

4.2　　*Enter* FALSTAFF *and* MISTRESS FORD.

FALSTAFF　Mistress Ford, your sorrow hath eaten up my sufferance. I see you are obsequious in your love, and I profess requital to a hair's breadth, not only, Mistress Ford, in the simple office of love, but in all the accoutrement, complement, and ceremony of it. 5 But are you sure of your husband now?

MISTRESS FORD　He's a-birding, sweet Sir John.

MISTRESS PAGE　[*within*]　What ho, gossip Ford! What ho!

MISTRESS FORD　Step into th' chamber, Sir John.
　　　　　　　　　　　　　　　　　　　　Exit Falstaff.

Enter MISTRESS PAGE.

MISTRESS PAGE　How now, sweetheart, who's at home 10 besides yourself?

MISTRESS FORD　Why, none but mine own people.

MISTRESS PAGE　Indeed?

MISTRESS FORD　No, certainly. – [*aside to her*] Speak louder. 15

MISTRESS PAGE　Truly, I am so glad you have nobody here.

MISTRESS FORD　Why?

MISTRESS PAGE　Why, woman, your husband is in his old lines again: he so takes on yonder with my husband; so 20 rails against all married mankind; so curses all Eve's daughters, of what complexion soever; and so buffets himself on the forehead, crying, 'Peer out, peer out!', that any madness I ever yet beheld seemed but tameness, civility, and patience to this his distemper he 25 is in now. I am glad the fat knight is not here.

MISTRESS FORD　Why, does he talk of him?

MISTRESS PAGE　Of none but him, and swears he was carried out, the last time he searched for him, in a basket; protests to my husband he is now here, and 30 hath drawn him and the rest of their company from their sport, to make another experiment of his suspicion. But I am glad the knight is not here; now he shall see his own foolery.

MISTRESS FORD　How near is he, Mistress Page? 35

MISTRESS PAGE　Hard by, at street end; he will be here anon.

MISTRESS FORD　I am undone: the knight is here.

MISTRESS PAGE　Why, then, you are utterly shamed, and he's but a dead man. What a woman are you? Away 40 with him, away with him; better shame than murder.

MISTRESS FORD　Which way should he go? How should I bestow him? Shall I put him into the basket again?

Enter FALSTAFF.

FALSTAFF　No, I'll come no more i'th' basket. May I not go out ere he come? 45

MISTRESS PAGE　Alas, three of Master Ford's brothers watch the door with pistols, that none shall issue out; otherwise you might slip away ere he came. But what make you here?

FALSTAFF　What shall I do? I'll creep up into the 50 chimney.

MISTRESS FORD　There they always use to discharge their birding-pieces. Creep into the kill-hole.

FALSTAFF　Where is it?

55 MISTRESS FORD   He will seek there, on my word. Neither press, coffer, chest, trunk, well, vault, but he hath an abstract for the remembrance of such places and goes to them by his note. There is no hiding you in the house.

60 FALSTAFF   I'll go out, then.

MISTRESS PAGE   If you go out in your own semblance, you die, Sir John – unless you go out disguised.

MISTRESS FORD   How might we disguise him?

MISTRESS PAGE   Alas the day, I know not: there is no
65 woman's gown big enough for him; otherwise he might put on a hat, a muffler, and a kerchief, and so escape.

FALSTAFF   Good hearts, devise something: any extremity rather than a mischief.

70 MISTRESS FORD   My maid's aunt, the fat woman of Brainford, has a gown above.

MISTRESS PAGE   On my word, it will serve him. She's as big as he is; and there's her thrummed hat, and her muffler too. Run up, Sir John.

75 MISTRESS FORD   Go, go, sweet Sir John; Mistress Page and I will look some linen for your head.

MISTRESS PAGE   Quick, quick! We'll come dress you straight; put on the gown the while.   *Exit Falstaff.*

MISTRESS FORD   I would my husband would meet him
80 in this shape. He cannot abide the old woman of Brainford; he swears she's a witch, forbade her my house, and hath threatened to beat her.

MISTRESS PAGE   Heaven guide him to thy husband's cudgel; and the devil guide his cudgel afterwards!

85 MISTRESS FORD   But is my husband coming?

MISTRESS PAGE   Ay, in good sadness, is he, and talks of the basket too, howsoever he hath had intelligence.

MISTRESS FORD   We'll try that: for I'll appoint my men to carry the basket again, to meet him at the door with
90 it, as they did last time.

MISTRESS PAGE   Nay, but he'll be here presently; let's go dress him like the witch of Brainford.

MISTRESS FORD   I'll first direct my men what they shall do with the basket. Go up; I'll bring linen for him
95 straight.

MISTRESS PAGE   Hang him, dishonest varlet, we cannot misuse him enough.
     We'll leave a proof, by that which we will do,
     Wives may be merry and yet honest too.
100 We do not act that often jest and laugh;
     'Tis old, but true: 'Still swine eats all the draff'.
                                                        Exit.

Enter JOHN *and* ROBERT.

MISTRESS FORD   Go, sirs, take the basket again on your shoulders. Your master is hard at door; if he bid you set it down, obey him. Quickly, dispatch.   *Exit.*
105 JOHN   Come, come, take it up.

ROBERT   Pray heaven it be not full of knight again.

JOHN   I hope not; I had as lief bear so much lead.

Enter FORD, PAGE, SHALLOW, CAIUS *and* EVANS.

FORD   Ay, but if it prove true, Master Page, have you any way then to unfool me again? – Set down the basket, villain! Somebody call my wife. Youth in a basket! O
110 you pandarly rascals, there's a knot, a ging, a pack, a conspiracy against me. Now shall the devil be shamed. – What, wife, I say! Come, come forth: behold what honest clothes you send forth to bleaching!

PAGE   Why, this passes, Master Ford; you are not to go
115 loose any longer, you must be pinioned.

EVANS   Why, this is lunatics; this is mad as a mad dog.

SHALLOW   Indeed, Master Ford, this is not well, indeed.

FORD   So say I too, sir.

Enter MISTRESS FORD.

Come hither, Mistress Ford – Mistress Ford, the
120 honest woman, the modest wife, the virtuous creature, that hath the jealous fool to her husband! I suspect without cause, mistress, do I?

MISTRESS FORD   Heaven be my witness you do, if you suspect me in any dishonesty.
125 FORD   Well said, brazen-face, hold it out. – Come forth, sirrah! [*pulling clothes out of the basket*]

PAGE   This passes!

MISTRESS FORD   Are you not ashamed? Let the clothes alone.
130 FORD   I shall find you anon.

EVANS   'Tis unreasonable; will you take up your wife's clothes? Come, away.

FORD   Empty the basket, I say!

MISTRESS FORD   Why, man, why?
135 FORD   Master Page, as I am a man, there was one conveyed out of my house yesterday in this basket: why may not he be there again? In my house I am sure he is; my intelligence is true, my jealousy is reasonable. Pluck me out all the linen.
140 MISTRESS FORD   If you find a man there, he shall die a flea's death.

PAGE   Here's no man.

SHALLOW   By my fidelity, this is not well, Master Ford; this wrongs you.
145 EVANS   Master Ford, you must pray, and not follow the imaginations of your own heart: this is jealousies.

FORD   Well, he's not here I seek for.

PAGE   No, nor nowhere else but in your brain.

FORD   Help to search my house this one time. If I find
150 not what I seek, show no colour for my extremity; let me for ever be your table-sport; let them say of me, 'As jealous as Ford, that searched a hollow walnut for his wife's leman'. Satisfy me once more; once more search with me.
155 *Exeunt John and Robert with the basket.*

MISTRESS FORD   What, ho, Mistress Page, come you and the old woman down; my husband will come into the chamber.

FORD   Old woman? What old woman's that?

MISTRESS FORD   Why, it is my maid's aunt of Brainford.

FORD   A witch, a quean, an old cozening quean! Have I
not forbid her my house? She comes of errands,
does she? We are simple men; we do not know what's
brought to pass under the profession of fortune-
telling. She works by charms, by spells, by th' figure,
and such daubery as this is, beyond our element; we
know nothing. Come down, you witch, you hag, you;
come down, I say!

MISTRESS FORD   Nay, good, sweet husband! – Good
gentlemen, let him not strike the old woman.

Enter FALSTAFF *in woman's clothes, and* MISTRESS PAGE.

MISTRESS PAGE   Come, Mother Prat, come, give me your
hand.

FORD   I'll prat her. [*beating him*] Out of my door, you
witch, you rag, you baggage, you polecat, you
runnion, out, out! I'll conjure you, I'll fortune-tell
you.   *Exit Falstaff.*

MISTRESS PAGE   Are you not ashamed? I think you have
killed the poor woman.

MISTRESS FORD   Nay, he will do it. 'Tis a goodly credit
for you!

FORD   Hang her, witch!

EVANS   By yea and no, I think the 'oman is a witch
indeed. I like not when a 'oman has a great peard; I spy
a great peard under his muffler.

FORD   Will you follow, gentlemen? I beseech you,
follow; see but the issue of my jealousy; if I cry out
thus upon no trail, never trust me when I open
again.

PAGE   Let's obey his humour a little further: come
gentlemen.

Exeunt Ford, Page, Shallow, Caius and Evans.

MISTRESS PAGE   Trust me, he beat him most pitifully.

MISTRESS FORD   Nay, by th' mass, that he did not: he
beat him most unpitifully, methought.

MISTRESS PAGE   I'll have the cudgel hallowed and hung
o'er the altar; it hath done meritorious service.

MISTRESS FORD   What think you: may we, with the
warrant of womanhood and the witness of a good
conscience, pursue him with any further revenge?

MISTRESS PAGE   The spirit of wantonness is sure scared
out of him; if the devil have him not in fee-simple,
with fine and recovery, he will never, I think, in the
way of waste attempt us again.

MISTRESS FORD   Shall we tell our husbands how we have
served him?

MISTRESS PAGE   Yes, by all means – if it be but to scrape
the figures out of your husband's brains. If they can
find in their hearts the poor unvirtuous fat knight
shall be any further afflicted, we two will still be the
ministers.

MISTRESS FORD   I'll warrant they'll have him publicly
shamed; and methinks there would be no period to the
jest should he not be publicly shamed.

MISTRESS PAGE   Come, to the forge with it, then; shape
it: I would not have things cool.   *Exeunt.*

4.3   *Enter* Host *and* BARDOLPH.

BARDOLPH   Sir, the German desires to have three of
your horses: the Duke himself will be to-morrow at
court, and they are going to meet him.

HOST   What duke should that be comes so secretly? I
hear not of him in the court. Let me speak with the
gentlemen. They speak English?

BARDOLPH   Ay, sir; I'll call him to you.

HOST   They shall have my horses, but I'll make them
pay; I'll sauce them. They have had my house a week
at command; I have turned away my other guests.
They must come off; I'll sauce them. Come.   *Exeunt.*

4.4   *Enter* PAGE, FORD, MISTRESS PAGE,
MISTRESS FORD *and* EVANS.

EVANS   'Tis one of the best discretions of a 'oman as ever
I did look upon.

PAGE   And did he send you both these letters at an
instant?

MISTRESS PAGE   Within a quarter of an hour.

FORD   Pardon me, wife. Henceforth do what thou wilt:
I rather will suspect the sun with cold
Than thee with wantonness; now doth thy honour
stand,
In him that was of late an heretic,
As firm as faith.

PAGE   'Tis well, 'tis well; no more.
Be not as extreme in submission
As in offence.
But let our plot go forward: let our wives
Yet once again, to make us public sport,
Appoint a meeting with this old fat fellow,
Where we may take him, and disgrace him for it.

FORD   There is no better way than that they spoke of.

PAGE   How? To send him word they'll meet him in the
Park at midnight? Fie, fie, he'll never come.

EVANS   You say he has been thrown in the rivers, and has
been grievously peaten, as an old 'oman: methinks
there should be terrors in him that he should not
come; methinks his flesh is punished, he shall have no
desires.

PAGE   So think I too.

MISTRESS FORD
Devise but how you'll use him when he comes,
And let us two devise to bring him thither.

MISTRESS PAGE
There is an old tale goes that Herne the hunter,
Sometime a keeper here in Windsor Forest,
Doth all the winter-time, at still midnight,
Walk round about an oak, with great ragg'd horns,
And there he blasts the tree, and takes the cattle,
And makes milch-kine yield blood, and shakes a
chain

In a most hideous and dreadful manner.

35   You have heard of such a spirit, and well you know
     The superstitious idle-headed eld
     Receiv'd, and did deliver to our age,
     This tale of Herne the hunter for a truth.
PAGE   Why, yet there want not many that do fear
40   In deep of night to walk by this Herne's oak.
     But what of this?
MISTRESS FORD   Marry, this is our device,
     That Falstaff at that oak shall meet with us.
PAGE   Well, let it not be doubted but he'll come;
     And in this shape when you have brought him
          thither,
45   What shall be done with him? What is your plot?
MISTRESS PAGE
     That likewise have we thought upon, and thus:
     Nan Page (my daughter) and my little son
     And three or four more of their growth we'll dress
     Like urchins, ouphs, and fairies, green and white,
50   With rounds of waxen tapers on their heads,
     And rattles in their hands; upon a sudden,
     As Falstaff, she, and I are newly met,
     Let them from forth a sawpit rush at once
     With some diffused song; upon their sight,
55   We two in great amazedness will fly;
     Then let them all encircle him about,
     And fairy-like to pinch the unclean knight,
     And ask him why, that hour of fairy revel,
     In their so sacred paths he dares to tread
     In shape profane.
60 MISTRESS FORD   And till he tell the truth,
     Let the supposed fairies pinch him sound,
     And burn him with their tapers.
MISTRESS PAGE   The truth being known,
     We'll all present ourselves, dis-horn the spirit,
     And mock him home to Windsor.
FORD   The children must
65   Be practis'd well to this, or they'll ne'er do 't.
EVANS   I will teach the children their behaviours; and I
     will be like a jack-an-apes also, to burn the knight with
     my taber.
FORD   That will be excellent. I'll go buy them vizards.
MISTRESS PAGE
70   My Nan shall be the queen of all the fairies,
     Finely attired in a robe of white.
PAGE   That silk will I go buy. – [*aside*] And in that time
     Shall Master Slender steal my Nan away,
     And marry her at Eton. – Go, send to Falstaff
          straight.
75 FORD   Nay, I'll to him again in name of Brook;
     He'll tell me all his purpose. Sure, he'll come.
MISTRESS PAGE   Fear not you that. Go get us properties
     And tricking for our fairies.
EVANS   Let us about it: it is admirable pleasures and fery
80   honest knaveries.   *Exeunt Page, Ford and Evans.*
MISTRESS PAGE   Go, Mistress Ford,
     Send quickly to Sir John to know his mind.

                                         Exit Mistress Ford.

     I'll to the Doctor, he hath my good will,
     And none but he to marry with Nan Page.
     That Slender, though well landed, is an idiot;   85
     And he my husband best of all affects.
     The Doctor is well money'd, and his friends
     Potent at court: he, none but he, shall have her,
     Though twenty thousand worthier come to crave her.
                                              Exit.

4.5   *Enter* Host *and* SIMPLE.

HOST   What wouldst thou have, boor? What, thick-skin?
     Speak, breathe, discuss; brief, short, quick, snap.
SIMPLE   Marry, sir, I come to speak with Sir John
     Falstaff from Master Slender.
HOST   There's his chamber, his house, his castle, his   5
     standing-bed, and truckle-bed; 'tis painted about
     with the story of the Prodigal, fresh and new. Go,
     knock and call; he'll speak like an Anthropophaginian
     unto thee; knock, I say.
SIMPLE   There's an old woman, a fat woman, gone up   10
     into his chamber. I'll be so bold as stay, sir, till she
     come down; I come to speak with her, indeed.
HOST   Ha? A fat woman? The knight may be robbed;
     I'll call. – Bully knight, bully Sir John! Speak from
     thy lungs military. Art thou there? It is thine host,   15
     thine Ephesian, calls.
FALSTAFF [*above*]   How now, mine host?
HOST   Here's a Bohemian-Tartar tarries the coming
     down of thy fat woman. Let her descend, bully, let
     her descend; my chambers are honourable. Fie!   20
     Privacy? Fie!
                    Enter FALSTAFF.
FALSTAFF   There was, mine host, an old fat woman even
     now with me, but she's gone.
SIMPLE   Pray you, sir, was't not the wise woman of
     Brainford?   25
FALSTAFF   Ay, marry, was it, mussel-shell: what would
     you with her?
SIMPLE   My master, sir, my master Slender, sent to her,
     seeing her go thorough the streets, to know, sir,
     whether one Nym, sir, that beguiled him of a chain,   30
     had the chain or no.
FALSTAFF   I spake with the old woman about it.
SIMPLE   And what says she, I pray, sir?
FALSTAFF   Marry, she says that the very same man that
     beguiled Master Slender of his chain cozened him of   35
     it.
SIMPLE   I would I could have spoken with the woman
     herself; I had other things to have spoken with her too,
     from him.
FALSTAFF   What are they? Let us know.   40
HOST   Ay, come; quick.
SIMPLE   I may not conceal them, sir.
HOST   Conceal them, or thou diest.
SIMPLE   Why, sir, they were nothing but about Mistress
     Anne Page, to know if it were my master's fortune to   45

have her or no.

FALSTAFF 'Tis, 'tis his fortune.

SIMPLE What, sir?

FALSTAFF To have her, or no. Go; say the woman told
me so.

SIMPLE May I be bold to say so, sir?

FALSTAFF Ay, sir; like who more bold.

SIMPLE I thank your worship; I shall make my master
glad with these tidings.   *Exit.*

HOST Thou art clerkly, thou art clerkly, Sir John. Was
there a wise woman with thee?

FALSTAFF Ay, that there was, mine host; one that hath
taught me more wit than ever I learned before in my
life; and I paid nothing for it neither, but was paid for
my learning.

Enter BARDOLPH.

BARDOLPH Out, alas sir, cozenage, mere cozenage!

HOST Where be my horses? Speak well of them,
varletto.

BARDOLPH Run away with the cozeners: for so soon as I
came beyond Eton, they threw me off, from behind
one of them, in a slough of mire; and set spurs and
away, like three German devils, three Doctor
Faustuses.

HOST They are gone but to meet the Duke, villain; do
not say they be fled. Germans are honest men.

Enter EVANS.

EVANS Where is mine host?

HOST What is the matter, sir?

EVANS Have a care of your entertainments: there is a
friend of mine come to town tells me there is three
cozen-Germans that has cozened all the hosts of
Readins, of Maidenhead, of Colebrook, of horses and
money. I tell you for good will, look you; you are wise,
and full of gibes and vlouting-stocks, and 'tis not
convenient you should be cozened. Fare you well.
                                            Exit.

Enter CAIUS.

CAIUS Vere is mine host de Jarteer?

HOST Here, Master Doctor, in perplexity and doubtful
dilemma.

CAIUS I cannot tell vat is dat; but it is tell-a me dat you
make grand preparation for a Duke de Jamanie: by my
trot, dere is no Duke that the court is know to come.
I tell you for good will; adieu.   *Exit.*

HOST Hue and cry, villain, go! – Assist me, knight, I am
undone! – Fly, run, hue and cry, villain, I am
undone!   *Exeunt Host and Bardolph.*

FALSTAFF I would all the world might be cozened, for I
have been cozened and beaten too. If it should come to
the ear of the court how I have been transformed, and
how my transformation hath been washed and
cudgelled, they would melt me out of my fat drop by
drop, and liquor fishermen's boots with me; I

warrant they would whip me with their fine wits till I
were as crest-fallen as a dried pear. I never prospered
since I forswore myself at primero. Well, if my wind
were but long enough, I would repent.

Enter MISTRESS QUICKLY.

Now, whence come you?   100

QUICKLY From the two parties, forsooth.

FALSTAFF The devil take one party, and his dam the
other, and so they shall be both bestowed. I have
suffered more for their sakes – more than the
villainous inconstancy of man's disposition is able to   105
bear.

QUICKLY And have not they suffered? Yes, I warrant,
speciously one of them: Mistress Ford, good heart, is
beaten black and blue, that you cannot see a white spot
about her.   110

FALSTAFF What tell'st thou me of black and blue? I was
beaten myself into all the colours of the rainbow; and
I was like to be apprehended for the witch of
Brainford. But that my admirable dexterity of wit,
my counterfeiting the action of an old woman,   115
delivered me, the knave constable had set me i'th'
stocks, i'th' common stocks, for a witch.

QUICKLY Sir, let me speak with you in your chamber:
you shall hear how things go and, I warrant, to your
content. Here is a letter will say somewhat. Good   120
hearts, what ado here is to bring you together! Sure,
one of you does not serve heaven well, that you are so
crossed.

FALSTAFF Come up into my chamber.   *Exeunt.*

4.6   *Enter* FENTON *and* Host.

HOST Master Fenton, talk not to me, my mind is heavy.
I will give over all.

FENTON Yet hear me speak. Assist me in my purpose
And, as I am a gentleman, I'll give thee
A hundred pound in gold more than your loss.   5

HOST I will hear you, Master Fenton; and I will, at the
least, keep your counsel.

FENTON From time to time I have acquainted you
With the dear love I bear to fair Anne Page,
Who mutually hath answer'd my affection,   10
So far forth as herself might be her chooser,
Even to my wish. I have a letter from her
Of such contents as you will wonder at,
The mirth whereof so larded with my matter
That neither singly can be manifested   15
Without the show of both. Fat Falstaff
Hath a great scene; the image of the jest
I'll show you here at large. Hark, good mine host.
To-night at Herne's oak, just 'twixt twelve and one,
Must my sweet Nan present the Fairy Queen –   20
The purpose why, is here – in which disguise,
While other jests are something rank on foot,
Her father hath commanded her to slip

25   Away with Slender, and with him at Eton
     Immediately to marry; she hath consented.
     Now, sir, her mother, even strong against that match,
     And firm for Doctor Caius, hath appointed
     That he shall likewise shuffle her away,
30   While other sports are tasking of their minds,
     And at the dean'ry, where a priest attends,
     Straight marry her; to this her mother's plot
     She seemingly obedient likewise hath
     Made promise to the Doctor. Now, thus it rests:
     Her father means she shall be all in white;
35   And in that habit, when Slender sees his time
     To take her by the hand and bid her go,
     She shall go with him: her mother hath intended,
     The better to denote her to the Doctor –
     For they must all be mask'd and vizarded –
40   That quaint in green she shall be loose enrob'd,
     With ribands pendant flaring 'bout her head;
     And when the Doctor spies his vantage ripe,
     To pinch her by the hand, and, on that token,
     The maid hath given consent to go with him.
45 HOST   Which means she to deceive, father or mother?
FENTON   Both, my good host, to go along with me:
     And here it rests – that you'll procure the vicar
     To stay for me at church, 'twixt twelve and one,
     And, in the lawful name of marrying,
50   To give our hearts united ceremony.
HOST   Well, husband your device; I'll to the vicar.
     Bring you the maid, you shall not lack a priest.
FENTON   So shall I evermore be bound to thee;
     Besides, I'll make a present recompense.   *Exeunt.*

5.1   *Enter* FALSTAFF *and* MISTRESS QUICKLY.

FALSTAFF   Prithee no more prattling; go. I'll hold. This
     is the third time; I hope good luck lies in odd numbers.
     Away, go! They say there is divinity in odd numbers,
     either in nativity, chance, or death. Away!
5 QUICKLY   I'll provide you a chain, and I'll do what I can
     to get you a pair of horns.
FALSTAFF   Away, I say, time wears; hold up your head,
     and mince.   *Exit Mistress Quickly.*

Enter FORD *as Brook*

     How now, Master Brook? Master Brook, the matter
     will be known to-night, or never. Be you in the Park
10   about midnight, at Herne's oak, and you shall see
     wonders.
FORD   Went you not to her yesterday, sir, as you told me
     you had appointed?
15 FALSTAFF   I went to her, Master Brook, as you see, like
     a poor old man, but I came from her, Master Brook,
     like a poor old woman. That same knave Ford, her
     husband, hath the finest mad devil of jealousy in him,
     Master Brook, that ever governed frenzy. I will tell
20   you he beat me grievously, in the shape of a woman;

     for in the shape of man, Master Brook, I fear not
     Goliath with a weaver's beam, because I know also
     life is a shuttle. I am in haste; go along with me: I'll
     tell you all, Master Brook. Since I plucked geese,
25   played truant, and whipped top, I knew not what 'twas
     to be beaten, till lately. Follow me; I'll tell you
     strange things of this knave Ford, on whom to-night
     I will be revenged, and I will deliver his wife into
     your hand. Follow. Strange things in hand, Master
     Brook! Follow.   *Exeunt.*   30

5.2   *Enter* PAGE, SHALLOW *and* SLENDER.

PAGE   Come, come, we'll couch i'th' castle-ditch till we
     see the light of our fairies. Remember, son Slender, my
     daughter.
SLENDER   Ay, forsooth; I have spoke with her, and we
     have a nay-word how to know one another: I come to   5
     her in white, and cry 'mum'; she cries 'budget'; and by
     that we know one another.
SHALLOW   That's good too; but what needs either your
     'mum' or her 'budget'? The white will decipher her
     well enough. It hath struck ten o'clock.   10
PAGE   The night is dark; light and spirits will become it
     well. Heaven prosper our sport! No man means evil
     but the devil, and we shall know him by his horns.
     Let's away; follow me.   *Exeunt.*

5.3   *Enter* MISTRESS PAGE, MISTRESS FORD
         and DOCTOR CAIUS.

MISTRESS PAGE   Master doctor, my daughter is in green:
     when you see your time, take her by the hand, away
     with her to the deanery, and dispatch it quickly. Go
     before into the Park; we two must go together.
CAIUS   I know vat I have to do. Adieu.   *Exit.*   5
MISTRESS PAGE   Fare you well, sir. – My husband will
     not rejoice so much at the abuse of Falstaff as he will
     chafe at the Doctor's marrying my daughter; but 'tis
     no matter: better a little chiding than a great deal of
     heartbreak.   10
MISTRESS FORD   Where is Nan now? And her troop of
     fairies? And the Welsh devil Hugh?
MISTRESS PAGE   They are all couched in a pit hard by
     Herne's oak, with obscured lights, which, at the very
     instant of Falstaff's and our meeting, they will at once   15
     display to the night.
MISTRESS FORD   That cannot choose but amaze him.
MISTRESS PAGE   If he be not amazed, he will be mocked;
     if he be amazed, he will every way be mocked.
MISTRESS FORD   We'll betray him finely.   20
MISTRESS PAGE
     Against such lewdsters and their lechery
     Those that betray them do no treachery.
MISTRESS FORD   The hour draws on. To the oak, to the
     oak!   *Exeunt.*

5.4   *Enter* EVANS *disguised and* WILLIAM
            and other children as fairies.

EVANS   Trib, trib, fairies; come; and remember your
parts. Be pold, I pray you; follow me into the pit; and
when I give the watch-'ords, do as I pid you. Come,
come; trib, trib.   *Exeunt.*

5.5   *Enter* FALSTAFF *disguised as Herne*
            wearing a buck's head.

FALSTAFF   The Windsor bell hath struck twelve; the
minute draws on. Now, the hot-blooded gods assist
me! Remember, Jove, thou wast a bull for thy Europa;
love set on thy horns. O powerful love, that in some
respects makes a beast a man; in some other, a man a   5
beast. You were also, Jupiter, a swan for the love of
Leda. O omnipotent love, how near the god drew to
the complexion of a goose! A fault done first in the
form of a beast: O Jove, a beastly fault! And then
another fault in the semblance of a fowl: think on't,   10
Jove, a foul fault! When gods have hot backs, what
shall poor men do? For me, I am here a Windsor
stag, and the fattest, I think, i'th' forest. Send me a
cool rut-time, Jove, or who can blame me to piss my
tallow? – Who comes here? My doe?   15

        Enter MISTRESS FORD *and* MISTRESS PAGE.

MISTRESS FORD   Sir John! Art thou there, my deer, my
male deer?
FALSTAFF   My doe with the black scut? Let the sky rain
potatoes; let it thunder to the tune of 'Greensleeves',
hail kissing-comfits, and snow eringoes; let there   20
come a tempest of provocation, I will shelter me here.
MISTRESS FORD   Mistress Page is come with me,
sweetheart.
FALSTAFF   Divide me like a bribed buck, each a haunch;
I will keep my sides to myself, my shoulders for the   25
fellow of this walk – and my horns I bequeath your
husbands. Am I a woodman, ha? Speak I like Herne
the hunter? Why, now is Cupid a child of
conscience: he makes restitution. As I am a true
spirit, welcome!   [*Noise of horns within.*]   30
MISTRESS PAGE   Alas, what noise?
MISTRESS FORD   Heaven forgive our sins!
FALSTAFF   What should this be?
MISTRESS FORD, MISTRESS PAGE   Away, Away!
                                  They run off.
FALSTAFF   I think the devil will not have me damned,   35
lest the oil that's in me should set hell on fire; he
would never else cross me thus.

  Enter EVANS *disguised as before;* PISTOL *as Hobgoblin;*
  MISTRESS QUICKLY *as the Fairy Queen;* ANNE PAGE
       and Children as fairies with tapers.

QUICKLY   Fairies, black, gray, green, and white,
You moonshine revellers, and shades of night,

You orphan heirs of fixed destiny,   40
Attend your office and your quality.
Crier Hobgoblin, make the fairy oyes.
PISTOL   Elves, list your names; silence, you airy toys.
Cricket, to Windsor chimneys shalt thou leap;
Where fires thou find'st unrak'd and hearths
  unswept,   45
There pinch the maids as blue as bilberry:
Our radiant Queen hates sluts and sluttery.
FALSTAFF
They are fairies; he that speaks to them shall die.
I'll wink and couch: no man their works must eye.
[*Lies face downwards.*]
EVANS
Where's Bead? Go you, and where you find a maid   50
That ere she sleep has thrice her prayers said
Raise up the organs of her fantasy,
Sleep she as sound as careless infancy;
But those as sleep and think not on their sins,
Pinch them, arms, legs, backs, shoulders, sides, and
  shins.   55
QUICKLY   About, about;
Search Windsor Castle, elves, within and out;
Strew good luck, ouphs, on every sacred room
That it may stand till the perpetual doom
In state as wholesome as in state 'tis fit,   60
Worthy the owner, and the owner it;
The several chairs of order look you scour
With juice of balm and every precious flower;
Each fair instalment, coat, and sev'ral crest,
With loyal blazon, evermore be blest;   65
And nightly, meadow-fairies, look you sing,
Like to the Garter's compass, in a ring:
Th' expressure that it bears, green let it be,
More fertile-fresh than all the field to see;
And *Honi soit qui mal y pense* write   70
In em'rald tufts, flowers purple, blue, and white,
Like sapphire, pearl, and rich embroidery
Buckled below fair knighthood's bending knee:
Fairies use flowers for their charactery.
Away, disperse; but till 'tis one o'clock,   75
Our dance of custom round about the oak
Of Herne the hunter, let us not forget.
EVANS
Pray you, lock hand in hand; yourselves in order set;
And twenty glow-worms shall our lanterns be
To guide our measure round about the tree.   80
But, stay, I smell a man of middle earth!
FALSTAFF   Heavens defend me from that Welsh fairy,
lest he transform me to a piece of cheese!
PISTOL
Vile worm, thou wast o'erlook'd even in thy birth.
QUICKLY   With trial-fire touch me his finger-end: 85
If he be chaste, the flame will back descend,
And turn him to no pain; but if he start,
It is the flesh of a corrupted heart.

PISTOL   A trial, come.

EVANS   Come, will this wood take fire?

[*They burn him with their tapers.*]

90 FALSTAFF   Oh, oh, oh!

QUICKLY

Corrupt, corrupt, and tainted in desire!

About him, fairies, sing a scornful rhyme;

And, as you trip, still pinch him to your time.

Song.

Fie on sinful fantasy,

95   Fie on lust and luxury!

Lust is but a bloody fire,

Kindled with unchaste desire,

Fed in heart, whose flames aspire,

As thoughts do blow them, higher and higher.

100   Pinch him, fairies, mutually;

Pinch him for his villainy;

Pinch him, and burn him, and turn him about,

Till candles and starlight and moonshine be out.

During this song they pinch Falstaff. DOCTOR CAIUS
comes one way, and steals away a fairy in green;
SLENDER *another way, and takes off a fairy in white; and*
FENTON *comes, and steals away Anne Page. A noise of
hunting is heard within. The fairies run away. Falstaff
pulls off his buck's head, and rises.*

Enter PAGE, FORD, MISTRESS PAGE *and* MISTRESS FORD.

PAGE

Nay, do not fly; I think we have watch'd you now.

105   Will none but Herne the hunter serve your turn?

MISTRESS PAGE

I pray you, come, hold up the jest no higher.

Now, good Sir John, how like you Windsor wives?

[*pointing to the horns*] See you these, husband? Do not
these fair yokes

Become the forest better than the town?

110 FORD   Now, sir, who's a cuckold now? Master Brook,
Falstaff's a knave, a cuckoldly knave; here are his
horns, Master Brook; and, Master Brook, he hath
enjoyed nothing of Ford's but his buck-basket, his
cudgel, and twenty pounds of money, which must be
115   paid to Master Brook; his horses are arrested for it,
Master Brook.

MISTRESS FORD   Sir John, we have had ill luck: we could
never meet. I will never take you for my love again,
but I will always count you my deer.

120 FALSTAFF   I do begin to perceive that I am made an ass.

FORD   Ay, and an ox too: both the proofs are extant.

FALSTAFF   And these are not fairies? I was three or four
times in the thought they were not fairies; and yet the
guiltiness of my mind, the sudden surprise of my
125   powers, drove the grossness of the foppery into a
received belief, in despite of the teeth of all rhyme
and reason, that they were fairies. See now how wit
may be made a Jack-a-Lent, when 'tis upon ill
employment!

EVANS   Sir John Falstaff, serve Got, and leave your   130
desires, and fairies will not pinse you.

FORD   Well said, fairy Hugh.

EVANS   And leave you your jealousies too, I pray you.

FORD   I will never mistrust my wife again, till thou art
able to woo her in good English.   135

FALSTAFF   Have I laid my brain in the sun and dried it,
that it wants matter to prevent so gross o'er-reaching
as this? Am I ridden with a Welsh goat too? Shall I
have a cockscomb of frieze? 'Tis time I were choked
with a piece of toasted cheese.   140

EVANS   Seese is not good to give putter; your belly is all
putter.

FALSTAFF   'Seese' and 'putter'? Have I lived to stand at
the taunt of one that makes fritters of English? This is
enough to be the decay of lust and late-walking   145
through the realm.

MISTRESS PAGE   Why, Sir John, do you think, though we
would have thrust virtue out of our hearts by the
head and shoulders, and have given ourselves
without scruple to hell, that ever the devil could   150
have made you our delight?

FORD   What, a hodge-pudding? A bag of flax?

MISTRESS PAGE   A puffed man?

PAGE   Old, cold, withered, and of intolerable entrails?

FORD   And one that is as slanderous as Satan?   155

PAGE   And as poor as Job?

FORD   And as wicked as his wife?

EVANS   And given to fornications, and to taverns, and
sack, and wine, and metheglins, and to drinkings, and
swearings, and starings, pribbles and prabbles?   160

FALSTAFF   Well, I am your theme: you have the start of
me. I am dejected; I am not able to answer the Welsh
flannel; ignorance itself is a plummet o'er me; use
me as you will.

FORD   Marry, sir, we'll bring you to Windsor to one   165
Master Brook that you have cozened of money, to
whom you should have been a pandar. Over and
above that you have suffered, I think to repay that
money will be a biting affliction.

PAGE   Yet be cheerful, knight: thou shalt eat a posset   170
to-night at my house, where I will desire thee to
laugh at my wife that now laughs at thee. Tell her
Master Slender hath married her daughter.

MISTRESS PAGE [*aside*]   Doctors doubt that; if Anne Page
be my daughter, she is, by this, Doctor Caius' wife.   175

Enter SLENDER.

SLENDER   Whoa, ho, ho, father Page!

PAGE   Son, how now? How now, son? Have you
dispatched?

SLENDER   Dispatched? I'll make the best in Gloucestershire know on't; would I were hanged, la, else!   180

PAGE   Of what, son?

SLENDER   I came yonder at Eton to marry Mistress
Anne Page, and she's a great lubberly boy. If it had not

been i'th' church, I would have swinged him, or he
should have swinged me. If I did not think it had
been Anne Page, would I might never stir – and 'tis a
postmaster's boy!

PAGE   Upon my life, then, you took the wrong.

SLENDER   What need you tell me that? I think so, when
I took a boy for a girl. If I had been married to him,
for all he was in woman's apparel, I would not have
had him.

PAGE   Why, this is your own folly. Did not I tell you how
you should know my daughter by her garments?

SLENDER   I went to her in white, and cried 'mum', and
she cried 'budget', as Anne and I had appointed; and
yet it was not Anne, but a postmaster's boy.

MISTRESS PAGE   Good George, be not angry: I knew of
your purpose, turned my daughter into green, and
indeed she is now with the Doctor at the deanery,
and there married.

Enter CAIUS.

CAIUS   Vere is Mistress Page? By gar, I am cozened: I ha'
married *un garçon*, a boy; *un paysan,* by gar; a boy; it is
not Anne Page; by gar, I am cozened.

MISTRESS PAGE   Why, did you take her in green?

CAIUS   Ay, by gar, and 'tis a boy; by gar, I'll raise all
Windsor.   *Exit.*

FORD   This is strange. Who hath got the right Anne?

PAGE   My heart misgives me: here comes Master
Fenton.

Enter FENTON *and* ANNE PAGE.

How now, Master Fenton?

ANNE   Pardon, good father; good my mother, pardon.

PAGE   Now, mistress, how chance you went not with
Master Slender?

MISTRESS PAGE
    Why went you not with Master Doctor, maid?

FENTON   You do amaze her. Hear the truth of it.
    You would have married her most shamefully,
    Where there was no proportion held in love.
    The truth is, she and I, long since contracted,
    Are now so sure that nothing can dissolve us.
    Th' offence is holy that she hath committed,
    And this deceit loses the name of craft,
    Of disobedience, or unduteous title,
    Since therein she doth evitate and shun
    A thousand irreligious cursed hours
    Which forced marriage would have brought upon
      her.

FORD   Stand not amaz'd; here is no remedy.
    In love the heavens themselves do guide the state;
    Money buys lands, and wives are sold by fate.

FALSTAFF   I am glad, though you have ta'en a special
    stand to strike at me, that your arrow hath glanced.

PAGE
    Well, what remedy? Fenton, heaven give thee joy!
    What cannot be eschew'd must be embrac'd.

FALSTAFF
    When night-dogs run, all sorts of deer are chas'd.

MISTRESS PAGE
    Well, I will muse no further. Master Fenton,
    Heaven give you many, many merry days!
    Good husband, let us every one go home,
    And laugh this sport o'er by a country fire,
    Sir John and all.

FORD   Let it be so. – Sir John,
    To Master Brook you yet shall hold your word,
    For he to-night shall lie with Mistress Ford. *Exeunt.*

A Midsummer Night's Dream

This play first appeared in print in 1600 in a text which may possibly be based on an authorial manuscript, since it contains a number of spellings which have been identified as Shakespearean and which might have been normalized by a scribe making a copy. The First Quarto was followed by a second in 1619 (an illicit edition, falsely dated 1600) and then by the First Folio in 1623. *A Midsummer Night's Dream* is listed amongst Shakespeare's comedies by Francis Meres in *Palladis Tamia* (1598) and it is generally thought to date from 1594 or 1595, putting it probably after *Love's Labour's Lost* and more certainly before *The Merchant of Venice* in the chronology of the comedies. It seems to have been written very close in time to *Romeo and Juliet*; the play-within-the-play of 'Pyramus and Thisbe' provides a parody of the ending of that love-tragedy. More surprisingly, perhaps, its lyrical language has stylistic affinities with that of *Richard II*, also written around this time.

A Midsummer Night's Dream is relatively unusual in the Shakespeare canon in not having a readily identifiable main source; rather it assembles heterogeneous materials and links them narratively and thematically. Shakespeare could have read about Theseus in Thomas North's translation of Plutarch's *Lives of the Noble Grecians and Romans* (1579), as well as in Chaucer's *Knight's Tale* (c. 1385), which he also adapted loosely for the plot of the four young lovers. (He was to use this poem again for *The Two Noble Kinsmen* at the very end of his career.) He probably used Arthur Golding's translation of Ovid's *Metamorphoses* (1565) for the story of Pyramus and Thisbe, and he drew on folklore for Puck (Robin Goodfellow) and the fairies. He seems in this play to be thinking about the nature of artistic illusion itself,

notably in Theseus' speech about 'The lunatic, the lover, and the poet' in 5.1 and in the courtiers' comments on the mechanicals' performance. This final scene has parallels with the show of the Nine Worthies at the end of *Love's Labour's Lost*, though Bottom and his colleagues are less perturbed by their unsympathetic audience.

Many scholars and editors have supposed that the play was written to celebrate some aristocratic marriage and performed privately, but there is no external evidence to support this theory, and the title-page of the 1600 Quarto claims that *A Midsummer Night's Dream* had been 'sundry times publicly acted' by the Lord Chamberlain's Men, Shakespeare's regular company. There are few records of pre-Restoration performances, but it became popular in the eighteenth and nineteenth centuries, usually in adapted form with the addition of music and dancing. It has inspired two operas: Henry Purcell's *The Fairy Queen* (1692) and Benjamin Britten's *A Midsummer Night's Dream* (1960); Felix Mendelssohn wrote extensive music for it (1842). The Victorian tradition encumbered the play with lavish spectacle; twentieth-century productions have been less elaborate and have included the revolutionary 1970 version directed by Peter Brook for the Royal Shakespeare Company with its 'white box' set, gymnastic actors and rediscovery of the play's darker side. Films have included a 1935 Hollywood version directed by Max Reinhardt with James Cagney as Bottom, and Woody Allen's more recent adaptation, *A Midsummer Night's Sex Comedy* (1982), which combined the Shakespearean source with influences from Ingmar Bergman's film *Smiles of a Summer Night* (1955).

The Arden text is based on the 1600 First Quarto.

THESEUS	*Duke of Athens*
HIPPOLYTA	*Queen of the Amazons, betrothed to Theseus*
LYSANDER	*young courtiers in love with Hermia*
DEMETRIUS	
HERMIA	*in love with Lysander*
HELENA	*in love with Demetrius*
EGEUS	*Hermia's father*
PHILOSTRATE	*Theseus' Master of the Revels*
OBERON	*King of the Fairies*
TITANIA	*Queen of the Fairies*
FAIRY	*in Titania's service*
PUCK	*or Robin Goodfellow, Oberon's jester and lieutenant*
PEASEBLOSSOM	
COBWEB	*fairies, in Titania's service*
MOTH	
MUSTARDSEED	
Peter QUINCE	*a carpenter;* PROLOGUE *in the Interlude*
Nick BOTTOM	*a weaver;* PYRAMUS *in the Interlude*
Francis FLUTE	*a bellows-mender;* THISBE *in the Interlude*
Tom SNOUT	*a tinker;* WALL *in the Interlude*
SNUG	*a joiner;* LION *in the Interlude*
Robin STARVELING	*a tailor;* MOONSHINE *in the Interlude*

Other Fairies attending on Oberon and Titania
Lords and Attendants to Theseus and Hippolyta

888

A Midsummer Night's Dream

Enter THESEUS, HIPPOLYTA *and* PHILOSTRATE,
with attendants.

THESEUS   Now, fair Hippolyta, our nuptial hour
   Draws on apace; four happy days bring in
   Another moon: but O, methinks, how slow
   This old moon wanes! She lingers my desires,
5   Like to a step-dame or a dowager
   Long withering out a young man's revenue.
HIPPOLYTA
   Four days will quickly steep themselves in night;
   Four nights will quickly dream away the time;
   And then the moon, like to a silver bow
10   New bent in heaven, shall behold the night
   Of our solemnities.
THESEUS   Go, Philostrate,
   Stir up the Athenian youth to merriments;
   Awake the pert and nimble spirit of mirth;
   Turn melancholy forth to funerals;
15   The pale companion is not for our pomp.
                Exit Philostrate.

   Hippolyta, I woo'd thee with my sword,
   And won thy love doing thee injuries;
   But I will wed thee in another key,
   With pomp, with triumph, and with revelling.

    Enter EGEUS *and his daughter* HERMIA,
    and LYSANDER *and* DEMETRIUS.

20 EGEUS   Happy be Theseus, our renowned Duke!
THESEUS
   Thanks, good Egeus. What's the news with thee?
EGEUS   Full of vexation come I, with complaint
   Against my child, my daughter Hermia.
   Stand forth Demetrius. My noble lord,
25   This man hath my consent to marry her.
   Stand forth Lysander. And, my gracious Duke,
   This hath bewitch'd the bosom of my child.
   Thou, thou, Lysander, thou hast given her rhymes,
   And interchang'd love-tokens with my child:
30   Thou hast by moonlight at her window sung
   With faining voice verses of feigning love,
   And stol'n the impression of her fantasy
   With bracelets of thy hair, rings, gauds, conceits,
   Knacks, trifles, nosegays, sweetmeats (messengers
35   Of strong prevailment in unharden'd youth):
   With cunning hast thou filch'd my daughter's heart,
   Turn'd her obedience (which is due to me)
   To stubborn harshness. And, my gracious Duke,
   Be it so she will not here, before your Grace,
40   Consent to marry with Demetrius,
   I beg the ancient privilege of Athens:
   As she is mine, I may dispose of her;
   Which shall be either to this gentleman,
   Or to her death, according to our law
45   Immediately provided in that case.
THESEUS
   What say you, Hermia? Be advis'd, fair maid.

   To you your father should be as a god:
   One that compos'd your beauties, yea, and one
   To whom you are but as a form in wax
   By him imprinted, and within his power   50
   To leave the figure, or disfigure it.
   Demetrius is a worthy gentleman.
HERMIA   So is Lysander.
THESEUS   In himself he is;
   But in this kind, wanting your father's voice,
   The other must be held the worthier.   55
HERMIA   I would my father look'd but with my eyes.
THESEUS
   Rather your eyes must with his judgement look.
HERMIA   I do entreat your Grace to pardon me.
   I know not by what power I am made bold,
   Nor how it may concern my modesty   60
   In such a presence here to plead my thoughts,
   But I beseech your Grace that I may know
   The worst that may befall me in this case,
   If I refuse to wed Demetrius.
THESEUS   Either to die the death, or to abjure   65
   For ever the society of men.
   Therefore, fair Hermia, question your desires,
   Know of your youth, examine well your blood,
   Whether, if you yield not to your father's choice,
   You can endure the livery of a nun,
   For aye to be in shady cloister mew'd,   70
   To live a barren sister all your life,
   Chanting faint hymns to the cold fruitless moon.
   Thrice blessed they that master so their blood
   To undergo such maiden pilgrimage;   75
   But earthlier happy is the rose distill'd
   Than that which, withering on the virgin thorn,
   Grows, lives, and dies, in single blessedness.
HERMIA   So will I grow, so live, so die, my lord,
   Ere I will yield my virgin patent up   80
   Unto his lordship whose unwished yoke
   My soul consents not to give sovereignty.
THESEUS
   Take time to pause; and by the next new moon,
   The sealing-day betwixt my love and me
   For everlasting bond of fellowship,   85
   Upon that day either prepare to die
   For disobedience to your father's will,
   Or else to wed Demetrius, as he would,
   Or on Diana's altar to protest,
   For aye, austerity and single life.   90
DEMETRIUS   Relent, sweet Hermia; and Lysander, yield
   Thy crazed title to my certain right.
LYSANDER   You have her father's love, Demetrius:
   Let me have Hermia's; do you marry him.
EGEUS   Scornful Lysander, true, he hath my love;   95
   And what is mine my love shall render him;
   And she is mine, and all my right of her
   I do estate unto Demetrius.
LYSANDER   I am, my lord, as well deriv'd as he,
   As well possess'd; my love is more than his;   100

My fortunes every way as fairly rank'd,
If not with vantage, as Demetrius';
And, which is more than all these boasts can be,
I am belov'd of beauteous Hermia.
105 Why should not I then prosecute my right?
Demetrius, I'll avouch it to his head,
Made love to Nedar's daughter, Helena,
And won her soul: and she, sweet lady, dotes,
Devoutly dotes, dotes in idolatry,
110 Upon this spotted and inconstant man.
THESEUS I must confess that I have heard so much,
And with Demetrius thought to have spoke thereof;
But, being over-full of self-affairs,
My mind did lose it. But, Demetrius, come,
115 And come, Egeus; you shall go with me:
I have some private schooling for you both.
For you, fair Hermia, look you arm yourself
To fit your fancies to your father's will;
Or else the law of Athens yields you up
120 (Which by no means we may extenuate)
To death, or to a vow of single life.
Come, my Hippolyta; what cheer, my love?
Demetrius and Egeus, go along;
I must employ you in some business
125 Against our nuptial, and confer with you
Of something nearly that concerns yourselves.
EGEUS With duty and desire we follow you.

Exeunt all but Lysander and Hermia.

LYSANDER
How now, my love? Why is your cheek so pale?
How chance the roses there do fade so fast?
130 HERMIA Belike for want of rain, which I could well
Beteem them from the tempest of my eyes.
LYSANDER Ay me! For aught that I could ever read,
Could ever hear by tale or history,
The course of true love never did run smooth;
135 But either it was different in blood –
HERMIA O cross! too high to be enthrall'd to low.
LYSANDER Or else misgraffed in respect of years –
HERMIA O spite! too old to be engag'd to young.
LYSANDER
Or else it stood upon the choice of friends –
140 HERMIA O hell! to choose love by another's eyes.
LYSANDER Or, if there were a sympathy in choice,
War, death, or sickness did lay siege to it,
Making it momentany as a sound,
Swift as a shadow, short as any dream,
145 Brief as the lightning in the collied night,
That, in a spleen, unfolds both heaven and earth,
And, ere a man hath power to say 'Behold!',
The jaws of darkness do devour it up:
So quick bright things come to confusion.
150 HERMIA If then true lovers have been ever cross'd,
It stands as an edict in destiny.
Then let us teach our trial patience,
Because it is a customary cross,
As due to love as thoughts and dreams and sighs,

Wishes and tears, poor fancy's followers. 155
LYSANDER
A good persuasion; therefore hear me, Hermia.
I have a widow aunt, a dowager
Of great revenue, and she hath no child –
From Athens is her house remote seven leagues –
And she respects me as her only son. 160
There, gentle Hermia, may I marry thee,
And to that place the sharp Athenian law
Cannot pursue us. If thou lov'st me then,
Steal forth thy father's house tomorrow night;
And in the wood, a league without the town 165
(Where I did meet thee once with Helena
To do observance to a morn of May),
There will I stay for thee.
HERMIA   My good Lysander,
I swear to thee by Cupid's strongest bow,
By his best arrow with the golden head, 170
By the simplicity of Venus' doves,
By that which knitteth souls and prospers loves,
And by that fire which burn'd the Carthage queen
When the false Trojan under sail was seen;
By all the vows that ever men have broke 175
(In number more than ever women spoke),
In that same place thou hast appointed me,
Tomorrow truly will I meet with thee.
LYSANDER
Keep promise, love. Look, here comes Helena.

Enter HELENA.

HERMIA God speed fair Helena! Whither away? 180
HELENA Call you me fair? That fair again unsay!
Demetrius loves your fair: O happy fair!
Your eyes are lode-stars, and your tongue's sweet air
More tuneable than lark to shepherd's ear,
When wheat is green, when hawthorn buds appear. 185
Sickness is catching; O were favour so,
Yours would I catch, fair Hermia, ere I go:
My ear should catch your voice, my eye your eye,
My tongue should catch your tongue's sweet melody.
Were the world mine, Demetrius being bated, 190
The rest I'd give to be to you translated.
O, teach me how you look, and with what art
You sway the motion of Demetrius' heart.
HERMIA I frown upon him; yet he loves me still.
HELENA
O that your frowns would teach my smiles such skill! 195
HERMIA I give him curses; yet he gives me love.
HELENA O that my prayers could such affection move!
HERMIA The more I hate, the more he follows me.
HELENA The more I love, the more he hateth me.
HERMIA His folly, Helena, is no fault of mine. 200
HELENA
None but your beauty; would that fault were mine!
HERMIA Take comfort: he no more shall see my face;
Lysander and myself will fly this place.
Before the time I did Lysander see,

Seem'd Athens as a paradise to me.
O then what graces in my love do dwell,
That he hath turn'd a heaven unto a hell!
LYSANDER Helen, to you our minds we will unfold:
Tomorrow night, when Phoebe doth behold
Her silver visage in the wat'ry glass,
Decking with liquid pearl the bladed grass
(A time that lovers' flights doth still conceal),
Through Athens' gates have we devis'd to steal.
HERMIA And in the wood, where often you and I
Upon faint primrose beds were wont to lie,
Emptying our bosoms of their counsel sweet,
There my Lysander and myself shall meet;
And thence from Athens turn away our eyes,
To seek new friends, and stranger companies.
Farewell, sweet playfellow; pray thou for us,
And good luck grant thee thy Demetrius!
Keep word, Lysander; we must starve our sight
From lovers' food, till morrow deep midnight.

Exit Hermia.

LYSANDER I will, my Hermia. Helena, adieu;
As you on him, Demetrius dote on you!

Exit Lysander.

HELENA How happy some o'er other some can be!
Through Athens I am thought as fair as she.
But what of that? Demetrius thinks not so;
He will not know what all but he do know;
And as he errs, doting on Hermia's eyes,
So I, admiring of his qualities.
Things base and vile, holding no quantity,
Love can transpose to form and dignity:
Love looks not with the eyes, but with the mind,
And therefore is wing'd Cupid painted blind;
Nor hath Love's mind of any judgement taste:
Wings, and no eyes, figure unheedy haste.
And therefore is Love said to be a child,
Because in choice he is so oft beguil'd.
As waggish boys, in game, themselves forswear,
So the boy Love is perjur'd everywhere;
For, ere Demetrius look'd on Hermia's eyne,
He hail'd down oaths that he was only mine;
And when this hail some heat from Hermia felt,
So he dissolv'd and show'rs of oaths did melt.
I will go tell him of fair Hermia's flight:
Then to the wood will he, tomorrow night,
Pursue her; and for this intelligence
If I have thanks, it is a dear expense.
But herein mean I to enrich my pain,
To have his sight thither and back again.   *Exit.*

1.2   *Enter* QUINCE, *the carpenter; and* SNUG,
        the joiner; and BOTTOM, *the weaver; and* FLUTE,
        the bellows-mender; and SNOUT, *the tinker;*
        and STARVELING, *the tailor.*

QUINCE Is all our company here?
BOTTOM You were best to call them generally, man by
man, according to the scrip.
QUINCE Here is the scroll of every man's name which is
thought fit through all Athens to play in our interlude
before the Duke and the Duchess, on his wedding-day
at night.
BOTTOM First, good Peter Quince, say what the play
treats on; then read the names of the actors; and so
grow to a point.
QUINCE Marry, our play is 'The most lamentable
comedy, and most cruel death of Pyramus and
Thisbe'.
BOTTOM A very good piece of work, I assure you, and a
merry. Now, good Peter Quince, call forth your
actors by the scroll. Masters, spread yourselves.
QUINCE Answer as I call you. Nick Bottom, the weaver?
BOTTOM Ready. Name what part I am for, and proceed.
QUINCE You, Nick Bottom, are set down for Pyramus.
BOTTOM What is Pyramus? A lover, or a tyrant?
QUINCE A lover, that kills himself most gallant for love.
BOTTOM That will ask some tears in the true
performing of it. If I do it, let the audience look to
their eyes: I will move storms, I will condole in some
measure. To the rest – yet my chief humour is for a
tyrant. I could play Ercles rarely, or a part to tear a cat
in, to make all split.

        The raging rocks,
        And shivering shocks,
        Shall break the locks
            Of prison-gates;
        And Phibbus' car
        Shall shine from far
        And make and mar
            The foolish fates.

This was lofty. Now name the rest of the players.
This is Ercles' vein, a tyrant's vein: a lover is more
condoling.
QUINCE Francis Flute, the bellows-mender?
FLUTE Here, Peter Quince.
QUINCE Flute, you must take Thisbe on you.
FLUTE What is Thisbe? A wandering knight?
QUINCE It is the lady that Pyramus must love.
FLUTE Nay, faith, let not me play a woman: I have a
beard coming.
QUINCE That's all one: you shall play it in a mask; and
you may speak as small as you will.
BOTTOM And I may hide my face, let me play Thisbe
too. I'll speak in a monstrous little voice: 'Thisne,
Thisne!' – 'Ah, Pyramus, my lover dear! thy Thisbe
dear, and lady dear!'
QUINCE No, no, you must play Pyramus; and Flute, you
Thisbe.
BOTTOM Well, proceed.
QUINCE Robin Starveling, the tailor?

STARVELING   Here, Peter Quince.

QUINCE   Robin Starveling, you must play Thisbe's mother. Tom Snout, the tinker?

SNOUT   Here, Peter Quince.

QUINCE   You, Pyramus' father; myself, Thisbe's father; Snug the joiner, you the lion's part. And I hope here is a play fitted.

SNUG   Have you the lion's part written? Pray you, if it be, give it me; for I am slow of study.

QUINCE   You may do it extempore, for it is nothing but roaring.

BOTTOM   Let me play the lion too. I will roar, that I will do any man's heart good to hear me. I will roar, that I will make the Duke say: 'Let him roar again; let him roar again!'

QUINCE   And you should do it too terribly, you would fright the Duchess and the ladies, that they would shriek: and that were enough to hang us all.

ALL   That would hang us, every mother's son.

BOTTOM   I grant you, friends, if you should fright the ladies out of their wits, they would have no more discretion but to hang us. But I will aggravate my voice so, that I will roar you as gently as any sucking dove; I will roar you and 'twere any nightingale.

QUINCE   You can play no part but Pyramus: for Pyramus is a sweet-faced man; a proper man as one shall see in a summer's day; a most lovely, gentleman-like man: therefore you must needs play Pyramus.

BOTTOM   Well, I will undertake it. What beard were I best to play it in?

QUINCE   Why, what you will.

BOTTOM   I will discharge it in either your straw-colour beard, your orange-tawny beard, your purple-in-grain beard, or your French-crown-colour beard, your perfect yellow.

QUINCE   Some of your French crowns have no hair at all, and then you will play bare-faced. But, masters, here are your parts; and I am to entreat you, request you, and desire you, to con them by tomorrow night; and meet me in the palace wood, a mile without the town, by moonlight; there will we rehearse, for if we meet in the city, we shall be dogged with company, and our devices known. In the meantime I will draw a bill of properties, such as our play wants. I pray you fail me not.

BOTTOM   We will meet, and there we may rehearse most obscenely and courageously. Take pains, be perfect: adieu!

QUINCE   At the Duke's oak we meet.

BOTTOM   Enough: hold, or cut bow-strings.   *Exeunt.*

2.1   *Enter a* Fairy *at one door, and* PUCK *at another.*

PUCK   How now, spirit! Whither wander you?

FAIRY   Over hill, over dale,
                Thorough bush, thorough briar,
            Over park, over pale,

            Thorough flood, thorough fire,
            I do wander everywhere,
            Swifter than the moon's sphere;
            And I serve the Fairy Queen,
            To dew her orbs upon the green.
            The cowslips tall her pensioners be,
            In their gold coats spots you see;
            Those be rubies, fairy favours,
            In those freckles live their savours.
        I must go seek some dew-drops here,
        And hang a pearl in every cowslip's ear.
    Farewell, thou lob of spirits; I'll be gone;
    Our Queen and all her elves come here anon.

PUCK   The King doth keep his revels here tonight;
    Take heed the Queen come not within his sight;
    For Oberon is passing fell and wrath,
    Because that she as her attendant hath
    A lovely boy, stol'n from an Indian king –
    She never had so sweet a changeling;
    And jealous Oberon would have the child
    Knight of his train, to trace the forests wild:
    But she perforce withholds the loved boy,
    Crowns him with flowers, and makes him all her joy.
    And now they never meet in grove or green,
    By fountain clear, or spangled starlight sheen,
    But they do square; that all their elves for fear
    Creep into acorn-cups, and hide them there.

FAIRY   Either I mistake your shape and making quite,
    Or else you are that shrewd and knavish sprite
    Call'd Robin Goodfellow. Are not you he
    That frights the maidens of the villagery,
    Skim milk, and sometimes labour in the quern,
    And bootless make the breathless housewife churn,
    And sometime make the drink to bear no barm,
    Mislead night-wanderers, laughing at their harm?
    Those that Hobgoblin call you, and sweet Puck,
    You do their work, and they shall have good luck.
    Are not you he?

PUCK   Thou speak'st aright;
    I am that merry wanderer of the night.
    I jest to Oberon, and make him smile
    When I a fat and bean-fed horse beguile,
    Neighing in likeness of a filly foal;
    And sometime lurk I in a gossip's bowl
    In very likeness of a roasted crab,
    And when she drinks, against her lips I bob,
    And on her wither'd dewlap pour the ale.
    The wisest aunt, telling the saddest tale,
    Sometime for three-foot stool mistaketh me;
    Then slip I from her bum, down topples she,
    And 'tailor' cries, and falls into a cough;
    And then the whole quire hold their hips and loffe
    And waxen in their mirth, and neeze, and swear
    A merrier hour was never wasted there.
    But room, fairy! Here comes Oberon.

FAIRY
    And here my mistress. Would that he were gone!

Enter OBERON, *the King of Fairies, at one door, with his train; and* TITANIA, *the Queen, at another, with hers.*

OBERON   Ill met by moonlight, proud Titania.
TITANIA   What, jealous Oberon? Fairies, skip hence;
I have forsworn his bed and company.
OBERON   Tarry, rash wanton; am not I thy lord?
TITANIA   Then I must be thy lady; but I know
When thou hast stol'n away from fairy land,
And in the shape of Corin, sat all day
Playing on pipes of corn, and versing love
To amorous Phillida. Why art thou here,
Come from the farthest step of India,
But that, forsooth, the bouncing Amazon,
Your buskin'd mistress and your warrior love,
To Theseus must be wedded, and you come
To give their bed joy and prosperity?
OBERON   How canst thou thus, for shame, Titania,
Glance at my credit with Hippolyta,
Knowing I know thy love to Theseus?
Didst not thou lead him through the glimmering
    night
From Perigouna, whom he ravished;
And make him with fair Aegles break his faith,
With Ariadne and Antiopa?
TITANIA   These are the forgeries of jealousy:
And never, since the middle summer's spring,
Met we on hill, in dale, forest or mead,
By paved fountain, or by rushy brook,
Or in the beached margent of the sea,
To dance our ringlets to the whistling wind,
But with thy brawls thou has disturb'd our sport.
Therefore the winds, piping to us in vain,
As in revenge have suck'd up from the sea
Contagious fogs; which, falling in the land,
Hath every pelting river made so proud
That they have overborne their continents.
The ox hath therefore stretch'd his yoke in vain,
The ploughman lost his sweat, and the green corn
Hath rotted ere his youth attain'd a beard;
The fold stands empty in the drowned field,
And crows are fatted with the murrion flock;
The nine-men's-morris is fill'd up with mud,
And the quaint mazes in the wanton green
For lack of tread are undistinguishable.
The human mortals want their winter cheer:
No night is now with hymn or carol blest.
Therefore the moon, the governess of floods,
Pale in her anger, washes all the air,
That rheumatic diseases do abound.
And thorough this distemperature we see
The seasons alter: hoary-headed frosts
Fall in the fresh lap of the crimson rose;
And on old Hiems' thin and icy crown,
An odorous chaplet of sweet summer buds
Is, as in mockery, set; the spring, the summer,
The childing autumn, angry winter, change

Their wonted liveries; and the mazed world,
By their increase, now knows not which is which.
And this same progeny of evils comes   115
From our debate, from our dissension;
We are their parents and original.
OBERON   Do you amend it then: it lies in you.
Why should Titania cross her Oberon?
I do but beg a little changeling boy   120
To be my henchman.
TITANIA   Set your heart at rest:
The fairy land buys not the child of me.
His mother was a votress of my order;
And in the spiced Indian air, by night,
Full often hath she gossip'd by my side;   125
And sat with me on Neptune's yellow sands,
Marking th'embarked traders on the flood:
When we have laugh'd to see the sails conceive
And grow big-bellied with the wanton wind;
Which she, with pretty and with swimming gait 130
Following (her womb then rich with my young
    squire),
Would imitate, and sail upon the land
To fetch me trifles, and return again
As from a voyage rich with merchandise.
But she, being mortal, of that boy did die;   135
And for her sake do I rear up her boy;
And for her sake I will not part with him.
OBERON   How long within this wood intend you stay?
TITANIA   Perchance till after Theseus' wedding-day.
If you will patiently dance in our round,   140
And see our moonlight revels, go with us;
If not, shun me, and I will spare your haunts.
OBERON   Give me that boy, and I will go with thee.
TITANIA   Not for thy fairy kingdom. Fairies, away!
We shall chide downright if I longer stay.   145
                Exeunt Titania and her train.
OBERON
Well, go thy way; thou shalt not from this grove
Till I torment thee for this injury.
My gentle Puck, come hither. Thou rememb'rest
Since once I sat upon a promontory,
And heard a mermaid on a dolphin's back   150
Uttering such dulcet and harmonious breath
That the rude sea grew civil at her song
And certain stars shot madly from their spheres
To hear the sea-maid's music?
PUCK   I remember.
OBERON   That very time I saw (but thou couldst not), 155
Flying between the cold moon and the earth,
Cupid all arm'd: a certain aim he took
At a fair vestal, throned by the west,
And loos'd his love-shaft smartly from his bow
As it should pierce a hundred thousand hearts. 160
But I might see young Cupid's fiery shaft
Quench'd in the chaste beams of the watery moon;
And the imperial votress passed on,
In maiden meditation, fancy-free.

165 Yet mark'd I where the bolt of Cupid fell:
It fell upon a little western flower,
Before milk-white, now purple with love's wound:
And maidens call it 'love-in-idleness'.
Fetch me that flower; the herb I show'd thee once.
170 The juice of it, on sleeping eyelids laid,
Will make or man or woman madly dote
Upon the next live creature that it sees.
Fetch me this herb, and be thou here again
Ere the leviathan can swim a league.
175 PUCK   I'll put a girdle round about the earth
In forty minutes.   *Exit.*
OBERON   Having once this juice,
I'll watch Titania when she is asleep,
And drop the liquor of it in her eyes:
The next thing then she waking looks upon
180 (Be it on lion, bear, or wolf, or bull,
On meddling monkey, or on busy ape)
She shall pursue it with the soul of love.
And ere I take this charm from off her sight
(As I can take it with another herb)
185 I'll make her render up her page to me.
But who comes here? I am invisible;
And I will overhear their conference.

Enter DEMETRIUS, HELENA *following him.*

DEMETRIUS   I love thee not, therefore pursue me not.
Where is Lysander and fair Hermia?
190 The one I'll slay, the other slayeth me.
Thou told'st me they were stol'n unto this wood;
And here am I, and wood within this wood
Because I cannot meet my Hermia.
Hence, get thee gone, and follow me no more.
195 HELENA   You draw me, you hard-hearted adamant –
But yet you draw not iron, for my heart
Is true as steel. Leave you your power to draw,
And I shall have no power to follow you.
DEMETRIUS   Do I entice you? Do I speak you fair?
200 Or rather do I not in plainest truth
Tell you I do not, nor I cannot love you?
HELENA   And even for that do I love you the more.
I am your spaniel; and, Demetrius,
The more you beat me, I will fawn on you.
205 Use me but as your spaniel, spurn me, strike me,
Neglect me, lose me; only give me leave,
Unworthy as I am, to follow you.
What worser place can I beg in your love –
And yet a place of high respect with me –
210 Than to be used as you use your dog?
DEMETRIUS   Tempt not too much the hatred of my spirit;
For I am sick when I do look on thee.
HELENA   And I am sick when I look not on you.
DEMETRIUS   You do impeach your modesty too much
215 To leave the city and commit yourself
Into the hands of one that loves you not,
To trust the opportunity of night
And the ill counsel of a desert place

With the rich worth of your virginity.
HELENA   Your virtue is my privilege: for that
It is not night when I do see your face,   220
Therefore I think I am not in the night;
Nor doth this wood lack worlds of company,
For you, in my respect, are all the world;
Then how can it be said I am alone,   225
When all the world is here to look on me?
DEMETRIUS
I'll run from thee and hide me in the brakes,
And leave thee to the mercy of wild beasts.
HELENA   The wildest hath not such a heart as you.
Run when you will; the story shall be chang'd: 230
Apollo flies, and Daphne holds the chase;
The dove pursues the griffin, the mild hind
Makes speed to catch the tiger – bootless speed,
When cowardice pursues and valour flies!
DEMETRIUS   I will not stay thy questions; let me go,   235
Or if thou follow me, do not believe
But I shall do thee mischief in the wood.
HELENA   Ay, in the temple, in the town, the field,
You do me mischief. Fie, Demetrius!
Your wrongs do set a scandal on my sex.   240
We cannot fight for love, as men may do;
We should be woo'd, and were not made to woo.
                                    Exit Demetrius.
I'll follow thee, and make a heaven of hell,
To die upon the hand I love so well.   *Exit.*
OBERON
Fare thee well, nymph; ere he do leave this grove   245
Thou shalt fly him, and he shall seek thy love.

Enter PUCK.

Hast thou the flower there? Welcome, wanderer.
PUCK   Ay, there it is.
OBERON   I pray thee give it me.
I know a bank where the wild thyme blows,
Where oxlips and the nodding violet grows,   250
Quite over-canopied with luscious woodbine,
With sweet musk-roses, and with eglantine.
There sleeps Titania sometime of the night,
Lull'd in these flowers with dances and delight;
And there the snake throws her enamell'd skin,   255
Weed wide enough to wrap a fairy in;
And with the juice of this I'll streak her eyes,
And make her full of hateful fantasies.
Take thou some of it, and seek through this grove:
A sweet Athenian lady is in love   260
With a disdainful youth; anoint his eyes;
But do it when the next thing he espies
May be the lady. Thou shalt know the man
By the Athenian garments he hath on.
Effect it with some care, that he may prove   265
More fond on her than she upon her love:
And look thou meet me ere the first cock crow.
PUCK   Fear not, my lord, your servant shall do so.
                                    Exeunt.

2.2 *Enter* TITANIA, *Queen of Fairies, with her train.*

TITANIA   Come, now a roundel and a fairy song;
   Then for the third part of a minute, hence:
   Some to kill cankers in the musk-rose buds;
   Some war with reremice for their leathern wings,
5   To make my small elves coats; and some keep back
   The clamorous owl, that nightly hoots and wonders
   At our quaint spirits. Sing me now asleep;
   Then to your offices, and let me rest.
   [*The Fairies sing.*]
1 FAIRY   You spotted snakes with double tongue,
10   Thorny hedgehogs, be not seen;
      Newts and blind-worms, do no wrong,
      Come not near our fairy queen.
CHORUS   Philomel, with melody,
         Sing in our sweet lullaby;
15   Lulla, lulla, lullaby; lulla, lulla, lullaby;
         Never harm, nor spell, nor charm,
         Come our lovely lady nigh;
         So goodnight, with lullaby.
1 FAIRY   Weaving spiders, come not here;
20   Hence, you long-legg'd spinners, hence!
      Beetles black, approach not near;
      Worm nor snail, do no offence.
CHORUS   Philomel, with melody, etc.
   [*Titania sleeps.*]
2 FAIRY   Hence, away! Now all is well;
25   One aloof stand sentinel.   *Exeunt Fairies.*

Enter OBERON, *and squeezes the juice on
Titania's eyelids.*

OBERON   What thou seest when thou dost wake,
   Do it for thy true love take;
   Love and languish for his sake.
   Be it ounce, or cat, or bear,
30   Pard, or boar with bristled hair,
   In thy eye that shall appear
   When thou wak'st, it is thy dear.
   Wake when some vile thing is near.   *Exit.*

Enter LYSANDER *and* HERMIA.

LYSANDER
   Fair love, you faint with wand'ring in the wood,
5   And, to speak troth, I have forgot our way.
   We'll rest us, Hermia, if you think it good,
   And tarry for the comfort of the day.
HERMIA   Be it so, Lysander: find you out a bed,
   For I upon this bank will rest my head.
10 LYSANDER   One turf shall serve as pillow for us both;
   One heart, one bed, two bosoms, and one troth.
HERMIA   Nay, good Lysander; for my sake, my dear,
   Lie further off yet; do not lie so near.
LYSANDER   O take the sense, sweet, of my innocence!
5   Love takes the meaning in love's conference.
   I mean that my heart unto yours is knit,

So that but one heart we can make of it:
Two bosoms interchained with an oath,
So then, two bosoms and a single troth.
Then by your side no bed-room me deny;   50
For lying so, Hermia, I do not lie.
HERMIA   Lysander riddles very prettily.
   Now much beshrew my manners and my pride,
   If Hermia meant to say Lysander lied!
   But, gentle friend, for love and courtesy,   55
   Lie further off, in human modesty;
   Such separation as may well be said
   Becomes a virtuous bachelor and a maid,
   So far be distant; and good night, sweet friend:
   Thy love ne'er alter till thy sweet life end!   60
LYSANDER   Amen, amen, to that fair prayer say I;
   And then end life when I end loyalty!
   Here is my bed; sleep give thee all his rest.
HERMIA
   With half that wish the wisher's eyes be press'd.
   [*They sleep.*]

Enter PUCK.

PUCK   Through the forest have I gone;   65
      But Athenian found I none
      On whose eyes I might approve
      This flower's force in stirring love.
      Night and silence – Who is here?
      Weeds of Athens he doth wear: 70
      This is he my master said
      Despised the Athenian maid;
      And here the maiden, sleeping sound,
      On the dank and dirty ground.
      Pretty soul, she durst not lie   75
      Near this lack-love, this kill-courtesy.
      Churl, upon thy eyes I throw
      All the power this charm doth owe:
      When thou wak'st, let love forbid
      Sleep his seat on thy eyelid.   80
      So awake when I am gone;
      For I must now to Oberon.   *Exit.*

Enter DEMETRIUS *and* HELENA, *running.*

HELENA   Stay, though thou kill me, sweet Demetrius!
DEMETRIUS
   I charge thee, hence, and do not haunt me thus.
HELENA   O wilt thou darkling leave me? Do not so.   85
DEMETRIUS   Stay, on thy peril; I alone will go.   *Exit.*
HELENA   O, I am out of breath in this fond chase!
   The more my prayer, the lesser is my grace.
   Happy is Hermia, wheresoe'er she lies,
   For she hath blessed and attractive eyes.   90
   How came her eyes so bright? Not with salt tears;
   If so, my eyes are oftener wash'd than hers.
   No, no; I am as ugly as a bear,
   For beasts that meet me run away for fear:
   Therefore no marvel though Demetrius   95

Do, as a monster, fly my presence thus.
What wicked and dissembling glass of mine
Made me compare with Hermia's sphery eyne?
But who is here? Lysander, on the ground?
100 Dead, or asleep? I see no blood, no wound.
Lysander, if you live, good sir, awake!

LYSANDER [*waking*]
And run through fire I will for thy sweet sake!
Transparent Helena! Nature shows art,
That through thy bosom makes me see thy heart.
105 Where is Demetrius? O how fit a word
Is that vile name to perish on my sword!

HELENA   Do not say so, Lysander, say not so.
What though he love your Hermia? Lord, what
though?
Yet Hermia still loves you; then be content.

110 LYSANDER   Content with Hermia? No. I do repent
The tedious minutes I with her have spent.
Not Hermia, but Helena I love:
Who will not change a raven for a dove?
The will of man is by his reason sway'd,
115 And reason says you are the worthier maid.
Things growing are not ripe until their season:
So I, being young, till now ripe not to reason;
And, touching now the point of human skill,
Reason becomes the marshal to my will,
120 And leads me to your eyes, where I o'erlook
Love's stories, written in love's richest book.

HELENA   Wherefore was I to this keen mockery born?
When at your hands did I deserve this scorn?
Is't not enough, is't not enough, young man,
125 That I did never, no, nor never can
Deserve a sweet look from Demetrius' eye,
But you must flout my insufficiency?
Good troth, you do me wrong, good sooth, you do,
In such disdainful manner me to woo.
130 But fare you well; perforce I must confess
I thought you lord of more true gentleness.
O that a lady, of one man refus'd,
Should of another therefore be abus'd!   *Exit.*

LYSANDER
She sees not Hermia. Hermia, sleep thou there,
135 And never mayst thou come Lysander near!
For, as a surfeit of the sweetest things
The deepest loathing to the stomach brings;
Or as the heresies that men do leave
Are hated most of those they did deceive;
140 So thou, my surfeit and my heresy,
Of all be hated, but the most of me!
And, all my powers, address your love and might
To honour Helen, and to be her knight!   *Exit.*

HERMIA [*starting*]
Help me, Lysander, help me! Do thy best
145 To pluck this crawling serpent from my breast!
Ay me, for pity! What a dream was here!
Lysander, look how I do quake with fear.

Methought a serpent ate my heart away,
And you sat smiling at his cruel prey.
Lysander! What, remov'd? Lysander! lord!   150
What, out of hearing? Gone? No sound, no word?
Alack, where are you? Speak, and if you hear;
Speak, of all loves I swoon almost with fear.
No? Then I well perceive you are not nigh.
Either death or you I'll find immediately.   *Exit.*   155
[*Titania remains lying asleep.*]

3.1   *Titania still lying asleep. Enter* QUINCE, BOTTOM,
SNUG, FLUTE, SNOUT *and* STARVELING.

BOTTOM   Are we all met?

QUINCE   Pat, pat; and here's a marvellous convenient
place for our rehearsal. This green plot shall be our
stage, this hawthorn-brake our tiring-house; and we
will do it in action, as we will do it before the Duke.   5

BOTTOM   Peter Quince!

QUINCE   What sayest thou, bully Bottom?

BOTTOM   There are things in this comedy of Pyramus
and Thisbe that will never please. First, Pyramus must
draw a sword to kill himself; which the ladies cannot   10
abide. How answer you that?

SNOUT   Byrlakin, a parlous fear.

STARVELING   I believe we must leave the killing out,
when all is done.

BOTTOM   Not a whit; I have a device to make all well.   15
Write me a prologue, and let the prologue seem to say
we will do no harm with our swords, and that Pyramus
is not killed indeed; and for the more better assurance,
tell them that I, Pyramus, am not Pyramus, but
Bottom the weaver. This will put them out of fear.   20

QUINCE   Well, we will have such a prologue; and it shall
be written in eight and six.

BOTTOM   No, make it two more; let it be written in eight
and eight.

SNOUT   Will not the ladies be afeard of the lion?   25

STARVELING   I fear it, I promise you.

BOTTOM   Masters, you ought to consider with yourself;
to bring in (God shield us!) a lion among ladies is a
most dreadful thing; for there is not a more fearful
wild-fowl than your lion living; and we ought to look   30
to't.

SNOUT   Therefore another prologue must tell he is not a
lion.

BOTTOM   Nay, you must name his name, and half his
face must be seen through the lion's neck; and he   35
himself must speak through, saying thus, or to the
same defect: 'Ladies,' or 'Fair ladies, I would wish
you,' or 'I would request you,' or 'I would entreat you,
not to fear, not to tremble: my life for yours! If you
think I come hither as a lion, it were pity of my life.   40
No, I am no such thing; I am a man, as other men
are': and there, indeed, let him name his name, and
tell them plainly he is Snug the joiner.

QUINCE   Well, it shall be so. But there is two hard things: that is, to bring the moonlight into a chamber; for you know, Pyramus and Thisbe meet by moonlight.

SNOUT   Doth the moon shine that night we play our play?

BOTTOM   A calendar, a calendar! Look in the almanac; find out moonshine, find out moonshine!

QUINCE   Yes, it doth shine that night.

BOTTOM   Why, then may you leave a casement of the great chamber window, where we play, open; and the moon may shine in at the casement.

QUINCE   Ay; or else one must come in with a bush of thorns and a lantern, and say he comes to disfigure or to present the person of Moonshine. Then there is another thing: we must have a wall in the great chamber; for Pyramus and Thisbe, says the story, did talk through the chink of a wall.

SNOUT   You can never bring in a wall. What say you, Bottom?

BOTTOM   Some man or other must present Wall; and let him have some plaster, or some loam, or some roughcast about him, to signify wall; and let him hold his fingers thus, and through that cranny shall Pyramus and Thisbe whisper.

QUINCE   If that may be, then all is well. Come sit down, every mother's son, and rehearse your parts. Pyramus, you begin: when you have spoken your speech, enter into that brake; and so every one according to his cue.

Enter PUCK *behind.*

PUCK
What hempen homespuns have we swaggering here,
So near the cradle of the Fairy Queen?
What, a play toward? I'll be an auditor;
An actor too perhaps, if I see cause.

QUINCE   Speak, Pyramus; Thisbe, stand forth.

BOTTOM   *Thisbe, the flowers of odious savours sweet –*

QUINCE   'Odorous'! 'odorous'!

BOTTOM   　　　　　　　　*Odorous savours sweet;*
So hath thy breath, my dearest Thisbe dear.
But hark, a voice! Stay thou but here awhile,
And by and by I will to thee appear.　　　　　*Exit.*

PUCK   A stranger Pyramus than e'er played here! *Exit.*

FLUTE   Must I speak now?

QUINCE   Ay, marry, must you; for you must understand he goes but to see a noise that he heard, and is to come again.

FLUTE   *Most radiant Pyramus, most lily-white of hue,*
Of colour like the red rose on triumphant briar,
Most brisky juvenal, and eke most lovely Jew,
As true as truest horse that yet would never tire;
I'll meet thee, Pyramus, at Ninny's tomb.

QUINCE   'Ninus' tomb', man! Why, you must not speak that yet; that you answer to Pyramus. You speak all your part at once, cues and all. Pyramus, enter! Your cue is past; it is 'never tire'.

FLUTE
O – As true as truest horse that yet would never tire.

Enter PUCK, *and* BOTTOM *with the ass-head on.*

BOTTOM   *If I were fair, Thisbe, I were only thine.*

QUINCE   O monstrous! O strange! We are haunted! Pray, masters! Fly, masters! Help!

Exeunt Quince, Snug, Flute, Snout and Starveling.

PUCK   I'll follow you: I'll lead you about a round!   100
Through bog, through bush, through brake, through briar;
Sometime a horse I'll be, sometime a hound,
A hog, a headless bear, sometime a fire;
And neigh, and bark, and grunt, and roar, and burn,
Like horse, hound, hog, bear, fire, at every turn. *Exit.*   105

BOTTOM   Why do they run away? This is a knavery of them to make me afeard.

Enter SNOUT.

SNOUT   O Bottom, thou art changed! What do I see on thee?

BOTTOM   What do you see? You see an ass-head of your   110
own, do you?   *Exit Snout.*

Enter QUINCE.

QUINCE   Bless thee, Bottom, bless thee! Thou art translated.   *Exit.*

BOTTOM   I see their knavery: this is to make an ass of me, to fright me, if they could. But I will not stir from   115
this place, do what they can; I will walk up and down here, and I will sing, that they shall hear I am not afraid.
[*Sings.*]   The ousel cock, so black of hue,
　　　　　　　With orange-tawny bill,   120
　　　　　　　The throstle, with his note so true,
　　　　　　　The wren with little quill –
[*The singing awakens Titania.*]

TITANIA   What angel wakes me from my flowery bed?

BOTTOM [*Sings.*]
　　　　　　　The finch, the sparrow, and the lark,
　　　　　　　The plain-song cuckoo gray,   125
　　　　　　　Whose note full many a man doth mark,
　　　　　　　And dares not answer nay –
for indeed, who would set his wit to so foolish a bird?
Who would give a bird the lie, though he cry 'cuckoo'
never so?   130

TITANIA   I pray thee, gentle mortal, sing again:
Mine ear is much enamour'd of thy note;
So is mine eye enthralled to thy shape;
And thy fair virtue's force perforce doth move me
On the first view to say, to swear, I love thee.   135

BOTTOM   Methinks, mistress, you should have little reason for that. And yet, to say the truth, reason and love keep little company together nowadays. The more the pity that some honest neighbours will not make them friends. Nay, I can gleek upon occasion.   140

TITANIA   Thou art as wise as thou art beautiful.

BOTTOM   Not so neither; but if I had wit enough to get out of this wood, I have enough to serve mine own turn.

TITANIA   Out of this wood do not desire to go:

145   Thou shalt remain here, whether thou wilt or no.
I am a spirit of no common rate;
The summer still doth tend upon my state;
And I do love thee: therefore go with me.
I'll give thee fairies to attend on thee;
150   And they shall fetch thee jewels from the deep,
And sing, while thou on pressed flowers dost sleep:
And I will purge thy mortal grossness so,
That thou shalt like an airy spirit go.
Peaseblossom! Cobweb! Moth! and Mustardseed!

Enter four fairies: PEASEBLOSSOM, COBWEB,
MOTH *and* MUSTARDSEED.

PEASEBLOSSOM   Ready.

COBWEB   And I.

MOTH   And I.

MUSTARDSEED   And I.

155   ALL   Where shall we go?

TITANIA   Be kind and courteous to this gentleman;
Hop in his walks, and gambol in his eyes;
Feed him with apricocks and dewberries,
With purple grapes, green figs, and mulberries;
160   The honey-bags steal from the humble-bees,
And for night-tapers crop their waxen thighs,
And light them at the fiery glow-worms' eyes,
To have my love to bed, and to arise;
And pluck the wings from painted butterflies
165   To fan the moonbeams from his sleeping eyes.
Nod to him, elves, and do him courtesies.

PEASEBLOSSOM   Hail, mortal!

COBWEB   Hail!

MOTH   Hail!

170   MUSTARDSEED   Hail!

BOTTOM   I cry your worships mercy, heartily. I beseech your worship's name?

COBWEB   Cobweb.

BOTTOM   I shall desire you of more acquaintance, good
175   Master Cobweb: if I cut my finger, I shall make bold with you. Your name, honest gentleman?

PEASEBLOSSOM   Peaseblossom.

BOTTOM   I pray you, commend me to Mistress Squash, your mother, and to Master Peascod, your father.
180   Good Master Peaseblossom, I shall desire you of more acquaintance too. Your name, I beseech you sir?

MUSTARDSEED   Mustardseed.

BOTTOM   Good Master Mustardseed, I know your patience well. That same cowardly giant-like ox-beef
185   hath devoured many a gentleman of your house: I promise you, your kindred hath made my eyes water ere now. I desire you of more acquaintance, good Master Mustardseed.

TITANIA   Come, wait upon him; lead him to my bower.
190   The moon, methinks, looks with a watery eye,

And when she weeps, weeps every little flower,
Lamenting some enforced chastity.
Tie up my love's tongue, bring him silently.   *Exeunt.*

3.2   *Enter* OBERON, *King of Fairies.*

OBERON   I wonder if Titania be awak'd;
Then, what it was that next came in her eye,
Which she must dote on in extremity.

Enter PUCK.

Here comes my messenger. How now, mad spirit?
What night-rule now about this haunted grove?   5

PUCK   My mistress with a monster is in love.
Near to her close and consecrated bower,
While she was in her dull and sleeping hour,
A crew of patches, rude mechanicals,
That work for bread upon Athenian stalls,   10
Were met together to rehearse a play
Intended for great Theseus' nuptial day.
The shallowest thick-skin of that barren sort,
Who Pyramus presented in their sport,
Forsook his scene, and enter'd in a brake,   15
When I did him at this advantage take:
An ass's nole I fixed on his head.
Anon, his Thisbe must be answered,
And forth my mimic comes. When they him spy –
As wild geese that the creeping fowler eye,   20
Or russet-pated choughs, many in sort,
Rising and cawing at the gun's report,
Sever themselves, and madly sweep the sky
So, at his sight, away his fellows fly;
And at our stamp, here o'er and o'er one falls;   25
He murder cries, and help from Athens calls.
Their sense thus weak, lost with their fears thus strong,
Made senseless things begin to do them wrong:
For briars and thorns at their apparel snatch;
Some sleeves, some hats, from yielders all things catch.   30
I led them on in this distracted fear,
And left sweet Pyramus translated there;
When in that moment, so it came to pass,
Titania wak'd, and straightway lov'd an ass.

OBERON   This falls out better than I could devise.   35
But hast thou yet latch'd the Athenian's eyes
With the love-juice, as I did bid thee do?

PUCK   I took him sleeping – that is finish'd too –
And the Athenian woman by his side,
That when he wak'd, of force she must be ey'd.   40

Enter DEMETRIUS *and* HERMIA.

OBERON   Stand close: this is the same Athenian.

PUCK   This is the woman, but not this the man.
    [*They stand apart.*]

DEMETRIUS   O why rebuke you him that loves you so?
Lay breath so bitter on your bitter foe.

HERMIA   Now I but chide, but I should use thee worse,
  For thou, I fear, hast given me cause to curse.
  If thou hast slain Lysander in his sleep,
  Being o'er shoes in blood, plunge in the deep,
  And kill me too.
  The sun was not so true unto the day
  As he to me. Would he have stol'n away
  From sleeping Hermia? I'll believe as soon
  This whole earth may be bor'd, and that the moon
  May through the centre creep, and so displease
  Her brother's noon-tide with th'Antipodes.
  It cannot be but thou hast murder'd him:
  So should a murderer look, so dead, so grim.

DEMETRIUS
  So should the murder'd look, and so should I,
  Pierc'd through the heart with your stern cruelty;
  Yet you, the murderer, look as bright, as clear,
  As yonder Venus in her glimmering sphere.

HERMIA   What's this to my Lysander? Where is he?
  Ah, good Demetrius, wilt thou give him me?

DEMETRIUS
  I had rather give his carcase to my hounds.

HERMIA
  Out, dog! Out, cur! Thou driv'st me past the bounds
  Of maiden's patience. Hast thou slain him then?
  Henceforth be never number'd among men!
  O once tell true; tell true, even for my sake!
  Durst thou have look'd upon him, being awake,
  And hast thou kill'd him sleeping? O brave touch!
  Could not a worm, an adder, do so much?
  An adder did it; for with doubler tongue
  Than thine, thou serpent, never adder stung!

DEMETRIUS
  You spend your passion on a mispris'd mood:
  I am not guilty of Lysander's blood;
  Nor is he dead, for aught that I can tell.

HERMIA   I pray thee tell me then that he is well.

DEMETRIUS   And if I could, what should I get therefor?

HERMIA   A privilege, never to see me more.
  And from thy hated presence part I so:
  See me no more, whether he be dead or no.   *Exit.*

DEMETRIUS
  There is no following her in this fierce vein;
  Here therefore for a while I will remain.
  So sorrow's heaviness doth heavier grow
  For debt that bankrupt sleep doth sorrow owe;
  Which now in some slight measure it will pay,
  If for his tender here I make some stay.
  [*Lies down and sleeps. Oberon and Puck come forward.*]

OBERON
  What hast thou done? Thou hast mistaken quite,
  And laid the love-juice on some true love's sight;
  Of thy misprision must perforce ensue
  Some true love turn'd, and not a false turn'd true.

PUCK
  Then fate o'er-rules, that, one man holding troth,
  A million fail, confounding oath on oath.

OBERON   About the wood go swifter than the wind,
  And Helena of Athens look thou find;   95
  All fancy-sick she is, and pale of cheer
  With sighs of love, that costs the fresh blood dear.
  By some illusion see thou bring her here;
  I'll charm his eyes against she do appear.

PUCK   I go, I go, look how I go!   100
  Swifter than arrow from the Tartar's bow. *Exit.*

OBERON [*squeezing the juice on Demetrius' eyelids.*]
  Flower of this purple dye,
  Hit with Cupid's archery,
  Sink in apple of his eye.
  When his love he doth espy,   105
  Let her shine as gloriously
  As the Venus of the sky.
  When thou wak'st, if she be by,
  Beg of her for remedy.

Enter PUCK.

PUCK   Captain of our fairy band,   110
  Helena is here at hand;
  And the youth, mistook by me,
  Pleading for a lover's fee.
  Shall we their fond pageant see?
  Lord, what fools these mortals be!   115

OBERON   Stand aside. The noise they make
  Will cause Demetrius to awake.

PUCK   Then will two at once woo one:
  That must needs be sport alone;
  And those things do best please me   120
  That befall prepost'rously.

[*They stand aside.*]

Enter LYSANDER *and* HELENA.

LYSANDER
  Why should you think that I should woo in scorn?
  Scorn and derision never come in tears.
  Look when I vow, I weep; and vows so born,   125
  In their nativity all truth appears.
  How can these things in me seem scorn to you,
  Bearing the badge of faith to prove them true?

HELENA   You do advance your cunning more and more.
  When truth kills truth, O devilish-holy fray!
  These vows are Hermia's: will you give her o'er?   130
  Weigh oath with oath, and you will nothing weigh:
  Your vows to her and me, put in two scales,
  Will even weigh; and both as light as tales.

LYSANDER   I had no judgement when to her I swore.

HELENA   Nor none, in my mind, now you give her o'er.   135

LYSANDER   Demetrius loves her, and he loves not you.

DEMETRIUS [*waking*]
  O Helen, goddess, nymph, perfect, divine!
  To what, my love, shall I compare thine eyne?
  Crystal is muddy. O how ripe in show
  Thy lips, those kissing cherries, tempting grow!   140
  That pure congealed white, high Taurus' snow,
  Fann'd with the eastern wind, turns to a crow

When thou hold'st up thy hand. O let me kiss
This princess of pure white, this seal of bliss!

145   HELENA   O spite! O hell! I see you all are bent
To set against me for your merriment.
If you were civil, and knew courtesy,
You would not do me thus much injury.
Can you not hate me, as I know you do,
150   But you must join in souls to mock me too?
If you were men, as men you are in show,
You would not use a gentle lady so:
To vow, and swear, and superpraise my parts,
When I am sure you hate me with your hearts.
155   You both are rivals, and love Hermia;
And now both rivals to mock Helena.
A trim exploit, a manly enterprise,
To conjure tears up in a poor maid's eyes
With your derision! None of noble sort
160   Would so offend a virgin, and extort
A poor soul's patience, all to make you sport.

LYSANDER   You are unkind, Demetrius; be not so,
For you love Hermia; this you know I know:
And here, with all good will, with all my heart,
165   In Hermia's love I yield you up my part;
And yours of Helena to me bequeath,
Whom I do love, and will do till my death.

HELENA   Never did mockers waste more idle breath.

DEMETRIUS   Lysander, keep thy Hermia; I will none.
170   If ere I lov'd her, all that love is gone.
My heart to her but as guest-wise sojourn'd,
And now to Helen is it home return'd,
There to remain.

LYSANDER   Helen, it is not so.

DEMETRIUS
Disparage not the faith thou dost not know,
175   Lest to thy peril thou aby it dear.
Look where thy love comes; yonder is thy dear.

Enter HERMIA.

HERMIA
Dark night, that from the eye his function takes,
The ear more quick of apprehension makes;
Wherein it doth impair the seeing sense,
180   It pays the hearing double recompense.
Thou art not by mine eye, Lysander, found;
Mine ear, I thank it, brought me to thy sound.
But why unkindly didst thou leave me so?

LYSANDER
Why should he stay whom love doth press to go?

HERMIA
185   What love could press Lysander from my side?

LYSANDER
Lysander's love, that would not let him bide –
Fair Helena, who more engilds the night
Than all yon fiery oes and eyes of light.
Why seek'st thou me? Could not this make thee know
190   The hate I bare thee made me leave thee so?

HERMIA   You speak not as you think; it cannot be!

HELENA   Lo, she is one of this confederacy!
Now I perceive they have conjoin'd all three
To fashion this false sport in spite of me.
Injurious Hermia! Most ungrateful maid!   195
Have you conspir'd, have you with these contriv'd,
To bait me with this foul derision?
Is all the counsel that we two have shar'd,
The sisters' vows, the hours that we have spent
When we have chid the hasty-footed time   200
For parting us – O, is all forgot?
All school-days' friendship, childhood innocence?
We, Hermia, like two artificial gods,
Have with our needles created both one flower,
Both on one sampler, sitting on one cushion,   205
Both warbling of one song, both in one key,
As if our hands, our sides, voices and minds,
Had been incorporate. So we grew together,
Like to a double cherry, seeming parted,
But yet an union in partition,   210
Two lovely berries moulded on one stem;
So, with two seeming bodies, but one heart;
Two of the first, like coats in heraldry,
Due but to one, and crowned with one crest.
And will you rent our ancient love asunder   215
To join with men in scorning your poor friend?
It is not friendly, 'tis not maidenly;
Our sex, as well as I, may chide you for it,
Though I alone do feel the injury.

HERMIA   I am amazed at your passionate words: 220
I scorn you not; it seems that you scorn me.

HELENA   Have you not set Lysander, as in scorn,
To follow me, and praise my eyes and face;
And made your other love, Demetrius,
Who even but now did spurn me with his foot,   225
To call me goddess, nymph, divine and rare,
Precious, celestial? Wherefore speaks he this
To her he hates? And wherefore doth Lysander
Deny your love, so rich within his soul,
And tender me, forsooth, affection,   230
But by your setting on, by your consent?
What though I be not so in grace as you,
So hung upon with love, so fortunate,
But miserable most, to love unlov'd?
This you should pity rather than despise.   235

HERMIA   I understand not what you mean by this.

HELENA   Ay, do! Persever: counterfeit sad looks,
Make mouths upon me when I turn my back,
Wink each at other; hold the sweet jest up;
This sport, well carried, shall be chronicled.   240
If you have any pity, grace, or manners,
You would not make me such an argument.
But fare ye well; 'tis partly my own fault,
Which death, or absence, soon shall remedy.

LYSANDER   Stay, gentle Helena; hear my excuse;   245
My love, my life, my soul, fair Helena!

HELENA　O excellent!

HERMIA　　　　　Sweet, do not scorn her so.

DEMETRIUS　If she cannot entreat, I can compel.

LYSANDER
Thou canst compel no more than she entreat;
Thy threats have no more strength than her weak
　　prayers.
Helen, I love thee, by my life I do;
I swear by that which I will lose for thee
To prove him false that says I love thee not.

DEMETRIUS　I say I love thee more than he can do.

LYSANDER　If thou say so, withdraw and prove it too.

DEMETRIUS　Quick, come!

HERMIA　　　　　Lysander, whereto tends all this?

LYSANDER　Away, you Ethiope!

DEMETRIUS　　　　　No, no; he'll
Seem to break loose –
[*to Lysander*]　　　take on as you would follow,
But yet come not! You are a tame man, go!

LYSANDER
Hang off, thou cat, thou burr! Vile thing, let loose,
Or I will shake thee from me like a serpent.

HERMIA
Why are you grown so rude? What change is this,
Sweet love?

LYSANDER　Thy love? Out, tawny Tartar, out!
Out, loathed medicine! O hated potion, hence!

HERMIA　Do you not jest?

HELENA　　　　　Yes sooth, and so do you.

LYSANDER　Demetrius, I will keep my word with thee.

DEMETRIUS　I would I had your bond, for I perceive
A weak bond holds you; I'll not trust your word.

LYSANDER
What, should I hurt her, strike her, kill her dead?
Although I hate her, I'll not harm her so.

HERMIA　What, can you do me greater harm than hate?
Hate me? Wherefor? O me! what news, my love?
Am not I Hermia? Are not you Lysander?
I am as fair now as I was erewhile.
Since night you lov'd me; yet since night you left me.
Why, then you left me – O the gods forbid! –
In earnest, shall I say?

LYSANDER　　　　　Ay, by my life!
And never did desire to see thee more.
Therefore, be out of hope, of question, of doubt;
Be certain, nothing truer; 'tis no jest
That I do hate thee, and love Helena.

HERMIA　O me!
[*to Helena*]　You juggler! You canker-blossom!
You thief of love! What, have you come by night
And stol'n my love's heart from him?

HELENA　　　　　Fine, i'faith!
Have you no modesty, no maiden shame,
No touch of bashfulness? What, will you tear
Impatient answers from my gentle tongue?
Fie, fie, you counterfeit! You puppet you!

HERMIA
'Puppet'! Why, so? Ay, that way goes the game! 290
Now I perceive that she hath made compare
Between our statures; she hath urg'd her height;
And with her personage, her tall personage,
Her height, forsooth, she hath prevail'd with him.
And are you grown so high in his esteem
Because I am so dwarfish and so low? 295
How low am I, thou painted maypole? Speak:
How low am I? I am not yet so low
But that my nails can reach unto thine eyes.

HELENA　I pray you, though you mock me, gentlemen,
Let her not hurt me. I was never curst; 300
I have no gift at all in shrewishness;
I am a right maid for my cowardice;
Let her not strike me. You perhaps may think,
Because she is something lower than myself,
That I can match her.

HERMIA　　　　　'Lower'? Hark, again! 305

HELENA　Good Hermia, do not be so bitter with me.
I evermore did love you, Hermia,
Did ever keep your counsels, never wrong'd you,
Save that, in love unto Demetrius,
I told him of your stealth unto this wood. 310
He follow'd you; for love I follow'd him;
But he hath chid me hence, and threaten'd me
To strike me, spurn me, nay, to kill me too:
And now, so you will let me quiet go,
To Athens will I bear my folly back, 315
And follow you no further. Let me go:
You see how simple and how fond I am.

HERMIA　Why, get you gone! Who is't that hinders you?

HELENA　A foolish heart that I leave here behind.

HERMIA　What! with Lysander?

HELENA　　　　　With Demetrius. 320

LYSANDER
Be not afraid; she shall not harm thee, Helena.

DEMETRIUS
No sir, she shall not, though you take her part.

HELENA　O, when she is angry, she is keen and shrewd;
She was a vixen when she went to school,
And though she be but little, she is fierce. 325

HERMIA　'Little' again? Nothing but 'low' and 'little'?
Why will you suffer her to flout me thus?
Let me come to her!

LYSANDER　　　　　Get you gone, you dwarf;
You minimus, of hindering knot-grass made;
You bead, you acorn.

DEMETRIUS　　　　　You are too officious 330
In her behalf that scorns your services.
Let her alone; speak not of Helena;
Take not her part; for if thou dost intend
Never so little show of love to her,
Thou shalt aby it.

LYSANDER　　　　　Now she holds me not: 335
Now follow, if thou dar'st, to try whose right,
Of thine or mine, is most in Helena.

DEMETRIUS
  Follow? Nay, I'll go with thee, cheek by jowl.
                      Exeunt Lysander and Demetrius.
HERMIA   You, mistress, all this coil is long of you.
  Nay, go not back.
340 HELENA   I will not trust you, I,
  Nor longer stay in your curst company.
  Your hands than mine are quicker for a fray:
  My legs are longer though, to run away.   *Exit.*
HERMIA   I am amaz'd, and know not what to say.   *Exit.*
  [*Oberon and Puck come forward.*]
345 OBERON   This is thy negligence: still thou mistak'st,
  Or else committ'st thy knaveries wilfully.
PUCK   Believe me, king of shadows, I mistook.
  Did not you tell me I should know the man
  By the Athenian garments he had on?
350 And so far blameless proves my enterprise
  That I have 'nointed an Athenian's eyes:
  And so far am I glad it so did sort,
  As this their jangling I esteem a sport.
OBERON   Thou seest these lovers seek a place to fight.
355 Hie therefore, Robin, overcast the night;
  The starry welkin cover thou anon
  With drooping fog, as black as Acheron,
  And lead these testy rivals so astray
  As one come not within another's way.
360 Like to Lysander sometime frame thy tongue,
  Then stir Demetrius up with bitter wrong;
  And sometime rail thou like Demetrius:
  And from each other look thou lead them thus,
  Till o'er their brows death-counterfeiting sleep
365 With leaden legs and batty wings doth creep.
  Then crush this herb into Lysander's eye,
  Whose liquor hath this virtuous property,
  To take from thence all error with his might,
  And make his eyeballs roll with wonted sight.
370 When they next wake, all this derision
  Shall seem a dream and fruitless vision;
  And back to Athens shall the lovers wend,
  With league whose date till death shall never end.
  Whiles I in this affair do thee employ,
375 I'll to my queen, and beg her Indian boy;
  And then I will her charmed eye release
  From monster's view, and all things shall be peace.
PUCK   My fairy lord, this must be done with haste,
  For night's swift dragons cut the clouds full fast;
380 And yonder shines Aurora's harbinger,
  At whose approach, ghosts wandering here and there
  Troop home to churchyards. Damned spirits all,
  That in cross-ways and floods have burial,
  Already to their wormy beds are gone,
385 For fear lest day should look their shames upon:
  They wilfully themselves exil'd from light,
  And must for aye consort with black-brow'd night.
OBERON   But we are spirits of another sort:
  I with the Morning's love have oft made sport;
390 And like a forester the groves may tread

  Even till the eastern gate, all fiery-red,
  Opening on Neptune with fair blessed beams,
  Turns into yellow gold his salt green streams.
  But notwithstanding, haste, make no delay;
  We may effect this business yet ere day.   *Exit.*   395
PUCK   Up and down, up and down,
      I will lead them up and down;
      I am fear'd in field and town:
      Goblin, lead them up and down.
  Here comes one.   400

                      Enter LYSANDER.

LYSANDER
  Where art thou, proud Demetrius? Speak thou now.
PUCK   Here, villain, drawn and ready. Where art thou?
LYSANDER   I will be with thee straight.
PUCK   Follow me then
  To plainer ground.
                Exit Lysander, as following the voice.

                      Enter DEMETRIUS.

DEMETRIUS   Lysander, speak again.
  Thou runaway, thou coward, art thou fled?   405
  Speak! In some bush? Where dost thou hide thy
      head?
PUCK   Thou coward, art thou bragging to the stars,
  Telling the bushes that thou look'st for wars,
  And wilt not come? Come, recreant, come thou child!
  I'll whip thee with a rod; he is defil'd   410
  That draws a sword on thee.
DEMETRIUS   Yea, art thou there?
PUCK   Follow my voice; we'll try no manhood here.
                                            Exeunt.

                      Enter LYSANDER.

LYSANDER   He goes before me, and still dares me on;
  When I come where he calls, then he is gone.
  The villain is much lighter-heel'd than I: 415
  I follow'd fast; but faster he did fly,
  That fallen am I in dark uneven way,
  And here will rest me. [*Lies down.*]
                      Come thou gentle day:
  For if but once thou show me thy grey light,
  I'll find Demetrius, and revenge this spite. [*Sleeps.*] 420

                Enter PUCK *and* DEMETRIUS.

PUCK   Ho, ho, ho! Coward, why com'st thou not?
  [*They dodge about the stage.*]
DEMETRIUS   Abide me if thou dar'st, for well I wot
  Thou runn'st before me, shifting every place,
  And dar'st not stand, nor look me in the face.
  Where art thou now?
PUCK   Come hither; I am here.   425
DEMETRIUS
  Nay, then, thou mock'st me; thou shalt buy this dear
  If ever I thy face by daylight see:
  Now go thy way. Faintness constraineth me

To measure out my length on this cold bed.
[*Lies down.*]
By day's approach look to be visited. [*Sleeps.*]

Enter HELENA.

HELENA   O weary night, O long and tedious night,
Abate thy hours! Shine, comforts, from the east,
That I may back to Athens by daylight,
From these that my poor company detest.
And sleep, that sometimes shuts up sorrow's eye,
Steal me awhile from mine own company.
[*Lies down and sleeps.*]
PUCK   Yet but three? Come one more,
Two of both kinds makes up four.
Here she comes, curst and sad:
Cupid is a knavish lad
Thus to make poor females mad!

Enter HERMIA.

HERMIA   Never so weary, never so in woe,
Bedabbled with the dew, and torn with briars,
I can no further crawl, no further go;
My legs can keep no pace with my desires.
Here will I rest me till the break of day. [*Lies down.*]
Heavens shield Lysander, if they mean a fray! [*Sleeps.*]
PUCK   On the ground
Sleep sound;
I'll apply
To your eye,
Gentle lover, remedy.
[*Squeezes the juice on Lysander's eyelids.*]
When thou wak'st,
Thou tak'st
True delight
In the sight
Of thy former lady's eye;
And the country proverb known,
That every man should take his own,
In your waking shall be shown:
Jack shall have Jill,
Nought shall go ill;
The man shall have his mare again, and all shall be
well.   *Exit.*

4.1   *Lysander, Demetrius, Helena and Hermia, still*
lying asleep. Enter TITANIA, *Queen of Fairies, and*
BOTTOM; PEASEBLOSSOM, COBWEB, MOTH,
MUSTARDSEED *and other fairies;* OBERON, *the King,*
behind, unseen.

TITANIA   Come sit thee down upon this flowery bed,
While I thy amiable cheeks do coy,
And stick musk-roses in thy sleek smooth head,
And kiss thy fair large ears, my gentle joy.
BOTTOM   Where's Peaseblossom?
PEASEBLOSSOM   Ready.

BOTTOM   Scratch my head, Peaseblossom. Where's
Mounsieur Cobweb?
COBWEB   Ready.
BOTTOM   Mounsieur Cobweb, good mounsieur, get you
your weapons in your hand, and kill me a red-hipped
humble-bee on the top of a thistle; and good
mounsieur, bring me the honey-bag. Do not fret
yourself too much in the action, mounsieur; and good
mounsieur, have a care the honey-bag break not; I
would be loath to have you overflowen with a honey-
bag, signior. Where's Mounsieur Mustardseed?
MUSTARDSEED   Ready.
BOTTOM   Give me your neaf, Mounsieur Mustardseed.
Pray you, leave your courtesy, good mounsieur.
MUSTARDSEED   What's your will?
BOTTOM   Nothing, good mounsieur, but to help
Cavalery Cobweb to scratch. I must to the barber's,
mounsieur, for methinks I am marvellous hairy about
the face; and I am such a tender ass, if my hair do but
tickle me, I must scratch.
TITANIA
What, wilt thou hear some music, my sweet love?
BOTTOM   I have a reasonable good ear in music. Let's
have the tongs and the bones.
TITANIA   Or say, sweet love, what thou desir'st to eat?
BOTTOM   Truly, a peck of provender; I could munch
your good dry oats. Methinks I have a great desire to a
bottle of hay: good hay, sweet hay, hath no fellow.
TITANIA   I have a venturous fairy that shall seek
The squirrel's hoard, and fetch thee new nuts.
BOTTOM
I had rather have a handful or two of dried peas.
But I pray you, let none of your people stir me:
I have an exposition of sleep come upon me.
TITANIA   Sleep thou, and I will wind thee in my arms.
Fairies, be gone, and be all ways away. *Exeunt Fairies.*
So doth the woodbine the sweet honeysuckle
Gently entwist; the female ivy so
Enrings the barky fingers of the elm.
O how I love thee! How I dote on thee! [*They sleep.*]

Enter PUCK

OBERON [*advancing*]
Welcome, good Robin. Seest thou this sweet sight.
Her dotage now I do begin to pity;
For, meeting her of late behind the wood
Seeking sweet favours for this hateful fool,
I did upbraid her and fall out with her:
For she his hairy temples then had rounded
With coronet of fresh and fragrant flowers;
And that same dew, which sometime on the buds
Was wont to swell like round and orient pearls,
Stood now within the pretty flowerets' eyes
Like tears, that did their own disgrace bewail.
When I had at my pleasure taunted her,
And she in mild terms begg'd my patience,

I then did ask of her her changeling child;
Which straight she gave me, and her fairy sent
60 To bear him to my bower in fairy land.
And now I have the boy, I will undo
This hateful imperfection of her eyes.
And gentle Puck, take this transformed scalp
From off the head of this Athenian swain,
65 That he awaking when the other do,
May all to Athens back again repair,
And think no more of this night's accidents
But as the fierce vexation of a dream.
But first I will release the fairy queen.
[Squeezes the juice on her eyelids.]
70   Be as thou wast wont to be;
        See as thou wont to see:
        Dian's bud o'er Cupid's flower
        Hath such force and blessed power.
Now my Titania, wake you, my sweet queen.
TITANIA *[waking]*
75 My Oberon! What visions have I seen!
Methought I was enamour'd of an ass.
OBERON   There lies your love.
TITANIA   How came these things to pass?
O how mine eyes do loathe his visage now!
OBERON   Silence awhile. Robin, take off this head.
80 Titania, music call; and strike more dead
Than common sleep, of all these five the sense.
TITANIA   Music ho, music, such as charmeth sleep!
                                        [Soft music.]
PUCK *[taking the ass-head off Bottom]*
Now when thou wak'st, with thine own fool's eyes peep.
OBERON   Sound, music!   *[Music strikes into a dance.]*
        Come my queen, take hands with me,
85 And rock the ground whereon these sleepers be.
[Oberon and Titania dance.]
Now thou and I are new in amity,
And will to-morrow midnight, solemnly,
Dance in Duke Theseus' house triumphantly,
And bless it to all fair prosperity.
90 There shall the pairs of faithful lovers be
Wedded, with Theseus, all in jollity.
PUCK   Fairy king, attend and mark:
            I do hear the morning lark.
OBERON   Then my queen, in silence sad,
95   Trip we after night's shade:
            We the globe can compass soon,
            Swifter than the wandering moon.
TITANIA   Come my lord, and in our flight
            Tell me how it came this night
100   That I sleeping here was found
            With these mortals on the ground.
        Exeunt. The four lovers and Bottom still lie asleep.

    To the winding of horns within, enter THESEUS,
        HIPPOLYTA, EGEUS *and train.*

THESEUS   Go one of you, find out the forester;
        For now our observation is perform'd,

And since we have the vaward of the day,
My love shall hear the music of my hounds.   105
Uncouple in the western valley; let them go;
Dispatch I say, and find the forester.
                                    Exit an attendant.
We will, fair queen, up to the mountain's top,
And mark the musical confusion
Of hounds and echo in conjunction.   110
HIPPOLYTA   I was with Hercules and Cadmus once,
When in a wood of Crete they bay'd the bear
With hounds of Sparta; never did I hear
Such gallant chiding; for, besides the groves,
The skies, the fountains, every region near   115
Seem'd all one mutual cry; I never heard
So musical a discord, such sweet thunder.
THESEUS   My hounds are bred out of the Spartan kind,
So flew'd, so sanded; and their heads are hung
With ears that sweep away the morning dew;   120
Crook-knee'd and dewlapp'd like Thessalian bulls;
Slow in pursuit, but match'd in mouth like bells,
Each under each: a cry more tuneable
Was never holla'd to, nor cheer'd with horn,
In Crete, in Sparta, nor in Thessaly.   125
Judge when you hear. But soft, what nymphs are
    these?
EGEUS   My lord, this is my daughter here asleep,
And this Lysander; this Demetrius is,
This Helena, old Nedar's Helena.
I wonder of their being here together.   130
THESEUS   No doubt they rose up early, to observe
The rite of May; and hearing our intent,
Came here in grace of our solemnity.
But speak, Egeus; is not this the day
That Hermia should give answer of her choice?   135
EGEUS   It is, my lord.
THESEUS
Go, bid the huntsmen wake them with their horns.
[Shout within; winding of horns.]
[The lovers wake and start up.]
Good-morrow friends. Saint Valentine is past:
Begin these wood-birds but to couple now?
LYSANDER   Pardon, my lord. *[The lovers kneel.]*
THESEUS   I pray you all, stand up.   140
I know you two are rival enemies:
How comes this gentle concord in the world,
That hatred is so far from jealousy
To sleep by hate, and fear no enmity?
LYSANDER   My lord, I shall reply amazedly,   145
Half sleep, half waking; but as yet, I swear,
I cannot truly say how I came here.
But as I think – for truly would I speak –
And now I do bethink me, so it is:
I came with Hermia hither; our intent   150
Was to be gone from Athens, where we might,
Without the peril of the Athenian law –
EGEUS   Enough, enough, my lord; you have enough!
I beg the law, the law upon his head!

They would have stol'n away, they would,
   Demetrius,
Thereby to have defeated you and me:
You of your wife, and me of my consent,
Of my consent that she should be your wife.

DEMETRIUS
My lord, fair Helen told me of their stealth,
Of this their purpose hither to this wood;
And I in fury hither follow'd them,
Fair Helena in fancy following me.
But my good lord, I wot not by what power –
But by some power it is – my love to Hermia,
Melted as the snow, seems to me now
As the remembrance of an idle gaud
Which in my childhood I did dote upon;
And all the faith, the virtue of my heart,
The object and the pleasure of mine eye,
Is only Helena. To her, my lord,
Was I betroth'd ere I saw Hermia;
But like a sickness did I loathe this food:
But as in health, come to my natural taste,
Now I do wish it, love it, long for it,
And will for evermore be true to it.

THESEUS Fair lovers, you are fortunately met;
Of this discourse we more will hear anon.
Egeus, I will overbear your will;
For in the temple, by and by, with us,
These couples shall eternally be knit.
And, for the morning now is something worn,
Our purpos'd hunting shall be set aside.
Away, with us, to Athens: three and three,
We'll hold a feast in great solemnity.
Come, Hippolyta.

Exeunt Theseus, Hippolyta, Egeus and train.

DEMETRIUS
These things seem small and undistinguishable,
Like far-off mountains turned into clouds.

HERMIA Methinks I see these things with parted eye,
When everything seems double.

HELENA   So methinks;
And I have found Demetrius like a jewel,
Mine own, and not mine own.

DEMETRIUS   Are you sure
That we are awake? It seems to me
That yet we sleep, we dream. Do not you think
The Duke was here, and bid us follow him?

HERMIA Yea, and my father.

HELENA   And Hippolyta.

LYSANDER And he did bid us follow to the temple.

DEMETRIUS Why then, we are awake: let's follow him,
And by the way let us recount our dreams. *Exeunt.*

BOTTOM [*waking*] When my cue comes, call me and I
will answer. My next is 'Most fair Pyramus'. Heigh-
ho! Peter Quince? Flute, the bellows-mender? Snout,
the tinker? Starveling? God's my life! Stolen hence,
and left me asleep! I have had a most rare vision. I have
had a dream, past the wit of man to say what dream it
was. Man is but an ass if he go about to expound this
dream. Methought I was – there is no man can tell
what. Methought I was – and methought I had – but
man is but a patched fool if he will offer to say what
methought I had. The eye of man hath not heard, the
ear of man hath not seen, man's hand is not able to
taste, his tongue to conceive, nor his heart to report,
what my dream was. I will get Peter Quince to write a
ballad of this dream: it shall be called 'Bottom's
Dream', because it hath no bottom; and I will sing it
in the latter end of a play, before the Duke.
Peradventure, to make it the more gracious, I shall
sing it at her death. *Exit.*

4.2 *Enter* QUINCE, FLUTE, SNOUT *and* STARVELING.

QUINCE Have you sent to Bottom's house? Is he come
home yet?

STARVELING He cannot be heard of. Out of doubt he is
transported.

FLUTE If he come not, then the play is marred: it goes
not forward, doth it?

QUINCE It is not possible. You have not a man in all
Athens able to discharge Pyramus but he.

FLUTE No, he hath simply the best wit of any handicraft
man in Athens.

QUINCE Yea, and the best person too; and he is a very
paramour for a sweet voice.

FLUTE You must say paragon. A paramour is, God bless
us, a thing of naught.

Enter SNUG *the joiner.*

SNUG Masters, the Duke is coming from the temple,
and there is two or three lords and ladies more
married. If our sport had gone forward, we had all
been made men.

FLUTE O sweet bully Bottom! Thus hath he lost
sixpence a day during his life; he could not have
'scaped sixpence a day. And the Duke had not given
him sixpence a day for playing Pyramus, I'll be
hanged. He would have deserved it: sixpence a day in
Pyramus, or nothing.

Enter BOTTOM.

BOTTOM Where are these lads? Where are these hearts?

QUINCE Bottom! O most courageous day! O most happy
hour!

BOTTOM Masters, I am to discourse wonders: but ask
me not what; for if I tell you, I am not true Athenian.
I will tell you everything, right as it fell out.

QUINCE Let us hear, sweet Bottom.

BOTTOM Not a word of me. All that I will tell you is,
that the Duke hath dined. Get your apparel together,
good strings to your beards, new ribbons to your
pumps; meet presently at the palace; every man look
o'er his part: for the short and the long is, our play is

preferred. In any case, let Thisbe have clean linen; and let not him that plays the lion pare his nails, for they shall hang out for the lion's claws. And most dear actors, eat no onions nor garlic, for we are to utter sweet breath; and I do not doubt but to hear them say, it is a sweet comedy. No more words. Away! Go, away!

Exeunt.

5.1   *Enter* THESEUS, HIPPOLYTA; *lords and attendants, among them* PHILOSTRATE.

HIPPOLYTA
'Tis strange, my Theseus, that these lovers speak of.
THESEUS   More strange than true. I never may believe
These antique fables, nor these fairy toys.
Lovers and madmen have such seething brains,
Such shaping fantasies, that apprehend
More than cool reason ever comprehends.
The lunatic, the lover, and the poet
Are of imagination all compact:
One sees more devils than vast hell can hold;
That is the madman: the lover, all as frantic,
Sees Helen's beauty in a brow of Egypt:
The poet's eye, in a fine frenzy rolling,
Doth glance from heaven to earth, from earth to
        heaven;
And as imagination bodies forth
The forms of things unknown, the poet's pen
Turns them to shapes, and gives to airy nothing
A local habitation and a name.
Such tricks hath strong imagination,
That if it would but apprehend some joy,
It comprehends some bringer of that joy:
Or, in the night, imagining some fear,
How easy is a bush suppos'd a bear!
HIPPOLYTA   But all the story of the night told over,
And all their minds transfigur'd so together,
More witnesseth than fancy's images,
And grows to something of great constancy;
But howsoever, strange and admirable.

Enter the lovers: LYSANDER, DEMETRIUS,
HERMIA *and* HELENA.

THESEUS   Here come the lovers, full of joy and mirth.
Joy, gentle friends, joy and fresh days of love
Accompany your hearts!
LYSANDER   More than to us
Wait in your royal walks, your board, your bed!
THESEUS
Come now; what masques, what dances shall we
        have,
To wear away this long age of three hours
Between our after-supper and bed-time?
Where is our usual manager of mirth?
What revels are in hand? Is there no play
To ease the anguish of a torturing hour?
Call Philostrate.

PHILOSTRATE [*advancing*]   Here, mighty Theseus.
THESEUS
Say, what abridgement have you for this evening,
What masque, what music? How shall we beguile
The lazy time, if not with some delight?
PHILOSTRATE
There is a brief how many sports are ripe:
Make choice of which your Highness will see first.
[*giving a paper*]
THESEUS [*Reads.*]
The battle with the Centaurs, to be sung
By an Athenian eunuch to the harp?
We'll none of that; that have I told my love
In glory of my kinsman Hercules.
[*Reads.*] *The riot of the tipsy Bacchanals,*
Tearing the Thracian singer in their rage?
That is an old device, and it was play'd
When I from Thebes came last a conqueror.
[*Reads.*] *The thrice three Muses mourning for the death*
Of learning, late deceas'd in beggary?
That is some satire, keen and critical,
Not sorting with a nuptial ceremony.
[*Reads.*] *A tedious brief scene of young Pyramus*
And his love Thisbe, very tragical mirth?
Merry and tragical? Tedious and brief?
That is hot ice, and wondrous strange snow!
How shall we find the concord of this discord?
PHILOSTRATE
A play there is, my lord, some ten words long,
Which is as brief as I have known a play;
But by ten words, my lord, it is too long,
Which makes it tedious; for in all the play
There is not one word apt, one player fitted.
And tragical, my noble lord, it is,
For Pyramus therein doth kill himself;
Which, when I saw rehears'd, I must confess
Made mine eyes water; but more merry tears
The passion of loud laughter never shed.
THESEUS   What are they that do play it?
PHILOSTRATE
Hard-handed men that work in Athens here,
Which never labour'd in their minds till now;
And now have toil'd their unbreath'd memories
With this same play, against your nuptial.
THESEUS   And we will hear it.
PHILOSTRATE   No, my noble lord,
It is not for you: I have heard it over,
And it is nothing, nothing in the world;
Unless you can find sport in their intents,
Extremely stretch'd and conn'd with cruel pain
To do you service.
THESEUS   I will hear that play;
For never anything can be amiss
When simpleness and duty tender it.
Go bring them in; and take your places, ladies.

Exit Philostrate.

HIPPOLYTA   I love not to see wretchedness o'er-charg'd, 85
    And duty in his service perishing.
THESEUS   Why, gentle sweet, you shall see no such thing.
HIPPOLYTA   He says they can do nothing in this kind.
THESEUS
    The kinder we, to give them thanks for nothing.
    Our sport shall be to take what they mistake: 90
    And what poor duty cannot do, noble respect
    Takes it in might, not merit.
    Where I have come, great clerks have purposed
    To greet me with premeditated welcomes;
    Where I have seen them shiver and look pale, 95
    Make periods in the midst of sentences,
    Throttle their practis'd accent in their fears,
    And, in conclusion, dumbly have broke off,
    Not paying me a welcome. Trust me, sweet,
    Out of this silence yet I pick'd a welcome, 100
    And in the modesty of fearful duty
    I read as much as from the rattling tongue
    Of saucy and audacious eloquence.
    Love, therefore, and tongue-tied simplicity
    In least speak most, to my capacity. 105

Enter PHILOSTRATE.

PHILOSTRATE
    So please your grace, the Prologue is address'd.
THESEUS   Let him approach.

[*Flourish of trumpets.*]

Enter QUINCE *for the* PROLOGUE.

PROLOGUE   *If we offend, it is with our good will.*
    That you should think, we come not to offend,
    But with good will. To show our simple skill, 110
    That is the true beginning of our end.
    Consider then, we come but in despite.
    We do not come, as minding to content you,
    Our true intent is. All for your delight,
    We are not here. That you should here repent you, 115
    The actors are at hand; and by their show,
    You shall know all, that you are like to know.
THESEUS   This fellow doth not stand upon points.
LYSANDER   He hath rid his prologue like a rough colt; he
    knows not the stop. A good moral, my lord: it is not 120
    enough to speak, but to speak true.
HIPPOLYTA   Indeed he hath played on this prologue like
    a child on a recorder; a sound, but not in government.
THESEUS   His speech was like a tangled chain; nothing
    impaired, but all disordered. Who is next? 125

Enter, with a trumpeter before them, BOTTOM *as* PYRAMUS,
FLUTE *as* THISBE, SNOUT *as* WALL,
STARVELING *as* MOONSHINE *and* SNUG *as* LION.

PROLOGUE   *Gentles, perchance you wonder at this show;*
    But wonder on, till truth make all things plain.
    This man is Pyramus, if you would know;
    This beauteous lady Thisbe is certain.
    This man, with lime and rough-cast, doth present 130

    Wall, that vile wall which did these lovers sunder;
    And through Wall's chink, poor souls, they are content
    To whisper. At the which let no man wonder.
    This man, with lantern, dog, and bush of thorn,
    Presenteth Moonshine; for, if you will know, 135
    By moonshine did these lovers think no scorn
    To meet at Ninus' tomb, there, there to woo.
    This grisly beast, which Lion hight by name,
    The trusty Thisbe, coming first by night,
    Did scare away, or rather did affright; 140
    And as she fled, her mantle she did fall,
    Which Lion vile with bloody mouth did stain.
    Anon comes Pyramus, sweet youth and tall,
    And finds his trusty Thisbe's mantle slain;
    Whereat with blade, with bloody blameful blade, 145
    He bravely broach'd his boiling bloody breast;
    And Thisbe, tarrying in mulberry shade,
    His dagger drew, and died. For all the rest.
    Let Lion, Moonshine, Wall, and lovers twain
    At large discourse, while here they do remain. 150
        Exeunt Prologue, Pyramus, Thisbe, Lion
                and Moonshine.
THESEUS   I wonder if the lion be to speak?
DEMETRIUS   No wonder, my lord; one lion may when
    many asses do.
WALL   *In this same interlude it doth befall*
    That I, one Snout by name, present a wall; 155
    And such a wall as I would have you think
    That had in it a crannied hole, or chink,
    Through which the lovers, Pyramus and Thisbe,
    Did whisper often, very secretly.
    This loam, this rough-cast, and this stone doth show 160
    That I am that same wall; the truth is so:
    And this the cranny is, right and sinister,
    Through which the fearful lovers are to whisper.
THESEUS   Would you desire lime and hair to speak better?
DEMETRIUS   It is the wittiest partition that ever I heard 165
    discourse, my lord.

Enter PYRAMUS.

THESEUS   Pyramus draws near the wall; silence!
PYRAMUS   *O grim-look'd night! O night with hue so black!*
    O night, which ever art when day is not!
    O night, O night, alack, alack, alack, 170
    I fear my Thisbe's promise is forgot!
    And thou, O wall, O sweet, O lovely wall,
    That stand'st between her father's ground and mine;
    Thou wall, O wall, O sweet and lovely wall,
    Show me thy chink, to blink through with mine eyne. 175
    [*Wall stretches out his fingers.*]
    Thanks, courteous wall: Jove shield thee well for this!
    But what see I? No Thisbe do I see.
    O wicked wall, through whom I see no bliss,
    Curs'd thy stones for thus deceiving me!
THESEUS   The wall, methinks, being sensible, should 180
    curse again.
PYRAMUS   No, in truth sir, he should not. 'Deceiving

me' is Thisbe's cue: she is to enter now, and I am to
spy her through the wall. You shall see it will fall pat
185   as I told you: yonder she comes.

Enter THISBE.

THISBE   *O wall, full often hast thou heard my moans,*
     For parting my fair Pyramus and me!
     My cherry lips have often kiss'd thy stones,
     Thy stones with lime and hair knit up in thee.
190   PYRAMUS   *I see a voice; now will I to the chink,*
     To spy and I can hear my Thisbe's face.
     Thisbe?
THISBE   *My love thou art, my love I think!*
PYRAMUS   *Think what thou wilt, I am thy lover's grace;*
     And like Limander am I trusty still.
195   THISBE   *And I like Helen, till the Fates me kill.*
PYRAMUS   *Not Shafalus to Procrus was so true.*
THISBE   *As Shafalus to Procrus, I to you.*
PYRAMUS   *O kiss me through the hole of this vile wall.*
THISBE   *I kiss the wall's hole, not your lips at all.*
200   PYRAMUS   *Wilt thou at Ninny's tomb meet me straightway?*
THISBE   *'Tide life, 'tide death, I come without delay.*
             Exeunt Pyramus and Thisbe, severally.
WALL   *Thus have I, Wall, my part discharged so;*
     And, being done, thus Wall away doth go.   *Exit.*
THESEUS   Now is the mure rased between the two
205   neighbours.
DEMETRIUS   No remedy my lord, when walls are so
     wilful to hear without warning.
HIPPOLYTA   This is the silliest stuff that ever I heard.
THESEUS   The best in this kind are but shadows; and the
210   worst are no worse, if imagination amend them.
HIPPOLYTA   It must be your imagination then, and not
     theirs.
THESEUS   If we imagine no worse of them than they of
     themselves, they may pass for excellent men. Here
215   come two noble beasts in, a man and a lion.

Enter LION *and* MOONSHINE.

LION   *You ladies, you whose gentle hearts do fear*
     The smallest monstrous mouse that creeps on floor,
     May now, perchance, both quake and tremble here,
     When lion rough in wildest rage doth roar.
220   *Then know that I as Snug the joiner am*
     A lion fell, nor else no lion's dam;
     For if I should as lion come in strife
     Into this place, 'twere pity on my life.
THESEUS   A very gentle beast, and of a good conscience.
225   DEMETRIUS   The very best at a beast, my lord, that e'er
     I saw.
LYSANDER   This lion is a very fox for his valour.
THESEUS   True; and a goose for his discretion.
DEMETRIUS   Not so, my lord, for his valour cannot carry
230   his discretion; and the fox carries the goose.
THESEUS   His discretion, I am sure, cannot carry his
     valour; for the goose carries not the fox. It is well: leave
     it to his discretion, and let us listen to the moon.

MOONSHINE   *This lantern doth the horned moon present –*
DEMETRIUS   He should have worn the horns on his head.   235
THESEUS   He is no crescent, and his horns are invisible
     within the circumference.
MOONSHINE   *This lantern doth the horned moon present;*
     Myself the Man i'th' Moon do seem to be.
THESEUS   This is the greatest error of all the rest; the   240
     man should be put into the lantern. How is it else the
     Man i'the Moon?
DEMETRIUS   He dares not come there for the candle; for
     you see it is already in snuff.
HIPPOLYTA   I am aweary of this moon. Would he would   245
     change!
THESEUS   It appears by his small light of discretion that
     he is in the wane; but yet in courtesy, in all reason, we
     must stay the time.
LYSANDER   Proceed, Moon.   250
MOONSHINE   All that I have to say is, to tell you that the
     lantern is the moon; I the Man i'th' Moon; this thorn-
     bush my thorn-bush; and this dog my dog.
DEMETRIUS   Why, all these should be in the lantern, for
     all these are in the moon. But silence: here comes   255
     Thisbe.

Enter THISBE.

THISBE   *This is old Ninny's tomb. Where is my love?*
LION   *O – !*   *The Lion roars. Thisbe,*
             dropping her mantle, runs off.
DEMETRIUS   Well roared, Lion!
THESEUS   Well run, Thisbe!   260
HIPPOLYTA   Well shone, Moon! Truly, the moon shines
     with a good grace.
             The Lion worries the mantle, and exit.
THESEUS   Well moused, Lion!
DEMETRIUS   And then came Pyramus –
LYSANDER   And so the lion vanished.   265

Enter PYRAMUS.

PYRAMUS   *Sweet Moon, I thank thee for thy sunny beams;*
     I thank thee, Moon, for shining now so bright;
     For by thy gracious, golden, glittering gleams,
     I trust to take of truest Thisbe sight.
       But stay! O spite!   270
       But mark, poor knight,
       What dreadful dole is here?
       Eyes, do you see?
       How can it be?
     O dainty duck! O dear!   275
       Thy mantle good,
       What! Stain'd with blood?
     Approach, ye Furies fell!
       O Fates, come, come!
       Cut thread and thrum: 280
     Quail, crush, conclude, and quell.
THESEUS   This passion, and the death of a dear friend,
     would go near to make a man look sad.
HIPPOLYTA   Beshrew my heart, but I pity the man.

PYRAMUS   *O wherefore, Nature, didst thou lions frame,*
    Since lion vile hath here deflow'r'd my dear?
    Which is – no, no – which was the fairest dame
    That liv'd, that lov'd, that lik'd, that look'd with cheer.
        Come tears, confound!
        Out sword, and wound
        The pap of Pyramus;
        Ay, that left pap,
        Where heart doth hop: [*Stabs himself.*]
    Thus die I, thus, thus, thus!
        Now am I dead,
        Now am I fled;
    My soul is in the sky.
    Tongue, lose thy light;
    Moon, take thy flight!
                Exit Moonshine.
    Now die, die, die, die, die. [*Dies.*]

DEMETRIUS   No die, but an ace for him; for he is but one.

LYSANDER   Less than an ace, man; for he is dead, he is nothing.

THESEUS   With the help of a surgeon he might yet recover, and prove an ass.

HIPPOLYTA   How chance Moonshine is gone, before Thisbe comes back and finds her lover?

THESEUS   She will find him by starlight.

        Enter THISBE.

Here she comes, and her passion ends the play.

HIPPOLYTA   Methinks she should not use a long one for such a Pyramus; I hope she will be brief.

DEMETRIUS   A mote will turn the balance, which Pyramus, which Thisbe, is the better: he for a man, God warrant us; she for a woman, God bless us!

LYSANDER   She hath spied him already with those sweet eyes.

DEMETRIUS   And thus she means, videlicet –

THISBE   *Asleep, my love?*
    What, dead, my dove?
  O Pyramus, arise!
    Speak, speak! Quite dumb?
    Dead, dead? A tomb
  Must cover thy sweet eyes.
    These lily lips,
    This cherry nose,
  These yellow cowslip cheeks,
    Are gone, are gone!
    Lovers, make moan;
  His eyes were green as leeks.
    O Sisters Three,
    Come, come to me,
  With hands as pale as milk;
    Lay them in gore,
    Since you have shore
  With shears his thread of silk.
    Tongue, not a word:

    Come, trusty sword,
  Come, blade, my breast imbrue! [*Stabs herself.*]
    And farewell, friends;   340
    Thus Thisbe ends:
  Adieu, adieu, adieu! [*Dies.*]

THESEUS   Moonshine and Lion are left to bury the dead.

DEMETRIUS   Ay, and Wall too.   345

BOTTOM [*starting up*]   No, I assure you; the wall is down that parted their fathers. [*Flute rises.*] Will it please you to see the epilogue, or to hear a Bergomask dance between two of our company?

THESEUS   No epilogue, I pray you; for your play needs   350
no excuse. Never excuse; for when the players are all dead, there need none to be blamed. Marry, if he that writ it had played Pyramus, and hanged himself in Thisbe's garter, it would have been a fine tragedy – and so it is, truly, and very notably discharged. But   355
come, your Bergomask; let your epilogue alone.

    Enter QUINCE, SNUG, SNOUT *and* STARVELING
    two of whom dance a bergamask. Then exeunt
    handicraftsmen, including Flute and Bottom.

The iron tongue of midnight hath told twelve.
Lovers, to bed; 'tis almost fairy time.
I fear we shall outsleep the coming morn
As much as we this night have overwatch'd.   360
This palpable-gross play hath well beguil'd
The heavy gait of night. Sweet friends, to bed.
A fortnight hold we this solemnity
In nightly revels and new jollity.   *Exeunt.*

    Enter PUCK.

PUCK   Now the hungry lion roars,   365
    And the wolf behowls the moon;
    Whilst the heavy ploughman snores,
    All with weary task fordone.
    Now the wasted brands do glow,
    Whilst the screech-owl, screeching loud,   370
    Puts the wretch that lies in woe
    In remembrance of a shroud.
    Now it is the time of night
    That the graves, all gaping wide,
    Every one lets forth his sprite   375
    In the church-way paths to glide.
    And we fairies, that do run
    By the triple Hecate's team
    From the presence of the sun,
    Following darkness like a dream,   380
    Now are frolic; not a mouse
    Shall disturb this hallow'd house.
    I am sent with broom before
    To sweep the dust behind the door.

    Enter OBERON *and* TITANIA, *the King and*
    Queen of Fairies, with all their train.

385	OBERON	Through the house give glimmering light
		By the dead and drowsy fire;
		Every elf and fairy sprite
		Hop as light as bird from briar;
		And this ditty after me
390		Sing, and dance it trippingly.
	TITANIA	First rehearse your song by rote,
		To each word a warbling note;
		Hand in hand, with fairy grace,
		Will we sing, and bless this place.

[*Oberon leading, the Fairies sing and dance.*]

395	OBERON	Now, until the break of day,
		Through this house each fairy stray.
		To the best bride-bed will we,
		Which by us shall blessed be;
		And the issue there create
400		Ever shall be fortunate.
		So shall all the couples three
		Ever true in loving be;
		And the blots of Nature's hand
		Shall not in their issue stand:
405		Never mole, hare-lip, nor scar,
		Nor mark prodigious, such as are
		Despised in nativity,
		Shall upon their children be.
		With this field-dew consecrate,

Every fairy take his gait,   410
And each several chamber bless
Through this palace with sweet peace;
And the owner of it blest,
Ever shall in safety rest.
Trip away; make no stay;   415
Meet me all by break of day.

              Exeunt all but Puck.

PUCK [*to the audience*]
   If we shadows have offended,
   Think but this, and all is mended,
   That you have but slumber'd here
   While these visions did appear.   420
   And this weak and idle theme,
   No more yielding but a dream,
   Gentles, do not reprehend:
   If you pardon, we will mend.
   And, as I am an honest Puck,   425
   If we have unearned luck
   Now to 'scape the serpent's tongue,
   We will make amends ere long;
   Else the Puck a liar call.
   So, goodnight unto you all.   430
   Give me your hands, if we be friends,
   And Robin shall restore amends.   *Exit.*

Much Ado About Nothing

A Quarto edition of *Much Ado About Nothing* appeared in 1600, and the play was not reprinted until it was included in the First Folio in 1623 in a text based on the Quarto. A number of relatively minor inconsistencies in the text have been variously explained as errors in transmission or authorial loose ends. The title-page of the Quarto claims that the play had been 'sundry times publicly acted' by the Lord Chamberlain's Men, Shakespeare's regular company. Unless it is identified with the mysterious *Love's Labour's Won*, it does not occur in Francis Meres's list of Shakespeare's comedies in 1598; this has caused scholars to believe that it was written in the second half of 1598 or 1599. It cannot have been written later than 1599 as the Quarto sometimes uses the name of Will Kemp instead of Dogberry in speech-headings, and this famous comic actor left the company in that year. It probably came after *A Midsummer Night's Dream* and before *As You Like It* and *Twelfth Night*. Although we do not have records of early performances of the play, allusions to it indicate that it must have been well known, and it was revived for a Court performance at Whitehall before King James I's daughter Princess Elizabeth and her husband the Elector Palatine in May 1613.

The plot of the play combines the tragicomic story of the courtship of Hero and Claudio (in scenes written mainly in verse) with the witty sparring of Beatrice and Benedick (in scenes written mainly in prose). The latter pair are tricked into acknowledging that their posture of disliking each other conceals their love. Leonard Digges referred to the popularity of Beatrice and Benedick in his prefatory tribute to the 1640 edition of Shakespeare's poems, and King Charles I wrote 'Benedik and Betrice' as a kind of alternative title in his copy of the 1632

Second Folio; the 'merry war' between these two characters (reminiscent of that between Berowne and Rosaline in *Love's Labour's Lost*) usually dominates productions. *Much Ado* is also, however, of particular interest in that it contains Shakespeare's earliest version of the more serious story of the man who mistakenly believes his partner has been unfaithful to him. This story is an ancient one, and Shakespeare could have used a number of Renaissance versions as his source(s). The triangle of Don John (deceiving villain), Claudio (credulous lover or husband) and Hero (slandered fiancée or wife) reappears in Iago, Othello and Desdemona and again in Iachimo, Posthumus and Imogen (in *Cymbeline*). Like Othello and Posthumus, Claudio is held responsible for the death (or apparent death) of the woman, although he at least does not mean to kill her. Not surprisingly recent critics, especially feminists, have found it difficult to forgive such behaviour.

In the Restoration William Davenant amalgamated parts of *Much Ado* with parts of *Measure for Measure* to produce an adaptation called *The Law Against Lovers* (1662), and Shakespeare's play was performed only sporadically until David Garrick's acclaimed revival in 1748. Thereafter it continued to be popular on stage with actors such as Charles Kemble, Henry Irving and John Gielgud starring as Benedick, partnered respectively by Helen Faucit, Ellen Terry and Peggy Ashcroft as Beatrice. Not a text which had previously attracted many film-makers, it received a boost in its recent fortunes with the 1993 version directed by Kenneth Branagh and starring Branagh and Emma Thompson.

The Arden text is based on the 1600 Quarto.

DON PEDRO	*Prince of Aragon*
DON JOHN	*his bastard brother*
CLAUDIO	*a young lord of Florence*
BENEDICK	*a young lord of Padua*
LEONATO	*governor of Messina*
ANTONIO	*his brother*
BALTHASAR	*a singer, attendant on Don Pedro*
CONRADE	
BORACHIO	} *followers of Don John*
FRIAR FRANCIS	
DOGBERRY	*master constable*
VERGES	*a headborough*
FIRST WATCHMAN	
SECOND WATCHMAN	
SEXTON	
BOY	
LORD	
HERO	*daughter to Leonato*
BEATRICE	*niece to Leonato*
MARGARET	
URSULA	} *gentlewoman attending on Hero*

Messengers, Musicians, Watchmen, Attendants, etc.

Much Ado About Nothing

1.1 *Enter* LEONATO, *Governor of Messina,* HERO, *his daughter, and* BEATRICE, *his niece, with a* Messenger.

LEONATO I learn in this letter that Don Pedro of Aragon comes this night to Messina.

MESSENGER He is very near by this, he was not three leagues off when I left him.

LEONATO How many gentlemen have you lost in this action?

MESSENGER But few of any sort, and none of name.

LEONATO A victory is twice itself when the achiever brings home full numbers. I find here that Don Pedro hath bestowed much honour on a young Florentine called Claudio.

MESSENGER Much deserved on his part, and equally remembered by Don Pedro. He hath borne himself beyond the promise of his age, doing, in the figure of a lamb, the feats of a lion: he hath indeed better bettered expectation than you must expect of me to tell you how.

LEONATO He hath an uncle here in Messina will be very much glad of it.

MESSENGER I have already delivered him letters, and there appears much joy in him, even so much that joy could not show itself modest enough without a badge of bitterness.

LEONATO Did he break out into tears?

MESSENGER In great measure.

LEONATO A kind overflow of kindness: there are no faces truer than those that are so washed. How much better is it to weep at joy than to joy at weeping!

BEATRICE I pray you, is Signior Mountanto returned from the wars or no?

MESSENGER I know none of that name, lady, there was none such in the army of any sort.

LEONATO What is he that you ask for, niece?

HERO My cousin means Signior Benedick of Padua.

MESSENGER O, he's returned, and as pleasant as ever he was.

BEATRICE He set up his bills here in Messina and challenged Cupid at the flight; and my uncle's fool, reading the challenge, subscribed for Cupid, and challenged him at the bird-bolt. I pray you, how many hath he killed and eaten in these wars? But how many hath he killed? For indeed I promised to eat all of his killing.

LEONATO Faith, niece, you tax Signior Benedick too much, but he'll be meet with you, I doubt it not.

MESSENGER He hath done good service, lady, in these wars.

BEATRICE You had musty victual, and he hath holp to eat it: he is a very valiant trencher-man; he hath an excellent stomach.

MESSENGER And a good soldier too, lady.

BEATRICE And a good soldier to a lady; but what is he to a lord?

MESSENGER A lord to a lord, a man to a man, stuffed with all honourable virtues.

BEATRICE It is so indeed, he is no less than a stuffed man; but for the stuffing – well, we are all mortal.

LEONATO You must not, sir, mistake my niece. There is a kind of merry war betwixt Signior Benedick and her: they never meet but there's a skirmish of wit between them.

BEATRICE Alas, he gets nothing by that. In our last conflict four of his five wits went halting off, and now is the whole man governed with one: so that if he have wit enough to keep himself warm, let him bear it for a difference between himself and his horse, for it is all the wealth that he hath left, to be known a reasonable creature. Who is his companion now? He hath every month a new sworn brother.

MESSENGER Is't possible?

BEATRICE Very easily possible: he wears his faith but as the fashion of his hat, it ever changes with the next block.

MESSENGER I see, lady, the gentleman is not in your books.

BEATRICE No; and he were, I would burn my study. But I pray you, who is his companion? Is there no young squarer now that will make a voyage with him to the devil?

MESSENGER He is most in the company of the right noble Claudio.

BEATRICE O Lord, he will hang upon him like a disease; he is sooner caught than the pestilence, and the taker runs presently mad. God help the noble Claudio! If he have caught the Benedick, it will cost him a thousand pound ere a be cured.

MESSENGER I will hold friends with you, lady.

BEATRICE Do, good friend.

LEONATO You will never run mad, niece.

BEATRICE No, not till a hot January.

MESSENGER Don Pedro is approached.

Enter DON PEDRO, CLAUDIO, BENEDICK, BALTHASAR *and* DON JOHN *the Bastard.*

DON PEDRO Good Signior Leonato, are you come to meet your trouble? The fashion of the world is to avoid cost, and you encounter it.

LEONATO Never came trouble to my house in the likeness of your Grace, for trouble being gone, comfort should remain; but when you depart from me, sorrow abides, and happiness takes his leave.

DON PEDRO You embrace your charge too willingly. I think this is your daughter.

LEONATO Her mother hath many times told me so.

BENEDICK Were you in doubt, sir, that you asked her?

LEONATO Signior Benedick, no, for then were you a child.

DON PEDRO You have it full, Benedick; we may guess by this what you are, being a man. Truly the lady fathers herself. Be happy, lady, for you are like an honourable father.

BENEDICK If Signior Leonato be her father, she would

not have his head on her shoulders for all Messina, as
like him as she is. [*Don Pedro and Leonato talk aside.*]

BEATRICE   I wonder that you will still be talking, Signior
Benedick: nobody marks you.

BENEDICK   What, my dear Lady Disdain! Are you yet
living?

BEATRICE   Is it possible disdain should die, while she
hath such meet food to feed it as Signior Benedick?
Courtesy itself must convert to disdain, if you come in
her presence.

BENEDICK   Then is courtesy a turncoat. But it is certain
I am loved of all ladies, only you excepted; and I would
I could find in my heart that I had not a hard heart, for
truly I love none.

BEATRICE   A dear happiness to women, they would else
have been troubled with a pernicious suitor. I thank
God and my cold blood, I am of your humour for that;
I had rather hear my dog bark at a crow than a man
swear he loves me.

BENEDICK   God keep your ladyship still in that mind, so
some gentleman or other shall scape a predestinate
scratched face.

BEATRICE   Scratching could not make it worse, and
'twere such a face as yours were.

BENEDICK   Well, you are a rare parrot-teacher.

BEATRICE   A bird of my tongue is better than a beast of
yours.

BENEDICK   I would my horse had the speed of your
tongue, and so good a continuer. But keep your way, a
God's name, I have done.

BEATRICE   You always end with a jade's trick, I know you
of old.

DON PEDRO   That is the sum of all, Leonato. [*turning to
the company*] Signior Claudio and Signior Benedick,
my dear friend Leonato hath invited you all. I tell him
we shall stay here at the least a month, and he heartily
prays some occasion may detain us longer: I dare
swear he is no hypocrite, but prays from his heart.

LEONATO   If you swear, my lord, you shall not be
forsworn. [*to Don John*] Let me bid you welcome, my
lord, being reconciled to the Prince your brother: I
owe you all duty.

DON JOHN   I thank you: I am not of many words, but I
thank you.

LEONATO   Please it your Grace lead on?

DON PEDRO   Your hand, Leonato, we will go together.
                          Exeunt all but Benedick and Claudio.

CLAUDIO   Benedick, didst thou note the daughter of
Signior Leonato?

BENEDICK   I noted her not, but I looked on her.

CLAUDIO   Is she not a modest young lady?

BENEDICK   Do you question me as an honest man
should do, for my simple true judgement, or would
you have me speak after my custom, as being a
professed tyrant to their sex?

CLAUDIO   No, I pray thee speak in sober judgement.

BENEDICK   Why, i'faith, methinks she's too low for a
high praise, too brown for a fair praise, and too little
for a great praise: only this commendation I can afford
her, that were she other than she is, she were
unhandsome, and being no other but as she is, I do
not like her.

CLAUDIO   Thou thinkest I am in sport: I pray thee tell
me truly how thou lik'st her.

BENEDICK   Would you buy her, that you inquire after her?

CLAUDIO   Can the world buy such a jewel?

BENEDICK   Yea, and a case to put it into. But speak you
this with a sad brow, or do you play the flouting Jack,
to tell us Cupid is a good hare-finder, and Vulcan a
rare carpenter? Come, in what key shall a man take
you to go in the song?

CLAUDIO   In mine eye, she is the sweetest lady that ever
I looked on.

BENEDICK   I can see yet without spectacles, and I see no
such matter: there's her cousin, and she were not
possessed with a fury, exceeds her as much in beauty
as the first of May doth the last of December. But I
hope you have no intent to turn husband, have you?

CLAUDIO   I would scarce trust myself, though I had
sworn the contrary, if Hero would be my wife.

BENEDICK   Is't come to this? In faith, hath not the world
one man but he will wear his cap with suspicion? Shall
I never see a bachelor of threescore again? Go to, i'
faith, and thou wilt needs thrust thy neck into a yoke,
wear the print of it and sigh away Sundays. Look, Don
Pedro is returned to seek you.

                          Enter DON PEDRO.

DON PEDRO   What secret hath held you here, that you
followed not to Leonato's?

BENEDICK   I would your Grace would constrain me to tell.

DON PEDRO   I charge thee on thy allegiance.

BENEDICK   You hear, Count Claudio: I can be secret as a
dumb man, I would have you think so; but on my
allegiance, mark you this, on my allegiance – he is in
love. With who? Now that is your Grace's part.
Mark how short his answer is: with Hero, Leonato's
short daughter.

CLAUDIO   If this were so, so were it uttered.

BENEDICK   Like the old tale, my lord: 'It is not so, nor
'twas not so: but indeed, God forbid it should be so!'

CLAUDIO   If my passion change not shortly, God forbid
it should be otherwise.

DON PEDRO   Amen, if you love her, for the lady is very
well worthy.

CLAUDIO   You speak this to fetch me in, my lord.

DON PEDRO   By my troth, I speak my thought.

CLAUDIO   And in faith, my lord, I spoke mine.

BENEDICK   And by my two faiths and troths, my lord, I
spoke mine.

CLAUDIO   That I love her, I feel.

DON PEDRO   That she is worthy, I know.

BENEDICK   That I neither feel how she should be loved,
nor know how she should be worthy, is the opinion that

220   fire cannot melt out of me; I will die in it at the stake.

DON PEDRO   Thou wast ever an obstinate heretic in the despite of beauty.

CLAUDIO   And never could maintain his part, but in the force of his will.

225 BENEDICK   That a woman conceived me, I thank her: that she brought me up, I likewise give her most humble thanks: but that I will have a recheat winded in my forehead, or hang my bugle in an invisible baldrick, all women shall pardon me. Because I will
230 not do them the wrong to mistrust any, I will do myself the right to trust none: and the fine is, for the which I may go the finer, I will live a bachelor.

DON PEDRO   I shall see thee, ere I die, look pale with love.

BENEDICK   With anger, with sickness, or with hunger,
235 my lord, not with love: prove that ever I lose more blood with love than I will get again with drinking, pick out mine eyes with a ballad-maker's pen, and hang me up at the door of a brothel-house for the sign of blind Cupid.

240 DON PEDRO   Well, if ever thou dost fall from this faith, thou wilt prove a notable argument.

BENEDICK   If I do, hang me in a bottle like a cat and shoot at me, and he that hits me, let him be clapped on the shoulder and called Adam.

245 DON PEDRO   Well, as time shall try. 'In time the savage bull doth bear the yoke.'

BENEDICK   The savage bull may; but if ever the sensible Benedick bear it, pluck off the bull's horns and set them in my forehead, and let me be vilely painted, and
250 in such great letters as they write, 'Here is good horse to hire,' let them signify under my sign, 'Here you may see Benedick, the married man.'

CLAUDIO   If this should ever happen, thou wouldst be horn-mad.

255 DON PEDRO   Nay, if Cupid have not spent all his quiver in Venice, thou wilt quake for this shortly.

BENEDICK   I look for an earthquake too, then.

DON PEDRO   Well, you will temporize with the hours. In the meantime, good Signior Benedick, repair to
260 Leonato's, commend me to him, and tell him I will not fail him at supper; for indeed he hath made great preparation.

BENEDICK   I have almost matter enough in me for such an embassage; and so I commit you –

265 CLAUDIO   To the tuition of God. From my house, if I had it –

DON PEDRO   The sixth of July. Your loving friend, Benedick.

BENEDICK   Nay, mock not, mock not; the body of your discourse is sometime guarded with fragments, and
270 the guards are but slightly basted on neither. Ere you flout old ends any further, examine your conscience; and so I leave you.   *Exit.*

CLAUDIO   My liege, your Highness now may do me good.

DON PEDRO   My love is thine to teach: teach it but how,
275   And thou shalt see how apt it is to learn
  Any hard lesson that may do thee good.

CLAUDIO   Hath Leonato any son, my lord?

DON PEDRO   No child but Hero, she's his only heir.
  Dost thou affect her, Claudio?

CLAUDIO   O my lord,
  When you went onward on this ended action, 280
  I look'd upon her with a soldier's eye,
  That lik'd, but had a rougher task in hand
  Than to drive liking to the name of love:
  But now I am return'd, and that war-thoughts
  Have left their places vacant, in their rooms 285
  Come thronging soft and delicate desires,
  All prompting me how fair young Hero is,
  Saying I lik'd her ere I went to wars.

DON PEDRO   Thou wilt be like a lover presently,
  And tire the hearer with a book of words. 290
  If thou dost love fair Hero, cherish it,
  And I will break with her, and with her father,
  And thou shalt have her. Was't not to this end
  That thou began'st to twist so fine a story?

CLAUDIO   How sweetly you do minister to love 295
  That know love's grief by his complexion!
  But lest my liking might too sudden seem,
  I would have salv'd it with a longer treatise.

DON PEDRO
  What need the bridge much broader than the flood?
  The fairest grant is the necessity. 300
  Look what will serve is fit: 'tis once, thou lovest,
  And I will fit thee with the remedy.
  I know we shall have revelling tonight:
  I will assume thy part in some disguise,
  And tell fair Hero I am Claudio, 305
  And in her bosom I'll unclasp my heart,
  And take her hearing prisoner with the force
  And strong encounter of my amorous tale:
  Then after to her father will I break,
  And the conclusion is, she shall be thine. 310
  In practice let us put it presently.   *Exeunt.*

1.2   *Enter* LEONATO *and an old man,* ANTONIO, *brother to Leonato, meeting.*

LEONATO   How now, brother, where is my cousin, your son? Hath he provided this music?

ANTONIO   He is very busy about it. But brother, I can tell you strange news that you yet dreamt not of.

LEONATO   Are they good? 5

ANTONIO   As the event stamps them, but they have a good cover; they show well outward. The Prince and Count Claudio, walking in a thick-pleached alley in mine orchard, were thus much overheard by a man of mine: the Prince discovered to Claudio that he loved 10 my niece your daughter, and meant to acknowledge it this night in a dance; and if he found her accordant, he meant to take the present time by the top and instantly break with you of it.

LEONATO   Hath the fellow any wit that told you this? 15

ANTONIO   A good sharp fellow; I will send for him, and

question him yourself.

LEONATO No, no, we will hold it as a dream till it appear itself: but I will acquaint my daughter withal, that she may be the better prepared for an answer, if peradventure this be true. Go you and tell her of it.

                Exit Antonio.

Enter Antonio's Son, with a Musician and others.

Cousins, you know what you have to do. [*to the musician*] O, I cry you mercy, friend, go you with me and I will use your skill. Good cousin, have a care this busy time.   *Exeunt.*

1.3 *Enter* DON JOHN *the Bastard and* CONRADE, *his companion.*

CONRADE What the good-year, my lord, why are you thus out of measure sad?

DON JOHN There is no measure in the occasion that breeds, therefore the sadness is without limit.

CONRADE You should hear reason.

DON JOHN And when I have heard it, what blessing brings it?

CONRADE If not a present remedy, at least a patient sufferance.

DON JOHN I wonder that thou – being, as thou say'st thou art, born under Saturn – goest about to apply a moral medicine to a mortifying mischief. I cannot hide what I am: I must be sad when I have cause, and smile at no man's jests; eat when I have stomach, and wait for no man's leisure; sleep when I am drowsy, and tend on no man's business; laugh when I am merry, and claw no man in his humour.

CONRADE Yea, but you must not make the full show of this till you may do it without controlment. You have of late stood out against your brother, and he hath ta'en you newly into his grace, where it is impossible you should take true root but by the fair weather that you make yourself. It is needful that you frame the season for your own harvest.

DON JOHN I had rather be a canker in a hedge than a rose in his grace, and it better fits my blood to be disdained of all than to fashion a carriage to rob love from any: in this, though I cannot be said to be a flattering honest man, it must not be denied but I am a plain-dealing villain. I am trusted with a muzzle and enfranchised with a clog; therefore I have decreed not to sing in my cage. If I had my mouth I would bite; if I had my liberty I would do my liking: in the meantime, let me be that I am, and seek not to alter me.

CONRADE Can you make no use of your discontent?

DON JOHN I make all use of it, for I use it only. Who comes here?

Enter BORACHIO.

What news, Borachio?

BORACHIO I came yonder from a great supper. The Prince your brother is royally entertained by Leonato; and I can give you intelligence of an intended marriage.

DON JOHN Will it serve for any model to build mischief on? What is he for a fool that betroths himself to unquietness?

BORACHIO Marry, it is your brother's right hand.

DON JOHN Who, the most exquisite Claudio?

BORACHIO Even he.

DON JOHN A proper squire! And who, and who? Which way looks he?

BORACHIO Marry, on Hero, the daughter and heir of Leonato.

DON JOHN A very forward March-chick! How came you to this?

BORACHIO Being entertained for a perfumer, as I was smoking a musty room, comes me the Prince and Claudio, hand in hand in sad conference. I whipped me behind the arras, and there heard it agreed upon that the Prince should woo Hero for himself, and having obtained her, give her to Count Claudio.

DON JOHN Come, come, let us thither; this may prove food to my displeasure; that young start-up hath all the glory of my overthrow. If I can cross him any way, I bless myself every way. You are both sure, and will assist me?

CONRADE To the death, my lord.

DON JOHN Let us to the great supper; their cheer is the greater that I am subdued. Would the cook were o' my mind! Shall we go prove what's to be done?

BORACHIO We'll wait upon your lordship. *Exeunt.*

2.1 *Enter* LEONATO, ANTONIO, *his brother,* HERO, *his daughter, and* BEATRICE, *his niece,* MARGARET *and* URSULA.

LEONATO Was not Count John here at supper?

ANTONIO I saw him not.

BEATRICE How tartly that gentleman looks! I never can see him but I am heart-burned an hour after.

HERO He is of a very melancholy disposition.

BEATRICE He were an excellent man that were made just in the mid-way between him and Benedick: the one is too like an image and says nothing, and the other too like my lady's eldest son, evermore tattling.

LEONATO Then half Signior Benedick's tongue in Count John's mouth, and half Count John's melancholy in Signior Benedick's face –

BEATRICE With a good leg and a good foot, uncle, and money enough in his purse, such a man would win any woman in the world – if a could get her good will.

LEONATO By my troth, niece, thou wilt never get thee a husband, if thou be so shrewd of thy tongue.

ANTONIO In faith, she's too curst.

BEATRICE Too curst is more than curst: I shall lessen God's sending that way, for it is said, 'God sends a curst cow short horns', but to a cow too curst he sends none.

LEONATO So, by being too curst, God will send you no horns.

BEATRICE   Just, if he send me no husband, for the which
blessing I am at him upon my knees every morning
and evening. Lord, I could not endure a husband
with a beard on his face! I had rather lie in the
woollen.

LEONATO   You may light on a husband that hath no beard.

BEATRICE   What should I do with him? Dress him in my
apparel and make him my waiting-gentlewoman?
He that hath a beard is more than a youth, and he
that hath no beard is less than a man; and he that is
more than a youth is not for me; and he that is less
than a man I am not for him: therefore I will even take
sixpence in earnest of the bearward and lead his apes
into hell.

LEONATO   Well then, go you into hell?

BEATRICE   No, but to the gate, and there will the Devil
meet me like an old cuckold with horns on his head,
and say, 'Get you to heaven, Beatrice, get you to
heaven, here's no place for you maids.' So deliver I up
my apes, and away to Saint Peter, for the heavens; he
shows me where the bachelors sit, and there live we
as merry as the day is long.

ANTONIO   *[to Hero]*   Well, niece, I trust you will be ruled
by your father.

BEATRICE   Yes, faith, it is my cousin's duty to make
curtsy and say, 'Father, as it please you': but yet for all
that, cousin, let him be a handsome fellow, or else make
another curtsy and say, 'Father, as it please me'.

LEONATO   Well, niece, I hope to see you one day fitted
with a husband.

BEATRICE   Not till God make men of some other metal
than earth. Would it not grieve a woman to be over-
mastered with a piece of valiant dust, to make an
account of her life to a clod of wayward marl? No,
uncle, I'll none: Adam's sons are my brethren, and
truly I hold it a sin to match in my kindred.

LEONATO   Daughter, remember what I told you: if the
Prince do solicit you in that kind, you know your
answer.

BEATRICE   The fault will be in the music, cousin, if you
be not wooed in good time. If the Prince be too
important, tell him there is measure in everything, and
so dance out the answer. For hear me, Hero: wooing,
wedding, and repenting is as a Scotch jig, a measure,
and a cinque-pace: the first suit is hot and hasty like a
Scotch jig, and full as fantastical; the wedding
mannerly-modest as a measure, full of state and
ancientry; and then comes repentance and, with his
bad legs, falls into the cinque-pace faster and faster,
till he sink into his grave.

LEONATO   Cousin, you apprehend passing shrewdly.

BEATRICE   I have a good eye, uncle; I can see a church by
daylight.

LEONATO   The revellers are entering, brother; make
good room.   *[Leonato and the men of his company mask.]*

Enter DON PEDRO, CLAUDIO, BENEDICK, BALTHASAR,
BORACHIO, DON JOHN *and others, masked, with a drum.*

DON PEDRO   Lady, will you walk a bout with your friend?

HERO   So you walk softly, and look sweetly, and say
nothing, I am yours for the walk; and especially when I
walk away.

DON PEDRO   With me in your company?

HERO   I may say so, when I please.

DON PEDRO   And when please you to say so?

HERO   When I like your favour, for God defend the lute
should be like the case!

DON PEDRO   My visor is Philemon's roof;
            Within the house is Jove.

HERO   Why then your visor should be thatch'd.

DON PEDRO   Speak low, if you speak love.
   [They step aside.]

BALTHASAR   Well, I would you did like me.

MARGARET   So would not I for your own sake, for I have
many ill qualities.

BALTHASAR   Which is one?

MARGARET   I say my prayers aloud.

BALTHASAR   I love you the better; the hearers may cry
Amen.

MARGARET   God match me with a good dancer!

BALTHASAR   Amen.

MARGARET   And God keep him out of my sight when
the dance is done! Answer, clerk.

BALTHASAR   No more words; the clerk is answered.
   [They step aside.]

URSULA   I know you well enough, you are Signior
Antonio.

ANTONIO   At a word, I am not.

URSULA   I know you by the waggling of your head.

ANTONIO   To tell you true, I counterfeit him.

URSULA   You could never do him so ill-well, unless you
were the very man. Here's his dry hand up and down:
you are he, you are he.

ANTONIO   At a word, I am not.

URSULA   Come, come, do you think I do not know you
by your excellent wit? Can virtue hide itself? Go to,
mum, you are he: graces will appear, and there's an
end. *[They step aside.]*

BEATRICE   Will you not tell me who told you so?

BENEDICK   No, you shall pardon me.

BEATRICE   Nor will you not tell me who you are?

BENEDICK   Not now.

BEATRICE   That I was disdainful, and that I had my good
wit out of the 'Hundred Merry Tales' – well, this was
Signior Benedick that said so.

BENEDICK   What's he?

BEATRICE   I am sure you know him well enough.

BENEDICK   Not I, believe me.

BEATRICE   Did he never make you laugh?

BENEDICK   I pray you, what is he?

BEATRICE   Why, he is the Prince's jester, a very dull fool;

only his gift is in devising impossible slanders. None
but libertines delight in him, and the commendation
is not in his wit, but in his villainy; for he both pleases
men and angers them, and then they laugh at him and
beat him. I am sure he is in the fleet; I would he had
boarded me.

BENEDICK   When I know the gentleman, I'll tell him
what you say.

BEATRICE   Do, do, he'll but break a comparison or two
on me, which peradventure not marked, or not
laughed at, strikes him into melancholy, and then
there's a partridge wing saved, for the fool will eat no
supper that night. [*Music.*] We must follow the
leaders.

BENEDICK   In every good thing.

BEATRICE   Nay, if they lead to any ill, I will leave them
at the next turning.

Dance. Exeunt all but Don John, Borachio and Claudio.

DON JOHN   Sure my brother is amorous on Hero, and
hath withdrawn her father to break with him about it.
The ladies follow her, and but one visor remains.

BORACHIO   And that is Claudio: I know him by his
bearing.

DON JOHN   Are not you Signior Benedick?

CLAUDIO   You know me well, I am he.

DON JOHN   Signior, you are very near my brother in his
love. He is enamoured on Hero; I pray you, dissuade
him from her, she is no equal for his birth. You may do
the part of an honest man in it.

CLAUDIO   How know you he loves her?

DON JOHN   I heard him swear his affection.

BORACHIO   So did I too, and he swore he would marry
her tonight.

DON JOHN   Come, let us to the banquet.

Exeunt Don John and Borachio.

CLAUDIO   Thus answer I in name of Benedick,
But hear these ill news with the ears of Claudio.
'Tis certain so; the Prince woos for himself.
Friendship is constant in all other things
Save in the office and affairs of love:
Therefore all hearts in love use their own tongues;
Let every eye negotiate for itself,
And trust no agent; for beauty is a witch
Against whose charms faith melteth into blood.
This is an accident of hourly proof,
Which I mistrusted not. Farewell, therefore, Hero!

Enter BENEDICK.

BENEDICK   Count Claudio?

CLAUDIO   Yea, the same.

BENEDICK   Come, will you go with me?

CLAUDIO   Whither?

BENEDICK   Even to the next willow, about your own
business, County. What fashion will you wear the
garland of? About your neck, like an usurer's chain?
Or under your arm, like a lieutenant's scarf? You must
wear it one way, for the Prince hath got your Hero.

CLAUDIO   I wish him joy of her.

BENEDICK   Why, that's spoken like an honest drover: so
they sell bullocks. But did you think the Prince would
have served you thus?

CLAUDIO   I pray you, leave me.

BENEDICK   Ho, now you strike like the blind man! 'Twas
the boy that stole your meat, and you'll beat the post.

CLAUDIO   If it will not be, I'll leave you.   *Exit.*

BENEDICK   Alas, poor hurt fowl, now will he creep into
sedges. But that my Lady Beatrice should know me,
and not know me! The Prince's fool! Ha, it may be I
go under that title because I am merry. Yea, but so I
am apt to do myself wrong. I am not so reputed: it is
the base, though bitter, disposition of Beatrice that
puts the world into her person, and so gives me out.
Well, I'll be revenged as I may.

Enter the Prince, DON PEDRO, HERO, LEONATO.

DON PEDRO   Now, signior, where's the Count? Did you
see him?

BENEDICK   Troth, my lord, I have played the part of
Lady Fame. I found him here as melancholy as a lodge
in a warren. I told him, and I think I told him true,
that your Grace had got the good will of this young
lady, and I offered him my company to a willow-tree,
either to make him a garland, as being forsaken, or to
bind him up a rod, as being worthy to be whipped.

DON PEDRO   To be whipped? What's his fault?

BENEDICK   The flat transgression of a schoolboy, who,
being overjoyed with finding a bird's nest, shows it his
companion, and he steals it.

DON PEDRO   Wilt thou make a trust a transgression? The
transgression is in the stealer.

BENEDICK   Yet it had not been amiss the rod had been
made, and the garland too; for the garland he might
have worn himself, and the rod he might have bestowed
on you, who, as I take it, have stolen his bird's nest.

DON PEDRO   I will but teach them to sing, and restore
them to the owner.

BENEDICK   If their singing answer your saying, by my
faith you say honestly.

DON PEDRO   The Lady Beatrice hath a quarrel to you:
the gentleman that danced with her told her she is
much wronged by you.

BENEDICK   O, she misused me past the endurance of a
block! An oak but with one green leaf on it would have
answered her: my very visor began to assume life and
scold with her. She told me, not thinking I had been
myself, that I was the Prince's jester, that I was duller
than a great thaw, huddling jest upon jest with such
impossible conveyance upon me that I stood like a
man at a mark, with a whole army shooting at me. She
speaks poniards, and every word stabs: if her breath
were as terrible as her terminations, there were no
living near her, she would infect to the North Star. I
would not marry her, though she were endowed with
all that Adam had left him before he transgressed. She

would have made Hercules have turned spit, yea, and have cleft his club to make the fire too. Come, talk not of her, you shall find her the infernal Ate in good apparel. I would to God some scholar would conjure her, for certainly, while she is here, a man may live as quiet in hell as in a sanctuary, and people sin upon purpose, because they would go thither; so indeed all disquiet, horror, and perturbation follows her.

Enter CLAUDIO *and* BEATRICE.

DON PEDRO Look, here she comes.

BENEDICK Will your Grace command me any service to the world's end? I will go on the slightest errand now to the Antipodes that you can devise to send me on; I will fetch you a toothpicker now from the furthest inch of Asia; bring you the length of Prester John's foot; fetch you a hair off the great Cham's beard; do you any embassage to the Pygmies, rather than hold three words' conference with this harpy. You have no employment for me?

DON PEDRO None, but to desire your good company.

BENEDICK O God, sir, here's a dish I love not! I cannot endure my Lady Tongue. *Exit.*

DON PEDRO Come, lady, come, you have lost the heart of Signior Benedick.

BEATRICE Indeed, my lord, he lent it me awhile, and I gave him use for it, a double heart for his single one. Marry, once before he won it of me with false dice, therefore your Grace may well say I have lost it.

DON PEDRO You have put him down, lady, you have put him down.

BEATRICE So I would not he should do me, my lord, lest I should prove the mother of fools. I have brought Count Claudio, whom you sent me to seek.

DON PEDRO Why, how now, Count? Wherefore are you sad?

CLAUDIO Not sad, my lord.

DON PEDRO How then? Sick?

CLAUDIO Neither, my lord.

BEATRICE The Count is neither sad, nor sick, nor merry, nor well; but civil Count, civil as an orange, and something of that jealous complexion.

DON PEDRO I'faith, lady, I think your blazon to be true, though I'll be sworn, if he be so, his conceit is false. Here, Claudio, I have wooed in thy name, and fair Hero is won. I have broke with her father, and his good will obtained. Name the day of marriage, and God give thee joy!

LEONATO Count, take of me my daughter, and with her my fortunes; his Grace hath made the match, and all grace say Amen to it.

BEATRICE Speak, Count, 'tis your cue.

CLAUDIO Silence is the perfectest herald of joy; I were but little happy, if I could say how much. Lady, as you are mine, I am yours; I give away myself for you and dote upon the exchange.

BEATRICE Speak, cousin, or, if you cannot, stop his mouth with a kiss, and let not him speak neither.

DON PEDRO In faith, lady, you have a merry heart.

BEATRICE Yea, my lord, I thank it, poor fool, it keeps on the windy side of care. My cousin tells him in his ear that he is in her heart.

CLAUDIO And so she doth, cousin.

BEATRICE Good Lord, for alliance! Thus goes everyone to the world but I, and I am sunburnt. I may sit in a corner and cry 'Heigh-ho for a husband!'

DON PEDRO Lady Beatrice, I will get you one.

BEATRICE I would rather have one of your father's getting. Hath your Grace ne'er a brother like you? Your father got excellent husbands, if a maid could come by them.

DON PEDRO Will you have me, lady?

BEATRICE No, my lord, unless I might have another for working days: your Grace is too costly to wear every day. But I beseech your Grace pardon me, I was born to speak all mirth and no matter.

DON PEDRO Your silence most offends me, and to be merry best becomes you, for out o' question, you were born in a merry hour.

BEATRICE No, sure, my lord, my mother cried, but then there was a star danced, and under that was I born. Cousins, God give you joy!

LEONATO Niece, will you look to those things I told you of?

BEATRICE I cry you mercy, uncle. By your Grace's pardon. *Exit.*

DON PEDRO By my troth, a pleasant-spirited lady.

LEONATO There's little of the melancholy element in her, my lord; she is never sad but when she sleeps, and not ever sad then; for I have heard my daughter say she hath often dreamt of unhappiness and waked herself with laughing.

DON PEDRO She cannot endure to hear tell of a husband.

LEONATO O, by no means, she mocks all her wooers out of suit.

DON PEDRO She were an excellent wife for Benedick.

LEONATO O Lord, my lord, if they were but a week married, they would talk themselves mad.

DON PEDRO County Claudio, when mean you to go to church?

CLAUDIO Tomorrow, my lord: time goes on crutches till love have all his rites.

LEONATO Not till Monday, my dear son, which is hence a just seven-night, and a time too brief, too, to have all things answer my mind.

DON PEDRO Come, you shake the head at so long a breathing, but I warrant thee, Claudio, the time shall not go dully by us. I will, in the interim, undertake one of Hercules' labours, which is, to bring Signior Benedick and the Lady Beatrice into a mountain of affection th'one with th'other. I would fain have it a match, and I doubt not but to fashion it, if you three will but minister such assistance as I shall give you direction.

350 LEONATO My lord, I am for you, though it cost me ten
nights' watchings.

CLAUDIO And I, my lord.

DON PEDRO And you too, gentle Hero?

HERO I will do any modest office, my lord, to help my
355 cousin to a good husband.

DON PEDRO And Benedick is not the unhopefullest
husband that I know. Thus far can I praise him: he is
of a noble strain, of approved valour, and confirmed
honesty. I will teach you how to humour your cousin
360 that she shall fall in love with Benedick; and I, [*to
Leonato and Claudio*] with your two helps, will so
practise on Benedick that, in despite of his quick wit
and his queasy stomach, he shall fall in love with
Beatrice. If we can do this, Cupid is no longer an
365 archer; his glory shall be ours, for we are the only love-
gods. Go in with me, and I will tell you my drift.

Exeunt.

2.2 *Enter* DON JOHN *and* BORACHIO.

DON JOHN It is so, the Count Claudio shall marry the
daughter of Leonato.

BORACHIO Yea, my lord, but I can cross it.

DON JOHN Any bar, any cross, any impediment will be
5 medicinable to me. I am sick in displeasure to him, and
whatsoever comes athwart his affection ranges
evenly with mine. How canst thou cross this marriage?

BORACHIO Not honestly, my lord, but so covertly that
no dishonesty shall appear in me.

10 DON JOHN Show me briefly how.

BORACHIO I think I told your lordship, a year since, how
much I am in the favour of Margaret, the waiting-
gentlewoman to Hero.

DON JOHN I remember

15 BORACHIO I can, at any unseasonable instant of the
night, appoint her to look out at her lady's chamber-
window.

DON JOHN What life is in that, to be the death of this
marriage?

20 BORACHIO The poison of that lies in you to temper. Go
you to the Prince your brother; spare not to tell him
that he hath wronged his honour in marrying the
renowned Claudio – whose estimation do you
mightily hold up – to a contaminated stale, such a one
25 as Hero.

DON JOHN What proof shall I make of that?

BORACHIO Proof enough to misuse the Prince, to vex
Claudio, to undo Hero, and kill Leonato. Look you for
any other issue?

30 DON JOHN Only to despite them I will endeavour anything.

BORACHIO Go then, find me a meet hour to draw Don
Pedro and the Count Claudio alone: tell them that you
know that Hero loves me; intend a kind of zeal both to
35 the Prince and Claudio – as in love of your brother's
honour, who hath made this match, and his friend's
reputation, who is thus like to be cozened with the

semblance of a maid – that you have discovered thus.
They will scarcely believe this without trial: offer
them instances, which shall bear no less likelihood
than to see me at her chamber-window, hear me call 40
Margaret Hero, hear Margaret term me Claudio; and
bring them to see this the very night before the
intended wedding – for in the meantime I will so
fashion the matter that Hero shall be absent – and
there shall appear such seeming truth of Hero's 45
disloyalty that jealousy shall be called assurance and
all the preparation overthrown.

DON JOHN Grow this to what adverse issue it can, I will
put it in practice. Be cunning in the working this, and
thy fee is a thousand ducats. 50

BORACHIO Be you constant in the accusation, and my
cunning shall not shame me.

DON JOHN I will presently go learn their day of marriage.

Exeunt.

2.3 *Enter* BENEDICK *alone.*

BENEDICK Boy!

Enter Boy.

BOY Signior?

BENEDICK In my chamber-window lies a book; bring it
hither to me in the orchard.

BOY I am here already, sir. 5

BENEDICK I know that, but I would have thee hence and
here again. *Exit Boy.*

I do much wonder that one man, seeing how much
another man is a fool when he dedicates his
behaviours to love, will, after he hath laughed at such 10
shallow follies in others, become the argument of his
own scorn by falling in love: and such a man is Claudio.
I have known when there was no music with him but
the drum and the fife, and now had he rather hear the
tabor and the pipe. I have known when he would have 15
walked ten mile afoot to see a good armour, and now
will he lie ten nights awake carving the fashion of a new
doublet. He was wont to speak plain and to the
purpose, like an honest man and a soldier, and now is
he turned orthography – his words are a very 20
fantastical banquet, just so many strange dishes. May I
be so converted and see with these eyes? I cannot tell; I
think not. I will not be sworn but love may transform
me to an oyster, but I'll take my oath on it, till he have
made an oyster of me, he shall never make me such a 25
fool. One woman is fair, yet I am well; another is wise,
yet I am well; another virtuous, yet I am well; but till
all graces be in one woman, one woman shall not come
in my grace. Rich she shall be, that's certain; wise, or
I'll none; virtuous, or I'll never cheapen her; fair, or 30
I'll never look on her; mild, or come not near me;
noble, or not I for an angel; of good discourse, an
excellent musician, and her hair shall be – of what
colour it please God. Ha! the Prince and Monsieur
Love! I will hide me in the arbour. [*Withdraws.*] 35

Enter DON PEDRO, LEONATO, CLAUDIO *and* BALTHASAR
with music.

DON PEDRO　Come, shall we hear this music?

CLAUDIO　Yea, my good lord. How still the evening is,
As hush'd on purpose to grace harmony!

DON PEDRO　See you where Benedick hath hid himself?

CLAUDIO　O, very well, my lord. The music ended,
We'll fit the kid-fox with a pennyworth.

DON PEDRO
Come, Balthasar, we'll hear that song again.

BALTHASAR　O good my lord, tax not so bad a voice
To slander music any more than once.

DON PEDRO　It is the witness still of excellency
To put a strange face on his own perfection.
I pray thee sing, and let me woo no more.

BALTHASAR　Because you talk of wooing, I will sing,
Since many a wooer doth commence his suit
To her he thinks not worthy, yet he woos,
Yet will he swear he loves.

DON PEDRO　　　　　　　Nay pray thee, come,
Or if thou wilt hold longer argument,
Do it in notes.

BALTHASAR　　　　Note this before my notes;
There's not a note of mine that's worth the noting.

DON PEDRO
Why, these are very crotchets that he speaks!
Note notes, forsooth, and nothing!　　　　[*Music.*]

BENEDICK [*aside*]　Now, divine air! Now is his soul
ravished! Is it not strange that sheep's guts should hale
souls out of men's bodies? Well, a horn for my money,
when all's done.

The Song.

BALTHASAR　Sigh no more, ladies, sigh no more,
　　Men were deceivers ever:
　　One foot in sea, and one on shore,
　　To one thing constant never.
　Then sigh not so, but let them go,
　　And be you blithe and bonny,
　Converting all your sounds of woe
　　Into Hey nonny, nonny.

　Sing no more ditties, sing no moe,
　　Of dumps so dull and heavy:
　The fraud of men was ever so,
　　Since summer first was leavy.
　　Then sigh not so, etc.

DON PEDRO　By my troth, a good song.

BALTHASAR　And an ill singer, my lord.

DON PEDRO　Ha, no, no, faith; thou sing'st well enough
for a shift.

BENEDICK [*aside*]　And he had been a dog that should
have howled thus, they would have hanged him, and I
pray God his bad voice bode no mischief. I had as lief
have heard the night-raven, come what plague could
have come after it.

DON PEDRO　Yea, marry, dost thou hear, Balthasar? I
pray thee get us some excellent music; for tomorrow
night we would have it at the Lady Hero's chamber-
window.　　85

BALTHASAR　The best I can, my lord.

DON PEDRO　Do so: farewell.　　　*Exit Balthasar.*
Come hither, Leonato. What was it you told me of
today, that your niece Beatrice was in love with Signior
Benedick?　　90

CLAUDIO　O, ay! [*aside to Don Pedro*] Stalk on, stalk on,
the fowl sits. – I did never think that lady would have
loved any man.

LEONATO　No, nor I neither, but most wonderful that　95
she should so dote on Signior Benedick, whom she
hath in all outward behaviours seemed ever to abhor.

BENEDICK [*aside*]　Is't possible? Sits the wind in that
corner?

LEONATO　By my troth my lord, I cannot tell what to　100
think of it, but that she loves him with an enraged
affection, it is past the infinite of thought.

DON PEDRO　Maybe she doth but counterfeit.

CLAUDIO　Faith, like enough.

LEONATO　O God! Counterfeit? There was never　105
counterfeit of passion came so near the life of passion
as she discovers it.

DON PEDRO　Why, what effects of passion shows she?

CLAUDIO [*aside*]　Bait the hook well, this fish will bite.

LEONATO　What effects, my lord? She will sit you – you　110
heard my daughter tell you how.

CLAUDIO　She did indeed.

DON PEDRO　How, how, I pray you? You amaze me, I
would have thought her spirit had been invincible
against all assaults of affection.　　115

LEONATO　I would have sworn it had, my lord, especially
against Benedick.

BENEDICK [*aside*]　I should think this a gull, but that the
white-bearded fellow speaks it. Knavery cannot sure
hide himself in such reverence.　　120

CLAUDIO [*aside*]　He hath ta'en th'infection; hold it up.

DON PEDRO　Hath she made her affection known to
Benedick?

LEONATO　No, and swears she never will: that's her
torment.　　125

CLAUDIO　'Tis true indeed, so your daughter says: 'Shall
I,' says she, 'that have so oft encountered him with
scorn, write to him that I love him?'

LEONATO　This says she now when she is beginning to
write to him, for she'll be up twenty times a night, and　130
there will she sit in her smock till she have writ a sheet
of paper: my daughter tells us all.

CLAUDIO　Now you talk of a sheet of paper, I remember
a pretty jest your daughter told us of.

LEONATO　O, when she had writ it, and was reading it　135
over, she found 'Benedick' and 'Beatrice' between the
sheet?

CLAUDIO　That.

LEONATO   O, she tore the letter into a thousand
140   halfpence; railed at herself, that she should be so
immodest to write to one that she knew would flout
her. 'I measure him', says she, 'by my own spirit, for I
should flout him, if he writ to me, yea, though I love
him, I should.'

CLAUDIO   Then down upon her knees she falls, weeps,
145   sobs, beats her heart, tears her hair, prays, curses: 'O
sweet Benedick! God give me patience!'

LEONATO   She doth indeed, my daughter says so, and
the ecstasy hath so much overborne her that my
150   daughter is sometime afeard she will do a desperate
outrage to herself: it is very true.

DON PEDRO   It were good that Benedick knew of it by
some other, if she will not discover it.

CLAUDIO   To what end? He would make but a sport of it
155   and torment the poor lady worse.

DON PEDRO   And he should, it were an alms to hang
him. She's an excellent sweet lady, and, out of all
suspicion, she is virtuous.

CLAUDIO   And she is exceeding wise.

160   DON PEDRO   In everything but in loving Benedick.

LEONATO   O my lord, wisdom and blood combating in
so tender a body, we have ten proofs to one that blood
hath the victory. I am sorry for her, as I have just
cause, being her uncle and her guardian.

165   DON PEDRO   I would she had bestowed this dotage on
me, I would have daffed all other respects and made
her half myself. I pray you tell Benedick of it and hear
what a will say.

LEONATO   Were it good, think you?

170   CLAUDIO   Hero thinks surely she will die; for she says
she will die if he love her not, and she will die ere she
make her love known, and she will die if he woo her,
rather than she will bate one breath of her accustomed
crossness.

175   DON PEDRO   She doth well: if she should make tender of
her love, 'tis very possible he'll scorn it, for the man,
as you know all, hath a contemptible spirit.

CLAUDIO   He is a very proper man.

DON PEDRO   He hath indeed a good outward happiness.

180   CLAUDIO   Before God, and, in my mind, very wise.

DON PEDRO   He doth indeed show some sparks that are
like wit.

CLAUDIO   And I take him to be valiant.

DON PEDRO   As Hector, I assure you: and in the
185   managing of quarrels you may say he is wise; for either
he avoids them with great discretion, or undertakes
them with a most Christian-like fear.

LEONATO   If he do fear God, a must necessarily keep
peace: if he break the peace, he ought to enter into a
190   quarrel with fear and trembling.

DON PEDRO   And so will he do, for the man doth fear
God, howsoever it seems not in him by some large
jests he will make. Well, I am sorry for your niece.
Shall we go seek Benedick, and tell him of her love?

195   CLAUDIO   Never tell him, my lord, let her wear it out
with good counsel.

LEONATO   Nay, that's impossible, she may wear her
heart out first.

DON PEDRO   Well, we will hear further of it by your
daughter; let it cool the while. I love Benedick well,   200
and I could wish he would modestly examine himself,
to see how much he is unworthy so good a lady.

LEONATO   My lord, will you walk? Dinner is ready.

CLAUDIO   [*aside*]   If he do not dote on her upon this, I
will never trust my expectation.   205

DON PEDRO   [*aside*]   Let there be the same net spread for
her, and that must your daughter and her gentlewomen carry. The sport will be when they hold one an
opinion of another's dotage, and no such matter: that's
the scene that I would see, which will be merely a   210
dumb-show. Let us send her to call him in to dinner.
          Exeunt Don Pedro, Claudio and Leonato.

BENEDICK   [*coming forward*]   This can be no trick: the
conference was sadly borne; they have the truth of
this from Hero. They seem to pity the lady: it seems
her affections have their full bent. Love me? Why, it   215
must be requited. I hear how I am censured: they say
I will bear myself proudly, if I perceive the love come
from her; they say too that she will rather die than
give any sign of affection. I did never think to marry:
I must not seem proud: happy are they that hear their   220
detractions and can put them to mending. They say
the lady is fair – 'tis a truth, I can bear them witness;
and virtuous – 'tis so, I cannot reprove it; and wise,
but for loving me – by my troth, it is no addition to
her wit, nor no great argument of her folly, for I will   225
be horribly in love with her. I may chance have some
odd quirks and remnants of wit broken on me because
I have railed so long against marriage: but doth not
the appetite alter? A man loves the meat in his youth
that he cannot endure in his age. Shall quips and   230
sentences and these paper bullets of the brain awe a
man from the career of his humour? No, the world
must be peopled. When I said I would die a bachelor,
I did not think I should live till I were married. Here
comes Beatrice. By this day, she's a fair lady! I do spy   235
some marks of love in her.

          Enter BEATRICE.

BEATRICE   Against my will I am sent to bid you come in
to dinner.

BENEDICK   Fair Beatrice, I thank you for your pains.

BEATRICE   I took no more pains for those thanks than   240
you take pains to thank me; if it had been painful, I
would not have come.

BENEDICK   You take pleasure then in the message?

BEATRICE   Yea, just so much as you may take upon a
knife's point and choke a daw withal. You have no   245
stomach, signior, fare you well.   *Exit.*

BENEDICK   Ha! 'Against my will I am sent to bid you
come in to dinner' – there's a double meaning in that.
'I took no more pains for those thanks than you took

pains to thank me' – that's as much as to say, 'Any
pains that I take for you is as easy as thanks'. If I do
not take pity of her, I am a villain; if I do not love her,
I am a Jew. I will go get her picture.   *Exit.*

3.1   *Enter* HERO *and two gentlewomen,* MARGARET
and URSULA.

HERO   Good Margaret, run thee to the parlour;
There shalt thou find my cousin Beatrice
Proposing with the Prince and Claudio.
Whisper her ear, and tell her I and Ursley
Walk in the orchard, and our whole discourse
Is all of her; say that thou overheard'st us,
And bid her steal into the pleached bower
Where honeysuckles, ripen'd by the sun,
Forbid the sun to enter, like favourites,
Made proud by princes, that advance their pride
Against that power that bred it. There will she hide
    her
To listen our propose. This is thy office;
Bear thee well in it, and leave us alone.
MARGARET
I'll make her come, I warrant you, presently.   *Exit.*
HERO   Now, Ursula, when Beatrice doth come,
As we do trace this alley up and down,
Our talk must only be of Benedick.
When I do name him, let it be thy part
To praise him more than ever man did merit:
My talk to thee must be how Benedick
Is sick in love with Beatrice. Of this matter
Is little Cupid's crafty arrow made,
That only wounds by hearsay.

Enter BEATRICE *into the arbour.*

                               Now begin;
For look where Beatrice like a lapwing runs
Close by the ground, to hear our conference.
URSULA   The pleasant'st angling is to see the fish
Cut with her golden oars the silver stream,
And greedily devour the treacherous bait:
So angle we for Beatrice, who even now
Is couched in the woodbine coverture.
Fear you not my part of the dialogue.
HERO   Then go we near her, that her ear lose nothing
Of the false sweet bait that we lay for it.
[*approaching the arbour*] No, truly, Ursula, she is too
    disdainful;
I know her spirits are as coy and wild
As haggards of the rock.
URSULA   But are you sure
That Benedick loves Beatrice so entirely?
HERO   So says the Prince and my new-trothed lord.
URSULA   And did they bid you tell her of it, madam?
HERO   They did entreat me to acquaint her of it;
But I persuaded them, if they lov'd Benedick,
To wish him wrestle with affection,

And never to let Beatrice know of it.
URSULA   Why did you so? Doth not the gentleman
Deserve as full as fortunate a bed   45
As ever Beatrice shall couch upon?
HERO   O god of love! I know he doth deserve
As much as may be yielded to a man:
But Nature never fram'd a woman's heart
Of prouder stuff than that of Beatrice.   50
Disdain and scorn ride sparkling in her eyes,
Misprising what they look on, and her wit
Values itself so highly that to her
All matter else seems weak. She cannot love,
Nor take no shape nor project of affection,   55
She is so self-endeared.
URSULA   Sure, I think so;
And therefore certainly it were not good
She knew his love, lest she'll make sport at it.
HERO   Why, you speak truth. I never yet saw man,
How wise, how noble, young, how rarely featur'd,   60
But she would spell him backward: if fair-fac'd,
She would swear the gentleman should be her sister;
If black, why, Nature, drawing of an antic,
Made a foul blot; if tall, a lance ill-headed;
If low, an agate very vilely cut;   65
If speaking, why, a vane blown with all winds;
If silent, why, a block moved with none.
So turns she every man the wrong side out,
And never gives to truth and virtue that
Which simpleness and merit purchaseth.   70
URSULA   Sure, sure, such carping is not commendable.
HERO   No, not to be so odd and from all fashions
As Beatrice is, cannot be commendable:
But who dare tell her so? If I should speak,
She would mock me into air; O, she would laugh me   75
Out of myself, press me to death with wit!
Therefore let Benedick, like cover'd fire,
Consume away in sighs, waste inwardly.
It were a better death than die with mocks,
Which is as bad as die with tickling.   80
URSULA   Yet tell her of it; hear what she will say.
HERO   No; rather I will go to Benedick
And counsel him to fight against his passion;
And truly I'll devise some honest slanders
To stain my cousin with: one doth not know   85
How much an ill word may empoison liking.
URSULA   O, do not do your cousin such a wrong!
She cannot be so much without true judgement –
Having so swift and excellent a wit
As she is priz'd to have – as to refuse   90
So rare a gentleman as Signior Benedick.
HERO   He is the only man of Italy,
Always excepted my dear Claudio.
URSULA   I pray you be not angry with me, madam,
Speaking my fancy: Signior Benedick,   95
For shape, for bearing, argument, and valour,
Goes foremost in report through Italy.

HERO   Indeed he hath an excellent good name.

URSULA   His excellence did earn it ere he had it.
100   When are you married, madam?

HERO   Why, every day, tomorrow! Come, go in;
       I'll show thee some attires, and have thy counsel
       Which is the best to furnish me tomorrow.

URSULA [*aside*]
       She's lim'd, I warrant you! We have caught her,
           madam.

105 HERO [*aside*]   If it prove so, then loving goes by haps:
       Some Cupid kills with arrows, some with traps.
                                    Exeunt Hero and Ursula.

BEATRICE [*coming forward*]
       What fire is in mine ears? Can this be true?
           Stand I condemn'd for pride and scorn so much?
       Contempt, farewell, and maiden pride, adieu!
110   No glory lives behind the back of such.
       And, Benedick, love on, I will requite thee,
           Taming my wild heart to thy loving hand.
       If thou dost love, my kindness shall incite thee
           To bind our loves up in a holy band;
115   For others say thou dost deserve, and I
       Believe it better than reportingly.   *Exit.*

3.2   *Enter* DON PEDRO, CLAUDIO, BENEDICK
                  and LEONATO.

DON PEDRO   I do but stay till your marriage be con-
       summate, and then go I toward Aragon.

CLAUDIO   I'll bring you thither, my lord, if you'll vouchsafe
       me.

5 DON PEDRO   Nay, that would be as great a soil in the new
       gloss of your marriage as to show a child his new
       coat and forbid him to wear it. I will only be bold
       with Benedick for his company, for from the crown
       of his head to the sole of his foot he is all mirth. He
10   hath twice or thrice cut Cupid's bow-string, and the
       little hangman dare not shoot at him. He hath a
       heart as sound as a bell, and his tongue is the clapper;
       for what his heart thinks his tongue speaks.

BENEDICK   Gallants, I am not as I have been.

15 LEONATO   So say I; methinks you are sadder.

CLAUDIO   I hope he be in love.

DON PEDRO   Hang him, truant! There's no true drop of
       blood in him to be truly touched with love. If he be
       sad, he wants money.

20 BENEDICK   I have the toothache.

DON PEDRO   Draw it.

BENEDICK   Hang it!

CLAUDIO   You must hang it first, and draw it afterwards.

DON PEDRO   What? Sigh for the toothache?

25 LEONATO   Where is but a humour or a worm.

BENEDICK   Well, every one can master a grief but he that
       has it.

CLAUDIO   Yet say I, he is in love.

DON PEDRO   There is no appearance of fancy in him,
30   unless it be a fancy that he hath to strange disguises –

as to be a Dutchman today, a Frenchman tomorrow, or
in the shape of two countries at once, as a German
from the waist downward, all slops, and a Spaniard
from the hip upward, no doublet. Unless he have a
fancy to this foolery, as it appears he hath, he is no fool   35
for fancy, as you would have it appear he is.

CLAUDIO   If he be not in love with some woman, there is
no believing old signs; a brushes his hat o' mornings,
what should that bode?

DON PEDRO   Hath any man seen him at the barber's?   40

CLAUDIO   No, but the barber's man hath been seen with
him, and the old ornament of his cheek hath already
stuffed tennis-balls.

LEONATO   Indeed he looks younger than he did, by the
loss of a beard.   45

DON PEDRO   Nay, a rubs himself with civet; can you
smell him out by that?

CLAUDIO   That's as much as to say the sweet youth's in
love.

DON PEDRO   The greatest note of it is his melancholy.   50

CLAUDIO   And when was he wont to wash his face?

DON PEDRO   Yea, or to paint himself? For the which I
hear what they say of him.

CLAUDIO   Nay, but his jesting spirit, which is now crept
into a lute-string, and now governed by stops.   55

DON PEDRO   Indeed that tells a heavy tale for him:
conclude, conclude he is in love.

CLAUDIO   Nay, but I know who loves him.

DON PEDRO   That would I know too: I warrant, one that
knows him not.   60

CLAUDIO   Yes, and his ill conditions, and in despite of
all, dies for him.

DON PEDRO   She shall be buried with her face upwards.

BENEDICK   Yet is this no charm for the toothache. Old
signior, walk aside with me; I have studied eight or   65
nine wise words to speak to you, which these hobby-
horses must not hear.   *Exeunt Benedick and Leonato.*

DON PEDRO   For my life, to break with him about
Beatrice.

CLAUDIO   'Tis even so. Hero and Margaret have by this   70
played their parts with Beatrice, and then the two
bears will not bite one another when they meet.

                  Enter DON JOHN *the Bastard.*

DON JOHN   My lord and brother, God save you!

DON PEDRO   Good den, brother.

DON JOHN   If your leisure served, I would speak with you.   75

DON PEDRO   In private?

DON JOHN   If it please you; yet Count Claudio may hear,
for what I would speak of concerns him.

DON PEDRO   What's the matter?

DON JOHN [*to Claudio*]   Means your lordship to be   80
married tomorrow?

DON PEDRO   You know he does.

DON JOHN   I know not that, when he knows what I know.

CLAUDIO   If there be any impediment, I pray you
discover it.   85

DON JOHN   You may think I love you not: let that appear hereafter, and aim better at me by that I now will manifest. For my brother, I think he holds you well, and in dearness of heart hath holp to effect your ensuing marriage – surely suit ill spent, and labour ill bestowed.

DON PEDRO   Why, what's the matter?

DON JOHN   I came hither to tell you; and, circumstances shortened – for she has been too long a-talking of – the lady is disloyal.

CLAUDIO   Who, Hero?

DON JOHN   Even she – Leonato's Hero, your Hero, every man's Hero.

CLAUDIO   Disloyal?

DON JOHN   The word is too good to paint out her wickedness. I could say she were worse; think you of a worse title and I will fit her to it. Wonder not till further warrant: go but with me tonight, you shall see her chamber-window entered, even the night before her wedding-day. If you love her then, tomorrow wed her; but it would better fit your honour to change your mind.

CLAUDIO   May this be so?

DON PEDRO   I will not think it.

DON JOHN   If you dare not trust that you see, confess not that you know. If you will follow me, I will show you enough; and when you have seen more, and heard more, proceed accordingly.

CLAUDIO   If I see anything tonight why I should not marry her tomorrow, in the congregation, where I should wed, there will I shame her.

DON PEDRO   And as I wooed for thee to obtain her, I will join with thee to disgrace her.

DON JOHN   I will disparage her no farther till you are my witnesses. Bear it coldly but till midnight, and let the issue show itself.

DON PEDRO   O day untowardly turned!

CLAUDIO   O mischief strangely thwarting!

DON JOHN   O plague right well prevented! So will you say when you have seen the sequel.   *Exeunt.*

3.3   *Enter* DOGBERRY *and his compartner* VERGES, *with the* Watch.

DOGBERRY   Are you good men and true?

VERGES   Yea, or else it were pity but they should suffer salvation, body and soul.

DOGBERRY   Nay, that were a punishment too good for them, if they should have any allegiance in them, being chosen for the Prince's watch.

VERGES   Well, give them their charge, neighbour Dogberry.

DOGBERRY   First, who think you the most desartless man to be constable?

1 WATCHMAN   Hugh Oatcake, sir, or George Seacoal, for they can write and read.

DOGBERRY   Come hither, neighbour Seacoal. God hath blest you with a good name: to be a well-favoured man is the gift of fortune, but to write and read comes by nature.

2 WATCHMAN   Both which, Master Constable –

DOGBERRY   You have: I knew it would be your answer. Well, for your favour, sir, why, give God thanks, and make no boast of it; and for your writing and reading, let that appear when there is no need of such vanity. You are thought here to be the most senseless and fit man for the constable of the watch; therefore bear you the lantern. This is your charge: you shall comprehend all vagrom men; you are to bid any man stand, in the Prince's name.

2 WATCHMAN   How if a will not stand?

DOGBERRY   Why then, take no note of him, but let him go, and presently call the rest of the watch together, and thank God you are rid of a knave.

VERGES   If he will not stand when he is bidden, he is none of the Prince's subjects.

DOGBERRY   True, and they are to meddle with none but the Prince's subjects. You shall also make no noise in the streets: for, for the watch to babble and to talk is most tolerable, and not to be endured.

A WATCHMAN   We will rather sleep than talk; we know what belongs to a watch.

DOGBERRY   Why, you speak like an ancient and most quiet watchman, for I cannot see how sleeping should offend: only have a care that your bills be not stolen. Well, you are to call at all the ale-houses, and bid those that are drunk get them to bed.

A WATCHMAN   How if they will not?

DOGBERRY   Why then, let them alone till they are sober: if they make you not then the better answer, you may say they are not the men you took them for.

A WATCHMAN   Well, sir.

DOGBERRY   If you meet a thief, you may suspect him, by virtue of your office, to be no true man; and for such kind of men, the less you meddle or make with them, why, the more is for your honesty.

A WATCHMAN   If we know him to be a thief, shall we not lay hands on him?

DOGBERRY   Truly, by your office you may, but I think they that touch pitch will be defiled. The most peaceable way for you, if you do take a thief, is to let him show himself what he is, and steal out of your company.

VERGES   You have been always called a merciful man, partner.

DOGBERRY   Truly, I would not hang a dog by my will, much more a man who hath any honesty in him.

VERGES   If you hear a child cry in the night, you must call to the nurse and bid her still it.

A WATCHMAN   How if the nurse be asleep and will not hear us?

DOGBERRY   Why then, depart in peace, and let the child wake her with crying, for the ewe that will not hear her lamb when it baas will never answer a calf when he bleats.

70   VERGES   'Tis very true.

DOGBERRY   This is the end of the charge: you, constable, are to present the Prince's own person; if you meet the Prince in the night, you may stay him.

VERGES   Nay, by'r lady, that I think a cannot.

75   DOGBERRY   Five shillings to one on't, with any man that knows the statutes, he may stay him: marry, not without the Prince be willing, for indeed the watch ought to offend no man, and it is an offence to stay a man against his will.

80   VERGES   By'r lady, I think it be so.

DOGBERRY   Ha, ah ha! Well, masters, good night: and there be any matter of weight chances, call up me: keep your fellows' counsels and your own, and good night. Come, neighbour.

85   2 WATCHMAN   Well, masters, we hear our charge: let us go sit here upon the church-bench till two, and then all to bed.

DOGBERRY   One word more, honest neighbours. I pray you watch about Signior Leonato's door, for the wedding being there tomorrow, there is a great coil

90   tonight. Adieu! Be vigitant, I beseech you.

Exeunt Dogberry and Verges.

Enter BORACHIO *and* CONRADE.

BORACHIO   What, Conrade!

2 WATCHMAN [*aside*]   Peace! Stir not.

BORACHIO   Conrade, I say!

95   CONRADE   Here, man, I am at thy elbow.

BORACHIO   Mass, and my elbow itched; I thought there would a scab follow.

CONRADE   I will owe thee an answer for that: and now forward with thy tale.

100   BORACHIO   Stand thee close then under this penthouse, for it drizzles rain, and I will, like a true drunkard, utter all to thee.

2 WATCHMAN [*aside*]   Some treason, masters; yet stand close.

105   BORACHIO   Therefore know, I have earned of Don John a thousand ducats.

CONRADE   Is it possible that any villainy should be so dear?

BORACHIO   Thou shouldst rather ask if it were possible

110   any villainy should be so rich; for when rich villains have need of poor ones, poor ones may make what price they will.

CONRADE   I wonder at it.

BORACHIO   That shows thou art unconfirmed. Thou

115   knowest that the fashion of a doublet, or a hat, or a cloak, is nothing to a man.

CONRADE   Yes, it is apparel.

BORACHIO   I mean, the fashion.

CONRADE   Yes, the fashion is the fashion.

120   BORACHIO   Tush! I may as well say the fool's the fool. But seest thou not what a deformed thief this fashion is?

2 WATCHMAN [*aside*]   I know that Deformed; a has been a vile thief this seven year; a goes up and down like a gentleman: I remember his name.

BORACHIO   Didst thou not hear somebody?   125

CONRADE   No, 'twas the vane on the house.

BORACHIO   Seest thou not, I say, what a deformed thief this fashion is, how giddily a turns about all the hot bloods between fourteen and five-and-thirty, sometimes fashioning them like Pharaoh's soldiers in   130 the reechy painting, sometime like god Bel's priests in the old church-window, sometime like the shaven Hercules in the smirched worm-eaten tapestry, where his codpiece seems as massy as his club?

CONRADE   All this I see, and I see that the fashion wears   135 out more apparel than the man. But art not thou thyself giddy with the fashion too, that thou hast shifted out of thy tale into telling me of the fashion?

BORACHIO   Not so, neither; but know that I have tonight wooed Margaret, the Lady Hero's gentlewoman, by   140 the name of Hero; she leans me out at her mistress' chamber-window, bids me a thousand times good night – I tell this tale vilely – I should first tell thee how the Prince, Claudio, and my master, planted and placed and possessed by my master Don John, saw afar   145 off in the orchard this amiable encounter.

CONRADE   And thought they Margaret was Hero?

BORACHIO   Two of them did, the Prince and Claudio, but the devil my master knew she was Margaret; and partly by his oaths, which first possessed them, partly   150 by the dark night, which did deceive them, but chiefly by my villainy, which did confirm any slander that Don John had made, away went Claudio enraged; swore he would meet her as he was appointed next morning at the temple, and there, before the whole   155 congregation, shame her with what he saw o'ernight, and send her home again without a husband.

2 WATCHMAN   We charge you in the Prince's name, stand!

1 WATCHMAN   Call up the right Master Constable; we   160 have here recovered the most dangerous piece of lechery that ever was known in the commonwealth.

2 WATCHMAN   And one Deformed is one of them; I know him, a wears a lock.

CONRADE   Masters, masters –   165

1 WATCHMAN   You'll be made bring Deformed forth, I warrant you.

CONRADE   Masters –

2 WATCHMAN   Never speak, we charge you, let us obey you to go with us.   170

BORACHIO   We are like to prove a goodly commodity, being taken up of these men's bills.

CONRADE   A commodity in question, I warrant you. Come, we'll obey you.   *Exeunt.*

3.4   *Enter* HERO, MARGARET *and* URSULA.

HERO   Good Ursula, wake my cousin Beatrice, and desire her to rise.

URSULA   I will, lady.

HERO And bid her come hither.

URSULA Well.   *Exit.*

MARGARET Troth, I think your other rebato were better.

HERO No, pray thee good Meg, I'll wear this.

MARGARET By my troth 's not so good, and I warrant your cousin will say so.

HERO My cousin's a fool, and thou art another; I'll wear none but this.

MARGARET I like the new tire within excellently, if the hair were a thought browner; and your gown's a most rare fashion, i'faith. I saw the Duchess of Milan's gown that they praise so.

HERO O, that exceeds, they say.

MARGARET By my troth 's but a night-gown in respect of yours – cloth o' gold, and cuts, and laced with silver, set with pearls, down sleeves, side sleeves, and skirts, round underborne with a bluish tinsel: but for a fine, quaint, graceful, and excellent fashion, yours is worth ten on 't.

HERO God give me joy to wear it, for my heart is exceeding heavy.

MARGARET 'Twill be heavier soon by the weight of a man.

HERO Fie upon thee, art not ashamed?

MARGARET Of what, lady? Of speaking honourably? Is not marriage honourable in a beggar? Is not your lord honourable without marriage? I think you would have me say, saving your reverence, 'a husband'. And bad thinking do not wrest true speaking, I'll offend nobody. Is there any harm in 'the heavier for a husband'? None, I think, and it be the right husband, and the right wife; otherwise 'tis light, and not heavy. Ask my Lady Beatrice else; here she comes.

Enter BEATRICE.

HERO Good morrow, coz.

BEATRICE Good morrow, sweet Hero.

HERO Why, how now? Do you speak in the sick tune?

BEATRICE I am out of all other tune, methinks.

MARGARET Clap's into 'Light o' Love'; that goes without a burden. Do you sing it, and I'll dance it.

BEATRICE Ye light o' love with your heels! Then, if your husband have stables enough, you'll see he shall lack no barns.

MARGARET O illegitimate construction! I scorn that with my heels.

BEATRICE 'Tis almost five o'clock, cousin, 'tis time you were ready. By my troth, I am exceeding ill – heigh-ho!

MARGARET For a hawk, a horse, or a husband?

BEATRICE For the letter that begins them all, H.

MARGARET Well, and you be not turned Turk, there's no more sailing by the star.

BEATRICE What means the fool, trow?

MARGARET Nothing I, but God send everyone their heart's desire!

HERO These gloves the Count sent me, they are an excellent perfume.

BEATRICE I am stuffed, cousin, I cannot smell.

MARGARET A maid, and stuffed! There's goodly catching of cold.

BEATRICE O, God help me, God help me, how long have you professed apprehension?

MARGARET Ever since you left it. Doth not my wit become me rarely?

BEATRICE It is not seen enough, you should wear it in your cap. By my troth, I am sick.

MARGARET Get you some of this distilled *carduus benedictus*, and lay it to your heart; it is the only thing for a qualm.

HERO There thou prick'st her with a thistle.

BEATRICE *Benedictus*! Why *benedictus*? You have some moral in this *benedictus*.

MARGARET Moral? No, by my troth I have no moral meaning, I meant plain holy-thistle. You may think perchance that I think you are in love, nay by'r lady I am not such a fool to think what I list, nor I list not to think what I can, nor indeed I cannot think, if I would think my heart out of thinking, that you are in love, or that you will be in love, or that you can be in love. Yet Benedick was such another and now is he become a man: he swore he would never marry, and yet now in despite of his heart he eats his meat without grudging: and how you may be converted I know not, but methinks you look with your eyes as other women do.

BEATRICE What pace is this that thy tongue keeps?

MARGARET Not a false gallop.

Enter URSULA.

URSULA Madam, withdraw! The Prince, the Count, Signior Benedick, Don John, and all the gallants of the town are come to fetch you to church.

HERO Help to dress me, good coz, good Meg, good Ursula.   *Exeunt.*

3.5 *Enter* LEONATO *and the constable* DOGBERRY *and the headborough* VERGES.

LEONATO What would you with me, honest neighbour?

DOGBERRY Marry, sir, I would have some confidence with you, that decerns you nearly.

LEONATO Brief, I pray you, for you see it is a busy time with me.

DOGBERRY Marry, this it is, sir.

VERGES Yes, in truth it is, sir.

LEONATO What is it, my good friends?

DOGBERRY Goodman Verges, sir, speaks a little off the matter: an old man, sir, and his wits are not so blunt as, God help, I would desire they were, but, in faith, honest as the skin between his brows.

VERGES Yes, I thank God, I am as honest as any man living, that is an old man, and no honester than I.

DOGBERRY Comparisons are odorous: *palabras*, neighbour Verges.

LEONATO Neighbours, you are tedious.

DOGBERRY   It pleases your worship to say so, but we are the poor Duke's officers; but truly, for mine own part, if I were as tedious as a king, I could find in my heart to bestow it all of your worship.

LEONATO   All thy tediousness on me, ah?

DOGBERRY   Yea, and 'twere a thousand pound more than 'tis, for I hear as good exclamation on your worship as of any man in the city, and though I be but a poor man, I am glad to hear it.

VERGES   And so am I.

LEONATO   I would fain know what you have to say.

VERGES   Marry, sir, our watch tonight, excepting your worship's presence, ha' ta'en a couple of as arrant knaves as any in Messina.

DOGBERRY   A good old man, sir, he will be talking; as they say, 'When the age is in, the wit is out', God help us, it is a world to see! Well said, i'faith, neighbour Verges; well, God's a good man, and two men ride of a horse, one must ride behind. An honest soul, i'faith, sir, by my troth he is, as ever broke bread; but God is to be worshipped, all men are not alike, alas, good neighbour!

LEONATO   Indeed, neighbour, he comes too short of you.

DOGBERRY   Gifts that God gives.

LEONATO   I must leave you.

DOGBERRY   One word, sir: our watch, sir, have indeed comprehended two aspicious persons, and we would have them this morning examined before your worship.

LEONATO   Take their examination yourself, and bring it me; I am now in great haste, as it may appear unto you.

DOGBERRY   It shall be suffigance.

LEONATO   Drink some wine ere you go. Fare you well!

Enter a Messenger.

MESSENGER   My lord, they stay for you to give your daughter to her husband.

LEONATO   I'll wait upon them; I am ready.

Exit with Messenger.

DOGBERRY   Go, good partner, go, get you to Francis Seacoal, bid him bring his pen and inkhorn to the gaol: we are now to examination these men.

VERGES   And we must do it wisely.

DOGBERRY   We will spare for no wit, I warrant you; here's that shall drive some of them to a non-come. Only get the learned writer to set down our excommunication, and meet me at the gaol.   *Exeunt.*

4.1   *Enter* DON PEDRO, DON JOHN *the Bastard,*
LEONATO, FRIAR FRANCIS, CLAUDIO, BENEDICK, HERO,
BEATRICE *and attendants.*

LEONATO   Come, Friar Francis, be brief: only to the plain form of marriage, and you shall recount their particular duties afterwards.

FRIAR   You come hither, my lord, to marry this lady?

CLAUDIO   No.

LEONATO   To be married to her, friar: you come to marry her.

FRIAR   Lady, you come hither to be married to this Count?

HERO   I do.

FRIAR   If either of you know any inward impediment why you should not be conjoined, I charge you on your souls to utter it.

CLAUDIO   Know you any, Hero?

HERO   None, my lord.

FRIAR   Know you any, Count?

LEONATO   I dare make his answer, None.

CLAUDIO   O, what men dare do! What men may do! What men daily do, not knowing what they do!

BENEDICK   How now? Interjections? Why then, some be of laughing, as ah, ha, he!

CLAUDIO   Stand thee by, friar. Father, by your leave:
Will you with free and unconstrained soul
Give me this maid, your daughter?

LEONATO   As freely, son, as God did give her me.

CLAUDIO   And what have I to give you back whose worth
May counterpoise this rich and precious gift?

DON PEDRO   Nothing, unless you render her again.

CLAUDIO
Sweet Prince, you learn me noble thankfulness.
There, Leonato, take her back again.
Give not this rotten orange to your friend;
She's but the sign and semblance of her honour.
Behold how like a maid she blushes here!
O, what authority and show of truth
Can cunning sin cover itself withal!
Comes not that blood as modest evidence
To witness simple virtue? Would you not swear,
All you that see her, that she were a maid,
By these exterior shows? But she is none:
She knows the heat of a luxurious bed:
Her blush is guiltiness, not modesty.

LEONATO   What do you mean, my lord?

CLAUDIO   Not to be married, not to knit my soul
To an approved wanton.

LEONATO   Dear my lord, if you, in your own proof,
Have vanquish'd the resistance of her youth,
And made defeat of her virginity –

CLAUDIO
I know what you would say: if I have known her,
You will say she did embrace me as a husband,
And so extenuate the 'forehand sin.
No, Leonato.
I never tempted her with word too large,
But, as a brother to his sister, show'd
Bashful sincerity and comely love.

HERO   And seem'd I ever otherwise to you?

CLAUDIO   Out on thee, seeming! I will write against it.
You seem to me as Dian in her orb,
As chaste as is the bud ere it be blown;
But you are more intemperate in your blood
Than Venus, or those pamper'd animals
That rage in savage sensuality.

HERO   Is my lord well that he doth speak so wide?

LEONATO   Sweet Prince, why speak not you?

DON PEDRO   What should I speak?
I stand dishonour'd, that have gone about
To link my dear friend to a common stale.

LEONATO   Are these things spoken, or do I but dream?

DON JOHN
Sir, they are spoken, and these things are true.

BENEDICK   This looks not like a nuptial!

HERO   'True'? O God!

CLAUDIO   Leonato, stand I here?
Is this the Prince? Is this the Prince's brother?
Is this face Hero's? Are our eyes our own?

LEONATO   All this is so, but what of this, my lord?

CLAUDIO
Let me but move one question to your daughter,
And by that fatherly and kindly power
That you have in her, bid her answer truly.

LEONATO   I charge thee do so, as thou art my child.

HERO   O God defend me, how am I beset!
What kind of catechizing call you this?

CLAUDIO   To make you answer truly to your name.

HERO   Is it not Hero? Who can blot that name
With any just reproach?

CLAUDIO   Marry, that can Hero;
Hero itself can blot out Hero's virtue.
What man was he talk'd with you yesternight,
Out at your window betwixt twelve and one?
Now if you are a maid, answer to this.

HERO   I talk'd with no man at that hour, my lord.

DON PEDRO   Why, then are you no maiden. Leonato,
I am sorry you must hear: upon mine honour,
Myself, my brother, and this grieved Count
Did see her, hear her, at that hour last night,
Talk with a ruffian at her chamber-window,
Who hath indeed, most like a liberal villain,
Confess'd the vile encounters they have had
A thousand times in secret.

DON JOHN   Fie, fie, they are not to be nam'd, my lord,
Not to be spoke of!
There is not chastity enough in language
Without offence to utter them. Thus, pretty lady,
I am sorry for thy much misgovernment.

CLAUDIO   O Hero! What a Hero hadst thou been,
If half thy outward graces had been plac'd
About thy thoughts and counsels of thy heart!
But fare thee well, most foul, most fair! Farewell,
Thou pure impiety and impious purity!
For thee I'll lock up all the gates of love,
And on my eyelids shall conjecture hang,
To turn all beauty into thoughts of harm,
And never shall it more be gracious.

LEONATO   Hath no man's dagger here a point for me?
[*Hero swoons.*]

BEATRICE
Why, how now, cousin! Wherefore sink you down?

DON JOHN
Come, let us go. These things, come thus to light,   110
Smother her spirits up.
                Exeunt Don Pedro, Don John and Claudio.

BENEDICK   How doth the lady?

BEATRICE   Dead, I think. Help, uncle!
Hero! Why, Hero! Uncle! Signior Benedick! Friar!

LEONATO   O Fate, take not away thy heavy hand!
Death is the fairest cover for her shame   115
That may be wish'd for.

BEATRICE   How now, cousin Hero?

FRIAR   Have comfort, lady.

LEONATO   Dost thou look up?

FRIAR   Yea, wherefore should she not?

LEONATO
Wherefore? Why, doth not every earthly thing
Cry shame upon her? Could she here deny   120
The story that is printed in her blood?
Do not live, Hero, do not ope thine eyes;
For did I think thou wouldst not quickly die,
Thought I thy spirits were stronger than thy shames,
Myself would on the rearward of reproaches   125
Strike at thy life. Griev'd I, I had but one?
Chid I for that at frugal Nature's frame?
O, one too much by thee! Why had I one?
Why ever wast thou lovely in my eyes?
Why had I not with charitable hand   130
Took up a beggar's issue at my gates,
Who smirched thus, and mir'd with infamy,
I might have said, 'No part of it is mine;
This shame derives itself from unknown loins'?
But mine, and mine I lov'd, and mine I prais'd,   135
And mine that I was proud on – mine so much
That I myself was to myself not mine,
Valuing of her – why, she, O, she is fall'n
Into a pit of ink, that the wide sea
Hath drops too few to wash her clean again,   140
And salt too little which may season give
To her foul-tainted flesh!

BENEDICK   Sir, sir, be patient.
For my part I am so attir'd in wonder,
I know not what to say.

BEATRICE   O, on my soul my cousin is belied!   145

BENEDICK   Lady, were you her bedfellow last night?

BEATRICE   No, truly, not; although until last night,
I have this twelvemonth been her bedfellow.

LEONATO
Confirm'd, confirm'd! O, that is stronger made
Which was before barr'd up with ribs of iron.   150
Would the two princes lie, and Claudio lie,
Who lov'd her so, that, speaking of her foulness,
Wash'd it with tears? Hence from her, let her die!

FRIAR   Hear me a little;
For I have only been silent so long,   155
And given way unto this course of fortune,
By noting of the lady. I have mark'd

A thousand blushing apparitions
To start into her face, a thousand innocent shames
160 In angel whiteness beat away those blushes,
And in her eye there hath appear'd a fire
To burn the errors that these princes hold
Against her maiden truth. Call me a fool;
Trust not my reading nor my observations,
165 Which with experimental seal doth warrant
The tenor of my book; trust not my age,
My reverence, calling, nor divinity,
If this sweet lady lie not guiltless here
Under some biting error.
LEONATO   Friar, it cannot be.
170 Thou seest that all the grace that she hath left
Is that she will not add to her damnation
A sin of perjury: she not denies it.
Why seek'st thou then to cover with excuse
That which appears in proper nakedness?
175 FRIAR   Lady, what man is he you are accus'd of?
HERO   They know that do accuse me; I know none.
If I know more of any man alive
Than that which maiden modesty doth warrant,
Let all my sins lack mercy! O my father,
180 Prove you that any man with me convers'd
At hours unmeet, or that I yesternight
Maintain'd the change of words with any creature,
Refuse me, hate me, torture me to death!
FRIAR
There is some strange misprision in the princes.
185 BENEDICK   Two of them have the very bent of honour;
And if their wisdoms be misled in this,
The practice of it lives in John the bastard,
Whose spirits toil in frame of villainies.
LEONATO   I know not. If they speak but truth of her,
190 These hands shall tear her: if they wrong her honour,
The proudest of them shall well hear of it.
Time hath not yet so dried this blood of mine,
Nor age so eat up my invention,
Nor fortune made such havoc of my means,
195 Nor my bad life reft me so much of friends,
But they shall find, awak'd in such a kind,
Both strength of limb and policy of mind,
Ability in means and choice of friends,
To quit me of them throughly.
FRIAR   Pause awhile,
200 And let my counsel sway you in this case.
Your daughter here the princes left for dead,
Let her awhile be secretly kept in,
And publish it that she is dead indeed;
Maintain a mourning ostentation,
205 And on your family's old monument
Hang mournful epitaphs, and do all rites
That appertain unto a burial.
LEONATO
What shall become of this? What will this do?
FRIAR   Marry, this well carried shall on her behalf
210 Change slander to remorse; that is some good:

But not for that dream I on this strange course,
But on this travail look for greater birth.
She dying, as it must be so maintain'd,
Upon the instant that she was accus'd,
Shall be lamented, pitied, and excus'd   215
Of every hearer; for it so falls out
That what we have we prize not to the worth
Whiles we enjoy it, but being lack'd and lost,
Why then we rack the value, then we find
The virtue that possession would not show us   220
Whiles it was ours: so will it fare with Claudio.
When he shall hear she died upon his words,
Th'idea of her life shall sweetly creep
Into his study of imagination,
And every lovely organ of her life   225
Shall come apparell'd in more precious habit,
More moving-delicate and full of life,
Into the eye and prospect of his soul
Than when she liv'd indeed: then shall he mourn –
If ever love had interest in his liver –   230
And wish he had not so accused her:
No, though he thought his accusation true.
Let this be so, and doubt not but success
Will fashion the event in better shape
Than I can lay it down in likelihood.   235
But if all aim but this be levell'd false,
The supposition of the lady's death
Will quench the wonder of her infamy:
And if it sort not well, you may conceal her,
As best befits her wounded reputation.   240
In some reclusive and religious life,
Out of all eyes, tongues, minds, and injuries.
BENEDICK   Signior Leonato, let the friar advise you;
And though you know my inwardness and love
Is very much unto the Prince and Claudio,   245
Yet, by mine honour, I will deal in this
As secretly and justly as your soul
Should with your body.
LEONATO   Being that I flow in grief,
The smallest twine may lead me.
FRIAR   'Tis well consented. Presently away;   250
For to strange sores strangely they strain the cure.
Come, lady, die to live; this wedding-day
Perhaps is but prolong'd; have patience and endure.
                    Exeunt all but Benedick and Beatrice.
BENEDICK   Lady Beatrice, have you wept all this while?
BEATRICE   Yea, and I will weep a while longer.   255
BENEDICK   I will not desire that.
BEATRICE   You have no reason, I do it freely.
BENEDICK   Surely I do believe your fair cousin is
  wronged.
BEATRICE   Ah, how much might the man deserve of me   260
  that would right her!
BENEDICK   Is there any way to show such friendship?
BEATRICE   A very even way, but no such friend.
BENEDICK   May a man do it?
BEATRICE   It is a man's office, but not yours.   265

BENEDICK   I do love nothing in the world so well as you
– is not that strange?

BEATRICE   As strange as the thing I know not. It were as
possible for me to say I loved nothing so well as you,
but believe me not; and yet I lie not; I confess nothing,
nor I deny nothing. I am sorry for my cousin.

BENEDICK   By my sword, Beatrice, thou lovest me.

BEATRICE   Do not swear and eat it.

BENEDICK   I will swear by it that you love me, and I will
make him eat it that says I love not you.

BEATRICE   Will you not eat your word?

BENEDICK   With no sauce that can be devised to it. I
protest I love thee.

BEATRICE   Why then, God forgive me!

BENEDICK   What offence, sweet Beatrice?

BEATRICE   You have stayed me in a happy hour, I was
about to protest I loved you.

BENEDICK   And do it with all thy heart.

BEATRICE   I love you with so much of my heart that none
is left to protest.

BENEDICK   Come, bid me do anything for thee.

BEATRICE   Kill Claudio!

BENEDICK   Ha, not for the wide world!

BEATRICE   You kill me to deny it. Farewell.

BENEDICK   Tarry, sweet Beatrice.

BEATRICE   I am gone, though I am here; there is no love
in you; nay I pray you let me go.

BENEDICK   Beatrice –

BEATRICE   In faith, I will go.

BENEDICK   We'll be friends first.

BEATRICE   You dare easier be friends with me than fight
with mine enemy.

BENEDICK   Is Claudio thine enemy?

BEATRICE   Is a not approved in the height a villain, that
hath slandered, scorned, dishonoured my kinswoman?
O that I were a man! What, bear her in hand until
they come to take hands, and then with public
accusation, uncovered slander, unmitigated rancour
– O God that I were a man! I would eat his heart in the
market-place.

BENEDICK   Hear me, Beatrice –

BEATRICE   Talk with a man out at a window! A proper
saying!

BENEDICK   Nay, but Beatrice –

BEATRICE   Sweet Hero! She is wronged, she is
slandered, she is undone.

BENEDICK   Beat –

BEATRICE   Princes and counties! Surely a princely
testimony, a goodly count, Count Comfect, a sweet
gallant surely! O that I were a man for his sake, or that
I had any friend would be a man for my sake! But
manhood is melted into curtsies, valour into
compliment, and men are only turned into tongue,
and trim ones too: he is now as valiant as Hercules that
only tells a lie and swears it. I cannot be a man with
wishing, therefore I will die a woman with grieving.

BENEDICK   Tarry, good Beatrice. By this hand I love

thee.

BEATRICE   Use it for my love some other way than
swearing by it.

BENEDICK   Think you in your soul the Count Claudio
hath wronged Hero?

BEATRICE   Yea, as sure as I have a thought, or a soul.

BENEDICK   Enough! I am engaged, I will challenge him.
I will kiss your hand, and so I leave you. By this hand,
Claudio shall render me a dear account. As you hear of
me, so think of me. Go comfort your cousin; I must
say she is dead: and so farewell.   *Exeunt.*

4.2   *Enter the constables,* DOGBERRY *and* VERGES, *and
the* SEXTON *as town clerk in gowns,* BORACHIO, CONRADE
and the WATCH.

DOGBERRY   Is our whole dissembly appeared?

VERGES   O, a stool and a cushion for the sexton.

SEXTON   Which be the malefactors?

DOGBERRY   Marry, that am I and my partner.

VERGES   Nay, that's certain, we have the exhibition to
examine.

SEXTON   But which are the offenders that are to be
examined? Let them come before Master Constable.

DOGBERRY   Yea, marry, let them come before me. What
is your name, friend?

BORACHIO   Borachio.

DOGBERRY   Pray write down 'Borachio'. Yours, sirrah?

CONRADE   I am a gentleman, sir, and my name is
Conrade.

DOGBERRY   Write down 'Master gentleman Conrade'.
Masters, do you serve God?

CONRADE, BORACHIO   Yea, sir, we hope.

DOGBERRY   Write down that they hope they serve God:
and write 'God' first, for God defend but God should
go before such villains! Masters, it is proved already
that you are little better than false knaves, and it will
go near to be thought so shortly. How answer you for
yourselves?

CONRADE   Marry, sir, we say we are none.

DOGBERRY   A marvellous witty fellow, I assure you, but
I will go about with him. Come you hither, sirrah, a
word in your ear, sir; I say to you, it is thought you are
false knaves.

BORACHIO   Sir, I say to you we are none.

DOGBERRY   Well, stand aside. 'Fore God, they are both
in a tale. Have you writ down that they are none?

SEXTON   Master Constable, you go not the way to
examine; you must call forth the watch that are their
accusers.

DOGBERRY   Yea, marry, that's the eftest way. Let the
watch come forth. Masters, I charge you in the
Prince's name, accuse these men.

1 WATCHMAN   This man said, sir, that Don John the
Prince's brother was a villain.

DOGBERRY   Write down 'Prince John a villain'. Why, this
is flat perjury, to call a prince's brother villain.

BORACHIO   Master Constable –

DOGBERRY   Pray thee, fellow, peace, I do not like thy
look, I promise thee.

45 SEXTON   What heard you him say else?

2 WATCHMAN   Marry, that he had received a thousand
ducats of Don John for accusing the Lady Hero
wrongfully.

DOGBERRY   Flat burglary as ever was committed.

50 VERGES   Yea, by mass, that it is.

SEXTON   What else, fellow?

1 WATCHMAN   And that Count Claudio did mean, upon
his words, to disgrace Hero before the whole
assembly, and not marry her.

55 DOGBERRY   O villain! Thou wilt be condemned into
everlasting redemption for this.

SEXTON   What else?

A WATCHMAN   This is all.

SEXTON   And this is more, masters, than you can deny.
60 Prince John is this morning secretly stolen away:
Hero was in this manner accused, in this very
manner refused, and upon the grief of this suddenly
died. Master Constable, let these men be bound and
brought to Leonato's; I will go before and show him
65 their examination.   *Exit.*

DOGBERRY   Come, let them be opinioned.

VERGES   Let them be in the hands –

CONRADE   Off, coxcomb!

DOGBERRY   God's my life, where's the sexton? Let him
70 write down 'the Prince's officer coxcomb'. Come, bind
them. Thou naughty varlet!

CONRADE   Away! You are an ass, you are an ass.

DOGBERRY   Dost thou not suspect my place? Dost thou
not suspect my years? O that he were here to write me
75 down an ass! But masters, remember that I am an
ass: though it be not written down, yet forget not
that I am an ass. No, thou villain, thou art full of piety,
as shall be proved upon thee by good witness. I am a
wise fellow, and which is more, an officer, and which is
80 more, a householder, and which is more, as pretty a
piece of flesh as any is in Messina, and one that knows
the law, go to, and a rich fellow enough, go to, and a
fellow that hath had losses, and one that hath two
gowns, and everything handsome about him. Bring
85 him away! O that I had been writ down an ass!

                                                    Exeunt.

5.1   *Enter* LEONATO *and* ANTONIO.

ANTONIO   If you go on thus, you will kill yourself,
And 'tis not wisdom thus to second grief
Against yourself.

LEONATO   I pray thee cease thy counsel,
Which falls into mine ears as profitless
5 As water in a sieve. Give not me counsel,
Nor let no comforter delight mine ear
But such a one whose wrongs do suit with mine.
Bring me a father that so lov'd his child,
Whose joy of her is overwhelm'd like mine,
10 And bid him speak of patience;
Measure his woe the length and breadth of mine,
And let it answer every strain for strain,
As thus for thus, and such a grief for such,
In every lineament, branch, shape, and form.
15 If such a one will smile and stroke his beard,
Bid sorrow wag, cry 'Hem!' when he should groan,
Patch grief with proverbs, make misfortune drunk
With candle-wasters, bring him yet to me,
And I of him will gather patience.
20 But there is no such man: for, brother, men
Can counsel and speak comfort to that grief
Which they themselves not feel; but tasting it,
Their counsel turns to passion, which before
Would give preceptial medicine to rage,
25 Fetter strong madness in a silken thread,
Charm ache with air, and agony with words.
No, no, 'tis all men's office to speak patience
To those that wring under the load of sorrow,
But no man's virtue nor sufficiency
30 To be so moral when he shall endure
The like himself. Therefore give me no counsel:
My griefs cry louder than advertisement.

ANTONIO
Therein do men from children nothing differ.

LEONATO   I pray thee peace, I will be flesh and blood;
35 For there was never yet philosopher
That could endure the toothache patiently,
However they have writ the style of gods,
And made a push at chance and sufferance.

ANTONIO   Yet bend not all the harm upon yourself;
40 Make those that do offend you suffer too.

LEONATO   There thou speak'st reason: nay, I will do so.
My soul doth tell me Hero is belied;
And that shall Claudio know, so shall the Prince,
And all of them that thus dishonour her.

          Enter DON PEDRO *and* CLAUDIO.

ANTONIO   Here comes the Prince and Claudio hastily.   45

DON PEDRO   Good den, good den.

CLAUDIO   Good day to both of you.

LEONATO   Hear you, my lords –

DON PEDRO   We have some haste, Leonato.

LEONATO
Some haste, my lord? Well, fare you well, my lord!
Are you so hasty now? Well, all is one.

DON PEDRO
Nay, do not quarrel with us, good old man.   50

ANTONIO   If he could right himself with quarrelling,
Some of us would lie low.

CLAUDIO   Who wrongs him?

LEONATO
Marry, thou dost wrong me, thou dissembler, thou!
Nay, never lay thy hand upon thy sword,
I fear thee not.

CLAUDIO   Marry, beshrew my hand
  If it should give your age such cause of fear.
  In faith, my hand meant nothing to my sword.
LEONATO   Tush, tush, man, never fleer and jest at me!
  I speak not like a dotard nor a fool,
  As under privilege of age to brag
  What I have done being young, or what would do
  Were I not old. Know, Claudio, to thy head,
  Thou hast so wrong'd mine innocent child and me,
  That I am forc'd to lay my reverence by,
  And with grey hairs and bruise of many days
  Do challenge thee to trial of a man.
  I say thou hast belied mine innocent child;
  Thy slander hath gone through and through her
    heart,
  And she lies buried with her ancestors –
  O, in a tomb where never scandal slept,
  Save this of hers, fram'd by thy villainy!
CLAUDIO   My villainy?
LEONATO   Thine, Claudio; thine, I say.
DON PEDRO   You say not right, old man.
LEONATO   My lord, my lord,
  I'll prove it on his body if he dare,
  Despite his nice fence and his active practice,
  His May of youth and bloom of lustihood.
CLAUDIO   Away! I will not have to do with you.
LEONATO
  Canst thou so daff me? Thou hast kill'd my child;
  If thou kill'st me, boy, thou shalt kill a man.
ANTONIO   He shall kill two of us, and men indeed:
  But that's no matter, let him kill one first.
  Win me and wear me, let him answer me.
  Come follow me, boy, come, sir boy, come follow me,
  Sir boy, I'll whip you from your foining fence,
  Nay, as I am a gentleman, I will.
LEONATO   Brother –
ANTONIO
  Content yourself. God knows I lov'd my niece,
  And she is dead, slander'd to death by villains,
  That dare as well answer a man indeed
  As I dare take a serpent by the tongue.
  Boys, apes, braggarts, Jacks, milksops!
LEONATO   Brother Antony –
ANTONIO
  Hold you content. What, man! I know them, yea,
  And what they weigh, even to the utmost scruple,
  Scambling, outfacing, fashion-monging boys,
  That lie, and cog, and flout, deprave, and slander,
  Go anticly, and show outward hideousness,
  And speak off half a dozen dang'rous words,
  How they might hurt their enemies, if they durst,
  And this is all.
LEONATO   But brother Antony –
ANTONIO   Come, 'tis no matter;
  Do not you meddle, let me deal in this.
DON PEDRO
  Gentlemen both, we will not wake your patience.

My heart is sorry for your daughter's death;
  But on my honour she was charg'd with nothing
  But what was true, and very full of proof.   105
LEONATO   My lord, my lord –
DON PEDRO   I will not hear you.
LEONATO   No? Come, brother, away! I will be heard.
ANTONIO   And shall, or some of us will smart for it.
                    Exeunt Leonato and Antonio.

                    Enter BENEDICK.

DON PEDRO   See, see! Here comes the man we went to   110
  seek.
CLAUDIO   Now, signior, what news?
BENEDICK   Good day, my lord.
DON PEDRO   Welcome, signior; you are almost come to
  part almost a fray.   115
CLAUDIO   We had like to have had our two noses
  snapped off with two old men without teeth.
DON PEDRO   Leonato and his brother. What think'st
  thou? Had we fought, I doubt we should have been too
  young for them.   120
BENEDICK   In a false quarrel there is no true valour. I
  came to seek you both.
CLAUDIO   We have been up and down to seek thee, for
  we are high-proof melancholy, and would fain have it
  beaten away. Wilt thou use thy wit?   125
BENEDICK   It is in my scabbard; shall I draw it?
DON PEDRO   Dost thou wear thy wit by thy side?
CLAUDIO   Never any did so, though very many have
  been beside their wit. I will bid thee draw, as we do the
  minstrels – draw to pleasure us.   130
DON PEDRO   As I am an honest man, he looks pale. Art
  thou sick, or angry?
CLAUDIO   What, courage, man! What though care killed
  a cat, thou hast mettle enough in thee to kill care.
BENEDICK   Sir, I shall meet your wit in the career, and 135
  you charge it against me. I pray you choose another
  subject.
CLAUDIO   Nay then, give him another staff; this last was
  broke cross.
DON PEDRO   By this light, he changes more and more; I 140
  think he be angry indeed.
CLAUDIO   If he be, he knows how to turn his girdle.
BENEDICK   Shall I speak a word in your ear?
CLAUDIO   God bless me from a challenge!
BENEDICK [*aside to Claudio*]   You are a villain. I jest not; 145
  I will make it good how you dare, with what you dare,
  and when you dare. Do me right, or I will protest
  your cowardice. You have killed a sweet lady, and her
  death shall fall heavy on you. Let me hear from you.
CLAUDIO   Well, I will meet you, so I may have good cheer. 150
DON PEDRO   What, a feast, a feast?
CLAUDIO   I'faith I thank him, he hath bid me to a calf's
  head and a capon, the which if I do not carve most
  curiously, say my knife's naught. Shall I not find a
  woodcock too?   155
BENEDICK   Sir, your wit ambles well; it goes easily.

DON PEDRO I'll tell thee how Beatrice praised thy wit the other day. I said thou hadst a fine wit. 'True,' said she, 'a fine little one.' 'No,' said I, 'a great wit.'
160 'Right,' says she, 'a great gross one.' 'Nay,' said I, 'a good wit.' 'Just,' said she, 'it hurts nobody.' 'Nay,' said I, 'the gentleman is wise.' 'Certain,' said she, 'a wise gentleman.' 'Nay,' said I, 'he hath the tongues.' 'That I believe,' said she, 'for he swore a thing to me on
165 Monday night, which he forswore on Tuesday morning; there's a double tongue; there's two tongues.' Thus did she an hour together transshape thy particular virtues: yet at last she concluded with a sigh, thou wast the properest man in Italy.
170 CLAUDIO For the which she wept heartily and said she cared not.
DON PEDRO Yea, that she did; but yet for all that, and if she did not hate him deadly, she would love him dearly – the old man's daughter told us all.
175 CLAUDIO All, all; and moreover, God saw him when he was hid in the garden.
DON PEDRO But when shall we set the savage bull's horns on the sensible Benedick's head?
CLAUDIO Yea, and text underneath, 'Here dwells
180 Benedick, the married man'?
BENEDICK Fare you well, boy, you know my mind: I will leave you now to your gossip-like humour. You break jests as braggarts do their blades, which God be thanked hurt not. My lord, for your many courtesies I
185 thank you: I must discontinue your company. Your brother the bastard is fled from Messina. You have among you killed a sweet and innocent lady. For my Lord Lackbeard there, he and I shall meet; and till then, peace be with him.   *Exit.*
190 DON PEDRO He is in earnest.
CLAUDIO In most profound earnest, and, I'll warrant you, for the love of Beatrice.
DON PEDRO And hath challenged thee.
CLAUDIO Most sincerely.
195 DON PEDRO What a pretty thing man is when he goes in his doublet and hose and leaves off his wit!
CLAUDIO He is then a giant to an ape; but then is an ape a doctor to such a man.
DON PEDRO But, soft you, let me be: pluck up, my heart,
200 and be sad. Did he not say my brother was fled?

Enter constables DOGBERRY *and* VERGES, *and the* Watch, *with* CONRADE *and* BORACHIO.

DOGBERRY Come you, sir, if justice cannot tame you she shall ne'er weigh more reasons in her balance. Nay, and you be a cursing hypocrite once, you must be looked to.
DON PEDRO How now? Two of my brother's men
205 bound? Borachio one?
CLAUDIO Hearken after their offence, my lord.
DON PEDRO Officers, what offence have these men done?
DOGBERRY Marry, sir, they have committed false report, moreover they have spoken untruths, secondarily they
210 are slanders, sixth and lastly they have belied a lady,

thirdly they have verified unjust things, and to conclude, they are lying knaves.
DON PEDRO First I ask thee what they have done, thirdly I ask thee what's their offence, sixth and lastly why they are committed, and to conclude, what you 215 lay to their charge.
CLAUDIO Rightly reasoned, and in his own division; and by my troth there's one meaning well suited.
DON PEDRO Who have you offended, masters, that you are thus bound to your answer? This learned constable 220 is too cunning to be understood. What's your offence?
BORACHIO Sweet Prince, let me go no farther to mine answer. Do you hear me, and let this Count kill me. I have deceived even your very eyes: what your wisdoms could not discover, these shallow fools have brought to 225 light, who in the night overheard me confessing to this man, how Don John your brother incensed me to slander the Lady Hero, how you were brought into the orchard and saw me court Margaret in Hero's garments, how you disgraced her when you should 230 marry her. My villainy they have upon record, which I had rather seal with my death than repeat over to my shame. The lady is dead upon mine and my master's false accusation; and briefly, I desire nothing but the reward of a villain. 235
DON PEDRO Runs not this speech like iron through your blood?
CLAUDIO I have drunk poison whiles he utter'd it.
DON PEDRO But did my brother set thee on to this?
BORACHIO Yea, and paid me richly for the practice of it. 240
DON PEDRO He is compos'd and fram'd of treachery, And fled he is upon this villainy.
CLAUDIO Sweet Hero! Now thy image doth appear In the rare semblance that I lov'd it first.
DOGBERRY Come, bring away the plaintiffs. By this time 245 our sexton hath reformed Signior Leonato of the matter: and masters, do not forget to specify, when time and place shall serve, that I am an ass.
VERGES Here, here comes Master Signior Leonato, and the sexton too. 250

Enter LEONATO, ANTONIO *and the* Sexton.

LEONATO Which is the villain? Let me see his eyes, That when I note another man like him I may avoid him. Which of these is he?
BORACHIO
If you would know your wronger, look on me.
LEONATO
Art thou the slave that with thy breath hast kill'd 255
Mine innocent child?
BORACHIO   Yea, even I alone.
LEONATO No, not so, villain, thou beliest thyself.
Here stand a pair of honourable men –
A third is fled – that had a hand in it.
I thank you, Princes, for my daughter's death; 260
Record it with your high and worthy deeds;
'Twas bravely done, if you bethink you of it.

CLAUDIO   I know not how to pray your patience,
  Yet I must speak. Choose your revenge yourself,
  Impose me to what penance your invention
  Can lay upon my sin; yet sinn'd I not
  But in mistaking.
DON PEDRO   By my soul, nor I:
  And yet, to satisfy this good old man,
  I would bend under any heavy weight
  That he'll enjoin me to.
LEONATO   I cannot bid you bid my daughter live –
  That were impossible – but I pray you both,
  Possess the people in Messina here
  How innocent she died; and if your love
  Can labour aught in sad invention,
  Hang her an epitaph upon her tomb,
  And sing it to her bones, sing it tonight.
  Tomorrow morning come you to my house,
  And since you could not be my son-in-law,
  Be yet my nephew. My brother hath a daughter,
  Almost the copy of my child that's dead,
  And she alone is heir to both of us.
  Give her the right you should have giv'n her cousin,
  And so dies my revenge.
CLAUDIO   O noble sir,
  Your overkindness doth wring tears from me!
  I do embrace your offer, and dispose
  For henceforth of poor Claudio.
LEONATO   Tomorrow then I will expect your coming;
  Tonight I take my leave. This naughty man
  Shall face to face be brought to Margaret,
  Who I believe was pack'd in all this wrong,
  Hir'd to it by your brother.
BORACHIO   No, by my soul she was not,
  Nor knew not what she did when she spoke to me,
  But always hath been just and virtuous
  In anything that I do know by her.
DOGBERRY   Moreover, sir, which indeed is not under
  white and black, this plaintiff here, the offender, did
  call me ass; I beseech you let it be remembered in his
  punishment. And also the watch heard them talk of
  one Deformed; they say he wears a key in his ear and a
  lock hanging by it, and borrows money in God's name,
  the which he hath used so long, and never paid, that
  now men grow hard-hearted and will lend nothing for
  God's sake: pray you examine him upon that point.
LEONATO   I thank thee for thy care and honest pains.
DOGBERRY   Your worship speaks like a most thankful
  and reverent youth, and I praise God for you.
LEONATO   There's for thy pains.
DOGBERRY   God save the foundation!
LEONATO   Go, I discharge thee of thy prisoner, and I
  thank thee.
DOGBERRY   I leave an arrant knave with your worship,
  which I beseech your worship to correct yourself, for
  the example of others. God keep your worship! I
  wish your worship well. God restore you to health! I
  humbly give you leave to depart, and if a merry

meeting may be wished, God prohibit it! Come,
neighbour.   *Exeunt Dogberry and Verges.*
LEONATO   Until tomorrow morning, lords, farewell.
ANTONIO   Farewell, my lords, we look for you tomorrow.   320
DON PEDRO   We will not fail.
CLAUDIO   Tonight I'll mourn with Hero.
LEONATO [*to the Watch*]
  Bring you these fellows on. We'll talk with Margaret,
  How her acquaintance grew with this lewd fellow.
          Exeunt.

5.2   *Enter* BENEDICK *and* MARGARET, *meeting.*

BENEDICK   Pray thee, sweet Mistress Margaret, deserve
  well at my hands, by helping me to the speech of
  Beatrice.
MARGARET   Will you then write me a sonnet in praise of
  my beauty?   5
BENEDICK   In so high a style, Margaret, that no man
  living shall come over it, for in most comely truth thou
  deservest it.
MARGARET   To have no man come over me? Why, shall I
  always keep below stairs?   10
BENEDICK   Thy wit is as quick as the greyhound's
  mouth, it catches.
MARGARET   And yours as blunt as the fencer's foils,
  which hit, but hurt not.
BENEDICK   A most manly wit, Margaret, it will not hurt   15
  a woman. And so I pray thee call Beatrice; I give thee
  the bucklers.
MARGARET   Give us the swords, we have bucklers of our
  own.
BENEDICK   If you use them, Margaret, you must put in   20
  the pikes with a vice, and they are dangerous weapons
  for maids.
MARGARET   Well, I will call Beatrice to you, who I think
  hath legs.   *Exit.*
BENEDICK   And therefore will come.   25
  [*Sings.*]   The god of love,
              That sits above,
          And knows me, and knows me,
              How pitiful I deserve –
  I mean in singing; but in loving, Leander the good   30
  swimmer, Troilus the first employer of pandars, and a
  whole bookful of these quondam carpet-mongers,
  whose names yet run smoothly in the even road of a
  blank verse, why, they were never so truly turned
  over and over as my poor self in love. Marry, I   35
  cannot show it in rhyme; I have tried. I can find out no
  rhyme to 'lady' but 'baby' – an innocent rhyme; for
  'scorn', 'horn' – a hard rhyme; for 'school', 'fool' – a
  babbling rhyme; very ominous endings! No, I was not
  born under a rhyming planet, nor I cannot woo in   40
  festival terms.

          Enter BEATRICE

  Sweet Beatrice, wouldst thou come when I called
  thee?

BEATRICE   Yea, signior, and depart when you bid me.

45 BENEDICK   O, stay but till then!

BEATRICE   'Then' is spoken; fare you well now. And yet ere I go, let me go with that I came, which is, with knowing what hath passed between you and Claudio.

BENEDICK   Only foul words – and thereupon I will kiss

50 thee.

BEATRICE   Foul words is but foul wind, and foul wind is but foul breath, and foul breath is noisome; therefore I will depart unkissed.

BENEDICK   Thou hast frighted the word out of his right

55 sense, so forcible is thy wit. But I must tell thee plainly, Claudio undergoes my challenge, and either I must shortly hear from him, or I will subscribe him a coward. And I pray thee now tell me, for which of my bad parts didst thou first fall in love with me?

60 BEATRICE   For them all together, which maintained so politic a state of evil that they will not admit any good part to intermingle with them. But for which of my good parts did you first suffer love for me?

BENEDICK   'Suffer love' – a good epithet! I do suffer love

65 indeed, for I love thee against my will.

BEATRICE   In spite of your heart, I think. Alas, poor heart! If you spite it for my sake, I will spite it for yours, for I will never love that which my friend hates.

BENEDICK   Thou and I are too wise to woo peaceably.

70 BEATRICE   It appears not in this confession; there's not one wise man among twenty that will praise himself.

BENEDICK   An old, an old instance, Beatrice, that lived in the time of good neighbours. If a man do not erect in this age his own tomb ere he dies, he shall live no longer

75 in monument than the bell rings, and the widow weeps.

BEATRICE   And how long is that, think you?

BENEDICK   Question: why, an hour in clamour and a quarter in rheum. Therefore is it most expedient for the wise, if Don Worm, his conscience, find no

80 impediment to the contrary, to be the trumpet of his own virtues, as I am to myself. So much for praising myself, who I myself will bear witness is praiseworthy. And now tell me, how doth your cousin?

BEATRICE   Very ill.

85 BENEDICK   And how do you?

BEATRICE   Very ill too.

BENEDICK   Serve God, love me, and mend. There will I leave you too, for here comes one in haste.

Enter URSULA.

URSULA   Madam, you must come to your uncle –

90 yonder's old coil at home. It is proved my Lady Hero hath been falsely accused, the Prince and Claudio mightily abused, and Don John is the author of all, who is fled and gone. Will you come presently?

BEATRICE   Will you go hear this news, signior?

95 BENEDICK   I will live in thy heart, die in thy lap, and be buried in thy eyes; and moreover, I will go with thee to thy uncle's.   *Exeunt.*

5.3   *Enter* CLAUDIO, DON PEDRO *and three or four with tapers, followed by* BALTHASAR *and musicians.*

CLAUDIO   Is this the monument of Leonato?

LORD   It is, my lord.

Epitaph.

CLAUDIO [*reading from a scroll*]

'Done to death by slanderous tongues
   Was the Hero that here lies:
Death, in guerdon of her wrongs,   5
   Gives her fame which never dies:
So the life that died with shame
Lives in death with glorious fame.'
[*Hangs up the scroll.*]
Hang thou there upon the tomb,
   Praising her when I am dumb.   10
Now, music, sound, and sing your solemn hymn.

Song.

BALTHASAR
      Pardon, goddess of the night,
      Those that slew thy virgin knight;
      For the which, with songs of woe,
      Round about her tomb they go.   15
         Midnight, assist our moan,
         Help us to sigh and groan,
            Heavily, heavily:
         Graves, yawn and yield your dead,
         Till death be uttered,   20
            Heavily, heavily.

CLAUDIO   Now unto thy bones good night!
   Yearly will I do this rite.

DON PEDRO
Good morrow, masters; put your torches out.
   The wolves have prey'd, and look, the gentle day,   25
Before the wheels of Phoebus, round about
   Dapples the drowsy east with spots of grey.
Thanks to you all, and leave us. Fare you well.

CLAUDIO
Good morrow, masters – each his several way.

DON PEDRO
Come let us hence, and put on other weeds,   30
And then to Leonato's we will go.

CLAUDIO   And Hymen now with luckier issue speed's
Than this for whom we render'd up this woe!
                                          Exeunt.

5.4   *Enter* LEONATO, BENEDICK, BEATRICE, MARGARET, URSULA, ANTONIO, FRIAR FRANCIS *and* HERO.

FRIAR   Did I not tell you she was innocent?

LEONATO
So are the Prince and Claudio, who accus'd her
Upon the error that you heard debated.
But Margaret was in some fault for this,

Although against her will, as it appears
In the true course of all the question.
ANTONIO   Well, I am glad that all things sort so well.
BENEDICK   And so am I, being else by faith enforc'd
  To call young Claudio to a reckoning for it.
LEONATO   Well, daughter, and you gentlewomen all,
  Withdraw into a chamber by yourselves,
  And when I send for you, come hither mask'd.
                                        Exeunt Ladies.

  The Prince and Claudio promis'd by this hour
  To visit me. You know your office, brother:
  You must be father to your brother's daughter,
  And give her to young Claudio.
ANTONIO
  Which I will do with confirm'd countenance.
BENEDICK   Friar, I must entreat your pains, I think.
FRIAR   To do what, signior?
BENEDICK   To bind me, or undo me – one of them.
  Signior Leonato, truth it is, good signior,
  Your niece regards me with an eye of favour.
LEONATO
  That eye my daughter lent her, 'tis most true.
BENEDICK   And I do with an eye of love requite her.
LEONATO   The sight whereof I think you had from me,
  From Claudio and the Prince. But what's your will?
BENEDICK   Your answer, sir, is enigmatical:
  But for my will, my will is, your good will
  May stand with ours, this day to be conjoin'd
  In the state of honourable marriage;
  In which, good friar, I shall desire your help.
LEONATO   My heart is with your liking.
FRIAR   And my help.
  Here comes the Prince and Claudio.

  Enter DON PEDRO and CLAUDIO, and two or three others.

DON PEDRO   Good morrow to this fair assembly.
LEONATO
  Good morrow, Prince; good morrow, Claudio;
  We here attend you. Are you yet determin'd
  Today to marry with my brother's daughter?
CLAUDIO   I'll hold my mind were she an Ethiope.
LEONATO
  Call her forth, brother; here's the friar ready.
                                        Exit Antonio.

DON PEDRO
  Good morrow, Benedick. Why, what's the matter,
  That you have such a February face,
  So full of frost, of storm, and cloudiness?
CLAUDIO   I think he thinks upon the savage bull.
  Tush, fear not, man, we'll tip thy horns with gold,
  And all Europa shall rejoice at thee,
  As once Europa did at lusty Jove,
  When he would play the noble beast in love.
BENEDICK   Bull Jove, sir, had an amiable low,
  And some such strange bull leap'd your father's cow,
  And got a calf in that same noble feat
  Much like to you, for you have just his bleat.

  Enter ANTONIO, HERO, BEATRICE, MARGARET and
  URSULA, *the ladies masked.*

CLAUDIO
  For this I owe you: here comes other reck'nings.
  Which is the lady I must seize upon?
ANTONIO   This same is she, and I do give you her.
CLAUDIO
  Why then she's mine. Sweet, let me see your face.   55
LEONATO   No, that you shall not till you take her hand,
  Before this friar, and swear to marry her.
CLAUDIO   Give me your hand before this holy friar.
  I am your husband if you like of me.
HERO [*unmasking*]
  And when I liv'd, I was your other wife;   60
  And when you lov'd, you were my other husband.
CLAUDIO   Another Hero!
HERO   Nothing certainer:
  One Hero died defil'd, but I do live,
  And surely as I live, I am a maid.
DON PEDRO   The former Hero! Hero that is dead!   65
LEONATO
  She died, my lord, but whiles her slander liv'd.
FRIAR   All this amazement can I qualify,
  When after that the holy rites are ended
  I'll tell you largely of fair Hero's death.
  Meantime let wonder seem familiar,   70
  And to the chapel let us presently.
BENEDICK   Soft and fair, friar. Which is Beatrice?
BEATRICE [*unmasking*]
  I answer to that name. What is your will?
BENEDICK   Do not you love me?
BEATRICE   Why, no, no more than reason.
BENEDICK
  Why then, your uncle, and the Prince, and Claudio   75
  Have been deceiv'd – they swore you did.
BEATRICE   Do not you love me?
BENEDICK   Troth, no, no more than reason.
BEATRICE   Why then, my cousin, Margaret, and Ursula
  Are much deceiv'd, for they did swear you did.
BENEDICK
  They swore that you were almost sick for me.   80
BEATRICE
  They swore that you were well-nigh dead for me.
BENEDICK
  'Tis no such matter. Then you do not love me?
BEATRICE   No, truly, but in friendly recompense.
LEONATO
  Come, cousin, I am sure you love the gentleman.
CLAUDIO   And I'll be sworn upon't that he loves her,   85
  For here's a paper written in his hand,
  A halting sonnet of his own pure brain,
  Fashion'd to Beatrice.
HERO   And here's another,
  Writ in my cousin's hand, stol'n from her pocket,
  Containing her affection unto Benedick.   90
BENEDICK   A miracle! Here's our own hands against our

hearts. Come, I will have thee, but by this light I take thee for pity.

BEATRICE   I would not deny you, but by this good day I yield upon great persuasion, and partly to save your life, for I was told you were in a consumption.

BENEDICK   Peace! I will stop your mouth. [*Kisses her.*]

DON PEDRO
How dost thou, 'Benedick, the married man'?

BENEDICK   I'll tell thee what, Prince; a college of wit-crackers cannot flout me out of my humour. Dost thou think I care for a satire or an epigram? No: if a man will be beaten with brains, a shall wear nothing handsome about him. In brief, since I do purpose to marry, I will think nothing to any purpose that the world can say against it; and therefore never flout at me for what I have said against it; for man is a giddy thing, and this is my conclusion. For thy part, Claudio, I did think to have beaten thee, but in that thou art like to be my kinsman, live unbruised, and love my cousin.

CLAUDIO   I had well hoped thou wouldst have denied Beatrice, that I might have cudgelled thee out of thy single life, to make thee a double-dealer; which out of question thou wilt be, if my cousin do not look exceeding narrowly to thee.

BENEDICK   Come, come, we are friends. Let's have a dance ere we are married, that we may lighten our own hearts and our wives' heels.

LEONATO   We'll have dancing afterward.

BENEDICK   First, of my word! Therefore play, music. Prince, thou art sad; get thee a wife, get thee a wife! There is no staff more reverend than one tipped with horn.

Enter Messenger.

MESSENGER
My lord, your brother John is ta'en in flight,
And brought with armed men back to Messina.

BENEDICK   Think not on him till tomorrow; I'll devise thee brave punishments for him. Strike up, pipers!
Dance. Exeunt.

938

Othello

The traditional date for the composition of *Othello* is 1603–4, though the editor of the 1997 Arden 3 text would put it slightly earlier in 1601–2, mainly on the basis of some echoes of *Othello* in the 1603 'bad' quarto of *Hamlet*. It was performed in the Banqueting House at Whitehall before James I on 1 November 1604 and had presumably been performed earlier at the Globe. Two early texts of the play were both published after Shakespeare's death, the Quarto in 1622 and the First Folio in 1623 (as the ninth of the tragedies). They differ from each other in many hundreds of readings – in single-word variants and in longer passages, in spelling, verse lineation and punctuation. The Folio text is about 160 lines longer than the Quarto; it alone contains Desdemona's willow song (4.3), and it has a more extensive role for Emilia in the final scenes. Editors have generally assumed that both versions are 'authorial' and have chosen readings from both, blending them together as they saw fit; the 1997 Arden 3 editor argues that the Quarto broadly represents Shakespeare's first thoughts and the Folio his second thoughts, but that some variants can be ascribed to textual corruption rather than to authorial revision.

Whatever the precise date, it is generally agreed that *Othello* is one of a sequence of tragedies Shakespeare wrote between 1599 and 1608, coming after *Julius Caesar* and *Hamlet* and before *King Lear* and *Macbeth*. The main narrative source is a short story in Giraldi Cinthio's *Hecatommithi* (1565), a collection Shakespeare also drew on for the plot of *Measure for Measure*. For *Othello* he seems also to have used John Pory's 1600 translation of John Leo's *A Geographical History of Africa*, Philemon Holland's 1601 translation of Pliny's *History of the World* and Lewis Lewkenor's 1599 *The Commonwealth and Government of Venice*, mainly translated from a Latin text

by Cardinal Contarini. Despite its exotic setting and central character, it is more of a domestic tragedy than *Hamlet*, *Lear* or *Macbeth*, concentrating on the destruction of Othello's marriage and his murder of his wife rather than on affairs of state and the deaths of kings. In the past this narrower focus has sometimes resulted in the relative devaluing of *Othello*, but modern critics have found a lot to say about its foregrounding of issues of race, gender and sexuality.

The play has been one of Shakespeare's most popular tragedies on stage where, from the first performances by Richard Burbage until very recently, the title role has been played by a white actor in 'black' make-up; scholars have disagreed as to whether the 'Moor of Venice' should be a dark-skinned African or a light-skinned Arab. References in the play itself do not resolve the question, and while Shakespeare may have seen the light-skinned Moorish Ambassador to Elizabeth I in London in 1601–2, he was also familiar with the stage stereotype of the 'coal-black' Moor with 'woolly hair' and 'thick lips' which he drew on for Aaron in *Titus Andronicus*. The role of Iago is almost as important as that of Othello and some leading actors have preferred to play it; Iago has the soliloquies in this play and a good actor can steal the show from the hero. There has also been something of a stage tradition of two 'stars' alternating in the roles; this was most famously done by Henry Irving and Edwin Booth in 1881. The appalling speed with which the action unfolds (notoriously, there seems not literally to be time for Desdemona's supposed adultery to have taken place) makes it an exciting – almost unbearable – play to watch.

The Arden text is based on the 1623 First Folio but adopts readings from the 1622 Quarto.

OTHELLO	*the Moor, a general in the service of Venice*
BRABANTIO	*father to Desdemona, a Venetian senator*
CASSIO	*an honourable lieutenant, who serves under Othello*
IAGO	*a villain, Othello's ancient or ensign*
RODERIGO	*a gulled gentleman, of Venice*
DUKE	*of Venice*
SENATORS	*of Venice*
MONTANO	*governor of Cyprus, replaced by Othello*
GENTLEMEN	*of Cyprus*
LODOVICO *and*	} *two noble Venetians, Desdemona's cousin and uncle*
GRATIANO	
SAILOR	
CLOWN	
DESDEMONA	*wife to Othello, and Brabantio's daughter*
EMILIA	*wife to Iago*
BIANCA	*a courtesan, and Cassio's mistress*

Messenger, Herald, Officers, Gentlemen, Musicians and Attendants

1.1   Enter RODERIGO *and* IAGO.

RODERIGO

Tush, never tell me, I take it much unkindly
That thou, Iago, who hast had my purse
As if the strings were thine, shouldst know of this.

IAGO

'Sblood, but you'll not hear me. If ever I did dream
Of such a matter, abhor me.

RODERIGO   Thou told'st me
Thou didst hold him in thy hate.

IAGO   Despise me
If I do not. Three great ones of the city,
In personal suit to make me his lieutenant,
Off-capped to him, and by the faith of man
I know my price, I am worth no worse a place.
But he, as loving his own pride and purposes,
Evades them, with a bombast circumstance
Horribly stuffed with epithets of war,
And in conclusion
Nonsuits my mediators. For 'Certes,' says he,
'I have already chose my officer.'
And what was he?
Forsooth, a great arithmetician,
One Michael Cassio, a Florentine,
A fellow almost damned in a fair wife
That never set a squadron in the field
Nor the division of a battle knows
More than a spinster – unless the bookish theoric,
Wherein the toged consuls can propose
As masterly as he. Mere prattle without practice
Is all his soldiership – but he, sir, had th'election
And I, of whom his eyes had seen the proof
At Rhodes, at Cyprus and on other grounds,
Christian and heathen, must be be-leed and calmed
By debitor and creditor. This counter-caster
He, in good time, must his lieutenant be
And I, God bless the mark, his Moorship's ancient!

RODERIGO

By heaven, I rather would have been his hangman.

IAGO

Why, there's no remedy, 'tis the curse of service:
Preferment goes by letter and affection
And not by old gradation, where each second
Stood heir to th' first. Now sir, be judge yourself
Whether I in any just term am affined
To love the Moor.

RODERIGO   I would not follow him then.

IAGO   O sir, content you!
I follow him to serve my turn upon him.
We cannot all be masters, nor all masters
Cannot be truly followed. You shall mark
Many a duteous and knee-crooking knave
That, doting on his own obsequious bondage,
Wears out his time much like his master's ass
For nought but provender, and, when he's old,
    cashiered.

Whip me such honest knaves! Others there are
Who, trimmed in forms and visages of duty,
Keep yet their hearts attending on themselves   50
And, throwing but shows of service on their lords,
Do well thrive by them, and, when they have lined
    their coats,
Do themselves homage: these fellows have some soul
And such a one do I profess myself. For, sir,
It is as sure as you are Roderigo,   55
Were I the Moor, I would not be Iago.
In following him I follow but myself:
Heaven is my judge, not I for love and duty
But seeming so, for my peculiar end,
For when my outward action doth demonstrate   60
The native act and figure of my heart
In complement extern, 'tis not long after
But I will wear my heart upon my sleeve
For daws to peck at: I am not what I am.

RODERIGO   What a full fortune does the thicklips owe 65
If he can carry't thus!

IAGO   Call up her father,
Rouse him, make after him, poison his delight,
Proclaim him in the streets, incense her kinsmen,
And, though he in a fertile climate dwell,
Plague him with flies! Though that his joy be joy   70
Yet throw such changes of vexation on't
As it may lose some colour.

RODERIGO   Here is her father's house, I'll call aloud.

IAGO   Do, with like timorous accent and dire yell
As when by night and negligence the fire   75
Is spied in populous cities.

RODERIGO   What ho! Brabantio, Signior Brabantio ho!

IAGO

Awake, what ho, Brabantio! thieves, thieves, thieves!
Look to your house, your daughter and your bags!
Thieves, thieves!   80

BRABANTIO *appears above at a window.*

BRABANTIO

What is the reason of this terrible summons?
What is the matter there?

RODERIGO   Signior, is all your family within?

IAGO   Are your doors locked?

BRABANTIO   Why? Wherefore ask you this?

IAGO

Zounds, sir, you're robbed, for shame put on your
    gown!   85
Your heart is burst, you have lost half your soul,
Even now, now, very now, an old black ram
Is tupping your white ewe! Arise, arise,
Awake the snorting citizens with the bell
Or else the devil will make a grandsire of you,   90
Arise I say!

BRABANTIO   What, have you lost your wits?

RODERIGO

Most reverend signior, do you know my voice?

BRABANTIO   Not I, what are you?

RODERIGO   My name is Roderigo.

BRABANTIO   The worser welcome!

95   I have charged thee not to haunt about my doors:
In honest plainness thou hast heard me say
My daughter is not for thee; and now in madness,
Being full of supper and distempering draughts,
Upon malicious bravery dost thou come
100   To start my quiet?

RODERIGO   Sir, sir, sir –

BRABANTIO   But thou must needs be sure
My spirit and my place have in them power
To make this bitter to thee.

RODERIGO   Patience, good sir!

BRABANTIO
What tell'st thou me of robbing? This is Venice:
My house is not a grange.

105   RODERIGO   Most grave Brabantio,
In simple and pure soul I come to you –

IAGO   Zounds, sir, you are one of those that will not
serve God, if the devil bid you. Because we come to do
you service, and you think we are ruffians, you'll have
110   your daughter covered with a Barbary horse; you'll
have your nephews neigh to you, you'll have coursers
for cousins and jennets for germans!

BRABANTIO   What profane wretch art thou?

IAGO   I am one, sir, that comes to tell you your daughter
115   and the Moor are now making the beast with two backs.

BRABANTIO
Thou art a villain!

IAGO   You are a senator!

BRABANTIO
This thou shalt answer. I know thee, Roderigo!

RODERIGO
Sir, I will answer anything. But I beseech you,
If't be your pleasure and most wise consent,
120   As partly I find it is, that your fair daughter
At this odd-even and dull watch o'th' night,
Transported with no worse nor better guard
But with a knave of common hire, a gondolier,
To the gross clasps of a lascivious Moor –
125   If this be known to you, and your allowance,
We then have done you bold and saucy wrongs.
But if you know not this, my manners tell me
We have your wrong rebuke. Do not believe
That from the sense of all civility
130   I thus would play and trifle with your reverence.
Your daughter, if you have not given her leave,
I say again, hath made a gross revolt,
Tying her duty, beauty, wit and fortunes
In an extravagant and wheeling stranger
135   Of here and everywhere. Straight satisfy yourself:
If she be in her chamber or your house
Let loose on me the justice of the state
For thus deluding you.

BRABANTIO   Strike on the tinder, ho!
Give me a taper, call up all my people.

This accident is not unlike my dream,   140
Belief of it oppresses me already.
Light, I say, light!   *Exit above.*

IAGO   Farewell, for I must leave you.
It seems not meet, nor wholesome to my place,
To be produced, as, if I stay, I shall,
Against the Moor. For I do know the state,   145
However this may gall him with some check,
Cannot with safety cast him, for he's embarked
With such loud reason to the Cyprus wars,
Which even now stands in act, that for their souls
Another of his fathom they have none   150
To lead their business – in which regard,
Though I do hate him as I do hell-pains,
Yet for necessity of present life
I must show out a flag and sign of love,
Which is indeed but sign. That you shall surely find
him,   155
Lead to the Sagittary the raised search,
And there will I be with him. So farewell.   *Exit.*

Enter BRABANTIO *in his night-gown and servants with
torches.*

BRABANTIO   It is too true an evil, gone she is,
And what's to come of my despised time
Is nought but bitterness. Now Roderigo,   160
Where didst thou see her? – O unhappy girl! –
With the Moor, say'st thou? – Who would be a
father? –
How didst thou know 'twas she? – O, she deceives me
Past thought! – What said she to you? – Get more
tapers,
Raise all my kindred. Are they married, think you?   165

RODERIGO   Truly I think they are.

BRABANTIO
O heaven, how got she out? O treason of the blood!
– Fathers, from hence trust not your daughters'
minds
By what you see them act. – Is there not charms
By which the property of youth and maidhood   170
May be abused? Have you not read, Roderigo,
Of some such thing?

RODERIGO   Yes sir, I have indeed.

BRABANTIO
Call up my brother. – O, would you had had her!
Some one way, some another. – Do you know
Where we may apprehend her and the Moor?   175

RODERIGO   I think I can discover him, if you please
To get good guard and go along with me.

BRABANTIO   Pray you lead on. At every house I'll call,
I may command at most: get weapons, ho!
And raise some special officers of night.   180
On, good Roderigo, I'll deserve your pains.   *Exeunt.*

1.2   *Enter* OTHELLO, IAGO *and attendants with torches.*

IAGO   Though in the trade of war I have slain men
Yet do I hold it very stuff o'th' conscience

To do no contrived murder: I lack iniquity
    Sometimes to do me service. Nine or ten times
    I had thought t'have yerked him here, under the ribs.
OTHELLO   'Tis better as it is.
IAGO   Nay, but he prated
    And spoke such scurvy and provoking terms
    Against your honour,
    That with the little godliness I have
    I did full hard forbear him. But I pray, sir,
    Are you fast married? Be assured of this,
    That the magnifico is much beloved
    And hath in his effect a voice potential
    As double as the duke's: he will divorce you
    Or put upon you what restraint or grievance
    The law, with all his might to enforce it on,
    Will give him cable.
OTHELLO   Let him do his spite;
    My services, which I have done the signiory,
    Shall out-tongue his complaints. 'Tis yet to know –
    Which, when I know that boasting is an honour,
    I shall promulgate – I fetch my life and being
    From men of royal siege, and my demerits
    May speak unbonneted to as proud a fortune
    As this that I have reached. For know, Iago,
    But that I love the gentle Desdemona
    I would not my unhoused free condition
    Put into circumscription and confine
    For the sea's worth. But look, what lights come
    yond?

    Enter CASSIO, *with officers and torches.*

IAGO   Those are the raised father and his friends,
    You were best go in.
OTHELLO   Not I, I must be found.
    My parts, my title and my perfect soul
    Shall manifest me rightly. Is it they?
IAGO   By Janus, I think no.
OTHELLO
    The servants of the Duke? and my lieutenant?
    The goodness of the night upon you, friends.
    What is the news?
CASSIO   The duke does greet you, general,
    And he requires your haste-post-haste appearance,
    Even on the instant.
OTHELLO   What's the matter, think you?
CASSIO   Something from Cyprus, as I may divine;
    It is a business of some heat. The galleys
    Have sent a dozen sequent messengers
    This very night, at one another's heels,
    And many of the consuls, raised and met,
    Are at the duke's already. You have been hotly called
    for,
    When, being not at your lodging to be found,
    The Senate hath sent about three several quests
    To search you out.
OTHELLO   'Tis well I am found by you:
    I will but spend a word here in the house

And go with you.   *Exit.*
CASSIO   Ancient, what makes he here?
IAGO   Faith, he tonight hath boarded a land carrack: 50
    If it prove lawful prize, he's made for ever.
CASSIO   I do not understand.
IAGO   He's married.
CASSIO   To whom?
IAGO   Marry, to –

    Enter OTHELLO.

        Come, captain, will you go?
OTHELLO   Ha' with you.
CASSIO   Here comes another troop to seek for you.

Enter BRABANTIO, RODERIGO, *with officers and torches and weapons.*

IAGO   It is Brabantio: general, be advised,   55
    He comes to bad intent.
OTHELLO   Holla, stand there!
RODERIGO   Signior, it is the Moor.
BRABANTIO   Down with him, thief!
    [*They draw on both sides.*]
IAGO   You, Roderigo! come sir, I am for you.
OTHELLO
    Keep up your bright swords, for the dew will rust
    them.
    Good signior, you shall more command with years   60
    Than with your weapons.
BRABANTIO
    O thou foul thief, where hast thou stowed my
    daughter?
    Damned as thou art, thou hast enchanted her,
    For I'll refer me to all things of sense,
    If she in chains of magic were not bound,   65
    Whether a maid so tender, fair and happy,
    So opposite to marriage that she shunned
    The wealthy, curled darlings of our nation,
    Would ever have, t'incur a general mock,
    Run from her guardage to the sooty bosom   70
    Of such a thing as thou? to fear, not to delight.
    Judge me the world if 'tis not gross in sense
    That thou hast practised on her with foul charms,
    Abused her delicate youth with drugs or minerals
    That weakens motion: I'll have't disputed on,   75
    'Tis probable and palpable to thinking.
    I therefore apprehend and do attach thee
    For an abuser of the world, a practiser
    Of arts inhibited and out of warrant.
    Lay hold upon him; if he do resist   80
    Subdue him at his peril!
OTHELLO   Hold your hands,
    Both you of my inclining and the rest:
    Were it my cue to fight, I should have known it
    Without a prompter. Where will you that I go
    To answer this your charge?
BRABANTIO   To prison, till fit time   85
    Of law, and course of direct session

Call thee to answer.

OTHELLO   What if I do obey?
How may the duke be therewith satisfied,
Whose messengers are here about my side
90   Upon some present business of the state,
To bring me to him?

OFFICER   'Tis true, most worthy signior,
The duke's in council, and your noble self
I am sure is sent for.

BRABANTIO   How? the duke in council?
In this time of the night? Bring him away:
95   Mine's not an idle cause, the duke himself,
Or any of my brothers of the state,
Cannot but feel this wrong as 'twere their own.
For if such actions may have passage free
Bond-slaves and pagans shall our statesmen be.

Exeunt.

1.3   Enter DUKE *and* Senators, *set at a table, with*
lights and attendants.

DUKE   There is no composition in these news
That gives them credit.

1 SENATOR   Indeed, they are disproportioned.
My letters say a hundred and seven galleys.

DUKE   And mine a hundred forty.

2 SENATOR   And mine two hundred.
5   But though they jump not on a just account –
As in these cases, where the aim reports,
'Tis oft with difference – yet do they all confirm
A Turkish fleet, and bearing up to Cyprus.

DUKE   Nay, it is possible enough to judgement:
10   I do not so secure me in the error
But the main article I do approve
In fearful sense.

SAILOR [*within*]   What ho, what ho, what ho!

Enter Sailor.

OFFICER   A messenger from the galleys.

DUKE   Now? what's the business?

15   SAILOR   The Turkish preparation makes for Rhodes,
So was I bid report here to the state
By Signior Angelo.

DUKE   How say you by this change?

1 SENATOR   This cannot be,
By no assay of reason: 'tis a pageant
20   To keep us in false gaze. When we consider
Th'importancy of Cyprus to the Turk,
And let ourselves again but understand
That as it more concerns the Turk than Rhodes
So may he with more facile question bear it,
25   For that it stands not in such warlike brace
But altogether lacks th'abilities
That Rhodes is dressed in. If we make thought of this
We must not think the Turk is so unskilful
To leave that latest which concerns him first,
30   Neglecting an attempt of ease and gain

To wake and wage a danger profitless.

DUKE   Nay, in all confidence, he's not for Rhodes.

OFFICER   Here is more news.

Enter a Messenger.

MESSENGER   The Ottomites, reverend and gracious,
Steering with due course toward the isle of Rhodes,   35
Have there injointed with an after fleet –

1 SENATOR   Ay, so I thought; how many, as you guess?

MESSENGER   Of thirty sail; and now they do re-stem
Their backward course, bearing with frank
appearance
Their purposes toward Cyprus. Signior Montano,   40
Your trusty and most valiant servitor,
With his free duty recommends you thus
And prays you to relieve him.

DUKE   'Tis certain then for Cyprus.
Marcus Luccicos, is not he in town?   45

1 SENATOR   He's now in Florence.

DUKE   Write from us to him; post-post-haste, dispatch.

1 SENATOR
Here comes Brabantio and the valiant Moor.

Enter BRABANTIO, OTHELLO, CASSIO, IAGO, RODERIGO
and officers.

DUKE   Valiant Othello, we must straight employ you
Against the general enemy Ottoman.   50
[*to Brabantio*] I did not see you: welcome, gentle
signior,
We lacked your counsel and your help tonight.

BRABANTIO
So did I yours. Good your grace, pardon me,
Neither my place nor aught I heard of business
Hath raised me from my bed, nor doth the general
care   55
Take hold on me, for my particular grief
Is of so flood-gate and o'erbearing nature
That it englups and swallows other sorrows
And it is still itself.

DUKE   Why? What's the matter?

BRABANTIO
My daughter, O my daughter!

1 SENATOR   Dead?

BRABANTIO   Ay, to me: 60
She is abused, stolen from me and corrupted
By spells and medicines bought of mountebanks,
For nature so preposterously to err
Being not deficient, blind, or lame of sense,
Sans witchcraft could not.   65

DUKE   Whoe'er he be, that in this foul proceeding
Hath thus beguiled your daughter of herself,
And you of her, the bloody book of law
You shall yourself read, in the bitter letter,
After your own sense, yea, though our proper son   70
Stood in your action.

BRABANTIO   Humbly I thank your grace.

Here is the man, this Moor, whom now it seems
Your special mandate for the state affairs
Hath hither brought.

ALL   We are very sorry for't.

DUKE [*to Othello*]

75 What in your own part can you say to this?

BRABANTIO   Nothing, but this is so.

OTHELLO   Most potent, grave, and reverend signiors,
My very noble and approved good masters:
That I have ta'en away this old man's daughter

80 It is most true; true, I have married her.
The very head and front of my offending
Hath this extent, no more. Rude am I in my speech
And little blest with the soft phrase of peace,
For since these arms of mine had seven years' pith

85 Till now some nine moons wasted, they have used
Their dearest action in the tented field,
And little of this great world can I speak
More than pertains to feats of broil and battle,
And therefore little shall I grace my cause

In speaking for myself. Yet, by your gracious
90   patience,
I will a round unvarnished tale deliver
Of my whole course of love, what drugs, what
      charms,
What conjuration and what mighty magic –
For such proceeding I am charged withal –
I won his daughter.

95 BRABANTIO   A maiden never bold,
Of spirit so still and quiet that her motion
Blushed at herself; and she, in spite of nature,
Of years, of country, credit, everything,
To fall in love with what she feared to look on?

100 It is a judgement maimed and most imperfect
That will confess perfection so could err
Against all rules of nature, and must be driven
To find out practices of cunning hell
Why this should be. I therefore vouch again

105 That with some mixtures powerful o'er the blood
Or with some dram conjured to this effect
He wrought upon her.

DUKE   To vouch this is no proof,
Without more certain and more overt test
Than these thin habits and poor likelihoods

110 Of modern seeming do prefer against him.

1 SENATOR   But, Othello, speak:
Did you by indirect and forced courses
Subdue and poison this young maid's affections?
Or came it by request and such fair question
As soul to soul affordeth?

115 OTHELLO   I do beseech you,
Send for the lady to the Sagittary,
And let her speak of me before her father.
If you do find me foul in her report
The trust, the office I do hold of you

120 Not only take away, but let your sentence
Even fall upon my life.

DUKE   Fetch Desdemona hither.

OTHELLO
Ancient, conduct them, you best know the place.
And till she come, as truly as to heaven

Exeunt Iago and two or three.

I do confess the vices of my blood   125
So justly to your grave ears I'll present
How I did thrive in this fair lady's love
And she in mine.

DUKE   Say it, Othello.

OTHELLO   Her father loved me, oft invited me,
Still questioned me the story of my life   130
From year to year – the battles, sieges, fortunes
That I have passed.
I ran it through, even from my boyish days
To th' very moment that he bade me tell it,
Wherein I spake of most disastrous chances,   135
Of moving accidents by flood and field,
Of hair-breadth scapes i'th' imminent deadly breach,
Of being taken by the insolent foe
And sold to slavery; of my redemption thence
And portance in my travailous history;   140
Wherein of antres vast and deserts idle,
Rough quarries, rocks and hills whose heads touch
      heaven
It was my hint to speak – such was my process –
And of the cannibals that each other eat,
The Anthropophagi, and men whose heads   .   145
Do grow beneath their shoulders. This to hear
Would Desdemona seriously incline,
But still the house affairs would draw her thence,
Which ever as she could with haste dispatch
She'd come again, and with a greedy ear   150
Devour up my discourse; which I, observing,
Took once a pliant hour and found good means
To draw from her a prayer of earnest heart
That I would all my pilgrimage dilate,
Whereof by parcels she had something heard   155
But not intentively. I did consent,
And often did beguile her of her tears
When I did speak of some distressful stroke
That my youth suffered. My story being done
She gave me for my pains a world of sighs,   160
She swore in faith 'twas strange, 'twas passing strange,
'Twas pitiful, 'twas wondrous pitiful;
She wished she had not heard it, yet she wished
That heaven had made her such a man. She thanked
      me
And bade me, if I had a friend that loved her,   165
I should but teach him how to tell my story
And that would woo her. Upon this hint I spake:
She loved me for the dangers I had passed
And I loved her that she did pity them.
This only is the witchcraft I have used: 170

Enter DESDEMONA, IAGO, *attendants.*

Here comes the lady, let her witness it.

DUKE   I think this tale would win my daughter too.
     Good Brabantio, take up this mangled matter at the
     best:
     Men do their broken weapons rather use
     Than their bare hands.

175   BRABANTIO   I pray you, hear her speak.
     If she confess that she was half the wooer,
     Destruction on my head if my bad blame
     Light on the man. Come hither, gentle mistress:
     Do you perceive, in all this noble company,
     Where most you owe obedience?

180   DESDEMONA   My noble father,
     I do perceive here a divided duty.
     To you I am bound for life and education:
     My life and education both do learn me
     How to respect you; you are the lord of duty,

185   I am hitherto your daughter. But here's my husband:
     And so much duty as my mother showed
     To you, preferring you before her father,
     So much I challenge that I may profess
     Due to the Moor my lord.

190   BRABANTIO   God be with you, I have done.
     Please it your grace, on to the state affairs;
     I had rather to adopt a child than get it.
     Come hither, Moor:
     I here do give thee that with all my heart

195   Which, but thou hast already, with all my heart
     I would keep from thee. For your sake, jewel,
     I am glad at soul I have no other child,
     For thy escape would teach me tyranny
     To hang clogs on them. I have done, my lord.

200   DUKE   Let me speak like yourself, and lay a sentence
     Which as a grise or step may help these lovers
     Into your favour.
     When remedies are past the griefs are ended
     By seeing the worst which late on hopes depended.

205   To mourn a mischief that is past and gone
     Is the next way to draw new mischief on.
     What cannot be preserved when fortune takes,
     Patience her injury a mockery makes.
     The robbed that smiles steals something from the
     thief,

210   He robs himself that spends a bootless grief.

   BRABANTIO   So let the Turk of Cyprus us beguile,
     We lose it not so long as we can smile;
     He bears the sentence well that nothing bears
     But the free comfort which from thence he hears.

215   But he bears both the sentence and the sorrow
     That, to pay grief, must of poor patience borrow.
     These sentences to sugar or to gall,
     Being strong on both sides, are equivocal.
     But words are words: I never yet did hear

220   That the bruised heart was pierced through the ear.
     I humbly beseech you, proceed to th'affairs of state.

   DUKE   The Turk with a most mighty preparation makes
     for Cyprus. Othello, the fortitude of the place is best
     known to you, and, though we have there a substitute

of most allowed sufficiency, yet opinion, a sovereign 225
mistress of effects, throws a more safer voice on you.
You must therefore be content to slubber the gloss of
your new fortunes with this more stubborn and
boisterous expedition.

OTHELLO   The tyrant custom, most grave senators,   230
     Hath made the flinty and steel couch of war
     My thrice-driven bed of down. I do agnize
     A natural and prompt alacrity
     I find in hardness, and do undertake
     This present war against the Ottomites.   235
     Most humbly therefore, bending to your state,
     I crave fit disposition for my wife,
     Due reverence of place, and exhibition,
     With such accommodation and besort
     As levels with her breeding.   240

DUKE   Why, at her father's.

BRABANTIO   I'll not have it so.

OTHELLO   Nor I.

DESDEMONA   Nor would I there reside
     To put my father in impatient thoughts
     By being in his eye. Most gracious duke,   245
     To my unfolding lend your prosperous ear
     And let me find a charter in your voice
     T'assist my simpleness.

DUKE   What would you, Desdemona?

DESDEMONA   That I did love the Moor to live with him   250
     My downright violence and scorn of fortunes
     May trumpet to the world. My heart's subdued
     Even to the very quality of my lord:
     I saw Othello's visage in his mind,
     And to his honours and his valiant parts   255
     Did I my soul and fortunes consecrate,
     So that, dear lords, if I be left behind,
     A moth of peace, and he go to the war,
     The rites for which I love him are bereft me,
     And I a heavy interim shall support   260
     By his dear absence. Let me go with him.

OTHELLO   Let her have your voice.
     Vouch with me, heaven, I therefore beg it not
     To please the palate of my appetite,
     Nor to comply with heat, the young affects   265
     In me defunct, and proper satisfaction,
     But to be free and bounteous to her mind.
     And heaven defend your good souls that you think
     I will your serious and great business scant
     When she is with me. No, when light-winged toys   270
     Of feathered Cupid seel with wanton dullness
     My speculative and officed instrument,
     That my disports corrupt and taint my business,
     Let housewives make a skillet of my helm
     And all indign and base adversities   275
     Make head against my estimation.

DUKE   Be it as you shall privately determine,
     Either for her stay or going: th'affair cries haste
     And speed must answer it.

1 SENATOR   You must away tonight.

DESDEMONA   Tonight, my lord?

DUKE   This night.

OTHELLO   With all my heart.

DUKE   At nine i'th' morning here we'll meet again.
Othello, leave some officer behind
And he shall our commission bring to you,
And such things else of quality and respect
As doth import you.

OTHELLO   So please your grace, my ancient:
A man he is of honesty and trust.
To his conveyance I assign my wife,
With what else needful your good grace shall think
To be sent after me.

DUKE   Let it be so.
Good-night to everyone. And, noble signior,
If virtue no delighted beauty lack
Your son-in-law is far more fair than black.

1 SENATOR   Adieu, brave Moor, use Desdemona well.

BRABANTIO
Look to her, Moor, if thou hast eyes to see:
She has deceived her father, and may thee.

Exeunt Duke, Brabantio, Senators, officers.

OTHELLO   My life upon her faith. Honest Iago,
My Desdemona must I leave to thee:
I prithee, let thy wife attend on her
And bring them after in the best advantage.
Come, Desdemona, I have but an hour
Of love, of worldly matter and direction
To spend with thee. We must obey the time.

Exeunt Othello and Desdemona.

RODERIGO   Iago!

IAGO   What sayst thou, noble heart?

RODERIGO   What will I do, think'st thou?

IAGO   Why, go to bed and sleep.

RODERIGO   I will incontinently drown myself.

IAGO   If thou dost, I shall never love thee after. Why,
thou silly gentleman?

RODERIGO   It is silliness to live when to live is torment;
and then have we a prescription to die, when death is
our physician.

IAGO   O villainous! I have looked upon the world for
four times seven years, and since I could distinguish
betwixt a benefit and an injury I never found a man
that knew how to love himself. Ere I would say I would
drown myself for the love of a guinea-hen I would
change my humanity with a baboon.

RODERIGO   What should I do? I confess it is my shame
to be so fond, but it is not in my virtue to amend it.

IAGO   Virtue? a fig! 'tis in ourselves that we are thus, or
thus. Our bodies are gardens, to the which our wills
are gardeners. So that if we will plant nettles or sow
lettuce, set hyssop and weed up thyme, supply it with
one gender of herbs or distract it with many, either to
have it sterile with idleness or manured with industry
– why, the power and corrigible authority of this lies in
our wills. If the balance of our lives had not one scale
of reason to poise another of sensuality, the blood and
baseness of our natures would conduct us to most
preposterous conclusions. But we have reason to cool
our raging motions, our carnal stings, our unbitted
lusts; whereof I take this, that you call love, to be a sect
or scion.

RODERIGO   It cannot be.

IAGO   It is merely a lust of the blood and a permission of
the will. Come, be a man! drown thyself? drown cats
and blind puppies. I have professed me thy friend, and
I confess me knit to thy deserving with cables of
perdurable toughness. I could never better stead thee
than now. Put money in thy purse, follow thou the
wars, defeat thy favour with an usurped beard; I say,
put money in thy purse. It cannot be that Desdemona
should long continue her love to the Moor – put
money in thy purse – nor he his to her. It was a violent
commencement in her, and thou shalt see an
answerable sequestration – put but money in thy
purse. These Moors are changeable in their wills – fill
thy purse with money. The food that to him now is as
luscious as locusts shall be to him shortly acerb as
coloquintida. She must change for youth; when she is
sated with his body she will find the error of her
choice: she must have change, she must. Therefore,
put money in thy purse. If thou wilt needs damn
thyself, do it a more delicate way than drowning –
make all the money thou canst. If sanctimony, and a
frail vow betwixt an erring Barbarian and a super-
subtle Venetian, be not too hard for my wits and all the
tribe of hell, thou shalt enjoy her – therefore make
money. A pox of drowning thyself, it is clean out of the
way: seek thou rather to be hanged in compassing thy
joy than to be drowned and go without her.

RODERIGO   Wilt thou be fast to my hopes, if I depend on
the issue?

IAGO   Thou art sure of me – go, make money. I have told
thee often, and I re-tell thee again and again, I hate the
Moor. My cause is hearted, thine hath no less reason:
let us be conjunctive in our revenge against him. If
thou canst cuckold him, thou dost thyself a pleasure,
me a sport. There are many events in the womb of
time, which will be delivered. Traverse, go, provide thy
money: we will have more of this tomorrow. Adieu!

RODERIGO   Where shall we meet i'th' morning?

IAGO   At my lodging.

RODERIGO   I'll be with thee betimes.

IAGO   Go to, farewell. – Do you hear, Roderigo?

RODERIGO   What say you?

IAGO   No more of drowning, do you hear?

RODERIGO   I am changed. I'll sell all my land.   *Exit.*

IAGO   Go to, farewell, put money enough in your purse.
Thus do I ever make my fool my purse:
For I mine own gained knowledge should profane
If I would time expend with such a snipe
But for my sport and profit. I hate the Moor
And it is thought abroad that 'twixt my sheets
He's done my office. I know not if 't be true,

But I for mere suspicion in that kind
Will do as if for surety. He holds me well,
The better shall my purpose work on him.
390 Cassio's a proper man: let me see now,
To get his place, and to plume up my will
In double knavery. How? How? let's see:
After some time to abuse Othello's ear
That he is too familiar with his wife.
395 He hath a person and a smooth dispose
To be suspected, framed to make women false.
The Moor is of a free and open nature
That thinks men honest that but seem to be so,
And will as tenderly be led by th' nose
400 As asses are.
I have't, it is engendered! Hell and night
Must bring this monstrous birth to the world's light.
Exit.

2.1   *Enter* MONTANO *and two* Gentlemen.

MONTANO What from the cape can you discern at sea?
1 GENTLEMAN   Nothing at all, it is a high-wrought flood:
I cannot 'twixt the haven and the main
Descry a sail.
5 MONTANO   Methinks the wind hath spoke aloud at land,
A fuller blast ne'er shook our battlements:
If it hath ruffianed so upon the sea
What ribs of oak, when mountains melt on them,
Can hold the mortise? What shall we hear of this?
10 2 GENTLEMAN   A segregation of the Turkish fleet:
For do but stand upon the foaming shore,
The chidden billow seems to pelt the clouds,
The wind-shaked surge, with high and monstrous
        mane,
Seems to cast water on the burning bear
15 And quench the guards of th'ever-fired pole.
I never did like molestation view
On the enchafed flood.
MONTANO   If that the Turkish fleet
Be not ensheltered and embayed, they are drowned.
It is impossible to bear it out.

Enter a Third Gentleman.

20 3 GENTLEMAN   News, lads: our wars are done!
The desperate tempest hath so banged the Turks
That their designment halts. A noble ship of Venice
Hath seen a grievous wrack and sufferance
On most part of their fleet.
MONTANO   How? Is this true?
25 3 GENTLEMAN   The ship is here put in,
A Veronessa; Michael Cassio,
Lieutenant to the warlike Moor, Othello,
Is come on shore; the Moor himself at sea,
And is in full commission here for Cyprus.
30 MONTANO   I am glad on't, 'tis a worthy governor.
3 GENTLEMAN
But this same Cassio, though he speak of comfort

Enter CASSIO.

Touching the turkish loss, yet he looks sadly
And prays the Moor be safe, for they were parted
With foul and violent tempest.
MONTANO   Pray heavens he be,
For I have served him, and the man commands   35
Like a full soldier. Let's to the seaside, ho!
As well to see the vessel that's come in
As to throw out our eyes for brave Othello,
Even till we make the main and th'aerial blue
An indistinct regard.
3 GENTLEMAN   Come, let's do so,   40
For every minute is expectancy
Of more arrivance.
CASSIO   Thanks, you the valiant of this warlike isle
That so approve the Moor. O, let the heavens
Give him defence against the elements,   45
For I have lost him on a dangerous sea.
MONTANO   Is he well shipped?
CASSIO   His bark is stoutly timbered, and his pilot
Of very expert and approved allowance,
Therefore my hopes, not surfeited to death,   50
Stand in bold cure.
A VOICE [*within*]   A sail! a sail! a sail!
CASSIO   What noise?
2 GENTLEMAN
The town is empty: on the brow o'th' sea
Stand ranks of people, and they cry 'A sail!'
CASSIO
My hopes do shape him for the governor. [*a shot.*]   55
2 GENTLEMAN
They do discharge their shot of courtesy,
Our friends at least.
CASSIO   I pray you sir, go forth
And give us truth who 'tis that is arrived.
2 GENTLEMAN   I shall.   *Exit.*
MONTANO   But, good lieutenant, is your general wived?   60
CASSIO   Most fortunately: he hath achieved a maid
That paragons description and wild fame;
One that excels the quirks of blazoning pens
And in th'essential vesture of creation
Does tire the inginer.

Enter Second Gentleman.

                How now? Who has put in?   65
2 GENTLEMAN
'Tis one Iago, ancient to the general.
CASSIO   He's had most favourable and happy speed.
Tempests themselves, high seas, and howling winds,
The guttered rocks and congregated sands,
Traitors ensteeped to clog the guiltless keel,   70
As having sense of beauty, do omit
Their mortal natures, letting go safely by
The divine Desdemona.
MONTANO   What is she?

CASSIO

She that I spake of, our great captain's captain,

75 Left in the conduct of the bold Iago,

Whose footing here anticipates our thoughts

A se'nnight's speed. Great Jove, Othello guard,

And swell his sail with thine own powerful breath

That he may bless this bay with his tall ship,

80 Make love's quick pants in Desdemona's arms,

Give renewed fire to our extinced spirits

And bring all Cyprus comfort! –

Enter DESDEMONA, IAGO, RODERIGO *and* EMILIA.

O, behold,

The riches of the ship is come on shore:

You men of Cyprus, let her have your knees!

85 Hail to thee, lady, and the grace of heaven,

Before, behind thee, and on every hand

Enwheel thee round!

DESDEMONA   I thank you, valiant Cassio.

What tidings can you tell me of my lord?

CASSIO

He is not yet arrived, nor know I aught

90 But that he's well, and will be shortly here.

DESDEMONA   O, but I fear . . . how lost you company?

CASSIO   The great contention of the sea and skies

Parted our fellowship.

[*A voice within:* 'A sail! a sail!']

But hark! a sail!

[*A shot is heard.*]

2 GENTLEMAN

They give their greeting to the citadel:

This likewise is a friend.

95 CASSIO   See for the news.

Exit Gentleman.

Good ancient, you are welcome.

[*to Emilia*]   Welcome, mistress.

Let it not gall your patience, good Iago,

That I extend my manners; 'tis my breeding

That gives me this bold show of courtesy.

[*He kisses Emilia.*]

100 IAGO   Sir, would she give you so much of her lips

As of her tongue she oft bestows on me

You'd have enough.

DESDEMONA   Alas! she has no speech.

IAGO   In faith, too much!

I find it still when I have list to sleep.

105 Marry, before your ladyship, I grant,

She puts her tongue a little in her heart

And chides with thinking.

EMILIA   You have little cause to say so.

IAGO

Come on, come on, you are pictures out of doors,

110 Bells in your parlours, wild-cats in your kitchens,

Saints in your injuries, devils being offended,

Players in your housewifery, and housewives in . . .

Your beds!

DESDEMONA   O, fie upon thee, slanderer!

IAGO   Nay, it is true, or else I am a Turk:

You rise to play, and go to bed to work.   115

EMILIA   You shall not write my praise.

IAGO   No, let me not.

DESDEMONA

What wouldst thou write of me, if thou shouldst

praise me?

IAGO   O, gentle lady, do not put me to't,

For I am nothing if not critical.

DESDEMONA

Come on, assay. There's one gone to the harbour?   120

IAGO   Ay, madam.

DESDEMONA   I am not merry, but I do beguile

The thing I am by seeming otherwise.

Come, how wouldst thou praise me?

IAGO   I am about it, but indeed my invention   125

Comes from my pate as birdlime does from frieze,

It plucks out brains and all; but my muse labours

And thus she is delivered:

If she be fair and wise, fairness and wit,

The one's for use, the other useth it.   130

DESDEMONA

Well praised. How if she be black and witty?

IAGO   If she be black, and thereto have a wit,

She'll find a white that shall her blackness fit.

DESDEMONA   Worse and worse.

EMILIA   How if fair and foolish?   135

IAGO   She never yet was foolish that was fair,

For even her folly helped her to an heir.

DESDEMONA   These are old fond paradoxes to make

fools laugh i'th' alehouse. What miserable praise hast

thou for her that's foul and foolish?   140

IAGO   There's none so foul, and foolish thereunto,

But does foul pranks which fair and wise ones do.

DESDEMONA   O heavy ignorance, thou praisest the worst

best. But what praise couldst thou bestow on a

deserving woman indeed? One that in the authority of   145

her merit did justly put on the vouch of very malice

itself?

IAGO   She that was ever fair and never proud,

Had tongue at will, and yet was never loud,

Never lacked gold, and yet went never gay,   150

Fled from her wish, and yet said 'now I may',

She that, being angered, her revenge being nigh,

Bade her wrong stay, and her displeasure fly,

She that in wisdom never was so frail

To change the cod's head for the salmon's tail,   155

She that could think, and ne'er disclose her mind,

See suitors following, and not look behind,

She was a wight, if ever such wights were –

DESDEMONA   To do what?

IAGO   To suckle fools, and chronicle small beer.   160

DESDEMONA   O, most lame and impotent conclusion!

Do not learn of him, Emilia, though he be thy

husband. How say you, Cassio, is he not a most

profane and liberal counsellor?

CASSIO   He speaks home, madam, you may relish him   165

more in the soldier than in the scholar.

IAGO [*aside*] He takes her by the palm; ay, well said,
whisper. With as little a web as this will I ensnare as
great a fly as Cassio. Ay, smile upon her, do: I will gyve
thee in thine own courtesies. You say true, 'tis so
indeed. If such tricks as these strip you out of your
lieutenantry, it had been better you had not kissed
your three fingers so oft, which now again you are
most apt to play the sir in. Very good, well kissed, and
excellent courtesy: 'tis so indeed! Yet again, your
fingers to your lips? would they were clyster-pipes for
your sake! [*Trumpets within*]
The Moor! I know his trumpet!

CASSIO   'Tis truly so.

DESDEMONA
Let's meet him and receive him.

Enter OTHELLO *and attendants.*

CASSIO   Lo, where he comes!

OTHELLO   O my fair warrior!

DESDEMONA   My dear Othello!

OTHELLO   It gives me wonder great as my content
To see you here before me! O my soul's joy,
If after every tempest come such calms
May the winds blow till they have wakened death,
And let the labouring bark climb hills of seas,
Olympus-high, and duck again as low
As hell's from heaven. If it were now to die
'Twere now to be most happy, for I fear
My soul hath her content so absolute
That not another comfort like to this
Succeeds in unknown fate.

DESDEMONA   The heavens forbid
But that our loves and comforts should increase
Even as our days do grow.

OTHELLO   Amen to that, sweet powers!
I cannot speak enough of this content,
It stops me here, it is too much of joy.
And this, and this the greatest discords be [*They kiss.*]
That e'er our hearts shall make.

IAGO [*aside*]
O, you are well tuned now: but I'll set down
The pegs that make this music, as honest
As I am.

OTHELLO   Come, let us to the castle.
News, friends, our wars are done, the Turks are
drowned.
How does my old acquaintance of this isle?
Honey, you shall be well desired in Cyprus,
I have found great love amongst them. O my sweet,
I prattle out of fashion, and I dote
In mine own comforts. I prithee, good Iago,
Go to the bay and disembark my coffers.
Bring thou the master to the citadel,
He is a good one, and his worthiness
Does challenge much respect. Come, Desdemona;
Once more, well met at Cyprus.

Exeunt all but Iago and Roderigo.

IAGO   Do thou meet me presently at the harbour. Come
hither: if thou be'st valiant – as, they say, base men
being in love have then a nobility in their natures,
more than is native to them – list me. The lieutenant
tonight watches on the court of guard. First I must tell
thee this: Desdemona is directly in love with him.

RODERIGO   With him? why, 'tis not possible.

IAGO   Lay thy finger thus, and let thy soul be instructed.
Mark me with what violence she first loved the Moor,
but for bragging and telling her fantastical lies – and
will she love him still for prating? let not thy discreet
heart think it. Her eye must be fed, and what delight
shall she have to look on the devil? When the blood is
made dull with the act of sport, there should be, again
to inflame it, and to give satiety a fresh appetite,
loveliness in favour, sympathy in years, manners and
beauties, all which the Moor is defective in. Now for
want of these required conveniences, her delicate
tenderness will find itself abused, begin to heave the
gorge, disrelish and abhor the Moor – very nature will
instruct her in it and compel her to some second
choice. Now sir, this granted – as it is a most pregnant
and unforced position – who stands so eminent in the
degree of this fortune as Cassio does? a knave very
voluble, no farther conscionable than in putting on the
mere form of civil and humane seeming, for the better
compassing of his salt and most hidden loose affection.
Why none, why none: a slipper and subtle knave, a
finder out of occasions, that has an eye, can stamp and
counterfeit advantages, though true advantage never
present itself – a devilish knave; besides, the knave is
handsome, young, and hath all those requisites in him
that folly and green minds look after. A pestilent
complete knave, and the woman hath found him
already.

RODERIGO   I cannot believe that in her, she's full of most
blest condition.

IAGO   Blest fig's-end! The wine she drinks is made of
grapes. If she had been blest she would never have
loved the Moor. Blest pudding! Didst thou not see her
paddle with the palm of his hand? Didst not mark
that?

RODERIGO   Yes, that I did, but that was but courtesy.

IAGO   Lechery, by this hand: an index and obscure
prologue to the history of lust and foul thoughts. They
met so near with their lips that their breaths embraced
together. Villainous thoughts, Roderigo: when these
mutualities so marshal the way, hard at hand comes
the master and main exercise, th'incorporate
conclusion. Pish! But, sir, be you ruled by me. I have
brought you from Venice: watch you tonight. For the
command, I'll lay't upon you. Cassio knows you not,
I'll not be far from you, do you find some occasion to
anger Cassio, either by speaking too loud or tainting
his discipline, or from what other cause you please
which the time shall more favourably minister.

RODERIGO Well.

IAGO Sir, he's rash and very sudden in choler, and haply
270　　with his truncheon may strike at you: provoke him
　　that he may, for even out of that will I cause these of
　　Cyprus to mutiny, whose qualification shall come into
　　no true trust again but by the displanting of Cassio. So
　　shall you have a shorter journey to your desires, by the
275　　means I shall then have to prefer them, and the
　　impediment most profitably removed, without the
　　which there were no expectation of our prosperity.

RODERIGO I will do this, if you can bring it to any
　　opportunity.

280 IAGO I warrant thee. Meet me by and by at the citadel:
　　I must fetch his necessaries ashore. Farewell.

RODERIGO Adieu.　　　　　　　　　　　　　*Exit.*

IAGO That Cassio loves her, I do well believe it,
　　That she loves him, 'tis apt and of great credit.
285　The Moor, howbeit that I endure him not,
　　Is of a constant, loving, noble nature,
　　And I dare think he'll prove to Desdemona
　　A most dear husband. Now I do love her too,
　　Not out of absolute lust – though peradventure
290　I stand accountant for as great a sin –
　　But partly led to diet my revenge,
　　For that I do suspect the lusty Moor
　　Hath leaped into my seat, the thought whereof
　　Doth like a poisonous mineral gnaw my inwards . . .
295　And nothing can or shall content my soul
　　Till I am evened with him, wife for wife . . .
　　Or, failing so, yet that I put the Moor
　　At least into a jealousy so strong
　　That judgement cannot cure; which thing to do,
300　If this poor trash of Venice, whom I trash
　　For his quick hunting, stand the putting on,
　　I'll have our Michael Cassio on the hip,
　　Abuse him to the Moor in the rank garb –
　　For I fear Cassio with my night-cap too –
305　Make the Moor thank me, love me, and reward me
　　For making him egregiously an ass,
　　And practising upon his peace and quiet
　　Even to madness. 'Tis here, but yet confused:
　　Knavery's plain face is never seen, till used.　　*Exit.*

2.2　*Enter Othello's* Herald, *with a proclamation.*

HERALD [*Reads.*] *It is Othello's pleasure, our noble and
valiant general, that, upon certain tidings now arrived,
importing the mere perdition of the Turkish fleet, every
man put himself into triumph: some to dance, some to
make bonfires, each man to what sport and revels his
5　addiction leads him. For besides these beneficial news, it is
the celebration of his nuptial.* – So much was his
pleasure should be proclaimed. All offices are open,
and there is full liberty of feasting from this present
10　hour of five till the bell have told eleven. Heaven bless
the isle of Cyprus and our noble general Othello!
　　　　　　　　　　　　　　　　　　　Exit.

2.3　*Enter* OTHELLO, CASSIO *and* DESDEMONA.

OTHELLO
　Good Michael, look you to the guard tonight.
　Let's teach ourselves that honourable stop
　Not to outsport discretion.

CASSIO　Iago hath direction what to do,
　But notwithstanding with my personal eye　　5
　Will I look to't.

OTHELLO　　　　　Iago is most honest.
　Michael, good night. Tomorrow with your earliest
　Let me have speech with you. Come, my dear love,
　The purchase made, the fruits are to ensue:
　That profit's yet to come 'tween me and you.　　10
　Good-night.　　　*Exeunt Othello and Desdemona.*

　　　　　　　　Enter IAGO.

CASSIO Welcome, Iago, we must to the watch.

IAGO Not this hour, lieutenant, 'tis not yet ten o'th'
　clock. Our general cast us thus early for the love of his
　Desdemona – whom let us not therefore blame; he　　15
　hath not yet made wanton the night with her, and she
　is sport for Jove.

CASSIO She's a most exquisite lady.

IAGO And I'll warrant her full of game.

CASSIO Indeed she's a most fresh and delicate creature.　　20

IAGO What an eye she has! methinks it sounds a parley
　to provocation.

CASSIO An inviting eye; and yet methinks right modest.

IAGO And when she speaks is it not an alarum to love?

CASSIO She is indeed perfection.　　25

IAGO Well: happiness to their sheets! Come, lieutenant,
　I have a stoup of wine, and here without are a brace of
　Cyprus gallants that would fain have a measure to the
　health of black Othello.

CASSIO Not tonight, good Iago, I have very poor and　　30
　unhappy brains for drinking. I could well wish courtesy
　would invent some other custom of entertainment.

IAGO O, they are our friends. But one cup, I'll drink for
　you.

CASSIO I have drunk but one cup tonight, and that was　　35
　craftily qualified too, and behold what innovation it
　makes here! I am unfortunate in the infirmity, and
　dare not task my weakness with any more.

IAGO What, man, 'tis a night of revels, the gallants
　desire it.　　40

CASSIO Where are they?

IAGO Here, at the door, I pray you call them in.

CASSIO I'll do't, but it dislikes me.　　　　　*Exit.*

IAGO If I can fasten but one cup upon him,
　With that which he hath drunk tonight already　　45
　He'll be as full of quarrel and offence
　As my young mistress' dog. Now my sick fool,
　　Roderigo,
　Whom love hath turned almost the wrong side out,
　To Desdemona hath tonight caroused
　Potations pottle-deep, and he's to watch.　　50

Three else of Cyprus, noble swelling spirits
That hold their honours in a wary distance,
The very elements of this warlike isle,
Have I tonight flustered with flowing cups,
And the watch too. Now 'mongst this flock of
55   drunkards
Am I to put our Cassio in some action
That may offend the isle.

     Enter CASSIO, MONTANO *and* Gentlemen.

               But here they come.
If consequence do but approve my dream
My boat sails freely, both with wind and stream.
60 CASSIO   'Fore God, they have given me a rouse already.
MONTANO   Good faith, a little one, not past a pint, as
    I am a soldier.
IAGO   Some wine, ho!
    [*Sings*.]
           And let me the cannikin clink, clink,
65   And let me the cannikin clink.
              A soldier's a man,
              O, man's life's but a span,
            Why then let a soldier drink!
    Some wine, boys!
70 CASSIO   'Fore God, an excellent song!
IAGO   I learned it in England, where indeed they are
    most potent in potting. Your Dane, your German, and
    your swag-bellied Hollander – drink, ho! – are nothing
    to your English.
75 CASSIO   Is your Englishman so exquisite in his drinking?
IAGO   Why, he drinks you with facility your Dane dead
    drunk; he sweats not to overthrow your Almain; he
    gives your Hollander a vomit ere the next pottle can be
    filled.
80 CASSIO   To the health of our general!
MONTANO   I am for it, lieutenant, and I'll do you justice.
IAGO   O sweet England!
    [*Sings*.]
           King Stephen was and-a worthy peer,
             His breeches cost him but a crown,
85   He held them sixpence all too dear,
             With that he called the tailor lown.
           He was a wight of high renown
             And thou art but of low degree,
           'Tis pride that pulls the country down,
90   Then take thine auld cloak about thee.
    Some wine, ho!
CASSIO   'Fore God, this is a more exquisite song than
    the other!
IAGO   Will you hear't again?
95 CASSIO   No, for I hold him to be unworthy of his place
    that does . . . those things. Well, God's above all, and
    there be souls must be saved, and there be souls must
    not be saved.
IAGO   It's true, good lieutenant.
100 CASSIO   For mine own part, no offence to the general
    nor any man of quality, I hope to be saved.

IAGO   And so do I too, lieutenant.
CASSIO   Ay, but, by your leave, not before me. The
    lieutenant is to be saved before the ancient. Let's have
    no more of this, let's to our affairs. God forgive us our   105
    sins! Gentlemen, let's look to our business. Do not
    think, gentlemen, I am drunk: this is my ancient, this
    is my right hand, and this is my left. I am not drunk
    now: I can stand well enough, and I speak well enough.
GENTLEMAN   Excellent well.   110
CASSIO   Why, very well then; you must not think then
    that I am drunk.   *Exit*.
MONTANO
    To th' platform, masters, come, let's set the watch.
IAGO   You see this fellow that is gone before,
    He is a soldier fit to stand by Caesar   115
    And give direction. And do but see his vice,
    'Tis to his virtue a just equinox,
    The one as long as th'other. 'Tis pity of him:
    I fear the trust Othello puts him in
    On some odd time of his infirmity   120
    Will shake this island.
MONTANO   But is he often thus?
IAGO   'Tis evermore the prologue to his sleep:
    He'll watch the horologe a double set
    If drink rock not his cradle.
MONTANO   It were well
    The general were put in mind of it.   125
    Perhaps he sees it not, or his good nature
    Prizes the virtue that appears in Cassio
    And looks not on his evils: is not this true?

     Enter RODERIGO.

IAGO [*aside*]   How now, Roderigo?
    I pray you, after the lieutenant, go!   *Exit Roderigo.*   130
MONTANO   And 'tis great pity that the noble Moor
    Should hazard such a place as his own second
    With one of an ingraft infirmity.
    It were an honest action to say so
    To the Moor.
IAGO   Not I, for this fair island.   135
    I do love Cassio well, and would do much
    [*A cry within*: 'Help! help!']
    To cure him of this evil. But hark, what noise?

     Enter CASSIO *pursuing* RODERIGO.

CASSIO   Zounds, you rogue! you rascal!
MONTANO   What's the matter, lieutenant?
CASSIO   A knave teach me my duty? I'll beat the knave   140
    into a twiggen bottle!
RODERIGO   Beat me?
CASSIO   Dost thou prate, rogue?
MONTANO   Nay, good lieutenant! I pray you, sir, hold
    your hand.   145
CASSIO   Let me go, sir, or I'll knock you o'er the mazzard.
MONTANO   Come, come, you're drunk.
CASSIO   Drunk? [*They fight*.]

IAGO [*aside to Roderigo*]

150 Away, I say, go out and cry a mutiny.   *Exit Roderigo.*
     Nay, good lieutenant! God's will, gentlemen –
     Help ho! Lieutenant! sir – Montano – sir –
     Help, masters, here's a goodly watch indeed.
     [*A bell rings.*]
     Who's that which rings the bell? Diablo, ho!
     The town will rise, God's will, lieutenant, hold,
155 You will be shamed for ever!

          Enter OTHELLO *and attendants.*

OTHELLO   What is the matter here?
MONTANO   Zounds, I bleed still;
     I am hurt to th' death: he dies! [*Lunges at Cassio.*]
OTHELLO   Hold, for your lives!
IAGO
     Hold, ho! Lieutenant! sir – Montano – gentlemen –
     Have you forgot all sense of place and duty?
160 Hold, the general speaks to you: hold, for shame!
OTHELLO
     Why, how now, ho? From whence ariseth this?
     Are we turned Turks? and to ourselves do that
     Which heaven hath forbid the Ottomites?
     For Christian shame, put by this barbarous brawl;
165 He that stirs next, to carve for his own rage,
     Holds his soul light: he dies upon his motion.
     Silence that dreadful bell, it frights the isle
     From her propriety. What is the matter, masters?
     Honest Iago, that look'st dead with grieving,
170 Speak: who began this? on thy love I charge thee.
IAGO
     I do not know, friends all, but now, even now,
     In quarter and in terms like bride and groom
     Divesting them for bed; and then, but now,
     As if some planet had unwitted men,
175 Swords out, and tilting one at other's breasts
     In opposition bloody. I cannot speak
     Any beginning to this peevish odds,
     And would in action glorious I had lost
     Those legs that brought me to a part of it.
180 OTHELLO   How comes it, Michael, you are thus forgot?
CASSIO   I pray you pardon me, I cannot speak.
OTHELLO   Worthy Montano, you were wont to be civil:
     The gravity and stillness of your youth
     The world hath noted, and your name is great
185 In mouths of wisest censure. What's the matter
     That you unlace your reputation thus
     And spend your rich opinion for the name
     Of a night-brawler? Give me answer to it.
MONTANO   Worthy Othello, I am hurt to danger:
190 Your officer Iago can inform you,
     While I spare speech, which something now offends
          me,
     Of all that I do know; nor know I aught
     By me that's said or done amiss this night
     Unless self-charity be sometimes a vice,
195 And to defend ourselves it be a sin

     When violence assails us.
OTHELLO   Now, by heaven,
     My blood begins my safer guides to rule
     And passion, having my best judgement collied,
     Assays to lead the way. Zounds, if I once stir,
200 Or do but lift this arm, the best of you
     Shall sink in my rebuke. Give me to know
     How this foul rout began, who set it on,
     And he that is approved in this offence,
     Though he had twinned with me, both at a birth,
205 Shall lose me. What, in a town of war
     Yet wild, the people's hearts brimful of fear,
     To manage private and domestic quarrel?
     In night, and on the court and guard of safety?
     'Tis monstrous. Iago, who began't?
MONTANO   If partially affined or leagued in office   210
     Thou dost deliver more or less than truth
     Thou art no soldier.
IAGO   Touch me not so near.
     I had rather have this tongue cut from my mouth
     Than it should do offence to Michael Cassio,
     Yet I persuade myself to speak the truth   215
     Shall nothing wrong him. Thus it is, general:
     Montano and myself being in speech,
     There comes a fellow crying out for help
     And Cassio following him with determined sword
     To execute upon him. Sir, this gentleman   220
     Steps in to Cassio and entreats his pause,
     Myself the crying fellow did pursue
     Lest by his clamour, as it so fell out,
     The town might fall in fright. He, swift of foot,
     Outran my purpose, and I returned the rather   225
     For that I heard the clink and fall of swords
     And Cassio high in oath, which till tonight
     I ne'er might say before. When I came back,
     For this was brief, I found them close together
     At blow and thrust, even as again they were   230
     When you yourself did part them.
     More of this matter cannot I report.
     But men are men, the best sometimes forget;
     Though Cassio did some little wrong to him,
     As men in rage strike those that wish them best,   235
     Yet surely Cassio, I believe, received
     From him that fled some strange indignity
     Which patience could not pass.
OTHELLO   I know, Iago,
     Thy honesty and love doth mince this matter,
     Making it light to Cassio. Cassio, I love thee,   240

          Enter DESDEMONA, *attended.*

     But never more be officer of mine.
     Look if my gentle love be not raised up!
     I'll make thee an example.
DESDEMONA   What is the matter, dear?
OTHELLO   All's well now, sweeting,
     Come away to bed. – Sir, for your hurts   245
     Myself will be your surgeon. Lead him off.

Montano is led off.

Iago, look with care about the town
And silence those whom this vile brawl distracted.
Come, Desdemona: 'tis the soldier's life
250 To have their balmy slumbers waked with strife.

Exeunt all but Iago and Cassio.

IAGO   What, are you hurt, lieutenant?

CASSIO   Ay, past all surgery.

IAGO   Marry, God forbid!

CASSIO   Reputation, reputation, reputation! O, I have
255   lost my reputation, I have lost the immortal part of
    myself – and what remains is bestial. My reputation,
    Iago, my reputation!

IAGO   As I am an honest man I thought you had received
    some bodily wound; there is more of sense in that than
260   in reputation. Reputation is an idle and most false
    imposition, oft got without merit and lost without
    deserving. You have lost no reputation at all, unless you
    repute yourself such a loser. What, man, there are ways
    to recover the general again. You are but now cast in his
265   mood, a punishment more in policy than in malice,
    even so as one would beat his offenceless dog to affright
    an imperious lion. Sue to him again, and he's yours.

CASSIO   I will rather sue to be despised, than to deceive
    so good a commander with so slight, so drunken, and
270   so indiscreet an officer. Drunk? and speak parrot? and
    squabble? swagger? swear? and discourse fustian with
    one's own shadow? O thou invisible spirit of wine, if
    thou hast no name to be known by, let us call thee
    devil!

275 IAGO   What was he that you followed with your sword?
    What had he done to you?

CASSIO   I know not.

IAGO   Is't possible?

CASSIO   I remember a mass of things, but nothing
280   distinctly; a quarrel, but nothing wherefore. O God,
    that men should put an enemy in their mouths, to steal
    away their brains! that we should with joy, pleasance,
    revel and applause, transform ourselves into beasts!

IAGO   Why, but you are now well enough: how came
285   you thus recovered?

CASSIO   It hath pleased the devil drunkenness to give
    place to the devil wrath; one unperfectness shows me
    another, to make me frankly despise myself.

IAGO   Come, you are too severe a moraler. As the time,
290   the place and the condition of this country stands, I
    could heartily wish this had not befallen; but since it is
    as it is, mend it for your own good.

CASSIO   I will ask him for my place again, he shall tell me
    I am a drunkard: had I as many mouths as Hydra, such
295   an answer would stop them all. To be now a sensible
    man, by and by a fool, and presently a beast! O
    strange! – Every inordinate cup is unblest, and the
    ingredient is a devil.

IAGO   Come, come, good wine is a good familiar crea-
300   ture, if it be well used: exclaim no more against it.
    And, good lieutenant, I think you think I love you.

CASSIO   I have well approved it, sir. I drunk?

IAGO   You, or any man living, may be drunk at some
    time, man. I'll tell you what you shall do. Our
    general's wife is now the general. I may say so in this   305
    respect, for that he hath devoted and given up himself
    to the contemplation, mark and denotement of her
    parts and graces. Confess yourself freely to her,
    importune her help to put you in your place again.
    She is of so free, so kind, so apt, so blest a disposition   310
    that she holds it a vice in her goodness not to do more
    than she is requested. This broken joint between you
    and her husband entreat her to splinter – and my
    fortunes against any lay worth naming, this crack of
    your love shall grow stronger than it was before.   315

CASSIO   You advise me well.

IAGO   I protest, in the sincerity of love and honest
    kindness.

CASSIO   I think it freely, and betimes in the morning I will
    beseech the virtuous Desdemona to undertake for me. I   320
    am desperate of my fortunes if they check me here.

IAGO   You are in the right. Good-night, lieutenant, I
    must to the watch.

CASSIO   Good-night, honest Iago.   *Exit.*

IAGO   And what's he then that says I play the villain?   325
    When this advice is free I give and honest,
    Probal to thinking and indeed the course
    To win the Moor again? For 'tis most easy
    Th'inclining Desdemona to subdue
    In any honest suit. She's framed as fruitful   330
    As the free elements: and then for her
    To win the Moor, were't to renounce his baptism,
    All seals and symbols of redeemed sin,
    His soul is so enfettered to her love
    That she may make, unmake, do what she list,   335
    Even as her appetite shall play the god
    With his weak function. How am I then a villain
    To counsel Cassio to this parallel course
    Directly to his good? Divinity of hell!
    When devils will the blackest sins put on   340
    They do suggest at first with heavenly shows
    As I do now. For whiles this honest fool
    Plies Desdemona to repair his fortune,
    And she for him pleads strongly to the Moor,
    I'll pour this pestilence into his ear: 345
    That she repeals him for her body's lust.
    And by how much she strives to do him good
    She shall undo her credit with the Moor –
    So will I turn her virtue into pitch
    And out of her own goodness make the net   350
    That shall enmesh them all.

Enter RODERIGO.

How now, Roderigo?

RODERIGO   I do follow here in the chase not like a hound
    that hunts, but one that fills up the cry. My money is
    almost spent, I have been tonight exceedingly well
    cudgelled, and I think the issue will be I shall have so   355

much experience for my pains: and so, with no money
at all, and a little more wit, return again to Venice.

IAGO   How poor are they that have not patience!
What wound did ever heal but by degrees?
360   Thou know'st we work by wit and not by witchcraft,
And wit depends on dilatory time.
Does't not go well? Cassio hath beaten thee
And thou by that small hurt hast cashiered Cassio.
Though other things grow fair against the sun
365   Yet fruits that blossom first will first be ripe;
Content thyself a while. By the mass, 'tis morning:
Pleasure and action make the hours seem short.
Retire thee, go where thou art billeted,
Away, I say, thou shalt know more hereafter:
Nay, get thee gone.   *Exit Roderigo.*
370   Two things are to be done:
My wife must move for Cassio to her mistress,
I'll set her on.
Myself the while to draw the Moor apart
And bring him jump when he may Cassio find
375   Soliciting his wife: ay, that's the way!
Dull not device by coldness and delay!   *Exit.*

3.1   *Enter* CASSIO *and some* Musicians.

CASSIO   Masters, play here, I will content your pains;
Something that's brief, and bid 'Good morrow,
general.'

They play. Enter Clown.

CLOWN   Why, masters, have your instruments been in
Naples, that they speak i'th' nose thus?
5   1 MUSICIAN   How, sir? how?
CLOWN   Are these, I pray you, wind instruments?
1 MUSICIAN   Ay marry are they, sir.
CLOWN   O, thereby hangs a tail.
1 MUSICIAN   Whereby hangs a tail, sir?
10   CLOWN   Marry, sir, by many a wind instrument that I
know. But, masters, here's money for you, and the
general so likes your music that he desires you, for
love's sake, to make no more noise with it.
1 MUSICIAN   Well, sir, we will not.
15   CLOWN   If you have any music that may not be heard,
to't again. But, as they say, to hear music the general
does not greatly care.
1 MUSICIAN   We have none such, sir.
CLOWN   Then put up your pipes in your bag, for I'll
20   away. Go, vanish into air, away!   *Exeunt Musicians.*
CASSIO   Dost thou hear, mine honest friend?
CLOWN   No, I hear not your honest friend, I hear you.
CASSIO   Prithee keep up thy quillets; there's a poor piece
of gold for thee – if the gentlewoman that attends the
25   general's wife be stirring, tell her there's one Cassio
entreats her a little favour of speech. Wilt thou do this?
CLOWN   She is stirring, sir; if she will stir hither, I shall
seem to notify unto her.

Enter IAGO.

CASSIO   Do, good my friend.   *Exit Clown.*
                    In happy time, Iago.
IAGO   You have not been a-bed then?   30
CASSIO   Why no, the day had broke before we parted.
I have made bold, Iago, to send in
To your wife: my suit to her is that she will
To virtuous Desdemona procure me
Some access.
IAGO   I'll send her to you presently,   35
And I'll devise a mean to draw the Moor
Out of the way, that your converse and business
May be more free.
CASSIO   I humbly thank you for't.   *Exit Iago.*
                    I never knew
A Florentine more kind and honest.   40

Enter EMILIA.

EMILIA   Good morrow, good lieutenant. I am sorry
For your displeasure, but all will sure be well.
The general and his wife are talking of it,
And she speaks for you stoutly; the Moor replies
That he you hurt is of great fame in Cyprus   45
And great affinity,
And that in wholesome wisdom he might not but
Refuse you; but he protests he loves you
And needs no other suitor but his likings
To take the safest occasion by the front   50
To bring you in again.
CASSIO   Yet I beseech you,
If you think fit, or that it may be done,
Give me advantage of some brief discourse
With Desdemon alone.
EMILIA   Pray you come in,
I will bestow you where you shall have time   55
To speak your bosom freely.
CASSIO   I am much bound to you.
                    Exeunt.

3.2   *Enter* OTHELLO, IAGO *and* Gentlemen.

OTHELLO   These letters give, Iago, to the pilot,
And by him do my duties to the Senate;
That done, I will be walking on the works,
Repair there to me.
IAGO   Well, my good lord, I'll do't.
OTHELLO   This fortification, gentlemen, shall we see't?   5
1 GENTLEMAN   We'll wait upon your lordship.   *Exeunt.*

3.3   *Enter* DESDEMONA, CASSIO *and* Emilia.

DESDEMONA   Be thou assured, good Cassio, I will do
All my abilities in thy behalf.
EMILIA
Good madam, do, I warrant it grieves my husband
As if the cause were his.
DESDEMONA
O, that's an honest fellow. Do not doubt, Cassio,   5
But I will have my lord and you again

As friendly as you were.

CASSIO   Bounteous madam,
Whatever shall become of Michael Cassio,
He's never anything but your true servant.

DESDEMONA

10   I know't, I thank you. You do love my lord,
You have known him long, and be you well assured
He shall in strangeness stand no farther off
Than in a politic distance.

CASSIO   Ay, but, lady,
That policy may either last so long,

15   Or feed upon such nice and waterish diet,
Or breed itself so out of circumstance,
That, I being absent and my place supplied,
My general will forget my love and service.

DESDEMONA   Do not doubt that: before Emilia here

20   I give thee warrant of thy place. Assure thee,
If I do vow a friendship I'll perform it
To the last article. My lord shall never rest,
I'll watch him tame and talk him out of patience,
His bed shall seem a school, his board a shrift,

25   I'll intermingle everything he does
With Cassio's suit: therefore be merry, Cassio,
For thy solicitor shall rather die
Than give thy cause away.

Enter OTHELLO *and* IAGO.

EMILIA   Madam, here comes my lord.

30   CASSIO   Madam, I'll take my leave.

DESDEMONA   Why, stay and hear me speak.

CASSIO   Madam, not now; I am very ill at ease,
Unfit for mine own purposes.

DESDEMONA   Well, do your discretion.   *Exit Cassio.*

IAGO   Ha, I like not that.

35   OTHELLO   What dost thou say?

IAGO   Nothing, my lord; or if – I know not what.

OTHELLO   Was not that Cassio parted from my wife?

IAGO   Cassio, my lord? no, sure, I cannot think it
That he would steal away so guilty-like
Seeing you coming.

40   OTHELLO   I do believe 'twas he.

DESDEMONA   How now, my lord?
I have been talking with a suitor here,
A man that languishes in your displeasure.

OTHELLO   Who is't you mean?

DESDEMONA

45   Why, your lieutenant, Cassio. Good my lord,
If I have any grace or power to move you
His present reconciliation take:
For if he be not one that truly loves you,
That errs in ignorance and not in cunning,

50   I have no judgement in an honest face.
I prithee, call him back.

OTHELLO   Went he hence now?

DESDEMONA   Yes, faith, so humbled
That he hath left part of his grief with me
To suffer with him. Good love, call him back.

OTHELLO   Not now, sweet Desdemon, some other time.   55

DESDEMONA   But shall't be shortly?

OTHELLO   The sooner, sweet, for you.

DESDEMONA   Shall't be tonight, at supper?

OTHELLO   No, not tonight.

DESDEMONA   Tomorrow dinner then?

OTHELLO   I shall not dine at home.
I meet the captains at the citadel.

DESDEMONA

Why then, tomorrow night, or Tuesday morn;   60
On Tuesday, noon or night; on Wednesday morn!
I prithee name the time, but let it not
Exceed three days: i'faith, he's penitent,
And yet his trespass, in our common reason
– Save that they say the wars must make examples   65
Out of their best – is not, almost, a fault
T'incur a private check. When shall he come?
Tell me, Othello. I wonder in my soul
What you would ask me that I should deny
Or stand so mamm'ring on? What, Michael Cassio   70
That came a-wooing with you? and so many a time
When I have spoke of you dispraisingly
Hath ta'en your part, to have so much to do
To bring him in? By'r lady, I could do much! –

OTHELLO

Prithee, no more. Let him come when he will,   75
I will deny thee nothing.

DESDEMONA   Why, this is not a boon,
'Tis as I should entreat you wear your gloves,
Or feed on nourishing dishes, or keep you warm,
Or sue to you to do a peculiar profit
To your own person. Nay, when I have a suit   80
Wherein I mean to touch your love indeed
It shall be full of poise and difficult weight
And fearful to be granted.

OTHELLO   I will deny thee nothing.
Whereon I do beseech thee, grant me this,
To leave me but a little to myself.   85

DESDEMONA   Shall I deny you? No, farewell, my lord.

OTHELLO

Farewell, my Desdemona, I'll come to thee straight.

DESDEMONA

Emilia, come. – Be as your fancies teach you:
Whate'er you be, I am obedient.

                         Exeunt Desdemona and Emilia.

OTHELLO   Excellent wretch! perdition catch my soul   90
But I do love thee! and when I love thee not
Chaos is come again.

IAGO   My noble lord –

OTHELLO   What dost thou say, Iago?

IAGO   Did Michael Cassio, when you wooed my lady,
Know of your love?

OTHELLO   He did, from first to last.   95
Why dost thou ask?

IAGO   But for a satisfaction of my thought,
No further harm.

OTHELLO   Why of thy thought, Iago?

IAGO   I did not think he had been acquainted with her.

100   OTHELLO   O yes, and went between us very oft.

IAGO   Indeed?

OTHELLO

Indeed? Ay, indeed. Discern'st thou aught in that?
Is he not honest?

IAGO   Honest, my lord?

105   OTHELLO   Honest? Ay, honest.

IAGO   My lord, for aught I know.

OTHELLO   What dost thou think?

IAGO   Think, my lord?

OTHELLO   Think, my lord! By heaven, thou echo'st me

110   As if there were some monster in thy thought
Too hideous to be shown. Thou dost mean
   something,
I heard thee say even now thou lik'st not that
When Cassio left my wife: what didst not like?
And when I told thee he was of my counsel

115   In my whole course of wooing, thou criedst 'Indeed?'
And didst contract and purse thy brow together
As if thou then hadst shut up in thy brain
Some horrible conceit. If thou dost love me
Show me thy thought.

IAGO   My lord, you know I love you.

120   OTHELLO   I think thou dost.
And for I know thou'rt full of love and honesty
And weigh'st thy words before thou giv'st them
   breath,
Therefore these stops of thine fright me the more.
For such things in a false disloyal knave

125   Are tricks of custom, but in a man that's just
They're close delations, working from the heart,
That passion cannot rule.

IAGO   For Michael Cassio,
I dare be sworn, I think, that he is honest.

OTHELLO   I think so too.

IAGO   Men should be what they seem,

130   Or those that be not, would they might seem none.

OTHELLO   Certain, men should be what they seem.

IAGO   Why then I think Cassio's an honest man.

OTHELLO   Nay, yet there's more in this:
I prithee speak to me, as to thy thinkings,
As thou dost ruminate, and give thy worst of
   thoughts

135   The worst of words.

IAGO   Good my lord, pardon me;
Though I am bound to every act of duty
I am not bound to that all slaves are free to –
Utter my thoughts? Why, say they are vile and false?

140   As where's that palace whereinto foul things
Sometimes intrude not? Who has a breast so pure
But some uncleanly apprehensions
Keep leets and law-days and in session sit
With meditations lawful?

145   OTHELLO   Thou dost conspire against thy friend, Iago,
If thou but think'st him wronged and mak'st his ear
A stranger to thy thoughts.

IAGO   I do beseech you,
Though I perchance am vicious in my guess
– As I confess it is my nature's plague

150   To spy into abuses, and oft my jealousy
Shapes faults that are not – that your wisdom
From one that so imperfectly conceits
Would take no notice, nor build yourself a trouble
Out of his scattering and unsure observance:

155   It were not for your quiet nor your good
Nor for my manhood, honesty and wisdom
To let you know my thoughts.

OTHELLO   Zounds! What dost thou mean?

IAGO   Good name in man and woman, dear my lord,
Is the immediate jewel of their souls:
Who steals my purse steals trash – 'tis something-
   nothing,

160   'Twas mine, 'tis his, and has been slave to thousands –
But he that filches from me my good name
Robs me of that which not enriches him
And makes me poor indeed.

OTHELLO   By heaven, I'll know thy thoughts!

165   IAGO   You cannot, if my heart were in your hand,
Nor shall not whilst 'tis in my custody.

OTHELLO   Ha!

IAGO   O beware, my lord, of jealousy!
It is the green-eyed monster, which doth mock
The meat it feeds on. That cuckold lives in bliss

170   Who, certain of his fate, loves not his wronger,
But O, what damned minutes tells he o'er
Who dotes yet doubts, suspects yet strongly loves!

OTHELLO   O misery!

IAGO   Poor and content is rich, and rich enough,

175   But riches fineless is as poor as winter
To him that ever fears he shall be poor.
Good God, the souls of all my tribe defend
From jealousy.

OTHELLO   Why – why is this?

180   Think'st thou I'd make a life of jealousy
To follow still the changes of the moon
With fresh suspicions? No: to be once in doubt
Is once to be resolved. Exchange me for a goat
When I shall turn the business of my soul

185   To such exsufflicate and blown surmises,
Matching thy inference. 'Tis not to make me jealous
To say my wife is fair, feeds well, loves company,
Is free of speech, sings, plays and dances well:
Where virtue is, these are more virtuous.

190   Nor from mine own weak merits will I draw
The smallest fear or doubt of her revolt,
For she had eyes and chose me. No, Iago,
I'll see before I doubt, when I doubt, prove,
And on the proof there is no more but this:

195   Away at once with love or jealousy!

IAGO   I am glad of this, for now I shall have reason
To show the love and duty that I bear you
With franker spirit: therefore, as I am bound,
Receive it from me. I speak not yet of proof:

200   Look to your wife, observe her well with Cassio.
       Wear your eyes thus, not jealous nor secure;
       I would not have your free and noble nature
       Out of self-bounty be abused: look to't.
       I know our country disposition well –
205   In Venice they do let God see the pranks
       They dare not show their husbands; their best
             conscience
       Is not to leave't undone, but keep't unknown.
OTHELLO   Dost thou say so?
IAGO   She did deceive her father, marrying you,
210   And when she seemed to shake, and fear your looks,
       She loved them most.
OTHELLO   And so she did.
IAGO   Why, go to then:
       She that so young could give out such a seeming
       To seel her father's eyes up, close as oak –
       He thought 'twas witchcraft. But I am much to blame,
215   I humbly do beseech you of your pardon
       For too much loving you.
OTHELLO   I am bound to thee for ever.
IAGO   I see this hath a little dashed your spirits.
OTHELLO   Not a jot, not a jot.
IAGO   I'faith, I fear it has.
220   I hope you will consider what is spoke
       Comes from my love. But I do see you're moved;
       I am to pray you not to strain my speech
       To grosser issues nor to larger reach
       Than to suspicion.
OTHELLO   I will not.
225   IAGO   Should you do so, my lord,
       My speech should fall into such vile success
       As my thoughts aimed not at: Cassio's my worthy
             friend.
       My lord, I see you're moved.
OTHELLO   No, not much moved.
       I do not think but Desdemona's honest.
230   IAGO   Long live she so; and long live you to think so.
OTHELLO   And yet how nature, erring from itself –
IAGO   Ay, there's the point: as, to be bold with you,
       Not to affect many proposed matches
       Of her own clime, complexion and degree,
235   Whereto we see, in all things, nature tends –
       Foh! one may smell in such a will most rank,
       Foul disproportion, thoughts unnatural.
       But pardon me, I do not in position
       Distinctly speak of her, though I may fear
240   Her will, recoiling to her better judgement,
       May fall to match you with her country forms,
       And happily repent.
OTHELLO   Farewell, farewell.
       If more thou dost perceive, let me know more:
       Set on thy wife to observe. Leave me, Iago.
IAGO   My lord, I take my leave.
245   OTHELLO   Why did I marry?
       This honest creature doubtless
       Sees and knows more – much more – than he unfolds.

IAGO   My lord, I would I might entreat your honour
       To scan this thing no farther. Leave it to time;
       Although 'tis fit that Cassio have his place,   250
       For sure he fills it up with great ability,
       Yet if you please to hold him off a while
       You shall by that perceive him, and his means:
       Note if your lady strain his entertainment
       With any strong or vehement importunity,   255
       Much will be seen in that. In the meantime
       Let me be thought too busy in my fears
       – As worthy cause I have to fear I am –
       And hold her free, I do beseech your honour.
OTHELLO   Fear not my government.   260
IAGO   I once more take my leave.   *Exit.*
OTHELLO
       This fellow's of exceeding honesty
       And knows all qualities, with a learned spirit,
       Of human dealings. If I do prove her haggard,
       Though that her jesses were my dear heart-strings,   265
       I'd whistle her off and let her down the wind
       To prey at fortune. Haply for I am black
       And have not those soft parts of conversation
       That chamberers have, or for I am declined
       Into the vale of years – yet that's not much –   270
       She's gone, I am abused, and my relief
       Must be to loathe her. O curse of marriage
       That we can call these delicate creatures ours
       And not their appetites! I had rather be a toad
       And live upon the vapour of a dungeon   275
       Than keep a corner in the thing I love
       For others' uses. Yet 'tis the plague of great ones,
       Prerogatived are they less than the base;
       'Tis destiny unshunnable, like death –
       Even then this forked plague is fated to us   280
       When we do quicken.

               Enter DESDEMONA *and* EMILIA.

                          Look where she comes:
       If she be false, O then heaven mocks itself,
       I'll not believe't.
DESDEMONA   How now, my dear Othello?
       Your dinner, and the generous islanders
       By you invited, do attend your presence.   285
OTHELLO   I am to blame.
DESDEMONA   Why do you speak so faintly?
       Are you not well?
OTHELLO   I have a pain upon my forehead, here.
DESDEMONA
       Faith, that's with watching, 'twill away again.
       Let me but bind it hard, within this hour   290
       It will be well.
OTHELLO   Your napkin is too little.
       [*She drops her handkerchief.*]
       Let it alone. Come, I'll go in with you.
DESDEMONA
       I am very sorry that you are not well.
                          Exeunt Othello and Desdemona.

EMILIA

95 I am glad I have found this napkin,
    This was her first remembrance from the Moor.
    My wayward husband hath a hundred times
    Wooed me to steal it, but she so loves the token
    – For he conjured her she should ever keep it –
    That she reserves it evermore about her
00 To kiss and talk to. I'll have the work ta'en out
    And give't Iago: what he will do with it
    Heaven knows, not I,
    I nothing, but to please his fantasy.

                   Enter IAGO.

IAGO   How now! What do you here alone?
05 EMILIA   Do not you chide, I have a thing for you –
IAGO   You have a thing for me? it is a common thing –
EMILIA   Ha?
IAGO   To have a foolish wife.
EMILIA   O, is that all? What will you give me now
    For that same handkerchief?
10 IAGO   What handkerchief?
EMILIA   What handkerchief?
    Why, that the Moor first gave to Desdemona,
    That which so often you did bid me steal.
IAGO   Hast stolen it from her?
15 EMILIA   No, faith, she let it drop by negligence
    And, to th'advantage, I being here, took't up.
    Look, here it is.
IAGO   A good wench, give it me.
EMILIA
    What will you do with't, that you have been so
       earnest
    To have me filch it?
IAGO [*snatching it*]   Why, what's that to you?
20 EMILIA   If it be not for some purpose of import
    Give't me again. Poor lady, she'll run mad
    When she shall lack it.
IAGO   Be not acknown on't,
    I have use for it. Go, leave me.   *Exit Emilia.*
    I will in Cassio's lodging lose this napkin
25 And let him find it. Trifles light as air
    Are to the jealous confirmations strong
    As proofs of holy writ. This may do something.
    The Moor already changes with my poison:
    Dangerous conceits are in their natures poisons
30 Which at the first are scarce found to distaste
    But with a little art upon the blood
    Burn like the mines of sulphur.

                 Enter OTHELLO.

                          I did say so:
    Look where he comes. Not poppy nor mandragora
    Nor all the drowsy syrups of the world
35 Shall ever medicine thee to that sweet sleep
    Which thou owedst yesterday.
OTHELLO   Ha! Ha! false to me?
IAGO   Why, how now, general? No more of that.

OTHELLO
    Avaunt, be gone, thou hast set me on the rack!
    I swear 'tis better to be much abused
    Than but to know't a little.
IAGO   How now, my lord?   340
OTHELLO
    What sense had I of her stolen hours of lust?
    I saw't not, thought it not, it harmed not me,
    I slept the next night well, fed well, was free and
       merry;
    I found not Cassio's kisses on her lips;
    He that is robbed, not wanting what is stolen,   345
    Let him not know't, and he's not robbed at all.
IAGO   I am sorry to hear this.
OTHELLO   I had been happy if the general camp,
    Pioneers and all, had tasted her sweet body,
    So I had nothing known. O now for ever   350
    Farewell the tranquil mind, farewell content!
    Farewell the plumed troops and the big wars
    That makes ambition virtue! O farewell,
    Farewell the neighing steed and the shrill trump,
    The spirit-stirring drum, th'ear-piercing fife,   355
    The royal banner, and all quality,
    Pride, pomp and circumstance of glorious war!
    And, O you mortal engines whose rude throats
    Th'immortal Jove's dread clamours counterfeit,
    Farewell: Othello's occupation's gone.   360
IAGO   Is't possible? my lord?
OTHELLO   Villain, be sure thou prove my love a whore,
    Be sure of it, give me the ocular proof,
    [*catching hold of him*]
    Or by the worth of man's eternal soul
    Thou hadst been better have been born a dog   365
    Than answer my waked wrath!
IAGO   Is't come to this?
OTHELLO   Make me to see't, or at the least so prove it
    That the probation bear no hinge nor loop
    To hang a doubt on, or woe upon thy life!
IAGO   My noble lord –   370
OTHELLO   If thou dost slander her and torture me
    Never pray more, abandon all remorse;
    On horror's head horrors accumulate,
    Do deeds to make heaven weep, all earth amazed,
    For nothing canst thou to damnation add   375
    Greater than that!
IAGO   O grace! O heaven forgive me!
    Are you a man? have you a soul, or sense?
    God buy you, take mine office. O wretched fool
    That lov'st to make thine honesty a vice!
    O monstrous world! Take note, take note, O world,   380
    To be direct and honest is not safe.
    I thank you for this profit, and from hence
    I'll love no friend, sith love breeds such offence.
OTHELLO   Nay, stay, thou shouldst be honest.
IAGO   I should be wise, for honesty's a fool   385
    And loses that it works for.
OTHELLO   By the world,

I think my wife be honest, and think she is not,
I think that thou art just, and think thou art not.
I'll have some proof. Her name, that was as fresh
390 As Dian's visage, is now begrimed and black
As mine own face. If there be cords or knives,
Poison, or fire, or suffocating streams,
I'll not endure it. Would I were satisfied!
IAGO I see, sir, you are eaten up with passion.
395 I do repent me that I put it to you.
You would be satisfied?
OTHELLO   Would? nay, and I will!
IAGO And may – but how? how satisfied, my lord?
Would you, the supervisor, grossly gape on?
Behold her topped?
OTHELLO   Death and damnation! O!
400 IAGO It were a tedious difficulty, I think,
To bring them to that prospect. Damn them then
If ever mortal eyes do see them bolster
More than their own. What then? how then?
What shall I say? where's satisfaction?
405 It is impossible you should see this
Were they as prime as goats, as hot as monkeys,
As salt as wolves in pride, and fools as gross
As ignorance made drunk. But yet, I say,
If imputation and strong circumstances
410 Which lead directly to the door of truth
Will give you satisfaction, you may have't.
OTHELLO Give me a living reason she's disloyal.
IAGO I do not like the office.
But sith I am entered in this cause so far,
415 Pricked to't by foolish honesty and love,
I will go on. I lay with Cassio lately
And being troubled with a raging tooth
I could not sleep. There are a kind of men
So loose of soul that in their sleeps will mutter
420 Their affairs – one of this kind is Cassio.
In sleep I heard him say 'Sweet Desdemona,
Let us be wary, let us hide our loves,'
And then, sir, would he gripe and wring my hand,
Cry 'O sweet creature!' and then kiss me hard
425 As if he plucked up kisses by the roots
That grew upon my lips, lay his leg o'er my thigh,
And sigh, and kiss, and then cry 'Cursed fate
That gave thee to the Moor!'
OTHELLO   O monstrous! monstrous!
IAGO Nay, this was but his dream.
430 OTHELLO But this denoted a foregone conclusion.
IAGO 'Tis a shrewd doubt, though it be but a dream,
And this may help to thicken other proofs
That do demonstrate thinly.
OTHELLO I'll tear her all to pieces!
435 IAGO Nay, yet be wise, yet we see nothing done,
She may be honest yet. Tell me but this,
Have you not sometimes seen a handkerchief
Spotted with strawberries, in your wife's hand?
OTHELLO I gave her such a one, 'twas my first gift.
440 IAGO I know not that, but such a handkerchief,

I am sure it was your wife's, did I today
See Cassio wipe his beard with.
OTHELLO   If it be that –
IAGO If it be that, or any that was hers,
It speaks against her with the other proofs.
OTHELLO O that the slave had forty thousand lives! 445
One is too poor, too weak for my revenge.
Now do I see 'tis true. Look here, Iago,
All my fond love thus do I blow to heaven:
'Tis gone!
Arise, black vengeance, from the hollow hell, 450
Yield up, O love, thy crown and hearted throne
To tyrannous hate! Swell, bosom, with thy fraught,
For 'tis of aspics' tongues!
IAGO   Yet be content!
OTHELLO O blood, blood, blood! [*Othello kneels.*]
IAGO Patience, I say, your mind perhaps may change. 455
OTHELLO Never, Iago. Like to the Pontic sea
Whose icy current and compulsive course
Ne'er keeps retiring ebb but keeps due on
To the Propontic and the Hellespont:
Even so my bloody thoughts with violent pace 460
Shall ne'er look back, ne'er ebb to humble love
Till that a capable and wide revenge
Swallow them up. Now by yond marble heaven
In the due reverence of a sacred vow
I here engage my words.
IAGO   Do not rise yet. [*Iago kneels.*] 465
Witness, you ever-burning lights above,
You elements that clip us round about,
Witness that here Iago doth give up
The execution of his wit, hands, heart,
To wronged Othello's service. Let him command 470
And to obey shall be in me remorse
What bloody business ever.
OTHELLO   I greet thy love
Not with vain thanks but with acceptance bounteous,
And will upon the instant put thee to't.
Within these three days let me hear thee say 475
That Cassio's not alive.
IAGO   My friend is dead,
'Tis done – at your request. But let her live.
OTHELLO
Damn her, lewd minx: O damn her, damn her!
Come, go with me apart; I will withdraw
To furnish me with some swift means of death 480
For the fair devil. Now art thou my lieutenant.
IAGO I am your own for ever.   *Exeunt.*

3.4   Enter DESDEMONA, EMILIA *and* Clown.

DESDEMONA Do you know, sirrah, where lieutenant
Cassio lies?
CLOWN I dare not say he lies anywhere.
DESDEMONA Why, man?
CLOWN He's a soldier, and for me to say a soldier lies,
'tis stabbing. 5
DESDEMONA Go to, where lodges he?

CLOWN   To tell you where he lodges is to tell you where
I lie.

DESDEMONA   Can anything be made of this?

CLOWN   I know not where he lodges, and for me to
devise a lodging and say he lies here, or he lies there,
were to lie in mine own throat.

DESDEMONA   Can you enquire him out and be edified by
report?

CLOWN   I will catechize the world for him, that is, make
questions and by them answer.

DESDEMONA   Seek him, bid him come hither, tell him I
have moved my lord on his behalf, and hope all will be
well.

CLOWN   To do this is within the compass of man's wit,
and therefore I will attempt the doing it.   *Exit.*

DESDEMONA
Where should I lose that handkerchief, Emilia?

EMILIA   I know not, madam.

DESDEMONA
Believe me, I had rather have lost my purse
Full of crusadoes; and but my noble Moor
Is true of mind, and made of no such baseness
As jealous creatures are, it were enough
To put him to ill-thinking.

EMILIA   Is he not jealous?

DESDEMONA
Who, he? I think the sun where he was born
Drew all such humours from him.

EMILIA   Look where he comes.

Enter OTHELLO.

DESDEMONA   I will not leave him now till Cassio
Be called to him. How is't with you, my lord?

OTHELLO
Well, my good lady. [*aside*] O hardness to dissemble! –
How do you, Desdemona?

DESDEMONA   Well, my good lord.

OTHELLO
Give me your hand. This hand is moist, my lady.

DESDEMONA
It yet hath felt no age, nor known no sorrow.

OTHELLO   This argues fruitfulness and liberal heart:
Hot, hot, and moist. This hand of yours requires
A sequester from liberty, fasting and prayer,
Much castigation, exercise devout,
For here's a young and sweating devil, here,
That commonly rebels. 'Tis a good hand,
A frank one.

DESDEMONA   You may indeed say so,
For 'twas that hand that gave away my heart.

OTHELLO   A liberal hand. The hearts of old gave hands
But our new heraldry is hands, not hearts.

DESDEMONA
I cannot speak of this. Come, now, your promise.

OTHELLO   What promise, chuck?

DESDEMONA
I have sent to bid Cassio come speak with you.

OTHELLO   I have a salt and sullen rheum offends me,
Lend me thy handkerchief.

DESDEMONA   Here, my lord.

OTHELLO   That which I gave you.

DESDEMONA   I have it not about me.   55

OTHELLO   Not?

DESDEMONA   No, faith, my lord.

OTHELLO   That's a fault. That handkerchief
Did an Egyptian to my mother give,
She was a charmer and could almost read
The thoughts of people. She told her, while she kept
    it   60
'Twould make her amiable and subdue my father
Entirely to her love; but if she lost it
Or made a gift of it, my father's eye
Should hold her loathed and his spirits should hunt
After new fancies. She, dying, gave it me   65
And bid me, when my fate would have me wive,
To give it her. I did so, and – take heed on't!
Make it a darling, like your precious eye! –
To lose't or give't away were such perdition
As nothing else could match.

DESDEMONA   Is't possible?   70

OTHELLO
'Tis true, there's magic in the web of it.
A sibyl that had numbered in the world
The sun to course two hundred compasses,
In her prophetic fury sewed the work;
The worms were hallowed that did breed the silk,   75
And it was dyed in mummy, which the skilful
Conserved of maidens' hearts.

DESDEMONA   I'faith, is't true?

OTHELLO   Most veritable, therefore look to't well.

DESDEMONA
Then would to God that I had never seen't!

OTHELLO   Ha! wherefore?   80

DESDEMONA   Why do you speak so startingly and rash?

OTHELLO   Is't lost? Is't gone? Speak, is't out o'the way?

DESDEMONA   Heaven bless us!

OTHELLO   Say you?

DESDEMONA   It is not lost, but what an if it were?   85

OTHELLO   How?

DESDEMONA   I say it is not lost.

OTHELLO   Fetch't, let me see't.

DESDEMONA   Why, so I can, sir; but I will not now.
This is a trick to put me from my suit.
Pray you, let Cassio be received again.   90

OTHELLO
Fetch me the handkerchief, my mind misgives.

DESDEMONA   Come, come,
You'll never meet a more sufficient man.

OTHELLO   The handkerchief!

DESDEMONA   I pray, talk me of Cassio.

OTHELLO   The handkerchief!

DESDEMONA   A man that all his time   95
Hath founded his good fortunes on your love,
Shared dangers with you –

OTHELLO   The handkerchief!

DESDEMONA   I'faith, you are to blame.

OTHELLO   Zounds!   *Exit.*

100 EMILIA   Is not this man jealous?

DESDEMONA   I ne'er saw this before,
     Sure there's some wonder in this handkerchief;
     I am most unhappy in the loss of it.

EMILIA   'Tis not a year or two shows us a man.
105 They are all but stomachs, and we all but food:
     They eat us hungerly, and when they are full
     They belch us.

                    Enter IAGO *and* CASSIO.

                    Look you, Cassio and my husband.

IAGO   There is no other way, 'tis she must do't,
     And lo, the happiness! go and importune her.

DESDEMONA
110 How now, good Cassio, what's the news with you?

CASSIO   Madam, my former suit. I do beseech you
     That by your virtuous means I may again
     Exist, and be a member of his love
     Whom I, with all the office of my heart
115 Entirely honour. I would not be delayed:
     If my offence be of such mortal kind
     That nor my service past nor present sorrows
     Nor purposed merit in futurity
     Can ransom me into his love again,
120 But to know so must be my benefit;
     So shall I clothe me in a forced content
     And shut myself up in some other course
     To fortune's alms.

DESDEMONA   Alas, thrice-gentle Cassio,
     My advocation is not now in tune;
125 My lord is not my lord, nor should I know him
     Were he in favour as in humour altered.
     So help me every spirit sanctified
     As I have spoken for you all my best
     And stood within the blank of his displeasure
130 For my free speech. You must awhile be patient:
     What I can do I will, and more I will
     Than for myself I dare. Let that suffice you.

IAGO   Is my lord angry?

EMILIA   He went hence but now,
     And certainly in strange unquietness.

135 IAGO   Can he be angry? I have seen the cannon
     When it hath blown his ranks into the air
     And like the devil, from his very arm,
     Puffed his own brother – and can he be angry?
     Something of moment then. I will go meet him,
140 There's matter in't indeed, if he be angry.

DESDEMONA
     I prithee do so.   *[Exit Iago.]*
                    Something sure of state
     Either from Venice, or some unhatched practice
     Made demonstrable here in Cyprus to him,
     Hath puddled his clear spirit, and in such cases
145 Men's natures wrangle with inferior things

Though great ones are their object. 'Tis even so,
     For let our finger ache and it indues
     Our other healthful members even to that sense
     Of pain. Nay, we must think men are not gods
150 Nor of them look for such observancy
     As fits the bridal. Beshrew me much, Emilia,
     I was, unhandsome warrior as I am,
     Arraigning his unkindness with my soul,
     But now I find I had suborned the witness
     And he's indicted falsely.

EMILIA   Pray heaven it be
155 State matters, as you think, and no conception
     Nor no jealous toy, concerning you.

DESDEMONA   Alas the day, I never gave him cause.

EMILIA   But jealous souls will not be answered so:
     They are not ever jealous for the cause,
160 But jealous for they're jealous. It is a monster
     Begot upon itself, born on itself.

DESDEMONA
     Heaven keep that monster from Othello's mind!

EMILIA   Lady, amen.

DESDEMONA
     I will go seek him. Cassio, walk here about,
165 If I do find him fit I'll move your suit
     And seek to effect it to my uttermost.

CASSIO   I humbly thank your ladyship.
                    Exeunt Desdemona and Emilia.

                    Enter BIANCA.

BIANCA   Save you, friend Cassio!

CASSIO   What make you from home?
     How is't with you, my most fair Bianca?
170 I'faith, sweet love, I was coming to your house.

BIANCA   And I was going to your lodging, Cassio.
     What, keep a week away? seven days and nights?
     Eight score eight hours? and lovers' absent hours
     More tedious than the dial, eight score times!
175 O weary reckoning!

CASSIO   Pardon me, Bianca,
     I have this while with leaden thoughts been pressed,
     But I shall in a more continuate time
     Strike off this score of absence. Sweet Bianca,
     [giving her Desdemona's handkerchief]
     Take me this work out.

BIANCA   O Cassio, whence came this? 180
     This is some token from a newer friend!
     To the felt absence now I feel a cause:
     Is't come to this? Well, well.

CASSIO   Go to, woman,
     Throw your vile guesses in the devil's teeth
     From whence you have them! You are jealous now 185
     That this is from some mistress, some remembrance:
     No, by my faith, Bianca.

BIANCA   Why, whose is it?

CASSIO   I know not neither, I found it in my chamber.
     I like the work well: ere it be demanded,
     As like enough it will, I'd have it copied. 190

Take it, and do't, and leave me for this time.

BIANCA   Leave you? Wherefore?

CASSIO   I do attend here on the general

And think it no addition, nor my wish,

To have him see me womaned.

BIANCA   Why, I pray you?

CASSIO   Not that I love you not.

BIANCA   But that you do not love me.

I pray you, bring me on the way a little,

And say if I shall see you soon at night.

CASSIO   'Tis but a little way that I can bring you

For I attend here, but I'll see you soon.

BIANCA   'Tis very good: I must be circumstanced.

Exeunt.

4.1   Enter OTHELLO *and* IAGO.

IAGO   Will you think so?

OTHELLO   Think so, Iago?

IAGO   What,

To kiss in private?

OTHELLO   An unauthorized kiss!

IAGO   Or to be naked with her friend in bed

An hour or more, not meaning any harm?

OTHELLO   Naked in bed, Iago, and not mean harm?

It is hypocrisy against the devil:

They that mean virtuously, and yet do so,

The devil their virtue tempts, and they tempt

heaven.

IAGO   So they do nothing, 'tis a venial slip;

But if I give my wife a handkerchief –

OTHELLO   What then?

IAGO   Why, then 'tis hers, my lord, and being hers

She may, I think, bestow't on any man.

OTHELLO   She is protectress of her honour too:

May she give that?

IAGO   Her honour is an essence that's not seen,

They have it very oft that have it not.

But for the handkerchief –

OTHELLO

By heaven, I would most gladly have forgot it!

Thou said'st – O, it comes o'er my memory

As doth the raven o'er the infectious house

Boding to all – he had my handkerchief.

IAGO   Ay, what of that?

OTHELLO   That's not so good now.

IAGO

What if I had said I had seen him do you wrong?

Or heard him say – as knaves be such abroad

Who, having by their own importunate suit

Or voluntary dotage of some mistress

Convinced or supplied them, cannot choose

But they must blab –

OTHELLO   Hath he said anything?

IAGO   He hath, my lord, but be you well assured

No more than he'll unswear.

OTHELLO   What hath he said?

IAGO

Faith, that he did – I know not what. He did –

OTHELLO   What? what?

IAGO   Lie.

OTHELLO   With her?

IAGO   With her, on her, what you will.

OTHELLO   Lie with her? lie on her? We say lie on her   35

when they belie her! Lie with her, zounds, that's

fulsome! – Handkerchief! confessions! handkerchief!

– To confess, and be hanged for his labour! First to be

hanged, and then to confess: I tremble at it. Nature

would not invest herself in such shadowing passion   40

without some instruction. It is not words that shakes

me thus. Pish! Noses, ears, and lips. Is't possible?

Confess! handkerchief! O devil! [*He falls in a trance*].

IAGO   Work on,

My medicine, work! Thus credulous fools are caught,   45

And many worthy and chaste dames even thus,

All guiltless, meet reproach. – What ho! my lord!

My lord, I say! Othello!

Enter CASSIO.

How now, Cassio?

CASSIO   What's the matter?

IAGO   My lord is fallen into an epilepsy;   50

This is his second fit, he had one yesterday.

CASSIO   Rub him about the temples.

IAGO   No, forbear:

The lethargy must have his quiet course,

If not, he foams at mouth, and by and by

Breaks out to savage madness. Look, he stirs;   55

Do you withdraw yourself a little while,

He will recover straight. When he is gone

I would on great occasion speak with you.

Exit Cassio.

How is it, general? have you not hurt your head?

OTHELLO   Dost thou mock me?

IAGO   I mock you? no, by heaven!   60

Would you would bear your fortune like a man!

OTHELLO   A horned man's a monster, and a beast.

IAGO   There's many a beast then in a populous city,

And many a civil monster.

OTHELLO   Did he confess it?

IAGO   Good sir, be a man,   65

Think every bearded fellow that's but yoked

May draw with you. There's millions now alive

That nightly lie in those unproper beds

Which they dare swear peculiar: your case is better.

O, 'tis the spite of hell, the fiend's arch-mock,   70

To lip a wanton in a secure couch

And to suppose her chaste. No, let me know,

And, knowing what I am, I know what she shall be.

OTHELLO   O, thou art wise, 'tis certain.

IAGO   Stand you a while apart,   75

Confine yourself but in a patient list.

Whilst you were here o'erwhelmed with your grief

– A passion most unsuiting such a man –

Cassio came hither. I shifted him away
80 And laid good 'scuse upon your ecstasy,
Bade him anon return and here speak with me,
The which he promised. Do but encave yourself
And mark the fleers, the gibes and notable scorns
That dwell in every region of his face;
85 For I will make him tell the tale anew
Where, how, how oft, how long ago, and when
He hath and is again to cope your wife.
I say, but mark his gesture; marry, patience,
Or I shall say you're all in all in spleen
And nothing of a man.
90 OTHELLO   Dost thou hear, Iago?
I will be found most cunning in my patience
But – dost thou hear? – most bloody.
IAGO   That's not amiss,
But yet keep time in all. Will you withdraw?
[*Othello withdraws.*]
Now will I question Cassio of Bianca,
95 A housewife that by selling her desires
Buys herself bread and clothes: it is a creature
That dotes on Cassio – as 'tis the strumpet's plague
To beguile many and be beguiled by one.
He, when he hears of her, cannot refrain
100 From the excess of laughter. Here he comes.

Enter CASSIO.

As he shall smile, Othello shall go mad.
And his unbookish jealousy must construe
Poor Cassio's smiles, gestures and light behaviour
Quite in the wrong. How do you now, lieutenant?
105 CASSIO   The worser, that you give me the addition
Whose want even kills me.
IAGO   Ply Desdemona well, and you are sure on't.
[*speaking lower*] Now if this suit lay in Bianca's power
How quickly should you speed!
CASSIO   Alas, poor caitiff!
110 OTHELLO   Look how he laughs already!
IAGO   I never knew a woman love man so.
CASSIO   Alas, poor rogue, I think i'faith she loves me.
OTHELLO   Now he denies it faintly, and laughs it out.
IAGO   Do you hear, Cassio?
OTHELLO   Now he importunes him
115 To tell it o'er; go to, well said, well said.
IAGO   She gives it out that you shall marry her;
Do you intend it?
CASSIO   Ha, ha, ha!
OTHELLO   Do ye triumph, Roman, do you triumph?
120 CASSIO   I marry! What, a customer! prithee bear some
charity to my wit, do not think it so unwholesome. Ha,
ha, ha!
OTHELLO   So, so, so, so: they laugh that win.
IAGO   Faith, the cry goes that you shall marry her.
125 CASSIO   Prithee say true!
IAGO   I am a very villain else.
OTHELLO   Have you stored me? Well.
CASSIO   This is the monkey's own giving out. She is

persuaded I will marry her, out of her own love and
flattery, not out of my promise.   130
OTHELLO   Iago beckons me: now he begins the story.
CASSIO   She was here even now, she haunts me in every
place. I was the other day talking on the sea-bank with
certain Venetians, and thither comes the bauble and,
by this hand, falls me thus about my neck –   135
OTHELLO   Crying 'O dear Cassio!' as it were: his gesture
imports it.
CASSIO   So hangs and lolls and weeps upon me, so
shakes and pulls me! Ha, ha, ha!
OTHELLO   Now he tells how she plucked him to my   140
chamber. O, I see that nose of yours, but not that dog
I shall throw it to.
CASSIO   Well, I must leave her company.
IAGO   Before me! look where she comes!

Enter BIANCA.

CASSIO   'Tis such another fitchew; marry, a perfumed   145
one. What do you mean by this haunting of me?
BIANCA   Let the devil and his dam haunt you! What did
you mean by that same handkerchief you gave me even
now? I was a fine fool to take it – I must take out the
work! A likely piece of work, that you should find it in   150
your chamber and know not who left it there! This is
some minx's token, and I must take out the work?
There, give it your hobby-horse; wheresoever you had
it, I'll take out no work on't!
CASSIO   How now, my sweet Bianca, how now, how now? 155
OTHELLO   By heaven, that should be my handkerchief!
BIANCA   If you'll come to supper tonight, you may; if
you will not, come when you are next prepared for.
                                                            Exit.
IAGO   After her, after her!
CASSIO   Faith, I must, she'll rail in the streets else.   160
IAGO   Will you sup there?
CASSIO   Faith, I intend so.
IAGO   Well, I may chance to see you, for I would very
fain speak with you.
CASSIO   Prithee come, will you?   165
IAGO   Go to, say no more.   *Exit Cassio.*
OTHELLO   How shall I murder him, Iago?
IAGO   Did you perceive how he laughed at his vice?
OTHELLO   O Iago!
IAGO   And did you see the handkerchief?   170
OTHELLO   Was that mine?
IAGO   Yours, by this hand: and to see how he prizes the
foolish woman your wife! She gave it him, and he hath
given it his whore.
OTHELLO   I would have him nine years a-killing. A fine   175
woman, a fair woman, a sweet woman!
IAGO   Nay, you must forget that.
OTHELLO   Ay, let her rot and perish and be damned
tonight, for she shall not live. No, my heart is turned
to stone: I strike it, and it hurts my hand. O, the world 180
hath not a sweeter creature: she might lie by an
emperor's side and command him tasks.

IAGO   Nay, that's not your way.

OTHELLO   Hang her, I do but say what she is: so delicate
with her needle, an admirable musician. O, she will
sing the savageness out of a bear! of so high and
plenteous wit and invention!

IAGO   She's the worse for all this.

OTHELLO   O, a thousand, a thousand times: and then of
so gentle a condition.

IAGO   Ay, too gentle.

OTHELLO   Nay, that's certain. But yet the pity of it, Iago
– O, Iago, the pity of it, Iago!

IAGO   If you are so fond over her iniquity, give her
patent to offend, for if it touch not you it comes near
nobody.

OTHELLO   I will chop her into messes! Cuckold me!

IAGO   O, 'tis foul in her.

OTHELLO   With mine officer!

IAGO   That's fouler.

OTHELLO   Get me some poison, Iago, this night. I'll not
expostulate with her, lest her body and beauty
unprovide my mind again. This night, Iago.

IAGO   Do it not with poison, strangle her in her bed –
even the bed she hath contaminated.

OTHELLO   Good, good, the justice of it pleases; very
good!

IAGO   And for Cassio, let me be his undertaker. You shall
hear more by midnight.

OTHELLO   Excellent good. [*A trumpet within.*] What
trumpet is that same?

IAGO   I warrant something from Venice.

Enter LODOVICO, DESDEMONA *and attendants.*

'Tis Lodovico, this, comes from the duke.
See, your wife's with him.

LODOVICO   God save you, worthy general.

OTHELLO   With all my heart, sir.

LODOVICO
The duke and senators of Venice greet you.
[*Gives him a letter.*]

OTHELLO   I kiss the instrument of their pleasures.
[*Opens the letter and reads.*]

DESDEMONA
And what's the news, good cousin Lodovico?

IAGO   I am very glad to see you, signior.
Welcome to Cyprus.

LODOVICO   I thank you. How does Lieutenant Cassio?

IAGO   Lives, sir.

DESDEMONA
Cousin, there's fallen between him and my lord
An unkind breach, but you shall make all well –

OTHELLO   Are you sure of that?

DESDEMONA   My lord?

OTHELLO [*Reads.*]   *This fail you not to do, as you will* –

LODOVICO   He did not call, he's busy in the paper.
Is there division 'twixt my lord and Cassio?

DESDEMONA   A most unhappy one: I would do much
T'atone them, for the love I bear to Cassio.

OTHELLO   Fire and brimstone!

DESDEMONA   My lord?

OTHELLO   Are you wise?

DESDEMONA   What, is he angry?

LODOVICO   Maybe the letter moved him.
For, as I think, they do command him home,   235
Deputing Cassio in his government.

DESDEMONA   By my troth, I am glad on't.

OTHELLO   Indeed!

DESDEMONA   My lord?

OTHELLO   I am glad . . . to see you mad.

DESDEMONA   Why, sweet Othello?

OTHELLO   Devil! [*striking her*]

DESDEMONA   I have not deserved this.   240

LODOVICO
My lord, this would not be believed in Venice
Though I should swear I saw't. 'Tis very much;
Make her amends, she weeps.

OTHELLO   O devil, devil!
If that the earth could teem with woman's tears
Each drop she falls would prove a crocodile: 245
Out of my sight!

DESDEMONA   I will not stay to offend you.

LODOVICO   Truly, an obedient lady.
I do beseech your lordship, call her back.

OTHELLO   Mistress!

DESDEMONA   My lord?   250

OTHELLO   What would you with her, sir?

LODOVICO   Who, I, my lord?

OTHELLO
Ay, you did wish that I would make her turn.
Sir, she can turn, and turn, and yet go on
And turn again. And she can weep, sir, weep.
And she's obedient: as you say, obedient,   255
Very obedient. – Proceed you in your tears. –
Concerning this, sir – O well-painted passion! –
I am commanded home. – Get you away.
I'll send for you anon. – Sir, I obey the mandate
And will return to Venice. – Hence, avaunt! –   260
                                                          Exit Desdemona.
Cassio shall have my place. And, sir, tonight
I do entreat that we may sup together.
You are welcome, sir, to Cyprus. Goats and monkeys!
                                                          Exit.

LODOVICO
Is this the noble Moor whom our full senate
Call all in all sufficient? This the nature   265
Whom passion could not shake? whose solid virtue
The shot of accident nor dart of chance
Could neither graze nor pierce?

IAGO   He is much changed.

LODOVICO   Are his wits safe? Is he not light of brain?

IAGO   He's that he is: I may not breathe my censure   270
What he might be; if what he might, he is not,
I would to heaven he were!

LODOVICO   What! strike his wife!

IAGO   Faith, that was not so well; yet would I knew

That stroke would prove the worst.

LODOVICO   Is it his use?
275   Or did the letters work upon his blood
       And new-create this fault?
IAGO   Alas, alas!
       It is not honesty in me to speak
       What I have seen and known. You shall observe him,
       And his own courses will denote him so
280   That I may save my speech. Do but go after
       And mark how he continues.
LODOVICO
       I am sorry that I am deceived in him.   *Exeunt.*

4.2   Enter OTHELLO *and* EMILIA.

OTHELLO   You have seen nothing, then?
EMILIA   Nor ever heard, nor ever did suspect.
OTHELLO
       Yes, you have seen Cassio and . . . she together.
EMILIA   But then I saw no harm, and then I heard
5   Each syllable that breath made up between them.
OTHELLO   What, did they never whisper?
EMILIA   Never, my lord.
OTHELLO   Nor send you out o'th' way?
EMILIA   Never.
OTHELLO
       To fetch her fan, her gloves, her mask, nor nothing?
10   EMILIA   Never, my lord.
OTHELLO   That's strange.
EMILIA   I durst, my lord, to wager she is honest,
       Lay down my soul at stake: if you think other
       Remove your thought, it doth abuse your bosom.
15   If any wretch have put this in your head
       Let heaven requite it with the serpent's curse,
       For if she be not honest, chaste and true
       There's no man happy: the purest of their wives
       Is foul as slander.
OTHELLO   Bid her come hither; go.
                                              Exit Emilia.
20   She says enough; yet she's a simple bawd
       That cannot say as much. This is a subtle whore,
       A closet, lock and key, of villainous secrets;
       And yet she'll kneel and pray, I have seen her do't.

                 Enter DESDEMONA *and* EMILIA.

DESDEMONA   My lord, what is your will?
OTHELLO   Pray, chuck, come hither.
DESDEMONA   What is your pleasure?
25   OTHELLO   Let me see your eyes.
       Look in my face.
DESDEMONA   What horrible fancy's this?
OTHELLO [*to Emilia*]   Some of your function, mistress,
       Leave procreants alone and shut the door;
       Cough, or cry hem, if anybody come.
30   Your mystery, your mystery: nay, dispatch!
                                              Exit Emilia.
DESDEMONA
       Upon my knees, what doth your speech import?

I understand a fury in your words
       But not the words.
OTHELLO   Why, what art thou?
DESDEMONA
       Your wife, my lord: your true and loyal wife.   35
OTHELLO   Come, swear it, damn thyself,
       Lest, being like one of heaven, the devils themselves
       Should fear to seize thee: therefore be double-
          damned,
       Swear thou art honest!
DESDEMONA   Heaven doth truly know it.
OTHELLO
       Heaven truly knows that thou art false as hell.   40
DESDEMONA
       To whom, my lord? with whom? how am I false?
OTHELLO   Ah, Desdemon, away, away, away!
DESDEMONA   Alas the heavy day, why do you weep?
       Am I the motive of these tears, my lord?
       If haply you my father do suspect   45
       An instrument of this your calling back,
       Lay not your blame on me: if you have lost him
       Why, I have lost him too.
OTHELLO   Had it pleased heaven
       To try me with affliction, had they rained
       All kinds of sores and shames on my bare head,   50
       Steeped me in poverty to the very lips,
       Given to captivity me and my utmost hopes,
       I should have found in some place of my soul
       A drop of patience; but, alas, to make me
       The fixed figure for the time of scorn   55
       To point his slow and moving finger at!
       Yet could I bear that too, well, very well:
       But there where I have garnered up my heart,
       Where either I must live or bear no life,
       The fountain from the which my current runs   60
       Or else dries up – to be discarded thence!
       Or keep it as a cistern for foul toads
       To knot and gender in! Turn thy complexion there,
       Patience, thou young and rose-lipped cherubin,
       Ay, here look, grim as hell!   65
DESDEMONA   I hope my noble lord esteems me honest.
OTHELLO   O, ay, as summer flies are in the shambles,
       That quicken even with blowing. O thou weed
       Who art so lovely fair and smell'st so sweet
       That the sense aches at thee, would thou hadst ne'er
          been born!   70
DESDEMONA
       Alas, what ignorant sin have I committed?
OTHELLO   Was this fair paper, this most goodly book
       Made to write 'whore' upon? What committed!
       Committed? O thou public commoner!
       I should make very forges of my cheeks   75
       That would to cinders burn up modesty
       Did I but speak thy deeds. What committed!
       Heaven stops the nose at it, and the moon winks,
       The bawdy wind that kisses all it meets
       Is hushed within the hollow mine of earth   80

And will not hear't. What committed!
  Impudent strumpet!
DESDEMONA   By heaven, you do me wrong.
OTHELLO   Are not you a strumpet?
DESDEMONA   No, as I am a Christian.
  If to preserve this vessel for my lord
  From any hated foul unlawful touch
  Be not to be a strumpet, I am none.
OTHELLO   What, not a whore?
DESDEMONA   No, as I shall be saved.
OTHELLO   Is't possible?
DESDEMONA   O heaven, forgive us!
OTHELLO   I cry you mercy then,
  I took you for that cunning whore of Venice
  That married with Othello. You! Mistress!

                Enter EMILIA.

  That have the office opposite to Saint Peter
  And keep the gates of hell – you, you, ay you!
  We have done our course, there's money for your
      pains,
  I pray you turn the key and keep our counsel.   *Exit.*
EMILIA   Alas, what does this gentleman conceive?
  How do you, madam? how do you, my good lady?
DESDEMONA   Faith, half asleep.
EMILIA   Good madam, what's the matter with my lord?
DESDEMONA   With whom?
EMILIA   Why, with my lord, madam.
DESDEMONA   Who is thy lord?
EMILIA   He that is yours, sweet lady.
DESDEMONA   I have none. Do not talk to me, Emilia;
  I cannot weep, nor answers have I none
  But what should go by water. Prithee, tonight
  Lay on my bed my wedding sheets; remember,
  And call thy husband hither.
EMILIA   Here's a change indeed!
                                              Exit.
DESDEMONA   'Tis meet I should be used so, very meet.
  How have I been behaved that he might stick
  The small'st opinion on my greatest misuse?

                Enter IAGO *and* EMILIA.

IAGO
  What is your pleasure, madam? How is't with you?
DESDEMONA
  I cannot tell. Those that do teach young babes
  Do it with gentle means and easy tasks.
  He might have chid me so, for, in good faith,
  I am a child to chiding.
IAGO   What is the matter, lady?
EMILIA   Alas, Iago, my lord hath so bewhored her,
  Thrown such despite and heavy terms upon her
  That true hearts cannot bear it.
DESDEMONA   Am I that name, Iago?
IAGO   What name, fair lady?
DESDEMONA   Such as she said my lord did say I was.
EMILIA   He called her whore. A beggar in his drink

Could not have laid such terms upon his callat.
IAGO   Why did he so?
DESDEMONA   I do not know; I am sure I am none such.   125
IAGO   Do not weep, do not weep: alas the day!
EMILIA   Hath she forsook so many noble matches,
  Her father, and her country, and her friends,
  To be called whore? would it not make one weep?
DESDEMONA   It is my wretched fortune.
IAGO   Beshrew him for't,   130
  How comes this trick upon him?
DESDEMONA   Nay, heaven doth know.
EMILIA   I will be hanged if some eternal villain
  Some busy and insinuating rogue,
  Some cogging, cozening slave, to get some office,
  Have not devised this slander, I'll be hanged else!   135
IAGO   Fie, there is no such man, it is impossible.
DESDEMONA   If any such there be, heaven pardon him.
EMILIA   A halter pardon him, and hell gnaw his bones!
  Why should he call her whore? who keeps her
      company?
  What place, what time, what form, what likelihood?   140
  The Moor's abused by some most villainous knave,
  Some base notorious knave, some scurvy fellow.
  O heaven, that such companions thou'dst unfold
  And put in every honest hand a whip
  To lash the rascals naked through the world   145
  Even from the east to th' west.
IAGO   Speak within doors.
EMILIA   O fie upon them! some such squire he was
  That turned your wit the seamy side without
  And made you to suspect me with the Moor.
IAGO   You are a fool, go to.
DESDEMONA   O God, Iago,   150
  What shall I do to win my lord again?
  Good friend, go to him, for, by this light of heaven,
  I know not how I lost him. Here I kneel:
  If e'er my will did trespass 'gainst his love
  Either in discourse of thought or actual deed,   155
  Or that mine eyes, mine ears or any sense
  Delighted them in any other form,
  Or that I do not yet, and ever did,
  And ever will – though he do shake me off
  To beggarly divorcement – love him dearly,   160
  Comfort forswear me! Unkindness may do much,
  And his unkindness may defeat my life
  But never taint my love. I cannot say whore:
  It does abhor me now I speak the word;
  To do the act that might the addition earn   165
  Not the world's mass of vanity could make me.
IAGO   I pray you, be content, 'tis but his humour;
  The business of the state does him offence
  And he does chide with you.
DESDEMONA   If 'twere no other –
IAGO   'Tis but so, I warrant.   170
                                        [*Trumpets.*]
  Hark how these instruments summon to supper:
  The messengers of Venice stay the meat,

Go in, and weep not; all things shall be well.
                    Exeunt Desdemona and Emilia.

                    Enter RODERIGO.

How now, Roderigo?

175   RODERIGO   I do not find that thou deal'st justly with me.

     IAGO   What in the contrary?

     RODERIGO   Every day thou doff'st me with some device, Iago, and rather, as it seems to me now, keep'st from me all conveniency than suppliest me with the least

180   advantage of hope. I will indeed no longer endure it; nor am I yet persuaded to put up in peace what already I have foolishly suffered.

     IAGO   Will you hear me, Roderigo?

     RODERIGO   Faith, I have heard too much; and your

185   words and performances are no kin together.

     IAGO   You charge me most unjustly.

     RODERIGO   With nought but truth. I have wasted myself out of my means. The jewels you have had from me to deliver to Desdemona would half have corrupted a

190   votarist. You have told me she hath received them, and returned me expectations and comforts of sudden respect and acquittance, but I find none.

     IAGO   Well, go to; very well.

     RODERIGO   'Very well,' 'go to'! I cannot go to, man, nor

195   'tis not very well. By this hand, I think it is scurvy, and begin to find myself fopped in it.

     IAGO   Very well.

     RODERIGO   I tell you, 'tis not very well! I will make myself known to Desdemona: if she will return me my

200   jewels I will give over my suit and repent my unlawful solicitation; if not, assure yourself I will seek satisfaction of you.

     IAGO   You have said now.

     RODERIGO   Ay, and said nothing but what I protest

205   intendment of doing.

     IAGO   Why, now I see there's mettle in thee, and even from this instant do build on thee a better opinion than ever before. Give me thy hand, Roderigo. Thou hast taken against me a most just exception – but yet I

210   protest I have dealt most directly in thy affair.

     RODERIGO   It hath not appeared.

     IAGO   I grant indeed it hath not appeared, and your suspicion is not without wit and judgement. But, Roderigo, if thou hast that in thee indeed which I have

215   greater reason to believe now than ever – I mean purpose, courage, and valour – this night show it. If thou the next night following enjoy not Desdemona, take me from this world with treachery and devise engines for my life.

220   RODERIGO   Well – what is it? Is it within reason and compass?

     IAGO   Sir, there is especial commission come from Venice to depute Cassio in Othello's place.

     RODERIGO   Is that true? Why, then Othello and

225   Desdemona return again to Venice.

     IAGO   O no, he goes into Mauretania and taketh away with him the fair Desdemona, unless his abode be lingered here by some accident – wherein none can be so determinate as the removing of Cassio.

     RODERIGO   How do you mean, removing of him?   230

     IAGO   Why, by making him uncapable of Othello's place: knocking out his brains.

     RODERIGO   And that you would have me to do!

     IAGO   Ay, if you dare do yourself a profit and a right. He sups tonight with a harlotry, and thither will I go to   235 him. He knows not yet of his honourable fortune: if you will watch his going thence – which I will fashion to fall out between twelve and one – you may take him at your pleasure. I will be near to second your attempt, and he shall fall between us. Come, stand not amazed   240 at it, but go along with me: I will show you such a necessity in his death that you shall think yourself bound to put it on him. It is now high supper time, and the night grows to waste: about it.

     RODERIGO   I will hear further reason for this.   245

     IAGO   And you shall be satisfied.   *Exeunt.*

4.3   Enter OTHELLO, LODOVICO, DESDEMONA, EMILIA
                    and attendants.

LODOVICO
   I do beseech you, sir, trouble yourself no further.

OTHELLO   O, pardon me, 'twill do me good to walk.

LODOVICO
   Madam, good night: I humbly thank your ladyship.

DESDEMONA   Your honour is most welcome.

OTHELLO   Will you walk, sir?
   O, Desdemona –

DESDEMONA   My lord?

OTHELLO   Get you to bed   5
   On th'instant, I will be returned forthwith.
   Dismiss your attendant there: look't be done.

DESDEMONA   I will, my lord.
            Exeunt Othello, Lodovico and attendants.

EMILIA
   How goes it now? He looks gentler than he did.

DESDEMONA   He says he will return incontinent,   10
   And hath commanded me to go to bed
   And bid me to dismiss you.

EMILIA   Dismiss me?

DESDEMONA
   It was his bidding; therefore, good Emilia,
   Give me my nightly wearing, and adieu.
   We must not now displease him.   15

EMILIA   Ay. – Would you had never seen him!

DESDEMONA
   So would not I: my love doth so approve him
   That even his stubbornness, his checks, his frowns
   – Prithee unpin me – have grace and favour.

EMILIA
   I have laid those sheets you bade me on the bed.   20

DESDEMONA
   All's one. Good faith, how foolish are our minds!

If I do die before thee, prithee shroud me
In one of these same sheets.

EMILIA   Come, come, you talk.

DESDEMONA
My mother had a maid called Barbary,
She was in love, and he she loved proved mad
And did forsake her. She had a song of 'willow',
An old thing 'twas, but it expressed her fortune
And she died singing it. That song tonight
Will not go from my mind. I have much to do
But to go hang my head all at one side
And sing it like poor Barbary. Prithee dispatch.

EMILIA   Shall I go fetch your night-gown?

DESDEMONA   No, unpin me here.

EMILIA   This Lodovico is a proper man. A very
handsome man.

DESDEMONA   He speaks well.

EMILIA   I know a lady in Venice would have walked
barefoot to Palestine for a touch of his nether lip.

DESDEMONA [*Sings.*]
The poor soul sat sighing by a sycamore tree,
    Sing all a green willow:
Her hand on her bosom, her head on her knee,
    Sing willow, willow, willow.
The fresh streams ran by her and murmured her
    moans,
    Sing willow, willow, willow:
Her salt tears fell from her and softened the stones,
    Sing willow, willow, willow.
[*Speaks.*] Lay by these.
    Willow, willow –
[*Speaks.*] Prithee hie thee: he'll come anon.
Sing all a green willow must be my garland.
Let nobody blame him, his scorn I approve –
[*Speaks.*] Nay, that's not next. Hark, who is't that
    knocks?

EMILIA   It's the wind.

DESDEMONA [*Sings.*]
I called my love false love; but what said he then?
    Sing willow, willow, willow:
If I court moe women, you'll couch with moe men.
[*Speaks.*] So, get thee gone; good night. Mine eyes do
    itch,
Doth that bode weeping?

EMILIA   'Tis neither here nor there.

DESDEMONA
I have heard it said so. O, these men, these men!
Dost thou in conscience think – tell me, Emilia –
That there be women do abuse their husbands
In such gross kind?

EMILIA   There be some such, no question.

DESDEMONA
Wouldst thou do such a deed for all the world?

EMILIA   Why, would not you?

DESDEMONA   No, by this heavenly light!

EMILIA   Nor I neither, by this heavenly light:
I might do't as well i'th' dark.

DESDEMONA
Wouldst thou do such a deed for all the world?

EMILIA   The world's a huge thing: it is a great price
For a small vice.

DESDEMONA   Good troth, I think thou wouldst not.

EMILIA   By my troth, I think I should, and undo't when 70
I had done. Marry, I would not do such a thing for a
joint-ring, nor for measures of lawn, nor for gowns,
petticoats, nor caps, nor any petty exhibition. But for
all the whole world? ud's pity, who would not make
her husband a cuckold to make him a monarch? I 75
should venture purgatory for't.

DESDEMONA   Beshrew me, if I would do such a wrong
For the whole world!

EMILIA   Why, the wrong is but a wrong i'th' world; and
having the world for your labour, 'tis a wrong in your 80
own world, and you might quickly make it right.

DESDEMONA   I do not think there is any such woman.

EMILIA   Yes, a dozen, and as many to th' vantage as
would store the world they played for.
But I do think it is their husbands' faults 85
If wives do fall. Say that they slack their duties
And pour our treasures into foreign laps;
Or else break out in peevish jealousies,
Throwing restraint upon us; or say they strike us,
Or scant our former having in despite, 90
Why, we have galls: and though we have some grace
Yet have we some revenge. Let husbands know
Their wives have sense like them: they see, and smell,
And have their palates both for sweet and sour
As husbands have. What is it that they do 95
When they change us for others? Is it sport?
I think it is. And doth affection breed it?
I think it doth. Is't frailty that thus errs?
It is so too. And have not we affections?
Desires for sport? and frailty, as men have? 100
Then let them use us well: else let them know,
The ills we do, their ills instruct us so.

DESDEMONA
Good night, good night. God me such usage send
Not to pick bad from bad, but by bad mend!

                                    Exeunt.

5.1   *Enter* IAGO *and* RODERIGO.

IAGO
Here, stand behind this bulk, straight will he come.
Wear thy good rapier bare, and put it home;
Quick, quick, fear nothing, I'll be at thy elbow.
It makes us or it mars us, think on that
And fix most firm thy resolution. 5

RODERIGO   Be near at hand, I may miscarry in't.

IAGO   Here, at thy hand: be bold, and take thy stand.
[*Retires.*]

RODERIGO   I have no great devotion to the deed
And yet he hath given me satisfying reasons:
'Tis but a man gone. Forth, my sword: he dies. 10

IAGO

    I have rubbed this young quat almost to the sense
    And he grows angry. Now, whether he kill Cassio
    Or Cassio him, or each do kill the other,
    Every way makes my gain. Live Roderigo,
15   He calls me to a restitution large
    Of gold and jewels that I bobbed from him
    As gifts to Desdemona:
    It must not be. If Cassio do remain
    He hath a daily beauty in his life
20   That makes me ugly; and besides, the Moor
    May unfold me to him – there stand I in much peril.
    No, he must die. Be't so! I hear him coming.

Enter CASSIO.

RODERIGO   I know his gait, 'tis he. Villain, thou diest!
    [*Makes a thrust at Cassio.*]
CASSIO   That thrust had been mine enemy indeed
25   But that my coat is better than thou know'st:
    I will make proof of thine.
    [*Draws, and wounds Roderigo.*]
RODERIGO   O, I am slain!
    [*Iago from behind wounds Cassio in the leg, and exit.*]
CASSIO
    I am maimed for ever! Help, ho! murder! murder!

Enter OTHELLO.

OTHELLO   The voice of Cassio. Iago keeps his word.
RODERIGO   O, villain that I am!
OTHELLO   It is even so.
30 CASSIO   O, help ho! light! a surgeon!
OTHELLO   'Tis he. O brave Iago, honest and just,
    That hast such noble sense of thy friend's wrong!
    Thou teachest me. Minion, your dear lies dead,
    And your unblest fate hies; strumpet, I come.
    Forth of my heart those charms, thine eyes, are
35   blotted,
    Thy bed, lust-stained, shall with lust's blood be
      spotted.   *Exit.*

Enter LODOVICO *and* GRATIANO.

CASSIO
    What ho, no watch, no passage? murder, murder!
GRATIANO
    'Tis some mischance, the voice is very direful.
CASSIO   O help!
40 LODOVICO   Hark!
RODERIGO   O wretched villain!
LODOVICO   Two or three groan. It is a heavy night;
    These may be counterfeits, let's think't unsafe
    To come in to the cry without more help.
45 RODERIGO   Nobody come? then shall I bleed to death.

Enter IAGO, *with a light.*

LODOVICO   Hark!
GRATIANO
    Here's one comes in his shirt, with light and weapons.

IAGO
    Who's there? Whose noise is this that cries on
      murder?
LODOVICO   We do not know.
IAGO   Did not you hear a cry?
CASSIO   Here, here! for heaven's sake help me!
IAGO   What's the matter?   50
GRATIANO   This is Othello's ancient, as I take it.
LODOVICO   The same indeed, a very valiant fellow.
IAGO   What are you here that cry so grievously?
CASSIO   Iago? O, I am spoiled, undone by villains!
    Give me some help.   55
IAGO   O me, lieutenant! What villains have done this?
CASSIO   I think that one of them is hereabout
    And cannot make away.
IAGO   O treacherous villains!
    What are you there? Come in, and give some help.
RODERIGO   O, help me here!   60
CASSIO   That's one of them.
IAGO   O murderous slave! O villain!
    [*Stabs Roderigo.*]
RODERIGO   O damned Iago! O inhuman dog!
IAGO
    Kill men i'th' dark? Where be these bloody thieves?
    How silent is this town! Ho, murder, murder!
    What may you be? Are you of good or evil?   65
LODOVICO   As you shall prove us, praise us.
IAGO   Signior Lodovico?
LODOVICO   He, sir.
IAGO   I cry you mercy: here's Cassio hurt by villains.
GRATIANO   Cassio?   70
IAGO   How is't, brother?
CASSIO   My leg is cut in two.
IAGO   Marry, heaven forbid!
    Light, gentlemen, I'll bind it with my shirt.

Enter BIANCA.

BIANCA   What is the matter, ho? who is't that cried?
IAGO   Who is't that cried?
BIANCA   O my dear Cassio!   75
    My sweet Cassio! O Cassio, Cassio, Cassio!
IAGO   O notable strumpet! Cassio, may you suspect
    Who they should be that have thus mangled you?
CASSIO   No.
GRATIANO   I am sorry to find you thus;   80
    I have been to seek you.
IAGO   Lend me a garter. So. – O for a chair
    To bear him easily hence!
BIANCA   Alas, he faints! O Cassio, Cassio, Cassio!
IAGO   Gentlemen all, I do suspect this trash   85
    To be a party in this injury.
    Patience awhile, good Cassio. Come, come,
    Lend me a light. Know we this face, or no?
    Alas, my friend and my dear countryman,
    Roderigo? No – yes sure! – O heaven, Roderigo!   90
GRATIANO   What, of Venice?
IAGO   Even he, sir. Did you know him?

GRATIANO   Know him? Ay.

IAGO   Signior Gratiano? I cry you gentle pardon:
These bloody accidents must excuse my manners
That so neglected you.

GRATIANO   I am glad to see you.

IAGO   How do you, Cassio? O, a chair, a chair!

GRATIANO   Roderigo?

IAGO
He, he, 'tis he. [*A chair is brought in.*]
                    O, that's well said, the chair.
Some good man bear him carefully from hence,
I'll fetch the general's surgeon. [*to Bianca.*]
                                        For you, mistress,
Save you your labour. – He that lies slain here,
    Cassio,
Was my dear friend. What malice was between you?

CASSIO   None in the world, nor do I know the man.

IAGO [*to Bianca*]
What, look you pale? – O, bear him out o'th' air.
– Stay you, good gentlemen. – Look you pale,
    mistress?
– Do you perceive the gastness of her eye?
– Nay, if you stare we shall hear more anon.
– Behold her well, I pray you, look upon her:
Do you see, gentlemen? nay, guiltiness will speak
Though tongues were out of use.

Enter EMILIA.

EMILIA   'Las, what's the matter?
What's the matter, husband?

IAGO   Cassio hath here been set on in the dark
By Roderigo and fellows that are 'scaped:
He's almost slain, and Roderigo dead.

EMILIA   Alas, good gentleman! alas, good Cassio!

IAGO   This is the fruits of whoring. Prithee, Emilia,
Go know of Cassio where he supped tonight.
What, do you shake at that?

BIANCA
He supped at my house, but I therefore shake not.

IAGO   O, did he so? I charge you, go with me.

EMILIA   O fie upon thee, strumpet!

BIANCA   I am no strumpet
But of life as honest as you, that thus
    Abuse me.

EMILIA   As I? Foh, fie upon thee!

IAGO
Kind gentlemen, let's go see poor Cassio dressed.
Come, mistress, you must tell's another tale.
Emilia, run you to the citadel
And tell my lord and lady what hath happed.
– Will you go on afore? – This is the night
That either makes me or fordoes me quite.   *Exeunt.*

5.2   *Enter* OTHELLO, *with a light.* DESDEMONA *in her bed asleep.*

OTHELLO   It is the cause, it is the cause, my soul!
Let me not name it to you, you chaste stars,
It is the cause. Yet I'll not shed her blood
Nor scar that whiter skin of hers than snow
And smooth as monumental alabaster: 5
Yet she must die, else she'll betray more men.
Put out the light, and then put out the light!
If I quench thee, thou flaming minister,
I can again thy former light restore
Should I repent me. But once put out thy light,   10
Thou cunning'st pattern of excelling nature,
I know not where is that Promethean heat
That can thy light relume: when I have plucked the
    rose
I cannot give it vital growth again,
It needs must wither. I'll smell thee on the tree;   15
O balmy breath, that dost almost persuade
Justice to break her sword! Once more, once more:
Be thus when thou art dead and I will kill thee
And love thee after. Once more, and that's the last.
[*He smells, then kisses her.*]
So sweet was ne'er so fatal. I must weep,   20
But they are cruel tears. This sorrow's heavenly,
It strikes where it doth love. She wakes.

DESDEMONA   Who's there? Othello?

OTHELLO   Ay, Desdemona.

DESDEMONA   Will you come to bed, my lord?

OTHELLO   Have you prayed tonight, Desdemon?

DESDEMONA   Ay, my lord.   25

OTHELLO   If you bethink yourself of any crime
Unreconciled as yet to heaven and grace,
Solicit for it straight.

DESDEMONA
Alack, my lord, what may you mean by that?

OTHELLO
Well, do it, and be brief; I will walk by.   30
I would not kill thy unprepared spirit,
No, heaven forfend, I would not kill thy soul.

DESDEMONA   Talk you of killing?

OTHELLO   Ay, I do.

DESDEMONA   Then, heaven,
Have mercy on me!

OTHELLO   Amen, with all my heart.

DESDEMONA   If you say so, I hope you will not kill me.   35

OTHELLO   Hum!

DESDEMONA   And yet I fear you, for you're fatal then
When your eyes roll so. Why I should fear I know
    not,
Since guiltiness I know not. But yet I feel I fear.

OTHELLO   Think on thy sins.

DESDEMONA   They are loves I bear to you.   40

OTHELLO   Ay, and for that thou diest.

DESDEMONA
That death's unnatural that kills for loving.
Alas, why gnaw you so your nether lip?
Some bloody passion shakes your very frame,
These are portents: but yet I hope, I hope   45
They do not point on me.

OTHELLO   Peace, and be still.

DESDEMONA   I will. So: what's the matter?

OTHELLO   That handkerchief
Which I so loved and gave thee, thou gavest
To Cassio.

DESDEMONA   No, by my life and soul:
Send for the man and ask him.

50   OTHELLO   Sweet soul, take heed,
Take heed of perjury. Thou art on thy death-bed.

DESDEMONA   I? – but not yet to die!

OTHELLO   Yes, presently.
Therefore confess thee freely of thy sin,
For to deny each article with oath
55   Cannot remove nor choke the strong conception
That I do groan withal. Thou art to die.

DESDEMONA   Then Lord have mercy on me.

OTHELLO   I say amen.

DESDEMONA   And have you mercy too. I never did
Offend you in my life, never loved Cassio
60   But with such general warranty of heaven
As I might love: I never gave him token.

OTHELLO   By heaven, I saw my handkerchief in's hand!
O perjured woman, thou dost stone my heart
And makest me call what I intend to do
65   A murder, which I thought a sacrifice!
I saw the handkerchief.

DESDEMONA   He found it then,
I never gave it him. Send for him hither,
Let him confess the truth.

OTHELLO   He hath confessed.

DESDEMONA   What, my lord?

OTHELLO   That he hath – ud's death! – used thee.

DESDEMONA   How? unlawfully?

OTHELLO   Ay.

70   DESDEMONA   He will not say so.

OTHELLO   No, his mouth is stopped. Honest Iago
Hath ta'en order for't.

DESDEMONA   O, my fear interprets!
What, is he dead?

OTHELLO   Had all his hairs been lives
My great revenge had stomach for them all.

75   DESDEMONA   Alas, he is betrayed, and I undone.

OTHELLO
Out, strumpet, weep'st thou for him to my face?

DESDEMONA   O, banish me, my lord, but kill me not!

OTHELLO   Down, strumpet!

DESDEMONA   Kill me tomorrow, let me live tonight!

80   OTHELLO   Nay, if you strive –

DESDEMONA   But half an hour!

OTHELLO   Being done, there is no pause –

DESDEMONA   But while I say one prayer!

OTHELLO   It is too late.

DESDEMONA   O Lord! Lord! Lord! [*He smothers her.*]

EMILIA [*within*]
My lord, my lord! what ho, my lord, my lord!

OTHELLO
85   What noise is this? Not dead? not yet quite dead?
I that am cruel am yet merciful,

I would not have thee linger in thy pain.
So, so.

EMILIA [*within*]   What ho! my lord! my lord!

OTHELLO   Who's there?

EMILIA [*within*]
O good my lord, I'd speak a word with you.   90

OTHELLO   Yes. 'Tis Emilia. –
[*to Emilia*]   By and by. – She's dead.
'Tis like she comes to speak of Cassio's death,
The noise was high. Ha, no more moving?
Still as the grave. Shall she come in? were't good?
I think she stirs again. No – what's best to do?   95
If she come in, she'll sure speak to my wife.
My wife, my wife! what wife? I have no wife.
O insupportable, O heavy hour!
Methinks it should be now a huge eclipse
Of sun and moon, and that th'affrighted globe   100
Should yawn at alteration.

EMILIA [*within*]   I do beseech you
That I may speak with you! O good my lord!

OTHELLO   I had forgot thee: O come in, Emilia.
Soft, by and by. Let me the curtains draw.
Where art thou? What's the matter with thee now?   105
[*He unlocks the door.*]

Enter EMILIA.

EMILIA   O my good lord, yonder's foul murders done!

OTHELLO   What? Now?

EMILIA   But now, my lord.

OTHELLO   It is the very error of the moon,
She comes more nearer earth than she was wont   110
And makes men mad.

EMILIA   Cassio, my lord, hath killed
A young Venetian, called Roderigo.

OTHELLO   Roderigo killed? and Cassio killed?

EMILIA   No, Cassio is not killed.

OTHELLO   Not Cassio killed?
Then murder's out of tune, and sweet revenge   115
Grows harsh.

DESDEMONA   O falsely, falsely murdered!

EMILIA   O lord, what cry is that?

OTHELLO   That? what?

EMILIA
Out and alas, that was my lady's voice:
[*She draws the bed-curtains.*]
Help, help, ho, help! O lady, speak again,   120
Sweet Desdemona, O sweet mistress, speak!

DESDEMONA   A guiltless death I die.

EMILIA   O, who hath done
This deed?

DESDEMONA   Nobody. I myself. Farewell.
Commend me to my kind lord – O, farewell!   125
[*She dies.*]

OTHELLO   Why, how should she be murdered?

EMILIA   Alas, who knows?

OTHELLO   You heard her say herself it was not I.

EMILIA   She said so; I must needs report the truth.

OTHELLO   She's like a liar gone to burning hell:
   'Twas I that killed her.
EMILIA   O, the more angel she,
   And you the blacker devil!
OTHELLO   She turned to folly, and she was a whore.
EMILIA   Thou dost belie her, and thou art a devil.
OTHELLO   She was false as water.
EMILIA   Thou art rash as fire to say
   That she was false. O, she was heavenly true!
OTHELLO   Cassio did top her: ask thy husband else.
   O, I were damned beneath all depth in hell
   But that I did proceed upon just grounds
   To this extremity. Thy husband knew it all.
EMILIA   My husband?
OTHELLO   Thy husband.
EMILIA   That she was false?
   To wedlock?
OTHELLO   Ay, with Cassio. Had she been true,
   If heaven would make me such another world
   Of one entire and perfect chrysolite,
   I'd not have sold her for it.
EMILIA   My husband?
OTHELLO
   Ay, 'twas he that told me on her first;
   An honest man he is, and hates the slime
   That sticks on filthy deeds.
EMILIA   My husband!
OTHELLO   What needs
   This iterance, woman? I say thy husband.
EMILIA
   O mistress, villainy hath made mocks with love!
   My husband say she was false?
OTHELLO   He, woman;
   I say thy husband: dost understand the word?
   My friend thy husband, honest, honest Iago.
EMILIA   If he say so, may his pernicious soul
   Rot half a grain a day! he lies to th' heart:
   She was too fond of her most filthy bargain!
OTHELLO   Ha!
EMILIA   Do thy worst:
   This deed of thine is no more worthy heaven
   Than thou wast worthy her.
OTHELLO   Peace, you were best!
EMILIA
   Thou hast not half that power to do me harm.
   As I have to be hurt. O gull, O dolt,
   As ignorant as dirt! Thou hast done a deed
   [*He threatens her with his sword.*]
   – I care not for thy sword, I'll make thee known
   Though I lost twenty lives. Help, help, ho, help!
   The Moor hath killed my mistress! Murder, murder!

        Enter MONTANO, GRATIANO *and* IAGO.

MONTANO   What is the matter? How now, general?
EMILIA   O, are you come, Iago? you have done well
   That men must lay their murders on your neck.
GRATIANO   What is the matter?

EMILIA   Disprove this villain, if thou be'st a man;   170
   He says thou told'st him that his wife was false,
   I know thou didst not, thou'rt not such a villain.
   Speak, for my heart is full.
IAGO   I told him what I thought, and told no more
   Than what he found himself was apt and true.   175
EMILIA   But did you ever tell him she was false?
IAGO   I did.
EMILIA   You told a lie, an odious, damned lie!
   Upon my soul, a lie, a wicked lie!
   She false with Cassio? Did you say with Cassio?   180
IAGO   With Cassio, mistress. Go to, charm your tongue.
EMILIA
   I will not charm my tongue, I am bound to speak:
   My mistress here lies murdered in her bed.
ALL   O heavens forfend!
EMILIA   And your reports have set the murder on.   185
OTHELLO   Nay, stare not, masters, it is true indeed.
GRATIANO   'Tis a strange truth.
MONTANO   O monstrous act!
EMILIA   Villainy, villainy, villainy!
   I think upon't, I think I smell't, O villainy!   190
   I thought so then: I'll kill myself for grief!
   O villainy, villainy!
IAGO   What, are you mad? I charge you, get you home.
EMILIA
   Good gentlemen, let me have leave to speak.
   'Tis proper I obey him – but not now.   195
   Perchance, Iago, I will ne'er go home.
OTHELLO   O! O! O! [*Othello falls on the bed.*]
EMILIA   Nay, lay thee down and roar
   For thou hast killed the sweetest innocent
   That e'er did lift up eye.
OTHELLO   O, she was foul.   200
   I scarce did know you, uncle: there lies your niece
   Whose breath, indeed, these hands have newly
     stopped;
   I know this act shows horrible and grim.
GRATIANO
   Poor Desdemon, I am glad thy father's dead;
   Thy match was mortal to him, and pure grief   205
   Shore his old thread in twain. Did he live now
   This sight would make him do a desperate turn,
   Yea, curse his better angel from his side
   And fall to reprobance.
OTHELLO   'Tis pitiful; but yet Iago knows   210
   That she with Cassio hath the act of shame
   A thousand times committed. Cassio confessed it,
   And she did gratify his amorous works
   With that recognizance and pledge of love
   Which I first gave her: I saw it in his hand,   215
   It was a handkerchief, an antique token
   My father gave my mother.
EMILIA   O God, O heavenly God!
IAGO   Zounds, hold your peace!
EMILIA   'Twill out, 'twill out! I peace?
   No, I will speak as liberal as the north.   220

Let heaven and men and devils, let them all,
All, all cry shame against me, yet I'll speak.

IAGO   Be wise, and get you home.

EMILIA   I will not. [*Iago tries to stab Emilia.*]

GRATIANO   Fie! Your sword upon a woman?

EMILIA
225   O thou dull Moor, that handkerchief thou speak'st of
I found by fortune and did give my husband,
For often, with a solemn earnestness
– More than indeed belonged to such a trifle –
He begged of me to steal't.

IAGO   Villainous whore!

EMILIA   She give it Cassio? No, alas, I found it
230   And I did give't my husband.

IAGO   Filth, thou liest!

EMILIA   By heaven I do not, I do not, gentlemen!
O murderous coxcomb, what should such a fool
Do with so good a wife?
[*Othello runs at Iago. Iago stabs his wife.*]

OTHELLO   Are there no stones in heaven
235   But what serves for the thunder? Precious villain!

GRATIANO
The woman falls, sure he hath killed his wife.

EMILIA
Ay, ay; O lay me by my mistress' side.   *Exit Iago.*

GRATIANO   He's gone, but his wife's killed.

MONTANO
'Tis a notorious villain. Take you this weapon
240   Which I have here recovered from the Moor;
Come, guard the door without, let him not pass
But kill him rather. I'll after that same villain,
For 'tis a damned slave.
                    Exeunt Montano and Gratiano.

OTHELLO   I am not valiant neither,
But every puny whipster gets my sword.
245   But why should honour outlive honesty?
Let it go all.

EMILIA   What did thy song bode, lady?
Hark, canst thou hear me? I will play the swan
And die in music. [*Sings.*] Willow, willow, willow.
– Moor, she was chaste, she loved thee, cruel Moor,
250   So come my soul to bliss as I speak true!
So speaking as I think, alas, I die. [*She dies.*]

OTHELLO   I have another weapon in this chamber,
It is a sword of Spain, the ice-brook's temper;
O, here it is. Uncle, I must come forth.

GRATIANO [*within*]
255   If thou attempt it it will cost thee dear;
Thou hast no weapon, and perforce must suffer.

OTHELLO
Look in upon me then, and speak with me,
Or, naked as I am, I will assault thee.

Enter GRATIANO.

GRATIANO   What is the matter?

OTHELLO   Behold, I have a weapon,
260   A better never did itself sustain

Upon a soldier's thigh. I have seen the day
That with this little arm and this good sword
I have made my way through more impediments
Than twenty times your stop: but, O vain boast,
Who can control his fate? 'Tis not so now.   265
Be not afraid, though you do see me weaponed:
Here is my journey's end, here is my butt
And very sea-mark of my utmost sail.
Do you go back dismayed? 'tis a lost fear:
Man but a rush against Othello's breast   270
And he retires. Where should Othello go?
Now: how dost thou look now? O ill-starred wench,
Pale as thy smock. When we shall meet at compt
This look of thine will hurl my soul from heaven
And fiends will snatch at it. Cold, cold, my girl,   275
Even like thy chastity. O cursed, cursed slave!
Whip me, ye devils,
From the possession of this heavenly sight!
Blow me about in winds, roast me in sulphur,
Wash me in steep-down gulfs of liquid fire!   280
O Desdemon! dead, Desdemon. Dead! O, O!

Enter LODOVICO, MONTANO, *officers with* IAGO, *prisoner,
and* CASSIO *in a chair.*

LODOVICO
Where is this rash and most unfortunate man?

OTHELLO   That's he that was Othello? here I am.

LODOVICO   Where is that viper? bring the villain forth.

OTHELLO
I look down towards his feet, but that's a fable.   285
If that thou be'st a devil, I cannot kill thee.
[*Wounds Iago.*]

LODOVICO   Wrench his sword from him.

IAGO   I bleed, sir, but not killed.

OTHELLO   I am not sorry neither, I'd have thee live:
For in my sense 'tis happiness to die.

LODOVICO
O thou Othello, that wert once so good,   290
Fallen in the practice of a cursed slave,
What shall be said to thee?

OTHELLO   Why, anything;
An honourable murderer, if you will,
For nought I did in hate, but all in honour.

LODOVICO
This wretch hath part confessed his villainy.   295
Did you and he consent in Cassio's death?

OTHELLO   Ay.

CASSIO   Dear general, I never gave you cause.

OTHELLO   I do believe it, and I ask your pardon.
Will you, I pray, demand that demi-devil   300
Why he hath thus ensnared my soul and body?

IAGO
Demand me nothing. What you know, you know.
From this time forth I never will speak word.

LODOVICO   What, not to pray?

GRATIANO   Torments will ope your lips.

OTHELLO   Well, thou dost best.   305

LODOVICO
Sir, you shall understand what hath befallen,
Which, as I think, you know not. Here is a letter
Found in the pocket of the slain Roderigo,
And here another: the one of them imports
The death of Cassio, to be undertook
By Roderigo.

OTHELLO O villain!

CASSIO Most heathenish and most gross!

LODOVICO Now here's another discontented paper
Found in his pocket too, and this, it seems,
Roderigo meant t'have sent this damned villain
But that, belike, Iago in the nick
Came in, and satisfied him.

OTHELLO
O thou pernicious caitiff!
How came you, Cassio, by that handkerchief
That was my wife's?

CASSIO I found it in my chamber,
And he himself confessed but even now
That there he dropped it for a special purpose
Which wrought to his desire.

OTHELLO O fool, fool, fool!

CASSIO There is besides in Roderigo's letter
How he upbraids Iago, that he made him
Brave me upon the watch, whereon it came
That I was cast; and even but now he spake,
After long seeming dead, Iago hurt him,
Iago set him on.

LODOVICO [*to Othello*]
You must forsake this room and go with us.
Your power and your command is taken off
And Cassio rules in Cyprus. For this slave,
If there be any cunning cruelty
That can torment him much and hold him long,
It shall be his. You shall close prisoner rest
Till that the nature of your fault be known
To the Venetian state. Come, bring him away.

OTHELLO
Soft you, a word or two before you go.
I have done the state some service, and they know't:

No more of that. I pray you, in your letters,
When you shall these unlucky deeds relate,
Speak of me as I am. Nothing extenuate,
Nor set down aught in malice. Then must you speak
Of one that loved not wisely, but too well;
Of one not easily jealous, but, being wrought,
Perplexed in the extreme; of one whose hand,
Like the base Indian, threw a pearl away
Richer than all his tribe; of one whose subdued eyes,
Albeit unused to the melting mood,
Drops tears as fast as the Arabian trees
Their medicinable gum. Set you down this,
And say besides that in Aleppo once,
Where a malignant and a turbanned Turk
Beat a Venetian and traduced the state,
I took by th' throat the circumcised dog
And smote him – thus! [*He stabs himself.*]

LODOVICO O bloody period!

GRATIANO All that's spoke is marred.

OTHELLO
I kissed thee ere I killed thee: no way but this,
Killing myself, to die upon a kiss.
[*Kisses Desdemona, and dies.*]

CASSIO
This did I fear, but thought he had no weapon,
For he was great of heart.

LODOVICO [*to Iago*] O Spartan dog,
More fell than anguish, hunger, or the sea,
Look on the tragic loading of this bed:
This is thy work. The object poisons sight,
Let it be hid. Gratiano, keep the house
And seize upon the fortunes of the Moor
For they succeed to you. To you, lord governor,
Remains the censure of this hellish villain,
The time, the place, the torture: O, enforce it!
Myself will straight aboard, and to the state
This heavy act with heavy heart relate. *Exeunt.*

340

345

350

355

360

365

370

Pericles

Pericles, Prince of Tyre had been performed before 20 May 1608, when Edward Blount entered it for publication in the Register of the Stationers' Company. The earliest two known Quartos are both dated 1609 and it reached a sixth edition by 1635. It remains unclear why *Pericles* was not included in the First Folio in 1623: perhaps it was known to be of collaborative authorship (favoured candidates as part-author include George Wilkins); perhaps no better text was readily available to replace the unsatisfactory and in places garbled text printed in 1609. In 1664, *Pericles* was the first of seven plays attributed to Shakespeare which were added as a supplement to a reissue of the 1663 Third Folio. Alone of the seven, it was gradually accepted into the Shakespeare canon, because of unmistakable signs of Shakespeare's late style in acts 3–5, but also because of other resemblances to the late romances, especially *The Winter's Tale*. Apparently a great success in its own time (Ben Jonson could complain, as late as 1629, of the continued popularity of such a 'mouldy tale'), *Pericles* is now the least performed of the romances.

In his opening speech, the Chorus, in the person of the fourteenth-century poet John Gower, introduces the story with the claim that '*bonum quo antiquius eo melius*', the older a good thing is the better it is. The romance of Apollonius of Tyre is indeed old, originating in the eastern Mediterranean in the fifth century AD. Its many English retellings stretch from a fragmentary Old English translation, by way of Gower's *Confessio Amantis* (late 1380s), to a prose novel by Laurence Twyne, *The Pattern of Painful Adventures . . . that Befell unto Prince Apollonius*, written in the 1570s. In the play – and in a prose narrative by George Wilkins published in 1608 and apparently influenced by seeing the play in performance – the protagonist becomes Pericles, a name which may recall the great Athenian statesman but which is more directly derived from 'Pyrocles', one of the two heroes of Sir Philip Sidney's vastly popular and much imitated romance, *Arcadia* (1590).

Pericles tells its old story with great directness and with remarkable fidelity to the sequence of events in Gower and Twyne. The travels and tribulations of Pericles are echoed, fourteen years later, by those of his lost (and supposedly dead) daughter, Marina, so named because she was born in a storm at sea in which her mother Thaisa died. The name Marina also originates in the play, and strikingly resembles those of other heroines of late Shakespearean romance – Perdita, 'the lost one', and Miranda, 'wonderful'. The Job-like despair and catatonic withdrawal of Pericles are cured, in the play's climactic scene, by reunion with his daughter, a cure effected both by the example of her patience in extremity and by their discovery of each other's identity. As a bonus, a vision of the goddess Diana leads Pericles and Marina to Ephesus where the family reunion is completed by the discovery of Thaisa, long supposed dead but providentially resuscitated by the sage Cerimon and preserved as a nun in the temple of Diana (circumstances which recall the dénouement of *The Comedy of Errors*, written some fourteen years earlier).

The Arden text is based on the 1609 First Quarto.

LIST OF ROLES

ANTIOCHUS	*King of Antioch*
PERICLES	*Prince of Tyre*
HELICANUS	*two lords of Tyre*
ESCANES	
SIMONIDES	*King of Pentapolis*
CLEON	*governor of Tharsus*
LYSIMACHUS	*governor of Mytilene*
CERIMON	*a lord of Ephesus*
THALIARD	*a lord of Antioch*
PHILEMON	*a servant to Cerimon*
LEONINE	*a servant to Dionyza*
MARSHAL	
PANDAR	
BOULT	*his servant*
DAUGHTER	*of Antiochus*
DIONYZA	*wife to Cleon*
THAISA	*daughter to Simonides*
MARINA	*daughter to Pericles and Thaisa*
LYCHORIDA	*nurse to Marina*
BAWD	

Lords, Ladies, Knights, Gentlemen, Sailors, Pirates, Fishermen and Messengers

DIANA	
GOWER	*as Chorus*

Pericles

1.Ch.   *Enter GOWER.*

GOWER   To sing a song that old was sung,
From ashes ancient Gower is come,
Assuming man's infirmities,
To glad your ear, and please your eyes.
It hath been sung at festivals,   5
On ember-eves and holy-ales;
And lords and ladies in their lives
Have read it for restoratives:
The purchase is to make men glorious,
Et bonum quo antiquius eo melius.   10
If you, born in these latter times,
When wit's more ripe, accept my rimes,
And that to hear an old man sing
May to your wishes pleasure bring,
I life would wish, and that I might   15
Waste it for you like taper-light.
This Antioch, then, Antiochus the Great
Built up, this city, for his chiefest seat,
The fairest in all Syria –
I tell you what mine authors say.   20
This king unto him took a peer,
Who died and left a female heir,
So buxom, blithe and full of face
As heaven had lent her all his grace;
With whom the father liking took,   25
And her to incest did provoke.
Bad child, worse father, to entice his own
To evil should be done by none.
But custom what they did begin
Was with long use account'd no sin.   30
The beauty of this sinful dame
Made many princes thither frame,
To seek her as a bed-fellow,
In marriage-pleasures play-fellow;
Which to prevent he made a law,   35
To keep her still, and men in awe;
That whoso ask'd her for his wife,
His riddle told not, lost his life.
So for her many a wight did die,
As yon grim looks do testify.   40
[*pointing to the heads*]
What now ensues, to the judgement of your eye
I give my cause, who best can justify.   *Exit.*

1.1   *Enter* ANTIOCHUS, PRINCE PERICLES *and*
attendants.

ANTIOCHUS
Young prince of Tyre, you have at large receiv'd
The danger of the task you undertake.
PERICLES   I have, Antiochus, and, with a soul
Embolden'd with the glory of her praise,
Think death no hazard in this enterprise.
ANTIOCHUS   Music!   [*Music.*]
Bring in our daughter, clothed like a bride,
For the embracements even of Jove himself;

At whose conception, till Lucina reign'd,
Nature this dowry gave: to glad her presence,   10
The senate-house of planets all did sit
To knit in her their best perfections.

Enter Antiochus' Daughter.

PERICLES
See, where she comes apparell'd like the spring,
Graces her subjects, and her thoughts the king
Of every virtue gives renown to men!   15
Her face the book of praises, where is read
Nothing but curious pleasures, as from thence
Sorrow were ever raz'd, and testy wrath
Could never be her mild companion.
You gods, that made me man, and sway in love,   20
That have inflam'd desire in my breast
To taste the fruit of yon celestial tree
Or die in the adventure, be my helps,
As I am son and servant to your will,
To compass such a boundless happiness!   25
ANTIOCHUS   Prince Pericles –
PERICLES   That would be son to great Antiochus.
ANTIOCHUS   Before thee stands this fair Hesperides,
With golden fruit, but dangerous to be touch'd;
For death-like dragons here affright thee hard.   30
Her face, like heaven, enticeth thee to view
Her countless glory, which desert must gain;
And which, without desert because thine eye
Presumes to reach, all the whole heap must die.
Yon sometimes famous princes, like thyself,   35
Drawn by report, advent'rous by desire,
Tell thee, with speechless tongues and semblance
    pale,
That without covering save yon field of stars,
Here they stand martyrs slain in Cupid's wars;
And with dead cheeks advise thee to desist   40
For going on death's net, whom none resist.
PERICLES   Antiochus, I thank thee, who hath taught
My frail mortality to know itself,
And by those fearful objects to prepare
This body, like to them, to what I must;   45
For death remember'd should be like a mirror,
Who tells us life's but breath, to trust it error.
I'll make my will then; and, as sick men do,
Who know the world, see heaven, but feeling woe
Gripe not at earthly joys as erst they did: 50
So I bequeath a happy peace to you
And all good men, as every prince should do;
My riches to the earth from whence they came;
[*to the Princess*] But my unspotted fire of love to you.
Thus ready for the way of life or death,   55
I wait the sharpest blow, Antiochus.
ANTIOCHUS   Scorning advice, read the conclusion then:
[*Angrily throws down the riddle.*]
Which read and not expounded, 'tis decreed,
As these before thee thou thyself shalt bleed.

DAUGHTER

60   Of all, 'say'd yet, may'st thou prove prosperous!
      Of all, 'say'd yet, I wish thee happiness.
PERICLES   Like a bold champion I assume the lists,
      Nor ask advice of any other thought
      But faithfulness and courage. [*He reads the riddle.*]
65   *I am no viper, yet I feed*
          On mother's flesh which did me breed.
          I sought a husband, in which labour
          I found that kindness in a father.
          He's father, son, and husband mild;
70   *I mother, wife, and yet his child:*
          How they may be, and yet in two,
          As you will live, resolve it you.
      [*aside*] Sharp physic is the last: but, O you powers
      That gives heaven countless eyes to view men's acts:
75   Why cloud they not their sights perpetually,
      If this be true, which makes me pale to read it?
      Fair glass of light, I lov'd you, and could still,
      Were not this glorious casket stor'd with ill.
      But I must tell you, now my thoughts revolt;
80   For he's no man on whom perfections wait
      That, knowing sin within, will touch the gate.
      You are a fair viol, and your sense the strings,
      Who, finger'd to make man his lawful music,
      Would draw heaven down and all the gods to
          hearken;
85   But being play'd upon before your time,
      Hell only danceth at so harsh a chime.
      [*turning towards the Princess*]
      Good sooth, I care not for you.
ANTIOCHUS   Prince Pericles, touch not, upon thy life,
      For that's an article within our law
90   As dangerous as the rest. Your time's expir'd:
      Either expound now or receive your sentence.
PERICLES   Great king,
      Few love to hear the sins they love to act;
      'Twould braid yourself too near for me to tell it.
95   Who has a book of all that monarchs do,
      He's more secure to keep it shut than shown;
      For vice repeated is like the wand'ring wind,
      Blows dust in others' eyes, to spread itself;
      And yet the end of all is bought thus dear,
100   The breath is gone, and the sore eyes see clear
      To stop the air would hurt them. The blind mole
          casts
      Copp'd hills towards heaven, to tell the earth is
          throng'd
      By man's oppression; and the poor worm doth die
          for't.
      Kings are earth's gods; in vice their law's their will;
105   And if Jove stray, who dares say Jove doth ill?
      It is enough you know; and it is fit,
      What being more known grows worse, to smother it.
      All love the womb that their first being bred,
      Then give my tongue like leave to love my head.

ANTIOCHUS [*aside*]
      Heaven, that I had thy head! he has found the meaning;   110
      But I will gloze with him.
      [*aloud*]   Young prince of Tyre,
      Though by the tenour of our strict edict,
      Your exposition misinterpreting,
      We might proceed to cancel of your days,
      Yet hope, succeeding from so fair a tree   115
      As your fair self, doth tune us otherwise:
      Forty days longer we do respite you;
      If by which time our secret be undone,
      This mercy shows we'll joy in such a son;
      And until then your entertain shall be   120
      As doth befit our honour and your worth.
                          Exeunt all but Pericles.
PERICLES   How courtesy would seem to cover sin,
      When what is done is like an hypocrite,
      The which is good in nothing but in sight!
      If it be true that I interpret false,   125
      Then were it certain you were not so bad
      As with foul incest to abuse your soul;
      Where now you're both a father and a son,
      By your uncomely claspings with your child, –
      Which pleasures fits a husband, not a father;   130
      And she an eater of her mother's flesh,
      By the defiling of her parent's bed;
      And both like serpents are, who though they feed
      On sweetest flowers, yet they poison breed.
      Antioch, farewell! for wisdom sees, those men   135
      Blush not in actions blacker than the night,
      Will shew no course to keep them from the light.
      One sin, I know, another doth provoke;
      Murder's as near to lust as flame to smoke.
      Poison and treason are the hands of sin,   140
      Ay, and the targets, to put off the shame:
      Then, lest my life be cropp'd to keep you clear,
      By flight I'll shun the danger which I fear.   *Exit.*

                    Enter ANTIOCHUS.

ANTIOCHUS   He hath found the meaning,
      For which we mean to have his head. He must   145
      Not live to trumpet forth my infamy,
      Nor tell the world Antiochus doth sin
      In such a loathed manner;
      And therefore instantly this prince must die;
      For by his fall my honour must keep high.   150
      Who attends us there?

                    Enter THALIARD.

THALIARD   Doth your highness call?
ANTIOCHUS   Thaliard,
      You are of our chamber, Thaliard, and our mind
          partakes
      Her private actions to your secrecy;
      And for your faithfulness we will advance you.   155
      Thaliard, behold here's poison, and here's gold;
      We hate the prince of Tyre, and thou must kill him:

It fits thee not to ask the reason why:
Because we bid it. Say, is it done?
THALIARD   My lord, 'tis done.
160 ANTIOCHUS   Enough.

Enter a Messenger.

Let your breath cool yourself, telling your haste.
MESSENGER   My lord, prince Pericles is fled.   *Exit.*
ANTIOCHUS   As thou wilt live, fly after; and like an
arrow shot from a well-experienc'd archer hits the
165   mark his eye doth level at, so thou never return unless
thou say 'Prince Pericles is dead'.
THALIARD   My lord, if I can get him within my pistol's
length, I'll make him sure enough: so, farewell to your
highness.
ANTIOCHUS   Thaliard, adieu!   *Exit Thaliard.*
170   Till Pericles be dead
My heart can lend no succour to my head.   *Exit.*

1.2   *Enter* PERICLES *with his* Lords.

PERICLES   Let none disturb us.   *The Lords withdraw.*
Why should this change of thoughts,
The sad companion, dull-ey'd melancholy,
Be my so us'd a guest, as not an hour
5   In the day's glorious walk or peaceful night,
The tomb where grief should sleep, can breed me
quiet?
Here pleasures court mine eyes, and mine eyes shun
them,
And danger, which I fear'd, is at Antioch,
Whose arm seems far too short to hit me here;
10   Yet neither pleasure's art can joy my spirits,
Nor yet the other's distance comfort me.
Then it is thus: the passions of the mind,
That have their first conception by mis-dread,
Have after-nourishment and life by care;
15   And what was first but fear what might be done,
Grows elder now and cares it be not done.
And so with me: the great Antiochus,
'Gainst whom I am too little to contend,
Since he's so great can make his will his act,
20   Will think me speaking, though I swear to silence;
Nor boots it me to say I honour him,
If he suspect I may dishonour him;
And what may make him blush in being known,
He'll stop the course by which it might be known.
25   With hostile forces he'll o'erspread the land,
And with th'ostent of war will look so huge,
Amazement shall drive courage from the state,
Our men be vanquish'd ere they do resist,
And subjects punish'd that ne'er thought offence:
30   Which care of them, not pity of myself, –
Who am no more but as the tops of trees
Which fence the roots they grow by and defend
them –
Makes both my body pine and soul to languish,
And punish that before that he would punish.

Enter HELICANUS *and all the* Lords *to Pericles.*

1 LORD   Joy and all comfort in your sacred breast!   35
2 LORD   And keep your mind, till you return to us,
Peaceful and comfortable!
HELICANUS   Peace, peace, and give experience tongue.
They do abuse the king that flatter him,
For flattery is the bellows blows up sin;   40
The thing the which is flatter'd but a spark,
To which that blast gives heat and stronger glowing;
Whereas reproof, obedient and in order,
Fits kings, as they are men, for they may err.
When Signior Sooth here does proclaim a peace,   45
He flatters you, makes war upon your life.
Prince, pardon me, or strike me, if you please;
I cannot be much lower than my knees. [*He kneels.*]
PERICLES   All leave us else; but let your cares o'erlook
What shipping and what lading's in our haven,   50
And then return to us.   *Exeunt Lords.*
Helicanus,
Thou hast mov'd us; what seest thou in our looks?
HELICANUS   An angry brow, dread lord.
PERICLES   If there be such a dart in princes' frowns,
How durst thy tongue move anger to our face?   55
HELICANUS
How dares the plants look up to heaven, from
whence
They have their nourishment?
PERICLES   Thou know'st I have power
To take thy life from thee.
HELICANUS   I have ground the axe myself;
Do but you strike the blow.
PERICLES   Rise, prithee, rise;
Sit down; thou art no flatterer;   60
I thank thee for't; and heaven forbid
That kings should let their ears hear their faults hid!
Fit counsellor and servant for a prince,
Who by thy wisdom makes a prince thy servant,
What would'st thou have me do?
HELICANUS   To bear with patience   65
Such griefs as you do lay upon yourself.
PERICLES   Thou speak'st like a physician, Helicanus,
That ministers a potion unto me
That thou wouldst tremble to receive thyself.
Attend me then: I went to Antioch,   70
Whereas thou know'st, against the face of death
I sought the purchase of a glorious beauty,
From whence an issue I might propagate,
Are arms to princes and bring joys to subjects.
Her face was to mine eye beyond all wonder;   75
The rest, hark in thine ear, as black as incest;
Which by my knowledge found, the sinful father
Seem'd not to strike, but smooth; but thou know'st
this:
'Tis time to fear when tyrants seem to kiss.
Which fear so grew in me, I hither fled,   80
Under the covering of a careful night,
Who seem'd my good protector; and, being here,

Bethought me what was past, what might succeed.
I knew him tyrannous; and tyrants' fears

85 Decrease not, but grow faster than the years.
And should he doubt, as no doubt he doth,
That I should open to the list'ning air
How many worthy princes' bloods were shed,
To keep his bed of blackness unlaid ope,

90 To lop that doubt he'll fill his land with arms,
And make pretence of wrong that I have done him;
When all, for mine if I may call offence,
Must feel war's blow, who spares not innocence:
Which love to all, of which thyself art one,
Who now reprov'dst me for't, –

95 HELICANUS   Alas, sir!
PERICLES
    Drew sleep out of mine eyes, blood from my cheeks,
    Musings into my mind, with thousand doubts
    How I might stop this tempest ere it came;
    And finding little comfort to relieve them,

100   I thought it princely charity to grieve them.
HELICANUS
    Well, my lord, since you have given me leave to
       speak,
    Freely will I speak. Antiochus you fear,
    And justly too, I think, you fear the tyrant,
    Who either by public war or private treason

105   Will take away your life.
    Therefore, my lord, go travel for a while,
    Till that his rage and anger be forgot,
    Or till the Destinies do cut his thread of life.
    Your rule direct to any; if to me,

110   Day serves not light more faithful than I'll be.
PERICLES   I do not doubt thy faith;
    But should he wrong my liberties in my absence?
HELICANUS
    We'll mingle our bloods together in the earth,
    From whence we had our being and our birth.
PERICLES

115 Tyre, I now look from thee then, and to Tharsus
    Intend my travel, where I'll hear from thee,
    And by whose letters I'll dispose myself.
    The care I had and have of subjects' good
    On thee I lay, whose wisdom's strength can bear it.

120   I'll take thy word for faith, not ask thine oath;
    Who shuns not to break one will crack both.
    But in our orbs we'll live so round and safe,
    That time of both this truth shall ne'er convince,
    Thou show'dst a subject's shine, I a true prince'.
                          Exeunt.

1.3   *Enter* THALIARD *alone.*

    THALIARD   So this is Tyre, and this the court. Here
       must I kill King Pericles; and if I do it not, I am
       sure to be hang'd at home: 'tis dangerous. Well, I
       perceive he was a wise fellow and had good

5   discretion that, being bid to ask what he would of

the king, desir'd he might know none of his secrets:
now do I see he had some reason for't; for if a king
bid a man be a villain, he's bound by the indenture
of his oath to be one. Husht! here comes the lords
of Tyre.   10

       Enter HELICANUS *and* ESCANES *with other lords.*

HELICANUS   You shall not need, my fellow peers of Tyre,
    Further to question of your king's departure.
    His seal'd commission, left in trust with me,
    Doth speak sufficiently he's gone to travel.
THALIARD [*aside*]   How? the king gone?   15
HELICANUS   If further yet you will be satisfied
    Why, as it were unlicens'd of your loves,
    He would depart, I'll give some light unto you.
    Being at Antioch –
THALIARD [*aside*]   What from Antioch?
HELICANUS
    Royal Antiochus, on what cause I know not,   20
    Took some displeasure at him; at least he judg'd so;
    And doubting lest he had err'd or sinn'd,
    To show his sorrow he'd correct himself;
    So puts himself unto the shipman's toil,
    With whom each minute threatens life or death.   25
THALIARD [*aside*]   Well, I perceive I shall not be hang'd
    now, although I would.
    But since he's gone, the king's ears it must please,
    He 'scap'd the land, to perish at the seas.
    I'll present myself. [*aloud*] Peace to the lords of Tyre!   30
HELICANUS   Lord Thaliard from Antiochus is welcome.
THALIARD   From him I come
    With message unto princely Pericles;
    But since my landing I have understood
    Your lord has betook himself to unknown travels,   35
    My message must return from whence it came.
HELICANUS   We have no reason to desire it,
    Commended to our master, not to us;
    Yet ere you shall depart, this we desire,
    As friends to Antioch, we may feast in Tyre. *Exeunt.* 40

1.4   *Enter* CLEON, *the governor of Tharsus, with*
               his wife DIONYZA *and attendants.*

CLEON   My Dionyza, shall we rest us here,
    And by relating tales of others' griefs,
    See if 'twill teach us to forget our own?
DIONYZA   That were to blow at fire in hope to quench it;
    For who digs hills because they do aspire   5
    Throws down one mountain to cast up a higher.
    O my distressed lord, even such our griefs are;
    Here they are but felt, and seen with mischief's eyes,
    But like to groves, being topp'd, they higher rise.
CLEON   O Dionyza,   10
    Who wanteth food, and will not say he wants it,
    Or can conceal his hunger till he famish?
    Our tongues and sorrows to sound deep?
    Our woes into the air, our eyes to weep,

15   Till lungs fetch breath that may proclaim them
          louder?
      That, if heaven slumber while their creatures want,
      They may awake their helps to comfort them.
      I'll then discourse our woes, felt several years,
      And wanting breath to speak help me with tears.
20 DIONYZA   I'll do my best, sir.
    CLEON
      This Tharsus, o'er which I have the government,
      A city on whom plenty held full hand,
      For riches strew'd herself even in her streets;
      Whose towers bore heads so high they kiss'd the
          clouds,
25   And strangers ne'er beheld but wond'red at;
      Whose men and dames so jetted and adorn'd,
      Like one another's glass to trim them by –
      Their tables were stor'd full to glad the sight,
      And not so much to feed on as delight:
30   All poverty was scorn'd, and pride so great,
      The name of help grew odious to repeat.
    DIONYZA   O, 'tis too true.
    CLEON   But see what heaven can do by this our change:
      These mouths, who but of late earth, sea and air,
35   Were all too little to content and please,
      Although they gave their creatures in abundance,
      As houses are defil'd for want of use,
      They are now starv'd for want of exercise;
      Those palates who, not yet two summers younger,
40   Must have inventions to delight the taste,
      Would now be glad of bread, and beg for it;
      Those mothers who, to nuzzle up their babes
      Thought nought too curious, are ready now
      To eat those little darlings whom they lov'd.
45   So sharp are hunger's teeth, that man and wife
      Draw lots who first shall die to lengthen life.
      Here stands a lord, and there a lady weeping;
      Here many sink, yet those which see them fall
      Have scarce strength left to give them burial.
50   Is not this true?
    DIONYZA   Our cheeks and hollow eyes do witness it.
    CLEON   O, let those cities that of plenty's cup
      And her prosperities so largely taste,
      With their superfluous riots, hear these tears!
55   The misery of Tharsus may be theirs.

Enter a Lord.

    LORD   Where's the lord governor?
    CLEON   Here.
      Speak out thy sorrows which thou bring'st in haste,
      For comfort is too far for us to expect.
60 LORD   We have descried, upon our neighbouring shore,
      A portly sail of ships make hitherward.
    CLEON   I thought as much.
      One sorrow never comes but brings an heir
      That may succeed as his inheritor;
65   And so in ours: some neighbouring nation,
      Taking advantage of our misery,

      Hath stuff'd the hollow vessels with their power,
      To beat us down, the which are down already,
      And make a conquest of unhappy men,
      Whereas no glory's got to overcome.   70
    LORD   That's the least fear; for, by the semblance
      Of their white flags display'd, they bring us peace,
      And come to us as favourers, not as foes.
    CLEON   Thou speak'st like him's untutor'd to repeat:
      Who makes the fairest show means most deceit.   75
      But bring they what they will and what they can,
      What need we fear?
      Our ground's the lowest, and we are half-way here.
      Go tell their general we attend him here, to know for
      what he comes, and whence he comes, and what he   80
      craves.
    LORD   I go, my lord.   *Exit.*
    CLEON   Welcome is peace, if he on peace consist;
      If wars, we are unable to resist.

Enter Lord, *with* PERICLES *and attendants.*

    PERICLES   Lord governor, for so we hear you are,   85
      Let not our ships and number of our men
      Be like a beacon fir'd t'amaze your eyes.
      We have heard your miseries as far as Tyre,
      And seen the desolation of your streets;
      Nor come we to add sorrow to your tears,   90
      But to relieve them of their heavy load;
      And these our ships, you happily may think
      Are like the Trojan horse was stuff'd within
      With bloody veins expecting overthrow,
      Are stor'd with corn to make your needy bread,   95
      And give them life whom hunger starv'd half dead.
    ALL   The gods of Greece protect you!
      [*Cleon, Dionyza and lords of Tharsus kneel.*]
      And we'll pray for you.
    PERICLES   Arise, I pray you, rise;
      We do not look for reverence, but for love
      And harbourage for ourself, our ships and men.   100
    CLEON   The which when any shall not gratify,
      Or pay you with unthankfulness in thought,
      Be it our wives, our children, or ourselves,
      The curse of heaven and men succeed their evils!
      Till when, – the which I hope shall ne'er be seen –   105
      Your grace is welcome to our town and us.
    PERICLES
      Which welcome we'll accept; feast here awhile,
      Until our stars that frown lend us a smile.   *Exeunt.*

2.Ch.   *Enter* GOWER

    GOWER
      Here have you seen a mighty king
      His child, I wis, to incest bring;
      A better prince and benign lord
      That will prove awful both in deed and word.
      Be quiet then, as men should be   5
      Till he hath pass'd necessity.

I'll show you those in troubles reign,
Losing a mite, a mountain gain.
The good in conversation,
10 To whom I give my benison,
Is still at Tharsus, where each man
Thinks all is writ he spoken can;
And, to remember what he does,
Build his statue to make him glorious.
15 But tidings to the contrary
Are brought your eyes; what need speak I?

Dumb Show.

Enter, at one door, PERICLES, talking with CLEON; all the
train with them. Enter, at another door, a gentleman, with
a letter to Pericles; Pericles shows the letter to Cleon;
Pericles gives the messenger a reward and knights him.
Exit Pericles at one door, and Cleon at another.

Good Helicane hath stay'd at home,
Not to eat honey like a drone
From others' labours; for he strives
20 To killen bad, keep good alive;
And to fulfil his prince' desire,
Sends word of all that haps in Tyre:
How Thaliard came full bent with sin
And hid intent to murder him;
25 And that in Tharsus was not best
Longer for him to make his rest.
He, doing so, put forth to seas,
Where when men been, there's seldom ease;
For now the wind begins to blow;
30 Thunder above and deeps below
Makes such unquiet that the ship
Should house him safe is wrack'd and split;
And he, good prince, having all lost,
By waves from coast to coast is toss'd.
35 All perishen of men, of pelf,
Ne aught escapend but himself;
Till fortune, tir'd with doing bad,
Threw him ashore, to give him glad:
And here he comes. What shall be next,
40 Pardon old Gower, – this 'longs the text.   *Exit.*

2.1   *Enter* PERICLES, *wet.*

PERICLES   Yet cease your ire, you angry stars of heaven!
Wind, rain, and thunder, remember, earthly man
Is but a substance that must yield to you;
And I, as fits my nature, do obey you.
5 Alas, the seas hath cast me on the rocks,
Wash'd me from shore to shore, and left me breath
Nothing to think on but ensuing death.
Let it suffice the greatness of your powers
To have bereft a prince of all his fortunes;
10 And having thrown him from your wat'ry grave,
Here to have death in peace is all he'll crave.

Enter three Fishermen.

1 FISHERMAN   What, ho, Pilch!
2 FISHERMAN   Ha, come and bring away the nets!
1 FISHERMAN   What, Patch-breech, I say!
3 FISHERMAN   What say you, master?   15
1 FISHERMAN   Look how thou stirr'st now! come away,
  or I'll fetch'th with a wanion.
3 FISHERMAN   Faith, master, I am thinking of the poor
  men that were cast away before us even now.
1 FISHERMAN   Alas, pour souls, it griev'd my heart to   20
  hear what pitiful cries they made to us to help them,
  when, well-a-day, we could scarce help ourselves.
3 FISHERMAN   Nay, master, said not I as much when I
  saw the porpoise, how he bounc'd and tumbled? they
  say they're half fish, half flesh; a plague on them, they   25
  ne'er come but I look to be wash'd! Master, I marvel
  how the fishes live in the sea.
1 FISHERMAN   Why, as men do a-land: the great ones eat
  up the little ones. I can compare our rich misers to
  nothing so fitly as to a whale: 'a plays and tumbles,   30
  driving the poor fry before him, and at last devours
  them all at a mouthful. Such whales have I heard on
  a'th' land, who never leave gaping till they swallow'd
  the whole parish, church, steeple, bells, and all.
PERICLES [*aside*]   A pretty moral.   35
3 FISHERMAN   But, master, if I had been the sexton, I
  would have been that day in the belfry.
2 FISHERMAN   Why, man?
3 FISHERMAN   Because he should have swallow'd me too;
  and when I had been in his belly, I would have kept   40
  such a jangling of the bells, that he should never have
  left till he cast bells, steeple, church, and parish up
  again. But if the good King Simonides were of my
  mind –
PERICLES [*aside*]   Simonides?   45
3 FISHERMAN   We would purge the land of these drones,
  that rob the bee of her honey.
PERICLES [*aside*]   How from the finny subject of the sea
  These fishers tell the infirmities of men;
  And from their wat'ry empire recollect   50
  All that may men approve or men detect! –
  Peace be at your labour, honest fishermen.
2 FISHERMAN
  Honest! good fellow, what's that? If it be a day fits you,
  search out of the calendar, and nobody look after it.
PERICLES   May see the sea hath cast upon your coast –   55
2 FISHERMAN
  What a drunken knave was the sea to cast thee in our
  way!
PERICLES   A man whom both the waters and the wind,
  In that vast tennis-court, hath made the ball
  For them to play upon, entreats you pity him;   60
  He asks of you, that never us'd to beg.
1 FISHERMAN   No, friend, cannot you beg? here's them
  in our country of Greece gets more with begging than
  we can do with working.
2 FISHERMAN   Canst thou catch any fishes then?   65
PERICLES   I never practis'd it.

2 FISHERMAN   Nay, then thou wilt starve, sure; for here's
nothing to be got now-a-days, unless thou canst fish
for't.

70 PERICLES   What I have been I have forgot to know;
But what I am, want teaches me to think on:
A man throng'd up with cold. My veins are chill,
And have no more of life than may suffice
To give my tongue that heat to ask your help;
75 Which if you shall refuse, when I am dead,
For that I am a man, pray you see me buried.

1 FISHERMAN   Die, quoth-a? Now gods forbid't, and I
have a gown here, come, put it on; keep thee warm.
Now, afore me, a handsome fellow! come, thou shalt go
80 home, and we'll have flesh for holidays, fish for
fasting-days, and moreo'er puddings and flap-jacks;
and thou shalt be welcome.

PERICLES   I thank you, sir.

2 FISHERMAN   Hark you, my friend; you said you could
85 not beg.

PERICLES   I did but crave.

2 FISHERMAN   But crave? then I'll turn craver too, and so
I shall 'scape whipping.

PERICLES   Why, are your beggars whipp'd then?

90 2 FISHERMAN   O, not all, my friend, not all; for if all your
beggars were whipp'd, I would wish no better office
than to be beadle. But, master, I'll go draw up the net.

Exeunt Second and Third Fishermen.

PERICLES [*aside*]   How well this honest mirth becomes
their labour!

95 1 FISHERMAN   Hark you, sir; do you know where ye are?

PERICLES   Not well.

1 FISHERMAN   Why, I'll tell you: this is call'd Pentapolis,
and our king, the good Simonides.

PERICLES   The good Simonides, do you call him?

100 1 FISHERMAN   Ay, sir; and he deserves so to be call'd for
his peacable reign and good government.

PERICLES   He is a happy king, since he gains from his
subjects the name of good by his government. How far
is his court distant from this shore?

105 1 FISHERMAN   Marry, sir, half a day's journey. And I'll
tell you, he hath a fair daughter, and to-morrow is her
birthday; and there are princes and knights come
from all parts of the world to joust and tourney for
her love.

110 PERICLES   Were my fortunes equal to my desires, I could
wish to make one there.

1 FISHERMAN   O, sir, things must be as they may; and
what a man cannot get, he may lawfully deal for his
wife's soul.

Enter Second and Third Fishermen, *drawing up a net.*

115 2 FISHERMAN   Help, master, help! here's a fish hangs in
the net, like a poor man's right in the law; 'twill hardly
come out. Ha, bots on't, 'tis come at last, and 'tis
turn'd to a rusty armour.

PERICLES   An armour, friends! I pray you, let me see it.
120 Thanks, Fortune, yet, that after all thy crosses

Thou giv'st me somewhat to repair myself;
And though it was mine own, part of mine heritage,
Which my dead father did bequeath to me,
With this strict charge, even as he left his life:
125 'Keep it, my Pericles; it hath been a shield
'Twixt me and death;' – and pointed to his brace –
'For that it sav'd me, keep it; in like necessity,
The which the gods protect thee from, may defend
thee!'
It kept where I kept – I so dearly lov'd it –
130 Till the rough seas, that spares not any man,
Took it in rage, though calm'd hath given't again.
I thank thee for't; my shipwreck now's no ill,
Since I have here my father gave in his will.

1 FISHERMAN   What mean you, sir?

PERICLES
135 To beg of you, kind friends, this coat of worth,
For it was sometime target to a king;
I know it by this mark. He lov'd me dearly,
And for his sake I wish the having of it;
And that you'd guide me to your sovereign's court,
140 Where with it I may appear a gentleman;
And if that ever my low fortunes better,
I'll pay your bounties; till then rest your debtor.

1 FISHERMAN   Why, wilt thou tourney for the lady?

PERICLES   I'll show the virtue I have borne in arms.

145 1 FISHERMAN   Why, di'e take it; and the gods give thee
good on't!

2 FISHERMAN   Ay, but hark you, my friend; 'twas we that
made up this garment through the rough seams of the
waters: there are certain condolements, certain vails. I
150 hope, sir, if you thrive, you'll remember from whence
you had them.

PERICLES   Believe't, I will.
By your furtherance I am cloth'd in steel;
And spite of all the rapture of the sea
155 This jewel holds his building on my arm.
Unto thy value I will mount myself
Upon a courser, whose delightful steps
Shall make the gazer joy to see him tread.
Only, my friend, I yet am unprovided of a pair of
160 bases.

2 FISHERMAN   We'll sure provide; thou shalt have my
best gown to make thee a pair, and I'll bring thee to the
court myself.

PERICLES   Then honour be but equal to my will,
165 This day I'll rise, or else add ill to ill.   *Exeunt.*

2.2   *Enter* SIMONIDES, *with* Lords *and*
attendants and THAISA.

SIMONIDES
Are the knights ready to begin the triumph?

1 LORD   They are, my liege,
And stay your coming to present themselves.

SIMONIDES
Return them we are ready; and our daughter,

In honour of whose birth these triumphs are,
Sits here like Beauty's child, whom Nature gat
For men to see, and seeing wonder at.   *Exit a Lord.*
[*Simonides and Thaisa take seats in the pavilion, facing
the public way.*]

THAISA   It pleaseth you, my royal father, to express
My commendations great, whose merit's less.

SIMONIDES   It's fit it should be so; for princes are
A model which heaven makes like to itself:
As jewels lose their glory if neglected,
So princes their renowns if not respected.
'Tis now your honour, daughter, to entertain
The labour of each knight in his device.

THAISA   Which, to preserve mine honour, I'll perform.
[*The first knight passes by, and his squire presents
his shield to the Princess.*]

SIMONIDES   Who is the first that doth prefer himself?

THAISA   A knight of Sparta, my renowned father;
And the device he bears upon his shield
Is a black Ethiop reaching at the sun;
The word, *Lux tua vita mihi.*
[*She hands the shield to Simonides who returns it
through her to the page.*]

SIMONIDES   He loves you well that holds his life of you.
[*The second knight passes.*]
Who is the second that presents himself?

THAISA   A prince of Macedon, my royal father;
And the device he bears upon his shield
Is an arm'd knight that's conquer'd by a lady;
The motto thus, in Spanish, *Più per dolcezza che per
forza.*
[*The third knight passes.*]

SIMONIDES   And what's the third?

THAISA   The third of Antioch;
And his device, a wreath of chivalry;
The word, *Me pompae provexit apex.*
[*The fourth knight passes.*]

SIMONIDES   What is the fourth?

THAISA   A burning torch that's turned upside down;
The word, *Qui me alit, me extinguit.*

SIMONIDES
Which shows that beauty hath his power and will,
Which can as well inflame as it can kill.
[*The fifth knight passes.*]

THAISA   The fifth, an hand environed with clouds,
Holding out gold that's by the touchstone tried;
The motto thus, *Sic spectanda fides.*
[*The sixth knight, Pericles, passes in rusty armour,
without shield, and unaccompanied. He presents his
device directly to Thaisa.*]

SIMONIDES
And what's the sixth and last, the which the knight
himself
With such a graceful courtesy deliver'd?

THAISA   He seems to be a stranger; but his present is
A wither'd branch, that's only green at top;
The motto, *In hac spe vivo.*

SIMONIDES   A pretty moral;
From the dejected state wherein he is,
He hopes by you his fortunes yet may flourish.

1 LORD
He had need mean better than his outward show
Can any way speak in his just commend;
For by his rusty outside he appears
To have practis'd more the whipstock than the lance.

2 LORD   He well may be a stranger, for he comes
To an honour'd triumph strangely furnished.

3 LORD   And on set purpose let his armour rust
Until this day, to scour it in the dust.

SIMONIDES   Opinion's but a fool, that makes us scan
The outward habit by the inward man.
But stay, the knights are coming;
We will withdraw into the gallery.   *Exeunt.*
[*Great shouts and all cry, 'The mean knight!'*]

2.3   *Enter* SIMONIDES, THAISA, Marshal, *ladies,
lords,* Knights *from tilting and attendants.*

SIMONIDES   Knights,
To say you're welcome were superfluous.
To place upon the volume of your deeds,
As in a title-page, your worth in arms,
Were more than you expect, or more than's fit,
Since every worth in show commends itself.
Prepare for mirth, for mirth becomes a feast.
You are princes and my guests.

THAISA   But you, my knight and guest;
To whom this wreath of victory I give,
And crown you king of this day's happiness.

PERICLES   'Tis more by fortune, lady, than my merit.

SIMONIDES   Call it by what you will, the day is yours;
And here, I hope, is none that envies it.
In framing an artist, art hath thus decreed:
To make some good, but others to exceed;
And you are her labour'd scholar. Come, queen o'th'
feast –
For, daughter, so you are – here take your place;
Marshal, the rest, as they deserve their grace.

KNIGHTS   We are honour'd much by good Simonides.

SIMONIDES
Your presence glads our days; honour we love,
For who hates honour hates the gods above.

MARSHAL   Sir, yonder is your place.

PERICLES   Some other is more fit.

1 KNIGHT   Contend not, sir; for we are gentlemen
Have neither in our hearts nor outward eyes
Envied the great nor shall the low despise.

PERICLES   You are right courteous knights.

SIMONIDES   Sit, sir, sit.
[*aside*] By Jove, I wonder, that is king of thoughts,
These cates resist me, he not thought upon.

THAISA [*aside*]   By Juno, that is queen of marriage,
All viands that I eat do seem unsavoury,
Wishing him my meat.

[*to Simonides*]   Sure he's a gallant gentleman.

SIMONIDES [*to Thaisa*] He's but a country gentleman;
   Has done no more than other knights have done;
35   Has broken a staff or so; so let it pass.

THAISA [*aside*] To me he seems like diamond to glass.

PERICLES [*aside*]
   Yon king's to me like to my father's picture,
   Which tells me in that glory once he was;
   Had princes sit like stars about his throne,
40   And he the sun, for them to reverence.
   None that beheld him but, like lesser lights,
   Did vail their crowns to his supremacy;
   Where now his son's like a glow-worm in the night,
   The which hath fire in darkness, none in light:
45   Whereby I see that Time's the king of men;
   He's both their parent, and he is their grave,
   And gives them what he will, not what they crave.

SIMONIDES What, are you merry, knights?

1 KNIGHT Who can be other in this royal presence?

SIMONIDES
50   Here, with a cup that's stor'd unto the brim, –
   As you do love, fill to your mistress' lips, –
   We drink this health to you.

KNIGHTS   We thank your grace.

SIMONIDES Yet pause awhile;
   Yon knight doth sit too melancholy,
55   As if the entertainment in our court
   Had not a show might countervail his worth.
   Note it not you, Thaisa?

THAISA What is't to me, my father?

SIMONIDES O attend, my daughter:
60   Princes, in this, should live like gods above,
   Who freely give to every one that come to honour
     them;
   And princes not doing so are like to gnats
   Which make a sound, but kill'd are wonder'd at.
   Therefore to make his entrance more sweet,
65   Here say we drink this standing-bowl of wine to him.

THAISA Alas, my father, it befits not me
   Unto a stranger knight to be so bold;
   He may my proffer take for an offence,
   Since men take women's gifts for impudence.

70 SIMONIDES How?
   Do as I bid you, or you'll move me else!

THAISA [*aside*]
   Now, by the gods, he could not please me better.

SIMONIDES Furthermore tell him, we desire to know
   Of whence he is, his name and parentage.

75 THAISA The king my father, sir, has drunk to you.

PERICLES I thank him.

THAISA Wishing it so much blood unto your life.

PERICLES
   I thank both him and you, and pledge him freely.

THAISA And further he desires to know of you
80   Of whence you are, your name and parentage.

PERICLES A gentleman of Tyre; my name, Pericles;
   My education been in arts and arms;

   Who, looking for adventures in the world,
   Was by the rough seas reft of ships and men,
   And after shipwreck driven upon this shore.   85

THAISA He thanks your grace; names himself Pericles,
   A gentleman of Tyre,
   Who only by misfortune of the seas
   Bereft of ships and men, cast on this shore.

SIMONIDES Now, by the gods, I pity his misfortune,   90
   And will awake him from his melancholy.
   Come, gentlemen, we sit too long on trifles,
   And waste the time, which looks for other revels.
   Even in your armours, as you are address'd,
   Will well become a soldier's dance.   95
   I will not have excuse with saying this:
   Loud music is too harsh for ladies' heads,
   Since they love men in arms as well as beds.
   [*The Knights dance.*]
   So this was well ask'd, 'twas so well perform'd.
   Come, sir, here's a lady that wants breathing too;   100
   And I have heard, you knights of Tyre
   Are excellent in making ladies trip,
   And that their measures are as excellent.

PERICLES In those that practise them they are, my lord.

SIMONIDES O, that's as much as you would be denied   105
   Of your fair courtesy.
   [*The Knights and ladies dance.*]
             Unclasp, unclasp!
   Thanks, gentlemen, to all; all have done well,
   [*to Pericles*] But you the best. Pages and lights, to
    conduct
   These knights unto their several lodgings!
   Yours, sir, we have given order be next our own.   110

PERICLES I am at your grace's pleasure.

SIMONIDES Princes, it is too late to talk of love,
   And that's the mark I know you level at.
   Therefore each one betake him to his rest;
   To-morrow all for speeding do their best.   *Exeunt.*

2.4   *Enter* HELICANUS *and* ESCANES.

HELICANUS No, Escanes, know this of me,
   Antiochus from incest liv'd not free;
   For which, the most high gods not minding longer
   To withhold the vengeance that they had in store,
   Due to this heinous capital offence,   5
   Even in the height and pride of all his glory,
   When he was seated in a chariot
   Of an inestimable value, and his daughter with him,
   A fire from heaven came and shrivell'd up
   Their bodies, even to loathing; for they so stunk,   10
   That all those eyes ador'd them ere their fall
   Scorn now their hand should give them burial.

ESCANES 'Twas very strange.

HELICANUS   And yet but justice; for though
   This king were great, his greatness was no guard
   To bar heaven's shaft, but sin had his reward.   15

ESCANES 'Tis very true.

Enter three Lords.

1 LORD   See, not a man in private conference
    Or council has respect with him but he.
2 LORD   It shall no longer grieve without reproof.
20   3 LORD   And curs'd be he that will not second it.
1 LORD   Follow me then. Lord Helicane, a word.
HELICANUS
    With me? and welcome; happy day, my lords.
1 LORD   Know that our griefs are risen to the top,
    And now at length they overflow their banks.
HELICANUS
    Your griefs! for what? wrong not your prince you
25   love.
1 LORD   Wrong not yourself then, noble Helicane;
    But if the prince do live, let us salute him,
    Or know what ground's made happy by his breath.
    If in the world he live, we'll seek him out;
30   If in his grave he rest, we'll find him there;
    And be resolv'd he lives to govern us,
    Or dead, gives cause to mourn his funeral
    And leaves us to our free election,
2 LORD
    Whose death indeed the strongest in our censure,
35   And knowing this kingdom is without a head –
    Like goodly buildings left without a roof
    Soon fall to ruin – your noble self,
    That best know how to rule and how to reign,
    We thus submit unto – our sovereign.
40   ALL   Live, noble Helicane!
HELICANUS   By honour's cause, forbear your suffrages;
    If that you love Prince Pericles, forbear.
    Take I your wish, I leap into the seas,
    Where's hourly trouble for a minute's ease.
45   A twelvemonth longer, let me entreat you
    To forbear the absence of your king;
    If in which time expir'd he not return,
    I shall with aged patience bear your yoke.
    But if I cannot win you to this love,
50   Go search like nobles, like noble subjects,
    And in your search spend your adventurous worth;
    Whom if you find and win unto return,
    You shall like diamonds sit about his crown.
1 LORD   To wisdom he's a fool that will not yield;
55   And since Lord Helicane enjoineth us,
    We with our travels will endeavour it.
HELICANUS
    Then you love us, we you, and we'll clasp hands:
    When peers thus knit, a kingdom ever stands.
                               Exeunt.

2.5   *Enter* SIMONIDES, *reading of a letter at one door;*
        the Knights *meet him.*

1 KNIGHT   Good morrow to the good Simonides.
SIMONIDES
    Knights, from my daughter this I let you know,

That for this twelvemonth she'll not undertake
A married life.
Her reason to herself is only known,   5
Which from her by no means can I get.
2 KNIGHT   May we not get access to her, my lord?
SIMONIDES   Faith, by no means; she has so strictly tied
    Her to her chamber that 'tis impossible.
    One twelve moons more she'll wear Diana's livery;   10
    This by the eye of Cynthia hath she vow'd,
    And on her virgin honour will not break it.
3 KNIGHT   Loath to bid farewell, we take our leaves.
                       Exeunt Knights.
SIMONIDES   So,
    They are well dispatch'd; now to my daughter's
      letter: 15
    She tells me here, she'll wed the stranger knight,
    Or never more to view nor day nor light.
    'Tis well, mistress; your choice agrees with mine;
    I like that well: nay, how absolute she's in't,
    Not minding whether I dislike or no!   20
    Well, I do commend her choice,
    And will no longer have it be delay'd.
    Soft, here he comes: I must dissemble it.

Enter PERICLES.

PERICLES   All fortune to the good Simonides!
SIMONIDES   To you as much: sir, I am beholding to you   25
    For your sweet music this last night. I do
    Protest my ears were never better fed
    With such delightful pleasing harmony.
PERICLES   It is your grace's pleasure to commend;
    Not my desert.
SIMONIDES   Sir, you are music's master.   30
PERICLES   The worst of all her scholars, my good lord.
SIMONIDES   Let me ask you one thing:
    What do you think of my daughter, sir?
PERICLES   A most virtuous princess.
SIMONIDES   And she is fair too, is she not?   35
PERICLES   As a fair day in summer, wondrous fair.
SIMONIDES   Sir, my daughter thinks very well of you;
    Ay, so well, that you must be her master,
    And she will be your scholar: therefore look to it.
PERICLES   I am unworthy for her schoolmaster.   40
SIMONIDES   She thinks not so; peruse this writing else.
PERICLES [*aside*]   What's here?
    A letter that she loves the knight of Tyre!
    'Tis the king's subtlety to have my life. –
    [*Kneels.*] O, seek not to entrap me, gracious lord,   45
    A stranger and distressed gentleman,
    That never aim'd so high to love your daughter,
    But bent all offices to honour her.
SIMONIDES
    Thou hast bewitch'd my daughter, and thou art
    A villain.
PERICLES   By the gods, I have not: 50
    Never did thought of mine levy offence;

Nor never did my actions yet commence
A deed might gain her love or your displeasure.
SIMONIDES   Traitor, thou liest.
PERICLES   Traitor?
SIMONIDES   Ay, traitor.
55 PERICLES   Even in his throat – unless it be the king –
That calls me traitor, I return the lie.
SIMONIDES [*aside*]
Now, by the gods, I do applaud his courage.
PERICLES   My actions are as noble as my thoughts,
That never relish'd of a base descent.
60 I came unto your court for honour's cause,
And not to be a rebel to her state;
And he that otherwise accounts of me,
This sword shall prove he's honour's enemy.
SIMONIDES   No?
65 Here comes my daughter, she can witness it.

Enter THAISA.

PERICLES   Then, as you are as virtuous as fair,
Resolve your angry father, if my tongue
Did e'er solicit, or my hand subscribe
To any syllable that made love to you.
70 THAISA   Why, sir, say if you had, who takes offence
At that would make me glad?
SIMONIDES   Yea, mistress, are you so peremptory?
[*aside*] I am glad on't with all my heart. –
I'll tame you, I'll bring you in subjection.
75 Will you, not having my consent,
Bestow your love and your affections
Upon a stranger? [*aside*] who, for aught I know,
May be (nor can I think the contrary)
As great in blood as I myself. –
80 Therefore hear you, mistress: either frame
Your will to mine; and you, sir, hear you:
Either be rul'd by me, or I'll make you –
Man and wife.
Nay, come, your hands and lips must seal it too;
85 And being join'd, I'll thus your hopes destroy,
And for further grief, – God give you joy!
What, are you both pleas'd?
THAISA   Yes, if you love me, sir.
PERICLES   Even as my life my blood that fosters it.
SIMONIDES   What, are you both agreed?
90 BOTH   Yes, if't please your majesty.
SIMONIDES
It pleaseth me so well, that I will see you wed;
And then, with what haste you can, get you to bed.
                                        Exeunt.

3.Ch.   *Enter* GOWER.

GOWER
Now sleep y-slacked hath the rout;
No din but snores the house about,
Made louder by the o'er-fed breast
Of this most pompous marriage-feast.

The cat, with eyne of burning coal,   5
Now couches 'fore the mouse's hole;
And crickets at the oven's mouth
Sing the blither for their drouth.
Hymen hath brought the bride to bed,
Where by the loss of maidenhead   10
A babe is moulded. Be attent,
And time that is so briefly spent
With your fine fancies quaintly eche;
What's dumb in show I'll plain with speech.

Dumb Show

Enter PERICLES *and* SIMONIDES *at one door, with
attendants; a messenger meets them, kneels, and gives
Pericles a letter; Pericles shows it to Simonides; the lords
kneel to him. Then enter* THAISA *with child, with*
LYCHORIDA, *a nurse; the King shows her the letter; she
rejoices; she and Pericles take leave of her father, and
depart with Lychorida and their attendants. Then exeunt
Simonides and the rest.*

By many a dern and painful perch   15
Of Pericles the careful search,
By the four opposing coigns
Which the world together joins,
Is made with all due diligence
That horse and sail and high expense   20
Can stead the quest. At last from Tyre,
Fame answering the most strange inquire,
To th' court of King Simonides
Are letters brought, the tenour these:
Antiochus and his daughter dead,   25
The men of Tyrus on the head
Of Helicanus would set on
The crown of Tyre, but he will none;
The mutiny he there hastes t'appease;
Says to 'em, if King Pericles   30
Come not home in twice six moons,
He, obedient to their dooms,
Will take the crown. The sum of this,
Brought hither to Pentapolis,
Y-ravished the regions round,   35
And every one with claps can sound,
'Our heir-apparent is a king!
Who dream'd, who thought of such a thing?'
Brief, he must hence depart to Tyre.
His queen with child makes her desire –   40
Which who shall cross? – along to go.
Omit we all their dole and woe.
Lychorida, her nurse, she takes,
And so to sea. Their vessel shakes
On Neptune's billow; half the flood   45
Hath their keel cut; but fortune's mood
Varies again; the grisled north
Disgorges such a tempest forth,
That, as a duck for life that dives,
So up and down the poor ship drives.   50

The lady shrieks and well-a-near
Does fall in travail with her fear;
And what ensues in this fell storm
Shall for itself itself perform.
55 I nill relate, action may
Conveniently the rest convey;
Which might not what by me is told.
In your imagination hold
This stage the ship, upon whose deck
60 The sea-tost Pericles appears to speak.   *Exit.*

3.1   *Enter* PERICLES, *on shipboard.*

PERICLES
The god of this great vast, rebuke these surges,
Which wash both heaven and hell; and thou that hast
Upon the winds command, bind them in brass,
Having call'd them from the deep! O, still
5 Thy deaf'ning, dreadful thunders; gently quench
Thy nimble sulphurous flashes! O, how, Lychorida,
How does my queen? Thou stormest venomously;
Wilt thou spit all thyself? The seaman's whistle
Is as a whisper in the ears of death,
10 Unheard. Lychorida! – Lucina, O
Divinest patroness, and midwife gentle
To those that cry by night, convey thy deity
Aboard our dancing boat; make swift the pangs
Of my queen's travails! Now, Lychorida!

Enter LYCHORIDA, *with an infant.*

15 LYCHORIDA   Here is a thing too young for such a place,
Who, if it had conceit, would die, as I
Am like to do. Take in your arms this piece
Of your dead queen.
PERICLES   How? how, Lychorida?
LYCHORIDA   Patience, good sir; do not assist the storm.
20 Here's all that is left living of your queen,
A little daughter: for the sake of it,
Be manly, and take comfort.
PERICLES   O you gods!
Why do you make us love your goodly gifts,
And snatch them straight away? We here below
25 Recall not what we give, and therein may
Use honour with you.
LYCHORIDA   Patience, good sir,
Even for this charge.
PERICLES   Now, mild may be thy life!
For a more blusterous birth had never babe;
Quiet and gentle thy conditions! for
30 Thou art the rudeliest welcome to this world
That e'er was prince's child. Happy what follows!
Thou hast as chiding a nativity
As fire, air, water, earth, and heaven can make,
To herald thee from the womb. Poor inch of nature!
35 Even at the first thy loss is more than can
Thy portage quit, with all thou canst find here.
Now the good gods throw their best eyes upon't!

Enter two Sailors.

1 SAILOR   What courage, sir? God save you!
PERICLES   Courage enough: I do not fear the flaw;
It hath done to me the worst. Yet for the love   40
Of this poor infant, this fresh-new seafarer,
I would it would be quiet.
1 SAILOR   Slack the bolins there! Thou wilt not, wilt
thou? Blow, and split thyself.
2 SAILOR   But sea-room, and the brine and cloudy billow   45
kiss the moon, I care not.
1 SAILOR   Sir, your queen must overboard; the sea works
high, the wind is loud, and will not lie till the ship be
clear'd of the dead.
PERICLES   That's your superstition.   50
1 SAILOR   Pardon us, sir; with us at sea it hath been still
observ'd; and we are strong in custom. Therefore
briefly yield 'er, for she must overboard straight.
PERICLES   As you think meet. Most wretched queen!
LYCHORIDA   Here she lies, sir.   55
PERICLES   A terrible childbed hast thou had, my dear;
No light, no fire: th'unfriendly elements
Forgot thee utterly; nor have I time
To give thee hallow'd to thy grave, but straight
Must cast thee, scarcely coffin'd, in the ooze;   60
Where, for a monument upon thy bones,
And e'er-remaining lamps, the belching whale
And humming water must o'erwhelm thy corpse,
Lying with simple shells. O Lychorida,
Bid Nestor bring me spices, ink and paper,   65
My casket and my jewels; and bid Nicander
Bring me the satin coffer; lay the babe
Upon the pillow; hie thee, whiles I say
A priestly farewell to her: suddenly, woman.
                                    Exit Lychorida.
2 SAILOR   Sir, we have a chest beneath the hatches,   70
caulked and bitumed ready.
PERICLES   I thank thee. Mariner, say what coast is this?
2 SAILOR   We are near Tharsus.
PERICLES   Thither, gentle mariner,
Alter thy course from Tyre. When canst thou reach it?   75
2 SAILOR   By break of day, if the wind cease.
PERICLES   O, make for Tharsus!
There will I visit Cleon, for the babe
Cannot hold out to Tyrus; there I'll leave it
At careful nursing. Go thy ways, good mariner;   80
I'll bring the body presently.   *Exeunt.*

3.2   *Enter Lord* CERIMON, *with a* Servant *and
            another poor man, both storm-beaten.*

CERIMON   Philemon, ho!

Enter PHILEMON.

PHILEMON   Doth my lord call?
CERIMON   Get fire and meat for these poor men;
'T has been a turbulent and stormy night.
                                    Exit Philemon.

SERVANT   I have been in many; but such a night as this,
Till now, I ne'er endur'd.

CERIMON   Your master will be dead ere you return;
There's nothing can be minister'd to nature
That can recover him.
[*to poor man*]   Give this to the 'pothecary
And tell me how it works.

          Exeunt Servant and poor man.

          Enter two Gentlemen.

1 GENTLEMAN   Good morrow.

2 GENTLEMAN   Good morrow to your lordship.

CERIMON   Gentlemen, why do you stir so early?

1 GENTLEMAN   Sir,
Our lodgings, standing bleak upon the sea,
Shook as th'earth did quake. The very principals
Did seem to rend and all to topple. Pure
Surprise and fear made me to quit the house.

2 GENTLEMAN
That is the cause we trouble you so early;
'Tis not our husbandry.

CERIMON   O, you say well.

1 GENTLEMAN
But I much marvel that your lordship, having
Rich tire about you, should at these early hours
Shake off the golden slumber of repose.
'Tis most strange,
Nature should be so conversant with pain,
Being thereto not compell'd.

CERIMON   I hold it ever,
Virtue and cunning were endowments greater
Than nobleness and riches; careless heirs
May the two latter darken and expend,
But immortality attends the former,
Making a man a god. 'Tis known I ever
Have studied physic, through which secret art,
By turning o'er authorities, I have,
Together with my practice, made familiar
To me and to my aid the blest infusions
That dwells in vegetives, in metals, stones;
And can speak of the disturbances that
Nature works, and of her cures; which doth give me
A more content in course of true delight
Than to be thirsty after tottering honour,
Or tie my treasure up in silken bags,
To please the fool and death.

2 GENTLEMAN
Your honour has through Ephesus pour'd forth
Your charity, and hundreds call themselves
Your creatures, who by you have been restor'd;
And not your knowledge, your personal pain, but
    even
Your purse, still open, hath built Lord Cerimon
Such strong renown as time shall never raze.

     Enter two or three Servants *with a chest.*

1 SERVANT   So; lift there.

CERIMON   What's that?

1 SERVANT   Sir, even now
Did the sea toss up upon our shore this chest;
'Tis of some wreck.

CERIMON   Set't down; let's look upon't.

2 GENTLEMAN   'Tis like a coffin, sir.

CERIMON   Whate'er it be,
'Tis wondrous heavy. Wrench it open straight.
If the sea's stomach be o'ercharg'd with gold,
'Tis a good constraint of fortune
It belches upon us.

2 GENTLEMAN   'Tis so, my lord.

CERIMON   How close 'tis caulked and bitumed! Did the
sea cast it up?

1 SERVANT   I never saw so huge a billow, sir, as tossed it
upon shore.

CERIMON   Wrench it open: soft! it smells most sweetly in
my sense.

2 GENTLEMAN   A delicate odour.

CERIMON   As ever hit my nostril. So, up with it.
O you most potent gods! what's here? a corse!

1 GENTLEMAN   Most strange!

CERIMON   Shrouded in cloths of state; balmed and
entreasured with full bags of spices! A passport too!
Apollo, perfect me in the characters!
[*Reads from a scroll.*]
     Here I give to understand,
     If e'er this coffin drives a-land,
     I, King Pericles, have lost
     This queen, worth all our mundane cost.
     Who finds her, give her burying;
     She was the daughter of a king.
     Besides this treasure for a fee,
     The gods requite his charity!
If thou livest, Pericles, thou hast a heart
That even cracks for woe! This chanc'd to-night.

2 GENTLEMAN   Most likely, sir.

CERIMON   Nay, certainly to-night;
For look how fresh she looks! They were too rough
That threw her in the sea. Make a fire within;
Fetch hither all my boxes in my closet.

          Exit a Servant.

Death may usurp on nature many hours,
And yet the fire of life kindle again
The o'erpress'd spirits. I heard of an Egyptian
That had nine hours lien dead,
Who was by good appliance recovered.

   Enter Servant, *with boxes, napkins, and fire.*

Well said, well said; the fire and cloths.
The still and woeful music that we have,
Cause it to sound, beseech you.   [*Music.*]
The viol once more; how thou stirr'st, thou block!
The music there!   [*Music.*]
          I pray you, give her air.
Gentlemen, this queen will live.
Nature awakes a warm breath out of her.

She hath not been entranc'd above five hours;
See, how she 'gins to blow into life's flower again!

1 GENTLEMAN
The heavens, through you, increase our wonder,
And set up your fame forever.

CERIMON   She is alive!
100 Behold, her eyelids, cases to those
Heavenly jewels which Pericles hath lost,
Begin to part their fringes of bright gold.
The diamonds of a most praised water
Doth appear to make the world twice rich. Live,
105 And make us weep to hear your fate, fair creature,
Rare as you seem to be. [*She moves.*]

THAISA   O dear Diana,
Where am I? Where's my lord? What world is this?

2 GENTLEMAN   Is not this strange?

1 GENTLEMAN   Most rare.

110 CERIMON   Hush, my gentle neighbours!
Lend me your hands; to the next chamber bear her;
Get linen: now this matter must be look'd to,
For her relapse is mortal. Come, come;
And Aesculapius guide us!

Exeunt, carrying Thaisa away.

3.3   *Enter* PERICLES *with* CLEON *and* DIONYZA,
and LYCHORIDA *with* MARINA *in her arms.*

PERICLES   Most honour'd Cleon, I must needs be gone;
My twelve months are expir'd, and Tyrus stands
In a litigious peace. You and your lady,
Take from my heart all thankfulness! the gods
Make up the rest upon you!

5 CLEON   Your strokes of fortune,
Though they hurt you mortally, yet glance
Full woundingly on us.

DIONYZA   O your sweet queen!
That the strict fates had pleas'd you had brought her
    hither,
To have bless'd mine eyes with her!

PERICLES   We cannot but obey
10 The powers above us. Could I rage and roar
As doth the sea she lies in, yet the end
Must be as 'tis. My gentle babe Marina,
Whom, for she was born at sea, I have nam'd so, here
I charge your charity withal; leaving her
15 The infant of your care; beseeching you
To give her princely training, that she may
Be manner'd as she is born.

CLEON   Fear not, my lord, but think
Your grace, that fed my country with your corn,
For which the people's prayers still fall upon you,
20 Must in your child be thought on. If neglection
Should therein make me vile, the common body,
By you reliev'd, would force me to my duty.
But if to that my nature need a spur,
The gods revenge it upon me and mine,
To the end of generation!

PERICLES   I believe you; 25
Your honour and your goodness teach me to't,
Without your vows. Till she be married, madam,
By bright Diana, whom we honour, all
Unscissor'd shall this hair of mine remain,
Though I show ill in't. So I take my leave. 30
Good madam, make me blessed in your care
In bringing up my child.

DIONYZA   I have one myself,
Who shall not be more dear to my respect
Than yours, my lord.

PERICLES   Madam, my thanks and prayers.

CLEON
We'll bring your grace e'en to the edge o'th' shore, 35
Then give you up to the mask'd Neptune and
The gentlest winds of heaven.

PERICLES   I will embrace
Your offer. Come, dearest madam. O, no tears,
Lychorida, no tears;
Look to your little mistress, on whose grace 40
You may depend hereafter. Come, my lord.   *Exeunt.*

3.4   *Enter* CERIMON *and* THAISA.

CERIMON   Madam, this letter and some certain jewels
Lay with you in your coffer; which are
At your command. Know you the character?

THAISA   It is my lord's. That I was shipp'd at sea
I well remember, even on my eaning time; 5
But whether there deliver'd, by the holy gods,
I cannot rightly say. But since King Pericles,
My wedded lord, I ne'er shall see again,
A vestal livery will I take me to,
And never more have joy. 10

CERIMON   Madam, if this you purpose as ye speak,
Diana's temple is not distant far,
Where you may abide till your date expire.
Moreover, if you please, a niece of mine
Shall there attend you. 15

THAISA   My recompense is thanks, that's all;
Yet my good will is great, though the gift small.

Exeunt.

4.Ch.   *Enter* GOWER.

GOWER
Imagine Pericles arriv'd at Tyre,
Welcom'd and settled to his own desire.
His woeful queen we leave at Ephesus,
Unto Diana there's a votaress.
Now to Marina bend your mind, 5
Whom our fast-growing scene must find
At Tharsus, and by Cleon train'd
In music's letters; who hath gain'd
Of education all the grace,
Which makes her both the heart and place 10
Of general wonder. But, alack,
That monster envy, oft the wrack

Of earned praise, Marina's life
Seeks to take off by treason's knife;
And in this kind hath our Cleon
One daughter and a wench full-grown,
Even ripe for marriage-rite. This maid
Hight Philoten; and it is said
For certain in our story, she
Would ever with Marina be:
Be't when she weav'd the sleided silk
With fingers long, small, white as milk;
Or when she would with sharp neele wound
The cambric, which she made more sound
By hurting it; or when to th' lute
She sung, and made the night-bird mute
That still records with moan; or when
She would with rich and constant pen
Vail to her mistress Dian; still
This Philoten contends in skill
With absolute Marina: so
With dove of Paphos might the crow
Vie feathers white. Marina gets
All praises, which are paid as debts,
And not as given. This so darks
In Philoten all graceful marks,
That Cleon's wife with envy rare
A present murderer does prepare
For good Marina, that her daughter
Might stand peerless by this slaughter.
The sooner her vile thoughts to stead,
Lychorida, our nurse, is dead;
And cursed Dionyza hath
The pregnant instrument of wrath
Prest for this blow. The unborn event
I do commend to your content;
Only I carried winged time
Post on the lame feet of my rime;
Which never could I so convey,
Unless your thoughts went on my way.
Dionyza does appear,
With Leonine, a murtherer.   *Exit.*

4.1   *Enter* DIONYZA *with* LEONINE.

DIONYZA   Thy oath remember; thou hast sworn to do't.
  'Tis but a blow, which never shall be known.
  Thou canst not do a thing in the world so soon,
  To yield thee so much profit. Let not conscience,
  Which is but cold, or flaming love thy bosom
  Enslave too nicely; nor let pity, which
  Even women have cast off, melt thee, but be
  A soldier to thy purpose.
LEONINE   I will do't; but yet she is a goodly creature.
DIONYZA   The fitter then the gods should have her.
  Here she comes weeping for her only mistress' death.
  Thou art resolv'd?
LEONINE   I am resolv'd.

          Enter MARINA, *with a basket of flowers.*

MARINA   No, I will rob Tellus of her weed,
  To strew thy green with flowers; the yellows, blues,
  The purple violets, and marigolds,   15
  Shall as a carpet hang upon thy grave,
  While summer-days doth last. Ay me! poor maid,
  Born in a tempest, when my mother died,
  This world to me is as a lasting storm,
  Whirring me from my friends.   20
DIONYZA   How now, Marina! why do you keep alone?
  How chance my daughter is not with you?
  Do not consume your blood with sorrowing:
  Have you a nurse of me! Lord, how your favour's
  Chang'd with this unprofitable woe!   25
  Come, give me your flowers. On the sea-margent
  Walk with Leonine; the air is quick there,
  And it pierces and sharpens the stomach.
  Come, Leonine, take her by the arm, walk with her.
MARINA
  No, I pray you; I'll not bereave you of your servant.   30
DIONYZA   Come, come;
  I love the king your father and yourself
  With more than foreign heart. We every day
  Expect him here; when he shall come and find
  Our paragon to all reports thus blasted,   35
  He will repent the breadth of his great voyage;
  Blame both my lord and me, that we have taken
  No care to your best courses. Go, I pray you,
  Walk, and be cheerful once again; reserve
  That excellent complexion, which did steal   40
  The eyes of young and old. Care not for me;
  I can go home alone.
MARINA   Well, I will go;
  But yet I have no desire to it.
DIONYZA   Come, come, I know 'tis good for you.
  Walk half an hour, Leonine, at the least.   45
  Remember what I have said.
LEONINE   I warrant you, madam.
DIONYZA   I'll leave you, my sweet lady, for a while.
  Pray, walk softly, do not heat your blood.
  What! I must have care of you.
MARINA   My thanks, sweet madam.
                Exit Dionyza.
  Is this wind westerly that blows?
LEONINE   South-west.   50
MARINA   When I was born, the wind was north.
LEONINE   Was't so?
MARINA   My father, as nurse says, did never fear,
  But cried 'Good seamen!' to the sailors, galling
  His kingly hands, haling ropes;
  And, clasping to the mast, endur'd a sea   55
  That almost burst the deck.
LEONINE   When was this?
MARINA   When I was born.
  Never was waves nor wind more violent;
  And from the ladder-tackle washes off   60
  A canvas-climber. 'Ha!' says one, 'wolt out?'
  And with a dropping industry they skip

From stem to stern; the boatswain whistles, and
The master calls and trebles their confusion.

65 LEONINE Come, say your prayers.

MARINA What mean you?

LEONINE If you require a little space for prayer,
I grant it. Pray, but be not tedious;
For the gods are quick of ear, and I am sworn
To do my work with haste.

70 MARINA   Why will you kill me?

LEONINE To satisfy my lady.

MARINA Why would she have me kill'd?
Now, as I can remember, by my troth,
I never did her hurt in all my life.

75 I never spake bad word, nor did ill turn
To any living creature; believe me la,
I never kill'd a mouse, nor hurt a fly;
I trod upon a worm against my will,
But I wept for't. How have I offended,

80 Wherein my death might yield her any profit,
Or my life imply her any danger?

LEONINE My commission
Is not to reason of the deed, but do't.

MARINA You will not do't for all the world, I hope.

85 You are well favour'd, and your looks foreshow
You have a gentle heart. I saw you lately,
When you caught hurt in parting two that fought.
Good sooth, it show'd well in you. Do so now.
Your lady seeks my life; come you between,
And save poor me, the weaker.

90 LEONINE   I am sworn,
And will dispatch. [*Seizes her.*]

Enter Pirates.

1 PIRATE Hold, villain!   *Leonine runs away.*

2 PIRATE A prize! a prize!

3 PIRATE Half-part, mates, half-part! Come, let's have

95 her aboard suddenly.   *Exeunt Pirates with Marina.*

Enter LEONINE.

LEONINE
These roguing thieves serve the great pirate Valdes;
And they have seiz'd Marina. Let her go;
There's no hope she'll return. I'll swear she's dead
And thrown into the sea. But I'll see further;

100 Perhaps they will but please themselves upon her,
Not carry her aboard. If she remain,
Whom they have ravish'd must by me be slain. *Exit.*

4.2   *Enter* Pandar, Bawd *and* BOULT.

PANDAR Boult!

BOULT Sir?

PANDAR Search the market narrowly; Mytilene is full of
gallants. We lost too much money this mart by being

5 too wenchless.

BAWD We were never so much out of creatures. We have
but poor three, and they can do no more than they can
do; and they with continual action are even as good as
rotten.

10 PANDAR Therefore let's have fresh ones, whate'er we
pay for them. If there be not a conscience to be us'd in
every trade, we shall never prosper.

BAWD Thou say'st true; 'tis not our bringing up of poor
bastards, as I think I have brought up some eleven –

15 BOULT Ay, to eleven; and brought them down again.
But shall I search the market?

BAWD What else, man? The stuff we have, a strong wind
will blow it to pieces, they are so pitifully sodden.

PANDAR Thou sayest true; there's two unwholesome, a'
20 conscience. The poor Transylvanian is dead, that lay
with the little baggage.

BOULT Ay, she quickly poop'd him; she made him
roast-meat for worms. But I'll go search the market.
Exit.

PANDAR Three or four thousand chequins were as
25 pretty a proportion to live quietly, and so give over.

BAWD Why to give over, I pray you? is it a shame to get
when we are old?

PANDAR O, our credit comes not in like the commodity,
nor the commodity wages not with the danger;
30 therefore, if in our youths we could pick up some
pretty estate, 'twere not amiss to keep our door
hatch'd. Besides, the sore terms we stand upon with
the gods will be strong with us for giving o'er.

BAWD Come, other sorts offend as well as we.

35 PANDAR As well as we? ay, and better too; we offend
worse. Neither is our profession any trade; it's no
calling. But here comes Boult.

Enter BOULT, *with the* Pirates *and* MARINA.

BOULT Come your ways, my masters; you say she's a
virgin?

40 1 PIRATE O, sir, we doubt it not.

BOULT Master, I have gone through for this piece you
see. If you like her, so; if not, I have lost my earnest.

BAWD Boult, has she any qualities?

BOULT She has a good face, speaks well, and has
45 excellent good clothes; there's no farther necessity of
qualities can make her be refus'd.

BAWD What's her price, Boult?

BOULT I cannot be bated one doit of a thousand pieces.

PANDAR Well, follow me, my masters; you shall have
50 your money presently. Wife, take her in; instruct her
what she has to do, that she may not be raw in her
entertainment.   *Exeunt Pandar and Pirates.*

BAWD Boult, take you the marks of her, the colour of her
hair, complexion, height, her age, with warrant of
55 her virginity, and cry 'He that will give most shall have
her first.' Such a maidenhead were no cheap thing, if
men were as they have been. Get this done as I
command you.

BOULT Performance shall follow.   *Exit.*

60 MARINA Alack that Leonine was so slack, so slow!

He should have struck, not spoke; or that these
   pirates
Not enough barbarous, had not o'erboard
Thrown me for to seek my mother!

BAWD   Why lament you, pretty one?

MARINA   That I am pretty.

BAWD   Come, the gods have done their part in you.

MARINA   I accuse them not.

BAWD   You are light into my hands, where you are like
to live.

MARINA   The more my fault
To 'scape his hands where I was like to die.

BAWD   Ay, and you shall live in pleasure.

MARINA   No.

BAWD   Yes, indeed shall you, and taste gentlemen of all
fashions. You shall fare well; you shall have the
difference of all complexions. What do you stop your
ears?

MARINA   Are you a woman?

BAWD   What would you have me be, and I be not a
woman?

MARINA   An honest woman, or not a woman.

BAWD   Marry, whip thee, gosling; I think I shall have
something to do with you. Come, you're a young
foolish sapling, and must be bow'd as I would have
you.

MARINA   The gods defend me!

BAWD   If it please the gods to defend you by men, then
men must comfort you, men must feed you, men stir
you up. Boult's return'd.

Enter BOULT.

Now, sir, hast thou cried her through the market?

BOULT   I have cried her almost to the number of her
hairs; I have drawn her picture with my voice.

BAWD   And I prithee tell me, how dost thou find the
inclination of the people, especially of the younger
sort?

BOULT   Faith, they listen'd to me as they would have
hearken'd to their father's testament. There was a
Spaniard's mouth water'd and he went to bed to her
very description.

BAWD   We shall have him here to-morrow with his best
ruff on.

BOULT   To-night, to-night. But, mistress, do you know
the French knight that cowers i'the hams?

BAWD   Who? Monsieur Verolles?

BOULT   Ay, he; he offer'd to cut a caper at the
proclamation; but he made a groan at it, and swore he
would see her to-morrow.

BAWD   Well, well; as for him, he brought his disease
hither: here he does but repair it. I know he will
come in our shadow, to scatter his crowns in the sun.

BOULT   Well, if we had of every nation a traveller, we
should lodge them with this sign.

BAWD   [*to Marina*] Pray you, come hither awhile. You
have fortunes coming upon you. Mark me: you must

seem to do that fearfully which you commit willingly;   115
despise profit where you have most gain. To weep that
you live as ye do makes pity in your lovers: seldom but
that pity begets you a good opinion, and that opinion
a mere profit.

MARINA   I understand you not.   120

BOULT   O, take her home, mistress, take her home; these
blushes of hers must be quench'd with some present
practice.

BAWD   Thou sayest true, i'faith, so they must; for your
bride goes to that with shame which is her way to go   125
with warrant.

BOULT   Faith, some do, and some do not. But, mistress,
if I have bargain'd for the joint, –

BAWD   Thou mayst cut a morsel off the spit.

BOULT   I may so?   130

BAWD   Who should deny it? Come, young one, I like
the manner of your garments well.

BOULT   Ay, by my faith, they shall not be chang'd yet.

BAWD   Boult, spend thou that in the town; report what a
sojourner we have; you'll lose nothing by custom.   135
When nature fram'd this piece, she meant thee a good
turn; therefore say what a paragon she is, and thou
hast the harvest out of thine own report.

BOULT   I warrant you, mistress, thunder shall not so
awake the bed of eels as my giving out her beauty   140
stirs up the lewdly inclin'd. I'll bring home some
to-night.

BAWD   Come your ways; follow me.

MARINA   If fires be hot, knives sharp, or waters deep,
Untied I still my virgin knot will keep.   145
Diana, aid my purpose!

BAWD   What have we to do with Diana? Pray you, will
you go with us?   *Exeunt.*

4.3   *Enter* CLEON *and* DIONYZA.

DIONYZA   Why are you foolish? Can it be undone?

CLEON   O Dionyza, such a piece of slaughter
The sun and moon ne'er look'd upon!

DIONYZA   I think you'll turn child again.

CLEON   Were I chief lord of all this spacious world,   5
I'd give it to undo the deed. A lady,
Much less in blood than virtue, yet a princess
To equal any single crown o'th' earth
I'th' justice of compare! O villain Leonine!
Whom thou hast poison'd too.   10
If thou hadst drunk to him, 't had been a kindness
Becoming well thy fact. What canst thou say
When noble Pericles shall demand his child?

DIONYZA   That she is dead. Nurses are not the fates,
To foster it, not ever to preserve.   15
She died at night; I'll say so. Who can cross it?
Unless you play the pious innocent,
And for an honest attribute cry out
'She died by foul play.'

CLEON   O, go to. Well, well.

Of all the faults beneath the heavens, the gods
Do like this worst.

DIONYZA   Be one of those that thinks
The petty wrens of Tharsus will fly hence,
And open this to Pericles. I do shame
To think of what a noble strain you are,
And of how coward a spirit.

CLEON   To such proceeding
Who ever but his approbation added,
Though not his prime consent, he did not flow
From honourable sources.

DIONYZA   Be it so, then.
Yet none does know but you how she came dead,
Nor none can know, Leonine being gone.
She did distain my child, and stood between
Her and her fortunes. None would look on her,
But cast their gazes on Marina's face,
Whilst ours was blurted at and held a malkin
Not worth the time of day. It pierc'd me through;
And though you call my course unnatural, –
You not your child well loving – yet I find
It greets me as an enterprise of kindness
Perform'd to your sole daughter.

CLEON   Heavens forgive it!

DIONYZA   And as for Pericles,
What should he say? we wept after her hearse,
And yet we mourn. Her monument
Is almost finish'd, and her epitaphs
In glitt'ring golden characters express
A general praise to her, and care in us
At whose expense 'tis done.

CLEON   Thou art like the harpy,
Which, to betray, dost with thine angel's face,
Seize with thine eagle's talons.

DIONYZA   Ye're like one that superstitiously
Do swear to th' gods that winter kills the flies;
But yet I know you'll do as I advise.   *Exeunt.*

4.4   *Enter* GOWER.

GOWER
Thus time we waste, and long leagues make short;
Sail seas in cockles, have and wish but for't;
Making, to take our imagination,
From bourn to bourn, region to region.
By you being pardon'd, we commit no crime
To use one language in each several clime
Where our scene seems to live. I do beseech you
To learn of me, who stand i'th' gaps to teach you
The stages of our story. Pericles
Is now again thwarting the wayward seas,
Attended on by many a lord and knight,
To see his daughter, all his life's delight.
Old Helicanus goes along. Behind
Is left to govern it, you bear in mind,
Old Escanes, whom Helicanus late
Advanc'd in time to great and high estate.

Well-sailing ships and bounteous winds have brought
This king to Tharsus – think his pilot thought;
So with his steerage shall your thoughts grow on –
To fetch his daughter home, who first is gone.
Like motes and shadows see them move awhile;
Your ears unto your eyes I'll reconcile.

                       Dumb Show.

Enter PERICLES *at one door, with all his train;* CLEON *and*
DIONYZA *at the other. Cleon shows Pericles the tomb;*
whereat Pericles makes lamentation, puts on sackcloth, and
in a mighty passion departs. Then exeunt Cleon, Dionyza
                    and the rest.

See how belief may suffer by foul show!
This borrow'd passion stands for true-ow'd woe;
And Pericles, in sorrow all devour'd,
With sighs shot through and biggest tears
    o'ershower'd,
Leaves Tharsus and again embarks. He swears
Never to wash his face, nor cut his hairs.
He puts on sackcloth, and to sea. He bears
A tempest, which his mortal vessel tears,
And yet he rides it out. Now please you wit
The epitaph is for Marina writ
By wicked Dionyza.
[*Reads the inscription on Marina's monument.*]
The fairest, sweet'st and best, lies here,
Who wither'd in her spring of year.
She was of Tyrus the king's daughter,
On whom foul death hath made this slaughter.
Marina was she call'd; and at her birth,
Thetis, being proud, swallow'd some part o'th' earth.
Therefore the earth, fearing to be o'erflow'd,
Hath Thetis' birth-child on the heavens bestow'd;
Wherefore she does, and swears she'll never stint,
Make raging battery upon shores of flint.
No visor does become black villainy
So well as soft and tender flattery.
Let Pericles believe his daughter's dead,
And bear his courses to be ordered
By Lady Fortune; while our scene must play
His daughter's woe and heavy well-a-day
In her unholy service. Patience, then,
And think you now are all in Mytilen.   *Exit.*

4.5   *Enter, from the brothel, two* Gentlemen.

1 GENTLEMAN   Did you ever hear the like?

2 GENTLEMAN   No, nor never shall do in such a place as
this, she being once gone.

1 GENTLEMAN   But to have divinity preach'd there! did
you ever dream of such a thing?

2 GENTLEMAN   No, no. Come, I am for no more bawdy-
houses. Shall's go hear the vestals sing?

1 GENTLEMAN   I'll do anything now that is virtuous; but
I am out of the road of rutting for ever.   *Exeunt.*

4.6   *Enter* Pandar, Bawd *and* BOULT.

PANDAR   Well, I had rather than twice the worth of her
she had ne'er come here.

BAWD   Fie, fie upon her! she's able to freeze the god
Priapus, and undo a whole generation. We must
either get her ravish'd or be rid of her. When she
should do for clients her fitment and do me the
kindness of our profession, she has me her quirks, her
reasons, her master-reasons, her prayers, her knees;
that she would make a puritan of the devil, if he would
cheapen a kiss of her.

BOULT   Faith, I must ravish her, or she'll disfurnish us
of all our cavalleria, and make our swearers priests.

PANDAR   Now, the pox upon her green-sickness for me!

BAWD   Faith, there's no way to be rid on't but by the way
to the pox. Here comes the Lord Lysimachus, disguis'd.

BOULT   We should have both lord and lown, if the
peevish baggage would but give way to customers.

Enter LYSIMACHUS.

LYSIMACHUS   How now! How a dozen of virginities?

BAWD   Now, the gods to bless your honour!

BOULT   I am glad to see your honour in good health.

LYSIMACHUS   You may so; 'tis the better for you that
your resorters stand upon sound legs. How now,
wholesome iniquity, have you that a man may deal
withal, and defy the surgeon?

BAWD   We have here one, sir, if she would – but there
never came her like in Mytilene.

LYSIMACHUS   If she'd do the deeds of darkness, thou
wouldst say.

BAWD   Your honour knows what 'tis to say well enough.

LYSIMACHUS   Well, call forth, call forth.

BOULT   For flesh and blood, sir, white and red, you shall
see a rose; and she were a rose indeed, if she had but –

LYSIMACHUS   What, prithee?

BOULT   O, sir, I can be modest.

LYSIMACHUS   That dignifies the renown of a bawd no
less than it gives a good report to a number to be
chaste.   *Exit Boult.*

BAWD   Here comes that which grows to the stalk; never
pluck'd yet, I can assure you.

Enter BOULT *with* MARINA.

Is she not a fair creature?

LYSIMACHUS   Faith, she would serve after a long voyage
at sea. Well, there's for you; leave us.

BAWD   I beseech your honour, give me leave a word, and
I'll have done presently.

LYSIMACHUS   I beseech you, do.

BAWD [*to Marina*]   First, I would have you note, this is
an honourable man.

MARINA   I desire to find him so, that I may worthily note
him.

BAWD   Next, he's the governor of this country, and a
man whom I am bound to.

MARINA   If he govern the country, you are bound to him
indeed; but how honourable he is in that I know not.

BAWD   Pray you, without any more virginal fencing, will   55
you use him kindly? he will line your apron with gold.

MARINA   What he will do graciously, I will thankfully
receive.

LYSIMACHUS   Ha' you done?

BAWD   My lord, she's not pac'd yet; you must take some   60
pains to work her to your manage. Come, we will leave
his honour and her together. Go thy ways.
                Exeunt Bawd, Pandar, and Boult.

LYSIMACHUS   Now, pretty one, how long have you been
at this trade?

MARINA   What trade, sir?   65

LYSIMACHUS   Why, I cannot name't but I shall offend.

MARINA   I cannot be offended with my trade. Please you
to name it.

LYSIMACHUS   How long have you been of this profession?

MARINA   E'er since I can remember.   70

LYSIMACHUS   Did you go to't so young? Were you a
gamester at five or at seven?

MARINA   Earlier too, sir, if now I be one.

LYSIMACHUS   Why, the house you dwell in proclaims
you to be a creature of sale.   75

MARINA   Do you know this house to be a place of such
resort, and will come into't? I hear say you're of
honourable parts and are the governor of this place.

LYSIMACHUS   Why, hath your principal made known
unto you who I am?   80

MARINA   Who is my principal?

LYSIMACHUS   Why, your herb woman; she that sets
seeds and roots of shame and iniquity. O, you have
heard something of my power, and so stand aloof for
more serious wooing. But I protest to thee, pretty one,   85
my authority shall not see thee, or else look friendly
upon thee. Come, bring me to some private place;
come, come.

MARINA   If you were born to honour, show it now;
If put upon you, make the judgement good   90
That thought you worthy of it.

LYSIMACHUS
How's this? how's this? Some more; be sage.

MARINA   For me,
That am a maid, though most ungentle fortune
Have plac'd me in this sty, where, since I came,
Diseases have been sold dearer than physic –   95
That the gods
Would set me free from this unhallow'd place,
Though they did change me to the meanest bird
That flies i'th' purer air!

LYSIMACHUS   I did not think
Thou couldst have spoke so well; ne'er dreamt thou
couldst.   100
Had I brought hither a corrupted mind,
Thy speech had alter'd it. Hold, here's gold for thee.
Persever in that clear way thou goest,

And the gods strengthen thee!

105 MARINA   The good gods preserve you!

LYSIMACHUS   For me, be you thoughten
  That I came with no ill intent; for to me
  The very doors and windows savour vilely.
  Fare thee well. Thou art a piece of virtue, and
110   I doubt not but thy training hath been noble.
  Hold, here's more gold for thee.
  A curse upon him, die he like a thief,
  That robs thee of thy goodness! If thou dost
  Hear from me, it shall be for thy good.

Enter BOULT.

115 BOULT   I beseech your honour, one piece for me.

LYSIMACHUS
  Avaunt thou damned door-keeper! Your house,
  But for this virgin that doth prop it,
  Would sink and overwhelm you. Away!   *Exit.*

BOULT   How's this? We must take another course with
120   you. If your peevish chastity, which is not worth a
  breakfast in the cheapest country under the cope, shall
  undo a whole household, let me be gelded like a
  spaniel. Come your ways.

MARINA   Whither would you have me?

125 BOULT   I must have your maidenhead taken off, or the
  common hangman shall execute it. Come your ways.
  We'll have no more gentlemen driven away. Come
  your ways, I say.

Enter Bawd *and* Pandar.

BAWD   How now! what's the matter?

130 BOULT   Worse and worse, mistress; she has here spoken
  holy words to the Lord Lysimachus.

BAWD   O abominable!

BOULT   She makes our profession as it were to stink
  afore the face of the gods.

135 BAWD   Marry, hang her up for ever!

BOULT   The nobleman would have dealt with her like a
  nobleman, and she sent him away as cold as a
  snowball; saying his prayers too.

BAWD   Boult, take her away; use her at thy pleasure.
140   Crack the glass of her virginity, and make the rest
  malleable.

BOULT   And if she were a thornier piece of ground than
  she is, she shall be plough'd.

MARINA   Hark, hark, you gods!

145 BAWD   She conjures: away with her! Would she had
  never come within my doors! Marry, hang you! She's
  born to undo us. Will you not go the way of women-
  kind? Marry, come up, my dish of chastity with
  rosemary and bays!   *Exeunt Bawd and Pandar.*

150 BOULT   Come, mistress; come your ways with me.

MARINA   Whither wilt thou have me?

BOULT   To take from you the jewel you hold so dear.

MARINA   Prithee, tell me one thing first.

BOULT   Come now, your one thing.

155 MARINA   What canst thou wish thine enemy to be?

BOULT   Why, I could wish him to be my master, or
  rather, my mistress.

MARINA   Neither of these are so bad as thou art,
  Since they do better thee in their command.
  Thou hold'st a place, for which the pained'st fiend   160
  Of hell would not in reputation change;
  Thou art the damned door-keeper to every
  Coistrel that comes inquiring for his Tib;
  To the choleric fisting of every rogue
  Thy ear is liable; thy food is such   165
  As hath been belch'd on by infected lungs.

BOULT   What would you have me do? go to the wars,
  would you? where a man may serve seven years for the
  loss of a leg, and have not money enough in the end to
  buy him a wooden one?   170

MARINA   Do any thing but this thou doest. Empty
  Old receptacles, or common shores, of filth;
  Serve by indenture to the common hangman:
  Any of these ways are yet better than this;
  For what thou professest, a baboon, could he speak,   175
  Would own a name too dear. That the gods
  Would safely deliver me from this place!
  Here, here's gold for thee.
  If that thy master would gain by me,
  Proclaim that I can sing, weave, sew, and dance,   180
  With other virtues, which I'll keep from boast;
  And will undertake all these to teach.
  I doubt not but this populous city will
  Yield many scholars.

BOULT   But can you teach all this you speak of?   185

MARINA   Prove that I cannot, take me home again,
  And prostitute me to the basest groom
  That doth frequent your house.

BOULT   Well, I will see what I can do for thee; if I can
  place thee, I will.   190

MARINA   But amongst honest women.

BOULT   Faith, my acquaintance lies little amongst them.
  But since my master and mistress hath bought you,
  there's no going but by their consent; therefore I will
  make them acquainted with your purpose, and I doubt   195
  not but I shall find them tractable enough. Come, I'll
  do for thee what I can; come your ways.   *Exeunt.*

5.Ch.   *Enter* GOWER.

GOWER
  Marina thus the brothel 'scapes, and chances
  Into an honest house, our story says.
  She sings like one immortal, and she dances
  As goddess-like to her admired lays.
  Deep clerks she dumbs, and with her neele composes   5
  Nature's own shape, of bud, bird, branch, or berry,
  That even her art sisters the natural roses;
  Her inkle, silk, twin with the rubied cherry:
  That pupils lacks she none of noble race,
  Who pour their bounty on her; and her gain   10
  She gives the cursed bawd. Here we her place,

And to her father turn our thoughts again,
Where we left him on the sea. We there him lost,
Whence, driven before the winds, he is arriv'd
Here where his daughter dwells; and on this coast
Suppose him now at anchor. The city striv'd
God Neptune's annual feast to keep; from whence
Lysimachus our Tyrian ship espies,
His banners sable, trimm'd with rich expense;
And to him in his barge with fervour hies.
In your supposing once more put your sight;
Of heavy Pericles, think this his bark,
Where what is done in action, more, if might,
Shall be discover'd; please you sit and hark.   *Exit.*

5.1   *Enter* HELICANUS, *to him two* Sailors,
one belonging to the Tyrian vessel, the other to the barge.

TYRIAN SAILOR
   Where is Lord Helicanus? he can resolve you.
   O, here he is.
   [*to Helicanus*] Sir, there is a barge put off from
      Mytilene,
   And in it is Lysimachus the governor,
   Who craves to come aboard. What is your will?
HELICANUS   That he have his. Call up some gentlemen.
TYRIAN SAILOR   Ho, gentlemen! my lord calls.

               Enter two or three Gentlemen.

1 GENTLEMAN   Doth your lordship call?
HELICANUS   Gentlemen, there is some of worth would
   come aboard; I pray, greet him fairly.
[*Gentlemen and Sailors descend, and go on board the barge.*]

         Enter from thence LYSIMACHUS *and* Lords; *with*
                  them the gentlemen and sailors.

TYRIAN SAILOR   Sir,
   This is the man that can, in aught you would,
   Resolve you.
LYSIMACHUS   Hail, reverend sir! the gods preserve you!
HELICANUS   And you, to outlive the age I am,
   And die as I would do.
LYSIMACHUS   You wish me well.
   Being on shore, honouring of Neptune's triumphs,
   Seeing this goodly vessel ride before us,
   I made to it to know of whence you are.
HELICANUS   First, what is your place?
LYSIMACHUS
   I am the governor of this place you lie before.
HELICANUS   Sir,
   Our vessel is of Tyre, in it the king;
   A man who for this three months hath not spoken
   To any one, nor taken sustenance
   But to prorogue his grief.
LYSIMACHUS   Upon what ground is his distemperature?
HELICANUS   'Twould be too tedious to repeat;
   But the main grief springs from the loss
   Of a beloved daughter and a wife.
LYSIMACHUS   May we not see him?

HELICANUS   You may;
   But bootless is your sight; he will not speak
   To any.
LYSIMACHUS   Yet let me obtain my wish.   35
HELICANUS   Behold him.

               PERICLES *discovered.*

                        This was a goodly person,
   Till the disaster that, one mortal night,
   Drove him to this.
LYSIMACHUS   Sir king, all hail! the gods preserve you!
   Hail, royal sir!   40
HELICANUS   It is in vain; he will not speak to you.
1 LORD   Sir,
   We have a maid in Mytilene, I durst wager,
   Would win some words of him.
LYSIMACHUS   'Tis well bethought.
   She, questionless, with her sweet harmony   45
   And other chosen attractions, would allure,
   And make a batt'ry through his deafen'd ports,
   Which now are midway stopp'd.
   She is all happy as the fairest of all,
   And with her fellow maids is now upon   50
   The leavy shelter that abuts against
   The island's side.
            [*Whispers a Lord, who goes off in the barge of*
                                          Lysimachus.]
HELICANUS   Sure, all effectless; yet nothing we'll omit
   That bears recovery's name. But, since your kindness
   We have stretch'd thus far, let us beseech you   55
   That for our gold we may provision have,
   Wherein we are not destitute for want,
   But weary for the staleness.
LYSIMACHUS   O, sir, a courtesy
   Which, if we should deny, the most just God
   For every graff would send a caterpillar,   60
   And so inflict our province. Yet once more
   Let me entreat to know at large the cause
   Of your king's sorrow.
HELICANUS   Sit, sir, I will recount it to you.
   But see, I am prevented.

            Enter Lord *from the barge, with* MARINA
                  and one of her companions.

LYSIMACHUS   O, here's the lady that I sent for.   65
   Welcome, fair one! Is't not a goodly presence?
HELICANUS   She's a gallant lady.
LYSIMACHUS   She's such a one that, were I well assur'd
   Came of gentle kind and noble stock,
   I'd wish no better choice, and think me rarely wed.   70
   Fair one, all goodness that consists in beauty,
   Expect even here, where is a kingly patient,
   If that thy prosperous and artificial feat
   Can draw him but to answer thee in aught,
   Thy sacred physic shall receive such pay   75
   As thy desires can wish.
MARINA   Sir, I will use

My utmost skill in his recovery, provided
That none but I and my companion maid
Be suffer'd to come near him.

LYSIMACHUS   Come, let us leave her;
80   And the gods make her prosperous!
     [*They withdraw. Marina sings.*]
     Mark'd he your music?

MARINA   No, nor look'd on us.

LYSIMACHUS   See, she will speak to him.

MARINA   Hail, sir! my lord, lend ear.

PERICLES   Hum, ha! [*pushing her back.*]

85   MARINA   I am a maid,
     My lord, that ne'er before invited eyes,
     But have been gaz'd on like a comet; she speaks,
     My lord, that, may be, hath endur'd a grief
     Might equal yours, if both were justly weigh'd.
90   Though wayward fortune did malign my state,
     My derivation was from ancestors
     Who stood equivalent with mighty kings;
     But time hath rooted out my parentage,
     And to the world and awkward casualties
95   Bound me in servitude. [*aside*] I will desist;
     But there is something glows upon my cheek,
     And whispers in mine ear 'Go not till he speak'.

PERICLES   My fortunes – parentage – good parentage –
     To equal mine – was it not thus? what say you?

100 MARINA   I said, my lord, if you did know my parentage,
     You would not do me violence.

PERICLES
     I do think so. Pray you, turn your eyes upon me.
     You're like something that – What countrywoman?
     Here of these shores?

MARINA   No, nor of any shores;
105 Yet I was mortally brought forth, and am
     No other than I appear.

PERICLES   I am great with woe
     And shall deliver weeping. My dearest wife
     Was like this maid, and such a one
     My daughter might have been: my queen's square
          brows;
110 Her stature to an inch; as wand-like straight;
     As silver-voic'd; her eyes as jewel-like
     And cas'd as richly; in pace another Juno;
     Who starves the ears she feeds, and makes them
          hungry
     The more she gives them speech. Where do you live?

115 MARINA   Where I am but a stranger; from the deck
     You may discern the place.

PERICLES   Where were you bred?
     And how achiev'd you these endowments which
     You make more rich to owe?

MARINA   If I should tell my history, 'twould seem
     Like lies, disdain'd in the reporting.

120 PERICLES   Prithee, speak;
     Falseness cannot come from thee, for thou look'st
     Modest as Justice, and thou seem'st a palace
     For the crown'd Truth to dwell in. I will believe thee,
     And make my senses credit thy relation
     To points that seem impossible; for thou look'st   125
     Like one I lov'd indeed. What were thy friends?
     Didst thou not say when I did push thee back,
     Which was when I perceiv'd thee, that thou cam'st
     From good descending?

MARINA   So indeed I did.

PERICLES   Report thy parentage. I think thou said'st   130
     Thou hadst been toss'd from wrong to injury,
     And that thou thought'st thy griefs might equal
          mine,
     If both were open'd.

MARINA   Some such thing I said,
     And said no more but what my thoughts
     Did warrant me was likely.

PERICLES   Tell thy story;   135
     If thine consider'd prove the thousandth part
     Of my endurance, thou art a man, and I
     Have suffer'd like a girl; yet thou dost look
     Like Patience gazing on kings' graves, and smiling
     Extremity out of act. What were thy friends?   140
     How lost thou them? Thy name, my most kind
          virgin?
     Recount, I do beseech you. Come, sit by me.

MARINA   My name is Marina.

PERICLES   O, I am mock'd,
     And thou by some incensed god sent hither
     To make the world to laugh at me.

MARINA   Patience, good sir,   145
     Or here I'll cease.

PERICLES   Nay, I'll be patient.
     Thou little know'st how thou dost startle me,
     To call thyself Marina.

MARINA   The name
     Was given me by one that had some power,
     My father and a king.

PERICLES   How, a king's daughter?   150
     And call'd Marina?

MARINA   You said you would believe me;
     But, not to be a troubler of your peace,
     I will end here.

PERICLES   But are you flesh and blood?
     Have you a working pulse, and are no fairy
     Motion? Well, speak on. Where were you born,   155
     And wherefore call'd Marina?

MARINA   Call'd Marina
     For I was born at sea.

PERICLES   At sea! what mother?

MARINA   My mother was the daughter of a king;
     Who died the minute I was born,
     As my good nurse Lychorida hath oft   160
     Deliver'd weeping.

PERICLES   O, stop there a little!
     This is the rarest dream that e'er dull'd sleep
     Did mock sad fools withal; this cannot be
     My daughter, buried; well; where were you bred?
     I'll hear you more, to th' bottom of your story,   165

And never interrupt you.

MARINA
You scorn; believe me, 'twere best I did give o'er.

PERICLES   I will believe you by the syllable
Of what you shall deliver. Yet, give me leave:
70   How came you in these parts? where were you bred?

MARINA   The king my father did in Tharsus leave me,
Till cruel Cleon, with his wicked wife,
Did seek to murder me; and having woo'd
A villain to attempt it, who having drawn to do't,
75   A crew of pirates came and rescu'd me;
Brought me to Mytilene. But, good sir,
Whither will you have me? Why do you weep? It may
be
You think me an impostor: no, good faith;
I am the daughter to King Pericles,
80   If good King Pericles be.

PERICLES   Ho, Helicanus!

HELICANUS   Calls my lord?

PERICLES   Thou art a grave and noble counsellor,
Most wise in general. Tell me, if thou canst,
85   What this maid is, or what is like to be,
That thus hath made me weep?

HELICANUS   I know not;
But here's the regent, sir, of Mytilene,
Speaks nobly of her.

LYSIMACHUS   She never would tell
Her parentage; being demanded that,
90   She would sit still and weep.

PERICLES   O Helicanus, strike me, honour'd sir!
Give me a gash, put me to present pain,
Lest this great sea of joys rushing upon me
O'erbear the shores of my mortality,
95   And drown me with their sweetness. O, come hither,
Thou that beget'st him that did thee beget;
Thou that wast born at sea, buried at Tharsus,
And found at sea again. O Helicanus,
Down on thy knees! thank the holy gods as loud
100   As thunder threatens us: this is Marina.
What was thy mother's name? tell me but that,
For truth can never be confirm'd enough,
Though doubts did ever sleep.

MARINA   First, sir, I pray, what is your title?

105   PERICLES   I am Pericles of Tyre: but tell me now
My drown'd queen's name, as in the rest you said
Thou hast been godlike perfect, the heir of
kingdoms,
And another life to Pericles thy father.

MARINA   Is it no more to be your daughter than
110   To say my mother's name was Thaisa?
Thaisa was my mother, who did end
The minute I began.

PERICLES   Now, blessing on thee! rise; thou art my child.
Give me fresh garments. Mine own, Helicanus,
115   She is not dead at Tharsus, as she should have been,
By savage Cleon; she shall tell thee all,
When thou shalt kneel, and justify in knowledge

She is thy very princess. Who is this?

HELICANUS   Sir, 'tis the governor of Mytilene,
Who, hearing of your melancholy state,   220
Did come to see you.

PERICLES   I embrace you.
Give me my robes; I am wild in my beholding.
O heavens bless my girl! But hark, what music?
Tell Helicanus, my Marina, tell him
O'er point by point, for yet he seems to doubt,   225
How sure you are my daughter.   [*Music.*]
                         But what music?

HELICANUS   My lord, I hear none.

PERICLES   None?
The music of the spheres! List, my Marina.

LYSIMACHUS   It is not good to cross him; give him way.   230

PERICLES   Rarest sounds! Do ye not hear?

LYSIMACHUS   Music, my Lord? I hear.

PERICLES   Most heavenly music!
It nips me unto list'ning, and thick slumber
Hangs upon mine eyes; let me rest. [*Sleeps.*]

LYSIMACHUS   A pillow for his head. So, leave him all.   235
Well, my companion friends,
If this but answer to my just belief,
I'll well remember you.   *Exeunt all but Pericles.*

DIANA *appears to* Pericles *in a vision.*

DIANA   My temple stands in Ephesus; hie thee thither,
And do upon mine altar sacrifice.   240
There, when my maiden priests are met together,
[   ] before the people all,
Reveal how thou at sea didst lose thy wife.
To mourn thy crosses, with thy daughter's, call
And give them repetition to the life.   245
Or perform my bidding, or thou liv'st in woe;
Do't, and happy; by my silver bow!
Awake, and tell thy dream.   *Disappears.*

PERICLES   Celestial Dian, goddess argentine,
I will obey thee. Helicanus!

Enter LYSIMACHUS, HELICANUS *and* MARINA.

HELICANUS   Sir?   250

PERICLES   My purpose was for Tharsus, there to strike
The inhospitable Cleon; but I am
For other service first; toward Ephesus
Turn our blown sails: eftsoons I'll tell thee why.
Shall we refresh us, sir, upon your shore,   255
And give you gold for such provision
As our intents will need?

LYSIMACHUS   Sir,
With all my heart; and when you come ashore,
I have another suit.

PERICLES   You shall prevail,   260
Were it to woo my daughter; for it seems
You have been noble towards her.

LYSIMACHUS   Sir, lend me your arm.

PERICLES   Come, my Marina.
                                   Exeunt.

5.2　　　　　　　*Enter* GOWER.

The temple of Diana at Ephesus; THAISA *standing near the altar, as high priestess; a number of virgins on each side;* CERIMON *and other inhabitants of Ephesus attending.*

GOWER Now our sands are almost run;
　　　　More a little, and then dumb.
　　　　This, my last boon, give me,
　　　　For such kindness must relieve me,
5　　　 That you aptly will suppose
　　　　What pageantry, what feats, what shows,
　　　　What minstrelsy and pretty din,
　　　　The regent made in Mytilin
　　　　To greet the king. So he thriv'd,
10　　 That he is promis'd to be wiv'd
　　　　To fair Marina; but in no wise
　　　　Till he had done his sacrifice,
　　　　As Dian bade: whereto being bound,
　　　　The interim, pray you, all confound.
15　　 In feather'd briefness sails are fill'd,
　　　　And wishes fall out as they're will'd.
　　　　At Ephesus the temple see
　　　　Our king and all his company.
　　　　That he can hither come so soon,
20　　 Is by your fancies' thankful doom.　　　*Exit.*

5.3　　　　*Enter* PERICLES, *with his train;*
　　　　　　 LYSIMACHUS, HELICANUS *and* MARINA.

PERICLES　 Hail, Dian! to perform thy just command,
　　　　I here confess myself the king of Tyre;
　　　　Who, frighted from my country, did wed
　　　　At Pentapolis the fair Thaisa.
5　　　 At sea in childbed died she, but brought forth
　　　　A maid-child call'd Marina; who, O goddess,
　　　　Wears yet thy silver livery. She at Tharsus
　　　　Was nurs'd with Cleon, who at fourteen years
　　　　He sought to murder; but her better stars
10　　 Brought her to Mytilene; 'gainst whose shore
　　　　Riding, her fortunes brought the maid aboard us,
　　　　Where, by her own most clear remembrance, she
　　　　Made known herself my daughter.
THAISA　　　　　　　　　　Voice and favour!
　　　　You are, you are – O royal Pericles! [*Faints.*]
PERICLES
15　　 What means the nun? she dies, help, gentlemen!
CERIMON　 Noble sir,
　　　　If you have told Diana's altar true,
　　　　This is your wife.
PERICLES　　　　　 Reverend appearer, no:
　　　　I threw her overboard with these very arms.
CERIMON　 Upon this coast, I warrant you.
20　　 PERICLES　　　　　　　　　　'Tis most certain.
CERIMON　 Look to the lady. O, she's but o'erjoy'd.
　　　　Early one blustering morn this lady was
　　　　Thrown upon this shore. I op'd the coffin,
　　　　Found there rich jewels; recover'd her, and plac'd her

Here in Diana's temple.
PERICLES　　　　　　　 May we see them?　　　　25
CERIMON
　　　　Great sir, they shall be brought you to my house,
　　　　Whither I invite you. Look, Thaisa is
　　　　Recovered.
THAISA　　　　 O, let me look!
　　　　If he be none of mine, my sanctity
　　　　Will to my sense bend no licentious ear,　　　30
　　　　But curb it, spite of seeing. O, my lord,
　　　　Are you not Pericles? Like him you spake,
　　　　Like him you are. Did you not name a tempest,
　　　　A birth and death?
PERICLES　　　　　 The voice of dead Thaisa!
THAISA　 That Thaisa am I, supposed dead　　　35
　　　　And drown'd.
PERICLES　 Immortal Dian!
THAISA　　　　　　　　 Now I know you better.
　　　　When we with tears parted Pentapolis,
　　　　The king my father gave you such a ring.
　　　　[*Points to his ring.*]
PERICLES
　　　　This, this: no more. You gods, your present kindness　40
　　　　Makes my past miseries sports. You shall do well,
　　　　That on the touching of her lips I may
　　　　Melt and no more be seen. O come, be buried
　　　　A second time within these arms.
MARINA　　　　　　　　　　My heart
　　　　Leaps to be gone into my mother's bosom.　　　45
　　　　[*Kneels to Thaisa.*]
PERICLES
　　　　Look, who kneels here, flesh of thy flesh, Thaisa;
　　　　Thy burden at the sea, and call'd Marina
　　　　For she was yielded there.
THAISA　　　　　　　　 Bless'd, and mine own!
HELICANUS　 Hail, madam, and my queen!
THAISA　　　　　　　　　　I know you not.
PERICLES
　　　　You have heard me say, when I did fly from Tyre,　50
　　　　I left behind an ancient substitute;
　　　　Can you remember what I call'd the man?
　　　　I have nam'd him oft.
THAISA　　　　　　 'Twas Helicanus then.
PERICLES　 Still confirmation!
　　　　Embrace him, dear Thaisa; this is he.　　　55
　　　　Now do I long to hear how you were found,
　　　　How possibly preserv'd, and who to thank,
　　　　Besides the gods, for this great miracle.
THAISA　 Lord Cerimon, my lord; this man,
　　　　Through whom the gods have shown their power;
　　　　　that can　　　60
　　　　From first to last resolve you.
PERICLES　　　　　　　　 Reverend sir,
　　　　The gods can have no mortal officer
　　　　More like a god than you. Will you deliver
　　　　How this dead queen re-lives?
CERIMON　　　　　　　 I will, my lord.

65 Beseech you, first go with me to my house,
Where shall be shown you all was found with her;
How she came plac'd here in the temple;
No needful thing omitted.

PERICLES   Pure Dian,
I bless thee for thy vision, and will offer
70 Night-oblations to thee. Thaisa,
This prince, the fair betrothed of your daughter,
Shall marry her at Pentapolis. And now
[   ] this ornament
Makes me look dismal will I clip to form;
75 And what this fourteen years no razor touch'd
To grace thy marriage-day I'll beautify.

THAISA   Lord Cerimon hath letters of good credit, sir,
My father's dead.

PERICLES
Heavens make a star of him! Yet there, my queen,
80 We'll celebrate their nuptials, and ourselves
Will in that kingdom spend our following days.
Our son and daughter shall in Tyrus reign.
Lord Cerimon, we do our longing stay
To hear the rest untold: sir, lead's the way.   *Exeunt*.

EPILOGUE

Enter GOWER.

GOWER
In Antiochus and his daughter you have heard
Of monstrous lust the due and just reward.
In Pericles, his queen and daughter, seen,
Although assail'd with fortune fierce and keen,
Virtue preserv'd from fell destruction's blast,   5
Led on by heaven, and crown'd with joy at last.
In Helicanus may you well descry
A figure of truth, of faith, of loyalty.
In reverend Cerimon there well appears
The worth that learned charity aye wears.   10
For wicked Cleon and his wife, when fame
Had spread his cursed deed to th' honour'd name
Of Pericles, to rage the city turn,
That him and his they in his palace burn:
The gods for murder seemed so content   15
To punish; although not done, but meant.
So on your patience evermore attending,
New joy wait on you! Here our play has ending.
                                                            Exit.

Romeo and Juliet

Romeo and Juliet was among the first plays Shakespeare wrote as a leading member of the Chamberlain's Men, of which he was a founder-member in 1594. A drastically abbreviated text, printed in Quarto in 1597, was superseded in 1599 by a Quarto representing the play, 'newly corrected, augmented, and amended', much as we know it and in the form in which it was reprinted in the 1623 Folio. *A Midsummer Night's Dream*, written in 1594-5, is usually thought of as following Romeo, mainly on the grounds that the mechanicals' play of 'Pyramus and Thisbe' parodies the tragic theme of feuding families and star-crossed lovers.

Unlike most of Shakespeare's tragedies, *Romeo and Juliet* (in common with *Othello*) is based on a fiction, a *novella* written in Italy in the late fifteenth century, that he knew in English versions including Arthur Brooke's pedestrian verse narrative, *Romeus and Juliet* (1562), which Shakespeare transformed into an unrivalled tragedy of young love. The transformation involved abbreviation, increasing sympathy for the lovers by decreasing their ages, building up the contrasting roles of the Nurse and the Friar, inventing that of Mercutio and reducing the element of explicit moralizing. The play is one of several in which Shakespeare openly challenges neoclassical assumptions about genre. It might almost be described as setting its tragic action in the world of comedy.

The celebrity of *Romeo and Juliet* derives largely from the love scenes, but the play which contains them is not confined to lyricism. It includes a wide spectrum of views on love, sex and marriage, so that impulsive adolescent passion gains sympathy by contrast with the prudential arguments of the parents and of Friar Lawrence, the obscenity and homosocial jealousy of Mercutio and the Nurse's moral relativism. The involvement of love in the family feud intensifies both love and danger: despite an emphasis on the lovers' disaster as fated, the outcome of the action as constructed by Shakespeare is as much the result of their own impulsiveness in marrying and in believing the worst as it is of the unexplained feud into which they were born.

Romeo and Juliet is the earliest of Shakespeare's plays to have imparted mythic status to its characters, to the extent that 'Juliet's balcony' (itself an eighteenth-century substitution for the window required by Shakespeare's text) is among the tourist sites of modern Verona. Also in the eighteenth century, David Garrick adapted the ending to allow the revived Juliet a final dialogue with the dying Romeo before her suicide. Nineteenth-century sensibilities were protected by removal of the play's pervasive sexual jesting and by suppression of Romeo's initial love for Rosaline. Famous Romeos of that time included the American actress, Charlotte Cushman.

The play was a powerful inspiration to composers of the romantic period and since, and is now widely known in the form of Sergei Prokofiev's ballet (1935), or as the source of orchestral compositions by Hector Berlioz (1839) and Peter Ilitsch Tchaikovsky (1869). It has been reworked in countless other plays, novels and films – most famously in Leonard Bernstein's musical *West Side Story* (1957) – and its theme of love destroyed by irrational inherited hate remains painfully familiar in the events of our own time.

The Arden text is based on the 1599 Second Quarto, with addition of some stage directions from the 1597 First Quarto.

Escalus, PRINCE of Verona

MERCUTIO	a young gentleman and kinsman to the Prince, friend of Romeo
PARIS	a noble young kinsman to the Prince
PAGE	to Paris
MONTAGUE	head of a Veronese family at feud with the Capulets
LADY MONTAGUE	
ROMEO	Montague's son
BENVOLIO	Montague's nephew and friend of Romeo and Mercutio
ABRAM	a servant to Montague
BALTHASAR	Romeo's servant
CAPULET	head of a Veronese family at feud with the Montagues
LADY CAPULET	
JULIET	Capulet's daughter
TYBALT	Lady Capulet's nephew
COUSIN CAPULET	an old gentleman
NURSE	a Capulet servant, Juliet's foster-mother
PETER	a Capulet servant attending on the nurse

SAMPSON
GREGORY
ANTHONY   } of the Capulet household
POTPAN
SERVINGMEN

FRIAR LAURENCE
FRIAR JOHN   } of the Franciscan Order

APOTHECARY   of Mantua
THREE MUSICIANS   (Simon Catling, Hugh Rebeck, James Soundpost)

CHORUS

Members of the Watch, Citizens of Verona, Masquers, Torchbearers, Pages, Servants

PROLOGUE

Enter CHORUS.

CHORUS   Two households both alike in dignity
(In fair Verona, where we lay our scene)
From ancient grudge break to new mutiny,
Where civil blood makes civil hands unclean.
From forth the fatal loins of these two foes
A pair of star-cross'd lovers take their life,
Whose misadventur'd piteous overthrows
Doth with their death bury their parents' strife.
The fearful passage of their death-mark'd love
And the continuance of their parents' rage,
Which, but their children's end, nought could
    remove,
Is now the two hours' traffic of our stage;
The which, if you with patient ears attend,
What here shall miss, our toil shall strive to mend.

Exit.

1.1   *Enter* SAMPSON *and* GREGORY, *with swords
and bucklers, of the house of Capulet.*

SAMPSON   Gregory, on my word we'll not carry coals.

GREGORY   No, for then we should be colliers.

SAMPSON   I mean, and we be in choler, we'll draw.

GREGORY   Ay, while you live, draw your neck out of
collar.

SAMPSON   I strike quickly being moved.

GREGORY   But thou art not quickly moved to strike.

SAMPSON   A dog of the house of Montague moves me.

GREGORY   To move is to stir, and to be valiant is to
stand: therefore if thou art moved thou runn'st away.

SAMPSON   A dog of that house shall move me to stand. I
will take the wall of any man or maid of Montague's.

GREGORY   That shows thee a weak slave, for the weakest
goes to the wall.

SAMPSON   'Tis true, and therefore women, being the
weaker vessels, are ever thrust to the wall; therefore I
will push Montague's men from the wall, and thrust
his maids to the wall.

GREGORY   The quarrel is between our masters and us
their men.

SAMPSON   'Tis all one. I will show myself a tyrant: when
I have fought with the men I will be civil with the
maids, I will cut off their heads.

GREGORY   The heads of the maids?

SAMPSON   Ay, the heads of the maids, or their
maidenheads; take it in what sense thou wilt.

GREGORY   They must take it in sense that feel it.

SAMPSON   Me they shall feel while I am able to stand,
and 'tis known I am a pretty piece of flesh.

GREGORY   'Tis well thou art not fish; if thou hadst, thou
hadst been Poor John. Draw thy tool – here comes of
the house of Montagues.

Enter two other servingmen, ABRAM *and* BALTHASAR.

SAMPSON   My naked weapon is out. Quarrel, I will back
thee.

GREGORY   How, turn thy back and run?   35

SAMPSON   Fear me not.

GREGORY   No, marry! I fear thee!

SAMPSON   Let us take the law of our sides: let them
begin.

GREGORY   I will frown as I pass by, and let them take it   40
as they list.

SAMPSON   Nay, as they dare. I will bite my thumb at
them, which is disgrace to them if they bear it.

ABRAM   Do you bite your thumb at us, sir?

SAMPSON   I do bite my thumb, sir.   45

ABRAM   Do you bite your thumb at us, sir?

SAMPSON   Is the law of our side if I say ay?

GREGORY   No.

SAMPSON   No sir, I do not bite my thumb at you, sir, but
I bite my thumb, sir.   50

GREGORY   Do you quarrel, sir?

ABRAM   Quarrel, sir? No, sir.

SAMPSON   But if you do, sir, I am for you. I serve as good
a man as you.

ABRAM   No better.   55

SAMPSON   Well, sir.

Enter BENVOLIO.

GREGORY   Say 'better', here comes one of my master's
kinsmen.

SAMPSON   Yes, better, sir.

ABRAM   You lie.   60

SAMPSON   Draw if you be men. Gregory, remember thy
washing blow. [*They fight.*]

BENVOLIO   Part, fools, put up your swords, you know
not what you do.

Enter TYBALT.

TYBALT
What, art thou drawn among these heartless hinds?   65
Turn thee, Benvolio, look upon thy death.

BENVOLIO   I do but keep the peace, put up thy sword,
Or manage it to part these men with me.

TYBALT
What, drawn, and talk of peace? I hate the word,
As I hate hell, all Montagues, and thee: 70
Have at thee, coward. [*They fight.*]

Enter three or four Citizens *with clubs or partisans.*

CITIZENS   Clubs, bills and partisans! Strike! Beat them
down! Down with the Capulets! Down with the
Montagues!

Enter old CAPULET *in his gown, and* LADY CAPULET.

CAPULET
What noise is this? Give me my long sword, ho!   75

LADY CAPULET
A crutch, a crutch! Why call you for a sword?

Enter old MONTAGUE *and* LADY MONTAGUE.

CAPULET   My sword I say! Old Montague is come,
And flourishes his blade in spite of me.
MONTAGUE
Thou villain Capulet! Hold me not! Let me go!
LADY MONTAGUE
80   Thou shalt not stir one foot to seek a foe.

Enter Prince ESCALUS *with his train.*

PRINCE   Rebellious subjects, enemies to peace,
Profaners of this neighbour-stained steel –
Will they not hear? What ho! You men, you beasts!
That quench the fire of your pernicious rage
85   With purple fountains issuing from your veins,
On pain of torture from those bloody hands
Throw your mistemper'd weapons to the ground
And hear the sentence of your moved prince.
Three civil brawls bred of an airy word
90   By thee, old Capulet, and Montague,
Have thrice disturb'd the quiet of our streets
And made Verona's ancient citizens
Cast by their grave-beseeming ornaments
To wield old partisans, in hands as old,
95   Canker'd with peace, to part your canker'd hate.
If ever you disturb our streets again
Your lives shall pay the forfeit of the peace.
For this time all the rest depart away;
You, Capulet, shall go along with me,
100   And Montague, come you this afternoon,
To know our farther pleasure in this case,
To old Freetown, our common judgement-place.
Once more, on pain of death, all men depart.
Exeunt all but Montague, Lady Montague
and Benvolio.
MONTAGUE   Who set this ancient quarrel new abroach?
105   Speak, nephew, were you by when it began?
BENVOLIO   Here were the servants of your adversary
And yours, close fighting ere I did approach.
I drew to part them; in the instant came
The fiery Tybalt, with his sword prepar'd,
110   Which, as he breath'd defiance to my ears
He swung about his head and cut the winds,
Who nothing hurt withal, hiss'd him in scorn.
While we were interchanging thrusts and blows
Came more and more, and fought on part and part,
115   Till the Prince came, who parted either part.
LADY MONTAGUE
O where is Romeo, saw you him today?
Right glad I am he was not at this fray.
BENVOLIO   Madam, an hour before the worshipp'd sun
Peer'd forth the golden window of the east
120   A troubled mind drive me to walk abroad,
Where underneath the grove of sycamore
That westward rooteth from this city side
So early walking did I see your son.
Towards him I made, but he was ware of me,

And stole into the covert of the wood.   125
I, measuring his affections by my own,
Which then most sought, where most might not be
found,
Being one too many by my weary self,
Pursu'd my humour, not pursuing his,
And gladly shunn'd who gladly fled from me.   130
MONTAGUE
Many a morning hath he there been seen,
With tears augmenting the fresh morning's dew,
Adding to clouds more clouds with his deep sighs;
But all so soon as the all-cheering sun
Should in the farthest east begin to draw   135
The shady curtains from Aurora's bed,
Away from light steals home my heavy son
And private in his chamber pens himself,
Shuts up his windows, locks fair daylight out
And makes himself an artificial night.   140
Black and portentous must this humour prove
Unless good counsel may the cause remove.
BENVOLIO   My noble uncle, do you know the cause?
MONTAGUE   I neither know it nor can learn of him.
BENVOLIO   Have you importun'd him by any means?   145
MONTAGUE   Both by myself and many other friends.
But he, his own affections' counsellor,
Is to himself – I will not say how true –
But to himself so secret and so close,
So far from sounding and discovery,   150
As is the bud bit with an envious worm
Ere he can spread his sweet leaves to the air
Or dedicate his beauty to the sun.
Could we but learn from whence his sorrows grow,
We would as willingly give cure as know.   155

Enter ROMEO.

BENVOLIO
See where he comes. So please you step aside;
I'll know his grievance or be much denied.
MONTAGUE   I would thou wert so happy by thy stay
To hear true shrift. Come, madam, let's away.
Exeunt Montague and Lady Montague.
BENVOLIO   Good morrow, cousin.
ROMEO   Is the day so young?   160
BENVOLIO   But new struck nine.
ROMEO   Ay me, sad hours seem long.
Was that my father that went hence so fast?
BENVOLIO
It was. What sadness lengthens Romeo's hours?
ROMEO
Not having that which, having, makes them short.
BENVOLIO   In love?   165
ROMEO   Out.
BENVOLIO   Of love?
ROMEO   Out of her favour where I am in love.
BENVOLIO   Alas that love so gentle in his view
Should be so tyrannous and rough in proof.   170
ROMEO   Alas that love whose view is muffled still

Should without eyes see pathways to his will.
Where shall we dine? O me! What fray was here?
Yet tell me not, for I have heard it all.
175 Here's much to do with hate, but more with love.
Why then, O brawling love, O loving hate,
O anything of nothing first create!
O heavy lightness, serious vanity,
Misshapen chaos of well-seeming forms!
180 Feather of lead, bright smoke, cold fire, sick health,
Still-waking sleep that is not what it is!
This love feel I that feel no love in this.
Dost thou not laugh?
BENVOLIO   No coz, I rather weep.
ROMEO   Good heart, at what?
BENVOLIO   At thy good heart's oppression.
185 ROMEO   Why such is love's transgression.
Griefs of mine own lie heavy in my breast,
Which thou wilt propagate to have it press'd
With more of thine. This love that thou hast shown
Doth add more grief to too much of mine own.
190 Love is a smoke made with the fume of sighs;
Being purg'd, a fire sparkling in lovers' eyes;
Being vex'd, a sea nourish'd with lovers' tears;
What is it else? A madness most discreet,
A choking gall, and a preserving sweet.
Farewell, my coz.
195 BENVOLIO   Soft, I will go along;
And if you leave me so, you do me wrong.
ROMEO   Tut, I have lost myself, I am not here.
This is not Romeo, he's some other where.
BENVOLIO   Tell me in sadness who is that you love?
200 ROMEO   What, shall I groan and tell thee?
BENVOLIO   Groan? Why no, but sadly tell me who.
ROMEO   Bid a sick man in sadness make his will?
A word ill-urg'd to one that is so ill.
In sadness, cousin, I do love a woman.
205 BENVOLIO   I aim'd so near when I suppos'd you lov'd.
ROMEO   A right good markman; and she's fair I love.
BENVOLIO   A right fair mark, fair coz, is soonest hit.
ROMEO   Well, in that hit you miss; she'll not be hit
With Cupid's arrow, she hath Dian's wit,
210 And in strong proof of chastity well arm'd
From love's weak childish bow she lives uncharm'd.
She will not stay the siege of loving terms
Nor bide th'encounter of assailing eyes
Nor ope her lap to saint-seducing gold;
215 O she is rich in beauty, only poor
That when she dies, with beauty dies her store.
BENVOLIO
Then she hath sworn that she will still live chaste?
ROMEO
She hath, and in that sparing makes huge waste.
For beauty starv'd with her severity
220 Cuts beauty off from all posterity.
She is too fair, too wise, wisely too fair,
To merit bliss by making me despair.
She hath forsworn to love, and in that vow

Do I live dead, that live to tell it now.
BENVOLIO   Be rul'd by me, forget to think of her.   225
ROMEO   O teach me how I should forget to think.
BENVOLIO   By giving liberty unto thine eyes:
Examine other beauties.
ROMEO   'Tis the way
To call hers, exquisite, in question more.
These happy masks that kiss fair ladies' brows,   230
Being black, puts us in mind they hide the fair.
He that is strucken blind cannot forget
The precious treasure of his eyesight lost.
Show me a mistress that is passing fair;
What doth her beauty serve but as a note   235
Where I may read who pass'd that passing fair?
Farewell, thou canst not teach me to forget.
BENVOLIO   I'll pay that doctrine or else die in debt.

Exeunt.

1.2   *Enter* CAPULET, PARIS *and a* Servant.

CAPULET   But Montague is bound as well as I,
In penalty alike, and 'tis not hard I think
For men so old as we to keep the peace.
PARIS   Of honourable reckoning are you both,
And pity 'tis you lived at odds so long.   5
But now my lord, what say you to my suit?
CAPULET   But saying o'er what I have said before.
My child is yet a stranger in the world,
She hath not seen the change of fourteen years.
Let two more summers wither in their pride   10
Ere we may think her ripe to be a bride.
PARIS   Younger than she are happy mothers made.
CAPULET
And too soon marr'd are those so early made.
Earth hath swallow'd all my hopes but she;
She is the hopeful lady of my earth.   15
But woo her, gentle Paris, get her heart,
My will to her consent is but a part,
And she agreed, within her scope of choice
Lies my consent and fair according voice.
This night I hold an old accustom'd feast   20
Whereto I have invited many a guest
Such as I love, and you among the store:
One more, most welcome, makes my number more.
At my poor house look to behold this night
Earth-treading stars that make dark heaven light.   25
Such comfort as do lusty young men feel
When well-apparell'd April on the heel
Of limping winter treads, even such delight
Among fresh female buds shall you this night
Inherit at my house. Hear all, all see,   30
And like her most whose merit most shall be;
Which, on more view of many, mine, being one,
May stand in number, though in reckoning none.
Come go with me.
[*To servant*]   Go sirrah, trudge about
Through fair Verona, find those persons out   35

Whose names are written there, and to them say,
My house and welcome on their pleasure stay.

Exeunt Capulet and Paris.

SERVANT   Find them out whose names are written here.
It is written that the shoemaker should meddle with
his yard, and the tailor with his last, the fisher with his
pencil, and the painter with his nets, but I am sent to
find those persons whose names are here writ, and can
never find what names the writing person hath here
writ. I must to the learned. In good time.

Enter BENVOLIO *and* ROMEO.

BENVOLIO
Tut man, one fire burns out another's burning,
One pain is lessen'd by another's anguish;
Turn giddy, and be holp by backward turning.
One desperate grief cures with another's languish;
Take thou some new infection to thy eye
And the rank poison of the old will die.
ROMEO   Your plantain leaf is excellent for that.
BENVOLIO   For what, I pray thee?
ROMEO   For your broken shin.
BENVOLIO   Why, Romeo, art thou mad?
ROMEO   Not mad, but bound more than a madman is:
Shut up in prison, kept without my food,
Whipp'd and tormented and – good e'en, good
    fellow.
SERVANT   God gi' good e'en; I pray, sir, can you read?
ROMEO   Ay, mine own fortune in my misery.
SERVANT   Perhaps you have learned it without book.
But I pray can you read anything you see?
ROMEO   Ay, if I know the letters and the language.
SERVANT   Ye say honestly; rest you merry.
ROMEO   Stay, fellow, I can read. [*He reads the letter.*]
Signor Martino and his wife and daughters;
County Anselm and his beauteous sisters;
The lady widow of Utruvio;
Signor Placentio and his lovely nieces;
Mercutio and his brother Valentine;
Mine uncle Capulet, his wife and daughters;
My fair niece Rosaline and Livia;
Signor Valentio and his cousin Tybalt;
Lucio and the lively Helena.
A fair assembly. Whither should they come?
SERVANT   Up.
ROMEO   Whither to supper?
SERVANT   To our house.
ROMEO   Whose house?
SERVANT   My master's.
ROMEO   Indeed I should have asked you that before.
SERVANT   Now I'll tell you without asking. My master is
the great rich Capulet, and if you be not of the house
of Montagues I pray come and crush a cup of wine.
Rest you merry.   *Exit.*
BENVOLIO   At this same ancient feast of Capulet's
Sups the fair Rosaline, whom thou so loves,
With all the admired beauties of Verona.

Go thither and with unattainted eye
Compare her face with some that I shall show
And I will make thee think thy swan a crow.
ROMEO   When the devout religion of mine eye   90
Maintains such falsehood, then turn tears to fire,
And these who, often drown'd, could never die,
Transparent heretics, be burnt for liars.
One fairer than my love! The all-seeing sun
Ne'er saw her match since first the world begun.   95
BENVOLIO   Tut, you saw her fair, none else being by:
Herself pois'd with herself in either eye.
But in that crystal scales let there be weigh'd
Your lady's love against some other maid
That I will show you shining at this feast,   100
And she shall scant show well that now seems best.
ROMEO   I'll go along, no such sight to be shown,
But to rejoice in splendour of mine own.   *Exeunt.*

1.3   *Enter* LADY CAPULET *and* Nurse.

LADY CAPULET
Nurse, where's my daughter? Call her forth to me.
NURSE   Now by my maidenhead at twelve year old,
I bade her come. What, lamb. What, ladybird.
God forbid. Where's this girl? What, Juliet!

Enter JULIET.

JULIET   How now, who calls?
NURSE   Your mother.   5
JULIET   Madam, I am here, what is your will?
LADY CAPULET
This is the matter. Nurse, give leave awhile,
We must talk in secret. Nurse, come back again,
I have remember'd me, thou's hear our counsel.
Thou knowest my daughter's of a pretty age.   10
NURSE   Faith, I can tell her age unto an hour.
LADY CAPULET   She's not fourteen.
NURSE   I'll lay fourteen of my teeth –
And yet, to my teen be it spoken, I have but four –
She's not fourteen. How long is it now
To Lammas-tide?
LADY CAPULET   A fortnight and odd days.   15
NURSE   Even or odd, of all days in the year,
Come Lammas Eve at night shall she be fourteen.
Susan and she – God rest all Christian souls –
Were of an age. Well, Susan is with God;
She was too good for me. But as I said,   20
On Lammas Eve at night shall she be fourteen.
That shall she; marry, I remember it well.
'Tis since the earthquake now eleven years,
And she was wean'd – I never shall forget it –
Of all the days of the year upon that day.   25
For I had then laid wormwood to my dug,
Sitting in the sun under the dovehouse wall.
My lord and you were then at Mantua –
Nay I do bear a brain. But as I said,
When it did taste the wormwood on the nipple   30

Of my dug and felt it bitter, pretty fool,
To see it tetchy and fall out with the dug.
Shake! quoth the dovehouse. 'Twas no need, I trow,
To bid me trudge.
35   And since that time it is eleven years.
For then she could stand high-lone, nay, by th'rood,
She could have run and waddled all about;
For even the day before she broke her brow,
And then my husband – God be with his soul,
40   A was a merry man – took up the child,
'Yea', quoth he, 'dost thou fall upon thy face?
Thou wilt fall backward when thou hast more wit,
Wilt thou not, Jule?' And by my holidame,
The pretty wretch left crying and said 'Ay'.
45   To see now how a jest shall come about.
I warrant, and I should live a thousand years
I never should forget it. 'Wilt thou not, Jule?' quoth he,
And, pretty fool, it stinted, and said 'Ay'.
LADY CAPULET   Enough of this, I pray thee, hold thy peace.
50   NURSE   Yes, madam, yet I cannot choose but laugh
To think it should leave crying and say 'Ay';
And yet I warrant it had upon it brow
A bump as big as a young cockerel's stone,
A perilous knock, and it cried bitterly.
55   'Yea', quoth my husband, 'fall'st upon thy face?
Thou wilt fall backward when thou comest to age,
Wilt thou not, Jule?' It stinted, and said 'Ay'.
JULIET   And stint thou too, I pray thee, Nurse, say I.
NURSE   Peace, I have done. God mark thee to his grace,
60   Thou wast the prettiest babe that e'er I nurs'd.
And I might live to see thee married once,
I have my wish.
LADY CAPULET   Marry, that marry is the very theme
I came to talk of. Tell me, daughter Juliet,
65   How stands your dispositions to be married?
JULIET   It is an honour that I dream not of.
NURSE   An honour. Were not I thine only nurse
I would say thou hadst suck'd wisdom from thy teat.
LADY CAPULET
Well, think of marriage now. Younger than you
70   Here in Verona, ladies of esteem,
Are made already mothers. By my count
I was your mother much upon these years
That you are now a maid. Thus then in brief:
The valiant Paris seeks you for his love.
75   NURSE   A man, young lady. Lady, such a man
As all the world – why, he's a man of wax.
LADY CAPULET
Verona's summer hath not such a flower.
NURSE   Nay, he's a flower, in faith a very flower.
LADY CAPULET
What say you, can you love the gentleman?
80   This night you shall behold him at our feast;
Read o'er the volume of young Paris' face

And find delight writ there with beauty's pen.
Examine every married lineament
And see how one another lends content;
And what obscur'd in this fair volume lies,   85
Find written in the margent of his eyes.
This precious book of love, this unbound lover,
To beautify him only lacks a cover.
The fish lives in the sea; and 'tis much pride
For fair without the fair within to hide.   90
That book in many's eyes doth share the glory
That in gold clasps locks in the golden story.
So shall you share all that he doth possess,
By having him, making yourself no less.
NURSE   No less, nay bigger. Women grow by men.   95
LADY CAPULET
Speak briefly, can you like of Paris' love?
JULIET   I'll look to like if looking liking move,
But no more deep will I endart mine eye
Than your consent gives strength to make it fly.

Enter a Servingman.

SERVINGMAN   Madam, the guests are come, supper   100
served up, you called, my young lady asked for, the
Nurse cursed in the pantry, and everything in
extremity. I must hence to wait, I beseech you follow
straight.   *Exit.*
LADY CAPULET
We follow thee; Juliet, the County stays.
NURSE   Go, girl, seek happy nights to happy days.   105
Exeunt.

1.4   *Enter* ROMEO, MERCUTIO, BENVOLIO, *with
five or six other masquers and torchbearers.*

ROMEO
What, shall this speech be spoke for our excuse?
Or shall we on without apology?
BENVOLIO   The date is out of such prolixity.
We'll have no Cupid hoodwink'd with a scarf,
Bearing a Tartar's painted bow of lath,   5
Scaring the ladies like a crowkeeper,
Nor no without-book prologue, faintly spoke
After the prompter, for our entrance.
But let them measure us by what they will,
We'll measure them a measure and be gone.   10
ROMEO   Give me a torch, I am not for this ambling.
Being but heavy I will bear the light.
MERCUTIO
Nay, gentle Romeo, we must have you dance.
ROMEO   Not I, believe me. You have dancing shoes
With nimble soles, I have a soul of lead   15
So stakes me to the ground I cannot move.
MERCUTIO   You are a lover, borrow Cupid's wings
And soar with them above a common bound.
ROMEO   I am too sore enpierced with his shaft
To soar with his light feathers, and so bound   20

I cannot bound a pitch above dull woe.
Under love's heavy burden do I sink.

MERCUTIO
And, to sink in it, should you burden love –
Too great oppression for a tender thing.

25 ROMEO   Is love a tender thing? It is too rough,
Too rude, too boisterous, and it pricks like thorn.

MERCUTIO
If love be rough with you, be rough with love;
Prick love for pricking and you beat love down.
Give me a case to put my visage in:
30 A visor for a visor. What care I
What curious eye doth quote deformities?
Here are the beetle brows shall blush for me.

BENVOLIO   Come, knock and enter, and no sooner in
But every man betake him to his legs.

35 ROMEO   A torch for me. Let wantons light of heart
Tickle the senseless rushes with their heels,
For I am proverb'd with a grandsire phrase –
I'll be a candle-holder and look on.
The game was ne'er so fair, and I am done.

MERCUTIO
40 Tut, dun's the mouse, the constable's own word.
If thou art dun, we'll draw thee from the mire
Of – save your reverence – love, wherein thou
        stickest
Up to the ears. Come, we burn daylight, ho.

ROMEO   Nay, that's not so.

MERCUTIO   I mean sir, in delay
45 We waste our lights in vain, light lights by day.
Take our good meaning, for our judgement sits
Five times in that ere once in our five wits.

ROMEO   And we mean well in going to this masque,
But 'tis no wit to go.

MERCUTIO   Why, may one ask?

ROMEO   I dreamt a dream tonight.

50 MERCUTIO   And so did I.

ROMEO   Well what was yours?

MERCUTIO   That dreamers often lie.

ROMEO   In bed asleep, while they do dream things true.

MERCUTIO
O then I see Queen Mab hath been with you.
She is the fairies' midwife, and she comes
55 In shape no bigger than an agate stone
On the forefinger of an alderman,
Drawn with a team of little atomi
Over men's noses as they lie asleep.
Her chariot is an empty hazelnut
60 Made by the joiner squirrel or old grub,
Time out o' mind the fairies' coachmakers;
Her waggon-spokes made of long spinners' legs,
The cover of the wings of grasshoppers,
Her traces of the smallest spider web,
65 Her collars of the moonshine's watery beams,
Her whip of cricket's bone, the lash of film,
Her waggoner a small grey-coated gnat,
Not half so big as a round little worm

Prick'd from the lazy finger of a maid;
And in this state she gallops night by night   70
Through lovers' brains, and then they dream of love;
O'er courtiers' knees, that dream on curtsies straight;
O'er lawyers' fingers who straight dream on fees;
O'er ladies' lips, who straight on kisses dream,
Which oft the angry Mab with blisters plagues   75
Because their breaths with sweetmeats tainted are.
Sometime she gallops o'er a courtier's nose
And then dreams he of smelling out a suit;
And sometimes comes she with a tithe-pig's tail,
Tickling a parson's nose as a lies asleep;   80
Then dreams he of another benefice.
Sometime she driveth o'er a soldier's neck
And then dreams he of cutting foreign throats,
Of breaches, ambuscados, Spanish blades,
Of healths five fathom deep; and then anon   85
Drums in his ear, at which he starts and wakes,
And being thus frighted swears a prayer or two
And sleeps again. This is that very Mab
That plaits the manes of horses in the night
And bakes the elf-locks in foul sluttish hairs,   90
Which, once untangled, much misfortune bodes.
This is the hag, when maids lie on their backs,
That presses them and learns them first to bear,
Making them women of good carriage.
This is she –

ROMEO   Peace, peace, Mercutio, peace.   95
Thou talk'st of nothing.

MERCUTIO   True, I talk of dreams,
Which are the children of an idle brain,
Begot of nothing but vain fantasy,
Which is as thin of substance as the air
And more inconstant than the wind, who woos   100
Even now the frozen bosom of the north
And, being anger'd, puffs away from thence
Turning his side to the dew-dropping south.

BENVOLIO
This wind you talk of blows us from ourselves:
Supper is done and we shall come too late.   105

ROMEO   I fear too early, for my mind misgives
Some consequence yet hanging in the stars
Shall bitterly begin his fearful date
With this night's revels, and expire the term
Of a despised life clos'd in my breast   110
By some vile forfeit of untimely death.
But he that hath the steerage of my course
Direct my suit. On, lusty gentlemen.

BENVOLIO   Strike, drum.

1.5   *They march about the stage, and*
                 Servingmen *come forth with napkins.*

1 SERVINGMAN   Where's Potpan that he helps not to take
    away? He shift a trencher! He scrape a trencher!
2 SERVINGMAN   When good manners shall lie all in one
    or two men's hands, and they unwashed too, 'tis a foul
    thing.   5

1 SERVINGMAN　Away with the joint-stools, remove the
court-cupboard, look to the plate. Good thou, save me
a piece of marchpane, and as thou loves me, let the
porter let in Susan Grindstone and Nell – Anthony,
and Potpan!

10

3 SERVINGMAN　Ay boy, ready.

1 SERVINGMAN　You are looked for and called for, asked
for and sought for, in the great chamber.

4 SERVINGMAN　We cannot be here and there too.

15

Cheerly, boys! Be brisk awhile, and the longer liver
take all.　　　　　　　　　　　　*Exeunt servingmen.*

Enter CAPULET, LADY CAPULET, JULIET, TYBALT, Nurse
and all the guests and gentlewomen to the masquers.

CAPULET

Welcome, gentlemen, ladies that have their toes
Unplagu'd with corns will walk a bout with you.
Ah my mistresses, which of you all

20

Will now deny to dance? She that makes dainty,
She I'll swear hath corns. Am I come near ye now?
Welcome, gentlemen. I have seen the day
That I have worn a visor and could tell
A whispering tale in a fair lady's ear,

25

Such as would please. 'Tis gone, 'tis gone, 'tis gone,
You are welcome, gentlemen: come, musicians, play.
A hall, a hall, give room! And foot it girls!
　　　　　　　　　　　[Music plays and they dance.]
More light, you knaves, and turn the tables up.
And quench the fire, the room is grown too hot.

30

Ah sirrah, this unlook'd-for sport comes well.
Nay sit, nay sit, good cousin Capulet,
For you and I are past our dancing days.
How long is't now since last yourself and I
Were in a masque?

COUSIN CAPULET　　By'r Lady, thirty years.

CAPULET

35

What, man, 'tis not so much, 'tis not so much.
'Tis since the nuptial of Lucentio,
Come Pentecost as quickly as it will,
Some five and twenty years: and then we masqu'd.

COUSIN CAPULET

'Tis more, 'tis more, his son is elder, sir:
His son is thirty.

40

CAPULET　　　　Will you tell me that?
His son was but a ward two years ago.

ROMEO　What lady's that which doth enrich the hand
Of yonder knight?

SERVANT　　　　I know not, sir.

ROMEO　O, she doth teach the torches to burn bright.

45

It seems she hangs upon the cheek of night
As a rich jewel in an Ethiop's ear –
Beauty too rich for use, for earth too dear.
So shows a snowy dove trooping with crows
As yonder lady o'er her fellows shows.

50

The measure done, I'll watch her place of stand,
And touching hers, make blessed my rude hand.
Did my heart love till now? Forswear it, sight.

For I ne'er saw true beauty till this night.

TYBALT　This by his voice should be a Montague.
Fetch me my rapier, boy.　　　　*Exit boy.*
　　　　　　　　What, dares the slave

55

Come hither, cover'd with an antic face,
To fleer and scorn at our solemnity?
Now by the stock and honour of my kin,
To strike him dead I hold it not a sin.

CAPULET

Why how now, kinsman, wherefore storm you so?

60

TYBALT　Uncle, this is a Montague, our foe:
A villain that is hither come in spite
To scorn at our solemnity this night.

CAPULET　Young Romeo is it?

TYBALT　　　　'Tis he, that villain Romeo.

CAPULET　Content thee, gentle coz, let him alone,

65

A bears him like a portly gentleman;
And, to say truth, Verona brags of him
To be a virtuous and well-govern'd youth.
I would not for the wealth of all this town
Here in my house do him disparagement.

70

Therefore be patient, take no note of him.
It is my will, the which if thou respect,
Show a fair presence and put off these frowns,
An ill-beseeming semblance for a feast.

TYBALT　It fits when such a villain is a guest:

75

I'll not endure him.

CAPULET　　　　He shall be endur'd.
What, goodman boy! I say he shall! Go to,
Am I the master here or you? Go to.
You'll not endure him! God shall mend my soul,
You'll make a mutiny among my guests,

80

You will set cock-a-hoop, you'll be the man!

TYBALT　Why, uncle, 'tis a shame.

CAPULET　　　　　　Go to, go to.
You are a saucy boy. Is't so indeed?
This trick may chance to scathe you. I know what.
You must contrary me. Marry, 'tis time –

85

Well said, my hearts – You are a princox, go
Be quiet, or – More light! More light! – For shame,
I'll make you quiet. What, cheerly, my hearts!

TYBALT　Patience perforce with wilful choler meeting
Makes my flesh tremble in their different greeting.

90

I will withdraw; but this intrusion shall
Now seeming sweet, convert to bitt'rest gall.　*Exit.*

ROMEO　If I profane with my unworthiest hand
This holy shrine, the gentle sin is this:
My lips, two blushing pilgrims, ready stand

95

To smooth that rough touch with a tender kiss.

JULIET

Good pilgrim, you do wrong your hand too much,
Which mannerly devotion shows in this;
For saints have hands that pilgrims' hands do touch,
And palm to palm is holy palmers' kiss.

100

ROMEO　Have not saints lips, and holy palmers too?

JULIET　Ay, pilgrim, lips that they must use in prayer.

ROMEO　O then, dear saint, let lips do what hands do:

They pray: grant thou, lest faith turn to despair.

JULIET

105 Saints do not move, though grant for prayer's sake.

ROMEO

Then move not, while my prayer's effect I take.

[*He kisses her.*]

Thus from my lips, by thine, my sin is purg'd.

JULIET Then have my lips the sin that they have took.

ROMEO Sin from my lips? O trespass sweetly urg'd.

Give me my sin again. [*He kisses her.*]

110 JULIET You kiss by th' book.

NURSE Madam, your mother craves a word with you.

ROMEO What is her mother?

NURSE Marry bachelor,

Her mother is the lady of the house,

And a good lady, and a wise and virtuous.

115 I nurs'd her daughter that you talk'd withal.

I tell you, he that can lay hold of her

Shall have the chinks.

ROMEO Is she a Capulet?

O dear account. My life is my foe's debt.

BENVOLIO Away, be gone, the sport is at the best.

120 ROMEO Ay, so I fear; the more is my unrest.

CAPULET Nay, gentlemen, prepare not to be gone,

We have a trifling foolish banquet towards.

[*They whisper in his ear.*]

Is it e'en so? Why then, I thank you all;

I thank you honest gentlemen, good night.

125 More torches here. Come on then, let's to bed.

Ah sirrah, by my fay, it waxes late,

I'll to my rest. *Exeunt Capulet, Lady Capulet,*

guests, gentlewomen and masquers.

JULIET Come hither Nurse. What is yond gentleman?

NURSE The son and heir of old Tiberio.

130 JULIET What's he that now is going out of door?

NURSE Marry, that I think be young Petruchio.

JULIET

What's he that follows here, that would not dance?

NURSE I know not.

JULIET Go ask his name. If he be married,

135 My grave is like to be my wedding bed.

NURSE His name is Romeo, and a Montague,

The only son of your great enemy.

JULIET My only love sprung from my only hate.

Too early seen unknown, and known too late.

140 Prodigious birth of love it is to me

That I must love a loathed enemy.

NURSE What's this? What's this?

JULIET A rhyme I learn'd even now

Of one I danc'd withal. [*One calls within:* 'Juliet'.]

NURSE Anon, anon!

Come let's away, the strangers all are gone. *Exeunt.*

2.Ch. *Enter* CHORUS.

CHORUS Now old desire doth in his deathbed lie

And young affection gapes to be his heir;

That fair for which love groan'd for and would die,

With tender Juliet match'd, is now not fair.

Now Romeo is belov'd and loves again, 5

Alike bewitched by the charm of looks,

But to his foe suppos'd he must complain

And she steal love's sweet bait from fearful hooks.

Being held a foe, he may not have access

To breathe such vows as lovers use to swear; 10

And she as much in love, her means much less

To meet her new beloved anywhere.

But passion lends them power, time means, to meet,

Tempering extremities with extreme sweet. *Exit.*

2.1 *Enter* ROMEO *alone.*

ROMEO Can I go forward when my heart is here?

Turn back, dull earth, and find thy centre out.

[*Withdraws.*]

Enter BENVOLIO *with* MERCUTIO.

BENVOLIO Romeo! My cousin Romeo! Romeo!

MERCUTIO He is wise,

And on my life hath stol'n him home to bed.

BENVOLIO He ran this way and leapt this orchard wall. 5

Call, good Mercutio.

MERCUTIO Nay, I'll conjure too:

Romeo! Humours! Madman! Passion! Lover!

Appear thou in the likeness of a sigh,

Speak but one rhyme and I am satisfied.

Cry but 'Ay me!' Pronounce but 'love' and 'dove', 10

Speak to my gossip Venus one fair word,

One nickname for her purblind son and heir,

Young Abraham Cupid, he that shot so trim

When King Cophetua lov'd the beggar maid.

He heareth not, he stirreth not, he moveth not: 15

The ape is dead and I must conjure him.

I conjure thee by Rosaline's bright eyes,

By her high forehead and her scarlet lip,

By her fine foot, straight leg, and quivering thigh,

And the demesnes that there adjacent lie, 20

That in thy likeness thou appear to us.

BENVOLIO And if he hear thee, thou wilt anger him.

MERCUTIO This cannot anger him. 'Twould anger him

To raise a spirit in his mistress' circle

Of some strange nature, letting it there stand 25

Till she had laid it and conjur'd it down:

That were some spite. My invocation

Is fair and honest; in his mistress' name

I conjure only but to raise up him.

BENVOLIO

Come, he hath hid himself among these trees 30

To be consorted with the humorous night.

Blind is his love, and best befits the dark.

MERCUTIO If love be blind, love cannot hit the mark.

Now will he sit under a medlar tree

And wish his mistress were that kind of fruit 35

As maids call medlars when they laugh alone.

O Romeo, that she were, O that she were
An open-arse and thou a poperin pear!
Romeo, good night. I'll to my truckle-bed.
40 This field-bed is too cold for me to sleep.
Come, shall we go?
BENVOLIO Go then, for 'tis in vain
To seek him here that means not to be found.
Exeunt Benvolio and Mercutio.

2.2

[*Romeo comes forward.*]
ROMEO He jests at scars that never felt a wound.

Enter JULIET *above.*

But soft, what light through yonder window breaks?
It is the east and Juliet is the sun!
Arise fair sun and kill the envious moon
5 Who is already sick and pale with grief
That thou her maid art far more fair than she.
Be not her maid since she is envious,
Her vestal livery is but sick and green
And none but fools do wear it. Cast it off.
10 It is my lady, O it is my love!
O that she knew she were!
She speaks, yet she says nothing. What of that?
Her eye discourses, I will answer it.
I am too bold. 'Tis not to me she speaks.
15 Two of the fairest stars in all the heaven,
Having some business, do entreat her eyes
To twinkle in their spheres till they return.
What if her eyes were there, they in her head?
The brightness of her cheek would shame those stars
20 As daylight doth a lamp. Her eyes in heaven
Would through the airy region stream so bright
That birds would sing and think it were not night.
See how she leans her cheek upon her hand.
O that I were a glove upon that hand,
That I might touch that cheek.
JULIET Ay me.
25 ROMEO She speaks.
O speak again bright angel, for thou art
As glorious to this night, being o'er my head,
As is a winged messenger of heaven
Unto the white-upturned wondering eyes
30 Of mortals that fall back to gaze on him
When he bestrides the lazy-puffing clouds
And sails upon the bosom of the air.
JULIET O Romeo, Romeo, wherefore art thou Romeo?
Deny thy father and refuse thy name.
35 Or if thou wilt not, be but sworn my love
And I'll no longer be a Capulet.
ROMEO Shall I hear more, or shall I speak at this?
JULIET 'Tis but thy name that is my enemy:
Thou art thyself, though not a Montague.
40 What's Montague? It is nor hand nor foot
Nor arm nor face nor any other part

Belonging to a man. O be some other name.
What's in a name? That which we call a rose
By any other word would smell as sweet;
45 So Romeo would, were he not Romeo call'd,
Retain that dear perfection which he owes
Without that title. Romeo, doff thy name,
And for thy name, which is no part of thee,
Take all myself.
ROMEO I take thee at thy word.
50 Call me but love, and I'll be new baptis'd:
Henceforth I never will be Romeo.
JULIET
What man art thou that thus bescreen'd in night
So stumblest on my counsel?
ROMEO By a name
I know not how to tell thee who I am:
55 My name, dear saint, is hateful to myself
Because it is an enemy to thee.
Had I it written, I would tear the word.
JULIET My ears have yet not drunk a hundred words
Of thy tongue's uttering, yet I know the sound.
60 Art thou not Romeo, and a Montague?
ROMEO Neither, fair maid, if either thee dislike.
JULIET
How cam'st thou hither, tell me, and wherefore?
The orchard walls are high and hard to climb,
And the place death, considering who thou art,
65 If any of my kinsmen find thee here.
ROMEO
With love's light wings did I o'erperch these walls,
For stony limits cannot hold love out,
And what love can do, that dares love attempt:
Therefore thy kinsmen are no stop to me.
70 JULIET If they do see thee, they will murder thee.
ROMEO Alack, there lies more peril in thine eye
Than twenty of their swords. Look thou but sweet
And I am proof against their enmity.
JULIET I would not for the world they saw thee here.
75 ROMEO I have night's cloak to hide me from their eyes,
And but thou love me, let them find me here.
My life were better ended by their hate
Than death prorogued, wanting of thy love.
JULIET
By whose direction found'st thou out this place?
80 ROMEO By love, that first did prompt me to enquire.
He lent me counsel, and I lent him eyes.
I am no pilot, yet wert thou as far
As that vast shore wash'd with the farthest sea,
I should adventure for such merchandise.
85 JULIET Thou knowest the mask of night is on my face,
Else would a maiden blush bepaint my cheek
For that which thou hast heard me speak tonight.
Fain would I dwell on form; fain, fain deny
What I have spoke. But farewell, compliment.
90 Dost thou love me? I know thou wilt say 'Ay',
And I will take thy word. Yet, if thou swear'st,
Thou mayst prove false. At lovers' perjuries,

They say, Jove laughs. O gentle Romeo,
If thou dost love, pronounce it faithfully.
95   Or, if thou think'st I am too quickly won,
I'll frown and be perverse and say thee nay,
So thou wilt woo; but else, not for the world.
In truth, fair Montague, I am too fond,
And therefore thou mayst think my haviour light,
100   But trust me, gentleman, I'll prove more true
Than those that have more cunning to be strange.
I should have been more strange, I must confess,
But that thou overheard'st, ere I was ware,
My true-love passion; therefore pardon me,
105   And not impute this yielding to light love
Which the dark night hath so discovered.
ROMEO   Lady, by yonder blessed moon I vow,
That tips with silver all these fruit-tree tops –
JULIET   O swear not by the moon, th'inconstant moon,
110   That monthly changes in her circled orb,
Lest that thy love prove likewise variable.
ROMEO   What shall I swear by?
JULIET   Do not swear at all.
Or if thou wilt, swear by thy gracious self,
Which is the god of my idolatry,
And I'll believe thee.
115   ROMEO   If my heart's dear love –
JULIET   Well, do not swear. Although I joy in thee,
I have no joy of this contract tonight:
It is too rash, too unadvis'd, too sudden,
Too like the lightning, which doth cease to be
120   Ere one can say 'It lightens'. Sweet, good night.
This bud of love, by summer's ripening breath,
May prove a beauteous flower when next we meet.
Good night, good night. As sweet repose and rest
Come to thy heart as that within my breast.
125   ROMEO   O wilt thou leave me so unsatisfied?
JULIET   What satisfaction canst thou have tonight?
ROMEO
Th'exchange of thy love's faithful vow for mine.
JULIET   I gave thee mine before thou didst request it,
And yet I would it were to give again.
ROMEO
130   Wouldst thou withdraw it? For what purpose, love?
JULIET   But to be frank and give it thee again;
And yet I wish but for the thing I have.
My bounty is as boundless as the sea,
My love as deep: the more I give to thee
135   The more I have, for both are infinite.
I hear some noise within. Dear love, adieu.
[*Nurse calls within.*]
Anon, good Nurse – Sweet Montague be true.
Stay but a little, I will come again.   *Exit Juliet.*
ROMEO   O blessed blessed night. I am afeard,
140   Being in night, all this is but a dream,
Too flattering sweet to be substantial.

Enter JULIET *above.*

JULIET
Three words, dear Romeo, and good night indeed.
If that thy bent of love be honourable,
Thy purpose marriage, send me word tomorrow
By one that I'll procure to come to thee,   145
Where and what time thou wilt perform the rite,
And all my fortunes at thy foot I'll lay,
And follow thee my lord throughout the world.
NURSE [*within*]   Madam.
JULIET   I come, anon – But if thou meanest not well   150
I do beseech thee –
NURSE [*within*]   Madam.
JULIET   By and by I come –
To cease thy strife and leave me to my grief.
Tomorrow will I send.
ROMEO   So thrive my soul –
JULIET   A thousand times good night.   *Exit Juliet.*
ROMEO   A thousand times the worse, to want thy light.   155
Love goes toward love as schoolboys from their
books,
But love from love, toward school with heavy looks.

Enter JULIET *above again.*

JULIET   Hist! Romeo, hist! O for a falconer's voice
To lure this tassel-gentle back again.
Bondage is hoarse and may not speak aloud,   160
Else would I tear the cave where Echo lies
And make her airy tongue more hoarse than mine
With repetition of my Romeo's name.
ROMEO   It is my soul that calls upon my name.
How silver-sweet sound lovers' tongues by night,   165
Like softest music to attending ears.
JULIET   Romeo.
ROMEO   My nyas.
JULIET   What o'clock tomorrow
Shall I send to thee?
ROMEO   By the hour of nine.
JULIET   I will not fail. 'Tis twenty year till then.
I have forgot why I did call thee back.   170
ROMEO   Let me stand here till thou remember it.
JULIET   I shall forget, to have thee still stand there,
Remembering how I love thy company.
ROMEO   And I'll still stay to have thee still forget,
Forgetting any other home but this.   175
JULIET   'Tis almost morning, I would have thee gone,
And yet no farther than a wanton's bird,
That lets it hop a little from his hand
Like a poor prisoner in his twisted gyves,
And with a silken thread plucks it back again,   180
So loving-jealous of his liberty.
ROMEO   I would I were thy bird.
JULIET   Sweet, so would I:
Yet I should kill thee with much cherishing.

Good night, good night. Parting is such sweet sorrow
That I shall say good night till it be morrow.   185
                                          Exit Juliet.
ROMEO
Sleep dwell upon thine eyes, peace in thy breast.
Would I were sleep and peace so sweet to rest.
The grey-ey'd morn smiles on the frowning night,
Chequering the eastern clouds with streaks of light;
And darkness fleckled like a drunkard reels   190
From forth day's pathway, made by Titan's wheels.
Hence will I to my ghostly Sire's close cell,
His help to crave and my dear hap to tell.   *Exit.*

2.3   *Enter* FRIAR LAURENCE *alone with a basket.*

FRIAR LAURENCE
Now, ere the sun advance his burning eye
The day to cheer, and night's dank dew to dry,
I must upfill this osier cage of ours
With baleful weeds and precious-juiced flowers.
The earth that's nature's mother is her tomb: 5
What is her burying grave, that is her womb;
And from her womb children of divers kind
We sucking on her natural bosom find.
Many for many virtues excellent,
None but for some, and yet all different.   10
O, mickle is the powerful grace that lies
In plants, herbs, stones, and their true qualities.
For naught so vile that on the earth doth live
But to the earth some special good doth give;
Nor aught so good but, strain'd from that fair use,   15
Revolts from true birth, stumbling on abuse.
Virtue itself turns vice being misapplied,
And vice sometime's by action dignified.

                      Enter ROMEO.

Within the infant rind of this weak flower
Poison hath residence, and medicine power: 20
For this, being smelt, with that part cheers each part;
Being tasted, stays all senses with the heart.
Two such opposed kings encamp them still
In man as well as herbs: grace and rude will;
And where the worser is predominant   25
Full soon the canker death eats up that plant.
ROMEO   Good morrow, father.
FRIAR LAURENCE   Benedicite.
What early tongue so sweet saluteth me?
Young son, it argues a distemper'd head
So soon to bid good morrow to thy bed.   30
Care keeps his watch in every old man's eye,
And where care lodges sleep will never lie,
But where unbruised youth with unstuff'd brain
Doth couch his limbs, there golden sleep doth reign.
Therefore thy earliness doth me assure   35
Thou art uprous'd with some distemperature;
Or, if not so, then here I hit it right:
Our Romeo hath not been in bed tonight.

ROMEO   That last is true. The sweeter rest was mine.
FRIAR LAURENCE
God pardon sin. Wast thou with Rosaline?   40
ROMEO   With Rosaline! My ghostly father, no.
I have forgot that name, and that name's woe.
FRIAR LAURENCE
That's my good son. But where hast thou been then?
ROMEO   I'll tell thee ere thou ask it me again.
I have been feasting with mine enemy,   45
Where on a sudden one hath wounded me
That's by me wounded. Both our remedies
Within thy help and holy physic lies.
I bear no hatred, blessed man, for lo,
My intercession likewise steads my foe.   50
FRIAR LAURENCE
Be plain, good son, and homely in thy drift;
Riddling confession finds but riddling shrift.
ROMEO   Then plainly know my heart's dear love is set
On the fair daughter of rich Capulet.
As mine on hers, so hers is set on mine,   55
And all combin'd save what thou must combine
By holy marriage. When, and where, and how
We met, we woo'd, and made exchange of vow
I'll tell thee as we pass; but this I pray,
That thou consent to marry us today.   60
FRIAR LAURENCE
Holy Saint Francis! What a change is here!
Is Rosaline, that thou didst love so dear,
So soon forsaken? Young men's love then lies
Not truly in their hearts but in their eyes.
Jesu Maria! What a deal of brine   65
Hath wash'd thy sallow cheeks for Rosaline.
How much salt water thrown away in waste
To season love, that of it doth not taste.
The sun not yet thy sighs from heaven clears,
Thy old groans yet ring in mine ancient ears.   70
Lo here upon thy cheek the stain doth sit
Of an old tear that is not wash'd off yet.
If ere thou wast thyself, and these woes thine,
Thou and these woes were all for Rosaline.
And art thou chang'd? Pronounce this sentence then: 75
Women may fall when there's no strength in men.
ROMEO   Thou chid'st me oft for loving Rosaline.
FRIAR LAURENCE
For doting, not for loving, pupil mine.
ROMEO   And bad'st me bury love.
FRIAR LAURENCE   Not in a grave
To lay one in, another out to have.   80
ROMEO   I pray thee chide me not, her I love now
Doth grace for grace and love for love allow.
The other did not so.
FRIAR LAURENCE   O, she knew well
Thy love did read by rote that could not spell.
But come young waverer, come, go with me,   85
In one respect I'll thy assistant be.
For this alliance may so happy prove
To turn your households' rancour to pure love.

ROMEO   O let us hence: I stand on sudden haste.

FRIAR LAURENCE

90   Wisely and slow; they stumble that run fast.   *Exeunt.*

2.4   *Enter* BENVOLIO *and* MERCUTIO.

MERCUTIO   Where the devil should this Romeo be? Came he not home tonight?

BENVOLIO   Not to his father's; I spoke with his man.

MERCUTIO   Why, that same pale hard-hearted wench, that Rosaline, torments him so that he will sure run mad.

BENVOLIO   Tybalt, the kinsman to old Capulet, hath sent a letter to his father's house.

MERCUTIO   A challenge, on my life.

10   BENVOLIO   Romeo will answer it.

MERCUTIO   Any man that can write may answer a letter.

BENVOLIO   Nay, he will answer the letter's master, how he dares, being dared.

MERCUTIO   Alas poor Romeo, he is already dead, stabbed with a white wench's black eye, run through the ear with a love song, the very pin of his heart cleft with the blind bow-boy's butt-shaft. And is he a man to encounter Tybalt?

BENVOLIO   Why, what is Tybalt?

20   MERCUTIO   More than Prince of Cats. O, he's the courageous captain of compliments: he fights as you sing pricksong, keeps time, distance and proportion. He rests his minim rests, one, two, and the third in your bosom: the very butcher of a silk button – a duellist, a duellist, a gentleman of the very first house, of the first and second cause. Ah, the immortal passado, the punto reverso, the hay!

BENVOLIO   The what?

30   MERCUTIO   The pox of such antic lisping affecting phantasimes, these new tuners of accent. By Jesu, a very good blade, a very tall man, a very good whore! Why, is not this a lamentable thing, grandsire, that we should be thus afflicted with these strange flies, these fashion-mongers, these 'pardon-me's', who stand so much on the new form that they cannot sit at ease on the old bench? O their bones, their bones!

Enter ROMEO.

BENVOLIO   Here comes Romeo, here comes Romeo!

MERCUTIO   Without his roe, like a dried herring. O flesh, flesh, how art thou fishified. Now is he for the numbers that Petrarch flowed in. Laura, to his lady, was a kitchen wench – marry, she had a better love to berhyme her – Dido a dowdy, Cleopatra a gypsy, Helen and Hero hildings and harlots, Thisbe a grey eye or so, but not to the purpose. Signor Romeo, bonjour. There's a French salutation to your French slop. You gave us the counterfeit fairly last night.

ROMEO   Good morrow to you both. What counterfeit did I give you?

MERCUTIO   The slip sir, the slip. Can you not conceive?

ROMEO   Pardon, good Mercutio, my business was great, 50 and in such a case as mine a man may strain courtesy.

MERCUTIO   That's as much as to say, such a case as yours constrains a man to bow in the hams.

ROMEO   Meaning to curtsy.

MERCUTIO   Thou hast most kindly hit it.   55

ROMEO   A most courteous exposition.

MERCUTIO   Nay, I am the very pink of courtesy.

ROMEO   Pink for flower.

MERCUTIO   Right.

ROMEO   Why, then is my pump well flowered.   60

MERCUTIO   Sure wit, follow me this jest now, till thou hast worn out thy pump, that when the single sole of it is worn, the jest may remain after the wearing solely singular.

ROMEO   O single-soled jest, solely singular for the 65 singleness.

MERCUTIO   Come between us, good Benvolio, my wits faints.

ROMEO   Switch and spurs, switch and spurs, or I'll cry a match!   70

MERCUTIO   Nay, if our wits run the wild-goose chase I am done. For thou hast more of the wild-goose in one of thy wits than I am sure I have in my whole five. Was I with you there for the goose?

ROMEO   Thou wast never with me for anything, when 75 thou wast not there for the goose.

MERCUTIO   I will bite thee by the ear for that jest.

ROMEO   Nay, good goose, bite not.

MERCUTIO   Thy wit is a very bitter sweeting, it is a most sharp sauce.   80

ROMEO   And is it not then well served in to a sweet goose?

MERCUTIO   O here's a wit of cheveril, that stretches from an inch narrow to an ell broad.

ROMEO   I stretch it out for that word 'broad', which, 85 added to the goose, proves thee far and wide a broad goose.

MERCUTIO   Why, is not this better now than groaning for love? Now art thou sociable, now art thou Romeo; now art thou what thou art, by art as well as by nature. 90 For this drivelling love is like a great natural that runs lolling up and down to hide his bauble in a hole.

BENVOLIO   Stop there, stop there.

MERCUTIO   Thou desirest me to stop in my tale against the hair.   95

BENVOLIO   Thou wouldst else have made thy tale large.

MERCUTIO   O, thou art deceived; I would have made it short; for I was come to the whole depth of my tale and meant indeed to occupy the argument no longer.

ROMEO   Here's goodly gear.   100

Enter Nurse *and her man* PETER.

A sail! A sail!

MERCUTIO   Two. Two. A shirt and a smock.

NURSE   Peter.

PETER   Anon.

105 NURSE   My fan, Peter.

MERCUTIO   Good Peter, to hide her face, for her fan's the fairer face.

NURSE   God ye good morrow, gentlemen.

MERCUTIO   God ye good e'en, fair gentlewoman.

110 NURSE   Is it good e'en?

MERCUTIO   'Tis no less, I tell ye; for the bawdy hand of the dial is now upon the prick of noon.

NURSE   Out upon you. What a man are you?

ROMEO   One, gentlewoman, that God hath made, 115 himself to mar.

NURSE   By my troth it is well said; 'for himself to mar' quoth a? Gentlemen, can any of you tell me where I may find the young Romeo?

ROMEO   I can tell you; but young Romeo will be older 120 when you have found him than he was when you sought him. I am the youngest of that name, for fault of a worse.

NURSE   You say well.

MERCUTIO   Yea, is the worst well? Very well took i'faith. Wisely, wisely.

125 NURSE   If you be he sir, I desire some confidence with you.

BENVOLIO   She will endite him to some supper.

MERCUTIO   A bawd! A bawd! A bawd! So ho.

130 ROMEO   What hast thou found?

MERCUTIO   No hare, sir, unless a hare, sir, in a lenten pie, that is something stale and hoar ere it be spent.
[*He walks by them and sings.*]
An old hare hoar,
And an old hare hoar,
135 Is very good meat in Lent.
But a hare that is hoar
Is too much for a score
When it hoars ere it be spent.
Romeo, will you come to your father's? We'll to 140 dinner thither.

ROMEO   I will follow you.

MERCUTIO   Farewell, ancient lady, farewell, lady, lady, lady.   *Exeunt Mercutio and Benvolio.*

NURSE   I pray you, sir, what saucy merchant was this, 145 that was so full of his ropery?

ROMEO   A gentleman, Nurse, that loves to hear himself talk, and will speak more in a minute than he will stand to in a month.

NURSE   And a speak anything against me I'll take him 150 down, and a were lustier than he is, and twenty such jacks. And if I cannot, I'll find those that shall. Scurvy knave! I am none of his flirt-gills, I am none of his skains-mates. [*She turns to Peter her man.*] And thou must stand by too and suffer every knave to use me at 155 his pleasure!

PETER   I saw no man use you at his pleasure; if I had, my weapon should quickly have been out. I warrant you, I dare draw as soon as another man, if I see occasion in a good quarrel, and the law on my side.

160 NURSE   Now afore God I am so vexed that every part about me quivers. Scurvy knave. Pray you, sir, a word – and as I told you, my young lady bid me enquire you out. What she bid me say, I will keep to myself. But first let me tell ye, if ye should lead her in a fool's 165 paradise, as they say, it were a very gross kind of behaviour, as they say; for the gentlewoman is young. And therefore, if you should deal double with her, truly it were an ill thing to be offered to any gentlewoman, and very weak dealing.

170 ROMEO   Nurse, commend me to thy lady and mistress. I protest unto thee –

NURSE   Good heart, and i'faith I will tell her as much. Lord, Lord, she will be a joyful woman.

ROMEO   What wilt thou tell her, Nurse? Thou dost not 175 mark me.

NURSE   I will tell her, sir, that you do protest – which, as I take it, is a gentlemanlike offer.

ROMEO   Bid her devise
Some means to come to shrift this afternoon,
And there she shall at Friar Laurence' cell   180
Be shriv'd and married. Here is for thy pains.

NURSE   No truly, sir; not a penny.

ROMEO   Go to, I say you shall.

NURSE   This afternoon, sir? Well, she shall be there.

ROMEO   And stay, good Nurse, behind the abbey wall.   185
Within this hour my man shall be with thee,
And bring thee cords made like a tackled stair,
Which to the high topgallant of my joy
Must be my convoy in the secret night.
Farewell, be trusty, and I'll quit thy pains;   190
Farewell. Commend me to thy mistress.

NURSE   Now God in heaven bless thee. Hark you, sir.

ROMEO   What say'st thou, my dear Nurse?

NURSE   Is your man secret? Did you ne'er hear say,
Two may keep counsel, putting one away?   195

ROMEO   I warrant thee my man's as true as steel.

NURSE   Well, sir, my mistress is the sweetest lady. Lord, Lord! When 'twas a little prating thing – O, there is a nobleman in town, one Paris, that would fain lay knife aboard; but she, good soul, had as lief see a toad, a very 200 toad, as see him. I anger her sometimes and tell her that Paris is the properer man, but I'll warrant you, when I say so she looks as pale as any clout in the versal world. Doth not rosemary and Romeo begin both with a letter?   205

ROMEO   Ay, Nurse, what of that? Both with an 'R'.

NURSE   Ah, mocker! That's the dog's name, 'R' is for the – No, I know it begins with some other letter; and she hath the prettiest sententious of it, of you and rosemary, that it would do you good to hear it.   210

ROMEO   Commend me to thy lady.   *Exit Romeo.*

NURSE   Ay, a thousand times. Peter!

PETER   Anon.

NURSE   Before, and apace.   *Exeunt.*

2.5   *Enter* JULIET.

JULIET
The clock struck nine when I did send the Nurse,
In half an hour she promis'd to return.
Perchance she cannot meet him. That's not so.
O, she is lame. Love's heralds should be thoughts
5   Which ten times faster glides than the sun's beams
Driving back shadows over lowering hills.
Therefore do nimble-pinion'd doves draw Love,
And therefore hath the wind-swift Cupid wings.
Now is the sun upon the highmost hill
10 Of this day's journey, and from nine till twelve
Is three long hours, yet she is not come.
Had she affections and warm youthful blood
She would be as swift in motion as a ball:
My words would bandy her to my sweet love,
15 And his to me.
But old folks, many feign as they were dead –
Unwieldy, slow, heavy, and pale as lead.

Enter Nurse *and* PETER.

O God she comes. O honey Nurse, what news?
Hast thou met with him? Send thy man away.
NURSE
20 Peter, stay at the gate.   *Exit Peter.*
JULIET
Now good sweet Nurse – O Lord why look'st thou
    sad?
Though news be sad, yet tell them merrily,
If good, thou sham'st the music of sweet news
By playing it to me with so sour a face.
25 NURSE   I am aweary, give me leave awhile.
Fie, how my bones ache. What a jaunce have I!
JULIET   I would thou hadst my bones and I thy news.
Nay come, I pray thee, speak: good, good Nurse,
    speak.
NURSE   Jesu, what haste. Can you not stay awhile?
30 Do you not see that I am out of breath?
JULIET
How art thou out of breath when thou hast breath
To say to me that thou art out of breath?
The excuse that thou dost make in this delay
Is longer than the tale thou dost excuse.
35 Is thy news good or bad? Answer to that,
Say either, and I'll stay the circumstance.
Let me be satisfied: is't good or bad?
NURSE   Well, you have made a simple choice. You know
    not how to choose a man. Romeo? No, not he. Though
40 his face be better than any man's, yet his leg excels all
    men's, and for a hand and a foot and a body, though
    they be not to be talked on, yet they are past compare.
    He is not the flower of courtesy, but I'll warrant him
    as gentle as a lamb. Go thy ways, wench, serve God.
45 What, have you dined at home?
JULIET   No, no. But all this did I know before.
What says he of our marriage? What of that?

NURSE   Lord, how my head aches! What a head have I:
It beats as it would fall in twenty pieces.
My back o' t'other side – ah, my back, my back!   50
Beshrew your heart for sending me about
To catch my death with jauncing up and down.
JULIET   I'faith I am sorry that thou art not well.
Sweet, sweet, sweet Nurse, tell me, what says my
    love?
NURSE   Your love says like an honest gentleman,   55
And a courteous, and a kind, and a handsome,
And I warrant a virtuous – Where is your mother?
JULIET   Where is my mother? Why, she is within.
Where should she be? How oddly thou repliest.
'Your love says, like an honest gentleman,   60
"Where is your mother?"'
                              O God's lady dear,
Are you so hot? Marry, come up, I trow.
Is this the poultice for my aching bones?
Henceforward do your messages yourself.
JULIET   Here's such a coil. Come, what says Romeo?   65
NURSE   Have you got leave to go to shrift today?
JULIET   I have.
NURSE   Then hie you hence to Friar Laurence' cell.
There stays a husband to make you a wife.
Now comes the wanton blood up in your cheeks.   70
They'll be in scarlet straight at any news.
Hie you to church. I must another way
To fetch a ladder by the which your love
Must climb a bird's nest soon when it is dark.
I am the drudge, and toil in your delight,   75
But you shall bear the burden soon at night.
Go. I'll to dinner. Hie you to the cell.
JULIET   Hie to high fortune! Honest Nurse, farewell.
                                          Exeunt.

2.6   *Enter* FRIAR LAURENCE *and* ROMEO.

FRIAR LAURENCE
So smile the heavens upon this holy act
That after-hours with sorrow chide us not.
ROMEO   Amen, amen, but come what sorrow can,
It cannot countervail the exchange of joy
That one short minute gives me in her sight.   5
Do thou but close our hands with holy words,
Then love-devouring death do what he dare:
It is enough I may but call her mine.
FRIAR LAURENCE
These violent delights have violent ends
And in their triumph die, like fire and powder,   10
Which as they kiss consume. The sweetest honey
Is loathsome in his own deliciousness,
And in the taste confounds the appetite.
Therefore love moderately; long love doth so.
Too swift arrives as tardy as too slow.   15

Enter JULIET *somewhat fast and embraces Romeo.*

Here comes the lady. O, so light a foot

Will ne'er wear out the everlasting flint.
A lover may bestride the gossamers
That idles in the wanton summer air

20 And yet not fall; so light is vanity.
JULIET   Good even to my ghostly confessor.
FRIAR LAURENCE
Romeo shall thank thee, daughter, for us both.
JULIET   As much to him, else is his thanks too much.
ROMEO   Ah, Juliet, if the measure of thy joy

25 Be heap'd like mine, and that thy skill be more
To blazon it, then sweeten with thy breath
This neighbour air, and let rich music's tongue
Unfold the imagin'd happiness that both
Receive in either by this dear encounter.

30 JULIET   Conceit more rich in matter than in words
Brags of his substance, not of ornament.
They are but beggars that can count their worth,
But my true love is grown to such excess
I cannot sum up sum of half my wealth.

FRIAR LAURENCE
35 Come, come with me and we will make short work
For, by your leaves, you shall not stay alone
Till holy church incorporate two in one.   *Exeunt.*

3.1   *Enter* MERCUTIO, BENVOLIO *and men.*

BENVOLIO   I pray thee, good Mercutio, let's retire;
The day is hot, the Capels are abroad,
And if we meet we shall not 'scape a brawl,
For now these hot days is the mad blood stirring.

5 MERCUTIO   Thou art like one of these fellows that, when
he enters the confines of a tavern, claps me his sword
upon the table and says 'God send me no need of
thee!' and by the operation of the second cup draws
him on the drawer, when indeed there is no need.

10 BENVOLIO   Am I like such a fellow?
MERCUTIO   Come, come, thou art as hot a Jack in thy
mood as any in Italy; and as soon moved to be moody,
and as soon moody to be moved.
BENVOLIO   And what to?

15 MERCUTIO   Nay, and there were two such, we should
have none shortly, for one would kill the other. Thou?
Why, thou wilt quarrel with a man that hath a hair
more or a hair less in his beard than thou hast. Thou
wilt quarrel with a man for cracking nuts, having no

20 other reason but because thou hast hazel eyes. What
eye but such an eye would spy out such a quarrel? Thy
head is as full of quarrels as an egg is full of meat, and
yet thy head hath been beaten as addle as an egg for
quarrelling. Thou hast quarrelled with a man for

25 coughing in the street, because he hath wakened thy
dog that hath lain asleep in the sun. Didst thou not fall
out with a tailor for wearing his new doublet before
Easter; with another for tying his new shoes with old
riband? And yet thou wilt tutor me from quarrelling!

30 BENVOLIO   And I were so apt to quarrel as thou art, any
man should buy the fee simple of my life for an hour
and a quarter.

MERCUTIO   The fee simple! O simple!

Enter TYBALT, PETRUCHIO *and others.*

BENVOLIO   By my head, here comes the Capulets.
MERCUTIO   By my heel, I care not.   35
TYBALT   Follow me close, for I will speak to them.
Gentlemen, good e'en: a word with one of you.
MERCUTIO   And but one word with one of us? Couple it
with something, make it a word and a blow.
TYBALT   You shall find me apt enough to that, sir, and   40
you will give me occasion.
MERCUTIO   Could you not take some occasion without
giving?
TYBALT   Mercutio, thou consortest with Romeo.
MERCUTIO   Consort? What, dost thou make us   45
minstrels? And thou make minstrels of us, look to hear
nothing but discords. Here's my fiddlestick, here's
that shall make you dance. Zounds, consort!
BENVOLIO   We talk here in the public haunt of men.
Either withdraw unto some private place,   50
Or reason coldly of your grievances,
Or else depart. Here all eyes gaze on us.
MERCUTIO
Men's eyes were made to look, and let them gaze.
I will not budge for no man's pleasure, I.

Enter ROMEO.

TYBALT
Well, peace be with you, sir, here comes my man.   55
MERCUTIO
But I'll be hang'd, sir, if he wear your livery.
Marry, go before to field, he'll be your follower.
Your worship in that sense may call him 'man'.
TYBALT   Romeo, the love I bear thee can afford
No better term than this: thou art a villain.   60
ROMEO   Tybalt, the reason that I have to love thee
Doth much excuse the appertaining rage
To such a greeting: villain am I none,
Therefore farewell. I see thou knowest me not.
TYBALT   Boy, this shall not excuse the injuries   65
That thou hast done me, therefore turn and draw.
ROMEO   I do protest I never injuried thee,
But love thee better than thou canst devise
Till thou shalt know the reason of my love.
And so, good Capulet, which name I tender   70
As dearly as mine own, be satisfied.
MERCUTIO   O calm, dishonourable, vile submission:
Alla stoccata carries it away! [*He draws.*]
Tybalt, you rat-catcher, will you walk?
TYBALT   What wouldst thou have with me?   75
MERCUTIO   Good King of Cats, nothing but one of your
nine lives. That I mean to make bold withal, and, as
you shall use me hereafter, dry-beat the rest of the
eight. Will you pluck your sword out of his pilcher by
the ears? Make haste, lest mine be about your ears ere   80
it be out.
TYBALT   I am for you. [*He draws.*]

ROMEO　Gentle Mercutio, put thy rapier up.

MERCUTIO　Come sir, your passado. [*They fight.*]

85 ROMEO　Draw, Benvolio, beat down their weapons.
　Gentlemen, for shame, forbear this outrage.
　Tybalt, Mercutio! The Prince expressly hath
　Forbid this bandying in Verona streets.
　Hold, Tybalt! Good Mercutio!
　[*Tybalt under Romeo's arm thrusts Mercutio in.*]

90 A FOLLOWER　Away Tybalt.
　　　　　　　　　　　Exit Tybalt with his followers.

MERCUTIO　I am hurt.
　A plague o' both your houses. I am sped.
　Is he gone, and hath nothing?

BENVOLIO　　　　　　　What, art thou hurt?

MERCUTIO
95　Ay, ay, a scratch, a scratch. Marry, 'tis enough.
　Where is my page? Go villain, fetch a surgeon.
　　　　　　　　　　　Exit Page.

ROMEO　Courage, man, the hurt cannot be much.

MERCUTIO　No, 'tis not so deep as a well, nor so wide as
　a church door, but 'tis enough, 'twill serve. Ask for
　me tomorrow and you shall find me a grave man. I am
100　peppered, I warrant, for this world. A plague o' both
　your houses. Zounds, a dog, a rat, a mouse, a cat, to
　scratch a man to death. A braggart, a rogue, a villain,
　that fights by the book of arithmetic – why the devil
　came you between us? I was hurt under your arm.

105 ROMEO　I thought all for the best.

MERCUTIO　Help me into some house, Benvolio,
　Or I shall faint. A plague o' both your houses,
　They have made worms' meat of me.
　I have it, and soundly too. Your houses!
　　　　　　　　　　Exit Mercutio with Benvolio.

110 ROMEO　This gentleman, the Prince's near ally,
　My very friend, hath got this mortal hurt
　In my behalf – my reputation stain'd
　With Tybalt's slander – Tybalt that an hour
　Hath been my cousin. O sweet Juliet,
115　Thy beauty hath made me effeminate
　And in my temper soften'd valour's steel.

Enter BENVOLIO.

BENVOLIO　O Romeo, Romeo, brave Mercutio is dead,
　That gallant spirit hath aspir'd the clouds
　Which too untimely here did scorn the earth.

120 ROMEO　This day's black fate on mo days doth depend:
　This but begins the woe others must end.

Enter TYBALT.

BENVOLIO　Here comes the furious Tybalt back again.

ROMEO　Again, in triumph, and Mercutio slain.
　Away to heaven respective lenity,
125　And fire-ey'd fury be my conduct now!
　Now, Tybalt, take the 'villain' back again
　That late thou gav'st me, for Mercutio's soul
　Is but a little way above our heads,
　Staying for thine to keep him company.

Either thou, or I, or both must go with him. 130

TYBALT
　Thou wretched boy, that didst consort him here,
　Shalt with him hence.

ROMEO　　　　　　This shall determine that.
　[*They fight. Tybalt falls.*]

BENVOLIO　Romeo, away, be gone,
　The citizens are up, and Tybalt slain!
　Stand not amaz'd. The Prince will doom thee death 135
　If thou art taken. Hence, be gone, away!

ROMEO　O, I am fortune's fool.

BENVOLIO　　　　　　　Why dost thou stay?
　　　　　　　　　　　Exit Romeo.

Enter Citizens.

CITIZEN　Which way ran he that kill'd Mercutio?
　Tybalt, that murderer, which way ran he?

BENVOLIO　There lies that Tybalt.

CITIZEN　　　　　　Up, sir, go with me. 140
　I charge thee in the Prince's name obey.

Enter PRINCE, MONTAGUE, CAPULET,
their wives and all.

PRINCE　Where are the vile beginners of this fray?

BENVOLIO　O noble Prince, I can discover all
　The unlucky manage of this fatal brawl.
　There lies the man, slain by young Romeo, 145
　That slew thy kinsman brave Mercutio.

LADY CAPULET
　Tybalt, my cousin, O my brother's child!
　O Prince, O husband, O, the blood is spill'd
　Of my dear kinsman. Prince, as thou art true,
　For blood of ours shed blood of Montague. 150
　O cousin, cousin.

PRINCE　Benvolio, who began this bloody fray?

BENVOLIO
　Tybalt, here slain, whom Romeo's hand did slay.
　Romeo, that spoke him fair, bid him bethink
　How nice the quarrel was, and urg'd withal 155
　Your high displeasure. All this uttered
　With gentle breath, calm look, knees humbly bow'd,
　Could not take truce with the unruly spleen
　Of Tybalt, deaf to peace, but that he tilts
　With piercing steel at bold Mercutio's breast, 160
　Who, all as hot, turns deadly point to point
　And, with a martial scorn, with one hand beats
　Cold death aside, and with the other sends
　It back to Tybalt, whose dexterity
　Retorts it. Romeo, he cries aloud 165
　'Hold, friends! Friends part!' and swifter than his
　　tongue
　His agile arm beats down their fatal points
　And 'twixt them rushes; underneath whose arm
　An envious thrust from Tybalt hit the life
　Of stout Mercutio; and then Tybalt fled, 170
　But by and by comes back to Romeo,
　Who had but newly entertain'd revenge,

And to't they go like lightning: for, ere I
Could draw to part them, was stout Tybalt slain,
75 And as he fell did Romeo turn and fly.
This is the truth, or let Benvolio die.

LADY CAPULET   He is a kinsman to the Montague.
Affection makes him false. He speaks not true.
Some twenty of them fought in this black strife
80 And all those twenty could but kill one life.
I beg for justice, which thou, Prince, must give.
Romeo slew Tybalt. Romeo must not live.

PRINCE   Romeo slew him, he slew Mercutio.
Who now the price of his dear blood doth owe?

MONTAGUE
85 Not Romeo, Prince, he was Mercutio's friend;
His fault concludes but what the law should end,
The life of Tybalt.

PRINCE   And for that offence
Immediately we do exile him hence.
I have an interest in your hearts' proceeding;
90 My blood for your rude brawls doth lie a-bleeding.
But I'll amerce you with so strong a fine
That you shall all repent the loss of mine.
I will be deaf to pleading and excuses;
Nor tears nor prayers shall purchase out abuses.
95 Therefore use none. Let Romeo hence in haste,
Else, when he is found, that hour is his last.
Bear hence this body, and attend our will.
Mercy but murders, pardoning those that kill.

Exeunt.

3.2   *Enter* JULIET *alone.*

JULIET   Gallop apace, you fiery-footed steeds,
Towards Phoebus' lodging. Such a waggoner
As Phaeton would whip you to the west
And bring in cloudy night immediately.
5 Spread thy close curtain, love-performing night,
That runaway's eyes may wink, and Romeo
Leap to these arms untalk'd-of and unseen.
Lovers can see to do their amorous rites
By their own beauties; or, if love be blind,
10 It best agrees with night. Come, civil night,
Thou sober-suited matron, all in black,
And learn me how to lose a winning match
Play'd for a pair of stainless maidenhoods.
Hood my unmann'd blood, bating in my cheeks,
15 With thy black mantle, till strange love grow bold,
Think true love acted simple modesty.
Come night, come Romeo, come thou day in night,
For thou wilt lie upon the wings of night
Whiter than new snow upon a raven's back.
20 Come gentle night, come loving black-brow'd night,
Give me my Romeo; and when I shall die
Take him and cut him out in little stars,
And he will make the face of heaven so fine
That all the world will be in love with night,
25 And pay no worship to the garish sun.

O, I have bought the mansion of a love
But not possess'd it, and though I am sold,
Not yet enjoy'd. So tedious is this day
As is the night before some festival
To an impatient child that hath new robes   30
And may not wear them. O, here comes my Nurse.

Enter Nurse *with cords, wringing her hands.*

And she brings news, and every tongue that speaks
But Romeo's name speaks heavenly eloquence.
Now, Nurse, what news? What hast thou there?
The cords that Romeo bid thee fetch?

NURSE   Ay, ay, the cords.   35

JULIET
Ay me, what news? Why dost thou wring thy hands?

NURSE   Ah weraday, he's dead, he's dead, he's dead!
We are undone, lady, we are undone.
Alack the day, he's gone, he's kill'd, he's dead.

JULIET   Can heaven be so envious?

NURSE   Romeo can,   40
Though heaven cannot. O Romeo, Romeo,
Who ever would have thought it? Romeo!

JULIET   What devil art thou that dost torment me thus?
This torture should be roar'd in dismal hell.
Hath Romeo slain himself? Say thou but 'Ay'   45
And that bare vowel 'I' shall poison more
Than the death-darting eye of cockatrice.
I am not I if there be such an 'I',
Or those eyes shut that makes thee answer 'Ay'.
If he be slain say 'Ay', or if not, 'No'.   50
Brief sounds determine of my weal or woe.

NURSE   I saw the wound, I saw it with mine eyes
– God save the mark – here on his manly breast.
A piteous corse, a bloody piteous corse,
Pale, pale as ashes, all bedaub'd in blood,   55
All in gore-blood. I swounded at the sight.

JULIET
O break, my heart. Poor bankrupt, break at once.
To prison, eyes, ne'er look on liberty.
Vile earth to earth resign, end motion here,
And thou and Romeo press one heavy bier.   60

NURSE   O Tybalt, Tybalt, the best friend I had.
O courteous Tybalt, honest gentleman.
That ever I should live to see thee dead.

JULIET   What storm is this that blows so contrary?
Is Romeo slaughter'd and is Tybalt dead?   65
My dearest cousin and my dearer lord?
Then dreadful trumpet sound the general doom,
For who is living if those two are gone?

NURSE   Tybalt is gone and Romeo banished.
Romeo that kill'd him, he is banished.   70

JULIET
O God! Did Romeo's hand shed Tybalt's blood?

NURSE   It did, it did, alas the day, it did.

JULIET   O serpent heart, hid with a flowering face.
Did ever dragon keep so fair a cave?
Beautiful tyrant, fiend angelical,   75

Dove-feather'd raven, wolvish-ravening lamb!
Despised substance of divinest show!
Just opposite to what thou justly seem'st!
A damned saint, an honourable villain!
80   O nature what hadst thou to do in hell
When thou didst bower the spirit of a fiend
In mortal paradise of such sweet flesh?
Was ever book containing such vile matter
So fairly bound? O, that deceit should dwell
In such a gorgeous palace.

NURSE   There's no trust,
85   No faith, no honesty in men. All perjur'd,
All forsworn, all naught, all dissemblers.
Ah, where's my man? Give me some aqua vitae.
These griefs, these woes, these sorrows make me old.
Shame come to Romeo.

JULIET   Blister'd be thy tongue
90   For such a wish. He was not born to shame.
Upon his brow shame is asham'd to sit,
For 'tis a throne where honour may be crown'd
Sole monarch of the universal earth.
95   O, what a beast was I to chide at him.

NURSE
Will you speak well of him that kill'd your cousin?

JULIET   Shall I speak ill of him that is my husband?
Ah, poor my lord, what tongue shall smooth thy
    name
When I thy three-hours wife have mangled it?
100   But wherefore, villain, didst thou kill my cousin?
That villain cousin would have kill'd my husband.
Back, foolish tears, back to your native spring,
Your tributary drops belong to woe
Which you mistaking offer up to joy.
105   My husband lives, that Tybalt would have slain,
And Tybalt's dead, that would have slain my
    husband.
All this is comfort. Wherefore weep I then?
Some word there was, worser than Tybalt's death,
That murder'd me. I would forget it fain,
110   But O, it presses to my memory
Like damned guilty deeds to sinners' minds.
Tybalt is dead and Romeo – banished.
That 'banished', that one word 'banished',
Hath slain ten thousand Tybalts: Tybalt's death
115   Was woe enough, if it had ended there.
Or if sour woe delights in fellowship
And needly will be rank'd with other griefs,
Why follow'd not, when she said 'Tybalt's dead',
Thy father or thy mother, nay or both,
120   Which modern lamentation might have mov'd?
But with a rearward following Tybalt's death,
'Romeo is banished': to speak that word
Is father, mother, Tybalt, Romeo, Juliet,
All slain, all dead. Romeo is banished,
125   There is no end, no limit, measure, bound,
In that word's death. No words can that woe sound.
Where is my father and my mother, Nurse?

NURSE   Weeping and wailing over Tybalt's corse.
Will you go to them? I will bring you thither.

JULIET
Wash they his wounds with tears? Mine shall be
    spent   130
When theirs are dry, for Romeo's banishment.
Take up those cords. Poor ropes, you are beguil'd,
Both you and I, for Romeo is exil'd.
He made you for a highway to my bed,
But I, a maid, die maiden-widowed.   135
Come, cords, come, Nurse, I'll to my wedding bed,
And death, not Romeo take my maidenhead.

NURSE   Hie to your chamber. I'll find Romeo
To comfort you. I wot well where he is.
Hark ye, your Romeo will be here at night.   140
I'll to him. He is hid at Laurence' cell.

JULIET   O find him, give this ring to my true knight
And bid him come to take his last farewell.   *Exeunt.*

3.3   *Enter* FRIAR LAURENCE.

FRIAR LAURENCE
Romeo, come forth, come forth, thou fearful man.
Affliction is enamour'd of thy parts
And thou art wedded to calamity.

                    Enter ROMEO.

ROMEO   Father, what news? What is the Prince's doom?
What sorrow craves acquaintance at my hand   5
That I yet know not?

FRIAR LAURENCE   Too familiar
Is my dear son with such sour company.
I bring thee tidings of the Prince's doom.

ROMEO
What less than doomsday is the Prince's doom?

FRIAR LAURENCE
A gentler judgement vanish'd from his lips: 10
Not body's death but body's banishment.

ROMEO   Ha! Banishment! Be merciful, say 'death'.
For exile hath more terror in his look,
Much more than death. Do not say 'banishment'.

FRIAR LAURENCE
Hence from Verona art thou banished.   15
Be patient, for the world is broad and wide.

ROMEO   There is no world without Verona walls
But purgatory, torture, hell itself;
Hence 'banished' is banish'd from the world,
And world's exile is death. Then 'banished'   20
Is death, misterm'd. Calling death 'banished'
Thou cut'st my head off with a golden axe
And smilest upon the stroke that murders me.

FRIAR LAURENCE   O deadly sin, O rude unthankfulness.
Thy fault our law calls death, but the kind Prince,   25
Taking thy part, hath rush'd aside the law
And turn'd that black word 'death' to banishment.
This is dear mercy and thou seest it not.

ROMEO   'Tis torture and not mercy. Heaven is here

Where Juliet lives, and every cat and dog
And little mouse, every unworthy thing,
Live here in heaven and may look on her,
But Romeo may not. More validity,
More honourable state, more courtship lives
In carrion flies than Romeo. They may seize
On the white wonder of dear Juliet's hand
And steal immortal blessing from her lips,
Who, even in pure and vestal modesty
Still blush, as thinking their own kisses sin.
But Romeo may not, he is banished.
Flies may do this, but I from this must fly.
They are free men but I am banished.
And say'st thou yet that exile is not death?
Hadst thou no poison mix'd, no sharp-ground knife,
No sudden mean of death, though ne'er so mean,
But 'banished' to kill me? 'Banished'?
O Friar, the damned use that word in hell.
Howling attends it. How hast thou the heart,
Being a divine, a ghostly confessor,
A sin-absolver, and my friend profess'd,
To mangle me with that word 'banished'?
FRIAR LAURENCE
　Thou fond mad man, hear me a little speak.
ROMEO　O, thou wilt speak again of banishment.
FRIAR LAURENCE
　I'll give thee armour to keep off that word,
　Adversity's sweet milk, philosophy,
　To comfort thee though thou art banished.
ROMEO　Yet 'banished'? Hang up philosophy.
　Unless philosophy can make a Juliet,
　Displant a town, reverse a Prince's doom,
　It helps not, it prevails not. Talk no more.
FRIAR LAURENCE
　O, then I see that mad men have no ears.
ROMEO
　How should they when that wise men have no eyes?
FRIAR LAURENCE
　Let me dispute with thee of thy estate.
ROMEO
　Thou canst not speak of that thou dost not feel.
　Wert thou as young as I, Juliet thy love,
　An hour but married, Tybalt murdered,
　Doting like me, and like me banished,
　Then mightst thou speak, then mightst thou tear thy
　　hair
　And fall upon the ground as I do now,
　Taking the measure of an unmade grave. [*knock*]
FRIAR LAURENCE
　Arise, one knocks. Good Romeo, hide thyself.
ROMEO　Not I, unless the breath of heartsick groans
　Mist-like infold me from the search of eyes. [*knock*]
FRIAR LAURENCE
　Hark how they knock. – Who's there? – Romeo, arise,
　Thou wilt be taken. – Stay awhile. – Stand up.
　[*knock*]
　Run to my study. – By and by. – God's will,

What simpleness is this? – I come, I come. [*knock*]
Who knocks so hard?
Whence come you, what's your will?
NURSE [*within*]
　Let me come in and you shall know my errand.　　80
　I come from Lady Juliet.
FRIAR LAURENCE　　　　　　Welcome then.

　　　　　　　Enter Nurse.

NURSE　O holy Friar, O, tell me, holy Friar,
　Where is my lady's lord, where's Romeo?
FRIAR LAURENCE
　There on the ground, with his own tears made
　　drunk.
NURSE　O, he is even in my mistress' case,　　　　85
　Just in her case. O woeful sympathy,
　Piteous predicament. Even so lies she,
　Blubbering and weeping, weeping and blubbering.
　Stand up, stand up. Stand, and you be a man.
　For Juliet's sake, for her sake, rise and stand.　　90
　Why should you fall into so deep an O? [*He rises.*]
ROMEO　Nurse.
NURSE　　　　　　Ah sir, ah sir, death's the end of all.
ROMEO　Spak'st thou of Juliet? How is it with her?
　Doth not she think me an old murderer
　Now I have stain'd the childhood of our joy　　95
　With blood remov'd but little from her own?
　Where is she? And how doth she? And what says
　My conceal'd lady to our cancell'd love?
NURSE　O, she says nothing, sir, but weeps and weeps,
　And now falls on her bed, and then starts up,　　100
　And Tybalt calls, and then on Romeo cries,
　And then down falls again.
ROMEO　　　　　　　　As if that name,
　Shot from the deadly level of a gun,
　Did murder her, as that name's cursed hand
　Murder'd her kinsman. O, tell me, Friar, tell me,　　105
　In what vile part of this anatomy
　Doth my name lodge? Tell me that I may sack
　The hateful mansion.
FRIAR LAURENCE　　　　　Hold thy desperate hand.
　Art thou a man? Thy form cries out thou art.
　Thy tears are womanish, thy wild acts denote　　110
　The unreasonable fury of a beast.
　Unseemly woman in a seeming man,
　And ill-beseeming beast in seeming both!
　Thou hast amaz'd me. By my holy order,
　I thought thy disposition better temper'd.　　115
　Hast thou slain Tybalt? Wilt thou slay thyself?
　And slay thy lady that in thy life lives,
　By doing damned hate upon thyself?
　Why rail'st thou on thy birth, the heaven and earth?
　Since birth, and heaven, and earth all three do meet　　120
　In thee at once; which thou at once wouldst lose.
　Fie, fie, thou sham'st thy shape, thy love, thy wit,
　Which, like a usurer, abound'st in all,
　And usest none in that true use indeed

125   Which should bedeck thy shape, thy love, thy wit.
     Thy noble shape is but a form of wax
     Digressing from the valour of a man;
     Thy dear love sworn but hollow perjury,
     Killing that love which thou hast vow'd to cherish;
130   Thy wit, that ornament to shape and love,
     Misshapen in the conduct of them both,
     Like powder in a skilless soldier's flask
     Is set afire by thine own ignorance,
     And thou dismember'd with thine own defence.
135   What, rouse thee, man. Thy Juliet is alive,
     For whose dear sake thou wast but lately dead.
     There art thou happy. Tybalt would kill thee,
     But thou slew'st Tybalt. There art thou happy.
     The law that threaten'd death becomes thy friend
140   And turns it to exile. There art thou happy.
     A pack of blessings light upon thy back;
     Happiness courts thee in her best array;
     But like a mishav'd and a sullen wench
     Thou pouts upon thy fortune and thy love.
145   Take heed, take heed, for such die miserable.
     Go, get thee to thy love as was decreed,
     Ascend her chamber – hence, and comfort her.
     But look thou stay not till the Watch be set,
     For then thou canst not pass to Mantua,
150   Where thou shalt live till we can find a time
     To blaze your marriage, reconcile your friends,
     Beg pardon of the Prince and call thee back,
     With twenty hundred thousand times more joy
     Than thou wentst forth in lamentation.
155   Go before, Nurse. Commend me to thy lady
     And bid her hasten all the house to bed,
     Which heavy sorrow makes them apt unto.
     Romeo is coming.
     NURSE   O lord, I could have stay'd here all the night
160   To hear good counsel. O, what learning is.
     My lord, I'll tell my lady you will come.
     ROMEO   Do so, and bid my sweet prepare to chide.
     [*Nurse offers to go in and turns again.*]
     NURSE   Here sir, a ring she bid me give you, sir.
     Hie you, make haste, for it grows very late.   *Exit.*
165   ROMEO   How well my comfort is reviv'd by this.
     FRIAR LAURENCE
     Go hence, good night, and here stands all your state:
     Either be gone before the Watch be set,
     Or by the break of day disguis'd from hence.
     Sojourn in Mantua. I'll find out your man,
170   And he shall signify from time to time
     Every good hap to you that chances here.
     Give me thy hand. 'Tis late. Farewell. Good night.
     ROMEO   But that a joy past joy calls out on me,
     It were a grief so brief to part with thee.
175   Farewell.   *Exeunt.*

3.4   *Enter* CAPULET, LADY CAPULET *and* PARIS.

CAPULET   Things have fallen out, sir, so unluckily
     That we have had no time to move our daughter.

     Look you, she lov'd her kinsman Tybalt dearly,
     And so did I. Well, we were born to die.
     'Tis very late. She'll not come down tonight.   5
     I promise you, but for your company,
     I would have been abed an hour ago.
PARIS   These times of woe afford no times to woo.
     Madam, good night. Commend me to your daughter.
LADY CAPULET
     I will, and know her mind early tomorrow.   10
     Tonight she's mew'd up to her heaviness.
     [*Paris offers to go in and Capulet calls him again.*]
CAPULET   Sir Paris, I will make a desperate tender
     Of my child's love. I think she will be rul'd
     In all respects by me; nay, more, I doubt it not.
     Wife, go you to her ere you go to bed,   15
     Acquaint her here of my son Paris' love,
     And bid her – mark you me? – on Wednesday next –
     But soft – what day is this?
PARIS   Monday, my lord.
CAPULET
     Monday! Ha ha! Well, Wednesday is too soon.
     A Thursday let it be, a' Thursday, tell her,   20
     She shall be married to this noble earl.
     Will you be ready? Do you like this haste?
     We'll keep no great ado – a friend or two.
     For, hark you, Tybalt being slain so late,
     It may be thought we held him carelessly,   25
     Being our kinsman, if we revel much.
     Therefore we'll have some half a dozen friends
     And there an end. But what say you to Thursday?
PARIS
     My lord, I would that Thursday were tomorrow.
CAPULET   Well, get you gone. A' Thursday be it then.   30
     Go you to Juliet ere you go to bed,
     Prepare her, wife, against this wedding day.
     Farewell, my lord. – Light to my chamber, ho!
     Afore me, it is so very late that we
     May call it early by and by. Good night.   *Exeunt.*   35

3.5   *Enter* ROMEO *and* JULIET *aloft at the window.*

JULIET   Wilt thou be gone? It is not yet near day.
     It was the nightingale and not the lark
     That pierc'd the fearful hollow of thine ear.
     Nightly she sings on yond pomegranate tree.
     Believe me, love, it was the nightingale.   5
ROMEO   It was the lark, the herald of the morn,
     No nightingale. Look, love, what envious streaks
     Do lace the severing clouds in yonder east.
     Night's candles are burnt out, and jocund day
     Stands tiptoe on the misty mountain tops.   10
     I must be gone and live, or stay and die.
JULIET   Yond light is not daylight, I know it, I.
     It is some meteor that the sun exhales
     To be to thee this night a torchbearer
     And light thee on thy way to Mantua.   15
     Therefore stay yet: thou need'st not to be gone.
ROMEO   Let me be ta'en, let me be put to death,

I am content, so thou wilt have it so.
I'll say yon grey is not the morning's eye,
'Tis but the pale reflex of Cynthia's brow.
Nor that is not the lark whose notes do beat
The vaulty heaven so high above our heads.
I have more care to stay than will to go.
Come death, and welcome. Juliet wills it so.
How is't, my soul? Let's talk. It is not day.

JULIET   It is, it is. Hie hence, begone, away.
It is the lark that sings so out of tune,
Straining harsh discords and unpleasing sharps.
Some say the lark makes sweet division.
This doth not so, for she divideth us.
Some say the lark and loathed toad change eyes.
O, now I would they had chang'd voices too,
Since arm from arm that voice doth us affray,
Hunting thee hence with hunt's-up to the day.
O now be gone, more light and light it grows.

ROMEO
More light and light: more dark and dark our woes.

Enter Nurse *hastily.*

NURSE   Madam.
JULIET   Nurse?
NURSE   Your lady mother is coming to your chamber.
The day is broke, be wary, look about.   *Exit.*
JULIET   Then, window, let day in and let life out.
ROMEO   Farewell, farewell, one kiss and I'll descend.
[*He goes down.*]
JULIET
Art thou gone so? Love, lord, ay husband, friend,
I must hear from thee every day in the hour,
For in a minute there are many days.
O, by this count I shall be much in years
Ere I again behold my Romeo.

ROMEO   Farewell.
I will omit no opportunity
That may convey my greetings, love, to thee.
JULIET   O think'st thou we shall ever meet again?
ROMEO   I doubt it not, and all these woes shall serve
For sweet discourses in our times to come.
JULIET   O God, I have an ill-divining soul!
Methinks I see thee, now thou art so low,
As one dead in the bottom of a tomb.
Either my eyesight fails, or thou look'st pale.
ROMEO   And trust me, love, in my eye so do you.
Dry sorrow drinks our blood. Adieu, adieu.   *Exit.*
JULIET   O Fortune, Fortune! All men call thee fickle;
If thou art fickle, what dost thou with him
That is renown'd for faith? Be fickle, Fortune,
For then I hope thou wilt not keep him long,
But send him back.

Enter LADY CAPULET.

LADY CAPULET   Ho, daughter, are you up?
JULIET   Who is't that calls? It is my lady mother.
Is she not down so late, or up so early?

What unaccustom'd cause procures her hither?
[*She goeth down from the window.*]
LADY CAPULET   Why, how now Juliet?

Enter JULIET.

JULIET   Madam, I am not well.
LADY CAPULET
Evermore weeping for your cousin's death?
What, wilt thou wash him from his grave with tears?   70
And if thou couldst, thou couldst not make him live.
Therefore have done: some grief shows much of love,
But much of grief shows still some want of wit.
JULIET   Yet let me weep for such a feeling loss.
LADY CAPULET
So shall you feel the loss but not the friend   75
Which you weep for.
JULIET   Feeling so the loss,
I cannot choose but ever weep the friend.
LADY CAPULET
Well, girl, thou weepst not so much for his death
As that the villain lives which slaughter'd him.
JULIET   What villain, madam?
LADY CAPULET   That same villain Romeo.   80
JULIET   Villain and he be many miles asunder.
God pardon him. I do with all my heart.
And yet no man like he doth grieve my heart.
LADY CAPULET
That is because the traitor murderer lives.
JULIET
Ay madam, from the reach of these my hands.   85
Would none but I might venge my cousin's death.
LADY CAPULET
We will have vengeance for it, fear thou not.
Then weep no more. I'll send to one in Mantua,
Where that same banish'd runagate doth live,
Shall give him such an unaccustom'd dram   90
That he shall soon keep Tybalt company;
And then I hope thou wilt be satisfied.
JULIET   Indeed I never shall be satisfied
With Romeo, till I behold him – dead –
Is my poor heart so for a kinsman vex'd.   95
Madam, if you could find out but a man
To bear a poison, I would temper it –
That Romeo should upon receipt thereof
Soon sleep in quiet. O, how my heart abhors
To hear him nam'd, and cannot come to him   100
To wreak the love I bore my cousin
Upon his body that hath slaughter'd him.
LADY CAPULET
Find thou the means and I'll find such a man.
But now I'll tell thee joyful tidings, girl.
JULIET   And joy comes well in such a needy time.   105
What are they, I beseech your ladyship?
LADY CAPULET
Well, well, thou hast a careful father, child;
One who to put thee from thy heaviness
Hath sorted out a sudden day of joy,

110   That thou expects not, nor I look'd not for.
JULIET   Madam, in happy time. What day is that?
LADY CAPULET
    Marry, my child, early next Thursday morn
    The gallant, young, and noble gentleman,
    The County Paris, at Saint Peter's Church,
115   Shall happily make thee there a joyful bride.
JULIET   Now by Saint Peter's Church, and Peter too,
    He shall not make me there a joyful bride.
    I wonder at this haste, that I must wed
    Ere he that should be husband comes to woo.
120   I pray you tell my lord and father, madam,
    I will not marry yet. And when I do, I swear
    It shall be Romeo, whom you know I hate,
    Rather than Paris. These are news indeed.
LADY CAPULET
    Here comes your father, tell him so yourself,
125   And see how he will take it at your hands.

       Enter CAPULET *and* Nurse.

CAPULET
    When the sun sets the earth doth drizzle dew,
    But for the sunset of my brother's son
    It rains downright.
    How now, a conduit, girl? What, still in tears?
130   Evermore showering? In one little body
    Thou counterfeits a bark, a sea, a wind.
    For still thy eyes, which I may call the sea,
    Do ebb and flow with tears. The bark thy body is,
    Sailing in this salt flood, the winds thy sighs,
135   Who raging with thy tears and they with them,
    Without a sudden calm will overset
    Thy tempest-tossed body. How now, wife?
    Have you deliver'd to her our decree?
LADY CAPULET
    Ay sir, but she will none, she gives you thanks.
140   I would the fool were married to her grave.
CAPULET
    Soft. Take me with you, take me with you, wife.
    How? Will she none? Doth she not give us thanks?
    Is she not proud? Doth she not count her blest,
    Unworthy as she is, that we have wrought
145   So worthy a gentleman to be her bride?
JULIET
    Not proud you have, but thankful that you have.
    Proud can I never be of what I hate,
    But thankful even for hate that is meant love.
CAPULET
    How, how, how, how? Chopp'd logic? What is this?
150   'Proud' and 'I thank you' and 'I thank you not'
    And yet 'not proud'? Mistress minion you,
    Thank me no thankings nor proud me no prouds,
    But fettle your fine joints 'gainst Thursday next
    To go with Paris to Saint Peter's Church,
155   Or I will drag thee on a hurdle thither.
    Out, you green-sickness carrion! Out, you baggage!
    You tallow-face!

LADY CAPULET   Fie, fie. What, are you mad?
JULIET   Good father, I beseech you on my knees.
    [*She kneels down.*]
    Hear me with patience but to speak a word.
CAPULET
    Hang thee young baggage, disobedient wretch!   160
    I tell thee what – get thee to church a' Thursday
    Or never after look me in the face.
    Speak not, reply not, do not answer me.
    My fingers itch. Wife, we scarce thought us blest
    That God had lent us but this only child;   165
    But now I see this one is one too much,
    And that we have a curse in having her.
    Out on her, hilding.
NURSE   God in heaven bless her.
    You are to blame, my lord, to rate her so.
CAPULET
    And why, my Lady Wisdom? Hold your tongue,   170
    Good Prudence! Smatter with your gossips, go.
NURSE   I speak no treason.
CAPULET   O God 'i' good e'en!
NURSE   May not one speak?
CAPULET   Peace, you mumbling fool!
    Utter your gravity o'er a gossip's bowl,
    For here we need it not.
LADY CAPULET   You are too hot.   175
CAPULET
    God's bread, it makes me mad! Day, night, work,
      play,
    Alone, in company, still my care hath been
    To have her match'd. And having now provided
    A gentleman of noble parentage,
    Of fair demesnes, youthful and nobly lign'd,   180
    Stuff'd, as they say, with honourable parts,
    Proportion'd as one's thought would wish a man –
    And then to have a wretched puling fool,
    A whining mammet, in her fortune's tender,
    To answer 'I'll not wed, I cannot love,   185
    I am too young, I pray you pardon me!'
    But, and you will not wed, I'll pardon you!
    Graze where you will, you shall not house with me.
    Look to't, think on't, I do not use to jest.
    Thursday is near. Lay hand on heart. Advise.   190
    And you be mine I'll give you to my friend;
    And you be not, hang! Beg! Starve! Die in the
      streets!
    For by my soul I'll ne'er acknowledge thee,
    Nor what is mine shall never do thee good.
    Trust to't, bethink you. I'll not be forsworn.   *Exit.*   195
JULIET   Is there no pity sitting in the clouds
    That sees into the bottom of my grief?
    O sweet my mother, cast me not away,
    Delay this marriage for a month, a week,
    Or if you do not, make the bridal bed   200
    In that dim monument where Tybalt lies.
LADY CAPULET
    Talk not to me, for I'll not speak a word.

Do as thou wilt, for I have done with thee.   *Exit.*

JULIET   O God, O Nurse, how shall this be prevented?

My husband is on earth, my faith in heaven.

How shall that faith return again to earth

Unless that husband send it me from heaven

By leaving earth? Comfort me, counsel me.

Alack, alack, that heaven should practise stratagems

Upon so soft a subject as myself.

What sayst thou? Hast thou not a word of joy?

Some comfort, Nurse.

NURSE   Faith, here it is.

Romeo is banish'd, and all the world to nothing

That he dares ne'er come back to challenge you.

Or if he do, it needs must be by stealth.

Then, since the case so stands as now it doth,

I think it best you married with the County.

O, he's a lovely gentleman.

Romeo's a dishclout to him. An eagle, madam,

Hath not so green, so quick, so fair an eye

As Paris hath. Beshrew my very heart,

I think you are happy in this second match,

For it excels your first; or, if it did not,

Your first is dead, or 'twere as good he were

As living here and you no use of him.

JULIET   Speakest thou from thy heart?

NURSE   And from my soul too, else beshrew them both.

JULIET   Amen.

NURSE   What?

JULIET

Well, thou hast comforted me marvellous much.

Go in, and tell my lady I am gone,

Having displeas'd my father, to Laurence' cell,

To make confession and to be absolv'd.

NURSE   Marry, I will; and this is wisely done.   *Exit.*

JULIET   Ancient damnation! O most wicked fiend,

Is it more sin to wish me thus forsworn,

Or to dispraise my lord with that same tongue

Which she hath prais'd him with above compare

So many thousand times? Go, counsellor.

Thou and my bosom henceforth shall be twain.

I'll to the Friar to know his remedy.

If all else fail, myself have power to die.   *Exit.*

4.1   *Enter* FRIAR LAURENCE *and* PARIS.

FRIAR LAURENCE

On Thursday, sir? The time is very short.

PARIS   My father Capulet will have it so,

And I am nothing slow to slack his haste.

FRIAR LAURENCE

You say you do not know the lady's mind.

Uneven is the course. I like it not.

PARIS   Immoderately she weeps for Tybalt's death,

And therefore have I little talk'd of love,

For Venus smiles not in a house of tears.

Now sir, her father counts it dangerous

That she do give her sorrow so much sway,

And in his wisdom hastes our marriage

To stop the inundation of her tears

Which, too much minded by herself alone,

May be put from her by society.

Now do you know the reason of this haste.   15

FRIAR LAURENCE

I would I knew not why it should be slow'd –

Look sir, here comes the lady toward my cell.

Enter JULIET.

PARIS   Happily met, my lady and my wife.

JULIET   That may be, sir, when I may be a wife.

PARIS   That may be, must be, love, on Thursday next.   20

JULIET   What must be, shall be.

FRIAR LAURENCE   That's a certain text.

PARIS   Come you to make confession to this father?

JULIET   To answer that, I should confess to you.

PARIS   Do not deny to him that you love me.

JULIET   I will confess to you that I love him.   25

PARIS   So will ye, I am sure, that you love me.

JULIET   If I do so, it will be of more price

Being spoke behind your back than to your face.

PARIS   Poor soul, thy face is much abus'd with tears.

JULIET   The tears have got small victory by that,   30

For it was bad enough before their spite.

PARIS

Thou wrong'st it more than tears with that report.

JULIET   That is no slander, sir, which is a truth,

And what I spake, I spake it to my face.

PARIS   Thy face is mine, and thou hast slander'd it.   35

JULIET   It may be so, for it is not mine own. –

Are you at leisure, holy father, now,

Or shall I come to you at evening mass?

FRIAR LAURENCE

My leisure serves me, pensive daughter, now. –

My lord, we must entreat the time alone.   40

PARIS   God shield I should disturb devotion.

Juliet, on Thursday early will I rouse ye;

Till then, adieu, and keep this holy kiss.   *Exit.*

JULIET   O shut the door, and when thou hast done so,

Come weep with me, past hope, past cure, past help!   45

FRIAR LAURENCE   O Juliet, I already know thy grief;

It strains me past the compass of my wits.

I hear thou must – and nothing may prorogue it –

On Thursday next be married to this County.

JULIET   Tell me not, Friar, that thou hearest of this,   50

Unless thou tell me how I may prevent it.

If in thy wisdom thou canst give no help,

Do thou but call my resolution wise,

And with this knife I'll help it presently.

God join'd my heart and Romeo's, thou our hands;   55

And ere this hand, by thee to Romeo's seal'd,

Shall be the label to another deed,

Or my true heart with treacherous revolt

Turn to another, this shall slay them both.

Therefore, out of thy long-experienc'd time   60

Give me some present counsel, or behold:

'Twixt my extremes and me this bloody knife
Shall play the umpire, arbitrating that
Which the commission of thy years and art
65   Could to no issue of true honour bring.
Be not so long to speak. I long to die
If what thou speak'st speak not of remedy.
FRIAR LAURENCE
Hold, daughter. I do spy a kind of hope
Which craves as desperate an execution
70   As that is desperate which we would prevent.
If, rather than to marry County Paris,
Thou hast the strength of will to slay thyself,
Then is it likely thou wilt undertake
A thing like death to chide away this shame,
75   That cop'st with death himself to scape from it.
And if thou dar'st, I'll give thee remedy.
JULIET
O, bid me leap, rather than marry Paris,
From off the battlements of any tower,
Or walk in thievish ways, or bid me lurk
80   Where serpents are. Chain me with roaring bears,
Or hide me nightly in a charnel-house
O'ercover'd quite with dead men's rattling bones,
With reeky shanks and yellow chapless skulls.
Or bid me go into a new-made grave,
85   And hide me with a dead man in his shroud –
Things that, to hear them told, have made me
    tremble –
And I will do it without fear or doubt,
To live an unstain'd wife to my sweet love.
FRIAR LAURENCE
Hold then. Go home, be merry, give consent
90   To marry Paris. Wednesday is tomorrow;
Tomorrow night look that thou lie alone.
Let not the Nurse lie with thee in thy chamber.
Take thou this vial, being then in bed,
And this distilling liquor drink thou off;
95   When presently through all thy veins shall run
A cold and drowsy humour, for no pulse
Shall keep his native progress, but surcease:
No warmth, no breath shall testify thou livest,
The roses in thy lips and cheeks shall fade
100   To wanny ashes, thy eyes' windows fall
Like death when he shuts up the day of life.
Each part depriv'd of supple government
Shall stiff and stark and cold appear, like death,
And in this borrow'd likeness of shrunk death
105   Thou shalt continue two and forty hours
And then awake as from a pleasant sleep.
Now when the bridegroom in the morning comes
To rouse thee from thy bed, there art thou, dead.
Then as the manner of our country is,
110   In thy best robes, uncover'd on the bier
Thou shall be borne to that same ancient vault
Where all the kindred of the Capulets lie.
In the meantime, against thou shalt awake,
Shall Romeo by my letters know our drift

And hither shall he come, and he and I   115
Will watch thy waking, and that very night
Shall Romeo bear thee hence to Mantua,
And this shall free thee from this present shame,
If no inconstant toy nor womanish fear
Abate thy valour in the acting it.   120
JULIET   Give me, give me! O tell not me of fear.
FRIAR LAURENCE
Hold. Get you gone. Be strong and prosperous
In this resolve. I'll send a friar with speed
To Mantua with my letters to thy lord.
JULIET
Love give me strength, and strength shall help
    afford.   125
Farewell, dear father.   *Exeunt.*

4.2   *Enter* CAPULET, LADY CAPULET, Nurse
         and two or three Servingmen.

CAPULET   So many guests invite as here are writ.
                              Exit Servingman.
Sirrah, go hire me twenty cunning cooks.
SERVINGMAN
You shall have none ill, sir, for I'll try if they can lick
their fingers.
CAPULET   How! Canst thou try them so?   5
SERVINGMAN
Marry sir, 'tis an ill cook that cannot lick his own
fingers; therefore he that cannot lick his fingers goes
not with me.
CAPULET   Go, be gone.   *Exit Servingman.*
We shall be much unfurnish'd for this time.   10
What, is my daughter gone to Friar Laurence?
NURSE   Ay, forsooth.
CAPULET   Well, he may chance to do some good on her.
A peevish self-will'd harlotry it is.

                    Enter JULIET

NURSE
See where she comes from shrift with merry look.   15
CAPULET
How now, my headstrong: where have you been
    gadding?
JULIET   Where I have learnt me to repent the sin
Of disobedient opposition
To you and your behests, and am enjoin'd
By holy Laurence to fall prostrate here,   20
To beg your pardon. Pardon, I beseech you.
Henceforward I am ever rul'd by you.
[*She kneels down.*]
CAPULET   Send for the County, go tell him of this.
I'll have this knot knit up tomorrow morning.
JULIET   I met the youthful lord at Laurence' cell,   25
And gave him what becomed love I might,
Not stepping o'er the bounds of modesty.
CAPULET   Why, I am glad on't. This is well. Stand up.
This is as't should be. Let me see the County.

Ay, marry. Go, I say, and fetch him hither.
Now afore God, this reverend holy Friar,
All our whole city is much bound to him.
JULIET   Nurse, will you go with me into my closet,
To help me sort such needful ornaments
As you think fit to furnish me tomorrow?
LADY CAPULET
No, not till Thursday. There is time enough.
CAPULET
Go, Nurse, go with her. We'll to church tomorrow.
Exeunt Juliet and Nurse.
LADY CAPULET   We shall be short in our provision,
'Tis now near night.
CAPULET   Tush I will stir about,
And all things shall be well, I warrant thee, wife.
Go thou to Juliet, help to deck up her.
I'll not to bed tonight, let me alone.
I'll play the housewife for this once. – What ho! –
They are all forth. Well, I will walk myself
To County Paris, to prepare up him
Against tomorrow. My heart is wondrous light
Since this same wayward girl is so reclaim'd. *Exeunt.*

4.3   *Enter* JULIET *and* NURSE.

JULIET   Ay, those attires are best. But, gentle Nurse,
I pray thee leave me to myself tonight,
For I have need of many orisons
To move the heavens to smile upon my state,
Which, well thou know'st, is cross and full of sin.

Enter LADY CAPULET.

LADY CAPULET
What, are you busy, ho? Need you my help?
JULIET   No madam, we have cull'd such necessaries
As are behoveful for our state tomorrow.
So please you, let me now be left alone
And let the Nurse this night sit up with you,
For I am sure you have your hands full all
In this so sudden business.
LADY CAPULET   Good night.
Get thee to bed and rest, for thou hast need.
Exeunt Lady Capulet and Nurse.
JULIET
Farewell. God knows when we shall meet again.
I have a faint cold fear thrills through my veins
That almost freezes up the heat of life.
I'll call them back again to comfort me.
– Nurse! – What should she do here?
My dismal scene I needs must act alone.
Come, vial.
What if this mixture do not work at all?
Shall I be married then tomorrow morning?
No! No! This shall forbid it. Lie thou there.
[She lays down a knife.]
What if it be a poison which the Friar
Subtly hath minister'd to have me dead,

Lest in this marriage he should be dishonour'd,
Because he married me before to Romeo?
I fear it is. And yet methinks it should not,
For he hath still been tried a holy man.
How if, when I am laid into the tomb,   30
I wake before the time that Romeo
Come to redeem me? There's a fearful point!
Shall I not then be stifled in the vault,
To whose foul mouth no healthsome air breathes in,
And there die strangled ere my Romeo comes?   35
Or, if I live, is it not very like,
The horrible conceit of death and night
Together with the terror of the place,
As in a vault, an ancient receptacle
Where for this many hundred years the bones   40
Of all my buried ancestors are pack'd,
Where bloody Tybalt yet but green in earth
Lies festering in his shroud; where, as they say,
At some hours in the night spirits resort –
Alack, alack! Is it not like that I   45
So early waking, what with loathsome smells,
And shrieks like mandrakes torn out of the earth,
That living mortals, hearing them, run mad –
O, if I wake, shall I not be distraught,
Environed with all these hideous fears,   50
And madly play with my forefathers' joints,
And pluck the mangled Tybalt from his shroud,
And, in this rage, with some great kinsman's bone
As with a club dash out my desperate brains?
O look, methinks I see my cousin's ghost   55
Seeking out Romeo that did spit his body
Upon a rapier's point! Stay, Tybalt, stay!
Romeo, Romeo, Romeo, here's drink! I drink to thee!
[She falls upon her bed within the curtains.]

4.4   *Enter* LADY CAPULET *and* Nurse.

LADY CAPULET
Hold, take these keys and fetch more spices, Nurse.
NURSE   They call for dates and quinces in the pastry.

Enter CAPULET.

CAPULET
Come, stir, stir, stir, the second cock hath crow'd!
The curfew bell hath rung, 'tis three o'clock.
Look to the bak'd meats, good Angelica: 5
Spare not for cost.
NURSE   Go, you cot-quean, go,
Get you to bed. Faith, you'll be sick tomorrow
For this night's watching.
CAPULET
No, not a whit. What, I have watch'd ere now
All night for lesser cause, and ne'er been sick. 10
LADY CAPULET
Ay, you have been a mouse-hunt in your time;
But I will watch you from such watching now.
Exeunt Lady Capulet and Nurse.

CAPULET   A jealous-hood, a jealous-hood!

Enter three or four Servingmen *with spits
and logs and baskets.*

Now fellow, what is there?

1 SERVINGMAN
    Things for the cook, sir, but I know not what.
CAPULET   Make haste, make haste!

Exit First Servingman.

15   – Sirrah, fetch drier logs!
    Call Peter, he will show thee where they are.
2 SERVINGMAN   I have a head, sir, that will find out logs
    And never trouble Peter for the matter.
CAPULET
    Mass and well said! A merry whoreson, ha.
    Thou shalt be loggerhead!   *Exit Second Servingman.*
20   – Good faith! 'Tis day!

[*Play music.*]

    The County will be here with music straight,
    For so he said he would. I hear him near.
    Nurse! Wife! What ho! What, Nurse I say!

Enter Nurse.

    Go waken Juliet, go, and trim her up.
25   I'll go and chat with Paris. Hie, make haste,
    Make haste! The bridegroom he is come already.
    Make haste I say.   *Exeunt Capulet and servingmen.*

4.5

[*Nurse goes to curtains.*]
NURSE
    Mistress! What, mistress! Juliet! Fast, I warrant her,
        she.
    Why, lamb, why, lady, fie! You slug-abed!
    Why, love I say! Madam! Sweetheart! Why, bride!
    What, not a word? You take your pennyworths now.
5   Sleep for a week; for the next night, I warrant,
    The County Paris hath set up his rest
    That you shall rest but little! God forgive me!
    Marry and amen. How sound is she asleep!
    I needs must wake her. Madam, madam, madam!
10   Ay, let the County take you in your bed,
    He'll fright you up, i'faith. Will it not be?
    What, dress'd, and in your clothes, and down again?
    I must needs wake you. Lady! Lady! Lady!
    Alas, alas! Help, help! My lady's dead!
15   O weraday that ever I was born.
    Some aqua vitae, ho! My lord! My lady!

Enter LADY CAPULET.

LADY CAPULET   What noise is here?
NURSE   O lamentable day!
LADY CAPULET   What is the matter?
NURSE   Look, look! O heavy day!
LADY CAPULET   O me, O me! My child, my only life.
20   Revive, look up, or I will die with thee.
    Help, help! Call help!

Enter CAPULET.

CAPULET
    For shame, bring Juliet forth, her lord is come.
NURSE
    She's dead, deceas'd! She's dead! Alack the day!
LADY CAPULET
    Alack the day! She's dead, she's dead, she's dead!
CAPULET   Ha! Let me see her. Out alas. She's cold,   25
    Her blood is settled and her joints are stiff.
    Life and these lips have long been separated.
    Death lies on her like an untimely frost
    Upon the sweetest flower of all the field.
NURSE   O lamentable day!
LADY CAPULET   O woeful time!   30
CAPULET
    Death, that hath ta'en her hence to make me wail
    Ties up my tongue and will not let me speak.

Enter FRIAR LAURENCE *and* PARIS *and* Musicians.

FRIAR LAURENCE
    Come, is the bride ready to go to church?
CAPULET   Ready to go, but never to return.
    O son, the night before thy wedding day   35
    Hath Death lain with thy wife. There she lies,
    Flower as she was, deflowered by him.
    Death is my son-in-law, Death is my heir.
    My daughter he hath wedded. I will die,
    And leave him all: life, living, all is Death's.   40
PARIS   Have I thought long to see this morning's face,
    And doth it give me such a sight as this?
LADY CAPULET
    Accurs'd, unhappy, wretched, hateful day.
    Most miserable hour that e'er time saw
    In lasting labour of his pilgrimage.   45
    But one, poor one, one poor and loving child,
    But one thing to rejoice and solace in,
    And cruel Death hath catch'd it from my sight.
NURSE   O woe! O woeful, woeful, woeful day.
    Most lamentable day. Most woeful day   50
    That ever, ever I did yet behold.
    O day, O day, O day, O hateful day.
    Never was seen so black a day as this.
    O woeful day, O woeful day.
PARIS   Beguil'd, divorced, wronged, spited, slain.   55
    Most detestable Death, by thee beguil'd,
    By cruel, cruel thee quite overthrown.
    O love! O life! Not life, but love in death!
CAPULET   Despis'd, distressed, hated, martyr'd, kill'd.
    Uncomfortable time, why cam'st thou now   60
    To murder, murder our solemnity?
    O child, O child! My soul and not my child,
    Dead art thou. Alack, my child is dead,
    And with my child my joys are buried.
FRIAR LAURENCE
    Peace, ho, for shame. Confusion's cure lives not   65
    In these confusions. Heaven and yourself
    Had part in this fair maid, now heaven hath all,

And all the better is it for the maid.
Your part in her you could not keep from death,
But heaven keeps his part in eternal life.
The most you sought was her promotion,
For 'twas your heaven she should be advanc'd,
And weep ye now, seeing she is advanc'd
Above the clouds, as high as heaven itself?
O, in this love you love your child so ill
That you run mad, seeing that she is well.
She's not well married that lives married long,
But she's best married that dies married young.
Dry up your tears, and stick your rosemary
On this fair corse, and, as the custom is,
All in her best array bear her to church.
For though fond nature bids us all lament,
Yet nature's tears are reason's merriment.

CAPULET   All things that we ordained festival
Turn from their office to black funeral:
Our instruments to melancholy bells,
Our wedding cheer to a sad burial feast;
Our solemn hymns to sullen dirges change,
Our bridal flowers serve for a buried corse,
And all things change them to the contrary.

FRIAR LAURENCE
Sir, go you in, and madam, go with him,
And go, Sir Paris. Every one prepare
To follow this fair corse unto her grave.
The heavens do lour upon you for some ill;
Move them no more by crossing their high will.

Exeunt all but the Nurse and Musicians, casting
rosemary on Juliet and shutting the curtains.

1 MUSICIAN   Faith, we may put up our pipes and be gone.

NURSE   Honest good fellows, ah put up, put up,
For well you know this is a pitiful case.

1 MUSICIAN   Ay, by my troth, the case may be amended.
Exit Nurse.

Enter PETER.

PETER   Musicians, O musicians, 'Heart's ease', 'Heart's
ease'! O, and you will have me live, play 'Heart's ease'.

1 MUSICIAN   Why 'Heart's ease'?

PETER   O musicians, because my heart itself plays 'My
heart is full'. O play me some merry dump to comfort
me.

1 MUSICIAN   Not a dump we! 'Tis no time to play now.

PETER   You will not then?

1 MUSICIAN   No.

PETER   I will then give it you soundly.

1 MUSICIAN   What will you give us?

PETER   No money, on my faith, but the gleek! I will give
you the minstrel.

1 MUSICIAN   Then will I give you the serving-creature.

PETER   Then will I lay the serving-creature's dagger on
your pate. I will carry no crotchets. I'll re you, I'll fa
you. Do you note me?

1 MUSICIAN   And you re us and fa us, you note us.

2 MUSICIAN   Pray you put up your dagger and put out
your wit.

PETER   Then have at you with my wit. I will dry-beat   120
you with an iron wit, and put up my iron dagger.
Answer me like men.
'When griping griefs the heart doth wound,
And doleful dumps the mind oppress,
Then music with her silver sound' –   125
Why 'silver sound'? Why 'music with her silver
sound'? What say you, Simon Catling?

1 MUSICIAN
Marry, sir, because silver hath a sweet sound.

PETER   Prates. What say you, Hugh Rebeck?

2 MUSICIAN   I say 'silver sound' because musicians   130
sound for silver.

PETER   Prates too. What say you, James Soundpost?

3 MUSICIAN   Faith, I know not what to say.

PETER   O, I cry you mercy, you are the singer. I will say
for you. It is 'music with her silver sound' because   135
musicians have no gold for sounding.
'Then music with her silver sound
With speedy help doth lend redress.'   *Exit.*

1 MUSICIAN   What a pestilent knave is this same.

2 MUSICIAN   Hang him, Jack. Come, we'll in here, tarry   140
for the mourners, and stay dinner.   *Exeunt.*

5.1   *Enter ROMEO.*

ROMEO   If I may trust the flattering truth of sleep
My dreams presage some joyful news at hand.
My bosom's lord sits lightly in his throne
And all this day an unaccustom'd spirit
Lifts me above the ground with cheerful thoughts.   5
I dreamt my lady came and found me dead –
Strange dream that gives a dead man leave to think! –
And breath'd such life with kisses in my lips
That I reviv'd and was an emperor.
Ah me, how sweet is love itself possess'd   10
When but love's shadows are so rich in joy.

Enter BALTHASAR, Romeo's man, booted.

News from Verona! How now, Balthasar,
Dost thou not bring me letters from the Friar?
How doth my lady? Is my father well?
How doth my Juliet? That I ask again,   15
For nothing can be ill if she be well.

BALTHASAR
Then she is well and nothing can be ill.
Her body sleeps in Capels' monument,
And her immortal part with angels lives.
I saw her laid low in her kindred's vault   20
And presently took post to tell it you.
O pardon me for bringing these ill news,
Since you did leave it for my office, sir.

ROMEO   Is it e'en so? Then I defy you, stars!
Thou know'st my lodging. Get me ink and paper,   25
And hire posthorses. I will hence tonight.

BALTHASAR   I do beseech you sir, have patience.

Your looks are pale and wild and do import
Some misadventure.

ROMEO   Tush, thou art deceiv'd.

30 Leave me, and do the thing I bid thee do.
Hast thou no letters to me from the Friar?

BALTHASAR   No, my good lord.

ROMEO   No matter. Get thee gone.
And hire those horses. I'll be with thee straight.

Exit Balthasar.

Well, Juliet, I will lie with thee tonight.

35 Let's see for means. O mischief thou art swift
To enter in the thoughts of desperate men.
I do remember an apothecary –
And hereabouts 'a dwells – which late I noted
In tatter'd weeds, with overwhelming brows,

40 Culling of simples. Meagre were his looks,
Sharp misery had worn him to the bones,
And in his needy shop a tortoise hung,
An alligator stuff'd, and other skins
Of ill-shap'd fishes; and about his shelves

45 A beggarly account of empty boxes,
Green earthen pots, bladders, and musty seeds,
Remnants of packthread, and old cakes of roses
Were thinly scatter'd to make up a show.
Noting this penury, to myself I said,

50 'And if a man did need a poison now,
Whose sale is present death in Mantua,
Here lives a caitiff wretch would sell it him'.
O, this same thought did but forerun my need,
And this same needy man must sell it me.

55 As I remember, this should be the house.
Being holiday, the beggar's shop is shut.
What ho! Apothecary!

Enter Apothecary.

APOTHECARY   Who calls so loud?

ROMEO   Come hither, man. I see that thou art poor.
Hold, there is forty ducats. Let me have

60 A dram of poison, such soon-speeding gear
As will disperse itself through all the veins,
That the life-weary taker may fall dead,
And that the trunk may be discharg'd of breath
As violently as hasty powder fir'd

65 Doth hurry from the fatal cannon's womb.

APOTHECARY
Such mortal drugs I have, but Mantua's law
Is death to any he that utters them.

ROMEO   Art thou so bare and full of wretchedness,
And fear'st to die? Famine is in thy cheeks,

70 Need and oppression starveth in thy eyes,
Contempt and beggary hangs upon thy back.
The world is not thy friend, nor the world's law;
The world affords no law to make thee rich;
Then be not poor, but break it, and take this.

75 APOTHECARY   My poverty, but not my will consents.

ROMEO   I pay thy poverty and not thy will.

APOTHECARY   Put this in any liquid thing you will

And drink it off and if you had the strength
Of twenty men it would dispatch you straight.

ROMEO
There is thy gold – worse poison to men's souls,   80
Doing more murder in this loathsome world
Than these poor compounds that thou mayst not sell.
I sell thee poison, thou hast sold me none.
Farewell, buy food, and get thyself in flesh.
Come, cordial, and not poison, go with me   85
To Juliet's grave, for there must I use thee.   *Exeunt.*

5.2   *Enter* FRIAR JOHN.

FRIAR JOHN   Holy Franciscan Friar, Brother, ho!

Enter FRIAR LAURENCE.

FRIAR LAURENCE
This same should be the voice of Friar John.
Welcome from Mantua. What says Romeo?
Or, if his mind be writ, give me his letter.

FRIAR JOHN   Going to find a barefoot brother out,   5
One of our order, to associate me,
Here in this city visiting the sick,
And finding him, the searchers of the town,
Suspecting that we both were in a house
Where the infectious pestilence did reign,   10
Seal'd up the doors and would not let us forth,
So that my speed to Mantua there was stay'd.

FRIAR LAURENCE   Who bare my letter then to Romeo?

FRIAR JOHN   I could not send it – here it is again –
Nor get a messenger to bring it thee,   15
So fearful were they of infection.

FRIAR LAURENCE
Unhappy fortune! By my brotherhood,
The letter was not nice but full of charge,
Of dear import, and the neglecting it
May do much danger. Friar John, go hence,   20
Get me an iron crow and bring it straight
Unto my cell.

FRIAR JOHN   Brother, I'll go and bring it thee.   *Exit.*

FRIAR LAURENCE   Now must I to the monument alone.
Within this three hours will fair Juliet wake.
She will beshrew me much that Romeo   25
Hath had no notice of these accidents,
But I will write again to Mantua,
And keep her at my cell till Romeo come.
Poor living corse, clos'd in a dead man's tomb.   *Exit.*

5.3   *Enter* PARIS *and his* Page, *with flowers*
                    and sweet water.

PARIS   Give me thy torch, boy. Hence and stand aloof.
Yet put it out, for I would not be seen.
Under yond yew trees lay thee all along,
Holding thy ear close to the hollow ground;
So shall no foot upon the churchyard tread,   5
Being loose, unfirm, with digging up of graves,
But thou shalt hear it. Whistle then to me

As signal that thou hear'st something approach.
Give me those flowers. Do as I bid thee. Go.

PAGE   I am almost afraid to stand alone
Here in the churchyard. Yet I will adventure.
[*Retires. Paris strews the tomb with flowers.*]

PARIS
Sweet flower, with flowers thy bridal bed I strew.
O woe, thy canopy is dust and stones
Which with sweet water nightly I will dew,
Or wanting that, with tears distill'd by moans.
The obsequies that I for thee will keep
Nightly shall be to strew thy grave and weep.
[*Page whistles.*]
The boy gives warning something doth approach.
What cursed foot wanders this way tonight,
To cross my obsequies and true love's rite?
What, with a torch? Muffle me, night, awhile.
[*Paris retires.*]

Enter ROMEO *and* BALTHASAR *with a torch,
a mattock and a crow of iron.*

ROMEO   Give me that mattock and the wrenching iron.
Hold, take this letter. Early in the morning
See thou deliver it to my lord and father.
Give me the light. Upon thy life I charge thee,
Whate'er thou hear'st or seest, stand all aloof
And do not interrupt me in my course.
Why I descend into this bed of death
Is partly to behold my lady's face
But chiefly to take thence from her dead finger
A precious ring, a ring that I must use
In dear employment. Therefore hence, be gone.
But if thou jealous dost return to pry
In what I farther shall intend to do,
By heaven I will tear thee joint by joint,
And strew this hungry churchyard with thy limbs.
The time and my intents are savage-wild,
More fierce and more inexorable far
Than empty tigers or the roaring sea.

BALTHASAR   I will be gone, sir, and not trouble ye.

ROMEO
So shalt thou show me friendship. Take thou that.
Live, and be prosperous, and farewell, good fellow.

BALTHASAR   For all this same, I'll hide me hereabout.
His looks I fear, and his intents I doubt.
[*Balthasar retires.*]

ROMEO   Thou detestable maw, thou womb of death
Gorg'd with the dearest morsel of the earth,
Thus I enforce thy rotten jaws to open,
And in despite I'll cram thee with more food.
[*Romeo opens the tomb.*]

PARIS   This is that banish'd haughty Montague
That murder'd my love's cousin – with which grief
It is supposed the fair creature died –
And here is come to do some villainous shame
To the dead bodies. I will apprehend him.
Stop thy unhallow'd toil, vile Montague.

Can vengeance be pursu'd further than death?   55
Condemned villain, I do apprehend thee.
Obey, and go with me, for thou must die.

ROMEO   I must indeed, and therefore came I hither.
Good gentle youth, tempt not a desperate man.
Fly hence and leave me. Think upon these gone.   60
Let them affright thee. I beseech thee, youth,
Put not another sin upon my head
By urging me to fury. O be gone.
By heaven I love thee better than myself,
For I come hither arm'd against myself.   65
Stay not, be gone, live, and hereafter say
A mad man's mercy bid thee run away.

PARIS   I do defy thy conjuration
And apprehend thee for a felon here.

ROMEO   Wilt thou provoke me? Then have at thee, boy!   70
[*They fight.*]

PAGE   O Lord, they fight! I will go call the Watch.
                                                    Exit Page.

PARIS   O, I am slain! If thou be merciful,
Open the tomb, lay me with Juliet. [*Paris dies.*]

ROMEO   In faith I will. Let me peruse this face.
Mercutio's kinsman, noble County Paris!   75
What said my man, when my betossed soul
Did not attend him, as we rode? I think
He told me Paris should have married Juliet.
Said he not so? Or did I dream it so?
Or am I mad, hearing him talk of Juliet,   80
To think it was so? O, give me thy hand,
One writ with me in sour misfortune's book.
I'll bury thee in a triumphant grave.
A grave? O no, a lantern, slaughter'd youth.
For here lies Juliet, and her beauty makes   85
This vault a feasting presence, full of light.
Death, lie thou there, by a dead man interr'd.
How oft when men are at the point of death
Have they been merry! Which their keepers call
A lightning before death. O how may I   90
Call this a lightning? O my love, my wife,
Death that hath suck'd the honey of thy breath
Hath had no power yet upon thy beauty.
Thou art not conquer'd. Beauty's ensign yet
Is crimson in thy lips and in thy cheeks,   95
And Death's pale flag is not advanced there.
Tybalt, liest thou there in thy bloody sheet?
O, what more favour can I do to thee
Than with that hand that cut thy youth in twain
To sunder his that was thine enemy?   100
Forgive me, cousin. Ah, dear Juliet,
Why art thou yet so fair? Shall I believe
That unsubstantial Death is amorous,
And that the lean abhorred monster keeps
Thee here in dark to be his paramour?   105
For fear of that I still will stay with thee,
And never from this palace of dim night
Depart again. Here, here, will I remain
With worms that are thy chambermaids. O here

110 Will I set up my everlasting rest
And shake the yoke of inauspicious stars
From this world-wearied flesh. Eyes, look your last.
Arms, take your last embrace! And lips, O you
The doors of breath, seal with a righteous kiss
115 A dateless bargain to engrossing Death.
Come, bitter conduct, come unsavoury guide,
Thou desperate pilot now at once run on
The dashing rocks thy seasick weary bark.
Here's to my love! [*He drinks.*] O true apothecary,
120 Thy drugs are quick. Thus with a kiss I die.
[*He falls.*]

Enter FRIAR LAURENCE *with lantern, crow and spade.*

FRIAR LAURENCE
Saint Francis be my speed. How oft tonight
Have my old feet stumbled at graves. Who's there?
BALTHASAR
Here's one, a friend, and one that knows you well.
FRIAR LAURENCE
Bliss be upon you. Tell me, good my friend,
125 What torch is yond that vainly lends his light
To grubs and eyeless skulls? As I discern,
It burneth in the Capels' monument.
BALTHASAR
It doth so, holy sir, and there's my master,
One that you love.
FRIAR LAURENCE   Who is it?
BALTHASAR   Romeo.
FRIAR LAURENCE   How long hath he been there?
130 BALTHASAR   Full half an hour.
FRIAR LAURENCE   Go with me to the vault.
BALTHASAR   I dare not, sir.
My master knows not but I am gone hence,
And fearfully did menace me with death
If I did stay to look on his intents.
FRIAR LAURENCE
135 Stay then, I'll go alone. Fear comes upon me.
O, much I fear some ill unthrifty thing.
BALTHASAR   As I did sleep under this yew tree here
I dreamt my master and another fought,
And that my master slew him.
FRIAR LAURENCE   Romeo!
[*Friar stoops and looks on the blood and weapons.*]
140 Alack, alack, what blood is this which stains
The stony entrance of this sepulchre?
What mean these masterless and gory swords
To lie discolour'd by this place of peace?
Romeo! O, pale! Who else? What, Paris too?
145 And steep'd in blood? Ah what an unkind hour
Is guilty of this lamentable chance?
The lady stirs.

JULIET rises.

JULIET   O comfortable Friar, where is my lord?
I do remember well where I should be,

And there I am. Where is my Romeo? 150
FRIAR LAURENCE
I hear some noise. Lady, come from that nest
Of death, contagion, and unnatural sleep.
A greater power than we can contradict
Hath thwarted our intents. Come, come away.
Thy husband in thy bosom there lies dead, 155
And Paris too. Come, I'll dispose of thee
Among a sisterhood of holy nuns.
Stay not to question, for the Watch is coming.
Come, go, good Juliet. I dare no longer stay.
JULIET   Go, get thee hence, for I will not away. 160
Exit Friar Laurence.
What's here? A cup clos'd in my true love's hand?
Poison, I see, hath been his timeless end.
O churl. Drunk all, and left no friendly drop
To help me after? I will kiss thy lips.
Haply some poison yet doth hang on them 165
To make me die with a restorative. [*She kisses him.*]
Thy lips are warm!
WATCHMAN [*within*]   Lead, boy. Which way?
JULIET   Yea, noise? Then I'll be brief. O happy dagger.
This is thy sheath. There rust, and let me die.
[*She stabs herself and falls.*]

Enter Page *and* Watchmen.

PAGE
This is the place. There, where the torch doth burn. 170
1 WATCHMAN
The ground is bloody. Search about the churchyard.
Go, some of you: whoe'er you find, attach.
Exeunt some watchmen.
Pitiful sight! Here lies the County slain
And Juliet bleeding, warm, and newly dead,
Who here hath lain this two days buried. 175
Go tell the Prince. Run to the Capulets.
Raise up the Montagues. Some others search.
Exeunt some watchmen.
We see the ground whereon these woes do lie,
But the true ground of all these piteous woes
We cannot without circumstance descry. 180

Enter several Watchmen *with* BALTHASAR.

2 WATCHMAN   Here's Romeo's man. We found him in
the churchyard.
1 WATCHMAN
Hold him in safety till the Prince come hither.

Enter another Watchmen *with* FRIAR LAURENCE.

3 WATCHMAN
Here is a friar that trembles, sighs and weeps.
We took this mattock and this spade from him 185
As he was coming from this churchyard's side.
1 WATCHMAN   A great suspicion. Stay the friar too.

Enter the PRINCE *and attendants.*

PRINCE   What misadventure is so early up,
    That calls our person from our morning rest?

Enter CAPULET *and* LADY CAPULET *and servants.*

190 CAPULET   What should it be that is so shriek'd abroad?

LADY CAPULET   O, the people in the street cry 'Romeo',
    Some 'Juliet', and some 'Paris', and all run
    With open outcry toward our monument.

PRINCE   What fear is this which startles in our ears?

195 1 WATCHMAN
    Sovereign, here lies the County Paris slain,
    And Romeo dead, and Juliet, dead before,
    Warm, and new kill'd.

PRINCE
    Search, seek, and know how this foul murder comes.

1 WATCHMAN
200   Here is a friar, and slaughter'd Romeo's man,
    With instruments upon them fit to open
    These dead men's tombs.

CAPULET
    O heavens! O wife, look how our daughter bleeds!
    This dagger hath mista'en, for lo, his house
205   Is empty on the back of Montague,
    And it mis-sheathed in my daughter's bosom.

LADY CAPULET
    O me! This sight of death is as a bell
    That warns my old age to a sepulchre.

Enter MONTAGUE *and servants.*

PRINCE   Come, Montague, for thou art early up
    To see thy son and heir now early down.

210 MONTAGUE   Alas, my liege, my wife is dead tonight.
    Grief of my son's exile hath stopp'd her breath.
    What further woe conspires against mine age?

PRINCE   Look, and thou shalt see.

MONTAGUE   O thou untaught! What manners is in this,
215   To press before thy father to a grave?

PRINCE   Seal up the mouth of outrage for a while
    Till we can clear these ambiguities
    And know their spring, their head, their true descent,
    And then will I be general of your woes
220   And lead you, even to death. Meantime forbear,
    And let mischance be slave to patience.
    Bring forth the parties of suspicion.

FRIAR LAURENCE   I am the greatest, able to do least,
    Yet most suspected, as the time and place
225   Doth make against me, of this direful murder.
    And here I stand, both to impeach and purge
    Myself condemned and myself excus'd.

PRINCE   Then say at once what thou dost know in this.

FRIAR LAURENCE
    I will be brief, for my short date of breath
230   Is not so long as is a tedious tale.
    Romeo, there dead, was husband to that Juliet,
    And she, there dead, that Romeo's faithful wife.
    I married them, and their stol'n marriage day
    Was Tybalt's doomsday, whose untimely death

    Banish'd the new-made bridegroom from this city;   235
    For whom, and not for Tybalt, Juliet pin'd.
    You, to remove that siege of grief from her,
    Betroth'd and would have married her perforce
    To County Paris. Then comes she to me
    And with wild looks bid me devise some mean   240
    To rid her from this second marriage,
    Or in my cell there would she kill herself.
    Then gave I her – so tutor'd by my art –
    A sleeping potion, which so took effect
    As I intended, for it wrought on her   245
    The form of death. Meantime I writ to Romeo
    That he should hither come as this dire night
    To help to take her from her borrow'd grave,
    Being the time the potion's force should cease.
    But he which bore my letter, Friar John,   250
    Was stay'd by accident, and yesternight
    Return'd my letter back. Then all alone
    At the prefixed hour of her waking
    Came I to take her from her kindred's vault,
    Meaning to keep her closely at my cell   255
    Till I conveniently could send to Romeo.
    But when I came, some minute ere the time
    Of her awakening, here untimely lay
    The noble Paris and true Romeo dead.
    She wakes; and I entreated her come forth   260
    And bear this work of heaven with patience,
    But then a noise did scare me from the tomb
    And she, too desperate, would not go with me
    But, as it seems, did violence on herself.
    All this I know; and to the marriage   265
    Her Nurse is privy; and if aught in this
    Miscarried by my fault, let my old life
    Be sacrific'd some hour before his time
    Unto the rigour of severest law.

PRINCE   We still have known thee for a holy man.   270
    Where's Romeo's man? What can he say to this?

BALTHASAR
    I brought my master news of Juliet's death,
    And then in post he came from Mantua
    To this same place, to this same monument.
    This letter he early bid me give his father   275
    And threaten'd me with death, going in the vault,
    If I departed not and left him there.

PRINCE   Give me the letter, I will look on it.
    Where is the County's Page that rais'd the Watch?
    Sirrah, what made your master in this place?   280

PAGE   He came with flowers to strew his lady's grave
    And bid me stand aloof, and so I did.
    Anon comes one with light to ope the tomb
    And by and by my master drew on him,
    And then I ran away to call the Watch.   285

PRINCE   This letter doth make good the Friar's words:
    Their course of love, the tidings of her death,
    And here he writes that he did buy a poison
    Of a poor pothecary, and therewithal
    Came to this vault to die and lie with Juliet.   290

Where be these enemies? Capulet, Montague,
See what a scourge is laid upon your hate,
That heaven finds means to kill your joys with love;
And I, for winking at your discords too,
295 Have lost a brace of kinsmen. All are punish'd.
CAPULET   O brother Montague, give me thy hand.
This is my daughter's jointure, for no more
Can I demand.
MONTAGUE   But I can give thee more,
For I will raise her statue in pure gold,
300 That whiles Verona by that name is known,

There shall no figure at such rate be set
As that of true and faithful Juliet.
CAPULET   As rich shall Romeo's by his lady's lie,
Poor sacrifices of our enmity.
PRINCE   A glooming peace this morning with it brings: 305
The sun for sorrow will not show his head.
Go hence to have more talk of these sad things.
Some shall be pardon'd, and some punished,
For never was a story of more woe
Than this of Juliet and her Romeo.   *Exeunt.*   310

The Taming of the Shrew

The text of *The Taming of the Shrew* printed in the First Folio in 1623 as the eleventh of the comedies stands in close, but ill-defined, relation to a play printed in 1594 with the similar title of *The Taming of a Shrew*. Once regarded as Shakespeare's source for *The Shrew*, *A Shrew* is perhaps better understood as a garbled and abbreviated adaptation of it in which the 'taming' plot follows very similar lines and includes verbal reminiscences, the 'Bianca' plot is radically rewritten and draws heavily on quotations from Marlowe's plays, and the framing device of Sly is sustained to the end of the play, where it affords an ironic epilogue in which Sly, sober, sets off home to tame his wife too. The likely period of composition of *The Shrew* is between about 1590 and 1594.

Shrew-taming stories and ballads, originating in folktales, were widely known in the sixteenth century and no single original for the play has been identified. Similarly, the device of gulling a beggar into the belief that he is a king or lord is an ancient and widespread narrative motif, best known today from *The Arabian Nights' Entertainment*. The story of Bianca and her suitors has an immediate dramatic source in *Supposes* (1566), George Gascoigne's English version of a prose comedy, *I Suppositi* (1509), by Lodovico Ariosto. The skilful weaving of these three into a complex action is among the play's notable achievements.

The Taming of the Shrew has had a long and successful stage history, both in its full form and in successive adaptations and abridgements, of which David Garrick's *Catherine and Petruchio* (1756) had the longest life. The play shares with *The Merchant of Venice* the unhappy distinction of giving general offence to late twentieth-century sensibilities. However, Shakespeare's portrayal of the 'taming' of Katherina tones down the coarseness and physical violence of contemporary analogues, substituting a course of psychological homeopathy to cure her of her shrewishness. A feminist repartee was delivered as early as 1611 by John Fletcher in his comedy *The Woman's Prize, or the Tamer Tamed*. In it, Petruchio is subjected to four acts of frustration and humiliation by a second wife, Maria (who is evidently acquainted with the *Lysistrata* of Aristophanes), before wounded male pride is restored at the end by her voluntary reversion to wifely good behaviour.

The modern response of indignation at the taming plot is understandable – even inevitable – but it runs the risk of ignoring the wholly speculative and fictional scheme of things in which Shakespeare's 'supposes' – hypothetical propositions about men and women as much as disguised or substituted characters – are presented for the entertainment of Sly and of ourselves. Katherina and Petruchio are at once differentiated from the rest of the characters by force of personality and by an evident emotional compatibility: the roles have been relished by generations of star performers, among them Richard Burton and Elizabeth Taylor on film. Their interchanges anticipate the 'merry war' of Beatrice and Benedick, both in their witty surface and in the underlying seriousness of the tussle for power in marriage. Sly's disappearance at the end of the first act of the Folio text is perplexing: some modern productions have made effective use of his later interventions borrowed from *A Shrew*. The disappearance of Sly leaves the end of the play more open to the various reactions of an audience, whereas his epilogue can increase a sense of that ending as no more than a male fantasy of unattainable control.

The Arden text is based on the 1623 First Folio.

LIST OF ROLES

INDUCTION

Christopher SLY	*a tinker*
HOSTESS	
LORD	
PAGE, HUNTSMEN *and* SERVANTS	*attending on the lord*
A company of PLAYERS	

THE TAMING OF THE SHREW

BAPTISTA Minola	*a rich citizen of Padua*
KATHERINA	*the Shrew, elder daughter of Baptista*
PETRUCHIO	*a gentleman of Verona, suitor to Katherina*
GRUMIO	*Petruchio's personal servant*
CURTIS	*Petruchio's chief servant at his country house*
TAILOR	
HABERDASHER	
Five other SERVANTS *of Petruchio*	
BIANCA	*younger daughter of Baptista*
GREMIO	*rich old citizen of Padua, suitor to Bianca*
HORTENSIO	*a gentleman of Padua, suitor to Bianca*
LUCENTIO	*a gentleman of Pisa, suitor to Bianca*
TRANIO	*personal servant to Lucentio*
BIONDELLO	*servant to Lucentio*
VINCENTIO	*rich citizen of Pisa, father of Lucentio*
PEDANT	*of Mantua*
WIDOW	
SERVANTS	*attending on Baptista*

The Taming of the Shrew

Ind.1 *Enter* CHRISTOPHER SLY *and the* Hostess.

SLY I'll feeze you, in faith.

HOSTESS A pair of stocks, you rogue.

SLY Y'are a baggage, the Slys are no rogues. Look in the Chronicles, we came in with Richard Conqueror. Therefore *paucas pallabris*, let the world slide. Sessa! 5

HOSTESS You will not pay for the glasses you have burst?

SLY No, not a denier. Go by, Saint Jeronimy, go to thy cold bed and warm thee.

HOSTESS I know my remedy, I must go fetch the third-borough. *Exit.* 10

SLY Third, or fourth, or fifth borough, I'll answer him by law. I'll not budge an inch, boy. Let him come, and kindly. [*Falls asleep.*]

Wind horns. Enter a Lord *from hunting, with his train.*

LORD

Huntsman, I charge thee, tender well my hounds. 15
Breathe Merriman, the poor cur is emboss'd,
And couple Clowder with the deep-mouth'd brach.
Saw'st thou not, boy, how Silver made it good
At the hedge corner, in the coldest fault?
I would not lose the dog for twenty pound. 20

1 HUNTSMAN

Why, Belman is as good as he, my lord.
He cried upon it at the merest loss,
And twice today pick'd out the dullest scent.
Trust me, I take him for the better dog.

LORD Thou art a fool. If Echo were as fleet, 25
I would esteem him worth a dozen such.
But sup them well, and look unto them all.
Tomorrow I intend to hunt again.

1 HUNTSMAN I will, my lord.

LORD

What's here? One dead, or drunk? See, doth he
breathe? 30

2 HUNTSMAN

He breathes, my lord. Were he not warm'd with ale,
This were a bed but cold to sleep so soundly.

LORD O monstrous beast, how like a swine he lies!
Grim death, how foul and loathsome is thine image!
Sirs, I will practise on this drunken man. 35
What think you, if he were convey'd to bed,
Wrapp'd in sweet clothes, rings put upon his fingers,
A most delicious banquet by his bed,
And brave attendants near him when he wakes,
Would not the beggar then forget himself? 40

1 HUNTSMAN

Believe me, lord, I think he cannot choose.

2 HUNTSMAN

It would seem strange unto him when he wak'd.

LORD Even as a flatt'ring dream or worthless fancy.
Then take him up, and manage well the jest.
Carry him gently to my fairest chamber, 45
And hang it round with all my wanton pictures.

Balm his foul head in warm distilled waters,
And burn sweet wood to make the lodging sweet.
Procure me music ready when he wakes,
To make a dulcet and a heavenly sound. 50
And if he chance to speak, be ready straight
And with a low submissive reverence
Say 'What is it your honour will command?'
Let one attend him with a silver basin
Full of rose-water and bestrew'd with flowers, 55
Another bear the ewer, the third a diaper,
And say 'Will't please your lordship cool your
hands?'
Some one be ready with a costly suit,
And ask him what apparel he will wear.
Another tell him of his hounds and horse, 60
And that his lady mourns at his disease.
Persuade him that he hath been lunatic,
And when he says he is, say that he dreams,
For he is nothing but a mighty lord.
This do, and do it kindly, gentle sirs. 65
It will be pastime passing excellent,
If it be husbanded with modesty.

1 HUNTSMAN

My lord, I warrant you we will play our part
As he shall think by our true diligence
He is no less than what we say he is. 70

LORD Take him up gently, and to bed with him,
And each one to his office when he wakes.
Sly is carried off. Sound trumpets.
Sirrah, go see what trumpet 'tis that sounds –
Exit Servingman.
Belike some noble gentleman that means,
Travelling some journey, to repose him here. 75

Enter Servingman.

How now? Who is it?

SERVINGMAN An't please your honour, players
That offer service to your lordship.

LORD Bid them come near.

Enter Players.

Now, fellows, you are welcome.

PLAYERS We thank your honour.

LORD Do you intend to stay with me tonight? 80

1 PLAYER

So please your lordship to accept our duty.

LORD With all my heart. This fellow I remember
Since once he play'd a farmer's eldest son.
'Twas where you woo'd the gentlewoman so well.
I have forgot your name; but, sure, that part 85
Was aptly fitted and naturally perform'd.

2 PLAYER

I think 'twas Soto that your honour means.

LORD 'Tis very true, thou didst it excellent.
Well, you are come to me in happy time,
The rather for I have some sport in hand 90
Wherein your cunning can assist me much.

There is a lord will hear you play tonight;
But I am doubtful of your modesties,
Lest over-eyeing of his odd behaviour–
95 For yet his honour never heard a play–
You break into some merry passion
And so offend him; for I tell you, sirs,
If you should smile, he grows impatient.

1 PLAYER
Fear not, my lord, we can contain ourselves,
100 Were he the veriest antic in the world.

LORD   Go, sirrah, take them to the buttery,
And give them friendly welcome every one.
Let them want nothing that my house affords.

Exit one with the Players.

Sirrah, go you to Barthol'mew my page,
105 And see him dress'd in all suits like a lady.
That done, conduct him to the drunkard's chamber,
And call him 'madam', do him obeisance.
Tell him from me, as he will win my love,
He bear himself with honourable action,
110 Such as he hath observ'd in noble ladies
Unto their lords, by them accomplished.
Such duty to the drunkard let him do,
With soft low tongue and lowly courtesy,
And say 'What is't your honour will command,
115 Wherein your lady and your humble wife
May show her duty and make known her love?'
And then with kind embracements, tempting kisses,
And with declining head into his bosom,
Bid him shed tears, as being overjoy'd
120 To see her noble lord restor'd to health,
Who for this seven years hath esteemed him
No better than a poor and loathsome beggar.
And if the boy have not a woman's gift
To rain a shower of commanded tears,
125 An onion will do well for such a shift,
Which in a napkin being close convey'd,
Shall in despite enforce a watery eye.
See this dispatch'd with all the haste thou canst,
Anon I'll give thee more instructions.

Exit a Servingman.

130 I know the boy will well usurp the grace,
Voice, gait, and action of a gentlewoman.
I long to hear him call the drunkard husband,
And how my men will stay themselves from laughter
When they do homage to this simple peasant.
135 I'll in to counsel them. Haply my presence
May well abate the over-merry spleen
Which otherwise would grow into extremes. *Exeunt.*

Ind.2 *Enter aloft* SLY, *with attendants; some with apparel,
basin and ewer, and other appurtenances; and* Lord.

SLY   For God's sake, a pot of small ale.

1 SERVINGMAN   Will't please your lordship drink a cup
of sack?

2 SERVINGMAN   Will't please your honour taste of these
conserves?   5

3 SERVINGMAN   What raiment will your honour wear
today?

SLY   I am Christophero Sly, call not me 'honour' nor
'lordship'. I ne'er drank sack in my life. And if you
give me any conserves, give me conserves of beef.   10
Ne'er ask me what raiment I'll wear, for I have no
more doublets than backs, no more stockings than
legs, nor no more shoes than feet – nay, sometime
more feet than shoes, or such shoes as my toes look
through the overleather.   15

LORD   Heaven cease this idle humour in your honour!
O, that a mighty man of such descent,
Of such possessions, and so high esteem,
Should be infused with so foul a spirit!

SLY   What, would you make me mad? Am not I   20
Christopher Sly, old Sly's son of Burton-heath, by
birth a pedlar, by education a cardmaker, by
transmutation a bear-herd, and now by present
profession a tinker? Ask Marian Hacket, the fat ale-
wife of Wincot, if she know me not. If she say I am not 25
fourteen pence on the score for sheer ale, score me up
for the lying'st knave in Christendom. [*A Servant
brings him a pot of ale.*] What! I am not bestraught.
Here's – [*He drinks.*]

3 SERVINGMAN
O, this it is that makes your lady mourn.   30

2 SERVINGMAN
O, this is it that makes your servants droop.

LORD
Hence comes it that your kindred shuns your house,
As beaten hence by your strange lunacy.
O noble lord, bethink thee of thy birth,
Call home thy ancient thoughts from banishment,   35
And banish hence these abject lowly dreams.
Look how thy servants do attend on thee,
Each in his office ready at thy beck.
Wilt thou have music? Hark, Apollo plays,   [*Music.*]
And twenty caged nightingales do sing.   40
Or wilt thou sleep? We'll have thee to a couch
Softer and sweeter than the lustful bed
On purpose trimm'd up for Semiramis.
Say thou wilt walk; we will bestrew the ground.
Or wilt thou ride? Thy horses shall be trapp'd,   45
Their harness studded all with gold and pearl.
Dost thou love hawking? Thou hast hawks will soar
Above the morning lark. Or wilt thou hunt?
Thy hounds shall make the welkin answer them
And fetch shrill echoes from the hollow earth.   50

1 SERVINGMAN
Say thou wilt course, thy greyhounds are as swift
As breathed stags, ay, fleeter than the roe.

2 SERVINGMAN
Dost thou love pictures? We will fetch thee straight
Adonis painted by a running brook,
And Cytherea all in sedges hid,   55
Which seem to move and wanton with her breath

Even as the waving sedges play with wind.
LORD   We'll show thee Io as she was a maid,
And how she was beguiled and surpris'd,
60   As lively painted as the deed was done.
3 SERVINGMAN
Or Daphne roaming through a thorny wood,
Scratching her legs that one shall swear she bleeds,
And at that sight shall sad Apollo weep,
So workmanly the blood and tears are drawn.
65   LORD   Thou art a lord, and nothing but a lord.
Thou hast a lady far more beautiful
Than any woman in this waning age.
1 SERVINGMAN
And till the tears that she hath shed for thee
Like envious floods o'er-run her lovely face,
70   She was the fairest creature in the world;
And yet she is inferior to none.
SLY   Am I a lord, and have I such a lady?
Or do I dream? Or have I dream'd till now?
I do not sleep. I see, I hear, I speak.
75   I smell sweet savours and I feel soft things.
Upon my life, I am a lord indeed,
And not a tinker nor Christophero Sly.
Well, bring our lady hither to our sight,
And once again a pot o'th' smallest ale.
2 SERVINGMAN
80   Will't please your mightiness to wash your hands?
O, how we joy to see your wit restor'd!
O, that once more you knew but what you are!
These fifteen years you have been in a dream,
Or when you wak'd, so wak'd as if you slept.
85   SLY   These fifteen years! By my fay, a goodly nap.
But did I never speak of all that time?
1 SERVINGMAN   O yes, my lord, but very idle words,
For though you lay here in this goodly chamber,
Yet would you say ye were beaten out of door,
90   And rail upon the hostess of the house,
And say you would present her at the leet,
Because she brought stone jugs and no seal'd quarts.
Sometimes you would call out for Cicely Hacket.
SLY   Ay, the woman's maid of the house.
3 SERVINGMAN
95   Why, sir, you know no house, nor no such maid,
Nor no such men as you have reckon'd up,
As Stephen Sly, and old John Naps of Greece,
And Peter Turph, and Henry Pimpernell,
And twenty more such names and men as these,
100   Which never were nor no man ever saw.
SLY   Now Lord be thanked for my good amends.
ALL   Amen.

Enter Page *as a lady, with attendants.*
One gives Sly a pot of ale.

SLY   I thank thee, thou shalt not lose by it.
PAGE   How fares my noble lord?
105   SLY   Marry, I fare well, for here is cheer enough.
Where is my wife?

PAGE   Here, noble lord, what is thy will with her?
SLY
Are you my wife, and will not call me husband?
My men should call me 'lord', I am your goodman.
PAGE
My husband and my lord, my lord and husband;   110
I am your wife in all obedience.
SLY   I know it well. What must I call her?
LORD   Madam.
SLY   Alice madam, or Joan madam?
LORD   Madam and nothing else, so lords call ladies.   115
SLY   Madam wife, they say that I have dream'd
And slept above some fifteen year or more.
PAGE   Ay, and the time seems thirty unto me,
Being all this time abandon'd from your bed.
SLY   'Tis much. Servants, leave me and her alone.   120
Exeunt attendants.
Madam, undress you and come now to bed.
PAGE   Thrice noble lord, let me entreat of you
To pardon me yet for a night or two;
Or, if not so, until the sun be set.
For your physicians have expressly charg'd,   125
In peril to incur your former malady,
That I should yet absent me from your bed.
I hope this reason stands for my excuse.
SLY   Ay, it stands so that I may hardly tarry so long. But
I would be loath to fall into my dreams again. I will   130
therefore tarry in despite of the flesh and the blood.

Enter a Messenger.

MESSENGER
Your honour's players, hearing your amendment,
Are come to play a pleasant comedy;
For so your doctors hold it very meet,
Seeing too much sadness hath congeal'd your blood,   135
And melancholy is the nurse of frenzy.
Therefore they thought it good you hear a play
And frame your mind to mirth and merriment,
Which bars a thousand harms and lengthens life.
SLY   Marry, I will. Let them play it. Is not a comonty   140
A Christmas gambol or a tumbling-trick?
PAGE   No, my good lord, it is more pleasing stuff.
SLY   What, household stuff?
PAGE   It is a kind of history.
SLY
Well, we'll see't. Come, madam wife, sit by my side
And let the world slip, we shall ne'er be younger.   145

1.1   *Flourish. Enter* LUCENTIO *and his man* TRANIO.

LUCENTIO
Tranio, since for the great desire I had
To see fair Padua, nursery of arts,
I am arriv'd for fruitful Lombardy,
The pleasant garden of great Italy,
And by my father's love and leave am arm'd   5
With his good will and thy good company,

My trusty servant well approv'd in all,
Here let us breathe and haply institute
A course of learning and ingenious studies.
10   Pisa renowned for grave citizens
Gave me my being and my father first,
A merchant of great traffic through the world,
Vincentio, come of the Bentivolii.
Vincentio's son, brought up in Florence,
15   It shall become to serve all hopes conceiv'd
To deck his fortune with his virtuous deeds.
And therefore, Tranio, for the time I study
Virtue, and that part of philosophy
Will I apply that treats of happiness
20   By virtue specially to be achiev'd.
Tell me thy mind, for I have Pisa left
And am to Padua come as he that leaves
A shallow plash to plunge him in the deep,
And with satiety seeks to quench his thirst.
25   TRANIO   *Mi perdonato*, gentle master mine.
I am in all affected as yourself,
Glad that you thus continue your resolve
To suck the sweets of sweet philosophy.
Only, good master, while we do admire
30   This virtue and this moral discipline,
Let's be no stoics nor no stocks, I pray,
Or so devote to Aristotle's checks
As Ovid be an outcast quite abjur'd.
Balk logic with acquaintance that you have,
35   And practise rhetoric in your common talk,
Music and poesy use to quicken you,
The mathematics and the metaphysics
Fall to them as you find your stomach serves you.
No profit grows where is no pleasure ta'en.
40   In brief, sir, study what you most affect.
LUCENTIO   Gramercies, Tranio, well dost thou advise.
If, Biondello, thou wert come ashore,
We could at once put us in readiness,
And take a lodging fit to entertain
45   Such friends as time in Padua shall beget.
But stay awhile, what company is this?
TRANIO   Master, some show to welcome us to town.

Lucentio and Tranio stand by.

Enter BAPTISTA *with his two daughters* KATHERINA *and*
BIANCA, GREMIO, *a pantaloon*, HORTENSIO, *suitor to*
Bianca.

BAPTISTA   Gentlemen, importune me no farther,
For how I firmly am resolv'd you know;
50   That is, not to bestow my youngest daughter
Before I have a husband for the elder.
If either of you both love Katherina,
Because I know you well and love you well,
Leave shall you have to court her at your pleasure.
55   GREMIO   To cart her rather. She's too rough for me.
There, there, Hortensio, will you any wife?
KATHERINA   I pray you, sir, is it your will
To make a stale of me amongst these mates?

HORTENSIO
Mates, maid, how mean you that? No mates for you
Unless you were of gentler, milder mould.   60
KATHERINA   I'faith, sir, you shall never need to fear.
Iwis it is not half way to her heart.
But if it were, doubt not her care should be
To comb your noddle with a three-legg'd stool,
And paint your face, and use you like a fool.   65
HORTENSIO   From all such devils, good Lord deliver us!
GREMIO   And me too, good Lord!
TRANIO
Husht, master, here's some good pastime toward.
That wench is stark mad or wonderful froward.
LUCENTIO   But in the other's silence do I see   70
Maid's mild behaviour and sobriety.
Peace, Tranio.
TRANIO   Well said, master. Mum! and gaze your fill.
BAPTISTA   Gentlemen, that I may soon make good
What I have said – Bianca, get you in.   75
And let it not displease thee, good Bianca,
For I will love thee ne'er the less, my girl.
KATHERINA   A pretty peat! it is best put finger in the
eye, and she knew why.
BIANCA   Sister, content you in my discontent.   80
Sir, to your pleasure humbly I subscribe.
My books and instruments shall be my company,
On them to look and practise by myself.
LUCENTIO
Hark, Tranio, thou may'st hear Minerva speak.
HORTENSIO   Signor Baptista, will you be so strange?   85
Sorry am I that our good will effects
Bianca's grief.
GREMIO   Why, will you mew her up,
Signor Baptista, for this fiend of hell,
And make her bear the penance of her tongue?
BAPTISTA   Gentlemen, content ye. I am resolv'd.   90
Go in, Bianca.   *Exit Bianca.*
And for I know she taketh most delight
In music, instruments, and poetry,
Schoolmasters will I keep within my house
Fit to instruct her youth. If you, Hortensio,   95
Or Signor Gremio, you, know any such,
Prefer them hither; for to cunning men
I will be very kind, and liberal
To mine own children in good bringing-up.
And so farewell. Katherina, you may stay,   100
For I have more to commune with Bianca.   *Exit.*
KATHERINA   Why, and I trust I may go too, may I not?
What, shall I be appointed hours, as though, belike, I
knew not what to take and what to leave? Ha?   *Exit.*
GREMIO   You may go to the devil's dam. Your gifts are so
good here's none will hold you. Their love is not so   105
great, Hortensio, but we may blow our nails together,
and fast it fairly out. Our cake's dough on both sides.
Farewell. Yet, for the love I bear my sweet Bianca, if I
can by any means light on a fit man to teach her that   110
wherein she delights, I will wish him to her father.

HORTENSIO So will I, Signor Gremio. But a word, I
pray. Though the nature of our quarrel yet never
brooked parle, know now, upon advice, it toucheth us
115 both – that we may yet again have access to our fair
mistress and be happy rivals in Bianca's love – to
labour and effect one thing specially.

GREMIO What's that, I pray?

HORTENSIO Marry, sir, to get a husband for her sister.

120 GREMIO A husband? A devil.

HORTENSIO I say a husband.

GREMIO I say a devil. Thinkest thou, Hortensio, though
her father be very rich, any man is so very a fool to be
married to hell?

125 HORTENSIO Tush, Gremio. Though it pass your
patience and mine to endure her loud alarums, why,
man, there be good fellows in the world, and a man
could light on them, would take her with all faults, and
money enough.

130 GREMIO I cannot tell. But I had as lief take her dowry
with this condition, to be whipped at the high cross
every morning.

HORTENSIO Faith, as you say, there's small choice in
rotten apples. But come, since this bar in law makes us
135 friends, it shall be so far forth friendly maintained
till by helping Baptista's eldest daughter to a husband
we set his youngest free for a husband, and then have
to't afresh. Sweet Bianca! Happy man be his dole. He
that runs fastest gets the ring. How say you, Signor
140 Gremio?

GREMIO I am agreed, and would I had given him the
best horse in Padua to begin his wooing that would
thoroughly woo her, wed her, and bed her, and rid
the house of her. Come on.

Exeunt Gremio and Hortensio.

145 TRANIO I pray, sir, tell me, is it possible
That love should of a sudden take such hold?

LUCENTIO O Tranio, till I found it to be true,
I never thought it possible or likely.
But see, while idly I stood looking on,
150 I found the effect of love in idleness,
And now in plainness do confess to thee,
That art to me as secret and as dear
As Anna to the Queen of Carthage was,
Tranio, I burn, I pine, I perish, Tranio,
155 If I achieve not this young modest girl.
Counsel me, Tranio, for I know thou canst.
Assist me, Tranio, for I know thou wilt.

TRANIO Master, it is no time to chide you now;
Affection is not rated from the heart.
160 If love have touch'd you, naught remains but so,
Redime te captum quam queas minimo.

LUCENTIO Gramercies, lad. Go forward, this contents.
The rest will comfort, for thy counsel's sound.

TRANIO Master, you look'd so longly on the maid,
165 Perhaps you mark'd not what's the pith of all.

LUCENTIO O yes. I saw sweet beauty in her face,
Such as the daughter of Agenor had,
That made great Jove to humble him to her hand,
When with his knees he kiss'd the Cretan strand.

TRANIO
Saw you no more? Mark'd you not how her sister   170
Began to scold and raise up such a storm
That mortal ears might hardly endure the din?

LUCENTIO Tranio, I saw her coral lips to move,
And with her breath she did perfume the air.
Sacred and sweet was all I saw in her.   175

TRANIO Nay, then 'tis time to stir him from his trance.
I pray, awake, sir. If you love the maid,
Bend thoughts and wits to achieve her. Thus it
stands:
Her elder sister is so curst and shrewd
That till the father rid his hands of her,   180
Master, your love must live a maid at home,
And therefore has he closely mew'd her up,
Because she will not be annoy'd with suitors.

LUCENTIO Ah, Tranio, what a cruel father's he!
But art thou not advis'd he took some care   185
To get her cunning schoolmasters to instruct her?

TRANIO Ay, marry, am I, sir – and now 'tis plotted.

LUCENTIO I have it, Tranio.

TRANIO   Master, for my hand,
Both our inventions meet and jump in one.

LUCENTIO Tell me thine first.

TRANIO   You will be schoolmaster,   190
And undertake the teaching of the maid.
That's your device.

LUCENTIO   It is. May it be done?

TRANIO Not possible. For who shall bear your part
And be in Padua here Vincentio's son,
Keep house and ply his book, welcome his friends,   195
Visit his countrymen and banquet them?

LUCENTIO *Basta*, content thee, for I have it full.
We have not yet been seen in any house,
Nor can we be distinguish'd by our faces
For man or master. Then it follows thus: 200
Thou shalt be master, Tranio, in my stead,
Keep house, and port, and servants, as I should;
I will some other be, some Florentine,
Some Neapolitan, or meaner man of Pisa.
'Tis hatch'd, and shall be so. Tranio, at once   205
Uncase thee, take my colour'd hat and cloak.
When Biondello comes, he waits on thee,
But I will charm him first to keep his tongue.

TRANIO So had you need.
In brief, sir, sith it your pleasure is,   210
And I am tied to be obedient –
For so your father charg'd me at our parting,
'Be serviceable to my son' quoth he,
Although I think 'twas in another sense –
I am content to be Lucentio,   215
Because so well I love Lucentio.

LUCENTIO Tranio, be so, because Lucentio loves;
And let me be a slave, t'achieve that maid
Whose sudden sight hath thrall'd my wounded eye.

Enter BIONDELLO.

220   Here comes the rogue. Sirrah, where have you been?
BIONDELLO
      Where have I been? Nay, how now, where are you?
      Master, has my fellow Tranio stol'n your clothes,
      Or you stol'n his, or both? Pray, what's the news?
LUCENTIO   Sirrah, come hither. 'Tis no time to jest,
225   And therefore frame your manners to the time.
      Your fellow Tranio here, to save my life,
      Puts my apparel and my countenance on,
      And I for my escape have put on his.
      For in a quarrel since I came ashore
230   I kill'd a man, and fear I was descried.
      Wait you on him, I charge you, as becomes,
      While I make way from hence to save my life.
      You understand me?
BIONDELLO   I, sir? Ne'er a whit.
LUCENTIO   And not a jot of Tranio in your mouth.
235   Tranio is chang'd into Lucentio.
BIONDELLO   The better for him. Would I were so too.
TRANIO
      So could I, faith, boy, to have the next wish after,
      That Lucentio indeed had Baptista's youngest
            daughter.
      But, sirrah, not for my sake but your master's I
            advise
      You use your manners discreetly in all kind of
240   companies.
      When I am alone, why then I am Tranio,
      But in all places else your master Lucentio.
LUCENTIO   Tranio, let's go.
      One thing more rests, that thyself execute,
      To make one among these wooers. If thou ask me
245   why,
      Sufficeth my reasons are both good and weighty.
                                            Exeunt.

[*The presenters above speak.*]
1 SERVINGMAN
      My lord, you nod, you do not mind the play.
SLY   Yes, by Saint Anne, do I. A good matter, surely.
      Comes there any more of it?
250 PAGE   My lord, 'tis but begun.
SLY   'Tis a very excellent piece of work, madam lady.
      Would 'twere done. [*They sit and mark.*]

1.2   *Enter* PETRUCHIO *and his man* GRUMIO.

PETRUCHIO   Verona, for a while I take my leave,
      To see my friends in Padua, but of all
      My best beloved and approved friend,
      Hortensio; and I trow this is his house.
5   Here, sirrah Grumio, knock, I say.
GRUMIO   Knock, sir? Whom should I knock? Is there
      any man has rebused your worship?
PETRUCHIO   Villain, I say, knock me here soundly.
GRUMIO   Knock you here, sir? Why, sir, what am I, sir,
10   that I should knock you here, sir?

PETRUCHIO   Villain, I say, knock me at this gate,
      And rap me well, or I'll knock your knave's pate.
GRUMIO
      My master is grown quarrelsome. I should knock you
            first,
      And then I know after who comes by the worst.
PETRUCHIO   Will it not be?   15
      Faith, sirrah, and you'll not knock, I'll ring it.
      I'll try how you can solfa and sing it.
      [*He wrings him by the ears.*]
GRUMIO   Help, masters, help! My master is mad.
PETRUCHIO   Now knock when I bid you, sirrah villain.

Enter HORTENSIO.

HORTENSIO   How now, what's the matter? My old friend   20
      Grumio, and my good friend Petruchio? How do you
      all at Verona?
PETRUCHIO
      Signor Hortensio, come you to part the fray?
      Con tutto il cuore ben trovato, may I say.
HORTENSIO   *Alla nostra casa ben venuto, molto honorato*   25
      signor mio Petrucio.
      Rise, Grumio, rise. We will compound this quarrel.
GRUMIO   Nay, 'tis no matter, sir, what he 'leges in Latin.
      If this be not a lawful cause for me to leave his service,
      look you, sir. He bid me knock him and rap him   30
      soundly, sir. Well, was it fit for a servant to use his
      master so, being perhaps, for aught I see, two and
      thirty, a pip out?
      Whom would to God I had well knock'd at first,
      Then had not Grumio come by the worst.   35
PETRUCHIO   A senseless villain. Good Hortensio,
      I bade the rascal knock upon your gate,
      And could not get him for my heart to do it.
GRUMIO   Knock at the gate? O heavens! Spake you not
      these words plain, 'Sirrah, knock me here, rap me   40
      here, knock me well, and knock me soundly'? And
      come you now with 'knocking at the gate'?
PETRUCHIO   Sirrah, be gone, or talk not, I advise you.
HORTENSIO   Petruchio, patience, I am Grumio's pledge.
      Why, this a heavy chance 'twixt him and you,   45
      Your ancient, trusty, pleasant servant Grumio.
      And tell me now, sweet friend, what happy gale
      Blows you to Padua here from old Verona?
PETRUCHIO
      Such wind as scatters young men through the world
      To seek their fortunes farther than at home,   50
      Where small experience grows. But in a few,
      Signor Hortensio, thus it stands with me:
      Antonio, my father, is deceas'd,
      And I have thrust myself into this maze,
      Haply to wive and thrive as best I may.   55
      Crowns in my purse I have, and goods at home,
      And so am come abroad to see the world.
HORTENSIO
      Petruchio, shall I then come roundly to thee,
      And wish thee to a shrewd ill-favour'd wife?

60 Thou'dst thank me but a little for my counsel,
And yet I'll promise thee she shall be rich,
And very rich. But th'art too much my friend,
And I'll not wish thee to her.

PETRUCHIO
Signor Hortensio, 'twixt such friends as we
65 Few words suffice; and therefore, if thou know
One rich enough to be Petruchio's wife –
As wealth is burden of my wooing dance –
Be she as foul as was Florentius' love,
As old as Sibyl, and as curst and shrewd
70 As Socrates' Xanthippe, or a worse,
She moves me not, or not removes at least
Affection's edge in me, were she as rough
As are the swelling Adriatic seas.
I come to wive it wealthily in Padua;
75 If wealthily, then happily in Padua.

GRUMIO Nay, look you, sir, he tells you flatly what his
mind is. Why, give him gold enough and marry him to
a puppet or an aglet-baby, or an old trot with ne'er a
tooth in her head, though she have as many diseases as
80 two and fifty horses. Why, nothing comes amiss, so
money comes withal.

HORTENSIO Petruchio, since we are stepp'd thus far in,
I will continue that I broach'd in jest.
I can, Petruchio, help thee to a wife
85 With wealth enough, and young and beauteous,
Brought up as best becomes a gentlewoman.
Her only fault, and that is faults enough,
Is that she is intolerable curst,
And shrewd, and froward, so beyond all measure
90 That, were my state far worser than it is,
I would not wed her for a mine of gold.

PETRUCHIO
Hortensio, peace. Thou know'st not gold's effect.
Tell me her father's name and 'tis enough.
For I will board her though she chide as loud
95 As thunder when the clouds in autumn crack.

HORTENSIO Her father is Baptista Minola,
An affable and courteous gentleman.
Her name is Katherina Minola,
Renown'd in Padua for her scolding tongue.

100 PETRUCHIO I know her father, though I know not her,
And he knew my deceased father well.
I will not sleep, Hortensio, till I see her,
And therefore let me be thus bold with you
To give you over at this first encounter,
105 Unless you will accompany me thither.

GRUMIO I pray you, sir, let him go while the humour
lasts. O' my word, and she knew him as well as I do,
she would think scolding would do little good upon
him. She may perhaps call him half a score knaves or
110 so. Why, that's nothing; and he begin once, he'll rail in
his rope-tricks. I'll tell you what, sir, and she stand
him but a little, he will throw a figure in her face, and
so disfigure her with it that she shall have no more
eyes to see withal than a cat. You know him not, sir.

HORTENSIO Tarry, Petruchio, I must go with thee, 115
For in Baptista's keep my treasure is.
He hath the jewel of my life in hold,
His youngest daughter, beautiful Bianca,
And her withholds from me and other more,
Suitors to her and rivals in my love, 120
Supposing it a thing impossible,
For those defects I have before rehears'd,
That ever Katherina will be woo'd.
Therefore this order hath Baptista ta'en,
That none shall have access unto Bianca 125
Till Katherine the curst have got a husband.

GRUMIO Katherine the curst,
A title for a maid of all titles the worst.

HORTENSIO
Now shall my friend Petruchio do me grace,
And offer me disguis'd in sober robes 130
To old Baptista as a schoolmaster
Well seen in music, to instruct Bianca,
That so I may by this device at least
Have leave and leisure to make love to her,
And unsuspected court her by herself. 135

GRUMIO Here's no knavery. See, to beguile the old folks,
how the young folks lay their heads together.

Enter GREMIO, *and* LUCENTIO *disguised.*

Master, master, look about you. Who goes there, ha?

HORTENSIO Peace, Grumio. It is the rival of my love.
Petruchio, stand by awhile. 140

GRUMIO A proper stripling and an amorous.

GREMIO O, very well; I have perus'd the note.
Hark you, sir, I'll have them very fairly bound –
All books of love, see that at any hand –
And see you read no other lectures to her. 145
You understand me. Over and beside
Signor Baptista's liberality,
I'll mend it with a largess. Take your paper too,
And let me have them very well perfum'd,
For she is sweeter than perfume itself 150
To whom they go to. What will you read to her?

LUCENTIO Whate'er I read to her, I'll plead for you
As for my patron, stand you so assur'd,
As firmly as yourself were still in place,
Yea, and perhaps with more successful words 155
Than you, unless you were a scholar, sir.

GREMIO O this learning, what a thing it is!

GRUMIO O this woodcock, what an ass it is!

PETRUCHIO Peace, sirrah.

HORTENSIO
Grumio, mum! God save you, Signor Gremio. 160

GREMIO And you are well met, Signor Hortensio.
Trow you whither I am going? To Baptista Minola.
I promis'd to enquire carefully
About a schoolmaster for the fair Bianca,
And by good fortune I have lighted well 165
On this young man, for learning and behaviour
Fit for her turn, well read in poetry

And other books, good ones, I warrant ye.

HORTENSIO   'Tis well. And I have met a gentleman
170   Hath promis'd me to help me to another,
     A fine musician to instruct our mistress.
     So shall I no whit be behind in duty
     To fair Bianca, so belov'd of me.

GREMIO   Belov'd of me, and that my deeds shall prove.

175   GRUMIO   And that his bags shall prove.

HORTENSIO   Gremio, 'tis now no time to vent our love.
     Listen to me, and if you speak me fair,
     I'll tell you news indifferent good for either.
     Here is a gentleman whom by chance I met,
180   Upon agreement from us to his liking,
     Will undertake to woo curst Katherine,
     Yea, and to marry her, if her dowry please.

GREMIO   So said, so done, is well.
     Hortensio, have you told him all her faults?

185   PETRUCHIO   I know she is an irksome brawling scold.
     If that be all, masters, I hear no harm.

GREMIO
     No, say'st me so, friend? What countryman?

PETRUCHIO   Born in Verona, old Antonio's son.
     My father dead, my fortune lives for me,
190   And I do hope good days and long to see.

GREMIO
     O sir, such a life with such a wife were strange.
     But if you have a stomach, to't a God's name,
     You shall have me assisting you in all.
     But will you woo this wildcat?

PETRUCHIO   Will I live?

195   GRUMIO   Will he woo her? Ay, or I'll hang her.

PETRUCHIO   Why came I hither but to that intent?
     Think you a little din can daunt mine ears?
     Have I not in my time heard lions roar?
     Have I not heard the sea, puff'd up with winds,
200   Rage like an angry boar chafed with sweat?
     Have I not heard great ordnance in the field,
     And heaven's artillery thunder in the skies?
     Have I not in a pitched battle heard
     Loud 'larums, neighing steeds, and trumpets' clang?
205   And do you tell me of a woman's tongue,
     That gives not half so great a blow to hear
     As will a chestnut in a farmer's fire?
     Tush, tush, fear boys with bugs!

GRUMIO   For he fears none.

GREMIO   Hortensio, hark.
210   This gentleman is happily arriv'd,
     My mind presumes, for his own good and yours.

HORTENSIO   I promis'd we would be contributors
     And bear his charge of wooing, whatsoe'er.

GREMIO   And so we will, provided that he win her.

215   GRUMIO   I would I were as sure of a good dinner.

Enter TRANIO *brave, and* BIONDELLO.

TRANIO   Gentlemen, God save you. If I may be bold,
     Tell me, I beseech you, which is the readiest way
     To the house of Signor Baptista Minola?

BIONDELLO
     He that has the two fair daughters, is't he you mean?

TRANIO   Even he, Biondello.   220

GREMIO   Hark you, sir, you mean not her too?

TRANIO
     Perhaps him and her, sir. What have you to do?

PETRUCHIO
     Not her that chides, sir, at any hand, I pray.

TRANIO   I love no chiders, sir. Biondello, let's away.

LUCENTIO
     Well begun, Tranio.

HORTENSIO   Sir, a word ere you go.   225
     Are you a suitor to the maid you talk of, yea or no?

TRANIO   And if I be, sir, is it any offence?

GREMIO
     No, if without more words you will get you hence.

TRANIO   Why, sir, I pray, are not the streets as free
     For me as for you?

GREMIO   But so is not she.   230

TRANIO   For what reason, I beseech you?

GREMIO   For this reason, if you'll know,
     That she's the choice love of Signor Gremio.

HORTENSIO   That she's the chosen of Signor Hortensio.

TRANIO   Softly, my masters. If you be gentlemen,
     Do me this right; hear me with patience.   235
     Baptista is a noble gentleman,
     To whom my father is not all unknown,
     And were his daughter fairer than she is,
     She may more suitors have, and me for one.
     Fair Leda's daughter had a thousand wooers,   240
     Then well one more may fair Bianca have.
     And so she shall. Lucentio shall make one,
     Though Paris came, in hope to speed alone.

GREMIO   What, this gentleman will out-talk us all!

LUCENTIO
     Sir, give him head, I know he'll prove a jade.   245

PETRUCHIO   Hortensio, to what end are all these words?

HORTENSIO   Sir, let me be so bold as ask you,
     Did you yet ever see Baptista's daughter?

TRANIO   No, sir, but hear I do that he hath two:
     The one as famous for a scolding tongue   250
     As is the other for beauteous modesty.

PETRUCHIO   Sir, sir, the first's for me, let her go by.

GREMIO   Yea, leave that labour to great Hercules,
     And let it be more than Alcides' twelve.

PETRUCHIO   Sir, understand you this of me in sooth,   255
     The youngest daughter whom you hearken for
     Her father keeps from all access of suitors,
     And will not promise her to any man
     Until the elder sister first be wed.
     The younger then is free, and not before.   260

TRANIO   If it be so, sir, that you are the man
     Must stead us all and me amongst the rest,
     And if you break the ice and do this feat,
     Achieve the elder, set the younger free
     For our access, whose hap shall be to have her   265
     Will not so graceless be to be ingrate.

HORTENSIO

    Sir, you say well, and well you do conceive.

    And since you do profess to be a suitor,

    You must, as we do, gratify this gentleman,

270   To whom we all rest generally beholding.

TRANIO   Sir, I shall not be slack. In sign whereof,

    Please ye we may contrive this afternoon,

    And quaff carouses to our mistress' health,

    And do as adversaries do in law,

275   Strive mightily, but eat and drink as friends.

GRUMIO, BIONDELLO

    O excellent motion! Fellows, let's be gone.

HORTENSIO   The motion's good indeed, and be it so.

    Petruchio, I shall be your *ben venuto*.   *Exeunt.*

2.1   *Enter* KATHERINA *and* BIANCA.

BIANCA

    Good sister, wrong me not, nor wrong yourself,

    To make a bondmaid and a slave of me.

    That I disdain. But for these other gawds,

    Unbind my hands, I'll pull them off myself,

5   Yea, all my raiment, to my petticoat,

    Or what you will command me will I do,

    So well I know my duty to my elders.

KATHERINA   Of all thy suitors here I charge thee tell

    Whom thou lov'st best. See thou dissemble not.

10   BIANCA   Believe me, sister, of all the men alive

    I never yet beheld that special face

    Which I could fancy more than any other.

KATHERINA   Minion, thou liest. Is't not Hortensio?

BIANCA   If you affect him, sister, here I swear

15   I'll plead for you myself but you shall have him.

KATHERINA   O then belike you fancy riches more.

    You will have Gremio to keep you fair.

BIANCA   Is it for him you do envy me so?

    Nay then you jest, and now I well perceive

20   You have but jested with me all this while.

    I prithee, sister Kate, untie my hands.

KATHERINA   If that be jest, then all the rest was so.

    [*Strikes her.*]

Enter BAPTISTA.

BAPTISTA

    Why, how now, dame, whence grows this insolence?

    Bianca, stand aside. Poor girl, she weeps.

25   Go ply thy needle; meddle not with her.

    For shame, thou hilding of a devilish spirit,

    Why dost thou wrong her that did ne'er wrong thee?

    When did she cross thee with a bitter word?

KATHERINA   Her silence flouts me, and I'll be reveng'd.

    [*Flies after Bianca.*]

30   BAPTISTA   What, in my sight? Bianca, get thee in.

    Exit Bianca.

KATHERINA

    What, will you not suffer me? Nay, now I see

    She is your treasure, she must have a husband,

    I must dance barefoot on her wedding-day,

    And for your love to her lead apes in hell.

    Talk not to me, I will go sit and weep,   35

    Till I can find occasion of revenge.   *Exit.*

BAPTISTA   Was ever gentleman thus griev'd as I?

    But who comes here?

Enter GREMIO, LUCENTIO *disguised as Cambio in the habit of a mean man;* PETRUCHIO, *with* HORTENSIO *disguised as Litio; and* TRANIO *disguised as Lucentio, with his boy* BIONDELLO, *bearing a lute and books.*

GREMIO   Good morrow, neighbour Baptista.

BAPTISTA   Good morrow, neighbour Gremio. God save   40

    you, gentlemen.

PETRUCHIO

    And you, good sir. Pray, have you not a daughter

    Call'd Katherina, fair and virtuous?

BAPTISTA   I have a daughter, sir, call'd Katherina.

GREMIO   You are too blunt, go to it orderly.   45

PETRUCHIO

    You wrong me, Signor Gremio, give me leave.

    I am a gentleman of Verona, sir,

    That hearing of her beauty and her wit,

    Her affability and bashful modesty,

    Her wondrous qualities and mild behaviour,   50

    Am bold to show myself a forward guest

    Within your house, to make mine eye the witness

    Of that report which I so oft have heard.

    And for an entrance to my entertainment

    I do present you with a man of mine,   55

    [*Presents Hortensio.*]

    Cunning in music and the mathematics,

    To instruct her fully in those sciences,

    Whereof I know she is not ignorant.

    Accept of him, or else you do me wrong.

    His name is Litio, born in Mantua.   60

BAPTISTA

    Y'are welcome, sir, and he for your good sake.

    But for my daughter Katherine, this I know,

    She is not for your turn, the more my grief.

PETRUCHIO   I see you do not mean to part with her,

    Or else you like not of my company.   65

BAPTISTA   Mistake me not, I speak but as I find.

    Whence are you, sir? What may I call your name?

PETRUCHIO   Petruchio is my name, Antonio's son,

    A man well known throughout all Italy.

BAPTISTA

    I know him well. You are welcome for his sake.   70

GREMIO   Saving your tale, Petruchio, I pray

    Let us that are poor petitioners speak too.

    Baccare! You are marvellous forward.

PETRUCHIO   O pardon me, Signor Gremio, I would fain

    be doing.   75

GREMIO   I doubt it not, sir, but you will curse your

    wooing. Neighbour, this is a gift very grateful, I am

    sure of it. To express the like kindness, myself, that

    have been more kindly beholding to you than any,

80 freely give unto you this young scholar [*Presents Lucentio.*], that hath been long studying at Rheims; as cunning in Greek, Latin, and other languages, as the other in music and mathematics. His name is Cambio. Pray accept his service.

85 BAPTISTA A thousand thanks, Signor Gremio. Welcome, good Cambio. [*to Tranio*] But, gentle sir, methinks you walk like a stranger. May I be so bold to know the cause of your coming?

TRANIO Pardon me, sir, the boldness is mine own,
90 That, being a stranger in this city here,
Do make myself a suitor to your daughter,
Unto Bianca, fair and virtuous.
Nor is your firm resolve unknown to me
In the preferment of the eldest sister.
95 This liberty is all that I request,
That, upon knowledge of my parentage,
I may have welcome 'mongst the rest that woo,
And free access and favour as the rest.
And toward the education of your daughters
100 I here bestow a simple instrument,
And this small packet of Greek and Latin books.
If you accept them, then their worth is great.

BAPTISTA Lucentio is your name? Of whence, I pray?

TRANIO Of Pisa, sir, son to Vincentio.

105 BAPTISTA A mighty man of Pisa. By report
I know him well. You are very welcome, sir.
[*to Hortensio*] Take you the lute,
[*to Lucentio*] and you the set of books.
You shall go see your pupils presently.
Holla, within!

Enter a Servant.

Sirrah, lead these gentlemen
110 To my daughters, and tell them both
These are their tutors. Bid them use them well.
Exeunt Servant, Hortensio, Lucentio, Biondello.
We will go walk a little in the orchard,
And then to dinner. You are passing welcome,
And so I pray you all to think yourselves.

115 PETRUCHIO Signor Baptista, my business asketh haste,
And every day I cannot come to woo.
You knew my father well, and in him me,
Left solely heir to all his lands and goods,
Which I have better'd rather than decreas'd.
120 Then tell me, if I get your daughter's love,
What dowry shall I have with her to wife?

BAPTISTA After my death the one half of my lands,
And in possession twenty thousand crowns.

PETRUCHIO And for that dowry I'll assure her of
125 Her widowhood, be it that she survive me,
In all my lands and leases whatsoever.
Let specialties be therefore drawn between us,
That covenants may be kept on either hand.

BAPTISTA Ay, when the special thing is well obtain'd,
130 That is, her love; for that is all in all.

PETRUCHIO Why, that is nothing. For I tell you, father,

I am as peremptory as she proud-minded;
And where two raging fires meet together,
They do consume the thing that feeds their fury.
Though little fire grows great with little wind, 135
Yet extreme gusts will blow out fire and all.
So I to her, and so she yields to me,
For I am rough and woo not like a babe.

BAPTISTA
Well mayst thou woo, and happy be thy speed.
But be thou arm'd for some unhappy words. 140

PETRUCHIO
Ay, to the proof, as mountains are for winds,
That shakes not, though they blow perpetually.

Enter HORTENSIO *with his head broke.*

BAPTISTA
How now, my friend, why dost thou look so pale?

HORTENSIO For fear, I promise you, if I look pale.

BAPTISTA
What, will my daughter prove a good musician? 145

HORTENSIO I think she'll sooner prove a soldier.
Iron may hold with her, but never lutes.

BAPTISTA
Why then, thou canst not break her to the lute?

HORTENSIO Why no, for she hath broke the lute to me.
I did but tell her she mistook her frets, 150
And bow'd her hand to teach her fingering,
When, with a most impatient devilish spirit,
'Frets, call you these?' quoth she, 'I'll fume with them.'
And with that word she struck me on the head,
And through the instrument my pate made way, 155
And there I stood amazed for a while,
As on a pillory, looking through the lute,
While she did call me rascal fiddler
And twangling Jack, with twenty such vile terms,
As had she studied to misuse me so. 160

PETRUCHIO Now, by the world, it is a lusty wench.
I love her ten times more than e'er I did.
O, how I long to have some chat with her.

BAPTISTA Well, go with me, and be not so discomfited.
Proceed in practice with my younger daughter; 165
She's apt to learn and thankful for good turns.
Signor Petruchio, will you go with us,
Or shall I send my daughter Kate to you?

PETRUCHIO I pray you do.
Exeunt all except Petruchio.
I'll attend her here,
And woo her with some spirit when she comes. 170
Say that she rail, why then I'll tell her plain
She sings as sweetly as a nightingale.
Say that she frown, I'll say she looks as clear
As morning roses newly wash'd with dew.
Say she be mute and will not speak a word, 175
Then I'll commend her volubility,
And say she uttereth piercing eloquence.
If she do bid me pack, I'll give her thanks,

As though she bid me stay by her a week.
180 If she deny to wed, I'll crave the day
When I shall ask the banns, and when be married.
But here she comes, and now, Petruchio, speak.

Enter KATHERINA.

Good morrow, Kate, for that's your name, I hear.
KATHERINA
Well have you heard, but something hard of hearing;
185 They call me Katherine that do talk of me.
PETRUCHIO
You lie, in faith, for you are call'd plain Kate,
And bonny Kate, and sometimes Kate the curst;
But Kate, the prettiest Kate in Christendom,
Kate of Kate Hall, my super-dainty Kate,
190 For dainties are all Kates, and therefore, Kate,
Take this of me, Kate of my consolation,
Hearing thy mildness prais'd in every town,
Thy virtues spoke of, and thy beauty sounded,
Yet not so deeply as to thee belongs,
195 Myself am mov'd to woo thee for my wife.
KATHERINA
Mov'd, in good time! Let him that mov'd you hither
Remove you hence. I knew you at the first
You were a movable.
PETRUCHIO   Why, what's a movable?
KATHERINA   A joint-stool.
PETRUCHIO   Thou hast hit it. Come, sit on me.
200 KATHERINA   Asses are made to bear, and so are you.
PETRUCHIO   Women are made to bear, and so are you.
KATHERINA   No such jade as you, if me you mean.
PETRUCHIO   Alas, good Kate, I will not burden thee!
For, knowing thee to be but young and light –
205 KATHERINA   Too light for such a swain as you to catch,
And yet as heavy as my weight should be.
PETRUCHIO   Should be? Should – buzz!
KATHERINA   Well ta'en, and like a buzzard.
PETRUCHIO
O slow-wing'd turtle, shall a buzzard take thee?
KATHERINA   Ay, for a turtle, as he takes a buzzard.
PETRUCHIO
210 Come, come, you wasp; i'faith, you are too angry.
KATHERINA   If I be waspish, best beware my sting.
PETRUCHIO   My remedy is then to pluck it out.
KATHERINA   Ay, if the fool could find it where it lies.
PETRUCHIO
Who knows not where a wasp does wear his sting?
In his tail.
KATHERINA   In his tongue.
215 PETRUCHIO   Whose tongue?
KATHERINA   Yours, if you talk of tales, and so farewell.
PETRUCHIO
What, with my tongue in your tail? Nay, come again,
Good Kate. I am a gentleman –
KATHERINA   That I'll try.
[*She strikes him.*]
PETRUCHIO   I swear I'll cuff you, if you strike again.

KATHERINA   So may you lose your arms.   220
If you strike me, you are no gentleman,
And if no gentleman, why then no arms.
PETRUCHIO   A herald, Kate? O, put me in thy books.
KATHERINA   What is your crest, a coxcomb?
PETRUCHIO   A combless cock, so Kate will be my hen.   225
KATHERINA
No cock of mine, you crow too like a craven.
PETRUCHIO
Nay, come, Kate, come; you must not look so sour.
KATHERINA   It is my fashion when I see a crab.
PETRUCHIO
Why, here's no crab, and therefore look not sour.
KATHERINA   There is, there is.   230
PETRUCHIO   Then show it me.
KATHERINA   Had I a glass, I would.
PETRUCHIO   What, you mean my face?
KATHERINA   Well aim'd of such a young one.
PETRUCHIO
Now, by Saint George, I am too young for you.
KATHERINA   Yet you are wither'd.
PETRUCHIO   'Tis with cares.
KATHERINA   I care not.
PETRUCHIO
Nay, hear you, Kate – in sooth, you scape not so.   235
KATHERINA   I chafe you, if I tarry. Let me go.
PETRUCHIO   No, not a whit. I find you passing gentle.
'Twas told me you were rough, and coy, and sullen,
And now I find report a very liar;
For thou art pleasant, gamesome, passing courteous,   240
But slow in speech, yet sweet as spring-time flowers.
Thou canst not frown, thou canst not look askance,
Nor bite the lip, as angry wenches will,
Nor hast thou pleasure to be cross in talk.
But thou with mildness entertain'st thy wooers,   245
With gentle conference, soft and affable.
Why does the world report that Kate doth limp?
O slanderous world! Kate like the hazel-twig
Is straight and slender, and as brown in hue
As hazel-nuts and sweeter than the kernels.   250
O, let me see thee walk. Thou dost not halt.
KATHERINA
Go, fool, and whom thou keep'st command.
PETRUCHIO   Did ever Dian so become a grove
As Kate this chamber with her princely gait?
O be thou Dian, and let her be Kate,   255
And then let Kate be chaste and Dian sportful.
KATHERINA
Where did you study all this goodly speech?
PETRUCHIO   It is extempore, from my mother-wit.
KATHERINA   A witty mother, witless else her son.
PETRUCHIO   Am I not wise?
KATHERINA   Yes, keep you warm.   260
PETRUCHIO
Marry, so I mean, sweet Katherine, in thy bed.
And therefore, setting all this chat aside,
Thus in plain terms: your father hath consented

265 That you shall be my wife; your dowry 'greed on;
And will you, nill you, I will marry you.
Now, Kate, I am a husband for your turn,
For by this light, whereby I see thy beauty,
Thy beauty that doth make me like thee well,
Thou must be married to no man but me.

270 For I am he am born to tame you, Kate,
And bring you from a wild Kate to a Kate
Conformable as other household Kates.

Enter BAPTISTA, GREMIO *and* TRANIO.

Here comes your father. Never make denial;
I must and will have Katherine to my wife.

BAPTISTA
Now, Signor Petruchio, how speed you with my
275   daughter?

PETRUCHIO   How but well, sir? How but well?
It were impossible I should speed amiss.

BAPTISTA
Why, how now, daughter Katherine? In your dumps?

KATHERINA   Call you me daughter? Now I promise you
280 You have show'd a tender fatherly regard
To wish me wed to one half lunatic,
A madcap ruffian and a swearing Jack,
That thinks with oaths to face the matter out.

PETRUCHIO   Father, 'tis thus: yourself and all the world
285 That talk'd of her have talk'd amiss of her.
If she be curst it is for policy,
For she's not froward, but modest as the dove.
She is not hot, but temperate as the morn.
For patience she will prove a second Grissel,
290 And Roman Lucrece for her chastity.
And to conclude, we have 'greed so well together
That upon Sunday is the wedding-day.

KATHERINA   I'll see thee hang'd on Sunday first.

GREMIO
Hark, Petruchio, she says she'll see thee hang'd first.

TRANIO
295 Is this your speeding? Nay then, good night our part.

PETRUCHIO
Be patient, gentlemen, I choose her for myself.
If she and I be pleas'd, what's that to you?
'Tis bargain'd 'twixt us twain, being alone,
That she shall still be curst in company.
300 I tell you 'tis incredible to believe
How much she loves me. O, the kindest Kate!
She hung about my neck, and kiss on kiss
She vied so fast, protesting oath on oath,
That in a twink she won me to her love.
305 O, you are novices. 'Tis a world to see
How tame, when men and women are alone,
A meacock wretch can make the curstest shrew.
Give me thy hand, Kate, I will unto Venice,
To buy apparel 'gainst the wedding-day.
310 Provide the feast, father, and bid the guests.
I will be sure my Katherine shall be fine.

BAPTISTA
I know not what to say, but give me your hands.
God send you joy, Petruchio, 'tis a match.

GREMIO, TRANIO   Amen, say we. We will be witnesses.

PETRUCHIO   Father, and wife, and gentlemen, adieu,   315
I will to Venice; Sunday comes apace.
We will have rings, and things, and fine array,
And kiss me, Kate, we will be married o' Sunday.

        Exeunt Petruchio and Katherina.

GREMIO   Was ever match clapp'd up so suddenly?

BAPTISTA
Faith, gentlemen, now I play a merchant's part,   320
And venture madly on a desperate mart.

TRANIO   'Twas a commodity lay fretting by you,
'Twill bring you gain, or perish on the seas.

BAPTISTA   The gain I seek is quiet in the match.

GREMIO   No doubt but he hath got a quiet catch.   325
But now, Baptista, to your younger daughter;
Now is the day we long have looked for.
I am your neighbour, and was suitor first.

TRANIO   And I am one that love Bianca more
Than words can witness or your thoughts can guess.   330

GREMIO   Youngling, thou canst not love so dear as I.

TRANIO   Greybeard, thy love doth freeze.

GREMIO   But thine doth fry.
Skipper, stand back, 'tis age that nourisheth.

TRANIO   But youth in ladies' eyes that flourisheth.

BAPTISTA
Content you, gentlemen, I will compound this strife.   335
'Tis deeds must win the prize, and he of both
That can assure my daughter greatest dower
Shall have my Bianca's love.
Say, Signor Gremio, what can you assure her?

GREMIO   First, as you know, my house within the city   340
Is richly furnished with plate and gold,
Basins and ewers to lave her dainty hands,
My hangings all of Tyrian tapestry.
In ivory coffers I have stuff'd my crowns,
In cypress chests my arras counterpoints,   345
Costly apparel, tents, and canopies,
Fine linen, Turkey cushions boss'd with pearl,
Valance of Venice gold in needlework,
Pewter and brass, and all things that belongs
To house or housekeeping. Then at my farm   350
I have a hundred milch-kine to the pail,
Six score fat oxen standing in my stalls,
And all things answerable to this portion.
Myself am struck in years, I must confess,
And if I die tomorrow this is hers,   355
If whilst I live she will be only mine.

TRANIO   That 'only' came well in. Sir, list to me:
I am my father's heir and only son.
If I may have your daughter to my wife,
I'll leave her houses three or four as good,   360
Within rich Pisa walls, as any one
Old Signor Gremio has in Padua,

Besides two thousand ducats by the year
Of fruitful land, all which shall be her jointure.
What, have I pinch'd you, Signor Gremio?   265

GREMIO   Two thousand ducats by the year of land!
[*aside*] My land amounts not to so much in all. –
That she shall have, besides an argosy
That now is lying in Marseilles road.   270
What, have I chok'd you with an argosy?

TRANIO   Gremio, 'tis known my father hath no less
Than three great argosies, besides two galliasses
And twelve tight galleys. These I will assure her,
And twice as much whate'er thou off'rest next.

GREMIO   Nay, I have offer'd all, I have no more,   275
And she can have no more than all I have.
If you like me, she shall have me and mine.

TRANIO   Why, then the maid is mine from all the world
By your firm promise. Gremio is outvied.

BAPTISTA   I must confess your offer is the best,   280
And let your father make her the assurance,
She is your own; else, you must pardon me,
If you should die before him, where's her dower?

TRANIO   That's but a cavil. He is old, I young.

GREMIO   And may not young men die as well as old?   285

BAPTISTA   Well, gentlemen,
I am thus resolv'd: on Sunday next you know
My daughter Katherine is to be married;
Now, on the Sunday following shall Bianca
Be bride to you, if you make this assurance;   290
If not, to Signor Gremio.
And so I take my leave, and thank you both.

GREMIO   Adieu, good neighbour.   *Exit Baptista.*
                 Now, I fear thee not.
Sirrah, young gamester, your father were a fool
To give thee all, and in his waning age   295
Set foot under thy table. Tut, a toy!
An old Italian fox is not so kind, my boy.   *Exit.*

TRANIO   A vengeance on your crafty wither'd hide!
Yet I have fac'd it with a card of ten.
'Tis in my head to do my master good.   300
I see no reason but suppos'd Lucentio
Must get a father, call'd suppos'd Vincentio.
And that's a wonder. Fathers commonly
Do get their children; but in this case of wooing
A child shall get a sire, if I fail not of my cunning.   305
                         Exit.

3.1   *Enter* LUCENTIO, HORTENSIO *and* BIANCA.

LUCENTIO   Fiddler, forbear. You grow too forward, sir.
Have you so soon forgot the entertainment
Her sister Katherine welcom'd you withal?

HORTENSIO   But, wrangling pedant, this is
The patroness of heavenly harmony.   5
Then give me leave to have prerogative,
And when in music we have spent an hour,
Your lecture shall have leisure for as much.

LUCENTIO   Preposterous ass, that never read so far

To know the cause why music was ordain'd!   10
Was it not to refresh the mind of man
After his studies or his usual pain?
Then give me leave to read philosophy,
And while I pause serve in your harmony.

HORTENSIO
Sirrah, I will not bear these braves of thine.   15

BIANCA   Why, gentlemen, you do me double wrong
To strive for that which resteth in my choice.
I am no breeching scholar in the schools,
I'll not be tied to hours nor 'pointed times,
But learn my lessons as I please myself.   20
And, to cut off all strife, here sit we down.
Take you your instrument, play you the whiles;
His lecture will be done ere you have tun'd.

HORTENSIO   You'll leave his lecture when I am in tune?

LUCENTIO   That will be never. Tune your instrument.   25

BIANCA   Where left we last?

LUCENTIO   Here, madam:
       Hic ibat Simois, hic est Sigeia tellus,
       Hic steterat Priami regia celsa senis.

BIANCA   Construe them.   30

LUCENTIO   *Hic ibat*, as I told you before – *Simois*, I am
Lucentio – *hic est*, son unto Vincentio of Pisa – *Sigeia
tellus*, disguised thus to get your love – *Hic steterat*,
and that Lucentio that comes a-wooing – *Priami*, is my
man Tranio – *regia*, bearing my port – *celsa senis*, that   35
we might beguile the old pantaloon.

HORTENSIO   Madam, my instrument's in tune.

BIANCA   Let's hear. O fie! The treble jars.

LUCENTIO   Spit in the hole, man, and tune again.

BIANCA   Now let me see if I can construe it: *Hic ibat*   40
Simois, I know you not – *hic est Sigeia tellus*, I trust you
not – *Hic steterat Priami*, take heed he hear us not –
regia, presume not – *celsa senis*, despair not.

HORTENSIO   Madam, 'tis now in tune.

LUCENTIO   All but the bass.

HORTENSIO
The bass is right, 'tis the base knave that jars.   45
[*aside*] How fiery and forward our pedant is.
Now, for my life, the knave doth court my love.
Pedascule, I'll watch you better yet.

BIANCA   In time I may believe, yet I mistrust.

LUCENTIO   Mistrust it not – for, sure, Aeacides   50
Was Ajax, call'd so from his grandfather.

BIANCA   I must believe my master, else, I promise you,
I should be arguing still upon that doubt.
But let it rest. Now, Litio, to you.
Good master, take it not unkindly, pray,   55
That I have been thus pleasant with you both.

HORTENSIO [*to Lucentio*]
You may go walk, and give me leave a while.
My lessons make no music in three parts.

LUCENTIO   Are you so formal, sir? Well, I must wait –
[*aside*] And watch, withal, for, but I be deceiv'd,   60
Our fine musician groweth amorous.

HORTENSIO   Madam, before you touch the instrument

To learn the order of my fingering,
I must begin with rudiments of art,
65 To teach you gamut in a briefer sort,
More pleasant, pithy, and effectual,
Than hath been taught by any of my trade.
And there it is in writing fairly drawn.
BIANCA   Why, I am past my gamut long ago.
70 HORTENSIO   Yet read the gamut of Hortensio.
BIANCA   *Gamut I am, the ground of all accord –*
A re, to plead Hortensio's passion –
B mi, Bianca, take him for thy lord –
C fa ut, that loves with all affection –
75 *D sol re, one clef, two notes have I –*
E la mi, show pity or I die.
Call you this gamut? Tut, I like it not!
Old fashions please me best. I am not so nice
To change true rules for odd inventions.

Enter a Servant.

SERVANT
80 Mistress, your father prays you leave your books,
And help to dress your sister's chamber up.
You know tomorrow is the wedding-day.
BIANCA   Farewell, sweet masters both, I must be gone.
Exeunt Bianca and Servant.
LUCENTIO   Faith, mistress, then I have no cause to stay.
Exit.
85 HORTENSIO   But I have cause to pry into this pedant.
Methinks he looks as though he were in love.
Yet if thy thoughts, Bianca, be so humble
To cast thy wandering eyes on every stale,
Seize thee that list. If once I find thee ranging,
90 Hortensio will be quit with thee by changing.   *Exit.*

3.2   *Enter* BAPTISTA, GREMIO, TRANIO, KATHERINA,
BIANCA, LUCENTIO *and others, attendants.*

BAPTISTA   Signor Lucentio, this is the 'pointed day
That Katherine and Petruchio should be married,
And yet we hear not of our son-in-law.
What will be said? What mockery will it be
5 To want the bridegroom when the priest attends
To speak the ceremonial rites of marriage!
What says Lucentio to this shame of ours?
KATHERINA
No shame but mine. I must forsooth be forc'd
To give my hand, oppos'd against my heart,
10 Unto a mad-brain rudesby, full of spleen,
Who woo'd in haste and means to wed at leisure.
I told you, I, he was a frantic fool,
Hiding his bitter jests in blunt behaviour.
And to be noted for a merry man
15 He'll woo a thousand, 'point the day of marriage,
Make feast, invite friends, and proclaim the banns,
Yet never means to wed where he hath woo'd.
Now must the world point at poor Katherine,
And say 'Lo, there is mad Petruchio's wife,

If it would please him come and marry her.'   20
TRANIO   Patience, good Katherine, and Baptista too.
Upon my life, Petruchio means but well,
Whatever fortune stays him from his word.
Though he be blunt, I know him passing wise;
Though he be merry, yet withal he's honest.   25
KATHERINA
Would Katherine had never seen him though.
Exit weeping followed by Bianca and attendants.
BAPTISTA   Go, girl, I cannot blame thee now to weep,
For such an injury would vex a saint,
Much more a shrew of thy impatient humour.

Enter BIONDELLO.

BIONDELLO   Master, master, news! And such old news as   30
you never heard of.
BAPTISTA   Is it new and old too? How may that be?
BIONDELLO   Why, is it not news to hear of Petruchio's
coming?
BAPTISTA   Is he come?   35
BIONDELLO   Why, no, sir.
BAPTISTA   What then?
BIONDELLO   He is coming.
BAPTISTA   When will he be here?
BIONDELLO   When he stands where I am and sees you   40
there.
TRANIO   But say, what to thine old news?
BIONDELLO   Why, Petruchio is coming in a new hat and
an old jerkin; a pair of old breeches thrice turned; a
pair of boots that have been candle-cases, one buckled,   45
another laced; an old rusty sword ta'en out of the
town armoury, with a broken hilt, and chapeless; with
two broken points; his horse hipped – with an old
mothy saddle and stirrups of no kindred – besides,
possessed with the glanders and like to mose in the   50
chine, troubled with the lampass, infected with the
fashions, full of windgalls, sped with spavins, rayed
with the yellows, past cure of the fives, stark spoiled
with the staggers, begnawn with the bots, swayed in
the back and shoulder-shotten, near-legged before,   55
and with a half-cheeked bit and a headstall of sheep's
leather, which, being restrained to keep him from
stumbling, hath been often burst and new-repaired
with knots; one girth six times pieced, and a woman's
crupper of velure, which hath two letters for her name   60
fairly set down in studs, and here and there pieced
with pack-thread.
BAPTISTA   Who comes with him?
BIONDELLO   O sir, his lackey, for all the world
caparisoned like the horse; with a linen stock on one   65
leg, and a kersey boot-hose on the other, gartered with
a red and blue list; an old hat, and the humour of forty
fancies pricked in't for a feather; a monster, a very
monster in apparel, and not like a Christian footboy or
a gentleman's lackey.   70
TRANIO
'Tis some odd humour pricks him to this fashion.

Yet oftentimes he goes but mean-apparell'd.

BAPTISTA   I am glad he's come, howsoe'er he comes.

BIONDELLO   Why, sir, he comes not.

BAPTISTA   Didst thou not say he comes?

BIONDELLO   Who? That Petruchio came?

BAPTISTA   Ay, that Petruchio came.

BIONDELLO   No, sir. I say his horse comes, with him on
his back.

BAPTISTA   Why, that's all one.

BIONDELLO   Nay, by Saint Jamy,
                I hold you a penny,
                A horse and a man
                Is more than one,
                And yet not many.

Enter PETRUCHIO *and* GRUMIO.

PETRUCHIO
Come, where be these gallants? Who's at home?

BAPTISTA   You are welcome, sir.

PETRUCHIO   And yet I come not well.

BAPTISTA   And yet you halt not.

TRANIO   Not so well apparell'd as I wish you were.

PETRUCHIO   Were it not better I should rush in thus?
But where is Kate? Where is my lovely bride?
How does my father? Gentles, methinks you frown.
And wherefore gaze this goodly company,
As if they saw some wondrous monument,
Some comet, or unusual prodigy?

BAPTISTA   Why, sir, you know this is your wedding-day.
First were we sad, fearing you would not come,
Now sadder that you come so unprovided.
Fie, doff this habit, shame to your estate,
An eyesore to our solemn festival!

TRANIO   And tell us what occasion of import
Hath all so long detain'd you from your wife
And sent you hither so unlike yourself.

PETRUCHIO   Tedious it were to tell, and harsh to hear.
Sufficeth I am come to keep my word,
Though in some part enforced to digress,
Which at more leisure I will so excuse
As you shall well be satisfied withal.
But where is Kate? I stay too long from her.
The morning wears, 'tis time we were at church.

TRANIO   See not your bride in these unreverent robes,
Go to my chamber, put on clothes of mine.

PETRUCHIO   Not I, believe me. Thus I'll visit her.

BAPTISTA   But thus, I trust, you will not marry her.

PETRUCHIO
Good sooth, even thus. Therefore ha' done with
    words;
To me she's married, not unto my clothes.
Could I repair what she will wear in me
As I can change these poor accoutrements,
'Twere well for Kate and better for myself.
But what a fool am I to chat with you,
When I should bid good morrow to my bride,
And seal the title with a lovely kiss.

Exeunt Petruchio and Grumio.

TRANIO   He hath some meaning in his mad attire.
We will persuade him, be it possible,   125
To put on better ere he go to church.

BAPTISTA   I'll after him and see the event of this.
Exeunt Baptista, Gremio, Biondello, attendants.

TRANIO   But, sir, to love concerneth us to add
Her father's liking, which to bring to pass,
As I before imparted to your worship,   130
I am to get a man – whate'er he be
It skills not much, we'll fit him to our turn –
And he shall be Vincentio of Pisa,
And make assurance here in Padua
Of greater sums than I have promised.   135
So shall you quietly enjoy your hope
And marry sweet Bianca with consent.

LUCENTIO   Were it not that my fellow schoolmaster
Doth watch Bianca's steps so narrowly,
'Twere good methinks to steal our marriage,   140
Which once perform'd, let all the world say no,
I'll keep mine own despite of all the world.

TRANIO   That by degrees we mean to look into,
And watch our vantage in this business.
We'll overreach the greybeard Gremio,   145
The narrow-prying father Minola,
The quaint musician, amorous Litio;
All for my master's sake, Lucentio.

Enter GREMIO.

Signor Gremio, came you from the church?

GREMIO   As willingly as e'er I came from school.   150

TRANIO
And is the bride and bridegroom coming home?

GREMIO   A bridegroom, say you? 'Tis a groom indeed,
A grumbling groom, and that the girl shall find.

TRANIO   Curster than she? Why, 'tis impossible.

GREMIO   Why, he's a devil, a devil, a very fiend.   155

TRANIO   Why, she's a devil, a devil, the devil's dam.

GREMIO   Tut! She's a lamb, a dove, a fool to him.
I'll tell you, Sir Lucentio, when the priest
Should ask if Katherine should be his wife,
'Ay, by gogs-wouns,' quoth he, and swore so loud   160
That all amaz'd the priest let fall the book,
And as he stoop'd again to take it up,
The mad-brain'd bridegroom took him such a cuff
That down fell priest and book, and book and priest.
'Now take them up,' quoth he, 'if any list.'   165

TRANIO   What said the wench when he rose up again?

GREMIO
Trembled and shook. For why, he stamp'd and swore
As if the vicar meant to cozen him.
But after many ceremonies done
He calls for wine. 'A health!' quoth he, as if   170
He had been aboard, carousing to his mates
After a storm; quaff'd off the muscadel,
And threw the sops all in the sexton's face,
Having no other reason

175 But that his beard grew thin and hungerly
And seem'd to ask him sops as he was drinking.
This done, he took the bride about the neck,
And kiss'd her lips with such a clamorous smack
That at the parting all the church did echo.
180 And I, seeing this, came thence for very shame,
And after me, I know, the rout is coming.
Such a mad marriage never was before.
Hark, hark! I hear the minstrels play.   [*Music plays.*]

Enter PETRUCHIO, KATHERINA, BIANCA, BAPTISTA,
HORTENSIO *with* GRUMIO *and attendants.*

PETRUCHIO
Gentlemen and friends, I thank you for your pains.
185 I know you think to dine with me today,
And have prepar'd great store of wedding cheer,
But so it is, my haste doth call me hence,
And therefore here I mean to take my leave.
BAPTISTA   Is't possible you will away tonight?
190 PETRUCHIO   I must away today before night come.
Make it no wonder. If you knew my business,
You would entreat me rather go than stay.
And honest company, I thank you all
That have beheld me give away myself
195 To this most patient, sweet, and virtuous wife.
Dine with my father, drink a health to me,
For I must hence, and farewell to you all.
TRANIO   Let us entreat you stay till after dinner.
PETRUCHIO   It may not be.
GREMIO   Let me entreat you.
PETRUCHIO   It cannot be.
KATHERINA   Let me entreat you.
200 PETRUCHIO   I am content.
KATHERINA   Are you content to stay?
PETRUCHIO   I am content you shall entreat me stay;
But yet not stay, entreat me how you can.
KATHERINA   Now if you love me, stay.
PETRUCHIO   Grumio, my horse.
GRUMIO
205 Ay, sir, they be ready; the oats have eaten the horses.
KATHERINA   Nay then,
Do what thou canst, I will not go today,
No, nor tomorrow, not till I please myself.
The door is open, sir, there lies your way,
210 You may be jogging whiles your boots are green.
For me, I'll not be gone till I please myself.
'Tis like you'll prove a jolly surly groom,
That take it on you at the first so roundly.
PETRUCHIO   O Kate, content thee, prithee be not angry.
215 KATHERINA   I will be angry; what hast thou to do?
Father, be quiet; he shall stay my leisure.
GREMIO   Ay, marry, sir, now it begins to work.
KATHERINA   Gentlemen, forward to the bridal dinner.
I see a woman may be made a fool
220 If she had not a spirit to resist.
PETRUCHIO
They shall go forward, Kate, at thy command.

Obey the bride, you that attend on her.
Go to the feast, revel and domineer,
Carouse full measure to her maidenhead,
Be mad and merry, or go hang yourselves.   225
But for my bonny Kate, she must with me.
Nay, look not big, nor stamp, nor stare, nor fret;
I will be master of what is mine own.
She is my goods, my chattels, she is my house,
My household stuff, my field, my barn,   230
My horse, my ox, my ass, my any thing,
And here she stands. Touch her whoever dare!
I'll bring mine action on the proudest he
That stops my way in Padua. Grumio,
Draw forth thy weapon, we are beset with thieves,   235
Rescue thy mistress if thou be a man.
Fear not, sweet wench, they shall not touch thee,
    Kate.
I'll buckler thee against a million.
            Exeunt Petruchio, Katherina and Grumio.
BAPTISTA   Nay, let them go, a couple of quiet ones.
GREMIO
Went they not quickly, I should die with laughing.   240
TRANIO   Of all mad matches never was the like.
LUCENTIO
Mistress, what's your opinion of your sister?
BIANCA   That being mad herself, she's madly mated.
GREMIO   I warrant him, Petruchio is Kated.
BAPTISTA
Neighbours and friends, though bride and
    bridegroom wants   245
For to supply the places at the table,
You know there wants no junkets at the feast.
Lucentio, you shall supply the bridegroom's place,
And let Bianca take her sister's room.
TRANIO   Shall sweet Bianca practise how to bride it?   250
BAPTISTA
She shall, Lucentio. Come, gentlemen, let's go.
                                            Exeunt.

4.1   *Enter* GRUMIO.

GRUMIO   Fie, fie on all tired jades, on all mad masters,
and all foul ways! Was ever man so beaten? Was ever
man so rayed? Was ever man so weary? I am sent
before to make a fire, and they are coming after to
warm them. Now, were I not a little pot and soon hot,   5
my very lips might freeze to my teeth, my tongue to
the roof of my mouth, my heart in my belly, ere I
should come by a fire to thaw me. But I with blowing
the fire shall warm myself, for, considering the
weather, a taller man than I will take cold. Holla, ho! 10
Curtis!

                Enter CURTIS.

CURTIS   Who is that calls so coldly?
GRUMIO   A piece of ice. If thou doubt it, thou mayst
slide from my shoulder to my heel with no greater a

run but my head and my neck. A fire, good Curtis.

CURTIS   Is my master and his wife coming, Grumio?

GRUMIO   O ay, Curtis, ay – and therefore fire, fire, cast on no water.

CURTIS   Is she so hot a shrew as she's reported?

GRUMIO   She was, good Curtis, before this frost. But thou know'st winter tames man, woman, and beast; for it hath tamed my old master, and my new mistress, and myself, fellow Curtis.

CURTIS   Away, you three-inch fool! I am no beast.

GRUMIO   Am I but three inches? Why, thy horn is a foot, and so long am I at the least. But wilt thou make a fire, or shall I complain on thee to our mistress, whose hand, she being now at hand, thou shalt soon feel, to thy cold comfort, for being slow in thy hot office?

CURTIS   I prithee, good Grumio, tell me how goes the world?

GRUMIO   A cold world, Curtis, in every office but thine; and therefore fire. Do thy duty, and have thy duty, for my master and mistress are almost frozen to death.

CURTIS   There's fire ready, and therefore, good Grumio, the news.

GRUMIO   Why, 'Jack, boy, ho, boy!' and as much news as wilt thou.

CURTIS   Come, you are so full of cony-catching.

GRUMIO   Why, therefore, fire, for I have caught extreme cold. Where's the cook? Is supper ready, the house trimmed, rushes strewed, cobwebs swept, the servingmen in their new fustian, their white stockings, and every officer his wedding-garment on? Be the Jacks fair within, the Jills fair without, the carpets laid, and everything in order?

CURTIS   All ready; and therefore, I pray thee, news.

GRUMIO   First know my horse is tired, my master and mistress fallen out.

CURTIS   How?

GRUMIO   Out of their saddles into the dirt, and thereby hangs a tale.

CURTIS   Let's ha't, good Grumio.

GRUMIO   Lend thine ear.

CURTIS   Here.

GRUMIO   There. [*Strikes him.*]

CURTIS   This 'tis to feel a tale, not to hear a tale.

GRUMIO   And therefore 'tis called a sensible tale; and this cuff was but to knock at your ear and beseech listening. Now I begin. *Imprimis*, we came down a foul hill, my master riding behind my mistress –

CURTIS   Both of one horse?

GRUMIO   What's that to thee?

CURTIS   Why, a horse.

GRUMIO   Tell thou the tale. But hadst thou not crossed me, thou shouldst have heard how her horse fell, and she under her horse; thou shouldst have heard in how miry a place, how she was bemoiled, how he left her with the horse upon her, how he beat me because her horse stumbled, how she waded through the dirt to pluck him off me, how he swore, how she prayed that

never prayed before, how I cried, how the horses ran away, how her bridle was burst, how I lost my crupper, with many things of worthy memory, which now shall die in oblivion, and thou return unexperienced to thy grave.

CURTIS   By this reckoning he is more shrew than she.

GRUMIO   Ay, and that thou and the proudest of you all shall find when he comes home. But what talk I of this? Call forth Nathaniel, Joseph, Nicholas, Philip, Walter, Sugarsop, and the rest. Let their heads be slickly combed, their blue coats brushed, and their garters of an indifferent knit. Let them curtsy with their left legs, and not presume to touch a hair of my master's horse-tail till they kiss their hands. Are they all ready?

CURTIS   They are.

GRUMIO   Call them forth.

CURTIS   Do you hear, ho? You must meet my master to countenance my mistress.

GRUMIO   Why, she hath a face of her own.

CURTIS   Who knows not that?

GRUMIO   Thou, it seems, that calls for company to countenance her.

CURTIS   I call them forth to credit her.

GRUMIO   Why, she comes to borrow nothing of them.

Enter four or five Servingmen.

NATHANIEL   Welcome home, Grumio.

PHILIP   How now, Grumio.

JOSEPH   What, Grumio.

NICHOLAS   Fellow Grumio.

NATHANIEL   How now, old lad.

GRUMIO   Welcome, you. How now, you. What, you. Fellow, you. And thus much for greeting. Now, my spruce companions, is all ready, and all things neat?

NATHANIEL   All things is ready. How near is our master?

GRUMIO

E'en at hand, alighted by this. And therefore be not
– Cock's passion, silence! I hear my master.

Enter PETRUCHIO *and* KATHERINA.

PETRUCHIO

Where be these knaves? What, no man at door
To hold my stirrup nor to take my horse?
Where is Nathaniel, Gregory, Philip?

ALL SERVINGMEN   Here, here sir, here sir.

PETRUCHIO   Here sir, here sir, here sir, here sir!
You logger-headed and unpolish'd grooms!
What, no attendance? No regard? No duty?
Where is the foolish knave I sent before?

GRUMIO   Here sir, as foolish as I was before.

PETRUCHIO

You peasant swain! You whoreson malt-horse drudge!
Did I not bid thee meet me in the park,
And bring along these rascal knaves with thee?

GRUMIO   Nathaniel's coat, sir, was not fully made,
And Gabriel's pumps were all unpink'd i' th' heel;

There was no link to colour Peter's hat,
And Walter's dagger was not come from sheathing.
There were none fine but Adam, Rafe, and Gregory,
125 The rest were ragged, old, and beggarly;
Yet, as they are, here are they come to meet you.
PETRUCHIO   Go, rascals, go, and fetch my supper in.
Exeunt Servingmen.
[*Sings.*]   Where is the life that late I led?
Where are those –
130 Sit down, Kate, and welcome. Food, food, food, food!

Enter servants with supper.

Why, when, I say? Nay, good sweet Kate, be merry.
Off with my boots, you rogues! You villains, when?
[*Sings.*]   It was the friar of orders grey,
As he forth walked on his way –
135 Out, you rogue! You pluck my foot awry.
Take that, and mend the plucking off the other.
[*Strikes him.*]
Be merry, Kate. Some water here. What ho!

Enter one with water.

Where's my spaniel Troilus? Sirrah, get you hence,
And bid my cousin Ferdinand come hither.
One, Kate, that you must kiss and be acquainted
140 with.
Where are my slippers? Shall I have some water?
Come, Kate, and wash, and welcome heartily.
You whoreson villain, will you let it fall?
[*Strikes servant.*]
KATHERINA
Patience, I pray you, 'twas a fault unwilling.
PETRUCHIO
145 A whoreson beetle-headed, flap-ear'd knave!
Come, Kate, sit down, I know you have a stomach.
Will you give thanks, sweet Kate, or else shall I?
What's this? Mutton?
1 SERVINGMAN   Ay.
PETRUCHIO   Who brought it?
PETER   I.
PETRUCHIO   'Tis burnt, and so is all the meat.
150 What dogs are these! Where is the rascal cook?
How durst you, villains, bring it from the dresser
And serve it thus to me that love it not?
There, take it to you, trenchers, cups, and all.
[*He throws the food and dishes at them.*]
You heedless jolt-heads and unmanner'd slaves!
155 What, do you grumble? I'll be with you straight.
Exeunt servants.
KATHERINA   I pray you, husband, be not so disquiet.
The meat was well, if you were so contented.
PETRUCHIO
I tell thee, Kate, 'twas burnt and dried away,
And I expressly am forbid to touch it,
160 For it engenders choler, planteth anger;
And better 'twere that both of us did fast,
Since, of ourselves, ourselves are choleric,

Than feed it with such over-roasted flesh.
Be patient, tomorrow 't shall be mended,
And for this night we'll fast for company.   165
Come, I will bring thee to thy bridal chamber.
Exeunt.

Enter Servants *severally.*

NATHANIEL   Peter, didst ever see the like?
PETER   He kills her in her own humour.

Enter CURTIS.

GRUMIO   Where is he?
CURTIS   In her chamber,   170
Making a sermon of continency to her,
And rails, and swears, and rates, that she, poor soul,
Knows not which way to stand, to look, to speak,
And sits as one new risen from a dream.
Away, away, for he is coming hither.   *Exeunt.*   175

Enter PETRUCHIO.

PETRUCHIO   Thus have I politicly begun my reign,
And 'tis my hope to end successfully.
My falcon now is sharp and passing empty,
And till she stoop she must not be full-gorg'd,
For then she never looks upon her lure.   180
Another way I have to man my haggard,
To make her come and know her keeper's call,
That is, to watch her, as we watch these kites
That bate and beat and will not be obedient.
She ate no meat today, nor none shall eat;   185
Last night she slept not, nor tonight she shall not.
As with the meat, some undeserved fault
I'll find about the making of the bed,
And here I'll fling the pillow, there the bolster,
This way the coverlet, another way the sheets.   190
Ay, and amid this hurly I intend
That all is done in reverend care of her.
And in conclusion she shall watch all night,
And if she chance to nod I'll rail and brawl,
And with the clamour keep her still awake.   195
This is a way to kill a wife with kindness,
And thus I'll curb her mad and headstrong humour.
He that knows better how to tame a shrew,
Now let him speak: 'tis charity to show.   *Exit.*

4.2   *Enter* TRANIO *and* HORTENSIO.

TRANIO   Is't possible, friend Litio, that Mistress Bianca
Doth fancy any other but Lucentio?
I tell you, sir, she bears me fair in hand.
HORTENSIO   Sir, to satisfy you in what I have said,
Stand by and mark the manner of his teaching.   5

Enter BIANCA *and* LUCENTIO.

LUCENTIO   Now, mistress, profit you in what you read?
BIANCA   What, master, read you? First resolve me that.
LUCENTIO   I read that I profess, *The Art to Love.*

BIANCA   And may you prove, sir, master of your art.

LUCENTIO

While you, sweet dear, prove mistress of my heart.

HORTENSIO

Quick proceeders, marry! Now tell me, I pray,
You that durst swear that your mistress Bianca
Lov'd none in the world so well as Lucentio.

TRANIO   O despiteful love, unconstant womankind!
I tell thee, Litio, this is wonderful.

HORTENSIO   Mistake no more, I am not Litio,
Nor a musician as I seem to be,
But one that scorn to live in this disguise,
For such a one as leaves a gentleman
And makes a god of such a cullion.
Know, sir, that I am call'd Hortensio.

TRANIO   Signor Hortensio, I have often heard
Of your entire affection to Bianca,
And since mine eyes are witness of her lightness,
I will with you, if you be so contented,
Forswear Bianca and her love for ever.

HORTENSIO

See how they kiss and court! Signor Lucentio,
Here is my hand, and here I firmly vow
Never to woo her more, but do forswear her,
As one unworthy all the former favours
That I have fondly flatter'd her withal.

TRANIO   And here I take the like unfeigned oath,
Never to marry with her though she would entreat.
Fie on her! See how beastly she doth court him.

HORTENSIO

Would all the world but he had quite forsworn!
For me, that I may surely keep mine oath,
I will be married to a wealthy widow
Ere three days pass, which hath as long lov'd me
As I have lov'd this proud disdainful haggard.
And so farewell, Signor Lucentio.
Kindness in women, not their beauteous looks,
Shall win my love; and so I take my leave,
In resolution as I swore before.   *Exit.*

TRANIO   Mistress Bianca, bless you with such grace
As 'longeth to a lover's blessed case!
Nay, I have ta'en you napping, gentle love,
And have forsworn you with Hortensio.

BIANCA

Tranio, you jest. But have you both forsworn me?

TRANIO   Mistress, we have.

LUCENTIO   Then we are rid of Litio.

TRANIO   I'faith, he'll have a lusty widow now,
That shall be woo'd and wedded in a day.

BIANCA   God give him joy.

TRANIO   Ay, and he'll tame her.

BIANCA   He says so, Tranio.

TRANIO   Faith, he is gone unto the taming-school.

BIANCA

The taming-school? What, is there such a place?

TRANIO   Ay, mistress, and Petruchio is the master,
That teacheth tricks eleven and twenty long,

To tame a shrew and charm her chattering tongue.

Enter BIONDELLO.

BIONDELLO   O master, master, I have watch'd so long
That I am dog-weary, but at last I spied   60
An ancient angel coming down the hill
Will serve the turn.

TRANIO   What is he, Biondello?

BIONDELLO   Master, a mercatante, or a pedant,
I know not what; but formal in apparel,
In gait and countenance surely like a father.   65

LUCENTIO   And what of him, Tranio?

TRANIO   If he be credulous and trust my tale,
I'll make him glad to seem Vincentio,
And give assurance to Baptista Minola
As if he were the right Vincentio.   70
Take in your love, and then let me alone.

Exeunt Lucentio and Bianca.

Enter a Pedant.

PEDANT   God save you, sir.

TRANIO   And you, sir. You are welcome.
Travel you far on, or are you at the farthest?

PEDANT   Sir, at the farthest for a week or two,
But then up farther, and as far as Rome,   75
And so to Tripoli, if God lend me life.

TRANIO   What countryman, I pray?

PEDANT   Of Mantua.

TRANIO   Of Mantua, sir? Marry, God forbid!
And come to Padua, careless of your life?

PEDANT   My life, sir? How, I pray? For that goes hard.   80

TRANIO   'Tis death for any one in Mantua
To come to Padua. Know you not the cause?
Your ships are stay'd at Venice, and the Duke,
For private quarrel 'twixt your Duke and him,
Hath publish'd and proclaim'd it openly.   85
'Tis marvel, but that you are but newly come,
You might have heard it else proclaim'd about.

PEDANT   Alas, sir, it is worse for me than so!
For I have bills for money by exchange
From Florence, and must here deliver them.   90

TRANIO   Well, sir, to do you courtesy,
This will I do, and this I will advise you:
First tell me, have you ever been at Pisa?

PEDANT   Ay, sir, in Pisa have I often been,
Pisa renowned for grave citizens.   95

TRANIO   Among them know you one Vincentio?

PEDANT   I know him not, but I have heard of him,
A merchant of incomparable wealth.

TRANIO   He is my father, sir, and sooth to say,
In countenance somewhat doth resemble you.   100

BIONDELLO [*aside*]

As much as an apple doth an oyster, and all one.

TRANIO   To save your life in this extremity,
This favour will I do you for his sake,
And think it not the worst of all your fortunes
That you are like to Sir Vincentio: 105

His name and credit shall you undertake,
And in my house you shall be friendly lodg'd.
Look that you take upon you as you should.
You understand me, sir. So shall you stay
110 Till you have done your business in the city.
If this be courtesy, sir, accept of it.
PEDANT O sir, I do, and will repute you ever
The patron of my life and liberty.
TRANIO Then go with me to make the matter good.
115 This, by the way, I let you understand;
My father is here look'd for every day
To pass assurance of a dower in marriage
'Twixt me and one Baptista's daughter here.
In all these circumstances I'll instruct you.
120 Go with me to clothe you as becomes you. *Exeunt.*

4.3 *Enter* KATHERINA *and* GRUMIO.

GRUMIO No, no, forsooth, I dare not for my life.
KATHERINA
The more my wrong, the more his spite appears.
What, did he marry me to famish me?
Beggars that come unto my father's door
5 Upon entreaty have a present alms,
If not, elsewhere they meet with charity.
But I, who never knew how to entreat,
Nor never needed that I should entreat,
Am starv'd for meat, giddy for lack of sleep,
10 With oaths kept waking, and with brawling fed.
And that which spites me more than all these wants,
He does it under name of perfect love,
As who should say, if I should sleep or eat,
'Twere deadly sickness or else present death.
15 I prithee go and get me some repast,
I care not what, so it be wholesome food.
GRUMIO What say you to a neat's foot?
KATHERINA 'Tis passing good, I prithee let me have it.
GRUMIO I fear it is too choleric a meat.
20 How say you to a fat tripe finely broil'd?
KATHERINA I like it well. Good Grumio, fetch it me.
GRUMIO I cannot tell, I fear 'tis choleric.
What say you to a piece of beef and mustard?
KATHERINA A dish that I do love to feed upon.
25 GRUMIO Ay, but the mustard is too hot a little.
KATHERINA
Why then, the beef, and let the mustard rest.
GRUMIO
Nay then, I will not. You shall have the mustard,
Or else you get no beef of Grumio.
KATHERINA Then both, or one, or anything thou wilt.
30 GRUMIO Why then, the mustard without the beef.
KATHERINA
Go, get thee gone, thou false deluding slave,
[*Beats him.*]
That feed'st me with the very name of meat.
Sorrow on thee and all the pack of you
That triumph thus upon my misery!

Go, get thee gone, I say. 35

Enter PETRUCHIO *and* HORTENSIO, *with meat.*

PETRUCHIO
How fares my Kate? What, sweeting, all amort?
HORTENSIO Mistress, what cheer?
KATHERINA   Faith, as cold as can be.
PETRUCHIO
Pluck up thy spirits, look cheerfully upon me.
Here, love, thou seest how diligent I am
To dress thy meat myself and bring it thee. 40
I am sure, sweet Kate, this kindness merits thanks.
What, not a word? Nay then, thou lov'st it not,
And all my pains is sorted to no proof.
Here, take away this dish.
KATHERINA   I pray you, let it stand.
PETRUCHIO The poorest service is repaid with thanks, 45
And so shall mine before you touch the meat.
KATHERINA I thank you, sir.
HORTENSIO Signor Petruchio, fie! You are to blame.
Come, Mistress Kate, I'll bear you company.
PETRUCHIO [*aside*]
Eat it up all, Hortensio, if thou lov'st me. – 50
Much good do it unto thy gentle heart.
Kate, eat apace. And now, my honey love,
We will return unto thy father's house,
And revel it as bravely as the best,
With silken coats and caps, and golden rings, 55
With ruffs and cuffs and farthingales and things,
With scarfs and fans, and double change of bravery,
With amber bracelets, beads, and all this knavery.
What, hast thou din'd? The tailor stays thy leisure,
To deck thy body with his ruffling treasure. 60

Enter Tailor.

Come, tailor, let us see these ornaments.
Lay forth the gown.

Enter Haberdasher.

              What news with you, sir?
HABERDASHER
Here is the cap your worship did bespeak.
PETRUCHIO Why, this was moulded on a porringer!
A velvet dish! Fie, fie! 'Tis lewd and filthy. 65
Why, 'tis a cockle or a walnut-shell,
A knack, a toy, a trick, a baby's cap.
Away with it! Come, let me have a bigger.
KATHERINA I'll have no bigger. This doth fit the time,
And gentlewomen wear such caps as these. 70
PETRUCHIO
When you are gentle, you shall have one too,
And not till then.
HORTENSIO [*aside*] That will not be in haste.
KATHERINA Why, sir, I trust I may have leave to speak,
And speak I will. I am no child, no babe.
Your betters have endur'd me say my mind, 75
And if you cannot, best you stop your ears.

My tongue will tell the anger of my heart,
Or else my heart concealing it will break,
And rather than it shall, I will be free
Even to the uttermost, as I please, in words.

PETRUCHIO   Why, thou say'st true. It is a paltry cap,
A custard-coffin, a bauble, a silken pie.
I love thee well in that thou lik'st it not.

KATHERINA   Love me or love me not, I like the cap,
And it I will have, or I will have none.

PETRUCHIO
Thy gown? Why, ay. Come, tailor, let us see't.

                 Exit Haberdasher.

O mercy, God! What masquing stuff is here?
What's this? A sleeve? 'Tis like a demi-cannon.
What, up and down, carv'd like an apple tart?
Here's snip and nip and cut and slish and slash,
Like to a censer in a barber's shop.
Why, what a devil's name, tailor, call'st thou this?

HORTENSIO [*aside*]
I see she's like to have neither cap nor gown.

TAILOR   You bid me make it orderly and well,
According to the fashion and the time.

PETRUCHIO   Marry, and did. But if you be remember'd,
I did not bid you mar it to the time.
Go, hop me over every kennel home,
For you shall hop without my custom, sir.
I'll none of it. Hence, make your best of it.

KATHERINA   I never saw a better-fashion'd gown,
More quaint, more pleasing, nor more commendable.
Belike you mean to make a puppet of me.

PETRUCHIO
Why, true, he means to make a puppet of thee.

TAILOR   She says your worship means to make a puppet
of her.

PETRUCHIO
O monstrous arrogance! Thou liest, thou thread, thou
    thimble,
Thou yard, three-quarters, half-yard, quarter, nail,
Thou flea, thou nit, thou winter-cricket thou!
Brav'd in mine own house with a skein of thread?
Away, thou rag, thou quantity, thou remnant,
Or I shall so bemete thee with thy yard
As thou shalt think on prating whilst thou liv'st.
I tell thee, I, that thou hast marr'd her gown.

TAILOR   Your worship is deceiv'd; the gown is made
Just as my master had direction.
Grumio gave order how it should be done.

GRUMIO   I gave him no order, I gave him the stuff.

TAILOR   But how did you desire it should be made?

GRUMIO   Marry, sir, with needle and thread.

TAILOR   But did you not request to have it cut?

GRUMIO   Thou hast faced many things.

TAILOR   I have.

GRUMIO   Face not me. Thou hast braved many men,
brave not me. I will neither be faced nor braved. I say
unto thee, I bid thy master cut out the gown, but I did

not bid him cut it to pieces. Ergo, thou liest.

TAILOR   Why, here is the note of the fashion to testify.

PETRUCHIO   Read it.

GRUMIO   The note lies in's throat if he say I said so.   130

TAILOR [*Reads.*]   *Imprimis, a loose-bodied gown.*

GRUMIO   Master, if ever I said loose-bodied gown, sew
me in the skirts of it, and beat me to death with a
bottom of brown thread. I said a gown.

PETRUCHIO   Proceed.   135

TAILOR   *With a small compassed cape.*

GRUMIO   I confess the cape.

TAILOR   *With a trunk sleeve.*

GRUMIO   I confess two sleeves.

TAILOR   *The sleeves curiously cut.*   140

PETRUCHIO   Ay, there's the villainy.

GRUMIO   Error i'th' bill, sir, error i'th' bill! I
commanded the sleeves should be cut out, and sewed
up again; and that I'll prove upon thee, though thy
little finger be armed in a thimble.   145

TAILOR   This is true that I say; and I had thee in place
where, thou shouldst know it.

GRUMIO   I am for thee straight. Take thou the bill, give
me thy mete-yard, and spare not me.

HORTENSIO   God-a-mercy, Grumio, then he shall have   150
no odds.

PETRUCHIO   Well sir, in brief, the gown is not for me.

GRUMIO   You are i'th' right, sir, 'tis for my mistress.

PETRUCHIO   Go, take it up unto thy master's use.

GRUMIO   Villain, not for thy life! Take up my mistress'   155
gown for thy master's use!

PETRUCHIO   Why sir, what's your conceit in that?

GRUMIO   O sir, the conceit is deeper than you think for.
Take up my mistress' gown to his master's use! O fie,
fie, fie!   160

PETRUCHIO [*aside*]   Hortensio, say thou wilt see the
tailor paid. – Go take it hence, be gone, and say no
more.

HORTENSIO [*aside*]
Tailor, I'll pay thee for thy gown tomorrow.
Take no unkindness of his hasty words.   165
Away, I say, commend me to thy master.   *Exit Tailor.*

PETRUCHIO
Well, come, my Kate, we will unto your father's
Even in these honest mean habiliments.
Our purses shall be proud, our garments poor,
For 'tis the mind that makes the body rich,   170
And as the sun breaks through the darkest clouds,
So honour peereth in the meanest habit.
What, is the jay more precious than the lark
Because his feathers are more beautiful?
Or is the adder better than the eel   175
Because his painted skin contents the eye?
O no, good Kate; neither art thou the worse
For this poor furniture and mean array.
If thou account'st it shame, lay it on me.
And therefore frolic. We will hence forthwith,   180

To feast and sport us at thy father's house.
[*to Grumio*] Go call my men, and let us straight to
                him;
And bring our horses unto Long-lane end,
There will we mount, and thither walk on foot.
185   Let's see, I think 'tis now some seven o'clock,
And well we may come there by dinner-time.
KATHERINA   I dare assure you, sir, 'tis almost two,
And 'twill be supper-time ere you come there.
PETRUCHIO   It shall be seven ere I go to horse.
190   Look what I speak, or do, or think to do,
You are still crossing it. Sirs, let 't alone,
I will not go today, and ere I do,
It shall be what o'clock I say it is.
HORTENSIO
Why, so this gallant will command the sun.   *Exeunt.*

4.4   *Enter* TRANIO, *and the* Pedant *dressed like*
                    VINCENTIO.

TRANIO   Sir, this is the house. Please it you that I call?
PEDANT   Ay, what else? And but I be deceiv'd
Signor Baptista may remember me
Near twenty years ago in Genoa,
5   Where we were lodgers at the Pegasus.
TRANIO   'Tis well, and hold your own, in any case,
With such austerity as 'longeth to a father.
PEDANT   I warrant you.

                    Enter BIONDELLO.

                    But sir, here comes your boy.
'Twere good he were school'd.
10   TRANIO   Fear you not him. Sirrah Biondello,
Now do your duty thoroughly, I advise you.
Imagine 'twere the right Vincentio.
BIONDELLO   Tut, fear not me.
TRANIO   But hast thou done thy errand to Baptista?
15   BIONDELLO   I told him that your father was at Venice,
And that you look'd for him this day in Padua.
TRANIO   Th'art a tall fellow. Hold thee that to drink.
Here comes Baptista. Set your countenance, sir.

                    Enter BAPTISTA *and* LUCENTIO.

Signor Baptista, you are happily met. –
20   Sir, this is the gentleman I told you of.
I pray you stand good father to me now,
Give me Bianca for my patrimony.
PEDANT   Soft, son.
Sir, by your leave, having come to Padua
25   To gather in some debts, my son Lucentio
Made me acquainted with a weighty cause
Of love between your daughter and himself.
And, for the good report I hear of you,
And for the love he beareth to your daughter,
30   And she to him, to stay him not too long,
I am content, in a good father's care,
To have him match'd; and, if you please to like

No worse than I, upon some agreement
Me shall you find ready and willing
With one consent to have her so bestow'd.   35
For curious I cannot be with you,
Signor Baptista, of whom I hear so well.
BAPTISTA   Sir, pardon me in what I have to say.
Your plainness and your shortness please me well.
Right true it is your son Lucentio here   40
Doth love my daughter, and she loveth him,
Or both dissemble deeply their affections.
And therefore if you say no more than this,
That like a father you will deal with him,
And pass my daughter a sufficient dower,   45
The match is made, and all is done,
Your son shall have my daughter with consent.
TRANIO   I thank you, sir. Where then do you know best
We be affied and such assurance ta'en
As shall with either part's agreement stand?   50
BAPTISTA   Not in my house, Lucentio, for you know
Pitchers have ears, and I have many servants.
Besides, old Gremio is hearkening still,
And happily we might be interrupted.
TRANIO   Then at my lodging, and it like you.   55
There doth my father lie; and there this night
We'll pass the business privately and well.
Send for your daughter by your servant here.
My boy shall fetch the scrivener presently.
The worst is this, that at so slender warning   60
You are like to have a thin and slender pittance.
BAPTISTA   It likes me well. Cambio, hie you home,
And bid Bianca make her ready straight.
And, if you will, tell what hath happened:
Lucentio's father is arriv'd in Padua,   65
And how she's like to be Lucentio's wife.
                                    Exit Lucentio.
BIONDELLO   I pray the gods she may with all my heart.
TRANIO   Dally not with the gods, but get thee gone.
                                    Exit Biondello.

                    Enter PETER, *a servingman.*

Signor Baptista, shall I lead the way?
Welcome. One mess is like to be your cheer.   70
Come sir, we will better it in Pisa.
BAPTISTA   I follow you.   *Exeunt.*

                    Enter LUCENTIO *and* BIONDELLO.

BIONDELLO   Cambio.
LUCENTIO   What sayest thou, Biondello?
BIONDELLO   You saw my master wink and laugh upon
you?   75
LUCENTIO   Biondello, what of that?
BIONDELLO   Faith, nothing. But 'has left me here
behind to expound the meaning or moral of his signs
and tokens.
LUCENTIO   I pray thee moralize them.   80
BIONDELLO   Then thus: Baptista is safe, talking with the
deceiving father of a deceitful son.

LUCENTIO   And what of him?

BIONDELLO   His daughter is to be brought by you to the supper.

LUCENTIO   And then?

BIONDELLO   The old priest at Saint Luke's church is at your command at all hours.

LUCENTIO   And what of all this?

BIONDELLO   I cannot tell, except they are busied about a counterfeit assurance. Take you assurance of her, *cum privilegio ad imprimendum solum*. To th' church! Take the priest, clerk, and some sufficient honest witnesses. If this be not that you look for, I have no more to say, But bid Bianca farewell for ever and a day.

LUCENTIO   Hear'st thou, Biondello –

BIONDELLO   I cannot tarry. I knew a wench married in an afternoon as she went to the garden for parsley to stuff a rabbit. And so may you, sir; and so adieu, sir. My master hath appointed me to go to Saint Luke's, to bid the priest be ready to come against you come with your appendix.   *Exit.*

LUCENTIO   I may and will, if she be so contented.
She will be pleas'd, then wherefore should I doubt?
Hap what hap may, I'll roundly go about her:
It shall go hard if Cambio go without her.   *Exit.*

4.5   *Enter* PETRUCHIO, KATHERINA, HORTENSIO *and servants.*

PETRUCHIO
Come on, a God's name, once more toward our
   father's.
Good Lord, how bright and goodly shines the moon!

KATHERINA
The moon? The sun! It is not moonlight now.

PETRUCHIO   I say it is the moon that shines so bright.

KATHERINA   I know it is the sun that shines so bright.

PETRUCHIO
Now by my mother's son, and that's myself,
It shall be moon, or star, or what I list,
Or e'er I journey to your father's house. –
[*to servants*] Go on, and fetch our horses back
   again. –
Evermore cross'd and cross'd, nothing but cross'd.

HORTENSIO   Say as he says, or we shall never go.

KATHERINA   Forward, I pray, since we have come so far,
And be it moon, or sun, or what you please.
And if you please to call it a rush-candle,
Henceforth I vow it shall be so for me.

PETRUCHIO   I say it is the moon.

KATHERINA   I know it is the moon.

PETRUCHIO   Nay, then you lie. It is the blessed sun.

KATHERINA   Then, God be blest, it is the blessed sun.
But sun it is not, when you say it is not,
And the moon changes even as your mind.
What you will have it nam'd, even that it is,
And so it shall be so for Katherine.

HORTENSIO   Petruchio, go thy ways, the field is won.

PETRUCHIO
Well forward, forward. Thus the bowl should run,
And not unluckily against the bias.   25
But soft, company is coming here.

Enter VINCENTIO.

[*to Vincentio*] Good morrow, gentle mistress, where
   away?
Tell me, sweet Kate, and tell me truly too,
Hast thou beheld a fresher gentlewoman?
Such war of white and red within her cheeks!   30
What stars do spangle heaven with such beauty
As those two eyes become that heavenly face?
Fair lovely maid, once more good day to thee.
Sweet Kate, embrace her for her beauty's sake.

HORTENSIO
'A will make the man mad, to make the woman of
   him.   35

KATHERINA
Young budding virgin, fair, and fresh, and sweet,
Whither away, or where is thy abode?
Happy the parents of so fair a child,
Happier the man whom favourable stars
Allots thee for his lovely bedfellow.   40

PETRUCHIO
Why, how now, Kate, I hope thou art not mad.
This is a man, old, wrinkled, faded, wither'd,
And not a maiden, as thou say'st he is.

KATHERINA   Pardon, old father, my mistaking eyes,
That have been so bedazzled with the sun   45
That everything I look on seemeth green.
Now I perceive thou art a reverend father.
Pardon, I pray thee, for my mad mistaking.

PETRUCHIO
Do, good old grandsire, and withal make known
Which way thou travellest: if along with us,   50
We shall be joyful of thy company.

VINCENTIO   Fair sir, and you my merry mistress,
That with your strange encounter much amaz'd me,
My name is call'd Vincentio, my dwelling Pisa,
And bound I am to Padua, there to visit   55
A son of mine, which long I have not seen.

PETRUCHIO   What is his name?

VINCENTIO   Lucentio, gentle sir.

PETRUCHIO   Happily met; the happier for thy son.
And now by law, as well as reverend age,
I may entitle thee my loving father.   60
The sister to my wife, this gentlewoman,
Thy son by this hath married. Wonder not,
Nor be not griev'd, she is of good esteem,
Her dowry wealthy, and of worthy birth;
Beside, so qualified as may beseem   65
The spouse of any noble gentleman.
Let me embrace with old Vincentio,
And wander we to see thy honest son,
Who will of thy arrival be full joyous.

VINCENTIO   But is this true, or is it else your pleasure, 70

Like pleasant travellers, to break a jest
Upon the company you overtake?

HORTENSIO   I do assure thee, father, so it is.

PETRUCHIO   Come, go along and see the truth hereof,
75   For our first merriment hath made thee jealous.

Exeunt all but Hortensio.

HORTENSIO   Well, Petruchio, this has put me in heart.
Have to my widow! And if she be froward,
Then hast thou taught Hortensio to be untoward.

Exit.

5.1   *Enter* BIONDELLO, LUCENTIO *and* BIANCA.
GREMIO is out before.

BIONDELLO   Softly and swiftly, sir, for the priest is
ready.

LUCENTIO   I fly, Biondello. But they may chance to need
thee at home, therefore leave us.   *Exit with Bianca.*

5   BIONDELLO   Nay, faith, I'll see the church a' your back,
and then come back to my master's as soon as I can.

Exit.

GREMIO   I marvel Cambio comes not all this while.

Enter PETRUCHIO, KATHERINA, VINCENTIO, GRUMIO, *with
attendants.*

PETRUCHIO
Sir, here's the door, this is Lucentio's house.
My father's bears more toward the market-place.
10   Thither must I, and here I leave you, sir.

VINCENTIO
You shall not choose but drink before you go.
I think I shall command your welcome here,
And by all likelihood some cheer is toward. [*Knocks.*]

GREMIO
They're busy within. You were best knock louder.

Pedant looks out of the window.

15   PEDANT   What's he that knocks as he would beat down
the gate?

VINCENTIO   Is Signor Lucentio within, sir?

PEDANT   He's within, sir, but not to be spoken withal.

VINCENTIO   What if a man bring him a hundred pound
20   or two to make merry withal?

PEDANT   Keep your hundred pounds to yourself. He
shall need none so long as I live.

PETRUCHIO   Nay, I told you your son was well beloved in
Padua. Do you hear, sir? To leave frivolous
25   circumstances, I pray you tell Signor Lucentio that his
father is come from Pisa, and is here at the door to
speak with him.

PEDANT   Thou liest. His father is come from Mantua,
and here looking out at the window.

30   VINCENTIO   Art thou his father?

PEDANT   Ay, sir, so his mother says, if I may believe her.

PETRUCHIO [*to Vincentio*]   Why, how now, gentleman!
Why, this is flat knavery, to take upon you another
man's name.

PEDANT   Lay hands on the villain. I believe a means to   35
cozen somebody in this city under my countenance.

Enter BIONDELLO.

BIONDELLO   I have seen them in the church together.
God send 'em good shipping! But who is here? Mine
old master Vincentio! Now we are undone and
brought to nothing.   40

VINCENTIO [*to Biondello*]   Come hither, crack-hemp.

BIONDELLO   I hope I may choose, sir.

VINCENTIO   Come hither, you rogue. What, have you
forgot me?

BIONDELLO   Forgot you? No, sir. I could not forget you,   45
for I never saw you before in all my life.

VINCENTIO   What, you notorious villain, didst thou
never see thy master's father, Vincentio?

BIONDELLO   What, my old worshipful old master? Yes,
marry, sir. See where he looks out of the window.   50

VINCENTIO   Is't so, indeed? [*He beats Biondello.*]

BIONDELLO   Help, help, help! Here's a madman will
murder me.   *Exit.*

PEDANT   Help, son! Help, Signor Baptista!

Exit from the window.

PETRUCHIO   Prithee, Kate, let's stand aside and see the   55
end of this controversy.

Enter Pedant *with servants,* BAPTISTA, TRANIO.

TRANIO   Sir, what are you that offer to beat my servant?

VINCENTIO   What am I, sir? Nay, what are you, sir? O
immortal   gods! O fine villain! A silken doublet, a
velvet hose, a scarlet cloak, and a copatain hat! O, I am   60
undone, I am undone! While I play the good husband
at home, my son and my servant spend all at the
university.

TRANIO   How now, what's the matter?

BAPTISTA   What, is the man lunatic?   65

TRANIO   Sir, you seem a sober ancient gentleman by
your habit, but your words show you a madman. Why,
sir, what 'cerns it you if I wear pearl and gold? I
thank my good father, I am able to maintain it.

VINCENTIO   Thy father? O villain! He is a sail-maker in   70
Bergamo.

BAPTISTA   You mistake, sir, you mistake, sir. Pray, what
do you think is his name?

VINCENTIO   His name? As if I knew not his name! I have
brought him up ever since he was three years old, and   75
his name is Tranio.

PEDANT   Away, away, mad ass! His name is Lucentio,
and he is mine only son, and heir to the lands of me,
Signor Vincentio.

VINCENTIO   Lucentio? O, he hath murdered his master!   80
Lay hold on him, I charge you, in the Duke's name. O,
my son, my son! Tell me, thou villain, where is my
son Lucentio?

TRANIO   Call forth an officer.

Enter an officer.

Carry this mad knave to the gaol. Father Baptista, I
charge you see that he be forthcoming.

VINCENTIO   Carry me to the gaol?

GREMIO   Stay, officer. He shall not go to prison.

BAPTISTA   Talk not, Signor Gremio. I say he shall go to
prison.

GREMIO   Take heed, Signor Baptista, lest you be cony-
catched in this business. I dare swear this is the right
Vincentio.

PEDANT   Swear, if thou dar'st.

GREMIO   Nay, I dare not swear it.

TRANIO   Then thou wert best say that I am not
Lucentio.

GREMIO   Yes, I know thee to be Signor Lucentio.

BAPTISTA   Away with the dotard, to the gaol with him!

VINCENTIO   Thus strangers may be haled and abused. O
monstrous villain!

Enter BIONDELLO, LUCENTIO *and* BIANCA.

BIONDELLO   O, we are spoiled, and yonder he is. Deny
him, forswear him, or else we are all undone.

LUCENTIO [*Kneels.*]   Pardon, sweet father.

VINCENTIO   Lives my sweet son?

Exeunt Biondello, Tranio and Pedant, as fast as may be.

BIANCA   Pardon, dear father.

BAPTISTA   How hast thou offended?
Where is Lucentio?

LUCENTIO   Here's Lucentio,
Right son to the right Vincentio,
That have by marriage made thy daughter mine,
While counterfeit supposes blear'd thine eyne.

GREMIO
Here's packing, with a witness, to deceive us all.

VINCENTIO   Where is that damned villain Tranio,
That fac'd and brav'd me in this matter so?

BAPTISTA   Why, tell me, is not this my Cambio?

BIANCA   Cambio is chang'd into Lucentio.

LUCENTIO   Love wrought these miracles. Bianca's love
Made me exchange my state with Tranio,
While he did bear my countenance in the town,
And happily I have arriv'd at the last
Unto the wished haven of my bliss.
What Tranio did, myself enforc'd him to;
Then pardon him, sweet father, for my sake.

VINCENTIO   I'll slit the villain's nose that would have
sent me to the gaol.

BAPTISTA   But do you hear, sir? Have you married my
daughter without asking my good will?

VINCENTIO   Fear not, Baptista, we will content you, go
to. But I will in, to be revenged for this villainy. *Exit.*

BAPTISTA   And I, to sound the depth of this knavery.
                                                        Exit.

LUCENTIO
Look not pale, Bianca; thy father will not frown.
                        Exeunt Lucentio and Bianca.

GREMIO
My cake is dough, but I'll in among the rest,   130
Out of hope of all, but my share of the feast.   *Exit.*

KATHERINA
Husband, let's follow to see the end of this ado.

PETRUCHIO   First kiss me, Kate, and we will.

KATHERINA   What, in the midst of the street?

PETRUCHIO   What, art thou ashamed of me?   135

KATHERINA   No, sir, God forbid; but ashamed to kiss.

PETRUCHIO
Why, then, let's home again. Come, sirrah, let's away.

KATHERINA
Nay, I will give thee a kiss. Now pray thee, love, stay.

PETRUCHIO   Is not this well? Come, my sweet Kate.
Better once than never, for never too late.   *Exeunt.*   140

5.2   *Enter* BAPTISTA, VINCENTIO, GREMIO, *the*
Pedant, LUCENTIO *and* BIANCA, PETRUCHIO *and*
KATHERINA, HORTENSIO *and* Widow; *the servingmen,*
with TRANIO, BIONDELLO, GRUMIO, *bringing in a banquet.*

LUCENTIO
At last, though long, our jarring notes agree,
And time it is, when raging war is done,
To smile at scapes and perils overblown.
My fair Bianca, bid my father welcome,
While I with self-same kindness welcome thine.   5
Brother Petruchio, sister Katherina,
And thou, Hortensio, with thy loving widow,
Feast with the best, and welcome to my house.
My banquet is to close our stomachs up
After our great good cheer. Pray you, sit down,   10
For now we sit to chat as well as eat.

PETRUCHIO   Nothing but sit and sit, and eat and eat!

BAPTISTA   Padua affords this kindness, son Petruchio.

PETRUCHIO   Padua affords nothing but what is kind.

HORTENSIO
For both our sakes I would that word were true.   15

PETRUCHIO
Now, for my life, Hortensio fears his widow.

WIDOW   Then never trust me if I be afeard.

PETRUCHIO
You are very sensible, and yet you miss my sense.
I mean Hortensio is afeard of you.

WIDOW   He that is giddy thinks the world turns round.   20

PETRUCHIO   Roundly replied.

KATHERINA   Mistress, how mean you that?

WIDOW   Thus I conceive by him.

PETRUCHIO
Conceives by me! How likes Hortensio that?

HORTENSIO
My widow says thus she conceives her tale.

PETRUCHIO
Very well mended. Kiss him for that, good widow.   25

KATHERINA
'He that is giddy thinks the world turns round' –
I pray you tell me what you meant by that.

WIDOW   Your husband, being troubled with a shrew,
   Measures my husband's sorrow by his woe.
30   And now you know my meaning.
KATHERINA   A very mean meaning.
WIDOW   Right, I mean you.
KATHERINA   And I am mean, indeed, respecting you.
PETRUCHIO   To her, Kate!
HORTENSIO   To her, widow!
PETRUCHIO
35   A hundred marks, my Kate does put her down.
HORTENSIO   That's my office.
PETRUCHIO   Spoke like an officer. Ha' to thee, lad.
   [*Drinks to Hortensio.*]
BAPTISTA   How likes Gremio these quick-witted folks?
GREMIO   Believe me, sir, they butt together well.
40 BIANCA   Head and butt! An hasty-witted body
   Would say your head and butt were head and horn.
VINCENTIO   Ay, mistress bride, hath that awaken'd you?
BIANCA
   Ay, but not frighted me, therefore I'll sleep again.
PETRUCHIO
   Nay, that you shall not. Since you have begun,
45   Have at you for a bitter jest or two.
BIANCA   Am I your bird? I mean to shift my bush,
   And then pursue me as you draw your bow.
   You are welcome all.
   Exeunt Bianca and Katherina and Widow.
PETRUCHIO
   She hath prevented me. Here, Signor Tranio,
50   This bird you aim'd at, though you hit her not;
   Therefore a health to all that shot and miss'd.
TRANIO   O sir, Lucentio slipp'd me like his greyhound,
   Which runs himself, and catches for his master.
PETRUCHIO
   A good swift simile, but something currish.
55 TRANIO   'Tis well, sir, that you hunted for yourself.
   'Tis thought your deer does hold you at a bay.
BAPTISTA   O, O, Petruchio! Tranio hits you now.
LUCENTIO   I thank thee for that gird, good Tranio.
HORTENSIO   Confess, confess, hath he not hit you here?
60 PETRUCHIO   'A has a little gall'd me, I confess;
   And as the jest did glance away from me,
   'Tis ten to one it maim'd you two outright.
BAPTISTA   Now, in good sadness, son Petruchio,
   I think thou hast the veriest shrew of all.
65 PETRUCHIO   Well, I say no. And therefore for assurance
   Let's each one send unto his wife,
   And he whose wife is most obedient,
   To come at first when he doth send for her,
   Shall win the wager which we will propose.
HORTENSIO   Content. What's the wager?
70 LUCENTIO   Twenty crowns.
PETRUCHIO   Twenty crowns?
   I'll venture so much of my hawk or hound,
   But twenty times so much upon my wife.
LUCENTIO   A hundred then.
HORTENSIO   Content.

PETRUCHIO   A match! 'Tis done.
HORTENSIO   Who shall begin? 75
LUCENTIO   That will I.
   Go, Biondello, bid your mistress come to me.
BIONDELLO   I go.   *Exit.*
BAPTISTA   Son, I'll be your half Bianca comes.
LUCENTIO   I'll have no halves. I'll bear it all myself. 80
   Enter BIONDELLO.
   How now, what news?
BIONDELLO   Sir, my mistress sends you word
   That she is busy and she cannot come.
PETRUCHIO   How? She's busy, and she cannot come?
   Is that an answer?
GREMIO   Ay, and a kind one too.
   Pray God, sir, your wife send you not a worse. 85
PETRUCHIO   I hope better.
HORTENSIO   Sirrah Biondello, go and entreat my wife
   To come to me forthwith.   *Exit Biondello.*
PETRUCHIO   O ho, entreat her!
   Nay, then she must needs come.
HORTENSIO   I am afraid, sir,
   Do what you can, yours will not be entreated. 90
   Enter BIONDELLO.
   Now, where's my wife?
BIONDELLO
   She says you have some goodly jest in hand.
   She will not come. She bids you come to her.
PETRUCHIO
   Worse and worse, she will not come! O vile,
   Intolerable, not to be endur'd! 95
   Sirrah Grumio, go to your mistress,
   Say I command her come to me.   *Exit Grumio.*
HORTENSIO   I know her answer.
PETRUCHIO   What?
HORTENSIO   She will not.
PETRUCHIO   The fouler fortune mine, and there an end.
   Enter KATHERINA.
BAPTISTA
   Now, by my holidame, here comes Katherina. 100
KATHERINA
   What is your will, sir, that you send for me?
PETRUCHIO   Where is your sister, and Hortensio's wife?
KATHERINA   They sit conferring by the parlour fire.
PETRUCHIO
   Go fetch them hither. If they deny to come,
   Swinge me them soundly forth unto their husbands. 105
   Away, I say, and bring them hither straight.
   Exit Katherina.
LUCENTIO   Here is a wonder, if you talk of a wonder.
HORTENSIO   And so it is. I wonder what it bodes.
PETRUCHIO
   Marry, peace it bodes, and love, and quiet life,
   An awful rule, and right supremacy, 110
   And, to be short, what not that's sweet and happy.

BAPTISTA   Now fair befall thee, good Petruchio!
    The wager thou hast won, and I will add
    Unto their losses twenty thousand crowns,
    Another dowry to another daughter,
    For she is chang'd, as she had never been.
PETRUCHIO   Nay, I will win my wager better yet,
    And show more sign of her obedience,
    Her new-built virtue and obedience.

            Enter KATHERINA, BIANCA *and* Widow.

    See where she comes, and brings your froward wives
    As prisoners to her womanly persuasion.
    Katherine, that cap of yours becomes you not.
    Off with that bauble, throw it under foot. [*She obeys.*]
WIDOW   Lord, let me never have a cause to sigh
    Till I be brought to such a silly pass.
BIANCA   Fie, what a foolish duty call you this?
LUCENTIO   I would your duty were as foolish too.
    The wisdom of your duty, fair Bianca,
    Hath cost me a hundred crowns since supper-time.
BIANCA   The more fool you for laying on my duty.
PETRUCHIO
    Katherine, I charge thee, tell these headstrong
        women
    What duty they do owe their lords and husbands.
WIDOW
    Come, come, you're mocking. We will have no telling.
PETRUCHIO   Come on, I say, and first begin with her.
WIDOW   She shall not.
PETRUCHIO   I say she shall. And first begin with her.
KATHERINA
    Fie, fie! Unknit that threatening unkind brow,
    And dart not scornful glances from those eyes,
    To wound thy lord, thy king, thy governor.
    It blots thy beauty as frosts do bite the meads,
    Confounds thy fame as whirlwinds shake fair buds,
    And in no sense is meet or amiable.
    A woman mov'd is like a fountain troubled,
    Muddy, ill-seeming, thick, bereft of beauty,
    And while it is so, none so dry or thirsty
    Will deign to sip or touch one drop of it.
    Thy husband is thy lord, thy life, thy keeper,
    Thy head, thy sovereign; one that cares for thee,
    And for thy maintenance; commits his body
    To painful labour both by sea and land,
    To watch the night in storms, the day in cold,
    Whilst thou liest warm at home, secure and safe;
    And craves no other tribute at thy hands
    But love, fair looks, and true obedience;
    Too little payment for so great a debt.
    Such duty as the subject owes the prince
    Even such a woman oweth to her husband.
    And when she is froward, peevish, sullen, sour,
    And not obedient to his honest will,
    What is she but a foul contending rebel,
    And graceless traitor to her loving lord?
    I am asham'd that women are so simple
    To offer war where they should kneel for peace,
    Or seek for rule, supremacy, and sway,
    When they are bound to serve, love, and obey.
    Why are our bodies soft, and weak, and smooth,
    Unapt to toil and trouble in the world,
    But that our soft conditions and our hearts
    Should well agree with our external parts?
    Come, come, you froward and unable worms,
    My mind hath been as big as one of yours,
    My heart as great, my reason haply more,
    To bandy word for word and frown for frown.
    But now I see our lances are but straws,
    Our strength as weak, our weakness past compare,
    That seeming to be most which we indeed least are.
    Then vail your stomachs, for it is no boot,
    And place your hands below your husband's foot.
    In token of which duty, if he please,
    My hand is ready, may it do him ease.
PETRUCHIO
    Why, there's a wench! Come on, and kiss me, Kate.
LUCENTIO
    Well, go thy ways, old lad, for thou shalt ha't.
VINCENTIO
    'Tis a good hearing, when children are toward.
LUCENTIO
    But a harsh hearing, when women are froward.
PETRUCHIO   Come, Kate, we'll to bed.
    We three are married, but you two are sped.
    [*to Lucentio*] 'Twas I won the wager, though you hit
        the white,
    And being a winner, God give you good night!
            Exeunt Petruchio and Katherina.
HORTENSIO
    Now go thy ways, thou hast tam'd a curst shrew.
LUCENTIO
    'Tis a wonder, by your leave, she will be tam'd so.
            Exeunt.

The Tempest

The Tempest was printed as the first comedy, and consequently the first play, in the Folio of 1623. It may have been granted such prominence as the last non-collaborative play Shakespeare wrote, but it must in any event have been highly regarded by the publishers of the Folio, and by his former colleagues John Hemmings and Henry Condell, who vouched for the authority and completeness of the volume, to appear first in it. Its full, descriptive stage directions may have been amplified by the scribe Ralph Crane, who transcribed the manuscript copy used by the printer. Its date of composition is fixed as 1610–11 by a performance at Court on 1 November 1611 and by its use of William Strachey's account (dated from Virginia on 15 July 1610 and known to have reached London no earlier than September) of the shipwreck of Sir William Somers on Bermuda in the summer of 1609. The play may have been designed for the Blackfriars playhouse, but no record of performance there or at the Globe has survived.

Like other plays from *Hamlet* onwards, *The Tempest* reflects Shakespeare's knowledge of the *Essays* of Montaigne, in John Florio's English version (1602). The essay 'Of the Cannibals' underlies Gonzalo's vision of an ideal commonwealth, raises questions about the distinction between civilization and barbarism and probably suggested Caliban's name. Virgil's *Aeneid* is a further influence, while Prospero's renunciation of magic, 5.1.33–57, is closely modelled on Medea's invocation in Ovid's *Metamorphoses*, 7.179–219.

The Tempest, in which Shakespeare observed the unities of place and time for the first time since *The Comedy of Errors*, is a work of synthesis and retrospection. The controlling role of Prospero may recall the Duke in *Measure for Measure*, who also prefers forgiveness to vindictive justice at the end. His magic harks back to Oberon in *A Midsummer Night's Dream*, just as Ariel's role recalls that of Puck. Its presentation of the pursuit of political power is equally reminiscent of the English histories and political tragedies. Stephano is the last, and most sinister, of Shakespeare's comic drunkards.

The Tempest was among the first of Shakespeare's plays to be adapted for the changed theatrical conditions of the Restoration. The version of it by Dryden and Davenant (1667) supplied it with a busier action, which introduced sisters for Miranda and Caliban, a female counterpart for Ariel, and Hippolyto, a man who has never seen a woman (a travesty role for an actress). The dreamlike quality of its action and the mythic symmetries of its cast have led to a wide and increasingly various array of interpretations of *The Tempest*. Nineteenth-century interest found its focus in Prospero, who was increasingly identified with Shakespeare; in the late twentieth century, attention has shifted towards Caliban and colonialism, or towards Miranda and the oppressions of patriarchy. The play has inspired many later literary and musical compositions, among them Hector Berlioz's symphonic fantasy *Lélio* (1832), Robert Browning's 'Caliban upon Setebos' (1864), Jean Sibelius's incidental music for the play, W. H. Auden's *The Sea and the Mirror* (1944) and Sir Michael Tippett's opera *The Knot Garden* (1969).

The Arden text is based on the 1623 First Folio.

LIST OF ROLES

ALONSO	*King of Naples*
SEBASTIAN	*his brother*
PROSPERO	*the right Duke of Milan*
ANTONIO	*his brother, the usurping Duke of Milan*
FERDINAND	*son to the King of Naples*
GONZALO	*an honest old councellor*
ADRIAN *and* FRANCISCO	*lords*
CALIBAN	*a salvage and deformed slave*
TRINCULO	*a jester*
STEPHANO	*a drunken butler*
MASTER	
BOATSWAIN	*of a ship*
MARINERS	
MIRANDA	*daughter to Prospero*
ARIEL	*an airy spirit*
IRIS	
CERES	
JUNO	*spirits*
NYMPHS	
REAPERS	

1.1 *Enter a* Ship-Master *and a* Boatswain.

MASTER   Boatswain!

BOATSWAIN   Here, master: what cheer?

MASTER   Good: speak to th' mariners: fall to't, yarely, or we run ourselves aground: bestir, bestir.   *Exit.*

Enter mariners.

BOATSWAIN   Heigh, my hearts! cheerly, cheerly, my hearts! yare, yare! Take in the topsail. Tend to th' master's whistle. Blow till thou burst thy wind, if room enough!

Enter ALONSO, SEBASTIAN, ANTONIO, FERDINAND, GONZALO *and others.*

ALONSO   Good boatswain, have care. Where's the master? Play the men.

BOATSWAIN   I pray now, keep below.

ANTONIO   Where is the master, boatswain?

BOATSWAIN   Do you not hear him? You mar our labour: keep your cabins: you do assist the storm.

GONZALO   Nay, good, be patient.

BOATSWAIN   When the sea is. Hence! What cares these roarers for the name of King? To cabin: silence! trouble us not.

GONZALO   Good, yet remember whom thou hast aboard.

BOATSWAIN   None that I more love than myself. You are a counsellor; if you can command these elements to silence, and work the peace of the presence, we will not hand a rope more; use your authority: if you cannot, give thanks you have lived so long, and make yourself ready in your cabin for the mischance of the hour, if it so hap. Cheerly, good hearts! Out of our way, I say.   *Exit.*

GONZALO   I have great comfort from this fellow: methinks he hath no drowning mark upon him; his complexion is perfect gallows. Stand fast, good Fate, to his hanging: make the rope of his destiny our cable, for our own doth little advantage. If he be not born to be hanged, our case is miserable.   *Exeunt.*

Re-enter Boatswain.

BOATSWAIN   Down with the topmast! yare! lower, lower! Bring her to try with main-course. [*a cry within*] A plague upon this howling! they are louder than the weather or our office.

Re-enter SEBASTIAN, ANTONIO *and* GONZALO.

Yet again! what do you here? Shall we give o'er, and drown? Have you a mind to sink?

SEBASTIAN   A pox o' your throat, you bawling, blasphemous, incharitable dog!

BOATSWAIN   Work you, then.

ANTONIO   Hang, cur! hang, you whoreson, insolent noisemaker. We are less afraid to be drowned than thou art.

GONZALO   I'll warrant him for drowning, though the ship were no stronger than a nutshell, and as leaky as an unstanched wench.

BOATSWAIN   Lay her a-hold, a-hold! set her two courses; off to sea again; lay her off.   50

Enter Mariners *wet.*

MARINERS   All lost, to prayers, to prayers! all lost!

BOATSWAIN   What, must our mouths be cold?

GONZALO
The King and Prince at prayers, let's assist them,
For our case is as theirs.

SEBASTIAN   I'm out of patience.

ANTONIO
We are merely cheated of our lives by drunkards: 55
This wide-chapp'd rascal, – would thou mightst lie drowning
The washing of ten tides!

GONZALO   He'll be hang'd yet,
Though every drop of water swear against it,
And gape at wid'st to glut him.
[*a confused noise within*]   'Mercy on us!' –
'We split, we split!' – 'Farewell, my wife and children!' –   60
'Farewell, brother!' – 'We split, we split, we split!'

ANTONIO   Let's all sink wi'th' King.

SEBASTIAN   Let's take leave of him.

Exeunt Antonio and Sebastian.

GONZALO   Now would I give a thousand furlongs of sea for an acre of barren ground, long heath, broom,   65 furze, anything. The wills above be done! but I would fain die a dry death.   *Exeunt.*

1.2   *Enter* PROSPERO *and* MIRANDA.

MIRANDA   If by your Art, my dearest father, you have
Put the wild waters in this roar, allay them.
The sky, it seems, would pour down stinking pitch,
But that the sea, mounting to th' welkin's cheek,
Dashes the fire out. O, I have suffered   5
With those that I saw suffer! a brave vessel,
(Who had, no doubt, some noble creature in her,)
Dash'd all to pieces. O, the cry did knock
Against my very heart! Poor souls, they perish'd!
Had I been any god of power, I would   10
Have sunk the sea within the earth, or ere
It should the good ship so have swallow'd, and
The fraughting souls within her.

PROSPERO   Be collected:
No more amazement: tell your piteous heart
There's no harm done.

MIRANDA   O, woe the day!

PROSPERO   No harm.   15
I have done nothing but in care of thee,
Of thee, my dear one; thee, my daughter, who
Art ignorant of what thou art; nought knowing
Of whence I am, nor that I am more better

20 Than Prospero, master of a full poor cell,
And thy no greater father.
MIRANDA   More to know
Did never meddle with my thoughts.
PROSPERO   'Tis time
I should inform thee farther. Lend thy hand,
And pluck my magic garment from me. – So:
[*Lays down his mantle.*]
Lie there, my Art. Wipe thou thine eyes; have
25   comfort.
The direful spectacle of the wrack, which touch'd
The very virtue of compassion in thee,
I have with such provision in mine Art
So safely ordered, that there is no soul –
30 No, not so much perdition as an hair
Betid to any creature in the vessel
Which thou heard'st cry, which thou saw'st sink.
        Sit down;
For thou must now know farther.
MIRANDA   You have often
Begun to tell me what I am, but stopp'd,
35 And left me to a bootless inquisition,
Concluding 'Stay: not yet.'
PROSPERO   The hour's now come;
The very minute bids thee ope thine ear;
Obey, and be attentive. Canst thou remember
A time before we came unto this cell?
40 I do not think thou canst, for then thou wast not
Out three years old.
MIRANDA   Certainly, sir, I can.
PROSPERO   By what? by any other house or person?
Of any thing the image tell me, that
Hath kept with thy remembrance.
MIRANDA   'Tis far off,
45 And rather like a dream than an assurance
That my remembrance warrants. Had I not
Four or five women once that tended me?
PROSPERO
Thou hadst, and more, Miranda. But how is it
That this lives in thy mind? What seest thou else
50 In the dark backward and abysm of time?
If thou remembrest aught ere thou cam'st here,
How thou cam'st here thou mayst.
MIRANDA   But that I do not.
PROSPERO
Twelve year since, Miranda, twelve year since,
Thy father was the Duke of Milan, and
A prince of power.
55 MIRANDA   Sir, are not you my father?
PROSPERO   Thy mother was a piece of virtue, and
She said thou wast my daughter; and thy father
Was Duke of Milan; and his only heir
And princess, no worse issued.
MIRANDA   O the heavens!
60 What foul play had we, that we came from thence?
Or blessed was't we did?
PROSPERO   Both, both, my girl:

By foul play, as thou say'st, were we heav'd thence,
But blessedly holp hither.
MIRANDA   O, my heart bleeds
To think o'th' teen that I have turn'd you to,
Which is from my remembrance! Please you, farther.   65
PROSPERO
My brother, and thy uncle, call'd Antonio, –
I pray thee, mark me, that a brother should
Be so perfidious! – he whom next thyself
Of all the world I lov'd, and to him put
The manage of my state; as at that time   70
Through all the signories it was the first,
And Prospero the prime duke, being so reputed
In dignity, and for the liberal Arts
Without a parallel; those being all my study,
The government I cast upon my brother,   75
And to my state grew stranger, being transported
And rapt in secret studies. Thy false uncle –
Dost thou attend me?
MIRANDA   Sir, most heedfully.
PROSPERO   Being once perfected how to grant suits,
How to deny them, who t'advance, and who   80
To trash for over-topping, new created
The creatures that were mine, I say, or chang'd 'em,
Or else new form'd 'em; having both the key
Of officer and office, set all hearts i'th' state
To what tune pleas'd his ear; that now he was   85
The ivy which had hid my princely trunk,
And suck'd my verdure out on't. Thou attend'st not?
MIRANDA   O, good sir, I do.
PROSPERO   I pray thee, mark me.
I, thus neglecting worldly ends, all dedicated
To closeness and the bettering of my mind   90
With that which, but by being so retir'd,
O'er-priz'd all popular rate, in my false brother
Awak'd an evil nature; and my trust,
Like a good parent, did beget of him
A falsehood in its contrary, as great   95
As my trust was; which had indeed no limit,
A confidence sans bound. He being thus lorded,
Not only with what my revenue yielded,
But what my power might else exact, like one
Who having into truth, by telling of it,   100
Made such a sinner of his memory,
To credit his own lie, he did believe
He was indeed the duke; out o'th' substitution,
And executing th'outward face of royalty,
With all prerogative; – hence his ambition growing, –   105
Dost thou hear?
MIRANDA   Your tale, sir, would cure deafness.
PROSPERO
To have no screen between this part he play'd
And him he play'd it for, he needs will be
Absolute Milan. Me, poor man, my library
Was dukedom large enough: of temporal royalties   110
He thinks me now incapable; confederates,
So dry he was for sway, wi'th' King of Naples

To give him annual tribute, do him homage,
Subject his coronet to his crown, and bend
115 The dukedom, yet unbow'd, – alas, poor Milan! –
To most ignoble stooping.
MIRANDA   O the heavens!
PROSPERO
Mark his condition, and th'event; then tell me
If this might be a brother.
MIRANDA   I should sin
To think but nobly of my grandmother:
Good wombs have borne bad sons.
120 PROSPERO   Now the condition.
This King of Naples, being an enemy
To me inveterate, hearkens my brother's suit;
Which was, that he, in lieu o'th' premises
Of homage and I know not how much tribute,
125 Should presently extirpate me and mine
Out of the dukedom, and confer fair Milan,
With all the honours, on my brother: whereon,
A treacherous army levied, one midnight
Fated to th' purpose, did Antonio open
130 The gates of Milan; and, i'th' dead of darkness,
The ministers for th' purpose hurried thence
Me and thy crying self.
MIRANDA   Alack, for pity!
I, not rememb'ring how I cried out then,
Will cry it o'er again: it is a hint
That wrings mine eyes to 't.
135 PROSPERO   Hear a little further,
And then I'll bring thee to the present business
Which now's upon's; without the which, this story
Were most impertinent.
MIRANDA   Wherefore did they not
That hour destroy us?
PROSPERO   Well demanded, wench:
140 My tale provokes that question. Dear, they durst not,
So dear the love my people bore me; nor set
A mark so bloody on the business; but
With colours fairer painted their foul ends.
In few, they hurried us aboard a bark,
145 Bore us some leagues to sea; where they prepared
A rotten carcass of a butt, not rigg'd,
Nor tackle, sail, nor mast; the very rats
Instinctively have quit it: there they hoist us,
To cry to th' sea that roar'd to us; to sigh
150 To th' winds, whose pity, sighing back again,
Did us but loving wrong.
MIRANDA   Alack, what trouble
Was I then to you!
PROSPERO   O, a cherubin
Thou wast that did preserve me. Thou didst smile,
Infused with a fortitude from heaven,
155 When I have deck'd the sea with drops full salt,
Under my burthen groan'd; which rais'd in me
An undergoing stomach, to bear up
Against what should ensue.
MIRANDA   How came we ashore?

PROSPERO   By Providence divine.
Some food we had, and some fresh water, that   160
A noble Neapolitan, Gonzalo,
Out of his charity, who being then appointed
Master of this design, did give us, with
Rich garments, linens, stuffs and necessaries,
Which since have steaded much; so, of his gentleness, 165
Knowing I lov'd my books, he furnish'd me
From mine own library with volumes that
I prize above my dukedom.
MIRANDA   Would I might
But ever see that man!
PROSPERO   Now I arise:
Sit still, and hear the last of our sea-sorrow.   170
Here in this island we arriv'd; and here
Have I, thy schoolmaster, made thee more profit
Than other princess' can, that have more time
For vainer hours, and tutors not so careful.
MIRANDA
Heavens thank you for't! And now, I pray you, sir,   175
For still 'tis beating in my mind, your reason
For raising this sea-storm?
PROSPERO   Know thus far forth.
By accident most strange, bountiful Fortune,
(Now my dear lady) hath mine enemies
Brought to this shore; and by my prescience   180
I find my zenith doth depend upon
A most auspicious star, whose influence
If now I court not, but omit, my fortunes
Will ever after droop. Here cease more questions:
Thou art inclin'd to sleep; 'tis a good dulness,   185
And give it way: I know thou canst not choose.
[*Miranda sleeps.*]
Come away, servant, come. I am ready now.
Approach, my Ariel, come.

Enter ARIEL.

ARIEL   All hail, great master! grave sir, hail! I come
To answer thy best pleasure; be't to fly,   190
To swim, to dive into the fire, to ride
On the curl'd clouds, to thy strong bidding task
Ariel and all his quality.
PROSPERO   Hast thou, spirit,
Perform'd to point the tempest that I bade thee?
ARIEL   To every article.   195
I boarded the king's ship; now on the beak,
Now in the waist, the deck, in every cabin,
I flam'd amazement: sometime I'd divide,
And burn in many places; on the topmast,
The yards and boresprit, would I flame distinctly,   200
Then meet and join. Jove's lightnings, the precursors
O'th' dreadful thunder-claps, more momentary
And sight-outrunning were not: the fire and cracks
Of sulphurous roaring the most mighty Neptune
Seem to besiege, and make his bold waves tremble,   205
Yea, his dread trident shake.
PROSPERO   My brave spirit!

Who was so firm, so constant, that this coil
Would not infect his reason?

ARIEL   Not a soul
210   But felt a fever of the mad, and play'd
Some tricks of desperation. All but mariners
Plung'd in the foaming brine, and quit the vessel,
Then all afire with me: the King's son, Ferdinand,
With hair up-staring, – then like reeds, not hair, –
Was the first man that leap'd; cried, 'Hell is empty,
And all the devils are here.'

215 PROSPERO   Why, that's my spirit!
But was not this nigh shore?

ARIEL   Close by, my master.

PROSPERO   But are they, Ariel, safe?

ARIEL   Not a hair perish'd;
On their sustaining garments not a blemish,
But fresher than before: and, as thou bad'st me.
220 In troops I have dispers'd them 'bout the isle.
The King's son have I landed by himself;
Whom I left cooling of the air with sighs
In an odd angle of the isle, and sitting,
His arms in this sad knot.

PROSPERO   Of the King's ship,
225 The mariners, say how thou hast dispos'd,
And all the rest o'th' fleet.

ARIEL   Safely in harbour
Is the King's ship; in the deep nook, where once
Thou call'dst me up at midnight to fetch dew
From the still-vex'd Bermoothes, there she's hid:
230 The mariners all under hatches stow'd;
Who, with a charm join'd to their suffer'd labour,
I have left asleep: and for the rest o'th' fleet,
Which I dispers'd, they all have met again,
And are upon the Mediterranean flote,
235 Bound sadly home for Naples;
Supposing that they saw the King's ship wrack'd,
And his great person perish.

PROSPERO   Ariel, thy charge
Exactly is perform'd: but there's more work.
What is the time o'th' day?

ARIEL   Past the mid season.

PROSPERO
240 At least two glasses. The time 'twixt six and now
Must by us both be spent most preciously.

ARIEL
Is there more toil? Since thou dost give me pains,
Let me remember thee what thou hast promis'd,
Which is not yet perform'd me.

PROSPERO   How now? moody?
What is 't thou canst demand?

245 ARIEL   My liberty.

PROSPERO   Before the time be out? no more!

ARIEL   I prithee,
Remember I have done thee worthy service;
Told thee no lies, made no mistakings, serv'd
Without or grudge or grumblings: thou did promise
To bate me a full year.

PROSPERO   Dost thou forget   250
From what a torment I did free thee?

ARIEL   No.

PROSPERO
Thou dost, and think'st it much to tread the ooze
Of the salt deep,
To run upon the sharp wind of the north,
To do me business in the veins o'th' earth   255
When it is bak'd with frost.

ARIEL   I do not, sir.

PROSPERO
Thou liest, malignant thing! Hast thou forgot
The foul witch Sycorax, who with age and envy
Was grown into a hoop? hast thou forgot her?

ARIEL   No, sir.

PROSPERO   Thou hast. Where was she born? speak;
tell me.   260

ARIEL   Sir, in Argier.

PROSPERO   O, was she so? I must
Once in a month recount what thou hast been,
Which thou forget'st. This damn'd witch Sycorax,
For mischiefs manifold, and sorceries terrible
To enter human hearing, from Argier,   265
Thou know'st, was banish'd: for one thing she did
They would not take her life. Is not this true?

ARIEL   Ay, sir.

PROSPERO
This blue-ey'd hag was hither brought with child,
And here was left by th' sailors. Thou, my slave,   270
As thou report'st thyself, was then her servant;
And, for thou wast a spirit too delicate
To act her earthy and abhorr'd commands,
Refusing her grand hests, she did confine thee,
By help of her more potent ministers,   275
And in her most unmitigable rage,
Into a cloven pine; within which rift
Imprison'd thou didst painfully remain
A dozen years; within which space she died,
And left thee there; where thou didst vent thy groans 280
As fast as mill-wheels strike. Then was this island –
Save for the son that she did litter here,
A freckled whelp hag-born – not honour'd with
A human shape.

ARIEL   Yes, Caliban her son.

PROSPERO   Dull thing, I say so; he, that Caliban,   285
Whom now I keep in service. Thou best know'st
What torment I did find thee in; thy groans
Did make wolves howl, and penetrate the breasts
Of ever-angry bears: it was a torment
To lay upon the damn'd, which Sycorax   290
Could not again undo: it was mine Art,
When I arriv'd and heard thee, that made gape
The pine, and let thee out.

ARIEL   I thank thee, master.

PROSPERO   If thou more murmur'st, I will rend an oak,
And peg thee in his knotty entrails, till   295
Thou hast howl'd away twelve winters.

ARIEL   Pardon, master:
    I will be correspondent to command,
    And do my spriting gently.
PROSPERO   Do so; and after two days
    I will discharge thee.
ARIEL   That's my noble master!
300   What shall I do? say what; what shall I do?
PROSPERO   Go make thyself like a nymph o'th' sea:
    Be subject to
    No sight but thine and mine; invisible
    To every eyeball else. Go take this shape,
305   And hither come in 't: go: hence
    With diligence.   *Exit Ariel.*
    Awake, dear heart, awake! thou hast slept well;
    Awake!
MIRANDA The strangeness of your story put
    Heaviness in me.
PROSPERO   Shake it off. Come on;
310   We'll visit Caliban my slave, who never
    Yields us kind answer.
MIRANDA   'Tis a villain, sir,
    I do not love to look on.
PROSPERO   But, as 'tis,
    We cannot miss him: he does make our fire,
    Fetch in our wood, and serves in offices
315   That profit us. What, ho! slave! Caliban!
    Thou earth, thou! speak.
CALIBAN [*within*]   There's wood enough within.
PROSPERO
    Come forth, I say! there's other business for thee;
    Come, thou tortoise! when?

        Re-enter ARIEL *like a water-nymph.*

    Fine apparition! My quaint Ariel,
    Hark in thine ear.
320 ARIEL   My lord, it shall be done.   *Exit.*
PROSPERO
    Thou poisonous slave, got by the devil himself
    Upon thy wicked dam, come forth!

        Enter CALIBAN.

CALIBAN   As wicked dew as e'er my mother brush'd
    With raven's feather from unwholesome fen
325   Drop on you both! a south-west blow on ye
    And blister you all o'er!
PROSPERO
    For this, be sure, to-night thou shalt have cramps,
    Side-stitches that shall pen thy breath up; urchins
    Shall, for that vast of night that they may work,
330   All exercise on thee; thou shalt be pinch'd
    As thick as honeycomb, each pinch more stinging
    Than bees that made 'em.
CALIBAN   I must eat my dinner.
    This island's mine, by Sycorax my mother,
    Which thou tak'st from me. When thou cam'st first,
    Thou strok'st me, and made much of me; wouldst
335   give me

Water with berries in 't; and teach me how
To name the bigger light, and how the less,
That burn by day and night: and then I lov'd thee,
And show'd thee all the qualities o'th' isle,
The fresh springs, brine-pits, barren place and
    fertile: 340
Curs'd be I that did so! All the charms
Of Sycorax, toads, beetles, bats, light on you!
For I am all the subjects that you have,
Which first was mine own King: and here you sty me
In this hard rock, whiles you do keep from me   345
The rest o'th' island.
PROSPERO   Thou most lying slave,
Whom stripes may move, not kindness! I have us'd
    thee,
Filth as thou art, with human care; and lodg'd thee
In mine own cell, till thou didst seek to violate
The honour of my child.   350
CALIBAN   O ho, O ho! would't had been done!
    Thou didst prevent me; I had peopled else
    This isle with Calibans.
MIRANDA   Abhorred slave,
    Which any print of goodness wilt not take,
    Being capable of all ill! I pitied thee,   355
    Took pains to make thee speak, taught thee each
      hour
    One thing or other: when thou didst not, savage,
    Know thine own meaning, but wouldst gabble like
    A thing most brutish, I endow'd thy purposes
    With words that made them known. But thy vile
      race,   360
    Though thou didst learn, had that in't which good
      natures
    Could not abide to be with; therefore wast thou
    Deservedly confin'd into this rock,
    Who hadst deserv'd more than a prison.
CALIBAN   You taught me language; and my profit on't   365
    Is, I know how to curse. The red plague rid you
    For learning me your language!
PROSPERO   Hag-seed, hence!
    Fetch us in fuel; and be quick, thou'rt best,
    To answer other business. Shrug'st thou, malice?
    If thou neglect'st, or dost unwillingly   370
    What I command, I'll rack thee with old cramps,
    Fill all thy bones with aches, make thee roar,
    That beasts shall tremble at thy din.
CALIBAN   No, 'pray thee.
    [*aside*] I must obey: his Art is of such pow'r,
    It would control my dam's god, Setebos,   375
    And make a vassal of him.
PROSPERO   So, slave; hence!
                         Exit Caliban.

    Re-enter ARIEL, *invisible, playing and singing;*
        FERDINAND *following.*

Ariel's Song.

ARIEL   Come unto these yellow sands,
                And then take hands:
          Courtsied when you have and kiss'd
380   The wild waves whist:
          Foot it featly here and there,
                And sweet sprites bear
          The burthen. Hark, hark.
          [*burthen dispersedly*] Bow-wow.
385 ARIEL   The watch dogs bark:
          [*burthen dispersedly*] Bow-wow.
     ARIEL   Hark, hark! I hear
          The strain of strutting chanticleer
          Cry
          [*burthen dispersedly*] Cock a diddle dow.
     FERDINAND
390   Where should this music be? i'th' air or th'earth?
          It sounds no more: and, sure, it waits upon
          Some god o'th' island. Sitting on a bank,
          Weeping again the King my father's wrack,
          This music crept by me upon the waters,
395   Allaying both their fury and my passion
          With its sweet air: thence I have follow'd it,
          Or it hath drawn me rather. But 'tis gone.
          No, it begins again.

Ariel's Song.

ARIEL Full fadom five thy father lies;
400   Of his bones are coral made;
          Those are pearls that were his eyes:
             Nothing of him that doth fade,
          But doth suffer a sea-change
          Into something rich and strange.
405   Sea-nymphs hourly ring his knell:
          [*burthen*] Ding-dong.
     ARIEL Hark! now I hear them, – Ding-dong, bell.

     FERDINAND
          The ditty does remember my drown'd father.
          This is no mortal business, nor no sound
410   That the earth owes: – I hear it now above me.
     PROSPERO   The fringed curtains of thine eye advance,
          And say what thou seest yond.
     MIRANDA   What is 't? a spirit?
          Lord, how it looks about! Believe me, sir,
          It carries a brave form. But 'tis a spirit.
     PROSPERO
415   No, wench; it eats and sleeps and hath such senses
          As we have, such. This gallant which thou seest
          Was in the wrack; and, but he's something stain'd
          With grief (that's beauty's canker) thou mightst call
             him
          A goodly person: he hath lost his fellows,
          And strays about to find 'em.
420 MIRANDA   I might call him
          A thing divine; for nothing natural
          I ever saw so noble.

PROSPERO [*aside*]   It goes on, I see,
     As my soul prompts it. Spirit, fine spirit! I'll free thee
     Within two days for this.
FERDINAND   Most sure the goddess
     On whom these airs attend! Vouchsafe my prayer   425
     May know if you remain upon this island;
     And that you will some good instruction give
     How I may bear me here: my prime request,
     Which I do last pronounce, is, O you wonder!
     If you be maid or no?
MIRANDA   No wonder, sir;   430
     But certainly a maid.
FERDINAND   My language! heavens!
     I am the best of them that speak this speech,
     Were I but where 'tis spoken.
PROSPERO   How? the best?
     What wert thou, if the King of Naples heard thee?
FERDINAND   A single thing, as I am now, that wonders   435
     To hear thee speak of Naples. He does hear me;
     And that he does I weep: myself am Naples,
     Who with mine eyes, never since at ebb, beheld
     The King my father wrack'd.
MIRANDA   Alack, for mercy!
FERDINAND
     Yes, faith, and all his lords; the Duke of Milan   440
     And his brave son being twain.
PROSPERO [*aside*]   The Duke of Milan
     And his more braver daughter could control thee,
     If now 'twere fit to do't. At the first sight
     They have chang'd eyes. Delicate Ariel,
     I'll set thee free for this. [*to Fer.*] A word, good sir; 445
     I fear you have done yourself some wrong: a word.
MIRANDA   Why speaks my father so ungently? This
     Is the third man that e'er I saw; the first
     That e'er I sigh'd for: pity move my father
     To be inclin'd my way!
FERDINAND   O, if a virgin,   450
     And your affection not gone forth, I'll make you
     The Queen of Naples.
PROSPERO   Soft, sir! one word more.
     [*aside*] They are both in either's pow'rs: but this swift
        business
     I must uneasy make, lest too light winning
     Make the prize light.
     [*to Ferdinand*]   One word more; I charge thee   455
     That thou attend me: thou dost here usurp
     The name thou ow'st not; and hast put thyself
     Upon this island as a spy, to win it
     From me, the lord on 't.
FERDINAND   No, as I am a man.
MIRANDA
     There's nothing ill can dwell in such a temple: 460
     If the ill spirit have so fair a house,
     Good things will strive to dwell with't.
PROSPERO   Follow me.
     Speak not you for him: he's a traitor. Come;
     I'll manacle thy neck and feet together:

Sea-water shalt thou drink; thy food shall be
465 The fresh-brook mussels, wither'd roots, and husks
Wherein the acorn cradled. Follow.

FERDINAND   No;
I will resist such entertainment till
Mine enemy has more pow'r.
[*He draws, and is charmed from moving.*]

MIRANDA   O dear father,
Make not too rash a trial of him, for
He's gentle, and not fearful.

470 PROSPERO   What! I say,
My foot my tutor? Put thy sword up, traitor;
Who mak'st a show, but dar'st not strike, thy
    conscience
Is so possess'd with guilt: come from thy ward;
For I can here disarm thee with this stick
And make thy weapon drop.

475 MIRANDA   Beseech you, father.

PROSPERO   Hence! hang not on my garments.

MIRANDA   Sir, have pity;
I'll be his surety.

PROSPERO   Silence! one word more
Shall make me chide thee, if not hate thee. What!
An advocate for an impostor! hush!
480 Thou think'st there is no more such shapes as he,
Having seen but him and Caliban: foolish wench!
To th' most of men this is a Caliban,
And they to him are angels.

MIRANDA   My affections
Are then most humble; I have no ambition
To see a goodlier man.

485 PROSPERO   Come on; obey:
Thy nerves are in their infancy again,
And have no vigour in them.

FERDINAND   So they are:
My spirits, as in a dream, are all bound up.
My father's loss, the weakness which I feel,
490 The wrack of all my friends, nor this man's threats,
To whom I am subdued, are but light to me,
Might I but through my prison once a day
Behold this maid: all corners else o'th' earth
Let liberty make use of; space enough
Have I in such a prison.

PROSPERO [*aside*]   It works.
495 [*to Ferdinand*]   Come on.
[*to Ariel*] Thou hast done well, fine Ariel! Follow me;
Hark what thou else shalt do me.

MIRANDA   Be of comfort;
My father's of a better nature, sir,
Than he appears by speech: this is unwonted
Which now came from him.

500 PROSPERO   Thou shalt be as free
As mountain winds: but then exactly do
All points of my command.

ARIEL   To th' syllable.

PROSPERO   Come, follow. Speak not for him.   *Exeunt.*

2.1 *Enter* ALONSO, SEBASTIAN, ANTONIO, GONZALO,
         ADRIAN, FRANCISCO *and others.*

GONZALO   Beseech you, sir, be merry; you have cause,
So have we all, of joy; for our escape
Is much beyond our loss. Our hint of woe
Is common; every day, some sailor's wife,
The masters of some merchant, and the merchant,   5
Have just our theme of woe; but for the miracle,
I mean our preservation, few in millions
Can speak like us: then wisely, good sir, weigh
Our sorrow with our comfort.

ALONSO   Prithee, peace.

SEBASTIAN [*aside to Antonio*]   He receives comfort like   10
cold porridge.

ANTONIO [*aside to Sebastian*]   The visitor will not give
him o'er so.

SEBASTIAN [*aside to Antonio*]   Look, he's winding up the
watch of his wit; by and by it will strike.   15

GONZALO   Sir, –

SEBASTIAN [*aside to Antonio*]   One: tell.

GONZALO   When every grief is entertain'd that's offer'd,
Comes to th'entertainer –

SEBASTIAN   A dollar.   20

GONZALO   Dolour comes to him, indeed: you have
spoken truer than you purpos'd.

SEBASTIAN   You have taken it wiselier than I meant you
should.

GONZALO   Therefore, my lord, –   25

ANTONIO   Fie, what a spendthrift is he of his tongue!

ALONSO   I prithee, spare.

GONZALO   Well, I have done: but yet, –

SEBASTIAN   He will be talking.

ANTONIO   Which, of he or Adrian, for a good wager,   30
first begins to crow?

SEBASTIAN   The old cock.

ANTONIO   The cockerel.

SEBASTIAN   Done. The wager?

ANTONIO   A laughter.   35

SEBASTIAN   A match!

ADRIAN   Though this island seem to be desert, –

ANTONIO   Ha, ha, ha!

SEBASTIAN   So: you're paid.

ADRIAN   Uninhabitable, and almost inaccessible, –   40

SEBASTIAN   Yet, –

ADRIAN   Yet, –

ANTONIO   He could not miss't.

ADRIAN   It must needs be of subtle, tender and delicate
temperance.   45

ANTONIO   Temperance was a delicate wench.

SEBASTIAN   Ay, and a subtle; as he most learnedly
deliver'd.

ADRIAN   The air breathes upon us here most sweetly.

SEBASTIAN   As if it had lungs, and rotten ones.   50

ANTONIO   Or as 'twere perfum'd by a fen.

GONZALO   Here is everything advantageous to life.

ANTONIO   True; save means to live.

SEBASTIAN   Of that there's none, or little.

55 GONZALO   How lush and lusty the grass looks! how green!

ANTONIO   The ground, indeed, is tawny.

SEBASTIAN   With an eye of green in't.

ANTONIO   He misses not much.

60 SEBASTIAN   No; he doth but mistake the truth totally.

GONZALO   But the rarity of it is, – which is indeed almost beyond credit, –

SEBASTIAN   As many vouch'd rarities are.

GONZALO   That our garments, being, as they were, drenched in the sea, hold, notwithstanding, their
65 freshness and glosses, being rather new-dyed than stained with salt water.

ANTONIO   If but one of his pockets could speak, would it not say he lies?

70 SEBASTIAN   Ay, or very falsely pocket up his report.

GONZALO   Methinks our garments are now as fresh as when we put them on first in Afric, at the marriage of the King's fair daughter Claribel to the King of Tunis.

SEBASTIAN   'Twas a sweet marriage, and we prosper well
75 in our return.

ADRIAN   Tunis was never grac'd before with such a paragon to their Queen.

GONZALO   Not since widow Dido's time.

ANTONIO   Widow! a pox o' that! How came that widow
80 in? widow Dido!

SEBASTIAN   What if he had said 'widower Aeneas' too? Good Lord, how you take it!

ADRIAN   'Widow Dido' said you? you make me study of that: she was of Carthage, not of Tunis.

85 GONZALO   This Tunis, sir, was Carthage.

ADRIAN   Carthage?

GONZALO   I assure you, Carthage.

ANTONIO   His word is more than the miraculous harp.

SEBASTIAN   He hath rais'd the wall, and houses too.

90 ANTONIO   What impossible matter will he make easy next?

SEBASTIAN   I think he will carry this island home in his pocket, and give it his son for an apple.

ANTONIO   And, sowing the kernels of it in the sea, bring
95 forth more islands.

GONZALO   Ay.

ANTONIO   Why, in good time.

GONZALO   Sir, we were talking that our garments seem now as fresh as when we were at Tunis at the marriage
100 of your daughter, who is now Queen.

ANTONIO   And the rarest that e'er came there.

SEBASTIAN   Bate, I beseech you, widow Dido.

ANTONIO   O, widow Dido! ay, widow Dido.

GONZALO   Is not, sir, my doublet as fresh as the first day
105 I wore it? I mean, in a sort.

ANTONIO   That sort was well fish'd for.

GONZALO   When I wore it at your daughter's marriage?

ALONSO   You cram these words into mine ears against The stomach of my sense. Would I had never
110 Married my daughter there! for, coming thence,

My son is lost, and, in my rate, she too,
Who is so far from Italy removed
I ne'er again shall see her. O thou mine heir
Of Naples and of Milan, what strange fish
Hath made his meal on thee?

FRANCISCO   Sir, he may live: 115
I saw him beat the surges under him,
And ride upon their backs; he trod the water,
Whose enmity he flung aside, and breasted
The surge most swoln that met him; his bold head
'Bove the contentious waves he kept, and oared   120
Himself with his good arms in lusty stroke
To th' shore, that o'er his wave-worn basis bowed,
As stooping to relieve him: I not doubt
He came alive to land.

ALONSO   No, no, he's gone.

SEBASTIAN
Sir, you may thank yourself for this great loss,   125
That would not bless our Europe with your daughter,
But rather loose her to an African;
Where she, at least, is banish'd from your eye,
Who hath cause to wet the grief on't.

ALONSO   Prithee, peace.

SEBASTIAN
You were kneel'd to, and importun'd otherwise,   130
By all of us; and the fair soul herself
Weigh'd between loathness and obedience, at
Which end o'th' beam should bow. We have lost your son,
I fear, for ever: Milan and Naples have
Mo widows in them of this business' making   135
Than we bring men to comfort them:
The fault's your own.

ALONSO   So is the dear'st o'th' loss.

GONZALO   My lord Sebastian,
The truth you speak doth lack some gentleness,
And time to speak it in: you rub the sore,   140
When you should bring the plaster.

SEBASTIAN   Very well.

ANTONIO   And most chirurgeonly.

GONZALO   It is foul weather in us all, good sir,
When you are cloudy.

SEBASTIAN   Fowl weather?

ANTONIO   Very foul.

GONZALO   Had I plantation of this isle, my lord, –   145

ANTONIO   He'd sow 't with nettle-seed.

SEBASTIAN   Or docks, or mallows.

GONZALO   And were the King on 't, what would I do?

SEBASTIAN   'Scape being drunk for want of wine.

GONZALO   I'th' commonwealth I would by contraries
Execute all things; for no kind of traffic   150
Would I admit; no name of magistrate;
Letters should not be known; riches, poverty,
And use of service, none; contract, succession,
Bourn, bound of land, tilth, vineyard, none;
No use of metal, corn, or wine, or oil;   155
No occupation; all men idle, all;

And women too, but innocent and pure:
No sovereignty; –

SEBASTIAN   Yet he would be King on't.

ANTONIO
The latter end of his commonwealth forgets the
beginning.

GONZALO
All things in common Nature should produce
Without sweat or endeavour: treason, felony,
Sword, pike, knife, gun, or need of any engine,
Would I not have; but Nature should bring forth,
Of it own kind, all foison, all abundance,
To feed my innocent people.

SEBASTIAN   No marrying 'mong his subjects?

ANTONIO   None, man; all idle; whores and knaves.

GONZALO   I would with such perfection govern, sir,
T'excel the Golden Age.

SEBASTIAN   'Save his Majesty!

ANTONIO   Long live Gonzalo!

GONZALO   And, – do you mark me, sir?

ALONSO   Prithee, no more: thou dost talk nothing to me.

GONZALO   I do well believe your highness; and did it to
minister occasion to these gentlemen, who are of such
sensible and nimble lungs that they always use to
laugh at nothing.

ANTONIO   'Twas you we laughed at.

GONZALO   Who in this kind of merry fooling am
nothing to you: so you may continue, and laugh at
nothing still.

ANTONIO   What a blow was there given!

SEBASTIAN   An it had not fallen flat-long.

GONZALO   You are gentlemen of brave mettle; you
would lift the moon out of her sphere, if she would
continue in it five weeks without changing.

Enter ARIEL, *invisible, playing solemn music.*

SEBASTIAN   We would so, and then go a bat-fowling.

ANTONIO   Nay, good my lord, be not angry.

GONZALO   No, I warrant you; I will not adventure my
discretion so weakly. Will you laugh me asleep, for I
am very heavy?

ANTONIO   Go sleep, and hear us.

[*All sleep except Alonso, Sebastian, and Antonio.*]

ALONSO   What, all so soon asleep! I wish mine eyes
Would, with themselves, shut up my thoughts: I find
They are inclin'd to do so.

SEBASTIAN   Please you, sir,
Do not omit the heavy offer of it:
It seldom visits sorrow; when it doth,
It is a comforter.

ANTONIO   We two, my lord,
Will guard your person while you take your rest,
And watch your safety.

ALONSO   Thank you. – Wondrous heavy.
Alonso sleeps. Exit Ariel.

SEBASTIAN   What a strange drowsiness possesses them!

ANTONIO   It is the quality o'th' climate.

SEBASTIAN   Why
Doth it not then our eyelids sink? I find not
Myself dispos'd to sleep.

ANTONIO   Nor I; my spirits are nimble.
They fell together all, as by consent;
They dropp'd, as by a thunder-stroke. What might,
Worthy Sebastian? – O, what might? – No more: –
And yet methinks I see it in thy face,
What thou shouldst be: th'occasion speaks thee; and
My strong imagination sees a crown
Dropping upon thy head.

SEBASTIAN   What, art thou waking?

ANTONIO   Do you not hear me speak?

SEBASTIAN   I do; and surely
It is a sleepy language, and thou speak'st
Out of thy sleep. What is it thou didst say?
This is a strange repose, to be asleep
With eyes wide open; standing, speaking, moving,
And yet so fast asleep.

ANTONIO   Noble Sebastian,
Thou let'st thy fortune sleep – die, rather; wink'st
Whiles thou art waking.

SEBASTIAN   Thou dost snore distinctly;
There's meaning in thy snores.

ANTONIO
I am more serious than my custom: you
Must be so too, if heed me; which to do
Trebles thee o'er.

SEBASTIAN   Well, I am standing water.

ANTONIO   I'll teach you how to flow.

SEBASTIAN   Do so: to ebb
Hereditary sloth instructs me.

ANTONIO   O,
If you but knew how you the purpose cherish
Whiles thus you mock it! how, in stripping it,
You more invest it! Ebbing men, indeed,
Most often do so near the bottom run
By their own fear or sloth.

SEBASTIAN   Prithee, say on:
The setting of thine eye and cheek proclaim
A matter from thee; and a birth, indeed,
Which throes thee much to yield.

ANTONIO   Thus, sir:
Although this lord of weak remembrance, this,
Who shall be of as little memory
When he is earth'd, hath here almost persuaded, –
For he's a spirit of persuasion, only
Professes to persuade, – the King his son's alive,
'Tis as impossible that he's undrown'd
As he that sleeps here swims.

SEBASTIAN   I have no hope
That he's undrown'd.

ANTONIO   O, out of that 'no hope'
What great hope have you! no hope that way is
Another way so high a hope, that even
Ambition cannot pierce a wink beyond,
But doubt discovery there. Will you grant with me

That Ferdinand is drown'd?

SEBASTIAN   He's gone.

245 ANTONIO   Then tell me,
   Who's the next heir of Naples?

SEBASTIAN   Claribel.

ANTONIO   She that is Queen of Tunis; she that dwells
   Ten leagues beyond man's life; she that from Naples
   Can have no note, unless the sun were post, –
250 The man i'th' moon's too slow, – till new-born chins
   Be rough and razorable; she that from whom
   We all were sea-swallow'd, though some cast again,
   And that by destiny, to perform an act
   Whereof what's past is prologue; what to come,
   In yours and my discharge.

255 SEBASTIAN   What stuff is this! how say you?
   'Tis true, my brother's daughter's Queen of Tunis;
   So is she heir of Naples; 'twixt which regions
   There is some space.

ANTONIO   A space whose ev'ry cubit
   Seems to cry out, 'How shall that Claribel
260 Measure us back to Naples? Keep in Tunis,
   And let Sebastian wake.' Say, this were death
   That now hath seiz'd them; why, they were no worse
   Than now they are. There be that can rule Naples
   As well as he that sleeps; lords that can prate
265 As amply and unnecessarily
   As this Gonzalo; I myself could make
   A chough of as deep chat. O, that you bore
   The mind that I do! what a sleep were this
   For your advancement! Do you understand me?

SEBASTIAN   Methinks I do.

270 ANTONIO   And how does your content
   Tender your own good fortune?

SEBASTIAN   I remember
   You did supplant your brother Prospero.

ANTONIO   True:
   And look how well my garments sit upon me;
   Much feater than before: my brother's servants
275 Were then my fellows; now they are my men.

SEBASTIAN   But for your conscience.

ANTONIO   Ay, sir; where lies that? if 'twere a kibe,
   'Twould put me to my slipper: but I feel not
   This deity in my bosom: twenty consciences,
280 That stand 'twixt me and Milan, candied be they,
   And melt, ere they molest! Here lies your brother,
   No better than the earth he lies upon,
   If he were that which now he 's like, that's dead;
   Whom I, with this obedient steel, three inches of it,
285 Can lay to bed for ever; whiles you, doing thus,
   To the perpetual wink for aye might put
   This ancient morsel, this Sir Prudence, who
   Should not upbraid our course. For all the rest,
   They'll take suggestion as a cat laps milk;
290 They'll tell the clock to any business that
   We say befits the hour.

SEBASTIAN   Thy case, dear friend,
   Shall be my precedent; as thou got'st Milan,

I'll come by Naples. Draw thy sword: one stroke
Shall free thee from the tribute which thou payest;
And I the King shall love thee.

ANTONIO   Draw together;   295
And when I rear my hand, do you the like,
To fall it on Gonzalo.

SEBASTIAN   O, but one word.
   [*They talk apart.*]

      Re-enter ARIEL, *invisible, with music and song.*

ARIEL   My master through his Art foresees the danger
   That you, his friend, are in; and sends me forth, –
   For else his project dies, – to keep them living.   300
   [*Sings in Gonzalo's ear.*]
            While you here do snoring lie,
            Open-ey'd conspiracy
               His time doth take.
            If of life you keep a care,
            Shake off slumber, and beware: 305
               Awake, Awake!

ANTONIO   Then let us both be sudden.

GONZALO [*waking*]   Now, good angels
   Preserve the King! [*The others wake.*]

ALONSO
   Why, how now? ho; awake? – Why are you drawn?
   Wherefore this ghastly looking?

GONZALO   What's the matter?   310

SEBASTIAN   Whiles we stood here securing your repose,
   Even now, we heard a hollow burst of bellowing
   Like bulls, or rather lions: did't not wake you?
   It struck mine ear most terribly.

ALONSO   I heard nothing.

ANTONIO   O, 'twas a din to fright a monster's ear,   315
   To make an earthquake! sure, it was the roar
   Of a whole herd of lions.

ALONSO   Heard you this, Gonzalo?

GONZALO   Upon mine honour, sir, I heard a humming,
   And that a strange one too, which did awake me:
   I shak'd you, sir, and cried: as mine eyes open'd,   320
   I saw their weapons drawn: – there was a noise,
   That's verily. 'Tis best we stand upon our guard,
   Or that we quit this place: let's draw our weapons.

ALONSO
   Lead off this ground; and let's make further search
   For my poor son.

GONZALO   Heavens keep him from these beasts!   325
   For he is, sure, i'th' island.

ALONSO   Lead away.

ARIEL   Prospero my lord shall know what I have done:
   So, King, go safely on to seek thy son.   *Exeunt.*

2.2   *Enter* CALIBAN *with a burthen of wood.*
            A noise of thunder heard.

CALIBAN   All the infections that the sun sucks up
   From bogs, fens, flats, on Prosper fall, and make him
   By inch-meal a disease! his spirits hear me,

And yet I needs must curse. But they'll nor pinch,
Fright me with urchin-shows, pitch me i'th' mire,
Nor lead me, like a firebrand, in the dark
Out of my way, unless he bid 'em: but
For every trifle are they set upon me;
Sometime like apes, that mow and chatter at me,
And after bite me; then like hedgehogs, which
Lie tumbling in my barefoot way, and mount
Their pricks at my footfall; sometime am I
All wound with adders, who with cloven tongues
Do hiss me into madness.

Enter TRINCULO.

                    Lo, now, lo!
Here comes a spirit of his, and to torment me
For bringing wood in slowly. I'll fall flat;
Perchance he will not mind me.

TRINCULO   Here's neither bush nor shrub, to bear off
any weather at all, and another storm brewing; I hear
it sing i'th' wind: yond same black cloud, yond huge
one, looks like a foul bombard that would shed his
liquor. If it should thunder as it did before, I know not
where to hide my head: yond same cloud cannot
choose but fall by pailfuls. What have we here? a man
or a fish? dead or alive? A fish: he smells like a fish; a
very ancient and fish-like smell; a kind of, not of the
newest Poor-John. A strange fish! Were I in England
now, as once I was, and had but this fish painted, not a
holiday fool there but would give a piece of silver:
there would this monster make a man; any strange
beast there makes a man: when they will not give a doit
to relieve a lame beggar, they will lay out ten to see a
dead Indian. Legg'd like a man! and his fins like arms!
Warm o' my troth! I do now let loose my opinion, hold
it no longer: this is no fish, but an islander, that hath
lately suffered by a thunderbolt. [*thunder*] Alas, the
storm is come again! my best way is to creep under his
gaberdine; there is no other shelter hereabout: misery
acquaints a man with strange bed-fellows. I will here
shroud till the dregs of the storm be past.

Enter STEPHANO, *singing: a bottle in his hand.*

STEPHANO   I shall no more to sea, to sea,
                    Here shall I die ashore, –
This is a very scurvy tune to sing at a man's funeral;
well, here's my comfort. [*Drinks.*]
[*Sings.*]
The master, the swabber, the boatswain, and I,
        The gunner, and his mate,
Lov'd Mall, Meg, and Marian, and Margery,
        But none of us car'd for Kate
        For she had a tongue with a tang,
        Would cry to a sailor, Go hang!
She lov'd not the savour of tar nor of pitch;
Yet a tailor might scratch her where'er she did itch.
        Then to sea, boys, and let her go hang!

This is a scurvy tune too: but here's my comfort.

[*Drinks.*]
CALIBAN   Do not torment me: – O!
STEPHANO   What's the matter? Have we devils here? Do
you put tricks upon 's with salvages and men of Ind,
ha? I have not scap'd drowning, to be afeard now of
your four legs; for it hath been said, As proper a man
as ever went on four legs cannot make him give
ground; and it shall be said so again, while Stephano
breathes at' nostrils.
CALIBAN   The spirit torments me: – O!
STEPHANO   This is some monster of the isle with four
legs, who hath got, as I take it, an ague. Where the
devil should he learn our language? I will give him
some relief, if it be but for that. If I can recover him,
and keep him tame, and get to Naples with him, he's a
present for any emperor that ever trod on neat's-
leather.
CALIBAN   Do not torment me, prithee; I'll bring my
wood home faster.
STEPHANO   He's in his fit now, and does not talk after
the wisest. He shall taste of my bottle: if he have never
drunk wine afore, it will go near to remove his fit. If I
can recover him, and keep him tame, I will not take too
much for him; he shall pay for him that hath him and
that soundly.
CALIBAN   Thou dost me yet but little hurt; thou wilt
anon, I know it by thy trembling: now Prosper works
upon thee.
STEPHANO   Come on your ways; open your mouth; here
is that which will give language to you, cat: open your
mouth; this will shake your shaking, I can tell you, and
that soundly: you cannot tell who's your friend: open
your chaps again.
TRINCULO   I should know that voice: it should be – but
he is drowned; and these are devils: – O defend me!
STEPHANO   Four legs and two voices, – a most delicate
monster! His forward voice, now, is to speak well of his
friend; his backward voice is to utter foul speeches
and to detract. If all the wine in my bottle will
recover him, I will help his ague. Come: – Amen!
I will pour some in thy other mouth.
TRINCULO   Stephano!
STEPHANO   Doth thy other mouth call me? Mercy,
mercy! This is a devil, and no monster: I will leave
him; I have no long spoon.
TRINCULO   Stephano! If thou beest Stephano, touch me,
and speak to me; for I am Trinculo, – be not afeard, –
thy good friend Trinculo.
STEPHANO   If thou beest Trinculo, come forth: I'll pull
thee by the lesser legs: if any be Trinculo's legs, these
are they. Thou art very Trinculo indeed! How cam'st
thou to be the siege of this moon-calf? can he vent
Trinculos?
TRINCULO   I took him to be kill'd with a thunder-stroke.
But art thou not drown'd, Stephano? I hope, now, thou
art not drown'd. Is the storm over-blown? I hid me

110   under the dead moon-calf's gaberdine for fear of the
storm. And art thou living, Stephano? O Stephano,
two Neapolitans scap'd!

STEPHANO   Prithee, do not turn me about; my stomach
is not constant.

115   CALIBAN [*aside*]   These be fine things, an if they be not
sprites. That's a brave god, and bears celestial liquor:
I will kneel to him.

STEPHANO   How didst thou scape? How cam'st thou
hither? swear, by this bottle, how thou cam'st hither. I

120   escap'd upon a butt of sack, which the sailors heaved
o'erboard, by this bottle! which I made of the bark of
a tree with mine own hands, since I was cast ashore.

CALIBAN   I'll swear, upon that bottle, to be thy true
subject; for the liquor is not earthly.

125   STEPHANO   Here; swear, then, how thou escap'dst.

TRINCULO   Swum ashore, man, like a duck: I can swim
like a duck, I'll be sworn.

STEPHANO   Here, kiss the book. Though thou canst
swim like a duck, thou art made like a goose.

130   TRINCULO   O Stephano, hast any more of this?

STEPHANO   The whole butt, man: my cellar is in a rock
by th' sea-side, where my wine is hid. How now,
moon-calf! how does thine ague?

CALIBAN   Hast thou not dropp'd from heaven?

135   STEPHANO   Out o' the moon, I do assure thee: I was the
man i'th' moon when time was.

CALIBAN   I have seen thee in her, and I do adore thee:
My mistress show'd me thee, and thy dog, and thy
bush.

140   STEPHANO   Come, swear to that; kiss the book: I will
furnish it anon with new contents: swear.

TRINCULO   By this good light, this is a very shallow
monster; I afeard of him? A very weak monster! The
man i'th' moon! A most poor credulous monster! Well

145   drawn, monster, in good sooth!

CALIBAN   I'll show thee every fertile inch o'th' island;
and I will kiss thy foot: I prithee, be my god.

TRINCULO   By this light, a most perfidious and drunken
monster! when 's god's asleep, he'll rob his bottle.

150   CALIBAN   I'll kiss thy foot; I'll swear myself thy subject.

STEPHANO   Come on, then; down, and swear.

TRINCULO   I shall laugh myself to death at this puppy-
headed monster. A most scurvy monster! I could find
in my heart to beat him, –

155   STEPHANO   Come, kiss.

TRINCULO   But that the poor monster's in drink. An
abominable monster!

CALIBAN
I'll show thee the best springs; I'll pluck thee berries;
I'll fish for thee, and get thee wood enough.

160   A plague upon the tyrant that I serve!
I'll bear him no more sticks, but follow thee,
Thou wondrous man.

TRINCULO   A most ridiculous monster, to make a
wonder of a poor drunkard!

CALIBAN
I prithee, let me bring thee where crabs grow;   165
And I with my long nails will dig thee pig-nuts;
Show thee a jay's nest, and instruct thee how
To snare the nimble marmoset; I'll bring thee
To clustering filberts, and sometimes I'll get thee
Young scamels from the rock. Wilt thou go with me?   170

STEPHANO   I prithee now, lead the way, without any
more talking. Trinculo, the King and all our company
else being drown'd, we will inherit here: here; bear my
bottle: fellow Trinculo, we'll fill him by and by
again.   175

CALIBAN [*Sings drunkenly.*]
     Farewell, master; farewell, farewell!

TRINCULO   A howling monster; a drunken monster!

CALIBAN   No more dams I'll make for fish;
     Nor fetch in firing
     At requiring;   180
     Nor scrape trenchering, nor wash dish:
     'Ban, 'Ban, Cacaliban
     Has a new master: – get a new man.
Freedom, high-day! high-day, freedom! freedom,
high-day, freedom!
  185

STEPHANO   O brave monster! lead the way.   *Exeunt.*

3.1   *Enter* FERDINAND, *bearing a log.*

FERDINAND
There be some sports are painful, and their labour
Delight in them sets off: some kinds of baseness
Are nobly undergone; and most poor matters
Point to rich ends. This my mean task
Would be as heavy to me as odious, but   5
The mistress which I serve quickens what's dead,
And makes my labours pleasures: O, she is
Ten times more gentle than her father's crabbed,
And he's compos'd of harshness. I must remove
Some thousands of these logs, and pile them up,   10
Upon a sore injunction: my sweet mistress
Weeps when she sees me work, and says, such
   baseness
Had never like executor. I forget:
But these sweet thoughts do even refresh my labours,
Most busilest when I do it.

Enter MIRANDA; *and* PROSPERO *at a distance, unseen.*

MIRANDA   Alas now, pray you,   15
Work not so hard: I would the lightning had
Burnt up those logs that you are enjoin'd to pile!
Pray, set it down, and rest you: when this burns,
'Twill weep for having wearied you. My father
Is hard at study; pray, now, rest yourself: 20
He's safe for these three hours.

FERDINAND   O most dear mistress,
The sun will set before I shall discharge
What I must strive to do.

MIRANDA   If you'll sit down,

I'll bear your logs the while: pray give me that;
I'll carry it to the pile.

FERDINAND   No, precious creature; 25
I had rather crack my sinews, break my back,
Than you should such dishonour undergo,
While I sit lazy by.

MIRANDA   It would become me
As well as it does you: and I should do it 30
With much more ease; for my good will is to it,
And yours it is against.

PROSPERO   Poor worm, thou art infected!
This visitation shows it.

MIRANDA   You look wearily.

FERDINAND
No, noble mistress: 'tis fresh morning with me
When you are by at night. I do beseech you, –
Chiefly that I might set it in my prayers, – 35
What is your name?

MIRANDA   Miranda. – O my father,
I have broke your hest to say so!

FERDINAND   Admir'd Miranda!
Indeed the top of admiration! worth
What's dearest to the world! Full many a lady
I have ey'd with best regard, and many a time 40
Th' harmony of their tongues hath into bondage
Brought my too diligent ear: for several virtues
Have I lik'd several women; never any
With so full soul, but some defect in her
Did quarrel with the noblest grace she ow'd, 45
And put it to the foil: but you, O you,
So perfect and so peerless, are created
Of every creature's best!

MIRANDA   I do not know
One of my sex; no woman's face remember,
Save, from my glass, mine own; nor have I seen 50
More that I may call men than you, good friend,
And my dear father: how features are abroad,
I am skilless of; but, by my modesty,
The jewel in my dower, I would not wish
Any companion in the world but you; 55
Nor can imagination form a shape,
Besides yourself, to like of. But I prattle
Something too wildly, and my father's precepts
I therein do forget.

FERDINAND   I am, in my condition,
A prince, Miranda; I do think, a King; 60
I would not so! – and would no more endure
This wooden slavery than to suffer
The flesh-fly blow my mouth. Hear my soul speak:
The very instant that I saw you, did
My heart fly to your service; there resides, 65
To make me slave to it; and for your sake
Am I this patient log-man.

MIRANDA   Do you love me?

FERDINAND
O heaven, O earth, bear witness to this sound,
And crown what I profess with kind event,
If I speak true! if hollowly, invert 70
What best is boded me to mischief! I,
Beyond all limit of what else i'th' world,
Do love, prize, honour you.

MIRANDA   I am a fool
To weep at what I am glad of.

PROSPERO   Fair encounter
Of two most rare affections! Heavens rain grace 75
On that which breeds between 'em!

FERDINAND   Wherefore weep you?

MIRANDA
At mine unworthiness, that dare not offer
What I desire to give; and much less take
What I shall die to want. But this is trifling;
And all the more it seeks to hide itself, 80
The bigger bulk it shows. Hence, bashful cunning!
And prompt me plain and holy innocence!
I am your wife if you will marry me;
If not, I'll die your maid: to be your fellow
You may deny me; but I'll be your servant, 85
Whether you will or no.

FERDINAND   My mistress, dearest;
And I thus humble ever.

MIRANDA   My husband, then?

FERDINAND   Ay, with a heart as willing
As bondage e'er of freedom: here's my hand.

MIRANDA
And mine, with my heart in't: and now farewell 90
Till half an hour hence.

FERDINAND   A thousand thousand!

Exeunt Ferdinand and Miranda severally.

PROSPERO   So glad of this as they I cannot be,
Who are surpris'd with all; but my rejoicing
At nothing can be more. I'll to my book;
For yet, ere supper-time, must I perform 95
Much business appertaining.   *Exit.*

3.2   *Enter* CALIBAN, STEPHANO *and* TRINCULO.

STEPHANO   Tell not me; – when the butt is out, we will
drink water; not a drop before: therefore bear up, and
board 'em. Servant-monster, drink to me.

TRINCULO   Servant-monster! the folly of this island!
They say there's but five upon this isle: we are three of 5
them; if th'other two be brain'd like us, the state
totters.

STEPHANO   Drink, servant-monster, when I bid thee:
thy eyes are almost set in thy head.

TRINCULO   Where should they be set else? he were a 10
brave monster indeed, if they were set in his tail.

STEPHANO   My man-monster hath drown'd his tongue
in sack: for my part, the sea cannot drown me; I swam,
ere I could recover the shore, five-and-thirty leagues
off and on. By this light, thou shalt be my lieutenant, 15
monster, or my standard.

TRINCULO   Your lieutenant, if you list; he's no standard.

STEPHANO   We'll not run, Monsieur Monster.

TRINCULO Nor go neither; but you'll lie, like dogs, and
20   yet say nothing neither.
STEPHANO Moon-calf, speak once in thy life, if thou
      beest a good moon-calf.
CALIBAN How does thy honour? Let me lick thy shoe:
      I'll not serve him, he is not valiant.
25 TRINCULO Thou liest, most ignorant monster: I am in
      case to justle a constable. Why, thou debosh'd fish,
      thou, was there ever man a coward that hath drunk so
      much sack as I to-day? Wilt thou tell a monstrous lie,
      being but half a fish and half a monster?
30 CALIBAN Lo, how he mocks me! wilt thou let him, my
      lord?
TRINCULO 'Lord', quoth he? That a monster should be
      such a natural!
CALIBAN Lo, lo, again! bite him to death, I prithee.
35 STEPHANO Trinculo, keep a good tongue in your head:
      if you prove a mutineer, – the next tree! The poor
      monster's my subject, and he shall not suffer
      indignity.
CALIBAN I thank my noble lord. Wilt thou be pleas'd to
40   hearken once again to the suit I made to thee?
STEPHANO Marry, will I: kneel and repeat it; I will
      stand, and so shall Trinculo.

Enter ARIEL, *invisible.*

CALIBAN As I told thee before, I am subject to a tyrant,
      a sorcerer, that by his cunning hath cheated me of the
45   island.
ARIEL Thou liest.
CALIBAN 'Thou liest', thou jesting monkey, thou!
      I would my valiant master would destroy thee!
      I do not lie.
50 STEPHANO Trinculo, if you trouble him any more in 's
      tale, by this hand, I will supplant some of your teeth.
TRINCULO Why, I said nothing.
STEPHANO Mum, then, and no more. Proceed.
CALIBAN I say, by sorcery he got this isle;
55   From me he got it. If thy greatness will
      Revenge it on him, – for I know thou dar'st,
      But this thing dare not, –
STEPHANO That's most certain.
CALIBAN Thou shalt be lord of it, and I'll serve thee.
60 STEPHANO How now shall this be compass'd? Canst
      thou bring me to the party?
CALIBAN Yea, yea, my lord: I'll yield him thee asleep,
      Where thou mayst knock a nail into his head.
ARIEL Thou liest; thou canst not.
65 CALIBAN What a pied ninny's this! Thou scurvy patch!
      I do beseech thy greatness, give him blows,
      And take his bottle from him: when that's gone,
      He shall drink nought but brine; for I'll not show
            him
      Where the quick freshes are.
70 STEPHANO Trinculo, run into no further danger:
      interrupt the monster one word further, and, by this
      hand, I'll turn my mercy out o' doors, and make a

stock-fish of thee.
TRINCULO Why, what did I? I did nothing. I'll go
      farther off.   75
STEPHANO Didst thou not say he lied?
ARIEL Thou liest.
STEPHANO Do I so? take thou that. [*Beats him.*] As you
      like this, give me the lie another time.
TRINCULO I did not give the lie. Out o' your wits, and   80
      hearing too? A pox o' your bottle! this can sack and
      drinking do. A murrain on your monster, and the
      devil take your fingers!
CALIBAN Ha, ha, ha!
STEPHANO Now, forward with your tale. – Prithee,   85
      stand further off.
CALIBAN Beat him enough: after a little time,
      I'll beat him too.
STEPHANO   Stand farther. – Come, proceed.
CALIBAN
      Why, as I told thee, 'tis a custom with him
      I'th' afternoon to sleep: there thou mayst brain him,   90
      Having first seiz'd his books; or with a log
      Batter his skull, or paunch him with a stake,
      Or cut his wezand with thy knife. Remember
      First to possess his books; for without them
      He's but a sot, as I am, nor hath not   95
      One spirit to command: they all do hate him
      As rootedly as I. Burn but his books.
      He has brave utensils, – for so he calls them, –
      Which, when he has a house, he'll deck withal.
      And that most deeply to consider is   100
      The beauty of his daughter; he himself
      Calls her a nonpareil: I never saw a woman,
      But only Sycorax my dam and she;
      But she as far surpasseth Sycorax
      As great'st does least.
STEPHANO   Is it so brave a lass?   105
CALIBAN Ay, lord; she will become thy bed, I warrant,
      And bring thee forth brave brood.
STEPHANO Monster, I will kill this man: his daughter
      and I will be king and queen, – save our graces! – and
      Trinculo and thyself shall be viceroys. Dost thou like   110
      the plot, Trinculo?
TRINCULO Excellent.
STEPHANO Give me thy hand: I am sorry I beat thee;
      but, while thou liv'st, keep a good tongue in thy head.
CALIBAN Within this half hour will he be asleep: 115
      Wilt thou destroy him then?
STEPHANO   Ay, on mine honour.
ARIEL This will I tell my master.
CALIBAN Thou mak'st me merry; I am full of pleasure:
      Let us be jocund: will you troll the catch
      You taught me but while-ere?   120
STEPHANO At thy request, monster, I will do reason,
      any reason. – Come on, Trinculo, let us sing.
      [*Sings.*]   Flout 'em and cout 'em,
                        And scout 'em and flout 'em;
                        Thought is free.   125

CALIBAN   That's not the tune.
[*Ariel plays the tune on a tabor and pipe.*]
STEPHANO   What is this same?
TRINCULO   This is the tune of our catch, played by the
picture of Nobody.
130   STEPHANO   If thou beest a man, show thyself in thy
likeness: if thou beest a devil, take't as thou list.
TRINCULO   O, forgive me my sins!
STEPHANO   He that dies pays all debts: I defy thee.
Mercy upon us!
135   CALIBAN   Art thou afeard?
STEPHANO   No, monster, not I.
CALIBAN   Be not afeard; the isle is full of noises,
Sounds and sweet airs, that give delight, and hurt
not.
Sometimes a thousand twangling instruments
140   Will hum about mine ears; and sometime voices,
That, if I then had wak'd after long sleep,
Will make me sleep again: and then, in dreaming,
The clouds methought would open, and show riches
Ready to drop upon me; that, when I wak'd,
145   I cried to dream again.
STEPHANO   This will prove a brave kingdom to me,
where I shall have my music for nothing.
CALIBAN   When Prospero is destroy'd.
STEPHANO   That shall be by and by: I remember the
150   story.
TRINCULO   The sound is going away; let's follow it, and
after do our work.
STEPHANO   Lead, monster; we'll follow. I would I could
see this taborer; he lays it on.
155   TRINCULO   Wilt come? I'll follow, Stephano.   *Exeunt.*

3.3   *Enter* ALONSO, SEBASTIAN, ANTONIO, GONZALO,
ADRIAN, FRANCISCO, *etc.*

GONZALO   By 'r lakin, I can go no further, sir;
My old bones ache: here's a maze trod, indeed,
Through forth-rights and meanders! By your
patience,
I needs must rest me.
ALONSO   Old lord, I cannot blame thee,
5   Whom am myself attach'd with weariness,
To th' dulling of my spirits: sit down, and rest.
Even here I will put off my hope, and keep it
No longer for my flatterer: he is drown'd
Whom thus we stray to find; and the sea mocks
10   Our frustrate search on land. Well, let him go.
ANTONIO [*aside to Sebastian*]
I am right glad that he's so out of hope.
Do not, for one repulse, forego the purpose
That you resolv'd t'effect.
SEBASTIAN [*aside to Antonio*]   The next advantage
Will we take throughly.
ANTONIO [*aside to Sebastian*]   Let it be to-night;
15   For, now they are oppress'd with travel, they

Will not, nor cannot, use such vigilance
As when they are fresh.
SEBASTIAN [*aside to Antonio*]   I say, to-night: no more.

Solemn and strange music; and PROSPER *on the top, invisible.
Enter several strange shapes, bringing in a banquet; and
dance about it with gentle actions of salutations; and
inviting the King, etc., to eat, they depart.*

ALONSO
What harmony is this? My good friends, hark!
GONZALO   Marvellous sweet music!
ALONSO
Give us kind keepers, heavens! – What were these?   20
SEBASTIAN   A living drollery. Now I will believe
That there are unicorns; that in Arabia
There is one tree, the phoenix' throne; one phoenix
At this hour reigning there.
ANTONIO   I'll believe both;
And what does else want credit, come to me,   25
And I'll be sworn 'tis true: travellers ne'er did lie,
Though fools at home condemn 'em.
GONZALO   If in Naples
I should report this now, would they believe me?
If I should say, I saw such islanders, –
For, certes, these are people of the island, –   30
Who, though they are of monstrous shape, yet, note,
Their manners are more gentle, kind, than of
Our human generation you shall find
Many, nay, almost any.
PROSPERO [*aside*]   Honest lord,
Thou hast said well; for some of you there present   35
Are worse than devils.
ALONSO   I cannot too much muse
Such shapes, such gesture, and such sound,
expressing –
Although they want the use of tongue – a kind
Of excellent dumb discourse.
PROSPERO [*aside*]   Praise in departing.
FRANCISCO   They vanish'd strangely.
SEBASTIAN   No matter, since   40
They have left their viands behind; for we have
stomachs. –
Will't please you taste of what is here?
ALONSO   Not I.
GONZALO
Faith, sir, you need not fear. When we were boys,
Who would believe that there were mountaineers
Dew-lapp'd like bulls, whose throats had hanging at
'em   45
Wallets of flesh? or that there were such men
Whose heads stood in their breasts? which now we
find
Each putter-out of five for one will bring us
Good warrant of.
ALONSO   I will stand to, and feed,
Although my last, no matter, since I feel   50

The best is past. Brother, my lord the duke,
Stand to, and do as we.

Thunder and lightning. Enter ARIEL *like a harpy;*
claps his wings upon the table; and, with
a quaint device, the banquet vanishes.

ARIEL   You are three men of sin, whom Destiny, –
That hath to instrument this lower world
55   And what is in't, – the never-surfeited sea
Hath caus'd to belch up you; and on this island,
Where man doth not inhabit, – you 'mongst men
Being most unfit to live. I have made you mad;
And even with such-like valour men hang and drown
Their proper selves.
[*Alonso, Sebastian, etc., draw their swords.*]
60   You fools! I and my fellows
Are ministers of Fate: the elements,
Of whom your swords are temper'd, may as well
Wound the loud winds, or with bemock'd-at stabs
Kill the still-closing waters, as diminish
65   One dowle that's in my plume: my fellow-ministers
Are like invulnerable. If you could hurt,
Your swords are now too massy for your strengths,
And will not be uplifted. But remember, –
For that's my business to you, – that you three
70   From Milan did supplant good Prospero:
Expos'd unto the sea, which hath requit it,
Him and his innocent child: for which foul deed
The powers, delaying, not forgetting, have
Incens'd the seas and shores, yea, all the creatures,
75   Against your peace. Thee of thy son, Alonso,
They have bereft; and do pronounce by me
Ling'ring perdition – worse than any death
Can be at once – shall step by step attend
You and your ways; whose wraths to guard you
     from, –
80   Which here, in this most desolate isle, else falls
Upon your heads, – is nothing but heart-sorrow
And a clear life ensuing.

He vanishes in thunder; then, to soft music, enter the shapes
again, and dance, with mocks and mows, and carrying out
the table.

PROSPERO   Bravely the figure of this Harpy hast thou
Perform'd, my Ariel; a grace it had devouring:
85   Of my instruction hast thou nothing bated
In what thou hadst to say: so, with good life
And observation strange, my meaner ministers
Their several kinds have done. My high charms
     work,
And these mine enemies are all knit up
90   In their distractions: they now are in my power;
And in these fits I leave them, while I visit
Young Ferdinand, – whom they suppose is
     drown'd, –
And his and mine lov'd darling.   *Exit.*

GONZALO
I'th' name of something holy, sir, why stand you
In this strange stare?
ALONSO   O, it is monstrous, monstrous!   95
Methought the billows spoke, and told me of it;
The winds did sing it to me; and the thunder,
That deep and dreadful organ-pipe, pronounc'd
The name of Prosper: it did bass my trespass.
Therefor my son i'th' ooze is bedded; and   100
I'll seek him deeper than e'er plummet sounded,
And with him there lie mudded.   *Exit.*
SEBASTIAN   But one fiend at a time,
I'll fight their legions o'er.
ANTONIO   I'll be thy second.
                    Exeunt Sebastian and Antonio.
GONZALO
All three of them are desperate: their great guilt,
Like poison given to work a great time after,   105
Now 'gins to bite the spirits. I do beseech you,
That are of suppler joints, follow them swiftly,
And hinder them from what this ecstasy
May now provoke them to.
ADRIAN   Follow, I pray you.
                              Exeunt omnes.

4.1   *Enter* PROSPERO, FERDINAND *and* MIRANDA.

PROSPERO   If I have too austerely punish'd you,
Your compensation makes amends; for I
Have given you here a third of mine own life,
Or that for which I live; who once again
I tender to thy hand: all thy vexations   5
Were but my trials of thy love, and thou
Hast strangely stood the test: here, afore Heaven,
I ratify this my rich gift. O Ferdinand,
Do not smile at me that I boast her off,
For thou shalt find she will outstrip all praise,   10
And make it halt behind her.
FERDINAND   I do believe it
Against an oracle.
PROSPERO   Then, as my gift, and thine own acquisition
Worthily purchas'd, take my daughter: but
If thou dost break her virgin-knot before   15
All sanctimonious ceremonies may
With full and holy rite be minister'd,
No sweet aspersion shall the heavens let fall
To make this contract grow; but barren hate,
Sour-ey'd disdain and discord shall bestrew   20
The union of your bed with weeds so loathly
That you shall hate it both: therefore take heed,
As Hymen's lamps shall light you.
FERDINAND   As I hope
For quiet days, fair issue and long life,
With such love as 'tis now, the murkiest den,   25
The most opportune place, the strong'st suggestion
Our worser genius can, shall never melt
Mine honour into lust, to take away

The edge of that day's celebration
When I shall think, or Phoebus' steeds are founder'd,
Or Night kept chain'd below.
PROSPERO   Fairly spoke.
　Sit, then, and talk with her; she is thine own.
　What, Ariel! my industrious servant, Ariel!

Enter ARIEL.

ARIEL　What would my potent master? here I am.
PROSPERO
　Thou and thy meaner fellows your last service
　Did worthily perform; and I must use you
　In such another trick. Go bring the rabble,
　O'er whom I give thee power, here to this place:
　Incite them to quick motion; for I must
　Bestow upon the eyes of this young couple
　Some vanity of mine Art: it is my promise,
　And they expect it from me.
ARIEL   Presently?
PROSPERO　Ay, with a twink.
ARIEL   Before you can say, 'come,' and 'go,'
　　　　　And breathe twice, and cry, 'so, so,'
　　　　　Each one, tripping on his toe,
　　　　　Will be here with mop and mow.
　　　　　Do you love me, master? no?
PROSPERO　Dearly, my delicate Ariel. Do not approach
　Till thou dost hear me call.
ARIEL   Well, I conceive.   *Exit.*
PROSPERO　Look thou be true; do not give dalliance
　Too much the rein: the strongest oaths are straw
　To th' fire i'th' blood: be more abstemious,
　Or else, good night your vow!
FERDINAND   I warrant you, sir;
　The white cold virgin snow upon my heart
　Abates the ardour of my liver.
PROSPERO   Well.
　Now come, my Ariel! bring a corollary,
　Rather than want a spirit: appear, and pertly!
　No tongue! all eyes! be silent.

[*Soft music.*]

Enter IRIS.

IRIS　*Ceres, most bounteous lady, thy rich leas*
　Of wheat, rye, barley, vetches, oats, and pease;
　Thy turfy mountains, where live nibbling sheep,
　And flat meads thatch'd with stover, them to keep;
　Thy banks with pioned and twilled brims,
　Which spongy April at thy hest betrims,
　To make cold nymphs chaste crowns; and thy broom-
　　　groves,
　Whose shadow the dismissed bachelor loves,
　Being lass-lorn; thy poll-clipt vineyard;
　And thy sea-marge, sterile and rocky-hard,
　Where thou thyself dost air; – the queen o'th' sky,
　Whose wat'ry arch and messenger am I,
　Bids thee leave these; and with her sovereign grace,

JUNO *descends.*

Here, on this grass-plot, in this very place,
To come and sport: – her peacocks fly amain:
Approach, rich Ceres, her to entertain.

Enter CERES.

CERES　*Hail, many-colour'd messenger, that ne'er*
　Dost disobey the wife of Jupiter;
　Who, with thy saffron wings, upon my flowers
　Diffusest honey-drops, refreshing showers;
　And with each end of thy blue bow dost crown
　My bosky acres and my unshrubb'd down,
　Rich scarf to my proud earth; why hath thy queen
　Summon'd me hither, to this short-grass'd green?
IRIS　*A contract of true love to celebrate;*
　And some donation freely to estate
　On the blest lovers.
CERES   *Tell me, heavenly bow,*
　If Venus or her son, as thou dost know,
　Do now attend the queen? Since they did plot
　The means that dusky Dis my daughter got,
　Her and her blind boy's scandal'd company
　I have forsworn.
IRIS   *Of her society*
　Be not afraid: I met her deity
　Cutting the clouds towards Paphos, and her son
　Dove-drawn with her. Here thought they to have done
　Some wanton charm upon this man and maid,
　Whose vows are, that no bed-right shall be paid
　Till Hymen's torch be lighted: but in vain;
　Mars's hot minion is return'd again;
　Her waspish-headed son has broke his arrows,
　Swears he will shoot no more, but play with sparrows,
　And be a boy right out.
CERES   *Highest queen of state,*
　Great Juno comes; I know her by her gait.
JUNO　*How does my bounteous sister? Go with me*
　To bless this twain, that they may prosperous be,
　And honour'd in their issue.
[*They sing.*]

JUNO　　*Honour, riches, marriage-blessing,*
　　　Long continuance, and increasing,
　　　Hourly joys be still upon you!
　　　Juno sings her blessings on you.
CERES　*Earth's increase, foison plenty,*
　　Barns and garners never empty;
　　Vines with clust'ring bunches growing;
　　Plants with goodly burthen bowing;
　　Spring come to you at the farthest
　　In the very end of harvest!
　　Scarcity and want shall shun you;
　　Ceres' blessing so is on you.
FERDINAND　This is a most majestic vision, and
　Harmonious charmingly. May I be bold
　To think these spirits?
PROSPERO   Spirits, which by mine Art
　I have from their confines call'd to enact
　My present fancies.

FERDINAND   Let me live here ever;
    So rare a wonder'd father and a wise
    Makes this place Paradise.
    [*Juno and Ceres whisper, and send Iris on employment.*]
PROSPERO   Sweet, now, silence!
125   Juno and Ceres whisper seriously;
    There's something else to do: hush, and be mute,
    Or else our spell is marr'd.
IRIS *You nymphs, call'd Naiads, of the windring brooks,*
    With your sedg'd crowns and ever-harmless looks,
130   *Leave your crisp channels, and on this green land*
    Answer your summons; Juno does command:
    Come, temperate nymphs, and help to celebrate
    A contract of true love; be not too late.

         Enter certain nymphs.

    You sunburn'd sicklemen, of August weary,
135   *Come hither from the furrow, and be merry:*
    Make holiday; your rye-straw hats put on,
    And these fresh nymphs encounter every one
    In country footing.

    Enter certain reapers, properly habited: they join with the
    nymphs in a graceful dance; towards the end whereof
    Prospero starts suddenly, and speaks; after which, to a
    strange, hollow, and confused noise, they heavily vanish.

PROSPERO [*aside*]   I had forgot that foul conspiracy
140   Of the beast Caliban and his confederates
    Against my life: the minute of their plot
    Is almost come.
    [*to the spirits*]   Well done! avoid; no more!
FERDINAND
    This is strange: your father's in some passion
    That works him strongly.
MIRANDA   Never till this day
145   Saw I him touch'd with anger, so distemper'd.
PROSPERO   You do look, my son, in a mov'd sort,
    As if you were dismay'd: be cheerful, sir.
    Our revels now are ended. These our actors,
    As I foretold you, were all spirits, and
150   Are melted into air, into thin air:
    And, like the baseless fabric of this vision,
    The cloud-capp'd towers, the gorgeous palaces,
    The solemn temples, the great globe itself,
    Yea, all which it inherit, shall dissolve,
155   And, like this insubstantial pageant faded,
    Leave not a rack behind. We are such stuff
    As dreams are made on; and our little life
    Is rounded with a sleep. Sir, I am vex'd;
    Bear with my weakness; my old brain is troubled:
160   Be not disturb'd with my infirmity:
    If you be pleas'd, retire into my cell,
    And there repose: a turn or two I'll walk,
    To still my beating mind.
FERDINAND, MIRANDA   We wish your peace.
               Exeunt.

PROSPERO
    Come with a thought. I thank thee. Ariel: come.

         Enter ARIEL.

ARIEL   Thy thoughts I cleave to. What's thy pleasure?
PROSPERO   Spirit,   165
    We must prepare to meet with Caliban.
ARIEL   Ay, my commander: when I presented Ceres,
    I thought to have told thee of it; but I fear'd
    Lest I might anger thee.
PROSPERO
    Say again, where didst thou leave these varlets?   170
ARIEL   I told you, sir, they were red-hot with drinking;
    So full of valour that they smote the air
    For breathing in their faces; beat the ground
    For kissing of their feet; yet always bending
    Towards their project. Then I beat my tabor;   175
    At which, like unback'd colts, they prick'd their ears,
    Advanc'd their eyelids, lifted up their noses
    As they smelt music: so I charm'd their ears,
    That, calf-like, they my lowing follow'd, through
    Tooth'd briers, sharp furzes, pricking goss, and
       thorns,   180
    Which enter'd their frail shins: at last I left them
    I'th' filthy-mantled pool beyond your cell,
    There dancing up to th' chins, that the foul lake
    O'erstunk their feet.
PROSPERO   This was well done, my bird.
    Thy shape invisible retain thou still: 185
    The trumpery in my house, go bring it hither,
    For stale to catch these thieves.
ARIEL   I go, I go.   *Exit.*
PROSPERO   A devil, a born devil, on whose nature
    Nurture can never stick; on whom my pains,
    Humanely taken, all, all lost, quite lost;   190
    And as with age his body uglier grows,
    So his mind cankers. I will plague them all,
    Even to roaring.

    Re-enter ARIEL, *loaden with glistering apparel, etc.*

         Come, hang them on this line.
[*Prospero and Ariel remain, invisible.*]

    Enter CALIBAN, STEPHANO *and* TRINCULO, *all wet.*

CALIBAN
    Pray you, tread softly, that the blind mole may not
    Hear a foot fall: we now are near his cell.   195
STEPHANO   Monster, your fairy, which you say is a
    harmless fairy, has done little better than played the
    Jack with us.
TRINCULO   Monster, I do smell all horse-piss; at which
    my nose is in great indignation.   200
STEPHANO   So is mine. Do you hear, monster? If I
    should take a displeasure against you, look you, –
TRINCULO   Thou wert but a lost monster.
CALIBAN   Good my lord, give me thy favour still.
    Be patient, for the prize I'll bring thee to   205

Shall hoodwink this mischance: therefore speak
   softly.
All's hush'd as midnight yet.

TRINCULO   Ay, but to lose our bottles in the pool, –

STEPHANO   There is not only disgrace and dishonour in
   that, monster, but an infinite loss.

TRINCULO   That's more to me than my wetting: yet this
   is your harmless fairy, monster.

STEPHANO   I will fetch off my bottle, though I be o'er
   ears for my labour.

CALIBAN
   Prithee, my King, be quiet. See'st thou here,
   This is the mouth o'th' cell: no noise, and enter.
   Do that good mischief which may make this island
   Thine own for ever, and I, thy Caliban,
   For aye thy foot-licker.

STEPHANO   Give me thy hand. I do begin to have bloody
   thoughts.

TRINCULO   O King Stephano! O peer! O worthy
   Stephano! look what a wardrobe here is for thee!

CALIBAN   Let it alone, thou fool; it is but trash.

TRINCULO   O, ho, monster! we know what belongs to a
   frippery. O King Stephano!

STEPHANO   Put off that gown, Trinculo; by this hand,
   I'll have that gown.

TRINCULO   Thy grace shall have it.

CALIBAN
   The dropsy drown this fool! what do you mean
   To dote thus on such luggage? Let't alone,
   And do the murther first: if he awake,
   From toe to crown he'll fill our skins with pinches,
   Make us strange stuff.

STEPHANO   Be you quiet, monster. Mistress line, is not
   this my jerkin? Now is the jerkin under the line: now,
   jerkin, you are like to lose your hair, and prove a bald
   jerkin.

TRINCULO   Do, do; we steal by line and level, an't like
   your grace.

STEPHANO   I thank thee for that jest; here's a garment
   for't: wit shall not go unrewarded while I am King of
   this country. 'Steal by line and level' is an excellent
   pass of pate; there's another garment for't.

TRINCULO   Monster, come, put some lime upon your
   fingers, and away with the rest.

CALIBAN   I will have none on't: we shall lose our time,
   And all be turn'd to barnacles, or to apes
   With foreheads villainous low.

STEPHANO   Monster, lay-to your fingers: help to bear
   this away where my hogshead of wine is, or I'll turn
   you out of my kingdom: go to, carry this.

TRINCULO   And this.

STEPHANO   Ay, and this.

A noise of hunters heard. Enter divers spirits, in shape of
dogs and hounds, hunting them about; Prospero
and Ariel setting them on.

PROSPERO   Hey, Mountain, hey!

ARIEL   Silver! there it goes, Silver!

PROSPERO   Fury, Fury! there, Tyrant, there! hark, hark!
   Caliban, Stephano, and Trinculo are driven out.
   Go charge my goblins that they grind their joints
   With dry convulsions; shorten up their sinews
   With aged cramps; and more pinch-spotted make
      them   260
   Than pard or cat o' mountain.

ARIEL   Hark, they roar!

PROSPERO   Let them be hunted soundly. At this hour
   Lies at my mercy all mine enemies:
   Shortly shall all my labours end, and thou
   Shalt have the air at freedom: for a little   265
   Follow, and do me service.   *Exeunt.*

5.1   *Enter* PROSPERO *in his magic robes, and* ARIEL.

PROSPERO   Now does my project gather to a head:
   My charms crack not; my spirits obey; and time
   Goes upright with his carriage. How's the day?

ARIEL
   On the sixth hour; at which time, my lord,
   You said our work should cease.

PROSPERO   I did say so,   5
   When first I rais'd the tempest. Say, my spirit,
   How fares the King and 's followers?

ARIEL   Confin'd together
   In the same fashion as you gave in charge,
   Just as you left them; all prisoners, sir,
   In the line-grove which weather-fends your cell;   10
   They cannot budge till your release. The King,
   His brother, and yours, abide all three distracted,
   And the remainder mourning over them,
   Brimful of sorrow and dismay; but chiefly
   Him you term'd, sir, 'The good old lord, Gonzalo';   15
   His tears runs down his beard, like winter's drops
   From eaves of reeds. Your charm so strongly works
      'em,
   That if you now beheld them, your affections
   Would become tender.

PROSPERO   Dost thou think so, spirit?

ARIEL   Mine would, sir, were I human.

PROSPERO   And mine shall.   20
   Hast thou, which art but air, a touch, a feeling
   Of their afflictions, and shall not myself,
   One of their kind, that relish all as sharply
   Passion as they, be kindlier mov'd than thou art?
   Though with their high wrongs I am struck to th'
      quick,   25
   Yet with my nobler reason 'gainst my fury
   Do I take part: the rarer action is
   In virtue than in vengeance: they being penitent,
   The sole drift of my purpose doth extend
   Not a frown further. Go release them, Ariel: 30
   My charms I'll break, their senses I'll restore,
   And they shall be themselves.

ARIEL   I'll fetch them, sir.
                                             Exit.

PROSPERO

    Ye elves of hills, brooks, standing lakes, and groves;

    And ye that on the sands with printless foot

35   Do chase the ebbing Neptune, and do fly him

    When he comes back; you demi-puppets that

    By moonshine do the green sour ringlets make,

    Whereof the ewe not bites; and you whose pastime

    Is to make midnight mushrooms, that rejoice

40   To hear the solemn curfew; by whose aid –

    Weak masters though ye be – I have bedimm'd

    The noontide sun, call'd forth the mutinous winds,

    And 'twixt the green sea and the azur'd vault

    Set roaring war: to the dread rattling thunder

45   Have I given fire, and rifted Jove's stout oak

    With his own bolt; the strong-bas'd promontory

    Have I made shake, and by the spurs pluck'd up

    The pine and cedar: graves at my command

    Have wak'd their sleepers, op'd, and let 'em forth

50   By my so potent Art. But this rough magic

    I here abjure; and, when I have requir'd

    Some heavenly music, – which even now I do, –

    To work mine end upon their senses, that

    This airy charm is for, I'll break my staff,

55   Bury it certain fadoms in the earth,

    And deeper than did ever plummet sound

    I'll drown my book.   [*Solemn music*]

Here enters ARIEL *before: then* ALONSO, *with a frantic*
gesture, attended by GONZALO; SEBASTIAN *and* ANTONIO
in like manner, attended by ADRIAN *and* FRANCISCO: *they*
all enter the circle which Prospero has made, and there
stand charm'd; which Prospero observing, speaks:

    A solemn air, and the best comforter

    To an unsettled fancy, cure thy brains,

60   Now useless, boil'd within thy skull! There stand,

    For you are spell-stopp'd.

    Holy Gonzalo, honourable man,

    Mine eyes, ev'n sociable to the show of thine,

    Fall fellowly drops. The charm dissolves apace;

65   And as the morning steals upon the night,

    Melting the darkness, so their rising senses

    Begin to chase the ignorant fumes that mantle

    Their clearer reason. O good Gonzalo,

    My true preserver, and a loyal sir

70   To him thou follow'st! I will pay thy graces

    Home both in word and deed. Most cruelly

    Didst thou, Alonso, use me and my daughter:

    Thy brother was a furtherer in the act.

    Thou art pinch'd for't now, Sebastian. Flesh and
        blood,

75   You, brother mine, that entertain'd ambition,

    Expell'd remorse and nature; whom, with
        Sebastian, –

    Whose inward pinches therefor are most strong, –

    Would here have kill'd your King; I do forgive thee,

    Unnatural though thou art. Their understanding

80   Begins to swell; and the approaching tide

    Will shortly fill the reasonable shore,

    That now lies foul and muddy. Not one of them

    That yet looks on me, or would know me: Ariel,

    Fetch me the hat and rapier in my cell:

    I will discase me, and myself present   85

    As I was sometime Milan: quickly, spirit;

    Thou shalt ere long be free.

ARIEL [*Sings, and helps to attire him.*]

    Where the bee sucks, there suck I:

    In a cowslip's bell I lie;

    There I couch when owls do cry.   90

    On the bat's back I do fly

    After summer merrily.

    Merrily, merrily shall I live now

    Under the blossom that hangs on the bough.

PROSPERO

    Why, that's my dainty Ariel! I shall miss thee;   95

    But yet thou shalt have freedom: so, so, so.

    To the King's ship, invisible as thou art:

    There shalt thou find the mariners asleep

    Under the hatches; the master and the boatswain

    Being awake, enforce them to this place,   100

    And presently, I prithee.

ARIEL   I drink the air before me, and return

    Or ere your pulse twice beat.   *Exit.*

GONZALO

    All torment, trouble, wonder and amazement

    Inhabits here: some heavenly power guide us   105

    Out of this fearful country!

PROSPERO   Behold, sir King,

    The wronged Duke of Milan, Prospero:

    For more assurance that a living Prince

    Does now speak to thee, I embrace thy body;

    And to thee and thy company I bid   110

    A hearty welcome.

ALONSO   Whether thou be'st he or no,

    Or some enchanted trifle to abuse me,

    As late I have been, I not know: thy pulse

    Beats, as of flesh and blood; and, since I saw thee,

    Th'affliction of my mind amends, with which,   115

    I fear, a madness held me: this must crave –

    An if this be at all – a most strange story.

    Thy dukedom I resign, and do entreat

    Thou pardon me my wrongs. – But how should
        Prospero

    Be living and be here?

PROSPERO   First, noble friend,   120

    Let me embrace thine age, whose honour cannot

    Be measur'd or confin'd.

GONZALO   Whether this be

    Or be not, I'll not swear.

PROSPERO   You do yet taste

    Some subtleties o'the isle, that will not let you

    Believe things certain. Welcome, my friends all!   125

    [*aside to Sebastian and Antonio*]

    But you, my brace of lords, were I so minded,

    I here could pluck his highness' frown upon you,

And justify you traitors: at this time
I will tell no tales.

SEBASTIAN [*aside*]   The devil speaks in him.

PROSPERO   No.
30 For you, most wicked sir, whom to call brother
Would even infect my mouth, I do forgive
Thy rankest fault, – all of them; and require
My dukedom of thee, which perforce, I know,
Thou must restore.

ALONSO   If thou be'st Prospero,
35 Give us particulars of thy preservation;
How thou hast met us here, whom three hours since
Were wrack'd upon this shore; where I have lost –
How sharp the point of this remembrance is! –
My dear son Ferdinand.

PROSPERO   I am woe for't, sir.

40 ALONSO   Irreparable is the loss; and patience
Says it is past her cure.

PROSPERO   I rather think
You have not sought her help, of whose soft grace
For the like loss I have her sovereign aid,
And rest myself content.

ALONSO   You the like loss!

45 PROSPERO   As great to me, as late; and, supportable
To make the dear loss, have I means much weaker
Than you may call to comfort you, for I
Have lost my daughter.

ALONSO   A daughter?
O heavens, that they were living both in Naples,
50 The King and Queen there! that they were, I wish
Myself were mudded in that oozy bed
Where my son lies. When did you lose your
      daughter?

PROSPERO   In this last tempest. I perceive, these lords
At this encounter do so much admire,
55 That they devour their reason, and scarce think
Their eyes do offices of truth, their words
Are natural breath: but, howsoe'er you have
Been justled from your senses, know for certain
That I am Prospero, and that very duke
60 Which was thrust forth of Milan; who most strangely
Upon this shore, where you were wrack'd, was
      landed,
To be the lord on't. No more yet of this;
For 'tis a chronicle of day by day,
Not a relation for a breakfast, nor
65 Befitting this first meeting. Welcome, sir;
This cell's my court: here have I few attendants,
And subjects none abroad: pray you, look in.
My dukedom since you have given me again,
I will requite you with as good a thing;
70 At least bring forth a wonder, to content ye
As much as me my dukedom.

Here Prospero discovers FERDINAND *and* MIRANDA
playing at chess.

MIRANDA   Sweet lord, you play me false.

FERDINAND   No, my dearest love,
I would not for the world.

MIRANDA
Yes, for a score of kingdoms you should wrangle,
And I would call it fair play.

ALONSO   If this prove   175
A vision of the island, one dear son
Shall I twice lose.

SEBASTIAN   A most high miracle!

FERDINAND
Though the seas threaten, they are merciful;
I have curs'd them without cause.

ALONSO   Now all the blessings
Of a glad father compass thee about!   180
Arise, and say how thou cam'st here.

MIRANDA   O, wonder!
How many goodly creatures are there here!
How beauteous mankind is! O brave new world,
That has such people in 't!

PROSPERO   'Tis new to thee.

ALONSO
What is this maid with whom thou wast at play?   185
Your eld'st acquaintance cannot be three hours:
Is she the goddess that hath sever'd us,
And brought us thus together?

FERDINAND   Sir, she is mortal;
But by immortal Providence she's mine:
I chose her when I could not ask my father   190
For his advice, nor thought I had one. She
Is daughter to this famous Duke of Milan,
Of whom so often I have heard renown,
But never saw before; of whom I have
Receiv'd a second life; and second father   195
This lady makes him to me.

ALONSO   I am hers:
But, O, how oddly will it sound that I
Must ask my child forgiveness!

PROSPERO   There, sir, stop:
Let us not burthen our remembrance with
A heaviness that's gone.

GONZALO   I have inly wept,   200
Or should have spoke ere this. Look down, you gods,
And on this couple drop a blessed crown!
For it is you that have chalk'd forth the way
Which brought us hither.

ALONSO   I say, Amen, Gonzalo!

GONZALO   Was Milan thrust from Milan, that his issue   205
Should become Kings of Naples? O, rejoice
Beyond a common joy! and set it down
With gold on lasting pillars: in one voyage
Did Claribel her husband find at Tunis,
And Ferdinand, her brother, found a wife   210
Where he himself was lost, Prospero his dukedom
In a poor isle, and all of us ourselves
When no man was his own.

ALONSO [*to Ferdinand and Miranda*]
                                    Give me your hands:
  Let grief and sorrow still embrace his heart
  That doth not wish you joy!

215 GONZALO   Be it so! Amen!

Re-enter ARIEL, *with the* Master *and* Boatswain
amazedly following.

  O, look, sir, look, sir! here is more of us:
  I prophesied, if a gallows were on land,
  This fellow could not drown. Now, blasphemy,
  That swear'st grace o'erboard, not an oath on shore?
220   Hast thou no mouth by land? What is the news?

BOATSWAIN   The best news is, that we have safely found
  Our King, and company; the next, our ship –
  Which, but three glasses since, we gave out split –
  Is tight and yare and bravely rigg'd, as when
  We first put out to sea.

225 ARIEL [*aside to Prospero*]   Sir, all this service
  Have I done since I went.

PROSPERO [*aside to Ariel*]   My tricksy spirit!

ALONSO   These are not natural events; they strengthen
  From strange to stranger. Say, how came you hither?

BOATSWAIN   If I did think, sir, I were well awake,
230   I'd strive to tell you. We were dead of sleep,
  And – how we know not – all clapp'd under hatches;
  Where, but even now, with strange and several noises
  Of roaring, shrieking, howling, jingling chains,
  And mo diversity of sounds, all horrible,
235   We were awak'd; straightway, at liberty;
  Where we, in all our trim, freshly beheld
  Our royal, good, and gallant ship; our master
  Cap'ring to eye her: – on a trice, so please you,
  Even in a dream, were we divided from them,
  And were brought moping hither.

240 ARIEL [*aside to Prospero*]   Was't well done?

PROSPERO [*aside to Ariel*]
  Bravely, my diligence. Thou shalt be free.

ALONSO   This is as strange a maze as e'er men trod;
  And there is in this business more than nature
  Was ever conduct of: some oracle
  Must rectify our knowledge.

245 PROSPERO   Sir, my liege,
  Do not infest your mind with beating on
  The strangeness of this business; at pick'd leisure
  Which shall be shortly single, I'll resolve you,
  Which to you shall seem probable, of every
250   These happen'd accidents; till when, be cheerful,
  And think of each thing well.

[*aside to Ariel*]   Come hither, spirit:
  Set Caliban and his companions free;
  Untie the spell.   *Exit Ariel.*
           How fares my gracious sir?
  There are yet missing of your company
255   Some few odd lads that you remember not.

Re-enter ARIEL, *driving in* CALIBAN, STEPHANO
and TRINCULO, *in their stolen apparel.*

STEPHANO   Every man shift for all the rest, and let no
  man take care for himself; for all is but fortune. –
  Coragio, bully-monster, coragio!

TRINCULO   If these be true spies which I wear in my
260   head, here's a goodly sight.

CALIBAN   O Setebos, these be brave spirits indeed!
  How fine my master is! I am afraid
  He will chastise me.

SEBASTIAN   Ha, ha!
  What things are these, my lord Antonio?
  Will money buy 'em?

ANTONIO   Very like; one of them
265   Is a plain fish, and, no doubt, marketable.

PROSPERO   Mark but the badges of these men, my lords,
  Then say if they be true. This mis-shapen knave,
  His mother was a witch; and one so strong
270   That could control the moon, make flows and ebbs,
  And deal in her command, without her power.
  These three have robb'd me; and this demi-devil –
  For he's a bastard one – had plotted with them
  To take my life. Two of these fellows you
275   Must know and own; this thing of darkness I
  Acknowledge mine.

CALIBAN   I shall be pinch'd to death.

ALONSO   Is not this Stephano, my drunken butler?

SEBASTIAN   He is drunk now: where had he wine?

ALONSO
  And Trinculo is reeling ripe: where should they
280   Find this grand liquor that hath gilded 'em? –
  How cam'st thou in this pickle?

TRINCULO   I have been in such a pickle, since I saw you
  last, that, I fear me, will never out of my bones: I shall
  not fear fly-blowing.

285 SEBASTIAN   Why, how now, Stephano!

STEPHANO   O, touch me not; – I am not Stephano, but a
  cramp.

PROSPERO   You'ld be King o'the isle, sirrah?

STEPHANO   I should have been a sore one, then.

290 ALONSO   This is a strange thing as e'er I look'd on.
  [*pointing to Caliban*]

PROSPERO   He is as disproportion'd in his manners
  As in his shape. Go, sirrah, to my cell;
  Take with you your companions; as you look
  To have my pardon, trim it handsomely.

295 CALIBAN   Ay, that I will; and I'll be wise hereafter,
  And seek for grace. What a thrice-double ass
  Was I, to take this drunkard for a god,
  And worship this dull fool!

PROSPERO   Go to; away!

ALONSO   Hence, and bestow your luggage where you
300   found it.

SEBASTIAN   Or stole it, rather.

PROSPERO   Sir, I invite your Highness and your train
  To my poor cell, where you shall take your rest
  For this one night; which, part of it, I'll waste
305   With such discourse as, I not doubt, shall make it
  Go quick away: the story of my life,

And the particular accidents gone by
Since I came to this isle: and in the morn
I'll bring you to your ship, and so to Naples,
Where I have hope to see the nuptial
Of these our dear-belov'd solemnized;
And thence retire me to my Milan, where
Every third thought shall be my grave.
ALONSO   I long
To hear the story of your life, which must
Take the ear strangely.
PROSPERO   I'll deliver all;
And promise you calm seas, auspicious gales,
And sail so expeditious, that shall catch
Your royal fleet far off.
[*aside to Ariel*]   My Ariel, chick,
That is thy charge: then to the elements
Be free, and fare thou well! Please you, draw near.
                                        Exeunt omnes.

EPILOGUE

Spoken by PROSPERO.

Now my charms are all o'erthrown,
And what strength I have's mine own,
Which is most faint: now, 'tis true,
I must be here confin'd by you,
Or sent to Naples. Let me not,   5
Since I have my dukedom got,
And pardon'd the deceiver, dwell
In this bare island by your spell;
But release me from my bands
With the help of your good hands: 10
Gentle breath of yours my sails
Must fill, or else my project fails,
Which was to please. Now I want
Spirits to enforce, Art to enchant;
And my ending is despair,   15
Unless I be reliev'd by prayer,
Which pierces so, that it assaults
Mercy itself, and frees all faults.
     As you from crimes would pardon'd be,
     Let your indulgence set me free.   *Exit.*   20

Timon of Athens

No reference to *The Life of Timon of Athens* is known to have survived from the years before its inclusion as the fourth of the tragedies in the First Folio of 1623. It is even questionable whether it would have been included in the Folio at all, had not need arisen to fill, at short notice, a gap in the sequence between *Romeo and Juliet* and *Julius Caesar*, created by the removal of *Troilus and Cressida* from that position after printing of it had started.

This is only the first of a succession of questions surrounding *Timon*. Others are: When was it written? Is it all by Shakespeare? Is it finished? Was it acted in Shakespeare's time? Orthodox arguments for dating would place it either around 1604–5, on the basis of linguistic and thematic links with *King Lear*, of which Coleridge described it as the 'stillborn twin', or about 1606–7, as a companion piece to the Plutarchan tragedies on Shakespeare's 'tragic frontier', *Antony and Cleopatra* and *Coriolanus*, but dates as late as 1613 have also been seriously proposed. Shakespeare's sole authorship was much questioned in the later nineteenth century, at a time of general doubt and undisciplined speculation about dramatic authorship. Work on the plays of Thomas Middleton since the 1960s and Middleton's marginal connection with *Macbeth* are currently leading to more substantial claims for Middleton as co-author of *Timon* (where his hand is most confidently identified in 1.2, 3.1–6, and in sections of 4.2 and 4.3, including those involving the steward Flavius). Act 1, scene 2 and the third act of *Timon* are close in tone and technique to the satirical comedies Middleton wrote for the boys' companies in the early years of James I. The unfinished nature of *Timon* is variously defined, either on the evidence of such internal loose ends as confusion of names and the inconsistent epitaphs for Timon, or in terms of lack of

development of some areas of the action, notably the role of Alcibiades in the first three acts. Ever since Thomas Shadwell wrote his own version of the subject in 1678, stagings of *Timon* have tended to entail major or minor reshaping and supplementation of the Folio text.

The story of 'critic Timon', as Shakespeare calls him in *Love's Labour's Lost*, is not the likeliest of tragic subjects. In 1605 Ben Jonson's treatment of the social and economic manifestations of greed took the form of a dark comedy in *Volpone*. *Timon of Athens* combines anecdotes about Timon from Plutarch's life of Mark Antony and more substantial matter from his life of Alcibiades (parallel to that of Coriolanus) with the satirical tradition originating in Lucian's dialogue, *Timon the Man-hater*, (as represented in English by the Inns of Court comedy of *Timon* (*c.* 1602)). Shakespeare is alone and innovative in laying equal emphasis on the two phases of Timon's career – as Lord Timon, the prodigal bankrupt, and as Timon *misanthropos*, the naked hermit ironically in command of a new store of gold. *Timon* begins as a mordant social satire and ends as a philosophical and political tragedy of pessimism. Like the character, described by the cynic philosopher Apemantus as lacking experience of 'the middle of humanity', the play itself seems to divide into two balancing and antithetical halves and to lack the expected enrichment of significance that might have arisen from more sustained development of human relationships. Even Timon's own awareness shows no signs of cumulative development and his death, from unexplained causes, is presented merely as his final negation of human value.

The Arden text is based on the 1623 First Folio.

TIMON of Athens

LUCIUS
LUCULLUS } *flattering lords*
SEMPRONIUS

VENTIDIUS   *one of Timon's false friends*

ALCIBIADES   *an Athenian captain*

APEMANTUS   *a churlish philosopher*

STEWARD   *to Timon*

FLAMINIUS
LUCILIUS } *servants to Timon*
SERVILIUS

CAPHIS
PHILOTUS
TITUS } *several servants to usurers*
HORTENSIUS

SERVANTS   *to Varro, Isidore and Lucius, usurers and Timon's creditors*

POET, PAINTER, JEWELLER, MERCHANT
HOSTILIUS *and two other* STRANGERS
OLD ATHENIAN
PAGE
FOOL
PHRYNIA
TIMANDRA } *mistress to Alcibiades*

Lords, Senators, Soldiers, Bandits and Attendants
Cupid and the Amazons in the Masque

1.1   *Enter* Poet, Painter, Jeweller,
            Merchant *at several doors.*

POET   Good day, sir.
PAINTER   I am glad y'are well.
POET   I have not seen you long; how goes the world?
PAINTER   It wears, sir, as it grows.
POET   Ay, that's well known.
   But what particular rarity, what strange,
   Which manifold record not matches? See,
   Magic of bounty, all these spirits thy power
   Hath conjur'd to attend! I know the merchant.
PAINTER   I know them both: th'other's a jeweller.
MERCHANT   O, 'tis a worthy lord.
JEWELLER   Nay, that's most fix'd.
MERCHANT
   A most incomparable man, breath'd, as it were,
   To an untirable and continuate goodness.
   He passes.
JEWELLER   I have a jewel here –
MERCHANT
   O pray, let's see't. For the Lord Timon, sir?
JEWELLER   If he will touch the estimate. But for that –
POET [*aside to Painter*]
   When we for recompense have prais'd the vild,
   It stains the glory in that happy verse
   Which aptly sings the good.
MERCHANT [*looking at the jewel*]   'Tis a good form.
JEWELLER   And rich. Here is a water, look ye.
PAINTER
   You are rapt, sir, in some work, some dedication
   To the great lord.
POET   A thing slipp'd idly from me.
   Our poesy is as a gum which oozes
   From whence 'tis nourish'd; the fire i'th' flint
   Shows not till it be struck: our gentle flame
   Provokes itself, and like the current flies
   Each bound it chases. What have you there?
PAINTER   A picture, sir. When comes your book forth?
POET   Upon the heels of my presentment, sir.
   Let's see your piece.
PAINTER   'Tis a good piece.
POET   So 'tis; this comes off well and excellent.
PAINTER   Indifferent.
POET   Admirable. How this grace
   Speaks his own standing! What a mental power
   This eye shoots forth! How big imagination
   Moves in this lip! To th' dumbness of the gesture
   One might interpret.
PAINTER   It is a pretty mocking of the life.
   Here is a touch: is't good?
POET   I will say of it,
   It tutors nature; artificial strife
   Lives in these touches, livelier than life.

       Enter certain senators, who go in to Timon.

PAINTER   How this lord is followed!

POET   The senators of Athens, happy men.   40
PAINTER   Look, moe!
POET
   You see this confluence, this great flood of visitors.
   I have in this rough work shap'd out a man,
   Whom this beneath world doth embrace and hug
   With amplest entertainment. My free drift   45
   Halts not particularly, but moves itself
   In a wide sea of wax: no levell'd malice
   Infects one comma in the course I hold,
   But flies an eagle flight, bold, and forth on,
   Leaving no tract behind.   50
PAINTER   How shall I understand you?
POET   I will unbolt to you.
   You see how all conditions, how all minds,
   As well of glib and slipp'ry creatures as
   Of grave and austere quality, tender down   55
   Their services to Lord Timon: his large fortune,
   Upon his good and gracious nature hanging,
   Subdues and properties to his love and tendance
   All sorts of hearts; yea, from the glass-fac'd flatterer
   To Apemantus, that few things loves better   60
   Than to abhor himself – even he drops down
   The knee before him, and returns in peace
   Most rich in Timon's nod.
PAINTER   I saw them speak together.
POET   Sir,
   I have upon a high and pleasant hill   65
   Feign'd Fortune to be thron'd. The base o'th' mount
   Is rank'd with all deserts, all kind of natures
   That labour on the bosom of this sphere
   To propagate their states. Amongst them all,
   Whose eyes are on this sovereign lady fix'd,   70
   One do I personate of Lord Timon's frame,
   Whom Fortune with her ivory hand wafts to her,
   Whose present grace to present slaves and servants
   Translates his rivals.
PAINTER   'Tis conceiv'd to scope.
   This throne, this Fortune, and this hill, methinks,   75
   With one man beckon'd from the rest below,
   Bowing his head against the steepy mount
   To climb his happiness, would be well express'd
   In our condition.
POET   Nay, sir, but hear me on: –
   All those which were his fellows but of late,   80
   Some better than his value, on the moment
   Follow his strides, his lobbies fill with tendance,
   Rain sacrificial whisperings in his ear,
   Make sacred even his stirrup, and through him
   Drink the free air.
PAINTER   Ay marry, what of these?   85
POET   When Fortune in her shift and change of mood
   Spurns down her late beloved, all his dependants
   Which labour'd after him to the mountain's top
   Even on their knees and hands, let him sit down,
   Not one accompanying his declining foot.   90
PAINTER   'Tis common.

A thousand moral paintings I can show
That shall demonstrate these quick blows of
 Fortune's
More pregnantly than words. Yet you do well
95 To show Lord Timon that mean eyes have seen
The foot above the head.

Trumpets sound. Enter LORD TIMON, *addressing himself*
courteously to every suitor; a Messenger *from Ventidius,*
talking with him; LUCILIUS *and other servants.*

TIMON   Imprison'd is he, say you?
MESSENGER   Ay, my good lord. Five talents is his debt;
His means most short, his creditors most strait.
100 Your honourable letter he desires
To those have shut him up, which failing
Periods his comfort.
TIMON   Noble Ventidius. Well,
I am not of that feather to shake off
My friend when he must need me. I do know him
105 A gentleman that well deserves a help,
Which he shall have: I'll pay the debt, and free him.
MESSENGER   Your lordship ever binds him.
TIMON   Commend me to him; I will send his ransom;
And being enfranchis'd, bid him come to me.
110 'Tis not enough to help the feeble up,
But to support him after. Fare you well.
MESSENGER   All happiness to your honour!   *Exit.*

Enter an Old Athenian.

OLD ATHENIAN   Lord Timon, hear me speak.
TIMON   Freely, good father.
OLD ATHENIAN   Thou hast a servant nam'd Lucilius.
115 TIMON   I have so. What of him?
OLD ATHENIAN
Most noble Timon, call the man before thee.
TIMON   Attends he here or no? Lucilius!
LUCILIUS   Here, at your lordship's service.
OLD ATHENIAN
This fellow here, Lord Timon, this thy creature,
120 By night frequents my house. I am a man
That from my first have been inclin'd to thrift,
And my estate deserves an heir more rais'd
Than one which holds a trencher.
TIMON   Well; what further?
OLD ATHENIAN   One only daughter have I, no kin else,
125 On whom I may confer what I have got.
The maid is fair, o'th' youngest for a bride,
And I have bred her at my dearest cost
In qualities of the best. This man of thine
Attempts her love. I prithee, noble lord,
130 Join with me to forbid him her resort;
Myself have spoke in vain.
TIMON   The man is honest.
OLD ATHENIAN   Therefore he will be, Timon.
His honesty rewards him in itself;
It must not bear my daughter.

TIMON   Does she love him?
135 OLD ATHENIAN   She is young and apt:
Our own precedent passions do instruct us
What levity's in youth.
TIMON [*to Lucilius*]   Love you the maid?
LUCILIUS   Ay, my good lord, and she accepts of it.
OLD ATHENIAN
If in her marriage my consent be missing,
140 I call the gods to witness, I will choose
Mine heir from forth the beggars of the world,
And dispossess her all.
TIMON   How shall she be endow'd
If she be mated with an equal husband?
OLD ATHENIAN
Three talents on the present; in future, all.
TIMON
145 This gentleman of mine hath serv'd me long.
To build his fortune I will strain a little,
For 'tis a bond in men. Give him thy daughter;
What you bestow, in him I'll counterpoise,
And make him weigh with her.
OLD ATHENIAN   Most noble lord,
150 Pawn me to this your honour, she is his.
TIMON   My hand to thee; mine honour on my promise.
LUCILIUS   Humbly I thank your lordship. Never may
That state or fortune fall into my keeping
Which is not owed to you.   *Exit.*
POET
155 Vouchsafe my labour, and long live your lordship!
TIMON   I thank you; you shall hear from me anon.
Go not away. What have you there, my friend?
PAINTER   A piece of painting, which I do beseech
Your lordship to accept.
TIMON   Painting is welcome.
160 The painting is almost the natural man:
For since dishonour traffics with man's nature,
He is but out-side; these pencill'd figures are
Even such as they give out. I like your work,
And you shall find I like it. Wait attendance
Till you hear further from me.
165 PAINTER   The gods preserve ye!
TIMON   Well fare you, gentleman. Give me your hand;
We must needs dine together. Sir, your jewel
Hath suffer'd under praise.
JEWELLER   What, my lord, dispraise?
TIMON   A mere satiety of commendations.
170 If I should pay you for't as 'tis extoll'd,
It would unclew me quite.
JEWELLER   My lord, 'tis rated
As those which sell would give; but you well know,
Things of like value, differing in the owners,
Are prized by their masters. Believe't, dear lord,
You mend the jewel by the wearing it.
175 TIMON   Well mock'd.

Enter APEMANTUS.

MERCHANT
  No, my good lord; he speaks the common tongue,
  Which all men speak with him.
TIMON   Look who comes here: will you be chid?
JEWELLER   We'll bear, with your lordship.
MERCHANT   He'll spare none.
TIMON   Good morrow to thee, gentle Apemantus.
APEMANTUS
  Till I be gentle, stay thou for thy good morrow,
  When thou art Timon's dog, and these knaves
      honest.
TIMON
  Why dost thou call them knaves, thou know'st them
      not?
APEMANTUS   Are they not Athenians?
TIMON   Yes.
APEMANTUS   Then I repent not.
JEWELLER   You know me, Apemantus?
APEMANTUS   Thou know'st I do, I call'd thee by thy
  name.
TIMON   Thou art proud, Apemantus.
APEMANTUS   Of nothing so much as that I am not like
  Timon.
TIMON   Whither art going?
APEMANTUS   To knock out an honest Athenian's brains.
TIMON   That's a deed thou'lt die for.
APEMANTUS   Right, if doing nothing be death by th' law.
TIMON   How lik'st thou this picture, Apemantus?
APEMANTUS   The best, for the innocence.
TIMON   Wrought he not well that painted it?
APEMANTUS   He wrought better that made the painter,
  and yet he's but a filthy piece of work.
PAINTER   Y'are a dog.
APEMANTUS   Thy mother's of my generation. What's
  she, if I be a dog?
TIMON   Wilt dine with me, Apemantus?
APEMANTUS   No; I eat not lords.
TIMON   And thou shouldst, thou'dst anger ladies.
APEMANTUS   O they eat lords; so they come by great
  bellies.
TIMON   That's a lascivious apprehension.
APEMANTUS   So thou apprehend'st it; take it for thy
  labour.
TIMON   How dost thou like this jewel, Apemantus?
APEMANTUS   Not so well as plain-dealing, which will
  not cast a man a doit.
TIMON   What dost thou think 'tis worth?
APEMANTUS   Not worth my thinking. How now Poet?
POET   How now Philosopher?
APEMANTUS   Thou liest.
POET   Art not one?
APEMANTUS   Yes.
POET   Then I lie not.
APEMANTUS   Art not a poet?
POET   Yes.
APEMANTUS   Then thou liest. Look in thy last work,
  where thou hast feign'd him a worthy fellow.

POET   That's not feign'd, he is so.
APEMANTUS   Yes, he is worthy of thee, and to pay thee
  for thy labour. He that loves to be flattered is worthy
  o'th' flatterer. Heavens, that I were a lord!   230
TIMON   What wouldst do then, Apemantus?
APEMANTUS   E'en as Apemantus does now: hate a lord
  with my heart.
TIMON   What, thyself?
APEMANTUS   Ay.   235
TIMON   Wherefore?
APEMANTUS   That I had no angry wit to be a lord. Art
  not thou a merchant?
MERCHANT   Ay, Apemantus.
APEMANTUS   Traffic confound thee, if the gods will not!   240
MERCHANT   If traffic do it, the gods do it.
APEMANTUS   Traffic's thy god, and thy god confound
  thee!

        Trumpet sounds. Enter a Messenger.

TIMON   What trumpet's that?
MESSENGER   'Tis Alcibiades, and some twenty horse,   245
  All of companionship.
TIMON   Pray entertain them, give them guide to us.
                              Exeunt some attendants.
  You must needs dine with me. Go not you hence
  Till I have thank'd you. When dinner's done
  Show me this piece. I am joyful of your sights.   250

        Enter ALCIBIADES, *and attendants.*

  Most welcome, sir!
APEMANTUS   So, so, there!
  Aches contract and starve your supple joints!
  That there should be small love amongst these sweet
      knaves,
  And all this courtesy! The strain of man's bred out
  Into baboon and monkey.   255
ALCIBIADES   Sir, you have sav'd my longing, and I feed
  Most hungerly on your sight.
TIMON   Right welcome, sir.
  Ere we depart, we'll share a bounteous time
  In different pleasures. Pray you, let us in.
                          Exeunt all but Apemantus.

        Enter two Lords.

1 LORD   What time o' day is't, Apemantus?   260
APEMANTUS   Time to be honest.
1 LORD   That time serves still.
APEMANTUS   The most accursed thou that still omitt'st
  it.
2 LORD   Thou art going to Lord Timon's feast?   265
APEMANTUS   Ay, to see meat fill knaves and wine heat
  fools.
2 LORD   Fare thee well, fare thee well.
APEMANTUS   Thou art a fool to bid me farewell twice.
2 LORD   Why, Apemantus?   270
APEMANTUS   Shouldst have kept one to thyself, for I
  mean to give thee none.

1 LORD Hang thyself!

APEMANTUS No, I will do nothing at thy bidding. Make
275   thy requests to thy friend.

2 LORD Away, unpeaceable dog, or I'll spurn thee hence!

APEMANTUS I will fly, like a dog, the heels o'th' ass.
                                                  Exit.

1 LORD He's opposite to humanity. Come, shall we in
        And taste Lord Timon's bounty? He out-goes
280   The very heart of kindness.

2 LORD He pours it out. Plutus the god of gold
        Is but his steward. No meed but he repays
        Seven-fold above itself: no gift to him
        But breeds the giver a return exceeding
        All use of quittance.

285 1 LORD   The noblest mind he carries
        That ever govern'd man.

2 LORD Long may he live in fortunes. Shall we in?
        I'll keep you company.   *Exeunt.*

1.2 *Hautboys playing loud music. A great banquet
     serv'd in; and then enter* LORD TIMON, *Athenian
     lords and senators;* VENTIDIUS *which Timon redeem'd
     from prison;* LUCULLUS *and* ALCIBIADES. *Steward
     and others in attendance. Then comes, dropping after
     all,* APEMANTUS, *discontentedly, like himself.*

VENTIDIUS Most honoured Timon,
        It hath pleas'd the gods to remember my father's age,
        And call him to long peace.
        He is gone happy, and has left me rich.
5   Then as in grateful virtue I am bound
        To your free heart, I do return those talents,
        Doubled with thanks and service, from whose help
        I deriv'd liberty.

TIMON   O by no means,
        Honest Ventidius. You mistake my love;
10   I gave it freely ever, and there's none
        Can truly say he gives, if he receives.
        If our betters play at that game, we must not dare
        To imitate them; faults that are rich are fair.

VENTIDIUS A noble spirit!

TIMON
15   Nay, my lords, ceremony was but devis'd at first
        To set a gloss on faint deeds, hollow welcomes,
        Recanting goodness, sorry ere 'tis shown;
        But where there is true friendship, there needs none.
        Pray, sit; more welcome are ye to my fortunes
20   Than my fortunes to me.

1 LORD My lord, we always have confess'd it.

APEMANTUS
        Ho, ho, confess'd it? Hang'd it, have you not?

TIMON O Apemantus, you are welcome.

APEMANTUS No, you shall not make me welcome:
25   I come to have thee thrust me out of doors.

TIMON Fie, th'art a churl, y'have got a humour there
        Does not become a man; 'tis much to blame.
        They say, my lords, *Ira furor brevis est,*

But yond man is very angry.
        Go, let him have a table by himself,   30
        For he does neither affect company,
        Nor is he fit for't, indeed.

APEMANTUS Let me stay at thine apperil, Timon;
        I come to observe: I give thee warning on't.

TIMON I take no heed of thee; th'art an Athenian, there-   35
        fore welcome. I myself would have no power; prithee
        let my meat make thee silent.

APEMANTUS I scorn thy meat; 'twould choke me, for I
        should ne'er flatter thee. O you gods! What a number
        of men eats Timon, and he sees 'em not! It grieves me   40
        to see so many dip their meat in one man's blood; and
        all the madness is, he cheers them up too. I wonder
        men dare trust themselves with men. Methinks they
        should invite them without knives: Good for their
        meat, and safer for their lives. There's much example   45
        for't; the fellow that sits next him, now parts bread
        with him, pledges the breath of him in a divided
        draught, is the readiest man to kill him. 'T'as been
        proved. If I were a huge man, I should fear to drink at
        meals,   50
        Lest they should spy my windpipe's dangerous notes,
        Great men should drink with harness on their
            throats.

TIMON My lord, in heart; and let the health go round.

2 LORD Let it flow this way, my good lord.

APEMANTUS Flow this way? A brave fellow. He keeps   55
        his tides well. Those healths will make thee and thy
        state look ill, Timon.
        Here's that which is too weak to be a sinner,
        Honest water, which ne'er left man i'th' mire.
        This and my food are equals, there's no odds;   60
        Feasts are too proud to give thanks to the gods.

                    Apemantus' Grace.

            Immortal gods, I crave no pelf;
            I pray for no man but myself.
            Grant I may never prove so fond,   65
            To trust man on his oath or bond;
            Or a harlot for her weeping,
            Or a dog that seems a-sleeping,
            Or a keeper with my freedom,
            Or my friends, if I should need 'em.   70
            Amen. So fall to't:
            Rich men sin, and I eat root.
        [*Eats and drinks.*]
        Much good dich thy good heart, Apemantus.

TIMON Captain Alcibiades, your heart's in the field
        now.   75

ALCIBIADES My heart is ever at your service, my lord.

TIMON You had rather be at a breakfast of enemies than
        a dinner of friends.

ALCIBIADES So they were bleeding new, my lord, there's
        no meat like 'em; I could wish my best friend at such   80
        a feast.

APEMANTUS Would all those flatterers were thine

enemies then, that then thou mightst kill 'em – and
bid me to 'em.

85   1 LORD   Might we but have that happiness, my lord,
that you would once use our hearts, whereby we
might express some part of our zeals, we should
think   ourselves for ever perfect.

TIMON   O no doubt, my good friends, but the gods
90   themselves have provided that I shall have much help
from you: how had you been my friends else? Why
have you that charitable title from thousands, did
not you chiefly belong to my heart? I have told more
of you to myself than you can with modesty speak in
95   your own behalf; and thus far I confirm you. O you
gods, think I, what need we have any friends, if we
should ne'er have need of 'em? They were the most
needless creatures living should we ne'er have use for
'em, and would most resemble sweet instruments
100   hung up in cases, that keeps their sounds to
themselves. Why, I have often wish'd myself poorer
that I might come nearer to you. We are born to do
benefits; and what better or properer can we call our
own than the riches of our friends? O what a precious
105   comfort 'tis to have so many like brothers
commanding one another's fortunes. O joy's e'en
made away ere't can be born! Mine eyes cannot hold
out water, methinks. To forget their faults, I drink to
you.

110   APEMANTUS   Thou weep'st to make them drink,
Timon.

2 LORD   Joy had the like conception in our eyes, And at
that instant like a babe sprung up.

APEMANTUS
Ho, ho: I laugh to think that babe a bastard.

115   3 LORD   I promise you, my lord, you mov'd me much.

APEMANTUS   Much.   [*Tucket sounded.*]

TIMON   What means that trump? How now?

Enter Servant.

SERVANT   Please you, my lord, there are certain ladies
most desirous of admittance.

TIMON   Ladies? What are their wills?

120   SERVANT   There comes with them a forerunner, my lord,
which bears that office to signify their pleasures.

TIMON   I pray let them be admitted.

Enter CUPID.

CUPID   Hail to thee, worthy Timon, and to all that of his
bounties taste! The five best senses acknowledge thee
125   their patron, and come freely to gratulate thy
plenteous bosom.
There, taste, touch, all, pleas'd from thy table rise;
They only now come but to feast thine eyes.

TIMON
They're welcome all; let 'em have kind admittance.
130   Music, make their welcome!   *Exit Cupid.*

LUCULLUS   You see, my lord, how ample y'are belov'd.

Music. Re-enter CUPID, *with a masque of ladies as
Amazons, with lutes in their hands, dancing and playing.*

APEMANTUS   Hoy-day!
What a sweep of vanity comes this way.
They dance? They are madwomen.
Like madness is the glory of this life,   135
As this pomp shows to a little oil and root.
We make ourselves fools, to disport ourselves,
And spend our flatteries to drink those men
Upon whose age we void it up again
With poisonous spite and envy.   140
Who lives that's not depraved or depraves?
Who dies that bears not one spurn to their graves
Of their friends' gift?
I should fear those that dance before me now
Would one day stamp upon me. 'T'as been done.   145
Men shut their doors against a setting sun.

*The Lords rise from table, with much adoring of Timon,
and to show their loves each single out an Amazon, and
all dance, men with women, a lofty strain or two to the
hautboys, and cease.*

TIMON
You have done our pleasures much grace, fair ladies,
Set a fair fashion on our entertainment,
Which was not half so beautiful and kind;
You have added worth unto't and lustre,   150
And entertain'd me with mine own device.
I am to thank you for't.

1 LADY   My lord, you take us even at the best.

APEMANTUS   Faith, for the worst is filthy; and would
not hold taking, I doubt me.   155

TIMON   Ladies, there is an idle banquet attends you;
Please you to dispose yourselves.

ALL LADIES   Most thankfully, my lord.
         Exeunt Cupid and Ladies.

TIMON   Flavius!

STEWARD   My lord?

TIMON   The little casket bring me hither.

STEWARD   Yes, my lord. [*aside*] More jewels yet!   160
There is no crossing him in's humour,
Else I should tell him well, i'faith, I should,
When all's spent, he'd be cross'd then, and he could.
'Tis pity bounty had not eyes behind,
That man might ne'er be wretched for his mind.   165
         Exit.

1 LORD   Where be our men?

SERVANT   Here, my lord, in readiness.

2 LORD   Our horses!

Re-enter Steward, *with the casket.*

TIMON   O my friends, I have one word
To say to you: look you, my good lord,
I must entreat you honour me so much   170
As to advance this jewel; accept it and wear it,
Kind my lord.

1 LORD   I am so far already in your gifts –

ALL   So are we all.

Enter a Servant.

175   SERVANT   My lord, there are certain nobles of the senate
newly alighted, and come to visit you.
TIMON   They are fairly welcome.   *Exit Servant.*
STEWARD   I beseech your honour, vouchsafe me a word;
it does concern you near.
180   TIMON   Near? Why, then, another time I'll hear thee. I
prithee, let's be provided to show them entertainment.
STEWARD [*aside*]   I scarce know how.

Enter another Servant.

2 SERVANT
May it please your honour, Lord Lucius,
Out of his free love, hath presented to you
185   Four milk-white horses, trapp'd in silver.
TIMON   I shall accept them fairly. Let the presents
Be worthily entertain'd.   *Exit Servant.*

Enter a third Servant.

How now? What news?

3 SERVANT
Please you, my lord, that honourable gentleman Lord
Lucullus entreats your company tomorrow, to hunt
190   with him, and has sent your honour two brace of
greyhounds.
TIMON   I'll hunt with him; and let them be receiv'd,
Not without fair reward.
STEWARD [*aside*]   What will this come to?
He commands us to provide, and give great gifts,
195   And all out of an empty coffer;
Nor will he know his purse, or yield me this,
To show him what a beggar his heart is,
Being of no power to make his wishes good.
His promises fly so beyond his state
200   That what he speaks is all in debt; he owes for ev'ry
word:
He is so kind that he now pays interest for't;
His land's put to their books. Well, would I were
Gently put out of office before I were forc'd out!
Happier is he that has no friend to feed
205   Than such that do e'en enemies exceed.
I bleed inwardly for my lord.   *Exit.*
TIMON   You do yourselves much wrong,
You bate too much of your own merits.
Here, my lord, a trifle of our love.
210   2 LORD   With more than common thanks I will receive
it.
3 LORD   O he's the very soul of bounty.
TIMON   And now I remember, my lord, you gave good
words the other day of a bay courser I rode on. 'Tis
215   yours, because you lik'd it.
3 LORD   O I beseech you pardon me, my lord, in that.
TIMON
You may take my word, my lord, I know no man
Can justly praise but what he does affect.

I weigh my friend's affection with mine own,
I'll tell you true. I'll call to you.   220
ALL LORDS   O none so welcome.
TIMON   I take all and your several visitations
So kind to heart, 'tis not enough to give:
Methinks I could deal kingdoms to my friends,
And ne'er be weary. Alcibiades,   225
Thou art a soldier, therefore seldom rich;
It comes in charity to thee: for all thy living
Is 'mongst the dead, and all the lands thou hast
Lie in a pitch'd field.
ALCIBIADES   Ay, defil'd land, my lord.   230
1 LORD   We are so virtuously bound –
TIMON   And so am I to you.
2 LORD   So infinitely endear'd –
TIMON   All to you. Lights, more lights!
1 LORD   The best of happiness, honour and fortunes,   235
Keep with you, Lord Timon!
TIMON   Ready for his friends.
                    Exeunt all but Timon, Apemantus.
APEMANTUS   What a coil's here,
Serving of becks and jutting-out of bums!
I doubt whether their legs be worth the sums
That are given for 'em. Friendship's full of dregs;   240
Methinks false hearts should never have sound legs.
Thus honest fools lay out their wealth on curtsies.
TIMON   Now Apemantus, if thou wert not sullen,
I would be good to thee.
APEMANTUS   No, I'll nothing; for if I should be brib'd 245
too, there would be none left to rail upon thee, and
then thou wouldst sin the faster. Thou giv'st so long,
Timon, I fear me thou wilt give away thyself in paper
shortly. What needs these feasts, pomps, and vain-
glories?   250
TIMON   Nay, and you begin to rail on society once, I am
sworn not to give regard to you. Farewell, and come
with better music.   *Exit.*
APEMANTUS   So. Thou wilt not hear me now; thou shalt
not then. I'll lock thy heaven from thee.   255
O that men's ears should be
To counsel deaf, but not to flattery.   *Exit.*

2.1   *Enter a* Senator.

SENATOR
And late, five thousand; to Varro and to Isidore
He owes nine thousand, besides my former sum,
Which makes it five and twenty. Still in motion
Of raging waste? It cannot hold, it will not.
If I want gold, steal but a beggar's dog   5
And give it Timon – why, the dog coins gold;
If I would sell my horse and buy twenty moe
Better than he – why, give my horse to Timon;
Ask nothing, give it him, it foals me straight
And able horses. No porter at his gate,   10
But rather one that smiles and still invites
All that pass by. It cannot hold; no reason
Can sound his state in safety. Caphis, ho!
Caphis, I say!

Enter CAPHIS.

CAPHIS   Here, sir, what is your pleasure?
SENATOR

15   Get on your cloak, and haste you to Lord Timon;
        Importune him for my moneys; be not ceas'd
        With slight denial, nor then silenc'd when
        'Commend me to your master' and the cap
        Plays in the right hand, thus – but tell him,
20   My uses cry to me; I must serve my turn
        Out of mine own; his days and times are past,
        And my reliances on his fracted dates
        Have smit my credit. I love and honour him,
        But must not break my back to heal his finger.
25   Immediate are my needs, and my relief
        Must not be toss'd and turn'd to me in words,
        But find supply immediate. Get you gone;
        Put on a most importunate aspect,
        A visage of demand: for I do fear,
30   When every feather sticks in his own wing,
        Lord Timon will be left a naked gull,
        Which flashes now a phoenix. Get you gone.
CAPHIS   I go, sir.
SENATOR   Ay, go sir! Take the bonds along with you,
        And have the dates in. Come.
CAPHIS   I will, sir.
35   SENATOR   Go.   *Exeunt.*

2.2   *Enter* Steward, *with many bills in his hand.*

STEWARD   No care, no stop; so senseless of expense,
        That he will neither know how to maintain it,
        Nor cease his flow of riot. Takes no accompt
5   How things go from him, nor resumes no care
        Of what is to continue. Never mind
        Was to be so unwise, to be so kind.
        What shall be done? He will not hear, till feel.
        I must be round with him, now he comes from
           hunting.
        Fie, fie, fie, fie!

Enter CAPHIS *and the* Servants *of Isidore and Varro.*

10   CAPHIS   Good even, Varro; what, you come for money?
VARRO'S SERVANT   Is't not your business too?
CAPHIS   It is; and yours too, Isidore?
ISIDORE'S SERVANT   It is so.
CAPHIS   Would we were all discharg'd!
15   VARRO'S SERVANT   I fear it.
CAPHIS   Here comes the lord.

Enter TIMON *and his train, and* ALCIBIADES.

TIMON   So soon as dinner's done, we'll forth again,
        My Alcibiades.
        [*to Caphis*]   With me? What is your will?
CAPHIS   My lord, here is a note of certain dues.
TIMON   Dues? Whence are you?
CAPHIS   Of Athens here, my lord.

TIMON   Go to my steward.
CAPHIS   Please it your lordship, he hath put me off
        To the succession of new days this month.
        My master is awak'd by great occasion
        To call upon his own, and humbly prays you   25
        That with your other noble parts you'll suit,
        In giving him his right.
TIMON   Mine honest friend,
        I prithee but repair to me next morning.
CAPHIS   Nay, good my lord –
TIMON   Contain thyself, good friend.
VARRO'S SERVANT   One Varro's servant, my good lord –   30
ISIDORE'S SERVANT   From Isidore; he humbly prays your
        speedy payment.
CAPHIS   If you did know, my lord, my master's wants –
VARRO'S SERVANT   'Twas due on forfeiture, my lord, six
        weeks and past.   35
ISIDORE'S SERVANT   Your steward puts me off, my lord,
        and I am sent expressly to your lordship.
TIMON
        Give me breath.
        I do beseech you, good my lords, keep on;
        I'll wait upon you instantly.
                        Exeunt Alcibiades and Lords.
        [*to Steward*]   Come hither. Pray you,   40
        How goes the world, that I am thus encounter'd
        With clamorous demands of debt, broken bonds,
        And the detention of long since due debts
        Against my honour?
STEWARD   [*to Caphis and other Servants*]
                        Please you, gentlemen,
        The time is unagreeable to this business.   45
        Your importunacy cease till after dinner,
        That I may make his lordship understand
        Wherefore you are not paid.
TIMON   Do so, my friends.
        See them well entertain'd.   *Exit.*
STEWARD   Pray draw near.   *Exit.*

Enter APEMANTUS *and* Fool.

CAPHIS   Stay, stay; here comes the fool with Apemantus: 50
        let's ha' some sport with 'em.
VARRO'S SERVANT   Hang him, he'll abuse us!
ISIDORE'S SERVANT   A plague upon him, dog!
VARRO'S SERVANT   How dost, fool?
APEMANTUS   Dost dialogue with thy shadow?   55
VARRO'S SERVANT   I speak not to thee.
APEMANTUS   No, 'tis to thyself. [*to the Fool*] Come
        away.
ISIDORE'S SERVANT [*to Varro's Servant*]   There's the fool
        hangs on your back already.   60
APEMANTUS   No, thou stand'st single; th'art not on him
        yet.
CAPHIS   Where's the fool now?
APEMANTUS   He last ask'd the question. Poor rogues,
        and usurers' men, bawds between gold and want!   65
ALL SERVANTS   What are we, Apemantus?

APEMANTUS   Asses.

ALL SERVANTS   Why?

APEMANTUS   That you ask me what you are, and do not
70   know yourselves. Speak to 'em, fool.

FOOL   How do you, gentlemen?

ALL SERVANTS   Gramercies, good fool. How does your
      mistress?

FOOL   She's e'en setting on water to scald such chickens
75   as you are. Would we could see you at Corinth!

APEMANTUS   Good! Gramercy.

              Enter Page.

FOOL   Look you, here comes my master's page.

PAGE [*to the Fool*]   Why, how now, captain? What do
      you in this wise company? How dost thou,
80   Apemantus?

APEMANTUS   Would I had a rod in my mouth, that I
      might answer thee profitably.

PAGE   Prithee, Apemantus, read me the superscription
      of these letters: I know not which is which.

85   APEMANTUS   Canst not read?

PAGE   No.

APEMANTUS   There will little learning die then that day
      thou art hang'd. This is to Lord Timon; this to
      Alcibiades. Go, thou wast born a bastard, and thou'lt
90   die a bawd.

PAGE   Thou wast whelp'd a dog, and thou shalt famish a
      dog's death. Answer not; I am gone.   *Exit.*

APEMANTUS   E'en so thou outrun'st grace. Fool, I will
      go with you to Lord Timon's.

95   FOOL   Will you leave me there?

APEMANTUS   If Timon stay at home. You three serve
      three usurers?

ALL SERVANTS   Ay; would they serv'd us.

APEMANTUS   So would I – as good a trick as ever
100   hangman serv'd thief.

FOOL   Are you three usurers' men?

ALL SERVANTS   Ay, fool.

FOOL   I think no usurer but has a fool to his servant; my
      mistress is one, and I am her fool. When men come
105   to borrow of your masters, they approach sadly, and go
      away merry; but they enter my master's house merrily,
      and go away sadly. The reason of this?

VARRO'S SERVANT   I could render one.

APEMANTUS   Do it then, that we may account thee a
110   whoremaster and a knave; which notwithstanding,
      thou shalt be no less esteemed.

VARRO'S SERVANT   What is a whoremaster, fool?

FOOL   A fool in good clothes, and something like thee.
      'Tis a spirit; sometime 't appears like a lord, sometime
115   like a lawyer, sometime like a philosopher, with two
      stones moe than's artificial one. He is very often like a
      knight; and generally in all shapes that man goes up
      and down in, from fourscore to thirteen, this spirit
      walks in.

120   VARRO'S SERVANT   Thou art not altogether a fool.

FOOL   Nor thou altogether a wise man. As much foolery

as I have, so much wit thou lack'st.

APEMANTUS   That answer might have become Apemantus.

ALL SERVANTS   Aside, aside; here comes Lord Timon.

              Re-enter TIMON *and* Steward.

APEMANTUS   Come with me, fool, come.   125

FOOL   I do not always follow lover, elder brother and
      woman; sometime the philosopher.

STEWARD
      Pray you, walk near: I'll speak with you anon.
              Exeunt Apemantus, Fool and Servants.

TIMON
      You make me marvel wherefore ere this time
      Had you not fully laid my state before me,   130
      That I might so have rated my expense
      As I had leave of means.

STEWARD   You would not hear me.
      At many leisures I propos'd –

TIMON   Go to.
      Perchance some single vantages you took,
      When my indisposition put you back,   135
      And that unaptness made your minister
      Thus to excuse yourself.

STEWARD   O my good lord,
      At many times I brought in my accompts,
      Laid them before you; you would throw them off,
      And say you found them in mine honesty.   140
      When for some trifling present you have bid me
      Return so much, I have shook my head and wept:
      Yea, 'gainst th'authority of manners, pray'd you
      To hold your hand more close. I did endure
      Not seldom, nor no slight checks, when I have   145
      Prompted you in the ebb of your estate
      And your great flow of debts. My lov'd lord,
      Though you hear now, too late, yet now's a time:
      The greatest of your having lacks a half
      To pay your present debts.

TIMON   Let all my land be sold.   150

STEWARD   'Tis all engag'd, some forfeited and gone,
      And what remains will hardly stop the mouth
      Of present dues. The future comes apace.
      What shall defend the interim, and at length
      How goes our reck'ning?   155

TIMON   To Lacedaemon did my land extend.

STEWARD   O my good lord, the world is but a word:
      Were it all yours, to give it in a breath,
      How quickly were it gone!

TIMON   You tell me true.

STEWARD   If you suspect my husbandry or falsehood,   160
      Call me before th'exactest auditors,
      And set me on the proof. So the gods bless me,
      When all our offices have been oppress'd
      With riotous feeders, when our vaults have wept
      With drunken spilth of wine, when every room   165
      Hath blaz'd with lights and bray'd with minstrelsy,
      I have retir'd me to a wasteful cock
      And set mine eyes at flow.

TIMON   Prithee no more.
STEWARD   Heavens, have I said, the bounty of this lord!
170   How many prodigal bits have slaves and peasants
      This night englutted! Who is not Timon's?
      What heart, head, sword, force, means, but is Lord
          Timon's,
      Great Timon, noble, worthy, royal Timon?
      Ah, when the means are gone that buy this praise,
175   The breath is gone whereof this praise is made.
      Feast-won, fast-lost; one cloud of winter show'rs,
      These flies are couch'd.
TIMON   Come, sermon me no further.
      No villainous bounty yet hath pass'd my heart;
      Unwisely, not ignobly, have I given.
      Why dost thou weep? Canst thou the conscience
180   lack,
      To think I shall lack friends? Secure thy heart.
      If I would broach the vessels of my love,
      And try the arguments of hearts by borrowing,
      Men and men's fortunes could I frankly use
      As I can bid thee speak.
185   STEWARD   Assurance bless your thoughts.
TIMON
      And in some sort these wants of mine are crown'd,
      That I account them blessings; for by these
      Shall I try friends. You shall perceive how you
      Mistake my fortunes; I am wealthy in my friends.
190   Within there! Flaminius! Servilius!

      Enter FLAMINIUS, SERVILIUS *and another* Servant.

ALL SERVANTS   My lord, my lord.
TIMON   I will dispatch you severally: [*to Servilius*] you
      to Lord Lucius; [*to Flaminius*] to Lord Lucullus you
      (I hunted with his honour to-day); [*to Third Servant*]
195   you, to Sempronius. Commend me to their loves;
      and I am proud, say, that my occasions have found
      time to use 'em toward a supply of money. Let the
      request be fifty talents.
FLAMINIUS   As you have said, my lord.
                              Exeunt Servants.
200   STEWARD [*aside*]   Lord Lucius and Lucullus? Humh!
TIMON [*to Steward*]   Go you, sir, to the senators,
      Of whom, even to the state's best health, I have
      Deserv'd this hearing: bid 'em send o'th' instant
      A thousand talents to me.
STEWARD   I have been bold,
205   For that I knew it the most general way,
      To them to use your signet and your name;
      But they do shake their heads, and I am here
      No richer in return.
TIMON   Is't true? can't be?
STEWARD   They answer in a joint and corporate voice
210   That now they are at fall, want treasure, cannot
      Do what they would, are sorry; you are honourable,
      But yet they could have wish'd – they know not;
      Something hath been amiss – a noble nature
      May catch a wrench – would all were well – 'tis pity –

And so, intending other serious matters,   215
After distasteful looks, and these hard fractions,
With certain half-caps, and cold-moving nods,
They froze me into silence.
TIMON   You gods reward them!
      Prithee, man, look cheerly. These old fellows
      Have their ingratitude in them hereditary;   220
      Their blood is cak'd, 'tis cold, it seldom flows;
      'Tis lack of kindly warmth they are not kind;
      And nature, as it grows again toward earth,
      Is fashion'd for the journey, dull and heavy.
      Go to Ventidius. Prithee, be not sad,   225
      Thou art true and honest; ingeniously I speak,
      No blame belongs to thee. Ventidius lately
      Buried his father, by whose death he's stepp'd
      Into a great estate. When he was poor,
      Imprison'd, and in scarcity of friends,   230
      I clear'd him with five talents. Greet him from me,
      Bid him suppose some good necessity
      Touches his friend, which craves to be remember'd
      With those five talents. That had, give't these fellows
      To whom 'tis instant due. Ne'er speak or think   235
      That Timon's fortunes 'mong his friends can sink.
STEWARD   I would I could not think it.
      That thought is bounty's foe;
      Being free itself, it thinks all others so.   *Exeunt.*

3.1   FLAMINIUS *waiting to speak with Lucullus*
      from his master. Enter a Servant *to him.*

SERVANT   I have told my lord of you; he is coming down
      to you.
FLAMINIUS   I thank you, sir.

             Enter LUCULLUS.

SERVANT   Here's my lord.
LUCULLUS [*aside*]   One of Lord Timon's men? A gift, I   5
      warrant. Why, this hits right: I dreamt of a silver basin
      and ewer to-night. – Flaminius, honest Flaminius, you
      are very respectively welcome, sir. Fill me some
      wine.   [*Exit Servant.*]
      And how does that honourable, complete, free-   10
      hearted gentleman of Athens, thy very bountiful good
      lord and master?
FLAMINIUS   His health is well, sir.
LUCULLUS   I am right glad that his health is well, sir.
      And what hast thou there under thy cloak, pretty 15
      Flaminius?
FLAMINIUS   Faith, nothing but an empty box, sir, which,
      in my lord's behalf, I come to entreat your honour to
      supply; who, having great and instant occasion to
      use fifty talents, hath sent to your lordship to furnish 20
      him, nothing doubting your present assistance
      therein.
LUCULLUS   La, la, la, la: 'nothing doubting', says he?
      Alas, good lord; a noble gentleman 'tis, if he would not
      keep so good a house. Many a time and often I ha'   25

din'd with him, and told him on't, and come again to
supper to him of purpose to have him spend less; and
yet he would embrace no counsel, take no warning by
my coming. Every man has his fault, and honesty is
30   his. I ha'told him on't, but I could ne'er get him
from't.

Re-enter Servant, *with wine.*

SERVANT   Please your lordship, here is the wine.

LUCULLUS   Flaminius, I have noted thee always wise.
Here's to thee.

35   FLAMINIUS   Your lordship speaks your pleasure.

LUCULLUS   I have observed thee always for a towardly
prompt spirit, give thee thy due, and one that knows
what belongs to reason; and canst use the time well, if
the time use thee well. Good parts in thee. [*to the*
40   *Servant*] Get you gone, sirrah.   [*Exit Servant.*]
Draw nearer, honest Flaminius. Thy lord's a bountiful
gentleman: but thou art wise, and thou know'st well
enough, although thou com'st to me, that this is no
time to lend money, especially upon bare friendship,
45   without security. Here's three solidares for thee; good
boy, wink at me, and say thou saw'st me not. Fare thee
well.

FLAMINIUS

Is't possible the world should so much differ,
And we alive that lived? Fly, damned baseness,
50   To him that worships thee!
[*throwing the money back at Lucullus*]

LUCULLUS

Ha? Now I see thou art a fool, and fit for thy master.
                                    Exit.

FLAMINIUS

May these add to the number that may scald thee!
Let molten coin be thy damnation,
Thou disease of a friend, and not himself!
55   Has friendship such a faint and milky heart
It turns in less than two nights? O you gods!
I feel my master's passion. This slave unto his
    honour
Has my lord's meat in him:
Why should it thrive and turn to nutriment
60   When he is turn'd to poison?
O may diseases only work upon't,
And when he's sick to death, let not that part of
    nature
Which my lord paid for, be of any power
To expel sickness, but prolong his hour!   *Exit.*

3.2   *Enter* LUCIUS, *with* HOSTILIUS *and two
other* Strangers.

LUCIUS   Who, the Lord Timon? He is my very good
friend and an honourable gentleman.

1 STRANGER   We know him for no less, though we are
but strangers to him. But I can tell you one thing, my
5   lord, and which I hear from common rumours: now

Lord Timon's happy hours are done and past, and his
estate shrinks from him.

LUCIUS   Fie, no, do not believe it; he cannot want for
money.

HOSTILIUS   But believe you this, my lord, that not long   10
ago, one of his men was with the Lord Lucullus, to
borrow so many talents, nay, urg'd extremely for't, and
showed what necessity belong'd to't, and yet was
denied.

LUCIUS   How?   15

HOSTILIUS   I tell you, denied, my lord.

LUCIUS   What a strange case was that! Now before the
gods, I am asham'd on't. Denied that honourable man?
There was very little honour show'd in't. For my own
part, I must needs confess I have received some small   20
kindnesses from him, as money, plate, jewels, and such
like trifles – nothing comparing to his; yet had he
mistook him, and sent to me, I should ne'er have
denied his occasion so many talents.

Enter SERVILIUS.

SERVILIUS   See, by good hap, yonder's my lord; I have   25
sweat to see his honour. My honour'd lord!

LUCIUS   Servilius? You are kindly met, sir. Fare thee
well; commend me to thy honourable virtuous lord,
my very exquisite friend.

SERVILIUS   May it please your honour, my lord hath   30
sent –

LUCIUS   Ha? What has he sent? I am so much endeared
to that lord; he's ever sending. How shall I thank him,
think'st thou? And what has he sent now?

SERVILIUS   H'as only sent his present occasion now, my   35
lord: requesting your lordship to supply his instant
use with so many talents.

LUCIUS   I know his lordship is but merry with me,
He cannot want fifty – five hundred talents.

SERVILIUS

But in the meantime he wants less, my lord.   40
If his occasion were not virtuous,
I should not urge it half so faithfully.

LUCIUS

Dost thou speak seriously, Servilius?

SERVILIUS

Upon my soul, 'tis true, sir.

LUCIUS   What a wicked beast was I to disfurnish myself   45
against such a good time, when I might ha'shown
myself honourable! How unluckily it happen'd, that I
should purchase the day before for a little part, and
undo a great deal of honour! Servilius, now before
the gods, I am not able to do (the more beast, I say!)   50
– I was sending to use Lord Timon myself, these
gentlemen can witness; but I would not, for the
wealth of Athens, I had done't now. Commend me
bountifully to his good lordship; and I hope his
honour will conceive the fairest of me, because I have   55
no power to be kind. And tell him this from me: I
count it one of my greatest afflictions, say, that I

cannot pleasure such an honourable gentleman. Good
Servilius, will you befriend me so far as to use mine
own words to him?

SERVILIUS Yes, sir, I shall.   *Exit.*

LUCIUS [*calling out after him*] I'll look you out a good
    turn, Servilius.
    [*to the others*] True, as you said, Timon is shrunk
    indeed;
    And he that's once denied will hardly speed.   *Exit.*

1 STRANGER Do you observe this, Hostilius?

HOSTILIUS Ay, too well.

1 STRANGER   Why, this is the world's soul,
    And just of the same piece
    Is every flatterer's sport. Who can call him his friend
    That dips in the same dish? For in my knowing
    Timon has been this lord's father,
    And kept his credit with his purse;
    Supported his estate; nay, Timon's money
    Has paid his men their wages. He ne'er drinks
    But Timon's silver treads upon his lip;
    And yet – O see the monstrousness of man,
    When he looks out in an ungrateful shape! –
    He does deny him, in respect of his,
    What charitable men afford to beggars.

2 STRANGER Religion groans at it.

1 STRANGER   For mine own part,
    I never tasted Timon in my life,
    Nor came any of his bounties over me,
    To mark me for his friend. Yet I protest,
    For his right noble mind, illustrious virtue,
    And honourable carriage,
    Had his necessity made use of me,
    I would have put my wealth into donation,
    And the best half should have return'd to him,
    So much I love his heart. But I perceive
    Men must learn now with pity to dispense,
    For policy sits above conscience.   *Exeunt.*

3.3 *Enter Timon's third Servant with* SEMPRONIUS,
    another of Timon's friends.

SEMPRONIUS Must he needs trouble me in't? Humh!
    'Bove all others?
    He might have tried Lord Lucius, or Lucullus;
    And now Ventidius is wealthy too,
    Whom he redeem'd from prison. All these
    Owes their estates unto him.

3 SERVANT   My lord,
    They have all been touch'd and found base metal,
    For they have all denied him.

SEMPRONIUS How? Have they denied him?
    Has Ventidius and Lucullus denied him?
    And does he send to me? Three? Humh?
    It shows but little love or judgment in him.
    Must I be his last refuge? His friends, like physicians,
    Thrive, give him over; must I take th' cure upon me?
    H'as much disgrac'd me in't; I'm angry at him

That might have known my place. I see no sense for't
But his occasions might have wooed me first:
For, in my conscience, I was the first man
That e'er received gift from him.
And does he think so backwardly of me now,
That I'll requite it last? No:
So it may prove an argument of laughter
To th' rest, and 'mongst lords I be thought a fool.
I'd rather than the worth of thrice the sum,
H'ad sent to me first, but for my mind's sake;
I'd such a courage to do him good. But now return,
And with their faint reply this answer join:
Who bates mine honour shall not know my coin.
                                 Exit.

3 SERVANT Excellent: your lordship's a goodly villain.
    The devil knew not what he did when he made man
    politic; he crossed himself by't: and I cannot think but
    in the end the villainies of man will set him clear. How
    fairly this lord strives to appear foul! Takes virtuous
    copies to be wicked, like those that under hot ardent
    zeal would set whole realms on fire: of such a nature is
    his politic love.
    This was my lord's best hope; now all are fled
    Save only the gods. Now his friends are dead,
    Doors that were ne'er acquainted with their wards
    Many a bounteous year, must be employ'd
    Now to guard sure their master.
    And this is all a liberal course allows:
    Who cannot keep his wealth must keep his house.
                                    Exit.

3.4 *Enter* VARRO'S *two* Servants, *meeting other
    servants of Timon's creditors, to wait for his
    coming out. Then enter Lucius'* Servant;
    then TITUS *and* HORTENSIUS.

VARRO'S 1 SERVANT
    Well met; good morrow, Titus and Hortensius.

TITUS The like to you, kind Varro.

HORTENSIUS   Lucius!
    What, do we meet together?

LUCIUS' SERVANT   Ay, and I think
    One business does command us all; for mine
    Is money.

TITUS So is theirs and ours.

Enter PHILOTUS.

LUCIUS' SERVANT And, sir, Philotus too!

PHILOTUS Good day at once.

LUCIUS' SERVANT   Welcome, good brother.
    What do you think the hour?

PHILOTUS   Labouring for nine.

LUCIUS' SERVANT So much?

PHILOTUS   Is not my lord seen yet?

LUCIUS' SERVANT   Not yet.

PHILOTUS
    I wonder on't; he was wont to shine at seven.

LUCIUS' SERVANT
  Ay, but the days are wax'd shorter with him:
  You must consider that a prodigal course
  Is like the sun's,
  But not, like his, recoverable. I fear
15 'Tis deepest winter in Lord Timon's purse;
  That is, one may reach deep enough, and yet
  Find little.
PHILOTUS   I am of your fear, for that.
TITUS
  I'll show you how t'observe a strange event.
  Your lord sends now for money?
HORTENSIUS   Most true, he does.
20 TITUS   And he wears jewels now of Timon's gift,
  For which I wait for money.
HORTENSIUS   It is against my heart.
LUCIUS' SERVANT   Mark how strange it shows,
  Timon in this should pay more than he owes:
  And e'en as if your lord should wear rich jewels,
25 And send for money for 'em.
HORTENSIUS
  I'm weary of this charge, the gods can witness;
  I know my lord hath spent of Timon's wealth,
  And now ingratitude makes it worse than stealth.
VARRO'S 1 SERVANT
  Yes, mine's three thousand crowns;
  What's yours?
30 LUCIUS' SERVANT   Five thousand mine.
VARRO'S 1 SERVANT
  'Tis much deep: and it should seem by th' sum,
  Your master's confidence was above mine,
  Else, surely, his had equall'd.

Enter FLAMINIUS.

TITUS   One of Lord Timon's men.
35 LUCIUS' SERVANT   Flaminius? Sir, a word. Pray is my
  lord ready to come forth?
FLAMINIUS   No, indeed he is not.
TITUS   We attend his lordship; pray signify so much.
FLAMINIUS   I need not tell him that; he knows you are
40 too diligent.   *Exit.*

Enter Steward *in a cloak, muffled.*

LUCIUS' SERVANT
  Ha, is not that his steward muffled so?
  He goes away in a cloud: call him, call him.
TITUS   Do you hear, sir?
VARRO'S 2 SERVANT   By your leave, sir –
45 STEWARD   What do ye ask of me, my friend?
TITUS   We wait for certain money here, sir.
STEWARD   Ay,
  If money were as certain as your waiting,
  'Twere sure enough.
  Why then preferr'd you not your sums and bills
50 When your false masters eat of my lord's meat?
  Then they could smile, and fawn upon his debts,

  And take down th'int'rest into their glutt'nous
    maws.
  You do yourselves but wrong, to stir me up;
  Let me pass quietly.
  Believe't, my lord and I have made an end;   55
  I have no more to reckon, he to spend.
LUCIUS' SERVANT   Ay, but this answer will not serve.
STEWARD   If 'twill not serve, 'tis not so base as you,
  For you serve knaves.   *Exit.*
VARRO'S 1 SERVANT   How? What does his cashier'd   60
  worship mutter?
VARRO'S 2 SERVANT   No matter what; he's poor, and
  that's revenge enough. Who can speak broader than he
  that has no house to put his head in? Such may rail
  against great buildings.   65

Enter SERVILIUS.

TITUS   O, here's Servilius; now we shall know some
  answer.
SERVILIUS   If I might beseech you, gentlemen, to repair
  some other hour, I should derive much from't; for,
  take't of my soul, my lord leans wondrously to   70
  discontent. His comfortable temper has forsook him,
  he's much out of health, and keeps his chamber.
LUCIUS' SERVANT
  Many do keep their chambers are not sick;
  And if it be so far beyond his health,
  Methinks he should the sooner pay his debts,   75
  And make a clear way to the gods.
SERVILIUS   Good gods!
TITUS   We cannot take this for answer, sir.
FLAMINIUS [*within*]   Servilius, help! My lord, my lord!

Enter TIMON, *in a rage.*

TIMON
  What, are my doors oppos'd against my passage?
  Have I been ever free, and must my house   80
  Be my retentive enemy, my gaol?
  The place which I have feasted, does it now,
  Like all mankind, show me an iron heart?
LUCIUS' SERVANT   Put in now, Titus.
TITUS   My lord, here is my bill.   85
LUCIUS' SERVANT   Here's mine.
HORTENSIUS   And mine, my lord.
1, 2 VARRO'S SERVANTS   And ours, my lord.
PHILOTUS   All our bills.
TIMON   Knock me down with 'em: cleave me to the
  girdle.   90
LUCIUS' SERVANT   Alas, my lord –
TIMON   Cut my heart in sums.
TITUS   Mine, fifty talents.
TIMON   Tell out my blood.
LUCIUS' SERVANT   Five thousand crowns, my lord.   95
TIMON
  Five thousand drops pays that. What yours? And yours?
VARRO'S 1 SERVANT   My lord –
VARRO'S 2 SERVANT   My lord –

TIMON   Tear me, take me, and the gods fall upon you!

Exit.

100 HORTENSIUS   Faith, I perceive our masters may throw their caps at their money; these debts may well be call'd desperate ones, for a madman owes 'em.

Exeunt.

Re-enter TIMON *and* Steward.

TIMON

They have e'en put my breath from me, the slaves.
Creditors? Devils!

STEWARD   My dear lord –

TIMON   What if it should be so?

105 STEWARD   My lord –

TIMON   I'll have it so. My steward?

STEWARD   Here, my lord.

TIMON   So fitly? Go, bid all my friends again,
Lucius, Lucullus and Sempronius: all.
I'll once more feast the rascals.

STEWARD   O my lord,

110 You only speak from your distracted soul;
There's not so much left to furnish out
A moderate table.

TIMON   Be it not in thy care.
Go, I charge thee, invite them all, let in the tide
Of knaves once more; my cook and I'll provide.

Exeunt.

3.5   *Enter three* Senators *at one door,* ALCIBIADES
meeting them with attendants.

1 SENATOR

My lord, you have my voice to't; the fault's
Bloody; 'tis necessary he should die;
Nothing emboldens sin so much as mercy.

2 SENATOR   Most true; the law shall bruise 'em.

ALCIBIADES

5 Honour, health and compassion to the Senate!

1 SENATOR   Now, captain?

ALCIBIADES   I am an humble suitor to your virtues;
For pity is the virtue of the law,
And none but tyrants use it cruelly.

10 It pleases time and fortune to lie heavy
Upon a friend of mine, who in hot blood
Hath stepp'd into the law, which is past depth
To those that, without heed, do plunge into't.
He is a man, setting his fate aside,

15 Of comely virtues;
Nor did he soil the fact with cowardice
(An honour in him which buys out his fault)
But with a noble fury and fair spirit,
Seeing his reputation touch'd to death,

20 He did oppose his foe;
And with such sober and unnoted passion
He did behove his anger, ere 'twas spent,
As if he had but prov'd an argument.

1 SENATOR   You undergo too strict a paradox,

Striving to make an ugly deed look fair.   25
Your words have took such pains as if they labour'd
To bring manslaughter into form, and set quarrelling
Upon the head of valour; which indeed
Is valour misbegot, and came into the world
When sects and factions were newly born.   30
He's truly valiant that can wisely suffer
The worst that man can breathe,
And make his wrongs his outsides,
To wear them like his raiment, carelessly,
And ne'er prefer his injuries to his heart,   35
To bring it into danger.
If wrongs be evils and enforce us kill,
What folly 'tis to hazard life for ill!

ALCIBIADES   My lord –

1 SENATOR   You cannot make gross sins look clear;   40
To revenge is no valour, but to bear.

ALCIBIADES   My lords, then, under favour, pardon me,
If I speak like a captain.
Why do fond men expose themselves to battle,
And not endure all threats? Sleep upon't,   45
And let the foes quietly cut their throats
Without repugnancy? If there be
Such valour in the bearing, what make we
Abroad? Why then, women are more valiant
That stay at home, if bearing carry it,   50
And the ass more captain than the lion,
The fellow loaden with irons wiser than the judge,
If wisdom be in suffering. O my lords,
As you are great, be pitifully good.
Who cannot condemn rashness in cold blood?   55
To kill, I grant, is sin's extremest gust,
But in defence, by mercy, 'tis most just.
To be in anger is impiety;
But who is man that is not angry?
Weigh but the crime with this.   60

2 SENATOR   You breathe in vain.

ALCIBIADES   In vain? His service done
At Lacedaemon and Byzantium
Were a sufficient briber for his life.

1 SENATOR   What's that?

ALCIBIADES   Why I say, my lords, h'as done fair service, 65
And slain in fight many of your enemies.
How full of valour did he bear himself
In the last conflict, and made plenteous wounds!

2 SENATOR   He has made too much plenty with 'em;
He's a sworn rioter; he has a sin   70
That often drowns him and takes his valour prisoner.
If there were no foes, that were enough
To overcome him. In that beastly fury
He has been known to commit outrages
And cherish factions; 'tis inferr'd to us,   75
His days are foul and his drink dangerous.

1 SENATOR   He dies.

ALCIBIADES   Hard fate! He might have died in war.
My lords, if not for any parts in him –
Though his right arm might purchase his own time,   80

And be in debt to none – yet, more to move you,
Take my deserts to his, and join 'em both;
And for I know your reverend ages love
Security, I'll pawn my victories, all
85   My honour to you, upon his good returns.
If by this crime he owes the law his life,
Why, let the war receive 't in valiant gore,
For law is strict, and war is nothing more.

1 SENATOR
    We are for law; he dies: urge it no more,
90   On height of our displeasure. Friend or brother,
He forfeits his own blood that spills another.

ALCIBIADES   Must it be so? It must not be.
My lords, I do beseech you know me.

2 SENATOR   How?

ALCIBIADES   Call me to your remembrances.

3 SENATOR   What!

95 ALCIBIADES   I cannot think but your age has forgot me;
It could not else be I should prove so base,
To sue and be denied such common grace.
My wounds ache at you.

1 SENATOR   Do you dare our anger?
'Tis in few words, but spacious in effect:
We banish thee for ever.

100 ALCIBIADES   Banish me?
Banish your dotage, banish usury,
That makes the Senate ugly!

1 SENATOR
    If after two days' shine Athens contain thee,
Attend our weightier judgment.
105   And, not to swell our spirit,
He shall be executed presently.   *Exeunt Senators.*

ALCIBIADES
    Now the gods keep you old enough, that you may
        live
Only in bone, that none may look on you!
I'm worse than mad: I have kept back their foes,
110   While they have told their money, and let out
Their coin upon large interest; I myself
Rich only in large hurts. All those, for this?
Is this the balsam that the usuring Senate
Pours into captains' wounds? Banishment!
115   It comes not ill. I hate not to be banish'd;
It is a cause worthy my spleen and fury,
That I may strike at Athens. I'll cheer up
My discontented troops, and lay for hearts.
'Tis honour with most lands to be at odds;
120   Soldiers should brook as little wrongs as gods.
                                                    Exit.

3.6   *Enter divers of Timon's* Friends *and senators*
                        at several doors.

1 LORD   The good time of day to you, sir.

2 LORD   I also wish it to you. I think this honourable lord
did but try us this other day.

1 LORD   Upon that were my thoughts tiring when we
encounter'd. I hope it is not so low with him as he   5
made it seem in the trial of his several friends.

2 LORD   It should not be, by the persuasion of his new
feasting.

1 LORD   I should think so. He hath sent me an earnest
inviting, which many my near occasions did urge me   10
to put off; but he hath conjur'd me beyond them, and
I must needs appear.

2 LORD   In like manner was I in debt to my importunate
business, but he would not hear my excuse. I am sorry,
when he sent to borrow of me, that my provision was   15
out.

1 LORD   I am sick of that grief too, as I understand how
all things go.

2 LORD   Every man here's so. What would he have
borrowed of you?   20

1 LORD   A thousand pieces.

2 LORD   A thousand pieces?

1 LORD   What of you?

2 LORD   He sent to me, sir – Here he comes.

                Enter TIMON *and attendants.*

TIMON   With all my heart, gentlemen both; and how   25
fare you?

1 LORD   Ever at the best, hearing well of your lordship.

2 LORD   The swallow follows not summer more willing
than we your lordship.

TIMON [*aside*]   Nor more willingly leaves winter; such   30
summer birds are men. – Gentlemen, our dinner will
not recompense this long stay. Feast your ears with the
music awhile, if they will fare so harshly o'th'
trumpet's sound; we shall to't presently.

1 LORD   I hope it remains not unkindly with your   35
lordship that I return'd you an empty messenger.

TIMON   O sir, let it not trouble you.

2 LORD   My noble lord –

TIMON   Ah my good friend, what cheer?
    [*The banquet brought in.*]

2 LORD   My most honourable lord, I am e'en sick of   40
shame, that when your lordship this other day sent to
me I was so unfortunate a beggar.

TIMON   Think not on't, sir.

2 LORD   If you had sent but two hours before –

TIMON   Let it not cumber your better remembrance. –   45
Come, bring in all together.

2 LORD   All cover'd dishes.

1 LORD   Royal cheer, I warrant you.

3 LORD   Doubt not that, if money and the season can
yield it.   50

1 LORD   How do you? What's the news?

3 LORD   Alcibiades is banish'd: hear you of it?

1 AND 2 LORDS   Alcibiades banish'd?

3 LORD   'Tis so, be sure of it.

1 LORD   How? How?   55

2 LORD   I pray you, upon what?

TIMON   My worthy friends, will you draw near?

3 LORD   I'll tell you more anon. Here's a noble feast
toward.

2 LORD   This is the old man still.

3 LORD   Will't hold? Will't hold?

2 LORD   It does; but time will – and so –

3 LORD   I do conceive.

TIMON   Each man to his stool, with that spur as he
would to the lip of his mistress. Your diet shall be in all
places alike. Make not a City feast of it, to let the meat
cool ere we can agree upon the first place. Sit, sit. The
gods require our thanks.

You great benefactors, sprinkle our society with
thankfulness. For your own gifts, make yourselves
prais'd; but reserve still to give, lest your deities be
despis'd. Lend to each man enough, that one need not
lend to another; for were your godheads to borrow of
men, men would forsake the gods. Make the meat be
belov'd, more than the man that gives it. Let no assembly
of twenty be without a score of villains. If there sit twelve
women at the table, let a dozen of them be as they are.
The rest of your fees, O gods, the Senators of Athens,
together with the common leg of people – what is amiss
in them, you gods, make suitable for destruction. For
these my present friends, as they are to me nothing, so in
nothing bless them, and to nothing are they welcome.
Uncover, dogs, and lap.

[*The dishes are uncovered and seen to be full of warm water.*]

SOME   What does his lordship mean?

OTHERS   I know not.

TIMON   May you a better feast never behold,
You knot of mouth-friends! Smoke and lukewarm
water
Is your perfection. This is Timon's last;
Who, stuck and spangled with your flatteries,
Washes it off, and sprinkles in your faces
Your reeking villainy. [*throwing the water in their faces*]
                                        Live loath'd, and long,
Most smiling, smooth, detested parasites,
Courteous destroyers, affable wolves, meek bears,
You fools of fortune, trencher-friends, time's flies,
Cap-and-knee slaves, vapours, and minute-jacks!
Of man and beast the infinite malady
Crust you quite o'er! What, dost thou go?
Soft, take thy physic first – thou too – and thou!
Stay, I will lend thee money, borrow none.
                                        Drives them out.
What? All in motion? Henceforth be no feast,
Whereat a villain's not a welcome guest.
Burn, house! Sink, Athens! Henceforth hated be
Of Timon, man and all humanity!   *Exit.*

Re-enter the Lords *and senators.*

1 LORD   How now, my lords?

2 LORD   Know you the quality of Lord Timon's fury?

3 LORD   Push, did you see my cap?

4 LORD   I have lost my gown.

1 LORD   He's but a mad lord, and nought but humours
sways him. He gave me a jewel th'other day, and now
he has beat it out of my hat. Did you see my jewel?

3 LORD   Did you see my cap?   110

2 LORD   Here 'tis.

4 LORD   Here lies my gown.

1 LORD   Let's make no stay.

2 LORD   Lord Timon's mad.

3 LORD   I feel't upon my bones.

4 LORD
One day he gives us diamonds, next day stones.   115
                                        Exeunt.

4.1   *Enter* TIMON.

TIMON   Let me look back upon thee. O thou wall
That girdles in those wolves, dive in the earth
And fence not Athens! Matrons, turn incontinent!
Obedience fail in children! Slaves and fools,
Pluck the grave wrinkled senate from the bench,   5
And minister in their steads! To general filths
Convert, o'th' instant, green virginity!
Do't in your parents' eyes! Bankrupts, hold fast;
Rather than render back, out with your knives,
And cut your trusters' throats! Bound servants, steal! 10
Large-handed robbers your grave masters are,
And pill by law. Maid, to thy master's bed;
Thy mistress is o'th' brothel! Son of sixteen,
Pluck the lin'd crutch from thy old limping sire;
With it beat out his brains! Piety and fear,   15
Religion to the gods, peace, justice, truth,
Domestic awe, night-rest and neighbourhood,
Instruction, manners, mysteries and trades,
Degrees, observances, customs and laws,
Decline to your confounding contraries;   20
And yet confusion live! Plagues incident to men,
Your potent and infectious fevers heap
On Athens ripe for stroke! Thou cold sciatica,
Cripple our senators, that their limbs may halt
As lamely as their manners! Lust and liberty   25
Creep in the minds and marrows of our youth,
That 'gainst the stream of virtue they may strive,
And drown themselves in riot! Itches, blains,
Sow all th'Athenian bosoms, and their crop
Be general leprosy! Breath infect breath,   30
That their society, as their friendship, may
Be merely poison! Nothing I'll bear from thee
But nakedness, thou detestable town!
Take thou that too, with multiplying bans!
Timon will to the woods, where he shall find   35
Th'unkindest beast more kinder than mankind.
The gods confound – hear me, you good gods all –
Th'Athenians both within and out that wall;
And grant, as Timon grows, his hate may grow
To the whole race of mankind, high and low!   40
Amen.   *Exit.*

4.2   *Enter* Steward, *with two or three* Servants.

1 SERVANT
Hear you, master steward, where's our master?
Are we undone, cast off, nothing remaining?

STEWARD   Alack, my fellows, what should I say to you?
Let me be recorded by the righteous gods,
I am as poor as you.

1 SERVANT   Such a house broke?
So noble a master fall'n, all gone, and not
One friend to take his fortune by the arm,
And go along with him.

2 SERVANT   As we do turn our backs
From our companion thrown into his grave,
So his familiars to his buried fortunes
Slink all away, leave their false vows with him,
Like empty purses pick'd; and his poor self,
A dedicated beggar to the air,
With his disease of all-shunn'd poverty,
Walks like contempt, alone. More of our fellows.

Enter other Servants.

STEWARD   All broken implements of a ruin'd house.

3 SERVANT   Yet do our hearts wear Timon's livery,
That see I by our faces; we are fellows still,
Serving alike in sorrow. Leak'd is our bark,
And we, poor mates, stand on the dying deck,
Hearing the surges threat; we must all part
Into this sea of air.

STEWARD   Good fellows all,
The latest of my wealth I'll share amongst you.
Wherever we shall meet, for Timon's sake
Let's yet be fellows. Let's shake our heads, and say,
As 'twere a knell unto our master's fortunes,
'We have seen better days'. Let each take some;
[*giving them money*]
Nay, put out all your hands. Not one word more;
Thus part we rich in sorrow, parting poor.
Embrace, and part several ways.
O the fierce wretchedness that glory brings us!
Who would not wish to be from wealth exempt,
Since riches point to misery and contempt?
Who would be so mock'd with glory, or to live
But in a dream of friendship,
To have his pomp and all what state compounds
But only painted like his varnish'd friends?
Poor honest lord, brought low by his own heart,
Undone by goodness; strange, unusual blood,
When man's worst sin is he does too much good!
Who then dares to be half so kind again?
For bounty, that makes gods, do still mar men.
My dearest lord, bless'd to be most accurs'd,
Rich only to be wretched – thy great fortunes
Are made thy chief afflictions. Alas, kind lord,
He's flung in rage from this ingrateful seat
Of monstrous friends;
Nor has he with him to supply his life,

Or that which can command it.
I'll follow and enquire him out.
I'll ever serve his mind, with my best will;   50
Whilst I have gold I'll be his steward still.   *Exit.*

4.3   *Enter* TIMON.

TIMON   O blessed breeding sun, draw from the earth
Rotten humidity; below thy sister's orb
Infect the air! Twinn'd brothers of one womb,
Whose procreation, residence and birth
Scarce is dividant – touch them with several
    fortunes,   5
The greater scorns the lesser. Not nature,
To whom all sores lay siege, can bear great fortune,
But by contempt of nature.
Raise me this beggar, and deny't that lord,
The senators shall bear contempt hereditary,   10
The beggar native honour.
It is the pasture lards the brother's sides,
The want that makes him lean. Who dares, who
    dares,
In purity of manhood stand upright,
And say this man's a flatterer? If one be,   15
So are they all, for every grise of fortune
Is smooth'd by that below: the learned pate
Ducks to the golden fool; all's obliquy;
There's nothing level in our cursed natures
But direct villainy. Therefore be abhorr'd   20
All feasts, societies, and throngs of men!
His semblable, yea himself, Timon disdains.
Destruction fang mankind! Earth, yield me roots.
[*digging*]
Who seeks for better of thee, sauce his palate
With thy most operant poison. What is here?   25
Gold? Yellow, glittering, precious gold?
No, gods, I am no idle votarist.
Roots, you clear heavens! Thus much of this will
    make
Black, white; foul, fair; wrong, right;
Base, noble; old, young; coward, valiant.   30
Ha, you gods! Why this? What this, you gods? Why,
    this
Will lug your priests and servants from your sides,
Pluck stout men's pillows from below their heads.
This yellow slave
Will knit and break religions, bless th'accurs'd,   35
Make the hoar leprosy ador'd, place thieves,
And give them title, knee and approbation
With senators on the bench. This is it
That makes the wappen'd widow wed again:
She whom the spital-house and ulcerous sores   40
Would cast the gorge at, this embalms and spices
To th'April day again. Come, damn'd earth,
Thou common whore of mankind, that puts odds
Among the rout of nations, I will make thee
Do thy right nature.   [*March afar off.*]

45   Ha? A drum? Th'art quick,
But yet I'll bury thee. Thou'lt go, strong thief,
When gouty keepers of thee cannot stand.
Nay, stay thou out for earnest. [*keeping some gold*]

Enter ALCIBIADES, *with drum and fife, in warlike*
manner; and PHRYNIA *and* TIMANDRA.

ALCIBIADES   What art thou there? Speak.

TIMON

50   A beast as thou art. The canker gnaw thy heart,
For showing me again the eyes of man!

ALCIBIADES

What is thy name? Is man so hateful to thee
That art thyself a man?

TIMON   I am *Misanthropos*, and hate mankind.

55   For thy part, I do wish thou wert a dog,
That I might love thee something.

ALCIBIADES   I know thee well;
But in thy fortunes am unlearn'd and strange.

TIMON

I know thee too, and more than that I know thee
I not desire to know. Follow thy drum;

60   With man's blood paint the ground, gules, gules.
Religious canons, civil laws are cruel;
Then what should war be? This fell whore of thine
Hath in her more destruction than thy sword,
For all her cherubin look.

PHRYNIA   Thy lips rot off!

65   TIMON   I will not kiss thee; then the rot returns
To thine own lips again.

ALCIBIADES

How came the noble Timon to this change?

TIMON   As the moon does, by wanting light to give.
But then renew I could not like the moon;

70   There were no suns to borrow of.

ALCIBIADES

Noble Timon, what friendship may I do thee?

TIMON   None, but to maintain my opinion.

ALCIBIADES   What is it, Timon?

TIMON   Promise me friendship, but perform none. If

75   thou wilt not promise, the gods plague thee, for thou
art a man! If thou dost perform, confound thee, for
thou art a man!

ALCIBIADES   I have heard in some sort of thy miseries.

TIMON   Thou saw'st them when I had prosperity.

80   ALCIBIADES   I see them now; then was a blessed time.

TIMON   As thine is now, held with a brace of harlots.

TIMANDRA   Is this th'Athenian minion whom the world
Voic'd so regardfully?

TIMON   Art thou Timandra?

TIMANDRA   Yes.

TIMON

Be a whore still. They love thee not that use thee.

85   Give them diseases, leaving with thee their lust.
Make use of thy salt hours; season the slaves
For tubs and baths; bring down rose-cheek'd youth

To the tub-fast and the diet.

TIMANDRA   Hang thee, monster!

ALCIBIADES   Pardon him, sweet Timandra, for his wits
Are drown'd and lost in his calamities.

90   I have but little gold of late, brave Timon,
The want whereof doth daily make revolt
In my penurious band. I have heard and griev'd
How cursed Athens, mindless of thy worth,
Forgetting thy great deeds, when neighbour states,

95   But for thy sword and fortune, trod upon them –

TIMON   I prithee beat thy drum, and get thee gone.

ALCIBIADES   I am thy friend, and pity thee, dear Timon.

TIMON

How dost thou pity him whom thou dost trouble?
I had rather be alone.

ALCIBIADES   Why, fare thee well:

100   Here is some gold for thee.

TIMON   Keep it, I cannot eat it.

ALCIBIADES   When I have laid proud Athens on a heap –

TIMON   Warr'st thou 'gainst Athens?

ALCIBIADES   Ay, Timon, and have cause.

TIMON   The gods confound them all in thy conquest,

105   And thee after, when thou hast conquer'd!

ALCIBIADES   Why me, Timon?

TIMON   That by killing of villains
Thou wast born to conquer my country.
Put up thy gold. Go on. Here's gold. Go on.
Be as a planetary plague, when Jove

110   Will o'er some high-vic'd city hang his poison
In the sick air. Let not thy sword skip one.
Pity not honour'd age for his white beard:
He is an usurer. Strike me the counterfeit matron:
It is her habit only that is honest,

115   Herself's a bawd. Let not the virgin's cheek
Make soft thy trenchant sword: for those milk-paps,
That through the window-bars bore at men's eyes,
Are not within the leaf of pity writ,
But set them down horrible traitors. Spare not the babe

120   Whose dimpled smiles from fools exhaust their mercy:
Think it a bastard, whom the oracle
Hath doubtfully pronounc'd the throat shall cut,
And mince it sans remorse. Swear against objects.
Put armour on thine ears and on thine eyes

125   Whose proof nor yells of mothers, maids, nor babes,
Nor sight of priests in holy vestments bleeding
Shall pierce a jot. There's gold to pay thy soldiers.
Make large confusion; and, thy fury spent,
Confounded be thyself! Speak not, be gone.

130   ALCIBIADES

Hast thou gold yet? I'll take the gold thou givest me,
Not all thy counsel.

TIMON

Dost thou, or dost thou not, heaven's curse upon thee!

PHRYNIA, TIMANDRA
  Give us some gold, good Timon: hast thou more?
TIMON
135 Enough to make a whore forswear her trade,
  And to make whores a bawd. Hold up, you sluts,
  Your aprons mountant. You are not oathable,
  Although I know you'll swear, terribly swear
  Into strong shudders and to heavenly agues
140 Th'immortal gods that hear you. Spare your oaths:
  I'll trust to your conditions. Be whores still;
  And he whose pious breath seeks to convert you,
  Be strong in whore, allure him, burn him up;
  Let your close fire predominate his smoke,
145 And be no turncoats: yet may your pains, six months,
  Be quite contrary. And thatch
  Your poor thin roofs with burthens of the dead –
  Some that were hang'd, no matter;
  Wear them, betray with them. Whore still;
150 Paint till a horse may mire upon your face:
  A pox of wrinkles!
PHRYNIA, TIMANDRA Well, more gold. What then?
  Believe't that we'll do anything for gold.
TIMON Consumptions sow
155 In hollow bones of man; strike their sharp shins,
  And mar men's spurring. Crack the lawyer's voice,
  That he may never more false title plead,
  Nor sound his quillets shrilly. Hoar the flamen,
  That scolds against the quality of flesh,
160 And not believes himself. Down with the nose,
  Down with it flat, take the bridge quite away
  Of him that, his particular to foresee,
  Smells from the general weal. Make curl'd-pate
    ruffians bald,
  And let the unscarr'd braggarts of the war
165 Derive some pain from you. Plague all,
  That your activity may defeat and quell
  The source of all erection. There's more gold.
  Do you damn others, and let this damn you,
  And ditches grave you all!
PHRYNIA, TIMANDRA
170 More counsel with more money, bounteous Timon.
TIMON
  More whore, more mischief first; I have given you
    earnest.
ALCIBIADES
  Strike up the drum towards Athens! Farewell,
    Timon:
  If I thrive well, I'll visit thee again.
TIMON If I hope well, I'll never see thee more.
175 ALCIBIADES I never did thee harm.
TIMON Yes, thou spok'st well of me.
ALCIBIADES   Call'st thou that harm?
TIMON Men daily find it. Get thee away, and take
  Thy beagles with thee.
ALCIBIADES   We but offend him. Strike!
  Drum beats. Exeunt Alcibiades, Phrynia and Timandra.
TIMON That nature, being sick of man's unkindness,

180 Should yet be hungry! Common mother, thou
  [*digging*]
  Whose womb unmeasurable and infinite breast
  Teems and feeds all; whose self-same mettle,
  Whereof thy proud child, arrogant man, is puff'd,
  Engenders the black toad and adder blue,
185 The gilded newt and eyeless venom'd worm,
  With all th'abhorred births below crisp heaven
  Whereon Hyperion's quick'ning fire doth shine:
  Yield him, who all the human sons do hate,
  From forth thy plenteous bosom, one poor root.
190 Ensear thy fertile and conceptious womb;
  Let it no more bring out ingrateful man.
  Go great with tigers, dragons, wolves and bears;
  Teem with new monsters, whom thy upward face
  Hath to the marbled mansion all above
195 Never presented. O, a root; dear thanks!
  Dry up thy marrows, vines and plough-torn leas,
  Whereof ingrateful man, with liquorish draughts
  And morsels unctuous, greases his pure mind,
  That from it all consideration slips –

        Enter APEMANTUS.

200 More man? Plague, plague!
APEMANTUS I was directed hither. Men report
  Thou dost affect my manners, and dost use them.
TIMON 'Tis then because thou dost not keep a dog
  Whom I would imitate. Consumption catch thee!
205 APEMANTUS This is in thee a nature but infected,
  A poor unmanly melancholy sprung
  From change of future. Why this spade? This place?
  This slave-like habit, and these looks of care?
  Thy flatterers yet wear silk, drink wine, lie soft,
210 Hug their diseas'd perfumes, and have forgot
  That ever Timon was. Shame not these woods
  By putting on the cunning of a carper.
  Be thou a flatterer now, and seek to thrive
  By that which has undone thee. Hinge thy knee,
215 And let his very breath whom thou'lt observe
  Blow off thy cap; praise his most vicious strain,
  And call it excellent. Thou wast told thus.
  Thou gav'st thine ears, like tapsters that bade
    welcome,
  To knaves, and all approachers. 'Tis most just
220 That thou turn rascal; hadst thou wealth again,
  Rascals should have't. Do not assume my likeness.
TIMON Were I like thee I'd throw away myself.
APEMANTUS
  Thou hast cast away thyself, being like thyself
  A madman so long, now a fool. What, think'st
225 That the bleak air, thy boisterous chamberlain,
  Will put thy shirt on warm? Will these moist trees,
  That have outliv'd the eagle, page thy heels
  And skip when thou point'st out? Will the cold
    brook,
  Candied with ice, caudle thy morning taste
230 To cure thy o'er-night's surfeit? Call the creatures

Whose naked natures live in all the spite
Of wreakful heaven, whose bare unhoused trunks,
To the conflicting elements expos'd,
Answer mere nature; bid them flatter thee.
O thou shalt find –

235   TIMON   A fool of thee. Depart.

APEMANTUS   I love thee better now than e'er I did.

TIMON   I hate thee worse.

APEMANTUS   Why?

TIMON   Thou flatter'st misery.

APEMANTUS   I flatter not, but say thou art a caitiff.

TIMON   Why dost thou seek me out?

APEMANTUS   To vex thee.

240   TIMON   Always a villain's office, or a fool's.
       Dost please thyself in't?

APEMANTUS   Ay.

TIMON   What, a knave too?

APEMANTUS   If thou didst put this sour cold habit on
       To castigate thy pride 'twere well; but thou
       Dost it enforcedly. Thou'dst courtier be again
245   Wert thou not beggar. Willing misery
       Outlives incertain pomp, is crown'd before;
       The one is filling still, never complete,
       The other, at high wish. Best state, contentless,
       Hath a distracted and most wretched being,
250   Worse than the worst, content.
       Thou shouldst desire to die, being miserable.

TIMON   Not by his breath that is more miserable.
       Thou art a slave, whom Fortune's tender arm
       With favour never clasp'd, but bred a dog.
255   Hadst thou like us from our first swath proceeded
       The sweet degrees that this brief world affords
       To such as may the passive drugs of it
       Freely command, thou wouldst have plung'd thyself
       In general riot, melted down thy youth
260   In different beds of lust, and never learn'd
       The icy precepts of respect, but followed
       The sugar'd game before thee. But myself –
       Who had the world as my confectionary,
       The mouths, the tongues, the eyes and hearts of men
265   At duty, more than I could frame employment:
       That numberless upon me stuck, as leaves
       Do on the oak, have with one winter's brush
       Fell from their boughs and left me open, bare,
       For every storm that blows – I, to bear this,
270   That never knew but better, is some burthen.
       Thy nature did commence in sufferance, time
       Hath made thee hard in't. Why shouldst thou hate
          men?
       They never flatter'd thee. What hast thou given?
       If thou wilt curse, thy father (that poor rag)
275   Must be thy subject, who in spite put stuff
       To some she-beggar and compounded thee
       Poor rogue hereditary. Hence, be gone!
       If thou hadst not been born the worst of men,
       Thou hadst been a knave and flatterer.

APEMANTUS   Art thou proud yet?

TIMON   Ay, that I am not thee.

APEMANTUS   I, that I was   280
       No prodigal.

TIMON   I, that I am one now.
       Were all the wealth I have shut up in thee,
       I'ld give thee leave to hang it. Get thee gone.
       That the whole life of Athens were in this!
       Thus would I eat it. [*eating a root*]

APEMANTUS   Here, I will mend thy feast.   285
[*offering food*]

TIMON First mend my company, take away thyself.

APEMANTUS
       So I shall mend mine own, by th' lack of thine.

TIMON   'Tis not well mended so, it is but botch'd;
       If not, I would it were.

APEMANTUS   What wouldst thou have to Athens?   290

TIMON   Thee thither in a whirlwind. If thou wilt,
       Tell them there I have gold; look, so I have.

APEMANTUS   Here is no use for gold.

TIMON   The best and truest;
       For here it sleeps, and does no hired harm.

APEMANTUS   Where liest a nights, Timon?

TIMON   Under that's above me.   295
       Where feed'st thou a days, Apemantus?

APEMANTUS   Where my stomach finds meat; or, rather,
       where I eat it.

TIMON   Would poison were obedient and knew my mind!

APEMANTUS   Where wouldst thou send it?   300

TIMON   To sauce thy dishes.

APEMANTUS   The middle of humanity thou never
       knewest, but the extremity of both ends. When thou
       wast in thy gilt and thy perfume, they mock'd thee for
       too much curiosity; in thy rags thou know'st none, but   305
       art despis'd for the contrary. There's a medlar for thee;
       eat it.

TIMON   On what I hate I feed not.

APEMANTUS   Dost hate a medlar?

TIMON   Ay, though it look like thee.   310

APEMANTUS   And th' hadst hated meddlers sooner, thou
       shouldst have loved thyself better now. What man
       didst thou ever know unthrift that was beloved after
       his means?

TIMON   Who, without those means thou talk'st of, didst   315
       thou ever know belov'd?

APEMANTUS   Myself.

TIMON   I understand thee; thou hadst some means to
       keep a dog.

APEMANTUS   What things in the world canst thou   320
       nearest compare to thy flatterers?

TIMON   Women nearest, but men – men are the things
       themselves. What wouldst thou do with the world,
       Apemantus, if it lay in thy power?

APEMANTUS   Give it the beasts, to be rid of the men.   325

TIMON   Wouldst thou have thyself fall in the confusion
       of men, and remain a beast with the beasts?

APEMANTUS   Ay, Timon.

TIMON   A beastly ambition, which the gods grant thee

330 t'attain to. If thou wert the lion, the fox would beguile thee; if thou wert the lamb, the fox would eat thee; if thou wert the fox, the lion would suspect thee, when peradventure thou wert accus'd by the ass; if thou wert
335 the ass, thy dulness would torment thee, and still thou liv'dst but as a breakfast to the wolf; if thou wert the wolf, thy greediness would afflict thee, and oft thou shouldst hazard thy life for thy dinner; wert thou the unicorn, pride and wrath would confound thee and make thine own self the conquest of thy fury; wert
340 thou a bear, thou wouldst be kill'd by the horse; wert thou a horse, thou wouldst be seiz'd by the leopard; wert thou a leopard, thou wert germane to the lion, and the spots of thy kindred were jurors on thy life. All thy safety were remotion, and thy defence absence.
345 What beast couldst thou be that were not subject to a beast? And what a beast art thou already, that seest not thy loss in transformation!

APEMANTUS   If thou couldst please me with speaking to me, thou mightst have hit upon it here; the commonwealth of Athens is become a forest of beasts.
350
TIMON   How has the ass broke the wall, that thou art out of the city?

APEMANTUS   Yonder comes a poet and a painter. The plague of company light upon thee! I will fear to catch
355 it, and give way. When I know not what else to do, I'll see thee again.

TIMON   When there is nothing living but thee, thou shalt be welcome. I had rather be a beggar's dog than Apemantus.
360
APEMANTUS   Thou art the cap of all the fools alive.

TIMON   Would thou wert clean enough to spit upon!

APEMANTUS   A plague on thee, thou art too bad to curse.

TIMON   All villains that do stand by thee are pure.

APEMANTUS
There is no leprosy but what thou speak'st.
365
TIMON   If I name thee.
I'll beat thee, but I should infect my hands.

APEMANTUS   I would my tongue could rot them off!

TIMON   Away, thou issue of a mangy dog!
Choler does kill me that thou art alive;
370 I swound to see thee.

APEMANTUS   Would thou wouldst burst!

TIMON
Away, thou tedious rogue, I am sorry I shall lose a stone by thee. [*throwing a stone at him*]

APEMANTUS   Beast!
375
TIMON   Slave!

APEMANTUS   Toad!

TIMON   Rogue, rogue, rogue!
I am sick of this false world, and will love nought
But even the mere necessities upon't.
380 Then, Timon, presently prepare thy grave;
Lie where the light foam of the sea may beat
Thy grave-stone daily: make thine epitaph,
That death in me at others' lives may laugh.
[*looking on the gold*]

O thou sweet king-killer, and dear divorce
'Twixt natural son and sire, thou bright defiler   385
Of Hymen's purest bed, thou valiant Mars,
Thou ever young, fresh, loved and delicate wooer,
Whose blush doth thaw the consecrated snow
That lies on Dian's lap! Thou visible god,
That sold'rest close impossibilities,   390
And mak'st them kiss; that speak'st with every
      tongue,
To every purpose! O thou touch of hearts,
Think thy slave Man rebels, and by thy virtue
Set them into confounding odds, that beasts
May have the world in empire!

APEMANTUS   Would 'twere so!   395
But not till I am dead. I'll say th' hast gold.
Thou wilt be throng'd to shortly.

TIMON   Throng'd to?

APEMANTUS   Ay.

TIMON   Thy back, I prithee.

APEMANTUS   Live, and love thy misery.

TIMON   Long live so, and so die! I am quit.

APEMANTUS
Moe things like men! Eat, Timon, and abhor them.   400
                                              Exit.

Enter the Banditti.

1 BANDIT   Where should he have this gold? It is some poor fragment, some slender ort of his remainder. The mere want of gold, and the falling-from of his friends, drove him into this melancholy.

2 BANDIT   It is nois'd he hath a mass of treasure.   405

3 BANDIT   Let us make the assay upon him. If he care not for't, he will supply us easily; if he covetously reserve it, how shall's get it?

2 BANDIT   True; for he bears it not about him: 'tis hid.

1 BANDIT   Is not this he?   410

ALL   Where?

2 BANDIT   'Tis his description.

3 BANDIT   He; I know him.

ALL   Save thee, Timon.

TIMON   Now, thieves?   415

ALL   Soldiers, not thieves.

TIMON   Both too; and women's sons.

ALL   We are not thieves, but men that much do want.

TIMON   Your greatest want is, you want much of meat.
Why should you want? Behold the earth hath roots;
Within this mile break forth a hundred springs;   420
The oaks bear mast, the briers scarlet hips;
The bounteous housewife nature on each bush
Lays her full mess before you. Want? Why want?

1 BANDIT   We cannot live on grass, on berries, water,
As beasts and birds and fishes.   425

TIMON
Nor on the beasts themselves, the birds and fishes;
You must eat men. Yet thanks I must you con
That you are thieves profess'd, that you work not

In holier shapes; for there is boundless theft
30 In limited professions. Rascal thieves,
Here's gold. Go, suck the subtle blood o'th' grape,
Till the high fever seethe your blood to froth,
And so 'scape hanging. Trust not the physician;
His antidotes are poison, and he slays
35 Moe than you rob. Take wealth and lives together.
Do villainy, do, since you protest to do't,
Like workmen. I'll example you with thievery:
The sun's a thief, and with his great attraction
Robs the vast sea; the moon's an arrant thief,
40 And her pale fire she snatches from the sun;
The sea's a thief, whose liquid surge resolves
The moon into salt tears; the earth's a thief,
That feeds and breeds by a composture stol'n
From gen'ral excrement; each thing's a thief.
45 The laws, your curb and whip, in their rough power
Has uncheck'd theft. Love not yourselves; away,
Rob one another. There's more gold. Cut throats.
All that you meet are thieves. To Athens go;
Break open shops: nothing can you steal
50 But thieves do lose it. Steal less for this I give you,
And gold confound you howsoe'er! Amen.
                                              Withdraws.

3 BANDIT H'as almost charm'd me from my
profession, by persuading me to it.
1 BANDIT 'Tis in the malice of mankind that he thus
55 advises us; not to have us thrive in our mystery.
2 BANDIT I'll believe him as an enemy, and give over my
trade.
1 BANDIT Let us first see peace in Athens. There is no
time so miserable but a man may be true.
                                       Exeunt Bandits.

                      Enter Steward.

460 STEWARD O you gods!
Is yond despis'd and ruinous man my lord?
Full of decay and failing? O monument
And wonder of good deeds evilly bestow'd!
What an alteration of honour has desp'rate want
made!
465 What vilder thing upon the earth than friends
Who can bring noblest minds to basest ends!
How rarely does it meet with this time's guise,
When man was wish'd to love his enemies!
Grant I may ever love, and rather woo
470 Those that would mischief me than those that do!
H'as caught me in his eye: I will present
My honest grief unto him; and, as my lord,
Still serve him with my life. My dearest master!

                  TIMON *comes forward.*

TIMON Away! What art thou?
STEWARD   Have you forgot me, sir?
475 TIMON Why dost ask that? I have forgot all men.
Then, if thou grant'st th'art a man,
I have forgot thee.

STEWARD An honest poor servant of yours.
TIMON Then I know thee not.
I never had honest man about me, I; all   480
I kept were knaves, to serve in meat to villains.
STEWARD The gods are witness,
Ne'er did poor steward wear a truer grief
For his undone lord than mine eyes for you.
TIMON
What, dost thou weep? Come nearer; then I love
thee,   485
Because thou art a woman, and disclaim'st
Flinty mankind, whose eyes do never give
But thorough lust and laughter. Pity's sleeping.
Strange times, that weep with laughing, not with
weeping!
STEWARD I beg of you to know me, good my lord,   490
T'accept my grief and whilst this poor wealth lasts
To entertain me as your steward still.
TIMON Had I a steward
So true, so just, and now so comfortable?
It almost turns my dangerous nature mild.   495
Let me behold thy face. Surely this man
Was born of woman.
Forgive my general and exceptless rashness,
You perpetual-sober gods! I do proclaim
One honest man. Mistake me not, but one.   500
No more, I pray – and he's a steward.
How fain would I have hated all mankind,
And thou redeem'st thyself. But all, save thee,
I fell with curses.
Methinks thou art more honest now than wise;   505
For, by oppressing and betraying me,
Thou mightst have sooner got another service;
For many so arrive at second masters
Upon their first lord's neck. But tell me true –
For I must ever doubt, though ne'er so sure –   510
Is not thy kindness subtle, covetous,
A usuring kindness, and as rich men deal gifts,
Expecting in return twenty for one?
STEWARD No, my most worthy master, in whose breast
Doubt and suspect, alas, are plac'd too late!   515
You should have fear'd false times when you did
feast;
Suspect still comes where an estate is least.
That which I show, heaven knows, is merely love,
Duty and zeal to your unmatched mind,
Care of your food and living; and believe it,   520
My most honour'd lord,
For any benefit that points to me,
Either in hope, or present, I'd exchange
For this one wish, that you had power and wealth
To requite me, by making rich yourself.   525
TIMON Look thee, 'tis so. Thou singly honest man,
Here, take: the gods out of my misery
Has sent thee treasure. Go, live rich and happy,
But thus condition'd: thou shalt build from men;
Hate all, curse all, show charity to none,   530

But let the famish'd flesh slide from the bone
Ere thou relieve the beggar; give to dogs
What thou deniest to men; let prisons swallow 'em,
Debts wither 'em to nothing; be men like blasted
    woods;
535   And may diseases lick up their false bloods!
And so farewell, and thrive.
STEWARD   O let me stay and comfort you, my master.
TIMON   If thou hat'st curses
Stay not; fly, whilst thou art bless'd and free:
540   Ne'er see thou man, and let me ne'er see thee.

                          Exit Steward; Timon withdraws.

5.1   *Enter* Poet *and* Painter.

PAINTER   As I took note of the place, it cannot be far
    where he abides.
POET   What's to be thought of him? Does the rumour
    hold for true that he's so full of gold?
5   PAINTER   Certain. Alcibiades reports it; Phrynia and
    Timandra had gold of him. He likewise enrich'd poor
    straggling soldiers with great quantity. 'Tis said he
    gave unto his steward a mighty sum.
POET   Then this breaking of his has been but a try for
10   his friends.
PAINTER   Nothing else. You shall see him a palm in
    Athens again, and flourish with the highest. Therefore
    'tis not amiss we tender our loves to him, in this
    suppos'd distress of his: it will show honestly in us,
15   and is very likely to load our purposes with what they
    travail for, if it be a just and true report that goes of his
    having.
POET   What have you now to present unto him?
PAINTER   Nothing at this time but my visitation; only I
20   will promise him an excellent piece.
POET   I must serve him so too, tell him of an intent that's
    coming toward him.
PAINTER   Good as the best. Promising is the very air o'
    th' time; it opens the eyes of expectation. Performance
25   is ever the duller for his act; and, but in the plainer
    and simpler kind of people, the deed of saying is quite
    out of use. To promise is most courtly and fashionable;
    performance is a kind of will or testament which
    argues a great sickness in his judgment that makes it.

                    Enter TIMON *from his cave.*

30   TIMON [*aside*]   Excellent workman, thou canst not paint
    a man so bad as is thyself.
POET   I am thinking what I shall say I have provided for
    him. It must be a personating of himself; a satire
    against the softness of prosperity, with a discovery of
35   the infinite flatteries that follow youth and opulency.
TIMON [*aside*]   Must thou needs stand for a villain in
    thine own work? Wilt thou whip thine own faults in
    other men? Do so, I have gold for thee.
POET   Nay, let's seek him:

Then do we sin against our own estate,   40
When we may profit meet, and come too late.
PAINTER   True.
When the day serves, before black-corner'd night
Find what thou want'st, by free and offer'd light.
Come.   45
TIMON [*aside*]
I'll meet you at the turn. What a god's gold,
That he is worshipp'd in a baser temple
Than where swine feed?
'Tis thou that rigg'st the bark and plough'st the
    foam,
Settlest admired reverence in a slave: 50
To thee be worship; and thy saints for aye
Be crown'd with plagues, that thee alone obey!
Fit I meet them. [*coming forward*]
POET   Hail, worthy Timon!
PAINTER   Our late noble master!
TIMON   Have I once liv'd to see two honest men?   55
POET   Sir,
Having often of your open bounty tasted,
Hearing you were retir'd, your friends fall'n off,
Whose thankless natures (O abhorred spirits!)
Not all the whips of heaven are large enough –   60
What, to you,
Whose star-like nobleness gave life and influence
To their whole being! I am rapt, and cannot cover
The monstrous bulk of this ingratitude
With any size of words.   65
TIMON   Let it go naked, men may see't the better.
You that are honest, by being what you are,
Make them best seen and known.
PAINTER   He and myself
Have travail'd in the great show'r of your gifts,
And sweetly felt it.
TIMON   Ay, you are honest men.   70
PAINTER   We are hither come to offer you our service.
TIMON
Most honest men! Why, how shall I requite you?
Can you eat roots and drink cold water, no?
BOTH   What we can do, we'll do, to do you service.
TIMON
Y'are honest men. Y' have heard that I have gold;   75
I am sure you have; speak truth, y'are honest men.
PAINTER   So it is said, my noble lord; but therefore
Came not my friend nor I.
TIMON   Good honest men! Thou draw'st a counterfeit
Best in all Athens: th'art indeed the best;   80
Thou counterfeit'st most lively.
PAINTER   So, so, my lord.
TIMON   E'en so, sir, as I say. And, for thy fiction,
Why, thy verse swells with stuff so fine and smooth
That thou art even natural in thine art.
But, for all this, my honest-natur'd friends,   85
I must needs say you have a little fault;
Marry, 'tis not monstrous in you, neither wish I

You take much pains to mend.

BOTH　　　　　　　　　　　Beseech your honour
To make it known to us.

TIMON　　　　　　　　You'll take it ill.

BOTH　Most thankfully, my lord.

90 TIMON　　　　　　　　　　Will you indeed?

BOTH　Doubt it not, worthy lord.

TIMON　There's never a one of you but trusts a knave,
That mightily deceives you.

BOTH　　　　　　　　　　Do we, my lord?

TIMON　Ay, and you hear him cog, see him dissemble,
95　Know his gross patchery, love him, feed him,
Keep in your bosom; yet remain assur'd
That he's a made-up villain.

PAINTER　I know none such, my lord.

POET　　　　　　　　　　　Nor I.

TIMON　Look you, I love you well; I'll give you gold,
100　Rid me these villains from your companies;
Hang them or stab them, drown them in a draught,
Confound them by some course, and come to me,
I'll give you gold enough.

BOTH　Name them, my lord; let's know them.

TIMON

105　You that way and you this, but two in company;
Each man apart, all single and alone,
Yet an arch-villain keeps him company.
[*to one*] If, where thou art, two villains shall not be,
Come not near him.
110　[*to the other*] If thou wouldst not reside
But where one villain is, then him abandon.
Hence, pack! There's gold; you came for gold, ye
slaves.
[*to Poet*] You have work for me, there's payment:
hence!
[*to Painter*] You are an alchemist, make gold of that!
115　Out, rascal dogs!　　　*Drives them out and then retires.*

Enter Steward *and two* Senators.

STEWARD　It is vain that you would speak with Timon;
For he is set so only to himself,
That nothing but himself, which looks like man,
Is friendly with him.

1 SENATOR　　　　　　Bring us to his cave.
120　It is our part and promise to th'Athenians
To speak with Timon.

2 SENATOR　　　　　　At all times alike
Men are not still the same. 'Twas time and griefs
That fram'd him thus: time with his fairer hand
Offering the fortunes of his former days
125　The former man may make him. Bring us to him,
And chance it as it may.

STEWARD　　　　　　　Here is his cave.
Peace and content be here! Lord Timon! Timon!
Look out, and speak to friends. Th'Athenians
By two of their most reverend senate greet thee.
130　Speak to them, noble Timon.

Re-enter TIMON *from his cave.*

TIMON

Thou sun, that comforts, burn! Speak and be hang'd;
For each true word, a blister; and each false
Be as a cauterizing to the root o'th' tongue,
Consuming it with speaking!

1 SENATOR　　　　　　　Worthy Timon –

TIMON　Of none but such as you, and you of Timon.　135

1 SENATOR　The senators of Athens greet thee, Timon.

TIMON

I thank them; and would send them back the plague,
Could I but catch it for them.

1 SENATOR　　　　　　　O forget
What we are sorry for ourselves in thee.
The senators, with one consent of love,　　　　140
Entreat thee back to Athens, who have thought
On special dignities which vacant lie
For thy best use and wearing.

2 SENATOR　　　　　　They confess
Toward thee forgetfulness too general gross;
Which now the public body, which doth seldom　145
Play the recanter, feeling in itself
A lack of Timon's aid, hath sense withal
Of it own fall, restraining aid to Timon,
And send forth us, to make their sorrowed render
Together with a recompense more fruitful　　　150
Than their offence can weigh down by the dram –
Ay, even such heaps and sums of love and wealth
As shall to thee blot out what wrongs were theirs,
And write in thee the figures of their love,
Ever to read them thine.

TIMON　　　　　　　You witch me in it;　155
Surprise me to the very brink of tears.
Lend me a fool's heart and a woman's eyes,
And I'll beweep these comforts, worthy senators.

1 SENATOR　Therefore so please thee to return with us,
And of our Athens, thine and ours, to take　　160
The captainship, thou shalt be met with thanks,
Allowed with absolute power, and thy good name
Live with authority. So soon we shall drive back
Of Alcibiades th'approaches wild,
Who like a boar too savage doth root up　　　165
His country's peace.

2 SENATOR　　　　　And shakes his threat'ning sword
Against the walls of Athens.

1 SENATOR　　　　　　Therefore Timon –

TIMON　Well, sir, I will; therefore, I will, sir, thus:
If Alcibiades kill my countrymen,
Let Alcibiades know this of Timon,　　　　170
That Timon cares not. But if he sack fair Athens,
And take our goodly aged men by th' beards,
Giving our holy virgins to the stain
Of contumelious, beastly, mad-brain'd war,
Then let him know (and tell him Timon speaks it,　175
In pity of our aged and our youth)
I cannot choose but tell him, that I care not,

And let him take't at worst – for their knives care not
While you have throats to answer. For myself,
180 There's not a whittle in th'unruly camp
But I do prize it at my love before
The reverend'st throat in Athens. So I leave you
To the protection of the prosperous gods,
As thieves to keepers.
STEWARD   Stay not; all's in vain.
185 TIMON   Why, I was writing of my epitaph;
It will be seen to-morrow. My long sickness
Of health and living now begins to mend,
And nothing brings me all things. Go, live still;
Be Alcibiades your plague, you his,
And last so long enough.
190 1 SENATOR   We speak in vain.
TIMON   But yet I love my country, and am not
One that rejoices in the common wrack,
As common bruit doth put it.
1 SENATOR   That's well spoke.
TIMON   Commend me to my loving countrymen.
1 SENATOR
These words become your lips as they pass through
195   them.
2 SENATOR   And enter in our ears like great triumphers
In their applauding gates.
TIMON   Commend me to them,
And tell them that, to ease them of their griefs,
Their fears of hostile strokes, their aches, losses,
200 Their pangs of love, with other incident throes
That nature's fragile vessel doth sustain
In life's uncertain voyage, I will some kindness do
        them:
I'll teach them to prevent wild Alcibiades' wrath.
1 SENATOR   I like this well; he will return again.
205 TIMON   I have a tree which grows here in my close,
That mine own use invites me to cut down,
And shortly must I fell it; tell my friends,
Tell Athens, in the sequence of degree,
From high to low throughout, that whoso please
210 To stop affliction, let him take his haste,
Come hither, ere my tree hath felt the axe,
And hang himself. I pray you, do my greeting.
STEWARD
Trouble him no further; thus you still shall find him.
TIMON   Come not to me again; but say to Athens,
215 Timon hath made his everlasting mansion
Upon the beached verge of the salt flood,
Who once a day with his embossed froth
The turbulent surge shall cover. Thither come,
And let my grave-stone be your oracle.
220 Lips, let four words go by and language end:
What is amiss, plague and infection mend!
Graves only be men's works and death their gain;
Sun, hide thy beams, Timon hath done his reign.
                                        Exit.
1 SENATOR   His discontents are unremoveably

Coupled to nature.   225
2 SENATOR   Our hope in him is dead. Let us return,
And strain what other means is left unto us
In our dear peril.
1 SENATOR   It requires swift foot.   *Exeunt.*

5.2   *Enter two other* Senators *with a* Messenger.

3 SENATOR   Thou hast painfully discover'd; are his files
As full as thy report?
MESSENGER   I have spoke the least;
Besides, his expedition promises
Present approach.
4 SENATOR
We stand much hazard if they bring not Timon.   5
MESSENGER   I met a courier, one mine ancient friend,
Whom, though in general part we were oppos'd,
Yet our old love made a particular force,
And made us speak like friends. This man was riding
From Alcibiades to Timon's cave,   10
With letters of entreaty, which imported
His fellowship i'th' cause against your city,
In part for his sake mov'd.

        Enter the two other Senators.

3 SENATOR   Here come our brothers.
1 SENATOR   No talk of Timon, nothing of him expect.
The enemy's drum is heard, and fearful scouring   15
Doth choke the air with dust. In, and prepare.
Ours is the fall, I fear; our foes' the snare.   *Exeunt.*

5.3   *Enter a* Soldier.

SOLDIER   By all description this should be the place.
Who's here? Speak, ho! No answer? What is this?
Timon is dead, who hath outstretch'd his span:
Some beast read this; there does not live a man.
Dead, sure; and this his grave. What's on this tomb 5
I cannot read. The character I'll take with wax;
Our captain hath in every figure skill,
An ag'd interpreter, though young in days.
Before proud Athens he's set down by this,
Whose fall the mark of his ambition is.   *Exit.*   10

5.4   *Trumpets sound. Enter* ALCIBIADES
                with his powers.

ALCIBIADES   Sound to this coward and lascivious town
Our terrible approach.   [*Sounds a parley.*]

        The Senators *appear upon the walls.*

Till now you have gone on, and fill'd the time
With all licentious measure, making your wills
The scope of justice; till now, myself and such   5
As slept within the shadow of your power
Have wander'd with our travers'd arms, and breath'd

Our sufferance vainly. Now the time is flush,
When crouching marrow, in the bearer strong,
Cries, of itself, 'No more'. Now breathless wrong
Shall sit and pant in your great chairs of ease,
And pursy insolence shall break his wind
With fear and horrid flight.

1 SENATOR   Noble, and young:
When thy first griefs were but a mere conceit,
Ere thou hadst power or we had cause of fear,
We sent to thee, to give thy rages balm,
To wipe out our ingratitude, with loves
Above their quantity.

2 SENATOR   So did we woo
Transformed Timon to our city's love
By humble message and by promis'd means.
We were not all unkind, nor all deserve
The common stroke of war.

1 SENATOR   These walls of ours
Were not erected by their hands from whom
You have receiv'd your grief; nor are they such
That these great tow'rs, trophies, and schools should
    fall
For private faults in them.

2 SENATOR   Nor are they living
Who were the motives that you first went out;
Shame, that they wanted cunning in excess,
Hath broke their hearts. March, noble lord,
Into our city with thy banners spread;
By decimation and a tithed death,
If thy revenges hunger for that food
Which nature loathes, take thou the destin'd tenth,
And by the hazard of the spotted die
Let die the spotted.

1 SENATOR   All have not offended.
For those that were, it is not square to take
On those that are, revenge: crimes, like lands,
Are not inherited. Then, dear countryman,
Bring in thy ranks, but leave without thy rage;
Spare thy Athenian cradle and those kin
Which in the bluster of thy wrath must fall
With those that have offended; like a shepherd,
Approach the fold and cull th'infected forth,
But kill not all together.

2 SENATOR   What thou wilt,
Thou rather shalt enforce it with thy smile
Than hew to't with thy sword.

1 SENATOR   Set but thy foot
Against our rampir'd gates, and they shall ope,
So thou wilt send thy gentle heart before,

To say thou'lt enter friendly.

2 SENATOR   Throw thy glove,
Or any token of thine honour else,   50
That thou wilt use the wars as thy redress
And not as our confusion, all thy powers
Shall make their harbour in our town, till we
Have seal'd thy full desire.

ALCIBIADES   Then there's my glove.
Descend, and open your uncharged ports.   55
Those enemies of Timon's and mine own
Whom you yourselves shall set out for reproof
Fall, and no more; and, to atone your fears
With my more noble meaning, not a man
Shall pass his quarter or offend the stream   60
Of regular justice in your city's bounds
But shall be remedied to your public laws
At heaviest answer.

BOTH   'Tis most nobly spoken.

ALCIBIADES   Descend, and keep your words.

Enter a Soldier.

SOLDIER   My noble general, Timon is dead,   65
Entomb'd upon the very hem o'th' sea;
And on his grave-stone this insculpture which
With wax I brought away, whose soft impression
Interprets for my poor ignorance.

ALCIBIADES [*reading the Epitaph*]
Here lies a wretched corse, of wretched soul bereft: 70
Seek not my name. A plague consume you, wicked
    caitiffs left!
Here lie I, Timon, who, alive, all living men did hate.
Pass by and curse thy fill, but pass and stay not here thy
    gait.
These well express in thee thy latter spirits.
Though thou abhorr'dst in us our human griefs,   75
Scorn'dst our brains' flow and those our droplets
    which
From niggard nature fall, yet rich conceit
Taught thee to make vast Neptune weep for aye
On thy low grave, of faults forgiven. Dead
Is noble Timon, of whose memory   80
Hereafter more. Bring me into your city,
And I will use the olive with my sword,
Make war breed peace, make peace stint war, make
    each
Prescribe to other, as each other's leech.
Let our drums strike.   *Exeunt*   85

Titus Andronicus

The only recorded copy of a 1594 Quarto edition of *The Most Lamentable Roman Tragedy of Titus Andronicus* was found in Sweden in 1904. It survives from the earliest known printed edition of any of Shakespeare's plays and is now a treasured item in the collection of the Folger Shakespeare Library. Before its discovery the play was known from the Quartos of 1600 and 1611 and from the First Folio of 1623, where it is the second of the tragedies and gains a whole scene, 3.2, not present in the Quartos. This scene, which appears to be authentic, may well have been added at some date later than 1594. The 1594 title-page records performance by the Earl of Derby, Earl of Pembroke and Earl of Sussex's Men, whether consecutively or in combination (the play makes heavy casting demands). Five performances at the Rose playhouse between 23 January and 12 June 1594 are recorded in Philip Henslowe's accounts, three by Sussex's Men, two by the Lord Chamberlain's (i.e. Derby's) Men. Proposed dates of composition range from 1589 to 1593–4: the Arden 3 editor puts forward arguments for the later date. Long regarded as a play of dubious authorship, *Titus* is now generally accepted as Shakespeare's, despite continuing claims that act 1, which shows signs of revision to incorporate the killings of Alarbus and Mutius, was originally the work of George Peele. A drawing of characters from the play by Henry Peacham (see p. 6) appears to combine moments from different scenes, if indeed it relates directly to performance at all. Once dated 1595, this well-known drawing may in fact have been made as late as 1615 (the date on it admitting of more than one interpretation).

Despite the presence of many motifs familiar from Ovid's *Metamorphoses* (a book used in its action), Seneca's tragedies and the plays of Marlowe, the plot of *Titus* appears to be original. A ballad and prose history once identified as its sources are better accounted for as derivative spin-offs, occasioned by the sustained success of the play (whose continued popularity Ben Jonson mocked as late as 1614).

A long period of infrequent revival and generally low esteem followed the attempt of Edward Ravenscroft to rewrite *Titus* for audiences in the Restoration. Modern theatrical interest began in the 1920s and received much stimulus from the worldwide success of Peter Brook's production starring Laurence Olivier and Vivien Leigh, which was first presented at Stratford-upon-Avon in 1955. Recent productions have used a less thoroughly rearranged text than that of Brook, who cut it heavily and reordered its action to inhibit intrusive laughter.

It is easy to caricature *Titus* as violent melodrama, but it exercises great power in the theatre and shows Shakespeare already engaged with tragic characters and situations to which he would return as late as *Antony and Cleopatra* and *Coriolanus* (alluded to at 4.4.62–7), which again dramatize the opposition of the values of an ostensibly civilized and honourable Rome to those of threatening barbarians. Titus adumbrates both the crafty madness of Hamlet and the passionate madness of Lear; the villainous Moor, Aaron, combines qualities which were to separate into Othello and Iago; but it is supremely Lavinia, mutilated and mute, who first realizes the pathos of female victims of violence which is so distinctive a feature of Shakespeare's tragic writing.

The Arden text is based on the unique copy of the 1594 First Quarto, with a few corrections from the 1600 Second Quarto and the addition of 3.2 from the 1623 First Folio. Passages unique to the Second Quarto and the First Folio are designated by superscript Q2 or F at the beginning and end of them.

ROMANS

SATURNINUS	*eldest son of the recently deceased Emperor of Rome, later Emperor*
BASSIANUS	*younger brother of Saturninus*
TITUS Andronicus	*a Roman nobleman, general against the Goths*
MARCUS Andronicus	*a tribune of the people, brother of Titus*
LUCIUS	
QUINTUS	*the surviving sons of Titus Andronicus*
MARTIUS	*(in descending order of age)*
MUTIUS	
LAVINIA	*only daughter of Titus Andronicus, betrothed to Bassianus*
Young Lucius, *a* BOY	*son of Lucius*
PUBLIUS	*son of Marcus Andronicus*
SEMPRONIUS	
CAIUS	*kinsmen of the Andronici*
VALENTINE	
EMILLIUS	*a Roman*
CAPTAIN	
MESSENGER	
NURSE	
CLOWN	
Other ROMANS	*including senators, tribunes, soldiers and attendants*

GOTHS

TAMORA	*Queen of the Goths and later Empress of Rome by marriage to Saturninus*
ALARBUS	
DEMETRIUS	*the sons of Tamora (in descending order of age)*
CHIRON	
AARON	*a Moor in the service of Tamora, her lover*
Other GOTHS	*forming an army*

Titus Andronicus

1.1 *Flourish. Enter the Tribunes including* MARCUS
Andronicus and Senators aloft. And then enter below
SATURNINUS *and his followers at one door, and* BASSIANUS
and his followers at the other, with drums and colours.

SATURNINUS   Noble patricians, patrons of my right,
Defend the justice of my cause with arms.
And countrymen, my loving followers,
Plead my successive title with your swords.
I am his first-born son that was the last
That wore the imperial diadem of Rome:
Then let my father's honours live in me,
Nor wrong mine age with this indignity.

BASSIANUS
Romans, friends, followers, favourers of my right,
If ever Bassianus, Caesar's son,
Were gracious in the eyes of royal Rome,
Keep then this passage to the Capitol,
And suffer not dishonour to approach
The imperial seat, to virtue consecrate,
To justice, continence and nobility;
But let desert in pure election shine,
And, Romans, fight for freedom in your choice.

MARCUS [*aloft, with the crown*]
Princes, that strive by factions and by friends
Ambitiously for rule and empery,
Know that the people of Rome, for whom we stand
A special party, have by common voice
In election for the Roman empery
Chosen Andronicus, surnamed Pius
For many good and great deserts to Rome.
A nobler man, a braver warrior,
Lives not this day within the city walls.
He by the senate is accited home
From weary wars against the barbarous Goths,
That with his sons, a terror to our foes,
Hath yoked a nation strong, trained up in arms.
Ten years are spent since first he undertook
This cause of Rome and chastised with arms
Our enemies' pride; five times he hath returned
Bleeding to Rome, bearing his valiant sons
In coffins from the field ^{Q2}and at this day
To the monument of the Andronici
Done sacrifice of expiation,
And slain the noblest prisoner of the Goths^{Q2}.
And now at last, laden with honour's spoils,
Returns the good Andronicus to Rome,
Renowned Titus, flourishing in arms.
Let us entreat, by honour of his name
Whom worthily you would have now succeed,
And in the Capitol and senate's right,
Whom you pretend to honour and adore,
That you withdraw you and abate your strength,
Dismiss your followers and, as suitors should,
Plead your deserts in peace and humbleness.

SATURNINUS
How fair the tribune speaks to calm my thoughts.

BASSIANUS   Marcus Andronicus, so I do affy   50
In thy uprightness and integrity,
And so I love and honour thee and thine,
Thy noble brother Titus and his sons,
And her to whom my thoughts are humbled all,
Gracious Lavinia, Rome's rich ornament,   55
That I will here dismiss my loving friends
And to my fortune's and the people's favour
Commit my cause in balance to be weighed.
                    Exeunt his soldiers.

SATURNINUS
Friends that have been thus forward in my right,
I thank you all and here dismiss you all,   60
And to the love and favour of my country
Commit myself, my person and the cause.
                    Exeunt his soldiers.
Rome, be as just and gracious unto me
As I am confident and kind to thee.
Open the gates and let me in.   65

BASSIANUS   Tribunes, and me, a poor competitor.
        Flourish. They go up into the Senate House.

            Enter a Captain.

CAPTAIN   Romans, make way: the good Andronicus,
Patron of virtue, Rome's best champion,
Successful in the battles that he fights,
With honour and with fortune is returned   70
From where he circumscribed with his sword
And brought to yoke the enemies of Rome.

Sound drums and trumpets, and then enter two of Titus'
sons, and then two men bearing a coffin covered with black,
then two other sons, then TITUS ANDRONICUS, *and then, as*
prisoners, TAMORA, *the Queen of Goths, and her three sons,*
ALARBUS, CHIRON *and* DEMETRIUS, *with* AARON *the Moor,*
and others as many as can be. Then set down the coffin and
                Titus speaks.

TITUS   Hail, Rome, victorious in thy mourning weeds!
Lo, as the bark that hath discharged his freight
Returns with precious lading to the bay   75
From whence at first she weighed her anchorage,
Cometh Andronicus, bound with laurel boughs,
To resalute his country with his tears,
Tears of true joy for his return to Rome.
Thou great defender of this Capitol,   80
Stand gracious to the rites that we intend.
Romans, of five-and-twenty valiant sons,
Half of the number that King Priam had,
Behold the poor remains, alive and dead:
These that survive, let Rome reward with love;   85
These that I bring unto their latest home,
With burial amongst their ancestors.
Here Goths have given me leave to sheathe my sword.
Titus, unkind and careless of thine own,
Why suffer'st thou thy sons unburied yet   90
To hover on the dreadful shore of Styx?

Make way to lay them by their brethren.
[*They open the tomb.*]
There greet in silence, as the dead are wont,
And sleep in peace, slain in your country's wars.
95 O sacred receptacle of my joys,
Sweet cell of virtue and nobility,
How many sons hast thou of mine in store
That thou wilt never render to me more!
LUCIUS   Give us the proudest prisoner of the Goths,
100 That we may hew his limbs and on a pile
Ad manes fratrum sacrifice his flesh
Before this earthly prison of their bones,
That so the shadows be not unappeased,
Nor we disturbed with prodigies on earth.
105 TITUS   I give him you, the noblest that survives,
The eldest son of this distressed queen.
TAMORA [*kneeling*]
Stay, Roman brethren, gracious conqueror,
Victorious Titus, rue the tears I shed,
A mother's tears in passion for her son!
110 And if thy sons were ever dear to thee,
O, think my son to be as dear to me.
Sufficeth not that we are brought to Rome
To beautify thy triumphs, and return
Captive to thee and to thy Roman yoke?
115 But must my sons be slaughtered in the streets
For valiant doings in their country's cause?
O, if to fight for king and commonweal
Were piety in thine, it is in these.
Andronicus, stain not thy tomb with blood.
120 Wilt thou draw near the nature of the gods?
Draw near them then in being merciful.
Sweet mercy is nobility's true badge:
Thrice noble Titus, spare my first-born son.
TITUS   Patient yourself, madam, and pardon me.
125 These are their brethren whom your Goths beheld
Alive and dead, and for their brethren slain,
Religiously they ask a sacrifice.
To this your son is marked, and die he must,
T'appease their groaning shadows that are gone.
130 LUCIUS   Away with him, and make a fire straight,
And with our swords upon a pile of wood
Let's hew his limbs till they be clean consumed.
Exeunt Titus' sons with Alarbus.
TAMORA [*rising*]   O cruel, irreligious piety!
CHIRON   Was never Scythia half so barbarous!
135 DEMETRIUS   Oppose not Scythia to ambitious Rome.
Alarbus goes to rest and we survive
To tremble under Titus' threatening look.
Then, madam, stand resolved, but hope withal
The self-same gods that armed the queen of Troy
140 With opportunity of sharp revenge
Upon the Thracian tyrant in his tent
May favour Tamora, the queen of Goths
(When Goths were Goths and Tamora was queen),
To quit the bloody wrongs upon her foes.

Enter the Sons *of Andronicus again.*

LUCIUS   See, lord and father, how we have performed   145
Our Roman rites: Alarbus' limbs are lopped
And entrails feed the sacrificing fire,
Whose smoke like incense doth perfume the sky.
Remaineth nought but to inter our brethren
And with loud 'larums welcome them to Rome.   150
TITUS   Let it be so, and let Andronicus
Make this his latest farewell to their souls.
[*Sound trumpets, and lay the coffin in the tomb.*]
In peace and honour rest you here, my sons;
Rome's readiest champions, repose you here in rest,
Secure from worldly chances and mishaps.   155
Here lurks no treason, here no envy swells,
Here grow no damned drugs, here are no storms,
No noise, but silence and eternal sleep:
In peace and honour rest you here, my sons.

Enter LAVINIA.

LAVINIA   In peace and honour, live Lord Titus long: 160
My noble lord and father, live in fame!
Lo, at this tomb my tributary tears
I render for my brethren's obsequies,
[*kneeling*] And at thy feet I kneel with tears of joy
Shed on this earth for thy return to Rome.   165
O bless me here with thy victorious hand,
Whose fortunes Rome's best citizens applaud.
TITUS   Kind Rome, that hast thus lovingly reserved
The cordial of mine age to glad my heart.
Lavinia live, outlive thy father's days   170
And fame's eternal date, for virtue's praise.
[*Lavinia rises.*]

Enter MARCUS *below.*

MARCUS   Long live Lord Titus, my beloved brother,
Gracious triumpher in the eyes of Rome!
TITUS   Thanks, gentle tribune, noble brother Marcus.
MARCUS
And welcome, nephews, from successful wars,   175
You that survive and you that sleep in fame.
Fair lords, your fortunes are alike in all
That in your country's service drew your swords;
But safer triumph is this funeral pomp
That hath aspired to Solon's happiness   180
And triumphs over chance in honour's bed.
Titus Andronicus, the people of Rome,
Whose friend in justice thou hast ever been,
Send thee by me, their tribune and their trust,
This palliament of white and spotless hue,   185
And name thee in election for the empire
With these our late-deceased emperor's sons.
Be *candidatus* then and put it on,
And help to set a head on headless Rome.
[*Offers robe.*]
TITUS   A better head her glorious body fits   190
Than his that shakes for age and feebleness.

What, should I don this robe and trouble you?
Be chosen with proclamations today,
Tomorrow yield up rule, resign my life
195 And set abroad new business for you all?
Rome, I have been thy soldier forty years,
And led my country's strength successfully,
And buried one-and-twenty valiant sons,
Knighted in field, slain manfully in arms
200 In right and service of their noble country:
Give me a staff of honour for mine age,
But not a sceptre to control the world.
Upright he held it, lords, that held it last.
MARCUS   Titus, thou shalt obtain and ask the empery.
SATURNINUS [*aloft*]
205 Proud and ambitious tribune, canst thou tell?
TITUS   Patience, prince Saturninus.
SATURNINUS [*aloft*]   Romans, do me right.
Patricians, draw your swords and sheathe them not
Till Saturninus be Rome's emperor.
210 Andronicus, would thou were shipped to hell
Rather than rob me of the people's hearts.
LUCIUS   Proud Saturnine, interrupter of the good
That noble-minded Titus means to thee.
TITUS   Content thee, prince, I will restore to thee
The people's hearts, and wean them from
215   themselves.
BASSIANUS [*aloft*]   Andronicus, I do not flatter thee,
But honour thee, and will do till I die.
My faction if thou strengthen with thy friends,
I will most thankful be, and thanks to men
220 Of noble minds is honourable meed.
TITUS   People of Rome, and people's tribunes here,
I ask your voices and your suffrages.
Will ye bestow them friendly on Andronicus?
TRIBUNES [*aloft*]   To gratify the good Andronicus
225 And gratulate his safe return to Rome,
The people will accept whom he admits.
TITUS   Tribunes, I thank you, and this suit I make,
That you create our emperor's eldest son,
Lord Saturnine, whose virtues will, I hope,
230 Reflect on Rome as Titan's rays on earth,
And ripen justice in this commonweal –
Then if you will elect by my advice,
Crown him and say, 'Long live our emperor!'
MARCUS   With voices and applause of every sort,
235 Patricians and plebeians, we create
Lord Saturninus Rome's great emperor,
And say, 'Long live our emperor Saturnine!'
                    [*A long flourish till they come down.*]
SATURNINUS   Titus Andronicus, for thy favours done
To us in our election this day,
240 I give thee thanks in part of thy deserts,
And will with deeds requite thy gentleness.
And for an onset, Titus, to advance
Thy name and honourable family,
Lavinia will I make my empress,

Rome's royal mistress, mistress of my heart,   245
And in the sacred Pantheon her espouse.
Tell me, Andronicus, doth this motion please thee?
TITUS   It doth, my worthy lord, and in this match
I hold me highly honoured of your grace,
And here in sight of Rome to Saturnine,   250
King and commander of our commonweal,
The wide world's emperor, do I consecrate
My sword, my chariot and my prisoners,
Presents well worthy Rome's imperious lord:
Receive them then, the tribute that I owe,   255
Mine honour's ensigns humbled at thy feet.
[*Titus' sword and prisoners are handed over to Saturninus.*]
SATURNINUS   Thanks, noble Titus, father of my life.
How proud I am of thee and of thy gifts,
Rome shall record, and when I do forget
The least of these unspeakable deserts,   260
Romans forget your fealty to me.
TITUS [*to Tamora*]
Now, madam, are you prisoner to an emperor,
To him that for your honour and your state
Will use you nobly and your followers.
SATURNINUS   A goodly lady, trust me, of the hue 265
That I would choose were I to choose anew.
[*to Tamora*] Clear up, fair queen, that cloudy
      countenance:
Though chance of war hath wrought this change of
      cheer,
Thou com'st not to be made a scorn in Rome;
Princely shall be thy usage every way.   270
Rest on my word, and let not discontent
Daunt all your hopes; madam, he comforts you
Can make you greater than the queen of Goths.
Lavinia, you are not displeased with this?
LAVINIA   Not I, my lord, sith true nobility   275
Warrants these words in princely courtesy.
SATURNINUS   Thanks, sweet Lavinia. Romans, let us go.
Ransomless here we set our prisoners free;
Proclaim our honours, lords, with trump and drum.
                    [*Sound drums and trumpets.*
      Tamora, Chiron, Demetrius and Aaron are released.]
BASSIANUS [*seizing Lavinia*]
Lord Titus, by your leave, this maid is mine.   280
TITUS   How, sir? Are you in earnest then, my lord?
BASSIANUS   Ay, noble Titus, and resolved withal
To do myself this reason and this right.
MARCUS   *Suum cuique* is our Roman justice:
This prince in justice seizeth but his own.   285
LUCIUS [*joining Bassianus*]
And that he will, and shall, if Lucius live.
TITUS   Traitors, avaunt! Where is the emperor's guard?
Treason, my lord – Lavinia is surprised.
SATURNINUS   Surprised? By whom?
BASSIANUS   By him that justly may
Bear his betrothed from all the world away.   290
MUTIUS   Brothers, help to convey her hence away,
And with my sword I'll keep this door safe.

Bassianus, Marcus and Titus' sons
bear Lavinia out of one door.

TITUS   Follow, my lord, and I'll soon bring her back.

Saturninus does not follow, but exit at the other
door with Tamora, her two sons and Aaron the Moor.

MUTIUS   My lord, you pass not here.

295 TITUS   What, villain boy, barr'st me my way in Rome?
[*He kills him.*]

MUTIUS   Help, Lucius, help!

LUCIUS [*returning*]
My lord, you are unjust, and more than so:
In wrongful quarrel you have slain your son.

TITUS   Nor thou, nor he, are any sons of mine:
300 My sons would never so dishonour me.
Traitor, restore Lavinia to the emperor.

LUCIUS   Dead if you will, but not to be his wife
That is another's lawful promised love.   *Exit.*

Enter aloft the Emperor *with* TAMORA *and her two sons*
and AARON *the Moor.*

SATURNINUS [*aloft*]
No, Titus, no, the emperor needs her not,
305 Nor her, nor thee, nor any of thy stock.
I'll trust by leisure him that mocks me once,
Thee never, nor thy traitorous haughty sons,
Confederates all thus to dishonour me.
Was none in Rome to make a stale
310 But Saturnine? Full well, Andronicus,
Agree these deeds with that proud brag of thine
That saidst I begged the empire at thy hands.

TITUS
O monstrous! What reproachful words are these?

SATURNINUS [*aloft*]
But go thy ways, go give that changing piece
315 To him that flourished for her with his sword.
A valiant son-in-law thou shalt enjoy,
One fit to bandy with thy lawless sons,
To ruffle in the commonwealth of Rome.

TITUS   These words are razors to my wounded heart.

SATURNINUS [*aloft*]
320 And therefore, lovely Tamora, queen of Goths,
That like the stately Phoebe 'mongst her nymphs
Dost overshine the gallant'st dames of Rome,
If thou be pleased with this my sudden choice,
Behold, I choose thee, Tamora, for my bride,
325 And will create thee empress of Rome.
Speak, queen of Goths, dost thou applaud my
choice?
And here I swear by all the Roman gods,
Sith priest and holy water are so near,
And tapers burn so bright, and everything
330 In readiness for Hymenaeus stand,
I will not resalute the streets of Rome,
Or climb my palace, till from forth this place
I lead espoused my bride along with me.

TAMORA [*aloft*]
And here in sight of heaven to Rome I swear,

If Saturnine advance the queen of Goths,   335
She will a handmaid be to his desires,
A loving nurse, a mother to his youth.

SATURNINUS [*aloft*]
Ascend, fair queen, Pantheon. Lords, accompany
Your noble emperor and his lovely bride,
Sent by the heavens for prince Saturnine,   340
Whose wisdom hath her fortune conquered.
There shall we consummate our spousal rites.

Exeunt omnes except Titus.

TITUS   I am not bid to wait upon this bride.
Titus, when wert thou wont to walk alone,
Dishonoured thus and challenged of wrongs?   345

Enter MARCUS *and Titus' three remaining* Sons.

MARCUS   O Titus, see! O see what thou hast done!
In a bad quarrel slain a virtuous son.

TITUS   No, foolish tribune, no. No son of mine,
Nor thou, nor these, confederates in the deed
That hath dishonoured all our family –   350
Unworthy brother and unworthy sons.

LUCIUS   But let us give him burial as becomes;
Give Mutius burial with our brethren.

TITUS   Traitors, away! He rests not in this tomb.
This monument five hundred years hath stood,   355
Which I have sumptuously re-edified.
Here none but soldiers and Rome's servitors
Repose in fame; none basely slain in brawls.
Bury him where you can, he comes not here.

MARCUS   My lord, this is impiety in you;   360
My nephew Mutius' deeds do plead for him,
He must be buried with his brethren.

2, 3 SONS   And shall, or him we will accompany.

TITUS   And shall? What villain was it spake that word?

2 SON   He that would vouch it in any place but here.   365

TITUS   What, would you bury him in my despite?

MARCUS   No, noble Titus, but entreat of thee
To pardon Mutius and to bury him.

TITUS   Marcus, even thou hast struck upon my crest,
And with these boys mine honour thou hast
wounded.   370
My foes I do repute you every one,
So trouble me no more, but get you gone.

3 SON   He is not with himself, let us withdraw.

2 SON   Not I, till Mutius' bones be buried.
[*The brother and the sons kneel.*]

MARCUS
Brother, for in that name doth nature plead –   375

2 SON   Father, and in that name doth nature speak –

TITUS   Speak thou no more, if all the rest will speed.

MARCUS   Renowned Titus, more than half my soul –

LUCIUS   Dear father, soul and substance of us all –

MARCUS   Suffer thy brother Marcus to inter   380
His noble nephew here in virtue's nest,
That died in honour and Lavinia's cause.
Thou art a Roman, be not barbarous.
The Greeks upon advice did bury Ajax

That slew himself, and wise Laertes' son
Did graciously plead for his funerals:
Let not young Mutius then, that was thy joy,
Be barred his entrance here.

TITUS   Rise, Marcus, rise. [*They rise.*]
The dismall'st day is this that e'er I saw:
To be dishonoured by my sons in Rome!
Well, bury him, and bury me the next.
[*They put him in the tomb.*]

LUCIUS
There lie thy bones, sweet Mutius, with thy friends',
Till we with trophies do adorn thy tomb.

MARCUS & TITUS' SONS [*kneeling*]
No man shed tears for noble Mutius:
He lives in fame that died in virtue's cause.
                    Exeunt all but Marcus and Titus.

MARCUS   My lord – to step out of these dreary dumps –
How comes it that the subtle queen of Goths
Is of a sudden thus advanced in Rome?

TITUS   I know not, Marcus, but I know it is –
Whether by device or no, the heavens can tell.
Is she not then beholden to the man
That brought her for this high good turn so far?

FMARCUS   Yes – and will nobly him remunerate.F

Flourish. Enter the Emperor, TAMORA *and her two sons,*
with the Moor at one door. Enter at the other door
BASSIANUS *and* LAVINIA, *with Titus' three Sons.*

SATURNINUS
So, Bassianus, you have played your prize.
God give you joy, sir, of your gallant bride.

BASSIANUS   And you of yours, my lord. I say no more,
Nor wish no less, and so I take my leave.

SATURNINUS
Traitor, if Rome have law or we have power,
Thou and thy faction shall repent this rape.

BASSIANUS
'Rape' call you it, my lord, to seize my own,
My true betrothed love, and now my wife?
But let the laws of Rome determine all;
Meanwhile am I possessed of that is mine.

SATURNINUS   'Tis good, sir. You are very short with us.
But if we live we'll be as sharp with you.

BASSIANUS   My lord, what I have done, as best I may,
Answer I must, and shall do with my life.
Only thus much I give your grace to know:
By all the duties that I owe to Rome,
This noble gentleman, Lord Titus here,
Is in opinion and in honour wronged,
That in the rescue of Lavinia
With his own hand did slay his youngest son
In zeal to you, and highly moved to wrath
To be controlled in that he frankly gave.
Receive him then to favour, Saturnine,
That hath expressed himself in all his deeds
A father and a friend to thee and Rome.

TITUS   Prince Bassianus, leave to plead my deeds;
'Tis thou and those that have dishonoured me.
[*He kneels.*]
Rome and the righteous heavens be my judge
How I have loved and honoured Saturnine!

TAMORA [*to Saturninus*]   My worthy lord, if ever Tamora
Were gracious in those princely eyes of thine,
Then hear me speak indifferently for all,
And at my suit, sweet, pardon what is past.

SATURNINUS   What, madam, be dishonoured openly,
And basely put it up without revenge?

TAMORA   Not so, my lord. The gods of Rome forfend
I should be author to dishonour you.
But on mine honour dare I undertake
For good Lord Titus' innocence in all,
Whose fury not dissembled speaks his griefs.
Then at my suit look graciously on him;
Lose not so noble a friend on vain suppose,
Nor with sour looks afflict his gentle heart.
[*aside to Saturninus*]
My lord, be ruled by me, be won at last,
Dissemble all your griefs and discontents.
You are but newly planted in your throne;
Lest then the people, and patricians too,
Upon a just survey take Titus' part,
And so supplant you for ingratitude,
Which Rome reputes to be a heinous sin,
Yield at entreats – and then let me alone:
I'll find a day to massacre them all,
And raze their faction and their family,
The cruel father and his traitorous sons
To whom I sued for my dear son's life,
And make them know what 'tis to let a queen
Kneel in the streets and beg for grace in vain.
[*aloud*] Come, come, sweet emperor – come,
                    Andronicus –
Take up this good old man, and cheer the heart
That dies in tempest of thy angry frown.

SATURNINUS
Rise, Titus, rise: my empress hath prevailed.

TITUS [*rising*]   I thank your majesty and her, my lord;
These words, these looks, infuse new life in me.

TAMORA   Titus, I am incorporate in Rome,
A Roman now adopted happily,
And must advise the emperor for his good.
This day all quarrels die, Andronicus;
And let it be mine honour, good my lord,
That I have reconciled your friends and you.
For you, Prince Bassianus, I have passed
My word and promise to the emperor
That you will be more mild and tractable.
And fear not, lords, and you, Lavinia:
By my advice, all humbled on your knees,
You shall ask pardon of his majesty.
[*Titus' sons kneel.*]

LUCIUS   We do, and vow to heaven and to his highness
That what we did was mildly as we might,

Tendering our sister's honour and our own.

MARCUS [*kneeling*]

That on mine honour here do I protest.

SATURNINUS   Away, and talk not; trouble us no more.

TAMORA

Nay, nay, sweet emperor, we must all be friends;

485   The tribune and his nephews kneel for grace;

I will not be denied: sweet heart, look back.

SATURNINUS

Marcus, for thy sake, and thy brother's here,

And at my lovely Tamora's entreats,

I do remit these young men's heinous faults.

[*Marcus and Titus' sons stand up.*]

490   Lavinia, though you left me like a churl,

I found a friend, and sure as death I swore

I would not part a bachelor from the priest.

Come, if the emperor's court can feast two brides,

You are my guest, Lavinia, and your friends.

495   This day shall be a love-day, Tamora.

TITUS   Tomorrow, and it please your majesty

To hunt the panther and the hart with me,

With horn and hound we'll give your grace *bonjour*.

SATURNINUS   Be it so, Titus, and gramercy too.

Sound trumpets. Exeunt all except the Moor.

[2.1]

500   AARON   Now climbeth Tamora Olympus' top,

Safe out of fortune's shot, and sits aloft,

Secure of thunder's crack or lightning flash,

Advanced above pale envy's threatening reach.

[5]   As when the golden sun salutes the morn

505   And, having gilt the ocean with his beams,

Gallops the zodiac in his glistering coach

And overlooks the highest-peering hills,

So Tamora.

[10]   Upon her wit doth earthly honour wait,

510   And virtue stoops and trembles at her frown.

Then, Aaron, arm thy heart and fit thy thoughts

To mount aloft with thy imperial mistress,

And mount her pitch whom thou in triumph long

[15]   Hast prisoner held, fettered in amorous chains

515   And faster bound to Aaron's charming eyes

Than is Prometheus tied to Caucasus.

Away with slavish weeds and servile thoughts!

I will be bright, and shine in pearl and gold

[20]   To wait upon this new-made empress.

520   To wait, said I? – to wanton with this queen,

This goddess, this Semiramis, this nymph,

This siren that will charm Rome's Saturnine

And see his shipwreck and his commonweal's.

[25]   Hallo, what storm is this?

Enter CHIRON *and* DEMETRIUS, *braving.*

DEMETRIUS

525   Chiron, thy years want wit, thy wits want edge

And manners to intrude where I am graced

And may, for aught thou knowest, affected be.

CHIRON   Demetrius, thou dost overween in all,

And so in this, to bear me down with braves.   [30]

'Tis not the difference of a year or two   530

Makes me less gracious, or thee more fortunate:

I am as able and as fit as thou

To serve, and to deserve my mistress' grace,

And that my sword upon thee shall approve,   [35]

And plead my passions for Lavinia's love.   535

AARON [*aside*]

Clubs, clubs! These lovers will not keep the peace.

DEMETRIUS

Why, boy, although our mother, unadvised,

Gave you a dancing-rapier by your side,

Are you so desperate grown to threat your friends?   [40]

Go to, have your lath glued within your sheath   540

Till you know better how to handle it.

CHIRON   Meanwhile, sir, with the little skill I have,

Full well shalt thou perceive how much I dare.

DEMETRIUS   Ay boy, grow ye so brave? [*They draw.*]

AARON   Why, how now, lords?   [45]

So near the emperor's palace dare ye draw   545

And maintain such a quarrel openly?

Full well I wot the ground of all this grudge.

I would not for a million of gold

The cause were known to them it most concerns,   [50]

Nor would your noble mother for much more   550

Be so dishonoured in the court of Rome.

For shame, put up.

DEMETRIUS   Not I, till I have sheathed

My rapier in his bosom, and withal

Thrust those reproachful speeches down his throat   [55]

That he hath breathed in my dishonour here.   555

CHIRON   For that I am prepared and full resolved,

Foul-spoken coward, that thunderest with thy

tongue,

And with thy weapon nothing dar'st perform.

AARON   Away, I say.   [60]

Now, by the gods that warlike Goths adore,   560

This petty brabble will undo us all.

Why, lords, and think you not how dangerous

It is to jet upon a prince's right?

What, is Lavinia then become so loose,   [65]

Or Bassianus so degenerate,   565

That for her love such quarrels may be broached

Without controlment, justice, or revenge?

Young lords, beware – and should the empress know

This discord's ground, the music would not please.   [70]

CHIRON   I care not, I, knew she and all the world: 570

I love Lavinia more than all the world.

DEMETRIUS

Youngling, learn thou to make some meaner choice;

Lavinia is thine elder brother's hope.

AARON   Why, are ye mad? Or know ye not in Rome   [75]

How furious and impatient they be,   575

And cannot brook competitors in love?

I tell you, lords, you do but plot your deaths

By this device.

CHIRON Aaron, a thousand deaths would I propose
  T'achieve her whom I love.
AARON   T'achieve her how?
DEMETRIUS   Why makes thou it so strange?
  She is a woman, therefore may be wooed;
  She is a woman, therefore may be won;
  She is Lavinia, therefore must be loved.
  What, man, more water glideth by the mill
  Than wots the miller of, and easy it is
  Of a cut loaf to steal a shive, we know.
  Though Bassianus be the emperor's brother,
  Better than he have worn Vulcan's badge.
AARON [*aside*]   Ay, and as good as Saturninus may.
DEMETRIUS
  Then why should he despair that knows to court it
  With words, fair looks and liberality?
  What, hast not thou full often struck a doe
  And borne her cleanly by the keeper's nose?
AARON   Why then, it seems some certain snatch or so
  Would serve your turns.
CHIRON   Ay, so the turn were served.
DEMETRIUS   Aaron, thou hast hit it.
AARON   Would you had hit it too,
  Then should not we be tired with this ado.
  Why, hark ye, hark ye, and are you such fools
  To square for this? Would it offend you then
  That both should speed?
CHIRON   Faith, not me.
DEMETRIUS   Nor me, so I were one.
AARON   For shame, be friends, and join for that you jar.
  'Tis policy and stratagem must do
  That you affect, and so must you resolve
  That what you cannot as you would achieve,
  You must perforce accomplish as you may.
  Take this of me: Lucrece was not more chaste
  Than this Lavinia, Bassianus' love.
  A speedier course than lingering languishment
  Must we pursue, and I have found the path.
  My lords, a solemn hunting is in hand;
  There will the lovely Roman ladies troop.
  The forest walks are wide and spacious,
  And many unfrequented plots there are,
  Fitted by kind for rape and villainy.
  Single you thither then this dainty doe,
  And strike her home by force, if not by words:
  This way or not at all stand you in hope.
  Come, come, our empress, with her sacred wit
  To villainy and vengeance consecrate,
  Will we acquaint withal what we intend,
  And she shall file our engines with advice
  That will not suffer you to square yourselves,
  But to your wishes' height advance you both.
  The emperor's court is like the house of Fame,
  The palace full of tongues, of eyes and ears;
  The woods are ruthless, dreadful, deaf and dull:
  There speak and strike, brave boys, and take your
      turns;

  There serve your lust, shadowed from heaven's eye,   630
  And revel in Lavinia's treasury.
CHIRON   Thy counsel, lad, smells of no cowardice.
DEMETRIUS   *Sit fas aut nefas*, till I find the stream
  To cool this heat, a charm to calm these fits,   [135]
  Per Stygia, per manes vehor.   *Exeunt.*   635

2.1 [2.2] *Enter* TITUS ANDRONICUS *and his three sons, and* MARCUS, *making a noise with hounds and horns.*

TITUS   The hunt is up, the morn is bright and grey,
  The fields are fragrant and the woods are green.
  Uncouple here, and let us make a bay
  And wake the emperor and his lovely bride,
  And rouse the prince, and ring a hunter's peal,   5
  That all the court may echo with the noise.
  Sons, let it be your charge, as it is ours,
  To attend the emperor's person carefully.
  I have been troubled in my sleep this night,
  But dawning day new comfort hath inspired.   10

Here a cry of hounds, and wind horns in a peal; then enter
SATURNINUS, TAMORA, BASSIANUS, LAVINIA, CHIRON,
DEMETRIUS *and their attendants.*

  Many good morrows to your majesty;
  Madam, to you as many and as good.
  I promised your grace a hunter's peal.
SATURNINUS   And you have rung it lustily, my lords,
  Somewhat too early for new-married ladies.   15
BASSIANUS   Lavinia, how say you?
LAVINIA   I say no:
  I have been broad awake two hours and more.
SATURNINUS
  Come on then, horse and chariots let us have,
  And to our sport.
  [*to Tamora*]   Madam, now shall ye see
  Our Roman hunting.
MARCUS   I have dogs, my lord,   20
  Will rouse the proudest panther in the chase
  And climb the highest promontory top.
TITUS   And I have horse will follow where the game
  Makes way and runs like swallows o'er the plain.
DEMETRIUS [*aside*]
  Chiron, we hunt not, we, with horse nor hound,   25
  But hope to pluck a dainty doe to ground.   *Exeunt.*

2.2 [2.3] *Enter* AARON *alone, with a money-bag.*

AARON   He that had wit would think that I had none,
  To bury so much gold under a tree
  And never after to inherit it.
  Let him that thinks of me so abjectly
  Know that this gold must coin a stratagem   5
  Which, cunningly effected, will beget
  A very excellent piece of villainy.
  And so repose, sweet gold, for their unrest
  That have their alms out of the empress' chest.
  [*Hides the money-bag.*]

Enter TAMORA *alone, to the Moor.*

10 TAMORA   My lovely Aaron, wherefore look'st thou sad
          When everything doth make a gleeful boast?
          The birds chant melody on every bush,
          The snakes lies rolled in the cheerful sun,
          The green leaves quiver with the cooling wind
15   And make a chequered shadow on the ground.
          Under their sweet shade, Aaron, let us sit,
          And whilst the babbling echo mocks the hounds,
          Replying shrilly to the well-tuned horns
          As if a double hunt were heard at once,
20   Let us sit down and mark their yellowing noise;
          And after conflict such as was supposed
          The wandering prince and Dido once enjoyed,
          When with a happy storm they were surprised
          And curtained with a counsel-keeping cave,
25   We may, each wreathed in the other's arms,
          Our pastimes done, possess a golden slumber,
          Whiles hounds and horns and sweet melodious birds
          Be unto us as is a nurse's song
          Of lullaby to bring her babe asleep.
30 AARON   Madam, though Venus govern your desires,
          Saturn is dominator over mine.
          What signifies my deadly-standing eye,
          My silence and my cloudy melancholy,
          My fleece of woolly hair that now uncurls
35   Even as an adder when she doth unroll
          To do some fatal execution?
          No, madam, these are no venereal signs;
          Vengeance is in my heart, death in my hand,
          Blood and revenge are hammering in my head.
40   Hark, Tamora, the empress of my soul,
          Which never hopes more heaven than rests in thee,
          This is the day of doom for Bassianus,
          His Philomel must lose her tongue today,
          Thy sons make pillage of her chastity
45   And wash their hands in Bassianus' blood.
          Seest thou this letter? Take it up, I pray thee,
          [*Gives letter.*]
          And give the king this fatal-plotted scroll.
          Now question me no more: we are espied.
          Here comes a parcel of our hopeful booty,
50   Which dreads not yet their lives' destruction.

Enter BASSIANUS *and* LAVINIA.

    TAMORA   Ah, my sweet Moor, sweeter to me than life!
    AARON   No more, great empress: Bassianus comes.
          Be cross with him, and I'll go fetch thy sons
          To back thy quarrels, whatsoe'er they be.   *Exit.*
55 BASSIANUS   Who have we here? Rome's royal empress,
          Unfurnished of her well-beseeming troop?
          Or is it Dian, habited like her,
          Who hath abandoned her holy groves
          To see the general hunting in this forest?
60 TAMORA   Saucy controller of my private steps,
          Had I the power that some say Dian had,

          Thy temples should be planted presently
          With horns, as was Actaeon's, and the hounds
          Should drive upon thy new-transformed limbs,
          Unmannerly intruder as thou art.   65
    LAVINIA   Under your patience, gentle empress,
          'Tis thought you have a goodly gift in horning,
          And to be doubted that your Moor and you
          Are singled forth to try experiments.
          Jove shield your husband from his hounds today: 70
          'Tis pity they should take him for a stag.
    BASSIANUS   Believe me, queen, your swart Cimmerian
          Doth make your honour of his body's hue,
          Spotted, detested and abominable.
          Why are you sequestered from all your train,   75
          Dismounted from your snow-white goodly steed,
          And wandered hither to an obscure plot,
          Accompanied but with a barbarous Moor,
          If foul desire had not conducted you?
    LAVINIA   And being intercepted in your sport,   80
          Great reason that my noble lord be rated
          For sauciness. [*to Bassianus*] I pray you, let us hence,
          And let her joy her raven-coloured love.
          This valley fits the purpose passing well.
    BASSIANUS   The king my brother shall have note of this. 85
    LAVINIA   Ay, for these slips have made him noted long:
          Good king, to be so mightily abused!
    TAMORA   Why, I have patience to endure all this.

Enter CHIRON *and* DEMETRIUS.

    DEMETRIUS
          How now, dear sovereign and our gracious mother,
          Why doth your highness look so pale and wan?   90
    TAMORA   Have I not reason, think you, to look pale?
          These two have 'ticed me hither to this place:
          A barren detested vale you see it is;
          The trees, though summer, yet forlorn and lean,
          O'ercome with moss and baleful mistletoe;   95
          Here never shines the sun, here nothing breeds
          Unless the nightly owl or fatal raven.
          And when they showed me this abhorred pit,
          They told me here at dead time of the night
          A thousand fiends, a thousand hissing snakes,   100
          Ten thousand swelling toads, as many urchins,
          Would make such fearful and confused cries
          As any mortal body hearing it
          Should straight fall mad, or else die suddenly.
          No sooner had they told this hellish tale,   105
          But straight they told me they would bind me here
          Unto the body of a dismal yew
          And leave me to this miserable death.
          And then they called me foul adulteress,
          Lascivious Goth, and all the bitterest terms   110
          That ever ear did hear to such effect.
          And had you not by wondrous fortune come,
          This vengeance on me had they executed.
          Revenge it as you love your mother's life,
          Or be ye not henceforth called my children.   115

DEMETRIUS   This is a witness that I am thy son.
    [*Stabs him.*]
CHIRON
    And this for me, struck home to shew my strength.
    [*He also stabs Bassianus, who dies.*]
LAVINIA   Ay, come, Semiramis, nay, barbarous Tamora,
    For no name fits thy nature but thy own.
TAMORA
120   Give me the poniard. You shall know, my boys,
    Your mother's hand shall right your mother's wrong.
DEMETRIUS   Stay, madam, here is more belongs to her:
    First thrash the corn, then after burn the straw.
    This minion stood upon her chastity,
125   Upon her nuptial vow, her loyalty,
    And with that quaint hope braves your mightiness.
    And shall she carry this unto her grave?
CHIRON   And if she do, I would I were an eunuch.
    Drag hence her husband to some secret hole
130   And make his dead trunk pillow to our lust.
TAMORA   But when ye have the honey we desire,
    Let not this wasp outlive, us both to sting.
CHIRON   I warrant you, madam, we will make that sure.
    Come, mistress, now perforce we will enjoy
135   That nice-preserved honesty of yours.
LAVINIA   O Tamora, thou bearest a woman's face –
TAMORA   I will not hear her speak; away with her!
LAVINIA   Sweet lords, entreat her hear me but a word.
DEMETRIUS [*to Tamora*]
    Listen, fair madam, let it be your glory
140   To see her tears, but be your heart to them
    As unrelenting flint to drops of rain.
LAVINIA
    When did the tiger's young ones teach the dam?
    O, do not learn her wrath: she taught it thee.
    The milk thou suckst from her did turn to marble;
145   Even at thy teat thou hadst thy tyranny.
    Yet every mother breeds not sons alike:
    [*to Chiron*] Do thou entreat her show a woman's pity.
CHIRON
    What, wouldst thou have me prove myself a bastard?
LAVINIA   'Tis true, the raven doth not hatch a lark.
150   Yet have I heard – O, could I find it now –
    The lion, moved with pity, did endure
    To have his princely paws pared all away.
    Some say that ravens foster forlorn children
    The whilst their own birds famish in their nests.
155   O be to me, though thy hard heart say no,
    Nothing so kind, but something pitiful.
TAMORA   I know not what it means; away with her!
LAVINIA   O, let me teach thee for my father's sake,
    That gave thee life when well he might have slain thee.
160   Be not obdurate, open thy deaf ears.
TAMORA   Hadst thou in person ne'er offended me,
    Even for his sake am I pitiless.
    Remember, boys, I poured forth tears in vain
    To save your brother from the sacrifice,
165   But fierce Andronicus would not relent.

    Therefore away with her and use her as you will:
    The worse to her, the better loved of me.
LAVINIA [*clinging to Tamora*]
    O Tamora, be called a gentle queen,
    And with thine own hands kill me in this place.
    For 'tis not life that I have begged so long;   170
    Poor I was slain when Bassianus died.
TAMORA
    What begg'st thou then, fond woman? Let me go!
LAVINIA   'Tis present death I beg, and one thing more
    That womanhood denies my tongue to tell.
    O, keep me from their worse-than-killing lust,   175
    And tumble me into some loathsome pit
    Where never man's eye may behold my body.
    Do this, and be a charitable murderer.
TAMORA   So should I rob my sweet sons of their fee.
    No, let them satisfy their lust on thee.   180
DEMETRIUS [*to Lavinia*]
    Away, for thou hast stayed us here too long.
LAVINIA
    No grace? No womanhood? Ah, beastly creature,
    The blot and enemy to our general name,
    Confusion fall –
CHIRON   Nay then, I'll stop your mouth.
    [*Grabs her, covering her mouth.*]
    [*to Demetrius*] Bring thou her husband: 185
    This is the hole where Aaron bid us hide him.
              Demetrius throws Bassianus' body into the pit,
              he and Chiron then exeunt, dragging Lavinia.
TAMORA
    Farewell, my sons; see that you make her sure.
    Ne'er let my heart know merry cheer indeed
    Till all the Andronici be made away.
    Now will I hence to seek my lovely Moor,   190
    And let my spleenful sons this trull deflower.   *Exit.*

    Enter AARON *with two of Titus' sons,* QUINTUS
              and MARTIUS.

AARON   Come on, my lords, the better foot before.
    Straight will I bring you to the loathsome pit
    Where I espied the panther fast asleep.
QUINTUS   My sight is very dull, whate'er it bodes.   195
MARTIUS
    And mine, I promise you; were it not for shame,
    Well could I leave our sport to sleep awhile.
    [*Falls into the pit.*]
QUINTUS
    What, art thou fallen? What subtle hole is this,
    Whose mouth is covered with rude-growing briers
    Upon whose leaves are drops of new-shed blood   200
    As fresh as morning dew distilled on flowers?
    A very fatal place it seems to me.
    Speak, brother, hast thou hurt thee with the fall?
MARTIUS [*from below*]
    O brother, with the dismall'st object hurt
    That ever eye with sight made heart lament.   205

AARON [*aside*]
   Now will I fetch the king to find them here,
   That he thereby may have a likely guess
   How these were they that made away his brother. *Exit.*
MARTIUS [*from below*]
   Why dost not comfort me and help me out
210   From this unhallowed and bloodstained hole?
QUINTUS   I am surprised with an uncouth fear;
   A chilling sweat o'erruns my trembling joints;
   My heart suspects more than mine eye can see.
MARTIUS [*from below*]
   To prove thou hast a true-divining heart,
215   Aaron and thou look down into this den,
   And see a fearful sight of blood and death.
QUINTUS   Aaron is gone and my compassionate heart
   Will not permit mine eyes once to behold
   The thing whereat it trembles by surmise.
220   O tell me who it is, for ne'er till now
   Was I a child to fear I know not what.
MARTIUS [*from below*]
   Lord Bassianus lies berayed in blood
   All on a heap, like to a slaughtered lamb,
   In this detested, dark, blood-drinking pit.
225 QUINTUS   If it be dark, how dost thou know 'tis he?
MARTIUS [*from below*]
   Upon his bloody finger he doth wear
   A precious ring that lightens all this hole,
   Which like a taper in some monument
   Doth shine upon the dead man's earthy cheeks
230   And shows the ragged entrails of this pit.
   So pale did shine the moon on Pyramus
   When he by night lay bathed in maiden blood.
   O brother, help me with thy fainting hand –
   If fear hath made thee faint, as me it hath –
235   Out of this fell devouring receptacle,
   As hateful as Cocytus' misty mouth.
QUINTUS [*Reaches into pit.*]
   Reach me thy hand that I may help thee out
   Or, wanting strength to do thee so much good,
   I may be plucked into the swallowing womb
240   Of this deep pit, poor Bassianus' grave.
   I have no strength to pluck thee to the brink –
MARTIUS [*from below*]
   Nor I no strength to climb without thy help.
QUINTUS   Thy hand once more; I will not loose again
   Till thou art here aloft or I below.
245   Thou canst not come to me – I come to thee.
   [*Falls into the pit.*]

Enter the Emperor *and* AARON *the Moor, with attendants.*

SATURNINUS   Along with me! I'll see what hole is here
   And what he is that now is leapt into it.
   [*Speaks into the pit.*]
   Say, who art thou that lately didst descend
   Into this gaping hollow of the earth?
MARTIUS [*from below*]
250   The unhappy sons of old Andronicus,

   Brought hither in a most unlucky hour
   To find thy brother Bassianus dead.
SATURNINUS
   My brother dead? I know thou dost but jest;
   He and his lady both are at the lodge
   Upon the north side of this pleasant chase.   255
   'Tis not an hour since I left them there.
MARTIUS [*from below*]
   We know not where you left them all alive,
   But, out alas, here have we found him dead.

Enter TAMORA, TITUS ANDRONICUS *and* LUCIUS.

TAMORA   Where is my lord the king?
SATURNINUS
   Here, Tamora, though gride with killing grief.   260
TAMORA   Where is thy brother Bassianus?
SATURNINUS
   Now to the bottom dost thou search my wound:
   Poor Bassianus here lies murdered.
TAMORA   Then all too late I bring this fatal writ,
   The complot of this timeless tragedy,   265
   And wonder greatly that man's face can fold
   In pleasing smiles such murderous tyranny.
   [*She giveth Saturnine a letter.*]
SATURNINUS [*Reads.*]
   And if we miss to meet him handsomely,
   Sweet huntsman – Bassianus 'tis we mean –
   Do thou so much as dig the grave for him.   270
   Thou know'st our meaning. Look for thy reward
   Among the nettles at the elder tree
   Which overshades the mouth of that same pit
   Where we decreed to bury Bassianus.
   Do this, and purchase us thy lasting friends.   275
   O Tamora, was ever heard the like?
   This is the pit and this the elder tree.
   Look, sirs, if you can find the huntsman out
   That should have murdered Bassianus here.
AARON [*finding the money-bag*]
   My gracious lord, here is the bag of gold.   280
SATURNINUS [*to Titus*]
   Two of thy whelps, fell curs of bloody kind,
   Have here bereft my brother of his life.
   Sirs, drag them from the pit unto the prison.
   There let them bide until we have devised
   Some never-heard-of torturing pain for them.   285
TAMORA   What, are they in this pit? O wondrous thing!
   How easily murder is discovered.
   [*Attendants pull Quintus, Martius and*
   Bassianus' body from the pit.]
TITUS [*kneeling*]   High emperor, upon my feeble knee
   I beg this boon with tears not lightly shed:
   That this fell fault of my accursed sons,   290
   Accursed if the fault be proved in them –
SATURNINUS   If it be proved? You see it is apparent.
   Who found this letter? Tamora, was it you?
TAMORA   Andronicus himself did take it up.
TITUS   I did, my lord, yet let me be their bail,   295

For by my fathers' reverend tomb I vow
They shall be ready at your highness' will
To answer their suspicion with their lives.
SATURNINUS
Thou shalt not bail them. See thou follow me.
Some bring the murdered body, some the murderers.
Let them not speak a word: the guilt is plain;
For, by my soul, were there worse end than death
That end upon them should be executed.
TAMORA   Andronicus, I will entreat the king;
Fear not thy sons, they shall do well enough.
TITUS [*rising*]
Come, Lucius, come; stay not to talk with them.
Exeunt, some taking the body, some guarding the prisoners.

2.3 [2.4]   *Enter* the Empress' Sons *with* LAVINIA,
her hands cut off and her tongue cut out, and ravished.

DEMETRIUS   So, now go tell, and if thy tongue can speak,
Who 'twas that cut thy tongue and ravished thee.
CHIRON   Write down thy mind, bewray thy meaning so,
And if thy stumps will let thee, play the scribe.
DEMETRIUS
See how with signs and tokens she can scrawl.
CHIRON   Go home, call for sweet water, wash thy hands.
DEMETRIUS
She hath no tongue to call, nor hands to wash,
And so let's leave her to her silent walks.
CHIRON   And 'twere my cause, I should go hang myself.
DEMETRIUS
If thou hadst hands to help thee knit the cord.
Exeunt Chiron and Demetrius.

Wind horns. Enter MARCUS *from hunting.*
Lavinia runs away.

MARCUS   Who is this – my niece that flies away so fast?
Cousin, a word. Where is your husband?
[*Lavinia turns.*]
If I do dream, would all my wealth would wake me;
If I do wake, some planet strike me down
That I may slumber an eternal sleep.
Speak, gentle niece, what stern ungentle hands
Hath lopped and hewed and made thy body bare
Of her two branches, those sweet ornaments
Whose circling shadows kings have sought to sleep in
And might not gain so great a happiness
As half thy love. Why dost not speak to me?
[*Lavinia opens her mouth.*]
Alas, a crimson river of warm blood,
Like to a bubbling fountain stirred with wind,
Doth rise and fall between thy rosed lips,
Coming and going with thy honey breath.
But sure some Tereus hath deflowered thee
And, lest thou shouldst detect him, cut thy tongue.
Ah, now thou turn'st away thy face for shame,
And notwithstanding all this loss of blood,
As from a conduit with three issuing spouts,

Yet do thy cheeks look red as Titan's face,
Blushing to be encountered with a cloud.
Shall I speak for thee? Shall I say 'tis so?
O that I knew thy heart, and knew the beast,
That I might rail at him to ease my mind!   35
Sorrow concealed, like an oven stopped,
Doth burn the heart to cinders where it is.
Fair Philomela, why she but lost her tongue,
And in a tedious sampler sewed her mind;
But, lovely niece, that mean is cut from thee.   40
A craftier Tereus, cousin, hast thou met,
And he hath cut those pretty fingers off,
That could have better sewed than Philomel.
O, had the monster seen those lily hands
Tremble like aspen leaves upon a lute   45
And make the silken strings delight to kiss them,
He would not then have touched them for his life.
Or had he heard the heavenly harmony
Which that sweet tongue hath made,
He would have dropped his knife and fell asleep,   50
As Cerberus at the Thracian poet's feet.
Come, let us go and make thy father blind,
For such a sight will blind a father's eye.
One hour's storm will drown the fragrant meads:
What will whole months of tears thy father's eyes?   55
Do not draw back, for we will mourn with thee;
O, could our mourning ease thy misery!   *Exeunt.*

3.1   *Enter the Tribunes as judges and the senators, with*
Titus' two sons QUINTUS *and* MARTIUS *bound, passing to*
the place of execution, and TITUS *going before pleading.*

TITUS   Hear me, grave fathers; noble tribunes, stay!
For pity of mine age, whose youth was spent
In dangerous wars whilst you securely slept;
For all my blood in Rome's great quarrel shed,
For all the frosty nights that I have watched,   5
And for these bitter tears which now you see
Filling the aged wrinkles in my cheeks,
Be pitiful to my condemned sons,
Whose souls is not corrupted as 'tis thought.
For two-and-twenty sons I never wept,   10
Because they died in honour's lofty bed.
[*Andronicus lieth down, and the judges pass by him.*]
For these two, tribunes, in the dust I write
My heart's deep languor and my soul's sad tears.
Let my tears staunch the earth's dry appetite;
My sons' sweet blood will make it shame and blush.   15
Exeunt all but Titus.
O earth, I will befriend thee more with rain
That shall distil from these two ancient ruins
Than youthful April shall with all his showers.
In summer's drought I'll drop upon thee still;
In winter with warm tears I'll melt the snow   20
And keep eternal springtime on thy face,
So thou refuse to drink my dear sons' blood.

Enter LUCIUS *with his weapon drawn.*

O reverend tribunes, O gentle aged men,
Unbind my sons, reverse the doom of death,
25   And let me say, that never wept before,
My tears are now prevailing orators.
LUCIUS   O noble father, you lament in vain:
The tribunes hear you not, no man is by,
And you recount your sorrows to a stone.
30   TITUS   Ah Lucius, for thy brothers let me plead.
Grave tribunes, once more I entreat of you –
LUCIUS   My gracious lord, no tribune hears you speak.
TITUS   Why, 'tis no matter, man: if they did hear,
They would not mark me, or if they did mark,
35   They would not pity me; yet plead I must,
And bootless unto them.
Therefore I tell my sorrows to the stones,
Who, though they cannot answer my distress,
Yet in some sort they are better than the tribunes
40   For that they will not intercept my tale.
When I do weep, they humbly at my feet
Receive my tears and seem to weep with me,
And were they but attired in grave weeds
Rome could afford no tribunes like to these.
A stone is soft as wax, tribunes more hard than
45   stones;
A stone is silent and offendeth not,
And tribunes with their tongues doom men to death.
But wherefore stand'st thou with thy weapon drawn?
LUCIUS   To rescue my two brothers from their death,
50   For which attempt the judges have pronounced
My everlasting doom of banishment.
TITUS [*rising*]
O happy man, they have befriended thee!
Why, foolish Lucius, dost thou not perceive
That Rome is but a wilderness of tigers?
55   Tigers must prey, and Rome affords no prey
But me and mine. How happy art thou then
From these devourers to be banished.
But who comes with our brother Marcus here?

Enter MARCUS *with* LAVINIA.

MARCUS   Titus, prepare thy aged eyes to weep,
60   Or if not so, thy noble heart to break:
I bring consuming sorrow to thine age.
TITUS   Will it consume me? Let me see it then.
MARCUS   This was thy daughter.
TITUS   Why, Marcus, so she is.
65   LUCIUS [*falling to his knees*]   Ay me, this object kills me.
TITUS   Faint-hearted boy, arise and look upon her.
[*Lucius rises.*]
Speak, Lavinia, what accursed hand
Hath made thee handless in thy father's sight?
What fool hath added water to the sea?
70   Or brought a faggot to bright-burning Troy?
My grief was at the height before thou cam'st,
And now like Nilus it disdaineth bounds.
Give me a sword, I'll chop off my hands too,
For they have fought for Rome, and all in vain;

And they have nursed this woe in feeding life;   75
In bootless prayer have they been held up,
And they have served me to effectless use.
Now all the service I require of them
Is that the one will help to cut the other.
'Tis well, Lavinia, that thou hast no hands,   80
For hands to do Rome service is but vain.
LUCIUS   Speak, gentle sister: who hath martyred thee?
MARCUS   O, that delightful engine of her thoughts,
That blabbed them with such pleasing eloquence,
Is torn from forth that pretty hollow cage   85
Where, like a sweet melodious bird, it sung
Sweet varied notes, enchanting every ear.
LUCIUS   O, say thou for her: who hath done this deed?
MARCUS   O, thus I found her, straying in the park,
Seeking to hide herself, as doth the deer   90
That hath received some unrecuring wound.
TITUS   It was my dear, and he that wounded her
Hath hurt me more than had he killed me dead.
For now I stand as one upon a rock,
Environed with a wilderness of sea,   95
Who marks the waxing tide grow wave by wave,
Expecting ever when some envious surge
Will in his brinish bowels swallow him.
This way to death my wretched sons are gone;
Here stands my other son, a banished man,   100
And here my brother, weeping at my woes.
But that which gives my soul the greatest spurn
Is dear Lavinia, dearer than my soul.
Had I but seen thy picture in this plight,
It would have madded me; what shall I do   105
Now I behold thy lively body so?
Thou hast no hands to wipe away thy tears,
Nor tongue to tell me who hath martyred thee;
Thy husband he is dead, and for his death
Thy brothers are condemned, and dead by this.   110
Look, Marcus, ah, son Lucius, look on her!
When I did name her brothers, then fresh tears
Stood on her cheeks, as doth the honey-dew
Upon a gathered lily almost withered.
MARCUS
Perchance she weeps because they killed her
     husband,   115
Perchance because she knows them innocent.
TITUS   If they did kill thy husband, then be joyful,
Because the law hath ta'en revenge on them.
No, no, they would not do so foul a deed:
Witness the sorrow that their sister makes.   120
Gentle Lavinia, let me kiss thy lips
Or make some sign how I may do thee ease.
Shall thy good uncle and thy brother Lucius
And thou and I sit round about some fountain,
Looking all downwards to behold our cheeks,   125
How they are stained like meadows yet not dry,
With miry slime left on them by a flood?
And in the fountain shall we gaze so long
Till the fresh taste be taken from that clearness

130   And made a brine pit with our bitter tears?
       Or shall we cut away our hands like thine?
       Or shall we bite our tongues and in dumb shows
       Pass the remainder of our hateful days?
       What shall we do? Let us that have our tongues
135   Plot some device of further misery
       To make us wondered at in time to come.
       LUCIUS   Sweet father, cease your tears, for at your grief
       See how my wretched sister sobs and weeps.
       MARCUS
       Patience, dear niece; good Titus, dry thine eyes.
       [*Gives handkerchief.*]
140   TITUS   Ah Marcus, Marcus, brother, well I wot
       Thy napkin cannot drink a tear of mine,
       For thou, poor man, hast drowned it with thine own.
       LUCIUS   Ah, my Lavinia, I will wipe thy cheeks.
       TITUS   Mark, Marcus, mark! I understand her signs:
145   Had she a tongue to speak, now would she say
       That to her brother which I said to thee.
       His napkin with his true tears all bewet
       Can do no service on her sorrowful cheeks.
       O, what a sympathy of woe is this;
150   As far from help as limbo is from bliss.

       Enter AARON *the Moor alone.*

       AARON   Titus Andronicus, my lord the emperor
       Sends thee this word: that if thou love thy sons,
       Let Marcus, Lucius, or thyself, old Titus,
       Or any one of you, chop off your hand
155   And send it to the king, he for the same
       Will send thee hither both thy sons alive –
       And that shall be the ransom for their fault.
       TITUS   O gracious emperor, O gentle Aaron!
       Did ever raven sing so like a lark
160   That gives sweet tidings of the sun's uprise?
       With all my heart I'll send the emperor my hand.
       Good Aaron, wilt thou help to chop it off?
       LUCIUS   Stay, father, for that noble hand of thine
       That hath thrown down so many enemies
165   Shall not be sent. My hand will serve the turn.
       My youth can better spare my blood than you,
       And therefore mine shall save my brothers' lives.
       MARCUS
       Which of your hands hath not defended Rome
       And reared aloft the bloody battleaxe,
170   Writing destruction on the enemy's casque?
       O, none of both but are of high desert.
       My hand hath been but idle: let it serve
       To ransom my two nephews from their death,
       Then have I kept it to a worthy end.
175   AARON   Nay, come, agree whose hand shall go along,
       For fear they die before their pardon come.
       MARCUS   My hand shall go.
       LUCIUS   By heaven it shall not go.
       TITUS
       Sirs, strive no more. Such withered herbs as these
       Are meet for plucking up – and therefore mine.

180   LUCIUS   Sweet father, if I shall be thought thy son,
       Let me redeem my brothers both from death.
       MARCUS   And for our father's sake and mother's care,
       Now let me show a brother's love to thee.
       TITUS   Agree between you: I will spare my hand.
185   LUCIUS   Then I'll go fetch an axe.
       MARCUS   But I will use the axe.
                                   Exeunt Lucius and Marcus.
       TITUS   Come hither, Aaron. I'll deceive them both:
       Lend me thy hand and I will give thee mine.
       AARON [*aside*]   If that be called deceit, I will be honest
190   And never whilst I live deceive men so.
       But I'll deceive you in another sort,
       And that you'll say ere half an hour pass.
       [*He cuts off Titus' hand.*]

       Enter LUCIUS *and* MARCUS *again.*

       TITUS
       Now stay your strife; what shall be is dispatched.
       Good Aaron, give his majesty my hand.
195   Tell him it was a hand that warded him
       From thousand dangers, bid him bury it:
       More hath it merited; that let it have.
       As for my sons, say I account of them
       As jewels purchased at an easy price,
200   And yet dear too, because I bought mine own.
       AARON   I go, Andronicus, and for thy hand
       Look by and by to have thy sons with thee.
       [*aside*] Their heads I mean. O, how this villainy
       Doth fat me with the very thoughts of it.
205   Let fools do good and fair men call for grace,
       Aaron will have his soul black like his face.   *Exit.*
       TITUS   O, here I lift this one hand up to heaven
       And bow this feeble ruin to the earth. [*Kneels.*]
       If any power pities wretched tears,
       To that I call. [*Lavinia kneels.*]
                             What, wouldst thou kneel with me?   210
       Do then, dear heart, for heaven shall hear our
           prayers,
       Or with our sighs we'll breathe the welkin dim
       And stain the sun with fog, as sometime clouds
       When they do hug him in their melting bosoms.
       MARCUS   O brother, speak with possibility,   215
       And do not break into these deep extremes.
       TITUS   Is not my sorrows deep, having no bottom?
       Then be my passions bottomless with them.
       MARCUS   But yet let reason govern thy lament.
       TITUS   If there were reason for these miseries,   220
       Then into limits could I bind my woes.
       When heaven doth weep, doth not the earth o'erflow?
       If the winds rage, doth not the sea wax mad,
       Threatening the welkin with his big-swollen face?
       And wilt thou have a reason for this coil?   225
       I am the sea. Hark how her sighs doth blow.
       She is the weeping welkin, I the earth.
       Then must my sea be moved with her sighs,
       Then must my earth with her continual tears

230 Become a deluge overflowed and drowned,
For why my bowels cannot hide her woes,
But like a drunkard must I vomit them.
Then give me leave, for losers will have leave
To ease their stomachs with their bitter tongues.

Enter a Messenger *with two heads and a hand.*

[*Titus and Lavinia may rise here.*]

235 MESSENGER   Worthy Andronicus, ill art thou repaid
For that good hand thou sent'st the emperor.
Here are the heads of thy two noble sons,
And here's thy hand in scorn to thee sent back:
Thy grief their sports, thy resolution mocked,
240 That woe is me to think upon thy woes
More than remembrance of my father's death.
Sets down heads and hand, exit.

MARCUS   Now let hot Etna cool in Sicily,
And be my heart an ever-burning hell!
These miseries are more than may be borne.
245 To weep with them that weep doth ease some deal,
But sorrow flouted at is double death.

LUCIUS
Ah, that this sight should make so deep a wound
And yet detested life not shrink thereat!
That ever death should let life bear his name,
250 Where life hath no more interest but to breathe!
[*Lavinia kisses the heads.*]

MARCUS   Alas, poor heart, that kiss is comfortless
As frozen water to a starved snake.

TITUS   When will this fearful slumber have an end?

MARCUS   Now farewell flattery, die Andronicus.
255 Thou dost not slumber. See thy two sons' heads,
Thy warlike hand, thy mangled daughter here,
Thy other banished son with this dear sight
Struck pale and bloodless, and thy brother, I,
Even like a stony image, cold and numb.
260 Ah, now no more will I control thy griefs:
Rend off thy silver hair, thy other hand
Gnawing with thy teeth, and be this dismal sight
The closing up of our most wretched eyes.
Now is a time to storm. Why art thou still?

265 TITUS   Ha, ha, ha!

MARCUS   Why dost thou laugh? It fits not with this hour.

TITUS   Why? I have not another tear to shed.
Besides, this sorrow is an enemy
And would usurp upon my watery eyes
270 And make them blind with tributary tears.
Then which way shall I find Revenge's cave?
For these two heads do seem to speak to me
And threat me I shall never come to bliss
Till all these mischiefs be returned again
275 Even in their throats that hath committed them.
Come, let me see what task I have to do.
You heavy people, circle me about,
That I may turn me to each one of you
And swear unto my soul to right your wrongs.
[*They make a vow.*]

The vow is made. Come, brother, take a head, 280
And in this hand the other will I bear.
And, Lavinia, thou shalt be employed:
Bear thou my hand, sweet wench, between thy teeth.
As for thee, boy, go get thee from my sight:
Thou art an exile and thou must not stay; 285
Hie to the Goths and raise an army there,
And if ye love me, as I think you do,
Let's kiss and part, for we have much to do.
They kiss. Exeunt. Lucius remains.

LUCIUS   Farewell, Andronicus, my noble father,
The woefull'st man that ever lived in Rome. 290
Farewell, proud Rome, till Lucius come again;
He loves his pledges dearer than his life.
Farewell, Lavinia, my noble sister,
O would thou wert as thou tofore hast been!
But now nor Lucius nor Lavinia lives 295
But in oblivion and hateful griefs.
If Lucius live, he will requite your wrongs
And make proud Saturnine and his empress
Beg at the gates like Tarquin and his queen.
Now will I to the Goths and raise a power, 300
To be revenged on Rome and Saturnine. *Exit Lucius.*

F3.2   *A banquet. Enter* TITUS ANDRONICUS, MARCUS,
LAVINIA *and the* Boy, *Young Lucius.*

TITUS   So, so, now sit, and look you eat no more
Than will preserve just so much strength in us
As will revenge these bitter woes of ours. [*They sit.*]
Marcus, unknit that sorrow-wreathen knot.
Thy niece and I, poor creatures, want our hands 5
And cannot passionate our tenfold grief
With folded arms. This poor right hand of mine
Is left to tyrannize upon my breast,
Who, when my heart, all mad with misery,
Beats in this hollow prison of my flesh, 10
Then thus I thump it down.
[*to Lavinia*]
Thou map of woe, that thus dost talk in signs,
When thy poor heart beats with outrageous beating,
Thou canst not strike it thus to make it still.
Wound it with sighing, girl, kill it with groans, 15
Or get some little knife between thy teeth
And just against thy heart make thou a hole,
That all the tears that thy poor eyes let fall
May run into that sink and, soaking in,
Drown the lamenting fool in sea-salt tears. 20

MARCUS   Fie, brother, fie! Teach her not thus to lay
Such violent hands upon her tender life.

TITUS   How now, has sorrow made thee dote already?
Why, Marcus, no man should be mad but I.
What violent hands can she lay on her life? 25
Ah, wherefore dost thou urge the name of hands
To bid Aeneas tell the tale twice o'er
How Troy was burnt and he made miserable?
O handle not the theme, to talk of hands,
Lest we remember still that we have none. 30

Fie, fie, how frantically I square my talk,
As if we should forget we had no hands
If Marcus did not name the word of hands.
Come, let's fall to, and, gentle girl, eat this.

35   Here is no drink! Hark, Marcus, what she says:
I can interpret all her martyred signs –
She says she drinks no other drink but tears,
Brewed with her sorrow, mashed upon her cheeks.
Speechless complainer, I will learn thy thought.

40   In thy dumb action will I be as perfect
As begging hermits in their holy prayers.
Thou shalt not sigh, nor hold thy stumps to heaven,
Nor wink, nor nod, nor kneel, nor make a sign,
But I of these will wrest an alphabet

45   And by still practice learn to know thy meaning.
BOY   Good grandsire, leave these bitter deep laments;
Make my aunt merry with some pleasing tale.
MARCUS   Alas, the tender boy in passion moved
Doth weep to see his grandsire's heaviness.

50 TITUS   Peace, tender sapling, thou art made of tears,
And tears will quickly melt thy life away.
[*Marcus strikes the dish with a knife.*]
What dost thou strike at, Marcus, with thy knife?
MARCUS   At that that I have killed, my lord – a fly.
TITUS   Out on thee, murderer. Thou kill'st my heart.

55   Mine eyes are cloyed with view of tyranny;
A deed of death done on the innocent
Becomes not Titus' brother. Get thee gone;
I see thou art not for my company.
MARCUS   Alas, my lord, I have but killed a fly.

60 TITUS   'But'?
How if that fly had a father and a mother?
How would he hang his slender gilded wings
And buzz lamenting doings in the air.
Poor harmless fly,

65   That with his pretty buzzing melody
Came here to make us merry, and thou hast killed him.
MARCUS   Pardon me, sir, it was a black ill-favoured fly,
Like to the empress' Moor. Therefore I killed him.
TITUS   Oh, Oh, Oh!

70   Then pardon me for reprehending thee,
For thou hast done a charitable deed.
Give me thy knife; I will insult on him,
Flattering myself as if it were the Moor
Come hither purposely to poison me.
[*Takes knife and strikes.*]

75   There's for thyself, and that's for Tamora.
Ah, sirrah!
Yet I think we are not brought so low
But that between us we can kill a fly
That comes in likeness of a coal-black Moor.

80 MARCUS   Alas, poor man! Grief has so wrought on him
He takes false shadows for true substances.
TITUS   Come, take away. Lavinia, go with me;
I'll to thy closet and go read with thee
Sad stories chanced in the times of old.

85   Come, boy, and go with me; thy sight is young,

And thou shalt read when mine begin to dazzle.
Exeunt.[F]

4.1   *Enter Lucius' son* YOUNG LUCIUS *and* LAVINIA
running after him, and the BOY *flies from her with his*
books under his arm. He drops the books. Enter TITUS *and*
MARCUS.

BOY   Help, grandsire, help! My aunt Lavinia
Follows me everywhere, I know not why.
Good uncle Marcus, see how swift she comes.
Alas, sweet aunt, I know not what you mean.
MARCUS   Stand by me, Lucius; do not fear thine aunt.   5
TITUS   She loves thee, boy, too well to do thee harm.
BOY   Ay, when my father was in Rome she did.
MARCUS   What means my niece Lavinia by these signs?
TITUS
Fear her not, Lucius – somewhat doth she mean.
MARCUS   See, Lucius, see how much she makes of thee;   10
Somewhither would she have thee go with her.
Ah, boy, Cornelia never with more care
Read to her sons than she hath read to thee
Sweet poetry and Tully's *Orator*.
Canst thou not guess wherefore she plies thee thus?   15
BOY   My lord, I know not, I, nor can I guess,
Unless some fit or frenzy do possess her.
For I have heard my grandsire say full oft
Extremity of griefs would make men mad,
And I have read that Hecuba of Troy   20
Ran mad for sorrow. That made me to fear,
Although, my lord, I know my noble aunt
Loves me as dear as e'er my mother did,
And would not but in fury fright my youth,
Which made me down to throw my books and fly,   25
Causeless perhaps. But pardon me, sweet aunt,
And, madam, if my uncle Marcus go,
I will most willingly attend your ladyship.
MARCUS   Lucius, I will. [*Lavinia turns over the books.*]
TITUS   How now, Lavinia? Marcus, what means this?   30
Some book there is that she desires to see.
Which is it, girl, of these? Open them, boy.
[*to Lavinia*]
But thou art deeper read and better skilled:
Come and take choice of all my library,
And so beguile thy sorrow till the heavens   35
Reveal the damned contriver of this deed.
Why lifts she up her arms in sequence thus?
MARCUS
I think she means that there were more than one
Confederate in the fact. Ay, more there was –
Or else to heaven she heaves them for revenge.   40
TITUS   Lucius, what book is that she tosseth so?
BOY   Grandsire, 'tis Ovid's *Metamorphosis*;
My mother gave it me.
MARCUS   For love of her that's gone,
Perhaps she culled it from among the rest.
TITUS   Soft, so busily she turns the leaves! [*Helps her.*]   45

What would she find? Lavinia, shall I read?
This is the tragic tale of Philomel,
And treats of Tereus' treason and his rape –
And rape, I fear, was root of thy annoy.
MARCUS
50   See, brother, see: note how she quotes the leaves.
TITUS   Lavinia, wert thou thus surprised, sweet girl,
Ravished and wronged as Philomela was,
Forced in the ruthless, vast and gloomy woods?
[*Lavinia nods.*] See, see!
55   Ay, such a place there is where we did hunt –
O, had we never, never hunted there! –
Patterned by that the poet here describes,
By nature made for murders and for rapes.
MARCUS   O, why should nature build so foul a den,
60   Unless the gods delight in tragedies?
TITUS
   Give signs, sweet girl – for here are none but friends –
What Roman lord it was durst do the deed.
Or slunk not Saturnine, as Tarquin erst,
That left the camp to sin in Lucrece' bed?
MARCUS
65   Sit down, sweet niece. Brother, sit down by me.
[*They sit.*] Apollo, Pallas, Jove or Mercury
Inspire me, that I may this treason find.
My lord, look here; look here, Lavinia.
[*He writes his name with his staff,*
and guides it with feet and mouth.]
This sandy plot is plain. Guide, if thou canst,
70   This after me. I here have writ my name
Without the help of any hand at all.
Cursed be that heart that forced us to this shift.
Write thou, good niece, and here display at last
What God will have discovered for revenge.
75   Heaven guide thy pen to print thy sorrows plain,
That we may know the traitors and the truth.
[*She takes the staff in her mouth,*
and guides it with her stumps, and writes.]
O do ye read, my lord, what she hath writ?
TITUS   *Stuprum – Chiron – Demetrius.*
MARCUS   What, what? The lustful sons of Tamora
80   Performers of this heinous bloody deed?
TITUS   *Magni dominator poli,*
   Tam lentus audis scelera, tam lentus vides?
MARCUS   O calm thee, gentle lord, although I know
There is enough written upon this earth
85   To stir a mutiny in the mildest thoughts
And arm the minds of infants to exclaims.
My lord, kneel down with me; Lavinia, kneel;
And kneel, sweet boy, the Roman Hector's hope,
[*They kneel.*]
And swear with me – as, with the woeful fere
90   And father of that chaste dishonoured dame,
Lord Junius Brutus swore for Lucrece' rape –
That we will prosecute by good advice
Mortal revenge upon these traitorous Goths,
And see their blood, or die with this reproach.

[*They rise.*]
TITUS   'Tis sure enough, and you knew how.   95
But if you hunt these bear-whelps, then beware:
The dam will wake, and if she wind ye once
She's with the lion deeply still in league,
And lulls him whilst she playeth on her back,
And when he sleeps will she do what she list.   100
You are a young huntsman, Marcus. Let alone,
And come, I will go get a leaf of brass
And with a gad of steel will write these words,
And lay it by. The angry northern wind
Will blow these sands like Sibyl's leaves abroad,   105
And where's our lesson then? Boy, what say you?
BOY   I say, my lord, that if I were a man
Their mother's bedchamber should not be safe
For these base bondmen to the yoke of Rome.
MARCUS   Ay, that's my boy! Thy father hath full oft   110
For his ungrateful country done the like.
BOY   And, uncle, so will I, and if I live.
TITUS   Come, go with me into mine armoury:
Lucius, I'll fit thee, and withal my boy
Shall carry from me to the empress' sons   115
Presents that I intend to send them both.
Come, come, thou'lt do my message, wilt thou not?
BOY   Ay, with my dagger in their bosoms, grandsire.
TITUS   No, boy, not so; I'll teach thee another course.
Lavinia, come; Marcus, look to my house;   120
Lucius and I'll go brave it at the court.
Ay, marry, will we, sir, and we'll be waited on.
                        Exeunt all but Marcus.
MARCUS   O heavens, can you hear a good man groan
And not relent or not compassion him?
Marcus, attend him in his ecstasy   125
That hath more scars of sorrow in his heart
Than foemen's marks upon his battered shield,
But yet so just that he will not revenge.
Revenge the heavens for old Andronicus!   *Exit.*

4.2   *Enter* AARON, CHIRON *and* DEMETRIUS *at one*
   door, and at the other door YOUNG LUCIUS *and another,*
   with a bundle of weapons, and verses writ upon them.

CHIRON   Demetrius, here's the son of Lucius:
He hath some message to deliver us.
AARON
   Ay, some mad message from his mad grandfather.
BOY   My lords, with all the humbleness I may,
I greet your honours from Andronicus –   5
[*aside*] And pray the Roman gods confound you both.
DEMETRIUS
   Gramercy, lovely Lucius. What's the news?
BOY [*aside*]
   That you are both deciphered, that's the news,
For villains marked with rape.
   [*to them*]   May it please you,
My grandsire, well advised, hath sent by me   10
The goodliest weapons of his armoury

To gratify your honourable youth,
The hope of Rome, for so he bid me say,
And so I do, and with his gifts present
Your lordships that, whenever you have need,   15
You may be armed and appointed well.
[*Attendant presents the weapons.*]
And so I leave you both [*aside*] like bloody villains.
Exit with attendant.

DEMETRIUS
What's here? A scroll, and written round about?
Let's see: 20
[*Reads.*] *Integer vitae, scelerisque purus,*
Non eget Mauri iaculis, nec arcu.
CHIRON   O, 'tis a verse in Horace, I know it well:
I read it in the grammar long ago.
AARON   Ay, just – a verse in Horace, right, you have it.   25
[*aside*] Now what a thing it is to be an ass.
Here's no sound jest! The old man hath found their
guilt,
And sends them weapons wrapped about with lines
That wound beyond their feeling to the quick.
But were our witty empress well afoot
She would applaud Andronicus' conceit.   30
But let her rest in her unrest awhile.
[*to them*] And now, young lords, was't not a happy star
Led us to Rome, strangers and, more than so,
Captives, to be advanced to this height?
It did me good before the palace gate   35
To brave the tribune in his brother's hearing.
DEMETRIUS   But me more good to see so great a lord
Basely insinuate and send us gifts.
AARON   Had he not reason, Lord Demetrius?
Did you not use his daughter very friendly?   40
DEMETRIUS   I would we had a thousand Roman dames
At such a bay, by turn to serve our lust.
CHIRON   A charitable wish, and full of love.
AARON   Here lacks but your mother for to say amen.
CHIRON
And that would she, for twenty thousand more.   45
DEMETRIUS   Come, let us go and pray to all the gods
For our beloved mother in her pains.
AARON   Pray to the devils; the gods have given us over.
[*Trumpets sound.*]
DEMETRIUS
Why do the emperor's trumpets flourish thus?
CHIRON   Belike for joy the emperor hath a son.   50
DEMETRIUS   Soft, who comes here?

Enter Nurse *with a blackamoor child.*

NURSE   Good morrow, lords.
O tell me, did you see Aaron the Moor?
AARON   Well, more or less, or ne'er a whit at all:
Here Aaron is, and what with Aaron now?   55
NURSE   O gentle Aaron, we are all undone.
Now help, or woe betide thee evermore!
AARON   Why, what a caterwauling dost thou keep!
What dost thou wrap and fumble in thy arms?

NURSE   O, that which I would hide from heaven's eye,   60
Our empress' shame and stately Rome's disgrace:
She is delivered, lords, she is delivered.
AARON   To whom?
NURSE   I mean she is brought abed.
AARON
Well, God give her good rest. What hath he sent her?   65
NURSE   A devil.
AARON   Why then, she is the devil's dam: a joyful issue.
NURSE   A joyless, dismal, black and sorrowful issue.
Here is the babe, as loathsome as a toad
Amongst the fair-faced breeders of our clime.   70
The empress sends it thee, thy stamp, thy seal,
And bids thee christen it with thy dagger's point.
AARON   Zounds, ye whore, is black so base a hue?
[*to the baby*] Sweet blowze, you are a beauteous
blossom, sure.
DEMETRIUS   Villain, what hast thou done?   75
AARON   That which thou canst not undo.
CHIRON   Thou hast undone our mother.
AARON   Villain, I have done thy mother.
DEMETRIUS
And therein, hellish dog, thou hast undone her.
Woe to her chance and damned her loathed choice,   80
Accursed the offspring of so foul a fiend.
CHIRON   It shall not live.
AARON   It shall not die.
NURSE   Aaron, it must: the mother wills it so.
AARON   What, must it, nurse? Then let no man but I   85
Do execution on my flesh and blood.
DEMETRIUS
I'll broach the tadpole on my rapier's point.
Nurse, give it me; my sword shall soon dispatch it.
AARON   Sooner this sword shall plough thy bowels up.
[*Draws his sword and takes the child.*]
Stay, murderous villains, will you kill your brother?   90
Now, by the burning tapers of the sky
That shone so brightly when this boy was got,
He dies upon my scimitar's sharp point
That touches this, my first-born son and heir.
I tell you, younglings, not Enceladus   95
With all his threatening band of Typhon's brood,
Nor great Alcides, nor the god of war,
Shall seize this prey out of his father's hands.
What, what, ye sanguine, shallow-hearted boys,
Ye white-limed walls, ye alehouse painted signs!   100
Coal-black is better than another hue
In that it scorns to bear another hue;
For all the water in the ocean
Can never turn the swan's black legs to white,
Although she lave them hourly in the flood.   105
Tell the empress from me I am of age
To keep mine own, excuse it how she can.
DEMETRIUS   Wilt thou betray thy noble mistress thus?
AARON   My mistress is my mistress, this myself,
The vigour and the picture of my youth.   110
This before all the world do I prefer,

This maugre all the world will I keep safe,
Or some of you shall smoke for it in Rome.
DEMETRIUS   By this our mother is for ever shamed.
115   CHIRON   Rome will despise her for this foul escape.
NURSE   The emperor in his rage will doom her death.
CHIRON   I blush to think upon this ignomy.
AARON   Why, there's the privilege your beauty bears.
Fie, treacherous hue, that will betray with blushing
120   The close enacts and counsels of thy heart.
Here's a young lad framed of another leer:
Look how the black slave smiles upon the father,
As who should say, 'Old lad, I am thine own.'
He is your brother, lords, sensibly fed
125   Of that self blood that first gave life to you,
And from that womb where you imprisoned were
He is enfranchised and come to light.
Nay, he is your brother by the surer side,
Although my seal be stamped in his face.
130   NURSE   Aaron, what shall I say unto the empress?
DEMETRIUS   Advise thee, Aaron, what is to be done
And we will all subscribe to thy advice.
Save thou the child, so we may all be safe.
AARON   Then sit we down and let us all consult.
135   My son and I will have the wind of you.
Keep there. [*They sit.*]
                  Now talk at pleasure of your safety.
DEMETRIUS [*to the Nurse*]
How many women saw this child of his?
AARON   Why, so, brave lords, when we join in league
I am a lamb – but if you brave the Moor,
140   The chafed boar, the mountain lioness,
The ocean, swells not so as Aaron storms.
[*to the Nurse*] But say again, how many saw the child?
NURSE   Cornelia the midwife, and myself,
And no one else but the delivered empress.
145   AARON   The empress, the midwife and yourself.
Two may keep counsel when the third's away.
Go to the empress, tell her this I said: [*He kills her.*]
'Wheak, wheak!' – so cries a pig prepared to the spit.
[*All stand up.*]
DEMETRIUS
What mean'st thou, Aaron? Wherefore didst thou
     this?
150   AARON   O Lord, sir, 'tis a deed of policy:
Shall she live to betray this guilt of ours?
A long-tongued, babbling gossip? No, lords, no.
And now be it known to you, my full intent.
Not far one Muly lives, my countryman:
155   His wife but yesternight was brought to bed;
His child is like to her, fair as you are.
Go pack with him and give the mother gold,
And tell them both the circumstance of all,
And how by this their child shall be advanced
160   And be received for the emperor's heir,
And substituted in the place of mine,
To calm this tempest whirling in the court;
And let the emperor dandle him for his own.

Hark ye, lords, you see I have given her physic,
And you must needs bestow her funeral;   165
The fields are near and you are gallant grooms.
This done, see that you take no longer days,
But send the midwife presently to me.
The midwife and the nurse well made away,
Then let the ladies tattle what they please.   170
CHIRON   Aaron, I see thou wilt not trust the air
With secrets.
DEMETRIUS   For this care of Tamora,
Herself and hers are highly bound to thee.
     Exeunt Chiron and Demetrius, with the Nurse's body.
AARON   Now to the Goths, as swift as swallow flies,
There to dispose this treasure in mine arms   175
And secretly to greet the empress' friends.
Come on, you thick-lipped slave, I'll bear you hence,
For it is you that puts us to our shifts.
I'll make you feed on berries and on roots,
And fat on curds and whey, and suck the goat,   180
And cabin in a cave, and bring you up
To be a warrior and command a camp.   *Exit.*

4.3 *Enter* TITUS, OLD MARCUS, YOUNG LUCIUS, *and*
     other gentlemen, Marcus' son PUBLIUS; *kinsmen of the*
     Andronici, CAIUS *and* SEMPRONIUS *with bows; and Titus*
     bears the arrows with letters on the ends of them.

TITUS   Come, Marcus, come; kinsmen, this is the way.
Sir Boy, let me see your archery.
Look ye draw home enough, and 'tis there straight.
Terras Astraea reliquit: be you remembered, Marcus,
She's gone, she's fled. Sirs, take you to your tools.   5
You, cousins, shall go sound the ocean
And cast your nets:
Happily you may catch her in the sea;
Yet there's as little justice as at land.
No, Publius and Sempronius, you must do it,   10
'Tis you must dig with mattock and with spade,
And pierce the inmost centre of the earth.
Then, when you come to Pluto's region,
I pray you deliver him this petition.
Tell him it is for justice and for aid,   15
And that it comes from old Andronicus,
Shaken with sorrows in ungrateful Rome.
Ah, Rome! Well, well, I made thee miserable
What time I threw the people's suffrages
On him that thus doth tyrannize o'er me.   20
Go, get you gone, and pray be careful all,
And leave you not a man-of-war unsearched:
This wicked emperor may have shipped her hence,
And, kinsmen, then we may go pipe for justice.
MARCUS   O Publius, is not this a heavy case,   25
To see thy noble uncle thus distract?
PUBLIUS   Therefore, my lords, it highly us concerns
By day and night t'attend him carefully
And feed his humour kindly as we may,
Till time beget some careful remedy.   30

MARCUS   Kinsmen, his sorrows are past remedy,
But let us live in hope that Lucius will
Join with the Goths and with revengeful war
Take wreak on Rome for this ingratitude,
35 And vengeance on the traitor Saturnine.
TITUS   Publius, how now? How now, my masters?
What, have you met with her?
PUBLIUS   No, my good lord, but Pluto sends you word
If you will have Revenge from hell, you shall.
40 Marry, for Justice, she is so employed,
He thinks with Jove in heaven or somewhere else,
So that perforce you must needs stay a time.
TITUS   He doth me wrong to feed me with delays.
I'll dive into the burning lake below
45 And pull her out of Acheron by the heels.
Marcus, we are but shrubs, no cedars we,
No big-boned men framed of the Cyclops' size,
But metal, Marcus, steel to the very back,
Yet wrung with wrongs more than our backs can
      bear.
50 And sith there's no justice in earth nor hell,
We will solicit heaven and move the gods
To send down Justice for to wreak our wrongs.
Come, to this gear. You are a good archer, Marcus:
[*He gives them the arrows.*]
'*Ad Jovem*', that's for you; here, '*ad Apollinem*';
55 '*Ad Martem*', that's for myself;
Here, boy, 'to Pallas'; here, 'to Mercury';
'To Saturn', Caius – not to Saturnine:
You were as good to shoot against the wind.
To it, boy; Marcus, loose when I bid.
60 Of my word, I have written to effect:
There's not a god left unsolicited.
MARCUS   Kinsmen, shoot all your shafts into the court;
We will afflict the emperor in his pride.
TITUS   Now, masters, draw. [*They shoot.*]
                                    O, well said, Lucius,
65 Good boy: in Virgo's lap! Give it Pallas.
MARCUS   My lord, I aimed a mile beyond the moon:
Your letter is with Jupiter by this.
TITUS   Ha, ha! Publius, Publius, what hast thou done?
See, see, thou hast shot off one of Taurus' horns.
MARCUS
70 This was the sport, my lord: when Publius shot,
The Bull, being galled, gave Aries such a knock
That down fell both the Ram's horns in the court,
And who should find them but the empress' villain!
She laughed and told the Moor he should not choose
75 But give them to his master for a present.
TITUS
Why, there it goes; God give his lordship joy.

Enter the Clown *with a basket and two pigeons in it.*

News, news, from heaven! Marcus, the post is come.
Sirrah, what tidings? Have you any letters?
Shall I have justice? What says Jupiter?
80 CLOWN   Ho, the gibbet-maker? He says that he hath

taken them down again, for the man must not be
hanged till the next week.
TITUS   But what says Jupiter, I ask thee?
CLOWN
Alas, sir, I know not Jubiter, I never drank with him in
all my life.   85
TITUS   Why, villain, art not thou the carrier?
CLOWN   Ay, of my pigeons, sir – nothing else.
TITUS   Why, didst thou not come from heaven?
CLOWN   From heaven? Alas, sir, I never came there. God
forbid I should be so bold to press to heaven in my   90
young days. Why, I am going with my pigeons to the
tribunal plebs to take up a matter of brawl betwixt my
uncle and one of the emperal's men.
MARCUS [*to Titus*]   Why, sir, that is as fit as can be to
serve for your oration, and let him deliver the pigeons   95
to the emperor from you.
TITUS   Tell me, can you deliver an oration to the
emperor with a grace?
CLOWN   Nay, truly, sir, I could never say grace in all
my life.   100
TITUS   Sirrah, come hither; make no more ado,
But give your pigeons to the emperor.
By me thou shalt have justice at his hands.
Hold, hold – meanwhile here's money for thy
      charges.
Give me pen and ink. [*Writes.*]   105
Sirrah, can you with a grace deliver up a supplication?
CLOWN   Ay, sir.
TITUS [*Gives letter.*]   Then here is a supplication for
you, and when you come to him, at the first approach
you must kneel, then kiss his foot, then deliver up your   110
pigeons, and then look for your reward. I'll be at hand,
sir; see you do it bravely.
CLOWN   I warrant you, sir, let me alone.
TITUS   Sirrah, hast thou a knife? Come, let me see it.
Here, Marcus, fold it in the oration;   115
[*to the Clown*] For thou must hold it like an humble
      suppliant,
And when thou hast given it to the emperor,
Knock at my door and tell me what he says.
CLOWN   God be with you, sir. I will.   *Exit.*
TITUS   Come, Marcus, let us go; Publius, follow me.   120
                                                              Exeunt.

4.4   *Enter* Emperor *and* Empress *and her two sons, and*
attendants. The Emperor brings the arrows in his hand that
                    Titus shot at him.

SATURNINUS
Why, lords, what wrongs are these! Was ever seen
An emperor in Rome thus overborne,
Troubled, confronted thus, and for the extent
Of equal justice used in such contempt?
My lords, you know, as know the mightful gods,   5
However these disturbers of our peace
Buzz in the people's ears, there nought hath passed

But even with law against the wilful sons
Of old Andronicus. And what and if
His sorrows have so overwhelmed his wits?
Shall we be thus afflicted in his wreaks,
His fits, his frenzy and his bitterness?
And now he writes to heaven for his redress.
See, here's 'to Jove', and this 'to Mercury',
This 'to Apollo', this 'to the god of war':
Sweet scrolls to fly about the streets of Rome!
What's this but libelling against the senate
And blazoning our injustice everywhere?
A goodly humour, is it not, my lords?
As who would say, in Rome no justice were.
But if I live, his feigned ecstasies
Shall be no shelter to these outrages,
But he and his shall know that justice lives
In Saturninus' health, whom, if she sleep,
He'll so awake as she in fury shall
Cut off the proud'st conspirator that lives.

TAMORA   My gracious lord, my lovely Saturnine,
Lord of my life, commander of my thoughts,
Calm thee and bear the faults of Titus' age,
Th'effects of sorrow for his valiant sons
Whose loss hath pierced him deep and scarred his
      heart;
And rather comfort his distressed plight
Than prosecute the meanest or the best
For these contempts.
   [*aside*]   Why, thus it shall become
High-witted Tamora to gloze withal.
But, Titus, I have touched thee to the quick;
Thy life-blood out, if Aaron now be wise,
Then is all safe, the anchor in the port.

Enter Clown.

How now, good fellow, wouldst thou speak with us?

CLOWN
Yea, forsooth, and your mistress-ship be emperial.

TAMORA   Empress I am, but yonder sits the emperor.

CLOWN   'Tis he. God and Saint Stephen give you good
e'en. I have brought you a letter and a couple of
pigeons here. [*Saturninus reads the letter.*]

SATURNINUS   Go, take him away and hang him presently!

CLOWN   How much money must I have?

TAMORA   Come, sirrah, you must be hanged.

CLOWN   Hanged, by'Lady? Then I have brought up a
neck to a fair end. *Exit under guard.*

SATURNINUS   Despiteful and intolerable wrongs!
Shall I endure this monstrous villainy?
I know from whence this same device proceeds.
May this be borne as if his traitorous sons,
That died by law for murder of our brother,
Have by my means been butchered wrongfully?
Go, drag the villain hither by the hair:
Nor age nor honour shall shape privilege.
For this proud mock I'll be thy slaughterman,
Sly frantic wretch that holp'st to make me great

In hope thyself should govern Rome and me.

Enter EMILLIUS, *a messenger.*

What news with thee, Emillius?

EMILLIUS
Arm, arm, my lords! Rome never had more cause:
The Goths have gathered head, and with a power
Of high-resolved men bent to the spoil
They hither march amain under conduct
Of Lucius, son to old Andronicus,
Who threats in course of this revenge to do
As much as ever Coriolanus did.

SATURNINUS
Is warlike Lucius general of the Goths?
These tidings nip me and I hang the head
As flowers with frost or grass beat down with storms.
Ay, now begins our sorrows to approach.
'Tis he the common people love so much;
Myself hath often heard them say,
When I have walked like a private man,
That Lucius' banishment was wrongfully,
And they have wished that Lucius were their
      emperor.

TAMORA   Why should you fear? Is not your city strong?

SATURNINUS   Ay, but the citizens favour Lucius
And will revolt from me to succour him.

TAMORA
King, be thy thoughts imperious like thy name.
Is the sun dimmed, that gnats do fly in it?
The eagle suffers little birds to sing,
And is not careful what they mean thereby,
Knowing that with the shadow of his wings
He can at pleasure stint their melody:
Even so mayst thou the giddy men of Rome.
Then cheer thy spirit, for know thou, emperor,
I will enchant the old Andronicus
With words more sweet and yet more dangerous
Than baits to fish or honey-stalks to sheep,
When as the one is wounded with the bait,
The other rotted with delicious feed.

SATURNINUS   But he will not entreat his son for us.

TAMORA   If Tamora entreat him, then he will,
For I can smooth and fill his aged ears
With golden promises that, were his heart
Almost impregnable, his old ears deaf,
Yet should both ear and heart obey my tongue.
[*to Emillius*] Go thou before to be our ambassador:
Say that the emperor requests a parley
Of warlike Lucius, and appoint the meeting
Even at his father's house, the old Andronicus.

SATURNINUS   Emillius, do this message honourably,
And if he stand in hostage for his safety,
Bid him demand what pledge will please him best.

EMILLIUS   Your bidding shall I do effectually.   *Exit.*

TAMORA   Now will I to that old Andronicus,
And temper him with all the art I have
To pluck proud Lucius from the warlike Goths.

And now, sweet emperor, be blithe again
And bury all thy fear in my devices.
SATURNINUS   Then go incessantly and plead to him.
Exeunt by different doors.

5.1 *Flourish. Enter* LUCIUS *with an army of* Goths *with drums and soldiers.*

LUCIUS   Approved warriors and my faithful friends,
I have received letters from great Rome
Which signifies what hate they bear their emperor,
And how desirous of our sight they are.
Therefore, great lords, be as your titles witness,   5
Imperious, and impatient of your wrongs,
And wherein Rome hath done you any scath
Let him make treble satisfaction.
1 GOTH   Brave slip sprung from the great Andronicus,
Whose name was once our terror, now our comfort,   10
Whose high exploits and honourable deeds
Ingrateful Rome requites with foul contempt,
Be bold in us. We'll follow where thou lead'st,
Like stinging bees in hottest summer's day
Led by their master to the flowered fields,   15
And be avenged on cursed Tamora.
ALL GOTHS   And as he saith, so say we all with him.
LUCIUS   I humbly thank him, and I thank you all.
But who comes here, led by a lusty Goth?

Enter a Goth, *leading of* AARON *with his child in his arms.*

2 GOTH   Renowned Lucius, from our troops I strayed   20
To gaze upon a ruinous monastery,
And as I earnestly did fix mine eye
Upon the wasted building, suddenly
I heard a child cry underneath a wall.
I made unto the noise, when soon I heard   25
The crying babe controlled with this discourse:
'Peace, tawny slave, half me and half thy dame!
Did not thy hue bewray whose brat thou art,
Had nature lent thee but thy mother's look,
Villain, thou mightst have been an emperor.   30
But where the bull and cow are both milk-white,
They never do beget a coal-black calf.
Peace, villain, peace,' – even thus he rates the babe –
'For I must bear thee to a trusty Goth
Who, when he knows thou art the empress' babe,   35
Will hold thee dearly for thy mother's sake.'
With this my weapon drawn, I rushed upon him,
Surprised him suddenly, and brought him hither
To use as you think needful of the man.
LUCIUS   O worthy Goth, this is the incarnate devil   40
That robbed Andronicus of his good hand;
This is the pearl that pleased your empress' eye,
And here's the base fruit of her burning lust.
[*to Aaron*] Say, wall-eyed slave, whither wouldst thou convey

This growing image of thy fiend-like face?   45
Why dost not speak? What, deaf? Not a word?
A halter, soldiers! Hang him on this tree,
And by his side his fruit of bastardy.
AARON   Touch not the boy, he is of royal blood.
LUCIUS   Too like the sire for ever being good.   50
First hang the child, that he may see it sprawl:
A sight to vex the father's soul withal.
Get me a ladder.
[*A Goth brings a ladder, which Aaron is made to climb; another Goth takes the child.*]
AARON   Lucius, save the child,
And bear it from me to the empress.
If thou do this, I'll show thee wondrous things   55
That highly may advantage thee to hear.
If thou wilt not, befall what may befall,
I'll speak no more but 'Vengeance rot you all!'
LUCIUS
Say on, and if it please me which thou speak'st,
Thy child shall live and I will see it nourished.   60
AARON   And if it please thee? Why, assure thee, Lucius,
'Twill vex thy soul to hear what I shall speak:
For I must talk of murders, rapes and massacres,
Acts of black night, abominable deeds,
Complots of mischief, treasons, villainies,   65
Ruthful to hear yet piteously performed;
And this shall all be buried in my death
Unless thou swear to me my child shall live.
LUCIUS   Tell on thy mind; I say thy child shall live.
AARON   Swear that he shall and then I will begin.   70
LUCIUS
Who should I swear by? Thou believest no god.
That granted, how canst thou believe an oath?
AARON   What if I do not? as indeed I do not –
Yet for I know thou art religious
And hast a thing within thee called conscience,   75
With twenty popish tricks and ceremonies
Which I have seen thee careful to observe,
Therefore I urge thy oath; for that I know
An idiot holds his bauble for a god,
And keeps the oath which by that god he swears,   80
To that I'll urge him, therefore thou shalt vow
By that same god, what god soe'er it be
That thou adorest and hast in reverence,
To save my boy, to nurse and bring him up,
Or else I will discover nought to thee.   85
LUCIUS   Even by my god I swear to thee I will.
AARON   First know thou I begot him on the empress.
LUCIUS   O most insatiate and luxurious woman!
AARON   Tut, Lucius, this was but a deed of charity
To that which thou shalt hear of me anon.   90
'Twas her two sons that murdered Bassianus;
They cut thy sister's tongue and ravished her
And cut her hands and trimmed her as thou sawest.
LUCIUS
O detestable villain, call'st thou that trimming?

AARON

Why, she was washed and cut and trimmed, and
95   'twas
Trim sport for them which had the doing of it.
LUCIUS   O barbarous, beastly villains, like thyself!
AARON   Indeed, I was their tutor to instruct them.
That codding spirit had they from their mother,
100   As sure a card as ever won the set.
That bloody mind I think they learned of me,
As true a dog as ever fought at head.
Well, let my deeds be witness of my worth:
I trained thy brethren to that guileful hole
105   Where the dead corpse of Bassianus lay;
I wrote the letter that thy father found,
And hid the gold within that letter mentioned,
Confederate with the queen and her two sons;
And what not done that thou hast cause to rue
110   Wherein I had no stroke of mischief in it?
I played the cheater for thy father's hand,
And when I had it, drew myself apart
And almost broke my heart with extreme laughter;
I pried me through the crevice of a wall
115   When for his hand he had his two sons' heads,
Beheld his tears and laughed so heartily
That both mine eyes were rainy like to his;
And when I told the empress of this sport,
She sounded almost at my pleasing tale
120   And for my tidings gave me twenty kisses.
1 GOTH   What, canst thou say all this and never blush?
AARON   Ay, like a black dog, as the saying is.
LUCIUS   Art thou not sorry for these heinous deeds?
AARON   Ay, that I had not done a thousand more.
125   Even now I curse the day – and yet I think
Few come within the compass of my curse –
Wherein I did not some notorious ill,
As kill a man or else devise his death,
Ravish a maid or plot the way to do it,
130   Accuse some innocent and forswear myself,
Set deadly enmity between two friends,
Make poor men's cattle break their necks,
Set fire on barns and haystacks in the night
And bid the owners quench them with their tears.
135   Oft have I digged up dead men from their graves
And set them upright at their dear friends' door,
Even when their sorrows almost was forgot,
And on their skins, as on the bark of trees,
Have with my knife carved in Roman letters,
140   'Let not your sorrow die though I am dead'.
Tut, I have done a thousand dreadful things
As willingly as one would kill a fly,
And nothing grieves me heartily indeed
But that I cannot do ten thousand more.
145   LUCIUS   Bring down the devil, for he must not die
So sweet a death as hanging presently.
   [*Aaron is made to climb down.*]
AARON   If there be devils, would I were a devil,
To live and burn in everlasting fire,

So I might have your company in hell
But to torment you with my bitter tongue.   150
LUCIUS
Sirs, stop his mouth and let him speak no more.
   [*Aaron is gagged.*]

                  Enter EMILLIUS.

A GOTH   My lord, there is a messenger from Rome
Desires to be admitted to your presence.
LUCIUS   Let him come near.
Welcome, Emillius: what's the news from Rome?   155
EMILLIUS   Lord Lucius and you princes of the Goths,
The Roman emperor greets you all by me,
And for he understands you are in arms,
He craves a parley at your father's house,
Willing you to demand your hostages   160
And they shall be immediately delivered.
1 GOTH   What says our general?
LUCIUS   Emillius, let the emperor give his pledges
Unto my father and my uncle Marcus,
And we will come.   *Flourish. They march away.*   165

5.2   *Enter* TAMORA *and her two* Sons, *disguised.*

TAMORA   Thus, in this strange and sad habiliment,
I will encounter with Andronicus
And say I am Revenge, sent from below
To join with him and right his heinous wrongs.
Knock at his study, where they say he keeps   5
To ruminate strange plots of dire revenge;
Tell him Revenge is come to join with him
And work confusion on his enemies.

         They knock, and TITUS *aloft with papers,*
                  opens his study door.

TITUS [*aloft*]   Who doth molest my contemplation?
Is it your trick to make me ope the door,   10
That so my sad decrees may fly away
And all my study be to no effect?
You are deceived, for what I mean to do
See here in bloody lines I have set down,
And what is written shall be executed.   15
TAMORA   Titus, I am come to talk with thee.
TITUS [*aloft*]   No, not a word. How can I grace my talk,
Wanting a hand to give it action?
Thou hast the odds of me, therefore no more.
TAMORA
If thou didst know me, thou wouldst talk with me.   20
TITUS [*aloft*]   I am not mad, I know thee well enough:
Witness this wretched stump, witness these crimson
      lines,
Witness these trenches made by grief and care,
Witness the tiring day and heavy night,
Witness all sorrow, that I know thee well   25
For our proud empress, mighty Tamora.
Is not thy coming for my other hand?
TAMORA   Know, thou sad man, I am not Tamora:

She is thy enemy and I thy friend.
I am Revenge, sent from th'infernal kingdom
To ease the gnawing vulture of thy mind
By working wreakful vengeance on thy foes.
Come down and welcome me to this world's light,
Confer with me of murder and of death.
There's not a hollow cave or lurking place,
No vast obscurity or misty vale
Where bloody murder or detested rape
Can couch for fear, but I will find them out,
And in their ears tell them my dreadful name,
Revenge, which makes the foul offender quake.

TITUS [*aloft*]
Art thou Revenge? And art thou sent to me
To be a torment to mine enemies?

TAMORA   I am, therefore come down and welcome me.

TITUS [*aloft*]   Do me some service ere I come to thee.
Lo by thy side where Rape and Murder stands;
Now give some surance that thou art Revenge:
Stab them or tear them on thy chariot wheels,
And then I'll come and be thy waggoner,
And whirl along with thee about the globe,
Provide thee two proper palfreys, black as jet,
To hale thy vengeful waggon swift away
And find out murderers in their guilty caves;
And when thy car is loaden with their heads,
I will dismount and by thy waggon wheel
Trot like a servile footman all day long,
Even from Hyperion's rising in the east
Until his very downfall in the sea.
And day by day I'll do this heavy task,
So thou destroy Rapine and Murder there.

TAMORA   These are my ministers, and come with me.

TITUS [*aloft*]
Are these thy ministers? What are they called?

TAMORA   Rape and Murder, therefore called so
'Cause they take vengeance of such kind of men.

TITUS [*aloft*]
Good Lord, how like the empress' sons they are,
And you the empress! But we worldly men
Have miserable, mad, mistaking eyes.
O sweet Revenge, now do I come to thee,
And if one arm's embracement will content thee,
I will embrace thee in it by and by.   *Exit aloft.*

TAMORA   This closing with him fits his lunacy.
Whate'er I forge to feed his brainsick humours
Do you uphold and maintain in your speeches,
For now he firmly takes me for Revenge,
And, being credulous in this mad thought,
I'll make him send for Lucius his son,
And whilst I at a banquet hold him sure,
I'll find some cunning practice out of hand
To scatter and disperse the giddy Goths,
Or at the least make them his enemies.
See, here he comes, and I must ply my theme.

Enter TITUS, *below.*

TITUS   Long have I been forlorn, and all for thee.
Welcome, dread Fury, to my woeful house;
Rapine and Murder, you are welcome too.
How like the empress and her sons you are!
Well are you fitted, had you but a Moor;   85
Could not all hell afford you such a devil?
For well I wot the empress never wags
But in her company there is a Moor,
And would you represent our queen aright
It were convenient you had such a devil.   90
But welcome as you are. What shall we do?

TAMORA   What wouldst thou have us do, Andronicus?

DEMETRIUS   Show me a murderer, I'll deal with him.

CHIRON   Show me a villain that hath done a rape,
And I am sent to be revenged on him.   95

TAMORA
Show me a thousand that hath done thee wrong,
And I will be revenged on them all.

TITUS [*to Demetrius*]
Look round about the wicked streets of Rome,
And when thou find'st a man that's like thyself,
Good Murder, stab him: he's a murderer.   100
[*to Chiron*] Go thou with him, and when it is thy hap
To find another that is like to thee,
Good Rapine, stab him: he is a ravisher.
[*to Tamora*] Go thou with them, and in the emperor's
   court,
There is a queen attended by a Moor –   105
Well shalt thou know her by thine own proportion,
For up and down she doth resemble thee –
I pray thee, do on them some violent death:
They have been violent to me and mine.

TAMORA   Well hast thou lessoned us; this shall we do.   110
But would it please thee, good Andronicus,
To send for Lucius, thy thrice-valiant son,
Who leads towards Rome a band of warlike Goths,
And bid him come and banquet at thy house?
When he is here, even at thy solemn feast,   115
I will bring in the empress and her sons,
The emperor himself and all thy foes,
And at thy mercy shall they stoop and kneel,
And on them shalt thou ease thy angry heart.
What says Andronicus to this device?   120

TITUS   Marcus, my brother! 'Tis sad Titus calls.

Enter MARCUS.

Go, gentle Marcus, to thy nephew Lucius;
Thou shalt enquire him out among the Goths.
Bid him repair to me and bring with him
Some of the chiefest princes of the Goths.   125
Bid him encamp his soldiers where they are.
Tell him the emperor and the empress too
Feast at my house, and he shall feast with them.
This do thou for my love, and so let him,
As he regards his aged father's life.   130

MARCUS   This will I do, and soon return again.   *Exit.*

TAMORA   Now will I hence about thy business,

And take my ministers along with me.
TITUS   Nay, nay, let Rape and Murder stay with me –
135   Or else I'll call my brother back again
And cleave to no revenge but Lucius.
TAMORA [*aside to her sons*]
What say you, boys, will you abide with him
Whiles I go tell my lord the emperor
How I have governed our determined jest?
140   Yield to his humour, smooth and speak him fair,
And tarry with him till I turn again.
TITUS [*aside*]
I knew them all, though they supposed me mad,
And will o'erreach them in their own devices –
A pair of cursed hellhounds and their dam.
145   DEMETRIUS   Madam, depart at pleasure, leave us here.
TAMORA   Farewell, Andronicus: Revenge now goes
To lay a complot to betray thy foes.
TITUS   I know thou dost – and sweet Revenge, farewell.
Exit Tamora.
CHIRON   Tell us, old man, how shall we be employed?
150   TITUS   Tut, I have work enough for you to do.
Publius, come hither; Caius and Valentine.

Enter PUBLIUS, CAIUS *and* VALENTINE.

PUBLIUS   What is your will?
TITUS   Know you these two?
PUBLIUS
The empress' sons I take them: Chiron, Demetrius.
155   TITUS   Fie, Publius, fie, thou art too much deceived.
The one is Murder and Rape is the other's name,
And therefore bind them, gentle Publius;
Caius and Valentine, lay hands on them.
Oft have you heard me wish for such an hour,
160   And now I find it; therefore bind them sure,
And stop their mouths if they begin to cry.   *Exit.*
CHIRON   Villains, forbear! We are the empress' sons.
PUBLIUS
And therefore do we what we are commanded.
[*They bind and gag them.*]
Stop close their mouths; let them not speak a word.
165   Is he sure bound? Look that you bind them fast.

Enter TITUS ANDRONICUS *with a knife, and* LAVINIA *with
a basin.*

TITUS   Come, come, Lavinia: look, thy foes are bound.
Sirs, stop their mouths; let them not speak to me,
But let them hear what fearful words I utter.
O villains, Chiron and Demetrius,
Here stands the spring whom you have stained with
170   mud,
This goodly summer with your winter mixed.
You killed her husband, and for that vile fault
Two of her brothers were condemned to death,
My hand cut off and made a merry jest,
175   Both her sweet hands, her tongue, and that more dear
Than hands or tongue, her spotless chastity,
Inhuman traitors, you constrained and forced.

What would you say if I should let you speak?
Villains, for shame you could not beg for grace.
Hark, wretches, how I mean to martyr you: 180
This one hand yet is left to cut your throats,
Whiles that Lavinia 'tween her stumps doth hold
The basin that receives your guilty blood.
You know your mother means to feast with me,
And calls herself Revenge and thinks me mad.   185
Hark, villains, I will grind your bones to dust,
And with your blood and it I'll make a paste,
And of the paste a coffin I will rear,
And make two pasties of your shameful heads,
And bid that strumpet, your unhallowed dam,   190
Like to the earth swallow her own increase.
This is the feast that I have bid her to,
And this the banquet she shall surfeit on:
For worse than Philomel you used my daughter,
And worse than Progne I will be revenged.   195
And now, prepare your throats. Lavinia, come,
Receive the blood, and when that they are dead
Let me go grind their bones to powder small,
And with this hateful liquor temper it,
And in that paste let their vile heads be baked.   200
Come, come, be everyone officious
To make this banquet, which I wish may prove
More stern and bloody than the Centaurs' feast.
[*He cuts their throats.*]
So, now bring them in, for I'll play the cook,
And see them ready against their mother comes.   205
Exeunt with the bodies.

5.3   *Enter* LUCIUS, MARCUS *and the* Goths, *with*
AARON *prisoner and one carrying his child.*

LUCIUS   Uncle Marcus, since 'tis my father's mind
That I repair to Rome, I am content.
1 GOTH   And ours with thine, befall what fortune will.
LUCIUS   Good uncle, take you in this barbarous Moor,
This ravenous tiger, this accursed devil;   5
Let him receive no sustenance, fetter him
Till he be brought unto the empress' face
For testimony of her foul proceedings.
And see the ambush of our friends be strong:
I fear the emperor means no good to us.   10
AARON   Some devil whisper curses in my ear,
And prompt me that my tongue may utter forth
The venomous malice of my swelling heart.
LUCIUS   Away, inhuman dog, unhallowed slave!
Sirs, help our uncle to convey him in.   15
Exit Aaron under guard. Sound trumpets.
The trumpets show the emperor is at hand.

Enter Emperor *and* Empress, *with tribunes and others
including* EMILLIUS.

SATURNINUS
What, hath the firmament more suns than one?
LUCIUS   What boots it thee to call thyself a sun?

MARCUS

    Rome's emperor, and nephew, break the parle;

20   These quarrels must be quietly debated.

    The feast is ready which the careful Titus

    Hath ordained to an honourable end,

    For peace, for love, for league and good to Rome,

    Please you therefore, draw nigh and take your places.

25 SATURNINUS   Marcus, we will.

Trumpets sounding, a table brought in. They sit. Enter
TITUS *like a cook, placing the dishes, and* LAVINIA *with a*
veil over her face and YOUNG LUCIUS.

TITUS

    Welcome, my gracious lord; welcome, dread queen;

    Welcome, ye warlike Goths; welcome, Lucius;

    And welcome, all. Although the cheer be poor,

    'Twill fill your stomachs. Please you, eat of it.

30 SATURNINUS   Why art thou thus attired, Andronicus?

TITUS   Because I would be sure to have all well

    To entertain your highness and your empress.

TAMORA   We are beholden to you, good Andronicus.

TITUS   And if your highness knew my heart you were.

35   My lord the emperor, resolve me this:

    Was it well done of rash Virginius

    To slay his daughter with his own right hand,

    Because she was enforced, stained and deflowered?

SATURNINUS   It was, Andronicus.

TITUS   Your reason, mighty lord?

SATURNINUS

40   Because the girl should not survive her shame,

    And by her presence still renew his sorrows.

TITUS   A reason mighty, strong, and effectual;

    A pattern, precedent, and lively warrant

    For me, most wretched, to perform the like.

    [*Unveils Lavinia.*]

45   Die, die, Lavinia, and thy shame with thee,

    And with thy shame thy father's sorrow die.

    [*He kills her.*]

SATURNINUS

    What hast thou done, unnatural and unkind?

TITUS

    Killed her for whom my tears have made me blind.

    I am as woeful as Virginius was,

50   And have a thousand times more cause than he

    To do this outrage, and it now is done.

SATURNINUS

    What, was she ravished? Tell who did the deed.

TITUS

    Will't please you eat? Will't please your highness feed?

TAMORA

    Why hast thou slain thine only daughter thus?

55 TITUS   Not I, 'twas Chiron and Demetrius:

    They ravished her and cut away her tongue,

    And they, 'twas they, that did her all this wrong.

SATURNINUS

    Go, fetch them hither to us presently.

TITUS   Why, there they are, both baked in this pie,

    Whereof their mother daintily hath fed,   60

    Eating the flesh that she herself hath bred.

    'Tis true, 'tis true, witness my knife's sharp point.

    [*He stabs the Empress.*]

SATURNINUS   Die, frantic wretch, for this accursed deed.

    [*He kills Titus.*]

LUCIUS   Can the son's eye behold his father bleed?

    There's meed for meed, death for a deadly deed.   65

    [*He kills Saturninus. Uproar. The Goths protect the*
    Andronici, who go aloft.]

MARCUS [*aloft*]

    You sad-faced men, people and sons of Rome,

    By uproars severed, as a flight of fowl

    Scattered by winds and high tempestuous gusts,

    O let me teach you how to knit again

    This scattered corn into one mutual sheaf,   70

    These broken limbs again into one body.

A ROMAN LORD   Let Rome herself be bane unto herself,

    And she whom mighty kingdoms curtsy to,

    Like a forlorn and desperate castaway,

    Do shameful execution on herself!   75

    But if my frosty signs and chaps of age,

    Grave witnesses of true experience,

    Cannot induce you to attend my words,

    Speak, Rome's dear friend, as erst our ancestor

    When with his solemn tongue he did discourse   80

    To lovesick Dido's sad-attending ear

    The story of that baleful burning night

    When subtle Greeks surprised King Priam's Troy.

    Tell us what Sinon hath bewitched our ears,

    Or who hath brought the fatal engine in   85

    That gives our Troy, our Rome, the civil wound.

MARCUS [*aloft*]

    My heart is not compact of flint nor steel,

    Nor can I utter all our bitter grief,

    But floods of tears will drown my oratory

    And break my utterance even in the time   90

    When it should move ye to attend me most,

    And force you to commiseration.

    Here's Rome's young captain: let him tell the tale,

    While I stand by and weep to hear him speak.

LUCIUS [*aloft*]

    Then, gracious auditory, be it known to you   95

    That Chiron and the damned Demetrius

    Were they that murdered our emperor's brother,

    And they it were that ravished our sister;

    For their fell faults our brothers were beheaded,

    Our father's tears despised and basely cozened   100

    Of that true hand that fought Rome's quarrel out

    And sent her enemies unto the grave;

    Lastly myself, unkindly banished,

    The gates shut on me, and turned weeping out

    To beg relief among Rome's enemies,   105

    Who drowned their enmity in my true tears

    And oped their arms to embrace me as a friend.

    I am the turned-forth, be it known to you,

    That have preserved her welfare in my blood,

110 And from her bosom took the enemy's point,
Sheathing the steel in my adventurous body.
Alas, you know I am no vaunter, I;
My scars can witness, dumb although they are,
That my report is just and full of truth.
115 But soft, methinks I do digress too much,
Citing my worthless praise. O pardon me,
For when no friends are by, men praise themselves.

MARCUS [*aloft*]   Now is my turn to speak.
  [*Points to Aaron's baby.*]   Behold the child:
Of this was Tamora delivered,
120 The issue of an irreligious Moor,
Chief architect and plotter of these woes.
The villain is alive in Titus' house,
And as he is to witness this is true,
Now judge what cause had Titus to revenge
125 These wrongs unspeakable, past patience,
Or more than any living man could bear.
Now have you heard the truth: what say you,
  Romans?
Have we done aught amiss, show us wherein,
And from the place where you behold us pleading,
130 The poor remainder of Andronici
Will hand in hand all headlong hurl ourselves
And on the ragged stones beat forth our souls
And make a mutual closure of our house.
Speak, Romans, speak, and if you say, we shall,
135 Lo, hand in hand, Lucius and I will fall.

EMILLIUS   Come, come, thou reverend man of Rome,
And bring our emperor gently in thy hand,
Lucius, our emperor, for well I know
The common voice do cry it shall be so.
140 MARCUS [*aloft*]   Lucius, all hail, Rome's royal emperor!
[*to others*] Go, go into old Titus' sorrowful house
And hither hale that misbelieving Moor
To be adjudged some direful slaughtering death
As punishment for his most wicked life.
  [*Exeunt some into the house. A long flourish till the*
  Andronici come down.]
145 ALL ROMANS   Lucius, all hail, Rome's gracious governor!
LUCIUS   Thanks, gentle Romans. May I govern so
To heal Rome's harms and wipe away her woe.
But, gentle people, give me aim awhile,
For nature puts me to a heavy task.
150 Stand all aloof, but, uncle, draw you near
To shed obsequious tears upon this trunk.
  [*Kisses Titus.*]
O, take this warm kiss on thy pale cold lips,
These sorrowful drops upon thy bloodstained face,
The last true duties of thy noble son.
MARCUS [*Kisses Titus.*]
155 Tear for tear and loving kiss for kiss,

Thy brother Marcus tenders on thy lips.
O, were the sum of these that I should pay
Countless and infinite, yet would I pay them.
LUCIUS [*to his son*]
Come hither, boy, come, come and learn of us
160 To melt in showers. Thy grandsire loved thee well:
Many a time he danced thee on his knee,
Sung thee asleep, his loving breast thy pillow;
Many a story hath he told to thee,
And bid thee bear his pretty tales in mind
165 And talk of them when he was dead and gone.
MARCUS
How many thousand times hath these poor lips,
When they were living, warmed themselves on thine!
O now, sweet boy, give them their latest kiss:
Bid him farewell, commit him to the grave;
170 Do them that kindness and take leave of them.
BOY [*Kisses Titus.*]
O grandsire, grandsire, e'en with all my heart
Would I were dead, so you did live again.
O Lord, I cannot speak to him for weeping,
My tears will choke me if I ope my mouth.

  Enter AARON *under guard.*

A ROMAN   You sad Andronici, have done with woes,
175 Give sentence on this execrable wretch
That hath been breeder of these dire events.
LUCIUS   Set him breast-deep in earth and famish him;
There let him stand and rave and cry for food.
If anyone relieves or pities him,
180 For the offence he dies. This is our doom;
Some stay to see him fastened in the earth.
AARON
Ah, why should wrath be mute and fury dumb?
I am no baby, I, that with base prayers
I should repent the evils I have done.
185 Ten thousand worse than ever yet I did
Would I perform if I might have my will.
If one good deed in all my life I did
I do repent it from my very soul.
LUCIUS
Some loving friends convey the emperor hence,
190 And give him burial in his fathers' grave;
My father and Lavinia shall forthwith
Be closed in our household's monument;
As for that ravenous tiger, Tamora,
No funeral rite, nor man in mourning weed,
195 No mournful bell shall ring her burial,
But throw her forth to beasts and birds to prey:
Her life was beastly and devoid of pity,
And being dead, let birds on her take pity.
  Exeunt with the bodies.

Troilus and Cressida

Published in quarto in 1609 as *The Famous History of Troilus and Cressida*, the play was to have followed *Romeo and Juliet* as the fourth of the tragedies in the First Folio of 1623, and its first three pages had been printed before it was removed and replaced by *Timon of Athens*. It does not appear in the table of contents, and some copies of the Folio had already gone on sale without it before it was hastily printed and inserted between *King Henry VIII*, last of the histories, and *Coriolanus*, first of the tragedies, in a text which adds the Prologue and shows minor but frequent variation of word or phrase from that of the Quarto, of which the version printed in the Folio is possibly a revision. The play was written about 1601–2, in the aftermath of the abortive rising of the Earl of Essex and his execution in February 1601. It may be in part the Chamberlain's Men's response to an earlier play on the subject by Thomas Dekker and Henry Chettle performed by the rival Admiral's Men in 1599 (now known only from a damaged stage 'plot').

A first setting of the title-page of the 1609 Quarto claimed that the play had been acted by the King's Men at the Globe – a claim retracted when that title-page was cancelled and replaced, deleting all reference to performance, and an epistle 'from a never writer to an ever reader' was added, in which the play, 'never clapper-clawed by the palms of the vulgar', is praised as a comedy which readers are lucky to see in print, contrary to the will of its 'grand possessors'. This epistle has given rise to the hypothesis that the play was written for a private occasion, although no positive evidence exists for such a performance. The epilogue, which may not have been included in all performances, has struck some scholars as more appropriate to an audience of lawyers at one of the Inns of Court than to public performance at the Globe. This chequered history of publication may result from disputes over copyright, or it may reflect the political sensitivity of its subject at a time when the association of Essex with Achilles was commonplace.

Many English plays (now lost) had been written on the 'matter of Troy' before *Troilus and Cressida*, which presents a sour, minor-key variation on familiar themes

and characters. Shakespeare himself had often alluded to Troy in earlier works, notably *Lucrece*, which contains a lengthy discourse on a painting of the Fall of Troy, *The Merchant of Venice*, which alludes to the separation of Troilus and Cressida, and *Hamlet*, where it supplies apt and familiar material for the Player's tragic speech. Medieval mythology derived the British people from the Trojan line of Aeneas, and London could still be popularly referred to as Troynovant or New Troy. The Troy story reached Shakespeare in part through George Chapman's translation of seven books of the *Iliad* (1598) but more importantly through medieval retellings and expansions. The play makes use of at least two of them. For the love story, itself a medieval addition to the 'matter of Troy', he adapted Chaucer's *Troylus and Criseyde* (c. 1385) (earlier a minor source for *Romeo and Juliet*, whose love story is sourly parodied by that of *Troilus and Cressida*) and, for the war plot, William Caxton's *Recuyell of the Histories of Troy* (1474). Shakespeare was the first to balance the war story against the love story, although unevenly, as the war story occupies two thirds of his action and the love story only one third. Whether history, tragedy or comedy, the play offers a destructive analysis of chivalric honour and romantic love which culminates in the double shock to Troilus of the infidelity of Cressida with Diomedes and of the murder of Hector by Achilles' Myrmidons.

After an adaptation by John Dryden which attempted to turn it into an exemplary tragedy, *Troilus and Cressida* disappeared from the stage for some two hundred years. Its disillusioned tone and inconclusive action have recommended it to the twentieth century and it has been regularly revived in productions many of which have urged its topicality by setting it in the historical periods of all the major wars since the Crimean War and the American Civil War.

The 1982 Arden text reprinted here is based on the 1609 Quarto, supplemented and corrected from the 1623 First Folio.

PROLOGUE

PRIAM — *King of Troy*

HECTOR
TROILUS
PARIS — } *sons of Priam*
DEIPHOBUS
HELENUS

MARGARELON — *a bastard son of Priam*

AENEAS
ANTENOR — } *Trojan commanders*

CALCHAS — *a Trojan priest taking part with the Greeks*

PANDARUS — *uncle to Cressida*

AGAMEMNON — *the Greek general*

MENELAUS — *his brother*

ACHILLES
AJAX
ULYSSES
NESTOR — } *Greek commanders*
DIOMEDES
PATROCLUS

THERSITES — *a deformed and scurrilous Greek*

ALEXANDER — *servant to Cressida*

SERVANT — *to Troilus*

SERVANT — *to Paris*

SERVANT — *to Diomedes*

HELEN — *wife to Menelaus*

ANDROMACHE — *wife to Hector*

CASSANDRA — *daughter to Priam; a prophetess*

CRESSIDA — *daughter to Calchas*

Trojan and Greek soldiers
Attendants

PROLOGUE

1.1 *Enter* PANDARUS *and* TROILUS.

TROILUS   Call here my varlet, I'll unarm again.
    Why should I war without the walls of Troy,
    That find such cruel battle here within?
    Each Trojan that is master of his heart
    Let him to field: Troilus, alas, hath none.

PANDARUS   Will this gear ne'er be mended?

TROILUS
    The Greeks are strong, and skilful to their strength,
    Fierce to their skill, and to their fierceness valiant;
    But I am weaker than a woman's tear,
    Tamer than sleep, fonder than ignorance,
    Less valiant than the virgin in the night,
    And skilless as unpractis'd infancy.

PANDARUS   Well, I have told you enough of this: for my
    part I'll not meddle nor make no farther. He that will
    have a cake out of the wheat must tarry the grinding.

TROILUS   Have I not tarried?

PANDARUS   Ay, the grinding; but you must tarry the
    bolting.

TROILUS   Have I not tarried?

PANDARUS   Ay, the bolting; but you must tarry the
    leavening.

TROILUS   Still have I tarried.

PANDARUS   Ay, to the leavening; but here's yet in the
    word 'hereafter' the kneading, the making of the cake,
    the heating of the oven, and the baking: nay, you
    must stay the cooling too, or you may chance burn
    your lips.

TROILUS   Patience herself, what goddess e'er she be,
    Doth lesser blench at suff'rance than I do.
    At Priam's royal table do I sit,
    And when fair Cressid comes into my thoughts –
    So, traitor! 'When she comes!' When is she thence?

PANDARUS
    Well, she looked yesternight fairer than ever I
    saw her look, or any woman else.

TROILUS   I was about to tell thee: when my heart,
    As wedged with a sigh, would rive in twain,
    Lest Hector or my father should perceive me,
    I have, as when the sun doth light a storm,
    Buried this sigh in wrinkle of a smile;
    But sorrow that is couch'd in seeming gladness
    Is like that mirth fate turns to sudden sadness.

PANDARUS   And her hair were not somewhat darker than
    Helen's – well, go to, there were no more com-
    parison between the women. But for my part, she is
    my kinswoman; I would not, as they term it, praise
    her, but I would somebody had heard her talk
    yesterday as I did. I will not dispraise your sister
    Cassandra's wit, but –

TROILUS   O Pandarus – I tell thee Pandarus –
    When I do tell thee there my hopes lie drown'd,
    Reply not in how many fathoms deep
    They lie indrench'd. I tell thee I am mad

In Cressid's love: thou answer'st, 'She is fair';
    Pour'st in the open ulcer of my heart
    Her eyes, her hair, her cheek, her gait, her voice;   55
    Handlest in thy discourse – O – that her hand,
    In whose comparison all whites are ink,
    Writing their own reproach, to whose soft seizure
    The cygnet's down is harsh, and spirit of sense
    Hard as the palm of ploughman. This thou tell'st me.   60
    As true thou tell'st me, when I say I love her.
    But saying thus, instead of oil and balm,
    Thou lay'st in every gash that love hath given me
    The knife that made it.

PANDARUS   I speak no more than truth.   65

TROILUS   Thou dost not speak so much.

PANDARUS   Faith, I'll not meddle in it – let her be as she
    is: if she be fair, 'tis the better for her; and she be not,
    she has the mends in her own hands.

TROILUS   Good Pandarus – how now, Pandarus?   70

PANDARUS   I have had my labour for my travail, ill
    thought on of her, and ill thought on of you; gone
    between and between, but small thanks for my labour.

TROILUS   What, art thou angry, Pandarus? What, with me?   75

PANDARUS   Because she's kin to me, therefore she's not
    so fair as Helen. And she were not kin to me, she
    would be as fair o' Friday as Helen is o' Sunday. But
    what care I? I care not and she were a blackamoor, 'tis
    all one to me.   80

TROILUS   Say I she is not fair?

PANDARUS   I do not care whether you do or no. She's a
    fool to stay behind her father; let her to the Greeks,
    and so I'll tell her the next time I see her. For my
    part I'll meddle nor make no more i'th' matter.   85

TROILUS   Pandarus –

PANDARUS   Not I.

TROILUS   Sweet Pandarus –

PANDARUS   Pray you speak no more to me; I will leave all
    as I found it, and there an end.   90

                                 Exit. Sound alarum.

TROILUS
    Peace, you ungracious clamours! Peace, rude sounds!
    Fools on both sides, Helen must needs be fair
    When with your blood you daily paint her thus.
    I cannot fight upon this argument;
    It is too starv'd a subject for my sword.   95
    But Pandarus – O gods, how do you plague me!
    I cannot come to Cressid but by Pandar,
    And he's as tetchy to be woo'd to woo
    As she is stubborn-chaste against all suit.
    Tell me, Apollo, for thy Daphne's love,   100
    What Cressid is, what Pandar, and what we.
    Her bed is India; there she lies, a pearl.
    Between our Ilium and where she resides,
    Let it be call'd the wild and wand'ring flood,
    Ourself the merchant, and this sailing Pandar   105
    Our doubtful hope, our convoy and our bark.

                  Alarum. Enter AENEAS.

AENEAS
How now, Prince Troilus, wherefore not afield?
TROILUS
Because not there. This woman's answer sorts,
For womanish it is to be from thence.
110   What news, Aeneas, from the field today?
AENEAS   That Paris is returned home and hurt.
TROILUS   By whom, Aeneas?
AENEAS   Troilus, by Menelaus.
TROILUS   Let Paris bleed, 'tis but a scar to scorn:
Paris is gor'd with Menelaus' horn.   [*Alarum.*]
115   **AENEAS**   Hark what good sport is out of town today.
TROILUS
Better at home, if 'would I might' were 'may'.
But to the sport abroad – are you bound thither?
AENEAS   In all swift haste.
TROILUS   Come, go we then together. *Exeunt.*

1.2   *Enter* CRESSIDA *and her man* ALEXANDER.

CRESSIDA   Who were those went by?
ALEXANDER   Queen Hecuba and Helen.
CRESSIDA   And whither go they?
ALEXANDER   Up to the eastern tower,
Whose height commands as subject all the vale,
To see the battle. Hector, whose patience
5   Is as a virtue fix'd, today was mov'd:
He chid Andromache and struck his armourer,
And like as there were husbandry in war,
Before the sun rose he was harness'd light
And to the field goes he, where every flower
10   Did as a prophet weep what it foresaw
In Hector's wrath.
CRESSIDA   What was his cause of anger?
ALEXANDER
The noise goes, this: there is among the Greeks
A lord of Trojan blood, nephew to Hector;
They call him Ajax.
CRESSIDA   Good, and what of him?
15   **ALEXANDER**   They say he is a very man *per se*
And stands alone.
CRESSIDA   So do all men, unless they are drunk, sick, or
have no legs.
ALEXANDER   This man, lady, hath robbed many beasts
20   of their particular additions. He is as valiant as the
lion, churlish as the bear, slow as the elephant: a man
into whom nature hath so crowded humours that his
valour is crushed into folly, his folly sauced with
discretion. There is no man hath a virtue that he hath
25   not a glimpse of, nor any man an attaint but he carries
some stain of it. He is melancholy without cause and
merry against the hair; he hath the joints of
everything, but everything so out of joint that he is a
gouty Briareus, many hands and no use, or purblind
30   Argus, all eyes and no sight.
CRESSIDA   But how should this man, that makes me
smile, make Hector angry?
ALEXANDER   They say he yesterday coped Hector in the

battle and struck him down, the disdain and shame
whereof hath ever since kept Hector fasting and   35
waking.

Enter PANDARUS.

CRESSIDA   Who comes here?
ALEXANDER   Madam, your uncle Pandarus.
CRESSIDA   Hector's a gallant man.
ALEXANDER   As may be in the world, lady.   40
PANDARUS   What's that? What's that?
CRESSIDA   Good morrow, uncle Pandarus.
PANDARUS   Good morrow, cousin Cressid; what do you
talk of? – Good morrow, Alexander – How do you,
cousin? When were you at Ilium?   45
CRESSIDA   This morning, uncle.
PANDARUS   What were you talking of when I came? Was
Hector armed and gone ere you came to Ilium? Helen
was not up, was she?
CRESSIDA   Hector was gone but Helen was not up.   50
PANDARUS   E'en so: Hector was stirring early.
CRESSIDA   That were we talking of, and of his anger.
PANDARUS   Was he angry?
CRESSIDA   So he says here.
PANDARUS   True, he was so; I know the cause too: he'll lay   55
about him today, I can tell them that,   *Exit Alexander.*
and there's Troilus will not come far behind him: let
them take heed of Troilus, I can tell them that too.
CRESSIDA   What, is he angry too?
PANDARUS   Who, Troilus? Troilus is the better man of   60
the two.
CRESSIDA   O Jupiter, there's no comparison.
PANDARUS   What, not between Troilus and Hector? Do
you know a man if you see him?
CRESSIDA   Ay, if I ever saw him before and knew him.   65
PANDARUS   Well, I say Troilus is Troilus.
CRESSIDA   Then you say as I say, for I am sure he is not
Hector.
PANDARUS   No, nor Hector is not Troilus in some
degrees.   70
CRESSIDA   'Tis just to each of them; he is himself.
PANDARUS   Himself? Alas poor Troilus, I would he were –
CRESSIDA   So he is.
PANDARUS   – Condition I had gone barefoot to India.
CRESSIDA   He is not Hector.   75
PANDARUS   Himself? No, he's not himself, would a were
himself. Well, the gods are above, time must friend or
end. Well, Troilus, well, I would my heart were in her
body. No, Hector is not a better man than Troilus.
CRESSIDA   Excuse me.   80
PANDARUS   He is elder.
CRESSIDA   Pardon me, pardon me.
PANDARUS   Th'other's not come to 't, you shall tell me
another tale when th'other's come to 't. Hector shall
not have his wit this year.   85
CRESSIDA   He shall not need it if he have his own.
PANDARUS   Nor his qualities.
CRESSIDA   No matter.

PANDARUS   Nor his beauty.

CRESSIDA   'Twould not become him, his own's better.

PANDARUS   You have no judgement, niece. Helen herself swore th'other day that Troilus, for a brown favour – for so 'tis, I must confess – not brown neither –

CRESSIDA   No, but brown.

PANDARUS   Faith, to say truth, brown and not brown.

CRESSIDA   To say truth, true and not true.

PANDARUS   She praised his complexion above Paris.

CRESSIDA   Why, Paris hath colour enough.

PANDARUS   So he has.

CRESSIDA   Then Troilus should have too much. If she praised him above, his complexion is higher than his: he having colour enough, and the other higher, is too flaming a praise for a good complexion. I had as lief Helen's golden tongue had commended Troilus for a copper nose.

PANDARUS   I swear to you I think Helen loves him better than Paris.

CRESSIDA   Then she's a merry Greek indeed.

PANDARUS   Nay, I am sure she does: she came to him th'other day into the compassed window – and you know he has not past three or four hairs on his chin –

CRESSIDA   Indeed a tapster's arithmetic may soon bring his particulars therein to a total.

PANDARUS   Why, he is very young, and yet will he within three pound lift as much as his brother Hector.

CRESSIDA   Is he so young a man, and so old a lifter?

PANDARUS   But to prove to you that Helen loves him, she came and puts me her white hand to his cloven chin –

CRESSIDA   Juno have mercy, how came it cloven?

PANDARUS   Why, you know 'tis dimpled: I think his smiling becomes him better than any man in all Phrygia.

CRESSIDA   O, he smiles valiantly.

PANDARUS   Does he not?

CRESSIDA   O yes, and 'twere a cloud in autumn.

PANDARUS   Why, go to then. But to prove to you that Helen loves Troilus –

CRESSIDA   Troilus will stand to the proof if you'll prove it so.

PANDARUS   Troilus? Why, he esteems her no more than I esteem an addle egg.

CRESSIDA   If you love an addle egg as well as you love an idle head you would eat chickens i'th' shell.

PANDARUS   I cannot choose but laugh to think how she tickled his chin: indeed she has a marvell's white hand, I must needs confess –

CRESSIDA   Without the rack.

PANDARUS   And she takes upon her to spy a white hair on his chin.

CRESSIDA   Alas poor chin, many a wart is richer.

PANDARUS   But there was such laughing: Queen Hecuba laughed that her eyes ran o'er –

CRESSIDA   With millstones.

PANDARUS   And Cassandra laughed. 145

CRESSIDA   But there was a more temperate fire under the pot of her eyes. Did her eyes run o'er too?

PANDARUS   And Hector laughed.

CRESSIDA   At what was all this laughing?

PANDARUS   Marry, at the white hair that Helen spied on 150 Troilus' chin.

CRESSIDA   And't had been a green hair I should have laughed too.

PANDARUS   They laughed not so much at the hair as at his pretty answer. 155

CRESSIDA   What was his answer?

PANDARUS   Quoth she, 'Here's but two and fifty hairs on your chin, and one of them is white.'

CRESSIDA   This is her question.

PANDARUS   That's true, make no question of that. 'Two 160 and fifty hairs,' quoth he, 'and one white: that white hair is my father, and all the rest are his sons.' 'Jupiter,' quoth she, 'which of these hairs is Paris my husband?' 'The forked one,' quoth he, 'pluck't out and give it him.' But there was such laughing, and Helen 165 so blushed, and Paris so chafed, and all the rest so laughed that it passed.

CRESSIDA   So let it now, for it has been a great while going by.

PANDARUS   Well cousin, I told you a thing yesterday; 170 think on't.

CRESSIDA   So I do.

PANDARUS   I'll be sworn 'tis true; he will weep you and 'twere a man born in April.

CRESSIDA   And I'll spring up in his tears and 'twere a 175 nettle against May.   [*Sound a retreat.*]

PANDARUS   Hark! they are coming from the field. Shall we stand up here and see them as they pass toward Ilium? Good niece, do, sweet niece Cressida.

CRESSIDA   At your pleasure. 180

PANDARUS   Here, here, here's an excellent place, here we may see most bravely. I'll tell you them all by their names as they pass by, but mark Troilus above the rest.

Enter AENEAS *and passes over.*

CRESSIDA   Speak not so loud.

PANDARUS   That's Aeneas, is not that a brave man? He's 185 one of the flowers of Troy, I can tell you. But mark Troilus; you shall see anon.

Enter ANTENOR *and passes over.*

CRESSIDA   Who's that?

PANDARUS   That's Antenor: he has a shrewd wit, I can tell you, and he's a man good enough; he's one o' th' 190 soundest judgements in Troy whosoever, and a proper man of person. When comes Troilus? I'll show you Troilus anon: if he see me, you shall see him nod at me.

CRESSIDA   Will he give you the nod? 195

PANDARUS   You shall see.

CRESSIDA If he do, the rich shall have more.

Enter HECTOR *and passes over.*

PANDARUS That's Hector, that, that, look you, that; there's a fellow! Go thy way, Hector – there's a brave man, niece – O brave Hector! Look how he looks, there's a countenance: is't not a brave man? 200

CRESSIDA O, a brave man.

PANDARUS Is a not? It does a man's heart good. Look you what hacks are on his helmet – look you yonder, do you see? Look you there: there's no jesting, there's 205 laying on, take't off who will, as they say: there be hacks.

CRESSIDA Be those with swords?

PANDARUS Swords, anything, he cares not: and the devil come to him, it's all one. By God's lid it does one's 210 heart good.

Enter PARIS *and passes over.*

Yonder comes Paris, yonder comes Paris: look ye yonder, niece, is't not a gallant man too, is't not? Why, this is brave now: who said he came hurt home today? He's not hurt. Why, this will do Helen's heart good 215 now, ha? Would I could see Troilus now: you shall see Troilus anon.

Enter HELENUS *and passes over.*

CRESSIDA Who's that?

PANDARUS That's Helenus – I marvel where Troilus is – that's Helenus – I think he went not forth today – 220 that's Helenus.

CRESSIDA Can Helenus fight, uncle?

PANDARUS Helenus? No – yes, he'll fight indifferent well – I marvel where Troilus is. Hark, do you not hear the people cry 'Troilus'? – Helenus is a priest. 225

CRESSIDA What sneaking fellow comes yonder?

Enter TROILUS *and passes over.*

PANDARUS Where? Yonder? That's Deiphobus. – 'Tis Troilus! There's a man, niece! Hem! Brave Troilus, the prince of chivalry!

CRESSIDA Peace, for shame, peace. 230

PANDARUS Mark him, note him. O brave Troilus! Look well upon him, niece, look you how his sword is bloodied, and his helm more hacked than Hector's, and how he looks, and how he goes! O admirable youth; he never saw three and twenty. Go thy way, 235 Troilus, go thy way. Had I a sister were a grace, or a daughter a goddess, he should take his choice. O admirable man! Paris? Paris is dirt to him, and I warrant Helen, to change, would give an eye to boot.

Enter common soldiers and pass over.

CRESSIDA Here comes more. 240

PANDARUS Asses, fools, dolts, chaff and bran, chaff and bran; porridge after meat. I could live and die in the eyes of Troilus. Ne'er look, ne'er look, the eagles are gone: crows and daws, crows and daws. I had rather be such a man as Troilus, than Agamemnon and all 245 Greece.

CRESSIDA There is amongst the Greeks Achilles, a better man than Troilus.

PANDARUS Achilles? A drayman, a porter, a very camel.

CRESSIDA Well, well. 250

PANDARUS Well, well? Why, have you any discretion? Have you any eyes? Do you know what a man is? Is not birth, beauty, good shape, discourse, manhood, learning, gentleness, virtue, youth, liberality and such like, the spice and salt that season a man? 255

CRESSIDA Ay, a minced man; and then to be baked with no date in the pie, for then the man's date is out.

PANDARUS You are such a woman, a man knows not at what ward you lie.

CRESSIDA Upon my back, to defend my belly; upon my 260 wit, to defend my wiles; upon my secrecy, to defend mine honesty; my mask, to defend my beauty; and you, to defend all these; and at all these wards I lie, at a thousand watches.

PANDARUS Say one of your watches. 265

CRESSIDA Nay, I'll watch you for that, and that's one of the chiefest of them too. If I cannot ward what I would not have hit, I can watch you for telling how I took the blow, unless it swell past hiding, and then it's past watching. 270

PANDARUS You are such another.

Enter Boy.

BOY Sir, my lord would instantly speak with you.

PANDARUS Where?

BOY At your own house, there he unarms him.

PANDARUS Good boy, tell him I come. *Exit Boy.* 275
I doubt he be hurt. Fare ye well, good niece.

CRESSIDA Adieu, uncle.

PANDARUS I will be with you, niece, by and by.

CRESSIDA To bring, uncle?

PANDARUS Ay, a token from Troilus. *Exit Pandarus.* 280

CRESSIDA By the same token, you are a bawd.
Words, vows, gifts, tears, and love's full sacrifice
He offers in another's enterprise;
But more in Troilus thousand-fold I see
Than in the glass of Pandar's praise may be; 285
Yet hold I off. Women are angels, wooing:
Things won are done; joy's soul lies in the doing.
That she belov'd knows naught that knows not this:
Men prize the thing ungain'd more than it is.
That she was never yet that ever knew 290
Love got so sweet as when desire did sue.
Therefore this maxim out of love I teach:
'Achievement is command; ungain'd, beseech'.
Then though my heart's content firm love doth bear,
Nothing of that shall from mine eyes appear. *Exit.* 295

1.3   *Sennet. Enter* AGAMEMNON, NESTOR, ULYSSES,
      DIOMEDES, MENELAUS, *with others.*

AGAMEMNON   Princes:
  What grief hath set these jaundies on your cheeks?
  The ample proposition that hope makes
  In all designs begun on earth below
  Fails in the promis'd largeness: checks and disasters
  Grow in the veins of actions highest rear'd,
  As knots, by the conflux of meeting sap,
  Infects the sound pine and diverts his grain
  Tortive and errant from his course of growth.
  Nor, princes, is it matter new to us
  That we come short of our suppose so far
  That after seven years' siege yet Troy walls stand,
  Sith every action that hath gone before
  Whereof we have record, trial did draw
  Bias and thwart, not answering the aim
  And that unbodied figure of the thought
  That gave't surmised shape. Why then, you princes,
  Do you with cheeks abash'd behold our works,
  And call them shames which are indeed naught else
  But the protractive trials of great Jove
  To find persistive constancy in men,
  The fineness of which metal is not found
  In fortune's love? For then the bold and coward,
  The wise and fool, the artist and unread,
  The hard and soft, seem all affin'd and kin;
  But in the wind and tempest of her frown,
  Distinction, with a broad and powerful fan
  Puffing at all, winnows the light away,
  And what hath mass or matter by itself
  Lies rich in virtue and unmingled.
NESTOR   With due observance of thy godlike seat,
  Great Agamemnon, Nestor shall apply
  Thy latest words. In the reproof of chance
  Lies the true proof of men. The sea being smooth,
  How many shallow bauble boats dare sail
  Upon her patient breast, making their way
  With those of nobler bulk;
  But let the ruffian Boreas once enrage
  The gentle Thetis, and anon behold
  The strong ribb'd bark through liquid mountains cut,
  Bounding between the two moist elements
  Like Perseus' horse. Where's then the saucy boat
  Whose weak untimber'd sides but even now
  Co-rivall'd greatness? Either to harbour fled,
  Or made a toast for Neptune. Even so
  Doth valour's show and valour's worth divide
  In storms of fortune; for in her ray and brightness
  The herd hath more annoyance by the breese
  Than by the tiger; but when the splitting wind
  Makes flexible the knees of knotted oaks,
  And flies flee under shade, why then the thing of
    courage,
  As rous'd with rage, with rage doth sympathize,
  And, with an accent tun'd in self-same key,

  Retires to chiding fortune.
ULYSSES   Agamemnon,
  Thou great commander, nerves and bone of Greece,   55
  Heart of our numbers, soul and only sprite,
  In whom the tempers and the minds of all
  Should be shut up, hear what Ulysses speaks.
  Besides th'applause and approbation
  [*to Agamemnon*] The which, most mighty for thy
    place and sway,   60
  [*to Nestor*] And thou, most reverend for thy
    stretch'd-out life,
  I give to both your speeches, which were such
  As Agamemnon and the hand of Greece
  Should hold up high in brass; and such again
  As venerable Nestor, hatch'd in silver,   65
  Should with a bond of air, strong as the axletree
  On which heaven rides, knit all the Greekish ears
  To his experienc'd tongue – yet let it please both,
  Thou great, and wise, to hear Ulysses speak.
AGAMEMNON
  Speak, Prince of Ithaca, and be't of less expect   70
  That matter needless, of importless burden,
  Divide thy lips, than we are confident
  When rank Thersites opes his mastic jaws
  We shall hear music, wit, and oracle.
ULYSSES   Troy yet upon his basis had been down   75
  And the great Hector's sword had lack'd a master
  But for these instances.
  The specialty of rule hath been neglected,
  And look how many Grecian tents do stand
  Hollow upon this plain, so many hollow factions.   80
  When that the general is not like the hive
  To whom the foragers shall all repair,
  What honey is expected? Degree being vizarded,
  Th'unworthiest shows as fairly in the mask.
  The heavens themselves, the planets, and this centre   85
  Observe degree, priority, and place,
  Insisture, course, proportion, season, form,
  Office, and custom, in all line of order.
  And therefore is the glorious planet Sol
  In noble eminence enthron'd and spher'd   90
  Amidst the other; whose med'cinable eye
  Corrects the influence of evil planets,
  And posts like the commandment of a king,
  Sans check, to good and bad. But when the planets
  In evil mixture to disorder wander,   95
  What plagues and what portents, what mutiny,
  What raging of the sea, shaking of earth,
  Commotion in the winds, frights, changes, horrors,
  Divert and crack, rend and deracinate
  The unity and married calm of states   100
  Quite from their fixture! O, when degree is shak'd,
  Which is the ladder of all high designs,
  The enterprise is sick. How could communities,
  Degrees in schools, and brotherhoods in cities,
  Peaceful commerce from dividable shores,   105

The primogenity and the due of birth,
Prerogative of age, crowns, sceptres, laurels,
But by degree stand in authentic place?
Take but degree away, untune that string,
110 And hark what discord follows. Each thing melts
In mere oppugnancy; the bounded waters
Should lift their bosoms higher than the shores,
And make a sop of all this solid globe;
Strength should be lord of imbecility,
115 And the rude son should strike his father dead;
Force should be right – or rather, right and wrong,
Between whose endless jar justice resides,
Should lose their names, and so should justice too.
Then everything includes itself in power,
120 Power into will, will into appetite,
And appetite, an universal wolf,
So doubly seconded with will and power,
Must make perforce an universal prey,
And last eat up himself. Great Agamemnon,
125 This chaos, when degree is suffocate,
Follows the choking;
And this neglection of degree it is
That by a pace goes backward, with a purpose
It hath to climb. The general's disdain'd
130 By him one step below, he by the next,
The next by him beneath: so every step,
Exampled by the first pace that is sick
Of his superior, grows to an envious fever
Of pale and bloodless emulation.
135 And 'tis this fever that keeps Troy on foot,
Not her own sinews. To end a tale of length,
Troy in our weakness stands, not in her strength.
NESTOR   Most wisely hath Ulysses here discover'd
The fever whereof all our power is sick.
AGAMEMNON
140 The nature of the sickness found, Ulysses,
What is the remedy?
ULYSSES   The great Achilles, whom opinion crowns
The sinew and the forehand of our host,
Having his ear full of his airy fame,
145 Grows dainty of his worth, and in his tent
Lies mocking our designs: with him Patroclus
Upon a lazy bed in the livelong day
Breaks scurril jests,
And with ridiculous and awkward action,
150 Which, slanderer, he imitation calls,
He pageants us. Sometime, great Agamemnon,
Thy topless deputation he puts on,
And like a strutting player, whose conceit
Lies in his hamstring and doth think it rich
155 To hear the wooden dialogue and sound
'Twixt his stretch'd footing and the scaffoldage,
Such to-be-pitied and o'er-wrested seeming
He acts thy greatness in; and when he speaks,
'Tis like a chime a-mending, with terms unsquar'd,
160 Which, from the tongue of roaring Typhon dropp'd,
Would seem hyperboles. At this fusty stuff

The large Achilles, on his press'd bed lolling,
From his deep chest laughs out a loud applause:
Cries 'Excellent! 'Tis Agamemnon right!
Now play me Nestor: hem and stroke thy beard, 165
As he being dress'd to some oration.'
That's done, as near as the extremest ends
Of parallels, as like as Vulcan and his wife;
Yet god Achilles still cries 'Excellent!
'Tis Nestor right: now play him me, Patroclus, 170
Arming to answer in a night alarm.'
And then, forsooth, the faint defects of age
Must be the scene of mirth, to cough and spit,
And with a palsy fumbling on his gorget
Shake in and out the rivet: and at this sport 175
Sir Valour dies, cries 'O, enough, Patroclus,
Or give me ribs of steel: I shall split all
In pleasure of my spleen.' And in this fashion
All our abilities, gifts, natures, shapes,
Severals and generals of grace exact, 180
Achievements, plots, orders, preventions,
Excitements to the field, or speech for truce,
Success or loss, what is or is not, serves
As stuff for these two to make paradoxes.
NESTOR   And in the imitation of these twain, 185
Who, as Ulysses says, opinion crowns
With an imperial voice, many are infect.
Ajax is grown self-will'd, and bears his head
In such a rein, in full as proud a place
As broad Achilles; keeps his tent like him; 190
Makes factious feasts; rails on our state of war
Bold as an oracle; and sets Thersites,
A slave whose gall coins slanders like a mint,
To match us in comparisons with dirt
To weaken and discredit our exposure, 195
How rank soever rounded in with danger.
ULYSSES   They tax our policy and call it cowardice,
Count wisdom as no member of the war,
Forestall prescience, and esteem no act
But that of hand. The still and mental parts, 200
That do contrive how many hands shall strike
When fitness calls them on and know by measure
Of their observant toil the enemy's weight –
Why, this hath not a finger's dignity.
They call this bed-work, mapp'ry, closet-war; 205
So that the ram that batters down the wall,
For the great swinge and rudeness of his poise,
They place before his hand that made the engine,
Or those that with the fineness of their souls
By reason guide his execution. 210
NESTOR   Let this be granted, and Achilles' horse
Makes many Thetis' sons.   [*Tucket.*]
AGAMEMNON   What trumpet? Look, Menelaus.
MENELAUS   From Troy.

Enter AENEAS.

AGAMEMNON   What would you 'fore our tent?
AENEAS   Is this great Agamemnon's tent, I pray you? 215

AGAMEMNON   Even this.

AENEAS   May one that is a herald and a prince
    Do a fair message to his kingly eyes?

AGAMEMNON   With surety stronger than Achilles' arm
220   'Fore all the Greekish lords, which with one voice
    Call Agamemnon head and general.

AENEAS   Fair leave and large security. How may
    A stranger to those most imperial looks
    Know them from eyes of other mortals?

AGAMEMNON   How?

225 AENEAS   Ay:
    I ask, that I might waken reverence,
    And bid the cheek be ready with a blush
    Modest as morning when she coldly eyes
    The youthful Phoebus.
230   Which is that god in office, guiding men?
    Which is the high and mighty Agamemnon?

AGAMEMNON
    This Trojan scorns us, or the men of Troy
    Are ceremonious courtiers.

AENEAS   Courtiers as free, as debonair, unarm'd,
235   As bending angels: that's their fame in peace;
    But when they would seem soldiers, they have galls,
    Good arms, strong joints, true swords, and – Jove's
        accord –
    Nothing so full of heart. But peace, Aeneas,
    Peace, Trojan, lay thy finger on thy lips.
240   The worthiness of praise distains his worth
    If that the prais'd himself bring the praise forth;
    But what the repining enemy commends,
    That breath fame blows; that praise, sole pure,
        transcends.

AGAMEMNON
    Sir you of Troy, call you yourself Aeneas?

245 AENEAS   Ay, Greek, that is my name.

AGAMEMNON   What's your affairs, I pray you?

AENEAS   Sir, pardon, 'tis for Agamemnon's ears.

AGAMEMNON
    He hears naught privately that comes from Troy.

AENEAS
250   Nor I from Troy come not to whisper with him.
    I bring a trumpet to awake his ear,
    To set his sense on the attentive bent,
    And then to speak.

AGAMEMNON   Speak frankly as the wind.
    It is not Agamemnon's sleeping hour:
    That thou shalt know, Trojan, he is awake,
    He tells thee so himself.

255 AENEAS   Trumpet, blow loud:
    Send thy brass voice through all these lazy tents,
    And every Greek of mettle, let him know
    What Troy means fairly shall be spoke aloud.
                        [*Sound trumpet.*]
    We have, great Agamemnon, here in Troy
260   A prince call'd Hector – Priam is his father –
    Who in this dull and long-continu'd truce
    Is resty grown. He bade me take a trumpet

And to this purpose speak: kings, princes, lords,
    If there be one among the fair'st of Greece
    That holds his honour higher than his ease,   265
    That feeds his praise more than he fears his peril,
    That knows his valour and knows not his fear,
    That loves his mistress more than in confession
    With truant vows to her own lips he loves,
    And dare avow her beauty and her worth   270
    In other arms than hers – to him this challenge:
    Hector, in view of Trojans and of Greeks,
    Shall make it good, or do his best to do it,
    He hath a lady wiser, fairer, truer,
    Than ever Greek did couple in his arms;   275
    And will tomorrow with his trumpet call
    Midway between your tents and walls of Troy
    To rouse a Grecian that is true in love.
    If any come, Hector shall honour him:
    If none, he'll say in Troy, when he retires,   280
    The Grecian dames are sunburnt and not worth
    The splinter of a lance. Even so much.

AGAMEMNON
    This shall be told our lovers, Lord Aeneas.
    If none of them have soul in such a kind,
    We left them all at home; but we are soldiers,   285
    And may that soldier a mere recreant prove
    That means not, hath not, or is not in love.
    If then one is, or hath, or means to be,
    That one meets Hector: if none else, I am he.

NESTOR   Tell him of Nestor, one that was a man   290
    When Hector's grandsire suck'd. He is old now;
    But if there be not in our Grecian host
    A noble man that hath no spark of fire
    To answer for his love, tell him from me
    I'll hide my silver beard in a gold beaver,   295
    And in my vambrace put my wither'd brawns,
    And, meeting him, will tell him that my lady
    Was fairer than his grandam, and as chaste
    As may be in the world. His youth in flood,
    I'll prove this troth with my three drops of blood. 300

AENEAS   Now heavens forfend such scarcity of youth.

ULYSSES   Amen.

AGAMEMNON
    Fair Lord Aeneas, let me touch your hand:
    To our pavilion shall I lead you, sir.
    Achilles shall have word of this intent;   305
    So shall each lord of Greece, from tent to tent.
    Yourself shall feast with us before you go,
    And find the welcome of a noble foe.
                Exeunt all but Ulysses and Nestor.

ULYSSES   Nestor.

NESTOR   What says Ulysses?   310

ULYSSES   I have a young conception in my brain:
    Be you my time to bring it to some shape.

NESTOR   What is't?

ULYSSES   This 'tis:
    Blunt wedges rive hard knots; the seeded pride   315
    That hath to this maturity blown up

In rank Achilles must or now be cropp'd,
        Or, shedding, breed a nursery of like evil
        To overbulk us all.
320   NESTOR   Well, and how?
      ULYSSES   This challenge that the gallant Hector sends,
        However it is spread in general name,
        Relates in purpose only to Achilles.
      NESTOR   True: the purpose is perspicuous as substance
325   Whose grossness little characters sum up;
        And in the publication make no strain
        But that Achilles, were his brain as barren
        As banks of Libya – though, Apollo knows,
        'Tis dry enough – will with great speed of
            judgement,
330   Ay, with celerity, find Hector's purpose
        Pointing on him.
      ULYSSES   And wake him to the answer, think you?
      NESTOR   Why, 'tis most meet: who may you else oppose
        That can from Hector bring his honour off
335   If not Achilles? Though't be a sportful combat,
        Yet in the trial much opinion dwells;
        For here the Trojans taste our dear'st repute
        With their fin'st palate; and trust to me, Ulysses,
        Our imputation shall be oddly pois'd
340   In this vile action; for the success,
        Although particular, shall give a scantling
        Of good or bad unto the general,
        And in such indexes, although small pricks
        To their subsequent volumes, there is seen
345   The baby figure of the giant mass
        Of things to come at large. It is suppos'd
        He that meets Hector issues from our choice;
        And choice, being mutual act of all our souls,
        Makes merit her election, and doth boil,
350   As 'twere from forth us all, a man distill'd
        Out of our virtues: who miscarrying,
        What heart receives from hence a conquering part
        To steel a strong opinion to themselves? –
        Which entertain'd, limbs are his instruments,
355   In no less working than are swords and bows
        Directive by the limbs.
      ULYSSES   Give pardon to my speech: therefore 'tis meet
        Achilles meet not Hector. Let us like merchants
        First show foul wares, and think perchance they'll sell:
360   If not,
        The lustre of the better shall exceed
        By showing the worse first. Do not consent
        That ever Hector and Achilles meet,
        For both our honour and our shame in this
365   Are dogg'd with two strange followers.
      NESTOR
        I see them not with my old eyes: what are they?
      ULYSSES   What glory our Achilles shares from Hector,
        Were he not proud, we all should share with him;
        But he already is too insolent,
370   And it were better parch in Afric sun
        Than in the pride and salt scorn of his eyes,

Should he 'scape Hector fair. If he were foil'd,
        Why then we did our main opinion crush
        In taint of our best man. No, make a lott'ry,
        And by device let blockish Ajax draw   375
        The sort to fight with Hector. Among ourselves
        Give him allowance for the better man;
        For that will physic the great Myrmidon,
        Who broils in loud applause, and make him fall
        His crest that prouder than blue Iris bends.   380
        If the dull brainless Ajax come safe off,
        We'll dress him up in voices: if he fail,
        Yet go we under our opinion still
        That we have better men. But, hit or miss,
        Our project's life this shape of sense assumes: 385
        Ajax employ'd plucks down Achilles' plumes.
      NESTOR   Ulysses,
        Now I begin to relish thy advice,
        And I will give a taste thereof forthwith
        To Agamemnon: go we to him straight.   390
        Two curs shall tame each other: pride alone
        Must tar the mastiffs on, as 'twere their bone.
                                                    Exeunt.

2.1   *Enter* AJAX *and* THERSITES.

AJAX   Thersites –
THERSITES   Agamemnon – how if he had boils, full, all
    over, generally?
AJAX   Thersites –
THERSITES   And those boils did run – say so – did not   5
    the general run then? Were not that a botchy core?
AJAX   Dog!
THERSITES   Then would come some matter from him: I
    see one now.
AJAX   Thou bitch-wolf's son, canst thou not hear? Feel   10
    then. [*Strikes him.*]
THERSITES   The plague of Greece upon thee, thou
    mongrel beef-witted lord!
AJAX   Speak then, thou vinewed'st leaven, speak! I will
    beat thee into handsomeness!   15
THERSITES   I shall sooner rail thee into wit and holiness,
    but I think thy horse will sooner con an oration than
    thou learn a prayer without book. Thou canst strike,
    canst thou? – A red murrain o' thy jade's tricks.
AJAX   Toadstool! Learn me the proclamation.   20
THERSITES   Dost thou think I have no sense, thou
    strikest me thus?
AJAX   The proclamation.
THERSITES   Thou art proclaimed fool, I think.
AJAX   Do not, porpentine, do not, my fingers itch –   25
THERSITES   I would thou didst itch from head to foot:
    and I had the scratching of thee, I would make thee
    the loathsomest scab in Greece. When thou art forth
    in the incursions thou strikest as slow as another.
AJAX   I say the proclamation.   30
THERSITES   Thou grumblest and railest every hour on
    Achilles, and thou art as full of envy at his greatness

as Cerberus is at Proserpina's beauty – ay, that thou
bark'st at him.

AJAX   Mistress Thersites!

THERSITES   Thou shouldst strike him.

AJAX   Cobloaf!

THERSITES   He would pun thee into shivers with his fist,
as a sailor breaks a biscuit.

AJAX   You whoreson cur! [*Beats him.*]

THERSITES   Do! do!

AJAX   Thou stool for a witch!

THERSITES   Ay, do! do! thou sodden-witted lord, thou
hast no more brain than I have in mine elbows: an
asinico may tutor thee. Thou scurvy-valiant ass, thou
art here but to thrash Trojans, and thou art bought
and sold among those of any wit, like a barbarian slave.
If thou use to beat me, I will begin at thy heel, and tell
what thou art by inches, thou thing of no bowels thou!

AJAX   You dog!

THERSITES   You scurvy lord!

AJAX   You cur! [*Beats him.*]

THERSITES   Mars his idiot! do, rudeness: do, camel: do,
do!

Enter ACHILLES *and* PATROCLUS.

ACHILLES   Why, how now, Ajax, wherefore do ye thus?
How now, Thersites, what's the matter man?

THERSITES   You see him there, do you?

ACHILLES   Ay: what's the matter?

THERSITES   Nay look upon him.

ACHILLES   So I do: what's the matter?

THERSITES   Nay but regard him well.

ACHILLES   Well? – why, so I do.

THERSITES   But yet you look not well upon him, for
who-somever you take him to be, he is Ajax.

ACHILLES   I know that, fool.

THERSITES   Ay, but that fool knows not himself.

AJAX   Therefore I beat thee.

THERSITES   Lo, lo, lo, lo, what modicums of wit he
utters – his evasions have ears thus long. I have
bobbed his brain more than he has beat my bones. I
will buy nine sparrows for a penny, and his pia mater
is not worth the ninth part of a sparrow. This lord,
Achilles – Ajax, who wears his wit in his belly and his
guts in his head – I'll tell you what I say of him.

ACHILLES   What?

THERSITES   I say, this Ajax – [*Ajax offers to strike him.*]

ACHILLES   Nay, good Ajax.

THERSITES   Has not so much wit –

ACHILLES   Nay, I must hold you.

THERSITES   As will stop the eye of Helen's needle, for
whom he comes to fight.

ACHILLES   Peace, fool!

THERSITES   I would have peace and quietness, but the
fool will not: he there, that he: look you there.

AJAX   O thou damned cur, I shall –

ACHILLES   Will you set your wit to a fool's?

THERSITES   No I warrant you, the fool's will shame it.

PATROCLUS   Good words, Thersites.

ACHILLES   What's the quarrel?

AJAX   I bade the vile owl go learn me the tenor of the   90
proclamation, and he rails upon me.

THERSITES   I serve thee not.

AJAX   Well, go to, go to.

THERSITES   I serve here voluntary.

ACHILLES   Your last service was suff'rance – 'twas not   95
voluntary, no man is beaten voluntary: Ajax was here
the voluntary, and you as under an impress.

THERSITES   E'en so – a great deal of your wit too lies in
your sinews, or else there be liars. Hector shall have a
great catch and a knock out either of your brains: a   100
were as good crack a fusty nut with no kernel.

ACHILLES   What, with me too, Thersites?

THERSITES   There's Ulysses, and old Nestor, whose wit
was mouldy ere your grandsires had nails on their
toes, yoke you like draught-oxen and make you plough   105
up the wars.

ACHILLES   What? what?

THERSITES   Yes, good sooth: to, Achilles: to, Ajax: to –

AJAX   I shall cut out your tongue.

THERSITES   'Tis no matter, I shall speak as much wit as   110
thou afterwards.

PATROCLUS   No more words, Thersites; peace.

THERSITES   I will hold my peace when Achilles' brach
bids me, shall I?

ACHILLES   There's for you, Patroclus.   115

THERSITES   I will see you hanged like clotpolls ere I
come any more to your tents: I will keep where there
is wit stirring, and leave the faction of fools.   *Exit.*

PATROCLUS   A good riddance.

ACHILLES
Marry, this, sir, is proclaim'd through all our host,   120
That Hector, by the fifth hour of the sun,
Will with a trumpet 'twixt our tents and Troy,
Tomorrow morning, call some knights to arms
That hath a stomach, and such a one that dare
Maintain – I know not what – 'tis trash – Farewell.   125

AJAX   Farewell: who shall answer him?

ACHILLES   I know not, 'tis put to lott'ry: otherwise
He knew his man.

AJAX   Oh, meaning you? I will go learn more of it.
Exeunt.

2.2   *Enter* PRIAM, HECTOR, TROILUS, PARIS
and HELENUS.

PRIAM   After so many hours, lives, speeches spent,
Thus once again says Nestor from the Greeks:
'Deliver Helen, and all damage else –
As honour, loss of time, travail, expense,
Wounds, friends, and what else dear that is consum'd   5
In hot digestion of this cormorant war –
Shall be struck off.' Hector, what say you to't?

HECTOR
    Though no man lesser fears the Greeks than I,
    As far as toucheth my particular,
10 Yet, dread Priam,
    There is no lady of more softer bowels,
    More spongy to suck in the sense of fear,
    More ready to cry out 'Who knows what follows?'
    Than Hector is. The wound of peace is surety,
15 Surety secure; but modest doubt is call'd
    The beacon of the wise, the tent that searches
    To th'bottom of the worst. Let Helen go.
    Since the first sword was drawn about this question
    Every tithe soul 'mongst many thousand dismes
20 Hath been as dear as Helen – I mean, of ours.
    If we have lost so many tenths of ours
    To guard a thing not ours nor worth to us
    (Had it our name) the value of one ten,
    What merit's in that reason which denies
    The yielding of her up?
25 TROILUS   Fie, fie, my brother:
    Weigh you the worth and honour of a king
    So great as our dread father's in a scale
    Of common ounces? Will you with counters sum
    The past-proportion of his infinite,
30 And buckle in a waist most fathomless
    With spans and inches so diminutive
    As fears and reasons? Fie for godly shame!
HELENUS
    No marvel though you bite so sharp of reasons,
    You are so empty of them. Should not our father
35 Bear the great sway of his affairs with reason
    Because your speech hath none that tell him so?
TROILUS
    You are for dreams and slumbers, brother priest,
    You fur your gloves with reason; here are your
        reasons:
    You know an enemy intends you harm,
40 You know a sword employ'd is perilous,
    And reason flies the object of all harm.
    Who marvels then when Helenus beholds
    A Grecian and his sword, if he do set
    The very wings of reason to his heels,
45 And fly like chidden Mercury from Jove,
    Or like a star disorb'd? Nay, if we talk of reason,
    Let's shut our gates and sleep: manhood and honour
    Should have hare hearts, would they but fat their
        thoughts
    With this cramm'd reason: reason and respect
50 Make livers pale, and lustihood deject.
HECTOR   Brother,
    She is not worth what she doth cost the keeping.
TROILUS   What's aught but as 'tis valued?
HECTOR   But value dwells not in particular will:
55 It holds his estimate and dignity
    As well wherein 'tis precious of itself
    As in the prizer. 'Tis mad idolatry

    To make the service greater than the god;
    And the will dotes that is attributive
    To what infectiously itself affects,   60
    Without some image of th'affected merit.
TROILUS   I take today a wife, and my election
    Is led on in the conduct of my will:
    My will enkindled by mine eyes and ears,
    Two traded pilots 'twixt the dangerous shores   65
    Of will and judgement – how may I avoid,
    Although my will distaste what it elected,
    The wife I choose? There can be no evasion
    To blench from this and to stand firm by honour.
    We turn not back the silks upon the merchant   70
    When we have soil'd them, nor the remainder viands
    We do not throw in unrespective sieve
    Because we now are full. It was thought meet
    Paris should do some vengeance on the Greeks;
    Your breath with full consent bellied his sails;   75
    The seas and winds, old wranglers, took a truce
    And did him service: he touch'd the ports desir'd,
    And for an old aunt whom the Greeks held captive,
    He brought a Grecian queen, whose youth and
        freshness
    Wrinkles Apollo's, and makes stale the morning.   80
    Why keep we her? – The Grecians keep our aunt.
    Is she worth keeping? – Why, she is a pearl
    Whose price hath launch'd above a thousand ships,
    And turn'd crown'd kings to merchants.
    If you'll avouch 'twas wisdom Paris went –   85
    As you must needs, for you all cried 'Go, go':
    If you'll confess he brought home worthy prize –
    As you must needs, for you all clapp'd your hands
    And cried 'Inestimable!': why do you now
    The issue of your proper wisdoms rate,   90
    And do a deed that never Fortune did –
    Beggar the estimation which you priz'd
    Richer than sea and land? O theft most base,
    That we have stol'n what we do fear to keep;
    But thieves unworthy of a thing so stol'n,   95
    That in their country did them that disgrace
    We fear to warrant in our native place.
CASSANDRA [*within*]   Cry, Trojans, cry!
PRIAM   What noise, what shriek is this?
TROILUS   'Tis our mad sister, I do know her voice.
CASSANDRA [*within*]   Cry, Trojans!   100
HECTOR   It is Cassandra.

            Enter CASSANDRA, *raving.*

CASSANDRA
    Cry, Trojans, cry! Lend me ten thousand eyes,
    And I will fill them with prophetic tears.
HECTOR   Peace, sister, peace.
CASSANDRA
    Virgins and boys, mid-age and wrinkled eld,   105
    Soft infancy, that nothing canst but cry,
    Add to my clamours! Let us pay betimes

A moiety of that mass of moan to come.
Cry, Trojans, cry! Practise your eyes with tears!
Troy must not be, nor goodly Ilion stand:
Our firebrand brother Paris burns us all.
Cry, Trojans, cry! A Helen and a woe:
Cry, cry! Troy burns, or else let Helen go.   *Exit.*

HECTOR
Now, youthful Troilus, do not these high strains
Of divination in our sister work
Some touches of remorse? Or is your blood
So madly hot, that no discourse of reason,
Nor fear of bad success in a bad cause,
Can qualify the same?

TROILUS   Why, brother Hector,
We may not think the justness of each act
Such and no other than event doth form it,
Nor once deject the courage of our minds
Because Cassandra's mad: her brain-sick raptures
Cannot distaste the goodness of a quarrel
Which hath our several honours all engag'd
To make it gracious. For my private part,
I am no more touch'd than all Priam's sons;
And Jove forbid there should be done amongst us
Such things as might offend the weakest spleen
To fight for and maintain.

PARIS   Else might the world convince of levity
As well my undertakings as your counsels.
But I attest the gods, your full consent
Gave wings to my propension, and cut off
All fears attending on so dire a project.
For what, alas, can these my single arms?
What propugnation is in one man's valour
To stand the push and enmity of those
This quarrel would excite? Yet I protest,
Were I alone to pass the difficulties,
And had as ample power as I have will,
Paris should ne'er retract what he hath done,
Nor faint in the pursuit.

PRIAM   Paris, you speak
Like one besotted on your sweet delights.
You have the honey still, but these the gall:
So to be valiant is no praise at all.

PARIS   Sir, I propose not merely to myself
The pleasures such a beauty brings with it,
But I would have the soil of her fair rape
Wip'd off in honourable keeping her.
What treason were it to the ransack'd queen,
Disgrace to your great worths, and shame to me,
Now to deliver her possession up
On terms of base compulsion! Can it be,
That so degenerate a strain as this
Should once set footing in your generous bosoms?
There's not the meanest spirit on our party
Without a heart to dare or sword to draw
When Helen is defended: nor none so noble
Whose life were ill bestow'd, or death unfam'd,

Where Helen is the subject. Then, I say,
Well may we fight for her whom we know well
The world's large spaces cannot parallel.

HECTOR   Paris and Troilus, you have both said well,
And on the cause and question now in hand   165
Have gloz'd, but superficially – not much
Unlike young men, whom Aristotle thought
Unfit to hear moral philosophy.
The reasons you allege do more conduce
To the hot passion of distemper'd blood   170
Than to make up a free determination
'Twixt right and wrong: for pleasure and revenge
Have ears more deaf than adders to the voice
Of any true decision. Nature craves
All dues be render'd to their owners: now   175
What nearer debt in all humanity
Than wife is to the husband? If this law
Of nature be corrupted through affection,
And that great minds, of partial indulgence
To their benumbed wills, resist the same,   180
There is a law in each well-order'd nation
To curb those raging appetites that are
Most disobedient and refractory.
If Helen then be wife to Sparta's king,
As it is known she is, these moral laws   185
Of nature and of nations speak aloud
To have her back return'd: thus to persist
In doing wrong extenuates not wrong,
But makes it much more heavy. Hector's opinion
Is this in way of truth: yet ne'ertheless,   190
My spritely brethren, I propend to you
In resolution to keep Helen still
For 'tis a cause that hath no mean dependence
Upon our joint and several dignities.

TROILUS   Why, there you touch'd the life of our design: 195
Were it not glory that we more affected
Than the performance of our heaving spleens,
I would not wish a drop of Trojan blood
Spent more in her defence. But, worthy Hector,
She is a theme of honour and renown,   200
A spur to valiant and magnanimous deeds,
Whose present courage may beat down our foes,
And fame in time to come canonize us;
For I presume brave Hector would not lose
So rich advantage of a promis'd glory   205
As smiles upon the forehead of this action
For the wide world's revenue.

HECTOR   I am yours,
You valiant offspring of great Priamus.
I have a roisting challenge sent amongst
The dull and factious nobles of the Greeks   210
Will strike amazement to their drowsy spirits.
I was advertis'd their great general slept
Whilst emulation in the army crept:
This, I presume, will wake him.   *Exeunt.*

2.3   *Enter* THERSITES *alone.*

THERSITES   How now, Thersites! What, lost in the
labyrinth of thy fury? Shall the elephant Ajax carry it
thus? He beats me, and I rail at him. O worthy
satisfaction! Would it were otherwise – that I could
beat him, whilst he railed at me. 'Sfoot, I'll learn to
conjure and raise devils but I'll see some issue of my
spiteful execrations. Then there's Achilles: a rare
enginer. If Troy be not taken till these two
undermine it, the walls will stand till they fall of
themselves. O thou great thunder-darter of Olympus,
forget that thou art Jove the king of gods: and Mercury,
lose all the serpentine craft of thy caduceus, if ye take
not that little little less than little wit from them that
they have; which short-armed ignorance itself knows is
so abundant scarce, it will not in circumvention deliver
a fly from a spider without drawing their massy irons
and cutting the web. After this, the vengeance on the
whole camp – or rather, the Neapolitan bone-ache; for
that methinks is the curse depending on those that war
for a placket. I have said my prayers, and devil Envy say
'Amen'. What ho! my Lord Achilles!

PATROCLUS [*within*]   Who's there? – Thersites? Good
Thersites, come in and rail.

THERSITES   If I could a' remembered a gilt counterfeit,
thou couldst not have slipped out of my
contemplation: but it is no matter – thyself upon
thyself! The common curse of mankind, folly and
ignorance, be thine in great revenue: Heaven bless
thee from a tutor, and discipline come not near thee!
Let thy blood be thy direction till thy death: then if
she that lays thee out says thou art a fair corse, I'll be
sworn and sworn upon't, she never shrouded any but
lazars. Amen.

Enter PATROCLUS.

Where's Achilles?

PATROCLUS   What, art thou devout? Wast thou in
prayer?

THERSITES   Ay, the heavens hear me!

PATROCLUS   Amen.

ACHILLES [*within*]   Who's there?

PATROCLUS   Thersites, my lord.

ACHILLES [*within*]   Where? where? – O where? – Art
thou come?

Enter ACHILLES.

Why, my cheese, my digestion, why hast thou not
served thyself in to my table so many meals?
Come, what's Agamemnon?

THERSITES   Thy commander, Achilles: then tell me
Patroclus, what's Achilles?

PATROCLUS   Thy lord, Thersites: then tell me I pray
thee, what's Thersites?

THERSITES   Thy knower, Patroclus: then tell me
Patroclus, what art thou?

PATROCLUS   Thou mayst tell that knowest.

ACHILLES   O tell, tell.

THERSITES   I'll decline the whole question. Agamemnon
commands Achilles, Achilles is my lord, I am
Patroclus' knower, and Patroclus is a fool.

PATROCLUS   You rascal!

THERSITES   Peace, fool, I have not done.

ACHILLES   He is a privileged man: proceed, Thersites.

THERSITES   Agamemnon is a fool, Achilles is a fool,
Thersites is a fool, and, as aforesaid, Patroclus is a
fool.

ACHILLES   Derive this: come.

THERSITES   Agamemnon is a fool to offer to command
Achilles, Achilles is a fool to be commanded of
Agamemnon, Thersites is a fool to serve such a fool,
and this Patroclus is a fool positive.

PATROCLUS   Why am I a fool?

THERSITES   Make that demand of the Creator, it suffices
me thou art. Look you, who comes here?

Enter AGAMEMNON, ULYSSES, NESTOR, DIOMEDES
and AJAX.

ACHILLES   Patroclus, I'll speak with nobody. Come in
with me, Thersites.   *Exit.*

THERSITES   Here is such patchery, such juggling, and
such knavery! All the argument is a whore and a
cuckold: a good quarrel to draw emulous factions, and
bleed to death upon. Now the dry serpigo on the
subject, and war and lechery confound all!   *Exit.*

AGAMEMNON   Where is Achilles?

PATROCLUS   Within his tent, but ill dispos'd, my lord.

AGAMEMNON   Let it be known to him that we are here.
He sate our messengers, and we lay by
Our appertainings, visiting of him.
Let him be told so, lest perchance he think
We dare not move the question of our place,
Or know not what we are.

PATROCLUS   I shall say so to him.   *Exit.*

ULYSSES   We saw him at the opening of his tent: He is
not sick.

AJAX   Yes, lion-sick – sick of proud heart. You may call
it melancholy if you will favour the man, but by my
head 'tis pride. But why? why? Let him show us a
cause. A word, my lord. [*Takes Agamemnon aside.*]

NESTOR   What moves Ajax thus to bay at him?

ULYSSES   Achilles hath inveigled his fool from him.

NESTOR   Who, Thersites?

ULYSSES   He.

NESTOR   Then will Ajax lack matter, if he have lost his
argument.

ULYSSES   No: you see, he is his argument, that has his
argument, Achilles.

NESTOR   All the better: their fraction is more our wish
than their faction; but it was a strong composure a
fool could disunite.

ULYSSES   The amity that wisdom knits not, folly may
easily untie.

Enter PATROCLUS.

Here comes Patroclus.

NESTOR　　　　　　　　　No Achilles with him.

ULYSSES
The elephant hath joints, but none for courtesy:
His legs are legs for necessity, not for flexure.

PATROCLUS　Achilles bids me say he is much sorry
If any thing more than your sport and pleasure 　　　10
Did move your greatness and this noble state
To call upon him; he hopes it is no other
But for your health and your digestion sake,
An after-dinner's breath.

AGAMEMNON　　　　　　　Hear you, Patroclus:
We are too well acquainted with these answers; 　　　15
But his evasion, wing'd thus swift with scorn,
Cannot outfly our apprehensions.
Much attribute he hath, and much the reason
Why we ascribe it to him; yet all his virtues,
Not virtuously on his own part beheld, 　　　20
Do in our eyes begin to lose their gloss –
Yea, like fair fruit in an unwholesome dish,
Are like to rot untasted. Go and tell him
We come to speak with him, and you shall not sin
If you do say we think him over-proud 　　　25
And under-honest, in self-assumption greater
Than in the note of judgement; and worthier than
　　himself
Here tend the savage strangeness he puts on,
Disguise the holy strength of their command,
And underwrite in an observing kind 　　　30
His humorous predominance – yea, watch
His course and time, his ebbs and flows, as if
The passage and whole stream of this
　　commencement
Rode on his tide. Go tell him this, and add
That if he overhold his price so much 　　　35
We'll none of him, but let him, like an engine
Not portable, lie under this report:
'Bring action hither, this cannot go to war.'
A stirring dwarf we do allowance give
Before a sleeping giant. Tell him so. 　　　40

PATROCLUS　I shall, and bring his answer presently.
　　　　　　　　　　　　　　　　　　　Exit.

AGAMEMNON　In second voice we'll not be satisfied:
We come to speak with him. Ulysses, enter you.
　　　　　　　　　　　　　　　　　Exit Ulysses.

AJAX　What is he more than another?

AGAMEMNON　No more than what he thinks he is. 　　　145

AJAX　Is he so much? Do you not think he thinks
himself a better man than I am?

AGAMEMNON　No question.

AJAX　Will you subscribe his thought, and say he is?

AGAMEMNON　No, noble Ajax; you are as strong, as 　　　150
valiant, as wise; no less noble, much more gentle, and
altogether more tractable.

AJAX　Why should a man be proud? How doth pride
grow? I know not what pride is.

AGAMEMNON　Your mind is the clearer, Ajax, and your 　　　155
virtues the fairer. He that is proud eats up himself:
pride is his own glass, his own trumpet, his own
chronicle; and whatever praises itself, but in the deed,
devours the deed in the praise.

Enter ULYSSES.

AJAX　I do hate a proud man as I do hate the engender- 　　　160
ing of toads.

NESTOR [*aside*]　And yet he loves himself: is't not strange?

ULYSSES　Achilles will not to the field tomorrow.

AGAMEMNON　What's his excuse?

ULYSSES　　　　　　　　　　He doth rely on none,
But carries on the stream of his dispose 　　　165
Without observance or respect of any,
In will peculiar and in self-admission.

AGAMEMNON　Why will he not, upon our fair request,
Untent his person, and share th'air with us?

ULYSSES
Things small as nothing, for request's sake only, 　　　170
He makes important; possess'd he is with greatness,
And speaks not to himself but with a pride
That quarrels at self-breath. Imagin'd worth
Holds in his blood such swol'n and hot discourse
That 'twixt his mental and his active parts 　　　175
Kingdom'd Achilles in commotion rages
And batters down himself. What should I say?
He is so plaguy proud that the death-tokens of it
Cry 'No recovery'.

AGAMEMNON　　　　　　Let Ajax go to him.
Dear lord, go you and greet him in his tent. 　　　180
'Tis said he holds you well, and will be led
At your request a little from himself.

ULYSSES　O Agamemnon, let it not be so!
We'll consecrate the steps that Ajax makes
When they go from Achilles. Shall the proud lord 　　　185
That bastes his arrogance with his own seam
And never suffers matter of the world
Enter his thoughts, save such as do revolve
And ruminate himself – shall he be worshipp'd
Of that we hold an idol more than he? 　　　190
No: this thrice worthy and right valiant lord
Shall not so stale his palm, nobly acquir'd,
Nor, by my will, assubjugate his merit –
As amply titled as Achilles is –
By going to Achilles. 　　　195
That were to enlard his fat-already pride
And add more coals to Cancer when he burns
With entertaining great Hyperion.
This lord go to him? Jupiter forbid,
And say in thunder 'Achilles, go to him!' 　　　200

NESTOR [*aside*]　O, this is well: he rubs the vein of him.

DIOMEDES [*aside*]
And how his silence drinks up this applause!

AJAX　If I go to him, with my armed fist
I'll pash him o'er the face.

AGAMEMNON　O no, you shall not go. 　　　205

AJAX   And a be proud with me, I'll feeze his pride:
  Let me go to him.
ULYSSES
  Not for the worth that hangs upon our quarrel.
AJAX   A paltry, insolent fellow!
210 NESTOR [*aside*]   How he describes himself!
AJAX   Can he not be sociable?
ULYSSES [*aside*]   The raven chides blackness.
AJAX   I'll let his humours blood.
AGAMEMNON [*aside*]   He will be the physician that
215   should be the patient.
AJAX   And all men were o' my mind –
ULYSSES [*aside*]   Wit would be out of fashion.
AJAX   – a should not bear it so, a should eat swords
  first. Shall pride carry it?
220 NESTOR [*aside*]   And 'twould, you'd carry half.
ULYSSES [*aside*]   A would have ten shares.
AJAX   I will knead him, I'll make him supple.
NESTOR [*aside*]   He's not yet through warm. Force him
  with praises – pour in, pour in, his ambition is dry.
ULYSSES [*to Agamemnon*]
225   My lord, you feed too much on this dislike.
NESTOR   Our noble general, do not do so.
DIOMEDES   You must prepare to fight without Achilles.
ULYSSES   Why, 'tis this naming of him does him harm.
  Here is a man – but 'tis before his face,
  I will be silent.
230 NESTOR   Wherefore should you so?
  He is not emulous, as Achilles is.
ULYSSES   Know the whole world, he is as valiant –
AJAX   A whoreson dog, that shall palter with us thus.
  Would he were a Trojan!
235 NESTOR   What a vice were it in Ajax now –
ULYSSES   If he were proud –
DIOMEDES   Or covetous of praise –
ULYSSES   Ay, or surly borne –
DIOMEDES   Or strange, or self-affected.
  ULYSSES
240   Thank the heavens, lord, thou art of sweet composure,
  Praise him that gat thee, she that gave thee suck;
  Fam'd be thy tutor, and thy parts of nature
  Thrice fam'd beyond, beyond all erudition;
  But he that disciplin'd thine arms to fight,
245   Let Mars divide eternity in twain
  And give him half; and, for thy vigour,
  Bull-bearing Milo his addition yield
  To sinewy Ajax. I will not praise thy wisdom,
  Which like a bourn, a pale, a shore, confines
250   Thy spacious and dilated parts. Here's Nestor,
  Instructed by the antiquary times –
  He must, he is, he cannot but be wise;
  But pardon, father Nestor, were your days
  As green as Ajax', and your brain so temper'd,
255   You should not have the eminence of him,
  But be as Ajax.
AJAX [*to Nestor*]   Shall I call you father?
NESTOR   Ay, my good son.

DIOMEDES   Be rul'd by him, Lord Ajax.
ULYSSES   There is no tarrying here: the hart Achilles
  Keeps thicket. Please it our great general   260
  To call together all his state of war:
  Fresh kings are come to Troy. Tomorrow
  We must with all our main of power stand fast;
  And here's a lord – come knights from east to west
  And cull their flower – Ajax shall cope the best.   265
AGAMEMNON   Go we to council: let Achilles sleep.
  Light boats sail swift, though greater hulks draw
    deep.   *Exeunt.*

3.1   *Enter* PANDARUS *and a* Servant.

                              [*Music sounds within.*]
PANDARUS   Friend, you, pray you, a word: do you not
  follow the young Lord Paris?
SERVANT   Ay sir, when he goes before me.
PANDARUS   You depend upon him, I mean.
SERVANT   Sir, I do depend upon the Lord.   5
PANDARUS   You depend upon a notable gentleman, I
  must needs praise him.
SERVANT   The Lord be praised!
PANDARUS   You know me, do you not?
SERVANT   Faith, sir, superficially.   10
PANDARUS   Friend, know me better: I am the Lord
  Pandarus.
SERVANT   I hope I shall know your honour better.
PANDARUS   I do desire it.
SERVANT   You are in the state of grace?   15
PANDARUS   Grace? Not so, friend: honour and lordship
  are my titles. What music is this?
SERVANT   I do but partly know, sir: it is music in parts.
PANDARUS   Know you the musicians?
SERVANT   Wholly, sir.   20
PANDARUS   Who play they to?
SERVANT   To the hearers, sir.
PANDARUS   At whose pleasure, friend?
SERVANT   At mine, sir, and theirs that love music.
PANDARUS   Command, I mean, friend.   25
SERVANT   Who shall I command, sir?
PANDARUS   Friend, we understand not one another: I am
  too courtly, and thou art too cunning. At whose
  request do these men play?
SERVANT   That's to't indeed, sir: marry, sir, at the   30
  request of Paris my lord, who is there in person; with
  him, the mortal Venus, the heart-blood of beauty,
  love's visible soul –
PANDARUS   Who, my cousin Cressida?
SERVANT   No, sir, Helen: could not you find out that by   35
  her attributes?
PANDARUS   It should seem, fellow, that thou hast not
  seen the Lady Cressida. I come to speak with Paris
  from the Prince Troilus: I will make a complimental
  assault upon him, for my business seethes.   40
SERVANT [*aside*]   Sodden business: there's a stewed
  phrase indeed!

Enter PARIS *and* HELEN *with attendants.*

PANDARUS   Fair be to you, my lord, and to all this fair
company; fair desires in all fair measure fairly guide
them – especially to you, fair queen: fair thoughts be
your fair pillow.

HELEN   Dear lord, you are full of fair words.

PANDARUS   You speak your fair pleasure, sweet queen.
Fair prince, here is good broken music.

PARIS   You have broke it, cousin, and by my life you
shall make it whole again: you shall piece it out with a
piece of your performance.

HELEN   He is full of harmony.

PANDARUS   Truly, lady, no.

HELEN   O sir –

PANDARUS   Rude, in sooth: in good sooth, very rude.

PARIS   Well said, my lord; well, you say so in fits.

PANDARUS   I have business to my lord, dear queen. My
lord, will you vouchsafe me a word?

HELEN   Nay, this shall not hedge us out: we'll hear you
sing, certainly.

PANDARUS   Well, sweet queen, you are pleasant with me.
– But marry, thus, my lord: my dear lord and most
esteemed friend, your brother Troilus –

HELEN   My Lord Pandarus, honey-sweet lord –

PANDARUS   Go to, sweet queen, go to – commends
himself most affectionately to you –

HELEN   You shall not bob us out of our melody; if you
do, our melancholy upon your head.

PANDARUS   Sweet queen, sweet queen, that's a sweet
queen, i'faith.

HELEN   And to make a sweet lady sad is a sour offence.

PANDARUS   Nay, that shall not serve your turn; that shall
it not, in truth, la. Nay, I care not for such words: no,
no. – And my lord, he desires you that if the King call
for him at supper, you will make his excuse.

HELEN   My Lord Pandarus.

PANDARUS   What says my sweet queen, my very very
sweet queen?

PARIS   What exploit's in hand? Where sups he tonight?

HELEN   Nay, but my lord –

PANDARUS   What says my sweet queen? – My cousin will
fall out with you: you must not know where he sups.

PARIS   I'll lay my life, with my disposer Cressida.

PANDARUS   No, no, no such matter, you are wide: come,
your disposer is sick.

PARIS   Well, I'll make's excuse.

PANDARUS   Ay, good my lord: why should you say
Cressida? No, your poor disposer's sick.

PARIS   I spy.

PANDARUS   You spy? What do you spy? – Come, give me
an instrument. Now, sweet queen.

HELEN   Why, this is kindly done.

PANDARUS   My niece is horribly in love with a thing you
have, sweet queen.

HELEN   She shall have it, my lord, if it be not my Lord
Paris.

PANDARUS   He? No, she'll none of him: they two are
twain.

HELEN   Falling in after falling out may make them three.   100

PANDARUS   Come, come, I'll hear no more of this: I'll
sing you a song now.

HELEN   Ay, ay, prithee, now. By my troth, sweet lord,
thou hast a fine forehead.

PANDARUS   Ay, you may, you may.   105

HELEN   Let thy song be love: this love will undo us all.
O Cupid, Cupid, Cupid!

PANDARUS   Love? Ay, that it shall, i'faith.

PARIS   Ay, good now, love, love, nothing but love.

PANDARUS   In good troth it begins so.   110
[*Sings.*]
Love, love, nothing but love, still love, still more!
    For O love's bow
    Shoots buck and doe;
    The shaft confounds
    Not that it wounds,   115
But tickles still the sore.
These lovers cry O ho, they die!
    Yet that which seems the wound to kill
Doth turn O ho, to Ha, ha, he!
    So dying love lives still.   120
O ho, a while, but Ha, ha, ha!
O ho, groans out for Ha, ha, ha! – Heigh ho!

HELEN   In love, i'faith, to the very tip of the nose.

PARIS   He eats nothing but doves, love, and that breeds
hot blood, and hot blood begets hot thoughts, and   125
hot thoughts beget hot deeds, and hot deeds is love.

PANDARUS   Is this the generation of love? Hot blood, hot
thoughts, and hot deeds? Why, they are vipers. Is love
a generation of vipers? Sweet lord, who's afield today?

PARIS   Hector, Deiphobus, Helenus, Antenor, and all   130
the gallantry of Troy. I would fain have armed today,
but my Nell would not have it so. How chance my
brother Troilus went not?

HELEN   He hangs the lip at something: you know all,
Lord Pandarus.   135

PANDARUS   Not I, honey-sweet queen; I long to hear
how they sped today. – You'll remember your
brother's excuse?

PARIS   To a hair.

PANDARUS   Farewell, sweet queen.   140

HELEN   Commend me to your niece.

PANDARUS   I will, sweet queen.
                                    Exit. Sound a retreat.

PARIS
They're come from the field: let us to Priam's hall
To greet the warriors. Sweet Helen, I must woo you
To help unarm our Hector. His stubborn buckles,   145
With these your white enchanting fingers touch'd,
Shall more obey than to the edge of steel
Or force of Greekish sinews: you shall do more
Than all the island kings – disarm great Hector.

HELEN   'Twill make us proud to be his servant, Paris.   150
Yea, what he shall receive of us in duty

Gives us more palm in beauty than we have,
Yea, overshines ourself.
PARIS   Sweet, above thought I love thee.   *Exeunt.*

3.2   *Enter* PANDARUS *and Troilus' Man, meeting.*

PANDARUS   How now, where's thy master? At my cousin
Cressida's?
MAN   No sir, he stays for you to conduct him thither.

Enter TROILUS.

5 PANDARUS   O here he comes! How now, how now?
TROILUS   Sirrah, walk off.   *Exit Man.*
PANDARUS   Have you seen my cousin?
TROILUS   No, Pandarus. I stalk about her door
   Like a strange soul upon the Stygian banks
10   Staying for waftage. O be thou my Charon,
   And give me swift transportance to those fields
   Where I may wallow in the lily beds
   Propos'd for the deserver! O gentle Pandar,
   From Cupid's shoulder pluck his painted wings
   And fly with me to Cressid!
15 PANDARUS   Walk here i'th' orchard, I'll bring her straight.
                                              Exit.
TROILUS   I am giddy: expectation whirls me round.
   Th'imaginary relish is so sweet
   That it enchants my sense: what will it be
   When that the wat'ry palate tastes indeed
20   Love's thrice-repured nectar? Death, I fear me,
   Sounding destruction, or some joy too fine,
   Too subtle-potent, tun'd too sharp in sweetness
   For the capacity of my ruder powers.
   I fear it much; and I do fear besides
25   That I shall lose distinction in my joys,
   As doth a battle, when they charge on heaps
   The enemy flying.

Enter PANDARUS.

PANDARUS   She's making her ready, she'll come straight.
   You must be witty, now: she does so blush, and
30   fetches her wind so short, as if she were frayed with a
   spirit! I'll fetch her: it is the prettiest villain; she
   fetches her breath as short as a new-ta'en sparrow.
                                              Exit.
TROILUS   Even such a passion doth embrace my bosom.
   My heart beats thicker than a feverous pulse,
35   And all my powers do their bestowing lose,
   Like vassalage at unawares encount'ring
   The eye of majesty.

Enter PANDARUS *and* CRESSIDA.

PANDARUS   Come, come, what need you blush? Shame's
   a baby. Here she is now; swear the oaths now to her
40   that you have sworn to me. – What, are you gone
   again? – You must be watched ere you be made tame,
   must you? Come your ways, come your ways: and you
   draw backward we'll put you i'th' fills. Why do you

not speak to her? Come, draw this curtain, and let's see
your picture – alas the day, how loath you are to offend   45
daylight! And 'twere dark, you'd close sooner. So, so;
rub on and kiss the mistress. How now, a kiss in fee-
farm! Build there, carpenter, the air is sweet. – Nay,
you shall fight your hearts out ere I part you: the
falcon as the tercel, for all the ducks i'th' river – go to,   50
go to.
TROILUS   You have bereft me of all words, lady.
PANDARUS   Words pay no debts, give her deeds; but
she'll bereave you o'th' deeds too, if she call your
activity in question. – What, billing again? Here's   55
'In witness whereof the parties interchangeably – '
Come in, come in: I'll go get a fire.   *Exit Pandarus.*
CRESSIDA   Will you walk in, my lord?
TROILUS   O Cressid, how often have I wished me thus.
CRESSIDA   Wished, my lord? The gods grant – O my   60
lord –
TROILUS   What should they grant? What makes this
pretty abruption? What too curious dreg espies my
sweet lady in the fountain of our love?
CRESSIDA   More dregs than water, if my fears have eyes.   65
TROILUS   Fears make devils of cherubins; they never see
truly.
CRESSIDA   Blind fear, that seeing reason leads, finds
safer footing than blind reason stumbling without fear.
To fear the worst oft cures the worse.   70
TROILUS   O let my lady apprehend no fear: in all
Cupid's pageant there is presented no monster.
CRESSIDA   Nor nothing monstrous neither?
TROILUS   Nothing but our undertakings, when we vow
to weep seas, live in fire, eat rocks, tame tigers;   75
thinking it harder for our mistress to devise
imposition enough than for us to undergo any
difficulty imposed. This is the monstruosity in love,
lady: that the will is infinite, and the execution
confined: that the desire is boundless, and the act a   80
slave to limit.
CRESSIDA   They say all lovers swear more performance
than they are able, and yet reserve an ability that they
never perform: vowing more than the perfection of ten,
and discharging less than the tenth part of one. They   85
that have the voice of lions and the act of hares, are they
not monsters?
TROILUS   Are there such? Such are not we. Praise us as
we are tasted, allow us as we prove. Our head shall go
bare till merit cover it: no perfection in reversion shall   90
have a praise in present. We will not name desert
before his birth, and, being born, his addition shall be
humble. Few words to fair faith: Troilus shall be such
to Cressid as what envy can say worst shall be a mock
for his truth, and what truth can speak truest, not   95
truer than Troilus.
CRESSIDA   Will you walk in, my lord?

Enter PANDARUS.

PANDARUS   What, blushing still? Have you not done

talking yet?

CRESSIDA   Well, uncle, what folly I commit, I dedicate to 100
you.

PANDARUS   I thank you for that: if my lord get a boy of
you, you'll give him me. Be true to my lord: if he
flinch, chide me for it.

TROILUS   You know now your hostages: your uncle's 105
word, and my firm faith.

PANDARUS   Nay, I'll give my word for her too: our
kindred, though they be long ere they be wooed, they
are constant being won. They are burs, I can tell you:
they'll stick where they are thrown. 110

CRESSIDA
Boldness comes to me now, and brings me heart:
Prince Troilus, I have lov'd you night and day
For many weary months.

TROILUS   Why was my Cressid then so hard to win?

CRESSIDA   Hard to seem won; but I was won, my lord, 115
With the first glance that ever – Pardon me:
If I confess much you will play the tyrant.
I love you now, but till now not so much
But I might master it. In faith I lie –
My thoughts were like unbridled children, grown 120
Too headstrong for their mother. – See, we fools!
Why have I blabb'd? Who shall be true to us
When we are so unsecret to ourselves? –
But though I lov'd you well, I woo'd you not;
And yet, good faith, I wish'd myself a man, 125
Or that we women had men's privilege
Of speaking first. Sweet, bid me hold my tongue,
For in this rapture I shall surely speak
The thing I shall repent. See, see, your silence,
Cunning in dumbness, from my weakness draws 130
My very soul of counsel. Stop my mouth.

TROILUS   And shall, albeit sweet music issues thence.
   [*Kisses her.*]

PANDARUS   Pretty, i'faith.

CRESSIDA   My lord, I do beseech you pardon me:
'Twas not my purpose thus to beg a kiss. 135
I am asham'd. O heavens, what have I done?
For this time I will take my leave, my lord.

PANDARUS   Leave? – And you take leave till tomorrow
morning –

CRESSIDA   Pray you, content you. 140

TROILUS   What offends you, lady?

CRESSIDA   Sir, mine own company.

TROILUS   You cannot shun yourself.

CRESSIDA   Let me go and try.
I have a kind of self resides with you, 145
But an unkind self, that itself will leave
To be another's fool. I would be gone:
Where is my wit? I know not what I speak.

TROILUS
Well know they what they speak that speak so wisely.

CRESSIDA
Perchance, my lord, I show more craft than love, 150

And fell so roundly to a large confession
To angle for your thoughts. But you are wise,
Or else you love not; for to be wise and love
Exceeds man's might: that dwells with gods above.

TROILUS   O that I thought it could be in a woman – 155
As, if it can, I will presume in you –
To feed for aye her lamp and flames of love;
To keep her constancy in plight and youth,
Outliving beauty's outward, with a mind
That doth renew swifter than blood decays! 160
Or that persuasion could but thus convince me
That my integrity and truth to you
Might be affronted with the match and weight
Of such a winnow'd purity in love –
How were I then uplifted! But alas, 165
I am as true as truth's simplicity,
And simpler than the infancy of truth.

CRESSIDA   In that I'll war with you.

TROILUS   O virtuous fight,
When right with right wars who shall be most right!
True swains in love shall, in the world to come, 170
Approve their truth by Troilus; when their rhymes,
Full of protest, of oath, and big compare,
Wants similes, truth tir'd with iteration
(As true as steel, as plantage to the moon,
As sun to day, as turtle to her mate, 175
As iron to adamant, as earth to th'centre)
Yet, after all comparisons of truth,
As truth's authentic author to be cited,
'As true as Troilus' shall crown up the verse
And sanctify the numbers.

CRESSIDA   Prophet may you be! 180
If I be false, or swerve a hair from truth,
When time is old and hath forgot itself,
When water-drops have worn the stones of Troy,
And blind oblivion swallow'd cities up,
And mighty states characterless are grated 185
To dusty nothing – yet let memory,
From false to false, among false maids in love,
Upbraid my falsehood. When they've said 'As false
As air, as water, wind, or sandy earth,
As fox to lamb, or wolf to heifer's calf, 190
Pard to the hind, or stepdame to her son' –
Yea, let them say, to stick the heart of falsehood,
'As false as Cressid'.

PANDARUS   Go to, a bargain made: seal it, seal it, I'll be
the witness. Here I hold your hand, here my cousin's. 195
If ever you prove false one to another, since I have
taken such pains to bring you together, let all pitiful
goers-between be called to the world's end after my
name: call them all Pandars: let all constant men be
Troiluses, all false women Cressids, and all brokers- 200
between Pandars. Say 'Amen'.

TROILUS   Amen.

CRESSIDA   Amen.

PANDARUS   Amen. Whereupon I will show you a

<table>
<tr><td>

205

5

10

15

20

25

30

35

40
</td><td>

chamber with bed, which bed, because it shall not
speak of your pretty encounters, press it to death.
Away.   *Exeunt Troilus and Cressida.*
And Cupid grant all tongue-tied maidens here
Bed, chamber, pander to provide this gear!   *Exit.*

3.3   *Flourish. Enter* AGAMEMNON, ULYSSES,
DIOMEDES, NESTOR, MENELAUS, AJAX
and CALCHAS.

CALCHAS
    Now, princes, for the service I have done,
    Th'advantage of the time prompts me aloud
    To call for recompense. Appear it to your mind
    That, through the sight I bear in things to come,
    I have abandon'd Troy, left my possession,
    Incurr'd a traitor's name, expos'd myself
    From certain and possess'd conveniences
    To doubtful fortunes, sequest'ring from me all
    That time, acquaintance, custom, and condition
    Made tame and most familiar to my nature;
    And here, to do you service, am become
    As new into the world, strange, unacquainted.
    I do beseech you, as in way of taste,
    To give me now a little benefit
    Out of those many register'd in promise
    Which, you say, live to come in my behalf.
AGAMEMNON
    What would'st thou of us, Trojan? Make demand.
CALCHAS   You have a Trojan prisoner call'd Antenor,
    Yesterday took: Troy holds him very dear.
    Oft have you – often have you thanks therefor –
    Desir'd my Cressid in right great exchange,
    Whom Troy hath still denied; but this Antenor,
    I know, is such a wrest in their affairs
    That their negotiations all must slack,
    Wanting his manage; and they will almost
    Give us a prince of blood, a son of Priam,
    In change of him. Let him be sent, great princes,
    And he shall buy my daughter; and her presence
    Shall quite strike off all service I have done
    In most accepted pain.
AGAMEMNON   Let Diomedes bear him,
    And bring us Cressid hither: Calchas shall have
    What he requests of us. Good Diomed,
    Furnish you fairly for this interchange;
    Withal, bring word if Hector will tomorrow
    Be answer'd in his challenge: Ajax is ready.
DIOMEDES   This shall I undertake, and 'tis a burden
    Which I am proud to bear.
                        Exeunt Diomedes and Calchas.

    ACHILLES *and* PATROCLUS *stand in their tent.*

ULYSSES   Achilles stands i'th' entrance of his tent.
    Please it our general pass strangely by him
    As if he were forgot; and, princes all,
</td><td>

Lay negligent and loose regard upon him.
I will come last. 'Tis like he'll question me
Why such unplausive eyes are bent, why turn'd on him.
If so, I have derision medicinable
To use between your strangeness and his pride,
Which his own will shall have desire to drink.
It may do good: pride hath no other glass
To show itself but pride; for supple knees
Feed arrogance, and are the proud man's fees.
AGAMEMNON   We'll execute your purpose, and put on
    A form of strangeness as we pass along.
    So do each lord, and either greet him not
    Or else disdainfully, which shall shake him more
    Than if not look'd on. I will lead the way.
    [*They cross the stage.*]
ACHILLES   What, comes the general to speak with me?
    You know my mind: I'll fight no more 'gainst Troy.
AGAMEMNON
    What says Achilles? Would he aught with us?
NESTOR   Would you, my lord, aught with the general?
ACHILLES   No.
NESTOR   Nothing, my lord.
AGAMEMNON   The better.
                    Exeunt Agamemnon and Nestor.
ACHILLES   Good day, good day.
MENELAUS   How do you? How do you?   *Exit.*
ACHILLES   What, does the cuckold scorn me?
AJAX   How now, Patroclus.
ACHILLES   Good morrow, Ajax.
AJAX   Ha?
ACHILLES   Good morrow.
AJAX   Ay, and good next day too.   *Exit.*
ACHILLES
    What mean these fellows? Know they not Achilles?
PATROCLUS
    They pass by strangely. They were us'd to bend,
    To send their smiles before them to Achilles,
    To come as humbly as they use to creep
    To holy altars.
ACHILLES   What, am I poor of late?
    'Tis certain, greatness once fall'n out with fortune
    Must fall out with men too. What the declin'd is,
    He shall as soon read in the eyes of others
    As feel in his own fall; for men, like butterflies,
    Show not their mealy wings but to the summer,
    And not a man, for being simply man,
    Hath any honour, but honour for those honours
    That are without him – as place, riches, and favour:
    Prizes of accident as oft as merit –
    Which when they fall, as being slippery standers,
    The love that lean'd on them, as slippery too,
    Doth one pluck down another, and together
    Die in the fall. But 'tis not so with me:
    Fortune and I are friends; I do enjoy
    At ample point all that I did possess,
    Save these men's looks; who do, methinks, find out
    Something not worth in me such rich beholding
</td><td>

45

50

55

60

65

70

75

80

85

90
</td></tr>
</table>

As they have often given. Here is Ulysses:
I'll interrupt his reading.
How now, Ulysses!

ULYSSES   Now, great Thetis' son.

ACHILLES   What are you reading?

ULYSSES   A strange fellow here
95
Writes me, that man, how dearly ever parted,
How much in having, or without or in,
Cannot make boast to have that which he hath,
Nor feels not what he owes, but by reflection,
As, when his virtues shining upon others
100
Heat them, and they retort that heat again
To the first giver.

ACHILLES   This is not strange, Ulysses.
The beauty that is borne here in the face
The bearer knows not, but commends itself
To others' eyes; nor doth the eye itself,
105
That most pure spirit of sense, behold itself,
Not going from itself; but eye to eye oppos'd
Salutes each other with each other's form;
For speculation turns not to itself
Till it hath travell'd and is mirror'd there
110
Where it may see itself. This is not strange at all.

ULYSSES   I do not strain at the position –
It is familiar – but at the author's drift,
Who in his circumstance expressly proves
That no man is the lord of anything,
115
Though in and of him there be much consisting,
Till he communicate his parts to others;
Nor doth he of himself know them for aught,
Till he behold them form'd in the applause
Where th'are extended; who, like an arch, reverb'rate
120
The voice again; or, like a gate of steel
Fronting the sun, receives and renders back
His figure and his heat. I was much rapt in this,
And apprehended here immediately
Th'unknown Ajax. Heavens, what a man is there!
125
A very horse, that has he knows not what!
Nature, what things there are
Most abject in regard and dear in use!
What things again most dear in the esteem
And poor in worth! Now shall we see tomorrow –
130
An act that very chance doth throw upon him –
Ajax renown'd. O heavens, what some men do,
While some men leave to do!
How some men creep in skittish Fortune's hall,
While others play the idiots in her eyes!
135
How one man eats into another's pride,
While pride is fasting in his wantonness!
To see these Grecian lords! – why, even already
They clap the lubber Ajax on the shoulder,
As if his foot were on brave Hector's breast,
140
And great Troy shrieking.

ACHILLES   I do believe it, for they pass'd by me
As misers do by beggars, neither gave to me
Good word nor look. What, are my deeds forgot?

ULYSSES   Time hath, my lord, a wallet at his back
145
Wherein he puts alms for oblivion,
A great-siz'd monster of ingratitudes.
Those scraps are good deeds past, which are devour'd
As fast as they are made, forgot as soon
As done. Perseverance, dear my lord,
150
Keeps honour bright: to have done is to hang
Quite out of fashion, like a rusty mail
In monumental mockery. Take the instant way;
For honour travels in a strait so narrow
Where one but goes abreast. Keep then the path;
155
For emulation hath a thousand sons
That one by one pursue; if you give way,
Or hedge aside from the direct forthright,
Like to an enter'd tide they all rush by
And leave you hindmost;
160
Or, like a gallant horse fall'n in first rank,
Lie there for pavement for the abject rear,
O'er-run and trampled on. Then what they do in present,
Though less than yours in past, must o'er-top yours;
For Time is like a fashionable host
165
That slightly shakes his parting guest by th'hand,
And with his arms out-stretch'd, as he would fly,
Grasps in the comer. Welcome ever smiles,
And farewell goes out sighing. O let not virtue seek
Remuneration for the thing it was;
170
For beauty, wit,
High birth, vigour of bone, desert in service,
Love, friendship, charity, are subjects all
To envious and calumniating Time.
One touch of nature makes the whole world kin –
175
That all with one consent praise new-born gauds,
Though they are made and moulded of things past,
And give to dust that is a little gilt
More laud than gilt o'er-dusted.
The present eye praises the present object:
180
Then marvel not, thou great and complete man,
That all the Greeks begin to worship Ajax,
Since things in motion sooner catch the eye
Than what stirs not. The cry went once on thee,
And still it might, and yet it may again
185
If thou wouldst not entomb thyself alive
And case thy reputation in thy tent,
Whose glorious deeds but in these fields of late
Made emulous missions 'mongst the gods themselves,
And drave great Mars to faction.

ACHILLES   Of this my privacy
190
I have strong reasons.

ULYSSES   But 'gainst your privacy
The reasons are more potent and heroical:
'Tis known, Achilles, that you are in love
With one of Priam's daughters.

ACHILLES   Ha, known?

ULYSSES   Is that a wonder?
The providence that's in a watchful state
195

Knows almost every grain of Pluto's gold,
Finds bottom in th'uncomprehensive deep,
Keeps place with thought, and (almost like the gods)
Do thoughts unveil in their dumb cradles.

200   There is a mystery, with whom relation
Durst never meddle, in the soul of state,
Which hath an operation more divine
Than breath or pen can give expressure to.
All the commerce that you have had with Troy

205   As perfectly is ours as yours, my lord;
And better would it fit Achilles much
To throw down Hector than Polyxena.
But it must grieve young Pyrrhus now at home,
When Fame shall in our islands sound her trump

210   And all the Greekish girls shall tripping sing
'Great Hector's sister did Achilles win,
But our great Ajax bravely beat down him'.
Farewell, my lord: I as your lover speak.
The fool slides o'er the ice that you should break.

                                          Exit.

215 PATROCLUS   To this effect, Achilles, have I mov'd you.
A woman impudent and mannish grown
Is not more loath'd than an effeminate man
In time of action. I stand condemn'd for this:
They think my little stomach to the war

220   And your great love to me restrains you thus.
Sweet, rouse yourself; and the weak wanton Cupid
Shall from your neck unloose his amorous fold,
And, like a dew-drop from the lion's mane,
Be shook to air.

ACHILLES   Shall Ajax fight with Hector?
PATROCLUS
225   Ay, and perhaps receive much honour by him.
ACHILLES   I see my reputation is at stake:
My fame is shrewdly gor'd.
PATROCLUS   O then beware:
Those wounds heal ill that men do give themselves.
Omission to do what is necessary

230   Seals a commission to a blank of danger;
And danger, like an ague, subtly taints
Even then when we sit idly in the sun.
ACHILLES   Go call Thersites hither, sweet Patroclus.
I'll send the fool to Ajax, and desire him

235   T'invite the Trojan lords after the combat
To see us here unarm'd. I have a woman's longing,
An appetite that I am sick withal,
To see great Hector in his weeds of peace,

             Enter THERSITES.

To talk with him, and to behold his visage
240   Even to my full of view. A labour sav'd.
THERSITES   A wonder.
ACHILLES   What?
THERSITES
Ajax goes up and down the field, asking for himself.
ACHILLES   How so?

THERSITES   He must fight singly tomorrow with Hector, 245
and is so prophetically proud of an heroical cudgelling
that he raves in saying nothing.
ACHILLES   How can that be?
THERSITES   Why, a stalks up and down like a peacock, a
stride and a stand; ruminates like an hostess that 250
hath no arithmetic but her brain to set down her
reckoning; bites his lip with a politic regard, as who
should say 'There were wit in this head, and 'twould
out' – and so there is; but it lies as coldly in him as fire
in a flint, which will not show without knocking. The 255
man's undone for ever, for if Hector break not his neck
i'th' combat, he'll break't himself in vainglory. He
knows not me: I said 'Good morrow, Ajax,' and he
replies 'Thanks, Agamemnon'. – What think you of
this man, that takes me for the general? He's grown a 260
very land-fish, languageless, a monster. A plague of
opinion! A man may wear it on both sides, like a
leather jerkin.
ACHILLES   Thou must be my ambassador to him,
Thersites. 265
THERSITES   Who, I? Why, he'll answer nobody: he
professes not answering; speaking is for beggars, he
wears his tongue in's arms. I will put on his
presence: let Patroclus make demands to me. You shall
see the pageant of Ajax. 270
ACHILLES   To him, Patroclus. Tell him I humbly desire
the valiant Ajax to invite the valorous Hector to
come unarmed to my tent, and to procure safe-
conduct for his person, of the magnanimous, and most
illustrious, six or seven times honoured captain- 275
general of the Grecian army, Agamemnon, et cetera.
Do this.
PATROCLUS   Jove bless great Ajax!
THERSITES   Hum!
PATROCLUS   I come from the worthy Achilles – 280
THERSITES   Ha?
PATROCLUS   Who most humbly desires you to invite
Hector to his tent –
THERSITES   Hum?
PATROCLUS   And to procure safe-conduct from 285
Agamemnon.
THERSITES   Agamemnon?
PATROCLUS   Ay, my lord.
THERSITES   Ha!
PATROCLUS   What say you to't? 290
THERSITES   God buy you, with all my heart!
PATROCLUS   Your answer, sir.
THERSITES   If tomorrow be a fair day, by eleven of the
clock it will go one way or other. Howsoever, he shall
pay for me ere he has me. 295
PATROCLUS   Your answer, sir.
THERSITES   Fare ye well, with all my heart.
ACHILLES   Why, but he is not in this tune, is he?
THERSITES   No, but out of tune thus. What music will
be in him when Hector has knocked out his brains, I 300

know not – but I am sure, none, unless the fiddler
Apollo get his sinews to make catlings on.

ACHILLES   Come, thou shalt bear a letter to him straight.

THERSITES   Let me bear another to his horse, for that's
305   the more capable creature.

ACHILLES   My mind is troubled, like a fountain stirr'd,
And I myself see not the bottom of it.

Exeunt Achilles and Patroclus.

THERSITES   Would the fountain of your mind were clear
again, that I might water an ass at it: I had rather be a
tick in a sheep than such a valiant ignorance.   *Exit.*

4.1   *Enter on one side* AENEAS, *and servant*
with a torch; on the other, PARIS, DEIPHOBUS,
ANTENOR, DIOMEDES *and others with torches.*

PARIS   See, ho! who is that there?

DEIPHOBUS   It is the Lord Aeneas.

AENEAS   Is the prince there in person?
Had I so good occasion to lie long
5   As you, Prince Paris, nothing but heavenly business
Should rob my bed-mate of my company.

DIOMEDES
That's my mind, too. Good morrow, Lord Aeneas.

PARIS   A valiant Greek, Aeneas: take his hand;
Witness the process of your speech, wherein
10   You told how Diomed a whole week by days
Did haunt you in the field.

AENEAS   Health to you, valiant sir,
During all question of the gentle truce;
But when I meet you arm'd, as black defiance
As heart can think or courage execute.

15   DIOMEDES   The one and other Diomed embraces.
Our bloods are now in calm, and, so long, health!
But when contention and occasion meet,
By Jove, I'll play the hunter for thy life
With all my force, pursuit, and policy.

20   AENEAS   And thou shalt hunt a lion that will fly
With his face backward. In human gentleness,
Welcome to Troy! Now by Anchises' life,
Welcome indeed! By Venus' hand I swear
No man alive can love in such a sort
25   The thing he means to kill, more excellently.

DIOMEDES   We sympathize. Jove, let Aeneas live –
If to my sword his fate be not the glory –
A thousand complete courses of the sun!
But in mine emulous honour let him die
30   With every joint a wound, and that tomorrow!

AENEAS   We know each other well.

DIOMEDES   We do, and long to know each other worse.

PARIS   This is the most despiteful gentle greeting,
The noblest hateful love, that e'er I heard of.
35   What business, lord, so early?

AENEAS
I was sent for to the King; but why, I know not.

PARIS
His purpose meets you: 'twas to bring this Greek

To Calchas' house, and there to render him,
For the enfreed Antenor, the fair Cressid.
Let's have your company, or, if you please,
40   Haste there before us. [*aside*] I constantly believe,
Or rather, call my thought a certain knowledge,
My brother Troilus lodges there tonight.
Rouse him, and give him note of our approach,
With the whole quality wherefore: I fear
45   We shall be much unwelcome.

AENEAS [*aside*]   That I assure you:
Troilus had rather Troy were borne to Greece
Than Cressid borne from Troy.

PARIS [*aside*]   There is no help:
The bitter disposition of the time
Will have it so. [*aloud*] On, lord, we'll follow you.   50

AENEAS   Good morrow, all.   *Exit Aeneas with servant.*

PARIS   And tell me, noble Diomed, faith, tell me true,
Even in the soul of sound goodfellowship,
Who in your thoughts deserves fair Helen best –
Myself, or Menelaus?

DIOMEDES   Both alike: 55
He merits well to have her that doth seek her,
Not making any scruple of her soilure,
With such a hell of pain and world of charge;
And you as well to keep her that defend her,
Not palating the taste of her dishonour,   60
With such a costly loss of wealth and friends.
He, like a puling cuckold, would drink up
The lees and dregs of a flat tamed piece;
You, like a lecher, out of whorish loins
Are pleas'd to breed out your inheritors.   65
Both merits pois'd, each weighs nor less nor more,
But he as thee, each heavier for a whore.

PARIS   You are too bitter to your country-woman.

DIOMEDES   She's bitter to her country: hear me, Paris –
For every false drop in her bawdy veins   70
A Grecian's life hath sunk; for every scruple
Of her contaminated carrion weight
A Trojan hath been slain. Since she could speak,
She hath not given so many good words breath
As for her Greeks and Trojans suffer'd death.   75

PARIS   Fair Diomed, you do as chapmen do,
Dispraise the thing that they desire to buy;
But we in silence hold this virtue well,
We'll not commend, that not intend to sell.
Here lies our way.   *Exeunt.*   80

4.2   *Enter* TROILUS *and* CRESSIDA.

TROILUS   Dear, trouble not yourself; the morn is cold.

CRESSIDA
Then, sweet my lord, I'll call mine uncle down;
He shall unbolt the gates.

TROILUS   Trouble him not:
To bed, to bed! Sleep kill those pretty eyes,
And give as soft attachment to thy senses   5
As infants empty of all thought.

CRESSIDA   Good morrow, then.

TROILUS   I prithee now, to bed.

CRESSIDA   Are you aweary of me?

TROILUS   O Cressida, but that the busy day,
    Wak'd by the lark, hath rous'd the ribald crows,
10   And dreaming night will hide our joys no longer,
    I would not from thee.

CRESSIDA   Night hath been too brief.

TROILUS
    Beshrew the witch! With venomous wights she stays
    As tediously as hell, but flies the grasps of love
    With wings more momentary-swift than thought.
    You will catch cold, and curse me.

15 CRESSIDA   Prithee, tarry.
    You men will never tarry.
    O foolish Cressid, I might have still held off,
    And then you would have tarried. Hark: there's one
    up.

PANDARUS [*within*]   What's all the doors open here?

20 TROILUS   It is your uncle.

            Enter PANDARUS.

CRESSIDA
    A pestilence on him! now will he be mocking:
    I shall have such a life.

PANDARUS
    How now, how now, how go maidenheads? Here, you,
    maid – where's my cousin Cressid?

CRESSIDA
25 Go hang yourself, you naughty mocking uncle!
    You bring me to do – and then you flout me too!

PANDARUS   To do what? To do what? Let her say what.
    What have I brought you to do?

CRESSIDA   Come, come, beshrew your heart: you'll ne'er
30 be good, nor suffer others.

PANDARUS   Ha, ha! Alas, poor wretch! Ah, poor
    capocchia! Has't not slept tonight? Would he not – ah,
    naughty man – let it sleep? A bugbear take him!

CRESSIDA   Did not I tell you? Would he were knock'd
35 i'th' head! [*One knocks.*]
    Who's that at door? Good uncle, go and see.
    My lord, come you again into my chamber. –
    You smile and mock me, as if I meant naughtily.

TROILUS   Ha, ha!

CRESSIDA
40 Come, you are deceiv'd: I think of no such thing.
    How earnestly they knock: pray you, come in.
    [*knock*] I would not for half Troy have you seen here.

            Exeunt Troilus and Cressida.

PANDARUS   Who's there? What's the matter? Will you
    beat down the door? [*opening it*] How now, what's the
45 matter?

            Enter AENEAS.

AENEAS   Good morrow, lord, good morrow.

PANDARUS   Who's there? My Lord Aeneas? By my troth,
    I knew you not. What news with you so early?

AENEAS   Is not Prince Troilus here?

PANDARUS   Here? What should he do here?   50

AENEAS   Come, he is here, my lord; do not deny him. It
    doth import him much to speak with me.

PANDARUS   Is he here, say you? It's more than I know, I'll
    be sworn. For my own part, I came in late. What
    should he do here?   55

AENEAS   Ho, nay then! Come, come, you'll do him
    wrong ere you are ware, you'll be so true to him to be
    false to him. Do not you know of him, but yet go fetch
    him hither: go.

            Enter TROILUS.

TROILUS   How now, what's the matter?   60

AENEAS   My lord, I scarce have leisure to salute you,
    My matter is so rash: there is at hand
    Paris your brother, and Deiphobus,
    The Grecian Diomed, and our Antenor
    Deliver'd to us; and for him forthwith,   65
    Ere the first sacrifice, within this hour,
    We must give up to Diomedes' hand
    The Lady Cressida.

TROILUS   Is it so concluded?

AENEAS   By Priam and the general state of Troy.
    They are at hand, and ready to effect it.   70

TROILUS   How my achievements mock me!
    I will go meet them; and, my Lord Aeneas,
    We met by chance: you did not find me here.

AENEAS   Good, good, my lord: the secrets of nature
    Have not more gift in taciturnity.   75

            Exeunt Troilus and Aeneas.

PANDARUS   Is't possible? No sooner got but lost? The
    devil take Antenor! The young prince will go mad.
    A plague upon Antenor! I would they had broke's neck!

            Enter CRESSIDA.

CRESSIDA   How now? What's the matter? Who was here?

PANDARUS   Ah, ah!   80

CRESSIDA   Why sigh you so profoundly? Where's my
    lord? Gone?
    Tell me, sweet uncle, what's the matter?

PANDARUS   Would I were as deep under the earth as I am
    above.   85

CRESSIDA   O the gods, what's the matter?

PANDARUS   Pray thee get thee in: would thou hadst ne'er
    been born! I knew thou wouldst be his death.
    O poor gentleman! A plague upon Antenor!

CRESSIDA   Good uncle, I beseech you, on my knees I   90
    beseech you, what's the matter?

PANDARUS   Thou must be gone, wench, thou must be
    gone: thou art changed for Antenor. Thou must to thy
    father, and be gone from Troilus: 'twill be his death,
    'twill be his bane; he cannot bear it.   95

CRESSIDA   O you immortal gods! I will not go.

PANDARUS   Thou must.

CRESSIDA   I will not, uncle. I have forgot my father;
    I know no touch of consanguinity,

No kin, no love, no blood, no soul so near me 　100
As the sweet Troilus! O you gods divine,
Make Cressid's name the very crown of falsehood
If ever she leave Troilus! Time, force, and death,
Do to this body what extremes you can; 　　105
But the strong base and building of my love
Is as the very centre of the earth,
Drawing all things to it. I'll go in and weep –
PANDARUS　Do, do.
CRESSIDA
　– Tear my bright hair, and scratch my praised
　　cheeks, 　　　　　　110
Crack my clear voice with sobs, and break my heart
With sounding 'Troilus'. I will not go from Troy.
　　　　　　　　　　　　Exeunt.

4.3　　*Enter* PARIS *and* TROILUS, *with* AENEAS,
　　　　DEIPHOBUS, ANTENOR *and* DIOMEDES.

PARIS　It is great morning; and the hour prefix'd
For her delivery to this valiant Greek
Comes fast upon. – Good my brother Troilus,
Tell you the lady what she is to do,
And haste her to the purpose.
TROILUS　　　　　　　　Walk into her house. 　5
I'll bring her to the Grecian presently;
And to his hand when I deliver her,
Think it an altar, and thy brother Troilus
A priest, there off'ring to it his own heart.　*Exit.*
PARIS　I know what 'tis to love, 　　　　10
And would, as I shall pity, I could help.
Please you walk in, my lords?　　　*Exeunt.*

4.4　　*Enter* PANDARUS *and* CRESSIDA.

PANDARUS　Be moderate, be moderate.
CRESSIDA　Why tell you me of moderation?
The grief is fine, full, perfect, that I taste,
And violenteth in a sense as strong
As that which causeth it: how can I moderate it? 　5
If I could temporize with my affection,
Or brew it to a weak and colder palate,
The like allayment could I give my grief.
My love admits no qualifying dross,
No more my grief, in such a precious loss. 　　10

　　　　Enter TROILUS.

PANDARUS　Here, here, here he comes. Ah, sweet ducks!
CRESSIDA　O Troilus, Troilus! [*Embraces him.*]
PANDARUS　What a pair of spectacles is here! Let me
　embrace, too. 'O heart', as the goodly saying is,
　　　O heart, heavy heart, 　　　　15
　　　Why sigh'st thou without breaking?
　where he answers again
　　　Because thou canst not ease thy smart
　　　By friendship nor by speaking.
There was never a truer rhyme. Let us cast away 　20
nothing, for we may live to have need of such a verse:

we see it, we see it. How now, lambs?
TROILUS　Cressid, I love thee in so strain'd a purity
That the blest gods, as angry with my fancy,
More bright in zeal than the devotion which 　25
Cold lips blow to their deities, take thee from me.
CRESSIDA　Have the gods envy?
PANDARUS　Ay, ay, ay, ay, 'tis too plain a case.
CRESSIDA　And is it true that I must go from Troy?
TROILUS　A hateful truth.
CRESSIDA　　　　　　What, and from Troilus too? 　30
TROILUS　From Troy and Troilus.
CRESSIDA　　　　　　　　Is't possible?
TROILUS　And suddenly; where injury of chance
Puts back leave-taking, jostles roughly by
All time of pause, rudely beguiles our lips
Of all rejoindure, forcibly prevents 　　35
Our lock'd embrasures, strangles our dear vows
Even in the birth of our own labouring breath.
We two, that with so many thousand sighs
Did buy each other, must poorly sell ourselves
With the rude brevity and discharge of one. 　40
Injurious Time now with a robber's haste
Crams his rich thiev'ry up, he knows not how;
As many farewells as be stars in heaven,
With distinct breath and consign'd kisses to them,
He fumbles up into a loose adieu, 　　45
And scants us with a single famish'd kiss
Distasted with the salt of broken tears.
AENEAS [*within*]　My lord, is the lady ready?
TROILUS　Hark, you are call'd. Some say the Genius
Cries so to him that instantly must die. 　50
Bid them have patience: she shall come anon.
PANDARUS　Where are my tears? Rain, to lay this wind,
　or my heart will be blown up by th' root.　*Exit.*
CRESSIDA　I must then to the Grecians?
TROILUS　　　　　　　　　No remedy.
CRESSIDA　A woeful Cressid 'mongst the merry Greeks: 　55
When shall we see again?
TROILUS
Hear me, my love: be thou but true of heart –
CRESSIDA　I, true? How now, what wicked deem is this?
TROILUS　Nay, we must use expostulation kindly,
For it is parting from us. 　　　　60
I speak not 'Be thou true' as fearing thee –
For I will throw my glove to Death himself
That there's no maculation in thy heart –
But 'Be thou true' say I to fashion in
My sequent protestation: be thou true, 　65
And I will see thee.
CRESSIDA　O you shall be expos'd, my lord, to dangers
As infinite as imminent! But I'll be true.
TROILUS
And I'll grow friend with danger: wear this sleeve.
CRESSIDA　And you this glove: when shall I see you? 　70
TROILUS　I will corrupt the Grecian sentinels
To give thee nightly visitation.
But yet be true.

CRESSIDA   O heavens – 'be true' again?

TROILUS   Hear why I speak it, love.

75   The Grecian youths are full of quality,
        Their loving well compos'd, with gift of nature
              flowing,
        And swelling o'er with arts and exercise.
        How novelty may move, and parts with person,
        Alas, a kind of godly jealousy –
80   Which I beseech you call a virtuous sin –
        Makes me afeard.

CRESSIDA   O heavens, you love me not!

TROILUS   Die I a villain then!
        In this I do not call your faith in question
        So mainly as my merit: I cannot sing,
85   Nor heel the high lavolt, nor sweeten talk,
        Nor play at subtle games – fair virtues all,
        To which the Grecians are most prompt and
              pregnant;
        But I can tell that in each grace of these
        There lurks a still and dumb-discoursive devil
90   That tempts most cunningly. But be not tempted.

CRESSIDA   Do you think I will?

TROILUS   No.
        But something may be done that we will not;
        And sometimes we are devils to ourselves,
        When we will tempt the frailty of our powers,
95   Presuming on their changeful potency.

AENEAS [*within*]   Nay, good my lord!

TROILUS   Come, kiss, and let us part.

PARIS [*within*]   Brother Troilus!

TROILUS [*aloud*]   Good brother, come you hither,
        And bring Aeneas and the Grecian with you.

CRESSIDA   My lord, will you be true?

100   TROILUS   Who, I? – alas, it is my vice, my fault.
        Whiles others fish with craft for great opinion,
        I with great truth catch mere simplicity;
        Whilst some with cunning gild their copper crowns,
        With truth and plainness I do wear mine bare.

                Enter AENEAS, PARIS, ANTENOR,
                DEIPHOBUS *and* DIOMEDES.

105   Fear not my truth: the moral of my wit
        Is 'Plain and true'; there's all the reach of it.
        Welcome, Sir Diomed: here is the lady
        Which for Antenor we deliver you.
        At the port, lord, I'll give her to thy hand,
110   And by the way possess thee what she is.
        Entreat her fair, and by my soul, fair Greek,
        If e'er thou stand at mercy of my sword,
        Name Cressid, and thy life shall be as safe
        As Priam is in Ilion.

DIOMEDES   Fair Lady Cressid,
115   So please you, save the thanks this prince expects.
        The lustre in your eye, heaven in your cheek,
        Pleads your fair usage; and to Diomed
        You shall be mistress, and command him wholly.

TROILUS   Grecian, thou dost not use me courteously,

To shame the zeal of my petition to thee   120
In praising her. I tell thee, lord of Greece,
She is as far high-soaring o'er thy praises
As thou unworthy to be call'd her servant.
I charge thee use her well, even for my charge;
For, by the dreadful Pluto, if thou dost not,   125
Though the great bulk Achilles be thy guard,
I'll cut thy throat.

DIOMEDES   O, be not mov'd, Prince Troilus.
Let me be privileg'd by my place and message
To be a speaker free. When I am hence
I'll answer to my lust. And know you, lord,   130
I'll nothing do on charge: to her own worth
She shall be priz'd. But that you say 'Be't so' –
I'll speak it in my spirit and honour, 'No!'

TROILUS   Come, to the port. I'll tell thee, Diomed,
This brave shall oft make thee to hide thy head.   135
Lady, give me your hand, and, as we walk,
To our own selves bend we our needful talk.
              Exeunt Troilus, Cressida, and Diomedes.
                                    [*Sound trumpet.*]

PARIS   Hark, Hector's trumpet!

AENEAS   How have we spent this morning!
The prince must think me tardy and remiss,
That swore to ride before him to the field.   140

PARIS
'Tis Troilus' fault: come, come, to field with him.

DEIPHOBUS   Let us make ready straight.

AENEAS   Yea, with a bridegroom's fresh alacrity
Let us address to tend on Hector's heels.
The glory of our Troy doth this day lie   145
On his fair worth and single chivalry.   *Exeunt.*

4.5   *Enter* AJAX *armed*, AGAMEMNON,
                ACHILLES, PATROCLUS, MENELAUS,
                ULYSSES, NESTOR *and others.*

AGAMEMNON
Here art thou in appointment fresh and fair
Anticipating time with starting courage.
Give with thy trumpet a loud note to Troy,
Thou dreadful Ajax, that the appalled air
May pierce the head of the great combatant,   5
And hale him hither.

AJAX   Thou, trumpet, there's my purse.
Now, crack thy lungs, and split thy brazen pipe;
Blow, villain, till thy sphered bias cheek
Out-swell the colic of puff'd Aquilon.
Come, stretch thy chest, and let thy eyes spout blood: 10
Thou blowest for Hector.   [*Flourish.*]

ULYSSES   No trumpet answers.

ACHILLES   'Tis but early days.

AGAMEMNON
Is not yond Diomed, with Calchas' daughter?

ULYSSES   'Tis he, I ken the manner of his gait:
He rises on the toe; that spirit of his   15
In aspiration lifts him from the earth.

Enter DIOMEDES *and* CRESSIDA.

AGAMEMNON   Is this the Lady Cressid?

DIOMEDES   Even she.

AGAMEMNON
  Most dearly welcome to the Greeks, sweet lady.
  [*Kisses her.*]

NESTOR   Our general doth salute you with a kiss.

20 ULYSSES   Yet is the kindness but particular;
  'Twere better she were kiss'd in general.

NESTOR   And very courtly counsel: I'll begin.
  So much for Nestor. [*Kisses her.*]

ACHILLES   I'll take that winter from your lips, fair lady:

25   [*Kisses her.*] Achilles bids you welcome.

MENELAUS   I had good argument for kissing, once.

PATROCLUS   But that's no argument for kissing now;
  For thus popp'd Paris in his hardiment,
  [*Steps between.*]
  And parted thus you and your argument. [*Kisses her.*]

ULYSSES [*aside*]

30   O deadly gall, and theme of all our scorns!
  For which we lose our heads to gild his horns.

PATROCLUS   The first was Menelaus' kiss: this, mine;
  [*Kisses her again.*] Patroclus kisses you.

MENELAUS   O, this is trim.

PATROCLUS   Paris and I kiss evermore for him.

35 MENELAUS   I'll have my kiss, sir. Lady, by your leave.

CRESSIDA   In kissing, do you render or receive?

MENELAUS   Both take and give.

CRESSIDA   I'll make my match to live,
  The kiss you take is better than you give:
  Therefore, no kiss.

MENELAUS

40   I'll give you boot, I'll give you three for one.

CRESSIDA   You are an odd man: give even or give none.

MENELAUS   An odd man, lady? – Every man is odd.

CRESSIDA   No, Paris is not, for you know 'tis true
  That you are odd, and he is even with you.

MENELAUS   You fillip me o'th' head.

45 CRESSIDA   No, I'll be sworn.

ULYSSES   It were no match, your nail against his horn.
  May I, sweet lady, beg a kiss of you?

CRESSIDA   You may.

ULYSSES   I do desire it.

CRESSIDA   Why, beg two.

ULYSSES   Why then, for Venus' sake, give me a kiss

50   When Helen is a maid again, and his.

CRESSIDA   I am your debtor; claim it when 'tis due.

ULYSSES   Never's my day, and then a kiss of you.

DIOMEDES   Lady, a word: I'll bring you to your father.
                 Exeunt Diomedes and Cressida.

NESTOR   A woman of quick sense.

ULYSSES   Fie, fie upon her!

55   There's language in her eye, her cheek, her lip –
  Nay, her foot speaks; her wanton spirits look out
  At every joint and motive of her body.
  O, these encounterers, so glib of tongue,

  That give accosting welcome ere it comes,
  And wide unclasp the tables of their thoughts   60
  To every ticklish reader: set them down
  For sluttish spoils of opportunity
  And daughters of the game.   [*Flourish.*]

ALL   The Trojan's trumpet.

AGAMEMNON   Yonder comes the troop.

Enter HECTOR *armed*, AENEAS, TROILUS, PARIS,
DEIPHOBUS *and attendants.*

AENEAS
  Hail, all the state of Greece! What shall be done   65
  To him that victory commands? Or do you purpose
  A victor shall be known – will you the knights
  Shall to the edge of all extremity
  Pursue each other – or shall they be divided
  By any voice or order of the field?   70
  Hector bade ask.

AGAMEMNON   Which way would Hector have it?

AENEAS   He cares not: he'll obey conditions.

AGAMEMNON   'Tis done like Hector.

ACHILLES   But securely done,
  A little proudly, and great deal misprizing
  The knight oppos'd.

AENEAS   If not Achilles, sir,   75
  What is your name?

ACHILLES   If not Achilles, nothing.

AENEAS   Therefore Achilles. But whate'er, know this:
  In the extremity of great and little,
  Valour and pride excel themselves in Hector;
  The one almost as infinite as all,   80
  The other blank as nothing. Weigh him well,
  And that which looks like pride is courtesy.
  This Ajax is half made of Hector's blood;
  In love whereof, half Hector stays at home:
  Half heart, half hand, half Hector comes to seek   85
  This blended knight, half Trojan and half Greek.

ACHILLES   A maiden battle, then? O, I perceive you.

Enter DIOMEDES.

AGAMEMNON   Here is Sir Diomed. Go, gentle knight,
  Stand by our Ajax. As you and Lord Aeneas
  Consent upon the order of their fight,   90
  So be it: either to the uttermost,
  Or else a breath. The combatants being kin
  Half stints their strife before their strokes begin.
  [*Ajax and Hector enter the lists.*]

ULYSSES   They are oppos'd already.

AGAMEMNON
  What Trojan is that same that looks so heavy?   95

ULYSSES   The youngest son of Priam, a true knight;
  Not yet mature, yet matchless; firm of word,
  Speaking in deeds, and deedless in his tongue;
  Not soon provok'd, nor, being provk'd, soon calm'd;
  His heart and hand both open and both free;   100
  For what he has he gives, what thinks he shows,
  Yet gives he not till judgement guide his bounty,

Nor dignifies an impare thought with breath;
Manly as Hector, but more dangerous;
105   For Hector in his blaze of wrath subscribes
To tender objects, but he in heat of action
Is more vindicative than jealous love.
They call him Troilus, and on him erect
A second hope as fairly built as Hector.
110   Thus says Aeneas, one that knows the youth
Even to his inches, and with private soul
Did in great Ilion thus translate him to me.
[*Alarum. Hector and Ajax fight.*]
AGAMEMNON   They are in action.
NESTOR   Now, Ajax, hold thine own!
TROILUS   Hector, thou sleep'st: awake thee!
115   AGAMEMNON   His blows are well dispos'd. There, Ajax!
[*Trumpets cease.*]
DIOMEDES   You must no more.
AENEAS   Princes, enough, so please you.
AJAX   I am not warm yet; let us fight again.
DIOMEDES   As Hector pleases.
HECTOR   Why then, will I no more.
Thou art, great lord, my father's sister's son,
120   A cousin-german to great Priam's seed;
The obligation of our blood forbids
A gory emulation 'twixt us twain.
Were thy commixtion Greek and Trojan so
That thou could'st say 'This hand is Grecian all,
125   And this is Trojan: the sinews of this leg
All Greek, and this, all Troy: my mother's blood
Runs on the dexter cheek, and this sinister
Bounds in my father's' – by Jove multipotent,
Thou shouldst not bear from me a Greekish member
130   Wherein my sword had not impressure made
Of our rank feud; but the just gods gainsay
That any drop thou borrow'dst from thy mother,
My sacred aunt, should by my mortal sword
Be drain'd! Let me embrace thee, Ajax.
135   By him that thunders, thou hast lusty arms;
Hector would have them fall upon him thus.
Cousin, all honour to thee!
AJAX   I thank thee, Hector.
Thou art too gentle and too free a man.
I came to kill thee, cousin, and bear hence
140   A great addition earned in thy death.
HECTOR   Not Neoptolemus so mirable,
On whose bright crest Fame with her loud'st Oyes
Cries 'This is he', could promise to himself
A thought of added honour torn from Hector.
145   AENEAS   There is expectance here from both the sides
What further you will do.
HECTOR   We'll answer it:
The issue is embracement. Ajax, farewell.
AJAX   If I might in entreaties find success –
As seld I have the chance – I would desire
150   My famous cousin to our Grecian tents.
DIOMEDES   'Tis Agamemnon's wish; and great Achilles
Doth long to see unarm'd the valiant Hector.

HECTOR   Aeneas, call my brother Troilus to me,
And signify this loving interview
To the expecters of our Trojan part: 155
Desire them home. Give me thy hand, my cousin;
I will go eat with thee, and see your knights.
[*Agamemnon and the rest come forward.*]
AJAX   Great Agamemnon comes to meet us here.
HECTOR
The worthiest of them, tell me name by name;
But for Achilles, my own searching eyes   160
Shall find him by his large and portly size.
AGAMEMNON   Worthy all arms! as welcome as to one
That would be rid of such an enemy –
But that's no welcome. Understand more clear:
What's past and what's to come is strew'd with husks   165
And formless ruin of oblivion;
But in this extant moment, faith and troth,
Strain'd purely from all hollow bias-drawing,
Bids thee with most divine integrity
From heart of very heart, great Hector, welcome.   170
HECTOR   I thank thee, most imperious Agamemnon.
AGAMEMNON [*to Troilus*]
My well-fam'd lord of Troy, no less to you.
MENELAUS
Let me confirm my princely brother's greeting:
You brace of warlike brothers, welcome hither.
HECTOR   Who must we answer?
AENEAS   The noble Menelaus.   175
HECTOR   O, you my lord: by Mars his gauntlet, thanks!
Mock not that I affect th'untraded oath:
Your quondam wife swears still by Venus' glove.
She's well, but bade me not commend her to you.
MENELAUS
Name her not now, sir; she's a deadly theme.   180
HECTOR   O, pardon: I offend.
NESTOR   I have, thou gallant Trojan, seen thee oft,
Labouring for destiny, make cruel way
Through ranks of Greekish youth; and I have seen
    thee,
As hot as Perseus, spur thy Phrygian steed,   185
Despising many forfeits and subduements,
When thou hast hung thy advanced sword i'th' air,
Not letting it decline on the declin'd,
That I have said to some my standers-by
'Lo, Jupiter is yonder, dealing life';   190
And I have seen thee pause, and take thy breath,
When that a ring of Greeks have shrap'd thee in,
Like an Olympian wrestling. This have I seen,
But this thy countenance, still lock'd in steel,
I never saw till now. I knew thy grandsire,   195
And once fought with him: he was a soldier good;
But by great Mars, the captain of us all,
Never like thee. O, let an old man embrace thee,
And, worthy warrior, welcome to our tents.
AENEAS   'Tis the old Nestor.   200
HECTOR   Let me embrace thee, good old chronicle,
That hast so long walk'd hand in hand with Time;

Most reverend Nestor, I am glad to clasp thee.
NESTOR
  I would my arms could match thee in contention
205   As they contend with thee in courtesy.
HECTOR   I would they could.
NESTOR   Ha?
  By this white beard, I'd fight with thee tomorrow.
  Well, welcome, welcome: I have seen the time.
210 ULYSSES   I wonder now how yonder city stands
  When we have here her base and pillar by us?
HECTOR   I know your favour, Lord Ulysses, well.
  Ah, sir, there's many a Greek and Trojan dead,
  Since first I saw yourself and Diomed
215   In Ilion on your Greekish embassy.
ULYSSES   Sir, I foretold you then what would ensue.
  My prophecy is but half his journey yet;
  For yonder walls that pertly front your town,
  Yon towers, whose wanton tops do buss the clouds,
  Must kiss their own feet.
220 HECTOR   I must not believe you.
  There they stand yet; and modestly I think
  The fall of every Phrygian stone will cost
  A drop of Grecian blood. The end crowns all;
  And that old common arbitrator, Time,
  Will one day end it.
225 ULYSSES   So to him we leave it.
  Most gentle and most valiant Hector, welcome.
  After the general, I beseech you next
  To feast with me, and see me at my tent.
ACHILLES   I shall forestall thee, Lord Ulysses, thou!
230   Now, Hector, I have fed mine eyes on thee;
  I have with exact view perus'd thee, Hector,
  And quoted joint by joint.
HECTOR   Is this Achilles?
ACHILLES   I am Achilles.
HECTOR   Stand fair, I pray thee; let me look on thee.
ACHILLES   Behold thy fill.
235 HECTOR   Nay, I have done already.
ACHILLES   Thou art too brief: I will the second time,
  As I would buy thee, view thee limb by limb.
HECTOR   O, like a book of sport thou'lt read me o'er;
  But there's more in me than thou understand'st.
240   Why dost thou so oppress me with thine eye?
ACHILLES
  Tell me, you heavens, in which part of his body
  Shall I destroy him – whether there, or there, or there –
  That I may give the local wound a name,
  And make distinct the very breach whereout
245   Hector's great spirit flew? Answer me, heavens!
HECTOR   It would discredit the blest gods, proud man,
  To answer such a question. Stand again.
  Think'st thou to catch my life so pleasantly
  As to prenominate in nice conjecture
  Where thou wilt hit me dead?
250 ACHILLES   I tell thee yea.
HECTOR   Wert thou an oracle to tell me so,
  I'd not believe thee. Henceforth guard thee well;

For I'll not kill thee there, nor there, nor there;
But, by the forge that stithied Mars his helm,
I'll kill thee everywhere, yea, o'er and o'er.   255
You wisest Grecians, pardon me this brag:
His insolence draws folly from my lips;
But I'll endeavour deeds to match these words,
Or may I never –
AJAX   Do not chafe thee, cousin;
  And you, Achilles, let these threats alone   260
  Till accident or purpose bring you to't.
  You may have every day enough of Hector,
  If you have stomach. The general state, I fear,
  Can scarce entreat you to be odd with him.
HECTOR   I pray you, let us see you in the field;   265
  We have had pelting wars since you refus'd
  The Grecians' cause.
ACHILLES   Dost thou entreat me, Hector?
  Tomorrow do I meet thee, fell as death;
  Tonight, all friends.
HECTOR   Thy hand upon that match.
AGAMEMNON
  First, all you peers of Greece, go to my tent;   270
  There in the full convive we; afterwards,
  As Hector's leisure and your bounties shall
  Concur together, severally entreat him.
  Beat loud the taborins, let the trumpets blow,
  That this great soldier may his welcome know.   275
    Flourish and drums. Exeunt all but Troilus and Ulysses.
TROILUS   My Lord Ulysses, tell me I beseech you,
  In what place of the field doth Calchas keep?
ULYSSES   At Menelaus' tent, most princely Troilus.
  There Diomed doth feast with him tonight,
  Who neither looks upon the heaven nor earth,   280
  But gives all gaze and bent of amorous view
  On the fair Cressid.
TROILUS   Shall I, sweet lord, be bound to you so much,
  After we part from Agamemnon's tent,
  To bring me thither?
ULYSSES   You shall command me, sir.   285
  As gentle tell me, of what honour was
  This Cressida in Troy? Had she no lover there
  That wails her absence?
TROILUS   O sir, to such as boasting show their scars
  A mock is due. Will you walk on, my lord?   290
  She was belov'd, she lov'd; she is, and doth;
  But still sweet love is food for fortune's tooth.
    Exeunt.

5.1   *Enter* ACHILLES *and* PATROCLUS.

ACHILLES
I'll heat his blood with Greekish wine tonight,
Which with my scimitar I'll cool tomorrow.
Patroclus, let us feast him to the height.

    Enter THERSITES.

PATROCLUS   Here comes Thersites.
ACHILLES   How now, thou core of envy!

5   Thou crusty botch of nature, what's the news?

THERSITES   Why, thou picture of what thou seemest, and
      idol of idiot-worshippers, here's a letter for thee.

ACHILLES   From whence, fragment?

THERSITES   Why, thou full dish of fool, from Troy.

10 PATROCLUS   Who keeps the tent now?

THERSITES   The surgeon's box or the patient's wound.

PATROCLUS   Well said, adversity! And what needs these
      tricks?

THERSITES   Prithee be silent, boy, I profit not by thy
15   talk; thou art said to be Achilles' male varlet.

PATROCLUS   Male varlet, you rogue? What's that?

THERSITES   Why, his masculine whore. Now the rotten
      diseases of the south, the guts-griping, ruptures,
      catarrhs, loads o' gravel i'th' back, lethargies, cold
20   palsies, raw eyes, dirt-rotten livers, whissing lungs,
      bladders full of impostume, sciaticas, lime-kilns i'th'
      palm, incurable bone-ache, and the rivelled fee-simple
      of the tetter, take and take again such preposterous
      discoveries!

25 PATROCLUS   Why, thou damnable box of envy, thou,
      what means thou to curse thus?

THERSITES   Do I curse thee?

PATROCLUS   Why, no, you ruinous butt, you whoreson
      indistinguishable cur, no.

30 THERSITES   No? Why art thou then exasperate, thou
      idle immaterial skein of sleave silk, thou green
      sarsenet flap for a sore eye, thou tassel of a prodigal's
      purse, thou: ah, how the poor world is pestered with
      such water-flies, diminutives of nature!

35 PATROCLUS   Out, gall!

THERSITES   Finch egg!

ACHILLES   My sweet Patroclus, I am thwarted quite
      From my great purpose in tomorrow's battle.
      Here is a letter from Queen Hecuba,
40   A token from her daughter, my fair love,
      Both taxing me, and gaging me to keep
      An oath that I have sworn. I will not break it.
      Fall, Greeks: fail, fame: honour, or go or stay;
      My major vow lies here, this I'll obey.
45   Come, come, Thersites, help to trim my tent;
      This night in banqueting must all be spent.
      Away, Patroclus!   *Exit with Patroclus.*

THERSITES   With too much blood and too little brain
      these two may run mad, but if with too much brain
50   and too little blood they do, I'll be a curer of madmen.
      Here's Agamemnon: an honest fellow enough, and
      one that loves quails, but he has not so much brain as
      ear-wax; and the goodly transformation of Jupiter
      there, his brother the bull, the primitive statue and
55   oblique memorial of cuckolds, a thrifty shoeing-horn
      in a chain at his brother's leg: to what form but that he
      is, should wit larded with malice and malice forced
      with wit turn him to? To an ass were nothing: he is
      both ass and ox; to an ox were nothing: he is both ox
60   and ass. To be a dog, a mule, a cat, a fitchook, a toad,
      a lizard, an owl, a puttock, or a herring without a roe,

I would not care; but to be Menelaus I would conspire
against destiny. Ask me not what I would be, if I were
not Thersites; for I care not to be the louse of a lazar,
so I were not Menelaus. – Hey-day! sprites and fires!   65

Enter HECTOR, TROILUS, AJAX, AGAMEMNON,
ULYSSES, NESTOR, MENELAUS *and* DIOMEDES,
with lights.

AGAMEMNON   We go wrong, we go wrong.

AJAX   No, yonder 'tis:
      There, where we see the lights.

HECTOR   I trouble you.

AJAX   No, not a whit.

Enter ACHILLES.

ULYSSES   Here comes himself to guide you.

ACHILLES
      Welcome, brave Hector; welcome, princes all.

AGAMEMNON
      So now, fair prince of Troy, I bid good night.   70
      Ajax commands the guard to tend on you.

HECTOR
      Thanks and good night to the Greeks' general.

MENELAUS   Good night, my lord.

HECTOR   Good night, sweet Lord Menelaus.

THERSITES [*aside*]   Sweet draught! 'sweet', quoth a?
      Sweet sink, sweet sewer!   75

ACHILLES
      Good night and welcome both at once, to those
      That go or tarry.

AGAMEMNON   Good night.
                              Exeunt Agamemnon and Menelaus.

ACHILLES   Old Nestor tarries; and you too, Diomed,
      Keep Hector company an hour or two.

DIOMEDES   I cannot, lord: I have important business,   80
      The tide whereof is now. Good night, great Hector.

HECTOR   Give me your hand.

ULYSSES [*aside to Troilus*]
      Follow his torch, he goes to Calchas' tent;
      I'll keep you company.

TROILUS [*aside to Ulysses*]   Sweet sir, you honour me.   85

HECTOR   And so, good night.
            Exit Diomedes; Ulysses and Troilus following.

ACHILLES   Come, come, enter my tent.
                              Exeunt all but Thersites.

THERSITES   That same Diomed's a false-hearted rogue,
      a most unjust knave: I will no more trust him when
      he leers than I will a serpent when he hisses. He will   90
      spend his mouth and promise, like Brabbler the
      hound; but when he performs, astronomers foretell it,
      it is prodigious, there will come some change. The sun
      borrows of the moon when Diomed keeps his word. I
      will rather leave to see Hector than not to dog him;   95
      they say he keeps a Trojan drab, and uses the traitor
      Calchas' tent. I'll after. Nothing but lechery:
      all incontinent varlets!   *Exit.*

5.2   *Enter* DIOMEDES.

DIOMEDES   What, are you up here, ho? Speak.
CALCHAS [*within*]   Who calls?
DIOMEDES
    Diomed. Calchas, I think? Where's your daughter?
CALCHAS [*within*]   She comes to you.

Enter TROILUS *and* ULYSSES *at a distance;*
after them THERSITES.

5   ULYSSES   Stand where the torch may not discover us.

Enter CRESSIDA.

TROILUS   Cressid comes forth to him.
DIOMEDES   How now, my charge.
CRESSIDA
    Now, my sweet guardian. Hark, a word with you.
    [*Whispers.*]
TROILUS   Yea, so familiar?
ULYSSES   She will sing any man at first sight.
10 THERSITES   And any man may sing her, if he can take
    her clef: she's noted.
DIOMEDES   Will you remember?
CRESSIDA   Remember? Yes.
DIOMEDES   Nay, but do, then,
15   And let your mind be coupled with your words.
TROILUS   What shall she remember?
ULYSSES   List!
CRESSIDA
    Sweet honey Greek, tempt me no more to folly.
THERSITES   Roguery.
20 DIOMEDES   Nay then –
CRESSIDA   I'll tell you what –
DIOMEDES   Fo, fo, come, tell a pin; you are forsworn.
CRESSIDA
    In faith, I cannot: what would you have me do?
THERSITES   A juggling trick: to be secretly open.
DIOMEDES
25   What did you swear you would bestow on me?
CRESSIDA   I prithee, do not hold me to mine oath;
    Bid me do anything but that, sweet Greek.
DIOMEDES   Good night.
TROILUS   Hold, patience!
30 ULYSSES   How now, Trojan?
CRESSIDA   Diomed.
DIOMEDES   No, no, good night; I'll be your fool no more.
TROILUS   Thy better must.
CRESSIDA   Hark, a word in your ear.
35 TROILUS   O plague and madness!
ULYSSES   You are mov'd, prince: let us depart, I pray,
    Lest your displeasure should enlarge itself
    To wrathful terms. This place is dangerous,
    The time right deadly: I beseech you, go.
TROILUS   Behold, I pray you.
40 ULYSSES   Nay, good my lord, go off;
    You flow to great distraction: come, my lord.
TROILUS   I prithee, stay.
ULYSSES   You have not patience; come.

TROILUS
    I pray you, stay: by hell and all hell's torments,
    I will not speak a word.
DIOMEDES   And so, good night.
CRESSIDA   Nay, but you part in anger.
TROILUS   Doth that grieve thee?   45
    O wither'd truth!
ULYSSES   How now, my lord?
TROILUS   By Jove,
    I will be patient.
CRESSIDA   Guardian! Why, Greek!
DIOMEDES   Fo, fo, adieu, you palter.
CRESSIDA   In faith I do not. Come hither once again.
ULYSSES
    You shake, my lord, at something; will you go?   50
    You will break out.
TROILUS   She strokes his cheek.
ULYSSES   Come, come.
TROILUS   Nay, stay: by Jove, I will not speak a word.
    There is between my will and all offences
    A guard of patience: stay a little while.
THERSITES   How the devil Luxury, with his fat rump and   55
    potato finger, tickles these together! Fry, lechery, fry.
DIOMEDES   But will you then?
CRESSIDA   In faith I will, la; never trust me else.
DIOMEDES   Give me some token for the surety of it.
CRESSIDA   I'll fetch you one.   *Exit.*   60
ULYSSES   You have sworn patience.
TROILUS   Fear me not, my lord;
    I will not be myself, nor have cognition
    Of what I feel: I am all patience.

Enter CRESSIDA.

THERSITES   Now the pledge: now, now, now!
CRESSIDA   Here, Diomed, keep this sleeve.   65
TROILUS   O beauty, where is thy faith?
ULYSSES   My lord!
TROILUS   I will be patient; outwardly I will.
CRESSIDA   You look upon that sleeve; behold it well.
    He lov'd me – O false wench! – Give't me again!
    [*Takes the sleeve.*]
DIOMEDES   Whose was't?   70
CRESSIDA   It is no matter, now I ha't again.
    I will not meet with you tomorrow night;
    I prithee, Diomed, visit me no more.
THERSITES   Now she sharpens: well said, whetstone.
DIOMEDES   I shall have it.
CRESSIDA   What, this?
DIOMEDES   Ay, that.   75
CRESSIDA   O all you gods! O, pretty, pretty pledge!
    Thy master now lies thinking on his bed
    Of thee and me, and sighs, and takes my glove,
    And gives memorial dainty kisses to it,
    As I kiss thee – Nay, do not snatch it from me: 80
    [*Diomedes snatches the sleeve.*]
    He that takes that doth take my heart withal.
DIOMEDES   I had your heart before: this follows it.

TROILUS   I did swear patience.

CRESSIDA
    You shall not have it, Diomed: faith, you shall not.
85   I'll give you something else.

DIOMEDES   I will have this. Whose was it?

CRESSIDA   It is no matter.

DIOMEDES   Come, tell me whose it was.

CRESSIDA
    'Twas one's that lov'd me better than you will.
    But now you have it, take it.

90 DIOMEDES   Whose was it?

CRESSIDA   By all Diana's waiting-women yond,
    And by herself, I will not tell you whose.

DIOMEDES   Tomorrow will I wear it on my helm,
    And grieve his spirit that dares not challenge it.

TROILUS
    Wert thou the devil, and wor'st it on thy horn,
95   It should be challeng'd.

CRESSIDA
    Well, well, 'tis done, 'tis past – and yet it is not:
    I will not keep my word.

DIOMEDES   Why then, farewell:
    Thou never shalt mock Diomed again.

CRESSIDA   You shall not go; one cannot speak a word
    But it straight starts you.

100 DIOMEDES   I do not like this fooling.

TROILUS   Nor I, by Pluto, but that that likes not you
    Pleases me best.

DIOMEDES   What, shall I come? the hour?

CRESSIDA
    Ay, come: O Jove, do come: I shall be plagu'd.

DIOMEDES   Farewell till then.

CRESSIDA   Good night; I prithee come.
                      Exit Diomedes.

105   Troilus, farewell! One eye yet looks on thee,
    But with my heart the other eye doth see.
    Ah, poor our sex! this fault in us I find:
    The error of our eye directs our mind.
    What error leads must err; O, then conclude,
110   Minds sway'd by eyes are full of turpitude.   *Exit.*

THERSITES
    A proof of strength she could not publish more,
    Unless she said 'My mind is now turn'd whore'.

ULYSSES   All's done, my lord.

TROILUS   It is.

ULYSSES   Why stay we then?

TROILUS   To make a recordation to my soul
115   Of every syllable that here was spoke.
    But if I tell how these two did co-act,
    Shall I not lie, in publishing a truth?
    Sith yet there is a credence in my heart,
    An esperance so obstinately strong,
120   That doth invert th'attest of eyes and ears,
    As if those organs had deceptious functions,
    Created only to calumniate.
    Was Cressid here?

ULYSSES   I cannot conjure, Trojan.

TROILUS   She was not, sure.

ULYSSES   Most sure she was.

TROILUS   Why, my negation hath no taste of madness.   125

ULYSSES
    Nor mine, my lord: Cressid was here but now.

TROILUS   Let it not be believ'd for womanhood.
    Think, we had mothers; do not give advantage
    To stubborn critics, apt, without a theme
    For depravation, to square the general sex   130
    By Cressid's rule: rather, think this not Cressid.

ULYSSES
    What hath she done, prince, that can soil our
      mothers?

TROILUS   Nothing at all, unless that this were she.

THERSITES   Will a swagger himself out on's own eyes?

TROILUS   This she? – No, this is Diomed's Cressida.   135
    If beauty have a soul, this is not she;
    If souls guide vows, if vows be sanctimonies,
    If sanctimony be the gods' delight,
    If there be rule in unity itself,
    This is not she. O madness of discourse,   140
    That cause sets up with and against itself!
    Bifold authority! where reason can revolt
    Without perdition, and loss assume all reason
    Without revolt. This is, and is not, Cressid.
    Within my soul there doth conduce a fight   145
    Of this strange nature, that a thing inseparate
    Divides more wider than the sky and earth;
    And yet the spacious breadth of this division
    Admits no orifex for a point as subtle
    As Ariachne's broken woof to enter.   150
    Instance, O instance! strong as Pluto's gates:
    Cressid is mine, tied with the bonds of heaven.
    Instance, O instance! strong as heaven itself:
    The bonds of heaven are slipp'd, dissolv'd, and
      loos'd;
    And with another knot, five-finger-tied,   155
    The fractions of her faith, orts of her love,
    The fragments, scraps, the bits, and greasy relics
    Of her o'er-eaten faith are given to Diomed.

ULYSSES   May worthy Troilus be half attach'd
    With that which here his passion doth express?   160

TROILUS   Ay, Greek; and that shall be divulged well
    In characters as red as Mars his heart
    Inflam'd with Venus. Never did young man fancy
    With so eternal and so fix'd a soul.
    Hark, Greek: as much as I do Cressid love,   165
    So much by weight hate I her Diomed.
    That sleeve is mine that he'll bear on his helm;
    Were it a casque compos'd by Vulcan's skill
    My sword should bite it. Not the dreadful sprout
    Which shipmen do the hurricano call,   170
    Constring'd in mass by the almighty sun,
    Shall dizzy with more clamour Neptune's ear
    In his descent than shall my prompted sword

Falling on Diomed.

75 THERSITES   He'll tickle it for his concupy.

TROILUS   O Cressid! O false Cressid! false, false, false!
Let all untruths stand by thy stained name,
And they'll seem glorious.

ULYSSES   O, contain yourself:
Your passion draws ears hither.

Enter AENEAS.

80 AENEAS   I have been seeking you this hour, my lord;
Hector by this is arming him in Troy.
Ajax your guard stays to conduct you home.

TROILUS
Have with you, prince. My courteous lord, adieu.
Farewell, revolted fair! and Diomed,

85 Stand fast, and wear a castle on thy head!

ULYSSES   I'll bring you to the gates.

TROILUS   Accept distracted thanks.

Exeunt Troilus, Aeneas and Ulysses.

THERSITES   Would I could meet that rogue Diomed! – I
would croak like a raven: I would bode, I would
bode. Patroclus will give me anything for the
90 intelligence of this whore; the parrot will not do
more for an almond than he for a commodious drab.
Lechery, lechery, still wars and lechery! Nothing else
holds fashion. A burning devil take them!   *Exit.*

5.3   *Enter* HECTOR *and* ANDROMACHE.

ANDROMACHE
When was my lord so much ungently temper'd
To stop his ears against admonishment?
Unarm, unarm, and do not fight today.

HECTOR   You train me to offend you; get you in.
By all the everlasting gods, I'll go.

ANDROMACHE
My dreams will, sure, prove ominous to the day.

HECTOR   No more, I say.

Enter CASSANDRA.

CASSANDRA   Where is my brother Hector?

ANDROMACHE   Here, sister, arm'd, and bloody in intent.
Consort with me in loud and dear petition,
Pursue we him on knees; for I have dreamt
Of bloody turbulence, and this whole night
Hath nothing been but shapes and forms of
   slaughter.

CASSANDRA   O, 'tis true.

HECTOR   Ho! Bid my trumpet sound!

CASSANDRA
No notes of sally, for the heavens, sweet brother.

HECTOR   Be gone, I say: the gods have heard me swear.

CASSANDRA   The gods are deaf to hot and peevish vows;
They are polluted offerings, more abhorr'd
Than spotted livers in the sacrifice.

ANDROMACHE   O, be persuaded: do not count it holy
To hurt by being just. It is as lawful,

For we would give much, to use violent thefts,
And rob in the behalf of charity.

CASSANDRA   It is the purpose that makes strong the vow;
But vows to every purpose must not hold:
Unarm, sweet Hector.

HECTOR   Hold you still, I say.   25
Mine honour keeps the weather of my fate:
Life every man holds dear, but the dear man
Holds honour far more precious-dear than life.

Enter TROILUS.

How now, young man; mean'st thou to fight today?

ANDROMACHE   Cassandra, call my father to persuade.   30

Exit Cassandra.

HECTOR
No, faith, young Troilus; doff thy harness, youth.
I am today i'th' vein of chivalry:
Let grow thy sinews till their knots be strong
And tempt not yet the brushes of the war.
Unarm thee, go; and doubt thou not, brave boy,   35
I'll stand today for thee and me and Troy.

TROILUS   Brother, you have a vice of mercy in you,
Which better fits a lion than a man.

HECTOR
What vice is that? Good Troilus, chide me for it.

TROILUS   When many times the captive Grecian falls   40
Even in the fan and wind of your fair sword,
You bid them rise, and live.

HECTOR   O, 'tis fair play.

TROILUS   Fool's play, by heaven, Hector.

HECTOR   How now, how now?

TROILUS   For th' love of all the gods,
Let's leave the hermit pity with our mother;   45
And when we have our armours buckled on
The venom'd vengeance ride upon our swords,
Spur them to ruthful work, rein them from ruth!

HECTOR   Fie, savage, fie.

TROILUS   Hector, then 'tis wars.

HECTOR   Troilus, I would not have you fight today.   50

TROILUS   Who should withhold me?
Not fate, obedience, nor the hand of Mars
Beckoning with fiery truncheon my retire;
Not Priamus and Hecuba on knees,
Their eyes o'er-galled with recourse of tears;   55
Nor you, my brother, with your true sword drawn,
Oppos'd to hinder me, should stop my way,
But by my ruin.

Enter PRIAM *and* CASSANDRA.

CASSANDRA   Lay hold upon him, Priam, hold him fast:
He is thy crutch. Now if thou lose thy stay,   60
Thou on him leaning, and all Troy on thee,
Fall all together.

PRIAM   Come, Hector, come: go back.
Thy wife hath dreamt; thy mother hath had visions;
Cassandra doth foresee; and I myself
Am, like a prophet, suddenly enrapt   65

To tell thee that this day is ominous.
Therefore, come back.

HECTOR   Aeneas is afield,
And I do stand engag'd to many Greeks,
Even in the faith of valour, to appear
This morning to them.

70   PRIAM   Ay, but thou shalt not go.

HECTOR   I must not break my faith.
You know me dutiful; therefore, dear sir,
Let me not shame respect, but give me leave
To take that course, by your consent and voice,

75   Which you do here forbid me, royal Priam.

CASSANDRA   O Priam, yield not to him.

ANDROMACHE   Do not, dear father.

HECTOR   Andromache, I am offended with you:
Upon the love you bear me, get you in.

                        Exit Andromache.

TROILUS   This foolish, dreaming, superstitious girl
Makes all these bodements.

80   CASSANDRA   O, farewell, dear Hector.
Look how thou diest: look how thy eye turns pale:
Look how thy wounds do bleed at many vents;
Hark how Troy roars, how Hecuba cries out,
How poor Andromache shrills her dolours forth;

85   Behold! distraction, frenzy, and amazement
Like witless antics one another meet,
And all cry 'Hector! Hector's dead! O, Hector!'

TROILUS   Away, away!

CASSANDRA
Farewell – yet soft: Hector, I take my leave;

90   Thou dost thyself and all our Troy deceive.   *Exit.*

HECTOR   You are amaz'd, my liege, at her exclaim.
Go in and cheer the town: we'll forth and fight,
Do deeds worth praise, and tell you them at night.

PRIAM   Farewell: the gods with safety stand about thee.

        Exeunt severally Priam and Hector. Alarums.

95   TROILUS   They are at it, hark! Proud Diomed, believe
I come to lose my arm, or win my sleeve.

                Enter PANDARUS.

PANDARUS   Do you hear, my lord, do you hear?

TROILUS   What now?

PANDARUS   Here's a letter come from yond poor girl.

100   TROILUS   Let me read.

PANDARUS   A whoreson tisick, a whoreson rascally
tisick, so troubles me, and the foolish fortune of this
girl, and what one thing, what another, that I shall
leave you one o'th' days; and I have a rheum in mine

105   eyes, too, and such an ache in my bones that unless a
man were cursed I cannot tell what to think on't. What
says she there?

TROILUS
Words, words, mere words, no matter from the heart;
Th'effect doth operate another way. [*Tears the letter.*]

110   Go, wind, to wind: there turn and change together.
My love with words and errors still she feeds,
But edifies another with her deeds.   *Exeunt severally.*

5.4   *Excursions. Enter* THERSITES.

THERSITES   Now they are clapper-clawing one another, I'll
go look on. That dissembling abominable varlet
Diomed has got that same scurvy, doting, foolish
knave's sleeve of Troy there in his helm. I would fain see
them meet, that that same young Trojan ass, that loves   5
the whore there, might send that Greekish
whoremasterly villain with the sleeve back to the
dissembling luxurious drab of a sleeveless errand. O'th'
other side, the policy of those crafty swearing rascals –
that stale old mouse-eaten dry cheese Nestor, and that   10
same dog-fox Ulysses – is not proved worth a blackberry.
They set me up in policy that mongrel cur Ajax, against
that dog of as bad a kind Achilles; and now is the cur Ajax
prouder than the cur Achilles, and will not arm today;
whereupon the Grecians begin to proclaim barbarism,   15
and policy grows into an ill opinion.

      Enter DIOMEDES, TROILUS *following.*

Soft: here comes sleeve, and t'other.

TROILUS   Fly not, for shouldst thou take the river Styx
I would swim after.

DIOMEDES   Thou dost miscall retire: 20
I do not fly; but advantageous care
Withdrew me from the odds of multitude.
Have at thee!

THERSITES   Hold thy whore, Grecian! Now for thy
whore, Trojan! Now the sleeve, now the sleeve!   25

      Exeunt Diomedes and Troilus, fighting.

             Enter HECTOR.

HECTOR   What art thou, Greek? Art thou for Hector's
match? Art thou of blood and honour?

THERSITES   No, no: I am a rascal, a scurvy railing knave:
a very filthy rogue.

HECTOR   I do believe thee: live.   *Exit.*   30

THERSITES   God-a-mercy that thou wilt believe me, but
a plague break thy neck for frighting me. – What's
become of the wenching rogues? I think they have
swallowed one another. I would laugh at that miracle;
yet in a sort lechery eats itself. I'll seek them.   *Exit.*   35

5.5   *Enter* DIOMEDES *and* Servant.

DIOMEDES   Go, go, my servant, take thou Troilus' horse;
Present the fair steed to my Lady Cressid.
Fellow, commend my service to her beauty;
Tell her I have chastis'd the amorous Trojan,
And am her knight by proof.

SERVANT   I go, my lord.   *Exit.*   5

           Enter AGAMEMNON.

AGAMEMNON   Renew, renew! The fierce Polydamas
Hath beat down Menon; bastard Margarelon
Hath Doreus prisoner,
And stands colossus-wise, waving his beam,
Upon the pashed corses of the kings   10

Epistrophus and Cedius. Polixenes is slain;
Amphimacus and Thoas deadly hurt;
Patroclus ta'en or slain; and Palamedes
Sore hurt and bruis'd; the dreadful Sagittary
Appals our numbers. Haste we, Diomed,
To reinforcement, or we perish all.

Enter NESTOR *and soldiers.*

NESTOR   Go bear Patroclus' body to Achilles,
And bid the snail-pac'd Ajax arm, for shame.
There is a thousand Hectors in the field;
Now here he fights on Galathe his horse
And here lacks work: anon he's there afoot,
And there they fly, or die, like scaled sculls
Before the belching whale; then is he yonder,
And there the strawy Greeks, ripe for his edge,
Fall down before him like a mower's swath.
Here, there, and everywhere, he leaves and takes,
Dexterity so obeying appetite
That what he will he does, and does so much
That proof is call'd impossibility.

Enter ULYSSES.

ULYSSES   O, courage, courage, princes: great Achilles
Is arming, weeping, cursing, vowing vengeance:
Patroclus' wounds have rous'd his drowsy blood,
Together with his mangled Myrmidons
That noseless, handless, hack'd and chipp'd, come to
   him,
Crying on Hector. Ajax hath lost a friend,
And foams at mouth, and he is arm'd and at it,
Roaring for Troilus, who hath done today
Mad and fantastic execution,
Engaging and redeeming of himself
With such a careless force and forceless care
As if that lust, in very spite of cunning,
Bade him win all.

Enter AJAX.

AJAX   Troilus! thou coward Troilus!   *Exit.*
DIOMEDES   Ay, there, there!   *Exit.*
NESTOR   So, so, we draw together.

Enter ACHILLES.

ACHILLES   Where is this Hector?
Come, come, thou boy-queller, show thy face;
Know what it is to meet Achilles angry.
Hector! where's Hector? I will none but Hector.
                              Exeunt.

5.6   *Enter* AJAX.

AJAX   Troilus! thou coward Troilus! show thy head.

Enter DIOMEDES.

DIOMEDES   Troilus, I say! Where's Troilus?
AJAX   What wouldst thou?
DIOMEDES   I would correct him.

AJAX   Were I the general, thou shouldst have my office
Ere that correction. Troilus, I say! What, Troilus!   5

Enter TROILUS.

TROILUS
O traitor Diomed! Turn thy false face, thou traitor,
And pay the life thou ow'st me for my horse.
DIOMEDES   Ha, art thou there?
AJAX   I'll fight with him alone: stand, Diomed.
DIOMEDES   He is my prize. I will not look upon.   10
TROILUS
Come, both you cogging Greeks: have at you both!
        Exit Troilus, with Ajax and Diomedes, fighting.

Enter HECTOR.

HECTOR
Yea, Troilus? O, well fought, my youngest brother!

Enter ACHILLES.

ACHILLES
Now do I see thee – Ha! have at thee, Hector!
[*They fight.*]
HECTOR   Pause, if thou wilt.
ACHILLES   I do disdain thy courtesy, proud Trojan.   15
Be happy that my arms are out of use:
My rest and negligence befriends thee now,
But thou anon shalt hear of me again;
Till when, go seek thy fortune.   *Exit.*
HECTOR   Fare thee well.
I would have been much more a fresher man,   20
Had I expected thee.

Enter TROILUS.

                         How now, my brother?
TROILUS   Ajax hath ta'en Aeneas: shall it be?
No! by the flame of yonder glorious heaven,
He shall not carry him! I'll be ta'en too
Or bring him off. Fate, hear me what I say: 25
I reck not, though thou end my life today.   *Exit.*

Enter one in sumptuous armour.

HECTOR
Stand, stand, thou Greek; thou art a goodly mark.
No? wilt thou not? I like thy armour well:
I'll frush it and unlock the rivets all
But I'll be master of it. Wilt thou not, beast, abide?   30
                              Exit Greek.
Why then, fly on; I'll hunt thee for thy hide.   *Exit.*

5.7   *Enter* ACHILLES, *with Myrmidons.*

ACHILLES   Come here about me, you my Myrmidons;
Mark what I say. Attend me where I wheel,
Strike not a stroke, but keep yourselves in breath;
And when I have the bloody Hector found,
Empale him with your weapons round about;   5
In fellest manner execute your arms.
Follow me, sirs, and my proceedings eye:

It is decreed Hector the great must die. *Exeunt.*

Enter MENELAUS *and* PARIS, *fighting; then* THERSITES.

10 THERSITES   The cuckold and the cuckold-maker are at it. Now, bull! Now, dog! 'Loo, Paris, 'loo! – Now, my double-horned Spartan! 'Loo, Paris, 'loo! The bull has the game: ware horns, ho! *Exeunt Paris and Menelaus.*

Enter MARGARELON.

MARGARELON   Turn, slave, and fight.
THERSITES   What are thou?
15 MARGARELON   A bastard son of Priam's.
THERSITES   I am a bastard, too: I love bastards. I am bastard begot, bastard instructed, bastard in mind, bastard in valour, in everything illegitimate. One bear will not bite another, and wherefore should one
20 bastard? Take heed: the quarrel's most ominous to us – if the son of a whore fight for a whore, he tempts judgement. Farewell, bastard. *Exit.*
MARGARELON   The devil take thee, coward. *Exit.*

5.8   *Enter* HECTOR.

HECTOR   Most putrefied core, so fair without,
   Thy goodly armour thus hath cost thy life.
   Now is my day's work done: I'll take my breath.
   Rest, sword; thou hast thy fill of blood and death.
   [*Disarms.*]

Enter ACHILLES *and* Myrmidons.

5 ACHILLES   Look, Hector, how the sun begins to set,
   How ugly night comes breathing at his heels;
   Even with the vail and dark'ning of the sun
   To close the day up, Hector's life is done.
HECTOR   I am unarm'd: forego this vantage, Greek.
10 ACHILLES   Strike, fellows, strike: this is the man I seek.
   [*Hector falls.*]
   So, Ilion, fall thou next! Come, Troy, sink down!
   Here lies thy heart, thy sinews, and thy bone.
   On, Myrmidons, and cry you all amain
   'Achilles hath the mighty Hector slain'.   [*Retreat.*]
15 Hark: a retire upon our Grecian part.
MYRMIDONS
   The Trojan trumpets sound the like, my lord.
ACHILLES
   The dragon wing of night o'er-spreads the earth
   And, stickler-like, the armies separates.
   My half-supp'd sword, that frankly would have fed,
20 Pleas'd with this dainty bait, thus goes to bed.
   Come: tie his body to my horse's tail;
   Along the field I will the Trojan trail.
                    Exeunt. Retreat.

5.9   *Enter* AGAMEMNON, AJAX, MENELAUS, NESTOR, DIOMEDES *and the rest, marching. Shouts within.*

AGAMEMNON   Hark, hark: what shout is that?
NESTOR   Peace, drums.   [*Drums cease.*]
SOLDIERS [*within*]
   Achilles! Achilles! Hector's slain! Achilles!
DIOMEDES   The bruit is, Hector's slain, and by Achilles.
AJAX   If it be so, yet bragless let it be: 5
   Great Hector was as good a man as he.
AGAMEMNON   March patiently along. Let one be sent
   To pray Achilles see us at our tent.
   If in his death the gods have us befriended,
   Great Troy is ours, and our sharp wars are ended.   10
                    Exeunt.

5.10   *Enter* AENEAS, PARIS, ANTENOR *and* DEIPHOBUS.

AENEAS   Stand, ho! yet are we masters of the field.
   Never go home: here starve we out the night.

Enter TROILUS.

TROILUS   Hector is slain.
ALL   Hector? The gods forbid.
TROILUS   He's dead, and at the murderer's horse's tail
   In beastly sort dragg'd through the shameful field.   5
   Frown on, you heavens: effect your rage with speed;
   Sit, gods, upon your thrones, and smile at Troy.
   I say at once let your brief plagues be mercy,
   And linger not our sure destructions on.
AENEAS   My lord, you do discomfort all the host.   10
TROILUS   You understand me not that tell me so.
   I do not speak of flight, of fear, of death,
   But dare all imminence that gods and men
   Address their dangers in. Hector is gone.
   Who shall tell Priam so, or Hecuba?   15
   Let him that will a screech-owl aye be call'd
   Go into Troy, and say there 'Hector's dead'.
   There is a word will Priam turn to stone,
   Make wells and Niobes of the maids and wives,
   Cold statues of the youth, and, in a word,   20
   Scare Troy out of itself. But march away.
   Hector is dead: there is no more to say. –
   Stay yet: you vile abominable tents,
   Thus proudly pight upon our Phrygian plains,
   Let Titan rise as early as he dare,   25
   I'll through and through you! and thou great-siz'd coward,
   No space of earth shall sunder our two hates:
   I'll haunt thee like a wicked conscience still,
   That mouldeth goblins swift as frenzy's thoughts.
   Strike a free march to Troy! With comfort go: 30
   Hope of revenge shall hide our inward woe.
                    Exeunt all but Troilus.

Enter PANDARUS.

PANDARUS   But hear you, hear you!

TROILUS   Hence, broker-lackey! Ignomy and shame
    Pursue thy life, and live aye with thy name!   *Exit.*

PANDARUS   A goodly medicine for my aching bones! O
    world, world, world! Thus is the poor agent despised.
    O traitors and bawds, how earnestly are you set awork,
    and how ill requited. Why should our endeavour be so
    loved and the performance so loathed? What verse for
    it, what instance for it? –
    Let me see:
        Full merrily the humble-bee doth sing
        Till he hath lost his honey and his sting;
        And being once subdu'd in armed tail,
        Sweet honey and sweet notes together fail.
    Good traders in the flesh, set this in your painted
        cloths:
    As many as be here of Pandar's hall,
    Your eyes, half out, weep out at Pandar's fall;
    Or if you cannot weep, yet give some groans,
    Though not for me, yet for your aching bones.
    Brethren and sisters of the hold-door trade,
    Some two months hence my will shall here be made.
    It should be now, but that my fear is this:
    Some galled goose of Winchester would hiss.
    Till then I'll sweat and seek about for eases,
    And at that time bequeath you my diseases.   *Exit.*

Twelfth Night

Twelfth Night, or What You Will was first printed in 1623 as the thirteenth of the comedies in the First Folio. Probably written in 1601, it was acted in the hall of the Middle Temple on 2 February 1602, Candlemas Day, the end of the Christmas season of revels. A law student, John Manningham, noted approvingly in his diary that it was 'much like the *Comedy of Errors*, or *Menaechmi* in Plautus, but most like and near to that in Italian called *Inganni*'. *Gl'Ingannati* (*The Deceived Ones*), an Italian comedy acted in Siena (1531) and printed in Venice (1537), provides the main lines of the love plot, whether directly or through sixteenth-century imitations and rewritings, one of which, the tale of Apolonius and Silla in Barnaby Rich's *Rich his Farewell to Military Profession* (1581), Shakespeare knew. Manningham applauded the gulling of the steward Malvolio into believing his mistress, the countess Olivia, to be in love with him as 'a good practice'. No source for this element in the plot has been identified, but its intrigue resembles the comic method of Ben Jonson. The play was revived at Court, under the title of 'Malvolio', on Candlemas Day 1623 and has that title substituted by hand in a copy of the Second Folio once in the library of Charles I.

Twelfth Night everywhere recalls Shakespeare's own earlier comedies: if the twins recall *The Comedy of Errors*, then the plight of 'Cesario' (the only name by which Viola is known until the final scene) echoes the disguise of Julia as 'Sebastian', and her predicament as servant to the man she loves, in *The Two Gentlemen of Verona*. The love of Antonio for Sebastian parallels the equally self-sacrificing love of another Antonio for Bassanio in *The Merchant of Venice*. The gulling of Malvolio resembles that of Ajax in *Troilus and Cressida*, while Sir Toby Belch and Sir Andrew Aguecheek are models for the more lethal relationship between Iago and Roderigo in *Othello*. The clown, Feste, has a line in logic-chopping and verbal dexterity which links him with Touchstone in *As You Like It* as well as with the sourer clowning of Thersites in *Troilus*, of Lavatch in *All's Well That Ends Well* and of Lear's Fool, whose paradoxes about wisdom and folly he anticipates. It is often claimed that these roles were all written for Robert Armin, from 1599 the company's leading comic actor.

Twelfth Night remains among Shakespeare's best loved and most frequently revived plays. Its peculiar mood, poised between broad comedy and pathos, has led to a variety of emphasis in performance. The most praised modern productions have endeavoured to 'sound all the notes that are there' (to quote the director John Barton). The play pushes its multiple deceptions beyond safe laughter to an awareness of the real pain and damage to which the games could lead. Its ending epitomizes the precariousness of the action's holiday licence: two couples of near strangers are married or betrothed, while Maria wins a marriage above her station, an aspiration thwarted in Malvolio. Malvolio departs with an impotent threat of future vengeance and he – like Sir Andrew, Antonio and Feste – stands apart from the final celebration, whose focus is on the mutual recognition of Viola and her brother rather than the resolution of tangled loves. Feste's last song is an epilogue which serves the usual function of returning the audience from the holiday mood of drama to the workaday world – a return doubly unwelcome at the end of the Christmas festivities to which the title alludes.

In the eighteenth century *Twelfth Night* was enjoyed mainly for its comic scenes, especially those of Malvolio, but the nineteenth century saw the restoration to favour of the romantic side of the play. An influential production was Granville Barker's at the Savoy Theatre in London in 1912, which simplified the setting in the interests of pace and clarity of performance of the full text and rejected the Victorian practice of scenic elaboration. Among many fine modern productions, John Barton's for the Royal Shakespeare Company in 1969–71, with Judi Dench as Viola and Donald Sinden as Malvolio, was memorable for its strong cast and its sensitivity to the play's shifting moods and opalescent tones.

The Arden text is based on the 1623 First Folio.

ORSINO	*Duke of Illyria*
VALENTINE	
CURIO	} *gentlemen attending on the Duke*
FIRST OFFICER	
SECOND OFFICER	} *in the service of the Duke*
VIOLA	*later disguised as Cesario*
SEBASTIAN	*her twin brother*
CAPTAIN	*of the wrecked ship, befriending Viola*
ANTONIO	*another sea-captain, befriending Sebastian*
OLIVIA	*a countess*
MARIA	*Olivia's waiting-gentlewoman*
SIR TOBY Belch	*Olivia's kinsman*
SIR ANDREW Aguecheek	*Sir Toby's companion*
MALVOLIO	*Olivia's steward*
FABIAN	*a member of Olivia's household*
CLOWN (Feste)	*jester to Olivia*
SERVANT	*to Olivia*
PRIEST	

Musicians, Lords, Sailors, Attendants

1.1 *Music. Enter* ORSINO, *Duke of Illyria,* CURIO
and other lords.

ORSINO   If music be the food of love, play on,
Give me excess of it, that, surfeiting,
The appetite may sicken, and so die.
That strain again, it had a dying fall:
O, it came o'er my ear like the sweet sound   5
That breathes upon a bank of violets,
Stealing and giving odour. Enough, no more;
'Tis not so sweet now as it was before.
O spirit of love, how quick and fresh art thou,
That notwithstanding thy capacity   10
Receiveth as the sea, nought enters there,
Of what validity and pitch soe'er,
But falls into abatement and low price,
Even in a minute! So full of shapes is fancy,
That it alone is high fantastical.   15
CURIO   Will you go hunt, my lord?
ORSINO   What, Curio?
CURIO   The hart.
ORSINO   Why so I do, the noblest that I have.
O, when mine eyes did see Olivia first,
Methought she purg'd the air of pestilence;   20
That instant was I turn'd into a hart,
And my desires, like fell and cruel hounds,
E'er since pursue me.

Enter VALENTINE.

                         How now? what news from her?
VALENTINE
So please my lord, I might not be admitted,
But from her handmaid do return this answer: 25
The element itself, till seven years' heat,
Shall not behold her face at ample view;
But like a cloistress she will veiled walk,
And water once a day her chamber round
With eye-offending brine: all this to season   30
A brother's dead love, which she would keep fresh
And lasting, in her sad remembrance.
ORSINO   O, she that hath a heart of that fine frame
To pay this debt of love but to a brother,
How will she love, when the rich golden shaft   35
Hath kill'd the flock of all affections else
That live in her; when liver, brain, and heart,
These sovereign thrones, are all supplied, and fill'd
Her sweet perfections with one self king!
Away before me to sweet beds of flowers!   40
Love-thoughts lie rich when canopied with bowers.

                                        Exeunt.

1.2   *Enter* VIOLA, *a* Captain *and sailors.*

VIOLA   What country, friends, is this?
CAPTAIN   This is Illyria, lady.
VIOLA   And what should I do in Illyria?
My brother he is in Elysium.
Perchance he is not drown'd: what think you, sailors?   5

CAPTAIN   It is perchance that you yourself were sav'd.
VIOLA
O my poor brother! and so perchance may he be.
CAPTAIN
True, madam, and to comfort you with chance,
Assure yourself, after our ship did split,
When you and those poor number sav'd with you   10
Hung on our driving boat, I saw your brother,
Most provident in peril, bind himself
(Courage and hope both teaching him the practice)
To a strong mast that liv'd upon the sea;
Where, like Arion on the dolphin's back,   15
I saw him hold acquaintance with the waves
So long as I could see.
VIOLA   For saying so, there's gold:
Mine own escape unfoldeth to my hope,
Whereto thy speech serves for authority,   20
The like of him. Know'st thou this country?
CAPTAIN   Ay, madam, well, for I was bred and born
Not three hours' travel from this very place.
VIOLA   Who governs here?
CAPTAIN   A noble duke, in nature as in name.   25
VIOLA   What is his name?
CAPTAIN   Orsino.
VIOLA   Orsino! I have heard my father name him.
He was a bachelor then.
CAPTAIN   And so is now, or was so very late;   30
For but a month ago I went from hence,
And then 'twas fresh in murmur (as, you know,
What great ones do, the less will prattle of)
That he did seek the love of fair Olivia.
VIOLA   What's she?   35
CAPTAIN   A virtuous maid, the daughter of a count
That died some twelvemonth since; then leaving her
In the protection of his son, her brother,
Who shortly also died; for whose dear love
(They say) she hath abjur'd the company   40
And sight of men.
VIOLA   O that I serv'd that lady,
And might not be deliver'd to the world,
Till I had made mine own occasion mellow,
What my estate is.
CAPTAIN   That were hard to compass,
Because she will admit no kind of suit,   45
No, not the Duke's.
VIOLA   There is a fair behaviour in thee, Captain;
And though that nature with a beauteous wall
Doth oft close in pollution, yet of thee
I will believe thou hast a mind that suits   50
With this thy fair and outward character.
I prithee (and I'll pay thee bounteously)
Conceal me what I am, and be my aid
For such disguise as haply shall become
The form of my intent. I'll serve this duke;   55
Thou shalt present me as an eunuch to him.
It may be worth thy pains; for I can sing,
And speak to him in many sorts of music,

That will allow me very worth his service.
60 What else may hap, to time I will commit;
Only shape thou thy silence to my wit.
CAPTAIN   Be you his eunuch, and your mute I'll be:
When my tongue blabs, then let mine eyes not see.
VIOLA   I thank thee. Lead me on.   *Exeunt.*

1.3   *Enter* SIR TOBY BELCH *and* MARIA.

SIR TOBY   What a plague means my niece to take the
death of her brother thus? I am sure care's an enemy
to life.
MARIA   By my troth, Sir Toby, you must come in earlier
5   o' nights: your cousin, my lady, takes great exceptions
to your ill hours.
SIR TOBY   Why, let her except, before excepted.
MARIA   Ay, but you must confine yourself within the
modest limits of order.
10 SIR TOBY   Confine? I'll confine myself no finer than I
am. These clothes are good enough to drink in, and so
be these boots too: and they be not, let them hang
themselves in their own straps.
MARIA   That quaffing and drinking will undo you: I
15 heard my lady talk of it yesterday; and of a foolish
knight that you brought in one night here to be her
wooer.
SIR TOBY   Who, Sir Andrew Aguecheek?
MARIA   Ay, he.
20 SIR TOBY   He's as tall a man as any's in Illyria.
MARIA   What's that to th' purpose?
SIR TOBY   Why, he has three thousand ducats a year.
MARIA   Ay, but he'll have but a year in all these ducats.
He's a very fool, and a prodigal.
25 SIR TOBY   Fie, that you'll say so! he plays o'th' viol-de-
gamboys, and speaks three or four languages word for
word without book, and hath all the good gifts of
nature.
MARIA   He hath indeed all, most natural: for besides that
30 he's a fool, he's a great quarreller; and but that he hath
the gift of a coward to allay the gust he hath in
quarrelling, 'tis thought among the prudent he would
quickly have the gift of a grave.
SIR TOBY   By this hand, they are scoundrels and
35 substractors that say so of him. Who are they?
MARIA   They that add, moreover, he's drunk nightly in
your company.
SIR TOBY   With drinking healths to my niece: I'll drink
to her as long as there is a passage in my throat, and
40 drink in Illyria: he's a coward and a coistrel that will
not drink to my niece till his brains turn o'th' toe, like
a parish top. What, wench! *Castiliano vulgo:* for here
comes Sir Andrew Agueface.

Enter SIR ANDREW AGUECHEEK.

SIR ANDREW   Sir Toby Belch! How now, Sir Toby Belch?
45 SIR TOBY   Sweet Sir Andrew!
SIR ANDREW   Bless you, fair shrew.

MARIA   And you too, sir.
SIR TOBY   Accost, Sir Andrew, accost.
SIR ANDREW   What's that?
SIR TOBY   My niece's chambermaid.   50
SIR ANDREW   Good Mistress Accost, I desire better
acquaintance.
MARIA   My name is Mary, sir.
SIR ANDREW   Good Mistress Mary Accost –
SIR TOBY   You mistake, knight. 'Accost' is front her,   55
board her, woo her, assail her.
SIR ANDREW   By my troth, I would not undertake her in
this company. Is that the meaning of 'accost'?
MARIA   Fare you well, gentlemen.
SIR TOBY   And thou let part so, Sir Andrew, would thou   60
might'st never draw sword again!
SIR ANDREW   And you part so, mistress, I would I might
never draw sword again. Fair lady, do you think you
have fools in hand?
MARIA   Sir, I have not you by th' hand.   65
SIR ANDREW   Marry, but you shall have, and here's my
hand.
MARIA   Now, sir, thought is free. I pray you bring your
hand to th' buttery bar and let it drink.
SIR ANDREW   Wherefore, sweetheart? What's your   70
metaphor?
MARIA   It's dry, sir.
SIR ANDREW   Why, I think so: I am not such an ass but I
can keep my hand dry. But what's your jest?
MARIA   A dry jest, sir.   75
SIR ANDREW   Are you full of them?
MARIA   Ay, sir, I have them at my fingers' ends: marry,
now I let go your hand, I am barren.   *Exit Maria.*
SIR TOBY   O knight, thou lack'st a cup of canary: when
did I see thee so put down?   80
SIR ANDREW   Never in your life, I think, unless you see
canary put me down. Methinks sometimes I have no
more wit than a Christian or an ordinary man has: but
I am a great eater of beef, and I believe that does harm
to my wit.   85
SIR TOBY   No question.
SIR ANDREW   And I thought that, I'd forswear it. I'll ride
home to-morrow, Sir Toby.
SIR TOBY   *Pourquoi,* my dear knight?
SIR ANDREW   What is *pourquoi?* Do, or not do? I would I   90
had bestowed that time in the tongues that I have in
fencing, dancing, and bear-baiting. O, had I but
followed the arts!
SIR TOBY   Then hadst thou had an excellent head of hair.
SIR ANDREW   Why, would that have mended my hair?   95
SIR TOBY   Past question, for thou seest it will not curl by
nature.
SIR ANDREW
But it becomes me well enough, does't not?
SIR TOBY   Excellent, it hangs like flax on a distaff; and I
hope to see a housewife take thee between her legs,   100
and spin it off.
SIR ANDREW   Faith, I'll home to-morrow, Sir Toby; your

niece will not be seen, or if she be, it's four to one
she'll none of me: the Count himself here hard by
woos her.

SIR TOBY   She'll none o'th' Count; she'll not match
above her degree, neither in estate, years, nor wit; I
have heard her swear't. Tut, there's life in't, man.

SIR ANDREW   I'll stay a month longer. I am a fellow o'th'
strangest mind i'th' world: I delight in masques and
revels sometimes altogether.

SIR TOBY   Art thou good at these kickshawses, knight?

SIR ANDREW   As any man in Illyria, whatsoever he be,
under the degree of my betters; and yet I will not
compare with an old man.

SIR TOBY   What is thy excellence in a galliard, knight?

SIR ANDREW   Faith, I can cut a caper.

SIR TOBY   And I can cut the mutton to't.

SIR ANDREW And I think I have the back-trick simply as
strong as any man in Illyria.

SIR TOBY   Wherefore are these things hid? Wherefore
have these gifts a curtain before 'em? Are they like to
take dust, like Mistress Mall's picture? Why dost thou
not go to church in a galliard, and come home in a
coranto? My very walk should be a jig; I would not so
much as make water but in a sink-a-pace. What dost
thou mean? Is it a world to hide virtues in? I did think,
by the excellent constitution of thy leg, it was formed
under the star of a galliard.

SIR ANDREW   Ay, 'tis strong, and it does indifferent well
in a damned coloured stock. Shall we set about some
revels?

SIR TOBY   What shall we do else? were we not born
under Taurus?

SIR ANDREW   Taurus? That's sides and heart.

SIR TOBY   No, sir, it is legs and thighs. Let me see thee
caper. Ha, higher! Ha, ha, excellent!   *Exeunt.*

1.4   *Enter* VALENTINE, *and* VIOLA *in man's attire.*

VALENTINE   If the Duke continue these favours towards
you, Cesario, you are like to be much advanced: he
hath known you but three days, and already you are no
stranger.

VIOLA   You either fear his humour, or my negligence,
that you call in question the continuance of his love. Is
he inconstant, sir, in his favours?

VALENTINE   No, believe me.

Enter DUKE, CURIO *and attendants.*

VIOLA   I thank you. Here comes the Count.

ORSINO   Who saw Cesario, ho?

VIOLA   On your attendance, my lord, here.

ORSINO [*to Curio and attendants*]
    Stand you awhile aloof. [*to Viola*] Cesario,
    Thou know'st no less but all: I have unclasp'd
    To thee the book even of my secret soul.
    Therefore, good youth, address thy gait unto her,
    Be not denied access, stand at her doors,
    And tell them, there thy fixed foot shall grow

Till thou have audience.

VIOLA   Sure, my noble lord,
    If she be so abandon'd to her sorrow
    As it is spoke, she never will admit me.

ORSINO   Be clamorous, and leap all civil bounds,
    Rather than make unprofited return.

VIOLA   Say I do speak with her, my lord, what then?

ORSINO   O then unfold the passion of my love,
    Surprise her with discourse of my dear faith;
    It shall become thee well to act my woes:
    She will attend it better in thy youth,
    Than in a nuncio's of more grave aspect.

VIOLA   I think not so, my lord.

ORSINO   Dear lad, believe it;
    For they shall yet belie thy happy years,
    That say thou art a man; Diana's lip
    Is not more smooth and rubious: thy small pipe
    Is as the maiden's organ, shrill and sound,
    And all is semblative a woman's part.
    I know thy constellation is right apt
    For this affair. Some four or five attend him;
    All, if you will: for I myself am best
    When least in company. Prosper well in this,
    And thou shalt live as freely as thy lord,
    To call his fortunes thine.

VIOLA   I'll do my best
    To woo your lady: [*aside*] yet, a barful strife!
    Whoe'er I woo, myself would be his wife.   *Exeunt.*

1.5   *Enter* MARIA *and* Clown.

MARIA   Nay, either tell me where thou hast been, or I
will not open my lips so wide as a bristle may enter, in
way of thy excuse: my lady will hang thee for thy
absence.

CLOWN   Let her hang me: he that is well hanged in this
world needs to fear no colours.

MARIA   Make that good.

CLOWN   He shall see none to fear.

MARIA   A good lenten answer. I can tell thee where that
saying was born, of 'I fear no colours.'

CLOWN   Where, good Mistress Mary?

MARIA   In the wars, and that may you be bold to say in
your foolery.

CLOWN   Well, God give them wisdom that have it; and
those that are fools, let them use their talents.

MARIA   Yet you will be hanged for being so long absent;
or to be turned away – is not that as good as a hanging
to you?

CLOWN   Many a good hanging prevents a bad marriage:
and for turning away, let summer bear it out.

MARIA   You are resolute then?

CLOWN   Not so, neither, but I am resolved on two
points.

MARIA   That if one break, the other will hold: or if both
break, your gaskins fall.

CLOWN   Apt, in good faith, very apt. Well, go thy way: if
Sir Toby would leave drinking, thou wert as witty a

piece of Eve's flesh as any in Illyria.

MARIA   Peace, you rogue, no more o' that. Here comes
30   my lady: make your excuse wisely, you were best.

Exit.

Enter Lady OLIVIA, *with* MALVOLIO *and attendants.*

CLOWN   Wit, and't be thy will, put me into good fooling!
Those wits that think they have thee, do very oft prove
fools: and I that am sure I lack thee, may pass for a
wise man. For what says Quinapalus? 'Better a witty
35   fool than a foolish wit.' God bless thee, lady!

OLIVIA   Take the fool away.

CLOWN   Do you not hear, fellows? Take away the lady.

OLIVIA   Go to, y'are a dry fool: I'll no more of you.
Besides, you grow dishonest.

40 **CLOWN**   Two faults, madonna, that drink and good
counsel will amend: for give the dry fool drink, then is
the fool not dry: bid the dishonest man mend himself,
if he mend, he is no longer dishonest; if he cannot, let
the botcher mend him. Anything that's mended is but
45   patched: virtue that transgresses is but patched with
sin, and sin that amends is but patched with virtue. If
that this simple syllogism will serve, so: if it will not,
what remedy? As there is no true cuckold but calamity,
so beauty's a flower. The lady bade take away the fool,
50   therefore I say again, take her away.

OLIVIA   Sir, I bade them take away you.

CLOWN   Misprision in the highest degree! Lady, *cucullus
non facit monachum*: that's as much to say, as I wear not
motley in my brain. Good madonna, give me leave to
55   prove you a fool.

OLIVIA   Can you do it?

CLOWN   Dexteriously, good madonna.

OLIVIA   Make your proof.

CLOWN   I must catechise you for it, madonna. Good my
60   mouse of virtue, answer me.

OLIVIA   Well sir, for want of other idleness, I'll bide
your proof.

CLOWN   Good madonna, why mourn'st thou?

OLIVIA   Good fool, for my brother's death.

65 **CLOWN**   I think his soul is in hell, madonna.

OLIVIA   I know his soul is in heaven, fool.

CLOWN   The more fool, madonna, to mourn for your
brother's soul, being in heaven. Take away the fool,
gentlemen.

70 **OLIVIA**   What think you of this fool, Malvolio, doth he
not mend?

MALVOLIO   Yes, and shall do, till the pangs of death
shake him. Infirmity, that decays the wise, doth ever
make the better fool.

75 **CLOWN**   God send you, sir, a speedy infirmity, for the
better increasing your folly! Sir Toby will be sworn
that I am no fox, but he will not pass his word for
twopence that you are no fool.

OLIVIA   How say you to that, Malvolio?

80 **MALVOLIO**   I marvel your ladyship takes delight in such
a barren rascal: I saw him put down the other day

with an ordinary fool, that has no more brain than a
stone. Look you now, he's out of his guard already:
unless you laugh and minister occasion to him, he is
gagged. I protest I take these wise men, that crow so at 85
these set kind of fools, no better than the fools' zanies.

OLIVIA   O, you are sick of self-love, Malvolio, and taste
with a distempered appetite. To be generous, guiltless,
and of free disposition, is to take those things for bird-
bolts that you deem cannon-bullets. There is no 90
slander in an allowed fool, though he do nothing but
rail; nor no railing in a known discreet man, though he
do nothing but reprove.

CLOWN   Now Mercury endue thee with leasing, for thou
speak'st well of fools! 95

Enter MARIA.

MARIA   Madam, there is at the gate a young gentleman
much desires to speak with you.

OLIVIA   From the Count Orsino, is it?

MARIA   I know not, madam: 'tis a fair young man, and
well attended. 100

OLIVIA   Who of my people hold him in delay?

MARIA   Sir Toby, madam, your kinsman.

OLIVIA   Fetch him off, I pray you: he speaks nothing but
madman. Fie on him!   *Exit Maria.*
Go you, Malvolio. If it be a suit from the Count, I am 105
sick, or not at home. What you will, to dismiss it.

Exit Malvolio.
Now you see, sir, how your fooling grows old, and
people dislike it.

CLOWN   Thou hast spoke for us, madonna, as if thy
eldest son should be a fool: whose skull Jove cram with 110
brains, for here he comes, one of thy kin has a most
weak *pia mater*.

Enter SIR TOBY.

OLIVIA   By mine honour, half drunk. What is he at the
gate, cousin?

SIR TOBY   A gentleman. 115

OLIVIA   A gentleman? What gentleman?

SIR TOBY   'Tis a gentleman here – [*Belches.*] A plague o'
these pickle-herring! How now, sot?

CLOWN   Good Sir Toby!

OLIVIA   Cousin, cousin, how have you come so early by 120
this lethargy?

SIR TOBY   Lechery? I defy lechery. There's one at the
gate.

OLIVIA   Ay, marry, what is he?

SIR TOBY   Let him be the devil and he will, I care not: 125
give me faith, say I. Well, it's all one.   *Exit.*

OLIVIA   What's a drunken man like, fool?

CLOWN   Like a drowned man, a fool, and a madman: one
draught above heat makes him a fool, the second mads
him, and a third drowns him. 130

OLIVIA   Go thou and seek the crowner, and let him sit o'
my coz: for he's in the third degree of drink; he's
drowned. Go look after him.

CLOWN   He is but mad yet, madonna, and the fool shall
   look to the madman.   *Exit.*

Enter MALVOLIO.

MALVOLIO   Madam, yond young fellow swears he will
   speak with you. I told him you were sick; he takes on
   him to understand so much, and therefore comes to
   speak with you. I told him you were asleep; he seems
   to have a foreknowledge of that too, and therefore
   comes to speak with you. What is to be said to him,
   lady? He's fortified against any denial.
OLIVIA   Tell him, he shall not speak with me.
MALVOLIO   'Has been told so: and he says he'll stand at
   your door like a sheriff's post, and be the supporter to
   a bench, but he'll speak with you.
OLIVIA   What kind o' man is he?
MALVOLIO   Why, of mankind.
OLIVIA   What manner of man?
MALVOLIO   Of very ill manner: he'll speak with you, will
   you or no.
OLIVIA   Of what personage and years is he?
MALVOLIO   Not yet old enough for a man, nor young
   enough for a boy: as a squash is before 'tis a peascod,
   or a codling when 'tis almost an apple. 'Tis with him
   in standing water, between boy and man. He is very
   well-favoured, and he speaks very shrewishly. One
   would think his mother's milk were scarce out of him.
OLIVIA   Let him approach. Call in my gentlewoman.
MALVOLIO   Gentlewoman, my lady calls.   *Exit.*

Enter MARIA.

OLIVIA   Give me my veil: come, throw it o'er my face.
   We'll once more hear Orsino's embassy.

Enter VIOLA.

VIOLA   The honourable lady of the house, which is she?
OLIVIA   Speak to me, I shall answer for her. Your will?
VIOLA   Most radiant, exquisite, and unmatchable beauty
   – I pray you tell me if this be the lady of the house, for
   I never saw her. I would be loath to cast away my
   speech: for besides that it is excellently well penned, I
   have taken great pains to con it. Good beauties, let me
   sustain no scorn; I am very comptible, even to the least
   sinister usage.
OLIVIA   Whence came you, sir?
VIOLA   I can say little more than I have studied, and that
   question's out of my part. Good gentle one, give me
   modest assurance if you be the lady of the house, that
   I may proceed in my speech.
OLIVIA   Are you a comedian?
VIOLA   No, my profound heart: and yet, by the very
   fangs of malice I swear, I am not that I play. Are you
   the lady of the house?
OLIVIA   If I do not usurp myself, I am.
VIOLA   Most certain, if you are she, you do usurp
   yourself: for what is yours to bestow is not yours to
   reserve. But this is from my commission. I will on

with my speech in your praise, and then show you the
   heart of my message.
OLIVIA   Come to what is important in't: I forgive you the
   praise.
VIOLA   Alas, I took great pains to study it, and 'tis
   poetical.
OLIVIA   It is the more like to be feigned; I pray you keep
   it in. I heard you were saucy at my gates, and allowed
   your approach rather to wonder at you than to hear
   you. If you be mad, be gone: if you have reason, be
   brief: 'tis not that time of moon with me to make one
   in so skipping a dialogue.
MARIA   Will you hoist sail, sir? Here lies your way.
VIOLA   No, good swabber, I am to hull here a little
   longer. Some mollification for your giant, sweet lady!
   Tell me your mind, I am a messenger.
OLIVIA   Sure you have some hideous matter to deliver,
   when the courtesy of it is so fearful. Speak your office.
VIOLA   It alone concerns your ear. I bring no overture of
   war, no taxation of homage; I hold the olive in my
   hand: my words are as full of peace, as matter.
OLIVIA   Yet you began rudely. What are you? What
   would you?
VIOLA   The rudeness that hath appeared in me have I
   learned from my entertainment. What I am, and what
   I would, are as secret as maidenhead: to your ears,
   divinity; to any other's, profanation.
OLIVIA   Give us the place alone: we will hear this
   divinity.   *Exeunt Maria and attendants.*
   Now, sir, what is your text?
VIOLA   Most sweet lady –
OLIVIA   A comfortable doctrine, and much may be said
   of it. Where lies your text?
VIOLA   In Orsino's bosom.
OLIVIA   In his bosom? In what chapter of his bosom?
VIOLA   To answer by the method, in the first of his
   heart.
OLIVIA   O, I have read it: it is heresy. Have you no more
   to say?
VIOLA   Good madam, let me see your face.
OLIVIA   Have you any commission from your lord to
   negotiate with my face? You are now out of your text:
   but we will draw the curtain and show you the picture.
   [*unveiling*] Look you, sir, such a one I was this present.
   Is't not well done?
VIOLA   Excellently done, if God did all.
OLIVIA   'Tis in grain, sir, 'twill endure wind and
   weather.
VIOLA   'Tis beauty truly blent, whose red and white
   Nature's own sweet and cunning hand laid on.
   Lady, you are the cruell'st she alive
   If you will lead these graces to the grave
   And leave the world no copy.
OLIVIA   O sir, I will not be so hard-hearted: I will give
   out divers schedules of my beauty. It shall be
   inventoried, and every particle and utensil labelled to
   my will. As, item, two lips indifferent red; item, two

grey eyes, with lids to them; item, one neck, one chin,
and so forth. Were you sent hither to praise me?

245 VIOLA   I see you what you are, you are too proud:
But if you were the devil, you are fair.
My lord and master loves you: O, such love
Could be but recompens'd, though you were crown'd
The nonpareil of beauty!

OLIVIA   How does he love me?

VIOLA   With adorations, fertile tears,
250 With groans that thunder love, with sighs of fire.

OLIVIA
Your lord does know my mind, I cannot love him.
Yet I suppose him virtuous, know him noble,
Of great estate, of fresh and stainless youth;
In voices well divulg'd, free, learn'd, and valiant,
255 And in dimension, and the shape of nature,
A gracious person. But yet I cannot love him:
He might have took his answer long ago.

VIOLA   If I did love you in my master's flame,
With such a suff'ring, such a deadly life,
260 In your denial I would find no sense,
I would not understand it.

OLIVIA   Why, what would you?

VIOLA   Make me a willow cabin at your gate,
And call upon my soul within the house;
Write loyal cantons of contemned love,
265 And sing them loud even in the dead of night;
Halloo your name to the reverberate hills,
And make the babbling gossip of the air
Cry out 'Olivia!' O, you should not rest
Between the elements of air and earth,
But you should pity me.

270 OLIVIA   You might do much.
What is your parentage?

VIOLA   Above my fortunes, yet my state is well:
I am a gentleman.

OLIVIA   Get you to your lord:
I cannot love him: let him send no more,
275 Unless, perchance, you come to me again,
To tell me how he takes it. Fare you well:
I thank you for your pains: spend this for me.

VIOLA   I am no fee'd post, lady; keep your purse;
My master, not myself, lacks recompense.
280 Love make his heart of flint that you shall love,
And let your fervour like my master's be,
Plac'd in contempt. Farewell, fair cruelty.   *Exit.*

OLIVIA   'What is your parentage?'
'Above my fortunes, yet my state is well;
285 I am a gentleman.' I'll be sworn thou art:
Thy tongue, thy face, thy limbs, actions, and spirit
Do give thee five-fold blazon. Not too fast: soft! soft!
Unless the master were the man. How now?
Even so quickly may one catch the plague?
290 Methinks I feel this youth's perfections
With an invisible and subtle stealth
To creep in at mine eyes. Well, let it be.
What ho, Malvolio!

Enter MALVOLIO.

MALVOLIO   Here, madam, at your service.

OLIVIA   Run after that same peevish messenger
The County's man: he left this ring behind him,   295
Would I or not; tell him, I'll none of it.
Desire him not to flatter with his lord,
Nor hold him up with hopes: I am not for him.
If that the youth will come this way to-morrow,
I'll give him reasons for't. Hie thee, Malvolio.   300

MALVOLIO   Madam, I will.   *Exit.*

OLIVIA   I do I know not what, and fear to find
Mine eye too great a flatterer for my mind.
Fate, show thy force; ourselves we do not owe.
What is decreed, must be: and be this so.   *Exit.*   305

2.1   *Enter* ANTONIO *and* SEBASTIAN.

ANTONIO   Will you stay no longer? nor will you not that
I go with you?

SEBASTIAN   By your patience, no: my stars shine darkly
over me; the malignancy of my fate might perhaps
distemper yours; therefore I shall crave of you your   5
leave that I may bear my evils alone. It were a bad
recompense for your love, to lay any of them on you.

ANTONIO   Let me yet know of you whither you are
bound.

SEBASTIAN   No, sooth, sir: my determinate voyage is   10
mere extravagancy. But I perceive in you so excellent
a touch of modesty, that you will not extort from me
what I am willing to keep in: therefore it charges me in
manners the rather to express myself. You must know
of me then, Antonio, my name is Sebastian, which I   15
called Roderigo; my father was that Sebastian of
Messaline whom I know you have heard of. He left
behind him myself and a sister, both born in an hour:
if the heavens had been pleased, would we had so
ended! But you, sir, altered that, for some hour before   20
you took me from the breach of the sea was my sister
drowned.

ANTONIO   Alas the day!

SEBASTIAN   A lady, sir, though it was said she much
resembled me, was yet of many accounted beautiful: 25
but though I could not with such estimable wonder
overfar believe that, yet thus far I will boldly publish
her, she bore a mind that envy could not but call fair.
She is drowned already, sir, with salt water, though I
seem to drown her remembrance again with more.   30

ANTONIO   Pardon me, sir, your bad entertainment.

SEBASTIAN   O good Antonio, forgive me your trouble.

ANTONIO   If you will not murder me for my love, let me
be your servant.

SEBASTIAN   If you will not undo what you have done,   35
that is, kill him whom you have recovered, desire it
not. Fare ye well at once; my bosom is full of kindness,
and I am yet so near the manners of my mother, that
upon the least occasion more mine eyes will tell tales
of me. I am bound to the Count Orsino's court: 40

farewell.   *Exit.*

ANTONIO   The gentleness of all the gods go with thee!
  I have many enemies in Orsino's court,
  Else would I very shortly see thee there:
45 But come what may, I do adore thee so,
  That danger shall seem sport, and I will go.   *Exit.*

2.2   *Enter* VIOLA *and* MALVOLIO, *at several doors.*

MALVOLIO   Were not you ev'n now with the Countess
  Olivia?
VIOLA   Even now, sir; on a moderate pace, I have since
  arrived but hither.
5 MALVOLIO   She returns this ring to you, sir: you might
  have saved me my pains, to have taken it away yourself.
  She adds, moreover, that you should put your lord
  into a desperate assurance she will none of him.
  And one thing more, that you be never so hardy to
10 come again in his affairs, unless it be to report your
  lord's taking of this. Receive it so.
VIOLA   She took the ring of me, I'll none of it.
MALVOLIO   Come sir, you peevishly threw it to her: and
  her will is, it should be so returned. If it be worth
15 stooping for, there it lies, in your eye: if not, be it his
  that finds it.   *Exit.*
VIOLA   I left no ring with her: what means this lady?
  Fortune forbid my outside have not charm'd her!
  She made good view of me, indeed so much,
20 That methought her eyes had lost her tongue,
  For she did speak in starts distractedly.
  She loves me, sure; the cunning of her passion
  Invites me in this churlish messenger.
  None of my lord's ring? Why, he sent her none.
25 I am the man: if it be so, as 'tis,
  Poor lady, she were better love a dream.
  Disguise, I see thou art a wickedness,
  Wherein the pregnant enemy does much.
  How easy is it for the proper false
30 In women's waxen hearts to set their forms!
  Alas, our frailty is the cause, not we,
  For such as we are made of, such we be.
  How will this fadge? My master loves her dearly,
  And I, poor monster, fond as much on him,
35 And she, mistaken, seems to dote on me:
  What will become of this? As I am man,
  My state is desperate for my master's love:
  As I am woman (now alas the day!)
  What thriftless sighs shall poor Olivia breathe?
40 O time, thou must untangle this, not I,
  It is too hard a knot for me t'untie.   *Exit.*

2.3   *Enter* SIR TOBY *and* SIR ANDREW.

SIR TOBY   Approach, Sir Andrew; not to be abed after
  midnight, is to be up betimes; and *diluculo surgere,*
  thou know'st –
SIR ANDREW   Nay, by my troth, I know not: but I know,
5 to be up late, is to be up late.

SIR TOBY   A false conclusion: I hate it as an unfilled can.
  To be up after midnight, and to go to bed then, is
  early: so that to go to bed after midnight, is to go to
  bed betimes. Does not our life consist of the four
10 elements?
SIR ANDREW   Faith, so they say, but I think it rather
  consists of eating and drinking.
SIR TOBY   Th'art a scholar; let us therefore eat and drink.
  Marian, I say! a stoup of wine!

Enter CLOWN.

SIR ANDREW   Here comes the fool, i'faith.   15
CLOWN   How now, my hearts? Did you never see the
  picture of 'we three'?
SIR TOBY   Welcome, ass. Now let's have a catch.
SIR ANDREW   By my troth, the fool has an excellent
  breast. I had rather than forty shillings I had such a   20
  leg, and so sweet a breath to sing, as the fool has. In
  sooth, thou wast in very gracious fooling last night,
  when thou spok'st of Pigrogromitus, of the Vapians
  passing the equinoctial of Queubus: 'twas very good,
  i'faith: I sent thee sixpence for thy leman: hadst it?   25
CLOWN   I did impeticos thy gratillity: for Malvolio's
  nose is no whipstock, my lady has a white hand, and
  the Myrmidons are no bottle-ale houses.
SIR ANDREW   Excellent! Why, this is the best fooling,
  when all is done. Now a song!   30
SIR TOBY   Come on, there is sixpence for you. Let's have
  a song.
SIR ANDREW   There's a testril of me too: if one knight
  give a –
CLOWN   Would you have a love-song, or a song of good   35
  life?
SIR TOBY   A love-song, a love-song.
SIR ANDREW   Ay, ay. I care not for good life.
CLOWN   [*Sings.*]
    O mistress mine, where are you roaming?
    O stay and hear, your true love's coming,   40
        That can sing both high and low.
    Trip no further, pretty sweeting:
    Journeys end in lovers meeting,
        Every wise man's son doth know.
SIR ANDREW   Excellent good, i'faith.   45
SIR TOBY   Good, good.
CLOWN
    What is love? 'Tis not hereafter,
    Present mirth hath present laughter:
        What's to come is still unsure.
    In delay there lies no plenty,   50
    Then come kiss me, sweet and twenty:
        Youth's a stuff will not endure.
SIR ANDREW   A mellifluous voice, as I am a true knight.
SIR TOBY   A contagious breath.
SIR ANDREW   Very sweet and contagious, i'faith.   55
SIR TOBY   To hear by the nose, it is dulcet in contagion.
  But shall we make the welkin dance indeed? Shall we

rouse the night-owl in a catch that will draw three souls out of one weaver? Shall we do that?

60   SIR ANDREW   And you love me, let's do't: I am dog at a catch.

CLOWN   By'r lady, sir, and some dogs will catch well.

SIR ANDREW   Most certain. Let our catch be, 'Thou knave'.

65   CLOWN   'Hold thy peace, thou knave', knight? I shall be constrained in't to call thee knave, knight.

SIR ANDREW   'Tis not the first time I have constrained one to call me knave. Begin, fool: it begins, 'Hold thy peace'.

70   CLOWN   I shall never begin if I hold my peace.

SIR ANDREW   Good, i'faith. Come, begin.   [*Catch sung.*]

Enter MARIA.

MARIA   What a caterwauling do you keep here? If my lady have not called up her steward Malvolio and bid him turn you out of doors, never trust me.

75   SIR TOBY   My lady's a Cataian, we are politicians, Malvolio's a Peg-a-Ramsey, and [*Sings.*] 'Three merry men be we.' Am not I consanguineous? Am I not of her blood? Tilly-vally! Lady! [*Sings.*] 'There dwelt a man in Babylon, Lady, Lady'.

80   CLOWN   Beshrew me, the knight's in admirable fooling.

SIR ANDREW   Ay, he does well enough, if he be disposed, and so do I too: he does it with a better grace, but I do it more natural.

SIR TOBY [*Sings.*]   'O'the twelfth day of December –'

85   MARIA   For the love o' God, peace!

Enter MALVOLIO.

MALVOLIO   My masters, are you mad? Or what are you? Have you no wit, manners, nor honesty, but to gabble like tinkers at this time of night? Do ye make an ale-house of my lady's house, that ye squeak out your coziers' catches without any mitigation or remorse of voice? Is there no respect of place, persons, nor time in you?

SIR TOBY   We did keep time, sir, in our catches. Sneck up!

MALVOLIO   Sir Toby, I must be round with you. My lady bade me tell you, that though she harbours you as her kinsman, she's nothing allied to your disorders. If you can separate yourself and your misdemeanours, you are welcome to the house: if not, and it would please you to take leave of her, she is very willing to bid you farewell.

100   SIR TOBY [*Sings.*]   Farewell, dear heart, since I must needs be gone.

MARIA   Nay, good Sir Toby.

CLOWN [*Sings.*]   His eyes do show his days are almost done.

MALVOLIO   Is't even so?

105   SIR TOBY [*Sings.*]   But I will never die.

CLOWN [*Sings.*]   Sir Toby, there you lie.

MALVOLIO   This is much credit to you.

SIR TOBY [*Sings.*]   Shall I bid him go?

CLOWN [*Sings.*]   What and if you do?

110   SIR TOBY [*Sings.*]   Shall I bid him go, and spare not?

CLOWN [*Sings.*]   O no, no, no, no, you dare not.

SIR TOBY   Out o' time, sir? ye lie! Art any more than a steward? Dost thou think because thou art virtuous, there shall be no more cakes and ale?

115   CLOWN   Yes, by Saint Anne, and ginger shall be hot i'th' mouth too.   *Exit.*

SIR TOBY   Th'art i'th' right. Go sir, rub your chain with crumbs. A stoup of wine, Maria!

MALVOLIO   Mistress Mary, if you prized my lady's favour at anything more than contempt, you would 120 not give means for this uncivil rule; she shall know of it, by this hand.   *Exit.*

MARIA   Go shake your ears.

SIR ANDREW   'Twere as good a deed as to drink when a man's a-hungry, to challenge him the field, and then to 125 break promise with him and make a fool of him.

SIR TOBY   Do't, knight. I'll write thee a challenge; or I'll deliver thy indignation to him by word of mouth.

MARIA   Sweet Sir Toby, be patient for to-night. Since the youth of the Count's was today with my lady, she 130 is much out of quiet. For Monsieur Malvolio, let me alone with him. If I do not gull him into a nayword, and make him a common recreation, do not think I have wit enough to lie straight in my bed: I know I can do it. 135

SIR TOBY   Possess us, possess us, tell us something of him.

MARIA   Marry sir, sometimes he is a kind of Puritan.

SIR ANDREW   O, if I thought that, I'd beat him like a dog.

SIR TOBY   What, for being a Puritan? Thy exquisite 140 reason, dear knight?

SIR ANDREW   I have no exquisite reason for't, but I have reason good enough.

MARIA   The devil a Puritan that he is, or anything constantly, but a time-pleaser, an affectioned ass, that 145 cons state without book, and utters it by great swarths: the best persuaded of himself, so crammed (as he thinks) with excellencies, that it is his grounds of faith that all that look on him love him: and on that vice in him will my revenge find notable cause to work. 150

SIR TOBY   What wilt thou do?

MARIA   I will drop in his way some obscure epistles of love, wherein by the colour of his beard, the shape of his leg, the manner of his gait, the expressure of his eye, forehead, and complexion, he shall find himself 155 most feelingly personated. I can write very like my lady your niece; on a forgotten matter we can hardly make distinction of our hands.

SIR TOBY   Excellent, I smell a device.

SIR ANDREW   I have't in my nose too. 160

SIR TOBY   He shall think by the letters that thou wilt drop that they come from my niece, and that she's in love with him.

MARIA   My purpose is indeed a horse of that colour.

SIR ANDREW   And your horse now would make him an 165 ass.

MARIA   Ass, I doubt not.

SIR ANDREW   O, 'twill be admirable!

MARIA   Sport royal, I warrant you: I know my physic
170   will work with him. I will plant you two, and let the
fool make a third, where he shall find the letter:
observe his construction of it. For this night, to bed,
and dream on the event. Farewell.   *Exit.*

SIR TOBY   Good night, Penthesilea.

175   SIR ANDREW   Before me, she's a good wench.

SIR TOBY   She's a beagle, true-bred, and one that adores
me: what o' that?

SIR ANDREW   I was adored once too.

SIR TOBY   Let's to bed, knight. Thou hadst need send
180   for more money.

SIR ANDREW   If I cannot recover your niece, I am a foul
way out.

SIR TOBY   Send for money, knight; if thou hast her not
i'th' end, call me cut.

185   SIR ANDREW   If I do not, never trust me, take it how you
will.

SIR TOBY   Come, come, I'll go burn some sack, 'tis too
late to go to bed now. Come, knight, come, knight.
Exeunt.

2.4   *Enter* DUKE, VIOLA, CURIO *and others.*

ORSINO
Give me some music. Now good morrow, friends.
Now, good Cesario, but that piece of song,
That old and antic song we heard last night;
Methought it did relieve my passion much,
5   More than light airs and recollected terms
Of these most brisk and giddy-paced times.
Come, but one verse.

CURIO   He is not here, so please your lordship, that
should sing it.

10   ORSINO   Who was it?

CURIO   Feste the jester, my lord, a fool that the Lady
Olivia's father took much delight in. He is about the
house.

ORSINO   Seek him out, and play the tune the while.
Exit Curio. Music plays.

15   Come hither, boy. If ever thou shalt love,
In the sweet pangs of it remember me:
For such as I am, all true lovers are,
Unstaid and skittish in all motions else,
Save in the constant image of the creature
20   That is belov'd. How dost thou like this tune?

VIOLA   It gives a very echo to the seat
Where love is thron'd.

ORSINO   Thou dost speak masterly.
My life upon't, young though thou art, thine eye
Hath stay'd upon some favour that it loves.
Hath it not, boy?

25   VIOLA   A little, by your favour.

ORSINO   What kind of woman is't?

VIOLA   Of your complexion.

ORSINO   She is not worth thee then. What years, i'faith?

VIOLA   About your years, my lord.

ORSINO   Too old, by heaven! Let still the woman take
An elder than herself; so wears she to him,   30
So sways she level in her husband's heart:
For boy, however we do praise ourselves,
Our fancies are more giddy and unfirm,
More longing, wavering, sooner lost and worn
Than women's are.

VIOLA   I think it well, my lord.   35

ORSINO   Then let thy love be younger than thyself,
Or thy affection cannot hold the bent:
For women are as roses, whose fair flower
Being once display'd, doth fall that very hour.

VIOLA   And so they are: alas, that they are so: 40
To die, even when they to perfection grow!

Enter CURIO *and* Clown.

ORSINO   O, fellow, come, the song we had last night.
Mark it, Cesario, it is old and plain;
The spinsters and the knitters in the sun,
And the free maids that weave their thread with
bones   45
Do use to chant it: it is silly sooth,
And dallies with the innocence of love,
Like the old age.

CLOWN   Are you ready, sir?

ORSINO   Ay, prithee sing.   [*Music.*]   50

The Clown's Song

CLOWN
Come away, come away death,
And in sad cypress let me be laid.
Fie away, fie away breath,
I am slain by a fair cruel maid:
My shroud of white, stuck all with yew,   55
O prepare it.
My part of death no one so true
Did share it.

Not a flower, not a flower sweet,
On my black coffin let there be strewn: 60
Not a friend, not a friend greet
My poor corpse, where my bones shall be thrown:
A thousand thousand sighs to save,
Lay me, O where
Sad true lover never find my grave,   65
To weep there.

ORSINO   There's for thy pains. [*giving him money*]

CLOWN   No pains, sir, I take pleasure in singing, sir.

ORSINO   I'll pay thy pleasure then.

CLOWN   Truly sir, and pleasure will be paid, one time or   70
another.

ORSINO   Give me now leave to leave thee.

CLOWN   Now the melancholy god protect thee, and the
tailor make thy doublet of changeable taffeta, for thy
mind is a very opal. I would have men of such   75
constancy put to sea, that their business might be

everything, and their intent everywhere, for that's it that always makes a good voyage of nothing. Farewell. *Exit.*

ORSINO

Let all the rest give place. *Exeunt Curio and others.*

80   Once more, Cesario,

Get thee to yond same sovereign cruelty.
Tell her my love, more noble than the world,
Prizes not quantity of dirty lands;
The parts that fortune hath bestow'd upon her,

85 Tell her I hold as giddily as fortune:
But 'tis that miracle and queen of gems
That nature pranks her in, attracts my soul.

VIOLA   But if she cannot love you, sir?

ORSINO   I cannot be so answer'd.

VIOLA   Sooth, but you must.

90 Say that some lady, as perhaps there is,
Hath for your love as great a pang of heart
As you have for Olivia: you cannot love her:
You tell her so. Must she not then be answer'd?

ORSINO   There is no woman's sides

95 Can bide the beating of so strong a passion
As love doth give my heart; no woman's heart
So big, to hold so much: they lack retention.
Alas, their love may be call'd appetite,
No motion of the liver, but the palate,

100 That suffers surfeit, cloyment, and revolt;
But mine is all as hungry as the sea,
And can digest as much. Make no compare
Between that love a woman can bear me
And that I owe Olivia.

VIOLA   Ay, but I know –

105 ORSINO   What dost thou know?

VIOLA   Too well what love women to men may owe:
In faith, they are as true of heart as we.
My father had a daughter lov'd a man,
As it might be perhaps, were I a woman,
I should your lordship.

110 ORSINO   And what's her history?

VIOLA   A blank, my lord: she never told her love,
But let concealment like a worm i'th' bud
Feed on her damask cheek: she pin'd in thought,
And with a green and yellow melancholy

115 She sat like Patience on a monument,
Smiling at grief. Was not this love indeed?
We men may say more, swear more, but indeed
Our shows are more than will: for still we prove
Much in our vows, but little in our love.

120 ORSINO   But died thy sister of her love, my boy?

VIOLA   I am all the daughters of my father's house,
And all the brothers too: and yet I know not.
Sir, shall I to this lady?

ORSINO   Ay, that's the theme.
To her in haste; give her this jewel; say

125 My love can give no place, bide no denay. *Exeunt.*

2.5   *Enter* SIR TOBY, SIR ANDREW *and* FABIAN.

SIR TOBY   Come thy ways, Signior Fabian.

FABIAN   Nay, I'll come: if I lose a scruple of this sport, let me be boiled to death with melancholy.

SIR TOBY   Would'st thou not be glad to have the niggardly rascally sheep-biter come by some notable shame?   5

FABIAN   I would exult, man: you know he brought me out o' favour with my lady, about a bear-baiting here.

SIR TOBY   To anger him we'll have the bear again, and we will fool him black and blue – shall we not, Sir Andrew?   10

SIR ANDREW   And we do not, it is pity of our lives.

Enter MARIA.

SIR TOBY   Here comes the little villain. How now, my metal of India?

MARIA   Get ye all three into the box-tree. Malvolio's   15 coming down this walk; he has been yonder i'the sun practising behaviour to his own shadow this half hour: observe him, for the love of mockery; for I know this letter will make a contemplative idiot of him. Close, in the name of jesting! [*As the men hide, she drops a letter.*]   20 Lie thou there: for here comes the trout that must be caught with tickling.   *Exit.*

Enter MALVOLIO.

MALVOLIO   'Tis but fortune, all is fortune. Maria once told me she did affect me, and I have heard herself come thus near, that should she fancy, it should be one   25 of my complexion. Besides, she uses me with a more exalted respect than any one else that follows her. What should I think on't?

SIR TOBY   Here's an overweening rogue!

FABIAN   O, peace! Contemplation makes a rare turkey-   30 cock of him: how he jets under his advanced plumes!

SIR ANDREW   'Slight, I could so beat the rogue!

SIR TOBY   Peace, I say!

MALVOLIO   To be Count Malvolio!

SIR TOBY   Ah, rogue!   35

SIR ANDREW   Pistol him, pistol him!

SIR TOBY   Peace, peace!

MALVOLIO   There is example for't. The Lady of the Strachy married the yeoman of the wardrobe.

SIR ANDREW   Fie on him, Jezebel!   40

FABIAN   O peace! now he's deeply in: look how imagination blows him.

MALVOLIO   Having been three months married to her, sitting in my state –

SIR TOBY   O for a stone-bow to hit him in the eye!   45

MALVOLIO   Calling my officers about me, in my branched velvet gown, having come from a day-bed, where I have left Olivia sleeping –

SIR TOBY   Fire and brimstone!

FABIAN   O peace, peace!   50

MALVOLIO   And then to have the humour of state; and

after a demure travel of regard, telling them I know
my place, as I would they should do theirs, to ask for
my kinsman Toby.

55 SIR TOBY   Bolts and shackles!

FABIAN   O peace, peace, peace! Now, now!

MALVOLIO   Seven of my people, with an obedient start,
make out for him. I frown the while, and perchance wind
up my watch, or play with my [*touching his chain*] – some
60 rich jewel. Toby approaches; curtsies there to me –

SIR TOBY   Shall this fellow live?

FABIAN   Though our silence be drawn from us with cars,
yet peace!

MALVOLIO   I extend my hand to him thus, quenching
65 my familiar smile with a austere regard of control –

SIR TOBY   And does not Toby take you a blow o'the lips
then?

MALVOLIO   Saying, 'Cousin Toby, my fortunes having
cast me on your niece give me this prerogative of
70 speech' –

SIR TOBY   What, what?

MALVOLIO   'You must amend your drunkenness.'

SIR TOBY   Out, scab!

FABIAN   Nay, patience, or we break the sinews of our plot.

75 MALVOLIO   'Besides, you waste the treasure of your time
with a foolish knight' –

SIR ANDREW   That's me, I warrant you.

MALVOLIO   'One Sir Andrew.'

SIR ANDREW   I knew 'twas I, for many do call me fool.

80 MALVOLIO [*seeing the letter*]   What employment have we
here?

FABIAN   Now is the woodcock near the gin.

SIR TOBY   O peace! and the spirit of humours intimate
reading aloud to him!

85 MALVOLIO [*taking up the letter*]   By my life, this is my
lady's hand: these be her very C's, her U's, and her
T's, and thus makes she her great P's. It is in contempt
of question her hand.

SIR ANDREW   Her C's, her U's, and her T's: why that?

90 MALVOLIO [*Reads.*]   *To the unknown beloved, this, and my
good wishes.* Her very phrases! By your leave, wax.
Soft! and the impressure her Lucrece, with which she
uses to seal: 'tis my lady! To whom should this be?
[*He opens the letter.*]

95 FABIAN   This wins him, liver and all.

MALVOLIO [*Reads.*]   *Jove knows I love;*
But who?
Lips, do not move,
No man must know.

'No man must know'! What follows? The numbers
100 altered! 'No man must know'! – If this should be thee,
Malvolio!

SIR TOBY   Marry, hang thee, brock!

MALVOLIO [*Reads.*]
I may command where I adore;
But silence, like a Lucrece knife,
105 *With bloodless stroke my heart doth gore;*
M.O.A.I. doth sway my life.

FABIAN   A fustian riddle!

SIR TOBY   Excellent wench, say I.

MALVOLIO   'M.O.A.I. doth sway my life.' – Nay, but first
110 let me see, let me see, let me see.

FABIAN   What dish o' poison has she dressed him!

SIR TOBY   And with what wing the staniel checks at it!

MALVOLIO   'I may command where I adore.' Why, she
may command me: I serve her, she is my lady. Why,
115 this is evident to any formal capacity. There is no
obstruction in this. And the end: what should that
alphabetical position portend? If I could make that
resemble something in me! Softly! 'M.O.A.I.' –

SIR TOBY   O ay, make up that! He is now at a cold scent.

120 FABIAN   Sowter will cry upon't for all this, though it be
as rank as a fox.

MALVOLIO   'M' – Malvolio! 'M'! Why, that begins my
name!

FABIAN   Did not I say he would work it out? the cur is
125 excellent at faults.

MALVOLIO   'M' – But then there is no consonancy in the
sequel; that suffers under probation: 'A' should follow,
but 'O' does.

FABIAN   And 'O' shall end, I hope.

130 SIR TOBY   Ay, or I'll cudgel him, and make him cry 'O'!

MALVOLIO   And then 'I' comes behind.

FABIAN   Ay, and you had any eye behind you, you might
see more detraction at your heels than fortunes before
you.

135 MALVOLIO   'M.O.A.I.' This simulation is not as the
former: and yet, to crush this a little, it would bow to
me, for every one of these letters are in my name.
Soft! here follows prose. [*Reads.*]   *If this fall into thy
hand, revolve. In my stars I am above thee, but be not
140 afraid of greatness. Some are born great, some achieve
greatness, and some have greatness thrust upon 'em. Thy
fates open their hands, let thy blood and spirit embrace
them, and to inure thyself to what thou art like to be, cast
thy humble slough, and appear fresh. Be opposite with a
145 kinsman, surly with servants. Let thy tongue tang
arguments of state; put thyself into the trick of singularity.
She thus advises thee, that sighs for thee. Remember who
commended thy yellow stockings, and wished to see thee
ever cross-gartered: I say, remember. Go to, thou art
150 made, if thou desir'st to be so. If not, let me see thee a
steward still, the fellow of servants, and not worthy to
touch Fortune's fingers. Farewell. She that would alter
services with thee,*

                                   The Fortunate Unhappy.

155 Daylight and champaign discovers not more!
This is open. I will be proud, I will read politic
authors, I will baffle Sir Toby, I will wash off gross
acquaintance, I will be point-device the very man. I do
not now fool myself, to let imagination jade me; for
160 every reason excites to this, that my lady loves me. She
did commend my yellow stockings of late, she did
praise my leg being cross-gartered, and in this she
manifests herself to my love, and with a kind of

injunction drives me to these habits of her liking. I
165 thank my stars, I am happy. I will be strange, stout, in
yellow stockings, and cross-gartered, even with the
swiftness of putting on. Jove and my stars be
praised! – Here is yet a postscript. [*Reads.*] *Thou
canst not choose but know who I am. If thou entertain'st
170 my love, let it appear in thy smiling, thy smiles become
thee well. Therefore in my presence still smile, dear my
sweet, I prithee.* Jove, I thank thee, I will smile, I will
do every thing that thou wilt have me.   *Exit.*

FABIAN   I will not give my part of this sport for a pension
175   of thousands to be paid from the Sophy.

SIR TOBY   I could marry this wench for this device.

SIR ANDREW   So could I too.

SIR TOBY   And ask no other dowry with her but such
another jest.

Enter MARIA.

180 SIR ANDREW   Nor I neither.

FABIAN   Here comes my noble gull-catcher.

SIR TOBY   Wilt thou set thy foot o' my neck?

SIR ANDREW   Or o' mine either?

SIR TOBY   Shall I play my freedom at tray-trip, and
185   become thy bond-slave?

SIR ANDREW   I'faith, or I either?

SIR TOBY   Why, thou hast put him in such a dream, that
when the image of it leaves him he must run mad.

MARIA   Nay, but say true, does it work upon him?

190 SIR TOBY   Like aqua-vitae with a midwife.

MARIA   If you will then see the fruits of the sport, mark
his first approach before my lady: he will come to her
in yellow stockings, and 'tis a colour she abhors, and
cross-gartered, a fashion she detests: and he will smile
195   upon her, which will now be so unsuitable to her
disposition, being addicted to a melancholy as she is,
that it cannot but turn him into a notable contempt. If
you will see it, follow me.

SIR TOBY   To the gates of Tartar, thou most excellent
200   devil of wit!

SIR ANDREW   I'll make one too.   *Exeunt.*

3.1 *Enter* VIOLA, *and* Clown *playing on pipe and tabor.*

VIOLA   Save thee, friend, and thy music! Dost thou live
by thy tabor?

CLOWN   No, sir, I live by the church.

VIOLA   Art thou a churchman?

5 CLOWN   No such matter, sir. I do live by the church, for
I do live at my house, and my house doth stand by the
church.

VIOLA   So thou may'st say the king lies by a beggar, if a
beggar dwell near him; or the church stands by thy
10   tabor, if thy tabor stand by the church.

CLOWN   You have said, sir. To see this age! A sentence is
but a chev'ril glove to a good wit – how quickly the
wrong side may be turned outward!

VIOLA   Nay, that's certain: they that dally nicely with
15   words may quickly make them wanton.

CLOWN   I would therefore my sister had had no name,
sir.

VIOLA   Why, man?

CLOWN   Why, sir, her name's a word, and to dally with
that word might make my sister wanton. But indeed,   20
words are very rascals, since bonds disgraced them.

VIOLA   Thy reason, man?

CLOWN   Troth, sir, I can yield you none without words,
and words are grown so false, I am loath to prove
reason with them.   25

VIOLA   I warrant thou art a merry fellow, and car'st for
nothing.

CLOWN   Not so, sir, I do care for something; but in my
conscience, sir, I do not care for you: if that be to
care for nothing, sir, I would it would make you   30
invisible.

VIOLA   Art not thou the Lady Olivia's fool?

CLOWN   No indeed sir, the Lady Olivia has no folly. She
will keep no fool, sir, till she be married, and fools are
as like husbands as pilchards are to herrings, the   35
husband's the bigger. I am indeed not her fool, but her
corrupter of words.

VIOLA   I saw thee late at the Count Orsino's.

CLOWN   Foolery, sir, does walk about the orb like the
sun, it shines everywhere. I would be sorry, sir, but the   40
fool should be as oft with your master as with my
mistress: I think I saw your wisdom there.

VIOLA   Nay, and thou pass upon me, I'll no more with
thee. Hold, there's expenses for thee.   [*giving a coin*]

CLOWN   Now Jove, in his next commodity of hair, send   45
thee a beard!

VIOLA   By my troth, I'll tell thee, I am almost sick for
one, [*aside*] though I would not have it grow on my
chin. – Is thy lady within?

CLOWN   Would not a pair of these have bred, sir?   50

VIOLA   Yes, being kept together, and put to use.

CLOWN   I would play Lord Pandarus of Phrygia, sir, to
bring a Cressida to this Troilus.

VIOLA   I understand you, sir, 'tis well begged.
[*giving another coin*]

CLOWN   The matter, I hope, is not great, sir, begging but   55
a beggar: Cressida was a beggar. My lady is within, sir.
I will conster to them whence you come; who you are
and what you would are out of my welkin. I might say
'element', but the word is overworn.   *Exit.*

VIOLA   This fellow is wise enough to play the fool,   60
And to do that well, craves a kind of wit:
He must observe their mood on whom he jests,
The quality of persons, and the time,
And like the haggard, check at every feather
That comes before his eye. This is a practice   65
As full of labour as a wise man's art:
For folly that he wisely shows is fit;
But wise men, folly-fall'n, quite taint their wit.

Enter SIR TOBY *and* SIR ANDREW.

SIR TOBY   Save you, gentleman.

VIOLA   And you, sir.

SIR ANDREW   *Dieu vous garde, monsieur.*

VIOLA   *Et vous aussi: votre serviteur.*

SIR ANDREW   I hope, sir, you are, and I am yours.

SIR TOBY   Will you encounter the house? My niece is
desirous you should enter, if your trade be to her.

VIOLA   I am bound to your niece, sir; I mean, she is the
list of my voyage.

SIR TOBY   Taste your legs, sir, put them to motion.

VIOLA   My legs do better understand me, sir, than I
understand what you mean by bidding me taste my
legs.

SIR TOBY   I mean, to go, sir, to enter.

VIOLA   I will answer you with gait and entrance; but we
are prevented.

Enter OLIVIA *and* MARIA.

Most excellent accomplished lady, the heavens rain
odours on you!

SIR ANDREW   That youth's a rare courtier: 'rain odours'
– well.

VIOLA   My matter hath no voice, lady, but to your own
most pregnant and vouchsafed ear.

SIR ANDREW   'Odours', 'pregnant', and 'vouchsafed': I'll
get 'em all three all ready.

OLIVIA   Let the garden door be shut, and leave me to my
hearing.   *Exeunt Sir Toby, Sir Andrew and Maria.*
Give me your hand, sir.

VIOLA   My duty, madam, and most humble service.

OLIVIA   What is your name?

VIOLA   Cesario is your servant's name, fair princess.

OLIVIA   My servant, sir? 'Twas never merry world
Since lowly feigning was call'd compliment:
Y'are servant to the Count Orsino, youth.

VIOLA   And he is yours, and his must needs be yours:
Your servant's servant is your servant, madam.

OLIVIA   For him, I think not on him: for his thoughts,
Would they were blanks, rather than fill'd with me.

VIOLA   Madam, I come to whet your gentle thoughts
On his behalf.

OLIVIA   O, by your leave, I pray you!
I bade you never speak again of him;
But would you undertake another suit,
I had rather hear you to solicit that,
Than music from the spheres.

VIOLA   Dear lady –

OLIVIA   Give me leave, beseech you. I did send,
After the last enchantment you did here,
A ring in chase of you. So did I abuse
Myself, my servant, and, I fear me, you.
Under your hard construction must I sit,
To force that on you in a shameful cunning
Which you knew none of yours. What might you think?
Have you not set mine honour at the stake,
And baited it with all th'unmuzzled thoughts
That tyrannous heart can think? To one of your
receiving

Enough is shown; a cypress, not a bosom,
Hides my heart: so, let me hear you speak.

VIOLA   I pity you.

OLIVIA   That's a degree to love.

VIOLA   No, not a grize: for 'tis a vulgar proof
That very oft we pity enemies.

OLIVIA   Why then methinks 'tis time to smile again.
O world, how apt the poor are to be proud!
If one should be a prey, how much the better
To fall before the lion than the wolf! [*Clock strikes.*]
The clock upbraids me with the waste of time.
Be not afraid, good youth, I will not have you,
And yet when wit and youth is come to harvest,
Your wife is like to reap a proper man.
There lies your way, due west.

VIOLA   Then westward ho!
Grace and good disposition attend your ladyship!
You'll nothing, madam, to my lord, by me?

OLIVIA   Stay:
I prithee tell me what thou think'st of me.

VIOLA   That you do think you are not what you are.

OLIVIA   If I think so, I think the same of you.

VIOLA   Then think you right; I am not what I am.

OLIVIA   I would you were as I would have you be.

VIOLA   Would it be better, madam, than I am?
I wish it might, for now I am your fool.

OLIVIA [*aside*]   O what a deal of scorn looks beautiful
In the contempt and anger of his lip!
A murd'rous guilt shows not itself more soon
Than love that would seem hid. Love's night is
noon. –
Cesario, by the roses of the spring,
By maidhood, honour, truth, and everything,
I love thee so, that maugre all thy pride,
Nor wit nor reason can my passion hide.
Do not extort thy reasons from this clause,
For that I woo, thou therefore hast no cause;
But rather reason thus with reason fetter:
Love sought is good, but given unsought is better.

VIOLA   By innocence I swear, and by my youth,
I have one heart, one bosom, and one truth,
And that no woman has; nor never none
Shall mistress be of it, save I alone.
And so adieu, good madam; never more
Will I my master's tears to you deplore.

OLIVIA   Yet come again: for thou perhaps mayst move
That heart which now abhors, to like his love. *Exeunt.*

3.2   *Enter* SIR TOBY, SIR ANDREW *and* FABIAN.

SIR ANDREW   No, faith, I'll not stay a jot longer.

SIR TOBY   Thy reason, dear venom, give thy reason.

FABIAN   You must needs yield your reason, Sir Andrew.

SIR ANDREW   Marry, I saw your niece do more favours to
the Count's serving-man than ever she bestowed upon
me: I saw't i'th' orchard.

SIR TOBY   Did she see thee the while, old boy, tell me that?

SIR ANDREW   As plain as I see you now.

10   FABIAN   This was a great argument of love in her toward
          you.

SIR ANDREW   'Slight! will you make an ass o' me?

FABIAN   I will prove it legitimate, sir, upon the oaths of
          judgment and reason.

15   SIR TOBY   And they have been grand-jurymen since
          before Noah was a sailor.

FABIAN   She did show favour to the youth in your sight
          only to exasperate you, to awake your dormouse
          valour, to put fire in your heart, and brimstone in your
20   liver. You should then have accosted her, and with
          some excellent jests, fire-new from the mint, you
          should have banged the youth into dumbness. This
          was looked for at your hand, and this was balked: the
          double gilt of this opportunity you let time wash off,
25   and you are now sailed into the north of my lady's
          opinion, where you will hang like an icicle on a
          Dutchman's beard, unless you do redeem it by some
          laudable attempt, either of valour or policy.

SIR ANDREW   And't be any way, it must be with valour,
30   for policy I hate: I had as lief be a Brownist as a
          politician.

SIR TOBY   Why then, build me thy fortunes upon the
          basis of valour. Challenge me the Count's youth to
          fight with him, hurt him in eleven places: my niece
35   shall take note of it; and assure thyself there is no love-
          broker in the world can more prevail in man's
          commendation with woman than report of valour.

FABIAN   There is no way but this, Sir Andrew.

SIR ANDREW   Will either of you bear me a challenge to
40   him?

SIR TOBY   Go, write it in a martial hand, be curst and
          brief: it is no matter how witty, so it be eloquent and
          full of invention. Taunt him with the licence of ink. If
          thou thou'st him some thrice, it shall not be amiss, and
45   as many lies as will lie in thy sheet of paper, although
          the sheet were big enough for the bed of Ware in
          England, set 'em down. Go, about it. Let there be gall
          enough in thy ink, though thou write with a goose-
          pen, no matter: about it.

50   SIR ANDREW   Where shall I find you?

SIR TOBY   We'll call thee at thy cubiculo. Go!

                                                Exit Sir Andrew.

FABIAN   This is a dear manikin to you, Sir Toby.

SIR TOBY   I have been dear to him, lad, some two
          thousand strong, or so.

55   FABIAN   We shall have a rare letter from him; but you'll
          not deliver't.

SIR TOBY   Never trust me then: and by all means stir on
          the youth to an answer. I think oxen and wainropes
          cannot hale them together. For Andrew, if he were
60   opened and you find so much blood in his liver as
          will clog the foot of a flea, I'll eat the rest of th'
          anatomy.

FABIAN   And his opposite, the youth, bears in his visage
          no great presage of cruelty.

                                Enter MARIA.

SIR TOBY   Look where the youngest wren of nine comes.   65

MARIA   If you desire the spleen, and will laugh
          yourselves into stitches, follow me. Yond gull Malvolio
          is turned heathen, a very renegado; for there is no
          Christian that means to be saved by believing rightly
          can ever believe such impossible passages of   70
          grossness. He's in yellow stockings!

SIR TOBY   And cross-gartered?

MARIA   Most villainously; like a pedant that keeps a
          school i'th' church. I have dogged him like his
          murderer. He does obey every point of the letter that I   75
          dropped to betray him: he does smile his face into
          more lines than is in the new map with the
          augmentation of the Indies: you have not seen such a
          thing as 'tis. I can hardly forbear hurling things at him.
          I know my lady will strike him: if she do, he'll smile,   80
          and take't for a great favour.

SIR TOBY   Come bring us, bring us where he is.

                                                Exeunt omnes.

3.3   *Enter* SEBASTIAN *and* ANTONIO.

SEBASTIAN   I would not by my will have troubled you,
          But since you make your pleasure of your pains,
          I will no further chide you.

ANTONIO   I could not stay behind you: my desire,
          More sharp than filed steel, did spur me forth: 5
          And not all love to see you (though so much
          As might have drawn one to a longer voyage)
          But jealousy what might befall your travel,
          Being skilless in these parts: which to a stranger,
          Unguided and unfriended, often prove   10
          Rough and unhospitable. My willing love,
          The rather by these arguments of fear,
          Set forth in your pursuit.

SEBASTIAN   My kind Antonio,
          I can no other answer make, but thanks,
          And thanks, and ever thanks; and oft good turns   15
          Are shuffled off with such uncurrent pay:
          But were my worth, as is my conscience, firm,
          You should find better dealing. What's to do?
          Shall we go see the relics of this town?

ANTONIO   To-morrow, sir; best first go see your lodging.   20

SEBASTIAN   I am not weary, and 'tis long to night.
          I pray you, let us satisfy our eyes
          With the memorials and the things of fame
          That do renown this city.

ANTONIO   Would you'd pardon me:
          I do not without danger walk these streets.   25
          Once in a sea-fight 'gainst the Count his galleys,
          I did some service, of such note indeed,
          That were I ta'en here it would scarce be answer'd.

SEBASTIAN   Belike you slew great number of his people.

ANTONIO   Th'offence is not of such a bloody nature,   30
          Albeit the quality of the time and quarrel
          Might well have given us bloody argument.

It might have since been answer'd in repaying
What we took from them, which for traffic's sake
35 Most of our city did. Only myself stood out,
For which, if I be lapsed in this place,
I shall pay dear.
SEBASTIAN   Do not then walk too open.
ANTONIO   It doth not fit me. Hold, sir, here's my purse.
In the south suburbs, at the Elephant,
40 Is best to lodge: I will bespeak our diet,
Whiles you beguile the time, and feed your
    knowledge
With viewing of the town: there shall you have me.
SEBASTIAN   Why I your purse?
ANTONIO   Haply your eye shall light upon some toy
45 You have desire to purchase: and your store,
I think, is not for idle markets, sir.
SEBASTIAN   I'll be your purse-bearer, and leave you for
An hour.
ANTONIO   To th'Elephant.
SEBASTIAN   I do remember.   *Exeunt separately.*

3.4   *Enter* OLIVIA *and* MARIA.

OLIVIA [*aside*]   I have sent after him, he says he'll come:
How shall I feast him? What bestow of him?
For youth is bought more oft than begg'd or
    borrow'd.
I speak too loud. –
5 Where's Malvolio? He is sad and civil,
And suits well for a servant with my fortunes:
Where is Malvolio?
MARIA   He's coming, madam, but in very strange
manner. He is sure possessed, madam.
10 OLIVIA   Why, what's the matter? Does he rave?
MARIA   No, madam, he does nothing but smile: your
ladyship were best to have some guard about you if he
come, for sure the man is tainted in's wits.
OLIVIA   Go call him hither.   *Exit Maria.*
          I am as mad as he
15 If sad and merry madness equal be.

Enter MALVOLIO *with* MARIA.

How now, Malvolio?
MALVOLIO   Sweet Lady, ho, ho!
OLIVIA   Smil'st thou? I sent for thee upon a sad occasion.
MALVOLIO   Sad, lady? I could be sad: this does make
20 some obstruction in the blood, this cross-gartering; but
what of that? If it please the eye of one, it is with me as
the very true sonnet is: 'Please one, and please all'.
OLIVIA   Why, how dost thou, man? What is the matter
with thee?
25 MALVOLIO   Not black in my mind, though yellow in my
legs. It did come to his hands, and commands shall be
executed. I think we do know the sweet Roman hand.
OLIVIA   Wilt thou go to bed, Malvolio?
MALVOLIO   To bed? Ay, sweetheart, and I'll come to
30 thee.

OLIVIA   God comfort thee! Why dost thou smile so, and
kiss thy hand so oft?
MARIA   How do you, Malvolio?
MALVOLIO   At your request? Yes, nightingales answer
daws!   35
MARIA   Why appear you with this ridiculous boldness
before my lady?
MALVOLIO   'Be not afraid of greatness': 'twas well writ.
OLIVIA   What mean'st thou by that, Malvolio?
MALVOLIO   'Some are born great' –   40
OLIVIA   Ha?
MALVOLIO   'Some achieve greatness' –
OLIVIA   What say'st thou?
MALVOLIO   'And some have greatness thrust upon
them.'   45
OLIVIA   Heaven restore thee!
MALVOLIO   'Remember who commended thy yellow
stockings' –
OLIVIA   Thy yellow stockings?
MALVOLIO   'And wished to see thee cross-gartered.'   50
OLIVIA   Cross-gartered?
MALVOLIO   'Go to, thou art made, if thou desir'st to be
so:' –
OLIVIA   Am I made?
MALVOLIO   'If not, let me see thee a servant still.'   55
OLIVIA   Why, this is very midsummer madness.

Enter Servant.

SERVANT   Madam, the young gentleman of the Count
Orsino's is returned; I could hardly entreat him back.
He attends your ladyship's pleasure.
OLIVIA   I'll come to him.   *Exit Servant.*   60
Good Maria, let this fellow be looked to. Where's my
cousin Toby? Let some of my people have a special
care of him; I would not have him miscarry for the half
of my dowry.
          Exeunt Olivia and Maria different ways.
MALVOLIO   O ho, do you come near me now? No worse   65
man than Sir Toby to look to me! This concurs
directly with the letter: she sends him on purpose, that
I may appear stubborn to him; for she incites me to
that in the letter. 'Cast thy humble slough,' says she;
'be opposite with a kinsman, surly with servants, let   70
thy tongue tang arguments of state, put thyself into
the trick of singularity': and consequently sets down
the manner how: as, a sad face, a reverend carriage, a
slow tongue, in the habit of some sir of note, and so
forth. I have limed her, but it is Jove's doing, and Jove   75
make me thankful! And when she went away now, 'Let
this fellow be looked to' – 'fellow'! – not Malvolio, nor
after my degree, but 'fellow'. Why, everything adheres
together, that no dram of a scruple, no scruple of a
scruple, no obstacle, no incredulous or unsafe   80
circumstance – what can be said? – nothing that can
be can come between me and the full prospect of my
hopes. Well, Jove, not I, is the doer of this, and he is
to be thanked.

Enter SIR TOBY, FABIAN *and* MARIA.

85 SIR TOBY   Which way is he, in the name of sanctity? If all the devils of hell be drawn in little, and Legion himself possessed him, yet I'll speak to him.

FABIAN   Here he is, here he is. How is't with you, sir? How is't with you, man?

90 MALVOLIO   Go off, I discard you. Let me enjoy my private. Go off.

MARIA   Lo, how hollow the fiend speaks within him! Did not I tell you? Sir Toby, my lady prays you to have a care of him.

95 MALVOLIO   [*aside*]   Ah ha! does she so?

SIR TOBY   Go to, go to: peace, peace, we must deal gently with him. Let me alone. How do you, Malvolio? How is't with you? What, man, defy the devil! Consider, he's an enemy to mankind.

100 MALVOLIO   Do you know what you say?

MARIA   La you, and you speak ill of the devil, how he takes it at heart! Pray God he be not betwitched!

FABIAN   Carry his water to th' wise woman.

MARIA   Marry, and it shall be done to-morrow morning, if I live. My lady would not lose him for more than I'll say.
105

MALVOLIO   How now, mistress?

MARIA   O Lord!

SIR TOBY   Prithee hold thy peace, this is not the way. Do you not see you move him? Let me alone with him.
110

FABIAN   No way but gentleness, gently, gently: the fiend is rough, and will not be roughly used.

SIR TOBY   Why, how now, my bawcock? How dost thou, chuck?

115 MALVOLIO   Sir!

SIR TOBY   Ay, biddy, come with me. What, man, 'tis not for gravity to play at cherry-pit with Satan. Hang him, foul collier!

MARIA   Get him to say his prayers, good Sir Toby, get him to pray.
120

MALVOLIO   My prayers, minx!

MARIA   No, I warrant you, he will not hear of godliness.

MALVOLIO   Go hang yourselves all: you are idle, shallow things, I am not of your element: you shall know more hereafter.   *Exit.*
125

SIR TOBY   Is't possible?

FABIAN   If this were played upon a stage now, I could condemn it as an improbable fiction.

SIR TOBY   His very genius hath taken the infection of the device, man.
130

MARIA   Nay, pursue him now, lest the device take air, and taint.

FABIAN   Why, we shall make him mad indeed.

MARIA   The house will be the quieter.

135 SIR TOBY   Come, we'll have him in a dark room and bound. My niece is already in the belief that he's mad: we may carry it thus for our pleasure, and his penance, till our very pastime, tired out of breath, prompt us to have mercy on him; at which time we will bring the device to the bar, and crown thee for a finder of madmen. But see, but see!
140

Enter SIR ANDREW.

FABIAN   More matter for a May morning!

SIR ANDREW   Here's the challenge, read it: I warrant there's vinegar and pepper in't.

FABIAN   Is't so saucy?
145

SIR ANDREW   Ay, is't, I warrant him: do but read.

SIR TOBY   Give me. [*Reads.*] *Youth, whatsoever thou art, thou art but a scurvy fellow.*

FABIAN   Good, and valiant.

SIR TOBY   *Wonder not, nor admire not in thy mind, why I do call thee so, for I will show thee no reason for't.*
150

FABIAN   A good note; that keeps you from the blow of the law.

SIR TOBY   *Thou com'st to the Lady Olivia, and in my sight she uses thee kindly: but thou liest in thy throat; that is not the matter I challenge thee for.*
155

FABIAN   Very brief, and to exceeding good sense [*aside*] –less.

SIR TOBY   *I will waylay thee going home, where if it be thy chance to kill me –*
160

FABIAN   Good.

SIR TOBY   *Thou kill'st me like a rogue and a villain.*

FABIAN   Still you keep o' th' windy side of the law: good.

SIR TOBY   *Fare thee well, and God have mercy upon one of our souls! He may have mercy upon mine, but my hope is better, and so look to thyself. Thy friend, as thou usest him, and thy sworn enemy,*
165

                                                          Andrew Aguecheek.

If this letter move him not, his legs cannot. I'll give't him.
170

MARIA   You may have very fit occasion for't: he is now in some commerce with my lady, and will by and by depart.

SIR TOBY   Go, Sir Andrew: scout me for him at the corner of the orchard, like a bum-baily. So soon as ever thou see'st him, draw, and as thou draw'st, swear horrible: for it comes to pass oft, that a terrible oath, with a swaggering accent sharply twanged off, gives manhood more approbation than ever proof itself would have earned him. Away!
175
180

SIR ANDREW   Nay, let me alone for swearing.   *Exit.*

SIR TOBY   Now will not I deliver his letter: for the behaviour of the young gentleman gives him out to be of good capacity and breeding: his employment between his lord and my niece confirms no less. Therefore this letter, being so excellently ignorant, will breed no terror in the youth: he will find it comes from a clodpole. But, sir, I will deliver his challenge by word of mouth, set upon Aguecheek a notable report of valour, and drive the gentleman (as I know his youth will aptly receive it) into a most hideous opinion of his rage, skill, fury, and impetuosity. This will so fright
185
190

them both that they will kill one another by the look,
like cockatrices.

Enter OLIVIA *and* VIOLA.

FABIAN   Here he comes with your niece: give them way
till he take leave, and presently after him.

SIR TOBY   I will meditate the while upon some horrid
message for a challenge.

Exeunt Sir Toby, Fabian and Maria.

OLIVIA   I have said too much unto a heart of stone,
And laid mine honour too unchary out:
There's something in me that reproves my fault:
But such a headstrong potent fault it is,
That it but mocks reproof.

VIOLA   With the same 'haviour that your passion bears
Goes on my master's griefs.

OLIVIA   Here, wear this jewel for me, 'tis my picture:
Refuse it not, it hath no tongue to vex you:
And I beseech you come again to-morrow.
What shall you ask of me that I'll deny,
That honour sav'd may upon asking give?

VIOLA   Nothing but this, your true love for my master.

OLIVIA   How with mine honour may I give him that
Which I have given to you?

VIOLA   I will acquit you.

OLIVIA   Well, come again to-morrow. Fare thee well;
A fiend like thee might bear my soul to hell.   *Exit.*

Enter SIR TOBY *and* FABIAN.

SIR TOBY   Gentleman, God save thee.

VIOLA   And you, sir.

SIR TOBY   That defence thou hast, betake thee to't. Of
what nature the wrongs are thou hast done him, I
know not: but thy intercepter, full of despite, bloody as
the hunter, attends thee at the orchard-end. Dismount
thy tuck, be yare in thy preparation, for thy assailant is
quick, skilful, and deadly.

VIOLA   You mistake, sir; I am sure no man hath any
quarrel to me: my remembrance is very free and clear
from any image of offence done to any man.

SIR TOBY   You'll find it otherwise, I assure you.
Therefore, if you hold your life at any price, betake
you to your guard: for your opposite hath in him what
youth, strength, skill, and wrath, can furnish man
withal.

VIOLA   I pray you, sir, what is he?

SIR TOBY   He is knight, dubbed with unhatched rapier,
and on carpet consideration, but he is a devil in private
brawl. Souls and bodies hath he divorced three, and
his incensement at this moment is so implacable that
satisfaction can be none but by pangs of death and
sepulchre. Hob, nob, is his word: give't or take't.

VIOLA   I will return again into the house, and desire
some conduct of the lady. I am no fighter. I have heard
of some kind of men that put quarrels purposely on
others to taste their valour: belike this is a man of that
quirk.

SIR TOBY   Sir, no: his indignation derives itself out of a
very competent injury; therefore get you on, and give
him his desire. Back you shall not to the house, unless
you undertake that with me which with as much safety
you might answer him; therefore on, or strip your
sword stark naked: for meddle you must, that's
certain, or forswear to wear iron about you.

VIOLA   This is as uncivil as strange. I beseech you, do
me this courteous office, as to know of the knight what
my offence to him is: it is something of my negligence,
nothing of my purpose.

SIR TOBY   I will do so. Signior Fabian, stay you by this
gentleman till my return.   *Exit Sir Toby.*

VIOLA   Pray you, sir, do you know of this matter?

FABIAN   I know the knight is incensed against you, even
to a mortal arbitrement, but nothing of the
circumstance more.

VIOLA   I beseech you, what manner of man is he?

FABIAN   Nothing of that wonderful promise, to read him
by his form, as you are like to find him in the proof of
his valour. He is indeed, sir, the most skilful, bloody,
and fatal opposite that you could possibly have found
in any part of Illyria. Will you walk towards him, I will
make your peace with him if I can.

VIOLA   I shall be much bound to you for't. I am one that
had rather go with sir priest than sir knight: I care not
who knows so much of my mettle.   *Exeunt.*

Enter SIR TOBY *and* SIR ANDREW.

SIR TOBY   Why, man, he's a very devil, I have not seen
such a firago. I had a pass with him, rapier, scabbard,
and all: and he gives me the stuck in with such a
mortal motion that it is inevitable; and on the answer,
he pays you as surely as your feet hits the ground they
step on. They say he has been fencer to the Sophy.

SIR ANDREW   Pox on't, I'll not meddle with him.

SIR TOBY   Ay, but he will not now be pacified: Fabian
can scarce hold him yonder.

SIR ANDREW   Plague on't, and I thought he had been
valiant, and so cunning in fence, I'd have seen him
damned ere I'd have challenged him. Let him let the
matter slip, and I'll give him my horse, grey Capilet.

SIR TOBY   I'll make the motion. Stand here, make a good
show on't: this shall end without the perdition of
souls. [*aside*] Marry, I'll ride your horse as well as I
ride you.

Enter FABIAN *and* VIOLA.

[*to Fabian*] I have his horse to take up the quarrel. I
have persuaded him the youth's a devil.

FABIAN   He is as horribly conceited of him, and pants
and looks pale, as if a bear were at his heels.

SIR TOBY [*to Viola*]   There's no remedy, sir, he will fight
with you for's oath sake. Marry, he hath better
bethought him of his quarrel, and he finds that now
scarce to be worth talking of. Therefore draw for the
supportance of his vow; he protests he will not hurt

you.

VIOLA [*aside*]   Pray God defend me! A little thing would
make me tell them how much I lack of a man.

FABIAN [*to Sir Andrew*]   Give ground if you see him
furious.

SIR TOBY   Come, Sir Andrew, there's no remedy, the
gentleman will for his honour's sake have one bout
with you; he cannot by the duello avoid it: but he has
promised me, as he is a gentleman and a soldier, he will
not hurt you. Come on, to't.

SIR ANDREW   Pray God he keep his oath!

Enter ANTONIO.

VIOLA   I do assure you, 'tis against my will.
[*Sir Andrew and Viola draw.*]

ANTONIO [*drawing*]
Put up your sword! If this young gentleman
Have done offence, I take the fault on me:
If you offend him, I for him defy you.

SIR TOBY   You, sir? Why, what are you?

ANTONIO   One, sir, that for his love dares yet do more
Than you have heard him brag to you he will.

SIR TOBY   Nay, if you be an undertaker, I am for you.
[*Draws.*]

Enter Officers.

FABIAN   O good Sir Toby, hold! here come the officers.

SIR TOBY [*to Antonio*]   I'll be with you anon.

VIOLA [*to Sir Andrew*]   Pray sir, put your sword up, if
you please.

SIR ANDREW   Marry, will I, sir: and for that I promised
you, I'll be as good as my word. He will bear you easily,
and reins well.

1 OFFICER   This is the man; do thy office.

2 OFFICER   Antonio, I arrest thee at the suit
Of Count Orsino.

ANTONIO   You do mistake me, sir.

1 OFFICER   No, sir, no jot: I know your favour well,
Though now you have no sea-cap on your head.
Take him away, he knows I know him well.

ANTONIO   I must obey.
[*to Viola*]   This comes with seeking you;
But there's no remedy, I shall answer it.
What will you do, now my necessity
Makes me to ask you for my purse? It grieves me
Much more for what I cannot do for you,
Than what befalls myself. You stand amaz'd,
But be of comfort.

2 OFFICER   Come, sir, away.

ANTONIO   I must entreat of you some of that money.

VIOLA   What money, sir?
For the fair kindness you have show'd me here,
And part being prompted by your present trouble,
Out of my lean and low ability
I'll lend you something. My having is not much;

I'll make division of my present with you.
Hold, there's half my coffer. [*Offers Antonio money.*]

ANTONIO   Will you deny me now? [*Refuses it.*]
Is't possible that my deserts to you
Can lack persuasion? Do not tempt my misery,
Lest that it make me so unsound a man
As to upbraid you with those kindnesses
That I have done for you.

VIOLA   I know of none,
Nor know I you by voice or any feature.
I hate ingratitude more in a man
Than lying, vainness, babbling drunkenness,
Or any taint of vice whose strong corruption
Inhabits our frail blood.

ANTONIO   O heavens themselves!

2 OFFICER   Come sir, I pray you go.

ANTONIO
Let me speak a little. This youth that you see here
I snatch'd one half out of the jaws of death,
Reliev'd him with such sanctity of love;
And to his image, which methought did promise
Most venerable worth, did I devotion.

1 OFFICER   What's that to us? The time goes by. Away!

ANTONIO   But O how vile an idol proves this god!
Thou hast, Sebastian, done good feature shame.
In nature there's no blemish but the mind:
None can be call'd deform'd but the unkind.
Virtue is beauty, but the beauteous evil
Are empty trunks, o'er-flourish'd by the devil.

1 OFFICER
The man grows mad, away with him! Come, come, sir.

ANTONIO   Lead me on.   *Exit with officers.*

VIOLA   Methinks his words do from such passion fly
That he believes himself; so do not I:
Prove true, imagination, O prove true,
That I, dear brother, be now ta'en for you!

SIR TOBY   Come hither, knight, come hither, Fabian.
We'll whisper o'er a couplet or two of most sage saws.

VIOLA   He nam'd Sebastian. I my brother know
Yet living in my glass; even such and so
In favour was my brother, and he went
Still in this fashion, colour, ornament,
For him I imitate. O if it prove,
Tempests are kind, and salt waves fresh in love! *Exit.*

SIR TOBY   A very dishonest paltry boy, and more a
coward than a hare; his dishonesty appears in leaving
his friend here in necessity, and denying him; and for
his cowardship, ask Fabian.

FABIAN   A coward, a most devout coward, religious in it.

SIR ANDREW   'Slid, I'll after him again, and beat him.

SIR TOBY   Do, cuff him soundly, but never draw thy
sword.

SIR ANDREW   And I do not –   *Exit.*

FABIAN   Come, let's see the event.

SIR TOBY   I dare lay any money 'twill be nothing yet.
                                        Exeunt

4.1   *Enter* SEBASTIAN *and* Clown.

CLOWN   Will you make me believe that I am not sent for
you?

SEBASTIAN   Go to, go to, thou art a foolish fellow,
Let me be clear of thee.

CLOWN   Well held out, i'faith! No, I do not know you,
nor I am not sent to you by my lady, to bid you come
speak with her; nor your name is not Master Cesario;
nor this is not my nose neither. Nothing that is so, is so.

SEBASTIAN   I prithee vent thy folly somewhere else,
Thou know'st not me.

CLOWN   Vent my folly! He has heard that word of some
great man, and now applies it to a fool. Vent my folly!
I am afraid this great lubber, the world, will prove a
cockney. I prithee now, ungird thy strangeness, and
tell me what I shall vent to my lady. Shall I vent to her
that thou art coming?

SEBASTIAN   I prithee, foolish Greek, depart from me.
There's money for thee: if you tarry longer,
I shall give worse payment.

CLOWN   By my troth, thou hast an open hand. These
wise men that give fools money get themselves a good
report – after fourteen years' purchase.

Enter SIR ANDREW, SIR TOBY *and* FABIAN.

SIR ANDREW   Now sir, have I met you again? There's for
you! [*Strikes Sebastian.*]

SEBASTIAN   Why, there's for thee, and there, and there!
[*Beats Sir Andrew.*] Are all the people mad?

SIR TOBY   Hold, sir, or I'll throw your dagger o'er the
house.

CLOWN   This will I tell my lady straight: I would not be
in some of your coats for twopence.   *Exit.*

SIR TOBY   Come on, sir, hold!

SIR ANDREW   Nay, let him alone, I'll go another way to
work with him: I'll have an action of battery against
him, if there be any law in Illyria; though I struck him
first, yet it's no matter for that.

SEBASTIAN   Let go thy hand!

SIR TOBY   Come, sir, I will not let you go. Come, my
young soldier, put up your iron: you are well fleshed.
Come on!

SEBASTIAN   I will be free from thee. What would'st thou
now?
If thou dar'st tempt me further, draw thy sword.
[*Draws.*]

SIR TOBY   What, what! Nay, then, I must have an ounce
or two of this malapert blood from you. [*Draws.*]

Enter OLIVIA.

OLIVIA   Hold, Toby! on thy life I charge thee, hold!

SIR TOBY   Madam!

OLIVIA   Will it be ever thus? Ungracious wretch,
Fit for the mountains and the barbarous caves,
Where manners ne'er were preach'd! Out of my sight!
Be not offended, dear Cesario.

Rudesby, be gone!
        Exeunt Sir Toby, Sir Andrew and Fabian.
                        I prithee, gentle friend,
Let thy fair wisdom, not thy passion, sway
In this uncivil and unjust extent
Against thy peace. Go with me to my house,
And hear thou there how many fruitless pranks   55
This ruffian hath botch'd up, that thou thereby
May'st smile at this. Thou shalt not choose but go:
Do not deny. Beshrew his soul for me,
He started one poor heart of mine, in thee.

SEBASTIAN   What relish is in this? How runs the stream?   60
Or I am mad, or else this is a dream:
Let fancy still my sense in Lethe steep;
If it be thus to dream, still let me sleep!

OLIVIA
Nay, come, I prithee; would thou'dst be rul'd by me!

SEBASTIAN   Madam, I will.

OLIVIA   O, say so, and so be. *Exeunt.*   65

4.2   *Enter* MARIA *and* Clown.

MARIA   Nay, I prithee put on this gown, and this beard;
make him believe thou art Sir Topas the curate; do it
quickly. I'll call Sir Toby the whilst.   *Exit.*

CLOWN   Well, I'll put it on, and I will dissemble myself
in't, and I would I were the first that ever dissembled   5
in such a gown. I am not tall enough to become the
function well, nor lean enough to be thought a good
student; but to be said an honest man and a good
housekeeper goes as fairly as to say a careful man and
a great scholar. The competitors enter.   10

Enter SIR TOBY *and* MARIA.

SIR TOBY   Jove bless thee, Master Parson.

CLOWN   *Bonos dies*, Sir Toby: for as the old hermit of
Prague, that never saw pen and ink, very wittily said to
a niece of King Gorboduc, 'That that is, is': so I, being
Master Parson, am Master Parson; for what is 'that'   15
but 'that'? and 'is' but 'is'?

SIR TOBY   To him, Sir Topas.

CLOWN   What ho, I say! Peace in this prison!

SIR TOBY   The knave counterfeits well: a good knave.

MALVOLIO *within.*

MALVOLIO   Who calls there?   20

CLOWN   Sir Topas the curate, who comes to visit
Malvolio the lunatic.

MALVOLIO   Sir Topas, Sir Topas, good Sir Topas, go to
my lady.

CLOWN   Out, hyperbolical fiend! how vexest thou this   25
man! Talkest thou nothing but of ladies?

SIR TOBY   Well said, Master Parson.

MALVOLIO   Sir Topas, never was man thus wronged.
Good Sir Topas, do not think I am mad. They have
laid me here in hideous darkness.   30

CLOWN   Fie, thou dishonest Satan! (I call thee by the

most modest terms, for I am one of those gentle ones that will use the devil himself with courtesy.) Say'st thou that house is dark?

MALVOLIO   As hell, Sir Topas.

CLOWN   Why, it hath bay-windows transparent as barricadoes, and the clerestories toward the south-north are as lustrous as ebony: and yet complainest thou of obstruction?

MALVOLIO   I am not mad, Sir Topas. I say to you, this house is dark.

CLOWN   Madman, thou errest. I say there is no darkness but ignorance, in which thou art more puzzled than the Egyptians in their fog.

MALVOLIO   I say this house is as dark as ignorance, though ignorance were as dark as hell; and I say there was never man thus abused. I am no more mad than you are: make the trial of it in any constant question.

CLOWN   What is the opinion of Pythagoras concerning wildfowl?

MALVOLIO   That the soul of our grandam might haply inhabit a bird.

CLOWN   What think'st thou of his opinion?

MALVOLIO   I think nobly of the soul, and no way approve his opinion.

CLOWN   Fare thee well: remain thou still in darkness. Thou shalt hold th' opinion of Pythagoras ere I will allow of thy wits, and fear to kill a woodcock lest thou dispossess the soul of thy grandam. Fare thee well.

MALVOLIO   Sir Topas, Sir Topas!

SIR TOBY   My most exquisite Sir Topas!

CLOWN   Nay, I am for all waters.

MARIA   Thou might'st have done this without thy beard and gown, he sees thee not.

SIR TOBY   To him in thine own voice, and bring me word how thou find'st him: I would we were well rid of this knavery. If he may be conveniently delivered, I would he were, for I am now so far in offence with my niece that I cannot pursue with any safety this sport to the upshot. Come by and by to my chamber.

Exit with Maria.

CLOWN [*singing*]
    Hey Robin, jolly Robin,
    Tell me how thy lady does.

MALVOLIO   Fool!

CLOWN   My lady is unkind, perdie.

MALVOLIO   Fool!

CLOWN   Alas, why is she so?

MALVOLIO   Fool, I say!

CLOWN   She loves another –
    Who calls, ha?

MALVOLIO   Good fool, as ever thou wilt deserve well at my hand, help me to a candle, and pen, ink, and paper: as I am a gentleman, I will live to be thankful to thee for't.

CLOWN   Master Malvolio?

MALVOLIO   Ay, good fool.

CLOWN   Alas, sir, how fell you besides your five wits?

MALVOLIO   Fool, there was never man so notoriously abused: I am as well in my wits, fool, as thou art.

CLOWN   But as well? Then you are mad indeed, if you be no better in your wits than a fool.

MALVOLIO   They have here propertied me: keep me in darkness, send ministers to me, asses, and do all they can to face me out of my wits.

CLOWN   Advise you what you say: the minister is here. [*as Sir Topas*] Malvolio, Malvolio, thy wits the heavens restore: endeavour thyself to sleep, and leave thy vain bibble babble.

MALVOLIO   Sir Topas!

CLOWN [*as Sir Topas*]   Maintain no words with him, good fellow! [*as himself*] Who, I, sir? not I, sir! God buy you, good Sir Topas! [*as Sir Topas*] Marry, amen! [*as himself*] I will, sir, I will.

MALVOLIO   Fool, fool, fool, I say!

CLOWN   Alas, sir, be patient. What say you, sir? I am shent for speaking to you.

MALVOLIO   Good fool, help me to some light and some paper: I tell thee I am as well in my wits as any man in Illyria.

CLOWN   Well-a-day that you were, sir!

MALVOLIO   By this hand, I am! Good fool, some ink, paper, and light, and convey what I will set down to my lady. It shall advantage thee more than ever the bearing of letter did.

CLOWN   I will help you to't. But tell me true, are you not mad indeed? or do you but counterfeit?

MALVOLIO   Believe me, I am not, I tell thee true.

CLOWN   Nay, I'll ne'er believe a madman till I see his brains. I will fetch you light, and paper, and ink.

MALVOLIO   Fool, I'll requite it in the highest degree: I prithee, be gone.

CLOWN [*singing*]
    I am gone, sir, and anon, sir,
      I'll be with you again,
    In a trice, like to the old Vice,
      Your need to sustain;
    Who, with dagger of lath, in his rage
             and his wrath,
      Cries, 'Ah, ha!' to the devil:
    Like a mad lad, 'Pare thy nails, dad.
      Adieu, goodman devil!'   *Exit.*

4.3   *Enter* SEBASTIAN.

SEBASTIAN   This is the air, that is the glorious sun,
This pearl she gave me, I do feel't, and see't,
And though 'tis wonder that enwraps me thus,
Yet 'tis not madness. Where's Antonio then?
I could not find him at the Elephant,
Yet there he was, and there I found this credit,
That he did range the town to seek me out.
His counsel now might do me golden service:
For though my soul disputes well with my sense
That this may be some error, but no madness,
Yet doth this accident and flood of fortune

So far exceed all instance, all discourse,
That I am ready to distrust mine eyes,
And wrangle with my reason that persuades me
To any other trust but that I am mad,
Or else the lady's mad; yet if 'twere so,
She could not sway her house, command her
    followers,
Take and give back affairs and their dispatch,
With such a smooth, discreet, and stable bearing
As I perceive she does. There's something in't
That is deceivable. But here the lady comes.

Enter OLIVIA *and* Priest.

OLIVIA Blame not this haste of mine. If you mean well,
  Now go with me, and with this holy man,
  Into the chantry by: there before him,
  And underneath that consecrated roof,
  Plight me the full assurance of your faith,
  That my most jealous and too doubtful soul
  May live at peace. He shall conceal it,
  Whiles you are willing it shall come to note,
  What time we will our celebration keep
  According to my birth. What do you say?
SEBASTIAN I'll follow this good man, and go with you,
  And having sworn truth, ever will be true.
OLIVIA
  Then lead the way, good father, and heavens so shine,
  That they may fairly note this act of mine! *Exeunt.*

5.1   *Enter* Clown *and* FABIAN.

FABIAN Now as thou lov'st me, let me see his letter.
CLOWN Good Master Fabian, grant me another request.
FABIAN Anything.
CLOWN Do not desire to see this letter.
FABIAN This is to give a dog, and in recompense desire
  my dog again.

Enter DUKE, VIOLA, CURIO *and lords.*

ORSINO Belong you to the Lady Olivia, friends?
CLOWN Ay, sir, we are some of her trappings.
ORSINO I know thee well. How dost thou, my good
  fellow?
CLOWN Truly, sir, the better for my foes, and the worse
  for my friends.
ORSINO Just the contrary: the better for thy friends.
CLOWN No, sir, the worse.
ORSINO How can that be?
CLOWN Marry, sir, they praise me, and make an ass of
  me. Now my foes tell me plainly I am an ass: so that
  by my foes, sir, I profit in the knowledge of myself, and
  by my friends I am abused. So that, conclusions to
  be as kisses, if your four negatives make your two
  affirmatives, why then the worse for my friends, and
  the better for my foes.
ORSINO Why, this is excellent.
CLOWN By my troth, sir, no: though it please you to be

one of my friends.
ORSINO Thou shalt not be the worse for me: there's gold.
CLOWN But that it would be double-dealing, sir, I would
  you could make it another.
ORSINO O, you give me ill counsel.
CLOWN Put your grace in your pocket, sir, for this once,
  and let your flesh and blood obey it.
ORSINO Well, I will be so much a sinner to be a double-
  dealer: there's another.
CLOWN *Primo, secundo, tertio*, is a good play, and the old
  saying is 'The third pays for all'; the triplex, sir, is a
  good tripping measure; or the bells of Saint Bennet,
  sir, may put you in mind – one, two, three.
ORSINO You can fool no more money out of me at this
  throw. If you will let your lady know I am here to speak
  with her, and bring her along with you, it may awake
  my bounty further.
CLOWN Marry, sir, lullaby to your bounty till I come
  again. I go, sir, but I would not have you to think that
  my desire of having is the sin of covetousness: but as
  you say, sir, let your bounty take a nap, I will awake it
  anon. *Exit.*

Enter ANTONIO *and* Officers.

VIOLA Here comes the man, sir, that did rescue me.
ORSINO That face of his I do remember well;
  Yet when I saw it last, it was besmear'd
  As black as Vulcan, in the smoke of war.
  A baubling vessel was he captain of,
  For shallow draught and bulk unprizable,
  With which such scathful grapple did he make
  With the most noble bottom of our fleet,
  That very envy and the tongue of loss
  Cried fame and honour on him. What's the matter?
1 OFFICER Orsino, this is that Antonio
  That took the Phoenix and her fraught from Candy,
  And this is he that did the Tiger board,
  When your young nephew Titus lost his leg.
  Here in the streets, desperate of shame and state,
  In private brabble did we apprehend him.
VIOLA He did me kindness, sir, drew on my side,
  But in conclusion put strange speech upon me,
  I know not what 'twas, but distraction.
ORSINO Notable pirate, thou salt-water thief,
  What foolish boldness brought thee to their mercies,
  Whom thou in terms so bloody and so dear
  Hast made thine enemies?
ANTONIO   Orsino, noble sir,
  Be pleas'd that I shake off these names you give me:
  Antonio never yet was thief, or pirate,
  Though I confess, on base and ground enough,
  Orsino's enemy. A witchcraft drew me hither:
  That most ingrateful boy there by your side,
  From the rude sea's enrag'd and foamy mouth
  Did I redeem. A wrack past hope he was.
  His life I gave him, and did thereto add
  My love, without retention or restraint,

All his in dedication. For his sake
80   Did I expose myself (pure for his love)
Into the danger of this adverse town;
Drew to defend him, when he was beset;
Where being apprehended, his false cunning
(Not meaning to partake with me in danger)
85   Taught him to face me out of his acquaintance,
And grew a twenty years' removed thing
While one would wink; denied me mine own purse,
Which I had recommended to his use
Not half an hour before.

VIOLA   How can this be?

90   ORSINO   When came he to this town?

ANTONIO   Today, my lord: and for three months before
No int'rim, not a minute's vacancy,
Both day and night did we keep company.

Enter OLIVIA *and attendants.*

ORSINO
Here comes the Countess: now heaven walks on
        earth.
95   But for thee, fellow – fellow, thy words are madness.
Three months this youth hath tended upon me;
But more of that anon. Take him aside.

OLIVIA
What would my lord, but that he may not have,
Wherein Olivia may seem serviceable?
100   Cesario, you do not keep promise with me.

VIOLA   [*speaking together*]   Madam
ORSINO   Gracious Olivia –

OLIVIA   What do you say, Cesario? Good my lord –

VIOLA   My lord would speak, my duty hushes me.

105   OLIVIA   If it be aught to the old tune, my lord,
It is as fat and fulsome to mine ear
As howling after music.

ORSINO   Still so cruel?

OLIVIA   Still so constant, lord.

ORSINO   What, to perverseness? You uncivil lady,
110   To whose ingrate and unauspicious altars
My soul the faithfull'st off'rings hath breath'd out
That e'er devotion tender'd – What shall I do?

OLIVIA
Even what it please my lord that shall become him.

ORSINO   Why should I not, had I the heart to do it,
115   Like to th'Egyptian thief at point of death,
Kill what I love? – a savage jealousy
That sometime savours nobly. But hear me this:
Since you to non-regardance cast my faith,
And that I partly know the instrument
120   That screws me from my true place in your favour,
Live you the marble-breasted tyrant still.
But this your minion, whom I know you love,
And whom, by heaven, I swear I tender dearly,
Him will I tear out of that cruel eye
125   Where he sits crowned in his master's spite.
Come, boy, with me; my thoughts are ripe in
        mischief:

I'll sacrifice the lamb that I do love,
To spite a raven's heart within a dove.

VIOLA   And I most jocund, apt, and willingly,
To do you rest, a thousand deaths would die.   130

OLIVIA   Where goes Cesario?

VIOLA   After him I love
More than I love these eyes, more than my life,
More, by all mores, than e'er I shall love wife.
If I do feign, you witnesses above
Punish my life, for tainting of my love.   135

OLIVIA   Ay me detested! how am I beguil'd!

VIOLA
Who does beguile you? Who does do you wrong?

OLIVIA   Hast thou forgot thyself? Is it so long?
Call forth the holy father.   *Exit an attendant.*

ORSINO   Come, away!

OLIVIA   Whither, my lord? Cesario, husband, stay!   140

ORSINO   Husband?

OLIVIA   Ay, husband. Can he that deny?

ORSINO   Her husband, sirrah?

VIOLA   No, my lord, not I.

OLIVIA   Alas, it is the baseness of thy fear
That makes thee strangle thy propriety.
Fear not, Cesario, take thy fortunes up,   145
Be that thou know'st thou art, and then thou art
As great as that thou fear'st.

Enter Priest.

                                O welcome, father!
Father, I charge thee by thy reverence
Here to unfold – though lately we intended
To keep in darkness what occasion now   150
Reveals before 'tis ripe – what thou dost know
Hath newly pass'd between this youth and me.

PRIEST   A contract of eternal bond of love,
Confirm'd by mutual joinder of your hands,
Attested by the holy close of lips,   155
Strengthen'd by interchangement of your rings,
And all the ceremony of this compact
Seal'd in my function, by my testimony;
Since when, my watch hath told me, toward my
        grave
I have travell'd but two hours.   160

ORSINO   O thou dissembling cub! What wilt thou be
When time hath sow'd a grizzle on thy case?
Or will not else thy craft so quickly grow
That thine own trip shall be thine overthrow?
Farewell, and take her, but direct thy feet   165
Where thou and I henceforth may never meet.

VIOLA   My lord, I do protest –

OLIVIA   O do not swear!
Hold little faith, though thou hast too much fear.

Enter SIR ANDREW.

SIR ANDREW   For the love of God, a surgeon! Send one
presently to Sir Toby.   170

OLIVIA   What's the matter?

SIR ANDREW 'Has broke my head across, and has given Sir
Toby a bloody coxcomb too. For the love of God, your
help! I had rather than forty pound I were at home.

OLIVIA Who has done this, Sir Andrew?   75

SIR ANDREW The Count's gentleman, one Cesario. We
took him for a coward, but he's the very devil incardinate.

ORSINO My gentleman, Cesario?

SIR ANDREW 'Od's lifelings, here he is! You broke my   80
head for nothing; and that that I did, I was set on to
do't by Sir Toby.

VIOLA Why do you speak to me? I never hurt you:
You drew your sword upon me without cause,
But I bespake you fair, and hurt you not.   85

Enter SIR TOBY *and* Clown.

SIR ANDREW If a bloody coxcomb be a hurt, you have
hurt me: I think you set nothing by a bloody coxcomb.
Here comes Sir Toby halting, you shall hear more: but
if he had not been in drink, he would have tickled you
othergates than he did.   90

ORSINO How now, gentleman? How is't with you?

SIR TOBY That's all one, 'has hurt me, and there's th'
end on't. Sot, didst see Dick Surgeon, sot?

CLOWN O, he's drunk, Sir Toby, an hour agone; his eyes
were set at eight i'th' morning.   95

SIR TOBY Then he's a rogue, and a passy measures
pavin: I hate a drunken rogue.

OLIVIA Away with him! Who hath made this havoc with
them?

SIR ANDREW I'll help you, Sir Toby, because we'll be   100
dressed together.

SIR TOBY Will you help? An ass-head, and a coxcomb,
and a knave, a thin-faced knave, a gull?

OLIVIA Get him to bed, and let his hurt be looked to.
Exeunt Clown, Fabian, Sir Toby and Sir Andrew.

Enter SEBASTIAN.

SEBASTIAN
I am sorry, madam, I have hurt your kinsman: 105
But had it been the brother of my blood,
I must have done no less with wit and safety.
You throw a strange regard upon me, and by that
I do perceive it hath offended you:
Pardon me, sweet one, even for the vows   110
We made each other but so late ago.

ORSINO
One face, one voice, one habit, and two persons!
A natural perspective, that is, and is not!

SEBASTIAN Antonio! O my dear Antonio,
How have the hours rack'd and tortur'd me,   115
Since I have lost thee!

ANTONIO Sebastian are you?

SEBASTIAN   Fear'st thou that, Antonio?

ANTONIO How have you made division of yourself?
An apple cleft in two is not more twin
Than these two creatures. Which is Sebastian?   120

OLIVIA Most wonderful!

SEBASTIAN Do I stand there? I never had a brother;
Nor can there be that deity in my nature
Of here and everywhere. I had a sister,
Whom the blind waves and surges have devour'd: 225
Of charity, what kin are you to me?
What countryman? What name? What parentage?

VIOLA Of Messaline: Sebastian was my father;
Such a Sebastian was my brother too:
So went he suited to his watery tomb.   230
If spirits can assume both form and suit,
You come to fright us.

SEBASTIAN   A spirit I am indeed,
But am in that dimension grossly clad
Which from the womb I did participate.
Were you a woman, as the rest goes even,   235
I should my tears let fall upon your cheek,
And say, 'Thrice welcome, drowned Viola.'

VIOLA My father had a mole upon his brow.

SEBASTIAN And so had mine.

VIOLA And died that day when Viola from her birth   240
Had number'd thirteen years.

SEBASTIAN O, that record is lively in my soul!
He finished indeed his mortal act
That day that made my sister thirteen years.

VIOLA If nothing lets to make us happy both,   245
But this my masculine usurp'd attire,
Do not embrace me, till each circumstance
Of place, time, fortune, do cohere and jump
That I am Viola; which to confirm,
I'll bring you to a captain in this town,   250
Where lie my maiden weeds; by whose gentle help
I was preserv'd to serve this noble count:
All the occurrence of my fortune since
Hath been between this lady and this lord.

SEBASTIAN [*to Olivia*] So comes it, lady, you have
been mistook.   255
But nature to her bias drew in that.
You would have been contracted to a maid;
Nor are you therein, by my life, deceiv'd:
You are betroth'd both to a maid and man.

ORSINO Be not amaz'd, right noble is his blood.   260
If this be so, as yet the glass seems true,
I shall have share in this most happy wreck.
[*to Viola*] Boy, thou hast said to me a thousand times
Thou never should'st love woman like to me.

VIOLA And all those sayings will I over-swear,   265
And all those swearings keep as true in soul
As doth that orbed continent the fire
That severs day from night.

ORSINO   Give me thy hand,
And let me see thee in thy woman's weeds.

VIOLA The captain that did bring me first on shore   270
Hath my maid's garments; he upon some action
Is now in durance, at Malvolio's suit,
A gentleman and follower of my lady's.

OLIVIA He shall enlarge him: fetch Malvolio hither.

275 And yet alas! now I remember me,
They say, poor gentleman, he's much distract.

Enter Clown *with a letter, and* FABIAN.

A most extracting frenzy of mine own
From my remembrance clearly banish'd his.
How does he, sirrah?

280 CLOWN   Truly, Madam, he holds Belzebub at the
stave's end as well as a man in his case may do; 'has
here writ a letter to you. I should have given't you
to-day morning, but as a madman's epistles are no
gospels, so it skills not much when they are
285 delivered.

OLIVIA   Open't, and read it.

CLOWN   Look then to be well edified, when the fool
delivers the madman. [*Reads.*] *By the Lord, madam, –*

OLIVIA   How now, art thou mad?

290 CLOWN   No, madam, I do but read madness: and your
ladyship will have it as it ought to be, you must allow *vox.*

OLIVIA   Prithee, read i'thy right wits.

CLOWN   So I do, madonna. But to read his right wits is to
read thus: therefore, perpend, my princess, and give ear.

295 OLIVIA [*to Fabian*]   Read it you, sirrah.

FABIAN [*Reads.*]   *By the Lord, madam, you wrong me, and
the world shall know it. Though you have put me into
darkness, and given your drunken cousin rule over me, yet
have I the benefit of my senses as well as your ladyship. I
300 have your own letter, that induced me to the semblance I put
on; with the which I doubt not but to do myself much right,
or you much shame. Think of me as you please. I leave my
duty a little unthought of, and speak out of my injury.*
                                      The madly-used Malvolio.

305 OLIVIA   Did he write this?

CLOWN   Ay, madam.

ORSINO   This savours not much of distraction.

OLIVIA   See him deliver'd, Fabian, bring him hither.
                                       Exit Fabian.

My lord, so please you, these things further thought
on,
310 To think me as well a sister, as a wife,
One day shall crown th'alliance on't, so please you,
Here at my house, and at my proper cost.

ORSINO   Madam, I am most apt t'embrace your offer.
[*to Viola*] Your master quits you; and for your service
done him,
315 So much against the mettle of your sex,
So far beneath your soft and tender breeding,
And since you call'd me master for so long,
Here is my hand; you shall from this time be
Your master's mistress.

OLIVIA   A sister! you are she.

Enter FABIAN *with* MALVOLIO.

ORSINO   Is this the madman?

320 OLIVIA   Ay, my lord, this same.
How now, Malvolio?

MALVOLIO   Madam, you have done me wrong,

Notorious wrong.

OLIVIA   Have I, Malvolio? No.

MALVOLIO   Lady, you have. Pray you, peruse that letter.
You must not now deny it is your hand:
Write from it, if you can, in hand, or phrase,   325
Or say 'tis not your seal, not your invention:
You can say none of this. Well, grant it then,
And tell me, in the modesty of honour,
Why you have given me such clear lights of favour,
Bade me come smiling and cross-garter'd to you,   330
To put on yellow stockings, and to frown
Upon Sir Toby, and the lighter people;
And acting this in an obedient hope,
Why have you suffer'd me to be imprison'd,
Kept in a dark house, visited by the priest,   335
And made the most notorious geck and gull
That e'er invention play'd on? Tell me, why?

OLIVIA   Alas, Malvolio, this is not my writing,
Though I confess much like the character:
But, out of question, 'tis Maria's hand.   340
And now I do bethink me, it was she
First told me thou wast mad; then cam'st in smiling,
And in such forms which here were presuppos'd
Upon thee in the letter. Prithee, be content;
This practice hath most shrewdly pass'd upon thee.   345
But when we know the grounds and authors of it,
Thou shalt be both the plaintiff and the judge
Of thine own cause.

FABIAN   Good madam, hear me speak,
And let no quarrel, nor no brawl to come,
Taint the condition of this present hour,   350
Which I have wonder'd at. In hope it shall not,
Most freely I confess, myself and Toby
Set this device against Malvolio here,
Upon some stubborn and uncourteous parts
We had conceiv'd against him. Maria writ   355
The letter, at Sir Toby's great importance,
In recompense whereof he hath married her.
How with a sportful malice it was follow'd
May rather pluck on laughter than revenge,
If that the injuries be justly weigh'd   360
That have on both sides pass'd.

OLIVIA   Alas, poor fool, how have they baffled thee!

CLOWN   Why, 'Some are born great, some achieve
greatness, and some have greatness thrown upon
them'. I was one, sir, in this interlude, one Sir Topas,   365
sir, but that's all one. 'By the Lord, fool, I am not mad.'
But do you remember, 'Madam, why laugh you at such
a barren rascal, and you smile not, he's gagged'? And
thus the whirligig of time brings in his revenges.

MALVOLIO   I'll be reveng'd on the whole pack of you!   370
                                         Exit.

OLIVIA   He hath been most notoriously abus'd.

ORSINO   Pursue him, and entreat him to a peace:
He hath not told us of the captain yet.   *Exit Fabian.*
When that is known, and golden time convents,
A solemn combination shall be made   375

Of our dear souls. Meantime, sweet sister,
We will not part from hence. Cesario, come;
For so you shall be while you are a man;
But when in other habits you are seen,
Orsino's mistress, and his fancy's queen.
      Exeunt all except Clown.

CLOWN [*Sings.*]
 When that I was and a little tiny boy,
  With hey, ho, the wind and the rain,
 A foolish thing was but a toy,
  For the rain it raineth every day.

 But when I came to man's estate,
  With hey, ho, the wind and the rain,
 'Gainst knaves and thieves men shut their gate,
  For the rain it raineth every day.

 But when I came, alas, to wive,
  With hey, ho, the wind and the rain, 390
 By swaggering could I never thrive,
  For the rain it raineth every day.

 But when I came unto my beds,
  With hey, ho, the wind and the rain,
 With toss-pots still 'had drunken heads, 395
  For the rain it raineth every day.

 A great while ago the world begun,
  With hey, ho, the wind and the rain,
 But that's all one, our play is done,
  And we'll strive to please you every day. *Exit.* 400

The Two Gentlemen of Verona

Although first printed in 1623 as the second (after *The Tempest*) of the comedies in the First Folio, *The Two Gentlemen of Verona* is thought to be among the earliest of Shakespeare's plays, perhaps even his first comedy, and to have been written no later than 1594. Details in it may come from Arthur Brooke's *Romeus and Juliet* (1562) but its plot is adapted from the Spanish romance *Diana* by George of Montemayor, translated into English by Bartholomew Yong, whose version Shakespeare must have read some years before its publication in 1598.

Shakespeare opened Montemayor's tragicomic love-triangle of two women and a faithless man out into a rectangle: his addition of Valentine allowed for a formal comic ending with a double wedding in prospect. His other illuminating change – germane to the play's comic scrutiny of the myth of the Petrarchan lover as servant to a cruel mistress – was the invention of the servants Speed and Launce, and of Launce's scapegrace dog, Crab, the only animal role in Shakespeare and an important source of the play's theatrical appeal. Julia is the first of Shakespeare's heroines in male disguise, a device whose usefulness to boy players Shakespeare would continue to exploit in later plays. Julia's predicament as the servant of the man she loves, employed by him to woo another woman, anticipates that of Viola in *Twelfth Night*, and the name she adopts in disguise, 'Sebastian', is that of Viola's twin brother.

The psychological implausibility of Proteus' sudden reform and, still more, of Valentine's real or apparent offer to cede Silvia to the penitent friend who has just attempted to rape her, has been a stumbling-block to appreciation of the play and has motivated attempts to rewrite the ending for performance, or to read it as a sustained satire on the stock Renaissance debate between the rival claims of love and friendship (which Shakespeare would later treat more obliquely in *The Merchant of Venice* and more directly in *The Two Noble Kinsmen*). The ending may as likely be perfunctory as satirical: at least it is evident that the major interest of the play lies in creating and complicating the predicaments of its characters rather than in resolving them. The open-eyed duplicity of Proteus is an adolescent premonition of the more dangerous insincerities of later lovers equally devoid of self-knowledge such as Bertram in *All's Well that Ends Well* or Angelo in *Measure for Measure*.

Franz Schubert's setting of 'Who is Silvia?' (1826) and Holman Hunt's painting of the play's dénouement (1851) testify to its favour in the nineteenth century. Revivals have taken place with some regularity since the middle of the eighteenth century, but seldom with marked success. Although among the least performed of the comedies in the late twentieth century, *The Two Gentlemen of Verona* was chosen, in the summer of 1996, as the first play to be staged at the reconstructed Globe in London, and it has succeeded as a musical with additional songs imported from the 1920s and 1930s.

The Arden text is based on the 1623 First Folio.

LIST OF ROLES

DUKE	*father to Silvia*
VALENTINE	*two gentlemen*
PROTEUS	
ANTONIO	*father to Proteus*
THURIO	*a foolish rival to Valentine*
EGLAMOUR	*agent for Silvia in her escape*
HOST	*where Julia lodges*
OUTLAWS	*with Valentine*
SPEED	*page to Valentine*
LAUNCE	*a clownish servant to Proteus*
PANTHINO	*servant to Antonio*
JULIA	*beloved of Proteus*
SILVIA	*beloved of Valentine*
LUCETTA	*waiting-woman to Julia*
SERVANT	*attending the Duke*

Musicians

The Two Gentlemen of Verona

Enter VALENTINE *and* PROTEUS.

VALENTINE   Cease to persuade, my loving Proteus;
  Home-keeping youth have ever homely wits.
  Were't not affection chains thy tender days
  To the sweet glances of thy honour'd love,
  I rather would entreat thy company
  To see the wonders of the world abroad
  Than (living dully sluggardis'd at home)
  Wear out thy youth with shapeless idleness.
  But since thou lov'st, love still, and thrive therein,
  Even as I would, when I to love begin.
PROTEUS   Wilt thou be gone? Sweet Valentine, adieu;
  Think on thy Proteus, when thou (haply) seest
  Some rare noteworthy object in thy travel.
  Wish me partaker in thy happiness,
  When thou dost meet good hap; and in thy danger
  (If ever danger do environ thee)
  Commend thy grievance to my holy prayers,
  For I will be thy beadsman, Valentine.
VALENTINE   And on a love-book pray for my success?
PROTEUS   Upon some book I love, I'll pray for thee.
VALENTINE   That's on some shallow story of deep love,
  How young Leander cross'd the Hellespont.
PROTEUS   That's a deep story, of a deeper love,
  For he was more than over shoes in love.
VALENTINE   'Tis true; for you are over boots in love,
  And yet you never swum the Hellespont.
PROTEUS   Over the boots? Nay, give me not the boots.
VALENTINE   No, I will not; for it boots thee not.
PROTEUS   What?
VALENTINE
  To be in love; where scorn is bought with groans;
  Coy looks, with heart-sore sighs; one fading
    moment's mirth,
  With twenty watchful, weary, tedious nights;
  If haply won, perhaps a hapless gain;
  If lost, why then a grievous labour won;
  How ever, but a folly bought with wit,
  Or else a wit by folly vanquished.
PROTEUS   So, by your circumstance, you call me fool.
VALENTINE
  So, by your circumstance, I fear you'll prove.
PROTEUS   'Tis Love you cavil at, I am not Love.
VALENTINE   Love is your master, for he masters you;
  And he that is so yoked by a fool
  Methinks should not be chronicled for wise.
PROTEUS   Yet writers say: as in the sweetest bud
  The eating canker dwells, so eating Love
  Inhabits in the finest wits of all.
VALENTINE   And writers say: as the most forward bud
  Is eaten by the canker ere it blow,
  Even so by Love the young and tender wit
  Is turn'd to folly, blasting in the bud,
  Losing his verdure, even in the prime,
  And all the fair effects of future hopes.
  But wherefore waste I time to counsel thee
  That art a votary to fond desire?

Once more adieu: my father at the road
Expects my coming, there to see me shipp'd.
PROTEUS   And thither will I bring thee, Valentine.   55
VALENTINE
  Sweet Proteus, no; now let us take our leave.
  To Milan let me hear from thee by letters
  Of thy success in love; and what news else
  Betideth here in absence of thy friend;
  And I likewise will visit thee with mine.   60
PROTEUS   All happiness bechance to thee in Milan.
VALENTINE   As much to you at home; and so farewell.
                                                   Exit.

PROTEUS   He after honour hunts, I after love;
  He leaves his friends, to dignify them more;
  I leave myself, my friends, and all, for love: 65
  Thou, Julia, thou hast metamorphos'd me;
  Made me neglect my studies, lose my time,
  War with good counsel, set the world at nought;
  Made wit with musing weak, heart sick with thought.

                Enter SPEED.

SPEED   Sir Proteus, 'save you; saw you my master?   70
PROTEUS
  But now he parted hence to embark for Milan.
SPEED   Twenty to one, then, he is shipp'd already,
  And I have play'd the sheep in losing him.
PROTEUS   Indeed a sheep doth very often stray,
  And if the shepherd be awhile away.   75
SPEED   You conclude that my master is a shepherd,
  then, and I a sheep?
PROTEUS   I do.
SPEED   Why, then my horns are his horns, whether I
  wake or sleep.   80
PROTEUS   A silly answer, and fitting well a sheep.
SPEED   This proves me still a sheep.
PROTEUS   True; and thy master a shepherd.
SPEED   Nay, that I can deny by a circumstance.
PROTEUS   It shall go hard but I'll prove it by another.   85
SPEED   The shepherd seeks the sheep, and not the sheep
  the shepherd; but I seek my master, and my master
  seeks not me: therefore I am no sheep.
PROTEUS   The sheep for fodder follow the shepherd, the
  shepherd for food follows not the sheep; thou for   90
  wages followest thy master, thy master for wages
  follows not thee: therefore thou art a sheep.
SPEED   Such another proof will make me cry 'baa'.
PROTEUS   But dost thou hear? Gavest thou my letter to
  Julia?   95
SPEED   Ay, sir; I (a lost mutton) gave your letter to her
  (a laced mutton) and she (a laced mutton) gave me
  (a lost mutton) nothing for my labour.
PROTEUS   Here's too small a pasture for such store of
  muttons.   100
SPEED   If the ground be over-charged, you were best
  stick her.
PROTEUS   Nay, in that you are astray; 'twere best pound
  you.

SPEED   Nay, sir, less than a pound shall serve me for
    carrying your letter.

PROTEUS   You mistake; I mean the pound, a pinfold.

SPEED   From a pound to a pin? Fold it over and over,
    'Tis threefold too little for carrying a letter to your
    lover.

PROTEUS   But what said she?

SPEED   [*first nodding*]   Ay.

PROTEUS   Nod – ay: why, that's 'noddy'.

SPEED   You mistook, sir: I say she did nod; and you ask
    me if she did nod, and I say 'Ay'.

PROTEUS   And that set together is 'noddy'.

SPEED   Now you have taken the pains to set it together,
    take it for your pains.

PROTEUS   No, no, you shall have it for bearing the letter.

SPEED   Well, I perceive I must be fain to bear with you.

PROTEUS   Why, sir, how do you bear with me?

SPEED   Marry, sir, the letter very orderly, having nothing
    but the word 'noddy' for my pains.

PROTEUS   Beshrew me, but you have a quick wit.

SPEED   And yet it cannot overtake your slow purse.

PROTEUS   Come, come, open the matter in brief: what
    said she?

SPEED   Open your purse, that the money and the matter
    may be both at once delivered.

PROTEUS   [*giving money*]   Well, sir; here is for your pains.
    What said she?

SPEED   Truly, sir, I think you'll hardly win her.

PROTEUS   Why, couldst thou perceive so much from
    her?

SPEED   Sir, I could perceive nothing at all from her; no,
    not so much as a ducat for delivering your letter; and
    being so hard to me that brought your mind, I fear
    she'll prove as hard to you in telling your mind. Give
    her no token but stones, for she's as hard as steel.

PROTEUS   What said she? Nothing?

SPEED   No, not so much as 'Take this for thy pains'. To
    testify your bounty, I thank you, you have testerned
    me; in requital whereof, henceforth carry your
    letters yourself; and so, sir, I'll commend you to my
    master.   *Exit.*

PROTEUS

    Go, go, be gone, to save your ship from wrack,
    Which cannot perish having thee aboard,
    Being destin'd to a drier death on shore.
    I must go send some better messenger:
    I fear my Julia would not deign my lines
    Receiving them from such a worthless post.   *Exit.*

1.2   *Enter* JULIA *and* LUCETTA.

JULIA   But say, Lucetta, now we are alone,
    Wouldst thou then counsel me to fall in love?

LUCETTA   Ay, madam, so you stumble not unheedfully.

JULIA   Of all the fair resort of gentlemen
    That every day with parle encounter me,
    In thy opinion which is worthiest love?

LUCETTA
    Please you repeat their names, I'll show my mind,
    According to my shallow simple skill.

JULIA   What think'st thou of the fair Sir Eglamour?

LUCETTA   As of a knight well-spoken, neat, and fine;
    But were I you, he never should be mine.

JULIA   What think'st thou of the rich Mercatio?

LUCETTA   Well of his wealth; but of himself, so so.

JULIA   What think'st thou of the gentle Proteus?

LUCETTA   Lord, Lord! to see what folly reigns in us!

JULIA
    How now? What means this passion at his name?

LUCETTA   Pardon, dear madam, 'tis a passing shame
    That I (unworthy body as I am)
    Should censure thus on lovely gentlemen.

JULIA   Why not on Proteus, as of all the rest?

LUCETTA   Then thus: of many good, I think him best.

JULIA   Your reason?

LUCETTA   I have no other but a woman's reason:
    I think him so, because I think him so.

JULIA   And wouldst thou have me cast my love on him?

LUCETTA   Ay; if you thought your love not cast away.

JULIA   Why, he, of all the rest, hath never mov'd me.

LUCETTA   Yet he, of all the rest, I think best loves ye.

JULIA   His little speaking shows his love but small.

LUCETTA   Fire that's closest kept burns most of all.

JULIA   They do not love that do not show their love.

LUCETTA
    O, they love least that let men know their love.

JULIA   I would I knew his mind.

LUCETTA   Peruse this paper, madam.

JULIA   'To Julia': say, from whom?

LUCETTA   That the contents will show.

JULIA   Say, say: who gave it thee?

LUCETTA
    Sir Valentine's page; and sent I think from Proteus.
    He would have given it you, but I being in the way
    Did in your name receive it: pardon the fault, I pray.

JULIA   Now, by my modesty, a goodly broker!
    Dare you presume to harbour wanton lines?
    To whisper, and conspire against my youth?
    Now trust me, 'tis an office of great worth,
    And you an officer fit for the place.
    There: take the paper; see it be return'd,
    Or else return no more into my sight.

LUCETTA
    To plead for love deserves more fee than hate.
    [*She drops the letter.*]

JULIA   Will ye be gone?

LUCETTA   That you may ruminate.   *Exit.*

JULIA   And yet I would I had o'erlook'd the letter.
    It were a shame to call her back again,
    And pray her to a fault for which I chid her.
    What fool is she, that knows I am a maid,
    And would not force the letter to my view!
    Since maids, in modesty, say 'no' to that
    Which they would have the profferer construe 'ay'.

Fie, fie; how wayward is this foolish love,
That (like a testy babe) will scratch the nurse,
And presently all humbled kiss the rod!
How churlishly I chid Lucetta hence,
When willingly I would have had her here!
How angerly I taught my brow to frown,
When inward joy enforc'd my heart to smile!
My penance is to call Lucetta back
And ask remission for my folly past.
What ho! Lucetta!

Enter LUCETTA.

LUCETTA   What would your ladyship?
JULIA   Is 't near dinner time?
LUCETTA   I would it were,
  That you might kill your stomach on your meat,
  And not upon your maid.
  [*She takes up Proteus' letter.*]
JULIA   What is 't that you took up so gingerly?
LUCETTA   Nothing.
JULIA   Why didst thou stoop then?
LUCETTA   To take a paper up that I let fall.
JULIA   And is that paper nothing?
LUCETTA   Nothing concerning me.
JULIA   Then let it lie, for those that it concerns.
LUCETTA   Madam, it will not lie where it concerns,
  Unless it have a false interpreter.
JULIA   Some love of yours hath writ to you in rhyme.
LUCETTA   That I might sing it, madam, to a tune.
  Give me a note; your ladyship can set.
JULIA   As little by such toys as may be possible:
  Best sing it to the tune of 'Light o' Love'.
LUCETTA   It is too heavy for so light a tune.
JULIA   Heavy? Belike it hath some burden then?
LUCETTA
  Ay; and melodious were it, would you sing it.
JULIA   And why not you?
LUCETTA   I cannot reach so high.
JULIA [*taking the letter*]
  Let's see your song. How now, minion?
LUCETTA   Keep tune there still: so you will sing it out.
  [*Julia strikes her.*]
  And yet methinks I do not like this tune.
JULIA   You do not?
LUCETTA   No, madam, 'tis too sharp.
JULIA   You, minion, are too saucy.
LUCETTA   Nay, now you are too flat;
  And mar the concord with too harsh a descant:
  There wanteth but a mean to fill your song.
JULIA   The mean is drown'd with your unruly bass.
LUCETTA   Indeed I bid the base for Proteus.
JULIA   This babble shall not henceforth trouble me.
  Here is a coil with protestation. [*She tears the letter.*]
  Go, get you gone; and let the papers lie.
  You would be fing'ring them, to anger me.
LUCETTA
  She makes it strange, but she would be best pleas'd

To be so anger'd with another letter.   *Exit.*
JULIA [*gathering up pieces of the letter*]
  Nay, would I were so anger'd with the same!   105
  O hateful hands, to tear such loving words;
  Injurious wasps, to feed on such sweet honey,
  And kill the bees that yield it, with your stings!
  I'll kiss each several paper, for amends.
  Look, here is writ 'kind Julia': unkind Julia!   110
  As in revenge of thy ingratitude,
  I throw thy name against the bruising stones,
  Trampling contemptuously on thy disdain.
  And here is writ 'love-wounded Proteus'.
  Poor wounded name: my bosom, as a bed,   115
  Shall lodge thee till thy wound be throughly heal'd;
  And thus I search it with a sovereign kiss.
  But twice, or thrice, was 'Proteus' written down:
  Be calm, good wind, blow not a word away,
  Till I have found each letter, in the letter,   120
  Except mine own name: that some whirlwind bear
  Unto a ragged, fearful, hanging rock,
  And throw it thence into the raging sea.
  Lo, here in one line is his name twice writ:
  'Poor forlorn Proteus', 'passionate Proteus'.   125
  'To the sweet Julia': that I'll tear away.
  And yet I will not, sith so prettily
  He couples it to his complaining names.
  Thus will I fold them, one upon another:
  Now kiss, embrace, contend, do what you will.   130

Enter LUCETTA.

LUCETTA
  Madam, dinner is ready; and your father stays.
JULIA   Well, let us go.
LUCETTA
  What, shall these papers lie, like tell-tales here?
JULIA   If you respect them, best to take them up.
LUCETTA   Nay, I was taken up, for laying them down.   135
  Yet here they shall not lie, for catching cold.
  [*She gathers up the letter.*]
JULIA   I see you have a month's mind to them.
LUCETTA
  Ay, madam, you may say what sights you see;
  I see things too, although you judge I wink.
JULIA   Come, come, will't please you go?   *Exeunt.*   140

1.3   *Enter* ANTONIO *and* PANTHINO.

ANTONIO   Tell me, Panthino, what sad talk was that
  Wherewith my brother held you in the cloister?
PANTHINO   'Twas of his nephew Proteus, your son.
ANTONIO   Why, what of him?
PANTHINO   He wonder'd that your lordship
  Would suffer him to spend his youth at home,   5
  While other men, of slender reputation,
  Put forth their sons, to seek preferment out:
  Some to the wars, to try their fortune there;
  Some, to discover islands far away;

10 Some, to the studious universities.
For any, or for all these exercises,
He said that Proteus, your son, was meet,
And did request me to importune you
To let him spend his time no more at home;
15 Which would be great impeachment to his age,
In having known no travel in his youth.

ANTONIO
Nor need'st thou much importune me to that
Whereon this month I have been hammering.
I have consider'd well his loss of time,
20 And how he cannot be a perfect man,
Not being tried and tutor'd in the world:
Experience is by industry achiev'd,
And perfected by the swift course of time.
Then tell me, whither were I best to send him?

25 PANTHINO   I think your lordship is not ignorant
How his companion, youthful Valentine,
Attends the Emperor in his royal court.

ANTONIO   I know it well.

PANTHINO
'Twere good, I think, your lordship sent him thither:
30 There shall he practise tilts and tournaments,
Hear sweet discourse, converse with noblemen,
And be in eye of every exercise
Worthy his youth and nobleness of birth.

ANTONIO   I like thy counsel: well hast thou advis'd.
35 And that thou mayst perceive how well I like it,
The execution of it shall make known.
Even with the speediest expedition,
I will dispatch him to the Emperor's court.

PANTHINO
To-morrow, may it please you, Don Alphonso
40 With other gentlemen of good esteem
Are journeying to salute the Emperor,
And to commend their service to his will.

ANTONIO   Good company: with them shall Proteus go.

Enter PROTEUS.

And in good time, now will we break with him.
45 PROTEUS [*aside*]   Sweet love, sweet lines, sweet life!
Here is her hand, the agent of her heart;
Here is her oath for love, her honour's pawn.
O that our fathers would applaud our loves
To seal our happiness with their consents!
50 O heavenly Julia!

ANTONIO
How now? What letter are you reading there?

PROTEUS
May 't please your lordship, 'tis a word or two
Of commendations sent from Valentine,
Deliver'd by a friend that came from him.

55 ANTONIO   Lend me the letter: let me see what news.

PROTEUS   There is no news, my lord, but that he writes
How happily he lives, how well-belov'd,
And daily graced by the Emperor;
Wishing me with him, partner of his fortune.

ANTONIO   And how stand you affected to his wish?   60

PROTEUS   As one relying on your lordship's will,
And not depending on his friendly wish.

ANTONIO   My will is something sorted with his wish.
Muse not that I thus suddenly proceed,
For what I will, I will, and there an end.   65
I am resolv'd that thou shalt spend some time
With Valentinus, in the Emperor's court:
What maintenance he from his friends receives,
Like exhibition thou shalt have from me.
To-morrow be in readiness to go.   70
Excuse it not, for I am peremptory.

PROTEUS   My lord, I cannot be so soon provided:
Please you deliberate a day or two.

ANTONIO
Look what thou want'st shall be sent after thee.
No more of stay; to-morrow thou must go.   75
Come on, Panthino; you shall be employ'd
To hasten on his expedition.

Exeunt Antonio and Panthino.

PROTEUS
Thus have I shunn'd the fire, for fear of burning,
And drench'd me in the sea, where I am drown'd.
I fear'd to show my father Julia's letter,   80
Lest he should take exceptions to my love,
And with the vantage of mine own excuse
Hath he excepted most against my love.
O, how this spring of love resembleth
The uncertain glory of an April day,   85
Which now shows all the beauty of the sun,
And by and by a cloud takes all away.

Enter PANTHINO.

PANTHINO   Sir Proteus, your father calls for you,
He is in haste, therefore I pray you go.

PROTEUS   Why, this it is: my heart accords thereto,   90
And yet a thousand times it answers 'no'.   *Exeunt*

2.1   *Enter* VALENTINE *and* SPEED.

SPEED   Sir, your glove.

VALENTINE   Not mine: my gloves are on.

SPEED   Why, then this may be yours; for this is but one.

VALENTINE   Ha! Let me see; ay, give it me, it's mine.
Sweet ornament, that decks a thing divine!   5
Ah, Silvia, Silvia!

SPEED   Madam Silvia! Madam Silvia!

VALENTINE   How now, sirrah?

SPEED   She is not within hearing, sir.

VALENTINE   Why, sir, who bade you call her?   10

SPEED   Your worship, sir, or else I mistook.

VALENTINE   Well, you'll still be too forward.

SPEED   And yet I was last chidden for being too slow.

VALENTINE
Go to, sir, tell me: do you know Madam Silvia?

SPEED   She that your worship loves?   15

VALENTINE   Why, how know you that I am in love?

SPEED Marry, by these special marks: first, you have learned (like Sir Proteus) to wreathe your arms like a malcontent; to relish a love-song, like a robin-redbreast; to walk alone, like one that had the pestilence; to sigh, like a schoolboy that had lost his ABC; to weep, like a young wench that had buried her grandam; to fast, like one that takes diet; to watch, like one that fears robbing; to speak puling, like a beggar at Hallowmas. You were wont, when you laughed, to crow like a cock; when you walked, to walk like one of the lions; when you fasted, it was presently after dinner; when you looked sadly, it was for want of money. And now you are metamorphosed with a mistress, that when I look on you, I can hardly think you my master.

VALENTINE Are all these things perceived in me?

SPEED They are all perceived without ye.

VALENTINE Without me? They cannot.

SPEED Without you? Nay, that's certain. For without you were so simple, none else would. But you are so without these follies that these follies are within you, and shine through you like the water in an urinal; that not an eye that sees you but is a physician to comment on your malady.

VALENTINE But tell me: dost thou know my lady Silvia?

SPEED She that you gaze on so, as she sits at supper?

VALENTINE Hast thou observed that? Even she I mean.

SPEED Why, sir, I know her not.

VALENTINE Dost thou know her by my gazing on her, and yet know'st her not?

SPEED Is she not hard-favoured, sir?

VALENTINE Not so fair, boy, as well-favoured.

SPEED Sir, I know that well enough.

VALENTINE What dost thou know?

SPEED That she is not so fair as, of you, well-favoured.

VALENTINE I mean that her beauty is exquisite, but her favour infinite.

SPEED That's because the one is painted, and the other out of all count.

VALENTINE How painted? And how out of count?

SPEED Marry, sir, so painted to make her fair that no man counts of her beauty.

VALENTINE How esteem'st thou me? I account of her beauty.

SPEED You never saw her since she was deformed.

VALENTINE How long hath she been deformed?

SPEED Ever since you loved her.

VALENTINE I have loved her ever since I saw her, and still I see her beautiful.

SPEED If you love her, you cannot see her.

VALENTINE Why?

SPEED Because Love is blind. O that you had mine eyes, or your own eyes had the lights they were wont to have, when you chid at Sir Proteus, for going ungartered.

VALENTINE What should I see then?

SPEED Your own present folly, and her passing deformity: for he, being in love, could not see to garter his hose; and you, being in love, cannot see to put on your hose. 75

VALENTINE Belike, boy, then you are in love, for last morning you could not see to wipe my shoes.

SPEED True, sir: I was in love with my bed. I thank you, you swinged me for my love, which makes me the 80 bolder to chide you for yours.

VALENTINE In conclusion, I stand affected to her.

SPEED I would you were set, so your affection would cease.

VALENTINE Last night she enjoined me to write some 85 lines to one she loves.

SPEED And have you?

VALENTINE I have.

SPEED Are they not lamely writ?

VALENTINE No, boy, but as well as I can do them. 90

Enter SILVIA.

Peace, here she comes.

SPEED [*aside*] O excellent motion! O exceeding puppet! Now will he interpret to her.

VALENTINE Madam and mistress, a thousand good-morrows. 95

SPEED [*aside*] O, 'give-ye-good-ev'n! Here's a million of manners.

SILVIA Sir Valentine, and servant, to you two thousand.

SPEED [*aside*] He should give her interest; and she gives it him. 100

VALENTINE As you enjoin'd me, I have writ your letter
Unto the secret, nameless friend of yours.
Which I was much unwilling to proceed in,
But for my duty to your ladyship. [*Gives her a letter.*]

SILVIA
I thank you, gentle servant. 'Tis very clerkly done. 105

VALENTINE Now trust me, madam, it came hardly off.
For being ignorant to whom it goes,
I writ at random, very doubtfully.

SILVIA
Perchance you think too much of so much pains?

VALENTINE No, madam; so it stead you, I will write 110
(Please you command) a thousand times as much.
And yet –

SILVIA A pretty period. Well, I guess the sequel;
And yet I will not name it; and yet I care not.
And yet take this again; and yet I thank you, 115
Meaning henceforth to trouble you no more.

SPEED [*aside*] And yet you will; and yet another 'yet'.

VALENTINE
What means your ladyship? Do you not like it?

SILVIA Yes, yes; the lines are very quaintly writ,
But (since unwillingly) take them again. 120
Nay, take them.

VALENTINE Madam, they are for you.

SILVIA Ay, ay. You writ them, sir, at my request,
But I will none of them: they are for you.
I would have had them writ more movingly. 125

VALENTINE [*taking the letter*]
    Please you, I'll write your ladyship another.
SILVIA   And when it's writ, for my sake read it over,
    And if it please you, so; if not, why, so.
VALENTINE   If it please me, madam? What then?
130 SILVIA   Why, if it please you, take it for your labour;
    And so good-morrow, servant.   *Exit.*
SPEED   O jest unseen, inscrutable, invisible,
    As a nose on a man's face, or a weathercock on a
      steeple!
    My master sues to her; and she hath taught her
      suitor,
135   He being her pupil, to become her tutor.
    O excellent device, was there ever heard a better?
    That my master being scribe, to himself should write
      the letter?
VALENTINE   How now, sir? What are you reasoning with
    yourself?
140 SPEED   Nay, I was rhyming; 'tis you that have the reason.
VALENTINE   To do what?
SPEED   To be a spokesman from Madam Silvia.
VALENTINE   To whom?
SPEED   To yourself. Why, she woos you by a figure.
145 VALENTINE   What figure?
SPEED   By a letter, I should say.
VALENTINE   Why, she hath not writ to me.
SPEED   What need she, when she hath made you write to
    yourself? Why, do you not perceive the jest?
150 VALENTINE   No, believe me.
SPEED   No believing you indeed, sir. But did you
    perceive her earnest?
VALENTINE   She gave me none, except an angry word.
SPEED   Why, she hath given you a letter.
155 VALENTINE   That's the letter I writ to her friend.
SPEED   And that letter hath she delivered, and there an
    end.
VALENTINE   I would it were no worse.
SPEED   I'll warrant you, 'tis as well.
160   For often have you writ to her, and she in modesty,
    Or else for want of idle time, could not again reply,
    Or fearing else some messenger, that might her mind
      discover,
    Herself hath taught her love himself to write unto
      her lover.
    All this I speak in print, for in print I found it.
165   Why muse you, sir? 'Tis dinner time.
VALENTINE   I have dined.
SPEED
    Ay, but hearken, sir: though the chameleon Love
    can feed on the air, I am one that am nourished by
    my victuals; and would fain have meat. O, be not
170   like your mistress, be moved, be moved.   *Exeunt.*

2.2   *Enter* PROTEUS *and* JULIA.

PROTEUS   Have patience, gentle Julia.
JULIA   I must where is no remedy.

PROTEUS   When possibly I can, I will return.
JULIA   If you turn not, you will return the sooner;   5
    Keep this remembrance for thy Julia's sake.
    [*She gives Proteus a ring.*]
PROTEUS
    Why then we'll make exchange; here, take you this.
    [*He gives Julia a ring.*]
JULIA   And seal the bargain with a holy kiss.
PROTEUS   Here is my hand, for my true constancy.
    And when that hour o'erslips me in the day   10
    Wherein I sigh not, Julia, for thy sake,
    The next ensuing hour some foul mischance
    Torment me for my love's forgetfulness.
    My father stays my coming. Answer not.
    The tide is now; nay, not thy tide of tears,   15
    That tide will stay me longer than I should.
    Julia, farewell.   *Exit Julia.*
        What, gone without a word?
    Ay, so true love should do: it cannot speak,
    For truth hath better deeds than words to grace it.

               Enter PANTHINO.

PANTHINO   Sir Proteus, you are stay'd for.
PROTEUS   Go; I come, I come.   20
    Alas, this parting strikes poor lovers dumb.   *Exeunt.*

2.3   *Enter* LAUNCE *with his dog Crab.*

LAUNCE   Nay, 'twill be this hour ere I have done
    weeping. All the kind of the Launces have this very
    fault. I have received my proportion, like the
    prodigious son, and am going with Sir Proteus to the
    Imperial's court. I think Crab my dog be the sourest-   5
    natured dog that lives: my mother weeping; my father
    wailing; my sister crying; our maid howling; our cat
    wringing her hands, and all our house in a great
    perplexity; yet did not this cruel-hearted cur shed one
    tear. He is a stone, a very pebble stone, and has no   10
    more pity in him than a dog. A Jew would have wept
    to have seen our parting. Why, my grandam, having no
    eyes, look you, wept herself blind at my parting. Nay,
    I'll show you the manner of it. This shoe is my father.
    No, this left shoe is my father; no, no, this left shoe is   15
    my mother; nay, that cannot be so neither. Yes, it is so,
    it is so: it hath the worser sole. This shoe with the hole
    in it is my mother; and this my father. A vengeance
    on't, there 'tis. Now, sir, this staff is my sister; for, look
    you, she is as white as a lily, and as small as a wand.   20
    This hat is Nan our maid. I am the dog. No, the dog is
    himself, and I am the dog. O, the dog is me, and I am
    myself. Ay; so, so. Now come I to my father: 'Father,
    your blessing.' Now should not the shoe speak a word
    for weeping; now should I kiss my father; well, he   25
    weeps on; now come I to my mother. O that she could
    speak now, like a wood woman! Well, I kiss her. Why,
    there 'tis: here's my mother's breath up and down.
    Now come I to my sister: mark the moan she makes.

Now the dog all this while sheds not a tear; nor speaks a word; but see how I lay the dust with my tears.

Enter PANTHINO.

PANTHINO   Launce, away, away; aboard; thy master is shipped, and thou art to post after with oars. What's the matter? Why weep'st thou, man? Away, ass, you'll lose the tide, if you tarry any longer.

LAUNCE   It is no matter if the tied were lost, for it is the unkindest tied that ever any man tied.

PANTHINO   What's the unkindest tide?

LAUNCE   Why, he that's tied here, Crab my dog.

PANTHINO   Tut, man. I mean thou'lt lose the flood, and in losing the flood, lose thy voyage, and in losing thy voyage, lose thy master, and in losing thy master, lose thy service, and in losing thy service – why dost thou stop my mouth?

LAUNCE   For fear thou shouldst lose thy tongue.

PANTHINO   Where should I lose my tongue?

LAUNCE   In thy tale.

PANTHINO   In my tail?

LAUNCE   Lose the tide, and the voyage, and the master, and the service, and the tied? Why, man, if the river were dry, I am able to fill it with my tears; if the wind were down, I could drive the boat with my sighs.

PANTHINO   Come; come away, man, I was sent to call thee.

LAUNCE   Sir, call me what thou dar'st.

PANTHINO   Wilt thou go?

LAUNCE   Well, I will go.   *Exeunt.*

2.4   *Enter* VALENTINE, SILVIA, THURIO *and* SPEED.

SILVIA   Servant, –

VALENTINE   Mistress?

SPEED   Master, Sir Thurio frowns on you.

VALENTINE   Ay, boy, it's for love.

SPEED   Not of you.

VALENTINE   Of my mistress, then.

SPEED   'Twere good you knocked him.

SILVIA   Servant, you are sad.

VALENTINE   Indeed, madam, I seem so.

THURIO   Seem you that you are not?

VALENTINE   Haply I do.

THURIO   So do counterfeits.

VALENTINE   So do you.

THURIO   What seem I that I am not?

VALENTINE   Wise.

THURIO   What instance of the contrary?

VALENTINE   Your folly.

THURIO   And how quote you my folly?

VALENTINE   I quote it in your jerkin.

THURIO   My jerkin is a doublet.

VALENTINE   Well, then, I'll double your folly.

THURIO   How!

SILVIA   What, angry, Sir Thurio? Do you change colour?

VALENTINE   Give him leave, madam, he is a kind of chameleon.   25

THURIO   That hath more mind to feed on your blood than live in your air.

VALENTINE   You have said, sir.

THURIO   Ay, sir, and done too for this time.   30

VALENTINE   I know it well, sir, you always end ere you begin.

SILVIA   A fine volley of words, gentlemen, and quickly shot off.

VALENTINE   'Tis indeed, madam: we thank the giver.   35

SILVIA   Who is that, servant?

VALENTINE   Yourself, sweet lady, for you gave the fire. Sir Thurio borrows his wit from your ladyship's looks, and spends what he borrows kindly in your company.

THURIO   Sir, if you spend word for word with me, I shall   40 make your wit bankrupt.

VALENTINE   I know it well, sir. You have an exchequer of words, and I think no other treasure to give your followers; for it appears by their bare liveries that they live by your bare words.   45

SILVIA   No more, gentlemen, no more. Here comes my father.

Enter DUKE.

DUKE   Now, daughter Silvia, you are hard beset.
Sir Valentine, your father is in good health.
What say you to a letter from your friends   50
Of much good news?

VALENTINE   My lord, I will be thankful
To any happy messenger from thence.

DUKE   Know ye Don Antonio, your countryman?

VALENTINE   Ay, my good lord, I know the gentleman
To be of worth, and worthy estimation,   55
And not without desert so well reputed.

DUKE   Hath he not a son?

VALENTINE   Ay, my good lord, a son that well deserves
The honour and regard of such a father.

DUKE   You know him well?   60

VALENTINE   I knew him as myself; for from our infancy
We have convers'd, and spent our hours together,
And though myself have been an idle truant,
Omitting the sweet benefit of time
To clothe mine age with angel-like perfection,   65
Yet hath Sir Proteus (for that's his name)
Made use and fair advantage of his days:
His years but young, but his experience old;
His head unmellow'd, but his judgment ripe;
And in a word (for far behind his worth   70
Comes all the praises that I now bestow)
He is complete in feature and in mind,
With all good grace to grace a gentleman.

DUKE   Beshrew me, sir, but if he make this good
He is as worthy for an empress' love   75
As meet to be an emperor's counsellor.
Well, sir; this gentleman is come to me
With commendation from great potentates,

And here he means to spend his time awhile:
80　　I think 'tis no unwelcome news to you.
VALENTINE
　　Should I have wish'd a thing, it had been he.
DUKE　　Welcome him then according to his worth.
　　Silvia, I speak to you, and you, Sir Thurio;
　　For Valentine, I need not cite him to it.
85　　I will send him hither to you presently.　　　　　*Exit.*
VALENTINE　　This is the gentleman I told your ladyship
　　Had come along with me, but that his mistress
　　Did hold his eyes lock'd in her crystal looks.
SILVIA　　Belike that now she hath enfranchis'd them
90　　Upon some other pawn for fealty.
VALENTINE
　　Nay, sure, I think she holds them prisoners still.
SILVIA　　Nay, then he should be blind, and being blind
　　How could he see his way to seek out you?
VALENTINE　　Why, lady, Love hath twenty pair of eyes.
95　　THURIO　　They say that Love hath not an eye at all.
VALENTINE　　To see such lovers, Thurio, as yourself:
　　Upon a homely object, Love can wink.

　　　　　　　　Enter PROTEUS.

SILVIA
　　Have done, have done: here comes the gentleman.
VALENTINE
　　Welcome, dear Proteus. Mistress, I beseech you
100　　Confirm his welcome, with some special favour.
SILVIA　　His worth is warrant for his welcome hither,
　　If this be he you oft have wish'd to hear from.
VALENTINE　　Mistress, it is; sweet lady, entertain him
　　To be my fellow-servant to your ladyship.
105　　SILVIA　　Too low a mistress for so high a servant.
PROTEUS　　Not so, sweet lady, but too mean a servant
　　To have a look of such a worthy mistress.
VALENTINE　　Leave off discourse of disability.
　　Sweet lady, entertain him for your servant.
110　　PROTEUS　　My duty will I boast of, nothing else.
SILVIA　　And duty never yet did want his meed.
　　Servant, you are welcome to a worthless mistress.
PROTEUS　　I'll die on him that says so but yourself.
SILVIA　　That you are welcome?
PROTEUS　　　　　　　　That you are worthless.

　　　　　　　　Enter a Servant.

SERVANT
115　　Madam, my lord your father would speak with you.
SILVIA　　I wait upon his pleasure. Come, Sir Thurio,
　　Go with me. Once more, new servant, welcome;
　　I'll leave you to confer of home affairs.
　　When you have done, we look to hear from you.
120　　PROTEUS　　We'll both attend upon your ladyship.
　　　　　　Exeunt Silvia, Thurio, Speed and Servant.
VALENTINE
　　Now tell me: how do all from whence you came?
PROTEUS
　　Your friends are well, and have them much

commended.
VALENTINE　　And how do yours?
PROTEUS　　　　　　　　　I left them all in health.
VALENTINE
　　How does your lady? And how thrives your love?
PROTEUS　　My tales of love were wont to weary you:　　125
　　I know you joy not in a love-discourse.
VALENTINE　　Ay, Proteus, but that life is alter'd now:
　　I have done penance for contemning Love,
　　Whose high imperious thoughts have punish'd me
　　With bitter fasts, with penitential groans,　　　　130
　　With nightly tears, and daily heart-sore sighs,
　　For in revenge of my contempt of Love,
　　Love hath chas'd sleep from my enthralled eyes,
　　And made them watchers of mine own heart's
　　　　sorrow.
　　O gentle Proteus, Love's a mighty lord,　　　　135
　　And hath so humbled me, as I confess
　　There is no woe to his correction,
　　Nor, to his service, no such joy on earth.
　　Now, no discourse, except it be of love;
　　Now can I break my fast, dine, sup, and sleep　　140
　　Upon the very naked name of Love.
PROTEUS　　Enough: I read your fortune in your eye.
　　Was this the idol that you worship so?
VALENTINE　　Even she; and is she not a heavenly saint?
PROTEUS　　No; but she is an earthly paragon.　　　145
VALENTINE　　Call her divine.
PROTEUS　　　　　　　　I will not flatter her.
VALENTINE　　O flatter me; for love delights in praises.
PROTEUS　　When I was sick, you gave me bitter pills,
　　And I must minister the like to you.
VALENTINE　　Then speak the truth by her: if not divine,　　150
　　Yet let her be a principality,
　　Sovereign to all the creatures on the earth.
PROTEUS　　Except my mistress.
VALENTINE　　　　　　　　Sweet, except not any,
　　Except thou wilt except against my love.
PROTEUS　　Have I not reason to prefer mine own?　　155
VALENTINE　　And I will help thee to prefer her too:
　　She shall be dignified with this high honour,
　　To bear my lady's train, lest the base earth
　　Should from her vesture chance to steal a kiss,
　　And of so great a favour growing proud,　　　160
　　Disdain to root the summer-swelling flower,
　　And make rough winter everlastingly.
PROTEUS　　Why, Valentine, what braggardism is this?
VALENTINE　　Pardon me, Proteus, all I can is nothing
　　To her whose worth makes other worthies nothing:　　165
　　She is alone.
PROTEUS　　Then let her alone.
VALENTINE
　　Not for the world. Why, man, she is mine own,
　　And I as rich in having such a jewel
　　As twenty seas, if all their sand were pearl,　　170
　　The water nectar, and the rocks pure gold.
　　Forgive me that I do not dream on thee,

Because thou seest me dote upon my love.
My foolish rival that her father likes
(Only for his possessions are so huge)   75
Is gone with her along, and I must after,
For love, thou know'st, is full of jealousy.

PROTEUS   But she loves you?

VALENTINE
Ay, and we are betroth'd; nay more, our marriage
      hour,
With all the cunning manner of our flight,   80
Determin'd of: how I must climb her window,
The ladder made of cords, and all the means
Plotted, and 'greed on for my happiness.
Good Proteus, go with me to my chamber,
In these affairs to aid me with thy counsel.   85

PROTEUS   Go on before; I shall enquire you forth.
I must unto the road, to disembark
Some necessaries that I needs must use,
And then I'll presently attend you.

VALENTINE   Will you make haste?   90

PROTEUS   I will.   *Exit Valentine.*
Even as one heat another heat expels,
Or as one nail by strength drives out another,
So the remembrance of my former love
Is by a newer object quite forgotten.   95
Is it mine eye, or Valentinus' praise,
Her true perfection, or my false transgression,
That makes me reasonless, to reason thus?
She is fair; and so is Julia that I love –
That I did love, for now my love is thaw'd,   00
Which like a waxen image 'gainst a fire
Bears no impression of the thing it was.
Methinks my zeal to Valentine is cold,
And that I love him not as I was wont.
O, but I love his lady too-too much,   05
And that's the reason I love him so little.
How shall I dote on her with more advice,
That thus without advice begin to love her?
'Tis but her picture I have yet beheld,
And that hath dazzled my reason's light;   10
But when I look on her perfections,
There is no reason but I shall be blind.
If I can check my erring love, I will;
If not, to compass her I'll use my skill.   *Exit.*

2.5   *Enter* SPEED *and* LAUNCE *with his dog.*

SPEED   Launce, by mine honesty, welcome to Padua.

LAUNCE   Forswear not thyself, sweet youth, for I am not
welcome. I reckon this always, that a man is never
undone till he be hanged, nor never welcome to a place
till some certain shot be paid, and the hostess say
'welcome'.

SPEED   Come on, you madcap: I'll to the ale-house with
you presently; where, for one shot of five pence, thou
shalt have five thousand welcomes. But, sirrah, how
did thy master part with Madam Julia?   10

LAUNCE   Marry, after they closed in earnest, they parted
very fairly in jest.

SPEED   But shall she marry him?

LAUNCE   No.

SPEED   How then? Shall he marry her?   15

LAUNCE   No, neither.

SPEED   What, are they broken?

LAUNCE   No; they are both as whole as a fish.

SPEED   Why then, how stands the matter with them?

LAUNCE   Marry, thus: when it stands well with him, it   20
stands well with her.

SPEED   What an ass art thou, I understand thee not.

LAUNCE   What a block art thou, that thou canst not! My
staff understands me.

SPEED   What thou say'st?   25

LAUNCE   Ay, and what I do too: look thee, I'll but lean,
and my staff understands me.

SPEED   It stands under thee indeed.

LAUNCE   Why, stand under and understand is all one.

SPEED   But tell me true, will't be a match?   30

LAUNCE   Ask my dog: if he say 'ay', it will; if he say 'no',
it will; if he shake his tail, and say nothing, it will.

SPEED   The conclusion is, then, that it will.

LAUNCE   Thou shalt never get such a secret from me but
by a parable.   35

SPEED   'Tis well that I get it so. But, Launce, how say'st
thou that my master is become a notable lover?

LAUNCE   I never knew him otherwise.

SPEED   Than how?

LAUNCE   A notable lubber; as thou reportest him to be.   40

SPEED   Why, thou whoreson ass, thou mistak'st me.

LAUNCE   Why, fool, I meant not thee, I meant thy
master.

SPEED   I tell thee, my master is become a hot lover.

LAUNCE   Why, I tell thee, I care not, though he burn   45
himself in love. If thou wilt, go with me to the alehouse; if not, thou art an Hebrew, a Jew, and not worth
the name of a Christian.

SPEED   Why?

LAUNCE   Because thou hast not so much charity in thee   50
as to go to the ale with a Christian. Wilt thou go?

SPEED   At thy service.   *Exeunt.*

2.6   *Enter* PROTEUS *alone.*

PROTEUS   To leave my Julia, shall I be forsworn;
To love fair Silvia, shall I be forsworn;
To wrong my friend, I shall be much forsworn.
And ev'n that power which gave me first my oath
Provokes me to this threefold perjury.   5
Love bade me swear, and Love bids me forswear.
O sweet-suggesting Love, if thou hast sinn'd,
Teach me (thy tempted subject) to excuse it.
At first I did adore a twinkling star,
But now I worship a celestial sun: 10
Unheedful vows may heedfully be broken,
And he wants wit that wants resolved will

To learn his wit t'exchange the bad for better.
Fie, fie, unreverend tongue, to call her bad
15   Whose sovereignty so oft thou hast preferr'd,
With twenty thousand soul-confirming oaths.
I cannot leave to love; and yet I do;
But there I leave to love, where I should love.
Julia I lose, and Valentine I lose;
20   If I keep them, I needs must lose myself;
If I lose them, thus find I by their loss:
For Valentine, myself; for Julia, Silvia.
I to myself am dearer than a friend,
For love is still most precious in itself,
25   And Silvia (witness heaven that made her fair)
Shows Julia but a swarthy Ethiope.
I will forget that Julia is alive,
Rememb'ring that my love to her is dead.
And Valentine I'll hold an enemy,
30   Aiming at Silvia as a sweeter friend.
I cannot now prove constant to myself,
Without some treachery us'd to Valentine.
This night he meaneth with a corded ladder
To climb celestial Silvia's chamber-window,
35   Myself in counsel, his competitor.
Now presently I'll give her father notice
Of their disguising and pretended flight;
Who, all enrag'd, will banish Valentine,
For Thurio he intends shall wed his daughter.
40   But Valentine being gone, I'll quickly cross,
By some sly trick, blunt Thurio's dull proceeding.
Love, lend me wings to make my purpose swift
As thou hast lent me wit to plot this drift.   *Exit.*

2.7   *Enter* JULIA *and* LUCETTA.

JULIA   Counsel, Lucetta; gentle girl, assist me,
And ev'n in kind love I do conjure thee,
Who art the table wherein all my thoughts
Are visibly character'd and engrav'd,
5   To lesson me, and tell me some good mean
How with my honour I may undertake
A journey to my loving Proteus.
LUCETTA   Alas, the way is wearisome and long.
JULIA   A true-devoted pilgrim is not weary
10   To measure kingdoms with his feeble steps,
Much less shall she that hath Love's wings to fly,
And when the flight is made to one so dear,
Of such divine perfection as Sir Proteus.
LUCETTA   Better forbear, till Proteus make return.
JULIA
15   O, know'st thou not his looks are my soul's food?
Pity the dearth that I have pined in,
By longing for that food so long a time.
Didst thou but know the inly touch of love,
Thou wouldst as soon go kindle fire with snow
20   As seek to quench the fire of love with words.
LUCETTA   I do not seek to quench your love's hot fire,
But qualify the fire's extreme rage,

Lest it should burn above the bounds of reason.
JULIA
The more thou damm'st it up, the more it burns:
The current that with gentle murmur glides,   25
Thou know'st, being stopp'd impatiently doth rage;
But when his fair course is not hindered,
He makes sweet music with th' enamell'd stones,
Giving a gentle kiss to every sedge
He overtaketh in his pilgrimage.   30
And so by many winding nooks he strays
With willing sport to the wild ocean.
Then let me go, and hinder not my course.
I'll be as patient as a gentle stream,
And make a pastime of each weary step,   35
Till the last step have brought me to my love,
And there I'll rest, as after much turmoil
A blessed soul doth in Elysium.
LUCETTA   But in what habit will you go along?
JULIA   Not like a woman, for I would prevent   40
The loose encounters of lascivious men:
Gentle Lucetta, fit me with such weeds
As may beseem some well-reputed page.
LUCETTA   Why, then your ladyship must cut your hair.
JULIA   No, girl, I'll knit it up in silken strings,   45
With twenty odd-conceited true-love knots:
To be fantastic may become a youth
Of greater time than I shall show to be.
LUCETTA
What fashion, madam, shall I make your breeches?
JULIA   That fits as well as 'Tell me, good my lord,   50
What compass will you wear your farthingale?'
Why, ev'n what fashion thou best likes, Lucetta.
LUCETTA
You must needs have them with a cod-piece, madam.
JULIA   Out, out, Lucetta, that will be ill-favour'd.
LUCETTA
A round hose, madam, now's not worth a pin   55
Unless you have a cod-piece to stick pins on.
JULIA   Lucetta, as thou lov'st me let me have
What thou think'st meet, and is most mannerly.
But tell me, wench, how will the world repute me
For undertaking so unstaid a journey?   60
I fear me it will make me scandalis'd.
LUCETTA
If you think so, then stay at home, and go not.
JULIA   Nay, that I will not.
LUCETTA   Then never dream on infamy, but go.
If Proteus like your journey, when you come,   65
No matter who's displeas'd, when you are gone.
I fear me he will scarce be pleas'd withal.
JULIA   That is the least, Lucetta, of my fear:
A thousand oaths, an ocean of his tears,
And instances of infinite of love,   70
Warrant me welcome to my Proteus.
LUCETTA   All these are servants to deceitful men.
JULIA   Base men, that use them to so base effect;
But truer stars did govern Proteus' birth,

His words are bonds, his oaths are oracles,
His love sincere, his thoughts immaculate,
His tears pure messengers sent from his heart,
His heart as far from fraud as heaven from earth.

LUCETTA
Pray heav'n he prove so when you come to him.

JULIA   Now, as thou lov'st me, do him not that wrong,
To bear a hard opinion of his truth.
Only deserve my love, by loving him,
And presently go with me to my chamber
To take a note of what I stand in need of,
To furnish me upon my longing journey.
All that is mine I leave at thy dispose,
My goods, my lands, my reputation,
Only, in lieu thereof, dispatch me hence.
Come; answer not; but to it presently,
I am impatient of my tarriance.   *Exeunt.*

3.1   *Enter* DUKE, THURIO *and* PROTEUS.

DUKE   Sir Thurio, give us leave, I pray, awhile,
We have some secrets to confer about.   *Exit Thurio.*
Now tell me, Proteus, what's your will with me?

PROTEUS
My gracious lord, that which I would discover
The law of friendship bids me to conceal,
But when I call to mind your gracious favours
Done to me, undeserving as I am,
My duty pricks me on to utter that
Which else no worldly good should draw from me.
Know, worthy prince, Sir Valentine my friend
This night intends to steal away your daughter;
Myself am one made privy to the plot.
I know you have determin'd to bestow her
On Thurio, whom your gentle daughter hates,
And should she thus be stol'n away from you,
It would be much vexation to your age.
Thus, for my duty's sake, I rather chose
To cross my friend in his intended drift,
Than, by concealing it, heap on your head
A pack of sorrows, which would press you down,
Being unprevented, to your timeless grave.

DUKE   Proteus, I thank thee for thine honest care,
Which to requite command me while I live.
This love of theirs myself have often seen,
Haply when they have judg'd me fast asleep,
And oftentimes have purpos'd to forbid
Sir Valentine her company and my court.
But fearing lest my jealous aim might err,
And so (unworthily) disgrace the man
(A rashness that I ever yet have shunn'd)
I gave him gentle looks, thereby to find
That which thyself hast now disclos'd to me.
And that thou mayst perceive my fear of this,
Knowing that tender youth is soon suggested,
I nightly lodge her in an upper tower,
The key whereof myself have ever kept,

And thence she cannot be convey'd away.

PROTEUS   Know, noble lord, they have devis'd a mean
How he her chamber-window will ascend,
And with a corded ladder fetch her down;
For which the youthful lover now is gone,
And this way comes he with it presently,
Where, if it please you, you may intercept him.
But, good my lord, do it so cunningly
That my discovery be not aimed at;
For love of you, not hate unto my friend,
Hath made me publisher of this pretence.

DUKE   Upon mine honour, he shall never know
That I had any light from thee of this.

PROTEUS   Adieu, my lord, Sir Valentine is coming.

Exit.

Enter VALENTINE.

DUKE   Sir Valentine, whither away so fast?

VALENTINE   Please it your grace, there is a messenger
That stays to bear my letters to my friends,
And I am going to deliver them.

DUKE   Be they of much import?

VALENTINE   The tenor of them doth but signify
My health, and happy being at your court.

DUKE   Nay then, no matter. Stay with me awhile;
I am to break with thee of some affairs
That touch me near; wherein thou must be secret.
'Tis not unknown to thee that I have sought
To match my friend Sir Thurio to my daughter.

VALENTINE
I know it well, my lord, and sure the match
Were rich and honourable. Besides, the gentleman
Is full of virtue, bounty, worth, and qualities
Beseeming such a wife as your fair daughter.
Cannot your grace win her to fancy him?

DUKE   No, trust me, she is peevish, sullen, froward,
Proud, disobedient, stubborn, lacking duty,
Neither regarding that she is my child,
Nor fearing me as if I were her father.
And may I say to thee, this pride of hers
(Upon advice) hath drawn my love from her,
And where I thought the remnant of mine age
Should have been cherish'd by her child-like duty,
I now am full resolv'd to take a wife,
And turn her out to who will take her in.
Then let her beauty be her wedding-dower;
For me and my possessions she esteems not.

VALENTINE
What would your grace have me to do in this?

DUKE   There is a lady in Verona here
Whom I affect; but she is nice, and coy,
And nought esteems my aged eloquence.
Now therefore would I have thee to my tutor
(For long agone I have forgot to court,
Besides the fashion of the time is chang'd)
How and which way I may bestow myself
To be regarded in her sun-bright eye.

VALENTINE

    Win her with gifts, if she respect not words:

90   Dumb jewels often in their silent kind,

    More than quick words, do move a woman's mind.

DUKE   But she did scorn a present that I sent her.

VALENTINE

    A woman sometime scorns what best contents her.

    Send her another; never give her o'er,

95   For scorn at first makes after-love the more.

    If she do frown, 'tis not in hate of you,

    But rather to beget more love in you.

    If she do chide, 'tis not to have you gone,

    For why, the fools are mad, if left alone.

100   Take no repulse, whatever she doth say,

    For 'get you gone' she doth not mean 'away!'.

    Flatter, and praise, commend, extol their graces;

    Though ne'er so black, say they have angels' faces;

    That man that hath a tongue, I say is no man,

105   If with his tongue he cannot win a woman.

DUKE   But she I mean is promis'd by her friends

    Unto a youthful gentleman of worth,

    And kept severely from resort of men,

    That no man hath access by day to her.

110 VALENTINE   Why, then I would resort to her by night.

DUKE   Ay, but the doors be lock'd, and keys kept safe,

    That no man hath recourse to her by night.

VALENTINE

    What lets but one may enter at her window?

DUKE   Her chamber is aloft, far from the ground,

115   And built so shelving that one cannot climb it

    Without apparent hazard of his life.

VALENTINE   Why, then a ladder quaintly made of cords

    To cast up, with a pair of anchoring hooks,

    Would serve to scale another Hero's tower,

120   So bold Leander would adventure it.

DUKE   Now, as thou art a gentleman of blood,

    Advise me where I may have such a ladder.

VALENTINE

    When would you use it? Pray, sir, tell me that.

DUKE   This very night; for Love is like a child

125   That longs for every thing that he can come by.

VALENTINE   By seven o'clock I'll get you such a ladder.

DUKE   But hark thee: I will go to her alone;

    How shall I best convey the ladder thither?

VALENTINE

    It will be light, my lord, that you may bear it

130   Under a cloak that is of any length.

DUKE   A cloak as long as thine will serve the turn?

VALENTINE   Ay, my good lord.

DUKE   Then let me see thy cloak,

    I'll get me one of such another length.

VALENTINE

    Why, any cloak will serve the turn, my lord.

135 DUKE   How shall I fashion me to wear a cloak?

    I pray thee let me feel thy cloak upon me.

    [*He takes Valentine's cloak, and finds with it a letter*

    and a corded ladder.]

What letter is this same? What's here? 'To Silvia'!

And here an engine fit for my proceeding.

I'll be so bold to break the seal for once.

[*Reads.*]

My thoughts do harbour with my Silvia nightly,   140

And slaves they are to me that send them flying.

O, could their master come and go as lightly,

Himself would lodge where (senseless) they are lying.

My herald thoughts in thy pure bosom rest them,

While I, their king, that thither them importune,   145

Do curse the grace that with such grace hath blest them,

Because myself do want my servants' fortune.

I curse myself for they are sent by me,

That they should harbour where their lord should be.

What's here?   150

Silvia, this night I will enfranchise thee.

'Tis so; and here's the ladder for the purpose.

Why, Phaëton, for thou art Merops' son

Wilt thou aspire to guide the heavenly car?

And with thy daring folly burn the world?   155

Wilt thou reach stars, because they shine on thee?

Go, base intruder, overweening slave,

Bestow thy fawning smiles on equal mates,

And think my patience (more than thy desert)

Is privilege for thy departure hence.   160

Thank me for this, more than for all the favours

Which (all too much) I have bestowed on thee.

But if thou linger in my territories

Longer than swiftest expedition

Will give thee time to leave our royal court,   165

By heaven, my wrath shall far exceed the love

I ever bore my daughter, or thyself.

Be gone, I will not hear thy vain excuse,

But as thou lov'st thy life, make speed from hence.

                                     Exit.

VALENTINE

And why not death, rather than living torment?   170

To die is to be banish'd from myself,

And Silvia is myself: banish'd from her

Is self from self. A deadly banishment.

What light is light, if Silvia be not seen?

What joy is joy, if Silvia be not by?   175

Unless it be to think that she is by

And feed upon the shadow of perfection.

Except I be by Silvia in the night,

There is no music in the nightingale.

Unless I look on Silvia in the day,   180

There is no day for me to look upon.

She is my essence, and I leave to be,

If I be not by her fair influence

Foster'd, illumin'd, cherish'd, kept alive.

I fly not death, to fly his deadly doom: 185

Tarry I here, I but attend on death,

But fly I hence, I fly away from life.

            Enter PROTEUS *and* LAUNCE.

PROTEUS   Run, boy, run, run, and seek him out.

LAUNCE So-ho, so-ho –

PROTEUS What seest thou?

LAUNCE Him we go to find. There's not a hair on's head but 'tis a Valentine.

PROTEUS Valentine?

VALENTINE No.

PROTEUS Who then? His spirit?

VALENTINE Neither.

PROTEUS What then?

VALENTINE Nothing.

LAUNCE Can nothing speak? Master, shall I strike?

PROTEUS Who wouldst thou strike?

LAUNCE Nothing.

PROTEUS Villain, forbear.

LAUNCE Why, sir, I'll strike nothing. I pray you –

PROTEUS
Sirrah, I say forbear. Friend Valentine, a word.

VALENTINE
My ears are stopp'd, and cannot hear good news,
So much of bad already hath possess'd them.

PROTEUS Then in dumb silence will I bury mine,
For they are harsh, untunable, and bad.

VALENTINE Is Silvia dead?

PROTEUS No, Valentine.

VALENTINE No Valentine indeed for sacred Silvia.
Hath she forsworn me?

PROTEUS No, Valentine.

VALENTINE No Valentine if Silvia have forsworn me.
What is your news?

LAUNCE
Sir, there is a proclamation that you are vanished.

PROTEUS
That thou art banish'd – O, that's the news –
From hence, from Silvia, and from me thy friend.

VALENTINE O, I have fed upon this woe already,
And now excess of it will make me surfeit.
Doth Silvia know that I am banished?

PROTEUS Ay, ay; and she hath offered to the doom
(Which unrevers'd stands in effectual force)
A sea of melting pearl, which some call tears;
Those at her father's churlish feet she tender'd,
With them, upon her knees, her humble self,
Wringing her hands, whose whiteness so became them
As if but now they waxed pale for woe.
But neither bended knees, pure hands held up,
Sad sighs, deep groans, nor silver-shedding tears
Could penetrate her uncompassionate sire;
But Valentine, if he be ta'en, must die.
Besides, her intercession chaf'd him so,
When she for thy repeal was suppliant,
That to close prison he commanded her,
With many bitter threats of biding there.

VALENTINE
No more; unless the next word that thou speak'st
Have some malignant power upon my life,
If so, I pray thee breathe it in mine ear,

As ending anthem of my endless dolour.

PROTEUS Cease to lament for that thou canst not help,
And study help for that which thou lament'st.
Time is the nurse and breeder of all good.
Here, if thou stay, thou canst not see thy love;
Besides, thy staying will abridge thy life.
Hope is a lover's staff: walk hence with that
And manage it, against despairing thoughts.
Thy letters may be here, though thou art hence,
Which, being writ to me, shall be deliver'd
Even in the milk-white bosom of thy love.
The time now serves not to expostulate.
Come, I'll convey thee through the city-gate,
And ere I part with thee, confer at large
Of all that may concern thy love-affairs.
As thou lov'st Silvia (though not for thyself)
Regard thy danger, and along with me.

VALENTINE
I pray thee, Launce, and if thou seest my boy,
Bid him make haste, and meet me at the North Gate.

PROTEUS Go, sirrah, find him out. Come, Valentine.

VALENTINE O my dear Silvia! Hapless Valentine!

Exeunt Proteus and Valentine.

LAUNCE I am but a fool, look you, and yet I have the wit to think my master is a kind of a knave; but that's all one, if he be but one knave. He lives not now that knows me to be in love, yet I am in love, but a team of horse shall not pluck that from me; nor who 'tis I love; and yet 'tis a woman; but what woman I will not tell myself; and yet 'tis a milk-maid; yet 'tis not a maid, for she hath had gossips; yet 'tis a maid, for she is her master's maid, and serves for wages. She hath more qualities than a water-spaniel, which is much in a bare Christian. [*taking out a paper*] Here is the cate-log of her conditions. 'Imprimis, she can fetch and carry': why, a horse can do no more; nay, a horse cannot fetch, but only carry, therefore is she better than a jade. 'Item, she can milk': look you, a sweet virtue in a maid with clean hands.

Enter SPEED.

SPEED How now, Signor Launce! What news with your mastership?

LAUNCE With my master's ship? Why, it is at sea.

SPEED Well, your old vice still: mistake the word. What news, then, in your paper?

LAUNCE The black'st news that ever thou heard'st.

SPEED Why, man, how black?

LAUNCE Why, as black as ink.

SPEED Let me read them.

LAUNCE Fie on thee, jolt-head, thou canst not read.

SPEED Thou lyest; I can.

LAUNCE I will try thee. Tell me this: who begot thee?

SPEED Marry, the son of my grandfather.

LAUNCE O illiterate loiterer! It was the son of thy grandmother. This proves that thou canst not read.

SPEED Come, fool, come; try me in thy paper.

LAUNCE [*giving him the paper*] There; and Saint Nicholas be thy speed.

295 SPEED *Imprimis, she can milk.*

LAUNCE Ay, that she can.

SPEED *Item, she brews good ale.*

LAUNCE And thereof comes the proverb: 'Blessing of your heart, you brew good ale.'

300 SPEED *Item, she can sew.*

LAUNCE That's as much as to say, 'Can she so?'

SPEED *Item, she can knit.*

LAUNCE What need a man care for a stock with a wench, when she can knit him a stock?

305 SPEED *Item, she can wash and scour.*

LAUNCE A special virtue; for then she need not be washed and scoured.

SPEED *Item, she can spin.*

LAUNCE Then may I set the world on wheels, when she can spin for her living.

310 SPEED *Item, she hath many nameless virtues.*

LAUNCE That's as much as to say 'bastard virtues'; that indeed know not their fathers; and therefore have no names.

315 SPEED *Here follow her vices.*

LAUNCE Close at the heels of her virtues.

SPEED *Item, she is not to be kissed fasting in respect of her breath.*

LAUNCE Well; that fault may be mended with a breakfast. Read on.

320 SPEED *Item, she hath a sweet mouth.*

LAUNCE That makes amends for her sour breath.

SPEED *Item, she doth talk in her sleep.*

LAUNCE It's no matter for that; so she sleep not in her talk.

325 SPEED *Item, she is slow in words.*

LAUNCE O villain, that set this down among her vices! To be slow in words is a woman's only virtue. I pray thee out with 't, and place it for her chief virtue.

330 SPEED *Item, she is proud.*

LAUNCE Out with that too: it was Eve's legacy, and cannot be ta'en from her.

SPEED *Item, she hath no teeth.*

LAUNCE I care not for that neither; because I love crusts.

335 SPEED *Item, she is curst.*

LAUNCE Well; the best is, she hath no teeth to bite.

SPEED *Item, she will often praise her liquor.*

LAUNCE If her liquor be good, she shall; if she will not, I will; for good things should be praised.

340 SPEED *Item, she is too liberal.*

LAUNCE Of her tongue she cannot, for that's writ down she is slow of; of her purse she shall not, for that I'll keep shut. Now, of another thing she may, and that cannot I help. Well, proceed.

345 SPEED *Item, she hath more hair than wit, and more faults than hairs, and more wealth than faults.*

LAUNCE Stop there. I'll have her. She was mine, and not mine, twice or thrice in that last article. Rehearse that once more.

350 SPEED *Item, she hath more hair than wit.*

LAUNCE More hair than wit: it may be. I'll prove it: the cover of the salt hides the salt, and therefore it is more than the salt; the hair that covers the wit is more than the wit; for the greater hides the less. What's next?

SPEED *And more faults than hairs.*

LAUNCE That's monstrous: O that were out!

SPEED *And more wealth than faults.*

360 LAUNCE Why, that word makes the faults gracious. Well, I'll have her. And if it be a match, as nothing is impossible –

SPEED What then?

LAUNCE Why, then will I tell thee that thy master stays for thee at the North Gate.

365 SPEED For me?

LAUNCE For thee? Ay, who art thou? He hath stayed for a better man than thee.

SPEED And must I go to him?

370 LAUNCE Thou must run to him; for thou hast stayed so long that going will scarce serve the turn.

SPEED Why didst not tell me sooner? 'Pox of your love-letters!   *Exit.*

375 LAUNCE Now will he be swinged for reading my letter; an unmannerly slave, that will thrust himself into secrets. I'll after, to rejoice in the boy's correction.
                                                                        Exit.

3.2   *Enter* DUKE *and* THURIO.

DUKE Sir Thurio, fear not but that she will love you
Now Valentine is banish'd from her sight.

THURIO Since his exile she hath despis'd me most,
Forsworn my company, and rail'd at me,
That I am desperate of obtaining her.   5

DUKE This weak impress of love is as a figure
Trenched in ice, which with an hour's heat
Dissolves to water, and doth lose his form.
A little time will melt her frozen thoughts,
And worthless Valentine shall be forgot.   10

                          Enter PROTEUS.

How now, Sir Proteus, is your countryman,
According to our proclamation, gone?

PROTEUS Gone, my good lord.

DUKE My daughter takes his going grievously?

PROTEUS A little time, my lord, will kill that grief.   15

DUKE So I believe; but Thurio thinks not so.
Proteus, the good conceit I hold of thee
(For thou hast shown some sign of good desert)
Makes me the better to confer with thee.

PROTEUS Longer than I prove loyal to your grace   20
Let me not live to look upon your grace.

DUKE Thou know'st how willingly I would effect
The match between Sir Thurio and my daughter?

PROTEUS I do, my lord.

DUKE   And also, I think, thou art not ignorant   25
    How she opposes her against my will?
PROTEUS   She did, my lord, when Valentine was here.
DUKE   Ay, and perversely she persevers so.
    What might we do to make the girl forget
    The love of Valentine, and love Sir Thurio?   30
PROTEUS   The best way is to slander Valentine,
    With falsehood, cowardice, and poor descent:
    Three things that women highly hold in hate.
DUKE   Ay, but she'll think that it is spoke in hate.
PROTEUS   Ay, if his enemy deliver it.   35
    Therefore it must with circumstance be spoken
    By one whom she esteemeth as his friend.
DUKE   Then you must undertake to slander him.
PROTEUS   And that, my lord, I shall be loath to do:
    'Tis an ill office for a gentleman,   40
    Especially against his very friend.
DUKE   Where your good word cannot advantage him,
    Your slander never can endamage him;
    Therefore the office is indifferent,
    Being entreated to it by your friend.   45
PROTEUS   You have prevail'd, my lord: if I can do it
    By aught that I can speak in his dispraise,
    She shall not long continue love to him.
    But say this wind her love from Valentine,
    It follows not that she will love Sir Thurio.   50
THURIO   Therefore, as you unwind her love from him,
    Lest it should ravel, and be good to none,
    You must provide to bottom it on me;
    Which must be done by praising me as much
    As you in worth dispraise Sir Valentine.   55
DUKE   And, Proteus, we dare trust you in this kind,
    Because we know (on Valentine's report)
    You are already Love's firm votary,
    And cannot soon revolt, and change your mind.
    Upon this warrant shall you have access   60
    Where you with Silvia may confer at large.
    For she is lumpish, heavy, melancholy,
    And, for your friend's sake, will be glad of you;
    Where you may temper her, by your persuasion,
    To hate young Valentine, and love my friend.   65
PROTEUS   As much as I can do, I will effect.
    But you, Sir Thurio, are not sharp enough:
    You must lay lime, to tangle her desires
    By wailful sonnets, whose composed rhymes
    Should be full-fraught with serviceable vows.   70
DUKE   Ay, much is the force of heaven-bred poesy.
PROTEUS   Say that upon the altar of her beauty
    You sacrifice your tears, your sighs, your heart.
    Write till your ink be dry; and with your tears
    Moist it again; and frame some feeling line   75
    That may discover such integrity.
    For Orpheus' lute was strung with poets' sinews,
    Whose golden touch could soften steel and stones,
    Make tigers tame, and huge leviathans
    Forsake unsounded deeps, to dance on sands.   80
    After your dire-lamenting elegies,

    Visit by night your lady's chamber-window
    With some sweet consort; to their instruments
    Tune a deploring dump: the night's dead silence
    Will well become such sweet complaining grievance. 85
    This, or else nothing, will inherit her.
DUKE   This discipline shows thou hast been in love.
THURIO   And thy advice, this night, I'll put in practice:
    Therefore, sweet Proteus, my direction-giver,
    Let us into the city presently   90
    To sort some gentlemen, well skill'd in music.
    I have a sonnet that will serve the turn
    To give the onset to thy good advice.
DUKE   About it, gentlemen.
PROTEUS   We'll wait upon your grace till after supper,   95
    And afterward determine our proceedings.
DUKE   Even now about it. I will pardon you.   *Exeunt.*

4.1   *Enter certain* Outlaws.

1 OUTLAW   Fellows, stand fast: I see a passenger.
2 OUTLAW
    If there be ten, shrink not, but down with 'em.

Enter VALENTINE *and* SPEED.

3 OUTLAW
    Stand, sir, and throw us that you have about ye.
    If not, we'll make you sit, and rifle you.
SPEED   Sir, we are undone; these are the villains   5
    That all the travellers do fear so much.
VALENTINE   My friends –
1 OUTLAW   That's not so, sir: we are your enemies.
2 OUTLAW   Peace; we'll hear him.
3 OUTLAW
    Ay, by my beard will we; for he is a proper man.   10
VALENTINE   Then know that I have little wealth to lose;
    A man I am, cross'd with adversity:
    My riches are these poor habiliments,
    Of which if you should here disfurnish me,
    You take the sum and substance that I have.   15
2 OUTLAW   Whither travel you?
VALENTINE   To Verona.
1 OUTLAW   Whence came you?
VALENTINE   From Milan.
3 OUTLAW   Have you long sojourned there?   20
VALENTINE
    Some sixteen months, and longer might have stay'd,
    If crooked fortune had not thwarted me.
1 OUTLAW   What, were you banished thence?
VALENTINE   I was.
2 OUTLAW   For what offence?   25
VALENTINE
    For that which now torments me to rehearse:
    I kill'd a man, whose death I much repent,
    But yet I slew him manfully, in fight,
    Without false vantage, or base treachery.
1 OUTLAW   Why, ne'er repent it, if it were done so;   30
    But were you banish'd for so small a fault?

VALENTINE   I was, and held me glad of such a doom.

2 OUTLAW   Have you the tongues?

VALENTINE
    My youthful travel therein made me happy,
35   Or else I often had been miserable.

3 OUTLAW   By the bare scalp of Robin Hood's fat friar,
    This fellow were a king for our wild faction.

1 OUTLAW   We'll have him. Sirs, a word.

SPEED   Master, be one of them: it's an honourable kind
40   of thievery.

VALENTINE   Peace, villain.

2 OUTLAW   Tell us this: have you anything to take to?

VALENTINE   Nothing but my fortune.

3 OUTLAW   Know, then, that some of us are gentlemen,
45   Such as the fury of ungovern'd youth
    Thrust from the company of awful men.
    Myself was from Verona banished,
    For practising to steal away a lady,
    An heir, and near allied unto the Duke.

50 2 OUTLAW   And I from Mantua, for a gentleman,
    Who, in my mood, I stabb'd unto the heart.

1 OUTLAW   And I, for such like petty crimes as these.
    But to the purpose: for we cite our faults,
    That they may hold excus'd our lawless lives;
55   And partly seeing you are beautified
    With goodly shape, and by your own report
    A linguist, and a man of such perfection
    As we do in our quality much want –

2 OUTLAW   Indeed because you are a banish'd man,
60   Therefore, above the rest, we parley to you:
    Are you content to be our general?
    To make a virtue of necessity,
    And live as we do in this wilderness?

3 OUTLAW
    What say'st thou? Wilt thou be of our consort?
65   Say 'ay', and be the captain of us all:
    We'll do thee homage, and be rul'd by thee,
    Love thee, as our commander, and our king.

1 OUTLAW   But if thou scorn our courtesy, thou diest.

2 OUTLAW
    Thou shalt not live to brag what we have offer'd.

70 VALENTINE   I take your offer, and will live with you,
    Provided that you do no outrages
    On silly women or poor passengers.

3 OUTLAW   No, we detest such vile base practices.
    Come, go with us, we'll bring thee to our crews,
75   And show thee all the treasure we have got;
    Which, with ourselves, all rest at thy dispose. *Exeunt.*

4.2   *Enter* PROTEUS.

PROTEUS   Already have I been false to Valentine,
    And now I must be as unjust to Thurio:
    Under the colour of commending him,
    I have access my own love to prefer.
5   But Silvia is too fair, too true, too holy,
    To be corrupted with my worthless gifts.

    When I protest true loyalty to her,
    She twits me with my falsehood to my friend;
    When to her beauty I commend my vows,
    She bids me think how I have been forsworn   10
    In breaking faith with Julia, whom I lov'd.
    And notwithstanding all her sudden quips,
    The least whereof would quell a lover's hope,
    Yet, spaniel-like, the more she spurns my love,
    The more it grows, and fawneth on her still.   15

Enter THURIO *and* Musicians.

    But here comes Thurio; now must we to her window,
    And give some evening music to her ear.

THURIO
    How now, Sir Proteus, are you crept before us?

PROTEUS   Ay, gentle Thurio, for you know that love
    Will creep in service where it cannot go.   20

THURIO   Ay, but I hope, sir, that you love not here.

PROTEUS   Sir, but I do; or else I would be hence.

THURIO   Who? Silvia?

PROTEUS   Ay, Silvia, for your sake.

THURIO
    I thank you for your own. Now, gentlemen,
    Let's tune; and to it lustily awhile.   25

Enter Host, *and* JULIA *in boy's clothes.*

HOST   Now, my young guest, methinks you're allycholy.
    I pray you, why is it?

JULIA   Marry, mine host, because I cannot be merry.

HOST   Come, we'll have you merry: I'll bring you where
    you shall hear music, and see the gentleman that you   30
    asked for.

JULIA   But shall I hear him speak?

HOST   Ay, that you shall.

JULIA   That will be music.   *[Music plays.]*

HOST   Hark, hark!   35

JULIA   Is he among these?

HOST   Ay; but peace, let's hear 'em.

Song.

    Who is Silvia? What is she
    That all our swains commend her?
    Holy, fair, and wise is she,   40
    The heaven such grace did lend her,
        That she might admired be.

    Is she kind as she is fair?
    For beauty lives with kindness.
    Love doth to her eyes repair,   45
    To help him of his blindness;
        And, being help'd, inhabits there.

    Then to Silvia let us sing,
    That Silvia is excelling;
    She excels each mortal thing   50
    Upon the dull earth dwelling.
        To her let us garlands bring.

HOST   How now? Are you sadder than you were before?
      How do you, man? The music likes you not.

JULIA   You mistake: the musician likes me not.   55

HOST   Why, my pretty youth?

JULIA   He plays false, father.

HOST   How, out of tune on the strings?

JULIA   Not so; but yet so false that he grieves my very
      heart-strings.   60

HOST   You have a quick ear.

JULIA   Ay, I would I were deaf: it makes me have a slow
      heart.

HOST   I perceive you delight not in music.

JULIA   Not a whit, when it jars so.   65

HOST   Hark, what fine change is in the music!

JULIA   Ay; that change is the spite.

HOST   You would have them always play but one thing?

JULIA   I would always have one play but one thing.
      But, host, doth this Sir Proteus, that we talk on,   70
      Often resort unto this gentlewoman?

HOST   I tell you what Launce his man told me, he loved
      her out of all nick.

JULIA   Where is Launce?

HOST   Gone to seek his dog, which to-morrow, by his   75
      master's command, he must carry for a present to his
      lady.   [*Music ceases.*]

JULIA   Peace, stand aside, the company parts.

PROTEUS   Sir Thurio, fear not you, I will so plead,
      That you shall say my cunning drift excels.   80

THURIO   Where meet we?

PROTEUS   At Saint Gregory's well.

THURIO   Farewell.
                    Exeunt Thurio and Musicians.

Enter SILVIA, *above.*

PROTEUS   Madam; good even to your ladyship.

SILVIA   I thank you for your music, gentlemen.
      Who is that that spake?

PROTEUS   One, lady, if you knew his pure heart's truth,   85
      You would quickly learn to know him by his voice.

SILVIA   Sir Proteus, as I take it.

PROTEUS   Sir Proteus, gentle lady, and your servant.

SILVIA   What's your will?

PROTEUS   That I may compass yours.

SILVIA   You have your wish: my will is even this,   90
      That presently you hie you home to bed.
      Thou subtle, perjur'd, false, disloyal man,
      Think'st thou I am so shallow, so conceitless,
      To be seduced by thy flattery,
      That hast deceiv'd so many with thy vows?   95
      Return, return, and make thy love amends.
      For me, by this pale queen of night I swear,
      I am so far from granting thy request,
      That I despise thee for thy wrongful suit;
      And by and by intend to chide myself,   100
      Even for this time I spend in talking to thee.

PROTEUS   I grant, sweet love, that I did love a lady,
      But she is dead.

JULIA [*aside*]   'Twere false, if I should speak it;
      For I am sure she is not buried.

SILVIA   Say that she be; yet Valentine thy friend   105
      Survives; to whom (thyself art witness)
      I am betroth'd; and art thou not asham'd
      To wrong him with thy importunacy?

PROTEUS   I likewise hear that Valentine is dead.

SILVIA   And so suppose am I; for in his grave,   110
      Assure thyself, my love is buried.

PROTEUS   Sweet lady, let me rake it from the earth.

SILVIA   Go to thy lady's grave and call hers thence,
      Or, at the least, in hers sepulchre thine.

JULIA [*aside*]   He heard not that.   115

PROTEUS   Madam: if your heart be so obdurate,
      Vouchsafe me yet your picture for my love,
      The picture that is hanging in your chamber:
      To that I'll speak, to that I'll sigh and weep;
      For since the substance of your perfect self   120
      Is else devoted, I am but a shadow;
      And to your shadow will I make true love.

JULIA [*aside*]
      If 'twere a substance, you would sure deceive it,
      And make it but a shadow, as I am.

SILVIA   I am very loath to be your idol, sir;   125
      But, since your falsehood shall become you well
      To worship shadows, and adore false shapes,
      Send to me in the morning, and I'll send it.
      And so, good rest.

PROTEUS   As wretches have o'ernight
      That wait for execution in the morn.   130
                    Exeunt Proteus and Silvia.

JULIA   Host, will you go?

HOST   By my halidom, I was fast asleep.

JULIA   Pray you, where lies Sir Proteus?

HOST   Marry, at my house. Trust me, I think 'tis almost
      day.   135

JULIA   Not so; but it hath been the longest night
      That e'er I watch'd, and the most heaviest.   *Exeunt.*

4.3   *Enter* EGLAMOUR.

EGLAMOUR   This is the hour that Madam Silvia
      Entreated me to call, and know her mind:
      There's some great matter she'd employ me in.
      Madam, madam!

Enter SILVIA, *above.*

SILVIA   Who calls?

EGLAMOUR   Your servant, and your friend;
      One that attends your ladyship's command.   5

SILVIA   Sir Eglamour, a thousand times good morrow.

EGLAMOUR   As many, worthy lady, to yourself.
      According to your ladyship's impose,
      I am thus early come, to know what service
      It is your pleasure to command me in.   10

SILVIA   O Eglamour, thou art a gentleman
      (Think not I flatter, for I swear I do not)

Valiant, wise, remorseful, well accomplish'd.
Thou art not ignorant what dear good will
15　I bear unto the banish'd Valentine;
Nor how my father would enforce me marry
Vain Thurio, whom my very soul abhorr'd.
Thyself hast lov'd, and I have heard thee say
No grief did ever come so near thy heart
20　As when thy lady and thy true love died,
Upon whose grave thou vow'dst pure chastity.
Sir Eglamour: I would to Valentine,
To Mantua, where I hear he makes abode;
And for the ways are dangerous to pass,
25　I do desire thy worthy company,
Upon whose faith and honour I repose.
Urge not my father's anger, Eglamour,
But think upon my grief, a lady's grief,
And on the justice of my flying hence,
30　To keep me from a most unholy match,
Which heaven and fortune still rewards with plagues.
I do desire thee, even from a heart
As full of sorrows as the sea of sands,
To bear me company, and go with me;
35　If not, to hide what I have said to thee,
That I may venture to depart alone.
EGLAMOUR　Madam, I pity much your grievances,
Which, since I know they virtuously are plac'd,
I give consent to go along with you,
40　Recking as little what betideth me,
As much I wish all good befortune you.
When will you go?
SILVIA　　　　　　　　This evening coming.
EGLAMOUR　Where shall I meet you?
SILVIA　　　　　　　　　　　At Friar Patrick's cell,
Where I intend holy confession.
45　EGLAMOUR　I will not fail your ladyship. Good morrow,
gentle lady.
SILVIA　Good morrow, kind Sir Eglamour.　　　*Exeunt.*

4.4　　　　　*Enter* LAUNCE *with his dog.*

LAUNCE　When a man's servant shall play the cur with
him, look you, it goes hard: one that I brought up of a
puppy; one that I saved from drowning, when three
or four of his blind brothers and sisters went to it. I
5　have taught him, even as one would say precisely
'Thus I would teach a dog'. I was sent to deliver him
as a present to Mistress Silvia, from my master; and
I came no sooner into the dining-chamber, but he
steps me to her trencher, and steals her capon's leg. O,
10　'tis a foul thing, when a cur cannot keep himself in all
companies: I would have (as one should say) one that
takes upon him to be a dog indeed, to be, as it were, a
dog at all things. If I had not had more wit than he, to
take a fault upon me that he did, I think verily he had
15　been hanged for't; sure as I live he had suffered for't.
You shall judge: he thrusts me himself into the
company of three or four gentleman-like dogs, under

the Duke's table; he had not been there (bless the
mark) a pissing while, but all the chamber smelt him.
'Out with the dog', says one; 'What cur is that?' says　20
another; 'Whip him out', says the third; 'Hang him
up', says the Duke. I, having been acquainted with the
smell before, knew it was Crab; and goes me to the
fellow that whips the dogs: 'Friend', quoth I, 'you
mean to whip the dog?' 'Ay, marry do I', quoth he.　25
'You do him the more wrong,' quoth I; ''twas I did the
thing you wot of.' He makes me no more ado, but
whips me out of the chamber. How many masters
would do this for his servant? Nay, I'll be sworn I have
sat in the stocks, for puddings he hath stolen,　30
otherwise he had been executed; I have stood on the
pillory for geese he hath killed, otherwise he had
suffered for't. Thou think'st not of this now. Nay, I
remember the trick you served me, when I took my
leave of Madam Silvia: did not I bid thee still mark me,　35
and do as I do? When didst thou see me heave up my
leg, and make water against a gentlewoman's
farthingale? Didst thou ever see me do such a trick?

Enter PROTEUS *and* JULIA.

PROTEUS　Sebastian is thy name? I like thee well,
And will employ thee in some service presently.　40
JULIA　In what you please; I'll do what I can.
PROTEUS　I hope thou wilt.
　[*to Launce*]　　　　How now, you whoreson peasant,
Where have you been these two days loitering?
LAUNCE　Marry, sir, I carried Mistress Silvia the dog
you bade me.　45
PROTEUS　And what says she to my little jewel?
LAUNCE　Marry, she says your dog was a cur, and tells
you currish thanks is good enough for such a present.
PROTEUS　But she received my dog?
LAUNCE　No, indeed did she not: here have I brought　50
him back again.
PROTEUS　What, didst thou offer her this from me?
LAUNCE　Ay, sir, the other squirrel was stolen from me
by the hangman boys in the market-place, and then I
offered her mine own, who is a dog as big as ten of　55
yours, and therefore the gift the greater.
PROTEUS　Go, get thee hence, and find my dog again,
Or ne'er return again into my sight.
Away, I say: stayest thou to vex me here?
A slave, that still an end turns me to shame!　60
　　　　　　　　　　　　　　　　Exit Launce.

Sebastian, I have entertained thee,
Partly that I have need of such a youth,
That can with some discretion do my business:
For 'tis no trusting to yond foolish lout;
But chiefly for thy face, and thy behaviour,　65
Which (if my augury deceive me not)
Witness good bringing up, fortune, and truth.
Therefore, know thou, for this I entertain thee.
Go presently, and take this ring with thee,
Deliver it to Madam Silvia;　70

She lov'd me well deliver'd it to me.
[*He gives her a ring.*]

JULIA   It seems you lov'd not her, to leave her token:
She is dead belike?

PROTEUS   Not so: I think she lives.

JULIA   Alas!

75   PROTEUS   Why dost thou cry 'Alas'?

JULIA   I cannot choose but pity her.

PROTEUS   Wherefore shouldst thou pity her?

JULIA   Because methinks that she lov'd you as well
As you do love your lady Silvia:

80   She dreams on him that has forgot her love,
You dote on her that cares not for your love.
'Tis pity love should be so contrary;
And thinking on it makes me cry 'Alas'.

PROTEUS   Well; give her that ring, and therewithal
This letter. [*He gives her a letter.*]

85   That's her chamber. Tell my lady,
I claim the promise for her heavenly picture.
Your message done, hie home unto my chamber,
Where thou shalt find me sad, and solitary.   *Exit.*

JULIA   How many women would do such a message?

90   Alas, poor Proteus, thou hast entertain'd
A fox, to be the shepherd of thy lambs.
Alas, poor fool, why do I pity him
That with his very heart despiseth me?
Because he loves her, he despiseth me,

95   Because I love him, I must pity him.
This ring I gave him, when he parted from me,
To bind him to remember my good will;
And now am I (unhappy messenger)
To plead for that which I would not obtain;

100 To carry that which I would have refus'd;
To praise his faith which I would have disprais'd.
I am my master's true confirmed love,
But cannot be true servant to my master,
Unless I prove false traitor to myself.

105 Yet will I woo for him, but yet so coldly,
As (heaven it knows) I would not have him speed.

Enter SILVIA.

Gentlewoman, good day. I pray you be my mean
To bring me where to speak with Madam Silvia.

SILVIA   What would you with her, if that I be she?

110 JULIA   If you be she, I do entreat your patience
To hear me speak the message I am sent on.

SILVIA   From whom?

JULIA   From my master, Sir Proteus, madam.

SILVIA   O, he sends you for a picture?

JULIA   Ay, madam.

SILVIA [*calling*]   Ursula, bring my picture there.
[*The picture is brought.*]

115 Go, give your master this. Tell him from me,
One Julia, that his changing thoughts forget,
Would better fit his chamber than this shadow.

JULIA   Madam, please you peruse this letter.
[*She gives her a letter.*]

Pardon me, madam, I have unadvis'd
Deliver'd you a paper that I should not;   120
This is the letter to your ladyship.
[*She gives another letter and takes back the first.*]

SILVIA   I pray thee let me look on that again.

JULIA   It may not be: good madam, pardon me.

SILVIA   There, hold.
I will not look upon your master's lines: 125
I know they are stuff'd with protestations,
And full of new-found oaths, which he will break
As easily as I do tear his paper.
[*She tears the second letter.*]

JULIA   Madam, he sends your ladyship this ring.
[*She offers the ring.*]

SILVIA   The more shame for him, that he sends it me;   130
For I have heard him say a thousand times
His Julia gave it him at his departure:
Though his false finger have profan'd the ring,
Mine shall not do his Julia so much wrong.

JULIA   She thanks you.   135

SILVIA   What say'st thou?

JULIA   I thank you, madam, that you tender her:
Poor gentlewoman, my master wrongs her much.

SILVIA   Dost thou know her?

JULIA   Almost as well as I do know myself.   140
To think upon her woes, I do protest
That I have wept a hundred several times.

SILVIA   Belike she thinks that Proteus hath forsook her?

JULIA   I think she doth; and that's her cause of sorrow.

SILVIA   Is she not passing fair?   145

JULIA   She hath been fairer, madam, than she is:
When she did think my master lov'd her well,
She, in my judgment, was as fair as you.
But since she did neglect her looking-glass,
And threw her sun-expelling mask away,   150
The air hath starv'd the roses in her cheeks,
And pinch'd the lily-tincture of her face,
That now she is become as black as I.

SILVIA   How tall was she?

JULIA   About my stature: for at Pentecost,   155
When all our pageants of delight were play'd,
Our youth got me to play the woman's part,
And I was trimm'd in Madam Julia's gown,
Which served me as fit, by all men's judgments,
As if the garment had been made for me;   160
Therefore I know she is about my height.
And at that time I made her weep agood,
For I did play a lamentable part.
Madam, 'twas Ariadne, passioning
For Theseus' perjury, and unjust flight;   165
Which I so lively acted with my tears,
That my poor mistress, moved therewithal,
Wept bitterly; and would I might be dead,
If I in thought felt not her very sorrow.

SILVIA   She is beholding to thee, gentle youth.   170
Alas, poor lady, desolate, and left;
I weep myself to think upon thy words.

Here, youth: there is my purse; I give thee this
For thy sweet mistress' sake, because thou lov'st her.
[*She gives her a purse.*]
175   Farewell.   *Exit.*

JULIA
And she shall thank you for't, if e'er you know her.
A virtuous gentlewoman, mild, and beautiful.
I hope my master's suit will be but cold,
Since she respects my mistress' love so much.
180   Alas, how love can trifle with itself!
Here is her picture: let me see; I think
If I had such a tire, this face of mine
Were full as lovely as is this of hers;
And yet the painter flatter'd her a little,
185   Unless I flatter with myself too much.
Her hair is auburn, mine is perfect yellow:
If that be all the difference in his love,
I'll get me such a colour'd periwig.
Her eyes are grey as glass, and so are mine;
190   Ay, but her forehead's low, and mine's as high.
What should it be that he respects in her,
But I can make respective in myself,
If this fond Love were not a blinded god?
Come, shadow, come, and take this shadow up,
195   For 'tis thy rival. O thou senseless form,
Thou shalt be worshipp'd, kiss'd, lov'd, and ador'd;
And were there sense in his idolatry,
My substance should be statue in thy stead.
I'll use thee kindly, for thy mistress' sake
200   That us'd me so; or else, by Jove I vow,
I should have scratch'd out your unseeing eyes,
To make my master out of love with thee.   *Exit.*

5.1   *Enter* EGLAMOUR.

EGLAMOUR   The sun begins to gild the western sky,
And now it is about the very hour
That Silvia at Friar Patrick's cell should meet me.
She will not fail; for lovers break not hours,
5   Unless it be to come before their time,
So much they spur their expedition.

Enter SILVIA.

See where she comes. Lady, a happy evening.
SILVIA   Amen, amen; go on, good Eglamour,
Out at the postern by the abbey wall;
10   I fear I am attended by some spies.
EGLAMOUR   Fear not: the forest is not three leagues off;
If we recover that, we are sure enough.   *Exeunt.*

5.2   *Enter* THURIO, PROTEUS *and* JULIA.

THURIO   Sir Proteus, what says Silvia to my suit?
PROTEUS   O sir, I find her milder than she was,
And yet she takes exceptions at your person.
THURIO   What? That my leg is too long?
5   PROTEUS   No, that it is too little.
THURIO   I'll wear a boot, to make it somewhat rounder.

JULIA [*aside*]
But love will not be spurr'd to what it loathes.
THURIO   What says she to my face?
PROTEUS   She says it is a fair one.
THURIO   Nay, then the wanton lies: my face is black.   10
PROTEUS   But pearls are fair; and the old saying is,
Black men are pearls, in beauteous ladies' eyes.
JULIA [*aside*]
'Tis true, such pearls as put out ladies' eyes,
For I had rather wink than look on them.
THURIO   How likes she my discourse?   15
PROTEUS   Ill, when you talk of war.
THURIO   But well, when I discourse of love and peace?
JULIA [*aside*]
But better, indeed, when you hold your peace.
THURIO   What says she to my valour?
PROTEUS   O sir, she makes no doubt of that.   20
JULIA [*aside*]
She needs not, when she knows it cowardice.
THURIO   What says she to my birth?
PROTEUS   That you are well derived.
JULIA [*aside*]   True: from a gentleman, to a fool.
THURIO   Considers she my possessions?   25
PROTEUS   O, ay; and pities them.
THURIO   Wherefore?
JULIA [*aside*]   That such an ass should owe them.
PROTEUS   That they are out by lease.
JULIA   Here comes the Duke.   30

Enter DUKE.

DUKE   How now, Sir Proteus! How now, Thurio!
Which of you saw Sir Eglamour of late?
THURIO   Not I.
PROTEUS   Nor I.
DUKE   Saw you my daughter?
PROTEUS   Neither.
DUKE
Why, then, she's fled unto that peasant, Valentine;
And Eglamour is in her company.   35
'Tis true: for Friar Laurence met them both
As he in penance wander'd through the forest.
Him he knew well; and guess'd that it was she,
But, being mask'd, he was not sure of it.
Besides, she did intend confession   40
At Patrick's cell this even, and there she was not.
These likelihoods confirm her flight from hence;
Therefore, I pray you, stand not to discourse,
But mount you presently, and meet with me
Upon the rising of the mountain foot   45
That leads toward Mantua, whither they are fled.
Dispatch, sweet gentlemen, and follow me.   *Exit.*
THURIO   Why, this it is to be a peevish girl,
That flies her fortune when it follows her.
I'll after; more to be reveng'd on Eglamour   50
Than for the love of reckless Silvia.   *Exit.*
PROTEUS   And I will follow, more for Silvia's love
Than hate of Eglamour that goes with her.   *Exit.*

JULIA   And I will follow, more to cross that love
55   Than hate for Silvia, that is gone for love.   *Exit.*

5.3   *Enter* SILVIA *and* Outlaws.

1 OUTLAW
    Come, come, be patient; we must bring you to our
       captain.
SILVIA   A thousand more mischances than this one
    Have learn'd me how to brook this patiently.
2 OUTLAW   Come, bring her away.
5   1 OUTLAW   Where is the gentleman that was with her?
    3 OUTLAW   Being nimble-footed, he hath outrun us,
    But Moyses and Valerius follow him.
    Go thou with her to the west end of the wood,
    There is our captain. We'll follow him that's fled;
10   The thicket is beset, he cannot 'scape.
                Exeunt Second and Third Outlaws.
1 OUTLAW
    Come, I must bring you to our captain's cave.
    Fear not: he bears an honourable mind,
    And will not use a woman lawlessly.
SILVIA   O Valentine! This I endure for thee.   *Exeunt.*

5.4   *Enter* VALENTINE.

VALENTINE   How use doth breed a habit in a man!
    This shadowy desert, unfrequented woods,
    I better brook than flourishing peopled towns:
    Here can I sit alone, unseen of any,
5   And to the nightingale's complaining notes
    Tune my distresses, and record my woes.
    O thou that dost inhabit in my breast,
    Leave not the mansion so long tenantless,
    Lest growing ruinous, the building fall,
10   And leave no memory of what it was.
    Repair me, with thy presence, Silvia:
    Thou gentle nymph, cherish thy forlorn swain.
    [*Shouts within.*]
    What halloing, and what stir is this to-day?
    These are my mates, that make their wills their law,
15   Have some unhappy passenger in chase.
    They love me well; yet I have much to do
    To keep them from uncivil outrages.
    Withdraw thee, Valentine; who's this comes here?
    [*Withdraws.*]

        Enter PROTEUS, SILVIA *and* JULIA.

PROTEUS   Madam, this service I have done for you
20   (Though you respect not aught your servant doth)
    To hazard life, and rescue you from him
    That would have forc'd your honour and your love.
    Vouchsafe me for my meed but one fair look:
    A smaller boon than this I cannot beg,
25   And less than this I am sure you cannot give.
VALENTINE [*aside*]
    How like a dream is this! I see, and hear:
    Love, lend me patience to forbear awhile.

SILVIA   O miserable, unhappy that I am!
PROTEUS   Unhappy were you, madam, ere I came;
    But by my coming I have made you happy.   30
SILVIA   By thy approach thou mak'st me most unhappy.
JULIA [*aside*]
    And me, when he approacheth to your presence.
SILVIA   Had I been seiz'd by a hungry lion,
    I would have been a breakfast to the beast,
    Rather than have false Proteus rescue me.   35
    O heaven be judge how I love Valentine,
    Whose life's as tender to me as my soul,
    And full as much (for more there cannot be)
    I do detest false perjur'd Proteus:
    Therefore be gone, solicit me no more.   40
PROTEUS   What dangerous action, stood it next to death,
    Would I not undergo, for one calm look?
    O 'tis the curse in love, and still approv'd,
    When women cannot love where they're belov'd.
SILVIA   When Proteus cannot love where he's belov'd: 45
    Read over Julia's heart, thy first best love,
    For whose dear sake thou didst then rend thy faith
    Into a thousand oaths; and all those oaths
    Descended into perjury, to love me.
    Thou hast no faith left now, unless thou'dst two,   50
    And that's far worse than none: better have none
    Than plural faith, which is too much by one.
    Thou counterfeit to thy true friend!
PROTEUS   In love,
    Who respects friend?
SILVIA   All men but Proteus.
PROTEUS   Nay, if the gentle spirit of moving words   55
    Can no way change you to a milder form,
    I'll woo you like a soldier, at arm's end,
    And love you 'gainst the nature of love: force ye.
SILVIA   O heaven!
PROTEUS   I'll force thee yield to my desire.
VALENTINE [*coming forward*]
    Ruffian! Let go that rude uncivil touch,   60
    Thou friend of an ill fashion.
PROTEUS   Valentine!
VALENTINE
    Thou common friend, that's without faith or love,
    For such is a friend now. Treacherous man,
    Thou hast beguil'd my hopes; nought but mine eye
    Could have persuaded me: now I dare not say   65
    I have one friend alive; thou wouldst disprove me.
    Who should be trusted now, when one's right hand
    Is perjured to the bosom? Proteus,
    I am sorry I must never trust thee more,
    But count the world a stranger for thy sake.   70
    The private wound is deepest: O time most accurst,
    'Mongst all foes that a friend should be the worst!
PROTEUS   My shame and guilt confounds me.
    Forgive me, Valentine: if hearty sorrow
    Be a sufficient ransom for offence,   75
    I tender't here; I do as truly suffer,
    As e'er I did commit.

VALENTINE   Then I am paid;
  And once again I do receive thee honest.
  Who by repentance is not satisfied,
80 Is nor of heaven, nor earth; for these are pleas'd:
  By penitence th'Eternal's wrath's appeas'd.
  And that my love may appear plain and free,
  All that was mine in Silvia I give thee.

JULIA O me unhappy! [*She swoons.*]

PROTEUS   Look to the boy.

VALENTINE   Why, boy!
85 Why, wag; how now? What's the matter? Look up;
  speak.

JULIA O good sir, my master charged me to deliver a
  ring to Madam Silvia; which (out of my neglect) was
  never done.

PROTEUS Where is that ring, boy?

90 JULIA   Here 'tis: this is it.
  [*She gives him a ring.*]

PROTEUS How! Let me see.
  Why, this is the ring I gave to Julia.

JULIA O, cry you mercy, sir, I have mistook:
  This is the ring you sent to Silvia.
  [*She shows another ring.*]

PROTEUS
95 But how cam'st thou by this ring? At my depart
  I gave this unto Julia.

JULIA And Julia herself did give it me,
  And Julia herself hath brought it hither.
  [*She reveals herself.*]

PROTEUS How! Julia!

100 JULIA Behold her that gave aim to all thy oaths,
  And entertain'd 'em deeply in her heart.
  How oft hast thou with perjury cleft the root!
  O Proteus, let this habit make thee blush.
  Be thou asham'd that I have took upon me
105 Such an immodest raiment; if shame live
  In a disguise of love!
  It is the lesser blot modesty finds,
  Women to change their shapes, than men their
    minds.

PROTEUS
  Than men their minds? 'Tis true: O heaven, were
    man
110 But constant, he were perfect. That one error
  Fills him with faults; makes him run through all th'
    sins;
  Inconstancy falls off, ere it begins.
  What is in Silvia's face but I may spy
  More fresh in Julia's, with a constant eye?

115 VALENTINE Come, come; a hand from either;
  Let me be blest to make this happy close:
  'Twere pity two such friends should be long foes.

PROTEUS Bear witness, heaven, I have my wish for ever.

JULIA And I mine.

Enter Outlaws, DUKE *and* THURIO.

OUTLAW   A prize, a prize, a prize!

VALENTINE
  Forbear, forbear, I say: it is my lord the Duke.   120
  Your grace is welcome to a man disgrac'd,
  Banish'd Valentine.

DUKE   Sir Valentine!

THURIO Yonder is Silvia; and Silvia's mine.

VALENTINE
  Thurio, give back; or else embrace thy death;
  Come not within the measure of my wrath;   125
  Do not name Silvia thine. If once again,
  Verona shall not hold thee. Here she stands,
  Take but possession of her with a touch:
  I dare thee but to breathe upon my love.

THURIO Sir Valentine, I care not for her, I: 130
  I hold him but a fool that will endanger
  His body for a girl that loves him not.
  I claim her not, and therefore she is thine.

DUKE The more degenerate and base art thou
  To make such means for her, as thou hast done,   135
  And leave her on such slight conditions.
  Now, by the honour of my ancestry,
  I do applaud thy spirit, Valentine,
  And think thee worthy of an empress' love:
  Know then, I here forget all former griefs,   140
  Cancel all grudge, repeal thee home again,
  Plead a new state in thy unrivall'd merit,
  To which I thus subscribe: Sir Valentine,
  Thou art a gentleman, and well deriv'd,
  Take thou thy Silvia, for thou hast deserv'd her.   145

VALENTINE
  I thank your grace; the gift hath made me happy.
  I now beseech you, for your daughter's sake,
  To grant one boon that I shall ask of you.

DUKE I grant it, for thine own, whate'er it be.

VALENTINE These banish'd men, that I have kept withal,   150
  Are men endu'd with worthy qualities:
  Forgive them what they have committed here,
  And let them be recall'd from their exile:
  They are reformed, civil, full of good,
  And fit for great employment, worthy lord.   155

DUKE Thou hast prevail'd, I pardon them and thee:
  Dispose of them as thou know'st their deserts.
  Come, let us go, we will include all jars,
  With triumphs, mirth, and rare solemnity.

VALENTINE And as we walk along, I dare be bold   160
  With our discourse to make your grace to smile.
  What think you of this page, my lord?

DUKE I think the boy hath grace in him, he blushes.

VALENTINE
  I warrant you, my lord, more grace than boy.

DUKE What mean you by that saying?   165

VALENTINE Please you, I'll tell you, as we pass along,
  That you will wonder what hath fortuned.
  Come, Proteus, 'tis your penance but to hear
  The story of your loves discovered.
  That done, our day of marriage shall be yours,   170
  One feast, one house, one mutual happiness. *Exeunt.*

The Two Noble Kinsmen

The Two Noble Kinsmen was printed in 1634 as the joint work of 'those memorable worthies of their time' John Fletcher and William Shakespeare, performed by the King's Men at the Blackfriars Theatre. These claims fit the likely date of composition, 1613–14, making it the latest surviving play in which Shakespeare had a hand. A dance from The Masque of the Inner Temple and Gray's Inn, by Fletcher's regular collaborator Francis Beaumont, which was presented at court on 20 February 1613 during the wedding celebrations of Princess Elizabeth and Frederick, Prince Palatine, supplied the characters (and presumably the costumes) for the morris dance in 3.5. Fletcher's major share in the authorship meant that until the nineteenth century the play remained within the printed canon of 'Beaumont and Fletcher' rather than Shakespeare. Interest in The Two Noble Kinsmen revived after collaborative authorship of King Henry VIII began to be seriously proposed in the mid-nineteenth century, and since the 1970s it has regularly appeared in collected editions of Shakespeare. The mode of collaboration is uncertain but the scenes in which Shakespeare's hand is most evident are mainly in the first and last acts (1.1–5; 2.1, 3[?]; 3.1–2; 4.3[?]; 5.1, 3–4), leaving to Fletcher the bulk of the central action and almost all of the sub-plot of the Jailer's daughter.

Though the story of the siege of Thebes is pervasive in classical Greek and Latin literature, the playwrights relied on a medieval accretion to it. Chaucer's version of the perplexities of the Theban cousins Palamon and Arcite in their rivalry for the love of Emilia, sister of the Amazon queen Hippolyta, bride of Theseus, is assigned to the Knight in The Canterbury Tales (c. 1385). Chaucer got the story from the Teseida of Giovanni Boccaccio (?late 1340s), behind which lies the Thebaid of Statius. Shakespeare had earlier used The Knight's Tale for his treatment of Theseus and Hippolyta in A Midsummer Night's Dream.

Like Chaucer's tale, the play sets up a series of moral and emotional dilemmas for its characters. Should Theseus proceed with his wedding, or postpone it until he has avenged the widowed queens? Should Palamon and Arcite fight for their native Thebes, or flee from the corruptions of its king, their uncle Creon? Should their friendship prevail over their rivalry in love for Emilia? Should the Jailer's daughter free Palamon at the risk of her father's life? Should Emilia choose between marriage and virginity – or between her equally unknown and unwelcome suitors? The struggles of the characters to resolve these dilemmas culminate in a scene, adapted from Chaucer, in which Arcite, Palamon and Emilia in turn invoke their tutelary gods, Mars, Venus and Diana. Thereafter, we increasingly see them as pawns in a divine chess-game. The outcome, in which accidental death robs Arcite of his victory in combat and leaves Emilia to the disconsolate Palamon, is well characterized by Emilia's cry, 'Is this winning?' Meanwhile the destructive passion of the Jailer's daughter for Palamon moves through suicidal despair and madness to the apparent possibility of transference to her faithful Wooer by a therapy involving sexual relations with him under the pretence that he is Palamon. It is unclear how fully audiences are invited to endorse the statement of Theseus that 'in the passage / The gods have been most equal', or his determinist conclusion,

> Let us be thankful
> For that which is, and with you leave dispute
> That are above our question.

The tone of the play varies sharply between elegaic solemnity and a brittle, even cynical, detachment. Since the 1970s, stage productions have proliferated after centuries of relative neglect. The play offers a powerful portrayal of the predicaments of women in a male-dominated world, and its unhappy open-endedness is congruous with the chastened mood of the end of the twentieth century.

The Arden text is based on the 1634 Quarto.

Speaker of the PROLOGUE

BOY	*singer in the wedding procession*
HYMEN	
Nymphs	*figures in the wedding procession*

ATHENIANS

THESEUS	*Duke of Athens*
PIRITHOUS	*friend of Theseus*
HIPPOLYTA	*bride of Theseus, an Amazon*
EMILIA	*sister of Hippolyta*
OFFICER (Artesius)	*officer of Theseus*
HERALD	
WAITING WOMAN	*to Emilia*
JAILER	
DAUGHTER	*to Jailer*
WOOER	*to Jailer's Daughter*
BROTHER	*to Jailer*
Two FRIENDS	*of Jailer*
DOCTOR	
MAID	*companion to Jailer's Daughter*
SCHOOLMASTER (Gerald)	
Five COUNTRYMEN	(*among them* Arcas, Rycas, Sennois)
TABORER (Timothy)	
Actor playing BAVIAN	
Five COUNTRYWOMEN	Barbary, Friz, Luce, Maudlin, Nell
GENTLEMEN	
EXECUTIONER	
Two MESSENGERS	

THEBANS

Three QUEENS	*widows of besiegers of Thebes*
ARCITE	
PALAMON	*cousins, nephews to Creon, King of Thebes*
VALERIUS	
Three KNIGHTS	*supporters of Arcite*
Three KNIGHTS	*supporters of Palamon*

Speaker of the EPILOGUE

Servants, Guards, Attendants, etc.

The Two Noble Kinsmen

PROLOGUE

Flourish. Enter Speaker of the Prologue.

New plays and maidenheads are near akin:
Much followed both, for both much money gi'en,
If they stand sound and well. And a good play,
Whose modest scenes blush on his marriage day
5   And shake to lose his honour, is like her
That after holy tie and first night's stir
Yet still is Modesty and still retains
More of the maid, to sight, than husband's pains.
We pray our play may be so, for I am sure
10   It has a noble breeder and a pure,
A learned, and a poet never went
More famous yet 'twixt Po and silver Trent.
Chaucer, of all admired, the story gives;
There, constant to eternity, it lives.
15   If we let fall the nobleness of this
And the first sound this child hear be a hiss,
How will it shake the bones of that good man
And make him cry from under ground, 'Oh, fan
From me the witless chaff of such a writer
20   That blasts my bays and my famed works makes
     lighter
Than Robin Hood!' This is the fear we bring;
For, to say truth, it were an endless thing
And too ambitious to aspire to him,
Weak as we are, and, almost breathless, swim
25   In this deep water. Do but you hold out
Your helping hands and we shall tack about
And something do to save us. You shall hear
Scenes, though below his art, may yet appear
Worth two hours' travel. To his bones sweet sleep;
30   Content to you. If this play do not keep
A little dull time from us, we perceive
Our losses fall so thick, we must needs leave.

Flourish. Exit.

1.1 *Music. Enter Hymen with a torch burning; a* Boy, *in
a white robe, before, singing and strewing flowers; after
Hymen, a Nymph encompassed in her tresses, bearing a
wheaten garland. Then* THESEUS *between two other
nymphs with wheaten chaplets on their heads. Then*
HIPPOLYTA *the bride, led by* PIRITHOUS *and another
holding a garland over her head (her tresses likewise
hanging). After her,* EMILIA, *holding up her train;
Artesius; attendants; musicians.*

BOY [*Sings.*]

Roses, their sharp spines being gone,
Not royal in their smells alone
    But in their hue;
Maiden pinks of odour faint,
5   Daisies smell-less yet most quaint,
    And sweet thyme true;

Primrose, first-born child of Ver,
Merry springtime's harbinger,

With harebells dim,
10   Oxlips in their cradles growing,
Marigolds on deathbeds blowing,
    Lark's-heels trim: [*Strews flowers.*]

All dear Nature's children sweet
Lie 'fore bride and bridegroom's feet,
15   Blessing their sense.
Not an angel of the air,
Bird melodious, or bird fair,
    Is absent hence.

The crow, the sland'rous cuckoo, nor
20   The boding raven, nor chough hoar,
    Nor chatt'ring 'pie,
May on our bride-house perch or sing,
Or with them any discord bring,
    But from it fly.

Enter three Queens *in black, with veils stained, with
imperial crowns. The First Queen falls down at the foot of
Theseus; the Second falls down at the foot of
Hippolyta; the Third before Emilia.*

1 QUEEN [*to Theseus*]
For pity's sake and true gentility's,   25
Hear and respect me.
2 QUEEN [*to Hippolyta*]   For your mother's sake
And as you wish your womb may thrive with fair
    ones,
Hear and respect me.
3 QUEEN [*to Emilia*]
Now, for the love of him whom Jove hath marked
The honour of your bed and for the sake   30
Of clear virginity, be advocate
For us and our distresses. This good deed
Shall raze you out o'th' book of trespasses
All you are set down there.
THESEUS   Sad lady, rise.
HIPPOLYTA   Stand up.
EMILIA   No knees to me!   35
What woman I may stead that is distressed
Does bind me to her.
THESEUS
What's your request?
[*to First Queen*]   Deliver you for all.
1 QUEEN
We are three queens whose sovereigns fell before
The wrath of cruel Creon, who endure   40
The beaks of ravens, talons of the kites
And pecks of crows, in the foul fields of Thebes.
He will not suffer us to burn their bones,
To urn their ashes, nor to take th'offence
Of mortal loathsomeness from the blest eye   45
Of holy Phoebus, but infects the winds
With stench of our slain lords. O pity, Duke;
Thou purger of the earth, draw thy feared sword
That does good turns to th' world; give us the bones
Of our dead kings that we may chapel them;   50

And of thy boundless goodness take some note
That for our crowned heads we have no roof,
Save this which is the lion's and the bear's
And vault to every thing.

THESEUS   Pray you, kneel not:

55 I was transported with your speech and suffered
Your knees to wrong themselves. I have heard the
    fortunes
Of your dead lords, which gives me such lamenting
As wakes my vengeance and revenge for 'em.
[*to First Queen*] King Capaneus was your lord. The
    day
60 That he should marry you, at such a season
As now it is with me, I met your groom.
By Mars's altar, you were that time fair!
Not Juno's mantle fairer than your tresses
Nor in more bounty spread her. Your wheaten
    wreath
65 Was then nor threshed nor blasted; Fortune at you
Dimpled her cheek with smiles. Hercules our
    kinsman,
Then weaker than your eyes, laid by his club;
He tumbled down upon his Nemean hide
And swore his sinews thawed. O, grief and time,
70 Fearful consumers, you will all devour!

1 QUEEN   O, I hope some god,
Some god hath put his mercy in your manhood,
Whereto he'll infuse power, and press you forth
Our undertaker.

THESEUS   O, no knees, none, widow.
75 Unto the helmeted Bellona use them,
And pray for me, your soldier.
Troubled I am. [*Turns away.*]

2 QUEEN   Honoured Hippolyta,
Most dreaded Amazonian, that hast slain
The scythe-tusked boar; that with thy arm, as strong
80 As it is white, wast near to make the male
To thy sex captive, but that this thy lord,
Born to uphold creation in that honour
First nature styled it in, shrunk thee into
The bound thou wast o'erflowing, at once subduing
85 Thy force and thy affection; soldieress,
That equally canst poise sternness with pity,
Whom now I know hast much more power on him
Than ever he had on thee, who ow'st his strength
And his love too, who is a servant for
90 The tenor of thy speech; dear glass of ladies:
Bid him that we, whom flaming war doth scorch,
Under the shadow of his sword may cool us.
Require him he advance it o'er our heads.
Speak't in a woman's key; like such a woman
95 As any of us three; weep ere you fail.
Lend us a knee;
But touch the ground for us no longer time
Than a dove's motion, when the head's plucked off.
Tell him, if he i'th' blood-sized field lay swollen,
100 Showing the sun his teeth, grinning at the moon,

What you would do.

HIPPOLYTA   Poor lady, say no more.
I had as lief trace this good action with you
As that whereto I am going, and never yet
Went I so willing way. My lord is taken
Heart-deep with your distress. Let him consider: 105
I'll speak anon. [*Second Queen rises.*]

3 QUEEN   O, my petition was
Set down in ice, which by hot grief uncandied
Melts into drops; so sorrow, wanting form,
Is pressed with deeper matter.

EMILIA   Pray, stand up;
Your grief is written in your cheek.

3 QUEEN   O, woe,   110
You cannot read it there. [*Rises.*]
                    There, through my tears,
Like wrinkled pebbles in a glassy stream,
You may behold 'em. Lady, lady, alack,
He that will all the treasure know o'th' earth
Must know the centre too; he that will fish   115
For my least minnow, let him lead his line
To catch one at my heart. O, pardon me;
Extremity, that sharpens sundry wits,
Makes me a fool.

EMILIA   Pray you, say nothing, pray you:
Who cannot feel nor see the rain, being in't,   120
Knows neither wet nor dry. If that you were
The ground-piece of some painter, I would buy you
T'instruct me 'gainst a capital grief, indeed
Such heart-pierced demonstration; but, alas,
Being a natural sister of our sex,   125
Your sorrow beats so ardently upon me
That it shall make a counter-reflect 'gainst
My brother's heart and warm it to some pity,
Though it were made of stone. Pray, have good
    comfort.

THESEUS   Forward to th' temple! Leave not out a jot   130
O'th' sacred ceremony.

1 QUEEN   O, this celebration
Will longer last and be more costly than
Your suppliants' war! Remember that your fame
Knolls in the ear o'th' world: what you do quickly
Is not done rashly; your first thought is more   135
Than others' laboured meditance; your
    premeditating
More than their actions; but, O Jove, your actions,
Soon as they move, as ospreys do the fish,
Subdue before they touch. Think, dear Duke, think
What beds our slain kings have!

2 QUEEN   What griefs our beds,   140
That our dear lords have none!

3 QUEEN   None fit for th' dead.
Those that with cords, knives, drams' precipitance,
Weary of this world's light, have to themselves
Been death's most horrid agents, human grace
Affords them dust and shadow –

1 QUEEN   But our lords   145

Lie blistering 'fore the visitating sun,
And were good kings when living.
THESEUS   It is true.
And I will give you comfort,
To give your dead lords graves – the which to do,
Must make some work with Creon.
150 1 QUEEN   And that work
Presents itself to th' doing.
Now 'twill take form; the heats are gone tomorrow.
Then, bootless toil must recompense itself
With its own sweat; now, he's secure,
155 Nor dreams we stand before your puissance
Rinsing our holy begging in our eyes
To make petition clear.
2 QUEEN   Now you may take him,
Drunk with his victory –
3 QUEEN   And his army full
Of bread and sloth.
THESEUS [*to officer*]   Artesius, that best knowest
160 How to draw out fit to this enterprise
The prim'st for this proceeding and the number
To carry such a business – forth and levy
Our worthiest instruments, whilst we dispatch
This grand act of our life, this daring deed
Of fate in wedlock.
1 QUEEN [*to Second and Third Queens*]
165   Dowagers, take hands.
Let us be widows to our woes; delay
Commends us to a famishing hope.
QUEENS   Farewell!
2 QUEEN
We come unseasonably; but when could grief
Cull forth, as unpanged judgement can, fitt'st time
For best solicitation?
170 THESEUS   Why, good ladies,
This is a service, whereto I am going,
Greater than any war; it more imports me
Than all the actions that I have foregone,
Or futurely can cope.
1 QUEEN   The more proclaiming
175 Our suit shall be neglected when her arms,
Able to lock Jove from a synod, shall
By warranting moonlight corslet thee. O, when
Her twinning cherries shall their sweetness fall
Upon thy taste-full lips, what wilt thou think
180 Of rotten kings or blubbered queens? What care
For what thou feel'st not, what thou feel'st being able
To make Mars spurn his drum? O, if thou couch
But one night with her, every hour in't will
Take hostage of thee for a hundred and
185 Thou shalt remember nothing more than what
That banquet bids thee to.
HIPPOLYTA   Though much unlike
You should be so transported, as much sorry
I should be such a suitor, yet I think,
Did I not, by th'abstaining of my joy
190 Which breeds a deeper longing, cure their surfeit

That craves a present med'cine, I should pluck
All ladies' scandal on me. Therefore, sir, [*Kneels.*]
As I shall here make trial of my prayers,
Either presuming them to have some force,
Or sentencing for aye their vigour dumb,   195
Prorogue this business we are going about and hang
Your shield afore your heart, about that neck
Which is my fee and which I freely lend
To do these poor queens service.
QUEENS [*to Emilia*]   Oh, help now.
Our cause cries for your knee.
EMILIA [*Kneels, to Theseus*]   If you grant not   200
My sister her petition in that force,
With that celerity and nature, which
She makes it in, from henceforth I'll not dare
To ask you anything nor be so hardy
Ever to take a husband.
THESEUS   Pray, stand up.   205
I am entreating of my self to do
That which you kneel to have me. [*They rise.*]
                      Pirithous,
Lead on the bride; get you and pray the gods
For success and return; omit not anything
In the pretended celebration. – Queens,   210
Follow your soldier.
[*to officer*]   As before – hence, you,
And at the banks of Aulis meet us with
The forces you can raise, where we shall find
The moiety of a number for a business
More bigger-looked.   *Exit officer.*
[*to Hippolyta*]   Since that our theme is haste,   215
I stamp this kiss upon thy current lip;
Sweet, keep it as my token. Set you forward,
For I will see you gone.
[*Procession moves toward the temple.*]
– Farewell, my beauteous sister. – Pirithous,
Keep the feast full; bate not an hour on't.
PIRITHOUS   Sir,   220
I'll follow you at heels; the feast's solemnity
Shall want till your return.
THESEUS   Cousin, I charge you,
Budge not from Athens. We shall be returning
Ere you can end this feast, of which I pray you
Make no abatement. Once more, farewell all.   225
             Exeunt all except Theseus and Queens.
1 QUEEN
Thus dost thou still make good the tongue o'th' world –
2 QUEEN   And earn'st a deity equal with Mars –
3 QUEEN   If not above him, for
Thou, being but mortal, mak'st affections bend
To godlike honours; they themselves, some say,   230
Groan under such a mast'ry.
THESEUS   As we are men,
Thus should we do; being sensually subdued,
We lose our human title. Good cheer, ladies:
Now turn we towards your comforts.
                     Flourish. Exeunt.

1.2   *Enter* PALAMON *and* ARCITE.

ARCITE   Dear Palamon, dearer in love than blood
And our prime cousin: yet unhardened in
The crimes of nature, let us leave the city
Thebes and the temptings in't, before we further
Sully our gloss of youth   5
And here to keep in abstinence we shame
As in incontinence; for not to swim
I'th' aid o'th' current, were almost to sink,
At least to frustrate striving, and to follow
The common stream, 'twould bring us to an eddy   10
Where we should turn or drown; if labour through,
Our gain but life and weakness.
PALAMON   Your advice
Is cried up with example. What strange ruins,
Since first we went to school, may we perceive
Walking in Thebes! Scars and bare weeds   15
The gain o'th' martialist, who did propound
To his bold ends honour and golden ingots,
Which, though he won, he had not – and now flurted
By Peace for whom he fought! Who then shall offer
To Mars's so scorned altar? I do bleed   20
When such I meet and wish great Juno would
Resume her ancient fit of jealousy
To get the soldier work, that Peace might purge
For her repletion and retain anew
Her charitable heart, now hard and harsher   25
Than strife or war could be.
ARCITE   Are you not out?
Meet you no ruin but the soldier in
The cranks and turns of Thebes? You did begin
As if you met decays of many kinds.
Perceive you none that do arouse your pity   30
But th'unconsidered soldier?
PALAMON   Yes, I pity
Decays where'er I find them, but such most
That, sweating in an honourable toil,
Are paid with ice to cool 'em.
ARCITE   'Tis not this
I did begin to speak of. This is virtue   35
Of no respect in Thebes. I spake of Thebes –
How dangerous, if we will keep our honours,
It is for our residing, where every evil
Hath a good colour; where every seeming good's
A certain evil; where not to be e'en jump   40
As they are here were to be strangers, and,
Such things to be, mere monsters.
PALAMON   'Tis in our power,
Unless we fear that apes can tutor's, to
Be masters of our manners. What need I
Affect another's gait, which is not catching   45
Where there is faith, or to be fond upon
Another's way of speech when by mine own
I may be reasonably conceived, saved too,
Speaking it truly? Why am I bound
By any generous bond to follow him   50

Follows his tailor, haply so long until
The followed make pursuit? Or let me know
Why mine own barber is unblessed, with him
My poor chin too, for 'tis not scissored just
To such a favourite's glass? What canon is there   55
That does command my rapier from my hip
To dangle't in my hand, or to go tiptoe
Before the street be foul? Either I am
The fore-horse in the team or I am none
That draw i'th' sequent trace. These poor slight
    sores   60
Need not a plantain; that which rips my bosom
Almost to th' heart's –
ARCITE   Our uncle Creon.
PALAMON   He.
A most unbounded tyrant, whose successes
Makes heaven unfeared and villainy assured
Beyond its power there's nothing; almost puts   65
Faith in a fever and deifies alone
Voluble Chance; who only attributes
The faculties of other instruments
To his own nerves and act; commands men service
And what they win in't, boot and glory; one   70
That fears not to do harm; good, dares not. Let
The blood of mine that's sib to him be sucked
From me with leeches, let them break and fall
 Off me with that corruption.
ARCITE   Clear-spirited cousin,
Let's leave his court, that we may nothing share   75
Of his loud infamy; for our milk
Will relish of the pasture and we must
Be vile or disobedient: not his kinsmen
In blood unless in quality.
PALAMON   Nothing truer:
I think the echoes of his shames have deafed   80
The ears of heavenly Justice. Widows' cries
Descend again into their throats and have not
Due audience of the gods.

Enter VALERIUS.

Valerius!
VALERIUS   The king calls for you; yet be leaden-footed
Till his great rage be off him. Phoebus, when   85
He broke his whipstock and exclaimed against
The horses of the sun, but whispered to
The loudness of his fury.
PALAMON   Small winds shake him.
But what's the matter?
VALERIUS
Theseus, who, where he threats, appals, hath sent   90
Deadly defiance to him and pronounces
Ruin to Thebes, who is at hand to seal
The promise of his wrath.
ARCITE   Let him approach.
But that we fear the gods in him, he brings not
A jot of terror to us. Yet what man   95
Thirds his own worth (the case is each of ours)

When that his action's dregged with mind assured
'Tis bad he goes about?

PALAMON   Leave that unreasoned.
Our services stand now for Thebes, not Creon.
Yet to be neutral to him were dishonour, 100
Rebellious to oppose; therefore we must
With him stand to the mercy of our fate,
Who hath bounded our last minute.

ARCITE   So we must.
[*to Valerius*] Is't said this war's afoot, or, it shall be,
On fail of some condition? 105

VALERIUS   'Tis in motion.
The intelligence of state came in the instant
With the defier.

PALAMON   Let's to the king – who, were he
A quarter-carrier of that honour which
His enemy come in, the blood we venture 110
Should be as for our health, which were not spent,
Rather laid out for purchase; but, alas,
Our hands advanced before our hearts, what will
The fall o'th' stroke do damage?

ARCITE   Let th'event,
That never-erring arbitrator, tell us
When we know all ourselves – and let us follow 115
The becking of our chance.   *Exeunt.*

1.3   *Enter* PIRITHOUS, HIPPOLYTA *and* EMILIA.

PIRITHOUS   No further.

HIPPOLYTA   Sir, farewell; repeat my wishes
To our great lord, of whose success I dare not
Make any timorous question; yet I wish him
Excess and overflow of power, an't might be
To dure ill-dealing fortune. Speed to him! 5
Store never hurts good governors.

PIRITHOUS   Though I know
His ocean needs not my poor drops, yet they
Must yield their tribute there.
[*to Emilia*]   My precious maid,
Those best affections that the heavens infuse
In their best-tempered pieces keep enthroned 10
In your dear heart.

EMILIA   Thanks, sir. Remember me
To our all-royal brother, for whose speed
The great Bellona I'll solicit; and,
Since in our terrene state petitions are not
Without gifts understood, I'll offer to her 15
What I shall be advised she likes. Our hearts
Are in his army, in his tent –

HIPPOLYTA   In's bosom.
We have been soldiers and we cannot weep
When our friends don their helms, or put to sea,
Or tell of babes broached on the lance, or women 20
That have sod their infants in (and after eat them)
The brine they wept at killing 'em. Then, if
You stay to see of us such spinsters, we
Should hold you here forever.

PIRITHOUS   Peace be to you
As I pursue this war, which shall be then 25
Beyond further requiring.   *Exit.*

EMILIA   How his longing
Follows his friend! Since his depart, his sports,
Though craving seriousness and skill, passed slightly
His careless execution, where nor gain
Made him regard or loss consider, but, 30
Playing one business in his hand, another
Directing in his head, his mind nurse equal
To these so-differing twins. Have you observed him,
Since our great lord departed?

HIPPOLYTA   With much labour,
And I did love him for't. They two have cabined 35
In many as dangerous as poor a corner,
Peril and want contending; they have skiffed
Torrents whose roaring tyranny and power
I'th' least of these was dreadful; and they have
Sought out together where Death's self was lodged; 40
Yet fate hath brought them off. Their knot of love,
Tied, weaved, entangled, with so true, so long,
And with a finger of so deep a cunning,
May be outworn, never undone. I think
Theseus cannot be umpire to himself, 45
Cleaving his conscience into twain and doing
Each side like justice, which he loves best.

EMILIA   Doubtless,
There is a best and reason has no manners
To say it is not you. I was acquainted
Once with a time when I enjoyed a play-fellow. 50
You were at wars when she the grave enriched,
Who made too proud the bed – took leave o'th' moon
(Which then looked pale at parting) when our count
Was each eleven.

HIPPOLYTA   'Twas Flavina.

EMILIA   Yes.
You talk of Pirithous' and Theseus' love. 55
Theirs has more ground, is more maturely seasoned,
More buckled with strong judgement, and their
  needs
The one of th'other may be said to water
Their intertangled roots of love – but I
And she I sigh and spoke of were things innocent, 60
Loved for we did and like the elements
That know not what nor why, yet do effect
Rare issues by their operance; our souls
Did so to one another. What she liked
Was then of me approved; what not, condemned – 65
No more arraignment. The flower that I would pluck
And put between my breasts (then but beginning
To swell about the blossom), O, she would long
Till she had such another, and commit it
To the like innocent cradle, where phoenix-like 70
They died in perfume. On my head no toy
But was her pattern; her affections – pretty,
Though happily her careless wear – I followed
For my most serious decking; had mine ear

75 Stol'n some new air or at adventure hummed one
From musical coinage, why, it was a note
Whereon her spirits would sojourn – rather, dwell
    on,
And sing it in her slumbers. This rehearsal,
Which fury-innocent wots well, comes in
80 Like old importment's bastard, has this end:
That the true love 'tween maid and maid may be
More than in sex dividual.
HIPPOLYTA   You're out of breath!
And this high-speeded pace is but to say
That you shall never, like the maid Flavina,
Love any that's called man.
85 EMILIA   I am sure I shall not.
HIPPOLYTA   Now, alack, weak sister,
I must no more believe thee in this point,
Though in't I know thou dost believe thy self,
Than I will trust a sickly appetite
90 That loathes even as it longs. But sure, my sister,
If I were ripe for your persuasion, you
Have said enough to shake me from the arm
Of the all-noble Theseus – for whose fortunes
I will now in and kneel, with great assurance
95 That we, more than his Pirithous, possess
The high throne in his heart.
EMILIA   I am not
Against your faith, yet I continue mine.   *Exeunt.*

1.4   *Cornets. A battle struck within; then a retreat.*
Flourish. Then enter THESEUS *as victor, with a* Herald,
other lords, and soldiers, PALAMON *and* ARCITE *on hearses.*
The three Queens *meet him and fall on*
their faces before him.

1 QUEEN   To thee no star be dark!
2 QUEEN   Both heaven and earth
Friend thee forever!
3 QUEEN   All the good that may
Be wished upon thy head, I cry 'Amen' to't!
THESEUS
Th'impartial gods, who from the mounted heavens
5 View us, their mortal herd, behold who err
And, in their time, chastise. Go and find out
The bones of your dead lords and honour them
With treble ceremony, rather than a gap
Should be in their dear rites. We would supply't,
10 But those we will depute, which shall invest
You in your dignities and even each thing
Our haste does leave imperfect. So adieu,
And heaven's good eyes look on you. *Exeunt Queens.*
[*Theseus notices the two hearses.*]   What are those?
HERALD   Men of great quality, as may be judged
15 By their appointment. Some of Thebes have told's
They are sisters' children, nephews to the King.
THESEUS   By th' helm of Mars, I saw them in the war,
Like to a pair of lions, smeared with prey,
Make lanes in troops aghast. I fixed my note
20 Constantly on them, for they were a mark

Worth a god's view. What prisoner was't that told me
When I enquired their names?
HERALD   Wi' leave, they're called
Arcite and Palamon.
THESEUS   'Tis right; those, those.
They are not dead?
HERALD   Nor in a state of life. Had they been taken   25
When their last hurts were given, 'twas possible
They might have been recovered; yet they breathe
And have the name of men.
THESEUS   Then like men use 'em.
The very lees of such, millions of rates,
Exceed the wine of others. All our surgeons   30
Convent in their behoof; our richest balms,
Rather than niggard, waste; their lives concern us
Much more than Thebes is worth. Rather than have
    'em
Freed of this plight and in their morning state,
Sound and at liberty, I would 'em dead;   35
But forty-thousandfold we had rather have 'em
Prisoners to us than death. Bear 'em speedily
From our kind air, to them unkind, and minister
What man to man may do, for our sake – more,
Since I have known frights, fury, friends' behests,   40
Love's provocations, zeal, a mistress' task,
Desire of liberty, a fever, madness,
Hath set a mark which nature could not reach to
Without some imposition, sickness in will
O'er-wrestling strength in reason. For our love   45
And great Apollo's mercy, all our best
Their best skill tender. Lead into the city,
Where having bound things scattered, we will post
To Athens 'fore our army.   *Flourish. Exeunt.*

1.5   *Music. Enter the* Queens *with the hearses*
of their knights, in a funeral solemnity.

The Dirge.

Urns and odours bring away;
Vapours, sighs, darken the day;
Our dole more deadly looks than dying –
Balms and gums and heavy cheers,
Sacred vials fill'd with tears,   5
And clamours through the wild air flying.
Come, all sad and solemn shows
That are quick-eyed Pleasure's foes;
We convent naught else but woes.
We convent naught else but woes.   10

3 QUEEN
This funeral path brings to your household's grave:
Joy seize on you again; peace sleep with him.
2 QUEEN   And this to yours.
1 QUEEN   Yours this way. Heavens lend
A thousand differing ways to one sure end.
3 QUEEN   This world's a city full of straying streets,   15
And death's the market-place where each one meets.
                              Exeunt severally.

2.1   *Enter* Jailer *and* Wooer.

JAILER I may depart with little while I live; something I may cast to you, not much. Alas, the prison I keep, though it be for great ones, yet they seldom come; before one salmon, you shall take a number of minnows. I am given out to be better lined than it can appear to me report is a true speaker. I would I were really that I am delivered to be. Marry, what I have, be it what it will, I will assure upon my daughter at the day of my death.

WOOER Sir, I demand no more than your own offer and I will estate your daughter in what I have promised.

JAILER Well, we will talk more of this when the solemnity is past. But have you a full promise of her?

Enter the Jailer's Daughter *carrying rushes.*

When that shall be seen, I tender my consent.

WOOER I have, Sir. Here she comes.

JAILER [*to his Daughter*] Your friend and I have chanced to name you here, upon the old business. But no more of that now; so soon as the court hurry is over, we will have an end of it. I'th' meantime, look tenderly to the two prisoners. I can tell you, they are princes.

DAUGHTER These strewings are for their chamber. 'Tis pity they are in prison and 'twere pity they should be out. I do think they have patience to make any adversity ashamed. The prison itself is proud of 'em and they have all the world in their chamber.

JAILER They are famed to be a pair of absolute men.

DAUGHTER By my troth, I think Fame but stammers 'em; they stand a grise above the reach of report.

JAILER I heard them reported in the battle to be the only doers.

DAUGHTER Nay, most likely, for they are noble sufferers. I marvel how they would have looked had they been victors, that with such a constant nobility enforce a freedom out of bondage, making misery their mirth and affliction a toy to jest at.

JAILER Do they so?

DAUGHTER It seems to me they have no more sense of their captivity than I of ruling Athens. They eat well, look merrily, discourse of many things, but nothing of their own restraint and disasters. Yet sometime a divided sigh, martyred, as 'twere, i'th' deliverance, will break from one of them – when the other presently gives it so sweet a rebuke that I could wish myself a sigh to be so chid, or at least a sigher to be comforted.

WOOER I never saw 'em.

JAILER The Duke himself came privately in the night and so did they.

Enter PALAMON *and* ARCITE, *above.*

What the reason of it is, I know not. Look, yonder they are; that's Arcite looks out.

DAUGHTER No, sir, no, that's Palamon. Arcite is the lower of the twain; you may perceive a part of him.

JAILER Go to, leave your pointing; they would not make us their object. Out of their sight.

DAUGHTER It is a holiday to look on them. Lord, the difference of men!   *Exeunt.*   55

2.2   *Enter* PALAMON *and* ARCITE *in prison.*

PALAMON How do you, noble cousin?

ARCITE   How do you, sir?

PALAMON Why, strong enough to laugh at misery
And bear the chance of war; yet we are prisoners,
I fear, forever, cousin.

ARCITE   I believe it
And to that destiny have patiently 5
Laid up my hour to come.

PALAMON   O, cousin Arcite,
Where is Thebes now? Where is our noble country?
Where are our friends and kindreds? Never more
Must we behold those comforts, never see
The hardy youths strive for the games of honour, 10
Hung with the painted favours of their ladies,
Like tall ships under sail – then start amongst 'em,
And as an east wind leave 'em all behind us,
Like lazy clouds, whilst Palamon and Arcite,
Even in the wagging of a wanton leg, 15
Outstripped the people's praises, won the garlands,
Ere they have time to wish 'em ours. O, never
Shall we two exercise, like twins of honour,
Our arms again and feel our fiery horses
Like proud seas under us; our good swords now 20
(Better the red-eyed god of war ne'er wore),
Ravished our sides, like age must run to rust
And deck the temples of those gods that hate us.
These hands shall never draw 'em out like lightning
To blast whole armies more.

ARCITE   No, Palamon, 25
Those hopes are prisoners with us. Here we are,
And here the graces of our youths must wither
Like a too-timely spring; here age must find us
And, which is heaviest, Palamon, unmarried.
The sweet embraces of a loving wife, 30
Loaden with kisses, armed with thousand Cupids,
Shall never clasp our necks; no issue know us;
No figures of ourselves shall we e'er see,
To glad our age, and like young eagles teach 'em
Boldly to gaze against bright arms and say, 35
'Remember what your fathers were, and conquer!'
The fair-eyed maids shall weep our banishments
And in their songs curse ever-blinded Fortune
Till she for shame see what a wrong she has done
To youth and nature. This is all our world. 40
We shall know nothing here but one another,
Hear nothing but the clock that tells our woes.
The vine shall grow but we shall never see it;
Summer shall come and with her all delights,
But dead-cold winter must inhabit here still. 45

PALAMON 'Tis too true, Arcite. To our Theban hounds
        That shook the aged forest with their echoes
        No more now must we hallow, no more shake
        Our pointed javelins whilst the angry swine
50   Flies like a Parthian quiver from our rages,
        Struck with our well-steeled darts. All valiant uses,
        The food and nourishment of noble minds,
        In us two here shall perish; we shall die,
        Which is the curse of honour, lastly,
        Children of grief and ignorance.
55 ARCITE   Yet, cousin,
        Even from the bottom of these miseries,
        From all that Fortune can inflict upon us,
        I see two comforts rising, two mere blessings,
        If the gods please: to hold here a brave patience
60   And the enjoying of our griefs together.
        While Palamon is with me, let me perish
        If I think this our prison!
    PALAMON   Certainly,
        'Tis a main goodness, cousin, that our fortunes
        Were twined together; 'tis most true, two souls
65   Put in two noble bodies, let 'em suffer
        The gall of hazard, so they grow together,
        Will never sink; they must not, say they could.
        A willing man dies sleeping and all's done.
    ARCITE   Shall we make worthy uses of this place
        That all men hate so much?
70 PALAMON   How, gentle cousin?
    ARCITE   Let's think this prison holy sanctuary,
        To keep us from corruption of worse men.
        We are young and yet desire the ways of honour,
        That liberty and common conversation,
75   The poison of pure spirits, might, like women,
        Woo us to wander from. What worthy blessing
        Can be but our imaginations
        May make it ours? And here being thus together,
        We are an endless mine to one another;
80   We are one another's wife, ever begetting
        New births of love; we are father, friends, acquaintance,
        We are, in one another, families;
        I am your heir and you are mine. This place
        Is our inheritance; no hard oppressor
85   Dare take this from us; here, with a little patience,
        We shall live long and loving. No surfeits seek us;
        The hand of war hurts none here, nor the seas
        Swallow their youth. Were we at liberty,
        A wife might part us lawfully, or business;
90   Quarrels consume us; envy of ill men
        Crave our acquaintance. I might sicken, cousin,
        Where you should never know it, and so perish
        Without your noble hand to close mine eyes,
        Or prayers to the gods. A thousand chances,
        Were we from hence, would sever us.
95 PALAMON   You have made me –
        I thank you, cousin Arcite – almost wanton
        With my captivity: what a misery

        It is to live abroad and everywhere!
        'Tis like a beast, methinks. I find the court here –
        I am sure, a more content; and all those pleasures   100
        That woo the wills of men to vanity,
        I see through now and am sufficient
        To tell the world 'tis but a gaudy shadow
        That old Time as he passes by takes with him.
        What had we been, old in the court of Creon,   105
        Where sin is justice, lust and ignorance
        The virtues of the great ones? Cousin Arcite,
        Had not the loving gods found this place for us,
        We had died as they do, ill old men, unwept,
        And had their epitaphs, the people's curses.   110
        Shall I say more?
    ARCITE   I would hear you still.
    PALAMON   You shall.
        Is there record of any two that loved
        Better than we do, Arcite?
    ARCITE   Sure there cannot.
    PALAMON   I do not think it possible our friendship
        Should ever leave us.
    ARCITE   Till our deaths it cannot.   115

                Enter EMILIA *and her* Woman.

        And after death our spirits shall be led
        To those that love eternally. [*Palamon sees Emilia.*]
                                    Speak on, sir.
    EMILIA   This garden has a world of pleasures in't.
        What flower is this?
    WOMAN   'Tis called narcissus, madam.
    EMILIA   That was a fair boy, certain, but a fool   120
        To love himself. Were there not maids enough?
    ARCITE [*to Palamon*] Pray, forward.
    PALAMON   Yes –
    EMILIA   Or were they all hard-hearted?
    WOMAN   They could not be to one so fair.
    EMILIA   Thou wouldst not.
    WOMAN   I think I should not, madam.
    EMILIA   That's a good wench.
        But take heed to your kindness, though.
    WOMAN   Why, madam?   125
    EMILIA   Men are mad things.
    ARCITE   Will ye go forward, cousin?
    EMILIA
        Canst not thou work such flowers in silk, wench?
    WOMAN   Yes.
    EMILIA   I'll have a gown full o' 'em, and of these.
        This is a pretty colour; will't not do
        Rarely upon a skirt, wench?
    WOMAN   Dainty, madam.   130
    ARCITE
        Cousin, cousin! how do you, sir? Why, Palamon!
    PALAMON   Never till now was I in prison, Arcite.
    ARCITE   Why, what's the matter, man?
    PALAMON [*Indicates Emilia.*]   Behold, and wonder!
        By heaven, she is a goddess.
    ARCITE [*Sees Emilia.*]   Ha!

PALAMON   Do reverence.
  She is a goddess, Arcite.
EMILIA   Of all flowers
  Methinks a rose is best.
WOMAN   Why, gentle madam?
EMILIA   It is the very emblem of a maid.
  For, when the west wind courts her gently,
  How modestly she blows and paints the sun
  With her chaste blushes! When the north comes near
    her,
  Rude and impatient, then, like chastity,
  She locks her beauties in her bud again
  And leaves him to base briars.
WOMAN   Yet, good madam,
  Sometimes her modesty will blow so far
  She falls for't. A maid,
  If she have any honour, would be loath
  To take example by her.
EMILIA   Thou art wanton.
ARCITE   She is wondrous fair.
PALAMON   She is all the beauty extant.
EMILIA
  The sun grows high; let's walk in. Keep these flowers.
  We'll see how near art can come near their colours.
  I am wondrous merry-hearted; I could laugh now.
WOMAN   I could lie down, I am sure.
EMILIA   And take one with you?
WOMAN   That's as we bargain, madam.
EMILIA   Well, agree then.
           Exeunt Emilia and Woman.
PALAMON   What think you of this beauty?
ARCITE   'Tis a rare one.
PALAMON   Is't but a rare one?
ARCITE   Yes, a matchless beauty.
PALAMON
  Might not a man well lose himself and love her?
ARCITE   I cannot tell what you have done; I have,
  Beshrew mine eyes for't; now I feel my shackles.
PALAMON   You love her then?
ARCITE   Who would not?
PALAMON   And desire her?
ARCITE   Before my liberty.
PALAMON   I saw her first.
ARCITE   That's nothing.
PALAMON   But it shall be.
ARCITE   I saw her too.
PALAMON   Yes, but you must not love her.
ARCITE   I will not as you do, to worship her
  As she is heavenly and a blessed goddess.
  I love her as a woman, to enjoy her:
  So both may love.
PALAMON   You shall not love at all.
ARCITE   Not love at all!
  Who shall deny me?
PALAMON   I that first saw her, I that took possession
  First with mine eye of all those beauties in her
  Revealed to mankind! If thou lovest her,

Or entertain'st a hope to blast my wishes,
Thou art a traitor, Arcite, and a fellow
False as thy title to her. Friendship, blood,
And all the ties between us, I disclaim,
If thou once think upon her.
ARCITE   Yes, I love her
  And, if the lives of all my name lay on it,
  I must do so; I love her with my soul:
  If that will lose ye, farewell, Palamon.
  I say again,
  I love her and in loving her maintain
  I am as worthy and as free a lover,
  And have as just a title to her beauty,
  As any Palamon, or any living
  That is a man's son.
PALAMON   Have I called thee friend?
ARCITE
  Yes, and have found me so; why are you moved thus?
  Let me deal coldly with you: am not I
  Part of your blood, part of your soul? you have told
    me
  That I was Palamon and you were Arcite.
PALAMON   Yes.
ARCITE   Am not I liable to those affections,
  Those joys, griefs, angers, fears, my friend shall
    suffer?
PALAMON   Ye may be.
ARCITE   Why then would you deal so cunningly,
  So strangely, so unlike a noble kinsman,
  To love alone? Speak truly: do you think me
  Unworthy of her sight?
PALAMON   No, but unjust
  If thou pursue that sight.
ARCITE   Because another
  First sees the enemy, shall I stand still
  And let mine honour down, and never charge?
PALAMON   Yes, if he be but one.
ARCITE   But say that one
  Had rather combat me?
PALAMON   Let that one say so,
  And use thy freedom. Else, if thou pursuest her,
  Be as that cursed man that hates his country,
  A branded villain.
ARCITE   You are mad.
PALAMON   I must be,
  Till thou art worthy, Arcite; it concerns me.
  And, in this madness, if I hazard thee
  And take thy life, I deal but truly.
ARCITE   Fie, sir!
  You play the child extremely. I will love her;
  I must, I ought, to do so, and I dare,
  And all this justly.
PALAMON   O that now, that now,
  Thy false self and thy friend had but this fortune:
  To be one hour at liberty and grasp
  Our good swords in our hands! I would quickly teach
    thee

What 'twere to filch affection from another;
Thou art baser in it than a cutpurse.
215 Put but thy head out of this window more
And, as I have a soul, I'll nail thy life to't.

ARCITE
Thou dar'st not, fool, thou canst not, thou art feeble.
Put my head out? I'll throw my body out
And leap the garden, when I see her next,
220 And pitch between her arms, to anger thee.

Enter Jailer.

PALAMON   No more; the keeper's coming. I shall live
To knock thy brains out with my shackles.
ARCITE   Do!
JAILER   By your leave, gentlemen.
PALAMON   Now, honest keeper?
JAILER   Lord Arcite, you must presently to th' Duke;
The cause I know not yet.
225 ARCITE   I am ready, keeper.
JAILER   Prince Palamon, I must awhile bereave you
Of your fair cousin's company.
Exeunt Arcite and Jailer.
PALAMON   And me too,
Even when you please, of life. – Why is he sent for?
It may be he shall marry her; he's goodly
230 And like enough the Duke hath taken notice
Both of his blood and body. But his falsehood –
Why should a friend be treacherous? If that
Get him a wife so noble and so fair,
Let honest men ne'er love again. Once more
235 I would but see this fair one. Blessed garden
And fruit and flowers more blessed that still blossom
As her bright eyes shine on ye: would I were
For all the fortune of my life hereafter
Yon little tree, yon blooming apricock!
240 How I would spread and fling my wanton arms
In at her window! I would bring her fruit
Fit for the gods to feed on; youth and pleasure
Still as she tasted should be doubled on her
And, if she be not heavenly, I would make her
245 So near the gods in nature, they should fear her,

Enter Jailer.

And then I am sure she would love me. – How now,
    keeper?
Where's Arcite?
JAILER   Banished. Prince Pirithous
Obtained his liberty, but never more
Upon his oath and life must he set foot
Upon this kingdom.
250 PALAMON   He's a blessed man.
He shall see Thebes again and call to arms
The bold young men that, when he bids 'em charge,
Fall on like fire. Arcite shall have a fortune,
If he dare make himself a worthy lover,
255 Yet in the field to strike a battle for her

And, if he lose her then, he's a cold coward;
How bravely may he bear himself to win her
If he be noble Arcite – thousand ways!
Were I at liberty, I would do things
Of such a virtuous greatness that this lady, 260
This blushing virgin, should take manhood to her
And seek to ravish me.
JAILER   My lord, for you
I have this charge to –
PALAMON   To discharge my life.
JAILER
No, but from this place to remove your lordship;
The windows are too open.
PALAMON   Devils take 'em 265
That are so envious to me! Prithee, kill me.
JAILER   And hang for't afterward!
PALAMON   By this good light,
Had I a sword I would kill thee.
JAILER   Why, my lord?
PALAMON
Thou bringst such pelting, scurvy news continually,
Thou art not worthy life. I will not go. 270
JAILER   Indeed you must, my lord.
PALAMON   May I see the garden?
JAILER   No.
PALAMON   Then I am resolved; I will not go.
JAILER
I must constrain you then and, for you are dangerous,
I'll clap more irons on you.
PALAMON   Do, good keeper!
I'll shake 'em so, ye shall not sleep; 275
I'll make ye a new morris. – Must I go?
JAILER   There is no remedy.
PALAMON   Farewell, kind window.
May rude winds never hurt thee! – O, my lady,
If ever thou hast felt what sorrow was,
Dream how I suffer! – Come, now bury me. 280
Exeunt Palamon and Jailer.

2.3   *Enter* ARCITE.

ARCITE   Banished the kingdom? 'Tis a benefit,
A mercy I must thank 'em for; but banished
The free enjoying of that face I die for –
Oh, 'twas a studied punishment, a death
Beyond imagination, such a vengeance 5
That, were I old and wicked, all my sins
Could never pluck upon me. Palamon,
Thou hast the start now; thou shalt stay and see
Her bright eyes break each morning 'gainst thy
    window
And let in life into thee; thou shalt feed 10
Upon the sweetness of a noble beauty
That nature ne'er exceeded nor ne'er shall.
Good gods, what happiness has Palamon!
Twenty to one, he'll come to speak to her
And, if she be as gentle as she's fair, 15

I know she's his; he has a tongue will tame
Tempests and make the wild rocks wanton.
Come what can come,
The worst is death; I will not leave the kingdom.
20   I know mine own is but a heap of ruins
And no redress there. If I go, he has her.
I am resolved another shape shall make me
Or end my fortunes. Either way I am happy:
I'll see her and be near her, or no more.

Enter four Countrymen, *and one with a garland
before them.* ARCITE *stands aside.*

25   1 COUNTRYMAN   My masters, I'll be there, that's certain.
2 COUNTRYMAN   And I'll be there.
3 COUNTRYMAN   And I.
4 COUNTRYMAN
Why then, have with ye, boys. 'Tis but a chiding.
Let the plough play today; I'll tickl't out
Of the jades' tails tomorrow.
30   1 COUNTRYMAN   I am sure
To have my wife as jealous as a turkey –
But that's all one: I'll go through; let her mumble.
2 COUNTRYMAN
Clap her aboard tomorrow night and stow her,
And all's made up again.
3 COUNTRYMAN   Ay, do but put
35   A fescue in her fist and you shall see her
Take a new lesson out and be a good wench.
Do we all hold against the Maying?
4 COUNTRYMAN   Hold?
What should ail us?
3 COUNTRYMAN   Arcas will be there.
2 COUNTRYMAN   And Sennois
40   And Rycas – and three better lads ne'er danced
Under green tree – and ye know what wenches, ha?
But will the dainty dominie, the schoolmaster,
Keep touch, do you think? For he does all, ye know.
3 COUNTRYMAN   He'll eat a hornbook ere he fail. Go to;
45   The matter's too far driven between him
And the tanner's daughter to let slip now;
And she must see the Duke and she must dance too.
4 COUNTRYMAN   Shall we be lusty?
2 COUNTRYMAN   All the boys in Athens
Blow wind i'th' breech on's. And here I'll be,
50   And there I'll be for our town and here again,
And there again – ha, boys, hey for the weavers!
1 COUNTRYMAN   This must be done i'th' woods.
4 COUNTRYMAN   O, pardon me.
2 COUNTRYMAN
By any means; our thing of learning says so –
Where he himself will edify the Duke
Most parlously in our behalfs. He's excellent i'th'
55   woods;
Bring him to th' plains, his learning makes no cry.
3 COUNTRYMAN
We'll see the sports, then every man to's tackle;
And, sweet companions, let's rehearse, by any means,

Before the ladies see us and do sweetly
And God knows what may come on't.   60
4 COUNTRYMAN
Content; the sports once ended, we'll perform.
Away, boys – and hold. [*Arcite comes forward.*]
ARCITE   By your leaves, honest friends:
Pray you, whither go you?
4 COUNTRYMAN   Whither?
Why, what a question's that?
ARCITE   Yes, 'tis a question,
To me that know not.
3 COUNTRYMAN   To the games, my friend.   65
2 COUNTRYMAN
Where were you bred, you know it not?
ARCITE   Not far, sir;
Are there such games today?
1 COUNTRYMAN   Yes, marry, are there
And such as you never saw; the Duke himself
Will be in person there.
ARCITE   What pastimes are they?
2 COUNTRYMAN
Wrestling and running. – 'Tis a pretty fellow.   70
3 COUNTRYMAN   Thou wilt not go along?
ARCITE   Not yet, sir.
4 COUNTRYMAN   Well, sir,
Take your own time. Come, boys.
1 COUNTRYMAN [*aside to the others*]
                        My mind misgives me,
This fellow has a vengeance trick o'th' hip;
Mark how his body's made for't.
2 COUNTRYMAN   I'll be hanged, though,
If he dare venture. Hang him, plum porridge!   75
He wrestle? He roast eggs! Come, let's be gone, lads.
                              Exeunt Countrymen.
ARCITE   This is an offered opportunity
I durst not wish for. Well I could have wrestled –
The best men called it excellent – and run
Swifter than wind upon a field of corn,   80
Curling the wealthy ears, never flew. I'll venture
And in some poor disguise be there; who knows
Whether my brows may not be girt with garlands
And happiness prefer me to a place,
Where I may ever dwell in sight of her?   *Exit.*   85

2.4   *Enter Jailer's* Daughter *alone.*

DAUGHTER
Why should I love this gentleman? 'Tis odds
He never will affect me: I am base,
My father the mean keeper of his prison,
And he a prince. To marry him is hopeless;
To be his whore is witless. Out upon't,   5
What pushes are we wenches driven to
When fifteen once has found us! – First, I saw him;
I, seeing, thought he was a goodly man;
He has as much to please a woman in him,
If he please to bestow it so, as ever   10

These eyes yet looked on. Next, I pitied him –
And so would any young wench, o' my conscience,
That ever dreamed, or vowed her maidenhead
To a young handsome man. Then, I loved him,
15 Extremely loved him, infinitely loved him!
And yet he had a cousin fair as he too,
But in my heart was Palamon and there,
Lord, what a coil he keeps! To hear him
Sing in an evening, what a heaven it is!
20 And yet his songs are sad ones. Fairer spoken
Was never gentleman. When I come in
To bring him water in a morning, first
He bows his noble body, then salutes me, thus:
'Fair, gentle maid, good morrow; may thy goodness
25 Get thee a happy husband.' Once, he kissed me.
I loved my lips the better ten days after:
Would he would do so every day! He grieves much –
And me as much to see his misery.
What should I do to make him know I love him?
30 For I would fain enjoy him. Say I ventured
To set him free? What says the law then?
Thus much for law or kindred! I will do it!
And this night, or tomorrow, he shall love me.   *Exit.*

2.5   *A short flourish of cornets and shouts within.*
Enter THESEUS, HIPPOLYTA, PIRITHOUS, EMILIA; ARCITE,
disguised as a countryman, with a garland;
attendants and spectators.

THESEUS   You have done worthily; I have not seen,
   Since Hercules, a man of tougher sinews.
   Whate'er you are, you run the best and wrestle,
   That these times can allow.
ARCITE   I am proud to please you.
THESEUS   What country bred you?
5 ARCITE   This; but far off, Prince.
THESEUS   Are you a gentleman?
ARCITE   My father said so
   And to those gentle uses gave me life.
THESEUS   Are you his heir?
ARCITE   His youngest, sir.
THESEUS   Your father
   Sure is a happy sire then. What profess you?
10 ARCITE   A little of all noble qualities.
   I could have kept a hawk and well have hallowed
   To a deep cry of dogs. I dare not praise
   My feat in horsemanship, yet they that knew me
   Would say it was my best piece; last and greatest,
   I would be thought a soldier.
15 THESEUS   You are perfect.
PIRITHOUS [*to Emilia*]   Upon my soul, a proper man.
EMILIA   He is so.
PIRITHOUS [*to Hippolyta*]   How do you like him, lady?
HIPPOLYTA   I admire him.
   I have not seen so young a man so noble,
   If he say true, of his sort.
EMILIA   Believe,

His mother was a wondrous handsome woman;   20
   His face, methinks, goes that way.
HIPPOLYTA   But his body
And fiery mind illustrate a brave father.
PIRITHOUS   Mark how his virtue, like a hidden sun,
   Breaks through his baser garments.
HIPPOLYTA   He's well got, sure.
THESEUS [*to Arcite*]   What made you seek this place, sir?
ARCITE   Noble Theseus,
   To purchase name and do my ablest service   25
   To such a well-found wonder as thy worth,
   For only in thy court, of all the world,
   Dwells fair-eyed Honour.
PIRITHOUS   All his words are worthy.
THESEUS [*to Arcite*]
   Sir, we are much indebted to your travel,   30
   Nor shall you lose your wish. Pirithous,
   Dispose of this fair gentleman.
PIRITHOUS   Thanks, Theseus.
   [*to Arcite*] Whate'er you are, you're mine, and I shall
      give you
   To a most noble service: to this lady,
   [*Leads him to Emilia.*]
   This bright young virgin; pray observe her goodness.   35
   You have honoured her fair birthday with your
      virtues
   And, as your due, you're hers; kiss her fair hand, sir.
ARCITE   Sir, you're a noble giver. – Dearest beauty,
   Thus let me seal my vowed faith. [*Kisses her hand.*]
                           When your servant,
   Your most unworthy creature, but offends you,   40
   Command him die: he shall.
EMILIA   That were too cruel.
   If you deserve well, sir, I shall soon see't.
   You're mine and somewhat better than your rank I'll
      use you.
PIRITHOUS   I'll see you furnished and, because you say
   You are a horseman, I must needs entreat you   45
   This afternoon to ride, but 'tis a rough one.
ARCITE   I like him better, Prince; I shall not then
   Freeze in my saddle.
THESEUS [*to Hippolyta*]   Sweet, you must be ready,
   And you, Emelia, and
   [*to Pirithous*]   you, friend, and all,
   Tomorrow by the sun, to do observance   50
   To flowery May, in Dian's wood.
   [*to Arcite*]   Wait well, sir,
   Upon your mistress. – Emily, I hope
   He shall not go afoot.
EMILIA   That were a shame, sir,
   While I have horses.
   [*to Arcite*]   Take your choice and what
   You want at any time, let me but know it;   55
   If you serve faithfully, I dare assure you
   You'll find a loving mistress.
ARCITE   If I do not,

Let me find that my father ever hated,
Disgrace and blows.

THESEUS   Go lead the way; you have won it
 It shall be so: you shall receive all dues   60
 Fit for the honour you have won; 'twere wrong else.
 – Sister, beshrew my heart, you have a servant,
 That, if I were a woman, would be a master.
 But you are wise.

EMILIA   I hope, too wise for that, sir.
         Flourish. Exeunt.

2.6 *Enter Jailer's* Daughter *alone.*

DAUGHTER Let all the dukes and all the devils roar,
 He is at liberty! I have ventured for him
 And out I have brought him; to a little wood
 A mile hence I have sent him, where a cedar
 Higher than all the rest spreads like a plane   5
 Fast by a brook, and there he shall keep close
 Till I provide him files and food, for yet
 His iron bracelets are not off. O, Love,
 What a stout-hearted child thou art! My father
 Durst better have endured cold iron than done it. 10
 I love him beyond love and beyond reason,
 Or wit, or safety; I have made him know it;
 I care not, I am desperate. If the law
 Find me and then condem me for't, some wenches,
 Some honest-hearted maids, will sing my dirge 15
 And tell to memory my death was noble,
 Dying almost a martyr. That way he takes,
 I purpose, is my way too. Sure he cannot
 Be so unmanly as to leave me here;
 If he do, maids will not so easily   20
 Trust men again. And yet he has not thanked me
 For what I have done, no, not so much as kissed me,
 And that methinks is not so well; nor scarcely
 Could I persuade him to become a free man,
 He made such scruples of the wrong he did 25
 To me and my father. Yet I hope,
 When he considers more, this love of mine
 Will take more root within him. Let him do
 What he will with me, so he use me kindly –
 For use me so he shall, or I'll proclaim him, 30
 And to his face, no man. I'll presently
 Provide him necessaries and pack my clothes up
 And where there is a path of ground I'll venture,
 So he be with me; by him, like a shadow,
 I'll ever dwell. Within this hour the hubbub 35
 Will be all o'er the prison: I am then
 Kissing the man they look for. Farewell, father!
 Get many more such prisoners and such daughters
 And shortly you may keep yourself. Now to him.
         Exit.

3.1 *Cornets in sundry places. Noise and hallooing*
  as people a-Maying. Enter ARCITE *alone.*

ARCITE The Duke has lost Hippolyta; each took

A several laund. This is a solemn rite
They owe bloomed May and the Athenians pay it
To th' heart of ceremony. O, Queen Emilia,
Fresher than May, sweeter   5
Than her gold buttons on the boughs, or all
Th'enamelled knacks o'th' mead, or garden – yea,
We challenge too the bank of any nymph
That makes the stream seem flowers: thou, oh jewel
O'th' wood, o'th' world, hast likewise blest a pace 10
With thy sole presence. In thy rumination,
That I, poor man, might eftsoons come between
And chop on some cold thought! Thrice blessed
 chance
To drop on such a mistress, expectation
Most guiltless on't! Tell me, O Lady Fortune 15
(Next, after Emily, my sovereign), how far
I may be proud. She takes strong note of me,
Hath made me near her and, this beauteous morn,
The prim'st of all the year, presents me with
A brace of horses: two such steeds might well 20
Be by a pair of kings backed, in a field
That their crowns' titles tried. Alas, alas,
Poor cousin Palamon, poor prisoner, thou
So little dream'st upon my fortune, that
Thou thinkst thyself the happier thing, to be 25
So near Emilia; me thou deem'st at Thebes,
And therein wretched, although free. But if
Thou knew'st my mistress breathed on me, and that
I eared her language, lived in her eye; O, coz,
What passion would enclose thee!

 Enter PALAMON *as out of a bush, with his shackles;*
   he bends his fist at Arcite.

PALAMON   Traitor kinsman, 30
 Thou shouldst perceive my passion, if these signs
 Of prisonment were off me and this hand
 But owner of a sword! By all oaths in one,
 I and the justice of my love would make thee
 A confessed traitor! O, thou most perfidious 35
 That ever gently looked, the void'st of honour
 That e'er bore gentle token, falsest cousin
 That ever blood made kin: call'st thou her thine?
 I'll prove it in my shackles, with these hands,
 Void of appointment, that thou liest, and art 40
 A very thief in love, a chaffy lord
 Not worth the name of villain. Had I a sword
 And these house-clogs away –

ARCITE   Dear cousin Palamon –

PALAMON Cosener Arcite, give me language such
 As thou hast showed me feat.

ARCITE   Not finding in 45
 The circuit of my breast any gross stuff
 To form me like your blazon holds me to
 This gentleness of answer. 'Tis your passion
 That thus mistakes, the which to you being enemy,
 Cannot to me be kind: honour and honesty 50

I cherish and depend on, howsoe'er
You skip them in me, and with them, fair coz,
I'll maintain my proceedings. Pray be pleased
To show in generous terms your griefs, since that
55　　Your question's with your equal, who professes
To clear his own way with the mind and sword
Of a true gentlemen.
PALAMON　　　　　　That thou durst, Arcite!
ARCITE　My coz, my coz, you have been well advertised
How much I dare; you've seen me use my sword
60　　Against th'advice of fear. Sure, of another
You would not hear me doubted, but your silence
Should break out, though i'th' sanctuary.
PALAMON　　　　　　　　　　Sir,
I have seen you move in such a place, which well
Might justify your manhood; you were called
A good knight and a bold. But the whole week's not
65　　　　fair
If any day it rain: their valiant temper
Men lose when they incline to treachery
And then they fight like compelled bears, would fly
Were they not tied.
ARCITE　　　　　Cousin, you might as well
70　　Speak this and act it in your glass as to
His ear which now disdains you.
PALAMON　　　　　　　Come up to me;
Quit me of those cold gyves; give me a sword,
Though it be rusty, and the charity
Of one meal lend me. Come before me then,
75　　A good sword in thy hand, and do but say
That Emily is thine – I will forgive
The trespass thou hast done me, yea, my life,
If then thou carry't, and brave souls in shades
That have died manly, which will seek of me
80　　Some news from earth, they shall get none but this:
That thou art brave and noble.
ARCITE　　　　　　　　　Be content.
Again betake you to your hawthorn house.
With counsel of the night, I will be here
With wholesome viands. These impediments
85　　Will I file off; you shall have garments and
Perfumes to kill the smell o'th' prison. After,
When you shall stretch yourself and say but, 'Arcite,
I am in plight', there shall be at your choice
Both sword and armour.
PALAMON　　　　　　O you heavens, dares any
90　　So nobly bear a guilty business? None
But only Arcite; therefore none but Arcite
In this kind but so bold.
ARCITE　　　　Sweet Palamon. [*Offers to embrace him.*]
PALAMON
I do embrace you and your offer; for
Your offer do't I only, sir; your person
95　　Without hypocrisy I may not wish
More than my sword's edge on't.
ARCITE　　　　　You hear the horns; [*Horns.*]
Enter your musit, lest this match between's

Be crossed ere met. Give me your hand; farewell.
I'll bring you every needful thing. I pray you
Take comfort and be strong.
PALAMON　　　　　Pray hold your promise　　100
And do the deed with a bent brow. Most certain
You love me not; be rough with me and pour
This oil out of your language. By this air,
I could for each word give a cuff, my stomach
Not reconciled by reason.
ARCITE　　　　　　Plainly spoken.　　105
Yet pardon me hard language. When I spur
My horse I chide him not; content and anger
In me have but one face.　　　　[*Horns again.*]
　　　　　　　Hark, sir, they call
The scattered to the banquet. You must guess
I have an office there.
PALAMON　　　　Sir, your attendance　　110
Cannot please heaven and I know your office
Unjustly is achieved.
ARCITE　　　　　'Tis a good title.
I am persuaded, this question, sick between 's,
By bleeding must be cured. I am a suitor
That to your sword you will bequeath this plea　　115
And talk of it no more.
PALAMON　　　　　But this one word:
You are going now to gaze upon my mistress –
For, note you, mine she is –
ARCITE　　　　　Nay, then –
PALAMON　　　　　　Nay, pray you!
You talk of feeding me to breed me strength.
You are going now to look upon a sun　　120
That strengthens what it looks on; there
You have a vantage on me. But enjoy't till
I may enforce my remedy. Farewell.　　　*Exeunt.*

3.2　　　　*Enter Jailer's* Daughter *alone.*

DAUGHTER
He has mistook the brake I meant, is gone
After his fancy. 'Tis now well-nigh morning.
No matter: would it were perpetual night,
And darkness lord o'th' world! – Hark, 'tis a wolf!
In me hath grief slain fear and but for one thing　　5
I care for nothing and that's Palamon.
I reck not if the wolves would jaw me, so
He had this file. What if I hallooed for him?
I cannot hallow. If I whooped – what then?
If he not answered, I should call a wolf,　　10
And do him but that service. I have heard
Strange howls this livelong night; why may't not be
They have made prey of him? He has no weapons;
He cannot run: the jangling of his gyves
Might call fell things to listen, who have in them　　15
A sense to know a man unarmed and can
Smell where resistance is. I'll set it down,
He's torn to pieces; they howled many together
And then they fed on him. So much for that:
Be bold to ring the bell. How stand I then?　　20

All's chared when he is gone – no, no, I lie.
My father's to be hanged for his escape,
Myself to beg, if I prized life so much
As to deny my act – but that I would not,
Should I try death by dozens. I am moped.
Food took I none these two days;
Sipped some water. I have not closed mine eyes,
Save when my lids scoured off their brine. Alas,
Dissolve, my life! Let not my sense unsettle,
Lest I should drown, or stab, or hang myself.
Oh, state of nature, fail together in me,
Since thy best props are warped! – So, which way
     now?
The best way is the next way to a grave:
Each errant step beside is torment. Lo,
The moon is down, the crickets chirp, the screech-
     owl
Calls in the dawn; all offices are done
Save what I fail in. But the point is this:
An end, and that is all.   *Exit.*

3.3   *Enter* ARCITE *with meat, wine and files.*

ARCITE
   I should be near the place. Ho! Cousin Palamon?
PALAMON [*from the bush*]
   Arcite?
ARCITE   The same. I have brought you food and files.
   Come forth and fear not; here's no Theseus.

          Enter PALAMON.

PALAMON   Nor none so honest, Arcite.
ARCITE   That's no matter.
   We'll argue that hereafter. Come, take courage!
   You shall not die thus beastly; here, sir, drink –
   I know you are faint – then I'll talk further with you.
PALAMON   Arcite, thou mightst now poison me.
ARCITE   I might,
   But I must fear you first. Sit down and, good now,
   No more of these vain parleys; let us not,
   Having our ancient reputation with us,
   Make talk for fools and cowards. To your health –
   [*Drinks.*]
PALAMON   Do!
ARCITE   Pray sit down then, and let me entreat you,
   By all the honesty and honour in you,
   No mention of this woman; 'twill disturb us.
   We shall have time enough.
PALAMON   Well, sir, I'll pledge you. [*Drinks.*]
ARCITE   Drink a good hearty draught: it breeds good
       blood, man.
   Do not you feel it thaw you?
PALAMON   Stay, I'll tell you
   After a draught or two more.
ARCITE   Spare it not;
   The Duke has more, coz. Eat now.
PALAMON   Yes.
ARCITE   I am glad

You have so good a stomach.
PALAMON   I am gladder
   I have so good meat to't.
ARCITE   Is't not mad lodging,
   Here in the wild woods, cousin?
PALAMON   Yes, for them
   That have wild consciences.
ARCITE   How tastes your victuals?
   Your hunger needs no sauce, I see.
PALAMON   Not much.
   But if it did, yours is too tart, sweet cousin.
   What is this?
ARCITE   Venison.
PALAMON   'Tis a lusty meat.
   Give me more wine. – Here, Arcite, to the wenches
   We have known in our days. The Lord Steward's
       daughter –
   Do you remember her?
ARCITE   After you, coz.
PALAMON   She loved a black-haired man –
ARCITE   She did so; well, sir?
PALAMON   And I have heard some call him Arcite, and –
ARCITE   Out with't, faith.
PALAMON   She met him in an arbour.
   What did she there, coz? play o'th' virginals?
ARCITE   Something she did, sir –
PALAMON   Made her groan a month for't.
   Or two, or three, or ten.
ARCITE   The Marshall's sister
   Had her share too, as I remember, cousin;
   Else there be tales abroad. You'll pledge her?
PALAMON   Yes.
ARCITE   A pretty brown wench 'tis. There was a time
   When young men went a-hunting, and a wood,
   And a broad beech; and thereby hangs a tale –
   Hey ho.
PALAMON   For Emily, upon my life! Fool,
   Away with this strained mirth! I say again,
   That sigh was breathed for Emily; base cousin,
   Dar'st thou break first?
ARCITE   You are wide.
PALAMON   By heaven and earth,
   There's nothing in thee honest.
ARCITE   Then I'll leave you;
   You are a beast now.
PALAMON   As thou mak'st me, traitor.
ARCITE
   There's all things needful – files and shirts, and
       perfumes;
   I'll come again some two hours hence, and bring
   That that shall quiet all –
PALAMON   A sword and armour.
ARCITE   Fear me not. You are now too foul; farewell.
   Get off your trinkets. You shall want nought.
PALAMON   Sirrah –
ARCITE   I'll hear no more.   *Exit.*
PALAMON   If he keep touch, he dies for't. *Exit.*

3.4   *Enter Jailer's Daughter.*

DAUGHTER   I am very cold and all the stars are out too,
      The little stars and all, that look like aglets;
      The sun has seen my folly. – Palamon! –
      Alas, no, he's in heaven; where am I now?
5   Yonder's the sea and there's a ship; how't tumbles!
      And there's a rock lies watching under water;
      Now, now, it beats upon it; now, now, now!
      There's a leak sprung, a sound one! How they cry!
      Run her before the wind, you'll lose all else.
10   Up with a course or two and tack about, boys!
      Good night, good night, you're gone. – I am very
          hungry.
      Would I could find a fine frog; he would tell me
      News from all parts o'th' world. Then would I make
      A carrack of a cockle shell and sail
15   By east and north-east to the king of pygmies,
      For he tells fortunes rarely. Now, my father
      Twenty to one is trussed up in a trice
      Tomorrow morning; I'll say never a word.
      [*Sings.*]
          For I'll cut my green coat, a foot above my knee
          And I'll clip my yellow locks, an inch below mine
              eye.
20   Hey, nonny, nonny, nonny,
          He's buy me a white cut, forth for to ride,
          And I'll go seek him through the world that is so
              wide,
          Hey, nonny, nonny, nonny.
25   O, for a prick now, like a nightingale,
      To put my breast against. I shall sleep like a top else.
                                        Exit.

3.5   *Enter Schoolmaster* GERALD *and*
                  five Countrymen.

SCHOOLMASTER   Fie, fie,
      What tediosity and disinsanity
      Is here among ye! Have my rudiments
      Been laboured so long with ye, milked unto ye
5   And, by a figure, even the very plum-broth
      And marrow of my understanding laid upon ye,
      And do ye still cry 'Where?' and 'How?' and
          'Wherefore?'
      You most coarse-frieze capacities, ye jean judgments,
      Have I said, 'Thus let be' and 'There let be'
10   And 'Then let be', and no man understand me?
      Proh Deum! Medius Fidius! Ye are all dunces.
      For why?
      Here stand I. Here the Duke comes; there are you,
      Close in the thicket; the Duke appears; I meet him
15   And unto him I utter learned things
      And many figures; he hears and nods and hums
      And then cries, 'Rare!' and I go forward. At length,
      I fling my cap up – mark there! Then do you,
      As once did Meleager and the boar,
20   Break comely out before him; like true lovers,

      Cast yourselves in a body decently
      And sweetly, by a figure, trace and turn, boys.
1 COUNTRYMAN
      And sweetly we will do it, Master Gerald.
2 COUNTRYMAN
      Draw up the company. Where's the taborer?
3 COUNTRYMAN   Why, Timothy!

                  Enter Taborer.

TABORER   Here, my mad boys, have at ye!   25
SCHOOLMASTER   But, I say, where's these women?
4 COUNTRYMAN   Here's Friz and Maudlin.

                  Enter five Countrywomen.

2 COUNTRYMAN
      And little Luce with the white legs and bouncing
          Barbary.
1 COUNTRYMAN
      And freckled Nell that never failed her master.
SCHOOLMASTER
      Where be your ribbons, maids? Swim with your
          bodies
      And carry it sweetly and deliverly   30
      And now and then a favour and a frisk.
NELL   Let us alone, sir.
SCHOOLMASTER   Where's the rest o'th' music?
3 COUNTRYMAN   Dispersed, as you commanded.
SCHOOLMASTER   Couple then
      And see what's wanting; where's the Bavian?
      – My friend, carry your tail without offence   35
      Or scandal to the ladies and be sure
      You tumble with audacity and manhood
      And, when you bark, do it with judgment.
BAVIAN   Yes, sir.
SCHOOLMASTER
      Quo usque tandem! Here's a woman wanting.
4 COUNTRYMAN
      We may go whistle; all the fat's i'th' fire.   40
SCHOOLMASTER
      We have, as learned authors utter, washed a tile.
      We have been *fatuus* and laboured vainly.
2 COUNTRYMAN
      This is that scornful piece, that scurvy hilding
      That gave her promise faithfully, she would be here –
      Cicely, the sempster's daughter.   45
      The next gloves that I give her shall be dogskin!
      Nay, an she fail me once – you can tell, Arcas,
      She swore by wine and bread, she would not break.
SCHOOLMASTER   An eel and woman,
      A learned poet says, unless by th' tail   50
      And with thy teeth thou hold, will either fail.
      In manners this was false position.
1 COUNTRYMAN   A fire ill take her; does she flinch now?
3 COUNTRYMAN   What
      Shall we determine, sir?
SCHOOLMASTER   Nothing.
      Our business is become a nullity,   55

Yea, and a woeful and a piteous nullity.

4 COUNTRYMAN
Now, when the credit of our town lay on it,
Now to be frampul, now to piss o'th' nettle!
Go thy ways, I'll remember thee, I'll fit thee.

Enter the Jailer's Daughter.

DAUGHTER [*Sings.*]
60   The George Alow came from the south
       From the coast of Barbary-a
       And there he met with brave gallants of war,
       By one, by two, by three-a.

65   'Well hailed, well hailed, you jolly gallants,
       And whither now are you bound-a?
       O let me have your company
       Till we come to the sound-a.'

There was three fools fell out about an howlet:

       The one he said it was an owl,
70   The other he said nay,
       The third he said it was a hawk,
       And her bells were cut away.

3 COUNTRYMAN
There's a dainty madwoman, Master,
Comes i'th' nick, as mad as a March hare.
75 If we can get her dance, we are made again;
I warrant her, she'll do the rarest gambols.

1 COUNTRYMAN   A madwoman? We are made, boys.

SCHOOLMASTER   And are you mad, good woman?

DAUGHTER   I would be sorry else.
Give me your hand.

SCHOOLMASTER   Why?

DAUGHTER   I can tell your fortune.
80 You are a fool. Tell ten. – I have posed him. Buzz!
   – Friend, you must eat no white bread; if you do,
   Your teeth will bleed extremely. – Shall we dance,
       ho?
   – I know you, you're a tinker; sirrah tinker,
   Stop no more holes but what you should.

SCHOOLMASTER   *Dii boni,*
A tinker, damsel?

85 DAUGHTER   Or a conjurer.
   Raise me a devil now and let him play
   Chi passa o'th' bells and bones.

SCHOOLMASTER   Go take her
And fluently persuade her to a peace.
Et opus exegi quod nec Jovis ira, nec ignis –
Strike up and lead her in.   [*Taborer plays.*]

90 2 COUNTRYMAN   Come, lass, let's trip it.

DAUGHTER   I'll lead. [*Dances.*]

3 COUNTRYMAN   Do, do!   [*Horns.*]

SCHOOLMASTER   Persuasively and cunningly.
Away, boys; I hear the horns. Give me some
   meditation –
And mark your cue.   *Exeunt all but Schoolmaster.*
       Pallas inspire me!

Enter THESEUS, PIRITHOUS, HIPPOLYTA, EMILIA
and train.

THESEUS   This way the stag took.

SCHOOLMASTER   Stay and edify!

THESEUS   What have we here?   95

PIRITHOUS   Some country sport, upon my life, sir.

THESEUS [*to Schoolmaster*]
Well, sir, go forward; we will 'edify'.
[*Chair and stools brought out.*]
Ladies, sit down; we'll stay it.
[*Theseus, Hippolyta and Emilia sit.*]

SCHOOLMASTER
Then, doughty Duke, all hail; all hail, sweet ladies –

THESEUS   This is a cold beginning.   100

SCHOOLMASTER
If you but favour, our country pastime made is.
We are a few of those collected here
That ruder tongues distinguish 'villager'.
And to say verity, and not to fable,
We are a merry rout, or else a *rable*,   105
Or company, or, by a figure, *chorus*,
That 'fore thy dignity will dance a morris.
And I that am the rectifier of all,
By title *pedagogus*, that let fall
The birch upon the breeches of the small ones   110
And humble with a ferula the tall ones,
Do here present this machine, or this frame,
And, dainty Duke, whose doughty dismal fame
From Dis to Daedalus, from post to pillar,
Is blown abroad, help me, thy poor well-willer,   115
And with thy twinkling eyes look right and straight
Upon this mighty 'Moor' of mickle weight.
'Is' now comes in, which, being glued together,
Makes 'Morris' and the cause that we came hither:
The body of our sport, of no small study.   120
I first appear, though rude and raw and muddy,
To speak before thy noble grace this tenor:
At whose great feet I offer up my penner.
The next the Lord of May and Lady bright;
The Chambermaid and Servingman, by night   125
That seek out silent hanging; then mine Host
And his fat Spouse that welcomes to their cost
The galled traveller and with a beck'ning
Informs the tapster to inflame the reck'ning.
Then the beest-eating Clown and next the Fool,   130
The Bavian with long tail and eke long tool,
Cum multis aliis that make a dance.
Say, 'Ay,' and all shall presently advance.

THESEUS   Ay, ay, by any means, dear *Domine.*

PIRITHOUS   Produce.   135

SCHOOLMASTER   *Intrate filii!* Come forth and foot it.
       [*Music. The villagers, with the Jailer's Daughter,
                      perform a morris dance.*]

SCHOOLMASTER
Ladies, if we have been merry
And have pleased ye with a derry,
And a derry, and a down,

140   Say the schoolmaster's no clown;
            Duke, if we have pleased thee too
            And have done as good boys should do,
            Give us but a tree or twain
            For a Maypole and again,
145   Ere another year run out,
            We'll make thee laugh and all this rout.

THESEUS
    Take twenty, Domine. – How does my sweetheart?
HIPPOLYTA   Never so pleased, sir.
EMILIA   'Twas an excellent dance
    And, for a preface, I never heard a better.
THESEUS
150   Schoolmaster, I thank you. One see 'em all rewarded.
PIRITHOUS
    And here's something to paint your pole withall.
    [*Gives Schoolmaster money.*]
THESEUS   Now to our sports again.
SCHOOLMASTER
            May the stag thou hunt'st stand long,
            And thy dogs be swift and strong;
155   May they kill him without lets
            And the ladies eat his dowsets.
                  Theseus and his party depart. Horns.
    Come, we are all made, *dii deaeque omnes.* Ye have
    danced rarely, wenches.   *Exeunt.*

3.6   *Enter* PALAMON *from the bush.*

PALAMON   About this hour my cousin gave his faith
    To visit me again and with him bring
    Two swords and two good armours. If he fail
    He's neither man nor soldier. When he left me
5   I did not think a week could have restored
    My lost strength to me, I was grown so low
    And crest-fall'n with my wants. I thank thee, Arcite:
    Thou art yet a fair foe; and I feel myself,
    With this refreshing, able once again
10   To outdure danger. To delay it longer
    Would make the world think, when it comes to
        hearing,
    That I lay fatting like a swine to fight
    And not a soldier. Therefore this blest morning
    Shall be the last and that sword he refuses,
15   If it but hold, I kill him with: 'tis justice.
    So love and fortune for me!

        Enter ARCITE *with armours and swords.*

                 O, good morrow.
ARCITE   Good morrow, noble kinsman.
PALAMON   I have put you
    To too much pains, sir.
ARCITE   That too much, fair cousin,
    Is but a debt to honour, and my duty.
PALAMON
20   Would you were so in all, sir; I could wish ye
    As kind a kinsman as you force me find

    A beneficial foe, that my embraces
    Might thank ye, not my blows.
ARCITE   I shall think either,
    Well done, a noble recompense.
PALAMON   Then I shall quit you.
ARCITE   Defy me in these fair terms, and you show   25
    More than a mistress to me. No more anger,
    As you love anything that's honourable!
    We were not bred to talk, man; when we are armed
    And both upon our guards, then let our fury,
    Like meeting of two tides, fly strongly from us;   30
    And then to whom the birthright of this beauty
    Truly pertains (without upbraidings, scorns,
    Despisings of our persons, and such poutings
    Fitter for girls and schoolboys) will be seen
    And quickly, yours or mine. Will't please you arm,
        sir?   35
    Or, if you feel yourself not fitting yet
    And furnished with your old strength, I'll stay,
        cousin,
    And every day discourse you into health,
    As I am spared. Your person I am friends with
    And I could wish I had not said I loved her,   40
    Though I had died; but, loving such a lady
    And justifying my love, I must not fly from't.
PALAMON   Arcite, thou art so brave an enemy
    That no man but thy cousin's fit to kill thee.
    I am well and lusty; choose your arms.
ARCITE   Choose you, sir.   45
PALAMON   Wilt thou exceed in all, or dost thou do it
    To make me spare thee?
ARCITE   If you think so, cousin,
    You are deceived, for, as I am a soldier,
    I will not spare you.
PALAMON   That's well said.
ARCITE   You'll find it.
PALAMON   Then, as I am an honest man and love,   50
    With all the justice of affection
    I'll pay thee soundly.
    [*Chooses armour.*]   This I'll take.
ARCITE [*Takes the other.*]   That's mine then.
    I'll arm you first.
PALAMON   Do. [*Arcite begins to arm him.*]
                Pray thee tell me, cousin,
    Where got'st thou this good armour?
ARCITE   'Tis the Duke's
    And, to say true, I stole it. Do I pinch you?
PALAMON   No.   55
ARCITE   Is't not too heavy?
PALAMON   I have worn a lighter,
    But I shall make it serve.
ARCITE   I'll buckl't close.
PALAMON   By any means.
ARCITE   You care not for a grand guard?
PALAMON   No, no, we'll use no horses; I perceive
    You would fain be at that fight.

ARCITE   I am indifferent.

PALAMON
    Faith, so am I. Good cousin, thrust the buckle
    Through far enough.

ARCITE   I warrant you.

PALAMON   My casque now.

ARCITE   Will you fight bare-armed?

PALAMON   We shall be the nimbler.

ARCITE
    But use your gauntlets, though. Those are o'th' least;
    Prithee take mine, good cousin.

PALAMON   Thank you, Arcite.
    How do I look? Am I fall'n much away?

ARCITE   Faith, very little; love has used you kindly.

PALAMON   I'll warrant thee, I'll strike home.

ARCITE   Do and spare not.
    I'll give you cause, sweet cousin.

PALAMON   Now to you, sir. [*Begins to arm Arcite.*]
    Methinks this armour's very like that, Arcite,
    Thou wor'st that day the three kings fell, but lighter.

ARCITE   That was a very good one. And that day,
    I well remember, you outdid me, cousin;
    I never saw such valour. When you charged
    Upon the left wing of the enemy,
    I spurred hard to come up and under me
    I had a right good horse.

PALAMON   You had indeed:
    A bright bay, I remember.

ARCITE   Yes, but all
    Was vainly laboured in me; you outwent me,
    Nor could my wishes reach you. Yet a little
    I did by imitation.

PALAMON   More by virtue.
    You are modest, cousin.

ARCITE   When I saw you charge first,
    Methought I heard a dreadful clap of thunder
    Break from the troop.

PALAMON   But still before that flew
    The lightning of your valour. – Stay a little:
    Is not this piece too strait?

ARCITE   No, no, 'tis well.

PALAMON
    I would have nothing hurt thee but my sword:
    A bruise would be dishonour.

ARCITE   Now I am perfect.

PALAMON   Stand off then.

ARCITE   Take my sword; I hold it better.

PALAMON   I thank ye, no; keep it, your life lies on it.
    Here's one: if it but hold, I ask no more
    For all my hopes. My cause and honour guard me!

ARCITE   And me my love!
    [*They bow several ways, then advance and stand.*]
                              Is there aught else to say?

PALAMON
    This only, and no more. Thou art mine aunt's son
    And that blood we desire to shed is mutual,
    In me thine and in thee mine; my sword

Is in my hand and if thou killest me
The gods and I forgive thee. If there be
A place prepared for those that sleep in honour,
I wish his weary soul that falls may win it.
Fight bravely, cousin; give me thy noble hand.

ARCITE   Here, Palamon. This hand shall never more
Come near thee with such friendship.

PALAMON   I commend thee.

ARCITE   If I fall, curse me, and say I was a coward,
For none but such dare die in these just trials.
Once more farewell, my cousin.

PALAMON   Farewell, Arcite.
[*They fight. Horns within. They stand.*]

ARCITE   Lo, cousin, lo, our folly has undone us!

PALAMON   Why?

ARCITE   This is the Duke, a-hunting as I told you;
If we be found, we are wretched. O, retire,
For honour's sake and safety, presently
Into your bush again. Sir, we shall find
Too many hours to die in! Gentle cousin,
If you be seen you perish instantly
For breaking prison and I, if you reveal me,
For my contempt. Then all the world will scorn us
And say we had a noble difference,
But base disposers of it.

PALAMON   No, no, cousin:
I will no more be hidden, nor put off
This great adventure to a second trial;
I know your cunning and I know your cause.
He that faints now, shame take him! Put thyself
Upon thy present guard –

ARCITE   You are not mad?

PALAMON   Or I will make the advantage of this hour
Mine own, and what to come shall threaten me
I fear less than my fortune. Know, weak cousin,
I love Emilia and in that I'll bury
Thee and all crosses else.

ARCITE   Then come what can come.
Thou shalt know, Palamon, I dare as well
Die as discourse or sleep. Only this fears me:
The law will have the honour of our ends.
Have at thy life!

PALAMON   Look to thine own well, Arcite.
[*They fight again.*]

Horns. Enter THESEUS, HIPPOLYTA, EMILIA, PIRITHOUS
and train.

THESEUS   What ignorant and mad malicious traitors
Are you, that 'gainst the tenor of my laws
Are making battle, thus like knights appointed,
Without my leave and officers of arms?
By Castor, both shall die!

PALAMON   Hold thy word, Theseus.
We are certainly both traitors, both despisers
Of thee and of thy goodness. I am Palamon
That cannot love thee, he that broke thy prison –
Think well what that deserves – and this is Arcite:

A bolder traitor never trod thy ground;
A falser ne'er seemed friend. This is the man
Was begged and banished; this is he contemns thee
And what thou dar'st do and in this disguise
145 Against thine own edict follows thy sister,
That fortunate bright star, the fair Emilia –
Whose servant, if there be a right in seeing
And first bequeathing of the soul to, justly
I am – and, which is more, dares think her his.
150 This treachery, like a most trusty lover,
I called him now to answer. If thou be'st
As thou art spoken, great and virtuous,
The true decider of all injuries,
Say, 'Fight again' and thou shalt see me, Theseus,
155 Do such a justice thou thyself wilt envy.
Then take my life; I'll woo thee to't.
PIRITHOUS   O heaven,
What more than man is this!
THESEUS   I have sworn.
ARCITE   We seek not
Thy breath of mercy, Theseus; 'tis to me
A thing as soon to die as thee to say it
And no more moved. Where this man calls me
160   traitor,
Let me say thus much: if in love be treason,
In service of so excellent a beauty,
As I love most, and in that faith will perish,
As I have brought my life here to confirm it,
165 As I have served her truest, worthiest,
As I dare kill this cousin that denies it,
So let me be most traitor and ye please me.
For scorning thy edict, Duke: ask that lady
Why she is fair, and why her eyes command me
170 Stay here to love her and, if she say 'traitor',
I am a villain fit to lie unburied.
PALAMON   Thou shalt have pity of us both, O Theseus,
If unto neither thou show mercy. Stop,
As thou art just, thy noble ear against us;
175 As thou art valiant – for thy cousin's soul,
Whose twelve strong labours crown his memory –
Let's die together, at one instant, Duke.
Only a little let him fall before me,
That I may tell my soul, he shall not have her.
THESEUS
180 I grant your wish, for, to say true, your cousin
Has ten times more offended, for I gave him
More mercy than you found, sir, your offences
Being no more than his. None here speak for 'em,
For, ere the sun set, both shall sleep for ever.
185 HIPPOLYTA   Alas the pity! Now or never, sister,
Speak not to be denied. That face of yours
Will bear the curses else of after ages
For these lost cousins.
EMILIA   In my face, dear sister,
I find no anger to 'em, nor no ruin;
190 The misadventure of their own eyes kill 'em.
Yet that I will be woman and have pity,

My knees shall grow to th' ground but I'll get mercy.
Help me, dear sister; in a deed so virtuous,
The powers of all women will be with us. [*Kneels.*]
Most royal brother –
HIPPOLYTA [*Kneels.*]   Sir, by our tie of marriage – 195
EMILIA   By your own spotless honour –
HIPPOLYTA   By that faith,
That fair hand and that honest heart you gave me –
EMILIA   By that you would have pity in another,
By your own virtues infinite –
HIPPOLYTA   By valour,
By all the chaste nights I have ever pleased you – 200
THESEUS   These are strange conjurings.
PIRITHOUS   Nay, then, I'll in too. [*Kneels.*]
By all our friendship, sir, by all our dangers,
By all you love most: wars, and this sweet lady –
EMILIA   By that you would have trembled to deny
A blushing maid –
HIPPOLYTA   By your own eyes, by strength, 205
In which you swore I went beyond all women,
Almost all men, and yet I yielded, Theseus –
PIRITHOUS   To crown all this, by your most noble soul,
Which cannot want due mercy, I beg first –
HIPPOLYTA   Next hear my prayers –
EMILIA   Last, let me entreat, sir – 210
PIRITHOUS   For mercy!
HIPPOLYTA   Mercy!
EMILIA   Mercy on these princes!
THESEUS   Ye make my faith reel. Say I felt
Compassion to 'em both, how would you place it?
[*Emilia, Hippolyta and Pirithous rise.*]
EMILIA   Upon their lives. But with their banishments.
THESEUS   You are a right woman, sister: you have pity 215
But want the understanding where to use it.
If you desire their lives, invent a way
Safer than banishment. Can these two live
And have the agony of love about 'em
And not kill one another? Every day 220
They'd fight about you; hourly bring your honour
In public question with their swords. Be wise then
And here forget 'em; it concerns your credit
And my oath equally. I have said they die.
Better they fall by th' law than one another. 225
Bow not my honour.
EMILIA   O, my noble brother,
That oath was rashly made and in your anger.
Your reason will not hold it; if such vows
Stand for express will, all the world must perish.
Besides, I have another oath 'gainst yours, 230
Of more authority, I am sure more love,
Not made in passion neither but good heed.
THESEUS   What is it, sister?
PIRITHOUS   Urge it home, brave lady.
EMILIA   That you would ne'er deny me anything
Fit for my modest suit and your free granting. 235
I tie you to your word now; if ye fail in't,
Think how you maim your honour. Tell me not

(For now I am set a-begging, sir, I am deaf
To all but your compassion) how their lives
240 Might breed the ruin of my name. Opinion!
Shall anything that loves me perish for me?
That were a cruel wisdom. Do men prune
The straight young boughs that blush with thousand
    blossoms,
Because they may be rotten? O, Duke Theseus,
245 The goodly mothers that have groaned for these
And all the longing maids that ever loved,
If your vow stand, shall curse me and my beauty
And in their funeral songs for these two cousins
Despise my cruelty and cry woe worth me,
250 Till I am nothing but the scorn of women.
For heaven's sake, save their lives and banish 'em.
THESEUS   On what conditions?
EMILIA   Swear 'em never more
To make me their contention, or to know me,
To tread upon thy dukedom, and to be,
255 Wherever they shall travel, ever strangers
To one another.
PALAMON   I'll be cut a-pieces
Before I take this oath! Forget I love her?
O, all ye gods, despise me then! Thy banishment
I not mislike, so we may fairly carry
260 Our swords and cause along; else, never trifle,
But take our lives, Duke; I must love and will
And, for that love, must and dare kill this cousin
On any piece the earth has.
THESEUS   Will you, Arcite,
Take these conditions?
PALAMON   He's a villain then.
265 PIRITHOUS   These are men!
ARCITE
No, never, Duke. 'Tis worse to me than begging
To take my life so basely. Though I think
I never shall enjoy her, yet I'll preserve
The honour of affection and die for her,
270 Make death a devil.
THESEUS
What may be done? For now I feel compassion.
PIRITHOUS   Let it not fall again, sir.
THESEUS   Say, Emilia,
If one of them were dead, as one must, are you
Content to take the other as your husband?
275 They cannot both enjoy you. They are princes
As goodly as your own eyes and as noble
As ever fame yet spoke of. Look upon 'em
And, if you can love, end this difference;
I give consent. Are you content too, princes?
PALAMON, ARCITE   With all our hearts.
280 THESEUS   He that she refuses
Must die then.
PALAMON, ARCITE
                    Any death thou canst invent, Duke.
PALAMON   If I fall from that mouth, I fall with favour
And lovers yet unborn shall bless my ashes.

ARCITE   If she refuse me, yet my grave will wed me
And soldiers sing my epitaph.
THESEUS [*to Emilia*]   Make choice, then.   285
EMILIA   I cannot, sir; they are both too excellent;
For me, a hair shall never fall of these men.
HIPPOLYTA   What will become of 'em?
THESEUS   Thus I ordain it
And by mine honour, once again, it stands,
Or both shall die. You shall both to your country   290
And each, within this month, accompanied
With three fair knights, appear again in this place,
In which I'll plant a pyramid; and whether,
Before us that are here, can force his cousin,
By fair and knightly strength, to touch the pillar,   295
He shall enjoy her; th'other lose his head,
And all his friends. Nor shall he grudge to fall,
Nor think he dies with interest in this lady.
Will this content ye?
PALAMON   Yes. There, cousin Arcite,
[*Offers his hand.*]
I am friends again, till that hour.
ARCITE   I embrace ye.   300
THESEUS   Are you content, sister?
EMILIA   Yes, I must, sir,
Else both miscarry.
THESEUS   Come, shake hands again, then,
And take heed, as you are gentlemen, this quarrel
Sleep till the hour prefixed, and hold your course.
[*Palamon and Arcite shake hands.*]
PALAMON   We dare not fail thee, Theseus.
THESEUS   Come, I'll give ye   305
Now usage like to princes and to friends.
When ye return, who wins, I'll settle here;
Who loses, yet I'll weep upon his bier.   *Exeunt.*

4.1   *Enter* Jailer *and* First Friend.

JAILER   Heard you no more? Was nothing said of me
Concerning the escape of Palamon?
Good sir, remember!
1 FRIEND   Nothing that I heard,
For I came home before the business
Was fully ended. Yet I might perceive,   5
Ere I departed, a great likelihood
Of both their pardons. For Hippolyta
And fair-eyed Emily, upon their knees,
Begged with such handsome pity that the Duke
Methought stood staggering whether he should
    follow   10
His rash oath or the sweet compassion
Of those two ladies; and, to second them,
That truly noble Prince Pirithous,
Half his own heart, set in too, that I hope
All shall be well. Neither heard I one question   15
Of your name or his 'scape.

                Enter Second Friend.

JAILER   Pray heaven it hold so.

2 FRIEND   Be of good comfort, man; I bring you news,
  Good news!
JAILER   They are welcome.
2 FRIEND   Palamon has cleared you,
  And got your pardon, and discovered how
  And by whose means he 'scaped – which was your
20   daughter's,
  Whose pardon is procured too; and the prisoner,
  Not to be held ungrateful to her goodness,
  Has given a sum of money to her marriage:
  A large one, I'll assure you.
JAILER   You're a good man
  And ever bring good news.
25 1 FRIEND   How was it ended?
2 FRIEND
  Why, as it should be. They that never begged
  But they prevailed had their suits fairly granted:
  The prisoners have their lives.
1 FRIEND   I knew 'twould be so.
2 FRIEND
  But there be new conditions, which you'll hear of
  At better time.
JAILER   I hope they are good.
30 2 FRIEND   They are honourable;
  How good they'll prove, I know not.

                    Enter Wooer.

1 FRIEND   'Twill be known.
WOOER [*to Jailer*]   Alas, sir, where's your daughter?
JAILER   Why do you ask?
WOOER   O, sir, when did you see her?
2 FRIEND   How he looks!
JAILER   This morning.
WOOER   Was she well? Was she in health? Sir,
  When did she sleep?
35 1 FRIEND   These are strange questions.
JAILER   I do not think she was very well, for now
  You make me mind her: but this very day
  I asked her questions, and she answered me
  So far from what she was, so childishly,
40 So sillily, as if she were a fool,
  An innocent, and I was very angry.
  But what of her, sir?
WOOER   Nothing but my pity.
  But you must know it, and as good by me
  As by another that less loves her.
JAILER   Well, sir?
1 FRIEND   Not right?
2 FRIEND   Not well?
45 WOOER   No sir, not well:
  'Tis too true: she is mad.
1 FRIEND   It cannot be!
WOOER   Believe, you'll find it so.
JAILER   I half suspected
  What you have told me. The gods comfort her!
  Either this was her love to Palamon,
50 Or fear of my miscarrying on his 'scape,

  Or both.
WOOER   'Tis likely.
JAILER   But why all this haste, sir?
WOOER   I'll tell you quickly. As I late was angling
  In the great lake that lies behind the palace,
  From the far shore, thick set with reeds and sedges,
  As patiently I was attending sport,   55
  I heard a voice, a shrill one, and attentive
  I gave my ear, when I might well perceive
  'Twas one that sung and, by the smallness of it,
  A boy or woman. I then left my angle
  To his own skill, came near, but yet perceived not   60
  Who made the sound, the rushes and the reeds
  Had so encompassed it. I laid me down
  And listened to the words she sung, for then,
  Through a small glade cut by the fishermen,
  I saw it was your daughter.
JAILER   Pray go on, sir.   65
WOOER   She sung much, but no sense; only I heard her
  Repeat this often: 'Palamon is gone,
  Is gone to th' wood to gather mulberries;
  I'll find him out tomorrow.'
1 FRIEND   Pretty soul!
WOOER   'His shackles will betray him, he'll be taken; 70
  And what shall I do then? I'll bring a bevy,
  A hundred black-eyed maids that love as I do,
  With chaplets on their heads of daffadillies,
  With cherry-lips and cheeks of damask roses,
  And all we'll dance an antic 'fore the Duke   75
  And beg his pardon.' Then she talked of you, sir:
  That you must lose your head tomorrow morning,
  And she must gather flowers to bury you,
  And see the house made handsome. Then she sung
  Nothing but 'Willow, willow, willow' and, between,   80
  Ever was 'Palamon, fair Palamon'
  And 'Palamon was a tall young man'. The place
  Was knee-deep where she sat; her careless tresses
  A wreath of bullrush rounded; about her stuck
  Thousand fresh water-flowers of several colours,   85
  That methought she appeared like the fair nymph
  That feeds the lake with waters, or as Iris
  Newly dropped down from heaven. Rings she made
  Of rushes that grew by and to 'em spoke
  The prettiest posies: 'Thus our true love's tied',   90
  'This you may loose, not me,' and many a one.
  And then she wept, and sung again, and sighed,
  And with the same breath smiled and kissed her
    hand.
2 FRIEND   Alas, what pity it is!
WOOER   I made in to her.
  She saw me, and straight sought the flood; I saved
    her,   95
  And set her safe to land, when presently
  She slipped away and to the city made,
  With such a cry and swiftness that, believe me,
  She left me far behind her. Three or four
  I saw from far off cross her – one of 'em   100

1264

I knew to be your brother – where she stayed
And fell, scarce to be got away. I left them with her,

Enter Jailer's Brother, *Jailer's* Daughter *and others.*

And hither came to tell you. Here they are.
DAUGHTER [*Sings.*]
        May you never more enjoy the light etc.
  Is not this a fine song?
105 BROTHER   O, a very fine one.
DAUGHTER   I can sing twenty more.
BROTHER   I think you can.
DAUGHTER   Yes, truly, can I. I can sing 'The Broom'
  And 'Bonny Robin'. Are not you a tailor?
BROTHER   Yes.
DAUGHTER   Where's my wedding gown?
BROTHER   I'll bring it tomorrow.
110 DAUGHTER   Do, very early. I must be abroad else
  To call the maids and pay the minstrels,
  For I must lose my maidenhead by cocklight;
  'Twill never thrive else.
  [*Sings.*]   O fair, O sweet etc.
BROTHER [*to Jailer*]
  You must e'en take it patiently.
115 JAILER   'Tis true.
DAUGHTER
  Good ev'n, good men; pray, did you ever hear
  Of one young Palamon?
JAILER   Yes, wench, we know him.
DAUGHTER   Is't not a fine young gentleman?
JAILER   'Tis, love.
BROTHER
  By no means cross her, she is then distempered
  Far worse than now she shows.
120 1 FRIEND [*to Daughter*]   Yes, he's a fine man.
DAUGHTER   O, is he so? You have a sister.
1 FRIEND   Yes.
DAUGHTER   But she shall never have him – tell her so –
  For a trick that I know; you'd best look to her,
  For if she see him once, she's gone; she's done,
125   And undone, in an hour. All the young maids
  Of our town are in love with him, but I laugh at 'em
  And let 'em all alone; is't not a wise course?
1 FRIEND   Yes.
DAUGHTER
  There is at least two hundred now with child by him –
  There must be four – yet I keep close for all this,
130   Close as a cockle; and all these must be boys
  (He has the trick on't) and at ten years old
  They must be all gelt for musicians
  And sing the wars of Theseus.
2 FRIEND   This is strange.
DAUGHTER   As ever you heard, but say nothing.
1 FRIEND   No.
DAUGHTER
135   They come from all parts of the dukedom to him.
  I'll warrant ye, he had not so few last night
  As twenty to dispatch – he'll tickle't up

In two hours, if his hand be in.
JAILER   She's lost
  Past all cure.
BROTHER   Heaven forbid, man!
DAUGHTER [*to Jailer*]   Come hither!
  You are a wise man.
1 FRIEND [*aside*]   Does she know him?
2 FRIEND [*aside*]   No.   140
  Would she did!
DAUGHTER   You are master of a ship?
JAILER   Yes.
DAUGHTER   Where's your compass?
JAILER   Here.
DAUGHTER   Set it to th' north.
  And now direct your course to th' wood, where Palamon
  Lies longing for me. For the tackling,
  Let me alone; come, weigh, my hearts, cheerily!   145
ALL [*severally*]
  Ugh! Ugh! Ugh!
  'Tis up! – The wind's fair! – Top the bowline! –
  Out with the mainsail! – Where's your whistle, master?
BROTHER   Let's get her in.
JAILER   Up to the top, boy.
BROTHER   Where's the pilot?
1 FRIEND   Here.   150
DAUGHTER   What kenn'st thou?
2 FRIEND   A fair wood.
DAUGHTER   Bear for it, master;
  Tack about!
  [*Sings.*] When Cynthia with her borrowed light etc.
          Exeunt.

4.2   *Enter* EMILIA *alone, with two pictures.*

EMILIA
  Yet I may bind those wounds up, that must open
  And bleed to death for my sake else; I'll choose,
  And end their strife. Two such young, handsome men
  Shall never fall for me; their weeping mothers,
  Following the dead cold ashes of their sons,   5
  Shall never curse my cruelty.
  [*Looks at one of the pictures.*] Good heaven,
  What a sweet face has Arcite! If wise Nature,
  With all her best endowments, all those beauties
  She sows into the births of noble bodies,
  Were here a mortal woman and had in her   10
  The coy denials of young maids, yet, doubtless,
  She would run mad for this man. What an eye,
  Of what a fiery sparkle and quick sweetness,
  Has this young prince! Here Love himself sits smiling;
  Just such another wanton Ganymede   15
  Set Jove afire with, and enforced the god
  Snatch up the goodly boy and set him by him,

A shining constellation. What a brow,
Of what a spacious majesty, he carries,
20   Arched like the great-eyed Juno's, but far sweeter,
Smoother than Pelops' shoulder! Fame and Honour,
Methinks, from hence, as from a promontory
Pointed in heaven, should clap their wings and sing,
To all the under-world, the loves and fights
Of gods and such men near 'em.
25   [*Looks at the other picture.*]   Palamon
Is but his foil; to him, a mere dull shadow;
He's swart and meagre, of an eye as heavy
As if he had lost his mother; a still temper;
No stirring in him, no alacrity;
30   Of all this sprightly sharpness, not a smile.
Yet these that we count errors may become him:
Narcissus was a sad boy, but a heavenly.
– 'O, who can find the bent of woman's fancy?'
I am a fool, my reason is lost in me,
35   I have no choice, and I have lied so lewdly
That women ought to beat me. On my knees,
I ask thy pardon, Palamon: thou art alone
And only beautiful, and these the eyes,
These the bright lamps of beauty, that command
And threaten love, and what young maid dare cross
40   'em?
What a bold gravity, and yet inviting,
Has this brown manly face! O Love, this only,
From this hour, is complexion!
[*Lays Arcite's picture down.*]   Lie there, Arcite;
Thou art a changeling to him, a mere gypsy,
45   And this the noble body. – I am sotted,
Utterly lost. My virgin's faith has fled me.
For if my brother but even now had asked me
Whether I loved, I had run mad for Arcite;
Now, if my sister, more for Palamon.
50   Stand both together. Now, come ask me, brother.
'Alas, I know not!' Ask me now, sweet sister.
'I may go look.' What a mere child is Fancy,
That, having two fair gauds of equal sweetness,
Cannot distinguish, but must cry for both!

Enter Gentleman.

How now, sir?
55   GENTLEMAN   From the noble Duke your brother,
Madam, I bring you news. The knights are come.
EMILIA   To end the quarrel?
GENTLEMAN   Yes.
EMILIA   Would I might end first!
What sins have I committed, chaste Diana,
That my unspotted youth must now be soiled
60   With blood of princes, and my chastity
Be made the altar where the lives of lovers –
Two greater and two better never yet
Made mothers joy – must be the sacrifice
To my unhappy beauty?

Enter THESEUS, HIPPOLYTA, PIRITHOUS
and attendants.

THESEUS   Bring 'em in
Quickly, by any means; I long to see 'em.   65
[*to Emilia*] Your two contending lovers are returned,
And with them their fair knights. Now, my fair sister,
You must love one of them.
EMILIA   I had rather both;
So neither for my sake should fall untimely.
THESEUS   Who saw 'em?
PIRITHOUS   I a while.
GENTLEMAN   And I.   70

Enter Messenger.

THESEUS   From whence come you, sir?
MESSENGER   From the knights.
THESEUS   Pray speak,
You that have seen them, what they are.
MESSENGER   I will, sir,
And truly what I think. Six braver spirits
Than these they have brought, if we judge by the
    outside,
I never saw nor read of. He that stands   75
In the first place with Arcite, by his seeming
Should be a stout man, by his face a prince,
His very looks so say him: his complexion
Nearer a brown than black, stern, and yet noble,
Which shows him hardy, fearless, proud of dangers.   80
The circles of his eyes show fire within him,
And as a heated lion so he looks.
His hair hangs long behind him, black and shining
Like ravens' wings; his shoulders broad and strong;
Armed long and round, and on his thigh a sword,   85
Hung by a curious baldrick, when he frowns,
To seal his will with. Better o' my conscience
Was never soldier's friend.
THESEUS   Thou hast well described him.
PIRITHOUS   Yet a great deal short,
Methinks, of him that's first with Palamon.   90
THESEUS   Pray, speak him, friend.
PIRITHOUS   I guess he is a prince too,
And, if it may be, greater; for his show
Has all the ornament of honour in't.
He's somewhat bigger than the knight he spoke of,
But of a face far sweeter. His complexion   95
Is, as a ripe grape, ruddy; he has felt
Without doubt what he fights for, and so apter
To make this cause his own. In's face appears
All the fair hopes of what he undertakes
And, when he's angry, then a settled valour,   100
Not tainted with extremes, runs through his body
And guides his arm to brave things. Fear he cannot;
He shows no such soft temper. His head's yellow,
Hard-haired, and curled, thick-twined like ivy tods,
Not to undo with thunder. In his face   105
The livery of the warlike maid appears,
Pure red and white, for yet no beard has blessed him;
And in his rolling eyes sits Victory,
As if she ever meant to court his valour.

His nose stands high, a character of honour;
His red lips, after fights, are fit for ladies.

EMILIA   Must these men die too?

PIRITHOUS   When he speaks, his tongue
Sounds like a trumpet. All his lineaments
Are as a man would wish 'em, strong and clean;
He wears a well-steeled axe, the staff of gold;
His age some five-and-twenty.

MESSENGER   There's another,
A little man, but of a tough soul, seeming
As great as any; fairer promises
In such a body yet I never looked on.

PIRITHOUS   O, he that's freckle-faced?

MESSENGER   The same, my lord.
Are they not sweet ones?

PIRITHOUS   Yes, they are well.

MESSENGER   Methinks,
Being so few and well disposed, they show
Great and fine art in nature. He's white-haired,
Not wanton white, but such a manly colour,
Next to an auburn; tough and nimble set,
Which shows an active soul; his arms are brawny,
Lined with strong sinews. To the shoulder piece,
Gently they swell, like women new-conceived,
Which speaks him prone to labour, never fainting
Under the weight of arms; stout-hearted, still,
But when he stirs, a tiger. He's grey-eyed,
Which yields compassion where he conquers; sharp
To spy advantages and, where he finds 'em,
He's swift to make 'em his. He does no wrongs,
Nor takes none; he's round-faced and when he smiles
He shows a lover; when he frowns, a soldier.
About his head he wears the winner's oak
And in it stuck the favour of his lady.
His age, some six-and-thirty. In his hand
He bears a charging-staff, embossed with silver.

THESEUS   Are they all thus?

PIRITHOUS   They are all the sons of honour.

THESEUS   Now, as I have a soul, I long to see 'em.
[*to Hippolyta*] Lady, you shall see men fight now.

HIPPOLYTA   I wish it,
But not the cause, my lord. They would show bravely
Fighting about the titles of two kingdoms.
'Tis pity love should be so tyrannous.
– O, my soft-hearted sister, what think you?
Weep not, till they weep blood. Wench, it must be.

THESEUS
You have steeled 'em with your beauty.
[*to Pirithous*]   Honoured friend,
To you I give the field; pray order it
Fitting the persons that must use it.

PIRITHOUS   Yes, sir.

THESEUS   Come, I'll go visit 'em! I cannot stay –
Their fame has fir'd me so; till they appear,
Good friend, be royal.

PIRITHOUS   There shall want no bravery.
                                        Exeunt all but Emilia.

EMILIA   Poor wench, go weep, for whosoever wins
Loses a noble cousin, for thy sins.   *Exit.*

4.3   *Enter* Jailer, Wooer *and* Doctor.

DOCTOR   Her distraction is more at some time of the
moon than at other some, is it not?

JAILER   She is continually in a harmless distemper:
sleeps little; altogether without appetite, save often
drinking; dreaming of another world and a better; and,
what broken piece of matter soe'er she's about, the
name Palamon lards it, that she farces every business
withall, fits it to every question.

                Enter Jailer's Daughter.

Look where she comes; you shall perceive her
behaviour.

DAUGHTER   I have forgot it quite. The burden on't was
'Down-a, down-a' and penned by no worse man than
Giraldo, Emilia's Schoolmaster; he's as fantastical too
as ever he may go upon's legs – for in the next world
will Dido see Palamon, and then will she be out of love
with Aeneas.

DOCTOR   What stuff's here? Poor soul!

JAILER   Even thus all day long.

DAUGHTER   Now for this charm that I told you of: you
must bring a piece of silver on the tip of your tongue,
or no ferry. Then if it be your chance to come where
the blessed spirits are, there's a sight now! We maids
that have our livers perished, cracked to pieces with
love, we shall come there and do nothing all day long
but pick flowers with Proserpine. Then will I make
Palamon a nosegay; then let him mark me – then.

DOCTOR   How prettily she's amiss! Note her a little
further.

DAUGHTER   Faith, I'll tell you, sometime we go to
barley-break, we of the blessed. Alas, 'tis a sore life
they have i'th' other place – such burning, frying,
boiling, hissing, howling, chattering, cursing: oh, they
have shrewd measure; take heed! If one be mad, or
hang or drown themselves, there they go – Jupiter
bless us! – and there shall we be put in a cauldron of
lead and usurers' grease, amongst a whole million of
cutpurses, and there boil like a gammon of bacon that
will never be enough.

DOCTOR   How her brain coins!

DAUGHTER   Lords and courtiers that have got maids
with child, they are in this place. They shall stand in
fire up to the navel and in ice up to the heart, and there
th'offending part burns and the deceiving part freezes.
In troth, a very grievous punishment, as one would
think, for such a trifle. Believe me, one would marry a
leprous witch to be rid on't, I'll assure you.

DOCTOR   How she continues this fancy! 'Tis not an
engrafted madness but a most thick and profound
melancholy.

DAUGHTER   To hear there a proud lady and a proud city

wife, howl together! I were a beast an I'd call it good
sport. One cries, 'O, this smoke!', another, 'This fire!'
One cries, 'O, that ever I did it behind the arras!' and
then howls; th'other curses a suing fellow and her
garden house.

Sings. I will be true, my stars, my fate etc.   *Exit.*

JAILER   What think you of her, sir?

DOCTOR   I think she has a perturbed mind, which I
cannot minister to.

JAILER   Alas, what then?

DOCTOR   Understand you she ever affected any man ere
she beheld Palamon?

JAILER   I was once, sir, in great hope she had fixed her
liking on this gentleman, my friend.

WOOER   I did think so too, and would account I had a
great penn'orth on't, to give half my state that both
she and I at this present stood unfeignedly on the same
terms.

DOCTOR   That intemperate surfeit of her eye hath
distempered the other senses; they may return and
settle again to execute their preordained faculties, but
they are now in a most extravagant vagary. This you
must do. Confine her to a place where the light may
rather seem to steal in than be permitted. Take upon
you, young sir her friend, the name of Palamon; say
you come to eat with her and to commune of love.
This will catch her attention, for this her mind beats
upon; other objects that are inserted 'tween her mind
and eye become the pranks and friskins of her
madness. Sing to her such green songs of love as she
says Palamon hath sung in prison. Come to her stuck
in as sweet flowers as the season is mistress of and
thereto make an addition of some other compounded
odours which are grateful to the sense. All this shall
become Palamon, for Palamon can sing, and Palamon
is sweet and every good thing. Desire to eat with her,
carve her, drink to her and, still among, intermingle
your petition of grace and acceptance into her favour.
Learn what maids have been her companions and
play-feres and let them repair to her with Palamon in
their mouths, and appear with tokens, as if they
suggested for him. It is a falsehood she is in, which is
with falsehoods to be combated. This may bring her to
eat, to sleep, and reduce what's now out of square in
her into their former law and regiment. I have seen it
approved, how many times I know not, but to make
the number more I have great hope in this. I will,
between the passages of this project, come in with my
appliance. Let us put it in execution and hasten the
success, which, doubt not, will bring forth comfort.

Exeunt.

5.1   *Flourish. Enter* THESEUS, PIRITHOUS, HIPPOLYTA,
attendants.

THESEUS   Now let 'em enter and before the gods
Tender their holy prayers. Let the temples

Burn bright with sacred fires and the altars
In hallowed clouds commend their swelling incense
To those above us. Let no due be wanting.
They have a noble work in hand, will honour
The very powers that love 'em.

Flourish of cornets. Enter PALAMON *and* ARCITE
and their knights.

PIRITHOUS   Sir, they enter.

THESEUS   You valiant and strong-hearted enemies,
You royal german foes, that this day come
To blow that nearness out that flames between ye:
Lay by your anger for an hour and, dove-like,
Before the holy altars of your helpers,
The all-feared gods, bow down your stubborn bodies.
Your ire is more than mortal; so your help be;
And, as the gods regard ye, fight with justice.
I'll leave you to your prayers and betwixt ye
I part my wishes.

PIRITHOUS   Honour crown the worthiest.

Exeunt Theseus and his train.

PALAMON   The glass is running now that cannot finish
Till one of us expire. Think you but thus:
That were there aught in me which strove to show
Mine enemy in this business, were't one eye
Against another, arm oppressed by arm,
I would destroy th'offender, coz, I would,
Though parcel of myself. Then from this gather
How I should tender you.

ARCITE   I am in labour
To push your name, your ancient love, our kindred
Out of my memory and i'th' selfsame place
To seat something I would confound. So hoist we
The sails that must these vessels port, even where
The heavenly limiter pleases.

PALAMON   You speak well.
Before I turn, let me embrace thee, cousin.
This I shall never do again.

ARCITE   One farewell.

PALAMON   Why, let it be so. Farewell, coz.

ARCITE   Farewell, sir.

Exeunt Palamon and his knights.

[*Arcite addresses his three knights.*]
Knights, kinsmen, lovers – yea, my sacrifices –
True worshippers of Mars, whose spirit in you
Expels the seeds of fear and th'apprehension
Which still is father of it: go with me
Before the god of our profession; there
Require of him the hearts of lions and
The breath of tigers, yea the fierceness too,
Yea, the speed also – to go on, I mean:
Else wish we to be snails. You know my prize
Must be dragged out of blood; force and great feat
Must put my garland on, where she sticks
The queen of flowers. Our intercession then
Must be to him that makes the camp a cistern
Brimmed with the blood of men. Give me your aid

And bend your spirits towards him.
[*They prostrate themselves before the altar, then kneel.*]
Thou mighty one, that with thy power hast turned
50 Green Neptune into purple; whose approach
Comets prewarn; whose havoc in vast field
Unearthed skulls proclaim; whose breath blows down
The teeming Ceres' foison; who dost pluck
With hand armipotent from forth blue clouds
55 The masoned turrets; that both mak'st and break'st
The stony girths of cities: me thy pupil,
Youngest follower of thy drum, instruct this day
With military skill, that to thy laud
I may advance my streamer and by thee
60 Be styled the lord o'th' day. Give me, great Mars,
Some token of thy pleasure.

[*Here they fall on their faces, as formerly, and there is
heard clanging of armour, with a short thunder, as the
burst of a battle, whereupon they all rise and bow
to the altar.*]

O great corrector of enormous times;
Shaker of o'er-rank states; thou grand decider
Of dusty and old titles, that heal'st with blood
65 The earth when it is sick and cur'st the world
O'th' pleurisy of people: I do take
Thy signs auspiciously and in thy name
To my design march boldly. Let us go.
                    Exeunt Arcite and his knights.

Enter PALAMON *and his knights, with the former
observance.*

PALAMON   Our stars must glister with new fire or be
70   Today extinct. Our argument is love,
Which, if the goddess of it grant, she gives
Victory too; then blend your spirits with mine,
You whose free nobleness do make my cause
Your personal hazard. To the goddess Venus
75   Commend we our proceeding and implore
Her power unto our party.
[*Here they kneel as formerly.*]
Hail, sovereign queen of secrets, who hast power
To call the fiercest tyrant from his rage
And weep unto a girl; that hast the might,
80   Even with an eye-glance, to choke Mars's drum
And turn th'alarm to whispers; that canst make
A cripple flourish with his crutch and cure him
Before Apollo; that mayst force the king
To be his subject's vassal and induce
85   Stale gravity to dance! The polled bachelor –
Whose youth, like wanton boys through bonfires,
Have skipped thy flame – at seventy, thou canst catch
And make him, to the scorn of his hoarse throat,
Abuse young lays of love. What godlike power
90   Hast thou not power upon? To Phoebus thou
Add'st flames hotter than his: the heavenly fires
Did scorch his mortal son, thine him; the huntress
All moist and cold, some say, began to throw

Her bow away and sigh. Take to thy grace
Me thy vowed soldier, who do bear thy yoke   95
As 'twere a wreath of roses, yet is heavier
Than lead itself, stings more than nettles.
I have never been foul-mouthed against thy law;
Ne'er revealed secret, for I knew none – would not,
Had I kenned all there were. I never practised   100
Upon man's wife nor would the libels read
Of liberal wits. I never at great feasts
Sought to betray a beauty, but have blushed
At simpering sirs that did. I have been harsh
To large confessors and have hotly asked them   105
If they had mothers – I had one, a woman,
And women 'twere they wronged. I knew a man
Of eighty winters, this I told them, who
A lass of fourteen brided. 'Twas thy power
To put life into dust: the aged cramp   110
Had screwed his square foot round;
The gout had knit his fingers into knots;
Torturing convulsions from his globy eyes
Had almost drawn their spheres, that what was life
In him seemed torture. This anatomy   115
Had by his young fair fere a boy, and I
Believed it was his, for she swore it was –
And who would not believe her? Brief, I am,
To those that prate and have done, no companion;
To those that boast and have not, a defier;   120
To those that would and cannot, a rejoicer.
Yea, him I do not love that tells close offices
The foulest way nor names concealments in
The boldest language. Such a one I am
And vow that lover never yet made sigh   125
Truer than I. O, then, most soft sweet goddess,
Give me the victory of this question, which
Is true love's merit, and bless me with a sign
Of thy great pleasure.
[*Here music is heard; doves are seen to flutter. They fall
again upon their faces, then rise to their knees.*]
O thou that from eleven to ninety reign'st   130
In mortal bosoms, whose chase is this world
And we in herds thy game: I give thee thanks
For this fair token, which, being laid unto
Mine innocent true heart, arms in assurance
My body to this business. Let us rise   135
And bow before the goddess. [*They rise and bow.*]
                    Time comes on.
                    Exeunt Palamon and his knights.

Still music of recorders. Enter EMILIA *in white, her hair
about her shoulders, wearing a wheaten wreath. One maid
in white holding up her train, her hair stuck with flowers.
One maid before her carrying a silver hind, in which is
conveyed incense and sweet odours, which being set upon the
altar, her maids standing aloof, she sets fire to it. Then they
curtsey and kneel.*

EMILIA   O sacred, shadowy, cold and constant queen,
      Abandoner of revels, mute contemplative,

Sweet, solitary, white as chaste, and pure
140 As wind-fanned snow, who to thy female knights
Allow'st no more blood than will make a blush,
Which is their order's robe: I here, thy priest,
Am humbled 'fore thine altar. O, vouchsafe
With that thy rare green eye, which never yet
145 Beheld thing maculate, look on thy virgin;
And, sacred silver mistress, lend thine ear,
Which ne'er heard scurrile term, into whose port
Ne'er entered wanton sound, to my petition
Seasoned with holy fear. This is my last
150 Of vestal office. I am bride-habited,
But maiden-hearted; a husband I have 'pointed,
But do not know him. Out of two, I should
Choose one and pray for his success, but I
Am guiltless of election. Of mine eyes,
155 Were I to lose one, they are equal precious;
I could doom neither: that which perished should
Go to't unsentenced. Therefore, most modest Queen,
He of the two pretenders that best loves me
And has the truest title in't, let him
160 Take off my wheaten garland, or else grant
The file and quality I hold I may
Continue in thy band.
[*Here the hind vanishes under the altar and in the place
ascends a rose tree, having one rose upon it.*]
See what our general of ebbs and flows,
Out from the bowels of her holy altar,
165 With sacred art advances: but one rose!
If well inspired, this battle shall confound
Both these brave knights and I, a virgin flower,
Must grow alone, unplucked.
[*Here is heard a sudden twang of instruments, and the
rose falls from the tree, which then descends.*]
The flower is fall'n; the tree descends. O, mistress,
170 Thou here dischargest me; I shall be gathered –
I think so – but I know not thine own will;
Unclasp thy mystery! – I hope she's pleased;
Her signs were gracious.   *They curtsey and exeunt.*

5.2   *Enter* Doctor, Jailer *and* Wooer *in the habit of
Palamon.*

DOCTOR
Has this advice I told you done any good upon her?
WOOER
O, very much. The maids that kept her company
Have half persuaded her that I am Palamon.
Within this half hour she came smiling to me
And asked me what I would eat and when I would
5   kiss her.
I told her, 'Presently!' and kissed her twice.
DOCTOR
'Twas well done. Twenty times had been far better,
For there the cure lies mainly.
WOOER   Then she told me
She would watch with me tonight, for well she knew

What hour my fit would take me.
DOCTOR   Let her do so.   10
And, when your fit comes, fit her home, and
presently.
WOOER   She would have me sing.
DOCTOR   You did so?
WOOER   No.
DOCTOR   'Twas very ill-done then;
You should observe her every way.
WOOER   Alas,
I have no voice, sir, to confirm her that way.   15
DOCTOR   That's all one, if ye make a noise.
If she entreat again, do anything.
Lie with her if she ask you.
JAILER   Whoa there, Doctor!
DOCTOR   Yes, in the way of cure.
JAILER   But first, by your leave,
I'th' way of honesty.
DOCTOR   That's but a niceness.   20
Ne'er cast your child away for honesty.
Cure her first this way; then if she will be honest,
She has the path before her.
JAILER   Thank ye, Doctor.
DOCTOR   Pray bring her in and let's see how she is.
JAILER   I will, and tell her   25
Her Palamon stays for her. But, Doctor,
Methinks you are i'th' wrong still.   *Exit Jailer.*
DOCTOR   Go, go,
You fathers are fine fools. Her honesty?
An we should give her physic till we find *that*!
WOOER   Why, do you think she is not honest, sir?   30
DOCTOR   How old is she?
WOOER   She's eighteen.
DOCTOR   She may be,
But that's all one, 'tis nothing to our purpose.
Whate'er her father says, if you perceive
Her mood inclining that way that I spoke of,
Videlicet, the 'way of flesh' – you have me?   35
WOOER   Yes, very well, sir.
DOCTOR   Please her appetite
And do it home, it cures her, *ipso facto*,
The melancholy humour that infects her.
WOOER   I am of your mind, Doctor.

                    Enter Jailer, Daughter *and maid.*

DOCTOR   You'll find it so. She comes; pray, humour her.   40
JAILER   Come, your love Palamon stays for you, child,
And has done this long hour, to visit you.
DAUGHTER   I thank him for his gentle patience;
He's a kind gentleman and I am much bound to him.
Did you ne'er see the horse he gave me?
JAILER   Yes.   45
DAUGHTER   How do you like him?
JAILER   He's a very fair one.
DAUGHTER   You never saw him dance?
JAILER   No.
DAUGHTER   I have, often.

He dances very finely, very comely,
And for a jig, come cut and long tail to him,
He turns ye like a top.

50 JAILER   That's fine indeed.

DAUGHTER
He'll dance the morris twenty mile an hour –
And that will founder the best hobby-horse,
If I have any skill, in all the parish –
And gallops to the tune of 'Light o' love'.
What think you of this horse?

55 JAILER   Having these virtues,
I think he might be brought to play at tennis.

DAUGHTER   Alas, that's nothing.

JAILER   Can he read and write too?

DAUGHTER
A very fair hand, and casts himself th'accounts
Of all his hay and provender. That ostler
60 Must rise betimes that cozens him. You know
The chestnut mare the Duke has?

JAILER   Very well.

DAUGHTER
She is horribly in love with him, poor beast!
But he is like his master, coy and scornful.

JAILER   What dowry has she?

DAUGHTER   Some two hundred bottles
65 And twenty strike of oats – but he'll ne'er have her.
He lisps in's neighing, able to entice
A miller's mare. He'll be the death of her.

DOCTOR   What stuff she utters!

JAILER   Make curtsey, here your love comes.
[*Wooer comes forward and bows.*]

WOOER   Pretty soul,
How do ye? [*She curtseys.*]

70   That's a fine maid! There's a curtsey!

DAUGHTER   Yours to command i'th' way of honesty.
How far is't now to th'end o'th' world, my masters?

DOCTOR   Why, a day's journey, wench.

DAUGHTER [*to Wooer*]   Will you go with me?

WOOER   What shall we do there, wench?

DAUGHTER   Why, play at stool-ball;
What is there else to do?

75 WOOER   I am content,
If we shall keep our wedding there.

DAUGHTER   'Tis true,
For there, I will assure you, we shall find
Some blind priest for the purpose, that will venture
To marry us, for here they are nice and foolish.
80 Besides, my father must be hanged tomorrow
And that would be a blot i'th' business.
Are not you Palamon?

WOOER   Do not you know me?

DAUGHTER   Yes, but you care not for me. I have nothing
But this poor petticoat and two coarse smocks.

WOOER   That's all one; I will have you.

85 DAUGHTER   Will you surely?

WOOER   Yes, by this fair hand, will I. [*Takes her hand.*]

DAUGHTER   We'll to bed then.

WOOER   E'en when you will. [*Kisses her.*]

DAUGHTER [*Rubs off the kiss.*]
                              O, sir, you would fain be nibbling.

WOOER   Why do you rub my kiss off?

DAUGHTER   'Tis a sweet one
And will perfume me finely against the wedding.
Is not this your cousin Arcite? [*Indicates the Doctor.*]

DOCTOR   Yes, sweetheart,   90
And I am glad my cousin Palamon
Has made so fair a choice.

DAUGHTER [*to Doctor*]   Do you think he'll have me?

DOCTOR   Yes, without doubt.

DAUGHTER [*to Jailer*]   Do you think so too?

JAILER   Yes.

DAUGHTER   We shall have many children.
[*to Doctor*]   Lord, how you're grown!
My Palamon, I hope, will grow too, finely,   95
Now he's at liberty. Alas, poor chicken,
He was kept down with hard meat and ill lodging!
But I'll kiss him up again.

Enter Messenger.

MESSENGER
What do you here? You'll lose the noblest sight
That e'er was seen.

JAILER   Are they i'th' field?

MESSENGER   They are.   100
You bear a charge there too.

JAILER   I'll away straight.
I must e'en leave you here.

DOCTOR   Nay, we'll go with you;
I will not lose the sight.

JAILER [*to Doctor*]   How did you like her?

DOCTOR
I'll warrant you, within these three or four days
I'll make her right again. *Exit Jailer with Messenger.*
[*to Wooer*]   You must not from her,   105
But still preserve her in this way.

WOOER   I will.

DOCTOR   Let's get her in.

WOOER [*to Daughter*]   Come, sweet, we'll go to dinner
And then we'll play at cards.

DAUGHTER   And shall we kiss too?

WOOER   An hundred times.

DAUGHTER   And twenty?

WOOER   Ay, and twenty.

DAUGHTER   And then we'll sleep together.

DOCTOR   Take her offer.   110

WOOER [*to Daughter*]   Yes, marry, will we.

DAUGHTER   But you shall not hurt me.

WOOER   I will not, sweet.

DAUGHTER   If you do, love, I'll cry. *Exeunt.*

5.3   *Flourish. Enter* THESEUS, HIPPOLYTA, EMILIA,
              PIRITHOUS *and attendants.*

EMILIA   I'll no step further.

PIRITHOUS   Will you lose this sight?

EMILIA   I had rather see a wren hawk at a fly
    Than this decision. Every blow that falls
    Threats a brave life; each stroke laments
5   The place whereon it falls and sounds more like
    A bell than blade. I will stay here.
    It is enough my hearing shall be punished
    With what shall happen, 'gainst the which there is
    No deafing, but to hear, not taint mine eye
    With dread sights it may shun.

10 PIRITHOUS [*to Theseus*]   Sir, my good lord,
    Your sister will no further.

THESEUS   O, she must.
    She shall see deeds of honour in their kind,
    Which sometime show well, pencilled. Nature now
    Shall make and act the story, the belief
    Both sealed with eye and ear.

15   [*to Emilia*]   You must be present:
    You are the victor's meed, the prize and garland
    To crown the question's title.

EMILIA   Pardon me;
    If I were there, I'd wink.

THESEUS   You must be there:
    This trial is as 'twere i'th' night, and you
    The only star to shine.

20 EMILIA   I am extinct.
    There is but envy in that light which shows
    The one the other. Darkness, which ever was
    The dam of horror, who does stand accursed
    Of many mortal millions, may even now,
25   By casting her black mantle over both
    That neither could find other, get herself
    Some part of a good name and many a murder
    Set off whereto she's guilty.

HIPPOLYTA   You must go.

EMILIA   In faith, I will not.

THESEUS   Why, the knights must kindle
30   Their valour at your eye. Know, of this war
    You are the treasure and must needs be by
    To give the service pay.

EMILIA   Sir, pardon me;
    The title of a kingdom may be tried
    Out of itself.

THESEUS   Well, well, then, at your pleasure.
35   Those that remain with you could wish their office
    To any of their enemies.

HIPPOLYTA   Farewell, sister.
    I am like to know your husband 'fore yourself
    By some small start of time; he whom the gods
    Do of the two know best, I pray them he
40   Be made your lot.   *Exeunt all but Emilia.*

EMILIA   Arcite is gently visaged, yet his eye
    Is like an engine bent, or a sharp weapon
    In a soft sheath; mercy and manly courage
    Are bedfellows in his visage. Palamon
45   Has a most menacing aspect; his brow
    Is graved and seems to bury what it frowns on,
    Yet sometime 'tis not so, but alters to
    The quality of his thoughts. Long time his eye
    Will dwell upon his object. Melancholy
    Becomes him nobly. So does Arcite's mirth.   50
    But Palamon's sadness is a kind of mirth,
    So mingled as if mirth did make him sad
    And sadness merry. Those darker humours that
    Stick misbecomingly on others, on them
    Live in fair dwelling.   55
                [*Cornets. Trumpets sound as to a charge.*]
    Hark how yon spurs to spirit do incite
    The princes to their proof! Arcite may win me
    And yet may Palamon wound Arcite to
    The spoiling of his figure. O, what pity
    Enough for such a chance? If I were by   60
    I might do hurt, for they would glance their eyes
    Toward my seat and in that motion might
    Omit a ward or forfeit an offence
    Which craved that very time. It is much better
    I am not there.
        [*Cornets; a great cry and noise within, crying,
                                    'A Palamon!'*]
                    O, better never born   65
    Than minister to such harm!

                Enter Servant.

                            What is the chance?

SERVANT   The cry's 'A Palamon!'

EMILIA   Then he has won.
    'Twas ever likely.
    He looked all grace and success and he is
    Doubtless the prim'st of men. I prithee, run   70
    And tell me how it goes.
            [*Shout, and cornets; cries of* 'A Palamon!']

SERVANT   Still 'Palamon'!

EMILIA   Run and enquire.   *Exit Servant.*
                    Poor servant, thou hast lost.
    Upon my right side still I wore thy picture,
    Palamon's on the left. Why so, I know not;
    I had no end in't else; chance would have it so.   75
    On the sinister side the heart lies. Palamon
    Had the best-boding chance.
            [*Another cry and shout within, and cornets.*]
                        This burst of clamour
    Is sure th'end o'th' combat.

                Enter Servant.

SERVANT   They said that Palamon had Arcite's body
    Within an inch o'th' pyramid, that the cry   80
    Was general, 'A Palamon!' But anon
    Th'assistants made a brave redemption and
    The two bold titlers at this instant are
    Hand to hand at it.

EMILIA   Were they metamorphosed
    Both into one! – O, why? There were no woman   85
    Worth so composed a man: their single share,
    Their nobleness peculiar to them, gives

The prejudice of disparity, value's shortness,
To any lady breathing.
            [*Cornets. Cry within, 'Arcite! Arcite!'*]
              More exulting?
'Palamon' still?
90 SERVANT   Nay, now the sound is 'Arcite!'
EMILIA   I prithee, lay attention to the cry.
      [*Cornets; a great shout and cry, 'Arcite! Victory!'*]
Set both thine ears to th' business.
SERVANT   The cry is
'Arcite and victory!' Hark! 'Arcite! Victory!'
The combat's consummation is proclaim'd
By the wind instruments.
95 EMILIA   Half-sights saw
That Arcite was no babe. God's lid, his richness
And costliness of spirit looked through him; it could
No more be hid in him than fire in flax,
Than humble banks can go to law with waters
100 That drift winds force to raging. I did think
Good Palamon would miscarry, yet I knew not
Why I did think so. Our reasons are not prophets
When oft our fancies are.   [*Cornets.*]
         They are coming off.
Alas, poor Palamon!

Enter THESEUS, HIPPOLYTA, PIRITHOUS, ARCITE
(as victor) and attendants.

105 THESEUS   Lo, where our sister is in expectation,
Yet quaking and unsettled. – Fairest Emily,
The gods by their divine arbitrament
Have given you this knight; he is a good one
As ever struck at head. Give me your hands:
110 Receive you her, you him, be plighted with
A love that grows as you decay.
ARCITE   Emilia,
To buy you, I have lost what's dearest to me,
Save what is bought; and yet I purchase cheaply,
As I do rate your value.
THESEUS   O, loved sister,
115 He speaks now of as brave a knight as e'er
Did spur a noble steed. Surely the gods
Would have him die a bachelor, lest his race
Should show i'th world too godlike. His behaviour
So charmed me that methought Alcides was
120 To him a sow of lead. If I could praise
Each part of him to th'all I have spoke, your Arcite
Did not lose by't. For he that was thus good
Encountered yet his better. I have heard
Two emulous Philomels beat the ear o'th' night
125 With their contentious throats, now one the higher,
Anon the other, then again the first,
And by and by out-breasted, that the sense
Could not be judge between 'em. So it fared
Good space between these kinsmen, till heavens did
Make hardly one the winner.
130 [*to Arcite*]   Wear the garland
With joy that you have won. – For the subdued,

Give them our present justice, since I know
Their lives but pinch 'em. Let it here be done.
The scene's not for our seeing; go we hence,
Right joyful, with some sorrow.
[*to Arcite*]   Arm your prize;   135
I know you will not loose her. – Hippolyta,
I see one eye of yours conceives a tear,
The which it will deliver.   [*Flourish.*]
EMILIA   Is this winning?
O, all you heavenly powers, where is your mercy?
But that your wills have said it must be so,   140
And charge me live to comfort this unfriended,
This miserable prince, that cuts away
A life more worthy from him than all women,
I should and would die too.
HIPPOLYTA   Infinite pity
That four such eyes should be so fixed on one   145
That two must needs be blind for't.
THESEUS   So it is.   *Exeunt.*

5.4   *Enter* PALAMON *and his* Knights, *pinioned;*
      Jailer, *executioner, guard and others, carrying*
               a block and axe.

PALAMON   There's many a man alive that has outlived
The love o'th' people; yea, i'th' selfsame state
Stands many a father with his child. Some comfort
We have by so considering. We expire
And not without men's pity; to live still,   5
Have their good wishes. We prevent
The loathsome misery of age, beguile
The gout and rheum that in lag hours attend
For grey approachers; we come towards the gods
Young and unwappered, not halting under crimes   10
Many and stale. That sure shall please the gods,
Sooner than such, to give us nectar with 'em,
For we are more clear spirits.
[*to Knights*]   My dear kinsmen,
Whose lives for this poor comfort are laid down,
You have sold 'em too, too cheap.
1 KNIGHT   What ending could be   15
Of more content? O'er us the victors have
Fortune, whose title is as momentary
As to us death is certain. A grain of honour
They not o'erweigh us.
2 KNIGHT   Let us bid farewell
And with our patience anger tottering Fortune,   20
Who at her certain'st reels. [*They embrace.*]
3 KNIGHT   Come, who begins?
PALAMON   E'en he that led you to this banquet shall
Taste to you all. [*to Jailer*] Aha, my friend, my
    friend,
Your gentle daughter gave me freedom once;
You'll see't done now forever. Pray, how does she?   25
I heard she was not well; her kind of ill
Gave me some sorrow.
JAILER   Sir, she's well restored

And to be married shortly.
PALAMON   By my short life,
    I am most glad on't. 'Tis the latest thing
30 I shall be glad of; prithee, tell her so.
    Commend me to her and, to piece her portion,
    Tender her this. [*Gives him his purse.*]
1 KNIGHT   Nay, let's be offerers all.
2 KNIGHT   Is it a maid?
PALAMON   Verily I think so.
    A right good creature, more to me deserving
35 Than I can 'quite or speak of.
THE KNIGHTS [*to Jailer*]   Commend us to her.
    [*They give their purses.*]
JAILER
    The gods requite you all and make her thankful.
PALAMON   Adieu; and let my life be now as short
    As my leave-taking. [*He lays his head on the block.*]
1 KNIGHT   Lead, courageous cousin.
2, 3 KNIGHT   We'll follow cheerfully.
    [*A great noise within, crying, 'Run, save, hold!'*]

Enter in haste a Messenger.

40 MESSENGER   Hold, hold! O, hold, hold, hold!

Enter PIRITHOUS *in haste.*

PIRITHOUS   Hold, ho! It is a cursed haste you made
    If you have done so quickly! – Noble Palamon,
    The gods will show their glory in a life
    That thou art yet to lead.
PALAMON   Can that be,
    When Venus, I have said, is false? How do things
45   fare?
PIRITHOUS   Arise, great sir, and give the tidings ear
    That are most rarely sweet and bitter.
PALAMON   What
    Hath waked us from our dream?
PIRITHOUS   List, then. Your cousin,
    Mounted upon a steed that Emily
50 Did first bestow on him, a black one, owing
    Not a hair-worth of white, which some will say
    Weakens his price and many will not buy
    His goodness with this note – which superstition
    Here finds allowance – on this horse is Arcite
55 Trotting the stones of Athens, which the calkins
    Did rather tell than trample; for the horse
    Would make his length a mile, if 't pleased his rider
    To put pride in him. As he thus went counting
    The flinty pavement, dancing as 'twere to th' music
60 His own hoofs made (for, as they say, from iron
    Came music's origin), what envious flint,
    Cold as old Saturn and, like him, possessed
    With fire malevolent, darted a spark,
    Or what fierce sulphur else, to this end made,
65 I comment not. The hot horse, hot as fire,
    Took toy at this and fell to what disorder
    His power could give his will; bounds, comes on end,
    Forgets school-doing, being therein trained

And of kind manage; pig-like he whines
At the sharp rowell, which he frets at rather   70
Than any jot obeys; seeks all foul means
Of boist'rous and rough jad'ry to disseat
His lord, that kept it bravely. When nought served –
When neither curb would crack, girth break, nor
    diff'ring plunges
Disroot his rider whence he grew, but that   75
He kept him 'tween his legs – on his hind hoofs
On end he stands,
That Arcite's legs, being higher than his head,
Seemed with strange art to hang. His victor's wreath
Even then fell off his head and presently   80
Backward the jade comes o'er and his full poise
Becomes the rider's load. Yet is he living,
But such a vessel 'tis, that floats but for
The surge that next approaches. He much desires
To have some speech with you. Lo, he appears.   85

Enter THESEUS, HIPPOLYTA, EMILIA, ARCITE
carried in a chair.

PALAMON   O miserable end of our alliance!
    The gods are mighty. Arcite, if thy heart,
    Thy worthy, manly heart, be yet unbroken,
    Give me thy last words. I am Palamon,
    One that yet loves thee dying.
ARCITE   Take Emilia   90
    And, with her, all the world's joy. Reach thy hand;
    Farewell. I have told my last hour. I was false
    Yet never treacherous. Forgive me, cousin.
    One kiss from fair Emilia. [*Emilia kisses Arcite.*]
                              'Tis done.
    Take her. I die.
PALAMON   Thy brave soul seek Elysium!   95
    [*Arcite dies.*]
EMILIA
    I'll close thine eyes, Prince; blessed souls be with thee.
    Thou art a right good man and, while I live,
    This day I give to tears.
PALAMON   And I to honour.
THESEUS   In this place first you fought: e'en very here
    I sundered you. Acknowledge to the gods   100
    Our thanks that you are living.
    His part is played and, though it were too short,
    He did it well; your day is lengthened and
    The blissful dew of heaven does arrose you.
    The powerful Venus well hath graced her altar   105
    And given you your love. Our master Mars
    Hath vouched his oracle and to Arcite gave
    The grace of the contention. So the deities
    Have showed due justice. Bear this hence.
PALAMON   O, cousin!
    That we should things desire, which do cost us   110
    The loss of our desire! That nought could buy
    Dear love, but loss of dear love!
    [*Arcite's body is carried out.*]
THESEUS   Never Fortune

Did play a subtler game. The conquered triumphs;
The victor has the loss; yet in the passage
115 The gods have been most equal. – Palamon,
Your kinsman hath confessed the right o'th' lady
Did lie in you, for you first saw her and
Even then proclaimed your fancy. He restored her
As your stol'n jewel and desired your spirit
120 To send him hence forgiven. The gods my justice
Take from my hand and they themselves become
The executioners. Lead your lady off
And call your lovers from the stage of death,
Whom I adopt my friends. A day or two
125 Let us look sadly and give grace unto
The funeral of Arcite, in whose end
The visages of bridegrooms we'll put on
And smile with Palamon – for whom an hour,
But one hour since, I was as dearly sorry
130 As glad of Arcite, and am now as glad
As for him sorry. O, you heavenly charmers,
What things you make of us! For what we lack
We laugh, for what we have are sorry, still
Are children in some kind. Let us be thankful
135 For that which is, and with you leave dispute
That are above our question. Let's go off
And bear us like the time.   *Flourish. Exeunt.*

EPILOGUE

Enter Speaker of the Epilogue.

I would now ask ye how ye like the play,
But, as it is with schoolboys, cannot say.
I am cruel fearful! Pray yet, stay a while,
And let me look upon ye. No man smile?
Then it goes hard, I see. He that has   5
Loved a young handsome wench, then, show his face –
'Tis strange if none be here – and, if he will,
Against his conscience let him hiss, and kill
Our market. 'Tis in vain, I see, to stay ye:
Have at the worst can come then! Now, what say ye?   10
And yet mistake me not: I am not bold;
We have no such cause. If the tale we have told
(For 'tis no other) any way content ye –
For to that honest purpose it was meant ye –
We have our end; and ye shall have ere long,   15
I dare say, many a better, to prolong
Your old loves to us. We, and all our might,
Rest at your service. Gentlemen, goodnight!
                                        Flourish. Exit.

The Winter's Tale

Shakespeare began his career in London as actor-dramatist in time to be denounced for his success by a rival playwright, the dying Robert Greene, in the autumn of 1592. Some eighteen years later, Greene's popular romance, *Pandosto, or The Triumph of Time* (1587) supplied Shakespeare with the plot of *The Winter's Tale*, while the roguery of Autolycus (among Shakespeare's main additions to the story) drew on anecdotes from Greene's popular pamphlets about the London underworld of the 1580s and 1590s. Shakespeare wrote *The Winter's Tale* and *Cymbeline* about 1609–10, perhaps during a lengthy closure of the theatres caused by the plague. No consensus exists about which came first, and both were seen at the Globe in the spring of 1611 by Simon Forman, whose notes surprisingly make reference neither to the bear that pursues Antigonus nor to the final scene of Hermione's resurrection.

In the First Folio *The Winter's Tale* appears as the last of the fourteen comedies, *Cymbeline* as the last of the tragedies (and so the last play in the book). Both are now commonly referred to as romances, or late plays, and attempts have been made to associate them with Jacobean politics and with the royal family. What is certain is that their tragicomic actions, like that of *Pericles*, make nostalgic reference to the romantic plays of the 1570s and 1580s derided by Sidney in his *Defence of Poetry* as 'mongrel tragicomedy'.

A winter's tale was the sort of story told round the fire to while away a long winter evening, hence simply an implausible romantic or fairytale fiction. The passage of time, human and seasonal, destructive and restorative, is among the major motifs of the play, whose cast includes characters of all ages from a newborn baby to a man of eighty. In *The Winter's Tale* Shakespeare simultaneously asserts the implausible conventionality of his story and invests it with a poetic and emotional power that transcends convention. The jealous Leontes may recall Othello, but the violence and irrational suddenness of his passion launch the action at a high pitch of tension. Time, as chorus, divides the play into balancing and antithetical halves when he turns his hourglass exactly in the middle of his speech. The sixteen-year gap in time between acts 3 and 4, more sharply defined than the fourteen years in the middle of *Pericles*, reflects the passage of the human seasons from the winter guilt and sadness of Leontes' court to the springtime innocence of his lost daughter Perdita and her lover Florizel. As in *The Comedy of Errors* and *Pericles*, the family reunion (promised by the oracle of Apollo) is capped by the reappearance of the supposedly dead mother, with the difference that this time the audience too have been persuaded of her death. The first half of the play ends with the pursuit of Antigonus by a bear, the second with the descent of the statue of Hermione from its plinth to be reunited with husband and daughter. Both are Shakespeare's additions to Greene's story, as is Paulina, the agent of Hermione's survival and the penitence of Leontes.

The Winter's Tale has had a long and successful stage history. An influential twentieth-century production was that by Harley Granville Barker at the Savoy Theatre in London in 1912, which restored the full text and simplified the setting in the interests of pace and clarity of performance. Today *The Winter's Tale* is, after *The Tempest*, the most frequently revived of the romances.

The Arden text is based on the 1623 First Folio.

LEONTES	*King of Sicilia*
MAMILLIUS	*young Prince of Sicilia*
CAMILLO	
ANTIGONUS	
CLEOMENES	*four lords of Sicilia*
DION	
POLIXENES	*King of Bohemia*
FLORIZEL	*Prince of Bohemia*
ARCHIDAMUS	*a lord of Bohemia*
Old SHEPHERD	*reputed father of Perdita*
CLOWN	*his son*
AUTOLYCUS	*a rogue*
MARINER	
GAOLER	
HERMIONE	*Queen to Leontes*
PERDITA	*daughter to Leontes and Hermione*
PAULINA	*wife to Antigonus*
EMILIA	*a lady attending on Hermione*
MOPSA	*shepherdesses*
DORCAS	

Other Lords and Gentlemen, Ladies, Officers, and Servants, Shepherds and Shepherdesses

TIME, as Chorus

1.1   *Enter* CAMILLO *and* ARCHIDAMUS.

ARCHIDAMUS   If you shall chance, Camillo, to visit Bohemia, on the like occasion whereon my services are now on foot, you shall see, as I have said, great difference betwixt our Bohemia and your Sicilia.

CAMILLO   I think, this coming summer, the King of Sicilia means to pay Bohemia the visitation which he justly owes him.

ARCHIDAMUS   Wherein our entertainment shall shame us: we will be justified in our loves: for indeed –

CAMILLO   Beseech you –

ARCHIDAMUS   Verily I speak it in the freedom of my knowledge: we cannot with such magnificence – in so rare – I know not what to say – We will give you sleepy drinks, that your senses (unintelligent of our insufficience) may, though they cannot praise us, as little accuse us.

CAMILLO   You pay a great deal too dear for what's given freely.

ARCHIDAMUS   Believe me, I speak as my understanding instructs me, and as mine honesty puts it to utterance.

CAMILLO   Sicilia cannot show himself over-kind to Bohemia. They were trained together in their childhoods, and there rooted betwixt them then such an affection which cannot choose but branch now. Since their more mature dignities and royal necessities made separation of their society, their encounters, though not personal, have been royally attorneyed with interchange of gifts, letters, loving embassies, that they have seemed to be together, though absent; shook hands, as over a vast; and embraced, as it were, from the ends of opposed winds. The heavens continue their loves!

ARCHIDAMUS   I think there is not in the world either malice or matter to alter it. You have an unspeakable comfort of your young prince Mamillius: it is a gentleman of the greatest promise that ever came into my note.

CAMILLO   I very well agree with you in the hopes of him: it is a gallant child; one that, indeed, physics the subject, makes old hearts fresh: they that went on crutches ere he was born desire yet their life to see him a man.

ARCHIDAMUS   Would they else be content to die?

CAMILLO   Yes; if there were no other excuse why they should desire to live.

ARCHIDAMUS   If the king had no son, they would desire to live on crutches till he had one.   *Exeunt.*

1.2   *Enter* LEONTES, HERMIONE, MAMILLIUS,
                POLIXENES, CAMILLO *and attendants.*

POLIXENES   Nine changes of the watery star hath been
The shepherd's note since we have left our throne
Without a burden. Time as long again
Would be fill'd up, my brother, with our thanks;
And yet we should, for perpetuity,
Go hence in debt: and therefore, like a cipher
(Yet standing in rich place) I multiply
With one 'We thank you' many thousands moe
That go before it.

LEONTES   Stay your thanks a while,
And pay them when you part.

POLIXENES   Sir, that's to-morrow.   10
I am question'd by my fears, of what may chance
Or breed upon our absence; that may blow
No sneaping winds at home, to make us say
'This is put forth too truly'. Besides, I have stay'd
To tire your royalty.

LEONTES   We are tougher, brother,   15
Than you can put us to't.

POLIXENES   No longer stay.

LEONTES   One seve'night longer.

POLIXENES   Very sooth, to-morrow.

LEONTES
We'll part the time between's then: and in that
I'll no gainsaying.

POLIXENES   Press me not, beseech you, so.
There is no tongue that moves, none, none i'th'
    world,   20
So soon as yours, could win me: so it should now,
Were there necessity in your request, although
'Twere needful I denied it. My affairs
Do even drag me homeward: which to hinder
Were (in your love) a whip to me; my stay,   25
To you a charge and trouble: to save both,
Farewell, our brother.

LEONTES   Tongue-tied our queen? speak you.

HERMIONE
I had thought, sir, to have held my peace until
You had drawn oaths from him not to stay. You, sir,
Charge him too coldly. Tell him, you are sure   30
All in Bohemia's well: this satisfaction
The by-gone day proclaim'd: say this to him,
He's beat from his best ward.

LEONTES   Well said, Hermione.

HERMIONE
To tell, he longs to see his son, were strong:
But let him say so then, and let him go;   35
But let him swear so, and he shall not stay,
We'll thwack him hence with distaffs.
Yet of your royal presence I'll adventure
The borrow of a week. When at Bohemia
You take my lord, I'll give him my commission   40
To let him there a month behind the gest
Prefix'd for's parting: yet, good deed, Leontes
I love thee not a jar o'th' clock behind
What lady she her lord. You'll stay?

POLIXENES   No, madam.

HERMIONE   Nay, but you will?

POLIXENES   I may not, verily.   45

HERMIONE   Verily!
You put me off with limber vows; but I,
Though you would seek t'unsphere the stars with

oaths,
Should yet say 'Sir, no going'. Verily,
50   You shall not go: a lady's Verily's
As potent as a lord's. Will you go yet?
Force me to keep you as a prisoner,
Not like a guest: so you shall pay your fees
When you depart, and save your thanks? How say
you?
55   My prisoner? or my guest? By your dread 'Verily',
One of them you shall be.

POLIXENES   Your guest then, madam:
To be your prisoner should import offending;
Which is for me less easy to commit
Than you to punish.

HERMIONE   Not your gaoler then,
60   But your kind hostess. Come, I'll question you
Of my lord's tricks, and yours, when you were boys.
You were pretty lordings then?

POLIXENES   We were, fair queen,
Two lads that thought there was no more behind,
But such a day to-morrow as to-day,
And to be boy eternal.

65   HERMIONE   Was not my lord
The verier wag o'th' two?

POLIXENES
We were as twinn'd lambs that did frisk i'th' sun,
And bleat the one at th'other: what we chang'd
Was innocence for innocence: we knew not
70   The doctrine of ill-doing, nor dream'd
That any did. Had we pursu'd that life,
And our weak spirits ne'er been higher rear'd
With stronger blood, we should have answer'd heaven
Boldly 'not guilty', the imposition clear'd
Hereditary ours.

75   HERMIONE   By this we gather
You have tripp'd since.

POLIXENES   O my most sacred lady,
Temptations have since then been born to 's: for
In those unfledg'd days was my wife a girl;
Your precious self had then not cross'd the eyes
Of my young play-fellow.

80   HERMIONE   Grace to boot!
Of this make no conclusion, lest you say
Your queen and I are devils. Yet go on;
Th'offences we have made you do, we'll answer,
If you first sinn'd with us, and that with us
85   You did continue fault, and that you slipp'd not
With any but with us.

LEONTES   Is he won yet?

HERMIONE   He'll stay, my lord.

LEONTES   At my request he would not.
Hermione, my dearest, thou never spok'st
To better purpose.

HERMIONE   Never?

LEONTES   Never but once.

HERMIONE
90   What! have I twice said well? when was't before?

I prithee tell me: cram's with praise, and make's
As fat as tame things: one good deed, dying
tongueless,
Slaughters a thousand, waiting upon that.
Our praises are our wages. You may ride's
With one soft kiss a thousand furlongs ere   95
With spur we heat an acre. But to th' goal:
My last good deed was to entreat his stay:
What was my first? It has an elder sister,
Or I mistake you: O, would her name were Grace!
But once before I spoke to th' purpose? when?   100
Nay, let me have't: I long!

LEONTES   Why, that was when
Three crabbed months had sour'd themselves to
death,
Ere I could make thee open thy white hand,
And clap thyself my love; then didst thou utter
'I am yours for ever.'

HERMIONE   'Tis Grace indeed.   105
Why lo you now; I have spoke to th' purpose twice:
The one, for ever earn'd a royal husband;
Th'other, for some while a friend.
[*giving her hand to Polixenes*]

LEONTES [*aside*]   Too hot, too hot!
To mingle friendship far, is mingling bloods.
I have *tremor cordis* on me: my heart dances,   110
But not for joy – not joy. This entertainment
May a free face put on, derive a liberty
From heartiness, from bounty, fertile bosom,
And well become the agent: 't may, I grant:
But to be paddling palms, and pinching fingers,   115
As now they are, and making practis'd smiles
As in a looking-glass; and then to sigh, as 'twere
The mort o'th' deer – O, that is entertainment
My bosom likes not, nor my brows. Mamillius,
Art thou my boy?

MAMILLIUS   Ay, my good lord.

LEONTES   I'fecks: 120
Why that's my bawcock. What! hast smutch'd thy
nose?
They say it is a copy out of mine. Come, captain,
We must be neat; not neat, but cleanly, captain:
And yet the steer, the heifer and the calf
Are all call'd neat. – Still virginalling   125
Upon his palm! – How now, you wanton calf!
Art thou my calf?

MAMILLIUS   Yes, if you will, my lord.

LEONTES
Thou want'st a rough pash and the shoots that I have
To be full like me: yet they say we are
Almost as like as eggs; women say so,   130
(That will say any thing): but were they false
As o'er-dy'd blacks, as wind, as waters; false
As dice are to be wish'd by one that fixes
No bourn 'twixt his and mine, yet were it true
To say this boy were like me. Come, sir page,   135
Look on me with your welkin eye: sweet villain!

Most dear'st, my collop! Can thy dam? – may't be? –
Affection! thy intention stabs the centre:
Thou dost make possible things not so held,
Communicat'st with dreams; – how can this be? –
With what's unreal thou coactive art,
And fellow'st nothing: then 'tis very credent
Thou may'st co-join with something; and thou dost,
(And that beyond commission) and I find it,
(And that to the infection of my brains
And hard'ning of my brows).

POLIXENES   What means Sicilia?

HERMIONE   He something seems unsettled.

POLIXENES   How, my lord?
What cheer? how is't with you, best brother?

HERMIONE   You look
As if you held a brow of much distraction:
Are you mov'd, my lord?

LEONTES   No, in good earnest.
How sometimes nature will betray its folly,
Its tenderness, and make itself a pastime
To harder bosoms! Looking on the lines
Of my boy's face, methoughts I did recoil
Twenty-three years, and saw myself unbreech'd,
In my green velvet coat; my dagger muzzl'd
Lest it should bite its master, and so prove,
As ornaments oft do, too dangerous:
How like, methought, I then was to this kernel,
This squash, this gentleman. Mine honest friend,
Will you take eggs for money?

MAMILLIUS   No, my lord, I'll fight.

LEONTES
You will? Why, happy man be's dole! My brother,
Are you so fond of your young prince, as we
Do seem to be of ours?

POLIXENES   If at home, sir,
He's all my exercise, my mirth, my matter:
Now my sworn friend, and then mine enemy;
My parasite, my soldier, statesman, all.
He makes a July's day short as December;
And with his varying childness cures in me
Thoughts that would thick my blood.

LEONTES   So stands this squire
Offic'd with me: we two will walk, my lord,
And leave you to your graver steps. Hermione,
How thou lov'st us, show in our brother's welcome;
Let what is dear in Sicily be cheap:
Next to thyself, and my young rover, he's
Apparent to my heart.

HERMIONE   If you would seek us,
We are yours i'th' garden: shall 's attend you there?

LEONTES
To your own bents dispose you: you'll be found,
Be you beneath the sky. [*aside*] I am angling now,
Though you perceive me not how I give line.
Go to, go to!
How she holds up the neb, the bill to him!
And arms her with the boldness of a wife

To her allowing husband!

Exeunt Polixenes, Hermione and attendants.
Gone already!
Inch-thick, knee-deep; o'er head and ears a fork'd
one.
Go, play, boy, play: thy mother plays, and I
Play too; but so disgrac'd a part, whose issue
Will hiss me to my grave: contempt and clamour
Will be my knell. Go, play, boy, play. There have
been,
(Or I am much deceiv'd) cuckolds ere now,
And many a man there is (even at this present,
Now, while I speak this) holds his wife by th' arm,
That little thinks she has been sluic'd in's absence
And his pond fish'd by his next neighbour, by
Sir Smile, his neighbour: nay, there's comfort in't,
Whiles other men have gates, and those gates open'd,
As mine, against their will. Should all despair
That have revolted wives, the tenth of mankind
Would hang themselves. Physic for't there's none;
It is a bawdy planet, that will strike
Where 'tis predominant; and 'tis powerful, think it,
From east, west, north, and south; be it concluded,
No barricado for a belly. Know't,
It will let in and out the enemy,
With bag and baggage: many thousand on's
Have the disease, and feel't not. How now, boy?

MAMILLIUS   I am like you, they say.

LEONTES   Why, that's some comfort.
What, Camillo there?

CAMILLO   Ay, my good lord.

LEONTES   Go play, Mamillius; thou'rt an honest man.
Exit Mamillius.
Camillo, this great Sir will yet stay longer.

CAMILLO   You had much ado to make his anchor hold:
When you cast out, it still came home.

LEONTES   Didst note it?

CAMILLO   He would not stay at your petitions; made
His business more material.

LEONTES   Didst perceive it?
[*aside*] They're here with me already; whisp'ring,
rounding
'Sicilia is a so-forth': 'tis far gone,
When I shall gust it last. – How cam't, Camillo,
That he did stay?

CAMILLO   At the good queen's entreaty.

LEONTES
At the queen's be't: 'good' should be pertinent,
But so it is, it is not. Was this taken
By any understanding pate but thine?
For thy conceit is soaking, will draw in
More than the common blocks: not noted, is't,
But of the finer natures? by some severals
Of head-piece extraordinary? lower messes
Perchance are to this business purblind? say!

CAMILLO   Business, my lord? I think most understand
Bohemia stays here longer.

LEONTES   Ha?

230   CAMILLO   Stays here longer.

LEONTES   Ay, but why?

CAMILLO   To satisfy your highness, and the entreaties
Of our most gracious mistress.

LEONTES   Satisfy?

Th'entreaties of your mistress? satisfy?

235   Let that suffice. I have trusted thee, Camillo,
With all the nearest things to my heart, as well
My chamber-counsels, wherein, priest-like, thou
Hast cleans'd my bosom: I from thee departed
Thy penitent reform'd. But we have been

240   Deceiv'd in thy integrity, deceiv'd
In that which seems so.

CAMILLO   Be it forbid, my lord!

LEONTES   To bide upon't: thou art not honest: or,
If thou inclin'st that way, thou art a coward,
Which hoxes honesty behind, restraining

245   From course requir'd: or else thou must be counted
A servant grafted in my serious trust,
And therein negligent; or else a fool,
That seest a game play'd home, the rich stake drawn,
And tak'st it all for jest.

CAMILLO   My gracious lord,

250   I may be negligent, foolish, and fearful;
In every one of these no man is free,
But that his negligence, his folly, fear,
Among the infinite doings of the world,
Sometime puts forth. In your affairs, my lord,

255   If ever I were wilful-negligent,
It was my folly: if industriously
I play'd the fool, it was my negligence,
Not weighing well the end: if ever fearful
To do a thing, where I the issue doubted,

260   Whereof the execution did cry out
Against the non-performance, 'twas a fear
Which oft infects the wisest: these, my lord,
Are such allow'd infirmities that honesty
Is never free of. But, beseech your Grace,

265   Be plainer with me; let me know my trespass
By its own visage: if I then deny it,
'Tis none of mine.

LEONTES   Ha' not you seen, Camillo?
(But that's past doubt: you have, or your eye-glass
Is thicker than a cuckold's horn) or heard?

270   (For to a vision so apparent rumour
Cannot be mute) or thought? (for cogitation
Resides not in that man that does not think)
My wife is slippery? If thou wilt confess,
Or else be impudently negative,

275   To have nor eyes, nor ears, nor thought, then say
My wife's a hobby-horse, deserves a name
As rank as any flax-wench that puts to
Before her troth-plight: say't and justify't!

CAMILLO   I would not be a stander-by, to hear

280   My sovereign mistress clouded so, without
My present vengeance taken: 'shrew my heart,

You never spoke what did become you less
Than this; which to reiterate were sin
As deep as that, though true.

LEONTES   Is whispering nothing?

Is leaning cheek to cheek? is meeting noses?   285
Kissing with inside lip? stopping the career
Of laughter with a sigh (a note infallible
Of breaking honesty)? horsing foot on foot?
Skulking in corners? wishing clocks more swift?
Hours, minutes? noon, midnight? and all eyes   290
Blind with the pin and web, but theirs; theirs only.
That would unseen be wicked? is this nothing?
Why then the world, and all that's in't, is nothing,
The covering sky is nothing, Bohemia nothing,
My wife is nothing, nor nothing have these nothings,   295
If this be nothing.

CAMILLO   Good my lord, be cur'd
Of this diseas'd opinion, and betimes,
For 'tis most dangerous.

LEONTES   Say it be, 'tis true.

CAMILLO   No, no, my lord.

LEONTES   It is: you lie, you lie:
I say thou liest, Camillo, and I hate thee,   300
Pronounce thee a gross lout, a mindless slave,
Or else a hovering temporizer that
Canst with thine eyes at once see good and evil,
Inclining to them both: were my wife's liver
Infected, as her life, she would not live   305
The running of one glass.

CAMILLO   Who does infect her?

LEONTES

Why, he that wears her like her medal, hanging
About his neck, Bohemia; who, if I
Had servants true about me, that bare eyes
To see alike mine honour as their profits,   310
Their own particular thrifts, they would do that
Which should undo more doing: ay, and thou
His cupbearer, – whom I from meaner form
Have bench'd and rear'd to worship, who may'st see
Plainly as heaven sees earth and earth sees heaven,   315
How I am gall'd, – might'st bespice a cup,
To give mine enemy a lasting wink;
Which draught to me were cordial.

CAMILLO   Sir, my lord,
I could do this, and that with no rash potion,
But with a ling'ring dram, that should not work   320
Maliciously, like poison: but I cannot
Believe this crack to be in my dread mistress
(So sovereignly being honourable).
I have lov'd thee, –

LEONTES   Make that thy question, and go rot!
Dost think I am so muddy, so unsettled,   325
To appoint myself in this vexation; sully
The purity and whiteness of my sheets,
(Which to preserve is sleep, which being spotted
Is goads, thorns, nettles, tails of wasps)
Give scandal to the blood o'th' prince, my son,   330

(Who I do think is mine and love as mine)
Without ripe moving to't? Would I do this?
Could man so blench?
CAMILLO   I must believe you, sir:
335   I do; and will fetch off Bohemia for't;
Provided, that when he's removed, your highness
Will take again your queen, as yours at first,
Even for your son's sake, and thereby for sealing
The injury of tongues in courts and kingdoms
Known and allied to yours.
LEONTES   Thou dost advise me
340   Even so as I mine own course have set down:
I'll give no blemish to her honour, none.
CAMILLO   My lord,
Go then; and with a countenance as clear
As friendship wears at feasts, keep with Bohemia,
345   And with your queen. I am his cupbearer:
If from me he have wholesome beverage,
Account me not your servant.
LEONTES   This is all:
Do't, and thou hast the one half of my heart;
Do't not, thou splitt'st thine own.
CAMILLO   I'll do't, my lord.
350 LEONTES   I will seem friendly, as thou hast advis'd me.
                                                 Exit.
CAMILLO   O miserable lady! But, for me,
What case stand I in? I must be the poisoner
Of good Polixenes, and my ground to do't
Is the obedience to a master; one
355   Who, in rebellion with himself, will have
All that are his, so too. To do this deed,
Promotion follows. If I could find example
Of thousands that had struck anointed kings
And flourish'd after, I'd not do't: but since
360   Nor brass, nor stone, nor parchment bears not one,
Let villainy itself forswear't. I must
Forsake the court: to do't, or no, is certain
To me a break-neck. Happy star reign now!
Here comes Bohemia.

                Enter POLIXENES.

POLIXENES   This is strange: methinks
365   My favour here begins to warp. Not speak?
Good day, Camillo.
CAMILLO   Hail, most royal sir!
POLIXENES   What is the news i'th' court?
CAMILLO   None rare, my lord.
POLIXENES   The king hath on him such a countenance
As he had lost some province, and a region
370   Lov'd as he loves himself: even now I met him
With customary compliment, when he,
Wafting his eyes to th' contrary, and falling
A lip of much contempt, speeds from me, and
So leaves me, to consider what is breeding
375   That changes thus his manners.
CAMILLO   I dare not know, my lord.

POLIXENES
How, dare not? do not? Do you know, and dare not?
Be intelligent to me: 'tis thereabouts:
For, to yourself, what you do know, you must,
And cannot say you dare not. Good Camillo,   380
Your chang'd complexions are to me a mirror
Which shows me mine chang'd too; for I must be
A party in this alteration, finding
Myself thus alter'd with't.
CAMILLO   There is a sickness
Which puts some of us in distemper, but   385
I cannot name the disease, and it is caught
Of you, that yet are well.
POLIXENES   How caught of me?
Make me not sighted like the basilisk.
I have look'd on thousands, who have sped the better
By my regard, but kill'd none so. Camillo, –   390
As you are certainly a gentleman, thereto
Clerk-like experienc'd, which no less adorns
Our gentry than our parents' noble names,
In whose success we are gentle, – I beseech you,
If you know aught which does behove my knowledge   395
Thereof to be inform'd, imprison't not
In ignorant concealment.
CAMILLO   I may not answer.
POLIXENES   A sickness caught of me, and yet I well?
I must be answer'd. Dost thou hear, Camillo?
I conjure thee, by all the parts of man   400
Which honour does acknowledge, whereof the least
Is not this suit of mine, that thou declare
What incidency thou dost guess of harm
Is creeping toward me; how far off, how near,
Which way to be prevented, if to be: 405
If not, how best to bear it.
CAMILLO   Sir, I will tell you;
Since I am charg'd in honour, and by him
That I think honourable. Therefore mark my
    counsel,
Which must be ev'n as swiftly follow'd as
I mean to utter it, or both yourself and me   410
Cry lost, and so good night!
POLIXENES   On, good Camillo.
CAMILLO   I am appointed him to murder you.
POLIXENES   By whom, Camillo?
CAMILLO   By the king.
POLIXENES   For what?
CAMILLO
He thinks, nay, with all confidence he swears,
As he had seen't, or been an instrument   415
To vice you to't, that you have touch'd his queen
Forbiddenly.
POLIXENES   O then, my best blood turn
To an infected jelly, and my name
Be yok'd with his that did betray the Best!
Turn then my freshest reputation to   420
A savour that may strike the dullest nostril
Where I arrive, and my approach be shunn'd,

Nay, hated too, worse than the great'st infection
That e'er was heard or read!
CAMILLO   Swear his thought over
425   By each particular star in heaven, and
By all their influences; you may as well
Forbid the sea for to obey the moon,
As or by oath remove or counsel shake
The fabric of his folly, whose foundation
430   Is pil'd upon his faith, and will continue
The standing of his body.
POLIXENES   How should this grow?
CAMILLO   I know not: but I am sure 'tis safer to
Avoid what's grown than question how 'tis born.
If therefore you dare trust my honesty,
435   That lies enclosed in this trunk; which you
Shall bear along impawn'd, away to-night!
Your followers I will whisper to the business,
And will by twos and threes, at several posterns,
Clear them o'th' city. For myself, I'll put
440   My fortunes to your service, which are here
By this discovery lost. Be not uncertain,
For by the honour of my parents, I
Have utter'd truth: which if you seek to prove,
I dare not stand by; nor shall you be safer
445   Than one condemned by the king's own mouth,
Thereon his execution sworn.
POLIXENES   I do believe thee:
I saw his heart in's face. Give me thy hand,
Be pilot to me, and thy places shall
Still neighbour mine. My ships are ready, and
450   My people did expect my hence departure
Two days ago. This jealousy
Is for a precious creature: as she's rare,
Must it be great; and, as his person's mighty,
Must it be violent; and, as he does conceive
455   He is dishonour'd by a man which ever
Profess'd to him; why, his revenges must
In that be made more bitter. Fear o'ershades me:
Good expedition be my friend, and comfort
The gracious queen, part of his theme, but nothing
460   Of his ill-ta'en suspicion! Come, Camillo,
I will respect thee as a father if
Thou bear'st my life off. Hence! let us avoid.
CAMILLO   It is in mine authority to command
The keys of all the posterns: please your highness
465   To take the urgent hour. Come sir, away.   *Exeunt.*

2.1   *Enter* HERMIONE, MAMILLIUS *and* Ladies.

HERMIONE   Take the boy to you: he so troubles me,
'Tis past enduring.
1 LADY   Come, my gracious lord,
Shall I be your play-fellow?
MAMILLIUS   No, I'll none of you.
1 LADY   Why, my sweet lord?
5   MAMILLIUS   You'll kiss me hard, and speak to me as if
I were a baby still. I love you better.

2 LADY   And why so, my lord?
MAMILLIUS   Not for because
Your brows are blacker; yet black brows, they say,
Become some women best, so that there be not
Too much hair there, but in a semicircle,   10
Or a half-moon, made with a pen.
2 LADY   Who taught' this!
MAMILLIUS
I learn'd it out of women's faces. Pray now,
What colour are your eyebrows?
1 LADY   Blue, my lord.
MAMILLIUS
Nay, that's a mock: I have seen a lady's nose
That has been blue, but not her eyebrows.
1 LADY   Hark ye,   15
The queen your mother rounds apace: we shall
Present our services to a fine new prince
One of these days, and then you'd wanton with us,
If we would have you.
2 LADY   She is spread of late
Into a goodly bulk: good time encounter her!   20
HERMIONE
What wisdom stirs amongst you? Come, sir, now
I am for you again: 'pray you, sit by us,
And tell 's a tale.
MAMILLIUS   Merry, or sad, shall't be?
HERMIONE   As merry as you will.
MAMILLIUS   A sad tale's best for winter: I have one   25
Of sprites and goblins.
HERMIONE   Let's have that, good sir.
Come on, sit down, come on, and do your best
To fright me with your sprites: you're powerful at it.
MAMILLIUS   There was a man –
HERMIONE   Nay, come sit down: then on.
MAMILLIUS   Dwelt by a churchyard: I will tell it softly, 30
Yond crickets shall not hear it.
HERMIONE   Come on then,
And giv't me in mine ear.

Enter LEONTES, *with* ANTIGONUS, Lords *and others.*

LEONTES
Was he met there? his train? Camillo with him?
A LORD   Behind the tuft of pines I met them, never
Saw I men scour so on their way: I ey'd them   35
Even to their ships.
LEONTES   How blest am I
In my just censure! in my true opinion!
Alack, for lesser knowledge! how accurs'd
In being so blest! There may be in the cup
A spider steep'd, and one may drink, depart,   40
And yet partake no venom (for his knowledge
Is not infected); but if one present
Th'abhorr'd ingredient to his eye, make known
How he hath drunk, he cracks his gorge, his sides,
With violent hefts. I have drunk, and seen the spider. 45
Camillo was his help in this, his pandar:
There is a plot against my life, my crown;

All's true that is mistrusted: that false villain,
Whom I employ'd, was pre-employ'd by him:
He has discover'd my design, and I
Remain a pinch'd thing; yea, a very trick
For them to play at will. How came the posterns
So easily open?

A LORD   By his great authority,
Which often hath no less prevail'd than so
On your command.

LEONTES   I know't too well.
Give me the boy: I am glad you did not nurse him:
Though he does bear some signs of me, yet you
Have too much blood in him.

HERMIONE   What is this? sport?

LEONTES
Bear the boy hence, he shall not come about her,
Away with him, and let her sport herself
With that she's big with; for 'tis Polixenes
Has made thee swell thus.

Exit Mamillius, with a Lady.

HERMIONE   But I'd say he had not;
And I'll be sworn you would believe my saying,
How e'er you lean to th' nay-ward.

LEONTES   You, my lords,
Look on her, mark her well: be but about
To say 'she is a goodly lady', and
The justice of your hearts will thereto add
''Tis pity she's not honest, honourable':
Praise her but for this her without-door form
(Which on my faith deserves high speech) and
     straight
The shrug, the hum or ha, these petty brands
That calumny doth use – O, I am out,
That mercy does; for calumny will sear
Virtue itself – these shrugs, these hum's and ha's,
When you have said 'she's goodly', come between,
Ere you can say 'she's honest': but be't known,
From him that has most cause to grieve it should be,
She's an adultress!

HERMIONE   Should a villain say so
(The most replenish'd villain in the world)
He were as much more villain: you, my lord,
Do but mistake.

LEONTES   You have mistook, my lady,
Polixenes for Leontes. O thou thing –
Which I'll not call a creature of thy place,
Lest barbarism, making me the precedent,
Should a like language use to all degrees,
And mannerly distinguishment leave out
Betwixt the prince and beggar. I have said
She's an adultress; I have said with whom:
More; she's a traitor, and Camillo is
A federary with her, and one that knows,
What she should shame to know herself
But with her most vile principal, that she's
A bed-swerver, even as bad as those
That vulgars give bold'st titles; ay, and privy

To this their late escape.

HERMIONE   No, by my life,
Privy to none of this. How will this grieve you,
When you shall come to clearer knowledge, that
You thus have publish'd me! Gentle my lord,
You scarce can right me throughly, then, to say
You did mistake.

LEONTES   No: if I mistake
In those foundations which I build upon,
The centre is not big enough to bear
A school-boy's top. Away with her, to prison!
He who shall speak for her is afar off guilty
But that he speaks.

HERMIONE   There's some ill planet reigns:
I must be patient till the heavens look
With an aspect more favourable. Good my lords,
I am not prone to weeping, as our sex
Commonly are; the want of which vain dew
Perchance shall dry your pities: but I have
That honourable grief lodg'd here which burns
Worse than tears drown: beseech you all, my lords,
With thoughts so qualified as your charities
Shall best instruct you, measure me; and so
The king's will be perform'd.

LEONTES   Shall I be heard?

HERMIONE
Who is't that goes with me? Beseech your highness,
My women may be with me, for you see
My plight requires it. Do not weep, good fools,
There is no cause: when you shall know your
     mistress
Has deserv'd prison, then abound in tears
As I come out: this action I now go on
Is for my better grace. Adieu, my lord:
I never wish'd to see you sorry; now
I trust I shall. My women, come; you have leave.

LEONTES   Go, do our bidding: hence!

Exit Queen, guarded; with Ladies.

A LORD   Beseech your highness, call the queen again.

ANTIGONUS
Be certain what you do, sir, lest your justice
Prove violence, in the which three great ones suffer,
Yourself, your queen, your son.

A LORD   For her, my lord,
I dare my life lay down, and will do't, sir,
Please you t'accept it, that the queen is spotless
I'th' eyes of heaven, and to you – I mean
In this which you accuse her.

ANTIGONUS   If it prove
She's otherwise, I'll keep my stables where
I lodge my wife; I'll go in couples with her;
Than when I feel and see her no farther trust her:
For every inch of woman in the world,
Ay, every dram of woman's flesh is false,
If she be.

LEONTES   Hold your peaces.

A LORD   Good my lord, –

ANTIGONUS   It is for you we speak, not for ourselves: 140
    You are abus'd, and by some putter-on
    That will be damn'd for't: would I knew the villain,
    I would land-damn him. Be she honour-flaw'd,
    I have three daughters: the eldest is eleven;
    The second and the third, nine and some five: 145
    If this prove true, they'll pay for't. By mine honour
    I'll geld 'em all; fourteen they shall not see
    To bring false generations: they are co-heirs,
    And I had rather glib myself, than they
    Should not produce fair issue.
LEONTES   Cease; no more. 150
    You smell this business with a sense as cold
    As is a dead man's nose: but I do see't and feel't,
    As you feel doing thus; and see withal
    The instruments that feel.
ANTIGONUS   If it be so,
    We need no grave to bury honesty: 155
    There's not a grain of it the face to sweeten
    Of the whole dungy earth.
LEONTES   What! lack I credit?
A LORD   I had rather you did lack than I, my lord,
    Upon this ground: and more it would content me
    To have her honour true than your suspicion, 160
    Be blam'd for't how you might.
LEONTES   Why, what need we
    Commune with you of this, but rather follow
    Our forceful instigation? Our prerogative
    Calls not your counsels, but our natural goodness
    Imparts this; which if you, or stupefied, 165
    Or seeming so, in skill, cannot or will not
    Relish a truth, like us, inform yourselves
    We need no more of your advice: the matter,
    The loss, the gain, the ord'ring on't, is all
    Properly ours.
ANTIGONUS   And I wish, my liege, 170
    You had only in your silent judgement tried it,
    Without more overture.
LEONTES   How could that be?
    Either thou art most ignorant by age,
    Or thou wert born a fool. Camillo's flight,
    Added to their familiarity, 175
    (Which was as gross as ever touch'd conjecture,
    That lack'd sight only, nought for approbation
    But only seeing, all other circumstances
    Made up to th' deed) doth push on this proceeding.
    Yet, for a greater confirmation 180
    (For in an act of this importance, 'twere
    Most piteous to be wild), I have dispatch'd in post
    To sacred Delphos, to Apollo's temple,
    Cleomenes and Dion, whom you know
    Of stuff'd sufficiency: now from the Oracle 185
    They will bring all; whose spiritual counsel had,
    Shall stop or spur me. Have I done well?
A LORD   Well done, my lord.
LEONTES   Though I am satisfied, and need no more
    Than what I know, yet shall the Oracle 190

    Give rest to th' minds of others; such as he
    Whose ignorant credulity will not
    Come up to th' truth. So have we thought it good
    From our free person she should be confined,
    Lest that the treachery of the two fled hence 195
    Be left her to perform. Come, follow us;
    We are to speak in public; for this business
    Will raise us all.
ANTIGONUS *[aside]*   To laughter, as I take it,
    If the good truth were known.   *Exeunt.*

2.2   *Enter* PAULINA, *a Gentleman and attendants.*

PAULINA   The keeper of the prison, call to him;
    Let him have knowledge who I am. Good lady,
    No court in Europe is too good for thee;
    What dost thou then in prison?

            Enter Gaoler.

                     Now good sir,
    You know me, do you not?
GAOLER   For a worthy lady 5
    And one who much I honour.
PAULINA   Pray you then,
    Conduct me to the queen.
GAOLER   I may not, madam:
    To the contrary I have express commandment.
PAULINA   Here's ado,
    To lock up honesty and honour from 10
    Th'access of gentle visitors! Is't lawful, pray you,
    To see her women? any of them? Emilia?
GAOLER   So please you, madam,
    To put apart these your attendants, I
    Shall bring Emilia forth.
PAULINA   I pray now, call her. 15
    Withdraw yourselves.
            Exeunt Gentleman and attendants.
GAOLER   And, madam,
    I must be present at your conference.
PAULINA   Well: be't so: prithee.   *Exit Gaoler.*
    Here's such ado to make no stain a stain
    As passes colouring.

          Enter Gaoler, *with* EMILIA.

                Dear gentlewoman, 20
    How fares our gracious lady?
EMILIA   As well as one so great and so forlorn
    May hold together: on her frights and griefs
    (Which never tender lady hath borne greater)
    She is, something before her time, deliver'd. 25
PAULINA   A boy?
EMILIA   A daughter; and a goodly babe,
    Lusty, and like to live: the queen receives
    Much comfort in't; says, 'My poor prisoner,
    I am innocent as you.'
PAULINA   I dare be sworn:
    These dangerous, unsafe lunes i'th' king, beshrew
       them! 30

He must be told on't, and he shall: the office
Becomes a woman best. I'll take't upon me:
If I prove honey-mouth'd, let my tongue blister,
And never to my red-look'd anger be
35 The trumpet any more. Pray you, Emilia,
Commend my best obedience to the queen:
If she dares trust me with her little babe,
I'll show't the king, and undertake to be
Her advocate to th' loud'st. We do not know
40 How he may soften at the sight o'th' child:
The silence often of pure innocence
Persuades, when speaking fails.

EMILIA   Most worthy madam,
Your honour and your goodness is so evident,
That your free undertaking cannot miss
45 A thriving issue: there is no lady living
So meet for this great errand. Please your ladyship
To visit the next room, I'll presently
Acquaint the queen of your most noble offer,
Who but to-day hammer'd of this design,
50 But durst not tempt a minister of honour,
Lest she should be denied.

PAULINA   Tell her, Emilia,
I'll use that tongue I have: if wit flow from't
As boldness from my bosom, let't not be doubted
I shall do good.

EMILIA   Now be you blest for it!
55 I'll to the queen: please you, come something nearer.

GAOLER
Madam, if't please the queen to send the babe,
I know not what I shall incur to pass it,
Having no warrant.

PAULINA   You need not fear it, sir:
This child was prisoner to the womb, and is
60 By law and process of great nature, thence
Free'd and enfranchis'd; not a party to
The anger of the king, nor guilty of
(If any be) the trespass of the queen.

GAOLER   I do believe it.
65 PAULINA   Do not you fear: upon mine honour, I
Will stand betwixt you and danger.   *Exeunt.*

2.3   LEONTES *discovered.*

LEONTES
Nor night, nor day, no rest: it is but weakness
To bear the matter thus: mere weakness. If
The cause were not in being, – part o'th' cause,
She th'adultress: for the harlot king
5 Is quite beyond mine arm, out of the blank
And level of my brain: plot-proof: but she
I can hook to me: say that she were gone,
Given to the fire, a moiety of my rest
Might come to me again.

Enter Servant.

Who's there?

SERVANT   My Lord!
LEONTES   How does the boy?
SERVANT   He took good rest to-night; 10
'Tis hop'd his sickness is discharg'd.
LEONTES   To see his nobleness,
Conceiving the dishonour of his mother!
He straight declin'd, droop'd, took it deeply,
Fasten'd and fix'd the shame on't in himself, 15
Threw off his spirit, his appetite, his sleep,
And downright languish'd. Leave me solely: go,
See how he fares.   *Exit Servant.*
          Fie, fie! no thought of him:
The very thought of my revenges that way
Recoil upon me: in himself too mighty, 20
And in his parties, his alliance; let him be
Until a time may serve. For present vengeance,
Take it on her. Camillo and Polixenes
Laugh at me; make their pastime at my sorrow:
They should not laugh if I could reach them, nor 25
Shall she, within my power.

Enter PAULINA, *carrying a baby, with* ANTIGONUS, Lords
and servants, who try to prevent her.

A LORD   You must not enter.
PAULINA   Nay rather, good my lords, be second to me:
Fear you his tyrannous passion more, alas,
Than the queen's life? a gracious innocent soul,
More free than he is jealous.
ANTIGONUS   That's enough. 30
SERVANT
Madam, he hath not slept to-night, commanded
None should come at him.
PAULINA   Not so hot, good sir;
I come to bring him sleep. 'Tis such as you,
That creep like shadows by him, and do sigh
At each his needless heavings; such as you 35
Nourish the cause of his awaking. I
Do come with words as medicinal as true,
Honest, as either, to purge him of that humour
That presses him from sleep.
LEONTES   What noise there, ho?
PAULINA   No noise, my lord; but needful conference 40
About some gossips for your highness.
LEONTES   How!
Away with that audacious lady! Antigonus,
I charg'd thee that she should not come about me.
I knew she would.
ANTIGONUS   I told her so, my lord,
On your displeasure's peril and on mine, 45
She should not visit you.
LEONTES   What! canst not rule her?
PAULINA   From all dishonesty he can: in this –
Unless he take the course that you have done,
Commit me for committing honour – trust it,
He shall not rule me.
ANTIGONUS   La you now, you hear: 50

When she will take the rein I let her run;
But she'll not stumble.

PAULINA   Good my liege, I come, –
And, I beseech you hear me, who professes
Myself your loyal servant, your physician,
Your most obedient counsellor, yet that dares   55
Less appear so, in comforting your evils,
Than such as most seem yours; – I say, I come
From your good queen.

LEONTES   Good queen!

PAULINA
Good queen, my lord, good queen: I say good queen,
And would by combat make her good, so were I   60
A man, the worst about you.

LEONTES   Force her hence.

PAULINA   Let him that makes but trifles of his eyes
First hand me: on mine own accord I'll off;
But first, I'll do my errand. The good queen
(For she is good) hath brought you forth a daughter;   65
Here 'tis: [*laying down the child*]
                         commends it to your blessing.

LEONTES   Out!
A mankind witch! Hence with her, out o' door:
A most intelligencing bawd!

PAULINA   Not so:
I am as ignorant in that, as you
In so entitling me: and no less honest   70
Than you are mad; which is enough, I'll warrant,
As this world goes, to pass for honest.

LEONTES   Traitors!
Will you not push her out? Give her the bastard,
Thou dotard! thou art woman-tir'd, unroosted
By thy dame Partlet here. Take up the bastard,   75
Take't up, I say; give't to thy crone.

PAULINA   For ever
Unvenerable be thy hands, if thou
Tak'st up the princess, by that forced baseness
Which he has put upon't!

LEONTES   He dreads his wife.

PAULINA
So I would you did; then 'twere past all doubt   80
You'd call your children yours.

LEONTES   A nest of traitors!

ANTIGONUS   I am none, by this good light.

PAULINA   Nor I; nor any
But one that's here, and that's himself; for he,
The sacred honour of himself, his queen's,
His hopeful son's, his babe's, betrays to slander,   85
Whose sting is sharper than the sword's; and will not
(For, as the case now stands, it is a curse
He cannot be compell'd to't) once remove
The root of his opinion, which is rotten
As ever oak or stone was sound.

LEONTES   A callat   90
Of boundless tongue, who late hath beat her
    husband,
And now baits me! This brat is none of mine;

It is the issue of Polixenes.
Hence with it, and together with the dam
Commit them to the fire!

PAULINA   It is yours;   95
And, might we lay th' old proverb to your charge,
So like you, 'tis the worse. Behold, my lords,
Although the print be little, the whole matter
And copy of the father: eye, nose, lip;
The trick of's frown; his forehead; nay, the valley,   100
The pretty dimples of his chin and cheek; his smiles;
The very mould and frame of hand, nail, finger:
And thou, good goddess Nature, which hast made
So like to him that got it, if thou hast
The ordering of the mind too, 'mongst all colours   105
No yellow in't, lest she suspect, as he does,
Her children not her husband's!

LEONTES   A gross hag!
And, lozel, thou art worthy to be hang'd,
That wilt not stay her tongue.

ANTIGONUS   Hang all the husbands
That cannot do that feat, you'll leave yourself   110
Hardly one subject.

LEONTES   Once more, take her hence.

PAULINA   A most unworthy and unnatural lord
Can do no more.

LEONTES   I'll ha' thee burnt.

PAULINA   I care not:
It is an heretic that makes the fire,
Not she which burns in't. I'll not call you tyrant;   115
But this most cruel usage of your queen –
Not able to produce more accusation
Than your own weak-hing'd fancy – something
    savours
Of tyranny, and will ignoble make you,
Yea, scandalous to the world.

LEONTES   On your allegiance,   120
Out of the chamber with her! Were I a tyrant,
Where were her life? she durst not call me so,
If she did know me one. Away with her!

PAULINA
I pray you, do not push me; I'll be gone.
Look to your babe, my lord: 'tis yours: Jove send her   125
A better guiding spirit! What needs these hands?
You, that are thus so tender o'er his follies,
Will never do him good, not one of you.
So, so: farewell; we are gone.   *Exit.*

LEONTES
Thou, traitor, hast set on thy wife to this.   130
My child? away with't! Even thou, that hast
A heart so tender o'er it, take it hence
And see it instantly consum'd with fire;
Even thou, and none but thou. Take it up straight:
Within this hour bring me word 'tis done,   135
And by good testimony, or I'll seize thy life,
With what thou else call'st thine. If thou refuse
And wilt encounter with my wrath, say so;
The bastard brains with these my proper hands

140 Shall I dash out. Go, take it to the fire;
For thou set'st on thy wife.
ANTIGONUS   I did not, sir:
These lords, my noble fellows, if they please,
Can clear me in't.
LORDS   We can: my royal liege,
He is not guilty of her coming hither.
145 LEONTES   You're liars all.
A LORD   Beseech your highness, give us better credit:
We have always truly serv'd you; and beseech'
So to esteem of us: and on our knees we beg
(As recompense of our dear services
150 Past and to come) that you do change this purpose,
Which being so horrible, so bloody, must
Lead on to some foul issue. We all kneel.
LEONTES   I am a feather for each wind that blows:
Shall I live on to see this bastard kneel
155 And call me father? better burn it now
Than curse it then. But be it: let it live.
It shall not neither. You sir, come you hither,
You that have been so tenderly officious
With Lady Margery, your midwife there,
160 To save this bastard's life – for 'tis a bastard,
So sure as this beard's grey – what will you
adventure
To save this brat's life?
ANTIGONUS   Anything, my lord,
That my ability may undergo,
And nobleness impose: at least thus much –
165 I'll pawn the little blood which I have left
To save the innocent: anything possible.
LEONTES   It shall be possible. Swear by this sword
Thou wilt perform my bidding.
ANTIGONUS   I will, my lord.
LEONTES   Mark and perform it: seest thou? for the fail
170 Of any point in't shall not only be
Death to thyself, but to thy lewd-tongu'd wife
(Whom for this time we pardon). We enjoin thee,
As thou art liege-man to us, that thou carry
This female bastard hence, and that thou bear it
175 To some remote and desert place, quite out
Of our dominions; and that there thou leave it
(Without more mercy) to it own protection
And favour of the climate. As by strange fortune
It came to us, I do in justice charge thee,
180 On thy soul's peril and thy body's torture,
That thou commend it strangely to some place
Where chance may nurse or end it. Take it up
ANTIGONUS   I swear to do this; though a present death
Had been more merciful. Come on, poor babe:
185 Some powerful spirit instruct the kites and ravens
To be thy nurses! Wolves and bears, they say,
Casting their savageness aside, have done
Like offices of pity. Sir, be prosperous
In more than this deed does require; and blessing
190 Against this cruelty, fight on thy side,
Poor thing, condemn'd to loss!   *Exit with the child.*

LEONTES   No: I'll not rear
Another's issue.

Enter a Servant.

SERVANT   Please your highness, posts
From those you sent to th'Oracle, are come
An hour since: Cleomenes and Dion,
Being well arriv'd from Delphos, are both landed, 195
Hasting to th'court.
A LORD   So please you, sir, their speed
Hath been beyond account.
LEONTES   Twenty-three days
They have been absent: 'tis good speed; foretells
The great Apollo suddenly will have
The truth of this appear. Prepare you, lords;
Summon a session, that we may arraign 200
Our most disloyal lady; for, as she hath
Been publicly accus'd, so shall she have
A just and open trial. While she lives
My heart will be a burden to me. Leave me.
And think upon my bidding.   *Exeunt.* 205

3.1   *Enter* CLEOMENES *and* DION.

CLEOMENES   The climate's delicate, the air most sweet,
Fertile the isle, the temple much surpassing
The common praise it bears.
DION   I shall report,
For most it caught me, the celestial habits
(Methinks I so should term them), and the reverence 5
Of the grave wearers. O, the sacrifice!
How ceremonious, solemn and unearthly
It was i'th' offering!
CLEOMENES   But of all, the burst
And the ear-deaf'ning voice o'th' Oracle,
Kin to Jove's thunder, so surpris'd my sense, 10
That I was nothing.
DION   If th'event o'th' journey
Prove as successful to the queen, – O be't so! –
As it hath been to us, rare, pleasant, speedy,
The time is worth the use on't.
CLEOMENES   Great Apollo
Turn all to th' best! These proclamations, 15
So forcing faults upon Hermione,
I little like.
DION   The violent carriage of it
Will clear or end the business: when the Oracle
(Thus by Apollo's great divine seal'd up)
Shall the contents discover, something rare 20
Even then will rush to knowledge. Go: fresh horses!
And gracious be the issue.   *Exeunt.*

3.2   *Enter* LEONTES, Lords *and* Officers.

LEONTES
This sessions (to our great grief we pronounce)
Even pushes 'gainst our heart: the party tried
The daughter of a king, our wife, and one

Of us too much belov'd. Let us be clear'd
5 Of being tyrannous, since we so openly
Proceed in justice, which shall have due course,
Even to the guilt or the purgation.
Produce the prisoner.
OFFICER It is his highness' pleasure that the queen
10 Appear in person, here in court. Silence!

Enter HERMIONE *guarded;* PAULINA *and ladies attending.*

LEONTES Read the indictment.
OFFICER [*Reads.*] *Hermione, queen to the worthy Leontes,*
king of Sicilia, thou art here accused and arraigned of
high treason, in committing adultery with Polixenes, king
15 *of Bohemia, and conspiring with Camillo to take away*
the life of our sovereign lord the king, thy royal husband:
the pretence whereof being by circumstances partly laid
open, thou, Hermione, contrary to the faith and allegiance
of a true subject, didst counsel and aid them, for their
20 *better safety, to fly away by night.*
HERMIONE Since what I am to say, must be but that
Which contradicts my accusation, and
The testimony on my part, no other
But what comes from myself, it shall scarce boot me
25 To say 'not guilty': mine integrity,
Being counted falsehood, shall, as I express it,
Be so receiv'd. But thus, if powers divine
Behold our human actions (as they do),
I doubt not then but innocence shall make
30 False accusation blush, and tyranny
Tremble at patience. You, my lord, best know
(Who least will seem to do so) my past life
Hath been as continent, as chaste, as true,
As I am now unhappy; which is more
35 Than history can pattern, though devis'd
And play'd to take spectators. For behold me,
A fellow of the royal bed, which owe
A moiety of the throne, a great king's daughter,
The mother to a hopeful prince, here standing
40 To prate and talk for life and honour 'fore
Who please to come and hear. For life, I prize it
As I weigh grief (which I would spare): for honour,
'Tis a derivative from me to mine,
And only that I stand for. I appeal
45 To your own conscience, sir, before Polixenes
Came to your court, how I was in your grace,
How merited to be so; since he came,
With what encounter so uncurrent I
Have strain'd t'appear thus: if one jot beyond
50 The bound of honour, or in act or will
That way inclining, harden'd be the hearts
Of all that hear me, and my near'st of kin
Cry fie upon my grave!
LEONTES   I ne'er heard yet
That any of these bolder vices wanted
55 Less impudence to gainsay what they did
Than to perform it first.
HERMIONE   That's true enough,
Though 'tis a saying, sir, not due to me.
LEONTES You will not own it.
HERMIONE   More than mistress of
Which comes to me in name of fault, I must not
At all acknowledge. For Polixenes,   60
With whom I am accus'd, I do confess
I lov'd him as in honour he requir'd,
With such a kind of love as might become
A lady like me; with a love, even such,
So, and no other, as yourself commanded: 65
Which, not to have done, I think had been in me
Both disobedience and ingratitude
To you, and toward your friend, whose love had
   spoke,
Even since it could speak, from an infant, freely,
That it was yours. Now, for conspiracy,   70
I know not how it tastes, though it be dish'd
For me to try how: all I know of it,
Is that Camillo was an honest man;
And why he left your court, the gods themselves
(Wotting no more than I) are ignorant.   75
LEONTES You knew of his departure, as you know
What you have underta'en to do in's absence.
HERMIONE Sir,
You speak a language that I understand not:
My life stands in the level of your dreams,   80
Which I'll lay down.
LEONTES   Your actions are my dreams.
You had a bastard by Polixenes,
And I but dream'd it! As you were past all shame
(Those of your fact are so) so past all truth,
Which to deny, concerns more than avails; for as   85
Thy brat hath been cast out, like to itself,
No father owning it (which is, indeed,
More criminal in thee than it), so thou
Shalt feel our justice; in whose easiest passage
Look for no less than death.
HERMIONE   Sir, spare your threats: 90
The bug which you would fright me with, I seek.
To me can life be no commodity;
The crown and comfort of my life, your favour,
I do give lost, for I do feel it gone,
But know not how it went. My second joy,   95
And first-fruits of my body, from his presence
I am barr'd, like one infectious. My third comfort
(Starr'd most unluckily) is from my breast
(The innocent milk in it most innocent mouth)
Hal'd out to murder; myself on every post   100
Proclaim'd a strumpet, with immodest hatred
The child-bed privilege denied, which 'longs
To women of all fashion; lastly, hurried
Here, to this place, i'th' open air, before
I have got strength of limit. Now, my liege,   105
Tell me what blessings I have here alive,
That I should fear to die? Therefore proceed.
But yet hear this: mistake me not: no life,
I prize it not a straw, but for mine honour,

Which I would free: if I shall be condemn'd
Upon surmises, all proofs sleeping else   110
But what your jealousies awake, I tell you
'Tis rigour and not law. Your honours all,
I do refer me to the Oracle:
Apollo be my judge!
A LORD   This your request   115
Is altogether just: therefore bring forth,
And in Apollo's name, his Oracle.

Exeunt certain Officers.

HERMIONE   The Emperor of Russia was my father:
O that he were alive, and here beholding
His daughter's trial! that he did but see   120
The flatness of my misery, yet with eyes
Of pity, not revenge!

Enter Officers, *with* CLEOMENES *and* DION.

OFFICER
You here shall swear upon this sword of justice,
That you, Cleomenes and Dion, have
Been both at Delphos, and from thence have brought   125
This seal'd-up Oracle, by the hand deliver'd
Of great Apollo's priest; and that since then
You have not dared to break the holy seal,
Nor read the secrets in't.
CLEOMENES, DION   All this we swear.
LEONTES   Break up the seals and read.   130
OFFICER   [Reads.]   *Hermione is chaste; Polixenes
blameless; Camillo a true subject; Leontes a jealous
tyrant; his innocent babe truly begotten; and the king shall
live without an heir, if that which is lost be not found.*
LORDS   Now blessed be the great Apollo!
HERMIONE   Praised!   135
LEONTES   Hast thou read truth?
OFFICER   Ay, my lord, even so
As it is here set down.
LEONTES   There is no truth at all i'th' Oracle:
The sessions shall proceed: this is mere falsehood.

Enter Servant.

SERVANT   My lord the king, the king!
LEONTES   What is the business?   140
SERVANT   O sir, I shall be hated to report it!
The prince your son, with mere conceit and fear
Of the queen's speed, is gone.
LEONTES   How! gone?
SERVANT   Is dead.
LEONTES   Apollo's angry, and the heavens themselves
Do strike at my injustice.
[*Hermione faints.*]   How now there?   145
PAULINA   This news is mortal to the queen: look down
And see what death is doing.
LEONTES   Take her hence:
Her heart is but o'ercharg'd: she will recover.
I have too much believ'd mine own suspicion:
Beseech you, tenderly apply to her   150
Some remedies for life.

Exeunt Paulina and Ladies, with Hermione.
                     Apollo, pardon
My great profaneness 'gainst thine Oracle!
I'll reconcile me to Polixenes,
New woo my queen, recall the good Camillo,
Whom I proclaim a man of truth, of mercy: 155
For being transported by my jealousies
To bloody thoughts and to revenge, I chose
Camillo for the minister to poison
My friend Polixenes: which had been done,
But that the good mind of Camillo tardied   160
My swift command; though I with death, and with
Reward, did threaten and encourage him,
Not doing it, and being done. He (most humane
And fill'd with honour) to my kingly guest
Unclasp'd my practice, quit his fortunes here   165
(Which you knew great) and to the certain hazard
Of all incertainties, himself commended,
No richer than his honour: how he glisters
Thorough my rust! and how his piety
Does my deeds make the blacker!

Enter PAULINA.

PAULINA   Woe the while!   170
O cut my lace, lest my heart, cracking it,
Break too!
A LORD   What fit is this, good lady?
PAULINA   What studied torments, tyrant, hast for me?
What wheels? racks? fires? what flaying? boiling?
In leads or oils? What old or newer torture   175
Must I receive, whose every word deserves
To taste of thy most worst? Thy tyranny,
Together working with thy jealousies
(Fancies too weak for boys, too green and idle
For girls of nine), O think what they have done,   180
And then run mad indeed: stark mad! for all
Thy by-gone fooleries were but spices of it.
That thou betray'dst Polixenes, 'twas nothing;
That did but show thee, of a fool, inconstant
And damnable ingrateful: nor was't much,   185
Thou would'st have poison'd good Camillo's honour,
To have him kill a king; poor trespasses,
More monstrous standing by: whereof I reckon
The casting forth to crows thy baby daughter,
To be or none or little; though a devil   190
Would have shed water out of fire, ere done't:
Nor is't directly laid to thee the death
Of the young prince, whose honourable thoughts
(Thoughts high for one so tender) cleft the heart
That could conceive a gross and foolish sire   195
Blemish'd his gracious dam: this is not, no,
Laid to thy answer: but the last – O lords,
When I have said, cry 'woe!' – the queen, the queen,
The sweet'st, dear'st creature's dead: and vengeance
     for't
Not dropp'd down yet.
A LORD   The higher powers forbid!   200

PAULINA

I say she's dead: I'll swear't. If word nor oath
Prevail not, go and see: if you can bring
Tincture, or lustre in her lip, her eye,
Heat outwardly or breath within, I'll serve you
205   As I would do the gods. But, O thou tyrant!
Do not repent these things, for they are heavier
Than all thy woes can stir: therefore betake thee
To nothing but despair. A thousand knees
Ten thousand years together, naked, fasting,
210   Upon a barren mountain, and still winter
In storm perpetual, could not move the gods
To look that way thou wert.

LEONTES   Go on, go on:
Thou canst not speak too much; I have deserv'd
All tongues to talk their bitt'rest.

A LORD   Say no more:
215   Howe'er the business goes, you have made fault
I'th' boldness of your speech.

PAULINA   I am sorry for't:
All faults I make, when I shall come to know them,
I do repent. Alas! I have show'd too much
The rashness of a woman: he is touch'd
220   To th' noble heart. What's gone and what's past help
Should be past grief. Do not receive affliction
At my petition; I beseech you, rather
Let me be punish'd, that have minded you
Of what you should forget. Now, good my liege,
225   Sir, royal sir, forgive a foolish woman:
The love I bore your queen – lo, fool again!
I'll speak of her no more, nor of your children:
I'll not remember you of my own lord
(Who is lost too): take your patience to you,
And I'll say nothing.

230   LEONTES   Thou didst speak but well
When most the truth: which I receive much better
Than to be pitied of thee. Prithee, bring me
To the dead bodies of my queen and son:
One grave shall be for both: upon them shall
235   The causes of their death appear, unto
Our shame perpetual. Once a day I'll visit
The chapel where they lie, and tears shed there
Shall be my recreation. So long as nature
Will bear up with this exercise, so long
240   I daily vow to use it. Come, and lead me
To these sorrows.   *Exeunt.*

3.3 *Enter* ANTIGONUS *with the babe, and a* Mariner.

ANTIGONUS

Thou art perfect, then, our ship hath touch'd upon
The deserts of Bohemia?

MARINER   Ay, my lord, and fear
We have landed in ill time: the skies look grimly,
And threaten present blusters. In my conscience,
5   The heavens with that we have in hand are angry,
And frown upon's.

ANTIGONUS

Their sacred wills be done! Go, get aboard;
Look to thy bark: I'll not be long before
I call upon thee.

MARINER   Make your best haste, and go not   10
Too far i'th' land: 'tis like to be loud weather;
Besides, this place is famous for the creatures
Of prey that keep upon't.

ANTIGONUS   Go thou away:
I'll follow instantly.

MARINER   I am glad at heart
To be so rid o'th' business.   *Exit.*

ANTIGONUS   Come, poor babe: 15
I have heard, but not believ'd, the spirits o'th' dead
May walk again: if such thing be, thy mother
Appear'd to me last night; for ne'er was dream
So like a waking. To me comes a creature,
Sometimes her head on one side, some another;   20
I never saw a vessel of like sorrow,
So fill'd, and so becoming: in pure white robes,
Like very sanctity, she did approach
My cabin where I lay: thrice bow'd before me,
And, gasping to begin some speech, her eyes   25
Became two spouts; the fury spent, anon
Did this break from her: 'Good Antigonus,
Since fate, against thy better disposition,
Hath made thy person for the thrower-out
Of my poor babe, according to thine oath,   30
Places remote enough are in Bohemia,
There weep, and leave it crying: and, for the babe
Is counted lost for ever, Perdita,
I prithee, call't. For this ungentle business,
Put on thee by my lord, thou ne'er shalt see   35
Thy wife Paulina more.' And so, with shrieks,
She melted into air. Affrighted much,
I did in time collect myself, and thought
This was so, and no slumber. Dreams are toys:
Yet for this once, yea, superstitiously,   40
I will be squar'd by this. I do believe
Hermione hath suffer'd death; and that
Apollo would, this being indeed the issue
Of King Polixenes, it should here be laid,
Either for life or death, upon the earth   45
Of its right father. Blossom, speed thee well!
There lie, and there thy character: there these,
Which may, if fortune please, both breed thee, pretty,
And still rest thine. The storm begins: poor wretch,
That for thy mother's fault art thus expos'd   50
To loss and what may follow! Weep I cannot,
But my heart bleeds; and most accurs'd am I
To be by oath enjoin'd to this. Farewell!
The day frowns more and more: thou'rt like to have
A lullaby too rough: I never saw   55
The heavens so dim by day. A savage clamour!
Well may I get aboard! This is the chase:
I am gone for ever!   *Exit, pursued by a bear.*

Enter a Shepherd.

SHEPHERD   I would there were no age between ten and three-and-twenty, or that youth would sleep out the rest; for there is nothing in the between but getting wenches with child, wronging the ancientry, stealing, fighting – Hark you now! Would any but these boiled-brains of nineteen and two-and-twenty hunt this weather? They have scared away two of my best sheep, which I fear the wolf will sooner find than the master: if anywhere I have them, 'tis by the sea-side, browzing of ivy. [*seeing the babe*] Good luck, and't be thy will, what have we here? Mercy on's, a barne! A very pretty barne! A boy or a child, I wonder? A pretty one; a very pretty one. Sure, some scape: though I am not bookish, yet I can read waiting-gentlewoman in the scape. This has been some stair-work, some trunk-work, some behind-door-work: they were warmer that got this than the poor thing is here. I'll take it up for pity: yet I'll tarry till my son come; he hallooed but even now. Whoa-ho-hoa!

Enter Clown.

CLOWN   Hilloa, loa!

SHEPHERD   What, art so near? If thou'lt see a thing to talk on when thou art dead and rotten, come hither. What ail'st thou man?

CLOWN   I have seen two such sights, by sea and by land! But I am not to say it is a sea, for it is now the sky: betwixt the firmament and it you cannot thrust a bodkin's point.

SHEPHERD   Why, boy, how is it?

CLOWN   I would you did but see how it chafes, how it rages, how it takes up the shore! But that's not to the point. O, the most piteous cry of the poor souls! sometimes to see 'em, and not to see 'em: now the ship boring the moon with her main-mast, and anon swallowed with yest and froth, as you 'd thrust a cork into a hogs-head. And then for the land-service, to see how the bear tore out his shoulder-bone, how he cried to me for help and said his name was Antigonus, a nobleman. But to make an end of the ship, to see how the sea flap-dragoned it: but first, how the poor souls roared, and the sea mocked them: and how the poor gentleman roared, and the bear mocked him, both roaring louder than the sea or weather.

SHEPHERD   Name of mercy, when was this, boy?

CLOWN   Now, now: I have not winked since I saw these sights: the men are not yet cold under water, nor the bear half dined on the gentleman: he's at it now.

SHEPHERD   Would I had been by, to have helped the old man!

CLOWN   I would you had been by the ship side, to have helped her: there your charity would have lacked footing.

SHEPHERD   Heavy matters! heavy matters! But look thee here, boy. Now bless thyself: thou met'st with things dying, I with things new-born. Here's a sight for thee; look thee, a bearing-cloth for a squire's child! look thee here; take up, take up, boy; open't. So, let's see: it was told me I should be rich by the fairies. This is some changeling: open't. What's within, boy?

CLOWN   You're a made old man: if the sins of your youth are forgiven you, you're well to live. Gold! all gold!

SHEPHERD   This is fairy gold, boy, and 'twill prove so; up with't, keep it close: home, home, the next way. We are lucky, boy; and to be so still requires nothing but secrecy. Let my sheep go: come, good boy, the next way home.

CLOWN   Go you the next way with your findings. I'll go see if the bear be gone from the gentleman, and how much he hath eaten; they are never curst but when they are hungry: if there be any of him left, I'll bury it.

SHEPHERD   That's a good deed. If thou mayest discern by that which is left of him what he is, fetch me to th' sight of him.

CLOWN   Marry, will I; and you shall help to put him i'th' ground.

SHEPHERD   'Tis a lucky day, boy, and we'll do good deeds on't.   *Exeunt.*

4.1   *Enter* TIME, *the Chorus.*

TIME   I that please some, try all: both joy and terror
Of good and bad, that makes and unfolds error,
Now take upon me, in the name of Time,
To use my wings. Impute it not a crime
To me, or my swift passage, that I slide
O'er sixteen years, and leave the growth untried
Of that wide gap, since it is in my power
To o'erthrow law, and in one self-born hour
To plant and o'erwhelm custom. Let me pass
The same I am, ere ancient'st order was,
Or what is now receiv'd. I witness to
The times that brought them in; so shall I do
To th' freshest things now reigning, and make stale
The glistering of this present, as my tale
Now seems to it. Your patience this allowing,
I turn my glass, and give my scene such growing
As you had slept between: Leontes leaving,
Th'effects of his fond jealousies so grieving
That he shuts up himself, imagine me,
Gentle spectators, that I now may be
In fair Bohemia, and remember well
I mentioned a son o'th' king's, which Florizel
I now name to you; and with speed so pace
To speak of Perdita, now grown in grace
Equal with wond'ring. What of her ensues
I list not prophesy; but let Time's news
Be known when 'tis brought forth. A shepherd's daughter,
And what to her adheres, which follows after,
Is th'argument of Time. Of this allow,
If ever you have spent time worse ere now;

If never, yet that Time himself doth say,
He wishes earnestly you never may.   *Exit.*

4.2   *Enter* POLIXENES *and* CAMILLO.

POLIXENES   I pray thee, good Camillo, be no more
importunate: 'tis a sickness denying thee anything; a
death to grant this.

CAMILLO   It is fifteen years since I saw my country:
though I have, for the most part, been aired abroad, I
desire to lay my bones there. Besides, the penitent
king, my master, hath sent for me; to whose feeling
sorrows I might be some allay (or I o'erween to think
so), which is another spur to my departure.

POLIXENES   As thou lov'st me, Camillo, wipe not out the
rest of thy services by leaving me now: the need I have
of thee, thine own goodness hath made; better not to
have had thee than thus to want thee. Thou, having
made me businesses, which none without thee can
sufficiently manage, must either stay to execute them
thyself, or take away with thee the very services thou
hast done: which if I have not enough considered (as
too much I cannot), to be more thankful to thee shall
be my study; and my profit therein, the heaping
friendships. Of that fatal country, Sicilia, prithee
speak no more; whose very naming punishes me with
the remembrance of that penitent (as thou call'st him)
and reconciled king, my brother; whose loss of his
most precious queen and children are even now to be
afresh lamented. Say to me, when sawest thou the
Prince Florizel, my son? Kings are no less unhappy,
their issue not being gracious, than they are in losing
them when they have approved their virtues.

CAMILLO   Sir, it is three days since I saw the prince.
What his happier affairs may be, are to me unknown:
but I have (missingly) noted, he is of late much retired
from court, and is less frequent to his princely
exercises than formerly he hath appeared.

POLIXENES   I have considered so much, Camillo, and
with some care; so far that I have eyes under my
service which look upon his removedness; from whom
I have this intelligence, that he is seldom from the
house of a most homely shepherd; a man, they say, that
from very nothing, and beyond the imagination of his
neighbours, is grown into an unspeakable estate.

CAMILLO   I have heard, sir, of such a man, who hath a
daughter of most rare note: the report of her is
extended more than can be thought to begin from
such a cottage.

POLIXENES   That's likewise part of my intelligence: but,
I fear, the angle that plucks our son thither. Thou shalt
accompany us to the place, where we will (not
appearing what we are) have some question with the
shepherd; from whose simplicity I think it not uneasy
to get the cause of my son's resort thither. Prithee, be
my present partner in this business, and lay aside the
thoughts of Sicilia.

CAMILLO   I willingly obey your command.

POLIXENES   My best Camillo! We must disguise
ourselves.   *Exeunt.*   55

4.3   *Enter* AUTOLYCUS, *singing.*

When daffodils begin to peer,
    With heigh! the doxy over the dale,
Why then comes in the sweet o'the year,
    For the red blood reigns in the winter's pale.

The white sheet bleaching on the hedge,   5
    With hey! the sweet birds, O how they sing!
Doth set my pugging tooth an edge;
    For a quart of ale is a dish for a king.

The lark, that tirra-lirra chants,
    With heigh! with heigh! the thrush and the jay,   10
Are summer songs for me and my aunts,
    While we lie tumbling in the hay.

I have served Prince Florizel, and in my time wore
three-pile, but now I am out of service.

    But shall I go mourn for that, my dear?   15
        The pale moon shines by night:
    And when I wander here and there,
        I then do most go right.

    If tinkers may have leave to live,
        And bear the sow-skin budget,   20
    Then my account I well may give,
        And in the stocks avouch it.

My traffic is sheets; when the kite builds, look to
lesser linen. My father named me Autolycus; who,
being as I am, littered under Mercury, was likewise a   25
snapper-up of unconsidered trifles. With die and
drab I purchased this caparison, and my revenue is
the silly cheat. Gallows and knock are too powerful on
the highway: beating and hanging are terrors to me:
for the life to come, I sleep out the thought of it. A   30
prize! a prize!

            Enter Clown.

CLOWN   Let me see: every 'leven wether tods; every tod
yields pound and odd shilling: fifteen hundred
shorn, what comes the wool to?

AUTOLYCUS [*aside*]   If the springe hold, the cock's mine.   35

CLOWN   I cannot do 't without counters. Let me see;
what am I to buy for our sheep-shearing feast? Three
pound of sugar, five pound of currants, rice – what
will this sister of mine do with rice? But my father
hath made her mistress of the feast, and she lays it on.   40
She hath made me four-and-twenty nosegays for the
shearers, three-man song-men all, and very good ones;
but they are most of them means and basses but one
puritan amongst them, and he sings psalms to horn-
pipes. I must have saffron to colour the warden pies;   45
mace; dates, none – that's out of my note; nutmegs,

seven; a race or two of ginger, but that I may beg; four pound of prunes, and as many of raisins o'th' sun.

50 AUTOLYCUS   O that ever I was born!

[grovelling on the ground]

CLOWN   I'th' name of me!

AUTOLYCUS   O, help me, help me! pluck but off these rags; and then, death, death!

55 CLOWN   Alack, poor soul! thou hast need of more rags to lay on thee, rather than have these off.

AUTOLYCUS   O sir, the loathsomeness of them offends me more than the stripes I have received, which are mighty ones and millions.

CLOWN   Alas, poor man! a million of beating may come
60   to a great matter.

AUTOLYCUS   I am robbed, sir, and beaten; my money and apparel ta'en from me, and these detestable things put upon me.

CLOWN   What, by a horseman, or a footman?

65 AUTOLYCUS   A footman, sweet sir, a footman.

CLOWN   Indeed, he should be a footman by the garments he has left with thee: if this be a horseman's coat, it hath seen very hot service. Lend me thy hand, I'll help thee: come, lend me thy hand.

70 AUTOLYCUS   O, good sir, tenderly, O!

CLOWN   Alas, poor soul!

AUTOLYCUS   O, good sir, softly, good sir! I fear, sir, my shoulder-blade is out.

CLOWN   How now? canst stand?

75 AUTOLYCUS   Softly, dear sir *[Picks his pocket.]*; good sir, softly. You ha' done me a charitable office.

CLOWN   Dost lack any money? I have a little money for thee.

AUTOLYCUS   No, good sweet sir; no, I beseech you, sir: I
80   have a kinsman not past three-quarters of a mile hence, unto whom I was going: I shall there have money, or anything I want: offer me no money, I pray you; that kills my heart.

CLOWN   What manner of fellow was he that robbed you?

85 AUTOLYCUS   A fellow, sir, that I have known to go about with troll-my-dames: I knew him once a servant of the prince: I cannot tell, good sir, for which of his virtues it was, but he was certainly whipped out of the court.

CLOWN   His vices, you would say; there's no virtue
90   whipped out of the court: they cherish it to make it stay there; and yet it will no more but abide.

AUTOLYCUS   Vices I would say, sir. I know this man well; he hath been since an ape-bearer, then a process-server (a bailiff), then he compassed a motion of the
95   Prodigal Son, and married a tinker's wife within a mile where my land and living lies; and, having flown over many knavish professions, he settled only in rogue. Some call him Autolycus.

CLOWN   Out upon him! prig, for my life, prig: he haunts
100   wakes, fairs, and bear-baitings.

AUTOLYCUS   Very true, sir; he, sir, he: that's the rogue that put me into this apparel.

CLOWN   Not a more cowardly rogue in all Bohemia: if you had but looked big and spit at him, he'd have run.

AUTOLYCUS   I must confess to you, sir, I am no fighter: 105
I am false of heart that way; and that he knew, I warrant him.

CLOWN   How do you now?

AUTOLYCUS   Sweet sir, much better than I was: I can stand, and walk: I will even take my leave of you, and 110 pace softly towards my kinsman's.

CLOWN   Shall I bring thee on the way?

AUTOLYCUS   No, good-faced sir; no, sweet sir.

CLOWN   Then fare-thee-well: I must go buy spices for our sheep-shearing.   *Exit.* 115

AUTOLYCUS   Prosper you, sweet sir! Your purse is not hot enough to purchase your spice. I'll be with you at your sheep-shearing too: if I make not this cheat bring out another, and the shearers prove sheep, let me be unrolled, and my name put in the book of virtue! 120

Song.
Jog on, jog on, the foot-path way,
   And merrily hent the stile-a:
A merry heart goes all the day,
   Your sad tires in a mile-a.   *Exit.*

4.4 *Enter* FLORIZEL *and* PERDITA *followed, at a little
distance, by* Shepherd, Clown; POLIXENES, CAMILLO,
disguised; MOPSA, DORCAS, *servants,
shepherds and shepherdesses.*

FLORIZEL
These your unusual weeds, to each part of you
Do give a life: no shepherdess, but Flora
Peering in April's front. This your sheep-shearing
Is as a meeting of the petty gods,
And you the queen on't.

PERDITA   Sir: my gracious lord,   5
To chide at your extremes, it not becomes me –
O pardon, that I name them! Your high self,
The gracious mark o'th' land, you have obscur'd
With a swain's wearing, and me, poor lowly maid,
Most goddess-like prank'd up: but that our feasts   10
In every mess have folly, and the feeders
Digest it with a custom, I should blush
To see you so attir'd; swoon, I think,
To show myself a glass.

FLORIZEL   I bless the time
When my good falcon made her flight across   15
Thy father's ground.

PERDITA   Now Jove afford you cause!
To me the difference forges dread (your greatness
Hath not been us'd to fear): even now I tremble
To think your father, by some accident
Should pass this way, as you did: O the Fates!   20
How would he look, to see his work, so noble,
Vilely bound up? What would he say? Or how
Should I, in these my borrowed flaunts, behold
The sternness of his presence?

FLORIZEL   Apprehend

25   Nothing but jollity. The gods themselves,
      Humbling their deities to love, have taken
      The shapes of beasts upon them: Jupiter
      Became a bull, and bellow'd; the green Neptune
      A ram, and bleated; and the fire-rob'd god,
30   Golden Apollo, a poor humble swain,
      As I seem now. Their transformations
      Were never for a piece of beauty rarer,
      Nor in a way so chaste, since my desires
      Run not before mine honour, nor my lusts
      Burn hotter than my faith.

35   PERDITA   O, but sir,
      Your resolution cannot hold when 'tis
      Oppos'd, as it must be, by th' power of the king:
      One of these two must be necessities,
      Which then will speak, that you must change this
            purpose,
      Or I my life.

40   FLORIZEL   Thou dearest Perdita,
      With these forc'd thoughts, I prithee, darken not
      The mirth o'th' feast. Or I'll be thine, my fair,
      Or not my father's. For I cannot be
      Mine own, nor anything to any, if
45   I be not thine. To this I am most constant,
      Though destiny say no. Be merry, gentle,
      Strangle such thoughts as these with anything
      That you behold the while. Your guests are coming:
      Lift up your countenance, as it were the day
50   Of celebration of that nuptial which
      We two have sworn shall come.

      PERDITA   O lady Fortune,
      Stand you auspicious!

            [*Shepherd, Clown, Mopsa, Dorcas and others come
            forward, with the disguised Polixenes and Camillo.*]

      FLORIZEL   See, your guests approach:
      Address yourself to entertain them sprightly,
      And let's be red with mirth.

      SHEPHERD
55   Fie, daughter! when my old wife liv'd, upon
      This day she was both pantler, butler, cook,
      Both dame and servant; welcom'd all, serv'd all;
      Would sing her song and dance her turn; now here
      At upper end o'th' table, now i'th' middle;
60   On his shoulder, and his; her face o'fire
      With labour, and the thing she took to quench it
      She would to each one sip. You are retired,
      As if you were a feasted one, and not
      The hostess of the meeting: pray you, bid
65   These unknown friends to's welcome; for it is
      A way to make us better friends, more known.
      Come, quench your blushes, and present yourself
      That which you are, Mistress o'th' Feast. Come on,
      And bid us welcome to your sheep-shearing,
      As your good flock shall prosper.

70   PERDITA [*to Polixenes*]   Sir, welcome:
      It is my father's will I should take on me

      The hostess-ship o'th' day.
      [*to Camillo*]   You're welcome, sir.
      Give me those flowers there, Dorcas. Reverend sirs,
      For you, there's rosemary, and rue; these keep
      Seeming and savour all the winter long: 75
      Grace and remembrance be to you both,
      And welcome to our shearing!

      POLIXENES   Shepherdess –
      A fair one are you – well you fit our ages
      With flowers of winter.

      PERDITA   Sir, the year growing ancient,
      Not yet on summer's death nor on the birth   80
      Of trembling winter, the fairest flowers o'th' season
      Are our carnations and streak'd gillyvors,
      Which some call nature's bastards: of that kind
      Our rustic garden's barren; and I care not
      To get slips of them.

      POLIXENES   Wherefore, gentle maiden,   85
      Do you neglect them?

      PERDITA   For I have heard it said
      There is an art which, in their piedness, shares
      With great creating nature.

      POLIXENES   Say there be;
      Yet nature is made better by no mean
      But nature makes that mean: so, over that art,   90
      Which you say adds to nature, is an art
      That nature makes. You see, sweet maid, we marry
      A gentler scion to the wildest stock,
      And make conceive a bark of baser kind
      By bud of nobler race. This is an art   95
      Which does mend nature – change it rather – but
      The art itself is nature.

      PERDITA   So it is.

      POLIXENES Then make your garden rich in gillyvors,
      And do not call them bastards.

      PERDITA   I'll not put
      The dibble in earth to set one slip of them;   100
      No more than, were I painted, I would wish
      This youth should say 'twere well, and only therefore
      Desire to breed by me. Here's flowers for you:
      Hot lavender, mints, savory, marjoram,
      The marigold, that goes to bed wi'th' sun   105
      And with him rises, weeping: these are flowers
      Of middle summer, and I think they are given
      To men of middle age. Y'are very welcome.
      [*She gives them flowers.*]

      CAMILLO I should leave grazing, were I of your flock,
      And only live by gazing.

      PERDITA   Out, alas!   110
      You'd be so lean that blasts of January
      Would blow you through and through.
      [*to Florizel*]   Now, my fair'st friend,
      I would I had some flowers o'th' spring, that might
      Become your time of day; and yours, and yours,
      [*to Mopsa and the other girls*] That wear upon your
            virgin branches yet   115
      Your maidenheads growing: O Proserpina,

For the flowers now that, frighted, thou let'st fall
From Dis's waggon! daffodils,
That come before the swallow dares, and take
120 The winds of March with beauty; violets, dim,
But sweeter than the lids of Juno's eyes
Or Cytherea's breath; pale primroses,
That die unmarried, ere they can behold
Bright Phoebus in his strength (a malady
125 Most incident to maids); bold oxlips and
The crown imperial; lilies of all kinds,
The flower-de-luce being one. O, these I lack,
To make you garlands of; and my sweet friend,
To strew him o'er and o'er!

FLORIZEL   What, like a corpse?
130 PERDITA   No, like a bank, for love to lie and play on:
Not like a corpse; or if – not to be buried,
But quick, and in mine arms. Come, take your
    flowers:
Methinks I play as I have seen them do
In Whitsun pastorals: sure this robe of mine
Does change my disposition.

135 FLORIZEL   What you do,
Still betters what is done. When you speak, sweet,
I'd have you do it ever: when you sing,
I'd have you buy and sell so, so give alms,
Pray so, and, for the ord'ring your affairs,
140 To sing them too: when you do dance, I wish you
A wave o'th' sea, that you might ever do
Nothing but that, move still, still so,
And own no other function. Each your doing,
So singular in each particular,
145 Crowns what you are doing, in the present deeds,
That all your acts are queens.

PERDITA   O Doricles,
Your praises are too large: but that your youth,
And the true blood which peeps fairly through't,
Do plainly give you out an unstain'd shepherd,
150 With wisdom I might fear, my Doricles,
You woo'd me the false way.

FLORIZEL   I think you have
As little skill to fear as I have purpose
To put you to't. But come; our dance, I pray,
Your hand, my Perdita: so turtles pair
That never mean to part.

155 PERDITA   I'll swear for 'em.
POLIXENES   This is the prettiest low-born lass that ever
Ran on the green-sward: nothing she does or seems
But smacks of something greater than herself,
Too noble for this place.

CAMILLO   He tells her something
160 That makes her blood look out: good sooth, she is
The queen of curds and cream.

CLOWN   Come on, strike up!
DORCAS   Mopsa must be your mistress: marry, garlic to
mend her kissing with!
165 MOPSA   Now, in good time!
CLOWN   Not a word, a word; we stand upon our

manners. Come, strike up!
    [*Music. Here a dance of shepherds and shepherdesses.*]
POLIXENES   Pray, good shepherd, what fair swain is this
Which dances with your daughter?

SHEPHERD   They call him Doricles; and boasts himself 170
To have a worthy feeding: but I have it
Upon his own report and I believe it;
He looks like sooth. He says he loves my daughter:
I think so too; for never gaz'd the moon
Upon the water as he'll stand and read 175
As 'twere my daughter's eyes: and, to be plain,
I think there is not half a kiss to choose
Who loves another best.

POLIXENES   She dances featly.
SHEPHERD   So she does any thing, though I report it
That should be silent. If young Doricles 180
Do light upon her, she shall bring him that
Which he not dreams of.

Enter Servant.

SERVANT   O master! if you did but hear the pedlar at the
door, you would never dance again after a tabor and
pipe; no, the bagpipe could not move you: he sings 185
several tunes, faster than you'll tell money; he utters
them as he had eaten ballads, and all men's ears grew
to his tunes.

CLOWN   He could never come better: he shall come in. I
love a ballad but even too well, if it be doleful matter 190
merrily set down; or a very pleasant thing indeed,
and sung lamentably.

SERVANT   He hath songs for man or woman, of all sizes:
no milliner can so fit his customers with gloves: he has
the prettiest love-songs for maids, so without bawdry 195
(which is strange); with such delicate burdens of
dildoes and fadings, jump her and thump her; and
where some stretch-mouthed rascal would, as it were,
mean mischief and break a foul gap into the matter, he
makes the maid to answer 'Whoop, do me no harm, 200
good man;' puts him off, slights him, with 'Whoop,
do me no harm, good man.'

POLIXENES   This is a brave fellow.
CLOWN   Believe me, thou talkest of an admirable
conceited fellow. Has he any unbraided wares? 205
SERVANT   He hath ribbons of all the colours i'th'
rainbow; points, more than all the lawyers in Bohemia
can learnedly handle, though they come to him by th'
gross; inkles, caddisses, cambrics, lawns: why, he
sings 'em over as they were gods or goddesses; you 210
would think a smock were a she-angel, he so chants
to the sleeve-hand and the work about the square on't.

CLOWN   Prithee bring him in; and let him approach
singing.
PERDITA   Forewarn him, that he use no scurrilous words 215
in's tunes.   *Exit Servant.*
CLOWN   You have of these pedlars that have more in
them than you'd think, sister.
PERDITA   Ay, good brother, or go about to think.

1297

Enter AUTOLYCUS, *singing.*

220   Lawn as white as driven snow,
    Cypress black as e'er was crow,
    Gloves as sweet as damask roses,
    Masks for faces and for noses:
    Bugle-bracelet, necklace amber,
225   Perfume for a lady's chamber:
    Golden quoifs and stomachers
    For my lads to give their dears:
    Pins, and poking-sticks of steel,
    What maids lack from head to heel:
230   Come buy of me, come! come buy! come buy!
    Buy, lads, or else your lasses cry.
    Come buy!

CLOWN   If I were not in love with Mopsa, thou shouldst
take no money of me; but being enthralled as I am, it
235 will also be the bondage of certain ribbons and gloves.

MOPSA   I was promised them against the feast; but they
come not too late now.

DORCAS   He hath promised you more than that, or there
be liars.

240 MOPSA   He hath paid you all he promised you: may be
he has paid you more, which will shame you to give
him again.

CLOWN   Is there no manners left among maids? Will
they wear their plackets where they should bear their
245 faces? Is there not milking-time, when you are going
to bed, or kiln-hole, to whistle of these secrets, but you
must be tittle-tattling before all our guests? 'Tis well
they are whispering: clamor your tongues, and not a
word more.

250 MOPSA   I have done. Come, you promised me a tawdry-
lace and a pair of sweet gloves.

CLOWN   Have I not told thee how I was cozened by the
way and lost all my money?

AUTOLYCUS   And indeed, sir, there are cozeners abroad;
255 therefore it behoves men to be wary.

CLOWN   Fear not thou, man, thou shalt lose nothing
here.

AUTOLYCUS   I hope so, sir; for I have about me many
parcels of charge.

260 CLOWN   What hast here? ballads?

MOPSA   Pray now, buy some: I love a ballad in print, a
life, for then we are sure they are true.

AUTOLYCUS   Here's one, to a very doleful tune, how a
usurer's wife was brought to bed of twenty money-
265 bags at a burden, and how she longed to eat adders'
heads and toads carbonadoed.

MOPSA   Is it true, think you?

AUTOLYCUS   Very true, and but a month old.

DORCAS   Bless me from marrying a usurer!

270 AUTOLYCUS   Here's the midwife's name to't, one
Mistress Tale-porter, and five or six honest wives that
were present. Why should I carry lies abroad?

MOPSA   Pray you now, buy it.

CLOWN   Come on, lay it by: and let's first see moe
ballads: we'll buy the other things anon.   275

AUTOLYCUS   Here's another ballad of a fish that
appeared upon the coast on Wednesday the fourscore
of April, forty thousand fathom above water, and sung
this ballad against the hard hearts of maids: it was
thought she was a woman, and was turned into a cold   280
fish for she would not exchange flesh with one that
loved her. The ballad is very pitiful, and as true.

DORCAS   Is it true too, think you?

AUTOLYCUS   Five justices' hands at it, and witnesses
more than my pack will hold.   285

CLOWN   Lay it by too: another.

AUTOLYCUS   This is a merry ballad, but a very pretty
one.

MOPSA   Let's have some merry ones.

AUTOLYCUS   Why, this is a passing merry one and goes   290
to the tune of 'Two maids wooing a man': there's
scarce a maid westward but she sings it; 'tis in request,
I can tell you.

MOPSA   We can both sing it: if thou'lt bear a part, thou
shalt hear; 'tis in three parts.   295

DORCAS   We had the tune on't a month ago.

AUTOLYCUS   I can bear my part; you must know 'tis my
occupation: have at it with you:

Song.

AUTOLYCUS   Get you hence, for I must go
    Where it fits not you to know.   300
      D. Whither? M. O whither? D. Whither?

MOPSA   It becomes thy oath full well,
    Thou to me thy secrets tell:
      D. Me too: let me go thither.

MOPSA   Or thou goest to th' grange or mill: 305

DORCAS   If to either, thou dost ill.
      A. Neither. D. What neither? A. Neither.

DORCAS   Thou hast sworn my love to be;

MOPSA   Thou hast sworn it more to me:
    Then whither goest? say whither?   310

CLOWN   We'll have this song out anon by ourselves: my
father and the gentlemen are in sad talk, and we'll
not trouble them. Come, bring away thy pack after
me. Wenches, I'll buy for you both. Pedlar, let's have
the first choice. Follow me, girls.   315

Exit with Dorcas and Mopsa.

AUTOLYCUS   And you shall pay well for 'em.

Song.

    Will you buy any tape,
    Or lace for your cape,
  My dainty duck, my dear-a?
    Any silk, any thread,   320
    Any toys for your head,
Of the new'st, and fin'st, fin'st wear-a?
    Come to the pedlar;
    Money's a meddler,

325   That doth utter all men's ware-a.   *Exit.*

Enter Servant.

SERVANT   Master, there is three carters, three shepherds,
three neat-herds, three swine-herds, that have made
themselves all men of hair, they call themselves
Saltiers, and they have a dance which the wenches say
330   is a gallimaufry of gambols, because they are not in't:
but they themselves are o'the mind (if it be not too
rough for some that know little but bowling) it will
please plentifully.

SHEPHERD   Away! we'll none on't: here has been too
335   much homely foolery already. I know, sir, we weary
you.

POLIXENES   You weary those that refresh us: pray, let's
see these four threes of herdsmen.

SERVANT   One three of them, by their own report, sir,
340   hath danced before the king; and not the worst of the
three but jumps twelve foot and a half by th' square.

SHEPHERD   Leave your prating: since these good men
are pleased, let them come in; but quickly now.

SERVANT   Why, they stay at door, sir.

    [*Here a dance of twelve Satyrs.*]

POLIXENES
345   O, father, you'll know more of that hereafter.
    [*to Camillo*] Is it not too far gone? 'Tis time to part
      them.
    He's simple and tells much.
    [*to Florizel*]   How now, fair shepherd!
    Your heart is full of something that does take
    Your mind from feasting. Sooth, when I was young
350   And handed love, as you do, I was wont
    To load my she with knacks: I would have ransack'd
    The pedlar's silken treasury, and have pour'd it
    To her acceptance: you have let him go,
    And nothing marted with him. If your lass
355   Interpretation should abuse, and call this
    Your lack of love or bounty, you were straited
    For a reply, at least if you make a care
    Of happy holding her.

FLORIZEL   Old sir, I know
    She prizes not such trifles as these are:
360   The gifts she looks from me are pack'd and lock'd
    Up in my heart, which I have given already,
    But not deliver'd. O hear me breathe my life
    Before this ancient sir, who, it should seem,
    Hath sometime lov'd. I take thy hand, this hand,
365   As soft as dove's down and as white as it,
    Or Ethiopian's tooth, or the fann'd snow that's bolted
    By th' northern blasts twice o'er.

POLIXENES   What follows this?
    How prettily the young swain seems to wash
    The hand was fair before! I have put you out:
370   But to your protestation: let me hear
    What you profess.

FLORIZEL   Do, and be witness to 't.

POLIXENES   And this my neighbour too?

FLORIZEL   And he, and more
    Than he, and men, the earth, the heavens, and all;
    That were I crown'd the most imperial monarch
    Thereof most worthy, were I the fairest youth   375
    That ever made eye swerve, had force and knowledge
    More than was ever man's, I would not prize them
    Without her love; for her, employ them all;
    Commend them and condemn them to her service,
    Or to their own perdition.

POLIXENES   Fairly offer'd.   380

CAMILLO   This shows a sound affection.

SHEPHERD   But my daughter,
    Say you the like to him?

PERDITA   I cannot speak
    So well, nothing so well; no, nor mean better:
    By th' pattern of mine own thoughts I cut out
    The purity of his.

SHEPHERD   Take hands, a bargain!   385
    And, friends unknown, you shall bear witness to 't.
    I give my daughter to him, and will make
    Her portion equal his.

FLORIZEL   O, that must be
    I'th' virtue of your daughter: one being dead,
    I shall have more than you can dream of yet;   390
    Enough then for your wonder. But come on,
    Contract us 'fore these witnesses.

SHEPHERD   Come, your hand;
    And, daughter, yours.

POLIXENES   Soft, swain, awhile, beseech you;
    Have you a father?

FLORIZEL   I have: but what of him?

POLIXENES   Knows he of this?

FLORIZEL   He neither does nor shall.   395

POLIXENES   Methinks a father
    Is at the nuptial of his son a guest
    That best becomes the table. Pray you once more,
    Is not your father grown incapable
    Of reasonable affairs? is he not stupid   400
    With age and alt'ring rheums? can he speak? hear?
    Know man from man? dispute his own estate?
    Lies he not bed-rid? and again does nothing
    But what he did being childish?

FLORIZEL   No, good sir;
    He has his health, and ampler strength indeed   405
    Than most have of his age.

POLIXENES   By my white beard,
    You offer him, if this be so, a wrong
    Something unfilial: reason my son
    Should choose himself a wife, but as good reason
    The father (all whose joy is nothing else   410
    But fair posterity) should hold some counsel
    In such a business.

FLORIZEL   I yield all this;
    But for some other reasons, my grave sir,
    Which 'tis not fit you know, I not acquaint

My father of this business.

POLIXENES   Let him know't.

FLORIZEL   He shall not.

POLIXENES   Prithee, let him.

FLORIZEL   No, he must not.

SHEPHERD

Let him, my son: he shall not need to grieve
At knowing of thy choice.

FLORIZEL   Come, come, he must not.
Mark our contract.

POLIXENES   Mark your divorce, young sir,
[*discovering himself*]
Whom son I dare not call; thou art too base
To be acknowledg'd: thou a sceptre's heir,
That thus affects a sheep-hook! Thou, old traitor,
I am sorry that by hanging thee I can
But shorten thy life one week. And thou, fresh piece
Of excellent witchcraft, who, of force, must know
The royal fool thou cop'st with, –

SHEPHERD   O, my heart!

POLIXENES

I'll have thy beauty scratch'd with briers and made
More homely than thy state. For thee, fond boy,
If I may ever know thou dost but sigh
That thou no more shalt see this knack (as never
I mean thou shalt), we'll bar thee from succession;
Not hold thee of our blood, no, not our kin,
Farre than Deucalion off: mark thou my words!
Follow us to the court. Thou churl, for this time,
Though full of our displeasure, yet we free thee
From the dead blow of it. And you, enchantment, –
Worthy enough a herdsman; yea, him too,
That makes himself, but for our honour therein,
Unworthy thee. If ever henceforth thou
These rural latches to his entrance open,
Or hoop his body more with thy embraces,
I will devise a death as cruel for thee
As thou art tender to't.   *Exit.*

PERDITA   Even here, undone,
I was not much afeard; for once or twice
I was about to speak, and tell him plainly,
The selfsame sun that shines upon his court
Hides not his visage from our cottage, but
Looks on alike. Will't please you, sir, be gone?
I told you what would come of this: beseech you,
Of your own state take care: this dream of mine –
Being now awake, I'll queen it no inch farther,
But milk my ewes, and weep.

CAMILLO   Why, how now, father!
Speak ere thou diest.

SHEPHERD   I cannot speak, nor think,
Nor dare to know that which I know. O sir!
You have undone a man of fourscore three,
That thought to fill his grave in quiet; yea,
To die upon the bed my father died,
To lie close by his honest bones: but now
Some hangman must put on my shroud and lay me

Where no priest shovels in dust. O cursed wretch,   460
That knew'st this was the prince, and wouldst
   adventure
To mingle faith with him! Undone! undone!
If I might die within this hour, I have liv'd
To die when I desire.   *Exit.*

FLORIZEL   Why look you so upon me?
I am but sorry, not afeard; delay'd,   465
But nothing alter'd: what I was, I am;
More straining on for plucking back; not following
My leash unwillingly.

CAMILLO   Gracious my lord,
You know your father's temper: at this time
He will allow no speech (which, I do guess,   470
You do not purpose to him) and as hardly
Will he endure your sight as yet, I fear:
Then, till the fury of his highness settle,
Come not before him.

FLORIZEL   I not purpose it.
I think – Camillo?

CAMILLO   Even he, my lord.   475

PERDITA   How often have I told you 'twould be thus!
How often said, my dignity would last
But till 'twere known!

FLORIZEL   It cannot fail, but by
The violation of my faith; and then
Let nature crush the sides o'th' earth together,   480
And mar the seeds within! Lift up thy looks:
From my succession wipe me, father; I
Am heir to my affection.

CAMILLO   Be advis'd.

FLORIZEL   I am: and by my fancy. If my reason
Will thereto be obedient, I have reason;   485
If not, my senses, better pleas'd with madness,
Do bid it welcome.

CAMILLO   This is desperate, sir.

FLORIZEL   So call it: but it does fulfill my vow;
I needs must think it honesty. Camillo,
Not for Bohemia, nor the pomp that may   490
Be thereat glean'd: for all the sun sees, or
The close earth wombs, or the profound seas hides
In unknown fathoms, will I break my oath
To this my fair belov'd. Therefore, I pray you,
As you have ever been my father's honour'd friend, 495
When he shall miss me, – as, in faith, I mean not
To see him any more, – cast your good counsels
Upon his passion: let myself and fortune
Tug for the time to come. This you may know,
And so deliver, I am put to sea   500
With her whom here I cannot hold on shore;
And most opportune to our need, I have
A vessel rides fast by, but not prepar'd
For this design. What course I mean to hold
Shall nothing benefit your knowledge, nor   505
Concern me the reporting.

CAMILLO   O my lord,
I would your spirit were easier for advice,

Or stronger for your need.

FLORIZEL   Hark, Perdita. [*drawing her aside*]
[*to Camillo*] I'll hear you by and by.

CAMILLO   He's irremoveable,
510 Resolv'd for flight. Now were I happy, if
His going I could frame to serve my turn,
Save him from danger, do him love and honour,
Purchase the sight again of dear Sicilia
And that unhappy king, my master, whom
515 I so much thirst to see.

FLORIZEL   Now good Camillo;
I am so fraught with curious business that
I leave out ceremony.

CAMILLO   Sir, I think
You have heard of my poor services, i'th' love
That I have borne your father?

FLORIZEL   Very nobly
520 Have you deserv'd: it is my father's music
To speak your deeds, not little of his care
To have them recompens'd as thought on.

CAMILLO   Well, my lord,
If you may please to think I love the king,
And through him what's nearest to him, which is
525 Your gracious self, embrace but my direction,
If your more ponderous and settled project
May suffer alteration. On mine honour,
I'll point you where you shall have such receiving
As shall become your highness; where you may
530 Enjoy your mistress; from the whom, I see,
There's no disjunction to be made, but by –
As heavens forefend! – your ruin. Marry her,
And with my best endeavours in your absence
Your discontenting father strive to qualify
And bring him up to liking.

FLORIZEL   How, Camillo,
535 May this, almost a miracle, be done?
That I may call thee something more than man
And after that trust to thee.

CAMILLO   Have you thought on
A place whereto you'll go?

FLORIZEL   Not any yet:
540 But as th' unthought-on accident is guilty
To what we wildly do, so we profess
Ourselves to be the slaves of chance, and flies
Of every wind that blows.

CAMILLO   Then list to me:
This follows, if you will not change your purpose,
545 But undergo this flight; make for Sicilia,
And there present yourself and your fair princess
(For so I see she must be) 'fore Leontes:
She shall be habited as it becomes
The partner of your bed. Methinks I see
550 Leontes opening his free arms and weeping
His welcomes forth; asks thee there 'Son,
          forgiveness!'
As 'twere i'th' father's person; kisses the hands
Of your fresh princess; o'er and o'er divides him

'Twixt his unkindness and his kindness; th'one
He chides to hell, and bids the other grow   555
Faster than thought or time.

FLORIZEL   Worthy Camillo,
What colour for my visitation shall I
Hold up before him?

CAMILLO   Sent by the king your father
To greet him and to give him comforts. Sir,
The manner of your bearing towards him, with   560
What you (as from your father) shall deliver,
Things known betwixt us three, I'll write you down:
The which shall point you forth at every sitting
What you must say; that he shall not perceive
But that you have your father's bosom there   565
And speak his very heart.

FLORIZEL   I am bound to you:
There is some sap in this.

CAMILLO   A course more promising
Than a wild dedication of yourselves
To unpath'd waters, undream'd shores; most certain
To miseries enough: no hope to help you,   570
But as you shake off one, to take another:
Nothing so certain as your anchors, who
Do their best office if they can but stay you
Where you'll be loath to be. Besides, you know
Prosperity's the very bond of love,   575
Whose fresh complexion and whose heart together
Affliction alters.

PERDITA   One of these is true:
I think affliction may subdue the cheek,
But not take in the mind.

CAMILLO   Yea? say you so?
There shall not, at your father's house, these seven
          years   580
Be born another such.

FLORIZEL   My good Camillo,
She is as forward of her breeding as
She is i'th' rear 'our birth.

CAMILLO   I cannot say 'tis pity
She lacks instructions, for she seems a mistress
To most that teach.

PERDITA   Your pardon, sir; for this   585
I'll blush you thanks.

FLORIZEL   My prettiest Perdita!
But O, the thorns we stand upon! Camillo,
Preserver of my father, now of me,
The medicine of our house, how shall we do?
We are not furnish'd like Bohemia's son,   590
Nor shall appear in Sicilia.

CAMILLO   My lord,
Fear none of this. I think you know my fortunes
Do all lie there: it shall be so my care
To have you royally appointed, as if
The scene you play were mine. For instance, sir,   595
That you may know you shall not want, – one word.
[*They talk aside.*]

Enter AUTOLYCUS.

AUTOLYCUS   Ha, ha! what a fool Honesty is! and Trust,
his sworn brother, a very simple gentleman! I have
sold all my trumpery: not a counterfeit stone, not a
ribbon, glass, pomander, brooch, table-book, ballad,
knife, tape, glove, shoe-tie, bracelet, horn-ring, to keep
my pack from fasting: they throng who should buy
first, as if my trinkets had been hallowed and brought
a benediction to the buyer: by which means I saw
whose purse was best in picture; and what I saw, to my
good use I remembered. My clown (who wants but
something to be a reasonable man) grew so in love
with the wenches' song, that he would not stir his
pettitoes till he had both tune and words; which so
drew the rest of the herd to me, that all their other
senses stuck in ears: you might have pinched a placket,
it was senseless; 'twas nothing to geld a codpiece of a
purse; I would have filed keys off that hung in chains:
no hearing, no feeling, but my sir's song, and admiring
the nothing of it. So that in this time of lethargy I
picked and cut most of their festival purses; and had
not the old man come in with a whoo-bub against his
daughter and the king's son, and scared my choughs
from the chaff, I had not left a purse alive in the
whole army.
[*Camillo, Florizel and Perdita come forward.*]

CAMILLO
  Nay, but my letters, by this means being there
  So soon as you arrive, shall clear that doubt.

FLORIZEL
  And those that you'll procure from King Leontes?

CAMILLO   Shall satisfy your father.

PERDITA   Happy be you!
  All that you speak shows fair.

CAMILLO [*seeing Autolycus*]   Who have we here?
  We'll make an instrument of this; omit
  Nothing may give us aid.

AUTOLYCUS   If they have overheard me now, – why,
hanging.

CAMILLO   How now, good fellow! why shakest thou so?
Fear not, man; here's no harm intended to thee.

AUTOLYCUS   I am a poor fellow, sir.

CAMILLO   Why, be so still; here's nobody will steal that
from thee: yet for the outside of thy poverty we must
make an exchange; therefore discase thee instantly,
– thou must think there's a necessity in't – and change
garments with this gentleman: though the
pennyworth on his side be the worst, yet hold thee,
there's some boot.

AUTOLYCUS   I am a poor fellow, sir. [*aside*] I know ye
well enough.

CAMILLO   Nay, prithee, dispatch: the gentleman is half
flayed already.

AUTOLYCUS   Are you in earnest, sir? [*aside*] I smell the
trick on't.

FLORIZEL   Dispatch, I prithee.

AUTOLYCUS   Indeed, I have had earnest; but I cannot
with conscience take it.

CAMILLO   Unbuckle, unbuckle.
[*Florizel and Autolycus exchange garments.*]
  Fortunate mistress, – let my prophecy
  Come home to ye! – you must retire yourself
  Into some covert: take your sweetheart's hat
  And pluck it o'er your brows, muffle your face,
  Dismantle you, and (as you can) disliken
  The truth of your own seeming; that you may
  (For I do fear eyes over) to shipboard
  Get undescried.

PERDITA   I see the play so lies
  That I must bear a part.

CAMILLO   No remedy.
  Have you done there?

FLORIZEL   Should I now meet my father
  He would not call me son.

CAMILLO   Nay, you shall have no hat.
[*giving it to Perdita*]
  Come, lady, come. Farewell, my friend.

AUTOLYCUS   Adieu, sir.

FLORIZEL   O Perdita, what have we twain forgot?
  Pray you, a word. [*They draw aside.*]

CAMILLO   What I do next, shall be to tell the king
  Of this escape and whither they are bound;
  Wherein my hope is I shall so prevail
  To force him after: in whose company
  I shall re-view Sicilia, for whose sight
  I have a woman's longing.

FLORIZEL   Fortune speed us!
  Thus we set on, Camillo, to th' sea-side.

CAMILLO   The swifter speed, the better.
              Exeunt Florizel, Perdita and Camillo.

AUTOLYCUS   I understand the business, I hear it. To
have an open ear, a quick eye, and a nimble hand, is
necessary for a cut-purse; a good nose is requisite also,
to smell out work for the other senses. I see this is the
time that the unjust man doth thrive. What an
exchange had this been without boot! What a boot is
here, with this exchange! Sure the gods do this year
connive at us, and we may do any thing extempore.
The prince himself is about a piece of iniquity
(stealing away from his father with his clog at his
heels): if I thought it were a piece of honesty to
acquaint the king withal, I would not do't: I hold it
the more knavery to conceal it; and therein am I
constant to my profession.

Enter Clown *and* Shepherd.

Aside, aside; here is more matter for a hot brain:
every lane's end, every shop, church, session, hanging,
yields a careful man work.

CLOWN   See, see; what a man you are now! There is no
other way but to tell the king she's a changeling, and
none of your flesh and blood.

SHEPHERD   Nay, but hear me.

CLOWN Nay, but hear me.

SHEPHERD Go to, then.

695 CLOWN She being none of your flesh and blood, your flesh and blood has not offended the king; and so your flesh and blood is not to be punished by him. Show those things you found about her (those secret things, all but what she has with her): this being
700 done, let the law go whistle: I warrant you.

SHEPHERD I will tell the king all, every word, yea, and his son's pranks too; who, I may say, is no honest man, neither to his father nor to me, to go about to make me the king's brother-in-law.

705 CLOWN Indeed, brother-in-law was the farthest off you could have been to him and then your blood had been the dearer by I know how much an ounce.

AUTOLYCUS [*aside*] Very wisely, puppies!

SHEPHERD Well, let us to the king: there is that in this
710 fardel will make him scratch his beard.

AUTOLYCUS [*aside*] I know not what impediment this complaint may be to the flight of my master.

CLOWN Pray heartily he be at' palace.

AUTOLYCUS [*aside*] Though I am not naturally honest, I
715 am so sometimes by chance; let me pocket up my pedlar's excrement. [*Takes off his false beard.*] How now, rustics! whither are you bound?

SHEPHERD To th' palace, and it like your worship.

AUTOLYCUS Your affairs there, what, with whom, the
720 condition of that fardel, the place of your dwelling, your names, your ages, of what having, breeding, and any thing that is fitting to be known, discover!

CLOWN We are but plain fellows, sir.

AUTOLYCUS A lie; you are rough and hairy. Let me have
725 no lying: it becomes none but tradesmen, and they often give us soldiers the lie; but we pay them for it with stamped coin, not stabbing steel; therefore they do not give us the lie.

CLOWN Your worship had like to have given us one, if
730 you had not taken yourself with the manner.

SHEPHERD Are you a courtier, and't like you, sir?

AUTOLYCUS Whether it like me or no, I am a courtier. Seest thou not the air of the court in these enfoldings? hath not my gait in it the measure of the court?
735 receives not thy nose court-odour from me? reflect I not on thy baseness, court-contempt? Think'st thou, for that I insinuate, or toaze from thee thy business, I am therefore no courtier? I am courtier *cap-a-pe*; and one that will either push on or pluck back thy business
740 there: whereupon I command thee to open thy affair.

SHEPHERD My business, sir, is to the king.

AUTOLYCUS What advocate hast thou to him?

SHEPHERD I know not, and't like you.

CLOWN Advocate's the court-word for a pheasant: say
745 you have none.

SHEPHERD None, sir; I have no pheasant, cock nor hen.

AUTOLYCUS
How blessed are we that are not simple men!
Yet nature might have made me as these are;

Therefore I will not disdain.

CLOWN This cannot be but a great courtier. 750

SHEPHERD His garments are rich, but he wears them not handsomely.

CLOWN He seems to be the more noble in being fantastical: a great man, I'll warrant; I know by the picking on's teeth. 755

AUTOLYCUS The fardel there? What's i'th' fardel? Wherefore that box?

SHEPHERD Sir, there lies such secrets in this fardel and box, which none must know but the king; and which he shall know within this hour, if I may come to th' 760 speech of him.

AUTOLYCUS Age, thou hast lost thy labour.

SHEPHERD Why, sir?

AUTOLYCUS The king is not at the palace; he is gone aboard a new ship to purge melancholy and air 765 himself: for, if thou be'st capable of things serious, thou must know the king is full of grief.

SHEPHERD So 'tis said, sir; about his son, that should have married a shepherd's daughter.

AUTOLYCUS If that shepherd be not in hand-fast, let 770 him fly: the curses he shall have, the tortures he shall feel, will break the back of man, the heart of monster.

CLOWN Think you so, sir?

AUTOLYCUS Not he alone shall suffer what wit can make heavy and vengeance bitter; but those that are 775 germane to him, though removed fifty times, shall all come under the hangman: which, though it be great pity, yet it is necessary. An old sheep-whistling rogue, a ram-tender, to offer to have his daughter come into grace! Some say he shall be stoned; but that death is 780 too soft for him, say I. Draw our throne into a sheepcote! All deaths are too few, the sharpest too easy.

CLOWN Has the old man e'er a son, sir, do you hear, and't like you, sir? 785

AUTOLYCUS He has a son, who shall be flayed alive, then 'nointed over with honey, set on the head of a wasps' nest, then stand till he be three quarters and a dram dead; then recovered again with aqua-vitae or some other hot infusion; then, raw as he is, and in the 790 hottest day prognostication proclaims, shall he be set against a brick wall, the sun looking with a southward eye upon him, where he is to behold him, with flies blown to death. But what talk we of these traitorly rascals, whose miseries are to be smiled at, 795 their offences being so capital? Tell me (for you seem to be honest plain men) what you have to the king: being something gently considered, I'll bring you where he is aboard, tender your persons to his presence, whisper him in your behalfs; and if it be in 800 man, besides the king, to effect your suits, here is man shall do it.

CLOWN He seems to be of great authority: close with him, give him gold; and though authority be a stubborn bear, yet he is oft led by the nose with gold: 805

show the inside of your purse to the outside of his
hand, and no more ado. Remember 'stoned', and
'flayed alive'!

810 SHEPHERD   And't please you, sir, to undertake the
business for us, here is that gold I have: I'll make it as
much more and leave this young man in pawn till I
bring it you.

AUTOLYCUS   After I have done what I promised?

SHEPHERD   Ay, sir.

815 AUTOLYCUS   Well, give me the moiety. Are you a party
in this business?

CLOWN   In some sort, sir: but though my case be a
pitiful one, I hope I shall not be flayed out of it.

AUTOLYCUS   O, that's the case of the shepherd's son:
820 hang him, he'll be made an example.

CLOWN   Comfort, good comfort! We must to the king
and show our strange sights: he must know 'tis none of
your daughter nor my sister; we are gone else. Sir, I
will give you as much as this old man does when the
825 business is performed, and remain, as he says, your
pawn till it be brought you.

AUTOLYCUS   I will trust you. Walk before toward the
sea-side; go on the right hand: I will but look upon the
hedge and follow you.

830 CLOWN   We are blest in this man, as I may say, even
blest.

SHEPHERD   Let's before, as he bids us: he was provided
to do us good.   *Exeunt Shepherd and Clown.*

AUTOLYCUS   If I had a mind to be honest, I see Fortune
835 would not suffer me: she drops booties in my mouth.
I am courted now with a double occasion – gold, and a
means to do the prince my master good; which who
knows how that may turn back to my advancement? I
will bring these two moles, these blind ones, aboard
840 him: if he think it fit to shore them again and that the
complaint they have to the king concerns him nothing,
let him call me rogue for being so far officious; for I
am proof against that title and what shame else
belongs to't. To him will I present them: there may be
845 matter in it.   *Exit.*

5.1   *Enter* LEONTES, CLEOMENES, DION, PAULINA
and servants.

CLEOMENES
Sir, you have done enough, and have perform'd
A saint-like sorrow: no fault could you make,
Which you have not redeem'd; indeed, paid down
More penitence than done trespass: at the last,
5 Do as the heavens have done, forget your evil;
With them, forgive yourself.

LEONTES   Whilst I remember
Her, and her virtues, I cannot forget
My blemishes in them, and so still think of
The wrong I did myself: which was so much,
10 That heirless it hath made my kingdom, and
Destroy'd the sweet'st companion that e'er man

Bred his hopes out of.

PAULINA   True, too true, my lord:
If, one by one, you wedded all the world,
Or from the all that are took something good,
To make a perfect woman, she you kill'd   15
Would be unparallel'd.

LEONTES   I think so. Kill'd!
She I kill'd! I did so: but thou strik'st me
Sorely, to say I did: it is as bitter
Upon thy tongue as in my thought. Now, good now,
Say so but seldom.

CLEOMENES   Not at all, good lady: 20
You might have spoken a thousand things that would
Have done the time more benefit and grac'd
Your kindness better.

PAULINA   You are one of those
Would have him wed again.

DION   If you would not so,
You pity not the state, nor the remembrance   25
Of his most sovereign name; consider little,
What dangers, by his highness' fail of issue,
May drop upon his kingdom, and devour
Incertain lookers on. What were more holy
Than to rejoice the former queen is well?   30
What holier than, for royalty's repair,
For present comfort, and for future good,
To bless the bed of majesty again
With a sweet fellow to't?

PAULINA   There is none worthy,
Respecting her that's gone. Besides, the gods   35
Will have fulfill'd their secret purposes;
For has not the divine Apollo said,
Is't not the tenor of his Oracle,
That King Leontes shall not have an heir,
Till his lost child be found? which, that it shall,   40
Is all as monstrous to our human reason
As my Antigonus to break his grave
And come again to me; who, on my life,
Did perish with the infant. 'Tis your counsel
My lord should to the heavens be contrary,   45
Oppose against their wills.
[to Leontes]   Care not for issue;
The crown will find an heir. Great Alexander
Left his to th' worthiest; so his successor
Was like to be the best.

LEONTES   Good Paulina,
Who hast the memory of Hermione,   50
I know, in honour, – O, that ever I
Had squar'd me to thy counsel! Then, even now,
I might have look'd upon my queen's full eyes,
Have taken treasure from her lips, –

PAULINA   And left them
More rich for what they yielded.

LEONTES   Thou speak'st truth.   55
No more such wives; therefore, no wife: one worse,
And better us'd, would make her sainted spirit
Again possess her corpse, and on this stage

(Were we offenders now) appear soul-vex'd,
And begin, 'Why to me?'

60 PAULINA   Had she such power,
She had just cause.

LEONTES   She had; and would incense me
To murder her I married.

PAULINA   I should so:
Were I the ghost that walk'd, I'd bid you mark
Her eye, and tell me for what dull part in't
65 You chose her: then I'd shriek, that even your ears
Should rift to hear me; and the words that follow'd
Should be 'Remember mine.'

LEONTES   Stars, stars,
And all eyes else, dead coals! Fear thou no wife;
I'll have no wife, Paulina.

PAULINA   Will you swear
70 Never to marry, but by my free leave?

LEONTES   Never, Paulina; so be blest my spirit!

PAULINA
Then, good my lords, bear witness to his oath.

CLEOMENES   You tempt him over-much.

PAULINA   Unless another,
As like Hermione as is her picture,
Affront his eye.

CLEOMENES   Good madam, –

75 PAULINA   I have done.
Yet, if my lord will marry, – if you will, sir;
No remedy but you will, – give me the office
To choose you a queen: she shall not be so young
As was your former, but she shall be such
80 As, walk'd your first queen's ghost, it should take joy
To see her in your arms.

LEONTES   My true Paulina,
We shall not marry till thou bid'st us.

PAULINA   That
Shall be when your first queen's again in breath:
Never till then.

Enter a Servant.

85 SERVANT   One that gives out himself Prince Florizel,
Son of Polixenes, with his princess (she
The fairest I have yet beheld) desires access
To your high presence.

LEONTES   What with him? he comes not
Like to his father's greatness: his approach
90 (So out of circumstance, and sudden) tells us
'Tis not a visitation fram'd, but forc'd
By need and accident. What train?

SERVANT   But few,
And those but mean.

LEONTES   His princess, say you, with him?

SERVANT   Ay, the most peerless piece of earth, I think,
That e'er the sun shone bright on.

95 PAULINA   O Hermione,
As every present time doth boast itself
Above a better gone, so must thy grave
Give way to what's seen now! Sir, you yourself

Have said, and writ so; but your writing now
Is colder than that theme: 'She had not been, 100
Nor was not to be equall'd'; – thus your verse
Flow'd with her beauty once: 'tis shrewdly ebb'd,
To say you have seen a better.

SERVANT   Pardon, madam:
The one I have almost forgot, – your pardon, –
The other, when she has obtain'd your eye, 105
Will have your tongue too. This is a creature,
Would she begin a sect, might quench the zeal
Of all professors else; make proselytes
Of who she but bid follow.

PAULINA   How! not women?

SERVANT   Women will love her, that she is a woman 110
More worth than any man; men, that she is
The rarest of all women.

LEONTES   Go, Cleomenes;
Yourself, assisted with your honour'd friends,
Bring them to our embracement.

Exeunt Cleomenes and others.
                    Still, 'tis strange
He thus should steal upon us.

PAULINA   Had our prince 115
(Jewel of children) seen this hour, he had pair'd
Well with this lord: there was not full a month
Between their births.

LEONTES   Prithee, no more; cease; thou know'st
He dies to me again, when talk'd of: sure,
When I shall see this gentleman, thy speeches 120
Will bring me to consider that which may
Unfurnish me of reason. They are come.

Enter FLORIZEL, PERDITA, CLEOMENES *and others.*

Your mother was most true to wedlock, prince;
For she did print your royal father off,
Conceiving you. Were I but twenty-one, 125
Your father's image is so hit in you,
His very air, that I should call you brother,
As I did him, and speak of something wildly
By us perform'd before. Most dearly welcome!
And your fair princess, – goddess! – O, alas! 130
I lost a couple, that 'twixt heaven and earth
Might thus have stood, begetting wonder, as
You, gracious couple, do: and then I lost –
All mine own folly – the society,
Amity too, of your brave father, whom 135
(Though bearing misery) I desire my life
Once more to look on him.

FLORIZEL   By his command
Have I here touch'd Sicilia, and from him
Give you all greetings that a king (at friend)
Can send his brother: and, but infirmity 140
(Which waits upon worn times) hath something
    seiz'd
His wish'd ability, he had himself
The lands and waters 'twixt your throne and his
Measur'd, to look upon you; whom he loves

145 (He bade me say so) more than all the sceptres
And those that bear them living.
LEONTES   O my brother, –
Good gentleman! – the wrongs I have done thee stir
Afresh within me; and these thy offices,
So rarely kind, are as interpreters
150 Of my behind-hand slackness! Welcome hither,
As is the spring to th'earth. And hath he too
Expos'd this paragon to th' fearful usage
(At least ungentle) of the dreadful Neptune,
To greet a man not worth her pains, much less
Th'adventure of her person?
155 FLORIZEL   Good my lord,
She came from Libya.
LEONTES   Where the warlike Smalus,
That noble honour'd lord, is fear'd and lov'd?
FLORIZEL
Most royal sir, from thence; from him, whose
     daughter
His tears proclaim'd his, parting with her: thence,
160 A prosperous south-wind friendly, we have cross'd,
To execute the charge my father gave me
For visiting your highness: my best train
I have from your Sicilian shores dismiss'd;
Who for Bohemia bend, to signify
165 Not only my success in Libya, sir,
But my arrival, and my wife's, in safety
Here, where we are.
LEONTES   The blessed gods
Purge all infection from our air whilst you
Do climate here! You have a holy father,
170 A graceful gentleman; against whose person
(So sacred as it is) I have done sin,
For which, the heavens (taking angry note)
Have left me issueless: and your father's blest
(As he from heaven merits it) with you,
175 Worthy his goodness. What might I have been,
Might I a son and daughter now have look'd on,
Such goodly things as you!

Enter a Lord.

LORD   Most noble sir,
That which I shall report will bear no credit,
Were not the proof so nigh. Please you, great sir,
180 Bohemia greets you from himself, by me;
Desires you to attach his son, who has –
His dignity and duty both cast off –
Fled from his father, from his hopes, and with
A shepherd's daughter.
LEONTES   Where's Bohemia? speak.
LORD
185 Here in your city; I now came from him.
I speak amazedly, and it becomes
My marvel and my message. To your court
Whiles he was hast'ning – in the chase, it seems,
Of this fair couple – meets he on the way

The father of this seeming lady and   190
Her brother, having both their country quitted
With this young prince.
FLORIZEL   Camillo has betray'd me;
Whose honour and whose honesty till now
Endur'd all weathers.
LORD   Lay't so to his charge:
He's with the king your father.
LEONTES   Who? Camillo?   195
LORD   Camillo, sir; I spake with him; who now
Has these poor men in question. Never saw I
Wretches so quake: they kneel, they kiss the earth;
Forswear themselves as often as they speak.
Bohemia stops his ears, and threatens them   200
With divers deaths in death.
PERDITA   O my poor father!
The heaven sets spies upon us, will not have
Our contract celebrated.
LEONTES   You are married?
FLORIZEL   We are not, sir, nor are we like to be:
The stars, I see, will kiss the valleys first: 205
The odds for high and low's alike.
LEONTES   My lord.
Is this the daughter of a king?
FLORIZEL   She is,
When once she is my wife.
LEONTES
That 'once', I see, by your good father's speed,
Will come on very slowly. I am sorry,   210
Most sorry, you have broken from his liking,
Where you were tied in duty; and as sorry
Your choice is not so rich in worth as beauty,
That you might well enjoy her.
FLORIZEL   Dear, look up:
Though Fortune, visible an enemy,   215
Should chase us, with my father, power no jot
Hath she to change our loves. Beseech you, sir,
Remember since you ow'd no more to time
Than I do now: with thought of such affections,
Step forth mine advocate: at your request,   220
My father will grant precious things as trifles.
LEONTES
Would he do so, I'd beg your precious mistress,
Which he counts but a trifle.
PAULINA   Sir, my liege,
Your eye hath too much youth in 't; not a month
'Fore your queen died, she was more worth such
     gazes   225
Than what you look on now.
LEONTES   I thought of her,
Even as these looks I made.
[*to Florizel*]   But your petition
Is yet unanswer'd. I will to your father:
Your honour not o'erthrown by your desires,
I am friend to them and you: upon which errand   230
I now go toward him; therefore follow me

And mark what way I make. Come, good my lord.

Exeunt.

5.2 *Enter* AUTOLYCUS *and a* Gentleman.

AUTOLYCUS Beseech you, sir, were you present at this relation?

1 GENTLEMAN I was by at the opening of the fardel, heard the old shepherd deliver the manner how he found it: whereupon, after a little amazedness, we were all commanded out of the chamber; only this, methought I heard the shepherd say he found the child.

AUTOLYCUS I would most gladly know the issue of it.

1 GENTLEMAN I make a broken delivery of the business; but the changes I perceived in the king and Camillo were very notes of admiration: they seemed almost, with staring on one another, to tear the cases of their eyes: there was speech in their dumbness, language in their very gesture; they looked as they had heard of a world ransomed, or one destroyed: a notable passion of wonder appeared in them; but the wisest beholder, that knew no more but seeing, could not say if th' importance were joy or sorrow; but in the extremity of the one it must needs be.

Enter another Gentleman.

Here comes a gentleman that haply knows more. The news, Rogero?

2 GENTLEMAN Nothing but bonfires: the Oracle is fulfilled; the king's daughter is found: such a deal of wonder is broken out within this hour, that ballad-makers cannot be able to express it.

Enter a third Gentleman.

Here comes the Lady Paulina's steward: he can deliver you more. How goes it now, sir? This news, which is called true, is so like an old tale that the verity of it is in strong suspicion. Has the king found his heir?

3 GENTLEMAN Most true, if ever truth were pregnant by circumstance: that which you hear you'll swear you see, there is such unity in the proofs. The mantle of Queen Hermione's, her jewel about the neck of it, the letters of Antigonus found with it, which they know to be his character; the majesty of the creature in resemblance of the mother, the affection of nobleness which nature shows above her breeding, and many other evidences proclaim her, with all certainty, to be the king's daughter. Did you see the meeting of the two kings?

2 GENTLEMAN No.

3 GENTLEMAN Then have you lost a sight which was to be seen, cannot be spoken of. There might you have beheld one joy crown another, so and in such manner that it seemed sorrow wept to take leave of them, for their joy waded in tears. There was casting up of eyes, holding up of hands, with countenance of such distraction, that they were to be known by garment, not by favour. Our king, being ready to leap out of himself for joy of his found daughter, as if that joy were now become a loss, cries 'O, thy mother, thy mother!' then asks Bohemia forgiveness; then embraces his son-in-law; then again worries he his daughter with clipping her; now he thanks the old shepherd, which stands by, like a weather-bitten conduit of many kings' reigns. I never heard of such another encounter, which lames report to follow it, and undoes description to do it.

2 GENTLEMAN What, pray you, became of Antigonus, that carried hence the child?

3 GENTLEMAN Like an old tale still, which will have matter to rehearse, though credit be asleep and not an ear open. He was torn to pieces with a bear: this avouches the shepherd's son; who has not only his innocence, which seems much, to justify him, but a handkerchief and rings of his that Paulina knows.

1 GENTLEMAN What became of his bark and his followers?

3 GENTLEMAN Wrecked the same instant of their master's death, and in the view of the shepherd: so that all the instruments which aided to expose the child were even then lost when it was found. But O, the noble combat that 'twixt joy and sorrow was fought in Paulina! She had one eye declined for the loss of her husband, another elevated that the Oracle was fulfilled: she lifted the princess from the earth, and so locks her in embracing as if she would pin her to her heart, that she might no more be in danger of losing.

1 GENTLEMAN The dignity of this act was worth the audience of kings and princes; for by such was it acted.

3 GENTLEMAN One of the prettiest touches of all, and that which angled for mine eyes (caught the water though not the fish) was, when at the relation of the queen's death (with the manner how she came to't bravely confessed and lamented by the king) how attentiveness wounded his daughter; till, from one sign of dolour to another, she did, with an 'Alas,' I would fain say, bleed tears, for I am sure my heart wept blood. Who was most marble, there changed colour; some swooned, all sorrowed: if all the world could have seen't, the woe had been universal.

1 GENTLEMAN Are they returned to the court?

3 GENTLEMAN No: the princess hearing of her mother's statue, which is in the keeping of Paulina, – a piece many years in doing and now newly performed by that rare Italian master, Julio Romano, who, had he himself eternity and could put breath into his work, would beguile Nature of her custom, so perfectly he is her ape: he so near to Hermione hath done Hermione, that they say one would speak to her and stand in hope of answer. Thither with all greediness of affection are they gone, and there they intend to sup.

2 GENTLEMAN I thought she had some great matter

there in hand; for she hath privately twice or thrice a day, ever since the death of Hermione, visited that removed house. Shall we thither, and with our company piece the rejoicing?

110 1 GENTLEMAN   Who would be thence that has the benefit of access? Every wink of an eye, some new grace will be born: our absence makes us unthrifty to our knowledge. Let's along.   *Exeunt Gentlemen.*

115 AUTOLYCUS   Now, had I not the dash of my former life in me, would preferment drop on my head. I brought the old man and his son aboard the prince; told him I heard them talk of a fardel and I know not what: but he at that time overfond of the shepherd's daughter (so he then took her to be), who began to be much sea-
120 sick, and himself little better, extremity of weather continuing, this mystery remained undiscovered. But 'tis all one to me; for had I been the finder out of this secret, it would not have relished among my other discredits.

Enter Shepherd *and* Clown.

125 Here come those I have done good to against my will, and already appearing in the blossoms of their fortune.

SHEPHERD   Come, boy; I am past moe children, but thy sons and daughters will be all gentlemen born.

130 CLOWN   You are well met, sir. You denied to fight with me this other day, because I was no gentleman born. See you these clothes? say you see them not and think me still no gentleman born: you were best say these robes are not gentleman born: give me the lie;
135 do; and try whether I am not now a gentleman born.

AUTOLYCUS   I know you are now, sir, a gentleman born.

CLOWN   Ay, and have been so any time these four hours.

SHEPHERD   And so have I, boy.

CLOWN   So you have: but I was a gentleman born before
140 my father; for the king's son took me by the hand, and called me brother; and then the two kings called my father brother; and then the prince, my brother, and the princess, my sister, called my father father; and so we wept; and there was the first gentleman-like tears
145 that ever we shed.

SHEPHERD   We may live, son, to shed many more.

CLOWN   Ay; or else 'twere hard luck, being in so preposterous estate as we are.

AUTOLYCUS   I humbly beseech you, sir, to pardon me all
150 the faults I have committed to your worship, and to give me your good report to the prince my master.

SHEPHERD   Prithee, son, do; for we must be gentle, now we are gentlemen.

CLOWN   Thou wilt amend thy life?
155 AUTOLYCUS   Ay, and it like your good worship.

CLOWN   Give me thy hand: I will swear to the prince thou art as honest a true fellow as any is in Bohemia.

SHEPHERD   You may say it, but not swear it.

CLOWN   Not swear it, now I am a gentleman? Let boors
160 and franklins say it, I'll swear it.

SHEPHERD   How if it be false, son?

CLOWN   If it be ne'er so false, a true gentleman may swear it in the behalf of his friend: and I'll swear to the prince thou art a tall fellow of thy hands and that thou wilt not be drunk; but I know thou art no tall
165 fellow of thy hands and that thou wilt be drunk: but I'll swear it, and I would thou would'st be a tall fellow of thy hands.

AUTOLYCUS   I will prove so, sir, to my power.

CLOWN   Ay, by any means prove a tall fellow: if I do not
170 wonder how thou dar'st venture to be drunk, not being a tall fellow, trust me not. Hark! the kings and the princes, our kindred, are going to see the queen's picture. Come, follow us: we'll be thy good masters.
                                                        Exeunt.

5.3   *Enter* LEONTES, POLIXENES, FLORIZEL,
        PERDITA, CAMILLO, PAULINA, *lords and attendants.*

LEONTES
   O grave and good Paulina, the great comfort
   That I have had of thee!
PAULINA   What, sovereign sir,
   I did not well, I meant well. All my services
   You have paid home: but that you have vouchsaf'd,
   With your crown'd brother and these your contracted   5
   Heirs of your kingdoms, my poor house to visit,
   It is a surplus of your grace, which never
   My life may last to answer.
LEONTES   O Paulina,
   We honour you with trouble: but we came
   To see the statue of our queen: your gallery   10
   Have we pass'd through, not without much content
   In many singularities; but we saw not
   That which my daughter came to look upon,
   The statue of her mother.
PAULINA   As she liv'd peerless,
   So her dead likeness, I do well believe,   15
   Excels whatever yet you look'd upon,
   Or hand of man hath done; therefore I keep it
   Lonely, apart. But here it is: prepare
   To see the life as lively mock'd as ever
   Still sleep mock'd death: behold, and say 'tis well. 20
   [*Paulina draws a curtain, and discovers Hermione
   standing like a statue.*]
   I like your silence, it the more shows off
   Your wonder: but yet speak; first you, my liege.
   Comes it not something near?
LEONTES   Her natural posture!
   Chide me, dear stone, that I may say indeed
   Thou art Hermione; or rather, thou art she   25
   In thy not chiding; for she was as tender
   As infancy and grace. But yet, Paulina,
   Hermione was not so much wrinkled, nothing
   So aged as this seems.
POLIXENES   O, not by much.
PAULINA   So much the more our carver's excellence,   30

Which lets go by some sixteen years and makes her
As she liv'd now.
LEONTES   As now she might have done,
  So much to my good comfort as it is
  Now piercing to my soul. O, thus she stood,
35 Even with such life of majesty, warm life,
  As now it coldly stands, when first I woo'd her!
  I am asham'd: does not the stone rebuke me
  For being more stone than it? O royal piece!
  There's magic in thy majesty, which has
40 My evils conjur'd to remembrance, and
  From thy admiring daughter took the spirits,
  Standing like stone with thee.
PERDITA   And give me leave,
  And do not say 'tis superstition, that
  I kneel, and then implore her blessing. Lady,
45 Dear queen, that ended when I but began,
  Give me that hand of yours to kiss.
PAULINA   O patience!
  The statue is but newly fix'd, the colour's
  Not dry.
CAMILLO   My lord, your sorrow was too sore laid on,
50 Which sixteen winters cannot blow away,
  So many summers dry: scarce any joy
  Did ever so long live; no sorrow
  But kill'd itself much sooner.
POLIXENES   Dear my brother,
  Let him that was the cause of this have power
55 To take off so much grief from you as he
  Will piece up in himself.
PAULINA   Indeed, my lord,
  If I had thought the sight of my poor image
  Would thus have wrought you – for the stone is
    mine –
  I'd not have show'd it.
LEONTES   Do not draw the curtain.
PAULINA
60 No longer shall you gaze on't, lest your fancy
  May think anon it moves.
LEONTES   Let be, let be!
  Would I were dead, but that methinks already –
  What was he that did make it? – See, my lord,
  Would you not deem it breath'd? and that those veins
  Did verily bear blood?
65 POLIXENES   Masterly done:
  The very life seems warm upon her lip.
LEONTES   The fixure of her eye has motion in't,
  As we are mock'd with art.
PAULINA   I'll draw the curtain:
  My lord's almost so far transported that
  He'll think anon it lives.
70 LEONTES   O sweet Paulina,
  Make me to think so twenty years together!
  No settled senses of the world can match
  The pleasure of that madness. Let't alone.
PAULINA   I am sorry, sir, I have thus far stirr'd you: but
  I could afflict you farther.

LEONTES   Do, Paulina;   75
  For this affliction has a taste as sweet
  As any cordial comfort. Still methinks
  There is an air comes from her. What fine chisel
  Could ever yet cut breath? Let no man mock me,
  For I will kiss her.
PAULINA   Good my lord, forbear: 80
  The ruddiness upon her lip is wet;
  You'll mar it if you kiss it, stain your own
  With oily painting. Shall I draw the curtain?
LEONTES   No: not these twenty years.
PERDITA   So long could I
  Stand by, a looker on.
PAULINA   Either forbear,   85
  Quit presently the chapel, or resolve you
  For more amazement. If you can behold it,
  I'll make the statue move indeed; descend,
  And take you by the hand: but then you'll think
  (Which I protest against) I am assisted   90
  By wicked powers.
LEONTES   What you can make her do,
  I am content to look on: what to speak,
  I am content to hear; for 'tis as easy
  To make her speak as move.
PAULINA   It is requir'd
  You do awake your faith. Then all stand still: 95
  Or – those that think it is unlawful business
  I am about, let them depart.
LEONTES   Proceed:
  No foot shall stir.
PAULINA   Music, awake her; strike!   [*Music.*]
  'Tis time; descend; be stone no more; approach;
  Strike all that look upon with marvel. Come!   100
  I'll fill your grave up: stir, nay, come away:
  Bequeath to death your numbness; for from him
  Dear life redeems you. You perceive she stirs:
  [*Hermione comes down.*]
  Start not; her actions shall be holy as
  You hear my spell is lawful.
  [*to Leontes*]   Do not shun her   105
  Until you see her die again; for then
  You kill her double. Nay, present your hand:
  When she was young you woo'd her; now, in age,
  Is she become the suitor?
LEONTES   O, she's warm!
  If this be magic, let it be an art   110
  Lawful as eating.
POLIXENES   She embraces him!
CAMILLO   She hangs about his neck!
  If she pertain to life, let her speak too!
POLIXENES
  Ay, and make it manifest where she has liv'd,
  Or how stolen from the dead!
PAULINA   That she is living,   115
  Were it but told you, should be hooted at
  Like an old tale: but it appears she lives,
  Though yet she speak not. Mark a little while.

     [*to Perdita*] Please you to interpose, fair madam,
       kneel
     And pray your mother's blessing.
120   [*to Hermione*]   Turn, good lady,
     Our Perdita is found.
     HERMIONE   You gods, look down,
     And from your sacred vials pour your graces
     Upon my daughter's head! Tell me, mine own,
     Where hast thou been preserv'd? where liv'd? how
       found
125   Thy father's court? for thou shalt hear that I,
     Knowing by Paulina that the Oracle
     Gave hope thou wast in being, have preserv'd
     Myself to see the issue.
     PAULINA   There's time enough for that;
     Lest they desire (upon this push) to trouble
130   Your joys with like relation. Go together,
     You precious winners all; your exultation
     Partake to every one. I, an old turtle,
     Will wing me to some wither'd bough, and there
     My mate (that's never to be found again)
     Lament, till I am lost.
135   LEONTES   O, peace, Paulina!

Thou shouldst a husband take by my consent,
As I by thine a wife: this is a match,
And made between's by vows. Thou hast found
   mine;
But how, is to be question'd; for I saw her,
As I thought, dead; and have in vain said many   140
A prayer upon her grave. I'll not seek far –
For him, I partly know his mind – to find thee
An honourable husband. Come, Camillo,
And take her by the hand; whose worth and honesty
Is richly noted; and here justified   145
By us, a pair of kings. Let's from this place.
[*to Hermione*] What! look upon my brother: both
   your pardons,
That e'er I put between your holy looks
My ill suspicion. This your son-in-law,
And son unto the king, whom, heavens directing,   150
Is troth-plight to your daughter. Good Paulina,
Lead us from hence, where we may leisurely
Each one demand, and answer to his part
Perform'd in this wide gap of time, since first
We were dissever'd: hastily lead away.   *Exeunt.*   155

Bibliography

SHAKESPEARE'S LIFE

Bentley, G.E., *Shakespeare: A Biographical Handbook*, New Haven: Yale University Press, 1961.
Chambers, E.K., *William Shakespeare: A Study of Facts and Problems*. 2 vols, Oxford: Clarendon Press, 1930, repr. 1988.
Dutton, Richard, *William Shakespeare: A Literary Life*, Basingstoke: Macmillan, 1989.
Eccles, Mark, *Shakespeare in Warwickshire*, Madison: University of Wisconsin Press, 1961.
Fraser, Russell, *Shakespeare, the Later Years*, New York: Columbia University Press, 1992.
Fraser, R., *Young Shakespeare*, New York: Columbia University Press, 1988.
Honigmann, E.A.J., *Shakespeare, the Lost Years*, Manchester: Manchester University Press, 1985.
Schoenbaum, Samuel, *Shakespeare's Lives*, 2nd edn, Oxford: Oxford University Press, 1991.
Schoenbaum, Samuel, *William Shakespeare: A Compact Documentary Life*, rev. edn, Oxford: Oxford University Press, 1987.
Schoenbaum, Samuel, *William Shakespeare: A Documentary Life*, Oxford: Oxford University Press; Ilkley, Yorks.: Scolar Press, 1975.
Schoenbaum, Samuel, *William Shakespeare: Records and Images*, London: Scolar Press, 1981.

SHAKESPEARE IN PERFORMANCE

Bate, Jonathan, and Jackson, Russell, *Shakespeare: An Illustrated Stage History*, Oxford: Oxford University Press, 1996.
Beckerman, Bernard, *Shakespeare at the Globe, 1599–1609*, New York: Macmillan, 1962.
Berry, Herbert, *Shakespeare's Playhouses*, New York: AMS Press, 1987.
Berry, Ralph, ed., *On Directing Shakespeare: Interviews with Contemporary Directors*, London and New York: Hamish Hamilton, 1989.
Bevington, David, *Action is Eloquence: Shakespeare's Language of Gesture*, Cambridge, Mass. and London: Harvard University Press, 1984.
Bulman, James C., ed., *Shakespeare, Theory and Performance*, New York and London: Routledge, 1996.
Bulman, James C., and Coursen, H.R., eds, *Shakespeare on Television*, Hanover, N.H. and London: University Press of New England, 1988.
Cook, Ann Jennalie, *The Privileged Playgoers of Shakespeare's London, 1576-1642*, Princeton and Guildford: Princeton University Press, 1981.
Dessen, Alan C., *Recovering Shakespeare's Theatrical Vocabulary*, Cambridge: Cambridge University Press, 1995.
Gurr, Andrew, *Playgoing in Shakespeare's London*, 2nd edn, Cambridge: Cambridge University Press, 1996.
Gurr, Andrew, *The Shakespearian Playing Companies*, Oxford: Clarendon Press, 1996.
Gurr, Andrew, *The Shakespearean Stage, 1574–1642*, 3rd edn, Cambridge: Cambridge University Press, 1992.
Gurr, Andrew and Orrell, John, *Rebuilding Shakespeare's Globe*, London: Weidenfeld & Nicolson, 1989.
Hogan, Charles B., *Shakespeare in the Theatre, 1701–1800*, 2 vols, Oxford: Clarendon Press, 1952, 1957.
Howard, Jean E., *Shakespeare's Art of Orchestration: Stage Technique and Audience Response*, Urbana: University of Illinois Press, 1984.
Jorgens, Jack J., *Shakespeare on Film*, Bloomington and London: Indiana University Press, 1979.
Joseph, Bertram, *Acting Shakespeare*, rev. edn, New York: Routledge, 1969.
Kennedy, Dennis, ed., *Foreign Shakespeare: Contemporary Performance*, Cambridge: Cambridge University Press, 1993.
King, T.J., *Casting Shakespeare's Plays: London Actors and Their Roles, 1590–1642*, Cambridge: Cambridge University Press, 1992.
King, T.J., *Shakespearean Staging, 1599–1642*, Cambridge, Mass.: Harvard University Press, 1971.
Knutson, Roslyn L., *The Repertory of Shakespeare's Company, 1594–1613*, Fayetteville: University of Arkansas Press, 1991.
Nungezer, Edwin, *A Dictionary of Actors and of Other Persons Associated with Public Representation of Plays in England before 1642*, New Haven: Yale University Press, 1929.
Odell, George C., *Shakespeare – From Betterton to Irving*, 2 vols, 1921; 2nd edn, New York: B. Blom, 1963.
Orrell, John, *The Quest for Shakespeare's Globe*, Cambridge: Cambridge University Press, 1983.
Shattuck, Charles H., *Shakespeare on the American Stage: From the Hallams to Edwin Booth*, Washington: Folger Shakespeare Library, 1976.
Speaight, Robert, *Shakespeare on the Stage: An Illustrated History of Shakespearian Performance*, Boston and Toronto: Little, Brown, 1973.
Sprague, Arthur Colby, *Shakespeare and the Actors: The Stage Business in His Plays, 1660–1905*, Cambridge, Mass.: Harvard University Press, 1944.
Styan, J.L., *Shakespeare's Stagecraft*, Cambridge: Cambridge University Press, 1967.
Thomson, Peter, *Shakespeare's Theatre*, 2nd edn, London: Routledge, 1992.
Trewin, J.C., *Shakespeare on the English Stage, 1900–1964*, London: Barrie & Rockliff, 1964.
Wiles, David, *Shakespeare's Clown: Actor and Text in the Elizabethan Playhouse*, Cambridge: Cambridge University Press, 1987.

THE EARLY TEXTS

Allen, Michael J.B. and Muir, Kenneth, eds, *Shakespeare's Plays in Quarto: A Facsimile Edition of Copies Primarily from the Henry E. Huntington Library*, Berkeley, Los Angeles and London: University of California Press, 1981.
Hinman, Charlton, ed., *The First Folio of Shakespeare: The Norton Facsimile*, 2nd edn, New York and London: W.W. Norton, 1996.

TEXTUAL STUDIES

Blayney, Peter W.M., *The First Folio of Shakespeare*, Washington: Folger Library Publications, 1991.
Blayney, Peter W.M., *The Texts of 'King Lear' and Their Origins*, vol. 1: *Nicholas Okes and the First Quarto*, Cambridge: Cambridge University Press, 1982.
Bowers, Fredson, *On Editing Shakespeare*, Charlottesville: University Press of Virginia, 1966.
De Grazia, Margreta, *Shakespeare Verbatim: The Reproduction of Authenticity and the 1790 Apparatus*, Oxford: Clarendon Press, 1991.
Greg, W.W., *The Editorial Problem in Shakespeare*, 3rd edn, Oxford: Clarendon Press, 1954 (1955).
Greg, W.W., *The Shakespeare First Folio: Its Bibliographical and Textual History*, Oxford: Clarendon Press, 1955.
Hinman, Charlton, *The Printing and Proof-reading of the First Folio of Shakespeare*, 2 vols, Oxford: Clarendon Press, 1963.
Honigmann, E.A.J., *The Stability of Shakespeare's Text*, London: Edward Arnold, 1965.
Honigmann, E.A.J., *The Texts of 'Othello' and Shakespearian Revision*, London and New York: Routledge, 1996.
Ioppolo, Grace, *Revising Shakespeare*, Cambridge, Mass.: Harvard University Press, 1991.
Irace, Kathleen O., *Reforming the 'Bad' Quartos: Performance and Provenance of Six Shakespearean First Editions*, Newark: University of Delaware Press, 1994.
Maguire, Laurie E., *Shakespearean Suspect Texts: The 'Bad' Quartos and Their Contexts*, Cambridge: Cambridge University Press, 1996.
Pollard, Alfred W., *Shakespeare Folio and Quartos: A Study in the Bibliography of Shakespeare's Plays, 1594–1685*, London: Methuen, 1909.
Taylor, Gary and Jowett, John, *Shakespeare Reshaped 1606–1623*, Oxford: Clarendon Press, 1991.
Walker, Alice, *Textual Problems of the First Folio*, Cambridge: Cambridge University Press, 1953.
Wells, Stanley, *Re-editing Shakespeare for the Modern Reader*, Oxford: Clarendon Press, 1984.
Wells, Stanley and Taylor, Gary, *Modernizing Shakespeare's Spelling, with Three Studies in the Text of 'Henry V'*, Oxford: Clarendon Press, 1979 (1980).
Wells, Stanley and Taylor, Gary, with Jowett, John and Montgomery, William, *William Shakespeare: A Textual Companion*, Oxford: Clarendon Press, 1987.
Wilson, F.P., *Shakespeare and the New Bibliography*, rev. and ed. Gardner, Helen, Oxford: Clarendon Press, 1970.

LANGUAGE AND STYLE

Dictionaries and concordances

Dent, R.W., *Shakespeare's Proverbial Language: An Index*, Berkeley, Los Angeles and London: University of California Press, 1981.
Onions, Charles T., *A Shakespeare Glossary*, 3rd edn., rev. and ed. Eagleson, Robert D., Oxford: Clarendon Press, 1986.
Partridge, Eric, *Shakespeare's Bawdy: A Literary and Psychological Essay and a Comprehensive Glossary*, 1968; 3rd edn, London; New York: Routledge, 1991.
Schmidt, Alexander, *Shakespeare Lexicon: A Complete Dictionary of All the English Words, Phrases and Constructions in the Work of the Poet*. 2 vols. 3rd edn, rev. and enl. by Gregor Sarrazin, New York: Dover, 1971.
Spevack, Marvin, *The Harvard Concordance to Shakespeare*, Hildesheim: Georg Olms and Cambridge, Mass.: Belknap Press, 1973 and 1974.
Spevack, Marvin, ed., *A Complete and Systematic Concordance to the Works of Shakespeare*, 9 vols, Hildesheim: Georg Olms, 1968-80.

Studies

Abbott, E.A., *A Shakespearian Grammar*, 1870; New York: Dover, 1966.
Blake, N.F., *Shakespeare's Language: An Introduction*, London: Macmillan, 1983.
Cercignani, Fausto, *Shakespeare's Works and Elizabethan Pronunciation*, Oxford: Clarendon Press, 1981.
Clemen, Wolfgang, *The Development of Shakespeare's Imagery*, 2nd edn, London: Methuen, 1977.
Donawerth, Jane, *Shakespeare and the Sixteenth-Century Study of Language*, Urbana: University of Illinois Press, 1984.
Doran, Madeleine, *Shakespeare's Dramatic Language*, Madison: University of Wisconsin Press, 1976.
Edwards, Philip, Ewbank, Inga-Stina and Hunter, G.K., eds, *Shakespeare's Styles: Essays in Honour of Kenneth Muir*, Cambridge: Cambridge University Press, 1980.
Hulme, Hilda H., *Explorations in Shakespeare's Language*, London and New York: Longman, 1962, repr. 1977.
Hussey, S.S., *The Literary Language of Shakespeare*, 2nd edn, London: Longman, 1992.
Kökeritz, Helge, *Shakespeare's Names: A Pronouncing Dictionary*, New Haven: Yale University Press, 1959, repr. 1985.
Kökeritz, Helge, *Shakespeare's Pronunciation*, New Haven: Yale University Press, 1953.
McDonald, Russ, ed., *Shakespeare Reread*, New York: Cornell University Press, 1994.
Mahood, M.M., *Shakespeare's Wordplay*, London: Methuen, 1957.
Miriam Joseph, Sister, *Shakespeare's Use of the Arts of Language*, New York: Columbia University Press, 1947.
Thompson, Ann and Thompson, John O., *Shakespeare: Meaning and Metaphor*, Brighton: Harvester, 1987.
Vickers, Brian, *The Artistry of Shakespeare's Prose*, London: Methuen, 1968.
Wright, George T., *Shakespeare's Metrical Art*, Berkeley, Los Angeles and London: University of California Press, 1988.

SHAKESPEARE'S SOURCES

Bate, Jonathan, *Shakespeare and Ovid*, Oxford: Oxford University Press, 1993.
Bullough, Geoffrey, ed., *Narrative and Dramatic Sources of Shakespeare*, 8 vols, London: Routledge & Kegan Paul, 1957-75.
Donaldson, E. Talbot, *The Swan at the Well: Shakespeare Reading Chaucer*, New Haven and London: Yale University Press, 1985.
Hart, Alfred, *Shakespeare and the Homilies*, 1934; New York: Octagon Books, 1970.
Martindale, Charles and Martindale, Michelle, *Shakespeare and the Uses of Antiquity: An Introductory Essay on Shakespeare and English Renaissance Classicism*, London and New York: Routledge, 1990.
Milward, Peter, *Shakespeare's Religious Background*, Bloomington and London: Indiana University Press, 1973.
Miola, Robert S., *Shakespeare and Classical Tragedy: The Influence of Seneca*, Oxford: Clarendon Press, 1992.
Muir, Kenneth, *The Sources of Shakespeare's Plays*, London: Methuen and New Haven: Yale University Press, 1977 and 1978.
Noble, Richmond S., *Shakespeare's Biblical Knowledge and Use of the Book Of Common Prayer*, 1935; New York: Gordon Press Publishers, 1972.
Pinciss, Gerald M. and Lockyer, Roger, eds, *Shakespeare's World: Background Readings in the English Renaissance*, New York: Continuum, 1989.
Shaheen, Naseeb, *Biblical References in Shakespeare's Comedies*, Newark, Del.: University of Delaware Press, 1993.
Shaheen, N., *Biblical References in Shakespeare's History Plays*, London: Associated University Press, 1989.
Shaheen, N., *Biblical References in Shakespeare's Tragedies*, London: Associated University Press, 1987.
Spencer, T.J.B., ed., *Shakespeare's Plutarch*, Harmondsworth: Penguin, 1964.
Thompson, Ann, *Shakespeare's Chaucer: A Study in Literary Origins*, Liverpool: Liverpool University Press, 1978.
Thomson, J.A.K., *Shakespeare and the Classics*, London: Allen & Unwin, 1952.

GENERAL CRITICISM

Anthologies of criticism

Calderwood, James L. and Toliver, Harold E., eds, *Essays in Shakespearean Criticism*, Englewood Cliffs, N.J.: Prentice-Hall, 1970.

Dollimore, Jonathan and Sinfield, Alan, eds, *Political Shakespeare: Essays in Cultural Materialism*, 1985; 2nd edn, Manchester: Manchester University Press, 1994.

Drakakis, John, ed., *Alternative Shakespeares*, London and New York: Methuen, 1985.

Hawkes, Terence, ed., *Alternative Shakespeares*, vol. 2, London and New York: Routledge, 1996.

Howard, Jean E. and O'Connor, Marion, eds, *Shakespeare Reproduced: The Text in History and Ideology*, London and New York: Methuen, 1987.

Lenz, Carolyn, Swift, Ruth, Greene, Gayle and Neely, Carol Thomas, eds, *The Woman's Part: Feminist Criticism of Shakespeare*, Urbana, Chicago and London: University of Illinois Press, 1980.

Parker, Patricia and Hartman, Geoffrey, eds, *Shakespeare and the Question of Theory*, London and New York: Methuen, 1985.

Schwartz, Murray M. and Kahn, Coppélia, eds, *Representing Shakespeare: New Psychoanalytic Essays*, Baltimore and London: Johns Hopkins University Press, 1980.

Thompson, Ann and Roberts, Sasha, eds, *Women Reading Shakespeare, 1660–1900*, Manchester: Manchester University Press and New York: St Martin's Press, 1997.

Individual critical studies

Adelman, Janet, *Suffocating Mothers: Fantasies of Maternal Origin in Shakespeare's Plays, 'Hamlet' to 'The Tempest'*, New York and London: Routledge, 1992.

Barroll, J. Leeds, *Politics, Plague, and Shakespeare's Theater: The Stuart Years*, Ithaca: Cornell University Press, 1991.

Berger, Harry, Jr, *Making Trifles of Terrors: Redistributing Complicities in Shakespeare*, ed. Erickson, Peter, Stanford: Stanford University Press, 1997.

Bristol, Michael D., *Big-time Shakespeare*, London and New York: Routledge, 1996.

Burckhardt, Sigurd, *Shakespearean Meanings*, Princeton: Princeton University Press, 1968.

Coleridge, Samuel Taylor, *Samuel Taylor Coleridge. Shakespearean Criticism*, 2 vols, ed. Raysor, T.M., 1960; Totowa, N.J.: Biblio Distribution Center, 1974, 1980.

Dusinberre, Juliet, *Shakespeare and the Nature of Women*, 2nd edn, Basingstoke: Macmillan, 1996.

Eagleton, Terry, *William Shakespeare*, Oxford: Blackwell, 1986.

Frye, Northrop, *Northrop Frye on Shakespeare*, ed. Sandler, Robert, New Haven and London: Yale University Press, 1986.

Garber, Marjorie, *Shakespeare's Ghost Writers: Literature as Uncanny Causality*, London and New York: Methuen, 1987.

Goldman, Michael, *Shakespeare and the Energies of Drama*, Princeton: Princeton University Press, 1972.

Greenblatt, Stephen J., *Shakespearean Negotiations: The Circulation of Social Energy in Renaissance England*, Oxford: Clarendon Press, 1988.

Hawkes, Terence, *That Shakespeherian Rag: Essays on a Critical Process*, London and New York: Methuen, 1986.

Jardine, Lisa, *Reading Shakespeare Historically*, London and New York: Routledge, 1996.

Johnson, Samuel, *Samuel Johnson on Shakespeare*, ed. Wouhuysen, H.R., London: Penguin, 1989.

Jones, Emrys, *Scenic Form in Shakespeare*, Oxford: Clarendon Press, 1971.

Kahn, Coppélia, *Man's Estate: Masculine Identity in Shakespeare*, Berkeley and Los Angeles: University of California Press, 1981.

Kastan, David Scott, *Shakespeare and the Shapes of Time*, London and Hanover, N.H.: University Press of New England and Macmillan, 1982.

Kernan, Alvin B, *The Playwright as Magician: Shakespeare's Image of the Poet in the English Public Theater*, New Haven and London: Yale University Press, 1979.

Kernan, A., *Shakespeare, the King's Playwright: Theater in the Stuart Court*, New Haven and London: Yale University Press, 1995.

Kott, Jan, *Shakespeare Our Contemporary*, trs. Taborski, Boleslaw, 2nd edn, London: Methuen, 1967.

Marcus, Leah, *Puzzling Shakespeare: Local Reading and Its Discontents*, Berkeley, Los Angeles and London: University of California Press, 1988.

Mullaney, Steven, *The Place of the Stage: License, Play, and Power in Renaissance England*, Chicago and London: University of Chicago Press, 1988.

Neely, Carol Thomas, *Broken Nuptials in Shakespeare's Plays*, New Haven and London: Yale University Press, 1985.

Orgel, Stephen, *Impersonations: The Performance of Gender in Shakespeare's England*, Cambridge: Cambridge University Press, 1996.

Parker, Patricia, *Shakespeare from the Margins: Language, Culture, Context*, Chicago: Chicago University Press, 1996.

Patterson, Annabel, *Shakespeare and the Popular Voice*, Oxford: Blackwell, 1989.

Rabkin, Norman, *Shakespeare and the Problem of Meaning*, Chicago: University of Chicago Press, 1981.

Rossiter, A.P., *Angel with Horns*, ed. Storey, Graham, 1961; re-issued, with an introduction by Peter Holland, London: Longman, 1989.

Shapiro, James, *Shakespeare and the Jews*, New York and Chichester: Columbia University Press, 1996.

Shaw, George Bernard, *Shaw on Shakespeare*, ed. Wilson, Edwin, 1961; Harmondsworth: Penguin, 1969.

Traub, Valerie, *Desire and Anxiety: Circulations of Sexuality in Shakespearean Drama*, London and New York: Routledge, 1992.

Weimann, Robert, *Shakespeare and the Popular Tradition in the Theater: Studies in the Social Dimension of Dramatic Form and Function*. trs. Schwartz, Robert, Baltimore and London: Johns Hopkins University Press, 1978.

Criticism of the comedies

Barber, C.L., *Shakespeare's Festive Comedy: A study of Dramatic Form and its Relation to Social Custom*, Princeton: Princeton University Press, 1957, repr. 1972.

Bradbrook, M.C., *The Growth and Structure of Elizabethan Comedy*, new edn, Cambridge: Cambridge University Press, 1979.

Carroll, William, *The Metamorphoses of Shakespearean Comedy*, Princeton and Guildford: Princeton University Press, 1985.

Evans, Betrand, *Shakespeare's Comedies*, Oxford: Clarendon Press, 1960.

Frye, Northrop, *The Myth of Deliverance: Reflections on Shakespeare's Problem Comedies*, Brighton: Harvester, 1983.

Frye, Northrop, *A Natural Perspective: The Development of Shakespearean Comedy and Romance*, New York and London: Columbia University Press, 1965.

Hunter, Robert Grams, *Shakespeare and the Comedy of Forgiveness*, New York and London: Columbia University Press, 1965.

Leggatt, Alexander, *Shakespeare's Comedy of Love*, London: Methuen, 1974.

Mowat, Barbara A., *The Dramaturgy of Shakespeare's Romances*, Athens, Ga.: University of Georgia Press, 1976.

Nevo, Ruth, *Shakespeare's Other Language*, London: Routledge, 1987.

Newman, Karen, *Shakespeare's Rhetoric of Comic Character*, New York and London: Methuen, 1985.

Salingar, Leo, *Shakespeare and the Traditions of Comedy*, Cambridge: Cambridge University Press, 1974.

Wheeler, Richard P., *Shakespeare's Development and the Problem Comedies: Turn and Counter-Turn*, Berkeley, Los Angeles and London: University of California Press, 1981.

Williamson, Marilyn, L., *The Patriarchy of Shakespeare's Comedies*, Detroit: Wayne State University Press, 1986.

Criticism of the history plays

Berry, Edward I., *Patterns of Decay: Shakespeare's Early Histories*, Charlottesville: University of Virginia Press, 1975.
Calderwood, James L., *Metadrama in Shakespeare's Henriad: 'Richard II' to 'Henry V'*, Berkeley, Los Angeles and London: University of California Press, 1979.
Campbell, Lily B., *Shakespeare's Histories: Mirrors of Elizabethan Policy*, 1947; London: Methuen, 1964.
Hodgdon, Barbara, *The End Crowns All: Closure and Contradiction in Shakespeare's History*, Princeton and Oxford: Princeton University Press, 1991.
Holderness, Graham, *Shakespeare's History*, New York: St Martin's Press, 1985.
Howard, Jean E. and Rackin, Phyllis, *Engendering a Nation: A Feminist Account of Shakespeare's English Histories*, London and New York: Routledge, 1997.
Jones, Emrys, *The Origins of Shakespeare*, Oxford: Clarendon Press, 1977.
Rackin, Phyllis, *Stages of History: Shakespeare's English Chronicles*, New York and London: Routledge, 1991.
Ribner, Irving, *The English History Play in the Age of Shakespeare*, 1957; rev. edn, London: Methuen, 1965.
Saccio, Peter, *Shakespeare's English Kings: History, Chronicle, and Drama*, Oxford: Oxford University Press, 1977.
Sprague, Arthur Colby, *Shakespeare's Histories: Plays for the Stage*, London: Society for Theatre Research, 1964.
Tillyard, E.M.W., *Shakespeare's History Plays*, London: Chatto & Windus, 1944, repr. 1980.

Criticism of the tragedies

Booth, Stephen, *'King Lear,' 'Macbeth', Indefinition, and Tragedy*, New Haven and London: Yale University Press, 1983.
Bradley, A.C., *Shakespearean Tragedy*, 3rd edn, with an introduction by John Russell Brown, Basingstoke and London: Macmillan, 1992
Brooke, Nicholas, *Shakespeare's Early Tragedies*, London: Methuen, 1968.
Danson, Lawrence, *Tragic Alphabet: Shakespeare's Drama of Language*, New Haven and London: Yale University Press, 1974.
Dollimore, Jonathan, *Radical Tragedy: Religion, Ideology and Power in the Drama of Shakespeare and his Contemporaries*, 1984; 2nd edn, New York and London: Harvester Wheatsheaf, 1989.
Everett, Barbara, *Young Hamlet: Essays on Shakespeare's Tragedies*, Oxford: Clarendon Press, 1990.
Felperin, Howard, *Shakespearean Representation: Mimesis and Modernity in Elizabethan Tragedy*, Princeton and Guildford: Princeton University Press, 1978.
Frye, Northrop, *Fools of Time: Studies in Shakespearean Tragedy*, London: Oxford University Press, 1967.
Garner, Shirley Nelson and Sprengnether, Madelon, eds, *Shakespearean Tragedy and Gender*, Bloomington: Indiana University Press, 1996.
Goldman, Michael, *Acting and Action in Shakespearean Tragedy*, Princeton and Guildford: Princeton University Press, 1985.
Honigmann, E.A.J., *Shakespeare, Seven Tragedies: The Dramatist's Manipulation of Response*, London: Macmillan, 1976.
Kahn, Coppélia, *Roman Shakespeare: Warriors, Wounds and Women*, New York and London: Routledge, 1997.
Knight, G. Wilson, *The Wheel of Fire: Interpretations of Shakespearian Tragedy*, 4th edn, London: Methuen, 1949, repr. 1960.
Miola, Robert S., *Shakespeare's Rome*, Cambridge: Cambridge University Press, 1983.
Muir, Kenneth, *Shakespeare's Tragic Sequence*, 1972; Liverpool: Liverpool University Press, 1979.

Hamlet criticism

Alexander, Nigel, *Poison, Play, and Duel: A Study in 'Hamlet'*, London: Routledge & Kegan Paul, 1971.
Calderwood, James L., *To Be and Not to Be: Negation and Metadrama in 'Hamlet'*, New York and Guildford: Columbia University Press, 1983.
Charney, Maurice, *Style in 'Hamlet'*, Princeton: Princeton University Press, 1969.
Clayton, Thomas, ed., *The 'Hamlet' First Published (Q1, 1603): Origins, Form, Intertextuality*, Newark, Del.: University of Delaware Press, 1992.
Frye, Roland Mushat, *The Renaissance 'Hamlet': Issues and Responses in 1600*, Princeton and Guildford: Princeton University Press, 1984.
Kastan, David Scott, ed., *Critical Essays on Shakespeare's Hamlet*, New York: G.K. Hall, 1995.
Levin, Harry, *The Question of Hamlet*, 1959; Oxford: Oxford University Press, 1970.
Prosser, Eleanor, *Hamlet and Revenge*, 2nd edn, Stanford: Stanford University Press, 1971.
Rosenberg, Marvin, *The Masks of 'Hamlet'*, 1961; Newark, Del.: University of Delaware Press, 1992.
Weitz, Morris, *Hamlet and the Philosophy of Literary Criticism*, London: Faber & Faber, 1965.

Othello criticism

Adamson, Jane, *'Othello' as Tragedy: Some Problems of Judgment and Feeling*, Cambridge: Cambridge University Press, 1980.
Calderwood, James L., *The Properties of 'Othello'*, Amherst: University of Massachusetts Press, 1989.
Heilman, Robert B., *Magic in the Web: Action and Language in 'Othello'*, Lexington: University of Kentucky Press, 1956.
Jones, Eldred, *Othello's Countrymen: The African in English Renaissance Drama*, London: Oxford University Press, 1965.
Rosenberg, Marvin, *The Masks of 'Othello': The Search for the Identity of Othello, Iago, and Desdemona by Three Centuries of Actors and Critics*, 1961; Newark, Del.: University of Delaware Press, 1993.
Vaughan, Virginia, *Othello: A Contextual History*, Cambridge: Cambridge University Press, 1994.

King Lear criticism

Colie, Rosalie L. and Flahiff, F.T. eds, *Some Facets of 'King Lear': Essays in Prismatic Criticism*, Toronto and Buffalo: Toronto University Press, 1974.
Elton, William R., *'King Lear' and the Gods*, 1966; Lexington: University of Kentucky Press, 1988.
Heilman, Robert B., *This Great Stage: Image and Structure in 'King Lear'*, Baton Rouge: Louisiana State University Press, 1948.
Lusardi, James P., and Schuleter, June. *Reading Shakespeare in Performance: 'King Lear'*, London: Associated University Press, 1991.
Mack, Maynard, *'King Lear' in Our Time*, Berkeley and Los Angeles: University of California Press, 1965.
Rosenberg, Marvin, *The Masks of 'King Lear'*, 1972; Newark, Del.: University of Delaware Press, 1993.
Taylor, Gary and Warren, Michael, eds, *The Division of the Kingdoms: Shakespeare's Two Versions of 'King Lear'*, Oxford: Clarendon Press, 1983.
Urkowitz, Steven, *Shakespeare's Revision of 'King Lear'*, Princeton and Guildford: Princeton University Press, 1980.

Macbeth criticism

Bartholomeusz, Dennis, *'Macbeth' and the Players*, Cambridge: Cambridge University Press, 1984.
Brown, John Russell, ed., *Focus on 'Macbeth'*, London: Routledge & Kegan Paul, 1982.
Calderwood, James L., *If It Were Done: 'Macbeth' and Tragic Action*, Amherst: University of Massachusetts Press, 1986.
Jorgensen, Paul, *Our Naked Frailties: Sensational Art and Meaning in 'Macbeth'*, Berkeley, Los Angeles and London: University of California Press, 1971.
Paul, Henry N., *The Royal Play of 'Macbeth'*, New York: Macmillan, 1950.
Rosenberg, Marvin, *The Masks of 'Macbeth'*, 1978; Newark, Del.: University of Delaware Press, 1993.

Criticism of nondramatic poetry

Baldwin, T.W., *On the Literary Genetics of Shakespeare's Poems and Sonnets*, Urbana: University of Illinois Press, 1950.

Booth, Stephen, *An Essay on Shakespeare's Sonnets*, New York and London: Yale University Press, 1969.

Bush, Douglas, *Mythology and the Renaissance Tradition in English Literature*, rev. ed, New York: W.W. Norton, 1963.

Dubrow, Heather, *Captive Victors: Shakespeare's Narrative Poems and Sonnets*, Ithaca, New York and London: Cornell University Press, 1987.

Fineman, Joel, *Shakespeare's Perjured Eye: The Invention of Poetic Subjectivity in the Sonnets*, Berkeley, Los Angeles and London: University of California Press, 1986.

Hammond, Gerald, *The Reader and Shakespeare's Young Man Sonnets*, London: Macmillan, 1981.

Hulse, Clark, *Metamorphic Verse: The Elizabethan Minor Epic*, Princeton and Guildford: Princeton University Press, 1981.

Knight, G. Wilson, *The Mutual Flame: On Shakespeare's Sonnets and 'The Phoenix and the Turtle'*, London: Methuen, 1955.

Kreiger, Murray, *A Window to Criticism: Shakespeare's Sonnets and Modern Poetics*, Princeton: Princeton University Press, 1964.

Leishman, J.B., *Themes and Variations in Shakespeare's Sonnets*, 1961; 2nd edn, London: Hutchinson, 1967.

Muir, Kenneth, *Shakespeare's Sonnets*, London: Allen & Unwin, 1979.

Smith, Hallett, *Elizabethan Poetry*, Cambridge, Mass.: Harvard University Press, 1952.

Vendler, Helen, *The Art of Shakespeare's Sonnets*, Cambridge, Mass.: Harvard University Press, 1997.

Index of first lines of sonnets

Index of first lines of songs

And let me the cannikin clink, clink *Oth* 2.3.64
And Robin Hood, Scarlet, and John *2H4* 5.3.103
And will 'a not come again *Ham* 4.5.188

Be merry, be merry, my wife has all *2H4* 5.3.32
Blow, blow, thou winter wind *AYL* 3.1.174
But shall I go mourn for that, my dear *WT* 4.3.15

Come away, come away death *TN* 2.4.51
Come o'er the bourn, Bessy, to me *KL* 3.6.25
Come, thou monarch of the vine *AC* 3.1.111
Come unto these yellow sands *Tem* 1.2.378
Cup of wine that's brisk and fine, A *2H4* 5.3.44

Do me right *2H4* 5.3.72
Do nothing but eat, and make good cheer *2H4* 5.3.17

Farewell, dear heart, since I must needs be gone *TN* 2.3.102
Fear no more the heat o'th' sun *Cym* 4.2.258
Fie on sinful fantasy *MW* 5.5.94
Fill the cup, and let it come *2H4* 5.3.52
Flout 'em and cout 'em *Tem* 3.3.123
Fools had ne'er less grace in a year *KL* 1.4.158
For bonny sweet Robin is all my joy *Ham* 4.5.184
For I'll cut my green coat, a foot above my knee *TNK* 3.4.19
Full fadom five thy father lies *Tem* 1.2.400

George Alow came from the south, The *TNK* 3.5.60
Get you hence, for I must go *WT* 4.4.299
God of love, The *MA* 5.2.26

Hark, hark, the lark at heaven's gate sings *Cym* 2.3.20
He that has and a little tiny wit *KL* 3.2.74
Hey Robin, jolly Robin *TN* 4.2.71
Hold thy peace *TN* 2.3.65
Honour, riches, marriage, blessing *Tem* 4.1.106
How should I your true love know *Ham* 4.5.23

I am gone, sir, and anon, sir *TN* 4.2.121
I shall no more to sea, to sea *Tem* 2.2.42
I will be true, my stars, my fate *TNK* 4.3.56
In youth when I did love, did love *Ham* 5.1.61
It was a lover and his lass *AYL* 5.3.15
It was the friar of orders grey *TS* 4.1.133

Jog on, jog on, the foot-path way *WT* 4.3.121

King Stephen was and-a worthy peer *Oth* 2.3.83

Lawn as white as driven snow *WT* 4.4.220

Love, love, nothing but love, still love, still more *TC* 3.1.112

Master, the swabber, the boatswain and I, The *Tem* 2.2.46
May you never more enjoy the light *TNK* 4.1.104

No more dams I'll make for fish *Tem* 2.2.179

O fair, o sweet *TNK* 4.1.114
O mistress mine, where are you roaming *TN* 2.3.39
O'the twelfth day of December *TN* 2.3.84
Old hare hoar, An *RJ* 2.4.133
One he said it was an owl, The *TNK* 3.5.69
Orpheus with his lute made trees *H8* 3.1.3
Ousel cock, so black of hue, The *MND* 3.1.119

Pardon, goddess of the night *MA* 5.3.12
Poor soul sat sighing by a sycamore tree, The *Oth* 4.3.39

Roses, their sharp spines being gone *TNK* 1.1.1

Sigh no more, ladies, sigh no more *MA* 2.3.61

Take, o take those lips away *MM* 4.1.1
Tell me where is Fancy bred *MV* 3.2.63
Then they for sudden joy did weep *KL* 1.4.175
There dwelt a man in Babylon *TN* 2.3.78
They bore him bare-fac'd on the bier *Ham* 4.5.164
Three merry men be we *TN* 2.3.76
To shallow rivers, to whose falls *MW* 3.1.16
Tomorrow is Saint Valentine's Day *Ham* 4.5.48

Under the greenwood tree *AYL* 1.3.69

Was this fair face the cause, quoth she *AW* 1.3.69
Wedding is great Juno's crown *AYL* 5.4.139
What shall he have that kill'd the deer *AYL* 4.2.10
When Arthur first in court *2H4* 2.4.33
When Cynthia with her borrowed light *TNK* 4.1.153
When daffodils begin to peer *WT* 4.3.1
When daisies pied and violets blue *LLL* 5.2.887
When icicles hang by the wall *LLL* 5.2.905
When that I was and a little tiny boy *TN* 5.1.387
Whenas I sat in Pabylon *MW* 3.1.23
Where is the life that late I led *TS* 4.1.128
Where the bee sucks, there suck I *Tem* 5.1.88
While you here do snoring lie *Tem* 2.1.301
Who is Silvia? what is she *TGV* 4.2.38
Will you buy any tape *WT* 4.4.317

You spotted snakes with double tongue *MND* 2.2.9

GLOSSARY

Abbreviations

(?)	possible meaning
adj.	adjective
adv.	adverb
cf.	compare
dial.	dialect
esp.	especially
Fr.	French
Gr.	Greek
int.	interjection
Ital.	Italian
Lat.	Latin
OE	Old English
prep.	preposition
sb.	substantive
Sp.	Spanish
v.	verb

'a, a he

a life on (my) life (an oath)

abate blunt; beat; shorten; deprive; except

abatement diminished amount; depreciation

Abel *see* **Cain**

abhor disgust; reject

abide stay temporarily; withstand, stand up to; pay the penalty for (*cf.* **aby**)

abject *sb.* servile person; *adj.* base, servile

able empower

abode *sb.* staying; *v.* forebode

abortive *sb.* premature birth; *adj.* deformed, horrible

abram auburn

abridgement shortening; passing of time, entertainment

abroad on the move; apart

abrook bear, tolerate

abruption interruption of speech

Absey book introductory book, primer

absolute perfect, complete, without limitation; determined

abuse *sb.* deception; *v.* deceive

aby pay the penalty for (*cf.* **abide**)

abysm abyss

accident incident

accite cite, call up; excite

accommodate equip

accommodation provision, delicacy

accomplice colleague

accomplish equip

accountant responsible

accoutred dressed

accusativo 'in the accusative case' (*Lat.*)

acerb bitter

ache *see* **H**

Acheron a river of the underworld

achieve win

Achilles' spear spear able both to wound and to cure those wounds with its rust

acknown aware, in the know

aconitum wolf's bane, a poisonous plant

acquit pay back; free

Actaeon hunter in myth who, seeing Diana bathing, was turned by her into a stag (creating connotations of cuckoldry, *see* **horn**) and hunted to death by his hounds

action-taking taking legal action, litigious

acture action

Ad manes fratrum to our brothers' spirits (*Lat.*)

Adam fallen man, wickedness; Adam Bell, an archer in folklore

adamant exceedingly hard metal; magnet

adder's sense *see* **sense**

addiction propensity

addition title granted in honour of some excellence

address prepare

admiral flagship

admiration amazement, wonder

admire wonder

admittance admissibility, fashion

adoptious bestowed

Adsum here I am (*Lat.*)

advantage *sb.* addition; interest; *v.* help, benefit

adventure *sb.* risk; *v.* take a risk

advertise make known, notify

advertisement advice, admonition; news

advice thought, reflection

advised careful

aedile Roman public officer

Aeneas Trojan prince who carried his father, Anchises, out of burning Troy and became the lover of Dido (*see* **Dido**) before abandoning her to found the Roman state

Aeolus god of the winds

aery *see* **eyrie**

Aesculapius god of healing

affect *sb.* passion, appetite; affection; *v.* admire, have affection for, favour; impersonate, put on

affectedly affectionately

affection feeling, disposition, propensity; passion; affectation

affeer'd assured

affiance trust

affined connected, bound

affront *sb.* attack; *v.* come face to face with, meet

affy affiance, betroth; place trust

after in the manner of

after-eye look after

again back, reciprocally

against before; in preparation for (when)

agate jewel sometimes carved with a small figure

Agenor father of Europa (*see* **Europa**)

aglet-baby (?) baby dressed with aglets (tags attached to clothes); (?) aglet in the shape of a small figure

agnize acknowledge

a-hold close to the wind

aidance help

aim *sb.* conjecture, idea; *v.* conjecture; **cry aim** = applaud, cheer; **give aim** = observe an archer's shots

Aio te, Aeacida, Romanos vincere posse the ambiguous answer Apollo gave Pyrrhus when he enquired whether he would vanquish Rome (*Lat.* = 'I affirm that thou, descendant of Aeacus, canst conquer the Romans' or 'I affirm that the Romans can vanquish thee, descendant of Aeacus')

Ajax Greek hero in the Trojan war

alarm noise; attack; *see* **alarum**

alarum call to arms

Alcides Hercules (*see* **Hercules**)

alderliefest dearest of all

Alecto one of the Furies, mythological hags with serpents in their hair

all amort downcast

all hid the game of hide and seek

all to altogether, utterly

Alla nostra casa ben venuto, molto honorato signor mio Petrucio 'Welcome to our house, my much-honoured Signor Petruchio' (*Ital.*)

Alla stoccato at the thrust (*Ital.*)

allay *sb.* calming influence; *v.* detract from

allegiant loyal

All-hallond Eve Hallowe'en (31 October)

All-hallowmas All Saints' Day (1 November)

All-hallown summer late season of fine weather

allicholy, allycholy melancholy

alligant Quickly's word for either 'elegant' or 'eloquent'

allons 'let's go' (*Fr.*)

allottery something allotted, share

allowance acknowledgement; approval, praise; permission

All-Souls' day 2 November

all-thing entirely

Almain German

alms-drink drink taken as charity

alow *see* **'loo**

alter exchange

Althaea Queen of Calydon who killed her son, Meleager, by burning a firebrand reserved for him by the Fates

amain aloud; at speed

amerce penalize

ames-ace two aces thrown at dice, the lowest score

Glossary

an *see* and

anatomize open up for inspection, dissect

anatomy skeleton

Anchises father of Aeneas (*see* Aeneas)

anchor religious recluse

ancient standard; standard-bearer; Ensign

and if

andirons props to support burning logs over a hearth

angel spirit; English gold coin depicting the archangel Michael

Anheers a form of address, possibly Dutch ('*Mynheers*') or Turkish ('*Ameers*', '*Emirs*')

Anna sister of Dido (*see* Dido)

annexment addition, appendage

annothanize (?) *see* anatomize; (?) annotate

annoy *sb.* torment, pain, injury; *v.* injure

anon in a moment; till anon = until a little later

Anthropophagi cannibals

Anthropophaginian cannibal

antic *sb.* grotesque figure, fool; grotesque pageant; *adj.* in grotesque disguise, masked; *v.* make grotesque

antre cave

ape mimic; fool; leading apes in hell = traditional punishment of old maids

Apollo god of song and music, of the sun, of healing and of the oracle at Delphi; he fell in love with Daphne who was transformed into a laurel as he chased her

appaid satisfied

apparently in open view

appeach impeach, accuse

appeal *sb.* formal challenge, accusation; *v.* impeach

appellant formal challenger

apple-john type of apple kept until shrivelled

appliance compliance; service; treatment

appointed equipped, armed

appointment equipment; resolution; direction

apprehensive possessing reason

approof proof, proving; sanction

approve prove; put to proof; be to one's credit

apt ready, inclined; probable, likely; impressionable

aqua-vitae strong spirits

Aquilon the North wind

Arabian bird the phoenix, a mythical bird supposed to be unique

arbitrament, arbitrement arbitration, decision

arch lord

argal see ergo

Argier Algiers

argo see ergo

argosy large trading vessel

argument theme, subject of controversy; proof, demonstration

Ariachne = Arachne, a weaver in mythology, metamorphosed to a spider

Ariadne beloved of Theseus, who abandoned her

Arion poet who charmed a dolphin into carrying him over the waves

arm bear, carry

arm-gaunt lean from bearing arms

Armigero from the title '*Armiger*' (*Lat.*), signifying entitlement to a coat of arms

armipotent mighty in arms

aroint thee, aroynt thee be off with you

arras curtain of woven tapestry

arrose sprinkle

Arthur's show an exhibition of archery given by an Arthurian society

articulate negotiate terms; set forth in detail

artificial relating to or skilled in any of the 'arts' (painting, medicine, witchcraft, *etc.*)

artist learned man

Ascanius son of Aeneas (*see* Aeneas)

asinico little ass (*Sp.*)

aspect gaze; image; (in astrology) planetary position

aspersion sprinkling, with connotations of benediction

aspicious Dogberry's word for 'suspicious'

assay *sb.* attempt; challenge; trial; *v.* try, test out, make trial of

assubjugate subdue

assurance transfer of property; guarantee, security; betrothal

assure betroth

Astraea goddess of justice

Atalanta maiden who outsprinted her suitors and put them to death

Ate goddess of confusion and strife

atomy atom, tiny particle; Quickly's word for 'anatomy' (*see* anatomy)

atone agree; set in agreement

atonement agreement

Atropos one of the Fates (*see* Fates)

attach arrest

attachment arrest

attainder accusation, taint, disgrace

attaint *sb.* disgrace; infection; weariness; *v.* condemn; stain

attasked taken to task

attribute esteem, character, reputation

attribution praise

aught anything

aunt old woman, crony; female beggar; prostitute

auricular relating to the ear, heard

avise advise

avoid leave; expel, get rid of; (in law) invalidate

awkward oblique, adverse

baby girl's doll

baccare stand back (*pseudo-Lat.*)

back saddle or ride (a horse)

back-friend false friend; police officer

backsword man fencer (backsword = single-stick, used in fencing)

back-trick backward step in dancing

baffle (of a knight) publicly disgrace

bait *sb.* light meal; *v.* harrass, terrorize, as with dogs; offer bait to, tempt, lure

baldrick belt, girdle

bale sorrow, misfortune

balk miss; lay up; balk logic = chop logic

ballow bring

ban *sb.* curse; *v.* curse

Banbury cheese proverbially thin cheese

ban-dog fierce dog

bandy toss, exchange; contend, brawl

bane poison; death, destruction

bank *sb.* shore; *v.* sail along the shore

banquet light refreshment; running banquet = light refreshment; whipping

Barbary breed of horse

Barbason a devil

barbed (of a horse) armed

barber-monger someone always at the barber's shop, vain person

barful full of difficulties

bark *sb.* ship; *v.* strip bark from

barley-break rustic chasing game in which the base was called 'hell'

barm yeast, head of froth

barne child

barnacle shellfish supposed to metamorphose into a goose

Barrabas murderer whose release from prison the Jews demanded instead of Christ's

Barson Barston or Barcheston (Warwickshire towns)

Bartholomew boar-pig roast pig eaten at Bartholomew Fair (*see* Bartholomew-tide)

Bartholomew-tide St Bartholomew's day (24 August), date of a popular fair

Basan biblical mountain famous for its bulls

base a chasing game; bid a base = challenge to a chase

base-court lower courtyard

bases knight's pleated skirt

Basilisco-like like Basilisco, a boastful knight in the play *Soliman and Perseda* (1592)

basilisk cockatrice (*see* cockatrice); large cannon

bass-viol stringed instrument, an early cello

basta enough (*Ital.*)

bastard sweet wine from Spain

bastinado cudgelling, hefty wallop

bate *sb.* strife; *v.* flutter the wings; abate, diminish; let off; lose; modify

bate-breeding mischief-making

bateless sharp

bat-fowling bird-catching at night by means of a strong light and sticks

batler paddle used to beat clothes being washed

batten gorge and grow fat

bauble toy, thing of trifling value; fool; fool's stick

baubling like a bauble, trifling

bavian baboon

bavin brushwood

bawcock fine chap

bawd hare; pimp

bay *sb.* space under the gable of a building; barking; *adj.* (of horses) reddish brown; *v.* chase with barking; trap, corner; at bay = cornered

bays poet's laurel wreath

beached of the beach

beachy *see* beached

beadle parish constable

beadsman person hired to pray for others

beam large piece of wood, mentioned by Christ as a metaphor for grave sinfulness (Matt. vii.3-5; Luke vi.41-2) (*cf.* mote)

bear win; bear in hand = lead on, deceive

bear-herd, bearherd *see* bearward

bearing-cloth cloth in which a child was carried to be christened

bearward bear-keeper

beated beaten

beaver helmet's visor

beck *sb.* beckoning; *v.* beckon

become be appropriate for, suit

bedded lying down

Bedlam hospital for the insane

bedlam *sb.* insane person; *adj.* insane, frantic

bed-swerver adulterous person

beest the unpalatable milk of a cow that has just given birth

beetle *sb.* sledge-hammer; *v.* jut out

beldam grandmother; crone

be-leed left without wind, high and dry

bell, book, and candle formula used in the ceremony of excommunication

Glossary

Bellona goddess of war

bell-wether sheep at the head of a flock

belock'd locked

bemadding causing madness

be-met met

bemete measure out

bemoiled covered with dirt

be-monster make hideous

bench *sb.* authority; *v.* raise to or occupy a position of authority

bench-hole hole in a privy

bend *sb.* look; obeisance; knot; *v.* turn; crease; tense

benetted netted, trapped

benevolence obligatory loan to the sovereign

benison blessing

bent limit, strain; direction, disposition; arch; sight

berayed stained, sullied

Bergomask from Bergamo in Italy, rustic

Bermoothes Bermudas

beshrew curse

besom brush, broom

Besonian ignoramus, beggarly person

besort *sb.* appropriate company; *v.* be appropriate for

beteem grant, allow

betid happened

betime soon, early

bevel oblique, zigzag

Bevis Bevis of Southampton, a legendary hero renowned for feats of arms

bewray betray, reveal, divulge

bezonian *see* **Besonian**

bias *adj.* convex; *adv.* crookedly; **of bias** = oblique, roundabout

bias-drawing deceit

bide stay, linger; endure

bifold twofold

bigamy marriage with someone previously married

biggen coarse nightcap

bilbo sword with a flexible blade

bilboes shackles used for prisoners on a ship

bill pike or halberd, painted brown to prevent rust; officer carrying a bill; written note; notice

bird-bolt flat-headed arrow for shooting birds

birding-piece gun for shooting birds

bis coctus cooked twice (*Lat.*)

bisson blind; obscuring the sight

bite the thumb make an insulting gesture

bitumed smeared with bitumen, made watertight

Black-Monday Easter Monday

blame blameworthy (in the phrase 'too blame')

blank *sb.* range, focus, target; *v.* make pale, drain of colour; **blank charter** = blank cheque

blastment blight

blazon *sb.* coat of arms; proclamation; description; *v.* proclaim; describe

blear dim or blur, especially with weeping

blench *sb.* sidelong glance; *v.* flinch, turn aside

blind-worm slow-worm

blister'd padded

block mould for shaping a hat; mounting-block (for mounting horses)

blood family; gallant man; character, disposition; appetite, passion; **in blood** = active, healthy

blood-bolter'd having hair caked and matted with blood

blood-sized glazed with blood (*cf.* **size**)

blow swell; (of plants) blossom; (of flies) lay eggs (on); **blow wind i'th' breech** = be unable to keep pace (with); break wind

blowse stocky, rosy-cheeked girl

blubbered with tear-stained face

bluebottle beadle, parish constable

blue-cap Scot

blurt scoff

board draw up alongside; attack

bob *sb.* jest; *v.* beat; cheat, diddle

bodement foreboding

bodkin short dagger; hair-pin; **God's bodkin** = by the Eucharist (God's little body) (an oath)

bodykins *see* **bodkin** (**God's bodkin**)

boggle take fright, swerve uncertainly

bolins bow-lines on a ship

boll'n swollen

bolt *sb.* arrow; shackle; *v.* sift, refine; shackle

bolter cloth for sifting meal

bolting-hutch sifting-bin

bombard wine vessel

bombast *sb.* cotton padding; *adj.* padded; bombastic, verbally over-elaborate

bona terra, mala gens a good land but bad people (*Lat.*)

bona-roba better class of prostitute (*Ital.*)

bones rustic musical instrument accompanied by bells or tongs; bone bobbins for lace-making

book-man scholar

boot *sb.* booty, spoil; something extra; advantage, help; *v.* give as something extra; help; **give the boots** = make a laughing-stock of

boot-hose long over-stocking

bootless useless, pointless

Boreas north wind

borrow *sb.* loan; *v.* take, adopt

borrowed taken, feigned, not genuine

bosky shrubby, woody

botcher one who patches old clothes

botchy carbuncular, ulcerous

bots maggot infection in horses

bottom *sb.* valley; ship's hold, ship; bobbin for winding thread; *v.* wind

bought and sold tricked, betrayed

bounce bang

bounden bound, obliged

bourn limit; burn, brook

bow-hand left-hand side of an archer

boy endow with the characteristics of a boy

brabble brawl

brace pair; armour to protect the arm; defensive position

brach bitch-hound

bragless without bragging

braid *adj.* false, deceitful *v.* upbraid, reproach

brainish deluded, frenzied

brain-pan skull

brake clump of bushes

branched bearing a pattern of leafy branches

brave *sb.* vaunt, boast; *adj.* fine, admirable; finely dressed; fearless, insolent; *v.* make brave, adorn; defy; **brave it** = swagger

bravery finery; flamboyance; defiant attitude

brawl French dance

brawn fattened boar; arm or leg muscle

break break up, disband; communicate; discipline; break across, **break cross** = (of a knight's lance) break awkwardly or unfairly; **break up** = open

break-neck disaster

breast singing voice

breathe talk, talk of; train, condition, accustom; allow to take a breath

breathing voice; excercise, activity; interval

breech breeches, trousers; **i'th' breech on** = behind, following

breed-bate trouble-maker (*cf.* **bate**)

breese, breeze gadfly

brewage brew

Briareus giant with a hundred arms and fifty heads

bribed (?) stolen; (?) obtained through bribery

bride-house house where a wedding takes place

brief *sb.* letter; list, summary; **brief in hand** = in need of attention

brinded patterned with streaks

bring off rescue

broach pierce; tap

brock badger

brogues heavy shoes

broke trade

broken fragmented; missing

teeth; **broken music** = music played by instruments of different families

broker go-between, pimp

brooch *sb.* ornament; *v.* decorate

brooded brooding

Brownist member of an English Puritan sect founded by Robert Browne

bruit *sb.* rumour; *v.* announce, report

bubuncle Fluellen's confusion of '*bubo*' (*Lat.* = 'abscess') and 'carbuncle'

buck stag; linen in the wash; **buck of the first head** = fully grown stag

bucking laundry

buckler *sb.* shield; *v.* protect, shield; **give the bucklers** = acknowledge defeat

Bucklersbury London street known for its apothecaries

buckram tough, stiff linen

buck-washing washing of linen

budget tinker's bag

buff hard-wearing leather worn by constables

bug bugbear, bogeyman

bugle black glass bead

bulk display stall at the front of a shop

bully fine man, friend

bum-baily bailiff

bung pickpocket

burden load; undersong; refrain; **at a burden** = at one birth

burgonet close-fitting helmet

burn heat up; light up; **burn daylight** = waste time

burthen *see* **burden**

buss *sb.* kiss; *v.* kiss

buttery bar hatch of a buttery (store room) where beer was served

butt-shaft strong, heavy arrow

buzzard insect; fool

by and by immediately; in due course

by-drinkings drinks between meals

by-peeping glancing sidelong

by'r lady by our Lady (an oath)

by'r lakin, byrlakin by our little Lady (an oath)

cabin *sb.* hut; den, cave; *v.* dwell, rest

cabinet small lodging

cacodemon malignant spirit

caddis ribbon for a garter

cade large barrel

cadent falling

Cadmus legendary founder of Thebes

caduceus Mercury's staff, wound about with two serpents

cage prison

Cain son of Adam and Eve, who murdered his brother Abel; **Cain-coloured** = red, the imagined colour of Cain's beard

caitiff, caitive *sb.* wretch; *adj.* captive; wretched

cake (of roses) compressed block used as perfume; **cake is dough** = plan has failed

calculate forecast by means of a horoscope; speculate upon the future

Caleno custore me Elizabethan version of '*cailin og a' stor*', the refrain of a popular Irish song, for Pistol a specimen of an incomprehensible foreign language

Calipolis character in Peele's *Battle of Alcazar* (1594), there presented with a lioness to eat

caliver light musket

calkins parts of a horse-shoe

call decoy

callat, callet slut

Cambyses a Persian king, subject of an early Elizabethan tragedy

can began

canary wine from the Canaries; Spanish dance

candidatus 'clad in a white robe', hence candidate (*Lat.*)

candied frosted, as if with sugar

candle-mine load of tallow

candle-waster book-worm

canker sore; wild rose; parasitic caterpillar

cannikin small drinking can

canon Church law, *hence* law, edict

cantle segment of a circle

canton song

canvas, canvass toss about

canzonet canzonetta, short song

capable responsive, appreciative; capacious; qualified to inherit

capacity mental capacity, mind

cap-a-pe, cap-à-pe 'head to foot' (*Old Fr.*)

capital mortal, fatal; chief, main

Capitol temple of Jupiter in Rome

capitulate come to terms

capocchia fool, simple person (*Ital.*)

capriccio caprice, fancy (*Ital.*)

captious capacious; deceitful

car cart, chariot

caract official marking

carbonado *sb.* fish or meat scored and grilled; *v.* score, slash

carcanet jewelled necklace

card *sb.* playing card; toothed instrument for combing out wool; compass; model; *v.* adulterate, dilute; **by the card** = correctly; **card of ten** = playing card worth ten points; **cooling card** = playing card that dashes an opponent's hopes; **pack cards with** = shuffle playing cards in favour of

cardecue small French coin (*quart d'écu*)

cardinally Elbow's word for 'carnally'

cardmaker maker of cards for wool (*see* **card**)

carduus benedictus 'holy thistle' (*Lat.*), a plant credited with healing properties

caret 'it is missing' (*Lat.*); interpreted by Quickly as 'carrot' (penis)

carl churl, rustic person

carlot rustic person

carnation rosy-pink

carpet *sb.* cover for chests and tables; **on carpet consideration** = at court rather than on the battle-field

carpet-monger knight more at home at court than in battle

carrack galleon, treasure ship

carriage carrying; ability to carry; conduct; deportment; purport

carry coals endure insults without retaliation

carry out a side fulfil a side of an agreement

carry-tale spy

carve *v.* compliment; **be one's own carver, carve for oneself** = be independent

case *sb.* question; body, skin or clothes; *v.* clothe, mask; skin; **in case** = in a position or mood; **on the case** = for some particular offence

cashiered discarded; (?) robbed

cast *adj.* cast off; *v.* vomit; discharge; examine; calculate; **cast the gorge** = vomit

casted *see* **cast** (*adj.*)

Castiliano vulgo Sir Toby's attempt to refer in Spanish and (?) Latin to (?) wine, (?) the devil

casual accidental; subject to misfortune

cat o' mountain, cat-a-mountain leopard

Cataian Cathaian (Chinese), used insultingly

cataplasm plaster

catastrophe final phase of action in classical drama

catch tune for several voices

cater-cousins close friends

caterpillar parasite

cates choice provisions, delicacies

catling catgut for stringed instruments

cautel wile, deception

cautelous deceitful

censer ornamental vessel for burning perfume

censure *sb.* judgement; opinion; *v.* judge; express an opinion

centre the earth's mid-point

century one hundred soldiers

Cerberus three-headed dog at the gate of the underworld, fought with by Hercules and charmed to sleep by Orpheus

cerecloth shroud

cerements shroud

Ceres goddess of agriculture and plenty

'cerns concerns

certes truly

cess ceasing, decease; **out of cess** = excessively

cesse cease

chair-days time of rest

chairs of order stalls in St George's Chapel, Windsor, for the Knights of the Order of the Garter

challenge *sb.* claim; legal objection; *v.* claim as due

chamberer wooer

chamber-lye urine

chambers small cannon

chamblet rich cloth of silk and goat's hair

champaign open countryside

champion challenge to fight

changeling turncoat; fairy child swapped for a human one (or vice versa)

chanson song

chanticleer cock

chape metal cap on the end of a scabbard

chapless with the lower jaw gone

chaplets garlands

chapman merchant

chaps chops, jaws

character *sb.* handwriting; *v.* write

charactery writing

chare *sb.* chore; *v.* accomplish, finish

charge-house school

charging-staff knight's lance

Charles' wain constellation of the Plough

charneco sweet wine

Charon ferryman of the underworld

chase hunt; (in tennis) bouncing ball

chat gossip about

chaudron entrails

che I; **che vor ye** = I warrant you; **ch'ill** = I will; **ch'ud** = I had (*dial.*)

cheapen bargain for

cheater officer in charge of estates forfeited to the crown

check *sb.* rebuke; *v.* come to a stop; rebuke

chequin gold coin

cherry-pit children's game of throwing cherry stones into a hole

cherubin cherub

cheval volant … qui a les narines de feu, le 'the flying horse … who has fiery nostrils' (*Fr.*)

cheveril, chev'ril kid leather, known for its stretching capacity

chewet jackdaw; minced-meat pie

Chi passa name of a popular dance tune (*Ital.* = 'Who is passing?')

chiding din

chien est retourné à son propre vomissement, et la truie lavée au bourbier, le 'The dog has returned to his own vomit and the washed sow to her mud' (*Fr.*, 2 Peter ii.22)

child girl

childe title used by young nobles aspiring to knighthood

childed having children

childing generative, fertile

ch'ill *see* **che**

chirurgeonly in the expert manner of a surgeon

choler one of the four humours (*see* **humour**); anger

chop *sb.* crack; *v.* crack; **chop on** = burst in on

chopine fashionable platform shoe

chopless *see* **chapless**

chough jackdaw

christom newly christened

chrysolite white or green gem

ch'ud *see* **che**

cicatrice mark, scar

cinque-pace quick dance

Cinque-ports five English ports; the barons of these places

cipher *sb.* the figure nought, zero; *v.* decipher; represent

Circe sorceress in Homer's *Odyssey* who transformed men into beasts

circummur'd walled round

cite summon, as to court; incite

citizen city-bred

cittern guitar with a carved head

civet perfume derived from a civet cat's anal glands

civil of citizens, urban; well-behaved; **civil doctor** = doctor of civil law

clack-dish begging bowl

clap pledge with a clasping of hands; **clap aboard** = board (a ship); **clap into** = begin promptly; **clap i'th' clout** = hit the bull's-eye (*cf.* clout); **clap up** = agree promptly

clapper-claw handle roughly

clepe call

clept called

clerestories upper windows in halls and churches

clerk cleric, scholar

clew ball of twine

climate *sb.* region of the earth or sky; *v.* live in a particular region

climatures inhabitants of a particular region

cling shrink up, wither

clinquant glittering

clip encircle, embrace

clipper one who trims coins for the metal

close *sb.* encounter; (in music) cadence; *adj.* confined; secret; secretive; *adv.* secretly; *v.* come to agreement

closure containment; conclusion

cloth o' gold, cloth-of-gold sumptuous, top-quality cloth

Glossary

clothier's yard a 'cloth-yard' length, the length of an arrow (*cf.* **yard**)

cloud (of horses) facial blemish

clout target in archery; cloth, rag; **babe of clouts** = rag doll; idiot

clouted patched; hobnailed

clown person from the country

clubs traditional cry for assistance in breaking up a brawl

clyster-pipe syringe inserted into the rectum or vagina

coat coat of arms

cobloaf small loaf

cock rowing boat towed behind a larger ship; weathercock; tap; (in oaths) God; **by cock and pie** = by God and pie (an oath) (*cf.* **pie**)

cockatrice legendary creature with a fatal stare

cockle cockleshell; weed; **cockle hat** = pilgrim's hat

cocklight first light, dawn

cockney person of affected manners

cock'red pampered

cockshut twilight

Cocytus a river of the underworld

cod husk

codding lascivious

codpiece prominent pouch at the front of a man's breeches to hold his genitals

coffin pie-crust

cog cheat

cognizance emblem worn by retainers

coif cap

coign corner

coil commotion, fuss

coistrel base person, scoundrel

Colbrand Danish giant in the English romance of Guy of Warwick

collect infer, learn

collection piecing together, understanding

collied darkened

collop slice of flesh

Colme-kill Iona

coloquintida colocynth, a bitter apple

Colossus gigantic statue of Apollo at Rhodes that stood over the harbour entrance

colour *sb.* appearance; pretext; sort, type; *v.* disguise

colourable plausible

colours military colours, banner

colt *sb.* young and foolish person; *v.* play the fool with, trick; **colt's tooth** = friskiness

combinate bound by pledge

come off withdraw; pay up

coming-on compliant

commeddled mingled

commit commit sins

commodity supply of merchandise; benefit, advantage; pledge against a loan

commoner prostitute

comonty Sly's word for 'comedy'

companion fellow, used insultingly

comparative *sb.* dealer in insults; *adj.* skilled at (insulting) comparisons

compeer *sb.* peer, companion; *v.* be the peer of, equal

competitor partner

complain bewail

complement outward appearance

complexion constitution, nature; face

complot *sb.* design, conspiracy; *v.* conspire

comply behave formally

compose reach agreement

compt account, reckoning; the Day of Judgement

comptible sensitive

con study, memorize; **con thanks** = acknowledge gratitude

Con tutto il cuore ben trovato 'With all my heart well met' (*Ital.*)

conceit *sb.* mental, imaginative or artistic conception; wit, intelligence; fancy article; *v.* conceive

conceited witty, inventive; **be conceited of** = conceive of

conceptious conceiving, fertile

concernancy relevance

conclusion experiment; judgement; riddle

concolinel (?) title of a song; (?) singer's preparatory warble

concupiscible concupiscent, lustful

concupy (?) concupiscence; (?) concubine

condition rank; disposition; compact, contract

condolement grieving; (?) confused with dole, portion

conference conversation, debate

confessors boasters

confiners inhabitants

congee, congie bow, take one's leave

congree agree together

conscience matter of conscience; mind, thoughts

conscionable governed by conscience

consider reward; (?) appreciate

consign subscribe, endorse

consist stand firm, insist

consolate console

conspectuity power of vision

constring'd drawn together, compressed

contain retain

contestation contention

continent *sb.* container, vessel; sum, summary; *adj.* restraining

contraction solemn agreement

control *sb.* compulsion; *v.* contradict; overpower

controller steward; critic

convenient fit, suitable

convent call together

conventicle secret assembly

conversation dealing; social conduct

converse associate, be in company (with)

conversion promotion; conversation

convert change

convertite penitent

convey manage discreetly; steal

conveyance dishonest dealing; (in law) transfer of property; escort

convict convicted

convince overpower; prove; prove guilty, convict

convive feast together

convoy means of transport

cony rabbit

cony-catch dupe, cheat

copatain hat hat with a high crown

cope *sb.* sky; *v.* encounter; have dealings; requite

copesmate companion

copp'd peaked

copy theme, copiously discussed; exemplar, model; copyhold, tenure

coragio courage (*Ital.*)

coram for 'quorum', justice whose particular presence was necessary for some cases

coranto dance with a running step

Corinth ancient city know for its licentiousness and partying

Corinthian one from Corinth (*see* **Corinth**)

corky dry, withered

Cornelia mother of the Gracchi (famous early Roman republicans)

cornet body of cavalry

cornuto horned beast, cuckold (*Ital.*) (*cf.* **horn**)

corollary excessive amount

corporal of the body, physical

correctioner one from the 'House of Correction'

corrigible corrective; susceptible of punishment

corroborate strengthened; Pistol's word for 'ruined'

corslet piece of body armour

costard large apple; the head

costermonger fruit seller, petty trader

cote *sb.* cottage; *v.* overtake

cot-quean man who meddles in domestic affairs

Cotsall the Cotswold hills

couch lie hidden; cause to shrink back

counsel reflection; secrets

countenance *sb.* face, outward appearance, demeanour; approval, patronage; *v.* behold; suit

counter *sb.* coin of negligible value; debtors' prison; *adv.* (in hunting) backwards, off course

counterchange exchange, reciprocation

counterfeit *sb.* image, reproduction; fake money; *adj.* painted, not real

Counter-gate gate of the Counter prison (*cf.* **counter**)

countermand contradict; prohibit

counterpoint counterpane, tapestry

countervail counterbalance, be equal to

county count

Couple a gorge Pistol's version of '*coupe la gorge*' (*Fr.* = 'cut the throat')

courage disposition

course sail of a ship

courser horse; **courser's hair** = horse's hair, supposed to turn into a serpent in water

court of guard guard room; body of soldiers on guard

court-cupboard sideboard

courthand handwriting used for legal contracts

cousin any near relation

coverture covering, shelter

cowish cowardly

cowl-staff wooden rod for carrying a cowl (tub)

cox cock's (God's) (*see* **cock**)

coxcomb jester's cap; the head

coy caress; show reluctance

coz cousin (*see* **cousin**)

cozen cheat

cozier cobbler

crab crab apple

crack *sb.* lad, rascal; partial fracture; *v.* boast; **cracked within the ring** = (of coins) nicked past the ring around the sovereign's head, and so no longer legal tender

crack-hemp one deserving to be hanged

crak'd cracked (*see* **crack**)

crank *sb.* winding passage; *v.* twist and turn

crants garland

craven *sb.* cock; coward; *v.* make cowardly

craze break, damage

credent believing; believable, plausible

credit credibility; belief, current opinion

crescive growing, having the power of growth

cressets fire-baskets, beacons

crestless not bearing a heraldic crest, not aristocratic

critic fault-finder, satirist

cross *sb.* an Elizabethan coin; *adj.* quarrelsome, thwarting; (of lightning) forked

cross'd freed from debts

Glossary

cross-gartered wearing garters above and below the knee (and so crossed behind)

cross-row the alphabet

crow-flower the ragged robin flower

crow-keeper, crowkeeper scarecrow; boy employed to shoo birds off crops

crown imperial the fritillary plant

crudy thick

crupper strap fixing the saddle to the horse's back end

crusado Portuguese coin

cry *sb.* barking pack of hounds; rumour; *v.* proclaim; **cried in the top of** = loudly exceeded; **cry aim** *see* **aim**; **cry out of** = cry out against; **cry up** = applaud

cubiculo bedroom

Cucullus non facit monachum 'The hood does not make the monk' (*Lat.*, proverbial)

cullion rascal

culverin small cannon

cum privilegio 'with privilege (*i.e.* immunity)' (*Lat.*); *cum privilegio ad imprimendum solum* = 'with the privilege for printing only' (*i.e.* 'with the sole right to print')

cunning *sb.* knowledge; skill; *adj.* skilful; ingenious

Cupid son of Venus, a winged boy, sometimes thought of as blind, whose arrows caused people to fall in (and out of) love; **Cupid's flower** = pansy

curate parish priest

curdied congealed

curiosity delicacy, scrupulousness

curious scrupulous, careful; elaborate, exquisite; anxious

currence flowing

curst fierce, cantankerous

curtal with a docked tail

curtle-axe short broadsword

cushes thigh-armour

Custalorum for '*Custos Rotulorum*' (*Lat.* = 'keeper of the rolls'), the highest justiciary office in a county

customer prostitute; prostitute's client

cut docked or gelded horse; female genitals; **cut and long-tail** = every kind; in any event; **draw cuts** = draw lots

cut-purse, cutpurse petty thief who snips purses from people's belts

cuttle (?) thief

Cyclops = Cyclopes, one-eyed giants who assisted in the manufacture of armour for the gods

cyme a medicinal plant

cynic foul-mouthed philosopher

Cynthia the goddess Diana when represented as the moon

cypress cypress wood; crape, linen

Cytherea the goddess Venus

Daedalus father of Icarus (*see* **Icarus**)

daff *see* **doff**

Dagonet King Arthur's fool

Daintry Daventry

dainty *adj.* particular, finicky; **make dainty** = hesitate primly

dam mother

Damascus traditional scene of Abel's murder (*see* **Cain**)

dan sir

dancing horse a famous Elizabethan performing horse

dancing-rapier ornamental sword worn when dancing

danger power to harm

Dansker Dane

Daphne *see* **Apollo**

dare (in bird-catching) dazzle, daze

darkling in the dark

darraign set in order, prepare

dash *sb.* mark, sign; *v.* crush, dishearten; **at first dash** = at the outset

date fixed term or limit

daub it put on a false show

daubery false pretence, trickery

day-bed couch

day-woman dairymaid

dear important; intense, ardent; grievous

dearth scarcity, *hence* high value

death-practised whose death has been plotted

deathsman executioner

death-token sign of the plague

debate *sb.* struggle, contention; *v.* contend; contend about

debile feeble

debitor and creditor account book; book-keeper

Deborah Israelite judge who incited an attack on Sisera, the general of the Canaanite king Jabin

debosh'd debauched

decerns Dogberry's word for 'concerns'

decimation execution of one man in ten

deck *sb.* deck of cards; *v.* adorn, cover

decoct boil up

deed performance, doing; contract; **deed of saying** = keeping promises

deep-fet fetched from deep down

deer animals

default fault, offence; **in the default** = (?) when necessary; (?) when you fail

defeat mar, destroy; defraud

defeature disfigurement

defence armour; fencing, swordplay

defend forbid

definement definition, description

defunct extinct, dead

defunction death

defunctive relating to death, funereal

degree order, hierarchy; step, stage

delations narrations, accusations

delicates luxuries, delicacies

deliverly nimbly

demean conduct, behave

demerit merit; deficiency, sin

demi-cannon large gun

demure *adj.* solemn, modest; *v.* look thoughtfully

denay *sb.* denial; *v.* deny

denier small copper coin

denunciation public announcement

depend be dependent; lean; hang, impend

dependency dependants; logical sequence; submissiveness

deplore talk woefully

depose take an oath; examine on oath

deputation appointment or office of a deputy (usually in high office)

deracinate uproot

derived descended

dern dark, wild

derogate *adj.* degenerate, debased; derogatory; *v.* degrade oneself

descant *sb.* sung variations; *v.* sing variations

descension descent

descry *sb.* discovery; *v.* discover

design *sb.* purpose, enterprise; *v.* designate, refer to

designment purpose, enterprise

determinate *adj.* at an end; decisive; planned; *v.* put an end to

determination end, expiry; decision

determine end, conclude; put an end to

Deucalion with his wife, the sole survivors of a great flood sent by Jupiter

deuce-ace a low score at dice

dewlap loose flesh around a cow's throat

dexter right

Di faciant laudis summa sit ista tuae 'The gods grant that this may be the peak of thy glory' (*Lat.*, Ovid)

diable devil (*Fr.*)

diablo devil (*Sp.*)

dial clock; sundial

Dian, Diana goddess of chastity, hunting and the moon (*cf.* **Cynthia**)

diapason bass accompaniment to a melody

diaper towel

dich (?) do it

Dickon Dick (Richard)

Dido Queen of Carthage, loved and abandoned by Aeneas (*see* **Aeneas**)

diet *sb.* prescribed course; food; *v.* prescribe a course for, condition

difference distinguishing mark in heraldry; distinction; variety; variance, strife

diffidence doubt, mistrust

digression deviation (from right)

dilate extend; relate or set out extensively

dildo artificial phallus, frequently mentioned in ballads

dilemma argument which always catches an opponent out

diluculo surgere 'to rise early [is very healthy]' (*Lat.*, proverbial)

dint impression, force

directitude mistake for (?) discrediture (disrepute); (?) dejectitude (misfortune)

Dis Pluto (*see* **Pluto**)

disable disqualify, disparage

disanimate dishearten

disappointed unprepared

disaster sign of ill-omen, as seen in the stars

disbranch break off, as from a tree trunk

discandy melt, thaw (*cf.* **candied**)

discase undress (*cf.* **case**)

discernings intellect

discomfortable having no word of comfort

discommend disapprove of

discontent discontented person, malcontent

discourse *sb.* talk, conversation; process or faculty of reasoning; *v.* talk

discover expose, reveal; distinguish

discovery revelation; exploration, reconnaissance

disdained disdainful

disease *sb.* unease, distress; *v.* make uneasy, trouble

disedg'd satisfied, with respect to appetite

disfurnish deprive, leave with nothing

disgracious lacking grace, unpleasant

disguise masque; wild drunkenness

dishabited dislodged, stripped

dishonest immodest

dishonesty unchastity

dislike displease; disapprove

disliken disguise

dislimn break up, smudge

disme tenth part

dismission dismissal

dismount (of swords) unsheathe; (of guns) lower

disorb'd thrown out of its place in the sky

dispark put (parkland) to other uses

Glossary

dispatch settle, conclude; kill; bereave, deprive

dispiteous merciless

disponge be sponged, drip

dispose *sb.* disposal; disposition; *v.* compose, make terms

disposer one who can do what he or she will with another

disposition arrangements

dispropertied dispossessed

dispursed disbursed, distributed

disputable disputatious, argumentative

dissembly Dogberry's word for 'assembly'

distain make colourless; stain, defile

distance (in fencing) correct space between the opponents

distaste be distasteful; make distasteful; find distasteful

distemper *sb.* lack of even temper, lack of balance; *v.* upset, disturb

distemperature constitutional disorder in the mind or body

distinctly separately, individually

distinguishment distinction

distract *adj.* separate; deranged, confused; *v.* divide; derange, confuse

distrain confiscate

distressful gained by misery and toil

dive-dapper dabchick, little grebe

divers several, various, different; perverse, evil

dividant separable, different

divided unfinished, broken

dividual separable

division musical notes that elaborate upon a basic melody; military arrangement

divulge openly proclaim

do him dead kill him

doctrine lesson

document lesson

doff take off; put off, dismiss

dog-apes baboons

dogged dog-like, cruel

doit small coin

dole grief; share; **happy man be his dole** = may his lot be that of a happy man (*i.e.* good luck to him)

dollar silver coin

domineer revel, feast

dominical red letter used to mark Sundays in almanacs

dominie schoolmaster

doom *sb.* judgement; day of judgement; *v.* judge, sentence

dotant senile person

double voucher testimony given by two independent parties

double-fatal fatal in two ways, as with the yew which was both poisonous and used for making bows

double-man supernatural apparition

doublet and hose vest and breeches (basic Elizabethan male dress)

doubt *sb.* suspicion; fear; *v.* suspect; fear

dout extinguish

dowlas coarse linen from Brittany

dowle small feather

down-gyved fallen down and resembling gyves (fetters)

down-roping falling in long strings

dowsets testicles

doxy female beggar

drab strumpet

drachma silver coin

draff pig-swill

draught sink, privy

draw withdraw; receive; drain; **draw dry-foot** = hunt by the scent

drawer tapster, waiter

dress prepare; adorn, cultivate

dribbling (in archery) weakly shot, ineffective

drift *sb.* intention, purpose; shower; *adj.* driving

drollery puppet show; comic painting

drum rallying-point

drumble be sluggish, lag

dry-beat bruise, beat

ducat gold coin

ducdame ostensibly nonsense but possibly Cymric ('Come to me') or Italian ('Lead him from me')

dudgeon haft, handle

due endue, grace

duello correct practice of duelling (*Ital.*)

dumb-discursive quietly seductive

dump tune, usually melancholy

dumps low spirits

dun *sb.* horse; log dragged out of an imaginary mire as a Christmas game; *adj.* dull grey-brown; **dun's the mouse** = be still

dung earth, the physical world

dupp'd opened

durance durable cloth or nature; imprisonment

each, at end to end

eager sharp, bitter

ean (of sheep) give birth

eanling new-born lamb

ear *v.* hear; plough; **by th'ears** = at odds; **in the ear** = in earshot; **shake your ears** = behave like the ass you are

earing ploughing

earn grieve

earnest initial payment of money as a deposit

earth'd laid in a grave

easy easily won over; small, light

eche augment, increase

ecstasy deranged mental state; unconsciousness

Edward shovel-board shilling from the reign of Edward VI later used in shovel-board (*see* shove-groat)

effectual conclusive

effigies likeness

effuse effusion

eftest Dogberry's word for 'aptest'

eftsoons afterwards

egall equal

egg worthless thing or person

egma Costard's word for 'enigma'

Ego et Rex meus I and my king (*Lat.*)

egregious outstanding, remarkable

eisel, eisell vinegar

eke also

elbow thrust back; **rub the elbow** = express pleasure

eld old age; people of a previous time

elder-gun pop-gun used for firing paper pellets

elect *sb.* people specially chosen; *v.* choose, accept

element one of the four universal substances (earth, water, air, fire); sky

elf *sb.* fairy, spirit; *v.* tangle or mat together

elf-locks hair tangled or matted together

Elizium, Elysium abode of the virtuous after death in the ancient world

elm tree used to train vines

emballing taking up the orb, a symbol of royalty

embare make bare

embarquements embargos, hindrances

embattail, embattle prepare for battle

embayed sheltered in a bay

emblaze set forth, as in heraldry

embossed hunted down, exhausted; bulging, swollen

embounded enclosed

embowel disembowel

embrasure embrace

eminence superiority, high rank

Emmanuel 'God with us', formula used to begin letters and documents

empale surround, encircle

empatron be patron to

emperial imperial

empery empire, sovereignty

empiric quack doctor

empiricutic characteristic of quack medicine

emulation envious rivalry

emulator petty rival, disparager

emulous envious

enciel'd screened

encompassment roundabout course

enew (in falconry) drive (the bird) into water

enfeoff surrender (property)

engage bind; pledge as security

engine plot, device; instrument; military machine

enginer contriver, plotter, creator; maker of military works or machines

englut devour

engraffed, engrafted attached; ingrained

engross fatten; amass, gather; monopolize; write large

enlard fatten

enlarge set free

enlargement liberty; liberation

enormous monstrous

enow enough

enround encircle

ensconce hide, tuck away

enseamed greasy (*cf.* seam)

ensear dry up, wither

enskied placed in heaven

ensteeped under water

entertain *sb.* entertainment; *v.* treat; employ; maintain

entertainment treatment; employment

entitled, entituled called; having a claim

entreat *sb.* entertainment; *v.* negotiate, ask; treat

entreatment negotiation

envy *sb.* malice, spite; *v.* bear ill will towards

enwheel encircle

Ephesian revelling companion

epicurism gluttony

epithet, epitheton adjective, expression

equal balanced, just, fair

equinox time of the year when day and night are of equal length

Ercles Hercules (*see* Hercules)

Erebus place of darkness on the way to the underworld

erection Quickly's word for 'direction' (instruction)

ergo therefore (*Lat.*)

eringo root of the sea-holly, a delicacy and aphrodisiac

erst once, formerly

escot provide for

esperance hope; the motto of the Percy family

espial spy

essay *see* assay

estimable esteemed, valuable; esteeming, admiring

estimation rate of esteem, worth; esteemed or valued object; reputation; valuation

estridge ostrich; goshawk

Et bonum quo antiquius eo melius 'And the older a good thing is, the better it is' (*Lat.*, proverbial)

eternize immortalize

Europa daughter of Agenor and loved by Jupiter, who transformed himself into a bull and carried her off to Crete

Glossary

even *sb.* the level truth; *v.* make even; keep up with; **even o'er** = make sense of; **go even** = agree
even-Christen fellow Christians
event outcome
ever always; **not ever** = not always; **ever among** = all the while
Evil, the the King's Evil (scrofula), supposed to be cured by the King's touch
evil (?) privy; (?) brothel
evitate avoid
exactly expressly
examine question
except take exception to; set aside; **except, before excepted** = legal phrase common in leases (*i.e.* 'with the aforesaid exceptions')
exception disapproval, objection
excitement exhortation
exclaim exclamation, outcry
exclamation reproach
excrement outgrowth from the body, particularly hair
excursion (in stage directions) skirmish
exempt separated, far away
exequies funeral ceremonies
exercise devotional exercise; homily
exhalation meteor, falling star
exhale draw out
exhaust draw out, elicit
exhibit submit, introduce; Gobbo's word for 'inhibit'
exhibition gift; allowance, maintenance; Verges' word for 'commission' (authority)
exigent critical moment
exion Quickly's word for 'action'
exorcise conjure up evil spirits
expectancy expectation, hope
expedience speed, expedition
expedient swift
expense expenditure
experimental of experience
expiate *adj.* terminated; *v.* extinguish
expostulate discuss, inquire into, argue
exposure exposure
express *adj.* well formed, well executed; *v.* show forth, make known
expressure expression; impression
exsufflicate (?) inflated, far-fetched
extemporal extempore
extend seize in satisfaction for a debt
extent behaviour; exercise; seizure (*cf.* **extend**)
extenuate mitigate, weaken the force of
extirp extirpate, root out
extracting drawing everything else away with it, absorbing
extraught extracted, derived
extravagancy vagrancy

extravagant straying beyond its proper bounds, vagrant
eyases young hawks, noted for their clamour
eyas-musket young sparrow-hawk
eye *sb.* spot; hole in a bowling ball; *v.* appear; **in the eye** = in sight
eye-glass lens of the eye
eye-strings muscles or tendons of the eye
eyne eyes
eyrie nest of a bird of prey

face *sb.* outward show; *v.* (of garments) trim with braid or velvet; bully; deceive; (in cards) call an opponent's bluff; **face down** = swear blind; **face out** = brazen out, intimidate, bluff
face-royal head depicted on a coin
Facile precor gelida quando pecus omne sub umbra Ruminat Holofernes's misquotation from a pastoral poem by Mantuanus (*Lat.* = '[Faustus], I pray, while all the herd chews the cud in the cold shade …')
facinerious facinorous, wicked
fact deed, crime; **in the fact** = red-handed
factious of or forming a faction, rebellious
factor agent, representative
faculty power; quality, nature
fadge turn out, succeed
fading word used in contemporary songs
fail *sb.* failure; failure to produce a son; death; *v.* fail in; die
fain *adj.* glad, well pleased, content; *adv.* gladly
fairings gifts bought at a fair
faithed believed
falchion curved broadsword
fall *sb.* cadence in music; *v.* let fall, bring down; befall; happen, turn out; waste away; **at fall** = at ebb; **fall from** = desert; **fall off** = revolt
falling-sickness epilepsy
falsing deceptive
fame *sb.* public image or opinion; *v.* make famous
familiar *sb.* spirit or demon; close friend; *adj.* native, accustomed
fan sift (*e.g.* grain) by means of an air current
fanatical frantic, outlandish
fancy *sb.* love; short piece of poetry or music, fantasia; *v.* love
fancy-free free from love
fancy-monger dealer in love
fangled pretentiously fashionable
fantastic *sb.* person given to flights of fancy; fop, gallant; *adj.* of the mind; given to or produced by extravagant flights of fancy, crazy

fantastical *see* **fantastic** (*adj.*)
fantasy imagination; imagining, fancy; self-delusion
fap drunk
farborough Sly's word for 'thirdborough' (*see* **thirdborough**)
farced stuffed
fardel pack
fare travel; feed; be, feel
far-fet far-fetched, highly cunning
farm rent; lease out profits from taxes in return for an immediate sum of cash; **in farm** = leased out
farrow pigs of a litter
farthingale petticoat stretched over whalebone hoops
fashions farcy, a disease in horses
fat stuffy; (?) sweating
Fates three deities who span the threads of human lives
fatigate fatigued, weary
faucet-seller seller of taps for wine-barrels
fault sin; misfortune; (in hunting) lost or 'cold' scent; **for fault of** = for want of
favour appearance, face, feature; charm; token of good will
fay faith
fazed tattered, frayed
feat *adj.* graceful; *adv.* gracefully, neatly; *v.* (?) make or render graceful
feature appearance of the body
federary *see* **feodary**
fee livestock; estate of a feudal lord; reward for services to a lord; **in fee** = outright; **in fee farm** = permanent
feeder servant; parasite
fee-grief particular grief, suggesting a large estate rented by a single tenant (*cf.* **fee**)
feeze beat
felicitate made happy
fell *sb.* skin, fleece; *adj.* terrible, savage
fellies parts of a wheel that form the rim
fence *sb.* defence; swordsmanship; *v.* shut in, defend
feodary confederate
fere companion; husband or wife
fern-seed seed supposed both to possess and to impart invisibility
ferret torment; search thoroughly
ferula teacher's cane for beating
fescue teacher's stick for pointing
festinate hurried, hasty
fetch *sb.* trick, evasion; *v.* make; strike; **fetch about** = change tack; **fetch in** = surround, catch; **fetch off** = rescue; get the better of, kill
fettle groom, prepare
few, in in short
fewness and truth the truth in short

fia see via
fico fig (*Ital.*) (*see* **fig**)
fidelicet Evans's word for 'videlicet' (*see* **videlicet**)
field-bed camp bed
fielded in the battle field
fifteens fifteenths (*see* **fifteenth**)
fifteenth tax of one-fifteenth levied on personal property
fig *sb.* contemptuous exclamation; obscene gesture sometimes called the 'fig of Spain'; *v.* make the 'fig' gesture
fights protective screens used on warships
fig's-end *see* **fig**
figure *sb.* numeral or letter; esoteric diagram; rhetorical device; imagining; *v.* express, represent; imagine
file *sb.* body of men, especially soldiers; list; *v.* defile; keep pace, as in marching
fill-horse horse used to draw a cart (*cf.* **fills**)
fills rods or shafts at the front of a cart
film gossamer
find find out; **find forth** = locate
fine *sb.* end; *adj.* refined; *v.* conclude; undertake to pay; make beautiful; **fine and recovery** = transfer of property
fineless boundless
firago virago, female warrior
fire-drake meteor
fire-new brand-new, as if fresh from the forge
firk beat, perhaps with connotations of 'fuck'
firstling first offspring
fisnomy physiognomy, face
fit *sb.* spasm; section of poetry or music; *v.* be appropriate (for)
fitchew polecat, known for its foul stench and sexual appetite
fitchook *see* **fitchew**
fitment that which is fitting; device
fives avives, a disease in horses
flamen ancient Roman priest
flap-dragon small fruit, floating in liquor, set alight and swallowed as a Christmas game
flap-jack pancake
flatness (?) completeness; (?) unrelieved expanse
flaunts fine clothes
flaw *sb.* fragment; gust or blast of wind; outburst; *v.* crack, break
fleckled spotted, blotchy
fledge fledged
fleer *sb.* sneer; *v.* grin, sneer
flesh (in hunting) awaken an appetite for bloodshed
fleshment first success
fleur-de-luce *see* **flower-de-luce**
flew'd big-jowled
fidge *see* **fledge**
flirt-gill easy woman
flote sea

Glossary

flourish *sb.* fanfare; decoration; *v.* sound a fanfare; decorate, embellish

flower-de-luce *fleur-de-lis* (iris), French heraldic device also used later by English kings

flurted scorned

flush ripe, full of vigour

flushing redness caused by weeping

flux something that flows

fluxive flowing, fluid

flying at the brook hunting for water-fowl with hawks

foil *sb.* defeat, disgrace; complementary setting or background; *v.* defeat, overthrow

foin *sb.* thrust of a sword; *v.* thrust or parry with a sword

foison plenty, abundance

fond *adj.* foolish; *v.* dote

fondling foolish person

fool jester; **fool's bolt** = allusion to the proverb 'a fool's bolt is soon shot'; **shrieve's fool** = penniless idiot in the custody of the sherrif (*cf.* **shrieve**)

fool-begg'd so idiotic that one might request custody of it from the courts

foot be or go on foot; kick; (of an eagle) snatch with the talons

foot-cloth *sb.* horse's decorative saddle-cloth; *adj.* equipped with a foot-cloth

foot-landrakers vagabond highwaymen

fop *sb.* fool; *v. see* **fub**

foppery, fopp'ry folly, foolery; cheating, trickery

foppish foolish

for for lack of; for fear of

forbid under a curse

force strengthen; care; urge, enforce; stuff; **force a straw** = care a straw for; **force perforce** = in spite of opposition, necessarily; **of force** = of importance; of necessity

fordo ruin, destroy

fordone tired out

forecast forethought

fore-end earlier part

foregone done previously

fore-hand, forehand leading position; **forehand shaft** = arrow shot with the target seen above the bow hand; **'forehand sin** = sin of acting prematurely

forehorse leading horse

fore-past previous

foresay determine, decree

forestall prevent, deny in advance

foreward vanguard

forgetive inventive

fork snake's tongue; arrow's head; leg or legs (where the body forks)

forked barbed; horned, cuckolded (*cf.* **horn**)

formal rational, sane; conventional, regular

former foremost

forsake give up; deny, decline

forslow delay

forspent wearied, exhausted

fortitude strength

fortuna de la guerra the chance of war (*Sp.?*)

foutre (*Fr.*) ruder version of 'fig' (*cf.* **fig**)

fox sword

foxship qualities of a fox, supposedly ingratitude and cunning

fracted broken

fraction breach, estrangement, quarrel; fragment

frame *sb.* systematic form; design; *v.* form, contrive, execute

frampold, frampul bad-tempered, full of peevishness

franchis'd free

franchise freedom from servitude

frank *sb.* sty for hogs; *adj.* generous; free from restraint; *v.* shut in a sty

franklin freeholder, rich yeoman

fraught *sb.* freight, cargo; *adj.* laden, supplied; *v.* burden

fraughtage freight, cargo

frayed frightened

French crown French gold coin; head bald through syphilis

frequent familiar, in company (with)

fresh freshwater spring

fret chafe, wear away; rot; ferment; adorn, ornament; equip with frets (*see* **frets**)

frets ridges on a lute to guide the fingering

fretten fretted, chafed

friend *sb.* family member; lover; *v.* befriend; **at friend, to friend** = friendly, as a friend

frieze coarse cloth

frippery old clothes shop

friskins leapings about

front *sb.* forehead, face; *v.* face, oppose; march in front

frontier rampart; border fortress

froward recalcitrant, awkward

frush beat, hammer

fub rob, cheat; **fub off** = fob off

fullam kind of false dice

fulsome full, abundant; foul

fumiter the fumitory plant, a weed

Furies mythological fiends who punished crimes

furnishings decorations, trimmings

furniture equipment; horse's gear

fury transcendental state; poetic inspiration

fury-innocent (?) one innocent of fury

fust become musty

fustian *sb.* coarse cloth; nonsense; *adj.* bombastic, highflown

fustilarian (?) fustilugs (a gross woman)

gaberdine cloak

gad spike; **upon the gad** = suddenly (as if pricked with a spike)

gage *sb.* pledge, especially to fight; *v.* pledge, engage, bind

gaingiving misgiving

gainsay deny, forbid

Galen famous Greek physician and author of medical textbooks

gall *sb.* suffering; indignation; *v.* vex, hurt

Gallian Gallic, French

galliard dance punctuated by capers (little leaps)

galliass large ship

gallimaufry jumble, mixture

gallow scare

Gallowglasses axe-wielding Irish soldiers

gallows person who will or should be hanged

gamut musical scale

Ganymede beautiful youth whom an enamoured Jupiter transported to heaven to be the cupbearer of the gods

garboil uproar, disturbance

Gargantua giant from French folklore, made famous by the work of Rabelais

garland crown; hero

garnish *sb.* clothes; *v.* clothe, decorate

gaskins wide breeches

gastness dread; ghastliness

gaud showy ornament, triviality

gaudy bright, ornate, festive

gaze thing gazed at; (in hunting) **at gaze** = distracted

gear purpose; matter, business

geck dupe

geminy pair, as of twins

gender *sb.* genus, sort; *v.* procreate, breed

generosity those of noble birth

generous of noble birth

genitivo 'in the genitive case' (*Lat.*)

genius spirit, especially a person's guardian spirit

gentility good birth and breeding; good manners

gentle *sb.* gentleman or gentlewoman; *adj.* noble, well bred; *adv.* nobly; *v.* ennoble

gentry nobility; noble behaviour

George badge of St George worn by Knights of the Order of the Garter

german, germane *sb.* close relative; *adj.* closely related

germen seed

gest stage in a journey, especially a royal progress; great deed, usually chivalric

get beget, sire

ghasted frightened

ghost *sb.* corpse; *v.* haunt

gib male cat

gift giving

gig spinning-top

giglet, giglot dizzy woman; strumpet

gillyvors gillyflowers

gimmaled made with gimmals (*see* **gimmer**)

gimmer gimmal, mechanical joint

ging gang, pack

gird *sb.* taunt, reproof; *v.* sneer or scoff (at)

glance *sb.* innuendo; *v.* rebound; make an oblique, usually disparaging, hint

glass *sb.* mirror; hour-glass; **glass eyes** = spectacles

glaze glare

gleek *sb.* scoff, gesture of contempt; *v.* scoff

glib geld, castrate

globe head; name of Shakespeare's theatre

glose, gloze *sb.* marginal comment; superficial word-play; *v.* interpret or comment as if with scholastic glosses; use false, attractive language

gloss attractive external appearance

glut swallow hungrily

go walk; **go to** = expression of scorn or disbelief (*cf.* go on, get away)

goatish lecherous, as goats were supposed to be

gobbet chunk of flesh

God dig-you-den, God gi' good e'en, God 'i' good e'en, God ye good e'en, God-den, good den (God give you) good evening

God 'ild (may) God yield (reward)

God's lid *see* **'Slid**

good good for credit, wealthy

good dild *see* **God 'ild**

goodly handsome

goodman title for people below the rank of gentleman; husband

good-year,' what the exclamation of surprise

goose tailor's iron; short for Winchester goose (= prostitute); sore caused by veneral disease

gorbellied bigbellied

Gordian knot according to legend, an impossibly complex knot to be untied only by he who would go on to rule Asia; Alexander the Great cut it with his sword

gore-blood clotted blood

gorge vomit

gorget throat armour

Gorgon one of three monsters, the most famous being Medusa, whose look turned the viewer to stone

Glossary

gospell'd instructed in the precepts of the gospel

goss gorse

gossip *sb.* godparent; merry, talkative woman; *v.* stand as a godparent; be merry in company

gourd kind of false dice

gout drop of liquid

government self-discipline, self-control; **in government** = under control

graceful blessed; favourable

graff, graft *sb.* grafted (*i.e.* hybrid) plant; *v.* graft, cross-breed by implanting a shoot into a plant of a different kind

grafter plant from which the shoot is taken for grafting (*see* **graff**)

grain, in fast dyed, ingrained; **purple-in-grain** = red

grained ingrained; bearing or displaying the grains found in timber

gramercy great thanks

grand guard heavy armour worn on horseback

grange farm house sometimes belonging to a religious establishment

grate vex, annoy

grateful pleasing

gratify reward; make pleasant

gratulate *adj.* gratifying; *v.* greet; gratify, satisfy

grave bury, entomb; carve, engrave

greasily obscenely

great morning broad daylight

'gree agree

greeing suitable

Greek reveller, person with relaxed moral standards

Greensleeves popular English ballad about an inconstant woman

grievance distress, trauma

grieve sorrow; offend

gripe *sb.* clutch; vulture or eagle; *v.* grip, clutch

grise, grize stair, step

groat coin; **ten groats** = an attorney's fee

ground (in heraldry) coloured background; (in music) air on which variations are sung or played

groundlings theatregoers who stood in front of the stage

ground-piece (?) exemplary painting

grow (of a sum of money) grow due; **grow to a point** = come to a stop; **grow upon** = encroach on

guardant guard; **Jack guardant** = petty official (*cf.* **Jack**)

guards trimmings of a garment; stars in the Ursa Minor constellation used for navigation

guidon pennant, flag

guilder gold coin

guiled deceitful, full of guile

guinea-hen (?) cunning woman; (?) prostitute

guise usual practice

gules (in heraldry) red

gull *sb.* nestling; credulous fool; hoax; *v.* trick, fool

gummed treated with gum, glossy

gurnet small fish considered a delicacy

gust *sb.* taste, appetite; *v.* get a taste of, realize

Guy, Sir Guy of Warwick, hero of an early English romance

gyve *sb.* fetter; *v.* fetter

H letter of the alphabet pronounced 'aitch', so sounding like the Elizabethan pronunciation of the word 'ache'

habiliment attire, dress

habit clothing, garments; bearing, disposition

habited dressed

habitude character, disposition

hack (?) associate with loose women

hackney prostitute

hade land part of the field where the plough turns around, and so planted last

haggard *sb.* wild hawk; *adj.* wild

haggled hacked

hag-seed offspring of a hag

hair sort, kind, nature; **against the hair** = against the grain

halberd battle-axe on a long pole; one armed with a halberd

halcyon kingfisher, supposed when hung up to turn its beak with the wind; **halcyon's days** = period of calm

half partner, wife

half-blooded having only one parent of noble blood

half-caps caps taken only half off, slight salutations

half-cheek profile

half-cheeked (of a horse's bit) giving insufficient control

half-face profile

half-faced showing a face in profile; pinched-faced

half-kirtle skirt portion of a kirtle (*see* **kirtle**)

half-sword very close quarters

halidom state of being holy; anything regarded as holy

halloo, hallow call, shout

Hallowmas All Saints' Day (1 November)

hand-fast custody; marriage contract

handsaw small saw; (?) heron

handy-dandy take your choice (from a children's game)

hanger straps attaching the sword to the girdle

haply by chance

happiness handsomeness

harbinger one who runs on ahead

hard-haired with tightly curled hair

hardiment valour; deeds of valour

hardness difficulty

harlot *sb.* person of loose life; beggar; *adj.* lewd

harlotry good-for-nothing

Harry ten shillings half-sovereign coined under Henry VII

hatch lower half of a divided door

hatchment tablet displaying a coat of arms

haud credo 'I do not believe' (*Lat.*)

haught haughty, arrogant

haughty high-pitched, ambitious

hautboy oboe

havoc signal for indiscriminate slaughter

hay country dance; (in fencing) thrust reaching the antagonist

hazard *sb.* dice game; risk; stake; *v.* risk

head *sb.* headland, promontory; subdivision; armed force, advance; *v.* behead; **head and front** = height

headstall part of the bridle that fits round the head

heady-rash impetuously violent

heap great company, crowd; **on a heap** = prostrate

heavy serious, grievous; sad; tiresome

hebenon poison

Hecate goddess of witchcraft

hectic fever

Hector Trojan hero

Hecuba Queen of Troy

hedge-pig hedgehog

hefts heavings, retchings

hempseed one deserving to be hanged

hent *sb.* seized opportunity; *v.* seize; instance

herb of grace rue

herblet small herb

Hercules legendary hero, supposedly a kinsman of Theseus; **Hercules and his load** = Hercules bearing the world on his shoulders, perhaps the sign at the Globe Theatre

Hero lover of Leander (*see* **Leander**)

Herod biblical tyrant

he's he shall

Hesperus the planet Venus

hest behest, command

hey-day, heyday exclamation of surprise or joy

Hic et ubique 'Here and everywhere' (*Lat.*)

Hic ibat Simois, hic est Sigeia tellus, / Hic steterat Priami regia celsa senis 'Here ran the

river Simois; here is the Sigeian land; here stood old Priam's lofty palace' (*Lat.*, Ovid)

hic jacet 'here lies' (*Lat.*)

Hiems Winter

high and low false dice

high-day *see* **hey-day**

high-lone alone, without support

high-proof in the highest degree

high-stomached high-spirited, haughty, stubborn

hight is called

hild held

hilding contemptible person of either sex, coward

hind female deer; rustic servant; boor

hint occasion, opportunity

hipped having a dislocated hip-bone

Hiren seductive woman (from the name of a character in a play by Peele)

hit agree; **hit of** = hit on

hive hat

hoar *adj.* mouldy; whitish; *v.* become mouldy; whiten (with disease)

hobby-horse character in the morris-dance; buffoon; loose woman

hodge-pudding pudding or sausage made of hodge (pigs' entrails)

holding consistency; refrain of a song

holidame *see* **halidom**

holp helped

holy-ales rural festivals on saints' days

holy-rood day feast of the Holy Cross (14 September)

holy-thistle *see* **carduus benedictus**

home thoroughly

honest worthy, decent; truthful; chaste

honesty uprightness, decency; chastity; generosity

honey-stalks clover flowers

honorificabilitudinitatibus stock comic example of a long (Latin) word

honour honourable deed

hood (of a hawk) blindfold

hoodman-blind blind man's buff

horn deer; sign of a cuckold

horn-book, hornbook child's primer (the alphabet on a leaf of paper protected by a translucent plate of horn)

horn-mad like a furious bull, with connotations of cuckoldry (*cf.* **horn**)

horologe clock

hose breeches; **French hose** = loose-fitting hose

host lodge

hot-house brothel

house-clogs shackles

housekeeper domestic woman; guard dog

housewife hussy, prostitute

howlet owlet or owl

hox hamstring

hoy small coasting vessel

hoy-day, hoyday *see* **hey-day**

hugger-mugger secrecy

hull float with sails furled

humorous damp; temperamental, capricious, whimsical (*see* **humour**)

humour dampness; one of the four physiological 'elements' (melancholy, blood, choler, phlegm) governing disposition, *hence* temperament, mood, inclination

Humphrey Hower (?) meal-time ('to dine with Duke Humphrey' = to solicit dinner invitations); (?) name of an unidentified contemporary individual

Hungarian needy, hungry

hunt's up morning song to awaken a newly married wife

hurricano waterspout

hurry commotion

husband *sb.* one who manages a household, accounts, etc.; *v.* cultivate; marry

husbandry management (*cf.* **husband**), thrift; farming, cultivation

huswife *see* **housewife**

Hybla mountain in Sicily famous for honey

Hydra legendary snake with many heads which grew back sevenfold when they were cut off

hyen hyena

Hymen, Hymenaeus god of marriage

hyperbole figure of speech used for exaggeration

Hyperion Phoebus, the sun god

Hyrcan, Hyrcanian from Hyrcania, a region on the shore of the Caspian sea famous for tigers

Hysterica passio type of hysteria in women (*Lat.*)

Icarus son of Daedalus who, with his father, used artificial wings to fly from Crete, where King Minos had imprisoned them; flying too near the sun, he melted the wax in his wings and so fell to his death in the sea

ice-brook stream of icy water, used in the tempering of sword blades

Iceland dog lap-dog from Iceland

idea image

ides of March 15 March in the Roman dating system

ignis fatuus (*Lat.*) will o'the wisp

ignominy, ignomy disgrace

Ilion, Ilium Troy; palace of Priam in Troy

ill-favoured ugly, unpleasant (*cf.* **favour**)

illness evil nature

ill-temper'd (of the humours in the blood) badly balanced (*see* **humour**)

illustrous not lustrous, lack-lustre

image archetypal image, perfect example

imaginary imagining, imaginative

imbecility feebleness

imbrue pierce; spill blood

imitari to imitate (*Lat.*)

immanity barbarity, ferocity

immediacy the position of being next in authority

immediate direct; next in succession

imminence impending danger

immoment of no moment, insignificant

immures enclosing walls

imp *sb.* young offshoot, *hence* child; *v.* repair (a wing) by grafting on new feathers

impale *see* **empale**

impare inappropriate, unworthy

impart say, reveal; provide

impartment speech, communication

impasted formed into a crust

impawn pledge, stake

impeach *sb.* charge, reproach; *v.* undermine, discredit

impeachment charge; impediment, hindrance

imperseverant (?) stubborn; (?) imperceptive

impertinency irrelevance, nonsense

impertinent Gobbo's word for 'pertinent'

impeticos (?) pocket

implorators implorers, beseechers

import *sb.* weighty significance; *v.* signify; involve, concern

importance significance, meaning; importunity, urgent request; question at issue

importancy significance, importance

important importunate, urgent

importless without significance, trivial

importment importance, significance

importune demand, urge

imposition command; accusation; penalty, burden

imposthume, impostume abscess

imprese allegorical representations used in heraldic decoration (*Ital.*)

impress *sb.* conscription; *v.* press into military service

imputation attribution, reputation

in capite 'at the head' (*Lat.*), used of tenants holding land direct from the king

In hac spe vivo 'In this hope I live' (*Lat.*)

incapable unable to take in; unable to understand, unaware

incardinate Aguecheek's word for 'incarnate'

incarnadine turn red

incarnation Gobbo's word for 'incarnate'

inch island; **Saint Colme's Inch** = Inchcomb, an island in the Firth of Forth

inclining *sb.* inclination, side; *adj.* ready to be persuaded

income gathering in

incomprehensible limitless

incontinent *adj.* lacking self-restraint; *adv.* immediately

incony darling; delicate

incorporate united in one body

incorps'd united into a single body

incorrect uncorrected, incorrigible

incredulous incredible, unbelievable

Ind, Inde India

indent *sb.* indentation; *v.* make an agreement; dart about

index table of contents at the beginning or end of a book

indifferency impartiality; unremarkable nature

indifferent impartial, lacking prejudice or interest; mediocre, moderate; identical

indigest *sb.* that which is amorphous; *adj.* crude, amorphous

indign disgraceful

indirect devious, wrongful

indirection injustice; oblique method

indirectly wrongly; obliquely; nonchalantly

indisposition unwillingness

indistinguishable of no recognized kind or function

indistinguished indistinguishable; limitless

individable (?) conforming to the dramatic unity of place; (?) not to be identified by divisions and subdivisions of genre

indrench'd drenched, overwhelmed

induction first step; opening scene

infamonize Armado's word for 'infamize' (make infamous, defame)

infect infected

infection Quickly's and Old Gobbo's word for 'affection' (*see* **affection**)

infer bring in; allege; imply

influence planetary emanation supposed to exert a determining effect upon people

inform take on a form; give form to, fashion, direct; report

informal deranged

infuse pour into or onto

ingenious mentally alert, responsive; crafty; crafted; appropriate

ingeniously ingenuously, candidly

inginer *see* **enginer**

ingraft *see* **engraffed**

inhabitable uninhabitable

inherit possess; put in possession of; take possession of

inhibited prohibited

inhibition prohibition, ban

initiate belonging to a beginner

injurious abusive, offensive

ink-horn small vessel for containing ink; **inkhorn mate** = bookish person

inkle tape or yarn

inland *sb.* interior of a land, especially its urban and prosperous parts

innocent *sb.* idiot, fool; *adj.* simple, foolish

inoculate graft a new shoot into (a plant)

insane causing insanity

insconce *see* **ensconce**

insensible unable to be sensed

insinuate flatter, wheedle; hint to

insinuation flattery, worming a way in

insisture (?) persistence; (?) moment of stasis

instalment installation; stall

instance proof, sign, evidence; motive

instruction information

insuppressive unable to be suppressed or contained

Integer vitae, scelerisque purus, / Non eget Mauri iaculis, nec arcu 'The man of upright life and free from crime does not need the javelins or bows of the Moor' (*Lat.*, Horace)

intellect message, meaning

intelligence communication; secret information; spies

intelligencer messenger; spy

intelligencing carrying information

intelligent carrying information; intelligible

intendment intention

intentively attentively

intercept interrupt

interested given a right to or share in

interest right to or share in

interlude short comedy

intervallum interval, pause

intitled, intituled *see* **entitled**

intreat *see* **entreat**

intrenchant unable to be cut

intrince intricate

intrinsicate intricate

investments robes; seiges

Invitis nubibus 'in spite of the opposition of the clouds' (*Lat.*)

Glossary

ipso facto 'by that very act' (*Lat.*)

Irā furor brevis est 'Anger is a brief madness' (*Lat.*, Horace)

Iris messenger of Juno, represented as a rainbow

irreconciled unreconciled (to God)

irregular lawless, unruly

irregulous *see* **irregular**

iterance repetition

iwis truly

Jack term of contempt, meaning fool or knave, also used in combinations, *e.g.* Jack-priest, Jack-slave

jack mechanized human figure that strikes a clock bell; small wooden block in a keyboard (wrongly used of the keys themselves); (in bowls) small bowl aimed at by the players; soldier's padded jacket; drinking vessel

Jack-a-Lent brightly dressed puppet stoned by fun-seeking children during Lent

jack-a-nape, jack-an-ape, jackanapes, jack'nape performing monkey; fool

jade *sb.* mangy or difficult horse; contemptuous term, usually for a woman; *v.* trick; harrass

jad'ry a horse's difficult behaviour (*cf.* **jade**)

jakes latrine

jaunce *sb.* (?) tiring business; *v.* prance

jaw devour

jay glamorous, immoral woman

jealous anxious; suspicious, doubtful

jealous-hood (?) jealous woman

jealousy anxiety; suspicion

jean kind of twilled cotton

jennet Spanish horse

jerk stroke, as of wit

jerkin jacket

jesses straps fastening a hawk's legs to the falconer's wrist

jet strut self-importantly; jut (*see* **jut**)

jig *sb.* merry tune or dance; *v.* sing or move in the manner of a jig

Jockey Jack (John)

John Drum's entertainment a good beating

jointress widow who inherits her husband's estate

joint-ring ring formed of two interlocking halves

joint-stool stool that has been properly crafted

jollity extravagant clothes

jolt-head, jolthead fool

jordan piss-pot

journal daily

Jove Jupiter (*see* **Jupiter**)

Jovial of Jupiter, hence kingly, liberal, *etc.*; **Jovial star** = the planet Jupiter

jowl strike, knock

Judas (Iscariot) apostle who betrayed Christ, identifying him to the authorities by kissing him; popular legend gave him red hair and says he hanged himself

Judas Maccabeus great Jewish warrior and freedom-fighter

Jug Joan

jump *sb.* risky move; *adv.* just, exactly; *v.* risk, chance; coincide, agree

junkets sweetmeats, dainties

Juno sister and wife of Jupiter, sometimes associated with marriage, otherwise imagined as formidably jealous and prone to anger

Jupiter principal god in classical mythology, brother and husband of Juno but given to affairs with mortals (*see* **Europa, Leda**)

just *sb.* jousting tournament; *adj.* precise; *adv.* precisely, indeed; **just distance** = half-way

justicer judge

justify verify; vindicate

jut overhang, encroach

jutty *sb.* part of a building that projects beyond the wall; *v.* overhang

kam awry, perverse

kecksies kexes, hollow stalks

keech rolled lump of fat

keel cool

ken *sb.* sight; *v.* see; know

Kendal green coarse cloth

kennel gutter, open drain

kern, Kerne Irish foot-soldier

kernel little seed

kersey plain, coarse cloth

kettle kettle-drum

key key for tuning a stringed instrument

kibe chilblain, sore on the heel

kickshaws fancy extra, trifle

kicky-wicky (?) wife

killen kill

kill-hole, kiln-hole opening of a kiln

kind *sb.* nature; lineage, family; way, manner; *adj.* natural; gracious

kindle incite; bring forth young

kindless unnatural

kindly *adj.* natural, in accordance with one's nature; *adv.* naturally; graciously; exactly

kirtle gown consisting of a bodice and skirt

kiss (in bowls) brush (the jack) with one's bowl

kissing-comfits sweetmeats (dried fruits, *etc.*) for sweetening the breath

kite bird of prey; whore

knack knick-knack, pretty artefact

knap knock; bite

knoll toll

knot gang, small group; folded arms; flower-bed

knot-grass plant supposed to inhibit growth

knotted laid with flower-beds (*cf.* **knot**)

knotty-pated block-headed

La fin couronne les oeuvres 'The end crowns the deeds' (*Fr.*, proverbial)

label append, as a codicil

labour'd employed in labour; accomplished with labour

laboursome finely worked; persistent

labras Pistol's word for '*labra*' (*Lat.* = 'lips')

lace interlace, embroider; laced mutton *see* **mutton**

lackey *sb.* page, footman; *v.* run around after, like a page

lade drain, bale out

lady-smock (?) cuckoo-flower

lag late, behind

Lammas-tide 1 August, an old harvest festival

lampass a disease in horses

land-damn (?) thrash; (?) scold

lank become thin

lantern turret with windows

lap wrap, clad

lapse *sb.* fall; *v.* slip, hence sin

lapsed (?) fallen; (?) apprehended; **laps'd in** = (?) having let slip by

lard baste, enrich; garnish

large liberal, unrestrained; **at large** = in full; full-size

lark's-heels larkspur

'larum, larum *see* **alarum**

latch catch, grasp; moisten

latest final

lath cheap wood

latten brass or tinplate

laud song of praise

laund cleared space in a wood

lavolt, lavolta dance involving high leaps

law-days court sessions

lay *sb.* wager; song; **lay aboard** = board (a ship); **lay by the heels** = put in fetters or stocks; **lay for** = waylay, beset

lazar leper

lead *sb.* lining of a wooden coffin; *v.* weight (a fishing line)

leading command

leads roof of a building

leaguer camp

Leander lover of Hero; every night he swam across the Hellespont and climbed up to her window to visit her

leaping-house brothel

learn teach

leash *sb.* (of hounds) group of three; *v.* keep (three hounds) on a leash

leasing falsehood, lying

leather-coats russet apples

lecture lesson

Leda maiden loved by Jupiter, who turned himself into a swan

to visit her, and the mother of Helen of Troy

leer cheek, complexion

lees sediment

leese loose

leet court held by a lord of the manor

Legion name of a host of evil spirits in the Bible (Mark v.9)

legitimation legitimacy

leiger resident ambassador

leman lover, sweetheart

lendings clothes; advance payment for soldiers

Lent in the Christian calendar, forty days before Easter marked by fasting and abstinence from meat (the slaughter of animals required a special licence)

lenten of Lent, *hence* thin, frugal

l'envoy epilogue of a poem

let *sb.* hindrance; *v.* hinder; forbear; (of blood) drain off; **let slip** = let (hounds) loose

Lethe a river of the underworld; its water caused drinkers to forget their past

letter, affect the resort to alliteration

lettered learned

level *sb.* line of fire, range; *adj.* unimpeded; *v.* aim; guess; **by line and level** *see* **line; level with** = equal

lewd base, wicked

lewdster rake, lecherous person

liable subject; suitable

libbard leopard

liberal refined; unrestrained

liberty right, prerogative; licence, licentiousness

lie live, lodge; **lie along** = lie stretched out

lief dear; **have as lief** = hold as dear, be as willing

liege lord

lieger *see* **leiger**

lifter thief

light *sb.* inkling; *v.* alight, descend, fall

lighten flash, as lightning; enlighten

like *adj.* likely; *adv.* alike, identically; *v.* please; liken; thrive

liking physique

limbeck alembic, a gourd-shaped vessel used in distillation

limber limp, flabby

Limbo region occupied by the souls of the virtuous who died before Christ (*Limbo Patrum*) or of unbaptized babies; prison

lime *sb.* birdlime, a kind of glue used to trap small birds; *v.* flavour with lime; smear or catch with birdlime; bind with mortar

limit *sb.* territory, precinct; appointed time; *v.* appoint; **strength of limit** = recovery after childbirth

Glossary

limitation time allotted

line *sb.* equator; category; *v.* picture, draw; strengthen; **by line and level** = according to rule

lined padded; financially provided for

line-grove grove of lime trees

linger protract

link torch, flare

linsey-woolsey mixture of wool and flax

linstock stick which held the lighted match for detonating a cannon

list *sb.* inclination; boundary; edge of a piece of cloth; *see* **lists**; *v.* desire; listen; hear

lists arena for a contest

lither unresisting

little, in in miniature

little, in a in brief

livelihood life, liveliness

lively living; lifelike

liver dweller; organ supposedly responsible for intense feeling, especially love; **liver vein** = vein or style of love

livery (in law) delivery or transfer of property

lob *sb.* lout, rustic; *v.* droop

lockram linen fabric

lode-star the Pole star

lodge flatten, beat down

loggets game of throwing pieces of wood at a target

London Stone a rounded block of stone in Cannon Street, London

'long, long belong

long purples kind of wild orchis

long-staff sixpenny strikers robbers who attack their victims with long poles

'loo, loo a shout of encouragement to dogs or hounds (*cf.* **halloo**)

loofed (?) aloof, at a distance

look before certain words is an idiomatic equivalent of adding 'ever', *e.g.* **look how** = however; **look what** = whatever

look upon stand by and watch

loon rogue, low-bred person

looped full of holes

loose *sb.* firing of an arrow; *adj.* unattached, independent; *v.* fire (an arrow); let loose, release

lop cuttings from a tree

Lord's sake, for the begging cry of prisoners at their windows

lose cause to lose; bring to ruin; let slip, forget

lots to blanks, it is (?) 'the chances are'

love-in-idleness pansy

lover friend

lown *see* **loon**

lozel rogue

lubber oaf; Quickly's word for 'leopard' (*cf.* **libbard**)

luce pike

Lucina goddess of childbirth, properly a surname of Juno (*see* **Juno**)

lucre gain, acquisition

Lud's town London, after King Lud, Cymbeline's grandfather

luggage baggage, encumbrance

lunes lunatic fits

Lupercal = Lupercalia, an ancient Roman festival at which participants ran around striking the citizens with animal skins

lurch rob

lure apparatus used by a falconer to recall his bird

lust pleasure

lustihood vigorous health

lustique in sprightly fashion

lusty cheerful; lustful

Lux tua vita mihi 'Thy light is life to me' (*Lat.*)

luxurious lecherous

luxury lechery

Ma foi '(by) my faith' (*Fr.*, an oath); *ma foi, il fait fort chaud. Je m'en vais voir à la court la grande affaire* = 'by my faith, it's very hot. I'm going to court, the great business'

Machiavel amoral intriguer, after the Italian politician, Niccolò Machiavelli

maculate spotted, blemished

maculation spot, blemish

madrigal song

magnanimious, magnanimous great-hearted, noble

Magni dominator poli, / Tam lentus audis scelera, tam lentus vides? 'Ruler of the great heavens, are you so slow to hear crimes, so slow to see?' (*Lat.*, after Seneca)

magnifico Venetian of high social standing

magot-pies magpies

Maid Marian a bawdy role in the morris-dance

mail *sb.* suit of armour; small bag; *v.* dress in armour; wrap (a hawk) in cloth

main *sb.* main part; sea; mainland; army; stake in a dice game; *adj.* strong; important; *v.* maim

main-course mainsail

mainly mightily; greatly

major basic premise in an argument

majority distinction, preeminence

make *sb.* partner; *v.* do; make fast, shut; make one's way, move; **make one** = join in

making bodily form

malapert insolent

malicho iniquity

malkin wench

malmsey strong, sweet wine

malt-horse, malthorse brewer's horse

malt-worms, maltworms beer drinkers

mammet doll

mammock tear into shreds

mamm'ring hestitating, stuttering

man tame; use as a weapon

manage *sb.* management; (of a horse) training, exercise; *v.* take control of (a horse)

mandragora the mandrake plant (*see* **mandrake**)

mandrake poisonous plant supposed to issue a fatal shriek when uprooted

man-enter'd entered like a man

manhood manliness, masculinity

mankind masculine, savage

manner, taken with the caught red-handed

mansionry dwelling

mantle scum resting on the surface of stagnant water

manu cita with ready hand (*Lat.*)

map image

mapp'ry map-reading

Marches, marches Welsh or Scottish borders

marchpane marzipan

margent margin, *hence* notes, accompanying explanation

mark marking, observation; quantity of money; (in archery) something aimed at

market profit

marry a mild oath, from the name of the Virgin Mary

Mars god of war and lover of Venus (*see* **Venus**)

Martial of Mars, *hence* warlike, *etc.*

Martin's summer, Saint good weather late in the year (St Martin's day = 11 November)

martlemas St Martin's day (*cf.* **Martin's summer, Saint**)

martlet swift or house-martin

Mary-buds marigolds

mast acorns, chestnuts and similar

mastic violently abusive

mate match; check, put at a loss

material of matter, substantial

maugre despite

maund basket

mazard, mazzard head

Me pompae provexit apex 'The crown of the triumph has led me on' (*Lat.*)

meacock tame, spiritless

meal'd mixed, of a piece

mean *sb.* middle position or course; middle voice in vocal or instrumental music; *v.* moan, lament

measurable fit, suitable

measure *sb.* dance or piece of music; punishment; *v.* tread, cross

mechanic, mechanical *sb.* manual labourer, artisan; *adj.* performing manual labour, common

Medea enchantress who rejuvenated her father-in-law Aeson and murdered her brother Absyrtus

Medice, teipsum physician, (heal) thyself (*Lat.*)

med'cinable, medicinable medicinal, curative

med'cine, medicine *sb.* doctor; drug, potion; (in alchemy) the elixir reputed to turn base metals into gold; *v.* heal; **med'cine potable** = drug containing gold

meditance meditating

medlar fruit eaten when almost rotten; prostitute

meed merit; payment

meetly fair, not bad

Mehercle by Hercules (*Lat.*)

meinie, meiny multitude; retinue

melancholy depression, associated with a thickening of the blood

Meleager Calydonian prince who, with Theseus and others, hunted down a local boar

mell associate, have intercourse

memorize make memorable

memory memorial, souvenir

mercatante merchant (*Ital.*)

Mercurial of Mercury, *hence* fleet of foot, *etc.*

Mercury the messenger god, associated with eloquence; he was depicted with winged sandals

mere utter, total

mered defined, marked out

merit reward, desert

mess serving of food; group of diners occupying a ranked position at table

metaphysical supernatural

mete judge; aim or level

metheglin potent spiced mead

method, by the in the same style

mew confine (a bird) in a cage

Mi perdonato excuse me (*Ital.*)

micher one who plays truant

miching lurking, stealthy

mickle great

microcosm man as the universe in miniature; **map of my microcosm** = my face

milch in milk, lactating

Mile-End Green drill-ground east of London for citizens under training and a place for fairs and shows

milk-livered chicken-hearted

milliner seller of gloves and fancy apparel

mill-sixpences silver sixpences

mince trivialize; walk or talk in an affected, gamesome manner

mind have in mind, mean; call to mind; notice

mineral poison; mine

Minerva goddess of wisdom and of arts and crafts

minikin high-pitched

minim basic short note-value in Tudor music

minime not in the least (*Lat.*)

minimus tiny creature

minion favourite or mistress; slut

Minotaur a monster, half bull and half man, placed in a labyrinth by Minos, King of Crete

minute-jacks clock figures (*cf.* **jack**)

minutely very frequent, by the minute

mirable admirable, marvellous

mirror pattern, example

Misanthropos man-hater (*Gr.*)

mischief *sb.* evil; misfortune; disease; *v.* harm

mis-dread fear of evil

miser wretched person

misgoverned unrestrained, rebellious

misgovernment misconduct

misgraffed ill-matched

misprision misunderstanding, blunder; disdain; false imprisonment

misproud arrogant, inappropriately proud

missive messenger

mistake take wrongly; misunderstand, misjudge

misthink think badly of, misjudge

mistress (in bowls) the jack

mo *see* **moe**

mobbled with face muffled

mockery, mock'ry semblance, imitation

model pattern; mould

modern trite, commonplace

modest moderate, sober

modestly moderately, restrainedly

modesty moderation

module pattern, image

moe more

moiety portion, sometimes a half

moldwarp mole

mome fool, ass

momentany momentary

Monarcho the name used by a famously vain contemporary Italian at the English court

Monmouth cap soldier's cap

monster make monstrous

monstruosity monstrosity

montant (in fencing) upward thrust (*Fr.*)

monument sign, omen

monumental serving as a sign or token (of identity, *etc.*)

mood anger; expression of feelings; (in music) scale, mode

moon-calf creature born deformed

Moor-ditch a notoriously filthy ditch in London

mop *sb.* grimace; *v.* grimace like a monkey

mope be or wander about in a daze, lack awareness

moralise, moralize expound morally or symbolically

Morisco morris-dancer

morris morris-dance

mort call of the hunting-horn announcing the death of the deer

mortified insensate, subdued

mortifying life-depriving

mortise part of a joint in carpentry

mose in the chine (?) display the symptoms of glanders (a disease in horses) in its final stages

mot motto, device

mote speck, mentioned by Christ as a metaphor for trivial sinfulness (*cf.* **beam**)

mother tenderness; *see Hysterica passio*

motion *sb.* puppet or puppet-show; appeal, proposal; impulse, feeling; *v.* move, propose; **upon the foot of motion** = at the stage of being expressed

motive mover, cause or instrument

motley pied garments of a jester

mould earth, clay, the mortal human body

moulten having moulted

mountebank swindle in the manner of a mountebank (a pedlar of quack medicines)

mouse *sb.* term of affection for a woman; *v.* treat as a cat treats a mouse

mouse-hunt one who hunts women, rake (*cf.* **mouse**)

mow *sb.* grimace; *v.* grimace mockingly

mulled dulled

mummer performer in a dumb-show

mummy dried human flesh used as the basis for a medicinal liquid

muniments military supplies or defences

murd'ring-piece cannon with a spraying shot

mure wall

murrain, murrion *sb.* plague in cattle or other animals; *adj.* infected

muscadel sweet wine

muse marvel (at); complain

musit hole in a hedge; hiding place

musk-cat musk-deer

muss game in which children scramble for objects thrown on the ground

mutine *sb.* mutineer; *v.* mutiny

mutiny *sb.* dispute; *v.* riot

mutton prostitute; **laced mutton** = prostitute

mutual shared, common; intimate

mutuality familiarity, intimacy

mutually together; reciprocally

Myrmidons followers of Achilles in the Trojan war; **the great Myrmidon** = Achilles (*see* **Achilles**)

mystery art or craft, calling

Nabuchadnezzar = Nebuchadnezzar, Babylonian king whom God punished by driving him into the wilderness where he ate grass like an ox

nail one-sixteenth of a yard

naked unarmed; **in naked bed** = undressed and in bed

napless worn, threadbare

Naso family name of the poet Ovid, from *nasus* (*Lat.* = 'nose')

native *sb.* natural source; *adj.* innate, natural; naturally connected

natural *sb.* congenital idiot; *adj.* idiotic

naturalize familiarize

naught *sb.* wrongdoing; *adj.* bad, worthless; **all to naught** = worthless; **be naught awhile** = petty insult

naughty bad, worthless

nave hub or boss of a wheel; navel

nay-ward direction of disbelief

nay-word, nayword password; byword

Nazarite Nazarene, *i.e.* Christ

ne intelligis domine? 'do you understand, sir?' (*Lat.*)

neaf fist (*dial.*)

Neapolitan bone-ache syphilis

near-legged knock-kneed

neat *sb.* ox; *adj.* trim, fancy

neb beak, nose or mouth

neeze sneeze

neglect cause to be neglected

Nemean of Nemea, where lived a fearsome lion; Hercules slew it and wore its hide

nephew cousin; descendant

Neptune god of the sea

Nereides benevolent sea-nymphs

Nero Roman emperor who had his mother murdered and was supposed to have played a harp while Rome burned

nerve nerve or sinew

nervy courageous; sinewy

Nessus centaur killed with a poisoned arrow by Hercules for abducting his wife; the bloodied shirt was later worn by Hercules who was driven to suicide by its residual poison

Nestor Hellenic king famed for his advanced age and wisdom

nether-stocks stockings for the lower legs

next closest

nice easy-going; delicate, particular; refined; slight

nicely subtly; strictly, particularly; daintily

niceness daintiness

nicety scruples

Nicholas, Saint patron saint of scholars; **Saint Nicholas' clerks** = highway robbers

nick *v.* (?) cut short; (?) emasculate; **in the nick** = at that point; **out of all nick** = beyond measure

nickname miscall; find new names for

niggard act meanly; stint

night-gown dressing-gown

night-rule affairs of the night

nimble-pinion'd swift-winged

nine-men's-morris rustic game played on a diagram cut in turf

Niobe mother of fourteen children slain by Apollo and Diana, transformed into stone as she wept

noble gold coin

noise *sb.* concert or small company of musicians; report, rumour; *v.* report, rumour; **noise it** = cry out

nole noddle, head

nonce, for the for the occasion, as the occasion requires

non-come Dogberry's word for '*non plus*' (*Lat.* = 'bewilderment'), confused with '*non compos*' (*Lat.* = 'mentally defective')

nonpareil unrivalled paragon

nonsuit reject, with respect to a suit

nook-shotten full of nooks and corners, misshapen

nose-herbs scented plants

note *sb.* mark of disgrace; mark, characteristic; notice, apprehension; record; *v.* mark with disgrace

notedly assuredly

nothing able to be pronounced 'noting' (= observing, tune, *etc.*); *sb.* triviality; *adv.* in no way

notion intellect, awareness

Novi hominem tanquam te 'I know the man as well as I know you' (*Lat.*)

novum dice game at which nine and five were high scores and perhaps interchangeable

noyance annoyance, harm

nuncio messenger

nursery care, nurturing

nut-hook, nuthook beadle

O spot; spangle, star; the Globe Theatre; vagina; sigh; prayer

oathable able to be placed under oath

ob. for '*obolus*' (*Lat.*), used in England of a half-penny

objection accusation or criminal charge

obligation contract

Glossary

obliged bound by contract

obliquy (?) obliquity, perversity; (?) *see* **obloquy**

oblivious causing oblivion or forgetfulness

obloquy slander, shame

obsequious of obsequies or funeral rites; loyal

observance observation; deference, respect; ritual

observant fawning attendant

observation performance of a rite; respectful attention

observe court; pay due respect to

obstruction lack of movement

occasion matter; need; fault; opportunity, proverbially represented as bearing a forelock (or 'front') which should be seized

occident the west

occulted concealed, secret

occupation labour, trade

occupy have sex

occurrents occurrences

oddly unevenly

'Od's, Od's 'God's' or 'God save' (in oaths)

oeillades meaningful, amorous looks

o'erblow blow away

o'ercount outnumber

o'ercrow triumph over

o'er-dy'd weak with overdyeing

o'er-eaten gnawed at and bitten

o'er-flourish'd elaborately carved or ornamented

o'er-galled made excessively sore

o'erlook, overlook look over, examine, read; curse, bewitch

o'ermaster make oneself master of

o'erparted assigned a theatrical part above one's capabilities

o'erpeer, over-peer, overpeer look down upon

o'erpicturing outdoing in pictorial qualities

o'er-posting passing over

o'er-raught, o'erraught o'erreached (*see* **o'erreach**)

o'erreach cheat; overtake

o'ersized smeared over, as with size (*see* **size**)

o'erteemed exhausted by bearing children

o'er-watch'd, o'erwatched exhausted through lack of sleep

o'erwhelm hang over

o'er-wrested overdone

off-cap take off one's cap or hat out of respect

offend trouble, injure

offer attempt; threaten violence

office *sb.* duty; official or body of officials; *v.* act as a servant; deter by means of one's station

offices servants' quarters, pantry, *etc.*

old plenty of; 'fine old'

omit neglect, disregard; forbear to use

omittance omission

omne bene all's well (*Lat.*)

onyers a grand-sounding title, possibly sherrifs owing debts to the king

ope open

open-arse the medlar fruit (*see* **medlar**)

operant working, effective

operation effective power

opinion reputation; general opinion; (adverse) judgement; (high) opinion of oneself

opposeless unable to be opposed

opposite *sb.* opponent; *adj.* opposed, antagonistic

opposition combat

oppress distress

oppression distress

oppugnancy antagonism, opposition

or ere, before; **or ... or** = either ... or

orb ring; earth; *see* **sphere**

ordinance that which is ordained by God, providence, tradition, *etc.*; order; ordnance, artillery

ordinant ordaining, directing

ordinary supper, as served in a tavern

orgulous haughty

orifex orifice, opening

orison prayer

ort left-over, scrap

orthography correct spelling, *hence* pedantic style of speaking

ostent appearance, show

ostentation public display, formal show

ostler groom, stable-boy

othergates in another way

Ottomite Ottoman, Turk

ouches gems, brooches

ought owed

ounce lynx

ouphs children of elves or fairies

ousel blackbird

outbrave outdo in bravery or splendour (*cf.* **brave**)

out-crafty outdo in craftiness

outdure outlast

out-peer excel

outvied outbidden

outward *sb.* outside, exterior; *adj.* on the outside of secret affairs

ovator one who receives ovations

overhear hear over

overhold value too highly

overlook *see* **o'erlook**

over-peer, overpeer *see* **o'erpeer**

overscutched worn out

overture opening, disclosure, declaration

Ovid Roman poet, author of *Metamorphoses*, a long poem telling stories of transformation, and erotic verse which may have contributed to his exile among the Getae (Goths)

owe own; bear

oyes = '*oyez*' (*Fr.*), a call for order before a public announcement

pace *sb.* horse's trained walk; way, passage; *v.* train or exercise (a horse) in walking

pack *sb.* conspiracy; *v.* conspire; be in league; pack off, go; pack cards with *see* **card**

packing intrigue

paddock toad

pageant *sb.* spectacular show or float; *v.* mimic, as in a pageant

pain *sb.* penalty; labour, pains; *v.* put to pains

painful involving labour; undergoing labour

painted hollow, false; **painted cloth** = decorative wall hanging painted with familiar figures

Pair-Taunt like as if possessing a winning hand at cards

pajock (?) peacock, supposed to be lecherous; (?) patchock (rogue)

palabras see **paucas pallabris**

pale *sb.* pallor; fence; rail; enclosure; *v.* make pale; enclose

palfrey small horse

palisadoes iron-pointed stakes

pall lose force; wrap

Pallas Greek goddess associated with law and wisdom

pallet basic bed

palliament candidate's gown

palmer pilgrim

palmy flourishing, victorious

palter equivocate, use deceit

pandar, pander *sb.* pimp, go-between; *v.* serve, as a pandar

Pandion father of Philomel and Progne (*see* **Philomel**)

pantaloon stock figure of the foolish old man in Italian comedy

Pantheon a temple in Rome

pantler servant in charge of the pantry

paper *sb.* statement of one's crime worn as a public penance; *v.* send a note to

Paracelsus innovative Swiss physician

paradox improbable or unusual proposition

paragon put forward as a paragon; surpass; parallel

Parca one of the *Parcae*, the Latin name for the Fates (*see* **Fates**)

parcel *sb.* group, band; item, part, bit; *v.* particularise

parcel-gilt partly gilded

pard leopard

Paris-balls tennis-balls

Parish top large spinning-top

Parish-garden Paris Garden in London where bear-baiting took place

paritor officer of the Ecclesiastical Courts

parle parley, talk

parlous perilous, dangerous

parmacity spermaceti, used as a medicinal treatment

part *sb.* ability, accompishment; quality; action; *v.* depart; **in part** = in part-payment

partake take sides; **partake to** = share with

partaker confederate

parted gifted, accomplished; (of the eyes) unfocused

partial of partiality

partialize make partial

partially by or with partiality

particular regard; personal concern, duty or motive

partisan pike-like weapon

Partlet traditional name for a hen

party-coated dressed in a fool's outfit (*cf.* **motley**)

party-verdict share in a joint decision

pash *sb.* head; *v.* bash

passado forward lunge with a sword

passant (in heraldry) walking position

passenger traveller

passion *sb.* strong emotion; suffering, *esp.* the final sufferings of Christ; passionate speech; *v.* suffer; express passion

passionate *adj.* compassionate; *v.* express passionately

passy measures pavin = passe-measure pavan, a stately dance

patch *sb.* jester, clown; *v.* make, as from patches

patchery fool's play, cheating

paten shallow metal dish, as used in Holy Communion

patent entitlement, licence

patience sufferance, permission

patronage patronise, defend

pattern *sb.* example, model; *v.* set a precedent (for)

paucas pallabris Sly's version of '*pocas palabras*' (*Sp.* = 'few words')

pauca verba few words (*Lat.*)

Paul's St Paul's Cathedral, London, a centre for trade and the hiring of servingmen

paunch rip or stab the belly

pax representation of Christ kissed by worshippers at Mass

peach *see* **appeach**

peak languish, become emaciated

pearl cataract

peat pet, sweetheart

peck *sb.* reasonable-sized vessel; *v. see* **pick**

peculiar own, personal, private

pedant schoolmaster

pedascule from '*pedasculus*' (*pseudo-Lat.* = little pedant)

peel'd shaven-headed, bald

Pegasus winged horse associated with the hero Perseus

peise weigh (down); balance

pelf possessions, booty

pelican bird supposed to feed its young with its own blood

Pelion like Ossa and Olympus, a

Glossary

famous mountain from Greek antiquity

Pelops boy to whom the gods gave an ivory shoulder

pelt scold

pelting trivial, petty, worthless

pencil paintbrush

pencilled painted

pendulous overhanging

Pene gelidus timor occupat artus 'Cold fear almost seizes the limbs' (*Lat.*)

penner pen-holder

penn'orth, pennyworth bargain (often in a bad sense)

pensioner royal attendant

Penthesilea an Amazon queen

Pepin French king of the eighth century

Per Stygia, per manes vehor 'I am carried through the Stygian regions, through the realm of shades' (*Lat.*, after Seneca) (*cf.* **Styx**)

peradventure perhaps

perdie by God (an oath)

perdition loss; ruin

perdu sentinel placed in a fatally exposed position

perdurable everlasting, imperishable

perdy *see* **perdie**

peregrinate like one who travels abroad

peremptory determined, obstinate, high-handed

perfect *adj.* matured; ripe, prepared; learned; *v.* finish; enlighten, instruct

perfection achievement, fulfilment

perfumer one who fumigates rooms with pleasant scents

perge continue (*Lat.*)

periapts amulets, charms

period *sb.* end-point, goal; full-stop, pause at the end of sentence; *v.* end

perjure *sb.* perjurer; *v.* force into perjury

perniciously fatally, to the point of death

peroration oration, speech

perpend weigh, consider

persistive persistent

perspective optical illusion or a glass device for producing one

pert quick, sharp

pervert divert

pester obstruct, trouble

petard bomb

pew-fellow companion at church

Phaëthon, Phaeton, Phaëton son of Phoebus (*see* **Phoebus**) and stepson of Merops; attempting to drive Phoebus' sun chariot, he failed to control its horses and almost crashed into the earth, whereupon Jupiter killed him with a lightning bolt

phantasma nightmare

phantisime person given to flights of fancy

Philip traditional name for a sparrow; **Philip and Jacob** = feast of SS. Philip and James (1 May)

Philippan from the Battle of Philippi, where Antony and Octavius defeated the republicans

Philomel, Philomela daughter of King Pandion, she was raped and mutilated by her brother-in-law Tereus but revealed her ordeal by depicting it in a tapestry; she was subsequently transformed into a nightingale (*cf.* **Progne**)

philosopher's stone means of transforming base metal into gold

Phoebe the goddess Diana when represented as the moon

Phoebus the god Apollo in his role as sun god and father of Phaeton (*see* **Phaëthon**)

phoenix fabulous bird supposed to be one of a kind and to rise again from its ashes

phraseless that defies the power of language

physic *sb.* medicine; *v.* mend, heal

physical healthy, therapeutic

pia mater membrane in the brain, *hence* brain

pick hurl

picked select; dandified, refined

pickers and stealers hands

pickthanks flatterers

Pickt-hatch seedy district of London

'pie magpie

pie church service book; *see* **'pie**

piece *sb.* coin; wine cask; masterpiece, paragon; insulting term for a woman; *v.* supplement; **piece out, piece up** = add to, increase

pigeon-liver'd incapable of anger

pight pitched; set, determined

pike pitchfork; spike set in the centre of shield

pilcher scabbard

pill pillage, take by force; peel, strip

Pillicock penis; **Pillicock Hill** = female genitals

pin nothing, an irrelevance; (in archery) bullseye; **pin and web** = cataracts

pinch *sb.* nip; *v.* vex, irritate; (of an animal) nip with the teeth

pinfold pound for stray animals

pinioned bound

pink'd porringer a fancy hat

pioned (?) covered in flowers; (?) dug out

pip spot on a playing card, *hence* one point

pipe-wine wine from a cask

Pippen *see* **Pepin**

pismire ant

pitch *sb.* height; **Pitch and pay** = 'cash only'

Più per dolcezza che per forza 'More by gentleness than by force' (*Ital.*)

place *sb.* safe place; (in falconry) a hawk's highest pitch; *v.* employ; **take place** = become respectable

placket skirt or slit in a skirt

plain-song basic melody

planched made of planks

plant sole of a foot

plantage plant growing

plantain plant used for basic first aid

plantation planting; colonization

plash puddle

plate *sb.* coin; *v.* dress in armour

plausible worthy of applause

plausibly with applause

plausive approved, worthy of applause; plausible

Plautus Roman writer of comedies

pleached intertwined, as the branches of a hedge; hedged

pleasant jesting

please-man flatterer

pleurisy inflamed excess

plight *sb.* pledge, promise; *v.* pledge, swear; **in plight** = physically fit

plume up (?) make a show of, as a bird ruffles its feathers

Pluto god of the underworld

Plutus personification of wealth, sometimes imagined as its god

point *sb.* lace for tying garments; sword; signal; pinnacle; *v.* appoint, assign; **at point** = ready, prepared; in every detail; about

point-device, point-devise *adj.* neat, exact; *adv.* exactly

poise *sb.* weight; *v.* weigh, consider; counterpoise

poke large bag

poking-sticks rods used for the stiffening of ruffs

Polack *sb.* Pole; *adj.* Polish

pole star; standard

polecat whore

policy politics; wisdom; strategy; stratagem

politic political

politician plotter, schemer

poll-clipt pruned

polled lopped, cleared; bald

pomander perfume ball

pomewater popular type of apple

Pomgarnet 'Pomegranate', the name of a room

pompous characterized by pomp, magnificent, stately

poop overcome

Poor-John dried, salted hake

popinjay parrot

popular common, of the people

popularity the people

porpentine porcupine

porridge soup, broth

port *sb.* portal, gate; (high) position in life; attitude, behaviour; *v.* bring to port

portable supportable

portage voyage (through life); porthole

portance attitude, behaviour

portion dowry

posied engraved with a posy (*see* **posy**)

position proposition, tenet advanced

possess give possession; tell, give to understand

posset *sb.* drink made by curdling hot milk with wine; *v.* curdle

post *sb.* messenger; horse; *adv.* quickly; *v.* hurry; **in post** = quickly; **post off** = defer

poster one who travels quickly

postern small side-gate

post-post-haste urgently

posy short motto engraved on a ring

potable *see* **med'cine**

potato supposed to be an aphrodisiac

potch jab, poke

potency power, authority

potential potent, commanding

potents potentates, rulers

pother uproar, riot

potting drinking

pottle half-gallon tankard

pouncet-box box containing perfume

powder pickle in salt

powdering-tub pickling barrel; Pistol's reference to the sweating tub (*see* **tub**)

power military force; person in authority; faculty

pox syphilis

practic practical

practice trick, machination; doing, performance

practisants accomplices

practise plot

praemunire writ issued against one who prefers papal to sovereign authority

praetor Roman magistrate

praise *sb.* virtue, merit; *v.* appraise; **praise in departing** = do not praise too soon

prank offensive act

preambulate walk before

precedence that which has preceded

precedent *sb.* example; sign; original; *adj.* earlier, previous

preceptial of precepts or moral instruction

precipitation precipitousness, sharpness of a drop

precise morally scrupulous, puritanical

precisian puritanical guide in religious matters

pre-contract future contract of marriage

precurrer precursor

precurse that which precedes by way of an omen

predicament category; situation

predominance ascendency, predominant influence (*see* **influence**)

predominant in the ascendent, a powerful planetary position

prefer bring forward; bring to attention, recommend; promote

pregnancy sharpness of intellect

pregnant skilful; ready, open; clear

prejudicate judge in advance

prejudice *sb.* detriment, disadvantage; *v.* harm

premeditation meditation on the future

premised predestined

prenominate *adj.* aforenamed; *v.* say in advance

pre-ordinance established rule

preparation military force; quality, gift

preposterous topsy-turvy, perverse

prerogative privilege, precedence

presage prediction, omen

prescript *sb.* order, instruction; *adj.* prescribed

prescription claim based on long standing possession

presence presence chamber, where royalty entertains visitors

present *sb.* present moment; document; *adj.* sudden, immediate; ready; *v.* act; lay before a court

presentation representation, image

presently at once

presentment presentation; representation

press *sb.* licence for conscription; cupboard; *v.* conscript; torture with crushing weights

pressure image, as if impressed on wax

Prester John legendary ruler of a medieval Eastern kingdom

presuppos'd previously laid down

pretence intention

pretend intend; claim; propose; show

prevent anticipate, pre-empt

prevention anticipation, forestalling

price value

prick *sb.* mark; point aimed at in archery; *v.* mark; urge; clothe

pricket two-year-old male deer

pricksong singing from printed music

pride highest pitch; splendour; lust

prig tinker, thief

prime *sb.* spring; *adj.* first, principal; sexually aroused

primero a card game

primogenity primogeniture, the inheritance rights of the oldest son

principal accomplice; corner-post of a house

principality one of the orders of angels

princox impertinent youth

Priscian Roman grammarian

pristine original, of old

prithee '(I) pray thee', please

private privacy; common subject; private communication

privilege *sb.* something that bestows a privilege; advantage; *v.* sanction, permit

prize *sb.* fight, bout; privilege; *v.* esteem, care for

prizer prizefighter

probal reasonable

probation proof; testing, trial

proceeders scholars

process sequence of events; relation, story; mandate, summons

procurator proxy, substitute

prodigious ominous; unnatural; Launce's word for 'prodigal'

proditor betrayer

proface an expression of welcome

profit *sb.* learning, advancement; *v.* learn, advance

progeny ancestry, lineage

Progne wife of Tereus and sister of Philomel (*see* **Philomel**); after learning of Philomel's rape she obtained revenge by serving Tereus the flesh of their son at dinner

prognostication prophecy; weather forecast

Proh Deum! Medius Fidius! 'By God! Holy Fidius (*i.e.* Jupiter) [help] me!' (*Lat.*)

project *sb.* thought, anticipation; *v.* present

projection scale

prolixious time-wasting

prolong'd postponed

Promethean of Prometheus (*see* **Prometheus**)

Prometheus legendary figure who stole fire from the gods to give to man and was punished by being shackled to a mountain where an eagle pecked at his liver

promulgate make publicly known

prone prostrate; eager, headstrong

proof testing, trial; tried and tested armour; success

propend incline

propension propensity, desire

proper personal, own; decent, fine

property *sb.* individual quality; instrument; *v.* obtain; exploit, treat as an object

proportion fortune; number, magnitude; **lay the proportions** = estimate the numbers needed

propose *sb.* talk; *v.* hold forth, talk

propriety true nature or identity

propugnation protection

prorogue postpone, put off; prolong

prosecution pursuit, attack

Proserpina, Proserpine maiden abducted by Pluto while she gathered flowers and then imprisoned in the underworld

prosperous favourable, leading to a desirable outcome

Proteus mythological figure able to change his shape

protractive delaying

proud resplendent, luxurious

provand *see* **provender**

prove test, try out, put on trial; ascertain

provender food, fodder

provincial subject to provincial jurisdiction; **Provincial rose** = (Provençal) rose with many petals

prune preen

psaltery stringed musical instrument

publish proclaim; publicly represent

pudder *see* **pother**

pudding stuffed intestine, sausage

pudency modesty

pueritia boyhood (*Lat.*)

pugging thieving

puissance strength; troops

puissant strong, overpowering

puke-stocking (wearing) heavy dark woollen stockings

pumpion pumpkin

punk whore, slut

punto (in fencing) thrust (*Ital.*); *punto reverso* = back-handed thrust (*Ital.*)

purblind blind or weak-sighted

purchase plunder; marketable value of a property, equal to twelve years' rent

purgation acquittal; confession and absolution

purl curl

purlieus vicinity of a forest

purpose talk; proposal

pursuivant herald's attendant

pursy flabby, short of breath

purveyor one who travels ahead of a party on the move to prepare for its arrival

push *sb.* crisis; action; *int.* 'pish'; **stand the push** = stand up to, tolerate

push-pin a children's game

putter-off investor who is repaid five-fold upon returning from a foreign voyage

putter-on one who instigates or incites

puttock kite

puzzel slut

pyramid obelisk, pillar

quail *sb.* whore; *v.* overpower; slacken

quaint skilful; ingenious, artful; dainty, pretty

qualify pacify; moderate; dilute

quality nature; accomplishment; rank; profession; company

quare why (*Lat.*)

quarry game killed in hunting

quarter military location, watch; relations

quat pimple

quatch (?) plump

quean slut

queasy dangerous; easily upset; sickened

quench cool down

quern (?) handmill; (?) churn

quest *sb.* jury, inquest; search; *v.* bark

question *sb.* conversation; trial, examination, consideration; *v.* talk (to), discuss; **in the loss of question** = for the sake of argument; **on the top of question** = with the maximum of contention

questionable which invites questioning

questrist seeker

Qui me alit, me extinguit 'Who feeds me extinguishes me' (*Lat.*)

quick living; pregnant; lively; fresh

quicken bring to life, fertilize; come to life, be conceived; make lively

quiddities quibbles

quietus clearing of accounts

quill, in the (?) in a body; (?) in order

quillets, quillities quibbles

quintain post for tilting practice

quis who (*Lat.*)

quit release from service; acquit; remit; pay; reward, requite

quite *see* **quit**

quiver nimble

Quo usque tandem 'How long?' (*Lat.*), expression of impatience

quoif *see* **coif**

quondam former (*Lat.*)

quoniam because (*Lat.*)

quote note; observe; set down

quotidian daily fever; **quotidian tertian** = (?) Quickly's confusion of two types of fever; (?) a severe fever of more than one strain

R letter meant to sound like the growling of a dog

rabbit-sucker baby rabbit

race hereditary nature; course; (of horses) stud; (of ginger) *see* **raze** (*sb.*)

Glossary

rack *sb.* cloud or bank of clouds; *v.* stretch, as on a rack; tax at an extortionate rate

racker torturer (*cf.* **rack**)

rage *sb.* poetic inspiration (*cf.* **fury**); *v.* enrage

raging-wood crazy with anger

raisins o'th' sun grapes dried naturally in the open air

ramp slut

rampallian rogue

ramping as heraldic 'rampant', rearing up in an aggressive stance

rampir'd barricaded or protected by ramparts

rangers gamekeepers

rank *sb.* journey; *adj.* excessively grown or swollen, bloated; sexually excited; *v.* tier

rankle make sore, aggravate

rankness excessive growth or swelling

ransack'd stolen, taken as plunder

rap possess, overcome

rapture violent seizure; paroxysm

rascal *sb.* young, skinny deer; *adj.* common

rash *adj.* sudden, hasty, violent; *adv.* hastily

rate *sb.* estimation, value; manner, style; *v.* berate, revile; estimate, evaluate; be valued at; give (a share)

rather, the all the sooner, all the more so

ratified brought into 'rate' or proportion

raught reached

ravel tangle; untangle

raven see **ravin** (*v.*)

ravin *adj.* ravenous; *v.* gulp, swallow eagerly

ravin'd (?) ravenous; (?) having gorged itself

ravish violate; seize, tear; enthrall

ravished seized from

rawness unprotected condition

rayed soiled

raze *sb.* (of ginger) root; *v.* scrape, cut

razure erasure, destruction

reach range of understanding

read lecture, tutor

re-answer repay

reason *sb.* something reasonable; talk, discourse; way of thinking; just cause; *v.* talk; ask, plead; argue rationally about; explain; **no reason** = nothing for it

reasonable of reason

reave deprive

rebate dampen

rebato type of stiff collar or ruff

rebeck an early ancestor of the violin

receipt something received; receptacle; volume; recipe

receiving apprehension, perception

recheat call on a hunting horn

reck care, take account of

reckless thoughtless, having no care for

reclaim overcome; domesticate (an animal)

recognizance bond acknowledging a debt; badge

recoil fall back, give way

recollect collect

recomforted comforted, reassured

recommend commend, entrust; report to

record sing

recordation record, memorial

Recorder civil magistrate of a city

recourse access; repeated flowing

recover revive, restore; obtain, reach; **recover the wind** = allow the hunted quarry to smell the hunt on the wind (*cf.* **wind**)

recoverable able to be recovered or retraced

recreation repast, refreshment

rector priest; ruler

rectorship sovereignty

recure cure, heal, repair

rede guidance, instruction

Redime te captum quam queas minimo 'Ransom yourself from captivity as cheaply as you can' (*Lat.*)

red-lattice an alternative to glass windows found in taverns

reduce bring or lead back

reechy grimy with smoke or grease

reed voice breaking, adolescent voice

re-edify rebuild

reek *sb.* smoke, fumes; *v.* be exhaled in the form of smoke or fumes

refel reject

reflect shine; look; rebound, throw back

refuge *sb.* (last) resort; *v.* screen, comfort

regard *sb.* face, expression, look; sight; consideration; heed; *v.* respect, pay attention to; tend

regiment authority

region stratum of the atmosphere, sky

regreet *sb.* greeting; reciprocal greeting; *v.* greet again

reguerdon *sb.* reward; *v.* reward

rehearsal account, repetition

rehearse tell, repeat

reins kidneys

rejoicer (?) encourager

rejoindure union; reunion

rejourn postpone

relation report

relative cogent, material

religion dutifulness, keen attention; superstition

religious dutiful, conscientious, assiduous

relinquish dismiss, abandon

relish *sb.* taste, quality; *v.* taste; flavour; please; sing elaborately

relume reignite

remainder someone remaining; money yet to be paid

remediate acting as a remedy

remember commemorate; remind; mention

remission pardon for an offence, *hence* desire or power to pardon; release from an obligation

remit give up

remonstrance manifestation

remorse compassion, sensitivity; (?) obligation

remorseful sensitive, compassionate

remotion relocation

remove raising of a siege

removedness withdrawal, absence

remover person who changes or withdraws

render *sb.* surrender; confession; (?) due service; *v.* surrender; report

rendezvous meeting place; home, refuge

renege deny; abandon

renew renew a battle

repair *sb.* act of making one's way; *v.* make one's way

repairing resilient

repasture food

repeal *sb.* recall (from exile); *v.* recall (from exile)

repetition utterance, narration; repetitive talk; talk of former events

repine fretting, vexation

repining grudging

replenished total, consummate

replication reply; repetition for the purposes of elaboration or illustration

reprisal booty

reprobance damnation

reprobate sinful

reproof condemnation; disproof

reprove deny, disprove

repugn repel, reject

repugnancy fighting back

repugnant recalcitrant, rebellious

repured refined

repute judge, hold; make a reputation (of), broadcast

requiring stern commands

requit requited

reremice bats

rescue forcible retrieval of a person or goods from custody

resemblance seeming

resist (?) repel, disgust

resolution certainty

resolve dissolve; solve, provide an answer; satisfy

resolvedly with clarification

respect *sb.* consideration; respectablity, worth; *v.* consider; value; **without respect** = absolutely

respective respectful; careful; equivalent, parallel

respectively respectfully

respice finem 'think on your end' (*Lat.*)

respite end of a period of respite

responsive appropriate, matching

'rest arrest

rest *sb.* stay, sojourn; *v.* remain; **above the rest** = above all; **in rest** = under arrest, detained; **set up one's rest** = resolve, stake all (from a card game)

resting changeless

restrain restrict, withold

restrained tightly drawn

resty lethargic, idle

retention detention; record, notebook; holding capacity

retentive restraining, detaining

retire *sb.* retreat; *v.* retreat; withdraw; **make retire** = withdraw

retort reject, throw back

retrograde (of a planet) moving backwards, *hence* contrary

return *sb.* reply; *v.* reply

reverb sound as a reverberation

reverberate reverberating, echoing

reverse '*punto reverso*' (*see* **punto**)

reversion inheritance or restoration of property to an original owner viewed as a future event

re-view, review see once more

revolt change or transfer (of allegiance); disgust; rebel

revolution turn, as of Fortune's or Time's wheel; turning of the thoughts

revolve consider, dwell on

rhapsody confused heap

Rhenish Rhine wine

rheum catarrhal or lachrymal discharge, seen in chronic cases as a morbid condition and sometimes linked with venereal disease

ribaudred (?) ribald (licentious); (?) 'ribald-rid' (ridden by a ribald man); (?) knackered with ribaldry

riggish licentious

right *adv.* straight; correctly; justly; **in right of** = in the name of

right-hand file aristocracy

rigol circle

rim peritoneum, abdominal membrane

ring, cracked within the *see* **crack**

ring-carrier bawd

ringlet fairy ring; fairy dance

riot revelling, partying

ripe *adj.* ready; urgent; of marriageable age; *v.* ripen

rivage shore

rival *sb.* fellow, colleague; *v.* compete

Glossary

rivality equality

rive burst, crack

rivelled wrinkled

rivo a cheer at drinking (*Sp.*)

road raid, inroad; leg of a journey; anchorage, harbour

robustious turbulent

rogue vagrant

roguing roving, vagrant

roguish vagabond's

roisting wild, boisterous

Roman (of handwriting) italic

rondure circle, sphere (*cf.* roundure)

ronyon mangy animal; term of abuse for a woman

rook crouch

ropery lewd jesting

Roscius great Roman actor

roted acquired or learnt by rote

round *sb.* earth; ring-dance; circular journey; rung; *adj.* direct; *adv.* thoroughly; *v.* surround; grow round; whisper mysteriously

roundel ring-dance

roundly without fuss or ceremony, directly; fluently; completely

roundure ring, circle (*cf.* rondure)

rouse *sb.* drink or drinking session; *v.* (in hunting) drive from cover

rowell spur

royal *sb.* coin worth ten shillings; **royal merchant** = successful merchant

royalty right granted to a subject by the king; crown

roynish scabby, dirty

rub *sb.* (in bowls) something that impedes or deflects the bowl from its course; *v.* sidetrack; **rub on** = roll on

rubious ruby-red

ruddock robin

rude rough, unskilled, unsophisticated

rudeness roughness, lack of skill or sophistication

rudesby ruffian

rue pity

ruffle *sb.* hectic activity and quarrels; *v.* brag; handle roughly; fight; **ruffle up** = enrage

rugged bristling

rug-headed having long, wild hair

ruinous in ruins, damaged

rummage busy activity, as on a ship

rumour confused din; rumoured character

rump-fed (?) fed on choice cuts; (?) having fat buttocks

runagate renegade, apostate

runnion *see* ronyon

russet reddish-brown, the colour of a coarse cloth worn by peasants

ruth repentance; pity

Saba the Queen of Sheba

sable *sb.* blackness; *adj.* black

sables magnificent dark furs

sack white wine, often sherry

sackbut brass instrument resembling the trombone

Sackerson a famous bear from the London bear-baiting scene

sacring bell small bell used in Protestant times to summon parishioners to prayers

sad serious, solemn; dark-coloured

sadly seriously, soberly

sadness seriousness; **in sadness** = in earnest, truly

safe *adj.* well, sound; *adv.* with regard to security; *v.* make safe

safety custody

saffron a dye used in both clothing and food

Sagittary a centaur that fought against the Greeks in the Trojan war

sail fleet

sain said

salad days youth

salamander species of lizard supposedly able to live in fire

sale-work ready-made goods

Salic law French law blocking females and their descendants from succession to the crown

sallet salad; light piece of armour for the head

salt *sb.* salt tears; *adj.* bitter; salacious, lustful; (of fish) salt-water

saltiers (?) woodland creatures that leap about, like satyrs

salute cheer, excite

sample example

sanctimonious holy

sanctimony holiness; something holy

sanctuarize provide with sanctuary or immunity from punishment

sand-blind partially blind

sanded sandy-coloured

sandy of sand, as used in an hour-glass

sanguine red, ruddy (the colour of blood); full-blooded

sans without (*Fr.*)

sapient wise

sarcenet, sarsenet thin, delicate silk

Sarum ancient city near Camelot

sate ignored

Satis quid sufficit Holofernes's version of '*satis quod sufficit*' (*Lat.* = 'enough is as good as a feast')

Saturn (in astrology) planet associated with old age, coldness, melancholy and evil

sauce season, spice, make hot

saucy highly seasoned; impudent; sexually bold or carefree

savagery profuse vegetation

savour *sb.* smell; nature; *v.* smack, smell; sense or relish

Savoy a great house on the Strand in London

saw wise saying

say *sb.* assay, evidence; kind of silk cloth; *v.* speak; speak truly or aptly

'say'd assayed, tried

'Sblood (by God)'s blood (an oath)

scab rogue

scaffoldage stage

scald scabby, scurvy

scale *sb.* mark used for measuring distance, height, *etc.*; *v.* weigh, judge

scamble scramble

scamels an unidentified type of bird

scandalis'd, scandaliz'd slandered; disgraced

scantling degree of capacity or ability; sample, specimen

scantly resentfully

'scape, scape *sb.* escape; escapade, transgression; *v.* escape

scarf sling; sash used to indicate rank in the army

scarre (?) snare

scathe *sb.* injury, damage; *v.* injure

scattering scattered, disordered

schedule paper, often a list or summary

school *sb.* university; *v.* teach (a lesson); govern, control

science (theoretical) knowledge

scion shoot or cutting from a plant

sconce small round fort; protective screen; head

scope target, purpose, aim; permission, opportunity; **scope of nature** = an event permitted by nature, a natural event

scorch cut, gash

score notch on a stick or post to mark an account, *hence* account; *v.* cut a notch, *hence* mark on an account

scorn, take scorn

scot small payment; **scot and lot** = in full

scotch *sb.* gash; *v.* gash

scour clean out (a pistol) with a ramrod; hurry

scrimers fencers

scrip script; shepherd's bag

scrippage Touchstone's coinage for 'shepherd's baggage' (*cf.* scrip)

scriptures (written) words

scroyles scabby scoundrels

scrubbed dwarfish

scruple doubt; a third of a dram

scrupulous full of scruples, hesitant

scullion kitchen servant of either sex

sculls schools (of fish)

scurril, scurrile scurrilous, filthy

scut tail of a rabbit or deer; female genitals

scutcheon cheap coat of arms used at funerals

'Sdeath (by God)'s death (an oath)

se offendendo Grave-digger's version of '*se defendendo*' (*Lat.* = 'in self-defence')

sea-coal superior type of coal transported to London by sea

seam grease

sea-maid mermaid

sea-monster creature to whom Laomedon, King of Troy, attempted to sacrifice his daughter Hesione; Hercules rescued her thinking to obtain some horses in payment

seamy showing the seams; **seamy side** = inner side (of a garment or glove)

sear *sb.* part of a gunlock; *v.* wrap in a cerecloth (shroud); brand; **tickle a'th' sear** = liable to go off (*cf.* tickle)

searchers public health officers similar to modern coroners

searching sharp, strong

second *sb.* supporter, as in a duel; *adj.* representative

seconds second-rate material

sect cutting; class, profession; political faction; sex

sectary adherent of a sect, disciple; **sectary astronomical** = disciple of astrologers

secure *adj.* over-confident; *v.* comfort; make over-confident; protect

securely with (false) confidence

security over-confidence

See, the the Holy See, the diocese of the Pope

seeded grown, matured

seedness state of being sown

seeing what one sees, appearance

seel sew up (the eyelids of a hawk in training)

seeming *sb.* appearance; likelihood; deception, falseness; *adj.* apparent; *adv.* in a seemly manner

seen qualified

seld seldom

self selfsame; relating to oneself, one's own

semblable *sb.* likeness; *adj.* matching

semblative similar in appearance to

Seneca Roman Stoic philosopher and writer of tragedies

sennet fanfare of trumpets or cornets

se'nnight, seve'night, seven-night, sev'n-night week

sense senses; sexual awareness; mind; **adder's sense** = senses

Glossary

'as deaf as an adder' (proverbial); **to the sense** = to the quick

senseless insensate, unresponsive; unconscious

sensible able to sense, having sensation; able to be sensed, material, evident

sensibly perceptibly; being alive and sensitive; with feeling

sentence opinion; decision, ruling; memorable saying

sententious memorable, using choice words; the Nurse's word for 'sentence'

Septentrion north

sequel that which follows

sequent *sb.* follower; *adj.* following, subsequent; successive

sequester *sb.* sequestration, removal; *v.* remove, divorce

sequestration removal, isolation; loss of property; (?) sequel, result

sere *sb.* dried-up condition; *adj.* dry

sergeant arresting officer

serpigo a skin disease popularly linked with venereal disease

servant lover

servanted to in the service of

service food served at table

set *sb.* twelve hours on a clock face; *adj.* seated; (of eyes) closed; lacking spontaneous wit; *v.* sit; put up a stake (in gambling); compose music for words; close (the eyes of the dead); **set a match** = plan a robbery; **set hand** = formal handwriting

setter thieves' informant

several *sb.* individual; particular; *adj.* different, various; individual, distinct; personal, (one's) own

severally individually

sewer chief servant, in charge of setting the table

'Sfoot (by God)'s foot (an oath)

shadow shade or shady spot; illusory image, picture; actor; spirit; ghost

shaft or a bolt on't, make a do it somehow

shag rough, untrimmed

shales husks, pods

shame natural modesty

shame-fac'd, shamefaced shy; full of shame

shard piece of broken pottery; cow-pat

shark up snatch indiscriminately, as a shark its food

shearman one involved in the manufacture of cloth

sheaved composed of sheaves (of straw)

sheep-biter dog or wolf that bites sheep, *hence* dangerous, sanctimonious person

sheep-biting dangerous, sanctimonious (*cf.* **sheep-biter**)

sheer pure

shent rebuked, scolded

sherris sherry

shift *sb.* expedient, trick; trickery; smock; *v.* make do, improvise, live on one's wits; change (clothing); **make shift** = use tricks or resourcefulness to achieve a purpose

ship-tire elaborate head-dress shaped like a ship or sails

shive slice

shoal area of shallow water

shock throw into confusion, meet force with force

shog be going; **shog off** = come away

shoon shoes

shot payment; account, bill; marksman, gunner

shotten (of a fish) having shot its roe (shed its eggs), lank

shoughs shag-haired dogs

shoulder-shotten having dislocated shoulders

shove-groat shovel-board, a game of propelling coins across a smooth board

shrewd sharp; cunning, mischievous, wicked

shrewdly sharply; sorely

shrieve sheriff; shrieve's fool *see* **fool**

shrift sacrament of Confession, *hence* confession, absolution or confessional

shrill-gorged shrill-sounding

shrine statue, icon

shrive hear confession and grant absolution

shroud *sb.* guard, protection; ropes of a ship's mast; *v.* hide, take cover

shuffle shift, make do; smuggle; cheat

Si fortuna me tormenta, spero me contenta see **Si fortune** (*etc.*)

Si fortune me tormente sperato me contento Pistol's expression, in a mixture of European languages, of the motto 'If fortune torments me, hope contents me'

Sic spectanda fides 'Thus is faithfulness to be shown' (*Lat.*)

sickle shekel, a Hebrew coin

siege seat, *esp.* of office or high rank; rank, status; excrement

sight aperture at the front of helmet; **of one's sight** = seeing one

sightless invisible; unpleasant to look at

silly simple; defenceless; meagre, trifling

simple *sb.* herb used as a medicine; ingredient; *adj.* unadulterated, pure

simpleness stupidity, nonsense; plain honesty; purity, state of being unadulterated

simplicity stupidity

simular *sb.* simulator, false representative; *adj.* specious

sinfully in a state of sin; **sinfully miscarry** = die without the last rites

single *adj.* alone, unaided; honest, direct; weak; *v.* (in hunting) select and pursue (an animal from the herd); **single bond** = (?) a contract without conditions; **single ten** = ten at cards

Singulariter nominativo 'in the nominative singular' (*Lat.*)

singularity personal qualities; odd behaviour; remarkable object

sinister left; irregular, wrong

sink *sb.* cesspit; *v.* go down to hell

sink-a-pace *see* **cinque-pace**

Sinon Greek who tricked the Trojans into receiving a wooden horse containing soldiers who went on to capture Troy

sirrah term of address to a social inferior

sir-reverence phrase used to apologize for foul talk; a euphemism for dung

sister *v.* closely resemble; neighbour; **Sisters Three** = the Fates (*see* **Fates**)

Sit fas aut nefas 'be it right or wrong' (*Lat.*)

sith since

sithence since

size a gelatinous glaze; allowance of food and drink

skains-mates cut-throat companions

skiffed travelled in a skiff (a light boat)

skill *sb.* discernment; need, reason; *v.* matter

skilless ignorant

skillet cooking pot

skimble-skamble incoherent, wild

skipper light-brained, skipping person

skirr run hastily

slab thick and slimy

slander *sb.* accusation; disgrace; disgraceful person; *v.* charge, accuse; disgrace, abuse

slanderous of accusation; bringing disgrace; ill-reputed

slave enslave

sleave a coarse silk

sledded riding in sledges

sleeve-hand cuff of a sleeve

sleided separated into loose threads

'Slid (by God)'s (eye-)lid (an oath)

sliding sin

'Slight (by God)'s light (an oath)

slip *sb.* cutting or graft from a plant; counterfeit coin; leash; *v.* unleash (a greyhound)

slipper slippery

slippery unstable, treacherous

slipshod wearing slippers

sliver split off

slobbery muddy, slimy

slop, slops large baggy breeches

slough old snake-skin

slovenry slovenliness, dirty untidiness

slubber smear, stain; carelessly hurry

smatch smack, whiff

smatter prattle, chat

smock petticoat; woman

smoke *sb.* fog; *v.* steam; smoke out, as in fox hunting; beat; disinfect

smooth *sb.* flatter, indulge; gloss over; *adj.* flattering

smug spruced-up; smooth, unruffled

sneap *sb.* snub, reprimand; *v.* bite, chill

sneck up an offensive insult

snipp'd-taffeta jagged silk (slashed to display the lining underneath)

snuff resentment; **in snuff** = (of candles) needing to be snuffed; **take in snuff** = take offence

sob rest, breather

sod sodden, boiled

soiled lively or skittish

soilure sullying, staining

sole singular

solely wholly

solemnity festal occasion, celebration (often of marriage)

solicit *sb.* suit, petition; *v.* urge, excite

solidares (?) *solidi* (Roman coins)

sometime, sometimes *adj.* former; *adv.* formerly, once

sonance sonorous sound

sonties, be God's by God's saints (an oath)

sooth *sb.* truth; appeasement, flattery; *adv.* truly

soothe flatter; play along with, indulge

soothers flatterers

sop hunk of bread soaked in wine

sophister clever arguer

sophisticated adulterated, no longer simple or natural

Sophy Shah (king) of Persia

sore four-year-old male deer

sorel three-year-old male deer

sort *sb.* rank; dress; lot; *v.* accord; find; conclude; keep company (with)

sortance accordance; **hold sortance** = accord

sotted made a sot (a fool)

sound faint; fathom

souse strike; (in hawking) swoop (upon)

soused pickled

Glossary

South Sea the Pacific; **South Sea of discovery** = a long, frustrating voyage

sow ingot, block

sowl seize roughly, drag

Sowter 'Cobbler', a dog's name

span-counter a children's game like marbles

spavin tumour on a horse's leg-joint

specialty contract; particular distinction

spectacles spyglasses (telescopes); eyes

speculation sight, observation

speculative of sight

sped ruined; *see* **speed**

speed *sb.* fate, lot; *v.* fare; meet with success; favour; **be one's speed** = bring one good fortune; **have the speed of** = match in speed; overtake; **speed you** = God speed (favour) you

speeding *sb.* fate, lot; success; *adj.* successful

spend speak; use up; **spend the mouth** = be in full cry, as a hunting hound

sphere (in Ptolomaic astronomy) one of the massive crystalline spheres around the earth in which the planets, stars, *etc.* were believed fixed; they revolved, generating harmonious music, inaudible on earth

spherical of a planet

spigot part of a tap on a barrel

spill destroy

spilth spilling

spin spurt

spines thorns

spinners (?) spiders; (?) craneflies

spinster woman spinning flax or wool

spital hospital, *esp.* for the lower classes

spleen organ supposedly responsible for fierce passion, laughter and melancholy, *hence* the abstract condition or a fit or bout of any of these moods

splinted splintered (*see* **splinter**)

splinter apply splints to (a broken limb)

spoil *sb.* sacking, carrying off booty; bloody end of a hunt; *v.* sack, rob, steal

spongy watery, dripping; full of drink

spot piece of embroidery; mark on a list; blemish

sprag smart, quick

spring bud, shoot, sapling

springe snare for catching birds

springhalt muscular disorder in horses causing them to jerk back their legs

spurn *sb.* blow, rude rejection; *v.* kick fiercely

square *sb.* measuring rule; breast-piece of a dress; *adj.* just, fair; *v.*

measure; regulate, direct; square up, adopt a hostile stance; **by the square** = precisely; **square of sense** = (?) part of the body or mind

squarer one who squares for a fight, brawler

squash unripe pea-pod

squier square (measuring rule)

squiny squint

staff quarterstaff, spear or lance; stanza; **set in one's staff** = take up residence

stagger falter, be unsure

staggers disease in horses causing staggering; reeling state

stain *sb.* blemish; tincture, hint; one whose superiority casts a shadow (stain) on others; *v.* eclipse

stair-work furtive business on the back stairs

stale *sb.* urine; decoy; whore; laughing-stock, *esp.* a risible lover; stalemate; *v.* make stale; cheapen, debase

stall enthrone; lodge, as in an animal's stall; **stall together** = (?) tolerate each other's presence

stamp *sb.* something created or minted; seal, official mark; *v.* create, manufacture, (of coins) mint; seal, authenticate

stand stand about; stand still; stand up to; **stand in an action** = be a party in a legal action

standard standard-bearer

standing-bed bed with legs

standing-bowl bowl with a foot or pedestal

staniel kestrel

staple texture of wool

stare *sb.* staring state; *v.* stand up stiffly

start *sb.* outburst; *v.* (in hunting) drive from cover; frighten

starting-hole bolt-hole, hiding place

starve destroy, *esp.* with cold, freeze; suffer or perish with cold

state standing position, stance; estate (property, condition or social position); chair of state, throne; court

states men of rank

station standing (still), posture

statist politician, man of affairs

statute document providing security to a creditor

statute-caps (?) academic caps; (?) apprentices' caps

stave's staff's (*see* **staff**)

staves staffs (*see* **staff**)

stay *sb.* support; ongoing condition; check, interruption; *v.* support, hold (up); **stay by't** = stand up to things, stand one's ground

stead help, serve the needs of; **stead up** = stand in for

stelled stellar, starry; fixed; (?) portrayed

stern helm

stew brothel

stick stick out; stickle, scruple; pierce, kill

stickler-like in the manner of a moderator, usher or umpire

stigmatic someone criminal (branded) or deformed

stigmatical deformed

still *adj.* constant; *adv.* always, constantly; **still an end** = constantly

stillitory apparatus used for distilling perfumes, *etc.*

stilly quietly

sting passionate urge

stint stop

stithy *sb.* smithy, forge; *v.* forge

stoccado (in fencing) thrust with the swordpoint

stock family; dowry; stocking; idiot; stoccado (*see* **stoccado**)

stock-fish, stockfish dried cod, haddock, *etc.*

stockish inanimate, insensible

stole robe, sometimes of religious significance

stomach *sb.* part of the body supposedly the seat of pride, ambition and courage; appetite; inclination; *v.* feel indignant (at)

stomacher piece of ladies' clothing worn over the breast

stone *sb.* testicle; thunderbolt; translucent stone used as a mirror; *v.* turn to stone

stone-bow catapult

stool-ball bat and ball game

stoop bow, bend over; (of a bird of prey) swoop down upon prey

stop (in horseriding) rapid switch from a gallop to a halt; point where the finger determines a note on a musical instrument

store *sb.* plenty; *v.* fill up

stoup flagon, tankard

stout proud; courageous

stoutness pride; courage

stover winter food for cattle

Strachy, The Lady of the (?) an unidentified lady of the day

straight-pight standing straight, upright

strain *sb.* inherited character; pitch, level; *v.* embrace; transgress; pervert; **make no strain** = do not doubt; **strain courtesy** = be unceremonious; hang back

strait narrow; severe

straited hard pushed

strange alien, foreign, unfamiliar; remarkable

strange-achieved (?) got by curious means; (?) got in distant lands

strangely like a foreigner or stranger; remarkably

strangeness aloofness

strappado a form of torture that involves breaking the arms

stratagem trick, plot; violent act

stray men wandering aimlessly; **make a stray** = stray, deviate

strength body of soldiers

strewments strewed flowers

stricture repression; strictness, rigour

strike *sb.* quantity of bushels; *v.* strike (lower) sail; (of a planet) ruin with evil influence; fight; **strike vessels** = (?) chink cups, as in a toast; (?) tap casks

strossers trousers

stubborn hard, rigid

stuck *see* **stoccado**

stuffed congested; full (of qualities or accomplishments)

stuprum rape (*Lat.*)

Stygian of the Styx (*see* **Styx**)

style appellation, title

Styx a river of the underworld

subduements men conquered

subjection allegiance, as required of a subject

submission confession

subscribe sign; proclaim; agree; admit

subscription support, allegiance

substractors subtractors, Sir Toby's word for 'detractors' (critics)

subtle deceptive, false

subtleties elaborate sugar sculptures

succeed follow; proceed; inherit; pass by succession

success outcome, upshot, result; succession

successfully potentially successful

succession that which follows; inheritors

successive hereditary

successively through succession or inheritance

sue make a petition, ask; woo

sufferance, suff'rance suffering; patience, endurance; permission

suffice feed, nourish; satisfy

sufficient competent; prosperous, well off; qualified to act as a guarantor

suggest tempt, woo, persuade (into sin or discontent)

suggestion prompting; temptation; craftiness

sumless countless

summoner officer who cited people to appear in an ecclesiastical court

sumpter horse used for carrying baggage

superflux unnecessary luxuries

supernal celestial, heavenly

superscript superscription, address at the head of a letter

super-serviceable anxious to do any kind of service

superstitious loving, in the manner of a religious worshipper

Glossary

supervise *sb.* inspection, reading; *v.* look over, inspect
suppliance filling-up, occupation
supply military reinforcement
supposal idea, notion
suppose *sb.* notion, estimate; *v.* guess at
supposition, in potential, unconfirmed
surcease *sb.* end, *hence* death; *v.* cease
sure safe; loyal; **make sure** = dispose of, kill; **surer side** = mother's side
surety *sb.* guarantor; guaranteeing; certainty; *v.* act as guarantor for
sur-reined overworked, exhausted
suspect suspicion
suspiration sighing
suspire respire, breath
sutler seller of provisions
Suum cuique 'To each his own' (*Lat.*)
swabber sailor in charge of keeping the ship clean
swaddling-clouts *see* **swathing-clothes**
swagger act like a bragging ruffian
swaggerer bragging ruffian
swart swarthy, dark
swarth *see* **swath**
swashers swashbucklers, loud ruffians
swashing swashbuckling, rough
swath swathe, heap (of mown grass); *see* **swathing-clothes**
swathing-clothes, swathling clothes baby clothes
sway *sb.* rule, authority, control; *v.* rule, exert influence; control oneself
swayed broken, deformed
swear make swear, exact an oath from; **swear out** = give up; **swear over** = attempt to repudiate with oaths
sweat *sb.* plague; *v.* use a sweating tub (*see* **tub**)
sweet *sb.* scent; flower; *adj.* scented
sweeting sweet apple, used as a term of affection
swim sail
swindg'd swinged (*see* **swinge**)
swinge beat
swinge-bucklers swashbucklers
Swithold (?) St Withold
swoopstake in the manner of a sweepstake (one who takes all the stakes in a game)
sword-and-buckler swashbuckling, boisterous
sworder soldier
swounded fainted (*cf.* **sound**)
'Swounds (by God)'s wounds (an oath)
sympathise, sympathize agree with or resemble (another) in

some quality; share; represent accurately
synod gathering, conference

table *sb.* wooden board for painting on; writing-tablet; palm (of the hand); *v.* write down
table-book book of writing-tablets
tables backgammon
tabor type of drum, usually played together with a pipe
taborins military drums, similar to tabors
tack about change direction (at sea)
tackled stair rope-ladder on a ship
taffeta, taffety type of silk
tag common people
tailor traditional exclamation when, upon going to sit down, one falls; (?) penis
taint *sb.* fault; discredit; *adj.* tainted; *v.* lose freshness; speak badly of
take take on (a role), feign; take fire; make an impression; encounter; enchant, possess; **take head** = rush away; **take on** = show anger; **take out** = copy; **take the heat** = show anger; act quickly
taking *sb.* panic; infection; *adj.* noxious, infectious
tale penis (*cf.* **tailor**); **in a tale** = agreed upon the same story
talent ancient unit of currency; talon
tall courageous; good-looking, dashing; **tall stockings** = long stockings
tally stick notched to keep an account
tamed exposed to the air
tang clang forth, as a bell
Tanta est erga te mentis integritas Regina serenissima 'Such is the honesty of mind towards you, fairest queen' (*Lat.*)
Tantaene animis coelestibus irae? 'Can heavenly spirits such great resentments feel?' (*Lat.*, Virgil)
tar *see* **tarre**
tardy off, come executed inadequately
targe shield
tarre urge (a dog) to fight
tarriance waiting
tarry await
Tartar Tartarus, the deepest region of the underworld; Mongol, an archer warrior from the East
task challenge; tax
tasking challenging
tassel-gentle *see* **tercel**
tawdry-lace coloured neckcloth
tax *sb.* charge; *v.* charge, reproach, condemn

taxation critical attacks; requirement
teem breed, *esp.* abundantly
teen misery, pain
tell count, count up to
temper *sb.* character as defined by the humours (*see* **humour**); stability of character, as from a balance of the humours; *v.* mix, concoct; dilute
Temperance a Christian name popular with Puritans
temperate well-tempered, balanced, modest
temporary temporal (rather than spiritual)
tempt attempt, make trial of
tenant someone dependent on a lord
tend attend
tendance attendance
tender *sb.* offer, token; concern; *v.* attend to; offer, lay (down); cherish; treat;
tender-hefted soft and gentle
tent *sb.* probe for a wound; canopy over a bed; *v.* probe (a wound) to clean or explore it
tercel male falcon
Tereus *see* **Philomel** and **Progne**
Termagant a blustering, villainous role in the Mystery plays
terminations terms, language
termless that defies the power of language (terms)
Terras Astraea reliquit 'Astraea has left the earth' (*Lat.*, Ovid) (*see* **Astraea**)
tester, testril small coin
tetchy touchy, irritable
tetter *sb.* disfiguring skin complaint; *v.* disfigure on the skin
text motto; sermon; **text B** = 'B' in formal script
Thane Scottish nobleman of middling rank
thankful deserving thanks
theoric (military) theory
therefor for that
Thessaly region of Greece terrorized by a fierce boar
Thetis sea-goddess and mother of Achilles
thews sinews, strength
thick *adj.* dull; numerous; *adv.* in a hectic manner, hurriedly
thin-belly having a thin waist
thing, a something
think be gloomily introspective
third achieve a third of
thirdborough officer similar to a constable
thought melancholy contemplation; **with a thought** = quick as a thought
Thracian from Thrace; **Thracian poet** = Orpheus, killed by followers of Bacchus; **Thracian tyrant** = Polymestor,

blinded by Hecuba for murdering her son
thrasonical like Thraso, a braggart soldier in a comedy by the Roman dramatist Terence
three-farthings coin featuring a rose behind the sovereign's ear
three-man song-men singers of music for three male voices
three-nooked divided into three, as a map of the world divided into Asian, European and African segments
three-pile thick, costly velvet
Threne *threnos* (*Gr.* = 'lament for the dead')
thrice-crowned queen the moon
thrift profit
thriftless unprofitable
throe (of giving birth) pain
thrum tuft of unwoven yarn
thunder-stone thunderbolt, believed to be a stone
thwart *adj.* churlish, obstreperous; *adv.* sideways; *v.* cross
tickle *adj.* unsteady; *v.* flatter; entertain; **tickle't up** = give sexual pleasure, bring to orgasm
tick-tack board game involving pegs and holes
tide full flood, chance for action; **high tides** = holidays
tidy well-fed
tight water-tight; skilful
tile, washed a wasted time, as one would by washing an oven tile (proverbial)
tilt spar, thrust
timeless untimely; taking no time, speedy
timely in good time, early
tinct alchemists' potion (*see* **med'cine**); colouring
tincture colour, *esp.* in heraldry; scent
tire *sb.* attire, *esp.* for the head; *v.* (of birds of prey) feed by pulling the flesh apart
tiring-house attiring-house, green-room
tisick phthisic, a cough associated with lung disease
Titan the sun
tithe *sb.* a tenth of one's produce or income paid to the church; *v.* take tithes
tithing parish
title entitlement, claim
titlers claimants
tittles little dots and dashes in writing
to cry of encouragement
toast fragment of toasted bread taken in wine
toaze tease
tod *sb.* unit of weight in wool-dealing; bush; *v.* amount to a tod of wool
tofore before
toge toga, gown

Glossary

toil *sb.* hunter's snare or net; *v.* exercise, put to work

tokens, the Lord's skin blemishes caused by the plague

toll for put up for sale

tomboys harlots, whores

tool blade; penis

top *sb.* height; *v.* mount, have sex with (*cf.* **tup**); take time by the top *see* **occasion**

topgallant platform on a ship's mast

topless supreme

tortive contorted

toss carry impaled on a pike; (of a book) (?) leaf through; (?) throw about

tottering swaying; ragged

touch *sb.* touchstone; brushstroke; facial feature; *v.* test, as a touchstone tests gold; refer to; **keep touch** = keep one's promise

touse dislocate

toy something trivial or imaginary; **take toy** = be seized by a mad impulse

trace succeed; attend, keep up with; roam

tract track, route; trace

trade traffic, business

traded skilled

trade-fallen out of work

train *sb.* bait, snare; *v.* lure, as towards a trap

traject an Italian ferry

trammel up entangle, as in a net

transfix pierce, impale; fix, imprint

translate convert, metamorphose; explain

transpose alter

trash keep (an eager hound) in check

travail, travel *sb.* labour; journey; *v.* labour

traverse (in fencing) dodge and weave; march

tray-trip a dice game (*cf.* **trey**)

treatise words, account, story

treble-dated long-living

tremor cordis 'trembling of the heart' (*Lat.*), palpitations

trench dig (a trench), gouge, cut

trencher wooden plate

trencher-friends friends won by feeding

trenchering trenchers (*see* **trencher**)

trencher-knight one who is brave only at the dinner table

trey winning throw of three at dice

tribunal platform for Roman magistrates; **tribunal plebs** = Clown's mistake for '*tribuni plebis*' (*Lat.* = 'tribunes of the people' (*see* **tribune**))

tribune Roman magistrate representing the interests of ~~..ry citizens~~

trick *sb.* trifle; knack; distinctive feature; *v.* (in heraldry) colour; dress

tricking adornments

Trigon triplicity, grouping of three zodiacal signs by element (*e.g.* fire)

trill roll

triple third

triple-turned three times unfaithful

tristful sorrowful

triumph pageant of processions and tournaments

triumphant of a triumph, triumphal

triumphantly in the spirit of a triumph

triumvirate a ruling coalition formed on two occasions in Roman history, first between Julius Caesar, Crassus and Pompey, subsequently between Octavius, Antony and Lepidus

triumviry *see* **triumvirate**

Trojan lad, bloke

troll sing heartily

troll-my-dames game taken round fairs

trophy monument, *esp.* of a battle; ornament; token

tropically metaphorically

trot crone, hag

troth truth; faith

trow suppose, believe; know; wish to know, wonder

Troyan *see* **Trojan**

truckle-bed small bed on wheels stored under a normal bed

truepenny good lad

trull whore

truncheon baton, symbol of military command

trundle-tail curly-tailed dog

trunk sleave large, wide sleave

try *sb.* test; *v.* test, prove; **try with main-course** = (of a ship) lie stationary

tub pickling barrel; sweating tub, for the treatment of venereal disease

tuck rapier; **standing tuck** = blade that has lost its resilience

tucket trumpet-call

tuition care

Tully (Marcus Tullius) Cicero, Roman politician, orator and writer of books on oratory

tun-dish type of funnel

tup (of a ram) mount, penetrate

turtle turtle dove, known for its faithfulness

tushes tusks

twiggen made of twigs, wicker-work

twire twinkle, glint

type mark, badge, title

tyrannically fiercely

tyranny violence, fierceness

tyrant fierce; **fowl of tyrant wing** = bird of prey

umber brown earth

umbrage shadow

unable powerless

unaccommodated not provided with the usual clothes or comforts

unacquainted unfamiliar

unadvised *adj.* unintentional; *adv.* carelessly, without thinking

unagreeable inappropriate

unanel'd not anointed with the holy oil of the last rites

unapproved false

unaptness unwillingness

unattainted not infected

unattempted unassailed

unavoided unable to be avoided, inevitable

unbarbed uncovered

unbated not blunted; lacking the protective 'button' normally used on the tip of a fencing weapon

unbent not frowning; not prepared, as the slack bow of an archer

unbid not asked for or invited

unbitted unrestrained

unblow'd cut before fully grown

unbolt open up

unbolted impure; (?) without a penis

unbonneted without one's hat; without having removed one's hat

unbookish ill-informed

unbraided still in good condition

unbreath'd unpractised

uncape uncover (? a fox)

uncase take off one's outer garments

uncharge exonerate, remove from suspicion

uncharged unassailed, still standing

unchary unsparingly, lavishly

uncheck'd not denied or refuted

unclasp open up, reveal

unclew undo, be the end of (*cf.* **clew**)

uncoined in its natural state, like gold bullion

uncomprehensive unimaginable; unfathomable

unconfirmed inexperienced; (?) not having had the sacrament of Confirmation

uncouth unfamiliar, unknown

uncovered without a hat; barefaced

uncross'd with debts not crossed off

unction ointment

uncurrent out of the ordinary

undeeded not having performed any deeds

under beneath the sun, worldly; of the underworld; **go under** = bear; seem, be called

underbear suffer under

underborne edged

undercrest have (a title) above one as one would a crest

undergo go under, bear, be subject to

underhand discreet

underskinker junior tapster (one who serves drink in an inn)

undertake take on; take in one's charge; take responsibility

undertaker one who takes on (a challenge)

undervalued of less value

underwrite accept

underwrought undermined

undeserving (?) *sb.* that which is undeserving; (?) *adj.* undeserved

undistinguished *see* **indistinguished**

undoubted free from doubt or fear

uneared unsown, as with ears of corn

uneath not easily, hardly

unexperient person without experience

unexpressive unable to be expressed

unfair make no longer fair

unfashionable lacking finished form

unfenced unbounded; unprotected

unfold open up, expose, reveal

unfolding star star at whose rising shepherds let their sheep out of the folds

unfurnished unprovided for, solitary, naked; unprepared

ungalled unwounded, safe

ungenitured sterile; (?) without genitals

ungor'd unwounded

unguem nail (*Lat.*), as used in the phrase '*ad unguem*' ('to the nail, exactly')

unhair'd without (facial) hair

unhandsome unskilful; (?) unsoldierly

unhappily, unhapp'ly unfortunately; adversely; with malice

unhappy unlucky, cursed

unhatched not yet hatched, embryonic

unhoused not occupying or used to occupying a house

unhousel'd not having received the eucharist in the last rites

unimproved unchecked, unrestrained

union pearl of fine quality; marriage

unjust false

unkennel unearth, uncover

unkind acting against one's family or the natural order

unlimited observing no dramatic unities

unluckily ominously

unmann'd (of a hawk) untrained

unmeet unsuitable

Glossary

unnerved enfeebled in sinew, strengthless

unow'd unowned

unpaved castrated

unpink'd with the decorative holes (pinks) either unfinished or worn out

unpitied merciless

unplausive disapproving

unpolicied lacking or outmanoeuvred in political skill

unpregnant slack, unresponsive

unprevailing pointless

unprizable of little value; of great value

unprized unvalued; priceless

unproper shared; indecent

unproportion'd unruly, unrestrained

unprovide disarm

unqualitied robbed of one's nature, unmanned

unquestionable irritable when spoken to

unquietness disquiet, perturbation

unrak'd (of a fire) not kept smouldering overnight

unrecalling irrevocable

unreclaimed untamed

unrecuring past curing, fatal

unrespective confused, without distinction or order; heedless

unrolled dismissed from a fraternity

unroosted knocked off the roost, henpecked

unrough without facial hair, adolescent; of good family

unscann'd unconsidered, rash

unseasoned raw, unready; untimely

unsecret open, forthcoming

unseminared seedless, castrated

unset unsown

unshape unsettle

unshaped fragmentary, incoherent

unsifted untried, inexperienced

unsisting (?) unresting; (?) insisting; (?) unassisting

unsorted inappropriate

unspeaking speechless, dumbfounded

unsphere knock from a sphere or spheres (*see* **sphere**)

unsquar'd unsuitable

unstanched *see* **unstaunched**

unstate rid of wealth and status

unstaunched leaking; unquenched

unsur'd unsure, uncertain

untainted untouched; uninjured; uncharged

untempering unable to melt or soften

untented too deep to be tented (*see* **tent**)

untoward perverse, unruly

untraded little used, unfamiliar

untrimmed sexually intact; stripped; set off balance

untrussing undoing laces

unvalu'd of no value; of inestimable value

unwappered unexhausted

unwarily unsuspectingly

unweighed unconsidered; light

unwitted made mad

unwrung not chafed by the saddle

unyok'd unbridled

up up in arms; imprisoned; **game is up** = game is afoot; **kill up** = kill off; **up and down** = absolutely, entirely

upcast (in bowls) throw

uproar turn to uproar or chaos

upshoot (in archery) the best shot until subsequently beaten

upspring wild dance

up-till up against

urchin hedgehog; goblin or elf, *esp.* in the shape of a hedgehog

urinal glass phial used to examine urine; (?) testicle

usance usury

use *sb.* custom, habit, way; interest; profit; *v.* be accustomed (to); keep company with; **in use** = in trust

utis holiday merriment; noise, din

utter advertise, sell

utterance furthest point

uttermost, to the (of a fight) to the death

vacancy spare time; air; the vacuum created by a removal of air

vade go away, fade

vagary wandering or erring state

vagrom Dogberry's word for 'vagrant'

vail *sb.* setting; *v.* lower, abase (oneself)

vails leftovers given to servants, tips

vain *sb.* vanity; *adj.* foolish; flattering

valanced decoratively draped

validity value, worth; strength, efficacy

valu'd discriminating, listing individual qualities

value evaluate, consider; compare; merit, be worth

vambrace defensive armour for the arms

Vanity a female role in the morality plays

vantage advantage; opportunity; **of vantage** = also, in addition

vara very (*dial.*)

varlet servant, page; often a term of abuse with occasional sexual overtones

varletry common people (*cf.* **varlet**)

vastidity vastness

vaulty vaulted, arched

vaunt *sb.* first part; *v.* rejoice

vaunt-couriers forerunners

vaward vanguard, front of an army

vein spirit, style; **rub the vein of** = encourage, flatter

velure velvet

velvet-guards those wearing fine clothes (*cf.* **guards**)

Venetia, Venetia, Chi non ti vede, non ti pretia 'Venice, Venice, he who does not see you does not prize you' (*Ital.*, proverbial)

veney *see* **venue**

vengeance *adj.* terrific; *adv.* terrifically

vent venting, discharge; (in hunting) scent, such as makes the hounds bark

ventages holes

ventricle chamber in the brain

venue (in fencing) round, assault

Venus goddess of love and lover of Mars (*see* **Mars**)

Ver spring

verbatim in speech

verge rim; area surrounding the court

Veronessa ship from Verona

vestal *sb.* virgin or nun, as the Roman virgins who tended the fire in the temple of Vesta; *adj.* relating to Vesta or virginity

via an expression of encouragement or impatience (*Ital.*)

viands food

Vice a comic villain in sixteenth-century moral interludes

vice *sb.* grasp; screw; *v.* force

vicegerent deputy (a royal title)

vicious wicked; blameworthy; mistaken

videlicet 'that is to say' (*Lat.*)

Videsne quis venit? Video, et gaudeo 'Do you see who comes? I see and rejoice' (*Lat.*)

vie vie with, rival; multiply; (at cards) put down a stake

vigil evening before a feast-day

Vilia miretur vulgus: mihi flavus Apollo / Pocula Castalia plena ministret aqua 'Let the common folk marvel at the everyday: golden Apollo shall serve me cups filled from the Castalian spring' (*Lat.*, Ovid)

villain, villein person of low birth, servant

villiago villain, rascal

vinewed'st mouldiest

viol stringed instrument, an early violin

viol-de-gamboys *see* **bass-viol**

violenteth rages

vir sapit qui pauca loquitur 'he is wise who says little' (*Lat.*, proverbial)

virginalling pressing with the fingers, as one would the keys of a virginal (an early keyboard)

virtue masculine virtue, courage; power; essence

virtuous fertile, breeding; powerful, effective; inherent, lying within

visitation infection

visited punished by God; infected

visitor one who visits the sick and distressed

visor, vizor mask

viva voce orally; speaking out loud (*Lat.*)

vizaments Evans's word for 'advisements'; **take your vizaments in that** = consider that

vizard *see* **visor**

vocativo 'in the vocative case' (*Lat.*)

vocatur '(it) is called' (*Lat.*)

voice *sb.* determining say, vote; *v.* vote, choose; **in voices** = reportedly

voiding lobby corridor for entrance or exit

Volquessen Rouen and district

voluble moving smoothly and swiftly, fluent

voluntary volunteer

votaress female votary (*cf.* **votarist**)

votarist, votary one under a vow, *esp.* in a religious order

vouch *sb.* allegation, evidence; *v.* testify

voyage enterprise

Vulcan god of fire and cuckolded husband of Venus, represented as a smith

vulgar *sb.* vernacular, native tongue; *adj.* of or among the ordinary people, common

waft wave; turn; carry by boat

waftage passage by boat

wafture waving gesture

wag go, go away, move

wage pay (a wage to); risk; stake; struggle, vie

wainropes waggon-ropes

waist middle of a ship's upper deck; garment for the waist

wake *sb.* parish festival; *v.* not sleep, stay up

wall-eyed glowering

wanion, with a a phrase used to emphasize a statement

wann'd became wan, paled

want lack; feel the lack of

wanton *sb.* exuberant joker; delicate youth; *adj.* vibrant, skittish; delicate; *v.* play

wappen'd sexually exhausted

ward *sb.* defence, defensive position; room in a prison; lock mechanism; *v.* defend

warden type of pear or apple

warder umpire's baton

ware *adj.* aware; wary; *v.* take heed of, beware

warp turn; change·

war-proof, of experienced in war

Glossary

warrant *sb.* licence; assurance; *v.* approve, license; assure, guarantee

warrantise, warrantize guarantee, pledge

warranty sanction, licence

warren enclosure for rabbits and other game

warrener one who protects rabbits from poachers

washing *see* **swashing**

wassail drinking session; **wassail candle** = thick candle

waste *sb.* damage done to a property by a tenant; *v.* consume, destroy

Wat traditional name for a hare

watch *sb.* fixed period of time; candle; watchword; *v.* catch by lying in wait for; train (a hawk) through sleep deprivation

watchful sleepless, of sleeplessness

water transparency in diamonds, used to grade their quality

water-galls minor types of rainbow

watering drinking

water-rugs rough-haired water dogs

waters, for all versatile, multi-talented

water-standing full of tears

waterwork painted imitation tapestry

wave waver

waxen *adj.* soft as wax; *v.* wax, increase

ways, come your come on your way, come

weal prosperity, well-being; state, society

wealsmen politicians

wealth prosperity, well-being (*cf.* **weal**)

wear *sb.* thing worn, fashion; *v.* wear out; be in fashion; adapt

weather, keep the be upwind, in a superior position

weather-fends defends from the weather

web and pin *see* **pin** (**pin and web**)

weed piece of clothing

week, in by the trapped, imprisoned

ween think

weet know, recognize

Weïrd Sisters goddesses of *wyrd* (*OE* = 'fate')

welkin *sb.* sky; *adj.* blue as the sky

well to live well off, well to do

well-a-day *sb.* saying 'alas', lament; *int.* alas

well-a-near alas (*cf.* **well-a-day**)

well-breath'd (?) well-trained; (?) breathing well

well-favoured good-looking, attractive

well-liking heavy

well-respected properly considered, not rash

Welsh hook a type of bill-hook or pike (without the 'cross' of a sword)

weraday *see* **well-a-day**

westward ho! Thames watermen's call for passengers heading west

wezand windpipe, throat

wharf river bank

wheel *sb.* sung refrain; *v.* move in an arc; **on wheels** = giddily; easily; **turn i'th' wheel** = (of dogs) tread a wheel to turn a spit

Wheeson Whitsun (*dial.*)

whelk boil

whelked resembling the shellfish, twisting round

when a cry of impatience

whether which (of two)

whey-face one blanching with fear

whiffler one who clears the path of an approaching procession

while until

while-ere a short time ago

whiles while (*see* **while**)

whilst while (*see* **while**)

whipping-cheer a bellyful of whipping

whipster whipper-snapper, boy

whip-stock, whipstock whip handle

whirligig spinning-top

whist silent, still

white *sb.* (in archery) bullseye; *adj.* afraid, cowardly

white-limed daubed with lime

whiting-time time for bleaching clothes

whitsters professional bleachers

whittle carving-knife

whoo-bub hubbub

whoreson bastard, used technically, offensively or affectionately

wide failing to hit, off course, wrong

widow provide (the widow) with the estate of the deceased

wight creature, person

Wild, the the Weald, an area of southern England

wild *sb.* desert, wasteland; *adj.* headstrong, unthinking; **wild mare** = boys' game of jumping on each other's backs

wilderness wildness, wild stock

wild-goose chase a type of horse race

wildly chaotically, haphazardly

wildness madness, distraction

wilful-blame blamable for too much self-will

will sexual organ

wimpled muffled, blindfolded

wince kick out

winch wince

Winchester goose *see* **goose**

Wincot a hamlet near Stratford-upon-Avon

wind *sb.* breath; (in hunting) direction of the wind and thus of scent; *v.* get wind of; wheedle; **wind up** = fill; tune (a stringed instrument) by tightening its pegs

windgalls tumours on the legs of horses

windlasses deviations

window-bars square patterns on a woman's bodice

windring both winding and wandering

wink *sb.* shutting the eyes; *v.* shut the eyes

winking with closed eyes

winnow sift, refine

winter'd during winter

winter-ground (?) *sb.* ground in winter; (?) *v.* insulate, keep warm

wipe branded stigma

wise *sb.* way, fashion; *adj.* in one's right mind; **wise woman** = expert in herbal medicine, witchcraft, *etc.*

wishtly wishfully and/or wistly (*see* **wistly**)

wisp of straw traditional target of a shrewish woman's hectoring

wistly earnestly, eagerly

wit *sb.* mind, intelligence, cleverness; *v.* know; **five wits** = five mental faculties; **wit, wither wilt?** = catchphrase used to shut someone up

wit-crackers teasers, jibers

withal, *prep.* with; *adv.* therewith, with (something specified); **do withal** = do anything about it

withers ridge between a horse's shoulders

withhold hold back, keep

without outside, beyond

without-door exterior

witting knowing

wittol husband who accepts his being cuckolded

witty mentally sound, intelligent, clever

wold open country

woman-tir'd prey to a woman (*see* **tire**)

wondered to be wondered at; capable of producing wonders

wond'ring wondering at

wood wild, frantic

woodbine honeysuckle or similar plant

woodcock a stupid, easily trapped bird

woodman hunter; hunter of women

woollen *adj.* dressed in coarse wool; **in the woollen** = in scratchy blankets

woolward wearing a woollen shirt without a vest to stop it scratching

woosel *see* **ousel**

woo't wilt (will you)

working *sb.* mental working, perception; deed; *adj.* moving

world *sb.* body (*cf.* **microcosm**); **go to the world** = reject the cloister, get married

worm snake

worn worn out

worship dignity

worshipped dignified

wort a plant of the cabbage family; unfermented beer

worthy *v.* make seem a hero; **the Worthies** = nine heroes from history and legend

wot know (*cf.* **wit**); wilt (*cf.* **woo't**)

wrack *sb.* wreck; wrecking; victim of a wreck; *v.* wreck

wrangler quarreller

wrath *sb.* raging passion; *adj.* wroth, furious

wreak *sb.* revenge; *v.* revenge

wrest tuning-key; peg for tightening a surgical ligature

wring twist, writhe

writ holy writ, scripture; any document or paper

writhled shrivelled, wrinkled

wroth misfortune, grief

wrying going astray

wry-neck'd with neck twisted, as was characteristic of fifers

Xanthippe notoriously bad-tempered wife of the philosopher Socrates

yard stick for measuring a yard; penis

yare light; quick; ready

Yaughan (?) for 'Johan', an unidentifed alehouse-keeper of the day

yaw sail unsteadily

y-clad clad, clothed

ycleped cleped, called

Yead Ed (*cf.* **Yedward**)

yea-forsooth given to using mild oaths in a servile manner

yearn grieve

Yedward Edward

yellowness jealousy

yellows jaundice in horses

yerk strike; kick

yest yeast, foam

yield bring forth; report; reward

yoke-devils devils working together

younger younger son, prodigal

younker young man, prodigal

y-ravished ravished, enraptured

y-slacked slacked, reduced to inactivity

zany clown's assistant

'zounds, zounds *see* **'Swounds**

zwaggered swaggered (*dial.*) (*see* **swagger**)